WORLD HISTORY

THE HUMAN EXPERIENCE

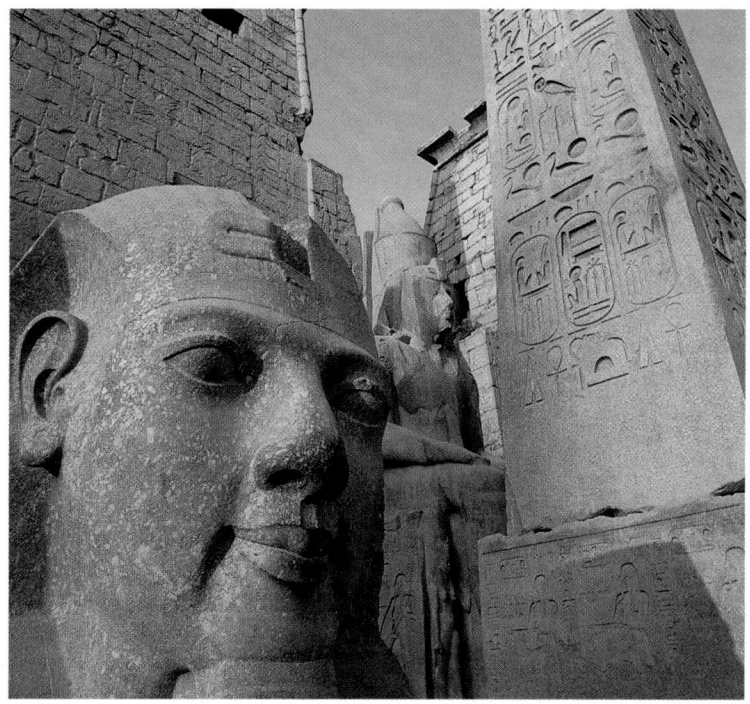

NATIONAL
GEOGRAPHIC
SOCIETY

Mounir A. Farah
Andrea Berens Karls

GLENCOE

McGraw-Hill

New York, New York   Columbus, Ohio   Woodland Hills, California   Peoria, Illinois

About the Authors

The **National Geographic Society**, founded in 1888 for the increase and diffusion of geographic knowledge, is the world's largest nonprofit scientific and educational organization. Since its earliest days, the Society has used sophisticated communication technologies and rich historical and archival resources to convey knowledge to a worldwide membership. The Educational Media Division supports the Society's mission by developing innovative educational programs—ranging from traditional print materials to multimedia programs including CD-ROMs, videodiscs, and software.

Mounir A. Farah, Ph.D. is a research historian and Associate Director of the Middle East Studies Program at the University of Arkansas, Fayetteville. Dr. Farah taught history and social science at New York University and Western Connecticut State University and has lectured at many teachers' conferences and workshops in the United States and abroad. He was a consultant to the Ministry of Education in Jordan and served as Coordinator of Social Studies in the Monroe, Connecticut public schools. Named Outstanding History Scholar-Teacher in New England and a recipient of the Connecticut Social Studies Annual Award, Dr. Farah is a past president of the Connecticut Council for the Social Studies and of the Middle East Outreach Council and a board member of the Arkansas Council for Social Studies. He is a contributing writer to several books and has authored numerous articles and reviews. Dr. Farah also is coauthor of Glencoe's *Global Insights*.

Andrea Berens Karls is an educator and coauthor of Glencoe's *Global Insights*. Educated at Wellesley College and Harvard University, she has taught at both the elementary and secondary levels. Ms. Karls was formerly Program Associate at Global Perspectives in Education, Inc., where she edited and wrote curriculum materials and worked with teachers. She is a member of the National Council for the Social Studies and the American Historical Association.

About the Cover

The temple of Amon-Ra—ancient Egypt's most important god—was the major building in Thebes, a city of Egypt. Between the 1300s B.C. and the 1100s B.C., Egyptian builders constructed the temple at the site of the present-day city of Luxor.

The part of the temple shown is an outer court, decorated with colossal images of the great Egyptian pharaoh Ramses II. A pair of granite obelisks covered with hieroglyphics also graced the outer court. One obelisk (shown in the cover photo) still stands. The other was removed to the Place de la Concorde in Paris, France, in 1831.

Glencoe/McGraw-Hill

A Division of The McGraw·Hill Companies

Design and Production: DECODE, Inc.
Cover photograph: Temple of Amon-Ra, Luxor, Egypt; Mark D. Phillips/Photo Researchers, Inc.

Send all inquiries to:
Glencoe/McGraw-Hill, 8787 Orion Place, Columbus, Ohio 43240

ISBN 0-07-821615-X (Student Edition) ISBN 0-07-821616-8 (Teacher's Wraparound Edition)

Printed in the United States of America.
1 2 3 4 5 6 7 8 9 10 071/043 05 04 03 02 01 00

Academic Consultants

Richard G. Boehm, Ph.D.
Professor of Geography
Southwest Texas State University
San Marcos, Texas

William Brinner, Ph.D.
Professor of History
Department of Near Eastern Studies
University of California
Berkeley, California

Stephen Chicoine
Author/Lecturer, World Affairs
Vice President
Bechtel Energy Resources Corporation
Houston, Texas

Paula Fredriksen, Ph.D.
Aurelio Professor of Scripture
Boston University
Boston, Massachusetts

Madhulika S. Khandelwal, Ph.D.
Research Historian
Asian/American Center
Queens College
City University of New York
New York City, New York

George Demetrius Knysh, Ph.D.
Associate Professor of Political Studies
University of Manitoba
Winnipeg, Manitoba
Canada

Frances Malino, Ph.D.
Professor of History
Wellesley College
Wellesley, Massachusetts

Shabbir Mansouri
Founding Director
Council on Islamic Education
Fountain Valley, California

Ali A. Mazrui, Ph.D.
Professor of History
State University of New York
Binghamton, New York

Jesus Mendez, Ph.D.
Associate Professor of History
Barry University
Miami Shores, Florida

Brendan Nagle, Ph.D.
Associate Professor
University of Southern California
Los Angeles, California

Al Naklowycz, Ph.D.
President, Ukrainian-American Academic
    Association of California
Carmichael, California

Donald Niewyk, Ph.D.
Professor of History
Southern Methodist University
Dallas, Texas

Boniface Obichere, Ph.D.
Professor of History
University of California
Los Angeles, California

Sayyid M. Syeed, Ph.D.
Secretary General
The Islamic Society of North America
Plainfield, Indiana

Frank De Varona
Region 1 Superintendent
Dade County Public Schools
Hialeah, Florida

Bluma Zuckerbrot-Finkelstein
Director, Special Projects
Middle Eastern Affairs
Anti-Defamation League of B'nai B'rith
St. Louis, Missouri

Teacher Reviewers

Christine Allen
North Salem High School
Salem, Oregon

John M. Arevalo
Harlandale High School
San Antonio, Texas

Mattie Collins
Pine Bluff High School
Pine Bluff, Arkansas

Janice Darley Dreyer
Vines High School
Plano, Texas

Louis Gallo
West High School
Knoxville, Tennessee

Mary Helen Haines
Richardson High School
Richardson, Texas

Mark Heinig
Reitz Memorial High School
Evansville, Indiana

Paul Horton
Williamsville East High School
East Amherst, New York

Jim Lloyd
Department Chair, History-Social Science
Bullard High School
Fresno, California

Patti Long
Forrest City High School
Forrest City, Arkansas

Willis M. Overton III
Warren Central High School
Indianapolis, Indiana

Table of Contents

Student Edition
Table of Contents T5

Professional Notes
Glencoe's Integrated Internet Support T12
Answering the Issue of Relevancy T14
The Story of History T16
Seeing the Big Picture T17
Visualizing History T18
Geography in History T20
Integrating Literature and
    Writing into History T21
Addressing Multiple Learning Styles T22
Implementing Block Scheduling T24
Utilizing Performance Assessment T25
Using Technology in the Classroom T26
Surfing the History Net T27
Correlation to NCSS Ten
    Thematic Strands T28
Six Alternative Course Outlines T30
Scope and Sequence Chart T32

Classroom Resources

Applications and Hands-On Activities
History Simulations T40
Historical Significance Chapter Activities T41
Skill Reinforcement Activities T42
People in World History T43

Review and Reinforcement Activities
Vocabulary Activities T44
Vocabulary PuzzleMaker Software T44
Guided Reading Activities T45
Reading Essentials and Study Guide T45
Time Line Activities T46
Chapter Themes: Graphic Organizers T47
Reteaching Activities T48

Spanish Language Resources T49

Geography Activities
Mapping History Activities T50
Geography and History Activities T51
Outline Map Resource Book T52
Student Desk Map T52

Interdisciplinary Connections
World Literature Selections T53
World Art and Music T54
World Music: Cultural Traditions T54
World History and Art Transparencies T55
Focus on World Art Prints T55

Enrichment and Extension Activities
Enrichment Activities T56
Critical Thinking Activities T57
Source Readings T58

Assessment and Evaluation
Performance Assessment Strategies
    and Activities T59
Section Quizzes T60
Chapter and Unit Tests: Forms A and B T61
Testmaker Software T61

Multimedia and Technology
Interactive Tutor Self-Assessment Software T62
MindJogger Videoquiz T63
Teaching Transparencies T64
Section Focus Transparencies T65

PRESENTATION *Plus!*
CD-ROM T65
Chapter Digests Audiocassettes T66

NATIONAL GEOGRAPHIC SOCIETY
Resources T67

ABCNEWS INTERACTIVE
Resources T72

A&E HOME VIDEO / THE HISTORY CHANNEL / Biography
Resources T72

Table of Contents

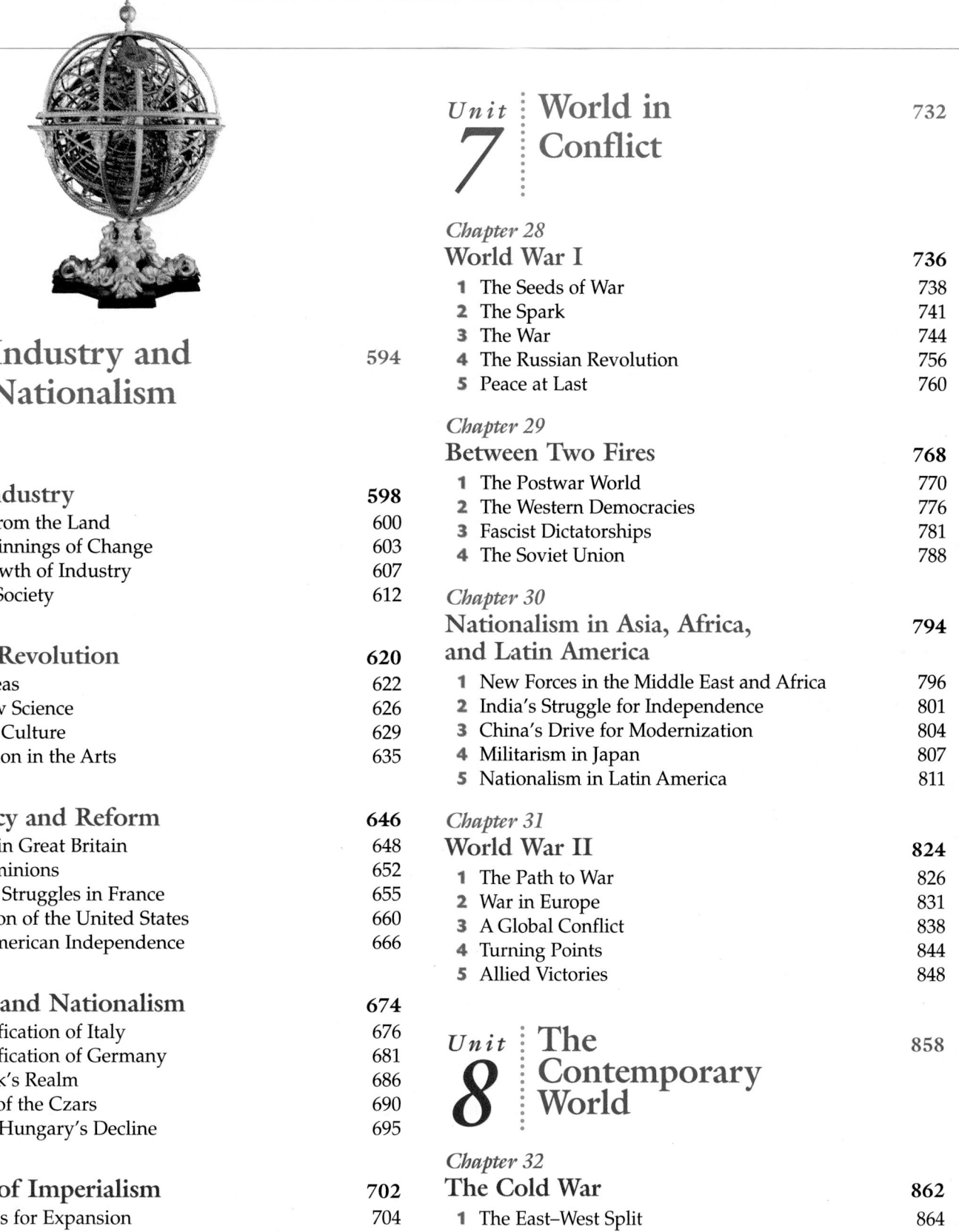

NATIONAL GEOGRAPHIC SOCIETY

TURNING POINT

The Spread of Ideas

Bridge to the Past — Literature

Images of the Times

Economics

Science and Technology

The Arts

Connections To...

Geography

Around the World

PRIMARY SOURCES
Library

Primary Sources Library

THE
PRINCETON
REVIEW

Standardized Test Practice

SKILLS

Social Studies Skills

Critical Thinking Skills

Study and Writing Skills

Technology Skills

Introducing the *World History W*
Integrated Internet Supp

World History Online boxes at point of use in the unit and chapter direct students to use Web curriculum as part of an integrated study of world history.

	You Need:	Current Content
✓	We Provide:	Updated Information and Current Event Resources via the Web
	You Need:	Help with Assessment
✓	We Provide:	Self-Check Quizzes and Interactive Puzzles
	You Need:	Integration of Web Resources into Your Lessons
✓	We Provide:	Complete Student Activities, Teacher Strategies, and Additional Links

Use our Web site for additional resources. All essential content is covered in the Student Edition.

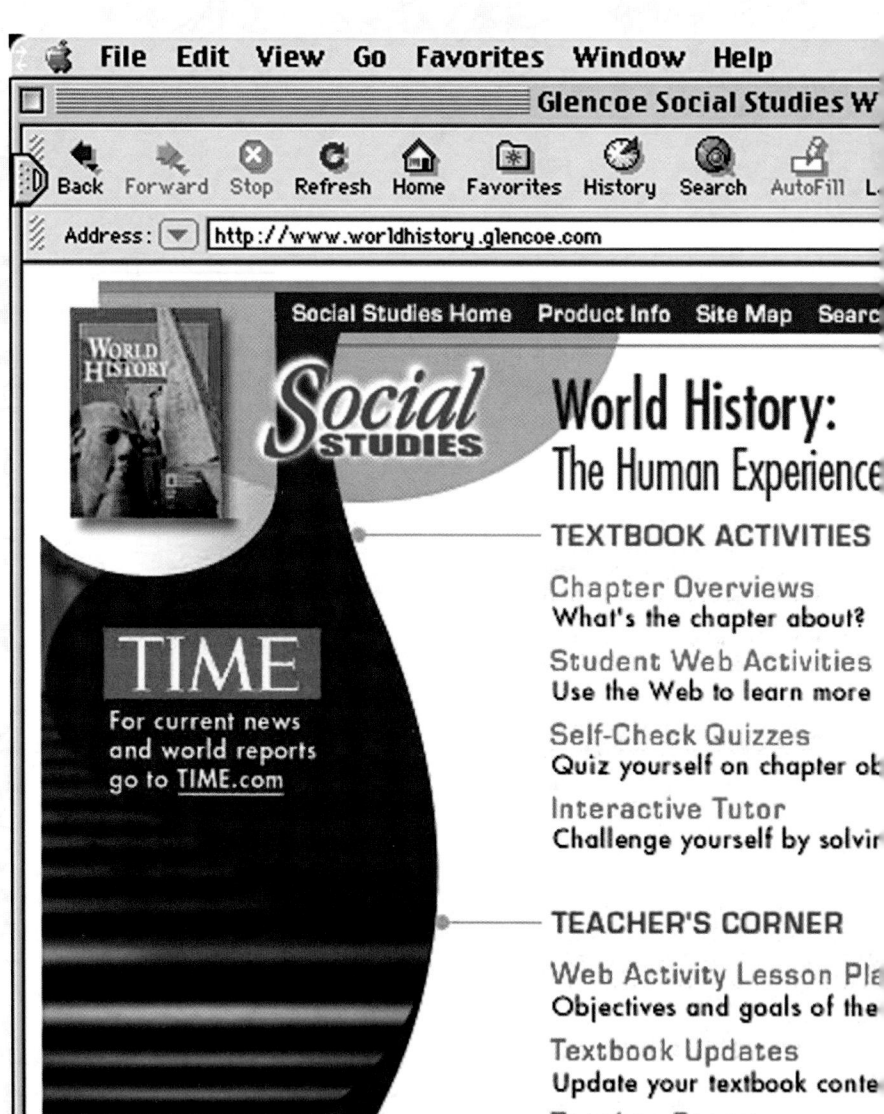

Our Pledge to You

Glencoe is committed to providing textbooks that are as error free and as accurate as possible. As part of this commitment, we will be updating critical time-sensitive data such as charts, graphs, and statistics along with the latest information in the field of world history on our Web site. In this way, you and your students will always have access to the most accurate information possible.

Chapter Overviews provide a quick preview or review of chapter content.

Student Web Activities enrich and extend chapter content.

Self-Check Quizzes help students prepare for chapter tests.

Answering the Issue of Relevancy

Links to Today

Revolution … expansion … imperialism … How do you get your students to see that these concepts changed the world before *and during* their lifetimes? It's true that, unless your students see relevant reasons to study about the history of the world, they will not learn the lessons that history reveals. Your challenge every day is to generate high enthusiasm for learning by making strong connections between today's reality and the most telling stories and messages of the past.

Glencoe's *World History: The Human Experience* is your primary tool for successful student motivation, second only to your masterful talents of instruction. It continually reminds students why the content *must* matter to them. Every unit opens with **Then & Now,** recognizing how history is directly embedded in our everyday lives. Each chapter and

section opens with **The Storyteller,** personalizing the historical period by disclosing the thoughts and ideas of people from that time in their own words. Pivotal questions pointing to the era's **Historical Significance** open each chapter, and the Chapter Assessment imparts more relevancy in **Linking Past and Present.**

Historical Significance

The Storyteller

Living the History

You want your students to *experience* history, to comprehend another's situation from a different perspective, and to develop more active empathy with people from another time. You raise the level of authentic instruction by increasing the students' interactions with the content and with each other. Your students begin and end the study of each chapter in Glencoe's *World History: The Human Experience* by writing in **Your History Journal,** where they explore real-world problems of another era, learning that no problem is totally objective and every point of view comes with a bias. **Footnotes to History** pique interest by revealing fascinating yet little-known facts about people, places, and events. And the classroom resource **History Simulations** take your students that much closer to actually being a part of history.

▪ For Further Professional Reading

Adams, D., and M. Hamm. 1994. *New Designs for Teaching and Learning: Promoting Active Learning in Tomorrow's Schools.* San Francisco: Jossey-Bass Publishers.

Bower, B., J. Lobdell, and L. Swenson. 1994. *History Alive! Engaging All Learners in the Diverse Classroom.* New York: Addison-Wesley Publishing Company.

Newmann, F. M., and G. G. Wehlage. 1993. "Five Standards of Authentic Instruction." *Educational Leadership* 50(7): 8–12.

Other Program Resources

Rely on these additional resources to help students understand the relevancy of world history.

Teacher's Wraparound Edition
- Then & Now
- Linking Past and Present
- Global Gourmet
- You Don't Say…

Classroom Resources
- Historical Significance Chapter Activities
- Turning Points in World History Videodisc
- National Geographic Society CD-ROMs
- World Music: Cultural Traditions

Linking Past and Present

The Story of History

Telling the Story

Students' world views are only as broad as their life experiences. Once your students hear the powerful stories of the world's peoples, you know their views will broaden further. What's magical about the history of the world is that each story is brought to a personal level at which your students can ponder their ancestors' options. Through this personal identification, students imagine what it was like for people in that particular time and place—and learn from it. They are touched by the magic of the past through authentic voices, showcased in **The Storyteller** in Glencoe's *World History: The Human Experience*, which dramatically open each new chapter study. Primary source quotations, integrated generously throughout the narrative, sustain the story's momentum. With so many stories to read and incredible people to learn about, students extend their world views and move toward acceptance of the many sides of the global story.

Other Program Resources

Rely on these additional resources to help students understand the world's many cultural perspectives.

Teacher's Wraparound Edition
- Cultural Diffusion
- Cultural Perspectives

Classroom Resources
- People in World History
- World Music: Cultural Traditions

The Storyteller

The caravan halted for the night. Chaghatai, the leader, before retiring posted a sign and fastened bells around the animals' necks. Maffeo, a young foreigner, wondered at these precautions. Chaghatai explained that strange things may happen in the Desert of Lop. "When a man is riding by night through this desert and something happens to make him ... lose touch with his companions ... he hears spirits talking.... Often these voices make him stray from the path.... For this reason bands of travellers make a point of keeping very close together.... And round the necks of all their beasts they fasten little bells, so that by listening to the sound they may prevent them from straying from the path."

—adapted from *The Travels of Marco Polo*, Marco Polo, translated by Ronald Latham, 1958

"What's going to be on the test?"

Seeing the Big Picture

Reading for Understanding

Your students want to know what is most important among the millions of facts, key figures, and significant events in world history. You want them to know what it *all* means—recognizing the common themes from era to era and relating this information to today's headlines. To help them read their textbooks effectively, structured reading strategies are offered on pages 12–13 of the student text. In addition, each lesson now opens with headings to help students read successfully. As coach and facilitator, your collaboration helps students become proficient in how to access information and derive meaning from it.

Guide to Reading

**Read to Find Out
Main Idea** *There were many social and political factors that caused the French Revolution.*

Who?What?Where?When?

Edith Cavell, an English nurse working in Belgium, was an Allied heroine of World War I. After the Germans occupied the country, she helped Belgian, French, and British soldiers escape. Arrested in 1915, she confessed and was sentenced to die by the firing squad. Her execution in October, though legally justified, aroused worldwide condemnation.

World History: The Human Experience provides depth of understanding by consistently reinforcing historical trends, themes, and concepts. Beginning the unit with **A Global Chronology**, students see the relationships among important political, scientific, and social and cultural events. The text consistently puts events in perspective with time lines at the beginning of each chapter and section, too.

A.D. 500   A.D. 800   A.D. 1100   A.D. 1400

c. A.D. 800s Khmer rulers establish empire in Cambodia.

A.D. 1185 Minamoto family rules in Japan.

A.D. 618 Tang dynasty comes to power in China.

A.D. 1392 Yi dynasty begins in Korea.

Visualizing History

Seeing Is Believing

Your students were raised on cable TV and remote controls. It's plain and simple from students' perspectives—if they can't see it, they *don't* believe it. But bringing the people, places, and events of world history to your students is what Glencoe's *World History: The Human Experience* does best. Interesting text and features are accompanied

by colorful illustrations, maps, charts, and photos. With the help of giants such as the National Geographic Society and ABCNews InterActive™, students witness the rich pageantry of the world's past through **STV Videodiscs**, **PictureShow CD-ROMs**, and **Turning Points in World History**. The *Picturing History* and *NGS Special Report* features in the student text are brought to you from the National Geographic Society, unveiling exciting visuals and high-interest descriptions.

Other Program Resources

Rely on these additional resources to help students visualize the spectacles of history.

Teacher's Wraparound Edition
- Visualizing History
- Images of the Times
- Making Connections Activities
- History & Art
- Curriculum Connection
- Connections: The Arts

Classroom Resources
- National Geographic Society Videodiscs
- NGS PictureShow CD-ROMs
- NGS Poster Sets and PicturePack Transparencies
- ABCNews InterActive™ Videodiscs
- Focus on World Art Prints
- Chapter Transparencies
- World History and Art Transparencies

Comprehending Concepts

The Spread of Ideas

You are convinced that knowing the "big picture" empowers students to learn more and to find new ways to learn. Investing them with the power of historians—to determine the essential questions, investigate for answers in a variety of sources, draw conclusions, and present their interpretations with vigor—builds critical thinkers, able researchers, and participating citizens. Through such work, students grasp the "big ideas" and understand how important they are in the study of history. Glencoe's *World History: The Human Experience* opens each unit with **The Spread of Ideas**, which identifies an important concept in world history and explains how people from different parts of the world learned and reacted to these ideas during the epoch. Questions at the end of the feature help students in **Linking the Ideas**. The program communicates concepts by identifying **Chapter Themes** at the beginning of the chapter and reinforcing them in **Understanding Themes** in the Chapter Assessment. Students start each section of study with a **Main Idea** question that channels their search for meaning.

Other Resources

Rely on these additional resources to help students see the "big picture."

Teacher's Wraparound Edition
- Section Theme Activity in Guided Practice
- Who?What?Where?When?

Classroom Resources
- Time Line Activities
- Chapter Themes: Graphic Organizers

For Further Professional Reading

Chuska, K. R. 1995. *Improving Classroom Questions: A Teacher's Guide to Increasing Student Motivation, Participation, and Higher-Level Thinking*. Bloomington, Ind.: Phi Delta Kappa Educational Foundation.

Thompson, L. J. 1995. *Habits of the Mind: Critical Thinking in the Classroom*. Lanham, Md.: University Press of America.

Williams, J. A. 1994. *Classroom in Conflict: Teaching Controversial Subjects in a Diverse Society*. Albany, N.Y.: State University of New York Press.

Geography in History

From the study of the emerging river valley civilizations in ancient times to the devastation of late twentieth-century natural disasters, the story of human history cannot be told without the influence of geographic features. Whether we talk about physical features—mountains blocking movement—or cultural features—dozens of ethnic groups and languages within a small region—geography has a significant impact on where and how people live.

Glencoe's *World History: The Human Experience* understands that there is no time to teach geography separately from world history. By integrating important geographic information and the five geographic themes within the narrative and providing in-depth focus on geography in **Connections: Geography** features, this program helps students see the undeniable tie between geography and history. The extensive map program and accompanying **Map Study** questions help students improve their map-reading skills while recognizing the importance of location, place, region, movement, and human/environment interaction. The **Geography in History** questions in the Chapter Assessment reinforce themes and key concepts. The best in the field—the National Geographic Society—offers special multimedia resources that extend the student text—CD-ROMs, videodiscs, transparencies, posters, related references to *National Geographic*, and more!

Other Program Resources

Rely on these additional resources to help students understand the importance of geography in history.

Teacher's Wraparound Edition
- Geography Connection
- Map Study

Classroom Resources
- Geography and History Activities
- Student Desk Map
- Mapping History Activities
- Mapping History Overlay Transparencies

Alexander's Empire 336–323 B.C.

Extent of empire
Alexander's routes of conquest
★ Major battles

Map Study

Alexander the Great united the Greeks and conquered an area stretching from Egypt to India.
1. **Movement** After freeing the Ionian city-states, in which direction did Alexander and his forces travel?
2. **Location** What key cities in the Persian Empire did Alexander conquer?

Integrating Literature and Writing into History

Concepts are better understood when information is presented in context rather than in unrelated bits and pieces. This means that integrating the important literature of particular eras and primary source documents within the study of history not only assists students in understanding the context of the people's lives but also reinforces verbal skills when completing writing assignments, such as **Your History Journal** at the start of each chapter.

Glencoe's *World History: The Human Experience* provides an extensive excerpt from world literature for each unit in **Literature: Bridge to the Past**. This selection represents the time, the people, and the issues of the period, exposing students to literature of interdisciplinary consequence. Discussions and activities related to the selection assist the student in understanding its **Historical Connection** and **Contemporary Connection**. In addition, a **Primary Source Document Library** concludes each unit, offering selected primary sources from the time period.

Other Program Resources

Rely on these additional resources to help students understand the importance of literature and writing in history.

Teacher's Wraparound Edition
- History and the Humanities
- About the Author
- Glencoe Literature Library— correlates units to literary works available from Glencoe.

Classroom Resources
- World Literature Selections
- Source Readings

■ For Further Professional Reading

Danks, C. 1995. "Using Holocaust Short Stories and Poetry in the Social Studies Classroom." *Social Education* 59(6): 358–61.

Irvin, J. L., J. P. Lunstrum, C. Lynch-Brown, and M. F. Shepard. 1995. *Enhancing Social Studies Through Literary Strategies*. Washington, D.C.: National Council for the Social Studies.

Addressing Multiple Learning Styles

With the advent of the 1980s and throughout the past 15 years, new discoveries about the inner workings and development of the brain and the nature of intelligence have replaced traditional beliefs that intelligence is entirely predetermined at birth. One of the most noted theories, advanced by Howard Gardner, is the theory of multiple intelligences, which contends that there are at least eight forms of intelligence that help us understand the world around us.

MULTIPLE LEARNING STYLES

Glencoe's *World History: The Human Experience* provides you with a chapter activity for eight types of intelligences in each **Chapter Planning Guide**.

1 Verbal/Linguistic Learners

Students who exhibit this intelligence can argue, persuade, entertain, or instruct others effectively with words. They read regularly, can write clearly, and easily understand the written word. They retain facts readily, and love to play with the sounds of language.

Teachers can help develop this intelligence by using overhead projectors to convey information, providing audiocassettes for Chapter Digests, as well as assigning reading and writing. Writing a journal, like the **Your History Journal** in *World History: The Human Experience*, will exercise linguistic intelligence.

2 Logical/ Mathematical Learners

Students who exhibit this intelligence demonstrate the ability to reason, sequence, identify cause and effect, and create hypotheses. They see numerical patterns and can spot conceptual irregularities. They generally have a very rational outlook toward life, and love to develop "what if" scenarios.

Teachers can help develop this intelligence by discussing the pros and cons of important decisions made in world history and eliciting rationales for each side. To exercise this intelligence, students, for example, could sequence events in the **Time Line Activities** booklet.

3 Visual/Spatial Learners

Students who exhibit this intelligence think in terms of pictures and images. They are acutely aware of visual details and need to draw or sketch their ideas graphically. They easily see three-dimensional space and can transform content into images.

Teachers can help develop this intelligence by planning videodisc and CD-ROM presentations or by assigning readings in the *NATIONAL GEOGRAPHIC Magazine*, which depicts historical events with beautiful illustrations.

4 Auditory/Musical Learners

Students who exhibit this intelligence can produce rhythms and melodies. They sing in tune, keep time to music, and listen perceptively to different kinds of music. They can discern subtle differences in sounds and have "good ears."

Teachers can help develop this intelligence by incorporating more technology into lessons. Having students listen to the **Chapter Digests Audiocassettes** will exercise this intelligence. CD-ROMs also provide students with instant auditory directions and feedback.

5 Kinesthetic Learners

Students who exhibit this intelligence coordinate their body movements well, must move their bodies frequently, and can maneuver objects with skill. They have good tactile sensitivity, needing to touch things in order to learn about them, and can sense with their physical body.

Teachers can help develop this intelligence by asking students to perform basic tasks, such as constructing models, charts, or graphs that apply new knowledge. Students also practice new skills by using the **Interactive Tutor Self-Assessment Software**.

6 Interpersonal Learners

Students who exhibit this intelligence understand and work well with other people. They demonstrate abilities to perceive others' moods, intentions, and desires. They can comfortably step into another's perspective of the world. Many class leaders have this intelligence.

Teachers can help develop this intelligence by integrating **History Simulations** and **Cooperative Learning Activities** into their plans. In such settings, students can seek help from another student or learn with a partner.

7 Intrapersonal Learners

Students who exhibit this intelligence can easily assess their own feelings, are very introspective, and enjoy meditation and soul-searching. They use their self-understanding to guide their lives and can be very goal-directed. They can be fiercely independent and highly self-disciplined. These students are likely to have opinions that set them apart from others and prefer to work alone. They take themselves very seriously yet have a realistic understanding of their strengths and weaknesses.

Teachers can help develop this intelligence by encouraging the use of a personal journal, asking for students' opinions on important issues, and encouraging the reading of autobiographies and biographies of important historical figures, such as those featured in **People in World History**. Analyzing the traits of figures who have been successful will help students analyze their own personal strengths.

8 Naturalist Learners

Students who exhibit this intelligence are able to observe, understand, and organize patterns in the natural environment. These skills of observing, collecting, and categorizing are also useful in the "human" environment to collect data and classify information.

Teachers can help develop this intelligence by integrating **Geography and History Activities, History Simulations,** and **Chapter Themes Graphic Organizers** into their plans.

What multiple intelligences mean to history teachers is that you must assign activities to students that accommodate their strongest intelligences but frequently exercise their weakest intelligences. Although students may experience some difficulty by engaging in work from a different domain, they can strengthen the weaker intelligence over time. And by stretching their comfort zones, you help them strengthen their overall thinking and problem-solving abilities.

The resources available in *World History: The Human Experience* guarantee that your classroom will be a multisensory environment, providing multiple paths for student learning.

Other Program Resources

Rely on these additional resources to help you provide for individual student needs.

Teacher's Wraparound Edition
- Multiple Learning Styles Chapter Activities
- Cooperative Learning Activities
- Key to Ability Levels
- Meeting Special Needs Activities

■ For Further Professional Reading

Armstrong, T. 1993. *Seven Kinds of Smart: Identifying and Developing Your Many Intelligences.* New York: Plume/Penguin Books Inc.

Csikszentmihalyi, M., K. Rathunde, and S. Whalen. 1993. *Talented Teenagers: The Roots of Success and Failure.* New York: Cambridge University Press.

Gardner, H. G. 1993. *Multiple Intelligences: The Theory in Practice.* New York: Basic Books, Inc.

Kagan, S. 1990. *Cooperative Learning: Resources for Teachers.* San Juan Capistrano, Calif.: Resources for Teachers.

Implementing Block Scheduling

Advantages for Schools

For the schools themselves, the greatest advantage of block scheduling is a better use of resources. The schedule change does not require additional teachers or classrooms. It eliminates half of the time needed for class changes, which results in fewer discipline problems. Schools also report an increase in the overall quality of teacher instruction and student's time on task.

Advantages for Teachers

With block scheduling, teachers instruct fewer students each term, so students and teachers get to know each other better, and relationships improve. Teachers have time to provide additional one-on-one help and other resources for meeting the individual needs of students. Because block scheduling cuts in half the time needed for introducing and closing classes, teachers have more time to teach the key concepts of their discipline and become more focused themselves. Some schools report improved teacher morale, increased teacher effectiveness, and decreased burn-out.

Block scheduling results in more frequent use of varied teaching approaches and more student-centered environments. Teachers venture away from discussion and lecture and use more productive models of teaching. Flexibility allows more opportunities for cooperative teaching strategies such as team teaching and interdisciplinary studies. Block scheduling also encourages activity-centered instruction; in Glencoe's *World History: The Human Experience* Teacher's Wraparound Edition, such activities and research projects are specially coded for block schedules.

Advantages for Students

Student success rate is greater in a block scheduling format because students interact more with their teachers and the content, learning more and retaining it longer. Students develop better problem-solving skills because they have more time to think.

In a block students study fewer subjects each term, making them better able to manage their workload.

Students experience fewer outside distractions and are better able to concentrate. They voice that there is more time to learn and more time to ask questions.

Students maximize use of the curriculum with a block schedule. They schedule required courses during the first term, and, if they do not pass the course, they can repeat it during the second term. Better students move ahead more quickly; block scheduling increases the number of students who take upper-level classes and earn advanced studies diplomas.

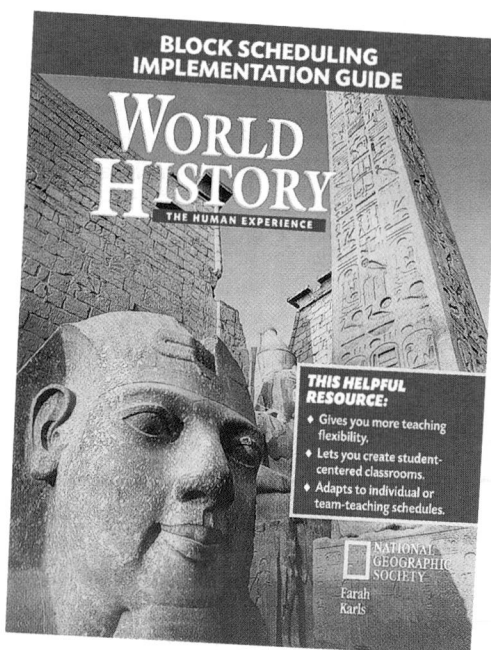

Utilizing Performance Assessment

Traditionally, in the social studies classroom, assessment has been at the end of study to measure how well students have learned the objectives of the unit of study. But today, in order to prepare students for future success in the adult world, more authentic forms of assessment, consisting of ongoing demonstrations of worthwhile, meaningful tasks, are in order.

Traditional Measures

Glencoe's *World History: The Human Experience* provides you with both types of assessment. Traditional forms—**Chapter and Unit Tests**, **Section Quizzes**, and **Testmaker Software**—are available to evaluate knowledge of factual content and some forms of thinking skills.

Performance Measures

The alternative measures most often utilized by classroom teachers are projects, teacher observation, performance-based essays, and portfolios.

Tasks may be divided into two broad types: teacher-directed tasks and student-directed tasks. In **teacher-directed tasks**, students may be guided step-by-step through various phases of a task. For example, the teacher leads the class in brainstorming, but when students realize that they do not have enough information in order to be successful, the teacher serves as coach or facilitator.

Student-directed tasks are typically used at the end of a unit of study in the place of or in concert with traditional tests. The teacher explains clearly what is expected of the students in process and product and makes known the essential criteria.

Journals are often used as performance assessment because they contain samples of students' work collected over a period of time—often an entire grading period or even a semester. **Your History Journal**, assigned at the beginning of every chapter, provides students an opportunity not only to find information but also to make sense of it and put that information in context. The most common form of assessing authentic performance is by rubric, or by percent or points. You determine the components of the product, process, or task, and weight the completion of each according to its merits.

A three-point rubric would show Score Point One as unacceptable performance and Score Point Three as completely successful. Each chapter's **Performance Assessment Activity**, suggested in *World History: The Human Experience*, is accompanied with possible rubric features to help you plan your assessment strategies.

Other Resources

Rely on these additional resources to help students prepare portfolio items for assessment.

Teacher's Wraparound Edition
- Performance Assessment Activities
- Extra Credit Project

Classroom Resources
- Performance Assessment Strategies and Activities
- Interactive Tutor Self-Assessment Software

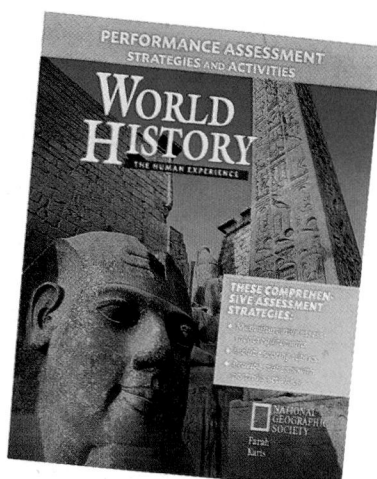

Using Technology in the Classroom

Advances in technology continually debut, and Glencoe has developed many programs for successful integration of technology into your classroom.

Software

Interactive Tutor Self-Assessment Software This new assessment product is a highly motivational program that allows students to check their comprehension by answering questions using the computer. If a student chooses a wrong answer, the computer explains why the choice is incorrect and the student tries again. This continues until the student answers correctly. Chapter Summaries and a Glossary are also integrated in this software. In addition, a robust Teacher Management System allows you to track student and class progress.

Testmaker Glencoe's Testmaker allows you to customize tests to fit your students' special needs. The software allows you to edit, reorder, and add questions as you desire and is available in Macintosh and DOS.

Vocabulary PuzzleMaker Vocabulary development and comprehension is an important part of social studies instruction. Glencoe has developed a special Vocabulary PuzzleMaker that helps you create high-interest crossword puzzles and word searches.

The National Geographic Society has prize-winning resources. Fascinating audio and video clips exhibit history, languages, music, and cultural traditions of nations and civilizations.

Picture Atlas of the World

PictureShow CD-ROMs
- **Egypt and the Fertile Crescent**
- **India and China**
- **Greece and Rome**
- **The Middle Ages**
- **The Renaissance**
- **Age of Exploration**

Videodiscs

If your school has a basic system consisting of a videodisc player and a television receiver, the videodiscs provide an effective and interesting tool for classroom presentations.

MindJogger Videoquiz The Mind-Jogger Videoquiz uses a game show format for review of key concepts. A bar code scanner allows you immediate access to specific chapters on the videodisc. The bar codes are placed on the Chapter Opener and Chapter Assessment pages of the Teacher's Wraparound Edition. The MindJogger Videoquiz is also available in a VHS format.

- **STV: World Geography**
- **STV: North America**
- **STV: Maya**

 The following videodiscs help students in their understanding of world history.

- **Turning Points in World History**
- **In the Holy Land**
- **Lessons of War**
- **Communism and the Cold War**

Computer Training for Teachers

You must have a general knowledge of computer operation, but you do not need to have a knowledge of internal hardware elements or programming languages. Call Glencoe's software hotline as your best resource when using any type of software.

■ For Further Professional Reading

Brady, H. R. 1994. "Overview of Computer Integration Into Social Studies Instruction." *Social Education* (58): 312.

Jonassen, D. H. 1996. *Computers in the Classroom: Mindtools for Critical Thinking.* Englewood Cliffs, N.J.: Prentice Hall

Surfing the History Net

You can join three history list servers:

- Send this message **Subscribe NCSS-L Your Name** to listproc2@bgu.edu to share information and ideas about K–12 social studies education, sponsored by the Instructional Technology Committee of the National Council for the Social Studies.
- Send **sub H-High-S Your Name Your School** to LIST SERV@msu.edu for inclusion in an ongoing discussion of curriculum, instructional strategies, and educational resources involved in teaching history.
- Send **Sub Histnews Your Name** to listserv@ukanvm. cc.ukans.edu for a newsletter for historians.

Access **Student Activities**, **Teaching Strategies**, and **Updated Information** at:

glencoe.socialstudies.com

The Internet

Think of the Internet as similar to using the telephone. If you know the name of the computer you want to contact, you look up its number, have your computer dial it, and talk to it. Sending messages from person to person is one of the Net's most popular uses. You can reach a specific person by using E-mail, be on a list server that sends information to its subscribers, or you can subscribe to bulletin boards where messages are posted for all to read. The Internet, however, is used for much more than just receiving and sending messages.

World Wide Web

Getting information through the Internet became much easier with the development of the World Wide Web in 1992. The Web is an exciting region of the Internet that contains pictures, sound, and video as well as text. You can scan the Web using "browsers"— programs such as Netscape and Mosaic. You can go directly to one of the million sources of information if you know an address called the Uniform Reference Locator (URL).

Online Resources

Each Chapter Planning Guide in *World History: The Human Experience* offers you easy-to-use Internet Connections. In addition to this unique feature, you may also wish to use the following Internet sites.

Online resources for world history teachers are limitless. Sites are listed below with their URLs. When you type the address, you will reach the organization's "homepage," which tells you what is available at its site. Some are clearinghouses for other sources.

- **Armadillo from Rice University**
  http://chico.rice.edu/ armadillo/about.html

- **CNN**
  http://www.cnn.com

- **ERIC Clearinghouses**
  http://ericir.syr.edu

- **Library of Congress**
  http://lcweb.loc.gov/ homepage/lchp.html

- **Western European Studies (since 1945) Homepage**
  http://www.pitt.edu/ ~wwwes/

- **Yahoo**
  http://www.yahoo.com/

The following sites are particularly relevant to world history:

- **Interactive Communication Simulations, which is geared for students of global education**
  http://ics.soe.umich.edu/

- **EuroDocs for primary historical documents**
  http://library.byu.edu/ ~rdh/eurodocs/

- **Medieval Studies**
  http://sunsite.berkeley. edu/OMACL/

- **Program in International Educational Resources**
  http://www.yale.edu/ pieris

- **Asian Institute of Technology, Bangkok, Thailand**
  http://www.ait.ac.th/

- **Resources on Japan**
  http://www.indiana.edu/ ~japan/odata.html

- **Resources on Africa**
  http://www.sas.upenn.edu /African_Studies/ Home_Page/Country.html

- **Resources on Egypt**
  http://www.egypt.com

- **Gateway to History**
  http://www.hartford-hwp.com/gateway/

Newspapers from other countries summarize daily news:

German News in English
http://www.mathematik. uni-ulm.de/germnews (in German)
http://www.mathematik. uni-ulm.de/de-news/ (in English)

China Daily
http://www.chinadaily. com.cn/

The Times (London)
http://www.the-times.co.uk/

Correlation to NCSS Ten Thematic Strands

In *Curriculum Standards for Social Studies: Expectations of Excellence,* the National Council for the Social Studies (NCSS) identified ten themes that serve as organizing strands for the social studies curriculum at every school level. These themes are interrelated and draw from all of the social science disciplines. Below is a correlation chart showing where the social studies themes are incorporated in *World History: The Human Experience.*

Social Studies Theme	Incorporated Within *World History: The Human Experience*			
I. Culture				
Human beings create, learn, and adapt culture. Human cultures are dynamic systems of beliefs, values, and traditions that exhibit both commonalities and differences. Understanding culture helps us understand ourselves and others.	Ch. 1; S. 2, 3 Ch. 2 Ch. 3 Ch. 4; S. 1, 4 Ch. 5 Ch. 6; S. 1, 3, 4 Ch. 7; S. 1, 2 Ch. 8 Ch. 9; S. 2, 3	Ch. 10; S. 1, 2, 3 Ch. 11; S. 1, 3 Ch. 12; S. 1, 3 Ch. 13; S. 1, 2, 4 Ch. 14 Ch. 15; S. 2, 3 Ch. 16 Ch. 17; S. 7 Ch. 18	Ch. 19; S. 1, 2, 3, 5 Ch. 20 Ch. 21; S. 1, 2, 4 Ch. 22; S. 2, 3, 4 Ch. 23; S. 1, 4 Ch. 24; S. 1, 3, 4 Ch. 25; S. 1, 3 Ch. 26; S. 3 Ch. 27; S. 1, 2	Ch. 29; S. 1, 4 Ch. 28; S. 4 Ch. 30; S. 2, 4 Ch. 32; S. 4 Ch. 33; S. 2, 5 Ch. 35; S. 2, 3 Ch. 36; S. 1 Ch. 37; S. 1, 4
II. Time, Continuity, and Change				
Human beings seek to understand their historic roots and to locate themselves in time. Such understanding involves knowing what things were like in the past and how things change and develop—allowing us to develop historic perspective and answer important questions about our current condition.	Ch. 1 Ch. 2 Ch. 3 Ch. 4; S. 1 Ch. 6; S. 1, 4 Ch. 7; S. 1 Ch. 8; S. 1 Ch. 9; S. 1	Ch. 10; S. 1 Ch. 11; S. 1 Ch. 12; S. 1 Ch. 14 Ch. 15 Ch. 16; S. 1 Ch. 17; S. 1, 3 Ch. 20	Ch. 21; S. 1, 3, 4 Ch. 22; S. 1, 3 Ch. 23 Ch. 24 Ch. 27; S. 1 Ch. 28; S. 1, 2, 4, 5 Ch. 29; S. 1 Ch. 30	Ch.31; S. 3, 5 Ch. 32; S. 1 Ch. 33; S. 1 Ch. 34; S. 1 Ch. 35; S. 3 Ch. 36; S. 1 Ch. 37
III. People, Places, and Environment				
Technological advancements have insured that students are aware of the world beyond their personal locations. As students study content related to this theme, they create their spatial views and geographic perspectives of the world; social, cultural, economic, and civic demands mean that students will need such knowledge, skills, and understandings to make informed and critical decisions about the relationship between human beings and their environment.	Ch. 33; S. 2 Ch. 34; S. 3 Ch. 35; S. 3 Ch. 36; S. 1 Ch. 37; S. 5 Ch. 7; S. 1, 3	Ch. 2 Ch. 3; S. 1, 2 Ch. 4; S. 1, 2, 3 Ch. 5; S. 3 Ch. 6; S. 1 Ch. 15; S. 1, 2	Ch. 10; S. 1, 3 Ch. 11; S. 1 Ch. 12; S. 2 Ch. 13; S. 2 Ch. 14; S. 1, 4 Ch. 32; S. 2	Ch. 21; S. 3 Ch. 23; S. 1, 2, 5 Ch. 24; S. 3 Ch. 26; S. 3, 5 Ch. 27; S. 1, 3
IV. Individual Development and Identity				
Personal identity is shaped by one's culture, by groups, and by institutional influences. Examination of various forms of human behavior enhances understanding of the relationships between social norms and emerging personal identities, the social processes which influence identity formation, and the ethical principles underlying individual action.	Ch. 1; S. 3 Ch. 2 Ch. 3 Ch. 4; S. 2 Ch. 5; S. 1, 2 Ch. 6; S. 3, 4 Ch. 7; S. 1 Ch. 8; S. 1, 2	Ch. 9; S. 2, 3 Ch. 10 Ch. 11; S. 1, 3 Ch. 12; S. 2, 3 Ch. 15 Ch. 16; S. 1, 4, 5 Ch. 17; S. 3 Ch. 20; S. 2, 3	Ch. 21; S. 1, 3, 4 Ch. 22; S. 2, 3 Ch. 23; S. 1, 3, 4 Ch. 24; S. 1, 3 Ch. 28; S. 1, 3, 4 Ch. 29; S. 1 Ch. 30 Ch. 31; S. 1, 3, 4	Ch. 32; S. 1 Ch. 34; S. 3 Ch. 35; S. 3 Ch. 36; S. 1 Ch. 37

Ch. = Chapter   S. = Section

V. Individuals, Groups, and Institutions

Institutions exert enormous influence over us. Institutions are organizational embodiments to further the core social values of those who comprise them. It is important for students to know how institutions are formed, what controls and influences them, how they control and influence individuals and culture, and how institutions can be maintained or changed.

Ch. 1; S. 3	Ch. 11; S. 1, 2	Ch. 21	Ch. 32
Ch. 2	Ch. 12; S. 1, 3, 4	Ch. 22	Ch. 33
Ch. 3	Ch. 13; S. 2, 3, 4	Ch. 23; S. 4	Ch. 34
Ch. 4; S. 2	Ch. 14	Ch. 25	Ch. 35
Ch. 6; S. 1, 3, 4	Ch. 15	Ch. 26	Ch. 36
Ch. 7; S. 1, 2	Ch. 16; S. 4, 5	Ch. 28; S. 4	Ch. 37
Ch. 8; S. 1, 3	Ch. 17; S. 2	Ch. 29; S. 2, 3, 4	
Ch. 9; S. 1	Ch. 18	Ch. 30	
Ch. 10; S. 2, 3	Ch. 19	Ch. 31; S.1, 3, 5	

VI. Power, Authority, and Governance

Understanding of the historical development of structures of power, authority, and governance and their evolving functions in contemporary society is essential for the emergence of civic competence.

Ch. 1; S. 3	Ch. 9; S. 1	Ch. 18	Ch. 29; S. 2, 3, 4
Ch. 2	Ch. 10	Ch. 19	Ch. 30
Ch. 3	Ch. 11; S. 2	Ch. 21	Ch. 32
Ch. 4	Ch. 12; S. 1, 4	Ch. 22	Ch. 33
Ch. 5; S. 3	Ch. 14	Ch. 25	Ch. 34
Ch. 6; S. 1, 2, 3, 5	Ch. 15	Ch. 26	Ch. 35
Ch. 7	Ch. 16; S. 1, 4, 5	Ch. 27; S. 2, 3, 4	
Ch. 8; S. 3	Ch. 17; S. 2	Ch. 28; S. 4	

VII. Production, Distribution, and Consumption

Decisions about exchange, trade, and economic policy and well-being are global in scope, and the role of government in policy making varies over time and from place to place. The systematic study of an interdependent world economy and the role of technology in economic decision making is essential.

Ch. 1; S. 3	Ch. 12; S. 2	Ch. 22; S. 1, 2, 4	Ch. 32
Ch. 2; S. 1, 2, 3	Ch. 13; S. 2	Ch. 23; S. 1, 2, 4	Ch. 33; S. 1, 3
Ch. 3; S. 1, 3	Ch. 14; S. 2, 4	Ch. 24; S. 1	Ch. 34; S. 2, 3
Ch. 4; S. 2, 3, 4	Ch. 15; S. 2, 3	Ch. 25; S. 4, 5	Ch. 35; S. 1, 2, 3
Ch. 6; S. 3, 5	Ch. 16; S. 1, 2	Ch. 26; S. 3	Ch. 36; S. 1, 2, 4
Ch. 7; S. 2	Ch. 17; S. 1, 3	Ch. 27; S. 1, 2	Ch. 37; S. 1, 2, 3, 5
Ch. 9; S. 1, 3	Ch. 18; S. 2, 3, 4	Ch. 28; S. 1, 4, 5	
Ch. 10; S. 2	Ch. 19; S. 1, 2, 3	Ch. 29	
Ch. 11; S. 3	Ch. 21; S. 1, 2, 3	Ch. 30; S. 4, 5	

VIII. Science, Technology, and Society

Technology is as old as the first crude tool invented by prehistoric humans, and modern life as we know it would be impossible without technology and the science which supports it. Today's technology forms the basis for some of our most difficult social choices.

Ch. 1; S. 2, 3	Ch. 10; S. 2	Ch. 20; S. 1, 2	Ch. 30; S. 4
Ch. 2; S. 1, 2	Ch. 11; S. 3	Ch. 22; S. 3	Ch. 31; S. 2, 4, 5
Ch. 3; S. 2, 3	Ch. 13; S. 3	Ch. 23; S. 1, 2, 3	Ch. 32; S. 3, 4
Ch. 4; S. 3	Ch. 14; S. 2	Ch. 24; S. 2, 3	Ch. 33; S. 1, 2
Ch. 5; S. 2, 3	Ch. 15; S. 2	Ch. 26; S. 3	Ch. 37; S. 5
Ch. 6; S. 3	Ch. 16; S. 1	Ch. 27; S. 4	
Ch. 8; S. 2, 3	Ch. 17; S. 1	Ch. 28; S. 3	
Ch. 9; S. 1, 3	Ch. 19; S. 5	Ch. 29; S. 1	

IX. Global Connections

The realities of global interdependence require understanding of the increasingly important and diverse global connections among world societies before there can be analysis leading to the development of possible solutions to persisting and emerging global issues.

Ch. 1	Ch. 7; S. 2, 3	Ch. 13; S. 1	Ch. 24; S. 4
Ch. 2	Ch. 8; S. 2	Ch. 14; S. 3	Ch. 3; S. 1, 3
Ch. 9; S. 3	Ch. 16; S. 2, 4	Ch. 25; S. 2	Ch. 27; S. 1
Ch. 4; S. 2	Ch. 10; S. 3	Ch. 17; S. 2	Ch. 33; S. 6
Ch. 5; S. 3	Ch. 11; S. 2, 3	Ch. 18; S. 2, 3, 4	Ch. 35; S. 3
Ch. 6; S. 3, 4	Ch. 12; S. 2, 3	Ch. 22; S. 4	Ch. 37; S. 5

X. Civic Ideals and Practices

All people have a stake in examining civic ideals and practices across time, in diverse societies, as well as in determining how to close the gap between present practices and the ideals upon which our democratic republic is based. An understanding of civic ideals and practices of citizenship is critical to full participation in society.

Ch. 2; S. 1, 2	Ch. 10; S. 1, 3	Ch. 20; S. 2, 3	Ch. 30
Ch. 3	Ch. 11; S. 1, 2	Ch. 21	Ch. 31; S. 1, 2, 3, 5
Ch. 4; S. 1, 2, 3	Ch. 12; S. 1, 2, 4	Ch. 22; S. 1, 2, 4	Ch. 32; S. 2, 3, 4
Ch. 5; S. 2, 3	Ch. 13; S. 2, 3	Ch. 25; S. 1, 2, 3, 5	Ch. 33; S. 1, 2, 5, 6
Ch. 6; S. 1, 2, 3, 5	Ch. 14	Ch. 26	Ch. 34; S. 1, 2
Ch. 7; S. 2	Ch. 15; S. 2, 3	Ch. 28; S. 2, 3, 4	Ch. 35
Ch. 9; S. 1, 2	Ch. 19	Ch. 29	Ch. 36

Six Alternative Course Outlines

World History: The Human Experience may be taught in a variety of courses.
Listed below are six examples.

OUTLINE 1 World History Survey

Unit 1 The Rise of Civilizations Chapters 1, 2, 3
Unit 2 Flowering of Civilizations Chapters 4, 5, 6, 7, 8, 9
Unit 3 Regional Civilizations Chapters 10, 11, 12, 13, 14, 15
Unit 4 Emergence of the Modern World Chapters 16, 17, 18, 19
Unit 5 Age of Revolution Chapters 20, 21, 22
Unit 6 Industry and Nationalism Chapters 23, 24, 25, 26, 27
Unit 7 World in Conflict Chapters 28, 29, 30, 31
Unit 8 The Contemporary World Chapters 32, 33, 34, 35, 36, 37

OUTLINE 2 Western Civilization

Unit 2 Flowering of Civilizations Chapters 4, 5, 6
Unit 3 Regional Civilizations Chapters 12, 13
Unit 4 Emergence of the Modern World Chapters 16, 17, 19
Unit 5 Age of Revolution Chapters 20, 21, 22
Unit 6 Industry and Nationalism Chapters 23, 24, 25, 26
Unit 7 World in Conflict Chapters 28, 29, 31
Unit 8 The Contemporary World Chapters 32, 37

OUTLINE 3 Non-Western Civilization

Unit 1 The Rise of Civilizations Chapters 1, 2, 3
Unit 2 Flowering of Civilizations Chapters 7, 8, 9
Unit 3 Regional Civilizations Chapters 10, 11, 14, 15
Unit 4 Emergence of the Modern World Chapter 18
Unit 6 Industry and Nationalism Chapter 27
Unit 7 World in Conflict Chapter 30
Unit 8 The Contemporary World Chapters 33 34, 35

Scope and Sequence

Historical Themes

Students need to understand and be able to recognize the themes that appear throughout history. Students also need to develop the ability to apply these themes as they examine the effect of the past on the present and the future.

The central theme highlighted in each section appears in red. Related themes are listed in black.

Content Knowledge

Students need to have a knowledge of the disciplines that play an integral role in the social studies: history, literature, art and culture, science and technology, government and civics, geography, economics, and religion. Students also need to develop a keen understanding of how these subjects interact with one another.

Skills

These are the skills taught in the Chapter *Skills*. Each skill is reinforced in the *Skill Practice* found in the Chapter Assessments and in the **Skill Reinforcement Activities** booklet in the TCR.

Chapter	1	2	3	4
Movement	Sections 1, 2	Sections 1, 2, 4	Sections 1, 3	Sections 1, 2
Innovation	Sections 2, 3	Sections 1, 2, 4	Sections 1, 2	Section 1
Conflict/ Cooperation		Sections 1, 2	Sections 2, 3	Sections 3, 4
Revolution/ Reaction		Section 1		Section 2
Change	Sections 2, 3	Section 1	Section 2	
Diversity/ Uniformity		Section 1	Sections 1, 2, 3	Section 1
Cultural Diffusion		Sections 1, 2, 3, 4	Sections 1, 3	Section 2
Relation to Environment	Sections 1, 2, 3	Sections 1, 2, 3, 4	Sections 1, 2	Sections 1, 2, 3
Regionalism/ Nationalism/ Internationalism		Sections 1, 2, 3, 4	Section 3	Sections 1, 3
Literature, Art, and Culture	Sections 2, 3	Sections 1, 2, 3, 4	Sections 1, 2, 3	Sections 1, 4
Science and Technology	Sections 2, 3	Sections 1, 2	Sections 2, 3	Section 3
Geography and Environment	Sections 1, 2, 3	Sections 1, 2, 3, 4	Sections 1, 2, 3	Sections 1, 2, 3
Economics	Section 3	Sections 1, 2, 3	Sections 1, 3	Sections 2, 3, 4
Government/ Civics	Section 3	Sections 1, 2, 3, 4	Sections 1, 2, 3	Sections 1, 2, 3
Religion	Section 2	Sections 1, 2, 3, 4	Sections 2, 3	Section 1
Skill Category	*Social Studies Skill*	*Critical Thinking Skill*	*Critical Thinking Skill*	*Critical Thinking Skill*
Specific Skill	Understanding Map Projections	Classifying Information	Problem Solving	Making Comparisons

5	6	7	8	9	10	11
Section 3	Sections 2, 3, 5	Section 1	Sections 1, 2, 3	Section 1	Section 3	Sections 1, 2
Sections 1, 2	Section 4	Section 3	Section 2	Section 2	Section 2	Section 1
Section 3	Sections 2, 5	Section 1		Section 1	Sections 1, 2	Sections 1, 2
	Section 5					
	Sections 1, 5				Section 3	
Section 3	Sections 1, 3	Section 3	Section 2	Section 1	Section 3	Section 2
Section 3	Sections 3, 4	Sections 2, 3	Sections 2, 3	Section 3	Section 3	Sections 2, 3
Section 3	Section 1	Sections 1, 3	Section 1		Sections 1, 3	Section 1
Section 3	Section 2		Section 3		Section 3	
Sections 1, 2, 3	Sections 1, 3	Section 1	Sections 1, 2, 3	Section 3	Sections 1, 2	Section 3
Sections 2, 3	Section 3		Sections 2, 3	Sections 1, 3	Section 2	Section 3
Section 3	Sections 1, 2	Sections 1, 2, 3	Section 1		Sections 1, 3	Section 1
	Sections 3, 5	Section 2		Sections 1, 3	Section 2	Section 3
Sections 2, 3	Sections 1, 2, 3, 5	Section 2	Section 3	Sections 1, 2	Sections 1, 3	Sections 1, 2
Section 1	Sections 1, 4	Sections 1, 2	Sections 1, 2, 3	Section 2	Sections 1, 2, 3	Section 1
Social Studies Skill	*Critical Thinking Skill*	*Critical Thinking Skill*	*Critical Thinking Skill*	*Critical Thinking Skill*	*Critical Thinking Skill*	*Social Studies Skill*
Finding Exact Location on a Map	Decision Making	Interpreting Point of View	Determining Cause and Effect	Identifying Central Issues	Distinguishing Between Fact and Opinion	Interpreting Demographic Data

Scope and Sequence

	12	13	14	15	16	17
Movement	Section 1		Sections 1, 2	Section 1	Sections 1, 2, 4, 5	Section 2
Innovation		Section 2	Section 4	Section 2	Section 1	Section 1
Conflict/ Cooperation	Sections 2, 3, 4	Sections 1, 3, 4	Sections 1, 3, 4		Sections 3, 4	Section 2
Revolution/ Reaction		Section 4			Section 5	Section 3
Change		Section 2		Section 3	Sections 1, 5	Section 3
Diversity/ Uniformity	Sections 1, 3	Section 3	Sections 2, 3			Section 2
Cultural Diffusion	Section 4	Section 1	Section 3		Sections 2, 4	Sections 1, 2
Relation to Environment	Section 2	Section 2	Sections 1, 4	Sections 1, 2		Sections 1, 2
Regionalism/ Nationalism/ Internationalism	Section 4	Sections 2, 3, 4	Section 1	Section 3		
Literature, Art, and Culture		Section 2	Sections 1, 2, 4	Section 2	Sections 1, 2, 3	
Science and Technology		Section 3	Section 2	Section 2	Section 1	Section 1
Geography and Environment	Section 2	Section 2	Sections 1, 4	Sections 1, 2		Sections 1, 2
Economics	Section 2	Section 2	Sections 2, 4	Sections 2, 3	Sections 1, 2	Sections 1, 3
Government/ Civics	Sections 1, 2, 4	Sections 2, 3	Sections 1, 2, 3, 4	Sections 2, 3	Section 1	Section 2
Religion	Sections 1, 3	Sections 1, 4	Sections 3, 4	Sections 2, 3	Sections 1, 2, 3, 4, 5	Section 3
Skill Category	*Critical Thinking Skill*	*Social Studies Skill*	*Critical Thinking Skill*	*Critical Thinking Skill*	*Critical Thinking Skill*	*Technology Skill*
Specific Skill	Making Inferences	Analyzing Historical Maps	Making Generalizations	Analyzing Primary and Secondary Sources	Identifying Evidence	Using a Computerized Card Catalog

18	19	20	21	22	23	24
Section 1	Section 3	Section 3	Section 2	Sections 4, 5	Sections 2, 3	Section 3
	Section 5	Sections 1, 2			Sections 2, 3	Sections 2, 3, 4
Section 1	Sections 1, 2, 3, 4, 5	Section 2	Sections 1, 3	Sections 2, 3, 4, 5	Section 4	
Sections 1, 3	Sections 4, 5	Section 3	Sections 2, 4	Sections 1, 3, 5	Sections 2, 3	
Sections 1, 4	Section 2	Section 1	Section 2	Sections 2, 3, 4	Sections 2, 3	Section 1
	Sections 1, 3					
Sections 2, 3, 4				Section 4		Section 4
			Section 3		Sections 1, 2, 5	Section 3
	Sections 1, 2, 3		Section 3	Sections 4, 5		
Section 2	Sections 2, 3	Section 3	Section 4	Sections 2, 3	Sections 1, 4	Sections 1, 3, 4
	Section 5	Sections 1, 2		Section 3	Sections 1, 2. 3, 4	Sections 2, 3
	Sections 4, 5		Section 3	Sections 4, 5	Sections 1, 2, 5	Section 3
Sections 2, 3, 4	Sections 1, 2, 3, 5		Sections 1, 2, 3	Sections 1, 2, 3, 4	Sections 1, 2, 4	Section 1
Sections 1, 2, 3	Sections 1, 2, 3, 4, 5	Sections 2, 3	Sections 1, 2, 3, 4	Sections 1, 2, 3, 4		Section 1
Sections 1, 3	Sections 1, 2, 3, 5	Sections 1, 2, 3	Sections 1, 2	Sections 2, 3, 4		
Technology Skill	*Critical Thinking Skill*	*Technology Skill*	*Study and Writing Skill*	*Social Studies Skill*	*Critical Thinking Skill*	*Technology Skill*
Using a Word Processor	Recognizing a Stereotype	Developing Multimedia Presentations	Outlining	Interpreting Graphs	Detecting Bias	Using E-Mail

Scope and Sequence

	25	26	27	28	29	30
Movement	Section 2		Sections 1, 2			Section 4
Innovation	Section 4	Section 3	Section 4	Section 3	Sections 1, 3	Section 4
Conflict/ Cooperation	Sections 2, 3, 4	Sections 1, 2, 4	Sections 3, 4	Sections 1, 2, 3, 4, 5		Sections 1, 2, 3, 4
Revolution/ Reaction	Section 3	Sections 4, 5	Section 3	Section 4		Section 3
Change	Sections 1, 4	Sections 3, 4	Section 2	Sections 4, 5	Section 2	Sections 2, 5
Diversity/ Uniformity		Section 5		Section 5	Sections 3, 4	
Cultural Diffusion	Section 2		Section 1			
Relation to Environment		Sections 3, 5	Sections 1, 3			
Regionalism/ Nationalism/ Internationalism	Section 5	Sections 1, 2	Sections 3, 4	Sections 1, 5	Section 1	Sections 1, 2, 5
Literature, Art, and Culture			Sections 2, 3		Sections 1, 4	Section 4
Science and Technology		Section 3	Section 4	Section 3	Section 1	Section 4
Geography and Environment	Sections 2, 4	Sections 3, 5	Sections 1, 3	Sections 3, 5		
Economics	Sections 4, 5	Section 3	Sections 1, 2	Sections 1, 4, 5	Sections 1, 2, 3, 4	Sections 4, 5
Government/ Civics	Sections 1, 2, 3, 5	Sections 1, 2, 3, 4, 5	Sections 1, 2, 3, 4,	Sections 2, 3, 4	Sections 1, 2, 3, 4	Sections 1, 2, 3, 4, 5
Religion	Sections 1, 3, 5	Section 3	Section 1	Section 4		Section 2
Skill Category	*Social Studies Skill*	*Study and Writing Skill*	*Technology Skill*	*Social Studies Skill*	*Critical Thinking Skill*	*Critical Thinking Skill*
Specific Skill	Reading a Cartogram	Selecting and Using Research Sources	Using the Internet	Interpreting Military Movements on Maps	Analyzing Political Cartoons	Identifying an Argument

31	32	33	34	35	36	37
Sections 1, 3				Section 2		Section 2
Section 5	Section 3					Section 5
Sections 2, 3, 4	Sections 1, 2, 4	Sections 3, 4, 5	Sections 1, 2	Sections 1, 2, 3	Sections 1, 2, 3, 4	Sections 1, 3, 4
		Section 2		Section 2	Sections 2, 3	Section 4
	Sections 1, 2, 4	Section 1	Sections 1, 2, 3		Sections 2, 4	Sections 1, 2
Section 3	Sections 2, 4	Section 5	Section 3			Sections 3, 5
		Section 6		Section 3		Section 5
	Section 2	Section 1	Section 3	Sections 1, 2	Section 1	Section 5
Section 1	Sections 2, 3, 4	Sections 3, 4, 6	Sections 1, 2, 3	Section 1	Sections 1, 2, 3, 4	Sections 1, 2, 3, 4, 5
	Section 4	Section 2		Section 3		Sections 1, 4
Sections 2, 4, 5	Sections 3, 4	Sections 1, 2				Section 5
	Sections 1, 2	Section 1	Section 3	Sections 1, 2	Section 1	Section 5
	Sections 1, 2, 3, 4	Sections 1, 3	Sections 2, 3	Sections 1, 2, 3	Sections 1, 2, 4	Sections 1, 2, 3, 5
Sections 1, 2, 5	Sections 2, 3, 4	Sections 1, 2, 5, 6	Sections 1, 2	Sections 1, 2, 3	Sections 1, 2, 3, 4	Sections 1, 2, 3, 4
		Section 5		Sections 2, 3	Section 1	Section 4
Critical Thinking Skill	*Social Studies Skill*	*Technology Skill*	*Study and Writing Skill*	*Study and Writing Skill*	*Technology Skill*	*Social Studies Skill*
Synthesizing Information	Understanding World Time Zones	Using a Spreadsheet	Writing a Research Report	Preparing a Bibliography	Developing a Database	Interpreting Statistics

World of Resources

NEW HELP for Teacher Planning!

Interactive Lesson Planner

Daily Lecture Notes
This free-standing desk accessory provides:

- detailed outline for each lesson
- lesson-extending background information
- discussion questions

The World – Physical/Political

GLENCOE

NSPARENCIES

INCLUDES:
- 147 high-interest transparencies
- Teaching Strategies
- Blackline Masters

World Music
Cultural Traditions

NSPARENCIES

THIS COMPREHENSIVE RESOURCE INCLUDES:
- 72 Mapping History Overlay Transparencies
- 37 Chapter Transp.
- 16 Unit Transp.
- Teaching and Act. transp.

GLENCOE
World Music
Cultural Traditions

World

ABCNEWS
INTERACTIVE

Lessons of War

ABCNEWS
INTERACTIVE

In the
Holy Land

ABCNEWS
INTERACTIVE

Communism and
the Cold War

ABCNEWS
INTERACTIVE

Turning Points in World H...

WORLD

WORLD
HISTORY
THE HUMAN EXPERIENCE

TEACHER'S ANNOTATED EDITION
BUILDING SKILLS IN
GEOGRAPHY

BUILDING SKILLS IN
GEOGRAPHY

FOODS
AROUND THE WORLD

WORLD LITERATURE
SELECTIONS
WORLD ART AND MUSIC
HISTORY SIMULATIONS
HISTORICAL SIGNIFICANCE
CHAPTER ACTIVITIES
SKILL REINFORCEMENT
ACTIVITIES
PEOPLE IN WORLD HISTORY
ENRICHMENT ACTIVITIES
CRITICAL THINKING ACTIVITIES
SOURCE READINGS
BLOCK SCHEDULING
REPRODUCIBLE LESSON PLANS
WORLD
HISTORY
THE HUMAN EXPERIENCE

PERFORMANCE ASSESSMENT
CHAPTER AND UNIT TESTS
FORMS A AND B
GUIDED READING ACTIVITIES
TIME LINE ACTIVITIES
CHAPTER THEMES
GRAPHIC ORGANIZERS
RETEACHING ACTIVITIES
VOCABULARY ACTIVITIES
MAPPING HISTORY ACTIVITIES
GEOGRAPHY AND HISTORY
ACTIVITIES
BAR CODE
CORRELATION GUIDE
WORLD
HISTORY
THE HUMAN EXPERIENCE

REPRODUCIBLE LESSON PLANS

WORLD
HISTORY
THE HUMAN EXPERIENCE

EASY-TO-USE PLANS LET YOU:
- Prepare for class in one easy step.
- Pinpoint chapter objectives.
- Integrate activities without extra preparation.

NATIONAL
GEOGRAPHIC
SOCIETY
Farah
Karls

Applications and Hands-On Activities

HISTORY SIMULATION 22

Where Do They Stand?

One of the reasons for France's difficulties during the late 1700s was the people's inability to reconcile the many different political opinions that existed. In this activity, students will examine a range of political opinions.

History Simulations:

- Make history relevant.
- Examine a variety of realistic problems.
- Provide opportunities for cooperative learning.

Name _____ Date _____ Class _____

HISTORY SIMULATION 22

HANDOUT MATERIAL

"Where Do They Stand?"—A Television Special

Select one of these individuals to be the subject of your interview:

- ☐ Louis XVI
- ☐ Maximilien Robespierre
- ☐ The Girondist leader
- ☐ One of the women who led the march for bread
- ☐ Napoleon Bonaparte
- ☐ George-Jacques Danton

Group Activity A	**Group Activity C**	**Group Activity E**
Draw your own version of the political opinion chart and any other visual materials you think would help your television special; fill in information on the chart as determined by your group.	Create questions to ask the person you will interview.	Select the news team who will conduct the interview.

Group Activity B	**Individual Activity D**	**Individual Activity F**
Write a description of the political position of the person your group selected to interview.	Select the person who acts as the political leader.	Select a timekeeper.

Group Assessment

When the activity is complete, your group will answer these questions:

1. Did the members of your group agree on the selection of the leader?
2. Did each member contribute ideas and participate in the activity?
3. Did group members work well together?
4. Was the information presented by the other groups clear to you? Why or why not?
5. Did you find this a helpful way to study this material? Why or why not?
6. What would you do to improve this assignment?

Name _____ Date _____ Class _____

Historical ActIVITY:22
Significance

Three Ways Napoleon Changed the World

Although assessments of Napoleon differ widely, no one denies that he was one of the most colorful and famous people in all of history. He was also among the most influential. Napoleon helped spread the ideas of the French Revolution throughout Europe. The passages below discuss three additional ways Napoleon changed the world. Read them and then answer the questions. Use a separate sheet of paper if necessary.

1. The Napoleonic Code

"One of Napoleon's reforms . . . was destined to have an impact far beyond the borders of France. That was the creation of the French civil code, the [Napoleonic Code]. In many ways the code embodied the ideals of the French Revolution. For example, under the code there were no privileges of birth, and all men were equal under the law. At the same time, the code was sufficiently close to the older French laws and customs to be acceptable to the French public and the legal profession. On the whole, the code was moderate, well organized, and written with commendable brevity and outstanding lucidity. As a result, the code has not only endured in France (the French civil code today is strikingly similar to the original [Napoleonic Code]) but has been adopted, with local modifications, in many other countries."

2. The Invasion of Spain

"Napoleon also had a large, though indirect, effect on the history of Latin America. His invasion of Spain so weakened the Spanish government that for a period of several years it lost effective control of its colonies in Latin America. It was during this period of *de facto* autonomy that the Latin American independence movements commenced."

3. The Louisiana Purchase

"Of all Napoleon's actions . . . the one that has perhaps had the most enduring and significant consequences was one that was almost irrelevant to his main plans. In 1803, Napoleon sold a vast tract of land to the United States. He realized that the French possessions in North America might be difficult to protect from British conquest, and besides he was short of cash. The Louisiana Purchase, perhaps the largest peaceful transfer of land in all of history, transformed the United States into a nation of near-continental size. It is difficult to say what the United States would have been like without the Louisiana Purchase; certainly it would have been a vastly different country than it is today. Indeed, it is doubtful whether the United States would have become a great power without the Louisiana Purchase.

Napoleon, of course, was not solely responsible for the Louisiana Purchase. The American government clearly played a role as well. But the French offer was such a bargain that it seems likely that any American government would have accepted it, while the decision of the French government to sell the Louisiana territory came about through the arbitrary judgment of a single individual, Napoleon Bonaparte."

— from *The 100: A Ranking of the Most Influential Persons in History* by Michael H. Hart. © 1978, Hart Publishing Company

1. Which change has affected the most people? Explain your answer.

2. Which change was the most significant one for your ancestors? Explain your answer.

3. Which has had the most significant effect on your life? Explain your answer.

4. Which change do you think is the most significant? Why?

Applications and Hands-On Activities

Name _____ Date _____ Class _____

SKILL REINFORCEMENT 22
Activity

Interpreting Graphs

Graphs can show a great deal of information in a single, easy-to-read format. The graph below illustrates an important aspect of the situation in France just prior to the revolution. To interpret the graph, follow these steps: First, read the title. Then, read the captions and text. Finally, determine the relationships among all sections of the graph. When you have done so, use the graph to answer the questions that follow. Use a separate sheet of paper for your answers.

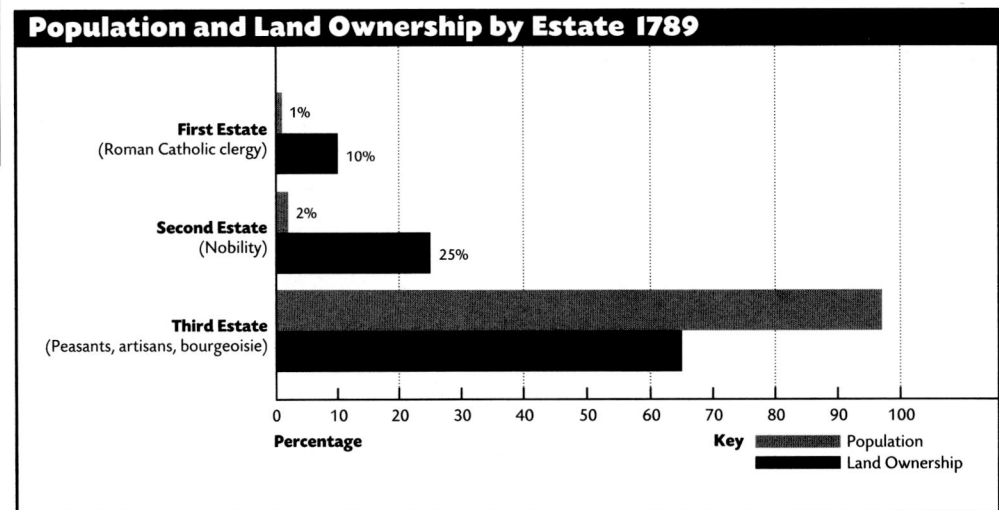

Population and Land Ownership by Estate 1789

First Estate (Roman Catholic clergy) — 1% / 10%

Second Estate (Nobility) — 2% / 25%

Third Estate (Peasants, artisans, bourgeoisie)

Percentage: 0 10 20 30 40 50 60 70 80 90 100

Key: ▨ Population ■ Land Ownership

1. What does the horizontal axis of the graph represent?

2. **a.** What percentage of the French population comprised the First Estate?

   b. What percentage of land did they own?

3. **a.** What percentage of the French population comprised the Second Estate?

   b. What percentage of land did they own?

4. **a.** Calculate the percentage of the French population that comprised the Third Estate. Write the value on the graph.

   b. Calculate the percentage of land owned by the Third Estate. Write the value on the graph.

5. Why was land a good measure of wealth at this time?

6. Which estate had the greatest land ownership in proportion to its population?

7. **a.** How was the relationship between population and land ownership fundamentally different in the Third Estate?

   b. How might this fact have helped lead to the Revolution?

Name _____ Date _____ Class _____

PEOPLE IN WORLD HISTORY *PROFILE* 41

Marie Antoinette (1755–1793)

Courage! I have shown it for years; think you I shall lose it at the moment when my sufferings are to end?
   —on the way to the guillotine, 1793

From childhood, Marie had been told that she would someday be a queen. At the age of 15, she was married to the French *dauphin,* or crown prince. In only four years, he became King Louis XVI, and Marie Antoinette—at the age when people today graduate from high school—became the queen of France.

Like many royal marriages of the day, the one between Marie and Louis was based not on love, but on politics. The marriage was arranged to strengthen France's ties to Marie's native Austria. Unhappy in her marriage, Marie sought comfort in elaborate balls at Versailles, horse races, expensive parties, and lavish theater productions. In her extravagance, Marie became an important symbol of royal excess and indifference. As such, her influence on the French Revolution was incalculable.

Marie's reputation was under attack for much of her reign, although not always justifiably. The quotation most commonly associated with Marie is "Let them eat cake." This was supposedly her unthinking reply to a courtier's remark that the peasants were rioting outside her palace because they had no bread. She never said these words, but the fact that people were willing to believe otherwise says much about the way she was perceived by the public. Many French citizens viewed Marie as simply frivolous. Others thought she was dangerous, an untrustworthy foreigner who would plot against France. Indeed, Marie tried constantly to influence French foreign policy to benefit her native Austria. When France went to war with Austria in 1792, Marie, who hoped for the defeat of the French revolutionaries, passed information to the enemy. Her treason gave the Republicans their reason to try and convict the queen. She was guillotined on October 16, 1793.

The last years of Marie's life were full of heartache. She spent four years as a virtual prisoner of the revolutionaries. In her final months, her husband was executed and her surviving son was taken from her. Surprisingly, the superficial queen demonstrated remarkable character during these tragedies. Accounts of the time portray her as courageous, steadfast, and above all else, dignified as she approached the guillotine. Her noble death, in such contrast to her frivolous life, is one reason why Marie Antoinette has intrigued people for generations.

Reviewing the Profile
Answer the following questions on a separate sheet of paper.

1. How did Marie Antoinette come to be queen of France?

2. Why was she so unpopular with the French people?

Critical Thinking
3. Evaluating Information Make a list of adjectives you think apply to Marie Antoinette.

4. Drawing Conclusions Does it surprise you that Marie Antoinette, famous for her frivolity, demonstrated such character toward the end of her life? Explain your answer.

World History: The Human Experience — People in World History **41**

Review and Reinforcement Activities

Name _____ Date _____ Class _____

Vocabulary Activity 22

Select and write the term that best completes each sentence.

1. Before the revolution, French society was divided into three _____ (estates/émigrés).

2. Although the Catholic Church in France used _____ (tithe/coup d'état) money for charitable activities, some of the money supported the grand lifestyles of the higher clergy.

3. The Constitution of 1791 created a _____ (unicameral legislature/ bicameral legislature), or one-house assembly, to represent the people.

4. In 1815, the Congress of Vienna established _____ (buffer states/tithes), or neutral territories, to isolate France.

5. As France grew more unstable, many nobles, called _____ (émigrés/plebiscites), fled France to live in neighboring countries.

6. The _____ (bourgeoisie/coup d'état), or French middle class, supported the revolution.

7. After the French armies suffered a string of losses, the leaders of the revolution were forced to adopt _____ (nationalism/conscription), or the draft.

8. The delegates of the Congress of Vienna were mostly _____ (liberals/reactionaries), who opposed change in Europe.

9. The popular general Napoleon Bonaparte seized control of France in a _____ (bourgeoisie/coup d'état).

10. To help secure his rule, Napoleon held a _____ (plebiscite/coup d'état), or popular vote, to ap...

11. The Congress of Vien... (nationalism/liberali... that celebrated indivi...

12. Although Napoleon t...

VOCABULARY PUZZLEMAKER SOFTWARE

WORLD HISTORY
THE HUMAN EXPERIENCE

VOCABULARY PUZZLEMAKER USER'S GUIDE

WORLD HISTORY
THE HUMAN EXPERIENCE

THIS UNIQUE RESOURCE:
- Reinforces vocabulary terms.
- Lets you create your own word puzzles.
- Includes DOS and Ma...

GLENCOE

Name _____ Date _____ Class _____

Guided Reading
Activity :22-1

The Old Order

As you read Section 1, answer the following questions.

1. What were the estates? _____
_____
_____

2. Who were the members of the First Estate? _____
_____

3. Who were the members of the Second Estate? _____
_____

4. Who were the members of the Third Estate? _____
_____

5. Which estate had the most members but the least money, rights, and privileges? _____

_____

6. Why was each group of the French population growing increasingly unhappy during the 1780s?

   a. peasants: _____

   b. artisans: _____

   c. bourgeoisie: _____

   d. nobility: _____

7. a. What financial crisis did King Louis XVI face? _____
_____

   b. Why did he call the Estates-General? _____
_____

8. How did the National Assembly form out of the Estates-General? _____
_____
_____

9. What led to the fall of the Bastille? _____
_____

10. What was the "Great Fear"? _____

Also available in Spanish

Guided Reading Activities help students:

• Master new material as they read each section.

• Read with a purpose.

• Prepare for quizzes and tests.

NEW!

Reading Essentials and Study Guide helps reluctant readers by:

• Condensing chapter content.

• Organizing students' reading with graphic organizers.

• Focusing on main concepts.

Review and Reinforcement Activities

Name _____ Date _____ Class _____

Time Line
Activity 22

The French Revolution

In France, the years from 1789 to 1815 were turbulent. You can trace the changes that took place during this time in French history on a time line. Read the time line below. Then answer the questions that follow, adding information to the time line as directed.

French Revolution 1789–1798
Directory 1795–1799
Consulate 1799–1804
Napoleonic Empire 1804–1815

1790   1795   1800   1805   1810   1815

Reign of Terror 1793–1794
National Convention 1792–1795
Legislative Assembly 1791–1792
Estates General and National Assembly 1789–1791

Time Line Activities help students:

- Put historical events in chronological perspective.
- Reinforce major events.
- Provide a visual/spatial learning strategy.

---

1. **a.** What event marked the beginning of the French Revolution? Add this point to the time line.

   _____

   b. How long did the French Revolution last? _____

2. **a.** What event marked the beginning of Napoleon's rule? Add this point to the time line.

   _____

   b. What event marked the end of Napoleon's rule? Add this point to the time line.

   _____

3. Napoleon ruled from 1799 to 1815. The Consulate accounts for the years 1799 to 1804. The remaining years are called the Napoleonic Empire. What 1804 event caused the change? Write your answer below, then mark this point on your time line.

   _____

   _____

4. A French historian once said that the French Revolution "turned out badly." How does your time line illustrate this concept?

   _____

   _____

Name _____ Date _____ Class _____

CHAPTER THEMES
GRAPHIC ORGANIZER 22

The French Revolution

The French Revolution is one of the great turning points in history. The years from 1789 to 1815 in France were chaotic. Change came swiftly and in unexpected ways. The chart below will help you understand and remember some of the major events of this time and the changes they caused. To complete the chart, identify at least one change that resulted from each event.

Event	Change(s) Resulting from Event
Meeting of the Estates-General	
The Great Fear	
The Declaration of Rights	
The March on Versailles	
The Reign of Terror	
Napoleon's coup d'état	
The Battle of Trafalgar	
The Invasion of Russia	
The Congress of Vienna	
The Concert of Europe	

Chapter Themes: Graphic Organizers help students:

- Learn in a visual way.
- Reinforce key chapter themes.
- Stimulate critical thinking.

Review and Reinforcement Activities

Name _____ Date _____ Class _____

Reteaching ACTIVITY...**22**

The French Revolution

The increasingly bitter division of French society in the late 1700s was a fundamental cause of the French Revolution. Understanding these divisions, then, is essential to your understanding of this turning point in history. To help you understand the divisions of French society, complete the activity below.

1. What were the estates? _____

2. Complete the diagram by copying each phrase into the appropriate space below.

- comprised about 1 percent of the population
- comprised about 2 percent of the population
- comprised about 97 percent of the population
- held high posts in government and the military
- made up of higher and lower Roman Catholic clergy
- made up of nobility
- made up of peasants, artisans, and the bourgeoisie

- main income was feudal dues
- most were very poor
- often enjoyed grand lifestyles paid for by tithe money
- owned 10 percent of French land
- owned 25 percent of French land
- owned 65 percent of French land

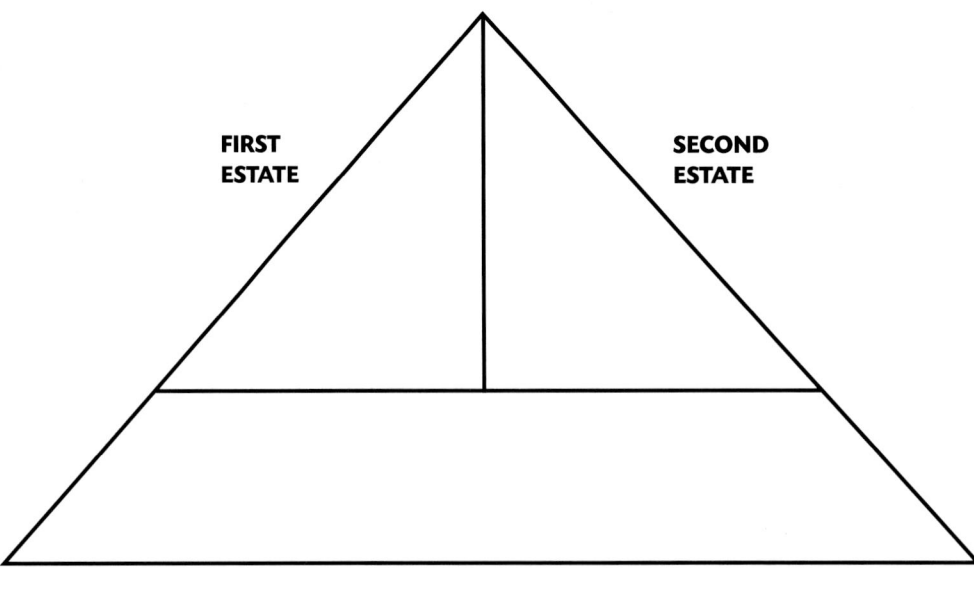

FIRST ESTATE

SECOND ESTATE

THIRD ESTATE

World History: The Human Experience

Spanish Language Resources

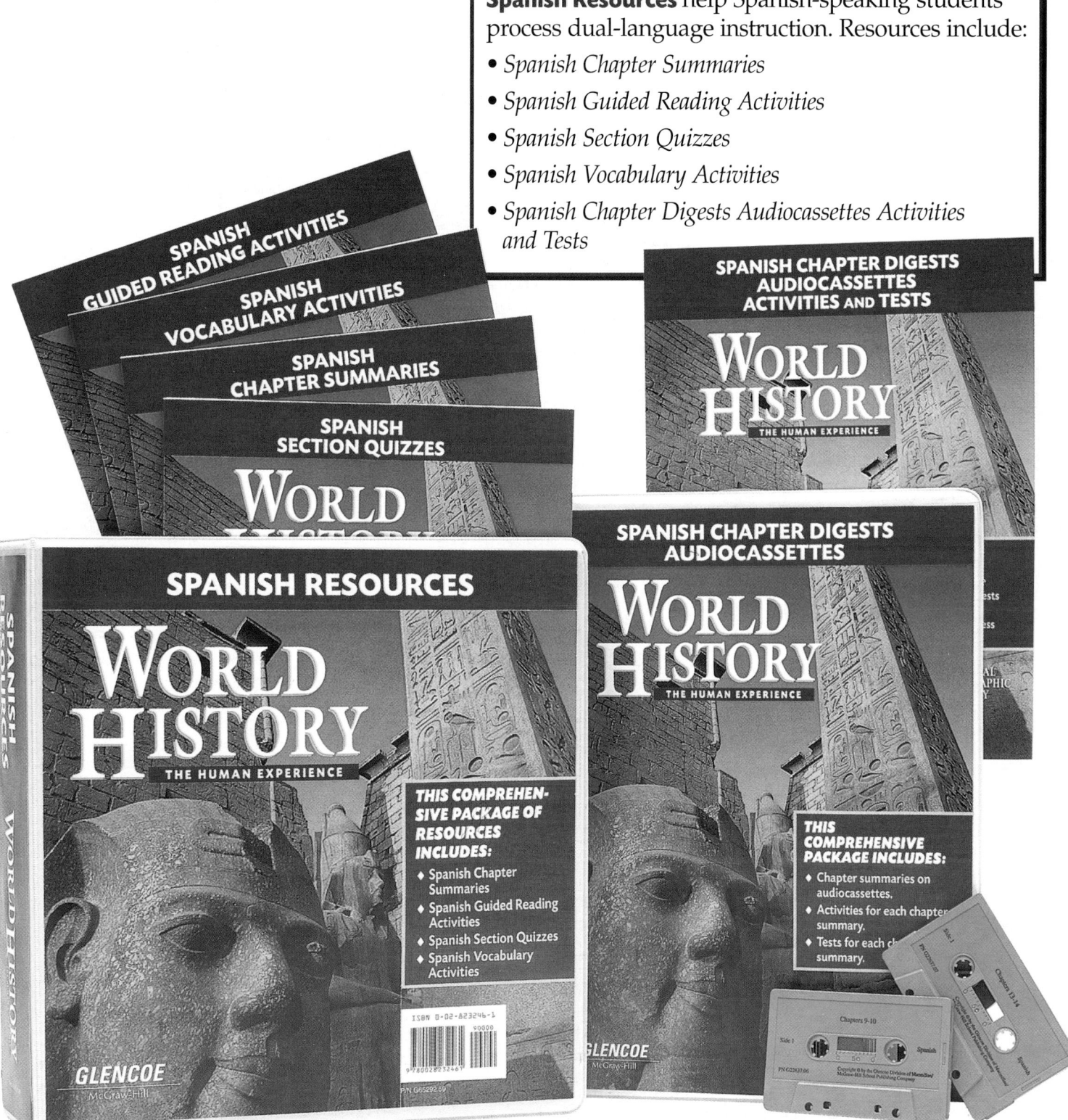

Spanish Resources help Spanish-speaking students process dual-language instruction. Resources include:

- *Spanish Chapter Summaries*
- *Spanish Guided Reading Activities*
- *Spanish Section Quizzes*
- *Spanish Vocabulary Activities*
- *Spanish Chapter Digests Audiocassettes Activities and Tests*

SPANISH
GUIDED READING ACTIVITIES

SPANISH
VOCABULARY ACTIVITIES

SPANISH
CHAPTER SUMMARIES

SPANISH
SECTION QUIZZES

SPANISH CHAPTER DIGESTS
AUDIOCASSETTES
ACTIVITIES AND TESTS

WORLD
HISTORY
THE HUMAN EXPERIENCE

SPANISH RESOURCES

WORLD
HISTORY
THE HUMAN EXPERIENCE

THIS COMPREHEN-
SIVE PACKAGE OF
RESOURCES
INCLUDES:

◆ Spanish Chapter
  Summaries
◆ Spanish Guided Reading
  Activities
◆ Spanish Section Quizzes
◆ Spanish Vocabulary
  Activities

ISBN 0-02-823246-1

GLENCOE
McGraw-Hill

SPANISH CHAPTER DIGESTS
AUDIOCASSETTES

WORLD
HISTORY
THE HUMAN EXPERIENCE

THIS
COMPREHENSIVE
PACKAGE INCLUDES:

◆ Chapter summaries on
  audiocassettes.
◆ Activities for each chapter
  summary.
◆ Tests for each chapter
  summary.

GLENCOE
McGraw-Hill

Geography Activities

Name _____ Date _____ Class _____

MAPPING HISTORY
Activity 22

The French Revolution

Napoleon so dominated Europe that the years 1800 to 1815 are often called "the Napoleonic Era." At the height of his power, Napoleon controlled virtually the entire continent. The map below illustrates the remarkable extent of his influence. Use it to complete the activities that follow. Write your answers on a separate sheet of paper.

Europe at Height of Napoleon's Power 1812

Mapping History Activities help students:

- Get hands-on practice using maps.
- Integrate world history with map skills.
- Make the history-geography connection.

1. **a.** In what year was Napoleon at the height of his power?

   b. What nations did he control?

   c. What nations did he make his allies?

2. What parts of Europe did he fail to conquer?

3. Napoleon's major battles are listed in the chart at right.

   a. Create a map symbol for a battle, and add the symbol to the map key.

   b. Using the symbol you created, mark the location of each battle on the map. Write the date of each battle next to its symbol.

   c. One historian said that between 1800 and 1815 "warfare ravaged Europe." Study the map. Do you agree? Explain your answer.

Battle	Date	Approximate Location
Marengo	1800	300 miles northwest of Rome
Trafalgar	1805	off the coast of Cape Trafalgar
Austerlitz	1805	250 miles southwest of Warsaw
Auerstedt	1806	just southwest of Leipzig
Jena	1806	just southeast of Auerstedt
Friedland	1807	extreme northern Poland, about 100 miles from the Baltic Sea
Peninsular War	1808–1814	throughout Spain
Wagram	1809	just north of Vienna
Aspern	1809	just northeast of Vienna
Borodino	1812	about 100 miles west of Moscow
Lützen	1813	about 100 miles west of Leipzig
Leipzig	1813	at Leipzig
Ligny	1815	about 100 miles southeast of Waterloo
Waterloo	1815	at Waterloo

Name .... Date .... Class ....

GEOGRAPHY and HISTORY 22
Activity

Movement: *A Doomed March to Russia*

Napoleon gathered troops from all quarters of his European empire in his quest to conquer the Russian Empire. By June 1812 his "Grand Army," numbering 600,000 men, confidently began to march east across the vast, level Russian plain. Yet six months later, these same troops were making a desperate escape from Russia—having lost more than 500,000 men. What caused this panicked retreat and massive loss of life?

Napoleon had underestimated the Russian troops and his most bitter rival, the fierce Russian winter. To resist Napoleon, the Russians used a new strategy. Instead of meeting the French in open battle, the Russian army retreated slowly, drawing the French army deeper and deeper into Russia.

In September, Napoleon's forces finally reached Moscow, which the Russians had evacuated. The day after the French entered Moscow, a huge fire, probably started by Russian patriots, destroyed the city. With the Russian winter looming, Napoleon faced a difficult decision. He could either chase the Russian army farther to the east or turn back to the west.

Napoleon waited too long to make his decision to retreat. Bitter cold and driving snow plagued the Grand Army as it crossed the vast Russian plain once again. Temperatures plunged and Russians began attacking French forces without mercy.

With the help of the severe winter of their homeland, Russian forces wiped out 80 percent of the Grand Army by the time it returned to Germany in December 1812.

The Grand Army's Retreat

The strongest threw into the river those who were weaker, and . . . trampled underfoot all the sick whom they found in their way. . . . Others, hoping to save themselves by swimming, were frozen in the middle of the river, or perished by placing themselves on pieces of ice, which sunk to the bottom. Thousands and thousands . . . were lost.

—French officer's account

Napoleon's Russian Campaign

1 In June 1812, Napoleon and his Grand Army of 600,000 men begin their march into Russia.

2 Bands of Russian troops destroy the French supply trains. The French leave more troops to guard their supply lines.

3 On September 14, the French army reaches Moscow. The city is stripped; fires add to the destruction. After five weeks, Napoleon finally orders a general retreat.

4 The Grand Army passes again over the battlefield of Borodino. The field is covered by 30,000 corpses half-eaten by wolves.

5 As temperatures plunge to 40 degrees below zero, some soldiers build shelters with frozen corpses.

6 On December 14, the Grand Army reaches the Prussian border. Only 30,000 men remain

BALTIC SEA — Koningsberg — Kovno — Vitebsk — Smolensk — Borodino — Moscow

Route to Moscow
Route of retreat from Moscow

0   50   100   150   200 miles
0   100   200   300 kilometers

World History: The Human Experience   Geography and History Activities   **43**

f barriers to

ately how rder to r this dis-

hing that conse- n leaders

6. How might geographical barriers to movement hinder a nation's development? How might they help it?

Activity
7. Research the settlement of the area in which you live. What factors encouraged settlement? What factors prohibited settlement? What affects the movement of people in and out of your area today?

Geography and History Activities:
• Show the important role of geography in history.
• Improve students' geography skills.
• Relate the five geography themes to world history.

Geography Activities

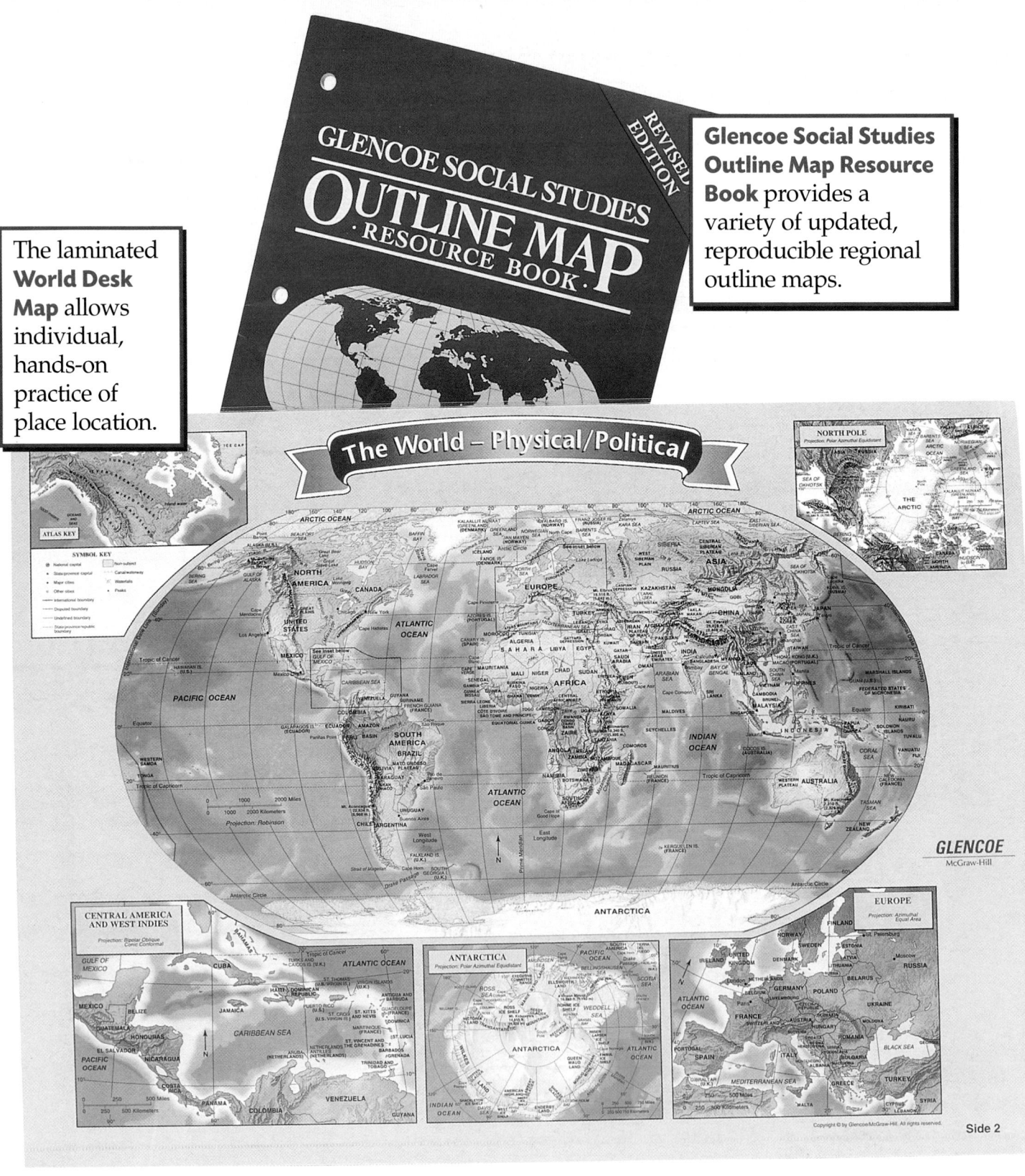

The laminated **World Desk Map** allows individual, hands-on practice of place location.

Glencoe Social Studies Outline Map Resource Book provides a variety of updated, reproducible regional outline maps.

Interdisciplinary Connections

Name _____ Date _____ Class _____

📖 WORLD LITERATURE SELECTION 22

Armed men and women flocked out of the Quarter so fast, and drew even these last dregs after them with such a force of suction, that within a quarter of an hour there was not a human creature in S... few old crones and...

No. They were a... choking the Hall of... where this old man... overflowing into the... adjacent open space... husband and wife, ... Three, were in the f...

*Use the information f...
answer the following...
sary, use a separate sh...
of paper.*

Interpreting the R...
1. Who are the De... their role in the Fre...

2. Why do you th... the mob against Fo...

3. Dickens person... hood of Saint A... seem like a pers... a place. Why d... does this?

Critical Thinking
4. Determining Ca...
    Effect Foulon h... starving people... Do you think h... his punishment...

World Literature Selections help students:
- Explore world cultures.
- Experience a variety of literature.
- Make cross-curricular connections.

Name _____ Date _____ Class _____

📖 WORLD LITERATURE SELECTION 22

distance from him in the Hall.
"See!" cried madame, pointing with her knife. "See the old villain bound with ropes. That was well done to tie a bunch of grass upon

one another, and themselves, to madness with the wildest cries and actions. Villain Foulon taken, my... Miscreant... score of ot... into the m... these, beat... and scream... the starvin... who told... when I ha... bread to g... Foulon wh... my baby i... suck grass... these brea... dry with... mother of... this Foulo... Heaven o... ing! Hear... dead baby... withered... swear on... it?"
  "News from the...
  "How, then?" cr... temptuously. "The c...
  "Does everyone... Foulon, who told th... that they might eat... died, and went to H...
  "Everybody!" fr...
  "The news is of... among us!"
  "Among us!" fr... throat again. "And...
  "Not dead! He... much—and with re... caused himself to be... had a grand mock-f... him alive, hiding in... brought him in. I ha... way to the Hôtel de... that he had reason t... reason?"
  Wretched old si... years and ten, if he... would have known... hearts if he could ha... answering cry.
  A moment of p... silence followed. De... his wife looked stea... one another. The Ve... stooped, and the jar... was heard as she m... her feet behind the...
  "Patriots!" said... a determined voice,

own friends until they dropped into a passionate swoon, and were only saved by the men

---

Name _____ Date _____ Class _____

📖 WORLD LITERATURE SELECTION 22

wine-shop, had been suddenly fired, a fast-spreading murmur came rushing along.
  "It is Defarge," ... patriots!"
  Defarge came i... off a red cap he wor... around him! "Lister... this Foulo... against a backgrou... mouths, formed out... in the wine-shop ha...
  "Say then, my h... it?"

ready?"
  Instantly Madame Defarge's knife was in her

Name _____ Date _____ Class _____

📖 WORLD LITERATURE SELECTION 22

A Tale of Two Cities was published serially and in book form in 1859. Dickens took his descriptions of the Revolution from his friend Thomas Carlyle's *French Revolution*. The two cities in question are Paris and London; the story follows a French doctor, his family, and their English friends, all caught up in the violence of the revolution. In this chapter, the author describes the rising tide of anger in a poor Parisian neighborhood.

ABOUT THE AUTHOR

The English author **Charles Dickens** (1812–1870) is one of the most popular writers in the history of literature, celebrated for his masterful storytelling, acute observation of people and places, and sharp social criticism. Dickens was a victim of social injustice himself. After his father's imprisonment for debt when Charles was 12, the child was forced to help support the family by working in a squalid factory. He never forgot the humiliation and hardship of unequal treatment, which is reflected in his story of the French Revolution, *A Tale of Two Cities*.

Guided Reading *As you read this excerpt from* A Tale of Two Cities, *think about how you might act in the same situation.*

A Tale of Two Cities: "The Sea Still Rises"

Haggard Saint Antoine[1] had had only one exultant week, in which to soften his modicum of hard and bitter bread to such extent as he could, with the relish of fraternal embraces and congratulations, when Madame Defarge sat at her counter, as usual, presiding over the customers. Madame Defarge wore no rose in her head, for the great brotherhood of Spies had become, even in one short week, extremely chary of trusting themselves to the saint's mercies. The lamps across his streets had a portentously elastic swing with them.

Madame Defarge, with her arms folded, sat in the morning light and heat, contemplating the wine-shop and the street. In both, there were several knots of loungers, squalid and miserable, but now with a manifest sense of power enthroned on their distress. The raggedest nightcap, awry on the wretchedest head, had this crooked significance in it: "I know how hard it has grown for me, the wearer of this, to support life in myself; but do you know how easy it has

grown for me, the wearer of this, to destroy life in you?" Every lean bare arm, that had been without work before, had this work always ready for it now, that it could strike. The fingers of the knitting women were vicious, with the experience that they could tear. There was a change in the appearance of Saint Antoine; the image had been hammered into this for hundreds of years, and the last finishing blows had told mightily of the expression.

Madame Defarge sat observing it, with such suppressed approval as was to be desired in the leader of the Saint Antoine women. One of her sisterhood knitted beside her. The short, rather plump wife of a starved grocer, the mother of two children withal, this lieutenant had already earned the complimentary name of The Vengeance.

"Hark!" said The Vengeance. "Listen, then! Who comes?"

As if a train of powder laid from the outermost bound of Saint Antoine Quarter to the

1. **Saint Antoine:** the Parisian neighborhood in which this chapter is set

Interdisciplinary Connections

**World Art and
Music** activities
and profiles:

- Tell the story of
history through
the arts.

- Introduce
important
personalities in
the arts.

- Make cross-
curricular
connections.

Name _____ Date _____ Class _____

WORLD ART and MUSIC 22
Activity

Jacques-Louis David

In the painting below, Jacques-Louis David depicts one of the turning
points in the history of Europe and of the world. Interestingly, the painting itself carries a historic importance all its own. Explore the painting's
many details. Pay particular attention to its formal style and the faces of the
individuals in the scene. Then read the accompanying article and respond to
the questions at the bottom of the next page.

The Consecration of Emperor Napoleon I and the Cor...

The painting you are looking at w... ...tual art
Napoleon's favorites. When he first sa... ...w other
exclaimed "How great! What relief! H... ...nfluence
This is not a painting; one can walk a... ...this one
this picture; life is everywhere!" ...XVI, direc-
...ary gov-
...n.
...nstrated
...man, he
...ndly
...t civiliza-
...leading pro-
...t.
...ovement that
...and Rome.
...their bal-

...vities

**World Music:
Cultural Traditions**
brings students
into contact with
music represent-
ing many cultures
and regions of the
world.

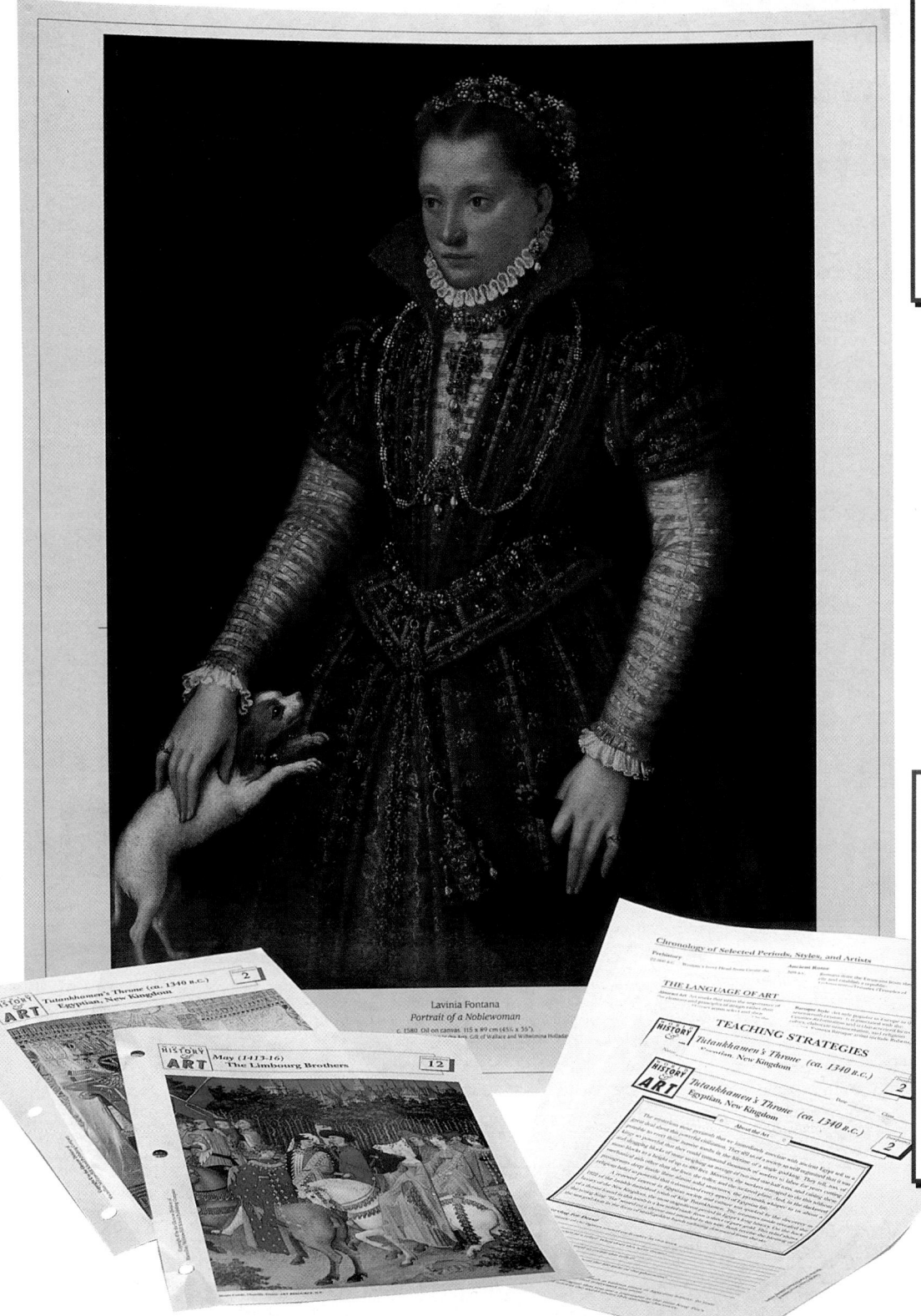

Lavinia Fontana
Portrait of a Noblewoman

c. 1580. Oil on canvas. 115 x 89 cm (45½ x 35"). Gift of Wallace and Wilhelmina Holladay

Focus on World Art Prints:

- Provides you with 25 display-quality prints, teaching strategies, and study activities.

- Offers your students a cultural perspective of history.

World History and Art Transparencies:

- Introduce your students to the world of fine art.

- Captivate students with the wonder, majesty, and intrigue of breathless works of art.

Enrichment and Extension Activities

Name _____ Date _____ Class _____

Enrichment Activity 22

The *Levée en Masse*

Four months after the French Revolutionaries proclaimed the first day of the "Year I of Liberty," they faced fierce attacks from European monarchies that feared the spread of the revolution. Desperate, the leaders of the revolution made a decision that would change the face of warfare forever. Read the excerpt below and answer the questions that follow.

Almost all of the monarchies of Europe [joined] their armies against France to stamp [out the] sacrilegious revolutionaries, and when [what] was left of the old royal army, aided by vol[unteer]s, proved unable to stem the attacks, the [Nationa]l Convention decided on conscription: [levée en masse.]

[. . .] the convention issued the call for a *levée [en mas]se* in August [1793]. By New Year's Day, [the] French armies numbered about 777,000 [. . . a]nd the wars of mass armies that ensued [shook] Europe for the next two decades.

Conscription was not an entirely new idea . . . but it had never really amounted to more than compulsory selection of an unfortunate minority, nor had it lasted long or been extended to an entire country. But the French Revolution, with its principles of liberty and equality, first stimulated and then exploited a fervent nationalism which made conscription acceptable. It also made French troops behave differently.

The "nation in arms" produced poorly trained soldiers . . . who had no time to master the intricate drill of close-order formations, but their enthusiasm and numbers made up for it: attacking in clouds of skirmishers and disorderly columns, they often simply overwhelmed their better-trained adversaries. . . . Battles rarely ended in draws any more—Carnot of the Committee of Public Safety instructed the French armies in 1794 "to act in mass formations and take the offensive. . . . Give battle on a large scale and pursue the enemy until he is utterly destroyed."

The basic principle underlying all this was that whereas the prerevolutionary regular soldiers had been scarce and expensive, the lives of conscripts were plentiful and cheap. The disdain for casualties grew even greater once Napoleon had seized control of France in 1799. "You cannot stop me," he boasted to Count Metternich, the Austrian diplomat. "I spend thirty thousand men a month." It was not an idle boast: the losses of France in 1793–1814 amounted to 1.7 million dead—almost all soldiers—out of a population of 29 million.

—from *War* by Gwynne Dyer. ©1985, Media Resources

1. Why did French revolutionary leaders institute the *levée en masse*? _____

2. How did the *levée en masse* change the French armies? _____
_____

3. What "basic principle" does the author refer to? _____
_____

4. France's enemies were reluctant to introduce conscription. Why do you think this was so?
_____

5. What do you think about Napoleon's statement? How do you think this reflects on him?
_____
_____

Enrichment Activities:

- Help you expand chapter themes.
- Stimulate critical thinking.
- Engage students in meaningful interpretations of history.

Name _____ Date _____ Class _____

CRITICAL THINKING 22
Activity

Analyzing Information

To the French people today, the Revolution of 1789 remains a lively topic of discussion and debate. No one disputes that it was a watershed in French—and human—history. In fact, historians generally agree that 1789 marks the beginning of the modern era. Yet the true meaning and legacy of the French Revolution continues to be debated. To sort through the many opinions about the French Revolution, or any historical event, you need to analyze information. Analyzing information means studying it carefully in order to learn as much as possible about what is being presented.

Below are three recent statements about the French Revolution. Answer the questions after each statement to help you analyze it. Then answer the final two questions, which will guide you in analyzing the quotations as a group. Use a separate sheet of paper for your answers.

> *The revolution is a complex whole, like life itself, with the inspiring and the unacceptable, with hope and fear, violence and fraternity.*
>
> —François Mitterrand, president of France, speaking at the Bicentennial Celebration of the French Revolution

1. Mitterrand said the Revolution included "the inspiring," "the unacceptable," "hope," "fear," "violence," and "fraternity." From your knowledge of the Revolution, identify at least one historical fact that fits each category.

2. What might have motivated Mitterrand to emphasize both the positive and negative aspects of the Revolution?

> *The French have come to realize that the revolution was a magnificent event that turned out badly."*
>
> —François Furet, historian at Paris's Ecole des Hautes Etudes

3. What do you think was "magnificent" about the French Revolution?

4. Why do you think Furet says it "turned out badly"?

> *One of my ancestors stormed the Bastille, and I feel both thrilled and proud to be French whenever I walk past the place where it once stood.*
>
> —Jacques Delmas, a lawyer from Reims

5. What is the source of Jacques Delmas's pride?

6. Do you think he would agree with Furet's statement? Why or why not?

7. Which of the three statements is the most positive statement about the Revolution? The most negative? Explain your choices.

8. Which one do you think best summarizes the Revolution? Why?

> **Critical Thinking Activities** help students:
> - Practice vital critical thinking skills.
> - Enrich essential chapter themes.

Enrichment and Extension Activities

Name _____ Date _____ Class _____

SOURCE READING 22

10. No one should be disturbed on account of his opinions, even religious, provided their manifestation does not trouble the public order as established by law.

11. The free communication of thoughts and opinions is one of the most precious of the rights of man; ever ____ write, and print fre ____ responsibility for t ____

tax is indispensable; it should be equally apportioned among all the citizens according to their means.

14. All citizens have the right to ascertain, by themselves or through their representatives, the necessary amount of public taxation, to

Source Readings:

- Reinforce and extend chapter content.
- Make connections across the curriculum.
- Let students experience the story of history.

Use information from th ____

1. What does the Dec ____
_____
_____

2. According to the D ____
from that in the An ____
_____
_____

3. If the Declaration h ____
_____
_____

Name _____ Date _____ Class _____

SOURCE READING 22

Declaration of the Rights of Man and of the Citizen

Although the French Revolution later turned to violence and terror, the first bold public statement of the revolutionary National Assembly echoes the high ideals of John Locke, the Enlightenment, and the American Declaration of Independence. The Declaration of the Rights of Man and of the Citizen was issued in August 1789.

Guided Reading *In this selection, read to learn what problems and rights the Declaration addresses.*

The representatives of the French people, constituted in National Assembly, considering that ignorance, forgetfulness, or contempt of the rights of man are the sole causes of public misfortunes and the corruption of governments, have resolved to set forth in a solemn declaration the natural, inalienable, and sacred rights of man so that this declaration, being constantly before all members of the social body, may unceasingly recall to them their rights and their duties; so that the acts of the legislative power and those of the executive power may always be compared with the true aim of political organization and thus may be more respected; and so that the demands of the citizens, founded henceforth upon simple and incontestable principles, may always be aimed at maintaining the constitution and the happiness of all.

In consequence, the National Assembly recognizes and declares, in the presence and under the auspices of the Supreme Being, the following rights of man and citizen.

1. Men are born and remain free and equal in rights. Social distinctions can be based only upon the common good.

2. The aim of every political association is the preservation of the natural and imprescriptible rights of man. These rights are liberty, property, security, and resistance to oppression.

3. The source of all sovereignty is essentially in the nation [that is, the people]; no body, no individual can exercise authority that does not emanate from it expressly.

4. Liberty consists in the power to do anything that does not injure others; accordingly, the exercise of the natural rights of each man has no limits except those that assure to the other members of society the enjoyment of these same rights. These limits can be determined only by law.

5. The law can forbid only such actions as are injurious to society. Nothing can be forbidden that is not forbidden by the law, and no one can be constrained to do that which it does not decree.

6. Law is the expression of the general will. All citizens have the right to take part personally, or by their representatives, in its enactment. It must be the same for all, whether it protects or punishes. All citizens being equal in its eyes, are equally eligible to all public dignities, places, and employments, according to their capacities, and without other distinction than that of their merits and their talents.

7. No man can be accused, arrested, or detained, except in the cases determined by the law and according to the forms which it has prescribed. Those who call for, expedite, execute, or cause to be executed arbitrary orders should be punished; but every citizen summoned or seized by virtue of the law ought to obey instantly; he makes himself culpable by resistance.

8. The law ought to establish only punishments that are strictly and obviously necessary, and no one should be punished except by virtue of a law established and promulgated prior to the offence and legally applied.

9. Every man being presumed innocent until he has been declared guilty, if it is judged indispensable to arrest him, all severity that may not be necessary to secure his person ought to be severely suppressed by law.

World History: The Human Experience

Source Readings

Name _____ Date _____ Class _____

PERFORMANCE ASSESSMENT 22
Activity

The French Revolution

Background
The Declaration of the Rights of Man and of the Citizen shocked the world. Its adoption by the National Assembly on August 26, 1789, trumpeted the success of the radical ideas of the revolutionary leaders. The inspiring document was to have dramatic effects beyond the borders of France. "This single page of print," the British statesman Lord Acton later said, "is stronger than all the armies of Napoleon." Today, the Declaration of Rights forms the preamble to the French Constitution and continues to serve as a model of liberal thought and government.

Task
You are a member of the National Assembly in the summer of 1789. You and other Assembly members are to compile a list of all the rights due to individuals and citizens.

Audience
Your audience is the people of France, present and future, and people around the world who will look to this document for inspiration as they struggle to end oppression in their own nations.

Purpose
The purpose is to determine the specific rights that will be included in the final Declaration of Rights adopted by the National Assembly.

Performance Assessment Strategies and Activities:

- Meet alternative assessment requirements.
- Include scoring rubrics.
- Provide students with activities to include in their portfolios.

Procedures

1. Working with a group, begin two lists. Title one list "Rights of Man"and the other list "Rights of the Citizen." (In the original document, the word *man* was used to refer to people in general, not to men only.)

2. Ask yourself, How do the rights of the individual (as a person) differ from the rights of a citizen (as a member of a nation)? Decide on the types of rights to be included in each list and write this at the beginning of each list.

3. Remember the historical situation: You are working in the National Assembly as feudalism is ending in France. Keeping this in mind, brainstorm a list of rights that you think all individuals should have. Then

brainstorm a list of rights that you think all citizens should have.

4. Review and revise your lists. Working together, decide whether to eliminate some rights and add others.

5. Combine your two lists into a single list titled "Rights of Man and of the Citizen." List the rights in order of importance.

6. Revise each right on the list so its meaning is clear.

7. Prepare a final copy of your list and post it. Compare your list to the text of the actual Declaration of the Rights of Man and of the Citizen.

Assessment and Evaluation

Name _____ Date _____ Class _____

Section: **Quiz 22-1**

Score _____

The Old Order

Matching
Match each item in Column A with an item in Column B by writing the correct letters in the blanks.
(3 points each)

Column A

_____ **1.** the middle class

_____ **2.** a Paris prison that symbolized the injustices of the French monarchy

_____ **3.** a lavish palace where French royalty lived

_____ **4.** the orders or classes of French society

_____ **5.** a tax paid by church members

Column B

a. estates

b. bourgeoisie

c. tithe

d. Versailles

e. the Bastille

Multiple Choice
In the blank at the left, write the letter of the choice that best completes the statement or answers the question. (4 points each)

_____ **6.** All of the following people belonged to the Third Estate EXCEPT

    a. peasants.

    b. artisans.

    c. members of the bourgeoisie.

    d. members of the nobility.

_____ **7.** The King of France during the French Revolution was

    a. Louis XIV.

    b. Louis XV.

    c. Louis XVI.

    d. Louis XVII.

_____ **8.** What was the Estates-General?

    a. a lavish palace in the French countryside

    b. an assembly of delegates

    c. a prison that was attacked by a French mob

    d. the court of the King of France

_____ **9.** Who took the Tennis Court Oath?

    a. representatives of the First Estate

    b. representatives of the Second Estate

    c. representatives of the Third Estate

    d. the King of France

_____ **10.** The violence that rocked the French countryside in 1789 was called the

    a. Terror.

    b. French Revolution.

    c. Great Fear.

    d. fall of the Bastille.

Assessment and Evaluation

Chapter and Unit Tests: Forms A and B:

- Evaluate student understanding of chapter ideas.
- Offer students a variety of question formats.
- Give you alternate tests to choose from.

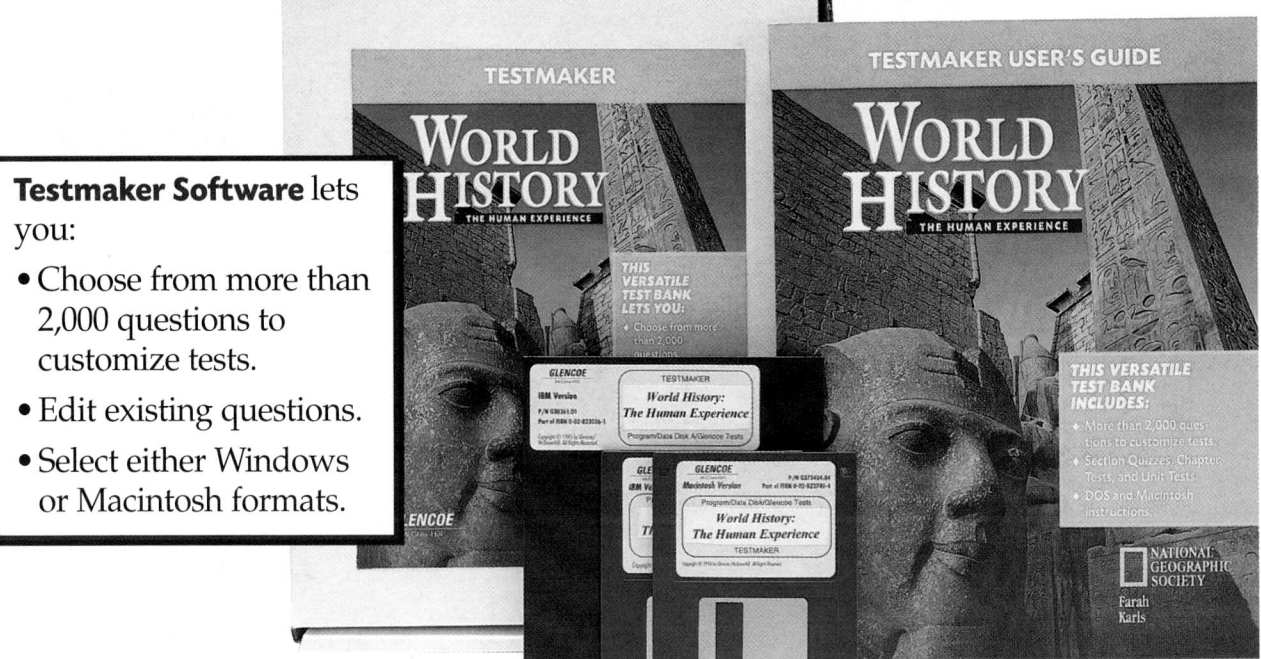

Form B (Chapter 22):

Name _____ Date _____ Class _____

Chapter 22 : Form
Test B

_____ 17. All of the following French leader
 a. Robespierre.
 b. Napoleon.

_____ 18. One of the National Assembly's m
 a. lower taxes on the nobility.
 b. abolish feudal dues.

_____ 19. A major goal of the Quadruple A
 a. encourage the spread of liberal
 b. abolish absolute monarchy.

_____ 20. Before the revolution, members o
 a. a smaller tax burden than the c

 b. a voice in government equal to
 First and Second Estates.

_____ 21. The Austrian chief minister who
 a. Prince Klemens von Metternich
 b. Frederick William III.

_____ 22. A major factor in Napoleon's failu
 a. the harsh Russian winter.
 b. Russian naval supremacy.

_____ 23. The attack on a Paris prison by e
 a. the storming of the Bastille.
 b. the Great Fear.

_____ 24. The Constitution of 1791 provided
 a. all male citizens.
 b. all male and female citizens.

_____ 25. All of the following contributed t
 a. lavish spending by Louis XV.
 b. French support for the
 American Revolution.

Essay
Answer one of the following questions on a sep

26a. Critical Thinking Describe the class str

26b. Critical Thinking Identify and describe
 influence outside of France.

88   Chapter and Unit Tests

Name _____ Date _____ Class _____

Chapter 22 : Form
Test B

Matching
Match each item in Column A with an item in
in the blanks.
Column A
_____ 1. doctors, lawyers, merchants
_____ 2. rivals of the Jacobins
_____ 3. ruled France during the Reign of
_____ 4. income tax placed on church mer
_____ 5. decision by popular vote
_____ 6. rarely called meeting of the three
_____ 7. regular meetings of the European
_____ 8. wanted to imprison royals and ab
 monarchy
_____ 9. a one-house assembly
_____ 10. money paid by France for war da

Multiple Choice
In the blank at the left, write the letter of the ch
(4 points each)
_____ 11. Napoleon's agreement with the C
 a. restored the authority of the lo
 b. acknowledged Catholicism wh
 maintaining religious tolerance

_____ 12. The nobility's main source of inc
 a. feudal dues collected from pea
 b. tithes collected from church mem

_____ 13. Members of the political faction f
 a. Girondists.
 b. royalists.

_____ 14. The neutral areas set up to surrou
 a. sans-culottes.
 b. buffer states.

_____ 15. King Louis XVI left Versailles for
 a. nobles demanding greater priv
 b. peasants demanding voting rig

_____ 16. By 1812, Napoleon had conquere
 a. Austria.
 b. England.

World History: The Human Experience

Name _____ Date _____ Class _____

Chapter 22 : Form
Test A

_____ 17. The old European monarchies wer
 a. Concert of Europe.
 b. National Assembly.

_____ 18. The resentment of foreign rule and
 characteristics of
 a. dictatorship.
 b. nationalism.

_____ 19. Louis XVI was executed after bein
 a. supporting universal suffrage.
 b. conspiring with foreign monarc

_____ 20. Pre-revolutionary French society
 a. inequality.
 b. harmony.

_____ 21. Napoleon seized power by overth
 a. First Estate.
 b. consulate.

_____ 22. Metternich's principle advocating
 a. legitimacy.
 b. balance-of-power.

_____ 23. The Declaration of the Rights of
 a. freedom of speech.
 b. equal rights for women.

_____ 24. Napoleon's invasion of Russia wa
 a. the creation of a French-British
 b. the defeat of the French fleet at

_____ 25. The fall of the Bastille led quickly
 a. a revolutionary government in
 b. the National Assembly.

Essay
Answer one of the following questions on a sep

26a. Critical Thinking Describe three factors
 France and its neighbors during the re

26b. Critical Thinking Describe the ways in
 reestablish the pre-revolutionary orde

86   Chapter and Unit Tests

Name _____

Chapter 22 : Form
Test A

Matching
Match each item in Column A with an item i
(3 points each)
Column A
_____ 1. included bishops and abbots
_____ 2. the unified French legal system
_____ 3. Paris prison stormed by a mob
_____ 4. type of French government before the revolution
_____ 5. group of extreme radicals
_____ 6. formed by those locked out of Estates-General
_____ 7. plan that forbade trade with Britain
_____ 8. repressive measures designed to stifle dissent
_____ 9. comprised 97% of the French population
_____ 10. those who continued to support the king

 c. monarchy
 d. royalists
 e. Carlsbad Decrees
 f. Jacobins
 g. National Assembly
 h. Continental System
 i. Napoleonic Code
 j. the higher clergy

Multiple Choice
In the blank at the left, write the letter of the choice that best completes the statement or answers the
question. (4 points each)
_____ 11. In 1789, King Louis XVI summoned the Estates-General primarily to
 a. eliminate feudal dues.   c. raise taxes to pay off growing debt.
 b. increase the influence of the peasants.   d. protect the privileges of the First
                                                  and Second Estates.

_____ 12. Robespierre's execution marked the end of
 a. the Reign of Terror.   c. the Enlightenment.
 b. the Directory.   d. the Napoleonic Code.

_____ 13. The largest social group included in the Third Estate was
 a. the bourgeoisie.   c. the peasants.
 b. the artisans.   d. the nobility.

_____ 14. Napoleon undertook all of the following actions EXCEPT
 a. placing education under government control.   c. restructuring the French legal
 b. requiring all citizens to pay taxes.   system.
                                                   d. prohibiting state censorship.

_____ 15. The policy of summoning civilian men into military service is
 a. conscription.   c. coup d'état.
 b. scorched-earth.   d. feudalism.

_____ 16. The Tennis Court Oath was made by
 a. a group of moderates known as Girondists.   c. Napoleon.
 b. King Louis XVI.   d. representatives of the Third Estate.

World History: The Human Experience   Chapter and Unit Tests   85

Testmaker Software lets you:

- Choose from more than 2,000 questions to customize tests.
- Edit existing questions.
- Select either Windows or Macintosh formats.

TESTMAKER

WORLD HISTORY
THE HUMAN EXPERIENCE

THIS VERSATILE TEST BANK LETS YOU:
- Choose from more than 2,000 questions

GLENCOE
IBM Version
P/N 03634L01
Part of ISBN 0-02-822036-1

TESTMAKER
World History:
The Human Experience
Program/Data Disk A/Glencoe Tests

GLENCOE
IBM Version
P/N 0374494.04
Macintosh Version   Part of ISBN 0-02-822740-4
Program/Data Disk/Glencoe Tests
World History:
The Human Experience
TESTMAKER

TESTMAKER USER'S GUIDE

WORLD HISTORY
THE HUMAN EXPERIENCE

THIS VERSATILE TEST BANK INCLUDES:
- More than 2,000 questions to customize tests.
- Section Quizzes, Chapter Tests, and Unit Tests.
- DOS and Macintosh instructions.

NATIONAL GEOGRAPHIC SOCIETY
Farah Karls

Multimedia and Technology

Available in Windows and Macintosh

Now with a user-friendly **Teacher-Management System** that allows you to easily track individual student and class progress.

WORLD HISTORY
THE HUMAN EXPERIENCE

EASY-TO-USE TECHNOLOGY HELPS STUDENTS:

GLENCOE
McGraw-Hill
IBM Version
P/N G23096.01
ISBN 0-02-823096-5
Copyright ©1995 Glencoe/
McGraw-Hill. All rights reserved.
*World History:
The Human Experience*

GLENCOE
McGraw-Hill
Macintosh Version
P/N G23097.01
Part of ISBN 0-02-823097-3
*World History:
The Human Experience*
Copyright © 1995 Glencoe/McGraw-Hill. All rights reserved.

MindJogger Videoquiz offers preview, review, and reinforcement of chapter content in a game-show format.

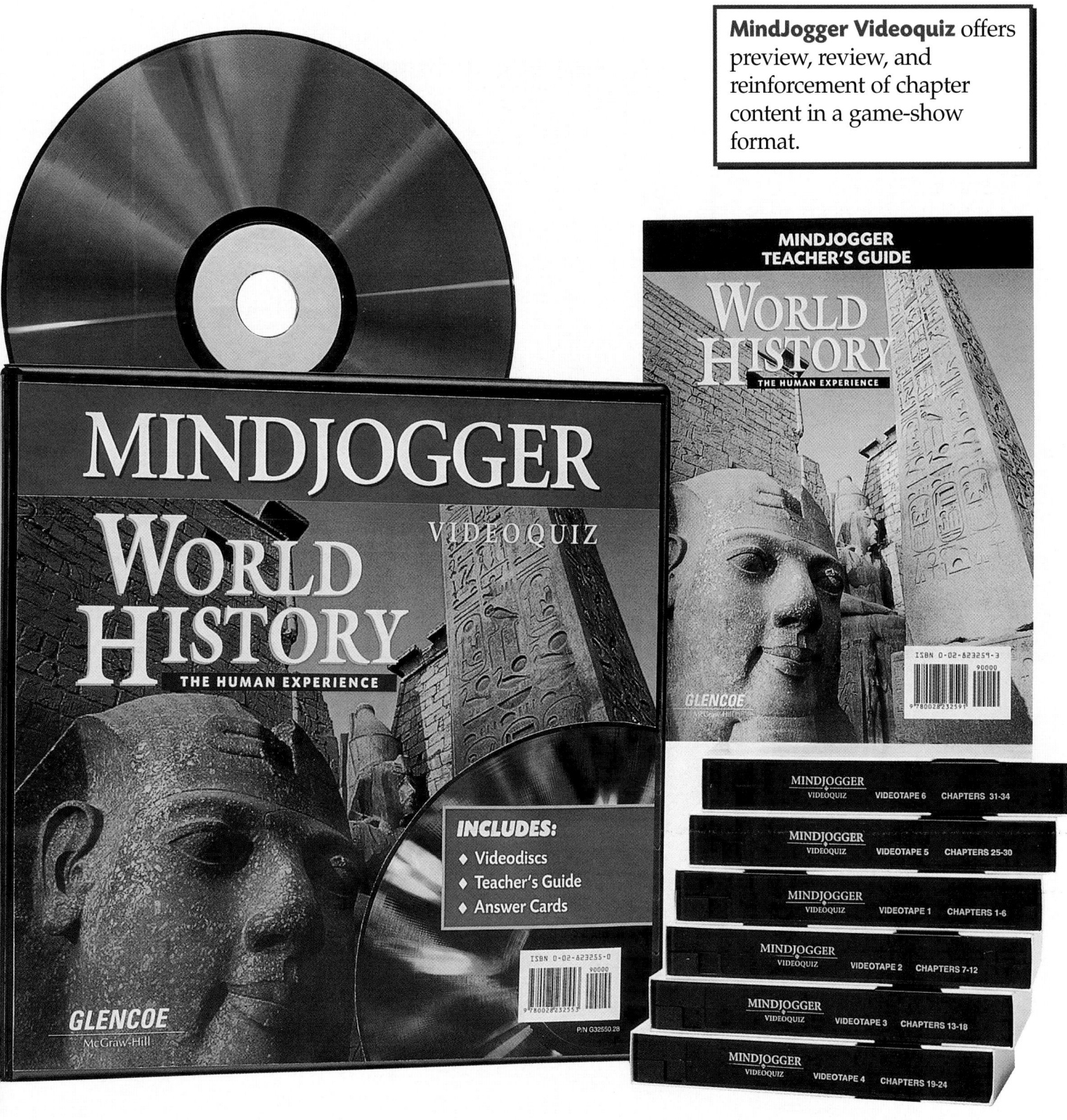

Multimedia and Technology

The following multiple-use **Teaching Transparencies** with teaching strategies and activities are included in this binder:

- Unit Digest Transparencies
- Mapping History Overlay Transparencies
- Chapter Transparencies

Presentation Plus! CD-ROM is an exciting new presentation tool that enables you to present dynamic lessons for every unit, chapter, and section of *World History: The Human Experience.* Presentation lessons include audio, graphics, links to videos, transparencies, content overviews, and much more. Use the provided lessons or customize for your classroom.

Section Focus Transparencies include 147 high-interest and colorful transparencies and blackline masters.

Multimedia and Technology

Chapter Digests Audiocassettes Activities and Tests:

- Includes activities to accompany the audiocassettes.
- Provides tests to assess comprehension of the audiocassettes.

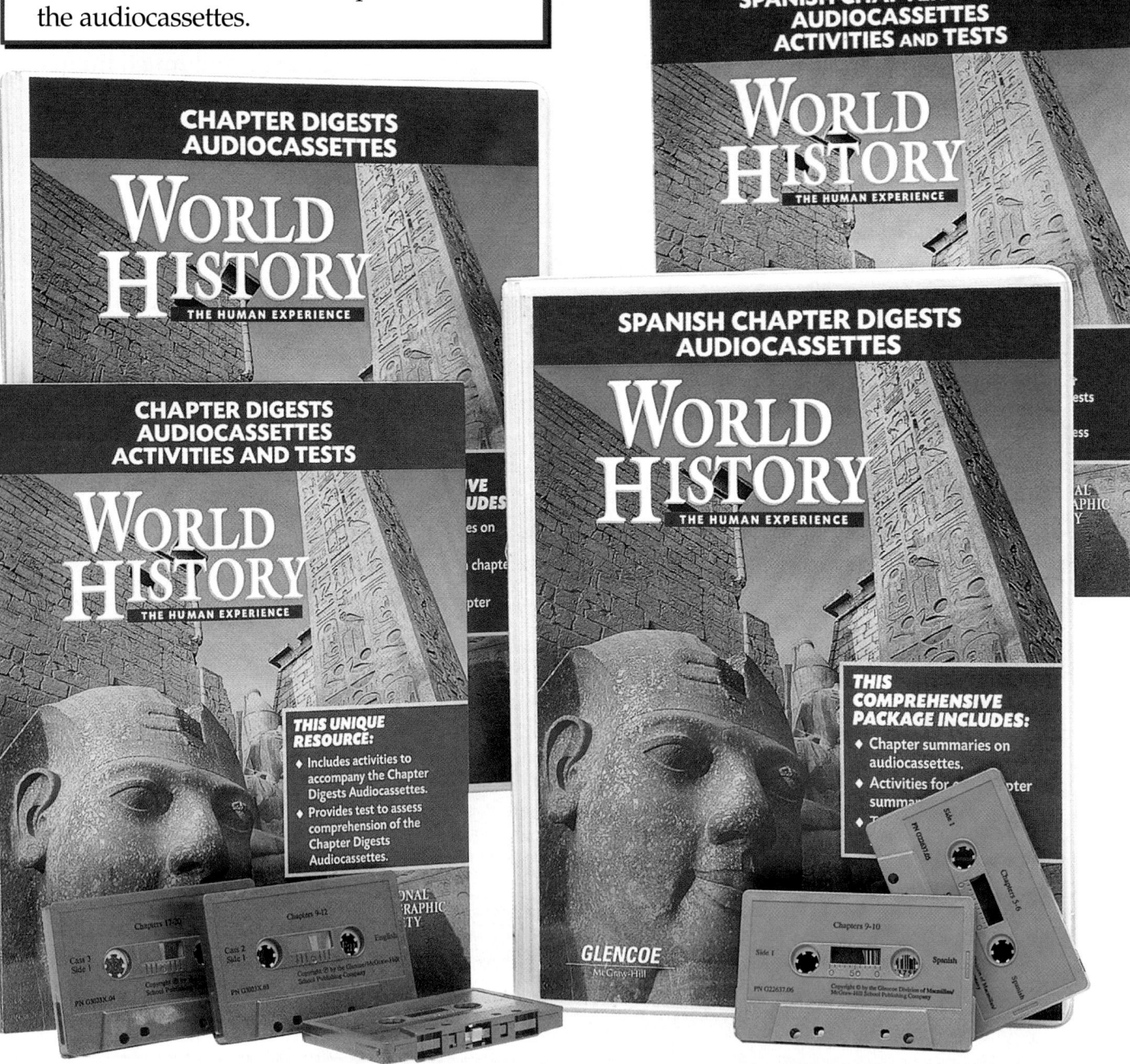

Also available in Spanish

SPANISH CHAPTER DIGESTS AUDIOCASSETTES ACTIVITIES AND TESTS

WORLD HISTORY
THE HUMAN EXPERIENCE

CHAPTER DIGESTS AUDIOCASSETTES

WORLD HISTORY
THE HUMAN EXPERIENCE

CHAPTER DIGESTS AUDIOCASSETTES ACTIVITIES AND TESTS

WORLD HISTORY
THE HUMAN EXPERIENCE

THIS UNIQUE RESOURCE:
- Includes activities to accompany the Chapter Digests Audiocassettes.
- Provides test to assess comprehension of the Chapter Digests Audiocassettes.

SPANISH CHAPTER DIGESTS AUDIOCASSETTES

WORLD HISTORY
THE HUMAN EXPERIENCE

THIS COMPREHENSIVE PACKAGE INCLUDES:
- Chapter summaries on audiocassettes.
- Activities for each chapter summary.

GLENCOE
McGraw-Hill

NATIONAL GEOGRAPHIC SOCIETY

The prestigious National Geographic Society has teamed with Glencoe to provide your students with a variety of interactive videodiscs, CD-ROMs, transparencies, and posters to extend and enrich the study of world history.

STV: Maya includes the National Geographic television special *Lost Kingdoms of the Maya* and more than 130 archival images.

Maya

SIDE 1

LEVEL ONE

STV

Maya

Contents
One Videodisc
Teacher's Guide
Activity Sheets

Maya

TEACHER'S GUIDE

NATIONAL GEOGRAPHIC SOCIETY

STV

Multimedia and Technology

STV: World Geography videodiscs opens the world to your students and allows them to see the environments in which the events they are studying took place. This series includes the following:

- *Volume 1: Asia and Australia*
- *Volume 2: Africa and Europe*
- *Volume 3: South America and Antarctica*

Also available is **STV: North America**.

NGS PictureShow™ CD-ROMs let students explore ancient civilizations, their powerful rulers, and their achievements in art, technology, and government.

- *New! Ancient Civilizations: Africa*
- *New! Ancient Civilizations Collection*
- *New! World War I Era*
- *New! World War II Era*
- *Ancient Civilizations: Egypt and the Fertile Crescent*
- *Ancient Civilizations: India and China*
- *Ancient Civilizations: Greece and Rome*
- *Ancient Civilizations: The Americas*
- *The Middle Ages*
- *The Renaissance*
- *Great Explorers, Parts 1 and 2*

Picture Atlas of the World CD-ROM is also available.

NATIONAL GEOGRAPHIC SOCIETY

NATIONAL GEOGRAPHIC SOCIETY

NGS PicturePack Transparency Sets and **Poster Sets** visually display the beauty and grandeur of the following:

PicturePack Transparencies

- *NEW! Africa*
- *NEW! Ancient Civilizations, Part I*
- *NEW! Ancient Civilizations, Part II*
- *NEW! World War I Era*
- *NEW! World War II Era*
- *Ancient Egypt*
- *The Fertile Crescent*
- *Ancient China*
- *Ancient India*
- *Ancient Greece*
- *Ancient Rome*
- *The Middle Ages*
- *The Renaissance*
- *Age of Exploration*

Physical Geography of the World Transparencies are also available.

Poster Sets

- *Ancient Egypt*
- *The Fertile Crescent*
- *Ancient Greece*
- *Ancient Rome*
- *The Middle Ages*
- *The Renaissance*
- *Age of Exploration*

ABCNews InterActive ™ videodiscs are excellent tools to aid students in visualizing and understanding history. The following titles are available:

- *In the Holy Land*
- *Lessons of War*
- *Communism and the Cold War*

ABCNEWS INTERACTIVE™

Turning Points in World History from ABCNews InterActive™ highlights the historical events that changed the world and its people.

Also available in VHS

THE HISTORY CHANNEL®

A&E Home Video®, THE HISTORY CHANNEL®, and Biography® provide a colorful means for students to view the rich history of the world.

REFERENCE ATLAS

NATIONAL
GEOGRAPHIC
SOCIETY

ATLAS KEY

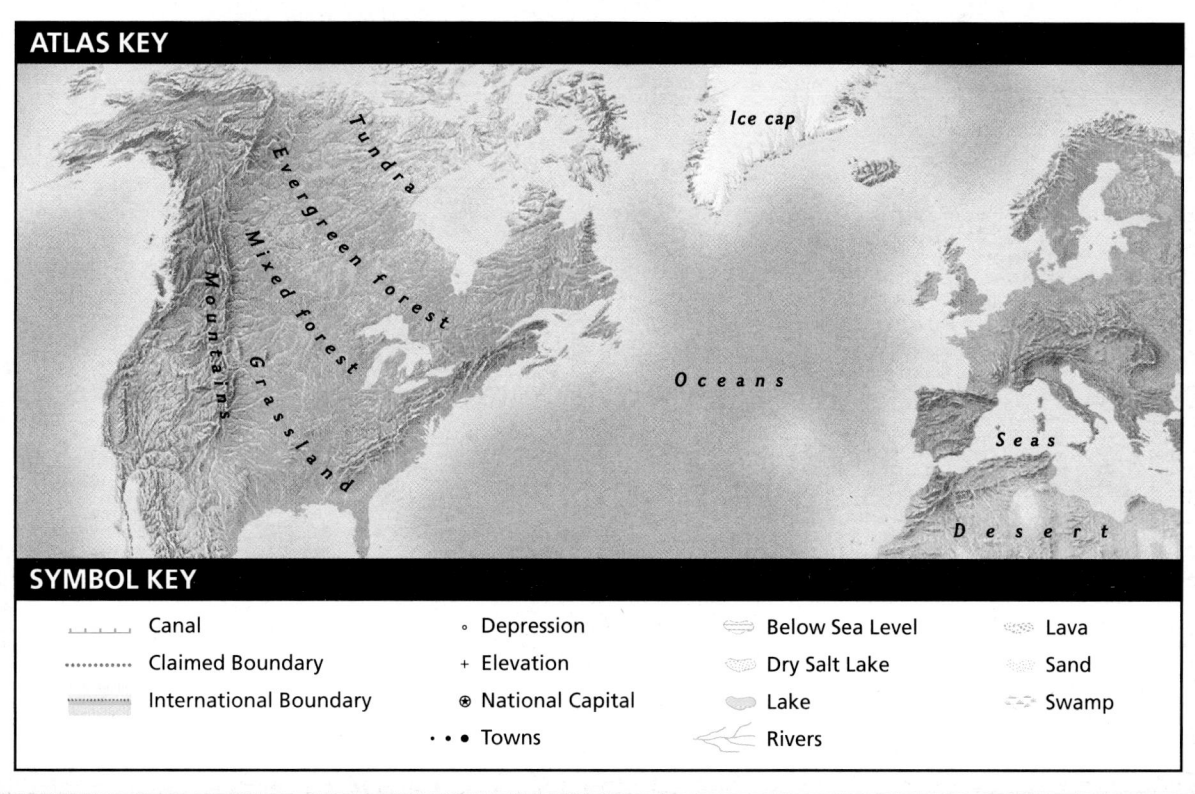

SYMBOL KEY

⋯⋯	Canal	∘	Depression	🞄 Below Sea Level		🞄 Lava
⋯⋯⋯	Claimed Boundary	+	Elevation	🞄 Dry Salt Lake		🞄 Sand
▦▦▦	International Boundary	⊛	National Capital	🞄 Lake		🞄 Swamp
		••••	Towns	⟨ Rivers		

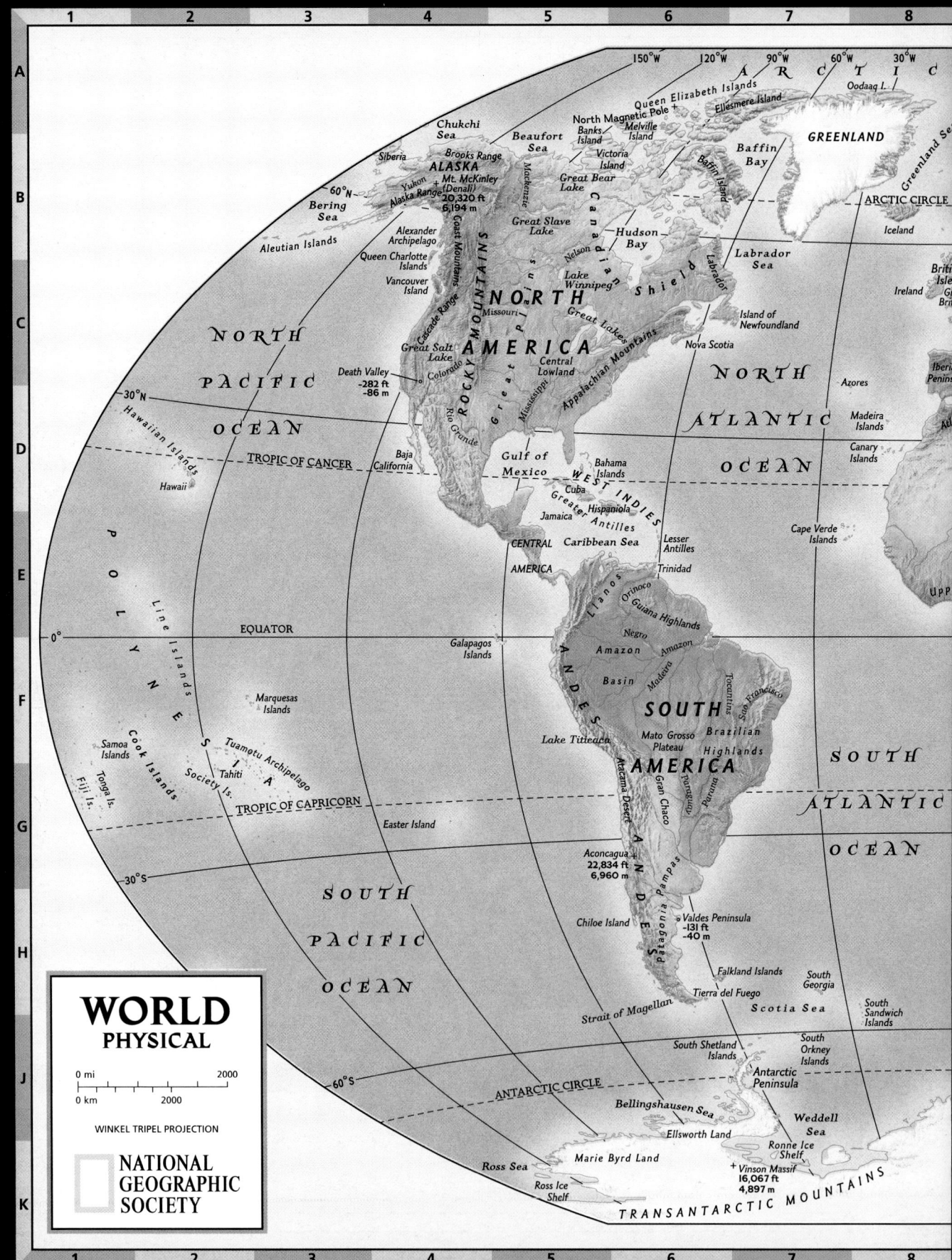

WORLD
PHYSICAL

0 mi   2000
0 km   2000

WINKEL TRIPEL PROJECTION

NATIONAL
GEOGRAPHIC
SOCIETY

9 10 11 12 13 14 15 16

A
B
C
D
E
F
G
H
J
K

30°E 60°E 90°E 120°E 150°E

O C E A N

Svalbard
Barents
Sea
Novaya Zemlya
Kara
Sea
Laptev Sea
East
Siberian Sea
egian Sea
Scandinavia
Northern European Plain
Ural Mountains
Ob
West
Siberian
Plain
Irtysh
Yenisey
Central
Siberian
Plateau
Angara
Lena
Lena
60°N
Bering
Sea
Kamchatka
Peninsula
Aleutian Is.

Baltic Sea
EUROPE
ASIA
Volga
The Steppes
Elbrus
18,510 ft
5,642 m
Aral
Sea
Altay Mountains
Lake
Baikal
Amur
Sea of
Okhotsk
Hokkaido
NORTH
Honshu
PACIFIC
30°N

Alps
Danube
Black Sea
Caucasus Mts.
Caspian
Sea
Tian Shan
Taklimakan
Desert
Kunlun Shan
GOBI A
Sea of
Japan
Korea
Yellow
North China Plain
Yellow
Sea
Japan
Nampo Shoto
OCEAN

Mediterranean Sea
Sicily
Cyprus
Zagros Mountains
Dead Sea
-1,349 ft
-411 m
ARABIAN
PENINSULA
Indus
Plateau of Tibet
HIMALAYA
Brahmaputra
Mt. Everest
29,035 ft
8,850 m
Ganges
Yangtze
East
China
Sea
Taiwan
Ryukyu Islands
Philippine
Sea
Philippine Islands

SAHARA
Red Sea
Nile
Arabian
Sea
INDIA
Deccan
Plateau
Bay of
Bengal
Salween
Mekong
Hainan
Luzon
South
China
Sea
Mariana
Islands
MICRONESIA

SAHEL
Gulf of Aden
Somali Peninsula
Andaman
Islands
Andaman Sea
Indochina
Peninsula
Marshall
Islands

AFRICA
Blue Nile
White Nile
Ethiopian
Highlands
Sri Lanka
Nicobar Is.
Malay
Peninsula

Congo
Lake
Victoria
Lower Guinea
Congo
Basin
Lake
Tanganyika
Kilimanjaro
19,340 ft
5,895 m
Seychelles
Maldive
Islands
EQUATOR
Sumatra
Borneo
Indonesia
Greater Sunda
Islands
Java
Celebes
Moluccas
New
Guinea
MELANESIA
Bismarck
Archipelago
Solomon
Islands
Gilbert
Islands

Namib Desert
Zambezi
Madagascar
Mascarene Islands
INDIAN
Arafura
Sea
Coral
Sea
Vanuatu
Fiji
Islands

Kalahari
Desert
Drakensberg
OCEAN
Great
Sandy Desert
AUSTRALIA
Lake Eyre
-52 ft, -16 m
Great
Victoria Desert
Great Dividing Range
New
Caledonia
SOUTH
PACIFIC
OCEAN

Kerguelen Islands
Murray
Darling
Mt. Kosciuszko
7,310 ft
2,228 m
Tasmania
Tasman
Sea
North Island
NEW
ZEALAND
South Island

Auckland
Islands

60°S
South
Magnetic
Pole

en Maud Land
ANTARCTICA
Transantarctic Mountains
Victoria Land
Ross Ice Shelf
Ross Sea

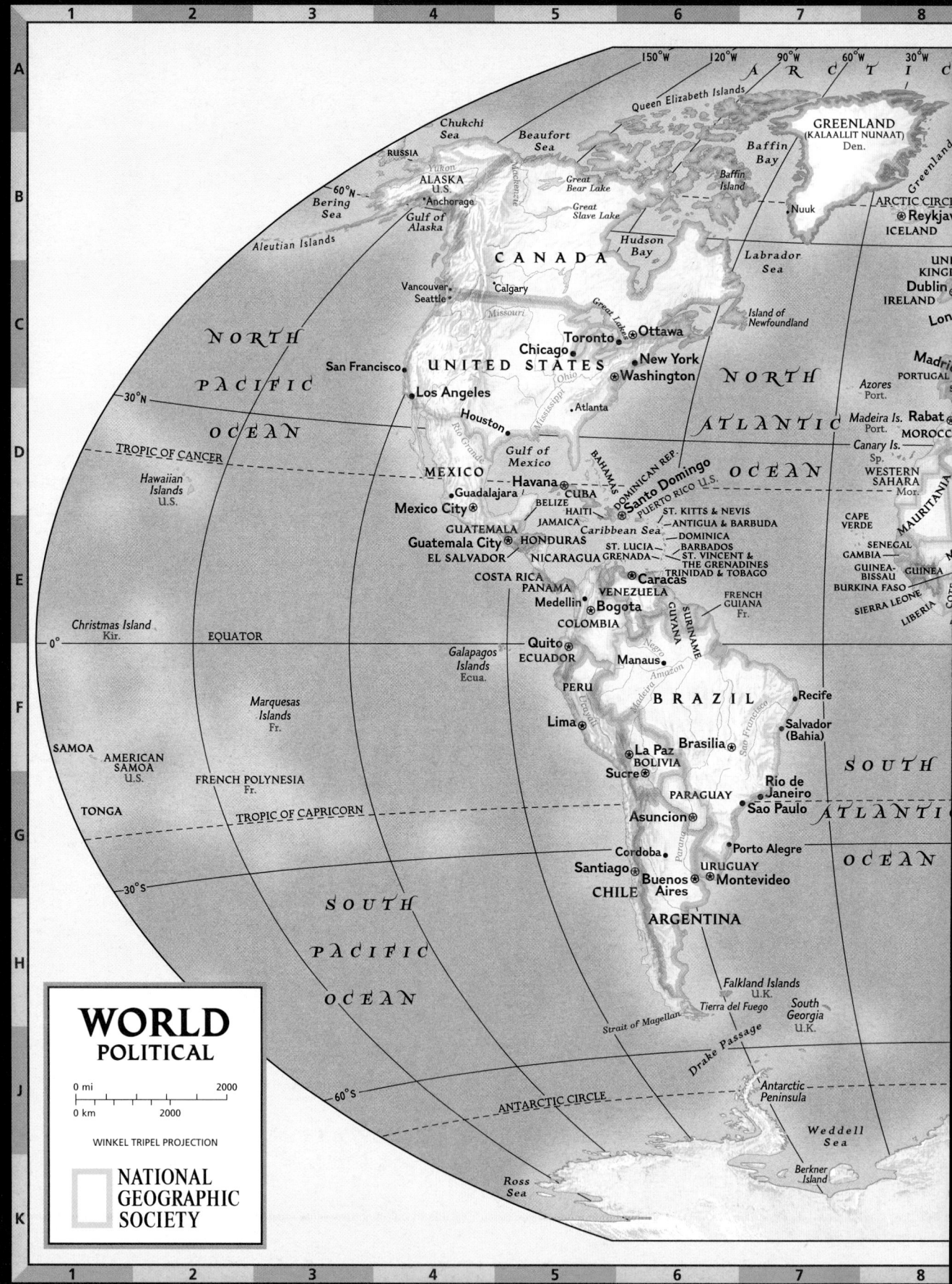

WORLD
POLITICAL

0 mi   2000

0 km   2000

WINKEL TRIPEL PROJECTION

NATIONAL GEOGRAPHIC SOCIETY

ABBREVIATIONS

AUST.	AUSTRIA
B.&H.	BOSNIA & HERZEGOVINA
BELG.	BELGIUM
CROAT.	CROATIA
CZECH REP.	CZECH REPUBLIC
DEM. REP. OF THE CONGO	DEMOCRATIC REPUBLIC OF THE CONGO
EQ. GUINEA	EQUATORIAL GUINEA
EST.	ESTONIA
HUNG.	HUNGARY
LITH.	LITHUANIA
MACED.	MACEDONIA
MOLD.	MOLDOVA
NETH.	NETHERLANDS
SLOV.	SLOVENIA
SWITZ.	SWITZERLAND
U.A.E.	UNITED ARAB EMIRATES
YUG.	YUGOSLAVIA

130°W 120°W 110°W 100°W 90°W 80°W 70°W 60°W 50°W 40°W 30°W

GREENLAND
(KALAALLIT NUNAAT)
Den.

70°N

20°W A

N

B

30°W

ARCTIC CIRCLE

50°N

C

UNITED
STATES
POLITICAL

0 mi — 600
0 km — 600

OBLIQUE AZIMUTHAL EQUIDISTANT PROJECTION

NATIONAL
GEOGRAPHIC
SOCIETY

40°W D

C A N A D A

E

40°N

50°W

MAINE
Montpelier   Augusta
NEW   Portland
MONTANA   NORTH   MINNESOTA   Lake Superior   YORK   Concord, N.H.
    DAKOTA   MICHIGAN   Boston, MASS.
Billings   Bismarck   Lake Huron   Albany   Providence, R.I.
    SOUTH   Minneapolis   St. Paul   Lansing   Lake   Hartford, CONN.
Helena   Pierre   DAKOTA   WISCONSIN   Milwaukee   Ontario   Buffalo
Casper   Madison   L. Erie   Detroit   Cleveland   PA.   New York
WYOMING   Sioux City   IOWA   Chicago   Toledo   Pittsburgh   Harrisburg   Trenton, N.J.
Cheyenne   NEBRASKA   Des Moines   IND.   OHIO   Philadelphia
    Lincoln   Omaha   ILLINOIS   Columbus   Baltimore   Dover, DEL.
Denver   Indianapolis   Dayton   W. VA.   Annapolis, MD.
COLORADO   Kansas City   Springfield   Cincinnati   Washington, D.C.
    Topeka   MISSOURI   Frankfort   Charleston   Richmond
Santa Fe   KANSAS   St. Louis   Louisville   Virginia Beach
    Jefferson City   KENTUCKY   VIRGINIA
        Nashville   Raleigh
    Tulsa   TENNESSEE   NORTH CAROLINA
Oklahoma City   ARKANSAS   Memphis   Charlotte
Albuquerque   OKLAHOMA   SOUTH   Columbia
NEW   Little Rock   Atlanta   CAROLINA
MEXICO   Birmingham   GEORGIA   Charleston
El Paso   Fort   MISS.   ALABAMA   Savannah
    Worth   Dallas   Montgomery
    TEXAS   LOUISIANA   Jackson   Jacksonville
Austin   Baton Rouge   Tallahassee
San Antonio   Houston   New Orleans   FLORIDA
        Tampa

F

Billings

50°N F

G

30°N

30°W

H

M E X I C O

Gulf of
Mexico

Miami

J

20°N

20°W

60°W

Bermuda Is.
U.K.

ATLANTIC OCEAN

Straits of Florida

CUBA

Caribbean

Sea   80°W   JAMAICA

100°W   90°W

BAHAMAS

ANTIGUA
& BARBUDA
ST. KITTS
& NEVIS

San Juan

HAITI   DOMINICAN
    REPUBLIC   PUERTO
        RICO
        U.S.   DOMINICA

70°W

K

UNITED STATES

**MIDDLE
AMERICA**
PHYSICAL/POLITICAL

0 mi   400

0 km   400

AZIMUTHAL EQUIDISTANT PROJECTION

NATIONAL
GEOGRAPHIC
SOCIETY

Tijuana
Mexicali
*Sonoran
Desert*
30°N
Baja California
Gulf of California
La Paz
False Cape
Mazatlan
20°N
*Revillagigedo Islands
Mex.*

Ciudad
Juarez
Chihuahua
M E X
Sierra Madre Occidental
Nuevo
Laredo
Monterrey
Matamoros
Rio Grande
Sierra Madre Oriental
I
San Luis
Potosi
Leon
C
Guadalajara
O
Mexico City
*Orizaba
18,855 ft
+5,747 m*
Popocatepetl†
17,802 ft
5,426 m
Veracruz
Ciudad Madero
Tampico
Bay of Campeche

Gulf of Mexico

Merida
*Cozumel
Island*
Yucatan
Peninsula
Belize
City
Belmopan
BELIZE *Gulf of
Hondur*
H O

Sierra Madre del Sur
Acapulco
*Isthmus of
Tehuantepec*
*Gulf of
Tehuantepec*
Sierra Madre
GUATEMALA
Guatemala City
EL SALVADOR
San Salvador
Tegucigalpa
Le

10°N

C E N T R A

A M E R I C A

P A C I F I C

O C E A N

Cocos Isla
C.R.

110°W   100°W   90°W

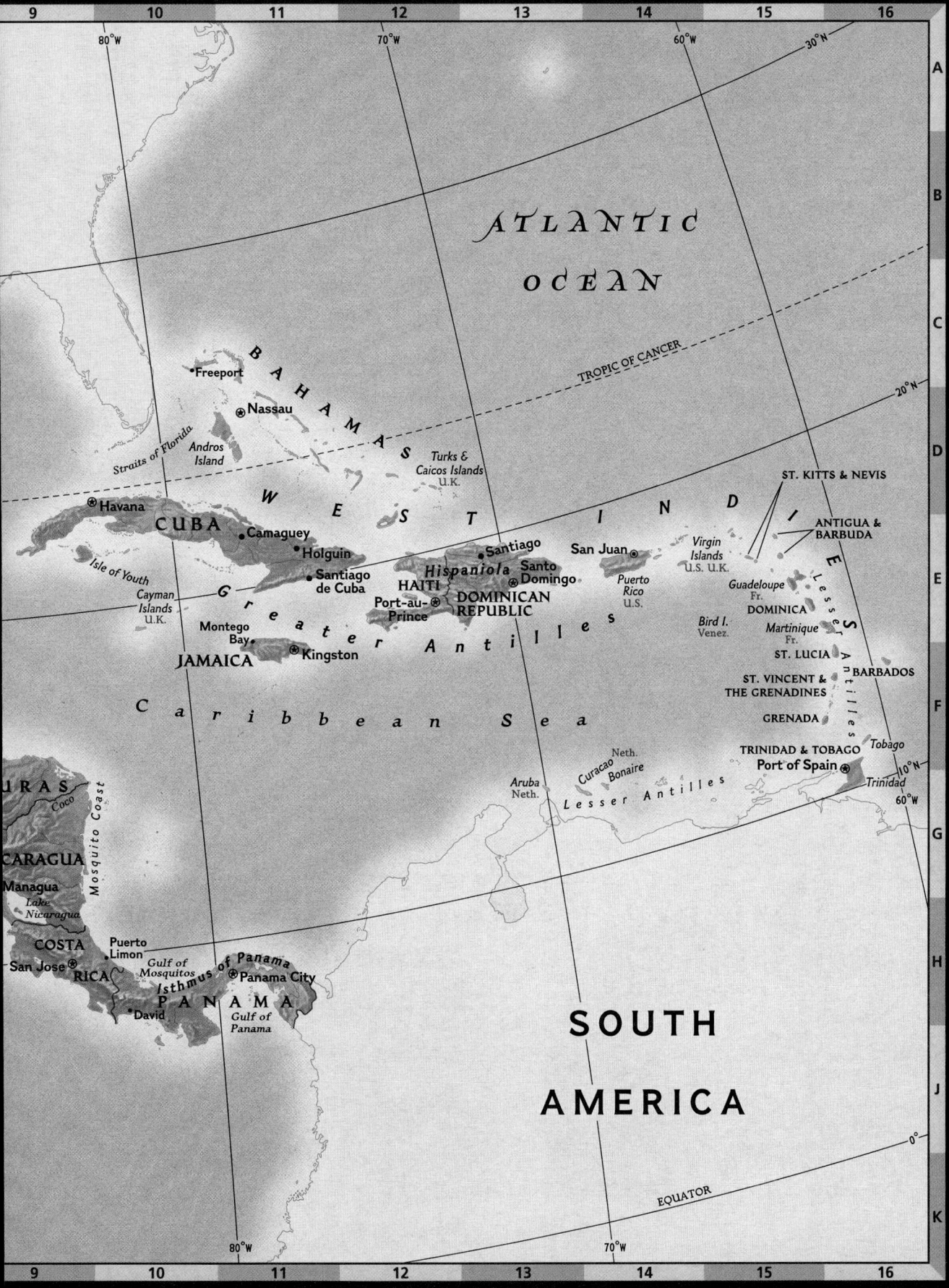

ATLANTIC OCEAN

30°N

TROPIC OF CANCER

20°N

•Freeport

⊛Nassau

B A H A M A S

Straits of Florida

Andros Island

W E S T

Turks & Caicos Islands U.K.

⊛Havana

CUBA

•Camaguey

•Holguin

Isle of Youth

Cayman Islands U.K.

•Santiago de Cuba

G r e a t e r

Hispaniola

•Santiago

Santo ⊛Domingo

San Juan ⊛

I N D I E

ST. KITTS & NEVIS

Virgin Islands U.S. U.K.

ANTIGUA & BARBUDA

HAITI

Port-au- ⊛ Prince

DOMINICAN REPUBLIC

Puerto Rico U.S.

Guadeloupe Fr.

DOMINICA

L e s s e r

Bird I. Venez.

Martinique Fr.

ST. LUCIA

Montego Bay

A n t i l l e s

⊛Kingston

JAMAICA

BARBADOS

ST. VINCENT & THE GRENADINES

A n t i l l e s

C a r i b b e a n   S e a

GRENADA

TRINIDAD & TOBAGO

Tobago

Neth.

Curacao Bonaire

Aruba Neth.

L e s s e r   A n t i l l e s

Port of Spain ⊛

Trinidad

10°N

60°W

RAS

Coco

Mosquito Coast

CARAGUA

Managua

Lake Nicaragua

Puerto Limon

Gulf of Mosquitos

Isthmus of Panama

⊛Panama City

COSTA

San Jose ⊛

RICA

P A N A M A

•David

Gulf of Panama

SOUTH

AMERICA

0°

EQUATOR

80°W

70°W

ASIA

ARCTIC OCEAN

Chukchi Sea

Bering Sea

Bering Strait

Point Barrow

North Magnetic Pole

Beaufort Sea

Banks Island

Queen Elizabeth Islands

Ellesmere Island

Parry Islands

Greenland Sea

EUROPE

GREENLAND (KALAALLIT NUNAAT) Den.

ALASKA U.S.

Victoria Island

Boothia Peninsula

Baffin Bay

Qeqertarsuaq

ARCTIC CIRCLE

Gulf of Alaska

YUKON TERRITORY

Great Bear Lake

NUNAVUT

Baffin Island

Davis Strait

Nuuk (Godthab)

NORTHWEST TERRITORIES

Southampton Island

Labrador Sea

PACIFIC

CANADA

Great Slave Lake

Hudson Bay

NEWFOUNDLAND

BRITISH COLUMBIA

Mackenzie

Athabasca

Churchill

QUEBEC

LABRADOR

Vancouver Island

ALBERTA

SASKATCHEWAN

MANITOBA

Lake Winnipeg

Seven

ONTARIO

Gulf of St. Lawrence

St.-Pierre & Miquelon Fr.

OCEAN

WASHINGTON

Missouri

P.E.I.

N.B.

NOVA SCOTIA

OREGON

MONTANA

NORTH DAKOTA

MINN.

Lake Superior

Lake Huron

Ottawa

ME.

VT.

N.H.

IDAHO

WYOMING

SOUTH DAKOTA

WIS.

MICHIGAN

Lake Michigan

L. Ontario

NEW YORK

MASS.

R.I.

CONN.

ATLANTIC

Great Salt Lake

NEVADA

NEBRASKA

IOWA

L. Erie

PA.

N.J.

OCEAN

CALIFORNIA

UTAH

COLORADO

KANSAS

MISSOURI

ILL.

IND.

OHIO

W.VA.

VA.

DEL.

MD.

Washington, D.C.

UNITED STATES

KENTUCKY

Bermuda Islands U.K.

ARIZONA

NEW MEXICO

OKLAHOMA

Arkansas

TENNESSEE

N.C.

ARK.

MISS.

ALA.

GEORGIA

S.C.

Guadalupe I. Mex.

TEXAS

LA.

Rio Grande

Mississippi

FLORIDA

TROPIC OF CANCER

MEXICO

BARBADOS

ANTIGUA AND BARBUDA

ST. KITTS AND NEVIS

BAHAMAS

Nassau

DOMINICAN REPUBLIC

Gulf of Mexico

Havana

CUBA

Santo Domingo

PUERTO RICO

U.S. DOMINICA

Mexico City

Cayman Is. U.K.

HAITI

Port-au-Prince

ST. LUCIA

ST. VINCENT AND THE GRENADINES

GRENADA

JAMAICA

Kingston

BELIZE

Belmopan

Caribbean Sea

TRINIDAD AND TOBAGO

GUATEMALA

Guatemala City

HONDURAS

Tegucigalpa

San Salvador

NICARAGUA

EL SALVADOR

Managua

Panama Canal

COSTA RICA

San Jose

PANAMA

Panama City

SOUTH AMERICA

Cocos I. C.R.

EQUATOR

NORTH AMERICA
POLITICAL

0 mi _____ 1000

0 km _____ 1000

AZIMUTHAL EQUIDISTANT PROJECTION

NATIONAL GEOGRAPHIC SOCIETY

SOUTH AMERICA POLITICAL

0 mi 800
0 km 800

AZIMUTHAL EQUIDISTANT PROJECTION

NATIONAL GEOGRAPHIC SOCIETY

Caribbean Sea

ATLANTIC OCEAN

PACIFIC OCEAN

Barranquilla
Santa Marta
Cartagena
Maracaibo
Barquisimeto
Caracas
Valencia
Lake Maracaibo
Ciudad Guayana
GUYANA
Georgetown
SURINAME
Paramaribo
Cayenne
FRENCH GUIANA
Fr.
VENEZUELA
Bucaramanga
San Cristobal
Medellin
Bogota
Cali
COLOMBIA
Boa Vista
Orinoco
Malpelo I. Col.
Negro
Boundary claimed by Suriname
Marajo Island
Belem
EQUATOR
Esmeraldas
Quito
ECUADOR
Guayaquil
AMAZON
Amazon
Santarem
Amazon (Solimoes)
Manaus
Iquitos
Marañon
BASIN
Madeira
Teresina
Fortaleza
Natal
Campina Grande
Recife
PERU
Purus
Tapajos
BRAZIL
Rio Branco
Porto Velho
Xingu
Tocantins
Sao Francisco
Callao
Lima
Machu Picchu
Cuzco
Ayacucho
Lake Titicaca
Trinidad
BOLIVIA
La Paz
Telés Pires
Salvador (Bahia)
Arequipa
Oruro
Santa Cruz
Goiania
Brasilia
Arica
Sucre
Uberlandia
Uberaba
Belo Horizonte
Iquique
Tarija
Campo Grande
PARAGUAY
Campinas
Nova Iguacu
Antofagasta
Londrina
Sao Paulo
Rio de Janeiro
Salta
Santos
San Felix I. San Ambrosio I. Chil.
Asuncion
Curitiba
San Miguel de Tucuman
Parana
Uruguaiana
Santa Maria
Porto Alegre
La Serena
Coquimbo
Cordoba
ARGENTINA
Juan Fernandez Is. Chil.
Rosario
Buenos Aires
URUGUAY
Montevideo
Valparaiso
Mendoza
La Plata
Rio de la Plata
Santiago
Concepcion
Mar del Plata
Bahia Blanca
Negro
Puerto Montt
ANDES
Comodoro Rivadavia
Falkland Islands (Islas Malvinas)
Stanley Administered by United Kingdom
(Claimed by Arg.)
Rio Gallegos
Strait of Magellan
TIERRA DEL FUEGO
Punta Arenas
South Georgia I. U.K.
Ushuaia
Cape Horn

EUROPE
POLITICAL

0 mi   400

0 km   400

AZIMUTHAL EQUIDISTANT PROJECTION

NATIONAL
GEOGRAPHIC
SOCIETY

Akureyri

⊛ Reykjavik
ICELAND

ARCTIC CIRCLE

Norwegian Sea

N

Tromso

Faroe Islands
Den.   Torshavn

Trondheim •

• Are   Um

Alesund •

Sundsvall •

Shetland
Islands
Lerwick •

Bergen •

Rockall
U.K.

Isle of Lewis

Orkney Islands

Stavanger •

Oslo ⊛

Uppsala •

Inverness •

Stockholm ⊛

Skagerrak

UNITED
SCOTLAND

• Aberdeen

Glasgow •

⊛ Edinburgh

• Goteborg

Gotland

NORTHERN
IRELAND   ⊛ Belfast

North
Sea

Arhus
•

DENMARK • Malmo
Copenhagen ⊛

IRELAND
Dublin ⊛

Irish
Sea

Liverpool •
• Manchester

KINGDOM

WALES

• Birmingham

• Kiel

Gdansk •

Celtic
Sea

Cardiff •

ENGLAND

• Hamburg

London ⊛

The
Hague ⊛

NETH.
⊛ Amsterdam

Berlin ⊛

Bydgoszcz •

Land's End

Southampton •

GERMANY

POLAN

**ATLANTIC
OCEAN**

English Channel

Brussels ⊛
BELGIUM

• Bonn

Rhine

Frankfurt •

Wroclaw •

Lodz

Le Havre •

LUX.

⊛ Prague

Brest •

CZECH REP.

Oder

• Rennes

⊛ Paris

Strasbourg •

Bratislava

SLOVAK

Nantes •

FRANCE

Munich •

LIECH.

Vienna •

La Rochelle •

Zurich •

Bern ⊛

AUSTRIA

Bay of
Biscay

Limoges •

SWITZERLAND

Budapest

Bordeaux •

Geneva •

Lyon •

SLOVENIA **HUNGAR**

A Coruna •

• Milan

Ljubljana ⊛

⊛ Zagreb

CROATIA

• Vigo

Turin •

Venice •

Donostia-
San Sebastian

Toulouse •

MONACO

Genoa •

**BOSNIA &
HERZEGOVIN**

Porto •

Bilbao •

Pyrenees

Nice •

SAN
MARINO

Sarajevo •

Valladolid •

ANDORRA

Marseille •

ITALY

MONTENEGR

Coimbra •

PORTUGAL

Madrid ⊛

Zaragoza •

Corsica
Fr.

**VATICAN
CITY**

⊛ Rome

Adriatic Sea

Lisbon ⊛

SPAIN

• Barcelona

Tira

ALBANI

Valencia •

Palma •

Sardinia
It.

• Naples

Cape
St. Vincent

• Cordoba

Balearic
Islands
Sp.

Cadiz •

• Seville

• Murcia

Tyrrhenian
Sea

GIBRALTAR
U.K.

• Malaga

• Cartagena

Cagliari •

Ionian
Sea

Strait of Gibraltar

M e d i t e r r a

Palermo •

Sicily

• Messina

• Catania

AFRICA

Valletta •
MALTA

10°W

0°

10°E

30°N

60°N

40°W

30°W

20°W

10°W

70°N

0°

10°E

50°N

30°W

30°W

20°W

40°N

20°W

ARCTIC CIRCLE

MERIDIAN OF GREENWICH (LONDON)

Balti

Gulf

30°E 40°E 70°N 50°E •Tobseda 70°E 60°N A

Barents Sea 80°E

PLAND •Murmansk

Ivalo• *Kola Peninsula* Pechora• URAL MOUNTAINS A commonly accepted division
between Asia and Europe—here
marked by a gray line—is
formed by the Ural Mountains,
Ural River, Caspian Sea, Caucasus
Mountains, and the Black Sea
with its outlets, the Bosporus
and the Dardanelles.

Kirovsk• •Umba *White Sea* B

Kem• •Archangel
Severodvinsk •Syktyvkar

Kemi F
I •Oulu N Europe-Asia
boundary ASIA C

asa L •Perm
•Kuopio *Lake Onega* A RUSSIA N 70°E

•Tampere *Lake Ladoga* •Kirov D 50°N D

urku ⊛Helsinki •St. Petersburg •Ufa

⊛Tallinn Velikiy
Novgorod •Kazan

ESTONIA •Yaroslavl K

⊛Riga •Tver Nizhniy
Novgorod •Samara A

LATVIA ⊛Moscow Orenburg• Z E

Daugavpils• •Ryazan •Penza A

THUANIA •Vitsyebsk •Smolensk •Saratov Oral• K 60°E

unas• ⊛Vilnius *Volga* H 40°N

⊛Minsk •Bryansk *Ural* S

BELARUS •Homyel •Kursk T F

saw •Chernihiv A

Sumy• •Volgograd N

Kiev ⊛ •Kharkiv •Astrakhan

•Lviv •Poltava *Caspian Sea* G

UKRAINE •Donetsk •Rostov 60°E

•Vinnytsya •Dnipropetrovsk •Stavropol 40°N

Dniester MOLDOVA ⊛Chisinau *Sea of Azov* •Groznyy

ROMANIA •Odesa •Kerch AZERBAIJAN G

DINA *Crimea* •Simferopol *Caucasus Mountains*
•Yalta GEORGIA ⊛Baku

rade ⊛Bucharest Sevastopol H

SLAVIA •Constanta *Black Sea*

Danube *Balkan Mts.* •Varna

BULGARIA *Bosporus*

⊛Sofia J

Skopje
ED. Istanbul• •Dardanelles

•Thessaloniki TURKEY J

ECE *Aegean Sea* ASIA

⊛Athens K

onnesus *Rhodes*

a •Iraklio 30°N
Crete 30°E 40°E 50°E K

ATLANTIC OCEAN

NORTH AMERICA

ARCTIC CIRCLE

Norwegian Sea

ARCT

Franz Josef Land
Russ.

Barents Sea

Kara S

Baltic Sea

EUROPE

⊗ Moscow

Europe-Asia
boundary

R

U

S

A commonly accepted division
between Asia and Europe—here
marked by a gray line—is
formed by the Ural Mountains,
Ural River, Caspian Sea, Caucasus
Mountains, and the Black Sea
with its outlets, the Bosporus
and the Dardanelles.

• Chelyabinsk

• Omsk

• Novosibirsk

•Istanbul   *Black
                Sea*

Ankara ⊗   TURKEY   GEORGIA
                            •Tbilisi
Nicosia •   ARMENIA
CYPRUS •Adana   •   •Yerevan AZERBAIJAN
LEBANON   Baku⊗
Beirut• •Damascus   •
Jerusalem• SYRIA   Caspian Sea
ISRAEL ⊗Amman
JORDAN
         •Baghdad   Tehran⊗
         IRAQ   Ashgabat⊗

                 Astana ⊗

KAZAKHSTAN

Aral
Sea

Syr Darya

TURKMENISTAN   UZBEKISTAN

⊗Tashkent •Bishkek
          •Almaty
          KYRGYZSTAN

SINK

•Dushanbe TAJIKISTAN Urum

AFGHANISTAN Hindu Kush   K U N L U

•Kabul ⊗   •

Islamabad⊗ KASHMIR

AFRICA

           SAUDI
Jeddah•   Riyadh⊗ Manama   Zahedan•
Makkah•   BAHRAIN •QATAR
(Mecca)   • Doha   Strait of
ARABIA   Abu Dhabi⊗ Hormuz
          UNITED ARAB
          EMIRATES
Sanaa⊗   Rub al Khali Muscat•

Basra•
KUWAIT•
Kuwait⊗

IRAN

PAKISTAN

Lahore •

Karachi•

Boundary
claimed
by India

TIB

Delhi•
New Delhi⊗
Jaipur •

Kathmandu⊗

HIMALA

NEPA

OMAN   Gulf of Oman

BOUNDARY UNDEFINED

YEMEN

Indore• •Bhopal

INDIA

•Aden
Gulf of Aden

*Arabian
Sea*

Mumbai•
(Bombay)

Godavari

Ganges

Calc
(Ko

Socotra
Yem.

Hyderabad B
                a

o

B e n

Bangalore•   •Chennai
             (Madras)

Lakshadweep
Ind.

Madurai•

Krishna

ASIA
POLITICAL

0 mi   1000

0 km   1000

TWO-POINT EQUIDISTANT PROJECTION

NATIONAL
GEOGRAPHIC
SOCIETY

EQUATOR

SRI LANKA
⊗Colombo

⊗Male
MALDIVES

INDIAN   OCEA

Chagos Archipelago
Brit. Ind. Oc. Terr.

9 10 11 12 13 14 15 16

NORTH AMERICA
Bering Strait

Chukchi
Sea

Wrangel I.

Gulf of Anadyr
•Anadyr

Bering
Sea

North Pole

OCEAN

East
Siberian
Sea

New Siberian Islands

Laptev Sea

Cherskiy Range

Kolyma Range

Commander Is.

Kamchatka Peninsula

Magadan•

Sea of Okhotsk

Yakutsk•

S I A

I A

Lena

Sakhalin

Kuril Islands

E R I A

Aldan

Lake Baikal

Amur

Hokkaido
•**Sapporo**

Irkutsk•

Sea of
Japan
•Vladivostok
Japan

JAPAN
⊛**Tokyo**

Marcus I.
Jap.

TROPIC
OF CANCER

Yenisey

MANCHURIA

Ulan Bator ⊛

MONGOLIA

Changchun•

Herlen

NORTH
KOREA

Honshu
Kyoto•

P A C I F I C O C E A N

TAY MTS.

Shenyang•

Pyongyang⊛

GOBI

Seoul
⊛
SOUTH
KOREA

Osaka
•**Hiroshima**

Bonin Is.
Jap.

Beijing ⊛

Kyushu

Volcano Is.
Jap.

Shijiazhuang•

Qingdao•

Yellow

Lanzhou•

Xuzhou•

Sea

Yellow

Xian•

East
China

•**Shanghai**

Ryukyu Islands

Okinawa

C H I N A

Nanjing•

Sea

Parece Vela
Jap.

Huang

Chengdu•

Nanchang•

Fuzhou•

⊛**Taipei**

Boundary
claimed
by China

Changsha•

Guiyang•

TAIWAN

Guangzhou•

The People's Republic of China claims
Taiwan as its 23rd province.

Kunming•

Hong Kong•
Macau•

Philippine

•**Luzon**

Sea

Hanoi ⊛ •Haiphong

South

MYANMAR
(BURMA)

LAOS

Hainan

Quezon City
⊛•**Manila**

Samar

BLADESH
ka

Yangon
(Rangoon)

Vientiane ⊛

Da Nang•

China

Mindoro

PHILIPPINES

Leyte

THAILAND

Sea

Panay
Negros

Bangkok⊛

CAMBODIA

VIETNAM

Palawan

Mindanao

Andaman
Islands
Ind.

Phnom Penh•
•**Ho Chi Minh City**

Biak•

Jayapura•

Andaman Sea

Bandar Seri
Begawan

SABAH

Morotai

New Guinea

Gulf of Thailand

BRUNEI

Halmahera

Kepi•

SARAWAK

Aru
Is.

Merauke•

Kuala•
Lumpur⊛

MALAYSIA

MALAYSIA

Buru

Ceram

Moluccas

Dolak•

Medan•

SINGAPORE⊛

Borneo

Celebes

bar
nds
d.

I N D O N E S I A

Following East Timor's vote for independence
from Indonesia, the United Nations,
in October 1999, established a UN transitional
administration to help East Timor's
870,000 people toward independence.

Sumatra

GREATER

Tanimbar
Is.

Jambi•

SUNDA ISLANDS

Mentawai
Islands

Java Sea

Dili•

EAST TIMOR
UN admin.

AUSTRALIA

Jakarta⊛

Java

Timor

Timor Sea

Kupang•

100°E   110°E   120°E   130°E   140°E   150°E

9 10 11 12 13 14 15 16

1   **2**   **3**   **4**   **5**   **6**   **7**   **8**

TROPIC OF CANCER

NORTH PACIFIC OCEAN

Wake Island
U.S.

NORTHERN
MARIANA
ISLANDS
U.S.

⊛ *Saipan*

GUAM ⊛ *Hagatna*
U.S.

Bikini Atoll

MARSHALL
ISLANDS

PALAU
Koror ⊛

Yap Islands

Truk Islands

Caroline Islands

⊛ *Palikir*
Pohnpei (Ponape)

⊛ *Majuro*

FEDERATED STATES
OF MICRONESIA

Tarawa

EQUATOR

Yaren ⊛
NAURU

SOLOMON
ISLANDS

TUVALU
Funafi

New Guinea

Mt. Wilhelm
14,793 ft
+ 4,509 m

New Britain

PAPUA
NEW GUINEA
Port Moresby ⊛
Torres Strait

Solomon Is.

⊛ *Honiara*

Santa Cruz Is.

Darwin •

Gulf of Carpentaria

CORAL SEA
ISLANDS
TERRITORY
Austral.

VANUATU
⊛ *Port-Vila*

Suva

Kimberley Plateau

NEW
CALEDONIA
Fr.

FIJI
ISLAN

• *Noumea*

TROPIC OF CAPRICORN

Macdonnell Ranges

AUSTRALIA

• Brisbane

Norfolk Island
Austral.

GREAT VICTORIA
DESERT

Lake Eyre ○
-52 ft
-16 m

Lord Howe Island
Austral.

• Perth

Darling

• Sydney

Great Australian Bight

Adelaide •

Murray

⊛ Canberra

Auckland •

Nor
Isla

+ *Mt. Kosciuszko*
7,310 ft
2,228 m

NEW
ZEALAND

Melbourne ⊛

Tasman Sea

Wellington ⊛

INDIAN OCEAN

Tasmania

• Hobart

Mt. Cook +
12,349 ft
3,764 m

Christchurch
South Island

Stewart Island

1   **2**   **3**   **4**   **5**   **6**   **7**   **8**

9   10   11   12   13   14   15   16

170°W   160°W   150°W   140°W   130°W   120°W

NORTH AMERICA

A

TROPIC OF CANCER

20°N

HAWAII
U.S.

B

Johnston Atoll
U.S.

N

10°N

Kingman Reef
U.S.

Palmyra Atoll
U.S.

C

P O L Y N E S I A

Howland Island
U.S.

Baker Island U.S.

Kiritimati
(Christmas I.)

EQUATOR

0°

D

RIBATI

Phoenix Is.

Jarvis I.
U.S.

Line Islands

OCEANIA
PHYSICAL/POLITICAL

0 mi   1000
0 km   1000

MERCATOR PROJECTION

NATIONAL GEOGRAPHIC SOCIETY

TOKELAU
N.Z.

AMERICAN SAMOA
U.S.

Marquesas Is.

10°S

E

SAMOA
Apia

Samoa Is.

⊕ Pago Pago

COOK ISLANDS
N.Z.

Tuamotu Archipelago

TONGA

Niue

Society Is.

Tahiti
⊙ Papeete

F

⊛ **Nukualofa**

FRENCH POLYNESIA
Fr.

Henderson I.
U.K.

20°S

TROPIC OF CAPRICORN

Austral Is.

Pitcairn I.
U.K.

Ducie I.
U.K.

G

adec
nds
Z.

30°S

INTERNATIONAL DATE LINE

H

S O U T H   P A C I F I C   O C E A N

40°S

J

Chatham Islands
N.Z.

K

170°W   160°W   150°W   140°W   130°W   120°W

50°S

9   10   11   12   13   14   15   16

AFRICA
POLITICAL

0 mi — 1000
0 km — 1000

AZIMUTHAL EQUIDISTANT PROJECTION

NATIONAL
GEOGRAPHIC
SOCIETY

ARCTIC OCEAN
PHYSICAL

0 mi 800
0 km 800

AZIMUTHAL EQUIDISTANT PROJECTION

NATIONAL GEOGRAPHIC SOCIETY

RUSSIA

Yenisey
Ob
Gulf of Ob
White Sea
GERMANY
LUX.
BELGIUM
DENMARK NETH.
FRANCE

Taymyr Peninsula
Kara Sea
Novaya Zemlya
Barents Sea
FINLAND
SWEDEN
NORWAY
North Sea
UNITED KINGDOM
IRELAND
50°N

Lena
Laptev Sea
120°E
90°E
60°E
30°E
North Land
Franz Josef Land
Svalbard
Norwegian Sea
ARCTIC CIRCLE
60°N
ICELAND
ATLANTIC OCEAN

Gr. 0°
Greenland Sea
Denmark Strait
70°N
80°

New Siberian Islands
150°E
ARCTIC
OCEAN
North Pole ★
Oodaaq Island
80°N
30°W

East Siberian Sea
Sea of Okhotsk
KAMCHATKA PENINSULA
180°
Lincoln Sea
GREENLAND

Wrangel Island
150°W
120°W
90°W
60°W
Queen
Ellesmere Island
Hayes Peninsula
Cape Farewell

Chukchi Sea
Chukchi Peninsula
Point Barrow
Elizabeth
Islands
Devon I.
Baffin Bay
Davis Strait

Bering Sea
St. Lawrence Island
Bering Strait
Seward Peninsula
Brooks Range
North Slope
Beaufort Sea
Banks Island
Melville Island
Prince of Wales I.
Somerset I.
Boothia Peninsula
Melville Peninsula
Foxe Basin
Baffin Island
Hudson Strait

Aleutian Islands
Nunivak Island
ALASKA
Yukon
Victoria Island
Southampton Island

PACIFIC OCEAN
Bristol Bay
Mackenzie
Great Bear Lake
CANADA
Hudson Bay

ANTARCTICA
PHYSICAL

0 mi 600
0 km 600

AZIMUTHAL EQUIDISTANT PROJECTION

NATIONAL GEOGRAPHIC SOCIETY

SOUTH ATLANTIC OCEAN
60°W
60°S
South Orkney Is.
45°W
30°W
15°W
0°
15°E
30°E
45°E
60°E
Fimbul Ice Shelf

South Shetland Islands
ANTARCTIC PENINSULA
ANTARCTIC CIRCLE
70°S
Ruser-Larsen Ice Shelf
QUEEN MAUD LAND
ENDERBY LAND
60°E

75°W
GRAHAM LAND
Larsen Ice Shelf
Mt. Jackson 13,747 ft 4,190 m
Weddell Sea
COATS LAND
Valkyrie Dome
INDIAN OCEAN
75°E

PALMER LAND
Alexander I.
Filchner Ice Shelf
Berkner Island
Ronne Ice Shelf
Amery Ice Shelf

SOUTH PACIFIC OCEAN
90°W
Bellingshausen Sea
ELLSWORTH LAND
Vinson Massif 16,067 ft 4,897 m
Ellsworth Mts.
ANTARCTICA
TRANSANTARCTIC MOUNTAINS
POLAR PLATEAU
★ South Pole
AMERICAN HIGHLAND
West Ice Shelf
90°E

WEST
ANTARCTICA
Bentley Subglacial Trench -8,327 ft -2,538 m
105°W
EAST
ANTARCTICA
Shackleton Ice Shelf
105°E

MARIE BYRD LAND
120°W
Ross Ice Shelf
Dome Circe
WILKES LAND
Dome Circe

Roosevelt I.
VICTORIA LAND
Ross I.
Mt. Erebus 12,448 ft 3,794 m
Talos Dome
150°E
INDIAN OCEAN

135°W
Ross Sea
150°W
165°W
180°
165°E
120°E
135°E

RUSSIA

Bering Sea

KAMCHATKA PENINSULA

Sea of Okhotsk

ALEUTIAN ISLANDS

Lake Baikal

Yablonovyy Range

Sakhalin

KURIL ISLANDS

Ulan Bator ⊛

MONGOLIA

ALTAY MOUNTAINS

GOBI

Greater Khingan Range

Manchurian Plain

Amur

Sikhote Alin Range

Hokkaido

Beijing ⊛

NORTH KOREA

Pyongyang ⊛

Sea of Japan

Honshu

JAPAN

⊛ Tokyo

NORTH PACIFIC

CHINA

Yellow

Seoul ⊛
SOUTH KOREA

Yellow Sea

Kyushu

Shikoku

Hawaii

Yangtze

Mekong

INDIA

East China Sea

⊛ Taipei

RYUKYU ISLANDS

TAIWAN

MYANMAR (BURMA)

⊛ Hanoi

Hainan

Luzon

PHILIPPINE ISLANDS

Philippine Sea

M I C R O N E S I A

MARIANA ISLANDS

NORTHERN MARIANA ISLANDS
U.S.

MARSHALL ISLANDS

Vientiane ⊛

VIETNAM

LAOS

South China Sea

Manila ⊛

PHILIPPINES

GUAM
U.S.

Ratak Chain

Yangon (Rangoon)

THAILAND
Bangkok ⊛

CAMBODIA

Phnom Penh ⊛

PALAU
Koror ⊛

CAROLINE ISLANDS

Ralik Chain

⊛ Majuro

Andaman Sea

Sulu Sea

Mindanao

⊛ Palikir

FEDERATED STATES OF MICRONESIA

Gilbert Islands

⊛ Tarawa

Bandar Seri Begawan

Celebes Sea

BRUNEI ⊛

KIRIBATI

Kuala Lumpur ⊛

MALAYSIA

Borneo

Celebes

MOLUCCAS

Yaren ⊛
NAURU

Phoenix Is.

⊛ SINGAPORE

Sumatra

INDONESIA

GREATER SUNDA ISLANDS

NEW GUINEA

M E L A N E S I A

SOLOMON ISLANDS

TUVALU
Funafuti ⊛

Tokelau
N.Z.

Jakarta ⊛

Java Sea

Celebes

Arafura Sea

PAPUA NEW GUINEA

Port ⊛
Moresby

Solomon Is.

⊛
Honiara

Santa Cruz Islands

WALLIS AND FUTUNA IS.
Fr.

AMERICAN SAMOA

SAMOA
⊛ Apia

Java

LESSER SUNDA ISLANDS

CORAL SEA ISLANDS TERRITORY
Austral.

VANUATU

NEW CALEDONIA
Fr.

⊛
Port-Vila

Suva ⊛

FIJI ISLANDS

TONGA

⊛ Nuku'alofa

TROPIC OF CAPRICORN

AUSTRALIA

Coral Sea

Darling

Norfolk Island
Austral.

Lord Howe Island
Austral.

Kermadec Islands
N.Z.

Great Australian Bight

⊛ Canberra

Tasman Sea

NEW ZEALAND

INDIAN

OCEAN

Tasmania

Wellington ⊛

Chatham Is.
N.Z.

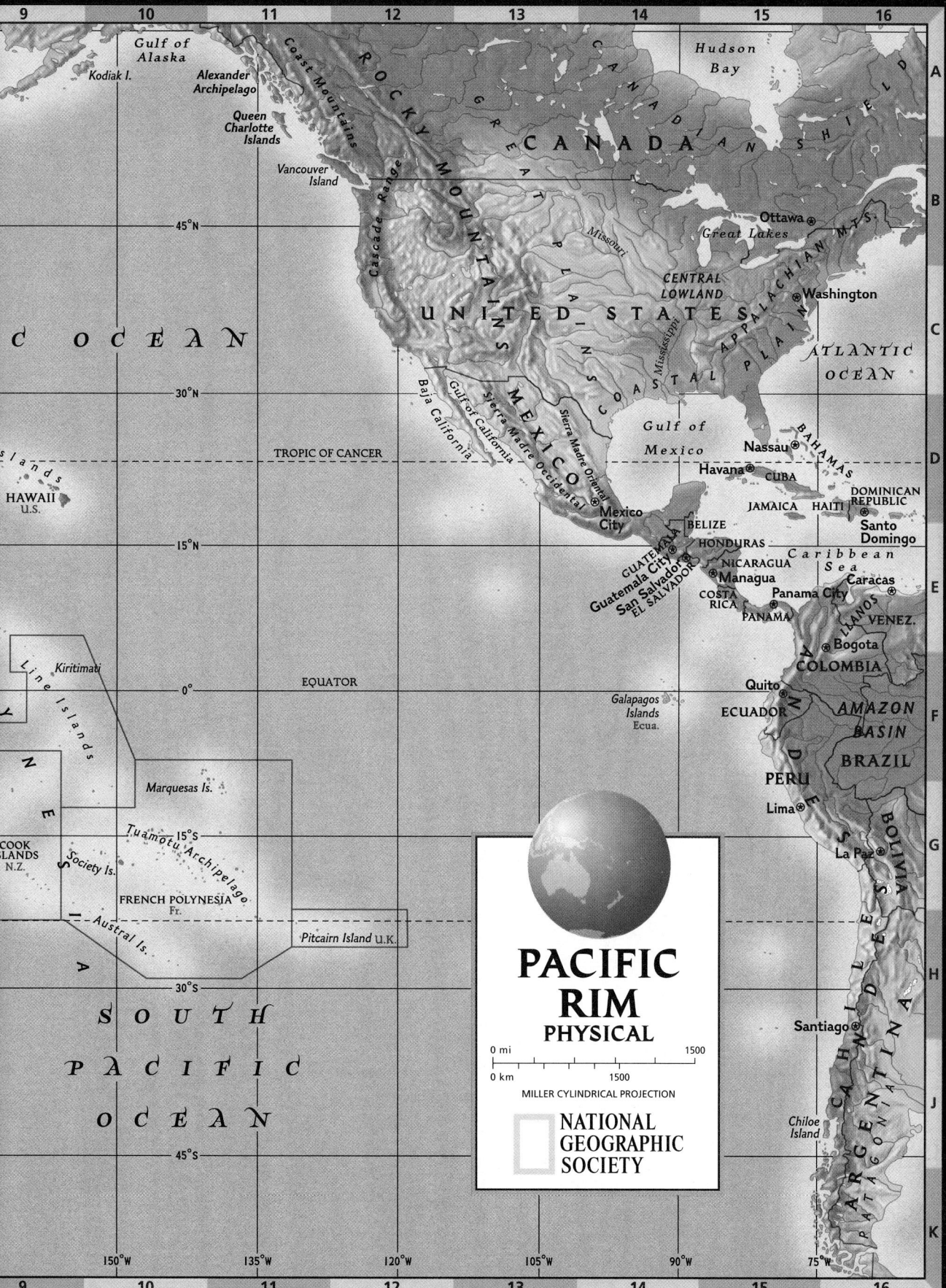

9 10 11 12 13 14 15 16

Gulf of
Alaska

Kodiak I.

Alexander
Archipelago

Queen
Charlotte
Islands

Vancouver
Island

Coast Mountains

ROCKY MOUNTAINS

Cascade Range

Hudson
Bay

C A N A D A   CANADIAN SHIELD

A

GREAT PLAINS

Missouri

Ottawa ⊛

Great Lakes

CENTRAL
LOWLAND

UNITED STATES

APPALACHIAN MTS.

⊛ Washington

B

45°N

OCEAN

30°N

C O A S T A L   P L A I N

ATLANTIC
OCEAN

C

TROPIC OF CANCER

Baja California

Gulf of California

Sierra Madre Occidental

M E X I C O

Sierra Madre Oriental

Gulf of
Mexico

Nassau ⊛

BAHAMAS

D

HAWAII
U.S.

Havana ⊛

CUBA

JAMAICA HAITI

DOMINICAN
REPUBLIC

⊛ Santo
Domingo

15°N

Mexico
City ⊛

BELIZE

HONDURAS

Caribbean
Sea

GUATEMALA

Guatemala City ⊛
San Salvador ⊛
EL SALVADOR

NICARAGUA

⊛ Managua

COSTA
RICA

Panama City ⊛

PANAMA

LLANOS

Caracas ⊛

VENEZ.

Bogota ⊛

COLOMBIA

E

Kiritimati

Line Islands

EQUATOR

0°

Galapagos
Islands
Ecua.

Quito ⊛

ECUADOR

ANDES

AMAZON
BASIN

BRAZIL

F

COOK
ISLANDS
N.Z.

Society Is.

Marquesas Is.

Tuamotu Archipelago

15°S

PERU

Lima ⊛

FRENCH POLYNESIA
Fr.

Austral Is.

Pitcairn Island U.K.

La Paz ⊛

BOLIVIA

G

30°S

S O U T H

P A C I F I C

O C E A N

45°S

Santiago ⊛

Chiloe
Island

ARGENTINA

ANDES

PATAGONIA

H

J

K

**PACIFIC
RIM**
PHYSICAL

0 mi   1500

0 km   1500

MILLER CYLINDRICAL PROJECTION

**NATIONAL
GEOGRAPHIC
SOCIETY**

150°W 135°W 120°W 105°W 90°W 75°W

9 10 11 12 13 14 15 16

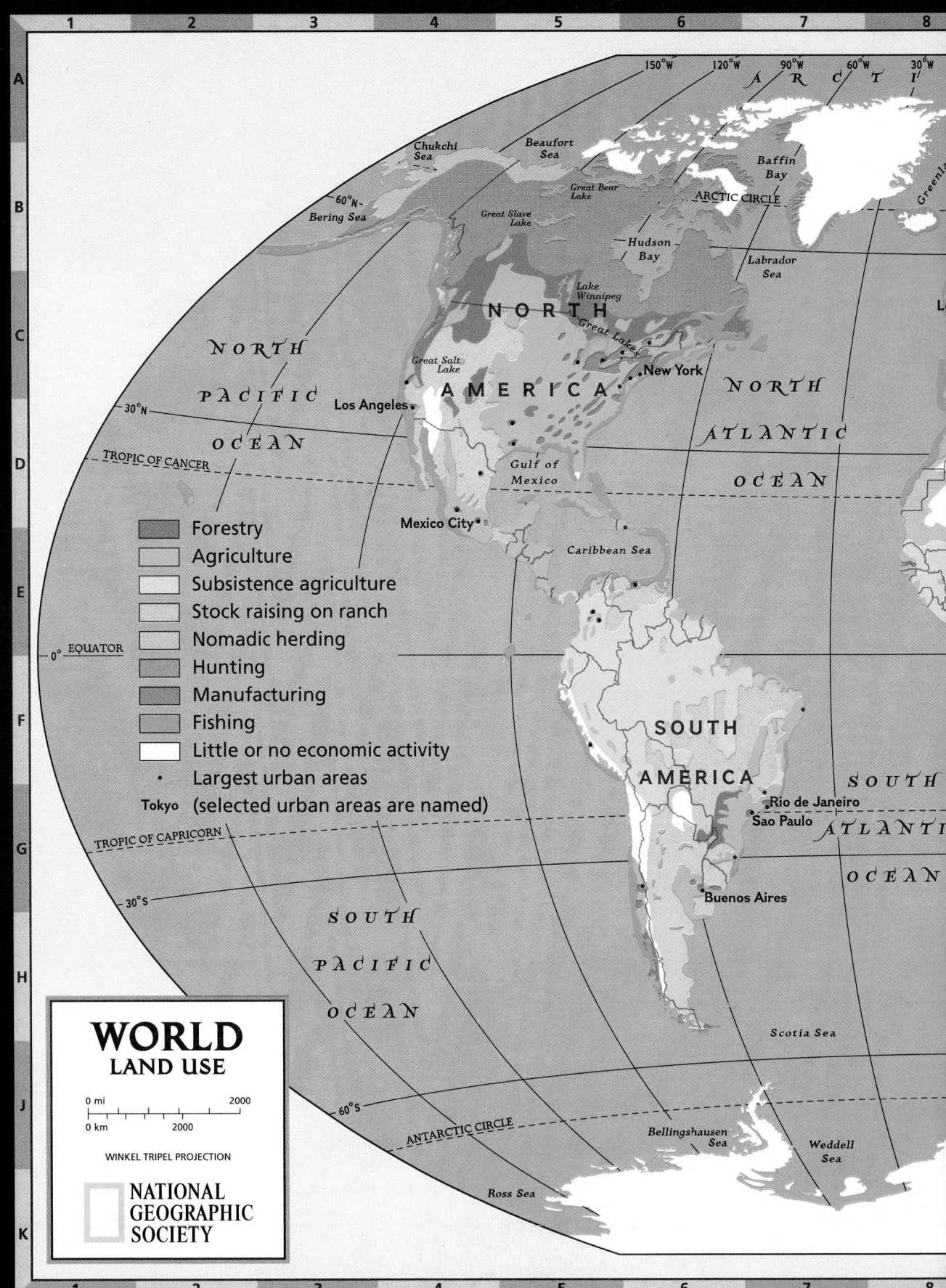

WORLD
LAND USE

Forestry
Agriculture
Subsistence agriculture
Stock raising on ranch
Nomadic herding
Hunting
Manufacturing
Fishing
Little or no economic activity
• Largest urban areas
Tokyo (selected urban areas are named)

0 mi 2000
0 km 2000

WINKEL TRIPEL PROJECTION

NATIONAL GEOGRAPHIC SOCIETY

30°E 60°E 90°E 120°E 150°E

C *E* *A* *N*

Kara
Sea

Laptev Sea

East Siberian Sea

Barents Sea

ian Sea

60°N

Bering Sea

Sea of
Okhotsk

Lake
Baikal

Moscow

Baltic Sea

U R O P E

A S I A

NORTH

Caspian
Sea

Aral
Sea

Black Sea

Sea of
Japan

Seoul

Tokyo

PACIFIC

Yellow
Sea

30°N

terranean Sea

Cairo

Shanghai
East
China
Sea

OCEAN

TROPIC OF CANCER

R E D

Red
Sea

Mumbai
Arabian
Sea

Calcutta

Bay of
Bengal

Andaman Sea

South
China
Sea

Philippine
Sea

F R I C A

Gulf of Aden

os

Lake
Victoria

Kinshasa

Lake
Tanganyika

EQUATOR 0°

Arafura
Sea

Coral
Sea

INDIAN

TROPIC OF CAPRICORN

OCEAN

AUSTRALIA

SOUTH

PACIFIC

OCEAN

Sydney

Tasman
Sea

60°S

N T A R C T I C A

Ross Sea

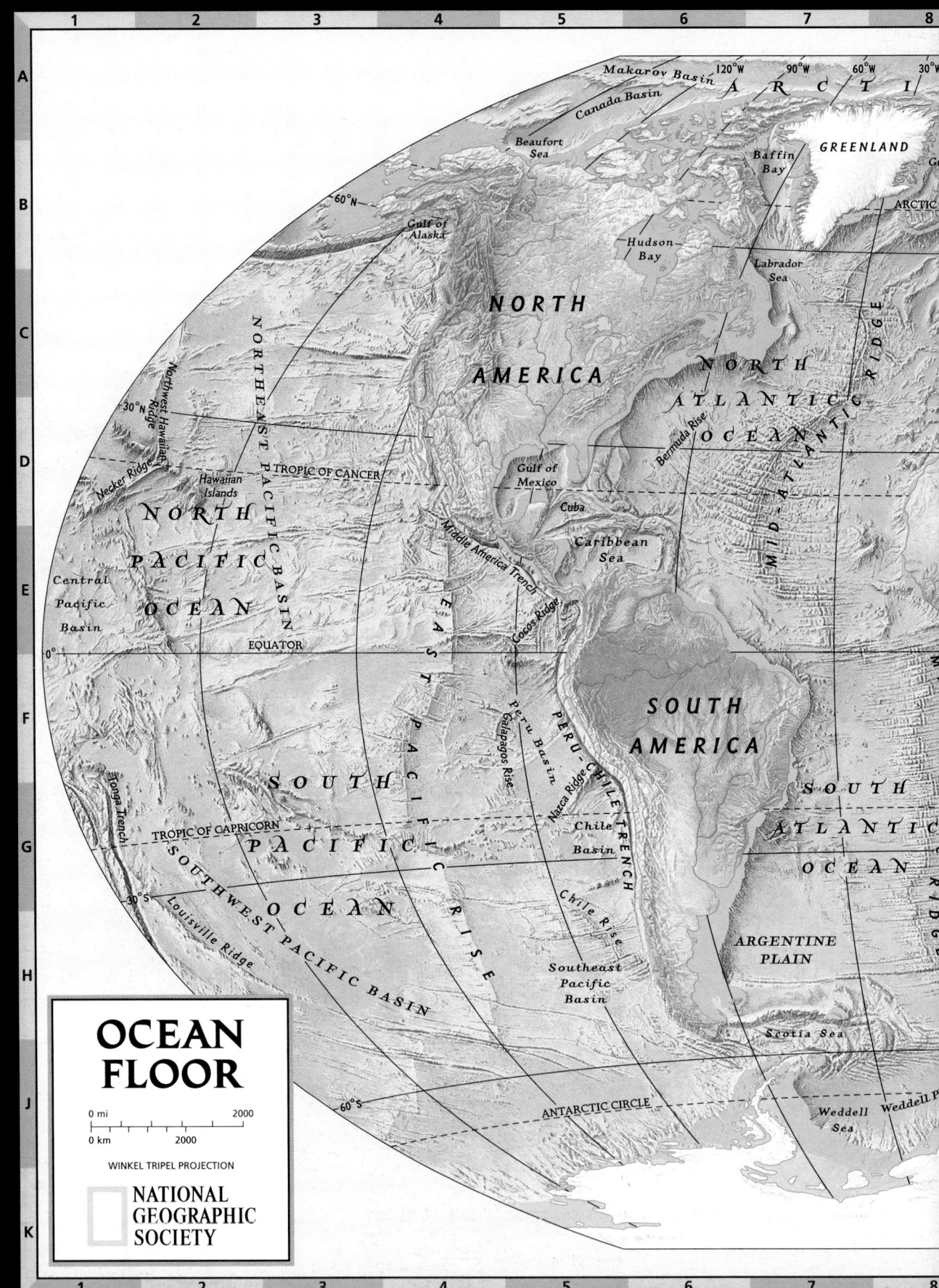

OCEAN
FLOOR

0 mi   2000
0 km   2000

WINKEL TRIPEL PROJECTION

NATIONAL
GEOGRAPHIC
SOCIETY

A

OCEAN

30°E　60°E　90°E　150°E

POLE PLAIN

Nansen Basin

Kara Sea

Laptev Sea

East Siberian Sea

Barents
Sea

orwegian
Sea

EUROPE

ASIA

Black Sea

Mediterranean Sea

Red Sea

AFRICA

Arabian
Sea

Arabian
Basin

Bay of
Bengal

Sea of
Okhotsk

Bering
Sea

60°N

Sea of
Japan

Kuril Trench

Northwest
Pacific
Basin

NORTH

PACIFIC

OCEAN

30°N

TROPIC OF CANCER

Ryukyu Trench

Kyushu-Palau Ridge

Philippine
Sea

Mariana
Trench

South
China
Sea

Central
Pacific
Basin

MID-INDIAN RIDGE

Mid-Indian
Basin

Investigator Ridge

Madagascar

idge

Borneo

EQUATOR

0°

Java Trench

New
Guinea

Coral
Sea

SOUTHWEST INDIAN RIDGE

INDIAN

Perth
Basin

AUSTRALIA

OCEAN

Crozet
Basin

SOUTHEAST INDIAN RIDGE

TROPIC OF CAPRICORN

SOUTH

PACIFIC

OCEAN

30°S

South
Australian
Basin

Tasmania

North Island

Tasman
Sea

South Island

Enderby Plain

South Indian
Basin

60°S

ANTARCTIC CIRCLE

NTARCTICA

World Facts

WHAT IS THE . . .	ANSWER	LOCATION	SIZE
largest continent?	Asia	Eastern Hemisphere	17,400,000 sq. miles
smallest continent?	Australia	South Pacific	2,941,290 sq. miles
largest nation?	Russia	Europe-Asia	6,592,800 sq. miles
smallest nation?	Vatican City	Europe	.17 sq. miles
largest ocean?	Pacific		64,186,300 sq. miles
longest river?	Nile	East Africa	4,160 miles long
largest lake?	Caspian Sea	Eurasia	143,244 sq. miles
deepest lake?	Baikal	Asia	5,315 feet deep
highest mountain?	Mt. Everest	Nepal-Tibet	29,035 feet high
highest waterfall?	Angel Falls	Venezuela	3,212 feet high
largest desert?	Sahara	North Africa	3,500,000 sq. miles
highest continental point?	Mt. Everest	Nepal-Tibet	29,035 feet high
lowest continental point?	Dead Sea	Israel-Jordan	1,312 feet below sea level

Historical Atlas AND World Data Bank

Early Civilizations 3500 B.C –1700s B.C.

Ancient Empires A.D. 1—A.D. 500

150°W 90°W 30°W 0° 30°E 90°E 150°E

ARCTIC OCEAN

60°N

NORTH AMERICA

EUROPE

ASIA

ATLANTIC OCEAN

Roman Empire A.D. 120

Sassanian Empire A.D. 250

Han Dynasty A.D. 100

30°N

PACIFIC OCEAN

Kush A.D. 250

Gupta Empire A.D. 400

Maya Civilization A.D. 250

Axum A.D. 400

0°

AFRICA

PACIFIC OCEAN

Moche Culture A.D. 400

SOUTH AMERICA

INDIAN OCEAN

AUSTRALIA

30°S

N
W—E
S

0   1,000   2,000 mi.
0   1,000   2,000 km
Miller Projection

60°S

ANTARCTICA

A New Global Age A.D. 800—A.D. 1500

150°W 90°W 30°W 0° 30°E 90°E 150°E

ARCTIC OCEAN

60°N

NORTH AMERICA

EUROPE

ASIA

ATLANTIC OCEAN

Mongol Empire 1300

30°N

Islamic Empire 750

PACIFIC OCEAN

Maya 800

Aztec 1500

Mali 1337

AFRICA

0°

SOUTH AMERICA

Inca 1500

Monomotapa 1400s

INDIAN OCEAN

AUSTRALIA

30°S

PACIFIC OCEAN

N
W—E
S

0   1,000   2,000 mi.
0   1,000   2,000 km
Miller Projection

60°S

ANTARCTICA

Age of Imperialism 1870–1914

Overseas Empires
- Belgium
- France
- Germany
- Great Britain
- Italy
- Netherlands
- Portugal
- Spain

ARCTIC OCEAN

NORTH AMERICA
United States
Mexico

PACIFIC OCEAN

ATLANTIC OCEAN

EUROPE
Russian Empire
Austria-Hungary
Ottoman Empire

ASIA
China
Japan

PACIFIC OCEAN

AFRICA

INDIAN OCEAN

SOUTH AMERICA
Brazil
Argentina

AUSTRALIA

N W E S

0   1,000   2,000 mi.
0   1,000   2,000 km
Miller Projection

ANTARCTICA

Global Civilization Today

ARCTIC OCEAN

NORTH AMERICA
Vancouver
Los Angeles
Chicago
Montreal
New York
Mexico City

EUROPE
London
Paris
Madrid
Berlin
Rome
Moscow
Algiers
Cairo
Baghdad
Tehran

ASIA
Beijing
Seoul
Shanghai
Hong Kong
Tokyo

PACIFIC OCEAN

ATLANTIC OCEAN

AFRICA
Dakar
Lagos
Kinshasa
Nairobi

Mumbai
Bangkok
Singapore
Jakarta

INDIAN OCEAN

SOUTH AMERICA
Caracas
Lima
Rio de Janeiro
Santiago
Buenos Aires

Cape Town

AUSTRALIA
Sydney

N W E S

0   1,000   2,000 mi.
0   1,000   2,000 km
Miller Projection

ANTARCTICA

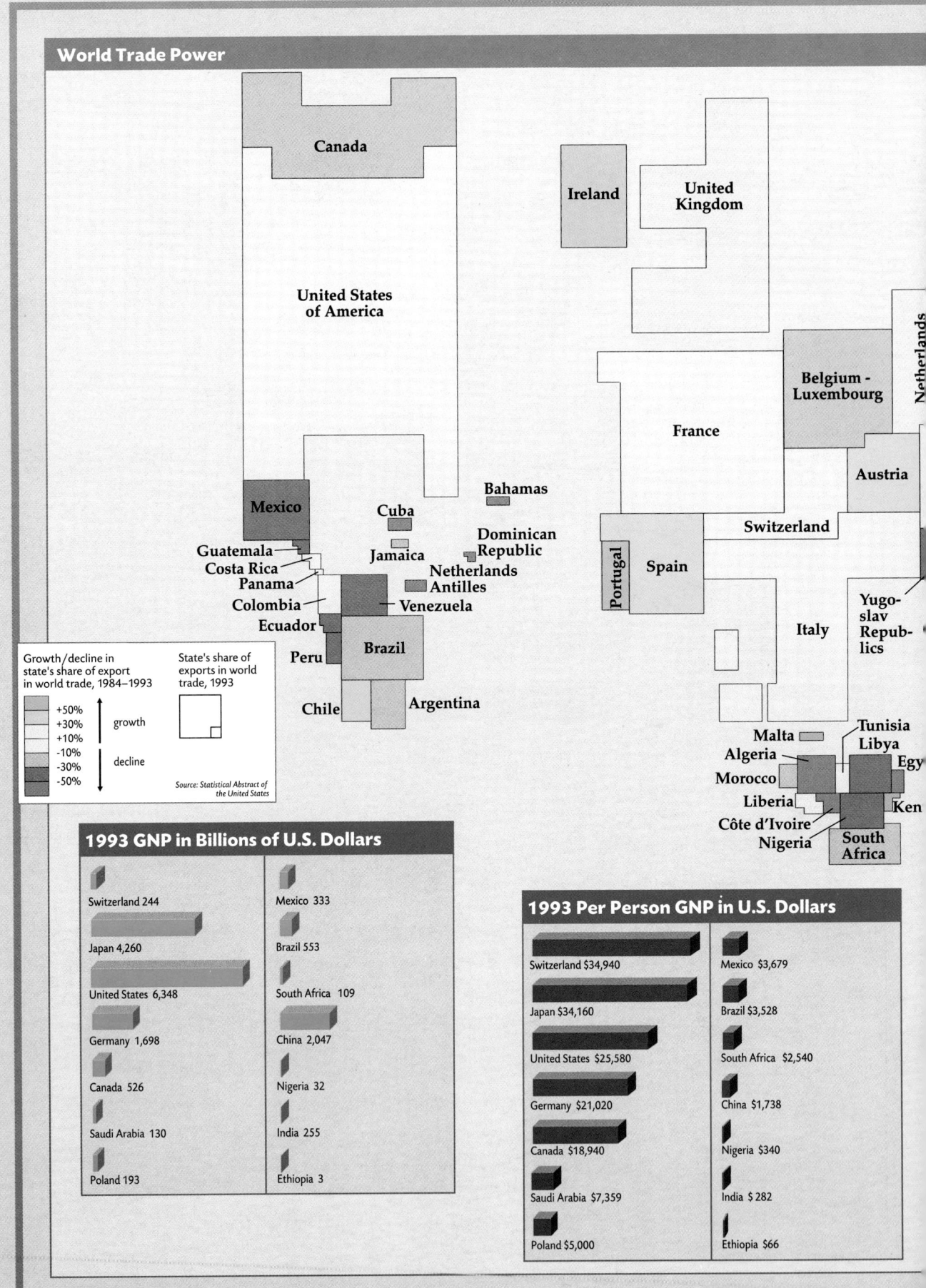

Canada

Ireland

United
Kingdom

Netherlands

United States
of America

Belgium -
Luxembourg

France

Austria

Bahamas

Mexico

Cuba

Switzerland

Dominican
Republic

Guatemala
Costa Rica
Panama

Jamaica

Portugal

Spain

Netherlands
Antilles

Colombia

Venezuela

Italy

Yugo-
slav
Repub-
lics

Ecuador

Peru

Brazil

Chile

Argentina

Malta

Tunisia
Libya

Algeria

Egy

Morocco

Ken

Liberia

Côte d'Ivoire
Nigeria

South
Africa

Growth/decline in
state's share of export
in world trade, 1984–1993

State's share of
exports in world
trade, 1993

+50%	
+30%	growth
+10%	
-10%	decline
-30%	
-50%	

*Source: Statistical Abstract of
the United States*

1993 GNP in Billions of U.S. Dollars

Switzerland 244

Mexico 333

Japan 4,260

Brazil 553

United States 6,348

South Africa 109

Germany 1,698

China 2,047

Canada 526

Nigeria 32

Saudi Arabia 130

India 255

Poland 193

Ethiopia 3

1993 Per Person GNP in U.S. Dollars

Switzerland $34,940

Mexico $3,679

Japan $34,160

Brazil $3,528

United States $25,580

South Africa $2,540

Germany $21,020

China $1,738

Canada $18,940

Nigeria $340

Saudi Arabia $7,359

India $ 282

Poland $5,000

Ethiopia $66

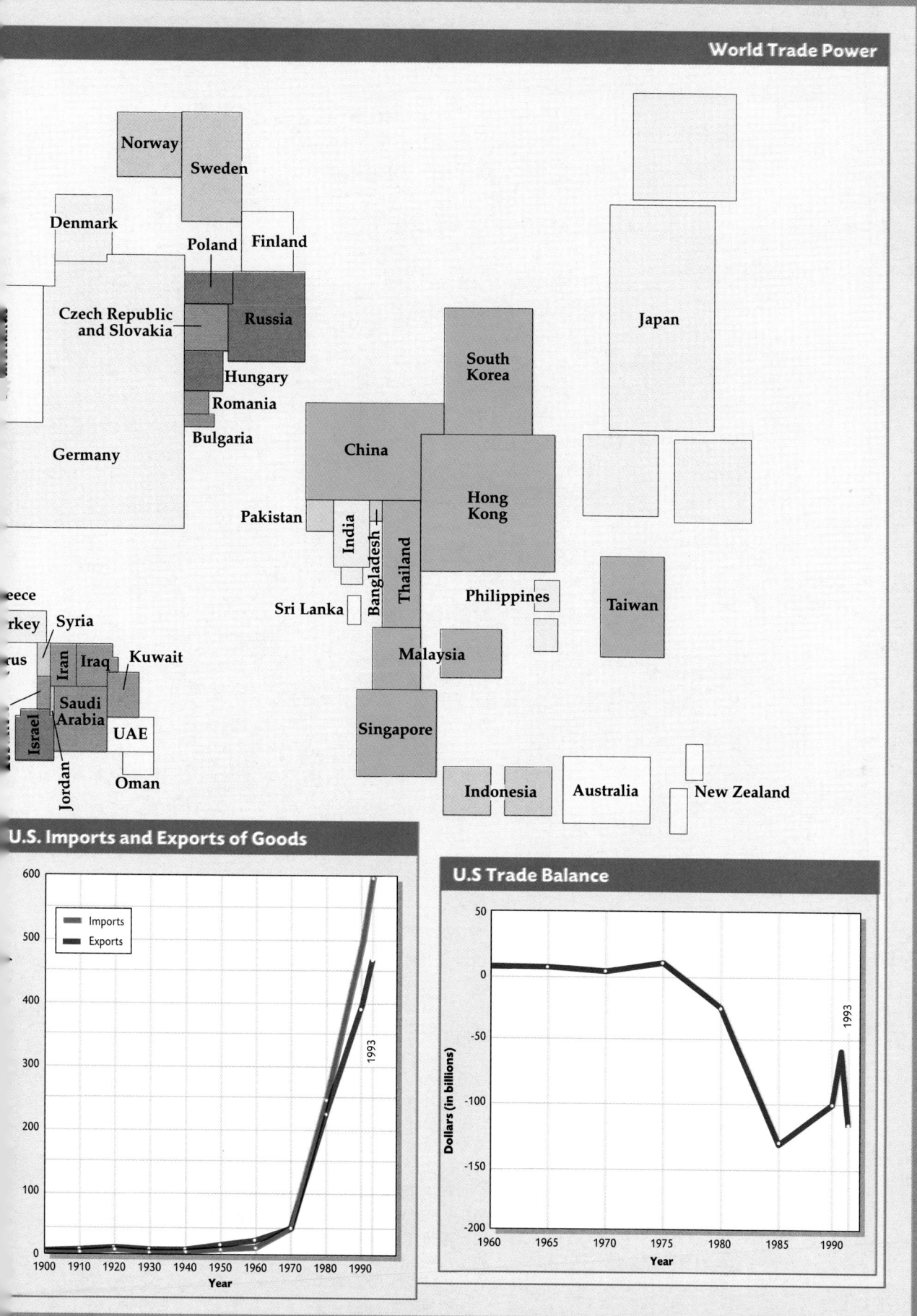

Norway
Sweden
Denmark
Poland
Finland
Czech Republic
and Slovakia
Russia
Hungary
Romania
Bulgaria
Germany
Japan
South
Korea
China
Hong
Kong
Pakistan
India
Bangladesh
Thailand
Taiwan
Sri Lanka
Philippines
eece
rkey
Syria
Kuwait
Iran
Iraq
us
Saudi
Arabia
Malaysia
Israel
UAE
Singapore
Jordan
Oman
Indonesia
Australia
New Zealand

U.S. Imports and Exports of Goods

Imports
Exports

600
500
400
300
200
100
0
1900 1910 1920 1930 1940 1950 1960 1970 1980 1990
Year
1993

U.S Trade Balance

50
0
-50
-100
-150
-200
1960 1965 1970 1975 1980 1985 1990
Year
Dollars (in billions)
1993

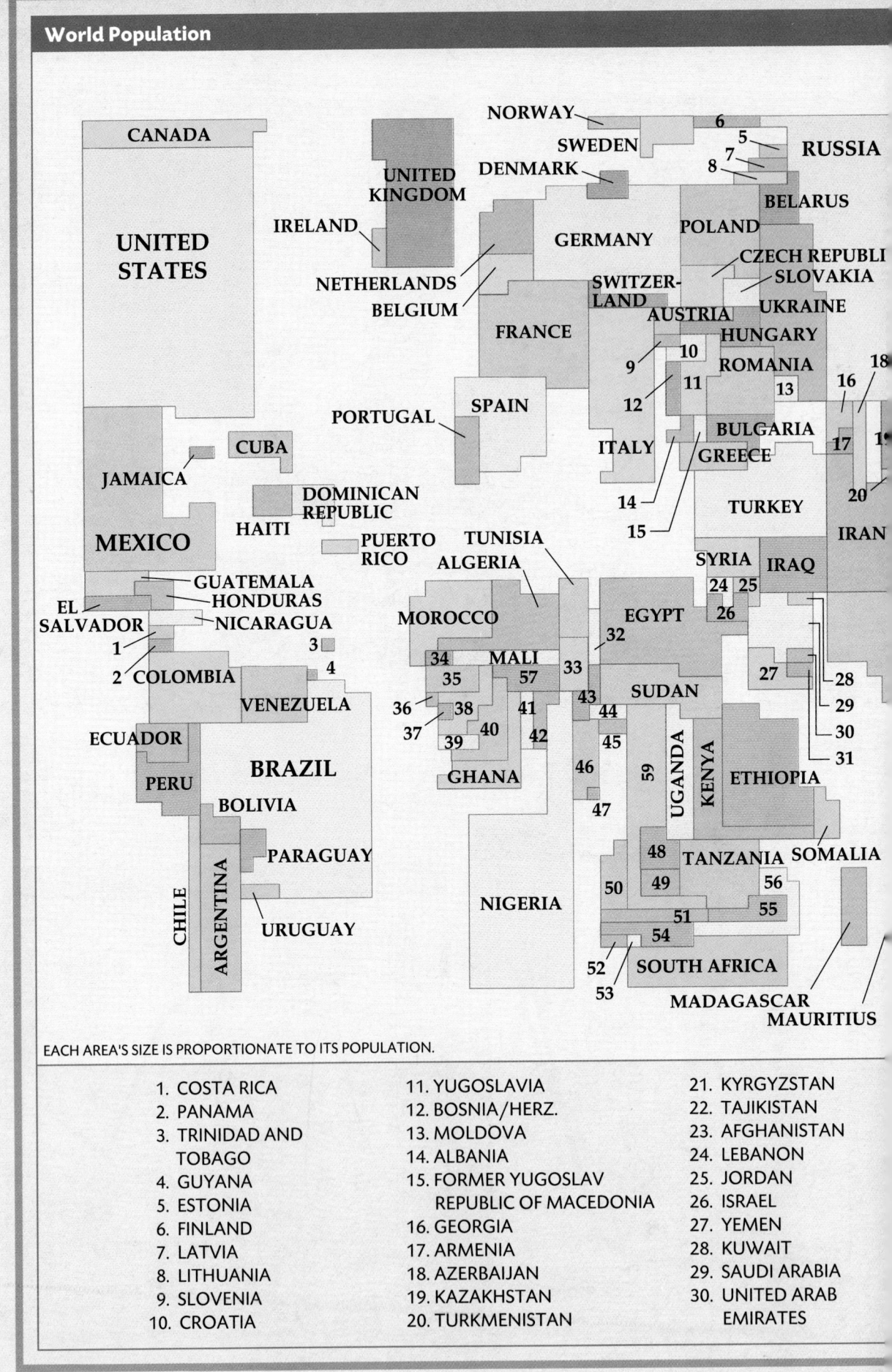

EACH AREA'S SIZE IS PROPORTIONATE TO ITS POPULATION.

1. COSTA RICA	11. YUGOSLAVIA	21. KYRGYZSTAN
2. PANAMA	12. BOSNIA/HERZ.	22. TAJIKISTAN
3. TRINIDAD AND TOBAGO	13. MOLDOVA	23. AFGHANISTAN
	14. ALBANIA	24. LEBANON
4. GUYANA	15. FORMER YUGOSLAV REPUBLIC OF MACEDONIA	25. JORDAN
5. ESTONIA		26. ISRAEL
6. FINLAND	16. GEORGIA	27. YEMEN
7. LATVIA	17. ARMENIA	28. KUWAIT
8. LITHUANIA	18. AZERBAIJAN	29. SAUDI ARABIA
9. SLOVENIA	19. KAZAKHSTAN	30. UNITED ARAB EMIRATES
10. CROATIA	20. TURKMENISTAN	

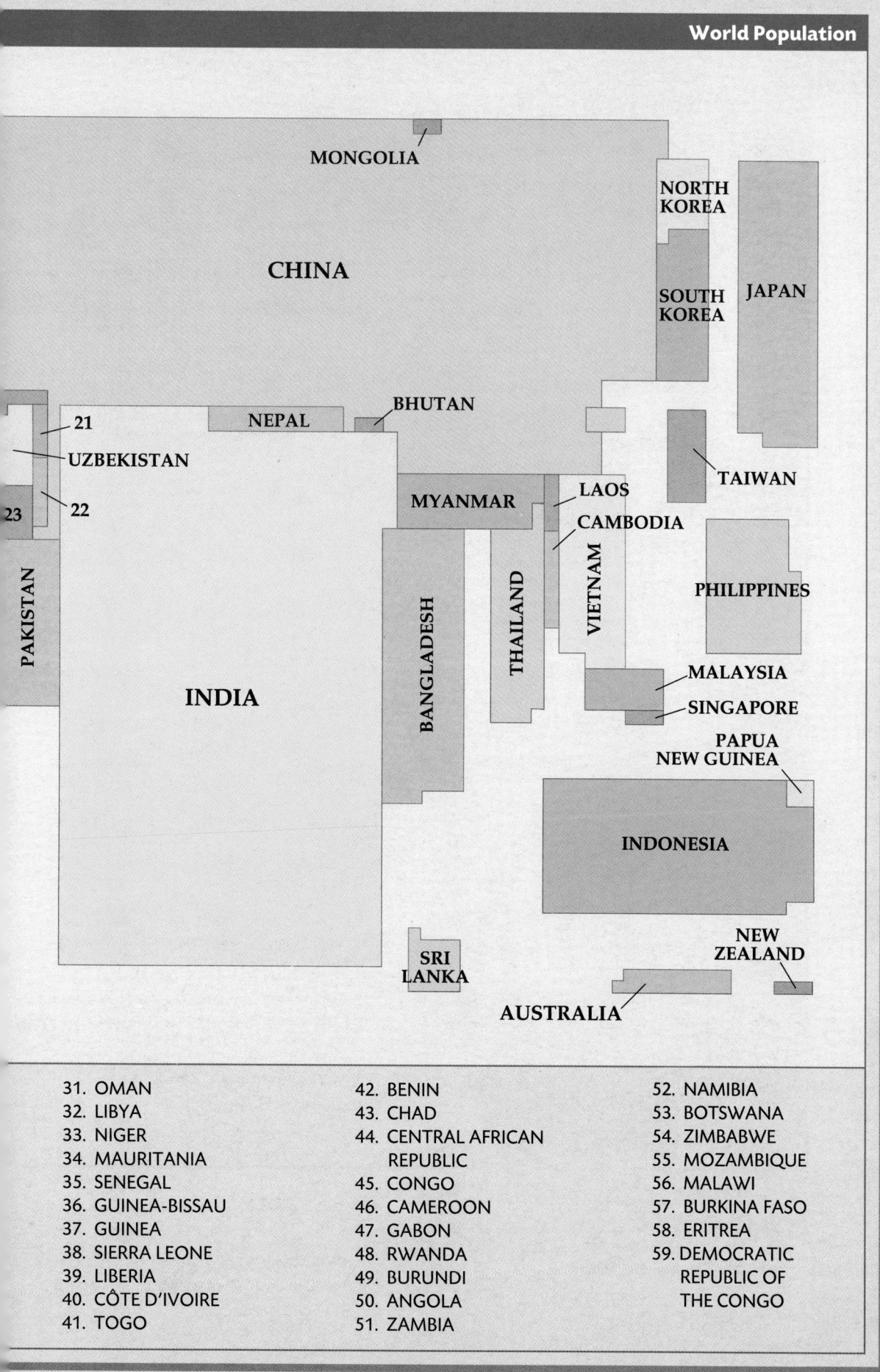

MONGOLIA

CHINA

NORTH KOREA

SOUTH KOREA

JAPAN

21

UZBEKISTAN

23

22

NEPAL

BHUTAN

TAIWAN

PAKISTAN

MYANMAR

LAOS

CAMBODIA

THAILAND

VIETNAM

PHILIPPINES

INDIA

BANGLADESH

MALAYSIA

SINGAPORE

PAPUA NEW GUINEA

INDONESIA

SRI LANKA

NEW ZEALAND

AUSTRALIA

31. OMAN	42. BENIN	52. NAMIBIA
32. LIBYA	43. CHAD	53. BOTSWANA
33. NIGER	44. CENTRAL AFRICAN	54. ZIMBABWE
34. MAURITANIA	REPUBLIC	55. MOZAMBIQUE
35. SENEGAL	45. CONGO	56. MALAWI
36. GUINEA-BISSAU	46. CAMEROON	57. BURKINA FASO
37. GUINEA	47. GABON	58. ERITREA
38. SIERRA LEONE	48. RWANDA	59. DEMOCRATIC
39. LIBERIA	49. BURUNDI	REPUBLIC OF
40. CÔTE D'IVOIRE	50. ANGOLA	THE CONGO
41. TOGO	51. ZAMBIA	

Introducing the Geography Handbook

Handbook Objectives

1. **Understand** the purpose and uses of globes and map projections.
2. **Identify** most commonly used geographic terms.
3. **Analyze** geographic factors that have shaped the course of historic events.

Vocabulary Pre-check

Survey the students' knowledge of geographic terms. Create three columns on the chalkboard with the following headings: *landforms*, *map elements*, and *bodies of water*.

List one term that fits each column, such as "canyon," "meridian," and "bay." Ask students to volunteer as many other terms for each column as they can.

Have students turn to page 4 and read the geographic dictionary. Then have them close their books and continue suggesting terms for each column on the chalkboard.

TEACH

NATIONAL GEOGRAPHIC SOCIETY

CD-ROM

PICTURE ATLAS OF THE WORLD

You and your students can see the challenges and solutions involved in making maps by viewing the Mapping Our World animation "Round Earth on Flat Paper."

What Is Geography?

The story of humanity begins with **geography**—the study of the earth in all of its variety. Geography concerns the earth's land, water, and plant and animal life. It also tells you about the people who live on the earth, the places they have created, and how these places differ. The earth is a planet of diverse groups of people. A study of geography can help you see why the people of the earth are so diverse.

The Five Themes of Geography

The study of geography can be organized around five themes: **location**, **place**, **human/environment interaction**, **movement**, and **region**. Geographers use these five themes to study and classify all parts of the earth and its variety of human activity.

Geography and World History

World geography is especially important to the study of world history. Historians use geography to explain connections between the past and the present. They study how places

Behaim's Globe

looked in the past, how places and patterns of human activity have changed over time, and how geographic forces have influenced these changes.

Globes

Photographs from space show the earth in its true form—a great ball spinning around the sun. The only accurate way to draw the earth is as a globe, or a round form. A globe gives a true picture of the earth's size and the shape of the earth's landmasses and bodies of water. Globes also show the true distances and true directions between places.

Maps

A map is a flat drawing of the earth's surface. People use maps to locate places, plot routes, and judge distances. Maps can also display useful information about the world's peoples.

What advantages does a map have over a globe? Unlike a globe, a map allows you to see all areas of the world at the same time. Maps also show much more detail and can be folded and more easily carried.

Maps, however, have their drawbacks. As you can imagine, drawing a round object on a flat surface is very difficult. Cartographers, or mapmakers, have drawn many **projections**, or kinds of maps. Each map projection is a different way of showing the round earth on a flat map. This is because it is impossible to draw a round planet on a flat surface without distorting or misrepresenting some parts of the earth. As a result, each kind of map projection has some distortion. Typical distortions involve distance, direction, shape, and/or area.

GEOGRAPHY HANDBOOK RESOURCES

📁 **Reproducible Masters**
- Glencoe Social Studies Outline Map Resource Book
- Building Skills in Geography Workbook

🔖 **Transparencies**
- NGS PicturePack Transparencies: Physical Geography of the World

Multimedia
- 📘 Student Desk Map
- 💾 Zip!Zap!Map! World
- 💾 Zip!Zap!Map! USA
- 💿 Picture Atlas of the World
- 📀 STV: World Geography:
  - Vol. 1: Asia and Australia

- Vol. 2: Africa and Europe
- Vol. 3: South America and Antarctica
- 📀 STV: North America

The Hemispheres

To determine location, distance, and direction on a map or globe, geographers have developed a network of imaginary lines that crisscross the earth. One of these lines, the **Equator**, circles the earth midway between the **North Pole** and the **South Pole**. It divides the earth into "half spheres," or **hemispheres**. The Northern Hemisphere includes all of the land and water between the Equator and the North Pole. The Southern Hemisphere includes all of the land and water between the Equator and the South Pole.

Another imaginary line running from north to south divides the earth into half spheres in the other direction. This line is called the **Prime Meridian**. Every place east of the Prime Meridian is in the Eastern Hemisphere. Every place west of the Prime Meridian is in the Western Hemisphere.

Latitude and Longitude

The Equator and the Prime Meridian are the starting points for two sets of lines used to find any location. The two sets measure distances north or south of the Equator, and east and west of the Prime Meridian.

One set of lines called **parallels** circle the earth and show **latitude**, which is distance measured in degrees (°) north and south of the Equator at 0° latitude. The letter *N* or *S* following the degree symbol tells you if the location is north or south of the Equator. The North Pole is at 90° North (*N*) latitude, and the South Pole is at 90° South (*S*) latitude.

Two important parallels in between the poles are the **Tropic of Cancer** at 23 1/2°N latitude and the **Tropic of Capricorn** at 23 1/2°S latitude. You can also find the **Arctic Circle** at 66 1/2°N latitude and the **Antarctic Circle** at 66 1/2°S latitude.

The second set of lines called **meridians** run north to south from the North Pole to the South Pole. These lines signify **longitude**, which is distance measured in degrees east (*E*) or west (*W*) of the Prime Meridian at 0° longitude. On the opposite side of the earth is the International Date Line, at about the 180° meridian.

The Grid System

Lines of latitude and longitude cross one another in the form of a **grid system**. You can use the grid system to find where places are exactly located on a map or globe. Each place on Earth has an address on the grid. This grid address is the place's **coordinates**—its degrees of latitude and longitude. For example, the coordinates of the city of San Francisco are 38°N latitude and 122°W longitude. This means that San Francisco lies about 38 degrees (°) north of the Equator and 122 degrees (°) west of the Prime Meridian. Where those two lines cross is called the **absolute location** of the city.

Map Symbols

Maps can direct you down the street, across the country, or around the world. There are as many different kinds of maps as there are uses for them. Being

Hemispheres

NORTHERN HEMISPHERE
North Pole

NORTH AMERICA

Equator

SOUTH AMERICA

South Pole
SOUTHERN HEMISPHERE

WESTERN HEMISPHERE
North Pole

NORTH AMERICA

Prime Meridian

SOUTH AMERICA

South Pole

EASTERN HEMISPHERE

EUROPE

AFRICA

ANTARCTICA

NORTHERN HEMISPHERE
North Pole

AFRICA

ASIA

Equator

AUSTRALIA

ANTARCTICA

South Pole
SOUTHERN HEMISPHERE

EASTERN HEMISPHERE
North Pole

ASIA

180°

AUSTRALIA

ANTARCTICA

WESTERN HEMISPHERE

NORTH AMERICA

PACIFIC OCEAN

South Pole

Geography Handbook

NATIONAL GEOGRAPHIC SOCIETY

CD-ROM

PICTURE ATLAS OF THE WORLD

Have students view the Mapping Our World animation "Where in the World," which introduces the concepts of latitude and longitude.

Skills Practice

Reading a Diagram Have students look at the illustrations on this page. What hemisphere contains most of the landmass of the earth? *(the Northern Hemisphere)* What continents are entirely in the Western Hemisphere? *(North America and South America)* What line divides the earth into the Northern and Southern Hemispheres? *(Equator)* What line divides the earth into the Eastern and Western Hemispheres? *(Prime Meridian)*

Cultural Perspectives

Universal Language The grid system provides a kind of universal language. Citizens of all countries, no matter how different their cultures, speak the same language of latitude and longitude.

COOPERATIVE LEARNING ACTIVITY

Game Have students prepare a game called "My Grid Address." Students should write out grid address question cards, with each card containing one multiple-choice question regarding the grid address of a well-known location—a city, lake, mountain, and so on. A sample question format is "My grid address is 36° north latitude and 140° east longitude. What city am I? a. Madrid b. Tokyo c. New York d. Cairo." After students have completed at least 30-40 cards, organize them into teams and play "My Grid Address." Allow five points for each correct answer. **L1**

Types of Maps

Types of Maps Explain that general purpose maps may include both physical and political information. Students should always carefully read the map title and key to determine the purpose of the map. Because of changes that occur in history, political maps should always identify the time period that they represent. If a political map does not identify a date, we usually assume that it is a current map.

Map Study

Have students look at the LANDSAT map and the San Francisco Bay Area map. Both maps are of the same general area.

Map Skills Practice

Reading a Map What is the value of the LANDSAT map? (*Changes to the earth's environment can be tracked by comparing LANDSAT maps over a period of time.*)

Have students each write a paragraph detailing the information about San Francisco that can be learned from the San Francisco Bay Area map. Have students read a detail from their paragraphs that they believe no other student recorded.

Who?What?Where?When?

Antarctica covers about 3.2 million square miles (8.3 million sq. km) of landmass. Including the islands and shelf ice, it is about 5.4 million square miles (14 million sq. km). No nation owns this territory. The Antarctica Treaty, signed by 16 nations, allows only the exploration of the continent.

GEOGRAPHY HANDBOOK

able to read a map begins with learning about its parts.

The **map key** explains the symbols used on the map. On a map of the world, for example, dots mark cities and towns. On a road map, various kinds of lines stand for paved roads, dirt roads, and interstate highways. A pine tree symbol may represent a state park, while an airplane is often the symbol for an airport.

An important first step in reading any map is to find the direction marker. A map has a symbol that tells you where the **cardinal directions**—north, south, east, and west—are positioned. Sometimes all of these directions are shown with a **compass rose**.

A measuring line, often called a **scale bar**, helps you find distance on the map. The map's **scale** tells you what distance on the earth is represented by the measurement on the scale bar. For example, 1 inch on a map may represent 100 miles on the earth. Knowing the scale allows you to visualize how large an area is, as well as to measure distances. Map scales are usually given in both miles and kilometers, a metric measurement of distance.

TYPES OF MAPS

Maps of many different kinds are used in this text to help you see the connection between world geography and the history of humanity.

General Purpose Maps

Maps that show a wide range of general information about an area are called **general purpose maps**. Two of the most common general purpose maps are physical maps and political maps. **Physical maps** show natural features, such as rivers and mountains. **Political maps** show places that people have created, such as cities or the boundaries of countries and states.

Special Purpose Maps

Special purpose maps show information on specific topics, such as climate, land use, or vegetation. Human activities, such as exploration routes, territorial expansion, or battle sites, also appear on special purpose maps. Colors and map key symbols are especially important on this type of map.

LANDSAT Maps

LANDSAT maps are made from photographs taken by camera-carrying LANDSAT satellites in space. The cameras record millions of energy waves invisible to the human eye. Computers then change this information into pictures of the earth's surface. With LANDSAT images, scientists can study whole mountain ranges, oceans, and geographic regions. Changes to the earth's environment can also be tracked using the satellite information.

LANDSAT map of San Francisco Bay area

San Francisco

San Francisco (38°N, 122°W)

San Francisco Bay Area

- Urbanized Area
- Park or Reservation
- City Boundary
- Highway, Street
- Bridge

122° 30' W San Pablo Bay

Golden Gate Bridge

Berkeley

Oakland

San Francisco Oakland Bay Bridge

San Francisco

San Francisco Bay

San Mateo

San Mateo Bridge

37° 30' N

PACIFIC OCEAN

Palo Alto

San Jose

COAST RANGES

SANTA CRUZ MOUNTAINS

122° W

0   5   10 mi.
0   5   10 km

MORE ABOUT...

Cartography British sea captain James Cook was the greatest explorer and cartographer of the eighteenth century. In three voyages, undertaken between 1769 and 1779, Cook surveyed and charted huge areas of the Pacific Ocean. He also verified the existence of the continent of Antarctica and provided a wealth of information about the south Atlantic, south Indian, and Arctic Oceans. Using the latest scientific developments, Cook created incredibly accurate charts of his journeys. These charts revolutionized cartographic knowledge and practices.

Geography Handbook

CONTINENTS

Geographers divide most of the earth's land surface into seven large landmasses called **continents**. The continents are North America, South America, Europe, Africa, Asia, Australia, and Antarctica. Asia is the largest continent in size, and Australia is the smallest.

LANDFORMS

Landforms cover about 30 percent of the surface of the earth. **Landforms**, or the natural features of the earth's surface, include **mountains**, **hills**, **plateaus**, and **plains**. Geographers describe each landform by its **elevation**, or height above sea level, and by its **relief**, or changes in height.

Mountains

Mountains are the highest of the world's landforms. They rise from about 2,000 feet (610 m) to more than 20,000 feet (6,100 m) above sea level. One of the peaks in the Himalaya mountain ranges of central Asia is Mount Everest, the world's highest mountain. It towers 29,028 feet (8,848 m) above sea level. Other mountains, such as the Appalachians in eastern North America, are not as high. Mountains generally have high relief.

Hills, Plateaus, and Plains

Hills are lower than mountains and generally rise from about 500 to 2,000 feet (152 to 610 m) above sea level. They generally have moderate relief.

Plateaus are raised areas of flat or almost flat land. Most plateaus have low relief and vary in elevation from about 300 to 3,000 feet (91 to 914 m) above sea level. The world's largest plateau area is the Tibetan Plateau in central Asia. It covers about 715,000 square miles (1,852,000 sq. km) and has an average altitude of 16,000 feet (4,877 m) above sea level.

Plains are large areas of flat or gently rolling land that generally rise less than 1,000 feet (305 m) above sea level and have low relief. The world's largest plain is the North European Plain, which stretches for more than 1,000 miles (1,609 km) from the western coast of France to the Ural Mountains in Russia.

BODIES OF WATER

About 70 percent of the earth's surface is covered with water. Geographers identify bodies of water by their shapes and sizes. The major types include oceans, seas, bays, gulfs, lakes, and rivers.

Oceans and Seas

The largest bodies of water in the world are the four saltwater **oceans**—the Pacific, the Atlantic, the Indian, and the Arctic. The Pacific Ocean is the largest ocean, covering about 64 million square miles (165,760,000 sq. km)—more than all the land areas of the earth combined.

Seas are smaller bodies of salt water that are usually in part surrounded by land. The world's largest sea is East Asia's South China Sea, with an area of 1,148,500 square miles (2,975,000 sq. km).

Bays and Gulfs

Still smaller bodies of salt water are gulfs and bays. **Bays** are extensions of a sea usually smaller than a **gulf**. The largest bay in the world measured by shoreline is Hudson Bay, Canada, with a shoreline of 7,623 miles (12,265 km) and an area of 476,000 square miles (1,233,000 sq. km). Measured by area, the Bay of Bengal, in the Indian Ocean and bordering South Asia and part of Southeast Asia, is larger at 839,000 square miles (2,173,000 sq. km).

Lakes and Rivers

Other water features of the earth include lakes and rivers. A **lake** is a body of water completely surrounded by land. The world's largest freshwater lake is Lake Superior, one of the five Great Lakes between the United States and Canada. It has an area of 31,820 square miles (82,414 sq. km). The world's largest inland body of water, however, is the Caspian Sea, often considered a saltwater lake. Lying between Europe and Asia and east of the Caucasus Mountains, the Caspian Sea has a total area of 143,550 square miles (371,795 sq. km).

A **river** is a waterway flowing through land and emptying into another body of water. The world's longest river is the Nile River in Africa, which flows into the Mediterranean Sea from the highlands of East Africa. The Nile's length is about 4,160 miles (6,690 km).

Geography Handbook 3

CURRICULUM CONNECTION

SCIENCE

It tastes really salty, but ocean water averages only about 3.5 percent salt. Of this, nearly 3 percent is sodium chloride (regular salt). The rest contains almost every chemical element on earth.

Landforms Mountains have fascinated people throughout history. They have provided refuge and asylum for those in danger; they have served as a buffer between warring states; they have challenged people for the sheer thrill of climbing them. How many mountain ranges or peaks can you name? Allow students a few minutes to list on the chalkboard several of the world's best known mountains. What historic event can you associate with any of the mountains on our list? *(Accept all legitimate answers such as Hannibal crossing the Alps, American settlers crossing the Rocky Mountains, the Inca building a refuge at Machu Picchu.)*

Cultural Perspectives

Terminology To promote communication, geographers the world over use the same terminology. The terms they use come from many different languages. For example, *tsunami* is a Japanese word meaning "overflowing wave," and *fjord* is a Norwegian word meaning "long, narrow bay."

TEACHER NOTES

_____

_____

_____

_____

_____

Geography Handbook

Labels on diagram: Mountain range, Mountain, Source of river, Valley, Hills, Low plain, Tributary, Plain, Plateau, Cliff, River, Canyon, Swamp, Bay, Seacoast, Delta, Cape, Mouth of river, Ocean or Sea

you don't say...

The word *longitude* comes from the Latin word for "length," and *latitude* comes from the Latin word "breadth."

Who? What? **Where?** When?

There is a point on Earth with **"no" latitude and "no" longitude**. The absolute location where the Prime Meridian and the Equator intersect, off the African coast in the Atlantic Ocean, is 0° N-S, 0° E-W.

CURRICULUM CONNECTION

COMPUTER LITERACY

Computers have revolutionized cartography. They reduce distortions and calculate changes at incredible speeds. They gather, process, and store data about contour reliefs, ethnicities, economics, waterways, and much more. They even produce animated "flow maps," such as those that show storm movement.

GEOGRAPHIC DICTIONARY

As you read about the world's geography and history, you will discover most of the terms listed and explained below. Many of the terms are pictured in the diagram above. Others you learned earlier in this Geography Handbook.

absolute location–exact location of a place on the earth described by global coordinates

basin–area of land drained by a given river and its branches; area of land surrounded by lands of higher elevations

bay–part of a large body of water that extends into a shoreline

canyon–deep and narrow valley with steep walls

cape–point of land surrounded by a body of water

channel–deep, narrow body of water that connects two larger bodies of water; deep part of a river or other waterway

cliff–steep, high wall of rock, earth, or ice

continent–one of the seven large landmasses on the earth

cultural feature–characteristic that humans have created in a place, such as language, religion, and history

delta–land built up from soil carried downstream by a river and deposited at its mouth

divide–stretch of high land that separates river basins

downstream–direction in which a river or stream flows from its source to its mouth

elevation–height of land above sea level

Equator–imaginary line that runs around the earth halfway between the North and South Poles; used as the starting point to measure degrees of north and south latitude

glacier–large, thick body of slowly moving ice, found in mountains and polar regions

globe–sphere-shaped model of the earth

gulf–part of a large body of water that extends into a shoreline, larger than a bay

harbor–a sheltered place along a shoreline where ships can anchor safely

highland–elevated land area with sloping sides such as a hill, mountain, or plateau, smaller than a mountain

island–land area, smaller than a continent, completely surrounded by water

isthmus–narrow stretch of land connecting two larger land areas

lake–a sizable inland body of water

latitude–distance north or south of the Equator, measured in degrees

longitude–distance east or west of the Prime Meridian, measured in degrees

lowland–land, usually level, at a low elevation

map–drawing of all or part of the earth shown on a flat surface

meridian–one of many lines on the global grid

MORE ABOUT...

Geographers work for the federal government in the Defense Mapping Agency, United States Geologic Survey, Central Intelligence Agency, Army Corps of Engineers, National Science Foundation, Smithsonian Institution, and Office of the Geographer in the Department of State.

State environmental and transportation agencies hire geographers as analysts, planners, and cartographers. In the private sector, geographers work as professors, researchers, and cartographers for high-tech computer mapmakers. Businesses as varied as fast-food chains and ski resorts consult geographers about optimal locations for new restaurants and effects of pollution on the slopes.

Mountain peak · Basin · Volcano · River basin · Lake · Upstream · Downstream · Highland · Glacier · Channel · Isthmus · Peninsula · Sound · Strait · Reef · Island

running from the North Pole to the South Pole, used to measure degrees of longitude

mesa–area of raised land with steep sides; smaller than a plateau

mountain–land with steep sides that rises sharply from surrounding land; larger and more rugged than a hill

mountain peak–pointed top of a mountain

mountain range–a series of connected mountains

mouth–(of a river) place where a stream or river flows into a larger body of water

ocean–one of the four major bodies of salt water that surrounds a continent

ocean current–stream of either cold or warm water that moves in a definite direction through an ocean

parallel–one of many lines on the global grid that circle the earth north or south of the Equator; used to measure degrees of latitude

peninsula–body of land almost surrounded by water

physical feature–characteristic of a place occurring naturally, such as a landform, body of water, climate pattern, or resource

plain–area of level land, usually at a low elevation

plateau–area of flat or rolling land at a high elevation

Prime Meridian–line of the global grid running from the North Pole to the South Pole at Greenwich, England; used as the starting point for measuring degrees of east and west longitude

relative location–position of a place on the earth in relation to other places

relief–changes in elevation, either few or many, that occur over a given area of land

river–large stream of water that runs through the land

sea–large body of water completely or partly surrounded by land

seacoast–land lying next to a sea or ocean

sea level–average level of an ocean's surface

sound–body of water between a shoreline and one or more islands off the coast

source–(of a river) place where a river or stream begins, often in high lands

strait–narrow stretch of water joining two larger bodies of water

tributary–small river or stream that flows into a large river or stream; a branch of the river

upstream–direction opposite the flow of a river; toward the source of a river or stream

valley–area of low land between hills or mountains

volcano–mountain created as liquid rock or ash are thrown up from inside the earth

---

Who? What? Where? When?

Flemish mathematician, geographer, and cartographer **Gerardus Mercator** created his well-known projection in 1568. This projection exaggerates areas as they increase in distance from the Equator, and has been favored by sailors for more than 400 years.

CURRICULUM CONNECTION

CIVICS

Geographic knowledge and perspectives help people be responsible citizens, especially when making decisions that affect their community, region, country, and world.

Who? What? Where? When?

One of the most violent **volcanic eruptions** in history occurred in 1883 on the island of Krakatau in Indonesia. The volcano collapsed from a height of 2,640 feet (692 meters) to 1,000 feet (300 meters) below sea level. Its collapse triggered a tidal wave that killed 36,000 people in nearby Java and Sumatra.

MORE ABOUT...

Geographic Information Systems (GIS) is a computer hardware and software system that can store, display, analyze, and map information. Geographers, urban planners, engineers, and utility companies use these systems. GIS are vital to planning because they enable us to combine data and look at layers of information at the same time. One GIS, for example, may begin with a digitized base map. A retailer wishing to make an informed decision about where to build a store may combine data such as population distribution, traffic movement, land availability, and real estate prices. Using the GIS, the retailer can see and analyze all this information at the same time.

GEOGRAPHY HANDBOOK

Linking Past and Present

Climate The early Greeks established a classification of climate based only on what they knew of differences between where they lived and lands to the north and south of Greece. They called their own climate *temperate* because it posed few problems of shelter and clothing. They believed that the area south of the Mediterranean became increasingly hotter, so they called these lands *torrid*. Stories told by travelers from the north and the cold winter winds that came from that direction led the Greeks to call that area *frigid*.

Map Study

Map Skills Practice

Reading a Map What are four classifications that may be used to describe climate today? (*tropical, mid-latitude, high latitude, and dry*) What projection is this map? (*Robinson*)

Who?What?**Where?**When?

Climatologists agree that the **United States** has the most varied climate on Earth. With its tornadoes, hurricanes, thunderstorms, and blizzards, the climate of the United States also is one of the most violent and unpredictable.

CLIMATE

Climate is the usual pattern of weather events that occurs in an area over a long period of time. Climate is determined by distance from the Equator, by location near large bodies of water, and sometimes by positions near mountain ranges.

The world's climates can be organized into four major regions: **tropical**, **mid-latitude**, **high latitude**, and **dry**. Some of these regions are determined by their latitude; others are based on the vegetation that grows in them.

Tropical Climates

Tropical climates get their name from the tropics, the areas along the Equator. Temperatures in the tropics change little from season to season. The warm tropical climate region can be separated into two types: tropical rain forest and tropical savanna.

The tropical rain forest climate region is wet in most months, with up to 100 inches (254 cm) of rain a year. In these areas, rain and heat produce lush vegetation and **rain forests**, dense forests that are home to millions of kinds of plant and animal life. The Amazon River basin in South America is the world's largest rain forest area.

The tropical **savanna** climate has two seasons—one wet and one dry. Savannas, or grasslands with few trees, occur in this region. Among the leading tropical savanna climate areas are southern India and eastern Africa.

Mid-Latitude Climates

Mid-latitude, or moderate, climates are found in the middle latitudes of the Northern and Southern Hemispheres. Most of the world's people live in this climate region. The mid-latitude region has a greater variety of climates than other regions. This variety results from the mix of air masses—warm air coming from the tropics and cool air coming from the polar regions. In most places, temperatures change with the seasons.

High Latitude Climates

High latitude, or polar, climate regions lie in the high latitudes of each hemisphere. Climates are cold everywhere in the high latitude regions, some more severe than others.

High latitude climate regions also include highland or mountainous regions even in lower

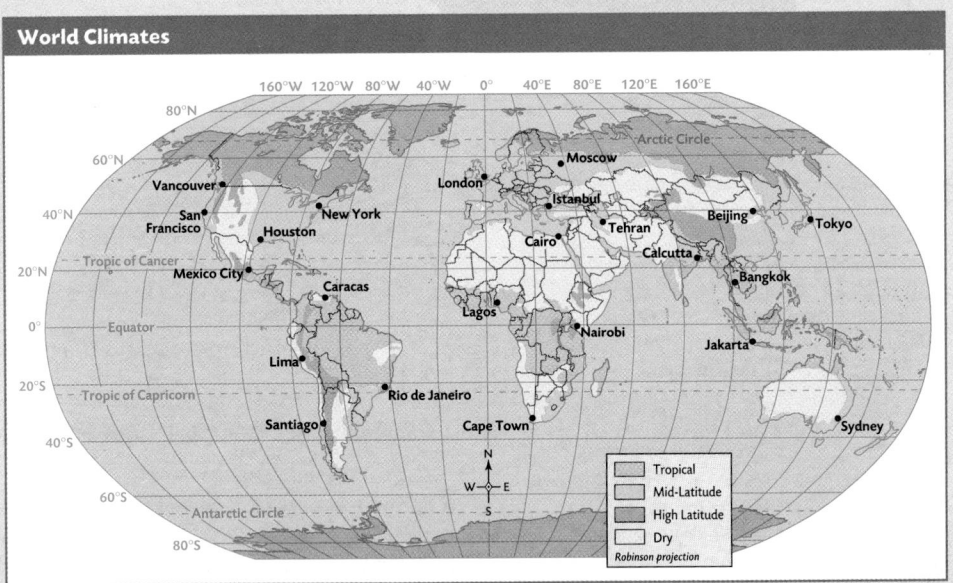

World Climates

Robinson projection

Legend: Tropical, Mid-Latitude, High Latitude, Dry

COOPERATIVE LEARNING ACTIVITY

Survival Strategy Organize students into four or more groups. Assign each group a climate type. Encourage group members to imagine that they will be stranded for one year in a remote area that has their assigned climate type. Have groups plan a survival strategy to live in that climate. Each group should identify at least the following: (1) the type of shelter they need and will be able to make or obtain; (2) the type of clothing they need and will be able to make; and (3) the way they will obtain food and water. Have each group present their survival plan to the class, and have the class challenge each plan with situations or conditions likely to arise in the climate region.
L2

World Land Use and Resources

Agriculture

Livestock farming	Nomadic herding
Little or no activity	Commercial farming
Subsistence farming	Forestry
Hunting and gathering	■ Manufacturing area

Resources

Coal	I Iron ore
Fishing	Petroleum

Robinson Projection

latitudes. The elevation of a place changes its climate dramatically. Higher into the mountains, the air becomes thinner. It cannot hold the heat from the sun, so the temperature drops. Even in the tropics, snow covers the peaks of high mountains.

Dry Climates

Dry climate refers to dry or partially dry areas that receive little or no rainfall. Temperatures can be extremely hot during the day and cold at night. Dry climates can also have severely cold winters.

Nearly an eighth of the world's land surface is dry, with a rainfall of less than 10 inches (25 cm) per year. The Sahara in North Africa is the largest desert in the world. The area covered by the Sahara—3,579,000 square miles (9,270,000 sq. km)—is about the size of the United States.

NATURAL RESOURCES

Natural resources refer to anything from the natural environment that people use to meet their needs. Natural resources include fertile soil, clean water, minerals, trees, and energy sources. Human skills and labor are also valuable natural resources.

Renewable Resources

Some natural resources can be replaced as they are used up. These renewable resources can be replaced naturally or grown fairly quickly. Forests, grasslands, plant and animal life, and rich soil all can be renewable resources if people manage them carefully. A lumber company concerned about future growth can replant as many trees as it cuts. Fishing and whaling fleets can limit the number of fish and whales they catch in certain parts of the ocean.

Nonrenewable Resources

Metals and other minerals found in the earth's crust are nonrenewable resources. They cannot be replaced because they were formed over millions of years by geologic forces within the earth.

One important group of nonrenewable resources is fossil fuels—coals, oil, and natural gas. Industries and people depend on these fuels for energy and as raw materials for plastics and other goods. We also use up large amounts of other metals and minerals, such as iron, aluminum, and phosphates. Some of these can be reused, but they cannot be replaced.

Geography Handbook 7

Natural Resources Forests are considered renewable natural resources, but they are renewable only if people manage them carefully. Depletion of forests causes changes to both ground and climate. What are the possible consequences of deforestation? (*Deforestation causes erosion. It might also cause a change in the world's heating balance or in its water cycle. It could cause many plants and animals to become extinct.*)

Map Study

Help students understand the uneven distribution of resources by studying the map on this page. Point out that the symbols show only the major concentrations of four resources. Why have coal and petroleum been important natural resources in the last 200 years? (*The Industrial Revolution depended on these energy sources for its development.*)

Explain that natural resources are only one factor in an area's standard of living. Japan, for example, must import most of its energy resources, yet it has one of world's highest standards of living. Technology, or the ability to use resources effectively, has been the key to development.

TEACHER NOTES

Geography Handbook

GEOGRAPHY HANDBOOK

Environmental Challenges Efforts to preserve a healthy environment date back hundreds of years. In A.D. 1253 the English Parliament placed bans on burning coal. The increasing use of fossil fuels, expanding populations, and the use of chemicals, however, present new challenges. Discuss the challenges presented on this page. Ask students to talk about how they view the future. Will people be able to preserve a healthy environment?

Who?What?Where?When?

Europe has few areas that have not been affected by human interaction. In recent years Europeans have taken steps to control pollution, despite the high costs. In some areas progress is slow. The estimated cost of cleaning up air pollution in eastern Europe ranges from $200 to $500 billion.

Geography's Impact on World History

Use the examples given for each unit as a launch pad for a general overview of world history.

Unit 1 Explain that most early civilizations developed near water. The Egyptians used the Nile, and many civilizations developed around the Mediterranean and near rivers in China. What are the essential needs that rivers and seas provided to early peoples? *(water for daily use, irrigation, transportation, fishing)*

Unit 2 Waves of Aryans from Europe swept into the Indus River valley around 1500 B.C. From there they spread into northern India. Why were river valleys good routes for early peoples to move from one

ENVIRONMENTAL CHALLENGES

When people use natural resources to make a living, they affect the environment. The unmanaged use of resources is a threat to the environment. Many human activities can cause pollution—putting impure or poisonous substances into the land, water, and air.

Land and Water

Only about 11 percent of the earth's surface has land good enough for farming. Chemicals that farmers use may improve their crops, but some also may damage the land. Pesticides, or chemicals that kill insects, can pollute rivers and groundwater, or water that fills tiny cracks in the rock layers below the earth's surface.

Other human activities also pollute soil and water. Oil spills from tanker ships threaten ocean coastal areas. Illegal dumping of dangerous waste products causes problems. Untreated sewage reaching rivers pollutes lakes and groundwater as well. Salt water can also pollute both soil and groundwater.

Air

Industries and vehicles that burn fossil fuels are the main sources of air pollution. Throughout the world, fumes from cars and other vehicles pollute the air. The chemicals in air pollution can seriously damage people's health.

These chemicals combined with precipitation may fall as acid rain, or rain carrying large amounts of sulfuric acid. Acid rain eats away the surfaces of buildings, kills fish, and can destroy entire forests.

Energy

All of the world nations need safe, dependable sources of energy. Fossil fuels are most often used to generate electricity, heat buildings, run machinery, and power vehicles. Fossil fuels, however, are non-renewable resources. In addition, they contribute to air pollution. So today

many countries are trying to discover new ways of using renewable energy sources. Two of these ways are hydroelectric power, the energy generated by falling water, and solar energy, or energy produced by the heat of the sun.

GEOGRAPHY'S IMPACT ON WORLD HISTORY

Geographic factors have shaped the outcome of historical events. Landforms, waterways, climate, and natural resources all have helped or hindered human activities. In many cases, people have learned either to adapt to their environment or to transform it to meet their needs.

Throughout the units of your text, you will discover how geography has shaped the course of events in world history. Here are some examples of the role that geographic factors have played in the story of humanity.

Unit 1 The Rise of Civilizations

Rivers contributed to the rise of many of the world's early civilizations. By 3000 B.C. the Sumerians of the Middle East had set up 12 prosperous city-states in the Tigris-Euphrates River valley. The Fertile Crescent, as the area is often called because of its relatively rich topsoil and its curved shape, was able to support city-state populations ranging from 20,000 to 250,000 people.

Unit 2 Flowering of Civilizations

Landforms and waterways also affected the political relationships of the world's ancient peoples. For example, the rugged landscape of Greece divided the ancient Greeks into separate city-states instead of uniting them into a single nation. Furthermore, closeness to the sea caused the Greek city-states to expand their trade, culture, and sense of civic pride to other parts of the Mediterranean world.

Unit 3 Regional Civilizations

From about A.D. 400 to A.D. 1500, regional civilizations developed at the crossroads of trade between different areas of the world. The city of Makkah (Mecca), in the Middle East's Arabian Peninsula, was a crossroads for caravans from North Africa, Palestine, and the

location to another? *(Before roads, rivers and the lowlands near rivers were the easiest routes to travel.)*

Unit 3 Large oceans helped to separate people into regional civilizations. The Atlantic, the Indian, and the Pacific Oceans kept civilizations in the Americas, Asia, and Africa from much contact

with each other. What people were most isolated from the rest of the world until the A.D. 1500s? *(the people in the Americas; some contact took place between Asia and Africa, Europe and Asia, and Europe and Africa in this period.)*

Unit 4 The modern world emerged largely as a result of

Persian Gulf. The religion of Islam established a firm base in Makkah, from which it spread to other areas of the Middle East, North Africa, South Asia, and Southeast Asia.

Unit 4 Emergence of the Modern World

The desire to control or to obtain scarce natural resources has encouraged trade and stimulated contact among the world's peoples. At the dawn of the modern era, Asians and Europeans came into contact with one another partly because Europeans wanted Asia's spices and silks. When the Asiatic people known as the Mongols could no longer guarantee safe passage for traders on overland routes, Europeans were forced to consider new water routes to Asia. This opened a new global age that brought the peoples of Europe, Asia, Africa, and the Americas into closer contact with each other.

Unit 5 Age of Revolution

Climate often affects the way a country behaves toward its neighbors. For example, many of Russia's harbors stay frozen during much of the year. In the past, Russia has often gone to war with other countries to capture land for warm water ports. Climate was also one reason why the Russians were able to stop the invasions of French ruler Napoleon Bonaparte in 1812 and the German dictator Adolf Hitler in 1941. The Russians were used to the bitter cold and snow of their country's winter, whereas the invaders were not.

Unit 6 Industry and Nationalism

Exploiting natural resources, such as coal and iron, was an important factor in the growth of the Industrial Revolution. Modern industry started in Great Britain, which had large amounts of coal and iron ore for making steel. Throughout Europe and North America, the rise of factories that turned raw materials into finished goods prompted people eager for employment to move from rural areas to urban centers.

Also, the availability of land and the discovery of minerals in the Americas, Australia, and South Africa caused hundreds of thousands of Europeans to move to these areas in hope of improving their lives. These mass migrations were possible because of improvements in

industrial technology and transportation that enabled people to overcome geographic barriers.

Unit 7 World in Conflict

Environmental disasters during the first part of the 1900s affected national economies in various parts of the world. For example, during the 1930s, winds blew away so much of the soil in the Great Plains of central North America that the area became known as the Dust Bowl. Ruined by the drought, many farmers packed up their belongings and headed west. It took many years of normal rainfall and improved farming techniques to transform the Great Plains from a Dust Bowl into productive land once again.

Unit 8 The Contemporary World

The world's peoples have become more aware of the growing scarcity of nonrenewable resources. Oil takes millions of years to form, and the earth's supply is limited. Industrialized countries like the United States consume far more oil than they produce and must import large amounts. Many experts believe that the world's fossil fuels will be used up if steps are not taken to limit their consumption and to find alternative sources of energy.

Geography and History Journal

You are about to journey to the past to learn about the people and events that have shaped the world you live in today. Throughout your course of study, keep a record of the events discussed above and any other events in world history that have been affected by geography. When you come to the last unit, you may also want to explore how geography impacts current events or issues: For example, how has geography influenced peacekeeping missions in Bosnia and other parts of the world, or what would happen to Canada geographically if the province of Quebec were to separate and form an independent nation? On a world map locate the places where these historical events have occurred, and identify the units of study in your text in which they are discussed.

helped to attract millions of people to the United States. How did the seemingly inexhaustible resources of the North American continent affect people's attitude toward these resources? *(Resources were exploited without much concern for their replacement or for the environment.)*

Unit 7 World War I grew out of national rivalries and the effects of imperialism. Imperialism was, in part, a quest for resources. What is a better way than conquest for a nation to obtain resources? *(Trade has been an effective means for Japan and many other nations.)*

Unit 8 As the world's population grows and more nations develop industrially, the demand for resources will increase. How can the world ensure adequate resources and avoid conflict over them? *(Science can research the use of alternative fuels; recycling can extend the use of resources; nations should consider the long-term costs and negative effects of war and explore the benefits of cooperation.)*

Using Your Geography and History Journal

An interesting and purposeful *Geography and History Journal* may be formatted using two columns in a notebook. For each chapter the student could list one or more events that were affected by specific geography listed in the first column. In the second column, the student could write a sentence explaining how geography helped shape history.

cultural exchange among people who had once been separated from each other. In what ways are cultural contacts increasing today? *(increased trade, travel, and telecommunications)*

Unit 5 Ideals of the American Revolution and the French Revolution affected people in

other lands. Within a few years revolution spread through Latin America. Why did ideals of these revolutions spread so quickly? *(People had overcome the barriers that had separated civilizations—oceans and communications.)*

Unit 6 Available land and abundant natural resources

To help illustrate the link between history and geography, geographers have identified five themes that can be used to examine the role that geography plays.

1 **Location** serves as a starting point by asking, "Where is it?" **Absolute location** refers to the exact location on the earth's surface as measured by latitude (lines north and south of the Equator) and longitude (lines east and west of the Prime Meridian). **Relative location** is less precise. It helps you orient yourself to a location that is relative to something else.

2 The idea of **Place** includes more than just where something is located. It includes those physical or human features and characteristics that give an area its own identity or personality.

3 **Human/Environment Interaction** focuses on how people respond to and alter their environment. To live comfortably or even to survive in many parts of the world, people must make changes in the environment or adapt to conditions they cannot change, or both.

4 The **Movement** of people and things between places means that events in other places can have an impact on you personally. Transportation routes, communication systems, and trade connections link people and places throughout the world. The movement of people is particularly important because they can spread ideas and cultural characteristics from one place to another.

5 A **Region** is an area that is unified by some geographic, cultural, economic, or political feature or a mixture of features. It is used to generalize about parts of the earth's surface in either physical or human terms.

Modern mapmaking uses photography as a tool. A LANDSAT satellite provided data for this image of Miami, Florida.

Geography's Impact on History

As you read *World History: The Human Experience*, pay special attention to the ways in which geography has influenced history and fashioned the world in which you live.

Themes IN WORLD HISTORY

World history is a record of the adventures of humankind—both the famous and the ordinary—throughout thousands of years. By studying world history—by gazing across time—you can understand the past and recognize its contribution to the present and the future. World history tells of significant people and events. It also encompasses broad historical themes that happen again and again, providing meaning for events in the past and showing how they affect contemporary life.

World History: The Human Experience introduces nine key historical themes. Each chapter highlights and develops several of these themes that demonstrate the interconnectedness of ideas and events. These events help organize your study of world history and make connections across time.

Cooperation/Conflict focuses on how people relate to each other throughout history—sometimes in cooperation, working together to accomplish a common goal, at other times in conflict, struggling against one another.

Revolution/Reaction deals with revolution, or the sudden overthrow of long-established ideas and organizations, contrasted with reaction, or the efforts to oppose new ideas and preserve traditional ways.

Change includes political, social, religious, cultural, and economic transformations that influence human activities throughout the centuries.

Diversity/Uniformity focuses on the diversity or variety of world peoples and customs, contrasted with the desire for uniformity or commonality in some societies.

Regionalism/Nationalism deals with a sense of loyalty and belonging, expressed in ties to a region, to a nation, or to the world as a whole—to the global community.

Innovation includes cultural, scientific, and technical breakthroughs that increase knowledge and impact the way people live and think.

Cultural Diffusion focuses on the spread of cultural expressions through a variety of means across nations, regions, and the world.

Movement involves the movement of people throughout history, including patterns of migration, exploration, and colonization as well as imperialism—people in one place on the globe exercising control over people in another place.

Relation to Environment emphasizes human-environment interchange—how people are affected by their environment and, in turn, how they affect that same environment.

Horn player, Benin

Reading for Information

Think about your textbook as a tool that helps you learn more about the world around you. It is an example of nonfiction writing—it describes real-life events, people, ideas, and places. Here is a menu of reading strategies that will help you become a better textbook reader. As you come to passages in your textbook that you don't understand, refer to these reading strategies for help.

✓ BEFORE YOU READ

Set a Purpose
- Why are you reading the textbook?
- How does the subject relate to your life?
- How might you be able to use what you learn in your own life?

Preview
- Read the chapter title to find what the topic will be.
- Read the subtitles to see what you will learn about the topic.
- Skim the photos, charts, graphs, or maps. How do they support the topic?
- Look for vocabulary words that are boldfaced. How are they defined?

Draw From Your Own Background
- What have you read or heard about concerning new information on the topic?
- How is the new information different from what you already know?
- How will the information that you already know help you understand the new information?

✓ AS YOU READ

Question
- What is the main idea?
- How do the photos, charts, graphs, and maps support the main idea?

Connect
- Think about people, places, and events in your own life. Are there any similarities with those in your textbook?
- Can you relate the textbook information to other areas of your life?

Predict
- Predict events or outcomes by using clues and information that you already know.
- Change your predictions as you read and gather new information.

Visualize
- Pay careful attention to details and descriptions.
- Create graphic organizers to show relationships that you find in the information.

LOOK FOR CLUES AS YOU READ

- **Comparison-and-Contrast Sentences:**

  Look for clue words and phrases that signal comparison, such as *similarly, just as, both, in common, also,* and *too.*

  Look for clue words and phrases that signal contrast, such as *on the other hand, in contrast to, however, different, instead of, rather than, but,* and *unlike.*

- **Cause-and-Effect Sentences:**

  Look for clue words and phrases such as *because, as a result, therefore, that is why, since, so, for this reason,* and *consequently.*

- **Chronological Sentences:**

  Look for clue words and phrases such as *after, before, first, next, last, during, finally, earlier, later, since,* and *then.*

✓ AFTER YOU READ

Summarize
- Describe the main idea and how the details support it.
- Use your own words to explain what you have read.

Assess
- What was the main idea?
- Did the text clearly support the main idea?
- Did you learn anything new from the material?
- Can you use this new information in other school subjects or at home?
- What other sources could you use to find more information about the topic?

0:00 **OUT OF TIME?**

If time does not permit teaching each chapter in Unit 1, you may use the Unit Digest Transparencies and Chapter Digest Audiocassettes with accompanying activities and tests.

Introducing the Unit

Unit 1 traces the development of humankind from prehistoric groups to early river valley civilizations in Egypt, the Fertile Crescent, the Indus Valley, and China. It then focuses on the kingdoms and empires of the ancient Middle East.

Unit Objectives

After reading Unit 1, students will be able to:

1. describe how prehistoric peoples lived, the development of agriculture and other technological achievements, and the growth of civilizations.

2. explain the achievements of early river valley civilizations in Egypt, the Fertile Crescent, and South Asia.

3. discuss the lasting contributions of ancient Middle Eastern peoples, including the development of monotheism.

History *and the* **Humanities**

- Focus on World Art Print 7, Egyptian. *Mask of Tutankhamen*
- World History and Art Transparency 1, *Woman's Head*; 3, *Terra-cotta Warriors*; 4, *Standard of Ur: Peace*

Unit **1**

Prehistory–500 B.C.

Rise of Civilizations

Chapter 1
Human Beginnings

Chapter 2
Early Civilizations

Chapter 3
Kingdoms and Empires in the Middle East

PRIMARY SOURCES
Library

See pages 96–97 for primary source readings that accompany Unit 1.

Then & Now Scholars have divided history into periods according to environmental changes on Earth and cultural developments of humanity. The Paleolithic period or Old Stone Age began about 2 million years ago and lasted until about 12,000 B.C. The earliest evidence of human cultural development was discovered by four teenagers, quite by accident. Jacques Marshal and three young friends entered a cave near Lascaux, France, in 1940 and found the most spectacular cave paintings from Ice Age Europe, created some 17,000 years ago. Cave paintings have been discovered in many parts of the world, but the Lascaux paintings provide the most dramatic and best preserved "snapshots" of early human life yet to be discovered.

A Global Chronology

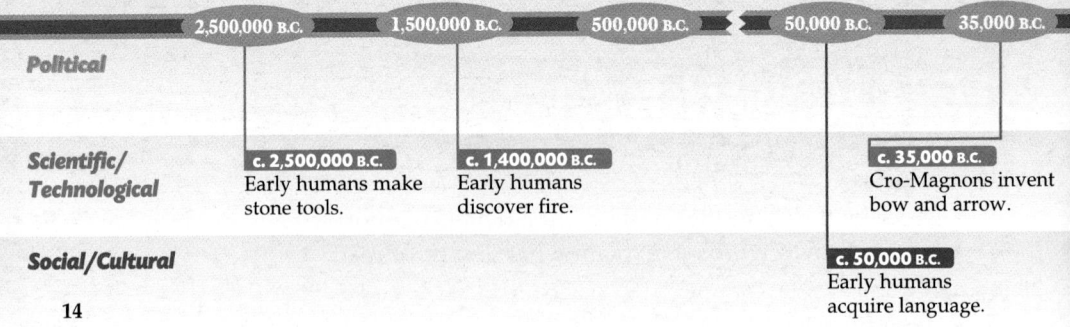

	2,500,000 B.C.	1,500,000 B.C.	500,000 B.C.	50,000 B.C.	35,000 B.C.
Political					
Scientific/ Technological	c. 2,500,000 B.C. Early humans make stone tools.	c. 1,400,000 B.C. Early humans discover fire.			c. 35,000 B.C. Cro-Magnons invent bow and arrow.
Social/Cultural				c. 50,000 B.C. Early humans acquire language.	

14

Then & Now **Art and Society** Unlike early river valley civilizations, which left pyramids and other large monuments, Paleolithic peoples left few traces. The paintings at Lascaux and other sites were not discovered until the twentieth century because they were hidden deep inside caves. The paintings show bison, reindeer, and other animals that Paleolithic peoples hunted. Because Stone Age peoples depended on these animals for food, the cave paintings were probably meant to bring success to the hunters. (See student page 29 for a discussion of cave paintings.) What things do you create that can be considered "art"? (*Answers may include drawings and doodles, homemade gifts such as Christmas or birthday cards, handmade clothing, jewelry, and so on.*) What do these artistic creations show about

Neolithic clay figure from archaeological excavations near Vinca, Serbia

ABCNEWS INTERACTIVE™

VIDEODISC
Turning Points in World History

Side One, Chapter 3

Title: *The Rise of Cities*
Subject: The inventions of the Sumerians in Mesopotamia enabled people to live together in communities for the first time.
Ask: What practice did the Sumerians create when they attempted to keep records of trading transactions? *(They created writing with symbols, which led to the creation of the alphabet.)*

History and You

Many historians believe that the Sumerians arrived in Mesopotamia around 3500 B.C. Scholars credit these people with being the first to create cities.

To better understand their contributions to Sumer, view videodisc Chapter 3: *The Rise of Cities* in Turning Points in World History.

History & Art Neolithic peoples sculpted figures from soft clay and then baked them rock-hard in ovens. These clay statuettes are the most common artifacts of early civilizations. Point out to students that most ancient art had symbolic or religious meaning.

GLENCOE TECHNOLOGY

Glencoe World History Primary Source Document Library
Use the CD-ROM to access primary source documents related to the rise of civilizations.

4000 B.C.	3000 B.C.	2000 B.C.	1000 B.C.

c. 3500 B.C. Sumerians build first cities.

c. 3000 B.C. Narmer unites Upper Egypt and Lower Egypt.

c. 1150 B.C. Olmec civilization begins in Mexico.

c. 3400 B.C. Corn and beans cultivated in the Americas.

c. 1700 B.C. Stonehenge monument is built.

c. 2000 B.C. Chinese write on oracle bones.

15

---

your lives? *(Current fashion trends and feelings about others, among other things.)* Do you create anything that has symbolic meaning, as the cave paintings did? *(Answers will vary, but students will probably say no.)* In the United States today, who creates art and symbols? *(Professional artists and performers, the media, the entertainment industry, sports, and companies produce most art and symbols today.)* Why do you think this is so? *(Answers may include that "art" has a broader meaning now than historically, and that the many common symbols of our culture originate in a variety of mediums.)*

The Spread of Ideas

TEACH

Introduction

This feature focuses on a revolutionary breakthrough in human history—the invention of agriculture. Before they learned to farm, our ancestors spent nearly all their time hunting and gathering food. Because farming is much more efficient than hunting, it created food surpluses that allowed people to live in larger, permanent communities and dedicate themselves to activities besides mere survival.

Who? What? Where? When?

Women and Agriculture
Many archaeologists believe that women invented the practice of agriculture. In hunter-gatherer societies, women collected fruit, nuts, and seeds. As they did so, women probably noticed that plants sprouted where seeds fell. Women probably invented the hoes they used to tend early farms. Only after the invention of the plow did men take over the job of raising crops.

Background Notes

Linking Past and Present

Farmers As farming methods have improved, fewer people are needed to produce the food we eat. In the nineteenth century, most Americans lived and worked on farms. Today, less than 10 percent of Americans are farmers. In developing countries, farming is still the primary occupation of most people. In China, India, and Nigeria, for example, more than half the people are farmers.

The Spread of Ideas

Farming and Civilization

Between 8,000 and 10,000 years ago, a quiet revolution took place. In scattered pockets of the Middle East, Asia, Africa, and the Americas, people learned to cultivate food-producing plants for the first time. As knowledge of farming gradually spread, it dramatically changed human culture. Farming encouraged the growth of permanent communities, which in turn became the seedbeds for the world's first civilizations.

The Middle East
Breadbasket of the Ancient World

Greek grain storage jar

Today only sparse vegetation covers the foothills of Iran's Zagros Mountains. Erosion and overgrazing by sheep and goats have taken their toll. Around 8000 B.C., however, wild wheat known as emmer covered the hills. Experts believe it was here that the world's first farmers may have watched seeds fall to earth and sprout. This observation led these ancient wanderers to plant seeds.

Over time, knowledge of farming spread in a broad arc of fertile land that curved from the Persian Gulf to the Mediterranean Sea. Farmers gradually added other foods to their diets—barley, chickpeas, lentils, figs, apricots, pistachios, walnuts, and more. A hunger for these foods kept people in one place. Hunting and gathering lifestyles changed as people began to develop new ideas and skills. Slowly—very slowly—farming settlements grew into cities. Known by names such as Ur, Babylon, and Jericho, these cities were the centers of Earth's oldest civilizations.

Foothills of the Zagros Mountains

16

COOPERATIVE LEARNING ACTIVITY

Research Organize the class into groups of four or five students. Have each group select an agricultural product, such as corn, wheat, rice, soybeans, apples, bananas, or potatoes. Using encyclopedias and other reference works, as well as outline maps of the world, each group should identify the regions of the world that produce the product they selected. After students have completed the unit, lead a discussion about the importance of agriculture in the development of civilization. Have students discuss which farm products are most important today in their region, and then rank the products they investigated. **L1**

The Americas
Mexico and Peru: Farming and Diversity

For much of world history, distance separated the Americas from the rest of the world. But the independent invention of farming in the areas of present-day Mexico and Peru created cities as sophisticated as those in other regions. The crops that spurred their growth, however, differed from crops elsewhere. Few of the wild grains found on other continents grew in the Americas. The first farmers in the Americas used the seeds of other plants, especially squash and beans. They also developed two high-yield foods unknown to the rest of the world—potatoes and maize (corn). When distant civilizations made contact, ideas about agriculture accompanied the wide distribution of foods that early peoples had developed and cultivated.

Corn Dance by Frank Reed Whiteside

Asia and Africa
Expansion of Earth's Gardens

The farming revolution did not happen just once. It occurred several times in widely separated regions. More than 6,000 years ago, farmers along the upper Huang He in present-day northern China started planting millet. About 5,000 years ago, farmers near the mouth of the Chang Jiang in southern China learned to grow rice. At roughly the same time, farmers along the Nile River in the northern part of Africa harvested their first crops of wheat and barley.

Like the gardens of the Middle East, the gardens of China and northern Africa grew more diverse. By 3000 B.C., farmers cultivated soybeans, bananas, and sugarcane. Supported by the harvests, people had more time to think and dream. Soon they created things that were used by the civilizations of the Middle East—calendars, systems of writing, forms of art and government.

Wood relief of farming activities, Yoruba peoples

LINKING THE IDEAS

1. How do experts think farming probably began?
2. Why is farming considered one of the most important inventions of human history?

Critical Thinking
3. **Cause and Effect** What is the connection between farming and the rise of ancient civilizations?

ANSWERS TO LINKING THE IDEAS

1. In the Middle East, people watched seeds sprout, then tried planting seeds themselves.
2. Farming produced food surpluses that allowed larger, permanent communities to develop, which became the world's first civilizations.
3. Early civilizations grew in areas that had pioneered farming and were well suited to agriculture because increasing numbers of people were freed to devote their time and energy to other pursuits.

The Spread of Ideas

Geography

Place Ask students to look at the small map on page 16. Ask them to locate the early American civilizations that developed farming. *(Modern-day Mexico and Peru)* Have them identify other continents and regions where early societies learned to farm. *(Middle East, China, Africa)* What crops were grown in each region? *(Americas: squash, beans, corn, potatoes; Middle East: wild wheat, barley, chickpeas, lentils; China: rice; Africa: wheat, barley, soybeans, bananas, sugarcane)* Then have students use larger, specialized world maps, such as relief and rainfall maps, to describe conditions in these areas that may have contributed to the development of agriculture.

Cultural Diffusion

The Columbian Exchange After 1492, Europe and the Americas exchanged plants, animals, and microbes. The potato, a tuber of the Americas, became a staple food in Ireland and other parts of Europe. The potato, like corn, yields far more food per acre than does wheat. The growth of Europe's population after 1500 is partly due to the introduction of nutritious, hardy crops of the Americas—such as the potato, corn, and manioc (also called cassava or tapioca).

A complete, 1-page lesson plan is provided for each section in the *Reproducible Lesson Plans* booklet.

Human Beginnings

CHAPTER RESOURCES

	Reproducible Resources	Multimedia Resources
Chapter Opener	📁 Chapter Themes: Graphic Organizer 1 📁 Historical Significance Chapter Activity 1	💿 MindJogger Videoquiz
Chapter Enrichment	📁 Vocabulary Activity 1* 📁 Time Line Activity 1 📁 Mapping History Activity 1 📁 History Simulation 1 📁 Geography and History Activity 1 📁 Source Reading 1 📁 Enrichment Activity 1 📁 Critical Thinking Activity 1 📁 Skill Reinforcement Activity 1 📁 Building Skills in Geography Workbook, Unit 1, Lesson 12 📁 Performance Assessment Activity 1 📁 Standardized Test Practice Workbook Activity 1 📁 Inclusion for the Social Studies Classroom Strategies and Activities	🎞 World History and Art Transparency 1, *Woman's Head* 🎞 Chapter Transparency 1 💿 Vocabulary PuzzleMaker Software 💿 Turning Points in World History: *The Rise of Cities* 💿 World History Primary Source Document Library
Chapter Review/Reteaching	📁 Reteaching Activity 1 📁 Skill Reinforcement Activity 1 📁 Spanish Chapter Summary 1	🎧 Chapter 1 Digest Audiocassette, Activity, Test* 💿 Vocabulary PuzzleMaker Software 💿 Interactive Tutor Self-Assessment Software 💿 MindJogger Videoquiz
Chapter Evaluation/Testing	📁 Performance Assessment Activity 1 📁 Chapter 1 Test, Forms A and B	💿 ExamView® Pro Testmaker

⏱ 0:00 **OUT OF TIME?** Assign the Chapter 1 Audiocassettes.

* Also available in Spanish

World History Primary Source Document Library
Make History Come Alive!
Engage your students with over 250 easily accessible primary source documents—available on this CD-ROM—that will give them real life insight into the important events of world history.

Block Schedule

Activities that are particularly suited to use within the block scheduling framework are identified throughout this chapter by the following designation. 📦

KEY TO ABILITY LEVELS

Teaching strategies are coded for varying learning styles.

L1 BASIC activities for all students

L2 AVERAGE activities for average to above-average students

L3 CHALLENGING activities for above-average students

LEP LIMITED ENGLISH PROFICIENCY activities

Use Glencoe's *Presentation Plus!* multimedia teacher tool to easily present dynamic lessons that visually excite your students. Using Microsoft PowerPoint® you can customize the presentations to create your own personalized lessons.

Interactive Lesson Planner

Planning has never been easier! Using this CD-ROM, organize your week, month, semester, or year with all the help you need. The **Interactive Lesson Planner** gives you access to all of the blackline masters that accompany *World History: The Human Experience.*

SECTION RESOURCES

Daily Objectives	Reproducible Resources	Multimedia Resources
Section 1 **Discovery of Early Humans in Africa** Explain how recent archaeological finds have contributed to our understanding of human origins.	Lecture Notes 1-1 Reproducible Lesson Plan 1-1 Guided Reading Activity 1-1* Time Line Activity 1 Section Quiz 1-1* Reading Essentials and Study Guide 1-1	Section Focus Transparency 1-1 Chapter Transparency 1 Vocabulary PuzzleMaker Software Interactive Tutor Self-Assessment Software Testmaker
Section 2 **The Appearance of *Homo Sapiens*** Describe some of the achievements of the earliest humans.	Lecture Notes 1-2 Reproducible Lesson Plan 1-2 Vocabulary Activity 1* Guided Reading Activity 1-2* History Simulation 1 Section Quiz 1-2* Reading Essentials and Study Guide 1-2	Section Focus Transparency 1-2 World History and Art Transparency 1, *Woman's Head* Interactive Tutor Self-Assessment Software Testmaker
Section 3 **Emergence of Civilization** Specify the kinds of economic, political, and social changes that resulted from the rise of cities.	Lecture Notes 1-3 Reproducible Lesson Plan 1-3 Guided Reading Activity 1-3* Reteaching Activity 1 Enrichment Activity 1 Section Quiz 1-3* Performance Assessment Activity 1 Spanish Chapter Summary 1 Reading Essentials and Study Guide 1-3	Section Focus Transparency 1-3 Vocabulary PuzzleMaker Software Interactive Tutor Self-Assessment Software Testmaker Turning Points in World History: *The Rise of Cities*

* Also available in Spanish

Chapter Activities

 Performance Assessment Activity

Planning a Documentary Have students take the roles of producers who must plan a documentary on early people. Have pairs of students prepare proposals for three thirty-minute segments, including where and when filming will take place, who will narrate, what types of people will be interviewed, what information will be presented and the manner in which it will be presented (interview, graph, photo, and so on). Students may present proposals either in written or oral form, and should keep in mind that their audience will be potential financial backers for the project.

Possible Rubric Features
Content information, concept attainment, decision-making skills, quality and clarity of product

• For an additional activity, refer to Activity 1 in the Performance Assessment Strategies and Activities booklet.

ACTIVITY

From the Classroom of...

Nancy Sue Romerdahl, EdD.
Everett High School
Everett, WA

An Archaeological "Dig"
Materials: Pen and paper, and a woman's purse, with most contents (except personal items) remaining.
Procedure: Ask students to brainstorm how people and particularly history book authors come to "know" what they know.

Explain that this simulation is designed to show how historians and archaeologists use artifacts to make observations and then inferences from those observations. The "dig" is a woman's purse. Have the class list and describe items in the purse. Next, see how many inferences students can make about the purse and its owner. For example, if the purse contains contact lens solution, they might infer that the owner wears contacts; however, she might also be holding the solution for a relative. The class would discuss which is the stronger possibility. Then, if there is also an optometrist appointment card with her name on it this, added to the lens solution "find," becomes stronger evidence that she wears contacts.

After all the items are cataloged, and all reasonable inferences listed, have students write a probable description of the woman.

Following this activity, help students understand how archaeologists generate knowledge about people who left no written record.

MULTIPLE LEARNING STYLES

Verbal/Linguistic
Have students read outside sources about the origin and development of writing. Ask one or more students to report orally on the information obtained.

Auditory/Musical
Have students identify and bring to class one or more musical selections that they think would provide suitable background music for a visit to a cave in which prehistoric paintings have been found.

Kinesthetic
Have students mime the movements of a Neanderthal hunter or gatherer or both. Ask students to explain how they decided what movements would be appropriate.

Interpersonal
Have students form a panel to discuss this question: *As a small group of cave dwellers who have just begun to grow a few crops for food, how shall we divide up the work necessary to keep us alive?*

 GLENCOE'S ASSESSMENT ADVANTAGE

Use the following to easily assess student learning in a variety of ways.

- Performance Assessment Strategies and Activities
- Section Quizzes
- Chapter and Unit Tests
- Interactive Tutor Self-Assessment Software
- Testmaker Software
- MindJogger Videoquiz
- SAT/SAT II Test Practice
- worldhistory.glencoe.com

Additional Resources

NATIONAL GEOGRAPHIC SOCIETY
Teacher's Corner

INDEX TO NATIONAL GEOGRAPHIC MAGAZINE

The following articles relate to this chapter:

- "The Power of Writing," by Joel L. Swerdlow, August 1999.
- "Journey to the Copper Age," by Katherine Ozment, April 1999.
- "The Dawn of Humans," by Lee Berger, August 1998.
- "The Dawn of Humans," by Rick Gore, September 1997.
- "The Dawn of Humans," by Rick Gore, July 1997.
- "The Dawn of Humans," by Rick Gore, May 1997.
- "Kingdom of Kush," by Timothy Kendall, November 1990.

NATIONAL GEOGRAPHIC SOCIETY PRODUCTS AVAILABLE FROM GLENCOE

To order the following, call Glencoe at 1-800-368-7344:

- *Picture Atlas of the World (CD-ROM)*
- *STV: World Geography (Videodisc)*

ADDITIONAL NATIONAL GEOGRAPHIC SOCIETY PRODUCTS

To order the following, call National Geographic at 1-800-368-2728:

- *National Geographic Atlas of World History (Book)*
- *Wonders of the Ancient World: National Geographic Atlas of Archaeology (Book)*
- *Read & Explore: "Painters of the Cave," by Patricia Lauber (Literature Kit)*

Access National Geographic's new dynamic MapMachine Web site and other geography resources at:

- http://www.nationalgeographic.com/
- http://www.nationalgeographic.com/maps/

BIBLIOGRAPHY

Literature About the Period
Auel, Jean M. *The Clan of the Cave Bear.* New York: Bantam, 1984 (paperback).

Readings for the Student
Johanson, Donald, and James Shreeve.
Lucy's Child: The Discovery of a Human Ancestor. New York: William Morrow and Company, Inc., 1989. An account of Johanson's return to Africa in 1986.

Readings for the Teacher
Gowlett, John. *Ascent to Civilization: The Archaeology of Early Man.* New York: Knopf, 1984. The rise and development of human culture as revealed by archaeological finds.

WORLD HISTORY Online

Use our Web site as an additional resource. All essential content is covered in the Student Edition.

You and your students can visit the *World History: The Human Experience* Web site at **worldhistory.glencoe.com** The student text directs students to the Web site for the following options:

- **Chapter Overviews**
- **Student Web Activities**
- **Self-Check Quizzes**

Answers are provided for you in a link entitled "Web Activity Lesson Plan." Additional Web Resources, Interactive Puzzles, and content updates are also available.

Visit the Glencoe Web site at **socialstudies.glencoe.com** for social studies activities, updates, and links to other resources.

LOCAL OBJECTIVES

_____
_____
_____
_____
_____
_____
_____
_____
_____
_____
_____
_____
_____
_____
_____
_____
_____

Introducing
Chapter 1

CHAPTER THEMES

Chapter Themes are listed by section on this chapter opening page of the Student Edition. A corresponding theme-based activity is available under "TEACH," and a theme-based question is asked in the Section and Chapter Assessments.

Historical Setting Finding the remains of the earliest hominids can be a daunting task. The famous anthropological team of Louis and Mary Leakey spent 30 years in Olduvai Gorge, Tanzania, before they finally found a hominid in 1959. (More than 60 hominids have since been found in the same general area.) The Leakeys felt certain they were searching in the right place, because they had been finding stone tools there—a sure sign of the presence of hominids. Their many discoveries in East Africa were the result of scientific knowledge, close observation, and perseverance.

Historical Significance

Answers: *Early people learned to make fire, clothing, and tools as they struggled to survive. They learned how to preserve food for future use. In time they learned to domesticate plants and animals.*

Early civilizations developed with the rise of cities. The cities grew because advances in agriculture—including irrigation—allowed specialization of labor, which led to advanced technology.

Have students use the **Chapter 1 Overview** at worldhistory. glencoe.com as a prereading and postreading exercise for understanding chapter content.

Chapter
1
Prehistory—1000 B.C.

Human Beginnings

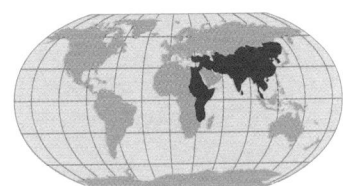

Chapter Themes

▶ **Movement** Migrations of prehistoric peoples result in their spread throughout the world. *Section 1*
▶ **Innovation** Early humans produce tools and domesticate animals and crops. *Section 2*
▶ **Change** The earliest civilizations begin with the evolution of farming settlements into the first cities. *Section 3*

The Storyteller

On the coast of southern Africa, in caves and rock shelters, lived some of the world's first communities of prehistoric people. The region enjoyed a mild climate and abundant food from both the land and the sea. Women gathered supplies, while men made longer journeys inland, hunting for big animals such as antelope, buffalo, and wildebeest. Both men and women searched the coast at each low tide for small sea animals.

The cave dwellers preserved food for times of scarcity by drying leftover meat in smoke from fires. They did not know that more than 70,000 years later scientists and other people exploring the same area would uncover the remains of their long-vanished way of life.

Historical Significance

How did early peoples develop skills that became the basic elements of human ways of life? What developments led to the rise of the world's first civilizations?

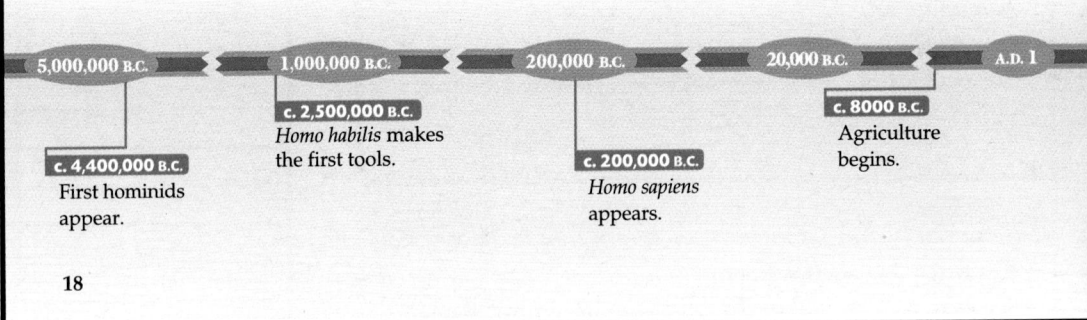

5,000,000 B.C. 1,000,000 B.C. 200,000 B.C. 20,000 B.C. A.D. 1

c. 4,400,000 B.C.
First hominids appear.

c. 2,500,000 B.C.
Homo habilis makes the first tools.

c. 200,000 B.C.
Homo sapiens appears.

c. 8000 B.C.
Agriculture begins.

18

GEOGRAPHY CONNECTION

Location Have students brainstorm a list of conditions that would have made it as easy as possible for early people to survive. (*Answers may include: warm climate all year long, plentiful water supply, abundant vegetation and wildlife.*) Next, have students use the Atlas of their text to locate areas of the world where these conditions exist. (*Answers may include: parts of South America, Africa, and South Asia.*) Finally, have students locate Ethiopia, northern Tanzania, and Kenya, where the remains of early people were actually found.

History & Art Cro-Magnon cave paintings from Vallon-Pont-d'Arc near Avignon, France

History & Art Paleolithic artists used three basic colors: black, red, and yellow. The pigments came from natural sources such as charcoal, clay, and minerals such as iron. How does this cave painting compare in color, composition, and technique to other art you have seen? *(fewer colors and simpler rendering of figures than in other paintings, but lively, with sense of movement and impression of three-dimensional form)*

✔ **Performance Assessment**

Refer to the activity on page 18C of the Planning Guide.

📁 For an additional activity, refer to Activity 1 in the *Performance Assessment Strategies and Activities* booklet.

WORLD HISTORY *Online*

Chapter Overview

Visit the *World History: The Human Experience* Web site at **worldhistory.glencoe.com** and click on ***Chapter 1—Chapter Overview*** to preview the chapter.

Your History Journal

Imagine that you and a friend are stranded on a large uninhabited island. You have no tools except a pocket knife. There are many species of small animals, a stream of fresh water, a sandy beach, and a dense forest. You must survive until rescued, perhaps a month later. Write a journal account of your first seven days.

Using Your History Journal

Journal entries may be in diary form. Remind students that the survival methods they use will parallel those of the earliest humans.

GLENCOE TECHNOLOGY

VIDEODISC
Use MindJogger to preview chapter content.

MindJogger Videoquiz
Chapter 1
Disc 1 Side A

 Also available in VHS.

Chapter 1 *Human Beginnings* **19**

➕ **EXTRA CREDIT PROJECT**

Essay Ask students why it is important to have an understanding of past events and their significance. Write on the chalkboard the following quotation from Cicero, a Roman statesman and orator: "To be ignorant of what happened before you were born is to be ever a child."

Have students write an essay in which they explain the meaning of Cicero's words. In the paper, have them explore the meaning and importance of history, discussing its relevance in today's world.

Timeline

5,000,000 B.C.   3,000,000 B.C.   1,000,000 B.C.

c. 4,400,000 B.C.
Earliest known human ancestor lives in East Africa.

c. 2,500,000 B.C.
Homo habilis develops first stone tools.

c. 1,700,000 B.C.
Homo erectus reaches Asia.

SECTION THEME

▶ **Movement** Migrations of prehistoric peoples result in their spread throughout the world.

Guide to Reading

For reading strategies to help students read effectively see pages 12–13. Have students think about the main head as they read the subheads.

Vocabulary Pre-check

🔲 Use the Vocabulary PuzzleMaker for Chapter 1 to create a crossword puzzle to reinforce section terms. **L1 LEP**

📁 Use Vocabulary Activity 1 to introduce vocabulary terms. **L1 LEP**

FOCUS

Section Objective

Explain how recent archaeological finds have contributed to our understanding of human origins.

BELLRINGER
Motivational Activity

Before taking roll at the beginning of the class period, project Section Focus Transparency 1-1 and have students answer the activity questions. Discuss students' responses.

📁 This activity is also available as a blackline master.

Section 1

Discovery of Early Humans in Africa

Guide to Reading

Read to Find Out
Main Idea *Recent archaeological finds have contributed to our understanding of human origins.*

▶ **Terms to Define**
prehistory, hominid, anthropologist, paleontologist, archaeologist, artifact, radiocarbon dating, nomad, culture, technology

▶ **People to Meet**
Gen Suwa, Tim D. White, Donald C. Johanson, Louis Leakey, Mary Leakey

▶ **Places to Locate**
Aramis, Hadar, Olduvai Gorge

The Storyteller

On the slab lies the shriveled corpse of a man.... Alongside him lies a long wooden stave with a fibrous end. Laid out on the slab ... are the other finds—the axe with its elbow-shafting and metal blade, a stone bead with a strange tassel of twisted hide thongs, the small dagger ... a wooden stick with holes in it, a scrap of leather, and a nut-sized stone.... Archaeologist Konrad Spindler's assessment: 'Roughly four thousand years old ... [or] even earlier.'

—adapted from *The Man in the Ice*, Konrad Spindler, 1994

Excavation of an ancient site in Lake Kinneret, Galilee

---

istory tells the story of humankind. Because historians mostly use written records to gather information about the past, history is said to begin with the invention of writing about 5,500 years ago. But the story of humankind really begins in the time *before* people developed writing—the period called **prehistory**.

Using the best available evidence, scientists have traced the existence of the first humanlike creatures back to about 4.4 million years ago in Africa. Human beings and the humanlike creatures that preceded them together belong to a group of beings named **hominids** (HAH•muh•nuhds). The scientific study of hominids—their physical features, development, and behavior—is called anthropology. Physical **anthropologists** (AN•thruh•PAH•luh•jihsts) compare hominid bones and other fossil remains, looking for changes in such features as brain size and posture. Anthropologists work closely with other scientists. **Paleontologists** (PAY•lee•AHN•TAH•luh•jihsts), for example, study fossil remains to determine the characteristics of various prehistoric periods. **Archaeologists** (AHR•kee•AH•luh•jihsts) investigate prehistoric life by unearthing and interpreting the objects left behind by prehistoric people. These **artifacts** include any objects that were shaped by human hands—tools, pots, and beads—as well as other remains of human life, such as bits of charcoal.

Dating Early Artifacts

As they carefully unearth the remains of prehuman and human settlements, archaeologists and physical anthropologists face the additional problem of dating what they find. It is easy to determine the relative sequence in which events happened.

SECTION RESOURCES

📁 **Reproducible Masters**
- Lecture Notes 1-1
- Reproducible Lesson Plan 1-1
- Guided Reading Activity 1-1
- Time Line Activity 1
- Section Quiz 1-1
- Reading Essentials and Study Guide 1-1

📽 **Transparencies**
- Section Focus Transparency 1-1
- Chapter Transparency 1

Multimedia
🔲 Vocabulary PuzzleMaker Software
🔲 Interactive Tutor Self-Assessment Software
🔲 Testmaker

More recent remains are usually found above older ones. The problem lies in assigning a definite age to fossil bones, tools, and other remains.

Among the techniques for determining age is radiocarbon dating. Once-living things contain small amounts of radioactive carbon. Because radioactive carbon decays at a known rate, archaeologists can measure how much the radioactive carbon has decayed in organic remains and figure out when the animal or plant died. In recent years, they also have used a dating technique that measures the rate of decay for chemical elements other than carbon.

Scientists have increased our understanding of the age of prehistoric peoples through the use of genetic evidence. They obtain genetic material called DNA from living people and compare it with DNA from other people and from living animals. Using computers, they calculate and analyze the rate of change in DNA over time. Although not error free, these studies have produced valuable information about the links between people today and their prehistoric ancestors.

Prehistoric Finds in Africa

On December 17, 1992, a paleontologist from Japan named **Gen Suwa** walked across the rugged desert landscape of Ethiopia in East Africa. At a site called **Aramis**, an object in the ground caught Suwa's eye. It turned out to be one of the oldest hominid teeth ever found—a link to the origins of our human ancestors!

The Oldest Human Ancestor

Over the next two years, Suwa, his colleague **Tim D. White** of the University of California, and a 20-person team uncovered additional remains. They came up with teeth, arm bones, and parts of a skull and jaw that belonged to 17 individuals. Analyzing the fossils, the scientists determined that they were about 4.4 million years old and came from the oldest direct human ancestor known. The small creatures would have weighed about 65 pounds (30 kg) and stood 4 feet (1.2 m) tall. Scientists have yet to determine whether they walked upright.

Discovery of Lucy

About 45 miles (73 km) north, at **Hadar**, two scientists—**Donald C. Johanson** and Tom Gray—in 1974 had uncovered the 3.2 million-year-old skeleton of a hominid nicknamed "Lucy." Lucy received her name from a popular Beatles song of the period,

"Lucy in the Sky with Diamonds." Hers was the most nearly complete skeleton of any erect-walking prehuman found up to that time.

Since then, Johanson and his team of researchers have made further discoveries. In 1994 they assembled, from other fossils found at the Hadar site, the first reasonably complete skull of a Lucy-like hominid. The scientists claimed that the skull provided evidence that males and females in this early hominid group were of significantly different sizes. The evidence also indicated that Lucy-like hominids spent some time climbing in trees and could also walk upright.

The earliest known direct evidence of upright walking comes from Kenya, where archaeologists in 1995 discovered a fossilized hominid shinbone about 4 million years old. The shape and size of the bone indicate upright walking.

Human Origins

Scientists disagree about many aspects of the story of human beginnings. As scientists unearth more clues, newer evidence may require them to reinterpret older evidence.

HISTORY AND SCIENCE
Human Origins: Differing Points of View

People disagree about the interpretation of the available data on human origins. The following are some examples of these differences.

Fossil record Fossils provide insights into human origins, but they do not give a complete or conclusive history of human development. Many gaps are present in the record, and fossils showing changes from one life-form to another are sometimes absent.

Fossil dating Scientists analyze many different samples, using as many different methods as possible because samples may not provide consistent results. Dating methods are constantly being refined to provide more accurate data.

Varying viewpoints A variety of ideas exist about the source of life. Many religions claim that a supreme being or a supernatural force created humans and other life-forms. Current scientific theories focus on chemical reactions in which organic materials have come together to form complex life-forms.

TEACH

Guided Practice

THEME Movement

Have students look at the map on page 22. Ask them to brainstorm a list of reasons why early *Homo sapiens* migrated from place to place. *(Answers may include: to find better sources of food; changes in climate; knowing how to make fire and clothing made life in colder climates possible.)* **L1**

Geography: Human/Environment Interaction Have students locate the middle latitudes on a world map or globe. *(30°N to 30°S)* Then ask a volunteer to point out Ethiopia on a classroom map. Discuss how the discoveries of Suwa, White, Johanson, and the Leakeys are consistent with the theory about where humans lived during the Ice Ages. *(Only the middle latitudes remained warm enough to support human and animal life.)* **L2**

 Chapter Transparency 1

COOPERATIVE LEARNING ACTIVITY

Bulletin Board Organize the class into three groups to prepare a bulletin board display showing the development of hominids from *Australopithecus* to *Homo habilis* to *Homo erectus*. Each group's contributions should include an illustration from a reliable source such as the *World Book Encyclopedia*, *Scientific American*, or *National Geographic*. Displays should also include an indication of the dates of the hominid category and a brief paragraph describing each type. Have students describe individual contributions and cite their sources before posting the bulletin board display. **L1**

Australopithecus The Latin word *australis* means "southern." It is familiar to many people only in the name *Australia* ("southern land"), so students may jump to the erroneous conclusion that *Australopithecus* lived in Australia. Point out that the diminutive "southern ape" was, like all the earliest hominids, native to Africa—specifically, as the name shows, to southern Africa.

Have students use the **Chapter 1 Student Web Activity** at worldhistory.glencoe.com for in-depth study of human beginnings.

Answers
1. *Asia and Australia*
2. *The two continents are so close at the Bering Strait that it is reasonable to assume they were once joined by a land bridge.*

A&E
HOME VIDEO.

The following videotape program is available from Glencoe:

• **The Secret Burial Mounds of Pre-Historic America**

To find classroom resources to accompany this video, check the following home page:

**A&E Television:
http://www.aetv.com**

The First Hominids

According to a generally accepted theory, the first prehuman hominids, such as those discovered in Ethiopia, date back about 4.4 million years. Known as *Australopithecus* (aw•STRAY•loh•PIH•thuh•kuhs), or "southern ape," they stood about 3.5 to 5.0 feet (1.1 to 1.6 m) tall and walked on two legs. They had large faces that jutted out, small brains, flat noses, and large teeth. The back teeth were suitable for grinding food.

Australopithecus lived in the humid forests of eastern and southern Africa, where they fed on fruits, leaves, and nuts. They probably also ate fish caught in streams and meat from animals killed by lions or other predators. *Australopithecus* were most likely nomads—moving constantly in search of food. Fossil evidence shows that family groups lived in temporary camps. No evidence exists showing that *Australopithecus* made or used tools. They may have used grass stems and twigs as tools and sticks or bones to dig roots, however.

Hominid Groups

Scientists use the Latin word *Homo*, which means "human," to name these hominids and all later human beings as well. Anthropologists today are still not certain whether a direct relationship connected *Australopithecus* and human beings or exactly when hominids became truly human. Scientists divided *Homo*—the genus of humans—into three species that differ somewhat in body structures. These three human or humanlike species arose at different times in prehistory. The earliest of the three was *Homo habilis*, or "person with ability," who lived until about 1.5 million years ago. After *Homo habilis* lived the second type

Student Web Activity 1

Visit the *World History: The Human Experience* Web site at **worldhistory.glencoe.com** and click on *Chapter 1—Student Web Activities* for an activity relating to human beginnings.

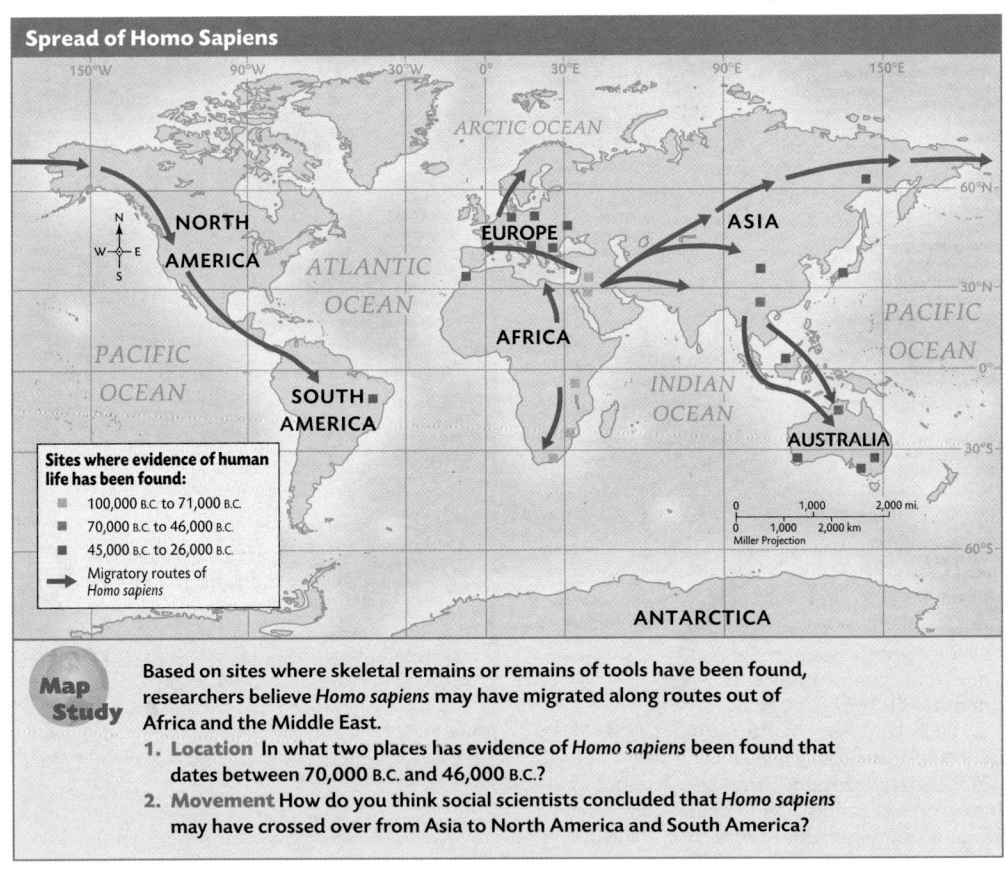

Spread of Homo Sapiens

Sites where evidence of human life has been found:
■ 100,000 B.C. to 71,000 B.C.
■ 70,000 B.C. to 46,000 B.C.
■ 45,000 B.C. to 26,000 B.C.
→ Migratory routes of Homo sapiens

Map Study Based on sites where skeletal remains or remains of tools have been found, researchers believe *Homo sapiens* may have migrated along routes out of Africa and the Middle East.
1. **Location** In what two places has evidence of *Homo sapiens* been found that dates between 70,000 B.C. and 46,000 B.C.?
2. **Movement** How do you think social scientists concluded that *Homo sapiens* may have crossed over from Asia to North America and South America?

22   Chapter 1   *Human Beginnings*

MEETING SPECIAL NEEDS ACTIVITY

Learning Style: Logical/Mathematical 4.4 million years—the approximate age of *Australopithecus*—may be hard for students to comprehend. Have them think of a grandmother-mother-daughter relationship. Three generations = 100 years. Add the word *great* to each previous generation—great-grandmother, great-great-grandmother, and so on. Have students calculate how many times *great* would have to be added to the word *grandmother* to name the ancestor that lived 1,000 years ago. *(27; the word great is not added for the first three generations)* Then have them figure how many times *great* would be used for a woman who lived 4.4 million years ago. *(132,000 less 3)* **L3**

© Bob Campbell

Hominid Hunter

Kenneth Garrett

Meave Leakey, daughter-in-law of famed fossil hunters Mary and Louis Leakey, sifts through soil near Lake Turkana in north-[ern] Kenya, a site in the East African [Rift] System famous for its treasury of [f]ossils of early humans. In recent [years] a wide range of scholars have [conti]nued to push back the date for [the] origin of the earliest humans. [Mole]cular biologists, through the [stud]y of human, chimpanzee, and gorilla genes and [cel]l proteins, speculate that hominids, or early humans, originated somewhere between five and seven million years ago. One of a number of scientists influenced by this research, Meave Leakey and her team began exploring for new evidence. They now theorize that a jawbone found near Lake Turkana in 1994 may be 4.1 million years old. Before that discovery there was little evidence of hominids older than 3.6 million years. Some researchers believe that a 5.6 million-year-old jaw fragment (left) discovered in 1967 may be the oldest hominid fossil yet found. ⊕

Chapter 1 *Human Beginnings* **23**

Tell students that in 1970 Meave Leakey found the first fossil hominid femur (thigh bone) to be recovered in Kenya. Her husband, Richard E. Leakey, a paleo-anthropologist, has written that before her discovery, he sometimes walked right past fossil leg bone fragments, as skulls, jaws, and teeth were easier to recognize. Skulls, jaws, and teeth can provide much interesting information, such as clues to diet and brain size. But they cannot tell the whole story. Ask students what information might be gained from a femur. *(A femur could provide information on the posture and movement of the hominid.)*

CURRICULUM CONNECTION

SCIENCE

Scientists have made great strides in dating fossil bones. Between 1908 and 1912, fragments of a supposed hominid were found in a gravel pit near Piltdown Common, England. Not until 1959, using fluorine tests and other analyses, was it proved conclusively that "Piltdown man" was a hoax.

Independent Practice

 Guided Reading Activity 1-1 **L1**

 Time Line Activity 1

Environment Have students draw pictures of and report on some of the giant mammals that became extinct as the Ice Age ended. These could include the mammoth, giant beaver, and giant sloth. **L1 LEP**

Archaeology Have students choose one of these archaeological sites to research: Altamira, Spain; Tassili n'Ajjer, Algeria; Stonehenge, England. Have them report their research in the form of a magazine article explaining site location and the importance of the discovery. **L2**

Linking Past and Present

Global warming is a topic of concern today. Some scientists predict gradual increases in world temperatures. Unlike the natural forming and melting of glaciers in prehistory, global warming stems from human activities, such as burning fossil fuels. The result is heat trapped in the atmosphere.

The First Australians

Australia, c. 200,000–30,000 B.C.
Early people traveled from Southeast Asia to Australia, crossing about 50 miles of open seas. A land bridge, formed during the Ice Ages, enabled them to make part of the journey by land. The early adventurers reached a landmass called Sahul, which consisted of Australia, New Guinea, and Tasmania. There they encountered animals such as kangaroos that were previously unknown to humans.

Australia

of early human—*Homo erectus,* or "person who walks upright"—who was, in turn, followed between 100,000 and 200,000 years ago by *Homo sapiens,* or "person who thinks." All people living today belong to the species *Homo sapiens.*

The Ice Ages

Climatic changes played an important part in the development of early humankind. Between 2 million and 10,000 years ago, Earth experienced four long periods of cold climate, known as the Ice Ages. During each such period, average temperatures in many parts of the world fell to below freezing, and massive glaciers spread out from the Poles, scarring the landforms over which they crept. The northern glaciers covered large portions of Europe, Asia, and North America, and the ice fields of Antarctica stretched over wide regions in the Southern Hemisphere. Only the middle latitudes remained warm enough to support human and animal life. Between glacial periods, Earth's climate warmed overall, and abundant rains brought lush plant growth—until the next glacial period began.

As the sheets of ice formed, the level of the oceans dropped more than 300 feet (90 m). As a result, some areas that are now separated by water were connected then by bridges of land. One such land bridge joined Japan and mainland Korea, another connected Great Britain and Ireland to western Europe, a third led from the Malay Peninsula through the Indonesian islands almost

all the way to Australia, and a fourth connected Asia and North America at the Bering Strait.

Early human beings responded to the environmental changes of the Ice Ages in several ways. Some migrated to warmer places. Others found strategies for keeping warm, such as clothing and fire. Those who could not adapt died from starvation or exposure.

Human Culture

Clothing and fire had become part of the culture, or way of life, of prehistoric people. Culture also includes the knowledge a people have, the language they speak, the ways in which they eat and dress, their religious beliefs, and their achievements in art and music.

Toolmaking

One of the earliest aspects of culture that people formed was the use of tools. At first they dug roots and tubers out of the ground with wooden digging sticks. Later, they made crude tools of stone, which enabled them to skin small animals and cut off pieces of meat. Improving their technology—the skills and useful knowledge available to them for collecting material and making the objects necessary for survival—early people began to create specialized tools, such as food choppers, skin scrapers, and spear points.

The Stone Age

The use of stone tools by early people led historians to apply the name Stone Age to the period before writing became established. Scholars divided the Stone Age into three shorter periods, depending on differences in toolmaking techniques. The earliest period, the Paleolithic (PAY•lee•uh•LIH•thihk) or Old Stone Age, began about 2.5 million years ago with the first toolmaking by *Homo habilis* and lasted until about 12,000 B.C. The Mesolithic (MEH•zuh•LIH•thihk) period or Middle Stone Age is usually dated from 12,000 B.C. to about 8000 B.C. The Neolithic (NEE•uh•LIH•thihk) period or New Stone Age lasted from about 8000 B.C. to 5000 B.C.

Paleolithic Hunter-Gatherers

Archaeologists as yet do not know a great deal about the culture of the early humans called *Homo habilis* and *Homo erectus.* Their knowledge, however, widens as new discoveries are made.

MAKING CONNECTIONS ACTIVITY

Environment For many years people thought the remains of a vast river system lay hidden under the Sahara. When scientists studied the radar scan of the Sahara by the space shuttle *Columbia* in 1981, they saw a network of waterways, floodplains, and broad river valleys throughout southern Egypt and northern Sudan. Prompted by these images, in 1982 an Egyptian-American team excavated along the banks of an ancient river. They found tools and other artifacts believed to have been used by *Homo erectus* who lived and hunted in the fertile Sahara 200,000 years ago. Have students research to find other areas in which the climate has changed markedly in the past 200,000 years. **L2**

Homo Habilis

Homo habilis lived during the first quarter of the Paleolithic period. It seems probable, however, that these prehistoric people are the oldest hominids known to manufacture tools. They lived in Africa from about 2.5 million to 1.5 million years ago, alongside *Australopithecus*. Their larger brains indicate physical and mental advances. Much of the evidence for *Homo habilis* has come from research by **Louis and Mary Leakey**, and later their son Richard, at **Olduvai** (OHL•duh•VY) **Gorge** in Tanzania and other sites in eastern Africa.

Homo Erectus

Scientists have gathered much more information about *Homo erectus* than about *Homo habilis*. *Homo erectus* first appeared in Africa and lived from 1.8 million years ago to about 30,000 years ago. Their living areas covered a variety of environments from woodlands and grasslands in Africa to forests and plains in Europe and Asia.

Homo erectus at first were mostly food gatherers. Scientists think the females gathered fruits, nuts, and seeds, and the males scavenged for meat—either searching for an animal that had died of natural causes or yelling and waving their arms to frighten carnivores away from a kill. By about 500,000 years ago, however, the males had become hunters, using spears and clubs to kill such small prey as deer, pigs, and rabbits. The females, whose movements were restricted by the constant demands of child care, continued to forage close to home for vegetable food.

Meanwhile, these early humans also had learned how to make fire. This discovery allowed them to keep warm, cook food, and scare away threatening animals. It also enabled them to live in caves. Before, they had protected themselves from the weather by digging shallow pits and covering these with branches. Now, they could drive animals out of caves and use the caves themselves.

Homo erectus by this time not only had fire but also made clothing. Initially they simply wrapped themselves in animal skins, having first scraped hair and tissue off the inner side of the skins. Later, they laced the skins together with strips of leather.

Migrations

Scientists disagree on when prehistoric peoples left Africa and moved to other parts of the world. Some experts believe that *Homo habilis* may have been the earliest to migrate to Europe and Asia; however, clear evidence to support this view is lacking. Scientists do know, however, that *Homo erectus* migrated from their native Africa to Europe and Asia. Skeletal remains found in Java have led anthropologists to conclude that *Homo erectus* reached the Indonesian islands about 1.6 to 1.8 million years ago. *Homo erectus* was clearly well established in China by 460,000 years ago, and the earliest skeletal traces in Europe may also date back around 400,000 years.

Language

To communicate, *Homo erectus* may have used little more than gestures and grunts. By 50,000 B.C., however, prehistoric peoples had developed speech. Language was one of humanity's greatest achievements. It enabled individuals to work with one another—to organize a hunting group, for example, or to give specific instructions about where to find a spring of fresh water. It allowed individuals to exchange ideas, such as what caused animals to migrate across the plains. Individuals could sit around a fire, eat together, and talk about the day's events. They could talk about the best way to fell a tree or build a shelter. Perhaps most significantly, spoken language made it possible for the older generation to pass its culture on to the younger generation, enabling new generations to build upon the knowledge of the past.

SECTION 1 ASSESSMENT

Main Idea
1. Use a chart like the one below to identify three important aspects of *Homo habilis* and *Homo erectus*.

Homo Habilis	Homo Erectus

Recall
2. **Define** prehistory, hominid, anthropologist, paleontologist, archaeologist, artifact, radiocarbon dating, nomad, culture, technology.
3. **Identify** Gen Suwa, Tim D. White, Donald C. Johanson, Louis Leakey, Mary Leakey.

Critical Thinking
4. **Making Comparisons** Compare and contrast the culture of *Homo habilis* and *Homo erectus*.

Understanding Themes
5. **Movement** How did changes in climate affect the migration of early peoples from one part of the world to another?

ASSESS

Check for Understanding

Assign Section 1 Assessment as homework or as an in-class activity.

 Use Interactive Tutor Self-Assessment Software to review Section 1.

Evaluate

Section Quiz 1-1

Use the Testmaker to create a customized quiz for Section 1.

Reteach

Discuss with students the meaning of the word *innovation*. Have them name innovations discussed in this section, and examine how each innovation changed the lives of prehistoric people.

Reading Essentials and Study Guide 1-1

Enrich

Have each student list what he or she thinks are the five most basic tools needed for human survival. Discuss and compare the lists.

CLOSE

Have students describe in their own words the migrations pictured on the map on page 22. Remind them to pay close attention to the symbols on the map that represent prehistoric time.

SECTION 1 ASSESSMENT ANSWERS

1. *Homo habilis:* lived in Africa from 2.5 to 1.5 million years ago; oldest hominids to make tools; more physically and mentally advanced than *Australopithecus*. *Homo erectus:* lived in Africa from 1.8 million to 30,000 years ago; food gatherers; made fire

2. All terms are defined in the Glossary.
3. Suwa, 21; Tim D. White, 21; Johanson, 21; Louis Leakey, 25; Mary Leakey, 25
4. *Homo habilis:* earliest toolmakers, may have migrated to Europe and Asia; *Homo erectus:* cave dwellers, made fire and clothing, migrated to Europe and Asia

5. **MOVEMENT** In Ice Ages, people migrated to warmer climates; answers should also mention land bridges during periods of glaciation.

100,000 B.C.   75,000 B.C.   50,000 B.C.   25,000 B.C.

c. 100,000 B.C. Neanderthals spread
from Africa into Europe and Asia.

c. 50,000 B.C.
Modern humans
originate in Africa.

c. 15,000 B.C.
World population
reaches about
2 million.

SECTION THEME

▶ **Innovation** Early humans produce tools and domesticate animals and crops.

Guide to Reading

For reading strategies to help
students read effectively see
pages 12–13.

Vocabulary Pre-check

🔲 Use the Vocabulary
PuzzleMaker for Chapter 1 to
create a crossword puzzle to
reinforce section terms. **L1 LEP**

📁 Use Vocabulary Activity 1
to introduce vocabulary terms.
L1 LEP

FOCUS

Section Objective

Describe some of the achievements of the earliest humans.

BELLRINGER
Motivational Activity

Before taking roll at the
beginning of the class
period, project Section
Focus Transparency 1-2
and have students answer
the activity questions. Discuss
students' responses.
📁 This activity is also available as a blackline master.

Section 2

The Appearance of *Homo Sapiens*

Guide to Reading

Read to Find Out
Main Idea *The earliest humans
achieved social and technological advances.*

▶ **Terms to Define**
domesticate, deity

▶ **People to Meet**
Neanderthals, Cro-Magnons

▶ **Places to Locate**
Neander Valley, Lascaux, Vallon-Pont-
d'Arc, Jericho, Çatal Hüyük

The Storyteller

*The first sign of animal domestication we
have discovered, at some of the earliest human settlements, is not of something that pulled a plow,
or was eaten; it is the dog. This creature, which
willingly chooses a human as the leader of its lifelong pack, was humankind's first friend, it seems,
as well as its best. Certain species began to thrive
under human care; and humans rearranged their
lives to care for the animals that now came to
depend on them.*

—adapted from *Women's Work: The
First 20,000 Years,* Elizabeth Wayland
Barber, 1994

Paleolithic scraper

26   Chapter 1   *Human Beginnings*

---

*H*omo erectus discovered, used, and
improved upon numerous aspects of
culture that are basic to present-day
life. These accomplishments occurred extremely
slowly, however, taking place over many thousands
of years. When *Homo sapiens*, the modern human
species, appeared, cultural changes began occurring with much greater frequency and took on
greater sophistication. In 1995 archaeologists
uncovered in the Democratic Republic of the
Congo, a number of 80,000-year-old barbed points
and blades. This find indicates that humans made
the first sophisticated tools in Africa and at a much
earlier date than had been believed.

The Neanderthals

Evidence of early *Homo sapiens* dates back
about 200,000 years. The first *Homo sapiens* probably
were the **Neanderthals** (nee•AN•duhr•TAWLZ).
Anthropologists named them after the **Neander
Valley** in Germany where their remains were first
discovered in the A.D. 1850s. Fossil evidence indicates that Neanderthal people may have originated
in Africa and began spreading into Europe and Asia
about 100,000 years ago.

Neanderthals stood about 5.5 feet (1.7 meters)
tall. Their brains were slightly larger than those of
modern human beings, and their bodies were
stocky, with thick bones and very muscular necks
and shoulders. Some scientists today believe that
these distinctive physical characteristics enabled
Neanderthals to adapt to colder climates.

Technological Skills

Like their predecessors, Neanderthals were
nomadic hunter-gatherers who used fire for
warmth and for cooking their food, but their tool-

SECTION RESOURCES

📁 Reproducible Masters
• Lecture Notes 1-2
• Reproducible Lesson Plan 1-2
• Vocabulary Activity 1
• Guided Reading Activity 1-2
• History Simulation 1
• Section Quiz 1-2
• Reading Essentials and Study Guide 1-2

📽 Transparencies
• Section Focus Transparency 1-2
• World History and Art Transparency 1,
Woman's Head

Multimedia
🔲 Interactive Tutor Self-Assessment
Software
🔲 Testmaker

making ability was more sophisticated than that of *Homo erectus.* Neanderthals skillfully crafted stone knives, spear points, and bone tools. Hide-cleaning and food-preparing tools were made of flakes struck from flint or whatever other kind of stone was available. The flakes were delicately shaped by chipping away small pieces from one or more edges of the stone.

Ways of Life

Most Neanderthals lived in small groups of 35 to 50 people. Because they were nomads, Neanderthals did not live in permanent homes. In good weather or warm climates, they lived in open-air camps along the shores of lakes or rivers. In several places, archaeologists have found the remains of Neanderthal shelters built of branches and animal skins. In colder climates, Neanderthals lived together in caves or under the overhangs of cliffs. Heavy clothing made from animal skins must have been worn to fight off the cold.

Culture and Beliefs

The Neanderthals were advanced culturally. They cared for their sick and aged, and may have been the first to practice medicine. A number of Neanderthal fossils show signs of serious injuries that had completely healed before death. Neanderthals also apparently had a belief in life after death. They covered the bodies of their dead with flowers and buried them in shallow graves with food, tools, and weapons.

Homo Sapiens Sapiens

Most scientists believe that modern humans, or *Homo sapiens sapiens,* originated in Africa about 50,000 years ago. Within 20,000 years, this new group dominated almost every continent in the world, including Australia and North America and

Visualizing History *Homo neanderthalensis* fossil skulls found in caves in France resemble the original fossil skull from the Neander Valley in Germany. Neanderthals were short, sturdy hunter-gatherers. *How did Neanderthals adapt to cold weather?*

South America. Many scientists believe that as *Homo sapiens sapiens* appeared in various places, they may have come into contact with Neanderthals and even *Homo erectus.* With the extinction of the Neanderthals and *Homo erectus, Homo sapiens sapiens* became the only hominids left on Earth.

The Cro-Magnons

The earliest *Homo sapiens sapiens* in Europe are called **Cro-Magnons,** after the rock shelter in France where their remains were first found in the A.D. 1860s. Since then, a wealth of Cro-Magnon remains have been found in other parts of Europe and in eastern and central Asia. Similar forms of modern humans have been discovered in Russia, China, Southeast Asia, and all over Africa.

The Cro-Magnons were taller but less robust than the Neanderthals. They brought with them improved technology and a more sophisticated

The First Razors
Archaeologists have unearthed evidence that prehistoric men were shaving as early as 18,000 B.C. Some Cro-Magnon cave paintings portray beardless men, and early Cro-Magnon grave sites contain sharpened shells that were the first razors. Later, people hammered razors out of bronze, and eventually, out of iron.

TEACH
Guided Practice

THEME Innovation

Write the word *innovation* on the chalkboard. Review its meaning with students. Elicit that an innovation can be more than just a device or contrivance. Have students give examples of various kinds of innovations that they are aware of from their own lifetime. Especially try to elicit examples of customs or methods of doing something. **L1**

Visualizing History The evolution of the brain, teeth, and jaw of hominids has determined the shape of the skull. From *Australopithecus* on, the teeth of hominids have become progressively smaller, the jaw less heavy, and the brain case larger (except for the Neanderthal brain, which was larger than that of modern humans).
Answer to Caption: *They lived together in caves and used animal skins for heavy clothing.*

Religion Have students discuss why the evidence of food, tools, and weapons at burial sites suggests to scientists a prehistoric belief in the afterlife. (*Answers might include the point that, since the articles would no longer be useful in the person's life, they must have been meant for an afterlife.*)
L2

COOPERATIVE LEARNING ACTIVITY

Role Play Have students work with partners. Have them role-play an interview with an archaeologist at one of the following sites: Neander Valley, Lascaux, Vallon-Pont-d'Arc, Jericho, Çatal Hüyük. To prepare for the interview, students should read the *archaeology* entry in a good encyclopedia. They should also find additional information on the particular site they have chosen. Have them write specific questions they would like to ask the archaeologist they are interviewing. Students can take turns being interviewer and interviewee. When all interviews have taken place, ask the class to summarize what they have learned from them. **L1**

**Chapter 1
Section 2**

Critical Thinking Have students discuss how people's attitudes toward their environment might have changed as they began to raise crops and domesticate animals. *(One conclusion that students might draw is that hunter-gatherers live in nature, but farmers set out to control nature.)* **L3**

 World History and Art Transparency 1, *Woman's Head*

Linking Past and Present

Beards Men's beards have gone in and out of fashion throughout history. The ancient Egyptians considered a clean-shaven face a symbol of high status. The ancient Persians, however, wore their beards long and curled.

 CURRICULUM CONNECTION

THE ARTS

Paleolithic cave painters used a variety of techniques, including painting with fingers, sticks, and pads of fur or moss. They daubed, dotted, and sketched, using charcoal or pigments from the earth. Sometimes they spray-painted through hollow bone. Painters of different eras often worked on the same cave walls. At Lascaux, 13 eras are evident.

culture. Although they still made their living by hunting and gathering, their methods of food gathering were more efficient, and their hunting techniques were more effective than those of earlier groups.

Cro-Magnon Technology

The many advances the Cro-Magnons made in their toolmaking technology transformed human life. Their blades were thinner and had sharper cutting edges than those of the Neanderthals. The Cro-Magnons used bone, antler, and ivory to make new kinds of tools—hammers, hoes, and pincers. Soon they were fishing with bone fishhooks and using bone needles to sew fitted leather clothes.

With the invention of the stone ax, Cro-Magnons could chop down trees and shape them into canoes. Soon they were traveling down rivers and along seacoasts. They may have used rafts to cross 50 miles (80 km) of sea to reach Australia.

Cro-Magnon hunters also invented long-distance weapons—the spear-thrower and the bow and arrow. Now they could hunt several animals at once and larger animals, too, such as woolly mammoths and bison. The food supply increased and with it the number of people on Earth. Anthropologists estimate that by 15,000 B.C., the world population of human beings stood at a little more than 2 million.

Social Life

The Cro-Magnons' increased food supply had political and social consequences as well. Because it was not possible for a lone band of Cro-Magnons to carry out a big-game hunt, it became necessary for four or five unrelated bands to cooperate, often for weeks at a time. The cooperating bands probably needed formal rules in order to get along, giving rise in turn to leaders who devised and enforced the rules. The evidence for Cro-Magnon leaders consists of high-status burials. Archaeologists have discovered certain Cro-Magnons buried with ivory daggers, amber beads, and other signs of high rank.

Cro-Magnons at first lived in a variety of temporary structures. Some lived inside cave

Images *of the* Times

Early Human Technology

Although they are difficult to date precisely, ancient artifacts provide important clues to early human life.

Discovered in France, this bison licking its flank was carved from bone during the Mesolithic period–12,000–8000 B.C.

A Paleolithic scraper, c. 70,000–50,000 B.C., flaked by repeated blows, helped ancient people dig up roots, shape wood, and cut meat.

28

Images *of the* Times Early Human Technology

Just as plastics are the wonder materials of the modern age, the Cro-Magnon era also had its wonder materials. Among these were bone, antler, and ivory. They were much more versatile than wood. They could be cut, carved, and shaped into implements from needles to shovels. They were strong and durable. They could be sharpened. Ivory could even be steamed and bent. Other Stone-Age wonder materials included flint, a type of quartz, and obsidian, a kind of glass formed when lava cools quickly. Both could be used to produce very sharp edges and were fashioned into knives, even razors.

entrances, while others built huts in forested areas. As better hunting methods developed, Cro-Magnons built more permanent homes. Long houses holding many families were made of stone blocks. There is archaeological evidence that communities of 30 to 100 people lived together.

Cave Paintings

To their technological advances, the Cro-Magnons added accomplished artistry. They created cave paintings like those found at **Lascaux** (la •SKOH) and **Vallon-Pont-d'Arc** (vah•YOHN pohn DAHRK), both in France, as well as those at numerous other cave sites in Spain and Africa. Researchers so far can only speculate on the purpose behind the mysterious wall images. Perhaps the hunting scenes were educational, designed to teach young hunters how to recognize prey. On the other hand, the Cro-Magnon painters may have been reaching out to the spiritual world, creating images meant to have mystical powers that would help the hunters.

Archaeologists have discovered some Cro-Magnon figures sculpted from clay or carved from reindeer antlers. They have also found figures of ivory and bone decorated with animal drawings and abstract designs. Some of these artifacts may well have been used in magic rituals.

The Neolithic Revolution

During the Neolithic period and immediately after, humanity made one of its greatest cultural advances. New environments had developed with the end of the last Ice Age, and forests and grasslands appeared in many areas. Over some 5,000 years, people gradually shifted from gathering and hunting food to producing food. Because new agricultural methods led to tremendous changes in peoples' lifestyles, this period is usually called the **Neolithic Revolution.**

Sumerian cuneiform laid the foundation of writing about 3000 B.C.

REFLECTING ON THE TIMES
1. What clue to early human life does the bison licking its flank provide?
2. How did people store information about the past before writing began?

29

Independent Practice

 Guided Reading Activity 1-2 **L1**

History Simulation 1

Art Have students research and report on the cave paintings of French, Spanish, or African sites such as Vallon-Pont-d'Arc in France or the Altamira Cave in Spain. They might include illustrations in the report. **L2**

Daily Life Have students use the information in the text as a guide to building a model of a Neolithic village such as the one discovered at Çatal Hüyük. **L2 LEP**

The Neolithic Revolution
How did the Neolithic Revolution change the way people lived?
The practice of farming and the domestication of animals enabled people to have a steady food supply and to settle in villages as they no longer had to travel to hunt and gather food.

ANSWERS TO REFLECTING ON THE TIMES
1. Early peoples had tools capable of fine carving.
2. by painting and drawing on cave walls and by memorizing stories and passing them on

The Arts Have students create comic strips illustrating their conception of Neolithic people's lives. Have them share their comic strips with the class. Then discuss these questions: What is the basis for the information presented in your comic strip? Is it based on your reading in this section? Is it completely imaginary? Does it reflect the popular media as represented by television *(The Flintstones)* or the movies *(History of the World–Part 1)*? **L3**

Chart Study

Answer
They can compare their ideas about prehistoric cultures with the records of more recent cultures–and with cultures from around the world today–to infer which social behaviors typically go along with specific technological innovations.

Practice

Reading a Chart How long ago did people learn to make tools out of bone? *(42,000–10,000 years ago)* What other technological innovation did bone tools make possible? *(sewing clothing, using a needle)*

ASSESS

Check for Understanding

Assign Section 2 Assessment as homework or as an in-class activity.

◉ Use Interactive Tutor Self-Assessment Software to review Section 2.

In a sense, the Mesolithic period was a forerunner of the Neolithic Revolution. Most of the cultural changes of the Mesolithic period came in methods of obtaining food. People domesticated, or tamed for human purposes, the dog and used it to help them hunt small game. They also domesticated the goat to use for meat and milk. Early farmers invented the sickle for cutting wild grains so that they could eat the seeds. Pottery, made from sun-hardened clay, was far more effective for carrying and storing food and water than the pouches of animal skin people had used previously.

The Dawn of Agriculture

The Neolithic Revolution not only took place slowly, but also began at different times in different parts of the world. Archaeologists have found evidence of agriculture in the Middle East dating as far back as 8000 B.C. In contrast, China and the Americas did not have agriculture until between 5000 B.C. and 4000 B.C.

The crops that Neolithic people domesticated varied from place to place, depending on the varieties of wild plants and on the crops best adapted to the region's climate—wheat and barley in the Middle East, rice in Southeast Asia, and corn in the Americas. Farmers in Africa cultivated bananas and yams, and farmers in South America grew potatoes. Neolithic people also domesticated animals. They used cattle, pigs, and sheep for meat and sometimes milk. Chickens provided eggs as well as meat.

Farming in many ways made life easier. It brought a steady food supply and enabled people to stay longer in one place. However, farmers had to work harder and longer than earlier hunters and gatherers.

Early Humans

	Homo Habilis	Homo Erectus	Homo Sapiens	
Years B.C.	2.5–1.5 million	1.8 million–30,000	200,000–35,000	40,000–8,000
			Neanderthal	Cro-Magnon
TECHNOLOGICAL INNOVATIONS	• Crude stone tools	• Hand axes and other flaked stone tools • Caves used and pits dug • Clothing of animal skins • Fire controlled for warmth, protection, and cooking	• Spear points and hide scrapers • Shelters built or caves improved • Skins laced for clothing	• Knives, chisel, spear-thrower, bow and arrow • Bone tools: needle, fish hook, harpoon • Fish nets, canoes • Sewed leather clothing • Sun-hardened pottery
SOCIAL BEHAVIORS	• Limited speech • Food gathering and scavenging	• Beginnings of language • Nomadic bands • Hunting-gathering	• Planned burials of dead • Care for disabled members of the community	• Cooperative big-game hunts • Status burials for leaders • Possible magic rituals with cave painting and carved, sculpted artifacts

Chart Study The category "Technological Innovations" describes items found in archaeological digs and dated to a specific period. Interpretation of likely prehistoric social behaviors, however, depends mostly on inferences made by archaeologists and anthropologists.
What evidence do researchers have to support the theory that the social behaviors listed above really existed?

MEETING SPECIAL NEEDS ACTIVITY

Language Delayed Play a "What's My Meaning?" word game. Organize students into two teams and have each team survey the section and list five terms to be defined. The first team gives a term for the second team to define or explain. The moderator (who can be the teacher) assigns points–from one to five for the answer given. The team with the most points is the winner. For the benefit of students with limited English proficiency, have a volunteer write the terms on the board as they are defined. Have students write the terms and their meanings in a notebook for future reference. **L1 LEP**

The First Villages

Now that they could produce food, many more people survived. Anthropologists estimate that by 4000 B.C. the world population had risen to 90 million. Once they had agriculture, people could also settle in communities instead of wandering as nomads. Soon, agricultural villages of about 200 or so inhabitants began to develop where soil was fertile and water abundant. Archaeologists date one of the earliest such villages—**Jericho**, in the modern West Bank—back to 8000 B.C. Another village, **Çatal Hüyük** (CHAH•tuhl hoo• YOOK), in present-day Turkey, dates from 7000 to 6300 B.C.

Çatal Hüyük is one of the largest Neolithic villages that archaeologists have so far discovered. Its people built rectangular, flat-roofed houses of mud bricks placed in wooden frames. Houses of several related families made up a compound with shared walls. People had to walk across roofs. The villagers of Çatal Hüyük also painted the interior walls of their windowless houses with vivid scenes of hunting and other activities.

Technological Advances

Neolithic farmers eventually made their agricultural work easier and more productive by inventing the plow and by training oxen to pull it. They also learned how to fertilize their fields with ashes, fish, and manure.

The relatively steady food supply quickened the pace of technological advance. Neolithic villagers invented the loom and began weaving textiles of linen and wool. They invented the wheel and used it for transportation. They found a way to bake clay bricks for construction. They learned how to hammer the metals copper, lead, and gold to make jewelry and weapons. In 1991, for example, the frozen body of a late Neolithic Age man was discovered in the Italian Alps. The 5,000-year-old "Iceman" wore well-made fur and leather clothing and shoes stuffed with grass. He carried a wooden backpack, a copper ax, a bow, and arrows.

Visualizing History This Neolithic flint knife and these cooking utensils are from Çatal Hüyük. *What evidence tends to show that these people enjoyed art?*

The agricultural way of life led to many other changes. People created calendars to measure the seasons and determine when to plant crops. Because their food supply depended on land ownership, people now cared about such matters as boundary lines and rules of inheritance. Warfare probably came into being as villages competed for land and water.

Neolithic people also believed in many deities, or gods and goddesses. The spirits that supposedly surrounded them throughout nature were transformed into humanlike gods and goddesses with the power to help or hurt people. The people of Çatal Hüyük, for example, set up shrines at which they offered gifts in honor of their deities.

SECTION 2 ASSESSMENT

Main Idea
1. Use a web diagram like the one below to identify four main achievements of the Cro-Magnons

Achievements of Cro-Magnons

Recall
2. **Define** domesticate, deity.
3. **Identify** Neanderthals, Cro-Magnons, Neolithic Revolution.

Critical Thinking
4. **Evaluating Information** Why does the use of agriculture by

Neolithic peoples deserve to be called a revolution?

Understanding Themes
5. **Innovation** Discuss how technological developments affected the food supplies of early peoples in various parts of the world.

SECTION 2 ASSESSMENT ANSWERS

1. made new kinds of tools; lived in communities of 30 to 100 people; created cave paintings; increased food supply and population
2. All terms are defined in the Glossary.
3. Neanderthals, 26; Cro-Magnons, 27; Neolithic Revolution, 29
4. because agriculture led to huge changes in people's lives, such as living in villages
5. **INNOVATION** Improved technology made farming easier, brought higher crop yields, and helped ensure a steady food supply.

Visualizing History Also found in Çatal Hüyük was the earliest known landscape painting. Created by a Neolithic artist, it consists of a series of squares representing the mud-brick houses of the city. An erupting volcano appears in the background. **Answer to Caption:** *the artistic shape and decoration of the knife and cooking utensils*

Evaluate

Section Quiz 1-2

Use the Testmaker to create a customized quiz for Section 2.

Reteach

Review students' understanding of the word *innovation*. Then have them name and discuss the significance of some of the innovations covered in this section. (*clothing, tools, agriculture, houses*)

Reading Essentials and Study Guide 1-2

Enrich

Have students obtain from the guidance office or library a course catalog of a university. Have them report to the class on some of the courses offered by the anthropology department.

CLOSE

Have students describe the progression in food-procurement methods discussed in this section. (*gathering, scavenging for meat, hunting, agriculture*) Then have them list innovations that helped in this progression. (*for example, knives, fishhooks, domestication of animals*)

10,000 B.C.		5000 B.C.		1000 B.C.
c. 10,000 B.C. Last Ice Age ends.	**c. 8000 B.C.** Agriculture begins in various places.	**c. 3500 B.C.** Cities develop along the Tigris and Euphrates Rivers.	**c. 1500 B.C.** First urban communities in East Asia appear.	

Section 3

Emergence of Civilization

Guide to Reading

Read to Find Out
Main Idea *Economic, political, and social changes resulted from the rise of cities.*

▶ **Terms to Define**
civilization, economy, artisan, cultural diffusion, myth

▶ **People to Meet**
the Sumerians

▶ **Places to Locate**
Nile, Tigris-Euphrates, Indus, and Huang River valleys

The Storyteller

Archaeological evidence leaves little doubt that women played key roles in every aspect of life in Old Europe. "In the temple workshops … females made and decorated quantities of various pots appropriate to different rites. Next to the altar of the temple stood a vertical loom on which were probably woven the sacred garments…. The most sophisticated creations of Old Europe—the most exquisite vases, sculptures, etc. now extant—were women's work."

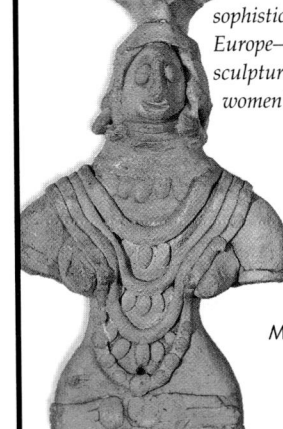

—from *The Early Civilizations of Europe,* (Monograph for Indo-European Studies, UCLA, 1980), Marija Gimbutas

Mohenjo-Daro mother goddess

Over thousands of years, some of the early farming villages evolved slowly into complex societies, known as civilizations. The people of a civilization lived in a highly organized society with an advanced knowledge of farming, trade, government, art, and science. The word *civilization* comes from the Latin word *civitas*, meaning "city," and most historians equate the rise of civilizations with the rise of cities. Because most city dwellers learned the art of writing, the development of cities also marks the beginning of history.

River Valley Civilizations

As with agriculture, cities formed at different times in different parts of the world. Many of the earliest civilizations, however, had one thing in common: They rose from farming settlements in river valleys like that of the **Nile** River in northeastern Africa. The earliest cities that archaeologists have uncovered so far lie in the valley of the **Tigris and Euphrates** (yoo•FRAYT•eez) Rivers in present-day Iraq and date back to about 3500 B.C. Cities arose in the **Indus** River valley in South Asia some 1,000 years later. The first urban communities in East Asia appeared about 1500 B.C. in the **Huang He** (HWONG HUH) valley. By about 1000 B.C. cities were flourishing in Europe and in the Americas, and by 750 B.C. in East Africa.

Early river valley civilizations also shared several other basic features. People's labor was specialized, with different men and women doing different jobs. The civilization depended on advanced technology, such as metalworking skills. Each civilization always had some form of government to coordinate large-scale cooperative efforts such as building irrigation systems. The people in each

Visualizing History Behind high baked-brick walls the people of the ancient city of Mohenjo-Daro, near the Indus River in Pakistan, used four-wheeled carts to carry grain to a large granary. *What was the value of surplus food to the development of a civilization?*

civilization also shared a complex system of values and beliefs.

Not all societies formed civilizations, however. Some people continued to live in small agricultural villages, while others lived by hunting and gathering. Some nomadic people built a specialized culture that relied on moving herds of domesticated animals in search of good pasture.

The Economy of a Civilization

The ways in which people use their environment to meet their material needs is known as an economy. The economy of early civilizations depended on their farmers' growing surplus food. With extra food, fewer men and women had to farm and more could earn their living in other ways.

First Irrigation Systems

A major reason that farmers could produce surpluses of grain crops was that early civilizations built massive irrigation systems. Neolithic farmers

had relied at first on rainfall to water their crops. Later, farmers transported water to grow the crops by digging ditches from a nearby river to their fields. Then they began building small canals and simple reservoirs.

Farmers also built earthen dikes and dams to control flooding in their valley by the river itself. They could now count on a reasonably steady flow of water and prevent destructive flooding.

Specialization of Labor

As men and women continued to specialize in ways of earning a living, artisans—workers skilled in a craft—became increasingly productive and creative. The longer they worked at one task, such as producing storage vessels, the more they learned about how to handle available materials, such as different types of clay. Gradually they turned out larger quantities of goods and improved the quality of their products.

Jewelry, eating utensils, weapons, and other goods were made by hammering copper, lead, and gold. Later, metalworkers in the early civilizations

Chapter 1 *Human Beginnings* 33

TEACH

Guided Practice

THEME Change

Have students list some of the changes that evolved in early civilizations. Discuss the results of these changes. *(Irrigation made food surpluses possible; metalworking provided tools and weapons; ships promoted long-distance trading.)* **L1**

Visualizing History Mohenjo-Daro was a great urban center that flourished from about 2500 B.C. to about 1500 B.C. A city with a perimeter of 3 miles (5 km), its streets were laid out in rectangular patterns. Houses, many of them two stories high, lined the streets. Drainage systems led into these brick-lined streets. The city had hilltop fortresses for protection and baths, probably for sacred rites.

Answer to Caption: *The economy depended on it; with surplus food fewer people had to farm and more could perform other types of work.*

Critical Thinking Have students explain why a system of writing that uses letters to represent sounds is superior to one that uses symbols or pictures to represent ideas or words. *(The former system is easier to encode and decode and is more efficient in communicating abstract ideas.)* **L3**

Independent Practice

 Guided Reading Activity 1-3 **L1**

History Have students research one topic about the Bronze Age and write a short report about it. Topics may include specific tools, hunting practices, ritual art objects, jewelry, food preparation, and so on. **L1**

Global Gourmet

Sumeria As methods of raising foods grew more sophisticated, so did methods of preparing it. The first ovens with burners on top were developed by the Sumerians. When Sir Leonard Woolley excavated the Sumerian city of Ur, he found one ancient stove so perfectly preserved that he was able to light it and prepare food on it.

POINT

The Rise of Cities
What led to the need for new forms of government in Mesopotamia?
population growth

VIDEODISC
Turning Points in World History

Side One
Chapter 3

Title: *The Rise of Cities*

---

learned to make alloys, or mixtures of metals. The most important alloy was bronze, a reddish-brown metal made by mixing melted copper and tin. Historians refer to the period that followed the Stone Age as the Bronze Age, when bronze replaced flint and stone as the chief material for weapons and tools.

Bronze, harder than either copper or tin alone, took a sharper cutting edge. Artisans also found it much easier to cast bronze, or shape the liquid metal by pouring it into a mold to harden. Because the copper- and tin-containing ores needed to make bronze were scarce, however, the metal was expensive and therefore used only by kings, priests, and soldiers.

Long-Distance Trade

The search for new sources of copper and tin is an example of the long-distance trade that accompanied the rise of early civilizations. At first farmers and artisans traded within their own communities. They eventually began traveling to nearby areas to exchange goods. After a while merchants, a specialized class of traders, began to handle trade, and expeditions soon were covering longer routes.

Some long-distance trade moved overland by means of animal caravans. Some goods were transported by water. People made rafts and boats for travel on rivers. After a time, people learned how to harness the force of the wind, and rivers and seacoasts became filled with sailing ships.

Along with goods, ideas were actively shared. This exchange of goods and ideas when cultures come in contact is known as cultural diffusion. Although early civilizations developed many similar ideas independently, other ideas arose in a few areas and then spread throughout the world by cultural diffusion. When ancient peoples learned about the technology and ideas of different civilizations, the new knowledge stimulated them to improve their own skills and way of life.

POINT

The Rise of Cities

Civilizations grew both more prosperous and more complex. Early cities had from 5,000 to 30,000 residents. A population of this size could not function in the same way that a Neolithic village of 200 inhabitants had.

Planning and Leadership

Ancient cities faced several problems unknown in the Neolithic period. Because city residents

---

depended on farmers for their food, they had to make certain that farmers regularly brought their surplus food to city markets. At the same time, farmers could not build dams, dig irrigation ditches, and maintain reservoirs on their own. As civilizations prospered, they drew the envy of nomadic groups, who would repeatedly raid and pillage farms and attack caravans. In short, the first cities needed a way of supervising and protecting agriculture and trade.

The early city dwellers found two solutions to these problems. First, ancient cities organized a group of government officials whose job it was to oversee the collection, storage, and distribution of farming surpluses. These officials also organized and directed the labor force needed for large-scale construction projects, such as irrigation systems and public buildings. Second, ancient cities hired professional soldiers to guard their territory and trade routes.

Government leaders, military officials, and priests belonged to a ruling class often led by a king, although women also held positions of authority. The ruling class justified its power by means of religion. According to ancient beliefs, the land produced food only if the gods and goddesses looked on the people with favor. One of the king's main functions, therefore, was to assist priests in carrying out religious ceremonies to ensure an abundant harvest. The first kings were probably elected, but in time they inherited their positions.

Levels of Social Standing

Archaeological evidence for the position of the ruling class can be found both in the treasures with which they were buried and in the physical layout of the ancient cities. At the city's center was an area that held the most imposing religious and government buildings. Nearby stood the residences of the ruling class. Next to these came the houses of the merchants. Farther out, the shops and dwellings of specific groups of artisans—such as weavers or smiths—were established in special streets or quarters. Farmers, as well as sailors and fishers, lived on the city's outskirts. Archaeological evidence suggests too that slaves, who were probably captured in battle, lived in many parts of the city.

Invention of Writing

Many archaeologists think that writing originated with the records that priests kept of the wheat, cloth, livestock, and other items they received as religious offerings. At first the priests used marks and pictures, called pictograms, to represent products. After a time they used the marks and pictures to represent abstract ideas and, later

---

still, to represent sounds. Priestly records listed the individual men and women who were heads of households, landowners, and merchants. Soon the priests were also recording such information as the king's battle victories, along with legal codes, medical texts, and observations of the stars.

Systems of Values

Among the materials recorded by the priesthoods in early civilizations were myths, traditional stories explaining how the world was formed, how people came into being, and what they owed their creator. The priests of the Sumerians in the Tigris-Euphrates River valley wrote their myth of creation, for example, on seven clay tablets.

According to the Sumerian story, before creation there were two gods, Apsu the First Father and Tiamat the First Mother. They married and had many children. "But each generation of gods grew taller than its parents … [and] the younger gods could do things their parents had never tried to do." Eventually Apsu's great-grandson Ea made a magic spell and killed Apsu. Ea's son Marduk killed Tiamat. Then:

    ❝Marduk turned again to the body of
       Tiamat.
    He slit her body like a shellfish into two parts.
    Half he raised on high and set it up as sky.…
    He marked the places for the stars.…
    He planned the days and nights, the months
       and years.
    From the lower half of Tiamat's body, Marduk
       made the earth.
    Her bones became its rocks.
    Her blood its rivers and oceans.…
    'We need creatures to serve us,' he said.
    'I will create man and woman who must
       learn to plow land to plant, and make
       the earth bring forth food and drink for us.
    I will make them of clay.'…❞

      —"Enuma Elish," Sumerian account
      of creation from *The Seven Tablets*
      of Creation, date unknown

CONNECTIONS

Geography

Migrations Then and Now

Little Diomedes Island, Bering Strait

One of the land bridges that formed during the Ice Ages joined Siberia, the easternmost part of Asia, with Alaska, the westernmost part of the Americas. Modern historians have named this land bridge Beringia, after the shallow Bering Strait that covers it today.

Approximately 40,000 years ago, groups of Cro-Magnons may have crossed Beringia from Asia to the Americas. According to some anthropologists, these groups were nomadic hunting bands in search of migrating herds of animals. We do not know whether the migrants crossed all at once or in successive waves.

From the north the migrants gradually moved south into new territory. Anthropologists estimate that their journey all the way to the southernmost tip of South America took about 600 generations. This equals a rate of migration of about 18 miles (29 kilometers) per generation, over 18,000 years.

Today, the availability of fast, safe, and mechanized transportation—by air and by water—makes migration easier and quicker from one place to another. As in the past, war, persecution, and disasters—such as famines and epidemics—have forced people to flee their homelands. At the same time, people have also been attracted to new places by economic opportunity—a better job and higher standards of living.

Linking Past and Present ACTIVITY

Research and write a brief essay comparing and contrasting prehistoric and modern migrations. Focus on methods and routes of travel, reasons for migrating, and the challenges faced in the new homeland.

Chapter 1 *Human Beginnings* 35

ASSESS

Check for Understanding

Assign Section 3 Assessment as homework or as an in-class activity.

 Use Interactive Tutor Self-Assessment Software to review Section 3.

Linking Past and Present

Migrations Then and Now

Although water now separates Siberia and Alaska, the Bering Strait is narrow enough (only about 55 miles wide) that small boats can easily cross it during the warmer months of the year.

ANSWER

Students might conclude that changes in technology have made migration today quicker and easier than in prehistoric times. Economic opportunity is a dominant motive—search for food (prehistory) and search for jobs and higher standards of living (modern). Prehistoric migrants had to adjust to the environmental challenges, while modern migrants deal with the challenges of adapting to a new culture, language, and so on.

MAKING CONNECTIONS ACTIVITY

Literature Have students engage in a roundtable discussion about creation myths from various civilizations, such as the story of Marduk in this section. Have students prepare by finding out as much as they can about these various creation myths. Each student should become a resource person for one myth. The myths can be discussed one at a time or thematically in class. Focus the discussion on the myths' similarities and differences. Have students speculate about the nature and beliefs of the different civilizations. Have excerpts from some of the myths read aloud in class. Creation myths from greatly differing civilizations will enhance this activity. For example: Greek theogony, Scandinavia's Ymir (or Imir), Ghana's Nyame, and China's cosmic egg. **L2**

Evaluate

 Section Quiz 1-3

⊙ Use the Testmaker to create a customized quiz for Section 3.

Reteach

Have students review the roles of the following people in early cities: farmers, merchants, artisans, soldiers, rulers, priests.

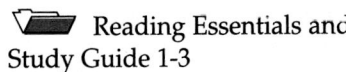 Reteaching Activity 1

Reading Essentials and Study Guide 1-3

Enrich

Have students research cuneiform writing. Direct them to find out how different pictograms evolved into abstract symbols and how people of modern times learned to decode and read cuneiform inscriptions.

 Enrichment Activity 1

CLOSE

Have students write four topic sentences that express main ideas about the first civilizations. (*Examples: The first civilizations began along river valleys. Farmers in early civilizations produced surpluses of food. Early civilizations traded with one another. City living created specialization of labor.*) Have students read and discuss their sentences in class.

Visualizing History **Statue of the god Abu and his consort from the temple at Tel Asmar.** *What god was worshiped by the ancient Sumerians as creator of the earth?*

After relating how the people drained marshes for farmland, built walled cities, learned to make bricks, and built a great temple at the center of their biggest city, the myth continues:

> **Daily they sang praises to Marduk, supreme among the gods**
> **He who created the vast spaces and fashioned earth and men;**
> **He who both creates and destroys; who is god of storms and of light;**
> **He who directs justice; a refuge for those in trouble;**
> **From whom no evil doer can escape;**
> **His wisdom is broad. His heart is wide. His sympathy is warm.**

Creation myths have been found in every civilization. Because these myths vary from place to place, historians often examine them for evidence of a people's customs and values. For example, the seven Sumerian clay tablets could easily imply information about Sumer's values and beliefs. The clay tablets reveal that Marduk, though not the first god, had become—at the time the tablets were recorded—the leading one by supplanting the goddess Tiamat. The Sumerians seemed to believe too that evil should—and would—be punished. Apparently they also thought it was effective to praise and worship Marduk. Of course, the inferences an archaeologist can reasonably make from a myth are often limited and leave many unanswered questions.

SECTION 3 ASSESSMENT

Main Idea
1. Use a chart like the one below to identify four changes that resulted from the rise of cities.

[Rise of Cities]

Recall
2. **Define** civilization, economy, artisan, cultural diffusion, myth.
3. **Identify** the Sumerians.

Critical Thinking
4. **Synthesizing Information** Imagine that you ruled a city in an early civilization. How would you improve living conditions?

Understanding Themes
5. **Change** How did technological changes of the first civilizations improve toolmaking and trade transportation?

SECTION 3 ASSESSMENT ANSWERS

1. government officials organized and directed the work force, collected and distributed farm supplies; professional soldiers were hired; ruling class justified power by religion; writing invented to keep records
2. All terms are defined in the Glossary.
3. a people who lived in the Tigris-Euphrates River valley and wrote their myth of creation on clay tablets
4. Students should consider basic needs of city's people. Answers may include issuing orders to build walls around the city and developing an adequate sewage system.
5. **CHANGE** toolmaking: ability to make alloys such as bronze; transportation: advances in boatbuilding, such as sails

Understanding Map Projections

Greenland appears to be a larger landmass than Australia on some maps, yet Australia actually has a larger land area than Greenland. Have you ever wondered why?

Learning the Skill

When mapmakers attempt to transfer the three-dimensional surface of Earth to a flat surface, some inaccuracies occur. To accomplish this mapmakers use *projections*—an image produced when light from within the globe projects the globe's surface on a flat paper. These projections may stretch or shrink Earth's features, depending on the map's intended use.

Projections create two major kinds of maps. A *conformal map* shows land areas in their true shapes, while distorting their actual size. An *equal-area map* shows land areas in correct proportion to one another, but distorts shapes.

The map on this page is a *Cylindrical Projection (Mercator)*. Imagine wrapping a paper cylinder around the globe. A light from within projects the globe's surface on the paper. The resulting conformal projection makes Alaska appear larger than Mexico. Distortion is greatest near the Poles.

A *Conic Projection* is formed by placing a cone of paper over a lighted globe. This produces a cross between a conformal and an equal-area

map. This projection is best when showing areas in middle latitudes.

To understand map projections use the following steps:
- Compare the map to a globe.
- Determine the type of projection used.
- Identify the purpose of the projection.

Practicing the Skill

Turn to the map of the world in the Atlas. Compare the sizes and shapes of the features on this map to those on a globe. Based on this comparison, answer the following questions:
1. What is the map's projection?
2. How does the map distort Earth's features?
3. In what way does the map accurately present Earth's features?
4. Why did the mapmaker use this projection?

Applying the Skill

Compare the size of Antarctica as it appears on a map with Antarctica on a globe.

For More Practice

Turn to the Skill Practice in the Chapter Assessment on page 43 for more practice in understanding map projections.

Cylindrical Projection *(Mercator): This projection is accurate along the line where the cylinder touches the globe, with great distortions near the Poles.*

 The **Glencoe Skillbuilder Interactive Workbook**, Level 2 provides instruction and practice in key social studies skills.

TEACH

Understanding Map Projections To help students see how maps distort our view of the world, have them plot the shortest, most direct route from New York City to Rome on a Mercator map. Then have them use a piece of string to do the same thing on a globe. Compare the two results. *(On the Mercator map, it looks like the route would be over the middle of the Atlantic Ocean, when in fact the shortest route is up the Canadian coast towards Greenland and down.)* Be sure to have a globe available while teaching this skill.

Additional Practice

📁 Skill Reinforcement Activity 1

📁 Building Skills in Geography Workbook, Unit 1, Lesson 12

GLENCOE
TECHNOLOGY

 Glencoe's **Skillbuilder Interactive Workbook, Level 2** This interactive CD-ROM promotes student mastery of key social studies skills.

ANSWERS TO PRACTICING THE SKILL

obinson projection (created recently by
erican cartographer Arthur Robinson)
e Robinson projection distorts Earth's
tures less than other projections have.
example, Australia looks as if it has a
ger land area than Greenland, which
eed it does.

3. The sizes and shapes of continents and the distances between places are fairly accurate, and visually disturbing distortions have been minimized.

4. The Robinson projection is a good compromise.

◻ NATIONAL
GEOGRAPHIC *Special Report*

Sygma

The Iceman

In 1991 two German hikers discovered the body of a pre-historic man who had been frozen in a glacier in the Alps.

Scientists determined that the "Iceman" was at least 5,000 years old.

The Iceman lived during the Copper Age, which in Europe lasted from 4000 to 2200 B.C.

From the Iceman's posses-sions we have learned that he was a member of a com-munity which knew how to sew, make finely hewn tools of metal and flint, and use natural substances to combat illness.

TEACH

Points to Discuss

After students have read the selection, discuss the following: What two methods did scientists use to determine the Iceman's age? Which of the two is more exact? *(estimating by style of ax, radiocarbon dating; the latter is more exact)* What factors led the Ice-man and others of his time to

O n September 19, 1991, Helmut and Erika Simon, a German couple hiking near the border between Austria and Italy, wandered slightly off the trail. Suddenly Erika Simon caught sight of a small head and pair of shoulders emerging from the ice. The Simons thought they had stumbled across a discarded doll. In fact, they had found the solitary

prehistoric traveler now known around the world as the Iceman.

At first the Iceman was thought to be 4,000 years old—which would have made the discovery remarkable enough. Scientists later discovered that the Iceman was at least 5,000 years old! In comparison, Tutankh-amen, Egypt's boy-king, was born some 2,000 years later.

The Iceman is the oldest body ever retrieved from an Alpine gla-cier; the next-oldest was only 400 years old. At 10,530 feet (3,210 m),

▧ *Overcome by fatigue and col mountaineer (above) lies down die high in the Alps. Some 5,00 years later, the discovery of his well-preserved body, along wit clothes and a copper ax, offers startling clues about how huma greeted the metal age in Europ*

▧ *The Iceman (top) emerges fr under a melting glacier.*

TEACHER NOTES

_____

_____

_____

_____

_____

Sygma

climb high into the Alps? (*climatic warming made higher and higher altitudes good locations for hunting game or pasturing sheep; large veins of copper found there*) How did the discovery of copper change life for the prehistoric people who lived in the Alps? (*led to the development of trade routes, and of new, specialized occupations such as smelters and axmakers*) What evidence is there that the Iceman had a spiritual life? (*He had tattoo-like marks in places that no one could see, which suggests they were to confer supernatural power; he carried two pieces of fungi on a leather thong, an artifact which also might have been believed to confer power or protection, as it has no other more utilitarian purpose.*)

Greg Harlin/Wood Ronsaville Harlin, Inc.

NGS Cartographic Division

e site where the Iceman lay is the ghest elevation in Europe in which ehistoric human remains have en found. Not even traces of a mpfire have ever been discovered that height.

The body of the Iceman was pre- ved through sheer luck. Shortly er he died, the rocky hollow here he lay filled with snow. For ousands of years a glacier covered is pocket of snow, only a few rds over the Iceman's head. More mmonly, a body caught in a gla- r would be crushed and torn by e movement of the ice. Instead, the eman was naturally mummified.

In the four days following the discovery, many well-meaning hikers and officials tried to free the Iceman from the glacier. They took turns hacking and prodding around the body with ice axes and ski poles. Unfortunately, they damaged the Iceman and the artifacts found with him—in ways that 5,000 years of glaciation had not. One of the "rescuers" seized a stick to dig with, breaking it in the process; the stick turned out to be part of the hazel-wood-and-larch frame of the Iceman's backpack, a type of ancient artifact never seen before. Workers also snapped off the top

▨ *The local coroner (above) and an assistant remove the corpse from his icy grave.*

▨ *The Iceman was found at an elevation of 10,530 feet (3,210 m) on the Austrian-Italian border. His tools and backpack frame were located near his body.*

Linking Past and Present

Archaeological Evidence Since the discovery of the Iceman, archaeologists have looked for other signs of prehistoric people in the high Alpine valleys where he died. They have found remains of campsites and flint tools from hunters who lived thousands of years before the Iceman. Many of these remains, as well as the Iceman's body, were found along a path which local shepherds still use.

FUN FACTS

- Although lung disease is often thought of as a symptom of modern life with its cigarette smoke and pollution, doctors found that the Iceman's lungs were as black as a smoker's. They attribute his condition to living in a shelter with an open fire.
- The development of metalworking increased contact between peoples, as the early metalsmiths were traveling specialists. The Iceman had large amounts of copper in his hair, and may have been such a traveling coppersmith.
- Copper is the first metal prehistoric people put to utilitarian use. The oldest known human-made metal is a copper pendant that dates from around 9500 B.C.
- Animals as well as humans have been preserved in ice. In Siberia, some 50 specimens of the long-extinct woolly mammoth have been found preserved in ice with their skin and flesh still intact.

CURRICULUM CONNECTION

MEDICINE

Doctors and scientists have used special instruments and techniques to study the Iceman's physical remains. Their studies have shown that he may have been in a weakened condition when he died, as he suffered from worms. X rays of the Iceman's shinbones revealed that he endured several periods of illness or extreme hunger during the course of his life that arrested his growth.

you don't say...

Copper Age The Copper Age is also sometimes called the Chalcolithic Age, which means "Copper-Stone" Age. This name is fitting because in the early stages of this period, copper was used mainly for small precious objects, while many tools continued to be made of stone. Some of the Iceman's tools, for example his dagger, were made of flint, not metal.

end of the Iceman's six-foot-long bow. What remained of the Iceman's clothing was torn off, as were parts of his body, and an officer using a jackhammer left a gaping hole in the Iceman's hip. To be sure, none of the salvagers suspected how old the Iceman was.

Not until five days after the discovery did an archaeologist examine the Iceman's body. Basing his estimate on the style of the ax found with the body, the archaeologist guessed that the Iceman was 4,000 years old.

Once officials knew the Iceman's approximate age, a rigorous effort to stabilize his condition began. The mummy was placed in a freezer, where the temperature was kept at a constant 21°F (-6°C) and the humidity at 98 percent—conditions much the same as those of the ice in which he had lain. The Iceman was not removed from the freezer for more than 20 minutes at a time, and then only for the most important scientific research. Part of that research was carbon-dating the Iceman to verify how old he was. Further chemical analysis revealed that the blade of his ax was not bronze, but nearly pure copper. He was, in fact, unique: a mummy from the Copper Age, which lasted in central Europe roughly from 4000 to 2200 B.C. Two different laboratories concluded that he was 5,000 to 5,500 years old.

THE ICEMAN'S DOMAIN was the Alps, stretching from southeast France to the Swiss-German border, and from Austria to northern Italy. Five thousand years ago these mountains were a vast wilderness. In the Copper Age, hardy voyagers trekked these ranges, and the goods they traded traveled even farther. We know from his tools and clothes that the Iceman was one of these

Iceman's artifacts photographed by Kenneth Garrett

rugged mountaineers.

The first half of the Copper Age was an era of climatic warming, when humans penetrated higher than ever into the Alps. The tree line climbed during the warming, game followed the forests, and hunters followed the game. Meadows above the tree line offered the best pastures for sheep, goats, and cattle and contained great green veins of a newly valued metal—which today we call copper. Copper changed the Alpine world forever, leading to the development of major trade routes between isolated valleys. Earlier, wealth was made through cattle or wheat. Copper was not only a form of portable wealth but also a stimulus for the development of specialized occupations. Men became smelters, axmakers, possibly even salesmen. The world's earliest known man-made copper objects—beads, pins,

A fragment of the Iceman's plaited-grass cape (above) was found next to his head.

This stone disk threaded with leather thong (inset, top right) may have been worn to protect against evil.

The Iceman's copper ax is the oldest ever found in Europe with its bindings and handle intact (inset, bottom right).

A fungus on a string may have been a first-aid kit (inset, above left).

and awls—were made about 8000 B.C. in Turkey and Iran. There is dence of copper mining in the Balkans by 5000 B.C. From there technology spread west, reaching the Alps a thousand years later.

TEACHER NOTES

copper ax may tell us most. Its yew-wood handle ends in a gnarled joint, where a notch holds the blade. Dark birch gum held the blade firmly in position beneath a tightly wrapped thong of rawhide. It is a ribbed ax, rather than the more primitive flat ax that archaeologists would have expected to find.

Researchers who reconstructed what remained of the Iceman's clothing observed that his garment had been skillfully stitched together with sinew. Cruder repairs had been made, probably by the Iceman himself on his travels. This led researchers to believe that the Iceman had been part of a community, although he was used to fending for himself. Also, tiny pieces of a wheat that grew only at low altitudes, and bits of charcoal from a variety of trees found throughout the Alps were discovered with the Iceman, indicating that he may have come from southern Tirol (in Austria).

Included among the Iceman's possessions were a stick with a tip of antler used to sharpen flint blades; a deerskin quiver that contained 14 arrows; and an unfinished bow. His small flint dagger was similar to those found at other Copper Age sites, but no one had ever seen the kind of delicately woven sheath that held the dagger.

Central Europe's oldest known plow is more than a thousand years younger than the Iceman. Yet Copper Age artists cut images of plows on rocks. Rows of furrows have been found preserved at a major Copper Age religious complex excavated in northwest Italy, though experts believe plowing was ritualistic rather than agricultural.

The Iceman also had tattoo-like marks that might imply something about his spiritual life. Located on normally hidden places—his lower back, behind his knee, and on his ankle—the marks were not for

The work of many researchers over the past 30 years tells us much about life during the Copper Age. Excavations have yielded bones that indicate that by around 5000 B.C. Alpine people had domesticated five animals: dogs, which were originally more important for food than companionship, cattle, sheep, goats, and pigs. Horses and chickens were still unknown in the Alps. Villagers grew wheat and barley and made linen clothes from flax. They had only recently discovered how to milk a cow and how to make cheese and butter. Their sheep may have been used for meat but not yet for wool. Many staple foods of today were still unknown, including potatoes, onions, and oats.

EVENTUALLY, THE ICEMAN'S possessions may tell us more than his body will. Of those possessions, his

Kenneth Garrett

☐ ***The Iceman's head was reconstructed by John Gurche, an anthropologically trained artist. He first sculpted a replica of the skull by using computer images, X rays, and CT scans of the Iceman. Gurche then added clay to duplicate the Iceman's mummified face, complete with smashed nose and lip. Next, he added muscles and fatty tissue, nasal cartilage, and glass eyes. Finally he made a new model of the head with soft urethane, tinted to suggest wind-burned skin. He completed the replica of the Iceman's head by adding human hair.***

show. Perhaps they were meant to confer supernatural power or protection. So might the pair of fungi he carried, each pierced by a leather thong. Archaeologists have never seen anything like this artifact from that period. The fungi contain chemical substances now known to be antibiotic. If the Iceman used them to counteract illness, perhaps they also seemed magical to him.

We may never know what drew the Iceman to the mountain pass where he died. Perhaps he was a shepherd, a trader, or an outcast. But, in the late 20th century, it is our good fortune to have the opportunity to learn from this ambassador of the Copper Age.

Chapter 1 *Human Beginnings* **41**

Copper From the time of the Iceman until the A.D. 1800s, methods for processing copper didn't change much. But in the late 1800s, the spread of telephone lines and electric power lines greatly increased the demand for copper, and deposits of high-grade ore were soon depleted. Around 1900, a new method for processing low-grade ore was invented by a young American engineer. Today, about 9 million short tons (8.3 million metric tons) of copper are mined each year.

Cultural Perspectives

Human Development The era in which the Iceman lived, the Copper Age, represented the first stage of human development beyond the Stone Age. In addition to the discovery of metalworking techniques, people made numerous other advances. In some communities of the time, people wore clothes of woven fabric, extracted oil from plants, ate out of stone and wooden bowls, and lived in houses.

MORE ABOUT...

Metal How did early people learn how to make metal? Scientists speculate that the discovery was probably made in a pottery kiln, because ordinary cooking fires do not get hot enough. Copper oxides in powdered form were sometimes used as a glaze on pots. After firing such a pot, a potter may have discovered a small piece of copper in his kiln. If this happened more than once, he might eventually figure out that it was made when the heat interacted with the copper oxide.

GLENCOE TECHNOLOGY

 VIDEODISC
Use MindJogger to review the chapter.

MindJogger Videoquiz

Chapter 1
Disc 1 Side A

Also available in VHS.

Answers

Using Key Terms

1. h	3. d	5. a
2. i	4. l	

Using Your History Journal

Students should understand that early humans had survival skills that people in industrialized societies seldom need; for example, how to make tools from stone and bone; how to start a fire without matches; how to hunt and fish without today's manufactured equipment.

Reviewing Facts

1. specialization of labor; made alloys such as bronze; need for copper and tin led to long-distance trade; trade handled by merchants; expeditions covered longer routes; river travel required rafts, boats, and sailing ships; spread of new ideas
2. connecting Japan and mainland Korea, Great Britain and Ireland to western Europe, the Malay Peninsula almost to Australia, Asia and North America at the Bering Strait
3. Europe and Asia
4. It enabled people to exchange

WORLD HISTORY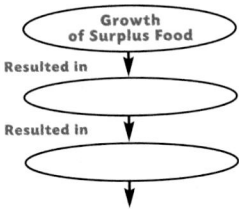
Online

Self-Check Quiz

Visit the *World History: The Human Experience* Web site at **worldhistory. glencoe.com** and click on **Chapter 1—Self-Check Quiz** to prepare for the Chapter Test.

Using Key Terms

Write the key term that completes each sentence. Then write a sentence for each term not chosen.

a. technology
b. artisan
c. myth
d. civilization
e. nomad
f. economy
g. anthropologist
h. prehistory
i. radiocarbon dating
j. archaeologist
k. artifact
l. cultural diffusion
m. culture

1. The period of time before people developed writing is called _____.
2. Among the techniques used by scientists for determining the age of organic remains is _____.
3. Over thousands of years, some of the early agricultural villages evolved into highly complex societies, known as _____ .
4. The exchange of goods and ideas when different peoples come in contact is known as _____.
5. _____ includes the skills and useful knowledge available to people for collecting materials and making objects necessary for survival.

Technology Activity

Using a Word Processor
Search the Internet for information on recent discoveries about early humans. Narrow your search by using words such as *archaeology* and *anthropology*. On your word processor, create a chart to organize your information. Include headings such as location, date of discovery, results of discovery, and approximate time period of remains. Then in a paragraph, theorize about what caused the extinction of early humans.

Reviewing Facts

1. **Innovation** Use a graphic like the one below to show how the ability of early civilizations to grow and supply food affected their lives in other ways.

> Growth of Surplus Food
> Resulted in ↓
> Resulted in ↓
> ↓

2. **Geography** Name the four land bridges used by prehistoric people during the Ice Ages.
3. **Geography** Locate the two places in which Cro-Magnons seem to have originated before spreading into other parts of the world.
4. **Culture** Explain why language is one of humanity's greatest achievements.
5. **Technology** Describe how the invention of the spear-thrower and the bow and arrow changed the Cro-Magnons' food supply.
6. **Culture** Explain the social, economic, and geographic factors that led to the rise of the world's first civilizations.
7. **History** State the ways archaeologists, anthropologists, historians, and geographers analyze limited evidence.

Critical Thinking

1. **Apply** What do you think are the three basic characteristics of a civilization?
2. **Analyze** What were the major cultural features of each period in the Stone Age?
3. **Synthesize** How do you think the invention of the stone ax might have changed the culture of a people who lived along the banks of a navigable river?

---

ideas and pass on culture.
5. They could hunt larger animals and more animals at a time.
6. early civilizations developed along fertile river valleys; extra food meant specialization of labor; advanced technology/political organization led to large-scale cooperative efforts
7. Archaeologists interpret objects left behind by prehistoric people; anthropologists compare hominid bones and other fossil remains;

historians analyze written documents; geographers study climate and landform changes.

Critical Thinking

1. highly organized society based on cities; economy based on a variety of activities and trade; a government that organizes social activities, provides law and order, regulates trade; clear system of beliefs and values
2. Paleolithic: hunting and food gathering, use

4. Evaluate What do you think was the most valuable skill that prehistoric people learned during the Paleolithic period? What was the most valuable skill learned during the Neolithic period?

Geography in History

1. Location Refer to the map below. What is the relative location of Mesopotamia?

2. Human/Environment Interaction Where in this area would ancient peoples have likely begun farming?

3. Human/Environment Interaction Why did early farmers build dikes and dams in the river valleys where they raised their crops?

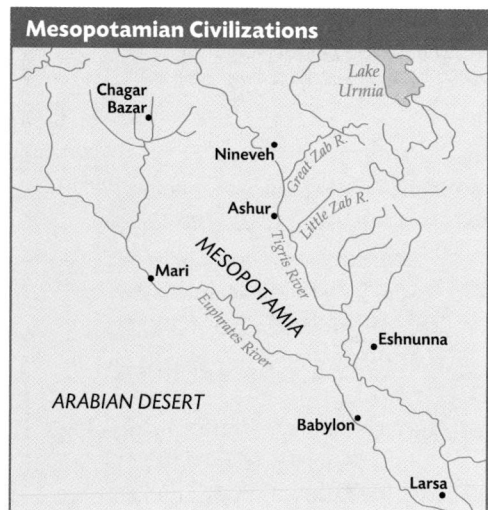

Mesopotamian Civilizations

Understanding Themes

1. Movement Describe the migrations of human beings from their places of origin to other parts of the world.

2. Innovation How did improvements in tool-making affect the way in which prehistoric people lived?

3. Change How did city life differ from village life in early civilizations?

Linking Past and Present

1. Many aspects of human culture are passed down from generation to generation. What cultural achievements of *Homo erectus*—from more than 200,000 years ago—do people still use today?

2. Government officials 5,000 years ago directed large-scale building projects, such as irrigation systems, and oversaw the collection, storage, and distribution of agricultural surpluses. Evaluate the effectiveness of their activities. How do government officials' activities in early civilizations compare with those of government officials in your community?

Skill Practice

Using a small tennis ball, place a dot on each side directly opposite one another to represent the North and South Poles. Cut paper strips in such a way that they could completely cover this "globe." (See the example below.)

1. Why are the cut strips shown on the example below wider at the middle than at each of the ends?

2. If the strips are laid down side-by-side on a flat surface, what object do they resemble or what pattern do they form?

3. What does this show about the problem of creating an accurate map of a round object on a flat surface?

4. The earth is a sphere, but it is somewhat pear-shaped—not a perfect sphere. What additional problem does this create for the cartographer who wants to make a very accurate map of the world?

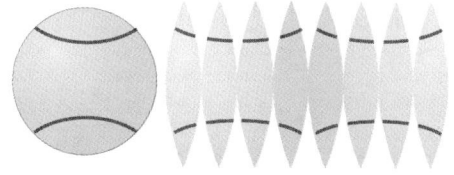

Chapter 1 Assessment

Europe and Asia and by land bridge to Americas; crossed to Australia by sea.

2. **INNOVATION** improvements in tools led to efficiency in hunting, fishing, making clothing, building homes, farming

3. **CHANGE** people in one place averaged 5,000 to 30,000 instead of 200; irrigation projects needed; labor more specialized; long-distance trade and large ruling class developed; writing invented

Linking Past and Present

1. hunting, making fire, wearing clothing, and talking

2. Careful supervision and cooperation enabled early civilizations to grow; the modern equivalents of supervision or protection of agriculture, building, and trade.

Skill Practice

1. The distance around the ball decreases as the strips get closer to the "poles."

2. a series of football shapes, joined at the middle

3. An accurate map may be difficult to read.

4. Even a projection such as the one described here would not reflect this slight deviation from a perfect sphere.

? Chapter Bonus Test Question

Ask students: In seeking the remains of early hominids, how does a paleontologist know where to look? *(It is important for the paleontologist to search in the right rock stratum [for geologic age], the right region [for habitable prehistoric climate], and the right area for fossilization [very rare, and determined by soil and environmental conditions].)*

---

of fire, making clothing, acquisition of language and religion, invention of tools; Mesolithic: domestication of dog and goat, pottery and sickle; Neolithic: agriculture, settled villages, plow, loom, wheel, calendar, rules of inheritance, belief in many deities

3. They could have made canoes, leading to trade and cultural diffusion.

4. Paleolithic: language; Neolithic: agriculture

Geography in History

1. between the Tigris and Euphrates Rivers
2. in the fertile river valleys
3. to control flooding and make the water supply steady

Understanding Themes

1. **MOVEMENT** Human beings originated in eastern Africa; spread by land to

A complete, 1-page lesson plan is provided for each section in the *Reproducible Lesson Plans* booklet.

Early Civilizations

CHAPTER RESOURCES

	Reproducible Resources	Multimedia Resources
Chapter Opener	Chapter Themes: Graphic Organizer 2 Historical Significance Chapter Activity 2	MindJogger Videoquiz
Chapter Enrichment	Vocabulary Activity 2* Time Line Activity 2 Mapping History Activity 2 History Simulation 2 Geography and History Activity 2 Source Reading 2 People in World History Profiles 1, 2 World Art and Music Activity 2 Enrichment Activity 2 Critical Thinking Activity 2 Skill Reinforcement Activity 2 Performance Assessment Activity 2 Standardized Test Practice Workbook 　　Activity 2 Inclusion for the Social Studies Classroom 　　Strategies and Activities	Focus on World Art Print 7, Egyptian. 　*Mask of Tutankhamen* World History and Art 　Transparencies 2, 3 Mapping History Overlay 　Transparencies 1, 2, 3 Chapter Transparency 2 NGS PicturePack Transparency Sets: 　*Ancient Egypt, The Fertile Crescent,* 　*Ancient China, Ancient India* Vocabulary PuzzleMaker Software NGS PictureShow CD-ROMS: *Egypt* 　*and the Fertile Crescent, India and* 　*China* Turning Points in World History: *The* 　*Code of Hammurabi* World History Primary Source 　Document Library
Chapter Review/Reteaching	Reteaching Activity 2 Skill Reinforcement Activity 2 Spanish Chapter Summary 2	Chapter 2 Digest Audiocassette, 　Activity, Test* Vocabulary PuzzleMaker Software Interactive Tutor Self-Assessment 　Software MindJogger Videoquiz
Chapter Evaluation/Testing	Performance Assessment Activity 2 Chapter 2 Test, Forms A and B	ExamView® Pro Testmaker

* Also available in Spanish

0:00 OUT OF TIME? Assign the Chapter 2 Audiocassettes.

World History Primary Source Document Library

Make History Come Alive!

Engage your students with over 250 easily accessible primary source documents—available on this CD-ROM—that will give them real life insight into the important events of world history.

Block Schedule

Activities that are particularly suited to use within the block scheduling framework are identified throughout this chapter by the following designation.

KEY TO ABILITY LEVELS

Teaching strategies are coded for varying learning styles.

L1　BASIC activities for all students
L2　AVERAGE activities for average to above-average students
L3　CHALLENGING activities for above-average students
LEP　LIMITED ENGLISH PROFICIENCY activities

Use Glencoe's *Presentation Plus!* multimedia teacher tool to easily present dynamic lessons that visually excite your students. Using Microsoft PowerPoint® you can customize the presentations to create your own personalized lessons.

Interactive Lesson Planner

Planning has never been easier! Using this CD-ROM, organize your week, month, semester, or year with all the help you need. The **Interactive Lesson Planner** gives you access to all of the blackline masters that accompany *World History: The Human Experience.*

SECTION RESOURCES

Daily Objectives	Reproducible Resources	Multimedia Resources
Section 1 The Nile Valley Understand why Egypt was called the "gift of the Nile."	Lecture Notes 2-1 Reproducible Lesson Plan 2-1 Guided Reading Activity 2-1* Section Quiz 2-1* Reading Essentials and Study Guide 2-1	Focus on World Art Print 7, Egyptian. *Mask of Tutankhamen* Section Focus Transparency 2-1 World History and Art Transparency 2, *Tutankhamen's Throne* Mapping History Overlay Transparency 2, *Ancient Egypt* Vocabulary PuzzleMaker Software Interactive Tutor Self-Assessment Software Testmaker Egypt and the Fertile Crescent
Section 2 The Fertile Crescent Summarize how Sumer's achievements enriched the early culture of the Middle East.	Lecture Notes 2-2 Reproducible Lesson Plan 2-2 Guided Reading Activity 2-2* Section Quiz 2-2* Reading Essentials and Study Guide 2-2	Section Focus Transparency 2-2 Mapping History Overlay Transparency 1, *River Valley Civilizations* Interactive Tutor Self-Assessment Software Testmaker Egypt and the Fertile Crescent Turning Points in World History: *The Code of Hammurabi*
Section 3 Early South Asia Relate how people of the Indus River valley civilization built cities.	Lecture Notes 2-3 Reproducible Lesson Plan 2-3 Vocabulary Activity 2* Guided Reading Activity 2-3* Reteaching Activity 2 Enrichment Activity 2 Section Quiz 2-3* Reading Essentials and Study Guide 2-3	Section Focus Transparency 2-3 Mapping History Overlay Transparency 3, *Ancient India and Ancient China* Interactive Tutor Self-Assessment Software Testmaker India and China
Section 4 Early China Examine the major contributions of early Chinese civilization.	Lecture Notes 2-4 Reproducible Lesson Plan 2-4 Guided Reading Activity 2-4* Reteaching Activity 2 Enrichment Activity 2 Section Quiz 2-4* Performance Assessment Activity 2 Spanish Chapter Summary 2 Reading Essentials and Study Guide 2-4	Section Focus Transparency 2-4 Mapping History Overlay Transparency 3, *Ancient India and Ancient China* World History and Art Transparency 3, *Terra-cotta Warriors* Ancient China Interactive Tutor Self-Assessment Software Testmaker India and China

* Also available in Spanish

Chapter Activities

 Performance Assessment Activity

Time Travel Have students assume the roles of time-traveling archaeologists who would like to go back in time to learn more about one of the civilizations in this chapter. Have students choose one of the civilizations and justify their decision with both facts and arguments. Tell them to indicate why they rejected the other civilizations as a choice. The final product should be a grant proposal for funding for the trip. It should include a rationale for the expenses incurred.

Possible Rubric Features
Accuracy and extent of content information, persuasiveness, organization and clarity, appropriateness of product for purpose, elaboration and detail
• *For an additional activity, refer to Activity 2 in the* Performance Assessment Strategies and Activities *booklet.*

ACTIVITY

From the Classroom of...

John Tabb
Central Hardin High
School, Cecilia, KY

Save the Temples
Before assigning reading from Chapter 2, present students with the following situation in modern-day Egypt: A new dam is nearly completed and water is beginning to rise behind it. In about two years it will flood temples built by Ramses II; archaeologists and others want to preserve the temples for posterity. Because Egypt needs the dam for hydroelectricity and irrigation, there is no chance the dam will be stopped before the area is flooded.

Students are instructed to write a short essay on how to save the temples. Have them consider such questions as what machinery to use or how to house the workers. Tell students that this was a real problem Egypt faced in the 1960s, but you would like to see how they would solve it today.

Have students read one another's work within small groups. One group member should briefly summarize for the class the idea selected by each group as its best plan to save the temples. Play the following video, "Touring Egypt," Chicago: Questar Video, 1988, which shows how the Temples of Abu Simbel were moved to higher ground (1964–1966).

MULTIPLE LEARNING STYLES

Verbal/Linguistic
Have students write and deliver a short oral presentation comparing and contrasting the earliest known deities. The speech should define and discuss monotheism and polytheism.

Logical/Mathematical
In a short oral or written report, have students speculate on the practical reasons why early civilizations showed a great interest in astronomy. Ask them to assess how important astronomy is to people today.

Visual/Spatial
Have students find examples of the art of early China. Then have them draw or paint a picture in the early Chinese style. Ask them to describe how this style differs from that of modern Western art.

Intrapersonal
Have students imagine themselves as a pharaoh in the Valley of the Kings. They are having a pyramid built that is bigger than all the other pyramids in Egypt. Have them explain, orally or in writing, why they have undertaken this massive project.

GLENCOE'S ASSESSMENT ADVANTAGE

Use the following to easily assess student learning in a variety of ways.

• Performance Assessment Strategies and Activities
• Section Quizzes
• Chapter and Unit Tests
• Interactive Tutor Self-Assessment Software
• Testmaker Software
• MindJogger Videoquiz
• SAT/SAT II Test Practice
• worldhistory.glencoe.com

Additional Resources

 NATIONAL GEOGRAPHIC SOCIETY **Teacher's Corner**

INDEX TO NATIONAL GEOGRAPHIC MAGAZINE

The following articles relate to this chapter:

- "Valley of the Mummies," by Donovan Webster, Oct. 1999.
- "Abusir Tomb," by Zahi Hawass, November 1998.
- "Valley of the Kings," by Kent R. Weeks, September 1998.
- "The Magic of Paper," by Jon R. Luoma, March 1997.
- "The Imperiled Nile Delta," by Peter Theroux, January 1997.
- "Ramses the Great," by Rick Gore, April 1991.

NATIONAL GEOGRAPHIC SOCIETY PRODUCTS AVAILABLE FROM GLENCOE

To order the following call Glencoe at 1-800-334-7344:

- *Picture Atlas of the World (CD-ROM)*
- *PictureShow:* Egypt and the Fertile Crescent *(CD-ROM)*
- *PictureShow:* India and China *(CD-ROM)*
- *Ancient Egypt (Transparencies, Poster Set)*
- *The Fertile Crescent (Transparencies, Poster Set)*

ADDITIONAL NATIONAL GEOGRAPHIC SOCIETY PRODUCTS

To order the following call National Geographic at 1-800-368-2728:

- *Egypt: Quest for Eternity (Video or Videodisc)*
- *Mr. Mummy (Video)*
- *Who Built the Pyramids? (Video)*
- *GeoKit: Ancient Egypt (Multimedia Teaching Module)*

Access National Geographic's new dynamic MapMachine Web site and other geography resources at:

- http://www.nationalgeographic.com/
- http://www.nationalgeographic.com/maps/

BIBLIOGRAPHY

Literature About the Period
Drury, Allen. *A God Against the Gods.* New York: Doubleday, 1976. Historical novel about the pharaoh Akhenaton.
Readings for the Student
Romer, John. *Ancient Lives: Daily Life in Egypt of the Pharaohs.* New York: Henry Holt, 1984. Social life and customs in the Valley of the Kings.
Readings for the Teacher
Hawkes, Jaquetta, ed. *Atlas of Ancient Archaeology.* New York: McGraw-Hill, 1974. Traces ancient cultures.

WORLD HISTORY Online

Use our Web site as an additional resource. All essential content is covered in the Student Edition.

You and your students can visit the *World History: The Human Experience* Web site at worldhistory.glencoe.com The student text directs students to the Web site for the following options:

- **Chapter Overviews**
- **Student Web Activities**
- **Self-Check Quizzes**

Answers are provided for you in a link entitled "Web Activity Lesson Plan." Additional Web Resources, Interactive Puzzles, and content updates are also available.

Visit the Glencoe Web site at socialstudies. glencoe.com for social studies activities, updates, and links to other resources.

LOCAL OBJECTIVES

_____
_____
_____
_____
_____
_____
_____
_____
_____
_____
_____
_____
_____
_____
_____
_____
_____
_____
_____
_____
_____
_____

Early Civilizations

CHAPTER THEMES

Chapter Themes are listed by section on this chapter opening page of the Student Edition. A corresponding theme-based activity is available under "TEACH," and a theme-based question is asked in the Section and Chapter Assessments.

 Storyteller

Historical Setting Although Khufu was responsible for the largest monument ever built, surprisingly little is known about him, except for the length of his reign. He ruled for 23 years, around 2500 B.C. Much can be said about the extraordinary dimensions of his pyramid, however. It was originally 481 feet (147 meters) high. At its base, which covers about 13 acres (5.3 hectares), it is almost perfectly square, 755 feet (230 meters) to a side. The more than 2 million blocks of limestone in the pyramid average more than 2.5 short tons (2.3 metric tons) each. Most of them came from nearby quarries.

Historical Significance

Answers: *Each civilization had unique features—Egypt, pyramids; Sumer, irrigation; Indus River valley, urban planning; China, metal casting. Although these four civilizations all developed in river valleys, worshiped many gods, and wrote with pictograms, they also differed in various ways, depending on climate, topography, and traditions. All contributed to the growth of cities, government, literacy, and technology—keys to the rise of a global civilization.*

 WORLD HISTORY *Online*

Have students use the **Chapter 2 Overview** at <u>worldhistory.glencoe.com</u> as a prereading and postreading exercise for understanding chapter content.

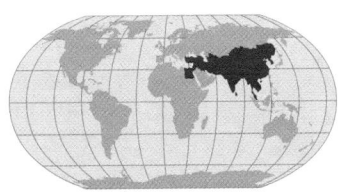

Chapter Themes

▶ **Relation to Environment** The Egyptians learn to control the floodwaters of the Nile River upon which their agriculture relies. *Section 1*

▶ **Cooperation** The peoples of the Fertile Crescent work together to build irrigation systems and cities. *Section 2*

▶ **Cultural Diffusion** Cities in early India develop close trading and cultural ties with the Fertile Crescent area. *Section 3*

▶ **Innovation** Early Chinese civilization excels in metal-casting. *Section 4*

Storyteller

Under the blazing sun, a gigantic stone structure began to take shape on the desert sands of Egypt in northeastern Africa. A hundred thousand men toiled together, building a burial pyramid for Khufu, a king of Egypt about 2500 B.C. Gangs of laborers dragged huge blocks of limestone up winding ramps of dirt and brick to pile layer upon layer of stone. Farmers during the rest of the year, these laborers were compelled to work for the 3 or 4 months during which the annual flooding of the Nile River made farming impossible. It would take 20 years of their forced labor and more than 2 million blocks of stone before the Egyptians completed the massive pyramid. Today, the Great Pyramid, built almost 5,000 years ago, still stands at Giza, near the city of Cairo.

Historical Significance

In what ways were each of the early civilizations unique? How were they different? How did the river valley civilizations lay the foundations for the global civilization that we know today?

5000 B.C.   3000 B.C.   1000 B.C.

3100 B.C.
The Sumerians invent cuneiform.

c. 5000 B.C. Hunter-gatherers migrate to the Nile River valley.

c. 2500 B.C.
Harappan civilization begins.

c. 1700 B.C.
Shang dynasty begins.

44

GEOGRAPHY CONNECTION

Location The civilizations discussed in this chapter arose along river valleys. Have students locate these historic rivers on the appropriate map in the Atlas of their text: Nile, Tigris, Euphrates, Indus, and Huang He. Why were river valleys vital to the development of civilizations? *(Water is essential to human life and agriculture. The flooding of rivers produced rich soil, which enabled farmers to grow more than they needed for their own consumption, thus permitting the rise of cities.)*

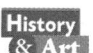 Fowling scene from a tomb at Thebes along the Nile River, Egypt

History & Art
Scenes depicting the sport of fowling are common in Egyptian tomb paintings. Here, a noble prepares to hurl a throwing stick at a flock of geese. Notice one woman holding the man's leg. What do you think this pose was intended to illustrate? *(personal attachment to the man; more than just a fowling scene, this is also a family scene)*

 Performance Assessment

Refer to the activity on page 44C of the Planning Guide.

For an additional activity, refer to Activity 2 in the *Performance Assessment Strategies and Activities* booklet.

WORLD HISTORY *Online*

Chapter Overview

Visit the *World History: The Human Experience* Web site at **worldhistory.glencoe.com** and click on *Chapter 2—Chapter Overview* to preview the chapter.

Your History Journal

Sumerian scribes studied at special schools called edubbas. *There they learned cuneiform writing. After reading Section 2, write a short creative account of a scribe's day at an* edubba.

Using Your History Journal

Advise students that an *edduba* was a very strict school. Sumerian youths attended from sunrise to sunset, and teachers used discipline.

GLENCOE TECHNOLOGY

 VIDEODISC
Use MindJogger to preview chapter content.

MindJogger Videoquiz

Chapter 2
Disc 1 Side A

Also available in VHS.

Chapter 2 *Early Civilizations* **45**

✚ EXTRA CREDIT PROJECT

Essay The invention of writing is part of the development of the four early civilizations in this chapter. Have students write an essay in which they compare and contrast Egyptian hieroglyphics, Sumerian cuneiform, Harappan pictograms, and Chinese written script. In their paper, students should explain why writing was important to the growth of these civilizations.

c. 3000 B.C.
King Narmer unifies Egypt.

c. 1700s B.C.
The Hyksos invade Egypt.

c. 1480 B.C.
Queen Hatshepsut comes to power.

c. 945 B.C.
Egypt enters long period of foreign rule.

SECTION THEME

▶ **Relation to Environment** The Egyptians learn to control the floodwaters of the Nile River upon which their agriculture relies.

Guide to Reading

For reading strategies to help students read effectively see pages 12–13. Have students think about the main head as they read the subheads.

Vocabulary Pre-check

▣ Use the Vocabulary PuzzleMaker for Chapter 2 to create a crossword puzzle to reinforce section terms. **L1 LEP**

▭ Use Vocabulary Activity 2 to introduce vocabulary terms. **L1 LEP**

FOCUS

Section Objective

Understand why Egypt was called the "gift of the Nile."

BELLRINGER
Motivational Activity

Before taking roll at the beginning of the class period, project Section Focus Transparency 2-1 and have students answer the activity questions. Discuss students' responses.
▭ This activity is also available as a blackline master.

Section 1

The Nile Valley

Guide to Reading

Read to Find Out
Main Idea *Egypt was called the "gift of the Nile."*

▶ **Terms to Define**
monarchy, dynasty, theocracy, bureaucracy, pharaoh, empire, polytheism, hieroglyphics

▶ **People to Meet**
Narmer, Hatshepsut, Thutmose III, Akhenaton, Ramses II

▶ **Places to Locate**
Nile River valley, Memphis, Thebes

The Storyteller

Live for today; the afterlife will come soon enough! The following message about the brief pleasures of this life demonstrates that Egyptian poets sometimes sang what their wealthy patrons liked to hear:

"The pharaohs, those ancient gods, rest now in their pyramids. The people who built houses; their walls have crumbled, as if they had never been! Listen! Put perfume upon your head, wear fine linen. Make holiday! … No one who has died has ever returned."

—freely adapted from
"Song of the Harper,"
Journal of Near Eastern Studies 4, 1945, translated by Miriam Lichtheim

King Narmer

One of the world's first civilizations developed along the banks of the Nile River in northeastern Africa. The **Nile River valley's** early inhabitants called their land *Kemet,* meaning "black land," after the dark soil. Later, the ancient Greeks would name the Nile area *Egypt.* Of the four early river valley civilizations, people today probably know the most about the ancient Egyptian civilization. People still marvel at its remains in modern Egypt—especially the enormous Sphinx, the wondrous pyramids, and the mummies buried in lavish tombs.

A River Valley and Its People

Running like a ribbon through great expanses of desert, the Nile River for thousands of years has shaped the lives of the Egyptians. The land of Egypt receives little rainfall, but its people have relied instead on the Nile's predictable yearly floods to bring them water.

At 4,160 miles (6,690 km) in length, the Nile River is the world's longest river. Several sources in the highlands of East Africa feed the Nile. The river then takes a northward route to the Mediterranean Sea. On its course through Egypt the Nile crosses six cataracts, or waterfalls. Because of the cataracts the Nile is not completely navigable until it reaches its last 650 miles (1,040 km). Before emptying into the Mediterranean, the Nile splits into many branches, forming a marshy, fan-shaped delta.

The Gifts of the River

The green Nile Valley contrasts sharply with the vast desert areas that stretch for hundreds of miles on either side. Rich black soil covers the river's banks and the Nile Delta. From late spring through summer, heavy tropical rains in central Africa and melting mountain snow in East Africa add to the Nile's volume. As a result the river overflows its banks and floods the land nearby. The

---

floodwaters recede in late fall, leaving behind thick deposits of silt.

As early as 5000 B.C., nomadic hunter-gatherers of northeastern Africa began to settle by the Nile. They took up a farming life regulated by the river's seasonal rise and fall, growing cereal crops such as wheat and barley. The Nile also provided these Neolithic farmers with ducks and geese in its marshlands and fish in its waters. The early Egyptians harvested papyrus growing wild along the banks of the Nile, using the long, thin reeds to make rope, matting, sandals, baskets, and later on, sheets of paperlike writing material.

Uniting Egypt

Protected from foreign invasion by deserts and cataracts, the early farming villages by the Nile prospered. In time a few strong leaders united villages into small kingdoms, or monarchies, each under the unrestricted rule of its king. The weaker kingdoms eventually gave way to the stronger. By 4000 B.C. ancient Egypt consisted of two large kingdoms: Lower Egypt in the north, in the Nile Delta, and Upper Egypt in the south, in the Nile Valley.

Around 3000 B.C., **Narmer**, also known as Menes (MEE•neez), a king of Upper Egypt, gathered the forces of the south and led them north to invade and conquer Lower Egypt. Narmer set up the first government that ruled all of the country. He governed both Lower Egypt and Upper Egypt from a capital city he had built at **Memphis**, near the border of the two kingdoms.

Narmer's reign marked the beginning of the first Egyptian dynasty, or line of rulers from one family. From 3000 B.C. until 332 B.C., a series of 30 dynasties ruled Egypt. Historians have organized the dynasties into three great periods: the Old Kingdom, the Middle Kingdom, and the New Kingdom.

The Old Kingdom

The Old Kingdom lasted from about 2700 B.C. to 2200 B.C. During the first centuries of the unified kingdom, Upper Egypt and Lower Egypt kept their separate identities as kingdoms. In time, however, Egypt built a strong national government under its kings. It also developed the basic features of its civilization.

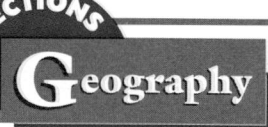

Geography

Stemming the Flood

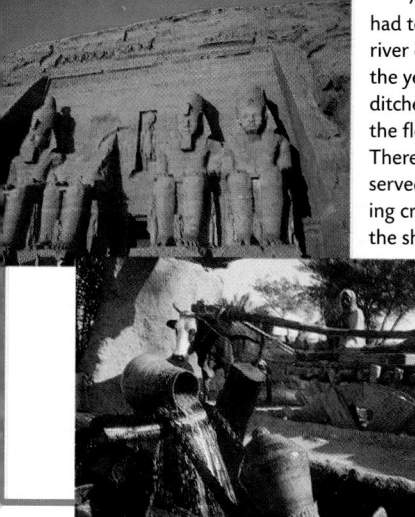

Ancient Egyptians had to take control of their river environment. Over the years farmers built ditches and canals to carry the floodwaters to basins. There the silt settled and served as fertilizer for planting crops. Machines, such as the shadoof, lifted water to cultivated land. Farmers eventually built dams and reservoirs, making year-round irrigation possible.

Built in the 1960s, the Aswan High Dam in southeastern Egypt trapped the waters of the Nile in a huge reservoir for later irrigation. When the rising waters of the Nile behind the dam threatened to destroy statues of Ramses II, engineers had to move the statues to higher ground. Today, the dam generates electrical power and protects against flooding. Because the dam prevents the Nile from flowing over the valley land, however, the floodwaters no longer deposit fertile silt annually. Farmers must add expensive chemical fertilizers to their fields. The absence of silt has also increased land erosion along the Nile.

 ACTIVITY

Describe ancient ways of controlling rivers. How are the Nile and other rivers "tamed" today? Why might people object to some modern methods of river control?

Chapter 2 *Early Civilizations* **47**

COOPERATIVE LEARNING ACTIVITY

A Play Have the class write and perform a play about one of the people listed in the section. Organize the class into small groups. Have each group be responsible for a specific task in the project, such as researching the person chosen and the way of life during his or her time, writing the script, acting, making costumes, finding props, writing and designing programs, and designing sets (if needed). At each stage of the project, all students should be given an opportunity to react to the group task. Then have the students present the play to other classes. **L1**

TEACH

Guided Practice

THEME Relation to Environment

On the map on page 48, have students trace the boundaries of the Old, Middle, and New Kingdoms. What is the position of the Nile in relation to the three kingdoms of Egypt? (*flows through the center of each of them*) **L1**

Geography: Location Have students study the map of ancient Egypt on page 48. Then ask them to use the Atlas in this text to find modern nations that fall within the boundaries of ancient Egypt during the New Kingdom. (*Egypt, Lebanon, Israel, Sudan, Cyprus, and part of Turkey*) **L1**

Stemming the Flood

Rivers typically overflow their usual channels about once every two years. At their worst, floods can destroy whole communities.

ANSWERS

Ancient peoples built ditches, canals, earthen dams, and reservoirs. Today, people build huge concrete dams for irrigation, electric power, and flood control. Dams are costly and may disturb the environment of a river, displacing people, causing erosion, and destroying areas of natural beauty.

Map Study

Answer

by supporting irrigation projects

Map Skills Practice

Reading a Map Why does the map suggest that ancient Egyptians made advances in transportation? *(parts of the New Kingdom are located across a large body of water, indicating ability to navigate and sail)*

NATIONAL GEOGRAPHIC SOCIETY

Use these materials to enrich student understanding of ancient Egyptian culture.

- **NGS PICTURESHOW CD-ROM**
  Egypt and the Fertile Crescent

- **NGS PICTUREPACK TRANSPARENCY SET**
  Ancient Egypt

- **ANCIENT CIVILIZATIONS POSTER SET**
  Ancient Egypt

HOME VIDEO.

The following videotape programs are available from Glencoe:

- **Mummies and the Wonders of Ancient Egypt**
- **Tomb of the Gods: The Great Pyramid**
- **The Secret Life of King Ramses II**
- **King Tut: The Face of Tutankhamen**

To find classroom resources to accompany these videos, check the following home page:

A&E Television: http://www.aetv.com

Ancient Egypt

Map Study

The Pyramids were constructed during the Old Kingdom near Memphis. Under the Middle Kingdom, the capital was moved south to Waset, later called Thebes by the Greeks.
Human/Environment Interaction How did Theban kings add thousands of acres to the land under cultivation?

The Egyptian Monarchy

The Egyptian people regarded their king as a god who ruled over all Egyptians. Such a government, in which the same person is both the religious leader and the political leader, is called a theocracy. As a god, the king performed many ritual acts believed to benefit the entire kingdom, such as cutting the first ripe grain to ensure a good harvest. As political leader, the king wielded absolute power, issuing commands regarded as the law of the land.

Unable to carry out all official duties himself,

the king delegated many responsibilities to a bureaucracy, a group of government officials headed by the king's vizier, or prime minister. Through the vizier and other bureaucrats the king controlled trade and collected taxes. He also indirectly supervised the building of dams, canals, and storehouses for grain—all crucial to survival for an agriculture-based civilization.

The Pyramids: A Lasting Legacy

To honor their god-kings and to provide them with an eternal place of rest, the Egyptians of the Old Kingdom built lasting monuments—the Pyramids. The Step Pyramid was built for King Djoser in the mid-2600s B.C. Overlooking Memphis, it was the first large, all-stone building in the world. Later the Egyptians constructed the three Pyramids at Giza, which stand today as testimony to Egyptian engineering skills. The Great Pyramid, the largest of the three, stands 481 feet (147 m) high. Long, narrow passageways lead to the king's burial chamber deep within the pyramid.

The Egyptians believed that a king's soul continued to guide the kingdom after death. Before entombing a dead king in his pyramid, they first preserved the king's body from decay by a procedure called embalming. Next they wrapped the dried, shrunken body—called a mummy—with long strips of linen and placed it in an elaborate coffin. Only then could the coffin lie in the burial chamber of the pyramid along with the king's clothing, weapons, furniture, and jewelry—personal possessions the king could enjoy in the afterlife.

The Middle Kingdom

Around 2200 B.C., the kings in Memphis began to lose their power as ambitious nobles fought each other for control of Egypt. The stable, ordered world of the Old Kingdom entered a period of upheaval and violence. Then, around 2050 B.C., a new dynasty reunited Egypt and moved the capital south to **Thebes**, a city in Upper Egypt. This new kingdom, known as the Middle Kingdom, would last until after 1800 B.C.

In time Theban kings became as powerful as the rulers of the Old Kingdom and brought unruly local governments under their control. They supported irrigation projects that added thousands of acres to the land already under cultivation. The Theban dynasty seized new territory for Egypt, setting up fortresses along the Nile to capture Nubia (part of modern Sudan) and launching military campaigns against Syria. Theban kings also ordered construction of a canal between the Nile and the Red Sea, and as a result, Egyptian ships traded along the coasts of the Arabian Peninsula and East Africa.

In the 1700s B.C., local leaders challenged the kings' power again, shattering the peace and prosperity of the Middle Kingdom. Egypt then also faced a serious threat—invasion by the Hyksos (HIHK•SAHS), a people from western Asia. The Hyksos swept into Egypt with new tools for war—bronze weapons and horse-drawn chariots. They easily conquered the Egyptians, who fought on foot with copper and stone weapons. The Hyksos established a new dynasty that ruled for 110 years.

The New Kingdom

To overthrow the despised Hyksos rule, the Egyptians learned to use Hyksos weapons and adopted the horse-drawn chariots of their conquerors. About 1600 B.C. Ahmose (ah•MOH•suh), an Egyptian prince, raised an army and drove the Hyksos out.

Pharaohs Rule an Empire

Ahmose founded the first dynasty of the New Kingdom. He and his successors took the title pharaoh, an Egyptian word meaning "great house of the king." Ahmose rebuilt Egypt, restored abandoned temples, and reopened avenues of trade. The pharaohs who followed him, however, used large armies to realize their dreams of conquest. They pressed farther to the east and into the rest of Africa than had previous kings.

Around 1480 B.C. Queen **Hatshepsut** (hat•SHEHP•soot) came to power in Egypt, first ruling with her husband and then on behalf of her stepson **Thutmose** (thoot•MOH•suh) **III**, who was too young to govern. Finally she had herself crowned pharaoh and assumed all the royal trappings of power, including the false beard traditionally worn by Egyptian kings. Hatshepsut carried out an extensive building program, which included a great funeral temple and a tomb built into the hills of what is now called the Valley of the Kings.

Thutmose III did reclaim the throne at Hatshepsut's death and marched with a large army out of Egypt toward the northeast. He conquered

Visualizing History The Great Pyramid (left), built for King Khufu (Cheops), rises on the Nile River's west bank in northern Egypt. The smaller pyramid (right) was constructed for King Khafre (Chephren). *Why did the Egyptians build pyramids for their kings?*

Syria and pushed the Egyptian frontier to the northern part of the Euphrates River. In a short time, Thutmose III had conquered an empire for Egypt, bringing many territories under one ruler.

The Egyptian Empire grew rich from commerce and tribute. The capital of Thebes, with its palaces, temples, and carved stone obelisks, reflected the wealth won by conquest. No longer isolated from other cultures, Egyptians benefited from cultural diffusion within their empire.

Akhenaton Founds a Religion

A new ruler, Amenhotep (AH•muhn•HOH•TEHP) IV, assumed power about 1370 B.C. Supported by his wife, Nefertiti, Amenhotep broke with the Egyptian tradition of worshiping many

Student Web Activity 2

Visit the *World History: The Human Experience* Web site at **worldhistory.glencoe.com** and click on *Chapter 2—Student Web Activities* for an activity relating to the New Kingdom.

Chapter 2 *Early Civilizations* **49**

Visualizing History Many pyramids had two temples that were connected by a long stone passageway. Funeral ceremonies were performed in these temples.
Answer to Caption: *They built the pyramids to honor the kings, believed to be gods, and to provide them with an eternal place of rest.*

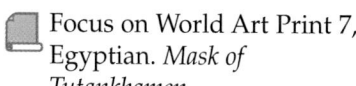
Focus on World Art Print 7, Egyptian. *Mask of Tutankhamen*

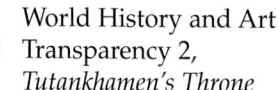
World History and Art Transparency 2, *Tutankhamen's Throne*

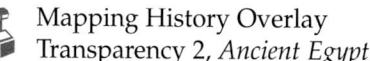
Mapping History Overlay Transparency 2, *Ancient Egypt*

Government Write this quotation from the Persian poet Sadi on the chalkboard: "[A King] requires a prudent and able man." Discuss the meaning of the quotation and how it applies to the pharaohs. Lead the class to consider how choosing wise people to help govern can ensure good government. Draw a parallel between the bureaucracy of Egypt and that of the United States today. **L2**

WORLD HISTORY *Online*

Have students use the **Chapter 2 Student Web Activity** at worldhistory.glencoe.com for in-depth study of the New Kingdom.

MAKING CONNECTIONS ACTIVITY

Technology In 1987 scientists from Egypt and the United States used advanced technology to view the remains of an ancient Egyptian boat that had been sealed inside a chamber for 4,600 years. To see inside without excavating and damaging the chamber, the scientists employed a special drill with technology invented for moon exploration. After drilling through the outer rock, they inserted a miniature video camera. Have students research other techniques used to handle and explore ancient Egyptian remains and report to the class on their findings. **L2**

TEACH

Not every well-preserved body from prehistoric times is a true mummy. Strictly speaking, a mummy is a dead body preserved by embalming. The technique of embalming seems to have been developed in Egypt about 2600 B.C. Bodies preserved from earlier times were the result of natural drying in the hot Egyptian sand. Mummification was costly, and at first only the wealthy could afford it. Still, mummified corpses of bulls, cats, and ibis have been found. Ask students why they think the Egyptians preserved these animals. *(The bull, cat, and ibis were sacred, associated with certain Egyptian gods.)*

CURRICULUM CONNECTION

ARCHAEOLOGY

One of the impressive temple sites of Ramses II is Abu Simbel, located near the Nile River about 762 miles south of Cairo. In the 1960s the High Dam at Aswan would have flooded the site, but 51 countries contributed funds to move the temples block by block to higher ground farther inland.

O. Louis Mazzatenta

Ramses the Great

O. Louis Mazzatenta

The mummy of Ramses the Great (above) lies in a display case on the second floor of the Egyptian Museum in Cairo. For many centuries before Ramses was brought to Cairo, the great pharaoh lay in his tomb near Luxor in a richly decorated coffin (left), embellished with symbols of Osiris, god of the afterlife. Ramses was nearly 90 when he died in 1237 B.C. His mummy has remained intact for the last 3,000 years.

Egyptians believed strongly in the afterlife took great care to preserve the bodies of the pharaohs. Embalmers spent 70 days preparing corpse of Ramses the Great. First they removed internal organs and placed them in sacred jars. heart was sealed in the body because Egypti believed that it was the source of intellect as wel feeling and was needed in the afterlife. The brain, the other hand, was thought to be useless, embalmers drew it out through the nose and thre away. The body was then dried with salt, wash coated with preserving resins, and wrapped in h dreds of yards of linen. Recent medical tests sh that Ramses suffered from arthritis, dental absces gum disease, and poor circulation. ⊕

deities. He declared that Egyptians should worship only Aton, the sun-disk god, as the one supreme deity. Claiming to be Aton's equal, Amenhotep changed his royal name to **Akhenaton** (AHK•NAH•tuhn), which means "spirit of Aton." To stress the break with the past, Akhenaton moved the capital from Thebes to a new city in central Egypt dedicated to Aton.

These controversial changes had an unsettling effect on Egypt. Many of the common people rejected the worship of Aton, a god without human form, and continued to believe in many deities. The priests of the old religion resented their loss of power. At the same time, the army was unhappy about Egypt's loss of territories under Akhenaton's weak rule.

After Akhenaton's death, the priests restored the old religion. They also made Akhenaton's successor, Tutankhamen, move the capital back to Thebes. Shortly thereafter, the head of the Egyptian army overthrew the dynasty and created a new one.

Recovery and Decline

During the 1200s B.C., the pharaohs worked to restore Egypt's prestige. Under **Ramses II**, or Ramses the Great, the Egyptians fought their neighbors, the Hittites, for control of Syria. The conflict, however, led to a standoff at the Battle of Kadesh in 1285 B.C. Later the two empires concluded a treaty—unique for its time—pledging to keep permanent peace with each other and to fight as allies against any enemy.

In Egypt, Ramses, who ruled for 67 years, erected large statues of himself and built many temples and tombs. In A.D. 1995, archaeologists uncovered one of the most significant Egyptian discoveries: a vast underground tomb believed to be the burial place of 50 of Ramses' 52 sons.

After the death of Ramses II in 1237 B.C., Egypt weakened under the attacks of Mediterranean sea raiders, and entered a period of decline. Beginning in 945 B.C., it came under the rule of foreigners—among them the Libyans from the west and the Kushites from the south.

Life in Ancient Egypt

At the height of its glory, ancient Egypt was home to some 5 million persons, most of whom lived in the Nile Valley and the Nile Delta. Even though Egyptian society was divided into classes, ambitious people in the lower classes could improve their social status somewhat.

Levels of Egyptian Society

Royalty, nobles, and priests formed the top of the social order. They controlled religious and political affairs. Members of the wealthy upper class lived in the cities or on estates along the Nile River. There they built large, elaborately decorated homes surrounded by magnificent gardens, pools, and orchards.

Below the upper class in social rank was the middle class. Its members—artisans, scribes, merchants, and tax collectors—carried out the business activities of Egypt. Middle-class homes—mostly in the cities—were comfortable but not elegant.

The majority of Egyptians belonged to the poor lower class. Many were farmers. For the land they farmed, they paid rent to the king—usually a large percentage of their crop. Farmers also worked on building projects for the king, and some members of the lower class served the priests and the nobles. They lived in small villages of simple huts on or near the large estates along the Nile.

Egyptian Families

In the cities and in the upper class the husband, wife, and children made up the family group.

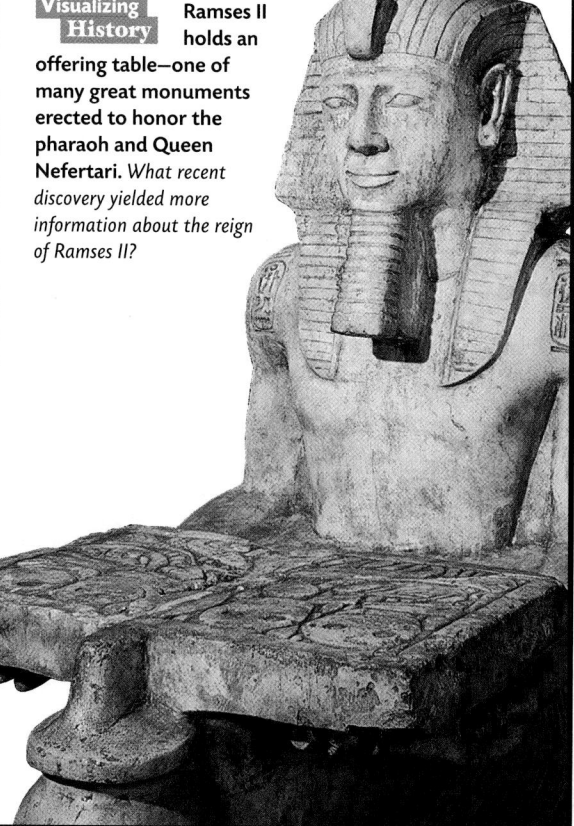

Visualizing History **Ramses II holds an offering table—one of many great monuments erected to honor the pharaoh and Queen Nefertari.** *What recent discovery yielded more information about the reign of Ramses II?*

Chapter 2
Section 1

Cultural Diffusion Have students locate Egypt on the map of the Middle East in the Atlas of this text. Discuss how Egypt's location at the crossroads between Africa and Asia provided opportunities for cultural diffusion. **L2**

Critical Thinking Remind students about the consensus that a writing system, a well-organized government, art and literature, and specialization of labor are the earmarks of civilization. Have students explain how ancient Egypt met these criteria. **L3**

Who?What?Where?When?

Nile Surroundings On the east bank of the Nile stood the commercial city of Thebes. On the west bank lay irrigated fields of black alluvium and green crops. At the edge of the fields rose a row of temples, each surrounded by a cluster of buildings. Several of these buildings were the homes of priests and scribes, but most were great storerooms holding the riches of the empire.

Visualizing History A modern historian calls the inscriptions on the monuments of Ramses II some of "the greatest propaganda pieces of all time." They impressed poets, too. "Ozymandias," the sonnet by Shelley, takes its title from the Greek name for Ramses.

Answer to Caption: *1995 discovery of tomb where 50 of 52 sons of Ramses II are believed to be buried.*

CRITICAL THINKING ACTIVITY

Making Generalizations In Chapter 1, students studied these themes as they relate to early human beings: movement, innovation, and change. The same three themes apply to many civilizations. Have students write a paragraph on each theme as it relates to ancient Egypt. Ask volunteers to read their paragraphs in class. Then discuss the question: How do these three themes also apply to the history of the United States? **L2**

Independent Practice

📂 Guided Reading Activity
2-1 **L1**

Economics Have students write a want ad for a vizier, a tax collector, an artisan, a scribe, or a construction laborer. Have them describe the qualifications needed for the job. Display the ads on a bulletin board. **L2**

Religion Have students write an editorial explaining their position on this question: Did religion play a greater role in Egyptian society than it does in our society today? Tell students to respond according to their perception of the role of religion in today's society. **L3**

ASSESS

Check for Understanding

Assign Section 1 Assessment as homework or as an in-class activity.

🖥 Use Interactive Tutor Self-Assessment Software to review Section 1.

Visualizing History Throughout Egyptian history, the falcon god Horus was personally identified with the ruler. Each pharaoh in turn used the name Horus as the first of his titles.

Answer to Caption: *They were rulers of the realm of the dead; Osiris was responsible for life, death, and rebirth of all living things.*

Outside the cities, especially among farmers and laborers, a family also included grandparents and other relatives, who took an active part in the life of the household. An Egyptian child was taught great respect for his or her parents, with a son particularly expected to maintain his father's tomb.

The status of Egyptian women changed somewhat as the centuries passed. Literature of the Old Kingdom portrayed women as the property of their husbands and as valued producers of children. Wise men reminded children to cherish their mothers for bearing them, nourishing them, and loving and caring for them. By the time of the empire, documents indicate that women's legal rights had improved. Women could buy, own, and sell property in their own names, testify in court, and start divorce and other legal proceedings. The lives of Hatshepsut and some of the queens of the later pharaohs, like Nefertiti, suggest that privileged women of the royalty could attain prominence.

Visualizing History The falcon god Horus served both as a protector and symbol of the pharaoh. Horus was the son of the deities Osiris and Isis. *What was the major role of Osiris and Isis?*

Worshiping Many Deities

Religion guided every aspect of Egyptian life. Egyptian religion was based on polytheism, or the worship of many deities, except during the controversial rule of Akhenaton. Gods and goddesses were often represented as part human and part animal—Horus, the sky god, had the head of a hawk. The Egyptians in each region worshiped local deities, but rulers and priests promoted the worship of specific gods and goddesses over all of Egypt. These deities included Ra, the sun god, whom the Theban pharaohs joined with their favorite god Amon to make one god, Amon-Ra.

The popular god Osiris, initially the powerful god of the Nile, became the god responsible for the life, death, and rebirth of all living things. The Egyptians worshiped Osiris and his wife, the goddess Isis, as rulers of the realm of the dead. They believed that Osiris determined a person's fate after death.

Because their religion stressed an afterlife, Egyptians devoted much time and wealth to preparing for survival in the next world. At first they believed that only kings and wealthy people could enjoy an afterlife. By the time of the New Kingdom, however, poor people could also hope for eternal life with Osiris's help.

Writing With Pictures

In their earliest writing system, called hieroglyphics, the Egyptians carved picture symbols onto pieces of slate. These picture symbols, or hieroglyphs, stood for objects, ideas, and sounds. For everyday business, however, the Egyptians used a cursive, or flowing, script known as hieratic, which simplified and connected the picture symbols.

Few people in ancient Egypt could read or write. Some Egyptians, though, did prepare at special schools for a career as a scribe in government or commerce. Scribes learned to write hieratic script on paper made from the papyrus reed.

MORE ABOUT...

Deciphering the Rosetta Stone Jean-François Champollion, who deciphered the Rosetta stone, had a thorough knowledge of Coptic, the modern Egyptian language. He knew Greek as well, so he was able to read the entire text of the stone. The stone's inscription is a decree by Ptolemy V Epiphanes, king of Egypt from 203 to 181 B.C. The two forms of Egyptian writing on the stone are hieroglyphics and Demotic, the language of Egypt at the time the stone was inscribed. The black basalt stone—3 feet 9 inches (114 centimeters) high, 2 feet 4 1/2 inches (72 centimeters) thick—is on view at the British Museum in London.

After the decline of ancient Egypt, hieroglyphs were no longer used, and their meaning remained a mystery to the world's scholars for nearly 2,000 years. Then in A.D. 1799 French soldiers in Egypt found a slab of stone dating to the 200s B.C. near the town of Rosetta. The stone was carved with Greek letters and two forms of Egyptian writing. In A.D. 1822 a French archaeologist named Jean-François Champollion (shahn•pawl•YOHN) figured out how the Greek text on the Rosetta stone matched the Egyptian texts. Using the Greek version, he was able to decipher the Egyptian hieroglyphics.

Some of the oldest writings from the Old Kingdom were carved on the inner walls of the Pyramids. Scribes also copied many prayers and hymns to deities. The Book of the Dead collected texts telling how to reach a happy afterlife, recording more than 200 prayers and magic formulas.

The ancient Egyptians also wrote secular, or nonreligious, works such as collections of proverbs. One vizier gave this advice: "Do not repeat slander; you should not hear it, for it is the result of hot temper. Repeat a matter seen, not what is heard." The Egyptians also enjoyed adventure stories, fairy tales, and love stories, as this excerpt shows:

> **Now I'll lie down inside**
> **and act as if I'm sick.**
> **My neighbors will come in to visit,**
> **and with them my girl.**
> **She'll put the doctors out,**
> **for she's the one to know my hurt.**
>
> –a love poem by a young Egyptian,
> date unknown

Achievements in Science

Pyramids, temples, and other monuments bear witness to the architectural and artistic achievement of Egyptian artisans. These works, however,

Stonehenge Religious Site

Salisbury Plain, England, c. 1700 B.C.
Ancient people created a religious monument in southwestern England by dragging huge stones from miles away and arranging them in giant circles. The work probably took hundreds of years to complete. The layout of stones suggests that they were used in ceremonies linked to the rising of the sun on the longest day of the year.

would not have been possible without advances in disciplines such as mathematics. The Egyptians developed a number system that enabled them to calculate area and volume, and they used principles of geometry to survey flooded land.

The Egyptians worked out an accurate 365-day calendar by basing their year not only on the movements of the moon but also on Sirius, the bright Dog Star. Sirius rises annually in the sky just before the Nile's flood begins.

Egyptians also developed medical expertise, having first learned about human anatomy in their practice of embalming. Egyptian doctors wrote directions on papyrus scrolls for using splints, bandages, and compresses when treating fractures, wounds, and diseases. Other ancient civilizations would acquire much of their medical knowledge from the Egyptians.

SECTION 1 ASSESSMENT

Main Idea
1. Use a chart like the one below to show how the Nile River affected life in ancient Egypt.

Cause	Nile River		
Effects			

Recall
2. **Define** monarchy, dynasty, theocracy, bureaucracy, pharaoh, empire, polytheism, hieroglyphics.
3. **Identify** Narmer, Hatshepsut, Thutmose III, Akhenaton, Ramses II.

Critical Thinking
4. **Evaluate** Was Thutmose III or Ramses II more successful in handling conflict?

Understanding Themes
5. **Relation to Environment** How did the ancient Egyptians use the environment to meet their needs?

Chapter 2 *Early Civilizations* **53**

Chapter 2
Section 1

Evaluate

📁 Section Quiz 2-1

🖥 Use the Testmaker to create a customized quiz for Section 1.

Reteach

Organize the class into groups and assign each one a topic, such as Old Kingdom, Middle Kingdom, New Kingdom, family and society, religion, writing, technology. Have each group devise review questions on their topic to ask the rest of the class.

📁 Reading Essentials and Study Guide 2-1

Enrich

Have students research Nefertiti and write a one-page biographical sketch.

CLOSE

Have students list factors that account for the growth and longevity (3,000 years) of civilization along the Nile River. (*fertile soil, favorable climate, easy transportation by boat, development of irrigation, presence of outlying desert and five cataracts as natural defense barriers, growth of strong national government, rise of cities, evolution of writing*) Discuss which of these factors can be found in any river valley and which are unique to Egypt's location or unrelated to geography.

SECTION 1 ASSESSMENT ANSWERS

1. yearly flood brought needed water; nomadic hunter-gatherers first settled by Nile; farmland around Nile produced wheat and barley; provided farmers with ducks, geese, and fish; papyrus along banks used for rope and writing material; early farming villages prospered; a canal between the Nile River and the Red Sea allowed Egyptian trade
2. All terms are defined in the Glossary.
3. Narmer, 47; Hatshepsut, 49; Thutmose III, 49; Akhenaton, 51; Ramses II, 51
4. Students might mention Thutmose's military skills in conquering an empire; Ramses's diplomatic skills in reaching peace rather than prolonging a war.
5. **RELATION TO ENVIRONMENT**
The ancient Egyptians grew crops in the soil and learned to control the Nile's floodwaters so they could farm year-round. They also used the lower Nile for travel and trade. They used stone from the nearby desert for the Pyramids and other buildings.

Special Report Summary

Discoveries at the Valley of the Kings in 1922 revealed the magnificence of ancient royalty in Egypt.

Discoveries made in 1988 and the early 1990s revealed details of lives of Egyptian commoners.

A bakery and skeletons reveal the diet and hard labor of the commoners.

Art, culture, and faith may have developed up from the average man and woman, rather than down from royalty.

TEACH

Points to Discuss

After students have read the feature, ask the following: What archaeological remains indicate differences in life for royalty and for commoners? *(Royal tombs and relics indicate great wealth; skeletons of workers reveal years of hard labor.)* Why would people be willing to spend a life of toil and perhaps injury to build monumental tombs for their

The Egyptians

T he Valley of the Kings has seen more than its share of visitors. For thousands of years, travelers, warriors, and more recently, archaeologists have descended on this area on the outskirts of what is now Luxor to marvel at the magnificence of ancient Egypt. It was thought that most of

what there was to discover had been found after British explorer Howard Carter opened up the tomb of Tutankhamen in 1922.

Then in 1988, plans were made to build a parking lot over the site of Tomb 5, which had been discovered—and looted—years earlier. Wanting to make sure that the parking facility would not seal off anything important, Egyptologist Kent Weeks of the American University of

Cairo decided to make one last exploration of the tomb. To his prise, beyond a few debris-chok rooms, he opened a door that le the mostly unexcavated tomb of perhaps 50 of the sons of Rams the powerful pharaoh who rule Egypt from 1279 to 1212 B.C.

Though the tomb was emptie valuables long ago, archaeologis consider Weeks's discovery a ma find. Scientists and researchers h

54 Chapter 2 *Early Civilizations*

Kenneth Garrett

Illustration by C.F. Payne

pharaohs? *(Some scholars believe that the divine aspect of Egyptian society was expressed through the pharaoh, and building a tomb for the leader may have been an act of religious faith for the workers.)* Why was the discovery of the bakery and the cemetery significant? *(These finds were rich sources of information about the life of common Egyptians.)*

📖 Focus on World Art Print 7, Egyptian. *Mask of Tutankhamen*

🖋 World History and Art Transparency 2, *Tutankhamen's Throne*

🖋 Mapping History Overlay Transparency 2, *Ancient Egypt*

---

that artifacts found in the tomb will provide clues about Egyptian civilization during Egypt's last golden age.

For students of Judeo-Christian history, any information on Ramses' oldest son, Amen-hir-khopshef, would be a most important discovery. Ramses was in power when, in retribution for the enslavement of the Israelites, according to the Book of Exodus, the Lord "...smote all the firstborn in the land of Egypt, from the firstborn of Pharaoh that sat on his throne unto the firstborn of the captive that was in the dungeon."

The tomb and pyramids of

ancient Egypt hold many answers: These stone monuments have certainly established the immortality of the pharaohs. But what about the commoners, who vastly outnumbered the royalty? What of the men and women who gave their strength, sweat, and lives to create Egypt's lasting monuments? The widespread fame of the Sphinx and the Pyramids at Giza make it easy to forget that basic questions about Egyptian history have remained unanswered. Only recently have Egyptologists begun to fill in those gaps.

SEVERAL YEARS AGO, archaeologists began to excavate two sites—located about half a mile from the Sphinx—searching for signs of the

🖼 *Offerings of food are carved in relief on an official's tomb (left).*

🖼 *Another pyramid nears completion about 2500 B.C. (above). Limestone facing blocks were quarried across the Nile and ferried to the work site. Teams then dragged the blocks to ramps made of rubble that were built around the pyramid during construction. Some experts believe that it took only 10,000 men—far below earlier estimates of up to 100,000—and 25 years to lay 5 million tons of rock. Half lion, half pharaoh, the Sphinx (in the foreground) is carved from an outcropping left unexcavated in a U-shaped quarry.*

Chapter 2 *Early Civilizations* **55**

- The Pyramids are one of the Seven Wonders of the Ancient World.
- A broken section of the head of the Great Sphinx indicates that it may have been used as a target for shooting practice at various times throughout history.

- The ancient Egyptians were among the first to use clocks and calendars, to produce books, and to devise formulas for finding the area and volume of geometric figures.
- One of the greatest treasures ever found

in ancient Egypt was the tomb of the boy-king Tutankhamen. When the tomb was opened in 1922, nearly 5,000 items from the fourteenth century B.C. came to light.

NATIONAL GEOGRAPHIC *Special Report*

Linking Past and Present

Tourism is an important economic activity in Egypt today. The warm, dry climate and magnificent relics from ancient times attract visitors from all over the world.

NATIONAL GEOGRAPHIC SOCIETY

Use these materials to enrich student understanding of ancient Egyptian culture.

- **NGS PICTURESHOW CD-ROM**
  Egypt and the Fertile Crescent
- **NGS PICTUREPACK TRANSPARENCY SET**
  Ancient Egypt
- **ANCIENT CIVILIZATIONS POSTER SET**
  Ancient Egypt

ordinary people who built the pyramids. Within months they uncovered the remains of many mud-brick buildings, including the oldest bakery yet discovered in Egypt.

This was a significant find. While the pyramids built Egypt by drawing its provinces together in a unified effort, it can be said that bread built the pyramids. For thousands of workers, a loaf of emmer–wheat bread—washed down with beer—was most likely the dietary staple.

At about the time the bakery was discovered, searchers also unearthed a cemetery of 600 graves of workers. Their skeletons revealed years of hard labor. Vertebrae were compressed and damaged from years of carrying heavy loads. Some skeletons were missing fingers and even limbs. A few of the tombs were adorned with mini-pyramids several feet high, made of mud brick. Nothing like these tiny pyramids had been found before. In the past, scholars believed that the pyramid form was invented as the shape for a royal tomb. However, Zahi Hawass, director general of the Giza Pyramids, thinks that the pyramid form actually may have arisen among the common people. He believes that the mini-pyramids evolved from sacred rectangular mounds found in tombs even older than the pharaohs' pyramids.

Life for most ancient Egyptians was hard. Society was built around a preoccupation with the pharaohs' immortality. But perhaps there were spiritual rewards for the common people in this devotion to their pharaohs. Some scholars think that ancient Egyptians believed not so much that the pharaoh was divine,

Hosul Kang, based on a drawing by Mark Lehner

Kenneth Garrett

■ *A drawing of an ancient bakery (top) was used to build this replica of an ancient Egyptian bakery near Saqqara, Egypt (bottom).*

but that through the pharaoh the divine nature of their society was expressed. Building a pyramid might have been an act of faith much as building a cathedral was in the Middle Ages.

Such recent discoveries about the life of the common people may lead to a new way of seeing ancient Egypt: not only as a brilliant civilization of the elite trickling down to the masses but also as a culture built

from the bottom up—a culture that stood on the daily toil of the workers and the beliefs of ordinary men and women.

Much of the emerging picture of daily life in ancient Egypt is one of arduous toil. The villages were crowded and dirty. Huts were made of thatch and mud brick. Men wore loincloths; women dressed in long sheaths with wide shoulder straps, and children went naked. On wooden sledges workers hauled the giant granite blocks that built the pyramids. Egypt created a vast agricultural empire, yet all the irrigation was done by hand. Farmers filled two heavy jars from the canals, then hung them from a yoke over their shoulders. Oxen dragging wooden plows tilled the fertile soil along the Nile, followed by lines of sowers who sang in cadence as they cast grains of emmer wheat from baskets.

There is much still to be learned and understood about daily life in ancient Egypt. The discovery of the bakery has provided insight into what sustained the masses; the bones in the commoners' graveyard tell us that life was not easy; the mini-pyramids illustrate that art, culture, and faith may have developed up from the average man and woman, rather than down from the royalty. For years Egyptologists have focused on the grandiose—and thereby disregarded most of Egyptian society. Eventually, however, our view of ancient Egyptian culture is broadening to encompass those responsible for creating it.

MORE ABOUT...

Recreation Although the ancient Egyptians were hard workers as farmers and pyramid builders, they also found time for leisure activities. Sailing on the Nile was a popular family pastime. Egyptians also enjoyed swimming and fishing on the Nile. Many Egyptians also liked to watch wrestling matches. The more adventurous hunted crocodiles, lions, hippopotamuses, and wild cattle with spears or bows and arrows. At home, Egyptians liked to play *senet*, a board game much like backgammon.

Kenneth Garrett

Kenneth Garrett

■ *A potter was hired to make replicas of the old baking pots. A local worker (top left) heats the tops in a wood fire in preparation for baking.*

■ *A kind of wheat known as emmer was supplied by a Californian who collects and grows ancient grains. The wet flour made from the emmer was left outside to collect free-floating native yeast spores and bacteria. (Store–bought yeast was not known to ancient Egyptians.) On baking day, the dough was placed into the pot bottoms and allowed to rise (bottom left). A hole for each pot was dug in the hot coals. The heated pot tops were then placed on the heated bottom halves and were placed in the coals to bake.*

■ *Success! For perhaps the first time in more than 4,000 years, a loaf of emmer bread popped out of an Old Kingdom-style pot. Edward Wood (above), who has been baking ancient breads for 50 years, holds up a perfect loaf.*

Chapter 2 *Early Civilizations* **57**

CURRICULUM CONNECTION

MATHEMATICS
The Pyramid of Khufu contains more than 2 million stone blocks that average 2 1/2 short tons (2.3 metric tons) each. The pyramid was originally 481 feet (147 meters) high. Its base covers about 13 acres (5 hectares).

Global 🌎 Gourmet

Egypt Just as emmer-wheat bread was the staple in the pyramid builders diet, most villagers and poor city dwellers today eat a simple diet based on bread and *fool* (broad beans). For a typical evening meal, each person dips bread into a large communal bowl of vegetable stew.

Portfolio Project

Tell students that the study of ancient Egypt is called "Egyptology." Have students choose one of the following categories—architecture, woodworking, metalworking, or written records, and list five facts that they have learned about life in ancient Egypt.

TEACHER NOTES

_____

_____

_____

_____

_____

_____

3000 B.C.	2000 B.C.	1000 B.C.

c. 3000 B.C.
Sumerians set up city-states.

c. 2300 B.C.
Akkadian king Sargon I begins conquests.

c. 1700 B.C.
Hammurabi develops code of laws.

Section 2

The Fertile Crescent

Guide to Reading

Read to Find Out
Main Idea *Sumer's achievements enriched the early culture of the Middle East.*

▶ **Terms to Define**
city-state, cuneiform

▶ **People to Meet**
the Sumerians, Sargon I, the Akkadians, Hammurabi

▶ **Places to Locate**
Fertile Crescent, Mesopotamia, Tigris and Euphrates Rivers

The Storyteller

Sumerians honored the sun god Shamash as a defender of the weak, giver of life, and even as a judge of business deals, as in this hymn:
"The whole of mankind bows to you,
Shamash the universe longs for your light....
As for him who declines a present, but
nevertheless takes the part of the weak,
It is pleasing to Shamash, and he will prolong
his life....
The merchant who practices
trickery as he holds the
balances...
He is disappointed in the matter
of profit and loses his capital.
The honest merchant who holds
the balances and gives good
weight—
Everything is presented to him in
good measure."

—from *Babylonian Wisdom Literature,* W. B. Lambert, in *Readings in Ancient History* (2nd ed.), N. Bailkey

Sumerian board game

Around 5000 B.C.—at about the same time as Egyptian nomads moved into the Nile River valley—groups of herders started to journey north from the Arabian Peninsula. Rainfall in the area had declined over the years, and the lakes and grasslands had begun to dry up. Other peoples—from the highlands near present-day Turkey—moved south at this time. Driven by poor weather, they also fled war and overpopulation.

Both groups of migrants headed into the crescent-shaped strip of fertile land that stretched from the Mediterranean Sea to the Persian Gulf, curving around northern Syria. Called the **Fertile Crescent,** this region included parts of the modern nations of Israel, Jordan, Lebanon, Turkey, Syria, and Iraq.

Many of the peoples migrating from the north and south chose to settle in **Mesopotamia** (MEH •suh•puh•TAY•mee•uh), the eastern part of the Fertile Crescent. Located on a low plain lying between the **Tigris and Euphrates Rivers,** the name *Mesopotamia* means "land between the rivers" in the Greek language. The two rivers begin in the hills of present-day eastern Turkey and later run parallel to each other through present-day Iraq on their way to the Persian Gulf. In this region, the newcomers built villages and farmed the land.

The Twin Rivers

Beginning with Neolithic farmers, people used the Tigris and Euphrates Rivers to water their crops. Unlike the Nile River, however, the twin rivers did not provide a regular supply of water. In the summer no rain fell, and the Mesopotamian plain was dry. As a result, water shortages often coincided with the fall planting season. By the spring harvest season, however, the rivers swelled with rain and melting snow. Clogged with deposits of silt, the Tigris and Euphrates Rivers often overflowed onto the plain. Strong floods sometimes

58 Chapter 2 *Early Civilizations*

swept away whole villages and fields. The time of year of such flooding, however, was never predictable, and the water level of the rivers often varied from year to year.

The early Mesopotamian villages cooperated in order to meet the rivers' challenges. Together they first built dams and escape channels to control the seasonal floodwaters and later constructed canals and ditches to bring river water to irrigate their fields. As a result of their determined efforts, Mesopotamian farmers were producing food, especially grain crops, in abundance by 4000 B.C.

The Sumerian Civilization

Around 3500 B.C. a people from either central Asia or Asia Minor—the Sumerians—arrived in Mesopotamia. They settled in the lower part of the Tigris-Euphrates river valley, known as Sumer. Sumer became the birthplace of what historians have considered the world's first cities.

The Sumerian City-States

By 3000 B.C. the Sumerians had formed 12 city-states in the Tigris-Euphrates valley, including Ur, Uruk, and Eridu. A typical Sumerian city-state consisted of the city itself and the land surrounding it.

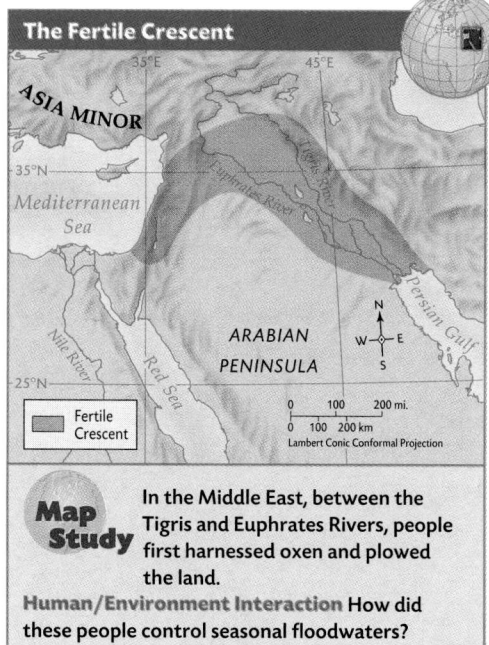

The Fertile Crescent

Map Study In the Middle East, between the Tigris and Euphrates Rivers, people first harnessed oxen and plowed the land.
Human/Environment Interaction How did these people control seasonal floodwaters?

The population of each city-state ranged from 20,000 to 250,000.

The people of Sumer shared a common culture, language, and religion. Sumerian city-states also shared some physical features. A ziggurat (ZIH•guh•RAT), or temple, made of sun-dried brick and decorated with colored tile, was built in each city-state. Sumerians built a ziggurat as a series of terraces, with each terrace smaller than the one below. A staircase climbed to a shrine atop the ziggurat. Only priests and priestesses were allowed to enter the shrine, which was dedicated to the city-state's chief deity. In form a ziggurat resembled a pyramid—both being massive stepped or peaked structures—but the feeling and emphasis of the two differed. A pyramid hid an inner tomb reachable only through passageways. A ziggurat raised a shrine to the sky, reached by mounting outer stairs.

Sumerian Government

Each Sumerian city-state usually governed itself independently of the others. In the city-state of Uruk, for example, a council of nobles and an assembly of citizens ran political affairs at first. But later, as city-states faced threats of foreign invaders and began to compete for land and water rights, the citizens of each city-state typically chose a military leader from among themselves. By 2700 B.C. the

Visualizing History Restored ziggurat at Ur, c. 2100 B.C. *What was the purpose of a ziggurat?*

Chapter 2 *Early Civilizations* **59**

TEACH

Guided Practice

THEME Cooperation

Ask why public works projects, such as dams and irrigation canals, require organization and cooperation. *(No one person can do them alone; they are too large, and many such projects require a number of different specialized skills.)* **L1**

Map Study

Answer
They built dams and escape channels.

Map Skills Practice

Reading a Map Using the Atlas in this text, name a state or states in the United States that are approximately the same distance from the Equator as is the Fertile Crescent. *(Possible answers include: Georgia, Alabama, Mississippi, Texas, Arizona, New Mexico, southern California)*

Visualizing History
 The sloping sides and terraces of ziggurats were often landscaped with trees and shrubs. The Hanging Gardens of Babylon, for example, were roof gardens that were laid out on a series of ziggurat terraces.
Answer to Caption: *It functioned as a temple and supported a shrine on top.*

COOPERATIVE LEARNING ACTIVITY

Team Presentation Organize the class into teams of five or six students. Have each team research one aspect of life in ancient Sumer, Akhad, or Babylon. Have teams prepare a class presentation, the subject and format of which they determine cooperatively. Students might include lifestyles, occupations, religious practices, or achievements. Formats may include skits, plays, and lectures. Assign specific tasks or have teams decide what role each team member will play in gathering and presenting the material. Provide time after each presentation for discussion and questions. Have a volunteer record on the board the main points brought out in the presentation. **L1**

Map Study

Answers

1. *Euphrates River*
2. *two rivers that supplied water, fertile land for farming*

Map Skills Practice

Reading a Map Have students locate the modern countries in the Fertile Crescent region in the Atlas in their text.

 Mapping History Overlay Transparency 1, *River Valley Civilizations*

Religion Three of the world's great religions—Judaism, Christianity, and Islam—originated in the Middle East. Several of the countries, peoples, regions, natural features, or cities mentioned in this section are also mentioned in the Bible or the Quran. Have students identify and describe three of these places. *(Ur, Uruk [Erech], Babylon)* **L3**

Independent Practice

Guided Reading Activity 2-2 **L1**

Time Line Have students create a time line of Mesopotamian history from 5000 B.C. (arrival of Akkadians) to 1600 B.C. (end of Hammurabi's empire). Encourage students to make the time line visually appealing by adding illustrations. **L1 LEP**

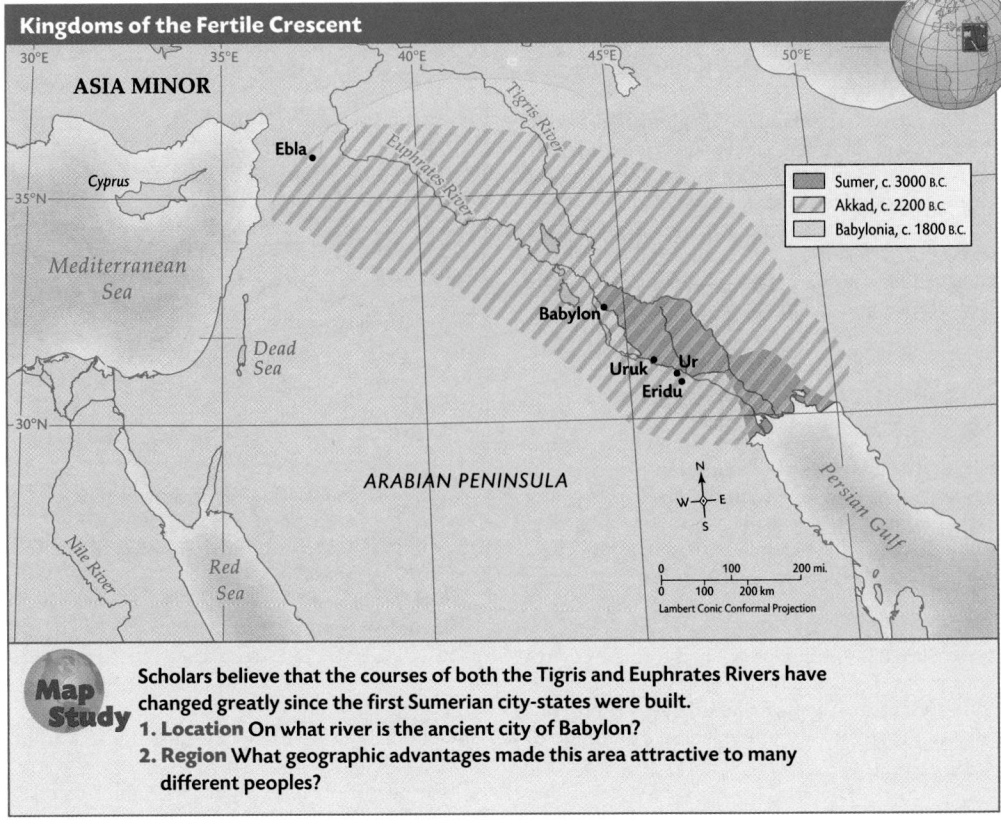

Kingdoms of the Fertile Crescent

Sumer, c. 3000 B.C.
Akkad, c. 2200 B.C.
Babylonia, c. 1800 B.C.

Map Study Scholars believe that the courses of both the Tigris and Euphrates Rivers have changed greatly since the first Sumerian city-states were built.
1. **Location** On what river is the ancient city of Babylon?
2. **Region** What geographic advantages made this area attractive to many different peoples?

---

leaders of several city-states ruled as kings. Soon after, the kingships became hereditary.

A Sumerian king served not only as military leader but as the high priest, who represented the city-state's deity. Thus the governments of the city-states were not only monarchies but theocracies. Because the Sumerians believed that much of the land belonged to a city-state's god or goddess, a king and his priests closely supervised farming. A king also enforced the law and set penalties for law-breakers. Most punishments consisted of fines and did not involve bodily injury or loss of life.

The Roles of Men and Women

Sumerian law extensively regulated family life and outlined the roles of men and women. As the heads of households, men exercised great authority over their wives and children. According to Sumerian law codes, a man could sell his wife or children into slavery if he needed the money to pay a debt. He could also divorce his wife for the slightest cause. For a Sumerian woman, in contrast, the

law codes made divorce much more difficult. Women did enjoy some legal rights, however. Like Egyptian women, they could buy and sell property. They could also operate their own businesses and own and sell their own slaves.

Writing on Clay Tablets

Commerce and trade dominated the Sumerian city-states. The Sumerians developed a system of writing so they could keep accounts and prepare documents. Archaeologists believe that the writing system the Sumerians invented is the oldest in the world, dating to about 3100 B.C. The **cuneiform** (kyoo•NEE•uh•FAWRM) system began with pictograms—as did Egyptian hieroglyphics—and consisted of hundreds of wedge-shaped markings made by pressing the end of a sharpened reed on wet clay tablets. Then the Sumerians dried or baked the tablets until they were hard. Eventually the pictograms developed into symbols representing complex ideas. In this way, cuneiform influenced later Mesopotamian writing systems.

MEETING SPECIAL NEEDS ACTIVITY

Study Strategy Have students who need help synthesizing and summarizing information research ancient Mesopotamian cities and write an in-depth report about one of them. Encourage students to illustrate the reports. These cities are possible research topics: Eridu, the first of the five cities that existed before the Flood; Uruk, the biblical city called Erech in Genesis; Ur, one of the important religious centers of ancient Sumer; Kish, the first seat of kingship after the Flood; Mari, a city on the trade route between Mesopotamia and Syria; Babylon, capital of the Amorite dynasty after the fall of the Ur empire. **L2**

Visualizing History Medical remedies are inscribed on this Sumerian clay tablet—a cuneiform writing tablet that was baked until hard. *How did cuneiform develop as a writing system?*

Sumerians wishing to learn cuneiform and become scribes studied for many years at special schools called *eddubas*. As educated professionals, scribes rose to high positions in Sumerian society. They produced business records, lists of historical dates, and literary works.

One of these literary works, the epic poem *Gilgamesh*, was written down about 1850 B.C. Scholars believe that the *Gilgamesh* epic may be the oldest story in the world. The scribes probably based the stories of Gilgamesh, a godlike man who performs heroic deeds, on an actual king of the city-state of Uruk.

Sumer's Many Deities

The Sumerians, like the Egyptians, practiced a polytheistic religion. Each Sumerian deity presided over a specific natural force—rain, moon, air—or over a human activity—plowing or brick making, for example. An, the highest Sumerian deity, was responsible for the seasons. Another important god—Enlil, god of winds and agriculture—created the hoe. Although Sumerians honored all the deities, each city-state claimed as its own one god or goddess, to whom its citizens prayed and offered sacrifices.

The Sumerians pictured their gods and goddesses as unpredictable, selfish beings who had little regard for human beings. The Sumerians believed that if deities became angry, they would cause misfortunes such as floods or famine. To appease their temperamental gods and goddesses, Sumerian priests and priestesses performed religious ceremonies and rituals.

Unlike the Egyptians, the Sumerians felt that humans had little control over their daily lives and could not look forward to a happy life after death. Only a grim underworld, without light or air, awaited them—an afterlife where the dead were only pale shadows.

Sumerian Inventions

Historians credit the Sumerians with numerous technological innovations. The Sumerians developed the wagon wheel, for example, to better transport people and goods, the arch to build sturdier buildings, the potter's wheel to shape containers, and the sundial to keep time. They developed a number system based on 60 and devised a 12-month calendar based on the cycles of the moon. The Sumerian civilization also was the first to make bronze out of copper and tin and to develop a metal plow. They produced an abundance of finely crafted metal work, some of which has been discovered in the Royal Cemetery at Ur. These and other Sumerian achievements have prompted one scholar to observe that "history begins at Sumer."

First Mesopotamian Empires

After a long period of conquest and reconquest, the Sumerian city-states eventually fell to foreign invaders in the 2000s B.C. The invaders of Sumer, like the Egyptians of the New Kingdom, were inspired by dreams of empire.

 The Umbrella
1400 B.C.—Umbrellas actually originated under the sunny skies of Mesopotamia. Sumerians used palm fronds or feather umbrellas to shield their heads from the harsh rays and scorching heat of the Middle Eastern sun.

Visualizing History Clay tablets with cuneiform writing on them have given us more information about Mesopotamia than any other artifact. They explain many aspects of Mesopotamian life.
Answer to Caption: *It began as pictograms, consisting of wedge-shaped markings. Eventually, the pictograms developed into symbols representing complex ideas.*

Technology Have students find out more about a Sumerian invention, such as the wagon wheel or the arch, and write a television commercial script about it. The script should explain the benefits of the invention to the Sumerian people. Have students write descriptions of the visuals that would accompany the script. **L3**

NATIONAL GEOGRAPHIC SOCIETY

Use these materials to enrich student understanding of Mesopotamian civilizations.

- **NGS PICTURESHOW CD-ROM**
  Egypt and the Fertile Crescent
- **NGS PICTUREPACK TRANSPARENCY SET**
  The Fertile Crescent
- **ANCIENT CIVILIZATIONS POSTER SET**
  The Fertile Crescent

MAKING CONNECTIONS ACTIVITY

Global Issues The Louvre in Paris owns and displays a stone pillar inscribed with Hammurabi's legal decisions. The British Museum in London has an extensive collection of Mesopotamian art. The University Museum at the University of Pennsylvania has a collection of early Sumerian literary works. Have students debate whether a museum should return artifacts such as these to their places of origin. **L1**

62

Linking Past and Present

Barley Most Sumerians were farmers. Indeed, the world's oldest agricultural manual was written in Sumer. It tells farmers how to grow barley, Mesopotamia's staple food. Barley is still an important crop throughout the world. It is the fourth most widely grown grain, after wheat, corn, and rice.

Critical Thinking Have students research Hammurabi's code of laws. Ask volunteers to present their findings in class. Students should understand that the code was an attempt to deal fairly with people in a political state made up of former independent states with different traditions. The code set up a social order based on individual rights. **L3**

Who?What?Where?When?

Cuneiform Whereas Egyptian hieroglyphics were used by a homogenous group of people, cuneiform was used by heterogenous groups who spoke different languages. Cuneiform served as the writing system for diverse cultures for some 3,000 years. Sumerians, Akkadians, Babylonians, Assyrians, Hittites, and Old Persians are among the peoples whose language was written in cuneiform. In its time, cuneiform was as widely used as the Latin alphabet is today.

Sargon Leads the Akkadians

The first empire builder in Mesopotamia—**Sargon I**—may have been born a herder or a farmer's son. According to legend his mother abandoned him as a baby, setting him out on the Euphrates River in a reed basket. Downstream a farmer irrigating his fields pulled Sargon ashore and raised him as his own.

Sargon's people, **the Akkadians**, were Semites, one of the nomadic groups that had migrated from the Arabian Peninsula to the Fertile Crescent around 5000 B.C. The Akkadians established a kingdom called Akkad (AH•KAHD) in northern Mesopotamia. When Sargon assumed power in Akkad around 2300 B.C., he immediately launched a military campaign of expansion. Sargon's conquests united all of the city-states of Mesopotamia in one empire, which predated the empire of the Egyptian New Kingdom by more than 800 years.

Under Sargon's rule the people of Mesopotamia began to use the Akkadian language instead of Sumerian. But the Akkadians adopted various Sumerian religious and farming practices. After Sargon's death and the successful rule of his grandson, however, the Akkadian Empire disintegrated.

The Kingdom of Ebla

No one really knows how far Sargon's empire extended. Historians do know, however, that Ebla, a kingdom located in what is now northern Syria, fought unsuccessfully against Sargon for control of the Euphrates River trade. When Sargon's grandson captured Ebla, he burned the royal archives. Yet fire did not destroy the thousands of clay tablets stored there. These tablets and other finds from Ebla have convinced historians that highly developed Semitic civilizations prospered in that area of Syria earlier than previously believed.

The overland trade that passed between Egypt and Mesopotamia made Ebla a wealthy and powerful city-state. Ebla controlled a number of neighboring towns, from which it exacted tribute.

The kings of Ebla were elected for seven-year terms. In addition to their political role, they looked

Images *of the* Times

Mesopotamia

For many centuries, beginning about 4000 B.C., enterprising civilizations rose and fell in the fertile valley of the Tigris and Euphrates Rivers.

The Royal Standard of Ur is an oblong decorated box with panels that represent scenes of war and peace. The war panel celebrates a military victory by the Sumerian city of Ur.

Images *of the* Times Mesopotamia

Our knowledge of life in Mesopotamia depends heavily on cuneiform studies. Translations were begun nearly 150 years ago and are still continuing. Tens of thousands of clay tablets have been found inscribed with the wedge-shaped script. They include business, legal, and administrative documents, as well as hymns, myths, epic tales, proverbs, fables, and essays. A thousand years before the Hebrews wrote their Bible or the Greeks their *Iliad* and *Odyssey*, writers in Mesopotamia had produced a rich and mature literature.

after the welfare of the poor. If the kings failed, they could be removed by a council. After 2000 B.C., Ebla declined and eventually was destroyed by the Amorites, a Semitic people from western Syria.

Hammurabi's Babylonian Empire

The Amorites also expanded beyond Syria. Their military forces poured into Mesopotamia, which was in decline after a short period of prosperity under the kings of Ur. The Amorites overran many Sumerian centers, including Babylon. The dynasty that they founded at Babylon later produced a ruler who would dominate Mesopotamia: **Hammurabi**.

Hammurabi used his might to put down other Mesopotamian rulers. He eventually brought the entire region under his control, reorganizing the tax system and ordering local officials to build and repair irrigation canals. Hammurabi organized a strong government and worked to increase the economic prosperity of his people. Under Hammurabi's rule, Babylon became a major trade center. Merchants from as far away as India and China paid gold and silver for the grain and cloth the Babylonians produced.

Hammurabi's Law Code

Historians consider Hammurabi's greatest achievement his effort "to make justice appear in the land." Hammurabi collected laws of the various Mesopotamian city-states and created a law code covering the entire region. When completed, Hammurabi's code consisted of 282 sections dealing with most aspects of daily life. It clearly stated which actions were considered violations and assigned a specific punishment for each. Hammurabi's code penalized wrongdoers more severely than did the old Sumerian laws. Instead of fining violators, it exacted what the Bible later expressed as "an eye for an eye, and a tooth for a tooth." According to the harsh approach of Hammurabi's code:

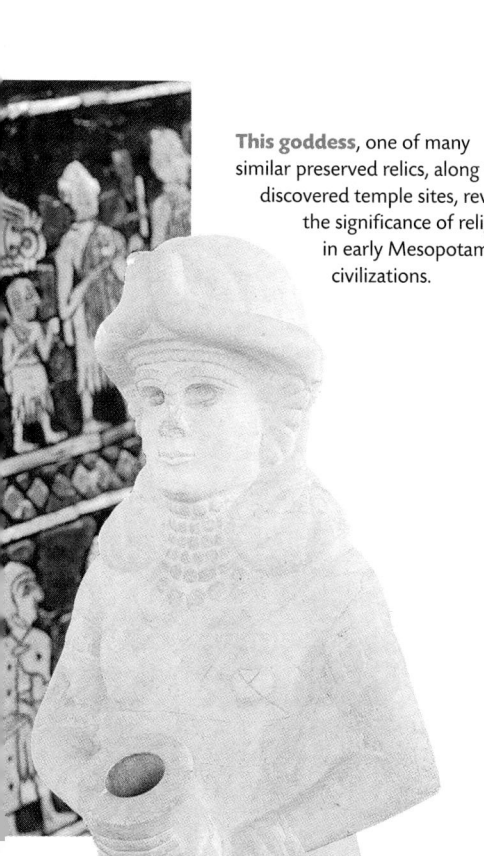

This goddess, one of many similar preserved relics, along with discovered temple sites, reveals the significance of religion in early Mesopotamian civilizations.

The Kassite stela fragment shows animals that were important to a vigorous agricultural people, the Kassites, who emerged as a dominant force after 2000 B.C.

REFLECTING ON THE TIMES

1. What evidence reveals the importance of religion in Mesopotamian cities?
2. What role might gods and goddesses have in times of war?

63

ANSWERS TO REFLECTING ON THE TIMES

1. Many religious relics have been found.
2. They could help ensure victory for their side, or, if angered, bring about defeat.

Hammurabi's Law Code
How were punishments for crimes decided?
Punishments were to fit the crimes, like the biblical saying, "an eye for an eye."

VIDEODISC
Turning Points in World History

Side One
Chapter 4

Title: *The Code of Hammurabi*

ASSESS

Check for Understanding
Assign Section 2 Assessment as homework or as an in-class activity.

Use Interactive Tutor Self-Assessment Software to review Section 2.

Evaluate
 Section Quiz 2-2

Use the Testmaker to create a customized quiz for Section 2.

Reteach
Have students write two sentences about each of the three Mesopotamian civilizations. Each sentence should present an important fact about the civilization being described. Ask students to read their sentences in class. Discuss.

 Reading Essentials and Study Guide 2-2

Enrich

Have students draw to scale an
Egyptian pyramid, a Sumerian
ziggurat, and a large building in
their area. Have them compare
the dimensions and report on
what they find.

CLOSE

Have students write a paragraph
about each of the three civilizations in this section—Sumerian,
Akkadian, and Babylonian—that
begins with this sentence: We
influenced the course of human
history. Have students summarize in these paragraphs the contributions of each civilization.
Ask volunteers to read their paragraphs aloud in class.

Visualizing History King Hammurabi stands in front of
the sun god Shamash at the top of
the stone slab upon which is inscribed Hammurabi's
code of laws. Shamash—the supreme judge—delivers
the laws to the king. *Why were Hammurabi's laws carved
in stone for public display?*

> **If a builder has built a house for a man
> and has not made his work sound, so that
> the house he has made falls down and
> causes the death of the owner of the
> house, that builder shall be put to death.
> If it causes the death of the son of the
> owner of the house, they shall kill the
> son of that builder.**

Other sections of Hammurabi's code covered
the property of married women, adoption and
inheritance, interest rates on loans, and damage to
fields by cattle. Some laws were attempts to protect
the less powerful—for example, protecting wives
against beatings or neglect by their husbands. The
development of written law in Mesopotamia was a
major advance toward justice and order. Before this
achievement, people who had been offended or
cheated often acted on their own and used violence
against their opponents. Now, crimes against people or property became the concern of the whole
community. Government assumed the responsibility of protecting its citizens in return for their loyalty and service.

Babylonian Society

Historians have been able to infer from
Hammurabi's code a threefold division of
Babylonian social classes—the kings, priests, and
nobles at the top; the artisans, small merchants,
scribes, and farmers next; and slaves as the lowest
group. His laws varied according to the class of the
person offended against, with more severe penalties for assaulting a landowner than for hurting a
slave. Most slaves had been captured in war or had
failed to pay their debts.

The Babylonians borrowed heavily from
Sumerian culture. They used the cuneiform script
for their Semitic language and wrote on clay tablets.
Babylonian literature was similar to that of Sumer.

Decline and Fall

After Hammurabi's death, the Babylonian
Empire declined, and Mesopotamia was again
divided into a number of small states. Hammurabi's dynasty finally ended and his empire fell
apart when the Hittites, a people from Asia Minor,
raided Babylon about 1600 B.C. Babylon, however,
would again play a role in Mesopotamian civilization in the 600s B.C. as the capital of a new empire
under the Chaldeans.

SECTION 2 ASSESSMENT

Main Idea
1. Use a chart like the one below
   to explain Sumer's achievements.

Political Life	Cultural Life	Inventions

Recall
2. **Define** city-state, cuneiform.
3. **Identify** the Sumerians, Gilgamesh, Sargon I, the Akkadians, Hammurabi.

Critical Thinking
4. **Making Comparisons**
   Contrast Hammurabi's code

with modern American law.
Which do you think serves
justice better? Why?

Understanding Themes
5. **Cooperation** Identify an economic or cultural achievement
of a Fertile Crescent civilization
that required skillful planning.

SECTION 2 ASSESSMENT ANSWERS

1. political life: city-states of 20,000 to
   250,000 people, theocratic rule; cultural
   life: ziggurats with shrines, cuneiform
   writing, literary works; inventions: wagon
   wheel, arch, potter's wheel, sundial
2. All terms are defined in the Glossary.

3. Sumerians, 59; Gilgamesh, 61; Sargon I,
   62; Akkadians, 62; Hammurabi, 63
4. Both examples spell out the rights of
   citizens as well as categories of violations
   and punishments; students will probably
   state that Hammurabi's code is harsher

in penalizing wrongdoers.
5. **COOPERATION** Answers may
   include: irrigating the land, governing
   city-states, building ziggurats, administering schools for scribes, conducting
   military operations.

Classifying Information

Imagine shopping in a store where products are all mixed together in piles. To find the item you need, you would have to comb through each pile. How frustrating!

Dealing with large quantities of information about a subject likewise can be frustrating. It is easier to understand information if you put it into groups, or classify it.

Learning the Skill

In classifying anything, we put together items with shared characteristics. For example, department stores put shoes and boots in the footwear department, while pots and pans are in the kitchen department.

We can classify written information in the same way.

1. As you read about a topic, look for items that have similar characteristics. List these items in separate columns or on separate note cards.
2. Give each list an appropriate label.
3. Add facts to the categories as you read.
4. Review the groups. If necessary, subdivide the categories into smaller groups or combine categories that overlap.

Once you have classified the material, look for patterns and relationships in the facts. Make comparisons, draw conclusions, and develop questions or hypotheses for further study.

Practicing the Skill

Use the information in the following passage to answer these questions:

1. The passage describes two groups of children in ancient Egypt. What are these groups?
2. Classify the educational opportunities available to each group.
3. Classify the occupations available to each group.
4. From your classifications, what conclusions can you draw about Egyptian society?

❝The royal children ... were privately tutored ... frequently joined by the sons of great noble families.... The most sought-after profession in Egypt was that of scribe.... The most important subjects were reading and writing ... history, literature, geography, [and] ethics. Arithmetic was almost certainly part of the curriculum.... Boys who were to specialize in medicine, law or religious liturgy would perhaps have devoted some of their time to elementary studies in these fields.

Formal education for [a son from] the lower classes ... was not selected for him because he wished to become an artist or goldsmith or a farmer ... he entered a trade because it was his father's work. The sons of artists and craftsmen were apprenticed and went to train at one of the temples or state workshops ... the sons of peasants would have joined their fathers in the field at an early age.❞

—A. Rosalie David,
The Egyptian Kingdoms, 1975

Applying the Skill

Find two newspaper or magazine articles about a topic that interests you. Classify the information on note cards or in a chart.

For More Practice

Turn to the Skill Practice in the Chapter Assessment on page 77 for more practice in classifying information.

The **Glencoe Skillbuilder Interactive Workbook,** Level 2 provides instruction and practice in key social studies skills.

TEACH

Classifying Information Elicit from students how they organize various aspects of their personal lives. You might mention such things as closets and bureau drawers; stamp, coin, or sports card collections; school papers, notes and assignments. Focus discussion on how they have grouped similar items together. The skills feature teaches a four-step process for classifying data. Emphasize how sorting items based on shared characteristics is a common method of classification and is simply part of being well organized.

Additional Practice

📁 Skill Reinforcement Activity 2

GLENCOE
TECHNOLOGY

Glencoe's **Skillbuilder Interactive Workbook, Level 2** This interactive CD-ROM promotes student mastery of key social studies skills.

ANSWERS TO PRACTICING THE SKILL

1. nobles' children, children of the lower classes
2. nobles: private tutoring in subjects such as reading , writing, history, ethics, literature, geography, arithmetic; lower classes: apprenticeships, field work, determined by their fathers' work
3. nobles: scribes, priests, doctors, lawyers; lower classes: artisans, farmers, craftspeople
4. It was rigidly divided by class.

2500 B.C.   2000 B.C.   1500 B.C.

c. 2500 B.C.
Settlements develop in
the Indus River valley.

c. 2300 B.C. Harappan people
trade with Mesopotamia.

c. 1500 B.C.
Indus Valley
civilization
declines.

SECTION THEME

▶ **Cultural Diffusion** Cities in
early India develop close trading and cultural ties with the
Fertile Crescent area.

Guide to Reading

For reading strategies to help
students read effectively see
pages 12–13.

Vocabulary Pre-check

 Use the Vocabulary
PuzzleMaker for Chapter 2 to
create a crossword puzzle to
reinforce section terms. **L1 LEP**

📁 Use Vocabulary Activity
2 to introduce vocabulary terms.
L1 LEP

FOCUS

Section Objective

Relate how people of the Indus
River valley civilization built cities.

BELLRINGER
Motivational Activity

 Before taking roll at the
beginning of the class
period, project Section
Focus Transparency 2-3
and have students answer
the activity questions. Discuss
students' responses.
📁 This activity is also
available as a blackline master.

Section 3

Early South Asia

Guide to Reading

Read to Find Out
Main Idea *People of the Indus River
valley civilization built well-organized cities.*

▶ **Terms to Define**
subcontinent, monsoon

▶ **People to Meet**
the Harappans

▶ **Places to Locate**
Indus River valley, Harappa,
Mohenjo-Daro

The Storyteller

*For a long time, it had been known that the
mounds of Mohenjo-Daro and Harappa contained
archaeological remains. But neighborhood construction workers actually used the ancient
mounds as sources for bricks, until practically
none remained above ground. As Sir Alexander
Cunningham, the first Director General of the
Archaeological Survey records, "Perhaps the best
idea of the extent of the ruined brick mounds of
Harappa may be formed from the fact that they
have more than sufficed to furnish brick ballast for
about 100 miles of Lahore and Multan Railway."*

—adapted from *Indus Valley
Civilization,* Ashim Kumar
Ron N.N. Gidwani
(Cunningham, 1875),
1982 and *Harappan
Civilization,* Gregory
Possehl, 1982

Harappan jar lid

A third civilization, larger than both
Egypt and Sumer in land area, arose
in the **Indus River valley** far to the
east, in South Asia. It reached its height at about the
time of the Akkadian and Babylonian Empires
between about 2500 B.C. and 1500 B.C.

The Subcontinent

Three modern nations—India, Pakistan, and
Bangladesh—trace their roots to the Indus Valley
civilization. These countries lie on the subcontinent of South Asia, a large, triangular-shaped landmass that juts into the Indian Ocean.

Bounded by Mountains

Natural barriers separate the South Asian subcontinent from the rest of Asia. Water surrounds the
landmass on the east and west. To the north rise
two lofty mountain ranges—the Himalayas and the
Hindu Kush. Throughout history, invaders entering the subcontinent by land have had to cross the
few high mountain passes of the Hindu Kush.

Plains sweep across the landscape to the south
of the mountains. Across the plains flow three
rivers, fed by rain and melting mountain snows.
The Indus River drains into the Arabian Sea, and
the Ganges (GAN•JEEZ) and Brahmaputra (BRAH
•muh•POO•truh) Rivers join and empty into the
Bay of Bengal, forming a wide delta. The Ganges-
Brahmaputra Delta and the Indus-Ganges plain are
formed from soils left by the rivers. Like the Nile
Valley and Delta and the Tigris-Euphrates plains,
fertile river areas of South Asia have supported vast
numbers of people over the ages.

Seasonal Winds

The northern mountains ensure generally
warm weather in South Asia. Like a wall, they
block blasts of cold air from central Asia. Two seasonal winds called monsoons affect the climate,

66 Chapter 2 *Early Civilizations*

SECTION RESOURCES

📁 **Reproducible Masters**
• Lecture Notes 2-3
• Reproducible Lesson Plan 2-3
• Vocabulary Activity 2
• Guided Reading Activity 2-3
• Section Quiz 2-3
• Reading Essentials and Study Guide 2-3

📊 **Transparencies**
• Section Focus Transparency 2-3
• Mapping History Overlay Transparency 3
• Ancient India

Multimedia
💻 Interactive Tutor Self-Assessment
Software
💿 Testmaker
🌐 India and China

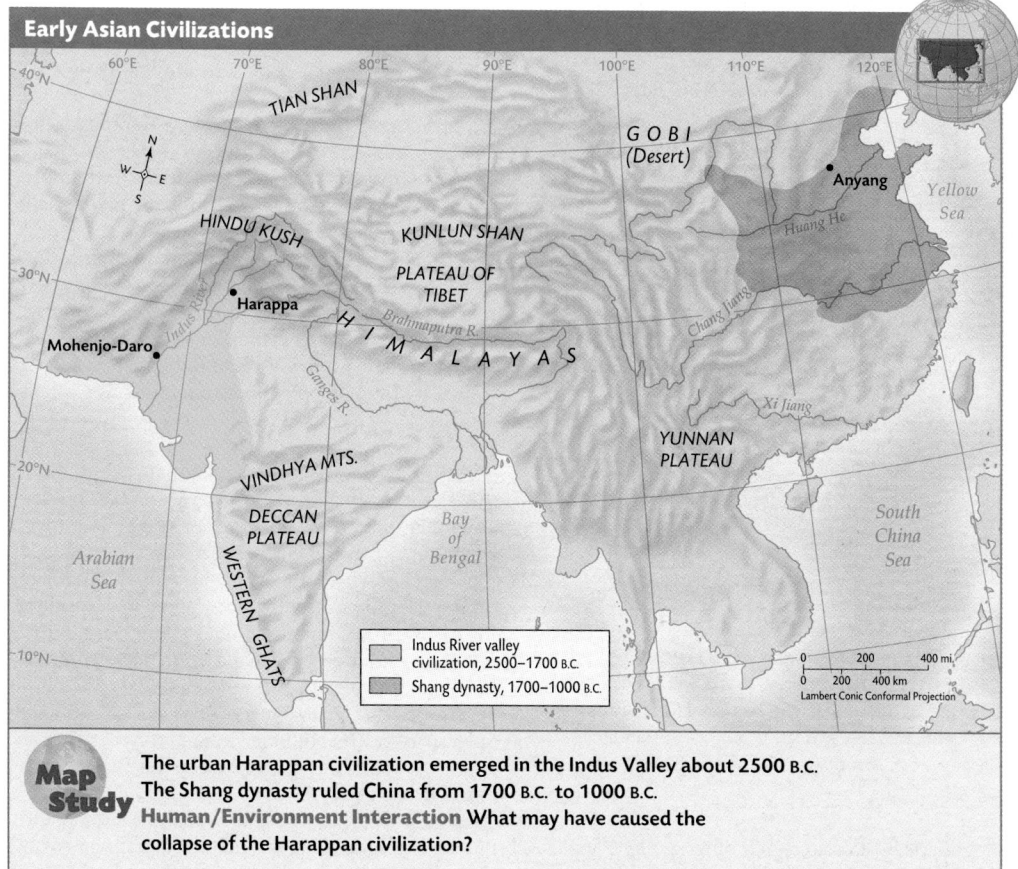

Early Asian Civilizations

Indus River valley civilization, 2500–1700 B.C.

Shang dynasty, 1700–1000 B.C.

0   200   400 mi.
0   200   400 km
Lambert Conic Conformal Projection

Map Study The urban Harappan civilization emerged in the Indus Valley about 2500 B.C. The Shang dynasty ruled China from 1700 B.C. to 1000 B.C. **Human/Environment Interaction** What may have caused the collapse of the Harappan civilization?

---

however, and shape the pattern of life on the subcontinent.

The northeast, or winter, monsoon blows from November to March; the southwest, or summer, monsoon from June to September. The northeast wind brings dry air from the mountains, and the average winter temperatures of the Indus-Ganges plain remain mild—about 70°F (21°C). By June, temperatures have soared, sometimes exceeding 100°F (38°C), and South Asians welcome the rain-bearing southwest wind blowing off the ocean.

Because of the heavy downpours of the southwest monsoon, the rivers swell rapidly, then widen across the flat plains and rush to the sea. The flooding enriches the soil, but in some years unusually heavy rains drown people and animals and destroy whole villages. In other years the monsoon arrives late or rainfall is light; then crops are poor and people go hungry. The people of the plains are dependent on the monsoons.

The Indus Valley Civilization

Less than a century ago, archaeologists working in the Indus River valley first identified an ancient civilization in South Asia. They dated this early civilization to about 2500 B.C.

Centrally Planned Cities

Archaeologists named the Indus Valley settlements "the Harappan civilization" after one of its major cities, **Harappa** (huh•RA•puh), located in present-day Pakistan. **Mohenjo-Daro** (moh •HEHN•joh DAHR•oh), another important Harappan city, lay nearer the Arabian Sea.

The ruins of Harappa and Mohenjo-Daro are outstanding examples of urban planning. A citadel, or fortress, built on a brick platform overlooked each city—possibly serving as a government and religious center. Below the citadel Harappan engineers skillfully laid out each city in a grid pattern of

Chapter 2 Early Civilizations **67**

TEACH

Guided Practice

THEME Cultural Diffusion

Using information in the text, have students trace on a relief map a possible route taken by the traders who traveled to Mesopotamia and brought ideas such as writing back to Harappa and Mohenjo-Daro. (*Routes should cross through a pass in the Hindu Kush.*) **L1 LEP**

Map Study

Answer

floods caused by climate changes, or violence—perhaps at the hands of invaders

Map Skills Practice

Reading a Map What features of physical geography, common to Egypt and Mesopotamia, were also vital to the Harappan and early Chinese civilizations? (*rivers*)

Independent Practice

 Guided Reading Activity 2-3 **L1**

 NATIONAL GEOGRAPHIC SOCIETY

Use these materials to enrich student understanding of Indus River valley civilizations.

- **NGS PICTURESHOW CD-ROM** India and China
- **NGS PICTUREPACK TRANSPARENCY SET** Ancient India

Visual Presentations Organize the class into groups of five or six students. Have each group choose a topic from this list of suggestions: religion, architecture, city planning, farming, textiles, arts and crafts, commerce, and geography. Have groups research their topic as it pertains to Harappan civilization. They should then prepare visuals illustrating what they have learned about their topic. The items may be labeled, but the emphasis should be on a visual presentation. Each group should decide what task the members of the group will perform. Provide space for the groups to display their completed work. Discussion of the displays should include a time for questions and answers. **L2**

Chapter 2 *Early Civilizations* **67**

Visualizing History Among the
many art objects from the Indus
River valley civilization are statuettes
made of soapstone and limestone,
square soapstone seals decorated
with a variety of animals, ceramic
storage jars, and toys with wheels.
Answer to Caption: *lack of written records from the Harappans*

ASSESS

Check for Understanding

Assign Section 3 Assessment as
homework or as an in-class
activity.

 Use Interactive Tutor Self-
Assessment Software to review
Section 3.

Evaluate

Section Quiz 2-3

Use the Testmaker to create a
customized quiz for Section 3.

Reteach

Have a discussion on the achievements of Harappan civilization.

Reading Essentials and
Study Guide 2-3

Enrich

Have students find out more
about monsoons, including their
causes, and write a one-page
report on the subject.

CLOSE

Have students write a paragraph
describing the features of Harappan civilization that made it
attractive to invaders, such as its
thriving agricultural enterprise.
Have students read their paragraphs in class.

Visualizing History Some fine jewelry crafted by
Harappan artisans has survived.
These pieces are now in the National Museum at
New Delhi, India. *Why is less known about Harappan
civilization than about Egypt and Mesopotamia?*

straight streets crossing each other at right angles.
The Harappans used oven-baked bricks to build
houses with flat wooden roofs, and some houses
rose to several stories and enclosed courtyards.
Almost every house had at least one bathroom,
with drains and chutes connected to a brick sewer
system beneath the streets.

Harappan Life

Most of the Harappan people worked the land.
In the fields of the Indus Valley floodplain they
grew wheat, barley, rice, and cotton. Farmers planted at the beginning or end of the flood season and
relied on the drenched land to provide the necessary water for their crops.

Supported by a food surplus, Harappan city
dwellers engaged in industry and commerce. Some
artisans worked bronze and copper into tools,
while others made silver vessels and gold, shell,
and ivory jewelry. The Harappans also mass-produced clay pots, and they spun and wove cotton
cloth. Merchants who handled these goods used
soapstone seals to identify bundles of merchandise.
The discovery by archaeologists of Harappan seals
in Mesopotamia indicates that Indus Valley people
traded with the people of Mesopotamia as early as
2300 B.C.

Language and Religion

The Harappans inscribed pictograms on the
seals they placed on packages of goods. Scientists
have yet to decipher these inscriptions—almost
the only known examples of the written language
of the Harappan civilization. Some believe that
the Harappans made their pictograms after
adopting the idea of writing from the people of
Mesopotamia.

The lack of written records has made it difficult
to learn as much about the Harappan civilization as
is known about Egypt and Mesopotamia. Artifacts
found in the ruins, however, have provided archaeologists with some clues. For example, animal and
humanlike figures suggest that the Harappans worshiped gods associated with natural forces.

Collapse of a Civilization

By 1500 B.C. the Harappan civilization had disappeared. Historians have many theories for what
caused this collapse. Evidence of floods, for example, suggests possible climate changes. In the
Mohenjo-Daro ruins are signs that some of its people may have met a violent end, possibly at the
hands of invaders.

SECTION 3 ASSESSMENT

Main Idea
1. Use a web diagram like the one
   below to identify details about
   the cities built by the people of
   the Indus River valley.

Cities of Indus
River Valley

Recall
2. **Define** subcontinent, monsoon.
3. **Identify** the Harappans.
Critical Thinking
4. **Analyzing Information**
   What do archaeological clues
   suggest about the decline of
   the Indus Valley civilization?

Understanding Themes
5. **Cultural Diffusion** How
   might the Indus Valley civilization at Mohenjo-Daro and the
   civilization at Harappa have
   been influenced by the
   Mesopotamian city-states and
   empires?

SECTION 3 ASSESSMENT ANSWERS

1. citadel on brick platform overlooked each
   city and served as governmental and religious center; grid layout of cities; houses
   built with bricks and included bathrooms;
   brick sewer systems
2. All terms are defined in the Glossary.
3. Harappans, 68

4. Historians theorize destructive natural disasters. At Mohenjo-Daro there are signs of
   a violent end.
5. **CULTURAL DIFFUSION** Trade existed
   between the Indus Valley and Mesopotamia;
   some believe the Harappans learned about
   writing from the people of Mesopotamia.

2500 B.C.	2000 B.C.	1500 B.C.	1000 B.C.

c. 2500 B.C. Lung-shan culture begins in China.

c. 2000 B.C. Yu founds the legendary Xia dynasty.

c. 1700 B.C. Tang establishes the Shang, the first historical dynasty.

c. 1000s B.C. The Zhou dynasty comes to power.

Section 4

Early China

Read to Find Out
Main Idea *Early Chinese civilization made major cultural contributions.*

▶**Terms to Define**
   mandate

▶**People to Meet**
   Yu the Great

▶**Places to Locate**
   Huang He valley, Anyang

The Storyteller

What would the oracle say this time? Tang tried not to lean too far forward to watch as the fortune-teller began to apply red-hot coals to the turtle shell. A man of his station should not appear too anxious: his confidence in divine support should be seen by all. On the shell was inscribed a question known only to him: "Shall I attack before harvest?" So much depended on the answer. There was nothing to do now but wait for the fire to work on the brittle shell covered with scratchings, containing the destiny of China.

—adapted from *Ancient Records of Assyria and Babylon*, Volume 1, edited by Daniel David Luckenbill, 1968

A tortoise shell oracle bone from the Shang Dynasty

Even as the Harappans were meeting their mysterious fate, China's first dynasty had begun to assert its power over another river valley. This fourth river valley civilization has endured to the present day.

For many centuries the Chinese lived in relative isolation from the rest of the world. They called their homeland *Zhong Guo* (JOONG GWAH), or "the Middle Kingdom." To them it was the center of the whole world and the one truly supreme civilization. The lack of outside contacts allowed the Chinese to develop one culture across many regions and a strong sense of national identity as well. As a result, China has the oldest continuous civilization in the world.

China's Geography

China's varied geography has affected its historical development. Mountains make up about one-third of China's area. The Himalayas close off China to the southwest, and on the western border rise the Kunlun Shan and Tian Shan ranges. To the east of the Tian Shan lie the vast desert wastes of the Gobi. These rugged physical features hindered cultural diffusion both into and out of China for many centuries.

On the east, China's coastline touches the Pacific Ocean. Although some Chinese became devoted seafarers, they mostly focused on developing the agriculture of eastern China's fertile river valleys and plains. Unlike the land to the west with its forbidding terrain, the east welcomed life. For centuries large numbers of Chinese have farmed in the region's North China Plain.

Three major rivers drain eastern China: the Huang He (HWONG HUH); the Chang Jiang (CHAHNG JYAHNG), known also as the Yangtze (YANG•SEE); and the Xi Jiang (SHEE JYAHNG), also called the West River. The Huang He flows more than 2,900 miles (4,640 km) from the northern

Chapter 2 *Early Civilizations* **69**

TEACH

Guided Practice

THEME Innovation

Have students explain in class the distinctive features of early Chinese writing and metal casting. *(writing: characters represented objects, ideas, or sounds; large number of written characters limited the number of people who could read and write; metal casting: Chinese produced some of finest objects ever made from bronze.)* **L1**

Independent Practice

📁 Guided Reading Activity 2-4 **L1**

Visualizing History Oracle-bone inscriptions were usually made on the shoulder blades of animals, mainly oxen, or else on turtle shells. The questions that were asked the priest concerned sacrifices, weather, war, hunting, travel, or luck. The form of the question had to yield a yes or no answer.

Answer to Caption: *to have a record of the king's question and the answer*

NATIONAL GEOGRAPHIC SOCIETY

Use these materials to enrich student understanding of early China.

💿 **NGS PICTURESHOW CD-ROM**
India and China

📷 **NGS PICTUREPACK TRANSPARENCY SET**
Ancient China

Visualizing History Oracle bones used to obtain advice about military campaigns were often inscribed with the question and answer and preserved as part of the king's records. *Why were such oracle bones stored by the rulers?*

highlands eastward to the Yellow Sea. On its way it cuts through thick layers of loess (LEHS), a rich yellow soil. The river carries away large amounts of loess, which it deposits farther downstream. The abundance of yellow soil in the Huang's waters gives it its name—Yellow River. The Chinese sometimes call the Huang He "the Great Sorrow" because of the tragedy brought by its floods. However, the silt deposits brought by the flooding river have made the North China Plain a rich agricultural area.

A favorable climate also contributes to successful farming on the North China Plain. Melting snow from the mountains and the monsoon rains between July and October feed the Huang He. Farmers of the region have long depended on the seasonal rhythm of temperature and rainfall.

The Shang Dynasty

Very little is known about the origins of Chinese civilization. In the A.D. 1920s, archaeologists in the Huang He valley uncovered traces of Neolithic life in China. The magnificent painted pots of the Yang-shao (YAHNG•SHOW) culture found by the archaeologists date back to 3000–1500 B.C. Archaeologists have discovered that the Lung-shan culture, from about 2500–2000 B.C., used a potter's wheel to make delicate pots and goblets. These and other Neolithic finds dated to earlier than 5000 B.C. make it clear that the **Huang He valley**, like the river valleys of Egypt, the Fertile Crescent, and South Asia, invited settlement from very early times.

Chinese Myths

Over the centuries the Chinese developed many myths to explain their remote past. One myth

tells how the universe was created from the body of a giant named Pan Gu (PAHN GOO), who hatched from an egg. Other legends celebrate the deeds of hero-kings. These larger-than-life rulers included Yao (YOW), a person in the form of a mountain, and Shun, the master of elephants. Another, **Yu the Great**, was a miraculous engineer. According to a myth about Yu:

❝ When widespread waters swelled to Heaven and serpents and dragons did harm, Yao sent Yu to control the waters and to drive out the serpents and dragons. The waters were controlled and flowed to the east. The serpents and dragons plunged to their places. ❞

The myth about Yu—written much later than the first oral tellings—may reflect stories about the attempts of one or many early rulers to channel the floodwaters of the Huang He.

According to tradition, Yu the Great founded China's first dynasty, named **Xia** (SYAH), around 2000 B.C. Archaeologists, however, have yet to find evidence of the legendary Xia. The first dynasty to be dated from written records in China is the **Shang** (SHAHNG). The Shang ruled China from about 1700 B.C. to 1000 B.C.

Early Religion

Though the Shang kings were political leaders, they also performed religious duties. As high priests, they could communicate with nature deities on behalf of the people. They prayed, made offerings, and performed sacrifices to gain a good harvest, a change in the weather, or victory in battle. Kings also had special powers for calling upon their ancestors. To do so, they had a priest scratch a question on an animal bone or sometimes on a

---

COOPERATIVE LEARNING ACTIVITY

Bulletin Board Have students prepare a bulletin board depicting the early history of China. Have the class discuss what should be included in the display. Possibilities are maps showing areas of China ruled by early dynasties, maps showing what crops were grown, drawings of artifacts, and illustrations of the layout of an excavated city or cities. After the topics have been determined, assign small groups to research and prepare each one. Group members should assume responsibility for a specific task in connection with their part of the display. When the parts are completed, have the class design the bulletin board display and assemble it. **L2** 📦

tortoise shell. The priest then applied intense heat to the bone. The bone would crack, and the priest would interpret the splintered pattern of cracks as the answer to the king's question. The bones helped the kings to predict the future. The scratchings on the oracle bones, as they are called, are the first known examples of writing in China.

Important Achievements

The priests writing on the oracle bones used a script with many characters. These characters represented objects, ideas, or sounds and were written in vertical columns. To use the script with ease, a writer had to memorize each character. Because only a small percentage of the population could master all the characters, few people in ancient China could read and write.

Not only did the Chinese of the Shang period develop a written script, but they also perfected their metal-casting skills and produced some of the finest bronze objects ever made. These included bronze daggers, figurines, and ritual urns. They built massive ceremonial cauldrons that stood on legs. Bronze fittings adorned hunting chariots, and warriors carried bronze daggers. Artisans also carved beautiful ivory and jade statues. They wove silk into elegantly colored cloth for the upper class and fashioned pottery from kaolin, a fine white clay.

The Chinese built their first cities under the Shang. Archaeologists today have identified seven capital cities, including the city of **Anyang**

(AHN•YAHNG). Their excavations reveal the general layout of Anyang. A palace and temple stood at the center of the city, as in the cities of other early civilizations, and public buildings and homes of government officials circled the royal sanctuary. Beyond the city's center stood various workshops and other homes.

Expansion and Decline

Shang kings at first ruled over a small area in northern China. Later, their armies, equipped with bronze weapons and chariots, conquered more distant territories and finally took over most of the Huang He valley.

The Shang dynasty lacked strong leaders, however, and in time grew weak. Around 1000 B.C., Wu, a ruler of a former Shang territory in the northwest, marshaled his forces and marched on the capital. Wu killed the Shang king and established a new dynasty. Wu's dynasty, known as the Zhou (JOH), ruled China for 800 years.

Many Centuries of Dynasties

From the beginning of its recorded history until the early 1900s, dynasties ruled China. When writing about China's past, Western historians have followed the Chinese practice of dividing Chinese history into periods based on the reigns of these ruling families.

The Chinese believed that their rulers governed according to a principle known as the **Mandate of Heaven**. If rulers were just and effective, they received a mandate, or authority to rule, from heaven. If rulers did not govern properly—as indicated by poor crops or losses in battle—they lost the mandate to someone else who then started a new dynasty. The principle first appeared during the Zhou dynasty. Indeed the Zhou, as did later rebels, probably found the Mandate of Heaven a convenient way to explain their overthrow of an unpopular dynasty.

SECTION 4 ASSESSMENT

Main Idea

1. Use a chart like the one below to show the major contributions of early Chinese civilization.

Culture	City Planning	Artistic	Military

Recall

2. **Define** mandate.
3. **Identify** Yu the Great, Xia dynasty, Shang dynasty, Mandate of Heaven.

Critical Thinking

4. **Making Comparisons** Compare the Mandate of Heaven

with the way Egyptian kings justified their rule.

Understanding Themes

5. **Innovation** Explain the basic features of the Chinese writing system as it developed in early times. How widespread was it under the early dynasties?

Chapter 2 *Early Civilizations* **71**

SECTION 4 ASSESSMENT ANSWERS

1. culture: script with characters to represent objects, ideas, and sounds; artistic: used potter's wheel, developed metal casting, made silk cloth; city planning: palace and temple in city center; military: armies used bronze weapons and chariots, conquered most of Huang He Valley

2. All terms are defined in the Glossary.
3. Yu the Great, 70; Xia dynasty, 70; Shang dynasty, 70; Mandate of Heaven, 71
4. Chinese rulers claimed their right to rule was given by the gods; Egyptian pharaohs claimed to be gods or descended from gods. Chinese rulers used the Mandate of Heaven to justify overthrowing an

unjust ruler. Egyptian pharaohs expected to be worshiped as gods.

5. **INNOVATION** consisted of many characters representing objects, ideas, or sounds; written in vertical columns. Very few people in ancient China could read or write.

ASSESS

Check for Understanding

Assign Section 4 Assessment as homework or as an in-class activity.

🖥 Use Interactive Tutor Self-Assessment Software to review Section 4.

Evaluate

📁 Section Quiz 2-4

🖥 Use the Testmaker to create a customized quiz for Section 4.

Reteach

Have students survey the chapter and make a list of questions to test their knowledge. Have students quiz partners.

📁 Reading Essentials and Study Guide 2-4

Enrich

Have students find out more about the Huang He and report their findings orally in class.

📁 Enrichment Activity 2

CLOSE

Write on the chalkboard this statement from page 69: *China has the oldest continuous civilization in the world.* Have students explain what this statement means. Ask students to consider how isolation has affected China. (*Possible answer: It has built a strong national identity.*)

Block Schedule

Team Teaching This excerpt from *Gilgamesh* may be presented in a team-teaching context, in conjunction with English or Language Arts.

Gilgamesh

Historical Connection

The story of Gilgamesh shows the variety of deities worshiped by the Sumerians and the humanlike emotions of these deities.

Background Information

Setting Storytellers set the Gilgamesh tales in the distant past. By the time the stories were written, they probably were different from the original versions.

Characters Gilgamesh: Sumerian hero based on a king of the city-state of Uruk who lived in about 2700 B.C. He was considered part human and part god. Utnapishtim: an elderly man chosen by the gods to survive the great flood sent to the city of Shurrupak.

Plot Utnapishtim tells Gilgamesh how the gods directed him to build a boat on which he and selected animals survived a great flood. After finishing the tale of horrible destruction, Utnapishtim considers how he might help Gilgamesh search for eternal life.

Literary Element The story of Gilgamesh is an epic, a long poem telling about a legendary figure. The *Iliad*, the *Odyssey*, and the *Song of Roland* are among the most famous epics in European

from
Gilgamesh

retold by Herbert Mason

*L*ike people today, ancient Sumerians loved adventure tales featuring extraordinary heroes battling the forces of evil. Many Sumerian myths featured a king, Gilgamesh, who lived around 2700 B.C. The earliest known written accounts of Gilgamesh's adventures date from about 1850 B.C., making them the oldest surviving examples of epic poetry. An epic is a long poem recalling the exploits of a legendary hero. Gilgamesh, after the death of his friend Enkidu, searched for the secret of eternal life, which he hoped to share with his departed friend. In the following excerpt, Gilgamesh, hoping to learn how to escape death, listens to a mysterious elderly man, Utnapishtim, recount how he survived a great flood.

*T*here was a city called Shurrupak
    On the bank of the Euphrates.
It was very old, and so many were the gods
Within it. They converged in their complex
    hearts
On the idea of creating a great flood.
There was Anu, their aging and weak-minded
    father,
The military Enlil, his adviser,
Ishtar, the sensation-craving one,
And all the rest. Ea, who was present
At their council, came to my house
And, frightened by the violent winds that filled
    the air,
Echoed all that they were planning and had said.
Man of Shurrupak, he said, tear down your
    house
And build a ship. Abandon your possessions
And the works that you find beautiful and crave,
And save your life instead. Into the ship
Bring the seed of all living creatures.

I was overawed, perplexed,
And finally downcast. I agreed to do
As Ea said, but I protested: What shall I say
To the city, the people, the leaders?

BOUT THE AUTHOR

It is not known who first told the story of Gilgamesh. In ancient civilizations, stories were passed orally from generation to generation. With the development of writing in Mesopotamia, people began to record stories. The earliest tablets inscribed with the tales of Gilgamesh date from 1850 B.C., but the most complete set of stories was found in a library that belonged to an Assyrian monarch, Ashurbanipal, who ruled Nineveh from about 669 to 630 B.C.

Tell them, Ea said, you have learned that Enlil
The war god despises you and will not
Give you access to the city anymore.
Tell them for this Ea will bring the rains.

This is the way gods think, he laughed. His tone
Of savage irony frightened Gilgamesh
Yet gave him pleasure, being his friend.
They only know how to compete or echo.
But who am I to talk? He sighed as if
Disgusted with himself; I did as he
Commanded me to do. I spoke to them,
And some came out to help me build the ship
Of seven stories, each with nine chambers.
The boat was cube in shape, and sound; it held
The food and wine and precious minerals
And seed of living animals we put
In it. My family then moved inside,
And all who wanted to be with us there:
The game of the field, the goats of the steppe,
The craftsmen of the city came, a navigator
Came. And then Ea ordered me to close
The door. The time of the great rains had come.
O there was ample warning, yes, my friend,
But it was terrifying still. Buildings
Blown by the winds for miles like desert brush.
People clung to branches of trees until
Roots gave way. New possessions, now debris,
Floated on the water with their special
Sterile vacancy. The riverbanks failed
To hold the water back. Even the gods
Cowered like dogs at what they had done.
Ishtar cried out like a woman at the height
Of labor: O how could I have wanted
To do this to my people! They were *hers*,
Notice. Even her sorrow was possessive.
Her spawn that she had killed too soon.
Old gods are terrible to look at when
They weep, all bloated like spoiled fish.
One wonders if they ever understand

OTHER WORKS ABOUT GILGAMESH

Gardner, John, and John Maier, trans.
Gilgamesh. New York: Knopf, 1984.
Konacs, Maureen Gallery, trans. *The Epic of
Gilgamesh.* Stanford: Stanford University
Press, 1989.
Silverberg, Robert. *Gilgamesh the King.*
New York: Arbor House, 1984.

Picard, Barbara Leonie. *Three Ancient Kings:
Gilgamesh, Hrolf Kraki, Conary.* New York:
Warne, 1972.
Westwood, Jennifer. *Gilgamesh and Other
Babylonian Tales.* New York: Coward-
McCann, 1970.

Literature

literature. Some modern movies, such as *Star Wars*, could be considered epics as well.

FOCUS

Ask students to consider the type of deities worshipped by the Sumerians. Tell students that the story of the flood suggests that gods and goddesses had human emotions. Point out that the story gives little explanation for why the floods came, other than "Enlil/The war god despised you."

TEACH

Comparison

Students may be familiar with the story of the great flood in the Bible: Noah built an ark and filled it with animals. Encourage students to compare the Sumerian and Hebrew accounts. (*Students may note, for example, that the line "O the dove, the swallow, and the raven/Found their land" seems to parallel the Bible's mention of the raven and dove.*)

Interpretation

Ask students how they interpret "Abandon your possessions/And the works that you find beautiful and crave,/And save your life instead." (*Some students may see this passage as evidence that the gods were angered by the materialism of Sumerian society. Others may argue that it shows that the gods cared little for human achievements.*)

Bridge to the Past
Literature

Clarification

Refer students to "Bodies lay like alewives ... , dead/And in the clay." Explain to students that alewives live in the Atlantic Ocean off the coast of North America and in the Great Lakes. Although alewives are not actually found in Mesopotamia, they are similar to small fish that are found there.

Evaluation

Ask students to evaluate Utnapishtim's questions about the flood: "Why? Why did they/Have to die? I couldn't understand. I asked/ Unanswerable questions a child asks/When a parent dies—for nothing." Point out that the gods chose to save someone who would ask questions rather than someone who was unconcerned.

World Literature
Selection 1

Visualizing History
The most complete version of the Gilgamesh tales, found in the library of the Assyrian king Ashurbanipal, consists of 12 tablets, totaling some 3,000 lines. Each tablet describes one adventure of the hero.
Answer to Caption: *He says that they shall be like gods.*

ASSESS

Assign **Responding to Literature** questions.

That they have caused their grief. When the
    seventh day
Came, the flood subsided from its slaughter
Like hair drawn slowly back
From a tormented face.
I looked at the earth and all was silence.
Bodies lay like alewives [a type of fish], dead
And in the clay. I fell down
On the ship's deck and wept. Why? Why did they
Have to die? I couldn't understand. I asked
Unanswerable questions a child asks
When a parent dies—for nothing. Only slowly
Did I make myself believe—or hope—they
Might all be swept up in their fragments
Together
And made whole again
By some compassionate hand.
But my hand was too small
To do the gathering.
I have only known this feeling since
When I look out across the sea of death,
This pull inside against a littleness—myself—
Waiting for an upward gesture.

O the dove, the swallow and the raven
Found their land. The people left the ship.
But I for a long time could only stay inside.
I could not face the deaths I knew were there.
Then I received Enlil, for Ea had *chosen* me;
The war god touched my forehead; he blessed
My family and said:
Before this you were just a man, but now
You and your wife shall be like gods. You
Shall live in the distance at the rivers' mouth,
At the source. I allowed myself to be
Taken far away from all that I had seen.
Sometimes even in love we yearn to leave mankind.
Only the loneliness of the Only One
Who never acts like gods
Is bearable.

Visualizing History Gilgamesh subdues a lion. By the 700s B.C. Gilgamesh had become a mythological hero. The real Gilgamesh ruled over ancient Uruk. *What blessing did the war god give Gilgamesh and his family?*

ADDITIONAL LITERARY WORKS OF THE PERIOD

The Torah. The first five books of the Bible cover the history of the Jews until about 1200 B.C. The written texts of the Torah were collected and organized in the 400s B.C.

I am downcast because of what I've seen,
Not what I still have hope to yearn for.
Lost youths restored to life,
Lost children to their crying mothers,
Lost wives, lost friends, lost hopes, lost homes,
I want to bring these back to them.
But now there is you.
We must find something for you.
How will you find eternal life
To bring back to your friend?
He pondered busily, as if
It were just a matter of getting down to work
Or making plans for an excursion.
Then he relaxed, as if there were no use
In this reflection. I would grieve
At all that may befall you still,
If I did not know you must return
And bury your own loss and build
Your world anew with your own hands.
I envy you your freedom.

As he listened, Gilgamesh felt tiredness again
Come over him, the words now so discouraging,
The promise so remote, so unlike what he sought.
He looked into the old man's face, and it seemed changed,
As if this one had fought within himself a battle
He would never know, that still went on.

RESPONDING TO LITERATURE

1. How did Utnapishtim of Shurrupak survive the great flood?
2. How were the reactions of the gods and of Utnapishtim similar?
3. What questions would you ask Utnapishtim if you could meet him?
4. **Applying Information** What aspects of this tale about the great flood in Mesopotamia might apply to other cultures in other places and at other times?

CLOSE

Discuss what the tale about Gilgamesh and the flood might mean for people today. For example, ask students to consider how people today react to disasters such as floods, earthquakes, or explosions. Also ask students how people today try to escape death. *(exercise, diet)*

Contemporary Connection

For hundreds of years before it was written down, the *Gilgamesh* epic was passed from generation to generation. Ask students what makes a good story and a good storyteller. **What modern equivalents are there to heroic epics such as *Gilgamesh*?** *(Students may name books or movies that deal with a big, important topic; a long time span; or characters that behave heroically.)*

Portfolio Project

Have students research the archaeological investigations that have attempted to determine whether the great flood mentioned in *Gilgamesh* and the Bible actually occurred. Then have students write an essay on their position. Instruct students to support their position with evidence from their research. This activity may be an appropriate method of authentic assessment.

ANSWERS TO RESPONDING TO LITERATURE

1. At the command of the god Ea, Utnapishtim tore down his house and built a ship.
2. Both the gods and Utnapishtim were horrified by the death and destruction the flood caused and wondered why it had happened.
3. Students might want to ask Utnapishtim why he thought he was selected to survive the flood, whether he tried to discourage the gods from causing the flood, and what he thought of Gilgamesh.
4. A terrible disaster happening for no apparent reason and the struggle for survival of one individual are themes that could apply to other cultures in other eras.

Chapter 2 Assessment

Have students use the **Chapter 2 Self-Check Quiz** at worldhistory.glencoe.com to prepare for the Chapter Test.

GLENCOE TECHNOLOGY

VIDEODISC
Use MindJogger to review the chapter.

MindJogger Videoquiz

Chapter 2
Disc 1 Side A

Also available in VHS.

Answers

Using Key Terms

1. d   3. c   5. e
2. f   4. b

Using Your History Journal

Tell students that their picture-writing will be personal and may be harder for others to translate than the more standardized cuneiform.

Reviewing Facts

1. strong government; Babylon a major trade center; a law code covered the entire region; reorganized tax system; local officials built and repaired irrigation canals
2. built dams and escape channels to prevent floods; constructed canals and ditches for irrigation
3. The pyramids were tombs; the ziggurats were temples.
4. They have uncovered and examined Harappan artifacts [soapstone seals] in Mesopotamia.
5. bronze figurines and urns; ivory and jade statues; pottery; silk cloth
6. protected Harappan and ancient Chinese civilizations
7. Old Kingdom: Unification of Egypt, building of Great Pyramid; Middle Kingdom: Capital moved

---

Self-Check Quiz

Visit the *World History: The Human Experience* Web site at **worldhistory.glencoe.com** and click on *Chapter 2—Self-Check Quiz* to prepare for the Chapter Test.

Using Key Terms

Write the key term that completes each sentence. Then write a sentence for each term not chosen.

a. bureaucracy	g. mandate
b. city-state	h. monarchy
c. cuneiform	i. monsoon
d. dynasty	j. pharaoh
e. empire	k. polytheism
f. hieroglyphics	l. theocracy

1. In ancient China, the first historical _____, or line of rulers from one family, was called the Shang.
2. The ancient Egyptians carved onto pieces of slate a variety of picture symbols, or _____, that stood for objects, ideas, and sounds.
3. The Sumerian form of writing, _____, consisted of hundreds of wedge-shaped markings made by pressing the end of a sharpened reed on wet clay tablets.
4. A typical Sumerian _____ included the city itself and surrounding land.
5. Sargon I united all of the Mesopotamian city-states in a single _____, which consisted of many different territories under one ruler.

Technology Activity

Using E-mail Search the Internet for the E-mail address of an Egyptologist from an international museum or university. Compose a letter requesting information about various aspects of ancient Egyptian culture such as architecture, religion, hieroglyphics, or medicine. From your response, write a short report of your findings. Share your report with the class.

Reviewing Facts

1. **Government** Use a diagram like the one below to summarize important details about Hammurabi's Babylonian empire.

Hammurabi's Babylonian Empire

2. **Technology** Explain how the early Mesopotamians controlled the Tigris and Euphrates Rivers.
3. **Culture** Describe the major difference between the pyramids of Egypt and the ziggurats of Mesopotamia.
4. **Economics** Explain why archaeologists believe that there was contact between Mesopotamian and Harappan cultures.
5. **Culture** List the achievements of the ancient Chinese that show their artistic innovation.
6. **Geography** Describe how the Himalayas affected two early river valley civilizations.
7. **History** Identify one event from each of the following periods: the Old Kingdom, the Middle Kingdom, and the New Kingdom.
8. **Government** Name the capital of Upper Egypt that was established in 2050 B.C.
9. **Government** Explain why Amenhotep changed his royal name to Akhenaton.
10. **Government** Describe the main powers and responsibilities of a typical king of a Sumerian city-state around 2700 B.C.
11. **Government** List four examples of the kinds of laws found in Hammurabi's code. Explain why the code was a significant development.

---

to Thebes, Hyksos invasion; New Kingdom: reigns of Hatshepsut and Thutmose III, Akhenaton founds new religion
8. Thebes
9. Amenhotep declared that Egyptians should worship only one god, Aton. To show he was equal to Aton, he changed his name to Akhenaton, which means "spirit of Aton."
10. military leader and high priest; he and his priests supervised farming, enforced the law,

and set penalties for offenders
11. laws governing property, the protection of women, adoption and inheritance, and finances; under Hammurabi's code, crimes became the concern of government

Critical Thinking

1. Deities were associated with natural forces.
2. Egyptian kings were regarded as gods, while Shang kings were not. Both were political

Critical Thinking

1. **Apply** What clues do artifacts found in the ruins at Harappa and Mohenjo-Daro provide about the Harappan religion?
2. **Compare** How did the powers of the Egyptian kings differ from those of the Shang kings? How were their powers the same?
3. **Synthesize** What reaction would you have had to Akhenaton's reforms if you had been a priest of Amon-Ra?
4. **Compare** How did life along the Tigris and Euphrates Rivers in Mesopotamia differ from life along the Nile River in Egypt?

Geography in History

1. **Location** Refer to the map below. What is the relative location of the Sinai Peninsula? Find this peninsula on the Middle East map in the Atlas. What is its absolute location?
2. **Place** Why was most agricultural production in ancient Egypt and in that nation today found along the Nile River?
3. **Movement** Why would travel in ancient Egypt have been easier for a person who was going from south to north than for a person going from east to west? What might make travel from east to west less difficult today?

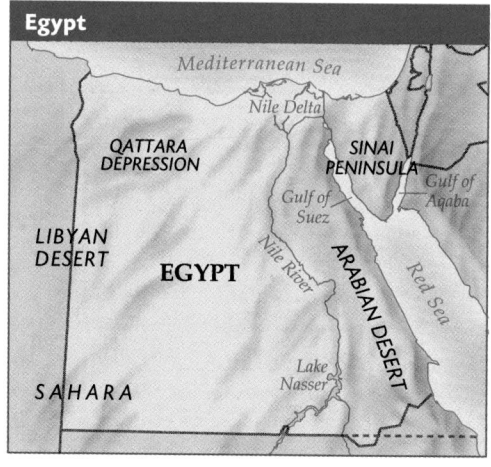

Skill Practice

Read about life in Harappan civilization in the Indus River valley on pages 67 and 68 in Section 3. Use this information to complete the following chart.

Harappan Life		
Occupations	**Artifacts**	**Theories of Decline**

Understanding Themes

1. **Relation to Environment** What flood-control methods of the ancient Egyptians and other river valley peoples are still in use today?
2. **Cooperation** In what areas of city life today is cooperation as important as it was when the Sumerians built the earliest cities?
3. **Cultural Diffusion** What advances in the twentieth century have made cultural diffusion easier and faster than in ancient times?
4. **Innovation** Why would you consider each of the following developments in ancient China an innovation: a writing script with many characters, bronze vessels and tools, pottery, and silk cloth?

Linking Past and Present

1. Examine Hatshepsut's role as a ruler of Egypt. How does her position and its influence compare with those of modern women holding high political office?
2. Why was early China largely isolated from the rest of the world? Do these same factors still affect modern China? In what ways have the modern Chinese increased contacts with other cultures? To what extent are they still isolated?

builder; artifacts: soapstone seals, jewelry, figurines; theories of decline: climate changes, destruction caused by invading peoples

Understanding Themes

1. **RELATION TO ENVIRONMENT** dams, canals, reservoirs
2. **COOPERATION** building and maintaining public buildings and areas, fighting societal problems (crime, poverty and drugs)
3. **CULTURAL DIFFUSION** telecommunications devices, computers, jet travel
4. **INNOVATION** a writing script with many characters: some represented sounds, unlike cuneiform; bronze vessels and tools: metal-casting skills were superior to those of other civilizations; pottery: artisans used a fine white clay called kaolin; silk cloth: earliest use of silk

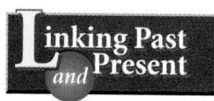
Linking Past and Present

1. Hatshepsut was a divine ruler; however, she had to be symbolically viewed as a man in order to carry out her role. Female rulers today, although not regarded as divinities, hold powerful positions in their own right as prime ministers and presidents.
2. mountains, deserts, plains, and seas; modern means of travel have largely overcome these barriers; increased global economic and cultural contacts, but Communist rulers are wary of outside influences challenging them

and religious leaders, and both performed ritual acts in order to benefit their people.
3. Priests resented the loss of their power.
4. The Nile yearly flooding was predictable and easy to "tame", while the Tigris-Euphrates' flooding was unpredictable and often brought hardships.

Geography in History
1. northeastern Egypt; 28°–31° N, 32°–35° E

2. The Nile River valley is fertile, while the rest of Egypt is desert.
3. south to north: could travel by boat or by land in Nile River valley; east to west: would have to cross vast desert; easier today because of modern roads and air travel

Skill Practice
occupations: farmer, trader, metalworker, pottery maker, weaver, jeweler, merchant, engineer,

? Chapter Bonus Test Question

Ask students: What factors can lead to the decline or fall of a civilization or dynasty? (*weak rulers, foreign invasion, natural disasters, climate changes*)

A complete, 1-page lesson plan is provided for each section in the *Reproducible Lesson Plans* booklet.

Kingdoms and Empires in the Middle East

CHAPTER RESOURCES

	Reproducible Resources	Multimedia Resources
Chapter Opener	Chapter Themes: Graphic Organizer 3 Historical Significance Chapter Activity 3	MindJogger Videoquiz
Chapter Enrichment	Vocabulary Activity 3* Time Line Activity 3 Mapping History Activity 3 History Simulation 3 Geography and History Activity 3 Source Reading 3 People in World History Profiles 3, 4 World Art and Music Activity 3 Enrichment Activity 3 Critical Thinking Activity 3 Skill Reinforcement Activity 3 Writer's Guidebook, Lesson 10 Performance Assessment Activity 3 Standardized Test Practice Workbook Activity 3 Inclusion for the Social Studies Classroom Strategies and Activities	Ancient Civilizations Poster Set: *The Fertile Crescent* Chapter Transparency 3 NGS PicturePack Transparency Set: *The Fertile Crescent* Vocabulary PuzzleMaker Software NGS PictureShow CD-ROM: *Egypt and the Fertile Crescent* World History Primary Source Document Library
Chapter Review/Reteaching	Reteaching Activity 3 Skill Reinforcement Activity 3 Spanish Chapter Summary 3	Chapter 3 Digest Audiocassette, Activity, Test* Vocabulary PuzzleMaker Software Interactive Tutor Self-Assessment Software MindJogger Videoquiz
Chapter Evaluation/Testing	Performance Assessment Activity 3 Chapter 3 Test, Forms A and B	ExamView® Pro Testmaker

* Also available in Spanish

0:00 **OUT OF TIME?** Assign the Chapter 3 Audiocassettes.

World History Primary Source Document Library

Make History Come Alive!

Engage your students with over 250 easily accessible primary source documents—available on this CD-ROM—that will give them real life insight into the important events of world history.

Block Schedule

Activities that are particularly suited to use within the block scheduling framework are identified throughout this chapter by the following designation.

KEY TO ABILITY LEVELS

Teaching strategies are coded for varying learning styles.

L1 **BASIC** activities for all students

L2 **AVERAGE** activities for average to above-average students

L3 **CHALLENGING** activities for above-average students

LEP **LIMITED ENGLISH PROFICIENCY** activities

Use Glencoe's *Presentation Plus!* multimedia teacher tool to easily present dynamic lessons that visually excite your students. Using Microsoft PowerPoint® you can customize the presentations to create your own personalized lessons.

Interactive Lesson Planner

Planning has never been easier! Using this CD-ROM, organize your week, month, semester, or year with all the help you need. The **Interactive Lesson Planner** gives you access to all of the blackline masters that accompany *World History: The Human Experience.*

SECTION RESOURCES

Daily Objectives	Reproducible Resources	Multimedia Resources
Section 1 **Trading Peoples** Explain how trading peoples influenced the development of the Middle East.	Lecture Notes 3-1 Reproducible Lesson Plan 3-1 Vocabulary Activity 3* Guided Reading Activity 3-1* Time Line Activity 3 Source Reading 3 Section Quiz 3-1* Reading Essentials and Study Guide 3-1	Section Focus Transparency 3-1 NGS PicturePack Transparency Set: *The Fertile Crescent* Interactive Tutor Self-Assessment Software Testmaker NGS PictureShow CD-ROM: *Egypt and the Fertile Crescent*
Section 2 **Early Israelites** Describe the role that slavery, exile, and return play in the history of the Israelites.	Lecture Notes 3-2 Reproducible Lesson Plan 3-2 Guided Reading Activity 3-2* Geography and History Activity 3 History Simulation 3 Mapping History Activity 3 Section Quiz 3-2* Reading Essentials and Study Guide 3-2	Section Focus Transparency 3-2 NGS PicturePack Transparency Set: *The Fertile Crescent* Vocabulary PuzzleMaker Software Interactive Tutor Self-Assessment Software Testmaker NGS PictureShow CD-ROM: *Egypt and the Fertile Crescent*
Section 3 **Empire Builders** Explain how a series of powerful empires extended their rule throughout the Middle East.	Lecture Notes 3-3 Reproducible Lesson Plan 3-3 Guided Reading Activity 3-3* Reteaching Activity 3 Enrichment Activity 3 Section Quiz 3-3* Performance Assessment Activity 3 Spanish Chapter Summary 3 Reading Essentials and Study Guide 3-3	Ancient Civilizations Poster Set: *The Fertile Crescent* Section Focus Transparency 3-3 NGS PicturePack Transparency Set: *The Fertile Crescent* Interactive Tutor Self-Assessment Software Testmaker NGS PictureShow CD-ROM: *Egypt and the Fertile Crescent*

* Also available in Spanish

Chapter Activities

 Performance Assessment Activity

Creating a Children's Book Have students take the roles of authors for a then-and-now children's book illustrating the concepts of trade, migration, cultural diffusion, and empires. Each set of facing pages should have an ancient example on the left accompanied by a modern-day example on the right. Illustrations and short explanatory paragraphs appropriate to an audience of young children should be included. Books may be sent to an elementary school.

Possible Rubric Features

Concept attainment, accuracy and extent of content information used, appropriateness to audience, visual appeal of product, clarity of text, relevance of modern-day examples

• *For an additional activity, refer to Activity 3 in the* Performance Assessment Strategies and Activities *booklet.*

ACTIVITY

From the Classroom of...

Terry Pollack
Shaker Heights High School
Shaker Heights, OH

Time Capsule

Make a "time capsule" by bringing in a wide-mouth bottle or a can and filling it with the following items, then covering all with sand:

1. a chart comparing several letters of the Hebrew, Greek, and German alphabets;
2. a map of early Israel and a map of modern Israel;
3. a copy of the Ten Commandments

Have students uncover the items one at a time and perform the following tasks:

1. Research the remaining letters in the alphabet and trace how many of them began their journey through the western world in ancient Israel.
2. Locate the cities of Jerusalem, Tyre, Sidon, and Petra on the maps of both modern and ancient Israel. Figure approximately how long these cities have been continuously occupied.
3. Discuss which commandments have been codified into contemporary law.

When students have completed the activities, discuss the many benefits the ancient Hebrews bestowed on the world.

MULTIPLE LEARNING STYLES

Verbal/Linguistic

Have students find copies of the Greek alphabet and the Hebrew alphabet. (Most dictionaries include these.) Ask students to make a chart displaying both alphabets, including both the symbol for each letter and the name of each letter. Discuss the similarities and differences between letters in these two alphabets and our own Roman alphabet.

Kinesthetic

Have students make a diorama portraying an event described in the chapter.

Interpersonal

Have students debate opposing sides of the following statement: The destruction of the Temple benefited the Jews.

Intrapersonal

Have students imagine that they are members of a people conquered by one of the kings described in the chapter. Ask them to write a short essay describing their experiences and emotions.

 GLENCOE'S ASSESSMENT ADVANTAGE

Use the following to easily assess student learning in a variety of ways.

- Performance Assessment Strategies and Activities
- Section Quizzes
- Chapter and Unit Tests
- Interactive Tutor Self-Assessment Software
- Testmaker Software
- MindJogger Videoquiz
- SAT/SAT II Test Practice
- worldhistory.glencoe.com

Additional Resources

NATIONAL GEOGRAPHIC SOCIETY

Teacher's Corner

INDEX TO NATIONAL GEOGRAPHIC MAGAZINE

The following articles relate to this chapter:

- "New Views of the Holy Land," by Richard Cleave and Technion-Israel Institute of Technology, June 1995.
- "Iraq: Crucible of Civilization," by Merle Severy, May 1991.
- "The Phoenicians: Sea Lords of Antiquity," by Samuel W. Mattews, August 1974.

NATIONAL GEOGRAPHIC SOCIETY PRODUCTS AVAILABLE FROM GLENCOE

To order the following, call Glencoe at 1-800-334-7344:

- *PictureShow: Egypt and the Fertile Crescent (CD-ROM)*
- *PicturePack: The Fertile Crescent (Transparencies)*
- *The Fertile Crescent (Poster Set)*
- *Picture Atlas of the World (CD-ROM)*

ADDITIONAL NATIONAL GEOGRAPHIC SOCIETY PRODUCTS

To order the following, call National Geographic at 1-800-368-2728:

- *Nations of the World Series, Israel (Video)*
- *Jerusalem: Within These Walls (Video)*

Access National Geographic's new dynamic MapMachine Web site and other geography resources at:

- http://www.nationalgeographic.com/
- http://www.nationalgeographic.com/maps/

BIBLIOGRAPHY

Literature About the Period
Tanakh—The Holy Scriptures. Philadelphia, New York, Jerusalem: The Jewish Publication Society, 1988. The standard Jewish Bible for the English-speaking world.

Readings for the Student
Saggs, H. W. *Everyday Life in Babylonia and Assyria.* New York: Dorset Press, 1987. Describes the life and customs of ancient Babylonians and Assyrians.

Readings for the Teacher
Pritchard, James B., ed. *Ancient Near Eastern Texts Relating to the Old Testament.* Princeton, NJ: Princeton University Press, 1969. Interesting parallels between Israelite culture and others.

WORLD HISTORY Online

Use our Web site as an additional resource. All essential content is covered in the Student Edition.

You and your students can visit the *World History: The Human Experience* Web site at worldhistory.glencoe.com The student text directs students to the Web site for the following options:

- **Chapter Overviews**
- **Student Web Activities**
- **Self-Check Quizzes**

Answers are provided for you in a link entitled "Web Activity Lesson Plan." Additional Web Resources, Interactive Puzzles, and content updates are also available.

Visit the Glencoe Web site at socialstudies.glencoe.com for social studies activities, updates, and links to other resources.

LOCAL OBJECTIVES

_____
_____
_____
_____
_____
_____
_____
_____
_____
_____
_____
_____
_____
_____
_____
_____
_____
_____
_____
_____

Chapter Themes are listed by section on this chapter opening page of the Student Edition. A corresponding theme-based activity is available under "TEACH," and a theme-based question is asked in the Section and Chapter Assessments.

The Storyteller

Historical Setting Archaeologists began to map the Assyrian city of Nineveh in 1820. During 1845–1851 British archaeologist Henry Layard studied the ruins of Nineveh. Layard brought back to England thousands of cuneiform tablets from the library of the palace of Ashurbanipal. The tablets provide examples of literature, religious thought, and administrative decrees. They also shed light on ancient Middle Eastern concepts of mathematics, botany, and chemistry. Scholars continue to learn about the ancient world by studying these tablets.

Historical Significance

Answers: *Traders spread languages, alphabets, commercial practices, customs, and ideas; religious thinkers introduced the concept of monotheism and ideas of human worth and accountability; empire builders developed methods of warfare, introduced legal systems, and organized complex societies.*
The alphabet, the concept of monotheism, and ethical laws that developed in the ancient Middle East have had lasting effects on civilization.

WORLD HISTORY Online

Have students use the **Chapter 3 Overview** at worldhistory. glencoe.com as a prereading and postreading exercise for understanding chapter content.

Chapter
3
2000–400 B.C.
Kingdoms and Empires in the Middle East

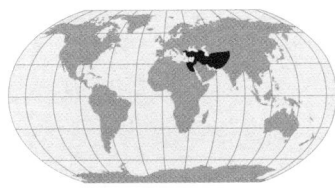

Chapter Themes

▶ **Cultural Diffusion** Aramaean and Phoenician merchants spread ideas throughout the Middle East. *Section 1*
▶ **Innovation** The Israelites contribute to the world the concept of monotheism. *Section 2*
▶ **Conflict** A series of empires— Hittite, then Assyrian, then Chaldean, then Persian—each conquers the previous one. *Section 3*

The Storyteller

Ashurbanipal, the last great Assyrian king, reigned in the mid-600s B.C. The dim rooms were almost still in Ashurbanipal's great palace at Nineveh, the splendid capital of his empire. Men with shoulder-length hair and squared-off beards glided in their tunics and sandals through the vast hallways. But the stone reliefs that decorated the palace walls told a less peaceful story. In intricately carved scenes, the impassive hunter in his chariot lets fly with a volley of arrows into a staggering lion, and the valiant general on the battlefield proudly waves his sword above the defeated enemy legions. Ashurbanipal followed a long line of ruthless Assyrian conquerors who boasted of their military exploits and cruelty.

Historical Significance

How did traders, religious thinkers, and empire builders shape the development of the ancient Middle East? How have their achievements influenced cultural and religious life today?

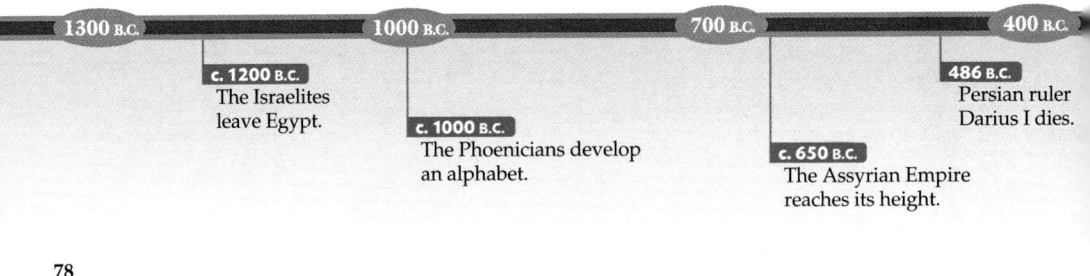

| 1300 B.C. | 1000 B.C. | 700 B.C. | 400 B.C. |

c. 1200 B.C. The Israelites leave Egypt.

c. 1000 B.C. The Phoenicians develop an alphabet.

c. 650 B.C. The Assyrian Empire reaches its height.

486 B.C. Persian ruler Darius I dies.

78

Location Using the Atlas in their texts, students should find the Middle East, including Iraq, Syria, Jordan, Israel, Turkey, Iran, Saudi Arabia, and Egypt, as well as the United States. How do the different countries compare in size with the states of the United States? *(Iraq: larger than California; Syria: slightly larger than North Dakota; Jordan: slightly larger than Indiana; Israel: about the size of New Jersey; Turkey: twice the size of California; Iran: slightly larger than Alaska; Saudi Arabia: one-third the size of the United States; Egypt: about the size of Texas, Oklahoma, and Arkansas combined)* Were boundaries in ancient times the same as those today? *(No.)*

History & Art Ashurbanipal hunting on horseback. Relief from the NW Palace at Nineveh, c. 640 B.C.

WORLD HISTORY Online

Chapter Overview

Visit the *World History: The Human Experience* Web site at **worldhistory.glencoe.com** and click on *Chapter 3—Chapter Overview* to preview the chapter.

Your History Journal

Early Middle Eastern accounts deal with the themes of peace and justice. Read the quotes on pages 86 and 93, and write similar verses describing events in the chapter that relate to these themes.

Chapter 3 *Kingdoms and Empires in the Middle East* **79**

History & Art Tell students that the main purpose of the designs on Assyrian reliefs was to glorify the king. Why do you think the Assyrian kings preferred scenes of military conquest or of hunting? *(to frighten their enemies)*

✔️ **Performance Assessment**

Refer to the activity on page 78C of the Planning Guide.

For an additional activity, refer to Activity 3 in the *Performance Assessment Strategies and Activities* booklet.

Using Your History Journal

Suggest to students that their verses focus on the achievements of individual biblical figures or of individual kings.

GLENCOE TECHNOLOGY

VIDEODISC
Use MindJogger to preview chapter content.

MindJogger Videoquiz

Chapter 3
Disc 1 Side A

 Also available in VHS.

➕ EXTRA CREDIT PROJECT

Research Report Have students research and report to the class on one or more of the gods worshiped by Assyrians, such as Ashur (chief god), Nabu (god of learning), Ninurta (god of war), and Ishtar (goddess of love). Suggested resources: H.W. Saggs, *Everyday Life in Babylonia and Assyria*.

1200 B.C.	1000 B.C.	800 B.C.	600 B.C.

c. 1200 B.C.
Aramaeans settle in central Syria.

c. 1100 B.C.
Phoenicians reach Spain and western Africa.

c. 600s B.C.
Lydians develop a wealthy kingdom in Asia Minor.

SECTION THEME

▶ **Cultural Diffusion** Aramaean and Phoenician merchants spread ideas throughout the Middle East.

Guide to Reading

For reading strategies to help students read effectively see pages 12–13. Have students think about the main head as they read the subheads.

Vocabulary Pre-check

▣ Use the Vocabulary PuzzleMaker for Chapter 3 to create a crossword puzzle to reinforce section terms. **L1 LEP**

📁 Use Vocabulary Activity 3 to introduce vocabulary terms. **L1 LEP**

FOCUS

Section Objective

Explain how trading peoples influenced the development of the Middle East.

BELLRINGER
Motivational Activity

Before taking roll at the beginning of the class period, project Section Focus Transparency 3-1 and have students answer the activity questions. Discuss students' responses.

📁 This activity is also available as a blackline master.

Section 1

Trading Peoples

Guide to Reading

Read to Find Out
Main Idea *Trading peoples influenced the development of the Middle East.*

▶ **Terms to Define**
confederation, alphabet, colony, barter

▶ **People to Meet**
the Aramaeans, the Phoenicians, the Lydians

▶ **Places to Locate**
Syria, Damascus, Tyre

𝓢 *The* toryteller

King Hiram was pleased. Tyre, his capital city, was a bustling seaport: sophisticated, cosmopolitan, and rich. Not only did the kings of Egypt and Babylon send ambassadors to Hiram's court, they also brought business to his land. Gold, copper, ivory, and linen from Egypt; precious stones from Babylon; silver from Asia Minor; and pottery from Crete enriched Tyre. In return, Tyre exchanged cedar, cut from the nearby mountains, and a vivid purple dye, harvested from murex shells found in the seas near the rocky coast. Hiram's people were Phoenicians, the people of the purple, the color—beautiful, costly, and rare—which throughout the ancient world marked an individual as one of immense wealth and high rank.

—adapted from *The Bible as History*, Werner Keller, translated by William Neil, 1969

Phoenician ship

The magnificent civilizations of Mesopotamia and Egypt greatly influenced neighboring peoples in the Fertile Crescent—among them **the Aramaeans** (AR•uh•MEE•uhnz) and **the Phoenicians** (fih•NEE•shuhnz). In turn, these trading peoples helped to spread their own cultures throughout the region and into much of the ancient world. Traveling on sailing ships and by caravan, traders from the Fertile Crescent brought languages, customs, and ideas along with their trade goods.

The Aramaeans

One of the most active peoples in early Middle Eastern trade, the Aramaeans settled in central **Syria** around 1200 B.C. Although Aramaean kings established a capital at **Damascus**, provincial leaders frequently challenged their authority. Despite political weaknesses, the Aramaeans gained control of the rich overland trade between Egypt and Mesopotamia.

Because Aramaean caravans crossed and recrossed the Fertile Crescent on business, people throughout the region learned Aramaic, the language of the Aramaeans. Until the A.D. 800s, the majority of the people living in the Fertile Crescent spoke Aramaic, a language closely related to Hebrew and Arabic. In addition, some parts of the Bible were written in Aramaic.

The Phoenicians

Between ancient Egypt and Syria lay the land of Canaan, today made up of Lebanon, Israel, and Jordan. The Phoenicians, one of the Semitic groups that migrated from the Arabian Peninsula about 3000 B.C., settled in the northern part of Canaan. Their neighbors in Canaan, the Philistines, came from the eastern Mediterranean. The Romans would

---

SECTION RESOURCES

📁 **Reproducible Masters**
- Lecture Notes 3-1
- Reproducible Lesson Plan 3-1
- Vocabulary Activity 3
- Guided Reading Activity 3-1
- Time Line Activity 3
- Source Reading 3

- Section Quiz 3-1
- Reading Essentials and Study Guide 3-1

📖 **Transparencies**
- Section Focus Transparency 3-1
- The Fertile Crescent

Multimedia
🖲 Interactive Tutor Self-Assessment Software
🖲 Testmaker
🌐 Egypt and the Fertile Crescent

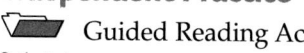

Merchants of the Mediterranean

In this illustration sturdy cargo boats dock in their North African home port of Carthage, and war galleys in the harbor lie in wait for any rivals caught in Phoenician waters. A captain bargains over the price of a bale of purple cloth for his next voyage as his crew unloads grain from Iberia and cedar logs from North Africa. Above sit clay jars of olive oil and wine; below, silver, gold, and ivory are stored. Departing vessels take on terra-cotta figurines, decorated ostrich eggshells, metal utensils, and perfume vials.

From their cities nestled along the coast of the eastern Mediterranean Sea, Phoenicians launched a trading empire. They soon became middlemen for their neighbors in Mesopotamia, Arabia, and Egypt. By 800 B.C., Phoenician trade had spread into the western Mediterranean. From Carthage and other Mediterranean cities, the Phoenicians manned supply depots, guarded sea lanes, and expanded their trading empire. ⊕

Chapter 3 *Kingdoms and Empires in the Middle East* **81**

TEACH

Guided Practice

THEME Cultural Diffusion

Ask students for a definition of the word *diffusion. (spreading or scattering widely)* Then ask if they know of other kinds of diffusion. *(scattering of light, spreading of different weather properties by air)* **L1**

Independent Practice

Guided Reading Activity 3-1 **L1**

←Picturing History

Ask students what is distinctive about the construction of the ships in the picture. *(The ships are much higher at the front and back; there is one large sail.)* As early as 1000 B.C. stemposts and sternposts were carved and painted as a way of identifying ships. Mediterranean peoples often placed a figurehead on the bow of their vessels. On Phoenician ships, the figurehead frequently was a carving of their principal god. The Carthaginians often featured a carving of their god Amon. The Phoenicians marked their trading route with lighthouses, which were illuminated by wood fires or torches.

NATIONAL GEOGRAPHIC SOCIETY

Use these materials to enrich student understanding of Phoenician culture.

🔘 **NGS PICTURESHOW CD-ROM**
Egypt and the Fertile Crescent

ASSESS

Check for Understanding

Assign Section 1 Assessment as homework or as an in-class activity.

 Use Interactive Tutor Self-Assessment Software to review Section 1.

Evaluate

Section Quiz 3-1

Use the Testmaker to create a customized quiz for Section 1.

Reteach

Have students summarize the business practices of the trading peoples discussed in this section and state how these practices made trade more efficient.

Reading Essentials and Study Guide 3-1

Enrich

Ask students to write a short scenario describing how using a system of record keeping could affect the relationship between trading partners.

CLOSE

Organize the class into two "nations": one with a bartering system and one with a monetary system. Ask each group to decide on a product to trade with the other group, the product's value, and a record-keeping system. Then ask them to role-play a trading situation, first using the bartering system and then the monetary system. Discuss the results.

---

later call southern Canaan *Palestine*, meaning "land of the Philistines."

In contrast to the Aramaeans, who trekked overland to reach their markets, the Phoenicians sailed the seas. On a narrow strip of land between the mountains of western Syria and the Mediterranean Sea, Phoenicia lacked enough arable land for farming, and many Phoenicians turned to the sea to earn a living. They harvested timber from nearby cedar forests to build strong, fast ships.

By 1200 B.C. the Phoenicians had built a string of cities and towns along their coast. Many of these scattered ports grew to become city-states, the largest of which were **Tyre**, Byblos, Sidon, and Berytus (modern Beirut). The city-state of Tyre often provided the leadership for what remained a confederation, or loose union, of independent Phoenician city-states. According to the Bible:

> ❝ Who was like Tyre.... In the midst of the sea? When your wares were unloaded from the seas, You satisfied many peoples; With your great wealth and merchandise You enriched the kings of the earth. ❞ —Ezekiel 27:32–33

The Phoenicians sailed from their coastal city-states throughout the Mediterranean. Expert navigators, they learned to plot their voyages with great accuracy by means of the sun and the stars. By 1100 B.C. Phoenicians reached the southern coast of Spain and the western coast of Africa. Some historians believe they even ventured as far as the British Isles in northwestern Europe.

Astute traders and businesspeople, the Phoenicians soon took charge of Mediterranean shipping and trade. At ports of call, they exchanged cedar logs, textiles dyed a beautiful purple, glass objects, and elegant jewelry for precious metals. They also brought new business practices, such as bills of sale and contracts.

An advantage that Phoenician merchants held over their competitors when keeping track of complex business deals was an improved alphabet—a series of written symbols that represent sounds. Phoenicians developed their efficient alphabet about 1000 B.C. from earlier, more complicated systems from southern Canaan and northwest Syria. The concise Phoenician alphabet used just 22 characters, each character representing a consonant sound. Readers mentally supplied vowels in the proper places.

The Phoenician system later became the foundation of several alphabets, including Greek, which in turn became the basis of all Western alphabets. Because the Phoenician alphabet did not require years of study to master, merchants no longer needed specially trained scribes to keep records.

To protect and resupply their ships, Phoenician sailors and traders set up along the coasts of the Mediterranean a network of temporary trading posts and colonies, or settlements of Phoenician emigrants. For example, about 814 B.C., people from Tyre founded a colony named Carthage on the coast of present-day Tunisia. Carthage eventually became the most powerful city in the western Mediterranean.

The Lydians

The **Lydians** (LIH•dee•uhnz) lived in Asia Minor—the peninsula jutting westward between the Mediterranean, Aegean, and Black Seas. Lydian merchants and artisans were well situated to prosper in the growing regional trade. By the late 600s B.C., the Lydians had developed a wealthy and independent kingdom famous for its rich gold deposits.

Most traders from neighboring cultures still relied on a system of barter for their transactions, exchanging their wares for other goods. The Lydians, however, began to set prices and developed a money system using coins as a medium of exchange. Soon Greek and Persian rulers began to stamp their own coins, and the concept of money spread beyond Lydia.

SECTION 1 ASSESSMENT

Main Idea
1. Use a chart like the one below to show how trading peoples affected development in the Middle East.

Aramaeans	Phoenicians	Lydians

Recall
2. **Define** confederation, alphabet, colony, barter.
3. **Identify** the Aramaeans, the Phoenicians, the Lydians.

Critical Thinking
4. **Evaluating Information** What geographic factors enabled the Phoenician city-states to remain independent and to prosper?

Understanding Themes
5. **Cultural Diffusion** Why was the Phoenician alphabet a significant development in world history?

SECTION 1 ASSESSMENT ANSWERS

1. Aramaeans: spread Aramaic, parts of Bible written in Aramaic; Phoenicians: great sailors, harvested timber, confederation of city-states, used bills of sale and contracts, improved alphabet, set up trading posts and colonies; Lydians: wealthy kingdom, set prices, used coins
2. All terms are defined in the Glossary.
3. Aramaeans, 80; Phoenicians, 80; Lydians, 82
4. their closeness to the sea and the sea trade they developed; their use and export of local resources, such as timber
5. **CULTURAL DIFFUSION** It was more efficient and easier to learn than the previous system.

2000 B.C.	1500 B.C.	1000 B.C.	500 B.C.

c. 1900 B.C.
Abraham settles in Canaan.

c. 1200 B.C.
The Israelites first celebrate Passover.

c. 1000 B.C.
David sets up capital at Jerusalem.

c. 530s B.C.
Jews rebuild the Temple in Jerusalem.

Section 2

Early Israelites

Guide to Reading

Read to Find Out
Main Idea *Slavery, exile, and return played an important part in the history of the Israelites.*

▶ **Terms to Define**
monotheism, prophet, covenant, exodus, Diaspora

▶ **People to Meet** the Israelites, Abraham, Moses, Deborah, David, Solomon

▶ **Places to Locate** Canaan, Jerusalem

The Storyteller

This battle would be decisive, Jael was certain. Before the sun set, the Israelites would be recognized as Yahweh's chosen people. Unlike the nomads who had passed through Canaan for generations, the 12 tribes of Israel now sought permanent settlement. However, to remain and prosper, the Israelites had to join together and defeat the threatening Canaanites. Several tribes of Israel, held together only by their common covenant with Yahweh, were sending armed men to battle. Jael, resolving to take action herself, if necessary, was sure that Yahweh would muster the heavens themselves to confound the enemies of the covenant, give victory to the Israelites, and bring peace to the land.

Mount Sinai

—adapted from the *Holy Bible,* Judges

*M*ost cultures of the ancient world worshiped many deities. The Phoenicians, for example, worshiped a chief god known as El, Baal, or Melqart; an earth-mother goddess called Astarte; and a young god of rebirth named Adonis.

The Israelites—another people living in **Canaan**—were an exception. They adhered to monotheism, the belief in one all–powerful God whose commands were revealed by prophets, or holy messengers. The Israelites believed that God, whom they called Yahweh, determined right and wrong and expected people to deal justly with each other and to accept moral responsibility for their actions. The teachings of the Israelites exist today as the religion of Judaism, which shares many beliefs with two other monotheistic religions—Christianity and Islam.

The Land of Canaan

The Bible remains one of the main sources of ancient history in the Fertile Crescent. As a record of the early Israelites, the Bible traces their origins to **Abraham**, a herder and trader who lived in the Mesopotamian city of Ur. Around 1900 B.C. Abraham and his household left Ur and settled in Canaan at the command of Yahweh, or God. The Israelites believed that God made a covenant, or agreement, with Abraham at this time. "I will make of you a great nation" was God's promise to bless Abraham and his descendants if they would remain faithful to God.

According to the Bible, once in the land of Canaan, the descendants of Abraham shared the land with other peoples, such as the Phoenicians and Philistines. Canaan contained rocky hills and desert, fertile plains and grassy slopes, with the best farming in the valley of the Jordan River. Many people lived as nomads herding sheep and goats.

Chapter 3 *Kingdoms and Empires in the Middle East* **83**

SECTION THEME

▶ **Innovation** The Israelites contribute to the world the concept of monotheism.

Guide to Reading

For reading strategies to help students read effectively see pages 12–13.

Vocabulary Pre-check

Use the Vocabulary PuzzleMaker for Chapter 3 to create a crossword puzzle to reinforce section terms. **L1 LEP**

Use Vocabulary Activity 3 to introduce vocabulary terms. **L1 LEP**

FOCUS

Section Objective

Describe the role that slavery, exile, and return play in the history of the Israelites.

BELLRINGER
Motivational Activity

Before taking roll at the beginning of the class period, project Section Focus Transparency 3-2 and have students answer the activity questions. Discuss students' responses.
This activity is also available as a blackline master.

SECTION RESOURCES

Reproducible Masters
- Lecture Notes 3-2
- Reproducible Lesson Plan 3-2
- Guided Reading Activity 3-2
- Geography and History Activity 3
- History Simulation 3
- Mapping History Activity 3

- Section Quiz 3-2
- Reading Essentials and Study Guide 3-2

Transparencies
- Section Focus Transparency 3-2
- The Fertile Crescent

Multimedia
- Vocabulary PuzzleMaker Software
- Interactive Tutor Self-Assessment Software
- Testmaker
- Egypt and the Fertile Crescent

TEACH

Guided Practice

THEME Innovation

Have students focus on the two Greek roots of the term for the early Israelites' major innovation: *monotheism*. After explaining that *monos* means "alone" or "single" and *theos* means "god," ask students for other words that incorporate either of the two roots. (*Answers may include* monogamy, monologue, monorail, *and* theocracy *and* theologian.) **L1**

The Exodus From Egypt
Why do Jews today celebrate Passover?
To commemorate their departure from bondage in Egypt.

Answer
Canaan lay northeast of Egypt and west of Babylon.

Use these materials to enrich student understanding of Mesopotamian cultures.

🔘 **NGS PICTURESHOW CD-ROM**
Egypt and the Fertile Crescent

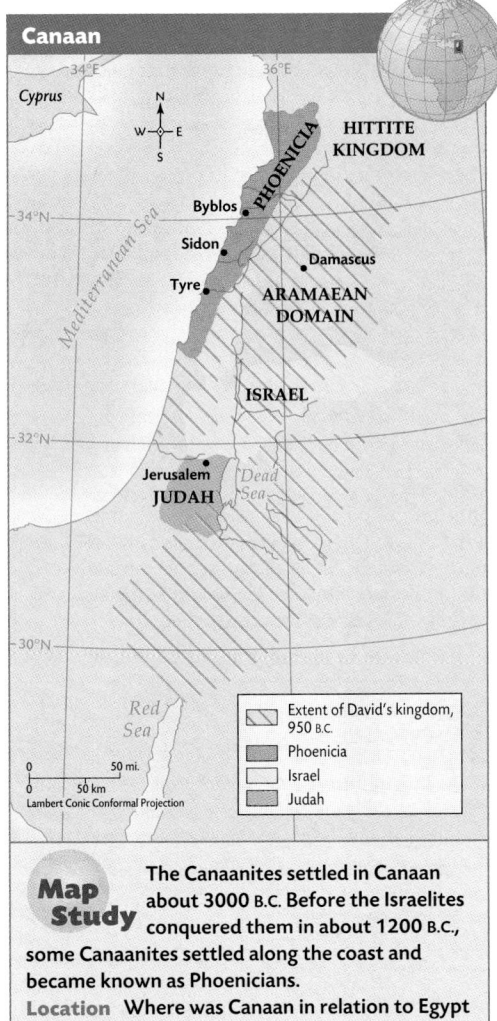

Canaan

Map Study The Canaanites settled in Canaan about 3000 B.C. Before the Israelites conquered them in about 1200 B.C., some Canaanites settled along the coast and became known as Phoenicians.
Location Where was Canaan in relation to Egypt and to Babylon?

Legend:
- Extent of David's kingdom, 950 B.C.
- Phoenicia
- Israel
- Judah

TURNING POINT

The Exodus From Egypt

Abraham's grandson Jacob, also known as Israel, raised 12 sons in Canaan, and each son led a separate family group, or tribe. These groups became the 12 tribes of Israel. To escape a severe famine, the Israelites migrated to Egypt. There they lived peacefully for several generations, until the Egyptians decided to enslave them.

In the 1200s B.C., the Israelite prophet **Moses** led his people out of Egypt in an exodus, or departure, into the Sinai Desert. Every year during the festival of Passover, Jews today retell the story of the Exodus from Egypt.

According to the Bible, during the long trek across the desert of the Sinai Peninsula, God renewed the covenant made with Abraham. Moses and the Israelites pledged to reject all gods other than the one true God and to obey God's laws, the most important of which would be called the Ten Commandments:

> **I the Lord am your God who brought you out of the land of Egypt, the house of bondage: You shall have no other gods beside Me.**
> **You shall not make for yourself a sculptured image....**
> **You shall not swear falsely by the name of the Lord your God....**
> **Remember the sabbath day and keep it holy....**
> **Honor your father and your mother, that you may long endure on the land that the Lord your God is giving you.**
> **You shall not murder.**
> **You shall not commit adultery.**
> **You shall not steal.**
> **You shall not bear false witness against your neighbor.**
> **You shall not covet ... anything that is your neighbor's.**
>
> —Exodus 20:2–14

In return for their loyalty, God promised the Israelites a safe return to the land of Canaan.

Settling the Land

Moses died before reaching Canaan, but his successor, Joshua, led the Israelites across the Jordan River into Canaan. For about 200 years, the Israelites fought the Philistines and the Canaanites who now occupied the land.

The Fighting Judges

Lack of unity among the 12 tribes of Israel prolonged the campaign to acquire Canaan. Leaders known as "judges" ruled each tribe. Serving as both judicial and military leaders, some of the judges attempted to rally the Israelites. The Bible relates how **Deborah**, a judge widely admired for her wisdom, planned an attack on a Canaanite army camped near Mount Tabor. The Israelites believed that through God's help, they won the battle.

84 Chapter 3 *Kingdoms and Empires in the Middle East*

COOPERATIVE LEARNING ACTIVITY

Reading and Summarizing Organize the class into small groups. Give each group a copy of *Exodus*: Chapters 1–13. Have all groups read Chapters 3–4 and summarize the points made in the dialogue between God and Moses. Divide the remaining chapters among the groups. Ask each group to read its section and work together to summarize the arguments Moses used to convince Pharaoh to let the Hebrews leave Egypt. Regroup students so that each chapter has been read by someone in each new group. Tell students to learn from other group members about the chapters they did not read. Ask students to write a paragraph comparing the arguments in later chapters with the original dialogue between God and Moses. **L2**

The Davidic Monarchy

Around 1020 B.C. continual warfare led most of the Israelite tribes to unite under one king, Saul. Although he was popular at first, Saul's power waned when he proved unable to defeat the Philistines. **David**, who had once fought the Philistine Goliath on Saul's behalf, took the throne in 1012 B.C. and ruled for the next 40 years. King David set up a capital at **Jerusalem**, organized a central government, and enlarged his kingdom's borders. During his reign, the Israelites enjoyed economic prosperity.

David's son **Solomon** succeeded his father in 961 B.C. Solomon founded new cities and lavished money on the construction of a magnificent temple to God in Jerusalem. The Israelites resented Solomon's high taxes and harsh labor requirements. After Solomon's death in 922 B.C., the 10 northern tribes broke away from the 2 tribes in the south. The northern tribes continued to call their kingdom Israel. The 2 southern tribes called their kingdom Judah, and kept Jerusalem as their capital. The word *Jew* comes from the name *Judah*.

Exile and Return

Although split politically, the people of Israel and Judah continued to share one religion. The 2 kingdoms, however, were too weak to resist invasions by powerful neighbors. In 722 B.C. the Assyrians of Mesopotamia swept in and conquered Israel, scattering the people of the 10 northern tribes throughout the Assyrian Empire. Then, in 586 B.C., another Mesopotamian people, the Chaldeans (kal•DEE•uhnz), gained control of Judah and destroyed the Temple in Jerusalem. They enslaved some of the city's residents and carried them off to exile in the Chaldean capital city of Babylon.

Exile in Babylon

During this difficult period, a series of prophets arose among the Israelites, who were called Jews after the Babylonian exile. Some prophets, such as Jeremiah, condemned abuses in society and blamed the exile on the Jews' forgetting their duties to God and to one another. The prophets also helped the Jews retain their religious culture during the exile.

While in Babylon, the Jews no longer had a temple. Instead, small groups of Jews began to meet on the Sabbath, the holy day of rest, for prayer and study. The rise of synagogues developed from these gatherings.

Rebuilding Jerusalem

Many Jews hoped to return to Jerusalem. Finally, in 539 B.C., the Persians conquered the

---

Science and Technology

Counting the Days

The modern week may trace its origins to the Jewish custom of observing a Sabbath day every seven days. Or it may have come from the Babylonian view that the number seven is sacred, a belief linked either to the four seven-day phases of the moon or to the seven planets then visible in the heavens. Ancient peoples developed lunar calendars, based on 29 days, the length of time it takes the moon to circle Earth. Of course, the lunar year of about 354 days did not match the solar year of 365 days. As a solution, the Babylonians added an extra month to certain years.

A modern sundial

Astronomers continued adjusting calendars to match the annual cycle of the seasons. In 46 B.C. the Roman ruler Julius Caesar decreed that months should be longer than a lunar month. He also introduced January 1 as the first day of a new year. But not until A.D. 1582 were errors in the Julian calendar corrected by Pope Gregory XIII, who formalized a self-correcting system of leap years. The Gregorian calendar used today by most people in the Western world closely matches the solar year.

Linking Past and Present ACTIVITY

Describe how our modern calendar differs from the ancient Babylonian calendar. Then, research current proposals for calendar reform. Would you support any of the proposed changes? Why or why not?

Independent Practice

Guided Reading Activity 3-2 **L1**

Daily Life Ask students to find out some differences between the Hebrew alphabet and the English alphabet. *(The Hebrew alphabet is read from right to left and has essentially no vowels.)* **L2**

Linking Past and Present

Counting the Days

Our names for the days of the week also can be traced back to ancient times. The Babylonians named each of the seven days after a god who ruled one of the seven planets then visible. The Romans and the Anglo-Saxons simply substituted the names of their gods. The Babylonian god that ruled Jupiter, for example, was Marduk, who gave his name to the fifth day. The ancient Romans gave the name Jove to this day (in French, it is *jeudi*). The Anglo-Saxons in turn called it after their god Thor—*Thursday*.

ANSWERS

Our months are one or two days longer than the lunar month, and we add a day each leap year. Calendar reform—two calendars have been proposed: The Fixed Calendar (13 months with four weeks each month) and The World Calendar (12 months of 30 or 31 days). Students may point out practical difficulties of switching to a new calendar; or they may state that the reform proposals are designed to simplify the present calendar.

ASSESS

Check for Understanding

Assign Section 2 Assessment as homework or as an in-class activity.

MEETING SPECIAL NEEDS ACTIVITY

Language Delayed Organize students with limited English proficiency into two groups. Have one group prepare a poster on King David and the other a poster on King Solomon. Explain that each poster should summarize information about the king. Have students work together to choose the information and then decide on a format for presenting it on the poster. Encourage the students to include copies of art depicting "their" king. Pair students from the two groups and have them describe their posters. **L1 LEP**

Visualizing History

To this day, after a scribe finishes copying the Torah onto parchment sheets, the sheets are sewn together with special thread made from animal muscles. The connected sheets are then attached to rollers.
Answer to Caption: *Micah envisioned a peaceful world.*

Evaluate

📁 Section Quiz 3-2

🖥 Use the Testmaker to create a customized quiz for Section 2.

Reteach

Have students select three major figures from early Hebrew history and write several paragraphs describing their contributions.

📁 Reading Essentials and Study Guide 3-2

Enrich

Have students research the Jewish festival of Passover and write a report on its origin and significance. Encourage them to interview a person of the Jewish faith to get a personal perspective.

CLOSE

Organize the class into small groups. Ask the groups to describe how Jews changed their rituals when they no longer had the Jerusalem Temple. Have them compare these methods of worship with those of other religions.

Chaldeans. The Persian king, Cyrus II, allowed the Jews to return to Judah and to rebuild the Temple. In the 400s B.C., Jewish holy writings were organized into the Torah, made up of the first five books of the Bible: Genesis, Exodus, Leviticus, Numbers, and Deuteronomy.

Many Jews, however, remained in Babylon, and some migrated to other areas in the Middle East. Ever since this time, communities of Jews have existed outside their homeland in what is known as the Diaspora, a Greek word meaning "scattered."

A Lasting Legacy

Their troubled history—with cycles of slavery, exile, and return—made the Jews keenly aware of their past. Seeing events as having a God-directed purpose, the Jews recorded their history and examined it for meaning. The Jewish Scriptures begin with the Torah, which states that God created the universe and that humans have infinite worth:

Visualizing History Scribes recopied the Torah carefully, from the original copy. *What was the prophet Micah's vision for the world?*

> **God created humankind in his image, in the image of God did he create it, male and female did he create them. God blessed them, God said to them: Bear fruit and be many and fill the earth and subdue it! Have dominion over the fish of the sea, the fowl of the heavens, and all living things that crawl upon the earth!**
>
> –Genesis 1:27–28

The Jewish Scriptures also include the writings of the prophets. The prophetic teachings state that humans work in partnership with God, striving to achieve a perfect world, and this link makes people accountable for what happens in the world. The prophet Micah expressed his vision for the world as follows:

> **And they shall beat their swords into plowshares, And their spears into pruning hooks. Nation shall not take up Sword against nation; They shall never again know war; But every man shall sit Under his grapevine or fig tree With no one to disturb him.**
>
> –Micah 4:3–4

As the Jews scattered beyond Canaan, they took their sacred writings with them. Jewish religious beliefs and ethical principles became an important part of the heritage of the West.

SECTION 2 ASSESSMENT

Main Idea
1. Use a chart like the one below to show the significance of three major events in Jewish history.

Event	Significance
1.	
2.	
3.	

Recall
2. Define monotheism, prophet, covenant, exodus, Diaspora.
3. Identify the Israelites, Abraham, Moses, Deborah, David, Solomon.

Critical Thinking
4. Analyzing Information Create a chronology of the migrations of the Israelites.

Understanding Themes
5. Innovation What religious beliefs set the Israelites apart from other ancient peoples?

SECTION 2 ASSESSMENT ANSWERS

1. Possibilities: exodus led to renewal of God's covenant; exile allowed for development of synagogues; return to Judah led to recording of Jewish history
2. All terms are defined in the Glossary.
3. the Israelites, 83; Abraham, 83; Moses, 84; Deborah, 84; David, 85; Solomon, 85
4. should begin with Abraham departing Mesopotamia about 1900 B.C. and end with the return to Judah under Cyrus
5. **INNOVATION** beliefs in one all-powerful God and moral responsibility; belief that their existence as a people had a God-directed purpose

Critical Thinking SKILLS

Problem Solving

You have just done poorly on a geography exam. You wonder why you can't do better since you always go to class, take notes, and study for exams. In order to improve your grades, you need to identify the specific problem, and then take actions to solve it.

Learning the Skill

There are six key steps that will help you through the problem-solving process.

1. Identify the problem. In this case, you are not doing well on geography exams.
2. Gather information. You know that you always go to class and take notes. You study by yourself for about two hours each day for two or three days before the exam. You also know that as you are taking the exam, you sometimes forget details or get confused.
3. List and consider options. For example, instead of studying by yourself, you might try a study group, or studying with a friend.
4. Consider the advantages and disadvantages of each option.
5. Once you have listed and considered the options, choose the best solution.
6. Evaluate the effectiveness of the solution. This will help you determine if you've solved the problem. If, on the next few geography exams, you earn better scores, you know that you have solved your problem.

Practicing the Skill

Reread the material in Section 1 on pages 80–82 about the trading peoples of the Middle East. Then, answer the following questions.

1. What problem did the Phoenicians encounter as they tried to farm the land of Phoenicia?
2. Summarize information the Phoenicians might have gathered after finding that they couldn't rely on farming as a means of survival.
3. List some of the options available to the Phoenicians. What were the advantages? What were the disadvantages?

4. Explain the solution the Phoenicians implemented to solve their problem.
5. Evaluate the effectiveness of their solution. Was it successful? How do you decide this?

Applying the Skill

The conservation club at your school has no money to continue its recycling project. The school district allocated money to the club at the beginning of the year, but that money has been spent. You might be able to get more funding if you can convince the school district that yours is a worthy project. As a member of the club, you have been asked to join a committee to save the conservation club and this project. Write an essay describing the problem, the list of options and their advantages and disadvantages, a solution, and an evaluation of the chosen solution.

For More Practice

Turn to the Skill Practice in the Chapter Assessment on page 95 for more practice with problem solving.

The **Glencoe Skillbuilder Interactive Workbook**, Level 2 provides instruction and practice in key social studies skills.

TEACH

Problem Solving Before students read the skill, ask them to describe some problems they have had and explain how they solved these problems. Then point out to the students that problem solving is similar to climbing a set of stairs. You start at the bottom and climb one step at a time to reach the top. Next, draw stairs with six steps. Write the following information on each step, starting with the bottom:

1. Identify problem.
2. Gather information.
3. List options.
4. Consider advantages and disadvantages of options.
5. Choose and implement a solution.
6. Evaluate effectiveness of solution.

Then have students read the skill and complete the questions.

Additional Practice

📁 Skill Reinforcement Activity 3

GLENCOE TECHNOLOGY

Glencoe's **Skillbuilder Interactive Workbook, Level 2**
This interactive CD-ROM promotes student mastery of key social studies skills.

ANSWERS TO PRACTICING THE SKILL

1. lack of arable land for farming
2. The text offers that Phoenicia had a long coastline near the Mediterranean Sea and had cedar forests on nearby slopes.
3. Possible options: herding, hunting, fishing, trading. <u>Advantages</u>: herding—possible on slopes; hunting—not dependent on arable land; fishing—located near the sea; trading—located near possible sea routes. <u>Disadvantages</u>: herding and hunting—needed to move to find food for animals or animals to hunt, so could not establish

permanent settlements; fishing—needed fishing boats; trading—needed strong, fast ships, goods to trade, people to trade with, and navigational skills.

4. They became traders to earn a living; harvested timber from the cedar forests to build strong, fast ships; established coastal city-states throughout the Mediterranean Sea; became expert navigators using the sun and the stars.
5. yes; they took charge of Mediterranean shipping and trade

For reading strategies to help students read effectively see pages 12–13.

SECTION THEME

▶ **Conflict** A series of empires—Hittite, then Assyrian, then Chaldean, then Persian—each conquers the previous one.

Guide to Reading

Vocabulary Pre-check

🔲 Use the Vocabulary PuzzleMaker for Chapter 3 to create a crossword puzzle to reinforce section terms. **L1 LEP**

📁 Use Vocabulary Activity 3 to introduce vocabulary terms. **L1 LEP**

FOCUS

Section Objective

Explain how a series of powerful empires extended their rule throughout the Middle East.

BELLRINGER
Motivational Activity

Before taking roll at the beginning of the class period, project Section Focus Transparency 3-3 and have students answer the activity questions. Discuss students' responses.

📁 This activity is also available as a blackline master.

2000 B.C.　　1500 B.C.　　1000 B.C.　　500 B.C.

c. 1600 B.C.
Hittite Empire reaches its height.

c. 605 B.C.
Nebuchadnezzar begins reign in Babylon.

525 B.C.
Persian armies conquer Egypt.

Section 3

Empire Builders

Guide to Reading

Read to Find Out
Main Idea *A series of powerful empires extended their rule throughout the Middle East.*

▶ **Terms to Define**
satrap

▶ **People to Meet**
the Hittites, the Assyrians, the Chaldeans, Nebuchadnezzar, the Persians, Cyrus II, Darius I, Zoroaster

▶ **Places to Locate** Anatolia, Babylon, Nineveh, Persepolis

The Storyteller

The scribe carefully recorded King Ashurbanipal II's proclamation. The royal archives would preserve an accurate account of the actions taken against the cities that had dared to revolt. The king dictated: "With the fury of my weapons I stormed the city. I flayed all the chief men who had revolted, and I covered a pillar with their skins. Some I impaled on the pillar on stakes.... I fashioned a heroic image of my royal self, my power and my glory I inscribed thereon...." Ashurbanipal called the gods to destroy all who opposed him, overthrowing their kingdoms and blotting out their names from the land.

Giant winged bull

—from *Ancient Records of Assyria and Babylonia*, Volume 1, edited by Daniel David Luckenbill, 1968

The Phoenicians, Aramaeans, Lydians, and Israelites gave the world their alphabets, languages, commercial practices, and religious beliefs. These peoples, however, lacked the military power of their neighbors, and the conquering armies of a series of warlike empires came to rule the Fertile Crescent.

The Hittites

Around 2000 B.C., **the Hittites**—perhaps coming from areas beyond the Black Sea—conquered the local people of Asia Minor. The Hittites set up several city-states on a central plateau called **Anatolia**, and by about 1650 B.C., they had built a well-organized kingdom. Archaeologists have deciphered the writing on some of the clay tablets found in the ruins of Hattusas, the Hittite capital. Other information about the Hittites comes from records of peoples they confronted as they expanded their empire. An Egyptian source, for example, described the Hittites' custom of wearing their hair in a long, thick pigtail that hung down in the back.

Hittite kings assembled a fearsome army—the first in the Middle East to wield iron weapons extensively. The army used light, spoked-wheel chariots that could carry two soldiers and a driver. This gave the Hittites a decided advantage in battle, because they were able to field twice as many troops as their foes in two-person chariots. Overwhelming any army that stood in their way, the Hittites pushed eastward and conquered the city of **Babylon** about 1595 B.C. The Hittite Empire—spanning Asia Minor, Syria, and part of Mesopotamia—lasted until about 1200 B.C.

The Hittites largely borrowed their culture from Mesopotamia and Egypt. However, they did contribute to Middle Eastern civilization a legal system considered less harsh than Hammurabi's code. Hittite law emphasized payments for damages rather than harsh punishments.

SECTION RESOURCES

📁 **Reproducible Masters**
- Lecture Notes 3-3
- Reproducible Lesson Plan 3-3
- Guided Reading Activity 3-3
- Reteaching Activity 3
- Enrichment Activity 3
- Section Quiz 3-3
- Performance Assessment Activity 3

- Spanish Chapter Summary 3
- Reading Essentials and Study Guide 3-3

📖 **Transparencies**
- Section Focus Transparency 3-3
- The Fertile Crescent

Multimedia
💻 The Fertile Crescent
🔲 Interactive Tutor Self-Assessment Software
🔲 Testmaker
🌐 Egypt and the Fertile Crescent

The Assyrians

The Assyrians, a people living in northern Mesopotamia, had faced constant invasions from adjoining Asia Minor—including those by the Hittites. About 900 B.C. the Assyrians finally became strong enough to repel attacks from the west. They also began to launch their own military campaigns to subdue their Mesopotamian neighbors.

A Powerful Army

The Assyrian army earned a reputation as the most lethal fighting force in the Middle East. The Assyrians organized their warriors into units of foot soldiers, charioteers, and fast-moving cavalry fighting on horseback. They were described as fighters "whose arrows were sharp and all their bows bent, the horses' hooves were like flint, and their [chariot] wheels like a whirlwind." The Assyrians fought with iron weapons and used battering rams against the walls of the cities they attacked.

The Assyrians treated conquered peoples cruelly. They burned cities and tortured and killed thousands of captives. The Assyrians routinely deported entire populations from their homelands. Resettling the land with people from other parts of the empire, the Assyrians forced these settlers to pay heavy taxes.

The Assyrian Empire

By about 650 B.C., the Assyrian kings governed an empire stretching from the Persian Gulf to Egypt and into Asia Minor. They divided their empire into provinces, each headed by a governor directly responsible to the king. Officials sent from the central government collected taxes to support the army and to fund building projects in **Nineveh**, the Assyrian capital. To improve communication, the Assyrians built a network of roads linking the provinces. Government messengers and Aramaean merchants traveled these roads, protected by soldiers from bandits.

In spite of these links, the Assyrian Empire eventually began to fracture as conquered peoples continually rebelled. In 612 B.C. **the Chaldeans**, who lived in the ancient city of Babylon, formed an alliance with the Medes from the east. The alliance captured Nineveh and brought down the Assyrian Empire.

The Chaldeans

Soon after the Assyrians fell, the Chaldean Empire succeeded in dominating the entire Fertile Crescent. Most of the Chaldeans—sometimes called the New Babylonians—were descended from people of Hammurabi's Babylonian Empire of the 1700s B.C.

The Chaldeans reached the height of their power during the reign of one of their greatest rulers, King **Nebuchadnezzar** (NEH•byuh•kuhd

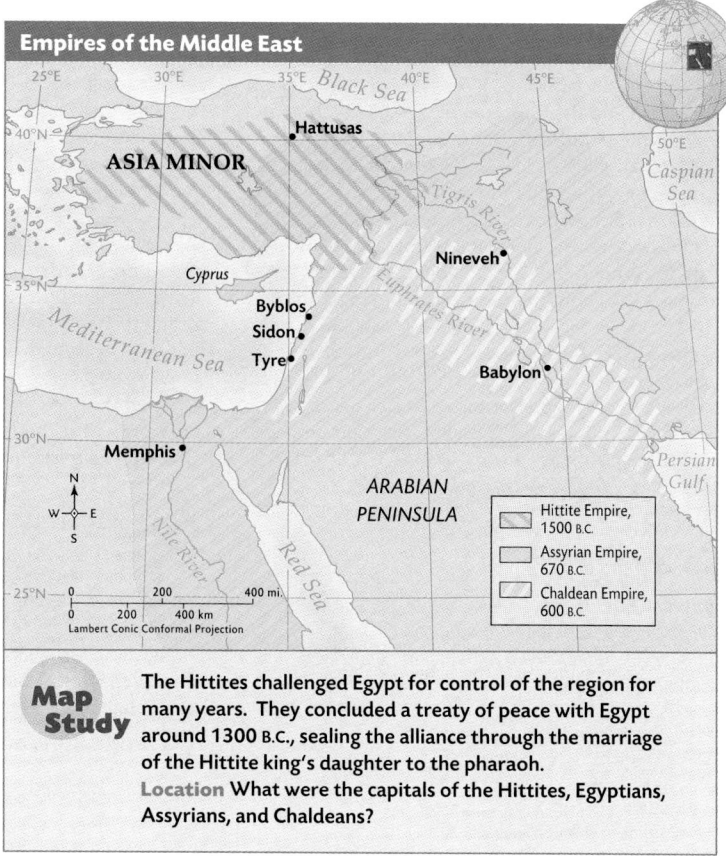

Empires of the Middle East

Map Study

The Hittites challenged Egypt for control of the region for many years. They concluded a treaty of peace with Egypt around 1300 B.C., sealing the alliance through the marriage of the Hittite king's daughter to the pharaoh.
Location What were the capitals of the Hittites, Egyptians, Assyrians, and Chaldeans?

Hittite Empire, 1500 B.C.
Assyrian Empire, 670 B.C.
Chaldean Empire, 600 B.C.

TEACH

Guided Practice

THEME Conflict
Have students compare the ways in which conquered peoples were treated by the Assyrians and the Persians. Discuss: Which methods are more likely to lead to conflict? **L1**

Critical Thinking Have students discuss if governments today might profit from certain principles of governmental organization of ancient Middle Eastern empires. **L3**

Geography: Movement Have students make travel plans for an ancient Greek who wants to visit one of the empires discussed in this section. Have them plot the route on an outline map, and then write a detailed description of it, including method of travel and a description of each site to be visited. **L2**

Map Study

Answer
Hittites: Hattusas; Egyptians: Memphis; Assyrians: Nineveh; Chaldeans: Babylon

Map Skills Practice

Reading a Map Which empire included the former Egyptian capital? *(Assyrian)*

Interview Organize the class into groups of four to six to plan interviews. Have students first work cooperatively to research and create a character who lived in Nebuchadnezzar's Babylon. Then have them plan an interview that elicits details about the character's life in the city of the Hanging Gardens. In planning and carrying out the interview, each student should assume one of these roles: interviewer, costume designer, editor, photographer, keyboardist, and interviewee. Tell students that the final product is to be a printed version of the interview with accompanying photographs. Display these on the bulletin board. **L2**

Independent Practice

 Guided Reading Activity 3-3 **L1**

Geography: Environment In the Hanging Gardens, Nebuchadnezzar put plants that would remind his wife of her home in the mountains of Media (northwestern Iran). Have students make a catalog of plants that Nebuchadnezzar might have placed in the Hanging Gardens had his wife come from the students' own region. **L1 LEP**

NATIONAL GEOGRAPHIC SOCIETY

Use these materials to enrich student understanding of Middle Eastern civilizations.

- **NGS PICTURESHOW CD-ROM**
  Egypt and the Fertile Crescent
- **NGS PICTUREPACK TRANSPARENCY SET**
  The Fertile Crescent
- **ANCIENT CIVILIZATIONS POSTER SET**
  The Fertile Crescent

WORLD HISTORY Online

Have students use the **Chapter 3 Student Web Activity** at worldhistory.glencoe.com for in-depth study of Babylon.

•NEH•zuhr), from 605 B.C. to 562 B.C. He extended the boundaries of the Chaldean Empire as far west as Syria and Canaan, conquering the city of Jerusalem and the Phoenician city-state of Tyre and forcing the people of the kingdom of Judah into a Babylonian exile in 586 B.C. Nebuchadnezzar also amassed great wealth and rebuilt Babylon into one of the most beautiful cities of the ancient world.

Historians of the time counted a feature of Babylon among the so-called Seven Wonders of the World—its Hanging Gardens. Nebuchadnezzar created the Hanging Gardens for his wife. Constructed on several levels and designed to be visible from any point in Babylon, the elaborate park was fed by water pumped from a nearby river. Another landmark of Babylon was an immense wall that snaked around the city, stood 50 feet (15 km) high, and bristled with watchtowers every 100 yards (90 m).

The Chaldeans were also noted for their interest in astrology. They recorded their observations of the stars and made maps that showed the position of the planets and the phases of the moon. Their studies laid the foundations for the science of astronomy.

After Nebuchadnezzar's death, a series of weak kings held the throne. Poor harvests and slow trade further sapped the strength of an empire whose people had been severely taxed and plundered. Then, in 539 B.C., **the Persians** under **Cyrus II** came from the mountains to the northeast, seized Babylon, and then conquered the rest of the Chaldean Empire.

The Persians

The Persians originated from a larger group of people now called Indo-Europeans. As warriors and cattle herders in search of new grasslands, the Persians and the Medes, another Indo-European group, left central Asia about 2000 B.C. They settled on a plateau between the Persian Gulf and the

Student Web Activity 3

Visit the *World History: The Human Experience* Web site at **worldhistory.glencoe.com** and click on *Chapter 3—Student Web Activities* for an activity relating to Babylon.

Images of the Times

Ancient Persepolis

The most luxurious palace of Darius was built at Persepolis. Completed by Xerxes, the palace was a monument to the king's power.

Alexander the Great destroyed most of the palace in 331 B.C., but the stone monumental gateways and terraces survived.

Bronze image of a Persian chariot

90

Images of the Times Ancient Persepolis

The location of Persepolis, in a remote and mountainous region, limited its use as a royal residence mainly to springtime. Among the cuneiform inscriptions archaeologists found cut in stone at Persepolis is one on the south retaining wall. The inscription gives Darius's prayer for his people: "God protect this country from foe, famine, and falsehood."

Caspian Sea, in the area of present-day Iran.

Cyrus's Conquests

During the 540s B.C., Cyrus had developed a strong army, conquered the Medes, and advanced into neighboring lands. He added northern Mesopotamia, Syria, Canaan, and the Phoenician cities to his empire. Cyrus also took over the kingdom of Lydia and the Greek city-states in Asia Minor. In 525 B.C. Cyrus's son Cambyses (kam•BY•seez) conquered Egypt, bringing all of the Middle East under Persian control.

The Persian Empire, then second to none, stretched from the Nile River to the Indus River, a distance of 3,000 miles (4,800 km). Within this immense empire, the Persians ruled more than 50 million people.

Darius's Empire

The best organizer among the Persian kings was **Darius I**, who reigned from 522 B.C. to 486 B.C. To administer his empire, Darius effectively divided the realm into provinces and assigned satraps, or provincial governors, to rule. Military officials and tax inspectors, chosen by the king from among the conquered people themselves, assisted the satraps in carrying out the king's decrees in the provinces. In addition, inspectors called "Eyes and Ears of the King" made unannounced tours of the provinces and reported directly to the king on the activities of officials. In this way, the king's court was able to keep watch on local government.

In contrast to the Assyrians, the Persians were tolerant rulers who allowed conquered peoples to retain their own languages, religions, and laws. The Persians won the loyalty of conquered peoples by respecting local customs. They believed that this loyalty could be won more easily with fairness than by fear or force. When faced with rebellion, however, the Persians did not hesitate to take extreme military measures.

Commerce and Roads

Darius brought artisans from many of his

Persian god and goddess protecting a palm tree

More than 1,000 years after Alexander destroyed Persepolis, the first curious travelers rediscovered the impressive remains of the city. The Apadana hall at the northern end of the palace contains stairways with beautiful reliefs of Persian nobles, guards, and tribute bearers.

REFLECTING ON THE TIMES

1. About what year did travelers rediscover Persepolis?
2. What ruins reveal the wealth of Persian kings?

91

The Arts Have students set up a gallery show of Persian art and architecture, using photocopies or sketches of actual artwork. Ask them to label and give background information on each item in the show. **L2**

Multicultural Have students read the following sections of the Hebrew Bible to see how the Israelites and the Hittites intermingled: Genesis 23, Genesis 26:34–35, II Samuel 11. Ask students to describe each interaction of the two peoples. **L2**

Who?What?Where?When?

Nineveh According to the Hebrew Bible, God sent the prophet Jonah to warn the people of Nineveh that they would be destroyed for their wickedness. The Ninevites repented, however, and God spared the city.

ANSWERS TO REFLECTING ON THE TIMES

1. Travelers rediscovered Persepolis after A.D. 670.
2. The ruins of Darius's palace at Persepolis reveal the wealth of Persian kings.

Map Study

Answer

Susa had a central location in the empire and was at the crossroads of the Royal Road and several trade routes; it was close to the Tigris and Euphrates rivers.

Map Skills Practice

Reading a Map What was the distance between Susa and Sardis along the Royal Road? *(It was about 1,400 miles or 2,253 kilometers.)*

Linking Past and Present

Zoroastrians The Parsees of the Bombay area in India are modern Zoroastrians. Their ancestors traveled to India from Iran in the A.D. 700s to avoid Muslim persecution. The Parsees represent an important economic group in India. From about 1850 on, they proved successful in industries such as shipbuilding and the railways.

ASSESS

Check for Understanding

Assign Section 3 Assessment as homework or as an in-class activity.

🖳 Use Interactive Tutor Self-Assessment Software to review Section 3.

Evaluate

 Section Quiz 3-3

🖳 Use the Testmaker to create a customized quiz for Section 3.

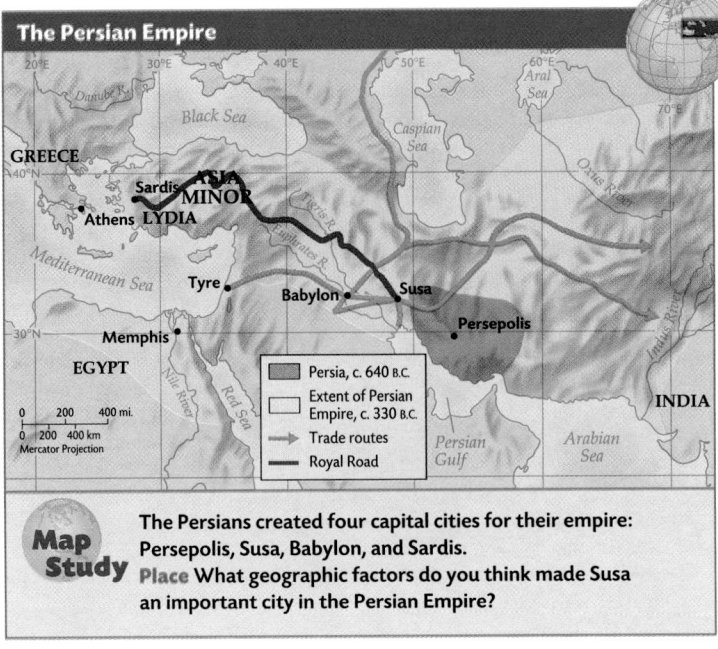

The Persian Empire

Persia, c. 640 B.C.
Extent of Persian Empire, c. 330 B.C.
Trade routes
Royal Road

Map Study The Persians created four capital cities for their empire: Persepolis, Susa, Babylon, and Sardis. **Place** What geographic factors do you think made Susa an important city in the Persian Empire?

conquered lands to build **Persepolis**, the most magnificent city in the empire. The Persians themselves did not engage in trade, which they considered an indecent occupation. However, they did encourage trade among the peoples of their empire. To advance trade throughout the empire and aid the movement of soldiers, Darius had Persian engineers improve and expand the network of roads first laid down by the Assyrians. Royal messengers also journeyed on the roads allowing "neither snow, nor rain, nor heat, nor the darkness of night to hinder them in the prompt completion of their … tasks."

The Royal Road, the most important thoroughfare in the Persian Empire, stretched more than 1,500 miles (2,400 km) from Persia to Asia Minor. Every 14 miles (22.4 km), stations along the Royal Road provided travelers with food, water, and fresh horses. Royal messengers could travel the length of the road in just seven days, a journey that had taken three months before the road was built.

A Persian Disaster

During his reign, Darius waged war against the Greeks over the control of city-states in Asia Minor. After Darius died, his son Xerxes (ZUHRK •SEEZ) led the forces of Persia in a disastrous campaign to conquer Greece in 480 B.C. Xerxes' defeat stopped Persian expansion into Europe.

Persian Religion and Culture

The Persians followed a strict moral code that stressed bravery and honesty. They taught their sons to "ride horses, to draw a bow, and to speak the truth." Before the 500s B.C., the Persian people worshiped many deities associated with the sky, sun, and fire. Then, about 570 B.C., a prophet named **Zoroaster** (ZOHR•uh•WAS•tuhr) began to call for reform of the Persian religion. Zoroaster preached that the world was divided by a struggle between good and evil. The god Ahura Mazda led the forces of good, and a lesser deity, Ahriman, represented the spirit of darkness. At the end of time, Ahura Mazda would triumph over Ahriman.

Zoroaster also taught that humans were caught up in this struggle and had to choose between good and evil. All humans who fought on the side of Ahura Mazda against evil would be rewarded with eternal life. Those who chose Ahriman would be condemned after death to eternal darkness and

Spread of Celtic Culture

Central Europe, c. 600 B.C.
The Hallstatt Celts spread their influence from Austria to the British Isles. They were among the first people in northern Europe to make iron. Their warlike chieftains relied on horses and slept on animal skins in crude houses. Their weapons and artifacts, however, were decorated with elaborate patterns. Celtic art featured highly stylized plants and animals.

Central Europe

MEETING SPECIAL NEEDS ACTIVITY

Learning Style: Visual/Spatial Have students trace the Chaldean Empire from the map (p. 89), including the labeled cities and the bodies of water abutting it. Ask them to name the rivers on which Babylon is located *(Euphrates)* and on which Nineveh is located *(Tigris)*, and the body of water into which the rivers empty *(Persian Gulf)*. Now have them use a ruler and the distance scale to figure out the distance Babylon-Nineveh. *(The distance is 3/4 of an inch, or, based on the distance scale, 300 miles.)* Ask them to compare the distances Babylon-Nineveh and New York-Los Angeles. *(New York and Los Angeles are 10 times farther apart.)*

Visualizing History This relief of King Darius and Xerxes is one of many at the palace of King Darius. *What do you think the appearance of these figures reveals about the Persian royal court?*

misery. These teachings were contained in a book called the Avesta.

Persian rulers believed that they ruled by the power of Ahura Mazda and were responsible to him alone. Darius I had the following statement carved on a cliff:

> **❝** On this account Ahura Mazda brought me health…. Because I was not wicked, nor was I a liar, nor was I a tyrant, neither I nor any of my line. We had ruled according to righteousness. **❞**

Zoroaster's teachings were eventually linked to the glorification of the Persian monarchy. Because the monarchy was viewed as a sacred institution, Persian kings commanded great respect and were surrounded by pomp and pageantry. This style of kingship later shaped the development of monarchies in the Western world.

Zoroaster's beliefs also may have shaped beliefs in the Mediterranean world. Some scholars believe that Zoroaster's teachings about paradise, hell, and the Last Judgment—or the separation of good and evil at the end of time—may have influenced Judaism, Christianity, and Islam. Other aspects of Persian culture lived on as well, and mixed with Greek culture when Alexander the Great absorbed the Persians into his own empire in the 300s B.C.

SECTION 3 ASSESSMENT

Main Idea
1. Use diagrams like the ones below to show how the Chaldeans and the Persians extended their rule.

Chaldeans ⟨
Persians ⟨

Recall
2. **Define** satrap.
3. **Identify** the Hittites, the Assyrians, the Chaldeans, Nebuchadnezzar, the Persians, Cyrus II, Darius I, Zoroaster.

Critical Thinking
4. **Evaluating Information** Why might religions have adopted parts of Zoroaster's beliefs?

Understanding Themes
5. **Conflict** How did the military exploits of the Hittites and the Assyrians change the way peoples of the time fought battles and dealt with conquered peoples?

SECTION 3 ASSESSMENT ANSWERS

1. Chaldeans: extended boundaries to Syria; forced people of Judah into exile; city wall protected Babylon. Persians: king's court controlled local government; tolerant rulers won respect of conquered people
2. All terms are defined in the Glossary.
3. Hittites, 88; Assyrians, 89; Chaldeans, 89; Nebuchadnezzar, 90; Persians, 90; Cyrus II, 90; Darius I, 91; Zoroaster, 92
4. Many people have found meaning in the idea of conflict between the forces of good and evil and a final day of judgment.
5. **CONFLICT** The Hittites introduced iron weapons; the Assyrians introduced cavalry. Both taxed conquered peoples heavily, a practice that endured.

Visualizing History The Persians operated a postal system along the Royal Road much like the American Pony Express. Postal stations were set up along the road a day's ride apart. At each station, a fresh rider and horse would wait to take the mail from the incoming rider.
Answer to Caption: *The figures, with their rigid posture and arrogant demeanor, reveal the grandeur and ceremony of the Persian royal court.*

Reteach

Prepare a chart on the chalkboard requesting the following information about each of the empires described in this section: beginning and ending dates, territorial extent of empire, names of rulers, significant achievements. Organize the class into four groups. Assign each group responsibility for filling in the chart of one of the four empires described in the section.

 Reteaching Activity 3

 Reading Essentials and Study Guide 3-3

Enrich

Have students find and summarize further information about ancient Susa (which the biblical book of Esther calls Shushan), where a stele containing the Code of Hammurabi was discovered.

 Enrichment Activity 3

CLOSE

Ask students to reflect on the transitory nature of the empires built by the Hittites, Assyrians, Chaldeans, and Persians. What remains of the original empire in each case? (*Little remains of these empires; students might discuss ways in which each empire has indirectly affected later cultures.*)

CHAPTER 3 ASSESSMENT

WORLD HISTORY Online

Have students use the **Chapter 3 Self-Check Quiz** at worldhistory.glencoe.com to prepare for the Chapter Test.

GLENCOE TECHNOLOGY

VIDEODISC
Use MindJogger to review the chapter.
MindJogger Videoquiz

Chapter 3
Disc 1 Side A

Also available in VHS.

Answers

Using Key Terms

1. g	3. h	5. i
2. j	4. f	

Using Your History Journal

Suggest that students use poetic conventions such as describing warfare and referring to the nation's gods.

Reviewing Facts

1. Phoenicians: loose union of city-states. King David: strong central government. Assyrians: provinces ruled by governors that reported to king. King Darius: provinces ruled by governors with officials and inspectors to carry out king's decrees
2. Aramaeans controlled overland trade between Egypt and Mesopotamia and traveled throughout the entire region.
3. bills of sale and contracts; alphabet allowed them to correspond with others and keep better track of business dealings
4. One God determined right and wrong, expected people to be morally responsible.
5. Philistines, Canaanites, Assyrians,

WORLD HISTORY Online

Self-Check Quiz

Visit the *World History: The Human Experience* Web site at **worldhistory.glencoe.com** and click on *Chapter 3—Self-Check Quiz* to prepare for the Chapter Test.

Using Key Terms

Write the key term that completes each sentence. Then write a sentence for each term not chosen.

a. alphabet	f. satraps
b. monotheism	g. exodus
c. colony	h. prophets
d. covenant	i. Diaspora
e. barter	j. confederation

1. In the 1200s B.C., the Israelite leader Moses rallied his people and led them out of Egypt in a(n)_____ into the Sinai Desert.
2. The Phoenicians were organized into a(n) _____ of independent city-states along the coast of northern Canaan.
3. Israelite _____ condemned abuses in society and urged people not to forget their duties to God and to one another.
4. Persian kings appointed a number of _____ to govern the provinces of the Persian Empire.
5. Jewish communities existing outside of their homeland have become known as the _____, after a Greek word meaning "scattered."

Technology Activity

Using a Word Processor
Search the Internet or your local library for information about the early Israelites and the Phoenicians. Using a word processor, create a chart comparing the two cultures. Include heads such as major contributions, cultural achievements, location, and time period. After comparing the contributions of both cultures, write a paragraph explaining how these contributions have affected your life.

Reviewing Facts

1. **Government** Use a chart like the one below to describe the systems of government of the Phoenicians, King David, the Assyrians, and the Persians under King Darius.

Phoenicians	King David	Assyrians	King Darius

2. **Culture** Explain how Aramaic came to be spoken throughout the Fertile Crescent.
3. **Technology** Identify the practices that the Phoenicians introduced to business and trade. What advantage did the Phoenicians have over their competitors?
4. **Culture** Describe how the Israelites interpreted and applied monotheism.
5. **History** List the peoples with whom the Israelites came into conflict after the Exodus from Egypt and the return to Canaan.
6. **Culture** Describe the role of Deborah in helping the Israelites settle Caanan.

Critical Thinking

1. **Apply** What natural resource supported the Lydians' development of a money system to replace the barter system?
2. **Analyze** How were the deities and beliefs of the Phoenicians, the Israelites, and the Persians different from one another?
3. **Analyze** What actions taken by Darius I made his rule so effective?

Chaldeans, Persians
6. She planned a successful Israelite attack on the Canaanites.

Critical Thinking
1. rich gold deposits
2. Phoenician: polytheistic, with three main deities; Hebrew: monotheistic, with God expecting moral behavior; Persian: polytheistic,

with gods of sky, sun, fire
3. divided Persian Empire into provinces; appointed officials from among conquered peoples; had surprise inspections of provinces; improved roads to encourage trade
4. It freed them from slavery in Egypt, strengthening their faith in the one God and their following of the Ten Commandments. This monotheistic belief and moral code later

4. Evaluate Why was the Exodus important to the Israelites? In what way did it shape the development of religion in the Western world?

Geography in History

1. Movement What event led to the establishment of a large Jewish community in Babylon after 586 B.C.?

2. Human/Environment Interaction How did the people of Babylon provide water to various locations inside the city walls?

3. Human/Environment Interaction How did the people of Babylon fortify the city against attack from outsiders?

Babylon c. 500s B.C.

Understanding Themes

1. Cultural Diffusion Based on your knowledge of the ancient trading peoples of the Middle East, what kinds of ideas might people be likely to adopt from other cultures?

2. Innovation From a modern perspective, do you see any advantages or disadvantages to the development of a religious belief system based on monotheism?

3. Conflict Make a list of what aims might have motivated conquerors such as the Hittites, Assyrians, Chaldeans, and Persians to incorporate their neighbors into empires.

Linking Past **and** Present

1. Does the legal system of our country parallel Hittite law or Hammurabi's code? Provide a brief explanation of your view.
2. The Persian Empire was made up of many different peoples. Evaluate the ways in which the Persians ruled their empire. How does the Persian experience compare or contrast with that of modern nations, such as the United States, that have diverse populations?
3. Solomon built a magnificent temple at Jerusalem. The last Jewish temple on the Temple Mount was destroyed in A.D. 70. What building stands on that site now?

Skill Practice

Reread pages 91–92 in Section 3 about Darius and his empire. Use that information to answer the following questions about the Persian Empire.

1. What problem hindered the expansion of the Persian Empire?
2. Write a short summary of the information the Persians might have gathered after deciding that trade was an indecent occupation in which to engage.
3. List the options that were available to the Persians. What were the advantages? What were the disadvantages?
4. What kind of solution did the Persians find to help in the expansion of the empire?
5. Evaluate and discuss the effectiveness of the solution. Why do you think it was, or was not, successful?

Linking Past **and** Present

1. Fines levied for misdemeanors resemble Hittite code; capital punishment parallels Hammurabi's code.
2. The Persian Empire treated its diverse peoples relatively well, but the empire ultimately rested on force. Many modern nations with diverse populations are democracies based on the rule of law and the consent of the governed.
3. the Dome of the Rock and al-Aqsa Mosque

Skill Practice

1. the problem of how to maintain and expand the empire
2. The Persians believed that it was indecent for them to engage in trade. However, they felt that it was okay for the people of the empire to do so. They knew that there was already a network of roads built by the Assyrians.
3. They could allow the empire's peoples to become traders. The Persians could improve and expand existing roads to advance trade and support the movement of soldiers and people.
4. They decided to allow the peoples of the empire to engage in trade and to improve and expand the roads throughout the empire.
5. It supported and expanded the empire without forcing the Persians to go against their beliefs. The Royal Road became vital in improving communications.

Chapter Bonus Test Question

Ask students: According to a well-known maxim, "the pen is mightier than the sword." What information in this chapter supports that view? (*The militarily weak ancient Hebrew culture, through its written scriptures, has made a lasting impact.*)

---

became a part of the West's religious heritage.

Geography in History
1. the Chaldeans' defeat of Judah in 586 B.C.
2. through a network of canals
3. a powerful double wall, reinforced by a moat

Understanding Themes
1. **CULTURAL DIFFUSION** ideas that simplify or improve daily life

2. **INNOVATION** Advantage: a single God who demands moral behavior of people is a better role model than a pantheon of gods who do not always act morally. Disadvantage: with one God responsible for both good and evil, people may have difficulty understanding why "bad things happen to good people."

3. **CONFLICT** desire for power, for enslaved persons, for more natural resources, for control of trade routes

FOCUS

Agriculture revolutionized human culture because people were able to settle in communities instead of migrating, which allowed many new developments to take place. Civilizations established specialized labor, trade networks, organized governments, and legal systems.

TEACH

Reinforcing Vocabulary

Point out the **Vocabulary Preview** to students alerting them to words they will encounter that might be unfamiliar.

The Iceman's World

Interpreting the Primary Source
Ask students how they interpret the comment that "some [of the] relics . . . were similar to" but also different from "those found at other Copper Age sites." (*This statement shows why the Iceman's tools are being used to date him to the Copper Age but also indicates that the evidence for that decision is somewhat limited.*)

Evaluating the Primary Source
This primary source is useful historically because it provides insight into the meaning of uncovered artifacts. The reliability of this source is determined by the reliability of its author. His statement that the artifact and thus the body are from the Copper Age is an interpretation. The author's comment that "[these tools] did . . . evoke vivid images of a distant time" indicates that he is speculating on the meaning of the artifacts. He is forming an opinion based on limited information.

Unit 1

For thousands of years prehistoric humans were migratory hunters and gatherers. With the development of agriculture, people no longer had to roam to find food, but could live in settled communities, learn specialized skills, and enjoy leisure pursuits.

Throughout the world, these communities grew into civilizations with cultures, organized governments, religions, and legal systems.

✦ VOCABULARY PREVIEW

smelters: workers who melt metals and mix them to create new metals

sovereign: supreme leader

tyrannously: in an unjust manner

For more primary sources to accompany this unit, use the *World History Primary Source Document Library CD-ROM.*

Chapter 1
The Iceman's World

Artifacts

A 1991 discovery shook the world of archaeology and made headlines around the world—an intact, five-thousand-year-old body was found frozen in the ice near the border between Austria and Italy. Around this Copper Age "Iceman" were scattered his tools, clothes, and other artifacts, all of which have opened an astonishing window into prehistoric life.

Geographically, the Iceman's domain was the Alps . . . Whatever else he was, the Iceman was a mountaineer: His very clothing and his tools proclaim as much.

. . . Some relics, such as a small flint dagger with an ash-wood handle, were similar to those found at other Copper Age sites. However, no one had ever seen the kind of delicately woven grass sheath that held the dagger.

These tools could not tell me who the Iceman was or what he was doing on a treacherous 10,530-foot-high pass. They did, however, evoke vivid images of a distant time.

. . . Copper was changing the Alpine world forever, stimulating the development of major trade routes between many isolated valleys.

"Before this moment," explained [archaeologist] Markus Egg, "there were only two ways for a man to be rich. He could have a great mass of cattle or a great mass of wheat. But these are not good treasures—you cannot carry them around."

Egg took the Iceman's copper ax blade in his hand. "This is a good treasure!" he said. "Moreover, you now need men to be miners, smelters, axmakers, maybe even salesmen. Now people have a real profession, a specialty. Before copper, everybody did everything. . . ."

The Revolt in Wei

Interpreting the Primary Source
Ask students how Chung Chung's opinion of Chou-hsü's violent tactics reflects the morals of this time period in China's history. How does Chung Chung think a ruler should behave in his or her position? (*Chung Chung's opinion shows disapproval over use of force to rule. He thinks it is a risky*

and immoral way to act and that rulers should rather "practice true virtue.")

Evaluating the Primary Source
This primary source is useful historically because it reveals both the ways some rulers used their power and also the ways the use of that power was viewed at that time. The reliability of this source is determined by

Chapter 2
The Revolt in Wei

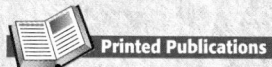
Printed Publications

In ancient China, rulers competed for greater power. This excerpt, from China's oldest history, the Tso chuan, describes a revolt in the kingdom of Wei in which Chou-hsü killed his half-brother to gain the throne. The duke of Lu, a neighboring ruler, discusses the situation with one of his officials.

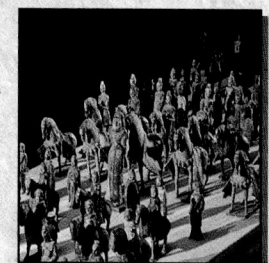
Statues of Chinese warriors
c. 6th century B.C.

The duke of Lu questioned Chung Chung, a high official of Lu, saying, "This Chou-hsü of Wei—will he succeed?"

Chung Chung replied, "I have heard of gaining the support of one's people through virtue, but I have never heard of doing so through violence. To try to do so through violence is like trying to straighten out threads by further tangling them. Now Chou-hsü relies on military force and is quite ready to resort to cruelty. Relying on military force, he has few followers; ever ready to resort to cruelty, he has few allies. Anyone whose followers turn against him and whose allies desert him will find it difficult to accomplish anything!

"Military force is like fire—if it is not kept in check, it will end by consuming the user. Chou-hsü has assassinated his sovereign and used his people tyrannously. And yet now he . . . hopes to achieve success through violence—he will never escape! . . ."

Chapter 3
Darius, King by the Grace of Ormazd

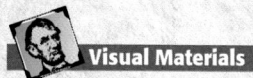
Visual Materials

The concept of the divine right of kings may have grown out of the Persian Empire's image of kingship. In the Behistun Inscriptions, which Darius of Persia had carved on a 1,700-foot-high rockface in 516 B.C., the king boasts of his divinely supported power and accomplishments.

6. Says Darius the king—These are the countries which have come to me; by the grace of Ormazd I have become king of them: Persia, Susiana, Babylonia, . . . in all twenty-three provinces.

Darius of Persia
r. 521–486 B.C.

7. Says Darius the king—These (are) the provinces which have come to me; by the grace of Ormazd they have become subject to me; they have brought tribute to me. . . .

8. Says Darius the king—Within these countries, the man who was good, him I have right well cherished. Whoever was evil, him have I utterly rooted out. . . .

9. Says Darius the king—Ormazd granted me the empire. Ormazd brought help to me, so that I gained this empire. By the grace of Ormazd I hold this empire. . . .

Interpreting Primary Sources

1. How did the discovery of copper change the way people lived?
2. What does Chung Chung say about the nature of power?
3. What is the purpose of the Behistun Inscriptions?
4. **CRITICAL THINKING:** What do the Behistun Inscriptions tell you about the connection between religion and political power in ancient Persia?

Applications Activity

Imagine you are a ruler in ancient China or Persia. Write a series of "inscriptions" that you would like carved in stone.

---

who wrote it and why. If the history was commissioned by the Duke of Lu, perhaps he wanted to highlight Chou-hsü's violence to make himself look more ethical. If it was written by a truly objective historian, then it may represent the situation fairly.

Darius, King by the Grace of Ormazd

Interpreting the Primary Source
Ask students how they think Darius's people were convinced that he was divinely chosen as king. Would the students be convinced in the same way? (*Many people probably viewed Darius's defeats as proof that Ormazd was on his side. Students may say they would not think Darius was divinely chosen but was rather just a good military leader; others may say that he was divinely chosen.*)

Evaluating the Primary Source
This primary source is a useful historical source because it reveals the types of justification a ruler could have used to establish his right to rule. The reliability of this source can be judged by assessing Darius's goals in having the Behistun Inscriptions written. Because he was trying to justify his right to rule, he may have exaggerated his successes to the writer in order to make a stronger impression. On the other hand, the writer of the inscriptions may also have given a fair account of Darius's defeats.

For the more complete version of each of these documents, see the World History Primary Source Document Library CD-ROM:

Document 2 *The Iceman*
Document 8 *Revolt in the Kingdom of Wei*
Document 14 *The Behistun Inscriptions of Darius*

ANSWER KEY

1. The invention of copper stimulated the development of major trade routes between isolated valleys, and people developed more specialized skills.
2. If not used wisely, power can destroy you. No one will support a ruler who relies on cruelty.
3. The Behistun Inscriptions were probably created to show Darius's power, influence, and accomplishments, as well as to immortalize him and spread knowledge of his achievements.
4. The inscriptions show that for thousands of years, rulers have claimed that their power comes from a god, and that that gives them the right to rule over others.

APPLICATIONS ACTIVITY: Answers will vary but should indicate that students have read the excerpts from the Behistun Inscriptions and that they understood the directions.

Answers and Analyses

1. **C** (Geography) According to the map, the only answer choice that is both a Neanderthal site and is northeast of Broken Hill is Skhul. Note that while Kostenki is northeast of Broken Hill, it is a Cro-Magnon site, not a Neanderthal site.

2. **G** (Geography) Map projections are discussed on page 37. There it states *A conformal map shows land areas in their true shapes, while distorting their actual size.* In the next paragraph it states that a Cylindrical Projection (Mercator) is a *conformal projection.*

 TEST-TAKING TIP

Remind students to use process of elimination and guess aggressively, even when their knowledge is incomplete. If a map did not show direction or location, it probably would not be very useful. Therefore choices F and H are unlikely choices.

3. **B** (Culture/Environment) The Neolithic Revolution is described on the top of page 29. There it states that *Over some 5,000 years, people shifted from gathering and hunting food to producing food.* This development was called the Neolithic Revolution.

Standardized Test Practice

Directions: Choose the *best* answer to each of the following multiple choice questions. If you have trouble answering a question, use the process of elimination to narrow your choices. Write your answers on a separate piece of paper.

Use the map below and your knowledge of history to answer questions 1 and 2.

1. Which Neanderthal site is northeast of Broken Hill?

A   Dolni Vestonice

B   Boskop

C   Skhul

D   Kostenki

> **Test-Taking Tip:** In order to determine *relative location*, look for a *compass rose* or an *arrow pointing to N (north)*. Since northeast is an *intermediate direction*, you will first need to determine *north* and *east*. Northeast will be in between these two directions.

2. This map is an example of a Mercator projection. This type of map CANNOT show

F   absolute location.

G   accurate size of continents.

H   true direction.

J   elevation.

> **Test-Taking Tip:** A *Mercator projection* is one way of representing a round Earth on a flat piece of paper. It is made by wrapping a piece of paper around a globe and tracing the features. The parts of the map that are farthest from the Equator become distorted on this type of map. However, it does show true direction (this type of map is often used by sailors) so answer H can be eliminated.

3. During the Neolithic Revolution, people settled in communities instead of wandering as nomads. Which of the following was the most important factor in bringing about this change?

A   The invention of stone hunting tools

B   The shift from a hunting to an agricultural society

C   The use of fire for cooking and warmth

D   The creation of calendars

> **Test-Taking Tip:** Remember to choose the *most important factor.* For example, the invention of hunting tools may have improved people's living conditions, but since hunters are usually nomadic—traveling to where the food supply is—answer A cannot be the *most important factor.*

4. The exchange of goods and ideas between different groups of people is known as cultural diffusion. Which of the following contributes the LEAST to cultural diffusion?

  F An established code of laws

  G The conquering of other civilizations

  H Trading between different civilizations

  J The development of written language

> **Test-Taking Tip:** Be careful—this question is looking for the *exception*. Do not quickly choose the first answer that "makes sense." For example, conquest and trade both contribute to cultural diffusion by exposing one civilization to another. Therefore, answers G and H cannot be the *exception* this question is looking for.

5. The Code of Law created by Mesopotamia's King Hammurabi contained 282 sections that addressed many aspects of both public and private life. In what way did this Code of Law strengthen Sumerian society?

  A It translated the Ten Commandments into Sumerian cuneiform.

  B It created a central body of law that applied to all citizens of Mesopotamia.

  C It punished wrongdoers more severely than did the old Sumerian laws.

  D It guaranteed freedom of religion for all citizens of Mesopotamia.

> **Test-Taking Tip:** Make sure that you read the entire question and *all* the answer choices carefully before choosing the best one. For example, although answer C is true, it is too narrow to be the best choice.

Use the map below **and** your knowledge of history to answer the following question.

Shang China

6. China has the world's oldest continuous civilization because of its development of a single, strong cultural identity. Early Chinese societies, like the Shang, were isolated from the rest of the world because

  F their crops and products were different from those of the other river valley civilizations.

  G the language spoken by the Chinese was not understood by the other river valley civilizations.

  H geographic features, such as mountains and deserts, separated this region from other early civilizations.

  J early Chinese dynasties were suspicious of the governments of other river valley civilizations.

> **Test-Taking Tip:** Eliminate answers that don't make sense. For example, people usually trade to *obtain* different crops and products—things that they cannot produce in their own lands. Therefore, you can easily eliminate answer F.

4. **F** (History) Cultural diffusion is discussed on page 34. There it states that the *exchange of goods and ideas when cultures come in contact is known as cultural diffusion.... When ancient peoples learned about the technology and ideas of different civilizations, the new knowledge stimulated them to improve their own skills and way of life.*

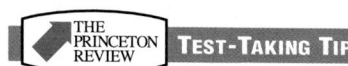

TEST-TAKING TIP

Students can often answer EXCEPT and NOT questions by association. All of these choices are associated with the idea of civilizations coming into contact with each other and sharing ideas, with the exception of choice F.

5. **B** (Civics) The Code of Hammurabi is discussed on page 63. There it states that Hammurabi made "justice appear in the land" because he *collected laws of the various Mesopotamian city-states and created a law code covering the entire region.* Choice C is also true, but it does not have the transformational effect of a universal code of laws on public and private life.

6. **H** (Geography) The Shang were surrounded by deserts, mountains, and water. These geographic features are the reason that they were cut off from other civilizations and lived in isolation from the rest of the world.

Tested Objectives	
Questions	**Objective**
1	Analyzing Information
2	Evaluating Information
3	Making Comparisons
4, 5	Making Generalizations
6	Determining Cause and Effect

0:00 OUT OF TIME?

If time does not permit teaching each chapter in Unit 2, you may use the Unit Digest Transparencies and Chapter Digest Audiocassettes with accompanying activities and tests.

Introducing the Unit

Unit 2 traces the growth of Hellenic civilization in Greece, the rise of Rome and of Christianity and their legacy to the West, and the development of civilizations in Africa, India, and China.

Unit Objectives

After reading Unit 2, students will be able to:

1. describe the development of the civilization of Greece.
2. give examples of the achievements of the ancient Greeks and tell how these were spread by Alexander.
3. explain the rise and decline of Rome and the spread of Roman culture, including Christianity, throughout Europe.
4. trace the rise of wealthy and powerful kingdoms in Africa.
5. summarize the development of Indian civilization and the importance of Hinduism and Buddhism.
6. discuss the achievements of Chinese civilization and the meaning of Confucianism and Daoism.

History _and the_ Humanities

📖 Focus on World Art Prints 6, 8, 9, 12
🖌 World History and Art Transparencies 5–11

Unit **2**

2500 B.C.–A.D. 500*

Flowering of Civilizations

PRIMARY SOURCES Library

See pages 236–237 for primary source readings that accompany Unit 2.

Then **& Now** As people developed agricultural technology, nomadic life gave way to living in communities. Emerging cities became centers of trade and commerce, characterized by highly organized social structures and governments. Commerce brought wealth that allowed more people time for leisure and study. Ancient civilizations contributed much that remains in the modern world. China developed a civil service system based on merit. The city of Alexandria in Egypt had a great library. The Greeks refined geometry to calculate the size of the earth. Architecture, theater, and education all have their roots in ancient civilizations.

✳ In A.D. 532, a Christian monk started a system of dating events, beginning with the year he believed Jesus was born. The years before Jesus' birth were called B.C. (before Christ). The years after this event were called A.D., an abbreviation for _anno Domini_, which is Latin for "in the year of the Lord." Today, some publications use B.C.E. (before the common era) instead of B.C., and C.E. (common era) instead of A.D. Note that unlike A.D., C.E. follows the year.

A Global Chronology

	2000 B.C.	1500 B.C.	1000 B.C.
Political		c. 1500 B.C. Aryans cross the Hindu Kush into South Asia.	
Scientific/ Technological	c. 1700 B.C. Babylonian Empire adopts Sumerian calendar.		
Social/Cultural	100		c. 1200 B.C. Vedic Age begins in India.

Then **& Now** **Classical Legacy** The influence of ancient civilizations, particularly the classical civilizations of Greece and Rome, is visible in many aspects of modern American society. Examples include the use of Latin mottoes such as _E pluribus unum_ inscribed on our currency, the neoclassical architecture of many public buildings, especially in Washington, D.C., and in state capitals, and even our form of government, which adopted the concepts of the senate and veto from the Roman Republic.

Have students brainstorm a list of things today that reflect the influence of ancient civilizations, prompting them from the examples above as necessary. Ask students why they think classical civilizations, especially Rome, have influenced the United States. Why was neoclassical

A gold mask found in the royal grave circle at Mycenae, National Archaeological Museum, Athens, Greece

History —and— YOU

 idea of democratic gov- ment, in which the major- rules but the minority still rights, developed in ens, Greece, almost 2,500 rs ago and is the basis of sent-day democracy.

To better understand origins and influence of ient concepts of democra- iew videodisc Chapter 5: *nocracy in Greece* in Turn- Points in World History.

ABCNEWS INTERACTIVE™

VIDEODISC
Turning Points in World History

Side One, Chapter 5

Title: *Democracy in Greece*
Subject: Athenian democracy laid the foundation for the concept of democratic government in which the majority rules, but the minority still has rights.
Ask: What are the basic ideals behind democracy? *(individual equality and freedom)*

Visualizing History

Some scholars once believed this to be the mask of King Agamemnon. According to Greek myth, Agamemnon was the brother of Menelaus, whose wife, Helen, was abducted by Paris. Agamemnon led the Mycenaean army that lay siege to Troy for 10 years. After the war, Agamemnon was murdered by his wife, Clytemnestra. The murder and its consequences are related by Aeschylus in the three-play cycle known as the *Oresteia*. What might be a prominent theme in this cycle of plays? *(revenge)*

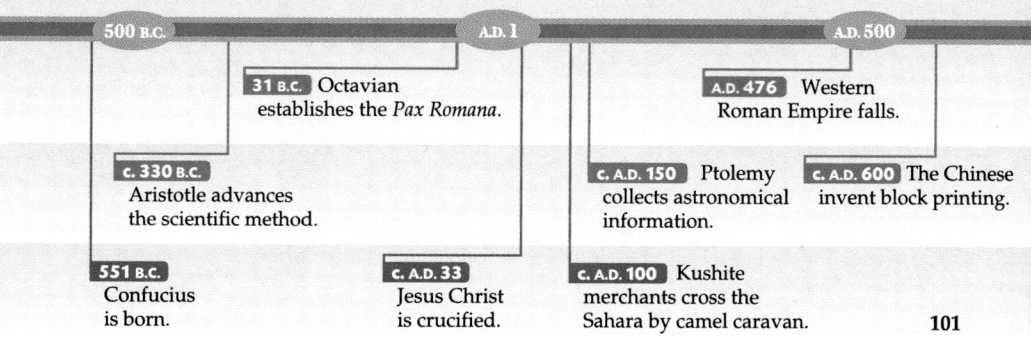

500 B.C.   **A.D. 1**   **A.D. 500**

31 B.C. Octavian establishes the *Pax Romana*.

c. 330 B.C. Aristotle advances the scientific method.

551 B.C. Confucius is born.

c. A.D. 33 Jesus Christ is crucified.

A.D. 476 Western Roman Empire falls.

c. A.D. 150 Ptolemy collects astronomical information.

c. A.D. 600 The Chinese invent block printing.

c. A.D. 100 Kushite merchants cross the Sahara by camel caravan.

101

architecture a popular style for public buildings? *(reflects power and solemnity, recalls the golden age of the Roman Republic)* Why was Latin often used for inscriptions and mottoes? *(Latin was the language of the learned for many centuries.)* Why do certain features of the federal and state governments stem from Roman institutions? *(Classical republican ideas influenced the Founders of the United States.)*

GLENCOE TECHNOLOGY

Glencoe World History Primary Source Document Library
Use the CD-ROM to access primary source documents related to ancient civilizations.

The Spread of Ideas

TEACH

Introduction

This feature focuses on the influence of Roman law and government on the development of legal and political systems in the West. Although the Greeks pioneered the idea of democratic government, it was Roman law, spread across Europe by Roman armies, that shaped the legal systems of most of the West.

Background Notes

Linking Past and Present

Roman history was a common reference point for educated American colonists. At the Constitutional Convention of 1787, delegates cited the fall of the Roman Republic as proof that a government allowing too much direct participation could not survive. Alexander Hamilton reminded delegates that when the Roman tribunes "levelled the boundary between the *patricians and plebeians*," disaster followed. The Constitution's limits on direct democracy reflect the fears of the founders that, as in Rome, too much democracy would destroy the new nation.

The Spread of Ideas

Systems of Law

L aw is a code of conduct and rights accepted or formally recognized by a society. Law provides social control, order, and justice. It enables people to know their rights and responsibilities. Law also forms the cornerstone of constitutional government. A constitutional government based upon law helps ensure justice, or the fair treatment of all citizens. "Where law ends, tyranny begins," said William Pitt, an English leader, in A.D. 1770.

Roman Empire
Laying the Foundation

Sometime around 451-450 B.C., a group of judges posted 12 tablets in Rome's main forum, or marketplace. According to legend, the common people of Rome had demanded that the laws be written down for all to see. People would then know their rights. The tablets listed the unwritten laws that guided judges. They also included penalties imposed on people who broke the law.

Although a group of invaders smashed the so-called Twelve Tables in 390 B.C., the basic code of law remained in effect for almost 1,000 years. When Roman armies marched out to conquer a huge empire, they carried their belief in law with them. By A.D. 120 Roman law governed the entire Mediterranean world and much of western Europe.

In theory, Roman law applied to all people, regardless of wealth or power. Not everyone honored Roman legal ideals. Nonetheless, the Romans developed an important democratic principle. They believed people should be ruled by law rather than by the whims of leaders. In A.D. 533-534 the Byzantine emperor Justinian consolidated all Roman law into a single written code. The Justinian Code became the foundation of the present civil law system. Civil law and common law, which originated in England, are two of the major legal systems in the world today.

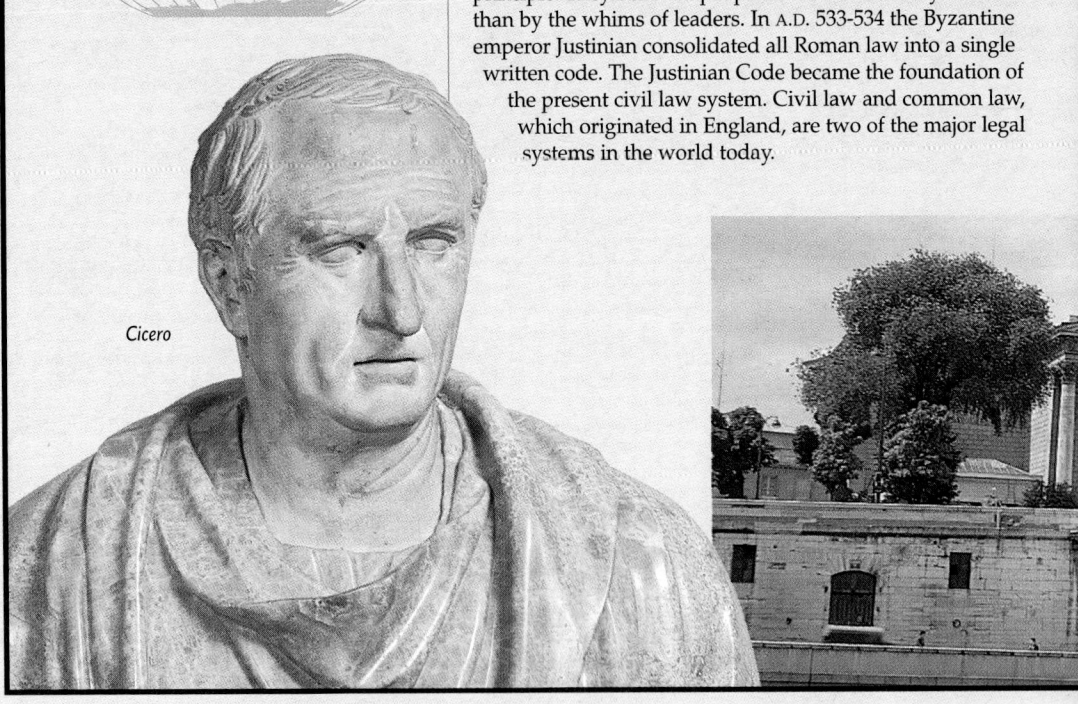

Cicero

COOPERATIVE LEARNING ACTIVITY

Writing a Constitution Ask students to imagine what school would be like if it had no rules. Ask students why rules are important for a nation or an organization. Then have students brainstorm a list of the most important rules that govern their behavior at school. Based on the list, have groups of students write a "Constitution" that embodies the school's "fundamental principles" and the goals these laws seek to accomplish. **L1**

The United States
A Model for Constitutional Government

The Founders of the United States knew about and admired the Romans. They understood what the Roman orator Cicero meant when he spoke of the need to limit the power of government. When it came time to draw up a plan of government, they wrote a constitution that balanced the powers of government among three branches.

To ensure that rulers did not place themselves above the law, the Framers included a provision that made the Constitution "the supreme law of the land." The Framers used the example of Rome to defend the Constitution. "The Roman republic attained … the utmost height of human greatness," declared Alexander Hamilton. He then explained how government under the Constitution would do the same.

A second system of legal justice, common law, evolved in England. Trial by jury, the right to petition the government, and many other rules governing trials originated in this system. Common law is not a written code but rather is based on written judicial decisions. Common law was established in the American colonies and continued to develop when the colonies became states of the United States.

Independence Hall, Philadelphia

France
Unifying the Law

In A.D. 1799 a French general named Napoleon Bonaparte set out to build an empire even larger than Rome's. By A.D. 1802 he had conquered much of Europe. Napoleon then tried to extend his reach into the Americas.

In seeking to rule this empire, Napoleon followed the Roman example. He took part in a commission to draw up a uniform code of laws. This code, known as the Napoleonic Code, was completed in A.D. 1804.

Although Napoleon ruled as emperor, the code named in his honor reaffirmed the principle that the same laws should be used to govern all people. In drafting these laws, Napoleon drew upon many of the legal precedents first introduced by the Romans. Under Napoleon, this code became applied in lands as far-flung as present-day Belgium, Quebec, Spain, and some Latin American nations.

Assemblée Nationale, Paris

LINKING THE IDEAS

1. What important democratic principle did the Romans develop?

Critical Thinking

2. How did the United States hope to ensure that rulers would not place themselves above the law?

Geography

Movement Have students look at the small map on page 102 and identify the areas that are highlighted. *(Roman Empire, France, U.S.)* How did Roman law spread through Europe? *(Roman armies carried the law with them to conquered regions.)* How did the influence of Roman law and government cross the Atlantic to the United States? *(The Founders knew about and admired the Roman Republic.)*

Cultural Diffusion

Roman Influence The influence of Roman law is evident today in American law schools and courthouses. The familiar vocabulary of the legal world, including *court, judge, jury, crime, verdict,* and *punish,* are all from Latin, the language of Rome. Lawyers often use terms taken directly from Latin, such as *stare decisis,* which means to follow precedent.

Despite the influence of Roman law, the U.S. legal system is based largely on the English common law tradition. The previous decisions of judges, together known as "case law," rather than legislative enactments or administrative codes, guide the decisions of the courts.

ANSWERS TO LINKING THE IDEAS

1. that people should be ruled by law rather than by the whims of rulers

2. They made the Constitution the supreme law of the land.

A complete, 1-page lesson plan is provided for each section in the *Reproducible Lesson Plans* booklet.

The Rise of Ancient Greece

CHAPTER RESOURCES

	Reproducible Resources	Multimedia Resources
Chapter Opener	Chapter Themes: Graphic Organizer 4 Historical Significance Chapter Activity 4	MindJogger Videoquiz
Chapter Enrichment	Vocabulary Activity 4* Time Line Activity 4 Mapping History Activity 4 History Simulation 4 Geography and History Activity 4 Source Reading 4 People in World History Profiles 5, 6 World Art and Music Activity 4 Enrichment Activity 4 Critical Thinking Activity 4 Skill Reinforcement Activity 4 Performance Assessment Activity 4 Standardized Test Practice Workbook Activity 4 Inclusion for the Social Studies Classroom Strategies and Activities	Focus on World Art Print 6, Early Cycladic II. *Cycladic Harpist* NGS Ancient Civilizations Poster Set: *Ancient Greece* World History and Art Transpar- ency 5, *Amphora from Vulci* Mapping History Overlay Transparency 4, *Ancient Greece* Chapter Transparency 4 NGS PicturePack Transparency Set: *Ancient Greece* Vocabulary PuzzleMaker Software NGS PictureShow CD-ROM: *Greece and Rome* Turning Points in World History: *Democracy in Greece* World History Primary Source Document Library
Chapter Review/Reteaching	Reteaching Activity 4 Skill Reinforcement Activity 4 Spanish Chapter Summary 4	Chapter 4 Digest Audiocassette, Activity, Test* Vocabulary PuzzleMaker Software Interactive Tutor Self-Assessment Software MindJogger Videoquiz
Chapter Evaluation/Testing	Performance Assessment Activity 4 Chapter 4 Test, Forms A and B	ExamView® Pro Testmaker

* Also available in Spanish

0:00 OUT OF TIME? Assign the Chapter 4 Audiocassettes.

World History Primary Source Document Library
Make History Come Alive!
Engage your students with over 250 easily accessible primary source documents—available on this CD-ROM—that will give them real life insight into the important events of world history.

Block Schedule

Activities that are particularly suited to use within the block scheduling framework are identified throughout this chapter by the following designation.

KEY TO ABILITY LEVELS

Teaching strategies are coded for varying learning styles.
L1 BASIC activities for all students
L2 AVERAGE activities for average to above-average students
L3 CHALLENGING activities for above-average students
LEP LIMITED ENGLISH PROFICIENCY activities

Use Glencoe's *Presentation Plus!* multimedia teacher tool to easily present dynamic lessons that visually excite your students. Using Microsoft PowerPoint® you can customize the presentations to create your own personalized lessons.

Interactive Lesson Planner

Planning has never been easier! Using this CD-ROM, organize your week, month, semester, or year with all the help you need. The **Interactive Lesson Planner** gives you access to all of the blackline masters that accompany *World History: The Human Experience.*

SECTION RESOURCES

Daily Objectives	Reproducible Resources	Multimedia Resources
Section 1 **Beginnings** Describe where and how the early civilizations of Greece developed.	Lecture Notes 4-1 Reproducible Lesson Plan 4-1 Vocabulary Activity 4* Guided Reading Activity 4-1* Time Line Activity 4 Section Quiz 4-1* Reading Essentials and Study Guide 4-1	Focus on World Art Transparency 6, Early Cycladic II. *Cycladic Harpist* Section Focus Transparency 4-1 Mapping History Overlay Transparency 4, *Ancient Greece* Interactive Tutor Self-Assessment Software Testmaker
Section 2 **The Polis** Explain how economic prosperity brought significant political and social changes to the Greek city-states.	Lecture Notes 4-2 Reproducible Lesson Plan 4-2 Guided Reading Activity 4-2* Mapping History Activity 4 Geography and History Activity 4 Section Quiz 4-2* Reading Essentials and Study Guide 4-2	Section Focus Transparency 4-2 Chapter Transparency 4 Vocabulary PuzzleMaker Software Interactive Tutor Self-Assessment Software Testmaker
Section 3 **Rivals** Differentiate between the values represented by Sparta and those represented by Athens.	Lecture Notes 4-3 Reproducible Lesson Plan 4-3 Vocabulary Activity 4* Guided Reading Activity 4-3* Source Reading 4 Section Quiz 4-3* Reading Essentials and Study Guide 4-3	NGS Ancient Civilizations Poster Set: *Ancient Greece* Section Focus Transparency 4-3 World History and Art Transparency 5, *Amphora from Vulci* Interactive Tutor Self-Assessment Software Testmaker NGS PictureShow CD-ROM: *Greece and Rome* Turning Points in World History: *Democracy in Greece*
Section 4 **War, Glory, and Decline** Discuss how the Persian and Peloponnesian Wars affected democracy in Greek city-states.	Lecture Notes 4-4 Reproducible Lesson Plan 4-4 Vocabulary Activity 4* Guided Reading Activity 4-4* Reteaching Activity 4 Enrichment Activity 4 Section Quiz 4-4* Performance Assessment Activity 4 Spanish Chapter Summary 4 Reading Essentials and Study Guide 4-4	Section Focus Transparency 4-4 Mapping History Overlay Transparency 4, *Ancient Greece* Interactive Tutor Self-Assessment Software Testmaker

* Also available in Spanish

Chapter Activities

 Performance Assessment Activity

Composing a Political Speech Have students take the roles of candidates running for a political office. They are interested in transforming American democracy so that it resembles the original Athenian state. Have them prepare and present a speech using information from the chapter—as well as problems from current events—to make connections between past theories and modern life. While students are presenting their speeches, their classmates should take the roles of voters who will fill out an "exit poll" regarding the nature of the speeches.

Possible Rubric Features

Persuasiveness, content information, clarity, relevance of current events, appropriateness to audience

• *For an additional activity, refer to Activity 4 in the* Performance Assessment Strategies and Activities *booklet.*

ACTIVITY

From the Classroom of...

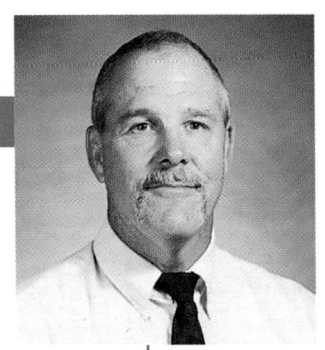

**Ray Barron
Heritage High School
Littleton, CO**

Comparing Pericles' *Funeral Oration* **and Lincoln's** *Gettysburg Address*

The purpose of this activity is to enable students to see the similarities among all civil wars and realize that there are connections between the American Civil War and that of the ancient Greeks.

Have students read both Pericles' *Funeral Oration* and Abraham Lincoln's *Gettysburg Address*. As they read each, have them list the qualities of individuals, government, and war that are mentioned. Next have them list those qualities of individuals, government, and war which seem to be mentioned in both orations. A Venn diagram is a helpful graphic organizer for this part of the activity. After they have done this, organize students into small groups and have each group reach a consensus as to which qualities are present in both orations and why this is so.

Have students write a paragraph explaining why these two speeches were made to the people of Greece and the United States, respectively, and summarize what we can learn about civil war from the speeches.

MULTIPLE LEARNING STYLES

Verbal/Linguistic

Have students write their own "Odyssey" in three or more pages, using prose or poetry. They should imagine a soldier traveling home from the Trojan War, and describe a few of his adventures.

Logical/Mathematical

Have students compute the distances, in miles and kilometers, between each of the Greek mainland cities shown on the map on page 107 and the following: Knossos, Phaestus, Troy.

Visual/Spatial

Have students prepare a class book about Minoan and Mycenaean culture, with each student contributing a page on some aspect of either culture: art, artifacts, clothing, food, transportation, and so on. Have each student sketch the chosen object.

Interpersonal

Have students research the prosecution against Aspasia. Then have them stage a hearing at which charges are brought against her, and she is successfully defended by Pericles.

GLENCOE'S ASSESSMENT ADVANTAGE

Use the following to easily assess student learning in a variety of ways.

• Performance Assessment Strategies and Activities
• Section Quizzes
• Chapter and Unit Tests
• Interactive Tutor Self-Assessment Software

• Testmaker Software
• MindJogger Videoquiz
• SAT/SAT II Test Practice
• worldhistory.glencoe.com

Additional Resources

NATIONAL GEOGRAPHIC SOCIETY

Teacher's Corner

INDEX TO NATIONAL GEOGRAPHIC MAGAZINE

The following articles may be used for research relating to this chapter:

- "Let the Games Begin," by Frank Deford, July 1996.
- "Oldest Known Shipwreck Reveals Splendors of the Bronze Age," by George F. Bass, December 1987.
- "The Quest for Ulysses," by Tim Severin, August 1986.
- "Drama of Death in a Minoan Temple," by Yannis Sakellarakis and Efi Sapouna-Sakellaraki, February 1981.

NATIONAL GEOGRAPHIC SOCIETY PRODUCTS AVAILABLE FROM GLENCOE

To order the following products for use with this chapter, contact your local Glencoe sales representative, or call Glencoe at 1-800-334-7344:

- *PictureShow: Greece and Rome (CD-ROM)*
- *Ancient Greece (Transparencies, Poster Set)*
- *Picture Atlas of the World (CD-ROM)*
- *PictureShow: Ancient Civilizations Library (CD-ROMs)*
- *PicturePack: Ancient Civilizations Library, Part I (Transparencies)*

ADDITIONAL NATIONAL GEOGRAPHIC SOCIETY PRODUCTS

Access National Geographic's new dynamic MapMachine Web site and other geography resources at:

- http://www.nationalgeographic.com/
- http://www.nationalgeographic.com/maps/

BIBLIOGRAPHY

Literature About the Period
Renault, Mary. *The King Must Die.* New York: Random House, 1988. Retells the legend of Theseus's struggle with the Minotaur.

Readings for the Student
Hamilton, Edith. *The Greek Way.* New York: Norton, 1983. The Greek spirit and mind as seen by great writers.

Readings for the Teacher
Grant, Michael. *The Rise of the Greeks.* New York: Scribner's, 1988. An examination of Greek civilization from the collapse of Mycenae to the Peloponnesian War.

WORLD HISTORY Online

Use our Web site as an additional resource. All essential content is covered in the Student Edition.

You and your students can visit the *World History: The Human Experience* Web site at worldhistory.glencoe.com The student text directs students to the Web site for the following options:

- **Chapter Overviews**
- **Student Web Activities**
- **Self-Check Quizzes**

Answers are provided for you in a link entitled "Web Activity Lesson Plan." Additional Web Resources, Interactive Puzzles, and content updates are also available.

Visit the Glencoe Web site at socialstudies.glencoe.com for social studies activities, updates, and links to other resources.

LOCAL OBJECTIVES

_____
_____
_____
_____
_____
_____
_____
_____
_____
_____
_____
_____
_____
_____
_____
_____
_____
_____
_____
_____

CHAPTER THEMES

Chapter Themes are listed by section on this chapter opening page of the Student Edition. A corresponding theme-based activity is available under "TEACH," and a theme-based question is asked in the Section and Chapter Assessments.

The Storyteller

Historical Setting The first European civilization, the Minoan, arose on the island of Crete, achieving a splendor comparable to the contemporary civilizations of Egypt and Mesopotamia. According to some ancient Greek legends, Zeus himself was born on Crete, died on the island, and was buried there.

Minoan Crete strongly influenced the early Greeks of the mainland and the classical culture that was to arise there.

Bulls were important in Minoan religion. Altars and shrine roofs were often surmounted by hornlike shapes, probably representing sacred bulls.

Historical Significance

Answers: *Governments of ancient Greece included kingdoms, aristocracies, tyrannies, oligarchies, and democracies. Most societies were based on trade and commerce, although Sparta emphasized militarism.*

The most important Greek political idea to influence later Western civilization was citizen participation in government.

Have students use the **Chapter 4 Overview** at worldhistory. glencoe.com as a prereading and postreading exercise for understanding chapter content.

The Rise of Ancient Greece

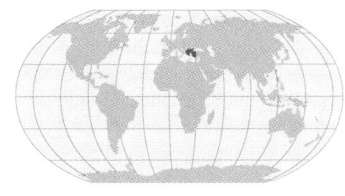

Chapter Themes

▶ **Relation to Environment** Closeness to the sea helps make the early Greeks seafarers. *Section 1*
▶ **Movement** The Greeks establish colonies throughout the area of the Mediterranean and Black Seas. *Section 2*
▶ **Regionalism** Two leading Greek city-states—Athens and Sparta—differ greatly from each other in their values, cultures, and achievements. *Section 3*
▶ **Conflict** Greek city-states together fight the Persians; then the city-states, led by rivals Athens and Sparta, fight each other. *Section 4*

The Storyteller

An eager crowd gathered in the sun-drenched sports arena just outside King Minos's palace at Knossos on the Aegean island of Crete. According to legend, Minos ruled over the Minoan civilization in the 2000s B.C. The Minoans' favorite event—bull leaping—was about to begin. The crowd gasped as a raging bull, representing the earthquakes that shook Crete, charged a young male gymnast who stood motionless. Just before the collision, the gymnast grabbed the bull's horns and somersaulted onto the bull's back. Then his body arched into the air, and he completed a back flip, landing in the arms of his female partner waiting nearby. The crowd cheered at the end of this spectacle, part sport and part religious ritual. By leaping over the bull, the gymnast had shown that no matter how much the earth trembled, the Minoans would stay on Crete.

Historical Significance

What kinds of governments and societies developed in ancient Greece? How have Greek political ideas shaped the development of Western civilization?

c. 1600 B.C. Minoan civilization reaches its peak.

c. 1100 B.C. Dorians invade Greece.

c. 700 B.C. Greeks found colonies in the Mediterranean area.

c. 460 B.C. Golden Age of Athens begins.

104

GEOGRAPHY CONNECTION

Place Have students locate the eastern Mediterranean region in the Atlas of their texts. On a wall map, point out the location of the Balkan Peninsula, the Aegean Sea, Asia Minor, and Crete while students follow along on their maps. How did geography affect the life of the ancient Greeks? *(Mountains protected the people from foreign attack, but limited communication within the region. Numerous harbors and the proximity of the sea led many people to take up fishing, trading, and piracy. Because of the mild climate, many activities were carried on outdoors.)*

History & Art This painting was created by the Minoans, the people of the ancient Aegean island of Crete. Much of what we know about this civilization comes from its art works; although the Minoans had a form of writing, it has not been deciphered. What can you guess about Minoan culture from looking at the painting? *(The Minoans enjoyed watching and participating in athletic events; they had skilled artists.)*

 Performance Assessment

Refer to the activity on page 104C of the Planning Guide.

For an additional activity, refer to Activity 4 in the *Performance Assessment Strategies and Activities* booklet.

Using Your History Journal

Students may want to refer to this essay as they read about later societies, especially those that were not democratic.

Minoan wall painting (fresco) of bull leaping. Archaeological Museum, Heraklion, Crete, Greece

WORLD HISTORY *Online*

Chapter Overview

Visit the *World History: The Human Experience* Web site at **worldhistory.glencoe.com** and click on *Chapter 4—Chapter Overview* to preview the chapter.

Your History Journal

Athens laid the foundation for the Western concept of democratic government. After reading about Athenian democracy, write an essay entitled "What Democracy Means to Me."

 GLENCOE TECHNOLOGY

VIDEODISC
Use MindJogger to preview chapter content.

MindJogger Videoquiz
Chapter 4
Disc 1 Side A

 Also available in VHS.

Chapter 4 *The Rise of Ancient Greece* **105**

✚ EXTRA CREDIT PROJECT

Report The Greek alphabet and the Greek language played an important role in the development of our own alphabet and language. Have students research and report to the class on some aspect of one of these topics. For example, one student might wish to report on Greek words in government *(aristocracy, democracy, politics)*, another on Greek words in science *(atom, botany, zoology)*, a third on Greek words in the arts *(architecture, music, poetry)*. Standard reference works, such as encyclopedias, should provide adequate information.

SECTION THEME

▶ **Relation to Environment**
Closeness to the sea helps make the early Greeks seafarers.

Guide to Reading

For reading strategies to help students read effectively see pages 12–13. Have students think about the main head as they read the subheads.

Vocabulary Pre-check

☐ Use the Vocabulary PuzzleMaker for Chapter 4 to create a crossword puzzle to reinforce section terms. **L1 LEP**

🗀 Use Vocabulary Activity 4 to introduce vocabulary terms. **L1 LEP**

FOCUS

Section Objective

Describe where and how the early civilizations of Greece developed.

BELLRINGER
Motivational Activity

Before taking roll at the beginning of the class period, project Section Focus Transparency 4-1 and have students answer the activity questions. Discuss students' responses.

🗀 This activity is also available as a blackline master.

Section 1

Beginnings

Guide to Reading

Read to Find Out
Main Idea *Greece developed a variety of early civilizations.*

▶ **Terms to Define**
labyrinth, bard

▶ **People to Meet**
Sir Arthur Evans, the Minoans, the Mycenaeans, Homer, Heinrich Schliemann

▶ **Places to Locate**
Crete, Mycenae

The Storyteller

The hero Sarpedon was a son of Zeus, but destined to die in the Trojan War. He held before him the perfect circle of his shield, a lovely thing of beaten bronze, which the bronze-smith had hammered out for him. On its inward side were stitched ox-hides in close folds with golden staples all around the circle.... And now Sarpedon spoke to Glaukos, son of Hippolochos: "Glaukos, why are we honored before others with the best seats, choice cuts of meat, brimming wine cups, and the best plots of land? Because we stand in the front line of blazing battle. Friend, if we could escape, and live forever ageless and immortal, I would not go on fighting, or encourage you to fight. But now, since the spirits of death stand close by us, let us go win glory for ourselves, or yield it to others."

Entrance to the ancient silver mines at Siphnos, Greece

—adapted from *The Iliad of Homer*, translated by Richmond Lattimore, 1951

The ancient Greeks became the people who set their stamp on the Mediterranean region and who also contributed greatly to the way we live today. Every time you go to the theater or watch the Olympic Games on television, you enjoy an activity that has its roots in ancient Greece. Modern public buildings often reflect Greek architectural styles. Above all, the ancient Greeks developed the Western concept of democracy.

The Aegean Area

Ancient Greece included the southern part of Europe's Balkan Peninsula and a group of small, rocky islands, most of which dot the Aegean (ih•JEE•uhn) Sea near Asia Minor. Low-lying, rugged mountains make up about three-fourths of the Greek mainland. Between the mountain ranges and along the coast lie fertile plains suitable for farming. Short, swift rivers flow from the interior to the sea, and the long, indented coastline provides many fine harbors. The climate is mild, with rainy winters. Afternoon breezes carrying cooler air from the sea offset the hot, dry summers.

The mountains both protected and isolated Greeks on the mainland. Besides making attacks by foreigners difficult, the mountains limited travel and communication between communities. The Greek people, therefore, never united under one government, although they spoke one language and practiced the same religion.

Because of the numerous harbors and since no place in Greece is more than 50 miles (80 km) from the coast, many Greeks turned to the sea to earn their living. They became fishers, traders, and even pirates.

In addition, the mild climate allowed the ancient Greeks to spend much of their time outdoors. People assembled for meetings in the public square, teachers met their students in public gardens, and actors performed plays in open-air theaters.

SECTION RESOURCES

🗀 **Reproducible Masters**
• Lecture Notes 4-1
• Reproducible Lesson Plan 4-1
• Vocabulary Activity 4
• Guided Reading Activity 4-1
• Time Line Activity 4
• Section Quiz 4-1
• Reading Essentials and Study Guide 4-1

🕯 **Transparencies**
• Section Focus Transparency 4-1
• Mapping History Overlay Transparency 4

Multimedia
📱 Focus on World Art Print 6
💻 Interactive Tutor Self-Assessment Software
💻 Testmaker

Visualizing History Chalices such as these are evidence that Mycenaean kings were rich and powerful.
What evidence suggests that these kings were meticulous about collecting taxes?

Aegean Civilizations

Greek myths referred to an early civilization on the island of **Crete**, southeast of the Greek mainland, but for a long time historians disputed this claim. Then, about A.D. 1900, British archaeologist **Sir Arthur Evans** unearthed remains of the Minoan civilization, which flourished from about 2500 B.C. to 1450 B.C.

The Minoans

At Knossos (NAH•suhs) on Crete, Evans uncovered the palace of legendary King Minos. Throughout the palace, passageways twist and turn in all directions to form a labyrinth, or maze. Brightly colored murals that decorate palace walls show that the Minoans—both men and women—curled their hair, bedecked themselves with gold jewelry, and set off their narrow waists with wide metal belts. The murals also show that they were fond of dancing and sporting events, such as boxing matches.

Minoan women apparently enjoyed a higher status than women in other early civilizations. For example, Minoan religion had more goddesses than gods. The chief deity of Crete was the Great Goddess, or Earth Mother, whom the Minoans believed caused the birth and growth of all living things.

The Minoans earned their living from sea trade. Crete's oak and cedar forests provided wood for ships. In addition, the island's location enabled Minoan traders to reach Egypt and Mesopotamia. By 2000 B.C., Minoan fleets dominated the eastern Mediterranean, carrying goods and keeping the seas free from pirates. The ships also guarded Crete

against outside attack, which explains why the Minoans did not build walls around their cities.

Minoan civilization reached its peak around 1600 B.C. About 250 years later it collapsed. Some historians think its cities were destroyed by huge tidal waves resulting from an undersea earthquake. Others think that a people from the Greek mainland, **the Mycenaeans** (MY•suh•NEE•uhnz), succeeded in invading Crete.

The Mycenaeans

The Mycenaeans originated among the Indo-European peoples of central Asia. About 2000 B.C., as a result of the rapid growth of their population, the Mycenaeans began moving out from their homeland. Upon entering the Balkan Peninsula, they gradually intermarried with the local people—known as Hellenes (HEH•leenz)—and set up a group of kingdoms.

Each Mycenaean kingdom centered around a hilltop on which was built a royal fortress. Stone walls circled the fortress, providing a shelter for the people in time of danger. Nobles lived on their estates outside the walls. They would turn out in armor when the king needed them to supply horse-drawn chariots. The slaves and tenants who farmed the land lived in villages on these estates.

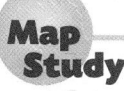

Aegean Civilizations 1400 B.C.

BALKAN PENINSULA
Mount Olympus
Hellespont
Troy
GREECE
Aegean Sea
ASIA MINOR
Mycenae
Attica
Ionian Sea
Peloponnesus
Mediterranean Sea
Knossos
Phaestus
Crete

☐ Aegean settlements

0   40   80 mi.
0   40   80 km
Lambert Azimuthal Equal-Area Projection

Map Study The Greek civilization grew out of the Minoan and Mycenaean civilizations that thrived in the Aegean area from about 3000 B.C. to 1000 B.C.
1. Location The remains of the Minoan civilization were discovered on what island?
2. Location Where did the Mycenaeans originate before settling in the Aegean area?

TEACH
Guided Practice

THEME Relation to Environment

Ask: **What geographical features offered protection to Minoan cities?** (*bodies of water*) **to Mycenaean cities?** (*mountains*) **How did the Minoans and Mycenaeans further protect their cities?** (*Minoans had ships to guard against attack; Mycenaeans built walls around their cities.*) **L1**

Visualizing History Other Mycenaean treasures include gold masks and jewelry.
Answer to Caption: *Government officials kept records of the wealth of everyone in the kingdom.*

Map Study

Answers
1. *Crete*
2. *central Asia*

Map Skills Practice

Reading a Map What bodies of water border mainland Greece on the west, east, and south? (*Ionian Sea, Aegean Sea, Mediterranean Sea*)

A&E HOME VIDEO

The following videotape programs are available from Glencoe:
• **Atlantis: The Lost Civilization**
• **Mystical Monuments of Ancient Greece**

To find classroom resources to accompany these videos, check the following home page:
**A&E Television:
http://www.aetv.com**

Class Presentation Organize the class into small groups and have each group find additional information about a Greek hero—either from the *Iliad* or the *Odyssey* or from myths. Each group should decide how best to present its information to the class and should assign tasks for the final presentation. Encourage students to be as inventive as possible. Some suggestions include: acting out a myth about a hero; recording information about the hero on audiotape; recording an oral/graphic presentation on videotape; delivering an oral/graphic presentation live; drawing and displaying posters that include a brief description of what is depicted. **L1**

Focus on World Art Print 6

 Mapping History Overlay Transparency 4

Visualizing History

After finding the rich tombs at Mycenae, Schliemann announced that they were the remains of the legendary king Agamemnon and his companions, from the time of the Trojan War. We now know that they are much older, dating from the 1500s B.C.
Answer to Caption: *fighting among the Mycenaeans themselves and invasions by the Dorians*

Independent Practice

📁 Guided Reading Activity 4-1 **L1**

📁 Time Line Activity 4 **L1**

Critical Thinking Have students write two paragraphs explaining why they would rather be a Mycenaean or a Minoan in the period before 1400 B.C. Have them consider such things as lifestyle, economics, and location. Ask several students to read their paragraphs aloud. **L2**

Who?What?Where?When?

The labyrinth, or maze, in the palace at Knossos was supposedly constructed by King Minos to house a dangerous monster, the Minotaur. A legendary hero named Theseus killed the Minotaur and married Ariadne, Minos's daughter.

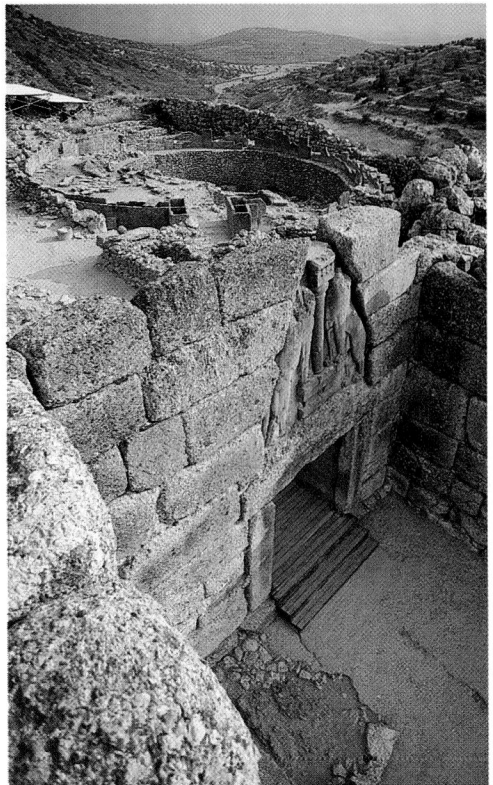

Visualizing History Heinrich Schliemann discovered six tombs at the royal grave circle near the lion gate at Mycenae. They contained 16 skeletons and a large hoard of gold. *What events ended Mycenaean civilization?*

The palaces in the city of **Mycenae** served as centers of both government administration and production. Inside, artisans tanned leather, sewed clothes, fashioned jars for storing wine and olive oil, and made bronze swords and ox-hide shields. To help in collecting taxes, government officials kept records of the wealth of every person in the kingdom. They collected taxes in the form of wheat, livestock, and honey, which were stored in the palace.

Minoan traders visited the Greek mainland soon after the Mycenaeans set up their kingdom. Gradually, the Mycenaeans adopted many elements of Minoan culture—metalworking and shipbuilding techniques and navigation by the sun and stars. The Mycenaeans worshiped the Minoan Earth Mother as well.

108   **Chapter 4**   *The Rise of Ancient Greece*

By the mid-1400s B.C., the Mycenaeans had conquered the Minoans and controlled the Aegean area. By 1100 B.C., however, fighting among the Mycenaeans had destroyed the great hilltop fortresses. Soon after, a new wave of invaders, the Greek-speaking Dorians, entered Greece from the north. Armed with iron weapons, the Dorians easily overran the mainland.

Historians call the next 300 years of Greek history a "dark age." During this period, overseas trade stopped, poverty increased, and people lost skills such as writing and craft making. Thousands of refugees fled the mainland and settled in Ionia—the west coast of Asia Minor and its adjoining islands.

By 750 B.C. the Ionians had reintroduced culture, crafts, and skills to their homeland, including the alphabet used by Phoenician traders. The "dark age" of the Dorians ended, and a new Greek civilization with Mycenaean elements emerged. The new civilization—called Hellenic, after the original people of Greece—flourished from about the 700s B.C. until 336 B.C.

Poets and Heroes

During the "dark age," bards, or singing storytellers, had kept alive Mycenaean traditions. With their new ability to write, the Greeks began to record the epic poems that the bards had passed from generation to generation.

The *Iliad* and the *Odyssey*

According to tradition, a blind poet named **Homer** who lived during the 700s B.C. composed the two most famous Greek epics—the *Iliad* and the *Odyssey*. Homer set the *Iliad* and the *Odyssey* during and after the legendary Trojan War. The Mycenaeans had supposedly fought the people of Troy in the mid-1200s B.C. In A.D. 1870 **Heinrich Schliemann**, a German archaeologist, claimed that Troy actually existed and was a major trading city in Asia Minor.

The *Iliad* begins when a Trojan prince named Paris falls in love with Helen, the wife of a Mycenaean king, and takes her with him to Troy. To avenge Helen's kidnapping, the Mycenaeans lay siege to Troy for 10 years, but they cannot capture the city. Finally, they trick the Trojans by building a huge, hollow wooden horse. The best Mycenaean soldiers hide inside the horse, while the rest board their ships and pretend to sail away. The joyful Trojans, thinking themselves victorious, bring the gift horse into the city. That night, the Greeks creep out of the horse, slaughter the Trojan men, enslave

---

MEETING SPECIAL NEEDS ACTIVITIES

Language Delayed Have students who find it hard to define and use larger words look for difficult words in the text and copy them into a notebook. Assign partners to work with them to define each word. Then use each word in another context to promote understanding. **L1**

Learning Style: Verbal/Linguistic For students who need a challenge, have them find and read sections of the *Iliad* or the *Odyssey* and present interpretations of what they have read to the class. Have students place the section they will interpret in context for their listeners. **L2**

Erich Lessing, Magnum

Trojan Horse

O n this Greek vase from the 600s B.C. the Trojan horse of myth and epic stands tall. According to the Greek poet Homer—who described the Trojan War in his epic poem *Iliad*—for ten long years the Mycenaeans of Greece [bat]led their enemies who lived within the walls of the [Turk]ish city of Troy. The two sides were so well [mat]ched that only a clever strategy of war could [prod]uce victory. So the Greeks came up with one: They [buil]t a great wooden horse, so large that a cargo of [sold]iers could hide in its belly. Then they set the horse [on w]heels and gave it to Troy as a "gift." Having tricked their way into Troy, the Greek soldiers leapt out of the horse and conquered their foe.

While time has blurred the line between historic fact and Homeric epic (written centuries after the struggle), an important war did take place in which a loose federation of Greek kings set out to conquer the city-state of Troy. Homer's epic reveals that piracy and plunder were part of that era's commerce. Archaeologists have uncovered the ruins of a mighty Turkish fortress that once commanded the narrows of the Hellespont. Modern opinions, however, differ as to whether or not this was the site of Homer's Troy.

Chapter 4 *The Rise of Ancient Greece* **109**

TEACH

Remind students that the *Iliad* and the *Odyssey* are epic poems, not reliable historic accounts of the Trojan War. According to scholars, Homer's totals—1,186 Greek ships carrying at least 60,000 soldiers who fought for 10 years—are gross exaggerations. Ask students why they think the poet, or poets, used those inflated figures. (*They wanted to make the heroes seem grand; the figures had probably been increased in oral retellings little by little over the years.*)

CURRICULUM CONNECTION

LITERATURE
The story of the Trojan horse is only touched upon in Homer; in its fullest version, it is found in the *Aeneid*, the Latin epic poem by Virgil. The hero, Aeneas, supposedly founded Rome after having fought in the Trojan War.

you don't say...

"Achilles' heel" is used to indicate a person's weak point. It is just one of several phrases still used in English derived from Greek legends about the Trojan War. When the Greek hero Achilles was a baby, his mother dipped him into a sacred river to make him invulnerable, but she did not wet the heel she held onto; it was in this heel that Achilles was mortally wounded at Troy.

Linking Past and Present

Tubs and Toilets The Minoans were one of the first civilizations to use bathtubs. They also had toilets. Both tubs and toilets bore a noticeable similarity to modern bathroom appointments.

Visualizing History No one knows what Homer looked like, or even if there was such a person. But because the ancient epics were so much admired, artists and sculptors have imagined the appearance of their author.
Answer to Caption: *The wife of a Mycenaean king, seized and taken to Troy; her kidnapping brought on the Trojan War.*

ASSESS

Check for Understanding

Assign Section 1 Assessment as homework or as an in-class activity.

◻ Use Interactive Tutor Self-Assessment Software to review Section 1.

---

the women and children, and burn the city to the ground.

The *Odyssey* describes the homeward wanderings of the Mycenaean king Odysseus after the fall of Troy. Because it took him 10 years to return to Greece, people refer to any long, adventure-filled journey as an *odyssey*.

Teaching Greek Values

Eventually, schools in ancient Greece used the *Iliad* and the *Odyssey* to present to students many of the values of Hellenic civilization. For example, in an exciting description of men marching to war, the *Iliad* taught students to be proud of their Greek heritage and their heroic ancestors:

❝ As a ravening fire blazes over a vast forest and the mountains, and its light is seen afar, so while they marched the sheen from their forest of bronze [spears] went up dazzling into high heaven.

As flocks of wildfowl on the wing, geese or cranes or long-necked swans fly this way and that way over the Asian meadows, proud of the power of their wings, and they settle on and on honking as they go until they fill the meadow with sound: so flocks of men poured out of their camp onwards over the Scamandrian plain, and the ground thundered terribly under the tramp of horses and of men. ❞

—Homer, from the *Iliad*, mid-700s B.C.

The *Iliad* and the *Odyssey* also represented other values of Hellenic civilization, such as a love for nature, the importance of husband-wife relationships and tender feelings, and loyalty between friends. Hellenic schools also used the two epics to teach students to always strive for excellence and to meet with dignity whatever fate had in store.

A Family of Deities

In Greek religion, the activities of gods and goddesses explained why people behaved the way they did and why their lives took one direction rather than another. The Greeks also believed that their powerful deities caused the events of the physical world to occur—such as the coming of spring or violent storms with thunder and lightning.

Most ancient peoples feared their deities. They believed that people were put on the earth only to obey and serve the gods and goddesses. The Greeks

110 **Chapter 4** *The Rise of Ancient Greece*

---

were the first people to feel differently. They placed importance on the worth of the individual. Because they believed in their own value, the Greeks had a great deal of self-respect. This allowed them to approach their gods with dignity.

Much more than other civilizations did, the Greeks humanized their deities. Unlike the half-animal gods and goddesses of Egypt, Greek deities had totally human forms. They behaved like humans, too—marrying, having children, lying, and murdering. Frequently jealous of one another, the Greek deities quarreled and sometimes played tricks on one another. They also possessed super-human powers. Since the Greeks saw their deities as sources of power, both physical and mental, they tried to be like them by doing everything to the best of their ability.

Gods and Goddesses

The gods and goddesses of ancient Greece combined features of both Minoan and Mycenaean deities. For example, different Greek goddesses took over different aspects of the Earth Mother. Athena became the goddess of wisdom and art, Demeter became the goddess of agriculture, and Aphrodite became the goddess of love and beauty. Each community chose a particular god or goddess as its patron and protector, but all Greeks worshiped as their chief deity the Mycenaean god Zeus.

Visualizing History The Greek poet Homer (below) wrote of the ancient Mycenaean king Agamemnon. Nineteenth-century discoveries raised Homer's work from the rank of myth to that of history. *Who was Helen of Troy?*

MAKING CONNECTIONS ACTIVITY

Religion Most peoples of the ancient world were polytheistic, worshiping many gods. Have students make three lists: one of the major gods of ancient Egypt, a second of the important Sumerian deities, and a third of the Greek gods. Have them point out similarities and differences. Both the Greeks and the Egyptians, for example, had a god of the sun, but Greek attitudes toward their gods differed from those of the Egyptians. **L2**

Visualizing History Dionysus shown riding a leopard. Greek tragedy was developed from the odes sung by choruses in honor of the god Dionysus. *Where were Greek dramas performed?*

Greeks believed that the 12 most important Greek deities lived on high Mount Olympus, an actual mountain in Greece. Each of the deities controlled a specific part of the natural world. For example, Zeus, the chief god, was thought to rule the sky, weather, and thunderstorms. His brother Pluto was thought to rule the underworld, where the dead spent eternity.

Zeus's son Apollo, the god of light, drove the sun across the sky every day in his chariot. Because the Greeks also considered Apollo to be the god of prophecy, they would bring gifts to the oracle at Delphi—a holy place to honor Apollo—and ask to have hidden knowledge revealed. Like the Shang in ancient China, the Greeks believed that oracles could predict the future. At the Delphic oracle, they would ask questions, and the priests and priestesses would interpret Apollo's replies.

Festivals

As Hellenic civilization developed, certain religious festivals became an important part of Greek life. Every four years the Greeks held a series of athletic contests "for the greater glory of Zeus." Because these contests were held at the city of Olympia, they were called the Olympic Games. The Greeks also originated the play—a celebration in honor of Dionysus, the god of wine and fertility. At these events, the audience sat on a hillside around an open space, where a chorus chanted a story about Dionysus and danced to the sound of a flute. As the years passed, cities began building permanent theaters, carving a hillside into a semicircle, adding rows of stone seats, and paving the stage area. Actors began to recite poems explaining the songs and dances of the chorus. The words they recited eventually evolved into dialogue.

SECTION 1 ASSESSMENT

Main Idea
1. Use a web diagram like the one below to identify details about where and how the early Greek civilization developed.

Development of Early Greece

Recall
2. **Define** labyrinth, bard.
3. **Identify** Sir Arthur Evans, the Minoans, the Mycenaeans, Homer, Heinrich Schliemann.

Critical Thinking
4. **Applying Information** Using Zeus, Athena, and Apollo as examples, illustrate how the ancient Greeks viewed their gods and goddesses.

Understanding Themes
5. **Relation to Environment** How did the geography and climate of Greece and the Aegean Islands affect the development of the Minoan and Mycenaean civilizations?

Chapter 4 *The Rise of Ancient Greece* **111**

SECTION 1 ASSESSMENT ANSWERS

1. Minoans: located on island of Crete; sea trade important; traders reached Egypt and Mesopotamia; ships guarded Crete from attack. Mycenaeans: from Central Asia; entered Balkan Peninsula and intermarried with Hellenes; government centered in city of Mycenae; conquered Minoans and controlled Aegean

2. All terms are defined in the Glossary.
3. Sir Arthur Evans, 107; Minoans, 107; Mycenaeans, 107; Homer, 108; Heinrich Schliemann, 108
4. Greeks believed that their deities caused the events of the physical world, and the activities of the gods explained the behavior of people.

5. **RELATION TO ENVIRONMENT**
Minoan civilization was strategically located for trade with Egypt, Mesopotamia, and the Greek mainland; the sea protected the island from invaders. The mainland offered Mycenaeans high places to build their cities. Warm climate meant activities outdoors.

700 B.C.

c. 700s B.C. Greek kings lose power to aristocrats.

600 B.C.

c. 600s B.C. Greeks learn coinage from the Lydians.

500 B.C.

c. 500 B.C. The rule of tyrants in Greek city-states ends.

Section 2

The Polis

Guide to Reading

Read to Find Out
Main Idea *Economic prosperity brought significant political and social changes to the Greek city-states.*

▶ **Terms to Define**
polis, citizen, aristocrat, phalanx, tyrant, oligarchy, democracy

▶ **Places to Locate**
Athens, Sparta

The Storyteller

An Athenian ruler had to be careful of plots hatched by jealous nobles. The tyrant Hippias, the once-mild ruler of Athens, learned this lesson. He was with his bodyguard, arranging a citywide parade, when two assassins approached. Pretending to take part in the procession, they had daggers ready, hidden behind their shields. Suddenly, seeing one of their accomplices casually talking with Hippias, they halted, thinking that he had betrayed the plot to the tyrant. Turning, they rushed within the gates, met Hippias's brother, and killed him. Afterward, Athenians found Hippias harsher, ever fearful of revolt.

The Parthenon on the Acropolis

—adapted from *The Peloponnesian War*, Thucydides, Crawley translation revised by T.E. Wick, 1892

he English language offers evidence of how ancient Greeks have influenced modern life. Words such as *police* and *politics*, for example, derive from the Greek word *polis*. The **polis**, or city-state, was the basic political unit of Hellenic civilization. Each polis developed its own pattern of life independently but shared certain features with other city-states.

The Typical Polis

A typical polis included a city and the surrounding villages, fields, and orchards. At the center of the city on the top of an acropolis (uh•KRAH•puh•luhs), or fortified hill, stood the temple of the local deity. At the foot of the acropolis the agora, or public square, served as the political center of the polis. Citizens—those who took part in government—gathered in the agora to carry out public affairs, choose their officials, and pass their laws. Artisans and merchants also conducted business in the agora.

The citizens of a polis had both rights and responsibilities. They could vote, hold public office, own property, and speak for themselves in court. In return, the polis expected them to serve in government and to defend the polis in time of war.

Citizens, however, made up only a minority of the residents of a polis. In Athens, slaves and those who were foreign-born were excluded from citizenship, and before 500 B.C. so were men who did not own land. Greek women had no political or legal rights.

Greek Colonies and Trade

The return of prosperity after the "dark age" led to an increase in Greece's population. By 700 B.C. Greek farmers no longer grew enough grain to feed everyone. As a result, each polis sent out groups of people to establish colonies in coastal areas around the Mediterranean and Black Seas.

112 **Chapter 4** *The Rise of Ancient Greece*

Colonies

Each colony kept close ties with its metropolis, or "parent city." A colony supplied its metropolis with grain—wheat and barley. Farmers on the Greek mainland produced wine, olive oil, and other cash crops for export. Because vineyards and olive groves needed fewer workers than did grain fields, many farmers moved to the cities, where they learned crafts. With more goods to sell, Greek merchants began trading throughout the Mediterranean region.

Economic Growth

During the 600s B.C. the Greeks replaced their barter system with a money economy, and their overseas trade expanded further. Merchants issued their own coins, but eventually individual city-states took over this responsibility.

The cities of Ionia in Asia Minor assumed leadership in a growing textile industry. Sheep in the interior of Asia Minor furnished the raw material. Purple dye obtained from mollusks, a type of shellfish, gave the woven materials color.

Pottery developed as a local industry wherever sufficient clay was found. Pottery made in Ionia was the earliest Greek pottery to be exported. Ionian pottery styles were based on Mycenaean and Middle Eastern influences. The artists who made and decorated the vases painted figures of birds and humans interspersed with line or geometric decorations.

Political and Social Change

Economic growth changed Greek political life. Greek communities at first were ruled by kings. By the 700s B.C., however, the kings had lost power to landholding aristocrats, or nobles, who as members of the upper class provided cavalry for the king's military ventures.

By 650 B.C. disputes arose between the aristocrats and the common people. Farmers often needed credit until harvest time. To obtain loans from the wealthy aristocrats, they had to pledge their fields as security. When they could not repay the loans, many farmers lost their land to the aristocrats and became either sharecroppers or day laborers in the cities. Some even had to sell themselves into slavery. In protest, farmers demanded political reforms.

CONNECTIONS

Geography

Sailing the Aegean

Because of their many natural harbors, the Greeks transported most goods by sea. Sea travel made good sense, given the rugged mountains of the Greek mainland. Besides, pack animals could carry only small loads short distances. Merchants found sea transport of bulky cargo—grain, timber, and even jugs of olive oil—to be practical and inexpensive.

Greek sailors could sail easily only when the wind was behind them. The prevailing northerly winds made the voyage from Athens to the Black Sea slow and difficult, but the return trip was quick and easy. Likewise, Greek ships could coast to Egypt, but they had to struggle to get home. Most ships managed only one round-trip per year.

Pottery jar showing a merchant ship

The typical Greek freighter was broad—about 25 feet (7.5 m) wide compared to a length of 80 feet (24 m). Rigged with a large square sail, this sturdy ship averaged only about 5 knots with the wind. Merchant ships usually sailed in fleets escorted by warships—galleys propelled by oarsmen.

Compare the ancient ships with today's diesel-driven giants. A container ship makes the round-trip between the United States and Europe in 21 days. It holds cargo in 1,000 containers—four of which are the size of one Greek freighter. Some things have not changed, however. The Greek merchant fleet of today ranks among the largest in the world.

Linking Past and Present ACTIVITY

Explain why the ancient Greeks relied on the sea for the transport of goods. In what kind of vessels did they sail? How has cargo transport changed since ancient times?

COOPERATIVE LEARNING ACTIVITY

Skit Have students write and produce a skit that shows typical activity in an agora, including parts for women, enslaved people, children, aristocrats, artisans, and merchants. Assign groups to handle various activities: scriptwriting; designing and producing a simple set, costumes, program, and promotional materials; acting; and directing.

The skit should clearly convey through dialogue and action the operation of democracy in the polis. After the skit, have students conduct a poll to see whether this aim was accomplished. **L1**

TEACH

Guided Practice

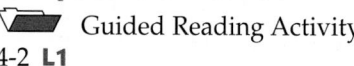 **Movement**

Ask: What types of movement resulted from colonization? *(Greeks left their poleis to establish colonies. Farmers on the mainland moved to cities. Greek traders sailed throughout the region.)* **L1**

Independent Practice

Guided Reading Activity 4-2 **L1**

 Linking Past and Present

Sailing the Aegean

Because Greek ships were small, they could carry very few provisions. As much as possible, ships hugged the coasts so that they could land frequently to take on food and water.

ANSWERS

They had excellent natural harbors, while rugged mountains hindered inland transportation. Greek sailors traveled on sturdy freighters with large square sails, sometimes escorted by warships. Cargo today is carried by giant diesel-driven container ships as well as by trains, planes, and trucks.

ASSESS

Check for Understanding

Assign Section 2 Assessment as homework or as an in-class activity.

Use Interactive Tutor Self-Assessment Software to review Section 2.

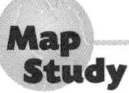

Map Study

Answer

wine and olive oil

Map Skills Practice

Reading a Map How far from Greece were the most distant Greek colonies? *(around 1,200 miles [about 1,900 kilometers])*

Evaluate

 Section Quiz 4-2

Use the Testmaker to create a customized quiz for Section 2.

Reteach

Have students summarize the chief political and social changes in Greece between 700 and 500 B.C.

Reading Essentials and Study Guide 4-2

Enrich

Have students write letters as if they were early Greek merchants promoting trade.

CLOSE

Ask students to compare the advantages and disadvantages of living in a Greek city-state with those of modern city life.

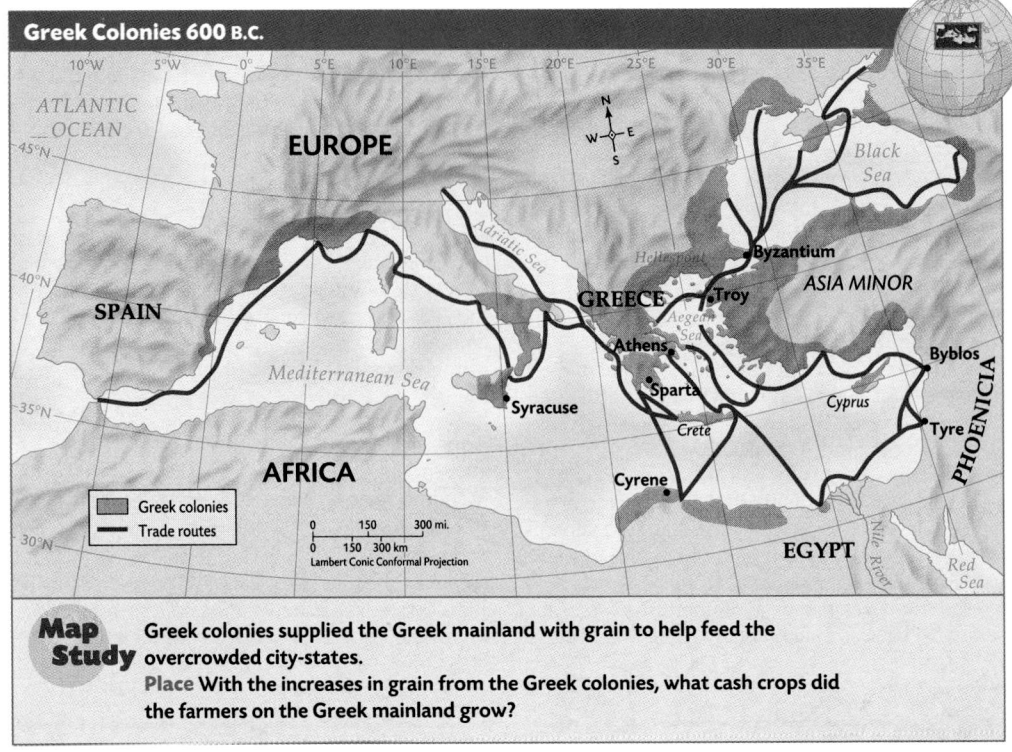

Greek Colonies 600 B.C.

Map Study Greek colonies supplied the Greek mainland with grain to help feed the overcrowded city-states.
Place With the increases in grain from the Greek colonies, what cash crops did the farmers on the Greek mainland grow?

The farmers, who were foot soldiers, were becoming more valuable to Greek armies than the aristocrats, who were cavalry. As Greek armies came to rely on the phalanx—rows of foot soldiers using their shields to form a wall—aristocrats began to lose influence. Middle-class, non-landowning merchants and artisans, thus far excluded from citizenship, wanted a voice in the government and joined the farmers in their demands. Merchants and artisans also wanted the polis to advance their interests by encouraging industry and by protecting profitable overseas trade routes.

As a result of the unrest, tyrannies arose. A tyranny was created when one man, called a tyrant, seized power and ruled the polis single-handedly. Although most tyrants ruled fairly, the harshness of a few gave *tyranny* its present meaning—rule by a cruel and unjust person.

Tyrants ruled various Greek city-states until about 500 B.C. From then until 336 B.C., most city-states became either oligarchies or democracies. In an oligarchy, a few wealthy people hold power. In a democracy, or government by the people, power lies in the hands of all the citizens. The democracy of **Athens** and the oligarchy of **Sparta** became the most famous of the Greek city-states.

SECTION 2 ASSESSMENT

Main Idea
1. Use a chart like the one below to show how economic prosperity caused political changes in Greek city-states.

Economic Prosperity → Political Changes

Recall
2. **Define** polis, citizen, aristocrat, phalanx, tyrant, oligarchy, democracy.
3. **Identify** Athens, Sparta.

Critical Thinking
4. **Synthesizing Information** What arguments might a citi-

zen of an ancient Greek polis present for or against changing citizenship?

Understanding Themes
5. **Movement** What kind of relationship existed between a Greek colony and its metropolis?

SECTION 2 ASSESSMENT ANSWERS

1. nobles became a powerful ruling class; political unrest by farmers, merchants, and artisans resulted in rise of tyrants; city-states became oligarchies and democracies
2. All terms are defined in the Glossary.
3. Athens, 114; Sparta, 114
4. Students might argue that citizenship

should be extended to foot soldiers, merchants, and artisans because of their contributions to the polis; or they might argue that the polis should follow tradition and continue to restrict citizenship.

5. **MOVEMENT** A Greek colony kept close religious, cultural, and eco-

nomic ties with its metropolis, usually supplying it with grain and buying products from its merchants.

650 B.C.   **600 B.C.**   **550 B.C.**   **500 B.C.**

c. 650 B.C.
Slaves revolt in Sparta.

621 B.C.
Draco enacts code of laws in Athens.

594 B.C. Solon becomes leader of Athens.

507 B.C.
Athens becomes a democracy.

Section 3

Rivals

Read to Find Out
Main Idea *Athens and Sparta each represented different Greek values.*

▶ **Terms to Define**
   constitution, rhetoric

▶ **People to Meet**
   Draco, Solon, Peisistratus, Cleisthenes

▶ **Places to Locate**
   Peloponnesus, Attica

Pausanias darted among the bushes to avoid the moonlight. Finally, stumbling, he plunged behind a large rock, his lungs heaving. Having managed to steal just one loaf of fresh bread, he knew that he must ration it out for at least two days. The ephors had declared that those caught with stolen food would be beaten severely. But, if he could just survive for two more days, he would finish the initiation and join the other young men in the barracks. He shivered quietly, trying to imagine where he might spend the next two cold nights.

—adapted from *The Ancient World*, edited by Esmond Wright, 1979

Spartan female athlete

The two leading city-states in ancient Greece—Sparta and Athens—stood in sharp contrast to each other. Though citizens of both Sparta and Athens participated in polis government, the two city-states differed greatly from each other in their values, cultures, and accomplishments.

Sparta

The descendants of the Dorian invaders of the dark age founded Sparta. It was located in the **Peloponnesus** (peh•luh•puh•NEE•suhs), a peninsula of southern Greece. Like other city-states, Sparta based its economy on agriculture.

Instead of founding overseas colonies, the Spartans invaded neighboring city-states and enslaved the local people. The polis of Sparta owned many slaves, known as helots (HEH•luhts), who farmed the estates of individual Spartans. In addition, a group of free individuals called *perioeci* (peh•REE•ee•sy)—artisans and merchants from the conquered territories—worked for the Spartans. Helots and *perioeci* together outnumbered Spartans by about 200,000 to 10,000.

Around 650 B.C., the helots revolted against their Spartan masters. It took 30 years, but the Spartans managed to suppress the revolt. They then decided that the only way they could maintain power was to establish a military society.

A Military Society

All life in Sparta revolved around the army. Spartan men strove to become first-rate soldiers, and Spartan women aspired to become mothers of soldiers. Spartans despised the other Greeks who lived behind city walls, believing that a city defended by Spartan soldiers did not need walls.

In Sparta, government officials examined newborn infants to see if they were healthy. If not, an official left the sickly infant on a hillside to die. At the age of 7, Spartan boys were taken away from their homes

Chapter 4 *The Rise of Ancient Greece* **115**

SECTION THEME

▶ **Regionalism** Two leading Greek city-states—Athens and Sparta—differ greatly from each other in their values, cultures, and achievements.

Guide to Reading

For reading strategies to help students read effectively see pages 12–13.

Vocabulary Pre-check

🔲 Use the Vocabulary PuzzleMaker for Chapter 4 to create a crossword puzzle to reinforce section terms. **L1 LEP**

📁 Use Vocabulary Activity 4 to introduce vocabulary terms. **L1 LEP**

FOCUS

Section Objective
Differentiate between the values represented by Sparta and those represented by Athens.

BELLRINGER
Motivational Activity

Before taking roll at the beginning of the class period, project Section Focus Transparency 4-3 and have students answer the activity questions. Discuss students' responses.
📁 This activity is also available as a blackline master.

SECTION RESOURCES

📁 **Reproducible Masters**
• Lecture Notes 4-3
• Reproducible Lesson Plan 4-3
• Vocabulary Activity 4
• Guided Reading Activity 4-3
• Source Reading 4
• Section Quiz 4-3
• Reading Essentials and Study Guide 4-3

🖋 **Transparencies**
• Section Focus Transparency 4-3
• World History and Art Transparency 5
• Ancient Greece

Multimedia
💻 Ancient Greece
🔲 Interactive Tutor Self-Assessment Software
🔲 Testmaker
🎵 Greece and Rome
🎞 Turning Points in World History

TEACH

Guided Practice

THEME Regionalism

Ask students to brainstorm definitions of the term *regionalism*. Then read this definition: "consciousness of and loyalty to a distinct region that has its own special characteristics." Ask students how this concept applies to their own lives and locality today. **L1**

Conflict Ask students to write a few sentences telling how they think 10,000 Spartans could keep many times that number of helots subjugated. Discuss the students' opinions. **L2**

 World History and Art Transparency 5

NATIONAL GEOGRAPHIC SOCIETY

Use these materials to enrich student understanding of ancient Greek culture.

- **NGS PICTURESHOW CD-ROM**
  Greece and Rome
- **NGS PICTUREPACK TRANSPARENCY SET**
  Ancient Greece
- **ANCIENT CIVILIZATIONS POSTER SET**
  Ancient Greece

---

and placed in military barracks. Their training included learning to read, write, and use weapons.

At age 20, Spartan men became soldiers and were sent to frontier areas. At age 30, they were expected to marry. But Spartan men could not closely supervise their family affairs. Instead, they spent their days in military drill until age 60, when they could retire from the army.

The Role of Women

The Spartans brought up women to be, like the Spartan men, as healthy and strong as possible. Female infants received as much food as their brothers, which was not the case elsewhere in Greece. Young Spartan girls trained in gymnastics, wrestling, and boxing. The women in Sparta married at age 19 rather than at 14—the average marrying age in most of Greece—which increased the likelihood that their children would be healthy.

Sparta gave its women more personal freedoms than the women of other Greek city-states received.

Spartan women could go shopping in the marketplace, attend dinners at which nonfamily members were present, own property, and express opinions on public issues. They could not, however, take part in government.

Sparta's Government

According to tradition, Sparta's government was set up by a lawmaker named Lycurgus during the 800s B.C. Two kings, who ruled jointly, officially governed Sparta. Except for leading the army and conducting religious services, however, Spartan kings had little power. The Assembly, made up of all male citizens over the age of 30, passed laws and made decisions concerning war and peace. Each year the Assembly elected five overseers, or ephors (EH•fuhrs), to administer public affairs. The ephors could also veto legislation. A Council of Elders, consisting of 28 men over the age of 60, proposed laws to the Assembly and served as a supreme court.

Images of the Times

The Glory of Greece

Archaeological treasures and architectural remains remind the world of the achievements of Greek civilization.

The Parthenon crowns the Acropolis at Athens.

Greek sculptors in the classical period depicted living and moving people in natural poses.

116

Images of the Times   The Glory of Greece

We tend to think of Greek buildings and sculptures as white or cream-colored—the color of old marble. In ancient times, however, they were much more colorful. The Greeks painted both buildings and statues in reds, blues, and other bright colors.

The Acropolis in Athens has suffered extensive damage in its long history. Over the centuries, various buildings were used as a mosque, an official residence, and a Turkish harem. At one time, when the Parthenon was being used as a powder magazine, it was hit by a bombardment that caused a huge explosion. Today air pollution poses a serious threat to the architectural remains.

Results of Militarism

The Spartans succeeded in maintaining control over their subject peoples for nearly 250 years. They paid a price, however. Suspicious of any new ideas that might bring change, the Spartans lagged far behind other Greek city-states in economic development. For example, Sparta used heavy iron bars instead of coins as currency. In this way, it hoped to discourage trade and to remain self-reliant. The Spartans also shunned philosophy, science, and the arts, while Athens and other city-states advanced in these fields. The Spartans, however, were exceptional Olympic athletes, and their soldiers played key roles in defending Greece against invaders.

Athens

Northeast of the Peloponnesus—on a peninsula of central Greece named **Attica**—people descended from the Mycenaeans established the city-state of Athens. They named their polis after the goddess Athena. Like the early rulers of the other city-states, Athenian kings and aristocrats in the 600s B.C. faced demands by small farmers, merchants, and artisans for economic and political reforms.

Around this time, the governing methods of Athens and Sparta diverged. Athens gradually expanded its definition of citizenship to encompass more people. Initially, only a man whose father and maternal grandfather had been citizens could be a citizen; however, non-landowning citizens could not participate in Athens's Assembly. Athenians called the many free (non-enslaved) foreigners who lived in Athens *metics*. These people could not own land or participate in government. By 507 B.C., however, the constitution, or plan of government, of Athens stated that all free, Athenian-born men were citizens regardless of what class they belonged to, and that they could participate in the Assembly regardless of whether they owned land. This political change reduced much of the friction between social classes and enabled Athens to forge ahead.

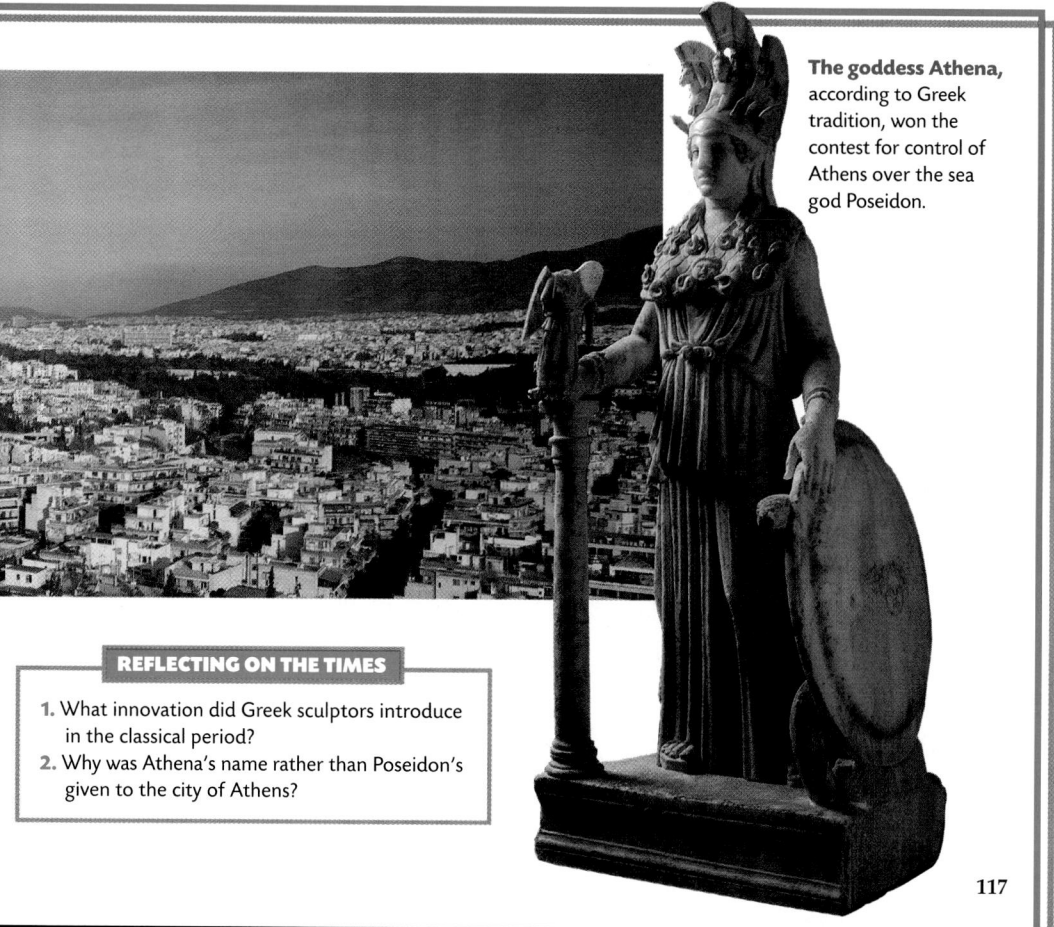

The goddess Athena, according to Greek tradition, won the contest for control of Athens over the sea god Poseidon.

REFLECTING ON THE TIMES

1. What innovation did Greek sculptors introduce in the classical period?
2. Why was Athena's name rather than Poseidon's given to the city of Athens?

117

Independent Practice

 Guided Reading Activity 4-3 **L1**

Source Reading 4

History Have students imagine that they are Athenian citizens organizing a protest march against the hated laws of the tyrant Draco. Have them create picket signs that express their points of view. Display the signs in the classroom. **L1 LEP**

City-States Have students research information about Greek city-states other than Athens and Sparta and report their findings to the class. Among the many that reward research are Argos, Corinth, Sicyon, Olympia, Delphi, Thebes, Miletus, and Ephesus. **L3**

Global Gourmet

Greece Olives were a staple of the Greek diet because olive trees grow well in dry, rocky soil. Olive oil was so important to the Greek economy that when the Spartans attacked Athens, their first move was to destroy the olive groves surrounding the city in order to weaken the Athenian economy.

ANSWERS TO REFLECTING ON THE TIMES

1. They depicted living and moving people in natural poses.
2. According to tradition, she defeated Poseidon in a contest for control of the city.

Visualizing History All important lawsuits tried anywhere in territories under Athenian control—including faraway colonies—could be appealed to the people's courts in Athens. **Answer to Caption:** *Athenians hoped that the large size would prevent jurors from being influenced by threats, bribes, or prejudice.*

Athenian Democracy
What is the meaning of democracy?
Democracy *literally means "rule by the people."*

VIDEODISC
Turning Points in World History

Side One
Chapter 5

Title: *Democracy in Greece*

Draco

Four successive leaders brought most of the changes in Athenian government. **Draco**, the first of these leaders, issued an improved code of laws in 621 B.C. The penalties given to offenders were extremely harsh. Even minor offenses, like stealing a cabbage, were punishable by death.

Over time, the word *draconian* has come to describe something that is very cruel and severe. On the other hand, because Draco's laws were written down, everyone knew exactly what the laws were. Aristocrats could no longer dictate what was legal and what was not.

Solon

The next series of reforms took place under the poet-lawmaker **Solon**, who became the leader of Athens in 594 B.C. To improve economic conditions, Solon canceled all land debts and freed debtors from slavery. He also placed limits on the amount of land any one individual could own. By urging farmers to grow cash crops rather than grain, Solon promoted trade. He also promoted industry by ordering fathers to teach their sons a skill and by extending citizenship to foreigners who would settle in Athens as skilled artisans.

Next, Solon introduced political reforms that moved Athens toward democracy while preserving some aristocratic control. He allowed citizens of all classes to participate in the Assembly and public law courts. An aristocratic Council of 400 was also established to draft measures that then went to the Assembly for approval.

Peisistratus

In 546 B.C. **Peisistratus** (pih•SIHS•truh•tuhs) took over the government of Athens. Peisistratus pushed reforms in an even more radical direction than had Solon. He divided large estates among landless farmers and extended citizenship to men who did not own land. Peisistratus provided the poor with loans and put many of them to work building temples and other public works.

Athenian Democracy

Cleisthenes (KLYS•thuh•NEEZ), the fourth leader to help reform Athens, came to power in 508 B.C. The following year he introduced a series of laws that established democracy for Athens. Through his reforms, Cleisthenes sought to end local rivalries, break the power of the aristocracy, and reorganize the structure of Athenian government.

Under Cleisthenes' constitution, the Assembly won increased powers and fully emerged as the major political body. All citizens could belong to the Assembly, in which they were considered equal before the law and guaranteed freedom of speech. In addition to passing laws, the Assembly served as a supreme court and appointed generals to run the military. A Council of 500, whose membership was open to any citizen, carried out daily government business.

Each year in a lottery, Athenian citizens chose members of the Council. They favored a lottery over a ballot, believing that all citizens were capable of holding public office. Elections, in their view, would unfairly favor the rich, who had the advantage of fame and training in public speaking. Besides, all citizens were supposed to take part in government.

Athenian democracy included a jury system to decide court cases. Juries contained from 201 to

Visualizing History A juror's token is shown above. Athenian courts demonstrated faith in the ordinary man's ability. Groups of hundreds of citizens sat on panels called *dicasteries* and decided cases by majority vote. *Why were juries so large?*

COOPERATIVE LEARNING ACTIVITY

Role Play Organize the class into groups of seven or eight. Have four or five in each group play the roles of typical residents of Athens and the remaining group members play newspaper reporters who ask them questions about their lives and times. Have the groups prepare by doing library research to find out all they can about an Athenian merchant, one of the tyrants, an upper-class woman, a priestess of Athena, or an enslaved person. Have the group work together to frame questions reporters might ask and answers that might be given. Each group should present its questions and answers to the whole class. Encourage students to strive for realism in their assumed roles. Have the audience take notes and write a summary. **L1**

1,001 members, with a majority vote needed to reach a verdict. The Athenians reasoned that the large size of their juries would keep jurors from being influenced by threats and bribes.

Athenian democracy also included a system called ostracism. Each year, citizens could write the name of an undesirable politician on a piece of baked clay called an ostracon. If a person's name appeared on 6,000 ostraca, he could be exiled.

Cleisthenes' democracy transformed Athens, but it affected only those 20 percent of Athenians who were citizens. Non-citizens—women, foreign-born males, and slaves—were still excluded from political life. In spite of these limitations, ancient Athens nevertheless laid the foundation for the Western concept of democratic government.

Athenian Education

The training an Athenian received depended on social and economic status. About a week after being born, a male child received a name and was enrolled as a citizen. Because Athens expected every citizen to hold public office at some time in his life, it required Athenian citizens to educate their sons. With few exceptions, Athenian girls—who would not participate in governing the democracy of Athens—did not receive a formal education. Instead, a girl learned household duties, such as weaving and baking, from her mother.

Private tutors educated the boys from wealthy upper-class families, while other students paid a small fee to attend a private school. Much of their education was picked up in the agora, through daily conversations and debates in the Assembly.

Athenian boys entered school at age 7 and graduated at 18. Their main textbooks were the *Iliad* and the *Odyssey*, which they learned by heart. They studied arithmetic, geometry, drawing, music, and gymnastics. When boys reached their teens, they added rhetoric, or the art of public speaking, to their studies. Because participants in a court case

were not represented by lawyers, an Athenian needed to be accomplished in rhetoric to argue his own position.

When Athenian men reached 18, they left for two years of military service. Before entering the army, they went with their fathers to the temple of Zeus to swear the following oath:

> 66 I will not bring dishonor upon my weapons nor desert the comrade by my side. I will strive to hand on my father-land greater and better than I found it. I will not consent to anyone's disobeying or destroying the constitution but will prevent him, whether I am with others or alone. I will honor the temples and the religion my forefathers established. 99
>
> —oath of enrollment in Epheboi corps, early 400s B.C.

Zapotec Temple Complex at Monte Albán

Mexico, c. 500 B.C.
Monte Albán in the valley of Oaxaca in southern Mexico became an important center of Zapotec culture. The Zapotecs flattened the mountaintop to create a large plaza, around which they designed a temple complex. They carved the slopes of the mountain into terraces for agriculture and housing. An estimated 5,000 people, or about 50 percent of the valley's population, lived at Monte Albán.

ASSESS

Check for Understanding
Assign Section 3 Assessment as homework or as an in-class activity.

☉ Use Interactive Tutor Self-Assessment Software to review Section 3.

Evaluate
🗁 Section Quiz 4-3

☉ Use the Testmaker to create a customized quiz for Section 3.

Reteach
Have students write a paragraph that explains in what areas Sparta failed to develop and why. *(trade, manufacturing, intellectual achievement; because they were suspicious of new ideas and devoted energies to becoming a military society)*

🗁 Reading Essentials and Study Guide 4-3

Enrich
Have students write a two-page essay that compares the Athenian practice of ostracism with the modern process of impeachment in the United States.

CLOSE

Write these headings on the chalkboard: *Sparta, Athens*. Have volunteers write facts about political, social, and economic life under the correct heading.

SECTION 3 ASSESSMENT

Main Idea
1. Use a chart like the one below to list the good citizenship criteria in Athens and Sparta.

Athenian Citizenship	Spartan Citizenship

Recall
2. **Define** constitution, rhetoric.
3. **Identify** Draco, Solon, Peisistratus, Cleisthenes.

Critical Thinking
4. **Evaluating Information** Were the reasons the Athenians gave for choosing government officials by lottery good ones? Why or why not?

Understanding Themes
5. **Regionalism** Contrast the city-states of Athens and Sparta in the areas of citizenship, education, and the status of women.

SECTION 3 ASSESSMENT ANSWERS

1. Athens: all citizens were expected to hold public office; men were expected to be educated and women to be trained in household duties; Sparta: men were expected to be first-rate soldiers and women to be mothers of soldiers; everyone was expected to be healthy and strong

2. All terms are defined in the Glossary.
3. Draco, 118; Solon, 118; Peisistratus, 118; Cleisthenes, 118
4. Yes: being rich or being a good speaker may win votes but may not reflect how good a job a person can do; or, no: different people have different abilities. Other methods might include choosing

officials from men who apply for the jobs or having the Assembly nominate and elect candidates.

5. **REGIONALISM** Athenian men received a broader education than Spartan men, but Athenian women had fewer rights than Spartan women.

546 B.C.
Persian armies
conquer Ionia.

490 B.C. Athenians
and Persians fight
the Battle of Marathon.

447 B.C. Pericles
begins rebuilding
of Athens.

431 B.C.
Peloponnesian
War begins.

Section 4

War, Glory, and Decline

Guide to Reading

**Read to Find Out
Main Idea** *The Persian Wars and the Peloponnesian War affected democracy in the Greek city-states.*

▶ **Terms to Define**
symposium, mercenary

▶ **People to Meet**
Darius I, Xerxes, Themistocles, Leonidas, Pericles, Aspasia

▶ **Places to Locate**
Ionia, Marathon, Thermopylae, Salamis, Delos

The **S**toryteller

The Greek historian Herodotus reported that during the Persian Wars, some Greek deserters approached the Persian king Xerxes. Questioned about what the Greeks were about to do, they told him the truth: The Olympic Games were being held. They were going to watch the athletic competitions and chariot races. When asked what the prize was for such contests, they responded that the Olympic prize was an olive wreath. Upon hearing this, a Persian noble cried out in fear: "What kind of men are these? How can we be expected to fight against men who compete with each other for no material reward, but only for honor!"

—adapted from *The Histories,* Herodotus, translated by Aubrey de Selincourt

Themistocles

As the 400s B.C. opened, the Persian Empire—then the strongest military power in the ancient world—stood poised to extend its influence into Europe. Surprisingly, the Greek city-states not only cooperated with each other in resisting the Persian attack, but they also succeeded in throwing Persia's armed forces back into Asia.

After their victory against Persia, the Greeks—especially the Athenians—enjoyed a "golden age" of remarkable cultural achievements. Then, the Greek city-states began to fight among themselves. This bitter and devastating war lasted for more than 27 years.

The Persian Wars

In 546 B.C. the Persian armies, led by Cyrus II, conquered the Greek city-states of **Ionia**, in Asia Minor. Despite the mildness of Persian rule, the Ionians disliked the conquerors. The Ionians considered the non-Greek-speaking Persians to be barbarians. In addition, an all-powerful king ruled the Persian Empire, whereas the Greek population of Ionia believed that citizens should choose their own government.

Finally, in 499 B.C., the Ionians revolted against the Persians. Even though Athens and another mainland polis sent some warships to help the Ionians, **Darius I** of Persia soon defeated the Ionians. Darius then decided to punish the mainland Greeks for helping the rebels.

Marathon

Darius first tried to send an army around the northern coast of the Aegean Sea. However, a storm destroyed his supply ships, forcing him to turn back. Two years later, in 490 B.C., Darius tried again.

This time he sent his fleet directly across the Aegean to the coastal plain of **Marathon**, about 25 miles (40 km) north of Athens. For several days the Persians awaited the Athenians. However, the Athenians, outnumbered 20,000 to 10,000, did nothing. Finally, the Persians decided to attack Athens directly. They loaded their ships with the cavalry—the strongest part of their army—and then began loading the infantry.

Not waiting for the Persians to take the offensive, the Athenians struck. The Athenian general ordered his well-disciplined foot soldiers to charge down the hills above Marathon at the Persian infantry, which stood in shallow water waiting to board the ships. This tactic astounded the Persians, who believed that infantrymen would fight only with the support of horsemen and archers. Marathon was a terrible defeat for the Persians, who reportedly lost 6,400 men compared to only 192 Greek casualties.

Salamis

After Marathon, the Persians withdrew to Asia Minor, but they returned 10 years later. In 480 B.C. Darius's son and successor, **Xerxes**, invaded Greece from the north, this time with 200,000 soldiers. Because so huge an army could not live off the land, offshore supply ships accompanied them.

Once again the Greeks, this time under the leadership of Sparta, faced the Persians. A few years before, the oracle at Delphi had said that Greece would be safe behind a "wooden wall." The Athenian general **Themistocles** (thuh•MIHS•tuh •KLEEZ) tried to convince his Greek allies that a "wooden wall" meant a fleet of ships and that the way to defeat the Persians was to challenge them at sea.

To do this, the Greek army had to set up a delaying action on land. They chose **Thermopylae** (thuhr•MAH•puh•lee) as the place—a mountain pass north of Athens. There, 7,000 Greeks led by King **Leonidas** of Sparta stood firm against the Persians for three days. Then a Greek traitor showed the enemy a trail over which they could attack the Greeks from the rear. Realizing that he would soon be surrounded, Leonidas sent off most of his troops. But he and 300 fellow Spartans remained obedient to the law of their polis—never

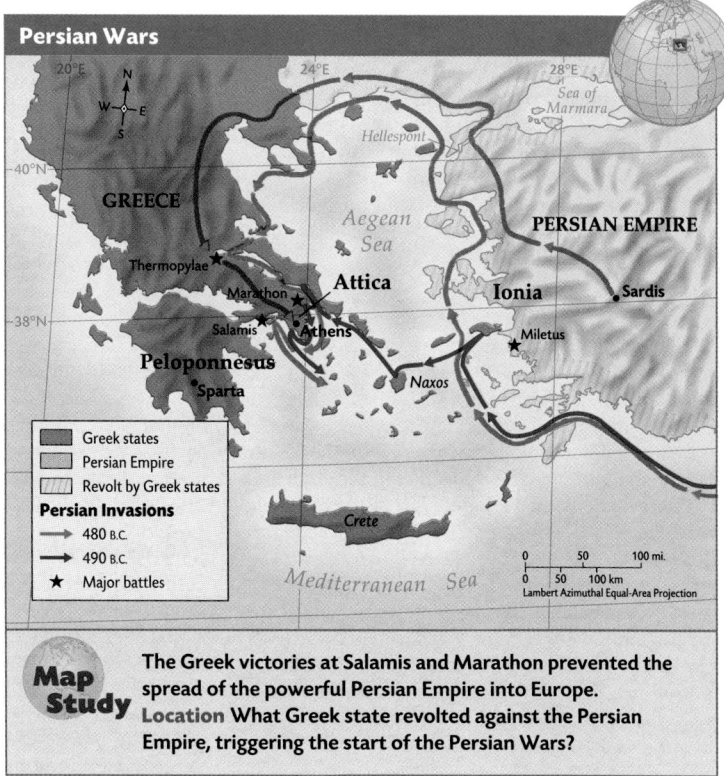

Persian Wars

Map Study

The Greek victories at Salamis and Marathon prevented the spread of the powerful Persian Empire into Europe.
Location What Greek state revolted against the Persian Empire, triggering the start of the Persian Wars?

Greek states
Persian Empire
Revolt by Greek states
Persian Invasions
→ 480 B.C.
→ 490 B.C.
★ Major battles

Footnotes to History

Marathon
According to legend, a messenger named Pheidippides (fy•DIH•puh•DEEZ) carried the news of the victory at Marathon back to Athens. Because Pheidippides had previously run 280 miles (448 km) in four days, he barely managed to reach the city and deliver his message before he fell to the ground, dead from exhaustion. Ever since, people have used the word *marathon* to describe a long-distance race.

Chapter 4 *The Rise of Ancient Greece* **121**

TEACH

Guided Practice

THEME Conflict

Have students name some of the reasons that other city-states came to resent Athens and eventually went to war with Athens. *(Answers should include: Pericles' use of Delian League money to build the Parthenon, his insistence that criminal cases be tried only in Athens, and his forcing other city-states to adopt the Athenian coinage system.)* **L1**

Map Study

Answers
Ionia

Map Skills Practice

Reading a Map How did Persian strategy in 480 B.C. differ from that in 490 B.C.? *(In 480 B.C., the Persians attacked from the north, rather than from the east. They also divided their forces in 480 B.C., with some on land and some at sea.)*

Pericles Point out that many great men and women have both positive and negative aspects to their lives and characters. Have students list positive and negative aspects of Pericles' life and accomplishments. *(positive: led Athens through its Golden Age, built the Parthenon and other buildings, spoke out for democracy; negative: used Delian League money to build Parthenon, tried to force other city-states to accept Athenian leadership, helped push Sparta to start Peloponnesian War)* **L2**

COOPERATIVE LEARNING ACTIVITY

Oral-Visual Presentations Organize the class into two groups for further study of the Persian Wars and the Peloponnesian War. Each group should prepare an oral and visual presentation for the other group. Organize each group into subgroups to research facets of the topic, such as the impact of geography on the battles and the leaders involved. Subgroups should also prepare visuals to add interest to the group presentation, including drawings of soldiers, weapons, battle formations, fortifications, and ships. Each group should prepare a large time line of the events. Have groups cooperatively decide how to present their completed report to the other group. Encourage them to use discussion rather than a written report. **L2**

📖 Mapping History Overlay
📼 Transparency 4

Independent Practice

📁 Guided Reading Activity
4-4 **L1**

Daily Life Have students draw floor plans for a typical Athenian home. Point out that most rooms looked inward to a courtyard, rather than outward to the noisy and smelly streets. **L1 LEP**

Editorial Have students imagine that they witnessed the battle of Salamis. Have them write a newspaper editorial glorifying the Greek victory. They may do outside reading. Editorials should be historically accurate but may reflect personal observations and feelings. **L3**

you don't say...

"Barbarians" is a word that goes back to the Greeks who applied the term to all non-Greeks. It was not a pejorative term, but simply a way of approximating a foreign language, which to the Greeks sounded like "bar-bar-bar."

Visualizing History Pericles gave his great funeral oration in 430 B.C., in honor of Athenian soldiers killed in the Peloponnesian War.
Answer to Caption: *Democracy meant that power was in the hands of the many, not the few.*

---

surrender on the battlefield, but fight until victory or death.

> ❝ They [the Spartans] defended themselves to the last, such as still had swords using them, and the others resisting with their hand and teeth; till the barbarians [Persians] ... overwhelmed and buried the remnant left beneath showers of missile weapons. ❞
>
> —Herodotus, from *History*, 400s B.C.

The heroic stand of Leonidas and the Spartans gave Themistocles time to carry out his plan. He drew the Persian fleet into the strait of Salamis, a narrow body of water between Athens and the island of **Salamis**. Themistocles reasoned that the heavy Persian ships would crowd together in the strait and make easy targets for the lighter but faster and more maneuverable Greek ships. The plan worked, and the outnumbered ships of the Greek navy destroyed almost the entire Persian fleet.

After the battle at Salamis, the Greeks gained the upper hand. By 479 B.C., the Persians had once again retreated to Asia Minor, this time for good. With the end of the Persian Wars, Athens emerged as a powerful and self-confident city-state, ready to embark on a new age of expansion.

The Golden Age of Athens

Greek culture reached its peak after the Persian Wars. Most historians refer to the period from 461

Visualizing History Pericles held virtual control over Athenian affairs for the last 15 years of his life, being elected each year as one of the 10 city generals. *How did Pericles identify his faith in democracy?*

B.C. to 429 B.C. as the Golden Age of Athens because most Greek achievements in the arts and sciences took place in Athens during this time.

Pericles in Charge

The Athenian general **Pericles**, beginning in the 450s B.C., led Athens through its Golden Age. The Persians had burned Athens during the Persian Wars, but beginning in 447 B.C., Pericles was determined to rebuild the city. When the rebuilt temples and palaces crowned its acropolis, Athens became the most beautiful city in Greece. The most famous structure built under Pericles, the Parthenon (the temple of Athena), still stands.

Pericles wanted the polis of Athens to stand for all that was best in Greek civilization. A persuasive speaker, he expressed his ideas in a famous funeral oration quoted by the Greek historian Thucydides (thoo•SIH•duh•DEEZ):

> ❝ We are called a democracy [because power] is in the hands of the many and not the few.... When it is a question of putting one person before another in positions of public responsibility, what counts is not membership of a particular class, but the actual ability which the man possesses.... We are prevented from doing wrong by respect ... for the laws.... We are lovers of the beautiful, yet simple in our tastes, and we cultivate the mind without loss of manliness.... To avow poverty with us is no disgrace; the true disgrace is in doing nothing to avoid it.... Athens is the school of Hellas [Greece]. ❞

Athenian Daily Life

Athenians lavished money on public buildings, but they kept their individual homes simple. The typical Athenian house contained two main rooms and several smaller ones built around a central courtyard. In one main room, the dining room, the men entertained guests and ate while reclining on couches. An Athenian woman joined her husband for dinner only if company was not invited. In the other main room, the wool room, the women spun and wove cloth. In the courtyard stood an altar, a wash basin, and sometimes a well. The courtyard also contained the family's chickens and goats.

Athenian men usually worked in the morning as farmers, artisans, and merchants. Then they spent the afternoon attending the Assembly or exercising in the gymnasium. Slaves—who were mostly foreigners and prisoners of war and who made up one-third of the population—did most of

---

MEETING SPECIAL NEEDS ACTIVITY

Learning Style: Logical/Mathematical Many students have trouble understanding dates. This is especially true in the pre-Christian era (B.C.), when numbers grow smaller as the time advances—just the opposite of what happens in more recent history when dates are A.D.

Have students reproduce the time line on page 120 and then add the following events in the appropriate places: battle of Salamis, Golden Age of Athens, Pericles' funeral oration, end of the Peloponnesian War. **L2** the heavy work in craft production and mining. Many slaves also worked as teachers and household servants. Most Athenian women spent their time at home, cooking and making wool cloth, but poor women worked in the open-air markets as food sellers and cloth weavers.

Upper-class Athenian men—as well as citizens from other city-states—enjoyed the symposium as a form of recreation. Wives were excluded from a symposium, which was a drinking session following a banquet. The men at a symposium were entertained and also spent much of the evening discussing literature, philosophy, and public issues.

Athenian Women

In spite of restrictions, many Athenian women were able to participate in public life—especially in city festivals—and learned to read and write. Public opinion allowed greater freedom to women of the *metic* class than to those of other groups. The most famous of *metic* women was **Aspasia**, who was known for her intelligence and personal charm. To her house came many of the women of Athens, and she apparently gave advice on home life while attempting to gain more education and greater freedom for Athenian women. Her views aroused great opposition among some Athenians of both sexes, and she was prosecuted on a charge of "impiety," or disloyalty to the gods. Aspasia was finally acquitted.

The Peloponnesian War

Even after the Persian Wars ended, the Persian threat remained. Athens persuaded most of the city-states—but not Sparta—to ally against the enemy. This alliance became known as the Delian League because the treasury was kept on the sacred island of **Delos**. Athens provided the principal naval and land forces, while the other city-states furnished money and ships. Over the next several decades, the Delian League freed Ionia from Persian rule and cleared the Aegean of pirates. Overseas trade expanded, and Greece grew richer.

The Athenian Empire

Athens gradually began to dominate the other city-states. Pericles, for example, used part of the Delian League's treasury to build the Parthenon. He insisted that criminal cases be tried only in Athens and that other city-states adopt the Athenian coinage system. He also sent Athenian troops to support revolts by commoners against aristocrats in other city-states. In short, the policies of Pericles more or less transformed the Delian League from what had been an anti-Persian defense

Visualizing History A Spartan soldier poised for battle. The Spartans developed a chain of orders to be shouted above the din of battle. *How did Sparta attain a navy?*

league into an Athenian empire.

As Athens's trade and political influence grew, several city-states reacted by forming an alliance opposed to Athens. Sparta, a long-standing Athenian rival, became the leader of the anti-Athens alliance. Since Sparta was located in the Peloponnesus, historians have called the war against Athens and its allies the Peloponnesian War.

The Conflict

The Peloponnesian War lasted from 431 B.C. to 404 B.C., excluding one brief period of peace. At first it seemed as if Athens could hold out indefinitely, since Sparta had no navy. Sparta's fear and jealousy of Athens, however, were so strong that the Spartans made a deal with the Persians to return Ionia to Persian control. In exchange, Sparta received gold to build its own fleet. Then, in 430 B.C., a disastrous

Student Web Activity 4

Visit the *World History: The Human Experience* Web site at **worldhistory.glencoe.com** and click on *Chapter 4—Student Web Activities* for an activity relating to Greek warfare.

Visualizing History Physical prowess alone was not responsible for Spartan military victories. Spartans also developed an early flame-throwing weapon.
Answer to Caption: *Persia gave Sparta enough gold to build its own fleet in exchange for being allowed to retake control of Ionia.*

Linking Past and Present

The Peloponnesian War demanded great sacrifice from Athens. It has been estimated that almost a third of its population was mobilized. By contrast, World War I mobilized 10 percent of the population of the countries involved.

ASSESS

Check for Understanding

Assign Section 4 Assessment as homework or as an in-class activity.

Use Interactive Tutor Self-Assessment Software to review Section 4.

Evaluate

Section Quiz 4-4

Use the Testmaker to create a customized quiz for Section 4.

WORLD HISTORY Online

Have students use the **Chapter 4 Student Web Activity** at worldhistory.glencoe.com for in-depth study of the Peloponnesian War.

MAKING CONNECTIONS ACTIVITY

Sports The first modern marathon—named after the battle that led to the famous run of Pheidippides—was held at the Olympic Games in Athens in 1896. The length of the marathon varied until it was officially set, in 1908, at 26 miles, 385 yards (42.19 kilometers). Have students research and report on famous marathons of today, such as those of Boston and New York City. Their reports should include the history of the event, the time and place in which it is staged, the average number of runners, the names of important recent winners, and the time it took these people to run the race. **L2**

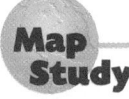

Chapter 4
Section 4

Map Study

Answers

1. *They feared and were jealous of Athens.*
2. *Ionia*

Map Skills Practice

Reading a Map What strategic advantage can you see in the geographic location of Sparta's allies? The allies of Athens? *(Sparta's allies not only surrounded Attica but also included a territory in the north (Macedonia), in the midst of regions linked to Athens. The allies of Athens dominated the Aegean Sea.)*

Reteach

Have students write two brief paragraphs describing Athenian political life, the first as it was before the Peloponnesian War, the second as it was after the war.

 Reteaching Activity 4

 Reading Essentials and Study Guide 4-4

Enrich

Have students research the clothing and weapons used by the typical Greek soldier.

 Enrichment Activity 4

CLOSE

Ask students which event discussed in this chapter was the most important for Greek civilization.

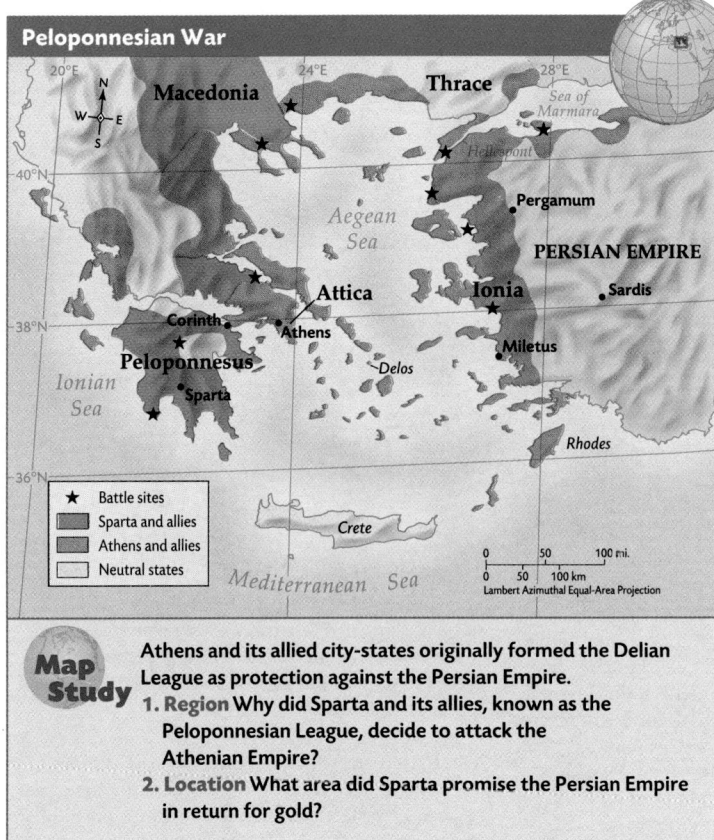

Peloponnesian War

Map Study
Athens and its allied city-states originally formed the Delian League as protection against the Persian Empire.
1. **Region** Why did Sparta and its allies, known as the Peloponnesian League, decide to attack the Athenian Empire?
2. **Location** What area did Sparta promise the Persian Empire in return for gold?

fleet. After the Spartans laid siege to Athens itself, the Athenians finally surrendered in 404 B.C.

Effects of the War

The Peloponnesian War brought disaster to the Greek city-states, both victors and vanquished. Many city-states declined in population. Fighting had destroyed much land. Unemployment was so widespread that thousands of young men emigrated and became mercenaries, or hired soldiers, in the Persian army.

Worst of all, the Greeks lost their ability to govern themselves. The length and cost of the war made people forget about the common good of their polis and think only about making money. Feelings between aristocrats and commoners grew increasingly bitter. Many Greeks, losing faith in democracy, even came to look down on free political discussion and began to believe that might makes right.

For a time, Sparta tried to rule the other city-states. Then, in 371 B.C., a new alliance of city-states led by Thebes overthrew the harsh, incompetent Spartan rulers. The Thebans, however, also made poor rulers and were also overthrown. As a result of almost continual fighting, the city-states became weaker than ever. When a new invader, the Macedonians, threatened Greece in the 350s B.C., the city-states were unable to resist.

plague—probably typhus—weakened Athens. Over a third of its population died, including Pericles.

After Pericles died in 429 B.C., some Athenians wanted to make peace with Sparta and its allies, while other Athenians wanted to keep on fighting. No decision was made, and the war continued deadlocked for many more years. Eventually, several allies of Athens switched sides and joined the Spartan-led alliance. Then, with their Persian-financed navy, the Spartans destroyed the Athenian

---

SECTION 4 ASSESSMENT

Main Idea
1. Use a diagram like the one below to show how the Peloponnesian War affected democracy in Greece.

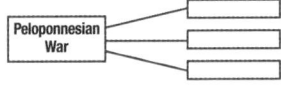

Recall
2. **Define** symposium, mercenary.
3. **Identify** Ionia, Darius I, Marathon, Xerxes, Themistocles, Thermopylae, Leonidas, Salamis, Pericles, Aspasia.

Critical Thinking
4. **Evaluating Information** Judge whether the rule of Peri-

cles was a "golden age" for Athens and its people. Why or why not?

Understanding Themes
5. **Conflict** What was the significance of the outcome of the Persian Wars? How did it affect both Greeks and Persians?

124 **Chapter 4** *The Rise of Ancient Greece*

SECTION 4 ASSESSMENT ANSWERS

1. Because the population of city-states declined, fighting destroyed fields and orchards, and there was widespread unemployment, the Greek city-states were weakened so that the Greeks could not govern themselves.
2. All terms are defined in the Glossary.
3. Ionia, 120; Darius, 120; Marathon, 121; Xerxes, 121; Themistocles, 121; Thermopylae, 121; Leonidas, 121; Salamis, 122; Pericles, 122; Aspasia, 123
4. Yes: he rebuilt Athens and extended Athenian power and influence; no: by transforming the Delian League into an Athenian Empire, he helped bring on the disastrous Peloponnesian War.

5. **CONFLICT** The Greeks gained the upper hand, and the Persians retreated to Asia Minor. Persian attempts to expand into Europe were blocked. The Greek victory encouraged the self-confidence of the city-states and prepared the way for many Greek cultural achievements.

Making Comparisons

In shopping for athletic shoes, you have narrowed your selection to two pairs. Which pair should you buy? You must compare to decide.

Learning the Skill

Making comparisons means finding similarities and differences. In the above example, you might first notice the similarities between the shoes. Both pairs are the same price and the same color. Then, you would look for differences. One pair extends above the ankle, the other pair does not. One pair is designed for jogging, the other for aerobics. Once you have compared the shoes, you can draw a conclusion about which pair will best suit your needs.

Apply the same method in comparing any two objects, groups, or concepts. First, determine what question you want to answer. Then determine the bases for comparison. In the shoe example, we compared on the bases of price, color, style, and athletic function. Then identify similarities and differences in each of these categories. Finally, use the comparison to draw conclusions or to answer your question.

Practicing the Skill

The excerpts on this page discuss the military strength of Sparta and Athens. Read the excerpts and answer the questions below.

1. Identify three bases for comparing the military strength of Athens and Sparta.
2. Do both city-states have armies and navies?
3. What are two differences in the military strength of Athens and Sparta?
4. Based on this comparison, which city-state has greater military strength? Why?

❝ We [Spartans] have many reasons to expect success,—first, superiority in numbers and in military experience, and second, our general and unvarying obedience in the execution of orders. ❞

❝ The naval strength which they [Athens] possess shall be raised by us from ... the monies at Olympia and Delphi. A loan from these enables us to seduce their foreign sailors by the offer of higher pay.... A single defeat at sea is in all likelihood their ruin. ❞

—Thucydides, account of a Corinthian envoy to the Congress at Sparta, 432 B.C.

❝ Personally engaged in the cultivation of their land, without funds either private or public, the Peloponnesians [Spartans] are also without experience in long wars across the sea.... Our naval skill is of more use to us for service on land, than their military skill for service at sea. Even if they were to ... try to seduce our foreign sailors by the temptation of higher pay ... none of our foreign sailors would consent to become an outlaw from his own country, and to take service with them. ❞

—Pericles, account to Athenian Ecclesia, 432 B.C.

Applying the Skill

Choose a topic or activity that interests you. Research two individuals, groups, or organizations involved in this activity. Make a chart outlining five similarities and five differences.

For More Practice

Turn to the Skill Practice in the Chapter Assessment on page 127.

The **Glencoe Skillbuilder Interactive Workbook**, Level 2 provides instruction and practice in key social studies skills.

TEACH

Making Comparisons Many television ads are based on comparisons. Have two volunteers with different preferences in morning cereal bring in the box or copy of the nutrition information, net weight, and price each displays. Other volunteers can transfer the nutritional data to the chalkboard. Then write on the chalkboard the price per ounce of the two cereals. Ask students to draw conclusions from the comparison.

Additional Practice

Skill Reinforcement Activity 4

GLENCOE TECHNOLOGY

Glencoe's **Skillbuilder Interactive Workbook, Level 2** This interactive CD-ROM promotes student mastery of key social studies skills.

ANSWERS TO PRACTICING THE SKILL

1. number of soldiers; experience; naval strength
2. yes
3. The Spartans claim to have a bigger army of more experienced soldiers; the Athenians claim to have a navy that is loyal and more skilled.
4. Students might make the case either for Sparta, with a better and larger army or for Athens, with a superior navy.

Chapter 4
Assessment

Answers

Using Key Terms

1. f	3. a	5. l
2. b	4. i	

Using Your History Journal

Students should consider how actions they take in their lives serve to maintain or achieve democracy.

Reviewing Facts

1. 800s B.C.: Sparta's government is set up; 650 B.C.: slave revolt in Sparta; 621 B.C.: Draco's laws issued; 594 B.C.: Solon leads Athens; 546 B.C.: Peisistratus leads Athens; 507 B.C.: Athens becomes a democracy; 490 B.C.: Battle of Marathon; 447 B.C.: Pericles rebuilds Athens; 431 B.C.: Peloponnesian War begins

2. metalworking techniques, shipbuilding, navigation by sun/stars, worship of the Earth Mother

3. pride in being Greek, love of life, desire for excellence, determination to meet fate with dignity

4. The Greeks humanized their deities and strived to achieve godlike power and excellence.

5. Sparta conquered neighboring

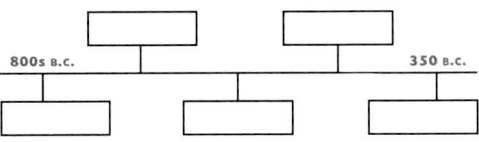

Self-Check Quiz

Visit the *World History: The Human Experience* Web site at **worldhistory.glencoe.com** and click on *Chapter 4—Self-Check Quiz* to prepare for the Chapter Test.

Using Key Terms

Write the key term that completes each sentence. Then write a sentence for each term not chosen.

a. aristocrats	h. tyrant
b. citizen	i. symposiums
c. democracy	j. labyrinth
d. oligarchy	k. phalanx
e. mercenary	l. bards
f. polis	m. constitution
g. rhetoric	

1. The _____, the basic political unit of ancient Greece, included a city and the surrounding villages, fields, and orchards.

2. A woman in ancient Greece was not considered to be a full _____ with the right to take part in political affairs.

3. By the 700s B.C., kings in Greece had lost power to landholding members of the upper class known as _____.

4. Athenian men entertained each other at _____, telling riddles and discussing literature, philosophy, and public issues.

5. _____, or singing storytellers, kept alive Mycenaean literary traditions during Greece's "dark age."

Technology Activity

Using a Spreadsheet Search the Internet or your local library for additional information about Greek gods and goddesses. Organize your findings by creating a spreadsheet. Include headings such as name of god or goddess, purpose of their existence, types of powers, and relationships to other gods or goddesses. Research further to find out and list the corresponding Roman names for Greek gods and goddesses.

Reviewing Facts

1. **History** Use a time line like the one below to show main events in the histories of Athens and Sparta.

800s B.C. _____ 350 B.C.

2. **Culture** List the elements of Minoan culture that were adopted by the Mycenaeans.

3. **Culture** State the values of the *Iliad* and the *Odyssey*.

4. **Culture** Explain how Greek attitudes toward their deities differ from those of the Egyptians.

5. **History** Explain how Sparta's response to the problems of increased population and a shortage of arable land differed from the response of most other Greek city-states.

6. **Citizenship** Trace the development of democracy in Athens, and describe citizens' rights and responsibilities. What groups were excluded from citizenship?

Critical Thinking

1. **Apply** How did Sparta's values affect its educational system?

2. **Analyze** How did the reforms of Cleisthenes in Athens affect the future development of government in the Western world?

3. **Synthesize** What might have been the outcome of the Persian Wars if Themistocles had not convinced the Greeks to build a fleet of ships?

---

city-states and enslaved the inhabitants. Other city-states set up colonies and expanded overseas trade.

6. Democracy developed through reforms that extended citizenship and the right to participate in government to all free Athenian-born males. Citizens could vote, hold public office, own property, and speak for themselves in court. They were expected to serve in government and to defend the polis; slaves, the

foreign-born, and women

Critical Thinking

1. Males learned how to use weapons so that they would be good soldiers. Females trained in gymnastics, wrestling, and boxing so they would be strong and bear healthy children.

2. They laid the basis for the development of democratic institutions in the West.

3. The Persians might have defeated the Greeks.

4. Analyze Shown below, the south porch of the Erechtheum near the Parthenon has figures of maidens in place of conventional columns. The buildings on the Acropolis are examples of early classical architecture and sculpture. What might these figures suggest about the role of women in Athenian life?

Understanding Themes

1. Relation to Environment What aspects of Crete's environment enabled the Minoans to become skilled seafarers?

2. Movement What role did trade play in the development of Greek civilization?

3. Regionalism What effect did Sparta's emphasis on military values have on its development as a city-state?

4. Conflict How did the Peloponnesian War affect Athens, Sparta, and the other Greek city-states?

Linking Past and Present

1. Why did tyrants seize power in ancient Athens during times of unrest? Do you think a tyrant could establish a dictatorship today in the United States in a time of crisis? Explain your answer.

2. Why might students at the United States Naval Academy study the Persian Wars?

Skill Practice

Reread Section 3 and compare the two leading city-states in ancient Greece.

1. What are two similarities in the education of young people in Athens and Sparta?

2. What are two differences in their educations in these two city-states?

3. What are two similarities in the political structure of Athens and Sparta?

4. What are two differences that can be identified in the political structure of these two Greek city-states?

5. What are two differences in the roles of women in Athens and Sparta?

6. What are two similarities in women's roles in these two city-states?

Geography in History

1. Place Although it is a small island without much land area, Crete contains what two distinct, but neighboring, landforms?

2. Location Refer to the map on page 124. What is the relative location of Crete? What is Crete's absolute location?

3. Location Where was the palace of the legendary king Minos?

4. Human/Environment Interaction Geography has an impact on how people live from day to day. How did the early people of Crete earn their living?

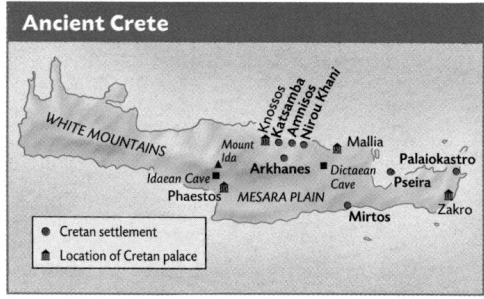

Ancient Crete

WHITE MOUNTAINS
Mount Ida
Knossos
Katsamba
Amnisos
Nirou Khani
Mallia
Palaiokastro
Arkhanes
Dictaean Cave
Pseira
Idaean Cave
Phaestos
MESARA PLAIN
Mirtos
Zakro

● Cretan settlement
⌂ Location of Cretan palace

4. They might suggest that women are powerful and respected enough to support an important building.

Understanding Themes

1. **RELATION TO ENVIRONMENT** It was an island, and it was located close to other centers of civilization.

2. **MOVEMENT** Minoan traders brought their culture to the Greek mainland.

Trade between the Greek city-states and their colonies flourished. The economic prosperity led those who made the goods traded to demand more rights. Democracy followed.

3. **REGIONALISM** It lagged behind other city-states in trade and manufacturing and created little in the way of intellectual, literary, and scientific accomplishments.

4. **CONFLICT** Athens was defeated, Sparta won, but, weakened by warfare, the

city-states were vulnerable to the Macedonians.

Linking Past and Present

1. Social and economic changes allowed for the rise of new leaders. Safeguards include constitutional checks against arbitrary power; a two-party system; and the influence of the media.

2. to learn about battle tactics

Skill Practice

1. All boys were educated; age 7.

2. Athens: more subjects were studied; Sparta: girls were trained in athletics

3. Both had an Assembly of all citizens; both had a Council.

4. Sparta had kings and ephors, while Athens did not.

5. Athens: women received no education and stayed at home. Sparta: women married later and had more personal rights.

6. inferior to men in status

Geography in History

1. mountains, plains

2. southeast of Greece and southwest of Ionia, 35°N latitude, 24°E longitude

3. at Knossos, on north coast

4. from sea trade

Chapter Bonus Test Question

Ask students: "Beware of Greeks bearing gifts" is a common expression. What event in Greek history or legend does it refer to, and what does it mean? When might someone today use this expression? *(the event is when a wooden horse was given to the Trojans that secretly contained Spartan soldiers. People should be wary of gifts coming from unlikely givers. People today might use this phrase in reference to the "free" gifts that businesses offer.)*

A complete, 1-page lesson plan is provided for each section in the Reproducible Lesson Plans booklet.

The Height of Greek Civilization

CHAPTER RESOURCES

	Reproducible Resources	Multimedia Resources
Chapter Opener	Chapter Themes: Graphic Organizer 5 Historical Significance Chapter Activity 5	MindJogger Videoquiz
Chapter Enrichment	Vocabulary Activity 5* Time Line Activity 5 Mapping History Activity 5 History Simulation 5 Geography and History Activity 5 Source Reading 5 People in World History Profiles 7, 8 World Art and Music Activity 5 Enrichment Activity 5 Critical Thinking Activity 5 Skill Reinforcement Activity 5 Building Skills in Geography Workbook, Unit 1, Lessons 3, 4, 5 Performance Assessment Activity 5 Standardized Test Practice Workbook Activity 5 Inclusion for the Social Studies Classroom Strategies and Activities	Focus on World Art Print 8, Greek. *Laocoön* Ancient Civilizations Poster Set: *Ancient Greece* World History and Art Transparency 6, *Nike of Samothrace* Mapping History Overlay Transparencies 4, 5 Chapter Transparency 5 NGS PicturePack Transparency Set: *Ancient Greece* Vocabulary PuzzleMaker Software NGS PictureShow CD-ROM: *Greece and Rome* World Music: Cultural Traditions, Lesson 3 World History Primary Source Document Library
Chapter Review/Reteaching	Reteaching Activity 5 Skill Reinforcement Activity 5 Spanish Chapter Summary 5	Chapter 5 Digest Audiocassette, Activity, Test* Vocabulary PuzzleMaker Software Interactive Tutor Self-Assessment Software MindJogger Videoquiz
Chapter Evaluation/Testing	Performance Assessment Activity 5 Chapter 5 Test, Forms A and B	ExamView® Pro Testmaker

0:00 OUT OF TIME? Assign the Chapter 5 Audiocassettes.

* Also available in Spanish

World History Primary Source Document Library

Make History Come Alive!

Engage your students with over 250 easily accessible primary source documents—available on this CD-ROM—that will give them real life insight into the important events of world history.

Block Schedule

Activities that are particularly suited to use within the block scheduling framework are identified throughout this chapter by the following designation.

KEY TO ABILITY LEVELS

Teaching strategies are coded for varying learning styles.

L1 **BASIC** activities for all students
L2 **AVERAGE** activities for average to above-average students
L3 **CHALLENGING** activities for above-average students
LEP **LIMITED ENGLISH PROFICIENCY** activities

Use Glencoe's *Presentation Plus!* multimedia teacher tool to easily present dynamic lessons that visually excite your students. Using Microsoft PowerPoint® you can customize the presentations to create your own personalized lessons.

Interactive Lesson Planner

Planning has never been easier! Using this CD-ROM, organize your week, month, semester, or year with all the help you need. The **Interactive Lesson Planner** gives you access to all of the blackline masters that accompany *World History: The Human Experience.*

SECTION RESOURCES

Daily Objectives	Reproducible Resources	Multimedia Resources
Section 1 **Quest for Beauty and Meaning** Describe how the Greeks expressed their love of beauty and meaning.	Lecture Notes 5-1 Reproducible Lesson Plan 5-1 Guided Reading Activity 5-1* Source Reading 5 World Art and Music Activity 5 Section Quiz 5-1* Reading Essentials and Study Guide 5-1	NGS Ancient Civilizations Poster Set: *Ancient Greece* Section Focus Transparency 5-1 World History and Art Transparency 6, *Nike of Samothrace* NGS PicturePack Transparency Set: *Ancient Greece* Vocabulary PuzzleMaker Software Interactive Tutor Self-Assessment Software Testmaker NGS PictureShow CD-ROM: *Greece and Rome* World Music: Cultural Traditions, Lesson 3
Section 2 **The Greek Mind** Identify the achievements of the ancient Greeks in philosophy, history, and science.	Lecture Notes 5-2 Reproducible Lesson Plan 5-2 Vocabulary Activity 5* Guided Reading Activity 5-2* People in World History Profiles 7, 8 History Simulation 5 Section Quiz 5-2* Reading Essentials and Study Guide 5-2	Section Focus Transparency 5-2 Mapping History Overlay Transparency 4, *Ancient Greece* Chapter Transparency 5 Interactive Tutor Self-Assessment Software Testmaker
Section 3 **Alexander's Empire** Outline Alexander's goals and evaluate his success in achieving them.	Lecture Notes 5-3 Reproducible Lesson Plan 5-3 Vocabulary Activity 5* Guided Reading Activity 5-3* Reteaching Activity 5 Enrichment Activity 5 Time Line Activity 5 Mapping History Activity 5 Geography and History Activity 5 Section Quiz 5-3* Performance Assessment Activity 5 Spanish Chapter Summary 5 Reading Essentials and Study Guide 5-3	Focus on World Art Print 8, Greek. *Laocoön* Section Focus Transparency 5-3 Mapping History Overlay Transparency 5, *Empire of Alexander the Great* Interactive Tutor Self-Assessment Software Testmaker

* Also available in Spanish

Chapter Activities

 Performance Assessment Activity

A Cultural Borrowing Portfolio Have students create a chapter portfolio of modern-day examples of Greek influence. Examples may come from library materials, magazines, television, multimedia, film, or newspapers—each cited and including a short explanation of how the event, process or item can be connected to ancient Greece. Portfolios should include at least ten examples. Students may work together in groups of up to four on the portfolios.

Possible Rubric Features

Accuracy of content information, concept attainment (cultural borrowing), relevancy of modern-day examples, organization of portfolio, clarity of text

• *For an additional activity, refer to Activity 5 in the* Performance Assessment Strategies and Activities *booklet.*

ACTIVITY

From the Classroom of...

Shannon Heck, Ladue Horton Watkins High School, St. Louis, MO

The Trial of Socrates

Students will simulate "democracy on trial." Socrates, at 70 years of age, in 399 B.C., is charged with 1) corrupting the youth of Athens and causing them to doubt the wisdom of Homer; 2) lack of reverence for the Greek gods; and 3) belief in his own gods. In his defense, Socrates claimed to be guided by an inner voice.

The roles in this simulation trial may include: "Cleon," an Athenian councilman fearful of Socrates' teachings; "Diodorus," a concerned father who believes that Socrates' teachings are undermining the youth; "Judge," presides over the trial; "Prosecutor," citizen attorney who accuses Socrates of the three crimes; "Defense," advises and counsels Socrates; "Plato" and "Xenophon," students of Socrates; "Agia," a worshiper of Athena.

Both teams should work out their strategies in the presentation of their cases. Attorneys for the teams should coach their witnesses for direct examination and prepare for cross-examinations also. The jurors and judge should prepare for the case by gaining background knowledge but should reserve judgment prior to the case. After the trial, discuss with students whether they think a case such as Socrates' could ever come to trial in the United States.

MULTIPLE LEARNING STYLES

Verbal/Linguistic

Have students contribute to a "Legacy of Ancient Greece" bulletin board. Ask each student to write on some aspect of architecture, art, history, literature, science, mathematics, or philosophy. They should illustrate their subjects and explain why each is an important contribution to Western civilization.

Logical/Mathematical

Have students construct a time line illustrating the Hellenic and Hellenistic eras. Have them include dates, events, and people. Students may begin with key dates from the chapter opener time line and add to their time line as they progress through the chapter. Have students work on poster-size paper.

Visual/Spatial

Have students draw a base map for the growth of Greek influence (see map on page 141). Then ask them to make two overlays on onionskin paper—one showing Hellenic Greece and its colonies (see map on page 114), the other, the Hellenistic region.

Kinesthetic

Have students find political cartoons in newspapers and magazines. Then have them prepare their own cartoons to illustrate the political philosophy of Plato or Aristotle, or to illustrate political issues from the days of ancient Greece.

 GLENCOE'S ASSESSMENT ADVANTAGE

Use the following to easily assess student learning in a variety of ways.

- Performance Assessment Strategies and Activities
- Section Quizzes
- Chapter and Unit Tests
- Interactive Tutor Self-Assessment Software
- Testmaker Software
- MindJogger Videoquiz
- SAT/SAT II Test Practice
- worldhistory.glencoe.com

Additional Resources

NATIONAL GEOGRAPHIC SOCIETY — Teacher's Corner

INDEX TO NATIONAL GEOGRAPHIC MAGAZINE

The following articles relate to this chapter:

- "Let the Games Begin," by Frank Deford, July 1996.
- "When the Greeks Went West," by Rick Gore, November 1994.
- "Warriors From a Watery Grave: Glorious Bronzes of Ancient Greece," by Joseph Alsop, June 1983.

NATIONAL GEOGRAPHIC SOCIETY PRODUCTS AVAILABLE FROM GLENCOE

To order the following, call Glencoe at 1-800-334-7344:

- *PictureShow: Greece and Rome (CD-ROM)*
- *Ancient Greece (Transparencies, Poster Set)*
- *PictureShow: Ancient Civilizations Library (CD-ROMs)*

ADDITIONAL NATIONAL GEOGRAPHIC SOCIETY PRODUCTS

Access National Geographic's new dynamic MapMachine Web site and other geography resources at:

- http://www.nationalgeographic.com/
- http://www.nationalgeographic.com/maps/

WORLD HISTORY Online

Use our Web site as an additional resource. All essential content is covered in the Student Edition.

You and your students can visit the *World History: The Human Experience* Web site at worldhistory. glencoe.com The student text directs students to the Web site for the following options:

- **Chapter Overviews**
- **Student Web Activities**
- **Self-Check Quizzes**

Answers are provided for you in a link entitled "Web Activity Lesson Plan." Additional Web Resources, Interactive Puzzles, and content updates are also available.

Visit the Glencoe Web site at socialstudies. glencoe.com for social studies activities, updates, and links to other resources.

LOCAL OBJECTIVES

_____
_____
_____
_____
_____
_____
_____
_____
_____
_____
_____
_____
_____
_____
_____
_____
_____
_____
_____

BIBLIOGRAPHY

Literature of the Period
Fagles, Robert, trans. *Sophocles: The Three Theban Plays.* New York: Penguin, 1984. Included are *Oedipus the King*, *Antigone*, and *Oedipus at Colonus*.
Hamilton, Edith, trans. *Three Greek Plays.* New York: Norton, 1958. Included are *The Trojan Women* by Euripides and *Prometheus Bound* and *Agamemnon* by Aeschylus.

Readings for the Student
Harris, Nathaniel. *Alexander the Great and the Greeks.* New York: Bookwright Press, 1986. Easy reading, but with well-researched detail about Alexander's contributions.

Readings for the Teacher
Grant, Michael. *The Classical Greeks.* New York: Scribner, 1989. Connects culture—art, architecture, philosophy, and drama—with historical events.

CHAPTER THEMES

Chapter Themes are listed by section on this chapter opening page of the Student Edition. A corresponding theme-based activity is available under "TEACH," and a theme-based question is asked in the Section and Chapter Assessments.

The Storyteller

Historical Setting Much of what we know about the life and teachings of Socrates comes to us from Socrates' most famous student, Plato. But Plato, according to some scholars, may have attributed ideas to Socrates that originated with Plato himself. Ask students why scholars might care whether the ideas should be attributed to Plato or Socrates. *(Scholars want to know how coherent and/or consistent their subject's ideas are, and how they relate to the work of others; uncertain provenance makes this task harder.)*

Historical Significance

Answers: *They valued moderation and balance, loved beauty, stressed the individual, and sought the truth through free inquiry.*

Western architects and sculptors have copied Greek works for centuries; Greek philosophers, historians, and scientists created traditions in these disciplines that are still valid today.

—WORLD HISTORY Online—

Have students use the **Chapter 5 Overview** at worldhistory. glencoe.com as a prereading and postreading exercise for understanding chapter content.

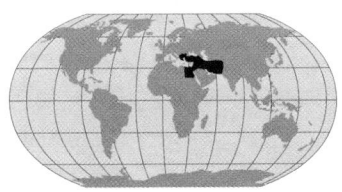

Chapter Themes

▶ **Innovation** The ancient Greeks develop a culture that becomes one of the foundations of Western civilization. *Section 1*

▶ **Innovation** Ancient Greek thinkers believe in reason and the importance of the individual. *Section 2*

▶ **Cultural Diffusion** Alexander's empire brings about a mix of Greek and Middle Eastern cultures. *Section 3*

The Storyteller

An outwardly unimpressive man, Socrates was nonetheless an intellectual giant in the Athens of the late 400s B.C. One of his devoted followers described Socrates' day: "At early morning he was to be seen betaking himself to one of the promenades or wrestling grounds; at noon he would appear with the gathering crowds in the marketplace; and as day declined, wherever the largest throng might be encountered, there was he to be found, talking for the most part, while anyone who chose might stop and listen." Socrates was a supreme questioner who succeeded in getting people to analyze their own behavior. Today, Socrates' reputation lives on as one of the greatest teachers of all time.

Historical Significance

What were the principal beliefs and values of the ancient Greeks? How did their achievements in art, philosophy, history, and science shape the growth of Western civilization?

800 B.C.	600 B.C.	400 B.C.	200 B.C.

776 B.C. Greeks hold first Olympic Games.

c. 585 B.C. Thales, first Greek scientist, studies astronomy.

c. 415 B.C. Euripides writes *The Trojan Women.*

336 B.C. Alexander becomes king of Macedonia.

128

GEOGRAPHY CONNECTION

Movement Using a wall map or text maps in Chapter 4, review with students the Mediterranean world of Hellenic civilization. Then, using a wall map or the text map on page 141, contrast it with the empire of Alexander. What are some of the modern countries that belonged, in whole or in part, to Alexander's empire? *(Greece, Serbia, Bulgaria, Turkey, Syria, Lebanon, Israel, Egypt, Libya, Iraq, Iran, Afghanistan, Pakistan)*

Plato's School, a mosaic from the Hellenistic period. National Museum, Naples, Italy.

WORLD HISTORY Online

Chapter Overview

Visit the *World History: The Human Experience* Web site at <u>worldhistory.glencoe.com</u> and click on *Chapter 5—Chapter Overview* to preview the chapter.

Your History Journal

The word thespian, *meaning "actor," derives from the Greek dramatist Thespis. Many Greek innovations in staging productions are still used today. Research the history of early Greek drama. Write a comparison with modern theater.*

Chapter 5 *The Height of Greek Civilization* **129**

History & Art
 The School of Plato, in Athens, was commonly referred to as the Academy. It was located in a grove of trees said to have belonged to a man named Academus, a hero of the Trojan War. Why do you think learning was important to the Greeks? *(They believed people could develop themselves by thinking clearly.)*

✔ Performance Assessment

Refer to the activity on page 128C of the Planning Guide.

 For an additional activity, refer to Activity 5 in the *Performance Assessment Strategies and Activities* booklet.

Using Your History Journal

Topics for comparison include the stage itself, scenery, music, dancing, and the actors (training, costumes, and so on).

GLENCOE TECHNOLOGY

VIDEODISC
Use MindJogger to preview chapter content.

MindJogger Videoquiz
 Chapter 5 Disc 1 Side B

Also available in VHS.

✚ EXTRA CREDIT PROJECT

Storytelling Greek writers produced many works other than dramas, although much of their output has been lost. Have students research and report on one of the Greek poets whose writings have survived: Archilochus, Pindar, or Sappho. Another writer who may be of special interest to students is Aesop, known for his fables. Have students prepare a storytelling session for young children, or for the class, using several of Aesop's best-known stories, such as the tale of the goose that laid the golden egg.

600 B.C.   500 B.C.   400 B.C.

c. 600 B.C.
Greeks perform
the earliest plays.

459 B.C. Aeschylus
writes the *Oresteia*.

432 B.C. Athenians
finish building the
Parthenon.

SECTION THEME

▶ **Innovation** The ancient Greeks
develop a culture that becomes
one of the foundations of Western civilization.

Guide to Reading

For reading strategies to help
students read effectively see
pages 12–13. Have students
think about the main head as
they read the subheads.

Vocabulary Pre-check

▣ Use the Vocabulary
PuzzleMaker for Chapter 5 to
create a crossword puzzle to reinforce section terms. **L1 LEP**

🗁 Use Vocabulary Activity 5
to introduce vocabulary terms.
L1 LEP

FOCUS

Section Objective
Describe how the Greeks
expressed their love of beauty
and meaning.

BELLRINGER
Motivational Activity

Before taking roll at the
beginning of the class
period, project Section
Focus Transparency 5-1
and have students answer
the activity questions. Discuss
student's responses.
🗁 This activity is also available as a blackline master.

Section 1

Quest for Beauty and Meaning

Guide to Reading

Read to Find Out
Main Idea *The Greeks expressed their
love of beauty and meaning through
aspects of their culture.*

▶ **Terms to Define**
classical, sanctuary, perspective,
amphora, tragedy, comedy

▶ **People to Meet**
Myron, Phidias, Praxiteles,
Aeschylus, Sophocles,
Euripides, Aristophanes

▶ **Places to Locate**
Olympia

The Storyteller

*An early Greek actor remembers performing in
his first tragedy: "I put on the robe of Zeus for the
prologue, a lovely thing, purple worked with golden
oak leaves.… The next thing I remember is sitting
enthroned down center on the god-walk, eagle on
left fist, scepter in right hand … and all the eyes of
Athens skinning me to the bone." The actor felt as
though he had sleepwalked into the scene. Gripped
by fear, he tried to remember his lines: "My father
would die of
shame.… He was
twice the artist I
am. At once my
lines came back
to me. I started
my speech.…"*

*Vase depicting
actors preparing
for a play*

—adapted from
*The Mask of
Apollo,* Mary
Renault, 1974

During the mid-400s B.C., Greek civilization reached its cultural peak, particularly in the city-state of Athens. This period
of brilliant cultural achievement has been called
ancient Greece's Golden Age. Artists of the Golden
Age excelled in architecture, sculpture, and painting. They created works characterized by beautiful
simplicity and graceful balance, an artistic style
now called **classical**.

Classical Greek art, copied soon after in Roman
artistic styles, set lasting standards of beauty still
admired today. The writers and thinkers of ancient
Greece also made enduring achievements in literature and drama, creating works read through the
centuries and still considered classics today. Many
cultural traditions of Western civilization—the civilization of Europe and those parts of the world
influenced by Europeans—began with Greece's
Golden Age.

Building for the Gods

The Greeks, wrote the Athenian leader Pericles,
were "lovers of the beautiful." Each Greek city-state
tried to turn its acropolis into an architectural treasure.

The Parthenon—the temple to Athena built on
the summit of the Acropolis in Athens—best exemplified classical Greek architecture. It was begun in
447 B.C. and finished in 432 B.C., under the rule of
Pericles. Because the Greeks worshiped either in
their homes or at outdoor altars, they did not need
large **sanctuaries**, or places of worship. Instead,
they built temples as places where their deities
would live.

The Parthenon has an ingeniously simple
design. It is a rectangle surrounded by 46 fluted
columns. At the same time, the Parthenon is
extremely beautiful. In the right light, because of

SECTION RESOURCES

🗁 **Reproducible Masters**
• Lecture Notes 5-1
• Reproducible Lesson Plan 5-1
• Guided Reading Activity 5-1
• Source Reading 5
• World Art and Music Activity 5
• Section Quiz 5-1
• Reading Essentials and Study Guide 5-1

🗋 **Transparencies**
• Section Focus Transparency 5-1
• World History and Art Transparency 6
• Ancient Greece

Multimedia
🖥 Ancient Greece
🖥 Vocabulary PuzzleMaker Software

▣ Interactive Tutor Self-Assessment
Software
▣ Testmaker
◉ Greece and Rome
🎵 World Music: Cultural Traditions,
Lesson 3

iron in its white marble, the Parthenon gleams a soft gold against the blue sky.

The Parthenon's graceful proportions perfectly balance width, length, and height. To the Greeks the Parthenon represented the ideal of "nothing to excess," an ideal sometimes called the "golden mean," or the midpoint between two extremes.

The architects of the Parthenon also understood optical illusions and perspective, or the artistic showing of distances between objects as they appear to the eye. Thus, they made the temple's columns thicker in the middle and thinner at the top so that the columns appeared straight when viewed from a distance. The steps leading up to the Parthenon, actually lower in the center than at either end, likewise appear straight. The Athenians wanted to create the impression of perfection—and they succeeded.

Greek Arts

The Greek love of beauty was expressed in the fine arts as well as in architecture. In both painting and sculpture, the Greeks—because they emphasized the individual—excelled at portraying the human form.

Painting on Vases

Although the Greeks painted murals, as had the Minoans, no originals have survived. We know of Greek murals only from written descriptions or Roman copies. But today we can still see examples of their work in the paintings on Greek vases.

The Greeks designed their pottery with different shapes that were suited for different functions. For example, Greek potters gave the *krater*—a small two-handled vase—a wide mouth in which it was easy to mix wine with water. On the other hand, they gave the *leythos* a narrow neck so that oil could be poured out slowly and in small quantities.

Most pottery remaining from ancient Greece is either red on a black background or black on a red background. The varied subjects of the paintings depended on the size and use of the vase. Potters usually decorated an *amphora*—a large vase for storing oil and other bulk supplies—with scenes from mythology. In contrast, a *kylix*—a wide, shallow two-handled drinking cup—showed scenes of everyday life: children attending school, shoemakers and carpenters plying their trades, a farmer guiding the plow behind a team of oxen, a merchant ship braving the winds. Greek potters skillfully adapted their designs and decorations to the curves and shape of the vase.

Sculpting the Human Body

Greek sculpture, like Greek architecture, reached its height in Athens during the time of Pericles. **Myron**, one of the greatest sculptors of Greece's Golden Age, portrayed in his statues idealized views of what people *should* look like rather than actual persons. When Myron sculpted his *Discus Thrower* poised to hurl the discus, he carved the lines of the body to indicate an athlete's excellent physical condition as well as his mental control over what he was doing.

The great sculptor **Phidias** (FIH•dee•uhs) was in charge of the Parthenon's sculptures. Phidias himself carved the towering statue of Athena that was placed inside the Parthenon. The statue, made of gold and ivory plates attached to a wooden framework, showed the goddess in her warlike aspect, carrying a shield, spear, and helmet.

Chapter 5 *The Height of Greek Civilization* **131**

Chapter 5
Section 1

TEACH

Guided Practice

THEME Innovation

Remind students that the word *innovation* means "something new." Ask them to recall innovations developed by earlier peoples. *(prehistoric: stone tools, agriculture, metalworking, boats; Egyptians: picture writing; Sumerians: cuneiform writing, wagon wheel, potter's wheel; early Chinese: picture writing, silk)* Then ask them what ancient Greek innovation they learned about in the last chapter. *(democracy)* **L1**

Visualizing History On his journey home after the Trojan War, Odysseus passed by the Sirens, half-bird half-woman creatures whose singing lured sailors to their death. He had his sailors stop their ears with wax and tie him to the mast in order to avoid temptation.
Answer to Caption: *amphoras*

The following videotape program is available from Glencoe:

• **Powerful Gods of Mt. Olympus**

To find classroom resources to accompany this video, check the following home page:
A&E Television:
http://www.aetv.com

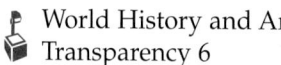
World History and Art
Transparency 6

Independent Practice
 Guided Reading Activity 5-1 **L1**

COOPERATIVE LEARNING ACTIVITY

Cultural Contributions Have students plan and execute a "Greek Heritage Day." Organize the class into groups. Assign or have each group choose a Greek creative achievement to demonstrate to the class. These may include drama (tragedy and comedy can be divided), painting, sculpture, and architecture. The groups may decide what form their demonstrations will take: an actual performance of part of a drama, a model of a vase, a model of a building, and so forth. Consult with the groups to make sure that each member has a specific assignment. **L1**

NATIONAL
GEOGRAPHIC
SOCIETY

Use these materials to enrich student understanding of ancient Greek culture.

- **NGS PICTURESHOW CD-ROM**
  Greece and Rome
- **NGS PICTUREPACK TRANSPARENCY SET**
  Ancient Greece
- **ANCIENT CIVILIZATIONS POSTER SET**
  Ancient Greece

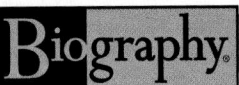
you don't say...

"Orchestra" is a Greek word from the verb "to dance" and was first used to describe the space between the stage and the audience where the chorus performed. In modern times, the term designates both the area in front of the stage and the group of musicians that plays there.

Biography

The following videotape program is available from Glencoe:
- **Hercules**

ASSESS

Check for Understanding

Assign Section 1 Assessment as homework or as an in-class activity.

AROUND THE
WORLD

Palace of Persepolis

Mesopotamia, mid-400s B.C.
The Persians completed a notable palace complex in their religious capital of Persepolis. Because Zoroastrianism did not require temples, the Persians built a group of adjoining buildings that included palaces, halls, chambers, and courtyards. Persian kings used a huge room, called the Hall of One Hundred Columns, as a reception area for visitors. The room was 250 feet (76 meters) square. Its vast beamed ceiling was supported by columns 60 feet (18 meters) high.

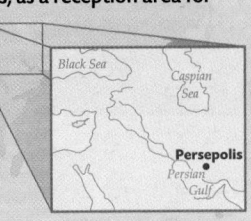

A hundred years after the Golden Age of Athens, the work of another famous Greek sculptor—**Praxiteles** (prak•SIH•tuhl•EEZ)—reflected the changes that had occurred in Greek life. The sculptures of Myron and Phidias had been full of power and striving for perfection, as befitted a people who had defeated the mighty Persian Empire. By the time of Praxiteles, the Greeks had suffered through the Peloponnesian War and had lost their self-confidence. Accordingly, Praxiteles and his colleagues favored life-sized statues rather than massive works. They emphasized grace rather than power. The sculptors of the Golden Age had carved only deities and heroes, but the sculptors of the 300s B.C. carved ordinary people too.

Drama and Theater

The Greeks also explored the human condition through theatrical dramas. They were the first people to write and perform plays, which they presented twice a year at festivals to honor Dionysus, the god of wine and fertility.

Aeschylus

The earliest Greek plays were tragedies. In a tragedy, the lead character struggles against fate only to be doomed—after much suffering—to an unhappy, or tragic, ending. **Aeschylus** (EHS•kuh •luhs), the first of the great writers of tragedies in the 400s B.C., wrote 90 plays. Seven have survived. His *Oresteia* is a trilogy—a set of three plays with a

---

related theme—and is famous for the grandeur of its language.

The *Oresteia* shows how the consequences of one's deeds are carried down from generation to generation. The first play in the trilogy tells about the return of King Agamemnon from the Trojan War and his murder by his wife Clytemnestra in revenge for Agamemnon's sacrifice of their daughter Iphigenia before the Greeks sailed for Troy. The second play describes how Agamemnon's son Orestes in turn avenges his father's death by killing his mother. The third play has Orestes standing trial in Athens for his bloody deed. When the jury splits six to six, the goddess Athena intervenes and casts the deciding vote in favor of mercy. The moral of the trilogy is that the law of the community, not personal revenge, should decide punishment.

Sophocles

The next great tragedian, **Sophocles** (SAH•fuh •KLEEZ), had served as a general in the Athenian army and had lived through most of the Peloponnesian War. Sophocles accepted human suffering as an unavoidable part of life. At the same time, he stressed human courage and compassion.

In one of his most famous plays, *Oedipus Rex*, Sophocles deals with the plight of Oedipus, a king who is doomed by the deities to kill his father and marry his mother. Despite Oedipus's efforts to avoid his fate, the deities' decree comes true. When Oedipus discovers what he has done, he blinds himself in despair and goes into exile.

Euripides

The last of the three great Greek tragedians— **Euripides** (yu•RIH•puh•DEEZ)—rarely dealt with the influence of the gods and goddesses on human lives. Instead, he focused on the qualities human beings possess that bring disaster on themselves.

Euripides also hated war, and many of his 19 surviving plays show the misery war brings. In *The Trojan Women*, the Trojan princess Cassandra explains why the Greeks, despite their victory, are not better off than the Trojans:

> 66 And when [the Greeks] came to the banks
>   of the Scamander those thousands died.
> And why?
> No man has moved their landmarks or
>   laid siege to their high-walled towns.
> But those whom war took never saw their
>   children.
> No wife with gentle hands shrouded them
>   for their grave.
> They lie in a strange land. And in their

Language Delayed To benefit students who need help in understanding the vocabulary and concepts in this section, have students create a crossword puzzle on a large laminated surface marked with a permanent grid. Have a student find a word to be included and write it on the grid. Have another student write a clue that defines or explains the word. Have students continue composing the puzzle as long as they can fit words together in crossword form or for a specific time period. Have students copy the puzzle from the large grid to refer to later or to challenge their friends or family. **L1**

Liberto Perugi

Greek Soldier

A Greek warrior, sculpted in bronze, gazes at the world with a determined stare. For more than 1,500 years, the soldier rested under the waters of the Mediterranean Sea. Then in an Italian chemist from Rome, diving off the coast uthern Italy, found this statue and a companion ze of an older Greek soldier. The statues were ably lost at sea en route to Rome—perhaps thrown board to lighten a storm-tossed ship. Rescued by s (upper left) and carefully restored, the statues stand guard in an Italian museum.

The Greeks began casting statues in bronze in the mid-500s B.C. Within a century ancient Greek civilization entered its Golden Age, the era in which Plato (427–347 B.C.) and Aristotle (384–322 B.C.) laid the foundations of Western philosophy; Sophocles (495–405 B.C.) wrote tragedies; Thucydides (471–c. 400 B.C.) recorded Greek history; and Phidias of Athens (500–431 B.C.) created statues—perhaps even these rare examples. It was an age in which sculptors created new modes of artistic expression and began to depict the human body with precision. ⊕

Chapter 5 *The Height of Greek Civilization* **133**

TEACH

Remind students that, by the time this statue was cast, ordinary Greek citizens had replaced aristocrats as the most valuable military men. Called *hoplites*, they were so heavily armed that they could fight well only in the tight formation of the phalanx, a group of soldiers close together with their shields overlapping. Ask the class why they think this statue was probably on its way to Rome. *(The Romans greatly admired Greek culture.)*

CURRICULUM CONNECTION

ARCHAEOLOGY
To the archaeologist, an ancient shipwreck like the one that yielded this statue is a sort of time capsule. Objects found under water are often very well preserved because of the lack of airborne bacteria.

Visualizing History The Greek sculptor Myron honored the Olympic discus thrower, shown here in a Roman marble copy. *How did the Greeks honor winners of the Olympic Games?*

> homes are sorrows, too, the very same. Lonely women who died, old men who waited for sons that never came—no son left to them to make the offering at their graves.
> That was the glorious victory they won. 🙶
>
> ——Euripides, from his tragedy *The Trojan Women*, c. 415 B.C.

A Comedy Tonight

Eventually the Greeks also wrote comedies, plays with humorous themes and happy endings. Aristophanes (ar•uh•STAH•fuh•NEEZ), the most famous writer of comedies, created imaginative social satire. In his works he made witty comments about leading figures—such as Euripides—and about issues of his day. In his play *The Clouds*, Aristophanes had a character named Strepsiades ask where Athens was on a map. When the polis's location was pointed out to him, Strepsiades replied: "Don't be ridiculous, that can't be Athens, for I can't see even a single law court in session."

The Olympic Games

Believing that healthy bodies made the best use of nature's gifts, the ancient Greeks stressed athletics in their school curriculum. Greek men who could afford the leisure time usually spent all or part of their afternoons practicing sports in their polis's gymnasiums.

The ancient Greeks held the Olympic Games—their best-known sporting event—in **Olympia** every four years. Because the Olympic Games were a religious festival in honor of Zeus, trading and fighting stopped while they were going on. The Greek calendar began with the supposed date of the first Olympic Games: 776 B.C.

Athletes came from all over the Greek-speaking world to compete in the Olympics. Only male athletes, however, were allowed to take part, and women were not permitted even as spectators. Games that honored the goddess Hera were held at a different location than Olympia and gave Greek women an opportunity to participate in races.

In line with the Greek emphasis on the individual, Olympic competition took the form of individual rather than team events. These consisted at first of only a footrace. Later other events—the broad jump, the discus throw, boxing, and wrestling—were added. An activity called the pentathlon (pehn•TATH•luhn) combined running, jumping, throwing the discus, wrestling, and hurling the javelin.

The Greeks crowned Olympic winners with wreaths of olive leaves and held parades in their honor. Some city-states even excused outstanding athletes from paying taxes.

SECTION 1 ASSESSMENT

Main Idea
1. Use a chart like the one below to list what Greeks expressed in their art and architecture.

Greek Art	Greek Architecture

Recall
2. **Define** classical, sanctuary, perspective, amphora, tragedy, comedy.
3. **Identify** Myron, Phidias, Praxiteles, Aeschylus, Sophocles, Euripides, Aristophanes.

Critical Thinking
4. **Applying Information** How did the Olympic Games and the arts demonstrate the Greek emphasis on the individual?

Understanding Themes
5. **Innovation** How did Greek drama reveal Greek values?

c. 500s B.C.
Pythagoras develops mathematical theories.

435 B.C.
Herodotus writes history of the Persian Wars.

399 B.C.
Athenians try Socrates for treason.

335 B.C.
Aristotle opens the Lyceum in Athens.

Section 2

The Greek Mind

Guide to Reading

Read to Find Out
Main Idea *The ancient Greeks achieved great things in philosophy, history, and science.*

▶ **Terms to Define**
   philosopher, logic, hygiene

▶ **People to Meet**
   Sophists, Socrates, Plato, Aristotle, Herodotus, Thucydides, Thales, Pythagoras, Hippocrates

The Storyteller

Socrates was on trial for his life, for crimes against religion and for corrupting the youth of Athens. He spoke in his own defense: "I have done nothing but try to persuade you all, young and old, not to be concerned with body or property first, but to care chiefly about improvement of the soul. I tell you that virtue does not come from money, but that money comes from virtue, as does every other good of man, public and private. This is my teaching, and if this corrupts the youth, then I am a mischievous person. O men of Athens, either acquit me or convict me; but whichever you do, understand that I shall never alter my ways, not even if I have to die many times."

—adapted from
The Apology of Socrates, Plato

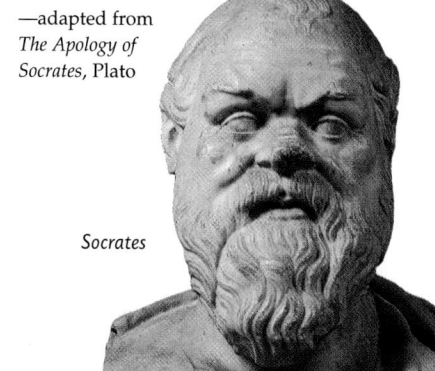

Socrates

The Greeks believed the human mind capable of understanding everything. As a result, the **philosophers**, or thinkers, of ancient Greece produced some of the most remarkable ideas the world has ever known. Through philosophy—which means "the seeking of wisdom"—they laid the foundations for such disciplines as history, political science, biology, and **logic**, or the science of reasoning.

The Sophists

In the 400s B.C. higher education was provided by professional teachers known as **Sophists**. Although Sophists traveled from polis to polis, many gathered in Athens, possibly for the freedom of speech allowed there. Sophists, meaning "knowers," claimed that they could find the answers to all questions.

Many Sophists rejected the belief that the gods and goddesses influenced human behavior. They also did not believe in absolute moral and legal standards. Instead, they asserted that "man is the measure of all things" and that truth is different for each individual.

Not only did Sophists challenge certain traditional Greek beliefs, they also took money for their teaching. Many of them seemed most intent on teaching young men how to win a political argument and get ahead in the world. Many Greeks, including two of Greece's greatest philosophers—**Socrates** (SAH•kruh•TEEZ) and his pupil **Plato**—criticized the Sophists severely.

Socrates

Socrates was born to a poor Athenian family in 470 B.C. Athough a sculptor by trade, he spent most of his time teaching. Unlike the Sophists, Socrates believed in absolute rather than relative truth. His

Chapter 5 *The Height of Greek Civilization* **135**

▶ **Innovation** Ancient Greek thinkers believe in reason and the importance of the individual.

Guide to Reading

For reading strategies to help students read effectively see pages 12–13.

Vocabulary Pre-check

 Use the Vocabulary PuzzleMaker for Chapter 5 to create a crossword puzzle to reinforce section terms. **L1 LEP**

Use Vocabulary Activity 5 to introduce vocabulary terms. **L1 LEP**

FOCUS

Section Objective

Identify the achievements of the ancient Greeks in philosophy, history, and science.

BELLRINGER
Motivational Activity

 Before taking roll at the beginning of the class period, project Section Focus Transparency 5-2 and have students answer the activity questions. Discuss students' responses.
   This activity is also available as a blackline master.

SECTION RESOURCES

Reproducible Masters
- Lecture Notes 5-2
- Reproducible Lesson Plan 5-2
- Vocabulary Activity 5
- Guided Reading Activity 5-2
- People in World History Profiles 7, 8
- History Simulation 5

- Section Quiz 5-2
- Reading Essentials and Study Guide 5-2

Transparencies
- Section Focus Transparency 5-2
- Mapping History Overlay Transparency 4
- Chapter Transparency 5

Multimedia
- Interactive Tutor Self-Assessment Software
- Testmaker

TEACH

Guided Practice

THEME Innovation

What two new ideas made the Sophists innovators in Greek thought? *(They rejected the notion that deities influenced human behavior, as well as belief in absolute moral and legal standards.)* **L1**

Philosophy Draw a rectangle on the chalkboard and label it *philosophy*. Have volunteers draw and label within it smaller rectangles to represent other disciplines founded on philosophy. *(history, political science, biology)* Use this graphic organizer to brainstorm with students some fundamental questions in each of these disciplines; questions which a philosopher might address. *(Examples are: Can people uncover the truth about the past? What form of government best serves justice? What qualities define "life"?)* **L2 LEP**

 Mapping History Overlay Transparency 4

 Chapter Transparency 5

Visualizing History For Plato, there was one criterion by which every public action and institution should be judged: whether or not it made people better than before.
Answer to Caption: *social disorder*

---

main interest did not lie in teaching rhetoric or in imparting information. Rather, Socrates was attracted to the process by which people learned how to think for themselves.

To encourage his students to clear away mistaken ideas and discover the truth, Socrates developed a teaching technique known as the Socratic method. He would ask students pointed questions without giving them answers and then oppose the students' answers with clear logical arguments. Through this method, he forced his students to defend their statements and to clarify their thinking. For example, in discussing the topic of justice, Socrates proceeded as follows:

> **Socrates: Does falsehood then exist among mankind?**
> **Euthydemus: It does assuredly.**
> **Socrates: Under which head [justice or injustice] shall we place it?**
> **Euthydemus: Under injustice, certainly.**
> **Socrates: Well then … if a father, when his son requires medicine, and refuses to take it, should deceive him, and give him the medicine as ordinary food, and, by adopting such deception, should restore him to health, under which head must we place such an act of deceit?**
> **Euthydemus: It appears to me that we must place it under [justice].… I retract what I said before.**
>
> —Xenophon, from *Memorabilia*, early 300s B.C.

Some prominent Athenians viewed Socrates' teachings as a threat to the polis. In 399 B.C. they accused him of "corrupting the young" and of "not worshiping the gods worshiped by the state" and had him brought to trial.

Socrates argued in his own defense that a person who *knew* what was right would always *do* what was right and that the intellectual search for truth was the most important thing in the world. "A man who is good for anything ought not to calculate the chance of living or dying; he ought only to consider whether … he is doing right or wrong."

Despite Socrates' eloquence, a jury of citizens found him guilty and sentenced him to death. Although Socrates had the right to ask for a lesser penalty, such as exile, he refused to do so. He had lived his life under the laws of his polis, and he would not avoid obeying them now.

Socrates carried out the sentence of his fellow citizens himself. He drank poisonous hemlock juice and died quietly among his grieving followers.

136 Chapter 5 *The Height of Greek Civilization*

Plato

Born an Athenian aristocrat, Plato thought at first of entering politics. However, after Socrates' death, Plato—at age 40—became a teacher and opened his Academy, a school that remained in existence until A.D. 529.

From memory Plato recorded dialogues, or conversations, between Socrates and fellow Athenians, and he also wrote the earliest book on political science, *The Republic*. In this book, he presented a plan for what he considered would be the ideal society and government.

Plato disliked Athenian democracy and preferred the government of Sparta. He gave more importance to the state than to the individual. Like the Spartans, he believed that each person should place service to the community above strictly personal goals. Plato also believed that the result of people having too much freedom is social disorder. He distrusted the lower classes and wanted only the most intelligent and best-educated citizens to participate in government. As he explained in *The Republic*:

> Until philosophers are kings, or the kings and princes of this world have the spirit and power of philosophy, and political greatness and wisdom meet in one, and those commoner natures who pursue either to the exclusion of the other are compelled to stand aside, cities will never have rest from their evils, no, nor the human race.

Visualizing History
Plato asked: What type of society is most likely to promote justice? In so doing, he helped to direct philosophy into the study of political science.
What did Plato believe would result from too much freedom?

COOPERATIVE LEARNING ACTIVITY

Radio Play Assign groups of six or seven students the task of writing and performing a ten-minute radio play about any aspect of Greek civilization presented in this section. For example, a group might choose as its theme Hippocrates and medicine. Encourage students to balance their plays with a mixture of narration and dialogue. Have them follow this plan: (1) choose a theme; (2) write a broad summary of the play; (3) decide on five or six scenes to tell the story; (4) write narration and dialogue for each scene; (5) agree on readers for the material; (6) present the play to the class. Encourage all students to participate in each step of the plan. **L1**

Plato's political views were part of an all-embracing philosophy by which he tried to search for "truth." Plato rejected the senses—seeing, hearing, touch, smell, and taste—as a source of truth, believing that the many things that could be perceived by these senses were only "appearance." Reality, the "real" world, was constructed from ideas, or ideal "forms," which could be understood through logical thought and reasoning.

Aristotle

The third great philosopher of ancient Greece was **Aristotle** (AR•uh•STAH•tuhl), who wrote more than 200 books on topics ranging from astronomy to political science. At his Athenian school known as the Lyceum, Aristotle taught the golden mean, an ethical principle that affirmed living moderately and avoiding extremes in one's actions.

Aristotle influenced later philosophers with his work on logic. He developed the syllogism, a means for presenting an argument in such a way that one can determine whether or not the conclusion follows logically from the premises, or basic statements.

Aristotle and Science

Aristotle also influenced scientific work. Unlike Plato, he stressed the value of knowledge gained through the senses. In his work *Physics*, Aristotle stated that the physical world's most striking feature is change, and that change basically consists of the same matter taking on new form. He was also the first person to observe facts, then classify them according to their similarities and their differences, and finally develop generalizations from his data. Some of his specific beliefs—notably, that Earth is the center of our solar system—were incorrect. Aristotle's views and his method of inquiry, however, would continue to dominate European scientific thinking for centuries.

Aristotle and Government

Many of Aristotle's writings focused on political science. Unlike Plato, he did not theorize about idealized principles of government. Instead, he examined the political structure of various city-states, analyzing their advantages and disadvantages. Only then did he spell out his conclusions in a book called *Politics*. Aristotle believed that the ideal form of government balanced monarchy, aristocracy, and democracy in one system. He preferred, however, to have power rest with the middle class, because they knew both how to command *and* obey.

Writers of History

The Greeks also used their intellectual skills in writing history. Until the 400s B.C. the Greeks had considered literary legends as history. **Herodotus** (hih•RAH•duh•tus), the first Greek historian, decided to separate fact from legend. Historians still consider him "the father of history."

Herodotus

Herodotus chose as his subject the Persian Wars and called his work the *Historia*, or "investigation." Herodotus traveled throughout the Persian Empire and also visited many Greek colonies. Everywhere he went, he asked questions, recorded answers, and checked the reliability of his sources. However, he accepted some statements that were not true, especially exaggerated numbers—such as how many Persians died at Marathon. He also sometimes offered supernatural explanations of events.

Herodotus did not limit himself to describing military and political events. He also wrote about outstanding individuals, social customs, and religious beliefs and practices. Later historians have learned a great deal from the *Historia* about the culture of the period and about the civilizations that Herodotus visited.

Thucydides

The second noted historian of ancient Greece, **Thucydides** (thoo•SIH•duh•DEEZ), wrote about the Peloponnesian War. Thucydides is regarded as the first scientific historian because he completely rejected the idea that the deities played a part in human history. Only human beings make history, Thucydides said. He also was as accurate and impartial as possible. He visited battle sites, carefully examined documents, and accepted only the evidence of actual eyewitnesses to events.

 Footnotes **to H**istory

The Atom
The Greek thinker Democritus came up with the idea of a solid particle of matter so small that it was both invisible and not divisible. He named this particle *atom*, meaning "indivisible." Today scientists know that atoms are in fact divisible and include many separate and smaller types of matter. But the basic idea of atomic physics can be traced back to Democritus.

Independent Practice

📁 Guided Reading Activity 5-2 **L1**

📁 People in World History Profiles 7, 8

📁 History Simulation 5

Biography Have students write a one- or two-page biography about any person discussed in this section. Students should research their subject to find information beyond that presented in the text. **L2**

Cultural Perspectives

Greek Influence The Romans borrowed heavily from Greek culture, especially after their conquest of Greece in 146 B.C. The poet Virgil, author of the *Aeneid*—the national epic of Rome—read and was inspired by Homer's works. Roman architects and sculptors imitated Greek styles. The Roman poet Horace put it this way: "Greece, taken captive, captured her savage conqueror."

ASSESS

Check for Understanding

Assign Section 2 Assessment as homework or as an in-class activity.

📀 Use Interactive Tutor Self-Assessment Software to review Section 2.

MEETING SPECIAL NEEDS ACTIVITY

Learning Disability Some students have difficulty dealing with abstract philosophical concepts, such as those discussed in this section. Organize the class into small groups and assign each one a statement from the text, such as the one summarizing the Sophists' belief that "truth is different for each individual." Have them restate the idea in other words (such as "Everyone has a special way of looking at things"). Then, using examples, they should agree or disagree. *(Yes, we each have a unique perspective on life. No, certain scientific truths, for example, are the same for everyone.)* **L1**

Visualizing History The medical school founded by Hippocrates published the world's first work on epidemics, as well as a treatise on epilepsy.
Answer to Caption: *proper hygiene, a sound diet, and plenty of rest*

Evaluate

 Section Quiz 5-2

⚙ Use the Testmaker to create a customized quiz for Section 2.

Reteach

Have students review the major innovations in thought discussed in this section.

 Reading Essentials and Study Guide 5-2

Enrich

Have students research the syllogism, the most common form of deductive logic, which Aristotle originated. Have them write and share syllogisms.

CLOSE

Have students discuss who they think was the single most important figure of all those treated in this section. Be sure they support their choice.

Visualizing History **Greek physicians observed the many symptoms of disease and concluded that illnesses have natural causes.** *What three prescriptions for health did Hippocrates suggest?*

Thucydides did not simply recite facts, however. He also offered explanations for why events took place and what motivated political leaders. He believed that future generations could learn from the past.

The First Scientists

The ancient Greeks believed that the world is ruled by natural laws and that human beings can discover these laws by using reason. Lacking scientific equipment, the Greek scientists made most of their discoveries by observation and thought. They then went on to develop general theories.

Greek Mathematicians

The Greeks became the first people to distin-guish mathematics as a pure science apart from everyday practical uses. They constructed systematic methods of reasoning to prove the truth of mathematical statements. Through the study of mathematics, Greek thinkers believed that they could find absolutely certain and eternal knowledge.

The first prominent Greek scientist was **Thales** (THAY•leez) of Miletus, a Greek city-state in Ionia. Born in the mid-600s B.C., Thales studied astronomy at Babylon and mathematics in Egypt and could foretell a solar eclipse. He also formulated a theory that water was the basic substance of which everything in the world is made.

During the 500s B.C., **Pythagoras** (puh•THA•guh•ruhs) tried to explain everything in mathematical terms. He explored the nature of numbers, especially whole numbers and their ratios. Students of geometry still learn the Pythagorean theorem about the relationship of sides of a right-angled triangle. Pythagoras also taught that the world was round and revolved around a fixed point.

Greek Medicine

Greek scientists also contributed to the field of medicine. Called "the father of medicine," the physician **Hippocrates** (hih•PAH•kruh•TEEZ) believed that diseases had natural, not supernatural, causes and that the body could heal itself. He was the first doctor to view medicine as a science.

Basing his work in the late 400s B.C. on observation, he diagnosed and treated illnesses all over Greece. He urged fellow doctors to record their cases and to exchange information with one another. He strongly advocated proper hygiene, or health care, a sound diet, and plenty of rest.

According to tradition, Hippocrates drafted a code for ethical medical conduct that has guided the practice of medicine for more than 2,000 years. Many doctors today recite the Hippocratic oath when they receive their medical degree.

SECTION 2 ASSESSMENT

Main Idea
1. Use a diagram like the one below to show Greek achievements in philosophy.

Greek Philosophy

Recall
2. **Define** philosopher, logic, hygiene.
3. **Identify** Sophists, Socrates, Plato, Aristotle, Herodotus, Thucydides, Thales, Pythagoras, Hippocrates.

Critical Thinking
4. **Making Comparisons** Compare Plato and Aristotle's views of politics and observations made through the senses.

Understanding Themes
5. **Innovation** How did Socrates and Hippocrates contribute to Greek intellectual life?

SECTION 2 ASSESSMENT ANSWERS

1. Sophists asserted that truth is different for each person; Socratic method; Plato gave more importance to state than to individual; Aristotle taught the golden mean
2. All terms are defined in the Glossary.
3. Sophists, 135; Socrates, 135; Plato, 135; Aristotle, 137; Herodotus, 137; Thucy-dides, 137; Thales, 138; Pythagoras, 138; Hippocrates, 138
4. Plato: government by educated citizens; Aristotle: ideal form of government balances monarchy, aristocracy, and democracy in one system, but power should rest with middle class. Plato: believed senses show only appearance, while reality is in ideas; Aristotle observed with his senses and classified what he observed as facts.
5. **INNOVATION** Socrates: developed Socratic method, forcing students to think clearly; Hippocrates: taught that diseases had natural causes and based his work on observation, thereby furthering the use of the scientific method.

Finding Exact Location on a Map

Your new friend invites you to her house. In giving directions, she says, "I live at the northwest corner of Vine Street and Oak Avenue." She has pinpointed her exact location. We use a similar system to identify the exact location of any place on Earth.

Learning the Skill

Over many centuries, cartographers developed a grid system of imaginary lines—the lines of latitude and lines of longitude. Lines of latitude run east and west around the earth. Because they always remain the same distance from each other, they are also called parallels. The parallel lines of latitude measure distance north and south of the Equator, located at 0° latitude. Each line of latitude is one degree, or 69 miles (110 km), from the next. There are 90 latitude lines between the Equator and each Pole. For example, New York City lies 41° north of the Equator, or 41° N.

Lines of longitude, or meridians, run north and south from Pole to Pole. Unlike lines of latitude, lines of longitude are not always the same distance from each other. Lines of longitude are farthest apart at the Equator and intersect at each Pole. Longitude measures distance east and west of the Prime Meridian, located at 0° longitude. That line runs through Greenwich, England, in western Europe and through western Africa. Longitude lines increase east and west of the Prime Meridian to 180°. This meridian runs through the Pacific Ocean. New York City, for example, lies 74° west of the Prime Meridian, or 74° W.

With this system, we can pinpoint the "grid address" of any place on Earth. On a map, find the nearest line of latitude to the designated place. Then follow along this line until it crosses the nearest line of longitude. The point where the lines intersect is the grid address. For example, New York City has this grid address: 41° N, 74° W.

Practicing the Skill

Use the map below to answer the following questions:
1. What is Babylon's approximate grid address?
2. What city sits at approximately 30° N, 31° E?
3. What is Nineveh's approximate grid address?
4. What is Tyre's approximate grid address?

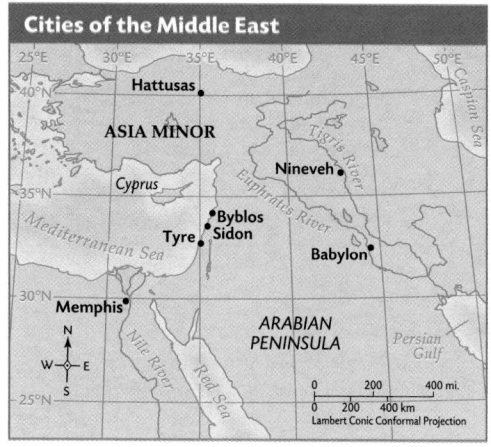

Cities of the Middle East

Applying the Skill

Create a travel itinerary for a tour of the ruins of ancient Egypt, Greece, or the Middle East. Choose at least 10 locations to visit. Draw a map of the region, including grid lines. On the map, identify each place's approximate grid location.

For More Practice

Turn to the Skill Practice in the Chapter Assessment on page 151 for more practice in finding exact location on a map.

The **Glencoe Skillbuilder Interactive Workbook**, Level 2 provides instruction and practice in key social studies skills.

TEACH

Finding Exact Location on a Map

Have one or more students draw on the chalkboard a simplified map of the area around your school or a nearby residential or business district. (The school, or some other landmark, should be at the center, labeled "0.") With north at the top, the map should include 3 or 4 streets to the north, south, east, and west of the central point. These should be labeled with the street name and with a grid location: 1, 2, and 3 north, 1, 2, and 3 east, and so on. Then ask students to give grid locations for several street intersections, and vice versa.

Additional Practice

Skill Reinforcement Activity 5

Building Skills in Geography Workbook, Unit 1, Lessons 3, 4, 5

GLENCOE
TECHNOLOGY

 Glencoe's **Skillbuilder Interactive Workbook, Level 2**
This interactive CD-ROM promotes student mastery of key social studies skills.

ANSWERS TO PRACTICING THE SKILL

1. 32°N, 44°E
2. Memphis
3. 36°N, 43°E
4. 33°N, 35°E

400 B.C.　　　300 B.C.　　　200 B.C.　　　100 B.C.

359 B.C.
Philip II becomes
king of Macedonia.

331 B.C. Alexander
the Great defeats the
Persians in the battle
of Gaugamela.

250 B.C.
Jewish scholars
translate the Hebrew
Bible into Greek.

c. 150 B.C.
Rome conquers
Greece.

Section 3

Alexander's Empire

Read to Find Out
Main Idea *Alexander had clear goals for his empire.*

▶ **Terms to Define**
　domain

▶ **People to Meet**
　Philip II, Demosthenes, Alexander the Great, Zeno, Menander, Eratosthenes, Euclid, Archimedes

▶ **Places to Locate**
　Macedonia, Alexandria

𝓢toryteller

Hellenistic poets who lived in bustling cities loved to tell simple fables about love in a countryside setting:

A bee once stung the god of love [Cupid]
　as he was stealing honey.
His fingertips began to smart,
　and he blew upon his hand,
　stamped and danced.
When he showed his wound to his mother,
　she laughed. "Aren't you just like the bee,
　　so small, yet inflicting great pain?"

　—adapted from *The Idylls of Theocritus,* (no. 19, "The Honey-Thief"), in *Greek Pastoral Poetry,* Anthony Holden, 1974

Cupid, wall painting, Pompeii, Italy

140　**Chapter 5**　*The Height of Greek Civilization*

𝓘n the early 400s B.C., the Persians under Darius I, and then under his son Xerxes, had tried to conquer the Greek city-states but failed. Some 150 years later the Macedonians, a people who lived north of Greece in the Balkan Peninsula, made a similar attempt—and succeeded.

Rise of Macedonia

The Macedonians, like the Spartans, were descended from the Dorians, and the Macedonian language incorporated many Greek words. The Greeks, however, looked down on the Macedonians as backward mountaineers.

In 359 B.C. **Philip II** became king of **Macedonia**. During his youth he had been a hostage for three years in the Greek city-state of Thebes. There he had learned to admire both Greek culture and military organization. As king, Philip determined to do three things: create a strong standing army, unify the quarreling Greek city-states under Macedonian rule, and destroy the Persian Empire.

Philip increased his army's fighting power by organizing his infantry into Greek-style phalanxes. Arrayed in close formation 16 rows deep, Philip's lance-bearing foot soldiers fought as a single unit.

For the next 23 years, Philip pursued his ambition. Sometimes he conquered a polis or bribed a polis's leaders to surrender. Sometimes he allied a polis through marriage; Philip had a total of six or seven wives.

The Greek city-states, weakened by the Peloponnesian War, would not cooperate in resisting Philip. The great Athenian orator **Demosthenes** (dih•MAHS•thuh•NEEZ) appealed to his fellow citizens to fight for their liberty. But Demosthenes' words were to no avail. By 338 B.C. Philip had conquered all of Greece except Sparta.

Philip then announced that he would lead the Greeks and Macedonians in a war against Persia. But in 336 B.C., just as he was ready to carry out his

Alexander's Empire 336–323 B.C.

Map Study
Alexander the Great united the Greeks and conquered an area stretching from Egypt to India.
1. **Movement** After freeing the Ionian city-states, in which direction did Alexander and his forces travel?
2. **Location** What key cities in the Persian Empire did Alexander conquer?

plans, Philip was murdered—either by a Persian agent or by an assassin hired by his first wife, Olympias. Olympias' son Alexander, later known as **Alexander the Great**, became king.

Alexander's Conquests

Alexander was only 20 when he became the ruler of Macedonia and Greece. A commander in the Macedonian army since he was 16, Alexander was highly respected by his soldiers for his courage and military skill. He was also extremely well educated, for his father had him tutored by Aristotle.

Conflict With Persia

In 334 B.C. Alexander led 30,000 soldiers and 5,000 cavalry into Asia to open his campaign of "West against East." The first major encounter with the Persians took place at the Granicus River in western Asia Minor. Alexander's forces won, and he sent 300 suits of Persian armor to Athens as an offering to the goddess Athena. He then marched along the coast of Asia Minor, freeing the Ionian city-states from Persian rule.

The second major battle between the Greeks

and Persians took place in 333 B.C. at Issus, Syria. Once again, Alexander's superb tactics resulted in victory, forcing the Persian king Darius III to flee.

Instead of pursuing Darius, Alexander and his troops moved south along the Mediterranean coast. First they captured the seaports of Phoenicia and cut off the Persian fleet from its main supply bases. The fleet soon surrendered. Next, turning west, they invaded Egypt where the people, discontented under Persian rule, welcomed them and declared Alexander a pharaoh. In Egypt, Alexander established a new city and named it **Alexandria** after himself.

Final Campaigns

In 331 B.C. Alexander again turned his attention eastward. He invaded Mesopotamia and smashed Darius's main army in the battle of Gaugamela near the Tigris River. He

Alexander the Great

COOPERATIVE LEARNING ACTIVITY

Making a Book Organize the class into groups to prepare pages or sections of a class book illustrating the exploits of Alexander the Great. Assign each group an area of conquest to research, including Thebes, the Granicus River, Issus, Egypt, Gaugamela, and the Indus River valley. Each finished product should include a description of the area, what happened there, and the dates on which the event(s) occurred. It should also include a map, with principal cities and features labeled. Groups may also include drawings showing costumes, weapons, and buildings. **L1**

Critical Thinking Have students identify the major strands of Hellenistic philosophy discussed in this section. *(Cynicism, Epicureanism, Stoicism)* Have them compare these philosophies with those of Plato and Aristotle. *(The Hellenistic philosophers cared more about individual well-being; the earlier philosophers cared about the well-being of the state.)* **L3**

 Focus on World Art Print 8

 Mapping History Overlay Transparency 5

Who?What?Where?When?

Achilles Alexander the Great's mother told him that Achilles was his ancestor, and the legendary Greek hero became Alexander's model.

Independent Practice

📁 Guided Reading Activity 5-3 **L1**

📁 Time Line Activity 5

📁 Mapping History Activity 5

📁 Geography and History Activity 5

Advertising Show students examples of advertisements for cities or regions from business or travel magazines. Have them write ad copy for a magazine, to be distributed throughout the Hellenistic world, that extols the virtues of living in Alexandria, Egypt. **L1**

— WORLD HISTORY *Online* **—**

Have students use the **Chapter 5 Student Web Activity** at worldhistory.glencoe.com for in-depth study of Alexander the Great.

went on to capture the key cities of the Persian Empire: Babylon, Persepolis, and Susa. When Darius was killed by one of his own generals, Alexander declared himself ruler of the Persian Empire.

Even this success was not enough for the young conqueror. In 327 B.C. he led his soldiers into India, and after three years they reached the Indus River valley. Alexander hoped to go farther yet, but his Macedonian veterans refused. Alexander therefore reluctantly turned around and went to Babylon, which he had made the capital of his empire. But the hardships of the journey had undermined his health, and he fell ill with a fever, probably malaria. In 323 B.C. Alexander the Great died at the age of 33.

— WORLD HISTORY *Online* **—**

Student Web Activity 5

Visit the *World History: The Human Experience* Web site at **worldhistory.glencoe.com** and click on *Chapter 5—Student Web Activities* for an activity relating to Alexander the Great.

Imperial Goals

When Alexander first set out with his army, his goal was to punish Persia for its invasion of Greece 150 years earlier. But as more and more territory came under his control, Alexander's views changed. His new vision was to create an empire that would unite Europe and Asia and combine the best of Greek and Persian cultures.

Alexander tried to promote this goal by example. He imitated Persian dress and royal court life. He married a daughter of Darius III and encouraged 10,000 of his soldiers to marry Persian women. He enrolled 30,000 Persians in his army. He also founded about 70 cities that served both as military outposts and as centers for spreading the Greek language and culture throughout his empire.

Divided Domain

Following Alexander's death, three of his generals—Ptolemy (TAH•luh•mee), Seleucus (suh•LOO•kuhs), and Antigonus (an•TIH•guh•nuhs)—eventually divided his vast empire into separate domains, or territories. Ptolemy and his descendants ruled Egypt, Libya, and part of Syria.

Images of the Times

The Hellenistic Age

Hellenistic culture blended mythology with real live heroes.

Bronze statuette of Hellenistic dancer, said to be from Alexandria.

This Pompeiian mosaic honors Alexander the Great, who extended his empire to the Indus River valley.

142

The Greeks retold tales of mythological figures on pottery. This scene shows the god of wine, Dionysus, in a boat.

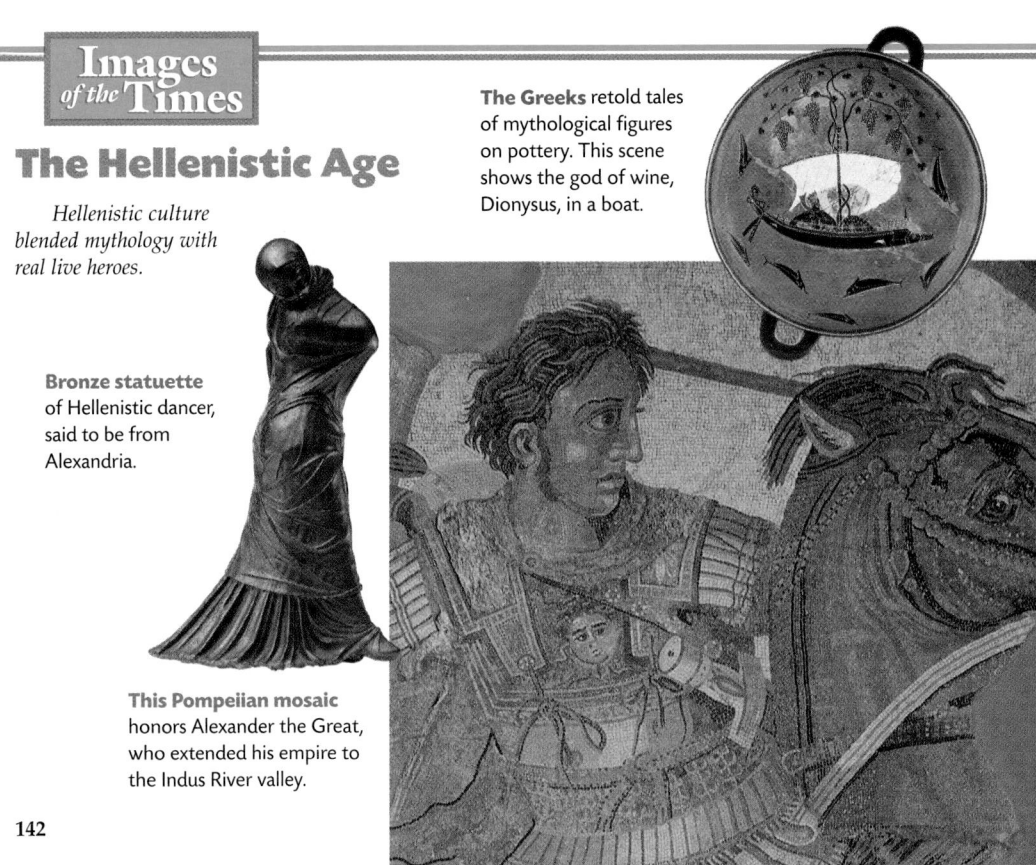

Images of the Times
The Hellenistic Age

The statue of the Winged Victory shown here is considered the greatest masterpiece of Hellenistic sculpture. It was discovered on the Aegean island of Samothrace in 1863. When found, the statue was in many fragments, which were later pieced together. Today it stands in the Louvre Museum in Paris.

The Winged Victory is just one of many military monuments and statues erected during this age that glorified armed conquest and commemorated victories. Hellenistic art was also characterized by a movement toward more realism in portraits. This reflected the growing tendency to look up to and even worship individuals who boasted great achievements.

The most famous Ptolemaic ruler was Cleopatra VII, who lost her kingdom to the Romans in 31 B.C.

Seleucus and his descendants—the Seleucids (suh•LOO•suhds)—at first controlled the rest of Syria, as well as Mesopotamia, Iran, and Afghanistan. After a while, however, they were forced to give up their eastern territory and withdraw to Syria. In 167 B.C. Jewish guerrillas led by Judah Maccabee challenged the Seleucid control of Palestine. The Seleucid Antiochus IV had ordered the Jews to worship the Greek deities, but many Jews refused to abandon their religion. In 165 B.C. Judah Maccabee succeeded in reoccupying Jerusalem and rededicating the Temple, an event commemorated by the Jewish festival of Hanukkah. The kingdom of Judah would remain independent until its defeat by Rome in 63 B.C. The Seleucids likewise ruled in Syria until the Romans came.

The domain of Antigonus and his heirs consisted at first of Macedonia and Greece. But the Greek city-states soon declared their independence and once again began fighting with each other. In the 100s B.C., the growing Roman Empire would conquer Macedonia and Greece.

Hellenistic Culture

The political unity of Alexander's empire disappeared with his death, but the Greek language and culture continued to spread and flourish in the lands he had conquered. There, Hellenic ways of life mixed with elements of Middle Eastern culture to form a new culture, called Hellenistic.

City Life

Hellenistic culture was concentrated in cities. The largest and wealthiest of these was Alexandria in Egypt. Alexandria's straight streets intersected each other at right angles, in contrast to the crooked streets of older cities. Its white stucco stone palaces and temples gleamed brilliantly in the sun.

The city's economic position benefited from a double harbor that could hold 1,200 ships at a time. Another asset to trade was the city's lighthouse, which was visible from 35 miles (56 km) out at sea.

Alexandria also was a major intellectual center. Its museum was the first ever and included a library of nearly a million volumes, an institute for scientific research, a zoo, and a botanical garden.

Science Have students work in pairs to find out more about and demonstrate one of Archimedes' inventions or innovations. These can be in addition to the ones mentioned in the section. The demonstrations may include models, prepared drawings, or "chalk talks" in which students illustrate their presentations on the chalkboard. **L2**

Multicultural Have students use what they have learned to prepare a chart that compares the roles of women in the Egyptian, Hellenic, and Hellenistic cultures. Headings could include main role, education, social life, and participation in government. **L3**

you don't say...

"Cynic" comes from the Greek *cynikos* meaning "like a dog." This term probably began as an insult, referring to the philosophers' aggressive manners. But they adopted it with pride, saying that they were the watchdogs of morality. Today the term refers to someone who is doubtful.

Woman and servant, a Hellenistic funerary stela from Kerameikos cemetery.

The Winged Victory of Samothrace, c. 200–100 B.C., was carved from a solid eight-foot block of marble.

REFLECTING ON THE TIMES

1. How did Greek pottery promote popular myths?
2. How are humans portrayed in Hellenistic art?

143

ANSWERS TO REFLECTING ON THE TIMES

1. It retold them in pictorial form.
2. Hellenistic art portrayed ordinary people in realistic situations as well as mythological or heroic figures.

ASSESS

Check for Understanding

Assign Section 3 Assessment as homework or as an in-class activity.

 Use Interactive Tutor Self-Assessment Software to review Section 3.

Evaluate

Section Quiz 5-3

 Use the Testmaker to create a customized quiz for Section 3.

Linking Past and Present

An Economic Region

The basic coin of Alexander's empire was the Athenian drachma. The term comes from the Greek word "handful" because the coin was originally the equivalent of a handful of arrows.

ANSWER

Numerous public works projects, thriving sea trade, and a uniform currency. Some students may suggest a region that extracts or produces particular resources or goods; others may describe a region with its trade, transport, business, and shopping/entertainment networks.

Scientists came from all over the Hellenistic world. Around 250 B.C. Jewish scholars in Alexandria translated the Hebrew Bible into Greek. This translation, known as the Septuagint (sehp•TOO•uh•juhnt), was later used by the apostle Paul and is still used in the Eastern Orthodox Church.

During Hellenic times, the Greeks had been intensely involved with their particular polis. In Hellenistic society, however, the Greeks formed the upper class of Alexandria and other cities in the Middle East and Asia Minor that were ruled by kings. Rather than being loyal to their king or kingdom, professional Greek soldiers and bureaucrats moved from place to place, wherever job opportunities were best.

In Alexandria and other Hellenistic cities, the social status of upper-class Greek women improved over their traditional status in the city-state of Athens. No longer secluded, these women could move about freely and enjoyed a certain amount of independence. They learned how to read and write and entered such occupations as real estate, banking, and government. Such social and economic opportunities were not, however, available to commoners.

Hellenistic Philosophers

Hellenistic philosophers focused on personal behavior, especially the question of how to achieve peace of mind. Three systems of thought attracted most Hellenistic intellectuals: Cynicism, Epicureanism (EH•pih•kyu•REE•uh•NIH•zuhm), and Stoicism.

The best known Cynic was Diogenes (dy•AH•juh•NEEZ). He criticized materialism and asserted that people would be happy if they gave up luxuries and lived simply, in accord with nature. The scholar Epicurus started the philosophy of Epicureanism. He argued that people should avoid both joy and pain by accepting the world as it was, ignoring politics, and living simply and quietly with a few close friends.

Zeno founded Stoicism. The name *Stoicism* comes from the *Stoa Poikile*, or "painted porch," in which Zeno lectured. The Stoics believed that what happened to people was governed by natural laws. Accordingly, people could gain happiness by ignoring their emotions, and instead following their reason. In this way, they were able to accept even the most difficult circumstances of life and do their duty. Stoicism later affected both Roman intellectuals and early Christian thinkers.

CONNECTIONS

Economics

An Economic Region

Geographers, historians, and economists often divide the world into regions based on economic factors, such as trade routes and uniform currency. The empire of Alexander the Great came to be one economic region.

Alexander and his successors used vast sums of gold and silver captured in Persia to finance public works projects, road construction, and harbor development. Extensive land routes helped maintain close economic links among the cities built by Alexander. A uniform currency also developed that held the empire together economically. International sea trade expanded greatly under Alexander's empire and its successor domains. Hellenistic sailors used monsoon winds to sail directly across the Indian Ocean between Africa and Asia

Coin bearing the face of Alexander the Great

instead of hugging the coast. As a result, luxury items from India and Arabia became common in Mediterranean cities. As in ancient times, the world today is made up of many different economic regions. For example, the American Midwest can be classified as an economic region because one of its economic characteristics is the production of corn, hogs, and cattle. Another example of an economic region is a large metropolitan area—such as that of Johannesburg, South Africa—in which a central urban area is joined to surrounding areas by transportation links, or by people's wants and needs, such as jobs, shopping, or entertainment.

 Linking Past and Present ACTIVITY

List three economic characteristics of Alexander's empire. Then, identify an economic region in which you live and list its characteristics.

MEETING SPECIAL NEEDS ACTIVITY

Learning Style: Visual/Spatial Many students have problems understanding distances. Have students, in pairs or small groups, "translate" some of the distances of Alexander's time into comparable distances in the United States today. For instance, the extent of Alexander's conquests in Asia, from the Aegean coast to the Indus Valley, is approximately 2,800 miles (4,505 kilometers)—about the same as the east-west distance across the United States. If possible, have students present their findings to the class using a wall map of the United States. **L1**

Hellenistic Art and Literature

During the Hellenistic era, artists departed from Hellenic styles. Instead of carving idealized individuals, Hellenistic sculptors showed people in the grip of powerful emotions. They also carved portrait heads, because art had become a business.

Hellenistic playwrights usually wrote comedies rather than tragedies. Like Hellenistic philosophers, they ignored the problems of the outside world as much as possible. **Menander,** the most renowned Hellenistic playwright, specialized in comedies about everyday life. Well-known lines from his works include "Whom the gods love die young" and "We live not as we will, but as we can."

Science, Medicine, and Mathematics

Although limited by their simple instruments, Hellenistic scientists performed many experiments and developed new theories. Aristarchus (AR•uh•STAHR•kuhs) of Samos concluded that the sun is larger than the earth, that the earth revolves around the sun, and that the stars lie at immense distances from both heavenly bodies. **Eratosthenes** (EHR•uh•TAHS•thuh•NEEZ) estimated the earth's circumference to within 1 percent of the correct figure. Hellenistic doctors dissected corpses in order to learn more about human anatomy. They discovered the body's nervous system, studied the brain and the liver, and learned how to use drugs to relieve pain.

The Hellenistic period also saw great developments and breakthroughs in mathematics and

 Actors preparing for a performance, a mosaic from the House of the Tragic Poet, Pompeii. National Museum, Naples, Italy
Why might people have had a work like this in their home?

physics. **Euclid** of Alexandria wrote *The Elements of Geometry,* a book that organized all information about geometry. **Archimedes** (AHR•kuh•MEE•deez) invented the compound pulley, which moves heavy objects easily, and the cylinder-screw, which is still used to lift water for irrigation. He also discovered the principle of buoyancy and demonstrated the principle of the lever.

History & Art This mosaic—a work formed by fitting together many small pieces of stone and/or glass—was found in Pompeii. The mosaic depicts many theater traditions that began with the Greeks, such as the wearing of masks by actors.
Answer to Caption: *They enjoyed attending plays, and so did their guests. Also, such a work displayed the wealth of those who commissioned it.*

Reteach

Have volunteers read each heading in this section. After each is read, have other volunteers summarize the main ideas under the heading.

📁 Reteaching Activity 5

📁 Reading Essentials and Study Guide 5-3

Enrich

Have students research achievements of other Greek scientists of the Hellenistic period, such as Hipparchus or Herophilus.

📁 Enrichment Activity 5

CLOSE

Organize the class into three teams to prepare questions and answers for a class quiz game called "It's Greek to Me." Each team takes a section of the chapter and prepares ten questions and answers. Each team also reviews the other two sections. Have teams quiz each other.

SECTION 3 ASSESSMENT

Main Idea
1. Use a web diagram like the one below to show Alexander the Great's goals for his empire.

Recall
2. **Define** domain.
3. **Identify** Philip II, Demosthenes, Alexander the Great, Zeno, Menander, Eratosthenes, Euclid, Archimedes.

Critical Thinking
4. **Analyzing Information** What were the most important

military exploits and conquests of Alexander the Great? Give reasons why.

Understanding Themes
5. **Cultural Diffusion** Explain how and why the arts of the Hellenistic period differ from the arts of the earlier Hellenic era.

Chapter 5 *The Height of Greek Civilization* **145**

SECTION 3 ASSESSMENT ANSWERS

1. To punish Persia for invading Greece 150 years before; to create empire uniting Europe with Asia and combine Greek and Persian cultures; to control lots of territory
2. All terms are defined in the Glossary.
3. Philip II, 140; Demosthenes, 140; Alexander the Great, 141; Zeno, 144; Menander, 145; Eratosthenes, 145;

Euclid, 145; Archimedes, 145;
4. Conquest at Granicus River freed the Ionian city-states from Persian rule; conquest at Issus forced Darius III to flee; conquest in Egypt made him a pharaoh over Alexandria; capture of key Mesopotamian cities made him ruler of Persian Empire.

5. **CULTURAL DIFFUSION**
Hellenistic sculptors created more emotional, less idealistic works. Hellenistic playwrights wrote comedies rather than tragedies. Causes for these changes may include: the absorption of different peoples into Alexander's empire; a tendency to be less involved in political life.

Block Schedule

Team Teaching This excerpt from *Antigone* may be presented in a team-teaching context, in conjunction with English or Language Arts.

Antigone

Historical Connection

Sophocles wrote during the Golden Age of Athens, an era in which Greek writers, philosophers, architects, and historians produced works that shaped all subsequent Western civilization. This excerpt from the play *Antigone* shows how thinkers of the time dealt with such basic issues as ethics and justice.

Background Information

Setting During the Golden Age of Athens, writers often set their works in the distant past. *Antigone* takes place in the city of Thebes in a mythological period long before Sophocles lived.

Characters Antigone: daughter of the deceased king of Thebes, niece of Creon, sister of Ismene, Polyneices, and Eteocles; Ismene: sister of Antigone; Creon: brother of the deceased king of Thebes.

Plot The main conflict is between Antigone, who wants to give her brother Polyneices an honorable burial, and Creon, her uncle, who argues that Polyneices was a traitor who does not deserve a burial. Antigone violates Creon's order and buries her brother. Antigone and Creon then debate the morality of her action.

from Antigone
by Sophocles

The Greek playwright Sophocles, who lived from about 495–405 B.C., wrote about the conflict between conscience and authority in his play *Antigone. After Antigone's two brothers died battling each other for the throne of Thebes, her uncle, Creon, became king. Creon allowed one brother, Eteocles, an honorable burial. He declared, however, that the other brother, Polyneices, was a traitor whose body should be left for the "birds and scavenging dogs." Anyone attempting to bury Polyneices, he warned, would be stoned to death. Antigone's sister, Ismene, obeys Creon. Antigone, however, out of respect for her brother, buries him.*

Creon [*slowly, dangerously*]. And you, Antigone,
You with your head hanging—do you confess this thing?

Antigone. I do. I deny nothing.

Creon [*to* SENTRY].　　　　　You may go.
[*Exit* SENTRY] [*To* ANTIGONE] Tell me, tell me briefly:
Had you heard my proclamation touching this matter?

Antigone. It was public. Could I help hearing it?

Creon. And yet you dared defy the law.

Antigone.　　　　　　　　　　I dared.
It was not God's proclamation. That final justice
That rules the world below makes no such laws.
Your edict, King, was strong,
But all your strength is weakness itself against
The immortal unrecorded laws of God.
They are not merely now: they were, and shall be,
Operative forever, beyond man utterly.

I knew I must die, even without your decree:
I am only mortal. And if I must die
Now, before it is my time to die,
Surely this is no hardship: can anyone
Living, as I live, with evil all about me,
Think death less than a friend? This death of mine
Is of no importance; but if I had left my brother
Lying in death unburied, I should have suffered.
Now I do not.
　　　　　You smile at me. Ah Creon.

ABOUT THE AUTHOR

Sophocles was born into a well-to-do family in ancient Greece. Many of his plays focused on one strong-willed individual who challenged authority, tradition, or the gods and goddesses. For example, Antigone defies the authority of the state to defend the honor of her brother. Although Sophocles wrote more than 100 plays, only 7 are known to exist today. Many of the lost plays won awards in the annual writing competition held in ancient Greece. In addition to writing, Sophocles served as a government administrator and a general in the Athenian army.

Think me a fool, if you like; but it may well be
That a fool convicts me of folly....
Creon, what more do you want than my death?

Creon.   Nothing.
That gives me everything.

Antigone.   Then I beg you: kill me.
This talking is a great weariness: your words
Are distasteful to me, and I am sure that mine
Seem so to you. And yet they should not seem so:
I should have praise and honor for what I have done.
All these men here would praise me
Were their lips not frozen shut with fear of you.
[*Bitterly*] Ah the good fortune of kings,
Licensed to say and do whatever they please!

Creon. You are alone here in that opinion.

Antigone. No, they are with me. But they keep their tongues
in leash.

Creon. Maybe. But you are guilty,
and they are not.

Antigone. There is no guilt in reverence for the dead.

Creon. But Eteocles—was he not
your brother too?

Antigone. My brother too.

Creon.   And you
insult his memory?

Antigone [*softly*]. The dead man
would not say that I insult it.

Creon. He would: for you honor a
traitor as much as him.

Antigone. His own brother, traitor or
not, and equal in blood.

Creon. He made war on his country.
Eteocles defended it.

Antigone. Nevertheless, there are
honors due all the dead.

History & Art Actors preparing for a performance
(detail), the House of the Tragic Poet,
Pompeii. National Museum, Naples, Italy
What is the theme of Antigone?

OTHER WORKS BY SOPHOCLES

Jebb, Richard Claverhouse, trans. *The
Complete Plays of Sophocles.* New York:
Bantam, 1982.
Knox, M. W., trans. *Oedipus the King.* New
York: Pocket Books, 1972.

Watling, E. F., trans. *Electra and Other Plays.*
New York: Penguin Books, 1954.
Williams, C. K., and Gregory W. Dickerson,
trans. *Women of Trachus.* New York: Oxford
University Press, 1978.

Literary Element Alliteration
occurs when words in a phrase
begin with a similar sound. The
first line by Creon uses alliteration, as in "head hanging." Later,
Antigone uses the phrase "a fool
convicts me of folly."

FOCUS

Before students read the excerpt,
list on the chalkboard people
who students feel have authority
over them, such as parents, teachers, and so on. Ask students to
describe hypothetical cases in
which they might choose to disobey a person having authority.
Help them see the difference
between ignoring authority and
principled disobedience.

TEACH

Interpretation

Ask students if they agree with
Antigone's claim that "All these
men here would praise me/Were
their lips not shut with fear of
you." Point out that ordinary
people may support a heroic
individual against a repressive
government. At other times, people see such an individual as a
threat to order and stability.

History & Art Pompeii was a
provincial Roman city buried in ash
and lava when the volcano Vesuvius
erupted in August of A.D. 79, killing
all its residents but preserving much
of the art and architecture.
Answer to Caption: *an individual
can stand up to an authority, but at a
price*

Clarification

The choragos is the leader of the chorus, who serves as a narrator to smooth the flow of the story and adds commentary from the author.

Evaluation

Discuss the role of women in Greek society as portrayed in this excerpt. Students might consider how the play would differ if Antigone had been male instead of female. (*She would have taken the throne instead of Creon.*)

History & Art

Roman art was strongly influenced by Hellenic styles. Wealthy Romans not only had artists copy Greek originals but also sometimes brought artists from Greece to decorate their homes. **Answer to Caption:** *Students may say that since Ismene feared to act, mere words cannot redeem her.*

Linking Past and Present

Greek Dramas *Antigone* and other tragedies by Sophocles, such as *Oedipus the King*, *Oedipus at Colonus*, and *Electra*, are often staged today by college theater groups and by local repertory companies. Some students may wish to attend a performance in your area.

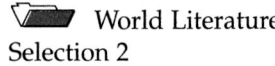 World Literature Selection 2

ASSESS

Assign **Responding to Literature** questions.

History & Art Wall painting of a Greek woman with flowers. National Museum, Naples, Italy
The Greeks admired beauty and virtue. *Does Ismene regain virtue by confessing a share in the crime?*

Creon. But not the same for the wicked as for the just.

Antigone. Ah Creon, Creon.
Which of us can say what the gods hold wicked?

Creon. An enemy is an enemy, even dead.

Antigone. It is my nature to join in love, not hate.

Creon [*finally losing patience*]. Go join them, then; if you must have your love,
Find it in hell!

Choragos [*leader of a group of 15 citizens*]. But see, Ismene comes:
[*Enter Ismene, guarded.*] Those tears are sisterly, the cloud
That shadows her eyes rains down gentle sorrow.

Creon. You too, Ismene,

ADDITIONAL LITERARY WORKS OF THE PERIOD

Book of Songs. A collection of 300 poems from China dating to 1000 B.C.
Homer. *Iliad* and *Odyssey.* Ancient Greek epic poems that have greatly influenced Western literature.
Laozi. *The Classic of the Way and the Virtue.*

Writings of the founder of Daoism, who lived in China in the 500s B.C.
Samhitas. Sacred Hindu hymns written in Sanskrit in India and compiled about 1000 B.C.

Snake in my ordered house, sucking my blood
Stealthily—and all the time I never knew
That these two sisters were aiming at my throne!

                              Ismene,
Do you confess your share in this crime, or deny it?
Answer me.

Ismene. Yes, if she will let me say so. I am guilty.

Antigone [*coldly*]. No, Ismene. You have no right to say so.
You would not help me, and I will not have you help me.

Ismene. But now I know what you meant; and I am here
To join you, to take my share of punishment.

Antigone. The dead man and the gods who rule the dead
Know whose act this was. Words are not friends.

Ismene. Do you refuse me, Antigone? I want to die with you:
I too have a duty that I must discharge to the dead.

Antigone. You shall not lessen my death by sharing it.

Ismene. What do I care for life when you are dead?

Antigone. Ask Creon. You're always hanging on his opinions.

Ismene. You are laughing at me. Why, Antigone?

Antigone. It's a joyless laughter, Ismene.

Ismene.   But can I do nothing?

Antigone. Yes. Save yourself. I shall not envy you.
There are those who will praise you; I shall have honor, too.

Ismene. But we are equally guilty!

Antigone.   No more, Ismene.
You are alive, but I belong to death.

RESPONDING TO LITERATURE

1. Explain what Antigone means when she says to Creon, "But all your strength is weakness itself against the immortal unrecorded laws of God."
2. Quote a passage that demonstrates Antigone's bravery.
3. Explain whether you would like to live in a society in which individuals followed only their consciences.
4. **Making Inferences** Predict whether Creon actually would have Antigone stoned to death.

CLOSE

Ask students to put themselves in the position of Antigone and Creon and have them describe what moral dilemmas each faced. (*As ruler, Creon may feel he cannot back down from sentencing Antigone to death, but as her uncle, he may be reluctant to carry out the punishment. Antigone does not wish to die, but she feels it is dishonorable to leave her brother unburied.*)

Contemporary Connection

One underlying theme of *Antigone* is loyalty to family. Discuss the idea with students, asking if they feel they have a duty to be loyal to their families. Ask students to consider how far loyalty to family should go.

Portfolio Project

Have students draw on their own experience to write a short essay, agreeing or disagreeing with this statement: *There is no value more important than loyalty to family.*

ANSWERS TO RESPONDING TO LITERATURE

1. Antigone believes that her duty to obey the laws of the gods and goddesses is more important than the laws of the state.
2. Her first line, "I do. I deny nothing," condemns her to die and so shows her courage.
3. Students may recognize that a society in which each person followed his or her conscience would be anarchic; on the other hand, they may sympathize with the right of individuals to determine what is right and wrong.
4. Based on the excerpt, some students may feel that Creon's hard posture implies that he will have Antigone executed; others may feel the fact that he enters into a discussion with her means that he might reconsider Antigone's punishment. At the end of the play, Creon banishes Antigone to a cave, where she commits suicide.

Chapter 5 Assessment

Have students use the **Chapter 5 Self-Check Quiz** at worldhistory.glencoe.com to prepare for the Chapter Test.

GLENCOE TECHNOLOGY

VIDEODISC

Use MindJogger to review the chapter.

MindJogger Videoquiz

Chapter 5
Disc 1 Side B

 Also available in VHS.

Answers

Using Key Terms

1. j   3. a   5. d
2. i   4. f

Using Your History Journal

Events might include: the trial or death of Socrates; a speech by Demosthenes; the murder of Philip II of Macedonia; Alexander's death.

Reviewing Facts

1. Science: made advances in astronomy and astrology; estimated circumference of earth; discovered body's nervous system. Mathematics: organized information about geometry; invented compound pulley and cylinder-screw
2. on the Acropolis in Athens as a temple to the goddess Athena
3. The Sophists believed in relative truth; Socrates believed in absolute truth. The Sophists emphasized the use of rhetoric in political arguments; Socrates aimed to teach people how to think for themselves.
4. observing facts, classifying them according to similarities and differences, and constructing generalizations from data

---

World History Online

Self-Check Quiz

Visit the *World History: The Human Experience* Web site at **worldhistory.glencoe.com** and click on *Chapter 5—Self-Check Quiz* to prepare for the Chapter Test.

Using Key Terms

Write the key term that completes each sentence. Then write a sentence for each term not chosen.

  a. classical   f. domains
  b. comedies   g. hygiene
  c. logic   h. sanctuaries
  d. philosophers   i. amphora
  e. tragedies   j. perspective

1. The architects of the Parthenon in Athens understood _____, the artistic representation of distances between objects as they appear to the eye.
2. Greek potters usually decorated an _____—a large vase for storing bulk supplies—with scenes from their mythology and legends.
3. Greek artists and architects created works characterized by a _____ style known for its beautiful simplicity and graceful balance.
4. After Alexander's death in 323 B.C., his large multicultural empire was divided into several _____.
5. Greek thinkers, or _____, developed the foundations for disciplines such as history, political science, and logic.

Technology Activity

Building a Database
Search the Internet or your local library for additional information about the Olympic Games. Build a database by collecting information about recent Olympic Game results of both summer and winter sporting events. Include headings such as name of the event, when it first became an event, if participated in by both sexes, and the number of medals each country obtained.

Using Your History Journal

The Greeks liked to relive historic events through drama. Each actor would wear a large mask to show the age, sex, and mood of each character. Write a short scene for a drama depicting an event from the chapter.

Reviewing Facts

1. **Science** Use a diagram like the one below to summarize important details about Hellenistic science and mathematics.

Hellenistic Culture	
Science	**Mathematics**

2. **Geography** Locate where the Parthenon was built and explain for what purpose.
3. **Culture** Describe the main philosophical differences between the Sophists and Socrates.
4. **Science** Name the main steps in the scientific method of inquiry developed by Aristotle.
5. **History/Culture** Explain why Thucydides is considered the first scientific historian.
6. **History** Discuss the ways in which Alexander's conquests changed Greek life.
7. **Culture** Identify the two major cultural areas that contributed to Hellenistic civilization.
8. **Science** State the contributions of Pythagorus, Archimedes, and Eratosthenes.

Critical Thinking

1. **Apply** How did the Peloponnesian War affect Greek drama and philosophy?
2. **Evaluate** Whose political ideas does the United States government more closely follow, those of Plato or those of Aristotle?
3. **Analyze** Why did conflicts develop in Alexander's empire after his death? Could they have been resolved peacefully? Why or why not?

---

5. because he rejected the idea that the deities play a part in human history; also, he was as accurate and impartial as possible
6. Greek culture mixed with that of the Middle East; the Greeks formed a ruling class in a multicultural empire and were less likely to place the interests of their communities above personal pursuits; upper-class Greek women enjoyed more social freedoms and entered occupations once closed to them.

7. the Greek world and the area dominated by Persian culture
8. Pythagorean theorem; the compound pulley and the cylinder-screw, principle of buoyancy, principle of the lever; Earth's circumference

Critical Thinking

1. Both Sophocles and Euripides wrote of human suffering and war's miseries.
2. those of Aristotle, because he favored a

Geography in History

1. **Place** Refer to the map "Alexander's Empire Divided." Who controlled the area of Macedonia?
2. **Location** What present-day countries make up the part of Alexander's empire ruled by Ptolemy?
3. **Place** Which of the Hellenistic lands do you think was the most difficult to govern, based on geographic factors? Explain.

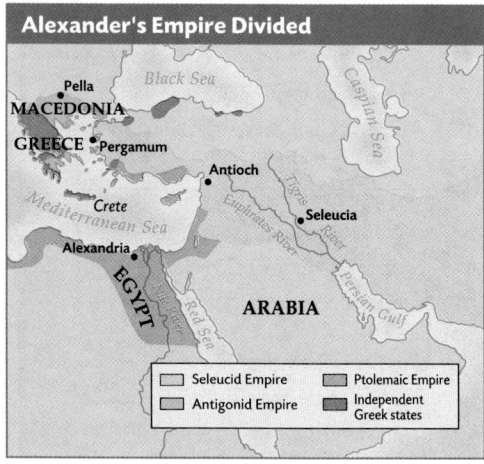

Alexander's Empire Divided

- Seleucid Empire
- Antigonid Empire
- Ptolemaic Empire
- Independent Greek states

Linking Past and Present

1. The Olympic Games were revived in 1896. In what ways do the modern Olympic Games resemble those of ancient Greece? In what ways do they differ?
2. The inclusion of diverse territories in Alexander the Great's empire led to widespread cultural diffusion. Besides military conquests, what factors promote cultural diffusion today?
3. Ideas of Greek civilization have affected much of American culture. Choose one area such as medicine, philosophy, politics, art, or architecture. Reread information about that area in your chapter. Then list as many examples of influences on American culture as you can. Ask friends, parents, or other family members to help complete the list.

Understanding Themes

1. **Innovation** What might contemporary theater be like if such great Hellenistic playwrights as Aristophanes and Menander had not lived and written about Greek society?
2. **Innovation** Do you think Herodotus deserves to be called the "father of history"? Explain your answer.
3. **Cultural Diffusion** How did Alexander the Great's founding of cities throughout his empire help spread Greek culture?

Skill Practice

Use the map "Greece and Persia" to answer the following questions.

1. What is the approximate location of Athens with regard to latitude and longitude?
2. Which body of water lies entirely north of 40° N latitude?
3. What is the approximate location of Sparta with regard to latitude and longitude?
4. What is the approximate location of Sardis with regard to longitude and latitude?
5. What is the relative location of Sardis?
6. What Mediterranean island lies along the 35th parallel?

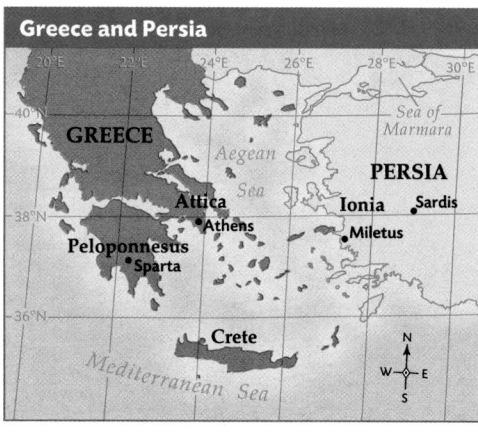

Greece and Persia

four years; today's events are the same as the ancient ones; winners are greatly honored. Today's Olympics feature athletes from all over the world, not just Greeks; women can watch and participate; many events have been added, including winter sports; today's winners can make millions of dollars by endorsements.
2. international travel, migration, and communications (Internet, movies, television, radio)
3. Answers will vary.

Understanding Themes

1. **INNOVATION** Perhaps the only type of play would be tragedy.
2. **INNOVATION** Yes, because he traveled widely, asked questions, and checked his sources; he also wrote about individuals, social customs, and religious practices and beliefs; or no, because he accepted some untrue statements; he also offered supernatural explanations for some events.
3. **CULTURAL DIFFUSION** Greek was spoken, and Greek culture flourished in these cities.

Skill Practice

1. 38°N, 24°E
2. Sea of Marmara
3. 37°N, 22°E
4. 38°N, 29°E
5. east of Ionia, south of the Sea of Marmara, northeast of Miletus
6. Crete

broader base of citizen participation in government than did Plato.
3. Conquered groups resisted attempts to make them accept Greek ways; the Greek city-states themselves opposed imperial rule and wanted independence. Students should focus on issues related to one dominant group ruling over other groups and to the difficulty of balancing unity and diversity in a vast territory made up of many different peoples.

Geography in History

1. Antigonid Empire
2. Egypt, Libya, and part of Syria
3. Students will probably mention the Seleucid Empire, because of its vast size.

Linking Past and Present

1. The modern Olympics are still held every

Chapter Bonus Test Question

Ask students: Which of the many philosophical outlooks discussed in this chapter do you think is most relevant to today's world? Why? *(Answers should include the basic tenets of philosopher or school.)*

A complete, 1-page lesson plan is provided for each section in the *Reproducible Lesson Plans* booklet.

Ancient Rome and Early Christianity

CHAPTER RESOURCES

	Reproducible Resources	Multimedia Resources
Chapter Opener	Chapter Themes: Graphic Organizer 6 Historical Significance Chapter Activity 6	MindJogger Videoquiz
Chapter Enrichment	Vocabulary Activity 6* Time Line Activity 6 Mapping History Activity 6 History Simulation 6 Geography and History Activity 6 Source Reading 6 People in World History Profiles 9, 10 World Art and Music Activity 6 Enrichment Activity 6 Critical Thinking Activity 6 Skill Reinforcement Activity 6 Performance Assessment Activity 6 Standardized Test Practice Workbook 　Activity 6 Inclusion for the Social Studies Classroom 　Strategies and Activities	Focus on World Art Print 9, Roman. 　*Girl With Writing Tablet* Ancient Civilizations Poster Set: 　*Ancient Rome* World History and Art Transparency 　7, *The Pantheon* Mapping History Overlay 　Transparency 6, *Roman Expansion* Chapter Transparency 6 NGS PicturePack Transparency Set: 　*Ancient Rome* Vocabulary PuzzleMaker Software NGS PictureShow CD-ROM: *Greece 　and Rome* Turning Points in World History: 　*Jerusalem: City of Three Faiths* In the Holy Land World History Primary Source 　Document Library
Chapter Review/Reteaching	Reteaching Activity 6 Skill Reinforcement Activity 6 Spanish Chapter Summary 6	Chapter 6 Digest Audiocassette, 　Activity, Test* Vocabulary PuzzleMaker Software Interactive Tutor Self-Assessment 　Software MindJogger Videoquiz
Chapter Evaluation/Testing	Performance Assessment Activity 6 Chapter 6 Test, Forms A and B	ExamView® Pro Testmaker

* Also available in Spanish

⏱ OUT OF TIME? Assign the Chapter 6 Audiocassettes.

World History Primary Source Document Library

Make History Come Alive!

Engage your students with over 250 easily accessible primary source documents—available on this CD-ROM—that will give them real life insight into the important events of world history.

Block Schedule

Activities that are particularly suited to use within the block scheduling framework are identified throughout this chapter by the following designation.

KEY TO ABILITY LEVELS

Teaching strategies are coded for varying learning styles.
L1 **BASIC** activities for all students
L2 **AVERAGE** activities for average to above-average students
L3 **CHALLENGING** activities for above-average students
LEP **LIMITED ENGLISH PROFICIENCY** activities

Use Glencoe's *Presentation Plus!* multimedia teacher tool to easily present dynamic lessons that visually excite your students. Using Microsoft PowerPoint® you can customize the presentations to create your own personalized lessons.

Interactive Lesson Planner

Planning has never been easier! Using this CD-ROM, organize your week, month, semester, or year with all the help you need. The **Interactive Lesson Planner** gives you access to all of the blackline masters that accompany *World History: The Human Experience.*

SECTION RESOURCES

Daily Objectives	Reproducible Resources	Multimedia Resources
Section 1 **The Roman Republic** Describe the structure of the Roman Republic and the ways it changed.	Lecture Notes 6-1 Reproducible Lesson Plan 6-1 Guided Reading Activity 6-1* Time Line Activity 6 History Simulation 6 Section Quiz 6-1* Reading Essentials and Study Guide 6-1	Focus on World Art Print 9, Roman. *Girl With Writing Tablet* Ancient Civilizations Poster Set: *Ancient Rome* Section Focus Transparency 6-1 Chapter Transparency 6 Vocabulary PuzzleMaker Software Interactive Tutor Self-Assessment Software
Section 2 **Expansion and Crisis** Outline the economic and social problems that ended the Roman Republic.	Lecture Notes 6-2 Reproducible Lesson Plan 6-2 Vocabulary Activity 6* Guided Reading Activity 6-2* Section Quiz 6-2* Reading Essentials and Study Guide 6-2	Section Focus Transparency 6-2 Mapping History Overlay Transparency 6, *Roman Expansion* NGS PicturePack Transparency Set: *Ancient Rome* Interactive Tutor Self-Assessment Software Testmaker
Section 3 **The Roman Empire** Characterize life under the *Pax Romana.*	Lecture Notes 6-3 Reproducible Lesson Plan 6-3 Vocabulary Activity 6* Guided Reading Activity 6-3* Section Quiz 6-3* Reading Essentials and Study Guide 6-3	Section Focus Transparency 6-3 World History and Art Transparency 7, *The Pantheon* Interactive Tutor Self-Assessment Software NGS PictureShow CD-ROM: *Greece and Rome*
Section 4 **The Rise of Christianity** Summarize the teachings of Jesus of Nazareth and the influence of early Christians on the later Roman Empire.	Lecture Notes 6-4 Reproducible Lesson Plan 6-4 Guided Reading Activity 6-4* Section Quiz 6-4* Reading Essentials and Study Guide 6-4	Section Focus Transparency 6-4 Vocabulary PuzzleMaker Software Interactive Tutor Self-Assessment Software Testmaker Turning Points in World History: *Jerusalem: City of Three Faiths In the Holy Land*
Section 5 **Roman Decline** List the reasons for the decline of the western Roman Empire.	Lecture Notes 6-5 Reproducible Lesson Plan 6-5 Vocabulary Activity 6* Guided Reading Activity 6-5* Reteaching Activity 6 Enrichment Activity 6 Section Quiz 6-5* Performance Assessment Activity 6 Spanish Chapter Summary 6 Reading Essentials and Study Guide 6-5	Section Focus Transparency 6-5 Interactive Tutor Self-Assessment Software Testmaker

* Also available in Spanish

Chapter Activities

Performance Assessment Activity

An Ad Campaign Have students take the roles of ad executives for a museum exhibit about ancient Rome. They should create a series of ten magazine ads (or billboards) showcasing the most important aspects of what can be learned by visiting the exhibit. Ads/billboards may be described or actually drawn and should be placed in priority order for an audience of potential contributors who may decide to fund only a portion of the campaign. Students should write a reflection in which they explain and support their ranking.

Possible Rubric Features
Accuracy of content information, decision-making skills, quality of product, extent of support

• *For an additional activity, refer to Activity 6 in the* Performance Assessment Strategies and Activities *booklet.*

ACTIVITY

From the Classroom of...

Lawrence J. Emsing
Arapahoe High School
Littleton, CO

The Collapse of the Roman Empire
The purpose of this simulation activity is to get students to analyze and to understand the underlying causes for the eventual collapse of the Roman Empire in the West. Students will appreciate that multiple causation is a more historically satisfying explanation for complex events than single causation theories. This activity is designed to encourage: critical analysis of a major historical event, collaborative decision making within a small group, and advocacy skills.

    Organize students into five groups, each representing a segment of the Roman population (wealthy landowners; urban poor in crowded Rome; rural poor in the provinces; the military; Christians, Jews, and other non-Roman religious sects). Groups will research and develop a plan for solving some of the many problems confronting the Empire. Each group will present its grievances and plans for addressing the grievances that will avert the fall as well as enhance their own position. The activity is designed to take 2-3 days depending on whether preparation time is included. After all groups have made their presentations, have students vote on which plan or plans for reform they would approve.

MULTIPLE LEARNING STYLES

Verbal/Linguistic
Have students write a detailed description of the Baths of Caracalla, one of the most elaborate of the Roman public baths.

Logical/Mathematical
Have students prepare a chart of Arabic numerals (1 through 15, then 20, 30, 40, 50, 60, 70, 80, 90, 100, 500, and 1,000), the corresponding Roman numerals, and the Latin names for the numerals. Have students research how Romans performed mathematical calculations using their numerals, and write a few simple examples.

Kinesthetic
Have students prepare a visual presentation of Roman architecture. They should present illustrations, diagrams, and pictures of some of the most important Roman structures from various periods, along with an explanation of each structure.

Intrapersonal
As students read Chapter 6, have them keep brief notes on each person mentioned. Then have them prepare a list of who they believe were the 10 most important Romans and briefly explain why they have chosen each person.

GLENCOE'S ASSESSMENT ADVANTAGE

Use the following to easily assess student learning in a variety of ways.

- Performance Assessment Strategies and Activities
- Section Quizzes
- Chapter and Unit Tests
- Interactive Tutor Self-Assessment Software
- Testmaker Software
- MindJogger Videoquiz
- SAT/SAT II Test Practice
- worldhistory.glencoe.com

Additional Resources

NATIONAL GEOGRAPHIC SOCIETY
Teacher's Corner

INDEX TO NATIONAL GEOGRAPHIC MAGAZINE

The following articles relate to this chapter:

- "Roman Shipwrecks," by Robert D. Ballard, April 1998.
- "Roman Legacy," by T. R. Reid, August 1997.
- "Brindisi Bronzes," by O. Louis Mazzatenta, April 1995.
- "The Day the World Ended at Kourion," by David Soren, July 1988.
- "The Eternal Etruscans," by Rick Gore, June 1988.
- "Caesarea Maritima: Herod the Great's City on the Sea," by Robert L. Hohlfelder, February 1987.
- "Arabia's Frankincense Trail," by Thomas J. Abercrombie, October 1985.

NATIONAL GEOGRAPHIC SOCIETY PRODUCTS AVAILABLE FROM GLENCOE

To order the following, call Glencoe at 1-800-334-7344:

- *PictureShow: Greece and Rome (CD-ROM)*
- *Ancient Rome (Transparencies, Poster Set)*

ADDITIONAL NATIONAL GEOGRAPHIC SOCIETY PRODUCTS

To order the following, call National Geographic at 1-800-368-2728:

- *In the Shadow of Vesuvius (Video or Videodisc)*
- *The Romans (Map)*

Access National Geographic's new dynamic MapMachine Web site and other geography resources at:

- http://www.nationalgeographic.com/
- http://www.nationalgeographic.com/maps/

BIBLIOGRAPHY

Literature of the Period
Virgil. *Aeneid.* Translated by John Dryden. Edited by Howard Clarke. University Park, PA: Pennsylvania State University, 1989. The national epic of Rome.

Readings for the Student
Wallace, Lewis. *Ben-Hur: A Tale of the Christ.* Uhrichsville, OH: Barbour and Co., 1985. A highly popular book, originally published in 1880, that has been twice made into a movie.

Readings for the Teacher
Hamilton, Edith. *The Roman Way.* New York: Norton, 1984. This famous work by an American classical scholar presents ancient Roman life as mirrored in its literature.

WORLD HISTORY Online

Use our Web site as an additional resource. All essential content is covered in the Student Edition.

You and your students can visit the *World History: The Human Experience* Web site at worldhistory. glencoe.com The student text directs students to the Web site for the following options:

- **Chapter Overviews**
- **Student Web Activities**
- **Self-Check Quizzes**

Answers are provided for you in a link entitled "Web Activity Lesson Plan." Additional Web Resources, Interactive Puzzles, and content updates are also available.

Visit the Glencoe Web site at socialstudies. glencoe.com for social studies activities, updates, and links to other resources.

LOCAL OBJECTIVES

_____
_____
_____
_____
_____
_____
_____
_____
_____
_____
_____
_____
_____
_____
_____
_____
_____
_____
_____

Ancient Rome and Early Christianity

CHAPTER THEMES

Chapter Themes are listed by section on this chapter opening page of the Student Edition. A corresponding theme-based activity is available under "TEACH," and a theme-based question is asked in the Section and Chapter Assessments.

The Storyteller

Historical Setting Romans admired and imitated the Greeks—their art, religion, architecture, philosophy, and science. Admiration led to an ambivalent approach to conquest. Rome conquered Greece shortly after 200 B.C., then proclaimed "the freedom of Greece." The Greeks proved to be recalcitrant, and the Romans finally subjugated Greece by destroying Corinth in 146 B.C. Greek influence in Roman culture, however, persisted.

Historical Significance

Answers: *Rome became the center of a vast empire by establishing a common Greco-Roman culture among the diverse peoples.*

Lasting legacies of the Roman Empire are its Latin language, which provided the roots of the Romance languages; its engineering skills; its transmission of Greek culture; and its development of Christianity.

WORLD HISTORY Online

Have students use the **Chapter 6 Overview** at <u>worldhistory.glencoe.com</u> as a prereading and postreading exercise for understanding chapter content.

Chapter Themes

▶ **Change** The Roman political system evolves as more people participate in government. *Section 1*
▶ **Conflict** Roman armies conquer most of the Mediterranean world. *Section 2*
▶ **Cultural Diffusion** The Roman empire spreads Latin culture. *Section 3*
▶ **Innovation** Christianity becomes the dominant religion in the West. *Section 4*
▶ **Change** Germanic invasions and cultural weaknesses destroy the Roman Empire. *Section 5*

The Storyteller

War trumpets rang over the cheers of the people of Rome who gathered to view the triumphal grand parade. Then sweating horses jerking at their harnesses rattled the victor's chariot over the paving stones, and the people's cries became louder. On this day in 146 B.C., the Romans were celebrating their conquest of the last of the free Greek city-states.

Ironically, however, over the next several centuries Greek culture would come to form the base of Roman culture and society. Texts written by Greeks would shape Roman knowledge in many areas of study. Even after years of Roman rule, the eastern Mediterranean world would retain Greek as its primary language.

Historical Significance

How did the small city-state of Rome become the center of a vast, diverse empire that spanned the Mediterranean world? What were Rome's lasting legacies to Europe, Africa, the Middle East, and other parts of the world?

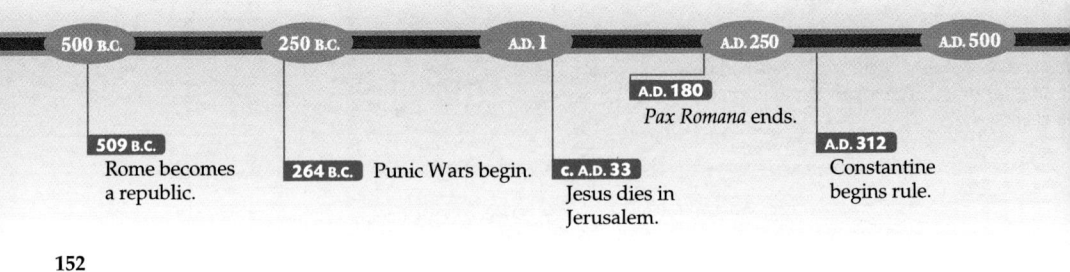

| 500 B.C. | 250 B.C. | A.D. I | A.D. 250 | A.D. 500 |

509 B.C. Rome becomes a republic.
264 B.C. Punic Wars begin.
c. A.D. 33 Jesus dies in Jerusalem.
A.D. 180 *Pax Romana* ends.
A.D. 312 Constantine begins rule.

152

GEOGRAPHY CONNECTION

Location Have students use the Atlas in their text to locate Europe, the Mediterranean Sea, Asia Minor, North Africa, and the Middle East—the regions controlled by the Roman Empire by A.D. 130. What problems might arise in governing such a vast area? (*delays in communications, need to provide defense against invaders and rebellions, tax collection*)

History & Art
Tell students that the Roman use of the cithera was another example of the pervasiveness of Greek culture. The cithera was one of two principal types of ancient Greek lyres, or stringed instruments with a sound box and two curved arms connected by a yoke. How does the painting suggest the cithera was played? *(held upright with the strings plucked by the fingers)* What common instrument derives its name from the cithera? *(guitar; also zither)*

✔ Performance Assessment
Refer to the activity on page 152C of the Planning Guide. 📁 For an additional activity, refer to Activity 6 in the *Performance Assessment Strategies and Activities* booklet.

History & Art
Woman playing the cithera, painted on the east wall of a room in the villa of Publius Fannius Synistor, Pompeii, Italy

Using Your History Journal
Suggest that students write from the perspective of Roman soldiers involved in the settlement of these outposts.

WORLD HISTORY Online

Chapter Overview

Visit the *World History: The Human Experience* Web site at **worldhistory.glencoe.com** and click on *Chapter 6—Chapter Overview* to preview the chapter.

Your History Journal

The European cities of Bonn, Vienna, London, and Paris were each founded by the Romans. Research the early history of one of these cities and describe the Roman influence on its early architecture and lifestyle.

GLENCOE TECHNOLOGY

VIDEODISC
Use MindJogger to preview chapter content.

MindJogger Videoquiz

Chapter 6
Disc 1 Side B

📼 Also available in VHS.

➕ EXTRA CREDIT PROJECT

Report Several studies focus on the importance of the military in the history of ancient Rome. Have students research and report to the class on the development of the professional army and the role military leaders played in Roman politics. Ask them to evaluate in their reports the importance of the military from the time of the republic through the rule of Constantine. Suggested resources: M. Mulvihill, *Roman Forts*; A. Ferrill, *The Fall of the Roman Empire: The Military Explanation*; and L. Keppie, *The Making of the Roman Army: From Republic to Empire.* 📁

800 B.C.			500 B.C.		200 B.C.
	c. 753 B.C. Romulus founds Rome.	**c. 620 B.C.** Etruscans gain control of Rome.	**451 B.C.** The patricians of Rome enact the Twelve Tables.	**287 B.C.** The plebeians begin to make laws for Rome.	

Section 1

The Roman Republic

SECTION THEME

▶ **Change** The Roman political system evolves as Rome allows more of its people to participate in government.

Guide to Reading

For reading strategies to help students read effectively see pages 12–13. Have students think about the main head as they read the subheads.

Vocabulary Pre-check

⬚ Use the Vocabulary PuzzleMaker for Chapter 6 to create a crossword puzzle to reinforce section terms. **L1 LEP**

📁 Use Vocabulary Activity 6 to introduce vocabulary terms. **L1 LEP**

FOCUS

Section Objective

Describe the structure of the Roman Republic and the ways it changed.

BELLRINGER
Motivational Activity

Before taking roll at the beginning of the class period, project Section Focus Transparency 6-1 and have students answer the activity questions. Discuss students' responses.

📁 This activity is also available as a blackline master.

Guide to Reading

Read to Find Out
Main Idea *Rome was governed as a republic, which changed over the years.*

▶ **Terms to Define**
patrician, republic, plebeian, consul, dictator, tribune

▶ **People to Meet**
the Etruscans, the Latins, Romulus, the Tarquins

▶ **Places to Locate**
Italy, Sicily, Rome

The Storyteller

The city of Rome was besieged by Lars Porsena, king of Clusium, and the time had come for decisive action. One young Roman hoped to break the siege by killing Porsena. After laying his plan before the Senate, he set out alone toward enemy lines. However, he was seized as a spy and dragged by guards before the very man he had hoped to kill—Porsena. He spoke boldly: "I am a Roman, my name is Gaius Mucius. I came here to kill you—my enemy. I have as much courage to die as to kill. It is our Roman way to do and to suffer bravely."

The Forum

—adapted from *Early History of Rome*, Titus Livy, in *The Global Experience, Readings in World History to 1500*, 1987

he peoples of **Italy** first came into contact with the Greeks around 900 B.C., when Greek traders sailed up both the east and west coasts of the Italian Peninsula. From about 750 B.C. to 500 B.C., the Greeks set up farming communities in southern Italy and in **Sicily**, an island southwest of the Italian Peninsula. These Greek colonists planted olive trees for the oil yielded and grapevines from which they could produce wine, thus introducing these two major products to Italy. The Greeks also introduced the Greek alphabet to the Italians.

The Italian Peninsula

The Greeks were interested in colonizing Italy for several reasons, one of which was Italy's central location in the Mediterranean. A narrow, boot-shaped peninsula, Italy extends from Europe toward the shores of Africa, dividing the Mediterranean almost in half. Thus, Italy was ideally situated to be the center of trade among three continents: Asia, Europe, and Africa. Italy's rich soil and mild, moist climate also attracted the Greek colonists. Beyond the mountains and foothills that covered three-quarters of the peninsula lay plains with soil enriched by the silt deposits of mountain streams.

However, the silt washing down Italy's short and shallow rivers blocked the mouths of many rivers, creating mosquito-infested swamps. The people of Italy suffered recurrent epidemics of malaria and other diseases carried by mosquitoes.

Because of Italy's mountains, the early inhabitants of the peninsula generally traded among themselves. Italy's only land connection—to the north—was cut off by the Alps. Furthermore, Italy's rocky and marshy coastline lacked good harbors. To increase trade, the Italians eventually turned to the sea, but until that time came, they remained attached to the land.

SECTION RESOURCES

📁 Reproducible Masters
- Lecture Notes 6-1
- Reproducible Lesson Plan 6-1
- Guided Reading Activity 6-1
- Time Line Activity 6
- History Simulation 6
- Section Quiz 6-1
- Reading Essentials and Study Guide 6-1

🖥 Transparencies
- Section Focus Transparency 6-1
- Chapter Transparency 6

Multimedia
- Focus on World Art Print 9
- Ancient Rome
- Vocabulary PuzzleMaker Software
- Interactive Tutor Self-Assessment Software
- Testmaker

Early Peoples

Archaeological evidence suggests that people lived in Italy long before the Greeks arrived or Roman civilization began. The remains of human settlements reveal that Neolithic cultures may have begun to form in Italy as early as about 5000 B.C. Early peoples in the Italian Peninsula built villages and farms, moving on whenever they had exhausted the land around their settlements.

Indo-Europeans

Between 2000 B.C. and 1000 B.C., waves of Indo-European immigrants arrived and overwhelmed these Neolithic peoples. By the time Greek colonists came to Italy, many peoples inhabited the peninsula—including Umbrians in the north, Latins in the central plain called Latium (LAY•shee•uhm), and Oscans in the south. Like the Greeks, most of these people spoke Indo-European languages.

The Etruscans

From about 900 B.C. to 500 B.C., one of these peoples, the Etruscans, ruled northern Italy from the plains of Etruria. Little is known about their origins, although the Etruscans did not speak an Indo-European language as did many of the peninsula's other inhabitants. The Etruscan alphabet came from the Greeks, but modern scholars have been able to decipher only a few Etruscan words.

Although Etruscan writings still baffle our understanding, Etruscan art is expressive, needing no translation. In wall paintings, Etruscan figures dance and play music, enjoying a rich and pleasant life. In Etruscan sculpture, men and women feast and converse, triumphant soldiers revel in their victories, and hauntingly beautiful deities smile and gesture.

Such sculptures ornamented the homes of the Etruscan upper classes. Historians believe that Etruscan society probably consisted of wealthy overlords, aristocratic priests, and a slave labor force made up of conquered peoples. Wealthy overlords enslaved these peoples to provide themselves with comforts, and aristocratic priests sacrificed prisoners of war or forced them to duel to the death to appease angry gods.

After repeated revolts, the Etruscan lower classes and the other Italian peoples under

---

The Arts

Murals: Etruscan and Modern

Although archaeologists have unearthed the remains of some Etruscan cities, these tell little about Etruscan culture. Murals unearthed in burial chambers, however, have provided significant clues about the Etruscans.

Etruscan mural

The murals show colorful and lively scenes of Etruscan daily life. Particularly popular subjects are scenes of wrestling matches, religious ceremonies, and people enjoying music and feasts.

Today, the desire to beautify urban areas has produced many striking murals in cities from Sydney, Australia, to Caracas, Venezuela. The boldly colored works appear on office, apartment, and supermarket walls. They usually are sponsored by municipal officials or businesses, and the artists employed draw inspiration from sources as varied as fashion magazines, cartoons, and modern art. Among their subjects are movie, TV, and sports celebrities as well as ordinary people involved in daily activities, such as shopping on a busy street or playing basketball at a neighborhood playground.

Linking Past and Present ACTIVITY

What subjects are popularly shown in Etruscan murals? Modern urban murals? What do Etruscan murals reveal about Etruscan life? What do urban murals today reveal about modern life?

COOPERATIVE LEARNING ACTIVITY

Wall Diagram The Romans borrowed extensively from other cultures, adapting Etruscan ritual duels, Etruscan and Greek deities, Greek styles of architecture and sculpture, and Greek medicine and science. Provide students with a wall-sized sheet of paper on which to show a composite of what Romans borrowed. Assign students to small groups. Have each group research one major topic and complete one portion of the wall diagram. Each group should divide tasks among its members: doing research, obtaining pictures or drawing illustrations, writing captions, explaining the group's work to the class. **L1**

TEACH

Guided Practice

THEME Change

Ask students to give two examples of conflict leading to change in ancient Rome. (*overthrow of Etruscan rule, struggle between patricians and plebeians over who ruled the republic*) **L1**

Geography: Region Have the class make a chart comparing the climates and physical characteristics of the Italian Peninsula and the region where you live. The chart should include climate, landforms, and agriculture. Then discuss with students how environmental factors have made their lives similar to or different from the lives of the people of Italy. **L2 LEP**

Murals: Etruscan and Modern

Basic questions about the Etruscans, such as their origin, will remain unanswered as long as scholars cannot translate the Etruscan language.

ANSWER

Etruscan: wrestling matches, religious ceremonies, and people enjoying music and feasts; Modern: celebrities and ordinary people involved in daily activities, such as shopping and playing sports. Students might say that the Etruscans enjoyed life (festivals, and other group activities), although there was a serious side to Etruscan life–religious celebrations and a concern about death (murals in burial chambers); modern murals reflect similar enjoyment of life by modern people, although the murals also reflect a serious concern to beautify urban areas that are considered unsightly.

NATIONAL GEOGRAPHIC SOCIETY

Use these materials to enrich student understanding of ancient Rome.

 ANCIENT CIVILIZATIONS POSTER SET
Ancient Rome

 Chapter Transparency 6

History Simulation 6

 Focus on World Art Print 9

Who?What?Where?When?

The legend of **Rome's founding** begins when the twin brothers Romulus and Remus were newborns. Their mother was a princess, their father the god Mars. The boys' great-uncle had the baby boys set adrift in a basket on the Tiber River. However, the twins did not die. A female wolf found them and nursed them. When they grew up, they set out to build a new city where they had been rescued from the Tiber.

Map Study

Answer

It would have enabled them to conquer the Etruscans more easily because a divided force can be easier to conquer than a united one.

Map Skills Practice

Reading a Map Why were the Latins ideally positioned to gain control of the entire Italian Peninsula? (*They were in a central location, at the mouth of the Tiber River.*)

Etruscan rule finally freed themselves from domination by these wealthy overlords and priests. Chief among those who overthrew the Etruscans were **the Latins**, whose center was the city of **Rome** in the central plain of Latium.

The Rise of Rome

According to legend, in 753 B.C., a stocky man named **Romulus** was building the wall of a city on a hill overlooking the Tiber River. His twin brother, Remus, came over from the hillside opposite, where he too had been laying the foundations for a city. The Roman historian Livy tells what happened next:

> ❝ Remus, by way of jeering at his brother, jumped over the half-built walls of the new settlement, whereupon Romulus killed him in a fit of rage, adding the threat, 'So perish whoever else shall overleap my battlements.' ❞
>
> —Livy, *Ab Urbe Condita*, 29 B.C.

Setting more stone on the stains of his brother's blood, Romulus is said to have continued his building. In time, his namesake city—Rome—grew to include his brother's hill and the other nearby hills. Romulus was so effective a military ruler, the myth tells us, that Rome became the greatest city in that part of the peninsula.

In fact, the origins of Rome were probably much less violent. At some time between 800 B.C. and 700 B.C., the Latins huddled in straw-roofed huts in the villages on the seven hills apparently agreed to join and form one community. It was this community that came to be called Rome.

Etruscan Rule

About 620 B.C. the Etruscans gained control of Rome. A wealthy Etruscan family, **the Tarquins**, provided kings to rule over the Romans. The Tarquins taught the Latins to build with brick and to roof their houses with tile. They drained the marshy lowlands around Rome and laid out city streets. At the center of the city they created a square called the Forum, which became the seat of Roman government. The Tarquins also built temples, taught the Romans many of the Etruscans' religious rituals, and elevated Rome to a position among the wealthiest cities in Italy.

Then in 534 B.C. Tarquin the Proud came to the throne. This king's cruelties so angered the Romans that in 509 B.C. they drove the Tarquins out. Skilled Etruscan artisans stayed on in Rome, however, helping the city continue to prosper.

Italy 500 B.C.

Greeks
Etruscans
Latins

Map Study
Notice on the map that Latium divides the Etruscan territory. **Region** What advantage might this location have provided the Latins when they set out to conquer the Etruscans?

Social Groups

Under Etruscan rule, a new wealthy aristocratic class had come into being in Rome—Latin nobles called patricians. Once the Etruscan rulers were driven out, the patricians declared Rome a republic, a community in which the people elect their leaders.

Most of Rome's inhabitants, however, were plebeians (plih•BEE•uhns), who included wealthy, nonaristocratic townspeople and landowners as well as merchants, shopkeepers, small farmers, and laborers. As citizens, both the plebeians and the patricians had rights, such as the right to vote, and responsibilities, such as paying taxes and serving in the military. Plebeians, however, could not hold public office as patricians could.

The Roman Republic

The patricians organized Rome's government into executive and legislative branches. The

---

Roman legislative branch at first consisted of the Assembly of Centuries and the Senate, both under patrician control. Members of the Assembly of Centuries (named for a military formation of 100 soldiers) elected officials of the executive branch. However, the Senate—a group of 300 patrician men who served for life—had much more power. They advised the consuls, debated foreign policy, proposed laws, and approved contracts for constructing roads, temples, and defenses.

The executive branch was headed by two patrician officials elected for one-year terms. These officials were called consuls because they had to consult each other before acting. Either consul could veto the other's decisions. The word *veto* is Latin for "I forbid." The consuls oversaw other executive officials, such as praetors, or judges, and censors, or keepers of tax and population records. Only a dictator, a leader whose word was law, could overrule the consuls. But dictators were temporarily appointed only in time of crisis.

The most admired Roman dictator was the legendary hero Cincinnatus (SIHN•suh•NA•tuhs). In 458 B.C., a powerful rival threatened Rome, and the Senate sent messengers to tell Cincinnatus that he had been named dictator to meet this emergency. The messengers found him plowing his fields. Always loyal to Rome, Cincinnatus immediately joined the army and led his forces into battle. He defeated the enemy, marched his army back to Rome, and then resigned as dictator. He returned to his plowing 16 days after taking command.

Plebeians Against Patricians

The plebeians resented their lack of power in the new republic—especially because they knew that the patricians could not maintain the republic without them. In 494 B.C., many plebeians refused to fight in the Roman army unless the patricians yielded to their demands for change.

Plebeian Victories

Frightened at the loss of their military forces, the patricians agreed to reforms. They recognized the plebeians' chosen representatives, the tribunes, granting them legal protections and the right to veto government decisions. The patricians also recognized the Assembly of Tribes, the body of plebeians who elected the tribunes. Eventually, the Assembly of Tribes even won the right to make laws.

In addition to political rights, the plebeians improved their social standing. Enslavement for debt was ended, and marriage between patricians and plebeians was allowed. However, the repub-

lic's social structure was still dominated by a small group of powerful and wealthy citizens. Through their struggles, though, the plebeians slowly moved Rome closer to democracy.

The Twelve Tables

The most significant plebeian victory was the creation of a written law code. Roman law rested largely on unwritten traditions that patrician judges often interpreted to favor their class. To make sure that the laws were applied fairly, the plebeians insisted that they be written down.

In 451 B.C. the patricians finally engraved the laws on 12 bronze tablets set in the Forum for all to see. The Twelve Tables, as these tablets were called, became the basis for all future Roman law. The Twelve Tables established the principle that all free citizens had a right to the law's protection.

Religion

Early Romans worshiped nature spirits. Under Etruscan influence, they came to think of these spirits as gods and goddesses. They also adopted the practice of foretelling the future. Priests known as soothsayers believed that they could gain knowledge of future events by observing the flight of birds or the intestines of animals.

For almost 500 years, Rome thrived as a republic. During this time, the Romans were influenced by Greek culture. They borrowed Greek deities, giving them Roman names. Aphrodite, the Greek

Student Web Activity 6

Visit the *World History: The Human Experience* Web site at **worldhistory.glencoe.com** and click on **Chapter 6—Student Web Activities** for an activity relating to Roman social status.

Footnotes to History

A Roman Dinner Party
In ancient Rome, dinner guests of wealthy Romans reclined on couches while slaves served them delicacies. Main courses might include boiled stingray garnished with hot raisins; boiled crane with turnips; roast hare in white sauce; leg of boar; wood pigeon baked in a pie; or roast flamingo cooked with dates, onions, honey, and wine.

Chapter 6 *Ancient Rome and Early Christianity* 157

Chapter 6
Section 1

Independent Practice

📁 Guided Reading Activity 6-1 **L1**

📁 Time Line Activity 6

Government Have students diagram the structure of republican government in Rome, showing the executive and legislative branches as well as the tribunes and Assembly of Tribes. Discuss in class the special powers of consuls and tribunes. **L2 LEP**

Linking Past and Present

Architecture Many shopping malls today have an atrium, a skylit central court. The atrium originated in ancient Rome, where it was the central room of a house. Open to the sky at the center, the atrium usually had a pool to collect rainwater.

ASSESS

Check for Understanding

Assign Section 1 Assessment as homework or as an in-class activity.

💻 Use Interactive Tutor Self-Assessment Software to review Section 1.

Have students use the **Chapter 6 Student Web Activity** at <u>worldhistory.glencoe.com</u> for in-depth study of Roman clothing.

MAKING CONNECTIONS ACTIVITIES

The Calendar Romans helped shape the modern calendar. Have students do research and write a report summarizing Roman contributions to the calendar, including the names of the months and the division of the year into 12 months. Suggest that they also describe the shortcomings leading to calendar reform in the late 1500s. **L1**

Public Speaking The Romans helped define rules of rhetoric, or the art of using words persuasively, for oratory—the art of eloquent speaking. Have students research the life of Cicero, focusing on his contributions to these arts and describing some of his most famous orations. Encourage students to rehearse and deliver parts of his best-known orations. **L2**

Evaluate

Section Quiz 6-1

Use the Testmaker to create a
customized quiz for Section 1.

Reteach

Have students work in small
groups to prepare time lines of
events covered in this section.
Then have groups present their
time lines to the class, explaining
the importance of each event.

Reading Essentials and
Study Guide 6-1

Enrich

The Roman goddess Vesta occupied a central role in the religious
lives of Roman families. Have
students research Vesta and write
a brief report on her origins, how
she was worshiped, and what
values she symbolized.

CLOSE

Ask half the class to imagine that
they are tribunes and the other
half to imagine that they are
senators in the year 250 B.C. Have
each group prepare a list of what
it thinks are the most important
accomplishments of Rome to that
time. After each group compares
and explains its list, allow one
group to challenge items on the
other's list. Group members
should be prepared to defend
the items on their own list.

Visualizing History An Etruscan farmer and his animals,
c. 300 B.C. Etruscan literature, music,
painting, metalwork, and jewelry were
admired by the Romans. *Why did the
Romans drive the wealthy Etruscan family,
the Tarquins, from the city?*

goddess of love, became the Roman goddess
Venus. Ares, the Greek god of war, became Mars.
They also made their old gods look Greek, giving
the Etruscan god Jupiter the characteristics of the
Greek Zeus.

Roman life remained distinctly Roman, however. Families privately worshiped their ancestral
spirits and their storeroom guardians, as well as
Vesta, goddess of the hearth.

Family

The family was the basic unit of Roman society.
Roman households were large and close-knit. They
included all unmarried children, married sons and
their families, all dependent relatives, and household slaves.

In Roman families the father was absolute head
of the household. He conducted the religious ceremonies, controlled property, and supervised the
education of his sons. He also had the power to sell
family members into slavery, or even kill them.
However, fathers also felt a deep sense of responsibility for the welfare of all family members.

Roman wives had few legal rights, but they
had more freedom than Greek women. They acted
as hostesses for parties, did their marketing, and
ran their households with little or no interference.
Occasionally, they did acquire their own property
and businesses. Wealthy women, with slaves to do
their work, could study Greek literature, arts, and
fashions. Lower-class women spent their time at
household tasks and in family-run shops.

In early Rome, parents taught children reading,
writing, and moral standards. Boys were trained by
their fathers to be farmers and soldiers. Mothers
taught their daughters how to run households.

Rich or poor, most Romans held the same values: thrift, discipline, self-sacrifice, and devotion to
the family and the republic. Long after the Roman
Republic ended, nostalgic reformers saw these as
traditional Roman values.

SECTION 1 ASSESSMENT

Main Idea
1. Use a chart like the one below
to identify characteristics of the
Roman Republic's government.

Roman Government Under Republic

Executive	Legislative

Recall
2. **Define** patrician, republic,
plebeian, consul, dictator,
tribune.
3. **Identify** the Etruscans, the
Latins, Romulus, the Tarquins.

Critical Thinking
4. **Evaluating Information** Did
the political struggle between

patricians and plebeians
strengthen or weaken the
Roman Republic? Give some
examples from the text to
support your case.

Understanding Themes
5. **Change** Why did political
change occur in the Roman
Republic?

SECTION 1 ASSESSMENT ANSWERS

1. Executive: patrician consuls; only dictator
could overrule consuls. Legislative: Assembly of Centuries, Senate under patrician
control; Senate more powerful
2. All terms are defined in the Glossary.
3. the Etruscans, 155; the Latins, 156; Romulus, 156, the Tarquins, 156
4. Strengthened: broadened citizen participa-

tion in government to include plebeians;
Weakened: plebeian refusal to fight and
patricians' slow recognition of plebeian
demands
5. **CHANGE** The plebeians wanted
a greater say in the government. Their key
role in the economy and military gave the
plebeians the clout to force change.

300 B.C.

c. 264 B.C. Rome rules the entire Italian Peninsula.

200 B.C.

202 B.C. Roman forces defeat Carthage at the battle of Zama.

100 B.C.

133 B.C. The reformer Tiberius Gracchus becomes tribune.

44 B.C. Group of senators assassinate Julius Caesar.

A.D. 1

Section 2

Expansion and Crisis

Read to Find Out
Main Idea *Economic and social problems brought down the Roman Republic.*

▶ **Terms to Define**
   indemnity, triumvirate

▶ **People to Meet**
   Hannibal, Scipio, Tiberius Gracchus, Gaius Gracchus, Marius, Sulla, Julius Caesar, Octavian, Marc Antony

▶ **Places to Locate**
   Carthage

The government of Rome had become cumbersome and corrupt. Maecenas, the richest man in Rome, was about to propose a radical change.

Marc Antony

Called before Mark Anthony, Marcus Lepidus, and Octavian, the most powerful men in Rome, he spoke persuasively. "Ever since we were led outside the peninsula, filling the whole earth with our power, nothing good has been our lot. Our city, like a great ship manned with a crew of every race and lacking a pilot, has been rolling and plunging as it has drifted in a heavy sea." Maecenas looked at his hearers. One of them must assume all authority. Rome had to cease being a republic.

—*from Roman History*, Dio Cassius, in *Readings in Ancient History from Gilgamesh to Diocletian*, 1969

From about 500 B.C. to 300 B.C., Rome faced threats from its many neighbors in Italy. To protect their republic, the Romans either conquered these opponents or forced them to ally with Rome. In this way the Romans subdued one rival after another, until by 264 B.C. Rome ruled the entire peninsula.

Roman forces, however, had faced a tough challenge from the Greek colonies in southern Italy. In 282 B.C. the Greek colonists received help from Pyrrhus (PIHR•uhs), a ruler in western Greece. Twice Pyrrhus's armies threw back the Romans, but each time suffered terrible losses. In 275 B.C. Roman forces finally pushed Pyrrhus's exhausted troops back to Greece. Since then, a victory won at too great a cost has been called a "Pyrrhic victory."

Roman Legions

Rome's success in war was due to its strong army. In the early days of the republic, every male citizen had to serve in the military when needed. Early Roman armies also used the tactics of Greek phalanx warfare. Roman generals, however, learned that phalanxes were too large and slow to be effective. They reorganized their troops into legions of 6,000 men and divided these further into small, mobile units of 60 to 120 soldiers. With this new organization, the Romans could shatter the phalanxes of their enemies.

Roman soldiers—called legionaries—were well trained, and deserters were punished by death. With such iron discipline, the legionaries would conquer an empire. In a time when victors routinely slaughtered or enslaved whole cities, Rome treated conquered foes remarkably well. Some conquered peoples were allowed to keep their own governments if they helped fight Rome's wars.

Chapter 6 *Ancient Rome and Early Christianity* **159**

SECTION THEME

▶ **Conflict** Roman armies conquer most of the Mediterranean world.

For reading strategies to help students read effectively see pages 12–13.

Vocabulary Pre-check

Use the Vocabulary PuzzleMaker for Chapter 6 to create a crossword puzzle to reinforce section terms. **L1 LEP**

Use Vocabulary Activity 6 to introduce vocabulary terms. **L1 LEP**

FOCUS

Section Objective
Outline the economic and social problems that ended the Roman Republic.

BELLRINGER
Motivational Activity

Before taking roll at the beginning of the class period, project Section Focus Transparency 6-2 and have students answer the activity questions. Discuss students' responses.

This activity is also available as a blackline master.

SECTION RESOURCES

Reproducible Masters
• Lecture Notes 6-2
• Reproducible Lesson Plan 6-2
• Vocabulary Activity 6
• Guided Reading Activity 6-2
• Section Quiz 6-2
• Reading Essentials and Study Guide 6-2

Transparencies
• Section Focus Transparency 6-2
• Mapping History Overlay Transparency 6
• Ancient Rome

Multimedia
Interactive Tutor Self-Assessment Software
Testmaker

TEACH

Guided Practice

THEME Conflict

Discuss with students various ways of resolving conflicts. *(negotiation, mediation, fighting)* **L1**

Visualizing History

The basic unit of the Roman legion was the maniple, which consisted of 120 men in 12 files and 10 ranks. The expression "rank and file," referring to common people, derives from this method of organizing Roman soldiers.

Answer to Caption: *Roman legionaries, well trained and highly disciplined, fought in small, mobile units that enabled them to defeat their enemies.*

Government The Roman Republic was founded to govern a city-state but floundered when Rome governed a vast empire. Have students list political changes occurring from about 300 B.C. that resulted from the growth of Roman territory. *(Rome created a system of proconsuls and publicans to rule non-Italian provinces; generals gained power controlling the provinces and took over government of the republic.)* **L2**

 Mapping History Overlay
 Transparency 6

A&E HOME VIDEO.

The following videotape program is available from Glencoe:

• **The Lost Legions of Rome**

To find classroom resources to accompany this video, check the following home page:

A&E Television:
http://www.aetv.com

Visualizing History Roman legionaries are shown in a mosaic, or picture made from bits of stone. *Why were legionaries so successful in their conquests?*

Rome gave other peoples partial rights, and to some peoples even granted citizenship.

The Romans set up permanent military settlements—called *coloniae*—throughout Italy to defend strategic heights and river crossings. To link these *coloniae*, the legions forged a chain of roads up and down the Italian Peninsula. As war yielded gradually to peace, some of these roads became major trade routes.

Rome Against Carthage

In Chapter 3 you read how **Carthage** became the Mediterranean area's wealthiest city. To expand their commerce, the Carthaginians had then gone on to conquer the Spanish coast and most of Sicily by about 300 B.C. The Romans decided to check the expansion of the Carthaginians—the *Punici*, as the Romans called them.

The First Punic War

In 264 B.C. Carthage threatened to seize the

Strait of Messina, a narrow passage between Sicily and Italy. When the Romans sent a force to secure the strategic waterway, a full-scale war erupted.

The Romans' strong army conquered most of Carthage's colonies in Sicily. However, the Carthaginians lashed out at the Romans with their huge and powerful fleet. For a time this naval superiority gave Carthage the advantage.

Undaunted, the Romans built a larger fleet. In a battle off the African coast, they stunned the Carthaginians with a new tactic. They snared the enemy's ships with grappling hooks, boarded them, and defeated the enemy in hand-to-hand combat. This enabled the Romans to fight on sea as well as they did on land. Thus, they were able to force the Carthaginians to retreat.

The war raged on until 241 B.C., but the Carthaginians never regained control of Sicily or the sea. Threatened with invasion of their homeland, they agreed to hand the Romans a huge indemnity, or payment for damages.

The Second Punic War

In 221 B.C. a young soldier named **Hannibal** became general of the Carthaginian army in Spain. In 219 B.C. Hannibal grabbed one of Rome's allied cities in Spain. His next move was even more audacious—to take the war into Italy itself. Leading 40,000 soldiers and about 40 elephants, he marched out of Spain, crossed southern Gaul, and started up the Alps. His soldiers, however, were terrified by the sight of those chilly heights, and their fears were well-founded. Before they reached Italy, cold, snow, hunger, sickness, and attacks by mountain peoples killed half of Hannibal's army and most of the elephants.

Although outnumbered, Hannibal's troops defeated the Roman armies sent against them. By 216 B.C., in a battle at Cannae in southeastern Italy, Hannibal's soldiers had nearly destroyed the Roman army. But the Romans rallied, refusing to admit defeat, and raised dozens of new volunteer legions. Their general, **Scipio** (SIH•pee•OH), attacked Carthage and forced Hannibal's recall to Africa.

In 202 B.C. Scipio's forces defeated Hannibal's army at Zama, near Carthage. At Scipio's demand, the Carthaginians gave up their lands in Spain, handed over most of their warships, and agreed to another indemnity.

The Third Punic War

After 50 years of peace, Carthage regained its prosperity but posed no threat to Rome. The Romans, however, decided to force war on

---

COOPERATIVE LEARNING ACTIVITY

Debate Organize the class into three groups and stage a debate on the following resolution: The wars with Carthage were worth the short-term and long-term cost. Have two of the groups take opposite sides in the debate. The third group should act as the audience, asking questions and voting for the more persuasive side. Assign one student as moderator and make sure each group member has specific responsibility for research, preparation, and presentation of arguments. Students in the audience should prepare questions in advance, as well as be encouraged to ask spontaneous questions. **L2**

Carthage. The most vindictive foe of Carthage was the Roman senator Cato, who always ended his speeches with the statement: *"Carthago delenda est"* (Carthage must be destroyed). In 146 B.C. the Romans burned Carthage, and sold its surviving population into slavery. Legend states that they even sowed salt in Carthage's soil so that no crops would grow. This victory gave Rome complete control of the western Mediterranean.

The Republic in Crisis

While Rome was fighting the Punic Wars in the west, its forces were also engaged in the east. Between 230 B.C. and 130 B.C., Rome brought the entire eastern Mediterranean area under its influence. As a result of this conquest, Romans began referring to the Mediterranean as *mare nostrum*— "our sea."

Rich, Poor, and Slavery

Although the Romans had triumphed militarily, they faced growing social discontent in their new empire. The conquered provinces, which paid tribute to Rome, complained of corrupt Roman officials stealing provincial wealth for personal gain. In Italy and throughout the empire, wealthy Romans acquired or seized land from war-ravaged small farmers who found it difficult to rebuild their farms, homes, and villages. Turning agriculture into a profitable business, these landowners created large estates called latifundia (LA•tuh•FUHN•dee •uh) that provided grain, sheep, olives, and fruits for urban markets. Labor for the latifundia was cheap because Rome's conquests brought thousands of captives and prisoners of war to work as slaves. By 100 B.C., slaves formed about 30 percent of Rome's people.

As slave labor replaced paid labor, thousands of small farmers and rural workers poured into the cities seeking employment. Jobs, however, were not readily available, and the new arrivals gradually formed into a class of urban, landless poor. Angry and without hope, the urban poor eked out a meager living and supported any politician who promised "bread and circuses," cheap food and free amusements.

As the gap between rich and poor steadily widened, upper-class Romans lived with the constant danger of revolts. To quell mounting unrest, Rome stationed legions in most provinces. Even Italy was not safe from uprisings. From 73 B.C. to 71 B.C., an army of 70,000 slaves led by the slave Spartacus plundered the Italian countryside in an effort to win freedom. With great difficulty, the Romans finally crushed the uprising and killed about 6,000 of Spartacus's followers. Putting down revolts cost Rome troops and money and placed a strain on its resources.

Visualizing History Rome's legions put down revolts in the provinces, but not without cost. Here, women funeral dancers mourn losses. *Why were the provinces not an endless source of wealth to Rome?*

Chapter 6 *Ancient Rome and Early Christianity* **161**

NATIONAL GEOGRAPHIC SOCIETY

Use these materials to enrich student understanding of ancient Rome.

 NGS PICTUREPACK
TRANSPARENCY SET
Ancient Rome

Independent Practice

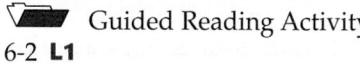 Guided Reading Activity 6-2 **L1**

Literature Have students work as individuals or in small groups to read and present to the class portions of Shakespeare's *Julius Caesar*. Suggest the following scenes: Caesar's assassination (III, i, 1–95); Marc Antony's address to the plebeians (III, ii); or the farewell of Brutus and Cassius (V, i, 70–125). **L2**

Multicultural Have students research various aspects of Carthage and its history and present short oral reports to the class. Suggest the following topics: the legend of Dido (its legendary queen) and Aeneas; the city's founding as a Phoenician colony; extent of the Carthaginian Empire; type of trade, culture, and religion; styles of art and architecture; famous leaders and rulers. **L3**

Visualizing History When the Roman legions finally suppressed the Jewish Revolt in A.D. 70, they had killed many thousands of Jews. Many legionaries also died in the five-year struggle.
Answer to Caption: *The cost of suppressing rebellions in the provinces began to strain Rome's resources.*

Chapter 6
Section 2

Linking Past and Present

Calendar More than 2,000 years after Caesar's death, our calendar continues to commemorate him. Already during his lifetime, Romans had changed the name of the month of Caesar's birth, Quintilis, to July in his honor.

Visualizing History

Even though Caesar's family traced its lineage back to the goddess Venus, the family was not snobbish, rich, or influential.

Answer to Caption: *Like the Greeks, the Romans sculpted heroic individuals; however, Roman sculpture is more realistic and lacks the spiritual quality of the Greek model.*

Biography

The following videotape program is available from Glencoe:

- **Cleopatra: Destiny's Queen**

ASSESS

Check for Understanding

Assign Section 2 Assessment as homework or as an in-class activity.

Reformers and Generals

Feuding among Rome's leading families also weakened the republic. As violence increased, some Romans proposed reforms to narrow the social gap and to stabilize society. In 133 B.C. the tribune **Tiberius Gracchus** proposed limiting the size of the latifundia and distributing land to the poor. But the Senate, made up of the wealthiest Romans, opposed him, and Tiberius was killed in street fighting. Ten years later, his brother **Gaius Gracchus** proposed the same reforms and was also murdered.

Crowding the Cities

After the death of the Gracchi, army leaders came to power in Rome. The first, the general **Marius**, became a consul in 107 B.C. after saving Rome from attack by Germanic tribes. Because the dwindling number of small farmers had made a citizen army obsolete, Marius turned to the unemployed urban poor to build a new army. Unlike the citizen soldiers, Marius's recruits were paid, given uniforms and equipment, and promised land when they were discharged. As a result of Marius's action, Rome for the first time had a professional army in which soldiers owed allegiance to their commander, not to the republic.

To advance their political ambitions, rival military and political leaders formed their own separate armies and used them against each other. From 88 B.C. to 82 B.C., Marius and a rival general named **Sulla** fought for control of Rome. Sulla finally drove Marius into exile and had himself appointed dictator. This practice of using the army to gain political power was copied by a rising young politician named Julius Caesar.

Julius Caesar

Born in Rome in about 100 B.C. of an aristocratic family, **Julius Caesar** became one of Rome's greatest generals and political leaders. Skillfully maneuvering himself through Rome's tumultuous game of politics, Caesar gradually rose to power. In 60 B.C. the ambitious aristocrat allied himself with the general Pompey and the politician Crassus. A year later, with their help he was elected consul. For the next decade, the three men ruled Rome as a triumvirate, or group of three persons with equal power. Through force and bribery, the triumvirate silenced government critics, bending senators and tribunes alike to its will.

Caesar's Military Campaigns

While serving as consul, Caesar realized he

162 Chapter 6 *Ancient Rome and Early Christianity*

---

needed military victories to advance his political career. In 59 B.C. he took a military command in Gaul, which was inhabited by Indo-Europeans known as Celts (KEHLTS). Caesar conquered the Celts and brought them under Roman rule. He also crossed the Rhine River to fight Germanic tribes and twice invaded Britain.

As a result of his victories, Caesar was hailed as a military hero by Rome's lower classes. But senators, alarmed at Caesar's growing popularity, regarded him as a political threat. By 50 B.C. the triumvirate itself had fallen apart: Crassus was dead, killed in battle while leading Roman forces in Asia, and Pompey had become Caesar's political rival.

In 49 B.C. the Senate, with Pompey's backing, ordered Caesar to give up his army and return to Rome. Caesar, however, had no intention of turning himself over to his enemies. He assembled 5,000 loyal troops and crossed the Rubicon, a stream that

Visualizing History Political strife following the murders of the Gracchi aided the rise of the young Julius Caesar, sculpted here in a heroic pose. *How do you think Roman sculpture differed from the Greek models on which it was based?*

MAKING CONNECTIONS ACTIVITIES

Human Rights Different cultures enslaved human beings for a variety of reasons. Have students use reference books to compare and contrast the practice of slavery in ancient Rome with that in ancient Egypt, ancient Greece, or ancient Israel. **L2**

Education Ancient Rome had no public schools, but most boys and some girls received some formal instruction. Have students use reference books to compare and contrast educational methods in ancient Rome with those in ancient Egypt, ancient Israel, ancient Greece, or ancient Persia. **L1**

divided his military provinces from Roman Italy. According to legend, Caesar had seen a vision that encouraged him to cross, and exclaimed to his troops, "Let us accept this as a sign from the gods, and follow where they beckon, in vengeance on our double-dealing enemies. The die is cast." By defying the Senate's order, Caesar realized there was no turning back; and a civil war was unavoidable. Ever since, "crossing the Rubicon" has meant making a decision that cannot be undone.

Caesar's army swiftly captured all of Italy and drove Pompey and his allies out. The fighting eventually spread east, with Caesar's troops defeating Pompey's at Pharsalus, Greece, in 48 B.C.

Caesar in Power

In 45 B.C. Caesar took over the government as dictator for life, to rule very much like a monarch. As absolute ruler, Caesar granted Roman citizenship to many people in the provinces outside of Italy. He added to the Senate representatives from the provinces who were loyal to him. In making these reforms, Caesar not only made the central government more responsive to Rome's newly conquered territories, he also strengthened his own power at the expense of the old patricians.

Caesar also carried out social reforms aimed to benefit the poor. To provide jobs, he set up public works programs and ordered slave-owning landowners to hire more free laborers. Colonies were founded throughout Rome's territories to provide land for the city's landless poor. Under Caesar, the government also continued its long-standing practice of distributing free grain but reduced the number of people eligible for it.

Caesar's most lasting reform was a new calendar based on the work of scholars in Alexandria. Replacing the old Roman lunar calendar, this new solar calendar counted 365 days in a year and 1 extra day every fourth year. Caesar's calendar, later

named Julian in honor of him, was used in western Europe until early modern times.

Caesar's Death

Many Romans believed that Caesar was a wise ruler who had brought order and peace to Rome. Others, however, considered him to be a tyrant who meant to make himself a king. According to ancient Roman law, anyone who plotted to become king could be killed without trial. Acting on this law, a group of senators, led by Brutus and Cassius, stabbed Caesar to death on March 15, 44 B.C.

End of the Republic

After the death of Julius Caesar, his 18-year-old grandnephew **Octavian** joined forces with **Marc Antony** and Marcus Lepidus, two of Caesar's top government officers. Together this second triumvirate defeated Caesar's assassins in 42 B.C. Then, while keeping up the appearance of republican government, these three generals divided the Roman world among themselves. Octavian ruled in Italy and the west, Antony in Greece and the east, and Lepidus in North Africa.

The second triumvirate did not last long, however. Octavian forced Lepidus to retire from political life. When Antony married Cleopatra, the queen of Egypt, Octavian persuaded the Romans that Antony intended to rule them with his foreign queen by his side, and so Octavian declared war on Antony in Rome's name. In 31 B.C. Octavian scattered the forces of his enemies in a critical naval battle at Actium in Greece. A year later, to evade capture by Octavian, Antony and Cleopatra committed suicide in Egypt. With Antony dead, Octavian became the undisputed ruler of Rome. Octavian's period of rule would mark the beginning of the Roman Empire.

 Use Interactive Tutor Self-Assessment Software to review Section 2.

Evaluate

Section Quiz 6-2

 Use the Testmaker to create a customized quiz for Section 2.

Reteach

Have students briefly summarize the importance of the Punic Wars, Hannibal, latifundia, *equites*, the Gracchi, Marius, Sulla, the triumvirate, Julius Caesar, and Octavian.

Reading Essentials and Study Guide 6-2

Enrich

Have students prepare an illustrated report on the Roman legions, focusing either on the army's structure and the legionaries' training and duties or on the legions' military siege machines.

CLOSE

Work with students to prepare a chronology of events and issues that led to the fall of the republic. Have students choose two or three events or issues that they think were the most significant.

SECTION 2 ASSESSMENT

Main Idea

1. Use a diagram like the one below to show which economic and social problems brought the Roman Republic to an end.

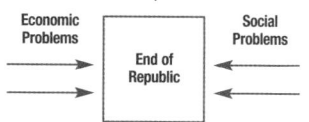

Recall

2. **Define** indemnity, triumvirate.
3. **Identify** Hannibal, Scipio, Tiberius Gracchus, Gaius Gracchus, Marius, Sulla, Julius Caesar, Octavian, Marc Antony.

Critical Thinking

4. **Analyzing Information** How did Julius Caesar's cross-

ing of the Rubicon help destroy the Roman Republic and create a dictatorship?

Understanding Themes

5. **Conflict** Explain how Roman military conquests overseas affected Rome's political, economic, and social development.

SECTION 2 ASSESSMENT ANSWERS

1. Economic problems: putting down revolts cost troops and money; wealthy Romans took land from small farmers. Social problems: corrupt Roman officials stole from conquered provinces; use of slave labor; growth of urban, landless poor
2. All terms are defined in the Glossary.

3. Hannibal, 160; Scipio, 160; Tiberius Gracchus, 162; Gaius Gracchus, 162; Marius, 162; Sulla, 162; Julius Caesar, 162; Octavian, 163; Marc Antony, 163
4. By crossing the Rubicon, Caesar defied Roman leaders, ended any chance of compromise, and made an all-out effort to seize power.

5. **CONFLICT** Political competition led to the use of armies to gain power. Provincial wealth was used to establish latifundia, displacing peasant farmers. A new social class, the *equites*, arose.

A.D. 1	A.D. 50	A.D. 100	A.D. 150	A.D. 200

A.D. 14
Augustus Caesar dies.

A.D. 79
Volcanic eruption
destroys Pompeii.

A.D. 96 Rule of the
Good Emperors begins.

A.D. 180
Pax Romana ends.

Section 3

The Roman Empire

SECTION THEME

▶ **Cultural Diffusion** The Romans build an empire and spread Latin culture.

Guide to Reading

For reading strategies to help students read effectively see pages 12–13.

Vocabulary Pre-check

 Use the Vocabulary PuzzleMaker for Chapter 6 to create a crossword puzzle to reinforce section terms. **L1 LEP**

 Use Vocabulary Activity 6 to introduce vocabulary terms. **L1 LEP**

FOCUS

Section Objective

Characterize life under the *Pax Romana*.

BELLRINGER
Motivational Activity

 Before taking roll at the beginning of the class period, project Section Focus Transparency 6-3 and have students answer the activity questions. Discuss students' responses.

 This activity is also available as a blackline master.

Guide to Reading

Read to Find Out
Main Idea *The Pax Romana brought order and peace to the Roman Empire.*

▶ **Terms to Define**
   aqueduct

▶ **People to Meet**
   Augustus, Tiberius, Claudius, Nero, Marcus Aurelius, Galen, Ptolemy, Virgil, Livy

▶ **Places to Locate**
   Appian Way

Storyteller

The visitor, Aelius Aristides, an educated and well-travelled man, had never seen anything to rival Rome. And it was not just the city—it was everything that Rome represented: military might, sensible government, and an elegant lifestyle. Who could help but admire an empire that commanded vast territories and diverse peoples, a military that conquered both armed forces and selfish ambition, a government where officials ruled not through arbitrary power but by law. Romans "measured out the world, bridged rivers, cut roads through mountains, filled the wastes with posting stations, introduced orderly and refined modes of life." They were, he declared, natural rulers.

Augustus Caesar

—adapted from *Oration on the Pax Romana*, Aelius Aristides, reprinted in *Sources of the Western Tradition*, Marvin Perry, 1991

Under the Roman Republic, laws had proven too weak to control social changes, while generals had taken power away from elected officials. Thus, Octavian believed that Rome needed one strong leader. The Senate agreed and appointed Octavian consul, tribune, and commander in chief for life in 27 B.C. Octavian gave himself the title *Augustus*, or "Majestic One."

The First Emperors

Augustus claimed to support the republic, but he actually laid the foundation for a new state called the Roman Empire. In practice, he became Rome's first emperor, or absolute ruler.

Augustus Caesar
In the 40 years of his reign—from 27 B.C. to A.D. 14—Augustus rebuilt the city of Rome and became a great patron of the arts. He also introduced many reforms to the empire. Proconsuls could no longer exploit the provinces. Publican tax collectors were replaced with permanent government employees. Grain was imported from North Africa so that all in Rome would be fed. New roads were built and old ones repaired. Magnificent public buildings were constructed throughout the empire. Augustus boasted that he had "found Rome a city of brick and left it a city of marble."

In 31 B.C. there began the *Pax Romana*, or Roman Peace, which lasted about 200 years. The only major disturbances during those years occurred when new emperors came to power. For, although Augustus chose his own successor carefully, he failed to devise any law for the selection of later emperors.

The Julio-Claudian Emperors
Historians call the four emperors who ruled from A.D. 14 to A.D. 68 the Julio-Claudians because

SECTION RESOURCES

 Reproducible Masters
- Lecture Notes 6-3
- Reproducible Lesson Plan 6-3
- Vocabulary Activity 6
- Guided Reading Activity 6-3
- Section Quiz 6-3
- Reading Essentials and Study Guide 6-3

 Transparencies
- Section Focus Transparency 6-3
- World History and Art Transparency 7

Multimedia
- Interactive Tutor Self-Assessment Software
- Testmaker
- Greece and Rome

Roman Expansion

North Sea · Hadrian's Wall · Britain · ATLANTIC OCEAN · Gaul · Rhine River · Spain · Italy · Rome · Adriatic Sea · Carthage · Actium ★ · Mediterranean Sea · Greece · ASIA MINOR · Black Sea · Danube River · Syria · Palestine · Tigris River · Euphrates River · Caspian Sea · Red Sea · Egypt · Nile River · AFRICA

	End of Punic Wars, 146 B.C.
	At Caesar's death, 44 B.C.
	At Augustus's death, A.D. 14
	Greatest extent of empire, A.D. 130
★	Battle site

0   200   400 mi.
0   200   400 km
Lambert Conic Conformal Projection

Map Study Most of the Roman Empire bordered the Mediterranean Sea, allowing Rome to have a stronghold on the Mediterranean region.
Region Why would control of the Mediterranean region be an advantage for Rome's economy?

each was a member of Augustus's family, known as the Julio-Claudians. Each showed promise when he became emperor, but later revealed great faults.

Augustus's adopted son **Tiberius**, who succeeded Augustus Caesar as emperor, spoiled his able leadership by accusing many innocent people of treason against him. Caligula, Tiberius's grandnephew and successor in A.D. 37, became mentally disturbed and was killed by a palace guard in A.D. 41. Caligula's uncle, **Claudius**, was a renowned scholar, but as he grew older he had difficulty focusing on affairs of state.

Nero, Claudius's stepson, who became emperor in A.D. 54, was cruel and probably insane. Nero was willing to bankrupt Rome to pay for his twin pleasures—horse racing and music. Suspecting others of plotting against him, he killed his wife and his mother and executed many senators. In A.D. 68 the Senate sentenced Nero to death for treason. Before he committed suicide, reportedly he cried, "What a loss I shall be to the arts!"

The Good Emperors

For 28 years following Nero's death, Rome was governed by a number of emperors who were backed by the army. Then, in A.D. 96 the Senate chose its own candidate for emperor: Nerva. Historians consider Nerva the first of the so-called Good Emperors; the others were Trajan, Hadrian, Antoninus Pius, and **Marcus Aurelius** (aw•REE•lee•uhs). The Good Emperors were known for their skills as effective administrators and their support of large building projects.

The Emperor Trajan increased the empire to its greatest size. Hadrian then strengthened Rome's frontiers, building Hadrian's Wall in Britain and other defense positions. Antoninus Pius succeeded him, maintaining the empire's prosperity. The philosopher-ruler Marcus Aurelius brought the empire to the height of its economic prosperity. All of these Good Emperors lived by the principle of Stoic philosophy best expressed by Marcus Aurelius in *Meditations*: "Every moment think steadily as a

Chapter 6 *Ancient Rome and Early Christianity* **165**

TEACH

Guided Practice

THEME Cultural Diffusion
Have students cite specific examples of cultural diffusion mentioned in this section. *(diffusion of Roman religion and law throughout the empire; Roman adaptation of Etruscan architecture, Egyptian astronomy, and Greek literature)* Discuss how Roman roads encouraged the diffusion of Roman culture throughout the empire, and ask what technologies in our world are important factors in cultural diffusion. *(satellite transmission of television signals; computer technology; ease and speed of world travel)* **L1**

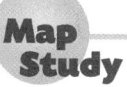
Map Study

Answer
It ensured access to a wide variety of resources and products, without the expense of foreign tariffs or the danger of naval attack.

Map Skills Practice

Reading a Map What is the distance of the farthest point of the empire from the city of Rome? *(about 2,500 miles, or 4,000 kilometers)*

The following videotape program is available from Glencoe:

• **Hadrian's Wall**

To find classroom resources to accompany this video, check the following home page:

A&E Television:
http://www.aetv.com

List Work with students to prepare a list of contributions Augustus Caesar made to the empire. Discuss how these contributions helped to establish the *Pax Romana.* **L2**

Government Discuss the ways in which Roman government in the days of the empire had changed from the government of the Roman Republic. *(Answers may include: emperor appointed governors rather than let Senate choose proconsuls; emperor ruled with absolute power for life, rather than elected consuls who served one-year terms.)* Explore with students the pros and cons of these changes in the structure of Roman government. **L3**

NATIONAL GEOGRAPHIC SOCIETY

Use these materials to enrich student understanding of everyday life in ancient Rome.

🌐 **NGS PICTURESHOW CD-ROM**
Greece and Rome

📖 World History and Art Transparency 7

Independent Practice

📁 Guided Reading Activity 6-3 **L1**

Geography: Place Have students trace a map of Italy. Ask them to research in an encyclopedia or other library reference books the Appian Way and other Roman roads and draw these on their maps. Have students include the names of the towns or cities connected by the Appian Way. **L2 LEP**

Roman and a human being how to do what you have in hand with perfect and simple dignity."

Roman Rule

By the time Augustus had come to power in 27 B.C., between 70 and 100 million people were living in the Roman Empire. To rule so many people effectively, Augustus had to make many changes in government.

Imperial Government

Augustus improved the working of the empire by carefully choosing professional governors rather than letting the Senate appoint inexperienced proconsuls every year. In some provinces, such as Judea, he left local kings in charge under his command. Augustus ordered new roads built so that he could keep in touch with all parts of the empire, and he personally inspected the provinces frequently.

Augustus also dignified his own position by serving as *pontifex maximus*, or chief priest of Rome. Thus he and each later emperor became the head of a national, unifying religion.

The Law

As the Romans won more provinces, they found that they needed a new kind of law that would apply to noncitizens. They therefore created the *jus gentium*, or law that dealt with noncitizens, as opposed to the *jus civile*, or citizen law. By the early A.D. 200s, however, emperors had granted citizenship to the peoples of so many nearby provinces that all free males in the empire had been made full citizens of Rome, and the two laws became one.

In their laws Romans generally stressed the authority of the state over the individual. They also accorded people definite legal rights, one of which was that an accused person should be considered innocent until proven guilty. The Roman system of law has formed the basis for the legal systems of many Western nations and of the Christian Church.

Images of the Times

Pompeii, A.D. 79

On August 23-25, A.D. 79, the volcano Vesuvius erupted in southern Italy. The city of Pompeii was buried in a single day.

A detail from the Villa of the Mysteries shows that life for many in Pompeii offered many comforts and pleasures.

166

Images of the Times Pompeii, A.D. 79

After the eruption of Vesuvius, Pompeii was buried under 19 to 23 feet (6 to 7 meters) of ash and debris. Herculaneum was covered by mud-lava to a depth of about 65 feet (20 meters).

An architect in the 1500s who was building a channel for drinking water discovered the ruins at Pompeii. Excavations of Herculaneum and Pompeii were begun in the 1700s and have continued, with interruptions, until the present. The earliest diggers were primarily treasure seekers, but in the mid-1800s archaeologists began to document their findings with care. Archaeologists have unearthed statue-covered public buildings, homes, shops, and luxurious villas.

An Imperial Army

Augustus and later emperors maintained the professional army. As conditions became more peaceful, however, Augustus reduced the number of legions and supplemented this fighting force with troops recruited from the provincial peoples. Even with forces combined, the emperor could count on having only about 300,000 troops, which was not enough to defend a border with a length of about 4,000 miles (6,440 km). Therefore, by A.D. 160, invasions by peoples outside the empire had become a continuing problem.

Roman Civilization

From about 31 B.C. to A.D. 180, the Roman world enjoyed a period of prosperity known as the *Pax Romana*, or Roman Peace. The stability of the *Pax Romana* boosted trade, raised standards of living, and generated many achievements in the arts. The Latin author Tertullian described this time:

> “ Everywhere roads are built, every district is known, every country is open to commerce ... the [fields] are planted; the marshes drained. There are now as many cities as there were once solitary cottages.... Wherever there is a trace of life, there are houses and human habitations, well-ordered governments, and civilized life. ”

—Tertullian, *Concerning the Soul*, c. A.D. 180

The Empire's Economy

Tertullian's description of economic growth under the empire was not exaggerated. In the first century A.D., artisans in Italy made pottery, woven cloth, blown glass, and jewelry for sale throughout the empire. The provinces in turn sent to Italy luxury items, such as silk cloth and spices, gathered in trade with China, India, and Southeast Asian countries. Dockworkers at Rome's harbor, Ostia, unloaded raw materials such as tin from Britain,

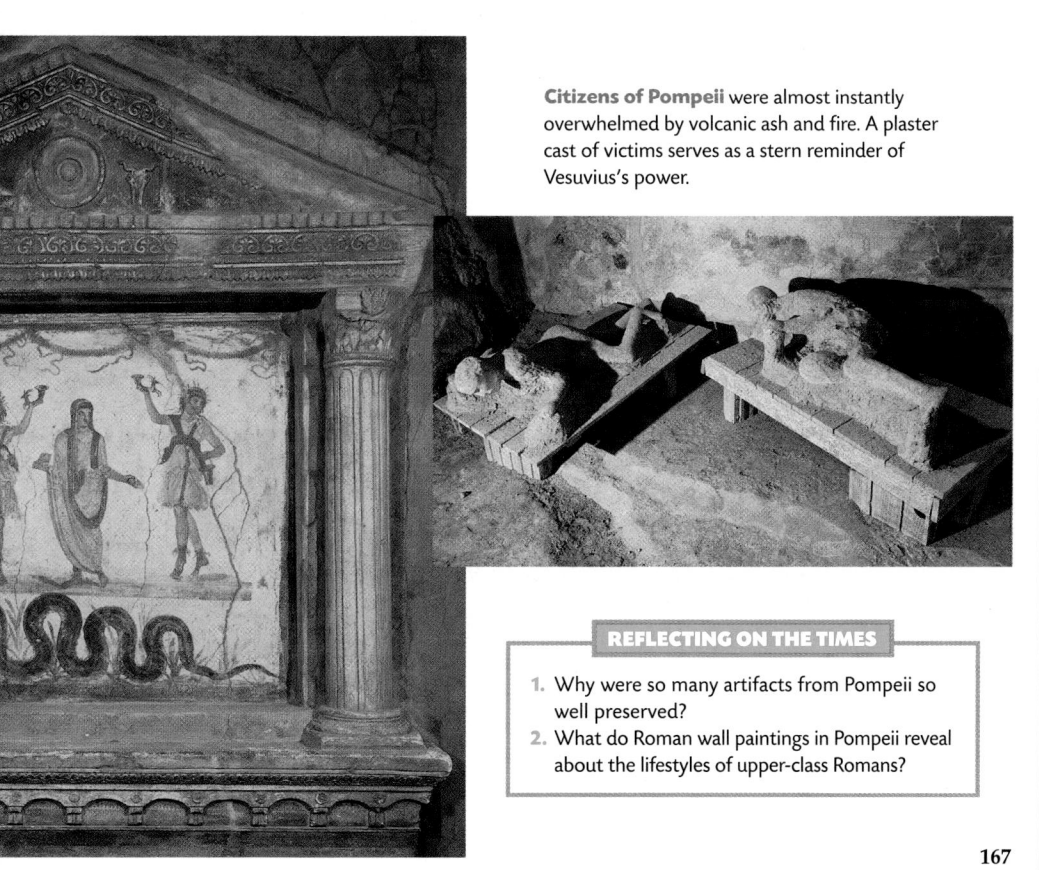

Citizens of Pompeii were almost instantly overwhelmed by volcanic ash and fire. A plaster cast of victims serves as a stern reminder of Vesuvius's power.

REFLECTING ON THE TIMES

1. Why were so many artifacts from Pompeii so well preserved?
2. What do Roman wall paintings in Pompeii reveal about the lifestyles of upper-class Romans?

167

ANSWERS TO REFLECTING ON THE TIMES

1. The remains at Pompeii were preserved intact when the volcanic ash covering them hardened.
2. Upper-class Romans had plenty of leisure time to enjoy music, literature, and entertainment.

Daily Life Have students choose the role of a person in the Roman Empire and then write a first-person narrative of a typical day. A student might choose to be a Roman legionary, a shopkeeper, a senator, a public official in the provinces, or an enslaved person. Students should research the daily life of the person they have chosen and include details of his or her occupational functions, family life, and social life. **L2**

Military History Although Romans made significant accomplishments during the *Pax Romana*, the period had its dark side as well. Have students research and report orally on gladiator matches, the behavior of Roman legions toward defeated enemies or provinces that revolted, or the practice of decimation (to select by lot and kill every tenth man) used to discipline cowardly or mutinous troops. **L3**

Who?What?Where?When?

Augustus had such handsome features that artists in the employ of Napoleon based their sculptures of the French ruler on busts of the Roman emperor crafted centuries earlier.

Linking Past and Present

Calendar The calendar used by much of the world today reflects the intervention of Augustus. During his lifetime, the Romans renamed the sixth month, Sextilis, in his honor. Some scholars believe that Augustus borrowed a day from February, reducing it to 28 days, so that the month named in his honor would have at least as many days as the month named for Julius Caesar.

Visualizing History

Although nothing but the site of the Circus Maximus remains today, it was one of the largest sports arenas ever constructed. In the fourth century A.D., under the emperor Constantine, it was enlarged to a seating capacity of about 250,000.

Answer to Caption: *concrete*

A&E HOME VIDEO.

The following videotape program is available from Glencoe:

• **The Incredible Monuments of Rome**

To find classroom resources to accompany this video, check the following home page:

A&E Television: http://www.aetv.com

---

iron from Gaul, and lead from Spain. Soon skillful Greek traders within the empire were doing business in distant areas, such as eastern Africa, Southeast Asia, and China.

Life During the *Pax Romana*

These economic changes brought changes in lifestyles. The family gradually became less significant than it had been during the republic. Romans had fewer children and were likely to divorce and remarry several times. Fathers lost some of the absolute power they had during the republic, and wives gained some legal rights. Society became less stable. Patricians might go bankrupt, wealthy military officers might sit in the Senate, and a poor man might even make a fortune in manufacturing.

Within each class, a consistent pattern of life formed. The wealthy often held public office, owned large farms outside the cities, ran factories, or directed trading firms. They lived comfortably in luxurious homes with marble walls, mosaic floors, running water, and baths.

The prosperity of the *Pax Romana* sometimes reached people of average means—shopkeepers and artisans. Although fewer people became very rich, more became moderately well off. The majority in Rome, however, were still poor. There were no private baths for them; instead they bathed at crowded public areas built under Augustus and later emperors. Most Romans lived in flimsy wooden apartment buildings of six or seven stories that readily collapsed or caught fire.

Public Amusements

Despite these trying conditions, the poor did not rebel against the government, because it offered them both free bread and free entertainment. By A.D. 160, Romans were celebrating 130 holidays a year. On some days, teams of charioteers competed in races in the Circus Maximus, an arena seating more than 150,000. On other holidays, crowds could watch gladiators fight each other to the death or battle wild animals in stadiums like the Colosseum.

Architecture, Engineering, and Science

The Romans erected many impressive buildings during the *Pax Romana* besides the Circus Maximus and the Colosseum. Between A.D. 118 and A.D. 128, Hadrian rebuilt the Pantheon, a temple for all the deities, with a soaring dome and a huge skylight. To build the Pantheon, the Romans mixed concrete—a new building material—with various kinds of stone.

The Romans also excelled in road building. The first major Roman road was the **Appian Way**. Constructed in the 300s B.C., it connected Rome and southeastern Italy. During the *Pax Romana*, a network of roads was built to link Rome with the provinces. Reaching a total length of 50,000 miles (80,000 km), the road network contributed to the empire's unity.

As they constructed public buildings and a vast network of roads, the Romans engineered aqueducts, or artificial channels for carrying water.

Visualizing History Entertainment at the giant arena Circus Maximus, depicted in this bas-relief, was free to Roman citizens. *What new building material did the Romans use to construct the Pantheon?*

168 **Chapter 6** *Ancient Rome and Early Christianity*

© Sonia Halliday Photographs

Roman Forum

The ruins of the Roman Forum are a major tourist attraction of modern Rome. In ancient times, the Forum was the center of both politics and commerce. The Forum contained a [num]ber of separate buildings: In the foreground the [tem]ple of Castor and Pollux, built in the 400s B.C., [reve]red Roman gods. Behind is the Arch of Titus, the [ ] whose military victory is enshrined in the arch [ ] about A.D 80. Beyond the Arch stand the walls of [the] Colosseum. The largest amphitheater built in ancient Rome, the Colosseum took a decade to construct and could seat 50,000. Here the Romans watched gladiators battle lions and later vanquish Christians.

The rise of the Roman state began with the city of Rome itself hundreds of years before the birth of Christ. Slowly the Romans consolidated control over Italy and built a great army. By 200 B.C. Rome had become a vast empire. Power brought wealth and great monuments such as these in the Forum.

Chapter 6 *Ancient Rome and Early Christianity* **169**

TEACH

Tell students that Castor and Pollux were twin brothers of the same mother (Leda) but different fathers. Castor was the son of a mortal (Tyndareus, Leda's husband), while Pollux was the son of Jupiter (the Roman name for Zeus), the king of the gods. According to legend, the twins brought the news to Rome of the Roman victory at the 496 B.C. battle of Lake Regillus.

Explain to students that the Arch of Titus commemorates the Roman victory in the Jewish war, in which one million Jews were said to have died. What do these buildings tell us about Roman society? (Possible answers: The Romans valued military conquests.) What buildings in our nation's capital do you think will still be standing 2,000 years from now, and what can they tell people about our country? (Answers may include the Capitol, the Washington Monument, the Lincoln and Jefferson Memorials; these buildings show that the United States values democratic government and honors those leaders who have built and supported it.)

CURRICULUM CONNECTION

ASTRONOMY

According to Greek myth, when Castor, who was mortal, died, Pollux refused immortality, which would have separated him from his brother. To unite them forever, Zeus transformed Castor and Pollux into the constellation Gemini, which means "twins" in Latin.

ASSESS

Check for Understanding

Assign Section 3 Assessment as homework or as an in-class activity.

 Use Interactive Tutor Self-Assessment Software to review Section 3.

Evaluate

Section Quiz 6-3

🖳 Use the Testmaker to create a customized quiz for Section 3.

Reteach

Have students work in small groups to make a list of the Roman emperors and the accomplishments of each.

Reading Essentials and Study Guide 6-3

Enrich

Have students imagine that they are contemporaries of one of the early Roman emperors and write a feature article about the life of that emperor. Students should research in the library the daily life of the emperor, as well as his contributions. Have students compile the completed reports into a "Book of Caesars" to be shared with the class.

CLOSE

Write these headings on the board: *Trade, Science and Technology, Literature, Government, Law, Religion, Entertainment, Military, Architecture*. Work with the class to describe the characteristics of each of these aspects of life during the *Pax Romana*.

These lofty arches built out of stone enabled water to flow into Rome from as far away as 57 miles (about 92 km). One Roman-built aqueduct in Segovia, Spain, was so well constructed that it is still used today—nearly 1,900 years after it was completed.

The Romans excelled at adapting the discoveries of others and using them in new and more practical ways. They made use of the Etruscan arch and dome to build aqueducts and the Pantheon, and borrowed the Greek design for columns to support porches built around city squares.

Roman scientists also relied upon information learned from other cultures. The ancient medical ideas compiled by the Greek physician **Galen** formed the basis of Roman medical science. The observations of the Egyptian astronomer **Ptolemy** formed the foundation of Roman astronomy. Galen's works influenced medical science for centuries, and Ptolemy's work allowed later astronomers to accurately predict the planets' motion.

Roman Education

The Romans studied their borrowed knowledge avidly. Wealthy boys and girls received private lessons at home. Young men from wealthy families went on to academies—where former Greek slaves often taught—to learn geometry, astronomy, philosophy, and oratory. The daughters of the wealthy did not attend academies. Many upper-class women continued to study at home, however, and often became as well educated as Roman men. People in the lower classes usually had at least a basic knowledge of reading, writing, and arithmetic.

Language and Literature

Latin, Rome's official language, had a vocabulary far smaller than that of Greek or modern English; thus, many words expressed several meanings. Nevertheless, Latin remained the *lingua franca*, or common language, of Europe as late as the A.D. 1500s. Latin also forms the basis of the so-called Romance languages, such as Italian, French, Spanish, Portuguese, and Romanian, and supplies the roots for more than half of English words.

Although Romans learned from Greek literature, during the reign of Augustus Latin literature achieved an elegance and power of its own. Cicero, a Roman senator, published beautifully written speeches. Ovid wrote the *Metamorphoses*, verses based on Greek mythology. Horace, a poet, wrote about the shortness of life and the rewards of companionship in his *Odes*. Horace's friend **Virgil** wrote the *Aeneid*, an epic poem comparable to those of Homer. In one passage of this poem, Virgil expresses both the humility and pride of Romans:

> 66 Others, no doubt, will better mould the bronze
> To the semblance of soft breathing, draw, from marble,
> The living countenance; and others plead
> With greater eloquence, or learn to measure,
> Better than we, the pathways of the heaven,
> The risings of the stars: remember, Roman,
> To rule the people under law, to establish
> The way of peace, to battle down the haughty,
> To spare the meek. Our fine arts, these, forever. 99
>
> —Virgil, the *Aeneid*, c. 20 B.C.

Livy, a later writer, wrote a monumental history of Rome that glorified the early Romans. The historian Tacitus, in contrast, condemned the tyranny of the Julio-Claudian emperors with subtle but scathing irony. In *Germania*, Tacitus contrasted the robust life of the Germans with what he felt was the weak and pleasure-loving life of the Romans.

SECTION 3 ASSESSMENT

Main Idea
1. Use a diagram like the one below to describe what lifestyles were like during the *Pax Romana*.

Recall
2. **Define** aqueduct.
3. **Identify** Augustus, *Pax Romana*, Tiberius, Claudius, Nero, Marcus Aurelius, Galen, Ptolemy, Virgil, Livy.

Critical Thinking
4. **Synthesizing Information** The expression "bread and circuses" has been used to describe measures taken by a government to prevent discontent among the poor. Do you think this expression applies to the modern United States? Why or why not?

Understanding Themes
5. **Change** What major new examples of architecture, engineering, and science appeared during the period of the *Pax Romana*?

SECTION 3 ASSESSMENT ANSWERS

1. family less significant; fathers less powerful; wives gained legal rights; families had fewer children; society less stable; prosperity reached to middle class; most Romans were poor
2. All terms are defined in the Glossary.
3. Augustus, 164; Tiberius, 165; Claudius, 165; Nero, 165; Marcus Aurelius, 165; *Pax Romana*, 167; Galen, 170; Ptolemy, 170; Virgil, 170; Livy, 170
4. Answers may include public welfare or televised professional sports displays as "bread and circuses."
5. **CHANGE** architecture: Pantheon; engineering: The Appian Way, road network, aqueducts; science: medical science and astronomy

A.D. 1

c. A.D. 30
Jesus preaches
in Palestine.

A.D. 150

A.D. 70 Jews in Palestine
unsuccessfully revolt
against Roman rule.

A.D. 300

A.D. 312
Constantine becomes
Roman emperor.

A.D. 450

A.D. 392
Christianity
becomes Rome's
official religion.

Section 4

The Rise of Christianity

Read to Find Out
Main Idea *Jesus of Nazareth's teachings and early Christianity influenced the later Roman Empire.*

▶ **Terms to Define**
   sect, messiah, disciple, martyr, bishop, patriarch, pope

▶ **People to Meet**
   Jesus, Paul, Peter, Constantine, Theodosius, Augustine

The Storyteller

How could Justin, a man well versed in philosophy and intellectual pursuits, explain to the emperor why he had embraced Christianity? He had opened a school to teach others about this religion, although most educated people dismissed it as a dangerous superstition. He had to convince the emperor that, just as the ancient philosophers had sought truth, Christians sought it too. Since both scholars and Christians shared this quest, following Christian teachings could only help in the search for understanding. He set his pen to paper and began to write a defense of the Christian faith.

—from *Apology*, Justin, reprinted in
Readings in Ancient History from Gilgamesh to Diocletian, Nels M. Bailkey, 1969

Mosaic of Jesus as shepherd

The early Romans worshiped nature spirits. Under Etruscan influence they came to think of these spirits as deities. Later, the Romans adopted much of Greek religion, identifying Greek deities with their own. Beginning with Augustus, the government also expected people to honor the emperor as Rome's chief priest. Nevertheless, the empire's people were still allowed to worship freely, and a variety of religions flourished.

Meanwhile, a new monotheistic religion called Christianity began to be practiced by some of the Jews in the eastern Mediterranean. At first, both the Romans and the earliest Christians thought of the new religion as a sect, or group, within Judaism. As Christians won over non-Jewish followers, however, the faith diverged from its Jewish roots and became a separate religion.

Judaism and the Empire

In A.D. 6 the Emperor Augustus turned the kingdom of Judah into the Roman province of Judea. The Romans in Judea still allowed the Jews to practice their religion, but they treated them cruelly. Many Jews therefore strengthened their hope that a messiah, or a deliverer chosen by God, would help them regain their freedom. The coming of a messiah had long been foretold by Jewish prophets.

Believing that God would intervene on their behalf, some Jews took matters into their own hands. In A.D. 66 they rebelled against the Romans and overpowered the small Roman army in Jerusalem. But only four years later, in A.D. 70, the Romans retook Jerusalem, destroying the Temple and killing thousands of Jews.

Then, after another unsuccessful rebellion in A.D. 132, the Romans banned the Jews from living

Chapter 6 *Ancient Rome and Early Christianity* **171**

Guide to Reading

For reading strategies to help students read effectively see pages 12–13.

Vocabulary Pre-check

 Use the Vocabulary PuzzleMaker for Chapter 6 to create a crossword puzzle to reinforce section terms. **L1 LEP**

Use Vocabulary Activity 6 to introduce vocabulary terms. **L1 LEP**

FOCUS

Section Objective

Summarize the teachings of Jesus of Nazareth and the influence of early Christians on the later Roman Empire.

BELLRINGER
Motivational Activity

Before taking roll at the beginning of the class period, project Section Focus Transparency 6-4 and have students answer the activity questions. Discuss students' responses.

This activity is also available as a blackline master.

SECTION RESOURCES

Reproducible Masters
- Lecture Notes 6-4
- Reproducible Lesson Plan 6-4
- Guided Reading Activity 6-4
- Section Quiz 6-4
- Reading Essentials and Study Guide 6-4

Transparencies
- Section Focus Transparency 6-4

Multimedia
- Vocabulary PuzzleMaker Software
- Interactive Tutor Self-Assessment Software
- Testmaker
- Turning Points in World History
- In the Holy Land

TEACH

Guided Practice

THEME Innovation

Review with students the meaning of innovation and the way in which Christianity grew out of Judaism. Ask students to explain how Christianity could be considered an innovation. (*Although like Judaism it was monotheistic and stressed ethical behavior, it was an innovation in teaching that Jesus was the Messiah and that the kingdom of God was close at hand.*) **L1 LEP**

Visualizing History The word *apostle* comes from the Greek for "one who is sent out." Jesus sent his original followers out into the world to preach the gospel, which literally means "good news."
Answer to Caption: *They formed churches for worship, fellowship, and instruction.*

ABCNEWS INTERACTIVE™

VIDEODISC
Turning Points in World History

Side One
Chapter 6

Title: *Jerusalem: City of Three Faiths*
Subject: Christian, Muslim, and Jewish scholars discuss the importance of Jerusalem to their three faiths.
Ask: Why is the land of Israel significant to Christianity? (*The events of Jesus' life took place there.*)

 Visualizing History An engraving of the apostles Peter and Paul decorates the sepulchre of the child Asellus. *Why did the apostles form churches?*

in Jerusalem. The Jews were forced to live in other parts of the Mediterranean and the Middle East. In their scattered communities, the Jews continued to study the Torah, the entire body of Jewish religious law and learning. They set up special academies called yeshivas to promote its study. Furthermore, between A.D. 200 and A.D. 500, rabbis—scholars trained in the yeshivas—assembled their various interpretations of the Torah into a book known as the Talmud. To this day the Talmud remains an important book of Jewish law.

Jesus of Nazareth

A few decades before the Jewish revolts, a Jew named **Jesus** grew up in the town of Nazareth. With deep spiritual fervor, Jesus traveled through Galilee and Judea from about A.D. 30 to A.D. 33, preaching a new message to his fellow Jews and winning disciples, or followers.

Proclaiming that God's rule was close at hand, Jesus urged people to turn away from their sins and practice deeds of kindness. He said that God was loving and forgiving toward all who repented, no matter what evil they had done or how lowly they were. In his teaching, Jesus often used parables, or symbolic stories. With the parable below, Jesus urged his followers to give up everything so that they would be ready for God's coming:

> 66 The kingdom of heaven is like treasure lying buried in a field. The man who found it, buried it again; and for sheer joy went and sold everything he had, and bought that field. 99
>
> —Matthew 13:44–46

Jesus' disciples believed that he was the messiah; other Jews, believing that the messiah had yet to come, disputed this claim. The growing controversy over Jesus troubled Roman officials in Palestine. They believed that anyone who aroused such strong public feelings could endanger Roman rule in the region. In about A.D. 33, the Roman governor Pontius Pilate arrested Jesus as a political rebel and ordered that he be crucified—hung from a cross until dead. This was a typical Roman way of punishing criminals.

The Spread of Christianity

After Jesus' death, his disciples proclaimed that he had risen from the dead and had appeared to them. They pointed to this as evidence that Jesus was the messiah. His followers began preaching that Jesus was the Son of God and the way of salvation. Small groups in the Hellenistic cities of the eastern Mediterranean world accepted this message. Jews and non-Jews who accepted Jesus and his teachings became known as Christians—*Christos* was Greek for "messiah." They formed churches—communities for worship, fellowship, and instruction.

A convert named **Paul** aided Christianity's spread, especially among non-Jews. He traveled widely and wrote on behalf of the new religion. Paul's letters to various churches were later combined with the Gospels, or stories about Jesus, and the writings of other early Christian leaders. Together, these works form the New Testament of the Bible.

Meanwhile, other apostles, or Christian missionaries, spread Christianity throughout the Roman world. It is believed that **Peter**, the leader of the group, came to Rome and helped found a church in that city. Other churches were set up in Greece, Asia Minor, Egypt, and later in Gaul and Spain.

COOPERATIVE LEARNING ACTIVITY

Religions Organize students into several groups. Have each group research one of the various religions practiced in the Roman Empire. Make sure each group member is responsible for either research, compiling information, providing illustrations, preparing answers for possible questions, or presentation to the class. Religions to be researched include the official religion of Rome, Judaism, and the Persian and Egyptian mystery religions, such as Mithraism and the cult of Isis. Have each group choose one of its members to deliver its report to the class. The entire group should act as a panel, answering questions from the class about the religion it studied. **L2**

Persecution and Competition

Christians taught that their religion was the only true faith. They refused to honor the emperor as a god and rejected military service. As a result, many Romans accused them of treason.

The Romans feared that Christian rejection of their deities would bring divine punishment. Therefore, although they did not hunt out the Christians, if local officials thought Christians were causing trouble, they might have the Christians killed. The Romans frequently threw these Christian martyrs—people who chose to die rather than give up their beliefs—into the stadiums to be killed by wild beasts in front of cheering crowds.

Such persecution, which lasted until the early A.D. 300s, kept many people from becoming Christians. To win converts, Christians had to overcome this obstacle. Christianity also had to compete for followers with polytheistic religions and mystery religions—so named for their mythical heroes and secret rituals—and with Judaism.

During the A.D. 200s and 300s, Christianity flourished in the Mediterranean world along with these other religions. Like Judaism, Christianity was mainly a religion of the cities, while traditional Roman religions retained their hold in the countryside. Even though the number of Christians was relatively small during this period, their strength in the cities of the Roman Empire gave Christianity an influence that was far beyond its size.

Romans Adopt Christianity

According to legend, in A.D. 312, as the Roman general **Constantine** led his army into battle, a flaming cross appeared in the sky and beneath it in fiery letters appeared the Latin words *In hoc signo vinces*: "With this as your standard you will have victory." Apparently because of this vision, Constantine ordered his soldiers to paint the Christian symbol of the cross on their shields. When his army won the battle, Constantine credited the victory to the Christian God.

Named emperor of Rome in A.D. 312, Constantine thus became a protector of Christianity. A year later, he issued the Edict of Milan, which decreed that all religious groups in the empire, including Christians, were free to worship as they pleased. Constantine attended meetings of Christian leaders and ordered churches to be built in Rome and Jerusalem.

Because of effective missionary work and growing government support, Christianity further increased in size and influence throughout the entire Roman world. It became as important in the western part of the empire as it was in the eastern part. In A.D. 392 the Emperor **Theodosius** (THEE•uh •DOH•shuhs) made Christianity the official religion of the Roman Empire. At the same time, he banned the old Hellenistic and Roman religions.

The Early Church

From early times Christians recognized that their organization, the Church, would prosper only if it was united. They also felt that Christian teachings had to be stated clearly to avoid differences of opinion that might divide the Church. Consequently, Christians turned to important religious thinkers who attempted to explain many Christian beliefs. Between A.D. 100 and A.D. 500, various scholars known as Church Fathers wrote books explaining Christian teachings. They greatly influenced later Christian thinkers.

Teachings of Augustine

Christians in the western part of the empire especially valued the work of **Augustine**, a scholar born in North Africa in A.D. 354. Augustine is considered to have written one of the world's first great autobiographies. In this work called *Confessions*, Augustine describes how he was converted to Christianity:

> ❝ I heard from a neighboring house a voice, as of a boy or girl, I know not, chanting, and oft repeating, 'Take up and read; Take up and read.'… So … I arose, interpreting it to be no other than a command from God, to open the book [the Bible], and read the first chapter I should find. ❞
>
> —Augustine, *Confessions*, c. A.D. 398

Visualizing History **Constantine became a defender of Christianity.** *How did the status of Christians living in the Roman Empire change under the rule of Constantine?*

VIDEODISC
In the Holy Land

Side One, Chapter 9
Frame: 9487
Title: *Ted Koppel: Three Religions*
Subject: Introduction to Islam, Christianity, and Judaism
Ask: Which of the three religious groups controls most of Israel today? *(Jewish religion)*

Romans Adopt Christianity
What caused Christianity to increase in size?
Its support by Constantine, the Edict of Milan, effective missionary work and increased government support.

Visualizing History Constantine believed he was God's chosen servant and responsible to God for good government of the Church.
Answer to Caption: *Christians gained complete freedom to worship as they pleased.*

ASSESS

Check for Understanding
Assign Section 4 Assessment as homework or as an in-class activity.

MEETING SPECIAL NEEDS ACTIVITY

Learning Style: Visual/Spatial Many movies have been made about the life of Jesus or the impact of Christianity on the people of imperial Rome. Have students who are visual learners or have limited English proficiency view a videotape of *The Robe, Ben Hur, The Silver Chalice,* or *The Greatest Story Ever Told* and then write a report. Instruct them to include descriptions of details about life under the *Pax Romana* (for example, in *Ben Hur*, the chariot races; in *The Silver Chalice*, the Greek artisan and enslaved person; in *The Robe*, the Roman legionaries). Ask students to deliver their reports to the rest of the class. **L1**

☑ Use Interactive Tutor Self-Assessment Software to review Section 4.

Evaluate

🗀 Section Quiz 6-4

☑ Use the Testmaker to create a customized quiz for Section 4.

Reteach

Work with students to create a time line on the chalkboard of significant events in Judaism and Christianity covered in this section.

🗀 Reading Essentials and Study Guide 6-4

Enrich

Have students interview a local Christian minister or priest or a Jewish rabbi about the Jewish roots of Christianity. Encourage students to tape-record the interview and to prepare a list of questions in advance. (Sample questions: What beliefs do Judaism and Christianity share? What are the significant differences?) Have students report orally on their interviews.

CLOSE

Have groups of five or six students summarize one of the following: the teachings of Jesus, the spread of Christianity throughout the Roman world, or the evolution of the early Church. Have each group present its summary.

Roman mural of Christian disciples

Characteristics of Christianity

- Christians acknowledge the God of the Jews as their God. The Christian Bible includes both the Jewish Scriptures (the Old Testament) and the New Testament.
- Most Christians believe that in one God are three Persons—the Father, the Son, and the Holy Spirit (the Trinity).
- Christianity affirms that Jesus is God the Son who became a human being, died, and rose from death to save humanity from sin. According to Christian belief, people receive eternal life by believing in Jesus and following his teachings.
- Christianity has had a major impact on the West, especially in the arts, philosophy, politics, and society.
- Today, Christianity, with more than 1.5 billion followers, is the world's largest religion. It is the major faith in Europe, the Americas, and Australia.
- Most Christians today belong to one of three major groups—Roman Catholic, Protestant, or Eastern Orthodox.

So powerful was Augustine's influence that he became a leading church official in North Africa. In this post he wrote books, letters, and sermons that shaped Christian thought. For instance, he wrote *City of God*—the first history of humanity from the Christian viewpoint.

Church Structure

By Augustine's time, Christian leaders had organized the Church as a hierarchy—into levels of authority, each level more powerful than the level below it. Local gatherings of Christians, called parishes, were led by priests. Priests conducted worship services and supervised parish activities. Several parishes together formed a diocese, each overseen by a bishop. Bishops interpreted Christian beliefs and administered regional church affairs. The most powerful bishops governed Christians in the empire's larger cities. The bishops of the five leading cities—Rome, Constantinople, Alexandria, Antioch, and Jerusalem—were called patriarchs

The bishops of the Christian Church met in councils to discuss questions and disputes about Christian beliefs. The decisions they reached at these councils, such as that at Nicaea in A.D. 325, came to be accepted as doctrine, or official teachings. The points of view the council did not accept were considered heresy, or false doctrine.

During the A.D. 400s, the bishop of Rome began to claim authority over the other patriarchs. Addressed by the Greek or Latin word *papa*, his name today is rendered *pope* in English. Latin-speaking Christians in the West regarded the pope as head of all of the churches. Greek-speaking Christians in the East, however, would not accept the authority of the pope. The bishops of Alexandria and Antioch claimed to exercise a paternal rule equal to that of the pope. Eventually these churches and those of the Latin West separated. In time, the Latin churches as a group became known as the Roman Catholic Church and the Greek churches as the Eastern Orthodox Church.

SECTION 4 ASSESSMENT

Main Idea

1. Use a diagram like the one below to identify the main points of Jesus' teachings.

Teachings of Jesus

Recall

2. **Define** sect, messiah, disciple, martyr, bishop, patriarch, pope.
3. **Identify** the Talmud, Jesus, Paul, Peter, Constantine, Theodosius, Augustine.

Critical Thinking

4. **Evaluating Information** Why might the Romans in Judea especially have responded harshly toward anyone arousing strong feelings among the Jewish people?

Understanding Themes

5. **Innovation** List some of the ways in which Christianity diverged from Judaism to become a distinct religion.

SECTION 4 ASSESSMENT ANSWERS

1. God's rule was close at hand; urged people to turn away from sins and practice forgiveness; God was loving and forgiving toward the repentant; taught with parables
2. All terms are defined in the Glossary.
3. Talmud, 172; Jesus, 172; Paul, 172; Peter, 172; Constantine, 173; Theodosius, 173; Augustine, 173

4. Romans feared a Jewish rebellion.
5. **INNOVATION** Unlike Jews, Christians believed Jesus was the Messiah. When Christianity spread to non-Jews, it changed from a Jewish sect into a separate religion.

A.D. 284
Diocletian becomes Roman emperor.

A.D. 330
Constantine moves capital to Byzantium, renamed Constantinople.

A.D. 395
Theodosius divides Roman Empire.

A.D. 476 German soldier Odoacer seizes Rome.

Section 5

Roman Decline

Read to Find Out
Main Idea *Political and economic causes led to the decline of the western Roman Empire.*

▶ **Terms to Define**
  inflation

▶ **People to Meet**
  Diocletian, Constantine, Theodosius I, Alaric, Attila, Odoacer

▶ **Places to Locate**
  Constantinople

The old world had ended. There was no longer any doubt of that. Gregory, whose family had for countless generations served Rome as Senators and consuls, looked out the window at the city which had once ruled the world. Now it was in the hands of warlike tribes who had no appreciation for Roman virtue, achievements, or culture.

"Cities are destroyed," he mused, "fortifications razed, fields devastated. Some men are led away captive, others are mutilated, others slain before our eyes." The pride of Rome was reduced to memories of a vanished glory.

—from Homiliarum in Ezechielem, Pope Gregory I, reprinted in Sources of the Western Tradition, Marvin Perry, Joseph Peden, and Theodore Von Laue, 1991

Marcus Aurelius

$\mathcal{D}$uring the A.D. 200s, while Christianity was spreading through the Roman Empire, Germanic tribes began to overrun the western half of the empire. Many inhabitants in this area reported widespread devastation and chaos. The Germanic tribes had always been a threat to the empire. Why were they so much more successful now than they were during the times of Marcus Aurelius?

The Empire's Problems

The Romans had a brief rest from political violence during the reign of the five Good Emperors. When Marcus Aurelius died in A.D. 180, however, a new period of violence and corruption brought the *Pax Romana* to an end.

Political Instability

The time of confusion began with the installation of Emperor Commodus, Marcus Aurelius's son. Like Nero, he spent so much state money on his own pleasures that he bankrupted the treasury. In A.D. 192 Commodus's own troops plotted to kill him.

From A.D. 192 to A.D. 284, army legions installed 28 emperors, only to kill most of them off in rapid succession. During this time of political disorder, Rome's armies were busier fighting each other than they were defending the empire's borders. Germanic tribes such as the Goths, the Alemanni, the Franks, and the Saxons repeatedly and successfully attacked the empire.

Economic Decline

Political instability led to economic decline. Warfare disrupted production and trade. For artisans and merchants, profits declined sharply, forcing many out of business. Warfare also destroyed farmland, causing food shortages that sent food prices soaring.

Chapter 6 *Ancient Rome and Early Christianity* **175**

SECTION THEME

▶ **Change** Germanic invasions and cultural weaknesses destroy the Roman Empire.

For reading strategies to help students read effectively see pages 12–13.

Vocabulary Pre-check
Use the Vocabulary PuzzleMaker for Chapter 6 to create a crossword puzzle to reinforce section terms. **L1 LEP**

Use Vocabulary Activity 6 to introduce vocabulary terms. **L1 LEP**

FOCUS

Section Objective
List the reasons for the decline of the western Roman Empire.

BELLRINGER
Motivational Activity

Before taking roll at the beginning of the class period, project Section Focus Transparency 6-5 and have students answer the activity questions. Discuss students' responses.
This activity is also available as a blackline master.

SECTION RESOURCES

Reproducible Masters
- Lecture Notes 6-5
- Reproducible Lesson Plan 6-5
- Vocabulary Activity 6
- Guided Reading Activity 6-5
- Reteaching Activity 6
- Enrichment Activity 6
- Section Quiz 6-5

- Performance Assessment Activity 6
- Spanish Chapter Summary 6
- Reading Essentials and Study Guide 6-5

Transparencies
- Section Focus Transparency 6-5

Multimedia
- Interactive Tutor Self-Assessment Software
- Testmaker

TEACH

Guided Practice

THEME Change

Work with students to make a list of some of the changes that took place in the empire from the days of the *Pax Romana* to the decline of the western empire. Then discuss with them which changes were positive and which contributed to the decline of the empire. *(positive: spread of Christianity, Constantinople established as eastern capital; negative: economic decline, Germanic invasions)* **L1**

Economics Have students name the economic reforms instituted by Diocletian and Constantine. For each, ask what specific problem(s) the reform was meant to solve. *(freezing wages and prices—inflation; ordering farmers not to leave their land or allowing land owners to chain them—farmers were leaving farms and food shortages were occurring; requiring people to stay at their jobs and making jobs hereditary—people leaving heavily taxed professions)* Have students suggest other methods the emperors might have used to solve these problems. **L2**

Critical Thinking Ask students how the lack of orderly succession affected the Roman Empire. *(political instability, process controlled by armies)* Ask how power is passed on in our country and what might happen if we did not have a method of selection. **L3**

To cope with falling incomes and rising prices, the government minted more coins. It hoped the increase would make it easier to pay its soldiers. However, because the government had already drained its stores of gold and silver, the new coins contained less of the precious metals—cutting their value. To continue getting the same return for their goods, merchants raised prices. Thus, the government's policy sparked severe inflation—a rise in prices corresponding to a decrease in the value of money.

The spiraling decline in wealth affected almost all parts of the empire. To sustain a fighting force, the Roman government had to continually raise soldiers' wages. Taxing landowners heavily seemed the only way to meet this expense, but as increased taxes made farming less profitable, more and more farmers abandoned their lands. As a result, the output of crops shrank even more, worsening the food shortage.

Unsuccessful Reforms

During the late A.D. 200s and early A.D. 300s, two emperors—**Diocletian** (DY•uh•KLEE•shuhn) and later, **Constantine**—struggled to halt the empire's decline. Their reforms preserved the government in the eastern part of the empire for more than 1,000 years. In the west, they succeeded only in briefly delaying the Germanic tribes' invasion of Rome.

Diocletian

General Diocletian came to power in A.D. 284 by slaying the murderer of the preceding emperor. To hold back invasions, he raised the number of legions in the army and spent his time traveling throughout the empire to oversee defenses. Recognizing, however, that the empire was too large for one person to govern, Diocletian divided the empire into two administrative units. Diocletian set himself up as coemperor of the eastern provinces and set up General Maximian as coemperor of the western provinces.

Diocletian also tried to stop the empire's economic decline. To slow inflation, he issued an order called the Edict of Prices. In this edict, Diocletian froze wages and set maximum prices for goods. Yet, even though the penalty for breaking the law was death, his effort failed completely. Citizens merely sold their goods through illegal trade. To stop farmers from leaving their lands and heavily taxed people from changing their

Visualizing History As this relief sculpture shows, tax collectors in Roman times were very visible. *Why did the Roman government have to increase taxes?*

176 Chapter 6 *Ancient Rome and Early Christianity*

COOPERATIVE LEARNING ACTIVITY

Role Play Organize the class into small groups and assign each group to role-play one of the following: Franks, Vandals, Visigoths, or Huns. Have each group research and prepare a presentation to the class on the group they are role-playing. The presentation should include information on the following: social structure and culture, homeland, methods of battle, and reasons for invading the empire. Make sure each group member is assigned a specific area of research and presentation. Have groups present their role plays to the class. Encourage them to use props such as maps and pictures in their presentations, and if they wish, to dress the part. Have the audience prepare questions in advance. **L1**

professions to avoid taxation, Diocletian required farmers who rented land never to leave their property and all workers to remain at the same job throughout their lives.

Constantine

When Diocletian retired in A.D. 305, civil wars broke out again. They continued until Constantine came to power in A.D. 312.

Constantine worked to stabilize the empire once more by reinforcing Diocletian's reforms. He made it legal for landowners to chain their workers to keep them on the farm. He declared most jobs hereditary; sons had to follow their fathers' occupations. In A.D. 330 he moved the capital of the eastern empire to the Greek town of Byzantium —an ideal site for trade and well protected by natural barriers—and renamed it **Constantinople**.

Theodosius

After Constantine's death in A.D. 337, civil war

Germanic Invasions A.D. 200–500

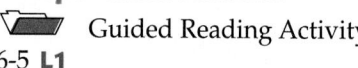

★ Battle site

◻ Empire of the West

◼ Empire of the East

→ Franks

→ Ostrogoths

→ Vandals

→ Angles/Saxons

→ Visigoths

→ Huns

Map Study Between A.D. 410 and A.D. 476 Visigoths, Huns, and Vandals invaded Italy.
Movement What was the area of origin and the destination of the Angles and Saxons during this period?

flared anew until **Theodosius I** succeeded Constantine. During Theodosius's rule, the empire still suffered internal problems, and again the western half suffered more. To lessen the problems, Theodosius willed upon his death that the eastern and western parts should be separate empires. In A.D. 395 this division came to pass. To distinguish the two, historians refer to the eastern empire as the Byzantine Empire—after Byzantium, the town that became the capital—and the western empire as the Roman Empire.

Barbarian Invasions

Germanic tribes entered the Roman Empire for many reasons. Beginning in the late A.D. 300s, large numbers of Germanic peoples migrated into the empire because they sought a warmer climate and

better grazing land. Others crossed the empire's borders wanting a share of Rome's wealth. Most, however, came because they were fleeing the Huns, fierce nomadic invaders from central Asia.

Warrior Groups

Germanic warriors lived mostly by raising cattle and farming small plots. Despite their interest in the empire's goods, they themselves had little surplus to trade and were poor compared to the Romans. Each warrior group consisted of warriors, their families, and a chief. This chief governed the group and also led the warriors into battle. As the bands of warriors were numerous, so too were the chiefs. Often the only unifying factor among these Germanic groups was their language, which to the Romans sounded like unintelligible babbling. The Romans labeled the Germanic peoples barbarians, a reference to the sounds they made.

Chapter 6   *Ancient Rome and Early Christianity*   **177**

Chapter 6
Section 5

Map Study

Answer
northern European mainland (present-day Denmark); Britain

Map Skills Practice

Reading a Map Which invading groups must have been skilled seafarers as well as warriors? *(Vandals, Angles/Saxons)*

Independent Practice

📂 Guided Reading Activity 6-5 **L1**

News Reports Have students imagine that they are anchorpersons for the Rome Evening News in August A.D. 410. The Visigoths, led by Alaric, are camped outside the walls ready to attack. Have students write news reports, including background information on Alaric and his Goths, and present their newscast to the class. **L2**

Economics Have students write an in-depth report on economic factors that led to the decline of the empire. Have students explain how the interaction of factors, such as increased taxes and inflation, caused further decline. Encourage students to discuss whether there are any similar economic problems today. **L3**

Linking Past and Present

The Vandals so thoroughly looted and destroyed Rome that today we call someone who willfully destroys valuable objects a *vandal* and deliberate destruction of property *vandalism*.

MEETING SPECIAL NEEDS ACTIVITY

Mixed Learners To make certain that students with learning difficulties understand the unsuccessful reforms that failed to halt the decline of the Roman Empire, have them imagine that they are farmers living in one of Rome's western provinces during the rule of Diocletian. Have them write letters to relatives in Rome describing the difficulties they are having and their worries. Then ask the students to read their letters to the rest of the class. **L2**

Chapter 6   *Ancient Rome and Early Christianity*   **177**

Chapter 6 Section 5

ASSESS

Check for Understanding

Assign Section 5 Assessment as homework or as an in-class activity.

 Use Interactive Tutor Self-Assessment Software to review Section 5.

Evaluate

 Section Quiz 6-5

 Use the Testmaker to create a customized quiz for Section 5.

Reteach

Work with students to create on the chalkboard a time line of significant events from A.D. 180–476.

 Reteaching Activity 6

 Reading Essentials and Study Guide 6-5

Enrich

Have students research to find out more about the culture of the Visigoths, Huns, and Vandals.

 Enrichment Activity 6

CLOSE

Have students summarize the factors that led to the fall of Rome and discuss their relative importance. For example, did invasions have a greater impact than economic problems?

 Sassanids Establish an Empire

Persia, A.D. 200s
Ardashir I, king of Persis, defeated the Parthian army in a decisive victory, then entered the capital of Ctesiphon in triumph. There he was crowned King of Kings and established the Sassanid Empire, which lasted until A.D. 651. Ardashir founded or rebuilt many cities and made Zoroastrianism the state religion. A rock carving at Naqshi-Rustam shows Ardashir taking the symbol of royalty from the supreme Zoroastrian god.

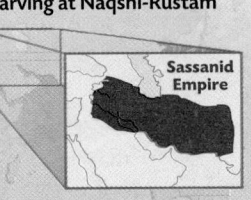

Sassanid Empire

The Visigoths

During the late A.D. 300s and A.D. 400s, a variety of Germanic groups extended their hold over much Roman territory. They were the Ostrogoths, Visigoths, Vandals, Franks, Angles, and Saxons. The Visigoths, at first, were the most important of these groups. In A.D. 378 they rebelled against Roman rule and defeated a large Roman army at Adrianople in the Balkan Peninsula, killing the eastern Roman emperor. To buy peace, his successor gave the Visigoths land in the Balkans. In A.D. 410 the Visigothic chief, **Alaric**, led his people into Italy, capturing and sacking Rome. After Alaric's death the Visigoths retreated into Gaul.

The Huns

The next threat to the empire was invasion by the Huns. This nomadic group streamed westward from the grasslands of central Asia. Led by their chief, **Attila**, the Huns raided the eastern empire;

then they moved north into Gaul. In A.D. 451 the Romans and the Visigoths combined to fight and stop the Huns in central Gaul. Foiled in the provinces, Attila turned upon Italy. There his horde plundered the larger cities. Eventually plague and famine took their toll on the Huns. After Attila died in A.D. 453, they retreated to eastern Europe.

The end of the Huns' empire brought the Romans new troubles. Wandering Germans, Slavs, Avars, and Persians battered continually at the Roman Empire's eastern frontier. Diplomacy, bribery, and warfare kept them at bay for only a short time.

End of the Western Empire

With the Huns gone and Italy devastated, nothing remained to prevent Germanic tribes from taking over. The Vandals raided and thoroughly sacked Rome in A.D. 455. Franks and Goths divided Gaul among themselves. Finally, in A.D. 476, a German soldier named **Odoacer** (OH•duh•WAY•suhr) seized control of Rome and overthrew the young emperor, Romulus Augustulus. Odoacer then named himself king of Italy.

Because Odoacer called himself king and never named a substitute emperor, people today refer to A.D. 476 as the year in which the Roman Empire "fell." However, this event no more signifies the collapse of the empire than any other event. Its end was caused by a complex interaction of events between A.D. 200 and A.D. 500.

More accurately, the western Roman Empire ended in the late A.D. 400s. Yet it did not mean the end of Roman culture, for the new Germanic rulers accepted the Latin language, Roman laws, and the Christian Church. In the Byzantine Empire, however, aspects of Roman culture were gradually supplanted by Hellenistic culture. By the A.D. 700s, Greek had even replaced Latin as the language of the Byzantine Empire.

SECTION 5 ASSESSMENT

Main Idea
1. Use a diagram like the one below to identify the political and economic causes of the decline of the Roman Empire.

Causes — Effect
Political
Economic → Decline of Roman Empire

Recall
2. **Define** inflation.
3. **Identify** Diocletian, Constantine, Theodosius I, Alaric, Attila, Odoacer.

Critical Thinking
4. **Synthesizing Information** Do you think that internal difficulties or outside invaders

had greater impact on the decline and fall of the western Roman Empire? Why? Give reasons from the text for your choice.

Understanding Themes
5. **Change** How did warfare create the Roman Empire and later destroy its western half?

---

178 **Chapter 6** *Ancient Rome and Early Christianity*

SECTION 5 ASSESSMENT ANSWERS

1. Political: from A.D. 192 to A.D. 284, army legions unseated 28 emperors; invaders successfully attacked empire. Economic: warfare disrupted production and travel; profits declined; businesses shut down; farmland destroyed during war; inflation; decline in wealth throughout empire; food shortages

2. All terms are defined in the Glossary.
3. Diocletian, 176; Constantine, 176; Theodosius I, 177; Alaric, 178; Attila, 178; Odoacer, 178
4. Answers will vary. Internal difficulties opened empire to outside invaders. Economic decline made maintaining armies difficult.

5. **CHANGE** Romans brought territories into the empire through warfare. The cost of maintaining armies and putting down rebellions weakened the empire. Outside invaders destroyed the empire through warfare.

Critical Thinking SKILLS

Decision Making

Suppose you have been given the choice of taking an art class or a music class during your free period at school. How will you decide which class to take?

Learning the Skill

When you make a decision, you are making a choice between alternatives. There are five key steps you should follow that will help you in the decision-making process.

1. Identify the problem. What are you being asked to choose between?
2. Identify and consider various alternatives that are possible.
3. Determine the consequences for each alternative. Identify both the positive and the negative consequences.
4. Evaluate the consequences. Consider both the positive and negative consequences for each alternative.
5. Ask yourself: Which alternative seems to have more positive consequences? Which seems to have more negative consequences? Then make your decision.

Practicing the Skill

Decisions throughout history have affected the outcome of events, and defined history. Identify the alternatives and describe their consequences for each of the following events that occurred during the time of ancient Rome. Each of these events took place as a result of a decision made by a person or a group of people.

1. The Twelve Tables became the basis for all future Roman law in 451 B.C.
2. During the Third Punic War, in 146 B.C., the Romans burned Carthage.
3. In 27 B.C., Augustus Caesar became Rome's first emperor.
4. The Emperor Theodosius made Christianity the official religion of the Roman Empire in A.D. 392.

5. Beginning in the late A.D. 300s, large numbers of Germanic peoples migrated into the Roman Empire.

Applying the Skill

Use a newspaper or magazine to find a current issue that directly affects your life. Identify the issue, and then review the facts. Identify various alternatives, and then determine the positive and negative consequences for each alternative. Make a sound decision about which alternative would be best for you.

For More Practice

Turn to the Skill Practice in the Chapter Assessment on page 181 for more practice in decision making.

 The **Glencoe Skillbuilder Interactive Workbook**, Level 2 provides instruction and practice in key social studies skills.

Critical Thinking SKILLS

TEACH

Decision Making Direct students to read the skill on page 179. Then help students follow the five-step decision-making process using the example in the textbook.

1. *Choose between taking an art class or a music class.*
2. *The alternatives are to take an art class or a music class.*
3. *Possible consequences for taking art: learning new art techniques, written exams, having work displayed in art show. Possible consequences for taking music: performing a solo, learning a new instrument, performing in another state.*
4. *One student might think it's good to have her work displayed but bad to have written exams. Another student may feel written exams are okay but doesn't want his work displayed.*
5. *Choose one of the classes.*

Additional Practice

📁 Skill Reinforcement Activity 6

GLENCOE TECHNOLOGY

 Glencoe's **Skillbuilder Interactive Workbook, Level 2** This interactive CD-ROM promotes student mastery of key social studies skills.

ANSWERS TO PRACTICING THE SKILL

1. Alternative: Roman law based on unwritten traditions interpreted by patrician judges. Consequence: Judges interpreted these laws to favor their class.
2. Alternative: Leave Carthage standing. Consequence: Carthage would have prospered. Rome would not have had complete control of the western Mediterranean.
3. Alternative: Rome under the rule of feuding generals. Consequence: Without strong leadership, Roman government

and society would have continued to weaken.
4. Alternative: Allow people to worship freely. Consequence: A variety of religions would have continued to flourish in the Roman Empire.
5. Alternative: Roman armies defend the Roman empire from Germanic invasions. Consequence: The Roman Empire could have continued to flourish.

Chapter 6 Assessment

GLENCOE TECHNOLOGY

VIDEODISC
Use MindJogger to review the chapter.

MindJogger Videoquiz

Chapter 6
Disc 1 Side B

  Also available in VHS.

Answers

Using Key Terms

1. g	**3.** a	**5.** c
2. i	**4.** d	

Using Your History Journal

Remind students who was emperor in A.D. 130 (Hadrian). Suggest they use reference books to amplify their knowledge of Rome's domestic and foreign policies at that time.

Reviewing Facts

1. late A.D. 300s: Germanic people migrate into empire; A.D. 378: Visigoths defeat Roman army; A.D. 410: Visigoth leader sacks Rome; A.D. 451: Romans and Visigoths fight Huns; A.D. 453: Attila dies, Huns retreat; A.D. 455: Vandals sack Rome; A.D. 476: Odoacer seizes Rome, makes himself king of Italy
2. used concrete and the arch in buildings, and aqueducts linked Rome and the provinces with roads; Roman scientists also influenced western science
3. Rome ceased to be a republic and became an empire.

WORLD HISTORY Online

Self-Check Quiz

Visit the *World History: The Human Experience* Web site at **worldhistory.glencoe.com** and click on *Chapter 6—Self-Check Quiz* to prepare for the Chapter Test.

Using Key Terms

Write the key term that completes each sentence. Then write a sentence for each term not chosen.

a. indemnity	h. patricians
b. bishop	i. triumvirate
c. plebeians	j. messiah
d. sect	k. pope
e. inflation	l. consul
f. aqueducts	m. dictator
g. republic	

1. After years of rule by kings, the Romans declared their city-state a _____, a form of government in which people elect their leaders.
2. In 60 B.C. Pompey, Crassus, and Julius Caesar formed a _____, a group of three persons with equal power, to control the government.
3. After their defeat, the people of Carthage agreed to pay the Romans a huge _____, or payment for damages.
4. Early Christianity was thought of as a _____, or group, within Judaism.
5. The majority of people in the Roman Republic were _____ —nonaristocratic landowners, merchants, shopkeepers, small farmers, and laborers.

Technology Activity

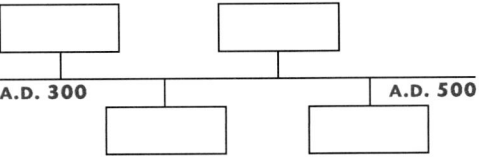

Creating a Multimedia Presentation Search a computerized card catalog or the Internet for information about the early Etruscans. Using multimedia tools, create a short presentation about the Etruscan culture. Incorporate images from the Internet. Before you begin, plan the type of presentation you want to develop and the steps you will take to make the presentation successful. Indicate tools you will need and cite all electronic resources.

Using Your History Journal

Imagine that you are either a young Roman legionary stationed in a remote outpost of the empire in A.D. 130 or you are a friend of the legionary, awaiting his return to Rome. Write a letter describing what you have been doing in the past week.

Reviewing Facts

1. **History** Use a time line like the one below to identify key events in the barbarian invasions of the Roman Empire.

A.D. 300   A.D. 500

2. **Science** Identify Roman achievements in science and engineering, and discuss their impact.
3. **Government** Describe how Rome's political system changed under Augustus Caesar.
4. **Citizenship** Trace the development of Roman law and its influence on Western civilization.
5. **Government** Discuss how Roman governors made provincial cities more like Rome.
6. **Geography** Explain the geographic factors that helped Rome to dominate the Mediterranean.

Critical Thinking

1. **Apply** In what ways did the Roman Republic, in its structure and growth, affect later governments in western Europe and America?
2. **Analyze** What evidence suggests that Roman society was more stable during the republic than during the time of the empire?
3. **Evaluate** In what ways did the Romans' treatment of the peoples they conquered differ from the ways in which other victors usually treated the peoples they conquered? How might Roman attitudes have strengthened the empire?

---

4. The Romans developed one law for citizens and another for noncitizens. Later, the two laws were made one. Their legal system is the basis for those of many Western nations and of the Christian Church.
5. used Roman engineering and architecture; staged Roman amusements
6. Rome's location provided an easy outreach to other areas; Italy's rich soil and mild climate encouraged growth of a civilization.

Critical Thinking

1. It was a model for later republican forms of government. Rome had executive and legislative branches of government.
2. During the republic the family unit was stable, and people held similar values.
3. Romans treated conquered people better, gave citizenship to some, and built cities; winning provincial loyalty.
4. unable to decipher Etruscan words

4. Analyze The vase shown here incorporates the Etruscan alphabet. Why have scholars been unable to tell the full story of Etruscan history?

Geography in History

1. **Location** Refer to the map below. Which area (east or west) was more heavily influenced by Christianity by A.D. 200?
2. **Movement** What major body of water did many early missionaries cross in their efforts to spread Christianity?
3. **Place** According to the map below, which city in western Europe had the largest concentration of Christians by A.D. 200?

The Spread of Christianity

Christian area, A.D. 200
Expansion of Christianity, A.D. 200–400

Black Sea

Rome
Constantinople
Antioch
Mediterranean Sea
Jerusalem
Red Sea
Alexandria

Understanding Themes

1. **Change** How did the Roman government change from the time of the Etruscans to Augustus Caesar?
2. **Conflict** Evaluate a conflict between nations that has occurred in the recent past, and analyze the ways in which it is similar to conflicts between the Romans and other peoples of the Mediterranean region.
3. **Cultural Diffusion** How might Roman roads have helped to foster cultural diffusion?
4. **Innovation** In what way did Constantine's victory in battle in A.D. 312 change the religious life of the Roman Empire? How did his religious policies later shape the future course of religion in Western civilization?
5. **Change** How did Roman architecture reflect the political and social changes that transformed Rome from a republic into an empire?

The United States government operates on the system of checks and balances, in which each branch of government limits the power of the other branches. Did this system operate in the Roman Republic? Why or why not? Use examples from Roman history to support your answer.

Skill Practice

Reread page 160 about the Punic Wars. For each of the three wars, identify the decision that affected the outcome of each. Explain the consequences of each decision, and how they affected the outcome. Examining the decisions and final outcomes of each war will help you see alternatives that might have been available to the decision makers at the time. Discuss some of the alternatives and their consequences for each war. How would history have changed if different decisions had been made?

5. **CHANGE** Roman buildings became monumental in size, reflecting the power and wealth that came with Rome's military conquests.

Students should point out existence of legislature, executive authority, and judicial system under the Republic; however, conquests and the army enhanced the executive's power.

Skill Practice

First Punic War: Roman force secured the Strait of Messina; Consequences: the Roman conquest of many of Carthage's colonies, the development of a large Roman fleet, and Carthage's indemnity payments to the Romans

Second Punic War: Hannibal's campaign in Spain, and his movement into Italy; Consequences: Hannibal's retreat to Africa, Carthage gave up its lands in Spain and paid more indemnity to Rome

Third Punic War: Decisive defeat of Carthage. Consequences: the burning of Carthage, the selling of its population into slavery, the sowing of salt into its soil, and Roman control of the western Mediterranean

? Chapter Bonus Test Question

Ask students: According to French philosopher Blaise Pascal, "Cleopatra's nose, had it been shorter, the whole face of the world would have been changed." How does this statement relate to this chapter? Do you agree with it? (*Antony's marriage to Cleopatra triggered events that led to the end of the republic and the rise of the empire; answers will vary as to the effect of beauty on love and of love on politics.*)

Geography in History
1. east
2. Mediterranean Sea
3. Rome

Understanding Themes
1. **CHANGE** It changed from a republic to an empire.
2. **CONFLICT** Students may choose examples in which nations have rivaled each other for territory or influence, or one nation has expanded (the Soviet Union after World War II, or China today with its holding of Tibet).
3. **CULTURAL DIFFUSION** Ease of travel between cities facilitated trade and travel.
4. **INNOVATION** Constantine credited the Christian God with his victory; and as a result, he became the protector of Christianity. Constantine's policies helped Christianity become the dominant religion of the West.

A complete, 1-page lesson plan is provided for each section in the *Reproducible Lesson Plans* booklet.

Flowering of African Civilizations

CHAPTER RESOURCES

	Reproducible Resources	Multimedia Resources
Chapter Opener	Chapter Themes: Graphic Organizer 7 Historical Significance Chapter Activity 7	MindJogger Videoquiz
Chapter Enrichment	Vocabulary Activity 7* Time Line Activity 7 Mapping History Activity 7 History Simulation 7 Geography and History Activity 7 Source Reading 7 People in World History Profiles 11, 12 World Art and Music Activity 7 Enrichment Activity 7 Critical Thinking Activity 7 Skill Reinforcement Activity 7 Writer's Guidebook, Lesson 7 Performance Assessment Activity 7 Standardized Test Practice Workbook Activity 7 Inclusion for the Social Studies Classroom Strategies and Activities	Focus on World Art Print 12, Fang, Gabon. *Ngi Society Mask* World History and Art Transparency 8, *Gold Pendant Mask* Mapping History Overlay Transparency 7, *African Regions* Chapter Transparency 7 NGS PicturePack Transparencies: Physical Geography of the World, *Africa South of the Sahara* Vocabulary PuzzleMaker Software STV: World Geography, Vol. 2, Africa and Europe: *Africa* World History Primary Source Document Library
Chapter Review/Reteaching	Reteaching Activity 7 Skill Reinforcement Activity 7 Spanish Chapter Summary 7	Chapter 7 Digest Audiocassette, Activity, Test* Vocabulary PuzzleMaker Software Interactive Tutor Self-Assessment Software MindJogger Videoquiz
Chapter Evaluation/Testing	Performance Assessment Activity 7 Chapter 7 Test, Forms A and B	ExamView® Pro Testmaker

* Also available in Spanish

0:00 OUT OF TIME? Assign the Chapter 7 Audiocassettes.

World History Primary Source Document Library

Make History Come Alive!

Engage your students with over 250 easily accessible primary source documents—available on this CD-ROM—that will give them real life insight into the important events of world history.

Block Schedule

Activities that are particularly suited to use within the block scheduling framework are identified throughout this chapter by the following designation.

KEY TO ABILITY LEVELS

Teaching strategies are coded for varying learning styles.

L1 **BASIC** activities for all students
L2 **AVERAGE** activities for average to above-average students
L3 **CHALLENGING** activities for above-average students
LEP **LIMITED ENGLISH PROFICIENCY** activities

Use Glencoe's *Presentation Plus!* multimedia teacher tool to easily present dynamic lessons that visually excite your students. Using Microsoft PowerPoint® you can customize the presentations to create your own personalized lessons.

SECTION RESOURCES

Daily Objectives	Reproducible Resources	Multimedia Resources
Section 1 **Early Africa** Investigate what kinds of societies emerged in early Africa.	Lecture Notes 7-1 Reproducible Lesson Plan 7-1 Guided Reading Activity 7-1* Time Line Activity 7 Source Reading 7 Section Quiz 7-1* Reading Essentials and Study Guide 7-1	Focus on World Art Print 12, Fang, Gabon. *Ngi Society Mask* Section Focus Transparency 7-1 Mapping History Overlay Transparency 7, *African Regions* Vocabulary PuzzleMaker Software Interactive Tutor Self-Assessment Software Testmaker STV: World Geography, Vol. 2: Africa and Europe: *Africa*
Section 2 **Kingdoms in West Africa** Describe how trade was carried out in West Africa.	Lecture Notes 7-2 Reproducible Lesson Plan 7-2 Vocabulary Activity 7* Guided Reading Activity 7-2* Mapping History Activity 7 Geography and History Activity 7 Section Quiz 7-2* Reading Essentials and Study Guide 7-2	Section Focus Transparency 7-2 Chapter Transparency 7 Interactive Tutor Self-Assessment Software Testmaker
Section 3 **African Trading Cities and States** Discuss how areas in East, Central, and South Africa developed as a result of inland and overseas trade.	Lecture Notes 7-3 Reproducible Lesson Plan 7-3 Vocabulary Activity 7* Guided Reading Activity 7-3* Reteaching Activity 7 Enrichment Activity 7 Section Quiz 7-3* Performance Assessment Activity 7 Spanish Chapter Summary 7 Reading Essentials and Study Guide 7-3	Section Focus Transparency 7-3 Mapping History Overlay Transparency 7, *African Regions* Interactive Tutor Self-Assessment Software Testmaker

* *Also available in Spanish*

Chapter Activities

Performance Assessment Activity

Creating a News Report Have students assume the roles of news reporters. They should create a fictitious news event set in a modern-day area once inhabited by early African civilizations. The task is then to create a short news segment of two to three minutes in which they inform the public of the significance and history of the area and how it relates to the event. The report may be submitted on audiotape or videotape, or as a written or oral presentation.

Possible Rubric Features

Accuracy of content information, clarity of presentation, appropriateness of inferences and connections

• *For an additional activity, refer to Activity 7 in the* Performance Assessment Strategies and Activities *booklet.*

ACTIVITY

From the Classroom of...

**Umbisa Kendeli-Gusa
Mifflin International
School
Columbus, OH**

Contemporary Lifestyle of African Teenagers

Have students make a direct link with a school in Africa and communicate one-on-one with an African teenager. This can be facilitated through E-mail, or by calling an African embassy in Washington, D.C., which will provide the link between the schools in Africa and the United States. It is recommended that students communicate with the English-speaking countries south of the Sahara.

Using their knowledge from Chapter 7, have students ask their African counterparts to focus on the way life is now as compared to the way it was in the past. Students should investigate in detail the interaction between the church, parents, the government, and any other agencies that affect the lives of youth from early childhood through adolescence. Students may also wish to inquire about age sets.

Have students write to the local newspaper and share this experience and their new knowledge with the community at large.

MULTIPLE LEARNING STYLES

Verbal/Linguistic
Have students think up words associated with daily life in early African cultures, such as *grasslands, cattle, gods, spirits, family,* and *traditions,* and record their responses on the chalkboard. Each student should write a poem using words from the list.

Visual/Spatial
Students may choose one African culture that they studied and create drawings that focus on a specific art form or aspect of that culture. Bind the artwork together to create a book.

Kinesthetic
Challenge students to create a dance through which they can teach others about some aspect of African culture. Dancing groups may have a narrator who helps interpret the symbolic meaning of their dance steps.

Intrapersonal
Have students write several paragraphs describing how their life would be different if our society were organized on matrilineal lines and stating whether they would prefer this type of social organization.

GLENCOE'S ASSESSMENT ADVANTAGE

Use the following to easily assess student learning in a variety of ways.

- Performance Assessment Strategies and Activities
- Section Quizzes
- Chapter and Unit Tests
- Interactive Tutor Self-Assessment Software
- Testmaker Software
- MindJogger Videoquiz
- SAT/SAT II Test Practice
- worldhistory.glencoe.com

Additional Resources

NATIONAL GEOGRAPHIC SOCIETY — Teacher's Corner

INDEX TO NATIONAL GEOGRAPHIC MAGAZINE

The following articles relate to this chapter:

- "Masai Passage to Manhood," by Carol Beckwith, September 1999.
- "Journey to the Heart of the Sahara," by Donovan Webster, March 1999.

NATIONAL GEOGRAPHIC SOCIETY PRODUCTS AVAILABLE FROM GLENCOE

To order the following, call Glencoe at 1-800-334-7344:

- *MapPack: Africa (Transparency Maps)*
- *STV: World Geography (Videodisc)*
- *Picture Atlas of the World (CD-ROM)*
- *PicturePack: Geography of Africa (Transparencies)*
- *PicturePack: Ancient Africa (Transparencies)*

ADDITIONAL NATIONAL GEOGRAPHIC SOCIETY PRODUCTS

To order the following, call National Geographic at 1-800-368-2728:

- *Physical Geography of the Continents Series: Africa (Video)*
- *Africa (Laminated Desk Maps)*

Access National Geographic's new dynamic MapMachine Web site and other geography resources at:

- http://www.nationalgeographic.com/
- http://www.nationalgeographic.com/maps/

BIBLIOGRAPHY

Literature About the Period
Davidson, Basil. *African Civilization Revisited.* Trenton: Africa World Press, 1991. Presents the story of Africa through a collection of historic chronicles and records.
Readings for the Student
Shinnie, Margaret. *Ancient African Kingdoms.* New York, St. Martin's Press, 1966. Combines archaeological and historical insights into the history of African states.
Readings for the Teacher
Davidson, Basil. *African Kingdoms.* New York, Time-Life Books, 1971. Reevaluation of the achievements of African civilizations from ancient Egypt through A.D. 1500.

WORLD HISTORY Online

Use our Web site as an additional resource. All essential content is covered in the Student Edition.

You and your students can visit the *World History: The Human Experience* Web site at worldhistory.glencoe.com The student text directs students to the Web site for the following options:

- **Chapter Overviews**
- **Student Web Activities**
- **Self-Check Quizzes**

Answers are provided for you in a link entitled "Web Activity Lesson Plan." Additional Web Resources, Interactive Puzzles, and content updates are also available.

Visit the Glencoe Web site at socialstudies.glencoe.com for social studies activities, updates, and links to other resources.

LOCAL OBJECTIVES

_____
_____
_____
_____
_____
_____
_____
_____
_____
_____
_____
_____
_____
_____
_____
_____

Chapter Themes are listed by section on this chapter opening page of the Student Edition. A corresponding theme-based activity is available under "TEACH," and a theme-based question is asked in the Section and Chapter Assessments.

The Storyteller

Historical Setting That the legend of Ogun is still told at festivals in West Africa illustrates how important the knowledge of iron technology was to African peoples. Both the Egyptians and the Kushites knew how to make iron, but they did little with the knowledge for many years. Only when the Kushites were attacked by the Assyrians, who were using superior iron weapons, did the Kushites begin making iron tools and weapons.

Historical Significance

Answers: *They traded their plentiful supplies of salt, gold, copper, iron ore, and ivory to obtain resources and goods they did not have. Through trade traffic, Islamic culture spread through much of Africa.*

Have students use the **Chapter 7 Overview** at <u>worldhistory.glencoe.com</u> as a prereading and postreading exercise for understanding chapter content.

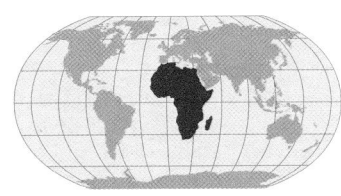

Chapter Themes

▶ **Movement** Migrations of Bantu-speaking people influence Africa's cultural development. *Section 1*

▶ **Cultural Diffusion** Africa's trade contacts with Europe and Asia affect African cultures. *Section 2*

▶ **Innovation** East African city-states develop a new culture based on African and Arab cultures. *Section 3*

The Storyteller

The Yoruba—West Africans living by the Niger River—gather each winter to hear storytellers recount a legend that tells of how their ancestors struggled to clear their land with tools made of wood and soft metal. Even orishas, or gods, could not cut through vines or trees with these tools until the god Ogun appeared, carrying his bush knife.

"He slashed through the heavy vines, felled the trees and cleared the forest from the land.... So [the people] made [Ogun] their ruler.... He built forges for them and showed them how to make spears, knives, hoes, and swords."

Legends such as this describe experiences that early people valued most. Early Africans built civilizations that have left rich traditions for today's peoples.

Historical Significance

How did early Africans use the natural resources of their environment to develop trade networks? What impact did their cultures have on other lands?

1500 B.C.

1000 B.C. Kush becomes an independent kingdom.

500 B.C. Nok civilization reaches its height.

A.D. 1

A.D. 800 Gold/salt trade crosses northern Africa.

A.D. 1500

A.D. 1312 Mansa Musa becomes king of Mali.

182

Location Ask students to locate the following physical features on a wall map or in the Atlas in their texts: the Nile, Niger, Senegal, Zambezi, and Limpopo Rivers; the Red Sea; the Sahara; the Sahel; and the Great Rift Valley. Why didn't Africa's rivers provide easy routes into and out of the interior? *(Many contain rapids and great waterfalls.)* Lead students to notice how few natural harbors are found on the African continent. Discuss the significance of this lack of harbors. *(The lack of protected harbors and navigable rivers would tend to isolate cultures and make land transport the major access route into the interior of the continent.)*

History & Art An early African people left a record of Stone Age life in the frescoes they carved and painted on rock walls at Tassili N'Ajjer Plateau in Algeria. These paintings were preserved by the dry air and the isolation of the plateau. What do these paintings reveal about conditions in the Sahara at the dawn of African culture? *(During this period, the Saharan region was a fertile land with abundant wildlife.)*

✔ **Performance Assessment**

Refer to the activity on page 182C of the Planning Guide.

📁 For an additional activity, refer to Activity 7 in the *Performance Assessment Strategies and Activities* booklet.

History & Art Prehistoric cave art from Tassili N'Ajjer Plateau, Algeria

Using Your History Journal

Have students name each civilization and share what they already know about it. Maps should include a title, legend, and the major African trade routes. Questions should be based on maps.

WORLD HISTORY *Online*

Chapter Overview

Visit the *World History: The Human Experience* Web site at **worldhistory.glencoe.com** and click on **Chapter 7—Chapter Overview** to preview the chapter.

Your History Journal

Consult a historical atlas, and draw an outline map of Africa showing early African kingdoms, the dates when they existed, and major trade routes. Write and answer questions based on the map's data.

GLENCOE TECHNOLOGY

VIDEODISC
Use MindJogger to preview chapter content.

MindJogger Videoquiz

 Chapter 7
Disc 1 Side B

 Also available in VHS.

➕ EXTRA CREDIT PROJECT

Investigate Ask students to select one culture on the African continent to research and investigate further. Specifically, have them find out in what ways the culture's heritage has survived to the present. Have them present their findings to the class, using photographs or other visual aids to accompany their reports.

c. 750 B.C. Kushite kings rule over Egypt.

c. 250 B.C. Merchants from Egypt, Rome, Persia, and India trade with Axum.

A.D. 330 Christianity becomes Axum's official religion.

SECTION THEME

▶ **Movement** Migrations of Bantu-speaking people influence Africa's cultural development.

Guide to Reading

For reading strategies to help students read effectively see pages 12–13. Have students think about the main head as they read the subheads.

Vocabulary Pre-check

 Use the Vocabulary PuzzleMaker for Chapter 7 to create a crossword puzzle to reinforce section terms. **L1 LEP**

Use Vocabulary Activity 7 to introduce vocabulary terms. **L1 LEP**

FOCUS

Section Objective

Investigate what kinds of societies emerged in early Africa.

BELLRINGER
Motivational Activity

 Before taking roll at the beginning of the class period, project Section Focus Transparency 7-1 and have students answer the activity questions. Discuss students' responses.

This activity is also available as a blackline master.

Section 1

Early Africa

Guide to Reading

Read to Find Out
Main Idea *A variety of societies and cultures emerged in early Africa.*

▶ **Terms to Define**
oral tradition, plateau, savanna, matrilineal, age set

▶ **People to Meet**
Piankhi, Ezana, the Nok

▶ **Places to Locate**
Nubia, Kush, Axum

The Storyteller

African oral tradition contained stories full of wisdom, to be enjoyed by all. For example, where did death come from? A myth from Madagascar gave this answer. One day God asked the first couple what kind of death they wanted, one like that of the moon, or that of the banana? The couple was puzzled. God explained: The banana creates young plants to take its place, but the moon itself comes back to life every month. After consideration, the couple prayed for children, because without children they would be lonely, would have to do all the work, and would have no one to provide for. Since that time, human life is short on this earth.

—freely adapted from
The Humanistic Tradition,
Gloria K. Fiero, 1992

Kilimanjaro

Africa's earliest civilizations left few written records of their existence. It was through oral traditions—legends and history passed by word of mouth from one generation to another—that early African peoples communicated knowledge about their culture. Thus, archaeologists and historians have had to rely on legends and artifacts to learn about the culture of African civilizations between 1100 B.C. and A.D. 1500.

Archaeologists have discovered that early African cultures developed technologies and trade based on regional natural resources. Civilizations rose and declined, and were influenced by the movement of people and by the way in which natural resources were developed.

Geography and Environment

Africa's geography and climate are a study in contrasts. Africa, the world's second-largest continent, is three times larger than the United States. Within its huge expanse lie desolate deserts, lofty mountains, rolling grasslands, and fertile river valleys.

Regions of Africa

The African continent can be divided into five regions based on location and environment: North Africa, East Africa, West Africa, Central Africa, and Southern Africa.

North Africa consists of a thin coastal plain, bordering the Mediterranean Sea, and an inland desert area. Coastal North Africa has mild temperatures and frequent rainfall. In contrast, the area south of this green belt is a vast expanse of sand: the Sahara, the world's largest desert. Extending more than 3,500 miles (5,630 km) across the continent, the Sahara is a region of shifting dunes and jagged rock piles.

SECTION RESOURCES

Reproducible Masters
- Lecture Notes 7-1
- Reproducible Lesson Plan 7-1
- Guided Reading Activity 7-1
- Time Line Activity 7
- Source Reading 7
- Section Quiz 7-1
- Reading Essentials and Study Guide 7-1

Transparencies
- Section Focus Transparency 7-1
- Mapping History Overlay Transparency 7, *African Regions*

Multimedia
- Focus on World Art Print 12
- Vocabulary PuzzleMaker Software
- Interactive Tutor Self-Assessment Software
- Testmaker
- STV: World Geography

History & Art Wall painting from the Metropolitan Museum of Art, New York City, New York. **Four late Bronze Age Nubian princes offer rings and gold to an Egyptian ruler.** *In what ways did Nubian culture resemble Egyptian culture?*

The Sahel

South of the Sahara, the continent of Africa is dominated by a great central plateau—a relatively high, flat area known as **the Sahel**. This region receives moderate rainfall to sustain the savannas, or treeless grasslands, that cover the plateau. The savannas south of the Sahara constitute about 40 percent of Africa's land area.

In East Africa, the Sahel descends into a deep crack known as the Great Rift Valley. The valley extends 40 miles (65 km) in width and 2,000 feet (610 m) in depth. It runs 3,000 miles (4,827 km) from the Red Sea in the north all the way to Southern Africa. Rising above the Sahel plateau east of the valley are two mountain peaks—Mount Kenya and Kilimanjaro. Kilimanjaro is Africa's highest mountain, with an elevation of 19,340 feet (5,895 m).

In West Africa, the Sahel descends to a narrow coastal plain that has a relatively unbroken coastline. The major rivers that do flow through the coastal plain—the Niger and the Zaire (Congo)—are navigable only for short distances. The few natural harbors and limited river travel isolated early African civilizations and made foreign invasions difficult in some areas.

Central Africa near the Equator has lush tropical rain forests so thick that sunlight cannot reach the forest floor. Although the rain forest climate is hot and humid, 1,500 miles (2,413 km) farther south the land again turns into a desert—the Kalahari. Still farther south, the Kalahari gives way to a cool, fertile highland in Southern Africa.

The African continent has provided rich resources for its people. Early cultures developed where rainfall was plentiful, or near lakes or along rivers like the Nile.

Nubia and Kush

By 3000 B.C., a people called the Nubians established a kingdom called **Nubia** in the southern part of the Nile River valley in present-day Sudan. The Nubian people mastered the bow and arrow and became warriors. With their military skills, they conquered smaller neighboring communities in the Nile Valley.

The Nubians maintained close contacts with Egypt to the north. Archaeologists have uncovered the tombs of Nubian kings, which contained precious stones, gold, jewelry, and pottery. These are as ornate as those found in Egypt from the same period. Some scholars believe that political ideas, such as monarchy, and various objects, like boats and eating utensils, reveal the early beginnings of the close cultural links between Nubia and Egypt.

By 2000 B.C., the Nubian river civilization had developed into the kingdom of **Kush**. After defeat in warfare, Kush was under Egyptian rule for 500 years. Egyptian pharaohs stationed soldiers in Kush to collect duties on goods moving through the region.

The people of Kush used their location along the Upper Nile River to develop a strong trade

Chapter 7 *Flowering of African Civilizations* **185**

TEACH
Guided Practice

THEME Movement

Ask students what the main reason for the Bantu migration was. *(population increase, leading to a shortage of arable land)* Discuss with students how this reason for moving compares with other reasons. Point out that an inability to provide for themselves and their families, whether due to natural disaster, climate changes, or lack of local resources, is a common reason people migrate.

📖 Focus on World Art Print 12

🔦 Mapping History Overlay Transparency 7

History & Art Egyptian civilization obtained luxury items such as gold, ivory, and ebony as tribute from Nubia to the south.
Answer to Caption: *Like the Egyptians, the Nubians built temples, pyramids, and monuments.*

 NATIONAL GEOGRAPHIC SOCIETY

VIDEODISC
STV: World Geography, Vol 2: Africa and Europe

Side One, Frames 00001-49739
Title: *Africa*
Subject: Geographic contrasts and how people and animals have affected the natural environment of Africa
Ask: What continues to happen geologically in the Great Rift Valley? *(volcanic activity)*

COOPERATIVE LEARNING ACTIVITY

Archaeology Organize the class into groups of three to four students. Have each group select one culture covered in this section—Kush, Axum, Nok, or Bantu—for further study. Each group should work together to write a journal of an imaginary archaeological expedition that has uncovered artifacts from the selected culture. Each member of the group should participate in collecting and recording the information, drawing pictures of the artifacts, and drawing the location of the finds on maps of the site. **L2**

Independent Practice

 Guided Reading Activity 7-1 **L1**

 Time Line Activity 7

Source Reading 7

Geography: Movement Have students imagine that they are West African farmers who moved during the Bantu migrations to the grassland plateau around Lake Chad. Have them write a story about their experiences. Ask them what might have affected them the most—meeting new cultures or adapting to a new environment. **L3**

Global Gourmet

Tropical Africa None of the food crops that today form the staple food supply of the forest regions of Africa was originally native to the continent. Bananas and yams were brought to Africa from Indonesia. Peanuts, maize, and cassava were introduced by Europeans from the Americas. Fou-fou, served in many African countries, is made from cassava root, yams, and rice or cornmeal. It has the consistency of pudding and is served as a main dish.

Visualizing History The kingdom of Axum was located in the northern part of modern Ethiopia. Emperor Haile Selassie was a member of Ethiopia's Amhara dynasty. Generations of this proud people are bound together by their Christian faith and traditional ways of life.
Answer to Caption: *When King Ezana of Axum converted to Christianity during the A.D. 300s, it became a state religion.*

economy. The Kushite cities of Napata and Meroë stood where trade caravans crossed the Nile, bringing gold, elephant tusks, and timber from the African interior. This strategic location brought wealth to the merchants and kings of Kush.

Around 1000 B.C. Kush broke away from Egypt and became politically independent. In time Kush grew strong enough that a Kushite king named **Piankhi** (pee•AHNK•hee) in 724 B.C. led a powerful army from Kush into Egypt and defeated the Egyptians. After this victory, Kushite kings ruled over both Egypt and Kush from their capital at Napata. The city boasted white sandstone temples, monuments, and pyramids fashioned in styles similar to those of the Egyptians.

In 671 B.C. the Assyrians invaded Egypt, easily defeating the Kushites, whose bronze weapons were no match against Assyrian iron swords. The Kushites were forced to leave Egypt and return to their home territory at the bend of the Upper Nile. In spite of their defeat, the Kushites learned from their enemies the technology of making iron. They built a new capital at Meroë that became a major center for iron production. Kush merchants traded iron, leopard skins, and ebony for goods from the Mediterranean and the Red Sea regions. They also conducted business throughout the Indian Ocean area. Meroë's merchants used their wealth to construct fine houses built around a central courtyard and public baths modeled after ones they had seen in Rome.

For about 150 years, the Kushite kingdom thrived. Then a new power—**Axum**, a kingdom located near the Red Sea—invaded Kush and ended Kushite domination of northeastern Africa.

Axum

Because of its location along the Red Sea, Axum also emerged as a trading power. During the 200s B.C., merchants from Egypt, Greece, Rome, Persia, and India sent ships laden with cotton cloth, brass, copper, and olive oil to Axum's main seaport at Adulis. Traders exchanged their goods for cargoes of ivory that the people of Axum hauled from Africa's interior.

Through trade Axum absorbed many elements of Roman culture, including a new religion:

Visualizing History Church of St. Mary of Zion. According to tradition, this church contains the original tablets of Moses, brought by King Menelik I to Axum. Menelik, the legendary founder of Axum's monarchy, was reputed to be the son of the Israelite king Solomon and the Arabian queen of Sheba. *How did Christianity come to Axum?*

186 **Chapter 7** *Flowering of African Civilizations*

Christianity. A remarkable event led to the conversion of Axum's King **Ezana** to Christianity. Shipwrecked off the coast of Ethiopia, two Christians from Syria were picked up and brought to King Ezana's court. Over time they convinced Ezana that he should become a Christian. About A.D. 330 he made Christianity Axum's official religion. At this time, Christianity also became dominant in other areas of northeastern Africa—Kush and Egypt.

Axum declined after the rise of Islam during the A.D. 600s. Its Red Sea ports lost their importance as links to the Mediterranean, and Axum's rulers—confined to the remote interior of East Africa—set up the Christian kingdom of Ethiopia.

South of the Sahara

Between 700 B.C. and 200 B.C., during Axum's rise to power, a West African culture called **the Nok** had already established itself in the fertile Niger and Benue River valleys. In the 1930s archaeologists working in present-day central Nigeria found terra-cotta, or baked clay, figurines that provided evidence of the Nok culture. Working in the Nok sites and other areas of West Africa, archaeologists also unearthed iron hoes and ax-heads. This latter discovery provided evidence that metal production had enabled African cultures south of the Sahara to farm their land more effectively.

As West African farmers used their iron tools to produce more food, the population increased. Arable land became scarce, causing widespread food shortages. Small groups of Africans began to migrate from West Africa to less populated areas. Over about a thousand years a great migration took place.

Bantu Migrations

Historians call this mass movement the Bantu migrations because descendants of the people who migrated throughout the continent share elements of a language group known as **Bantu**. The Bantu migrations did not follow a single pattern. Some villagers followed the Niger or other rivers, settling in one spot to farm for a few years and moving on as the soil became less fertile. Other groups penetrated the rain forests and grew crops along the riverbanks. Still others moved to the highland savannas of East Africa and raised cattle. Groups that settled on the eastern coastal plain grew new crops, such as bananas and yams that had been brought to East Africa by traders from Southeast Asia.

Map Study

Kush and Axum developed along the Nile River and the Red Sea. **Location** Because of its location, Axum was influenced by merchants and traders from what areas of the world?

As people pushed into new areas, they met other African groups that adopted their ways of life. In time, Bantu-speaking peoples became the dominant group in Africa south of the Sahara.

Village Life

Bantu-speaking Africans divided into hundreds of ethnic groups, each with its own religious beliefs, marriage and family customs, and traditions. Close-knit communities formed in which most families were organized into large households that included descendants of one set of grandparents.

Many villages were *matrilineal* societies in which villagers traced their descent through mothers rather than through fathers. However, when a girl married, she joined her husband's family. To compensate for the loss of a member, the bride's family received gifts of iron tools, goats, or cloth from the husband's family.

Student Web Activity 7

Visit the *World History: The Human Experience* Web site at **worldhistory.glencoe.com** and click on **Chapter 7—Student Web Activities** for an activity relating to Nubian women.

Map Study

Answer

Egypt, Greece, Rome, Persia, India, Arabia, and the African interior

Map Skills Practice

Reading a Map Where was Meroë located in relation to Thebes? With respect to Axum? *(south of Thebes; west of Axum)*

POINT

Bantu Migrations

How did the Bantu migrations affect the cultural development of early Africa? *They spread Bantu language to other parts of Africa. Later, the Bantu-speaking peoples became the dominant group in Africa south of the Sahara.*

Have students use the **Chapter 7 Student Web Activity** at **worldhistory.glencoe.com** for in-depth study of ancient Nubian women.

MAKING CONNECTIONS ACTIVITY

Geology When the first reliable world maps were made, several scientists noted the remarkable fit between the west coast of Africa and the east coast of South America. The suggestion was made that the two continents might once have been joined but had broken apart and moved to their present locations. Guide students to discover this for themselves by taking an outline map of the world, cutting out the continents, and fitting them together like a jigsaw puzzle. Then, by researching African and South American landforms, fossils, and natural resources, have students present evidence other than shapes of the continents that might confirm the idea that the continents were once joined. **L2**

ASSESS

Check for Understanding

Assign Section 1 Assessment as homework or as an in-class activity.

📀 Use Interactive Tutor Self-Assessment Software to review Section 1.

Evaluate

 Section Quiz 7-1

📀 Use the Testmaker to create a customized quiz for Section 1.

Reteach

Distribute outline maps of Africa. Have students indicate the name, dates, and approximate location of the following: the kingdoms of Kush and Axum, Nok culture, and the Bantu-speaking peoples. Students may use the text or historical atlases.

📁 Reading Essentials and Study Guide 7-1

Enrich

Have students read traditional African folktales. Have them work in groups of three or four to prepare an oral reading or dramatization of a tale they have read.

CLOSE

Have students create posters illustrating what they have learned about early African civilizations and ways of life. Display on a bulletin board.

 Rebuilding of the Kremlin

Moscow, A.D.1340
Many medieval Russian cities were built around a kremlin, or fortress, surrounded by a wall and a moat. The Moscow Kremlin originally was built of wood in A.D. 1156. In the A.D.1300s it was rebuilt in brick. It is triangular in shape and has four gateways. Its back gate conceals a secret passage to the Moscow River. Italian architects designed some of the Kremlin's impressive towers and cathedrals in the late A.D.1400s.

RUSSIA

Moscow •

Even before marriage, specific jobs were assigned to groups of males and females of a similar age, called age sets. Boys younger than 10 or 12 herded cattle; girls of that age helped their mothers plant, tend, and harvest crops. At about age 12, boys and girls took part in ceremonies initiating them into adulthood. A boy remained with his age set throughout his life. After marriage, a girl joined an age set in her husband's village.

Religious Beliefs

To most Africans, all social laws and traditions were made by a supreme god who created and ruled the universe. The god rewarded those who followed social rules with abundant harvests and healthy children, and punished those who violated tradition with accidents, crop failures, or illness.

Beneath the supreme god, many lesser deities influenced the daily affairs of men and women. These deities were present in natural phenomena such as storms, mountains, and trees. Many Africans also believed that spirits of dead ancestors lived with them and guided their destiny.

The religious beliefs and family loyalties of most Africans maintained village stability. Communities expected their members to obey social rules they believed to have come from the supreme god.

Although African communities relied heavily on religious and family traditions to maintain a stable social structure, outside influences through trade and learning still affected them. North Africans absorbed influences from the Arab world, whereas African people south of the Sahara adapted to Persian, Indian, and later, European influences. From these outsiders, African communities adopted many new customs, ideas, and languages.

The Arts

Various arts developed throughout Bantu-speaking Africa. African sculpture included figures, masks, decorated boxes, and objects for ceremonial and daily use. Most of these items were made of wood, bronze, ivory, or baked clay. The wearing of masks at ceremonial dances symbolized the link between the living and the dead. Those wearing the masks and performing the dances called upon ancestral spirits to guide the community.

Music rich in rhythm was interwoven with the fabric of everyday African life. It included choral singing, music performed at royal courts, and songs and dances for ceremonies. In villages, where many activities were performed by groups, music often provided the motivation and rhythm for various tasks, such as digging ditches or pounding grain. African musicians used a variety of drums as well as harps, flutes, pipes, horns, and xylophones.

Early Africa excelled in oral literature passed down from one generation to another. The stories included histories, fables, and proverbs. Oral literature not only recorded the past but also taught traditions and values.

SECTION 1 ASSESSMENT

Main Idea
1. Use a diagram like the one below to identify the major early African societies.

Early African Societies

Recall
2. **Define** oral tradition, plateau, savanna, matrilineal, age set.
3. **Identify** Sahel, Axum, Kush, the Nok, Piankhi, Nubia, Ezana, Bantu.

Critical Thinking
4. **Applying Information** Explain how trade with the

Mediterranean world influenced the economy of the kingdom of Axum.
Understanding Themes
5. **Movement** How do the migrations of Bantu-speaking peoples in early Africa compare with the Aryan migrations in early South Asia?

188 Chapter 7 *Flowering of African Civilizations*

SECTION 1 ASSESSMENT ANSWERS

1. Nubia, Kush, Axum, and Bantu
2. All terms are defined in the Glossary.
3. Sahel, 185; Nubia, 185; Kush, 185; Piankhi, 186; Axum, 186; Ezana, 187; the Nok, 187; Bantu, 187
4. Mediterranean trade brought many

resources and manufactured goods to Axum and stimulated the local production of ivory.
5. **MOVEMENT** Both migrations took place over long periods. The Bantu migration was peaceful, whereas the

Aryan one was the result of conquest. Both the Aryan and Bantu languages and customs blended with those of native peoples.

A.D. 300 Ghana begins to build a trading empire.

c. A.D. 1275 Mali conquers surrounding territory.

A.D. 1493 Askia Muhammad begins rule in Songhai.

Section 2

Kingdoms in West Africa

Guide to Reading

Read to Find Out
Main Idea *Trade was an important aspect of society in West Africa.*

▶ **Terms to Define**
monotheism, ghana, mosque

▶ **People to Meet**
Sundiata Keita, Mansa Musa, Askia Muhammad

▶ **Places to Locate**
Ghana, Mali, Timbuktu, Songhai

The Storyteller

The poets of Mali preserved the history of their people. Hear one speak: "I teach kings the history of their ancestors so that the lives of the ancients might serve them as an example, for the world is old, but the future springs from the past. My word is pure and free of all untruth…. Listen to my word, you who want to know, by my mouth, you will learn the history of Mali. By my mouth you will get to know the story of the ancestor of great Mali, the story of him who … surpassed even Alexander the Great…. Whoever knows the history of a country can read its future."

Horn player, Benin

—from Sundiata: An Epic of Old Mali in The Humanistic Tradition, Gloria K. Fiero, 1992

A diverse environment provided rich natural resources for the early kingdoms of West Africa. Africans living in this region between A.D. 300 and A.D. 1500 mined gold and other mineral resources. An active trade developed between them and peoples outside West Africa who practiced a religion called Islam. Islam preached monotheism, or the belief in one God, and spread throughout the Middle East, North Africa, and Spain during the A.D. 600s and A.D. 700s. Through their trade contacts with Muslims, the followers of Islam, African cultures gradually adopted Islamic cultural elements such as language and religion.

Kingdom of Ghana

The kingdom of **Ghana** became one of the richest trading civilizations in West Africa due to its location midway between Saharan salt mines and tropical gold mines. Between A.D. 300 and A.D. 1200 the kings of Ghana controlled a trading empire that stretched more than 100,000 square miles (260,000 sq. km). They prospered from the taxes they imposed on goods that entered or left their kingdom. Because the ghana, or king, ruled such a vast region, the land became known by the name of its ruler—Ghana.

There was two-way traffic by caravan between cities in North Africa and Ghana. Muslim traders from North Africa sent caravans loaded with cloth, metalware, swords, and salt across the western Sahara to northern settlements in Ghana. Large caravans from Ghana traveled north to Morocco, bringing kola nuts and farming produce. Ghanaian gold was traded for Saharan salt brought by Muslim traders.

Salt was an important trade item for the people of Ghana. They needed salt to preserve and flavor their foods. Using plentiful supplies of gold as a

Chapter 7 *Flowering of African Civilizations* **189**

▶ **Cultural Diffusion** Africa's trade contacts with Europe and Asia affect African cultures.

Guide to Reading

For reading strategies to help students read effectively see pages 12–13.

Vocabulary Pre-check

 Use the Vocabulary PuzzleMaker for Chapter 7 to create a crossword puzzle to reinforce section terms. **L1 LEP**

Use Vocabulary Activity 7 to introduce vocabulary terms. **L1 LEP**

FOCUS

Section Objective

Describe how trade was carried out in West Africa.

BELLRINGER Motivational Activity

 Before taking roll at the beginning of the class period, project Section Focus Transparency 7-2 and have students answer the activity questions. Discuss students' responses.

This activity is also available as a blackline master.

TEACH

Guided Practice

THEME Cultural Diffusion

Develop a working definition of the term *cultural diffusion* by asking students to think of ways they have changed as a result of contact with other persons or groups. *(the transfer of religion, customs, traditions, arts, and language from one people to another)* How did trade contacts with Arabs affect the development of African cultures? *(The Arabs brought with them the religion of Islam, written language, and other elements of Islamic culture that were adopted by West Africans.)* **L1 LEP**

Economics List the products the West Africans exchanged for Arab goods. *(gold, kola nuts, and farm produce)* Ask what Arab goods they chiefly traded for. *(cloth, metalware, swords, salt)* Challenge students to name items people use today that come from Africa. *(gold, diamonds for jewelry, agricultural products such as cocoa and coffee, petroleum, and carvings)* Discuss ways early and modern African trading patterns are similar. *(Africans still trade precious metals and agricultural products for items they need.)* **L3**

 Chapter Transparency 7

Who?What?Where?When?

The Silent Trade The trade exchange described by Masudi is also known as "the silent trade." It has been described by other writers, including Herodotus, as the method often used by peoples who have no common language.

medium of exchange, Ghanaian merchants traded the precious metal for salt and other goods from Morocco and Spain.

Masudi, a Muslim traveler, writing about A.D. 950, described how trade was conducted:

> ❝ The merchants … place their wares and cloth on the ground and then depart, and so the people of [Ghana] come bearing gold which they leave beside the merchandise and then depart. The owners of the merchandise then return, and if they are satisfied with what they have found, they take it. If not, they go away again, and the people of [Ghana] return and add to the price until the bargain is concluded. ❞

Ghana reached the height of its economic and political power as a trading kingdom in the A.D. 800s and A.D. 900s. The salt and gold trade moving through Ghana brought Islamic ideas and customs to the kingdom. Muslim influence increased and many Ghanaians converted to Islam.

At the end of the A.D. 1000s, an attack on the Ghanaian trade centers by **the Almoravids**, a Muslim group from North Africa, led to the decline of Ghana as a prosperous kingdom. Groups of Ghanaians broke away to form many small Islamic states.

Kingdom of Mali

Mali, one of the small states to break away from Ghana, became a powerful kingdom that eventually ruled much of West Africa. The word *Mali* means "where the king resides" and is an appropriate name for a kingdom that gained much of its power and influence from its kings. **Sundiata Keita**, one of Mali's early kings, defeated his leading rival in A.D. 1235 and began to conquer surrounding territories. By the late A.D. 1200s, Mali's territory included the old kingdom of Ghana.

Images of the Times

Africa's Religious Heritage

Religion played a central role in the development of African cultures. Islam became the dominant religion in the north.

The Great Mosque at Timbuktu
Founded around A.D. 1100, the city of Timbuktu became a major center of trade and site of an important Islamic school.

Altar of the Hand, Benin
Beginning in the A.D. 1200s the kingdom of Benin emerged as a wealthy trading state. The *oba*, or king, became the political, economic, and spiritual leader of the people.

190

Images of the Times
Africa's Religious Heritage

Africa's indigenous religious beliefs were not universal but ethnic in scope. Thus, each ethnic group had its own name for the supreme being, its own account of the creation and the origin of death, and its own magic, initiation rites, and rituals. Nearly all Africans, however, believed in a supreme being that was the origin of all things and presided over a realm of lesser beings and a host of animate and inanimate forces. These religious beliefs and practices permeated every phase of life on the African continent.

Sundiata worked to bring prosperity to his new empire. He restored the trans-Saharan trade in gold and salt that had been interrupted by the Almoravid attacks and he restored agricultural production. Sundiata ordered soldiers to clear large expanses of savanna and burn the grass that had been cleared to provide fertilizer for crops of peanuts, rice, sorghum, yams, beans, onions, and grains. With the benefit of rainfall, agriculture flourished in Mali. With larger tracts of land under cultivation, farmers produced surplus crops that Mali's kings collected as taxes.

Mali's greatest king was **Mansa Musa**, who ruled from A.D. 1312 to A.D. 1332. By opening trade routes and protecting trade caravans with a powerful standing army, Musa maintained the economic prosperity begun by Sundiata. He also introduced Islamic culture to Mali.

A Muslim himself, Musa enhanced the prestige and power of Mali through a famous pilgrimage to Makkah in A.D. 1324. Arab writers report that Musa traveled in grand style. He took with him 12,000 slaves, each dressed in silk or brocade and carrying bars of gold. Musa gave away so much gold on his journey that the world price of gold fell. At Makkah, Musa persuaded a Spanish architect to return with him to Mali. There the skilled architect built great mosques—Muslim houses of worship—and other fine buildings, including a palace for Musa in the capital of **Timbuktu** (TIHM•BUHK•TOO). Timbuktu became an important center of Muslim art and culture mainly through the efforts of Mansa Musa, who encouraged Muslim scholars to teach at his court. Two hundred years later, the North African scholar and traveler Hassan ibn Muhammad (known in the West as Leo Africanus) described Timbuktu's continuing intellectual brilliance:

> ❝ Here are great store of doctors, judges, priests, and other learned men that are bountifully maintained at the king's cost and charges. And hither are brought diverse manuscripts or written books out of [North Africa], which are sold for more money than any other merchandise. ❞

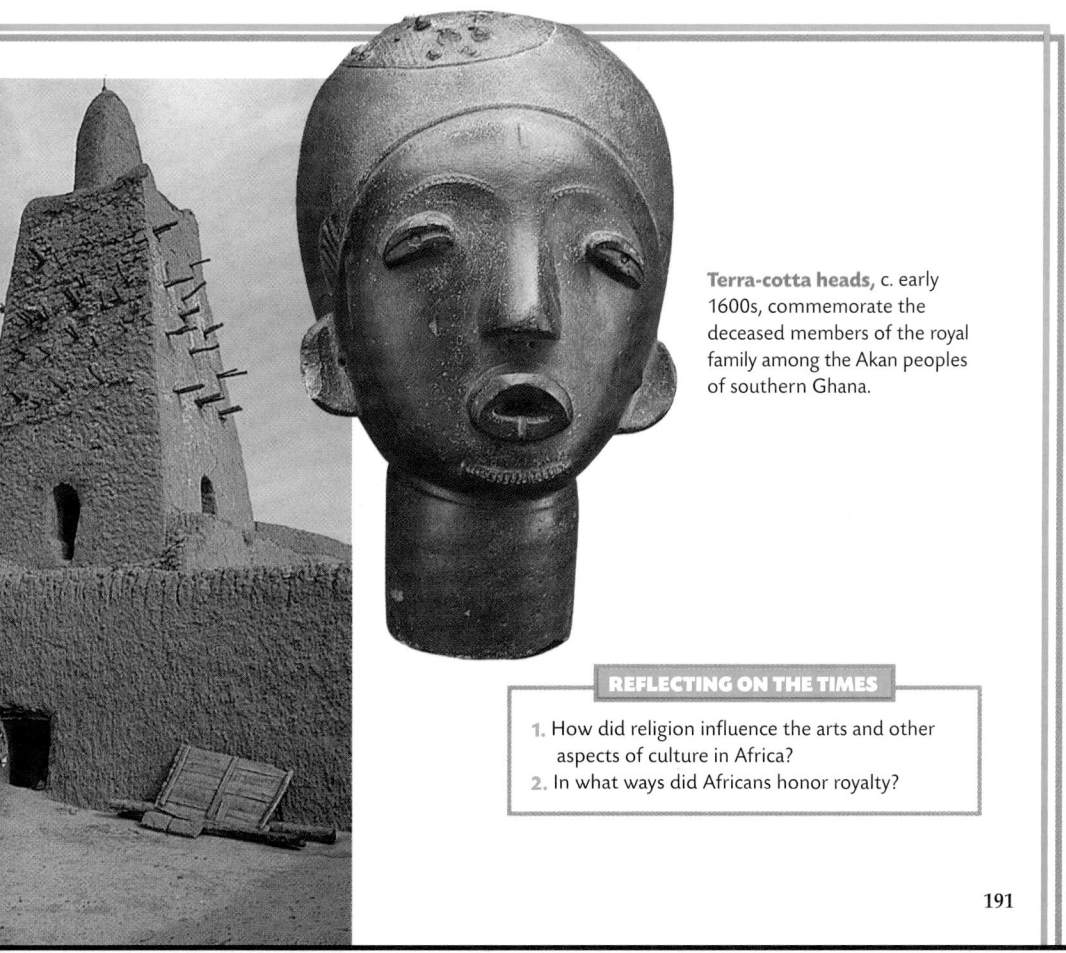

Terra-cotta heads, c. early 1600s, commemorate the deceased members of the royal family among the Akan peoples of southern Ghana.

REFLECTING ON THE TIMES

1. How did religion influence the arts and other aspects of culture in Africa?
2. In what ways did Africans honor royalty?

191

Chapter 7 Section 2

Independent Practice

📁 Guided Reading Activity 7-2 **L1**

📁 Mapping History Activity 7

📁 Geography and History Activity 7

A&E HOME VIDEO.

The following videotape program is available from Glencoe:

• **The Last Elephants of Timbuktu**

To find classroom resources to accompany this video, check the following home page:
A&E Television:
http://www.aetv.com

ASSESS

Check for Understanding

Assign Section 2 Assessment as homework or as an in-class activity.

💽 Use Interactive Tutor Self-Assessment Software to review Section 2.

Evaluate

📁 Section Quiz 7-2

💽 Use the Testmaker to create a customized quiz for Section 2.

ANSWERS TO REFLECTING ON THE TIMES

1. Africans made artifacts with religious themes and built places of worship. Islam especially promoted the growth of education.
2. African rulers were portrayed on artifacts; other members of royalty were also commemorated in the arts: for example, the Akan made terra-cotta heads of deceased members of their royal family.

☐ NATIONAL GEOGRAPHIC PICTURING HISTORY

TEACH

Tell students that the main religion of the Republic of Mali is still Islam. Today 90 percent of the people are of that faith. Another mosque has been built recently in Niomo, Mali, as a monument to Islam. What might have attracted a traveler like Battuta to Timbuktu? *(It was on an important caravan route and was a center of Islamic culture.)*

Who?What?**Where?**When?

Timbuktu was an important site for the gold-salt trade in the A.D. 1300s. Today it is the administrative center of Mali. Small salt caravans are still evident, but no gold trade exists. The city has air service, but it is more accessible by camel or boat.

CURRICULUM CONNECTION

GEOGRAPHY

Mali is within three climatic zones: the Sudanic of the south with temperatures of 75° to 86°F; the Sahel with temperatures of 73° to 97°F; and the Saharan area with temperatures ranging from 117°F in the daytime to 39°F at night.

West African Empire

This turreted mosque in Djenné, Mali, harks back to the A.D. 1300s, when the town thrived as a center of trade and Islamic learning. A masterpiece of African-Muslim architecture, the great mosque boasts massive mud ramparts broken by patterns of protruding beams. Its tall spires are crowned not with the traditional Islamic crescent but with ostrich eggs, symbol of fertility and fortune. Every year, after the rainy season, the town turns out 4,000 people to replaster the walls of the mosque with their bare hands. The job is done in a day.

Almost two centuries before Columbus set off for the Americas, an Arab traveler and author named Ibn Battuta began his travels in A.D. 1325 to the far corners of the Islamic world—from North Africa China and back. He returned home three decades l. as one of history's great travelers and travel writ His journeys totaled 75,000 miles (121,000 km three times the distance logged by his European decessor, Marco Polo. Ibn Battuta's final jour brought him here to the West African empire of M where he praised the piety of the Muslims. Batt sought out the ruler, Mansa Sulayman, at his cap but was not impressed with the king's generos Mansa Sulayman, he wrote, "is a miserly kir Battuta also traveled to Timbuktu—about a hunc years before the city really started to prosper. At height, in the A.D. 1500s, the city could boast th universities and perhaps 50,000 residents. ⊕

192   **Chapter 7**   *Flowering of African Civilizations*

After Mansa Musa died in A.D. 1332, the empire came under attack by Berbers, a people living in the Sahara region to the north. They raided Mali and captured Timbuktu. From the south, warriors from the rain forest also attacked Mali. Inside the kingdom, people living in the **Songhai** region of the Niger River valley resented losing control over their region and rebelled against the empire. By the middle of the A.D. 1500s, Mali had split into several independent states.

Kingdom of Songhai

The rebellious Songhai, who were skilled traders, farmers, and fishers, were led by strong leaders. During the late A.D. 1400s their ruler, Sunni Ali, fought many territorial wars and managed to conquer the cities of Timbuktu and Djenné, expanding his empire to include most of the West African savanna. Sunni Ali was Muslim, but when he died, rule fell to his non-Muslim son. Songhai's Muslim population overthrew Ali's son and brought a Muslim ruler to the throne.

Under the new ruler, **Askia Muhammad**, the Songhai Empire reached the height of its glory. Ruling from A.D. 1493 to A.D. 1528, Askia Muhammad divided Songhai into five huge provinces, each with a governor, a tax collector, a court of judges, and a trade inspector—very much like the government structure of China in the A.D. 1400s. The king maintained the peace and security of his realm with a cavalry and a navy. Timbuktu was a center of Muslim learning.

Devoted to Islam, Muhammad introduced laws based on the teachings of the holy book of Islam, the Quran (kuh•RAHN). Lesser crimes were sometimes overlooked, but those who committed major crimes such as robbery or idolatry received harsh punishments. Askia Muhammad appointed Muslim judges, assuring that Islamic laws would be upheld.

In A.D. 1528 Askia Muhammad was overthrown by his son. A series of struggles for the throne followed, leading to a weakened central government. Around A.D. 1589 the rulers of Morocco sent an army across the Sahara to attack Songhai gold-trading centers. Moroccan soldiers, armed with guns and cannons, easily defeated the Songhai forces fighting with only swords, spears, and bows and arrows. By A.D. 1600 the Songhai Empire had come to an end.

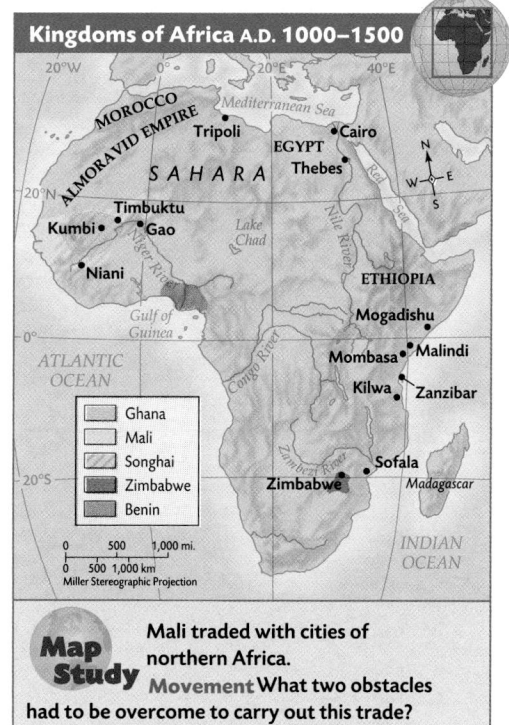

Kingdoms of Africa A.D. 1000–1500

Ghana
Mali
Songhai
Zimbabwe
Benin

Map Study Mali traded with cities of northern Africa. **Movement** What two obstacles had to be overcome to carry out this trade?

Map Study

Answer
the Sahara and attacks by the Almoravids

Map Skills Practice

Reading a Map Have students determine how far it is across the Sahara from Timbuktu north to Morocco. *(about 1,000 miles [1,700 km])* Discuss how long such a journey might have taken when traveling on foot or by camel.

Reteach

Hold a class discussion in which students compare the bartering practices of the Ghanaian and Arab traders with their own experiences buying and selling.

 Reading Essentials and Study Guide 7-2

Enrich

Have students use library resources to find interesting details and insights about early African leaders such as Sundiata Keita, Mansa Musa, Sunni Ali, or Askia Muhammad. Students may prepare oral or written reports on their findings.

CLOSE

Hold a class discussion about why the kingdoms of West Africa declined. *(Almoravid invaders, leadership struggles, interruption of vital trade routes, death of strong leaders)*

SECTION 2 ASSESSMENT

Main Idea
1. Use a diagram like the one below to list items traded in West Africa.

Trade in West Africa

Recall
2. **Define** monotheism, ghana, mosque.
3. **Identify** the Almoravids, Sundiata Keita, Mansa Musa, Askia Muhammad.

Critical Thinking
4. **Analyzing Information** Why was trade vital to the economies of the West African kingdoms?

Understanding Themes
5. **Cultural Diffusion** How did trade with other parts of the world influence the development of West African cultures between A.D. 900 and A.D. 1500?

SECTION 2 ASSESSMENT ANSWERS

1. gold, salt, metalware, swords, farm products, and cloth
2. All terms are defined in the Glossary.
3. Almoravids, 190; Sundiata Keita, 190; Mansa Musa, 191; Askia Muhammad, 193

4. They needed salt to preserve their food and could procure it only through trade.
5. **CULTURAL DIFFUSION** North African Arab merchants brought the teachings of the Quran and other Islamic customs and learning to West

Africa. Islamic scholars came to live there. Arab traders helped convert many West Africans to Islam.

A.D. 500

A.D. 1000

A.D. 1500

A.D. 900 Arab and Persian merchants trade in East Africa.

c. A.D. 1200 Kilwa thrives as East African coastal city-state.

c. A.D. 1300 People of Karanga build stone-walled fortresses.

SECTION THEME

▶ **Innovation** East African city-states develop a new culture based on African and Arab cultures.

Guide to Reading

For reading strategies to help students read effectively see pages 12–13.

Vocabulary Pre-check

🔲 Use the Vocabulary PuzzleMaker for Chapter 7 to create a crossword puzzle to reinforce section terms. **L1 LEP**

📁 Use Vocabulary Activity 7 to introduce vocabulary terms. **L1 LEP**

FOCUS

Section Objective

Discuss how areas in East, Central, and Southern Africa developed as a result of trade.

BELLRINGER
Motivational Activity

Before taking roll at the beginning of the class period, project Section Focus Transparency 7-3 and have students answer the activity questions. Discuss students' responses.
📁 This activity is also available as a blackline master.

Section 3

African Trading Cities and States

Guide to Reading

Read to Find Out
Main Idea *Areas in East, Central, and Southern Africa developed as a result of inland and overseas trade.*

▶ **Terms to Define**
monopoly, multicultural

▶ **Places to Locate**
Kilwa, Malindi, Mombasa, Sofala, Zanzibar, Karanga, Great Zimbabwe

The Storyteller

The first trained engineer ever to see the ruins of the Great Zimbabwe reported: "For fifty miles I saw the ruins…. The ruins are principally terraces, which rise up continually from the base to the apex of all the hills…. The terraces are all made very flat and of dry masonry…. The way the ancients seem to have levelled off the contours of the various hills around which the water courses are laid is very astonishing, as they seem to have been levelled with as much exactitude as we can accomplish with our best mathematical instruments."

Ruins of the Great Zimbabwe

—from *The Mystery of the Great Zimbabwe*, Wilfrid Mallows, 1984

194 Chapter 7 *Flowering of African Civilizations*

---

*D*uring the same time that West African kings ruled their empires, important trading communities developed along the coast of East Africa and in the interior of Central and Southern Africa. Inland African kingdoms mined copper and iron ore and traded these minerals and ivory with city-states that had developed along the East African coast. There Muslim traders brought cotton, silk, and Chinese porcelain from India and Southeast Asia to exchange for the products from Africa's interior. As in West Africa, trade contacts with the Muslim world enabled East African coastal areas to adopt the religion of Islam and Islamic cultural practices.

East Africa

As early as 500 B.C., coastal areas of East Africa were trading with the Arabian Peninsula and South Asia. Using dhows (Arab sailboats), East Africans sailed with the monsoon winds across the stretch of Indian Ocean separating Africa from India. By the A.D. 900s Arab and Persian merchants had settled on the East African coast and controlled the trade there. Traders from the interior of Africa brought ivory, gold, iron, and rhinoceros horn to the east coast to trade for Indian cloth and Chinese porcelain.

Coastal City-States

By A.D. 1200 small East African trading settlements had become thriving city-states taxing the goods that passed through their ports. The port of **Kilwa** had a virtual monopoly, or sole control or ownership, of the gold trade with the interior. **Malindi** and **Mombasa**, both ports farther north on the coast, were also important centers, as was **Sofala**, a port in what is present-day Mozambique. The iron mined in the surroundings of these three

---

city-states was widely used in the Arabian Peninsula and South Asia.

The island of **Zanzibar** was also an important center of trade. Sailors from the islands of Southeast Asia as well as India and China came to Zanzibar in search of ivory and gold, which was brought to Zanzibar ports from the coastal city-states of East Africa.

Blending of Cultures

By the A.D. 1300s, the city-states of East Africa had reached the height of their prosperity. They had become truly multicultural centers—populated by a variety of cultural groups. Within each city-state, Islamic and African cultures blended. For the most part, Arab and Persian merchants ruled the trading states. They converted many Africans to Islam.

Arab merchants married local women who had converted to Islam. Families having members with African and Islamic cultural backgrounds began speaking Swahili, a Bantu language that included Arabic and Persian words. The people of the East African coastal city-states also developed an Arabic form of writing that enabled them to record their history.

East African rulers were either Arab governors or African chieftains. They used coral from Indian Ocean reefs to build mosques, palaces, and forts.

The Bantu Kingdoms

The Indian Ocean trade was not limited to the coastal trading states. It reached far inland, contributing to the rise of wealthy Bantu kingdoms in Central and Southern Africa. The inland kingdoms mined rich deposits of copper and gold. During the A.D. 900s, traders from the East African coast made their way to the inland mining communities in Central Africa and began an active trade among the people living there. The traders brought silk and porcelain from China, glass beads from India, carpets from Arab lands, and fine pottery from Persia. They traded these goods for minerals, ivory, and coconut oil. They also acquired enslaved Africans for export.

Great Zimbabwe

The people of **Karanga**, a Bantu kingdom located on a high plateau between the Zambezi and Limpopo Rivers, built nearly 300 stone-walled fortresses throughout their territory between A.D.

Economics

East African Trading Cities

Port of Mombasa, Kenya

In the A.D. 700s Arab immigrants arrived on East Africa's coast to set up a flourishing trade in gold, ivory, and tortoise shells. Descendants of the Arab immigrants and the local African inhabitants became known as the Swahili (an Arabic word for "people of the coast"). By the late A.D. 1100s, thriving Swahili port cities, such as Kilwa, Malindi, and Mombasa, served as trading links between the gold and ivory producers of East Africa's interior and traders from India, Ceylon (Sri Lanka), and China. Cotton, porcelain, and pottery were the major imports. By the 1500s China's withdrawal from foreign trade and the coming of European rule to East Africa contributed to a serious decline in East Africa's international trade.

Today, the East African coast has become an important link in the global trading network. While preserving its old town and traditions, the modern city of Mombasa ranks as one of Africa's busiest seaports and the second-largest city in the nation of Kenya. It handles most of the international shipping of Kenya as well as that of the neighboring, land-locked nations of Uganda, Rwanda, and Burundi, to which it is linked by rail. East African agricultural products, such as coffee, tea, sisal (a plant fiber used for twine), cotton, sugar, and coconuts are exported from Mombasa, as well as petroleum products produced from the foreign oil refined at Mombasa's refinery.

Linking Past and Present ACTIVITY

Compare and contrast Mombasa's trade in the A.D. 1200s with that of the city today. What factors have contributed to any changes?

Chapter 7 *Flowering of African Civilizations* **195**

TEACH

Guided Practice

THEME Innovation
Ask students to identify some aspects of the East African or Bantu cultures that represented an innovation. **L1**

Independent Practice
Guided Reading Activity 7-3 **L1**

ASSESS

Check for Understanding
Assign Section 3 Assessment as homework or as an in-class activity.

Use Interactive Tutor Self-Assessment Software to review Section 3.

Evaluate
Section Quiz 7-3

Use the Testmaker to create a customized quiz for Section 3.

Linking Past and Present

East African Trading Cities

The organization of seagoing trade at first was largely in the hands of the visiting Arabs, Chinese, Persians, and Indians because the Africans had no ships of their own. Merchant trading cities such as Kilwa and Sofala, however, controlled early trade between interior and coastal Africa.

ANSWER
During the A.D. 1200s, Mombasa exported gold and ivory to Indian Ocean ports in India, Ceylon, and China in exchange for cotton, porcelain, and pottery. Today, Mombasa is a thriving modern city in a global trading network, exporting agricultural and petroleum products. Modern transportation has made Mombasa a vital outlet for Kenya and landlocked nations in East Africa.

Visualizing History The Great Zimbabwe is located in what was once the British colony of Rhodesia. When Rhodesia became independent, it took Zimbabwe as its new name.
Answer to Caption: *political and religious center; fortress*

Reteach

Have students make a resource map that presents the information in the section.

 Reteaching Activity 7

 Reading Essentials and Study Guide 7-3

Enrich

Have students research to learn more about the archaeological excavation of the Great Zimbabwe or similar stone building sites at Khami, Natetali, and Mapungubwe. Encourage artistic students to create visual representations.

 Enrichment Activity 7

CLOSE

Have students create a chart that compares the achievements of the early African cultures with another civilization that they have studied. Headings should include *Religion, Agriculture, Architecture, Literature, Trade Networks,* and *Science and Technology.*

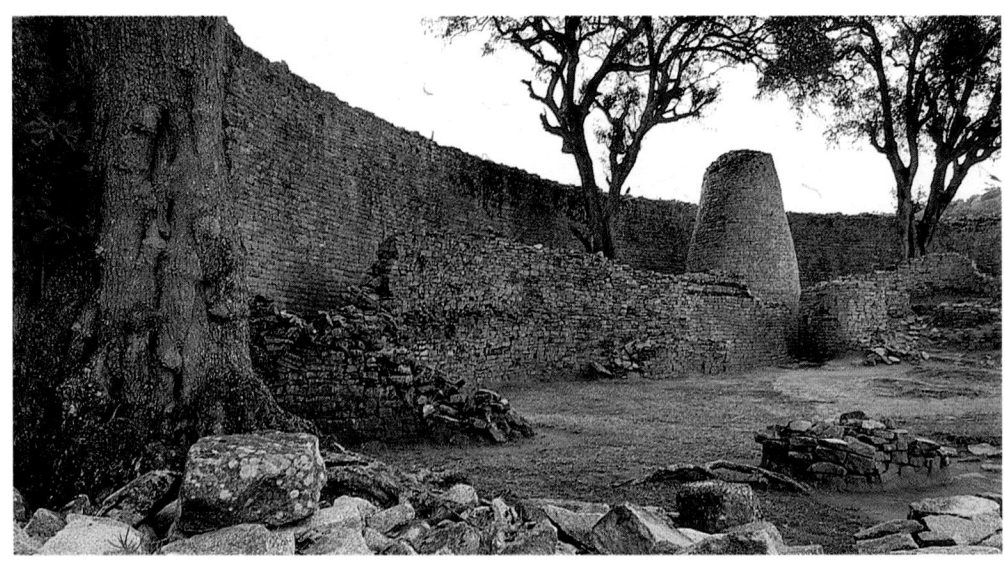

Visualizing History This view shows the circular stone ruins of the Great Zimbabwe with an exterior wall more than 800 feet in circumference. *What functions did this "stone house" serve?*

1000 and A.D. 1500. The largest was called the **Great Zimbabwe**—meaning "stone house"—and served as the political and religious center of the kingdom. The oval stone wall of the Zimbabwe enclosure was 30 feet (9.15 m) high. Within the wall was a maze of interior walls and hidden passages that protected the circular house of the Zimbabwe chief. Near the house, archaeologists have uncovered a platform with several upright stones that may have been the place where the chief held court.

Territorial Divisions

For nearly five centuries, Karanga and the other Bantu states grew wealthy from their control of the chief routes between the gold mines and the sea. However, during the A.D. 1400s, Bantu states in Southern Africa struggled in civil wars that brought disorder to the kingdoms and disrupted trade.

The Changamire Empire became stronger than the Monomotapa Empire. Changamire rulers took over Great Zimbabwe and built the fortress's largest structures. At the same time, European explorers arrived along the African coasts. Eager to control the sources of gold, ivory, and copper, the Europeans posed challenges to the survival of the African civilizations in the continent's interior.

SECTION 3 ASSESSMENT

Main Idea
1. Use a chart like the one below to show how inland and overseas trade affected areas in East, Central, and Southern Africa.

East Africa	Central Africa	Southern Africa

Recall
2. **Define** monopoly, multicultural.
3. **Identify** Kilwa, Malindi, Mombasa, Sofala, Zanzibar, Karanga, Great Zimbabwe.

Critical Thinking
4. **Synthesizing Information** If you were an Arab merchant visiting an East African coastal city-state in the A.D. 1300s, what aspects of the culture would be familiar or unfamiliar to you?

Understanding Themes
5. **Innovation** What new aspect of cultural life developed in the city-states of East Africa as a result of African and Middle Eastern contact?

---

196 **Chapter 7** *Flowering of African Civilizations*

SECTION 3 ASSESSMENT ANSWERS

1. East Africa: trading settlements became city-states; city-states became multicultural centers. Central and Southern Africa: Bantu states grew rich from control of chief routes between gold mines and sea.
2. All terms are defined in the Glossary.
3. Kilwa, 194; Malindi and Mombasa, 194; Sofala, 194; Zanzibar, 195; Karanga, 195; Great Zimbabwe, 196
4. Sample answer: The Arabs and Africans in the coastal city-states who practice Islam and speak Swahili would make you feel at home. Some of the exotic goods from the interior of Africa might seem strange.
5. **INNOVATION** the Swahili language, a Bantu language with a written form

Interpreting Point of View

Suppose you are interested in seeing a new science fiction movie, but you are hearing mixed reviews from your friends. People often have different opinions about the same people, events, or issues because they look at them from different points of view.

Learning the Skill

A point of view is a set of beliefs and values that affects a person's opinion. Many factors affect an individual's point of view, including age, sex, racial or ethnic background, economic class, and religion. In order to determine the accuracy of a description or the objectivity of an argument, first you must identify the speaker's point of view.

To interpret point of view in written material, read the material to identify the general subject. Then gather background information on that author that might reveal his or her point of view. Identify aspects of the topic that the author chooses to emphasize or exclude. Look for emotionally charged words such as *cruel, vicious, heartrending, drastic.*

If you are uncertain of an author's point of view, read a selection on the same topic by another author with a different background. Comparison may make both points of view clear.

Practicing the Skill

Read the following excerpt from Ross E. Dunn's book *The Adventures of Ibn Battuta* and then answer these questions.

1. What is the general subject of the excerpt?
2. What do you know about Ibn Battuta that might reveal his point of view?
3. What emotionally charged words and phrases indicate his point of view?
4. Which aspects of Islamic leadership are praised and which are not?

❝ Sulayman came close to matching his brother's [Mansa Musa's] reputation for Islamic leadership and piety. Moreover, he ruled Mali in prosperity and peace.

He was the sort of king from whom Ibn Battuta had come to expect an honorable and large-hearted reception. . . . Later, when Ibn Battuta had returned to his house, one of the scholars called to tell him that the sultan [Sulayman] had sent along the requisite welcoming gift.

'I got up, thinking that it would be robes of honor and money, but behold! It was three loaves of bread and a piece of beef fried in *gharti* [shea butter] and a gourd containing yoghurt. When I saw it I laughed, and was long astonished at their feeble intellect and their respect for mean things.' ❞

According to Dunn, Ibn Battuta found Sulayman to be "a miserly king from whom no great donation is to be expected," while Mansa Musa had been "generous and virtuous."

Applying the Skill

In a newspaper, find an editorial, column, or a letter to the editor that expresses a point of view that conflicts with your own. Write a brief paragraph analyzing the author's point of view and compare it to your point of view. Explain why you agree or disagree with the viewpoint of the author.

The Columbus Dispatch
An Independent Newspaper Serving Ohio Since July 1, 1871
JOHN F. WOLFE, Publisher, President and CEO
MICHAEL F. CURTIN, Editor
EDITORIALS
Ballot issue
Workers' comp to steal thunder from schools

For More Practice

Turn to the Skill Practice in the Chapter Assessment on page 199.

The **Glencoe Skillbuilder Interactive Workbook**, Level 2 provides instruction and practice in key social studies skills.

TEACH

Interpreting Point of View
Distribute copies of two reviews of the same movie, one favorable, one critical. After students have read both, ask them what the reviews reveal about the two critics' different perspectives, or points of view. Then have students read the skill and complete the practice questions.

Additional Practice
📁 Skill Reinforcement Activity 7

GLENCOE
TECHNOLOGY

Glencoe's **Skillbuilder Interactive Workbook, Level 2**
This interactive CD-ROM promotes student mastery of key social studies skills.

ANSWERS TO PRACTICING THE SKILL

1. a comparison of the Islamic rulers Mansa Musa and his brother Sulayman
2. Ibn Battuta had received generous gifts from Sulayman's brother, Mansa Musa, so Battuta had expected the same kinds of gifts from Sulayman.
3. *honorable, largehearted, but behold!, I laughed and was long astonished, feeble intellect, respect for mean things*
4. Aspects praised: Ruled in prosperity and peace. Aspects not praised: Sulayman is said to have a feeble intellect and is called a miserly king.

—WORLD HISTORY—
Online

Have students use the **Chapter 7 Self-Check Quiz** at worldhistory.glencoe.com to prepare for the Chapter Test.

GLENCOE TECHNOLOGY

VIDEODISC
Use MindJogger to review the chapter.

MindJogger Videoquiz

Chapter 7
Disc 1 Side B

  Also available in VHS.

Answers

Using Key Terms
1. c   3. d   5. a
2. f   4. g

Using Your History Journal
Encourage students to notice how many modern African states have taken the names of early kingdoms.

Reviewing Facts
1. North Africa: thin, coastal plain; Sahara desert. East Africa: Sahel descends into Great Rift Valley; east of valley are mounts Kenya and Kilimanjaro. West Africa: Sahel descends to narrow coastal plain; few natural harbors; limited river travel. Central Africa: tropical rain forests; south of rain forests is desert. Southern Africa: fertile highland
2. through oral traditions and artifacts
3. Located in central Nigeria, the Nok produced terra-cotta figurines and iron tools.
4. it taxed all goods that entered or left its territory
5. introduced Islamic culture to Mali; reopened trade routes and protected caravans

---

WORLD HISTORY
Online

Self-Check Quiz

Visit the *World History: The Human Experience* Web site at **worldhistory.glencoe.com** and click on *Chapter 7—Self-Check Quiz* to prepare for the Chapter Test.

Using Key Terms

Write the key term that completes each sentence. Then write a sentence for each term not chosen.

a. multicultural   f. oral traditions
b. matrilineal   g. monopoly
c. plateau   h. age sets
d. savanna   i. monotheism
e. ghana   j. mosque

1. Africa south of the Sahara includes a large central _____—a relatively high, flat area called the Sahel.
2. Early African peoples communicated knowledge about their culture through _____ —legends and history passed by word of mouth from one generation to another.
3. Much of Africa's landscape is covered by ____, or treeless grasslands.
4. The city-state of Kilwa had a near _____, or sole control, of the gold trade along the East African coast.
5. A society is said to be _____ when it has people of many different cultural backgrounds.

Technology Activity

Using a Computerized Card Catalog Choose a modern-day African country to research. Use a computerized card catalog to find information on that country from its early history to the present. Then create a bulletin board about that country, including an illustrated time line of significant events of the country's history. Display current information about culture, national resources, demographics, and government.

Using Your History Journal

On your map of Africa draw in the modern states where each ancient kingdom that you identified was located. Use the map of Africa in the Atlas of your text.

Reviewing the Facts

1. **Geography** Use a chart like the one below to identify key geographical features of North, East, West, Central, and Southern Africa.

North Africa	East Africa	West Africa	Central Africa	Southern Africa

2. **History** Discuss how archaeologists and historians have learned about early Africa.
3. **Culture** Identify the Nok people, their location, and their major cultural achievements.
4. **Economics** Explain Ghana's wealth.
5. **History** Summarize the major accomplishments of Mansa Musa in Mali.
6. **Culture** Name the city that became a major center of trade and learning in Mali.
7. **Government** Explain how Askia Muhammad kept order and control over his huge empire.
8. **Economics** List the products traded in the coastal city-states of East Africa.
9. **Culture** State how the language of Swahili originated.
10. **Geography** Name the three areas of Africa that prospered from the Indian Ocean trade.
11. **Culture** Identify Great Zimbabwe and discuss its importance to Karanga.

Critical Thinking

1. **Apply** How do climate and geography affect the development of a civilization?

---

6. Timbuktu
7. divided his kingdom into five provinces, each with its own governor, tax collector, court, and trade inspector
8. copper, iron ore, gold, ivory, rhinoceros horn, cotton, silk, and fine porcelain
9. From the intermarriage of Arab merchants and women from local Bantu-speaking groups on the east coast of Africa
10. trading communities along the coast and

inland kingdoms in Central and South Africa
11. the stone fortress that served as the political and religious center of the Karanga kingdom

Critical Thinking
1. They determine which crops can be grown, whether a community has resources useful to trade, and whether travel and exchanges with other civilizations are easy.
2. People encountered new environments and

2. **Evaluate** The Bantu languages changed as people moved into central, eastern, and southern regions of Africa. Why do you think this happened?

3. **Making Comparisons** Compare the causes for the decline of each of the three West African kingdoms.

4. **Synthesize** Discuss how family and social life in a typical Bantu-speaking village was organized around A.D. 1000.

5. **Analyze** What two cultural values does this artifact of a West African horn player reveal?

Horn player, Benin

Understanding Themes

1. **Movement** How did population movements affect the development of early Africa?

2. **Cultural Diffusion** What were major political and cultural developments in each of the following early African territories: Nubia, Axum, Songhai, Kilwa, and Karanga?

3. **Innovation** What two examples can you give that illustrate how the peoples of coastal East Africa and of the interior of Central Africa and Southern Africa made creative use of their resources?

Linking Past and Present

1. Gold helped make Ghana a powerful empire. Name another natural resource that has made African countries wealthy today.

2. Ancient peoples adapted to their environments in order to survive. Explain ways we adapt today.

3. How do strong central governments affect a nation's economic and social structures? What factors often lead to a weakening of central governments?

Skill Practice

Read the following African proverbs carefully. Then answer the questions for each proverb.
- Familiarity breeds contempt; distance breeds respect.
- When you follow in the path of your father, you learn to walk like him.

1. What is the general subject of each proverb?

2. Describe the point of view expressed in each proverb.

3. Do you agree with the point of view? Make sure you are able to support your answer.

Geography in History

1. How does the continent of Africa compare with the United States in land area?

2. Refer to the map below. Why has communication and travel always been difficult between the northwest African interior and northeast Africa?

3. Why has Egypt had nearly continual contact with peoples of Asia and Europe?

Africa

Songhai: well-organized government, Islamic legal reforms; Kilwa: city-state based on gold trade, Swahili language; Karanga: fortresses, ruled by chiefs.

3. **INNOVATION** Some used coral to produce mosques and palaces, others used stone to build Great Zimbabwe.

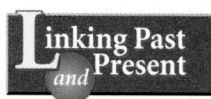

Linking Past and Present

1. diamond and gem mining

2. air conditioning, burn oil and gas for heat; build dams to irrigate

3. They may improve a nation's economy but may impose rigid controls; conflicts between groups can weaken a government.

Skill Practice

Proverb 1:

1. maintaining just the right distance from your surroundings

2. If you keep some distance between yourself and something/someone, you maintain your respect and positive feelings about it/them.

3. Answers will vary.

Proverb 2:

1. influences from your family

2. If you follow what your family teaches, you will be like them.

3. Answers will vary.

Geography in History

1. It is three times larger.

2. separated by the Sahara

3. Egypt had ports on the Mediterranean and Red Seas.

objects, which needed new words; they adopted the words from the peoples they met.

3. Ghana: Islamic peoples from the north attacked Ghanaian trade centers, Mali: attacked from north and south and faced internal rebellion; Songhai: the central government weakened and Morocco attacked

4. Households included descendants of one set of grandparents. Males and females joined age sets. When a girl married, she joined her husband's family and age set.

5. love of music, artistic skill

Understanding Themes

1. **MOVEMENT** They brought Bantu peoples, language, and culture to most of Africa south of the Sahara.

2. **CULTURAL DIFFUSION** Nubia: kingdom with pyramids, iron production; Axum: trading power, a center of Christianity;

Chapter Bonus Test Question

Ask students: How might the history of Africa have differed if the rivers of the West African coastal plain were easily navigable? *(Kingdoms might have had more outside contact and been attacked by foreign invaders more often.)*

A complete, 1-page lesson plan is provided for each section in the *Reproducible Lesson Plans* booklet.

India's Great Civilization

CHAPTER RESOURCES

	Reproducible Resources	Multimedia Resources
Chapter Opener	Chapter Themes: Graphic Organizer 8 Historical Significance Chapter Activity 8	MindJogger Videoquiz

Chapter Enrichment	Vocabulary Activity 8*
	Time Line Activity 8
	Mapping History Activity 8
	History Simulation 8
	Geography and History Activity 8
	Source Reading 8
	People in World History Profiles 13, 14
	World Art and Music Activity 8
	Enrichment Activity 8
	Critical Thinking Activity 8
	Skill Reinforcement Activity 8
	Performance Assessment Activity 8
	Standardized Test Practice Workbook
	   Activity 8
	Inclusion for the Social Studies
	   Classroom Strategies and Activities
		World History and Art Transparency 9, *Siva Nataraja*
		Chapter Transparency 8
		NGS PicturePack Transparency Set: *Ancient India*
		Vocabulary PuzzleMaker Software
		NGS PictureShow CD-ROM: *India and China*
		World Music: Cultural Traditions, Lesson 7
		World History Primary Source Document Library

Chapter Review/Reteaching	Reteaching Activity 8 Skill Reinforcement Activity 8 Spanish Chapter Summary 8	Chapter 8 Digest Audiocassette, Activity, Test* Vocabulary PuzzleMaker Software Interactive Tutor Self-Assessment Software MindJogger Videoquiz
Chapter Evaluation/Testing	Performance Assessment Activity 8 Chapter 8 Test, Forms A and B	ExamView® Pro Testmaker

* Also available in Spanish

0:00 OUT OF TIME? Assign the Chapter 8 Audiocassettes.

World History Primary Source Document Library

Make History Come Alive!

Engage your students with over 250 easily accessible primary source documents—available on this CD-ROM—that will give them real life insight into the important events of world history.

Block Schedule

Activities that are particularly suited to use within the block scheduling framework are identified throughout this chapter by the following designation.

KEY TO ABILITY LEVELS

Teaching strategies are coded for varying learning styles.

L1   **BASIC** activities for all students
L2   **AVERAGE** activities for average to above-average students
L3   **CHALLENGING** activities for above-average students
LEP   **LIMITED ENGLISH PROFICIENCY** activities

Use Glencoe's *Presentation Plus!* multimedia teacher tool to easily present dynamic lessons that visually excite your students. Using Microsoft PowerPoint® you can customize the presentations to create your own personalized lessons.

Interactive Lesson Planner

Planning has never been easier! Using this CD-ROM, organize your week, month, semester, or year with all the help you need. The **Interactive Lesson Planner** gives you access to all of the blackline masters that accompany *World History: The Human Experience.*

SECTION RESOURCES

Daily Objectives	Reproducible Resources	Multimedia Resources
Section 1 **Origins of Hindu India** Describe how the cultures of the Aryans and the peoples they conquered developed into the culture of Hindu India.	Lecture Notes 8-1 Reproducible Lesson Plan 8-1 Guided Reading Activity 8-1* Time Line Activity 8 Source Reading 8 Geography and History Activity 8 Section Quiz 8-1* Reading Essentials and Study Guide 8-1	Section Focus Transparency 8-1 World History and Art Transparency 9, *Siva Nataraja* Chapter Transparency 8 NGS PicturePack Transparency Set: *Ancient India* Vocabulary PuzzleMaker Software Interactive Tutor Self-Assessment Software Testmaker
Section 2 **Rise of Buddhism** Analyze why Buddhism appealed to many people in India, Southeast Asia, and East Asia.	Lecture Notes 8-2 Reproducible Lesson Plan 8-2 Vocabulary Activity 8* Guided Reading Activity 8-2* History Simulation 8 Section Quiz 8-2* Reading Essentials and Study Guide 8-2	Section Focus Transparency 8-2 Interactive Tutor Self-Assessment Software Testmaker
Section 3 **Indian Empires** List the cultural achievements of the Mauryan and Gupta Empires.	Lecture Notes 8-3 Reproducible Lesson Plan 8-3 Vocabulary Activity 8* Guided Reading Activity 8-3* Mapping History Activity 8 Reteaching Activity 8 Enrichment Activity 8 Section Quiz 8-3* Performance Assessment Activity 8 Spanish Chapter Summary 8 Reading Essentials and Study Guide 8-3	Section Focus Transparency 8-3 Interactive Tutor Self-Assessment Software Testmaker NGS PictureShow CD-ROM: *India and China* World Music: Cultural Traditions, Lesson 7

* Also available in Spanish

Chapter Activities

✔ Performance Assessment Activity

A Guide for India Have students take the roles of advisers hired to help educate employees of a company that is transferring many Americans to a newly opened branch in India. The company is very hopeful that the two cultures will be able to respect each other in order to create a well-functioning corporate operation. The students should work in groups to develop guides to be used in a course for the American employees. Included should be the information and concepts the students feel are most vital to developing true understanding. Students should work under the assumption that Hinduism is by far the dominant religion in India today.

Possible Rubric Features
Accuracy of content information, concept attainment, clarity, decision-making skills, collaborative skills

• *For an additional activity, refer to Activity 8 in the* Performance Assessment Strategies and Activities *booklet.*

ACTIVITY

From the Classroom of...

Mary Beth Craddock
Grandview Senior High School
Grandview, MO

Indian Wedding
Point out that in India many marriages are arranged through a family decision, just as they were centuries ago. Have students create an ad for a bride to be placed by a family in a newspaper in Mumbai (or other major Indian city). Discuss what qualities the family might advertise. *(education, caste,* jati*)* Also discuss the importance of the dowry (bride's price) the bride brings to the marriage. Then ask students what qualities might be stressed in an ad for a groom.

Have students use library resources to make a plan for a wedding. Have them detail who would come; what kinds of music, dance, and food would be involved; what the bride and groom would wear; what kinds of gifts would be given; and what rituals would be followed. If there are Indian families in the community, they might be asked for advice.

Conclude by having students generate a class list of qualities that make for good relationships and families. Discuss how arranged marriages might help or hinder building good family relationships. Have students consider to what degree parents in the United States indirectly have a role in arranging marriages.

MULTIPLE LEARNING STYLES

Verbal/Linguistic
Have one or more students lead a discussion on the early caste system in India. Suggest that they compare and contrast the ranking of social classes in a modern democracy.

Visual/Spatial
Have students illustrate, draw, paint, sketch, sculpt, or construct an image of the Buddha. This can be either representational (similar to existing Buddha images) or purely imaginative.

Kinesthetic
Have students make flash cards for their classmates to use in identifying and studying the terms, people, and places introduced in this chapter.

Intrapersonal
Point out that many people might find unappealing the idea of having one's marriage partner or future career largely determined by their family and the social position to which one is born. Have students consider all sides of these issues and write a paragraph in defense of one of these practices.

GLENCOE'S ASSESSMENT ADVANTAGE

Use the following to easily assess student learning in a variety of ways.

• Performance Assessment Strategies and Activities
• Section Quizzes
• Chapter and Unit Tests
• Interactive Tutor Self-Assessment Software
• Testmaker Software
• MindJogger Videoquiz
• SAT/SAT II Test Practice
• worldhistory.glencoe.com

Additional Resources

NATIONAL GEOGRAPHIC SOCIETY

Teacher's Corner

INDEX TO NATIONAL GEOGRAPHIC MAGAZINE

The following articles relate to this chapter:

- "India," by Geoffrey C. Ward, May 1997.
- "Banaras: India's City of Light," by Santha Rama Rau, February 1986.

NATIONAL GEOGRAPHIC SOCIETY PRODUCTS AVAILABLE FROM GLENCOE

To order the following, call Glencoe at 1-800-334-7344:

- *MapPack: Asia (Transparency Maps)*
- *Picture Atlas of the World (CD-ROM)*
- *PictureShow: Ancient Civilizations: India and China (CD-ROM)*
- *PicturePack: Ancient India (Transparencies)*
- *PictureShow: Geography of Asia (CD-ROM)*

ADDITIONAL NATIONAL GEOGRAPHIC SOCIETY PRODUCTS

To order the following, call National Geographic at 1-800-368-2728:

- *Physical Geography of the Continents Series: Asia (Video)*
- *Asia (Laminated Desk Maps)*

Access National Geographic's new dynamic MapMachine Web site and other geography resources at:

- http://www.nationalgeographic.com/
- http://www.nationalgeographic.com/maps/

BIBLIOGRAPHY

Literature About the Period
van Buitenen, J. A. B., trans. and ed. *The Mahabharata: I. The Book of the Beginning.* Chicago: University of Chicago Press, 1973. Indian and Hindu culture and history are represented in this epic Sanskrit poem that is a collection of legends, romance, theology, and ethics.

Readings for the Student
DeRoin, Nancy, ed. *Jataka Tales: Fables from the Buddha.* Boston: Houghton Mifflin, 1975. A retelling of 30 tales told by the Buddha.

Readings for the Teacher
Miller, Barbara Stolar, trans. *The Bhagavad Gita: Krishna's Council in Time of War.* New York: Columbia University Press, 1986. An Indian culture and Sanskrit literature scholar's translation of the philosophical dialogue between Krishna and Arjuna.

WORLD HISTORY Online

Use our Web site as an additional resource. All essential content is covered in the Student Edition.

You and your students can visit the *World History: The Human Experience* Web site at worldhistory. glencoe.com The student text directs students to the Web site for the following options:

- **Chapter Overviews**
- **Student Web Activities**
- **Self-Check Quizzes**

Answers are provided for you in a link entitled "Web Activity Lesson Plan." Additional Web Resources, Interactive Puzzles, and content updates are also available.

Visit the Glencoe Web site at socialstudies. glencoe.com for social studies activities, updates, and links to other resources.

LOCAL OBJECTIVES

_____
_____
_____
_____
_____
_____
_____
_____
_____
_____
_____
_____
_____
_____
_____
_____

CHAPTER THEMES

Chapter Themes are listed by section on this chapter opening page of the Student Edition. A corresponding theme-based activity is available under "TEACH," and a theme-based question is asked in the Section and Chapter Assessments.

S̃toryteller

Historical Setting The *Mahabharata*, a national epic of India and the world's longest poem, depicts heroes and their adventures and was the basis for the Hindus' religious, moral, and political duties. Some of these beliefs are still prevalent today. Ask students what other epic poems in world literature they know. *(Answers may include:* Iliad, Odyssey, Aeneid, Beowulf, Song of Roland.*)*

Historical Significance

Answers: *India's early civilization saw the introduction of Sanskrit; the evolution of hymns, epics, and holy books (Vedas); and the development of the caste system. Hinduism and Buddhism emerged in early India.*

— WORLD HISTORY —
Online

Have students use the **Chapter 8 Overview** at worldhistory. glencoe.com as a prereading and postreading exercise for understanding chapter content.

India's Great Civilization

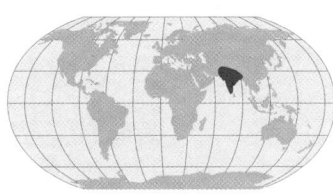

Chapter Themes

▶ **Movement** Aryans invade the Indian subcontinent and bring new ideas and practices. *Section 1*
▶ **Innovation** Hinduism and Buddhism emerge and become the dominant religions in much of Asia. *Section 2*
▶ **Cultural Diffusion** Mauryan and Gupta rulers bring unity to northern India and encourage cultural achievements. *Section 3*

S̃toryteller

The *Mahabharata, an epic poem of ancient India, relates an amazing event. A battle raged, but the prince Arjuna did not want to fight. After all, among his foes were relatives. Arjuna took his case to the god Krishna: "O Krishna, when I see my own people … eager for battle, my limbs shudder, my mouth is dry, my body shivers, and my hair stands on end.… I can see no good in killing my own kinsmen."*

Krishna answered, "As a [warrior], your duty is to fight a righteous battle.… Arise, O Arjuna, and be determined to fight. Get ready for battle without thought of pleasure and pain, gain and loss, victory and defeat."

As a warrior, Arjuna understood Krishna's words. A warrior must fight. It was his duty.

Historical Significance

What were the achievements of India's early civilization? What religions emerged from early India that have shaped the cultures of Asia and, in many ways, the rest of the world?

1500 B.C.		500 B.C.		A.D. 500

184 B.C.
The Mauryan Empire collapses.

c. 1500 B.C.
Aryans invade India.

c. 1000 B.C.
Aryan priests prepare *Rig-Veda*.

527 B.C.
Siddhartha Gautama introduces Buddhism.

A.D. 310 Gupta dynasty begins.

200

GEOGRAPHY CONNECTION

Location This chapter focuses on events that occurred in the Indian peninsula and parts of Central and Southeast Asia. Have students locate the Indus and Ganges Rivers, the Khyber Pass, the Deccan Plateau, and the Himalayas in the Atlas in their text and/or on a large wall map. Ask them to point out the following major cities and to specify their location within India: Delhi *(north central)*, Calcutta *(east)*, Mumbai *(west central)*, Hyderabad *(south central)*, Madras *(southeast)*, Bangalore *(south central)*.

Visualizing History Vishnu was usually depicted as blue in color, wearing a crown, and having four hands. He was often shown riding an eagle, as in this picture. Some worshipers regarded him as the supreme deity.

✔ **Performance Assessment**

Refer to the activity on page 200C of the Planning Guide.

📁 For an additional activity, refer to Activity 8 in the *Performance Assessment Strategies and Activities* booklet. 📦

Using Your History Journal

Students' charts should include the four religions with the greatest number of adherents worldwide. They are: Christianity (1,900,174,000), Islam (1,033,453,000), Hinduism (764,000,000), and Buddhism (338,621,000). 📦

Visualizing History Hindus communicated their beliefs through poems, tales, songs, and art. This painting of Vishnu on a bird honors one of the three main gods of Hinduism.

WORLD HISTORY Online

Chapter Overview

Visit the *World History: The Human Experience* Web site at **worldhistory.glencoe.com** and click *Chapter 8—Chapter Overview* to preview the chapter.

Your History Journal

Using a recent edition of an almanac, make a chart of the world's major religions, including the number of people who today are adherents of each religion.

GLENCOE TECHNOLOGY

 VIDEODISC Use MindJogger to preview chapter content.

MindJogger Videoquiz

 Chapter 8 Disc 1 Side B

 Also available in VHS.

➕ **EXTRA CREDIT PROJECT**

Quotation Booklet In this chapter students learn about the beginnings of two of the world's major religions: Hinduism and Buddhism. Have students compile a group of 20 quotations from the sacred texts of the world's four major religions: five quotations from the Holy Bible (Christianity), five quotations from the Quran (Islam), five quotations from the Vedas and/or *Upanishads* (Hinduism), and five quotations from the Sutras (Buddhism). If several students work on this project, have them combine their efforts to create a small booklet of the quotations they find. 📦

1500 B.C.   1000 B.C.   500 B.C.

c. 1200 B.C.
Vedic Age begins.

c. 1000 B.C.
Rig-Veda records
Aryan legends.

c. 700 B.C.
Religious thinkers
compile the *Upanishads.*

SECTION THEME

▶ **Movement** Aryans invade the Indian subcontinent and bring new ideas and practices.

Guide to Reading

For reading strategies to help students read effectively see pages 12–13. Have students think about the main head as they read the subheads.

Vocabulary Pre-check

 Use the Vocabulary PuzzleMaker for Chapter 8 to create a crossword puzzle to reinforce section terms. **L1 LEP**

Use Vocabulary Activity 8 to introduce vocabulary terms. **L1 LEP**

FOCUS

Section Objective

Describe how the cultures of the Aryans and the peoples they conquered developed into the culture of Hindu India.

BELLRINGER
Motivational Activity

Before taking roll at the beginning of the class period, project Section Focus Transparency 8-1 and have students answer the activity questions. Discuss students' responses.

This activity is also available as a blackline master.

Section 1

Origins of Hindu India

Guide to Reading

Read to Find Out

Main Idea *The cultures of the Aryans and the peoples they conquered developed into the culture of Hindu India.*

▶ **Terms to Define**
rajah, epic, *varna*, *jati*, dharma, reincarnation, karma, ahimsa

▶ **People to Meet**
the Aryans

▶ **Places to Locate**
Hindu Kush, Ganges Plain

The Storyteller

The bleeding warrior lay helpless with a broken arm. Only proper words and medicines could save him now. The priest, sprinkling him with water and herbs chanted: "He who drinks you, medicine, lives. Save the man. You are mender of wounds inflicted by club, arrow, or flame. Mend this man. O most beautiful one, go to the fracture." Next would come the grass and termite mud mixture to drink, then water in a cow's horn, and pepper-corns to eat. The warrior breathed quietly, thankful that he had found a healer who knew the ritual.

—adapted from *Religious Healing in the Veda,* Kenneth Zysk, 1985

Hindu Kush

Into the Indus River valley raced horse-drawn chariots carrying tall, light-skinned warriors. These warriors, known as **the Aryans**, were an Indo-European group from areas north of the Black and Caspian Seas. The invasion began around 1500 B.C. For several generations, waves of Aryans swept through passes in the mountains known as the **Hindu Kush** into the Indus River valley and from there into northern India.

Aryans

After conquering the people of the Indus River valley, the Aryans moved southeast into the **Ganges Plain**. There they subdued the local inhabitants and developed a new civilization that eventually spread over much of South Asia. Aspects of this civilization endure today.

Ways of Life

The Aryans were loosely organized into tribes of nomadic herders. Each tribe was led by a rajah, or chief. Ancient Aryan legends and hymns describe people who delighted in waging war, gambling on chariot races, and singing and dancing at festivals. Cattle were the basis of their diet and economy, even serving as money. Wealth was measured in cattle, and so the Aryans raided each other's herds. They were often at war.

The fertile Indus Valley was ideal for farming, and the Aryans soon settled down into an agricultural way of life. Dozens of Aryan words describe cattle, indicating their continued prominence in Aryan life. Cattle provided meat, fresh milk, and ghee, or liquid butter. The Aryans also hunted game and butchered sheep and goats from their herds. Later, their herds would be considered so sacred that a ban was placed on eating meat. The

---

Reproducible Masters
- Lecture Notes 8-1
- Reproducible Lesson Plan 8-1
- Guided Reading Activity 8-1
- Time Line Activity 8
- Source Reading 8
- Geography and History Activity 8

- Section Quiz 8-1
- Reading Essentials and Study Guide 8-1

Transparencies
- Section Focus Transparency 8-1
- World History and Art Transparency 9
- Chapter Transparency 8
- Ancient India

Multimedia
 Vocabulary PuzzleMaker Software
- Interactive Tutor Self-Assessment Software
- Testmaker

Aryans also ate cucumbers, bananas, and barley cakes.

Men dominated the Aryan world. Although a woman had some say in choosing a husband, the man she married expected no challenge to his authority. Even so, women took part in religious ceremonies and social affairs, and they were allowed to remarry if they were widowed—freedoms they would lose in the centuries to come. Both girls and boys from families of high rank attended school, where they learned Aryan traditions.

Language and Traditions

As a nomadic people, the Aryans had no written language. Sanskrit, their spoken language, evolved slowly and became one of the major languages of India. As part of the great Indo-European language family, Sanskrit has many of the same root words as English, Spanish, French, and German. It also includes many words from the languages of the peoples living in India before the Aryan invasions.

The Aryan warrior-herders sang rousing hymns and recited epics, long poems celebrating their heroes. For centuries these hymns and poems were passed by word of mouth from generation to generation. Families of warriors and priests were responsible for preserving this oral heritage. Over and over they repeated the legends, striving for complete accuracy.

Eventually, the Aryans developed a written form of Sanskrit. Priests collected the hymns, poems, legends, and religious rituals into holy books known as Vedas (VAY•duhz), or "Books of Knowledge," which formed the basis of Aryan religious practices.

Indeed, the Vedas are extremely valuable sources of knowledge, for without them historians would know little about the Aryans. Unlike the Indus River valley people, the Aryans left no artifacts or structures. Whatever we know of their life and culture we know from the Vedas. Indeed, Indian history from 1200 B.C. to 500 B.C. is known as the Vedic Age. The oldest of the four Vedas, the *Rig-Veda*, dates from around 1000 B.C. It records legends that tell us about Aryan life. The *Rig-Veda* is one of the world's oldest religious texts still in use.

Social Structure

The Vedas reveal the complex social system of ancient India. The invading Aryans brought a system of four main social classes, or *varnas*. At first the warriors, called Kshatriyas (KSHA•tree•uhz), were the most honored *varna*. They were followed by the priests, or Brahmans; merchants, artisans, and farmers, called Vaisyas (VYSH•yuhz); and

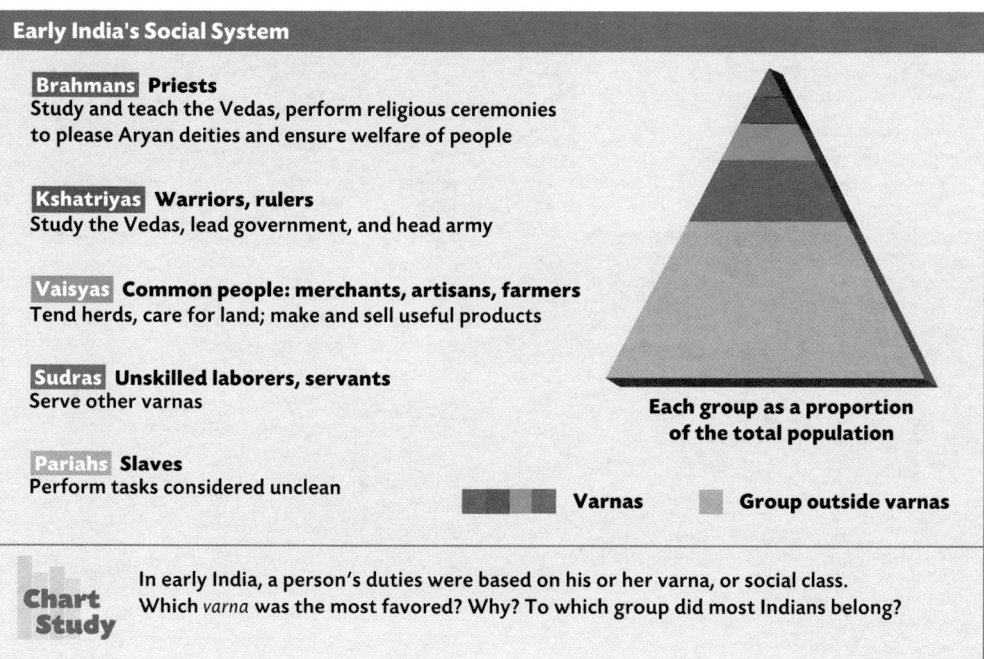

Early India's Social System

Brahmans Priests
Study and teach the Vedas, perform religious ceremonies to please Aryan deities and ensure welfare of people

Kshatriyas Warriors, rulers
Study the Vedas, lead government, and head army

Vaisyas Common people: merchants, artisans, farmers
Tend herds, care for land; make and sell useful products

Sudras Unskilled laborers, servants
Serve other varnas

Pariahs Slaves
Perform tasks considered unclean

Each group as a proportion of the total population

■ Varnas ■ Group outside varnas

Chart Study In early India, a person's duties were based on his or her varna, or social class. Which *varna* was the most favored? Why? To which group did most Indians belong?

TEACH

Guided Practice

THEME Movement

Have students locate India on a map (in the text Atlas or other resource) and trace the route of conquering Aryans from central Asia to the northwestern part of the South Asian subcontinent (*today's Pakistan and northern India*). Also have them locate the area to which the Indus River valley people fled to escape Aryan capture (*southern part of Indian peninsula*). **L1 LEP**

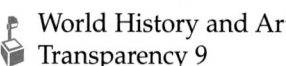 World History and Art
Transparency 9

 Chapter Transparency 8

 NATIONAL GEOGRAPHIC SOCIETY

Use these materials to enrich student understanding of ancient India.

 NGS PICTUREPACK TRANSPARENCY SET
Ancient India

Chart Study

Answer
Brahmans, who could read the Vedas and perform the religious rituals; most Indians were pariahs, outside of the varna system entirely, who performed tasks considered unclean.

Practice

Reading a Chart Why is a pyramid an appropriate geometric form to use for this chart? (*In going from the base to the peak, the number of people in each group decreases.*)

COOPERATIVE LEARNING ACTIVITY

Role Play Organize the class into the four *varnas* and the "untouchables" shown in the chart on this page. To assure fairness, be sure that students are put into groups at random, counting off 1-2-3-4-5 or pulling numbers out of a box. Have students discuss and write how the group members should act and what their duties and rights would be in their particular social group, according to ancient Indian beliefs. Also have each group discuss how its members should react to the following hypothetical situation: In ancient India, a cow from a small herd dies in a crowded street in front of a Hindu temple or shrine. Have one person from each group explain the group's responses to the entire class. **L1**

Adaptation Change occurs as people migrate, bringing ideas and customs with them and adapting to new surroundings. Over time, some traditions are adopted and some rejected. Remind students that the Aryans, formerly nomadic herders and hunters, became farmers. Ask what effects this had on Indian life, religion, and culture. Write answers on the chalkboard. *(Answers may include: Aryans settled in fertile valleys, began to farm, conquered Indus River valley people; brought caste system of* varnas; *beliefs changed as political and social organizations evolved.)* **L2**

Critical Thinking India is known for its rigid caste system. Sociologists in recent times have counted as many as 3,000 *jati*, some with marriage exclusions so strict that caste members cannot marry outside of 15 families. By contrast, the "American Dream" in the United States is based on the idea that everyone should have the opportunity to achieve a higher socioeconomic status. Have students discuss how different the United States is from India in terms of social mobility. **L3**

Independent Practice

📁 Guided Reading Activity 8-1 **L1**

📁 Time Line Activity 8

📁 Source Reading 8

📁 Geography and History Activity 8

unskilled laborers and servants, known as Sudras (SHOO•druhz).

Only priests and warrior families were allowed to hear and recite the Vedas. Over the years, rituals grew more secret and complex, and priests replaced warriors as the most honored members of society. The priests alone knew how to make sacrifices properly and to repeat the appropriate hymns. The social system changed to reflect the importance of priests.

Each *varna* had its own duties and took pride in doing them well. The Brahmans performed the elaborate rituals and studied the Vedas; only they could teach the Vedas. As warriors, Kshatriyas took charge of the army and the government. They led the councils of elders who ran small villages. Kshatriyas could study the Vedas but were not allowed to teach them. Vaisyas had the important tasks of tending the cattle, lending money, trading goods, and caring for the land. The Sudras' job was to serve the other varnas. They worked in the fields and acted as servants.

By 500 B.C. the division among the four *varnas* had become more rigid. Varnas were divided into smaller groups known as *jati*. Jati were formed according to occupations: shoemakers, potters, farmers, and so on. Priests were higher than cultivators, and cultivators were higher than carpenters, for example. *Jati* had their own rules for diet, marriage, and social customs. Groups lived in separate neighborhoods and did not mix socially with others.

Centuries later, Europeans named the Indian system of *varnas* and *jati* the caste system. The word *caste* has no one definition, but how it worked is clear. Within the system people were always ranked. They were born into a group, and that group could not be changed. People married within their own group. Moreover, that group determined a great deal about people's everyday lives. Members of the group lived in the same neighborhoods and did not mix socially with those outside.

Outside the system of *varnas* and *jati* were a group later called the pariahs. They did work that

Images of the Times

Hindu Beliefs

The three main gods of Hinduism are Brahma, Vishnu, and Siva. Brahma is creator of the world, Vishnu is preserver, and Siva is destroyer. These three are part of the same universal spirit.

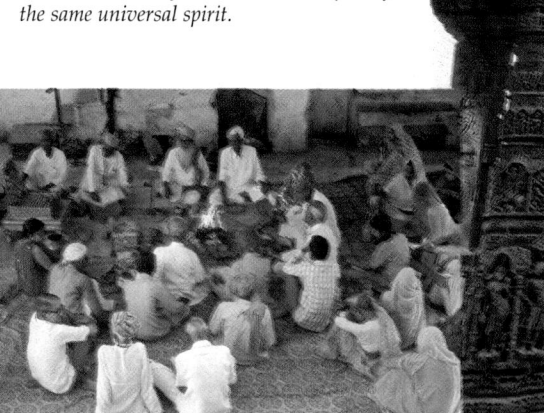

Meeting to read holy writings such as the *Mahabharata* is a long-standing custom among Hindus in India.

204

Images of the Times
Hindu Beliefs

The Hindu religion is polytheistic, which means that followers worship many gods. Early Hindus worshiped gods that represented powers in nature—the sun and the rain, for example. In time, some Hindus began to believe that gods appear in various forms, and that these separate forms are part of one universal spirit called Brahman. These Hindus believed that Brahman consists of many divinities. The creation of religious art was itself regarded as an act of worship. Many Hindu shrines are literally covered with stone sculptures of nymphs, dwarfs, serpents, and demons. Sometimes these figures represent one of the principal gods, often Vishnu or Siva.

was considered unclean, such as skinning animals and tanning their hides for leather. Sometimes called "outcastes" or "untouchables," the pariahs lived outside the villages and were shunned by most other people.

Concept of Duty

The Vedas outlined the dharma, or duties, of the males who belonged to each *varna*. Members of each *varna* were urged to do their duty. The epic poem called the *Mahabharata* (muh•HAH•BAH •ruh•tuh) makes the concept clear. One eloquent section, called the *Bhagavad Gita* (BAH•guh•VAHD GEE•tuh), or "Song of the Lord," includes the story you read at the beginning of this chapter. Arjuna's decision—to fight no matter what the personal cost—illustrates the importance of dharma in Indian life. As a warrior, Arjuna had to do his duty, even if it meant fighting against family.

The concept of dharma included doing what was proper for one's age. For instance, a male student would follow an occupation that was appropriate for his class. He then took a wife, and assumed responsibility for a family. In old age, he retired. As he neared death, he withdrew from his friends and family to pray. A woman was educated in household tasks. She married and served her husband and family until he died or retired, at which time she was expected to retire from active life and be taken care of by her sons and daughters-in-law. This concept of duty affected every member of society.

India's Two Epics

Two epics addressed the concepts of good and evil and became the spiritual forebears of India's main religions. The tale of Arjuna is a small part of the *Mahabharata*, which is 100,000 verses in length—as long as the first five books of the Bible. The epic—like the Bible—is a collection of writings by several authors. Some characters are historical, while others represent human ideals and various deities. Woven into the story of two families' struggle for power are discussions of religion and philosophy.

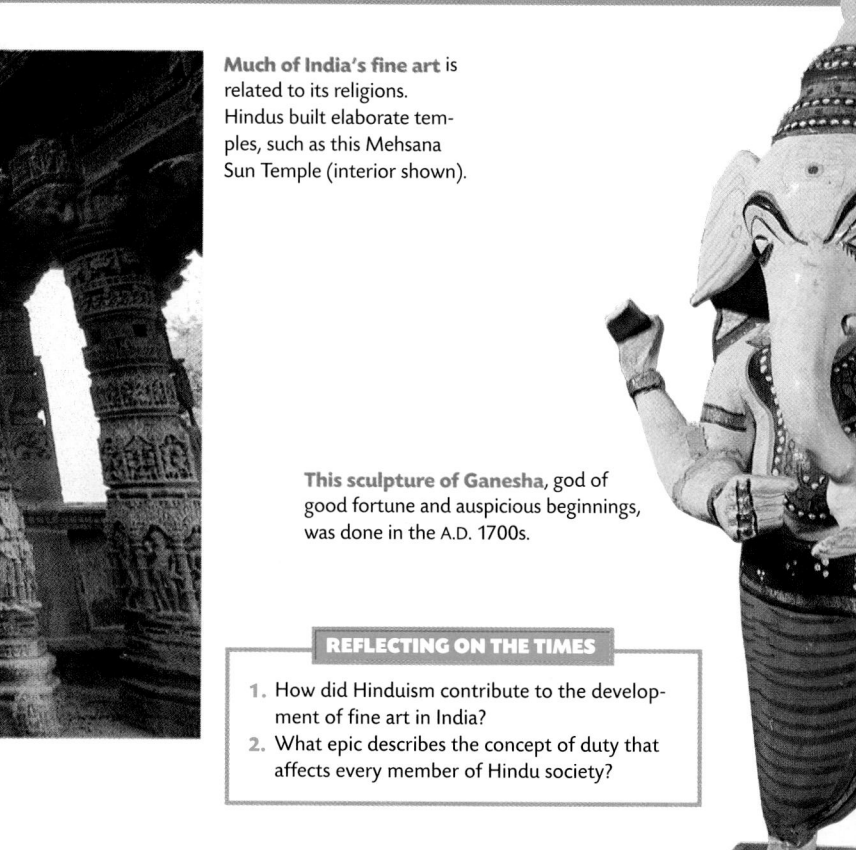

Much of India's fine art is related to its religions. Hindus built elaborate temples, such as this Mehsana Sun Temple (interior shown).

This sculpture of Ganesha, god of good fortune and auspicious beginnings, was done in the A.D. 1700s.

REFLECTING ON THE TIMES

1. How did Hinduism contribute to the development of fine art in India?
2. What epic describes the concept of duty that affects every member of Hindu society?

205

Daily Life Have students select one *varna*, or social group, to which they would want to belong (assuming they had a choice). Then have them tell or write a short explanation of why they chose the particular group. Students should mention the daily roles, rights, and duties of members of the category they have chosen. **L1 LEP**

Critical Thinking Have students write a short paper that supports or opposes Krishna's advice to Arjuna, "Get ready for battle without thought of pleasure and pain, gain and loss, victory and defeat." **L3**

Who?What?Where?When?

Concepts of Time Western and Hindu beliefs differ profoundly. Consider the concept of time. Westerners see time as a steady, fixed progression. To Westerners, when a moment is gone, it is gone forever. Hindus see time as a revolving, endless circle. To Hindus, everything that happens today has happened before and will happen again.

ASSESS

Check for Understanding

Assign Section 1 Assessment as homework or as an in-class activity.

 Use Interactive Tutor Self-Assessment Software to review Section 1.

Evaluate

Section Quiz 8-1

 Use the Testmaker to create a customized quiz for Section 1.

One passage tells of how the need for a king arose when dharma no longer guided people in everyday life:

> **Bhishma said: ... Neither kingship nor king was there in the beginning, neither scepter nor the bearer of the scepter. All people protected one another by means of righteous conduct (dharma). Thus, while protecting one another by means of righteous conduct, O Bharata, men eventually fell into a state of spiritual lassitude [weariness]. Then delusion overcame them ... their sense of righteous conduct was lost. When understanding was lost, all men ... became victims of greed.**

Later, the God Vishnu chooses "... that one person among mortals who alone is worthy of high eminence." A man named Virajas is brought forth, and he becomes the first king.

A second epic, the well-loved *Ramayana*, grew to 24,000 verses before it was written down. It presents the moving tale of Rama and Sita (SEE•tuh). Rama was the ideal king; Sita, his faithful wife. Vividly describing the struggle between good and evil, the *Ramayana* tells how the demon Ravana captures Sita. When Rama finds that she is missing, he cries:

> **Sita! Gentle Sita! If you have wanted to prove my love, if you are hiding from us, let the agony of my fear suffice. Come to me, my love, come to me!**
>
> **He stood there, both his arms held wide, as though half hoping she might run forward to his embrace. The country lay very still around him. Only the old tree shivered in every leafy spray and seemed to wring its hands for pity. Slowly that gleam of hope quite faded, and his arms fell to his sides.**

Rama at first doubts Sita; but later she is saved, and they reunite. Like other Indian epics, the *Ramayana* ends with good winning over evil.

Hinduism

The Aryan conquerors believed in many deities and thought their gods and goddesses had power over the forces of nature. They worshiped Agni, the god of fire; Indra, the god of thunder and war; and Usha, the goddess of dawn. Aryan priests created elaborate rituals and offered sacrifices to appease the gods and win their favor.

Over the centuries, as political and social organizations evolved, the Aryan religion slowly changed into Hinduism and became the national religion of India.

Universal Spirit

Hinduism was not founded on the teachings of one person, nor did it have one holy book. Instead it was based on different beliefs and practices, many of which had their roots in the Vedas and the Indian epics. As a result, Hinduism became a complex religion of many deities. Three gods, however, eventually emerged as the most important: Brahma, the Creator; Vishnu, the Preserver; and Siva, the Destroyer.

Other ideas that became part of Hinduism came from religious thinkers who looked for a single religious truth behind the many Hindu deities and rituals. Between 800 B.C. and 400 B.C., their personal searches and philosophies were reflected in the religious writings known as the *Upanishads* (oo•PAH•nih•SHAHDZ).

The *Upanishads* tell of a universal spirit present within all life, "a light that shines beyond all things on earth." According to these writings, all living things—including gods, humans, and animals—have souls. All souls, say the *Upanishads*, are part of the one eternal spirit, sometimes called Brahman Nerguna. Their bodies tie them to the material world, but only for a short time. To know true freedom, a soul must be separated from the material world and united with Brahman Nerguna: "As a lump of salt thrown in water dissolves, and cannot be taken out again as salt, though wherever we taste the water it is salt."

The authors of the *Upanishads* taught that forms of self-denial such as fasting helped people achieve union with the universal spirit. They encouraged the practice of yoga, a discipline that combines physical and mental exercises designed to help one achieve a state of tranquility.

Cycle of Rebirth

Another idea that came from the *Upanishads* was that of reincarnation, or the rebirth of the soul. Hindus believe the soul passes through many lifetimes before it finally achieves union with the universal spirit. The *Upanishads* offer this picture of rebirth:

> **As a caterpillar, having reached the end of a blade of grass, takes hold of another blade, then draws its body from the first,**

206   Chapter 8   *India's Great Civilization*

> so the Self, having reached the end of his body, takes hold of another body, then draws itself from the first. "

The cycle of rebirth is determined by a principle called karma. According to this principle, how a person lives his or her life determines what form the person will take in the next life. To move toward the universal spirit, one must live a good life and fulfill one's dharma. For example, a conscientious diplomat, a Kshatriya, might be reborn as a Brahman. The souls of those who fail to fulfill their dharma, however, might be reborn in a lower *varna*, or perhaps even as snakes or insects.

The concept of karma creates the desire to live a good life, for "By good deeds a man becomes what is good, by evil deeds what is bad." Out of that desire arose the practice of nonviolence toward all living things. Called ahimsa (uh•HIHM•SAH), this practice requires the believer to protect humans, animals, and even insects and plants.

The cycle of reincarnation continues until a person reaches *moksha*, or release from the pain and suffering of rebirth after rebirth. In *moksha* a person finds freedom from reincarnation in a state of complete oneness with Brahman Nerguna. Hindus teach that a life committed to prayer, religious rituals, strict self-denial, and rejection of all worldly possessions will help a person to achieve the final goal of *moksha*.

Jainism

As Hinduism evolved, many holy people stressed different aspects of Hindu belief and practice. The teacher Mahavira (muh•hah•VEE•ruh) placed a special emphasis on the practice of ahimsa. Born a noble in northern India, Mahavira gave up his wealthy lifestyle and traveled for many years throughout the country. About 500 B.C. Mahavira founded Jainism, a new religion that rejected sacrifices and rigid Hindu social divisions. Believing in

History & Art Siva, ringed by a circle of flames, dances on the back of the dwarf Apasmara. *Why do Hindus regard animals as sacred?*

the sacredness of all life, the Jains, as Mahavira's followers were called, used brooms to sweep aside insects so they would not step on them. They refused to farm for fear of plowing under living things. Instead, they turned to commerce and gained great wealth and influence.

Chapter 8 Section 1

History & Art Have students notice that in two of his four hands Siva holds symbols of his divine nature— the drum of creation and the flame of destruction. Apasmara, the dwarf beneath his foot, represents the illusions that Siva dispels. Why do you think Siva is ringed by flames? *(He is the god of destruction.)*
Answer to Caption: *Since all living things have souls, animals are sacred and cannot be killed.*

Reteach

Ask students to explain why Hinduism was not just a religion but a way of life for Indians. *(Answers may include: Religion was the basis for daily life, social groups, duties; religious texts explained life and culture; duty [dharma] was placed above all else; beliefs in self-denial and reincarnation influenced people's daily behavior.)*

📁 Reading Essentials and Study Guide 8-1

Enrich

Have students write a short essay supporting or rejecting the Hindu idea of ahimsa, the practice of nonviolence toward all living things.

CLOSE

Have students summarize the major Hindu beliefs and terms used in Section 1.

SECTION 1 ASSESSMENT

Main Idea
1. Use a diagram like the one below to show the elements of the society, culture, and religion of the Aryans that carried over to the culture of Hindu India.

Recall
2. **Define** rajah, epic, *varna, jati,* dharma, reincarnation, karma, ahimsa.
3. **Identify** the Aryans, Sanskrit, Vedas, *Mahabharata, Bhagavad Gita, Ramayana,* Hinduism, *Upanishads.*

Critical Thinking
4. **Applying Information** Explain the Hindu concept of dharma by telling the story of the warrior prince Arjuna.
Understanding Themes
5. **Movement** How did the Aryan invasion affect the later development of culture in South Asia?

Chapter 8 *India's Great Civilization* **207**

SECTION 1 ASSESSMENT ANSWERS

1. society: Aryan system of social classes became the caste system; culture: two epics addressing the concept of good and evil became the spiritual forebears of India's main religions; religion: Aryan conquerors believed in many gods and goddesses; over time Aryan religion changed into Hinduism
2. All terms are defined in the Glossary.
3. Aryans, 202; Sanskrit, 203; Vedas, 203; *Mahabharata*, 205; *Bhagavad Gita*, 205; *Ramayana*, 206; Hinduism, 206; *Upanishads*, 206
4. Sample answer: Dharma means doing whatever is required of one's *varna*; Arjuna was a Kshatriya, or warrior. He made a decision to fight even if it meant fighting against his family.
5. **MOVEMENT** brought new language, customs, and traditions to Indian society

| 600 B.C. | | 550 B.C. | | 500 B.C. |

c. 566 B.C.
Siddhartha
Gautama is born.

c. 540 B.C.
Gautama begins
spiritual search.

c. 500 B.C. Gautama
(the Buddha) dies.

Section 2
Rise of Buddhism

Guide to Reading

**Read to Find Out
Main Idea** *Buddhism appealed to many people in India, Southeast Asia, and East Asia.*

▶ **Terms to Define**
  nirvana, stupa

▶ **People to Meet**
  Siddhartha Gautama

The Storyteller

Siddhartha stood still, as if a snake lay in his path. Suddenly the icy thought stole over him: he must begin his life completely afresh. "I am no longer what I was, … I am no longer a hermit, no longer a priest, no longer a Brahmin. How can I return home? What would I do at home with my father? Study? Offer sacrifices? Practice meditation? All this is over for me now." He realized how alone he was. Now he was Siddhartha, the awakened. He must begin his life afresh. He began to walk quickly, no longer homewards, no longer looking back.

—from *Siddhartha*, Herman Hesse, translated by Hilda Rosner, 1957

Gautama, the Buddha

During the 500s B.C., changes occurred in Indian religious life. Many devout Hindus became dissatisfied with external rituals and wanted a more spiritual faith. They left the towns and villages and looked for solitude in the hills and forests. Through meditation, many of these religious seekers developed new insights and became religious teachers. Their ideas and practices often led to the rise of new religions. The most influential of the new religions was Buddhism.

The Buddha

Siddhartha Gautama (sih•DAHR•tuh GOW•tuh•muh), the founder of Buddhism, began his life as a Kshatriya prince. Born around 566 B.C., Gautama was raised in luxury. As a young man he continued to live a sheltered life, shielded from sickness and poverty. Tradition states that one day Gautama's charioteer drove him around his estates, and for the first time Gautama saw sickness, old age, and death. Shocked at these scenes of misery, Gautama decided to find out why people suffered and how suffering could be ended. Around the age of 29, he left his wife and newborn son and wandered throughout India.

For seven years Gautama lived as a hermit, seeking the truth through fasting and self-denial. This did not lead him to the truth, however. One day, while meditating under a tree, Gautama gained a flash of insight that he felt gave him an answer to the problem of suffering. He began to share with others the meaning of his "enlightenment." Dressed in a yellow robe, he preached his message to people and began to gather followers. His closest friends began calling him the Buddha, or "Enlightened One."

208 Chapter 8 *India's Great Civilization*

Rajesh Bedi

The Buddha's First Sermon

From this stupa, or domed shrine, in Isipatana, a village in northern India, the Buddha is said to have delivered his first sermon. Once a small village, Isipatana is now Sarnath, a sub- of the city of Varanasi. Here, Buddhists believe, c 500s B.C. the Buddha delivered his first ser- to five followers. A large monastery, which housed 1,500 monks, was founded on this d spot. Today the shrine stands empty.

The Buddha began India's second religion, after the far older Hindu religion had become entrenched. He lived in a unique moment of history. The 500s B.C. gave birth not only to Buddhism in India but also to Confucianism in China and to new rational- ist philosophies in Greece. Buddhism became one of the world's major religions and the Buddha one of the most notable spiritual leaders in the history of the world. ⊕

Chapter 8 *India's Great Civilization* **209**

TEACH

Guided Practice

THEME **Innovation**

Have students list the religious ideas taught by the Buddha that were different from Hindu beliefs. *(no sacrifices to gods; rejection of the* varna *system)* **L1 LEP**

 History Simulation 8

⟵ **Picturing History**

The site of the Buddha's first ser- mon can be identified, and so can the circumstances of his death— although both events are based on tradition. The story goes that the 80-year-old Buddha accepted a piece of pork from a dedicated fol- lower. Even though the Enlight- ened One knew the meat was spoiled, he ate it out of politeness. He sickened and died in a park, telling his followers in his last breath, "Work out your own salva- tion with diligence." What other famous person's last words do you know? *(Possible answers: Julius Caesar's "Et tu, Brute," Nathan Hale's "I only regret that I have but one life to lose for my country.")*

CURRICULUM CONNECTION

LITERATURE

Hermann Hesse's novel *Siddhartha*, published in 1922, is a poetic expression of Indian phi- losophy. Hesse, a German, nar- rates how his young hero, the Brahman Siddhartha, after encountering the Buddha, sets off in search of self-fulfillment. His goal is to conquer suffering and fear, to attain serene con- tentment, and to see the unity in seeming contrasts—in short, to reach nirvana.

Spread of Buddhism
To what other parts of Asia and the world did Buddhism spread?
It spread to China, Japan, Korea, and the Middle East.

Independent Practice

 Guided Reading Activity 8-2 **L1**

ASSESS

Check for Understanding

Assign Section 2 Assessment as homework or as an in-class activity.

◘ Use Interactive Tutor Self-Assessment Software to review Section 2.

Evaluate

Section Quiz 8-2

◘ Use the Testmaker to create a customized quiz for Section 2.

Reteach

Ask students to summarize in their own words the Four Noble Truths and the Eightfold Path.

Reading Essentials and Study Guide 8-2

Enrich

Have students write a brief statement in which they explain why they agree or disagree with the Buddha's teaching that desire causes suffering. Discuss answers.

CLOSE

Discuss possible reasons Buddhism did not flourish in India as Hinduism had. (*resistance from leaders, strength of caste system, strictness regarding poverty and nonviolence.*)

Four Noble Truths

The Buddha developed a new religious philosophy. He outlined his main ideas in the Four Noble Truths. First, as he had discovered, all people suffer and know sorrow. Next, said the Buddha, people suffer because their desires bind them to the cycle of rebirth. He told his followers:

> ❝ The thirst for existence leads from rebirth to rebirth; lust and pleasure follow. Power alone can satisfy lust. The thirst for power, the thirst for pleasure, the thirst for existence; there, O monks, is the origin of suffering. ❞

The third truth, said the Buddha, was that people could end their suffering by eliminating their desires. And according to the fourth truth, one could eliminate desire by following the Eightfold Path.

The Eightfold Path

The Buddha urged his disciples to do eight things: know the truth, resist evil, say nothing to hurt others, respect life, work for the good of others, free their minds of evil, control their thoughts, and practice meditation. By avoiding extremes and following the Eightfold Path, a person could attain *nirvana*, a state of freedom from the cycle of rebirth. Nirvana is not a place, like heaven, but a state of extinction. In fact, the root meaning of the word *nirvana* is a "blowing out," as of a candle. In nirvana, a person would be in a state of oneness with the universe.

The Buddha rejected the *varna* system. He taught that a person's place in life depended on the person, not on the person's birth. He taught that anyone, regardless of caste, could attain enlightenment. He did not believe in the Hindu deities. He believed in reincarnation but taught that one could escape the cycle of suffering and reach nirvana by following the Eightfold Path.

Spread of Buddhism

The Buddha spent 40 years teaching the Four Noble Truths and the Eightfold Path. He gathered thousands of disciples around him. After their master's death, traveling monks carried the new religion beyond India to other parts of Asia, especially to China, Japan, Korea, and the Middle East.

Architecture and the Arts

The rise of Buddhism led to a flowering of architecture and the arts. Buddhist architects built *stupas*, or large stone mounds, over the bones of Buddhist holy people. Stupas were known for their elaborately carved stone gateways. Paintings and statues of the Buddha, carved of polished stone or wood covered with gilt, adorned stupas and cave temples. Exquisite smaller statues were made from fine porcelain. Books about the Buddha's life and teachings were often beautifully illustrated.

Divisions

As Buddhism spread, disagreements developed among the Buddha's followers. Two distinct branches of Buddhism soon arose. One branch, known as Theravada, was established in South Asia and Southeast Asia. It remained fairly close in practice to the original teachings of the Buddha, regarding him as simply a teacher.

The other branch of Buddhism was known as Mahayana. It became dominant in China, Korea, and Japan. Mahayana encouraged the worship of the Buddha as a divine being and savior.

Today, only a few Indians are Buddhists. Most are Hindus. Muslims, Jains, Christians, and others make up the rest of the population. Recently, however, Buddhism has gained new followers in India, as well as in the West. ◣▬

SECTION 2 ASSESSMENT

Main Idea
1. Use a chart like the one below to identify teachings of Buddhism that appealed to people in India, Southeast Asia, and East Asia.

   ┌─────────────────────────┐
   │ Teachings of Buddhism   │
   │ _____   │
   │ _____   │
   │ _____   │
   └─────────────────────────┘

Recall
2. **Define** nirvana, stupa.
3. **Identify** Siddhartha Gautama, Four Noble Truths.

Critical Thinking
4. **Synthesizing Information** Compare the religions of Hinduism and Buddhism, explaining which Hindu beliefs and practices the Buddha accepted and which he rejected in his teachings.

Understanding Themes
5. **Innovation** Decide how your own life and goals would be different if you tried to live by the Four Noble Truths and the Eightfold Path.

SECTION 2 ASSESSMENT ANSWERS

1. rejection of the caste system; idea that all people could end their own suffering; idea that all people could attain a state of freedom from the cycle of rebirth
2. All terms are defined in the Glossary.
3. Siddhartha Gautama, 208; Four Noble Truths, 210
4. Hinduism: many gods, make sacrifices, *varnas*; Buddhism: no gods, sacrifices, or *varnas*, Eightfold Path. Both believe in rebirth, *moksha* for Hindus and nirvana for Buddhists; both believe in nonviolence.
5. **INNOVATION** Answers might include: less materialistic, less ambitious for worldly success, more compassionate.

Section 3

Indian Empires

Read to Find Out
Main Idea *The Mauryan and Gupta Empires made many cultural achievements.*

▶ **Terms to Define**
"Arabic numerals"

▶ **People to Meet**
Chandragupta Maurya, Asoka, Chandragupta I, Chandragupta II

▶ **Places to Locate**
Magadha

The Storyteller

It troubled King Asoka that criminals continued their wrongdoing within his empire. Therefore he was proud of his latest merciful decree, carved on stone monuments: "Thus speaks the Beloved of the Gods.... This is my instruction from now on: Men who are imprisoned or sentenced to death are

to be given three days respite. Thus their relations [relatives] may plead for their lives, or, if there is no one to plead for them, they may make their donations or undertake a fast for a better rebirth in the next life. For it is my wish that they should gain the next world."

—from *Asoka and the Decline of the Mauryas*, Romila Thapar, 1961

Lion-headed capital atop a Rock Edict pillar of Asoka

Despite the high mountain barriers in the north, India has never been completely cut off from other lands. The Aryans marched through the mountain passes to invade the Indus River valley; later, others followed. In the 500s B.C., Persian ruler Darius I conquered lands in the Indus River valley. Alexander the Great invaded the same area in 327 B.C., and Indian merchants carried on a busy trade with the Roman Empire. In all that time, however, no Indian king or foreign conqueror had ever succeeded in uniting the separate kingdoms into one Indian nation.

At the time of Darius's invasion, one Indian kingdom, **Magadha**, was expanding in the north. King Bimbisara, who ruled Magadha from 542 B.C. to 495 B.C., added to its territory by conquest and marriage. Although Magadha declined after Bimbisara's death, it was to become the center of India's first empire.

The Mauryan Empire

At the time of Alexander's invasion, Magadha was only one of many small warring states in northern India. Then, in 321 B.C., a military officer named **Chandragupta Maurya** (CHUHN•druh•GUP•tuh MAH•oor•yuh) overthrew the Magadhan king and proclaimed himself ruler.

Chandragupta Maurya was a skilled administrator whose achievements included the development of an efficient postal system. He kept control of his empire by maintaining a strong army and by using an extensive spy network. He founded a Mauryan kingdom that included most of northern and central India and lasted until 184 B.C.

Asoka's Enlightened Rule

Indian civilization blossomed during the reign of Chandragupta's grandson, **Asoka** (uh•SHOH•kuh). Asoka's rule began in 274 B.C. with fierce wars of conquest. His merciless armies hunted

Chapter 8 *India's Great Civilization* **211**

SECTION THEME

▶ **Cultural Diffusion** Mauryan and Gupta rulers bring unity to northern India and encourage cultural achievements.

Guide to Reading

For reading strategies to help students read effectively see pages 12–13.

Vocabulary Pre-check

 Use the Vocabulary PuzzleMaker for Chapter 8 to create a crossword puzzle to reinforce section terms. **L1 LEP**

Use Vocabulary Activity 8 to introduce vocabulary terms. **L1 LEP**

FOCUS

Section Objective

List the cultural achievements of the Mauryan and Gupta Empires.

BELLRINGER
Motivational Activity

Before taking roll at the beginning of the class period, project Section Focus Transparency 8-3 and have students answer the activity questions. Discuss students' responses.

This activity is also available as a blackline master.

SECTION RESOURCES

Reproducible Masters
- Lecture Notes 8-3
- Reproducible Lesson Plan 8-3
- Vocabulary Activity 8
- Guided Reading Activity 8-3
- Mapping History Activity 8
- Reteaching Activity 8
- Enrichment Activity 8

- Section Quiz 8-3
- Performance Assessment Activity 8
- Spanish Chapter Summary 8
- Reading Essentials and Study Guide 8-3

Transparencies
- Section Focus Transparency 8-3

Multimedia
- Interactive Tutor Self-Assessment Software
- Testmaker
- India and China
- World Music: Cultural Traditions, Lesson 7

TEACH

Guided Practice

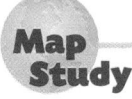 **THEME** Cultural Diffusion

Discuss how the cultures of the early Indian empires influenced the cultures of visitors from the West. **L2**

Map Study

Answers

1. *through the Khyber Pass in the Hindu Kush mountain range; from central Asia*
2. *Ganges River*

Map Skills Practice

Reading a Map What areas of India that the Mauryas had controlled did the Guptas fail to conquer? *(Indus Valley and the Deccan Plateau)*

Economics Discuss how rulers in both empires financed their governments and provided for Indian citizens. Remind students of the harsh policies of some rulers and the compassion of others. **L3**

♪ World Music: Cultural Traditions, Lesson 7

Have students use the **Chapter 8 Student Web Activity** at worldhistory.glencoe.com for in-depth study of King Asoka.

Indian Empires

- → Routes of Aryan invaders, 1200 B.C.
- ▢ Mauryan Empire, 250 B.C.
- ▨ Gupta Empire, A.D. 400

0   200   400 mi.
0   200   400 km
Lambert Conic Conformal Projection

Map Study Under Mauryan rule, India's borders expanded to include new territory; however, under Gupta rule India's unity was weakened.
1. **Movement** By what route did the Aryans invade India? Where did they come from?
2. **Place** On what river was Pataliputra located?

---

down and killed their enemies. He built an empire that covered two-thirds of the Indian subcontinent.

After one particularly brutal battle, Asoka rode out to view the battlefield. As he looked on the bloodied bodies of the dead and maimed, the Indian ruler was horrified. Determined never again to rule by force and terror, Asoka renounced war. Henceforth, he announced, he would follow the teachings of the Buddha and become a man of peace. During his reign, missionaries spread Buddhism throughout India and other parts of Asia.

Asoka issued laws stressing concern for other human beings. To make sure these laws became widely known, Asoka wrote them in the local languages rather than in Sanskrit. The laws, known today as the Rock Edicts, were carved on rocks and on tall stone pillars throughout the vast empire.

Asoka's public projects reflected the same care for people. He provided free hospitals and veterinary

---

clinics. He built fine roads, with rest houses and shade trees for the travelers' comfort.

Although he promoted Buddhism, Asoka permitted his subjects to practice Hinduism if they wished. The Hindu caste system continued.

Collapse of Mauryan Empire

The Mauryan Empire declined after Asoka's death in 232 B.C. His successors levied heavy taxes on the goods sold by merchants and seized large portions of the crops grown by peasants. Such harsh policies caused the people to turn against the Mauryas. When the last Mauryan ruler was murdered in 184 B.C., northern India again split into many small warring kingdoms.

The Gupta Empire

Five hundred years passed before much of India was again united. About A.D. 310, **Chandragupta I** began to build an empire. He was not related to Chandragupta Maurya, but like that earlier ruler he made Magadha the base of his kingdom.

Chandragupta I introduced the Gupta dynasty, which ruled northern India for more than 200 years. The arts and sciences flourished, and the Gupta period would later be called India's Golden Age.

The Guptas governed a much smaller empire than the Mauryas. They never gained control of the Indus Valley or of the Deccan, the broad plateau that forms most of India's southern peninsula. The Guptas did manage to build a strong state, however. They trained soldiers and used spies and political assassins. In short, they did whatever they felt had to be done to maintain power.

Gupta Religion

The Gupta rulers encouraged learning based on the *Upanishads*. They made Hinduism the religion of their empire. Hindu temples were built—elaborate structures with brightly painted sculptures depicting tales in the epics. Although each temple had its presiding god or goddess, the Hindus viewed the many deities as different ways of worshiping Brahman Nerguna, the eternal spirit.

Student Web Activity 8

Visit the *World History: The Human Experience* Web site at **worldhistory.glencoe.com** and click on *Chapter 8—Student Web Activities* for an activity relating to King Asoka.

COOPERATIVE LEARNING ACTIVITY

Debate Have students form two groups, one to support Asoka and his followers, who opposed war, and the other to defend the Gupta rulers and warriors, who wanted to conquer more land. Be sure the groups are balanced in research and communications skills. Have each group break into smaller teams to discuss such issues as politics, law, religion, and economics. Then have students rejoin the larger groups to discuss findings. Key ideas should be written down and presented to the class in oral arguments by one or two spokespersons. Following the debate, discuss the major points made by both sides. Take a poll to see if the debate changed students' minds about the rulers and the peace-versus-war issue. **L1** 📖

The Arts

Indian Music

Ravi Shankar

Like the other arts of India, Indian music has a long and rich history. It began in Hindu temples and the courts of Indian rulers centuries ago. Traditionally, Indian musicians play instruments and sing without using chords or other harmonies. A group of musicians starts out with a basic melody called a raga, which each player then develops with his or her own spontaneous arrangements. The musicians perform on a number of different instruments, including drums, flutes, and a stringed instrument known as a sitar. Their performances often go on for several hours at a time.

Probably the best-known modern Indian musician is Ravi Shankar, often called India's "sitar king" and the "godfather of world music." Shankar, almost as well known in the West as in India, has brought an appreciation of Indian music to Western audiences. He has worked with George Harrison of the Beatles and other musicians, such as violinist Yehudi Menuhin, flutist Jean-Pierre Rampal, and composer Philip Glass.

Linking Past and Present ACTIVITY

Discuss the origins of Indian music and its major characteristics. What contribution has Ravi Shankar made to world music?

Linking Past and Present

Indian Music

Indian music sometimes sounds strange to European and American listeners because it uses a different scale than that of the West. Westerners are used to listening to music that is based on chords and harmonies, which are not present in Indian music. Indian dancers use the position of their arms, hands, and fingers to tell stories and indicate moods.

ANSWER

Indian music has its origins in Hindu temples and the courts of Indian rulers. It is played without chords on a variety of instruments, including the sitar; a basic melody is interwoven with individual improvisations. Ravi Shankar has spurred an interest in Indian music in the West and has closely collaborated with Western musicians.

Gupta Life

The Gupta Empire reached its height under **Chandragupta II**, who ruled from A.D. 375 to A.D. 415. Faxian (FAH•SYEN), a Buddhist monk from China, traveled to India and recorded in his diary:

> " In the Gupta Empire, people are numerous and happy; only those who cultivate the royal land have to pay [in] grain.... If they want to go, they go; if they want to stay, they stay. The king governs without decapitation [cutting off heads] or corporal [bodily] punishment.... The leaders of Vaisya families have houses in the cities for dispensing charity and medicine. "

Faxian may have exaggerated the benefits of Gupta rule, but he provided a useful glimpse into Indian life. By easing tax burdens, Chandragupta II gave people more freedom. Of all the Gupta monarchs, he was the most chivalrous and heroic. Though he expanded the empire, he is remembered for more than conquest. Gupta rulers believed they had reached a high level of civilization. They began to write down rules for everything, from grammar to drama to politics. The Sanskrit of the Gupta court became the major language in the north.

In one respect, though, daily life did not improve during the Gupta period. The status of Indian women had declined since Aryan times. Aryan women at first often had a say about whom they would marry. By Gupta times, parents were choosing mates for their children, and child marriages were common. Women and mothers were

Footnotes to History

Highway Rest Stops
Asoka's highway rest stops were marked by stone pillars engraved with Buddhist teachings. On one of these pillars, Asoka explained:

I have ordered banyan trees to be planted along the roads to give shade to men and animals. I have ordered mango groves to be planted. I have ordered wells to be dug every [half-mile], and I have ordered rest houses built.

—The Edicts of Asoka

NATIONAL GEOGRAPHIC SOCIETY

Use these materials to enrich student understanding of ancient India.

🔘 **NGS PICTURESHOW CD-ROM**
India and China

Independent Practice

📁 Guided Reading Activity 8-3 **L1**

Politics Have students make lists of the "positive" (*public projects, art, learning*) and the "negative" (*wars, repression*) historical developments that occurred during the Mauryan and Gupta Empires. **L2**

MEETING SPECIAL NEEDS ACTIVITY

Learning Disability For students who need extra help and additional reinforcement with the material in this section, read aloud to them (or have other students read aloud) relevant entries about the Indian empires from a children's encyclopedia. *The World Book Encyclopedia* is a good choice. Ask students to explain in their own words the main points of some or all of the following entries: Mauryan Empire, Chandragupta Maurya, Asoka, Gupta dynasty, Sanskrit literature. **L1**

Visualizing
History
The monks carved out the Ajanta caves to serve as monasteries and temples. They first fashioned the ceilings of the chambers, then cut out the walls and floors. Sculptors and painters decorated cave entrances and interiors.
Answer to Caption: *In Gupta India, deep social divisions continued, and the status of women declined. However, the period was one of great economic prosperity and cultural achievement.*

ASSESS

Check for Understanding

Assign Section 3 Assessment as homework or as an in-class activity.

 Use Interactive Tutor Self-Assessment Software to review Section 3.

Evaluate

 Section Quiz 8-3

 Use the Testmaker to create a customized quiz for Section 3.

Reteach

Ask students to name the important people from this section and several contributions from each of the major empires.

 Reteaching Activity 8

 Reading Essentials and Study Guide 8-3

Enrich

Have students discuss some of the reasons that "golden ages" end, using the Mauryan and Gupta Empires as examples.

 Enrichment Activity 8

CLOSE

Ask students to speculate on why Hindu religion, social structure, and customs remain deeply embedded in Indian life, even though the Gupta rulers were India's last Hindu rulers.

Visualizing
History
Buddhist monks carved this 24-foot-long reclining Buddha on the wall of the Chai-tya-griha cave in the first century B.C. *What do the Ajanta carvings reveal about life in Gupta India?*

highly respected, but they had little power or independence.

Gupta Achievements

Learning flourished under the Guptas. The court welcomed poets, playwrights, philosophers, and scientists. Much of the writing was concentrated on religion, but folktales were also popular. A collection of tales called the *Panchatantra* presented moral lessons through animals who acted like humans. Many of these stories eventually spread to the Middle East and the West, where they were retold by other authors. Drama was also important during Gupta times. Kalidasa, the most famous playwright, wrote *Shakuntala*, a play about romantic love between a king and a forest maiden.

Gupta mathematicians contributed significantly to mathematics as it is today, making major advances in developing the principles of algebra. They also explained the concept of infinity and invented the concept of zero. The symbols they devised for the numbers 1 to 9 were adopted by traders from the Middle East and so came to be called "Arabic numerals" in the West.

Gupta astronomers used these mathematical discoveries to advance their understanding of the universe. They realized that the earth is round, and they had some knowledge of gravity. In medicine, Gupta doctors set bones, performed operations, and invented hundreds of medical instruments.

Many countries benefited from Gupta achievements, as both ideas and products traveled the land and sea trade routes that connected India to the rest of the world. Indian exporters traded such items as gems, spices, cotton, teak, and ebony for horses from Arabia and central Asia, silk from China, and gold from Rome.

The Golden Age Ends

After Chandragupta II's death in A.D. 415, the Gupta Empire began to fail. As the government weakened, the Guptas faced invasions along India's northwestern border. By A.D. 600, the Gupta Empire had dissolved into a collection of small states.

However, much of the culture that was uniquely Indian survived. Many aspects of India's life today grew out of the social structures and religions, the arts and sciences, that were born during the 2,000 years that followed the Aryan invasions.

SECTION I ASSESSMENT

Main Idea
1. Use a chart like the one below to show the cultural achievements of the Mauryan and Gupta Empires.

Cultural Achievements

Mauryan Empire	Gupta Empire

Recall
2. **Define** "Arabic numerals."
3. **Identify** Chandragupta Maurya, Asoka, Chandragupta I, Chandragupta II, *Panchatantra*, *Shakuntala*.

Critical Thinking
4. **Analyzing Information** How did India's rulers affect the religious life of the people?

Understanding Themes
5. **Cultural Diffusion** In what lasting ways have early Indian empires influenced the world?

SECTION 3 ASSESSMENT ANSWERS

1. Mauryan Empire: spread Buddhism; laws expressed concern for other human beings; freedom of religion for non-Buddhist subjects. Gupta Empire: arts and sciences flourished; developed principles of algebra and Arabic numerals; encouraged learning based on ideas in *Upanishads*; Hinduism the empire's religion

2. All terms are defined in the Glossary.

3. Chandragupta Maurya, 211; Asoka, 211; Chandragupta I, 212; Chandragupta II, 213; *Panchatantra*, 214; *Shakuntala*, 214

4. Asoka encouraged Buddhism; Guptas supported Hinduism.

5. **CULTURAL DIFFUSION** in religious, social, intellectual ways

Critical Thinking SKILLS

Determining Cause and Effect

As you read a mystery novel, you may try to figure out which events or actions caused the main character to act in specific ways. Understanding history is a similar process. Looking for cause-effect relationships unlocks the mystery of history.

Learning the Skill

To identify cause-effect relationships in history, first select an event. Then examine the situation before this event. How was it different? Look for related problems and actions. These are likely causes of the event. Suppose you select the following event: Asoka's renunciation of war. What events preceded Asoka's decision? In earlier years, Asoka was horrified by the bloody results of war. This caused him to renounce war altogether.

Now examine what happened after Asoka renounced war. He became a Buddhist, promoted Buddhist ideas of compassion, and passed laws based on this philosophy. He also built hospitals and roads. These were direct and indirect effects of Asoka's change of direction.

Buddha with halo, Gupta period

Certain words and phrases often indicate cause-effect relationships; these include *because, due to, therefore, as a result of, led to,* and *brought about.* It can be hard to determine causes and effects of historical events. Moreover, we can't test our ideas as we can in science experiments. Instead, we must rely on logic and common sense.

Practicing the Skill

Read the paragraph below. Then answer the questions that follow.

❝ **Cattle were the basis of the Aryan diet and economy, even serving as money. Wealth was measured in cattle, and so the Aryans raided each other's herds. They were often at war.... Dozens of Aryan words describe cattle, indicating their continued prominence in Aryan life. Later, their herds would be considered so sacred that a ban was placed on eating meat.** ❞

1. What were causes of conflict among Aryans?
2. How did the importance of cattle affect the culture and language of Aryans?

Applying the Skill

Reread Section 2, "Rise of Buddhism." Then describe causes of Buddhism's rise in India and its effects on India and other parts of the world.

For More Practice

Turn to the Skill Practice in the Chapter Assessment on page 217 for more practice in determining cause and effect.

The **Glencoe Skillbuilder Interactive Workbook,** Level 2 provides instruction and practice in key social studies skills.

Critical Thinking SKILLS

TEACH

Determining Cause and Effect
To show students a few clear-cut cases of cause and effect, use examples from biology. Have students explain how or why the following diseases occur in human beings: malaria *(bite of infected mosquito)*, rickets *(lack of vitamin D)*, beri-beri *(lack of thiamine)*, typhoid *(contaminated food or water)*, rabies *(bite of infected animal)*, scurvy *(lack of vitamin C)*. Ask how the causes of these diseases were discovered. *(observation, experimentation, logic)* Emphasize, as the text does, that cause-and-effect relationships in history may be less certain than those in science and medicine. Have students read the skill and complete the practice questions.

Additonal Practice
📁 Skill Reinforcement Activity 8

GLENCOE TECHNOLOGY

 Glencoe's **Skillbuilder Interactive Workbook, Level 2** This interactive CD-ROM promotes student mastery of key social studies skills.

ANSWERS TO PRACTICING THE SKILL

1. Aryans were nomadic herders who delighted in waging war. Since their wealth was measured in cattle, they often raided one another's herds.
2. Cattle became the basis of the Aryans' diet and economy. Their language had dozens of words to describe cattle. Cattle were so important that they would in time be considered sacred and could not be eaten.

WORLD HISTORY Online

Have students use the **Chapter 8 Self-Check Quiz** at worldhistory.glencoe.com to prepare for the Chapter Test.

GLENCOE TECHNOLOGY

VIDEODISC
Use MindJogger to review the chapter.

MindJogger Videoquiz

Chapter 8
Disc 1 Side B

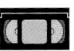

Also available in VHS.

Answers

Using Key Terms
1. j   3. e   5. d
2. h   4. i

Using Your History Journal

The 1998 *World Almanac* shows that 38,000 Buddhists live in Africa, 322 million in Asia, 1.6 million in Europe, 569,000 in Latin America, 920,000 in North America, and 200,000 in Oceania; of the world's Hindus, 2 million live in Africa, 787 million in Asia, 1.6 million in Europe, 760,000 in Latin America, 1.4 million in North America, and 323,000 in Oceania.

Reviewing Facts
1. Kshatriyas: warriors; led army, government, councils of elders. Brahmans: priests; performed religious rituals. Vaisyas: merchants, artisans, and farmers; cared for land; traded goods. Sudras: unskilled laborers, servants; served other castes
2. military officer who in 321 B.C. founded Mauryan Empire
3. All people suffer; people suffer because desire binds them to cycle of rebirth; eliminating desires will end suffering; desire is eliminated

WORLD HISTORY Online

Self-Check Quiz

Visit the *World History: The Human Experience* Web site at **worldhistory.glencoe.com** and click on *Chapter 8—Self-Check Quiz* to prepare for the Chapter Test.

Using Key Terms

Write the key term that completes each sentence. Then write a sentence for each term not chosen.

a. ahimsa	f. nirvana
b. dharma	g. rajah
c. epics	h. reincarnation
d. *jati*	i. stupas
e. karma	j. *varnas*

1. The invading Aryans brought to the Indian subcontinent a system of four main social classes, or _____.
2. Hindus believe in _____, a process of rebirth in which the soul resides in many bodies before it finally unites with Brahman Nerguna, or the universal spirit.
3. A person's _____ determines whether he or she will be closer to the universal spirit in the next life.
4. For purposes of prayer, Buddhist architects built large elaborate _____ over the remains of holy people.
5. Each *varna* was made up of social groups called _____ that were defined and ranked by different occupations.

Technology Activity

Using a Word Processor
Search the Internet or your local library to locate information about the following religions of India: Buddhism, Hinduism, Jainism, Sikhism, Christianity, and Islam. Use a word processor to organize your research into a fact sheet. Include headings such as religion, number of followers, basic beliefs, and major figures. Illustrate your chart with symbols of the different regions.

Using Your History Journal

Refer to a world almanac to determine how many Buddhists and how many Hindus live in each region of the world today. Build a graph or create a world map that illustrates this information.

Reviewing Facts

1. **Culture** Use a chart like the one below to identify the four main Hindu castes and their duties in the Indian caste system.

Caste Name	Duties
1.	
2.	
3.	
4.	

2. **History** Identify Chandragupta Maurya and his role in developing early Indian civilization.
3. **Culture** Explain in your own words the Four Noble Truths of Buddhism.
4. **Culture** Define *ahimsa* and describe how it is practiced in Indian society.
5. **Culture** Identify the *Bhagavad Gita*.
6. **Culture** Discuss the concept of dharma and how it affected Indian family life. What were the duties of husbands? Of wives?
7. **Science** List some of the achievements of Indian mathematicians during the Gupta Empire.
8. **History** Describe the achievements of Asoka's reign and their impact on Indian society.

Critical Thinking

1. **Apply** How could a person use the principle of nonviolence, or ahimsa, as a force for social change?
2. **Making Comparisons** In what ways are Buddhism and Christianity different? In what ways are they similar?
3. **Synthesize** What might have happened if Asoka had not been horrified while viewing the carnage after a fierce battle?

---

by following Eightfold Path.
4. Concept of karma creates desire to live a good life, and from that arose practice of nonviolence toward all living things, or ahimsa.
5. portion of the *Mahabharata*
6. Dharma refers to the duties of one's varna. A man took a wife and assumed responsibility for a family. A woman performed household tasks and served her husband and family.
7. advances in principles of algebra; explained

concept of infinity; invented concept of zero; devised symbols for numbers 1 to 9.
8. He renounced war, issued laws stressing concern for humans and written in local languages, built roads and hospitals, and promoted Buddhism, but also tolerance.

Critical Thinking
1. to force better treatment of humans
2. Differences: Christians believe in a personal

4. Analyze Here, two Brahman cattle stand in a street of Mumbai, India. Why do Hindus abstain from eating meat?

Understanding Themes

1. **Movement** How was India affected by the Aryan invasions?
2. **Innovation** What might make Buddhism attractive to people from different cultures?
3. **Cultural Diffusion** Why did Gupta achievements in science and the arts spread quickly to other parts of the world, both Eastern and Western?

1. The *varna* system created a huge underclass that Europeans called "the untouchables." How do you think this system created problems for modern India?
2. Religion has always had a major part in Indian society. How have religious differences hindered Indian unity in modern times?
3. Early in the 1900s, India applied the Hindu principle of nonviolence to help win its independence from Great Britain. Do you think people can still use nonviolence effectively to win freedom and human rights?

Geography in History

1. **Location** What mountain range forms India's northern border?
2. **Movement** What routes did the Aryan invaders take to the interior of India?
3. **Region** What effect did the invasion of the Aryans have on the developing culture of India?
4. **Human/Environment Interaction** What physical features made it difficult for one empire to unify all of northern and southern India?

Modern India

Skill Practice

Reread the discussion of "The Gupta Empire" in Section 3. Then answer the following questions.

1. What caused the Gupta rulers to use spies and assassins?
2. The Guptas adopted Hinduism as India's religion. What effects did this have on art and architecture?
3. What were the effects of Gupta science and mathematics on world civilization?
4. What caused the breakup of the Gupta Empire?

Chapter 8   *India's Great Civilization*   **217**

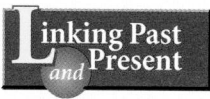

1. the *varna* system created vast social inequalities; it burdened the government with a large, needy underclass
2. Clashes between Hindus and Muslims have led to wars and tensions on the Indian subcontinent.
3. Students should weigh effects of violence against those of nonviolence in today's world.

Geography in History

1. Himalaya
2. through the passes in the Hindu Kush onto the Ganges Plain
3. The Aryans brought religious ideas and a rigid caste system to India as well as Sanskrit.
4. the Vindhya Range, the Godavari River, and the Thar Desert

Skill Practice

1. They wanted to maintain unquestioned authority.
2. beautiful temples were built, adorned with pictures and statues of Hindu gods and goddesses
3. Mathematicians made advances in algebra, invented the concept of zero, explained the concept of infinity, devised symbols for the numbers 1 to 9 we use today; astronomers knew the earth was round; doctors invented many surgical instruments.
4. The government began to fail and also faced invaders.

? Chapter Bonus Test Question

Ask students: The philosophy of nonviolence has been espoused by many Hindus. How do you reconcile this fact with the fact that Hindu India has been involved in many wars and armed struggles? (*not all Hindus believed in nonviolence, or some believed there could be instances of justifiable exceptions.*)

God, with Jesus as the way of salvation, while Buddhists do not believe in deities and affirm the Buddha as a teacher of enlightenment; Similarities: both stress compassion and doing good; they have influenced arts and thought in their respective regions.
3. Fierce wars might have continued to characterize the Indian empire; it would have encompassed more territory but had less cultural advancement.

4. Animals are considered sacred, and killing them is forbidden.

Understanding Themes

1. **MOVEMENT** cultural, social, linguistic influences
2. **INNOVATION** emphasis on nonviolence, social equality
3. **CULTURAL DIFFUSION** Trade extended achievements to other parts of the world.

A complete, 1-page lesson plan is provided for each section in the *Reproducible Lesson Plans* booklet.

China's Flourishing Civilization

CHAPTER RESOURCES

	Reproducible Resources	Multimedia Resources
Chapter Opener	📁 Chapter Themes: Graphic Organizer 9 📁 Historical Significance Chapter Activity 9	💿 MindJogger Videoquiz
Chapter Enrichment	📁 Vocabulary Activity 9* 📁 Time Line Activity 9 📁 Mapping History Activity 9 📁 History Simulation 9 📁 Geography and History Activity 9 📁 Source Reading 9 📁 People in World History Profiles 15, 16 📁 World Art and Music Activity 9 📁 Enrichment Activity 9 📁 Critical Thinking Activity 9 📁 Skill Reinforcement Activity 9 📁 Performance Assessment Activity 9 📁 Standardized Test Practice Workbook Activity 9 📁 Inclusion for the Social Studies Classroom Strategies and Activities	🔲 World History and Art Transparency 10, *Buddha*; 11, *Ming Phoenix Crown* 🔲 Chapter Transparency 9 🔲 NGS PicturePack Transparency Set: *Ancient China* 🔲 Vocabulary PuzzleMaker Software 💿 NGS PictureShow CD-ROM: *India and China* 🎵 World Music: Cultural Traditions, Lesson 8 💿 World History Primary Source Document Library
Chapter Review/Reteaching	📁 Reteaching Activity 9 📁 Skill Reinforcement Activity 9 📁 Spanish Chapter Summary 9	🎧 Chapter 9 Digest Audiocassette, Activity, Test* 🔲 Vocabulary PuzzleMaker Software 🔲 Interactive Tutor Self-Assessment Software 💿 MindJogger Videoquiz
Chapter Evaluation/Testing	📁 Performance Assessment Activity 9 📁 Chapter 9 Test, Forms A and B	🔲 💿 ExamView® Pro Testmaker

* Also available in Spanish

0:00 **OUT OF TIME?** Assign the Chapter 9 Audiocassettes.

World History Primary Source Document Library
Make History Come Alive!
Engage your students with over 250 easily accessible primary source documents—available on this CD-ROM—that will give them real life insight into the important events of world history.

Block Schedule

Activities that are particularly suited to use within the block scheduling framework are identified throughout this chapter by the following designation. 📦

KEY TO ABILITY LEVELS

Teaching strategies are coded for varying learning styles.
L1 **BASIC** activities for all students
L2 **AVERAGE** activities for average to above-average students
L3 **CHALLENGING** activities for above-average students
LEP **LIMITED ENGLISH PROFICIENCY** activities

Use Glencoe's *Presentation Plus!* multimedia teacher tool to easily present dynamic lessons that visually excite your students. Using Microsoft PowerPoint® you can customize the presentations to create your own personalized lessons.

Interactive Lesson Planner

Planning has never been easier! Using this CD-ROM, organize your week, month, semester, or year with all the help you need. The **Interactive Lesson Planner** gives you access to all of the blackline masters that accompany *World History: The Human Experience.*

SECTION RESOURCES

Daily Objectives	Reproducible Resources	Multimedia Resources
Section 1 **Three Great Dynasties** Summarize the major advances the Chinese made under the Zhou, the Qin, and the Han dynasties.	Lecture Notes 9-1 Reproducible Lesson Plan 9-1 Vocabulary Activity 9* Guided Reading Activity 9-1* Time Line Activity 9 Mapping History Activity 9 Section Quiz 9-1* Reading Essentials and Study Guide 9-1	Section Focus Transparency 9-1 Chapter Transparency 9 World History and Art Transparency 11, *Ming Phoenix Crown* Interactive Tutor Self-Assessment Software Testmaker
Section 2 **Three Ways of Life** Describe the philosophic ideals that helped to shape China's government.	Lecture Notes 9-2 Reproducible Lesson Plan 9-2 Vocabulary Activity 9* Guided Reading Activity 9-2* History Simulation 9 Geography and History Activity 9 Section Quiz 9-2* Reading Essentials and Study Guide 9-2	Section Focus Transparency 9-2 World History and Art Transparency 10, *Buddha* Interactive Tutor Self-Assessment Software Testmaker
Section 3 **Society and Culture** Explain how early Chinese society was organized and summarize the scientific and technological breakthroughs.	Lecture Notes 9-3 Reproducible Lesson Plan 9-3 Vocabulary Activity 9* Guided Reading Activity 9-3* Source Reading 9 People in World History Profiles 15, 16 World Art and Music Activity 9 Reteaching Activity 9 Enrichment Activity 9 Section Quiz 9-3* Performance Assessment Activity 9 Spanish Chapter Summary 9 Reading Essentials and Study Guide 9-3	Section Focus Transparency 9-3 NGS PicturePack Transparency Set: *Ancient China* Interactive Tutor Self-Assessment Software Testmaker World Music: Cultural Traditions, Lesson 8 NGS PictureShow CD-ROM: *India and China*

* Also available in Spanish

Chapter Activities

Performance Assessment Activity

A Last Will and Testament Have students take the roles of lawyers who help the philosophers and people of early China prepare wills in which they leave their artifacts, beliefs, and so on, to those nations, groups, or individuals in most need of them today. Students should use news media to find modern-day recipients in order to make connections with the past. Students should produce a document similar to an actual will and then present an oral "reading of the will" to classmates.

Possible Rubric Features

Concept attainment, content information, inferences and connections, decision-making skills, clarity, and appropriateness to purpose and audience

• *For an additional activity, refer to Activity 9 in the* Performance Assessment Strategies and Activities *booklet.*

ACTIVITY
From the Classroom of...

**Robert W. Gardner
New Canaan High
School
New Canaan, CT**

Ancient China

The purpose of this activity is to have students understand that Chinese civilization evolved as a result of varied political, social, economic, and geographic forces. It makes a good wrap-up activity for the chapter.

Organize students into groups of three or four and have them brainstorm four or five topics such as: the Great Wall, Confucianism, Daoism, the Silk Road, and the role of the family in Chinese culture. Students should take notes. Then give each student a copy of three short readings (either from periodicals or teacher-prepared), each one of which focuses on one of the three great dynasties. Have the class devote the remainder of the period to reading and studying them. The next day, have students write in-class essays of several paragraphs using assigned reading from the text, notes taken during brainstorming, and the teacher-provided readings. Pose essay questions that encourage students to integrate these sources. Samples: "To what degree did economic need and opportunity–along with the forces of geography–shape the political behavior of the great dynasties?" "What were the most outstanding aspects of Chinese culture and why did they develop at the time they did?"

MULTIPLE LEARNING STYLES

Verbal/Linguistic

Have students research myths and legends of the ancient Chinese and then write a series of stories recounting the myths in their own words.

Kinesthetic

Have students find an ancient Chinese nature painting that they admire. Then ask them to try painting a similar scene that is consistent with the Daoist emphasis on harmony with nature.

Interpersonal

Have students work in small groups to create a newsmagazine about this chapter. The magazine could carry news stories of significant events; profiles of important people; feature articles on family life, art, religion, and literature; and articles on significant achievements in science and technology. Have students illustrate the magazine with their own drawings or pictures cut from magazines.

Intrapersonal

Have students imagine that they are members of an ancient Chinese family. Ask them to keep a journal in which they recount interactions that reflect their position in their family.

GLENCOE'S ASSESSMENT ADVANTAGE

Use the following to easily assess student learning in a variety of ways.

• Performance Assessment Strategies and Activities
• Section Quizzes
• Chapter and Unit Tests
• Interactive Tutor Self-Assessment Software
• Testmaker Software
• MindJogger Videoquiz
• SAT/SAT II Test Practice
• worldhistory.glencoe.com

Additional Resources

NATIONAL GEOGRAPHIC SOCIETY — Teacher's Corner

INDEX TO NATIONAL GEOGRAPHIC MAGAZINE

The following articles relate to this chapter:

- "China's Terra-cotta Warriors," by O. Louis Mazzatenta, October 1996.
- "Pilgrimage to Buddhist Caves," by Reza, April 1996.
- "The Silk Road's Lost World," by Thomas B. Allen, March 1996.

NATIONAL GEOGRAPHIC SOCIETY PRODUCTS AVAILABLE FROM GLENCOE

To order the following, call Glencoe at 1-800-334-7344:

- *PictureShow: Ancient Civilizations: India and China (CD-ROM)*
- *PicturePack: Ancient China (Transparencies)*
- *PicturePack: Geography of Asia (Transparencies)*

ADDITIONAL NATIONAL GEOGRAPHIC SOCIETY PRODUCTS

To order the following, call National Geographic at 1-800-368-2728:

- *Physical Geography of the Continents: Asia (Video)*
- *China: Sichuan Province (Video)*
- *China: Beyond the Clouds (Video)*

Access National Geographic's new dynamic MapMachine Web site and other geography resources at:

- http://www.nationalgeographic.com/
- http://www.nationalgeographic.com/maps/

BIBLIOGRAPHY

Literature of the Period
Shih-Ching: The Classical Anthology Defined by Confucius. Translated by Ezra Pound. Cambridge: Harvard University Press, 1954. The *Book of Songs*, with songs and poetry from the 1100s to the 200s B.C.

Readings for the Student
Temple, Robert. *The Genius of China: 3,000 Years of Science, Discovery, and Invention.* New York: Simon and Schuster, 1989. Includes such inventions as the wheelbarrow, the stirrup, and the umbrella.

Readings for the Teacher
Fairbank, John King. *China: A New History.* Cambridge: Harvard University Press, 1992. A survey of Chinese history from antiquity to the Tiananmen Square protests.

WORLD HISTORY Online

Use our Web site as an additional resource. All essential content is covered in the Student Edition.

You and your students can visit the *World History: The Human Experience* Web site at worldhistory.glencoe.com The student text directs students to the Web site for the following options:

- **Chapter Overviews**
- **Student Web Activities**
- **Self-Check Quizzes**

Answers are provided for you in a link entitled "Web Activity Lesson Plan." Additional Web Resources, Interactive Puzzles, and content updates are also available.

Visit the Glencoe Web site at socialstudies.glencoe.com for social studies activities, updates, and links to other resources.

LOCAL OBJECTIVES

_____
_____
_____
_____
_____
_____
_____
_____
_____
_____
_____
_____
_____
_____
_____
_____
_____
_____

CHAPTER THEMES

Chapter Themes are listed by section on this chapter opening page of the Student Edition. A corresponding theme-based activity is available under "TEACH," and a theme-based question is asked in the Section and Chapter Assessments.

Storyteller

Historical Setting The family was the most important social unit in China, not only supplying basic human needs but also serving as the focus of religious practice through ancestor worship. Confucius was once asked why he did not take part in government. In response, he quoted from an ancient classic, the *Shu Ching* (Classic of History), "Simply by being a good son and friendly to his brothers a man can exert an influence upon government!" He thus made clear his belief that the public good is served by the practice of family ethics.

Historical Significance

Answers: *For centuries, Chinese society centered around the family and esteemed just government and ethical behavior, in keeping with the teachings of Confucius. Chinese arts have reflected the Daoist ideal of harmony with nature.*

Confucius's teachings served as a basis for Chinese society and government until the 1900s. The Daoist concept of yin and yang helped China accept new ideas, such as those of Buddhism, brought by traders and other foreigners.

— **WORLD HISTORY**
Online

Have students use the **Chapter 9 Overview** at worldhistory. glencoe.com as a prereading and postreading exercise for understanding chapter content.

China's Flourishing Civilization

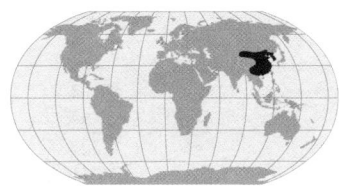

Chapter Themes

▶ **Uniformity** The Qin and Han dynasties establish and maintain a strong central government. *Section 1*
▶ **Innovation** The Chinese formulate ethical philosophies and make scientific and technological advances. *Section 2*
▶ **Cultural Diffusion** Traders carry ideas and products along the Silk Road. *Section 3*

Storyteller

Whom do you agree with in the following conversation, dating from the 500s B.C.? What is right, or "straightness," in this case?

The Governor of She said to Confucius: "In our village there is a man nicknamed Straight Body. When his father stole a sheep, he gave evidence against him." Confucius answered, "In our village those who are straight are quite different. Fathers cover up for their sons, and sons cover up for their fathers...."

This conversation involves a conflict between law and family. Confucius's view—that family should always take precedence—reflects an attitude toward families that was dominant in Chinese culture for a long time.

Historical Significance

How did the ideas of Confucius and other Chinese thinkers affect behavior in Chinese society for centuries? How have their ideas influenced China's development and its relationship with other parts of the world?

600 B.C.

551 B.C.
Confucius is born.

300 B.C.

202 B.C.
Liu Bang founds the Han dynasty.

126 B.C. Explorer Zhang Qian returns from the West.

A.D. 1

A.D. 220
Han dynasty falls.

A.D. 300

218

GEOGRAPHY CONNECTION

Place Have students locate China on a world map. How does China rank among the nations of the world in terms of size? *(third largest, after Russia and Canada)* What bodies of water encircle its coastline from north to south? (Yellow Sea, East China Sea, Taiwan Strait, South China Sea) With what countries does it share its land frontier to the south? *(Hong Kong, Vietnam, Laos, Myanmar)* To the southwest? *(India, Bhutan, Nepal, Kyrgyzstan, Tajikistan, Afghanistan)* To the north? *(Kazakhstan, Russia, Mongolia)* To the northeast? *(North Korea)*

Visualizing History Although the Chinese had built protective walls since the 600s B.C., Qin ruler Shihuangdi was, according to tradition, the first Chinese ruler to build a Great Wall to deter invasion. Most of the Qin wall, however, was north of the Great Wall tourists visit today, which was built mostly during the Ming dynasty (A.D. 1368–1644).

Visualizing History

The Great Wall of China at Huang Ya Guan, a view of a section of the 4,000-mile-long wall

Performance Assessment

Refer to the activity on page 219C of the Planning Guide.

For an additional activity, refer to Activity 9 in the *Performance Assessment Strategies and Activities* booklet.

Using Your History Journal

Instruct students to include the approximate date of the invention, the need that led to it, and the approximate date the invention made its way beyond China.

 WORLD HISTORY *Online*

Chapter Overview

Visit the *World History: The Human Experience* Web site at **worldhistory.glencoe.com** and click on *Chapter 9—Chapter Overview* to preview the chapter.

Your History Journal

Chinese inventions and discoveries include many "firsts" such as printed books, the compass, and gunpowder. Choose one Chinese invention or discovery reported in this chapter and write a short research report on its early history.

Chapter 9 *China's Flourishing Civilization* **219**

GLENCOE TECHNOLOGY

VIDEODISC
Use MindJogger to preview chapter content.

MindJogger Videoquiz

Chapter 9
Disc 2 Side A

 Also available in VHS.

✚ EXTRA CREDIT PROJECT

Research Over the course of history, China's Great Wall has been transformed from a defense against invaders to a lure for tourists. Have students research the history of the Great Wall from ancient times to the present.

Suggested resources: J. Fryer, *The Great Wall of China*; A. Waldron, *The Great Wall of China: From History to Myth*; C. Capa, ed., *Behind the Great Wall of China*.

1000 B.C.		500 B.C.		A.D. 1	A.D. 500

771 B.C. Zhou political power begins to decline.

221 B.C. Qin Shihuangdi founds the Qin dynasty.

141 B.C. Wudi becomes the sixth Han emperor.

Section 1

Three Great Dynasties

Guide to Reading

Read to Find Out
Main Idea *China made major advances under the Zhou, Qin, and Han dynasties.*

▶ **Terms to Define**
cavalry, civil service, mandarin

▶ **People to Meet**
Qin Shihuangdi, Liu Bang, Wudi, Zhang Qian

▶ **Places to Locate**
Great Wall of China, Silk Road

The **Storyteller**

Seeing the Marquis Chao of Han asleep on the cold floor, the keeper of the royal hat covered him with a robe. Upon awakening, the marquis demanded to know who had covered him. Learning the keeper of the hat was responsible, the marquis punished the keeper of the robe for failing to perform his duty. Then he punished the keeper of the hat for undertaking tasks not his to perform. The trespass of one official upon the duties of another was considered a great danger.

—adapted from *Basic Writing of Mo Tzu, Hsün Tzu, and Han Fei Tzu,* reprinted in *The Global Experience: Readings in World History to 1500,* 1987

Late Zhou jade dragon

Around 1100 B.C., the Chinese people were fashioning ideas that would result in a unique civilization. From then until the A.D. 200s, the Chinese lived under three dynasties, or ruling families—the Zhou (JOH), the Qin (CHIN), and the Han (HAHN). The first of these, the Zhou, ruled the nation for more than 800 years, longer than any other Chinese dynasty.

The Enduring Zhou

The Zhou conquered the last Shang dynasty king around 1028 B.C., claiming the Mandate of Heaven, or heaven's approval. They called their king the Son of Heaven, saying that the Shang had lost the mandate by ruling poorly.

Eventually, the Zhou held a vast realm. To control their holdings, Zhou kings set up an agricultural system in which nobles owned the land and peasants worked it. They appointed their relatives to govern, giving each one a city-state.

Each local lord had total authority on his own lands and built his own army. At first all the lords pledged allegiance to the Son of Heaven. In time, though, some grew strong enough to challenge the king's authority.

In 771 B.C. the Zhou suffered a severe defeat in a conflict with their enemies. After that, political power fell increasingly to local nobles. In the next centuries, the nobles fought small wars until by the 200s B.C., several city-states were locked in a struggle that ended the Zhou era.

Even though Zhou rulers lost their power, the Zhou are remembered for many technological advances. During the Zhou period the Chinese built roads and expanded foreign trade. They obtained horses from western nomads, forming a

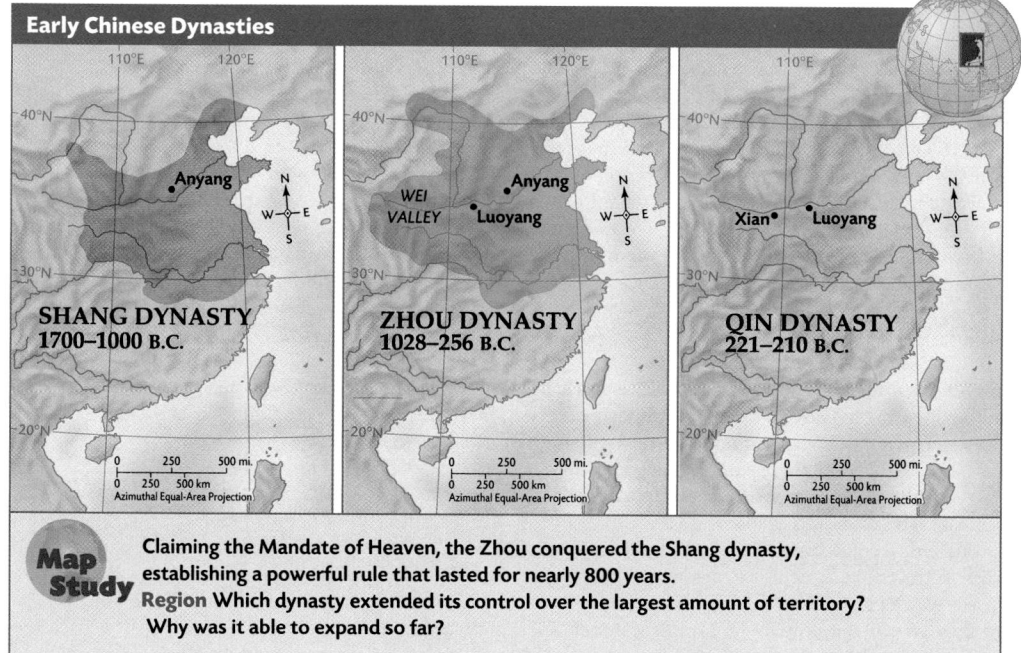

Early Chinese Dynasties

SHANG DYNASTY
1700–1000 B.C.
• Anyang

ZHOU DYNASTY
1028–256 B.C.
WEI VALLEY • Anyang • Luoyang

QIN DYNASTY
221–210 B.C.
Xian • • Luoyang

Map Study Claiming the Mandate of Heaven, the Zhou conquered the Shang dynasty, establishing a powerful rule that lasted for nearly 800 years.
Region Which dynasty extended its control over the largest amount of territory? Why was it able to expand so far?

cavalry, or group of mounted warriors, along with horse-drawn chariots. The Zhou also added a deadly weapon: the crossbow. They further elaborated the system of picture writing begun by the Shang, a system that is the ancestor of modern Chinese writing. Under the Zhou, iron plows were invented, irrigation systems were developed, and flood-control systems were initiated. These and other advances led to population growth, and Zhou China became the world's most densely populated country.

The Mighty Qin

Meanwhile, several small states were struggling for control in China. Among them was a state on the western border ruled by the Qin. By 221 B.C., the Qin had wiped out the Zhou and conquered the rest of northern China, uniting much of the nation under a strong central authority for the first time. Westerners would later call the nation *China* after the Qin, whose first ruler added the title Shihuangdi (SHUR•HWONG•DEE), or First Emperor, to his name.

A tireless ruler, **Qin Shihuangdi** set out to create a government directly under his control. He reorganized the empire into military districts, appointing officials to govern them. This system prevented local lords from becoming strong enough to challenge the power of the central government—the problem that had led to the downfall of the Zhou.

The First Emperor made other changes to further centralize his control. He devised a system of weights and measures to replace the various systems used in different regions. He standardized coins, instituted a uniform writing system, and set up a law code throughout China.

Qin had grandiose plans for his empire, and he used forced labor to accomplish them. Gangs of Chinese peasants dug canals and built roads.

Footnotes to History

Court Magic
A court magician made a potion for Wudi, claiming that it would give immortality. Before the emperor got the potion, a scholar drank it. The scholar was immediately sentenced to death but told Wudi that, if the potion was genuine, Wudi would not be able to kill him. If the potion was a fake, he had done no harm. Wudi had to agree. Needless to say, the scholar had exposed a fraud.

Chapter 9   *China's Flourishing Civilization*   **221**

TEACH

Guided Practice

THEME Uniformity
Have students assemble a list of the main features of the Qin empire. (*central government that controlled all districts, standardized system of weights and measures, uniform writing system, uniform law code, built roads and canals, began building Great Wall*) Help students to see how these features contributed to uniformity in China. **L1**

Map Study

Answer
the Qin dynasty; by centralizing control of the empire

Map Skills Practice

Reading a Map About how far apart were the Zhou capitals? (*more than 1/4" apart on the map, or about 130 to 170 miles apart*) The Qin capitals? (*slightly more than 1/4 of an inch apart on the map, or about 125 to 250 miles*)

Critical Thinking Have students name the many technological advances of the Zhou dynasty. (*roads, horses, crossbow, improved writing system, iron plows, irrigation systems, flood control*) Have students suggest ways these advances could have led to population growth. **L2**

 Chapter Transparency 9

 World History and Art Transparency 11

COOPERATIVE LEARNING ACTIVITY

An Interview Assign two groups of students the task of preparing a *Meet the Press* interview with either Qin Shihuangdi or the Han emperor Wudi. Remind students that each group member must contribute to the research effort. One student should play the person to be interviewed, and the other group members should act as reporters. All group members should prepare a list of questions, such as "What did you learn from your predecessors?" "What reforms are you planning and how will they affect the people?" Each group should work together to prepare answers for their questions. Have each group present their interview to the class. **L2**

Independent Practice

 Guided Reading Activity 9-1 **L1**

Time Line Activity 9

Mapping History Activity 9

Geography: Place Have students examine a physical map of China and then write a brief explanation of why the ancient Chinese thought of their country as the "Middle Country" or the center of the civilized world. (*China is isolated by geographic barriers.*) **L2**

Have students use the **Chapter 9 Student Web Activity** at worldhistory.glencoe.com for in-depth study of the Han Dynasty.

ASSESS

Check for Understanding

Assign Section 1 Assessment as homework or as an in-class activity.

🖵 Use Interactive Tutor Self-Assessment Software to review Section 1.

Evaluate

 Section Quiz 9-1

🖵 Use the Testmaker to create a customized quiz for Section 1.

Reteach

Work with students to make lists summarizing the main activities and contributions of the three dynasties in this section. Have students explain how each activity helped or harmed the country.

Reading Essentials and Study Guide 9-1

The Great Wall

To Qin, one building project seemed especially urgent—shoring up China's defenses to the north. Earlier rulers had built walls to prevent attacks by nomadic invaders. Qin ordered those walls connected. Over several years some 300,000 peasants toiled—and thousands died—to complete the more than 4,000-mile-long (6,437 km) wall. Rebuilt by later rulers, the **Great Wall of China** stands today as a monument to Qin's ambition and to the peasants who carried out their emperor's will.

Qin's Strict Rule

Qin Shihuangdi imposed a new order on China. He ended the power of the local lords by taking land from many of them and imposing a tax on landowners. He appointed educated men instead of nobles as officials to run his government.

Qin even imposed censorship, clamping down on scholars who discussed books and ideas. In 213 B.C. he ordered all books burned except those about "practical" subjects like agriculture, medicine, and magic. In this way he hoped to break people's ties to the past so they would not criticize the present. About 460 scholars resisted and were executed.

Qin's subjects saw him as a cruel tyrant who had lost the Mandate of Heaven. Nobles were angry because he had destroyed the aristocracy; scholars detested him for the burning of books; and peasants hated his forced-labor gangs. In 210 B.C. Qin died, and soon the dynasty itself came to an end. Even so, the rule of the Qin established foundations for the Chinese state that would last 2,000 years.

The Glorious Han

In 207 B.C. **Liu Bang** (LYOH BONG) overthrew the Qin. A military official from a peasant background, Liu defeated his most powerful rival in 202 B.C. and declared himself the emperor of a new dynasty, the Han. The Han governed China until A.D. 220, more than 400 years. The Han emperors used Qin forms of centralized power, but without the harshness of Qin rule. Han China rivaled the Roman Empire in its power and achievement.

Student Web Activity 9

Visit the *World History: The Human Experience* Web site at **worldhistory.glencoe.com** and click on *Chapter 9—Student Web Activities* for an activity relating to the Han dynasty.

Advances Under Wudi

The Han dynasty reached its peak during the reign of **Wudi** (WOO•DEE), who ruled from 141 B.C. to 87 B.C. Wudi, one of the most talented and dynamic rulers in Chinese history, personally supervised all aspects of his government.

An ambitious ruler, Wudi extended his empire. He sent huge armies against nomadic invaders and other non-Chinese peoples. He conquered lands to the north, including Korea and Manchuria, south into Southeast Asia, and west to northern India.

In 139 B.C. Wudi sent out an expedition led by **Zhang Qian** (JAHNG CHYEN), a general and explorer. Thirteen years later, Zhang staggered back. His troops had been nearly wiped out by barbarian attacks, and the general had endured more than 10 years of captivity.

Zhang brought back amazing tales heard on his travels. He told of a great empire to the west, with huge cities full of people "who cut their hair short, wear embroidered garments, and ride in very small chariots." Zhang, who was describing Rome, gave Han rulers their first hint of another civilization as advanced as their own.

Wudi's new interest in the West, fed by news of Zhang Qian's explorations, led to the expansion of trade routes later known as the **Silk Road**. Winding past deserts and through mountain passes, the Silk Road linked East and West. It allowed traders to exchange China's fine silk for Middle Eastern and European products, such as gold, glassware, and wool and linen fabrics.

Pax Sinica

Under the Han, China enjoyed a 400-year period of prosperity and stability, later referred to as the *Pax Sinica* (PAHKS SIH•nuh•kuh), the Chinese Peace. The *Pax Sinica* coincided with the *Pax Romana* in the West.

During the *Pax Sinica*, Wudi adopted an economic policy designed to prevent food shortages and high prices. Government agents stored surplus food during years of plenty and sold it when harvests were poor. Under this system, China was able to feed its growing population.

Before Wudi, emperors had chosen as their officials members of their families or of the aristocracy, a practice that led easily to corruption in government. Wudi wanted talented people to govern, and so he initiated changes. He asked people to recommend candidates, who then took long, difficult written examinations. After an official "graded" the tests, the emperor evaluated the results and appointed those with the highest scores.

Silk Road

A caravan of men and mules walk a trail that once formed part of the old Silk Road, a work of paths cutting across from the Pacific coast of [Chin]a to the Mediterranean Sea. [The] route, first traveled many years before the [Chri]stian era, was the passageway not only for Chinese [silk] but for a great range of products including jade and [gold], ideas and paintings. Today it is still possible to [see] how poles and rocks created the actual highway [over] which goods moved throughout many centuries— [befor]e ships, trains, buses, and airplanes replaced [mul]es and packs.

You can trace the length of the trip on the accompanying map. A trader setting forth from the Chinese city of Nanjing would soon leave Chinese territory and enter a world of Muslim ethnic groups and treacherous terrain. The trail loops south and north of the scorching Takla Makan Desert and rises high through mountain passes across the Pamir Mountains. The whole trip was far too long for a single caravan to undertake. Instead, Chinese or Persian merchants dealt with central Asian middlemen from lands such as Afghanistan and Turkestan. ⊕

Chapter 9 *China's Flourishing Civilization* **223**

Thomas J. Abercrombie
National Geographic Publications Art Division

TEACH

Tell students that for more than 2,000 years, the Silk Road and its extensions westward into Roman territory made up the world's longest road. The travel distance along the length of the road and its western extensions totaled 8,000 miles (12,800 km). Ask students in which direction the silk traveled. *(westward)* Point out to students that among the ideas China received via the road were Christianity and Buddhism.

CURRICULUM CONNECTION

ENGINEERING
Part of the Silk Road is currently in use as a paved highway linking Pakistan and Sinkiang Uihgur Autonomous Region, China. The ancient trade route was the inspiration for a United Nations' plan for a trans-Asian highway.

Map Study

Answer

China is isolated by mountains to the north and west, the Gobi to the northwest, and the sea to the east.

Map Skills Practice

Reading a Map From what regions does the Great Wall separate China? (*Manchuria, Mongolia, and the Gobi*)

Enrich

Students may wonder why the spelling of the names *Qin* and *Zhou*, as well as other Chinese personal and place names, appear in different spellings in different books. Have students research the Wade-Giles and pinyin systems for writing Chinese in languages using the Latin alphabet.

CLOSE

Organize the class into two teams. Appoint one person as scorekeeper. Have the teams take turns challenging each other by giving specific names or occurrences and having the other team identify the ruler or dynasty under which the person lived or the event occurred.

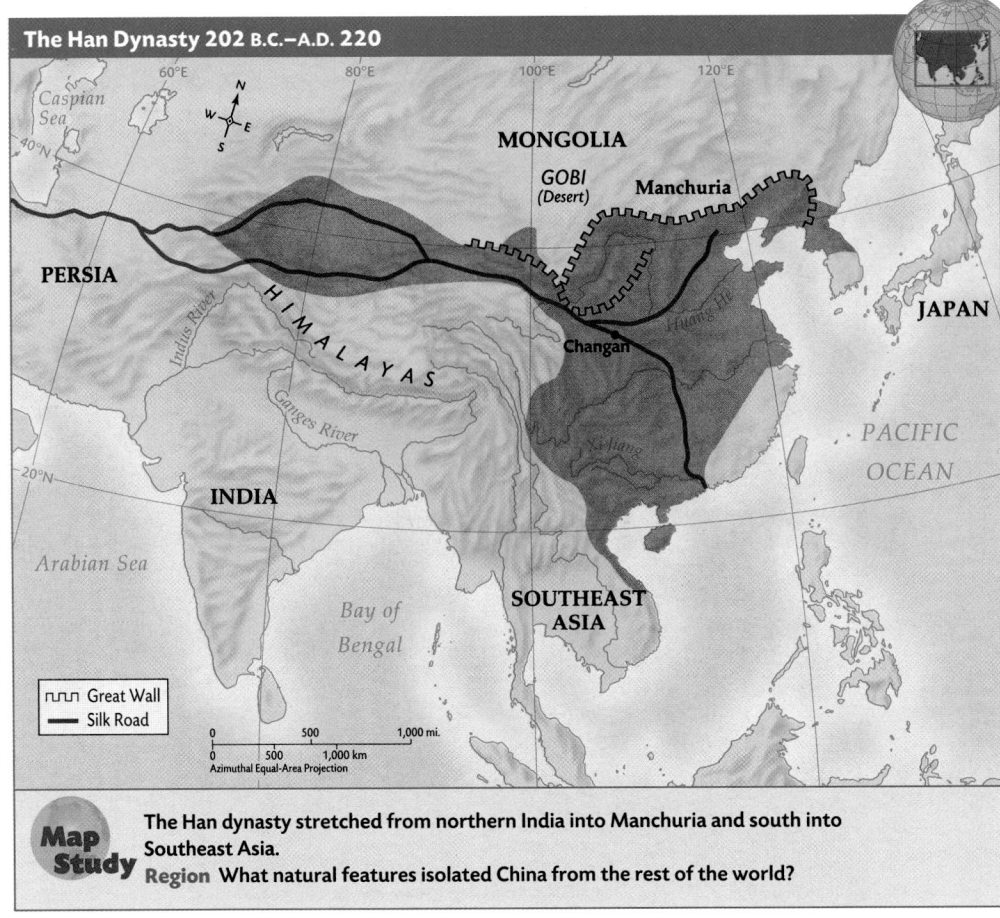

The Han Dynasty 202 B.C.–A.D. 220

Great Wall
Silk Road

0   500   1,000 mi.
0 500 1,000 km
Azimuthal Equal-Area Projection

Map Study The Han dynasty stretched from northern India into Manchuria and south into Southeast Asia.
Region What natural features isolated China from the rest of the world?

Wudi's examinations evolved into the civil service, a system that, in theory, allowed anyone with ability to attain public office. In practice, the system favored the wealthy, for usually only they could afford to obtain enough education to pass the exams.

The civil service system made scholars the most respected members of society. A new class of educated civil servants, called mandarins, controlled the government and would do so until the early 1900s.

After Wudi's reign, Han power declined until the dynasty eventually fell in A.D. 220. However, Han achievements in government, technology, science, and the arts were lasting.

SECTION 1 ASSESSMENT

Main Idea
1. Use a chart like the one below to list China's major advances under the Zhou, Qin, and Han dynasties.

Zhou	Qin	Han

Recall
2. **Define** cavalry, civil service, mandarin.
3. **Identify** Qin Shihuangdi, Liu Bang, Wudi, Zhang Qian.

Critical Thinking
4. **Analyzing Information** Did Wudi's civil service system offer equal opportunity to all people in the Chinese Empire? Give reasons from the text for your answer.

Understanding Themes
5. **Uniformity** How did Qin Shihuangdi politically unite China?

224 **Chapter 9** *China's Flourishing Civilization*

SECTION 1 ASSESSMENT ANSWERS

1. Zhou: built roads; expanded foreign trade; imported horses and formed cavalry; used the crossbow; expanded picture writing; developed irrigation systems; began flood control. Qin: devised system of weights and measures; standardized coins; uniform writing system; law code throughout China; built Great Wall of China. Han: extended empire; expanded trade routes through Silk Road; economic policies prevented food shortages and high prices

2. All terms are defined in the Glossary.
3. Qin Shihuangdi, 221; Liu Bang, 222; Wudi, 222; Zhang Qian, 222

4. No: it abolished the system whereby rulers chose family members as officials, but it discriminated against those who could not afford education in the classics.
5. **UNIFORMITY** standardized coins; uniform tax system, writing system, weights and measures

c. 522 B.C. Confucius begins to teach.

c. 500 B.C. Daoism emerges as a major Chinese philosophy.

c. A.D. 400 Buddhism becomes a popular religion in China.

Section 2

Three Ways of Life

Guide to Reading

Read to Find Out
Main Idea *China's philosophic ideals helped to shape its government.*

▶ **Terms to Define**
ethics, filial piety, yin and yang

▶ **People to Meet**
Confucius (Kongfuzi), Laozi

The Storyteller

One of the duties of Prince Wei-hui's cook was to slaughter cattle for the royal table. When he performed this task, all his movements were harmonious, like a dance. The prince was amazed and asked his servant how he was able to do such heavy work so effortlessly. The cook explained, "What your servant loves is the Tao, which I have applied to the skill of carving. I work with my mind, and not with my eyes." In this way, the toughest cuts yielded easily before his skill. He had learned how to nurture his spirit while maintaining his livelihood.

—adapted from *A Source Book in Chinese Philosophy,* reprinted in *Lives and Times: A World History Reader,* James P. Holoka and Jiu-Hwa L. Upshur, 1994

Confucius

During the late Zhou era, scholars sought solutions to the problems of political breakdown and social disorder that were paralyzing China. Their efforts led to the rise of major philosophies, such as Confucianism, Legalism, and Daoism. These philosophies dealt very little with the supernatural or with eternal life; instead, they focused on life in this world and how it should be lived. By the latter part of the Han dynasty, between A.D. 50 and A.D. 100, Buddhism had reached China, and the Chinese blended its insights with those of Confucianism and Daoism.

POINT

Confucianism

China's most influential scholar was **Kongfuzi** (KOONG•FOO•DZUH), known in the West as **Confucius**. Born about 551 B.C. to a peasant family, Confucius at first sought a political post but later became a teacher. In his teachings, Confucius stated that social harmony and good government would return to China if people lived according to principles of ethics—good conduct and moral judgment. When a student asked Confucius for a single word that could serve as a principle for conduct, he responded: "Perhaps the word *reciprocity* will do. Do not do unto others what you would not want others to do unto you." This rule is similar to a familiar teaching of Judaism and Christianity, sometimes called the Golden Rule: "Do unto others as you would have others do unto you."

The Five Relationships

Confucius stressed the importance of moral behavior in five basic relationships: ruler and subject, parent and child, husband and wife, old and young, and friend and friend. A code of proper conduct governed each of these relationships. For example, rulers had a duty to rule justly and to set

Chapter 9 *China's Flourishing Civilization* **225**

SECTION THEME

▶ **Innovation** The Chinese formulate ethical philosophies and make technological advances.

Guide to Reading

For reading strategies to help students read effectively see pages 12–13.

Vocabulary Pre-check

▣ Use the Vocabulary PuzzleMaker for Chapter 9 to create a crossword puzzle to reinforce section terms. **L1 LEP**

📁 Use Vocabulary Activity 9 to introduce vocabulary terms. **L1 LEP**

FOCUS
Section Objective

Describe the philosophic ideals that shaped China's government.

BELLRINGER
Motivational Activity

 Before taking roll, project Section Focus Transparency 9-2 and have students answer the activity questions.
📁 This activity is also available as a blackline master.

POINT

Confucianism How did Confucianism influence Chinese history? *It provided ethical guidelines for social and political life.*

SECTION RESOURCES

📁 Reproducible Masters
- Lecture Notes 9-2
- Reproducible Lesson Plan 9-2
- Vocabulary Activity 9
- Guided Reading Activity 9-2
- History Simulation 9
- Geography and History Activity 9

- Section Quiz 9-2
- Reading Essentials and Study Guide 9-2

📃 Transparencies
- Section Focus Transparency 9-2
- World History and Art Transparency 10

Multimedia
▣ Interactive Tutor Self-Assessment Software
▣ Testmaker

TEACH
Guided Practice

THEME Innovation

Have students explain the new ideas put forth by Confucius and Laozi. (*Confucius: filial piety, ethical conduct toward others, importance of accepting one's role in society, reverence for the past; Laozi: renouncing worldly ambitions, harmony with nature, yin/yang*) **L1**

Independent Practice

 Guided Reading Activity 9-2 **L1**

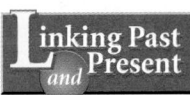
Linking Past and Present

Measuring Earthquakes

The seismograph in the picture is a model. Experts have been able to create one similar to Zhang Heng's based upon available descriptions.

ANSWER

The mechanism of the ancient seismograph included: a ball falling into a metal toad's mouth whenever a tremor occurred, with the side of the seismograph indicating the quake's direction and the ball's loudness, the tremor's strength. Modern seismographs have sensors that detect the seismic waves, producing wavy lines that reflect the size of the waves, with impressions registered on paper, film, or recording tape. The ancient Chinese believed earthquakes were caused by angry spirits and therefore looked for divine messages; modern scientific views state that earthquakes are caused by shifting in the earth's crust that sends out seismic waves.

ASSESS
Check for Understanding

Assign Section 2 Assessment as homework or as an in-class activity.

Use Interactive Tutor Self-Assessment Software to review Section 2.

---

an example of right living. In return, subjects should be loyal and obey the law.

The most basic relationships, however, concerned the family. Confucius cared especially about filial piety, or children's respect for their parents and elders. For Confucius, the family represented society in miniature. He said:

> **The superior man spreads his culture to the entire nation by remaining at home.... The teaching of filial piety is a preparation for serving the ruler of the state; the teaching of respect for one's elder brothers is a preparation for serving all the elders of the community; and the teaching of kindness in parents is a training for ruling over people....When individual families have learned kindness, then the whole nation has learned kindness.**

After Confucius died in 479 B.C., his teachings were collected in a work called the *Analects*. During the Han dynasty, Confucian ethics provided the basis for the civil service system. They would continue to shape Chinese society and government until the early 1900s.

Legalism

Opposition to Confucian ideas, however, came from scholars known as Legalists. Legalism, as their philosophy was called, rejected the Confucian idea of learning by example. Instead, it emphasized the importance of strict laws and harsh punishments.

Legalism developed from the teachings of Hanfeizi (HAHN•FAY•DZEE), a scholar who lived during the 200s B.C. According to Hanfeizi, humans were by nature evil and required a strong, forceful government to make them attend to their duties. Because of its justification of force and power, Legalism was favored by many nobles and became the official policy of the Qin dynasty that unified China during the 200s B.C. Legalism later gave way to Confucianism. However, Legalism's influence was reflected in the harsh laws and punishments often inflicted on China's peasant population.

Daoism

In spite of their differences, Confucianism and Legalism both stressed the importance of an orderly society. Another philosophy called Daoism, however,

---

CONNECTIONS
Science and Technology
Measuring Earthquakes

People in Han China believed that earthquakes were caused by angry spirits expressing their displeasure with society. Scholars studied quakes closely in hope of finding a divine message.

In A.D. 132 Zhang Heng invented the world's first seismograph, an instrument for detecting and measuring earthquakes. Zhang's device resembled a domed, cylindrical urn. Each of eight dragons around the top held a ball in its jaws. At the base of the urn sat eight toads with upturned heads and open mouths, each directly under a dragon.

Zhang Heng's seismograph

When a tremor occurred, a mechanism caused one of the balls to fall into a toad's mouth. This action showed that somewhere an earthquake was taking place. The side of the seismograph where that toad was sitting indicated the quake's direction. As the ball popped into the toad's mouth, the loudness indicated the tremor's strength.

Today we know that shifting in the earth's crust causes earthquakes. This movement sends seismic waves across the earth's surface much as dropping a pebble in a pond sends ripples across water. Modern seismographs have sensors that can detect ground motions caused by seismic waves from both near and distant earthquakes. The sensors produce wavy lines that reflect the size of seismic waves passing beneath them. Impressions of the waves are registered on paper, film, or recording tape, or are stored and displayed by computers.

Linking Past and Present **ACTIVITY**

Contrast the workings of ancient and modern seismographs. Then, examine the differences in ancient Chinese and modern views about the causes of earthquakes.

226   **Chapter 9**   *China's Flourishing Civilization*

COOPERATIVE LEARNING ACTIVITY

Panel Discussion Organize the class into three groups. Assign one of the following thinkers to each group: Confucius, Laozi, the Buddha. Have each group research the teachings of its thinker. (Alert students that they may find variant spellings: *Kongzi, Kungfuzi,* or *Kung-fu-tzu* for *Confucius; Tao* instead of *Dao;* and *Lao-tzu* or other variants for *Laozi.*) Ask each group to prepare for a panel discussion in which each thinker will explain how his ideas can benefit individuals and society. Each group should appoint one student to role-play the thinker. Other students should be prepared to ask questions of the panel members. You or a student should act as panel moderator. **L2**

emphasized living in harmony with nature. Daoism rejected formal social structures and the idea that people must fill specific roles in society.

Daoist Ideas

Daoism traced its origins to the teachings of a scholar named **Laozi** (LOW•DZUH), who is thought to have lived sometime around the 500s B.C. Laozi's ideas were recorded in the *Dao De Jing*, a Chinese classic. His followers, known as Daoists, believed that people should renounce worldly ambitions and turn to nature and the Dao, the universal force that guides all things. They used examples from nature to describe how one follows the Dao:

> ❝ The highest good is like water.
> Water gives life to the ten thousand things
>   and does not strive.
> It flows in places men reject and so is like
>   the Dao.
> In dwelling, be close to the land.
> In meditation, go deep in the heart.
> In dealing with others, be gentle and kind.
> In speech, be true.
> In ruling, be just. ❞

By emphasizing harmony with nature, Daoists deeply influenced Chinese painting and poetry.

Daoist simplicity seems to oppose Confucian formalism, but a person could be both a Confucianist and a Daoist. Confucianism provided the pattern for government and one's place in the social order, and Daoism emphasized harmony within the individual attuned to nature. Because the emphasis of each was different, a person could easily be both.

Yin and Yang

A Chinese theory related to Daoist ideas was the concept of yin and yang, the two opposing forces believed to be present in all nature. Yin was cool, dark, female, and submissive, while yang was warm, light, male, and aggressive. Everything had both elements. For harmony the two elements had

History & Art Laozi on his buffalo. Guimet Museum, Paris, France. *How did the teachings recorded in the* Dao De Jing *influence Chinese arts and poetry?*

to be in balance. Human life and natural events resulted from the interplay between yin and yang.

The concept of yin and yang helped the Chinese reconcile seeming opposites—like Dao simplicity and Confucian formalism. It also helped them accept Buddhist ideas brought to China by monks and traders from India.

Buddhism

Buddhism reached China just as the Han Empire was collapsing, and its emphasis on personal salvation in nirvana appealed to many people seeking an escape from suffering. Confucianists could follow its Eightfold Path, and Daoists admired its use of meditation. By the A.D. 400s, Buddhism was widely embraced in China.

SECTION 2 ASSESSMENT

Main Idea
1. Use a diagram like the one below to show what ideas of Confucianism and Legalism shaped China's government.

Confucianism	Legalism

Chinese Government

Recall
2. **Define** ethics, filial piety, yin and yang.
3. **Identify** Confucius, Laozi.

Critical Thinking
4. **Making Comparisons** Compare Confucianist and Daoist ideas and ways of life.

Understanding Themes
5. **Innovation** How did the concept of yin and yang help the Chinese people reconcile opposing ideas in the thought of Daoism that seemed opposed to Confucianism? Explain.

History & Art
Laozi was a scholar at the royal court of the Zhou dynasty. When he realized that the Zhou dynasty was in decline, he made a legendary voyage to the state of Qin. The guardian of the pass to the Qin state begged Laozi to write a book for him. The result was the *Dao De Jing*.
Answer to Caption: *Laozi's teachings influenced Chinese arts by emphasizing harmony with nature.*

Evaluate
📁 Section Quiz 9-2

💻 Use the Testmaker to create a customized quiz for Section 2.

Reteach
Have students meet in small groups to discuss the three belief systems of ancient China. Have the groups identify the primary teachings of each system.

📁 Reading Essentials and Study Guide 9-2

Enrich
Have students write a report on Buddhism today, describing each of the major traditions, its beliefs, and where it is practiced.

CLOSE

Have students explain how a Han Chinese family might have practiced Confucianism, Daoism, and Buddhism simultaneously.

SECTION 2 ASSESSMENT ANSWERS

1. Confucianism: ruler to rule justly and set example; subjects to be loyal and obey law. Legalism: harsh laws and punishments, especially for peasants
2. All terms are defined in the Glossary.
3. Confucius, 225; Laozi, 227

4. Confucianists were scholars and public officials concerned about a structured, orderly society, while Daoists were thinkers who discounted social roles and concentrated on achieving harmony with nature.

5. **INNOVATION** The concept of yin and yang taught that opposing forces were present in all of nature.

SECTION THEME

▶ **Cultural Diffusion** Traders carry ideas and products along the Silk Road.

Guide to Reading

For reading strategies to help students read effectively see pages 12–13.

Vocabulary Pre-check

 Use the Vocabulary PuzzleMaker for Chapter 9 to create a crossword puzzle to reinforce section terms. **L1 LEP**

📁 Use Vocabulary Activity 9 to introduce vocabulary terms. **L1 LEP**

FOCUS

Section Objective

Explain how early Chinese society was organized and summarize the scientific and technological breakthroughs.

BELLRINGER
Motivational Activity

 Before taking roll at the beginning of the class period, project Section Focus Transparency 9-3 and have students answer the activity questions. Discuss students' responses.

📁 This activity is also available as a blackline master.

1000 B.C. | **500 B.C.** | **A.D. 1**

1000 B.C. Chinese begin poems in the *Book of Songs*.

240 B.C. Chinese astronomers record appearance of Halley's comet.

c. 100 B.C. Chinese invent paper.

Section 3

Society and Culture

Guide to Reading

Read to Find Out

Main Idea *Many scientific and technological breakthroughs took place in early China.*

▶ **Terms to Define**
hierarchy, extended family, nuclear family, acupuncture

▶ **People to Meet**
Sima Qian

The Storyteller

Wu Phu was a physician, trained by Hua Tho, an outstanding medical theorist. Hua Tho impressed upon his pupils the importance of physical exercise as a means of obtaining good health. He compared an exercised body to running water, which never became stale. "When the body feels ill," he counseled, "one should do one of these exercises. After perspiring, one will sense the body grow light and the stomach will manifest hunger." There was merit in those recommendations. Wu Phu had carefully followed his master's regimen, and although he was past ninety years of age, his hearing, vision, and even his teeth were all still excellent.

Acupuncture chart

—adapted from "Hygiene and Preventive Medicine in Ancient China," reprinted in *Reflections on World Civilization*, edited by Ronald H. Fritze, James S. Olson, and Randy W. Roberts, 1994

Confucian values governed all aspects of personal and social life in Han China. "With harmony at home, there will be order in the nation," Confucius had said. "With order in the nation, there will be peace in the world." And indeed, the family was supreme in Chinese society. It was the focus of life, bound together strongly by mutual love, loyalty, and dependence.

Family Life

The members of a Chinese family of the Han era lived and worked together. In an ideal family every member knew his or her role and the duties that went with it.

Relationships

Family members did not relate to each other as equals; instead, the family was a strict hierarchy, organized into different levels of importance. The oldest male in the home, usually the father, was dominant. Next in rank was the oldest son, followed by all the younger sons and all the females. The mother came before the daughters, and finally—at the bottom—the youngest daughter or childless daughter-in-law. Each family member expected obedience from those who were further down in the hierarchy, and each obeyed and respected those who were above.

Family Rules

Strict rules governed the relationships between husbands and wives, parents and grandparents, uncles and aunts, brothers and sisters, and other relatives. Each family member knew his or her place and understood its duties, and each was careful not to bring dishonor on the family by failing in those duties. Moreover, the duty to family members did not stop at death; all were expected to pay respect to departed ancestors.

228 **Chapter 9** *China's Flourishing Civilization*

SECTION RESOURCES

📁 **Reproducible Masters**
- Lecture Notes 9-3
- Reproducible Lesson Plan 9-3
- Vocabulary Activity 9
- Guided Reading Activity 9-3
- Source Reading 9
- People in World History Profiles 15, 16
- World Art and Music Activity 9

- Reteaching Activity 9
- Enrichment Activity 9
- Section Quiz 9-3
- Performance Assessment Activity 9
- Spanish Chapter Summary 9
- Reading Essentials and Study Guide 9-3
📋 **Transparencies**
- Section Focus Transparency 9-3

- Ancient China
Multimedia
📀 Interactive Tutor Self-Assessment Software
📀 Testmaker
📀 World Music: Cultural Traditions, Lesson 8
📀 India and China

Typical homes in Han China did not have the extended families, or families of many generations living together, that would later be typical. Rather, they had what we call today nuclear families, each consisting of parents and their children. The father assigned his children's careers, determined their education, arranged their marriages, meted out rewards or punishments, and controlled the family finances. The family also provided support for members who themselves could not contribute—the aged, the young, the sick, and even the lazy.

No doubt the system offered many opportunities for exploiting those further down in the hierarchy. Nevertheless, few fathers were tyrants. Like other family members, they practiced ethical principles of kindness and compassion, either from genuine love or from fear of the disapproval of others and the scorn of their ancestors.

Status of Women

Under the Confucian social system, women were subordinate to men. Confucius himself had little regard for women, saying, "Women and uneducated people are the most difficult to deal with."

Girls began life subservient to their fathers and brothers. Later their husbands and in-laws were their superiors, and eventually even a mother came under the authority of her own sons. Parents valued baby girls far less than baby boys. A poor family had to work hard to raise and support a child, and if that child was a daughter, she left home to become part of her husband's family as soon as she married.

Some women were able to gain respect in Chinese homes. With marriage and motherhood, they became revered. Other opportunities for women, such as education, were limited. In spite of Confucianism's predominance, women fared far better under the Han than they would in later centuries. They could inherit property, even own it after they married, and they could remarry after a husband's death.

Society and Economy

Chinese society consisted of three main classes: landowners, peasants, and merchants. Landowning families were wealthy. They lived in tile-roofed mansions with courtyards and gardens. They surrounded their homes with walls to protect them from bandits. They filled their rooms with fine furniture and adorned them with silk wall hangings and carpets. Wealthy families feasted on a rich variety of foods.

The landholders' wealth was generally limited, however, and families rarely kept their holdings for

Aesop's Fables

Greece, c. 500 B.C.
A collection of stories told by an enslaved Greek named Aesop features animals who talk and act like people. Each of Aesop's fables ends with a proverb that teaches a moral. For example, the proverb "The Tortoise and the Hare" teaches that slow and steady wins the race. Aesop's fables were not written down until nearly three centuries after his death.

Greece

more than a few generations. When a family's land was divided, it went to all the sons, not just the oldest, with the result that in time individual landowners had less and less property.

Probably 90 percent of the Chinese people were peasants. The wealth that supported the lifestyles of the rich was gained from the hard labor of the peasants who cultivated the land. Unlike Western farmers, who usually lived on the land they farmed, most Chinese peasants lived in rural villages and worked fields outside their mud walls. Their homes were simple, and they ate a plain diet that featured millet, rice, beans, turnips, and fish.

The peasants raised livestock and toiled long hours in the grain fields. They faced constant threats from floods and from famines. As rent for the land, peasants turned over part of their produce to the landowner. The government required them to pay taxes and to work one month each year on public works projects such as road building. In times of conflict, peasants were drafted into the army as soldiers.

At the bottom of the social hierarchy were merchants—a group that included shopkeepers, traders, service workers, and even bankers. The merchants lived in towns and provided goods and services for the wealthy. In spite of the great wealth that many merchants accumulated, Chinese society generally held them in contempt. Confucianism taught that the pursuit of profit was an unworthy pastime for the "superior" individual. Merchants were not allowed to take the civil service examinations and enter government service.

Chapter 9 *China's Flourishing Civilization* **229**

TEACH

Guided Practice

THEME Cultural Diffusion

Have students list inventions and discoveries made by the ancient Chinese. Then have them list things in their homes that originated in China. (*Possible items: kite, firecrackers, abacus, paper, silk, compass, paper money, chinaware or porcelain.*) Have students compare their lists in class. Discuss how and why certain inventions might have spread to other cultures. **L1 LEP**

Social Class Work with students to organize a chart showing the social classes in ancient China. List the classes in order of hierarchy. Next to each class, list its characteristics. **L2**

World Music: Cultural Traditions, Lesson 8

Use these materials to enrich student understanding of Chinese culture.

NGS PICTURESHOW CD-ROM
India and China

COOPERATIVE LEARNING ACTIVITY

Making Posters Organize the class into small groups to create posters that illustrate the costumes and decorations worn by ancient Chinese of various social classes. Make sure each student is assigned a specific task, such as reading, drawing, designing, framing, and so on. Students should research costumes worn by groups such as mandarins, women of the royal family, peasants, merchants, and so on. Students should include a brief explanation under each illustration. Students may also illustrate groups' hair styles or personal grooming habits (such as makeup). Display the completed posters. **L1**

Independent Practice

📁 Guided Reading Activity
9-3 **L1**

📁 Source Reading 9

📁 People in World History
Profiles 15, 16

📁 World Art and Music
Activity 9

The Arts Have students research and write a report on some of the poetry and songs from the *Book of Songs* or *Shih Ching*. Have students share the poems or songs with the class. **L2**

Global 🍵 Gourmet

China The Chinese have been drinking tea since about 50 B.C. Tea was originally used as a medicine—to help keep awake and alert, or to counteract the effects of too much food or drink. But eventually the Chinese came to appreciate tea for its own merits, and an elaborate culture grew up around the drinking of tea.

NATIONAL GEOGRAPHIC SOCIETY

Use these materials to enrich student understanding of ancient Chinese culture.

📖 **NGS PICTUREPACK**
🎞 **TRANSPARENCY SET**
Ancient China

For all the people in Han society except merchants, the civil service system provided opportunities for advancement, though the expense of education blocked most of the poor from competing. Still, poor but talented individuals sometimes rose to positions of power and influence.

Literature

Although the Qin burned thousands of books, many survived in royal libraries and secret private collections. Particularly prized was a collection of books called the Five Classics, some of which were written before Confucius. All candidates for the civil service were required to master them. No better example is recorded of the Chinese reverence for history.

The oldest of the Five Classics, the *Book of Songs*, preserves 305 of the earliest Chinese poems, written between 1000 B.C. and 600 B.C. The poems deal with political themes, ritual, and romance. Many seem modern, with their everyday topics and simple, concrete imagery—this one, for example:

> ❝ Near the East Gate
> Young women go
> Like so many clouds all day.
> Like drifting clouds
> A thought of them
> Soon blows away.
>
> There. White robe
> and a blue scarf—
> she makes my day.
>
> Near the Great Tower and Wall
> Go slender girls
> Like reeds by river's edge:
> Like bending reeds
> A thought of them
> Soon passes by. ❞

The *Book of Documents* records political speeches and documents from early in the Zhou dynasty,

---

Images *of the* Times

Han China

The Han dynasty was a golden age of Chinese history. Important political, economic, and cultural changes took place.

Wudi's examinations developed into a civil service system, leading to a wealthy class of mandarins who controlled the government.

230

Images *of the* Times Han China

The terra-cotta horseman in the photograph is only one example of Han tomb sculpture. Han tombs were very elaborate, in many cases constructed of brick or stone and divided into several chambers. The tombs of Han emperors were enclosed in giant mounds of earth that are still visible today. In addition to statues, the tombs often contained bronze mirrors. The ancient Chinese believed that mirrors were sources of light and as such could brighten the darkness of the tomb through all eternity. A great deal of pottery has also been unearthed from Han tombs, including both household items and pots made especially for burial, called *ming ch'i,* or "spirit utensils."

including the earliest statement of the Mandate of Heaven. The *Book of Changes* presents a complex system for foretelling the future and choosing a course of action. In *Spring and Autumn Annals* Confucius reported major events that occurred in the state of Lu between 722 B.C. and 481 B.C.

The Five Classics were thought to carry solutions to most problems. Officials studied them closely to find support for their positions, such as the conduct of political leaders. Accounts of solar eclipses, meteor showers, and droughts were used to show what terrifying events and disasters could befall poor political leaders.

Another great collection of books, the Thirteen Classics, included the *Analects*—Confucius's sayings compiled by his students after his death. Many appeared as answers to questions. For example, Confucius was asked about the gentleman, or the "superior man." Among other replies he gave this one: "What the gentleman seeks, he seeks within himself; what the small man seeks, he seeks in others."

The Han Chinese encouraged literary pursuits and made literature available to everyone. An especially valuable work produced during the Han dynasty period was the *Historical Record*. Written by **Sima Qian** during the reign of Wudi, it is the first true history of ancient China.

Science and Technology

Besides literature and philosophy, China made major contributions in science and technology. By the 300s B.C., Chinese astronomers had calculated the length of the solar year as $365\frac{1}{4}$ days. They gazed through bronze tubes equipped with a device that divided the sky into measured segments, allowing them to make accurate measurements. They kept valuable records of solar and lunar eclipses and comet sightings. In 240 B.C. Chinese astronomers recorded the appearance of the object that would later be called Halley's comet—many centuries before Halley's birth.

ASSESS

Check for Understanding

Assign Section 3 Assessment as homework or as an in-class activity.

 Use Interactive Tutor Self-Assessment Software to review Section 3.

Evaluate

 Section Quiz 9-3

Use the Testmaker to create a customized quiz for Section 3.

Reteach

Have students work in pairs to make a chart summarizing the main topics of this section. Headings should include *Family Structure, Social Structure, Literature,* and *Science and Technology.* Have students list the important points and illustrate the chart.

Reteaching Activity 9

Reading Essentials and Study Guide 9-3

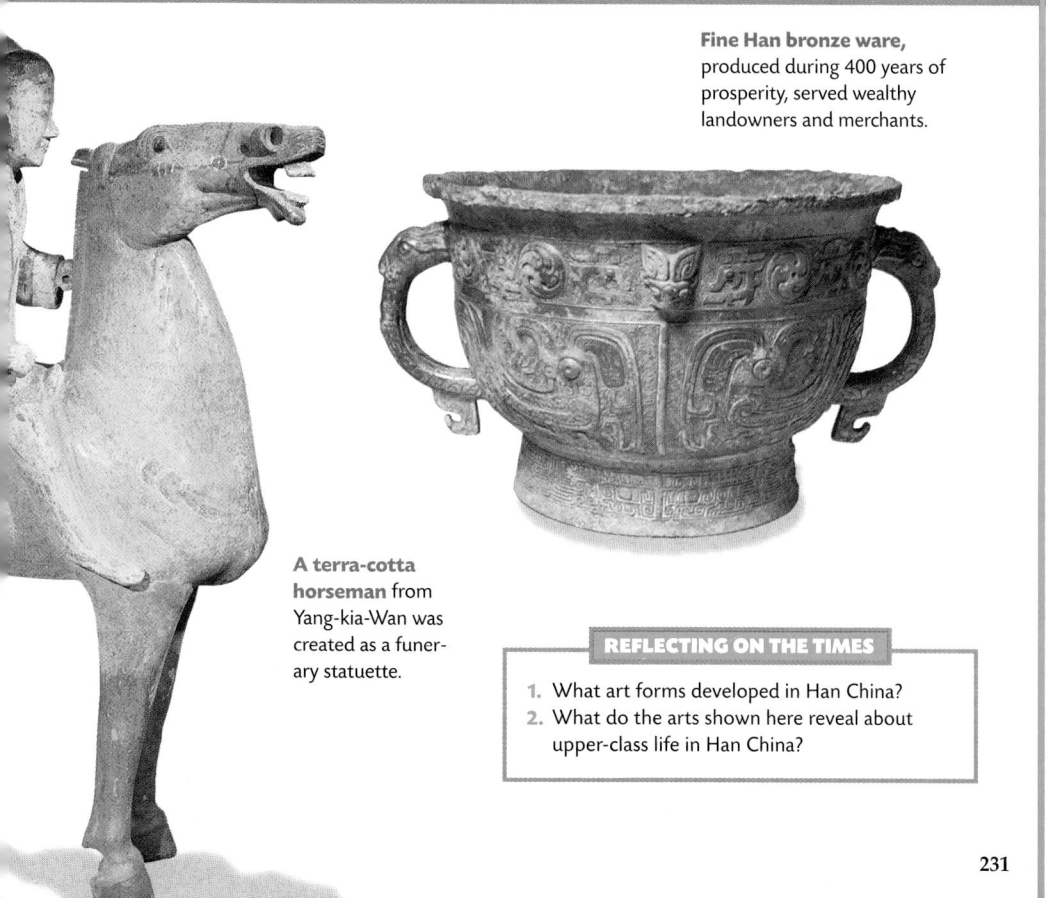

Fine Han bronze ware, produced during 400 years of prosperity, served wealthy landowners and merchants.

A terra-cotta horseman from Yang-kia-Wan was created as a funerary statuette.

REFLECTING ON THE TIMES

1. What art forms developed in Han China?
2. What do the arts shown here reveal about upper-class life in Han China?

231

ANSWERS TO REFLECTING ON THE TIMES

1. painting, pottery, and silk weaving
2. The arts reveal the high level of prosperity in Han China among the upper classes who had the money to patronize artists.

According to legend, in about 2700 B.C. Chinese emperor Huangdi ordered his wife to find out what was killing his mulberry trees. Finding white worms eating and spinning shiny cocoons on the leaves, she accidentally dropped a cocoon into hot water. When she removed a thin thread unwinding from the cocoon, she discovered silk. **Answer to Caption:** *through trade, especially over the Silk Road*

Enrich

Have students research the status of merchants in one or more other ancient civilizations. Ask students to prepare a report that summarizes their findings and highlights areas of comparison/contrast with the status of merchants in ancient China.

 Enrichment Activity 9

CLOSE

Ask students to imagine that they live in China in A.D. 200. Have them decide which family role (father, mother, eldest son, youngest son, daughter, daughter-in-law) they would like best and which they would like least. Ask them to explain why.

Visualizing History **Women prepare newly woven silk. Han weavers created beautiful damasks of many colors.** *How did Chinese arts and inventions spread to other civilizations?*

Medicine

Chinese physicians recognized nutrition as vital and realized that some diseases resulted from vitamin deficiencies. Although they did not identify vitamins as such, they discovered and prescribed foods that would correct some problems. They also understood that many herbs had medicinal value.

Chinese doctors treated ailments and relieved pain with acupuncture, a technique in which the skin is pierced with thin needles at vital points. They believed acupuncture restored the balance between yin and yang in a person's body.

Farming and Transport

Under the Han, many improvements occurred in agriculture and transportation. Complex irrigation systems drained swamps and diverted rivers to quench parched fields. Fertilizing crops helped farmers produce enough to feed China's popula-

tion. Veterinary medicine helped save many farm animals. New canals and improved roadways reduced the cost of distributing food and spread ideas rapidly.

Inventions

Many inventions in ancient China were vital to life and the economy. Made by the Chinese since prehistoric times, silk was in great demand as a trade item; its worth was attested to by the name of one of history's greatest trade routes—the Silk Road. Caravans carried the precious cargo as far as Rome.

Paper was probably invented by 100 B.C., although it was officially credited to an inventor of about 200 years later. Artisans pounded tree bark, hemp, or rags into a pulp. By treating it with gelatin, they could then make paper. Used first for wrapping and clothing, paper was soon recognized as an ideal writing material.

The invention of paper benefited the bureaucratic Han government. Its centralized structure resulted in an explosion in the number of documents. Most were written on strips of wood, which were fragile and cumbersome to work with. The use of paper had many obvious advantages.

Other inventions improved mining and construction. Miners, using iron drill bits driven by workers on seesaw-like levers, drilled boreholes to obtain salt from the earth. Another invention was the wheelbarrow, which was first used on building sites around 100 B.C.

These are only a few examples from a list of Chinese "firsts," which also includes the first printed books, the earliest technologies for casting bronze and iron, the suspension bridge, the compass, and gunpowder. Such achievements caused China to remain far ahead of Europe in science and technology until the A.D. 1300s.

SECTION 3 ASSESSMENT

Main Idea
1. Use a chart like the one below to identify the scientific and technological breakthroughs in early China.

Scientific	Technological

Recall
2. **Define** hierarchy, extended family, nuclear family, acupuncture.
3. **Identify** the Five Classics, *Spring and Autumn Annals*, the *Analects*, Sima Qian.

Critical Thinking
4. **Making Comparisons** Compare a typical Han Chinese family with families you consider typical of America today.

Understanding Themes
5. **Cultural Diffusion** What ideas and products from ancient China have become popular in the West in recent years? What factors account for their popularity among people in the West?

SECTION 3 ASSESSMENT ANSWERS

1. Scientific: astronomers calculated the length of the solar year; recorded solar and lunar eclipses and comet sightings. Technological: used bronze tubes to make measurements of the sky; irrigation system; iron drills; wheelbarrow
2. All terms are defined in the Glossary.

3. Five Classics, 230; *Spring and Autumn Annals*, 231; the *Analects*, 231; Sima Qian, 231
4. Answers will vary. Students may refer to the strict Han family hierarchy with the father at the top, obedience and respect due to those above, and limited oppor-

tunities available to women.
5. **CULTURAL DIFFUSION** Answers may include: acupuncture, herbal medicine, ancient philosophies; popularity linked to perception that Western products and ideas have failed to prevent social decline.

Identifying Central Issues

The saying "He can't see the forest for the trees" refers to someone so focused on separate details that he cannot see the entire situation. Sometimes we face this problem when studying history. It is easy to focus on details such as names, dates, and places, thus losing sight of the bigger picture. To avoid this, it is important to identify the central issues.

Learning the Skill

First, skim the material to identify its general subject. Look for headings and subheadings; often they highlight central issues. A central issue may also appear in the topic sentence of a paragraph. The other sentences in the paragraph usually explain and support the central issue.

When looking for central issues, ask yourself these questions: What is the general topic of this material? What ideas have the greatest emphasis? What main idea holds the details together? If I had to summarize this material in one sentence, what would it be?

Practicing the Skill

Read the passage about the *Book of Changes* and answer the questions that follow.

66 The *Book of Changes—I Ching* in Chinese—is unquestionably one of the most important books in the world's literature.... Nearly all that is greatest and most significant in the three thousand years of Chinese cultural history has either taken its inspiration from this book, or has exerted an influence on the interpretation of its text.... Indeed, not only the philosophy of China but its science and statecraft as well have never ceased to draw from the spring of wisdom in the *I Ching*.... Even the commonplaces of everyday life in China are saturated with its influence. In going

through the streets of a Chinese city, one will find, here and there at a street corner, a fortune teller sitting behind a neatly covered table, brush and tablet at hand.... 99

1. What is the general subject of the passage?
2. Which idea has the greatest emphasis?
3. What are some details that support this idea?
4. Which sentence states the central issue of the passage?

Applying the Skill

Find a newspaper or magazine article that interests you. Identify the central issues in this article and summarize them in your own words.

For More Practice

Turn to the Skill Practice in the Chapter Assessment on page 235 for more practice in identifying central issues.

The **Glencoe Skillbuilder Interactive Workbook**, Level 2 provides instruction and practice in key social studies skills.

TEACH

Identifying Central Issues Before asking students to read the skill, distribute copies of a newspaper editorial. Ask students which sentence best indicates the subject of the editorial. Ask them what such a sentence is called. *(topic sentence)* Have them restate the point of the topic sentence in their own words. Now ask them to identify sentences in the editorial that support the main point. After you are satisfied with the students' ability to locate the central issue, have students read the skill and complete the practice questions.

Additional Practice

 Skill Reinforcement Activity 9

GLENCOE TECHNOLOGY

GO TO Glencoe's **Skillbuilder Interactive Workbook, Level 2** This interactive CD-ROM promotes student mastery of key social studies skills.

ANSWERS TO PRACTICING THE SKILL

1. the *Book of Changes*, or *I Ching*
2. The book's influence has permeated all levels of Chinese life.
3. Fortune tellers on city streets base their message on the *I Ching*. Science and statecraft have drawn on the wisdom of the *I Ching*.
4. Students may name either the first sentence or the second sentence as the topic sentence. As long as students can argue convincingly to support their choice, either is an acceptable answer.

Chapter 9 Assessment

Have students use the **Chapter 9 Self-Check Quiz** at worldhistory.glencoe.com to prepare for the Chapter Test.

GLENCOE TECHNOLOGY

VIDEODISC
Use MindJogger to review the chapter.

MindJogger Videoquiz

Chapter 9
Disc 2 Side A

Also available in VHS.

Answers

Using Key Terms

1. c	3. g	5. h
2. a	4. e	

Using Your History Journal

Suggest that students also look at the Old Testament book of Proverbs, or at Benjamin Franklin's *Poor Richard's Almanack* for ideas.

Reviewing Facts

1. Landowners: lived in mansions surrounded by walls; varied diet; land divided among all sons; eventually had less and less land. Peasants: lived in rural villages; plain diet; gave part of produce as rent; drafted as soldiers. Merchants: traders, bankers, service workers; lived in towns; could not enter government service
2. a thinker from Zhou times who stressed order, ethics, and filial piety
3. as a result of civil service exams.
4. ruler-subject, parent-child, husband-wife, old-young, friend-friend
5. *Book of Songs*: oldest of Five Classics; *Spring and Autumn Annals*:

WORLD HISTORY Online

Self-Check Quiz

Visit the *World History: The Human Experience* Web site at **worldhistory.glencoe.com** and click on *Chapter 9—Self-Check Quiz* to prepare for the Chapter Test.

Using Key Terms

Write the key term that completes each sentence. Then write a sentence for each term not chosen.

a. acupuncture	f. mandarin
b. civil service	g. yin and yang
c. extended family	h. filial piety
d. hierarchy	i. cavalry
e. ethics	j. nuclear family

1. An _____ consists of parents, children, grandparents, and other relatives living together in one household.
2. Chinese doctors treated ailments and relieved pain with _____, a technique in which the skin is pierced with thin needles at vital points.
3. A Chinese theory related to Daoism was the concept of _____, the two opposing forces believed to be present in all of nature.
4. Confucius taught that individuals should live according to principles of _____.
5. The Chinese cared especially about _____, or children's respect for their parents.

Technology Activity

Building a Database The teachings of the ancient Chinese teacher Confucius date back to 479 B.C. Many of his teachings are still practiced in China today. Search the Internet or your local library for additional information about Confucius. Build a database of collected Confucian sayings, or analects. Organize analects by headings reflecting different categories according to Confucius's principles or ethics. Examples of categories would be a person's conduct or filial piety.

Using Your History Journal

Many of Confucius's sayings compiled after his death are similar to proverbs. Write a set of your own proverbs about everyday decisions and situations.

Reviewing Facts

1. **Culture** Use a diagram like the one below to show the organization of classes in early Chinese society.

2. **Culture** Identify Confucius and his ideas.
3. **Government** Explain how Mandarins came to shape China's government.
4. **Culture** List the five relationships in Chinese society that were identified by Confucius.
5. **Culture** Describe the *Book of Songs*, the *Spring and Autumn Annals*, and the *Historical Record*.
6. **History** Explain why Qin Shihuangdi ordered the construction of the Great Wall of China.
7. **Government** List the characteristics of China's government and politics under the Zhou, Qin, and Han dynasties.
8. **Government** Analyze how Confucius applied the idea of filial piety to governments.
9. **Culture** Explain why Qin rulers strongly opposed the teachings of Confucius, though Han rulers like Wudi later promoted Confucianism.
10. **Technology** List three Chinese inventions and state how they changed Chinese life.

Critical Thinking

1. **Synthesize** Create a time line showing major events in China from the Zhou to the Han dynasties.

Confucius's account of major events in state of Lu from 722 B.C. to 481 B.C.; *Historical Record*: first true history of ancient China, written by Sima Qian in Han era
6. to protect China's border from invaders
7. Zhou: local lords were powerful; Qin: strong central government; Han: mandarins controlled government
8. a ruler had to be ethical and set an example of right conduct for those beneath him

9. The Qin disliked the Confucian reverence for the past and emphasis on the need for rulers to exhibit ethical behavior.
10. silk helped boost Chinese trade abroad; paper helped the bureaucracy maintain documents; wheelbarrow was an asset in public works projects

Critical Thinking

1. Include founding and end dates of dynasties

2. **Evaluate** Was a strong family structure a positive or a negative influence on Chinese society?
3. **Apply** How does your society make use of the Han concept of appointing officials by ability?
4. **Synthesize** How would you respond if your government adopted the social policies of the Qin dynasty?
5. **Compare** How is Confucianism different from Christianity and Judaism? How is it similar?
6. **Synthesize** Think about how merchants were viewed in Han society and why. How might the United States be different if we felt that way about merchants?

Geography in History

1. **Movement** Refer to the map below. Buddhism came to China from which area of the world?
2. **Location** What cities became major Buddhist sites in China?
3. **Region** What large area was a major stronghold of Daoism?
4. **Region** What Daoist concepts made it possible for much of China to accept the teachings of Confucius, Laozi, and the Buddha into a unified belief system?

Buddhism and Daoism in China

Area embracing Daoism
Buddhist missionary activity
Spread of Buddhism
Buddhist sites

Understanding Themes

1. **Uniformity** What methods did Qin Shihuangdi use to unify China? What was their impact?
2. **Innovation** How did the ethical philosophy of Confucius influence Chinese society?
3. **Cultural Diffusion** How did Buddhism reach China?

Linking Past and Present

1. The Qin tried to control people's ideas by limiting the books they could read. Provide an example of a modern government that limits the information its people receive.
2. All candidates for China's civil service were required to master the Five Classics. Can you think of literature from our own culture that everyone should know? Why would it be difficult for Americans to agree on five classics?

Skill Practice

Read the passage below and answer the questions that follow.

❝Females should be strictly grave and sober, and yet adapted to the occasion. Whether in waiting on her parents, receiving or reverencing her husband, rising up or sitting down, when pregnant, in times of mourning, or when fleeing in war, she should be perfectly decorous. Rearing the silkworm and working cloth are the most important employments of the female; preparing food for the household and setting in order sacrifices follow next, each of which must be attended to. After that, study and learning can fill up the time.❞

Book of Changes (I Ching)

1. What is the general topic of this passage?
2. What details are offered on this topic?
3. Which sentence, if any, states the central issue of this passage?
4. State the central issue in your own words.

Understanding Themes

1. **UNIFORMITY** centralizing government; standardizing weights, measures, coins, writing; imposing censorship; Strict Qin rule led to unrest among many groups but established the foundations of the Chinese state.
2. **INNOVATION** Confucian emphasis on order made the Chinese obey authority.
3. **CULTURAL DIFFUSION** Buddhist monks and traders from India crossed mountains to bring their message to China.

1. Iran, Iraq, Syria, Libya, Singapore, China, Cuba
2. Answers might include works by Hawthorne, Thoreau, Emerson, Melville, Twain, etc.

Skill Practice

1. woman's role in society
2. Details are listed in the second through fourth sentences.
3. the first sentence
4. Accept well-phrased summaries.

Chapter Bonus Test Question

Ask Students: In ancient China, either birth or individual talent and achievement might be the basis for an individual's standing in society. How did Confucianism support these seemingly contradictory positions? *(One's standing was largely determined by one's family; a wealthy family gave a person the educational opportunities needed to prepare for the civil service exam. The civil service system gave one the chance to achieve public office on the basis of one's own performance.)*

---

and time periods of Confucius and Laozi.
2. positive: social order, loyalty, sense of duty; negative: low status of women, lack of individual choice, submissiveness to authority
3. federal and state civil service systems, jobs and promotions based on merit
4. Answers will vary.
5. Judaism and Christianity are based on belief in a personal God whose will is revealed in the words of prophets or a messiah; Confucianism basically does not deal with the supernatural or with eternal life, focusing instead on ethical relationships in this world.
6. The country might be less productive if merchants were held in contempt.

Geography in History
1. India
2. Wanfo-hsiu, Peking, Wutai Shan, O-mei Shan
3. China
4. the yin-yang concept

FOCUS

The establishment of powerful civilizations caused the spread of new ideas about rulership, religion, culture, and intellectual thought, the impact of which has lasted into modern times.

TEACH

Reinforcing Vocabulary

Point out the **Vocabulary Preview** to students alerting them to words they will encounter that might be unfamiliar.

Plague in Athens

Interpreting the Primary Source
Ask students to explain why Thucydides felt that the new arrivals in the city increased the hardship suffered by the Athenians during the Plague. *(Thucydides states that the overpopulation of Athens caused harsh living conditions which, added to the Plague, increased the death toll.)*

Evaluating the Primary Source
This primary source is an example of an attempt to avoid interpreting events subjectively, but rather to report them as objectively as possible. The reliability of this source is determined by how accurately and objectively Thucydides described the Plague in Athens. He avoided making subjective comments, so his presentation of the situation may be a very fair one. If students were to compare his description to another one from the time, they could better assess the accuracy of Thucydides' descriptions.

Unit 2

Between 2000 B.C. and A.D. 500

a number of powerful and influential civilizations developed in

different regions of the world.

The political systems, religions,

arts, and sciences of these ancient

civilizations continue to influ-

ence the civilizations of the

modern world.

◆ VOCABULARY PREVIEW

livid: discolored

profane: of this world; secular

lamentation: an expression of mourning

For more primary sources to accompany this unit, use the *World History Primary Source Document Library CD-ROM.*

Chapter 5
Plague in Athens

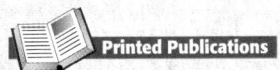
Printed Publications

Thucydides is regarded as the first scientific historian. In his account of the plague that broke out in Athens in 430 B.C., Thucydides simply presents the facts, describing the diseases's symptoms and impact on the city itself.

. . . Externally, the body was not so very warm to the touch; it was not pale, but reddish, livid, and breaking out in small blisters and ulcers. But internally it was consumed by such a heat that the patients could not bear to have on them the lightest coverings or linen sheets. . . .

But in addition to the trouble under which they already laboured, the Athenians suffered further hardship owing to the crowding into the city of the people from the country districts; and this affected the new arrivals especially. For since no houses were available for them and they had to live in huts that were stifling in the hot season, they perished in wild disorder. Bodies of dying men

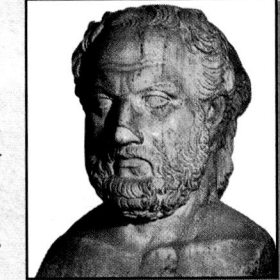
*Thucydides
471–c. 400 B.C.*

lay one upon another, and half-dead people rolled about in the streets and, in their longing for water, near all the fountains. . . . the calamity which weighed upon them was so overpowering that men, not knowing what was to become of them, became careless of all law, sacred as well as profane. And the customs which they had hitherto observed regarding burial were all thrown into confusion, and they buried their dead each one as he could . . .

Journey to the Land of Punt

Interpreting the Primary Source
Ask students to speculate why Queen Hatshepsut would have thought it important to send an expedition to another country and to document it in scenes and inscriptions. *(She may have thought that making it known— through the scenes and inscriptions—that she*

had made peaceful contact with another people would help underscore her power and wisdom as a ruler.)

Evaluating the Primary Source
This primary source provides insight into the ways in which a ruler might depict events that took place on an excursion she

Chapter 7
Journey to Punt
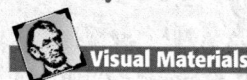
Visual Materials

Around 1480 B.C., Egyptian queen Hatshepsut assumed the title of pharaoh. On the walls of her temple were carved scenes from an expedition she had sent to the land of Punt, which show that the Egyptians regarded Punt as a holy land.

254. The voyage has been safely made, and the expedition has landed.
Over the Egyptians
255. [The arrival] of the king's-messenger in God's-Land, . . . with the army which is behind him, before the chiefs of Punt; dispatched with every good thing from the court . . . for Hathor, mistress of Punt; for the sake of the life, prosperity, and health of her majesty. . . .
Over the Puntites
257. They say, as they pray for peace: "Why have ye come thither unto this land, which the people know not? Did ye come down upon the ways of heaven, or did ye sail upon the waters, upon the sea of God's-Land? . . . Lo, as for the King of Egypt, is there no way to his majesty, that we may live by the breath which he gives?" . . .
Over the Vessels
265. The loading of the ships very heavily with marvels of the country of Punt; . . . with ebony and pure ivory, with green gold of Emu, . . . with cinnamon wood, khesyt wood, with ihmut-incense, sonter incense, eye-cosmetic, with apes, monkeys, dogs, and with skins of the southern panther . . . with natives and their children. Never was brought the like of this for any king who has been since the beginning. . . .

Chapter 8
The Buddha's Sermon
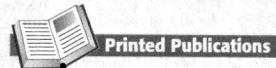
Printed Publications

Siddhartha Gautama, called the Buddha, achieved enlightenment in approximately 528 B.C. He gave sermons in India, but they were only written down after about 250 B.C. An excerpt from one of these follows.

(1) Now this, O monks, is the noble truth of pain: birth is painful, old age is painful, sickness is painful, death is painful, sorrow, lamentation, dejection, and despair are painful. Contact with unpleasant things is painful, not getting what one wishes is painful. In short the five khandhas of grasping are painful.

The Buddha ?563–483? B.C.

(2) Now this, O monks, is the noble truth of the cause of pain: that craving which leads to rebirth, combined with pleasure and lust, finding pleasure here and there, namely, the craving for passion, the craving for existence, the craving for non-existence.
(3) Now this, O monks, is the noble truth of the cessation of pain: the cessation without a remainder of that craving, abandonment, forsaking, release, non-attachment.
(4) Now this, O monks, is the noble truth of the way that leads to the cessation of pain: this is the noble Eightfold Path. . . .

Interpreting Primary Sources

1. According to Thucydides, what were the symptoms of the plague in Athens?
2. How did the Puntites react to the arrival of the Egyptian expedition?
3. What, according to the Buddha, is the cause of pain?
4. **CRITICAL THINKING:** According to the Buddha, how is it possible to escape pain?

Applications Activity
Write a first-person account of an event you have witnessed in the same objective style that Thucydides used to write his history.

had commissioned. The reliability of this source can be judged by assessing Queen Hatshepsut's reasons for having the events depicted in scenes and inscriptions. She may have been trying to strengthen the view of her as a powerful queen and thus may have exaggerated the glory of the trip. However, she may also have been hoping to document the encounter of a land much different than her own.

The Buddha's Sermon
Interpreting the Primary Source
Ask students to explain how they think the recording of the Buddha's sermons in writing may have increased the effect of his teachings. *(When the sermons were spoken, only those in attendance would have heard the words of the Buddha. Once they were written down, many more people could access the Buddha's ideas, and thus support for his teachings could spread.)*

Evaluating the Primary Source
This primary source reveals the teachings of the Buddha as he expressed them during his life. The reliability of this source is determined by the accuracy with which the Buddha's words were recorded and translated into English. If the document was written from memory, it is possible that words were remembered incorrectly or sections were paraphrased.

For the more complete version of each of these documents, see the *World History Primary Source Document Library CD-ROM:*

Document 20 *Plague in Athens*
Document 42 *Journey to the Land of Punt*
Document 46 *The Buddha's Sermon*

ANSWER KEY

1. Victims of the Plague felt intense fever and could not bear to be covered.
2. They were astonished, asking the Egyptians why they had come and how they had reached Punt.
3. According to the Buddha, craving, or desire, is the source of pain.
4. One can escape pain by destroying craving and by concentrating on "non-attachment."

APPLICATIONS ACTIVITY: Accounts will vary but should all depict the events in a factual manner without presenting bias or subjective viewpoints.

Answers and Analyses

1. C (Geography) On the map, a star can be found at approximately 39° N (39 degrees North) and 23° E. According to the legend, a star on the map indicates a battle site.

2. H (History) The Delian League is discussed on page 123. There it states that *Athens persuaded most of the city-states to ally against the enemy. This alliance became known as the Delian League.*

 TEST-TAKING TIP

When several choices seem possible, students should re-read the question and look for a key word in the question that will help make one answer choice better than others. In this case, what is the likely result of a war? A desire for protection. The most logical choice is H.

3. B (Civics) According to page 136, Plato preferred the government of Sparta because *he believed that each person should place service to the community above strictly personal goals and that the result of people having too much freedom is social disorder.*

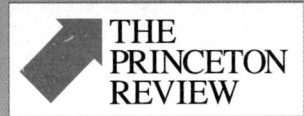
THE PRINCETON REVIEW

Standardized Test Practice

Directions: Choose the *best* answer to each of the following multiple choice questions. If you have trouble answering a question, use the process of elimination to narrow your choices. Write your answers on a separate piece of paper.

Use the map below <u>and</u> your knowledge of history to answer question 1.

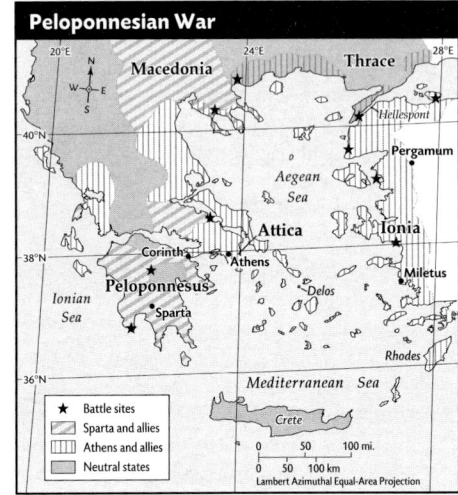

1. What is located at approximately 39°N and 23°E?

A Corinth

B A neutral state

C A battle site

D Athens

> **Test-Taking Tip:** Use the map's *legend*, or *key*, to understand how it is organized. You will need to *estimate* to find the approximate grid address mentioned in the question. Remember to double check all the answer choices against the information *on the map.*

2. Greek city-states formed the Delian League in order to

F create a unified, central government.

G promote trade among the city-states.

H provide protection against future Persian attacks.

J fund the building of the Parthenon.

> **Test-Taking Tip:** This question is asking for a *cause and effect* relationship. Remember, phrases such as *as a result of, because,* and *due to* can help you identify this type of question. Look for an answer that has a direct relationship to the *Persian Wars.*

3. Plato believed that Sparta's system of government was better than the system of government in Athens. What was his reason for this conclusion?

A The Athenian government failed to develop a strong military, leaving the city-state open to enemy attacks.

B The Spartan government gave citizens fewer rights, preventing civil unrest.

C Athenian citizens spent too much time in government service and did not develop a strong trading economy.

D The Spartan government focused more on physical strength and fitness, and therefore had a stronger society.

> **Test-Taking Tip:** Eliminate answers that don't make sense. Since Plato believed that community service was more important than personal goals, you can eliminate answer C.

4. During the *Pax Romana*, there was an increased interest in art, literature, and education throughout the Roman Empire. Which of the following was most responsible for the rise of the *Pax Romana*?

F   The influence of Greek culture on Roman life

G   The elimination of social classes in Roman society

H   The rise of the Roman Catholic and Eastern Orthodox churches

J   A strong economy and relatively few conflicts with enemy nations

---

Test-Taking Tip: You may remember that *Pax Romana* means "Roman Peace." Which answer fits *best* with this information?

---

5. In what way is Hinduism different from Judaism, Christianity, and Islam?

A   Hinduism has a set of writings about the religion.

B   Hinduism is generally a polytheistic religion, while the others are monotheistic religions.

C   Hinduism has had religious leaders and teachers.

D   Hinduism encourages physical and mental discipline for religious purposes.

Test-Taking Tip: This question is asking you to *compare* and *contrast*. First, think about what Judaism, Christianity, and Islam have in common. How is Hinduism *different*? Since the *Upanishads* are the religious writings of Hindu philosophers, answer A must be incorrect.

Use the graph below <u>and</u> your knowledge of history to answer question 6.

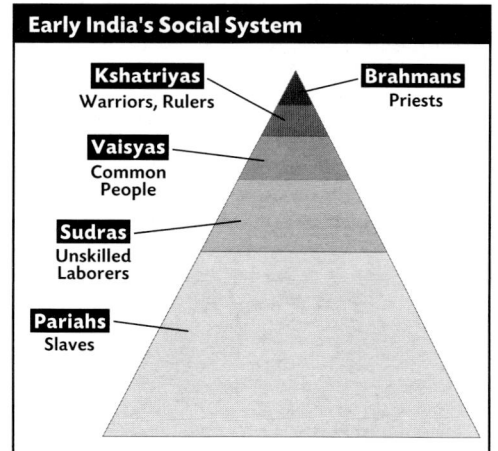

Early India's Social System

- **Kshatriyas** — Warriors, Rulers
- **Brahmans** — Priests
- **Vaisyas** — Common People
- **Sudras** — Unskilled Laborers
- **Pariahs** — Slaves

6. In which of the following ways were India's *varnas* similar to social classes in Europe?

F   There were far more people in the lower social classes than in the higher classes.

G   There were only nobles and peasants.

H   Only the higher classes practiced religion.

J   People could easily move to a higher class by marriage or hard work.

Test-Taking Tip: This question requires you to draw on knowledge beyond the graph. For example, you will need to remember that people remained in their *varna* for life. However, other answers can be eliminated by looking at the graph: answer G states that there were two main classes of people in Europe, but there are clearly more than two *varnas* on this graph. Therefore, answers G and J are both incorrect.

STOP

4. J (History) The *Pax Romana* is discussed on pages 167–168. No mention is made of Greek cultural influences, elimination of social classes, or the rise of the Church. Therefore choices F, G, and H can be eliminated. Economic prosperity, however, is mentioned on these pages.

THE PRINCETON REVIEW **TEST-TAKING TIP**

Process of elimination is very helpful for this question. Since classes were not abolished in Roman society, choice G cannot be the answer. Further, religion had very little to do with the *Pax Romana*, so choice H can also be eliminated. While choice F is tempting, choice J is better, since it discusses the lack of conflict.

---

5. B (History) According to page 206, *Hinduism was not founded on the teachings of one person… Instead it was based on different beliefs and practices… As a result, Hinduism became a complex religion of many deities.*

6. F (History) The caste system is described on pages 203–205. There it states that there were more than two classes, and that people *were born into a group, and the group could not be changed.* Therefore choices G and J can be eliminated. The chart on page 203 shows that there were far more people in the lower classes than in the higher ones.

Tested Objectives

Questions	Objective
1	Analyzing Information
2, 4	Determining Cause and Effect
3	Making Generalizations
5	Making Comparisons
6	Analyzing Information

0:00 OUT OF TIME?

If time does not permit teaching each chapter in Unit 3, you may use the Unit Digest Transparencies and Chapter Digest Audiocassettes with accompanying activities and tests.

Introducing the Unit

Unit 3 traces the economic, political, religious, and cultural development of Europe, the Middle East, Asia, and the Americas from A.D. 500 to 1500.

Unit Objectives

After reading Unit 3, students will be able to:

1. trace the rise and fall of the Byzantine Empire and the development of Slavic culture in Kiev and Moscow.
2. understand Islam and describe the spread of Islamic civilization.
3. define feudalism and discuss the influence of the Church in early medieval Europe.
4. explain the effects of the Crusades and the development of Europe in the later Middle Ages.
5. summarize the achievements of the Tang and Song dynasties and the influence of China on other Asian cultures.
6. describe the civilizations that arose in Mexico, Central America, and South America.

GLENCOE
TECHNOLOGY

Glencoe World History Primary Source Document Library
Use the CD-ROM to access primary source documents related to advanced civilizations.

Unit **3** A.D. 400–1500

Regional Civilizations

Chapter 10
Byzantines and Slavs

Chapter 11
Islamic Civilization

Chapter 12
The Rise of Medieval Europe

Chapter 13
Medieval Europe at Its Height

Chapter 14
East and South Asia

Chapter 15
The Americas

See pages 394–395 for primary source readings that accompany Unit 3.

Then **& Now** As this period opened, advanced civilizations began to develop in many regions of the world. Although some cultures were cut off from other regions, trade and migrations spread ideas across continents and among several different peoples. Emerging centers of trade and commerce brought more highly organized social structures and governments. These regional civilizations contributed many ideas that influenced the development of the modern world. Christianity, Islam, Confucianism, and Buddhism spread over wide areas. Scientific discoveries crossed cultures. Some contact between cultures caused conflict that lasted for decades or centuries.

A Global Chronology

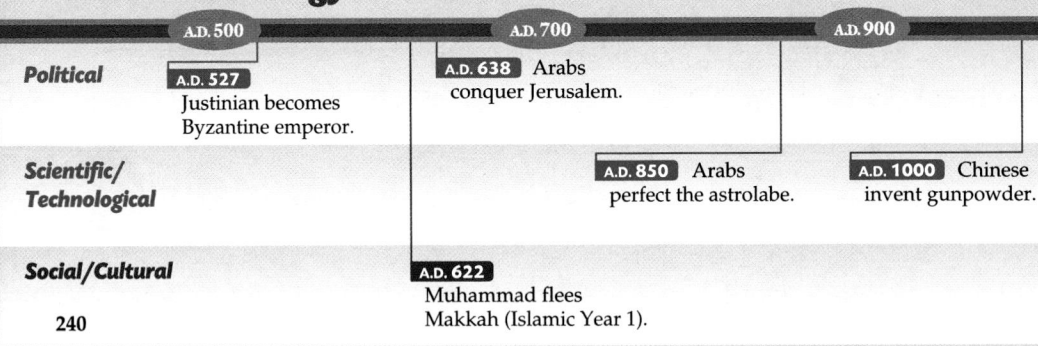

	A.D. 500	A.D. 700	A.D. 900
Political	A.D. 527 Justinian becomes Byzantine emperor.	A.D. 638 Arabs conquer Jerusalem.	
Scientific/ Technological		A.D. 850 Arabs perfect the astrolabe.	A.D. 1000 Chinese invent gunpowder.
Social/Cultural		A.D. 622 Muhammad flees Makkah (Islamic Year 1).	

240

Then **& Now** **Religion** One theme of this unit is contact and conflict between followers of different religions. Point out to students that in some epochs, people of different religions have interacted and lived side by side without conflict. At other times, during the spread of Islam and the Crusades, for example, religious differences led to violence and war.

Have students brainstorm a list of places in the world today where people of different religions live together in peace and other areas where there is religious conflict. In what areas does a

Mayan clay figurine of a man and a woman wrapped in a blanket, c. A.D. 700–1000. Campeche, Mexico

History and You

The Crusades left lasting effects on the economic and political development of western Europe, bringing new knowledge, increased trade, and new technology.

To better understand the influence of the Crusades on Europe, view videodisc Chapter 7: *The Crusades* in Turning Points in World History.

ABCNEWS INTERACTIVE™

 VIDEODISC
Turning Points in World History

 Side One
Chapter 7

Title: *The Crusades*
Subject: The Crusades affected Europe's economic and political development.
Ask: Why did the Crusades encourage western Europeans to increase trade? *(Increased knowledge of Middle Eastern civilizations led to an increase in demand for imported goods.)*

History & Art

The Maya produced remarkably detailed sculptures and relief carvings using only stone tools.

 ## History *and the* Humanities

Focus on World Art Prints
- 13 *Mantik et-Tayr*
- 14 *Bayeux Tapestry*
- 15 *Saint George and the Dragon*
- 17 *Saint Jerome in His Study*
- 11 *Presentation of Captives to a Maya Ruler*

World History and Art Transparencies
- 12 *Theodora and Attendants*
- 13 *Ukrainian Easter Eggs*
- 14 *Court of the Lions, the Alhambra*
- 15 *Cover of the Lindau Gospels*
- 16 *May*
- 17 *Angkor Wat*
- 18 *Mola Stitchery*
- 19 *Quilled Buckskin Robe*

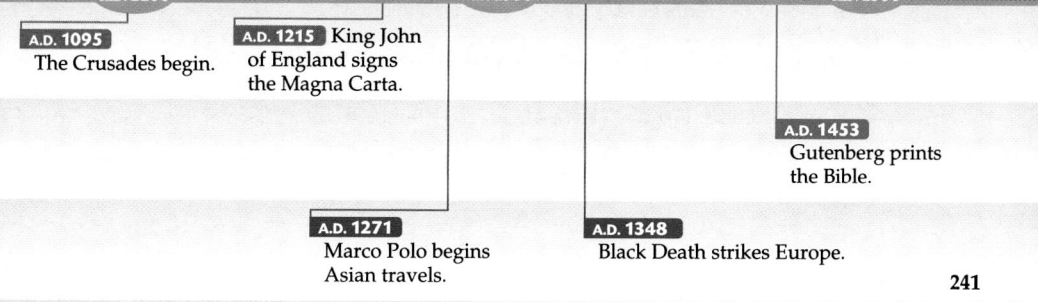

A.D. 1100   A.D. 1300   A.D. 1500

A.D. 1095 The Crusades begin.

A.D. 1215 King John of England signs the Magna Carta.

A.D. 1271 Marco Polo begins Asian travels.

A.D. 1348 Black Death strikes Europe.

A.D. 1453 Gutenberg prints the Bible.

241

history of religious conflict spur violence today? *(former Yugoslavia, Northern Ireland, Indian subcontinent, Middle East [Israel])* What factors besides religion may contribute to conflict among religious groups? *(differences in wealth in Northern Ireland and Middle East; issues of political power in all four regions)* In what countries do people of different religious backgrounds live together peacefully? *(United States, Argentina, most of Europe)* What explains the peaceful coexistence of different groups in those areas? *(Answers may include: traditions of pluralism, lessons learned from past intolerance.)*

TEACH

Introduction

This feature focuses on the contributions of Hindu and Arab mathematicians to Western civilization. To impress upon students the importance of the Hindu-Arab system, discuss the efficiencies of using only nine digits, place value, and zero as a placeholder. Have students invent and write numerals for the first 20 numbers without using place value or zero as a placeholder.

Background Notes

Linking Past and Present

Italian merchants were the first Europeans to adopt the Hindu-Arabic numerals. In Venice and other cities, schools of mathematics drew students from across Europe. A German father told his son "to rise early, go to church regularly, and pay attention to his arithmetic teacher." The schools focused on practical mathematics for use in business. Students had to learn the multiplication tables up to 99 x 99; they also learned to calculate interest, compute land areas, and handle fractions.

Geography

Movement Two great centers of learning developed in the Islamic world: one in Baghdad, in modern-day Iraq; the other in Córdoba, in Spain. The caliphs of Baghdad gathered mathematical and scientific works from Greece and India and had them translated into Arabic. These translations, as well as original works by Muslim scholars, then traveled across the Islamic world, often reaching Europeans through Spain.

Mathematics

The invention of mathematics changed the course of civilization. Astronomers used mathematics to account for the movements of the sun and moon so they could mark the seasons. Geometry enabled people to calculate the volume of a cylindrical granary. Mathematics supported travel, from the earliest sea travel to the development of the space program. It all began with the Sumerians.

Sumerian cuneiform tablet

Indus Valley
The Use of Numerals

The Sumerians devised one of the world's earliest numbering systems. They used two wedge-like symbols for counting. One symbol stood for 1, the other for 10. But these symbols—and others to follow—basically came from the Sumerian cuneiform. The wedges served double-duty for symbolizing words and figures.

Other early peoples who invented numbering systems used letters from their alphabets. Then, around A.D. 500, Hindu people in the Indus River valley abandoned the use of letters. They created instead special number symbols to stand for the figures 1 to 9. Although modernized over time, these 9 Hindu symbols are the ones we use today.

COOPERATIVE LEARNING ACTIVITY

Create a New Numeric System Have students discuss why Europe was so slow to adopt Hindu-Arabic numerals. Point out that the United States has still not converted to the metric system despite its simplicity and widespread use. Then organize students into two groups. Have one group create new symbols for the numbers 1–5, the other for 6–9 and zero. Combine the symbols and have volunteers attempt to carry out different mathematical functions with the new system. After students complete this activity, have them project how difficult it might be to switch numbering systems. **L1**

Persian astronomer

The Middle East
The Rise of Algebra

Trade introduced people in the Middle East to the Hindu number system. About A.D. 825 an Arab mathematician, al-Khowarizmi of Baghdad, wrote a book recommending the new system to everyone. In a second book, al-Khowarizmi showed how the system could be used. He called the book *al-jabr w'al-muqabalah*, which roughly means "the art of bringing together unknowns to match a known quantity." The word *algebra* comes from the key word in the title—*al-jabr*, or "bringing together."

The wonder of the system caught Arab imaginations. Arabs especially liked the concept of zero—developed by the Hindus after they created the symbols for 1-9. In explaining this concept, one Arab mathematician wrote: "When [in subtraction] nothing is left over, then write the little circle so that the place does not remain empty." With the use of zero, mathematicians could build numbers of astronomical size using just 10 symbols.

The astrolabe was used by Muslim astronomers and navigators to observe and calculate the position of stars and other heavenly bodies.

Europe
The Triumph of Arabic Numerals

Muslims ruled in Spain from the A.D. 700s to the A.D. 1400s. Their presence opened the door for European use of the new Hindu-Arabic number system. At first, many Europeans rejected it. They clung instead to Roman numerals. The Italian city-state of Florence even passed a law banning the use of the Hindu-Arabic system.

Later, however, "Arabic numerals," as they were called, proved a more powerful conqueror than Arab soldiers. European merchants found knowledge of the symbols necessary for dealings with merchants in Muslim ports. Europeans who learned the new arithmetic also found it easier to do their tallies. By the A.D. 1400s, the numbers could even be found in popular art.

As you will read in this unit, Europeans began to adopt other practices from the Middle East as well. The pace of change quickened as wars and trade brought more people in contact with each other.

Book of Hours *with Arabic numerals*

LINKING THE IDEAS

1. How did the Hindu system of numbers differ from earlier systems?
2. What was the importance of the invention of zero?

Critical Thinking

3. **Cause and Effect** What was the role of conquest and trade in spreading the use of the Hindu-Arabic number system?

Who?What?Where?When?

Al-Khowarizmi His short work on algebra, al-Khowarizmi said, was meant to be a practical guide for "the measuring of lands, the digging of canals, geometrical computation, and other objects of various sorts." The work became so widely known that for centuries Europeans assumed that al-Khowarizmi had invented Hindu-Arabic numerals. The word *algorithm* is derived from al-Khowarizmi's name.

Cultural Diffusion

The Spread of Arabic Numerals
Europeans resisted the use of Hindu-Arabic numerals well into the A.D. 1400s. An Italian bookkeeping manual insisted that Roman numerals "cannot be falsified as easily as those of the new art of computation, of which one can, with ease, make one out of another, such as turning the zero into a 6 or a 9."

During the age of exploration, Europeans came into contact with societies that used the more advanced numerals. For practical reasons they had to adopt the new system. The Portuguese author of a mathematics text published in 1519 explained: "I am printing this arithmetic because it is a thing so necessary in Portugal for transactions with the merchants of India, Persia, Arabia, Ethiopia, and other places." After A.D. 1450, the printing press helped spread the use of Hindu-Arabic numerals across Europe.

ANSWERS TO LINKING THE IDEAS

1. It used special number symbols instead of letters.
2. With zero, mathematicians could create large numbers using only 10 symbols.

3. With the Muslim conquest of Spain in the A.D. 700s, Hindu-Arabic numbers began to penetrate Europe. Merchants who traded with the Arab world hastened the process.

A complete, 1-page lesson plan is provided for each section in the *Reproducible Lesson Plans* booklet.

Byzantines and Slavs

CHAPTER RESOURCES

	Reproducible Resources	Multimedia Resources
Chapter Opener	Chapter Themes: Graphic Organizer 10 Historical Significance Chapter Activity 10	MindJogger Videoquiz
Chapter Enrichment	Vocabulary Activity 10* Time Line Activity 10 Mapping History Activity 10 History Simulation 10 Geography and History Activity 10 Source Reading 10 People in World History Profiles 17, 18 World Literature Selection 3 World Art and Music Activity 10 Enrichment Activity 10 Critical Thinking Activity 10 Skill Reinforcement Activity 10 Performance Assessment Activity 10 Standardized Test Practice Workbook Activity 10 Inclusion for the Social Studies Classroom Strategies and Activities	World History and Art Transparencies 12, *Theodora and Attendants*; 13, *Ukrainian Easter Eggs* Chapter Transparency 10 Vocabulary PuzzleMaker Software Picture Atlas of the World World Music: Cultural Traditions, Lesson 4 World History Primary Source Document Library
Chapter Review/Reteaching	Reteaching Activity 10 Skill Reinforcement Activity 10 Spanish Chapter Summary 10	Chapter 10 Digest Audiocassette, Activity, Test* Vocabulary PuzzleMaker Software Interactive Tutor Self-Assessment Software MindJogger Videoquiz
Chapter Evaluation/Testing	Performance Assessment Activity 10 Chapter 10 Test, Forms A and B	ExamView® Pro Testmaker

* Also available in Spanish

0:00 OUT OF TIME? Assign the Chapter 10 Audiocassettes.

World History Primary Source Document Library
Make History Come Alive!
Engage your students with over 250 easily accessible primary source documents—available on this CD-ROM—that will give them real life insight into the important events of world history.

Block Schedule
Activities that are particularly suited to use within the block scheduling framework are identified throughout this chapter by the following designation.

KEY TO ABILITY LEVELS
Teaching strategies are coded for varying learning styles.
L1 BASIC activities for all students
L2 AVERAGE activities for average to above-average students
L3 CHALLENGING activities for above-average students
LEP LIMITED ENGLISH PROFICIENCY activities

Use Glencoe's *Presentation Plus!* multimedia teacher tool to easily present dynamic lessons that visually excite your students. Using Microsoft PowerPoint® you can customize the presentations to create your own personalized lessons.

Interactive Lesson Planner

Planning has never been easier! Using this CD-ROM, organize your week, month, semester, or year with all the help you need. The **Interactive Lesson Planner** gives you access to all of the blackline masters that accompany *World History: The Human Experience.*

SECTION RESOURCES

Daily Objectives	Reproducible Resources	Multimedia Resources

Section 1
The New Rome
Explain what made the Byzantine Empire rich and powerful.
	Lecture Notes 10-1
	Reproducible Lesson Plan 10-1
	Guided Reading Activity 10-1*
	Geography and History Activity 10
	Time Line Activity 10
	History Simulation 10
	Section Quiz 10-1*
	Reading Essentials and Study Guide 10-1
		Section Focus Transparency 10-1
		
		Chapter Transparency 10
		World History and Art
		  Transparency 12, *Theodora and Attendants*
		Vocabulary PuzzleMaker Software
		Interactive Tutor Self-Assessment
		  Software
		Testmaker

Section 2
Byzantine Civilization
Investigate the role of Christianity in Byzantine and neighboring societies.
	Lecture Notes 10-2
	Reproducible Lesson Plan 10-2
	Guided Reading Activity 10-2*
	Section Quiz 10-2*
	Reading Essentials and Study Guide 10-2
		Section Focus Transparency 10-2
		World History and Art
		  Transparency 12
		Vocabulary PuzzleMaker Software
		Interactive Tutor Self-Assessment
		  Software
		Testmaker
		Picture Atlas of the World

Section 3
The Eastern Slavs
Describe how the Eastern Slavs developed separate cultures from those of western Europe.
	Lecture Notes 10-3
	Reproducible Lesson Plan 10-3
	Vocabulary Activity 10*
	Guided Reading Activity 10-3*
	Reteaching Activity 10
	Enrichment Activity 10
	Section Quiz 10-3*
	Performance Assessment Activity 10
	Spanish Chapter Summary 10
	Reading Essentials and Study Guide 10-3
		Section Focus Transparency 10-3
		World History and Art
		  Transparency 13, *Ukrainian Easter Eggs*
		Interactive Tutor Self-Assessment
		  Software
		Testmaker
		World Music: Cultural Traditions,
		  Lesson 4

* Also available in Spanish

Chapter Activities

 Performance Assessment Activity

An Itinerary for a Trip Have students assume the roles of travelers to the area of the world where the Byzantine and Slavic civilizations once existed. (Refer students to the maps on pages 247, 254, and 259 to identify these historical boundaries.) Then, using current maps and researching the geography of the area today, students should plan an itinerary that would take them to areas, cities, and landmarks of historic significance during a 5- to 10-day trip. Included should be a list of the types of artifacts or information that a traveler might hope to find at each stop. Students should be called on to explain their choices of destinations.

Possible Rubric Features
Accuracy and extent of content information, research skills, decision-making skills, organization

• *For an additional activity, refer to Activity 10 in the* Performance Assessment Strategies and Activities *booklet.*

ACTIVITY

From the Classroom of...

Bud Robertson
C.M. Russell High
School
Great Falls, MT

Cyrillic Alphabet
One of the easiest ways to introduce students to the Byzantine and Slavic cultures is to teach them the Cyrillic (Russian) alphabet. For a week or so before presenting the activity, spend a few minutes a day memorizing and practicing the alphabet.

Begin by showing students how to make the letters. Using all capital letters is easiest, and spelling the names of a few students helps pique interest. Here, for example, is John (Ivan) written in Cyrillic:

ИВАН

The name "Robertson" looks like this:

РОБЭРТСОН

Hand out copies of the alphabet. Allow students time to practice. By the end of one period, everyone should be able to write his or her name.

MULTIPLE LEARNING STYLES

Verbal/Linguistic
Have students think up words that describe Byzantine culture and record their responses on a flip chart. Each student should use these word lists to write a description of his or her impression of everyday life in the Byzantine Empire.

Visual/Spatial
Students may use colored stones or pieces of paper to create a mosaic portrait. They may choose a subject illustrated in the text or from another source and represent it in the Byzantine style.

Auditory/Musical
Have students find examples of music from the areas of study in this chapter. These might be Turkish folk tunes, Russian ballets, or religious music. Have the class listen and compare the different styles.

Interpersonal
Suggest that students imagine that they are visitors to Russia from the Byzantine Empire. Have them prepare the script for a speech to the Russians about the benefits of Byzantine civilization and present the speech to their classmates.

 GLENCOE'S ASSESSMENT ADVANTAGE

Use the following to easily assess student learning in a variety of ways.

- Performance Assessment Strategies and Activities
- Section Quizzes
- Chapter and Unit Tests
- Interactive Tutor Self-Assessment Software
- Testmaker Software
- MindJogger Videoquiz
- SAT/SAT II Test Practice
- worldhistory.glencoe.com

Additional Resources

NATIONAL GEOGRAPHIC SOCIETY — Teacher's Corner

INDEX TO NATIONAL GEOGRAPHIC MAGAZINE

The following articles relate to this chapter:

- "Hunting With Eagles," by Candice S. Millard, September 1999.
- "A Comeback for the Cossacks," by Mike Edwards, November 1998.
- "Searching for the Scythians," by Mike Edwards, September 1996.

NATIONAL GEOGRAPHIC SOCIETY PRODUCTS AVAILABLE FROM GLENCOE

To order the following, call Glencoe at 1-800-334-7344:

- *STV: World Geography, Vol. 2: Africa and Europe (Videodisc)*
- *Picture Atlas of the World (CD-ROM)*
- *PictureShow: The Middle Ages (CD-ROM)*
- *PicturePack: Physical Geography of the World (Transparencies)*
- *PicturePack: The Middle Ages (Transparencies, Posters)*

ADDITIONAL NATIONAL GEOGRAPHIC SOCIETY PRODUCTS

To order the following, call National Geographic at 1-800-368-2728:

- *The Mongols (Map)*
- *National Geographic Atlas of World History*

Access National Geographic's new dynamic MapMachine Web site and other geography resources at:

- http://www.nationalgeographic.com/
- http://www.nationalgeographic.com/maps/

BIBLIOGRAPHY

Literature About the Period
Procopius. *The Secret History.* Translated by G.A. Williamson. London: Penguin Books, 1966. Political commentaries by a contemporary historian.

Readings for the Student
Sherrard, Philip. *Byzantium.* New York: Time-Life Books, 1966. Traces the history of the Byzantine Empire from the establishment of New Rome to the fall of Constantinople.

Readings for the Teacher
Norwich, John Julius. *Byzantium: The Early Centuries.* New York: Knopf, 1989. Popular history of early Byzantine Empire.

WORLD HISTORY Online

Use our Web site as an additional resource. All essential content is covered in the Student Edition.

You and your students can visit the *World History: The Human Experience* Web site at worldhistory.glencoe.com The student text directs students to the Web site for the following options:

- **Chapter Overviews**
- **Student Web Activities**
- **Self-Check Quizzes**

Answers are provided for you in a link entitled "Web Activity Lesson Plan." Additional Web Resources, Interactive Puzzles, and content updates are also available.

Visit the Glencoe Web site at socialstudies.glencoe.com for social studies activities, updates, and links to other resources.

LOCAL OBJECTIVES

_____
_____
_____
_____
_____
_____
_____
_____
_____
_____
_____
_____
_____
_____
_____
_____
_____
_____

Introducing Chapter 10

The Storyteller

Historical Setting First built in A.D. 360, Hagia Sophia was twice destroyed by fire. The second time it was rebuilt, in A.D. 532–537, it was made fireproof. Earthquakes caused the dome to collapse in A.D. 558, but this, too, was rebuilt.

For a millennium, Hagia Sophia was the empire's spiritual center, first as a church and then as an Ottoman mosque. It remains an architectural masterpiece, presenting a magnificent interplay of stone and marble, light and color.

Historical Significance

Answers: *The old Roman laws were organized under Justinian, and they served as the foundation for the legal systems of Europe. By preserving the writings of ancient Greeks and Romans, the Byzantines made the learning of the past available to the Western world.*

The Byzantine Empire's greatest achievement may lie in the civilizing influence it exercised over all the peoples it encompassed. The Eastern Slavic peoples of the Balkans and Russia received written language, Christianity, and the basis of their art and culture from Byzantium.

Chapter 10

A.D. 400–1500

Byzantines and Slavs

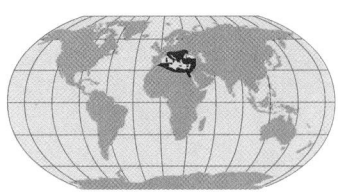

Chapter Themes

▶ **Conflict** Byzantines fight off invaders and struggle over use of icons. *Section 1*
▶ **Innovation** Byzantines develop Eastern Orthodox theology and distinctive art forms. *Section 2*
▶ **Cultural Diffusion** Trade routes and invasions spread beliefs and ideas. *Section 3*

The Storyteller

The awestruck visitor arriving in A.D. 600 in the city of Constantinople in southeastern Europe scarcely knew where to turn. Splendid public buildings as well as simple private homes lined the streets; the scent of rare spices perfumed the air; people dressed in fine silk thronged the church of Hagia Sophia. "One might imagine that one has chanced upon a meadow in full bloom," the Greek historian Procopius wrote about the newly built church. "For one would surely marvel at the purple hue of some [columns], the green of others, at those on which the crimson blooms, at those that flash with white, at those, too, which nature, like a painter, has varied with the most contrasting colors." The church's grandeur reflected that of Constantinople, "city of the world's desire," capital of a prosperous empire that controlled east-west trade and laid the basis for the Greek and Slavic cultures of modern Europe.

Historical Significance

What cultural achievements did the Byzantines pass on to western Europe? How did their civilization affect the development of the peoples of eastern Europe?

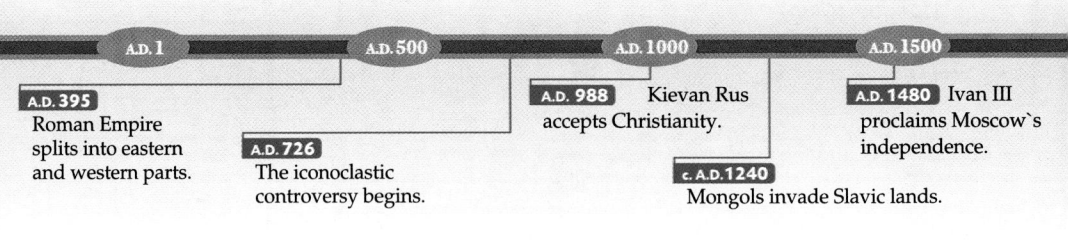

A.D. 1	A.D. 500	A.D. 1000	A.D. 1500

A.D. 395 Roman Empire splits into eastern and western parts.

A.D. 726 The iconoclastic controversy begins.

A.D. 988 Kievan Rus accepts Christianity.

c. A.D. 1240 Mongols invade Slavic lands.

A.D. 1480 Ivan III proclaims Moscow's independence.

244

GEOGRAPHY CONNECTION

Location Explain to students that they will be studying the Mediterranean area, focusing on the Balkan Peninsula, Asia Minor, ancient Russia, and the waterways from the Mediterranean Sea to the Black Sea. Have students locate the Balkan Peninsula, Asia Minor, and the Caucasus Mountains in the Atlas of their text and identify the seas bordering on those areas. Find the present-day site of Constantinople. *(Istanbul)* What made this site ideal for trade? *(It was situated on a natural harbor where Asia and Europe meet. By sailing north, contact could be made with ports on the Black Sea, and trade developed with Russia, India, and China. Turning south, ships could enter the Mediterranean Sea.)*

The archangel Gabriel, an icon on wood, from the
Russian State Museum, St. Petersburg, Russia

The word *icon* is
Greek for "image." In Byzantine art
the image on an icon is of a holy
person. The artist attempted to portray the person's sanctity. Icons can
be found in church frescoes,
mosaics, and paintings on wood
panels, such as this one of the
archangel Gabriel. What other religions that you have studied used
images of deities or holy people?
*(Answers may include ancient Sumerian,
Egyptian, Greek, and Roman religions.)*

✔ *Performance Assessment*

Refer to the activity on page
244C of the Planning Guide.

📁 For an additional activity, refer to Activity 10 in the
*Performance Assessment Strategies
and Activities* booklet.

Using Your History Journal

Entries should incorporate appropriate penalties for violations of the
chosen law. Illuminations may be full
page or use decorative capital letters
and margin adornments.

WORLD HISTORY Online

Chapter Overview

Visit the *World History: The Human Experience*
Web site at **worldhistory.glencoe.com** and
click on *Chapter 10—Chapter Overview* to
preview the chapter.

Your History Journal

*Find out about a specific law in
Justinian's Code in an encyclopedia or a
book on the history of legal systems. Write
the law as an illuminated manuscript,
an art form described in this chapter.*

Chapter 10 *Byzantines and Slavs* **245**

➕ EXTRA CREDIT PROJECT

Preparing a Biography Suggest that students do further library research about a
notable person introduced in this chapter, such
as Justinian, Constantine, Theodora, Sultan
Mehmet, Queen Tamara, Tiridates III, or
Alexander Nevsky. Ask students to prepare a
written report detailing what they have learned
about the life, politics, and contributions of this
person to Byzantine or Slavic history.

GLENCOE TECHNOLOGY

VIDEODISC
Use MindJogger to pre-
view chapter content.

MindJogger Videoquiz

Chapter 10
Disc 2 Side A

 Also available in VHS.

A.D. 300	A.D. 600	A.D. 900	A.D. 1200

A.D. 330 Constantine builds city of Constantinople.

A.D. 527 Justinian becomes eastern Roman emperor.

A.D. 787 Church council at Nicaea approves use of icons.

A.D. 1054 Eastern and Western Churches split.

SECTION THEME

▶ **Conflict** Byzantines fight off invaders and struggle over use of icons.

Guide to Reading

For reading strategies to help students read effectively see pages 12–13. Have students think about the main head as they read the subheads.

Vocabulary Pre-check

☐ Use the Vocabulary PuzzleMaker for Chapter 10 to create a crossword puzzle to reinforce section terms. **L1 LEP**

☐ Use Vocabulary Activity 10 to introduce vocabulary terms. **L1 LEP**

FOCUS

Section Objective

Explain what made the Byzantine Empire rich and powerful.

BELLRINGER
Motivational Activity

Before taking roll at the beginning of the class period, project Section Focus Transparency 10-1 and have students answer the activity questions. Discuss students' responses.

☐ This activity is also available as a blackline master.

Section 1

The New Rome

Guide to Reading

Read to Find Out
Main Idea *The Byzantine Empire became rich and powerful.*

▶ **Terms to Define**
clergy, laity, icon, iconoclast, schism

▶ **People to Meet**
Constantine, Justinian, Theodora, Leo III

▶ **Places to Locate**
Byzantine Empire, Constantinople

The Storyteller

Byzantium [Constantinople] was in flames. A mob was screaming insults at Emperor Justinian and Empress Theodora. The emperor swiftly ordered the imperial treasury loaded onto ships to prepare for escape. Half crazed and without hope, Justinian held a final council of a few loyal friends; Theodora was present. After the military generals expressed their fears, Theodora suddenly rose and broke the silence. "I do not choose to flee," she said. "Never shall I see the day when

I am not saluted as the empress.... You have the money, the ships are ready, the sea is open. As for me, I shall stay." Hearing her, the others took heart. That day, Theodora saved Justinian's throne.

—adapted from *Theodora, Empress of Byzantium,* Charles Diehl, 1972

Theodora, detail of mosaic

After the Roman Empire was divided in A.D. 395, the eastern half became known as the **Byzantine Empire**. At its height in the A.D. 500s, the Byzantine Empire included most of the Balkan Peninsula, Italy, southern Spain, Asia Minor, Syria and North Africa. Its major population group, the Greeks, lived mainly in the central part of the empire. Also included in the empire were Egyptians, Syrians, Arabs, Armenians, Jews, Persians, Slavs, and Turks. These varied peoples and cultures gave Byzantine civilization an international character.

Byzantine Foundations

The location of **Constantinople**, the Byzantine capital, reinforced this multicultural character. The city was located near the centers of early Christianity as well as on major trade routes.

A Strategic City

In A.D. 330 the Roman emperor **Constantine** built Constantinople at a strategic place where Europe and Asia meet. Located on a peninsula, Constantinople overlooked the Bosporus, the narrow strait between the Sea of Marmara and the Black Sea. A second strait, the Dardanelles, connects the Sea of Marmara and the Aegean Sea, which leads to the Mediterranean. These straits gave the occupiers of the peninsula control over movement between the Mediterranean and the Black Seas and, as a result, over the routes leading east to Asia and north to northern Europe. The site of Constantinople itself offered natural protection from attack at a time when Germanic invaders were assaulting Rome to the west. Water protected the city on three sides, and triple walls fortified the side open to attack by land. Eventually a huge chain was strung across the narrow mouth of the deep harbor on Constantinople's north side for still greater protection.

SECTION RESOURCES

Reproducible Masters
- Lecture Notes 10-1
- Reproducible Lesson Plan 10-1
- Guided Reading Activity 10-1
- Geography and History Activity 10
- Time Line Activity 10
- History Simulation 10

- Section Quiz 10-1
- Reading Essentials and Study Guide 10-1

Transparencies
- Section Focus Transparency 10-1
- Chapter Transparency 10
- World History and Art Transparency 12

Multimedia
- Vocabulary PuzzleMaker Software
- Interactive Tutor Self-Assessment Software
- Testmaker

The straits also made the peninsula a natural crossroads for trade. By A.D. 400 the Byzantine capital had become the wealthiest part of the Roman Empire, handling rich cargoes from Asia, Europe, and Africa.

Cultural Blend

After Rome's fall, the Byzantine Empire was regarded as heir to Roman power and traditions. Constantinople was known as the New Rome because its emperors were Romans who spoke Latin and many of its wealthy families came from Rome. Despite these ties, the Byzantine Empire was more than a continuation of the old Roman Empire.

Lands once part of the Greek world formed the heart of the Byzantine Empire. The Byzantine people not only spoke Greek but also stressed their Greek heritage. Eventually Byzantine emperors and officials also used Greek rather than Latin. Religious scholars expressed their ideas in Greek and developed a distinct form of Christianity known today as Eastern Orthodoxy. In addition to the Byzantine Empire's classical Greek heritage and Christian religion came cultural influences from eastern civilizations such as Persia. This mixture of cultures created a distinct Byzantine civilization. Between A.D. 500 and A.D. 1200, this civilization was one of the most advanced in the world and had a higher standard of living than western Europe.

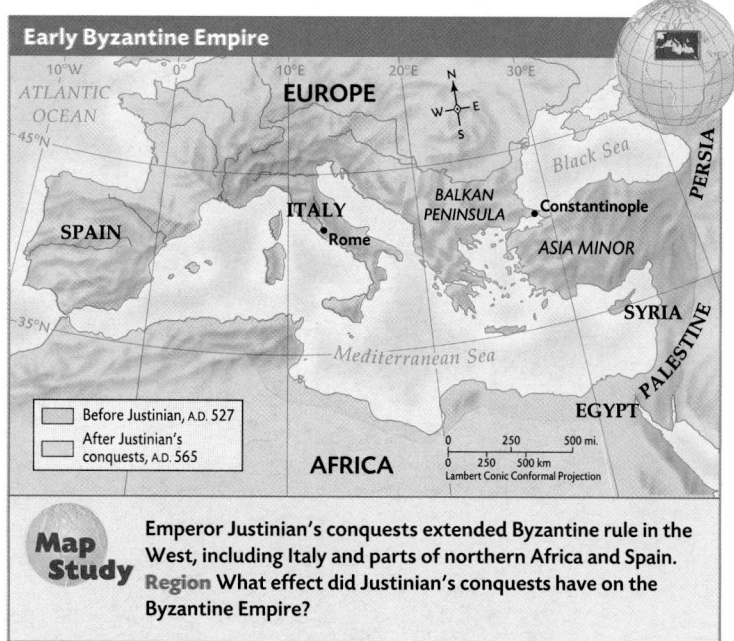

Early Byzantine Empire

Map Study

Emperor Justinian's conquests extended Byzantine rule in the West, including Italy and parts of northern Africa and Spain. **Region** What effect did Justinian's conquests have on the Byzantine Empire?

POINT

Justinian's Rule

At its height the Byzantine Empire was ruled by **Justinian**, the son of prosperous peasants from Macedonia in the western part of the empire. While a young man in the court of his uncle, Emperor Justin I, he worked late into the night at his studies. Justinian's enthusiasm for knowledge and hard work continued after he became emperor in A.D. 527, at age 44.

Theodora's Support

Justinian's wife, **Theodora**, was beautiful, intelligent, and ambitious. Justinian had married her in spite of court objections to her occupation as an actress—a profession held in low esteem in the empire. A capable empress, Theodora participated actively in government, rewarding friends with positions and using dismissals to punish enemies.

Theodora was especially concerned with improving the social standing of women. She persuaded Justinian to issue a decree giving a wife the right to own land equal in value to the wealth she brought with her at marriage. This land gave a widow the income she needed to support her children without the assistance of the government.

In A.D. 532 Theodora's political talents helped save Justinian's throne. When a revolt of taxpayers in Constantinople threatened the government, Justinian's advisers urged him to leave the city. As flames roared through Constantinople and the rebels battered at the palace gates, Justinian prepared to flee. Theodora, however, persuaded him to remain in control.

Inspired by his wife's determination, Justinian reasserted his power. His army crushed the rebels, killing 30,000 people. From that time until his death in A.D. 565, Justinian ruled without challenge.

Chapter 10 *Byzantines and Slavs* **247**

TEACH

Guided Practice

THEME Conflict

Have students name the various issues that led to conflict between the Eastern and Western Churches. Discuss which of these were primarily religious and which primarily political. *(religious: iconoclastic controversy, source of religious authority, points of doctrine; political: control over new churches in Balkans)* **L1**

Map Study

Answer
Justinian's conquests were very expensive. The empire had little money left to protect its eastern borders.

POINT

Justinian's Rule
How did Justinian's reign contribute to world civilization?
The Justinian Code became the basis for most European legal systems, and Byzantine art and architecture flourished under Justinian's rule.

Who?What?Where?When?

Justinian's wife, **Theodora**, had remarkable intellectual gifts and an indomitable will. She actively helped Justinian shape his policies. Theodora also built hospitals for the poor and homes for destitute women.

Mock Trial Have students research a section of the Justinian law code that interests them and work in small groups to prepare a mock court session in which someone is tried for breaking the chosen law. **L2**

Art Have students draw an icon. They should choose a subject from an illustration in the text or another source and copy it in the Byzantine manner. Students should try to use the same colors as those used by Byzantine artists. Ask students to observe the motionless aspect of the faces. **L2 LEP**

 Chapter Transparency 10

 World History and Art Transparency 12

Independent Practice

 Guided Reading Activity 10-1 **L1**

 History Simulation 10

 Time Line Activity 10

Geography and History Activity 10

 History & Art The Emperor Justinian, a mosaic from the A.D. 500s from Ravenna, Italy. *What architectural landmark did Justinian build?*

Military Campaigns

During Justinian's reign, the Byzantines faced a serious military threat from the East. The Sassanian Empire of Persia, under Chosroes (kaz•ROH•eez) I, grew in strength and threatened to conquer the eastern provinces of the Byzantine Empire. The Byzantines rallied their forces and threw back the Persians. Justinian gained a brief period of security for the eastern borders by agreeing to pay tribute in return for peace.

Justinian dreamed of restoring the Roman Empire. In A.D. 533 he began the reconquest of Italy, North Africa, and Spain—Roman lands that had fallen to Germanic invaders. Under the general Belisarius, the Byzantine armies were strengthened and reorganized. Between A.D. 533 and A.D. 555, they fought a series of wars against the Vandals in North Africa, the Ostrogoths in Italy, and the Visigoths in southern Spain. The Byzantines conquered these Germanic groups and extended Byzantine rule in the west.

The successful reconquest, however, proved costly for the empire. The wars exhausted most of the Byzantine resources. Funds were low for defending the eastern borders, which faced attack by an expanding Persian Empire. Justinian's conquests did not last. Within a generation of his death, the empire lost many of its outlying territories.

Code of Laws

Justinian's legal reforms did last, affecting Western law even today. Shortly after becoming emperor, Justinian appointed a commission to codify, or classify, the empire's Roman laws. For centuries, these laws had accumulated without organization or classification.

The commission was made up of 10 scholars headed by a legal expert named Tribonian. For more than 6 years, the commission collected and organized vast numbers of laws. It threw out the ones that were outdated, simplified many, and put the remainder into categories. The commission's work was recorded in a collection of books known as the *Corpus of Civil Law,* or the Justinian Code. This massive work preserved Rome's legal heritage and later became the basis for most European legal systems.

The Arts

Under Justinian, Byzantine art and architecture

MEETING SPECIAL NEEDS ACTIVITIES

Reading Comprehension Have students work in pairs to create comprehension questions for each part of the section. Students can then use these to quiz each other over section content. **L1**

Learning Style: Verbal/Linguistic Have students read the poem "Ozymandias" by Percy Bysshe Shelley. Direct them to use this as a springboard for writing a one-page paper on what kinds of accomplishments by a political leader endure the longest. Have them apply this question to Justinian's accomplishments. **L3**

thrived and achieved their distinct character. The emperor ordered the construction of new roads, fortresses, aqueducts, monasteries, and other buildings. His most famous project was the church of Hagia Sophia, "Holy Wisdom," in Constantinople. The largest and most beautiful church in the empire, Hagia Sophia still stands today as one of the world's great architectural landmarks. ◣

Byzantine Religion

Strong ties linked Byzantine emperors and the Church. The emperors were regarded as God's representatives on earth. Starting in the A.D. 400s, Byzantine emperors and empresses were crowned by the patriarch of Constantinople and took an oath to defend the Christian faith.

Church and State

Byzantine emperors frequently played a major role in church affairs. They appointed church officials, defined the style of worship, and used the wealth of the Church for government purposes.

Justinian strengthened this control over the Church by intervening in disputes over church beliefs. He also tried to unify the empire under one Christian faith, a practice that sometimes led to persecution of Jews and non-Greek Christians.

Religious Controversy

Both Byzantine clergy—church officials such as priests and bishops—and laity—church members who were not clergy—were intensely interested in religious matters. In their homes, markets, and shops, Byzantines often engaged in heated religious discussions. Visitors to Constantinople saw shoppers in the marketplaces having lively discussions about such topics as the exact relationship of Jesus the Son to God the Father. Such arguments often became political issues and led to fights and riots.

In the A.D. 700s, a dispute broke out over the use of icons (EYE•KAHNZ), or religious images, in worship. Although Christians had disagreed about this practice since the A.D. 400s, the use of icons in churches became a political issue by the A.D. 700s.

Those who objected to the use of icons in Christian worship argued that the Bible, in the Ten Commandments, prohibited such images. Defenders stressed that icons were symbols of

Check for Understanding

Assign Section 1 Assessment as homework or as an in-class activity.

🔲 Use Interactive Tutor Self-Assessment Software to review Section 1.

Linking Past and Present

Byzantine Architecture

Justinian ordered his architects to create the most spectacular building of all time. The construction of Constantinople's Hagia Sophia took five years. To an extent, Justinian succeeded in creating the greatest religious monument of his time. It was centuries before a building of equal size and splendor was built in the Mediterranean world.

ANSWER

Students may point out the use of domes, arches, and columns as well as embellishments (i.e. carvings of figures and objects) in Byzantine-style architecture, contrasting them with the streamlined simplicity and starkness of much modern architecture.

The Arts

Byzantine Architecture

Hagia Sophia

Hagia Sophia, completed in A.D. 537, was built to symbolize both Christianity's importance in the Byzantine Empire and the Byzantine emperor's authority. It also represented the beginning of what became known as the Byzantine style of architecture.

Early Byzantine churches featured a central dome on a flat roof supported by four arches springing from columns or piers. Often the dome was pierced by windows and covered with glittering mosaics. Light streamed into the church from all directions and reflected off the decorated surfaces.

The Byzantine style eventually spread to other lands, such as Ukraine and Russia, that accepted Eastern Christianity. Architects in these lands modified the original Byzantine model to suit their own needs. For example, the Russians, who lived in a cold climate with a lot of snow, replaced the flat roof and large central dome with sloping roofs and onion-shaped domes.

Today, Eastern Christians throughout the world still use some form of the Byzantine style. In cities and towns of North America, the descendants of Eastern Christian immigrants who came during the late 1800s and early 1900s have sometimes combined traditional Byzantine architectural principles with modern ones in their churches.

Linking Past and Present — ACTIVITY

Examine a church or other building in your community that is built in the Byzantine style. What elements of its architecture do you think reflect the basic Byzantine model? What elements do you think are modern or come from other cultural traditions?

Chapter 10 *Byzantines and Slavs* **249**

MAKING CONNECTIONS ACTIVITIES

Religion Since the schism of A.D. 1054, the Eastern Orthodox and Roman Catholic Churches have continued to develop their own doctrine and traditions. Have students research the principal differences in doctrine and religious practices between the two churches today and report their findings to the class. **L2**

The Arts Numerous conventions governed the painting of Byzantine icons to ensure that an icon would have a particular effect on its viewers. Have students research the conventions and report to the class on their findings. Have them illustrate their report with examples of Byzantine art. **L3**

Evaluate

Section Quiz 10-1

Use the Testmaker to create a customized quiz for Section 1.

Reteach

Have students create cards with questions and answers such as the following and encourage them to play a Jeopardy-style game with the question cards.

1. walled harbors and fortified gates (*What protected Byzantium from outside attack?*)
2. the iconoclast controversy (*What conflict involved the use of images in the Church?*)

Reading Essentials and Study Guide 10-1

Enrich

Have students research the epidemic of plague that struck Constantinople in A.D. 542. Encourage them to prepare an essay on the devastation caused by the epidemic and its impact on political affairs in the empire.

CLOSE

Discuss the importance of Christianity in the Byzantine Empire. Explain that the emperor was never questioned and that the emperor and the patriarch of the Church were very close. Organize a class discussion about how religious disagreements, such as the schism with Rome and the iconoclastic controversy, affected politics.

 Simplified Alphabet Becomes Popular

Japan, A.D. 860
The Japanese alphabet, hiragana, became popular around A.D. 860. It consisted of characters developed by simplifying the Chinese alphabet. Hiragana was popularized by women of the Heian court, who used the system in writing poetry, diaries, and novels. It was called "letters of women" because men continued to use kanji, or the Chinese system.

Japan

God's presence in human affairs. The Byzantine theologian John of Damascus wrote many religious articles defending the use of icons.

Believing that icons encouraged superstition and idol-worship, in A.D. 726 Emperor **Leo III** ordered all icons removed from the churches. The emperor's supporters—military leaders, government officials, and many people in Asia Minor—became known as iconoclasts, or image breakers.

Church leaders and other Byzantines resisted the order, and were supported by the Church in Rome, which was as important a center of Christianity as Constantinople. The Roman pope's involvement in the controversy strained relations between the Eastern and Western Churches.

Feeling his authority was being challenged, Leo asserted his power and suppressed demonstrations in favor of icons. Although several later emperors did the same, they were not supported by the people. In A.D. 787 a church council at Nicaea approved the use of icons. Soon after, the Empress Irene—the first woman to hold the Byzantine throne—allowed the use of icons as long as they were not given the worship due to God. The Eastern Church further settled the issue in A.D. 843, allowing the use of pictures, but not statues, in worship.

Conflict With Rome

Since the A.D. 300s, the Eastern and Western Churches had disagreed on a number of religious and political issues. As centuries passed, the disagreements intensified.

The iconoclastic controversy was but one of many reasons that divided the two churches. The most serious issue concerned the source of religious authority. The pope in Rome and the patriarch of Constantinople did not agree on their roles in the Christian Church. The pope stated that he was supreme leader of the Church; the patriarch of Constantinople opposed this claim. The two church leaders also disagreed over points of doctrine. They challenged each other for control of new churches in the Balkan Peninsula.

Relations between Eastern and Western Churches worsened in the A.D. 700s when the Germanic Lombards invaded central Italy. When the Byzantine emperor refused to give the pope in Rome military protection, the pope turned to the Franks, a Germanic Catholic people in western Europe. After the Franks defeated the Lombards, the pope gave the Frankish leader, Charlemagne, the title of emperor—a title which only the Byzantine ruler could legally grant. This action made the Byzantines even more bitter toward the pope and the Western Church.

By A.D. 1054 doctrinal, political, and geographical differences finally led to a schism (SIH•zuhm), or separation, of the Church into the Roman Catholic Church in the West and the Eastern Orthodox Church in the East. The split further weakened the Byzantine Empire, which had faced attacks from numerous peoples since its founding.

SECTION 1 ASSESSMENT

Main Idea
1. Use a diagram like the one below to identify ways in which the Byzantine Empire rose to power.

Causes

Effect → Powerful Byzantine Empire

Recall
2. **Define** clergy, laity, icon, iconoclast, schism.
3. **Identify** Constantine, Justinian, Theodora, Leo III.

Critical Thinking
4. **Analyzing Information** How were Byzantine emperors and the Christian Church linked?

Understanding Themes
5. **Conflict** How did religious disputes, such as the iconoclastic controversy, affect the political affairs of the Byzantine Empire?

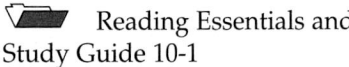 **SECTION 1 ASSESSMENT ANSWERS**

1. Constantinople's location enabled it to control trade routes to Asia and Northern Europe; Constantinople was protected from invasion; cultural mix resulted in advanced civilization; Byzantine rule was extended in west; legal reform; emperor-controlled church

2. All terms are defined in the Glossary.
3. Constantine, 246; Justinian, 247; Theodora, 247; Leo III, 250
4. Byzantine emperors played a major role in church affairs by appointing church officials, setting the style of worship, and intervening in church disputes.

5. **CONFLICT** Religious disputes such as the iconoclastic controversy helped produce the schism between the Eastern and Western Churches. This split weakened the Byzantine Empire.

A.D. 500   A.D. 1000   A.D. 1500

A.D. 550 Byzantines send expedition to China.

A.D. 863 Cyril develops alphabet for the Slavs.

A.D. 1184 Queen Tamara begins her reign in Georgia.

A.D. 1453 Constantinople falls to Ottoman Turks.

Chapter 10
Section 2

Section 2

Byzantine Civilization

Read to Find Out

Main Idea *Christianity played a significant role in Byzantine and neighboring societies.*

▶ **Terms to Define**
theology, regent, mosaic, illuminated manuscript, monastery, missionary

▶ **People to Meet**
Cyril, Methodius, the Seljuk Turks, the Ottoman Turks, Tiridates III, Tamara

▶ **Places to Locate**
Venice, Armenia, Georgia, Bulgaria, Serbia

toryteller

A bishop from Italy wrote home describing the Byzantine court: "In the audience-hall sat the Emperor on a throne before which stood an artificial tree, all gilded, on whose branches mechanical birds perched, singing. To either side of the throne stood a mighty lion, which, as the visitor approached, lashed the ground with its tail and from whose open jaws … there came a terrifying roar." The visitor threw himself to the ground three times, and looking up beheld the Emperor raised by an invisible mechanism to the roof of the hall, where he sat glittering among his jewels.

—adapted from Istanbul, Martin Heurlimann, 1958

Emperor Constantine IX

From A.D. 500 to A.D. 800, when western Europe was in decline, the Byzantine Empire was a brilliant center of civilization. Its scholars preserved Greek philosophy and literature, Roman political and legal ideas, and Christian theology, or religious teachings. The Byzantines also created new art forms and spread the religion of the Eastern Orthodox Church into eastern Europe.

Byzantine Life

Byzantine society was divided into a hierarchy of social groups. Yet, there were few barriers to prevent a person from moving from one group to another. This flexibility brought variety and change to Byzantine life.

Family Life

The family was the center of social life for most Byzantines. Both the Church and the government supported marriage as a sacred institution. Divorce was difficult to obtain, and the Church generally forbade more than one remarriage.

Byzantine women were expected to live partly in seclusion, and so rooms in homes and churches were set aside for their sole use. Nevertheless, women had gained some rights through Theodora's efforts. Like the empress herself, some women became well educated and influential in the government. Several governed as regents, or temporary rulers, and a few ruled in their own right as empresses.

The Economy

Most Byzantines made a living through farming, herding, or working as laborers. Farmers paid heavy taxes that supported the government.

Chapter 10 *Byzantines and Slavs* **251**

TEACH

Guided Practice

THEME Innovation

Refer students to the description of Byzantine architecture on page 249 and discuss Byzantine architectural innovation: the large central church dome. Explain that although domes were not a new architectural feature, Byzantine domes were used in a new geometrical setting—flanked by smaller domes—and were higher and wider than any previous domes. If possible, bring to class pictures of ancient Roman domed buildings for students to compare. **L1 LEP**

Daily Life Ask students to consider such aspects of Byzantine civilization as art, religion, the economy, education, politics, and family life. Have small groups of students each choose two areas of interest and examine how these areas affected Byzantine culture. Then ask groups to share their findings with their classmates. **L3**

World History and Art Transparency 12, *Theodora and Attendants*

Although the base of the Byzantine economy was agricultural, commerce thrived in cities such as Constantinople, which was the site of a natural crossroads for trade. Byzantine ships loaded with cargo sailed between the Mediterranean and Black Seas by way of the Bosporus and Dardanelles. At the eastern shore of the Black Sea, goods could be shipped overland through Asia. Rivers such as the Dnieper, which flows from the Baltic region south to the Black Sea, provided access to northern Europe.

Merchants traded Byzantine agricultural goods and furs and enslaved people from northern Europe for luxury goods from the East. To Constantinople's busy harbor, called the Golden Horn, ships brought cloves and sandalwood from the East Indies; pepper, copper, and gems from India and Ceylon (present-day Sri Lanka); and silk from China.

The major Byzantine industry was weaving silk. It developed after A.D. 550, when Justinian sent two monks to China, the center of the silk industry.

On a visit to a silk factory the monks stole some silkworm eggs, hid them in hollow bamboo canes, and smuggled their precious cargo out of China. Brought to Constantinople, the silkworms fed on mulberry leaves and spun the silk that made the empire wealthy.

Byzantine Art and Learning

Among the products of Byzantine culture were beautiful icons, jewel-encrusted crosses, and carved ivory boxes for sacred items. These art forms were adopted by eastern Europe and also influenced western Europe and the Middle East.

Art

Religious subjects were the sources of most Byzantine art. Icons, the most popular art form, portrayed saints and other religious figures. Icons were displayed on the walls of churches, homes, and shrines. Magnificent churches were

Images *of the* Times

Byzantine Art

Byzantine art reflected the strong influence of Christianity.

The Byzantine church of St. Kosmas at Loukas, Greece, displays a colorful mosaic.

The crucifix was a familiar Byzantine icon both in churches and in homes.

252

Images *of the* Times   Byzantine Art

The creative artists of the Byzantine Empire painted frescoes and icons, carved ivories, illuminated manuscripts, created reliquaries with precious jewels and metalwork, embroidered tapestries, and used tiny bits of stone and glass to produce superb mosaics. The mood of much of this art was reverent, with religious themes. But secular forms existed alongside the religious: sculptures, woven silk, textiles, dishes, enamelwork, and glass.

embellished with gold and silver, polished and carved marble, ivory, and jewels, as well as icons and other religious images.

The Byzantines also excelled in the art of mosaic, or pictures made of many tiny pieces of colored glass or flat stone set in plaster. The most masterly mosaics captured the finest gradations of skin tones and textures of clothing—a skill even painters found difficult to master. Byzantine emperor Constantine VII, historian, painter, and author, described one mosaic:

> **As you move, the figures seem to move, too. You could swear that their eyes are turning and shining and that their garments are rustling ... the Byzantine mosaicist has succeeded in creating the illusion that his jig-saw puzzle has come to life.**

Religious scholars of the Byzantine Empire created another art form, the illuminated manuscript.

These were books decorated with elaborate designs, beautiful lettering, and miniature paintings. The brilliantly colored paintings portrayed religious themes as well as scenes of Byzantine daily life. Adopted in western Europe, the art of illuminating manuscripts provided a vivid record of daily life between A.D. 300 and A.D. 1200.

Education

Schools and learning also played an important role in Byzantine culture. The government-supported University of Constantinople, established in A.D. 850, trained scholars and lawyers for government jobs; the Eastern Orthodox Church provided religious schools to train priests and theological scholars. Beyond the religious subjects that reflected the primary role of the Church, areas of study included medicine, law, philosophy, arithmetic, geometry, astronomy, grammar, and music. Wealthy people sometimes hired tutors to instruct their children, particularly their daughters, who were usually not admitted to schools and universities.

Beautiful illuminated manuscripts, such as this from St. Catherine's Monastery at Sinai, were the work of religious scholars. Monasteries were financed by the emperor and by wealthy citizens.

REFLECTING ON THE TIMES

1. How do these images reveal the prosperity of the Byzantine Empire?
2. Who paid to have much of the religious art at churches and monasteries created?

253

ANSWERS TO REFLECTING ON THE TIMES

1. Jewel-encrusted crosses and gold and glass mosaics reflected the great wealth of resources from the empire's trade.
2. The emperor and wealthy citizens financed this religious art.

Independent Practice

Guided Reading Activity 10-2 **L1**

The Arts Have students select a letter of the alphabet (one of their own initials, for example) to be illuminated. They will need to check resources for examples of illuminated manuscripts. Encourage students to be creative and decorate the letter with as much color and detail as possible. **L2 LEP**

Who?What?Where?When?

Education The Byzantine Empire provided free schools open to all children regardless of nationality or class as early as the eleventh century. Children of upper-class families, however, were often educated by private tutors.

Global Gourmet

Byzantine Empire Byzantine eating habits were similar to our own. Three meals a day (breakfast, midday, and supper) were common. Most people ate simply: bread and cheese, and vegetables cooked in olive oil. The wealthy enjoyed banquets of meats roasted or cooked in herbs and spices. A variety of meat, game, poultry, and fish was eaten. Soups and stews were often on the menu. Fruits such as apples, melon, figs, and dates were staple items of the diet.

Map Study

Answer

unending attacks by many peoples, both in the east and in the west; losing control of trade

Map Skills Practice

Reading a Map Between what latitudes on the map does Constantinople lie? *(between 40°N–45°N latitudes)*

Religion and the Arts Students may work in small groups to list specific examples of how Byzantine art and architecture were strongly influenced by religion. Have all students then write individual short essays explaining the relationship. **L3**

NATIONAL GEOGRAPHIC SOCIETY

CD-ROM
PICTURE ATLAS OF THE WORLD

You and your students can see the present-day skyline of Istanbul and the beautiful Hagia Sophia by clicking the "Photos" button of Istanbul, Turkey.

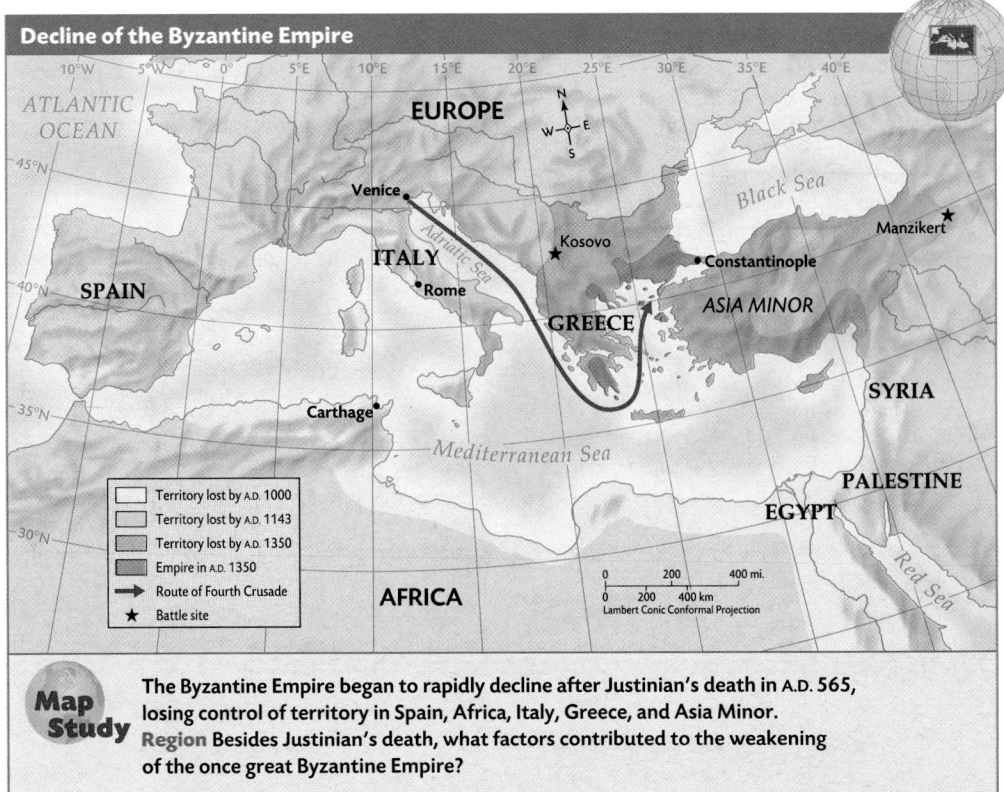

Decline of the Byzantine Empire

Territory lost by A.D. 1000
Territory lost by A.D. 1143
Territory lost by A.D. 1350
Empire in A.D. 1350
Route of Fourth Crusade
★ Battle site

Map Study The Byzantine Empire began to rapidly decline after Justinian's death in A.D. 565, losing control of territory in Spain, Africa, Italy, Greece, and Asia Minor. **Region** Besides Justinian's death, what factors contributed to the weakening of the once great Byzantine Empire?

Byzantine literature focused on salvation of the soul and obedience to God's will. Writers composed hymns and poems in praise of Christ and his mother, Mary. Instead of popular fiction, Byzantine authors wrote books about the lives of the saints, which provided readers with moral lessons as well as accounts of the saints' miracles and adventures.

The foremost occupation of Byzantine scholars, however, was copying the writings of the ancient Greeks and Romans. By preserving ancient works on science, medicine, and mathematics, the Byzantines helped spread classical knowledge to the Western world.

Spread of Christianity

Near the end of the A.D. 300s, devout Christians throughout the Byzantine Empire formed religious communities called monasteries. In the monasteries, men called monks sought to develop a spiritual way of life apart from the temptations of the world. At the same time, they could help other people by doing good deeds and by setting an example of Christian living. Christian women who did the same were called nuns and lived in quarters of their own known as convents.

Monasteries and convents soon played an important role in Byzantine life. They helped the poor and ran hospitals and schools for needy children. They also spread Byzantine arts and learning. Monasteries also sent missionaries—people who carry a religious message—to neighboring peoples to convert them to the Christian faith.

Footnotes to History

Greek Fire

In fighting their enemies, the Byzantines used a terrifying weapon known as Greek fire, one of the earliest uses of chemicals in warfare. This chemical mixture exploded when it came into contact with fire or water. The formula remains a mystery; it probably included highly flammable oil, pitch, quicklime, sulfur, and resin.

254 Chapter 10 *Byzantines and Slavs*

COOPERATIVE LEARNING ACTIVITY

Role Play Organize the class into two large groups—one representing citizens of the Byzantine Empire and the other representing visitors from northern Europe. Have each group prepare a presentation. The Byzantines should prepare a speech welcoming their visitors. The speech should stress the virtues and achievements of Byzantine culture. Then the visitors from northern Europe should respond by acknowledging their hosts' achievements and commenting on what they have seen during their visit. The visitors should compare features of their homeland with those of the Byzantine Empire. Conclude the presentations with a discussion of various social, religious, political, and economic concerns and conflicts facing both groups. **L1**

Among the most successful missionaries were the brothers **Cyril** and **Methodius**. They reasoned that Christianity would be more acceptable to the Slavic peoples who lived north of the empire if it were presented in their own language. About A.D. 863 Cyril devised an alphabet for the Slavic languages. Known today as the Cyrillic (suh•RIH•lihk) alphabet in honor of its inventor, this script is still used by Russians, Ukrainians, Bulgarians, and Serbs. When Cyril and Methodius presented the Slavs with Cyrillic translations of the Bible and church ceremonies, they won many converts.

Decline and Fall

From its founding, the Byzantine Empire suffered frequent attacks by invading armies. Among them were Germanic Lombards, Slavs, Avars, Bulgars, Persians, and Arabs.

Unending Attacks

After Justinian died in A.D. 565, the Germanic Lombards took over most of Italy, the Avars attacked the northern frontier, Slavic peoples moved into the Balkans, and the Persians resumed their attacks in the east. By A.D. 626 the Slavs were at the walls of Constantinople. Although a brilliant counterattack stopped their advance, a new enemy—the Arabs from the Middle East—entered the scene. Followers of the new religion of Islam, the Arabs sought to spread their faith and acquire wealth. By the A.D. 630s, they occupied Syria and Palestine and had expanded into Persia and across North Africa. The Byzantines stopped the Arabs at Constantinople, but could not regain the lost territories in the Middle East and North Africa.

By A.D. 700 the Byzantine Empire was reduced to the territories that were primarily Greek. The loss of the non-Greek lands actually helped strengthen the empire because it now had one religion, one language, and one culture.

Christian Conquest

In A.D. 1071 northern European people called Normans seized the Byzantine lands in southern Italy. **Venice**, an Italian trading city on the Adriatic Sea, agreed to help the Byzantines' effort to regain the lands in return for trading privileges in Constantinople. The attempt failed, however, and the Byzantines soon lost control of trade, badly weakening an economy already strained by war.

In the same year, **the Seljuk** (SEHL•JOOK) **Turks**, who had come from central Asia and converted to Islam, defeated the Byzantines at the town

Visualizing History St. Jacob holding script in the Cyrillic alphabet, a modified form of the Greek alphabet. *What peoples use the Cyrillic alphabet today?*

of Manzikert. As the invaders advanced, the Byzantine emperor asked the pope's help in defending Christianity. Expeditions sent by the pope against the Islamic forces were more interested in taking over Palestine.

In A.D. 1204 Christian soldiers from western Europe agreed to help the Venetians attack Constantinople. For three days the attackers burned and looted the city, stealing and destroying priceless manuscripts and works of art. Their actions were so brutal that Pope Innocent III publicly condemned them:

  ❝ These defenders of Christ, who should have turned their swords only against the infidels [followers of Islam], have bathed in Christian blood. They have respected neither religion, nor age, nor sex.... It was

Visualizing History The Russian language and other Slavic languages are closely related. The Cyrillic alphabet, which is based largely on the Greek alphabet and originally had 43 letters, eventually became the basis for the culture of the entire Slavic world.
Answer to Caption: *A modified form of the Cyrillic alphabet, containing 33 letters, is used by the Russians, Ukrainians, Bulgarians, and Serbs today.*

Politics Encourage students to consider the factors that led to the fall of the Byzantine Empire. Have them create a time line tracing the decline of the empire after the reign of Justinian. Students may need to do library research to fill in some of the details. Time lines should include the reigning emperor, economic factors, internal and external conflicts, and a list of territories lost at each stage. **L2**

MEETING SPECIAL NEEDS ACTIVITY

Language Delayed Encourage students who have difficulty defining terms to search through the text for new words and jot them down on index cards. Assign partners to work together to define the terms on the back of the cards. Have students use the words in another context to ensure understanding. The entire class can use the set of cards for review at the end of the chapter and before the unit test. **L1 LEP**

CURRICULUM CONNECTION

LITERATURE
Georgia enjoyed a golden age during the reign of Queen Tamara. Her court welcomed artists and poets, including Shota Rustaveli, whose epic poem, *The Knight in the Tiger Skin*, was dedicated to the queen. Set in Arabia, the poem tells a tale of courtly love, emphasizing courage, loyalty, and patriotism. It has been translated into French, Russian, Japanese, and other languages.

Visualizing History Mahmet set about rebuilding the newly renamed capital, Istanbul. He constructed new buildings and converted some of the city's finest churches into mosques.
Answer to Caption: *The city held out for six weeks under siege until their last emperor was slain.*

ASSESS

Check for Understanding

Assign Section 2 Assessment as homework or as an in-class activity.

⬛ Use Interactive Tutor Self-Assessment Software to review Section 2.

---

not enough for them to squander the treasures of the Empire and to rob private individuals, whether great or small.... They have dared to lay their hands on the wealth of the churches. They have been seen tearing from the altars the silver adornments, breaking them in fragments, over which they quarreled, violating the sanctuaries, carrying away the icons, crosses, and relics. 🙶

The western Christians established "a Latin empire" in Constantinople. The Byzantine people resisted this rule successfully and reestablished their own culture in A.D. 1261.

Fall of Constantinople

The years of fighting had severely weakened the Byzantine Empire. Soon Serbs and Bulgars took over Balkan territory. New invaders from central

Visualizing History **Portrait of Sultan Mahmet II, who conquered Constantinople and renamed it Istanbul.** *How long did the Byzantine city hold out against the sultan's siege?*

Asia, **the Ottoman Turks**, attacked the eastern provinces. By the late A.D. 1300s, the Byzantine Empire consisted of only Constantinople and part of Greece.

About 100,000 people still lived in the capital; food was scarce, and wealth was gone. In A.D. 1453 the Ottomans laid siege to Constantinople. For six weeks their huge cannon blasted away at the city's walls. The Byzantines fought fiercely until their last emperor was killed.

For a thousand years, the Byzantine Empire had protected the Christian lands to its north. With the fall of Constantinople, central Europe lay open to attack by Islamic forces. Despite the empire's fall, the Byzantine heritage lived on in the civilization developed by the Eastern Slavs.

Neighboring Kingdoms

During the time of the Byzantine Empire, four neighboring kingdoms went through periods of prosperity and decline. Northeast of the empire, and south of the Caucasus Mountains between the Black and Caspian Seas, lay the kingdoms of **Armenia** and **Georgia**. Northwest of Byzantine territory, in Europe's Balkan Peninsula, arose two other realms—**Bulgaria** and **Serbia**.

Armenia

Located at a crossroads between Europe and Asia, Armenia struggled against foreign invasions. Settling the area in the 700s B.C., the Armenians within 300 years had become part of the Persian Empire. When Alexander the Great conquered Persia in the 330s B.C., his armies acquired Armenia but allowed it some freedoms. King Tigran II, who came to power about 95 B.C., built an independent Armenian kingdom stretching from the Caspian Sea to the Mediterranean Sea. The Romans, however, defeated Tigran in 69 B.C., and Armenia became part of the Roman Empire.

In the early A.D. 300s, the Armenians, under King **Tiridates** (TEER•uh•DAH •teez) **III**, accepted Christianity. This decision made Armenia the first officially Christian country in the world. Christianity gave Armenians a sense of national identity. Mesrob (MEH•zrohb), an Armenian scholar-monk, developed the Armenian alphabet in the early A.D. 400s. In A.D. 451, the Armenians successfully

---

MAKING CONNECTIONS ACTIVITY

Daily Life Have students bring in works of folk art, literature, and music and examples of foods from the Balkan Peninsula and Slavic areas. Some might prepare recipes from Turkey, Armenia, and Russia. Other students can locate collections of folktales and perform a dramatic reading. Still others might play recordings of typical folk music of the region. Possibly someone from the community can share a traditional costume or perform a folk dance. **L1** 📦

defended their Christian state against the Persians in the Battle of Avarair (ah•vah•RAHR).

Arab armies invaded Armenia in the A.D. 600s, but they failed to conquer the entire country. An independent Armenian kingdom eventually arose in the northern region. In the A.D. 1000s the Seljuk Turks swept into Armenia, followed by the Ottoman Turks in the A.D. 1400s. Within 300 years, Armenia had become a battlefield among the Ottomans, Persians, and Russians. During the A.D. 1800s, it was divided between the Russian and Ottoman empires.

Georgia

Like Armenia, Georgia continually faced waves of foreign invasions. Ancient Georgia consisted of two kingdoms known as Colchis and Iberia. Both realms came under Roman rule in 65 B.C. The Roman conquerors built new roads and introduced their laws and customs to the region. The Silk Road, which passed through the Caucasus Mountains, allowed the Georgians to prosper from trade between Europe and Asia. Caravans of silk cloth, spices, and other goods reached ports on Georgia's Black Sea coast and continued on to the Middle East and Europe.

Georgia was converted to Christianity in the A.D. 300s by a Christian woman named Nino. Meanwhile, newly Christianized Georgia was attacked by rival Persian and Byzantine armies.

During the A.D. 1100s and early A.D. 1200s, Georgia enjoyed a golden age of freedom and culture under Queen **Tamara** (tah•MAH•rah). However, from the late A.D. 1200s to the A.D. 1700s, the Georgians again faced a series of conquerors, including the Mongols, the Persians, and the Ottomans. Turning northward to the Russians for military aid, Georgia by the early A.D. 1800s had become part of the Russian Empire.

Bulgaria

The Balkan Peninsula also underwent upheavals. Conquered by Roman armies, the region that is present-day Bulgaria became part of the Roman Empire in the A.D. 40s. When Rome fell about 400 years later, Slavs from east central Europe and Bulgars from central Asia settled Bulgaria, intermarrying to become the Bulgarians.

Influenced by Byzantine culture and religion, the first Bulgarian state arose in the A.D. 600s. It reached its peak 300 years later under King Simeon I, and finally fell prey to Byzantine conquest in A.D. 1018. Byzantine decline, however, enabled the Bulgarians to regain their freedom. This second Bulgarian kingdom survived from the late A.D. 1100s to the late A.D. 1300s, when Ottoman invaders from central Asia conquered it. Ottoman rule of Bulgaria lasted more than 500 years.

Serbia

Northwest of Bulgaria was the Slavic kingdom of Serbia. During the A.D. 500s and 600s, groups of Slavs settled in the Balkan Peninsula. By the 1100s, the Serbs, one of the most powerful of these groups, had accepted Eastern Orthodox Christianity and the Cyrillic alphabet. They also formed a state. The Serbian kingdom enjoyed its greatest period of prosperity in the A.D. 1300s under Stefan Dusán (STEH•fahn•doo•SHAHN), who assumed the title of emperor of the Serbs. Dusán's armies successfully fought the Byzantines, expanding Serbian rule throughout much of the Balkans.

After Dusán's death in 1355, his heirs lacked the skills to keep the Serbian kingdom united. The Serbs valiantly fought the Ottomans but were eventually defeated in 1389 in the Battle of Kosovo. Almost 500 years of Ottoman rule followed, but the desire to reverse the shame of Kosovo helped keep alive Serbian national pride.

SECTION 2 ASSESSMENT

Main Idea
1. Use a diagram like the one below to identify Christianity's role in Byzantine and neighboring societies.

Recall
2. **Define** theology, regent, mosaic, illuminated manuscript, monastery, missionary.
3. **Identify** Cyril, Methodius, the Seljuk Turks, the Ottoman Turks, Tiridates III, Tamara.

Critical Thinking
4. **Analyzing Information** How did the split between eastern and western Christians influence Byzantine decline?

Understanding Themes
5. **Innovation** What was the role of art and religion in the Byzantine and neighboring kingdoms? How did Christianity affect it?

Evaluate

 Section Quiz 10-2

🔲 Use the Testmaker to create a customized quiz for Section 2.

Reteach

Ask students to make a list of key elements of Byzantine culture during Emperor Justinian's time. *(religion, art, architecture, and trade)*

Reading Essentials and Study Guide 10-2

Enrich

Have students research the life of the Empress Theodora. Direct them to focus especially on what she did to improve the lives of women in the empire.

CLOSE

Help the class summarize the section by asking them to list three important contributions of Byzantine civilization. Ask whether they agree with historians that the Byzantine Empire transmitted the classical culture of ancient Greece and Rome to western Europe, and passed eastern Christianity along to the Slavs.

SECTION 2 ASSESSMENT ANSWERS

1. Byzantium: monasteries and convents ran hospitals and schools; missionary Cyril devised alphabet for Slavic language; Cyrillic translation of Bible won converts. Armenia: Christianity helped shape national identity; a scholarly monk developed an Armenian alphabet. Serbia: accepted Eastern Orthodox Christianity and Cyrillic alphabet
2. All terms are defined in the Glossary.
3. Cyril, 255; Methodius, 255; Seljuk Turks, 255; Manzikert, 255; Ottoman Turks, 256; Tiridates III, 256; Tamara, 257
4. Constant conflict and friction disrupted and distracted religious and political leadership, leading to an attack on Constantinople by western Christians.
5. **INNOVATION** Religion and art played a central role in these societies and helped give them a sense of identity and unity. Religious devotion stimulated and inspired cultural creativity.

A.D. 900 | A.D. 1100 | A.D. 1300 | A.D. 1500

A.D. 980 Vladimir becomes Grand Prince of Kiev.

A.D. 1240 Alexander Nevsky defeats the Swedes.

A.D. 1380 Moscow defeats Mongols at the Battle of Kulikovo.

A.D. 1472 Ivan III of Moscow takes title of czar.

Section 3

The Eastern Slavs

Read to Find Out
Main Idea *The Eastern Slavs developed separate cultures from those of western Europe.*

▶ **Terms to Define**
steppe, principality, boyar, czar

▶ **People to Meet**
the Slavs, Rurik, Olga, Vladimir, Yaroslav, the Mongols, Alexander Nevsky, Ivan III

▶ **Places to Locate**
Dnieper River, Kiev, Novgorod, Moscow

As a pagan prince, Vladimir behaved kindly; once he became a Christian, his generosity became unlimited. Beggars assembled in his courtyard every

Eastern Orthodox church

day for food, drink, clothing, and money. For the sick and weak, supply wagons were loaded up and driven around the city of Kiev. Once, when his friends showed disgust at having to eat with plain wooden spoons, Vladimir laughed and had silver ones cast for them. He was also the first Kiev prince to mint gold and silver coins. The first of these, made by inexperienced Russian crafts workers, were slightly lumpy and uneven, but bore Vladimir's picture and the inscription, "Here is Vladimir on his throne. And this is his gold."

—from *Vladimir the Russian Viking,*
Vladimir Volkoff, 1985

fter the fall of Constantinople in A.D. 1453, the leadership of the Eastern Orthodox world passed from the Byzantines to **the Slavs**. The Slavs were among the largest groups living in eastern Europe. Because of their location, the Slavs had been in close contact with the Byzantines since the A.D. 900s.

This relationship made a lasting mark on the development of Slavic history. The Slavs, especially those living in the areas that are today the Balkan Peninsula, Ukraine, Belarus, and Russia, borrowed much from the Byzantines. On the basis of Byzantine religion, law, and culture, the Slavs built a new civilization. They also borrowed heavily from western European and Asian cultures. As a result of these different influences, Russia—the farthest north and east of the Slavic lands—never became a completely European or completely Asian country.

The Setting

One of the Byzantine trade routes ran north across the Black Sea and up the **Dnieper River**, then overland to the Baltic Sea. From trading posts along the river grew the roots of early Slavic civilization.

The Steppe

North of the Black Sea are vast plains, thick forests, and mighty rivers. Much of the land is an immense plain called the steppe. Ukrainian author Nikolay Gogol vividly captures its spirit in his *Cossack Tales:*

❝ The farther the steppe went the grander it became ... one green uninhabited waste. No plow ever furrowed its immense wavy plains of wild plants; the wild horses, which herded there, alone trampled them down. The whole extent of the steppe was nothing but a green-gold ocean, whose surface seemed besprinkled with millions of different colored flowers. ❞

258 Chapter 10 *Byzantines and Slavs*

Although the steppe has rich black soil, the harsh climate makes farming difficult and crop failures common. Too far inland to be reached by moist ocean breezes, the steppe often has scanty rainfall. In addition, most of the land lies in the same latitudes as Canada and has the same short growing season. During the long, hard winter, blasts of Arctic air roar across the land and bury it deep in snow.

Forests and Rivers

North of the steppe stretch seemingly endless forests of evergreens, birch, oak, and other hardwoods. North–south flowing rivers such as the Dnieper, Dniester, and Volga cross the steppe and penetrate the forests, providing the easiest means of transportation. Yet travel is difficult for much of the year. In winter, deep drifts of snow cover the ground, and in the spring thaw the land turns to knee-deep mud.

The People

Historians know little about the origin of the first Slavic peoples. Some believe the Slavs came from present-day eastern Poland. Others think they may have been farmers in the Black Sea region. It is known that by about A.D. 500 the Slavs had formed into three distinct groups and had settled in different parts of eastern Europe.

Slavic Groups

One group, known as the West Slavs, lived in the marshlands, plains, and mountains of east-central Europe. They successfully fought the Germans to the west and the Scandinavians to the north for control of territory. Today the descendants of the West Slavs are the peoples of Poland, the Czech Republic, and Slovakia. Their religious ties came to be with the Roman Catholic Church, and their cultural ties were with western Europe.

Another group, known as the South Slavs, settled in the Balkan Peninsula, and had frequent contacts with the Byzantines. Today, their descendants are the Serbs, Croats, and Slovenes, whose languages and cultures were shaped by both the Roman Catholic West and the Orthodox East. One group of South Slavs—the Bosnians—were influenced by the religion of Islam from the Middle East.

The third and largest Slavic group, the Eastern Slavs, includes those now known as Ukrainians, Russians, and Belarussians. They lived north of the Black Sea between the Dnieper and Dniester Rivers and traded with the Byzantine Empire and northern Europe. From A.D. 500 to A.D. 800, some Eastern Slavs moved eastward toward the Volga River.

East Slavic Lands A.D. 1100s

Map Study

Trade with the Byzantine Empire helped build Kiev into a major city. **Movement** In what direction would traders have traveled from Kiev to Sweden?

Early Ways of Life

The early Eastern Slavs lived in villages made up of related families. They were farmers who hunted wild game and birds to supplement the wheat, rye, and oats they grew. In the forests they cleared land by cutting and burning trees and scattering the ash to enrich the soil. On the steppes they ignited a "sea of flame" to burn off the grass for planting.

Most farm homes were sturdy log houses. With knife, chisel, and ax the peasants skillfully shaped the logs, notching them so that they would fit together without nails. Many log houses had wooden gables and window frames decorated with painted carvings of flowers and animals. Skilled artisans also used wood to make furniture, cooking utensils, musical instruments, boats, and images of favorite deities.

The Eastern Slavs used the many rivers in their region for transportation and trade. They set up trading towns along the riverbanks. By the A.D. 800s, a trade route ran from the Baltic Sea in the north to the Black Sea in the south.

TEACH

Guided Practice

THEME Cultural Diffusion
Discuss with the class the influences of the Byzantines on early Slavic peoples: trade items such as silk, jewels, and food; the Cyrillic alphabet; and Christianity. Ask students to consider how the early Slavic people might have felt about these influences on their traditional culture and practices. **L1**

World History and Art Transparency 13

Map Study

Answer
Traders would have traveled northwest from Kiev to Sweden.

Map Skills Practice

Reading a Map How would Kiev's location have been favorable to Byzantine trade? *(Kiev was centrally located along the Dnieper River between Sweden and Constantinople.)*

Who?What?Where?When?

Slash-and-Burn A farming technique known as slash-and-burn was used by the Eastern Slavs to clear forests. After the trees were hauled away, remaining stumps and brush were set on fire. The ashes provided rich fertilizer that produced good harvests. After a few years the land was exhausted, however, and the Slavs were compelled to move to new locations at frequent intervals.

COOPERATIVE LEARNING ACTIVITY

Cultural Influences Organize the class into three groups—one representing the West Slavs, the second representing the South Slavs, and the third representing the Eastern Slavs. Group members should work together to research and prepare a family chronicle that reveals the cultural and religious influences on their group and then present the results of their work to the rest of the class. All members should participate in gathering and recording the information by using the text and library resources, preparing the chronicle, finding appropriate illustrations, and making the oral report. Conclude with a discussion of similarities and differences and any conflicts that divide the three groups. **L2**

Visualizing History This log house in Russian Siberia's Lake Baikal region evidences the decorative style of Eastern Slav houses. *How did these people build without nails?*

Kievan Rus

The early Eastern Slavs were not warlike. During the late A.D. 800s, they relied on Vikings, a group of warriors and traders from Scandinavia, to protect their trade routes. The Vikings also helped to lay the foundations of Slavic government.

The Vikings' arrival is recorded in the *Primary Chronicle*, a collection of Eastern Slavic history and tales written around A.D. 1100. According to the *Chronicle*, in about A.D. 860 the Slavic people from the northern village of Novgorod asked Vikings from Scandinavia for aid. The Viking leader **Rurik** accepted the request. The Slavs called the Vikings and the area they controlled *Rus*; the word *Russia* is probably derived from this name.

Rise of Kiev

In about A.D. 880, Rurik's successor, Prince Oleg, conquered the fortress-village of **Kiev** (Kyiv in Ukrainian) to the south. Built high on a bluff where the forest meets the steppe, Kiev prospered because it lay on the Dnieper River trade route. Some still call it the mother of Eastern Slavic cities.

Control of Kiev enabled Oleg to dominate the water trade route. Towns along the route were brought together under his leadership. Kiev soon

WORLD HISTORY *Online*

Student Web Activity 10

Visit the *World History: The Human Experience* Web site at **worldhistory.glencoe.com** and click on *Chapter 10—Student Web Activities* for an activity relating to the Vikings.

became the major city of a region of Slavic territories known as Kievan Rus. The rulers of Kiev, known as Grand Princes, conducted raids against Constantinople. They were attracted by the wealth and civilization of the Byzantine capital. In A.D. 911 a treaty ended these raids and established trade between the Byzantines and the Eastern Slavs. During the summer months, Slavic merchants carried furs, honey, and other forest products by boat to Constantinople. There they traded their goods for cloth, wine, weapons, and jewelry.

Kievan Government

By A.D. 900, Kievan Rus had organized into a collection of city-states and principalities, or territories ruled by princes. Each region enjoyed local self-government; however, they all paid tribute to the Grand Prince of Kiev to support his court and army. The major duties of these princes were to administer justice and to defend the frontiers. They were assisted by councils of wealthy merchants and landed nobles, who were known as boyars. Assemblies represented all free adult male citizens. They handled daily affairs and had the power to accept or remove princes.

These three institutions—the princely office, the council, and the assembly—varied in power from region to region. In the northeastern territories, the prince wielded a great deal of political power. In the southeastern areas, the boyars had the greatest political influence. In Novgorod and a few northern trading towns and cities, the assemblies overshadowed both princes and boyars. In these areas, the assemblies came close to establishing a tradition of representative government. However, later princes limited the powers of the assemblies.

Jim Brandenburg

Rurik the Rus

TEACH

Explain to students that the Vikings were capable sailors and had already been carrying out raids and expeditions to establish settlements beyond their own territory—present-day Scandinavia. They settled as far away as North America. After Rurik went to Novgorod, he took complete control. Twenty years later his successor Oleg set himself up as prince of Kiev but retained control of Novgorod. **Why would Novgorod have been a desirable place for the Vikings to become established?** *(It gave them control of and access to the trade route with Constantinople.)*

Linking Past and Present

St. Sophia Cathedral Kiev is the capital of the Republic of Ukraine. The St. Sofia Cathedral in Kiev, one of the city's oldest structures, dates back to Kievan Rus.

 CURRICULUM CONNECTION

ARCHAEOLOGY

Recent discoveries suggest that there was already a flourishing grain trade in Kiev when the Scandinavians took over. The native Slavs grew wheat, rye, barley, and oats.

This 19th-century statue of Kievan Rus's ruler Rurik stands in the center of the Russian city of Novgorod. The bronze Rurik, a mighty Prince, holds symbols of [mili]tary might and political power: a shield and [swor]d. His fur cape sweeps proudly over his shoul[ders.] Founder of nations, the Viking warrior pro[mise]s a glorious past.

[Ru]rik and his Viking warriors came from [Scan]dinavia to what is now Russia and Ukraine in [A].D. 800s, perhaps invited there by native Slavic tribes constantly warring with each other. The Eastern Slavs during the A.D. 800s had little political stability, which made farming and commerce difficult. The Vikings changed that. Trading with the strong, plundering the weak, they moved south from Novgorod to Kiev, where they founded a political state, and from there they moved on to Odessa on the shores of the Black Sea. It took them two centuries to complete their expansion. By then the Vikings had lost their Scandinavian ways and had become assimilated into the local cultures. ✎

Chapter 10 *Byzantines and Slavs* **261**

you don't say...

Pravda commonly means "truth," but during Yaroslav's reign it also meant "justice." The Kievan legal system that Yaroslav organized during his reign was known as the *Russkaya Pravda*. Yaroslav's *Pravda* was based on Byzantine models and was notable for being mild by medieval standards, not using corporal or capital punishment. The word *pravda* is familiar to the West through its association with the Moscow newspaper of the same name.

Visualizing History
Monasteries played a key role in the revival of Russian civilization, much as they did in medieval Europe. Early Russian monasteries were often built near cities, and many monks took part in local political, economic, or military activities outside the monastery.
Answer to Caption: *Legend states that Prince Vladimir sent observers abroad to examine various religions and, upon their recommendation, converted to Eastern Orthodoxy.*

Arrival of Christianity

Before the late A.D. 900s, the Eastern Slavs honored nature spirits and ancestors, and worshiped many deities. The most popular gods were Perun, god of thunder and lightning, and the Great Mother, goddess of the land and harvest. Images of the deities were built on the highest ground outside the villages.

Vladimir's Conversion

Because of contact with the Byzantine Empire, many Eastern Slavs were influenced by Eastern Orthodoxy. **Olga**, a princess of Kiev, became the first member of the Kievan nobility to accept the faith. Her grandson, Prince **Vladimir** of Kiev, decided to abandon the old beliefs and to adopt a new religion that he thought would help the Eastern Slavs become a more powerful civilization. An old Slavic legend states that Vladimir sent observers abroad to examine Judaism, Roman Catholicism, Eastern Orthodoxy, and Islam. Only the beautiful ceremony in the splendid Byzantine church of Hagia Sophia impressed the observers. In A.D. 988, after his own conversion to Eastern Orthodoxy, Vladimir ordered a mass baptism in the Dnieper River for his people.

Visualizing History This ancient monastery stands as a symbol of the influence of Byzantine Christianity. *How was Eastern Orthodoxy introduced in Kievan Rus?*

Effects of Conversion

The conversion to Eastern Orthodoxy brought Byzantine culture to Kievan Rus. Byzantine priests and bishops introduced the Eastern Slavs to colorful rituals and taught them the art of painting icons. The Eastern Slavs also learned to write their language in the Cyrillic alphabet. Schools were established in the towns for the sons of boyars, priests, and merchants. Byzantine architects arrived in Kiev to build stone churches with magnificent domes. Monasteries also were founded in the towns and countryside, and attracted many new converts.

Acceptance of Eastern Orthodoxy, however, tended to isolate the Eastern Slavs from the outside world. Following the split between the Eastern and Western Churches, Kievan Rus was separated from western Europe. Its people lost contact with developments that took place in that area after A.D. 1200. At the same time, the Byzantine practice of translating the Bible and Orthodox church services into local languages had an important impact. Because Kievan scholars had translations of some classical and Christian writings in their own language, they did not learn Greek or Latin. As a result, they did not deepen their knowledge of the heritage of western European civilization. Instead, they turned for inspiration to the traditions of their own local culture.

Kiev's Golden Age

Vladimir, who ruled from A.D. 980 to A.D. 1015, was one of the most important grand princes of Kiev. Known for his skills as a warrior, he successfully defended Kievan Rus's eastern frontiers against nomadic invaders. He also expanded its western borders by capturing lands in Poland and near the Baltic Sea.

Yaroslav's Reign

After a time of dynastic conflict, Vladimir's son **Yaroslav** became Grand Prince in A.D. 1019. Under Yaroslav's rule, Kievan culture reached its height. Yaroslav encouraged the spread of learning by establishing the first library in Kiev. Yaroslav also organized the Kievan legal system, drawing from Justinian's Code. Written primarily for the princes and merchants, the code treated crimes against property as well as against persons.

A skilled diplomat, Yaroslav arranged for his daughters and sisters to marry kings in Norway, Hungary, France, and Poland. To the Europeans, who were just arising from the isolation and disorder of the early Middle Ages, Kiev was a glittering capital whose culture outshone that of any in western Europe.

Kiev's Decline

After Yaroslav's death, Kiev declined in power and wealth for several reasons. First, Yaroslav began the practice of dividing up his lands among all his sons instead of willing them to one heir. Since no law established a clear line of succession, the heirs battled one another over control of Kiev. Second, the Latin Christian state created in Constantinople disrupted trade with the Byzantines and weakened Kiev's economy. Finally, in A.D. 1240 Mongol invaders from central Asia captured Kiev and completely destroyed it.

Mongol Rule

The Mongols, or Tatars, as the Slavs called them, defeated the armies of the Eastern Slavic princes and conquered most of the country except for Novgorod. They sacked towns and villages and killed thousands. Mongols sought to tax the peoples they conquered, rather than impose their culture. The Slavs were allowed to practice their Christian faith, but the Mongols required allegiance to the Mongol ruler and service in the Mongol army.

For two centuries, Mongol rule isolated most of the Eastern Slavs from European civilization. Although the occupation helped unify the Eastern Slavs, it also further distanced them from ideas and trends of the Western world.

Rise of Moscow

As city life in the south declined after the fall of Kiev, many Eastern Slavs—led by monks, farmers, and artisans—moved into the remote northern forests to escape Mongol rule. By the late A.D. 1200s, Vladimir–Suzdal and **Novgorod** were the strongest Eastern Slavic principalities.

Alexander Nevsky

The Mongols had never advanced as far north as Novgorod because the spring thaw turned the land into a swamp they could not cross. Instead, the city faced attacks in the Baltic Sea area from Swedes and Germans who wanted to convert the Eastern Slavs to Roman Catholicism. In a ferocious battle on the Neva River in A.D. 1240, Alexander,

Visualizing History Alexander Nevsky, ruler of Novgorod, fought the German Teutonic Knights in A.D. 1242. *Why did the Germans and Swedes attack the Eastern Slavs?*

prince of Novgorod, defeated the invading Swedes. This victory earned him the nickname **Alexander Nevsky**, Alexander "of the Neva," and his victory established Novgorod as a strong, independent principality.

Moscow's Beginnings

Daniel, the youngest son of Alexander Nevsky, became ruler of **Moscow**, a small but prosperous town located near vital land and water routes. Using war and diplomatic marriages, the princes of Moscow gradually expanded their state's territory. Moscow's importance grew in A.D. 1325 when the metropolitan, or leader of the Orthodox Church in the Eastern Slavic lands, was transferred there. By about A.D. 1350, Moscow had become the most powerful city. Cooperation with Mongol policies had kept it free from outside interference. Daniel's son, Prince Ivan I, became known as Money Bag because the Mongols even trusted him to collect taxes for them.

Muscovite forces defeated the Mongols at the Battle of Kulikovo in A.D. 1380. The tide had turned in favor of Moscow. Over the next hundred years, the Eastern Slavs steadily drove out the Mongols. In A.D. 1480 during the rule of **Ivan III**, Moscow

Visualizing History Nevsky defended his frontiers against Christian invaders but was forced to pay tribute to the Mongol Batu Khan, the grandson of Genghis Khan. **Answer to Caption:** *The Germans and Swedes wanted to convert the Eastern Slavs to Roman Catholicism.*

Global Gourmet

Russia The diet of the Russian peasant was very starchy. Staples included cabbage dishes; cooked grains such as barley, buckwheat, and millet; dark bread; and smoked and pickled herring.

TURNING POINT

Rise of Moscow
Why was the rise of Moscow a turning point in Russian history?
It strengthened the rule of the czars and laid the foundation of the Russian Empire, which was modeled after the Byzantine Empire.

ASSESS

Check for Understanding

Assign Section 3 Assessment as homework or as an in-class activity.

🖳 Use Interactive Tutor Self-Assessment Software to review Section 3.

Evaluate

📁 Section Quiz 10-3

🖳 Use the Testmaker to create a customized quiz for Section 3.

CRITICAL THINKING ACTIVITY

Synthesizing Information Have students think about the unique culture that developed among the Eastern Slavs and in Russia in particular. Have them create a chart that includes the following headings: *Geography, Religion, Economic Activities, Arts and Architecture,* and *Politics.* In each column, have students note the historic factors that influenced the development of Slavic culture. Ask students to identify which elements resulted from contacts with Asia and which came from the West. **L3**

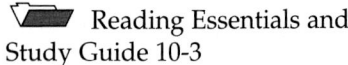 **Visualizing History** Throughout the disruptive invasions, the Church kept the people of Russia united. More than a dozen churches and cathedrals stood within the protective walls of the Kremlin.
Answer to Caption: *The Kremlin was a fortress located within the city of Moscow.*

Reteach

Ask students to explain the significance of waterways and mobility in early Russia.

 Reteaching Activity 10

 Reading Essentials and Study Guide 10-3

Enrich

Encourage students to research the history of the Kremlin and the role it has played as a symbol of Russian unity. Students may write essays or create posters.

 Enrichment Activity 10

CLOSE

Byzantine influence spread to Russia, and Ivan III declared a "Third Rome" as the final and eternal Rome of all the land. Ask the class to discuss Ivan's declaration. Ask how students view the Commonwealth of Independent States, its lands, and its governments today.

Visualizing History Gold-domed spires of the Church of the Annunciation reach toward the sky behind the Kremlin's walls. *What was the original purpose of the Kremlin?*

finally refused to pay taxes to the Mongols. The long submission to the Asian rulers was over. Today, Ivan is known as Ivan the Great because he was able to bring many of the Eastern Slavic principalities under his rule. His major gain was Novgorod, which controlled territory all the way east to the Ural Mountains.

The Third Rome

Other factors helped to strengthen the power of Moscow's rulers. After Constantinople fell to the Ottoman Turks in A.D. 1453, Moscow stood alone as the center of the Eastern Orthodox Church. In A.D. 1472 when Ivan III married Sophia, niece of the last Byzantine emperor, he took the title czar, or "caesar," the title used by the Roman and Byzantine emperors. Ivan also made the two-headed Byzantine eagle the symbol of his rule.

In A.D. 1493 Ivan added the title Sovereign of All Russia. The lands he ruled, eventually known as Russia, were a hundred times as large as the original Muscovite state. The people spoke one language, and the princes served one czar. The Russian Orthodox Church, which identified its interests with those of the Muscovite ruler, proclaimed that Moscow was the Third Rome. The Church regarded Ivan as both the successor of the Byzantine emperor and protector of the Eastern Orthodox Church, a claim all succeeding Russian czars would also make.

Moscow's Culture

Eastern Orthodoxy shaped the development of Moscow's culture. Its leaders stressed that obedience to the czar and the government was a Christian duty. Joseph Sanin, an influential church leader, wrote that "although the [ruler] was like other men in his physical characteristics, in his power he was similar to God in heaven."

Although western European influences reached Russia, they were transformed by local Russian styles and tastes. Instead of using Greek, Latin, or other classical languages, the Church used an early Slavic language in its worship and writings. Russia's religious leaders and political rulers also encouraged the development of a unique national style of icon painting and building construction. Ivan III had western European and Russian architects rebuild the Moscow Kremlin, or fortress. In spite of Western influences on its construction, the Kremlin became known for the typically Russian splendor of its beautiful onion-domed churches and ornately decorated palaces. Today the Kremlin in Moscow is still a center of government, religion, and culture for Russia.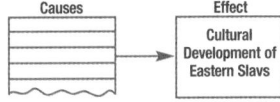

SECTION 3 ASSESSMENT

Main Idea
1. Use a chart like the one below to show the main reasons why Eastern Slavs developed separately from western Europe.

Causes		Effect
	→	Cultural Development of Eastern Slavs

Recall
2. **Define** steppe, principality, boyar, czar.
3. **Identify** the Slavs, Rurik, Olga, Vladimir, Yaroslav, the Mongols, Alexander Nevsky, Ivan III.

Critical Thinking
4. **Making Comparisons** Compare the role of the Orthodox Church in Kievan Rus and Moscow.

Understanding Themes
5. **Cultural Diffusion** What Roman traditions became part of Russia's culture? How did Russia's culture differ from the culture of western Europe? Why?

264 **Chapter 10** *Byzantines and Slavs*

SECTION 3 ASSESSMENT ANSWERS

1. conversion to Eastern Orthodoxy brought Byzantine culture to area and isolated Eastern Slavs from outside world; scholars did not learn Greek and Latin and did not deepen their knowledge of western European civilization; Mongol rule isolated Eastern Slavs from European civilization

2. All terms are defined in the Glossary.
3. the Slavs, 258; Rurik, 260; Olga, 262; Vladimir, 262; Yaroslav, 262; the Mongols, 263; Alexander Nevsky, 263; Ivan III, 263
4. Kiev saw the arrival of Christianity; Moscow became an important Christian center.

5. **CULTURAL DIFFUSION** Sample answers: Christian faith and title of Caesar; geography, differences in language, and the schism between Eastern and Western churches tended to isolate Russian culture, compounded by Russia's use of its native language rather than Greek or Latin.

Distinguishing Between Fact and Opinion

Imagine that you are watching two candidates for President debate the merits of the college loan program. One says, "In my view, the college loan program must be reformed. Sixty percent of students do not repay their loans on time."

The other replies, "College costs are skyrocketing, but only 30 percent of students default on their loans for more than one year. I believe we should spend more on this worthy program."

How can you tell who or what to believe? You must learn to distinguish fact from opinion.

Learning the Skill

A fact is a statement that can be proved to be true or false. In the example above, the statement "Sixty percent of students do not repay their loans on time" is a fact. By reviewing statistics on the number of student loan recipients who repay their loans, we can determine whether it is true or false. To identify facts, look for words and phrases indicating specific people, places, events, dates, times.

An opinion, on the other hand, expresses a personal belief, viewpoint, or emotion. Because opinions are subjective, we cannot prove or disprove them. In the opening example, most statements by the candidates are opinions.

Opinions often include qualifying words and phrases such as *I think, I believe, probably, seems to me, may, might, could, ought, in my judgment,* or *in my view.* Also, look for expressions of approval or disapproval such as *good, bad, poor,* and *satisfactory.* Be aware of superlatives such as *greatest, worst, finest,* and *best.* Notice words with negative meanings and implications such as *squander, contemptible,* and *disgrace.* Also, identify generalizations such as *none, every, always,* and *never.*

Practicing the Skill

For each pair of statements below, determine which is fact and which is opinion. Give a reason for each choice.

1. (a) The Byzantine Empire came to a pitiful end at the hands of the savage Turks.
(b) The Byzantine Empire ended when Constantine XI died while defending Constantinople in A.D. 1453.
2. (a) The alliance with the Byzantine Empire made Kiev a major trading link between Europe and Asia and between Scandinavia and the Middle East.
(b) In the A.D. 900s Kiev was the most isolated, uncivilized place and possessed little in the way of culture.
3. (a) The Byzantine culture was more advanced than any other of its day.
(b) Vladimir's conversion to Eastern Orthodoxy brought Byzantine culture to Kievan Rus.

Applying the Skill

In a newspaper, find a news article and an editorial on the same topic or issue. Identify five facts and five opinions from these sources.

For More Practice

Turn to the Skill Practice in the Chapter Assessment on page 267 for more practice in distinguishing between fact and opinion.

The **Glencoe Skillbuilder Interactive Workbook**, Level 2 provides instruction and practice in key social studies skills.

Distinguishing Between Fact and Opinion Point out to students that they are confronted with facts and opinions every day in newspapers and magazines. Ask where they would look for opinions in newspapers. (*editorial pages, book and movie reviews*) Where would solid facts be? (*news stories, sports scores, weather reports from day before*) Have students consider headlines and suggest that they bring in samples of fact and opinion headlines for a bulletin-board display.

Additional Practice

Skill Reinforcement Activity 10

GLENCOE TECHNOLOGY

GO TO

Glencoe's **Skillbuilder Interactive Workbook, Level 2** This interactive CD-ROM promotes student mastery of key social studies skills.

ANSWERS TO PRACTICING THE SKILL

1. (a) opinion: uses negative words *pitiful* and *savage* to imply disapproval
(b) fact: can be verified by reading a historical text
2. (a) fact: can be verified by studying reports of archaeologists in Sweden who have unearthed Arabic and Byzantine coins, evidence that extensive trade occurred

(b) opinion: uses negative words *uncivilized* and *little* with superlative *most*
3. (a) opinion: does not give any specific facts to prove statement or allow checking
(b) fact: can be verified by reading historical documents and studying arts of that era

Chapter 10 *Byzantines and Slavs* **265**

Chapter 10 Assessment

Answers

Using Key Terms
1. d   3. i   5. k
2. l   4. a

Using Your History Journal

Stories should incorporate information on how the law was administered in Justinian's time. Stories may show daily life at the time.

Reviewing Facts
1. A.D. 330: Constantinople built; A.D. 532: Justinian crushes revolt in Constantinople; A.D. 1054: church splits into Roman Catholic and Eastern Orthodox; A.D. 1204: Christian soldiers and Venetians attack Constantinople; A.D. 1261: Byzantium reestablishes own culture; A.D. 1453: fall of Constantinople
2. preserved the legal heritage of Rome; served as the basis for later European legal systems
3. icons, mosaics, illuminated manuscripts; religion, daily life
4. Byzantine court appointed church officials, built churches, intervened in doctrinal disputes.
5. Byzantine women were expected

WORLD HISTORY *Online*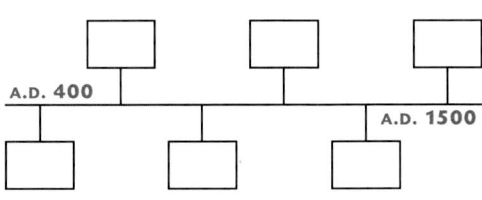

Self-Check Quiz

Visit the *World History: The Human Experience* Web site at **worldhistory.glencoe.com** and click on *Chapter 10—Self-Check Quiz* to prepare for the Chapter Test.

Using Key Terms

Write the key term that completes each sentence. Then write a sentence for each term not chosen.

a. boyars
b. clergy
c. mosaic
d. iconoclasts
e. monasteries
f. illuminated manuscripts
g. missionary
h. regent
i. schism
j. laity
k. czar
l. steppe

1. Wanting to prevent superstition and idol worship, _____, or image breakers, supported the removal of all images from churches.
2. North of the Black Sea are thick forests, mighty rivers, and a vast plain known as the _____.
3. In A.D. 1054 doctrinal, political, and geographic differences led to a _____ between the Roman Catholic Church in the West and the Eastern Orthodox Church in the East.
4. In Kievan Rus, wealthy nobles and landowners who assisted the princes were called _____.
5. In A.D. 1472 the Muscovite ruler Ivan III took the title _____, the title used by the Roman and Byzantine emperors.

Technology Activity

Using the Internet Locate a Web site dealing with the history of the Cyrillic written language. Focus your search by using phrases such as *Cyrillic language* and *Slavic languages*. Create a bulletin board showing examples of Cyrillic words with their English translations. When possible, include illustrations.

266 Chapter 10 *Byzantines and Slavs*

Reviewing Facts

1. **History** Use a time line like the one below to identify key events in Byzantine history.

A.D. 400   A.D. 1500

2. **Government** Explain the significance of Justinian's Code to later generations.
3. **Culture** Describe three major art forms that developed in the Byzantine Empire. What are the leading themes in Byzantine arts?
4. **Culture** Analyze how the Byzantine Empire promoted Christianity.
5. **Culture** Discuss the role of women in Byzantine society, especially in family life.
6. **Culture** Explain the contribution that Nino made to the development of Georgia.
7. **Geography** State the ways the early Eastern Slavs made use of their environment.
8. **History** Explain why the reign of Yaroslav is considered a golden age for Kievan Rus.
9. **History** Explain the effects of the Mongol invasions on Kievan Rus.
10. **History** Describe how Moscow's rise affected the Eastern Slavs.

Critical Thinking

1. **Analyze** Was the title of New Rome suitable or unsuitable for the city of Constantinople? Explain.

---

to live partly in seclusion, but they had some rights through Theodora's efforts.
6. Nino converted Iberia to Christianity.
7. they hunted game, grew oats and rye; wood was used to build log houses; rivers served as means of transportation and trade
8. cultural and economic prosperity; legal system was organized; contacts with western Europe were close
9. They caused widespread destruction of

cities, such as Kiev, caused Slavic populations and political power to shift northward, and helped isolate the Eastern Slavs.
10. The Muscovite state grew under the rule of the czars and absorbed neighboring Slavic principalities; it eventually became known as Russia.

Critical Thinking
1. the Roman heritage in government, language, and culture; also the influences of

2. **Evaluate** Why was the preservation of Greek and Roman learning a significant contribution of Byzantine civilization?

3. **Analyze** What do these Byzantine coins reveal about the level of development of Byzantine civilization?

4. **Analyze** What were the causes of the schism in the Christian Church? Could the split have been prevented? Explain.

5. **Evaluate** Would Justinian have been an effective ruler if he had not married Theodora? Explain.

6. **Analyze** How did trade affect the Byzantine Empire?

7. **Synthesize** What were the three parts of Kievan government? Why did representative government not develop in the East Slavic lands?

8. **Synthesize** Imagine you are a Russian boyar under Ivan III. Would you resist calling him Czar? Explain.

Understanding Themes

1. **Conflict** How does conflict—such as the iconoclastic controversy in the Byzantine Empire—weaken a government?

2. **Innovation** Using Byzantine civilization as an example, explain how one civilization's ideas can be adapted to other societies.

3. **Cultural Diffusion** How can two societies be enriched by sharing cultural aspects? Give examples from the cases of Kievan Rus and Moscow.

Linking Past and Present

1. Investigate the role the Bosporus played in World War I and World War II.
2. Explain the historical reasons why Russia has a continuing interest in the affairs of eastern European nations.
3. Investigate the historical roots of religious controversies in modern societies, such as Bosnia and Northern Ireland.

Skill Practice

Read the following statements. Determine which are facts and which are opinions. Give a reason for each choice.

1. The *Primary Chronicle* states that in A.D. 911 Grand Prince Oleg agreed on a peace treaty with the Byzantine emperors Leo and Alexander.
2. The Volga River is longer than the Danube River.
3. The Russian Orthodox Church is the most spiritually uplifting faith in the world.
4. Nomads wandered aimlessly throughout the steppes and lived in flimsy shelters.

Geography in History

1. **Location** Refer to the map below. By what year had the area around the Volga River been added to Moscow's holdings?
2. **Place** What geographic factors enabled the princes of Moscow to expand their territory?
3. **Region** By A.D. 1493 Moscow's ruler claimed to be "Sovereign of All Russia." About how far did Moscow's territory stretch from north to south in A.D. 1462?

The Rise of Moscow

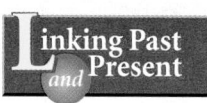

Lake Onega

Lake Ladoga

Ustyug

Vologda

Novgorod

Galich

Volokolamsk

Vladimir

Moscow

Volga River

Kasimov

Tula

N W-E S

| 0 | 100 | 200 mi. |
0 100 200 km
Lambert Conic Conformal Projection

- Moscow, A.D. 1300
- Acquisitions to A.D. 1340
- Acquisitions to A.D. 1389
- Acquisitions to A.D. 1425
- Acquisitions to A.D. 1462

Chapter 10 *Byzantines and Slavs* **267**

Chapter 10 Assessment

Understanding Themes

1. **CONFLICT** can distract leaders' attentions from other important matters and can cause divisions in society
2. **INNOVATION** The Byzantines used architectural ideas from Eastern sources.
3. **CULTURAL DIFFUSION** The cultures of both Kiev and Moscow were shaped by contact with Eastern Orthodoxy.

Linking Past and Present

1. During World War I, the Russians hoped to annex the Bosporus and Dardanelles Straits. In World War II, the Russians again pressed for control of the Turkish straits.
2. Both the Russians and the peoples of eastern Europe share a common past as Slavic peoples.
3. conflicts between Christians and Muslims in Bosnia; Catholics and Protestants in Northern Ireland

Skill Practice

1. fact—names specific people, dates, event
2. fact—can be proved by comparing measurements
3. opinion—contains a superlative; cannot be proved
4. opinion—contains words with judgmental connotations

Geography in History

1. by A.D. 1425
2. Moscow was located near rivers, making it a crossroads of trade.
3. about 600 miles

? Chapter Bonus Test Question

Ask students: Use your knowledge of the early history of either Georgia or Armenia to explain the turmoil that followed the 1990s breakup of the Soviet Union. *(Answers will vary according to student knowledge.)*

Greece and the Middle East that made the Byzantine Empire distinct from Rome.

2. served to unite people in a common heritage and provided the basis for further innovations
3. They reveal a civilization advanced in trade, metallurgy, mining, and religious thought.
4. use of icons, disagreements over the roles of the Roman pope and the Eastern patriarch. Compromise might have prevented the split; doubtful because of doctrinal differences.

5. Theodora's influence on Justinian suppressed the tax revolt and saved his throne; on the other side, Justinian had significant achievements in law and military conquest that did not involve Theodora.
6. It made the Byzantine Empire wealthy and prosperous, provided the funds for growth.
7. Prince, council, and assembly; the role of princes in limiting the power of assemblies
8. Yes; it implied a loss of power by the boyars.

A complete, 1-page lesson plan is provided for each section in the *Reproducible Lesson Plans* booklet.

Islamic Civilization

CHAPTER RESOURCES

	Reproducible Resources	Multimedia Resources
Chapter Opener	Chapter Themes: Graphic Organizer 11 Historical Significance Chapter Activity 11	MindJogger Videoquiz
Chapter Enrichment	Vocabulary Activity 11* Time Line Activity 11 Mapping History Activity 11 History Simulation 11 Geography and History Activity 11 Source Reading 11 People in World History Profiles 19, 20 World Art and Music Activity 11 Enrichment Activity 11 Critical Thinking Activity 11 Skill Reinforcement Activity 11 Performance Assessment Activity 11 Standardized Test Practice Workbook Activity 11 Inclusion for the Social Studies Classroom Strategies and Activities	Focus on World Art Print 13, Habib Allah. *Mantik et-Tayr* World History and Art Transparency 14, *Court of the Lions, The Alhambra* Chapter Transparency 11 Vocabulary PuzzleMaker Software World Music: Cultural Traditions, Lesson 5 Turning Points in World History: *Jerusalem: City of Three Faiths* In the Holy Land: Ted Koppel: *The Holy Land* In the Holy Land: Ted Koppel: *Three Religions* World History Primary Source Document Library
Chapter Review/Reteaching	Reteaching Activity 11 Skill Reinforcement Activity 11 Spanish Chapter Summary 11	Chapter 11 Digest Audiocassette, Activity, Test* Vocabulary PuzzleMaker Software Interactive Tutor Self-Assessment Software MindJogger Videoquiz
Chapter Evaluation/Testing	Performance Assessment Activity 11 Chapter 11 Test, Forms A and B	ExamView® Pro Testmaker

* Also available in Spanish

`0:00` **OUT OF TIME?** Assign the Chapter 11 Audiocassettes.

World History Primary Source Document Library
Make History Come Alive!
Engage your students with over 250 easily accessible primary source documents—available on this CD-ROM—that will give them real life insight into the important events of world history.

Block Schedule
Activities that are particularly suited to use within the block scheduling framework are identified throughout this chapter by the following designation.

KEY TO ABILITY LEVELS
Teaching strategies are coded for varying learning styles.
L1 BASIC activities for all students
L2 AVERAGE activities for average to above-average students
L3 CHALLENGING activities for above-average students
LEP LIMITED ENGLISH PROFICIENCY activities

Use Glencoe's *Presentation Plus!* multimedia teacher tool to easily present dynamic lessons that visually excite your students. Using Microsoft PowerPoint® you can customize the presentations to create your own personalized lessons.

Interactive Lesson Planner

Planning has never been easier! Using this CD-ROM, organize your week, month, semester, or year with all the help you need. The **Interactive Lesson Planner** gives you access to all of the blackline masters that accompany *World History: The Human Experience.*

SECTION RESOURCES

Daily Objectives	Reproducible Resources	Multimedia Resources
Section 1 **A New Faith** Identify the basic beliefs and practices of Islam.	Lecture Notes 11-1 Reproducible Lesson Plan 11-1 Guided Reading Activity 11-1* History Simulation 11 Time Line Activity 11 Section Quiz 11-1* Reading Essentials and Study Guide 11-1	Section Focus Transparency 11-1 Chapter Transparency 11 Vocabulary PuzzleMaker Software Interactive Tutor Self-Assessment Software Testmaker Turning Points in World History: *Jerusalem: City of Three Faiths* In the Holy Land: *Ted Koppel: The Holy Land* In the Holy Land: *Ted Koppel: Three Religions*
Section 2 **Spread of Islam** Explain how the Islamic state expanded and how it affected a variety of cultures.	Lecture Notes 11-2 Reproducible Lesson Plan 11-2 Vocabulary Activity 11* Guided Reading Activity 11-2* Mapping History Activity 11 Section Quiz 11-2* Reading Essentials and Study Guide 11-2	Section Focus Transparency 11-2 World History and Art Transparency 14, *Court of the Lions, the Alhambra* Interactive Tutor Self-Assessment Software Testmaker
Section 3 **Daily Life and Culture** Name the achievements of Islamic civilization and explain how they were spread to other parts of the world.	Lecture Notes 11-3 Reproducible Lesson Plan 11-3 Guided Reading Activity 11-3* Geography and History Activity 11 Reteaching Activity 11 Enrichment Activity 11 Section Quiz 11-3* Performance Assessment Activity 11 Spanish Chapter Summary 11 Reading Essentials and Study Guide 11-3	Focus on World Art Print 13, Habib Allah. *Mantik et-Tayr* Section Focus Transparency 11-3 Interactive Tutor Self-Assessment Software Vocabulary PuzzleMaker Software Testmaker World Music: Cultural Traditions, Lesson 5

* Also available in Spanish

Chapter Activities

 Performance Assessment Activity

A Cultural Contract Have small groups of students produce a contract for tolerance and understanding between their culture and the Islamic culture. Students should first research how Islamic life has changed since the time of early Islam. Groups should synthesize their information in order to produce a contract of conduct for both cultures to follow.

Possible Rubric Features Concept attainment, research skills, clarity and organization, content information

• *For an additional activity, refer to Activity 11 in the* Performance Assessment Strategies and Activities *booklet.*

ACTIVITY

From the Classroom of...

Eric Hahn
Ladue Horton Watkins
High School
St. Louis, MO

Lessons Through Islamic Literature

The purpose of this activity is to learn about history and social science concepts utilizing children's stories from *The Arabian Nights*. You will need a copy of *The Arabian Nights*, which is readily available in most libraries and many bookstores. If you can obtain multiple copies, students can read in groups.

Allow students to select a story from *The Arabian Nights*. There are many stories to choose from, but a few favorites include "Ali Baba and the Forty Thieves" and "Sinbad the Sailor and the Mudpies". After students read the story, ask them the following questions:

What does this story teach? Explain that these stories usually had a moral to them, just like *Aesop's Fables*, *Grimm's Fairy Tales*, or even Dr. Seuss stories.

What technologies are identified? (For example, Sinbad's ships are often described in detail, depending on the translation; the thieves in "Ali Baba" hide inside large containers of oil—ask students about the uses of oil.)

Finally, ask students for any comparisons they can make with recently studied units. This allows for some review and synthesis.

A great follow-up homework assignment is to have students write a short story utilizing the vocabulary learned in Chapter 11.

MULTIPLE LEARNING STYLES

Auditory/Musical
Ask students to modify any song they know by writing new lyrics that describe some aspect of Islamic history or culture presented in this chapter. Ask one student to accompany the singing by playing the tune on an instrument.

Kinesthetic
Have students draw poster-size pictures of calligraphy, arabesques, or a combination of the two for a bulletin-board display. They may find examples of Islamic art in reference materials to serve as a guide.

Interpersonal
Have students work together to make a wall map of the Islamic state at its peak. The map should include enough surrounding territory to show the context of the Islamic state. Students should label places discussed in Chapter 11, including Tours in France, Seville and Córdoba in Spain, the North African states, and India, and then show the path of Islamic expansion. Display the map for students to refer to as they study this chapter.

Intrapersonal
Ask students to research ceremonies involved in the hajj. Have them use their research to write a day-by-day journal account of their own imaginary participation in the hajj. Choose several journal accounts to be read aloud in class.

GLENCOE'S ASSESSMENT ADVANTAGE

Use the following to easily assess student learning in a variety of ways.

• Performance Assessment Strategies and Activities
• Section Quizzes
• Chapter and Unit Tests
• Interactive Tutor Self-Assessment Software
• Testmaker Software
• MindJogger Videoquiz
• SAT/SAT II Test Practice
• worldhistory.glencoe.com

Additional Resources

NATIONAL GEOGRAPHIC SOCIETY

Teacher's Corner

INDEX TO NATIONAL GEOGRAPHIC MAGAZINE

The following articles relate to this chapter:

- "The Three Faces of Jerusalem," by Alan Mairson, April 1996.
- "Ibn Battuta: Prince of Travelers," by Thomas J. Abercrombie, December 1991.
- "When the Moors Ruled Spain," by Thomas J. Abercrombie, July 1988.

NATIONAL GEOGRAPHIC SOCIETY PRODUCTS AVAILABLE FROM GLENCOE

To order the following, call Glencoe at 1-800-334-7344:

- *Picture Atlas of the World (CD-ROM)*

ADDITIONAL NATIONAL GEOGRAPHIC SOCIETY PRODUCTS

To order the following, call National Geographic at 1-800-368-2728

- *Jerusalem: Within These Walls (Video)*

Access National Geographic's new dynamic MapMachine Web site and other geography resources at:

- http://www.nationalgeographic.com/
- http://www.nationalgeographic.com/maps/

BIBLIOGRAPHY

Literature of the Period
Arabian Nights: The Thousand and One Nights. New York: Norton, 1990. The classic tales including those of Sinbad and Aladdin.
Readings for the Student
Gordon, Matthew S. *Islam.* New York: Facts on File, 1991. The history, religious practices, and political influence of Islamic sects.
Readings for the Teacher
Esposito, John L. *Islam: The Straight Path.* Expanded ed. New York: Oxford University Press, 1991. Clear, up-to-date survey of Islam.
Hourani, Albert. *A History of the Arab Peoples.* Cambridge: Harvard University Press, 1991. A comprehensive study.

WORLD HISTORY Online

Use our Web site as an additional resource. All essential content is covered in the Student Edition.

You and your students can visit the *World History: The Human Experience* Web site at worldhistory. glencoe.com The student text directs students to the Web site for the following options:

- **Chapter Overviews**
- **Student Web Activities**
- **Self-Check Quizzes**

Answers are provided for you in a link entitled "Web Activity Lesson Plan." Additional Web Resources, Interactive Puzzles, and content updates are also available.

Visit the Glencoe Web site at socialstudies. glencoe.com for social studies activities, updates, and links to other resources.

LOCAL OBJECTIVES

_____
_____
_____
_____
_____
_____
_____
_____
_____
_____
_____
_____
_____
_____
_____
_____
_____
_____
_____

CHAPTER THEMES

Chapter Themes are listed by section on this chapter opening page of the Student Edition. A corresponding theme-based activity is available under "TEACH," and a theme-based question is asked in the Section and Chapter Assessments.

The Storyteller

Historical Setting The woman quoted is describing her participation in the hajj, the pilgrimage to Makkah, the holy city in Saudi Arabia. The white-robed pilgrims the woman describes are wearing two white seamless sheets wrapped around the body. This special garb is prescribed for pilgrims when they are about 6 miles (10 kilometers) from the holy city, at which point they are said to enter the state of holiness and purity known as *ihram.* The white clothes symbolize not only the pilgrims' purity but also the equality of all members of the Muslim community.

Historical Significance

Answers: *Islamic principles include belief in one all-powerful, just, and merciful God, the belief that God's message was revealed to Muhammad and recorded in the Quran, and moral values similar to those of Christianity and Judaism.*

Islamic civilization has made significant contributions in fields ranging from mathematics and the physical and biological sciences to literature and the arts.

Have students use the **Chapter 11 Overview** at worldhistory. glencoe.com as a prereading and postreading exercise for understanding chapter content.

Islamic Civilization

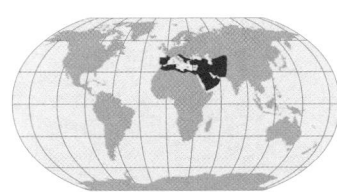

Chapter Themes

▶ **Innovation** The faith and principles of Islam become the basis of a new civilization. *Section 1*
▶ **Movement** Armies and merchants spread Islam through the Middle East and North Africa, and into Spain and Asia. *Section 2*
▶ **Cultural Diffusion** Contributions from many cultures and peoples enrich the Islamic state. *Section 3*

The Storyteller

"I was in Makkah at last," writes a devout Muslim woman about her pilgrimage to Makkah, the holiest city of the religion of Islam. She continues, "Before me was the Kaaba, a great black cube partly submerged in a torrent of white-robed pilgrims circling round and round. Around us, like a great dam containing the torrent, stood the massive walls and the seven slim minarets of the Sacred Mosque. High above, the muezzin began the evening call to prayer: 'Allahu Akbar! … God is Most Great!'…

"Around the Kaaba … repeating the customary prayers, swirled men and women of every race and nation, from every corner of the earth.…"

All believers of Islam hope to share in this event at least once in their lives. Since the a.d. 600s, it has been one of the unifying celebrations for all Muslims.

Historical Significance

What are the basic beliefs and principles of Islam? What contributions has Islamic civilization made to world knowledge and culture?

A.D. 500	A.D. 800	A.D. 1100	A.D. 1400

A.D. 830 Ma'mun founds House of Wisdom in Baghdad.

A.D. 570 Muhammad is born.

A.D. 661 Umayyads establish Islamic Empire.

A.D. 1258 Mongols attack Baghdad.

GEOGRAPHY CONNECTION

Location Have students locate a number of Arab nations on a map, including Iran, Saudi Arabia, and Egypt. Explain that, contrary to what many people believe, these countries are not home to the majority of the world's Muslims. The majority of the world's 1 billion Muslims are not Arab but rather Asian and African. Have students locate Indonesia, Bangladesh, Pakistan, India, central Asia, and Nigeria. Where are the world's largest Muslim communities found? *(in these regions)* Point out that there are also large Muslim communities in France and England, in Bosnia, and in the United States.

![WORLD HISTORY Online]

Chapter Overview

Visit the *World History: The Human Experience* Web site at **worldhistory.glencoe.com** and click on *Chapter 11—Chapter Overview* to preview the chapter.

Your History Journal

Choose a topic from the text headings on astronomy and geography, chemistry and medicine, or art and architecture in the Muslim world. Research the subject in a library and write a short report.

History & Art
Tell students that Islam, like Judaism and Christianity, includes a number of different branches. One of the two major Muslim groups—the Shiites—has a particular connection to Ali, who was the son-in-law of Muhammad, the prophet of Islam. The name "Shiite" derives from the Arabic words *shi'at Ali*, which means "party of Ali." Shiites revere Ali as the only true successor to Muhammad.

✔ Performance Assessment

Refer to the activity on page 268C of the Planning Guide.

📁 For an additional activity, refer to Activity 11 in the *Performance Assessment Strategies and Activities* booklet.

Using Your History Journal

Advise students to avoid overgeneralization in their reports by focusing on the work of an individual, such as Ibn Sina, or on a particular advance, such as algebra.

GLENCOE TECHNOLOGY

VIDEODISC
Use MindJogger to preview chapter content.

MindJogger Videoquiz

Chapter 11
Disc 2 Side A

 Also available in VHS.

➕ EXTRA CREDIT PROJECT

Compare and Contrast Students can learn about some of the similarities and differences between the Judeo-Christian tradition and the Islamic tradition by comparing and contrasting the Bible and the Quran. There are many translations of the latter, but A. J. Arberry's *The Koran* is the most poetic. Ask students to consider whether the Quran is tied to the history of a single nation in the way the Bible is. Suggest that they compare the accounts of Joseph, Moses, Noah, or Jonah in the Quran with those in the Bible's Old Testament. 📁

SECTION THEME

▶ **Innovation** The faith and principles of Islam become the basis of a new civilization.

Guide to Reading

For reading strategies to help students read effectively see pages 12–13. Have students think about the main head as they read the subheads.

Vocabulary Pre-check

🖳 Use the Vocabulary Puzzlemaker for Chapter 11 to create a crossword puzzle to reinforce section terms. **L1 LEP**

 Use Vocabulary Activity 11 to introduce vocabulary terms. **L1 LEP**

FOCUS

Section Objective

Identify the basic beliefs and practices of Islam.

BELLRINGER
Motivational Activity

Before taking roll at the beginning of the class period, project Section Focus Transparency 11-1 and have students answer the activity questions.

 This activity is also available as a blackline master.

| A.D. 600 | A.D. 625 | A.D. 650 |

A.D. 610 Muhammad has his first revelation.

A.D. 622 Muhammad and followers depart on the *Hijrah*.

A.D. 630 The people of Makkah accept Islam.

A.D. 632 Muhammad dies at Madinah.

Section 1

A New Faith

Guide to Reading

Read to Find Out
Main Idea *Muhammad established basic beliefs and practices for Islam.*

▶ **Terms to Define**
sheikh, revelation, *shari'ah*, mosque, imam, hajj

▶ **People to Meet**
Muhammad, Muslims

▶ **Places to Locate**
Arabian Peninsula, Makkah

The Storyteller

*(Allah) Most Gracious!
It is He Who has taught the Qur'an.
He has created man:
He has taught him speech (and Intelligence)
The sun and the moon follow courses (exactly) computed; And the herbs and the trees–both (alike) bow in adoration.
And the Firmament has He raised high and He has set up the balance (of Justice)
In order that you may not transgress (due) balance.
So establish weight with justice and fall not short in the balance. It is He Who has spread out the earth for (His) creatures:
Therein is fruit and date-palms producing spathes (enclosing dates);
Also corn with (its) leaves and stalk for fodder and sweet-smelling plants.*

—from *The Quran,* Chapter 55

Abu-Zayd preaching in the Mosque of Samarkand

South of Asia Minor lies the **Arabian Peninsula**, home of the Arabs. This location placed the Arabs at the margins of the great Middle Eastern civilizations. Like the ancient Israelites, Phoenicians, and Chaldeans, the Arabs were descended from Semitic tribes. Archaeologists have traced Arab civilizations in the Arabian Peninsula to at least 3000 B.C.

Arab Life

The relative geographic remoteness of the Arabian Peninsula kept the empires in the northern part of the region from invading Arab lands. Their isolation allowed the Arabs to create their own civilization.

The Setting

The Arabian Peninsula is a wedge of land of about 1 million square miles (2.6 million sq. km) between the Red Sea and the Persian Gulf. It is made up of two distinct regions. The southwestern area, across from the northeast coast of Africa, has well-watered valleys nestled between mountains. The rest of the peninsula, however, consists of arid plains and deserts.

Yet the peninsula is not entirely forbidding. Grass grows quickly during the showers of the rainy season, and oases, the fertile areas around springs and water holes, provide a permanent source of water for farmers, herders, and travelers. For centuries, nomadic herders and caravans have crisscrossed the desert, traveling from oasis to oasis.

Lives of the Bedouin

In ancient times many of the Arabs were bedouin (BEH•duh•wuhn), nomads who herded sheep, camels, and goats and lived in tents made of felt from camel or goat hair. They ate mainly fresh or dried dates, and they drank milk from their herds; on special occasions they also ate mutton.

SECTION RESOURCES

Reproducible Masters
- Lecture Notes 11-1
- Reproducible Lesson Plan 11-1
- Guided Reading Activity 11-1
- History Simulation 11
- Time Line Activity 11
- Section Quiz 11-1
- Reading Essentials and Study Guide 11-1

🖳 **Transparencies**
- Section Focus Transparency 11-1
- Chapter Transparency 11-1

Multimedia
- Vocabulary PuzzleMaker Software
- Interactive Tutor Self-Assessment Software
- Testmaker
- Jerusalem: City of Three Faiths
- Ted Koppel: The Holy Land
- Ted Koppel: Three Religions

The bedouin lived in tribes, each made up of related families. Arabs valued family ties because they ensured protection and survival in the harsh desert environment. Leading each tribe was a sheikh (SHAYK), or chief, appointed by the heads of the families. A council of elders advised the sheikh, who ruled as long as he had the tribe's consent. Warfare was part of bedouin life. The Arab tribes went on raids to gain camels and horses and battled one another over pastures and water holes, the most precious resources in the desert. To protect their honor and their possessions, the bedouin believed in retaliation—"an eye for an eye, and a tooth for a tooth."

For entertainment the bedouin enjoyed many activities. Camel and horse races and other games sharpened the men's abilities as warriors, and then everyone enjoyed an evening of storytelling around the campfires. Poets composed and recited poems about battles, deserts, camels and horses, and love. In these lines an Arab sheikh states his view of war:

> ❝ From the cup of peace
> drink your fill;
> but from the cup of war
> a sip will suffice. ❞

Growth of Towns

By the A.D. 500s, many tribes had settled around oases or in fertile valleys to pursue either farming or trade. Groups of merchants soon founded prosperous market towns. The most important of these towns was **Makkah**, a crossroads of commerce about 50 miles (80 km) inland from the Red Sea.

People from all over the Arabian Peninsula traveled to Makkah to trade animal products for weapons, dates, grain, spices, jewels, ivory, silk, and perfumes. Enormous caravans from the fertile southwest passed through Makkah en route to Syria, Iraq, and as far away as China. Arabs also visited Makkah to worship at the peninsula's holiest shrine, the Kaaba, which contained statues of the many Arab deities. The business the pilgrims brought to Makkah made its merchants wealthy.

Signs of Change

As business ties replaced tribal ties in the trading towns, the old tribal rules were no longer adequate. At the same time, the Byzantine and Persian Empires were threatening to take over Arab lands. The Arabs had a common language, but they lacked a sense of unity and had no central government to solve these new problems.

Religious ideas were also changing. Contacts with the Byzantines, the Persians, and the

Heraclius Recaptures the True Cross

Jerusalem, A.D. 630
In A.D. 622 the Emperor Heraclius set out from Constantinople to recapture what was believed to be the "True Cross" on which Christ died. The cross had been taken by the Persians when they conquered Jerusalem. Heraclius advanced on the Persian capital of Ctesiphon, demanding the return of the cross. In A.D. 630, a triumphant Heraclius restored the True Cross to the Church of the Holy Sepulchre in Jerusalem.

Ethiopians introduced the teachings of the monotheistic religions of Judaism and Christianity. Moreover, a number of Christian and Jewish Arabs lived in the peninsula. Dissatisfied with their old beliefs, many idol-worshiping Arabs searched for a new religion. Holy men known as hanifs (hah•NEEFS) denounced the worship of idols and believed in one god. They rejected Judaism and Christianity, however, preferring to find a uniquely Arab form of monotheism.

This ferment in Arab religious life contributed to the emergence of the religion known as Islam, which means "submission to the will of Allah (God)." This faith would bring the Arabs into contact with other civilizations and change Arab history.

Muhammad and His Message

The prophet of Islam, **Muhammad**, was born in the bustling city of Makkah around A.D. 570. Muslim traditions state that Muhammad was orphaned at an early age and raised by an uncle.

Life of Muhammad

During his teens, Muhammad worked as a caravan leader on a trade route. His reputation as an exceptionally honest and able person prompted his employer, a wealthy widow of 40 named Khadija (kuh•DEE•juh), to put him in charge of her business affairs. When Muhammad was about 25 years old, Khadija proposed marriage to him.

Muhammad's marriage to Khadija relieved

Chapter 11 *Islamic Civilization* **271**

TEACH

Guided Practice

THEME Innovation

Discuss how innovations can occur in any field—in religion as well as in science and technology. Ask students to name some of Muhammad's innovative ideas. *(belief in one God, the equality of all who believe in God, the responsibility of the wealthy to help the poor; placing loyalty to the Islamic community above tribal loyalty)* **L1**

VIDEODISC
In the Holy Land

Side One, Chapter 3
Title: *Ted Koppel: The Holy Land*
Subject: Introduction to the geography and history of the Holy Land
Ask: Where is the Holy Land located? *(in modern-day Israel)*

Side One, Chapter 9
Frame: 9487
Title: *Ted Koppel: Three Religions*
Subject: Introduction to Islam, Christianity, and Judaism
Ask: What is the hajj? *(annual pilgrimage to Makkah)*

COOPERATIVE LEARNING ACTIVITY

Oral Report Organize the class into three groups. Have each group research one of the three main holy places in Jerusalem—the Western Wall, the Church of the Holy Sepulchre, or the Dome of the Rock. Each group should present an oral report that traces the site's history and explains its importance to Jews, Christians, or Muslims. Suggest that students include drawings or photographs and a diagram of the city showing the site's location. After the presentations, ask why it is significant that these sites are all in the same city. Students should not only understand that the Middle East was the birthplace of three major world religions, but also consider the sensitive political question of who should control Jerusalem today. **L2**

Chapter 11
Section 1

Geography: Movement Have students draw or trace a map of the Arabian Peninsula. Have them locate and label Madinah, Makkah, the Red Sea, the Arabian Sea, and the Persian Gulf. Then ask students to look at the trade routes on the map on page 284. Why was the Arabian Peninsula a good starting point for the spread of Islam? (*near overland trade routes and Red Sea and Persian Gulf water routes*) **L2**

ABC NEWS INTERACTIVE™

VIDEODISC
Turning Points in World History

Side One
Chapter 6

Title: *Jerusalem: City of Three Faiths*
Subject: Discussion of the importance of the Holy City to three faiths
Ask: Why is Jerusalem important to Muslims? (*because Muhammad ascended from Jerusalem to heaven*)

Visualizing History The Ottomans controlled almost the whole of the Arab world from 1520 until the twentieth century. Ottoman architects skillfully used colored tiles to transform buildings into strikingly colorful edifices.
Answer to Caption: *to "rise and warn" the people about divine judgment*

him of financial worries and gave him time to reflect on the meaning of life. Muhammad was troubled by the greed of Makkah's wealthy citizens, the worship of idols, and the mistreatment of the poor. Seeking guidance, Muhammad spent time alone praying and fasting in a cave outside the city.

Revelation

Islamic tradition holds that, in A.D. 610, Muhammad experienced a revelation, or vision. He heard a voice calling him to be the apostle of the one true deity—Allah, the Arabic word for God. Three times the voice proclaimed, "Recite!" When Muhammad asked what he should recite, the voice replied:

> **Recite in the name of your Lord,
> the Creator,
> Who created man from clots of blood.
> Recite! Your Lord is the most bountiful
> One
> Who by the pen has taught mankind
> things they did not know.**

A second revelation commanded Muhammad to "rise and warn" the people about divine judgment. Although Muhammad had doubts about the revelations, he finally accepted his mission and returned to Makkah to preach.

In A.D. 613 Muhammad began sharing his revelations with his family and friends. He preached to the people of Makkah that there was only one God and that people everywhere must worship and obey him. He also declared that all who believed in God were equal. Therefore the rich should share their wealth with the poor. Muhammad also preached that God measured the worth of people by their devotion and good deeds. He told the people of Makkah to live their lives in preparation for the day of judgment, when God would punish evildoers and reward the just.

Muhammad made slow progress in winning converts. Khadija and members of Muhammad's family became the first **Muslims**, or followers of Islam. Many of the other converts came from Makkah's poor, who were attracted by Muhammad's call for social justice.

Opposition to Islam

Most Makkans rejected Muhammad's message. Wealthy merchants and religious leaders were upset by the prophet's attacks on the images at the Kaaba. They feared that monotheistic worship would end the pilgrimages to Makkah. Wealthy Makkans believed that this development would ruin the city's economy and lead to the loss of their prestige and wealth. Driven by these fears, the merchants persecuted Muhammad and the Muslims.

Muhammad persisted in his preaching until threats against his life forced him to seek help outside the city. He found it in Yathrib, a small town north of Makkah. In A.D. 622 Muhammad sent about 60 Muslim families from Makkah to Yathrib; soon after, he followed them in secret. His departure to Yathrib is known in Muslim history as the *Hijrah* (HIH•jruh), or emigration. The year in which the *Hijrah*

Visualizing History Nineteenth-century Turkish decorative tile with inscription "Allah is Great." The Ottoman Turks built an Islamic state that lasted until 1918. *What was the command Muhammad received in the second revelation?*

MEETING SPECIAL NEEDS ACTIVITY

Learning Style: Visual/Spatial Have students work individually to prepare posters that highlight aspects of daily life and culture in the Islamic Empire. Encourage them to embellish their drawings with decorative borders using a floral design similar to the one on the tile pictured on this page. Have students write brief captions to identify the subject of each scene. Display the completed posters in the classroom. **L1**

took place, A.D. 622, marks the beginning of the Islamic era and is recognized as the first year of the Muslim calendar.

The Islamic Community

Yathrib accepted Muhammad as God's prophet and their ruler. As the center of Islam, it became known as Madinat al-Nabi, "the city of the prophet," or Madinah (muh•DEE•nuh).

Origin of the Islamic State

Muhammad was a skilled political as well as religious leader. In the **Madinah Compact** of A.D. 624, Muhammad laid the foundation of an Islamic state. He decreed that all Muslims were to place loyalty to the Islamic community above loyalty to their tribe. Disputes were to be settled by Muhammad, who was declared the community's judge and commander in chief. All areas of life were placed under the divine law given to Muhammad and recorded in the Quran (kuh•RAHN), the holy scriptures of Islam. Muhammad also extended protection to Jews and Christians who accepted Islam's political authority.

Acceptance of Islam

Eventually the Makkans invaded Yathrib, forcing the Muslims to retaliate in self-defense. In the resulting battles, the Muslims defeated the Makkans, and the Muslims won the support of many Arab groups outside Madinah.

When Muhammad and his followers entered Makkah in A.D. 630, they faced little resistance. The Makkans accepted Islam and acknowledged Muhammad as God's prophet. The Muslims destroyed the idols in the Kaaba and turned the shrine into a place of worship believed to have been built by the prophet Abraham. Makkah became the spiritual capital of Islam, and Madinah remained its political capital.

The Muslims also expanded into new areas. By A.D. 631 their state included the entire Arabian Peninsula and was supported by a strong army representing each of the Arab tribes.

After a brief illness, Muhammad died at Madinah in A.D. 632. He left behind two major achievements. The first achievement was the formation of a religious community based on carefully preserved sacred writings. The second was the example of his life as an interpretive guide for Muslims to follow.

  Because the Quran was written in Arabic, Muslims of many cultures adopted Arabic as a universal language. *What does the name "Quran" mean?*

Beliefs and Practices of Islam

Muhammad established beliefs and practices for his followers based on his revelations. In spite of social and political changes, these Islamic beliefs and practices have remained remarkably stable through the centuries.

The Quran

According to Muslim tradition, the angel Gabriel revealed divine messages to Muhammad over a 22-year period. Faithful Muslims wrote down or memorized these messages, but they were not compiled into one written collection until after Muhammad died. Then his successor, Abu Bakr, ordered Muslims to retrieve these messages from wherever they could be found, from the "ribs of palm-leaves and tablets of white stone and from the breasts of men." It took 20 years before the messages were compiled into the **Quran**, whose name means "recital." For all Muslims, the Quran is the final authority in matters of faith and lifestyle.

Written in Arabic, the Quran is believed to contain God's message as revealed to Muhammad. This message is expressed in stories, teachings, and exhortations. Some of the stories—such as Noah's

Chapter 11 *Islamic Civilization* **273**

The Islamic Community
In what way was the creation of the Islamic community a turning point in history? *It politically unified the Arabs and enabled them to spread Islam to other parts of the Middle East and the world.*

Visualizing History

Arabic is the religious language of all Muslims. Although classical Arabic—the form of the language found in the Quran—is uniform throughout the Arab world, colloquial Arabic includes several different dialects.
Answer to Caption: *The name "Quran" means "recital."*

History Simulation 11

Chapter Transparency 11

Independent Practice
Guided Reading Activity 11-1 **L1**

MAKING CONNECTIONS ACTIVITIES

The Arts Muslims reproduced their sacred text, the Quran, in beautiful handwritten script. Other cultures have done likewise. Have students work together to create a bulletin-board display showing examples of how Christian, Jewish, and Islamic sacred scriptures have been written by scribes over the ages.
L2

Religion Have students research the Muslim celebration that occurs on the last day of Ramadan. Have them write short reports in which they compare customs for that holiday with those for Christmas or Hanukkah. **L2**

TEACH

Tell students that a minaret is always associated with a mosque. The mosque associated with the minaret in the picture, Samarra's Great Friday Mosque, is now in ruins, although the minaret itself still stands. Samarra was the Abbasid capital from 836, when the caliph al-Mutasim was forced to leave Baghdad, until 892. Ask students to describe the minaret in the picture. (*The tower is composed of thick, squat spiral ramps.*)

CURRICULUM CONNECTION

ARCHITECTURE

Minarets are not always constructed in the same form as the great minaret of Samarra. Some have very thin, delicate spires. The crowning feature also varies from minaret to minaret, ranging from a round dome to an open pavilion to a metal-covered cone.

Linking Past and Present

The **Islamic calendar** was instituted in A.D. 622 and is still used today by Muslims. The calendar is a lunar one, with 12 months and 354 days. The Muslim Era, which counts years from the year of the *Hijrah*, is the official era in Saudi Arabia, Yemen, and the Persian Gulf principalities. Even in Muslim countries where the Christian Era is in official use, people use the Muslim Era in private.

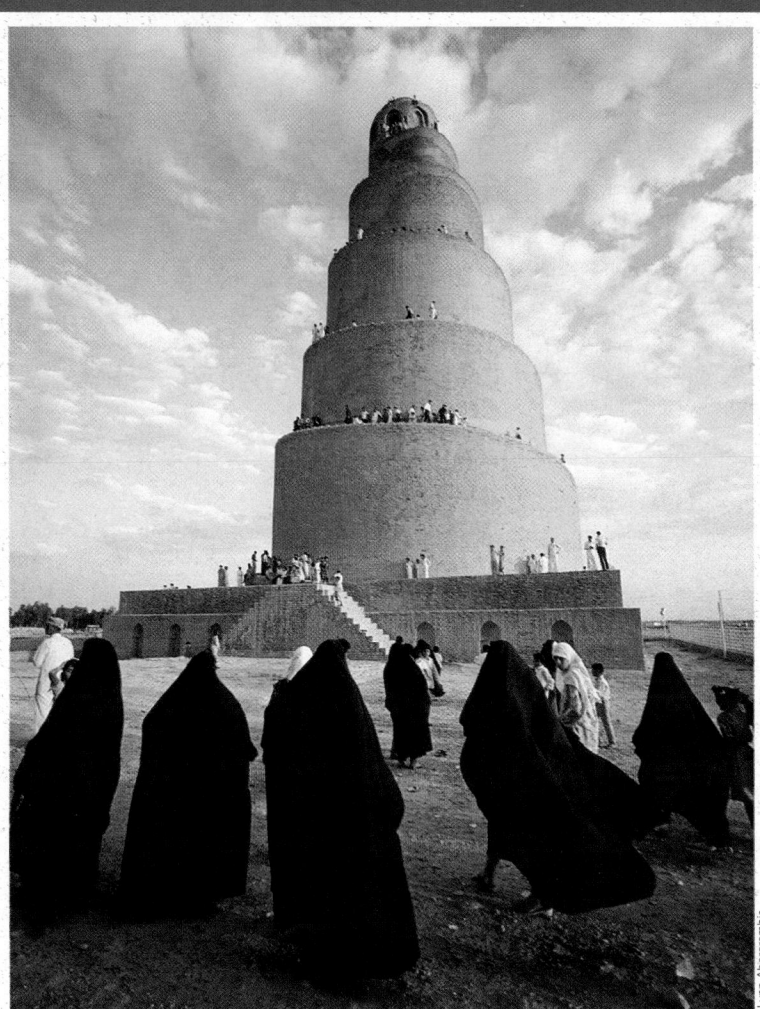

Lynn Abercrombie

Tower Mosque

In Samarra, Iraq, modern Muslim worshippers make their way up the spiral of a mosque built in the A.D. 800s. Some of the women, clothed from head to foot in black, are in purdah, or fully veiled from the public eye.

After Muhammad's death in A.D. 632, Islam spread through the Middle East, into Africa and Europe, and to the borders of India and China. This mosque was built during Islam's golden age, after the Abbasid caliphs assumed power over the Muslim Empire in A.D. The new rulers shifted the capital of the expanding Muslim Empire to the brand-new ci Baghdad and ended the legal distinctions bet Arab Muslims and non-Arab Muslims, a division had long deprived the non-Arabs of many legal ri The peoples of the empire were now given greater dom, and the Abbasids ruled over a period of grea tural flowering, peace, and order. ⊕

274 Chapter 11 *Islamic Civilization*

ark and Jonah in the belly of the whale—are variations of those found in the Bible.

Values

The Quran presents the basic moral values of Islam, which are similar to those of Judaism and Christianity. Muslims are commanded to honor their parents, show kindness to their neighbors, protect orphans and widows, and give generously to the poor. Murder, stealing, lying, and adultery are condemned.

The Quran also lays down specific rules to guide Muslims in their daily activities. It forbids gambling, eating pork, or drinking alcoholic beverages. It also contains rules governing marriage, divorce, family life, property inheritance, and business practices.

Law

Law cannot be separated from religion in Islamic society. Islam has no ranked order of clergy. Instead, generations of legal scholars have organized Islamic moral principles into a body of law known as the *shari'ah* (shuh•REE•uh). Based on the Quran and the Hadith (huh •DEETH), or sayings of Muhammad, the *shari'ah* covers all aspects of Muslim private and public life.

Five Pillars of Islam

The Quran presents the Five Pillars of Islam, or the five essential duties that all Muslims are to fulfill. They are the confession of faith, prayer, almsgiving, fasting, and the pilgrimage to Makkah.

Faith

The first pillar is the confession of faith: "There is no god but God, Muhammad is the messenger of God." It affirms the oneness of an all-powerful, just, and merciful God. All Muslims are required to submit to God's will as given in the Quran.

The confession stresses Muhammad's role as a prophet; he is not considered divine. Believing that at no time are humans without knowledge of God's will, Muslims view Muhammad as the last and greatest of several prophets whom God has sent to different peoples. Taking their lead from Muhammad, devout Muslims see their lives as a preparation for the Day of Judgement, when people will rise from death and be judged according to their actions. If they were faithful, they will be rewarded with eternal happiness in paradise. If they were not faithful, they will be condemned forever in hell.

To Muslims, Allah is the same god as the God of the Jews and the Christians. Adam, Abraham, Moses, and Jesus are considered prophets in the divine chain of messengers ending with Muhammad. As a result, Muslims have a great respect for the Bible, Judaism, and Christianity. They call Jews and Christians "People of the Book." Muslims believe the Arabs are descendants of Abraham through his son Ishmael and the Jews are descendants of Abraham through his son Isaac. The Quran also states that Jesus transmitted God's message and performed miracles.

Prayer

Muslims express their devotion in prayers offered five times each day—sunrise, noon, afternoon, sunset, and evening. Worshipers pray while facing Makkah, always using the same set of words and motions—kneeling, bowing, and

Visualizing History A Turkish pulpit tile from the A.D. 1600s depicts the plan of the Kaaba at Makkah. *What is the fifth pillar of Islam?*

Chapter 11 *Islamic Civilization* **275**

Time Line Activity 11

Daily Life Have students write a letter to a bedouin cousin from the viewpoint of a former bedouin who now lives in pre-Islamic Makkah. The letter should describe how the cousin's life has changed since the move to the city. **L1**

Visualizing History Muslims believe that the Kaaba is the place of worship that God commanded Abraham and his son Ishmael to build over four thousand years ago. **Answer to Caption:** *the annual pilgrimage, or hajj, to Makkah*

ASSESS

Check for Understanding

Assign Section 1 Assessment as homework or as an in-class activity.

⊡ Use Interactive Tutor Self-Assessment Software to review Section 1.

Evaluate

Section Quiz 11-1

⊡ Use the Testmaker to create a customized quiz for Section 1.

CRITICAL THINKING ACTIVITY

Making Comparisons Have students practice their skill at comparing and contrasting by devising a list of points on which various religions might be compared. The lists could include such things as the nature of God, worship, and religious leaders. Then have students use their lists to compare Islam, Christianity, and Judaism. **L2**

Reteach

Have students outline the central ideas in each of the five main divisions of this section. Discuss the outlines in class, correcting any misconceptions students have about the content.

📁 Reading Essentials and Study Guide 11-1

Enrich

Have students find out about the Feast of Sacrifice, or *Id al-Adha*, which concludes the hajj. Have them write a brief report summarizing what the sacrifice commemorates and symbolizes.

CLOSE

Explain to students that, in the next section, they will learn about the spread of Islam. Then ask students to name Muhammad's achievements as described in this section. Write the achievements on the chalkboard.

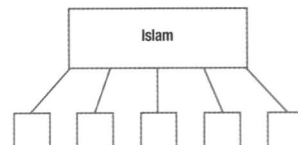

Lamp from the Sulmaniyeh Mosque in Istanbul, Turkey *How may a mosque serve in an Islamic community?*

touching one's forehead to the ground as a sign of submission to God.

Muslims can offer their daily prayers outside or inside, at work or at home. At noon on Fridays, many Muslims pray together in a mosque, a building that may serve as a place of worship, a school, a court of law, and a shelter.

An imam (ih•MAHM), or prayer leader, guides believers in prayer, and a sermon sometimes follows. Any male Muslim with the proper religious education can serve as an imam.

Alms

The third pillar of Islam is the giving of alms, or charity. It reflects the Islamic view that the wealthy should assist the poor and weak. Almsgiving is practiced privately through contributions to the needy and publicly through a state tax that supports schools and aids the poor.

Fasting

The fourth pillar of Islam, fasting, occurs in the month of Ramadan (RAH•muh•DAHN), the ninth month in the Muslim calendar. During Ramadan, Muhammad received the first revelation. From sunrise to sunset Muslims neither eat nor drink, although they work as usual. Children, pregnant women, travelers, and the sick are exempt from fasting. At sunset the call for prayer—and in large cities the sound of a cannon—announces the end of the fast. Muslims then sit down to eat their "evening breakfast." At the end of Ramadan, there is a three-day celebration for the end of the fast.

Pilgrimage

The fifth pillar of Islam is the annual pilgrimage, or hajj, to Makkah. Every able-bodied Muslim who can afford the trip is expected to make the pilgrimage at least once in his or her lifetime. Those who perform the hajj are especially honored in the community.

The hajj takes place two months and ten days after the Ramadan fast and involves three days of ceremony, prayer, and sacrifice. Today, hundreds of thousands of Muslims come together to worship at the Kaaba and other shrines of Islam in Makkah and Madinah. The hajj is more than a religious pilgrimage. A visible expression of Muslim unity, the hajj allows a continuing exchange of ideas among the peoples of Africa, Europe, Asia, and the Americas who follow Islam.

SECTION 1 ASSESSMENT

Main Idea
1. Use a web diagram like the one below to identify the Five Pillars of Islam.

```
        Islam
    ┌──┬──┼──┬──┐
   [ ][ ][ ][ ][ ]
```

Recall
2. **Define** sheikh, revelation, *shari'ah*, mosque, imam, hajj.
3. **Identify** Arabian Peninsula, Makkah, Muhammad, Muslims, *Hijrah*, Madinah Compact, Quran.

Critical Thinking
4. **Analyzing Information** How was Islam similar to and

different from other religions that were also founded in this region—Judaism and Christianity?

Understanding Themes
5. **Innovation** How did the Five Pillars of Islam and the Madinah Compact change ways of life throughout the Arabian Peninsula?

SECTION 1 ASSESSMENT ANSWERS

1. the confession of faith, which affirms that God is the only God and that Muhammad is his messenger; five daily prayers facing Makkah; the giving of alms; fasting during the month of Ramadan; annual pilgrimage to Makkah
2. All terms are defined in the Glossary.
3. Arabian Peninsula, 270; Makkah, 271; Muhammad, 271; Muslims, 272; *Hijrah*, 272; Madinah Compact, 273; Quran, 273
4. similar: monotheistic, stresses moral conduct, some stories in Quran similar to those in the Bible (Abraham, Jesus); different: affirms Muhammad as the last and greatest prophet and the Quran as the final scriptural revelation
5. **INNOVATION** Attention to the duties outlined by the Five Pillars replaced worship of many deities and a greedy lifestyle among the wealthy; loyalty to the Islamic community replaced tribal loyalty.

A.D. 600   A.D. 800   A.D. 1000   A.D. 1200

A.D. 632
Abu Bakr becomes the first caliph.

A.D. 732
Muslims and Christians fight the Battle of Tours.

A.D. 750
The Abbasid dynasty comes to power.

c. A.D. 1050 The Abbasids enter period of decline.

Section 2

Spread of Islam

Guide to Reading

Read to Find Out
Main Idea *The Islamic state expanded and affected a variety of cultures.*

▶ **Terms to Define**
   caliph, jihad

▶ **People to Meet**
   Abu Bakr, Ali, Mu'awiyah, Husayn, the Sunni, the Shiite, Harun al-Rashid

▶ **Places to Locate**
   Damascus, Baghdad

The Storyteller

From the far reaches of the Mediterranean to the Indus River valley, the faithful approached the holy city. All had the same objective—to worship together at the holiest shrine of Islam, the Kaaba in Makkah. One such traveler was Mansa Musa, king of Mali in western Africa. Musa had prepared carefully for the long journey he and his attendants would take. He was determined to go, not only for his own religious fulfillment, but also for recruiting teachers and leaders, so that his land could learn more of the Prophet's teachings.

—adapted from *The Chronicle of the Seeker*, Mahmud Kati, reprinted in *The Human Record*, Alfred J. Andrea and James H. Overfield, 1990

Pilgrimage to Makkah

When Muhammad died in A.D. 632, he had left no clear instructions about who was to succeed him as the leader of Islam. Muslims knew that no one could take Muhammad's place as the messenger of God. They realized, however, that the Islamic community needed a strong leader who could preserve its unity and guide its daily affairs. A group of prominent Muslims met and chose a new type of leader, whom they called *khalifah* (kuh•LEE•fuh) or caliph (KAY•luhf), meaning "successor."

"The Rightly Guided Caliphs"

The first four caliphs were chosen for life. All were close friends or relatives of Muhammad. The first caliph was Muhammad's father-in-law and close friend, **Abu Bakr** (uh•BOO BA•kuhr). The last, his son-in-law Ali, was married to Muhammad's daughter Fatimah (FAH•tuh•muh). The first four caliphs followed Muhammad's example, kept in close touch with the people, and asked the advice of other Muslim leaders. For these reasons, Muslims have called them "the Rightly Guided Caliphs."

Early Conquests

The Rightly Guided Caliphs sought to protect and spread Islam. Their military forces carried Islam beyond the Arabian Peninsula. In addition to religious motives, the Arabs were eager to acquire the agricultural wealth of the Byzantine and Persian Empires to meet the needs of their growing population.

Arab armies swept forth against the weakened Byzantine and Persian Empires. By A.D. 650, these armies had acquired Palestine, Syria, Iraq, Persia, and Egypt. The conquests reduced the Asian part of the Byzantine Empire to Asia Minor and the Constantinople area and brought the Persian Empire completely under Muslim control.

Chapter 11 *Islamic Civilization* **277**

SECTION THEME

▶ **Movement** Armies and merchants spread Islam through the Middle East and North Africa, and into Spain and Asia.

Guide to Reading

For reading strategies to help students read effectively see pages 12–13.

Vocabulary Pre-check

🔲 Use the Vocabulary PuzzleMaker for Chapter 11 to create a crossword puzzle to reinforce section terms. **L1 LEP**

📁 Use Vocabulary Activity 11 to introduce vocabulary terms. **L1 LEP**

FOCUS

Section Objective

Explain how the Islamic state expanded and affected a variety of cultures.

BELLRINGER
Motivational Activity

Before taking roll at the beginning of the class period, project Section Focus Transparency 11-2 and have students answer the activity questions. Discuss students' responses.
📁 This activity is also available as a blackline master.

SECTION RESOURCES

📁 **Reproducible Masters**
• Lecture Notes 11-2
• Reproducible Lesson Plan 11-2
• Vocabulary Activity 11
• Guided Reading Activity 11-2
• Mapping History Activity 11
• Section Quiz 11-2
• Reading Essentials and Study Guide 11-2

📘 **Transparencies**
• Section Focus Transparency 11-2
• World History and Art Transparency 14

Multimedia
🔲 Interactive Tutor Self-Assessment Software
🔲 Testmaker

TEACH

Guided Practice

THEME Movement

Ask students to what regions Islam spread under "the Rightly Guided Caliphs." *(Palestine, Syria, Iraq, Persia, Egypt, bringing the Persian Empire under Muslim control and reducing the Byzantine Empire)* Under the Umayyads? *(eastward to the borders of India and China, westward across North Africa and into Spain)* Ask why the Arabs were able to conquer such a vast, diverse area. *(religious duty to spread Islam to other peoples; promise of paradise for those who died in jihad; weakened condition of defeated empires)* **L1**

Critical Thinking Have students list reasons for the rise of the Abbasids. Have them single out the reason they consider most important and defend it in a written paragraph or in a class discussion. *(Choices might include Shiite opposition to the Umayyads, or non-Arab Muslims' dissatisfaction with Umayyad policies.)* **L2**

 World History and Art Transparency 14, *Court of the Lions, The Alhambra*

The Arab armies were successful for several reasons. First, they were united in the belief that they had a religious duty to spread Islam. The Islamic state, therefore, saw the conquests as a jihad (jih•HAHD), or holy struggle to bring Islam to other lands. In addition, continual warfare between the Byzantines and the Persians had weakened both of their empires and made them open to Arab attacks. Still another factor was the attempt of Byzantine and Persian rulers to impose religious unity on their peoples. Because of persecution, members of unofficial religions in both empires readily accepted Muslim rule.

Divisions Within Islam

While Muslim armies were achieving military success, rival groups fought for the caliphate, or the office of caliph. The struggle began when **Ali**, Muhammad's son-in-law, became the fourth caliph in A.D. 656. One of Ali's powerful rivals was **Mu'awiyah** (moo•UH•wee•uh), the governor of Syria. Mu'awiyah carried out conquests in Egypt and Iraq, steadily weakening Ali's hold on the caliphate. In A.D. 661, Ali was murdered by a disillusioned follower, and Mu'awiyah became the first caliph of the powerful Umayyad (oo•MY•uhd) dynasty. Ali's son **Husayn** (hoo•SAYN), however, refused to accept Umayyad rule and continued the struggle. In A.D. 680, Husayn and many of his followers were massacred by Umayyad troops in a battle at Karbala in present-day Iraq.

The murders of Ali and Husayn led to a significant division in the Islamic world. The majority of Muslims, known as **the Sunni** (SU•nee), or "followers of the way," believed that the caliph was primarily a leader, not a religious authority. They also claimed that any devout Muslim could serve in the office with the acceptance of the people. However, **the Shiite**, the smaller group of Muslims who followed Ali and Husayn, believed that the caliphate should be held only by descendants of Muhammad through his daughter Fatimah and her husband Ali. Shiite Muslims stressed the spiritual, rather than political, aspects of Islamic leadership. Because of

---

Images of the Times

Islamic Art and Architecture

Inspired by their faith, artists and architects of Islam created unequaled geometric designs, floral patterns, and calligraphy.

Carpets and other textiles were turned into fine art pieces by the skilled hands of Islamic weavers.

Ornate bookbinding reflected the importance of the book in Islamic civilization.

278

Images of the Times — Islamic Art and Architecture

Although the Quran neither prohibits nor allows the representation of living things, by the middle of the eighth century such a prohibition became a standard element of Islamic thought. In spite of this prohibition, Islamic artists produced elaborate arabesques and developed a stylistic form of calligraphy.

The Alhambra (in Arabic, "the red," probably from the color of the outer wall's bricks) was built in Granada, Spain, mainly between 1238 and 1358. The Alhambra has six courts, of which the Court of the Myrtles is the most famous. It leads into the huge Hall of Ambassadors.

their conflicts with Sunni leaders, the Shiite also came to regard suffering and martyrdom as signs of their devotion to Islam.

The split between Sunni and Shiite Muslims had a profound impact on Islam and has lasted into modern times. Today, about 90 percent of Muslims are Sunnis; the minority Shiites live primarily in Iran, Iraq, and Lebanon. The Shiite movement itself has divided into several groups. In spite of differences, all Sunni and Shiite Muslims believe in the oneness of God, regard the Quran as sacred scripture, and make the hajj, or the yearly sacred pilgrimage to Makkah.

During the struggle for the caliphate, other Muslims, dissatisfied with the worldliness of the Umayyads, developed a mystical form of Islam known as Sufism. The Sufis, as the followers of this movement were called, sought direct contact with God through prayer, meditation, fasting, and spiritual writing. In addition to their devotional activities, many Sufis carried out missionary work that helped in spreading Islam to remote areas of India, Central Asia, Turkey, and North Africa.

The Islamic State

The Umayyad dynasty, which was founded by Mu'awiyah, ruled from A.D. 661 to A.D. 750. The Umayyads moved the capital from Madinah to **Damascus**, Syria, which was more centrally located in the expanding state.

Umayyad Conquests

In the next century, Umayyad warriors carried Islam east, to the borders of India and China. In the west, they swept across North Africa and into Spain, the southernmost area of Christian western Europe.

By A.D. 716 the Muslims ruled almost all of Spain. They advanced halfway into France before the Frankish leader Charles Martel stopped them at the Battle of Tours in A.D. 732. This battle halted the spread of Islam into western Europe.

Life in the Umayyad State

The Umayyads built a powerful Islamic state that stressed the political, rather than the religious,

Court of the Myrtles, Alhambra, Granada, Spain, remains as a striking example of intricate Islamic architectural design.

REFLECTING ON THE TIMES

1. What details characterize the interior walls of the Court of the Myrtles?
2. Why do you think the decorative arts flourished in the Islamic world during this period?

279

Map Study

Answer

The Muslim defeat at the Battle of Tours prevented the spread of Islam into France.

Map Skills Practice

Reading a Map Which caliphs added most of the territory in Europe and North Africa? *(Umayyads)* Which added most of the territory in Asia and North Africa? *(the Rightly Guided Caliphs)*

Geography: Place Have students make a visual representation of their interpretation of Baghdad as described in this section. Have them use information from the diagram on page 281 and the text to illustrate a poster, develop a clay model, render a sketch, or complete another type of visual. **L2**

Poetry Have students compose a poem celebrating Mu'awiyah's achievements in a lofty style, suitable for delivery after one of his victories. **L3**

ASSESS

Check for Understanding

Assign Section 2 Assessment as homework or as an in-class activity.

▣ Use Interactive Tutor Self-Assessment Software to review Section 2.

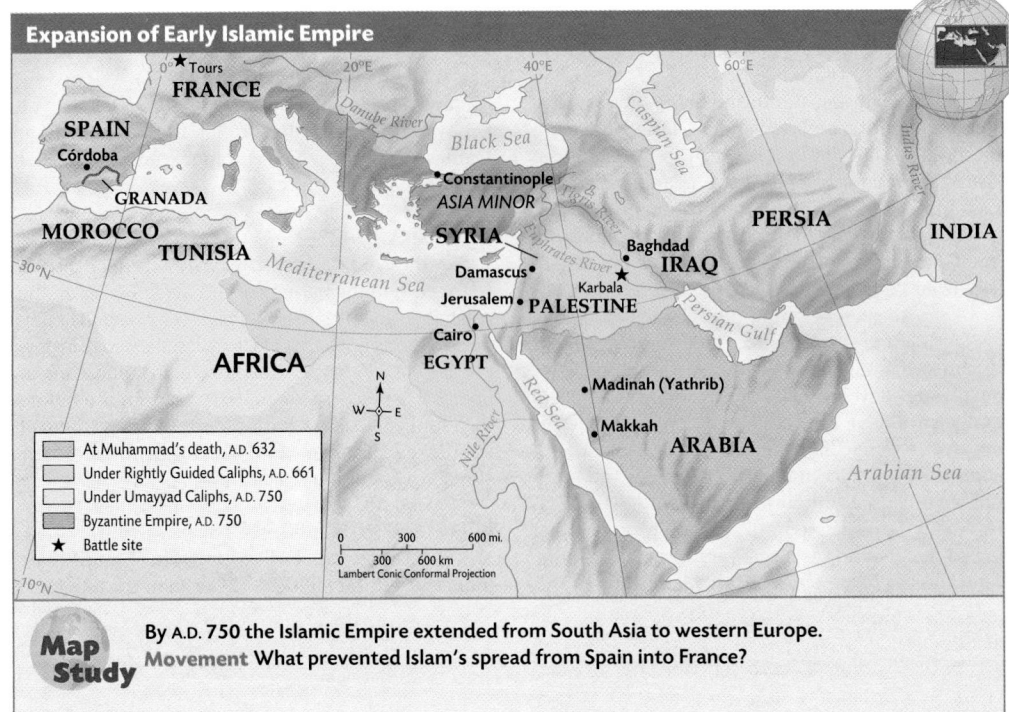

Expansion of Early Islamic Empire

- At Muhammad's death, A.D. 632
- Under Rightly Guided Caliphs, A.D. 661
- Under Umayyad Caliphs, A.D. 750
- Byzantine Empire, A.D. 750
- ★ Battle site

Map Study By A.D. 750 the Islamic Empire extended from South Asia to western Europe. **Movement** What prevented Islam's spread from Spain into France?

---

aspect of their office. As time went by, they ruled more like kings and less like the earlier caliphs.

The Umayyads did, however, help to unite the lands they ruled. They made Arabic the official language, minted the first Arabic currency, built roads, and established postal routes. Their administration depended on a civil service made up of well-trained bureaucrats who had served as officials in the Byzantine and Persian Empires.

Umayyad rule also improved conditions for many, particularly Jews and non-Greek Christians, who had often suffered under Byzantine rule. They had to pay a special tax, but they were tolerated because they believed in one God. The great Arab commander Khalid ibn al-Walid, who had led the conquest of Syria and Persia, described Muslim policy:

> ❝ In the name of Allah, the compassionate, the merciful, this is what Khalid ibn al-Walid would grant to the inhabitants of Damascus.... He promises to give them security for their lives, property and churches. Their city wall shall not be demolished, neither shall any Muslim be quartered in their houses. Thereunto we give to them the pact of Allah and the

protection of His Prophet, the Caliphs and the believers. So long as they pay the tax, nothing but good shall befall them. ❞

Opposition to Umayyad Rule

Despite this enlightened outlook, Umayyad rule caused dissatisfaction among non-Arab Muslims. They paid higher taxes, received lower wages in the army and government, and were discriminated against socially. Discontent was particularly strong in Iraq and Persia, the center of the Shiite opposition to Umayyad rule.

The Abbasids

In the year A.D. 747, the anti-Umayyad Arabs and the non-Arab Muslims in Iraq and Persia joined forces, built an army, and, in three years of fighting, overwhelmed the Umayyads. The new caliph, Abu'l-'Abbas, was a descendant of one of Muhammad's uncles. He established the Abbasid (uh•BA•suhd) dynasty, and his successor, al-Mansur, had a new city, **Baghdad**, built on the banks of the Tigris River. By the A.D. 900s, about 1.5 million people lived in Baghdad.

Baghdad lay at the crossroads of the land and

280 **Chapter 11** *Islamic Civilization*

COOPERATIVE LEARNING ACTIVITY

The Arts To understand the role and influence of Islamic decorative arts, have students form two groups. Have one group research and prepare a presentation on the different styles of art and architecture in the Islamic world. Ask students to offer illustrations of each kind of art and to explain the significance of the different styles. Have students choose two members of the group to present the material and lead a classroom discussion after their presentation. The second group of students should investigate the ways Islamic art influenced European art. They should organize their presentation in the same fashion as the first group. **L3**

water trade routes that stretched from the Mediterranean Sea to East Asia. The circular city was surrounded by walls. Highways led from Baghdad's center to different parts of the empire and divided the city into districts. At its heart stood the great mosque and the caliph's magnificent palace, where he ruled in splendor like the Persian rulers. Surrounding areas contained the luxurious homes of court members and army officials. Outer districts of the city were made up of the homes of the common people.

Abbasid Diversity

The Abbasid Empire reached its height under Caliph **Harun al-Rashid** (ha•ROON ahl•rah•SHEED), who ruled from A.D. 786 to A.D. 809. During this time, the Abbasids developed a sophisticated urban civilization based on the diversity of the empire's peoples. Harun and his successors worked to ensure equality among all Muslims, Arab and non-Arab. They set up a new ruling group that included Muslims of many nationalities. Persians became the dominant group in the government bureaucracy, while the Turks became the leading group in the army. Arabs, however, continued to control religious life and administration of law.

Breakup of the Islamic State

The Abbasids ruled the Islamic state from A.D. 750 to A.D. 1258; during this time, however, many of the lands that had been won by the Umayyads broke free from Baghdad. In central Asia, during the A.D. 800s, Persian Muslims set up the Samanid dynasty in the city of Bukhara (boo•KAHR•uh). Under Samanid rule, Bukhara and other central Asian cities, such as Samarkand and Tashkent, became major commercial, religious, and educational centers. Their wealth was based on caravans that traveled through the region, bringing silk, spices, and animal products from East Asia to European areas as far north as the Baltic Sea.

Independent states also emerged in other parts of the crumbling Abbasid Empire. One of the last Umayyad princes fled to Spain and continued Umayyad rule there. The Egyptian dynasty, the Fatimids, gained control over areas in North Africa and the Middle East, rivaling Baghdad for power. Much of Persia also came under the control of rival rulers. By the A.D. 1000s, the Abbasids ruled little more than the area around Baghdad.

During the next 200 years, Baghdad and its Abbasid rulers came under the control of the Seljuk Turks and later, the Mongols. In their ferocious assault on the city in A.D. 1258, the Mongols burned buildings and slaughtered 50,000 inhabitants, among them the last Abbasid caliph.

Baghdad A.D. 800s

Palace

Mosque

Markets

Tigris River

— Bridge
— Roads
⌐⌐⌐ Walls

0 ___ 1 mi.
0 ___ 1 km

Map Study
The Abbasids built a new capital in Iraq called Baghdad.
Region How was the city protected?

SECTION 2 ASSESSMENT

Main Idea
1. Use a diagram like the one below to identify ways the Islamic state had an impact on other cultures.

Impact of Islamic state	

Recall
2. **Define** caliph, jihad.
3. **Identify** Abu Bakr, Ali, Mu'awiyah, Husayn, the Sunni, the Shiite, the Umayyads, the Abbasids, Harun al-Rashid.

Critical Thinking
4. **Evaluating Information** What were the strengths and weaknesses of Umayyad rule?
Understanding Themes
5. **Movement** How did expansion affect the Islamic Empire's ethnic diversity and stability?

Chapter 11 *Islamic Civilization* **281**

SECTION 2 ASSESSMENT ANSWERS

1. united lands they ruled; Arabic as official language; built roads; postal routes; civil service; improved conditions for Jews and non-Greek Christians; harsh conditions for non-Arab Muslims
2. All terms are defined in the Glossary.
3. Abu Bakr, 277; Ali, 278; Mu'awiyah, 278; Husayn, 278; the Shiite, 278; the Sunni, 278; the Umayyads, 279; the Abbasids, 280; Harun al-Rashid, 281
4. strengths: efficient government, tolerance for non-Muslims; weaknesses: emphasis on politics over religion, discrimination against non-Arab Muslims
5. **MOVEMENT** Expansion increased diversity but led to instability.

Map Study

Answer
Walls surrounded the city.

Map Skills Practice

Reading a Map How far from the mosque was the palace? *(about 4 miles [6 km])* How far from the mosque were the markets? *(less than 2 miles [3 km])*

Evaluate

⬒ Section Quiz 11-2

⬒ Use the Testmaker to create a customized quiz for Section 2.

Reteach

Ask students to imagine they have moved to a foreign country. Have them speculate about the changes they would have to make in their lives to adapt to a new culture. What facets of the students' culture would people in the new environment be likely to absorb? Have them relate these concepts to the expansion of the Islamic state.

⬒ Reading Essentials and Study Guide 11-2

Enrich

Have students find out more about the four Rightly Guided Caliphs and write a two-page report about them.

CLOSE

Write these names from the section on the chalkboard: Abu Bakr, Ali, Umayyads, Abbasids. Have students identify the names and explain the importance of each in the history of Islam and the expansion of the Islamic state.

SECTION THEME

▶ **Cultural Diffusion** Contributions from many cultures and peoples enrich the Islamic state.

Guide to Reading

For reading strategies to help students read effectively see pages 12–13.

Vocabulary Pre-check

 Use the Vocabulary PuzzleMaker for Chapter 11 to create a crossword puzzle to reinforce section terms. **L1 LEP**

📁 Use Vocabulary Activity 11 to introduce vocabulary terms. **L1 LEP**

FOCUS

Section Objective

Name the achievements of Islamic civilization and explain how they were spread to other parts of the world.

BELLRINGER
Motivational Activity

 Before taking roll at the beginning of the class period, project Section Focus Transparency 11-3 and have students answer the activity questions. Discuss students' responses.

📁 This activity is also available as a blackline master.

A.D. 600	A.D. 800	A.D. 1000	A.D. 1200

c. A.D. 635 The Quran is compiled.

c. A.D. 830 Baghdad reaches its height as a major center of learning.

c. A.D. 910 Arab chronicler al Tabari writes a history of the world.

A.D. 1135 The Jewish philosopher Maimonides is born.

Section 3

Daily Life and Culture

Guide to Reading

Read to Find Out
Main Idea *The many achievements of Islamic civilization spread to and influenced other parts of the world.*

▶ **Terms to Define**
madrasa, bazaar, calligraphy, arabesque, chronicle

▶ **People to Meet**
Ma'mun, al-Razi, Ibn Sina, Omar Khayyám, Moses Maimonides, Ibn-Khaldun

The Storyteller

One hundred and twenty camels were required to transport Ismail's books as he prepared to move from Baghdad to Cairo. It was not that he would be unable to obtain books in Cairo. That city, like Baghdad, was lavishly supplied with both public and private libraries whose collections numbered in the tens of thousands. Like many scholars in the Muslim world, Ismail had amassed a collection of works on topics from poetry, history, and law to medicine, mathematics, and astronomy. Now it would take a major effort to move them.

—adapted from *The Mind of the Middle Ages*, Frederick B. Artz, 1990

An astrolabe

In the Abbasid state, the arts and learning flourished despite political disunity. The time of conquest had ended, and the people had enough leisure to enjoy cultural activities. Because Arabic was the language of the Quran, it became the common language. Its widespread use enabled scientists, rulers, and writers from different lands to communicate with one another. This blend of people and ideas gave the Islamic state a new multicultural character and created a golden age.

Family Life

Islam set the guidelines for the way people lived. It laid down rules for family life and business as well as for religious practices.

Role of Women

Early Islam stressed the equality of all believers before God; however, as in the case of contemporary Christian and Jewish communities, in Islamic communities men and women had distinct roles and rights. The Quran told Muslims that "men are responsible for women." A woman's social position was therefore largely defined by her relationship as wife, mother, daughter, or sister to the male members of her family.

Islam did, however, improve the position of women. It forbade the tribal custom of killing female infants and also limited polygamy (puh•LIH•guh •mee), or the practice that allowed a man to have more than one wife. A Muslim could have as many as four wives, but all were to be treated as equals and with kindness. Also, a woman had complete control over her own property. If she were divorced, she could keep the property she had brought with her when she married. A woman could also inherit property from her father and remarry.

SECTION RESOURCES

📁 **Reproducible Masters**
• Lecture Notes 11-3
• Reproducible Lesson Plan 11-3
• Guided Reading Activity 11-3
• Geography and History Activity 11
• Reteaching Activity 11
• Enrichment Activity 11
• Section Quiz 11-3

• Performance Assessment Activity 11
• Spanish Chapter Summary 11
• Reading Essentials and Study Guide 11-3

Transparencies
• Section Focus Transparency 11-3

Multimedia
📖 Focus on World Art Print 13
💻 Interactive Tutor Self-Assessment Software
💻 Vocabulary PuzzleMaker Software
💻 Testmaker
🎵 World Music: Cultural Traditions, Lesson 5

Most women's lives revolved around family and household. Other roles, however, were available to Muslim women, especially among the upper classes. Scholarship was a prominent way for women to win recognition, and many important teachers of Islamic knowledge were women. Women often used their control over property for investment in trade and in financing charitable institutions. The lists of Muslim rulers include a number of prominent women, both as members of the court and as leaders in their own right.

Many Muslim women made contributions in the arts, and several women in the caliph's court were renowned for their poetry. Some of them were not always happy with their lives, though, as indicated by this poem written by Maisuna, the bedouin wife of Mu'awiyah. Her comments made Mu'awiyah so furious that he sent her back to the desert:

> " The coarse cloth worn in the serenity
>   of the desert
> Is more precious to me than the luxurious
>   robes of a queen;
> I love the bedouin's tent, caressed by the
>   murmuring breeze, and standing amid
>   boundless horizons,
> More than the gilded halls of marble in
>   all their royal splendor.
> I feel more at ease with my simple crust,
> Than with the delicacies of the court;
> I prefer to rise early with the caravan,
> Rather than be in the golden glare of
>   the sumptuous escort.
> The barking of a watchdog keeping away
>   strangers
> Pleases me more than the sounds of the
>   tambourine played by the court
>   singers;
> I prefer a desert cavalier, generous and
>   poor,
> To a fat lout in purple living behind
>   closed doors. "

—Najib Ullah, *Islamic Literature*

Role of Men

In addition to politics and the army, Muslim men worked at a variety of businesses or in the fields. For leisure they visited public baths and meeting places where they relaxed and talked. Men also played chess and practiced gymnastics.

When Muslim boys reached age seven, they entered mosque schools, which cost little and were open to all boys. Wealthier families paid tuition, but many poor children were admitted without charge.

Being able to speak Arabic fluently and to write with grace and ease were skills that Muslims valued. For all but the sons of the wealthy, however, schooling ended with learning to read and write. Some young men continued their studies at *madrasas*, or theological schools. Those who were to become leaders in Muslim society studied the classical literature of Islam, memorized poetry, and learned to compose original verses.

City and Country

Most Arabs lived in rural or desert places. The leadership of the Islamic state, however, came from the cities.

Many cities, such as Damascus, in Syria, developed as trading centers even before the rise of Islam. Others, such as Kufa, in Iraq, developed from military towns set up during the early conquests. Muslim cities were divided into distinct business and residential districts. A maze of narrow streets, often covered to protect pedestrians from the scorching sun, separated the closely packed buildings.

Urban Centers

City homes were designed to provide maximum privacy and to keep the occupants cool in the blazing heat. Houses were centered around courtyards; in wealthy homes, these courtyards had fountains and gardens. Thick walls of dried mud or brick and few windows kept the interior dim and cool.

The interiors of most Muslim homes were plain with few pieces of furniture. They were decorated with beautiful carpets and small art objects. Most people sat on carpets or leaned on cushions or pillows. At mealtime, household members sat in a circle and ate from large trays of breads, meats, and fruits.

Footnotes to History

Magic Carpets
The magic carpet gliding through the air is a familiar form of transportation in *The Arabian Nights*. The real magic of Islamic carpets, however, is their glowing colors and intricate designs. During the Islamic Empire, carpets adorned both caliphs' palaces and shepherds' tents. Today, carpets from the Islamic world still give their magic to modern walls and floors.

TEACH

Guided Practice

THEME Cultural Diffusion
Write this sentence on the chalkboard: *Merchants traded freely throughout the Islamic world.* Have students give examples from the section to illustrate this statement. Then have them write two sentences explaining how such trade influenced Islamic civilization. Ask several students to read their sentences aloud. Students should conclude that contact with many different cultures modified and expanded the original Islamic civilization. **L1**

Social Life Have students write paragraphs defending or rebutting the following statement: "Outside the home, Islamic society was a man's world." Use students' paragraphs as a springboard for a class discussion of gender roles in Muslim society. **L2**

Daily Life Have students contrast their education with early Islamic education. How do public schools today differ from the Islamic schools of a thousand years ago? *(Islamic schools available only to boys, free only to boys from poor families, mission was to teach literacy only, advanced schooling mainly religious)* What conclusions about Islamic society can you draw from its educational system? *(Possible conclusion: No distinction was made between religious life and secular life.)* **L3**

🎵 World Music: Cultural Traditions, Lesson 5

📖 Focus on World Art Print 13, Habib Allah. *Mantik et-Tayr*

COOPERATIVE LEARNING ACTIVITY

Role Play Have students write and perform plays about life in Islamic society. Organize the class into small groups and have each group select a theme for its play. Themes could include family life, education, religion, business activities, or bazaars. Have students in each group pool their information and collectively decide what to use in the play. Some group members should be responsible for writing the play, including the dialogue. Other members should perform the play. Each group should choose a student to act as director, as well as an announcer to introduce the play by setting it in time and place. **L2**

Map Study

Answer

Trade routes from Baghdad to Asia include overland routes through Persia; to Europe, overland routes through Syria, Egypt, and the Byzantine Empire; across the Mediterranean Sea.

Map Skills Practice

Reading a Map About how far did a caravan travel overland to go from Makkah to Constantinople? *(about 1,600 miles [2,574 km])*

Independent Practice

📂 Guided Reading Activity 11-3 **L1**

📂 Geography and History Activity 11

Puzzle Have students make a crossword puzzle by using Islamic words from this section. The puzzle may include proper nouns, common nouns, adjectives, and verbs. Students should construct a grid for their puzzle and write short clues for the words. Have students solve each other's puzzles. **L2**

you don't say...

Originally, **"bazaar"** referred to the public market districts of Persian towns. The word spread from Persia to Arabia and other parts of the Islamic state, including Turkey, North Africa, and India. In current English usage it may mean a store offering many types of goods for sale, a sale of contributed articles to benefit a cause, or a Middle Eastern marketplace.

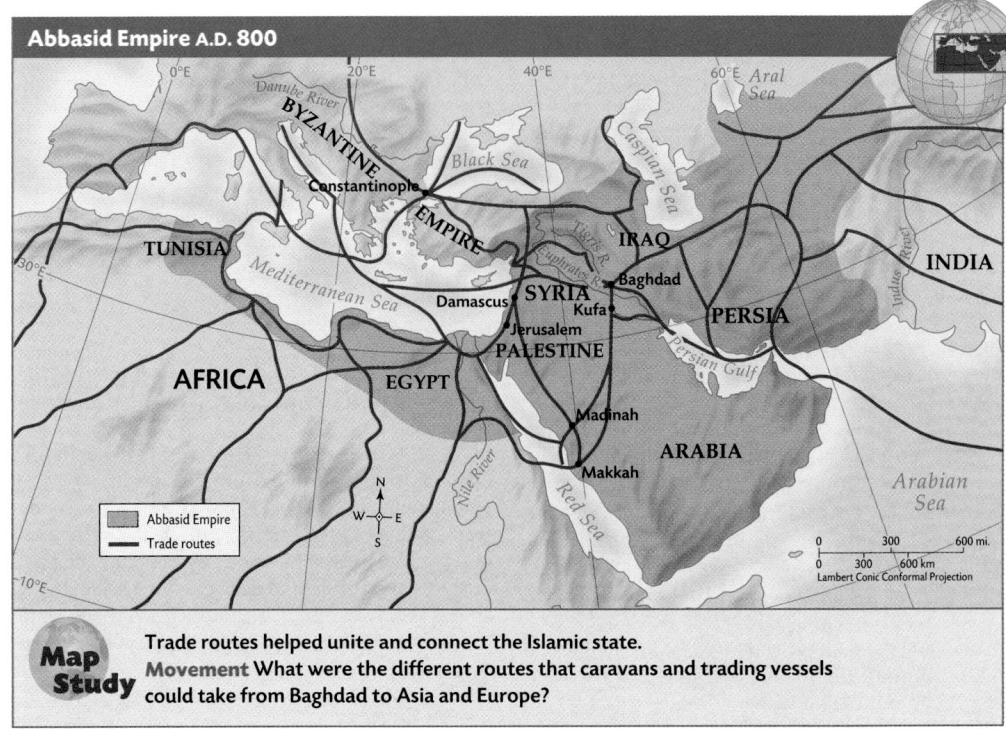

Abbasid Empire A.D. 800

Abbasid Empire
— Trade routes

Map Study Trade routes helped unite and connect the Islamic state.
Movement What were the different routes that caravans and trading vessels could take from Baghdad to Asia and Europe?

The main religious, government, and business buildings were at the center of the city. Dominating the skyline were graceful mosques and their slender minarets, or towers from which people were called to prayer. Mosques usually included a prayer hall where worshipers gathered on Fridays. At one end of this hall a mihrab, or niche, marked the direction of Makkah. Often mosques included schools and shelters for travelers.

Trade and the Bazaar

Muslim merchants dominated trade throughout the Middle East and North Africa until the A.D. 1400s. Caravans traveled overland from Baghdad to China. Muslim traders crossed the Indian Ocean gathering cargoes of rubies from India, silk from China, and spices from Southeast Asia. Gold, ivory, and enslaved people were brought from Africa, Asia, and Europe. From the Islamic world came spices, textiles, glass, and carpets.

The destination of these goods were the city bazaars, or marketplaces. In major cities, such as Baghdad, Damascus, and Cairo, the bazaars consisted of mazes of shops and stalls, often enclosed to shut out the glare of the sun. Buyers at the major bazaars included Europeans who purchased Asian goods,

shipped them across the Mediterranean Sea to Italy and then on to other parts of Europe. Men also met at the bazaars for conversation as well as business. Nearby were large warehouses and lodging houses that served traveling merchants.

Rural Areas

Because of the dry climate and the scarcity of water, growing food was difficult in many areas of the Islamic state. Farmers, however, made efficient use of the few arable areas. They produced good yields by irrigating their fields, rotating crops, and fertilizing the land. Most productive land was held by large landowners who received grants from the government. They had large estates and employed farmers from nearby villages to work the land. Muslim farms produced wheat, rice, beans, cucumbers, celery, and mint. Orchards provided almonds, blackberries, melons, apricots, figs, and olives. Farmers also cultivated flowers for perfume.

After Arab irrigation methods were introduced into Spain, Muslims there could cultivate valuable new crops, including cherries, apples, pears, and bananas. Seville, Córdoba, and other Spanish Islamic cities grew rich from the produce they sold in international trade.

284 Chapter 11 *Islamic Civilization*

MEETING SPECIAL NEEDS ACTIVITY

Learning Style: Verbal/Linguistic Ask students to imagine that they are followers of Muhammad in Madinah during his lifetime. Have them write letters to Muhammad praising him for the improved status of women under Islam. Letters should mention specific improvements, such as abolishing the killing of female infants. Proofread each student's letter individually, pointing out mistakes in grammar, fuzzy passages, and unclear statements. Give specific suggestions as to how to improve these weaknesses. **L2**

Islamic Achievements

The use of Arabic not only promoted trade but also encouraged communication among the different peoples in the Islamic state. From these peoples the Islamic state built a rich storehouse of knowledge and scientific discovery.

Between the A.D. 800s and A.D. 1300s, Islamic scientists made important contributions in several scientific areas, such as mathematics, astronomy, chemistry, and medicine. They based their work on two main intellectual traditions. The first, and most important, was that of Greece. The second was that of India, which came to the Arabs by way of Persia.

The House of Wisdom

The Islamic world experienced a scientific awakening under the Abbasids. During the A.D. 800s, Baghdad became a leading intellectual center.

According to Muslim tradition, the Abbasid caliph **Ma'mun** (mah•MOON) founded the House of Wisdom at Baghdad in A.D. 830. This research center specialized in the translation into Arabic of Greek, Persian, and Indian scientific texts. Ma'mun staffed the institute with Christian, Jewish, and Muslim scholars who shared ideas from different intellectual traditions. They performed scientific experiments, made mathematical calculations, and built upon the ideas of the ancients. The House of Wisdom sparked many of the mathematical and scientific achievements in the Islamic world.

Mathematics

As you read in Chapter 8, Gupta mathematicians in India devised the numerals we know as Arabic numerals and the concept of zero. Muslim mathematicians adopted these numerals and used them in a place-value system. In this system, today used worldwide, a number's value is determined by the position of its digits. The place-value system made possible great achievements in mathematics.

Muslim mathematicians invented algebra and expressed equations to define curves and lines. Their work in geometry led to the development of trigonometry, which was used to calculate the distance to a star and the speed of a falling object. Mathematicians also were interested in practical applications, such as devising pumps and fountains and applying their skills to building and surveying.

Astronomy and Geography

At Ma'mun's observatory in Baghdad, astronomers checked the findings of the ancient Greeks, made observations of the skies, and produced physical and mathematical models of the universe. They accurately described solar eclipses and proved that the moon affects the oceans.

Muslim astronomers improved on the Greek astrolabe, with which they determined the positions of stars, the movements of planets, and the time. The astrolabe made navigation easier and safer. It was also useful in religious practices, enabling Muslims to ascertain the direction of Makkah, the beginning of Ramadan, and the hours of prayer.

Using the astrolabe, Muslim geographers measured the size and circumference of the earth with accuracy unmatched until the 1900s. From such studies, geographers concluded that the earth was round, although most continued to accept the Greek theory that heavenly bodies revolve around the earth.

By the A.D. 1100s, Muslim geographers had determined the basic outlines of Asia, Europe, and North Africa and had produced the first accurate maps of the Eastern Hemisphere. They also traveled widely to gain firsthand knowledge of the earth's surface, its climates, and its peoples.

Chemistry and Medicine

Muslims developed alchemy, the branch of chemistry that attempted to change lead into gold. Although alchemists never succeeded in their goal, they did develop the equipment and methods that are still used in modern chemistry.

The renowned chemist and physician **al-Razi** (ahl•RAH•zee), who lived from A.D. 865 to A.D. 925, classified chemical substances as animal, mineral, or vegetable, a classification system that remains in use today. Al-Razi also made invaluable contributions to medicine. Among his nearly 200 works are a medical encyclopedia that describes the origin of disease and a handbook identifying the differences between smallpox and measles.

In the A.D. 900s, the doctor **Ibn Sina** (IH•buhn SEE•nuh) produced the *Canon of Medicine*, a monumental volume that attempted to summarize all the medical knowledge of that time. It described the functions of organs and offered diagnosis and treatment for many diseases.

Muslim physicians founded the science of optics, or the study of light and its effect on sight. Ibn al-Haytham, the founder of optics, discovered

Student Web Activity 11

Visit the *World History: The Human Experience* Web site at **worldhistory.glencoe.com** and click on *Chapter 11—Student Web Activities* for an activity relating to Islamic achievements.

Social Life Ask students to research the status of women in the Islamic state and in another culture such as that of Native Americans. Have students write a paper that compares the status and the relative freedom and independence of women in both cultures. Display the papers or have several students read their papers aloud in class. **L2**

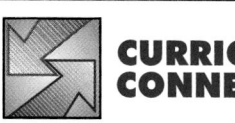

CURRICULUM CONNECTION

MATHEMATICS

About A.D. 825 al-Khowarizmi (ahl KWAHR•eez•mee), a teacher of mathematics in Baghdad, wrote a book titled *Kitab al-jabr wa al-muqabalah*. He presented what was known about algebra at the time. The Arab mathematician improved and expanded algebra. Al-Khowarizmi—and readers of his book—invented so many things that scholars consider algebra an Arab creation. Even the name *algebra* comes from part of the title of al-Khowarizmi's book—*al-jabr*.

Have students use the **Chapter 11 Student Web Activity** at worldhistory.glencoe.com for in-depth study of Islamic achievement.

MAKING CONNECTIONS ACTIVITY

Mathematics To help students appreciate the Muslim innovation of the place-value system, have them try adding the following Roman numerals without writing down their Arabic equivalents: CXLVIII + LXXXII + CCXXXVII. *(467)* You may need to review Roman numerals with students. (M=1,000, C=100, L=50, X=10, V=5) Then have them add these Arabic numbers : 342 + 79 + 175. *(596)* Have students make similar comparisons with multiplication and division. Discuss the results. **L3**

The following videotape program is available from Glencoe:

• **Legends of the Arabian Nights**

To find classroom resources to accompany this video, check the following home page:

A&E Television: http://www.aetv.com

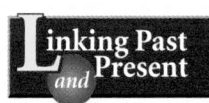

At the Doctor's

The accounts of Mansur's stomach distress and Muslim pioneering work in hygiene illustrate the contributions of physicians from the Islamic empire to the advancement of medicine. Not all the physicians in the empire were Muslim, however. Some, including Maimonides, whose religious work is described on pages 287–288, were Jewish, while others were Christian. An early physician was the ninth-century Persian al-Razi (Rhazes), whose most famous book described and distinguished between smallpox and measles. Ibn Sina, introduced on page 285, was also a Persian. His *Canon of Medicine* was used as late as 1650 in medical schools at Montpellier, France, and elsewhere.

ANSWER

Muslim doctors based their medical practices on scientific methods; western European doctors continued to rely on superstition to explain and treat illnesses until Islamic knowledge spread westward. Regarding today, answers will vary but may include organ transplants, vaccines against diseases such as polio, as well as treatments and diagnostic techniques based on technological breakthroughs, such as laser surgery, sonograms, and CAT scans.

---

that the eye sees because it receives light from the object seen. Earlier physicians had believed the opposite: that the eye sees because it produces rays that give light to the object seen. Muslim medicine, in fact, was centuries ahead of the medicine practiced in the West.

Art and Architecture

Like mathematics and science, Islamic art and architecture benefited from the cultural diversity of the Islamic Empire. Opposed to idol worship, Muslim scholars discouraged artists from making images or pictures of living creatures. Instead, artists used calligraphy (kuh•LIH•gruh•fee), or the art of elegant handwriting, to decorate the walls of mosques and other public buildings with passages from the Quran. Often the beautiful script of written Arabic was accompanied by geometric designs entwined with plant stems, leaves, flowers, and stars. These arabesques (AR•uh•BEHSKS) decorated books, carpets, swords, and entire walls.

Islamic architects and artists did their best work in architecture, particularly in building and decorating mosques. Gardens and water, both precious in the arid Islamic lands, became artistic objects. Sun-drenched courtyards in mosques, palaces, and wealthy homes had trees to provide cool shade and flowers to delight the eye and nose; splashing fountains and running water refreshed both eye and ear.

Literature

Until the A.D. 600s, Arabic literature consisted mostly of poetry passed orally from one generation to the next. After the rise of Islam, religion had much influence in the creation of Arabic literature. The Quran, the first and greatest work in Arabic prose, was familiar to every Muslim, and its style influenced Islamic writing.

During the A.D. 700s, nonreligious prose appeared that both taught and entertained. The most famous of these writings was *Kalila and Dimna*, a collection of animal fables that presented moral lessons.

During the Abbasid period, Islamic literature blossomed as a result of contact with Greek thought, Hindu legends, and Persian court epics.

CONNECTIONS
Science and Technology

At the Doctor's

Today we take it for granted that the doctor can make us better when we get sick. In A.D. 765, however, the caliph al-Mansur was not so fortunate. His personal physicians—the best in Baghdad—could find no remedy for his chronic indigestion.

The caliph had heard that physicians in a Persian medical school based their practices on rational Greek methods of treatment. Traditional Arab medicine was based mainly on magic or superstition.

When the caliph asked the medical school for help, the chief physician, a Christian named Jurjis ibn Bakhtishu, cured al-Mansur. This encouraged other Muslim doctors to practice medicine based on the methods of the Greeks and Persians. Muslim doctors were the first to

Medicinal herb from an Islamic manuscript

discover the functions of internal organs and to diagnose illnesses such as meningitis. They also advanced surgery, carrying out head and stomach operations with the aid of anesthetics such as opium.

Believing that medicine required long training, Muslim doctors studied in hospitals and medical schools. Doctors based their treatments upon careful observation of their patients rather than superstition. They also diagnosed diseases such as measles and smallpox, prescribed treatments, and performed surgery. Such practices were unknown in the West until the A.D. 1100s and A.D. 1200s, when Islamic knowledge reached western Europe.

ACTIVITY

Explain why Islamic medicine was far ahead of Western medicine during the Middle Ages. Then, research sources and list five new methods of treatment developed by doctors in the past 50 years.

CRITICAL THINKING ACTIVITY

Making Comparisons and Drawing Conclusions The Muslims made important contributions in many fields of human knowledge and endeavor: mathematics, astronomy, geography, chemistry, medicine, philosophy. Have students decide in which area they think Muslim contributions were the most significant. Have them write one-page papers defending their choice. Their arguments should include comparisons with Islamic achievements in other fields. **L2**

The upper classes valued elegant speech and the ability to handle words cleverly. Reading and appreciating literature became the sign of a good upbringing; every wealthy person took pride in having a well-stocked library. Córdoba, the Umayyad capital in Spain, had 70 libraries and more than half a million books. In contrast, at the time the center of European learning, held only a few hundred volumes.

In the A.D. 1000s, Persian became a second literary language in the Muslim world. Persian authors wrote epics about warrior-heroes, religious poetry, and verses about love. One of the best known works of this period is the *Rubaiyat* of **Omar Khayyám** (OH•MAHR KY•YAHM), a Persian mathematician and poet. You may also have heard some of the stories found in *A Thousand and One Nights*, also known as *The Arabian Nights*—stories such as "Sinbad the Sailor," "Aladdin and His Lamp," and "Ali Baba and the Forty Thieves." Originating in Arabia, India, Persia, Egypt, and other lands, the tales reflect the multinational character of the Islamic state.

Philosophy and History

Muslim philosophers tried to reconcile the Quran with Greek philosophy. They believed that religious truths could be analyzed and defended using logic. Many of their works were translated into Latin and later brought a new understanding of philosophy to western Europe. Ibn Sina, known in Europe as Avicenna, wrote numerous books on logic and theology as well as medicine. Ibn-Rushd, a judge in Córdoba, was the most noted Islamic philosopher. Christian schol-

ars in western Europe called him Averroës and used his commentaries on Aristotle.

Moses Maimonides (my•MAH•nuh•DEEZ), a Spanish Jew born in A.D. 1135, fled to North Africa to escape persecution from Spanish Christians. Maimonides became a leader in the Jewish community and a doctor to the Egyptian ruler. Like several Muslim scholars, Maimonides attempted to reconcile his faith with the teachings of Aristotle.

One of Maimonides' major contributions was the *Mishne Torah*, a 14-volume work on Jewish law

History & Art Turkish miniature depicting angels, from the *Ajac, ib Mahlukat* by Sururi, A.D. 1500s. British Museum, London, England *What cultural influences shaped the development of Islamic arts?*

Who?What?Where?When?

Kufic script is the earliest Islamic style of calligraphy used to transcribe the Quran. The script's name comes from the Iraqi city of Kufa, where it may have originated. Kufa was a center of Arab culture and learning from the eighth to the tenth centuries. From about the twelfth century, Kufic script was not generally used except as a decorative border around later scripts.

ASSESS

Check for Understanding

Assign Section 3 Assessment as homework or as an in-class activity.

Use Interactive Tutor Self-Assessment Software to review Section 3.

History & Art According to Islamic myth, God created angels from light before creating Adam from clay. With the exception of Iblis (Satan), all the angels obeyed God's order to bow down to Adam. Upon dying, a person is questioned by two angels. The archangel Israfil will blow a trumpet to awaken the dead for the day of resurrection.
Answer to Caption: *the influence of the religion of Islam itself; Greek, Hindu, and Persian cultural influences, especially in literature.*

MORE ABOUT...

Omar Khayyám and the *Rubaiyat* The name *Khayyám* refers to Omar's father's trade, tentmaking. Omar's fame as a scholar spread widely. One of eight experts chosen to revise the calendar, he also prepared astronomical tables and a book on algebra. The *Rubaiyat*, his collection of quatrains or *rubais* (four-line stanzas), was never popular in his own country. The English translation, discovered only after the death of the translator, Edward Fitzgerald (1809–1883), is

a masterpiece of English poetry. The most famous quatrain is:
A Book of Verses underneath the Bough,
A Jug of Wine, a Loaf of Bread—and Thou
Beside me singing in the Wilderness—
Oh, Wilderness were Paradise enow!

Visualizing History A modern Islamic mosque in Isfahan, Iran, one of the most magnificent cities in the early Muslim world. *What kind of writings traced the early historical events of Islam?*

and tradition, written in Hebrew. His other major religious work, *The Guide of the Perplexed,* was writ-ten in Arabic and later translated into Hebrew and Latin. After his death in A.D. 1204, Maimonides was recognized as one of the world's great philosophers.

Like Judaism and Christianity, Islam traces its origins to historical events. Therefore, Islamic scholars were interested in writing history. At first they wrote chronicles, or accounts in which events are arranged in the order in which they occurred. The most famous of the Islamic chroniclers were al Tabari (al tah•BAH•ree), who in the early A.D. 900s wrote a multivolume history of the world, and Ibn

al-Athir (IH•buhn ahl•ah•THEER), who wrote an extensive history during the early A.D. 1200s.

Later, historians began to organize their accounts around events in the lives of rulers and others. The first Muslim historian to examine histo-ry scientifically was a North African diplomat named **Ibn-Khaldun** (IH•buhn KAL•DOON). He looked for laws and cause-and-effect relationships to explain historical events. Ibn-Khaldun believed that history was a process in which human affairs were shaped by geography, climate, and econom-ics, as well as by moral and spiritual forces. His work later influenced European historical writing.

SECTION 3 ASSESSMENT

Main Idea
1. Use a chart like the one below to identify the achievements of Islamic civilization.

> Achievements of Islam
> _____
> _____
> _____
> _____
> _____

Recall
2. **Define** *madrasa,* bazaar, calligraphy, arabesque, chronicle.
3. **Identify** Ma'mun, House of Wisdom, al-Razi, Ibn Sina, Omar Khayyám, Moses Maimonides, Ibn-Khaldun.

Critical Thinking
4. **Evaluating Information** Most Muslim scholars objected

to the portrayal of living beings, but some Islamic art does show figures. Why is this so?

Understanding Themes
5. **Cultural Diffusion** What examples of cultural diffusion in the Islamic state can you find in the following areas: (a) art, (b) mathematics, (c) commerce, and (d) literature?

288 Chapter 11 *Islamic Civilization*

SECTION 3 ASSESSMENT ANSWERS

1. House of Wisdom; place-value system; proved moon affected oceans; measured size of the earth; alchemy; optics; calli-graphy; built mosques; wrote Hindu legends; chronicled historical events
2. All terms are defined in the Glossary.
3. Ma'mun, 285; House of Wisdom, 285; al-Razi, 285; Ibn Sina, 285; Omar Khayyám, 287;

Moses Maimonides, 287; Ibn-Khaldun, 288
4. The Islamic empire was very diverse, and each region that converted to Islam blended the new religion with its local artistic styles and cultural traditions.
5. **CULTURAL DIFFUSION** Answers may include (a) calligraphy; (b) algebra; (c) bazaars; (d) fables, legends.

Social Studies SKILLS

Interpreting Demographic Data

Demographic data are statistics about a population, or group of people. Demographic data can tell us a great deal about where and how people live.

Learning the Skill

Demographers measure populations in different ways. Sometimes they simply count the number of people living in a country or region. By comparing these numbers, we can determine which countries have more people than others.

Suppose, however, that country A and country B each has five million people, but country A has five times more land area than country B. Country B would be more crowded, or more densely populated, than country A. Population density measures the number of people living within a certain area. Population distribution measures the pattern of settlement within a country.

Demographic data also describe population growth. Zero population growth occurs when births equal deaths. If births exceed deaths, the population is growing; if deaths exceed births, the population is shrinking. Population growth is expressed as a percentage rate. Demographers use growth rates to predict the future size of a population. A population pyramid is a graph showing the age distribution of a population. If the pyramid is wider at the bottom than at the top, the population is growing. If a pyramid is smaller at the bottom, the population is shrinking.

Practicing the Skill

The graphs on this page show demographic data for seven countries in the modern Islamic world. Use the graphs to answer these questions.
1. What kind of demographic data is shown?
2. Which four populations are the largest?
3. Which four countries are growing fastest?
4. How is population size related to growth rates in the graphs of these countries?

Applying the Skill

At the library, find demographic data about your city or county and illustrate it in a table, graph, or map. You could show population increase or decrease, population distribution, population growth rates, or age distribution. Write a short paragraph or pose questions that can help in interpreting your data.

For More Practice

Turn to the Skill Practice in the Chapter Assessment on page 291 for more practice in interpreting demographic data.

The **Glencoe Skillbuilder Interactive Workbook**, Level 2 provides instruction and practice in key social studies skills.

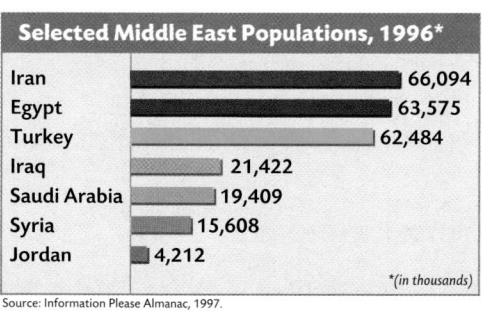

Selected Middle East Populations, 1996*

Iran	66,094
Egypt	63,575
Turkey	62,484
Iraq	21,422
Saudi Arabia	19,409
Syria	15,608
Jordan	4,212

*(in thousands)

Source: Information Please Almanac, 1997.

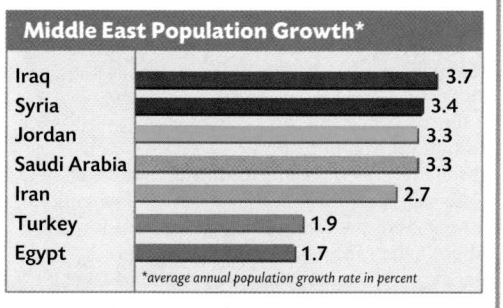

Middle East Population Growth*

Iraq	3.7
Syria	3.4
Jordan	3.3
Saudi Arabia	3.3
Iran	2.7
Turkey	1.9
Egypt	1.7

*average annual population growth rate in percent

TEACH

Interpreting Demographic Data
Ask students if they know the meaning of the word *demography*. *(the science of the statistics of populations)* Ask them what other words they can think of that share one of the two roots of the word *demography*. *(for example, democracy, geography, biography)* Then ask them what conclusions they might reach from the following information:
1. The number of students entering twelfth grade in the imaginary country of Utopia has been declining since 1990.
2. The number of students entering kindergarten in Utopia has been on the rise since 1995. *(They will probably conclude that after a decline in the birthrate for a number of years, Utopia is witnessing a rise in the birthrate.)* Now have students complete the skill lesson.

Additional Practice

📁 Skill Reinforcement Activity 11

📁 Building Skills in Geography Workbook, Unit 2, Lesson 4

GLENCOE TECHNOLOGY

Glencoe's **Skillbuilder Interactive Workbook, Level 2**
This interactive CD-ROM promotes student mastery of key social studies skills.

ANSWERS TO PRACTICING THE SKILL

1. The graph on the left presents a simple count of the number of people in each country. The graph on the right compares the rate of population growth in the same countries.
2. Iran, Turkey, Egypt
3. Iraq, Syria, Jordan, and Saudi Arabia
4. The four countries with the smallest populations are experiencing the highest rates of growth. The three countries with the largest populations are experiencing a lesser percentage rate of growth.

CHAPTER 11 ASSESSMENT

GLENCOE TECHNOLOGY

VIDEODISC
Use MindJogger to review the chapter.

MindJogger Videoquiz

Chapter 11
Disc 2 Side A

Also available in VHS.

Answers

Using Key Terms
1. k   3. b   5. a
2. j   4. f

Using Your History Journal

Encourage students to use one kind of calligraphy for the text and another as a border around the text.

Reviewing Facts
1. A.D. 650: Arab armies capture Palestine, Syria, Iraq, Persia, and Egypt; A.D. 661: Ali murdered, Umayyad dynasty begins; A.D. 716: Muslims rule most of Spain; A.D. 732: Battle of Tours halts Islam's spread into Europe; A.D. 750–1258: Abbasid rule; A.D. 1258: Mongol attack
2. growth of towns and trade; new religious ideas
3. called for loyalty to Islamic state
4. Muhammad himself served as judge and resolved disputes.
5. Umayyad discrimination against non-Arab Muslims
6. Women's social position was defined by their relationship to

---

WORLD HISTORY *Online*

Self-Check Quiz

Using Key Terms

Write the key term that completes each sentence. Then write a sentence for each term not chosen.

a. arabesques   h. bazaars
b. caliph   i. revelations
c. chronicle   j. calligraphy
d. hajj   k. *shari'ah*
e. imam   l. sheikh
f. jihad   m. mosque
g. *madrasa*

1. Islamic scholars and theologians organized Islamic moral rules into the _____, or code of law.
2. Islamic artists used the beautiful script of Arabic in _____, or the art of elegant handwriting.
3. After Muhammad's death in A.D. 632, a group of prominent Muslims chose a _____ to head the Muslim community.
4. Muslims believed they had a religious duty to struggle for their faith through conquests known as _____.
5. Islamic geometric designs entwined with plant stems, leaves, flowers, and stars that decorate walls, books, and various objects are known as _____.

Technology Activity

Building a Database Search a library or the Internet to find information about different modern Islamic countries. Build a database collecting information about all Islamic countries of the world. Include information about beliefs, practices, and demographics of each country. Include a world map and label all countries that have a large Muslim population.

Using Your History Journal

Calligraphy, an elegant form of handwriting, is still used as an art form. Look at samples of calligraphy in an encyclopedia. Then, in calligraphy, reproduce the beginning page of your short report on Muslim life.

Reviewing Facts

1. **History** Use a time line like the one below to identify key events in the spread and decline of the Islamic state.

A.D. 600 ———————————— A.D. 1300

2. **History** Identify the changes in the Arabian Peninsula during the A.D. 600s.
3. **Government** Explain how the Madinah Compact formed the basis for the Islamic state.
4. **Government** Discuss how disputes were resolved in the early Islamic community.
5. **Citizenship** Explain why some Muslims revolted against the Umayyads.
6. **Culture** Describe the role of women in the Islamic Empire.
7. **Science** Discuss some Islamic achievements in science and the changes they produced.
8. **Culture** Describe the career of Moses Maimonides. In what ways did he reflect the multicultural character of the Islamic Empire?
9. **Culture** Name the work in which a person would find tales such as "Sinbad the Sailor" and "Ali Baba and the Forty Thieves."
10. **History** Describe the change in writing history that was introduced by Ibn-Khaldun.

Critical Thinking

1. **Contrast** How did bedouin society differ from the society that formed under Islam?

---

male family members; however, some controlled property and in the upper classes excelled in scholarship and the arts.
7. the adoption of numerals and a place-value system; invention of algebra, trigonometry; astronomical and nautical aids (astrolabe); mapping of basic outlines of continents; scientific diagnosis and treatment of diseases; and anatomical studies. Their contributions changed theoretical knowledge and led to

many practical applications in technology; Islamic knowledge and the techniques based on it later spread to other parts of the world.
8. outstanding Jewish legal scholar and philosopher, physician to Egyptian ruler; born in Spain but later lived in Morocco and Egypt; a Jewish leader yet involved in the Muslim community
9. *The Arabian Nights*
10. first to examine scientifically the effects of geography, climate, and economics on history

2. Apply Would there have been a struggle for the caliphate if Muhammad had named a successor before his death?

3. Analyze Why do you think Abu Bakr wanted to compile Muhammad's revelations into one written collection?

4. Synthesize If the hajj was not among the Five Pillars of Islam, how might its omission have affected the Islamic state?

5. Evaluate How did Muslim scholars contribute to the world's knowledge?

6. Contrast How did the Islamic Empire under the Abbasids differ from the early Islamic community under Muhammad?

Geography in History

1. Movement Refer to the map below. Identify how far the Abbasid Empire had spread by A.D. 800 by naming the areas that it encompassed.

2. Place What was the capital city of the Abbasid Empire, and where was it located?

3. Location How did the city of Baghdad fortify itself against invasion?

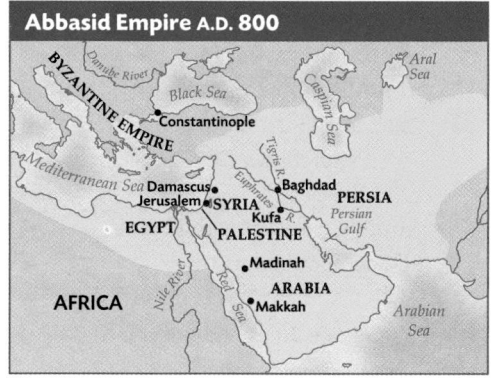

Abbasid Empire A.D. 800

Understanding Themes

1. Innovation What changes did the religion of Islam bring to the peoples of the Arabian Peninsula and the rest of the Middle East?

2. Movement How was the Umayyads' decision to move the nation's capital from Madinah to Damascus a result of Islamic expansion?

3. Cultural Diffusion How did the failure of the Umayyad government to embrace non-Arab Muslims destroy Umayyad rule?

Linking Past and Present

1. What evidence can you find in today's world of the split between the Sunni and the Shiite?

2. How have students today benefited from the work done at the House of Wisdom?

3. What words in the English language have their origins in the Arabic language?

Skill Practice

Study the population pyramid below and then answer these questions.

1. What is the general shape of the graph?

2. What percentage of the female population is between 10 and 19 years old?

3. Are there equal numbers of males and females in this population? How can you tell?

4. What conclusion can you draw about the growth rate in this population? On what data do you base this conclusion?

Age Distribution in Jordan

Age	% of Pop'n	Male	Female	% of Pop'n	Age
70+	0.8%			0.8%	70+
60-69	1.2%			1.1%	60-69
50-59	2.4%			2.2%	50-59
40-49	3.8%			3.4%	40-49
30-39	4.5%			4.2%	30-39
20-29	8.1%			7.3%	20-29
10-19	13.9%			12.4%	10-19
0-9	17.6%			16.3%	0-9
		640 320 0 320 640			

Total Population: 4,212,000
Total Male Population: 2,161,000
Total Female Population: 2,051,000
Life Expectancy (Male): 71 years
Life Expectancy (Female): 74 years

Sources: Broderbund Software, Inc., CIA World Factbook 1996.

Geography in History

1. Egypt, Arabia, Palestine, Syria, Persia

2. Baghdad, Iraq

3. surrounded city with walls

Understanding Themes

1. **INNOVATION** Arabs went from polytheism to monotheism; Islam became the spiritual basis of a new multicultural civilization in much of the Middle East as well as other regions.

2. **MOVEMENT** As the Islamic state expanded, its central location changed.

3. **CULTURAL DIFFUSION** Dissatisfaction among non-Arab Muslims was strong in Iraq and Persia, the center of Shiite opposition to Umayyad rule.

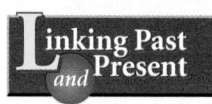
Linking Past and Present

1. Students may point to Iran's Shiite fundamentalists.

2. algebra and lab equipment

3. Answers may include *bazaar* and *algebra*.

Skill Practice

1. bottom-heavy pyramid

2. 12.4 percent

3. No, the male bars of the pyramid are longer.

4. The population growth rate is high; the population pyramid is much wider at the bottom than at the top.

? Chapter Bonus Test Question

Ask students: What role may Muhammad's personal life have played in making the Muslim attitude toward merchants different from that of the ancient Chinese? (*Since Muhammad was a successful merchant himself, Muslims respected merchants, while the ancient Chinese held them in contempt.*)

Critical Thinking

1. bedouins: polytheistic, tribal loyalty paramount; Muslims: monotheistic, loyalty to God and Islamic state

2. Possible answer: A successor appointed by Muhammad would not have encountered opposition, at least initially.

3. to prevent revelations from being lost or corrupted; to unify Islamic scripture

4. would have deprived state of its unifying effect and of the economic and cultural benefits travelers making the hajj provided

5. Translations into Arabic of Greek and Indian works transmitted previous knowledge; achievements in arts and sciences; House of Wisdom brought scholars together.

6. Early Islamic state mostly Arab; under Abbasids, population larger and diverse, and people had more leisure for cultural pursuits.

A complete, 1-page lesson plan is provided for each section in the *Reproducible Lesson Plans* booklet.

The Rise of Medieval Europe

CHAPTER RESOURCES

	Reproducible Resources	Multimedia Resources
Chapter Opener	Chapter Themes: Graphic Organizer 12 Historical Significance Chapter Activity 12	MindJogger Videoquiz
Chapter Enrichment	Vocabulary Activity 12* Time Line Activity 12 Mapping History Activity 12 History Simulation 12 Geography and History Activity 12 Source Reading 12 People in World History Profiles 21, 22 World Art and Music Activity 12 Enrichment Activity 12 Critical Thinking Activity 12 Performance Assessment Activity 12 Standardized Test Practice Workbook Activity 12 Inclusion for the Social Studies Classroom Strategies and Activities	Focus on World Art Print 14, French. *William Exhorts His Troops,* from the Bayeux Tapestry NGS Poster Set: *The Middle Ages* World History and Art Transparency 15, *Cover of the Lindau Gospels* Mapping History Overlay Transparency 9 Chapter Transparency 12 NGS PicturePack Transparency Set: *The Middle Ages* Vocabulary PuzzleMaker Software NGS PictureShow CD-ROM: *The Middle Ages* World History Primary Source Document Library
Chapter Review/Reteaching	Reteaching Activity 12 Skill Reinforcement Activity 12 Spanish Chapter Summary 12	Chapter 12 Digest Audiocassette, Activity, Test* Vocabulary PuzzleMaker Software Interactive Tutor Self-Assessment Software MindJogger Videoquiz
Chapter Evaluation/Testing	Performance Assessment Activity 12 Chapter 12 Test, Forms A and B	ExamView® Pro Testmaker

* *Also available in Spanish*

0:00 OUT OF TIME? Assign the Chapter 12 Audiocassettes.

World History Primary Source Document Library

Make History Come Alive!

Engage your students with over 250 easily accessible primary source documents—available on this CD-ROM—that will give them real life insight into the important events of world history.

Block Schedule

Activities that are particularly suited to use within the block scheduling framework are identified throughout this chapter by the following designation.

KEY TO ABILITY LEVELS

Teaching strategies are coded for varying learning styles.

L1 BASIC activities for all students

L2 AVERAGE activities for average to above-average students

L3 CHALLENGING activities for above-average students

LEP LIMITED ENGLISH PROFICIENCY activities

Use Glencoe's *Presentation Plus!* multimedia teacher tool to easily present dynamic lessons that visually excite your students. Using Microsoft PowerPoint® you can customize the presentations to create your own personalized lessons.

Interactive Lesson Planner

Planning has never been easier! Using this CD-ROM, organize your week, month, semester, or year with all the help you need. The **Interactive Lesson Planner** gives you access to all of the blackline masters that accompany *World History: The Human Experience.*

SECTION RESOURCES

Daily Objectives	Reproducible Resources	Multimedia Resources
Section 1 **Frankish Rulers** Explain what made Frankish rulers, such as Charlemagne, exceptional rulers for their time.	Lecture Notes 12-1 Reproducible Lesson Plan 12-1 Vocabulary Activity 12* Guided Reading Activity 12-1* Time Line Activity 12 Section Quiz 12-1* Reading Essentials and Study Guide 12-1	Section Focus Transparency 12-1 Chapter Transparency 12 Interactive Tutor Self-Assessment Software Testmaker
Section 2 **Medieval Life** Describe how loyalties were maintained in a divided and often violent Europe.	Lecture Notes 12-2 Reproducible Lesson Plan 12-2 Guided Reading Activity 12-2* Source Reading 12 History Simulation 12 Section Quiz 12-2* Reading Essentials and Study Guide 12-2	NGS Poster Set: *The Middle Ages* Section Focus Transparency 12-2 Vocabulary PuzzleMaker Software Interactive Tutor Self-Assessment Software Testmaker NGS PictureShow CD-ROM: *The Middle Ages*
Section 3 **The Medieval Church** Summarize the role of the Catholic Church in shaping the development of medieval Europe.	Lecture Notes 12-3 Reproducible Lesson Plan 12-3 Guided Reading Activity 12-3* People in World History Profiles 21, 22 World Art and Music Activity 12 Section Quiz 12-3* Reading Essentials and Study Guide 12-3	Section Focus Transparency 12-3 World History and Art Transparency 15, *Cover of the Lindau Gospels* NGS PicturePack Transparency Set: *The Middle Ages* Vocabulary PuzzleMaker Software Interactive Tutor Self-Assessment Software Testmaker NGS PictureShow CD-ROM: *The Middle Ages*
Section 4 **Rise of European Monarchy** Name the achievements of medieval European monarchs.	Lecture Notes 12-4 Reproducible Lesson Plan 12-4 Vocabulary Activity 12* Guided Reading Activity 12-4* Time Line Activity 12 Mapping History Activity 12 Geography and History Activity 12 Reteaching Activity 12 Enrichment Activity 12 Section Quiz 12-4* Performance Assessment Activity 12 Spanish Chapter Summary 12 Reading Essentials and Study Guide 12-4	Focus on World Art Print 14, French. *William Exhorts His Troops,* from the Bayeux Tapestry Section Focus Transparency 12-4 Mapping History Overlay Transparency 9, *Europe in A.D. 1160* Interactive Tutor Self-Assessment Software Testmaker

* *Also available in Spanish*

Chapter Activities

 Performance Assessment Activity

Writing a Historical Fiction Narrative Have students take the role of authors to develop a historical fiction story set in medieval Europe. Students should combine accounts of actual leaders with those of fictitious characters. You may wish to have on hand a dictionary of old English terms from which students can draw words to make their narratives more authentic. Have students share their narratives with the class.

Possible Rubric Features
Accuracy and extent of content information, concept attainment, elaboration and detail, clarity and organization

• *For an additional activity, refer to Activity 12 in the* Performance Assessment Strategies and Activities *booklet.*

ACTIVITY

From the Classroom of...

Amy Chevalier
Sun Prairie High School
Sun Prairie, WI

Be a Medieval
Have students identify with an individual from medieval Europe by assuming a role and communicating a message to another party.

Have students choose the character whose identity they will assume, the type of communication they wish to use, their audience, and the subject matter of the message they will convey. They may choose from the following list, or use ideas of their own.
Characters: a ruler (Clovis, Pepin, Charlemagne), a noble (a mayor of the palace, a knight, a lord or a lady), a member of the clergy (Pope Gregory, an abbot, monk, cardinal, or friar), a Viking, a serf
Communication: letter, poem, speech, decree, sermon, editorial, song
Audience: a family member (for example, a cousin in Constantinople), a church congregation, peasants on the manor, the king, the pope
Subject of Message: Viking raids, feudal battles, living conditions on the manor, change in taxation, new laws for the manor, heresy in the Church, life in the castle

Students may also choose to authenticate their document when they present it. For example, they may choose to write it in an old-style script.

MULTIPLE LEARNING STYLES

Verbal/Linguistic
As students study the people of the Middle Ages, read portraits from Chaucer's Prologue to *The Canterbury Tales* aloud. Discuss the details provided by Chaucer on the major characters in relation to information provided in the text.

Visual/Spatial
Have the class work together to create a mural in the fashion of the Bayeux Tapestry. Have them include portraits of people from the chapter, including details of their dress and objects that symbolize their station in life.

Kinesthetic
Have students research a key medieval ceremony, such as homage or the admission of a squire to knighthood. Then have them stage a reenactment, with a narrator explaining the steps in the ceremony.

Interpersonal
Have students work in groups to create advertisements for some of the many technological improvements that date from the Middle Ages. Students should work together to divide and coordinate the various tasks of researching, writing, and illustrating. Display the ads in the classroom as you cover Chapter 12.

 GLENCOE'S ASSESSMENT ADVANTAGE

Use the following to easily assess student learning in a variety of ways.

- Performance Assessment Strategies and Activities
- Section Quizzes
- Chapter and Unit Tests
- Interactive Tutor Self-Assessment Software
- Testmaker Software
- MindJogger Videoquiz
- SAT/SAT II Test Practice
- worldhistory.glencoe.com

Additional Resources

Teacher's Corner

INDEX TO NATIONAL GEOGRAPHIC MAGAZINE

The following articles may be used for research relating to this chapter:

- "The Basques," by Thomas J. Abercrombie, November 1995.
- "The Hanseatic League: Europe's First Common Market," by Edward Von Der Porten, October 1994.

NATIONAL GEOGRAPHIC SOCIETY PRODUCTS AVAILABLE FROM GLENCOE

To order the following, call Glencoe at 1-800-334-7344:

- *PictureShow: The Middle Ages (CD-ROM)*
- *PicturePack: The Middle Ages (Transparencies)*
- *MapPack: Europe (Transparency Maps)*

ADDITIONAL NATIONAL GEOGRAPHIC SOCIETY PRODUCTS

Access National Geographic's new dynamic MapMachine Web site and other geography resources at:

- http://www.nationalgeographic.com/
- http://www.nationalgeographic.com/maps/

BIBLIOGRAPHY

Literature of the Period
Sayers, Dorothy, trans. *The Song of Roland.* New York: Penguin, 1957. Chronicles the events and legends of Charlemagne's life and that of his young nephew Roland.

Readings for the Student
Guerber, H. A., ed. *Middle Ages.* New York: Avenel Books, 1985. From the Myths and Legends Series, covers Beowulf, Charlemagne, Arthur and his knights, and other tales of the Middle Ages.

Readings for the Teacher
Ehrenreich, Barbara, and Deirdre English. *Witches, Midwives, and Nurses: A History of Women Healers.* New York: Feminist Press, 1972. Covers the roles of women in medicine during the Middle Ages.

Power, Eileen. *Medieval People.* New York: Barnes and Noble, 1963. Includes detailed portraits of medieval people from different social classes, including peasants, merchants, and clergy.

WORLD HISTORY Online

Use our Web site as an additional resource. All essential content is covered in the Student Edition.

You and your students can visit the *World History: The Human Experience* Web site at worldhistory. glencoe.com The student text directs students to the Web site for the following options:

- **Chapter Overviews**
- **Student Web Activities**
- **Self-Check Quizzes**

Answers are provided for you in a link entitled "Web Activity Lesson Plan." Additional Web Resources, Interactive Puzzles, and content updates are also available.

Visit the Glencoe Web site at socialstudies. glencoe.com for social studies activities, updates, and links to other resources.

LOCAL OBJECTIVES

_____
_____
_____
_____
_____
_____
_____
_____
_____
_____
_____
_____
_____
_____
_____
_____
_____
_____
_____

CHAPTER THEMES

Chapter Themes are listed by section on this chapter opening page of the Student Edition. A corresponding theme-based activity is available under "TEACH," and a theme-based question is asked in the Section and Chapter Assessments.

S*toryteller*

Historical Setting Training for knighthood began early for boys of noble birth. When a boy reached the age of 7, he was usually sent away to the home of a nobleman or knight. There he served the lord of the manor and received formal training to become a squire and then a knight—learning to ride and manage a horse, to wield a heavy sword, to hurl a lance, to shoot a bow, and to clean and care for his armor.

Historical Significance

Answers: *A new European civilization took shape with the interaction of the influence of Roman Catholicism, the learning of classical times, and the political innovations of Frankish rulers.*

The civilization developed through a number of institutions, including feudalism, manorialism, and monasticism. Modern European countries had their beginnings in the Middle Ages.

— WORLD HISTORY *Online* —

Have students use the **Chapter 12 Overview** at worldhistory. glencoe.com as a prereading and postreading exercise for understanding chapter content.

Chapter
12
A.D. 500–1300
The Rise of Medieval Europe

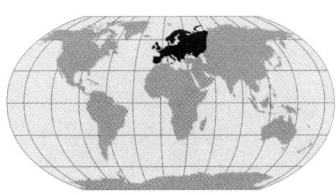

Chapter Themes

▶ **Movement** Invasions by Vikings, Magyars, and Muslims influence medieval Europe. *Section 1*
▶ **Cooperation** Nobles, church officials, and peasants develop ties of loyalty and service to one another. *Section 2*
▶ **Uniformity** The Catholic Church affects every aspect of medieval life. *Section 3*
▶ **Conflict** European kings, feudal lords, and popes struggle for political dominance. *Section 4*

S*toryteller*

It was tournament day. As trumpets flourished, the marshal shouted, "In the name of God and St. Michael, do your battle!" Knights on horseback thundered toward each other and met with a deafening clash. Lords and ladies cheered as their favorite unhorsed his opponents. The victor was awarded a prize from the lady whose colors he wore.

Such tournaments provided more than just entertainment. They also trained soldiers for combat. After the fall of Rome, wars were frequent. A professional warrior class—the knights— led the new, vigorous, competitive society that would reshape western Europe.

Historical Significance

How did Christianity, the classical heritage, and Germanic practices combine to form a new European civilization? How did this civilization develop and lay the foundation for modern European life?

A.D. 700   A.D. 900   A.D. 1100   A.D. 1300

A.D. 1066 William the Conqueror invades England.

A.D. 800 Charlemagne is crowned emperor.

A.D. 1210 Francis of Assisi preaches in Italy.

A.D. 1122 Concordat of Worms decides church appointments.

292

GEOGRAPHY CONNECTION

Movement Have students consult the map on page 297. Make sure that they understand the use of different colors to indicate movement by Vikings, Magyars, and Muslims. What region was the original home of the Vikings? *(Scandinavia)* On which continent did the Magyars originate? *(Asia)* In which direction did the Muslims travel to reach Europe? *(north)* What physical obstacles did the invaders have to overcome? *(mountains, seas)*

Apparition Before the Chapter of Arles by Giotto di Bondone. San Francesco, Assisi, Italy

WORLD HISTORY *Online*

Chapter Overview

Visit the *World History: The Human Experience* Web site at <u>worldhistory.glencoe.com</u> and click on *Chapter 12—Chapter Overview* to preview the chapter.

Your History Journal

Monarchies and representative assemblies arose in medieval Europe. Draw a time line of key events in the development of these institutions.

History & Art Florentine painter Giotto painted a series of frescoes on the life of St. Francis of Assisi. The frescoes are in the cathedral at Assisi, Italy. In September 1997 a severe earthquake damaged the cathedral and some of the frescoes.

✔ **Performance Assessment**

Refer to the activity on page 292C of the Planning Guide.

  For an additional activity, refer to Activity 12 in the *Performance Assessment Strategies and Activities* booklet.

Using Your History Journal

Key events should include the coronation of Charlemagne in 800, the invasion of England by William the Conqueror in 1066, the 1215 signing of the Magna Carta, the Model Parliament in 1295.

GLENCOE TECHNOLOGY

VIDEODISC
Use MindJogger to preview chapter content.

MindJogger Videoquiz

Chapter 12
Disc 2 Side A

  Also available in VHS.

➕ EXTRA CREDIT PROJECT

Music Among the best-loved figures of the Middle Ages were the poet-musicians known variously as minstrels, troubadours, minnesingers, skalds, or bards. Have students research the lives of these men, paying special attention to their role in society and the tales they sang or told. Students should write summaries of their research, then present them to the class. If possible, have them obtain and play recordings of music typical of the period. Then have students write their own lyrics to music composed in the medieval style. The songs may be presented live in class or audiotaped.

A.D. 400 · A.D. 600 · A.D. 800 · A.D. 1000

A.D. 496 Frankish King Clovis accepts Catholicism.

A.D. 768 Charlemagne becomes Frankish king.

A.D. 843 Treaty of Verdun divides Carolingian lands.

c. A.D. 850 Vikings begin explorations.

Section 1

Frankish Rulers

Guide to Reading

**Read to Find Out
Main Idea** *Frankish rulers, such as Charlemagne, were exceptional rulers for their time.*

▶ **Terms to Define**
mayor of the palace, count

▶ **People to Meet**
Clovis, Charles Martel, Pepin the Short, Charlemagne, the Vikings

▶ **Places to Locate**
Frankish Empire, Scandinavia

The **Storyteller**

The men of medieval times, including Charlemagne, loved hunting. It was a cruel sport, but at least it provided meat for the royal tables.

When Charlemagne sat down to dinner, the main course was usually a roast of game from the morning hunt. During the meal, one of the poets of the royal court might rise to read aloud a poem—to the dismay of the king's soldiers, who sometimes clapped their hands over their ears and glared at the poet until Charlemagne scolded them. With dinner, the king enjoyed "the wine of learning."

—freely adapted from *Charlemagne*, Richard Winston, 1968

Charlemagne

By A.D. 500, Germanic invasions had all but destroyed the urban world of the Roman Empire. Trade declined. Cities, bridges, and roads fell into disrepair and disuse. Law and order vanished, and education almost disappeared. Money was no longer used. For most people, life did not extend beyond the tiny villages where they were born, lived, and died.

Western Europe was so backward because of this decline that the early part of this period was once called "the Dark Ages." Scholars later combined the Latin terms *medium* (middle) and *aevum* (age) to form the term *medieval*, recognizing that this period was an era of transition between ancient and modern times. Out of this violent medieval period, or Middle Ages, a dynamic civilization arose. It combined elements of classical and Germanic cultures with Christian beliefs.

Merovingian Rulers

During the A.D. 400s the Franks, who settled in what is now France and western Germany, emerged as the strongest Germanic group. Their early rulers, known as Merovingian (MEHR•uh•VIHN•jee•uhn) kings for the ruler Merowig, held power until the early A.D. 700s.

Clovis

In A.D. 481 a brutal and wily warrior named **Clovis** became king of the Franks. Fifteen years later, Clovis became the first Germanic ruler to accept Catholicism. Clovis's military victories and his religious conversion gave his throne stability.

A century later the Frankish kingdom began to decline. Frankish kings had followed the custom of dividing the kingdom among their heirs. Heirs became rivals and fought each other for land. By A.D. 700 political power had passed from kings to government officials known as mayors of the palace.

Charles Martel

In A.D. 714 **Charles Martel**, or "Charles the Hammer," became mayor of the palace. When Muslim forces threatened Europe in A.D. 732, Charles led the successful defense of Tours, in France. This victory won him great prestige. As you read in Chapter 11, the victory ensured that Christianity would remain the dominant religion of Europe.

Pepin the Short

In A.D. 752, with the backing of nobles and church officials, **Pepin the Short**, the son of Charles Martel, became king of the Franks. The pope anointed, or put holy oil on, Pepin, making him a divinely chosen ruler in the eyes of the people.

In return for the Church's blessing, Pepin was expected to help the pope against his enemies. In A.D. 754 Pepin forced the Lombards, a Germanic people, to withdraw from Rome. He then gave the pope a large strip of Lombard land in central Italy. In appreciation, the pope cut his political ties to the Byzantine Empire and looked to the Franks as his protector. As a result, the fortunes of western Europe and Catholicism were bound more closely together.

Charlemagne's Empire

In A.D. 768 Pepin's son, **Charlemagne**, became the Frankish king. Charlemagne, or Charles the Great, was one of Europe's great monarchs. In Latin his name is written *Carolus Magnus*, which gave the name Carolingian to his dynasty. The king cut an imposing figure. His biographer, a monk named Einhard, described him this way:

> 66 Charles was large and strong, and of lofty stature, though not disproportionally tall … nose a little long, hair fair, and face laughing and merry…. He used to wear the national, that is to say, the Frankish, dress—next his skin a linen shirt and linen breeches, and above these a tunic fringed with silk; white hose fastened by bands covered his lower limbs and shoes his feet, and he protected his shoulders and chest in winter by a close-fitting coat of otter or marten skins. Over all he flung a blue cloak, and he always had a sword girt about him. 99

Charlemagne nearly doubled the borders of his kingdom to include Germany, France, northern Spain, and most of Italy. His enlarged domain became known as the **Frankish Empire**. For the

Visualizing History Shown here, a decorated Merovingian buckle. Gregory, bishop of Tours, wrote the best source of the history of the Merovingian kings. *Why did the political power of these kings fade?*

first time since the fall of Rome, most western Europeans were ruled by one government.

Because few western Europeans could read and write, Charlemagne wanted to revive learning. He set up a palace school at Aachen, his capital, to educate his officials. Alcuin (AL•kwihn), a scholar from England, ran the school and developed a program of study based on the Bible and Latin writings. Under Alcuin's direction, scholars preserved classical learning by copying ancient manuscripts. Charlemagne's school helped provide western Europeans with a common set of ideas.

A Christian Realm

One of the ideas that united western Europeans was the creation of a Christian Roman Empire. Church leaders believed that Charlemagne could turn this idea into reality. In A.D. 800 Charlemagne came to Rome to militarily defend Pope Leo III against the Roman nobles. To show his gratitude, Leo crowned Charlemagne the new Roman emperor. As protector of the Church and ruler of much of western Europe, Charlemagne wanted the title, but he had misgivings about receiving it from the pope. By crowning a monarch, the pope seemed to be saying that church officials were superior to rulers.

In spite of his concern, Charlemagne accepted his duties as emperor and worked to strengthen the empire. Because the central bureaucracy was small, he relied on local officials called counts to assist him. Each count was carefully instructed in the duties of office. The counts solved local problems, stopped feuds, protected the weak, and raised

TEACH

Guided Practice

THEME Movement

Ask students to list other movements of peoples they have already studied. *(those of the Dorians into Greece, the Aryans into the Indus Valley, and the Germanic tribes into the Roman Empire)* Then have them discuss some important population movements of the present day. *(famine victims or war refugees in Africa, war refugees in the former Yugoslav republics, immigration to the United States)* **L1 LEP**

Visualizing History The history written by Gregory of Tours, who lived in the A.D. 500s, included ancient chronicles, legends, and his own eyewitness observations. **Answer to Caption:** *because the Frankish kingdom was divided among rivals, and because of outside invasions*

Government Have students make a list on the chalkboard of Charlemagne's major personality traits, as described in the text. Then have them compare these with traits desirable in present-day politicians. What similarities and differences do they see? **L2**

Chapter Transparency 12

Who?What?Where?When?

Charlemagne was such an important ruler that legends about him soon spread. According to one legend, he did not die but was only sleeping, and would awake in the hour of his country's need.

COOPERATIVE LEARNING ACTIVITY

Role Play Have the class create a historical account of a medieval village under Viking attack. Some students should take on the roles of Vikings, keeping a record of their voyage, their intentions, and their strategies for attack. Other students may assume the roles of clergy members, keeping the village's official records. Still others may represent the villagers, recording the raid with drawings of the encounter. Encourage students to research and to include vivid details in their projects. Conclude the activity with a class presentation. **L1 LEP**

Map Study

Answer

France, Belgium, the Netherlands, most of Germany and Austria, northern Italy

Map Skills Practice

Reading a Map How far from north to south did the Frankish Empire stretch at its greatest extent? *(about 1,000 miles [1,600 kilometers])*

Independent Practice

  Guided Reading Activity 12-1 **L1**

  Time Line Activity 12

The following videotape program is available from Glencoe:

- **The Vikings in North America**

To find classroom resources to accompany this video, check the following home page:

A&E Television: http://www.aetv.com

ASSESS

Check for Understanding

Assign Section 1 Assessment as homework or as an in-class activity.

⬛ Use Interactive Tutor Self-Assessment Software to review Section 1.

Frankish Empire

ENGLAND
North Sea
Aachen
ATLANTIC
Paris
OCEAN
Tours ★
ITALY
Rome
Adriatic Sea
Mediterranean Sea

Clovis's kingdom
Added by Martel and Pepin
Added by Charlemagne
★ Battle site

0   150   300 mi.
0 150 300 km
Lambert Conic Conformal Projection

Map Study During the A.D. 400s, the Franks emerged as the strongest of all Germanic peoples.
Location What modern countries did the Franks control?

---

armies for the emperor. Each year royal messengers, the *missi dominici*, went on inspections in which they informed Charlemagne about the performance of the counts and other local administrators. The emperor also traveled throughout the empire observing the work of his officials firsthand.

Collapse of Charlemagne's Empire

More than anything else, Charlemagne's forceful personality held his empire together. His death in A.D. 814 left a void that his only surviving son, Louis the Pious, could not fill. After Louis's death, Charlemagne's three grandsons fought one another for control of the empire.

In A.D. 843 the three brothers agreed in the Treaty of Verdun to divide the Carolingian lands. Charles the Bald took the western part, which covered most of present-day France. Louis the German acquired the eastern portion, which today is Germany. Lothair, who became the Roman emperor, took a strip of land in the middle of the empire stretching from the North Sea southward to Italy.

Invasions Increase Disunity

While internal feuding weakened the Carolingian kingdoms, outside invasions nearly destroyed them. Muslims from North Africa seized parts of southern Italy and gained control of the western Mediterranean. The Slavs marched out of the east to invade central Europe. From Asia a new group of fierce nomads called Magyars galloped west, leaving a trail of destruction. The most threatening attacks, however, came from **the Vikings**, raiders from **Scandinavia** to the north.

Viking Invasions

In medieval Scandinavian, to go *a-viking* means to fight as a warrior. Viking warriors traveled in long, deckless ships with one sail that were designed to slide swiftly through the water propelled by long oars. These boats were sturdy enough to cross the Atlantic Ocean, shallow enough to navigate Europe's rivers, and light enough to be carried past fortified bridges. The Vikings became known for surprise attacks and speedy retreats. What they could not steal they burned. No place in Europe was safe from attack.

Boasting names like Eric Bloodax and Harald Bluetooth, the Vikings sought riches and adventure. In the A.D. 800s they left their overpopulated homeland, which later became the kingdoms of Norway, Denmark, and Sweden. Viking warriors fought ferociously and showed their victims no mercy.

Viking Trade

The Vikings, however, were more than just raiders. They were also explorers and settlers. Skilled in sailing and trading, they moved along the Atlantic and Mediterranean coasts of Europe. The Norwegians settled the North Atlantic islands of Greenland and Iceland, and even reached North America. The Danes temporarily held England and established the Viking state of Normandy in northwestern France. The Swedes settled in present-day Ukraine and Russia.

Viking Culture

In Scandinavia and their new homelands, the Vikings worshiped many deities. They were proud of their gods and told stories of the gods' great deeds. These stories became written poems called *Eddas*. The Vikings also made up sagas, or long tales. At first, storytellers recited them at special feasts. After A.D. 1100 the Vikings wrote down their sagas. By this time they had converted to Christianity. With their acceptance of the new religion, the Vikings began to write their languages with Roman letters.

MEETING SPECIAL NEEDS ACTIVITY

Study Strategy Ask students with strong organizational skills to work in small groups with students who are having difficulty understanding this material. Ask the groups to create descriptive flowcharts that show the movement of power from Clovis to the heirs of Charlemagne. Have students add boxed features that give biographical details, relationships to other rulers, major accomplishments, and important events for each ruler. Then ask the groups to compare their information in a class discussion. **L1 LEP**

Invasions of Europe A.D. 800–1000

Vikings
Magyars
Muslims
★ Battle site

ICELAND

ATLANTIC OCEAN

SCOTLAND
IRELAND
ENGLAND
London
GERMANY
Paris · Lechfeld
FRANCE
SPAIN
ITALY
Rome
AFRICA
Mediterranean Sea

SCANDINAVIA
North Sea
Baltic Sea

Kiev
Black Sea
Constantinople
BYZANTINE EMPIRE

ASIA
Aral Sea
Caspian Sea

0   250   500 mi.
0   250   500 km
Lambert Conic Conformal Projection

Map Study

Foreign invasions were a constant threat in western Europe at this time.
1. **Region** What effects did the invasions have on the Carolingian kingdoms?
2. **Human/Environment Interaction** What characteristic of the Vikings allowed no one in Europe to be safe from their attacks?

A New Europe

The people of western Europe suffered at the hands of Vikings and other invaders. These raids isolated communities and severely weakened the central authority of monarchs. Trade declined, and many areas faced economic collapse. As a result of royal weakness, nobles and local officials took over the local defense. Beginning in the A.D. 900s, a new political and social system brought more stability to western Europe.

SECTION 1 ASSESSMENT

Main Idea
1. Use a chart like the one below to identify reasons why Frankish rulers were exceptional for their time.

What Made Frankish Rulers Exceptional?
1.
2.

Recall
2. **Define** mayor of the palace, count.
3. **Identify** Clovis, Charles Martel, Pepin the Short, Charlemagne, Treaty of Verdun, the Vikings.

Critical Thinking
4. **Making Comparisons** How did Charlemagne work to

achieve European unity? How are European leaders trying to achieve the same goal in Europe today?

Understanding Themes
5. **Movement** Why did the Vikings, the Magyars, and the Slavs leave their homelands and invade western Europe?

Chapter 12 Section 1

Map Study

Answers
1. *They nearly destroyed them.*
2. *They attacked by surprise and retreated swiftly.*

Map Skills Practice

Reading a Map Name five European seas across or to which the Vikings traveled. (*Baltic, North, Mediterranean, Black, and Caspian*)

Evaluate

Section Quiz 12-1

Use the Testmaker to create a customized quiz for Section 1.

Reteach

Ask students to explain how each of the following influenced the early Middle Ages: Germanic invasions, the donation of papal states by Pepin to the pope, Charlemagne's dedication to education, the Viking raids.

Reading Essentials and Study Guide 12-1

Enrich

Have students sketch a Viking ship setting out on a raid.

CLOSE

Discuss the term "Middle Ages." What were the Middle Ages in the middle of? (*a dark age and the Renaissance*) Did people living at the time think of the era as the "middle"? (*no*)

A.D. 700   A.D. 900   A.D. 1100

c. A.D. 750 Charles Martel grants warriors landed estates with peasants.

c. A.D. 900 Feudalism takes hold in northern France.

c. A.D. 1000 Peasants begin to use three-field system in farming.

SECTION THEME

▶ **Cooperation** Nobles, church officials, and peasants develop ties of loyalty and service to one another.

Guide to Reading

For reading strategies to help students read effectively see pages 12–13.

Vocabulary Pre-check

🔲 Use the Vocabulary PuzzleMaker for Chapter 12 to create a crossword puzzle to reinforce section terms. **L1 LEP**

 Use Vocabulary Activity 12 to introduce vocabulary terms. **L1 LEP**

FOCUS

Section Objective

Describe how loyalties were maintained in a divided and often violent Europe.

BELLRINGER
Motivational Activity

Before taking roll at the beginning of the class period, project Section Focus Transparency 12-2 and have students answer the activity questions. Discuss students' responses.
This activity is also available as a blackline master.

Section 2

Medieval Life

Guide to Reading

Read to Find Out
Main Idea *Loyalties were maintained even in a divided and often violent Europe.*

▶ **Terms to Define**
  feudalism, fief, vassal, homage, tournament, chivalry, manorialism, serf

▶ **People to Meet**
  knights, lords, ladies, peasants

The Storyteller

Medieval law laid down rules for marriage. When a young woman arrived at marriageable age, one of her brothers or male relatives had to find her a suitable husband. If he did not, she could register a complaint, and her relative could be called to the king's court and given a year and a day to find her one. The husband had to be suited to her social status and property. If the relative did not do this, the king would step in and assign the woman a part of the family inheritance. Then she could marry whomever she wished.

—from *Women's Lives in Medieval Europe, A Sourcebook*, edited by Emile Amt, 1993

Medieval tournament

---

ith the weakening of central government, a new political system known as **feudalism** developed in western Europe. Feudalism was a highly decentralized form of government that stressed alliances of mutual protection between monarchs and nobles of varying degrees of power. The system was based on giving land to nobles in exchange for loyalty and military aid. With the land came peasants to farm it and many powers usually reserved for governments. Feudalism took hold in northern France around A.D. 900 and spread through the rest of western Europe by the A.D. mid-1000s.

Feudal Relationships

The tie between military service and land ownership that characterized feudalism began in the A.D. 700s. At that time, Charles Martel was fighting the Muslims. Unlike the Europeans, the Muslim soldiers used saddles with stirrups that enabled them to fight on horseback, using a sword or lance. Charles wanted to adopt the stirrup and develop a cavalry. However, the cost of keeping such a force required a new type of military system. To support the cavalry, Martel began granting warriors **fiefs**, or estates with peasants. From these fiefs, warriors got the income to buy horses and battle equipment.

Frankish kings later enlarged this system by giving fiefs to counts and local officials. In time, such nobles assumed many of the powers usually held by government: raising armies, dispensing justice, and in some cases even minting coins. In return, the nobles swore an oath of loyalty and pledged military support to the king.

By the A.D. 900s, such arrangements among nobles and monarchs emerged as feudalism. Lords who had been granted fiefs were allowed to pass their lands on to their heirs. In return, these nobles were to provide **knights**, or mounted warriors, for the royal army.

SECTION RESOURCES

📁 Reproducible Masters
- Lecture Notes 12-2
- Reproducible Lesson Plan 12-2
- Guided Reading Activity 12-2
- Source Reading 12
- History Simulation 12
- Section Quiz 12-2
- Reading Essentials and Study Guide 12-2

📊 Transparencies
- Section Focus Transparency 12-2

Multimedia
- 📖 The Middle Ages
- 🔲 Vocabulary PuzzleMaker Software
- 🔲 Interactive Tutor Self-Assessment Software
- 🔲 Testmaker
- ⏺ The Middle Ages

In theory, feudal relationships were like a pyramid. The king was at the top. In the middle were various ranks of lords. Each lord was a vassal—a noble who served a lord of the next higher rank. At the bottom were the knights. In practice, however, a noble might be both a lord and a vassal, since a noble could pledge his allegiance to more than one lord. In fact, one German warrior, Siboto of Falkenstein, was vassal to 20 different lords. Of course, conflicts of loyalty arose if one of a vassal's lords went to war with another.

Feudal Obligations

Ties between a lord and a vassal were made official in a solemn ceremony known as homage. In return for a fief, the vassal pledged to perform certain duties. The most important obligation was military service. The vassal agreed to provide his lord with a certain number of knights for battle during a period of 40 to 60 days each year. In addition, the vassal agreed to serve in the lord's court, to provide food and lodging when the lord came visiting, and to contribute funds when the lord's son became a knight or when his oldest daughter married. Vassals also pledged to pay ransom in the event of the lord's capture in battle.

Castles for Defense

Because of the lack of a strong central government, warfare occurred frequently in feudal society. As a result, every noble built a castle, or fortified manor house, for defense against enemies. The first castles were wooden buildings with high fences of logs or mounds of hard-packed earth around them. By the A.D. 1100s castles were built of stone, with thick walls and turrets, or small towers. Each castle was built on a hill or mound surrounded by a deep moat. Castles had a square tower called a keep. The keep, located in the strongest part of the castle, contained many rooms, a hall, and a dungeon. Surrounding the keep was a large open area called a bailey. Within the bailey were various buildings, including barracks, storerooms, workshops, and a chapel.

Life of the Nobility

Lords, ladies, and knights made up the nobility of the Middle Ages. Although the nobles lived much easier lives than the peasants who worked for them, their lives can hardly be called luxurious or glamorous. Castles were built for security, not comfort, and were largely cold, dingy, and damp places.

Within his fief, a **lord**, or nobleman, had almost total authority. He collected rents in goods from

 An illustration from the *Trés Riches Heures du Duc de Berry* shows peasants at work outside a castle. *Why did feudal lords need castles?*

peasants and settled disputes between his vassals. Any outside attempt to seize the land or control the inhabitants of his fief was met with violent resistance.

In contrast, a **lady**, or noblewoman, had few, if any, rights. A noblewoman could be wed as early as her twelfth birthday to a man her father selected. Her primary duties lay in bringing up children and taking care of the household. Noblewomen took pride in their needlework, turning out cloth and fine embroidery. They also learned to make effective medicines from plants and herbs. Some women shared the supervision of the estate with the lord and took over their husband's duties while the men were away at war.

Entertainment

Nobles looked forward to tournaments—mock battles between knights—as a show of military

---

TEACH

Guided Practice

THEME Cooperation
Review with students the political situation in Europe after the invasions that ended Frankish rule. *(no central authority; danger from marauding bands of thieves and murderers)* Why would cooperation be important at such a time? *(Individuals could not defend themselves on their own; they needed the strength of others to withstand attack.)* **L1 LEP**

Visualizing History
One of the most famous works of the Middle Ages, the *Trés Riches Heures du Duc de Berry* (Very Rich Hours of the Duke of Berry) is a book of hours, or devotional prayer book, illustrated by the Limbourg Brothers. It includes a beautiful painting for each of the twelve months of the year.
Answer to Caption: *They needed them because warfare was frequent, and, being fortified, castles provided defense against enemies.*

NATIONAL GEOGRAPHIC SOCIETY

Use these materials to enrich student understanding of the Middle Ages.

- **NGS PICTURESHOW CD-ROM**
  The Middle Ages
- **NGS POSTER SET**
  The Middle Ages

COOPERATIVE LEARNING ACTIVITY

Building Castles Have the class work in small groups to create plans for a medieval castle like those described in the text. Refer to David Macaulay's book *Castle* and the videocassette that accompanies it. Tasks may be divided in several ways: researching medieval architecture, organizing data, writing plans, and illustrating the finished design by blueprint and sketch on poster board. Special attention should be paid to the outer wall, the turrets, surrounding fields, the drawbridge, the keep and well, the chapel, and the great hall. **L1 LEP**

NATIONAL GEOGRAPHIC PICTURING HISTORY

PICTURING
HISTORY

TEACH

Tell students that the center of castle activity was the great hall, which changed greatly during the castle-building period. Though initially drafty, smoky, and dark, it gradually became more comfortable with tapestries on the walls and balconies for musicians. Ask students which part of the castle they think was the most important. *(Answers will vary. Without walls and a moat, a castle could be stormed. But without a well, livestock, and gardens, the inhabitants would starve during a siege.)*

CURRICULUM CONNECTION

LITERATURE

One of Europe's best-preserved castles is the Castle of Chillon, built in Switzerland on an island in Lake Geneva. A famous poem by Lord Byron, published in 1816, tells the story of "The Prisoner of Chillon," who was imprisoned in the castle for so long that he lost his desire for freedom.

Cultural Perspectives

Castles Medieval castles had their origins in the early Byzantine Empire. Byzantine general Belisarius constructed square forts with tall corner towers during his North African campaigns. Muslim conquerors of North Africa copied the idea and built similar structures in Spain. Castles spread from there to France during the tenth century, where they were first used as private fortresses.

1–Moat; 2–Drawbridge; 3–Guardroom; 4–Latrine; 5–Armory; 6–Soldiers' quarters; 7–Kitchen garden;
8–Storerooms and servants' quarters; 9–Kitchen; 10–Great hall; 11–Chapel; 12–Lord and lady's quarters; 13–Inner ward

Life in the Castle

The medieval castle was both fortress and home. The first castles, raised in the A.D. 900s, were square towers encircled by wooden ramparts. By the A.D. 1100s, castles had become mighty stone fortresses. From the towers and walls archers took aim and soldiers dumped boiling liquids on attackers. The castle was surrounded by a moat—a body of water encircling the castle—that could be crossed when a drawbridge was let down.

Inside it was crowded, smelly, dirty, and d_. The animals ate and slept with the people, an_ smell of animal and human waste was everyw_. The occupants of the castle had to contend with earthen or stone floors, drafty halls, smoky ro_ and windows without glass that let in cold and along with light. Not even the lord and lady had own private room. Grand but never comfortable castle's main purpose was military security. ⊕

300 Chapter 12 *The Rise of Medieval Europe*

skills. They also loved to hunt, and both men and women learned the art of falconry and archery. A dinner featuring several dishes of game and fish and entertainment by minstrels, or singers, might follow.

Becoming a Knight

A nobleman's son began training for knighthood at age 7. Beginning as a page, or assistant, in the house of a lord, he learned manners and the use of weapons. At 15, the page became a squire who assisted a knight and practiced using weapons. Once he proved himself in battle, the squire was knighted in an elaborate ceremony.

The behavior of knights was governed by a code of chivalry. This code called for knights to be brave in battle, fight fairly, keep promises, defend the Church, and treat women of noble birth in a courteous manner. Chivalry eventually became the basis of good manners in Western society.

The Manorial System

The wealth of a feudal lord came from the labor of the **peasants** who lived on and worked his land. Since the Roman Empire's end, many peasants had worked for large landowners, in part because they could not afford their own land and in part for protection. By the Middle Ages, European economic life centered around a system of agricultural production called manorialism. It provided lords and peasants with food, shelter, and protection.

Manors, or estates, varied in size from several hundred to several hundred thousand acres. Each included the lord's house, pastures for livestock, fields for crops, forest areas, and a peasant village. While feudalism describes the political relationships between nobles, manorialism concerns economic ties between nobles and peasants.

Visualizing History An English suit of armor made of steel, brass, and leather. *What knightly code became the basis of good manners in Western society?*

Work on a Manor

In return for protection, the peasants provided various services for the lord. Chief among these were farming the lord's land and making various payments of goods. For example, each time a peasant ground grain at the lord's mill, he was obligated to leave a portion for the lord. Peasants were also obligated to set aside a number of days each year to provide labor such as road or bridge repair.

Warfare and invasions made trade almost impossible, so the manor had to produce nearly everything its residents needed. Most of the peasants farmed or herded sheep. A few worked as skilled artisans, for each manor needed a blacksmith to make tools, a carpenter for building, a

Student Web Activity 12

Visit the *World History: The Human Experience* Web site at **worldhistory.glencoe.com** and click on *Chapter 12—Student Web Activities* for an activity relating to medieval knights.

Chapter 12 *The Rise of Medieval Europe* **301**

Visualizing History Early medieval armor, called chain mail, consisted of small metal rings linked closely together. With the development of more deadly weaponry—crossbows, maces, and axes—heavier protection was needed. By the 1300s, most knights wore plate armor.
Answer to Caption: *chivalry*

The following videotape program is available from Glencoe:
- **Lost Castles of England**
- **Knights and Armor**

To find classroom resources to accompany these videos, check the following home page:
A&E Television:
http://www.aetv.com

Independent Practice

 Guided Reading Activity 12-2 **L1**

 Source Reading 12

History Simulation 12

Women in History Have students research the roles of medieval women from different classes, compare them with those of women today, and write reports on what they find. **L3**

— **WORLD HISTORY Online** —

Have students use the **Chapter 12 Student Web Activity** at worldhistory.glencoe.com for in-depth study of medieval knights.

MEETING SPECIAL NEEDS ACTIVITY

Learning Style: Verbal/Linguistic Some students may have difficulty differentiating between feudalism, a political system, and manorialism, an economic system. Have students write on the chalkboard the headings *Political* and *Economic*. Then introduce various activities and ask students to place them in the appropriate column. Activities might include voting, shopping, baby-sitting, eating a restaurant meal, depositing a check, and writing a letter to the editor of the local paper.
L1

Who?What?Where?When?

Fairs served as centers of trade in medieval Europe, attracting merchants from all over the continent. There were four major fair seasons per year: one in the winter, one at Easter, one in midsummer, and one in October.

ASSESS

Check for Understanding

Assign Section 2 Assessment as homework or as an in-class activity.

 Use Interactive Tutor Self-Assessment Software to review Section 2.

Evaluate

Section Quiz 12-2

Use the Testmaker to create a customized quiz for Section 2.

Reteach

Have students review the political workings of feudalism.

Reading Essentials and Study Guide 12-2

Enrich

Have students read and report on one of the Arthurian legends.

CLOSE

Have students summarize the main advantages and disadvantages of the manorial system.

---

shoemaker, a miller to grind grain, a vintner to make wine, and a brewer to make beer. Peasant women made candles, sheared sheep, spun wool, and sewed clothing.

Peasants rarely left the manor. Most were **serfs**, people who were bound to the manor and could not leave it without permission. But the serfs were not slaves—they could not be "sold" off of the land they lived on.

Increased Production

The manorial system normally produced only enough food to support the peasants and the lord's household. However, a number of improvements gradually boosted productivity and eased the threat of famine.

The first improvement was the development of a new, heavier type of plow. The new plow made deeper cuts in the ground and had a device called a mould-board that pushed the soil sideways. The heavier plow meant less time in the fields for peasant farmers. As a result, farmers developed a better method of planting.

Instead of dividing plots of land into two fields, one of which lay fallow, or unsown, each year, farmers in the A.D. 1000s began to use a three-field system. One field might be planted with winter wheat, a second with spring wheat and vegetables, and a third left fallow. The next year, different crops were planted in the fallow field. One of the two remaining fields was planted, and the other one was left fallow. This system produced more crops than the old system and helped to preserve the soil.

Peasant Life

Poverty and hardship characterized peasant life, and few serfs lived beyond the age of 40. Famine and disease were constant dangers. In times of war, the peasants were the first and hardest hit.

Invading knights trampled crops and burned villages, causing famine and loss of life. To support the war, their lord might require additional payments of crops or labor. A monk of Canterbury described an English serf's account of his day:

> ❝ I work very hard. I go out at dawn, driving the oxen to the field, and I yoke them to the plough; however hard the winter I dare not stay home for fear of my master; but, having yoked the oxen and made the ploughshare and coulter fast to the plough, every day I have to plough a whole acre or more. ❞
>
> —Aelfric, *Colloquy*, A.D. 1005

Serfs like this man lived in tiny, one-room houses with dirt floors, no chimney, and one or two crude pieces of furniture. People slept huddled together for warmth. Coarse bread, a few vegetables from their gardens, and grain for porridge made up their usual diet. Meat was a rarity.

In spite of hardships, peasants were able to relax on Sundays and holy days. They enjoyed dancing, singing, and sports such as wrestling and archery. In addition, there were religious plays, pageants, and shows by minstrels.

Despite the obvious differences between serfs and nobles, the two groups did share a common interest in the land. Medieval Europeans believed that every person was equal in the "eyes of God." In practice, however, society was viewed as a hierarchy with ranked leaders. Each person—no matter what his or her place might be in the hierarchy—had certain duties that were attached to his or her position in life. In general, people did not question their standing or obligations. Although the manorial system seemed to lack freedom and opportunity for most of the people involved in it, it did create a stable and secure way of life during a time that was generally violent and uncertain.

SECTION 2 ASSESSMENT

Main Idea
1. Use a diagram like the one below to show the system of loyalties created under feudalism.

System of Loyalties

↑ ↓

↑ ↓

Recall
2. **Define** feudalism, fief, vassal, homage, tournament, chivalry, manorialism, serf.
3. **Identify** knight, lord, lady, peasant.

Critical Thinking
4. **Making Comparisons** Compare and contrast the feudal class structure in medieval Europe with the *varna* system in early India discussed in Chapter 8.

Understanding Themes
5. **Cooperation** Diagram the ways nobles, knights, and peasants cooperated during the medieval period.

SECTION 2 ASSESSMENT ANSWERS

1. kings gave land to nobles; nobles promised loyalty and military aid to kings; knights were provided by nobles for army
2. All terms are defined in the Glossary.
3. knight, 298; lord, 299; lady, 299; peasant, 301
4. Both systems clearly defined a person's place in society and attached certain duties to that position. The *varna* system, however, was based more on occupation, feudalism on political relationships.
5. **COOPERATION** Diagrams should emphasize interdependency while illustrating the various rights, responsibilities, levels, and relationships that characterized medieval life.

A.D. 500

A.D. 529 Benedict introduces rule for monasteries.

c. A.D. 650 Irish missionaries win converts in western Europe.

A.D. 900

A.D. 1073 The monk Hildebrand becomes Pope Gregory VII.

A.D. 1300

A.D. 1232 The Inquisition begins.

Section 3

The Medieval Church

Read to Find Out
Main Idea *The Catholic Church shaped the development of medieval Europe.*

▶ **Terms to Define**
sacrament, abbot, abbess, cardinal, lay investiture, heresy, excommunication, friar

▶ **People to Meet**
Benedict, Gregory I, Gregory VII, Innocent III, Francis of Assisi, Dominic

▶ **Places to Locate**
Monte Cassino, Cluny

The Storyteller

Alcuin, a Benedictine monk, arose to begin his day. The day's work in a monastery depended on sunlight hours, for candles were expensive and no one in medieval times had access to cheap artificial light. Because it was winter, Alcuin had to get up at 2:30 A.M., and go to bed at 6:30 P.M.
after sunset. Sometimes he was already tired by noon! His workday included reading, choir practice, bookbinding, sewing, gardening, and worship services—which were the only times during the day that he was permitted to break his vow of silence and speak.

—from *Monastic Life in Medieval England,* J.C. Dickinson, 1962

Ancient monastery in Glendalough, Ireland

*D*uring the Middle Ages, the Catholic Church was the dominant spiritual influence in western Europe. For most people, the Church was the center of their lives. A small number of Europeans, however, were Jews, Muslims, or non-Catholic Christians.

The Medieval Church

Although the Church's primary mission was spiritual, the decline of Rome in the A.D. 400s led the Church to assume many political and social tasks. During this time, the bishop of Rome, now called the pope, became the strongest political leader in western Europe. The pope claimed spiritual authority over all Christians, basing this claim on the belief that Peter the Apostle, Rome's first bishop, had been chosen by Jesus to lead the Church.

Religious Role

The Catholic Church taught that all people were sinners and dependent on God's grace, or favor. The only way to receive grace was by taking part in the sacraments, or church rituals: baptism, penance, eucharist, confirmation, matrimony, anointing of the sick, and holy orders. One of the most important sacraments was the eucharist, or holy communion, which commemorated Christ's death. People shared in the eucharist at a mass, or worship service. At each mass, the priest blessed wheat wafers and a cup of wine that stood on an altar. According to Catholic teaching, the priests and the worshippers received Jesus' invisible presence in the forms of the bread and the wine.

During the Middle Ages, people generally had a limited understanding of church rituals. Masses were said in Latin, a language few people understood. Also, many priests were poorly educated

Chapter 12 The Rise of Medieval Europe **303**

SECTION THEME

▶ **Uniformity** The Catholic Church affects every aspect of medieval life.

Guide to Reading

For reading strategies to help students read effectively see pages 12–13.

Vocabulary Pre-check

Use the Vocabulary PuzzleMaker for Chapter 12 to create a crossword puzzle to reinforce section terms. **L1 LEP**

Use Vocabulary Activity 12 to introduce vocabulary terms. **L1 LEP**

FOCUS

Section Objective
Summarize the role of the Catholic Church in shaping the development of medieval Europe.

BELLRINGER Motivational Activity

Before taking roll at the beginning of the class period, project Section Focus Transparency 12-3 and have students answer the activity questions. Discuss students' responses.
This activity is also available as a blackline master.

SECTION RESOURCES

Reproducible Masters
• Lecture Notes 12-3
• Reproducible Lesson Plan 12-3
• Guided Reading Activity 12-3
• People in World History Profiles 21, 22
• World Art and Music Activity 12
• Section Quiz 12-3
• Reading Essentials and Study Guide 12-3

Transparencies
• Section Focus Transparency 12-3
• World History and Art Transparency 15
• The Middle Ages

Multimedia
• Vocabulary PuzzleMaker Software
• Interactive Tutor Self-Assessment Software
• Testmaker
• The Middle Ages

TEACH

Guided Practice

The goal of the medieval Church was to unify western Europe in accordance with the teachings and beliefs of Christianity. Does the Catholic Church play the same role today in the Western world? (*No, because it is not the only Christian church, and there are other non-Christian religions as well.*) What factors tend to create uniformity in the United States today? (*Answers will vary but might include: the English language, our government under the Constitution, and the mass media.*) **L2**

 World History and Art Transparency 15, *Cover of the Lindau Gospels*

Global Gourmet

Southern Europe The knot-shaped pretzels that we enjoy today were the creation of medieval monks, given as rewards to children for memorizing their prayers. (The Latin word *pretiola* means "small reward.") The shape represented the folded arms of children at prayer.

NATIONAL GEOGRAPHIC SOCIETY

Use these materials to enrich student understanding of the culture of the Middle Ages.

- **NGS PICTURESHOW CD-ROM**
  The Middle Ages
- **NGS PICTUREPACK TRANSPARENCY SET**
  The Middle Ages

---

and did not preach effectively. Moreover, few worshippers could read or write. What the average person learned about the Christian faith came from the statues, paintings, and later the stained glass windows that adorned most medieval churches.

Church Organization

The church hierarchy, which was described in Chapter 6, remained largely the same during the Middle Ages. The contact most people had with the Church was through parish priests, who conducted services and oversaw the spiritual life of the community. Occasionally bishops visited a parish to supervise the priests.

The pope, bishops, and priests formed what is called the secular clergy because they lived *in saeculo*, a Latin phrase that means "in the world." Other clergy, known as regular clergy, lived by a *regula*, or rule. Regular clergy included monks and nuns who lived apart from society. These Christians played an important role in strengthening the medieval Church.

Benedict's Rule

In A.D. 529 a Roman official named **Benedict** founded a monastery at **Monte Cassino** in Italy. His monastery became a model for monks in other communities. Benedict drew up a list of rules that provided for manual work, meditation, and prayer. According to the Benedictine rule, monks could not own goods, must never marry, and were bound to obey monastic laws. Their life was one of poverty, chastity, and obedience to the directives of an abbot, or monastery head.

Monastic Life

Monks dressed in simple, long robes made of coarse material and tied at the waist by a cord. They ate one or two plain meals each day. Most monasteries had a rule of silence; monks could not converse with one another except for a short time each day. In some monasteries total silence was the rule. During meals, one monk might read passages from

---

Images of the Times

Monastic Life

Although monasteries were closed religious communities, they profoundly influenced European culture during the Middle Ages.

An illustrated page from a book copied by monks shows the careful, artistic writing that became the manuscript before printing was developed.

St. Benedict and his monks, like all those who lived at the monasteries, ate together in a refectory.

Mont St. Michel presents a view of the beautiful old monastery's lower ramparts.

304

Images of the Times

Monastic Life

According to St. Benedict's *Rule for Monasteries*, all monks took a vow of obedience to their abbot. This was intended to help them develop humility. Abbots, in turn, were responsible for the care of the souls of all the men in their monastery. It was their job to set a good example, to teach, coax, and admonish the monks so as to best ensure their spiritual development.

St. Benedict did much to foster the important social role monasteries were to play during the Middle Ages. "Let all guests who arrive be received like Christ ...," he wrote. "In the reception of the poor and of pilgrims the greatest care and solicitude should be shown."

the Bible while the others meditated.

Women took part in monastic life by living in a convent under the direction of an abbess. Known as nuns, they wore simple clothes and wrapped a white cloth called a wimple around their face and neck. They alternated prayer with spinning, weaving, and embroidering items such as tapestries and banners. They also taught needlework and the medicinal use of herbs to the daughters of nobles.

Influence of Monastics

Although monks and nuns lived apart from society, they were not completely isolated. Indeed, they played a crucial role in medieval intellectual and social life. Since few people could read or write, the regular clergy preserved ancient religious works and the classical writings. Scribes laboriously copied books by hand, working in a small drafty room with only a candle or small window for light. Illuminated manuscripts decorated with rich colors and intricate pictures indicate that, although the task was tedious, it was lovingly done.

Monasteries and convents provided schools for young people, hospitals for the sick, food for the needy, and guest houses for weary travelers. They taught peasants carpentry and weaving and made improvements in agriculture that they passed on to others. Some monks and nuns became missionaries who spread Christian teachings to non-Christians.

Missionary Efforts

Pope **Gregory I** was so impressed with the Benedictine Rule that he adopted it to spread Christianity in Europe. In A.D. 597 he sent monks to England, where they converted the Anglo-Saxons to Catholicism. From England, missionaries carried Christianity to northern Germany. During the A.D. 600s, monasteries in Ireland sent missionaries throughout the North Atlantic and western Europe. Although the Irish were isolated from the pope in Rome, their missionaries won many converts. By the A.D. mid-1000s, most western Europeans had become Catholics.

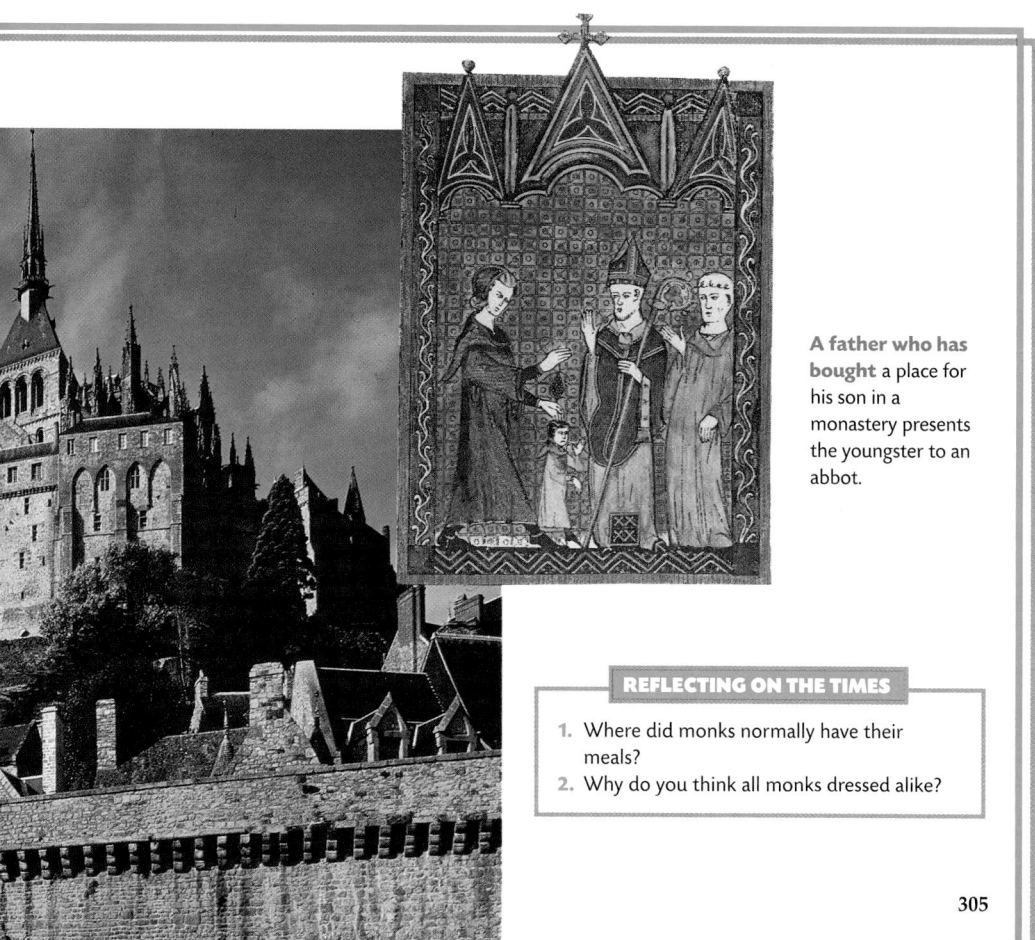

A father who has bought a place for his son in a monastery presents the youngster to an abbot.

REFLECTING ON THE TIMES

1. Where did monks normally have their meals?
2. Why do you think all monks dressed alike?

305

Independent Practice

📁 Guided Reading Activity 12-3 **L1**

Religion Have students speculate on what the various attractions of the monastic life might have been to young medieval men and women. *(Answers may include: opportunity to better serve and worship God; desire to study or to develop the particular skills used in monasteries and convents; for women, a chance to escape a life of childbearing and child rearing.)* Discuss which of these were spiritual in nature and which were worldly. **L3**

The Arts Have students create posters in the style of medieval stained glass to tell a story about people or events they have studied in this section. Possible subjects include Francis of Assisi, missionary efforts in Europe, a church ritual, or the Albigensian crusade. **L2 LEP**

Who?What?Where?When?

Iona The great center of Irish monasticism was the island of Iona, off the western coast of Scotland. From its monastery, founded in the A.D. 500s by St. Columba, missionaries traveled over northern Scotland, converting the Scots to Christianity.

ANSWERS TO REFLECTING ON THE TIMES

1. in a refectory
2. All were equal in the eyes of God.

Linking Past and Present

Electing a Pope The pope today is still elected by a gathering of cardinals, called a "conclave." They meet no later than the twentieth day after the death of a pope and vote by secret ballot until they can achieve a two-thirds majority on a given candidate.

Visualizing History
Relics were an important object of devotion in medieval times. Remains of the bodies or clothes of the saints, or splinters from Jesus' cross or his crown of thorns were housed in special receptacles called reliquaries. Reliquaries were often decorated with jewels and precious metals.
Answer to Caption: *He criticized the practice of lay investiture.*

Power of the Church

The medieval Catholic Church helped to govern western Europe. It had its own laws and courts that dealt with cases related to the clergy, doctrine, and marriage and morals. Disobedience to church laws resulted in severe penalties for a common person and ruler alike. For example, a lord or king who violated Church law could face an interdict, which banned an entire region or country from receiving the sacraments necessary to salvation.

The Church also had feudal ties that boosted its wealth and political power but often undermined its spiritual vitality. Many high church officials were nobles and held land from kings in return for military service. Because their religious duties prevented them from fighting, these church leaders gave some of their land to knights who would fight for them. The Church also received donations of land and money from nobles wanting to ensure their salvation. Nobles, however, began to influence church policies, especially by having relatives appointed to church positions. Many of these appointees had little devotion to their spiritual calling.

Visualizing History
A young boy, having obtained the office of bishop, carries sacred church relics. *How did Pope Gregory try to stop the selection of church officials by secular rulers?*

Church Reform

By the A.D. 900s, many devout Christians were calling for reform. The reform movement began in the monasteries and spread throughout much of western Europe. Most famous was the monastery at **Cluny** in eastern France, whose monks won respect for leading lives of pious simplicity. The abbots of Cluny sent representatives to other monasteries to help them undertake similar reforms.

Other church leaders tried to free the Church from the control of feudal lords. They wanted the Church, not the state, to be the final authority in Western society. In A.D. 1059 a church council declared that political leaders could no longer choose the pope. Instead, the pope would be elected by a gathering of cardinals—high church officials in Rome ranking directly below the pope. In addition, the reformers insisted that the pope, not secular rulers such as lords and kings, should be the one to appoint bishops and other officials to church offices.

In A.D. 1073 the cardinals elected a reform-minded monk named Hildebrand as Pope **Gregory VII**. Gregory believed that the pope should have complete jurisdiction over all church officials. He especially criticized the practice of lay investiture, in which secular rulers gave the symbols of office, such as a ring and a staff, to the bishops they had appointed.

Fighting Heresy

Innocent III, one of the most powerful popes, also tried to reform the Catholic Church. In A.D. 1215 he convened a council that condemned drunkenness, feasting, and dancing among the clergy. The council also laid down strict rules for stopping the spread of heresy, or the denial of basic church teachings. Heresy had increased as corruption and scandal had rocked the Church. In the Middle Ages, heresy was regarded as seriously as the crime of treason is viewed today.

At first, the Catholic Church tried to convert heretics, or those who challenged its teachings. When that failed, however, heretics were threatened with excommunication, or expulsion from the Church. An excommunicated person was not allowed to take part in the sacraments and was also outlawed from any contact with Christian society. Since receiving the sacraments was considered to be essential for salvation, banishment was an especially severe penalty.

Early in the A.D. 1200s, for example, the Church became concerned about a group of heretics in France known as Albigensians (AL•buh•JEHN •shuhnz). The Albigensians believed that the

COOPERATIVE LEARNING ACTIVITY

Role Play Organize the class into three groups. One group will represent missionaries who have been ordered by Pope Gregory I to convert the people of England, and should describe their thoughts and goals as they prepare to leave continental Europe. The second group will represent monks and nuns who teach the young and help the sick and needy, and should explain how their work benefits others. The third group will represent the regular clergy who copy books by hand in order to preserve ancient learning, and should portray the life of a scribe. The members of each group should explain why their work is important, what their goals are, and how their work reflects their Christian beliefs. **L2**

material world was evil and rejected church sacraments. To end this heresy, Pope Innocent III sent French knights to crush the group.

The Inquisition

In order to seek out and punish people suspected of heresy, the Church set up a court in A.D. 1232 known as the Inquisition. Those brought before the court were urged to confess their heresy and to ask forgiveness. Often, however, Inquisition officials accused people without sufficient proof; sometimes they even used torture to obtain confessions. The Church welcomed back those who repented, but those who did not repent were punished. Punishment ranged from imprisonment to loss of property and even execution. According to church officials, these punishments were needed to save the souls of the heretics.

Friars Inspire Reform

Other reformers of the Church during the early A.D. 1200s were friars, or wandering preachers. At a time when church leaders were criticized for their love of wealth and power, the friars depended on gifts of food and shelter to survive.

The friars followed monastic rules but did not isolate themselves from the rest of the Christian community. Instead, they lived in towns and preached Christianity. The best-known friars were the Franciscans and the Dominicans.

Francis of Assisi, the son of a wealthy Italian cloth merchant, founded the Franciscan friars about A.D. 1210. Francis and his followers sought to follow the simple life of Jesus and his disciples. They became known for their cheerful trust in God and their respect for nature as a divine gift.

A Spanish priest named **Dominic** organized the Dominican friars in A.D. 1215. Like the Franciscans, the Dominicans lived a life of poverty, simplicity, and service. In addition, they were well-educated and persuasive preachers.

The Jews

As the Church's power increased in medieval Europe, the position of the Jews worsened. In the early Middle Ages, Jews and Christians had lived peacefully together in most of Europe. Many Jews had become merchants, artisans, or landowners, and their contributions to society were valued by their Christian neighbors.

By the 1000s, however, many Christians increasingly saw the Jews as outsiders and a threat to society. They unfairly blamed the Jews for plagues, famines, and other social problems. Such false accusations gave mobs the excuse to attack and kill thousands of Jews.

The most powerful source of anti-Semitism, or hatred of the Jews, came from interpretations of Christian doctrine. Many church leaders and laity blamed the Jews for Jesus' death and resented the Jews' refusal to become Christians. With church approval, political leaders required Jews in certain areas to wear badges or special clothes that identified them as Jews. Jews were also forced to live in separate communities that became known as ghettos. They also lost the right to own land and to practice certain trades. To earn a living, many Jews became peddlers or money-lenders, jobs despised by medieval Christians.

Beginning in the late 1200s, rulers in England, France, and certain parts of central Europe even expelled their Jewish subjects. Many of the expelled Jews settled in eastern Europe, especially Poland, where they received protection. Over the centuries, the Jews of eastern Europe developed thriving communities based on their religious traditions.

Chapter 12 Section 3

ASSESS

Check for Understanding
Assign Section 3 Assessment as homework or as an in-class activity.

 Use Interactive Tutor Self-Assessment Software to review Section 3.

Evaluate
Section Quiz 12-3

 Use the Testmaker to create a customized quiz for Section 3.

Reteach
Ask students to summarize the contributions that monasteries and convents made to society during the Middle Ages.

Reading Essentials and Study Guide 12-3

Enrich
Have students research the life of St. Francis of Assisi or St. Dominic and present their findings to the class.

CLOSE

Have the class summarize the various elements of church reform mentioned in this section. Discuss which reform would seem to be the most effective and which the least effective.

SECTION 3 ASSESSMENT

Main Idea
1. Use a diagram like the one below to show the reforms made by the Catholic Church that affected the development of medieval Europe.

Reforms → → Development of Medieval Europe

Recall
2. **Define** sacrament, abbot, abbess, cardinal, lay investiture, heresy, excommunication, friar.
3. **Identify** Benedict, Gregory I, Gregory VII, Innocent III, Francis of Assisi, Dominic.

Critical Thinking
4. **Synthesizing Information** Imagine that you are a religious, but superstitious, peasant living during the Middle Ages. Invent an explanation for the famine that has struck your village.

Understanding Themes
5. **Uniformity** How effective were the actions of the Catholic Church in trying to make all western Europeans believe and practice one faith?

SECTION 3 ASSESSMENT ANSWERS

1. pope became strongest political leader in western Europe; heightened focus on sacraments; combating heresy; friars taught living simply and in service to God
2. All terms are defined in the Glossary.
3. Benedict, 304; Gregory I, 305; Gregory VII, 306; Innocent III, 306; Francis of Assisi, 307; Dominic, 307
4. Possible answer: It is a punishment from God because you and/or your neighbors have disobeyed the teachings of the Church.
5. **UNIFORMITY** In terms of maintaining uniformity, the Church's methods—persuasion and force—were largely effective. Small groups of Europeans, however, still refused to submit to church authority and often suffered hardships and persecution.

A.D. 700 — A.D. 871 Alfred the Great begins rule in England.

A.D. 900 — A.D. 955 German King Otto defeats the Magyars at Lechfeld.

A.D. 1100 — A.D. 1180 Philip Augustus becomes king of France.

A.D. 1300 — A.D. 1215 English King John and his barons sign the Magna Carta.

Section 4

Rise of European Monarchy

Guide to Reading

**Read to Find Out
Main Idea** *Medieval European monarchs made great achievements.*

▶ **Terms to Define**
common law, grand jury, petit jury, middle class

▶ **People to Meet**
Alfred the Great, William the Conqueror, Henry II, Thomas à Becket, Eleanor of Aquitaine, Philip Augustus, Henry IV

▶ **Places to Locate**
England, France, Germany

The Storyteller

The English throne was at stake as the Battle of Hastings approached. William decided to provoke Harold to fight in single combat and called on him to spare the blood of his followers. Under Norman law, personal combat decided difficult cases, looking for the judgment of God to settle the matter. Harold refused because he knew the cause was not personal, but national. It would take a full-scale invasion to decide who would wear the English crown.

—adapted from *William the Conqueror*, Edward A. Freeman, 1927

William the Conqueror

After the decline of Rome, central authority in western Europe disappeared. Except for Charlemagne's reign in the late A.D. 700s, kings were rulers in name only, their lands and power gradually lost to nobles. However, in the A.D. 1100s, many European monarchs began to build strong states.

England

After the Romans abandoned Britain in the A.D. 400s, the island was invaded by Germanic Angles, Saxons, and Jutes. These groups took over much of Britain from the native Celts (KEHLTZ) and set up several kingdoms. In the late A.D. 800s, the Danish Vikings from Scandinavia posed another threat. King Alfred of Wessex, known as **Alfred the Great**, united the Anglo-Saxon kingdoms and defeated the Danes in A.D. 886. His united kingdom eventually became known as "Angleland," or **England**.

The Anglo-Saxons

Alfred ruled Anglo-Saxon England from A.D. 871 to A.D. 899. Like Charlemagne, he was interested in the revival of learning. The English king founded schools and hired scholars to translate many books from Latin to Anglo-Saxon. He also had the scholars write a history of England, known as the *Anglo-Saxon Chronicle*.

The kings who followed Alfred were weak rulers. When the last Anglo-Saxon king, Edward the Confessor, died in A.D. 1066, three rivals claimed the throne.

The Norman Conquest

One of the claimants to the throne was William, the Duke of Normandy. A cousin of the late English king and vassal of the French king, William had a feudal stronghold in northwestern France. Gathering a force of several hundred boats and some 6,000 soldiers, he invaded England in A.D. 1066. At the Battle of Hastings, William defeated Harold Godwinson, the king chosen by the Anglo-Saxon nobles. The victory won William the English crown and the name **William the Conqueror**.

As king, William kept tight control over the government. He took Anglo-Saxon lands, kept some of the land for himself, and gave the rest to his Norman vassals in return for military service. He later made all landowners swear direct loyalty to him. William also set up a council of nobles to advise him and named local officials called sheriffs to collect taxes. To determine taxable wealth, William carried out the first census in western Europe since Roman times. Every person, manor, and farm animal became an entry in the *Domesday Book*.

Royal Power

Although William's court and nobles were French-speaking, England's population remained largely Anglo-Saxon. Over the next 300 years, however, Norman French and Anglo-Saxon ways blended to form a new English culture. During this time, William's successors further strengthened the monarchy. Henry I, William's son who ruled from A.D. 1100 to A.D. 1135, created a royal exchequer, or treasury, to collect taxes and gave royal courts greater authority. Henry's grandson, **Henry II**, set up a system of common law, using traveling judges to apply the law equally throughout the land. In each community, the judges met with a grand jury that submitted the names of suspects. A petit jury soon developed to establish the guilt or innocence of the accused.

Henry's plan to try clergy in the royal courts brought him into conflict with **Thomas à Becket**, the archbishop of Canterbury. In A.D. 1170 four of Henry's knights, who believed they were acting on the king's command, murdered Becket in his cathedral.

At the height of his power, Henry ruled western France as well as England. His wife, **Eleanor of Aquitaine**, once married to the French king, owned vast lands in southwestern France. Although Henry's relations with Eleanor soured, Eleanor continued to influence royal policies through their sons, Richard I (the Lionhearted) and John.

TEACH

Guided Practice

THEME Conflict

Discuss the word *conflict* as it applies to England in this section. What specific conflicts are mentioned in the text? *(military conflicts between the Anglo-Saxons and the Danes and between the English and the Normans; political conflicts between the monarchy and the Church and between the monarchy and the nobility)* **L1 LEP**

The following videotape is available from Glencoe:
- **Robin Hood: Outlaw of the Forest**

Linking Past and Present

Tapestries

The Bayeux Tapestry is named after the Norman town where, for many years, it was displayed annually in the cathedral. It is now preserved in the Bayeux Museum.

ANSWER

Students might identify themes based on religious, mythical, or historical events as well as point out any significant abstract renditions. They might also note the differences between the kinds of tapestries displayed in homes and those found in churches or other public buildings. Materials used in tapestries might be analyzed in terms of whether they are natural or synthetic.

The Arts

Tapestries

Bayeux Tapestry (detail)

The Bayeux Tapestry, made between A.D. 1073 and A.D. 1083, is a remarkable example of medieval art. It is a work of embroidery, a band of linen upon which pictures and patterns are stitched in colored wool. Twenty inches high and 230 feet long, it probably once decorated the walls of an entire room.

The 72 scenes on the tapestry illustrate William the Conqueror's invasion of England in A.D. 1066. Probably the work of William's wife, Matilda, and the ladies of her court, the tapestry tells the story of the invasion in a series of individual scenes, much as a story is told in a comic book today. The images are lively and simple and give a sense of movement and vitality. The tapestry even includes words to reveal what is happening in each scene.

The popularity of tapestries among the European nobility continued into the A.D. 800s and then declined. However, since World War II, interest in this art form has revived. Artists today experiment with materials and weaving to create many new kinds of wall tapestry. One of the most famous modern tapestries, "Christ in Glory," was done in 1962 by the English artist Graham Sutherland and hangs above the high altar in England's new Coventry Cathedral.

Linking Past and Present ACTIVITY

Visit an art museum in your community that has medieval and modern tapestries. Compare and contrast the tapestries of both time periods in terms of their themes, techniques, and the materials used to make them.

Chapter 12 *The Rise of Medieval Europe* **309**

COOPERATIVE LEARNING ACTIVITY

Pictorial Record Have students choose a historical event presented in this chapter and plan the presentation of a pictorial record. Organize the class into three groups. One group should determine the style and nature of the record and how it will be produced, choose particular scenes to present, and make recommendations during its execution. A second group should be responsible for the actual production. The third group should create a narrative to accompany the record. Have students select one person from each group to work together on a class presentation when the record is finished. **L2 LEP**

Map Study

Answers

1. *Holy Roman Empire*
2. *Kingdom of Poland, Kingdom of Hungary*

Map Skills Practice

Reading a Map What three kingdoms were located in what is now Spain? (*Aragon, Castile, and Navarre*)

Focus on World Art Print 14, French. *William Exhorts His Troops*, from the Bayeux Tapestry

Mapping History Overlay Transparency 9

POINT

The Magna Carta
How did the Magna Carta change the balance of power in government?
It placed clear limits on royal power and bound the king to law. For example, the king could no longer collect taxes without consent of the people's representatives, and it assured all freemen the right of trial by jury.

CURRICULUM CONNECTION

GOVERNMENT

Unlike the United States, the United Kingdom has no single written constitution. Instead, it is governed according to a series of laws and charters. The oldest of them is the Magna Carta.

Europe A.D. 1160

Map Study

In the A.D. 1100s Europe was divided into many separate kingdoms that eventually became nations.
1. **Region** According to the map, what kingdom controlled the most amount of land?
2. **Region** What kingdoms posed the greatest threat to the Holy Roman Empire?

POINT

The Magna Carta

During his reign, John lost some English land to France and became unpopular when he increased taxes and punished his enemies without trial. Alarmed at the loss of their feudal rights, a group of nobles met at Runnymede in A.D. 1215. They forced John to sign the Magna Carta, or Great Charter, one of the most important documents in the history of representative government.

The Magna Carta placed clear limits on royal power. The charter prevented the king from collecting taxes without the consent of the Great Council. It also assured freemen the right of trial by jury. Article 39 stated:

> **No freeman shall be taken, or imprisoned, or disseized [dispossessed], or outlawed, or exiled, or in any way harmed—nor will we go upon or send upon him—save by the lawful judgment of his peers [equals] or by the law of the land.**

The nobles intended the Magna Carta to protect their feudal rights. Over time, however, it guaranteed the rights of all English people.

Rise of Parliament

During the reign of John's son, Henry III, an increase in population encouraged the growth of towns. A new social class—the middle class—was emerging. The middle class did not fit in the medieval social order of nobles, clergy, and peas-

310 Chapter 12 *The Rise of Medieval Europe*

MEETING SPECIAL NEEDS ACTIVITY

Study Strategy Have students make a list of each of the major figures discussed in this section. In a second column, they should write the name of the person or group with which the first figure was in conflict. Then students should make a check mark next to the victor. For instance, Alfred the Great (checked) would be paired with Danes; William of Normandy (checked) with Harold Godwinson; and so on. **L1**

ants. Its income came from business and trade, not from the land. This group played an increasingly important role in government.

Recognizing the towns' growing power, Henry III added knights and burgesses, or important townspeople, to the Great Council that advised the king. By that time the Great Council was called Parliament, the name by which it is still known.

In A.D. 1295 Henry's son, Edward I, called into session the Model Parliament, which included representatives from the clergy, nobility, and burgesses. As England's government became more representative, Edward encouraged members of Parliament to advise him on business matters, submit petitions to him, and meet frequently.

By A.D. 1400 Parliament had divided into two chambers. Nobles and clergy met as the House of Lords, while knights and burgesses met as the House of Commons.

France

Like England, **France** developed a strong monarchy in the Middle Ages. The type of government that emerged in France, however, differed considerably from the increasingly representative government in England.

Beginnings of Central Government

After Charlemagne's death, the Frankish lands disintegrated into separate territories governed by feudal lords. These lords defended their own lands and were virtually independent rulers.

In A.D. 987 a noble named Hugh Capet seized the French throne from the weak Carolingian king. Capet controlled only the city of Paris and a strip of land between the Seine and Loire Rivers in northern France. The Capetian (kuh•PEE•shuhn) dynasty he established, however, lasted for more than three centuries. By the A.D. 1100s Capetian kings had established the principle of the eldest son inheriting the throne. The Capetians strengthened the power of the monarchy and brought French feudal lords under royal control.

As in England, the number of towns in France increased during the A.D. 1100s. Louis VI, who became king in A.D. 1108, used the townspeople to strengthen the royal government at the expense of the nobles. Louis awarded both the townspeople and the clergy positions on his court of advisers and also granted self-government to towns, freeing them from obligations to feudal lords. These measures led local officials to be loyal to the monarch rather than to feudal lords.

Strengthening the Monarchy

Philip II, known as **Philip Augustus**, ruled France from A.D. 1180 to A.D. 1223. Barely 15 when he succeeded to the throne, Philip was determined to strengthen the monarchy. During his 43-year reign Philip doubled the area of his domain, acquiring some territory through marriage and recapturing French land from England. By appointing local officials who were loyal to the king and forming a semipermanent royal army, Philip further weakened the power of feudal lords.

A Saintly Ruler

Philip's grandson became King Louis IX in A.D. 1226. Louis made royal courts dominant over feudal courts and decreed that only the king had the right to mint coins. Bans on private warfare and the bearing of arms further promoted the French monarch.

A very religious man, Louis was regarded as the ideal for his chivalry and high moral character. His advice to his son reveals these characteristics:

> ❝ [Have] a tender pitiful heart for the poor … [and] hold yourself steadfast and loyal toward your subjects and your vassals, without turning either to the right or to the left, but always straight, whatever may happen. And if a poor man have a quarrel with a rich man, sustain the poor rather than the rich, until the truth is made clear, and when you know the truth, do justice to them. ❞

Founding of Cairo

Egypt, A.D. 968
The Fatimids, who claimed to be descendants of Muhammad's daughter Fatima, conquered Egypt around A.D. 968. They founded the city of El Qahira, which means "The Victorious." The name of the city in English is Cairo. The Fatimids made Cairo their capital, and it soon became one of the most important cities in the Arab world. By the late Middle Ages, Cairo had a population of nearly 500,000.

Independent Practice
Guided Reading Activity 12-4 **L1**

News Report Assign students to prepare a TV report on Henry IV's plea before the gates of Gregory VII's castle. Designate a news anchor, reporters, Henry, Gregory, and passersby for on-the-spot interviews. Have students present the report to the class. **L2**

📁 Time Line Activity 12

📁 Mapping History Activity 12

📁 Geography and History Activity 12

Cultural Perspectives
Language For years after the Norman Conquest, two languages were spoken in England—Norman French by the upper classes and Anglo-Saxon English by the lower classes. This double heritage is preserved in the English language today. The words for animals in the field (in the Middle Ages, tended by the lower classes) are Anglo-Saxon: *ox, pig,* and *sheep.* The words for cooked meat (served to the upper classes) are French: *beef, pork,* and *mutton.*

MAKING CONNECTIONS ACTIVITIES

Religion The tomb of Thomas à Becket became a popular destination for pilgrims soon after Becket's murder. (It was the goal of the pilgrims in Chaucer's *The Canterbury Tales*.) Have students research other medieval pilgrimage sites that are still popular today, notably Rome, Italy, and Santiago de Compostela, Spain. Students should report on the nature of the pilgrimages in the Middle Ages, comparing them with journeys made today. **L2**

Government Hold a mock debate between representatives of the English monarchy and the Church of Rome. Organize the class into three groups. Have one group prepare arguments defending the position of the monarchy and another group defend the position of the Church. These two groups should make use of outside sources as well as information in the text. The third group should hear the arguments by both sides, determine the most persuasive position, and write a statement defending its decision. **L3**

ASSESS

Check for Understanding

Assign Section 4 Assessment as homework or as an in-class activity.

 Use Interactive Tutor Self-Assessment Software to review Section 4.

Evaluate

 Section Quiz 12-4

 Use the Testmaker to create a customized quiz for Section 4.

Reteach

Have students review the major theme of this section, conflict, as it applies to England, France, and the Holy Roman Empire.

 Reteaching Activity 12

 Reading Essentials and Study Guide 12-4

Enrich

Have students read and discuss T. S. Eliot's *Murder in the Cathedral*, a play about the martyrdom of Thomas à Becket.

 Enrichment Activity 12

CLOSE

Have students review the time lines for the four sections of Chapter 12 and discuss which one of the highlighted events on each time line was most important.

Signs of a Strong Monarchy

Louis IX's grandson, Philip IV, was so handsome he was nicknamed Philip the Fair. The blond, blue-eyed Philip increased France's territory and trade by defeating both England and Flanders in war. To pay for the wars, he raised taxes and taxed new groups, such as the clergy. Although Pope Boniface VIII opposed taxing the clergy, he could not force Philip to back down.

Before he died in A.D. 1314, Philip summoned the Estates-General, an assembly of nobles, clergy, and townspeople. He wanted to use the assembly to raise taxes on a national level rather than locally. The assembly, however, never became as powerful as Parliament in England.

The Holy Roman Empire

While monarchs in England and France were building strong central governments, rulers in **Germany** remained weak and often powerless. Among the major reasons were their disputes with the pope and with powerful German nobles.

"Emperor of the Romans"

During the A.D. 1000s and A.D. 1100s, German kings posed the biggest threat to the pope's authority. King Otto I, or Otto the Great, of Germany tried to restore Charlemagne's empire. After defeating the Magyars at the Battle of Lechfeld in A.D. 955, King Otto set his sights on Italy. In A.D. 962 Pope John XII sought Otto's help against Roman nobles who opposed the pope. In return for the help, the pope crowned Otto Holy Roman emperor.

Problems of the Holy Roman Empire

Otto and his successors claimed the right to intervene in the election of popes, and Otto himself appointed and deposed several popes. The pope, as you have read, claimed the right to anoint and depose kings. These two conflicting claims led to centuries of dispute between the Holy Roman emperors and the Roman Catholic popes.

Powerful German lords also prevented the Holy Roman emperors from building a strong, unified state. Numerous wars with the Slavic states—Poland and Bohemia—and with Hungary also weakened the Holy Roman emperor's power.

Emperor and Pope Collide

During the rule of **Henry IV**, a major quarrel broke out with Pope Gregory VII. In A.D. 1073 the pope condemned lay investiture, hoping to free the Church from secular control. Since the bishops supported Henry in his struggle with feudal lords, the emperor refused to halt the practice.

The pope promptly proclaimed Henry deposed and urged the German nobles to elect another ruler. Henry gave in. In A.D. 1077 he made his way southward in bitter January weather across the snowy mountains to Canossa, Italy. There he sought forgiveness from the pope. He showed his repentance by standing before the gate of the castle begging for mercy for three days.

Gregory pardoned Henry, but the struggle between the Holy Roman emperor and the pope resumed later. Finally, in A.D. 1122, church officials and representatives of the Holy Roman emperor reached a compromise at the German city of Worms. This agreement, known as the Concordat of Worms, allowed the emperor to name bishops and grant them land. It also gave the pope the right to reject unworthy candidates.

Popes and monarchs would continue to struggle over power and territory in the coming years. The increasing strength of Europe's monarchies not only threatened the authority of the Church, but it also paved the way for other changes on the European scene.

SECTION 4 ASSESSMENT

Main Idea

1. Use a chart like the one below to identify key achievements of four major medieval monarchs in England and France.

Monarch/Country	Achievements
1.	
2.	
3.	
4.	

Recall

2. **Define** common law, grand jury, petit jury, middle class.
3. **Identify** Alfred the Great, William the Conqueror, Henry II, Thomas à Becket, Eleanor of Aquitaine, Magna Carta, Philip Augustus, Henry IV.

Critical Thinking

4. **Evaluating Information** Judge the importance of the Magna Carta and the English Parliament in the development of representative government.

Understanding Themes

5. **Conflict** What caused conflicts between popes and monarchs? Could they have been avoided?

SECTION 4 ASSESSMENT ANSWERS

1. England: William the Conqueror made landowners swear direct loyalty to him, carried out first census; King John signed Magna Carta. France: Philip Augustus appointed local officials loyal to king, doubled domain; King Louis IV made royal courts dominant over feudal courts
2. All terms are defined in the Glossary.
3. Alfred the Great, 308; William the Conqueror, 309; Henry II, 309; Thomas à Becket, 309; Eleanor of Aquitaine, 309; Magna Carta, 310; Philip Augustus, 311; Henry IV, 312
4. The Magna Carta prevented royal collection of taxes without the consent of the Great Council. Parliament became more representative when townspeople were added to the nobles and clergy, and as it assumed additional functions.
5. **CONFLICT** Conflicts developed over whether ecclesiastical or secular leaders had supreme authority. Answers will vary as to whether conflicts could have been avoided.

Making Inferences

Just as you leave home to catch your school bus, you hear a news flash that firefighters are battling a blaze near the bus garage. Your bus arrives 45 minutes late. Though no one told you directly, you know that the fire disrupted the bus schedule.

Learning the Skill

In the situation above, you made an *inference*. That is, from the limited facts at hand, you formed a conclusion. You knew that the fire was near the garage. From past experience, you knew that fire trucks often create traffic jams. By combining immediate facts and general knowledge, you inferred that the fire trucks delayed your bus.

To make accurate inferences:

- Read or listen carefully for stated facts and ideas.
- Then review what you already know about the same topic or situation.
- Use logic and common sense to form a conclusion about the topic.
- If possible, find specific information that proves or disproves your inference. In the example above, you could determine whether your inference was correct by asking the bus driver why she was late.

Practicing the Skill

Read the passage about Pepin the Short and then answer the questions that follow.

> 66 Charles's son, Pepin the Short, succeeded his father and became mayor of the palace in A.D. 741. Pepin ... wished to be named king of the Franks. Since he had no blood claim to the throne, Pepin used his influence with the Frankish bishops and the pope to bring about a change in dynasties. In a show of support, the pope journeyed to France and anointed King Pepin I with holy oil.

In return for the Church's blessing, Pepin was to defend the pope against his enemies. In A.D. 754 the new king forced the Lombards, a Germanic people, to withdraw from Rome. Pepin seized a large tract of Lombard territory around Rome and gave it to the pope. 99

1. What facts are stated about Pepin the Short's acquisition of the title King of the Franks?
2. What inference can you make about the pope's power in Europe at this time?
3. What facts are stated about Pepin's actions on behalf of the pope?
4. What inference can you make about the Lombards' relations with the pope and the Franks?

Applying the Skill

Review the sections on "Monastic Life" and the "Influence of Monastics" on pages 304–305. Many men and women adopted the monastic lifestyle during the Middle Ages. What inferences can you make about their motivations? Also, do you think motivations were the same for men and women? How might you prove or disprove these inferences?

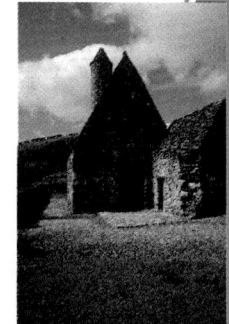

Ancient monastery

For More Practice

Turn to the Skill Practice in the Chapter Assessment on page 315 for more practice in making inferences.

The **Glencoe Skillbuilder Interactive Workbook**, Level 2 provides instruction and practice in key social studies skills.

TEACH

Making Inferences Bring to class a short news story from the local newspaper or, if appropriate, from the school newspaper. Duplicate and circulate it, or read it aloud to the class. Have students summarize the facts as stated, review what they already know about the situation, and then form one or more conclusions about the topic. If time permits, have the class follow up later if additional information appears to support or refute the conclusion(s).

Additional Practice

Skill Reinforcement Activity 12

GLENCOE TECHNOLOGY

 Glencoe's **Skillbuilder Interactive Workbook, Level 2** This interactive CD-ROM promotes student mastery of key social studies skills.

ANSWERS TO PRACTICING THE SKILL

1. He had no blood claim to the throne, but he persuaded Frankish bishops and the pope to make a change in dynasties. The pope anointed Pepin with holy oil.
2. The pope must have been powerful.
3. He forced the Lombards out of Rome and gave the pope territory.
4. The Lombards were enemies of the pope; they had more power than the pope. Relations with the Franks were hostile; the Franks exerted power over the Lombards.

WORLD HISTORY Online

Have students use the **Chapter 12 Self-Check Quiz** at worldhistory.glencoe.com to prepare for the Chapter Test.

WORLD HISTORY Online

Self-Check Quiz

Visit the *World History: The Human Experience* Web site at **worldhistory.glencoe.com** and click on *Chapter 12—Self-Check Quiz* to prepare for the Chapter Test.

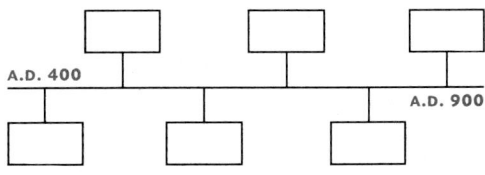

Using Your History Journal

The Church had a significant role in medieval life. Imagine living as a monk or a nun. Write a short diary entry called "Today at the Monastery" or "Today at the Convent," describing the life of a monk or a nun.

GLENCOE TECHNOLOGY

VIDEODISC

Use MindJogger to review the chapter.

MindJogger Videoquiz

Chapter 12
Disc 2 Side A

 Also available in VHS.

Answers

Using Key Terms

1. l	**3.** m	**5.** c
2. h	**4.** j	

Using Your History Journal

Encourage students to be as specific as possible about the work, duties, and daily life of monks or nuns.

Reviewing Facts

1. A.D. 481: Clovis king; A.D. 714: Charles Martel mayor of the palace; A.D. 732: Charles Martel defends Tours; A.D. 754: Pepin forces Lombards out; A.D. 768: Charlemagne king; A.D. 800: Charlemagne defends Pope Leo III; A.D. 814: Charlemagne dies; A.D. 843: Treaty of Verdun
2. Muslims, Slavs, Magyars, Vikings
3. Feudalism—a hierarchy of relationships among the noble ruling class that linked military service with landownership; manorialism—the agricultural system of medieval Europe in which land owned by nobles was farmed by communities of peasants.
4. Students might refer to the strong central government in

Using Key Terms

Write the key term that completes each sentence. Then write a sentence for each term not chosen.

a. counts	h. manorialism
b. cardinals	i. abbess
c. chivalry	j. common law
d. fief	k. excommunication
e. feudalism	l. sacraments
f. friars	m. serfs
g. heresy	n. vassal

1. _____ are formal church rituals, such as baptism, eucharist, confirmation, marriage, anointing of the sick, and holy orders.
2. During the Middle Ages, economic life in Europe centered around a system of agricultural production called _____.
3. Peasants in medieval Europe often were _____, people who were bound to the manor.
4. In place of old feudal rules, Henry II of England established a _____ that applied throughout his kingdom.
5. The code of _____ called for knights to be brave in battle, fight fairly, keep promises, defend the Church, and treat noblewomen courteously.

Technology Activity

Using a Word Processor

Use the draw program on your word processor, or software, to illustrate the layout of a typical medieval manor and surrounding fields. Include the lord's manor house, pastures for livestock, fields for crops, forest areas, and a village where peasants lived. Use a word processor to create a short story from a peasant's point of view, describing a typical day on a medieval manor.

Reviewing Facts

1. **History** Use a time line like the one below to highlight key events in the rise and fall of the Frankish Empire.

A.D. 400 ———————————————— A.D. 900

2. **History** List the invading groups that attacked the Carolingian Empire.
3. **History** Describe the major characteristics of feudalism and manorialism.
4. **History** Describe how medieval and ancient Roman life were similar and different.
5. **Culture** Outline briefly how missionaries carried Christianity across Europe.
6. **History/Culture** Describe the organization of the medieval Catholic Church.
7. **Culture** List the factors that helped maintain religious uniformity during medieval times.
8. **Culture** List several services that monasteries and convents provided for the community in medieval times.
9. **History** Explain why historians consider A.D. 1066 an important date.
10. **Culture** Describe the role of Eleanor of Aquitaine in medieval English history.

Critical Thinking

1. **Apply** Until the 1970s, "good manners" required a man to help a woman with her coat,

---

Roman times and the absence of a central political authority in medieval times; the relative order in the empire compared to the fragmentation after the western empire's fall.

5. Pope Gregory I sent missionaries to England; they traveled to northern Germany. Irish missionaries traveled throughout North Atlantic and western Europe.
6. A hierarchy headed by the pope; under the pope were bishops at the regional level and

priests at the local level; popes, bishops, and priests were secular clergy. Monks and nuns were regular clergy.

7. The Church used force through the Inquisition and persuasion through preaching.
8. preserved learning; provided schools, hospitals, and guest houses; taught skills to peasants; improved agriculture; did missionary work
9. William the Conqueror invaded England, was victorious at Hastings, and reorganization of

and push in her chair. How do these customs relate to chivalry?

2. **Evaluate** Every society has to develop ways to deal with ignorance, ill health, hunger, and homelessness. How did feudal society handle these problems compared to the way modern society handles them?

3. **Compare** How did medieval Europe treat its Jewish population? How have Europe's Jews fared in modern times?

Geography in History

1. **Place** Refer to the map below. Where did Leif Eriksson's journey lead him?

2. **Movement** What reasons did Vikings have for leaving Scandinavia and venturing out into the Atlantic?

3. **Human/Environment Interaction** Why did the Vikings sail across the far northern part of the Atlantic rather than through the warmer waters to the south?

4. **Location** After leaving Scandinavia, which landmasses did the Vikings explore?

Viking Exploration A.D. 1000

→ Route of Viking settlement
→ Route of Erik the Red (late 900s)
→ Route of Leif Eriksson (late 900s)
→ Viking trading route

Understanding Themes

1. **Movement** How can the movement of people both have created and crippled Frankish society?

2. **Cooperation** How were lords and peasants mutually dependent?

3. **Uniformity** How is uniformity implied in the term *regular clergy*?

4. **Conflict** How did the conflict between King John and the nobles, resolved in the Magna Carta, eventually have positive results for all English people?

Linking Past and Present

1. Common law, developed in England during the A.D. 1100s, later crossed the Atlantic Ocean and shaped the legal system of the United States. How does the American legal system today reveal the influence of English common law?

2. People often cherish a romantic view of medieval life: for example, medieval Europeans lived in elegant castles, wore beautiful clothes, and enjoyed festivals. Is such a view justified by historical evidence?

3. Improvements changed farming in Europe around A.D. 1000. What improvements today will increase farm productivity? What far-reaching effects will they have?

Skill Practice

Read the passage about knights. Use stated facts and your knowledge to answer the questions that follow.

> A knight cannot distinguish himself in [war] if he has not trained for it in tourneys. He must have seen his blood flow, heard his teeth crack under fist blows, felt his opponent's weight bear down upon him as he lay on the ground and, after being twenty times unhorsed, have risen twenty times to fight.

1. From this passage, what can you infer about the physical appearance of many European knights?

2. What fact(s) or observations helped you make this inference?

3. What can you infer about the average length of a knight's career?

3. Their homeland bordered the northern Atlantic.

4. Iceland, Greenland, North America

Understanding Themes

1. 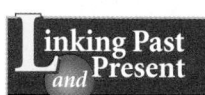 **MOVEMENT** Expansion increased power and wealth but made governing more difficult.

2. **COOPERATION** Without lords, peasants would not have had land or protection; without peasants, lords would not have had laborers.

3. **UNIFORMITY** All the members of a given order abided by its rule *(regula)*.

4. **CONFLICT** It limited the power of the monarch.

Linking Past and Present

1. the doctrine of precedent; the role of juries in determining the facts in important cases; the protection of individual rights by "due process of law" and observance of "the rule of law"

2. No, evidence shows that medieval life was harsh and difficult.

3. Hybridization and gene splicing will increase productivity; better pesticides will prevent crop loss. Both may reduce hunger.

Skill Practice

1. They probably looked scarred and battered.

2. The passage mentions blood flowing and teeth cracking.

3. It probably was not very long.

? Chapter Bonus Test Question

Ask students: Medieval society operated under a system of mutual obligations. What kinds of mutual obligations exist in our own society today? *(An example might be government: citizens pay taxes and in return are provided such services as defense.)*

English government began.

10. She became queen of England when she married Henry II. She influenced royal policies through her sons, Richard I and John.

Critical Thinking

1. They grew out of that part of the chivalric code that required knights to treat ladies of noble birth in a courteous manner.

2. In medieval times, most of these problems

were dealt with by the Church. Today, the responsibility is largely borne by government.

3. It isolated the Jews into separate areas and placed restrictions on their activities; anti-Jewish mobs often killed Jews; today, students might point out the Holocaust.

Geography in History

1. to Labrador and possibly Vinland

2. They sought riches, adventure, and land.

A complete, 1-page lesson plan is provided for each section in the *Reproducible Lesson Plans* booklet.

Medieval Europe at Its Height

CHAPTER RESOURCES

	Reproducible Resources	Multimedia Resources
Chapter Opener	Chapter Themes: Graphic Organizer 13 Historical Significance Chapter Activity 13	MindJogger Videoquiz
Chapter Enrichment	Vocabulary Activity 13* Time Line Activity 13 Mapping History Activity 13 History Simulation 13 Geography and History Activity 13 Source Reading 13 People in World History Profiles 23, 24 World Literature Selection 13 World Art and Music Activity 13 Enrichment Activity 13 Critical Thinking Activity 13 Skill Reinforcement Activity 13 Building Skills in Geography Workbook, Unit 1, Lesson 13 Performance Assessment Activity 13 Standardized Test Practice Workbook Activity 13 Inclusion for the Social Studies Classroom Strategies and Activities	Focus on World Art Prints 15, 17 NGS Poster Set: *The Middle Ages* World History and Art Transparency 16, *May* Mapping History Overlay Transparencies 8, 9 Chapter Transparency 13 NGS PicturePack Transparency Set: *The Middle Ages* Vocabulary PuzzleMaker Software NGS PictureShow CD-ROM: *The Middle Ages* Turning Points in World History: *The Crusades* World History Primary Source Document Library
Chapter Review/Reteaching	Reteaching Activity 13 Skill Reinforcement Activity 13 Spanish Chapter Summary 13	Chapter 13 Digest Audiocassette, Activity, Test* Vocabulary PuzzleMaker Software Interactive Tutor Self-Assessment Software MindJogger Videoquiz
Chapter Evaluation/Testing	Performance Assessment Activity 13 Chapter 13 Test, Forms A and B	ExamView® Pro Testmaker

* *Also available in Spanish*

0:00 OUT OF TIME? Assign the Chapter 13 Audiocassettes.

World History Primary Source Document Library

Make History Come Alive!

Engage your students with over 250 easily accessible primary source documents—available on this CD-ROM—that will give them real life insight into the important events of world history.

Block Schedule

Activities that are particularly suited to use within the block scheduling framework are identified throughout this chapter by the following designation.

KEY TO ABILITY LEVELS

Teaching strategies are coded for varying learning styles.

L1 **BASIC** activities for all students

L2 **AVERAGE** activities for average to above-average students

L3 **CHALLENGING** activities for above-average students

LEP **LIMITED ENGLISH PROFICIENCY** activities

Use Glencoe's *Presentation Plus!* multimedia teacher tool to easily present dynamic lessons that visually excite your students. Using Microsoft PowerPoint® you can customize the presentations to create your own personalized lessons.

Interactive Lesson Planner

Planning has never been easier! Using this CD-ROM, organize your week, month, semester, or year with all the help you need. The **Interactive Lesson Planner** gives you access to all of the blackline masters that accompany *World History: The Human Experience.*

SECTION RESOURCES

Daily Objectives	Reproducible Resources	Multimedia Resources
Section 1 **The Crusades** Summarize how the Crusades began and what their results were.	Lecture Notes 13-1 Reproducible Lesson Plan 13-1 Vocabulary Activity 13* Guided Reading Activity 13-1* Mapping History Activity 13 Time Line Activity 13 Section Quiz 13-1* Reading Essentials and Study Guide 13-1	NGS Poster Set: *The Middle Ages* Section Focus Transparency 13-1 Chapter Transparency 13 Mapping History Overlay Transparency 8, *Early Christian Communities* Interactive Tutor Self-Assessment Software Turning Points in World History: *The Crusades*
Section 2 **Economic and Cultural Revival** Explain how the growth of towns affected the society of medieval Europe.	Lecture Notes 13-2 Reproducible Lesson Plan 13-2 Guided Reading Activity 13-2* Geography and History Activity 13 Section Quiz 13-2* Reading Essentials and Study Guide 13-2	Focus on World Art Prints 15, 17 Section Focus Transparency 13-2 World History and Art Transparency 16, *May* Mapping History Overlay Transparency 9, *Europe in A.D. 1160* NGS PicturePack Transparency Set: *The Middle Ages* Vocabulary PuzzleMaker Software Interactive Tutor Self-Assessment Software NGS PictureShow CD-ROM: *The Middle Ages*
Section 3 **Strengthening of Monarchy** Describe how European monarchs increased their powers during the Middle Ages.	Lecture Notes 13-3 Reproducible Lesson Plan 13-3 Vocabulary Activity 13* Guided Reading Activity 13-3* Section Quiz 13-3* Reading Essentials and Study Guide 13-3	Section Focus Transparency 13-3 Interactive Tutor Self-Assessment Software
Section 4 **The Troubled Church** List the reasons the Church was under pressure to reform.	Lecture Notes 13-4 Reproducible Lesson Plan 13-4 Vocabulary Activity 13* Guided Reading Activity 13-4* History Simulation 13 Reteaching Activity 13 Enrichment Activity 13 Section Quiz 13-4* Performance Assessment Activity 13 Spanish Chapter Summary 13 Reading Essentials and Study Guide 13-4	Section Focus Transparency 13-4 Interactive Tutor Self-Assessment Software Testmaker

* Also available in Spanish

Chapter Activities

✔ Performance Assessment Activity

Starting a Modern-Day Crusade Have students expand their concept of *crusade* by researching modern-day crusades such as the women's movement, the March of Dimes crusade against polio, and so forth. After students have developed various perspectives on crusades, have them choose an issue for which they would "crusade." Students should take the roles of social activists and develop a plan for their crusade, including major events, strategies, people they would involve, and so on.

Students should also complete a reflection in which they compare their crusade to that of medieval times.

Possible Rubric Features
Accuracy of content information, research skills, organization of plan, decision-making skills

• *For an additional activity, refer to Activity 13 in the* Performance Assessment Strategies and Activities *booklet.*

ACTIVITY

From the Classroom of...

Hank Poehling
Central High School
La Crosse, Wisconsin

Compare and Contrast

The purpose of this project is to acquaint students with the historical impact of the Black Death on medieval European society. In comparing the Black Death to AIDS, students will understand the relevance of history as they also examine a contemporary problem. In addition, they receive beneficial AIDS education.

Have students produce a project comparing and contrasting the Black Death (bubonic plague) with AIDS, working either individually or in groups of up to four. The type of project can be left up to each individual or group—a display, a video newscast, a reenactment, a news-style magazine. Tell students that the following areas must be addressed in the project:

- causes of both diseases
- symptoms of both diseases
- how both are spread
- any known or possible cures for both
- the effects of each disease on the individual
- the effects of each disease on society

Allow about two weeks for the projects. On the due date, have all groups and individuals make a formal presentation of their projects to the class.

MULTIPLE LEARNING STYLES

Verbal/Linguistic
Have students prepare a talk show program about dissent within the medieval Church. The guests to be interviewed might include a corrupt clergyman, Pope Clement V, John Wycliffe, and Jan Hus. Some students may act the parts of each of these figures and others may serve as panel members and the host.

Visual/Spatial
Have the class create a mural in the fashion of medieval tapestries. First have them research the art of tapestry and the tapestries of the Middle Ages. Then they can design a tapestry depicting some motif or event from this chapter. Students may choose such themes as the Crusades, a medieval fair, or the Hundred Years' War. Display the tapestry designs in class.

Auditory/Musical
Have students present a short musical based on portraits from Chaucer's *The Canterbury Tales*. Students may write their lyrics either to medieval music or to contemporary music.

Intrapersonal
Have students write essays in which they state whether they would have supported or opposed Wycliffe or Hus during the late Middle Ages. Ask them to explain their reasoning.

GLENCOE'S ASSESSMENT ADVANTAGE

Use the following to easily assess student learning in a variety of ways.

- Performance Assessment Strategies and Activities
- Section Quizzes
- Chapter and Unit Tests
- Interactive Tutor Self-Assessment Software

- Testmaker Software
- MindJogger Videoquiz
- SAT/SAT II Test Practice
- worldhistory.glencoe.com

Additional Resources

NATIONAL GEOGRAPHIC SOCIETY

Teacher's Corner

INDEX TO NATIONAL GEOGRAPHIC MAGAZINE

The following articles relate to this chapter:

- "A World Together," by Erla Zwingle, August 1999.
- "The Power of Money," by Peter T. White, January 1993.
- "Retracing the First Crusade," by Tim Severin, September 1989.
- "A Castle Under the Louvre," by Peter Miller, July 1989.
- "The Gothic Revolution," by James L. Stanfield and Victor R. Boswell, Jr., July 1989.

NATIONAL GEOGRAPHIC SOCIETY PRODUCTS AVAILABLE FROM GLENCOE

To order the following, call Glencoe at 1-800-334-7344:

- *PictureShow: The Middle Ages (CD-ROM)*
- *PicturePack: The Middle Ages (Transparencies)*

ADDITIONAL NATIONAL GEOGRAPHIC SOCIETY PRODUCTS

To order the following, call National Geographic at 1-800-368-2728:

- *The Soul of Spain (Video)*
- *The Builders: Marvels of Engineering (Book)*
- *Europe (Laminated Desk Maps)*

Access National Geographic's new dynamic MapMachine Web site and other geography resources at:

- http://www.nationalgeographic.com/
- http://www.nationalgeographic.com/maps/

BIBLIOGRAPHY

Literature of the Period
Chaucer, Geoffrey. *The Canterbury Tales.* In *The Complete Poetry and Prose of Geoffrey Chaucer,* 2nd ed. New York: Holt, Rinehart and Winston, 1989. Masterpiece of English literature.
Readings for the Student
Gies, Frances and Joseph. *Life in a Medieval Village.* New York: HarperCollins, 1991. Describes everyday medieval life.
Readings for the Teacher
Armstrong, Karen. *Holy War: The Crusades and Their Impact on Today's World.* New York: Doubleday, 1991. Analyzes the effect of the Crusades on current relations among Christians, Jews, and Muslims.

WORLD HISTORY Online

Use our Web site as an additional resource. All essential content is covered in the Student Edition.

You and your students can visit the *World History: The Human Experience* Web site at worldhistory.glencoe.com The student text directs students to the Web site for the following options:

- **Chapter Overviews**
- **Student Web Activities**
- **Self-Check Quizzes**

Answers are provided for you in a link entitled "Web Activity Lesson Plan." Additional Web Resources, Interactive Puzzles, and content updates are also available.

Visit the Glencoe Web site at socialstudies.glencoe.com for social studies activities, updates, and links to other resources.

LOCAL OBJECTIVES

_____
_____
_____
_____
_____
_____
_____
_____
_____
_____
_____
_____
_____
_____
_____
_____
_____

Chapter 13

A.D. 1050–1500

Medieval Europe at Its Height

CHAPTER THEMES

Chapter Themes are listed by section on this chapter opening page of the Student Edition. A corresponding theme-based activity is available under "TEACH," and a theme-based question is asked in the Section and Chapter Assessments.

The Storyteller

Historical Setting In medieval Latin, the word *universitas* meant "corporation," and the earliest universities were corporations of students and masters. These corporations received charters from popes and emperors but were entitled to govern themselves as long as they stayed away from heretical or atheistic teachings. To support themselves the teachers had not only to charge fees but also to please those they taught. As the letter from the student to his father shows, students also had financial worries.

Historical Significance

Answers: *Modern nations, national languages, many of Europe's great cities, international trade networks, the predecessors of modern labor unions, the middle class, and the university all had their beginnings during the height of the Middle Ages.*

The Crusades, the breakdown of the feudal system and the growth of towns, the Hundred Years' War, and dissension within the Church changed European society during the High Middle Ages.

— WORLD HISTORY *Online* **—**

Have students use the **Chapter 13 Overview** at worldhistory. glencoe.com as a prereading and postreading exercise for understanding chapter content.

Chapter Themes

▶ **Cultural Diffusion** The Crusades increase European contact with other areas. *Section 1*
▶ **Innovation** Advances in commerce, learning, and the arts change Europe. *Section 2*
▶ **Conflict** England and France battle while their monarchs gain power. *Section 3*
▶ **Conflict** The Church faces a split from within and opposition from without. *Section 4*

The Storyteller

"Well-beloved father," wrote a medieval student, *"I have not a penny, nor can I get any save through you, for all things at the University are so dear: nor can I study in my [law books], for they are all tattered. Moreover, I owe ten crowns in dues to the [university administrator], and can find no man to lend them to me.*

"Well-beloved father, to ease my debts … at the baker's, with the doctor … and to pay … the laundress and the barber, I send you word of greetings and of money."

This letter from a medieval student sounds very much like something a modern student might write. At that time, however, the university was something new. It was part of the cultural awakening that took place in the High Middle Ages.

Historical Significance

What features of modern Western civilization had their beginnings during the height of the Middle Ages in western Europe? What new developments changed European society during the High Middle Ages?

A.D. 1100   A.D. 1300   A.D. 1500

c. A.D. 1150 First universities develop in Europe.

A.D. 1337 France and England begin Hundred Years' War.

A.D. 1455 Wars of the Roses begin in England.

A.D. 1412 Joan of Arc is born.

316

GEOGRAPHY CONNECTION

Movement Have students use a map to locate the city of Jerusalem (in the present country of Israel), as well as England, France, Germany, and Italy. Have students discuss some of the difficulties that physical geography presented to medieval armies traveling from Europe to Jerusalem. *(crossing the Alps, crossing the mountains of the Macedonian peninsula, traveling through the Syrian and Palestinian deserts, the dangers of open sea voyages on the Mediterranean)*

The Church Militant and Triumphant, a fresco from the A.D. 1300s by Andrea de Bonaiuto. The Spanish Chapel in Santa Maria Novella, Florence, Italy

History & Art
The church of Santa Maria Novella was founded by the Dominicans, who were named after a Spanish priest. But in Latin the words *Domini Canes* mean the "dogs of God." Why did de Bonaiuto include dogs in his fresco? *(The Dominicans served God in hunting out heresy like hounds served hunters by tracking prey.)*

✔ Performance Assessment

Refer to the activity on page 316C of the Planning Guide.

📁 For an additional activity, refer to Activity 13 in the *Performance Assessment Strategies and Activities* booklet.

WORLD HISTORY Online

Chapter Overview

Visit the *World History: The Human Experience* Web site at **worldhistory.glencoe.com** and click on *Chapter 13—Chapter Overview* to preview the chapter.

Your History Journal

Medieval literature contains epics that were put into writing for the first time. Read an excerpt from Beowulf, *the* Song of Roland, *or* The Canterbury Tales *and take notes about life in Europe at the time.*

Using Your History Journal

Suggest that students look for details of medieval life in the descriptions of the feasts in *Beowulf*; in the General Prologue to *The Canterbury Tales*; or in the description of the battle at Roncesvalles in the *Song of Roland*.

GLENCOE TECHNOLOGY

 VIDEODISC
Use MindJogger to preview chapter content.
MindJogger Videoquiz

 Chapter 13
Disc 2 Side B

 Also available in VHS.

Chapter 13 *Medieval Europe at Its Height* 317

✚ EXTRA CREDIT PROJECT

Research Report The Crusades are of interest from a military as well as a religious perspective. Ask students to prepare a report that compares and contrasts the organization, tactics, and effectiveness of the Crusader and Muslim armies. Suggested resources: R. C. Finucane, *Soldiers of the Faith: Crusaders and Moslems at War*; J. Godfrey, *1204: The Unholy Crusade*; H. E. Mayer, *The Crusades*; and J. Riley-Smith, *The Crusades: A Short History*.

A.D. 1050   A.D. 1150   A.D. 1250

A.D. 1095 Pope Urban II calls for First Crusade.

A.D. 1147 Second Crusade begins.

A.D. 1204 Crusaders sack Constantinople.

A.D. 1212 Children's Crusade begins.

SECTION THEME

▶ **Cultural Diffusion** The Crusades increased European contact with other areas.

Guide to Reading

For reading strategies to help students read effectively see pages 12–13. Have students think about the main head as they read the subheads.

Vocabulary Pre-check

☐ Use the Vocabulary PuzzleMaker for Chapter 13 to create a crossword puzzle to reinforce section terms. **L1 LEP**

 Use Vocabulary Activity 13 to introduce vocabulary terms. **L1 LEP**

FOCUS

Section Objective

Summarize how the Crusades began and what their results were.

BELLRINGER
Motivational Activity

Before taking roll at the beginning of the class period, project Section Focus Transparency 13-1 and have students answer the activity questions. Discuss students' responses.

This activity is also available as a blackline master.

Section 1

The Crusades

Guide to Reading

Read to Find Out
Main Idea *The Crusades had a variety of impacts on medieval society.*

▶ **Terms to Define**
the Crusades

▶ **People to Meet**
the Seljuk Turks, Pope Urban II, Saladin, Richard I

▶ **Places to Locate**
Jerusalem, Constantinople

The **Storyteller**

Geoffrey de Renneville was footsore, thirsty, and covered with dust. He had joined the Crusade as an adventure. The Crusaders had traveled for weeks and were beset by flies, bandits, disease, poor food, and limited drink. The cavalcade stopped and the weary men dropped into an uneasy slumber. Suddenly, they were startled awake by the cry "Help for the Holy Sepulchre!" One by one the knights took up the cry. Shouting with the others, Geoffrey was reminded of the Crusade's purpose.

—adapted from *The Dream and the Tomb*, Robert Payne, 1984

Leaving for the Crusades

Life in the Early Middle Ages was characterized by decentralized government, warfare, cultural isolation, famine, and wretched living conditions. Trade was sparse, and agricultural production—the mainstay of the European economy—was inefficient.

By A.D. 1100, however, conditions in Europe had begun to improve. Some European monarchs succeeded in building strong central governments. Better farming methods led to larger crop yields and a growth in population. Towns and trade began to reappear. The Church held a powerful sway over the emotions and energies of the people. Changes in religion, society, politics, and economics made the High Middle Ages—the period between A.D. 1050 and A.D. 1270—a springboard for a new and brilliant civilization in western Europe.

The transformation of medieval society began with a holy war over the city of **Jerusalem**. European Christians undertook a series of military expeditions—nine in all—to recover the Holy Land from the Muslims. These expeditions were called the Crusades, from the Latin word *crux*, meaning "cross." Those who fought were called Crusaders because they vowed to "take up the cross."

TURNING POINT

Call for a Crusade

Jerusalem was a holy city for people of three faiths. Jews treasured it as Zion, God's own city, and as the site of Solomon's temple. To Christians, the city was holy because it was the place where Jesus was crucified and resurrected. Muslims regarded Jerusalem as their third holiest city, after Makkah and Madinah. According to Muslim tradition, Muhammad ascended to heaven from Jerusalem.

Jerusalem and the entire region of Palestine fell to Arab invaders in the A.D. 600s. Mostly Muslims, the Arabs tolerated other religions. Christians and

---

SECTION RESOURCES

Reproducible Masters
- Lecture Notes 13-1
- Reproducible Lesson Plan 13-1
- Vocabulary Activity 13
- Guided Reading Activity 13-1
- Mapping History Activity 13
- Time Line Activity 13

- Section Quiz 13-1
- Reading Essentials and Study Guide 13-1

Transparencies
- Section Focus Transparency 13-1
- Chapter Transparency 13
- Mapping History Overlay Transparency 8

Multimedia
- The Middle Ages
- Interactive Tutor Self-Assessment Software
- Testmaker
- The Crusades

Jews were allowed to live in Jerusalem as long as they paid their taxes and followed certain regulations. European traders and religious pilgrims traveled to Palestine without interference.

In the late A.D. 1000s, **the Seljuk Turks**—a Muslim people from central Asia—took Jerusalem. Their conquest left Palestine in chaos, and the hazards of pilgrimage increased. Meanwhile, the Seljuks threatened the Byzantine Empire, especially **Constantinople**. The Byzantine emperor wrote to the pope in A.D. 1095 requesting military aid from the West. Concerns about the safety of Christian pilgrims gave added urgency to the emperor's request.

First Crusade

On a cold November day in A.D. 1095, **Pope Urban II** mounted a platform outside the church at Clermont, France. His voice shaking with emotion, he addressed the assembled throng, asking for a volunteer army to take Jerusalem and Palestine from the Seljuks:

> ❝ I exhort you ... to strive to expel that wicked race from our Christian lands.... Christ commands it. Remission of sins will be granted for those going thither.... Let those who are accustomed to wage private war wastefully even against believers go forth against the infidels.... Let those who have lived by plundering be soldiers of Christ; let those who formerly contended against brothers and relations rightly fight barbarians; let those who were recently hired for a few pieces of silver win their eternal reward. ❞

"Deus vult!" (God wills it!) shouted the crowd in response to the pope's plea. Knights and peasants alike vowed to join the expedition to the Holy Land. For knights, the Crusade was a welcome chance to employ their fighting skills. For peasants, the Crusade meant freedom from feudal bonds while on the Crusade. All were promised immediate salvation in heaven if they were killed freeing the Holy Land from non-Christians. Adventure and the possibility of wealth were other reasons to join the Crusade. In preparation for the holy war, red crosses of cloth were stitched on clothing as a symbol of service to God.

This First Crusade heightened already existing hatred of non-Christians and marked the onset of a long period of Christian persecution of the Jews. During the First Crusade, which began in A.D. 1096,

Pope Urban II arrives at the Council of Clermont. *What did the pope ask the people to do?*

three armies of Crusader knights and volunteers traveled separately from western Europe to the eastern Mediterranean. On the way, many of them killed Jews and sometimes massacred entire Jewish communities.

Led by French nobles, the three armies finally met in Constantinople in A.D. 1097. From there the Crusaders made their way to Jerusalem, enduring the hardships of desert travel as well as quarrels among their leaders. In June A.D. 1099, the Crusaders finally reached the city. After a siege of almost two months Jerusalem fell. Crusaders swarmed into the city and massacred most of its Muslim and Jewish inhabitants.

The success of the First Crusade reinforced the authority of the Church and strengthened the self-confidence of western Europeans. The religious zeal of the Crusaders soon cooled, however, and many knights returned home. Those who stayed set up feudal states in Syria and Palestine. Contact between the Crusaders and the relatively more sophisticated civilizations of the Byzantines and the Muslims would continue for the next 100 years and become a major factor in ending the cultural isolation of western Europe.

TEACH

Guided Practice

THEME Cultural Diffusion
Have students provide examples of cultural diffusion that resulted from the Crusades. *(exposure of Europe to classic texts preserved by the Muslims and Byzantines, to Muslim expertise in cartography and shipbuilding technology, and to many luxury goods from the East)* **L1**

 Chapter Transparency 13

 Mapping History Overlay Transparency 8, *Early Christian Communities*

Visualizing History When he was born to noble parents about 1035 in the Champagne region of France, the baby who would become pope some 53 years later was named Odo.
Answer to Caption: *to wage war against the infidels*

TURNING POINT

Call for a Crusade
How did the Crusades encourage Europeans to increase trade?
Increased knowledge of Asia's civilizations increased the demand for imported goods.

 VIDEODISC
Turning Points in World History

 Side One
Chapter 7

Title: *The Crusades*

Drawing Maps Have students work in small groups to research and prepare maps of the various routes used by the Crusaders to reach the Middle East. (For example, early Crusaders from France and Germany sailed from Italy to Greece or crossed Europe to Constantinople, then marched across present-day Turkey. Later Crusaders sailed from the Mediterranean coast to ports in Palestine.) Assign each student a task, such as tracing the area from western Europe to the Middle East, drawing in topographic features, drawing the routes used by the Crusaders, or illustrating maps with pictures pertaining to the Crusaders or dangers they encountered. Display and discuss the completed maps in class. **L2**

320 Chapter 13 Medieval Europe at Its Height

Map Study

Answer
about 1,875 miles (3,017 km)

Map Skills Practice

Reading a Map About how far did Crusaders on the First Crusade travel before reaching Jerusalem? *(about 2,000 miles [3,218 km])*

The following videotape program is available from Glencoe:

- **Richard the Lionheart**

Independent Practice

📁 Guided Reading Activity 13-1 **L1**

📁 Mapping History Activity 13

📁 Time Line Activity 13

Literature Have students read Sir Walter Scott's *Ivanhoe*, whose main character is a Crusader. Ask them to report to the class on the Christian-Jewish interactions depicted in the novel. **L3**

NATIONAL GEOGRAPHIC SOCIETY

Use these materials to enrich student understanding of the Middle Ages.

📖 **NGS POSTER SET**
The Middle Ages

ASSESS

Check for Understanding

Assign Section 1 Assessment as homework or as an in-class activity.

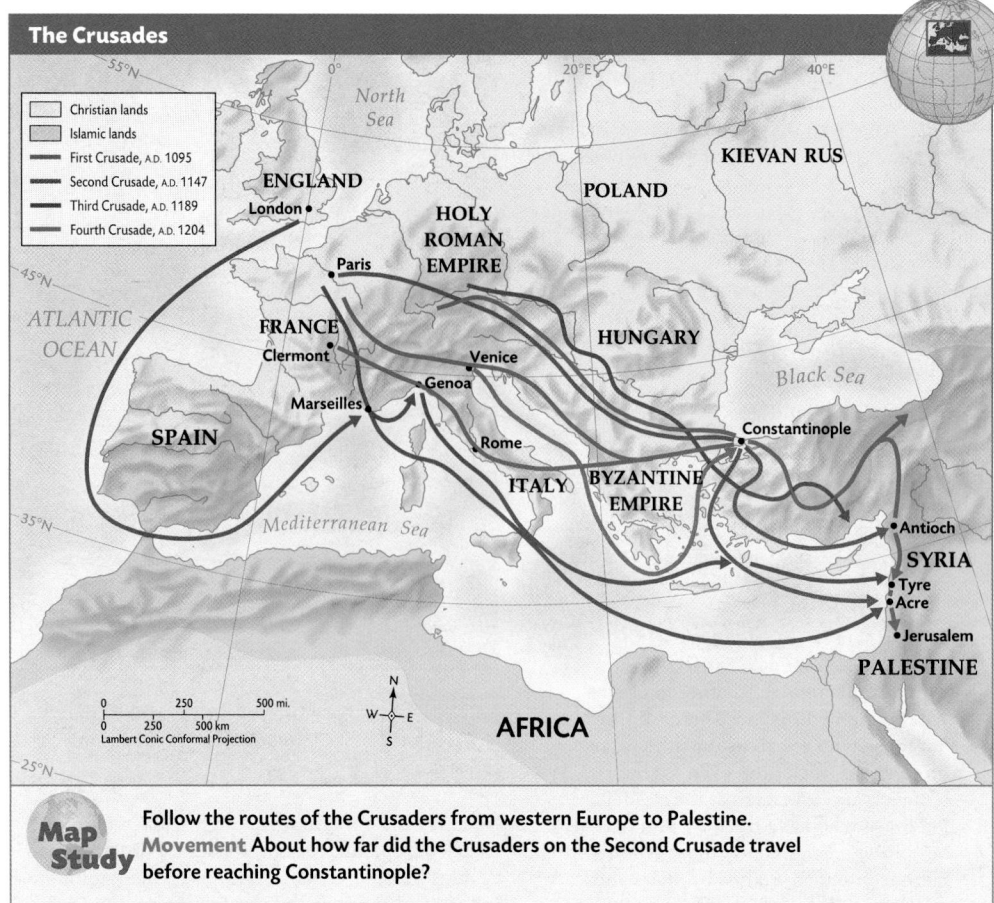

The Crusades

Christian lands
Islamic lands
First Crusade, A.D. 1095
Second Crusade, A.D. 1147
Third Crusade, A.D. 1189
Fourth Crusade, A.D. 1204

Map Study Follow the routes of the Crusaders from western Europe to Palestine.
Movement About how far did the Crusaders on the Second Crusade travel before reaching Constantinople?

Second Crusade

Less than 50 years after the First Crusade, the Seljuks conquered part of the Crusader states in Palestine. Pope Eugenius IV called for a Second Crusade to regain the territory. Eloquent sermons by the monk Bernard of Clairvaux (KLAR•VOH) persuaded King Louis VII of France and Holy Roman Emperor Conrad III to lead armies to Palestine. The Second Crusade, which lasted from A.D. 1147 to A.D. 1149, was unsuccessful. Louis VII and Conrad III quarreled constantly and were ineffective militarily. They were easily defeated by the Seljuks.

Third Crusade

A diplomatic and forceful leader named **Saladin** (SA•luh•DEEN) united the Muslim forces and then captured Jerusalem in A.D. 1187. The people of western Europe were stunned and horrified. Holy Roman Emperor Frederick Barbarossa of Germany, King Philip Augustus of France, and King **Richard I** of England assembled warriors for the Third Crusade. This "Crusade of Kings" lasted from A.D. 1189 to A.D. 1192 and was no more successful than the Second Crusade. Frederick Barbarossa died on the way to Palestine, and his army returned home. Philip Augustus returned to France before the army reached Jerusalem. Richard continued the struggle alone.

Although his army defeated the Muslims in several battles, Richard could not win a decisive victory over Saladin's well-trained and dedicated forces. After three years of fighting, Richard signed a truce with the Muslims and tried to persuade Saladin to return Jerusalem to the Christians. "Jerusalem," he wrote to the Muslim leader, "we are resolved not to renounce as long as we have a single man left." Saladin's reply to Richard showed his equal determination to keep the city:

320 Chapter 13 *Medieval Europe at Its Height*

MEETING SPECIAL NEEDS ACTIVITY

Learning Style: Visual/Spatial To reinforce the ideas presented in this section, have students who are visual learners draw a series of illustrations depicting important events and people. Illustrations could include Pope Urban II delivering his call for the First Crusade, a series of drawings depicting the journeys of Crusaders to the Holy Land, or a portrait of King Richard I of England. Ask the artists to work with other students to create text that explains their drawings. Display the completed drawings and accompanying text in the classroom. **L1 LEP**

> " To us Jerusalem is as precious, aye and more precious, than it is to you, in that it was the place whence our Prophet made his journey by night to heaven and is destined to be the gathering place of our nation at the last day. Do not dream that we shall give it up to you…. It belonged to us originally, and it is you who are the real aggressors. "

Although Saladin refused to turn over Jerusalem, he allowed Christian pilgrims access.

Other Crusades

Other Crusades followed in the A.D. 1200s, but none won permanent Christian control of Palestine. By this time, western Europeans had lost sight of the religious goal of the Crusades, being more concerned about political and economic gain.

In the Fourth Crusade of A.D. 1204, Crusaders put aside their goal of marching to Jerusalem and instead attacked the Christian city of Constantinople. They burned libraries, destroyed churches, and stole valuable treasures. Their actions left a lasting bitterness between the Eastern Orthodox world and western Europe. The Fourth Crusade seriously weakened the Byzantine Empire, making possible a later Muslim advance into eastern Europe.

Effects of the Crusades

Although Western Europeans failed to gain control of Palestine, the Crusades helped to speed the pace of changes already underway in western Europe. They helped break down feudalism and increase the authority of kings. European monarchs levied taxes, raised armies, and cooperated on a large scale. Some nobles died in battle without leaving heirs, and their lands passed to kings. To raise money for weapons and supplies, many lesser nobles sold their estates or allowed their serfs to

 Return from the Crusade by Karl Friedrich Lessing. Rheinland Museum, Bonn, Germany *How did the Crusades help to break down feudalism?*

buy their freedom to become freeholders on the land or artisans in the towns.

During the Crusades contact with the more advanced Byzantine and Muslim civilizations broadened European views of the world. The European presence in the East heightened demand at home for Eastern luxury goods: spices, sugar, melons, tapestries, silk, and other items. Commerce increased in the eastern Mediterranean area and especially benefited Italian trading cities, such as Venice and Genoa.

From the Muslims the Crusaders learned how to build better ships, make more accurate maps, use the magnetic compass to tell direction, and improve their weaponry. Religious military orders of knights primarily aided pilgrims, but they were also bankers for both princes and merchants.

The Crusades had less impact on the Muslims. Crusader states were relatively weak in an area divided among powerful Muslim rivals. The arrival of the Crusaders, however, helped unite the Muslims against a common enemy.

SECTION 1 ASSESSMENT

Main Idea
1. Use a diagram like the one below to identify causes and effects of the Crusades.

Crusades

Causes		Effects

Recall
2. **Define** the Crusades.
3. **Identify** the Seljuk Turks, Pope Urban II, Saladin, Richard I.

Critical Thinking
4. **Analyzing Information** In what ways were the Crusades both a success and a failure?

Could Christians and Muslims have resolved their differences peacefully? Explain.

Understanding Themes
5. **Cultural Diffusion** Describe how the Crusades contributed to cultural diffusion in western Europe and the Mediterranean.

SECTION 1 ASSESSMENT ANSWERS

1. causes: Muslim control of Holy Land, Christian pilgrims unsafe, political and economic gain; effects: broke down feudalism, increased authority of kings, increased commerce, united Muslims
2. All terms are defined in the Glossary.
3. Seljuk Turks, 319; Pope Urban II, 319; Saladin, 320; Richard I, 320
4. They brought new ideas/goods to western Europe, broke down feudalism/strengthened monarchies; they were costly in terms of human life and failed to achieve their goal; negotiations between Richard I and Saladin possible missed opportunity.
5. **CULTURAL DIFFUSION** Contact with eastern cultures affected European ways.

History & Art By bringing the knights of Christian Europe together in a joint undertaking sponsored by the Church, the Crusades did much to transform the Christian ideal of knightly behavior into reality.
Answer to Caption: *They weakened feudal lords, whose lands passed to kings when the lords died heirless in battle. The lords sometimes raised money for supplies by selling their estates or allowing their serfs to buy their freedom.*

▣ Use Interactive Tutor Self-Assessment Software to review Section 1.

Evaluate
Section Quiz 13-1

▣ Use the Testmaker to create a customized quiz for Section 1.

Reteach
Have students work in small groups to list the important features of each Crusade discussed in this section. Have the groups compare and discuss their lists.

Reading Essentials and Study Guide 13-1

Enrich
Have students read an account of Saladin and Richard I during the Third Crusade. Ask them to give a report comparing the character of the two men, their motives for fighting, and the regard in which they held each other.

CLOSE

Have students evaluate the positive and negative effects of the Crusades on Western civilization. *(gains: increased trade and knowledge; losses: heavy casualties, bitterness and distrust between Muslims and Christians)*

A.D. 1000   A.D. 1200   A.D. 1400

c. A.D. 1000 Europe's economy begins to revive.

c. A.D. 1150 French architects begin to build in the Gothic style.

c. A.D. 1348 The Black Death spreads throughout Europe.

c. A.D. 1386 Geoffrey Chaucer begins writing *The Canterbury Tales.*

SECTION THEME

▶ **Innovation** Advances in commerce, learning, and the arts change Europe.

Guide to Reading

For reading strategies to help students read effectively see pages 12–13.

Vocabulary Pre-check

 Use the Vocabulary PuzzleMaker for Chapter 13 to create a crossword puzzle to reinforce section terms. **L1 LEP**

Use Vocabulary Activity 13 to introduce vocabulary terms. **L1 LEP**

FOCUS

Section Objective

Explain how the growth of towns affected the society of medieval Europe.

BELLRINGER
Motivational Activity

Before taking roll at the beginning of the class period, project Section Focus Transparency 13-2 and have students answer the activity questions. Discuss students' responses.

This activity is also available as a blackline master.

Section 2

Economic and Cultural Revival

Guide to Reading

Read to Find Out
Main Idea *The growth of towns affected the society of medieval Europe.*

▶ **Terms to Define**
money economy, guild, master, apprentice, journeyman, charter, scholasticism, troubadour, vernacular

▶ **People to Meet**
Peter Abelard, Thomas Aquinas, Dante Alighieri, Geoffrey Chaucer

▶ **Places to Locate**
Venice, Flanders, Champagne, Bologna

The Storyteller

To help rebuild the cathedral, people for miles around brought their goods. So that the church might rise swiftly, larger and more beautiful than any they had seen, peasants, skilled workers, and even nobles pulled heavy carts filled with wood and stone. Religious fervor motivated the people, and the reward was a renewed spirit in the community. Perfect harmony reigned. During the night, the workers formed a camp with their wagons, and by the light of candles, they sang canticles and psalms. Everyone was doing penance and forgiving their enemies.

—adapted from *Chronique,* Robert de Torigni, in *Chartres,* Emil Mâle, translated by Sarah Wilson, 1983

Cathedral at Reims, France

The Crusades accelerated the transformation of western Europe from a society that was crude, backward, and violent—showing little cultural and technological advancement—to a civilization that exhibited some early features of modern Western civilization. Towns grew, trade expanded, and learning and the arts thrived.

Economic Expansion

The economy of western Europe had begun to show vigor around A.D. 1000. Agricultural production increased. Expanding opportunities in trade encouraged the growth of towns, and the lively atmosphere of the towns in turn stimulated creative thought and innovations in art.

Agricultural Advances

Plows during the Early Middle Ages were light and did not cut much below the surface of the soil. The invention of a new, heavier plow made it possible to cut through the rich, damp soils of northwestern Europe. This plow enabled farmers to produce more and to cultivate new lands, increasing food production. Nobles and freeholders—peasants not bound to the land—migrated to new areas, clearing forests, draining swamps, and building villages. In one of the largest migrations of the time, the Germans moved to areas of eastern Europe, doubling the territory they controlled.

About the same time, the collar harness replaced the ox yoke. Horses were choked by the ox yoke, but the new harness shifted weight off the neck and onto the shoulders, allowing farmers to replace oxen with horses. Horses pulled the plow faster than oxen, allowing farmers to plant and plow more crops.

SECTION RESOURCES

Reproducible Masters
- Lecture Notes 13-2
- Reproducible Lesson Plan 13-2
- Guided Reading Activity 13-2
- Geography and History Activity 13
- Section Quiz 13-2
- Reading Essentials and Study Guide 13-2

Transparencies
- Section Focus Transparency 13-2
- World History and Art Transparency 16
- Mapping History Overlay Transparency 9
- The Middle Ages

Multimedia
- Focus on World Art Prints 15, 17
- Vocabulary PuzzleMaker Software
- Interactive Tutor Self-Assessment Software
- Testmaker
- The Middle Ages

As you read in Chapter 12, the three-field system of planting also made the land more productive. As the land began to feed more people, the population naturally increased.

Expansion of Trade

The revival of towns caused a rapid expansion of trade. Soon the sea-lanes and roads were filled with traders carrying goods to market. Important sea and river routes connected western Europe with the Mediterranean, eastern Europe, and Scandinavia. The repaired and rebuilt Roman road system carried international traders to and from Europe.

Italian towns, such as **Venice**, Pisa, and Genoa controlled the Mediterranean trade after A.D. 1200, bringing silks and spices from Asia to Europe. **Flanders**, a region including present-day northern France and southwestern Belgium, became the center of trade on Europe's northern coast. Textiles produced there were sent by way of an eastern route to the Black Sea and then traded at Middle Eastern markets for porcelain, silk, and silver. Towns along the Baltic coast formed the Hanseatic League, which controlled trade between eastern Europe and the North Atlantic.

The merchandise for sale in a town was varied and seemingly endless. This was especially true during trade fairs. Each year hundreds of traders met at large trade fairs in places convenient to land and water routes. Feudal lords charged the merchants fees, charged taxes on goods, and offered protection to the merchants. The most famous fair was at **Champagne** in eastern France, located in almost the exact center of western Europe. For four to six weeks each year, Champagne was a distribution point for goods from around the world.

Banking

Early merchants used the barter system, trading goods without using money. Before long, however, merchants found this system impractical. Moreover, some of the merchants who supplied luxury goods such as silk would only accept money in payment. European merchants therefore needed a common medium of exchange.

The rise of a money economy, or an economy based on money, had far-reaching consequences. Initially, it led to the growth of banking. Since traders came from many countries, they carried different currencies with different values. Moneychangers—often Jews or Italians—determined the value of the various currencies and exchanged one currency for another. They also developed procedures for transferring funds from one place to another, received deposits, and arranged loans, thus becoming the first bankers

Italian bankers, from *Treatise on the Seven Vices: Avarice*. The Church viewed lending with the intent to charge interest as evil. *What is the origin of the term "bank"?*

in Europe. Indeed, the word *bank* comes from the *banca*, or bench, that the moneychangers set up at fairs.

As the money economy grew, it put the feudal classes in an economic squeeze. Kings, clergy, and nobles became dependent on money from banks to pay their expenses. To pay off their loans, they had to raise taxes, sell their lands, or demand money in place of traditional feudal services. As serfs became able to buy their freedom, the feudal system declined.

Growth of Towns

The number of towns in western Europe grew tremendously in the A.D. 1000s and A.D. 1100s. Many grew up beside well-traveled roads or near waterways. Although warfare had declined,

TEACH

Guided Practice

THEME Innovation

Have students give some examples of innovations that developed during the High Middle Ages. *(heavier plows and collar harnesses, trade fairs, money economy, universities)* **L1 LEP**

Economics Have students explain the consequences of the rise of a money economy. Ask how it affected banking. *(led to the growth of banking)* How did a money economy affect the feudal system? *(It weakened feudalism by forcing lords to become dependent on money for expenses and by enabling serfs to buy their freedom.)* **L2**

Visualizing History Medieval scholars associated the demon Mammon, whose name means "riches" in Aramaic, with the sin of avarice, or insatiable greed for riches.
Answer to Caption: *It derives from the* banca, *or bench, that money changers set up at medieval fairs.*

you don't say...

Burg The term *burg* originally meant a fortified town or castle. As part of town names, it appeared in the German -*burg*, the French -*bourg*, and the English -*borough* and -*bury*. Today in Europe one can find Hamburg, Strasbourg, Edinburgh, and Canterbury; in the United States there is Pittsburgh, Harrisburg, Jonesboro, and Salisbury.

COOPERATIVE LEARNING ACTIVITY

Role Play Have students write and present a brief play showing daily life in a medieval town. Assign small groups to research the daily work, clothing, food, and homes of townspeople. Assign each student a specific task such as selecting an event and characters, outlining and writing parts of the script, and obtaining or making props.

Students may choose to portray such characters as apprentices, journeymen, masters of various guilds, university students, clergy, moneychangers, or troubadours. When students have completed their research, writing, costumes, and set, have them present the play. If possible, videotape the play for viewing by students in other classes. **L2**

Critical Thinking Have students discuss the benefits of the guild system. How did guilds help not only guild members but also society at large? *(ensured high quality)* What were some disadvantages? *(Students may answer that guilds could fix prices at an unfair level or that discouraging competition also discouraged growth of business.)* **L3**

NATIONAL GEOGRAPHIC SOCIETY

Use these materials to enrich student understanding of the Middle Ages.

- **NGS PICTURESHOW CD-ROM**
  The Middle Ages
- **NGS PICTUREPACK TRANSPARENCY SET**
  The Middle Ages

- World History and Art Transparency 16, *May*

- Mapping History Overlay Transparency 9, *Europe in A.D. 1160*

- Focus on World Art Print 15, Master Guillebert de Mets and Others. *Saint George and the Dragon*

- Focus on World Art Print 17, Jan van Eyck. *Saint Jerome in His Study*

Biography

The following videotape program is available from Glencoe:

- **King Arthur: His Life and Legends**

---

settlements still faced bandits. To protect themselves, townspeople built walls around their towns. At first these enclosures were simple wooden fences. As the population grew, stone walls were built, with guard towers at the gates.

Inside the walls narrow, winding streets bustled with people, carts drawn by horses and oxen, and farm animals on the way to market. A din of noise and overpowering smells attacked the senses. Church bells chimed the hours; carts piled high with goods creaked and rumbled through streets that were little more than alleys. Shops lined the streets at ground level, and the shop owners often lived in quarters above. Most buildings were of wood and had thatch roofs, making fire a constant hazard.

Medieval towns had almost no sanitation, and a constant stench assailed the people from the garbage and sewage tossed into the streets. These conditions caused the rapid spread of diseases such as diphtheria, typhoid, influenza, and malaria. In crowded towns such diseases often turned into epidemics and took many lives. The worst of these epidemics—the bubonic plague—ravaged Europe between A.D. 1348 and 1350, killing one-third of the population and earning the name the Black Death.

Guilds

During the A.D. 1100s, merchants and artisans organized themselves into business associations called guilds. The primary function of the merchant guild was to maintain a monopoly of the local market for its members. To accomplish this end, merchant guilds severely restricted trading by foreigners in their city and enforced uniform pricing. The following regulations from Southampton, England, indicate the power of the merchant guilds:

❝ **And no one shall buy honey, fat, salt herrings, or any kind of oil, or millstones, or fresh hides, or any kind of fresh skins, unless he is a guildsman; nor keep a tavern for wine, nor sell cloth at retail, except in market or fair days …** ❞

Images *of the* Times

Medieval Life

The recovery of commerce and the beginnings of industries stimulated the growth of European towns.

Market scene in a medieval town is the subject of this fresco from Castello de Issogne, Val d' Aosta, Italy.

324

Images *of the* Times Medieval Life

Craft and merchant guilds often controlled different aspects of a given industry. In a wool-processing town, for example, the merchant guild would control the purchase of raw wool along with the production and sale of the processed fiber. The craft guilds, by contrast, would control such aspects of the industry as wool carding, dyeing, and weaving.

The word *romance* originally referred not to romantic love but to narratives written in the vernacular rather than in Latin. Although love stories often played a part in these tales of chivalric adventure, they were not essential to this literary genre.

Craft guilds, by contrast, regulated the work of artisans: carpenters, shoemakers, blacksmiths, masons, tailors, and weavers. Women working as laundresses, seamstresses and embroiderers, and maidservants had their own trade associations.

Craft guilds established strict rules concerning prices, wages, and employment. A member of the shoemakers' guild could not charge more (or less) for a pair of shoes than other shoemakers, nor could he advertise or in any way induce people to buy his wares. Although the guilds prohibited competition, they set standards of quality to protect the public from shoddy goods.

Craft guilds were controlled by masters, or artisans who owned their own shops and tools and employed less-skilled artisans as helpers. To become a master at a particular craft, an artisan served an apprenticeship, the length of which varied according to the difficulty of the craft. Apprentices worked for a master without pay. An apprentice then became a journeyman and received pay. However, a journeyman could only work under a master. To become a master, a journeyman submitted a special sample of his work—a masterpiece—to the guild for approval. If the sample was approved, the journeyman became a master and could set up his own shop.

Aside from business activities, guilds provided benefits for their members such as medical help and unemployment relief. Guilds also organized social and religious life by sponsoring banquets, holy day processions, and outdoor plays.

Rise of the Middle Class

The medieval town, or burg, created the name for a new class of people. In Germany they were called *burghers*; in France, the *bourgeoisie* (BURZH•WAH•ZEE); and in England, *burgesses*. The name originally referred to anyone living in a town. Gradually it came to mean the people who made money through the developing money economy. They were a middle class made up of merchants, bankers, and artisans who no longer had to rely on the land to make a living.

Global Gourmet

France The first important French cookbook was written during the Middle Ages. Taillevent, the chef of King Charles VI, wrote *Le Viander* around 1375. Although Taillevent is the name of one of the finest restaurants in modern Paris, the recipes in Taillevent's cookbook aim not at bringing out the flavor of food but rather at disguising it, since the lack of refrigeration often led to spoilage.

you don't say...

Journeyman Because a journeyman had proved his competence by serving an apprenticeship but still had to work under a master, today the word has come to mean an experienced and capable—but routine—worker or performer.

Who?What?Where?When?

Hospitals became more widespread during the Middle Ages. During the Crusades military hospitals were established along the Crusaders' routes and in the Holy Land. Although most medieval hospitals were established by Benedictine monks, cities and towns also began to set up health-care institutions.

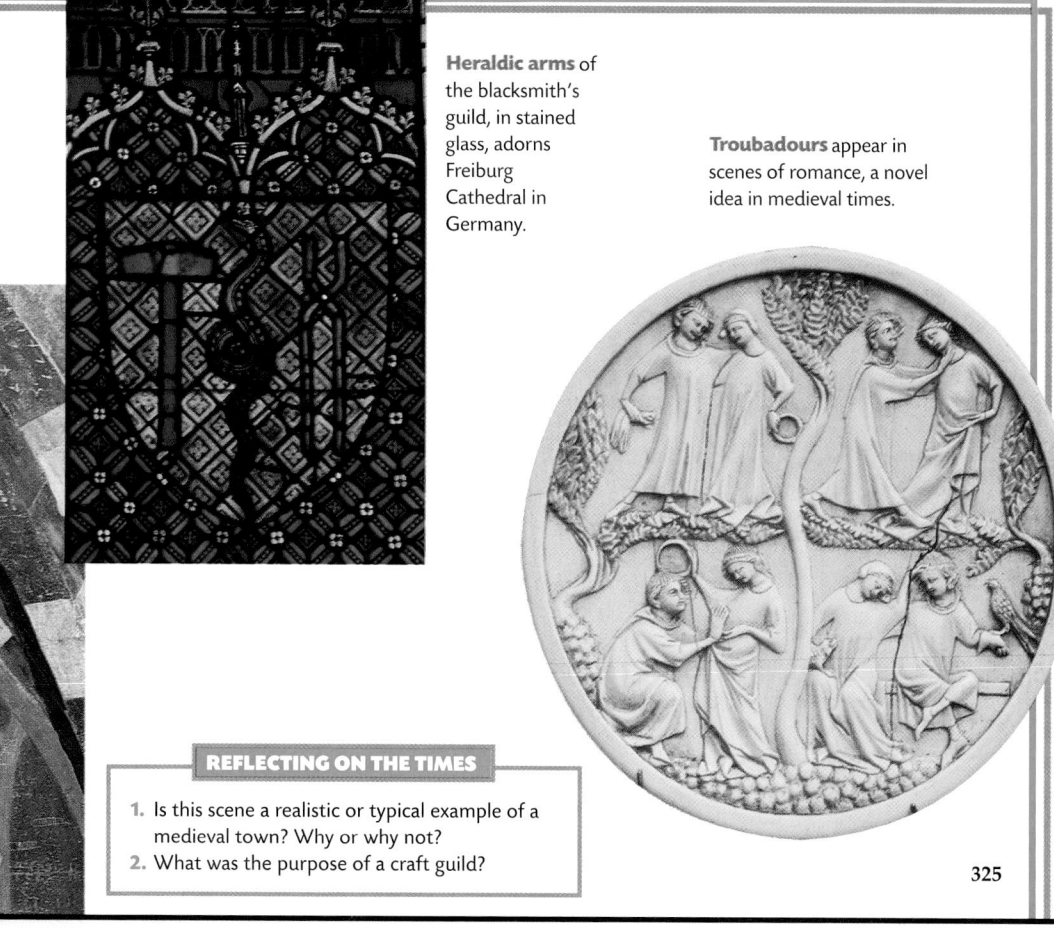

Heraldic arms of the blacksmith's guild, in stained glass, adorns Freiburg Cathedral in Germany.

Troubadours appear in scenes of romance, a novel idea in medieval times.

REFLECTING ON THE TIMES

1. Is this scene a realistic or typical example of a medieval town? Why or why not?
2. What was the purpose of a craft guild?

325

ANSWERS TO REFLECTING ON THE TIMES

1. Students may argue that the scene is not realistic because it doesn't show the crowding and poor sanitation of typical medieval towns.
2. Craft guilds regulated the work of artisans, establishing rules governing prices, wages, and employment; setting standards of quality; and providing other social benefits for their members.

THE HISTORY CHANNEL.

The following videotape program is available from Glencoe:

- **Cathedrals: Notre Dame to Washington's National Cathedral**

To find classroom resources to accompany this video, check the following home page:

The History Channel: http://www.historychannel.com

Independent Practice

📁 Guided Reading Activity 13-2 **L1**

Daily Life Have students write two paragraphs describing what it might have been like to live in a medieval town. Have them mention both advantages (*jobs, safety, intellectual opportunity*) and disadvantages (*crowded conditions, lack of sanitation, disease*). **L2**

Literature Have students read the General Prologue to Chaucer's *The Canterbury Tales* and write a character sketch of three different pilgrims. Select several students to read their character sketches aloud. **L3**

📁 Geography and History Activity 13

Cultural Perspectives

Early Universities Although modern universities had their origins in medieval Europe, Arabs had founded universities nearly 200 years earlier. The Fatimids founded Cairo's al-Azhar University in A.D. 970. It remains the world's chief center of Islamic and Arabic learning.

Kano Becomes a Walled City

Nigeria, A.D. 1150
Before Kano became a walled city, five generations of Kano's Hausa citizens endured warfare with neighboring chiefs. Hausa rulers developed the city into an urban center that attracted aristocrats, merchants, weavers, and scholars. Kano's third ruler began the walls, which were completed by his grandson Tsaraki in A.D. 1150. Kano later became part of the Songhai Empire.

The middle class helped turn towns into organized municipalities. Businessmen created councils to administer town affairs and gained political power for themselves. As the money economy spread, kings began to depend on the middle class for loans and for income from the taxes they paid. The leading merchants and bankers became advisers to lords and kings.

Town Government

Conflict gradually developed between the feudal classes and the burghers. City dwellers did not fit into the feudal system; they resented owing taxes and services to lords. They wanted to run their own affairs and have their own courts and laws. At the same time, feudal lords feared the growing wealth and power of the middle class. To try to keep the burghers in line, the lords began to strictly enforce feudal laws.

The money economy gave the towns the income and power they needed to win the struggle against the lords. In the A.D. 1000s Italian towns formed groups called communes. Using the political power they gained from the growing money economy, the communes ended the power of feudal lords and made the Italian towns into independent city-states. In other areas of Europe, kings and nobles granted townspeople charters, documents that gave them the right to control their own affairs. At the same time, many towns remained a part of a kingdom or feudal territory.

Education

During the Early Middle Ages, most people were illiterate. Education was controlled by the clergy. In monastery and cathedral schools, students prepared for monastery life or for work as church officials. In addition to religious subjects, students learned grammar, rhetoric, logic, arithmetic, geometry, astronomy, and music.

As towns grew, the need for educated officials stimulated a new interest in learning. The growth of courts and other legal institutions created a need for lawyers. As a result, around A.D. 1150, students and teachers began meeting away from monastery and cathedral schools. They formed organizations that became known as universities.

Universities

At first the university was not so much a place as it was a guild of scholars organized for learning. Classes were held in rented rooms, churches, or outdoors. Because books were scarce, a teacher read the text and discussed it, while students took notes on slates. Classes did, however, meet regularly, and university rules set down the obligations of students and teachers toward each other. To qualify as a teacher, students had to pass an examination leading to a degree, or certificate of completion.

By the end of the A.D. 1200s, universities had spread throughout Europe. Most southern European universities were modeled after the law school at **Bologna** (buh•LOH•nyuh), Italy, and specialized in law and medicine. Universities in northern Europe, on the other hand, specialized in liberal arts and theology. These were generally modeled after the University of Paris.

New Learning

Medieval scholars studied Roman law, the works of Aristotle, and Muslim writings. Much of this knowledge reached Europe by way of Muslim and Jewish scholars in European Muslim strongholds, such as Spain and Sicily. European contact with Muslim scientific thought sparked an interest in the physical world that eventually led to the rise of Western science.

Many church leaders opposed the study of Aristotle's works, fearing that his ideas threatened Christian teachings. In contrast, some scholars thought the new knowledge could be used to support Christian ideas. They applied Aristotle's philosophy to theological questions and developed a system of thought called scholasticism. This new type of learning emphasized reason as well as faith in the

---

MEETING SPECIAL NEEDS ACTIVITY

Learning Style: Auditory/Musical Medieval guilds did much more than regulate people's work lives. Ask students who are particularly sensitive to or have a special interest in music to listen to Richard Wagner's opera *Die Meistersinger von Nürnberg*. Ask them to prepare a presentation for the class including a description of the Meistersingers who arose among the burghers of late thirteenth-century Germany. Students also may describe selections from the opera, a summary of its libretto, and some biographical information about its main character, the German poet and composer Hans Sachs, who was the most famous of the Meistersingers. **L3** 📁

interpretation of Christian doctrine. Scholastics sought to reconcile classical philosophy with the Church's teachings. They believed all knowledge could be integrated into a coherent whole.

One early scholastic teacher, **Peter Abelard**, taught theology in Paris during the early A.D. 1100s. In his book *Sic et Non* (Yes and No), he collected statements from the Bible and the writings of early Christian leaders that showed both sides of controversial questions. Abelard then had his students reconcile the differences through logic.

In the A.D. 1200s the most important scholastic thinker was **Thomas Aquinas** (uh•KWY•nuhs). In his work *Summa Theologica*, Aquinas claimed that reason was God's gift that could provide answers to basic philosophical questions. Reason, he said, existed in harmony with faith, both pointing to God and the orderliness of creation. The Catholic Church later accepted and promoted Aquinas's way of thinking.

Medieval Literature and Art

The spread of universities and the revival of intellectual endeavor stimulated advances in literature and the arts. Songs and epics of the Early Middle Ages were put in writing for the first time.

Epics and Romances

One of the earliest surviving literary works of the feudal world was the Anglo-Saxon epic *Beowulf*. A tale of grim battle and gloomy scenery, *Beowulf* reveals the harshness of life in northern Europe. Handed down by oral tradition for two centuries, it was finally written down in Old English (Anglo-Saxon) by an unknown poet in about A.D. 700. In colorful verses and exciting narrative, the epic describes how the Anglo-Saxon warrior Beowulf defeats a horrible monster named Grendel.

French epics called *chansons de geste*, or songs of high deeds, celebrated the courage of feudal warriors. The *Song of Roland*, written around A.D. 1100, gives an account of the chivalrous defense of Christianity by Charlemagne's knights.

Romances about knights and ladies were also popular. In southern France in the A.D. 1100s and A.D. 1200s, traveling poet-musicians called troubadours composed lyric poems and songs about love and the feats of knights. They helped define the ideal chivalric knight.

Talented writers were also found among women in convents and at royal courts. The German abbess Hildegard of Bingen, known for her spiritual wisdom, wrote about religion, science, and medicine. She was also a noted composer of music. Another abbess, Herrad of Landsberg, assisted by her nuns,

Linking Past and Present

The Plague

In addition to the physical effects, the psychological effects of the Black Death were also significant. Many people, searching for answers to the scourge, turned to mysticism and superstitious practices. They often found little spiritual guidance among the clergy, who fell ill and died at the same alarming rate as the general population. As the number of educated priests declined, religious orders began to recruit less qualified individuals, which lowered the overall intellectual level of the Church.

ANSWERS

Students may discuss the advances in medicine during modern times that have helped control the spread of diseases and have lessened their economic impact. When people exposed to an infection in one part of the world travel to another part, they can infect people with whom they come into contact.

ASSESS

Check for Understanding

Assign Section 2 Assessment as homework or as an in-class activity.

🔲 Use Interactive Tutor Self-Assessment Software to review Section 2.

Geography — The Plague

The Black Death

The Black Death—known today as the bubonic plague—was the worst medieval epidemic. It began in China and spread across Asia. Trading ships carried the disease west to the Mediterranean and to Europe. During the worst phase of the plague—between A.D. 1348 and A.D. 1350—nearly 25 million Europeans died. Not until the early 1900s were rats carrying bacteria-infected fleas identified as the carriers of the plague.

The plague brought terror to many medieval Europeans, who saw it as God's punishment. As deaths increased, production declined, and prices and wages rose. To cut costs, many landowners switched from farming to sheep raising (which required less labor) and drove villagers off the land. Merchants in towns laid off workers and demanded laws to limit wages. These setbacks, as well as the fear of plague, sparked peasant and worker uprisings. It would take at least a century for western Europe to recover.

Today, plague occasionally occurs in developing areas of Asia, Africa, and South America. Knowledge of disease prevention and the development of vaccines, however, have largely isolated plague outbreaks and reduced their devastating impact on societies.

Linking Past and Present — ACTIVITY

Examine the effects of disease on medieval and modern societies. How is the spread of disease related to human movement?

Chapter 13 *Medieval Europe at Its Height* 327

MAKING CONNECTIONS ACTIVITIES

Health Have students research and write a short report on other plague epidemics, such as the biblical plague of Ashdod, reported in I Samuel; epidemics in ancient Greece and Rome; the plague in London in the mid-1600s; and the plague in China in the mid-1800s. **L2**

The Arts Have students peruse art books to find several styles of manuscript illumination, such as Byzantine, Indian, Islamic, and one or more of the styles of medieval Europe, including Gothic, Romanesque, and Irish. Encourage students to make photocopies of works that reveal the distinctive characteristics of each style. Have them put together illustrated reports and then display them in the classroom. **L2 LEP**

Evaluate

Section Quiz 13-2

Use the Testmaker to create
a customized quiz for Section 2.

Reteach

Have students prepare charts
describing the key people discussed in the chapter, as well
as innovations in agriculture,
economics, trade, education,
literature, and art.

Reading Essentials and
Study Guide 13-2

Enrich

Have students read David
Macaulay's *Cathedral: The Story
of Its Construction* and prepare
an oral report on how and why
cathedrals were built, with a
focus on the role of craft guilds.

CLOSE

Have students write summaries
of how the focus of medieval life
gradually shifted from the feudal
manor to the towns.

Have students use the **Chapter
13 Student Web Activity** at
worldhistory.glencoe.com for in-
depth study of medieval writers.

Visualizing History Interior of a Gothic cathedral at
Reims, France. *How did the Gothic style
differ from the Romanesque?*

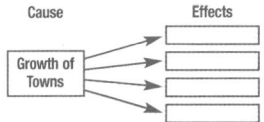

Student Web Activity 13

Visit the *World History: The Human Experience* Web
site at **worldhistory.glencoe.com** and click on
Chapter 13—Student Web Activities for an activity
relating to medieval writers.

---

compiled the *Garden of Delights*, an encyclopedia of
world history. Christine de Pisan, who grew up at the
French royal court, authored numerous love poems.

Vernacular Literature

By the late Middle Ages, most literature was
written in the vernacular, or the language of everyday speech. Instead of using the Latin, people spoke
the language of their own country—English, French,
German, Italian, or Spanish. In writing, these languages made literature accessible to more people.

Major literary works in the vernacular appeared during the A.D. 1300s. **Dante Alighieri**
(DAHN•tay A•luh•GYEHR•ee) wrote *The Divine
Comedy*, an epic poem in Italian that describes an
imaginary journey from hell to heaven. In England,
Geoffrey Chaucer produced *The Canterbury Tales*.
These narrative poems describe a varied group of
pilgrims who tell stories to amuse one another on
their way to Thomas à Becket's shrine at Canterbury.

Medieval Art

Early medieval churches were built in a style
called Romanesque, which combined features of
Roman and Byzantine structures. Romanesque
churches had thick walls, close-set columns, heavy
curved arches, and small windows. About A.D.
1150, French architects began to build in a new style
called Gothic. They replaced the heavy walls and
low arches with flying buttresses. These stone
beams, extending out from the walls, took the
weight of the building off the walls. This allowed the
walls to be thinner, with space for stained-glass windows. The ceiling inside was supported by pointed
arches made of narrow stone ribs reaching out from
tall pillars. These supports allowed architects to
build higher ceilings and more open interiors.

Medieval painters, by contrast, turned their
attention to a much smaller art form, the illuminated manuscript. Adorned with brilliantly colored
illustrations and often highlighted with gold leaf,
these works were miniature masterpieces.

SECTION 2 ASSESSMENT

Main Idea
1. Use a diagram like the one
below to show the effects of
the growth of towns on
medieval European society.

Cause   Effects

Growth of
Towns

Recall
2. **Define** money economy, guild,
master, apprentice, journeyman, charter, scholasticism,
troubadour, vernacular.
3. **Identify** Peter Abelard, Thomas
Aquinas, *Beowulf*, Dante
Alighieri, Geoffrey Chaucer.

Critical Thinking
4. **Synthesizing Information**
Create an imaginary medieval

town. Briefly explain its prominent physical characteristics.
Then describe what a typical
day for an artisan working
there would be like.

Understanding Themes
5. **Innovation** Choose one of the
following developments and
trace its effect on medieval
society: three-field system,
money economy, guilds.

328 Chapter 13 *Medieval Europe at Its Height*

SECTION 2 ASSESSMENT ANSWERS

1. built protective walls around town; lack of
sanitation spread disease and caused epidemics; rise of guilds to maintain trade
monopoly; rise of middle class; towns won
struggle against lords; self-government;
some towns became city-states; new interest in learning; achievements in literature
and arts

2. All terms are defined in the Glossary.
3. Abelard, 327; Aquinas, 327; *Beowulf*, 327;
Dante, 328; Chaucer, 328
4. Answers should refer to protective walls,
crowding, poor sanitation, markets, and
guilds.
5. **INNOVATION** Answers should
reflect chosen topic's significance.

A.D. 1300   A.D. 1400   A.D. 1500

A.D. 1346 France and England fight the Battle of Crécy.

A.D. 1469 Ferdinand of Aragon and Isabella of Castile marry.

c. A.D. 1485 Henry VII founds England's Tudor dynasty.

Section 3

Strengthening of Monarchy

Guide to Reading

Read to Find Out

Main Idea *European monarchs strengthened their powers during the Middle Ages.*

▶ **Terms to Define**
  cortes

▶ **People to Meet**
  Joan of Arc, Louis XI, Richard III, Henry VII, Ferdinand of Aragon, Isabella of Castile

▶ **Places to Locate**
  Crécy, Agincourt, Burgundy, Castile, Aragon

The Storyteller

A popular legend in English history is the story of the first Prince of Wales. Edward, King of England, desired to make the proud chieftains of Wales acknowledge his power. He campaigned against them, soon controlling their lands. The Welsh chiefs refused to accept Edward as their prince. They agreed, however, to serve a prince

The Tower of London

whom Edward would choose— provided he was noble and spoke neither English nor French. Edward accepted these terms and showed them their prince, his newborn son, who was indeed of noble birth and could speak neither language. The chiefs accepted the baby as their lawful lord, the Prince of Wales.

—adapted from *The Three Edwards*, Thomas Costain, 1964

uring the late Middle Ages, Europe's monarchs set up stronger central governments. They won the loyalty of their people and began to limit the powers of clergy and nobles. Gradually educated common people and laymen became royal advisers. At the outset, however, violent warfare engulfed western Europe.

The Hundred Years' War

Between A.D. 1337 and A.D. 1453, England and France fought a series of conflicts, known as the Hundred Years' War. For centuries, England's rulers had fought hard to keep the French lands inherited from the Normans. France's kings, however, wanted to unite these lands to their kingdom. In 1337 warfare began anew when England's Edward III laid claim to the French crown.

Major Battles

At first, the English were victorious—at **Crécy** in 1346 and **Agincourt** in 1415. Their success was primarily due to their weapons: a firearm that was the forerunner of the cannon and the longbow. About as tall as a man, the longbow could shoot arrows capable of piercing heavy armor at 300 yards (274 km). French historian Jean Froissart described the impact of the longbow at Crécy:

❝ **Then the English archers stept forth one pace and let fly their arrows so wholly [together] and so thick, that is seemed snow. When the [French soldiers] felt the [arrows piercing through heads, arms, and breasts, many of them cast down their cross-bows and did cut their strings and [retreated]... ❞**

Chapter 13   *Medieval Europe at Its Height*   **329**

SECTION THEME

▶ **Conflict** England and France battle while their monarchies gain power.

Guide to Reading

For reading strategies to help students read effectively see pages 12–13.

Vocabulary Pre-check

🔲 Use the Vocabulary PuzzleMaker for Chapter 13 to create a crossword puzzle to reinforce section terms. **L1 LEP**

📁 Use Vocabulary Activity 13 to introduce vocabulary terms. **L1 LEP**

FOCUS

Section Objective

Describe how European monarchs increased their powers during the Middle Ages.

BELLRINGER
Motivational Activity

Before taking roll at the beginning of the class period, project Section Focus Transparency 13-3 and have students answer the activity questions. Discuss students' responses.

📁 This activity is also available as a blackline master.

SECTION RESOURCES

📁 Reproducible Masters
- Lecture Notes 13-3
- Reproducible Lesson Plan 13-3
- Vocabulary Activity 13
- Guided Reading Activity 13-3
- Section Quiz 13-3
- Reading Essentials and Study Guide 13-3

📠 Transparencies
- Section Focus Transparency 13-3

Multimedia
🔲 Interactive Tutor Self-Assessment Software
🔲 Testmaker

TEACH

Guided Practice

THEME Conflict

Ask students to refer to pages 329–330, then give examples of conflicting claims and name the outright conflict that arose from those claims. *(dispute between France and England over lands in Normandy and southern France, and over the French throne, which led to the Hundred Years' War)* **L1**

Critical Thinking Have students recap the developments they learned about in Section 2 that led to the decline of feudalism. Then have them explain how the Hundred Years' War further hastened its decline. *(revival of trade and growth of towns; new ways of fighting led to need for standing armies rather than feudal soldiers)* **L3**

History & Art *La Pucelle* is French for "the Maid." How is Joan dressed? *(in men's clothes)* Among the charges of blasphemy brought against Joan in her trial was her wearing of men's clothes. **Answer to Caption:** *Her courage rallied the French around the king and drove the English out of France.*

 "La Pucelle!" Jeanne d' Arc Leads Her Army by Franck Craig, 1907. Musée d' Orsay, Paris, France *What did the "Maid of Orléans" accomplish for the French?*

Joan of Arc

Just as French fortunes had sunk to their lowest, a young woman helped bring about a dramatic reversal. In A.D. 1429, 17-year-old **Joan of Arc** appeared at the court of France's King Charles VII. She told the king that heavenly voices had called her to save France. With Charles's support, she inspired a French army to victory at Orléans, a town that had been placed under siege by the English. Soon after her triumph, Joan fell into English hands, was tried for witchcraft, and burned at the stake. Her courage, however, led the French to rally around their king and to gradually drive the English out of France. When the war ended in A.D. 1453, the port of Calais was the only French territory still in English hands.

Effects of the War

The Hundred Years' War deeply affected the peoples of France and England. France had suffered more severely than England, since the fighting had occurred on French soil. Yet victory gave the French a new sense of unity. England had been spared destruction, but its defeat led to bitterness among the nobles who had lost French lands. For the rest of the A.D. 1400s, England was divided by social conflict. In the long run, however, England's departure from France contributed to its unity and enabled the English to focus on problems at home.

The Hundred Years' War also hastened the decline of feudalism. The use of the longbow and firearms made feudal warfare based on castles and mounted knights outdated. Monarchs replaced feudal soldiers with national armies made up of hired soldiers. Maintaining these armies, however, was expensive. Monarchs turned to townspeople and the lower nobility for new sources of revenue. These groups willingly paid taxes and made loans in return for security and good government.

France

During the late 1400s, France's monarchy won much power and prestige. **Louis XI**, son of Charles VII, strengthened the bureaucracy, kept the nobles under royal control, and promoted trade and agriculture. Above all, he worked to unite all French feudal lands under his crown. Louis especially desired **Burgundy**, one of Europe's most prosperous areas. Burgundy's ruler, Charles the Bold, however, wanted to make his territory independent. Rather than fight Charles openly, Louis encouraged quarrels between Burgundy and the neighboring Swiss. After Charles's death in battle with the Swiss in A.D. 1477, Burgundy was divided between his daughter Mary and the French king.

COOPERATIVE LEARNING ACTIVITY

Readers' Theater Have groups of students prepare and present readings from the play *Saint Joan* by George Bernard Shaw, choosing suitable passages for presentation, assigning and reading the roles, preparing and presenting a synopsis of the play, and explaining the scenes.

Advanced students may prefer to present readings from Shakespeare's *Henry V*, Act IV, Scenes iii–viii, which dramatize the Battle of Agincourt from the English point of view. Much of the dialogue in this scene is in French; students taking French classes might especially enjoy the challenge. Make sure they use an edition with adequate footnotes, such as the Arden Shakespeare, and that they do not overlook the humor in Scene iv. **L3**

Adam Woolfitt

Cathedral of Chartres

The cathedral stands out against a lowering sky. The old town of Chartres, France, crowds the foreground, where artisans, merchants, bakers, and stonemasons once lived, [clus]tered near the great church. At the center of the [phot]ograph, the rose window provides a perfect exam[ple] of medieval stained glass. The two towers, one [orna]te, the other plain, were finished in different peri[ods]. They pierce the sky—giving form to the faith and [spiri]t of Europe's Middle Ages.

The cathedral reflects the technology of the High Middle Ages. Built before A.D. 1300, Chartres Cathedral, located about 50 miles southwest of Paris, is one of many works of Gothic architecture expressing both the fervor of the medieval era and the revival of the European economy, beginning around A.D. 1000. The growth of towns such as Chartres was a result of such changes. The combination of new building techniques, financial resources, and professional skills enabled the construction of the great cathedrals of Europe. ⊕

Chapter 13 *Medieval Europe at Its Height* **331**

TEACH

Tell students that the rose window (also called a wheel window) was a richly decorated circular window. Toward the mid-1100s the rose window began to be used widely in Gothic churches. Ask students to explain why stained glass art is not static. (*As sunlight changes in intensity, direction, and color during the day, the effect of the stained glass changes.*) Ask students which windows of Chartres Cathedral are the first to come fully to life. (*the east windows, because the sun rises in the east*)

CURRICULUM CONNECTION

RELIGION
Numerous street names in today's Chartres, such as *Rue aux Juifs*, recall the presence of an important medieval Jewish community there. The city's Saint-Hilaire Hospital probably originated as a synagogue.

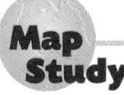
Map Study

Answer

Conflicting feudal claims to French lands and to the French throne fueled the Hundred Years' War.

Map Skills Practice

Reading a Map Why was control of Calais particularly important? *(It is the French port closest to England.)*

Independent Practice

📁 Guided Reading Activity 13-3 **L1**

The Arts When Ferdinand and Isabella captured the Moorish province of Granada, they gained some remarkable examples of Moorish art and architecture, such as the Alhambra. Have students research and report on the art and architecture of Moorish Spain. Have them give an oral summary, bringing pictures to share with the class. **L2**

Biography The French estates of Eleanor of Aquitaine were a source of dispute during the Hundred Years' War. An extraordinary woman in her own right, Eleanor was more than the wife and mother of French and English kings. Have students research the life of Eleanor of Aquitaine and write a brief summary of their findings. **L2**

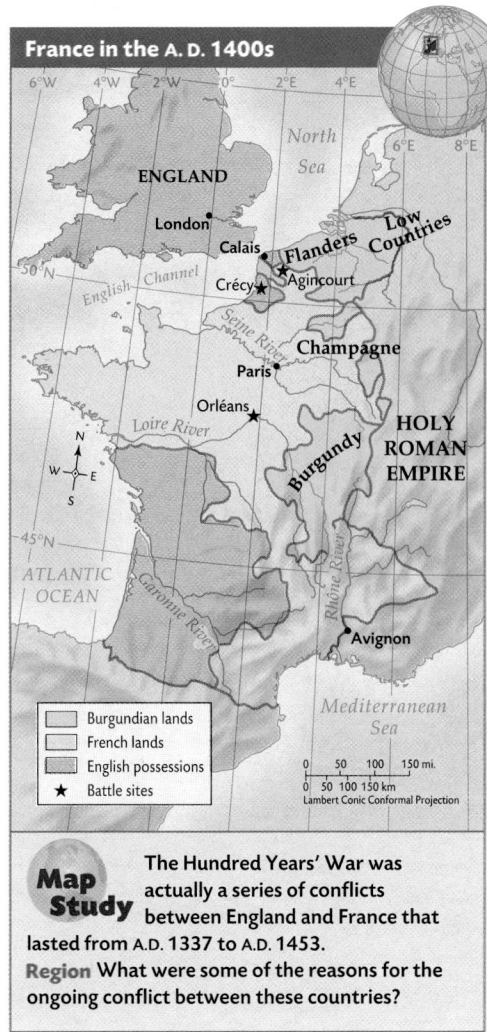

France in the A.D. 1400s

Burgundian lands
French lands
English possessions
★ Battle sites

★ **Map Study** The Hundred Years' War was actually a series of conflicts between England and France that lasted from A.D. 1337 to A.D. 1453.
Region What were some of the reasons for the ongoing conflict between these countries?

England

During the Hundred Years' War, the English monarchy's power was limited by Parliament, which had won the right to levy taxes, approve laws, and provide advice. Royal authority further eroded as a result of a struggle among the nobility for control of the throne. Begun in A.D. 1455, this conflict became known as the Wars of the Roses because of the symbols of the rival families involved. The royal house of Lancaster bore the red rose; its rival, the house of York, a white rose.

During the Wars of the Roses, Edward, duke of York, overthrew the weak Lancaster dynasty and became King Edward IV. As king, Edward worked

to strengthen royal government and to promote trade. His death in A.D. 1483 brought uncertainty to England. The heirs to the throne were the late king's two sons. Edward's brother, Richard, however had himself proclaimed king and locked his young nephews in the Tower of London, where they were probably murdered. **Richard III** tried to rule well but lacked widespread support. He finally fell to the forces of Henry Tudor, a Lancaster noble, on Bosworth Field in A.D. 1485.

Henry became **King Henry VII**, the first Tudor king. Henry eliminated royal claimants to the throne, avoided costly foreign wars, and increased royal power over the nobles. As a result, the English monarchy emerged from the Wars of the Roses strengthened and with few challengers.

Spain

During the late A.D. 1400s, Spain emerged as a leading European power. Even before Pope Urban's call for the Crusades, the Christian rulers of northern Spain had been fighting the *Reconquista* (RAY•kohn•KEES•tuh), or "reconquest," of Muslim areas in Spain. By A.D. 1250, the Iberian Peninsula consisted of three Christian realms: Portugal in the west, **Castile** in the center, and **Aragon** on the Mediterranean coast. Only Granada in the south remained in the hands of the Moors, or Spanish Muslims.

In A.D. 1469 **Ferdinand of Aragon** and **Isabella of Castile** were married. Their two kingdoms, however, maintained separate governments, and royal power was limited by local interests. Christians settling in formerly Muslim areas, as well as large Jewish and Muslim communities in Castile and Aragon, had their own laws and officials. Special royal charters allowed many towns to keep their courts and local customs. Finally, assemblies known as cortes, in which nobles were powerful, had the right to review royal policies.

In Castile, however, the two monarchs worked to strengthen royal power. They sent out officials to govern the towns and set up special courts in the countryside to enforce royal laws. In A.D. 1492 their armies forced the surrender of the last Moorish stronghold at Granada. Shortly afterward, Ferdinand and Isabella ended religious toleration. To unite Spain, they wanted all Spaniards to be Catholic. Spanish Jews and Moors were ordered to convert or to leave Spain. The persecution and departure of many Jews and Moors, known for their banking, business, and intellectual skills, weakened Spain's economy and culture.

Religion Not until 1990 did Spain officially overturn the 1492 order calling for the expulsion or conversion of the Jews. The 1990 accord places not only Judaism but also Protestantism on par with Roman Catholicism in Spain.

MEETING SPECIAL NEEDS ACTIVITY

Learning Style: Visual/Spatial Organize the class into small groups of three to five students. Each group should include one student who draws well. Have each group choose a topic related to medieval life and draw several designs for stained glass treatment. Each group should then select a single design to prepare for presentation using poster board and colored tissue paper. After the design has been sketched in pencil on the poster board, students should work together to cut out the design and glue the tissue paper to the back of the poster. Have each group present its finished project to the class. **L1 LEP**

The Spanish monarchy also set up the Spanish Inquisition to enforce Catholic teaching. The Inquisition believed that Jews and Moors who had converted to Catholicism were still practicing their old religions in secret. It tortured, tried, and punished anyone suspected of heresy. The fear created by the Inquisition further strengthened the power of Spanish monarchs over their people.

The Holy Roman Empire

During the Middle Ages, the Holy Roman Empire, made up largely of German, Italian, and Slavic lands, was Europe's largest political unit. Despite its size, the Empire was far from achieving unity under a strong monarch. While most European rulers came to power through family ties, the Holy Roman emperor was elected by a diet, or assembly of mostly German princes who governed their local territories as independent rulers.

In A.D. 1356 the number of princes taking part in imperial elections was limited to seven. Whenever an emperor died, these seven electors chose as his successor a politically weak noble with small landholdings. In the early 1400s, they began choosing emperors from the Hapsburgs, a family of nobles based in Austria. Once in power, Hapsburg emperors could not control the princes and unify the empire. Yet they were able to increase their prestige by securing other areas of Europe.

One of the most ambitious Hapsburg emperors was Maximilian I. Elected emperor in A.D. 1493, Maximilian married Mary of Burgundy and acquired the Low Countries (present-day Belgium, the Netherlands, and Luxembourg) as part of the Hapsburg inheritance. His grandson, Charles, born in A.D. 1500, later became king of Spain; German princes elected him Holy Roman emperor as Charles V. Under Charles, the Hapsburgs became the most powerful European royal family.

Eastern Europe

The Middle Ages also saw the rise of kingdoms in the area of eastern Europe between present-day Germany and Russia. The largest and most powerful of these lands were Poland and Hungary.

Poland

Formed in the A.D. 900s by West Slavs, Poland had accepted Roman Catholicism and close ties with western Europe. About A.D. 1000, the Poles began fighting groups of German warriors known as the Teutonic Knights for control of areas of Poland near the Baltic Sea.

During the A.D. 1300s, Poland enjoyed a golden age under King Casimir III, who reduced the power of local nobles and formed a strong central government. In A.D. 1386, a successor, Queen Jadwiga (yahd•VEE•gah), married Wladyslaw Jagiello (vwah•DIHS•wahv yahg•YEH•loh), duke of Lithuania. Their marriage unified Poland and Lithuania, creating one of the largest states in medieval Europe. With the added strength of Lithuania, Polish forces finally defeated the Teutonic Knights at the Battle of Tannenburg in A.D. 1410.

Hungary

South of Poland, the kingdom of Hungary was made up of Magyars, Germans, and Slavs. In A.D. 1000 King Stephen I became a Roman Catholic and introduced his people to western European ways.

In A.D. 1241 Mongols from central Asia invaded Hungary and caused widespread destruction. They soon withdrew, however, and the kingdom was able to rebuild. During the A.D. 1400s and A.D. 1500s, Hungary faced periodic attacks from the Ottoman Turks. In A.D. 1526 Hungary's King Louis II was defeated by the Ottoman ruler Suleiman I at the Battle of Mohacs (MOH•hahch). Most of Hungary came under the Ottomans; the rest was ruled by the Hapsburg emperors.

ASSESS

Check for Understanding

Assign Section 3 Assessment as homework or as an in-class activity.

 Use Interactive Tutor Self-Assessment Software to review Section 3.

Evaluate

Section Quiz 13-3

Use the Testmaker to create a customized quiz for Section 3.

Reteach

Have students prepare a time line of significant events in this section, including brief explanations.

Reading Essentials and Study Guide 13-3

Enrich

The son of the English king Edward III was known as the Black Prince because he wore black armor. Have students research the Black Prince and his role in the Hundred Years' War. Ask them to summarize his career in a brief written report.

CLOSE

Summarize how and why the monarchy was strengthened during the period covered in this section. Have students debate the advantages and disadvantages of a strong monarchy.

SECTION 3 ASSESSMENT

Main Idea
1. Use a chart like the one below to identify ways in which medieval European monarchs increased their power.

France	England	Spain	Holy Roman Empire

Recall
2. **Define** cortes.
3. **Identify** Joan of Arc, Louis XI, Richard III, Henry VII, Ferdinand of Aragon, Isabella of Castile.

Critical Thinking
4. **Applying Information** Relate how one European monarchy, such as that of the English, French, or Holy Roman Empire, changed during the Middle Ages.

Understanding Themes
5. **Conflict** Explain the reasons for the struggles between the various European monarchies.

SECTION 3 ASSESSMENT ANSWERS

1. France: Louis XI united feudal lords under his crown; England: Edward IX strengthened royal government and promoted trade; Henry VII increased power over nobles; Spain: Ferdinand and Isabella sent officials to enforce royal laws in towns, Spanish Inquisition; Holy Roman Empire: Hapsburgs increased prestige by seizing other areas in Europe

2. All terms are defined in the Glossary.

3. Joan of Arc, 330; Louis XI, 330; Richard III, 332; Henry VII, 332; Ferdinand, 332; Isabella, 332

4. Answers should describe that country's social, political, and economic life.

5. **CONFLICT** Answers should include analysis of feudalism and of shifting political interests during the Middle Ages.

A.D. 1300   **A.D. 1400** **A.D. 1500**

A.D. 1309 Pope's court moves to Avignon, France.

A.D. 1378 Great Schism in the Church occurs.

A.D. 1415 Church authorities burn Jan Hus as a heretic.

A.D. 1436 Compromise reached between the Church and Hussites.

Section 4

The Troubled Church

Guide to Reading

Read to Find Out
Main Idea *The Church came under pressure to reform.*

▶ **Terms to Define**
pilgrimage, simony

▶ **People to Meet**
Pope Clement V, John Wycliffe, the Lollards, Jan Hus, the Hussites

▶ **Places to Locate**
Avignon, Bohemia

The Storyteller

The situation was intolerable, Nicholas of Clèmanges thought angrily. The Church was increasingly corrupt. Greed, pride, and love of luxury prevailed in place of humility and charity. Comparing the current priests and bishops with the holy leaders of antiquity, he reflected, was like comparing mud to gold. What would come of such ills? "So great a flood of evils must assuredly be crushed and utterly

destroyed by God's most righteous judgment. It does not seem possible in any other way to chasten it." Nicholas prayed that the Church might be spared from complete destruction—that a little seed might remain in the world.

—adapted from *On the Ruin and the Repair of the Church*, Nicholas Clèmanges, reprinted in *Readings in Western Civilization*, 1986

The Church besieged by evil forces

During the upheavals of the Late Middle Ages—caused by warfare, the plague, and religious controversy—many people turned to the Church for comfort and reassurance. Religious ceremonies multiplied, and thousands of people went on religious pilgrimages, or journeys to holy places. In spite of this increase in religious devotion, the temporal authority of the Church was weakening due to the influence of strong monarchs and national governments. A growing middle class of educated townspeople and a general questioning of the Church's teachings also contributed to this decline.

Babylonian Captivity

During the early A.D. 1300s, the papacy came under the influence of the French monarchy. In A.D. 1305 a French archbishop was elected **Pope Clement V**. A few years later, Clement decided to move his court from Rome to **Avignon** (A•veen•YOHN), a small city in southern France, to escape the civil wars that were disrupting Italy. While in France, the pope appointed only French cardinals. Pope Clement V and his successors—all French—remained in Avignon until A.D. 1377.

This long period of the exile of the popes at Avignon came to be known as the Babylonian Captivity, after the period of the exile of the Jews in Babylon in the 500s B.C. For centuries, Rome had been the center of the western Church. With the pope in France, people feared that the papacy would be dominated by French monarchs. Others disliked the concern the Avignon popes showed for increasing church taxes and making church administration more efficient. They believed the popes had become corrupted by worldly power and were neglecting their spiritual duties. The Italian poet Petrarch complained:

❝ Here reign the successors of the poor fishermen of Galilee; they have strangely

> forgotten their origin. I am astounded ... to see these men loaded with gold and clad in purple, boasting of the spoils of princes and nations. "

The Great Schism

Finally, in A.D. 1377, Pope Gregory XI left Avignon and returned to Rome. After his death, Roman mobs forced the College of Cardinals to elect an Italian as pope. The cardinals later declared the election invalid, insisting they had voted under pressure. The cardinals then elected a second pope, who settled in Avignon. When the Italian pope refused to resign, the Church faced the dilemma of being led by two popes.

This controversy became known as the Great Schism because it caused serious divisions in the Church. The Great Schism lasted from A.D. 1378 until A.D. 1417 and seriously undermined the pope's authority. People wondered how they could regard the pope as the divinely chosen leader of Christianity when there was more than one person claiming to be the single, unquestioned head of the Church.

Calls for a Council

Many kings, princes, and church scholars called for a reform of church government. The most popular remedy was a general church council. However, this solution posed many problems. First, such councils were traditionally called by popes. No pope was willing to call a council that would limit his authority. However, the legality of a council would be questionable if it did not receive papal approval. Second, different rulers in Europe supported particular popes for political reasons. Such political divisions made it almost impossible to reach agreement on even the site of a council, let alone to reach agreement on the deeper and more important issues involved.

By A.D. 1400 many western Europeans were committed to the idea of a church council. In A.D. 1409 a council met at Pisa, Italy, to unite the Church behind one pope. It resulted in the election of a third pope, since neither the pope at Rome nor the pope at Avignon would resign. Finally, in A.D. 1414, another council met at Constance, Germany. It forced the resignation of all three popes and then elected Pope Martin V, ending the Great Schism. The long period of disunity, however, had seriously weakened the political influence of the Church. Moreover, many Europeans had come to feel a greater sense of loyalty to their monarchs than to the pope.

Calls for Reform

Church authority was also weakened by people's dislike of abuses within the Church. The clergy used many unpopular means to raise money. Fees were charged for almost every type of service the Church performed. Common people especially disliked *simony*—the selling of church positions—because the cost of buying these positions was passed on to them. The princely lifestyles of the clergy further eroded regard for the Church. Many Europeans called for reform. Two of the clearest voices belonged to an English scholar and a Bohemian preacher.

John Wycliffe

John Wycliffe (WIH•KLIHF), a scholar at England's Oxford University, criticized the Church's wealth, corruption among the clergy, and the pope's claim to absolute authority. He wanted secular rulers to remove church officials who were immoral or corrupt.

Wycliffe claimed that the Bible was the sole authority for religious truth. He began to translate the Bible from Latin into English so people could read it themselves. Since church doctrine held that only the clergy could interpret God's word in the Bible, this act was regarded as revolutionary. Some of Wycliffe's followers, known as **the Lollards**, angrily criticized the Church. They destroyed images of saints, ridiculed the Mass, and ate communion bread with onions to show that it was no different from ordinary bread.

Widespread antipapal feelings made it difficult for the English government to suppress Lollards. Wycliffe was persuaded to moderate his views and received only a mild punishment. He died peacefully in A.D. 1384, but his ideas spread.

Among those who supported the Lollards was Bohemian-born Queen Anne, the wife of King

---

Footnotes to History

Silver Spoons During the Middle Ages, pewter spoons became common utensils for eating. In the A.D. 1400s silver "apostle spoons," bearing the image of a child's patron saint, were favored gifts for newborns in Italy. Only the wealthy could afford such a luxury. From these apostle spoons came the saying that a privileged child is "born with a silver spoon in his or her mouth."

Chapter 13 *Medieval Europe at Its Height* 335

TEACH

Guided Practice

THEME Conflict

After students have read this section, ask them to name specific examples of conflict within the medieval Church that led to changes. (*Students should mention the teachings of John Wycliffe and the Lollards, and Jan Hus and the Hussites. Changes include the translation of the Bible into vernacular languages and some religious liberties for Hussites.*) **L1**

Philosophy Tell students that Wycliffe's belief that people could and should think for themselves was not original. Ask students to name other historical or contemporary figures who have advocated the same belief. (*Answers may include Socrates and Thoreau.*) **L3**

History Simulation 13

Independent Practice

Guided Reading Activity 13-4 **L1**

Political Cartoon Have students draw a political cartoon about an event or issue in this section, such as the Babylonian Captivity, the Great Schism, or the behavior of corrupted clergy. Display the cartoons in class. **L3**

ASSESS

Check for Understanding

Assign Section 4 Assessment as homework or as an in-class activity.

Use Interactive Tutor Self-Assessment Software to review Section 4.

COOPERATIVE LEARNING ACTIVITY

Role Play Have students work in small groups to write and present a play about an incident related in this section. Each student in the group should be responsible for a specific task, such as researching, writing dialogue, preparing props, or acting in the play itself. Students could present a play about the refusal of Urban VI to resign as pope, thus causing the Great Schism; Jan Hus defending his views to church leaders; John Wycliffe discussing his views with a group of his students; or some other incident related to this section. Encourage students to research the material thoroughly. Have students present their play for the class and, if possible, videotape their presentation. **L2**

**History
& Art**
 John of Gaunt (1340–1399) was the fourth son of the English king Edward III. His political aspirations were opposed by a group of powerful clergymen. In opposition to them, John formed an alliance with Wycliffe. *Gaunt* refers to Ghent, where John was born. **Answer to Caption:** *It encouraged people to search the Bible for religious truths on their own, rather than rely on the clergy.*

History & Art *John Wycliffe Reading His Translation of the Bible to John of Gaunt* by Ford Madox Brown. *Why was Wycliffe's translation of the Bible revolutionary?*

Evaluate

 Section Quiz 13-4

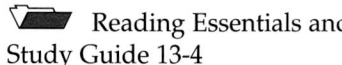 Use the Testmaker to create a customized quiz for Section 4.

Reteach

Have students identify two major events that destroyed people's confidence in the Church and two main dissenters who called for reform.

 Reteaching Activity 13

Reading Essentials and Study Guide 13-4

Enrich

Ask students to find out why Wycliffe's followers were called Lollards and to summarize their findings in a brief paragraph. *(from the Middle Dutch* lollaert, *"mumbler," a name given to earlier European groups considered heretical)*

Enrichment Activity 13

CLOSE

Lead a discussion about the problems within the medieval Church. Ask students to identify the most serious problems.

Richard II. Anne sent copies of Wycliffe's writings to her homeland in the Holy Roman Empire, where they influenced another great religious reformer.

Jan Hus

During the late A.D. 1300s and A.D. 1400s, the Slavs of **Bohemia**, known as Czechs, became more aware of their own national identity. They wanted to end German control of their country and backed sweeping reforms in the Catholic Church in Bohemia, which had many German clergy. Their religious and political grievances combined to produce an explosive situation.

The Czechs produced religious pamphlets and copies of the Bible in Czech and criticized the corruption of leading church officials, many of whom were German. The leader of the Czech religious reform movement was **Jan Hus**, a popular preacher and professor at the University of Prague. When Hus and his works were condemned by the Church

and political leaders, a violent wave of riots swept across Bohemia.

Faced with a possible full-scale rebellion against the Church, in A.D. 1415 the council at Constance demanded that Hus appear before them to defend his views. The Holy Roman emperor promised Hus safe conduct to Constance, Germany, but this guarantee was ignored. Hus was burned at the stake as a heretic, but his heroic death caused many Czechs to rally around their new martyr.

From A.D. 1420 to A.D. 1436, Hus's supporters, called **Hussites**, resisted the Church and the Holy Roman emperor, and the Church launched five crusades against the Hussites. All five failed. Using firearms and the tactic of forming movable walls with farm wagons, the Hussites defeated the crusading knights.

In A.D. 1436 representatives of the pope and the Holy Roman emperor reached a compromise with the Hussite leaders. They gave the Hussites certain religious liberties in return for their allegiance to the Church. The ideas of Jan Hus, however, continued to spread throughout Europe to influence later and more radical reformers. While this agreement gave the appearance that the Church had successfully met the challenges to its authority, the basic spiritual questions raised by Hus and others did not go away.

SECTION 4 ASSESSMENT

Main Idea
1. Use a web diagram like the one below to identify reasons why the church was under pressure to make reforms.

Reasons for Church Reform

Recall
2. **Define** pilgrimage, simony.
3. **Identify** Pope Clement V, Babylonian Captivity, Great Schism, John Wycliffe, the Lollards, Jan Hus, the Hussites.

Critical Thinking
4. **Synthesizing Information** Imagine you are a follower of

Jan Hus just after his execution. How would you feel about carrying on his work?

Understanding Themes
5. **Conflict** Explain the rise of dissent among many devout Europeans. Why were they against the Church and its leadership?

SECTION 4 ASSESSMENT ANSWERS

1. papacy influenced by French monarchy; Great Schism: two popes, one in Rome and one in Avignon; abuses within Church such as simony; in Bohemia, criticism of corrupt church leaders
2. All terms are defined in the Glossary.
3. Clement V, 334; Babylonian Captivity, 334; Great Schism, 335; Wycliffe, 335; Lollards, 335; Hus, 336; Hussites, 336
4. would have continued resistance to Church and Holy Roman Emperor in order to attain goal of ridding Bohemia of German influence
5. **CONFLICT** People were angered by corruption within Church and abuse of power by church leaders.

Analyzing Historical Maps

Walking through your town, you may see changes in progress. Change also takes place on a larger scale across nations and continents. Historical maps illustrate political, social, and cultural changes.

Learning the Skill

To analyze a historical map, first read the title to identify its theme. Then identify the chronology of events on the map. Many historical maps show changes in political boundaries over time. For example, the map below of the Frankish Empire uses colors to show land acquisitions under three different rulers. On the other map, however, colors represent areas controlled by different rulers at the same time. Read the map key, labels, and captions to determine what time periods and changes appear on the map.

To compare historical maps of the same region in different time periods, first identify the geographic location and time period of each map. Then identify which features have remained the same and which have changed. What groups control the area in each map? Has the country's size changed over time?

After analyzing the maps, draw conclusions about the causes and effects of these changes.

Practicing the Skill

The two maps on this page show the same region in different time periods. Study both maps and answer these questions.
1. What is the time period of each map?
2. How did the Frankish Empire change from A.D. 500 to A.D. 800?
3. Did France grow larger or smaller between A.D. 800 and A.D. 1400?
4. What other changes appear on these maps?

Applying the Skill

Compare a map of Europe today with a map of Europe in 1985 or earlier. Identify at least five changes that have occurred since the early 1980s.

For More Practice

Turn to the Skill Practice in the Chapter Assessment on page 339 for more practice in analyzing historical maps.

The **Glencoe Skillbuilder Interactive Workbook**, Level 2 provides instruction and practice in key social studies skills.

Frankish Empire A.D. 481–814

- [ ] Clovis's kingdom
- [ ] Added by Martel and Pepin
- [ ] Added by Charlemagne
- ★ Battle site

France in the A.D. 1400s

- [ ] Burgundian lands
- [ ] English possessions
- [ ] French lands
- ★ Battle sites

Chapter 13 *Medieval Europe at Its Height* 337

ANSWERS TO PRACTICING THE SKILL

1. The map on the left shows the Frankish Empire from A.D. 481 to A.D. 814; the map on the right shows France in the 1400s.
2. It spread eastward and south to include parts of present-day Spain, Italy, Switzerland, and the Benelux countries.
3. smaller
4. Answers may include that France was divided up among various rulers, that its boundaries changed over time, and so on.

Social Studies
SKILLS

TEACH

Analyzing Historical Maps Before students read the skill, ask them whether they think of maps as static or changing and to justify their answers. Then ask them to name some other kinds of maps with which they are familiar. (*Students might mention weather maps, topographic maps, astronomical maps.*) Ask them to indicate what kinds of changes those maps can illustrate. (*Weather maps clearly show changing weather patterns; changes in topographic maps of the same region over time might show the formation of a new island from vulcanism; changes in astronomical maps of the same region over time might show the appearance of a comet.*) When students are sufficiently familiar with the idea that maps of different kinds can serve as records of change, have them read the skill and complete the practice questions.

Additional Practice

📁 Skill Reinforcement Activity 13

📁 Building Skills in Geography Workbook, Unit 1, Lesson 13

GLENCOE TECHNOLOGY

Glencoe's **Skillbuilder Interactive Workbook**, Level 2
This interactive CD-ROM promotes student mastery of key social studies skills.

Chapter 13 Assessment

CHAPTER 13 ASSESSMENT

WORLD HISTORY *Online*

Have students use the **Chapter 13 Self-Check Quiz** at worldhistory. glencoe.com to prepare for the Chapter Test.

GLENCOE TECHNOLOGY

VIDEODISC
Use MindJogger to review the chapter.

MindJogger Videoquiz

Chapter 13
Disc 2 Side B

Also available in VHS.

Answers

Using Key Terms
1. d
3. b
5. g
2. i
4. l

Using Your History Journal

Students should consider how military or religious motives shaped the characters in these works.

Reviewing Facts

1. France: much suffering, new sense of unity; England: social conflict, contributed to unity, enabled England to focus on internal problems; other: decline of feudalism, national armies replaced knights, monarchs turned to townspeople and lower nobility for sources of revenue

2. First: 1096–1099, captured Jerusalem; Second: 1147–1149, attempt to regain territory in Palestine failed; Third: 1189–1192, failed to regain control of Jerusalem; others: 1200s, Muslims conquered remaining Christian territories in Palestine.

3. heavier plow, collar harness, three-field system

4. Working women served in guilds, while women in convents and royal courts wrote literature.

WORLD HISTORY *Online*

Self-Check Quiz

Visit the *World History: The Human Experience* Web site at **worldhistory.glencoe.com** and click on *Chapter 13—Self-Check Quiz* to prepare for the Chapter Test.

Using Key Terms

Write the key term that completes each sentence. Then write a sentence for each term not chosen.

a. apprentice
b. *cortes*
c. charter
d. scholasticism
e. Crusade
f. guilds
g. vernacular
h. simony
i. money economy
j. pilgrimages
k. master
l. troubadours

1. Church scholars developed a system of thought known as _____ that sought to reconcile faith and reason.
2. The rise of a _____ led to the growth of banking and put the feudal classes in an economic squeeze.
3. In Spain, assemblies known as _____ at first had the right to review the policies of Spanish monarchs.
4. In medieval France, traveling poet-musicians called _____ composed lyric poems and songs about love and the feats of knights.
5. During the Middle Ages, the rise of _____ languages gave each kingdom of Europe a separate identity.

Technology Activity

Using E-mail Locate an E-mail address for your local historical society or chamber of commerce. Write a letter requesting information about various styles and influences of medieval architecture found in your area. Using your response, create an illustrated tourist pamphlet of information about area structures. Include a map.

Using Your History Journal

From your notes on Beowulf, *the* Song of Roland, *or* The Canterbury Tales, *write a short description of the manners, customs, and values of the Europeans described in the work.*

Reviewing Facts

1. **History** Use a chart like the one below to identify the effects of the Hundred Years' War.

Effects of Hundred Years' War

England	France	Other

2. **History** List the various medieval Crusades and their results.
3. **Technology** Describe several agricultural improvements in the Middle Ages.
4. **Culture** Discuss the contributions made by women to the society of the Middle Ages.
5. **History** List the key events in the Hundred Years' War.
6. **Culture** Identify two church reformers and a major event in the life of each.
7. **Culture** Describe a typical medieval town.
8. **Economics** Identify the bourgeoisie and state their role in late medieval Europe.
9. **History** Discuss the impact of the Black Death.
10. **Government** Explain why townspeople and the lower nobility supported the rise of strong monarchies in western Europe.
11. **Culture** List the problems that the Catholic Church faced at the end of the Middle Ages.
12. **Government** State how Louis XI strengthened the French monarchy.
13. **History** Discuss the major result of the Wars of the Roses.
14. **History** Identify the *Reconquista*. How did it contribute to the unity of Spain?
15. **Economics** List new business methods that developed in Europe by the A.D. 1400s. How did they change European life?

---

5. English king claimed throne of France when French king died in 1328 without a direct heir; England won early battles but France eventually prevailed.
6. Wycliffe began translating Bible into English; Hus burned at stake as heretic.
7. dirty, crowded, smelly, noisy, constant threat of fire and disease
8. middle class, merchants; helped turn towns into cities, weakened feudal system, strengthened monarchies
9. wiped out about a third of Europe's population; disrupted warfare, business
10. They received freedom from feudal obligations by financially supporting monarchs.
11. decline in religious/political authority as result of Babylonian Captivity and Great Schism
12. strengthened bureaucracy, kept nobles under royal control, promoted trade/farming
13. English monarchy emerged strengthened.

Critical Thinking

1. **Apply** How did the medieval middle class change European society?
2. **Analyze** What various forces led to Europe's economic growth during the Middle Ages?
3. **Evaluate** How would Europe be different today if there had been no Crusades?
4. **Apply** How did European monarchies change during the Middle Ages? What were the effects of this change on culture, religion, and politics in Europe?

Geography in History

1. **Place** Refer to the map "Trade Routes A.D. 1400s." Name the major trading cities in western Europe during the 1400s.
2. **Human/Environment Interaction** Why did most European traders avoid overland routes whenever possible?
3. **Location** With which two areas to the east did the cities of Europe most want to trade?
4. **Movement** How did the desire for luxuries from the East lead to changes in transportation in the West?

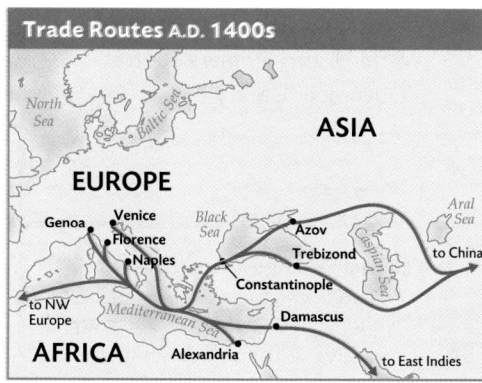

Trade Routes A.D. 1400s

Understanding Themes

1. **Cultural Diffusion** How did a mix of cultures affect medieval Europe?
2. **Innovation** Choose one medieval innovation and describe its influence on medieval society.

Do the same for a modern innovation and modern society.
3. **Conflict** How did continual conflict between England and France strengthen the monarchies of those countries?
4. **Conflict** Why was there religious dissent in the Catholic Church of the Late Middle Ages?

Linking Past and Present

1. The Crusades were a series of "holy wars" conducted by Christians against Muslims. Can you find examples of holy wars in modern times?
2. Compare the rise of towns in medieval Europe with the rise of towns in America.
3. How do medieval European universities compare to today's higher educational institutions?

Skill Practice

Study the map "Spread of the Black Death" and answer the questions below.

1. What is the topic and time period of this map?
2. What does color represent?
3. When and where did the Black Death begin?
4. In which direction did the Black Death spread? How does the map show this?
5. What factor do you think caused this pattern of the epidemic?`

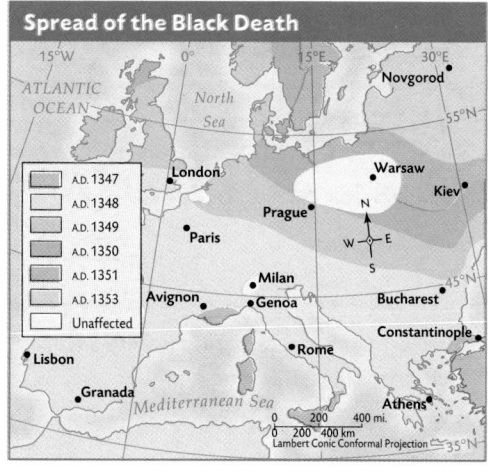

Spread of the Black Death

Understanding Themes

1. **CULTURAL DIFFUSION** brought new ideas and influences to political, technological, and social spheres
2. **INNOVATION** Improved plows increased medieval food production. Computer technology today has strengthened interdependence among nations.
3. **CONFLICT** Victory in the Hundred Years' War gave power to French monarchy. Civil war in England culminated in rise of strong Tudor monarchy.
4. **CONFLICT** Doctrinal differences as well as internal abuses of power led to dissent.

Linking Past and Present

1. Arab-Israeli conflicts.
2. similar process, with political, social, and economic growth leading to new opportunities
3. Medieval universities had to be careful not to offend the Church. Admission based on ability to pay. Only males admitted.

Skill Practice

1. spread of the Black Death in 1300s
2. where plague spread to at different times
3. China in 1347
4. north and west; colors correspond to dates, showing northern and westward movement
5. As ships sailed from Asia to Mediterranean, the plague spread from China to ports in southern Europe and beyond.

---

14. reconquest of Muslim lands in Spain; nearly all of Spain shared same religion
15. development of a money economy, banking; led to growth of towns, undermined feudalism

Critical Thinking
1. helped turn towns into organized municipalities; businessmen gained power; stimulated new interest in learning, founded universities
2. money economy, rise of middle class, improved agricultural methods
3. lack of cultural diffusion and hostility

between Christians and Muslims
4. Monarchies became stronger, leading to greater control over religion and politics, and to stronger national cultures.

Geography in History
1. Venice, Florence, Naples, Genoa
2. sea travel was safer and faster
3. East Indies and China
4. New sea and river routes were developed; the Roman road system was repaired and rebuilt.

Chapter Bonus Test Question

Ask students: How do you think the Church felt about the growth of medieval towns? *(positive—applauded the building of cathedrals; negative—disapproved of practices seen as avaricious)*

A complete, 1-page lesson plan is provided for each section in the *Reproducible Lesson Plans* booklet.

East and South Asia

CHAPTER RESOURCES

	Reproducible Resources	Multimedia Resources
Chapter Opener	Chapter Themes: Graphic Organizer 14 Historical Significance Chapter Activity 14	MindJogger Videoquiz
Chapter Enrichment	Vocabulary Activity 14* Time Line Activity 14 Mapping History Activity 14 History Simulation 14 Geography and History Activity 14 Source Reading 14 People in World History Profiles 25, 26 World Literature Selection 14 World Art and Music Activity 14 Enrichment Activity 14 Critical Thinking Activity 14 Skill Reinforcement Activity 14 Performance Assessment Activity 14 Standardized Test Practice Workbook Activity 14 Inclusion for the Social Studies Classroom Strategies and Activities	World History and Art Transparency 17, *Angkor Wat* Chapter Transparency 14 PicturePack Transparency Set: Physical Geography of the World Vocabulary PuzzleMaker Software Picture Atlas of the World World Music: Cultural Traditions, Lessons 8, 9 STV: World Geography, Vol. 1, *Asia* World History Primary Source Document Library
Chapter Review/Reteaching	Reteaching Activity 14 Skill Reinforcement Activity 14 Spanish Chapter Summary 14	Chapter 14 Digest Audiocassette, Activity, Test* Vocabulary PuzzleMaker Software Interactive Tutor Self-Assessment Software MindJogger Videoquiz
Chapter Evaluation/Testing	Performance Assessment Activity 14 Chapter 14 Test, Forms A and B	ExamView® Pro Testmaker

* Also available in Spanish

0:00 OUT OF TIME? Assign the Chapter 14 Audiocassettes.

World History Primary Source Document Library

Make History Come Alive!

Engage your students with over 250 easily accessible primary source documents—available on this CD-ROM—that will give them real life insight into the important events of world history.

Block Schedule

Activities that are particularly suited to use within the block scheduling framework are identified throughout this chapter by the following designation.

KEY TO ABILITY LEVELS

Teaching strategies are coded for varying learning styles.
- **L1 BASIC** activities for all students
- **L2 AVERAGE** activities for average to above-average students
- **L3 CHALLENGING** activities for above-average students
- **LEP LIMITED ENGLISH PROFICIENCY** activities

Use Glencoe's *Presentation Plus!* multimedia teacher tool to easily present dynamic lessons that visually excite your students. Using Microsoft PowerPoint® you can customize the presentations to create your own personalized lessons.

Interactive Lesson Planner

Planning has never been easier! Using this CD-ROM, organize your week, month, semester, or year with all the help you need. The **Interactive Lesson Planner** gives you access to all of the blackline masters that accompany *World History: The Human Experience.*

SECTION RESOURCES

Daily Objectives	Reproducible Resources	Multimedia Resources
Section 1 Central Asia Describe how the Mongols acquired the world's largest land empire.	Lecture Notes 14-1 Reproducible Lesson Plan 14-1 Vocabulary Activity 14* Guided Reading Activity 14-1* Time Line Activity 14 Section Quiz 14-1* Reading Essentials and Study Guide 14-1	Section Focus Transparency 14-1 Chapter Transparency 14 Interactive Tutor Self-Assessment Software Testmaker STV: World Geography, Vol. 1, *Asia*
Section 2 China Summarize the achievements of the Tang, Song, and Yuan dynasties.	Lecture Notes 14-2 Reproducible Lesson Plan 14-2 Vocabulary Activity 14* Guided Reading Activity 14-2* History Simulation 14 Section Quiz 14-2* Reading Essentials and Study Guide 14-2	Section Focus Transparency 14-2 Interactive Tutor Self-Assessment Software Testmaker World Music: Cultural Traditions, Lesson 8 Picture Atlas of the World
Section 3 Southeast Asia Explain how Southeast Asians were influenced by the cultures of China and India.	Lecture Notes 14-3 Reproducible Lesson Plan 14-3 Vocabulary Activity 14* Guided Reading Activity 14-3* Geography and History Activity 14 Section Quiz 14-3* Reading Essentials and Study Guide 14-3	Section Focus Transparency 14-3 World History and Art Transparency 17, *Angkor Wat* Interactive Tutor Self-Assessment Software Testmaker World Music: Cultural Traditions, Lesson 9 Picture Atlas of the World
Section 4 Korea and Japan Explain how the Koreans and Japanese accepted Chinese culture.	Lecture Notes 14-4 Reproducible Lesson Plan 14-4 Guided Reading Activity 14-4* Reteaching Activity 14 Enrichment Activity 14 Section Quiz 14-4* Performance Assessment Activity 14 Spanish Chapter Summary 14 Reading Essentials and Study Guide 14-4	Section Focus Transparency 14-4 Vocabulary PuzzleMaker Software Interactive Tutor Self-Assessment Software Testmaker

* *Also available in Spanish*

Chapter Activities

✔ *Performance Assessment Activity*

Modern-Day Dynasties and Empires Have students expand their understanding of the concepts of dynasty, empire, and kingdom by researching modern-day examples, such as publishing dynasties and entertainment empires. Have students work in pairs or trios to conduct their research and complete a collage, mural, or other complex visual to show the many examples. Students should also include information about dynasties, empires, and kingdoms from the chapter.

Possible Rubric Features

Concept attainment, accuracy of content information, research skills, relevance and appropriateness of examples, creative and visual appeal of product

• *For an additional activity, refer to Activity 14 in the* Performance Assessment Strategies and Activities *booklet.*

ACTIVITY

From the Classroom of...

**Ken Austin
Friends Academy
Locust Valley, NY**

Steppe People Mural and Time Line

Organize students into three groups—illustrators, historians, and scribes. The illustrators will create a 3' x 20' mural, beginning by drawing a map on the mural of East and South Asia. Meanwhile, the historians will gather facts concerning the steppe peoples' way of life, interests, and activities. They should also trace chronologically the rise and movement of these peoples. The historians will share their information with the illustrators, who will add drawings and pictures to the mural, and the scribes, who will prepare a time line and brief fact sheets to accompany the illustrations. Place the time line along the bottom of the mural and the fact sheets near appropriate illustrations.

MULTIPLE LEARNING STYLES

Verbal/Linguistic
Ask students to look for a collection of Chinese or Japanese myths or children's stories in the school or public library. Have them prepare a selection to present to the class.

Logical/Mathematical
Direct students to create a three-part time line of the major events that occurred in China, Korea, and Japan during the period covered in this chapter. Have them label each event as political, cultural, or other.

Visual/Spatial
Have students plan a special Asian Arts day when each person brings to class and displays or reports on the origin of an item from China, Japan, Korea, or Southeast Asia. Suggest items such as a musical recording, pottery, clothing, a special book, or even an ethnic food.

Kinesthetic
Remind students that Chinese writing was originally pictographic—it used pictures to convey the meaning of the words. Ask students to research Chinese writing and make a poster showing Chinese characters and their meanings.

GLENCOE'S ASSESSMENT ADVANTAGE

Use the following to easily assess student learning in a variety of ways.

• Performance Assessment Strategies and Activities
• Section Quizzes
• Chapter and Unit Tests
• Interactive Tutor Self-Assessment Software
• Testmaker Software
• MindJogger Videoquiz
• SAT/SAT II Test Practice
• worldhistory.glencoe.com

Additional Resources

NATIONAL GEOGRAPHIC SOCIETY
Teacher's Corner

INDEX TO NATIONAL GEOGRAPHIC MAGAZINE

The following articles may be used for research relating to this chapter:

- "Sumo," by T. R. Reid, July 1997.
- "Genghis Khan," by Mike Edwards, December 1996.
- "The Golden Hoard of Bactria," by Viktor Ivanovich Sarianidi, March 1990.
- "The Queen of Textiles," by Nina Hyde, January 1984.
- "Indonesia Rescues Ancient Borobudur," by W. Brown Morton III, January 1983.
- "The Lost Fleet of Kublai Khan," by Torao Mozai, November 1982.
- "The Temples of Angkor: Ancient Glory in Stone," by Peter T. White, May 1982.

NATIONAL GEOGRAPHIC SOCIETY PRODUCTS AVAILABLE FROM GLENCOE

To order the following, call Glencoe at 1-800-334-7344:

- *STV: World Geography, Vol. 1, Asia (Videodisc)*
- *Picture Atlas of the World (CD-ROM)*
- *MapPack: Asia (Transparency Maps)*

ADDITIONAL NATIONAL GEOGRAPHIC SOCIETY PRODUCTS

Access National Geographic's new dynamic MapMachine Web site and other geography resources at:

- http://www.nationalgeographic.com/
- http://www.nationalgeographic.com/maps/

BIBLIOGRAPHY

Literature of the Period
Murasaki, Shikibu. *The Tale of Genji.* New York: Knopf, 1992. Novel considered to be one of Japan's greatest works of fiction.
Readings for the Student
Van den Heuvel, Cor. *The Haiku Anthology.* Garden City, N.Y.: Anchor Press, 1974. A diverse collection of haiku poetry.
Readings for the Teacher
Bloodworth, Dennis. *The Chinese Looking Glass.* New York: Farrar, Straus and Giroux, 1980. A historical look at the Chinese people and their customs.

WORLD HISTORY Online

Use our Web site as an additional resource. All essential content is covered in the Student Edition.

You and your students can visit the *World History: The Human Experience* Web site at worldhistory. glencoe.com The student text directs students to the Web site for the following options:

- **Chapter Overviews**
- **Student Web Activities**
- **Self-Check Quizzes**

Answers are provided for you in a link entitled "Web Activity Lesson Plan." Additional Web Resources, Interactive Puzzles, and content updates are also available.

Visit the Glencoe Web site at socialstudies. glencoe.com for social studies activities, updates, and links to other resources.

LOCAL OBJECTIVES

CHAPTER THEMES

Chapter Themes are listed by section on this chapter opening page of the Student Edition. A corresponding theme-based activity is available under "TEACH," and a theme-based question is asked in the Section and Chapter Assessments.

The Storyteller

Historical Setting For more than 2,000 years, the Chinese used competitive exams as a way of selecting government workers. The civil service exam such as the one described here was the last in a series of tests a Chinese student had to pass in order to be offered a government post. First the student took a local exam. If he passed it, he took a provincial exam. The final step was an empirewide exam, given every three years. Applicants were tested on their knowledge of Chinese poetry and the writings of Confucius. Of the hundreds of thousands of men who took these exams, only a few hundred passed.

Historical Significance

Answer: *Indian culture strongly affected Southeast Asia, while Chinese civilization had a strong impact on Southeast Asia, Korea, and Japan. Many aspects of Asian culture reached other parts of the world during the time of the Mongol Empire.*

WORLD HISTORY Online

Have students use the **Chapter 14 Overview** at worldhistory. glencoe.com as a prereading and postreading exercise for understanding chapter content.

Chapter
14

500 B.C.–A.D. 1400

East and South Asia

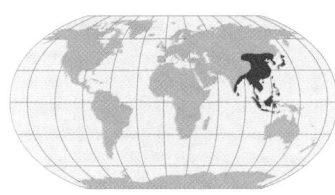

Chapter Themes

▶ **Movement** The Mongols of central Asia conquer China and parts of Europe. *Section 1*
▶ **Uniformity** A centralized government, religion, and a common language maintain China's cultural continuity. *Section 2*
▶ **Cultural Diffusion** The civilizations of Southeast Asia reflect the influences of India and China. *Section 3*
▶ **Innovation** Japan and Korea produce innovations from a blend of Chinese and local traditions. *Section 4*

The Storyteller

In China, in the year A.D. 1200, a lone student sat behind a desk in a room furnished only with a lamp, some paper, a writing brush, and an inkstone. He labored over a grueling government exam designed to test his knowledge of Confucian texts. He worried because examiners could fail a person for even a single misquotation. If he passed, he would be one of the Song emperor's officials. If he failed, he would have to hawk cheap goods in the streets.

Civil service examinations helped ancient China to maintain a consistent government no matter which dynasty was in power. Later, the neighboring countries of Korea and Japan adopted these civil service examinations as well as other aspects of Chinese culture.

Historical Significance

How did the civilizations of East and South Asia influence each other and the rest of the world?

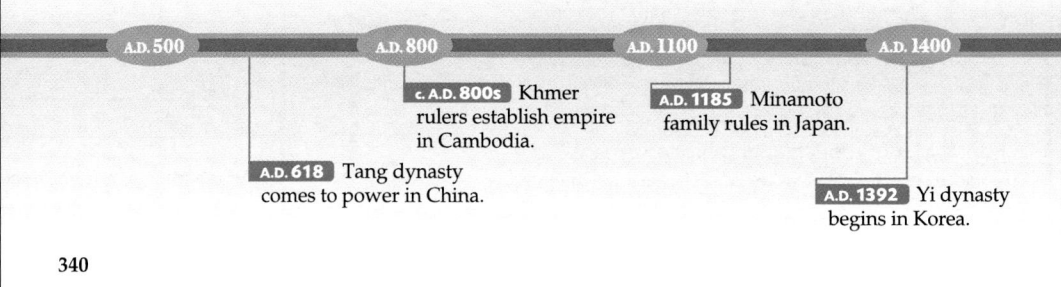

A.D. 500   A.D. 800   A.D. 1100   A.D. 1400

c. A.D. 800s Khmer rulers establish empire in Cambodia.

A.D. 618 Tang dynasty comes to power in China.

A.D. 1185 Minamoto family rules in Japan.

A.D. 1392 Yi dynasty begins in Korea.

340

GEOGRAPHY CONNECTION

Location Have students look at a wall map to locate the geographic boundaries of China, Southeast Asia, Korea, and Japan. *(China: the Gobi, the Tibetan plateau; Southeast Asia: water boundaries including the Bay of Bengal and the Pacific Ocean; Korea: Yellow Sea, Sea of Japan; Japan: Pacific Ocean, Sea of Japan)* Ask which boundaries might serve as barriers and which might encourage interaction. *(Difficult landforms tend to impede movement, while water encourages it.)*

A partial view of the summer palace constructed under Emperor Ch'ien Lung. Bibliothèque Nationale, Paris, France

Visualizing History Members of the Chinese imperial family lived in elaborate palace complexes. Secluded and sheltered from the outside world, most of them knew little about the lives of their subjects.

✔ Performance Assessment

Refer to the activity on page 340C of the Planning Guide.

📁 For an additional activity, refer to Activity 14 in the *Performance Assessment Strategies and Activities* booklet.

Using Your History Journal

Students may want to use different colors to represent different types of events, such as red for military engagements, blue for political matters (the founding of cities and/or dynasties), and so on.

WORLD HISTORY *Online*

Chapter Overview

Visit the *World History: The Human Experience* Web site at **worldhistory.glencoe.com** and click on **Chapter 14—Chapter Overview** to preview the chapter.

Your History Journal

Consult an atlas and create a map of East Asia. As you read the chapter, place 10 to 20 key events on your map in the countries or areas where they occurred. Include the dates of these events.

GLENCOE TECHNOLOGY

VIDEODISC
Use MindJogger to preview chapter content.

MindJogger Videoquiz

Chapter 14
Disc 2 Side B

 Also available in VHS.

➕ EXTRA CREDIT PROJECT

Martial Arts Asian civilizations developed several different systems of martial arts. Have students research one or more of these: tai chi chuan (Chinese), tae kwon do (Korean), or karate (Japanese). They should find out where, how, and when the discipline originated and what role it plays in society today. If possible, have students demonstrate or show pictures of some of the basic principles and movements of the system they choose. **L2**

A.D. 1200 — **c. A.D. 1206** Genghis Khan becomes ruler of all Mongol tribes.

A.D. 1300 — **c. A.D. 1279** The Mongols establish rule in China.

A.D. 1400 — **A.D. 1398** Timur Lenk (Tamerlane) sacks Delhi in central Asia.

Section 1

Central Asia

Guide to Reading

Read to Find Out
Main Idea *The Mongols acquired the world's largest land empire.*

▶ **Terms to Define**
clan, yurt, *yasa*, khan

▶ **People to Meet**
the Seljuk Turks, the Mongols, Genghis Khan, Batu, Helagu, Timur Lenk (Tamerlane)

▶ **Places to Locate**
Mongolia

The Storyteller

The caravan halted for the night. Chaghatai, the leader, before retiring posted a sign and fastened bells around the animals' necks. Maffeo, a young foreigner, wondered at these precautions. Chaghatai explained that strange things may happen in the Desert of Lop. "When a man is riding by night through this desert and something happens to make him … lose touch with his companions ... he hears spirits talking…. Often these voices make him stray from the path…. For this reason bands of travellers make a point of keeping very close together…. And round the necks of all their beasts they fasten little bells, so that by listening to the sound they may prevent them from straying from the path."

—adapted from *The Travels of Marco Polo*, Marco Polo, translated by Ronald Latham, 1958

Porcelain figure on camel

342 **Chapter 14** *East and South Asia*

From the A.D. 1000s to the A.D. 1400s, invaders from the steppe of central Asia conquered territories in eastern Asia, the Middle East, and eastern Europe. Originally nomads, the invaders settled in many of the conquered areas. They adapted to the local cultures, advanced trade, and encouraged the exchange of goods and ideas.

The Steppe Peoples

At the beginning of the A.D. 1000s, large numbers of nomadic groups roamed the steppe of central Asia. Loosely organized into clans, or groups based on family ties, they depended for their livelihood on the grazing of animals. To protect their pastures and provide for a growing population, they organized under powerful chiefs. The chiefs formed cavalry units of warriors armed with bows and arrows. The nomadic peoples became a military threat to neighboring territories that were more culturally developed. They carried out a series of invasions that transformed the cultures of eastern Asia, the Middle East, and eastern Europe.

The Seljuk Turks

The first people of the steppes to engage in conquest were the Turks. Around A.D. 800, weak Abbasid rulers centered in Baghdad hired Turkish warriors to fight in their armies. As a result, the Turks became powerful and soon controlled the Abbasid government. Later, about A.D. 1000, a group of Muslim Turks called **the Seljuk Turks** moved from central Asia into the Middle East. There they formed settlements and restored the Sunni caliphate. The Seljuks also gained control of the main trade routes between eastern Asia, the Middle East, and Europe. They benefited from this trade and used their wealth to build an empire.

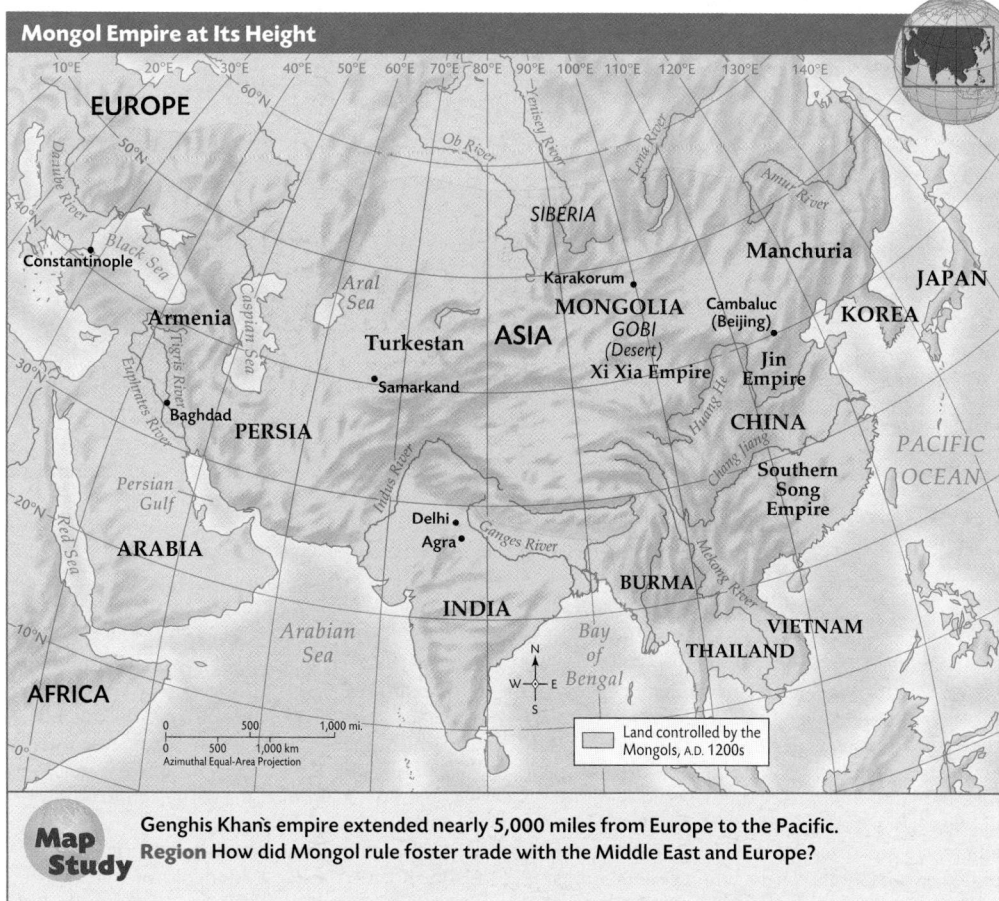

Mongol Empire at Its Height

Map
Study

Genghis Khan's empire extended nearly 5,000 miles from Europe to the Pacific.
Region How did Mongol rule foster trade with the Middle East and Europe?

TEACH

Guided Practice

THEME Movement

Explain that the steppes are a region of dry, treeless plains covered with grass. They are very hot in summer and bitter cold in winter. Why would this kind of topography encourage the movement of peoples? *(The harsh environment could not long support a large population; people would have to move to find new sources of food for themselves and their animals.)* **L1**

 Chapter Transparency 14

Map
Study

Answer
A large land empire joined distant areas.

Map Skills Practice

Reading a Map What Mongol settlement is today the capital of China? *(Cambaluc [Beijing])*

 NATIONAL
GEOGRAPHIC
SOCIETY

 VIDEODISC
STV: World Geography, Volume 1

Side One, Frames 13631–17712
Title: *Asia*
Subject: Interior and North Asia
Ask: What is the winter climate of the taiga like? *(Winters are long, very cold, and days are short.)*

Seljuk warriors also invaded the plains and highlands of Asia Minor. There they defeated the Byzantines at the Battle of Manzikert in A.D. 1071. The Byzantine emperor Alexius I Comnenus feared the loss of Byzantine territory to the Seljuks and appealed to the pope and the monarchs of western Europe for aid. About 20 years later, the Seljuk conquest of Palestine led to Pope Urban II's calling of the First Crusade.

Though the Seljuks were skilled warriors, they were unable to develop a well-organized government to rule their territories. Seljuk rulers lacked strong traditions of government administration and had difficulties holding the empire together. Local officials ignored the central government and acted like independent rulers. They began to fight each other for control of land. Weakened by internal upheavals, the Seljuks became prey to new nomadic invaders from central Asia.

The Mongols

During the late A.D. 1100s, **the Mongols** became the dominant nomadic group in central Asia. Their homeland was **Mongolia**, a region of forests and steppe northwest of China. In this wild and isolated area, they wandered from pasture to pasture with their herds of sheep, horses, and yaks, or long-haired oxen. Because of their nomadic life, the Mongols lived in movable tents called yurts. Their principal foods were meat and mare's milk. In a few fertile areas, Mongol farmers established small communities. There women raised grains while men herded animals.

Genghis Khan

Like other nomads, the Mongols at first were divided into clans. They were expert fighters on horseback, using bow and arrow. About A.D. 1206

Chapter 14 *East and South Asia* **343**

TV Interview Organize the class into five teams and assign each a Mongol leader: Genghis Khan, Ogadai, Batu, Helagu, Timur Lenk. One member of each team should play the role of announcer, one should act as interviewer, and one should be the guest. Team members should research the man to be interviewed and write questions and answers for the interview. Allow time for team members to share what they have learned and to plan the interview. Then have each team present its interview to the class. **L2**

Visualizing History Some modern yurts have stoves and wooden floors and are even equipped with electricity. **Answer to Caption:** *because the Mongols were nomads and yurts are easily moved*

Independent Practice

 Guided Reading Activity 14-1 **L1**

 Time Line Activity 14

TURNING POINT

Mongol Conquests
Why were the Mongol conquests so successful?
The Mongols were skilled horse riders who gained tribute and recruits from conquered peoples. From the Chinese, they adopted techniques of siege warfare. This combination enabled the Mongols to have the largest land empire in history.

Daily Life The horse was basic to the culture of the Mongols. Have one or more students research (a) the kind of horses the Mongols rode, and (b) what made the Mongols such good riders. **L2**

Linking Past and Present

Mogul Rule In the 1500s, a descendant of both Genghis Khan and Timur Lenk led a Mongol conquest of India. His people, who ruled India for 200 years, were called Moguls, from the Persian word for Mongol. A Mogul ruler named Shah Jahan built the Taj Mahal, one of the most beautiful buildings in the world.

Visualizing History Some people in Mongolia still live in yurts, circular domed tents of skins or felt stretched over a lattice frame. *Why did ancient Mongols choose this kind of housing?*

a Mongol leader named Temujin (teh•MOO•juhn) organized the scattered clans under one government. He brought together Mongol laws in a new code known as the *yasa*. Under Temujin's guidance, an assembly of tribal chiefs met for the first time to plan military campaigns.

Temujin's greatest achievement was in military affairs. He organized the Mongol armies into disciplined cavalry units. These units were then placed under the command of officers chosen for their abilities and not for their family ties. These changes made the Mongols the most skilled fighting force in the world at that time. As a result of his efforts, Temujin was recognized as khan, or absolute ruler. Now called **Genghis Khan** (JEHN•guhs KAHN), or "universal ruler," Temujin set out to create a large empire.

TURNING POINT

Mongol Conquests

The Mongol armies under Genghis Khan first conquered the other steppe peoples, most of whom were Turks. These victories brought tribute money to the Mongol state as well as new recruits for the Mongol armies. By A.D. 1211 the Mongols were strong enough to attack major civilizations. In that year, 100,000 Mongol horsemen invaded China. While fighting against the Chinese, the Mongols learned Chinese techniques of siege warfare. Using

gunpowder, storming ladders, and battering rams, they won significant victories against their opponents. In spite of Genghis Khan's death in A.D. 1227, the Mongols continued their advance. By A.D. 1279 all of China's territory was in their hands, and a Mongol dynasty ruled the entire country.

Under Ogadai (OH•guh•DY) Khan, the other Mongol forces moved westward. During the A.D. 1230s and A.D. 1240s, a Mongol army led by the commander **Batu** (bah•TOO) conquered East Slavic lands and then crossed the Carpathian Mountains into eastern and central Europe. Upon hearing of Ogadai's death, Batu's army returned to Russia. There they awaited the selection of a new khan. Meanwhile, Ogadai's widow ruled the Mongols.

During the same period, other Mongols invaded the Middle East. Using terror to subdue the region, the Mongols destroyed cities and killed many people. In A.D. 1258 the commander **Helagu** (heh•lah•GOO) captured Baghdad, the old Abbasid capital, and enslaved its inhabitants. The destruction of Baghdad represented a major setback to Islamic civilization. However, the Mongol advance was finally halted by the Mamluks, a Muslim military group that ruled Egypt.

The Mongol Empire

The Mongols created the largest land empire in history. Their territories extended from China to the frontiers of western Europe. Many of the great trade routes between Europe and Asia passed

344 Chapter 14 *East and South Asia*

MEETING SPECIAL NEEDS ACTIVITY

Language Delayed To help make studying easier for students with limited English proficiency, ask other students to record this chapter on tape for home study. Have several students divide the chapter, with each student recording a few paragraphs. Ask students who use the tapes to summarize orally the main ideas of each section. These same students could prepare questions about the chapter and quiz their classmates. **L1 LEP**

through Mongol lands. During the A.D. 1200s Mongol rule brought peace to the region. This advanced the growth of trade and encouraged closer cultural contacts between East and West.

The Mongols respected the highly advanced culture of conquered groups and learned from them. In China, Mongol rulers gradually adopted Chinese ideas and practices. In Persia and central Asia, Mongol settlers converted to Islam and intermarried with the local Turkish population. Turkish became the principal language of the region. The Mongols of Russia, however, kept their traditional customs and lived apart from the Slavs. They settled in the empty steppe region north of the Caspian Sea. From there, they controlled the Slavic principalities located in the northern forests.

The unity of the Mongol Empire did not last long. All Mongols gave allegiance to the khan in Mongolia, but local rulers became increasingly self-reliant. By the end of the A.D. 1200s, Mongol territories in Russia, central Asia, Persia, and China had each developed into independent domains.

Timur Lenk

About 100 years later, another powerful nomadic force emerged from central Asia. In the A.D. 1390s a Turkish-Mongol chief named **Timur Lenk** (in English, Tamerlane) rose to power in the region. He began as leader of a small nomadic tribe and extended his rule through numerous wars with neighboring tribes.

A devout Muslim, Timur hoped to spread Islam to new areas. Claiming descent from Genghis Khan, Timur united the Turkish-Mongols by conquest and eventually extended their rule over much of the Middle East.

Although Timur was ruthless, the people under his rule created important centers of civilization in central Asia. The most influential city in the region

TAMER LANE TIM

Visualizing History Timur Lenk, or Tamerlane, devoted much of his life to conquest. *What city was the center of his empire?*

was Samarkand. A wealthy trading and craft center, it became known for its beautifully decorated mosques and tombs.

In A.D. 1402 Timur and his armies swept into Asia Minor, defeating another Turkish group—the Ottomans—at Ankara. However, Timur's effort to gain territory in Asia Minor never succeeded. In A.D. 1405 Timur died and was buried at Samarkand. The huge empire that he had created soon collapsed. The Ottomans were then able to regain their lost lands and began the building of their state.

SECTION 1 ASSESSMENT

Main Idea
1. Use a chart like the one below to show how the Mongols acquired the world's largest land empire.

Causes		Effect
☐	→	World's Largest Land Empire
☐	→	
☐	→	

Recall
2. **Define** clan, yurt, *yasa*, khan.
3. **Identify** the Seljuk Turks, the Mongols, Genghis Khan, Batu, Helagu, Timur Lenk.

Critical Thinking
4. **Synthesizing Information** What factors led the steppe

peoples to expand their territories and to create empires?

Understanding Themes
5. **Movement** How did the Mongol conquests contribute to the spread of culture and ideas throughout Asia and parts of Europe?

SECTION 1 ASSESSMENT ANSWERS

1. Genghis Khan made Mongol armies a skilled fighting force, conquered steppe people and received tribute and recruits from them, invaded China; Ogadai Khan moved Mongols west; Mongols moved into eastern and central Europe, invaded Middle East, captured Baghdad; Timur Lenk extended rule over Middle East

2. All terms are defined in the Glossary.
3. Seljuk Turks, 342; Mongols, 343; Genghis Khan, 344; Batu, 344; Helagu, 344; Timur Lenk, 345
4. The steppe could not support an expanding population.
5. **MOVEMENT** by creating a large, peaceful empire.

— WORLD HISTORY Online —

Have students use the **Chapter 14 Student Web Activity** at worldhistory.glencoe.com for in-depth study of the Mongols.

History & Art The name Timur Lenk means "Timur the Lame." This Mongol leader was wounded by an arrow when he was a young man. **Answer to Caption:** *Samarkand*

ASSESS

Check for Understanding

Assign Section 1 Assessment as homework or as an in-class activity.

▣ Use Interactive Tutor Self-Assessment Software to review Section 1.

Evaluate

🗁 Section Quiz 14-1

▣ Use the Testmaker to create a customized quiz for Section 1.

Reteach

Have students summarize the main conquests of the Mongols.

🗁 Reading Essentials and Study Guide 14-1

Enrich

Have students research and report on present-day Mongolia, especially its people's way of life.

CLOSE

Ask students to summarize the positive and negative consequences of Mongol rule.

A.D. 600		A.D. 1000		A.D. 1400

c. A.D. 649 Empress Wu begins to control the Chinese Empire.

A.D. 907 Tang dynasty ends.

A.D. 1260 Kublai Khan begins reign.

A.D. 1368 Yuan dynasty collapses.

Section 2

China

Guide to Reading

Read to Find Out
Main Idea *The Tang, Song, and Yuan dynasties made significant achievements.*

▶ **Terms to Define**
meritocracy, mandarin

▶ **People to Meet**
Tai Cong, Empress Wu, Xuanzang, Duo Fu, Li Bo, Zhao Kuangyin, Kublai Khan, Marco Polo

▶ **Places to Locate**
Changan, Hangzhou

The Storyteller

Thoughtfully, Gui Xi considered the civil service examination. He was to select a single line of poetry and, using his finest calligraphy, write it on a silk scroll. Then he must create a painting linked to the chosen text, filling the scroll. To pass this vital test a man needed to be able to read, drawing conclusions and inferences. He also needed to demonstrate proficiency in the brush arts, a discipline requiring many years to master. Gui Xi recollected the steps essential to writing and painting. One must first find the spirit, rhythm, and thought, then one could seek to control the scenery, brush, and ink. For good work to result, mental and physical aspects must balance.

—adapted from *Record of Brush Methods: Essay on Landscape Painting*, Ching Hao, reprinted in *Varieties of Visual Experience*, 1991

Chinese calligraphy

346 **Chapter 14** *East and South Asia*

For more than 350 years after the collapse of the Han dynasty in A.D. 220, Chinese kingdoms and invaders from the north rivaled each other for control of China. Then in A.D. 589, a northern official named Yang Jian (YAHNG JYEN) united China by conquering both the north and the south. Yang Jian took the title Emperor Wen and founded the Sui (SWAY) dynasty. Emperor Wen renewed many of the goals and traditions that had been accepted during the reign of the Han dynasty. He organized public works projects such as the rebuilding of the former Han capital city at **Changan** (CHONG•ON), the repair of the Great Wall, and the construction of a Grand Canal to link northern and southern China. However, to accomplish these projects Emperor Wen used crews of forced laborers, which made him quite unpopular with the peasants.

The Tang Dynasty

In A.D. 618 peasant uprisings against the Sui dynasty enabled a rebellious lord named Li Yuan (LEE YOO•AHN) to take control of the country and proclaim himself emperor. He established the Tang (TONG) dynasty, which lasted from A.D. 618 to A.D. 907. Under the Tang, the Chinese Empire expanded its borders to include new territories.

Government and Society

The military genius behind the early Tang expansion was a son of Li Yuan who took the name **Tai Cong** (TIE TSOONG). Not only was Tai Cong a warrior, but he was also a shrewd administrator. By restoring a strong central government in China, he maintained control of his enormous empire while continuing to expand it.

To obtain a position in the Tang government, candidates had to pass civil service examinations. Under Tang rule, these tests measured the degree to which candidates had mastered Confucian principles. According to Confucianism, an individual was expected to obey the emperor just as a son was expected to obey his father.

Because almost any male could take these examinations, the Chinese government claimed that it was a **meritocracy**—a system in which people are chosen and promoted for their talents and performance. But in practice it did not meet that ideal. Few boys from poor families could afford to pay tutors to help them prepare for the exams. Most could not spare the time away from their labor to study on their own.

Nevertheless, some peasants benefited from the Tang dynasty's rule. The Tang government gave land to farmers and enforced the peace that enabled them to till their land. In the Chang Jiang (Yangtze River) region, farmers were able to experiment with new strains of rice and better methods for growing it—both of which led to greater crop yields. With more food available, the Chinese population increased as well.

Foreign Influences

Tang rulers also devoted resources to the construction of roads and waterways. These routes made travel within China and to neighboring countries much easier. New and improved routes helped government officials to perform their duties. They also enabled Chinese merchants to increase trade with people from Japan, India, and the Middle East.

Chinese luxury goods, such as silk and pottery, passed through central Asia along the Silk Road. Beginning in central China, traders' camel caravans traveled north to the Great Wall and then headed west, crossing into central Asia just north of the Tibetan plateau. Some traveled as far west as Syria. These caravans brought Chinese goods and ideas to other cultures and returned with foreign products and new ideas as well. The Buddhist, Christian, and Islamic religions came to China by way of the Silk Road. During the Tang dynasty, Buddhism especially became very popular in China.

As trade increased the wealth of the empire, the Tang capital at Changan grew into the largest city in the world. Dazzling tales attracted merchants and scholars from countries throughout Asia to this city of 2 million people. Visitors to Changan spoke of wide, tree-shaded avenues and two vast market squares where merchants sold goods from Asia and the Middle East. They said that acrobats, jugglers, and dancers performed in the streets and that wealthy Chinese—including women—played the Persian games of chess and polo.

The Arts

In A.D. 649 Gaozong (GOW•DZOONG) succeeded Tai Cong as emperor of China. But Gaozong's wife, **Empress Wu**, actually ruled the empire. She expanded the bureaucracy and strengthened China's military forces.

History & Art *Four Travelers on Horseback,* porcelain figures from the Tang dynasty **Chinese potters discovered how to make porcelain in the A.D. 800s by firing pieces at very high temperatures.** *What constructions helped merchants trade fine Chinese wares with other countries?*

TEACH

Guided Practice

THEME Uniformity

List on the chalkboard some of the factors that made for a uniform Chinese culture: a strong centralized government, good transportation between the different parts of the country, written literature available. Ask students who restored strong central government in China (*Tai Cong*), who improved transportation (*Emperor Wen, Tang rulers*), and what invention made it easier to make literature available to people in China (*block printing*). **L1**

Economy Ask students what three groups of people benefited under Tang rule and why. (*peasants: received land and, in Jiang region, benefited from farm improvements; government officials: improved travel routes; merchants: improved travel routes*) **L2**

Cultural Diffusion Ask students how religions—Buddhism, Christianity, Islam—might come to China "by way of the Silk Road."(*Answers will vary but might include via missionaries, by books, and by traders who practiced these religions.*) **L3**

World Music: Cultural Traditions, Lesson 8

History Simulation 14

History & Art Tang porcelain and other crafts were widely admired. In many Asian languages, the word for "Chinese" became a synonym for "superior."
Answer to Caption: *roads and waterways*

COOPERATIVE LEARNING ACTIVITY

Technology Organize the class into four groups. Ask each group to choose one of the technological advances of the Tang and Song dynasties: porcelain, block printing, the compass, or gunpowder. Have each group research its topic to learn more about when and how the invention came about, how it was used, and how knowledge of it spread. If possible, each group should find illustrations of its subject. Then have the groups present their findings to the class. **L2**

NATIONAL GEOGRAPHIC SOCIETY

CD-ROM
PICTURE ATLAS OF THE WORLD

You and your students can see the Grand Canal, the Great Wall, and the Silk Road by clicking China's "Photos" button.

Independent Practice

📁 Guided Reading Activity 14-2 **L1**

Literature Encourage students to find a poem by Duo Fu or Li Bo or another poet of the Tang or Song dynasty. Ask them to copy their selection so that it can be displayed on a bulletin board. **L1 LEP**

Biography Assign a brief written biography of Tai Cong, the Empress Wu, Kublai Khan, or Marco Polo. Students should use and cite several research sources. **L3**

China Chopsticks, the eating implements used by Asians, originated in China as early as the Shang dynasty. Most Asian food is served in bite-sized pieces making it easier to handle with the slender sticks. The Chinese word for chopsticks, *kuai-zi*, is a pun on the word *kuai*, which means both "quick" and "piece."

In A.D. 712 Empress Wu's grandson, **Xuanzang** (SEE•WAHN•DZONG), became emperor of China. Because he welcomed artists to his splendid court, the arts flourished during his reign. Tang artisans made porcelain, a fine translucent pottery that became known in the West as "china."

Two of China's greatest poets, **Duo Fu** (DWA FOO) and **Li Bo** (LEE BWAW), produced their works in Xuanzang's court. Scholars compiled encyclopedias, dictionaries, and official histories of China. Writers popularized stories about ghosts, crime, and love. And while European monks were still slowly and laboriously copying texts by hand, Chinese Buddhist monks invented the more efficient technique of block printing. They carved the text of a page into a block of wood, then inked the wood and pressed a piece of paper onto it.

Tang Decline

For a time the cultural splendor of Xuanzang's court masked its military weakness. However, the Tang ruler's vulnerability to attack was revealed in A.D. 755, when Turkish armies in central Asia successfully revolted against China. They cut off China's trade routes to the Middle East, and they put an end to the thriving exchange of goods and ideas along the Silk Road. Border wars with the Tibetans and rebellions in famine-stricken provinces plagued the Tang from A.D. 766 on. In A.D. 907 the Tang dynasty finally fell.

The Song Dynasty

From A.D. 907 to 960, China was ruled by military dynasties. Then a military general named **Zhao Kuangyin** (JOW KWONG•YIN) seized the throne and established the Song (SOONG) dynasty.

Song emperors kept peace with a group of Mongols in the north, the Khitan, by paying them generously in silver. But in A.D. 1127 the Jurchen, a

Footnotes to History

Pasta
Almost everyone associates noodles, or pasta, with Italy. But, according to tradition, the Chinese were the first to make noodles, and their recipes were brought to Italy in the A.D. 1200s by the Polos. Some recent historians, however, claim that pasta actually originated in Persia and from there spread east and west.

nomadic people, captured the Song capital of Kaifeng (KIE•FUHNG). The Song rulers set up their royal court in the southern city of **Hangzhou** (HONG•JOH).

Cultural Contributions

Song scholars, resentful of foreign influences, produced an official state philosophy called neo-Confucianism. This philosophy combined Confucian values with elements of Buddhism and Daoism.

Song rulers also more firmly entrenched the civil service system that the Tang had resurrected. They made determining one's knowledge of Confucian curriculum the main focus of these tests. The scholars who had passed the tests eventually formed a wealthy elite group, called mandarins by Westerners.

Rich and Poor

During the Song dynasty, China experienced unprecedented economic growth, partly because Song rulers used tax revenues to fund several public-works projects that benefited the economy. For example, they used these revenues to fund the digging of irrigation ditches and canals, which in turn helped farmers increase their crop yields.

The introduction of new crops from Southeast Asia, such as tea and a faster-growing rice plant, further boosted China's farming economy. The new crops also led to an increase in China's trade with India and Southeast Asia. With farming, trade, and commerce all thriving, urban centers prospered.

The urban wealthy lived in spacious homes and enjoyed going to teahouses, restaurants, and luxurious bathhouses. The capital of the dynasty, Hangzhou, grew to nearly 1 million residents.

Of course, the country still had many urban poor who lived in flimsy houses and hawked cheap goods, worked as manual laborers, begged, or stole.

Song Arts and Sciences

Song achievements in the arts and sciences were many. The cuisine which people recognize today as distinctively Chinese originated during the Song dynasty. Experts regard Song porcelain as the best ever made. Landscape painting reached its peak during Song rule. Song inventors perfected the compass, and they also produced gunpowder. Bamboo-tube rocket launchers charged with gunpowder made the Song army a powerful fighting force.

China's enemies, however, eventually obtained the secrets of Song military technology. Thus, using the Song Empire's own technology against it, the Mongols were able to completely capture northern China in A.D. 1234 and bring about the fall of the Song dynasty in southern China in A.D. 1279.

MEETING SPECIAL NEEDS ACTIVITY

Attention Deficiency Chinese food is very popular in the United States. Students who have trouble focusing their attention should enjoy learning more about some of their favorite dishes. They might use cookbooks or other library resources. (These students might be helped in their research by other students with longer attention spans.) If possible, a Chinese meal could be prepared for the class and presented along with informative commentary. **L2 LEP**

The Bodleian Library, Oxford, Ms. Bodl. 264, fol.219ᴿ

Kublai Khan and Marco Polo

his medieval English manuscript shows the Chinese emperor Kublai Khan presenting golden tablets to Marco Polo and his family to ensure their safe passage back to the West. A.D. 1297 Marco Polo wrote an account of a trip he [clai]med to have made to China, and his book eventu[ally] became popular with the small literate class in [Euro]pe. The painter who embellished this manuscript [had] never met Marco Polo nor had he ever seen a pic[ture] of an Asian. Maybe that's why the emperor looks [Euro]pean rather than Asian.

[T]he Mongol rulers of China put the country in [clos]er touch with the Middle East and Europe. The [Mon]golian khans were outsiders who distrusted, and were distrusted by, their Chinese subjects. The khans turned to outsiders to help them rule, especially after Kublai Khan moved the Chinese capital to Beijing. The Polos (Marco Polo's father and uncle accompanied him to China) were but three of hundreds of European and Muslim merchants and artisans who moved in and out of China. But Marco Polo became famous, both in his time and in ours, because he wrote a book about his adventures. The Polos may have brought Chinese noodles back to Europe, and other European and Muslim travelers brought Chinese inventions such as gunpowder and the compass back to the West. This transfer of technology had a major impact on the history of Europe.

Chapter 14 *East and South Asia* **349**

TEACH

Tell students that, after Marco Polo's return, he was captured and imprisoned by the Genoese, archrivals of the Venetians. There he dictated his book, known in English as the *Travels of Marco Polo*, to a fellow prisoner. It was instantly popular and soon known all over Europe (even though this was before the days of printing). Why do you think Europeans of Polo's time were eager to read his book? (*Answers will vary but should include the fact that East Asia was practically unknown to Europe at the time.*)

CURRICULUM CONNECTION

LITERATURE
One of the most famous poems of the English Romantic period is "Kubla Khan," by Samuel Taylor Coleridge. Published in 1816, it portrays Kublai Khan's court as a place of fantastic beauty.

Map Study

Answer

the mountain ranges of eastern Tibet

Map Skills Practice

Reading a Map At their greatest extent, how far did the domains of the Tang dynasty stretch from east to west? *(about 3,000 miles [4,825 kilometers])*

ASSESS

Check for Understanding

Assign Section 2 Assessment as homework or as an in-class activity.

◼ Use Interactive Tutor Self-Assessment Software to review Section 2.

Evaluate

▱ Section Quiz 14-2

◼ Use the Testmaker to create a customized quiz for Section 2.

Reteach

Have students recall one important contribution each from the Tang, Song, and Yuan dynasties.

▱ Reading Essentials and Study Guide 14-2

Enrich

Have students create a bulletin-board display of various Chinese porcelains and chinas.

CLOSE

Guide students in outlining this section. Put key headings on the chalkboard. Students can suggest entries under the headings. *(Example: I. Tang; A. Government and Society; B. Foreign Influences; C. The Arts)*

350 Chapter 14 *East and South Asia*

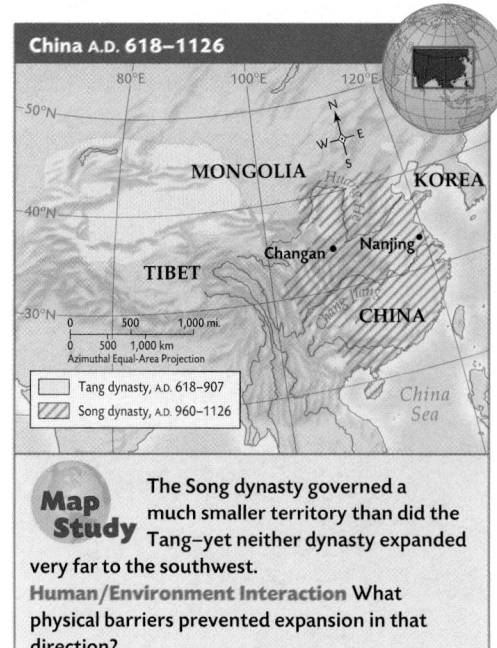

China A.D. 618–1126

MONGOLIA
KOREA
TIBET
Changan   Nanjing
CHINA
China Sea

0   500   1,000 mi.
0   500 1,000 km
Azimuthal Equal-Area Projection

☐ Tang dynasty, A.D. 618–907
▨ Song dynasty, A.D. 960–1126

Map Study The Song dynasty governed a much smaller territory than did the Tang—yet neither dynasty expanded very far to the southwest.
Human/Environment Interaction What physical barriers prevented expansion in that direction?

The Yuan Dynasty

During the A.D. 1200s, the Mongols overthrew the Jurchen and Song rulers. They established the Yuan (YOO•AHN), or Mongol, dynasty and became the first conquerors to rule most of the country.

WORLD HISTORY *Online*

Student Web Activity 14

Visit the *World History: The Human Experience* Web site at **worldhistory.glencoe.com** and click on *Chapter 14—Student Web Activities* for an activity relating to the Mongols.

SECTION 2 ASSESSMENT

Main Idea
1. Use a chart like the one below to identify the achievements of the Tang, Song, and Yuan dynasties.

Tang	Song	Yuan

Recall
2. **Define** meritocracy, mandarin.
3. **Identify** Tai Cong, Empress Wu, Xuanzang, Duo Fu, Li Bo, Zhao Kuangyin, Kublai Khan, Marco Polo.

Critical Thinking
4. **Evaluating Information** Do you think the Tang and Song

systems of government were true meritocracies? Give reasons for your answer.

Understanding Themes
5. **Uniformity** What methods did the rulers of the Tang, Song, and Yuan dynasties use to unite the territories of China?

350   **Chapter 14**   *East and South Asia*

Kublai Khan

The first great Mongol emperor of China was **Kublai Khan** (KOO•BLUH KAHN). A grandson of Genghis Khan, Kublai ruled from A.D. 1260 to A.D. 1294. Kublai Khan extended Mongol rule beyond China's borders. He conquered Korea and part of Southeast Asia. He twice tried to invade Japan, using Chinese and Korean ships, but failed because the Mongols were not skilled in naval warfare.

Although Kublai complied with some Chinese traditions to better control the Chinese, he tried to maintain Mongol culture. Government documents were written in Mongolian, then translated into Chinese. The highest positions in the emperor's court were given to Mongols or foreigners.

The most famous of these foreigners may have been a Venetian named **Marco Polo**. Polo claimed to have arrived in China about A.D. 1271 and to have stayed 17 years, traveling through Mongol territory on the Khan's missions. Whether true or not, Polo's tales of the splendor of Chinese civilization astounded Europeans.

Mongol Peace and Decline

Travel throughout China greatly improved because the Mongols enforced a relatively stable order. Merchants could safely travel the roads built by the Mongols. Mongol rule thus fostered trade and connections with Europe.

Through contact with the Middle East, Russia, and Europe, the Chinese obtained enslaved people as well as products such as glass, hides, clothes, silver, cotton, and carpets. In return, Europeans got exotic products such as silk, porcelain, and tea.

After Kublai Khan died in A.D. 1294, a series of weak successors took over the throne. The Chinese, still resentful of foreign rule, began to stage rebellions against these rulers. Finally, in A.D. 1368, a young Buddhist monk named Zhu Yuanzhang (JOO YOO•AHN•JAHNG) led an army against the capital and overthrew the Yuan dynasty.

SECTION 2 ASSESSMENT ANSWERS

1. Tang: strong central government, built roads and waterways, arts; Song: neo-Confucianism, civil service, mandarins, public works, landscape paintings, invented gunpowder; Yuan: extended Mongol rule out of China, stable order fostered outside connections
2. All terms are defined in the Glossary.
3. Tai Cong, 346; Empress Wu, 347; Xuanzang, 348; Duo Fu, 348; Li Bo, 348; Zhao Kuangyin, 348; Kublai Khan, 350; Marco Polo, 350
4. Civil service exams were open to all, but the time and money involved in studying for them favored the wealthy.
5. **UNIFORMITY** strong central governments, good roads, civil service system

A.D. 800　　　　**A.D. 1100**　　　　**A.D. 1400**

A.D. 802 The Khmer people establish capital at Angkor.

A.D. 938 The Vietnamese defeat the Chinese in the Battle of Bach Dang River.

c. A.D. 1200s The Mongols destroy Burman city of Pagan.

A.D. 1350 The Thai establish kingdom of Ayutthaya.

Section 3

Southeast Asia

Guide to Reading

Read to Find Out
Main Idea *Southeast Asians were influenced by the cultures of China and India.*

▶ **Terms to Define**
archipelago, animism

▶ **People to Meet**
the Khmer, Suryavarman II, Trung Trak, Trung Nhi, Ngo Quyen, Ramkhamhaeng

▶ **Places to Locate**
Angkor Wat, Pagan, Sukhothai, Ayutthaya, Melaka

The Storyteller

The situation was a general's nightmare, T'u Sui thought despairingly. His lord, the Chinese emperor, was determined to subjugate the land of Yueh [Vietnam]. T'u Sui had gladly accepted the command of five hundred thousand men of ability to complete the task. However, when he attacked the Yueh fled into the mountains and forests where it was impossible to fight them or even to find them. Gradually, the troops grew weary of their duties. The Yueh would then attack, inflicting great losses upon the powerful Chinese army.

—from *Huai Nan Tzu*, reprinted in *Ancient Vietnam*, Keith W. Taylor

Mountains of Vietnam

Although China was the most culturally diverse and influential society in Asia from about A.D. 220 until A.D. 1400, other Asian civilizations were creating distinct and influential cultures of their own at the same time. Southeast Asian cultures were among these new societies.

Crossroads of Asia

South of China and east of India is the region known as Southeast Asia. Southeast Asia includes the present-day countries of Myanmar (Burma), Thailand, Vietnam, Laos, Cambodia, Malaysia, Singapore, Brunei, Indonesia, and the Philippines. Located in the tropics, many of these countries have fertile soils, warm climates, and abundant rainfall. Geographically, Southeast Asia is divided into mainland and maritime Southeast Asia. The latter includes more than 10,000 islands of the Philippine and Indonesian **archipelagos**, or chains of islands.

During the A.D. 100s, an exchange of goods and ideas began between India and Southeast Asia. This exchange led Southeast Asia to adopt many elements of Indian culture. For instance, at that time, traveling Indian traders and scholars introduced to Southeast Asia the Sanskrit language and the religions of Hinduism and Buddhism. Indian epics such as the *Ramayana* were interwoven with Southeast Asian stories and legends. Indian architecture, law codes, and political ideas also deeply influenced the cultures of the region. As contact with India increased, Indian culture gradually spread throughout Southeast Asia.

Southeast Asians nevertheless retained many of their own traditions. They continued to perform the art of shadow puppetry, to make intricately patterned cloth called batik, and to play their own unique instruments and music. They also believed in **animism**, the idea that spirits inhabit living and nonliving things.

Chapter 14　*East and South Asia*　**351**

TEACH

Guided Practice

THEME Cultural Diffusion

Using a wall map if possible, point out the major origins of cultural influence *(India, China)*, the region affected *(the countries of Southeast Asia)*, and the water routes by which cultural elements traveled *(Bay of Bengal, South China Sea, Mekong River).* **L1 LEP**

Religion Review with students the major precepts of the religious and ethical teachings "imported" into Southeast Asia from India and China. *(Hinduism: Brahman as eternal spirit, reincarnation based on karma; Buddhism: Four Noble Truths and Eightfold Path; Confucianism: right conduct, especially filial piety; Daoism: harmony with nature)* **L2**

World History and Art Transparency 17, *Angkor Wat*

World Music: Cultural Traditions, Lesson 9

Who?What?Where?When?

Tran Hung Dao One of the greatest of all Vietnamese heroes is Tran Hung Dao, a military leader who defeated the Mongol forces of Kublai Khan. His biggest victory was a naval engagement in 1288. Kublai Khan's fleet was ripped apart by iron-tipped spears that Hung Dao had planted upright under water.

The Khmer

In A.D. 802 **the Khmer** (kuh•MEHR) people of the mainland Southeast Asian country of Cambodia established a great Hindu-Buddhist empire with its capital at Angkor. The Khmer Empire reached its height during the A.D. 1100s, when it conquered much of the land that now includes Laos, Thailand, and Vietnam.

The empire's wealth came primarily from its rice production. Elaborate hydraulic engineering projects enabled the Khmer to irrigate and produce three crops of rice a year. With the wealth from this bountiful harvest, Khmer rulers subsidized mammoth construction projects. Adapting Indian building techniques to create their own distinctive architecture, the Khmer built hundreds of temples that glorified Hindu and Buddhist religious figures. They also constructed roads, reservoirs, irrigation canals, harbors, and hospitals. Khmer rulers were known for the splendor of their court. Borrowing from the Indian idea of kingship, Khmer rulers presented themselves as incarnations of the Hindu gods or as future Buddhas, which served to enhance their power. They bedecked themselves in elaborate finery and filled their palaces with ornate thrones and beautiful furnishings. A Chinese traveler named Zhou Dakuan (JOH DAH•KWON) described the splendor of a Khmer king in dress and manner:

> **His crown of gold is high and pointed like those on the heads of the mighty gods. When he does not wear his crown, he wreathes his chignon [hair gathered in a bun] in garlands of sweet-scented jasmine. His neck is hung with ropes of huge pearls (they weigh almost three pounds); his wrists and ankles are loaded with bracelets and on his fingers are rings of gold set with cats' eyes. He goes barefoot—the soles of his feet, like the palms of his hands, are rouged with a red stuff. When he appears in public he carries the Golden Sword.**

Images *of the* Times

Angkor Wat

Angkor Wat (meaning "temple of the capital") was built in the A.D. 1100s by the Khmer ruler Suryavarman II. Suryavarman believed he was the incarnation of the Hindu god Vishnu.

The temple complex at Angkor Wat is encircled by a three-mile moat. The temples and monuments within the complex honored the god-king Suryavarman II and impressed visitors with their size and detailed ornamentation.

A bas–relief of the Bayon depicts a battle between the Khmer and the Chams.

Seen through a doorway, the pavilion and the central sanctuary reveal a five-headed Naga serpent.

352

Images *of the* Times Angkor Wat

The temple complex at Angkor Wat forms the largest single religious building in the world. Its builders were extraordinarily skilled. Modern research indicates that they designed and constructed Angkor Wat so carefully that its walls, built over great distances, deviate from straight lines less than .1 percent.

During the A.D. 1100s, under the rule of King **Suryavarman** (soor•yah•VAHR•mahn) **II**, the Khmer kingdom reached the height of its power. Having expanded Cambodia by conquest to include parts of areas known today as Laos, Vietnam, and Thailand, the king decided to glorify both the Hindu god Vishnu and himself. He ordered the construction of **Angkor Wat**, a temple complex covering nearly a square mile. Carvings depicting the Hindu gods cover the walls of Angkor Wat, and, at the center of the complex, the sanctuary stands 130 feet (40 m) high. Angkor Wat also was used as an astronomical observatory.

The Khmer king poured so much of the empire's wealth into building Angkor Wat, however, that he severely weakened the kingdom. This excess, along with rebellions against Khmer rule and infighting between members of the royal family, further crippled the empire. In A.D. 1431 the Thai, a neighboring Southeast Asian people, captured the capital city of Angkor, bringing an end to Khmer rule there.

Vietnam

East of Cambodia and south of China lies the area of present-day Vietnam. Because of Vietnam's proximity to China and because the Chinese dominated Vietnam for more than 1,000 years, Vietnam's culture in some ways came to resemble that of China.

The Vietnamese absorbed elements of Chinese belief systems such as Confucianism, Daoism, and Buddhism. The Vietnamese also adopted Chinese forms of writing and government. Just as in China, Vietnamese officials were selected through civil service exams based on Confucian principles.

The Vietnamese retained many of their own traditions, however. They adopted Chinese religions and beliefs, but they continued to believe in animism. The Vietnamese built a *dinh*, or spirit house, in each village. This tiny house served as the home for the guardian spirit of a village. The Vietnamese wore their hair long and tattooed their skin. They wrote and spoke their own Vietnamese

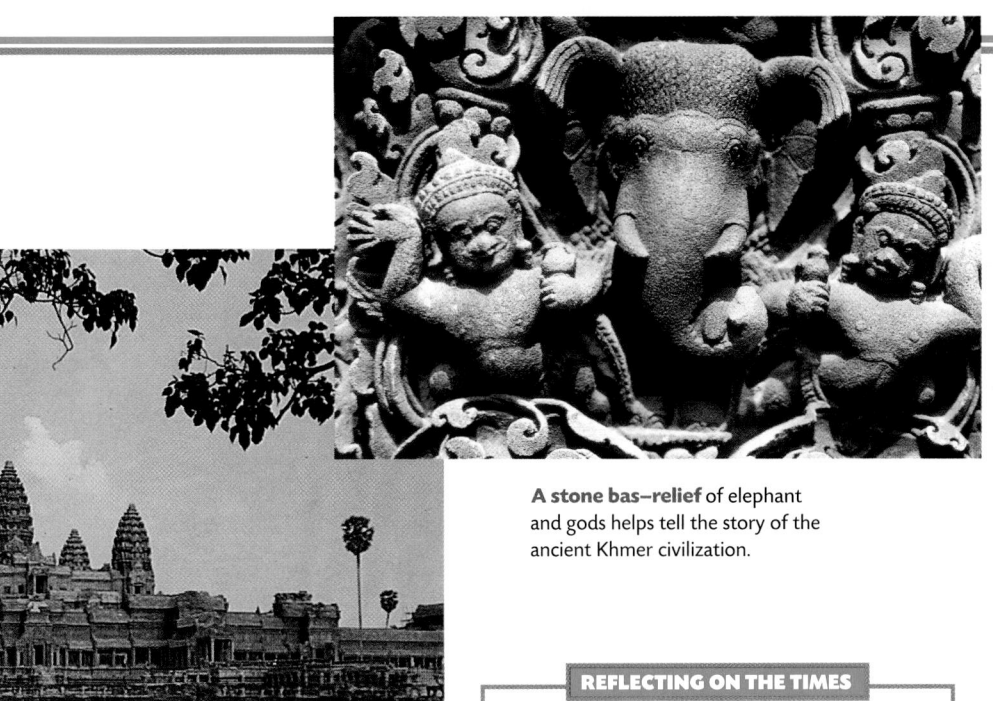

A stone bas–relief of elephant and gods helps tell the story of the ancient Khmer civilization.

REFLECTING ON THE TIMES

1. What values of the Khmer are reflected in these images?
2. How did Suryavarman attempt to impress upon visitors that he was an incarnation of Vishnu?

353

**Chapter 14
Section 3**

Independent Practice

📁 Guided Reading Activity 14-3 **L1**

Daily Life The cloth known as batik originated in Southeast Asia but is known in many other parts of the world. Have students report on the history of batik and how it is made. Ask a volunteer to bring a piece of batik cloth to class. **L2 LEP**

Religion Encourage students to find out more about animism, the beliefs and practices associated with it, and the areas where it has flourished. Have them compile their findings in a brief written report. **L3**

Architecture After the decline of the Khmer kingdom, the capital city of Angkor fell into ruins and was covered with rain forest growth. Have students research the rediscovery and rebuilding of Angkor, beginning in the late 1800s. **L2**

📁 Geography and History Activity 14

ANSWERS TO REFLECTING ON THE TIMES

1. the importance of religion, pride in the accomplishments of the Khmer, respect for the ruler
2. He built Angkor Wat to glorify both himself and Vishnu.

Map Study

Answer

fertile soil, a warm climate, and abundant rain

Map Study Practice

Reading a Map Why do you think Southeast Asia was never united under a single ruler or political system? (*It would be difficult to subdue, much less hold together, a region that includes so many peninsulas and islands scattered over a wide region.*)

Who?What?Where?When?

The city of **Pagan**, in what is now Myanmar, controlled a large area along the Irrawaddy River. Among the visitors to this kingdom was Marco Polo, who was impressed by its magnificent monasteries and temples.

Linking Past and Present

The **shadow puppet theater** of Java, called *wayang kulit*, developed hundreds of years ago. It is still very popular, with several thousand active puppeteers. A single puppeteer works the puppets, chants the story, sings, and recites dialogue. Performances last from 9:00 P.M. until almost dawn.

Western Pacific Rim A.D. 700

100°E 120°E 140°E
50°N
Hokkaido
Honshu
Silla JAPAN
Nara
KOREA Shikoku
Kyushu
CHINA
30°N
INDIA
PACIFIC OCEAN
INDOCHINA PENINSULA
(PHILIPPINES)
10°N
Strait of Malacca
MALAY PENINSULA
SUMATRA
0°
(INDONESIA)
INDIAN OCEAN
0 300 600 mi.
0 300 600 km
Azimuthal Equal-Area Projection
Borobudur
JAVA

Map Study Much of Southeast Asia (shown in purple on the map) lies in the tropics. **Region** What conditions in this region have made farming an important part of the economy?

language, although in writing it they used Chinese characters. Even though the Chinese controlled Vietnam almost continuously from about 200 B.C. to A.D. 939, the Vietnamese fought hard to retain—and then to regain—their independence.

> **❝** The Viets [Vietnamese] were very difficult to defeat. They did not come out to fight, but hid in their familiar mountains and used the jungle like a weapon. As a result, neither side could win.... The Viets would raid suddenly, rob and get away fast, so that just as our army obtained its supplies from the home base, the Viets obtained theirs from our army. **❞**
>
> —Chinese general, c. 200 B.C.

In A.D. 39 two Vietnamese sisters, **Trung Trak** and **Trung Nhi**, clad in armor and riding atop elephants, led a successful revolt against the Chinese. For two years Vietnam was independent of China. Then the Chinese returned in greater numbers and defeated the Vietnamese. Rather than surrender to the Chinese, the Trung sisters are said to have drowned themselves in a river.

During the confusion after the overthrow of the Tang dynasty, the Vietnamese took advantage of China's disunity to revolt again. The Chinese sent a fleet of warships to Vietnam to try to subdue the rebels. In A.D. 938, however, under the leadership of **Ngo Quyen** (noo chu•YEHN), the Vietnamese defeated the warships in the Battle of the Bach Dang River. Although Emperor Tai Cong countered this defeat by launching an invasion of Vietnam, the Vietnamese date their independence from the battle, because Tai Cong's invasion failed.

After the Song dynasty gained control of China, the Song emperor threatened the Vietnamese with invasion. To keep peace with China, the Vietnamese agreed to send tribute—gifts—to the Chinese emperor. In return, China agreed not to invade Vietnam. From then on, the Vietnamese ruler called himself emperor at home, but in his messages to the Chinese court he referred to himself merely as a king.

Myanmar

The westernmost area of mainland Southeast Asia today includes the country of Myanmar (Burma). The first peoples to extensively settle most of present-day Myanmar were the Mons and the Tibeto-Burmans. From 200 B.C. to A.D. 100, these two groups gradually occupied different parts of the country. The Mons established villages in southern Burma, while the Tibeto-Burmans lived along the Irrawaddy (IHR•uh•WAH•dee) River in the northern part of the country. Although they developed their own traditions, the Mons and the Tibeto-Burmans accepted Buddhism and other aspects of Indian culture from visiting South Asian sailors and traders.

During the A.D. 500s, the Tibeto-Burmans became the dominant group and pushed the Mons southward. In A.D. 849 they set up a capital city called **Pagan** (pah•GAHN), which eventually became a center of Buddhist learning and culture. By the A.D. 1200s, skilled architects had transformed Pagan from a small settlement into a city of elaborate Buddhist temples and monasteries.

During the A.D. 1200s, the Mongol armies of Kublai Khan captured Pagan and ended its glory. To escape Mongol rule, many Burmans moved into

COOPERATIVE LEARNING ACTIVITY

Class Presentation Organize the class into groups of four or five students to prepare a presentation comparing the early governments of Southeast Asian countries with governments in those countries today. After each group selects a country, group members should divide the tasks necessary to research the type of government formed in early years and that of today. Then have groups prepare a fact sheet for both periods and develop a short talk about the differences and similarities between the governments. Allow each group to give a five-minute presentation of their findings and answer any questions classmates have. **L2**

the southern part of Myanmar. There they founded fortified towns along the rivers between their ruined capital and the Andaman Sea. Although Burman culture was preserved, a united kingdom did not arise again in Myanmar until the A.D. 1500s.

The Thai

More than four out of every five people who live in the Southeast Asian country of Thailand today belong to the ethnic group called Thai. They are descendants of people who began migrating south from China about A.D. 700. About A.D. 1238 the Thai established their first kingdom at **Sukhothai** (SOO•kah•TY) in the north-central part of the country.

Sukhothai

The Sukhothai kingdom lasted only about 100 years, but it was known for its wise leaders. The kingdom's greatest monarch, King **Ramkhamhaeng** (rahm•KAHM•hong), ruled from A.D. 1275 to A.D. 1317. He made Sukhothai into a center of learning and the arts. During Ramkhamhaeng's reign, the Thai developed an alphabet and writing system based on the Khmer script. Artisans from China taught the making of porcelain, and Buddhist monks from South Asia won most of the Thai people to Buddhism. Beautiful Buddhist temples, with many levels of roofs, rose gracefully above the skyline of Sukhothai. Even during Ramkhamhaeng's lifetime, the Thai saw his reign as a golden age. A stone pillar erected in A.D. 1292 and still standing has the following words engraved on it:

> 66 This Sukhothai is good. In the water there are fish. In the fields there is rice. The king does not levy a [tax] on his people.... Who wants to trade in elephants, trades. Who wants to trade in horses, trades. Who wants to trade in gold and silver, trades.... 99

Ayutthaya

In A.D. 1350 a prince named Ramathibodi (rah•MAH•thee•BOH•dee) overthrew the last Sukhothai ruler and founded a new kingdom known as **Ayutthaya** (ah•YOO•thy•yuh). He set up his capital south of Sukhothai and up the Chao Phraya River (chow PRY•uh) from where Bangkok, the present Thai capital, is today.

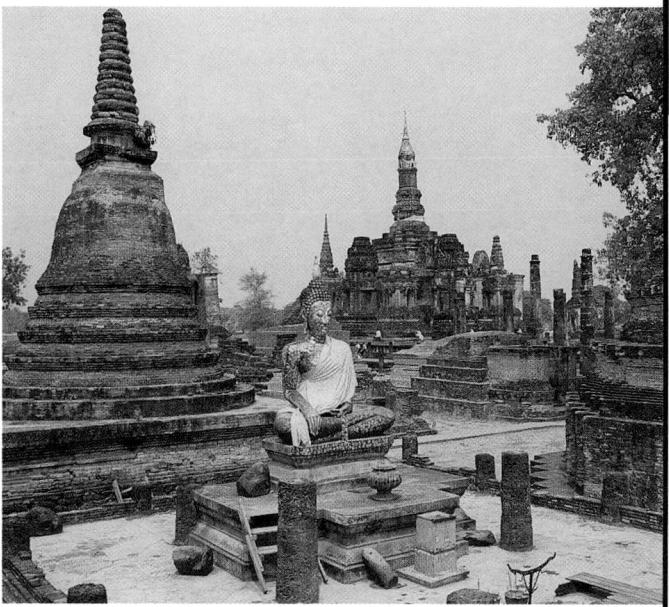

Visualizing History Wat Mahathat, an ancient Buddhist temple now restored, is in Sukhothai Historic Park, which was opened to the public in **1980.** *What was accomplished in Sukhothai's golden age?*

The Ayutthaya kingdom lasted for about 400 years, with a succession of 33 kings. At its height, it held control over large areas of Southeast Asia, including parts of Myanmar and the Malay Peninsula. Like Sukhothai, Ayutthaya was an important center of Buddhist learning and culture. Economically prosperous, Ayutthaya carried on trade in teakwood, salt, spices, and hides with China and neighboring Asian kingdoms.

Seafaring Kingdoms

Many kingdoms in early Southeast Asia developed around strategic ports. The Indonesian islands became a crossroads in the expanding international trade that stretched from the Arabian Peninsula to China. Merchants of many lands—Arabs, Chinese, Indians, and Persians—traded such products as porcelain, textiles, and silk for Southeast Asian spices and valuable woods.

The Srivijaya (SHREE•vih•JAY•uh) Empire arose on the islands of Java and Sumatra in present-day Indonesia. Lasting from about A.D. 600 to A.D. 1100, the Srivijaya Empire was one of the region's

---

Visualizing History The name Sukhothai means "Dawn of Happiness." According to the stone pillar of 1292, all citizens were treated equally and "all its citizenry, all chiefs and nobles, everyone everywhere, all men and women, all groups, believe in Buddhism."
Answer to Caption: *The kingdom became a center of learning and the arts and saw the development of an alphabet and writing system. People learned to make porcelain and built beautiful temples.*

Who?What?Where?When?

Borobudur Another magnificent religious complex in Southeast Asia, Borobudur, is located on the island of Java. Built about A.D. 800, it is not only a temple but also a representation of Buddhist doctrine. As visitors climb its five terraces, they pass from sculptural depictions of the ordinary world to those suggesting the profound truths of Buddhist enlightenment.

NATIONAL GEOGRAPHIC SOCIETY

CD-ROM
PICTURE ATLAS OF THE WORLD

Have students click the "Music" button of Vietnam, Cambodia, Thailand, Myanmar, Malaysia, and Indonesia to hear centuries-old songs played for emperors, rituals, and soldiers.

MEETING SPECIAL NEEDS ACTIVITY

Learning Style: Auditory/Musical Students who have difficulties reading and writing may enjoy staging a musical and/or dance presentation. Have them obtain recordings of gamelan music—the distinctive Indonesian art form that makes extensive use of percussion instruments, including gongs, cymbals, xylophones, and drums. Or, if possible, have them rent a video that combines this music with dance. **L1 LEP**

Visualizing History Temples are
everywhere in Bali—in villages, in
family courtyards, and on lakeshores
or sacred slopes in the countryside.
Answer to Caption: *It remained
Hindu when the rest of Indonesia adopted Islam.*

ASSESS

Check for Understanding

Assign Section 3 Assessment
as homework or as an in-class
activity.

 Use Interactive Tutor Self-
Assessment Software to review
Section 3.

Evaluate

Section Quiz 14-3

 Use the Testmaker to create a
customized quiz for Section 3.

Reteach

Have students identify the countries of Southeast Asia and summarize the major cultural
elements they adopted from
India (*Hinduism, Buddhism, Sanskrit*) and China (*Confucianism,
written language*).

Reading Essentials and
Study Guide 14-3

Enrich

Have students do necessary
research to create a travel
brochure for a Southeast Asian
country they would like to visit.

CLOSE

Have students summarize the
areas of Southeast Asian culture
in which the people retained their
own traditions. (*shadow puppetry,
batik, music, animism, architectural
styles, tattoos, Vietnamese hairstyle,
and language*)

Visualizing History The Hindu temple of Pura Ulun Danau on Lake Bratan in the
Central Mountains of Bali has a typical thatched roof. *How is
Bali's religious heritage different from that of the rest of Indonesia?*

great seafaring powers. It controlled shipping along
the Strait of Malacca that separates Sumatra from
the Malay Peninsula. By the end of the A.D. 1100s,
Srivijaya was reduced to a small kingdom, and the
Majapahit (mah•jah•PAH•heet) kingdom began to
dominate the Indonesian islands.

From the A.D. 400s to the A.D. 1400s, Buddhism
and Hinduism were the dominant religious influences that affected maritime Southeast Asian life.
During the early A.D. 1200s Muslim traders from
the Arabian Peninsula and India brought Islam to
the peoples of the Malay Peninsula and Indonesia.

The first major center of Islam in Southeast Asia
was **Melaka**, a port kingdom on the southwestern
coast of the Malay Peninsula.

From Melaka, Islam spread throughout the
Indonesian islands. The only island to remain outside of Muslim influence was Bali, which has kept
its Hindu religion and culture to the present day.

During the A.D. 1500s, a number of Muslim
trading kingdoms competed for control of the
Indonesian islands. European explorers, beginning
with the Portuguese in A.D. 1511, gradually won
control by setting local rulers against each other.

SECTION 3 ASSESSMENT

Main Idea
1. Use a diagram like the one
   below to show specific additions to Southeast Asian culture introduced from China
   and India.

Recall
2. **Define** archipelago, animism.
3. **Identify** the Khmer,
   Suryavarman II, Trung Trak,
   Trung Nhi, Ngo Quyen,
   Ramkhamhaeng.

Critical Thinking
4. **Synthesizing Information**
   How might Buddhism or

Confucianism complement a
belief in animism?

Understanding Themes
5. **Cultural Diffusion** Some
   aspects of Southeast Asian
   civilization were affected by
   China and India. What aspects
   of life in Southeast Asia did
   not change? Explain.

356 Chapter 14 *East and South Asia*

SECTION 3 ASSESSMENT ANSWERS

1. China: Confucianism, Daoism, and Buddhism, forms of government and writing,
   system of selecting officials; India: Hinduism, Buddhism, Sanskrit, Indian epics
   interwoven with Southeast Asian stories,
   architecture, law codes, political ideas
2. All terms are defined in the Glossary.
3. Khmer, 352; Suryavarman II, 353; Trung

Trak, 354; Trung Nhi, 354; Ngo Quyen,
354; Ramkhamhaeng, 355
4. Students should support their answers with
   facts about the religions in question.
5. **CULTURAL DIFFUSION** shadow
   puppetry, making batik, playing own instruments and music, animism, clothing and
   hair styles, alphabets

Making Generalizations

Have you heard statements such as "Only tall people play basketball well" or "Dogs make better pets than cats"? Do you consider the validity of such statements?

Learning the Skill

These statements, called generalizations, are broad statements about a topic. To be valid, a generalization must be based on accurate information. Let's examine the generalization "Only tall people play basketball well." Is this accurate? We can find many examples of tall basketball players. However, there are also many shorter players who excel at this sport.

In this case, we began with a generalization and looked for facts to support or disprove it. In other cases, you will make a generalization from a group of facts about a topic. To make a valid generalization, first collect facts—not opinions—relevant to the topic.

Suppose that you want to make a generalization about the relative danger of air and automobile travel. First, you would collect accident statistics involving airplanes and cars. Then classify the information into categories and look for relationships. For example, you might put the airplane and automobile statistics in separate categories. Finally, make a generalization that is consistent with most of the information.

Practicing the Skill

Read the passage about literature in the Tang dynasty and answer the questions that follow.

> ❝ Xuanzang welcomed artists to his splendid court.... Two of China's greatest poets, Duo Fu and Li Bo, produced their works in Xuanzang's court. Scholars compiled encyclopedias, dictionaries, and official histories of China. Writers popularized stories about ghosts, crime, and love. And while European monks were still slowly and laboriously copying texts by hand, Chinese Buddhist monks invented the more efficient technique of block printing. ❞

1. What facts about literature in the Tang dynasty are presented?
2. Organize these facts into categories.
3. How does the invention of block printing relate to the other facts?
4. What generalization can you make about literature during the Tang dynasty?

Applying the Skill

Chinese pouring vessel

Review the information in the chapter about religion in China, Cambodia, Vietnam, Korea, and Japan. Write a generalization about religion in East and Southeast Asia. Then support your generalization with at least five facts. Use your generalization and facts as the basis for an oral presentation to the class.

For More Practice

Turn to the Skill Practice in the Chapter Assessment on page 371 for more practice in making generalizations.

The **Glencoe Skillbuilder Interactive Workbook**, Level 2 provides instruction and practice in key social studies skills.

TEACH

Making Generalizations Write the following statement on the chalkboard: "Our school produces great football players [or hockey players or debaters, or whatever]." Ask students what information should be gathered in order to validate this generalization. *(number of team members who have won awards over the years; similar statistics for other schools in the area)* Then have students read the skill and complete the practice questions.

Additional Practice

⬦ Skill Reinforcement Activity 14

GLENCOE TECHNOLOGY

GO TO Glencoe's **Skillbuilder Interactive Workbook, Level 2**
This interactive CD-ROM promotes student mastery of key social studies skills.

ANSWERS TO PRACTICING THE SKILL

1. Xuanzang welcomed artists; two great poets wrote in his court; scholars compiled dictionaries and other works; writers popularized stories about ghosts, crime, and love; monks invented block printing.
2. patronage: emperor welcomes artists; types of works produced: encyclopedias, dictionaries, official histories, ghost stories, crime stories, love stories; technology: block printing
3. It made it easier to preserve and transmit writings of the period.
4. Literature flourished during the Tang dynasty.

A.D. 400 ——— A.D. 1000 ——— A.D. 1600

c. A.D. 400 Yamato clan founds Japanese imperial dynasty.

A.D. 668 The Silla kingdom conquers all of Korea.

A.D. 1274 Mongols make first attempt to invade Japan.

A.D. 1336 The Ashikaga family rules in Japan.

Section 4

Korea and Japan

Guide to Reading

Read to Find Out
Main Idea *The Koreans and the Japanese accepted some aspects of China's culture.*

▶ **Terms to Define**
shamanism, shogun, shogunate, samurai, daimyo, Bushido

▶ **People to Meet**
Amaterasu, Sejong, Yi-Sun-shin, Jimmu, Prince Shotoku, Lady Shikibu Murasaki, Yoritomo Minamoto

▶ **Places to Locate**
Heian (Kyoto)

The **Storyteller**

Zeami Motokiyo was adamant as he lectured his students. "Actors are not thoughtless mimics incapable of intellectualism or philosophy. We seek excellence, as do courtiers and men of letters." Motokiyo had been developing a new form of drama, the Noh play, that had uplifting stories and moral lessons, aspects that appealed to the educated upper classes. "Actors must always bear in mind the correct balance between mental and physical actions.

An actor, using his intelligence, will make his presentation seem beautiful." Motokiyo wanted his actors to think as well as to rehearse.

—adapted from *Sources of Japanese Tradition,* Ryusaku Tsunoda, reprinted in *Sources of World History,* Volume 1, edited by Mark A. Kishlansky, 1994

Noh theater mask

358 Chapter 14 *East and South Asia*

*L*ike the nations of Southeast Asia, Korea and Japan adopted elements of Chinese culture. But also like these other nations, they retained their own rich traditions.

Korea

A glance at Korea on the map on page 354 will reveal why a Korean proverb describes the country as "a shrimp between whales." Korea forms a peninsula on the east coast of Asia, extending south toward the western tip of Japan. Thus, it acts as a bridge between its two neighbors, China and Japan.

Early History

By legend, the Koreans claim descent from Tangun, the son of a bear and a god who supposedly founded the first Korean kingdom 5,000 years ago. Historians believe that the first Korean people were immigrants from northern Asia. These settlers lived in villages, grew rice, and made tools and other implements of bronze. They were animists who practiced shamanism, a belief that good and evil spirits inhabit both living and nonliving things. Shamans, or priests, interceded between the spirit world and humans.

In 109 B.C. China first invaded Korea, putting Korea under the control of the Han dynasty. From 109 B.C. until the fall of the Han dynasty in A.D. 220, Korea was dominated by China. But after the fall of the Han dynasty, Koreans regained control of their peninsula and, by A.D. 313, eventually formed three kingdoms—Silla, Paekche (pah•EHK•chee), and Koguryo. During the Three Kingdoms period, from A.D. 313 to A.D. 668, the Koreans adopted many elements of Chinese culture. Among these were Confucianism, Buddhism, calligraphy, and ideas about government.

Koreans also used Chinese knowledge of arts and sciences to make their own unique creations. For example, in the A.D. 300s, Koguryo artists produced mammoth cave art murals. In Silla, Queen Sondok built an astronomical observatory that still stands today and is the oldest observatory in Asia.

In A.D. 668 the kingdom of Silla conquered all of Korea, ushering in a period of peace, prosperity, and creativity. Korean potters produced superb porcelain decorated with flower designs. Koreans also created a unique mask dance that expressed sentiments of shamanism and Buddhism, which had been adopted as the state religion in A.D. 528. Over a 16-year period, Korean scholars compiled the *Tripitaka Koreana*, the largest collection of Buddhist scriptures in the world today. The *Tripitaka* has 81,258 large wooden printing plates.

The Yi Dynasty

In A.D. 1392 a dynasty called the Yi came to power in Korea. The Yi called their kingdom Choson and built Hanyang—today the city of Seoul—as their capital. They opened schools to teach Chinese classics to civil service candidates and made neo-Confucianism the state doctrine.

The adoption of Korean neo-Confucianism deeply affected people's roles and relationships. According to Korean Confucian doctrine, the eldest son in each family was bound by duty to serve his parents until their death. Korean women—who had been accorded high status under shamanism and Buddhism—were given much lower standing under Korean Confucianism. In fact, women from the higher ranks of society had to stay indoors until nightfall, when a great bell signaled the closing of the city gates. Even then, to go out they had to obtain permission from their husbands.

One of the greatest Yi rulers, King **Sejong**, had two significant accomplishments. He ordered bronze instruments to be used in measuring rain. As a result, Korea now has the oldest record of rainfall in the world. He and his advisers made a greater contribution by creating simplified writing to spread literacy. Together they devised *hangul*, an alphabet that uses 14 consonants and 10 vowels to represent Korean sounds. Although scholars continued to write with Chinese characters after the invention of *hangul*, writers began using *hangul* to transcribe folk tales and popular literature.

Although the Japanese tried to capture Korea in A.D. 1592, the Yi dynasty managed to successfully rebuff the Japanese invaders, mainly because of an invention created by Korea's Admiral **Yi-Sun-shin**. The admiral's ironclad warships, or "turtle ships," devastated the Japanese fleet. The Koreans won the war. However, in the years that followed, they increasingly avoided contact with the outside world

and isolated themselves so totally that Korea became known as the Hermit Kingdom.

Japan

Just 110 miles (204 km) east of Korea lies the Japanese archipelago. As the map on page 354 shows, Japan consists of four large islands—Honshu, Shikoku, Kyushu, and Hokkaido—and many smaller ones.

Visualizing History Shown here is the world's oldest astronomical observatory in Asia. It was built at Silla, Korea, from 365 stones. *How much territory did the kingdom of Silla hold by A.D. 668?*

Chapter 14 *East and South Asia* **359**

TEACH

Guided Practice

THEME Innovation

Explain the difference between a discovery and an innovation. *(To discover is to reveal or find for the first time; to innovate is to introduce something new, or to renew.)* Explain how an innovation can be based on someone else's discovery. What Korean innovations were based on knowledge gained from the Chinese? *(cave murals, observatory, new ways to decorate porcelain, mask dance)* **L1**

Technology Review the principles behind the Chinese system of writing. *(Hundreds of characters were needed to represent objects, ideas, and sounds.)* Why would an innovation like the Korean system of hangul be an improvement? *(Because it was alphabetic, requiring only 24 symbols. This made it much easier for the average person to learn.)* **L2**

Visualizing History When the kingdom of Silla dominated Korea, absolute monarchy flourished. Although the rulers granted land to aristocrats, the land reverted to the central government when the nobles died.
Answer to Caption: *all of Korea*

COOPERATIVE LEARNING ACTIVITY

Panel Presentation Organize the class into groups of four or five. Each group is to become a panel of experts on a Japanese topic. Subjects may include ikebana (flower arranging); the tea ceremony; Kabuki theater; architecture; the samurai; and various customs relating to food, clothing, manners, or holidays. Choose a leader for each group. Each member of each group should prepare a five-minute presentation on one aspect of the team's subject. **L2**

Visualizing History The graceful shape of Mount Fuji has made this volcanic mountain famous all over the world. The temples and shrines on its slopes—and even in its craters—draw hundreds of thousands of climbers every year.
Answer to Caption: *It inspired Japanese painters and poets with deep reverence for nature.*

Government Ask students to summarize the changes in Japan's form of government from Yamato times to the fourteenth century. *(clan rule: with Taika reforms, stronger central government; Nara: greater centralization; Heian: power struggles and rise of shogunate)* **L3**

Independent Practice

📁 Guided Reading Activity 14-4 **L1**

Cultural Perspectives

The Ainu Because of Japan's geographic isolation, the country today has very few minorities. There is, however, one group that may have descended from the very first inhabitants of Japan. They are called Ainu, and most of them live on the northernmost main island, Hokkaido. Although most of the 15,000 Ainu have intermarried with other Japanese, a few still live in isolated villages, where they follow their traditional way of life.

Visualizing History Mount Fuji and Lake Ashi at Hakone, Japan. *How did the physical beauty of the land affect Japanese art?*

Island Geography

Because of its island geography, Japanese culture formed mostly in isolation from mainland Asian cultures, except for that of China. Although the Japanese borrowed from Chinese civilization, their customs and traditions were different from those of most other Asian peoples.

The geography of these islands influenced the formation of Japanese culture in other ways as well. Because much of the land is mountainous—less than 20 percent of it is suitable for farming—the Japanese learned to get most of their food from the sea. They also learned to rely on the sea for protection from invaders—being a natural barrier to invasion from the mainland—and yet to regard it as a route of transport between the islands. The physical beauty of the land inspired deep reverence for nature in works by many Japanese painters and poets. Because these islands are located in an area where earthquakes, typhoons, floods, and volcanic eruptions are frequent, the Japanese long ago created a myth that helped to explain the stormy weather there.

Creation Myth

An ancient Japanese creation myth is the oldest explanation for the origins of Japan, its turbulent weather, and its first emperor. According to the myth, brother and sister gods Izanagi and Izanami dipped a spear into the churning sea. When they

pulled it out, the drops of brine that fell upon the water's surface became the islands of Japan. The two gods then created the sun goddess **Amaterasu**, and because they loved her best of all their children, they sent her to heaven to rule over the world. Next they created Tsuki-yumi, the moon god, and Susanowo, the storm god, to be her companions.

Amaterasu gave life to everything around her. But Susanowo, who had a fierce temper, ruined his sister's rice crop and so frightened her that she hid in a cave. Without her in heaven, the world became dark. The other gods placed a jewel and a mirror on a tree outside the cave to coax Amaterasu back outside. When she came out and told them why she had hidden, the other gods banished Susanowo to the earth.

According to the myth, Susanowo's descendants were the first inhabitants of Japan. Amaterasu sent her grandson, Ninigi, to govern these descendants on the island of Honshu. So that all would acknowledge his divine power, she sent with him her mirror, her jewel, and a great sword. According to legend, Ninigi's grandson, **Jimmu**, conquered the rest of Susanowo's descendants in 660 B.C., becoming the first emperor of Japan.

By tradition, each successive emperor has received Amaterasu's three gifts: a mirror, a jewel, and a sword. Also by tradition, each emperor—until Hirohito—has claimed to be Amaterasu's descendant. In 1945, after the Japanese defeat in

360 Chapter 14 *East and South Asia*

MEETING SPECIAL NEEDS ACTIVITY

Study Strategy For most Americans, the cultures of East and Southeast Asia are unfamiliar. Students may be helped in studying these peoples if they construct a table summarizing the basic information in the four sections of this chapter. They should put dates along one axis and main categories of information (politics, religion, and so on) along the other. **L2**

World War II, Emperor Hirohito announced that he did not possess divine status.

Early Inhabitants

Among the first people to inhabit the Japanese islands were hunter-gatherers who came there from the mainland more than 10,000 years ago. These people had developed the technology to make pottery but not to make bronze or iron. When Koreans and others from mainland Asia invaded Japan during the 200s B.C. and 100s B.C., they were easily able to defeat the early inhabitants by using iron and bronze weapons.

The invaders introduced the islanders to agricultural methods, such as how to grow rice in flooded paddies. Heavy summer rains in Japan made it the ideal place to grow rice, which soon became Japan's most important crop.

Between A.D. 200 and A.D. 300, another influx of mainlanders came to Japan. According to scholars, these armor-clad warriors who fought on horseback were probably the ancestors of the aristocratic warriors and imperial family of Japan referred to in the creation myth.

In early Japan, though, even before there was an emperor or an imperial family, separate clans ruled their own regions. Clan members practiced a form of animism called Shinto, meaning "the way of the gods." Each clan included a group of families descended from a common ancestor, often said to have been an animal or a god. The clan worshiped this ancestor as its special *kami*, or spirit. Practitioners of Shinto believed that *kami* dwelled within people, animals, and even nonliving objects such as rocks and streams. To honor this *kami*—and the *kami* of their ancestors—they held festivals and rituals. Often these ceremonies were conducted by the chief of the clan, who acted as both military leader and priest.

The Yamato Clan

By about A.D. 400, the military skill and prestige of the Yamato clan, which claimed descent from Amaterasu, enabled it to extend a loose rule over most of Japan. Although other clans continued to rule their own lands, they owed their loyalty to the Yamato chief. In effect, he became the emperor.

Initially, the emperor had a great deal of political power. By the A.D. mid-500s, however, the emperor had become more of a ceremonial figure who carried out religious rituals. The real political power was held by the members of the Soga

Music Have students find recordings of Korean or Japanese music to share with the class. Samples could include koto (a harplike instrument) or samisen (a three-stringed banjo) music, or a recording of folk songs. **L2 LEP**

Religion Many Japanese practice Shinto along with Buddhism. Have students write a report on Shinto, describing the beliefs and practices of this religion. **L2**

Linking Past and Present

Samurai Arts

The samurai's loyalty to his overlord was absolute. Nothing was to come before it—not duties to wife, parents, or children. Although the samurai and the European feudal knight had this tradition of loyalty to one's lord in common, the two were quite different in other ways. The samurai did not go to battle to defend a lady or for religious motives, as his European counterpart often did.

ANSWER

Students might suggest values, such as bravery, heroism, or the strength of the human spirit against adversity. They may note that these same values are expressed in the films.

Samurai Arts

Kiyomatsu, a samurai hero

In the A.D. 1100s the rise of military rule in Japan brought in a new style of art. Supported by daimyo and samurai, artists created paintings highlighting the skill and bravery of soldiers. These works show warriors in richly patterned clothing, riding magnificent horses and wielding long swords. The expressions of the riders and their horses often convey wild—but controlled—emotions.

Today in Japan the samurai artistic tradition is most prominent in movies and television. Many popular Japanese films are samurai tales set in feudal times and filled with action and adventure. Akira Kurosawa, one of the world's renowned directors, has made a number of samurai movies. His film *The Hidden Fortress*—about a brave general who leads an endangered princess to safety—helped inspire American director George Lucas to create the epic film *Star Wars*.

Linking Past and Present ACTIVITY

Study a painting with a samurai theme. What values are expressed in the painting? You might want to view the films *The Hidden Fortress* and *Star Wars*. In what ways do you think these films reflect samurai values? In what ways do you think they do not?

Chapter 14 *East and South Asia* **361**

MAKING CONNECTIONS ACTIVITIES

Religion Have students research the Japanese tea ceremony, focusing especially on the symbolism of the ritual. Encourage students to do a demonstration of a tea ceremony for the rest of the class. **L2**

The Arts Have students research ikebana, the Japanese art of flower arranging. On the basis of the information they find, have students create an arrangement that conforms to the principle of ikebana. Most libraries have books on the subject. **L3**

Politics Have students research the Taika reforms of the Fujiwara family. Ask them to use library resources to describe some of the reforms and draw conclusions about their effects. **L3**

Linking Past and Present

Nara Temples During the Nara period in Japan, hundreds of temples were built at the capital city of Nara. Today, 1,300 years later, many of these temples still stand. Their beauty and historic interest draw some 10 million visitors a year.

Who?What?Where?When?

Early Japanese Writings The earliest known Japanese books are the *Kojiki* (Records of Ancient Matters), completed in A.D. 712, and the *Nihon shoki* (Chronicles of Japan), completed in 720. The two works combine actual events with myths that trace the imperial family to the foundations of the world. Their purpose was to give the court—then under Chinese influence—a history that could compete with that of the Chinese.

The following videotape program is available from Glencoe:

• **Samurai!**

To find classroom resources to accompany this video, check the following home page:

A&E Television: http://www.aetv.com

---

family. The emperors kept their position as heads of Japan because people believed that only they could intercede with the gods. But the Soga family controlled the country.

Chinese Influences

In A.D. 552 a Korean king sent a statue of the Buddha and some Buddhist texts to the Japanese court. The king wrote, "This religion is the most excellent of all teachings" and suggested that the emperor make Buddhism the national religion. Buddhism had come to Korea from China, and its introduction to Japan made the Japanese open to Chinese culture. This curiosity about China was especially strong among Japan's nobles and scholars.

Through a kind of cultural exchange program that lasted four centuries, the Japanese learned much from the Chinese. Not only did they learn about the teachings of the Buddha, they also learned a great deal about Chinese art, medicine, astronomy, and philosophy. They incorporated much of this knowledge into Japanese culture. For instance, the Japanese adopted the Chinese characters for writing to create their own writing system.

Prince Shotoku was responsible for much of this cultural exchange. When he became the leading court official in A.D. 593, he instituted programs that encouraged further learning from Chinese civilization. He ordered the construction of Buddhist monasteries and temples and sent officials and students to China to study. When Shotoku heard about the Chinese Confucian ideas of government, he wrote a constitution for Japan in which he set forth

Temple of Kailasa

India, A.D. 760
Emperor Krishna of the Rashtrakuta dynasty ordered construction of the Kailasa Temple at Ellora. The temple, completed in A.D. 760, was cut from a single outcropping of rock. It was 165 feet (50 m) long and 96 feet (29 m) high. Kailasa was dedicated to the Hindu god Siva. Its elaborate carvings featured Hindu gods and mythological figures in various poses.

INDIA
• Ellora

---

general principles that explained how government officials should act.

After Shotoku's death, the Fujiwara family seized power in the name of the emperor and began to urge him to pattern the government more closely on that of China. China had a strong central government at that time.

In A.D. 646 government officials instituted the Taika reforms, or "Great Change." These reforms proclaimed that all the land was the property of the emperor rather than clan leaders. Clan leaders could oversee the peasants working the land, but they could no longer assign them land or collect taxes from them. Instead, government officials were to allocate plots to peasants and collect part of their harvest in taxes for the emperor.

In modeling their government on China, however, the Japanese did not always adopt Chinese ways. For example, civil service examinations were never accepted; instead officials gained their posts through family ties. Also, even after the Taika reforms, much of Japan remained under the control of regional clan leaders.

The Nara Period

Greater government centralization did not take place until A.D. 710, when Japan built its first permanent capital at Nara. A smaller version of China's Changan, Nara had an imperial palace, broad streets, large public squares, rows of Chinese-style homes, and Buddhist temples.

With the completion of the colossal Todaiji Temple at Nara in A.D. 752, Buddhist fervor in Japan reached its peak. Buddhism, however, did not replace Shinto, for each religion met different needs. Shinto linked the Japanese to nature and their homeland. Buddhism promised spiritual rewards to the good. Therefore, people practiced both.

During the Nara period, the Japanese also produced their first written literature. Scribes wrote histories of ancient Japan that combined the creation myths with actual events. Other writers compiled collections of Japanese poems.

The Heian Period

In A.D. 794 the Japanese established a new capital in **Heian,** later called **Kyoto.** For more than 1,000 years, this city remained the capital of Japan.

A century after the city was founded, Japan stopped sending cultural missions to China. In the period that followed, a small group of about 3,000 Japanese aristocrats, calling themselves "dwellers among the clouds," created Heian culture.

The focus of Heian court life was the pursuit of

CRITICAL THINKING ACTIVITY

Making Comparisons Although Korea and Japan have many things in common, there are also profound differences between them. Have students compare and contrast the two countries, perhaps using a double-column format with side headings such as: *mythological origins; major historical periods to about 1400; cultural borrowings from China;* and *native cultural contributions.* **L3**

The Lady Fujitsubo Watching Prince Genji Departing in the Moonlight by A. Hiroshige and U. Toyokuni, A.D. 1853. **What was a major theme of the Heian novel,** The Tale of Genji?

History & Art Lady Murasaki's novel depicts Prince Genji and his courtiers as refined members of the nobility. To succeed at court, an aristocrat had to be skilled as a musician, poet, and calligrapher, and be wise in the ways of elegant courtship. **Answer to Caption:** *the beauty of nature*

beauty. It pervaded all of life's activities, from wrapping presents to mixing perfumes and colors. People devoted hours each day to writing letters in the form of poems. Calligraphy was as important as the poem itself, for a person's handwriting was taken to be an indication of his or her character. People were even said to fall in love upon seeing each other's handwriting.

During the Heian period, women were the creators of Japan's first great prose literature. About A.D. 1010 **Lady Shikibu Murasaki** wrote *The Tale of Genji*, which some believe to be the world's first novel. The novelist chronicles the life and loves of a fictional prince named Genji. Filled with poems about the beauty of nature, *The Tale of Genji* quickly became very popular.

The Heian aristocrats were so deeply involved in their search for beauty, however, that they neglected tasks of government. Order began breaking down in the provinces. Warlike provincial leaders started running their estates as independent territories, ignoring the emperor's officials and refusing to pay taxes. Thus the Heian aristocrats eventually lost control of the empire completely.

The Way of the Warrior

As Heian power faded, two powerful court families, the Taira and the Minamoto, struggled for control. The families fought a decisive battle in A.D. 1185 in which the Taira were defeated. To **Yoritomo**

Minamoto, head of the Minamoto family, the emperor then gave the title shogun, or "general," and delegated to him most of the real political and military power. While the emperor remained with his court in the capital of Kyoto carrying on ritual tasks, Yoritomo and his soldiers ran a shogunate, or military government, from Kamakura near present-day Tokyo.

The shogunate proved to be quite strong. Even though Kublai Khan tried twice to invade Japan— once in A.D. 1274 and again in A.D. 1281—he did not succeed. On the first occasion, Japanese warriors and the threat of a storm forced the Mongols to withdraw. On the second occasion, 150,000 Mongol warriors came by ship, but a typhoon arose and destroyed the fleet. The Japanese thought of the storm as the *kamikaze*, or "divine wind," and took it to be confirmation that their islands were indeed sacred.

In A.D. 1336 the Ashikaga family gained control of the shogunate. But the family failed to get control of regional warriors. Japan soon broke into individual warring states, leaving the shogun and the emperor as mere figureheads.

The powerful landowner-warriors in the countryside were called samurai. The most powerful samurai became daimyo (DY•mee•OH), or lords. Like the medieval knights of feudal Europe who pledged their loyalty to lords, samurai pledged their loyalty and military service to their daimyo. There were many samurai and many daimyo. Poor

you don't say...

"Tycoon" is an English word that now applies mainly to business leaders. It comes to us from China by way of Japan. The Chinese term for "great prince," *ta kuin*, was adapted by the Japanese as *taikun* and used to describe the shogun.

Linking Past and Present

The *kamikaze*, or "divine wind" that saved Japan from Mongol defeat in 1281, never lost its importance for the Japanese. During World War II, Allied planes bombed Japan from aircraft carriers. Suicide pilots, their planes loaded with explosives, dived into the aircraft carriers in an effort to stave off defeat. Admired at home and feared by the Allies, they were known as kamikaze pilots.

Chapter 14 *East and South Asia* **363**

MORE ABOUT...

Lady Murasaki The author of *The Tale of Genji* was born about 978 and died around 1014. Her real name is unknown; the name by which she is called is that of the heroine of her novel. After the death of her husband, Fujiwara Nobutaka, Lady Murasaki served at court. It was during this time that she wrote *The Tale of Genji*. It has been recognized as a masterpiece ever since. In the thirteenth century, a 54-volume commentary appeared; more recently, a Japanese publisher issued a 1,200-page *Tale of Genji Encyclopedia*.

Visualizing History The Buddha himself did not believe in any god or gods. After his death, however, he was worshiped as a god, surrounded by lesser gods. Buddhism became a complex religion with temples, rituals, priests, monks, and nuns.

Answer to Caption: *by a Korean king who sent a statue of the Buddha and some Buddhist texts to the Japanese court*

ASSESS

Check for Understanding

Assign Section 4 Assessment as homework or as an in-class activity.

▣ Use Interactive Tutor Self-Assessment Software to review Section 4.

Evaluate

🗀 Section Quiz 14-4

▣ Use the Testmaker to create a customized quiz for Section 4.

Reteach

Ask the class to answer these questions:

1. What country acted as a bridge between China and Japan? (*Korea*)
2. What elements of Chinese culture became part of Korean and Japanese cultures? (*Confucianism, Buddhism, language, art of making porcelain, use of wood-block printing*)
3. What kind of military government and class of warriors were unique to Japan? (*shogunate and samurai*)

 Reteaching Activity 14

🗀 Reading Essentials and Study Guide 14-4

Visualizing History Friends mourn the death of the Buddha in this Japanese painting.
How was Buddhism introduced to Japan?

rice farmers paid high taxes for the right to farm a daimyo's lands. In return, that daimyo provided the farmers with protection. The system in which large landholders give protection to people in exchange for their services is called feudalism. Japanese feudalism was similar to European feudalism as described in Chapter 12.

The samurai fought on horseback with bows, arrows, and steel swords. They dressed in loose-fitting armor. The samurai followed a strict code of honor called **Bushido**, meaning "the way of the warrior." Bushido stressed bravery, self-discipline, and loyalty. It demanded that the samurai endure suffering and defend his honor at all costs. If a samurai was dishonored or defeated, he was expected to commit suicide.

Japanese women too could be warriors. This passage from *The Tale of the Heike* describes a female Minamoto samurai:

❝ Tomoe had long black hair and a fair complexion, and her face was very lovely; moreover she was a fearless rider whom neither the fiercest horse nor the roughest ground could dismay, and so dexterously did she handle sword and bow that she was a match for a thousand warriors and fit to meet either god or devil. Many times

364 Chapter 14 *East and South Asia*

had she … won matchless renown in encounters with the bravest captains, and so in this last fight, when all the others had been slain or had fled, among the last seven there rode Tomoe. ❞

—*The Tale of the Heike*, A.D. 1200s

Growth of a Merchant Class

Despite the political turmoil during its feudal period, Japan developed economically at this time. Workshops on daimyo estates produced arms, armor, and iron tools. Each region began to specialize in goods such as pottery, paper, textiles, and lacquerware. Trade increased between regions.

The increasing trade led to the growth of towns around the castles of the daimyos. Merchants and artisans formed guilds to promote their interests—just as they did in medieval Europe. These guilds, called *za* in Japan, benefited their members in many ways. A *za* might pay a fee to exempt its members from paying tolls for shipping their goods. Over a long period of time, this exemption would save the members quite a bit of money.

Japanese merchants began to trade with Chinese and Korean merchants. Chinese copper coins became the chief means of exchange. The Japanese exported raw materials such as lumber, pearls, and gold, as well as finished goods such as swords and painted fans. The Japanese imported items such as medicines, books, and pictures.

Religion and the Arts

By the A.D. 1200s Buddhism had spread from the nobles to the common people. The opening words of *The Tale of the Heike* describe the Buddhist sentiments that were prevalent in Japan during its feudal period:

❝ In the sound of the bell of the Gion Temple echoes the impermanence of all things. The pale hue of the flowers of the teak tree show the truth that they who prosper must fall. The proud do not last long, but vanish like a spring-night's dream. And the mighty ones too will perish in the end, like dust before the wind. ❞

During Japan's feudal age, Buddhist teachings were simplified and gave rise to many religious groups. The new varieties of Buddhism all taught about a personal afterlife in paradise. The way to paradise, they stated, was through simple trust in the Buddha. With salvation so easily available, the influence of priests, monks, and nuns declined. For

_____

_____

_____

_____

_____

Visualizing History Zen meditation aims at emptying the mind in order to achieve limitless receptivity.
Answer to Caption: *to free the mind and thus reach enlightenment*

Visualizing History

Zen Buddhist monks sit in a meditation garden at Ryoanji Temple in Kyoto, Japan.
To a Zen Buddhist, what is the purpose of meditation?

the first time, the common people began to play an important role in Buddhist life. With widespread support, Japanese Buddhist groups linked religion with patriotism. Some believed that Japanese Buddhism was the only true Buddhism and that Japan was the center of the universe.

While the common people turned to new forms of Buddhism, the samurai followed a form of Buddhism called Zen. The Japanese scholar Eisai had brought Zen to Japan from China late in the A.D. 1100s. Zen taught that the individual had to live in harmony with nature and that this harmony could be achieved through a deep religious understanding called enlightenment. The followers of Zen rejected book learning and logical thought, embracing instead bodily discipline and meditation. They believed that by meditation a student could free his mind and arrive at enlightenment.

Zen was particularly useful for warriors because it taught them to act instinctively, and thinking was a hindrance to action. Samurai could improve skills such as archery by freeing their minds from distractions to better concentrate on the object or target.

Zen also perfected art forms and rituals such as ikebana, or flower arranging, meditation gardens, and the tea ceremony. Ikebana grew out of the religious custom of placing flowers before images of the Buddha. The Zen practice of meditation gave rise to meditation gardens, consisting of carefully placed rocks surrounded by neatly raked sand.

Meditation also sparked the tea ceremony, an elegant, studied ritual for serving tea. One tea master said of the ceremony that it was intended to "cleanse the senses … so that the mind itself is cleansed from defilements." These and other arts and rituals derived from Buddhism are still popular in Japan today.

Enrich

Have students research the art of Japanese screens, bringing illustrations to class. Suggest that they also use watercolors to paint a facsimile screen.

 Enrichment Activity 14

CLOSE

Discuss the Korean and Japanese acceptance of aspects of Chinese culture that advanced their own cultures. Ask students to give examples. (*Answers may include: Korea: produced superb porcelain with flower designs, compiled world's largest collection of Buddhist scriptures and printed it with wooden plates; Japan: developed stronger central government based on Confucian ideals, used Chinese characters to create their own writing system*)

SECTION 4 ASSESSMENT

Main Idea
1. Use a chart like the one below to identify elements of Chinese culture accepted by Korea and Japan.

Chinese Culture in. . .	
Japan	Korea

Recall
2. **Define** shamanism, shogun, shogunate, samurai, daimyo.
3. **Identify** Sejong, Yi-Sun-shin, Amaterasu, Jimmu, Shinto, Prince Shotoku, Taika reforms, Lady Shikibu Murasaki, Yoritomo Minamoto, Bushido.

Critical Thinking
4. **Evaluating Information** Would you prefer to follow the ideals of the Heian court or the samurai code of Bushido? Why? What effects do you think each viewpoint might have had on the people of Japan?

Understanding Themes
5. **Innovation** Identify one Japanese or Korean invention from this period of Asian history, and explain why it was innovative.

SECTION 4 ASSESSMENT ANSWERS

1. Korea: Confucianism, Buddhism, calligraphy, ideas about government; knowledge of arts and sciences; civil service classes, neo-Confucianism; Japan: Buddhism, art, medicine, philosophy, astronomy, writing characters, Confucian ideas of government

2. All terms are defined in the Glossary.
3. Sejong, 359; Yi-Sun-shin, 359; Amaterasu, 360; Jimmu, 360; Shinto, 361; Prince Shotoku, 362; Taika reforms, 362; Lady Shikibu Murasaki, 363; Yoritomo Minamoto, 363; Bushido, 364
4. Answers will vary. Students choosing

Heian ideals should stress their aesthetic focus, while those who choose Bushido might mention its nobility or enforced self-discipline.

5. **INNOVATION** Answers will vary. Sample answer: Koreans built the world's oldest astronomical observatory.

Block Schedule

Team Teaching These poems of Li Bo may be presented in a team-teaching context, in conjunction with English or Language Arts.

Poetry of Li Bo

Historical Connection

Artistic, political, and economic advances often go together. The success of Li Bo was one indication of the prosperity of China during the Tang dynasty.

Background Information

Setting Li Bo often set his poems in natural surroundings. He traveled a great deal and, as a result, he was sensitive to variations in landscape and climate.

Literary Elements Allusion is a reference, often indirect, to something that the writer assumes the reader knows about. For example, in Li Bo's letter to his children, he notes that the silkworms "have now had three sleeps," assuming they would understand how long a time was indicated. When silkworms make their cocoons, they alternate between working and resting.

Simile is the direct comparison of two things. In "Taking Leave of a Friend," Li Bo writes "Sunset like the parting of old acquaintances." He is comparing the setting of the sun with the parting of friends.

Bridge to the Past
Literature

from

Four Poems
by Li Bo

L i Bo was born in A.D. 701 in western China. People began praising his beautiful poems even before he reached adulthood. Throughout his life he traveled extensively in China, amazing people with his ability to compose insightful, touching poems. He usually wrote about the world around him, the people he met, and the emotions he felt. By the time of his death in A.D. 762, he was regarded as one of China's greatest poets, a distinction he still holds today.

I n the following poem, Li Bo comments on an experience everyone faces at some time: parting with a close companion.

Taking Leave of a Friend

Blue mountains to the north of the walls,
White river winding about them;
Here we must make separation
And go out through a thousand miles
    of dead grass.

Mind like a floating wide cloud,
Sunset like the parting of old acquaintances
Who bow over their clasped hands at a distance.
Our horses neigh to each other
    as we are departing.

T he following poem is a favorite of many Chinese citizens who have left their homeland and settled in the United States or elsewhere.

On a Quiet Night

I saw the moonlight before my couch,
And wondered if it were not the frost
    on the ground.
I raised my head and looked out on the
    mountain moon;
I bowed my head and thought of my
    far-off home.

366 **Chapter 14** *East and South Asia*

ABOUT THE AUTHOR

Li Bo wrote more than 1,000 poems, which are still read today. Many were short poems composed as thank-you notes and gifts to friends. Other poems, usually longer, were more like folk songs. Li Bo wrote them in a traditional ballad style to accompany music. As a follower of Daoism, he believed in intuition and loved nature. According to legend, he died when he jumped out of a boat to grab the reflection of the moon on the water.

Li Bo lived in ancient China's greatest epoch for poetry. Three other revered poets, Wang Wei, Duo Fu, and Bo Juyi, also lived during the Tang dynasty.

𝓛i Bo used extensive symbolism in his writing. In the following poem, he compares life to a traveler on a journey.

Hard Is the Journey

Gold vessels of fine wines,
   thousands a gallon,
Jade dishes of rare meats,
   costing more thousands,

I lay my chopsticks down,
   no more can banquet,
And draw my sword and stare
   wildly about me:

Ice bars my way to cross
   the Yellow River,
Snows from dark skies to climb
   the T'ai-hang Mountains!

At peace I drop a hook
   into a brooklet,
At once I'm in a boat
   but sailing sunward …

   (Hard is the Journey,
   Hard is the Journey,
   So many turnings,
   And now where am I?)

So when a breeze breaks waves,
   bringing fair weather,
I set a cloud for sails,
   cross the blue oceans!

Visualizing History *Dawn Over Elixir Terrace* depicts a tranquil river scene. *How do the river and mountains present obstacles to the traveler in the poem?*

FOCUS

Before students read the first poem, describe Li Bo's life and his extensive travels. Ask students to predict what subjects a poet who traveled frequently might emphasize.

Visualizing History Landscape painting became popular in China during the Tang dynasty, the period when Li Bo lived. Artists of this time painted scenes of craggy mountains, rocks, streams, and trees.
Answer to Caption: *The river is iced over, and snow falls in the mountains.*

OTHER WORKS OF AND ABOUT CHINESE LITERATURE

Bynner, Witter, trans. *The Jade Mountain.* New York: Knopf, 1929, 1957.
Grousett, Rene. *The Rise and Splendor of the Chinese Empire.* Berkeley: University of California Press, 1953.
Obata, Shigeyoshi. *The Works of Li Po.* New York: Paragon, 1965.

Pound, Ezra. *Personae.* New York: New Directions, 1926.
Waley, Arthur, trans. *The Poetry and Career of Li Po.* New York: Macmillan, 1950.

TEACH

Evaluation

In "Taking Leave of a Friend," Li Bo uses hyperbole, or exaggeration. The "thousand miles of dead grass" is an exaggeration used for effect. Ask students if they think hyperbole works to convey the sense of bleakness one might feel if separated from a close friend.

Clarification

In "Hard Is the Journey," Li Bo refers to the Yellow River, now known as the Huang River. It flows through north and central China.

Interpretation

Ask students what the peach tree symbolizes in Li Bo's letter to his children. One view might be that it suggests the poet's role as provider for his family. Another interpretation might be that it symbolizes the changes that affected Li Bo's family during his three-year absence.

 World Literature Selection 3

History & Art
Artists and poets during the Tang dynasty used natural scenes to express their deepest feelings. "Outwardly, nature has been my teacher," said one Tang landscape painter, "but inwardly I follow the springs of my heart."
Answer to Caption: *spring*

Since Li Bo spent much of his time traveling, he was often separated from his family. He wrote and sent the following poem to his children.

Letter to His Two Small Children Staying in Eastern Lu at Wen Yang Village Under Turtle Mountain

Here in Wu Land mulberry leaves are green,
Silkworms in Wu have now had three sleeps:

My family, left in Eastern Lu,
Oh, to sow now Turtle-shaded fields,
Do the Spring things I can never join,
Sailing Yangtse always on my own—

Let the South Wind blow you back my heart,
Fly and land it in the Tavern court
Where, to the East, there are sprays and leaves
Of one peach-tree, sweeping the blue mist;

History & Art *Landscape of the Four Seasons by Shen Shih-Ch'ung. In what season did Li Bo write the above poem?*

ADDITIONAL LITERARY WORKS OF THE PERIOD

Bede, the Venerable. *Ecclesiastical History of the English Nation.* The first important account of English history, written in the early A.D. 700s.

Dante Alighieri. *The Divine Comedy.* Epic about Christian views of life after death, written in early A.D. 1300s.

Murasaki, Shikibu. *The Tale of Genji.* Japanese tale of romance and political intrigue, written about A.D. 1000.

Nibelungenlied. German epic poems written down in the A.D. 1200s; they formed the basis for several famous operas by Richard Wagner in the 1800s.

Visualizing History This winter scene is a detail from the Ming dynasty painting *Landscape of the Four Seasons*. *How many winters have passed since the author was at home?*

This is the tree I myself put in
When I left you, nearly three years past;
A peach-tree now, level with the eaves,
And I sailing cannot yet turn home!

Pretty daughter, P'ing-yang is your name,
Breaking blossom, there beside my tree,
Breaking blossom, you cannot see me
And your tears flow like the running stream;

And little son, Po-ch'in you are called,
Your big sister's shoulder you must reach
When you come there underneath my peach,
Oh, to pat and pet you too, my child!

I dreamt like this till my wits went wild,
By such yearning daily burned within;
So tore some silk, wrote this distant pang
From me to you living at Wen Yang....

RESPONDING TO LITERATURE

1. In "On a Quiet Night," why is the person unhappy?
2. In "Hard Is the Journey," what do the gold vessels and jade dishes symbolize?
3. What types of images did Li Bo use in each of his poems included here?
4. **Supporting an Opinion** Which poem do you like best? Explain why.

ANSWERS TO RESPONDING TO LITERATURE

1. The person is sad because he or she is far from home.
2. They symbolize the many pleasures, experiences, and fine things to enjoy in life.
3. Li Bo used images from nature: moonlight, frost, blue mountains, white river, mulberry leaves, ice, snow.
4. Students should explain what they like about the poem: for example, that "Hard Is the Journey" has an upbeat ending.

This painting was done centuries after Li Bo wrote. However, many painters of the Ming dynasty revived older artistic traditions.
Answer to Caption: *three*

ASSESS

Assign **Responding to Literature** questions.

CLOSE

Discuss with students whether Li Bo's poems are relevant today. Point out that people travel more than ever before, which may allow them to more easily identify with the themes in Li Bo's poetry. On the other hand, travel and communication are so much easier today that people may feel less separated from their families when traveling.

Contemporary Connection
Have students think about times they have been away from home or separated from family or friends in some way. Have them use the poem "On a Quiet Night" on page 366 as a model to write a short poem or a paragraph expressing how they felt.

Portfolio Project

Have students select another Chinese poem or a Japanese haiku and write a brief response to it. In their response students should summarize the poem's theme, explain what effects the poet achieves and how he or she achieves them, and discuss the poem's relevance to people today.

WORLD HISTORY Online

Have students use the **Chapter 14 Self-Check Quiz** at worldhistory.glencoe.com to prepare for the Chapter Test.

GLENCOE TECHNOLOGY

VIDEODISC
Use MindJogger to review the chapter.

MindJogger Videoquiz

Chapter 14
Disc 2 Side B

Also available in VHS.

Answers

Using Key Terms

1. b   3. i   5. c
2. f   4. d

Using Your History Journal

Students might use colors to represent different types of events.

Reviewing Facts

1. late A.D. 1100s: Mongols dominant nomadic group; A.D. 1206: Genghis Khan organizes clans under one government; A.D. 1211: invade China; A.D. 1279: rule all of China; A.D. 1230s–1240s: cross into eastern and central Europe; A.D. 1258: capture Baghdad; A.D. 1200s: peaceful empire; A.D. 1402: Timur defeats Ottomans; A.D. 1405: Timur dies, empire collapses
2. son of the Tang dynasty founder; expanded empire and restored strong central government
3. scientific: compass, gunpowder, rocket launchers; artistic: porcelain, landscape painting

---

WORLD HISTORY Online

Self-Check Quiz

Visit the *World History: The Human Experience* Web site at **worldhistory.glencoe.com** and click on *Chapter 14—Self-Check Quiz* to prepare for the Chapter Test.

Using Key Terms

Write the key term that completes each sentence. Then write a sentence for each term not chosen.

a. yurts   g. shogun
b. *yasa*   h. shogunate
c. daimyo   i. archipelago
d. meritocracy   j. mandarins
e. samurai   k. clans
f. shamanism

1. The Mongol warrior Temujin, later known as Genghis Khan, developed a code of law known as the _____.
2. The early Koreans practiced _____, a belief that priests could intercede between humans and spirits.
3. The Japanese _____ geographically consists of four large islands and many smaller ones.
4. Because of its examination system, the Chinese government claimed that it was a _____, or a system in which people are chosen and promoted for their talents and performance rather than for favors.
5. In return for protection, Japanese farmers farmed the lands of powerful landowner-warriors known as _____.

Technology Activity

Creating a Multimedia Presentation Search a computerized card catalog or the Internet to locate information about Genghis Khan. Using multimedia tools, create a presentation about the reign of Genghis Khan. Include information about Genghis Khan as a person and as a ruler. Incorporate images from the Internet in your presentation. Cite all electronic resources used for your final project.

Using Your History Journal

Choose one country from your map of East Asia. Draw that country on a separate sheet of paper. From the section of Chapter 14 that provides information on your chosen country, list 5 to 10 important facts or events beside your map.

Reviewing Facts

1. **History** Use a time line like the one below to identify key events in the rise and fall of the Mongol empire.

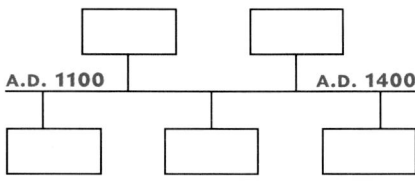

2. **History** Identify Tai Cong and name his important political achievements.
3. **Science/Culture** List the scientific and artistic accomplishments that took place during the Song dynasty.
4. **History** Explain the significance of the Battle of the Bach Dang River to the Vietnamese people and their country as a whole.
5. **History** Discuss the importance of the *kamikaze*, the "divine wind," in early Japanese history.
6. **Culture** Describe examples of female leadership in early East and South Asia.

Critical Thinking

1. **Apply** How did civil service examinations aid in the development of a strong central government in China?
2. **Analyze** Why did China's economy expand during Song rule?
3. **Synthesize** Do you think the strengths of Mongol society would benefit a nation today? Why or why not?
4. **Evaluate** In what ways did Chinese innovations change the cultures of Korea and Japan?

---

4. The Vietnamese won their independence from China.
5. The storm destroyed the Mongol fleet attempting to invade Japan and confirmed the Japanese belief that their islands were sacred.
6. China's Empress Wu in the A.D. 600s strengthened its central government. That same century, Korea's Queen Sondok built Asia's oldest observatory. In A.D. 39, the Trung sisters led a Vietnamese struggle

against the Chinese. About A.D. 1010, Lady Shikibu Murasaki wrote *The Tale of Genji.*

Critical Thinking

1. To pass the exams, students had to master Confucianism, which stressed obedience to the emperor; thus, government officials chosen by the exams were loyal to the emperor.
2. Population increased, making government able to collect more taxes; with increased

5. Analyze Japanese gardens show a love for nature and order. How did the geography of the islands influence Japanese arts and gardening?

Japanese garden

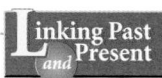

1. How has Japan's possession of Heian and samurai values helped it to become a world leader in industry today?
2. Confucianism spread to many East and South Asian countries. How do Confucian values benefit these countries today?

Skill Practice

Read the passage below and answer the questions that follow.

> ❝ Indian traders and scholars introduced to Southeast Asia the Sanskrit language and the religions of Hinduism and Buddhism. Indian epics such as the *Ramayana* were interwoven with Southeast Asian stories and legends. Indian architecture, law codes, and political ideas also deeply influenced the cultures of the region.... In A.D. 802 the Khmer people of Cambodia established a great Hindu-Buddhist empire.... Borrowing the Indian idea of kingship, Khmer rulers presented themselves as incarnations of the Hindu gods or as future Buddhas.... ❞

1. What facts are presented about India's influence on Southeast Asia in general?
2. What generalization can you make based on these facts?

Understanding Themes

1. **Movement** The Mongols were able to conquer a vast territory, but their empire survived for a relatively short time. Provide a hypothesis that might explain this situation.
2. **Uniformity** What elements of Chinese society remained the same during the Tang, Song, and Yuan dynasties? What effect did this stability have on China's culture?
3. **Cultural Diffusion** What are some of the similarities between Southeast Asian cultures and Chinese culture?
4. **Innovation** Identify one Chinese discovery and explain some of the ways in which it has been used by the Chinese and others. Name things in our culture that derive from this innovation.

Geography in History

1. **Place** Refer to the map below. What river formed a natural border between China and the kingdom of Koguryo?
2. **Region** How did geography contribute to Korea's becoming known as the Hermit Kingdom?

Korea in the Three Kingdoms Period

CHINA
Kungnae
Pyongyang
KOGURYO
Sea of Japan
Kaesong
Yellow Sea
Kwangju
Kongju
SILLA
Puyo
Kyongju
PAEKCHE
KAYA STATES (MIMANA)

0   50   100 mi.
0   50   100 km
Polyconic Projection

---

taxes, government built public works, which in turn helped expand trade and commerce.
3. Answers will vary, but the Mongols' major asset—military strength—is still regarded as necessary for a strong nation.
4. They altered almost every aspect of society: religion, philosophy, ideas about government, science, and the arts.
5. The islands' beauty inspired writers and artists with a reverence for nature.

1. Heian values, emphasizing taste and beauty, are reflected in simple, elegant design of Japanese buildings, goods, rituals. Bushido, stressing self-discipline and loyalty, may underlie Japanese work ethic.
2. Confucianism, with focus on deference for

Chapter 14 Assessment

authority, inspires respect for teachers and supervisors. Many Asian businesses have educated and efficient workforces.

Skill Practice

1. India contributed Sanskrit, two religions, great epics, architecture, law codes, and political ideas.
2. Indian civilization profoundly influenced Southeast Asia.

Understanding Themes

1. **MOVEMENT** Possible answers: they were skilled fighters but not good administrators, and so could not hold their domains together.
2. **UNIFORMITY** A strong central government, vigorous trade, highly developed art and science, and a common written language; stability meant that China's economy and cultural life were able to thrive.
3. **CULTURAL DIFFUSION** Confucian principles and civil service exams; writing; arts
4. **INNOVATION** One answer: the compass, used by Chinese mariners and later adopted throughout the world.

Geography in History

1. the Yalu
2. As a peninsula, Korea had little contact with other peoples.

Chapter Bonus Test Question

Ask students: How does cultural diffusion today differ from what it was in the period covered by this chapter? *(Answers will vary but should make the point that today it is affected by sophisticated systems of communication and transportation and thus happens much more quickly.)*

A complete, 1-page lesson plan is provided for each section in the *Reproducible Lesson Plans* booklet.

The Americas

CHAPTER RESOURCES

	Reproducible Resources	Multimedia Resources
Chapter Opener	Chapter Themes: Graphic Organizer 15 Historical Significance Chapter Activity 15	MindJogger Videoquiz
Chapter Enrichment	Vocabulary Activity 15* Time Line Activity 15 Mapping History Activity 15 History Simulation 15 Geography and History Activity 15 Source Reading 15 People in World History Profiles 27, 28 World Art and Music Activity 15 Enrichment Activity 15 Critical Thinking Activity 15 Skill Reinforcement Activity 15 Performance Assessment Activity 15 Standardized Test Practice Workbook Activity 15 Inclusion for the Social Studies Classroom Strategies and Activities	Focus on World Art Print 11 World History and Art Transparency 18, *Mola Stitchery*; 19, *Quilled Buckskin Robe* Chapter Transparency 15 NGS PicturePack Transparency Sets: *Middle America, South America* Vocabulary PuzzleMaker Software NGS PictureShow CD-ROM: *Native Americans, 1 & 2* World Music: Cultural Traditions, Lessons 1, 2 STV: Maya World History Primary Source Document Library
Chapter Review/Reteaching	Reteaching Activity 15 Skill Reinforcement Activity 15 Spanish Chapter Summary 15	Chapter 15 Digest Audiocassette, Activity, Test* Vocabulary PuzzleMaker Software Interactive Tutor Self-Assessment Software MindJogger Videoquiz
Chapter Evaluation/Testing	Performance Assessment Activity 15 Chapter 15 Test, Forms A and B	ExamView® Pro Testmaker

* Also available in Spanish

0:00 OUT OF TIME? Assign the Chapter 15 Audiocassettes.

World History Primary Source Document Library

Make History Come Alive!

Engage your students with over 250 easily accessible primary source documents—available on this CD-ROM—that will give them real life insight into the important events of world history.

Block Schedule

Activities that are particularly suited to use within the block scheduling framework are identified throughout this chapter by the following designation.

KEY TO ABILITY LEVELS

Teaching strategies are coded for varying learning styles.

L1 BASIC activities for all students
L2 AVERAGE activities for average to above-average students
L3 CHALLENGING activities for above-average students
LEP LIMITED ENGLISH PROFICIENCY activities

Use Glencoe's *Presentation Plus!* multimedia teacher tool to easily present dynamic lessons that visually excite your students. Using Microsoft PowerPoint® you can customize the presentations to create your own personalized lessons.

Interactive Lesson Planner

Planning has never been easier! Using this CD-ROM, organize your week, month, semester, or year with all the help you need. The **Interactive Lesson Planner** gives you access to all of the blackline masters that accompany *World History: The Human Experience.*

SECTION RESOURCES

Daily Objectives	Reproducible Resources	Multimedia Resources
Section 1 The Early Americas Describe how early Native Americans made use of their environment.	Lecture Notes 15-1 Reproducible Lesson Plan 15-1 Vocabulary Activity 15* Guided Reading Activity 15-1* Time Line Activity 15 Section Quiz 15-1* Reading Essentials and Study Guide 15-1	Section Focus Transparency 15-1 World History and Art Transparency 19, *Quilled Buckskin Robe* Chapter Transparency 15 NGS PicturePack Transparencies: Physical Geography of the World Interactive Tutor Self-Assessment Software Testmaker World Music: Cultural Traditions, Lesson 1
Section 2 Early Mesoamerican Cultures Explain how trade encouraged the growth of city-states and kingdoms in the areas of present-day Mexico and Central America.	Lecture Notes 15-2 Reproducible Lesson Plan 15-2 Vocabulary Activity 15* Guided Reading Activity 15-2* Section Quiz 15-2* Reading Essentials and Study Guide 15-2	Focus on World Art Print 11, Mayan. *Presentation of Captives to a Maya Ruler* Section Focus Transparency 15-2 Interactive Tutor Self-Assessment Software Testmaker World Music: Cultural Traditions, Lesson 2 STV: Maya
Section 3 The Aztec and Inca Empires List the factors that led to the rise and decline of the Aztec and Inca Empires.	Lecture Notes 15-3 Reproducible Lesson Plan 15-3 Guided Reading Activity 15-3* Reteaching Activity 15 Enrichment Activity 15 Section Quiz 15-3* Performance Assessment Activity 15 Spanish Chapter Summary 15 Reading Essentials and Study Guide 15-3	Section Focus Transparency 15-3 World History and Art Transparency 18, *Mola Stitchery* Vocabulary PuzzleMaker Software Interactive Tutor Self-Assessment Software Testmaker World Music: Cultural Traditions, Lesson 2

* Also available in Spanish

Chapter Activities

 Performance Assessment Activity

A Travel Brochure Have students demonstrate their understanding of the concept of adaptation to environment by taking roles of travel agents or advertising executives who have been commissioned to develop a series of travel brochures to entice people to visit areas of North, Central, and South America. Students should work in groups of three to research what the lifestyle is like in each area today and how the people have adapted. They should use both modern-day attractions and historic sites in their brochures, including reasons for visiting each site.

Possible Rubric Features
Concept attainment, extent and accuracy of content information, organization and clarity of product, collaborative skills, research skills, elaboration and detail

• *For an additional activity, refer to Activity 15 in the* Performance Assessment Strategies and Activities *booklet.*

ACTIVITY
From the Classroom of...

Sandra Blackman
Dana Center
San Diego, CA

A Woman's Point of View
This activity allows students to experience Cortés's conquest of Mexico from the Mexican perspective and to understand the religious and political influences affecting the decline of the Aztec Empire. Have students read the short novel *The Legend of La Llorona* by Rodolfo Anaya, which tells the story of the Spanish conquest from the point of view of Malintzin [Malinche], Cortés's interpreter and common-law wife whose actions played a significant role in the conquest.

As students read the novel, discuss some of the issues that arise: using religious belief to gain power; how oppressive rule hastens decline; historical truth vs. historical fiction; conflict of identity when two cultures meet; a woman's voice in history.

Have students write a letter from Malintzin to her friend in her village where she describes the burning of Cortés's ships, her participation in the march across Mexico into Tenochtitlán, the death of Montezuma, and the overthrow and enslavement of the Aztec people. In the letter have them answer the question: How does Malintzin explain the fall of the Aztec Empire?

MULTIPLE LEARNING STYLES

Verbal/Linguistic
Have students research the treatment of the young captive chosen by the Aztec each year to represent the god Tezcatlipoca. Have them keep a journal in which they record monthly entries by an imaginary captive during the year of captivity, culminating in the sacrifice.

Logical/Mathematical
Have students do further research on the complicated calendar used by the early Mesoamericans. Ask them to report to the class on the calendar's combination of a 260-day "year" with the 365-day solar year.

Visual/Spatial
Ask students to research several of the ruins of ancient Native American civilizations. Have them organize an album of photocopied photographs, including short captions describing each picture.

Kinesthetic
Have students design a set of illustrated cards for each of the North American cultures described in the first section. For each culture, include a card depicting geographical location, clothing, buildings and shelters, and crafts and weapons.

Use the following to easily assess student learning in a variety of ways.

- Performance Assessment Strategies and Activities
- Section Quizzes
- Chapter and Unit Tests
- Interactive Tutor Self-Assessment Software

- Testmaker Software
- MindJogger Videoquiz
- SAT/SAT II Test Practice
- worldhistory.glencoe.com

Additional Resources

NATIONAL GEOGRAPHIC SOCIETY — Teacher's Corner

INDEX TO NATIONAL GEOGRAPHIC MAGAZINE

The following articles relate to this chapter:

- "New Inca Mummies," by Johan Reinhard, 7/98.
- "The Royal Crypts of Copán," by George E. Stuart, 12/97.
- "The Most Ancient Americans," by Rick Gore, 10/97.
- "Maya Masterpiece Revealed at Bonampak," by Mary Miller, 2/95.
- "New Light on the Olmec," by George E. Stuart, 11/93.

NATIONAL GEOGRAPHIC SOCIETY PRODUCTS AVAILABLE FROM GLENCOE

To order the following, call Glencoe at 1-800-334-7344:

- *STV: Maya (Videodisc)*
- *PictureShow: Middle and South America (CD-ROM)*
- *PictureShow: Native Americans, 1 & 2 (CD-ROM)*
- *PicturePack: Native Americans, 1 & 2 (Transparencies)*
- *PicturePack: Ancient Civilizations: Middle America (Transparencies)*
- *PicturePack: Ancient Civilizations: South America (Transparencies)*

ADDITIONAL NATIONAL GEOGRAPHIC SOCIETY PRODUCTS

To order the following, call National Geographic at 1-800-368-2728:

- *Lost City of the Maya (Video)*
- *Lost Empire of Tiwanaku (Video)*
- *Mystery of the Inca Mummy (Video)*
- *Read & Explore: Discovering the Inca Ice Maiden, by Johan Reinhard (Literature Kit)*
- *The Mesoamericans (Map)*

Access National Geographic's new dynamic MapMachine Web site and other geography resources at:

- http://www.nationalgeographic.com/
- http://www.nationalgeographic.com/maps/

BIBLIOGRAPHY

Literature of the Period
Bierhorst, John, ed. *The Hungry Woman: Myths and Legends of the Aztecs.* New York: William Morrow, 1984. New illustrated versions of more than two dozen traditional tales.

Readings for the Student
Suzuki, David, and Peter Knudtson. *Wisdom of the Elders: Honoring Sacred Native Visions of Nature.* New York: Bantam, 1992. Comparison of Native American beliefs.

Readings for the Teacher
Coe, Michael, Dean Snow and Elizabeth Benson. *Atlas of Ancient America.* New York: Facts on File, 1986.

WORLD HISTORY Online

Use our Web site as an additional resource. All essential content is covered in the Student Edition.

You and your students can visit the *World History: The Human Experience* Web site at worldhistory.glencoe.com The student text directs students to the Web site for the following options:

- **Chapter Overviews**
- **Student Web Activities**
- **Self-Check Quizzes**

Answers are provided for you in a link entitled "Web Activity Lesson Plan." Additional Web Resources, Interactive Puzzles, and content updates are also available.

Visit the Glencoe Web site at socialstudies.glencoe.com for social studies activities, updates, and links to other resources.

LOCAL OBJECTIVES

_____
_____
_____
_____
_____
_____
_____
_____
_____
_____
_____
_____
_____
_____
_____
_____
_____
_____

Chapter

15

1500 B.C.–A.D. 1500

The Americas

S̃toryteller

Historical Setting Inti, the sun god, was the chief deity of the Inca civilization. Farmers adored him for warming the Andean earth and making their crops mature. Inti, who was depicted with a human face on a disk with rays emanating from it, was revered as the divine ancestor of the Inca. The best known Inca temple is the Sun Temple in Cuzco, Peru, where the Inca established their capital in the twelfth century.

Historical Significance

Answers: *Native Americans developed agricultural techniques, religious beliefs, trading networks, and an understanding of astronomy and mathematics.*

The development of the Americas was shaped by the reliance of Native Americans on their environment.

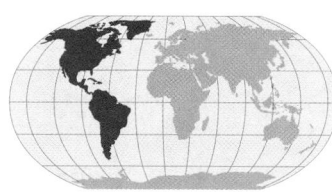

Chapter Themes

▶ **Relation to Environment** Native Americans in North America adapt to a variety of environments. *Section 1*

▶ **Innovation** The Mesoamerican civilizations develop an understanding of astronomy and mathematics. *Section 2*

▶ **Change** The Aztec and the Inca conquer neighboring territories and establish powerful empires in Mexico and South America. *Section 3*

S̃toryteller

In the Andes Mountains of South America, an Inca boy begs to hear how the Inca came to be. "The sun was unhappy with the world," the storyteller begins, "for he saw people living like wild beasts among the mountains and cliffs. He decided to send his son and daughter to teach them to adore the sun as their god. He gave special instructions: 'Each day that passes I go around all the world … to satisfy [men's] needs. Follow my example: Do unto all of them as a merciful father would do unto his well-beloved children; for I have sent you on earth for the good of men, that they might cease to live like wild animals.'"

This legend describes what the Inca people believed about the beginnings of their empire. Close to nature and deeply religious, the Inca were only one of a number of Native American groups who built powerful civilizations in the Americas.

Historical Significance

What were the achievements of Native Americans? How did Native American traditions shape the development of the Americas?

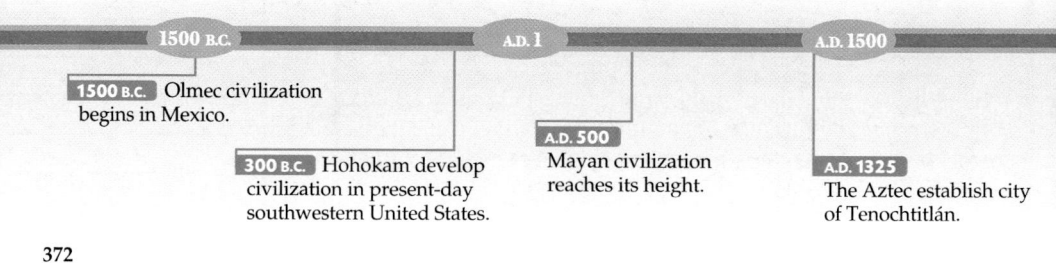

1500 B.C.		A.D. 1		A.D. 1500

1500 B.C. Olmec civilization begins in Mexico.

300 B.C. Hohokam develop civilization in present-day southwestern United States.

A.D. 500 Mayan civilization reaches its height.

A.D. 1325 The Aztec establish city of Tenochtitlán.

372

Aztec turquoise mosaic of double-headed serpent, Mexico

History & Art The art of mosaic in pre-Columbian Mexico and Central America was widespread and required great technical skill. Turquoise was a favorite material of lapidaries and was used in many religious objects. The stones were laid upon wood, stone, gold, shell, pottery, and perhaps leather and homemade paper, and held in place by a gum, pitch, or type of cement. What modern items have you seen that use the art of turquoise mosaic? *(Native American jewelry, belt buckles, vases, candleholders, and so on.)*

✔ Performance Assessment

Refer to the activity on page 372C of the Planning Guide.

📁 For an additional activity, refer to Activity 15 in the *Performance Assessment Strategies and Activities* booklet. 📦

Using Your History Journal

Students might wish to include maps with their time lines. 📦

WORLD HISTORY
Online

Chapter Overview

Visit the *World History: The Human Experience* Web site at **worldhistory.glencoe.com** and click on **Chapter 15—Chapter Overview** to preview the chapter.

Your History Journal

Using dates from section time lines and each section narrative, build a time line of important dates in Native American civilizations between 1500 B.C. and A.D. 1500.

GLENCOE
TECHNOLOGY

 VIDEODISC
Use MindJogger to preview chapter content.

MindJogger Videoquiz
 Chapter 15
Disc 2 Side B

 Also available in VHS.

➕ EXTRA CREDIT PROJECT

Report and Storytelling In addition to their sun god, Inti, the Inca revered a creator god, Viracocha. Have students research the Inca creation myth and prepare a brief report comparing the Inca account of creation with the creation stories in Genesis and Greek mythology.

Students should also be encouraged to present a storytelling session for the rest of the class in which they tell the Inca story of creation. Suggested resource: J. Bierhorst, ed., *Black Rainbow: Legends of the Incas and Myths of Ancient Peru.* **L2** 📦

| 5000 B.C. | 2500 B.C. | A.D. 1 | A.D. 2500 |

c. 5000 B.C. Hunter-gatherers first plant maize in the highlands of Mexico.

c. 3000 B.C. Native Americans make use of stone axes and digging sticks for farming.

c. A.D. 1500 Eastern Woodland peoples form the Iroquois League.

SECTION THEME

▶ **Relation to Environment**
Native Americans in North America adapt to a variety of environments.

Guide to Reading

For reading strategies to help students read effectively see pages 12–13. Have students think about the main head as they read the subheads.

Vocabulary Pre-check

▣ Use the Vocabulary PuzzleMaker for Chapter 15 to create a crossword puzzle to reinforce section terms. **L1 LEP**

📁 Use Vocabulary Activity 15 to introduce vocabulary terms. **L1 LEP**

FOCUS

Section Objective

Describe how early Native Americans made use of their environment.

BELLRINGER
Motivational Activity

Before taking roll at the beginning of the class period, project Section Focus Transparency 15-1 and have students answer the activity questions. Discuss students' responses.

📁 This activity is also available as a blackline master.

Section 1

The Early Americas

Guide to Reading

Read to Find Out
Main Idea *Early Native Americans made many uses of their environment.*

▶ **Terms to Define**
maize, weir, potlatch, confederation

▶ **People to Meet**
the Kwakiutl, the Hohokam, the Pueblo, the Apache, the Navajo, the Plains peoples, Mound Builders

▶ **Places to Locate**
Mexico, Great Plains

The Storyteller

A Navajo tale describes the origin of the twelve months of the year: First Man and First Woman built a hogan in which to live. Turquoise Boy and White Shell Girl came from the underworld to live with them. "It is not unwise that we plan for the time to come, how we shall live," said First Man. First Woman and First Man whispered together during many nights. They planned that there should be a sun, and day and night. Whenever Coyote, called First Angry, came to make trouble and asked them what they were doing, they told him: "Nothing whatsoever." He said, "So I see," and

went away. After he had gone, they planned the twelve months of the year.

—adapted from *The Portable North American Indian Reader*, edited by Frederick W. Turner III, 1974

Navajo rug

hen did the earliest humans come to the Americas? Until recently, archaeologists believed that humans arrived in the Western Hemisphere about 12,000 years ago. The theory was that tribes migrated from Asia to North America, following herds of bison and other game across the then-exposed land bridge that today is the Bering Strait.

New evidence, however, challenges this old theory. Archaeologists working in North America and South America have found sites that indicate the presence of humans as early as 40,000 years ago. New theories argue that humans arrived in more than one migratory wave. Some early humans may also have traveled by boat along the Pacific coast from Siberia to Alaska, then to South America.

Once in the Western Hemisphere, the peoples dispersed throughout North America and South America. As they adapted to particular environments, they developed distinct ways of life. Some remained nomadic, while others settled and developed complex civilizations.

The First Americans

Hunter-gatherers in the Americas used the resources of their environments for food, clothing, and shelter. People living along seacoasts collected mussels and snails. Those inland hunted game or fished in rivers and streams. Archaeologists have unearthed evidence of these ways of life in artifacts, such as rounded stones for grinding seeds, bone hooks for fishing, and heaps of shells at campsites.

By about 5000 B.C., a group of hunter-gatherers in a highland area of present-day **Mexico** had discovered that the seeds of maize, or corn, and other native plants could be planted and harvested, providing a reliable source of food. As this discovery

SECTION RESOURCES

📁 **Reproducible Masters**
- Lecture Notes 15-1
- Reproducible Lesson Plan 15-1
- Vocabulary Activity 15
- Guided Reading Activity 15-1
- Time Line Activity 15
- Section Quiz 15-1
- Reading Essentials and Study Guide 15-1

🔖 **Transparencies**
- Section Focus Transparency 15-1
- World History and Art Transparency 19
- Chapter Transparency 15
- Physical Geography of the World Transparencies 2, 3, 4, 6, 8, 9

Multimedia
▣ Interactive Tutor Self-Assessment Software
▣ Testmaker
📀 World Music: Cultural Traditions, Lesson 1

spread from Mexico into the southwestern United States, groups of early people began to settle in permanent villages. About 3000 B.C. farmers made use of stone axes to clear their fields and pointed digging sticks to plant improved varieties of maize, beans, and squash.

As the food supply improved, the population of the Americas grew. By the time Europeans arrived in North America around A.D. 1500, about 30 million to 100 million Native Americans belonging to more than 2,000 different groups were inhabiting the two continents. About 15 to 20 million of these early inhabitants lived in the present-day United States and various parts of Canada.

North Americans

Much of what we know about the early people of northern North America comes from the work of archaeologists. Archaeological digs have uncovered homes, burial mounds, pottery, baskets, stone tools, and the bones of people and animals in the Arctic and Northwest, California and the Great Basin, the Southwest, the Great Plains, and the Eastern Woodlands. By studying these artifacts, archaeologists discovered that there were distinct regional differences. People who settled in a particular region developed a common culture. Gradually the arts and crafts and religious customs of each region grew to be distinct from those of other regions, a pattern historians call cultural differentiation. In each region, culture reflected the local geography and natural resources.

The Arctic and Northwest

The early people of the Arctic lived in the cold northern regions of present-day Canada and Alaska. The severe climate of this region prohibited

Native American Cultures of North America

North American Peoples
- Arctic
- Subarctic
- Northwest Coast
- California-Great Basin
- Southwest
- Great Plains
- Eastern Woodlands

0   500   1,000 mi.
0   500   1,000 km
Albers Azimuthal Equal-Area Projection

Map Study Many of the first people to inhabit North America lived near the seacoast or made their homes in river valleys.
Place Why did Native Americans choose to settle in those locations?

farming. Thus, small bands of extended families moved about, hunting and fishing. By 6500 B.C. some Arctic people were living in small villages of pit houses, covered with dome-shaped roofs of whalebone and driftwood. Villagers hunted whales, sea lions, seals, and water birds. They ate the meat and used the skins to make warm, protective clothing.

In contrast to the cold and snow of the Arctic, the thickly forested seacoast of the Pacific Northwest had a milder climate. Rainfall was plentiful, and mild winters and warm ocean currents kept rivers and bays free of ice. Like the people of the Arctic, those who settled along the Pacific Coast—**the Kwakiutl**, for example—hunted whales, fish, and other sea animals as their main source of food. Forests of the Northwest provided additional sources of food—small forest animals and acorns. After about A.D. 500 the people of the Northwest used other resources from the surrounding forests

Chapter 15   *The Americas*   **375**

COOPERATIVE LEARNING ACTIVITY

Bulletin Board Organize the class into five groups, corresponding to the five different regions inhabited by native North Americans. Ask each group to select one of the peoples identified in the text as living in "their" region. Have them research and prepare a bulletin-board display on that people, highlighting aspects of daily life and customs. Among the topics students should consider are layout of villages and buildings, the development of crafts, food-gathering techniques, and religious ceremonies. Each group member should have a specific role to play in preparing the display.
L1 LEP

TEACH

Guided Practice

THEME Relation to Environment Using the map on this page, ask students how the climatic conditions differed for the various North American cultures. (*Arctic and Far North: long winters with subzero temperatures; Northwest: mild winters and a cool, rainy climate much of the year; California Great Basin: warm, mild climate, with rivers making farming possible for most of year; Southwest: dry, desert climate, making farming more difficult; Great Plains: hot summers, very cold winters; Eastern Woodlands: temperate climate*) **L1**

The First Americans
What discovery by the first Americans transformed life in the Western Hemisphere?
the discovery that seeds of maize and other native plants could be planted and harvested, providing a reliable source of food

Map Study

Answer
Rivers and coastal areas provided a supply of fish that people used for food. River valleys and coastlands also provided good land for farming. People living in these areas could use boats for travel and trade.

Map Skills Practice

Reading a Map What two natural boundaries marked the region of the Great Plains people? (*Rocky Mountains, Mississippi River*)

The following videotape program is available from Glencoe:

- **The Secret Burial Mounds of Pre-Historic America**

To find classroom resources to accompany this video, check the following home page:

A&E Television: http://www.aetv.com

 World History and Art Transparency 19, *Quilled Buckskin Robe*

 Chapter Transparency 15

 World Music: Cultural Traditions, Lesson 1

NATIONAL GEOGRAPHIC SOCIETY

TRANSPARENCIES

PHYSICAL GEOGRAPHY OF THE WORLD

Display the following to enrich student understanding of Native American environments.

2. Sonoran Desert, U.S.
3. Rocky Mountains, Canada
4. Grand Canyon, U.S.
6. Mississippi River, U.S.
8. Baffin Island, Canada
9. Appalachian Mountains, U.S.

Independent Practice

 Guided Reading Activity 15-1 **L1**

 Time Line Activity 15

and rivers. With stone and copper woodworking tools they split cedar, fir, and redwood trees into planks to make houses and canoes. They also harvested salmon with fiber nets, stone-tipped spears, and elaborate wooden traps called weirs.

Society among the Kwakiutl and other Northwest peoples was organized into lineages, each of which claimed to be descended from a mythical ancestor. A lineage group lived together in a single large house and owned the right to use or display special designs, songs, ceremonies, or prized possessions, such as patterned sheets of copper. A lineage maintained exclusive use of its own fishing area and berry-picking grounds. The wealth of each lineage was displayed and given away as gifts at festive gatherings called potlatches. At a potlatch a chief might give away canoes, blankets, and other goods. In turn, guests might bring the chief deerskins and food.

To obtain items they themselves could not make, some people of the Northwest developed trading networks with people living farther south.

Traders paddled redwood canoes along the coast, stopping at villages along the shore to exchange goods. Trade networks stretched from southern Alaska to northern California.

California–Great Basin

Native Americans living along the California coast enjoyed a warm climate and abundant food resources. Many communities ate only abalone and mussels. Near San Francisco Bay, archaeologists have found evidence of this diet in heaps of discarded shells that date from 2000 B.C. The first Californians also fished for sea bass, hunted seals, and gathered berries and nuts. The abundant resources made food gathering easier in this region.

Like other Native Americans, they developed elaborate religious ceremonies designed to worship nature spirits, especially those spirits related to animals or plants used for food. The Chumash, who lived in the area of present-day southern California, would gather together at harvest festivals to celebrate the goodness of the earth.

Native Americans

A variety of peoples have inhabited North America for thousands of years. Some mysteries of the earliest cultures have yet to be revealed.

Georgia's Etowa Mounds sheltered these two-foot high marble images of a man and a woman more than 500 years ago.

376

 Mound Builders

Native American mounds are found from the Great Lakes to the Gulf of Mexico, and from the Mississippi to the Appalachians. A number of different peoples built mounds over a period spanning hundreds of years. The mounds varied widely in size, shape, and function. Some cover more than 100 acres (40.5 hectares). Others were modest in size. In addition to the serpent-shaped mound shown here, there is one in Wisconsin shaped like an elephant. Other mounds were round; still others long and wall-like.

While many mounds were used as burial places, others served as foundations for temples or as fortresses. The purpose of some mounds, such as the Serpent Mound, is not clear.

People living farther inland scratched their living from a harsh desert and mountain environment. Great Basin people moved about in small bands, living in windbreak shelters and eating seeds, grasshoppers, and small animals.

Southwest

People who settled in the high desert regions of present-day Arizona, New Mexico, southern Colorado and Utah, and northern Mexico had fewer resources than those who settled along the Pacific Coast. Nevertheless, they adapted to their harsh environment by inventing techniques of irrigation to farm the land. For example, around 300 B.C., **the Hohokam** living in present-day Arizona dug an irrigation canal 3 miles (4.8 km) long to draw the waters of the Gila and Salt Rivers onto fields planted with maize, kidney beans, and squash.

Farther north the Anasazi and their descendants, **the Pueblo**, grew maize on flat-topped hills or on the plains. They built two- or three-story dwellings of adobe, a sun-dried brick. Some villages were constructed under ledges on the sides of cliffs to shade residents from the desert sun and to make the villages easier to defend.

Religious leaders governed these villages. In underground chambers called kivas, they held ceremonies to ensure harmony with the spiritual world. They believed that, if harmony existed, the spirits would provide rain for crops.

A group known as **the Apache** lived in areas that were unsuitable for farming. They hunted birds and rabbits and gathered plants. Sometimes they raided Pueblo fields; other times they traded meat and hides with Pueblo villagers for maize and other food supplies. A neighboring people, **the Navajo**, did manage to raise a breed of sheep that could live on the sparse desert vegetation.

Great Plains

In contrast to the sparse Southwestern environment, vast grasslands covered the **Great Plains**, stretching from the Rocky Mountains to the Mississippi River. This environment provided a dif-

Literature Have students find one or two examples of Native American poetry and stories in the library and share a reading of one with the class. Ask them to explain its purpose in the culture, such as its use in religious ceremonies or celebrations. **L2**

Science Have students research the Bighorn Medicine Wheel in Wyoming and the Anasazi sun dagger in New Mexico and summarize their findings. *(Both show sophisticated understanding of motions of sun and moon.)* **L3**

you don't say...

"Mississippi," the name of the principal river of the United States, comes from an Algonquian word meaning "big river."

Linking Past and Present

Lacrosse, a soccerlike ball game, developed from a war-training exercise called "baggataway" by Native Americans living in today's Canada. The original game was violent, with few rules, and sometimes involved as many as a thousand warriors. Today the game uses 10 players on a men's lacrosse team and 12 on a women's team.

ASSESS

Check for Understanding

Assign Section 1 Assessment as homework or as an in-class activity.

Use Interactive Tutor Self-Assessment Software to review Section 1.

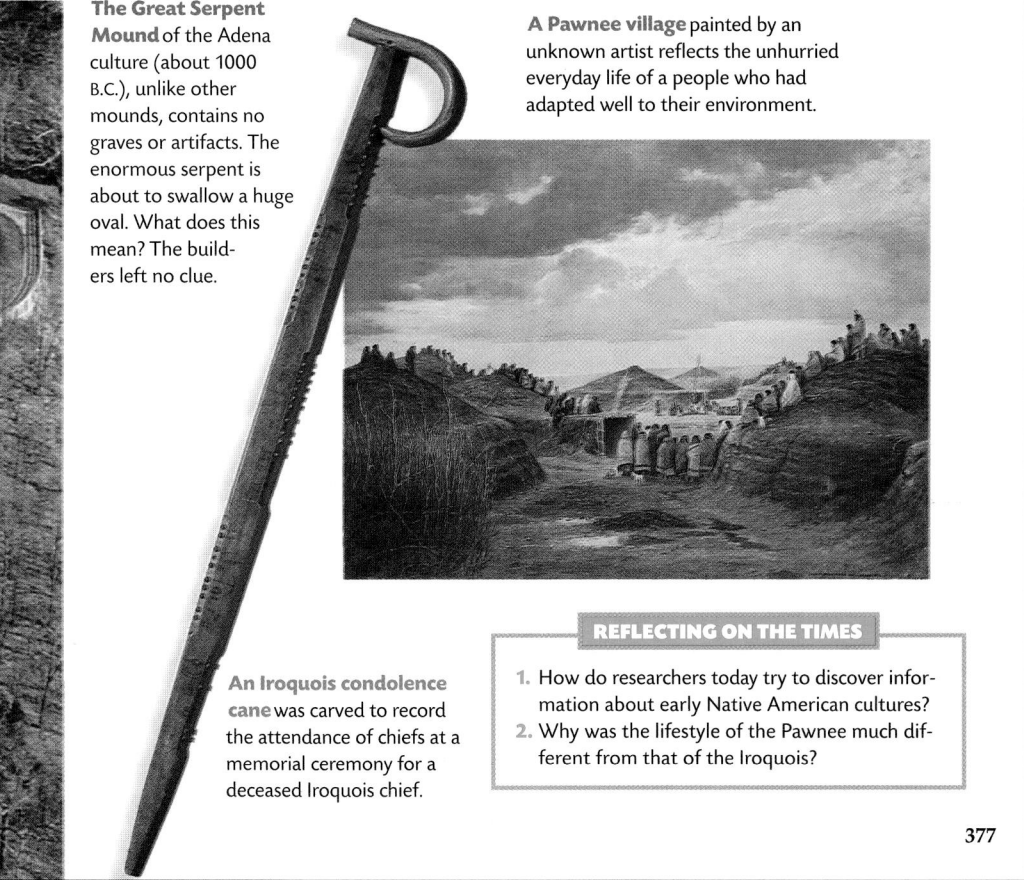

The Great Serpent Mound of the Adena culture (about 1000 B.C.), unlike other mounds, contains no graves or artifacts. The enormous serpent is about to swallow a huge oval. What does this mean? The builders left no clue.

A Pawnee village painted by an unknown artist reflects the unhurried everyday life of a people who had adapted well to their environment.

An Iroquois condolence cane was carved to record the attendance of chiefs at a memorial ceremony for a deceased Iroquois chief.

REFLECTING ON THE TIMES

1. How do researchers today try to discover information about early Native American cultures?
2. Why was the lifestyle of the Pawnee much different from that of the Iroquois?

377

ANSWERS TO REFLECTING ON THE TIMES

1. by conducting digs and studying the artifacts and bones they uncover
2. The plains environment of the Pawnee was very different from the temperate woodland environment of the Iroquois.

Visualizing History In the Northwest a totem was the symbol and protector of the group. *What does this totem reveal about its group?*

ferent challenge for its early inhabitants. Native Americans adapting to life on the plains needed a reliable source of food. Farming in the region was difficult, as the thick sod was hard to plow. Moreover, maize needs more water than is naturally available on most parts of the Great Plains.

Although some farming was done along streams, most of **the Plains peoples** depended on the great herds of bison, or buffalo, that roamed the plains. The Kiowa, Crow, Blackfoot, and other peoples of the plains used every part of the bison for their food, clothing, shelter, and tools.

Eastern Woodlands

Unlike the Plains peoples who depended on the bison, Native Americans of the woodlands east of the Mississippi River hunted deer, turkey, and other small game for food and clothing. Like the Plains peoples, Eastern Woodlands peoples used every part of the animals they killed. They ate deer meat, wore deerskin clothing, and made tools out of animal bones and antlers. Because of the warm summers, abundant rainfall, and fertile soil, the Woodlands peoples lived in farming villages and grew corn, squash, beans, and tobacco.

In the Ohio and Mississippi Valleys, groups of Native Americans known as **Mound Builders** erected large earthen mounds. Archaeologists today believe the mounds were ceremonial centers or tombs for leaders. A number of mounds were made in the shape of animals. The largest ceremonial center was Cahokia, in present-day Illinois. It had about 40,000 people and was probably also a political and commercial settlement.

Native Americans living in the northeastern forests cleared the land and built fenced-in villages of long houses, made of poles covered with tree bark. While the women farmed, the men hunted, warred, and governed. During the A.D. 1500s, five groups allied to form the Iroquois League—a confederation, or loose union. A council of male representatives from each group discussed and resolved disputes, but every clan had an elderly female known as a "clan mother," who named and deposed chiefs and council members.

Student Web Activity 15

Visit the *World History: The Human Experience* Web site at **worldhistory.glencoe.com** and click on *Chapter 15—Student Web Activities* for an activity relating to the Mound Builders.

SECTION 1 ASSESSMENT

Main Idea

1. Use a chart like the one below to identify ways in which early Native Americans made use of their environment for food, clothing, and shelter.

Food	Clothing	Shelter

Recall

2. **Define** maize, weir, potlatch, confederation.
3. **Identify** the Kwakiutl, the Hohokam, the Pueblo, the Apache, the Navajo, the Plains peoples, Mound Builders, Iroquois League.

Critical Thinking

4. **Analyzing Information** Compare the structure of the Iroquois League with that of the United States government.

Understanding Themes

5. **Environment** Give examples of artifacts archaeologists might find that reveal how Native Americans used natural resources.

500 B.C.　　　　　A.D. 500　　　　　A.D. 1500

c. 400 B.C. Olmec civilization declines.

c. A.D. 300 The Maya begin to expand their territory.

c. A.D. 800 Mayan civilization begins to decline.

Chapter 15
Section 2

Section 2

Early Mesoamerican Cultures

Guide to Reading

Read to Find Out

Main Idea *Trade, agriculture, and religion helped shape early Mesoamerican cultures.*

▸ **Terms to Define**
　slash-and-burn farming, obsidian

▸ **People to Meet**
　the Olmec, the Maya, the Teotihuacános, the Toltec

▸ **Places to Locate**
　San Lorenzo, La Venta, Yucatán Peninsula, Teotihuacán, Tula

The Storyteller

　How did the world begin? According to Mayan myth, "All was in suspense, all calm, in silence; all motionless, still.... There was nothing standing; only the calm water, the placid sea, alone and tranquil. Nothing existed. There was only silence in the darkness, in the night. Only the Creator[s] were there. By nature they were great thinkers. They decided: when day dawned for the first time, the human being must appear. Thus they spoke. "Let there be light, let there be dawn in the sky and on the earth."

　—adapted from *Sources of World History,* edited by Mark A. Kishlansky, 1995

Chichén Itzá temple figure

etween 1500 B.C. and A.D. 1200, a series of sophisticated civilizations emerged in the areas of present-day Mexico, Guatemala, Honduras, El Salvador, and Belize. Amid volcanic mountains, cool valleys, dense rain forests, and dry forested plains, early farmers developed methods that produced plentiful harvests and supported large populations. Maize was their basic crop.

　Ruins of ancient cities reveal an astonishing way of life. Ideas from earlier civilizations were adopted and modified by later ones. Although each culture had unique features, they shared common elements. Archaeologists have labeled them together as Mesoamerican civilizations. The prefix *meso-* means "middle" and refers to the fact that these people lived in the middle land area that joins North America and South America. Descendants of the early Mesoamericans continue to live in this region and maintain many of their early traditions.

The Olmec

　About 150 years before Tutankhamen ruled Egypt, **the Olmec** emerged as one of the earliest Mesoamerican civilizations. Between 1500 B.C. and 400 B.C., the Olmec flourished in the swampy, lowland river valleys near the Gulf of Mexico. Our knowledge of the Olmec way of life and Olmec beliefs has come primarily from excavations of two principal Olmec sites, **San Lorenzo** and **La Venta**, discovered in the late 1930s. Until then, Olmec culture had been buried by centuries of accumulated layers of earth and rain forest.

　Among the objects unearthed at San Lorenzo and La Venta were enormous stone heads carved from basalt, a volcanic rock. Some were more than 9 feet (2.7 m) tall and weighed as much as 40 tons.

Chapter 15 *The Americas* **379**

SECTION THEME

▸ **Innovation** The Mesoamerican civilizations develop astronomy and mathematics.

Guide to Reading

For reading strategies to help students read effectively see pages 12–13.

Vocabulary Pre-check

▣ Use the Vocabulary PuzzleMaker for Chapter 15 to create a crossword puzzle to reinforce section terms. **L1 LEP**

🗀 Use Vocabulary Activity 15 to introduce vocabulary terms. **L1 LEP**

FOCUS

Section Objective

Explain how trade encouraged the growth of city-states and kingdoms in the areas of present-day Mexico and Central America.

BELLRINGER Motivational Activity

Before taking roll at the beginning of the class period, project Section Focus Transparency 15-2 and have students answer the activity questions. Discuss students' responses.
　🗀 This activity is also available as a blackline master.

SECTION RESOURCES

🗀 Reproducible Masters
- Lecture Notes 15-2
- Reproducible Lesson Plan 15-2
- Vocabulary Activity 15
- Guided Reading Activity 15-2
- Section Quiz 15-2
- Reading Essentials and Study Guide 15-2

📦 Transparencies
- Section Focus Transparency 15-2

Multimedia
- 📖 Focus on World Art Print 11
- ▣ Interactive Tutor Self-Assessment Software
- ▣ Testmaker
- 🎵 World Music: Cultural Traditions, Lesson 2
- ◉ STV: Maya

TEACH

Guided Practice

THEME Innovation

Ask students to make a written list of the innovations of the Olmec, the Maya, the Teotihuacános, and the Toltec. Ask volunteers to read their lists and have the class point out any omissions. **L1**

Visualizing History The Olmec produced distinctive sculptures that are a combination of jaguars and human infants. Evidently the Olmec believed that in the distant past a union between a woman and a jaguar had produced a race of mythical creatures. What is distinctive about the head of the statue? *(It is cleft at the top; this is a typical feature of Olmec sculptures of mythical creatures.)*
Answer to Caption: *Jade carvings, figurines, and carved stone murals led them to make that inference.*

Economics Mayan farmers produced large surplus crops of maize that they brought to market to trade for other goods made by craftspeople. Ask students to explain what made Mayan trade successful. *(The Maya had trade routes throughout Mexico and Central America; merchants traveled by road, river, and sea.)* **L1**

Focus on World Art Print 11, Mayan. *Presentation of Captives to a Maya Ruler*

World Music: Cultural Traditions, Lesson 2

Visualizing History **This jade ceremonial ax in the form of a feline monster is from the pre-Columbian Olmec culture.** *Why do archaeologists believe that religion played an important role in Olmec life?*

These heads are believed to be portraits of rulers, and may have been part of larger monuments. Without the aid of wheels or beasts of burden, but perhaps using river rafts, the Olmec had moved the heads some 60 miles (97 km) from the mountains to the sites where they were discovered.

Evidence suggests that San Lorenzo and La Venta each had populations of only about 1,000 at their peak. Yet there was clearly organization, planning, and a division of labor. A hilltop at San Lorenzo was sheared off to create a central plaza for market and ceremonial purposes. Stone drains were built to direct water during the rainy season. Early forms of hieroglyphic writings were developed as well as an early calendar.

From jade carvings, figurines, and carved stone murals, archaeologists infer that religion played an important role in the lives of the Olmec. For instance, many carvings show an Olmec god with a human body and the face of a jaguar, the large spot-

ted wild cat that roamed the region. The Olmec believed the jaguar-god controlled their harvests.

Early Olmec farmers practiced what is known as slash-and-burn farming. To clear land, farmers cut down trees, let them dry, and then burned them. They planted maize among the fertile ashes. Since the soil became exhausted after a few years, farmers shifted fields and repeated the cycle on other lands.

Trade with other parts of Mesoamerica was common. Olmec artifacts have been found throughout the region, and Olmec ideas were echoed in later Mesoamerican civilizations.

The Maya

As early as 900 B.C., **the Maya** began to settle the **Yucatán Peninsula** of present-day Mexico. Mayan civilization reached its peak between A.D. 300 and A.D. 900. Mayan ruins can be found throughout the region in diverse terrains: highlands, lowlands, and coastal plains. The Maya adapted to their various environments, developing different farming practices, languages, and governments. The Maya were not unified in one empire. Instead, the patchwork of city-states and kingdoms were linked by culture, political ties, and trade.

Religion

Religion was at the center of Mayan life. The Maya believed in two levels of existence. One level was the daily physical life they lived. The second level was the Otherworld, a spiritual world peopled with gods, the souls of ancestors, and other supernatural creatures. The two levels were closely intertwined. Actions on each level could influence the other. Mayan myths explained the workings of this world and the Otherworld.

Mayan kings were spiritual leaders as well as political leaders. They were responsible for their people's understanding of the Otherworld and for their behaving in ways that would keep the gods pleased. Rulers performed rituals and ceremonies to satisfy the gods. In their great cities, the Maya constructed plazas, temples, and huge pyramids—symbolically sacred mountains—where thousands of people could gather for special religious ceremonies and festivals.

Images on Mayan temples, sacred objects, and pottery provide clues about Mayan beliefs and practices. The rain god, Chac, appears frequently. Images depict other gods in the form of trees, jaguars, birds, monkeys, serpents, reptiles, fish, and shells. Mythical creatures that combine parts of several animals are also shown.

COOPERATIVE LEARNING ACTIVITY

Chart Organize the class into five groups, corresponding to the five subheadings in the section covering the Maya. Distribute a large sheet of poster board to each group. The groups should use the poster board to display information about their subheading that is not found in the text. Each group should select a coordinator responsible for assigning specific tasks to every group member. When each group has filled in its piece of poster board with additional information, mount the display so that it forms a comprehensive chart presenting information on Mayan culture. One member of each group should present its findings to the rest of the class. **L2**

Blood symbols also appear. Human sacrifices and bloodletting rituals were part of Mayan practice. These ceremonies were considered important to appease the gods and to maintain and renew life.

Some festivals also included a ceremonial ball game called *pok-a-tok*. For this game, the Maya invented the use of solid rubber balls about the size of basketballs. Players wearing protective padding batted the balls back and forth across a walled court. These games recalled games played by mythical Mayan heroes.

Sciences

Like the ancient Greeks, the Maya believed that the movements of the sun, moon, and planets were journeys of gods across the sky. Since the gods controlled nature—including harvests—charting the movements of the celestial bodies was essential.

To do this charting, Mayan priests became excellent mathematicians and astronomers. The Maya built on the earlier work of the Olmec. The Maya developed a system of mathematics using the base 20. They used three symbols to represent numbers. A dot stood for the number one; a bar was five; and a shell figure symbolized zero. Rather than expressing place value with the highest place to the left, the Maya expressed their numbers vertically with the largest place at the top. The Maya also developed accurate calendars, a 260-day sacred calendar and another 365-day calendar. The calendars were used to predict eclipses, schedule religious ceremonies, and determine times to plant and harvest.

Economy

The Mayan economy was based on agriculture and trade. In addition to maize, farmers grew beans, squash, pumpkins, chili peppers, and tomatoes. Slash-and-burn farming continued in some areas. Elsewhere the Maya produced larger harvests by intensively farming raised plots surrounded by canals.

Perhaps as often as every five days, farmers brought surplus crops to the open-air markets of the major cities. Maize and other produce were traded for cotton cloth, jade ornaments, pottery, fish, deer meat, and salt.

Mayan merchants participated in long-distance trade throughout Mexico and Central America. Traders transported their cargoes by canoes on rivers and coastal waterways. Overland, goods were carried by humans, for wheeled vehicles and beasts of burden to haul them were unknown.

The Arts

Mayan Architecture

Temple-pyramid at Chichén Itzá

Mayan temple-pyramids were the religious and political centers of Mayan cities. Built of stone, these vast stepped structures were mainly platforms for religious ceremonies. Stone temples at the summit of the pyramids were erected to memorialize dead rulers by associating them with the gods. Religious sacrifices conducted by priests took place outside the temple on top of the pyramid platform.

Archaeologists believe the stepped levels of the pyramids may have represented the harmonious layers of the universe. Mayan astronomers and priests held high administrative positions. Much of a priest's power was in his ability to predict the movements of stars and planets. Thus, a priest would consult with astronomers before projects were undertaken to see when the heavens would favor such actions.

Since the mid-1900s, Mexican architects have combined Mayan and other Native American designs with modern construction methods. Their work includes the buildings of the University of Mexico and the National Museum of Anthropology in Mexico City, as well as many resorts along Mexico's Caribbean and Pacific coasts.

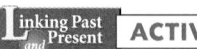

Linking Past and Present ACTIVITY

What purpose did the Mayan temple-pyramids serve? How might you compare Mayan temple-pyramids with public buildings today?

Chapter 15   *The Americas*   381

NATIONAL GEOGRAPHIC SOCIETY

 VIDEODISC
STV: Maya

Side 1
Frames 00002–34603
Title: *Who Were the Ancient Maya?*
Subject: Exploration and scientific excavation of Copán in an effort to rebuild
Ask: What lands did the Maya once occupy? *(Honduras, Guatemala, El Salvador, Belize, and Mexico)*

Independent Practice

Guided Reading Activity 15-2 **L1**

Daily Life Have students read the article on Teotihuacán in the December 1995 *NATIONAL GEOGRAPHIC*. Ask them to summarize some of the recent discoveries about that city that surprised archaeologists. **L2**

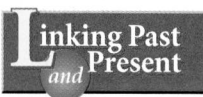
Linking Past and Present

Mayan Architecture

Ruined ancient Mayan monuments can still be viewed in such sites as Uxmal, 50 miles south of modern Mérida, Yucatán state, Mexico; Chichén Itzá, in south central Yucatán state; and Tikal, in the northwestern part of the department of Petén, Guatemala.

ANSWER

platforms for religious ceremonies; public buildings today are political, but not religious, centers of modern cities

TEACH

Tell students that the Mayan ball game was called *pok-a-tok*. The game, which originated not with the Maya but with the Olmec or possibly even earlier, was widespread throughout Mesoamerica, where it was called *ollama*. The ball court, or *tlachtli*, was shaped like a capital I. Oriented in a north-south or east-west direction, the court represented the heavens. Ask students what the ball in the picture resembles. *(the sun or another celestial object)* The serious nature of the sport is especially obvious in art decorating one of the several ball courts of El Tajin in eastern Mexico. Carvings on this court depict scenes in which a skeleton, representing the god of death, observes two men dressed in players' padded clothing.

**CURRICULUM
CONNECTION**

ARCHAEOLOGY

In the early sixteenth century, Spanish explorers in western Honduras near the Guatemalan border discovered the ruins of Copán, an ancient Mayan city. Between 1936 and 1950, archaeologists from the United States and Honduras worked on the ruins. Among the restored sites is a court for playing *pok-a-tok*.

Serious Sport

In this illustration of an ancient Mayan game a rubber ball bounces off the leather pad on the player's chest. The object was to drive the ball through a stone ring, but players could not throw or bat the ball. They had to hit it off a leather pad on their elbow, wrist, torso, or hip. Making a goal was so rare that when a player scored, crowds rewarded the hero with all their clothing and jewelry—unless they could first flee.

Scholars believe that these games were playe[d] only for sport but also on special holidays as r[ ] reenactments of Mayan raids. Large cities conta[in] numerous walled courts lined with images of wa[r] and sacrificial victims. According to Mayan reli[gious] beliefs, ordinary humans could never outwit d[ ] and so the Mayan ball court became a symbolic m[ ]ing ground—a kind of threshold between earth[and] the underworld. ⊕

Writings

The Maya were one of the first Native American peoples to develop a writing system. They wrote in accordion-folded books made of flattened bark covered with a thin layer of plaster. Four of these books have survived. They also carved inscriptions in clay, and on jade, bone, shells, and large stone monuments. Linguists have made major breakthroughs in translating Mayan writing. They have discovered that some inscriptions are phonetic syllables, while others are full words. The Maya recorded royal genealogies, mythology, history, ritual practices, and trade.

Collapse

By A.D. 900 the Maya in the lowlands showed signs of collapse. They stopped building and moved elsewhere. Why this happened is unclear. There is evidence of increasing conflict and warfare among Mayan families and with outsiders. Agricultural breakdown, perhaps caused by warfare or by erosion and over-farming, may have produced rising malnutrition, sickness, and death rates.

Other Mesoamericans

In a high fertile valley 30 miles (48 km) northeast of present-day Mexico City, **the Teotihuacános** (TAY•oh•TEE•wuh•KAHN•ohs) flourished for about 750 years. By A.D. 100, they dominated the centrally located Mexican Plateau. At its height their main city, **Teotihuacán**, had an estimated 120,000 to 200,000 inhabitants.

Teotihuacán was laid out on a grid. The most important buildings were built along the north-south axis. Excavations of the ruins have revealed 600 pyramids, 2,000 apartment compounds, 500 workshop areas, and a huge marketplace. A valuable source of obsidian was found near Teotihuacán. Obsidian, a volcanic glass, was used for sharp-edged tools, arrow points, and other objects. It was easily traded, because Teotihuacán lay on the trade routes east to the Gulf of Mexico.

Teotihuacán declined about A.D. 750. Historians still are uncertain about the reasons for its decline. Drought may have been the cause, or invasion by **the Toltec**, a people from the north.

With a powerful army, the Toltec conquered land as far south as the Yucatán Peninsula. The Toltec capital of **Tula** was the center of a powerful mining and trading empire. Their gods Quetzalcoatl (ket•suhl•KWAH•tuhl), the "plumed serpent" god of the air, and Tezcatlipoca (tehz•KAHT•lee•POH•kuh), the god of war, would be adopted by the Aztec, a later Mesoamerican group. When invaders destroyed Tula in A.D. 1170, the Toltec Empire collapsed.

Visualizing History The Teotihuacáno rain god Tlaloc is shown in an *incensario* (container for burning incense) from A.D. 400–700. *Where was the Teotihuacáno civilization located?*

Chapter 15 *The Americas* **383**

SECTION 2 ASSESSMENT

Main Idea
1. Use a diagram like the one below to identify the elements of trade and agriculture in the Mayan culture.

Mayan Culture
Trade	Agriculture

Recall
2. **Define** slash-and-burn farming, obsidian.
3. **Identify** the Olmec, the Maya, the Teotihuacános, the Toltec, Quetzalcoatl.

Critical Thinking
4. **Synthesizing Information** What did the Mesoamerican civilizations have in common?

Understanding Themes
5. **Innovation** What were some of the major achievements of the Mesoamerican civilizations?

SECTION 2 ASSESSMENT ANSWERS

1. trade: long-distance trade throughout Mexico and Central America; canoes used for water transport, humans for overland transport; agriculture: farmers grew maize, beans, squash, pumpkins; slash-and-burn farming; intensive farming of raised plots surrounded by canals
2. All terms are defined in the Glossary.
3. Olmec, 379; Maya, 380; Teotihuacános, 383; Toltec, 383; Quetzalcoatl, 383
4. maize as basic food; markets for trade; importance of religion; complex cultures
5. **INNOVATION** writing; folded books; sophisticated calendar; extensive astronomical knowledge

Visualizing History The Aztec borrowed the rain god Tlaloc from the Teotihuacános. At the center of the Aztec capital was a temple where victims were sacrificed to Tlaloc. **Answer to Caption:** *the Mexican Plateau*

ASSESS

Check for Understanding
Assign Section 2 Assessment as homework or as an in-class activity.

▣ Use Interactive Tutor Self-Assessment Software to review Section 2.

Evaluate
◣ Section Quiz 15-2

▣ Use the Testmaker to create a customized quiz for Section 2.

Reteach
Write on the board the following sentence from page 379: *Although each culture had unique features, they shared common elements.* Ask students to identify the unique features of each of the cultures covered in the section and the elements common to all of them.

◣ Reading Essentials and Study Guide 15-2

Enrich
Have students write a short report comparing Mayan hieroglyphics and pyramids with those of ancient Egypt.

CLOSE

Ask students how a culture is reflected in its art and architecture. Have them describe the types of art and architecture characteristic of the Mesoamerican civilizations.

Special Report Summary

In 1989 archaeologists went to Guatemala to learn why the great Mayan civilization vanished more than 1,000 years ago.

↓

Interpreting artifacts and hieroglyphs, they found that the rulers of the city of Dos Pilas had won control of other cities in the region.

↓

In A.D. 761 the subject kingdoms attacked Dos Pilas. The people of Dos Pilas tore down palaces to build defensive walls, but they were overrun.

↓

Scholars believe that the warfare among rival Mayan kings reduced farming, disrupted trade, and killed young people, contributing to the decline of Mayan civilization.

TEACH

Points to Discuss

After students have read the feature, ask: Why did a team of archaeologists go to Guatemala in 1989? *(to learn why the golden age of the Maya ended in the ninth century A.D.)* What did archaeologists use to learn more about the Maya? *(potsherds, bones, monuments, spearheads, trash, fortifications, and a hieroglyphic stairway)* How did the archaeological finds change our view of Mayan society? *(not a series of peaceful kingdoms with ceremonial centers, but wracked by battle and human sacrifice)*

The Maya

Some 2,000 years ago, the lowland Mayan civilization of what is now Central America flourished. A society dating to 1200 B.C., the Maya developed the most complex writing system in the Americas, built majestic temple-pyramids and palaces, and mastered astronomy and mathematics. Then suddenly, in the A.D. 800s, the record of life in the region fell silent: The people stopped erecting monuments, carving hieroglyphic texts, and making pottery. Their cities lay in ruins, their fields and villages were abandoned to the jungle, and the great civilization of the Maya vanished.

What happened to end the golden age of the Maya more th thousand years ago? To answer question, in 1989 an internation team of archaeologists, sponsore part by the National Geographic Society and Vanderbilt Universit went to the Petexbatún rain fore northern Guatemala. Amid the r of the ancient city of Dos Pilas, team set to work on one of arch ology's greatest mysteries.

_____
_____
_____
_____
_____

Enrico

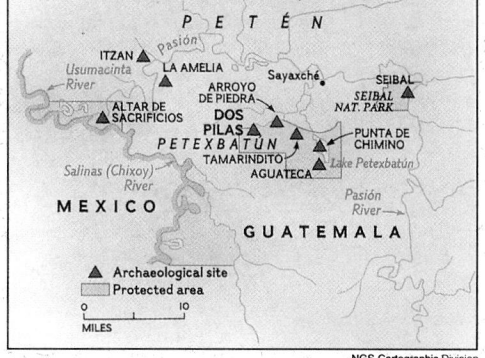

P E T É N

ITZAN — Pasión
Usumacinta — LA AMELIA — Sayaxché
River — ARROYO — SEIBAL
DE PIEDRA — SEIBAL
ALTAR DE — NAT. PARK
SACRIFICIOS — DOS
PILAS — PUNTA DE
PETEXBATÚN — CHIMINO
TAMARINDITO — Lake Petexbatún
Salinas (Chixoy) — AGUATECA
River
MEXICO — Pasión
River
GUATEMALA

▲ Archaeological site
□ Protected area
0   10
MILES

NGS Cartographic Division

Enrico Ferorelli

□ NATIONAL
GEOGRAPHIC   *Special Report*

History *and the*
Humanities

Focus on World Art Print
11, Mayan. *Presentation of
Captives to a Maya Ruler*

Cultural Perspectives
Mayan Innovations The Maya
learned to make a durable cement
using burnt lime, which they used
for temples and other structures.
The pyramids at Tikal rise to 230
feet. Mayan priests also made
exact calculations of dates; they
estimated the beginning of history
to have been August 10, 3113 B.C.

□ NATIONAL
GEOGRAPHIC
SOCIETY

VIDEODISC
STV: Maya

Side 2
Frames 15839–38987
Title: *End of Classic Period*
Subject: Evidence of warfare and
violence in Mayan society
Ask: What evidence found in
1990 proved that the Maya were
violent? *(hieroglyphic text that told of
battles)*

After setting up a fully function-
camp complete with a computer
and drafting workstations, scien-
began their task. They studied
usands of potsherds, scores of
numents, bone fragments, spear-
ds, trash heaps, and miles of for-
ations of Dos Pilas—built by
egades from the great Mayan
ter of Tikal—and nearby cities.
One spectacular find that told the
e of the Maya was a hieroglyphic
rway. Five limestone steps, about
feet wide, each with two rows of

glyphs carved on the risers, climb to
the base of the royal palace near the
main plaza at Dos Pilas. Experts at
deciphering glyphs were on hand to
translate each glyph as it was uncovered. The story on the steps
gives an account of the battles of
the first ruler of the Petexbatún
(referred to as Ruler 1) against his
brother at Tikal, some 65 miles
northeast of Dos Pilas.

One of the epigraphists summed
up the inscription: "It begins by
talking about the 60th birthday of

 *A Mayan warrior-king is por-
trayed on a stela carved in A.D. 731.
Discoveries at Dos Pilas have led to
new theories on the collapse of the
Mayan civilization along the border
of Guatemala and Mexico.*

*A stairway of five long steps
(top) came to light during excavations at the Dos Pilas site.*

Chapter 15 *The Americas* 385

NATIONAL GEOGRAPHIC SOCIETY

Use these materials to enrich student understanding of life in the ancient Americas.

- **NGS PICTURESHOW CD-ROM**
  The Americas
- **NGS PICTUREPACK TRANSPARENCY SET**
  Ancient Central America

Linking Past and Present

Mayan Ruins Until the mid-1800s most Mayan ruins lay hidden and unknown in the jungles of Mexico and Central America. When the sites were discovered, priceless sculptures were often looted and sold. Today, Mayan ruins are protected by the governments of Mexico, Guatemala, and Belize.

NATIONAL GEOGRAPHIC SOCIETY

VIDEODISC
STV: Maya

Side 2
Frames 25914–34042
Title: *Fall of Ancient Maya Cities*
Subject: An attempt to defend Dos Pilas
Ask: How did the Maya of Dos Pilas attempt to defend themselves? *(They built two walls to blockade the city.)*

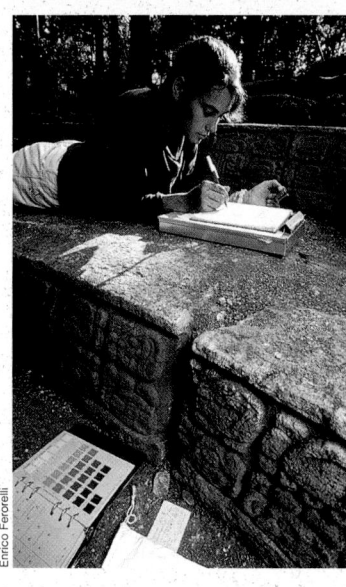

Enrico Ferorelli

🔲 *As Vanderbilt graduate student Stacy Symonds excavated a defensive wall, she discovered the hieroglyphic stairway beneath it. Here she records information about the glyphs.*

Ruler 1, that he danced a ritual dance. As you read down the steps, the glyphs give a historical sequence to his reign. We think Ruler 1 left Tikal and started a splinter kingdom at Dos Pilas. There's an emblem glyph—which is like a political title—for Tikal, and both brothers claimed it. Ruler 1 was defeated, but then there was another war. This time Dos Pilas won."

Although the glyphs told archaeologists about the origin of a dynasty, what was even more intriguing was a stone wall built on top of the stairs during the kingdom's fall. Less than a hundred years after memorializing their founder, the people of Dos Pilas threw a wall up over his monument in what must have been a desperate attempt to protect themselves. Why did the people of Dos Pilas build defensive walls, which are rarely found at Mayan sites?

The second and third rulers of Dos Pilas changed traditional warfare when they set forth on campaigns of expansion. Digging a 30-foot shaft into the burial temple of Ruler 2, archaeologists discovered hieroglyphs on fine pottery that offered more clues. These glyphs suggest that Ruler 2, who reigned from A.D. 698 to A.D. 726, expanded the influence of Dos Pilas and gained control of other cities through marriage and political alliances.

Ruler 3 went on to wed a royal lady from the city of Cancuén and to dominate the entire region. He traveled to the cities of Tamarindito, Aguateca, Seibal, and others to perform ceremonies and quell unrest. After Ruler 3 died in A.D. 741, Ruler 4 took control, living mostly at Aguateca—by then a twin capital—which rests on a limestone bluff high above Lake Petexbatún.

In A.D. 761 something went wrong. According to hieroglyphs, the kings of the Petexbatún had overextended their domain. There had been hints of trouble for more than a decade: Ruler 4 had spent much of his 20-year reign racing from one end of the realm to the other, performing bloodletting rituals, leading battles, and contracting alliances. He used every technique to sustain the kingdom, but to no avail.

Then the city of Tamarindito threw off the yoke of Dos Pilas. Hieroglyphs at Tamarindito tell us that its warriors attacked the capital and killed Ruler 4.

About that time the citizens of Dos Pilas made a valiant last stand. In desperation they ripped stones from temples and monuments, including the tomb of Ruler 2 and the hieroglyphic stairway. They tore

down much of the royal palace build two walls around the cen palaces and temples.

The surviving nobles deserte their citizens and fled to Aguate proclaiming themselves the nev rulers of the kingdom. They ch Aguateca as its final capital bec of its defensive location. The pe of Aguateca held out for about years, but disappeared in the ea A.D. 800s

IN A SPAN of only a few hundre years the kingdom rose, expand and collapsed as a succession of moved from limited conflict to v spread warfare. Scholars have ai that the Mayan civilization simpl grew its environment, exhaustin, soil and creating environmental economic stress. But another po ty is that intensive warfare force Maya, at least in the Petexbatún to move close to fortresses such Aguateca, where they would hav soon run out of fertile land. Perl farmers were limited to fortified near cities that could provide pr tion, forcing them to forsake trac al agricultural practices that had tained them for hundreds of yea The wars must have disrupted tr upset population distribution, destroyed crops, and killed your farmer-warriors, exacting a huge

Scholars have added greatly our view of Mayan society. On regarded as a network of cere al centers ruled by peaceful pr kings, Mayan civilization is no longer seen that way. Battle ar human sacrifice were aspects of Perhaps siege warfare was ulti ly too costly for the Maya. For to come, scientists will study th ruins in the Petexbatún rain fo researching changes that may contributed to the collapse of lowland Mayan civilization.

MORE ABOUT...

Mayan Women The archaeologist Tatiana Proskouriakoff (1909–1985) was a leading expert on Mayan civilization. Proskouriakoff pioneered research on the role of women in Mayan society by analyzing female figures in Mayan sculpture. She argued that Mayan women were often the founders of dynasties and suggested that descent among the Maya may have been matrilineal.

Before A.D. 761

A.D. 761

Enrico Ferorelli

CURRICULUM CONNECTION

LITERATURE

In the A.D. 1500s, Mayan myths were written down in an epic called *Popol Vuh*. The epic describes the universe before the creation of the earth: "There is not yet one person, one animal, bird, fish, crab, tree, rock, hollow, canyon, meadow, forest. Only the sky alone is there; the face of the earth is not clear. Only the sea alone is pooled under all the sky; there is nothing whatever gathered together. It is at rest; not a single thing stirs."

Enrico Ferorelli

Global Gourmet

Central America Corn and beans remain essential ingredients in the diet of the people of southern Mexico, Guatemala, and Belize. Corn is ground and pounded flat to make tortillas, the pancake-shaped bread popular throughout the region.

In proper Mayan style Dos Pilas's ceremonial precinct (above, top) featured palaces for rulers and temples to the gods. But an apparent golden age came to an abrupt end in A.D. 761 (above, bottom). After the killing of Ruler 4, warfare consumed the region. Residents tore down facades of temples and palaces to raise two walls. A cleared area between the walls likely served as a killing alley. Seeking refuge, farmers moved into the plaza and erected huts. Soon the city was abandoned.

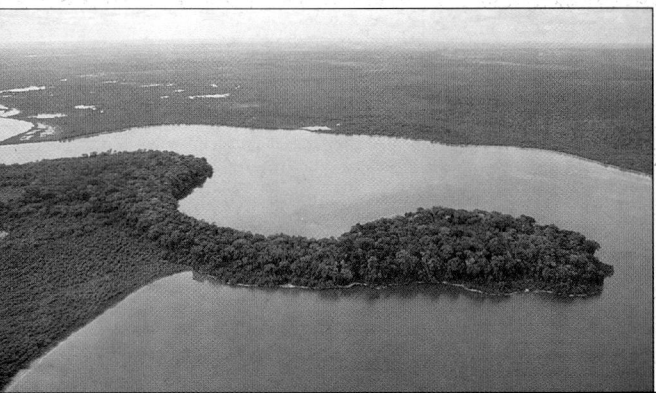

A peninsula became an island (left, top and bottom) as defenders of the Lake Petexbatún port dug three moats across the neck of land. At the tip of the island, a walled wharf protected a canoe landing. Perhaps the enemy proved too strong or conditions too harsh, for the outpost was abandoned.

Portfolio Project

Remind students of the importance of religion to the Maya. Then ask them to write a brief essay discussing how the people of Dos Pilas probably felt when they tore down temples and palaces to build defensive walls.

Chapter 15 *The Americas* 387

TEACHER NOTES

_____
_____
_____
_____
_____

A.D. 1300   A.D. 1400   A.D. 1500

A.D. 1325 The Aztec found their capital, Tenochtitlán.

A.D. 1438 The Inca emperor Pachacuti comes to power.

c. A.D. 1500 The Aztec control all of central and southern Mexico.

SECTION THEME

▶ **Change** The Aztec and the Inca conquer neighboring territories and establish powerful empires in Mexico and South America.

Guide to Reading

For reading strategies to help students read effectively see pages 12–13.

Vocabulary Pre-check

◉ Use the Vocabulary PuzzleMaker for Chapter 15 to create a crossword puzzle to reinforce section terms. **L1 LEP**

📁 Use Vocabulary Activity 15 to introduce vocabulary terms. **L1 LEP**

FOCUS

Section Objective

List causes of the rise and decline of the Aztec and Inca Empires.

BELLRINGER
Motivational Activity

Before taking roll at the beginning of the class period, project Section Focus Transparency 15-3 and have students answer the activity questions. Discuss students' responses.

📁 This activity is also available as a blackline master.

Section 3

The Aztec and Inca Empires

Guide to Reading

Read to Find Out
Main Idea *Multiple factors led to the rise and decline of the Aztec and the Inca Empires.*

▶ **Terms to Define**
   chinampas, hierarchy, quinoa

▶ **People to Meet**
   the Aztec, the Inca, the Moche, Pachacuti

▶ **Places to Locate**
   Tenochtitlán, Cuzco

The Storyteller

Cortés captured many Aztec cities. This Aztec song remembers how it was:
"Broken spears lie in the roads;
   we have torn our hair in our grief.
The houses are roofless now, and their walls
   are red with blood....
We have pounded our hands in despair against
   the adobe walls, for our inheritance, our
   city, is lost and dead.
   The shields of our warriors
      were its defense, but they
      could not save it.
   We have chewed dry twigs
      and salt grasses;
   We have filled our mouths
      with dust and bits of
      adobe; we have eaten
      lizards, rats and
      worms...."

Aztec Stone of the Sun calendar

—from *Sources of World History*, edited by Mark A. Kishlansky, 1995

388 **Chapter 15** *The Americas*

Like other Native American groups, **the Aztec** of Mexico and Central America and **the Inca** of South America lacked metal tools, large work animals, and a practical use of the wheel. Yet they were able to develop centralized governments, raise armies and conquer empires. Both civilizations, however, came to sudden ends in the early A.D. 1500s, when they were overwhelmed and destroyed by Spanish invaders from Europe.

The Aztec Empire

The early Aztec were hunters and warriors who moved from the north into central Mexico during the A.D. 1200s. In A.D. 1325 they founded a city in central Mexico named **Tenochtitlán** (tay•NAWCH•teet•LAHN), today the site of Mexico City. According to Aztec legend, Aztec priests told their people to settle in the area where they would find an eagle sitting on a cactus and holding a snake in its beak. After much wandering, the Aztecs finally saw on an island in Lake Texcoco what the priests had described. There, they established Tenochtitlán.

Tenochtitlán

The Aztec turned Tenochtitlán into an agricultural center and marketplace. Since land for farming was scarce on the island, they built *chinampas*, or artificial islands, by piling mud from the bottom of the lake onto rafts secured by stakes. These became floating gardens where farmers grew a variety of crops, including corn and beans. With a plentiful food supply, the population grew and people moved outside the city to the mainland. A network of canals, bridges, and causeways was built to connect the mainland with the capital city.

SECTION RESOURCES

Empire

Strengthened by early alliances with neighboring city-states, the Aztec then conquered more distant rivals. By A.D. 1500 their empire stretched from north-central Mexico to the border of Guatemala, and from the Atlantic Ocean to the Pacific Ocean. Conquered peoples had to pay heavy tribute in the form of food, clothing, raw materials, and prisoners for sacrifice.

As the Aztec Empire expanded, Tenochtitlán prospered. Estimates of the city's population by A.D. 1500 range from 120,000 to 200,000. Goods and tribute came to the city from all parts of the empire.

Government and Society

The Aztec civilization was organized as a hier-archy—divided into levels of authority, each level more powerful than the level below it. At the top was the emperor. His power came from his control of the army and was reinforced by religious beliefs.

The Aztec social order had four classes: nobili-ty, commoners, serfs, and slaves. Land could be owned by noble families and commoners. Commoners included priests, merchants, artisans, and farmers. Serfs were farmworkers tied to noble lands. The lowest class included criminals and debtors, as well as female and children prisoners of war. Male prisoners of war were sacrificed to the Aztec gods.

Religion and the Arts

Religion motivated the Aztecs to engage in war and sacrifice. Borrowing ideas from the Maya and the Toltec, the Aztecs believed that live human sacrifices were needed to keep the gods pleased and to prevent drought, floods and other natural disasters. The chief deity was the sun god Huitzilopochtli (wee•tsee•loh•POHKT•lee), whose giant pyramid-temple arose in the center of Tenochtitlán.

Priests used a 360-day religious calendar to determine appropriate days for activities, such as planting crops or going to war. The Aztec also had a 365-day solar calendar that consisted of 18 months of 20 days plus 5 extra days. One of the most famous surviving pieces of Aztec sculpture is a large, circular calendar stone that represents the Aztec universe, with carvings that stand for the days of the Aztec month.

Aztec artists decorated temple-pyramids with scenes of deities or battles. Writers glorified Aztec victories in their works. The empire, however, proved to be fragile. Revolts in outlying areas weakened Aztec control. In A.D. 1521 the rebels joined the Spaniards in destroying the Aztec heritage.

Chocolate Is Introduced to Europe

Spain, A.D. 1528
According to legend, the Aztec ruler Montezuma had served Hernán Cortés a beverage called *chocolatl*. When Cortés returned to Spain in A.D. 1528, he brought with him the beans of the cacao tree. Spaniards added sugar, vanilla, and cinnamon to sweeten the bitter drink. Chocolate became a favorite with the aristocracy and spread to Italy, France, Austria, and England.

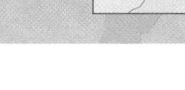

Spain

The Inca Empire

Other Native American civilizations arose in western South America. One of the earliest was **the Moche**, who lived on the north coast of present-day Peru between A.D. 100 and A.D. 600. In A.D. 1987 archaeologists discovered a noble's tomb that revealed the Moche had a social order based on ranks, skilled artisans who made metal ornaments, and rituals that included sacrifices.

Rise of the Inca

The Inca began as one of many small tribes competing for scarce fertile land in the valleys of the Andes mountain ranges. Around A.D. 1200 the Inca settled in **Cuzco** (KOOS•koh), which became their capital. They raided other tribes and slowly established a powerful empire.

The decisive period of Inca expansion began in A.D. 1438, when **Pachacuti**, the ninth Inca ruler, came to power. He and his son, Topa Inca Yupanqui, have been compared to Philip and Alexander the Great of Macedonia. By persuasion, threats, and force, they extended Inca boundaries far to the north and south.

The Inca Empire eventually included all of present-day Peru, much of Chile, and parts of Ecuador, Bolivia, and Argentina. It stretched more than 2,500 miles (4,020 km) through coastal deserts, dry highlands, fertile river valleys, and rain forests. Most of the Inca lived in the Andes highlands and adjusted to high altitudes. Cuzco was 11,600 feet (3,560 m) above sea level.

Chapter 15 *The Americas* **389**

TEACH

Guided Practice

THEME Change
Ask students to list the changes instituted by the Aztec and the Inca that enabled them to flour-ish. *(centralized government, productive farming techniques)* **L1**

Geography: Location Have students locate the Aztec and Inca Empires, as well as the Mayan civilization studied in the previous section, on a map of Latin America. Discuss why so many civilizations arose in the same area. **L2**

🔖 World History and Art Transparency 18, *Mola Stitchery*

🎵 World Music: Cultural Traditions, Lesson 2

Independent Practice

📁 Guided Reading Activity 15-3 **L1**

Science, Technology, and Society Encourage students to make a tabletop model or drawing of Aztec *chinampas*. Pair students with limited English proficiency with native English-speakers to help with research using an ency-clopedia or other resources. After research and completion of the model or drawing, have students summarize the importance of *chinampas*. **L2 LEP**

ASSESS

Check for Understanding

Assign Section 3 Assessment as homework or as an in-class activity.

💿 Use Interactive Tutor Self-Assessment Software to review Section 3.

COOPERATIVE LEARNING ACTIVITY

Model Organize the class into small groups. Propose the task of creating a model of an Aztec city. Groups should approach the task as if they were a city planning committee, including administra-tors, architects, construction teams, artisans, and researchers. Have groups determine what com-mercial, residential, governmental, educational, or religious buildings they want to include in addi-tion to water systems, sewers, and roads.

Advise groups to assign a task to each group member. When all the models are completed, have the class evaluate differences in interpretation and materials. Encourage students to consid-er difficulties the Aztec encountered in building their cities. **L2**

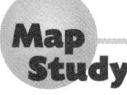

Map Study

Answer

They adjusted to high altitudes.

Map Skills Practice

Reading a Map Where was Machu Picchu located?
(in the Andes Mountains of central Peru, about 50 miles [80 kilometers] northwest of Cuzco)

Evaluate

 Section Quiz 15-3

 Use the Testmaker to create a customized quiz for Section 3.

Reteach

Have students make a chart on the chalkboard summarizing the religion, economy, and government of the Aztec and Inca.

 Reteaching Activity 15

 Reading Essentials and Study Guide 15-3

Enrich

Ask students to write reports comparing Pachacuti and his son, Topa Inca Yupanqui, to Philip and Alexander the Great of Macedonia.

 Enrichment Activity 15

CLOSE

Ask students to describe the social classes and hierarchy of government of the Aztec and Inca civilizations.

Government and Society

Pachacuti created a strong central government to control the vast realm. He permitted local rulers to continue governing conquered territories as long as they were loyal. Rebellious peoples were resettled elsewhere where they could pose less of a threat. Pachacuti instituted a complex system of tribute collections, courts, military posts, trade inspections, and local work regulations to bind outlying territories to the center. To further unite the diverse peoples, the Inca established a common imperial language—Quechua (KEH•chuh•wuh).

The Inca emperor and his officials closely regulated the lives of the common people. As a divine ruler, the emperor owned all land and carefully regulated the growing and distribution of foods, such as potatoes and quinoa (keen•wah), a protein-rich grain. To make good use of the limited arable land, Inca farmers cut step terraces into hillsides and built irrigation systems in the dry coastal plain. After harvest, part of their crops went to the government as taxes. Under the emperor's direction, work crews built roads and woven fiber suspension bridges that linked the regions of the empire.

The Inca believed in many deities, including the creator god Viracocha and the sun god Inti. Priests offered food, animals, and sometimes humans as sacrifices to please the deities. In A.D. 1995 archaeologists discovered in the Andes the frozen, preserved body of a teenage Inca girl. Food and pottery remains seemed to indicate that she was a sacrificial victim. Priests also served as doctors, using herbs to treat illnesses and performing an early form of brain surgery.

The Inca kept records by using *quipu*, a rope with knotted cords of different lengths and colors. Each knot represented an item or number. They also observed the heavens to predict seasonal changes. They were able to perform certain mathematical calculations that they used to design their buildings and roads.

Aztec, Inca, and Maya Empires

Map Study The Aztec, Inca, and Maya built powerful empires in the Americas. **Human/Environment Interaction** How did the Inca adapt to their environment in order to build their civilization?

Inca Decline

The Inca would prove to be no match for the Spanish conquerors who arrived in South America in the A.D. 1530s. In spite of fierce resistance, the Inca Empire eventually disappeared. Spanish forces slew those Inca who threatened their authority—an action that would be repeated in many parts of the Americas. Aspects of Inca culture, however, have survived among the Inca descendants living today in western areas of South America.

SECTION 3 ASSESSMENT

Main Idea
1. Use a diagram like the one below to identify the factors in the rise and fall of the Aztec Empire.

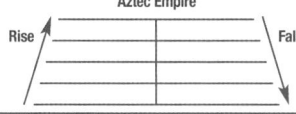

Recall
2. **Define** *chinampas*, hierarchy, quinoa.
3. **Identify** the Aztec, the Inca, the Moche, Pachacuti.

Critical Thinking
4. **Synthesizing Information** What do modern nations take as tribute after a war? How is

this the same as or different from the tribute paid by conquered peoples to the Aztec Empire?

Understanding Themes
5. **Change** Contrast the methods used by the Aztec and the Inca to expand and administer their vast empires.

SECTION 3 ASSESSMENT ANSWERS

1. Rise: plentiful food supply, growth of population, alliances with neighboring city-states, conquered distant rivals, Tenochtitlán prospered; Decline: revolts in outlying area weakened Aztec control, rebels joined Spaniards in destroying Aztec heritage

2. All terms are defined in the Glossary.
3. Aztec, 388; Inca, 388; Moche, 389; Pachacuti, 389
4. Answers about modern warfare will vary but may include monetary payments or guarantees of future nonaggression. Aztec demanded tribute of food, cloth-

ing, raw materials, and sacrificial victims.
5. **CHANGE** Aztec: heavy tribute imposed on conquered peoples; Inca: resettled rebellious peoples

Analyzing Primary and Secondary Sources

Y ou see a television interview with an eyewitness to a tornado. Later you read a newspaper account. Is one account more accurate than the other?

Learning the Skill

To determine the accuracy of an account, you must analyze its source. There are two main kinds of sources—primary and secondary. Primary sources are produced by eyewitnesses to events. Diaries, letters, autobiographies, interviews, artifacts, and paintings are primary sources. Secondary sources use information gathered from others. Textbooks and biographies are secondary sources. Because primary sources convey personal experiences, they often give emotions and opinions of participants in an event. Secondary sources, written at a later time, often help us to understand events in a larger context.

Determine the reliability of the source. For a primary source, find out who wrote it and when. An account written during or immediately after an event is more reliable than one written years later. For a secondary source, look for good documentation. Researchers should cite their sources in footnotes and bibliographies.

For both types of sources evaluate the author. Is this author biased? What background and authority does he or she have? Finally, compare two accounts of the same event. If they disagree, you should question their reliability.

Practicing the Skill

Read the sources and answer the questions.

&& Finally the two groups met...When all was ready Moctezuma placed his feet, shod in gold-soled, gem-studded sandals, on the carpeted pavement and... advanced to an encounter that would shape both his own destiny and that of his nation....Moctezuma had servants bring forward two necklaces of red

shells hung with life-size shrimps made of gold. These he placed around Cortés's neck. 99
—from *Cortés* by William Weber Johnson, 1975

&& When we had arrived at a place not far from the town, where several small towers rose together, the monarch raised himself in his sedan...Montezuma himself, according to his custom, was sumptuously attired, had on a species of half boot, richly set with jewels, and whose soles were made of solid gold.... Montezuma came up to Cortés, and taking him by the hand, conducted him himself into the apartments where he was to lodge, which had been beautifully decorated...He then hung about his neck a chaste necklace of gold, most curiously worked with figures all representing crabs. 99

—from an account by Conquistador Bernal Díaz del Castillo, 1519

1. What is the general topic of the two sources?
2. Which is a primary source and which is a secondary source? How can you tell?
3. What different technique does each quote use to approach the same topic?

Applying the Skill

Find two accounts of a recent event or a historical event. Analyze the reliability of each.

For More Practice

Turn to the Skill Practice in the Chapter Assessment on page 393.

The **Glencoe Skillbuilder Interactive Workbook**, Level 2 provides instruction and practice in key social studies skills.

ANSWERS TO PRACTICING THE SKILL

1. the meeting of Montezuma and Cortés
2. Source B is the primary source; it was excerpted from an account by the Conquistador Bernal Díaz del Castillo in 1519. Source A is a secondary source; it is excerpted from the book *Cortés* published in 1975.
3. Source A helps put the event in a larger context by stating that Montezuma "advanced to an encounter that would shape both his destiny and that of his nation." Source B is written as an eyewitness account, using the word *we*.

TEACH

Analyzing Primary and Secondary Sources Show the class several print advertisements and have students analyze the accuracy of the claims. Why is it important to analyze information in advertisements? *(Because ads try to sell products, they may not present the product objectively.)* Then tell students that, similarly, it is important to analyze the purpose and accuracy of all kinds of information.

Direct students to read the skill on page 391. What is the difference between a primary and secondary source? *(Primary sources are accounts or artifacts produced by eyewitnesses to events. Secondary sources use information gathered from others.)* What are some examples of primary sources? *(diaries, letters, autobiographies, interviews, artifacts, and paintings)* How can you analyze the content of a document? *(Identify the type of source, determine its reliability, determine who created it, identify when and where it was created, its topic, and its purpose. If possible, compare two accounts of the same event to determine reliability.)*

Additional Practice

📁 Skill Reinforcement Activity 15

GLENCOE
TECHNOLOGY

Glencoe's **Skillbuilder Interactive Workbook, Level 2** This interactive CD-ROM promotes student mastery of key social studies skills.

WORLD HISTORY Online

Have students use the **Chapter 15 Self-Check Quiz** at worldhistory.glencoe.com to prepare for the Chapter Test.

GLENCOE TECHNOLOGY

 VIDEODISC
Use MindJogger to review the chapter.

MindJogger Videoquiz

Chapter 15
Disc 2 Side B

 Also available in VHS.

Answers

Using Key Terms
1. d   3. h   5. f
2. a   4. j

Using Your History Journal

Suggest that students compare when similar achievements (such as the invention of writing or calendars) were made in different parts of the world.

Reviewing Facts
1. religion with idea of two levels of existence; kings as spiritual leaders; ceremonial ball game; base-20 mathematics; symbols for numbers; astronomical charting; calendar systems; economy based on agriculture and trade; writing system; books, inscriptions
2. California: abundant resources: fish, shellfish, berries, nuts; Great Basin: limited resources: seeds, grasshoppers, small animals
3. invented irrigation techniques; Pueblo terraced fields to check

---

Self-Check Quiz

Visit the *World History: The Human Experience* Web site at worldhistory.glencoe.com and click on *Chapter 15—Self-Check Quiz* to prepare for the Chapter Test.

Using Key Terms

Write the key term that completes each sentence. Then write a sentence for each term not chosen.

a. *chinampas*   f. obsidian
b. weirs   g. potlatches
c. quinoa   h. hierarchy
d. confederation   i. slash-and-burn farming
e. maize

1. Around A.D. 1500 the Cayuga, Mohawk, Oneida, Onondaga, and Seneca formed a _____, or loose union.
2. Because of the scarcity of land to farm, the Aztec devised a way of making _____, or artificial islands.
3. Among Native Americans of the Pacific Northwest, the wealth of each lineage group was displayed and given away as gifts at _____.
4. The early Olmec practiced a form of agriculture known as _____.
5. By about 5000 B.C., hunter-gatherers in the highland area of present-day Mexico had discovered that the seeds of _____ could be planted.

Technology Activity

Using the Internet Access the Internet to locate a Web site that has information about the ancient Inca Empire. Use a search engine to help focus your search by using phrases such as *inca empire, mesoamerican civilizations,* or *native americans*. Create a bulletin board using the information found, and incorporate illustrations of Inca culture and artifacts. Include captions with your photos and illustrations.

Using Your History Journal

Parallel to your time line of important dates in Native American civilizations, add a time line of significant civilizations and achievements in Africa, Asia, and Europe. Use dates from the Unit 3 Digest on pages 395–397.

Reviewing Facts

1. **Culture** Use a chart like the one below to identify key events in the development of the Mayan civilization.

Key Developments
1. _____
2. _____
3. _____

2. **Geography** Explain how the food resources of Native Americans along the California coast differed from those of Native Americans living in the Great Basin.
3. **Geography** Discuss how the people of southwestern North America adapted to the desert.
4. **Culture** Identify the purposes of the mounds left by the Mound Builders.
5. **History** Name the two principal sites where excavations have revealed an ancient Olmec culture.
6. **Culture** Describe the four books that have survived from the Mayan civilization.
7. **History** Identify the events in the early A.D. 1500s that were responsible for the sudden end to the Inca and the Aztec civilizations.
8. **Science/Technology** Explain how mathematical, technical, and scientific innovations affected Native Americans.
9. **Geography** State what was unique about the location of the Aztec city of Tenochtitlán.
10. **Citizenship** Discuss the ways in which the Inca served their emperor and the empire.

---

erosion, built with adobe; Navajo raised sheep adapted to desert
4. ceremonial centers, tombs for leaders
5. San Lorenzo and La Venta
6. plaster-covered, pleated, flattened bark
7. Aztec weakened by rebellions from outlying territories; both empires succumbed to the Spanish.
8. **Maya:** system of mathematics using base 20 for charting heavenly bodies and calendars

for dating religious ceremonies and other activities; **Aztec:** *chinampas,* or artificial islands, enabled farmers to grow a variety of crops; religious and solar calendars to determine appropriate days for activities; **Inca:** terraces and irrigation canals for farming; roads and fiber suspension bridges to link empire; early form of brain surgery
9. It was an island city.
10. Inca farmers provided a portion of their

Critical Thinking

1. **Analyze** How did the rise and decline of the Aztec and Inca Empires differ?
2. **Analyze** High in the Andes mountain ranges, the city of Machu Picchu was the last refuge of the Inca. Why did Inca rulers retreat to a city in such a remote location?

Ruins of Machu Picchu

Understanding Themes

1. **Relation to the Environment** How did Native Americans in the Eastern Woodlands differ from the Native Americans of the Great Plains? How were they similar?
2. **Innovation** What were some of the cultural achievements of the Mayan civilization?
3. **Change** How did Spaniards affect the Aztec and Inca civilizations?

Linking Past and Present

1. What impact do Native American traditions have on life in the Americas today? In what ways has modern civilization been affected by the early Native Americans?
2. Religion played an important role in early American and other ancient civilizations. What role does religion have in modern societies?

Skill Practice

Read the following excerpt and answer the questions.

❝The things the Incas built were copied from the older civilizations that they conquered. In their cities, fortresses, roads, terraces, temples, they did only what had been done before by the people around them, but a great deal more of it. The ornamentation, the woven fabrics, the work in gold they pursued so avidly as a symbol of the Sun, all were adopted by their predecessors. ❞

— from *The Last Americans: The Indian in American Culture* by the American historian, William Brandon, 1974

1. What is the topic of the source?
2. Is this a primary or a secondary source? Explain your answer.
3. What authority does the author have?

Geography in History

1. **Movement** Refer to the map below. In the A.D. 1500s and A.D. 1600s Native American civilizations declined as the whole region came under the rule of powerful European nation-states. The triangular trade linked four continents between A.D. 1600 and A.D. 1760. How did trade change the population of the Caribbean Islands?
2. **Human/Environment Interaction** How did farming change when crops such as sugarcane began to be raised for trade?
3. **Movement** What positive and negative changes resulted from the cultural contact of peoples from four different continents?

The Triangular Trade Route

Chapter 15 Assessment

3. **CHANGE** Both civilizations were destroyed.

Linking Past and Present

1. Native American traditions have left their impact on language, recreation (lacrosse, use of hammocks, canoeing), and diet. Respect for the environment, similar to the early Native Americans, has become a concern of modern society.
2. Many modern societies support the separation of church and state, although in others, such as Iran, religion and government are closely connected.

Skill Practice

1. how the things built by the Incas were copied from the civilizations that the Incas conquered
2. This is a secondary source; it came from a book written in 1974.
3. that he is an American historian

Geography in History

1. Enslaved Africans were imported; Europeans settled there.
2. Subsistence farming by native peoples gave way to commercial plantations worked by enslaved people.
3. positive: exchange of products, resources, ideas; negative: enslavement of native populations

Chapter Bonus Test Question

Ask students: What similarities do you see between the rise of urban civilization in the Americas and the rise of early urban civilizations in the Near East? *(Answers may include: location in areas that are warm year-round; the building of huge structures such as pyramids; development of astronomy and calendars.)*

crops as taxes; work crews carried out the building of roads and bridges.

Critical Thinking

1. Aztec demanded tribute of conquered peoples; Inca resettled rebellious peoples; Aztec decline hastened by alliance of conquered peoples with Spanish; fall of Inca to Spanish eased by obedient national character.
2. to escape the Spaniards

Understanding Themes

1. **RELATION TO ENVIRONMENT** differences: Great Plains: farming difficult, depended on bison; Eastern Woodlands: lived in farming villages, hunted variety of animals; similarity: made use of every part of animals they killed
2. **INNOVATION** understood concept of zero; developed accurate calendars; wrote books and left written records on monuments

FOCUS

During this time of growth and increased cultural contact, world-views—whether ethical, religious, social, or scientific—were changed. Some ideas become more in-grained, while others changed as a result of new concepts acquired from other parts of the world.

TEACH

Reinforcing Vocabulary

Point out the **Vocabulary Preview** to students alerting them to words they will encounter that might be unfamiliar.

The Quran

Interpreting the Primary Source
Ask students to describe the relationship between God (Allah) and his followers as depicted in this passage. *(The passage depicts a relationship of give and take, in which both Allah and his followers affirm their commitment to the covenant established between them.)*

Evaluating the Primary Source
This primary source depicts the establishment of a relationship between Allah and his followers and implies the way all followers should interact with the Deity. This source is a useful historical document because of its implied tolerance of and belief in a strong kinship with the other major monotheistic religions of the region.

Thomas Aquinas

Interpreting the Primary Source
Ask students to explain how Aquinas uses logic to assert that war can be moral even though in his initial argument he says that

---

PRIMARY SOURCES
Library

Unit 3

In many parts of the world, the period between A.D. 500 and A.D. 1500 was a time of turmoil and change. It was also a time of growth and exploration. Merchants and missionaries brought different areas into contact with one another and helped spread religious and scientific ideas.

✦ VOCABULARY PREVIEW

covenant: promise; agreement

belligerents: groups at war with each other

abject: low in spirit; hopeless

For more primary sources to accompany this unit, use the *World History Primary Source Document Library CD-ROM.*

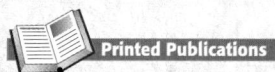

Chapter 11
The Quran

Muslims believe that the angel Gabriel carried a series of revelations from God (Allah) to Muhammad, which were collected in a book called the Quran, the sacred text of Islam. The following excerpts are from the Quran.

Section 9
81.   Behold! Allah took
The Covenant of the Prophets,
Saying: "I give you
A Book and Wisdom;
Then comes to you
A Messenger,
confirming
What is with you;
Do you believe in him
And render him
help."
Allah said: "Do ye agree,
And take this my Covenant
As binding on you?"
They said: "We agree."
He said: "Then bear witness,
and I am with you
Among the witnesses. . . ."

84.   Say: "We believe
In Allah, and in what
Has been revealed to us
And what was revealed
To Abraham Ism[ae]l;
Isaac, Jacob, and the Tribes,
And in (the Books)
Given to Moses, Jesus,
And the Prophets,
From their Lord:
We make no distinction
Between one and another
Among them, and to Allah do we
Bow our will (in Islam). . . ."

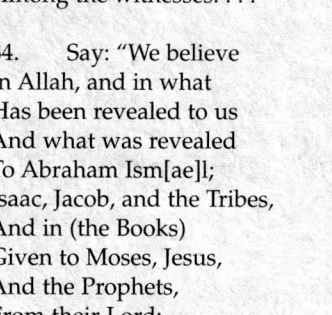

Muslims circl[e] the Ka'aba

---

war is a sin. *(Aquinas uses a passage in the Bible to reason that war can be moral; in his logic, if the Bible allows soldiering, then war must be just at least in certain cases, and that, he says, is because war can serve to achieve peace. He thus uses logic to refute his initial argument that war is contrary to peace and thus sinful.)*

Evaluating the Primary Source
This primary source presents logic as a means by which one can reason through moral concerns. This source offers insight into the way medieval people viewed warfare. It shows, since Aquinas addressed the issue, that it was an important and frequent occurrence. But at the same time, people

---

Chapter 13
Thomas Aquinas

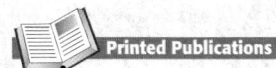
Printed Publications

Thomas Aquinas was a thinker of the Middle Ages. His Summa Theologica *(1273) applies logic to Christian beliefs. Here he discusses war.*

Whether It Is Always Sinful to Wage War?

Objection 1. It would seem that it is always sinful to wage war. Because punishment is not inflicted except for sin. Now those who wage war are threatened by Our Lord with punishment, according to Matth. xxvi. 52: All that take the sword shall perish with the sword. Therefore all wars are unlawful. . . .

Obj. 3. Further, nothing, except sin, is contrary to an act of virtue. But war is contrary to peace. Therefore war is always a sin. . . .

On the contrary, Augustine says . . . : If the Christian Religion forbade war altogether, those who sought . . . advice in the Gospel would rather have been counselled . . . to give up soldiering altogether. On the contrary, they were told: ". . . be content with your pay." If he commanded them to be content with their pay, he did not forbid soldiering.

I answer that, In order for a war to be just, three things are necessary. First, the authority of the sovereign by whose command the war is to be waged. . . .

Secondly, a just cause is required, . . .

Thirdly, it is necessary that the belligerents should have a rightful intention, so that they intend the advancement of good, or the avoidance of evil. . . .

Reply Obj. 3. Those who wage war justly aim at peace, and so they are not opposed to peace. . . . Hence Augustine says . . . : We do not seek peace in order to be at war, but we go to war that we may have peace. . . .

Chapter 14
The Tale of Genji

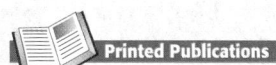
Printed Publications

Around A.D. 1010 Lady Shikibu Murasaki wrote The Tale of Genji, *a novel that is considered the greatest work of Japanese fiction. The tale follows the life and loves of a fictional prince named Genji. In this excerpt, Genji discusses the subject of women with his friend.*

". . . I divide women into three classes. Those of high rank and birth are made such a fuss of and their weak points are so completely concealed that we are certain to be told that they are paragons [models of perfection]. About those of the middle class everyone is allowed to express his own opinion, and we shall have much conflicting evidence to sift. As for the lower classes, they do not concern us."

Illustration from
The Tale of Genji

The completeness with which To no Chujo disposed of the question amused Genji, who said "It will not always be so easy to know into which of the three classes a woman ought to be put. For sometimes people of high rank sink to the most abject [low] positions; while others of common birth rise to . . . think themselves as good as anyone. How are we to deal with such cases? . . ."

Interpreting Primary Sources

1. What does the Quran say about the revelations to Moses and Jesus?
2. According to Aquinas, what is necessary for a "just" war?
3. Why does Genji disagree with To no Chujo?
4. **CRITICAL THINKING:** Why do you think a woman would write this passage from *The Tale of Genji?* Do you think the author believed what she wrote?

Applications Activity
Suppose you had to debate Thomas Aquinas over the issue of the morality of war. Write a speech rebutting Aquinas's arguments.

must also have been questioning the morality of killing others.

The Tale of Genji
Interpreting the Primary Source
Ask students to interpret the implication of the following phrase: "The completeness with which To no Chujo disposed of the question amused Genji. . . ." *(This phrase shows that Genji does not think To no Chujo has considered any other possible viewpoints on women than the one he has presented; Genji's amusement over this shows that he does not agree with To no Chujo's narrow viewpoint.)*

Evaluating the Primary Source
This primary source reveals one conception of how Japanese women were viewed by Japanese men during the time period in which the novel is set. The reliability of this source is determined by the goal of the author. Because the novel was written by a woman, her presentation of men's views is an interpretation. Why she chose to represent this particular interpretation depends on what message she hoped to reveal in this passage. Additionally, because the text is fiction, the author would have chosen to use whatever interpretation best suited her characters and her goal.

ANSWER KEY

1. that they are the same as, or as valid as, those given to Muhammad
2. permission of the sovereign; a just cause; good intentions
3. To no Chujo's classification of women is simplistic. Genji points out that women of low birth can rise to important positions, while women of high birth may sink to "the most abject positions," so one cannot know the true nature of a woman from her rank alone.
4. Lady Murasaki may have been poking fun at people who are very class-conscious. She probably was being ironic and did not literally believe what she made To no Chujo say.

APPLICATIONS ACTIVITY: Speeches will vary, but students should make a logical argument with supporting details and should make reference to specific statements from *Summa Theologica*.

For the more complete version of each of these documents, see the *World History Primary Source Document Library CD-ROM:*

Document 57 *The Quran*
Document 63 *Thomas Aquinas*
Document 71 *The Tale of Genji*

Answers and Analyses

1. **C** (Geography) According to the map, Manzikert was lost by 1143, and the empire still had some land on the Adriatic. Further, the crusaders left from Venice, and not from Rome. Therefore choices A, B, and D can be eliminated. Since the map shows that all of Italy had been lost by 1143, the best choice is C.

2. **J** (History) Islamic contributions to science and culture are described on pages 285–286. There it states that Muslims made important contributions in mathematics, astronomy, and optics.

THE PRINCETON REVIEW TEST-TAKING TIP

Remind students to read all of the answer choices. Choice F is true, but so are choices G and H. Therefore the best answer is J.

3. **A** (History) According to page 306, Church leaders *tried to free the Church from the control of feudal lords. They wanted the Church, not the state, to be the final authority in Western society . . . the reformers insisted that the pope, not secular rulers such as lords and kings, should be the one to appoint bishops and other officials to church offices.*

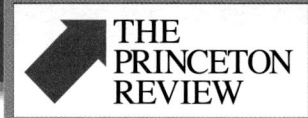
THE PRINCETON REVIEW

Standardized Test Practice

Directions: Choose the *best* answer to each of the following multiple choice questions. If you have trouble answering a question, eliminate answers you know are incorrect. Write your answers on a separate piece of paper.

Use the map below to answer question 1.

Decline of the Byzantine Empire

EUROPE
Venice
Adriatic Sea
ITALY
Rome
Black Sea
Kossovo
Manzikert
Constantinople
GREECE
ASIA MINOR
Carthage
SYRIA
Mediterranean Sea
PALESTINE
EGYPT
AFRICA
Red Sea

Territory lost by A.D. 1143
Territory lost by A.D. 1350
Empire in A.D. 1350
Route of Fourth Crusade
Battle site

0   200   400 mi.
0   200   400 km
Lambert Conic Conformal Projection

1. According to the map above, which of the following was true about the Byzantine Empire in 1143?

 A Manzikert was still a part of the empire.

 B The empire had no lands along the Black Sea.

 C Italy was no longer part of the empire.

 D Crusaders left Rome for Asia Minor.

> **Test-Taking Tip:** The map's *legend*, or *key*, explains how the map is organized. Make sure that you double check all answer choices against the information *on the map* to make sure that you have chosen the *best* answer.

2. Islamic contributions include

 F the invention of algebra.

 G the accurate description of solar eclipses.

 H the study of light and its effect on sight.

 J all of the above.

> **Test-Taking Tip:** Always read the question and *all* the answer choices. Do not simply choose the first answer that "makes sense"—especially when one of the choices is *all of the above* or *none of the above*.

3. The medieval Church introduced reforms to strengthen its influence. Which had the greatest impact on these reforms?

 A The Church's desire to free itself from feudal lords

 B The Church's desire to establish more monasteries on the manors of nobles

 C The need to make Roman Catholicism more accessible to serfs and to women

 D The fear of foreign invasion

> **Test-Taking Tip:** The word *reform* means "an improvement to correct faults." What *faults* existed in the Church? Notice also that the question asks you which answer had the *greatest* impact. When a question uses words like *greatest* or *least*, it means that more than one answer may seem correct—make sure you choose the most important.

4. During the Tang dynasty, the Chinese expanded trade and established a strong central government. To govern a large land area and many people, the Tang claimed to have developed a *meritocracy.* In a meritocracy, the government

F gives people government offices based on family ties.

G awards land ownership based on military service.

H gives people jobs based on talent and qualifications.

J gives people jobs based on religious affiliation.

Test-Taking Tip: At the root of the word *meritocracy* is the word *merit.* If you are not sure what *merit* means, think about other places you may have heard it—for example, *merit scholarship* or *merit badge.* People who receive these types of awards have earned them through outstanding performance and hard work. Becoming a government official based on family ties is not an example of merit, so you can eliminate answer F.

5. Which of the following demonstrates how the Native Americans of the Southwest adapted to their environment?

A Many of their legends told the story of the creation of mountains and sand dunes.

B They constructed elaborately decorated totem poles to honor their dead leaders.

C They held their religious ceremonies in underground chambers known as kivas.

D They invented techniques of irrigation to farm the land.

Test-Taking Tip: Make sure that your answer is directly related to *adapting to the environment.* Since answers B and C are not strongly related to the *environment,* you can eliminate them. Of the remaining choices, which answer shows an adaptation that would help people survive in this type of region?

Use the map below **and** your knowledge of history to answer question 6.

Korea in the Three Kingdoms Period

6. What physical feature characterizes the eastern coast of Korea?

F Plains

G Deserts

H Islands

J Mountains

Test-Taking Tip: Not all map features are identified by a legend or key. Rivers are shown by wavy lines (blue if the map is in color) that are *labeled,* so they can be distinguished from political borders. Mountains are shaded to show relief—they will look "bumpy." Different typefaces are used for cities, nations (kingdoms), and bodies of water. Familiarity with these standard map features will make map reading easier.

4. H (History) According to page 347, a meritocracy is *a system in which people are chosen and promoted for their talents and performance.*

5. D (Culture/Environment) According to page 377, *the Hohokam living in the area of present-day Arizona dug an irrigation canal 3 miles long to draw the waters of the Gila and Salt Rivers onto fields planted with maize, kidney beans, and squash.*

6. J (Geography) According to the map, a mountain range runs up the eastern coast of Korea.

 TEST-TAKING TIP

If students had a difficult time answering this question, they probably confused east and west. Remind them how to determine east and west after locating north.

MORE PRACTICE

For additional practice, assign practice pages from:

Glencoe Standardized Test Practice Workbook

Glencoe SAT/SAT II Practice Book

Tested Objectives

Questions	Objective
1	Analyzing Information
2	Summarizing Information
3	Evaluating Information
4, 5	Making Generalizations
6	Synthesizing Information

0:00 **OUT OF TIME?**

If time does not permit teaching each chapter in Unit 4, you may use the Unit Digest Transparencies and Chapter Digest Audiocassettes with accompanying activities and tests.

Introducing the Unit

Unit 4 focuses on how the Renaissance, the Reformation, and the age of exploration dramatically changed Europe and much of the rest of the world. The unit also explores the way Asian civilizations enriched their own cultures by adapting elements of Western culture.

Unit Objectives

Students will be able to:
1. explain how the Renaissance emphasized individualism and how the Protestant Reformation established new forms of Christianity.
2. understand how Europeans explored and colonized the Americas, Asia, and Africa.
3. trace the growing power of monarchs and the rise of strong nation-states in Europe from the 1500s to the 1700s.
4. examine the powerful Ottoman, Persian, Mogul, Chinese, and Japanese Empires and understand the cultural achievements of Asia.

GLENCOE
TECHNOLOGY

Glencoe World History Primary Source Document Library
Use the CD-ROM to access primary source documents related to modern civilizations.

Unit **4** 1400–1800

Emergence of the Modern World

Chapter 16
Renaissance and Reformation

Chapter 17
Expanding Horizons

Chapter 18
Empires of Asia

Chapter 19
Royal Power and Conflict

PRIMARY SOURCES
Library

See pages 506–507 for primary source readings that accompany Unit 4.

Then *& Now* The Renaissance and Reformation changed European culture and created powerful political alliances. Europeans set out on uncharted seas to explore the world as powerful European monarchs competed for trade, influence, and territory. While the peoples of the Americas struggled against European invaders, civilizations in Asia reached pinnacles of cultural achievement.

Every time you use paper money or write a check, you are trusting in a system based on banking that originated during this period. As European trade and commerce increased, merchants turned to bankers for the capital to finance their ventures. Wealthy banking families even made loans to European monarchs. By the 1600s government-chartered banks began to replace family-owned banks. These banks issued banknotes and checks that made trading in heavy coins obsolete.

A Global Chronology

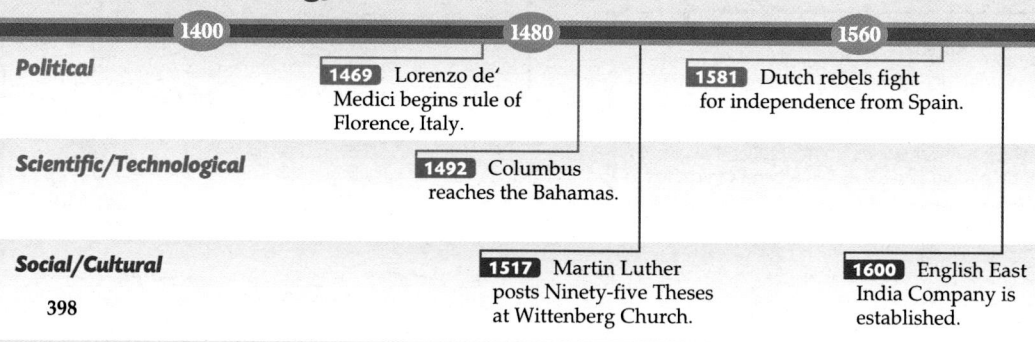

	1400	1480	1560
Political		**1469** Lorenzo de' Medici begins rule of Florence, Italy.	**1581** Dutch rebels fight for independence from Spain.
Scientific/Technological		**1492** Columbus reaches the Bahamas.	
Social/Cultural	398	**1517** Martin Luther posts Ninety-five Theses at Wittenberg Church.	**1600** English East India Company is established.

Then *& Now*

Power In this unit students will learn about the emergence of powerful and wealthy nation-states in Europe and the creation of European colonies in the Americas, Africa, and Asia. Explain that Spain, Portugal, France, Britain, and Holland were the leading commercial and naval powers of the Renaissance and Reformation.

Ask students to make a list of the most powerful nations in the world today, using wealth and

ABCNEWS INTERACTIVE™

VIDEODISC
Turning Points in World History

Side One
Chapter 9

Title: *Age of Exploration*
Subject: Western Europeans seek new routes to Asia.
Ask: In what ways was the age of exploration a turning point? *(Europeans gained territory and indigenous peoples mistreated; new crops were introduced to Europe.)*

History & Art

Galileo Galilei was an Italian scientist who embodied the Renaissance humanists' ideal of thinking independently.

Glencoe Literature Library

The following literature from the **Glencoe Literature Library** may enrich this unit:
Midsummer Night's Dream by W. Shakespeare
The Tempest by W. Shakespeare

History *and the* Humanities

Focus on World Art Prints
•16 *Portrait of a Noblewoman*
•20 *The Attributes of Painting*

World History and Art Transparencies
•20 *Mona Lisa* •22 *View of Toledo*
•24 Taj Mahal

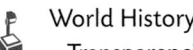

World Music: Cultural Traditions, Lessons 2, 3, 7

History and You

During the voyages of the Age of Exploration, European explorers gained new contacts for trade, expansion, and innovation that profoundly changed European culture.

To better understand the history of European exploration, view videodisc Chapter 9: *Age of Exploration* in Turning Points in World History.

Galileo's telescope

1640

1642 English Civil War begins.

1717 Lady Mary Wortley Montagu introduces inoculation against smallpox.

1608 First checks are used to replace cash in the Netherlands.

1720

1763 Peace of Paris ends Seven Years' War.

1764 Mozart writes his first symphony at age 8.

1800

1795 Russia, Prussia, and Austria divide Poland among themselves.

399

---

military power as their criteria. Are any countries on both lists? Which? *(Britain and France)* Why are some nations wealthy and powerful? *(They possess abundant natural resources, an industrial and technological base, and an educated population.)* What causes nations to lose their position as world leaders? *(loss of economic predominance, limited resources and population, competition of newly industrialized nations)*

The
Spread
of Ideas

TEACH

Introduction

This feature focuses on the spread of musical forms from Africa to the Americas as an unintended consequence of the Atlantic slave trade. In North America and the Caribbean, the distinctive African musical forms evolved into spirituals, blues, ragtime, jazz, rock and roll, rap, reggae, calypso, and salsa, among other styles.

Background Notes

Linking Past and Present

Several elements of African music have profoundly influenced modern popular forms, particularly rhythmic polyphony, a more complex and compelling rhythmic style than those of European origin. The minor third, a regular feature of West African music, also became an essential element of blues and rock and roll.

Geography

Movement After reaching North America, African-influenced music was at first found mainly in the Deep South. Early blues masters such as Robert Johnson and Blind Lemon Jefferson came from the Mississippi Basin, and New Orleans and Memphis emerged as centers of the new style. During the Great Depression, millions of African Americans moved north, and the blues traveled with them to St. Louis, Kansas City, Chicago, and New York.

Music

In the 1400s and 1500s, European ships edged into uncharted waters. These voyages set the stage for one of the greatest cultural exchanges in history, as people from Europe, Africa, and the Americas came face-to-face for the first time. One of the products of this exchange was the birth of "America music," a collection of styles deeply rooted in West Africa.

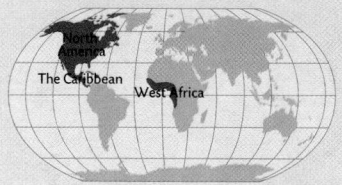

West Africa
Traditional Rhythms

"We are almost a nation of dancers, musicians, and poets," recalled a West African named Olaudah Equiano. "Every great event ... is celebrated ... with songs and music suited to the occasion."

Equiano's words highlighted the importance of music to everyday life among the varied peoples of West Africa. Here musicians won fame for the skill with which they played complicated rhythms on drums, flutes, whistles, and stringed instruments. People added the sounds of their voices to a rhythm known as a call-and-response pattern. A leader would sing out a short piece of music, and people would sing it back to the beat of a drum.

African-style drum

400   Unit 4   *Emergence of the Modern World*

COOPERATIVE LEARNING ACTIVITY

Map   Have students use a large outline map of the world to show the diffusion of musical forms from Africa to the Americas, Europe, and back to Africa. Have them label musical centers such as West Africa and New Orleans. Suggest that they use thumbtacks and colored thread to show the paths that music has traveled. Display the finished map in the classroom.

Also encourage students to bring in examples of older forms of music, such as ragtime, blues, jazz, and rhythm and blues, and try to identify similarities and differences in their musical styles.
L1 LEP

The Spread of Ideas

North America
New Musical Forms

The musical heritage of West Africa traveled to the Americas aboard European slave ships. To endure the pains of slavery, West Africans kept alive musical patterns that reminded them of their ancestral homelands. Because most West Africans came as laborers, work songs took root first. The rhythmic patterns of these songs set the pace for repetitious tasks. West African laborers added field hollers—long calls by a worker in which other workers answered back. Outside the fields, enslaved Africans cried out for freedom in religious folk songs known as spirituals.

Over hundreds of years, these musical forms came together to create new styles. The blues grew out of the field songs and spirituals of slavery. Ragtime echoed the complicated rhythms of West African music. On these foundations grew yet other styles—jazz, rock 'n' roll, and rap.

Chicago 1955 by Ben Shahn

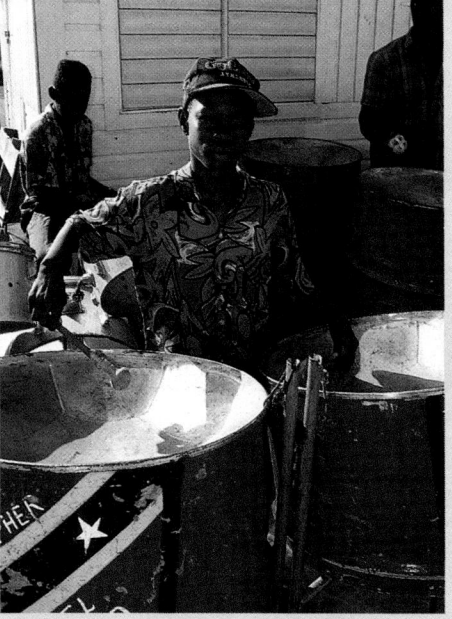

Steel drums of the Caribbean

The Caribbean
Afro-Caribbean Beats

The sounds of West Africa could be heard wherever large enslaved African populations lived in the Americas. On islands in the Caribbean, the beat of bongos, the conga, the tambour, and other West African drums became the soul of Afro-Caribbean music. Added to the drums were European instruments such as the Spanish guitar and a variety of Native American instruments such as the marimba (xylophone), maraca, and wooden rhythm sticks called claves. Out of this blend of influences emerged a range of styles as diverse as the Caribbean islands themselves—reggae, calypso, salsa, and more.

LINKING THE IDEAS

1. What are some of the features of West African music?
2. How did West African music influence musical styles in North America and the Caribbean?

Critical Thinking

3. **Evaluating Information** Which styles of music that you listen to at least once a week are influenced by West African musical patterns?

Unit 4   *Emergence of the Modern World*   **401**

Who?What?Where?When?

W. C. Handy was a pioneer of jazz and blues. The son of a minister, Handy became a musician over his father's protests. As a young man, he played the cornet in minstrel shows, later forming his own band. In 1912 he published "Memphis Blues," originally composed for a political campaign, and one of the first popular blues songs.

Cultural Diffusion

The Circle Is Unbroken The diffusion of African-influenced music continues. In the 1960s, British groups such as the Beatles, the Rolling Stones, and Led Zeppelin recorded blues and rhythm and blues classics written by Muddy Waters, Howlin' Wolf, and Willie Dixon, among others. The British versions of such songs as "Little Red Rooster" and "Seventh Son" became popular among American fans who had never heard the originals.

At the same time, blues and soul have traveled back across the Atlantic Ocean to influence Ali Farka Toure of Mali and other popular African musicians. Similarly, Caribbean musicians have incorporated elements of rap into merengue, from the Dominican Republic, and reggae, from Jamaica.

ANSWERS TO LINKING THE IDEAS

1. complicated rhythms and call-and-response patterns
2. Musical forms such as work songs, field hollers, and spirituals evolved into modern forms of music such as jazz, rock and roll, rap, salsa, reggae, and calypso.
3. Answers should explain the West African connection.

A complete, 1-page lesson plan is provided for each section in the *Reproducible Lesson Plans* booklet.

Renaissance and Reformation

CHAPTER RESOURCES

	Reproducible Resources	Multimedia Resources
Chapter Opener	Chapter Themes: Graphic Organizer 16 Historical Significance Chapter Activity 16	MindJogger Videoquiz
Chapter Enrichment	Vocabulary Activity 16* Time Line Activity 16 Mapping History Activity 16 History Simulation 16 Geography and History Activity 16 Source Reading 16 People in World History Profiles 29, 30 World Literature Selection 4 World Art and Music Activity 16 Enrichment Activity 16 Critical Thinking Activity 16 Skill Reinforcement Activity 16 Performance Assessment Activity 16 Standardized Test Practice Workbook Activity 16 Inclusion for the Social Studies Classroom Strategies and Activities	Focus on World Art Print 16, *Portrait of a Noblewoman* NGS Poster Set: *The Renaissance* World History and Art Transparency 20, *Mona Lisa*; 21, *Herzogenburg Monastery* Chapter Transparency 16 NGS PicturePack Transparency Set: *The Renaissance* Vocabulary PuzzleMaker Software NGS PictureShow CD-ROM: *The Renaissance* World Music: Cultural Traditions, Lesson 3 Turning Points in World History World History Primary Source Document Library
Chapter Review/Reteaching	Reteaching Activity 16 Skill Reinforcement Activity 16 Spanish Chapter Summary 16	Chapter 16 Digest Audiocassette, Activity, Test* Vocabulary PuzzleMaker Software Interactive Tutor Self-Assessment Software MindJogger Videoquiz
Chapter Evaluation/Testing	Performance Assessment Activity 16 Chapter 16 Test, Forms A and B	ExamView® Pro Testmaker

0:00 OUT OF TIME? Assign the Chapter 16 Audiocassettes.

* *Also available in Spanish*

World History Primary Source Document Library
Make History Come Alive!
Engage your students with over 250 easily accessible primary source documents—available on this CD-ROM—that will give them real life insight into the important events of world history.

Block Schedule
Activities that are particularly suited to use within the block scheduling framework are identified throughout this chapter by the following designation.

KEY TO ABILITY LEVELS
Teaching strategies are coded for varying learning styles.
L1 BASIC activities for all students
L2 AVERAGE activities for average to above-average students
L3 CHALLENGING activities for above-average students
LEP LIMITED ENGLISH PROFICIENCY activities

Use Glencoe's *Presentation Plus!* multimedia teacher tool to easily present dynamic lessons that visually excite your students. Using Microsoft PowerPoint® you can customize the presentations to create your own personalized lessons.

Interactive Lesson Planner

Planning has never been easier! Using this CD-ROM, organize your week, month, semester, or year with all the help you need. The **Interactive Lesson Planner** gives you access to all of the blackline masters that accompany *World History: The Human Experience.*

SECTION RESOURCES

Daily Objectives	Reproducible Resources	Multimedia Resources
Section 1 **The Italian Renaissance** Identify the factors that inspired the Renaissance.	Lecture Notes 16-1 Reproducible Lesson Plan 16-1 Vocabulary Activity 16* Guided Reading Activity 16-1* People in World History Profile 30 Geography and History Activity 16 Time Line Activity 16 History Simulation 16 Section Quiz 16-1* Reading Essentials and Study Guide 16-1	NGS Poster Set: *The Renaissance* Section Focus Transparency 16-1 Chapter Transparency 16 World History and Art Transparency 20, *Mona Lisa* NGS PicturePack Transparency Set: *The Renaissance* Interactive Tutor Self-Assessment Software NGS PictureShow CD-ROM: *The Renaissance*
Section 2 **The Northern Renaissance** Explain how the Renaissance reached northern Europe.	Lecture Notes 16-2 Reproducible Lesson Plan 16-2 Vocabulary Activity 16* Guided Reading Activity 16-2* Section Quiz 16-2* Reading Essentials and Study Guide 16-2	Focus on World Art Print 18, Pieter Brueghel. *The Wedding Dance* Section Focus Transparency 16-2 Interactive Tutor Self-Assessment Software Testmaker
Section 3 **The Protestant Reformation** Discuss how Luther's religious reforms led to Protestantism, a new branch of Christianity.	Lecture Notes 16-3 Reproducible Lesson Plan 16-3 Vocabulary Activity 16* Guided Reading Activity 16-3* People in World History Profile 29 Section Quiz 16-3* Reading Essentials and Study Guide 16-3	Section Focus Transparency 16-3 Interactive Tutor Self-Assessment Software Testmaker Turning Points in World History: *The Reformation*
Section 4 **The Spread of Protestantism** Identify the different forms of Protestantism that emerged in Europe as the Reformation spread.	Lecture Notes 16-4 Reproducible Lesson Plan 16-4 Vocabulary Activity 16* Guided Reading Activity 16-4* Section Quiz 16-4* Reading Essentials and Study Guide 16-4	Section Focus Transparency 16-4 Interactive Tutor Self-Assessment Software Testmaker
Section 5 **The Catholic Reformation** Describe how the Catholic Church tried to halt the spread of Protestantism.	Lecture Notes 16-5 Reproducible Lesson Plan 16-5 Guided Reading Activity 16-5* Reteaching Activity 16 Enrichment Activity 16 Section Quiz 16-5* Performance Assessment Activity 16 Spanish Chapter Summary 16 Reading Essentials and Study Guide 16-5	Focus on World Art Print 16 Section Focus Transparency 16-5 World History and Art Transparency 21, *Herzogenburg Monastery* Vocabulary PuzzleMaker Software Interactive Tutor Self-Assessment Software Testmaker

* Also available in Spanish

Chapter Activities

 Performance Assessment Activity

Renaissance and Reformation Have students take the roles of merchants, artisans, and other citizens of Italy and Germany during this era. Pair students and have them write a series of letters to each other in which they give details of the events happening at the time and express their feelings and attitudes regarding the developments and reforms. Each student should write at least five letters that are detailed, persuasive in tone and style, and responsive to the previous letter received.

Possible Rubric Features

Accuracy of content, persuasiveness, concept attainment, appropriateness of inferences and predictions, clarity of organization

• *For an additional activity, refer to Activity 16 in the* Performance Assessment Strategies and Activities *booklet.*

ACTIVITY

From the Classroom of...

Carla Eileen Heckstall
Franklin K. Lane High
School
Brooklyn, NY

Renaissance Art and Modern Art

Organize the class into two groups. Have one group review pictures of artwork from the Renaissance. (You may use pictures from the text.) Have the other group review pictures of modern art, preferably from the 1990s. (Use pictures from art magazines or museum or gallery catalogs.)

Ask both groups to select two or three pictures and try to identify values the artists were trying to depict. Have students compare the list of values from the Renaissance art with the list from the modern art.

MULTIPLE LEARNING STYLES

Verbal/Linguistic
Have students research and then debate the following statement: Without the Renaissance, the Reformation could never have taken place.

Logical/Mathematical
Have students create a timeline of major events that occurred during the Renaissance and Reformation.

Visual/Spatial
Have students design a bulletin-board display that identifies famous Renaissance paintings, sculptures, and buildings.

Auditory/Musical
Have students collect and present examples of court, church, and popular music that were common in Europe during the Renaissance and Reformation.

Kinesthetic
Have students research and reenact the meeting with Luther at the Diet of Worms in 1521. Remind them to clearly present and defend the points of view of the Catholic Church and of Martin Luther.

 ASSESSMENT ADVANTAGE

Use the following to easily assess student learning in a variety of ways.

- Performance Assessment Strategies and Activities
- Section Quizzes
- Chapter and Unit Tests
- Interactive Tutor Self-Assessment Software
- Testmaker Software
- MindJogger Videoquiz
- SAT/SAT II Test Practice
- worldhistory.glencoe.com

Additional Resources

NATIONAL GEOGRAPHIC SOCIETY
Teacher's Corner

INDEX TO NATIONAL GEOGRAPHIC MAGAZINE

The following articles may be used for research relating to this chapter:

- "Italy's Endangered Art," by Erla Zwingle, August 1999.
- "Venice," by Erla Zwingle, February 1995.
- "Out of the Darkness: Michelangelo's Last Judgment," by Meg Nottingham Walsh, May 1994.
- "A Renaissance for Michelangelo," by David Jeffrey, December 1989.
- "Restoration Reveals the Last Supper," by Carlo Bertelli, November 1983.
- "Carrara Marble: Touchstone of Eternity," by Cathy Newman, July 1982.

NATIONAL GEOGRAPHIC SOCIETY PRODUCTS AVAILABLE FROM GLENCOE

To order the following products for use with this chapter, contact your local Glencoe sales representative, or call Glencoe at 1-800-334-7344:

- *PictureShow: The Renaissance (CD-ROM)*
- *PicturePack: The Renaissance (Transparencies)*

ADDITIONAL NATIONAL GEOGRAPHIC SOCIETY PRODUCTS

Access National Geographic's new dynamic MapMachine Web site and other geography resources at:

- http://www.nationalgeographic.com/
- http://www.nationalgeographic.com/maps/

BIBLIOGRAPHY

Literature of the Period
Castiglione, Baldassare. *The Book of the Courtier.* Translated by George Bull. New York: Penguin, 1976. Contemporary handbook of courtly etiquette.

Readings for the Student
Rabb, Theodore K. *Renaissance Lives: Portraits of an Age.* New York: Pantheon, 1993. The Renaissance through the lives of fifteen Renaissance men and women.

Readings for the Teacher
Lucas, Henry. *The Renaissance and the Reformation.* New York: Harper, 1960. Historical survey of the Renaissance, Reformation, and the Catholic Reformation.

WORLD HISTORY *Online*

Use our Web site as an additional resource. All essential content is covered in the Student Edition.

You and your students can visit the *World History: The Human Experience* Web site at worldhistory.glencoe.com The student text directs students to the Web site for the following options:

- **Chapter Overviews**
- **Student Web Activities**
- **Self-Check Quizzes**

Answers are provided for you in a link entitled "Web Activity Lesson Plan." Additional Web Resources, Interactive Puzzles, and content updates are also available.

Visit the Glencoe Web site at socialstudies.glencoe.com for social studies activities, updates, and links to other resources.

LOCAL OBJECTIVES

_____
_____
_____
_____
_____
_____
_____
_____
_____
_____
_____
_____
_____
_____
_____
_____
_____

CHAPTER THEMES

Chapter Themes are listed by section on this chapter opening page of the Student Edition. A corresponding theme-based activity is available under "TEACH," and a theme-based question is asked in the Section and Chapter Assessments.

Storyteller

Historical Setting The House of Este, which ruled Ferrara from the 1200s through the 1500s, was one of the most influential families in Italian politics. Ercole I, father of Isabella d'Este, used marriage as a means of consolidating his position. He had married the daughter of the king of Naples. He had arranged Isabella's marriage to the Marquis of Mantua, Francesco Gonzaga, and his two other daughters married the rulers of Bologna and Milan.

Historical Significance

Answers: *During the Renaissance, interest in classical art, literature, and values caused Europeans to place emphasis on current life and on the individual, as well as to view themselves as part of a larger world.*

During the Reformation, many northern Europeans left the Catholic Church and joined new—often persecuted—Protestant religions. In some countries, the king became head of the church. In others, the church controlled the government.

Have students use the **Chapter 16 Overview** at worldhistory. glencoe.com as a prereading and postreading exercise for understanding chapter content.

Renaissance and Reformation

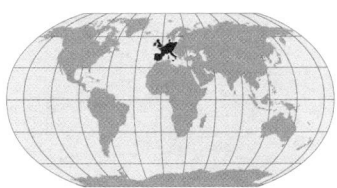

Chapter Themes

▶ **Innovation** The Renaissance leads to an artistic and intellectual awakening in Europe. *Section 1*
▶ **Cultural Diffusion** Renaissance ideas and artistic styles spread from Italy to northern Europe. *Section 2*
▶ **Conflict** Martin Luther's protests against the Catholic Church result in Protestantism. *Section 3*
▶ **Cultural Diffusion** Protestant religious groups spread reform through northern Europe. *Section 4*
▶ **Reaction** The Catholic Church enacts its own reform, the Catholic Reformation. *Section 5*

Storyteller

Isabella d'Este, married in 1490 at the age of 16 to the Marquis of Mantua, played a vital role in ruling the Italian city-state of Mantua. A brilliant and well-educated young woman who loved Latin literature, Isabella gathered a fashionable assemblage of artists and statesmen in her sparkling court. In a room decorated with ornately carved woodwork and paintings that illustrated Greek myths, Isabella entertained her guests to her own lute recitals and poetry readings. Isabella was one of the many Italians of her time who rediscovered and repopularized Greek and Roman classics, educating their contemporaries to the glories of their classical past after a thousand years of neglect. The word Renaissance, coming from the French word meaning "rebirth," was coined to refer to this rebirth of interest in classical ideas and culture.

Historical Significance

What happened during the Renaissance that changed Europeans' outlook on the world? How did the Reformation shape the religious and political life of Europe?

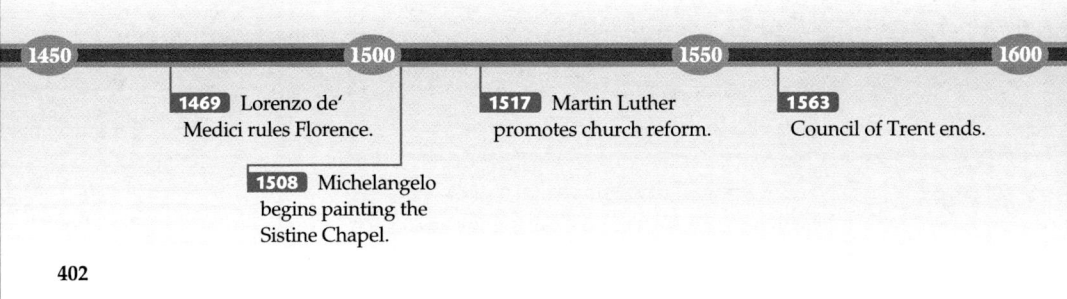

1450	1500	1550	1600

1469 Lorenzo de' Medici rules Florence.

1508 Michelangelo begins painting the Sistine Chapel.

1517 Martin Luther promotes church reform.

1563 Council of Trent ends.

402

GEOGRAPHY CONNECTION

Location Have students locate Italy, France, the Low Countries (present-day Belgium, Luxembourg, and the Netherlands), Germany, England, and Switzerland on a physical map of Europe in the Atlas of this book. What main geographic barrier separates Italy from these other countries? *(mountains: the Alps)* How could this barrier have affected the spread of new ideas? *(The mountains would have made overland travel difficult.)* **L1**

Detail of *The Court* by Andrea Mantegna.
Palazzo Ducale, Mantua, Italy

WORLD HISTORY Online

Chapter Overview

Visit the *World History: The Human Experience* Web site at **worldhistory.glencoe.com** and click on *Chapter 16—Chapter Overview* to preview the chapter.

Your History Journal

Choose a Renaissance sculptor, architect, or painter mentioned in this chapter. Research and write a short report on the work and influence of this person.

Chapter 16 *Renaissance and Reformation* **403**

History & Art
Tell students that Andrea Mantegna served as painter to the Gonzaga court at Mantua from 1460 until his death in 1506. Besides executing large frescoes for the palace, Mantegna painted smaller works for Isabella d'Este's study. How does the artist show Gonzaga's importance in this fresco? *(He is seated in an armchair, surrounded by family and servants, and is being consulted about some kind of business.)*

✔ Performance Assessment

Refer to the activity on page 402C of the Planning Guide.

📁 For an additional activity, refer to Activity 16 in the *Performance Assessment Strategies and Activities* booklet. 📦

Using Your History Journal

Have students use their journals to take notes, organize their ideas, and write a rough draft of the report. 📦

GLENCOE TECHNOLOGY

VIDEODISC
Use MindJogger to preview chapter content.

MindJogger Videoquiz

  Chapter 16
Disc 2 Side B

  Also available in VHS.

✚ EXTRA CREDIT PROJECT

Research First-person accounts and other information about the Renaissance and Reformation are available in many books. Have students research and report to the class on a person, event, or artwork from this historical period that is not detailed in the chapter. Suggest that students use vivid quotations from the first-person accounts and use descriptive language in their own explanations. 📦

SECTION THEME

▶ **Innovation** The Renaissance leads to an artistic and intellectual awakening in Europe.

Guide to Reading

For reading strategies to help students read effectively see pages 12–13. Have students think about the main head as they read the subheads.

Vocabulary Pre-check

 Use the Vocabulary PuzzleMaker for Chapter 16 to create a crossword puzzle to reinforce section terms. **L1 LEP**

Use Vocabulary Activity 16 to introduce vocabulary terms. **L1 LEP**

FOCUS

Section Objective

Identify the factors that inspired the Renaissance.

BELLRINGER
Motivational Activity

 Before taking roll at the beginning of the class period, project Section Focus Transparency 16-1 and have students answer the activity questions. Discuss students' responses.

This activity is also available as a blackline master.

Section **1**
....

The Italian Renaissance

Guide to Reading

Read to Find Out
Main Idea *An array of cultural factors inspired the Renaissance.*

▶ **Terms to Define**
humanism, secular, individualism, sonnet, doge

▶ **People to Meet**
Niccolò Machiavelli, Lorenzo de' Medici, Michelangelo Buonarroti, Leonardo da Vinci

▶ **Places to Locate**
Florence, Rome, Venice

The Storyteller

Michelangelo finished the Sistine Chapel in September 1512. Pope Julius came to see the completed work. One man had covered ten thousand square feet with the greatest wall painting in Italy. Michelangelo wrote to his father, "I have finished the chapel which I have been painting. The Pope is very satisfied.... Your Michelangelo, sculptor, in Rome." The artist, tired and in poor health, went home to Florence, hoping for rest and relaxation.

—adapted from *Michelangelo The Man*, Donald Lord Finlayson, 1935

Ancestors of Christ, detail from the Sistine Chapel

404 Chapter 16 *Renaissance and Reformation*

T he Renaissance—the period from about 1350 until 1600 during which western Europeans experienced a profound cultural awakening—was in many ways a continuation of the Middle Ages, but it also signaled the beginning of modern times. The Renaissance caused educated Europeans to develop new attitudes about themselves and the world around them.

The Renaissance began first in the city-states of Italy. Unlike other areas of Europe, Italy had largely avoided the economic crisis of the late Middle Ages. Italian towns remained important centers of Mediterranean trade and boosted their production of textiles and luxury goods.

More than other Europeans, Italians were attached to classical traditions. The ruins of ancient Roman buildings, arches, and amphitheaters constantly reminded them of their heritage. Moreover, through trade Italian towns remained in close contact with the Byzantine Empire, where scholars preserved the learning of ancient Greece.

Humanism

Through renewed contact with the classics, Italian scholars improved their understanding of Greek and Latin, studied old manuscripts, and copied the classical writing style. This interest in classical learning, however, was more than just a fascination with ancient times. It led to a new intellectual movement known as humanism that focused on secular, or worldly, themes rather than on the religious ideas that had concerned medieval thinkers. Humanists—the scholars who promoted humanism—accepted classical beliefs and wanted to use them to renew their own society. Among the most important beliefs was individualism, an emphasis on the dignity and worth of the individual person.

SECTION RESOURCES

Reproducible Masters
• Lecture Notes 16-1
• Reproducible Lesson Plan 16-1
• Vocabulary Activity 16
• Guided Reading Activity 16-1
• People in World History Profile 30
• Geography and History Activity 16
• Time Line Activity 16

• History Simulation 16
• Section Quiz 16-1
• Reading Essentials and Study Guide 16-1

Transparencies
• Section Focus Transparency 16-1
• Chapter Transparency 16
• World History and Art Transparency 20

• The Renaissance

Multimedia
📖 The Renaissance
💿 Interactive Tutor Self-Assessment Software
💿 Testmaker
💿 The Renaissance

Another was the idea of human improvement, that people should develop their talents through many activities: politics, sports, and the arts.

Education and Literature

Humanists believed that education could help people improve themselves. They opened schools that taught the *studia humanitas*, or humanities—Greek, Latin, history and philosophy, the subjects taught in ancient times. These schools became so popular that humanists began to replace the clergy as teachers of the sons of the wealthy.

Humanism also inspired new forms of literature written in the vernacular and focusing on personal feelings. During the 1300s, Francesco Petrarca, or Petrarch (PEE•TRAHRK), wrote sonnets, or short poems, that expressed his love for Laura, a woman who had died during the Black Death. His friend, Giovanni Boccaccio, in the work *Decameron,* described young people who tell stories to divert their attention from the plague's horrors.

As the Renaissance developed, writers also focused on the topics of individual ambition and success. During the 1500s, Benvenuto Cellini, a goldsmith and sculptor, glorified his achievements in one of the first modern autobiographies. In a popular manual, *The Book of the Courtier,* Baldassare Castiglione (bahl•dahs•SAHR•ray kahs•steel •YOHN•ay) gave advice to men and women on the Renaissance ideal of good behavior. Men were to be skilled in many activities; women were to be graceful, attractive, and courteous. The diplomat Niccolò Machiavelli (mak•ee•uh•VEHL•ee) wrote *The Prince,* a book that realistically analyzed the politics of Renaissance Italy. Rulers, Machiavelli said, should be ready to use force and deceit to hold power. Critics charged that *The Prince* justified immoral behavior in politics, but Machiavelli's book appealed to power-hungry Renaissance rulers. It also influenced the thought and actions of later political leaders.

Scholarship

Humanist scholars influenced more than just literature. With their independent thinking, they began to challenge long-accepted traditions, assumptions, and institutions. As they made all sorts of unsettling discoveries, it further validated their desire to challenge and question nearly everything—even long-standing church traditions. For example, in an exciting piece of Renaissance detective work, the scholar Lorenzo Valla determined that a document that supposedly provided the legal basis for the pope's supremacy over kings was actually a forgery.

Renaissance Italy 1400s

Notice the locations of the Italian city-states during the 1400s. **Location** Which city-state was in the best position to trade by land as well as by sea with the Byzantine Empire to the east?

Through their teaching and writing, humanists reawakened the educated public to classical values. They also encouraged a ferment of new ideas that eventually spread from Italy throughout Europe and reshaped European civilization.

City Life

Town life was stronger in Italy than in other parts of Europe. As a result, Italians could easily discard feudalism and other medieval institutions that had their origins in the rural north. Italy did not become unified as did France and England. Wealthy and successful, most Italian communes, or communities, resisted the efforts of emperors, kings, and nobles to control them. They became independent city-states, each of which included a walled urban center and the surrounding countryside.

Social Groups

The Italian city-states fashioned a new social order in which wealth and ability mattered more than aristocratic titles and ownership of land. Wealthy merchants and bankers replaced the

TEACH

Guided Practice

THEME Innovation

Ask students to volunteer examples from this section of innovations in literature and art that resulted from the influence of humanism. *(new forms of writing, such as sonnets and autobiography; literature in the common language instead of Latin; more lifelike art; classical as well as religious themes in painting and sculpture)* Write their suggestions on the chalkboard. **L1**

Map Study

Answer
Venice

Map Skills Practice

Reading a Map In which part of Italy were most of its great Renaissance cities located? *(north)*

NATIONAL GEOGRAPHIC SOCIETY

Use these materials to enrich student understanding of the Renaissance.

- **NGS PICTURESHOW CD-ROM**
  The Renaissance
- **NGS PICTUREPACK TRANSPARENCY SET**
  The Renaissance
- **NGS POSTER SET**
  The Renaissance

Geography: Movement Have students review a map of the Byzantine Empire to explain how Italy's trade routes helped maintain the influence of earlier cultures. *(Routes across the Adriatic, Ionian, and Mediterranean Seas led to Greece and Turkey as well as to other countries of the Byzantine Empire.)* **L1**

 Chapter Transparency 16

 World History and Art Transparency 20, *Mona Lisa*

 History Simulation 16

Who?What?Where?When?

Machiavelli's *The Prince* was roundly denounced by the Medici family, even though it had been dedicated to Lorenzo de' Medici. To express his political views to a wider audience, Machiavelli turned to writing plays. His comedy *Mandragola* is considered one of Italy's best Renaissance plays.

landed nobility as the most powerful social and political group—the upper class. Shopkeepers and artisans ranked below the wealthy merchants, forming a moderately prosperous middle class that employed large numbers of poor workers. Most of these workers—who were the majority of town dwellers—came to urban areas from the countryside. At the bottom of the social order were the peasants who worked on the country estates of the wealthy classes.

Government

During the Renaissance, Italy was not under one government, but instead consisted of individual city-states, each ruled by wealthy families whose fortunes came from commercial trading or banking. Workers often rebelled against the upper classes. Their demands for equal rights and lower taxes, however, were suppressed.

During the 1400s, social conflicts created upheaval so often that certain city-states felt it necessary to turn over all political authority to a single powerful leader to restore peace. These powerful political leaders were called signori (seen•YOHR•ee). Some signori ruled as dictators, using violence to maintain control. Others successfully ensured popular loyalty by improving city services, supporting the arts, and providing festivals and parades for the lower classes.

While dealing with internal unrest, city-states also fought with each other in territorial disputes. But the prosperous merchants and bankers, unlike the nobility they had supplanted, did not want to fight in these battles. Since military service would interfere with conducting business and trade, the signori chose to replace citizen-soldiers with hired soldiers known as condottieri (KAHN•duh•TYEHR•ee).

Hiring condottieri made wars very costly. To avoid this expense, signori began to seek territorial gain through negotiated agreements. To carry out this policy, they assembled the first modern diplomatic services. Permanent ambassadors were appointed to represent their city-states at foreign

Images of the Times

Art of the Italian Renaissance

The Italian Renaissance produced a host of great Italian artists and sculptors. Among the most notable of these were Michelangelo, Raphael, and Leonardo da Vinci.

Michelangelo created *David*, a gigantic marble sculpture, while at home in Florence between 1501 and 1504. A painter, architect, sculptor, and poet, he has had an unparalleled influence on Western art.

406

Images of the Times

Art of the Italian Renaissance

Leonardo da Vinci's *Mona Lisa* has fascinated art lovers and the general public for centuries. To this day, art critics and historians still do not know for sure who the woman in the painting is or why she is smiling. Some say that a wealthy Florentine merchant named Giocondo commissioned Leonardo to paint a portrait of his third wife. This painting became the famous *La Gioconda*, also known as *Mona Lisa*. Toward the end of his life, Leonardo sold the painting to Francis I, the king of France, who hung it in the Louvre in Paris where it can still be seen today.

courts. The city-states also worked out an agreement among all the city-states that no one city-state would be allowed enough power to threaten the others. During the 1500s other European states adopted similar agreements with one another and also began to practice diplomacy.

Although the Italian city-states had much in common, each developed its own characteristic life. Three cities in particular played leading roles in the Renaissance: **Florence**, **Rome**, and **Venice**.

Florence

Originally a republic, Florence in the 1400s came under the control of a prominent banking family known as the Medici (MEH•duh•chee). Medici rulers helped to foster the spirit of humanism among the city-state's scholars and artists. With this spirit alive throughout the city, Florence became the birthplace of the Italian Renaissance.

Cosimo de' Medici gained control of Florence in 1434. He worked to end worker uprisings by introducing an income tax that placed a heavier burden on wealthier citizens. He used the tax revenues to make city improvements, such as sewers and paved streets, that benefited everyone. Cosimo also worked to establish peaceful relations between the city and its neighbors.

Cosimo's grandson **Lorenzo de' Medici** ruled Florence from 1469 to 1492, and he continued policies like those of his grandfather. He used his wealth to support artists, philosophers, and writers and to sponsor public festivals. As a result of the city's prosperity and fame, Lorenzo was known as "the Magnificent."

During the 1490s Florence's economic prosperity, based mostly on the banking and textile industries, began to decline with increasing competition from English and Flemish cloth makers. Tired of the Medici rule, discontented citizens rallied in support of a Dominican friar named Girolamo Savonarola (SA•vuh•nuh•ROH•luh). In fiery sermons before hundreds of people, Savonarola attacked the Medici for promoting ideas that he claimed were causing the downfall of Florence:

Leonardo da Vinci painted the *Mona Lisa* during a period of intensive study in Florence in 1503. His talent was also expressed in sculpture, architecture, and engineering.

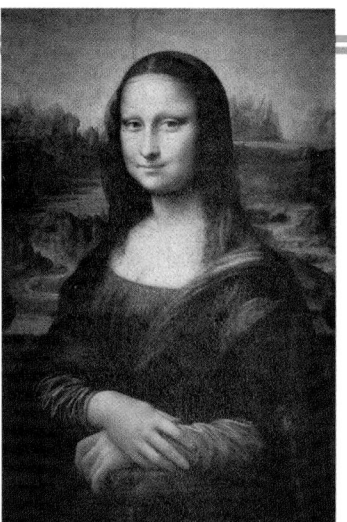

Raphael painted the *School of Athens* for Pope Julius II. When Raphael died in Rome on his 37th birthday, the whole city mourned. His funeral mass was celebrated at the Vatican.

REFLECTING ON THE TIMES

1. What Renaissance values are reflected in the paintings and sculpture shown in this feature?
2. Why are there many similarities in style and subject matter among works of the Italian Renaissance?

407

ANSWERS TO REFLECTING ON THE TIMES

1. lifelike, strong individuals; accurate and natural portrayal of the human form; balance and harmony of subject details
2. The Italian Renaissance artists were all influenced by humanism; because they studied and worked in the same cities, they were in contact with and came to influence one another.

Independent Practice

📁 Guided Reading Activity 16-1 **L1**

Daily Life Have students use outside sources to research one of the following types of Renaissance persons: wealthy banker or merchant, shopkeeper, artisan, manual worker, or peasant. Ask students to write a diary entry for a typical day in their person's life. **L2**

Biography

The following videotapes are available from Glencoe:

- **Michaelangelo: Artist and Man**
- **Leonardo da Vinci: Renaissance Master**

you don't say...

Penknife During the 1400s, penknives were just that—knives for trimming quill pens, whose points quickly became dull. After metal pen points were invented, *"penknife"* came to mean any small blade that could be carried in a pocket.

Linking Past and Present

Tunics, mid-thigh-length garments worn over tights, were fashionable attire for many young Renaissance men. Today, many women favor a similar style of clothing—a long, loose sweater or shirt worn over pants.

History & Art Brunelleschi's sculpture of the sacrifice of Isaac was a contest entry for the east doors of the Baptistry in Florence. *Brunelleschi lost but is remembered for what architectural feat?*

> 66 In the mansions of the great prelates and great lords there is no concern save for poetry and the oratorical art. Go … and see; [you] shall find them all with books of the humanities in their hands…. Arise and come to deliver [your] Church from the hands of the devils! 99

So many people were won over by Savonarola that the Medici family was forced to turn over the rule of Florence to his supporters. On Savonarola's advice, the city's new leaders imposed strict regulations on public behavior. Gambling, swearing, and horse racing were banned. Savonarola urged his listeners to repent of their "worldly" ways. He had crowds make bonfires to burn books, paintings, fancy clothes, and musical instruments.

Savonarola soon aroused a great deal of opposition to his preaching. His criticism of church officials angered the pope. Many people in Florence disliked his strict ways. In 1498 Savonarola was hanged for heresy, and the Medici family returned to power. By this time, however, Florence's greatness had passed.

408 Chapter 16 *Renaissance and Reformation*

Rome

During the 1500s Rome emerged as a leading Renaissance city. In Rome, the pope and the cardinals living in the Vatican made up the wealthiest and most powerful class.

Eager to increase their prestige, Renaissance popes rebuilt the ancient city. Architects constructed large churches and palaces, and artists created magnificent paintings and sculptures to decorate these buildings. Scholars came from all over Europe to study manuscripts and books in the Vatican Library.

Renaissance popes often placed political goals ahead of religious duties. In ruling Rome and its surroundings, they sent ambassadors to other lands, collected taxes, and fought wars. The most politically minded pope was Alexander VI. Elected pope in 1492, Alexander had bribed the College of Cardinals to vote for him. Once in office, he used the wealth of the Church to support his family, the Borgias. He especially encouraged his son Cesare, who raised an army and conquered much of central Italy.

After Alexander's death in 1503, his successors, Julius II and later Leo X, promoted artistic projects to beautify Rome. Their most notable effort was the rebuilding of St. Peter's Basilica, the largest church in the Christian world.

Venice

Another Renaissance center was Venice, the port city on the Adriatic Sea. Venice's economic power, enjoyed since the Crusades, was fading because of changing trade routes and Muslim invasions in the east. However, the city's role as a link between Asia and western Europe still drew traders from all over the world. Venetian shipyards also turned out huge galleys, and Venetian workshops produced high quality glass.

One benefit of Venice's prosperity was political stability. Venice's republican government was headed by an elected **doge**, (DOHJ), or leader. The doge officially ran the city, but the wealthiest merchants meeting in committee as the Council of Ten held the real power. This council passed laws, elected the doge, and even had to be consulted should the doge's son want to marry.

Influenced by Byzantine as well as western European culture, Venice was known for its artistic achievements. Painters, such as Titian, Tintoretto, and Giorgione, used brilliant oil colors to portray rural landscapes and classical and religious themes. Venetian architects, such as Sansovino and Palladio, erected buildings in the classical style.

Renaissance Arts

What were the unique characteristics of Renaissance art? The humanists' emphasis on cultivating individual talent inspired Italian artists to express their own values, emotions, and attitudes. No longer content with creating symbolic representations of their subjects, artists made their subjects as lifelike and captivating as possible. Although much of the art was still devoted to religious subjects, it had more secular, or worldly, overtones. Interest in ancient Greece and Rome moved artists to include classical mythology as well as biblical themes in their works.

To make their creations lifelike and captivating, artists experimented with new techniques. For example, they learned to create a sense of perspective, which gave their paintings depth. They studied anatomy so they could portray human figures more accurately and naturally. Artists also learned to depict subtleties of gesture and expression to convey human emotions. Much of their work consisted of frescoes, or paintings done on damp plaster.

The public in Renaissance Italy appreciated works of art and hailed great artists as geniuses. Nobles and townspeople used art to decorate homes as well as churches. They lavishly rewarded artists and gave them a prominent place in society.

Architecture

During the Middle Ages, cathedral architects had pointed soaring arches and spires heavenward for the glory of God. During the Renaissance, however, Italian architects returned to the classical style. They substituted domes and columns from classical Greek and Roman architecture for the medieval arches and spires. They sought both comfort and beauty in their buildings, adorning them with tapestries, paintings, statues, finely made furniture, and glass windows. Unlike the anonymous architects of the Middle Ages, Renaissance architects took credit for their fine buildings.

The most famous Italian Renaissance architect was Filippo Brunelleschi (BROO•nuhl•EHS•kee), best known for the dome he designed and completed in 1436 for the Cathedral of Florence. No one before had been able to design a dome large or strong enough to cover the cathedral without collapsing from its own weight. Brunelleschi's Roman-inspired design was considered to be the greatest engineering feat of the time.

Sculpture

Renaissance sculpture reflected a return to classical ideals. The free-standing statues of nude figures sculpted in bronze or marble during the Renaissance resembled ancient Greek and Roman sculptures much more than they did medieval sculptures. Human figures in medieval sculptures had usually been portrayed in a stiff, stylized manner.

Some of the best-known Renaissance sculptors—Donatello, Michelangelo, and Ghiberti (gee•BEHR•tee)—came from Florence. There the Medicis opened a school for sculptors. Donatello was the first sculptor since ancient times to cast a large, free-standing nude statue. Although the sculptor **Michelangelo Buonarroti** later went to Rome to sculpt works for the pope, he learned his craft in Florence. Florentine sculptor Lorenzo Ghiberti took 21 years to create 10 biblical scenes on bronze doors for Florence's cathedral baptistry.

Painting

Italian Renaissance painters departed from the flat, symbolic style of medieval painting to begin a more realistic style. This change first appeared in the early 1300s when the Florentine artist-sculptor-architect Giotto (jee•AH•toh) effectively captured human emotions in a series of frescoes portraying the life of Francis of Assisi. In the 1400s Florentine artist Masaccio (muh•ZAH•chee•oh) employed lighting and perspective in his paintings to give depth to the human body and to set off his figures from the background. He thus created an even greater sense of realism than Giotto had.

Timur Lenk Rebuilds Central Mosque

Samarkand, 1404
Timur Lenk (Tamerlane), the Mongol ruler, decided to rebuild the central mosque in Samarkand, making it grander than any in Asia. The Bibi Khanum mosque consisted of 4 vaulted halls. Its 480 marble pillars were carried by teams of elephants from quarries 25 miles (40 km) away. The vault of the central dome was so large that one of its gold inscriptions reportedly could be read a mile away. Shortly after completion the central dome collapsed.

Renaissance Arts
What changes did Renaissance artists bring to the arts of Europe?
They broke with medieval symbolism and brought a new realism to the arts, experimenting with new techniques, such as perspective; much Renaissance art was still devoted to religious topics, but Renaissance artists also turned to classical mythology.

Have students use the **Chapter 16 Student Web Activity** at worldhistory.glencoe.com for in-depth study of Renaissance art.

ASSESS

Check for Understanding
Assign Section 1 Assessment as homework or as an in-class activity.

▣ Use Interactive Tutor Self-Assessment Software to review Section 1.

MAKING CONNECTIONS ACTIVITY

Sports The Renaissance revived the Greek concept that an ideal person participated in a variety of activities, including sports. Have students research and report to the class on one of the following popular Renaissance games or sports: javelin hurling, tennis, chess, archery, fencing, boxing, falcony, hunting, and gambling. Tell students to explain how these sports or games are alike or different from the same activities today. Ask students to bring props for their reports and, if possible, to give a brief demonstration of the skills needed for their game or sport. **L2**

TEACH

Tell students that to show life and activity, Leonardo chose to illustrate the moment when Jesus says that one of his disciples will betray him. The disciples are caught as they ask, "Is it I?" Encourage students to compare this painting with religious paintings of the Middle Ages and to note the differences in style and subject matter.

More About . . .

The Last Supper A friend of Leonardo's suggested that he leave the face of Jesus incomplete so viewers would not compare Jesus to the disciples.

CURRICULUM CONNECTION

TECHNOLOGY

Because Leonardo believed that an artist's most important work was thinking and planning rather than the actual painting or brush strokes, he didn't use the standard fresco technique of painting on wet plaster, which required quick, certain strokes. Instead, he painted *The Last Supper* on dry plaster with tempera. That is why the painting soon started to deteriorate.

"The Last Supper"

Victor R. Boswell, Jr.

"One of you shall betray me," said Jesus, sitting amid the disciples gathered around in a flurry of worry, gossip, and fear. Between 1495 and 1497 Leonardo da Vinci painted *The Last Supper* on the walls of a monastery in Milan, Italy. Unstable paint and centuries of wear slowly destroyed the mural. In 1977 restoration of the painting began, as shown in the detail (above) depicting the apostles Matthew, Thaddeus, and Simon. The larger view of the master-piece (left) shows visitors clustered around restorers continue their work.

Da Vinci was one of the most famous pain the Italian Renaissance. During the Renaissan peoples of Europe began to see themselv Europeans rather than as members of the kingd Christendom whose single passport was belie Renaissance was a period of upheaval and cha religion, politics, and economy. The arts flour Writers began using the language of their own n instead of Latin. Painters, architects, and scu experimented with new techniques. Expressi belief in the newfound power of paintings, da boasted that the painter could "even induce m fall in love with a picture that does not portra living woman." Indeed, people throughout the have fallen in love with *The Last Supper*. ⊕

One of the greatest Renaissance artists was **Leonardo da Vinci** (VIHN•chee). A citizen of Florence, he did much of his work in Milan and Rome. Da Vinci is best known for the *Mona Lisa*, a portrait of a strangely smiling young woman of Florence, and *The Last Supper*, a wall painting of Jesus' last meal with his disciples. Da Vinci skillfully portrayed his subjects' personalities and feelings. He also made designs on astronomy, mathematics, and anatomy. These drawings often pictured parachutes, flying machines, and other mechanical inventions far ahead of his time.

Another outstanding Renaissance artist—Michelangelo Buonarroti—began his career as a sculptor in Florence. There he did a famous marble statue of David, after the heroic biblical king. Later in Rome he sculpted *La Pietà* (PEE•ay•TAH), which shows the dead Jesus in the arms of his mother, Mary. Most of Michelangelo's sculptures were awesome in size and suggested controlled but intense emotions.

In 1508 Pope Julius II hired Michelangelo to paint the Vatican's Sistine Chapel ceiling with scenes from the Bible. All Michelangelo's painted figures resembled sculptures. They had well-formed muscular bodies that expressed vitality and power. Michelangelo ended his career by designing the dome of the new St. Peter's Basilica.

Raphael Santi also worked at the Vatican. He completed a series of paintings on classical and religious themes for the pope's apartment. Raphael is most noted for his paintings of Mary, the mother of Jesus. These works reflected the Renaissance ideals of grace, harmony, and beauty.

Women and the Arts

Although Renaissance women had few roles independent of men, some of them did contribute to the arts. These women were either daughters of artists who trained in their fathers' workshops or children of noblemen, who were expected to have literary, musical, and artistic skills. Among the most celebrated female artists were the portrait painters

History & Art *La Pietà* by Michelangelo Buonarroti. St. Peter's Basilica, The Vatican, Rome, Italy
What is the subject of La Pietà*?*

Lavinia Fontana and Sofonisba Anguissola (soh•foh•NIHZ•bah ahn•gwee•SOH•lah). An Italian noblewoman, Anguissola became a painter at the Spanish royal court of King Philip II.

WORLD HISTORY Online

Student Web Activity 16

Visit the *World History: The Human Experience* Web site at **worldhistory.glencoe.com** and click on *Chapter 16—Student Web Activities* for an activity relating to Renaissance art.

SECTION 1 ASSESSMENT

Main Idea
1. Use a web diagram like the one below to show major factors that inspired the Renaissance.

Recall
2. **Define** humanism, secular, individualism, sonnet, doge.
3. **Identify** Niccolò Machiavelli, Lorenzo de' Medici, Savonarola, Michelangelo Buonarroti, Leonardo da Vinci.

Critical Thinking
4. **Making Comparisons** How does the role of female artists

today compare with the role of female artists during the Renaissance?

Understanding Themes
5. **Innovation** Identify one masterpiece in Renaissance literature or the arts. Explain how it reflects Renaissance ideals. Also state what subject is represented.

Chapter 16 *Renaissance and Reformation* **411**

---

c.1456 Johannes Gutenberg uses movable metal type in printing.

1494 Francis I of France invades Italy.

1509 Desiderius Erasmus writes *The Praise of Folly*.

Section 2

The Northern Renaissance

Read to Find Out
Main Idea *The Renaissance spread from Italy to northern Europe.*

▶ **Terms to Define**
   châteaux

▶ **People to Meet**
   Johannes Gutenberg, Michel de Montaigne, François Rabelais, Desiderius Erasmus, Jan and Hubert van Eyck, Pieter Brueghel, Thomas More, William Shakespeare

▶ **Places to Locate**
   the Low Countries

Storyteller

When Shakespeare's play Hamlet *opened in London, about 2,000 people crowded in to see the performance. Admission was one penny. Down in front of the stage, where it was standing room only,*

the crowd could be noisy. One writer complained: "Such heaving, and shoving, such pushing and shouldering— especially by the women! Such care for their clothes, that no one step on their dress;.... Such smiling and winking.... Never mind the stage—it is a comedy to watch them!"

—freely adapted from *Shakespeare: Of an Age For All Time,* The Yale University Festival Lectures, edited by Charles Tyler Prouty, 1954

William Shakespeare

During the late 1400s, Renaissance art and humanist ideas—characterized by a revival of interest in classical antiquity—began to filter northward from Italy to France, England, the Netherlands, and other European countries. War, trade, travel, and a newly invented method of printing helped to promote this cultural diffusion. The people of the Northern Renaissance adapted ideas of the Italian Renaissance to their own individual tastes, values, and needs.

Spreading Ideas

War, as usual, helped spread ideas by furthering contact between people of different cultures. After France invaded Italy in 1494, French kings and their warrior-nobles became fascinated by Italian Renaissance art and fashions. In 1517 King Francis I brought Leonardo da Vinci to his court in France, thus helping to promote the entry of Renaissance ideas into northern Europe. Other European monarchs also developed an enthusiasm for the Renaissance. Kings and queens so eagerly supported scholars and artists that the number of humanists in the north grew rapidly along with the popularity of humanist ideas.

At the same time, Italian traders living in the north set an example for northern European merchants, who began to appreciate wealth, beauty, personal improvement, and other Renaissance values. These northern merchants—having only recently become successful enough to afford lifestyles based upon such values—began to spend their wealth on education, fine houses, and material goods. Some northern Europeans began to travel to Italy to study with Italian masters. Thus began the emergence of a newly educated middle class.

412 Chapter 16 *Renaissance and Reformation*

This spread of knowledge among the middle class was aided by the invention of the printing press. By the 1400s, German engravers had developed movable type, in which the type was set into adjustable molds, inked, and then pressed onto a sheet of paper. In 1456 **Johannes Gutenberg** printed a complete edition of the Bible using movable metal type. As a result of this invention, books were published more quickly and less expensively. Production of humanist texts could now begin to match the newfound desire for such works.

Although Italian Renaissance ideas became quite popular in the north, they were not merely transplanted there. Rather, northern scholars interpreted them according to their own individual ways of thinking. Furthermore, the people of each northern culture adapted these ideas to suit their own needs and traditions.

The French Renaissance

The French Renaissance had a character all its own. French architects blended medieval Gothic towers and windows with the classical arches used by Italian architects to create châteaux (sha•TOHZ), or castles, for Francis I and his nobles. These country estates were erected mainly in the Loire valley.

Many French Renaissance writers borrowed extensively from the new literary forms of the Italian Renaissance. Inspired by Petrarch's sonnets, Pierre Ronsard (rohn•SAHR) wrote his own sonnets with common humanist themes such as love, the passing of youth, and the poet's immortality. **Michel de Montaigne** (mahn•TAYN) may have based his informal and direct style on Italian literary models. He cultivated the literary form called the personal essay, a short prose composition written to express clearly the personal view of a writer on a subject. In his essay "Of the Disadvantages of Greatness," Montaigne analyzed the authority of royalty:

> ❝ The most difficult occupation in the world, in my opinion, is to play the part of a king worthily. I excuse more of their faults than people commonly do, in consideration of the dreadful weight of their burden, which dazes me. It is difficult for a power so immoderate to observe moderation.... ❞

Physician-monk **François Rabelais** (RA•buh•LAY), France's most popular Renaissance author, wrote comic tales, satires, and parodies on a broad spectrum of contemporary life. He rejected the Middle Ages' focus on the afterlife and believed

Visualizing History *Erasmus* by Quentin Metsys. The "Prince of the Humanists" joined a love for the classics with respect for Christian values. *What reforms did Christian humanists promote?*

that people should enjoy life to the fullest. He also wrote on such subjects as law, medicine, politics, theology, botany, and navigation.

Northern Europe

The Italian Renaissance was enthusiastically accepted by the wealthy towns of Germany and **the Low Countries** (present-day Belgium, Luxembourg, and the Netherlands). Universities and schools promoted humanist learning, and printers produced a large quantity of books. Latin was still the main scholarly language, but writers increased their use of German and Dutch.

Christian Humanism

Unlike in Italy, the Renaissance in northern Europe had a more religious tone. Groups of scholars, known as Christian humanists, wanted reforms in Catholicism that would eliminate abuses and restore the simple piety of the early Church. They believed that humanist learning and Bible study were the best ways to promote these goals.

The most famous Christian humanist, **Desiderius Erasmus** (dehz•ih•DEER•ee•uhs ih•RAZ•muhs), inspired his colleagues to study Greek and Hebrew so that they could understand older versions of the Bible written in these lan-

Chapter 16 *Renaissance and Reformation* 413

TEACH

Guided Practice

THEME Cultural Diffusion

Ask students how ideas were transported during the time of the Northern Renaissance. *(war, as when France invaded Italy; traveling merchants; new, more affordable printed books)* **L1**

Visualizing History With the help of the printing press, Erasmus became a best-selling author.
Answer to Caption: *They wanted to eliminate abuses in the Catholic Church and restore piety through humanist learning and Bible study.*

Literature Have students identify the contributions of Ronsard, Montaigne, Erasmus, Thomas More, and Shakespeare. **L2**

📖 Focus on World Art Print 18, Pieter Brueghel. *The Wedding Dance*

Who?What?Where?When?

The Book of Manners by Giovanni della Casa stated, "Anyone whose legs are too thin, or exceptionally fat, ... should not wear vivid or parti-colored hose, in order not to attract attention to his defects."

Independent Practice

🗂 Guided Reading Activity 16-2 **L1**

Government Have students research to compare the views of Montaigne and Machiavelli on how a ruler should exercise authority. **L3**

History & Art

 Brueghel, disguised as a peasant, attended village fairs and recorded dances and children's games in his sketchbook.

Answer to Caption: *realistic portraits, religious themes, landscapes, and scenes of daily life*

ASSESS

Check for Understanding

Assign Section 2 Assessment as homework or as an in-class activity.

▣ Use Interactive Tutor Self-Assessment Software to review Section 2.

Evaluate

📁 Section Quiz 16-2

▣ Use the Testmaker to create a customized quiz for Section 2.

Reteach

Have students create a list on the chalkboard of specific accomplishments and innovations of the Northern Renaissance that show the influence of ideas from Italy.

📁 Reading Essentials and Study Guide

Enrich

Have students write a report using outside sources on criticisms of Renaissance society by Thomas More, Rabelais, or Montaigne.

CLOSE

Lead students in a brief discussion that summarizes major characteristics of Northern Renaissance literature, painting, and architecture.

History & Art *Peasant's Dance* by Pieter Brueghel the Elder. **The painting emphasizes the enjoyments of common people.** *What four subjects did northern European realistic artists paint?*

guages. Erasmus also used biting humor to make people take a more critical view of society. He specifically attacked the wealth of Renaissance popes, as in his noted work, *The Praise of Folly*:

> ❝ Scarce any kind of men live more [devoted to pleasure] or with less trouble.... To work miracles is … not in fashion now; to instruct the people, troublesome; to interpret the Scripture, [too bookish]; to pray, a sign one has little else to do … and lastly, to die, uncouth; and to be stretched on a cross, infamous. ❞

Northern European Painters

Artists in northern Europe developed a style of painting that relied more on medieval than classical models. In the early 1400s, a group of Flemish painters, led by the brothers **Jan and Hubert van Eyck** (EYEK), painted scenes from the Bible and daily life in sharp, realistic detail. They developed the technique of painting in oils. Oils provided artists with richer colors and allowed them to make changes on the painted canvas. Painting in oils soon spread to Italy. Meanwhile, Italian Renaissance art reached northern Europe. Artists such as Albrecht Dürer and **Pieter Brueghel** (BROY•guhl) combined Italian technique with the artistic traditions of their homelands. They painted realistic portraits, religious themes, landscapes, and scenes of daily life.

The English Renaissance

Renaissance ideas did not spread to England until 1485, when the Wars of the Roses—bloody conflicts over who was the rightful heir to the throne—ended. Ultimately, the Tudor family defeated the York family, bringing the Tudor king Henry VII to power. Henry invited Italian Renaissance scholars to England, where they taught humanist ideas and encouraged the study of classical texts.

English humanists expressed deep interest in social issues. **Thomas More**, a statesman and a friend of Erasmus, wrote a book that criticized the society of his day by comparing it with an ideal society in which all citizens are equal and prosperous. The book, written in Latin, was called *Utopia*.

The English Renaissance was especially known for drama. The best-known English playwrights were **William Shakespeare** and Christopher Marlowe. They drew ideas for their works from medieval legends, classical mythology, and the histories of England, Denmark, and ancient Rome. Shakespeare dealt with universal human qualities such as jealousy, ambition, love, and despair so effectively that his plays are still relevant to audiences today.

SECTION 2 ASSESSMENT

Main Idea
1. Use a diagram like the one below to show the ways in which the Italian Renaissance spread to northern Europe.

> Spread of Italian Renaissance to Northern Europe

Recall
2. **Define** châteaux.
3. **Identify** Johannes Gutenberg, Michel de Montaigne, François Rabelais, Desiderius Erasmus, Jan and Hubert van Eyck, Pieter Brueghel, Thomas More, William Shakespeare.

Critical Thinking
4. **Applying Information** Choose one northern European writer or artist and explain how his or her works reflected Renaissance ideas.

Understanding Themes
5. **Cultural Diffusion** In what ways did northern Europe alter Renaissance ideas?

414 Chapter 16 *Renaissance and Reformation*

SECTION 2 ASSESSMENT ANSWERS

1. war (France invaded Italy); trade; travel (northern Europeans traveled to Italy to study with Italian masters); Gutenberg's newly invented printing method; emergence of newly educated middle class in Europe
2. All terms are defined in the Glossary.
3. Johannes Gutenberg, 413; Michel de Montaigne, 413; François Rabelais, 413; Desiderius Erasmus, 413; Jan and Hubert van Eyck, 414; Pieter Brueghel, 414; Thomas More, 414; William Shakespeare, 414
4. Answers should incorporate humanistic themes of the Renaissance.
5. **CULTURAL DIFFUSION** it was more religious; art based on a medieval model

1517 Martin Luther preaches against indulgences.

1520 The Church condemns Luther's works.

c. 1550 Lutheranism spreads through northern Europe.

Section 3

The Protestant Reformation

SECTION THEME

▶ **Conflict** Martin Luther's protests against the Catholic Church result in Protestantism.

Guide to Reading

Read to Find Out
Main Idea *Luther's religious reforms led to Protestantism, a new branch of Christianity.*

▶ **Terms to Define**
   justification by faith, indulgences, vocation

▶ **People to Meet**
   Martin Luther, Pope Leo X

▶ **Places to Locate**
   Wittenberg, Worms

Guide to Reading

For reading strategies to help students read effectively see pages 12–13.

Vocabulary Pre-check

◉ Use the Vocabulary PuzzleMaker for Chapter 16 to create a crossword puzzle to reinforce section terms. **L1 LEP**

📁 Use Vocabulary Activity 16 to introduce vocabulary terms. **L1 LEP**

The Storyteller

In later years, Martin Luther remembered the fateful day he entered the monastery: "Afterwards I regretted my vow, and many of my friends tried to persuade me not to enter the monastery. I, however, was determined to go through with it.... I invited certain of my best men friends to a farewell party.... In tears they led me away; and my father was very angry ... yet I persisted in my determination. It never occurred to me to leave the monastery." Luther's break with the Church was an even bigger decision than the one to enter monastic life.

—adapted from *Luther and His Times*, E.G. Schweibert, 1950

Martin Luther

The Renaissance values of humanism and secularism stimulated widespread criticism of the Catholic Church's extravagance. By about 1500, educated Europeans began calling for a reformation—a change in the Church's ways of teaching and practicing Christianity. In Germany the movement for church reform eventually led to a split in the Church that produced a new form of Christianity known as Protestantism. The series of events that gave birth to Protestantism is known as the Protestant Reformation.

Martin Luther

The Protestant Reformation was begun by a German monk named **Martin Luther**, born in 1483, the son of middle-class townspeople. His father wanted him to become a lawyer, but Luther was interested in religion. In 1505 he was nearly struck by lightning in a thunderstorm. Terrified that the storm was God's way of punishing him, the law student knelt and prayed to Saint Anne. In return for protection, he promised to become a monk. Shortly thereafter, Luther entered a monastery.

As a young monk, Luther struggled to ensure his soul's salvation. He would confess his sins for hours at a time. Yet still he worried that God might not find him acceptable.

Then he read Saint Paul's Epistle to the Romans: "He who through faith is righteous shall live"—and Luther's worries dissolved. He interpreted this to mean that a person could be made just, or good, simply by faith in God's mercy and love. Luther's idea became known as justification by faith. Luther later stated that because of this discovery he felt as if he "had been born again and had entered Paradise through wide open gates."

FOCUS

Section Objective

Discuss how Luther's religious reforms led to Protestantism, a new branch of Christianity.

BELLRINGER
Motivational Activity

Before taking roll at the beginning of the class period, project Section Focus Transparency 16-3 and have students answer the activity questions. Discuss students' responses.
📁 This activity is also available as a blackline master.

SECTION RESOURCES

📁 **Reproducible Masters**
• Lecture Notes 16-3
• Reproducible Lesson Plan 16-3
• Vocabulary Activity 16
• Guided Reading Activity 16-3
• People in World History Profile 29
• Section Quiz 16-3
• Reading Essentials and Study Guide 16-3

🖋 **Transparencies**
• Section Focus Transparency 16-3

Multimedia
💻 Interactive Tutor Self-Assessment Software
💻 Testmaker
🌐 Turning Points in World History: *The Reformation*

TEACH

Guided Practice

THEME Conflict

Important historical events often occur when ideas come into conflict. Ask students to describe conflicting ideas that led to the development of Lutheranism. **L1**

Luther's Protest

How did Luther's protest affect European religious life?

His protest led to the rise of Protestantism. In challenging the pope's authority, Luther also contributed to ending the religious unity of western Europe.

VIDEODISC

Turning Points in World History

Side One
Chapter 8

Title: *The Reformation*

Ask: Who was Martin Luther?
(a professor and priest who founded Lutheranism)

Independent Practice

 Guided Reading Activity 16-3 **L1**

ANSWER

Books were printed at less cost and were able to circulate, aiding in the spread of ideas. The printing press got Luther's books quickly into readers' hands—spreading Protestantism; imprints from computer files, the development of the Internet and E-mail

---

Luther's Protest

Luther's ideas gradually matured and eventually brought him into conflict with the Church. At this time **Pope Leo X** was trying to raise money to rebuild St. Peter's Basilica in Rome. To this end, the pope sold church positions to his friends and also authorized sales of indulgences.

Indulgences were certificates issued by the Church that were said to reduce or even cancel punishment for a person's sins—as long as one also truly repented. People purchased indulgences believing that the document would assure them admission to heaven. John Tetzel, the Church's agent for selling indulgences in northern Germany, even went so far as to promise peasants that indulgences would relieve them of guilt for *future* sins. He also encouraged people to buy indulgences for the salvation of their dead relatives. Tetzel's sale of indulgences inspired a popular jingle: "Once you hear the money's ring, the soul from purgatory is free to spring." (According to church teaching, pur-

gatory is a place in the afterlife where people are made fit for heaven.)

Luther, a professor and priest in the town of **Wittenberg**, preached against the sale of indulgences. He also lectured against other church practices he believed were corrupt. Then, on October 31, 1517, Luther nailed on the door of the Wittenberg Church a placard with 95 theses, or statements, criticizing indulgences and other church policies.

Breaking With Rome

Printed copies of the Ninety-five Theses spread quickly all over Germany. Sales of indulgences declined sharply. Encouraged by this reaction, Luther published hundreds of essays advocating justification by faith and attacking church abuses.

Pope Leo X responded to the decline in indulgence sales by sending envoys to Germany to persuade Luther to withdraw his criticisms. But Luther refused. In 1520 the pope formally condemned Luther and banned his works. In 1521 Pope Leo X excommunicated Luther from the Church.

Shortly after Luther's excommunication, a diet, or council, of German princes met in **Worms**, Germany, to try to bring Luther back into the Church. They decided that Luther should take back his crit-

Science and Technology

Printing

Before the 1400s books had to be copied by hand—a time-consuming method. Consequently, books were rare, owned and read only by scholars and the wealthy. Gutenberg's invention of movable type changed all that: books could be produced faster at lower cost; more people were able to buy books and expand their knowledge; and traditional ideas were questioned. German printers quickly adopted Gutenberg's invention and set up similar printing presses in other European countries.

Martin Luther was one of the first authors to benefit from the new technology. Since his books could be reproduced inexpensively and in large quantities, they could be easily obtained throughout Europe shortly after Luther completed them. Thus, Luther was able to spread his ideas and

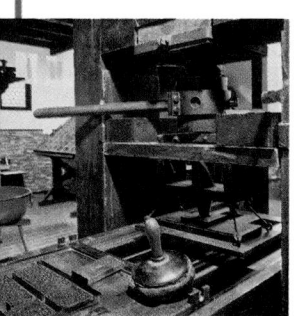

Gutenberg's press

gain widespread support before the Catholic Church could respond.

In the past few decades, more advances have been made in printing than in all the years since Gutenberg. Today high-speed machines and computer technology together have revolutionized the printing industry. Images are now transferred onto paper directly from computer files. The development of copy machines and laser printers has also made smaller printing jobs easier.

Linking Past and Present ACTIVITY

Describe how Gutenberg's printing press transformed European society during the 1400s and 1500s. How did Luther benefit from Gutenberg's invention? Explain how computer technology and other innovations have transformed printing and other means of communication today.

COOPERATIVE LEARNING ACTIVITY

Role Play Organize the class into five groups and have each group create a short television interview spot in which students interview either Tetzel on the sale of indulgences, Luther on his Ninety-five Theses, Pope Leo X on excommunicating Luther, Prince Frederick of Saxony on hiding Luther, or Luther on the teachings of Lutheranism. Encourage students to conduct research at the library. Have each group select a member to act as an interviewer and another member to be interviewed. All group members should prepare questions for the interview. After all interviews have been presented, have the class summarize the events that led to the Reformation. **L2**

History & Art

Luther Preaching to the Faithful, (artist unknown). National Museum, Copenhagen, Denmark *What was Luther's view of vocations?* (below) Indulgence box—an item that Luther opposed.

icisms of the papacy. Meanwhile, Luther traveled to Worms as crowds of cheering people lined the road. Luther strode into the assembly hall and, when asked to take back his teachings, gave this reply: "I am bound by the Sacred Scriptures I have cited … and my conscience is captive to the Word of God. I cannot and will not recant [take back] anything.… God help me." Luther, condemned as a heretic and outlaw, was rushed out of Worms and hidden at a castle in Wartburg by a friend, Prince Frederick of Saxony.

While in hiding, Luther translated the New Testament into German. Earlier German translations of the Bible were so rare and costly that few people had them. With Luther's more affordable translation, most people could now read the Bible.

Lutheranism

After Worms, Luther laid the foundation of the first Protestant faith: Lutheranism. While Catholicism stressed faith and good works in salvation and the importance of church teaching as a spiritual guide,

Lutheranism emphasized salvation by faith alone and the Bible's role as the only source of religious truth. Lutheran services centered on biblical preaching rather than ritual and were held in the language of the people instead of Latin. In this way people could understand and participate in the services. Luther and his followers also held that the Church was not a hierarchy of clergy, but a community of believers. All useful occupations, not just the priesthood, were vocations, or callings, in which people could serve God and neighbor.

Lutheranism brought a new religious message to Germany, but it also stirred social unrest among peasants wanting to end serfdom. When a major peasant revolt erupted in 1525, Luther, fearing social chaos, backed the princes against the peasants. The princes cruelly put down the uprising, killing thousands of people. Lutheranism became a more conservative movement as a result; however, it had already sown the seeds of more radical Protestant movements that would transform Europe's religious landscape.

SECTION 3 ASSESSMENT

Main Idea

1. Use a diagram like the one below to show Luther's actions that led to Church reform.

Luther's Actions

☐ → ☐ → Reform

Recall

2. **Define** justification by faith, indulgences, vocation.
3. **Identify** Protestant Reformation, Martin Luther, Pope Leo X.

Critical Thinking

4. **Synthesizing Information** If you wanted to protest against

something today, what medium would you use to communicate your cause? Why?

Understanding Themes

5. **Conflict** Why did Pope Leo X ask Martin Luther to recant his beliefs and then excommunicate him when Luther would not do so?

SECTION 3 ASSESSMENT ANSWERS

1. established belief in salvation by faith alone, Bible as only source of religious truth, Church as a community of believers, belief that all useful occupations were vocations to serve God, services with language of people, not Latin
2. All terms are defined in the Glossary.
3. Protestant Reformation, 415; Martin Luther,

415; Pope Leo X, 416

4. Possible answers might include television and newspapers, but students should give reasons for their choice of medium.
5. **CONFLICT** Possible answer: The pope exercised his authority as head of the Catholic Church in an attempt to stop criticism of a church practice.

Tell students that the painting illustrates many of Luther's beliefs: the importance of the sermon in services, having believers physically closer to the minister, baptism and the Lord's Supper as the only sacraments, simplified interior of churches.

Answer to Caption: *All occupations were vocations through which people could serve God and their neighbors.*

ASSESS

Check for Understanding

Assign Section 3 Assessment as homework or as an in-class activity.

🖳 Use Interactive Tutor Self-Assessment Software to review Section 3.

Evaluate

📁 Section Quiz 16-3

🖳 Use the Testmaker to create a customized quiz for Section 3.

Reteach

Ask students to explain the relevance of justification by faith and the sale of indulgences to Luther's break from the Catholic Church.

📁 Reading Essentials and Study Guide 16-3

Enrich

Have students imagine that they are living in Germany in the 1500s. Ask them to assert a Catholic or Lutheran point of view in a letter to the editor about the implications of Luther's reforms on the Catholic Church in Germany.

CLOSE

Have students list reasons that Lutheranism attracted many followers across Germany.

SECTION THEME

▶ **Cultural Diffusion** Protestant religious groups spread reform throughout northern Europe.

Guide to Reading

For reading strategies to help students read effectively see pages 12–13.

Vocabulary Pre-check

 Use the Vocabulary PuzzleMaker for Chapter 16 to create a crossword puzzle to reinforce section terms. **L1 LEP**

Use Vocabulary Activity 16 to introduce vocabulary terms. **L1 LEP**

FOCUS

Section Objective

Identify the different forms of Protestantism that emerged in Europe as the Reformation spread.

BELLRINGER
Motivational Activity

 Before taking roll at the beginning of the class period, project Section Focus Transparency 16-4 and have students answer the activity questions. Discuss students' responses.

This activity is also available as a blackline master.

Section 4

The Spread of Protestantism

Guide to Reading

**Read to Find Out
Main Idea** *Different forms of Protestantism emerged in Europe as the Reformation spread.*

▶ **Terms to Define**
theocracy, predestination

▶ **People to Meet**
Huldrych Zwingli, John Calvin, the Anabaptists, Henry VIII, Catherine of Aragon, Anne Boleyn, Edward VI, Mary, Elizabeth I

▶ **Places to Locate**
Zurich, Geneva

The Storyteller

Mary Queen of Scots was a prisoner for seventeen long years. What was she to do, as she and her keeper's wife sat together all that time? She could sew. Over the years, she and her attendant ladies embroidered seas of fabric: tablecloths, cushions, and hangings, every piece scattered with coats of arms and emblems, every piece sprinkled with gold and silver spangles to catch the light. Some became gifts; but occasionally her presents were rudely refused. Her own son, King James VI, returned a vest his mother had embroidered for him because she had addressed it to "The Prince of Scotland."

—adapted from *Mary Queen of Scots*, Roy Strong and Julia Trevelyan Oman, 1972

Mary Queen of Scots

418 Chapter 16 *Renaissance and Reformation*

---

lthough the Protestant Reformation spread throughout Europe in the 1500s, divisions began to appear within the movement soon after it had started. Not only did the Protestant reformers not believe in the same methods; they did not even agree on the same goals.

Swiss Reformers

After the rise of Lutheranism in Germany, many preachers and merchants in neighboring Switzerland separated from Rome and set up churches known as Reformed. **Huldrych Zwingli**, a Swiss priest who lived from 1484 to 1531, led the Protestant movement in Switzerland. Like Luther, Zwingli stressed salvation by faith alone and denounced many Catholic beliefs and practices, such as purgatory and the sale of indulgences. Unlike Luther, though, Zwingli wanted to break completely from Catholic tradition. He wanted to establish a theocracy, or church-run state, in the Swiss city of **Zurich**. By 1525 Zwingli had achieved this goal. But in 1531 war broke out over Protestant missionary activity in the Catholic areas of Switzerland. Zwingli and his force of followers were defeated by an army of Catholics.

In the mid-1500s **John Calvin**, another reformer, established the most powerful and influential Reformed group in the Swiss city of **Geneva**. Here Calvin set up a theocracy similar to Zwingli's rule in Zurich.

Born in 1509, Calvin grew up in Catholic France at the start of the Reformation. He received an education in theology, law, and humanism that prompted him to study the Bible very carefully and to formulate his own Protestant theology. In 1536 Calvin published his theology in *The Institutes of the Christian Religion*, soon one of the most

---

SECTION RESOURCES

Reproducible Masters
- Lecture Notes 16-4
- Reproducible Lesson Plan 16-4
- Vocabulary Activity 16
- Guided Reading Activity 16-4
- Section Quiz 16-4
- Reading Essentials and Study Guide 16-4

Transparencies
- Section Focus Transparency 16-4

Multimedia
- Interactive Tutor Self-Assessment Software
- Testmaker

popular books of its day, influencing religious reformers in Europe and later in North America.

The cornerstone of Calvin's theology was the belief that God possessed all-encompassing power and knowledge. Calvin contended that God alone directed everything that has happened in the past, that happens in the present, and that will happen in the future. Thus, he argued, God determines the fate of every person—a doctrine he called predestination.

To advance his views, Calvin tried to turn the city of Geneva into a model religious community. He began this project in 1541 by establishing the Consistory, a church council of 12 elders that was given the power to control almost every aspect of people's daily lives. All citizens were required to attend Reformed church services several times each week. The Consistory inspected homes annually to make sure that no one was disobeying the laws that forbade fighting, swearing, drunkenness, gambling, card playing, and dancing. It dispensed harsh punishments to those who disobeyed. This atmosphere earned Geneva the title "City of God" and attracted reformers from all over Europe.

Visitors to Geneva helped to spread Calvinism, or John Calvin's teaching, throughout Europe. Because the Calvinist church was led by local councils of ministers and elected church members, it was easy to establish in most countries. Furthermore, the somewhat democratic structure of this organization gave its participants a stake in its welfare and inspired their intense loyalty.

The people of the Netherlands and Scotland became some of Calvin's most ardent supporters. John Knox, a leader of the Reformation in Scotland, and other reformers used Calvin's teachings to encourage moral people to overthrow "ungodly" rulers. They preached, as Calvin had, "We must obey princes and others who are in authority, but only insofar as they do not deny to God, the supreme King, Father, and Lord, what is due Him." Calvinism thus became a dynamic social force in western Europe in the 1500s and contributed to the rise of revolutionary movements later in the 1600s and 1700s.

Radical Reformers

Several new Protestant groups in western Europe, called **the Anabaptists**, initiated the practice of baptizing, or admitting into their groups, only adult members. They based this practice on the belief that only people who could make a free and informed choice to become Christians should be allowed to do so. Catholic and established Protestant churches, in contrast, baptized infants.

Many Anabaptists denied the authority of local governments to direct their lives. They refused to hold office, bear arms, or swear oaths, and many lived separate from a society they saw as sinful. Consequently, they were often persecuted by government officials, forcing many Anabaptists to wander from country to country seeking refuge.

Although most Anabaptists were peaceful, others were fanatical in their beliefs. These zealots brought about the downfall of the rest. When in 1534 radical Anabaptists seized power in the German city of Münster and proceeded to burn books, seize private property, and practice polygamy, Lutherans and Catholics united to crush them. Together they killed the Anabaptist leaders and persecuted any surviving Anabaptist believers.

As a result, many Anabaptist groups left Europe for North America during the 1600s. In the Americas, the Anabaptists promoted two ideas that would become crucial in forming the United States of America: religious liberty and separation of church and state. Today, Protestant groups such as the Baptists, Mennonites, and Amish all trace their ancestry to the Anabaptists.

England's Church

Reformation ideas filtered into England during the 1500s. A serious quarrel between King **Henry VIII** and the pope brought them to the forefront.

The quarrel arose over succession to the throne. Of Henry's six children by **Catherine of Aragon**, only Mary survived. Henry wanted to leave a male heir to the throne to avoid civil war. Believing that Catherine was too old to have more children, the king decided to marry **Anne Boleyn**. In 1527 Henry asked the pope to agree to a divorce between himself and Catherine. But Catherine's nephew was the powerful Holy Roman Emperor Charles V, upon whom the pope depended for protection. Charles wanted Catherine to remain as queen of England in order to influence the country's policies in favor of

Footnotes to History

King Henry VIII

Henry VIII was a typical Renaissance ruler who tried to excel in many areas. He enjoyed tennis, jousting, music, and discussions about religion and the sciences. He wrote a book of theology and composed several pieces of music, one of which may have been the song "Greensleeves."

TEACH

Guided Practice

THEME Cultural Diffusion
Using a wall map, have students trace the spread of Protestantism from Germany to other European countries. **L1 LEP**

Politics Have students make a chart in which they show the country, leader, relation to government, and basic beliefs of Zwinglism, Calvinism, the Anabaptists, and Anglicanism. *(Example: Zwinglism—Zurich, Switzerland; Huldrych Zwingli; theocracy; salvation by faith alone.)* **L2**

Biography

The following videotapes are available from Glencoe:
- **Henry VIII**
- **Elizabeth I: The Virgin Queen**

Independent Practice
Guided Reading Activity 16-4 **L1**

ASSESS

Check for Understanding
Assign Section 4 Assessment as homework or as an in-class activity.

Use Interactive Tutor Self-Assessment Software to review Section 4.

COOPERATIVE LEARNING ACTIVITY

Panel Discussion Organize the class into five groups to prepare and present a panel discussion of Reformation movements in one of the following countries: Switzerland, Scotland, the Netherlands, England, or Germany (Anabaptists). Using outside sources, each group member should focus on a specific topic, such as leadership, religious beliefs, relationship to government, or important political events. Have each group appoint a member to serve as moderator or timekeeper. After each group member presents his or her topic, have the moderator summarize the panel's main points. After all panels have made their presentations, encourage the class to compare and contrast these Reformation movements. **L2**

History & Art Henry VIII was an absolute monarch. By placing his allies in positions of power in Parliament, he totally controlled England. **Answer to Caption:** *to show that breaking from the Catholic Church was the will of the English people, not merely a whim of his own*

Evaluate

Section Quiz 16-4

Use the Testmaker to create a customized quiz for Section 4.

Reteach

On the chalkboard, draw a time line from 1500 to 1600. On the time line, have volunteers mark important events from this section.

Reading Essentials and Study Guide 16-4

Enrich

Have students research the more recent history of one of the Protestant groups mentioned in this section. Have them prepare brief reports that include size of the sect today and where most members live, current beliefs and practices, and how the latter have evolved since the group's founding.

CLOSE

Ask students to compare the reasons that England became Protestant with the reasons Switzerland adopted Protestantism.

History & Art *Henry VIII,* a portrait by Hans Holbein, shows the king's splendid royal attire, reflecting his authority. *Why did Henry seek Parliament's support in breaking with the Catholic Church?*

his own interests. The pope refused Henry's request.

Henry would not be thwarted. With Parliament's support, he had a series of laws passed that separated the English Church from the pope. The most important law, the Act of Supremacy passed in 1534, made Henry head of the English Church instead of the pope. Despite this break with Rome, Henry was not a Protestant reformer. The new Church of England kept Catholic

doctrines and forms of worship. Devout Catholics, however, opposed the king's rule of the Church. The most noted Catholic, the humanist scholar Thomas More, was beheaded for treason in 1535. Henry took other measures against supporters of the old religion. Between 1536 and 1540, he closed monasteries and convents, seized their land, and shared the gains with nobles and other high officials. In this way, the king filled his treasury and ensured influential support for his religious policies.

Henry also worked to strengthen the succession to the throne. He had the Church of England end his marriage to Catherine and then wed Anne Boleyn. Anne bore him a daughter, Elizabeth. In the years that followed, Henry married four more times but had only one son, Edward. When Henry died in 1547, 9-year-old Edward succeeded him to the throne. The young king was dominated by devout Protestant officials who introduced Protestant doctrines into the Church of England.

When **Edward VI** died in his teens, his Catholic half sister **Mary** became queen. Mary tried to restore Catholicism in England and ended up burning hundreds of Protestants at the stake. This persecution earned her the nickname of "Bloody Mary" and only served to strengthen her people's support for Protestantism.

After Mary's death in 1558, her Protestant half sister, **Elizabeth I**, became queen. To unite her people, Elizabeth followed a moderate course in religion. She made the English Church Protestant with some Catholic features. Anglicanism, as this blend of Protestant belief and Catholic practice was called, pleased most English people. However, radical Protestants known as Puritans wanted to "purify" the English Church of Catholic rituals. Although at first small in numbers, the Puritans gradually became influential both in the Church of England and the English Parliament.

SECTION 4 ASSESSMENT

Main Idea
1. Use a diagram like the one below to identify different forms of Protestantism that arose during the Reformation.

Protestantism

Recall
2. **Define** theocracy, predestination.
3. **Identify** Huldrych Zwingli, John Calvin, the Anabaptists, Henry VIII, Catherine of Aragon, Anne Boleyn, Edward VI, Mary, Elizabeth I.

Critical Thinking
4. **Making Comparisons** How did Calvinist and Anabaptist attitudes differ about participating in government activities?
Understanding Themes
5. **Cultural Diffusion** Why did the Catholic Church want to stop the spread of Protestant ideas?

SECTION 4 ASSESSMENT ANSWERS

1. Zwingli's Reformed churches in Switzerland stressed salvation by faith alone; most powerful Reformed church, established in Geneva by Calvin, stressed that God had all encompassing power and knowledge; Anabaptists arose in western Europe and baptized adult members into group; Church of England established with king as its head

2. All terms are defined in the Glossary.
3. Huldrych Zwingli, 418; John Calvin, 418; the Anabaptists, 419; Henry VIII, 419; Catherine of Aragon, 419; Anne Boleyn, 419; Edward VI, 420; Mary, 420; Elizabeth I, 420
4. The Anabaptists denied the authority of

government in their lives and did not take part in government activities; the Calvinists set up a church-run state that had control over people's daily lives.

5. **CULTURAL DIFFUSION** Possible answer: The Catholic Church was losing members, money, and power, as well as influence over European governments.

Identifying Evidence

In a geography trivia game, you picked the following question: What is the longest river in the world? The game card says it is the Amazon River, but you think it is the Nile River. How can you prove you are right?

You must identify evidence that will establish your claim. In the example above, you could consult an atlas, almanac, or encyclopedia to find the lengths of both rivers. (The Nile River is 4,160 miles long, while the Amazon is 4,000 miles long.)

Learning the Skill

There are four basic kinds of evidence: 1) oral accounts (eyewitness testimony); 2) written documents (diaries, letters, books, articles); 3) objects (artifacts); and 4) visual items (photographs, videotapes, paintings). These kinds of evidence fall into one of two categories—primary evidence and secondary evidence.

Primary evidence is produced by participants or eyewitnesses to events. Eyewitness accounts or photographs of a fire are examples of primary evidence. Secondary evidence is produced later, by those who have not experienced the events directly. Textbooks and encyclopedias are examples of secondary evidence.

To identify evidence that proves a claim, first clearly define the claim. Search available information to find the kind of evidence that can prove or disprove the claim. Compare the pieces of evidence to see if they agree. Also, rate the objectivity of your evidence. If you consulted an atlas, almanac, or encyclopedia, these are all reliable sources of information. However, if you are using letters, diaries, and news accounts, carefully assess which evidence is most reliable.

Practicing the Skill

Read the claim below. Then read each piece of evidence that follows. Decide which pieces of evidence prove the claim to be true and explain why.

Claim: *Humanism's emphasis on the value of the individual led to artistic flowering in the Renaissance.*

1. In Renaissance Italy humanist scholars opened schools to promote the study of history, philosophy, Latin, and Greek.
2. Renaissance artists used painting and sculpture to convey human emotions and values.
3. In Rome, the pope and cardinals made up the wealthiest and most powerful class of people.
4. In England, William Shakespeare wrote plays that dealt with universal human qualities such as jealousy, ambition, love, and despair.
5. The invention of the printing press spread knowledge of humanism.

Applying the Skill

Think about this claim: Renaissance humanist values still dominate modern American culture. Find at least five pieces of evidence from newspapers, magazines, and other sources to prove or disprove this claim.

For More Practice

Turn to the Skill Practice in the Chapter Assessment on page 431.

The **Glencoe Skillbuilder Interactive Workbook**, Level 2 provides instruction and practice in key social studies skills.

ANSWERS TO PRACTICING THE SKILL

1. no
2. yes; tells that Renaissance artists showed human emotions in their works
3. no
4. yes; tells that Shakespeare wrote about human characteristics
5. no

TEACH

Identifying Evidence Show students a headline from a newspaper that states a claim or write the following headline on the chalkboard: *Worst Fire in City's History Kills 25.* Call on volunteers to explain what the headline is claiming. (*No other fire in the city's history has been as bad and that 25 people died in the fire.*) Ask students what kind of information they need to prove the claim made in the headline. (*information about previous fires; names of people who died in the fire*) Have students discuss where they might find this information. (*city histories, fire department records, interviews with long-time city residents*) Then ask which of these sources would be the most reliable. (*fire department records*) Tell students that identifying sources of evidence and determining their reliability are steps they should take when trying to prove a claim. Then have students complete the skill lesson.

Additional Practice

▭ Skill Reinforcement Activity 16

GLENCOE TECHNOLOGY

Glencoe's **Skillbuilder Interactive Workbook, Level 2** This interactive CD-ROM promotes student mastery of key social studies skills.

SECTION THEME

▶ **Reaction** The Catholic Church enacts its own reform, the Catholic Reformation.

Guide to Reading

For reading strategies to help students read effectively see pages 12–13.

Vocabulary Pre-check

🖉 Use the Vocabulary PuzzleMaker for Chapter 16 to create a crossword puzzle to reinforce section terms. **L1 LEP**

📁 Use Vocabulary Activity 16 to introduce vocabulary terms. **L1 LEP**

FOCUS

Section Objective

Describe how the Catholic Church tried to halt the spread of Protestantism.

BELLRINGER
Motivational Activity

Before taking roll at the beginning of the class period, project Section Focus Transparency 16-5 and have students answer the activity questions. Discuss students' responses.
📁 This activity is also available as a blackline master.

Section 5

The Catholic Reformation

Guide to Reading

Read to Find Out
Main Idea *The Catholic Church attempted to halt the spread of Protestantism.*

▶ **Terms to Define**
   seminary, baroque

▶ **People to Meet**
   Pope Paul III, the Jesuits, Ignatius of Loyola

▶ **Places to Locate**
   Trent

The Storyteller

The Inquisition sometimes used "ordeals" to determine guilt or innocence, confident that God would give victory to an innocent person and punish the guilty. In the "Trial of the Cross," both parties, accuser and accused, stood before a cross with arms outstretched. The first to drop his arms was judged guilty. In the "Trial by Hot Water," the accused lifted a stone from the bottom of a boiling cauldron. If, after three days, his wound had healed, he was innocent. In the "Trial by Cold Water," the accused was tied up and lowered into water. If he sank, he was innocent. If he floated, he was guilty.

—from *The Medieval Inquisition*, Albert Clement Shannon, 1983

Trial of Books *(detail)*

422 Chapter 16 *Renaissance and Reformation*

Most of the people in Spain, France, Italy, Portugal, Hungary, Poland, and southern Germany remained Catholic during the Protestant Reformation. Nevertheless, Catholicism's power was threatened by Protestantism's increasing popularity in northern Europe. To counter the Protestant challenge, Catholics decided to enact reforms. The Catholic Church had had a history of periodic reform since the Middle Ages. Thus, in the movement that came to be known as the Counter-Reformation, or Catholic Reformation, the Church eliminated many abuses, clarified its theology, and reestablished the pope's authority over church members.

TURNING POINT

Reaffirming Catholicism

During the 1530s and 1540s, **Pope Paul III** set out to reform the Church and stem the Protestant advance. To establish the goals of the Catholic Reformation, he called a council of bishops at **Trent**, Italy, in 1545.

The Council of Trent

The Council of Trent, which met in several sessions until 1563, reaffirmed Catholic teachings that had been challenged by the Protestants. Salvation, it declared, comes through faith and good works, and church tradition is equal to the Bible as a source of religious truth. The Latin Vulgate translation of the Bible was made the only acceptable version of scripture.

The Council also put an end to many church abuses. It forbade the selling of indulgences. Clergy were ordered to follow strict rules of behavior. The

---

SECTION RESOURCES

📁 **Reproducible Masters**
- Lecture Notes 16-5
- Reproducible Lesson Plan 16-5
- Guided Reading Activity 16-5
- Reteaching Activity 16
- Enrichment Activity 16
- Section Quiz 16-5

- Performance Assessment Activity 16
- Spanish Chapter Summary 16
- Reading Essentials and Study Guide 16-5

📷 **Transparencies**
- Section Focus Transparency 16-5
- World History and Art Transparency 21

Multimedia
- 📘 Focus on World Art Print 16
- 📀 Vocabulary PuzzleMaker Software
- 📀 Interactive Tutor Self-Assessment Software
- 📀 Testmaker

History & Art *The Council of Trent* by Titian. **Held off and on for about 20 years, this church council reaffirmed Catholic doctrine and introduced reforms.** *What Bible was made the only acceptable version?*

Council decided that each diocese had to establish a seminary, or theological school, to ensure a better-educated clergy.

The Inquisition

To deal with the Protestant threat, Pope Paul also strengthened the Inquisition. As you read in Chapter 12, the Inquisition was a church court set up to stamp out heresy. In addition to carrying out its traditional functions, the Inquisition in the 1500s introduced censorship to curtail humanist and Protestant thinking. In 1543 it published the Index of Forbidden Books, a list of works considered too immoral or irreligious for Catholics to read.

The Arts

The Church also used the arts to further the Catholic Reformation. The Council of Trent maintained the Church's elaborate art and ritual, and it declared that the Mass should be said only in Latin.

Church art and Latin ritual were to serve as sources of inspiration for educated and less educated Catholics alike. Many artists were influenced by the intensely emotional devotion of the Catholic Reformation. One of these was the Greek painter Domenikos Theotokopoulos, known in Spain as El Greco, or "The Greek." Residing in Spain, El Greco painted the saints in distorted figures that showed strong religious feelings.

As the Catholic Reformation spread through Europe, it helped spark a new style of art and architecture called baroque (buh•ROHK). The Renaissance arts had shown restraint, simplicity, and order, but the baroque arts stressed emotion, complexity, and exaggeration for dramatic effect. In painting, Peter Paul Rubens of Flanders was a master of the baroque style. He painted large altarpieces of emotional religious scenes as well as mythological subjects. Another master was the Spaniard Diego Velázquez, who painted portraits at the Spanish royal court. Among the most famous

Chapter 16 *Renaissance and Reformation* **423**

TEACH

Guided Practice

THEME Reaction

Ask students why the Catholic Reformation is also called the Counter-Reformation. (*The Catholic Church reacted to the challenges of the Protestant Reformation.*) **L1**

TURNING POINT

Reaffirming Catholicism
Why was the Council of Trent an important gathering in early modern Europe? *Council reforms enabled Catholicism to meet the challenge of the Protestant Reformation; it supported a new art form known as baroque that became widespread in Catholic Europe.*

The Arts Show students examples of work by baroque artists, such as Bernini, Caravaggio, Peter Paul Rubens, and Anthony Van Dyck. Have volunteers describe the works and comment on their effect on the viewer. **L2 LEP**

History & Art Wars, a plague in Trent, and the deaths of three popes, as well as many disagreements between delegates interrupted the sessions of the Council of Trent.
Answer to Caption: *the Latin Vulgate translation*

Focus on World Art Print 16, Lavinia Fontana. *Portrait of a Noblewoman*

World History and Art Transparency 21, *Herzogenburg Monastery*

COOPERATIVE LEARNING ACTIVITY

Visual Reports Organize the class into five groups. Using the map on page 424 as a guide, have one group create a large map showing the distribution of religions in Europe after the Council of Trent. Have the second group research the *Index of Forbidden Books* and make a list of well-known authors and books that were on the list over the years. Have the third group research the Inquisition and make drawings of the trials and punishments. Have the fourth group make an illustrated list of the main outcomes of the Council of Trent. Have the fifth group make a large world map showing areas of Jesuit missionary activities. Remind students to use library resources when needed. Have groups display their work on a Catholic Reformation bulletin-board display. **L1 LEP**

Map Study

Answer

Religious wars broke out.

Map Skills Practice

Reading a Map Which Protestant religion was a significant minority in largely Catholic France? *(Calvinism)*

Independent Practice

☐ Guided Reading Activity 16-5 **L1**

Foreign Affairs Have students choose an area where the Jesuits sent missionaries, such as China, Japan, or North America, and research the Jesuits' activities and accomplishments there. Let students share this information with the class. **L2**

Diplomacy Have students write a brief report on the safe-conducts issued to Protestants who addressed the Council of Trent. **L3**

Cultural Perspectives

No More Latin In the 1960s the Catholic Church convened the Second Vatican Council (the First Vatican Council had met in 1869 and 1870). One result was the decision to say Mass in the vernacular language of each country rather than in Latin.

ASSESS

Check for Understanding

Assign Section 5 Assessment as homework or as an in-class activity.

◉ Use Interactive Tutor Self-Assessment Software to review Section 5.

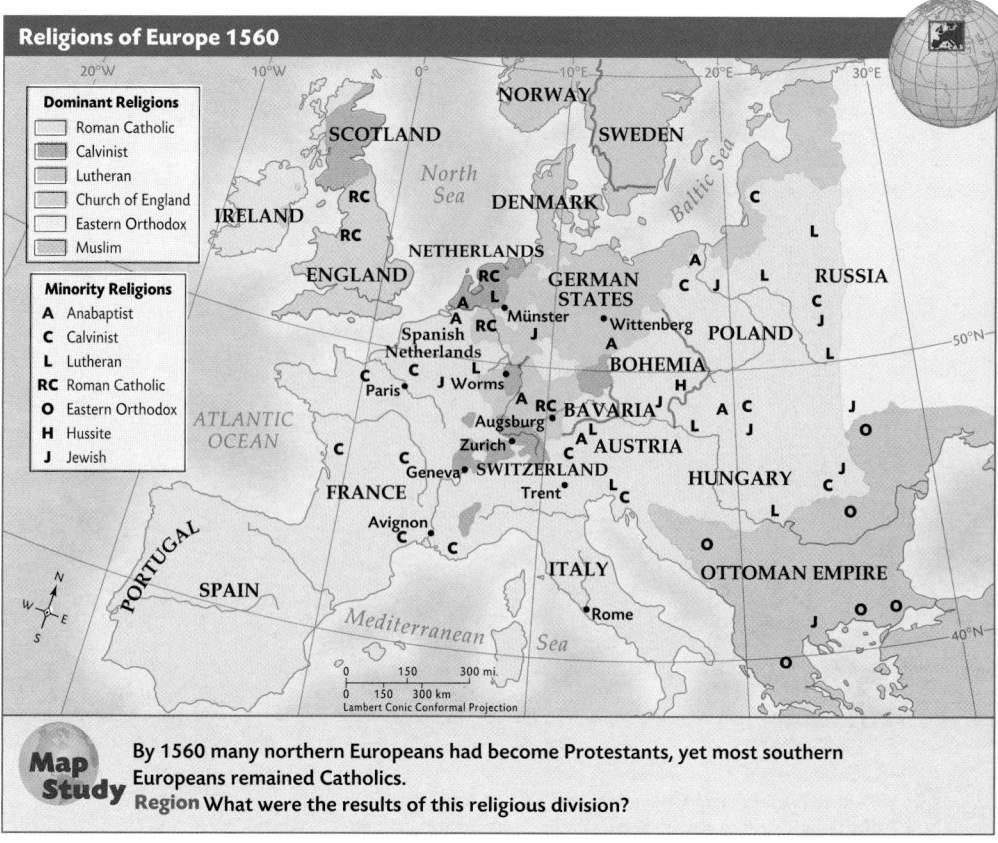

Religions of Europe 1560

Dominant Religions
- ☐ Roman Catholic
- ☐ Calvinist
- ☐ Lutheran
- ☐ Church of England
- ☐ Eastern Orthodox
- ☐ Muslim

Minority Religions
- **A** Anabaptist
- **C** Calvinist
- **L** Lutheran
- **RC** Roman Catholic
- **O** Eastern Orthodox
- **H** Hussite
- **J** Jewish

Map Study By 1560 many northern Europeans had become Protestants, yet most southern Europeans remained Catholics.
Region What were the results of this religious division?

baroque architects was the Italian artist Gian Lorenzo Bernini. His best known work is the public square of St. Peter's Basilica in Rome, which is enclosed by two great semicircles of columns.

Spreading Catholicism

The Church also set out to win converts and to strengthen the spiritual life of Catholics. Many religious orders and individuals in the Church became involved in these efforts.

Ignatius of Loyola

In 1540 the pope recognized a new religious order, the Society of Jesus, or **Jesuits**. Founded by **Ignatius of Loyola**, the Jesuits worked to spread Catholicism and combat heresy.

Ignatius was a Spanish noble whose military career had ended abruptly when he was wounded in battle. During a long recovery, he found comfort in the lives of the saints and vowed to serve God.

The outcome of his vow was the founding of the Jesuits, who followed a strict spiritual discipline and pledged absolute obedience to the pope.

The Jesuits wore the black robes of monks, lived simple lives, but did not withdraw from the world. They preached to the people, helped the poor, and set up schools. They also served as advisers in royal courts and founded universities. Jesuit centers of learning taught not only theology but also physics, astronomy, mathematics, archaeology, and other subjects.

As missionaries, the Jesuits helped strengthen Catholicism in southern Germany, Bohemia, Poland, and Hungary. They also carried their message to the Americas, Africa, and Asia. The Jesuit priest Matteo Ricci, for example, traveled to China and preached Christianity at the court of the Ming emperor. To make his message relevant to Chinese needs, Ricci learned to speak Chinese and dressed in Chinese clothing. Although he had little success in spreading his religious beliefs, Ricci shared with Chinese scholars his knowledge of European arts and sciences.

424 Chapter 16 *Renaissance and Reformation*

MEETING SPECIAL NEEDS ACTIVITY

Study Strategy Have students divide Section 5 into three parts according to the following headings: *Reforms in the Catholic Church, Missionary Activity of the Catholic Church, Results of the Reformation*. Then have students find similar headings in the text and write at least three outcomes under each heading. *(For example: Missionary Activity—Jesuit order formed; Jesuits retained church members in southern Germany, Bohemia, Hungary, and Poland; Jesuits establish universities throughout Europe.)* Tell students that *Reforms in the Catholic Church* corresponds with "Reaffirming Catholicism" in the text. **L2**

Teresa of Avila

Another supporter of Catholic renewal was the Spanish nun Teresa of Avila. Born to a noble family in 1515, Teresa entered a Carmelite convent. Daily life there, however, was not strict enough for the deeply religious Teresa, so she set up her own order of Carmelite nuns. Teresa later opened many new convents throughout Spain. Made a saint after her death, Teresa's spiritual writings rank as classics of Christianity.

A Divided Europe

While Catholicism carried out reforms, the Catholic Holy Roman Emperor Charles V tried, but failed, to stem the spread of Protestantism in his domains. Finally, in 1555, Charles and the German princes signed the Peace of Augsburg, which allowed each prince—whether Catholic or Lutheran—to choose the religion of his subjects.

This treaty set the stage for the division of Europe into a Protestant north and a Catholic south, a division that remains to this day. Northern Germany and Scandinavia were Lutheran. Areas of southern Germany, Switzerland, the Netherlands, and Scotland—with their economic wealth based in towns—held to Calvinism. England set up its own Anglican Church, a blend of Protestantism and Catholicism under royal control.

There were many reasons why Europeans in large numbers supported Protestantism. One reason was undoubtedly religious conviction. However, nonreligious factors were also involved. German princes often favored Protestantism in order to increase their power. They made Protestantism the official religion of their territories, placing it under their control. They also seized lands and wealth owned by the Catholic Church. Townspeople also rallied to the new faith, which supported their business practices. Above all, northern Europeans saw Protestantism as a way to

Visualizing History **Jesuit missionaries in Japan are depicted by a Japanese painter.** *Who founded the Society of Jesus?*

defy an Italian-controlled Catholic Church that drew so much money from their homelands.

During the 1500s and early 1600s, religious wars engulfed Europe, bringing widespread killing and destruction. In France, a struggle for the monarchy heightened bitter fighting between French Protestants, or Huguenots, and the Catholic majority. Both sides carried out terrible atrocities. The most infamous event was the Saint Bartholomew's Day Massacre. On that day—August 24, 1572—violence erupted that led to the killing of 3,000 Huguenots.

Religious bigotry also brought hard times to European Jews caught in the middle of the Christian feuding. One exception to this pattern of intolerance was the Netherlands, which took in Jews driven out of other areas of Europe.

SECTION 5 ASSESSMENT

Main Idea
1. Use a chart like the one below to show steps the Catholic Church took to stop the spread of Protestantism.

> Church's Efforts to
> Stop Protestantism
> _____
> _____
> _____

Recall
2. **Define** seminary, baroque.
3. **Identify** Pope Paul III, the Jesuits, Ignatius of Loyola.

Critical Thinking
4. **Analyzing Information** List any three of the reforms proposed by the Council of Trent.

Beside each reform, give the Protestant viewpoint to which it responded.

Understanding Themes
5. **Reaction** Which of the Catholic Church's actions against Protestantism were successful, and which were not?

Visualizing History In 1549 the Jesuits began their mission to Japan under the Spanish priest Francis Xavier. He learned Japanese and recommended that other missionaries follow local customs and use the native language.
Answer to Caption: *Ignatius of Loyola*

Evaluate

 Section Quiz 16-5

⬛ Use the Testmaker to create a customized quiz for Section 5.

Reteach

Have students summarize the Catholic Church's activities to halt the Protestant Reformation.

 Reteaching Activity 16

 Reading Essentials and Study Guide 16-5

Enrich

Have students do research on the Inquisition, the methods it employed, and how and why it eventually ended.

 Enrichment Activity 16

CLOSE

Have students make a wall chart summarizing the work of the Inquisition and the Council of Trent.

SECTION 5 ASSESSMENT ANSWERS

1. reaffirmed Catholicism: Council of Trent to reform church, strengthened Inquisition, used arts to further Catholic Reformation; spread Catholicism: set out to win converts, strengthened spiritual life of Catholics
2. All terms are defined in the Glossary.

3. Pope Paul III, 422; the Jesuits, 424; Ignatius of Loyola, 424
4. Sample answer: Council of Trent—salvation achieved through faith and works; Protestant viewpoint—salvation achieved by faith alone
5. **REACTION** Sample answer:

Catholic missionary activities were successful because they retained many church members; the Inquisition was unsuccessful because it aroused fears in Protestant countries of what might happen if Catholicism were restored.

The Prince

Historical Connection

Machiavelli's advice on how to rule a kingdom helps us to understand the way people in any age compete for power. He emphasizes how rulers really act, not how they should behave, a reflection of the focus on human behavior that began in Europe in the 1400s.

Background Information

Setting Machiavelli lived in a time of political instability in Italy. Tyranny, war, and corruption were common. Machiavelli believed that an effective ruler had to impose peace so that the country could progress.

Literary Elements Tone is the outlook of the writer toward his or her material. Machiavelli tries to achieve an objective tone. For example, when he describes "men in general" as "ungrateful, fickle, and deceitful," he neither condemns nor praises them for these traits.

Machiavelli's theme, the central idea in *The Prince*, is that the end justifies the means. The point of his handbook is to help a ruler stay in power at whatever cost.

from
The Prince
by Niccolò Machiavelli

Like many other Renaissance thinkers, Niccolò Machiavelli (1469–1527) analyzed human actions rather than spiritual issues. Unlike many of his contemporaries, however, he focused on the selfish side of human nature more than on humanity's potential for progress. Machiavelli observed how successful politicians won and secured power. He sent his thoughts to an Italian prince, hoping to win a position as an adviser. His ruthlessly honest look at how politicians act both confirms and challenges the views we have toward our leaders.

It is the custom of those who are anxious to find favor in the eyes of a prince to present him with such things as they value most highly or in which they see him take delight. Hence offerings are made of horses, arms, golden cloth, precious stones and such ornaments, worthy of the greatness of the Prince. Since therefore I am desirous of presenting myself to Your Magnificence with some token of my eagerness to serve you, I have been able to find nothing in what I possess which I hold more dear or in greater esteem than the knowledge of the actions of great men which has come to me through a long experience of present-day affairs and continual study of ancient times. And having pondered long and diligently on this knowledge and tested it well, I have reduced it to a little volume which I now send to Your Magnificence. Though I consider this work unworthy of your presence, nonetheless I have much hope that your kindness may find it acceptable, if it be considered that I could offer you no better gift than to give you occasion to learn in a very short space of time all that I have come to have knowledge and understanding of over many years and through many hardships and dangers. I have not adorned the work nor inflated it with lengthy clauses nor pompous or magnificent words, nor added any other refinement or extrinsic ornament wherewith many are wont to advertise or embellish their work, for it has been my wish either that no honor should be given it or that simply the truth of the material

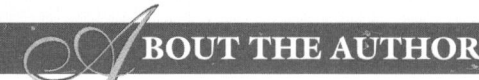

BOUT THE AUTHOR

Machiavelli was born into a poor family in Florence, Italy. For many years he served the ruler of Florence as an ambassador and military adviser. In 1512 Lorenzo de' Medici seized power in Florence and dismissed Machiavelli, who later settled in the countryside where he wrote *The Prince*. Machiavelli dedicated the book to Lorenzo de' Medici in the hope the ruler would forgive him and allow him back into the government.

In *The Prince*, Machiavelli says what many rulers believed but would never have dared declare in public. For centuries *Machiavelli* has been synonymous with amoral cunning.

and the gravity of the subject should make it acceptable....

As for the exercise of the mind, the prince should read the histories of all peoples and ponder on the actions of the wise men therein recorded, note how they governed themselves in time of war, examine the reasons for their victories or defeats in order to imitate the former and avoid the latter, and above all conduct himself in accordance with the example of some great man of the past....

We now have left to consider what should be the manners and attitudes of a prince toward his subjects and his friends. As I know that many have written on this subject I feel that I may be held presumptuous in what I have to say, if in my comments I do not follow the lines laid down by others. Since, however, it has been my intention to write something which may be of use to the understanding reader, it has seemed wiser to me to follow the real truth of the matter rather than what we imagine it to be. For imagination has created many principalities and republics that have never been seen or known to have any real existence, for how we live is so different from how we ought to live that he who studies what ought to be done rather than what is done will learn the way to his downfall rather than to his preservation. A man striving in every way to be good will meet his ruin among the great number who are not good. Hence it is necessary for a prince, if he wishes to remain in power, to learn how not to be good and to use his knowledge or refrain from using it as he may need....

Here the question arises; whether it is better to be loved than feared or feared than loved. The answer is that it would be desirable to be both

Visualizing History Machiavelli advised Lorenzo de' Medici, who became the ruler of Florence in 1513, to be as cunning as his grandfather, Lorenzo the Magnificent, shown here. *Why did Machiavelli believe it is better to be feared than loved?*

Chapter 16 *Renaissance and Reformation* **427**

OTHER WORKS OF OR ABOUT MACHIAVELLI

Bondanella, Peter, and Mark Musa, trans. *The Portable Machiavelli.* New York: Viking, 1979.

Detmold, Christian, trans. *Discourse on the First Ten Books of Livy.* New York: Modern Library, 1940.

History of Florence and the Affairs of Italy. Washington, DC: M. W. Dunne, 1901.

Hale, J.R., ed. and trans. *The Literary Works of Machiavelli.* New York: Oxford University Press, 1961.

FOCUS

Have students brainstorm a list of words that can be applied to politicians today. After they have come up with five or more words, ask them whether the connotations of each word are positive or negative.

Visualizing History The Medici were a leading family of Florence. Originally physicians—the family name means "doctors" in Italian—they later founded one of Italy's most important banking houses. **Answer to Caption:** *It is safer to be feared, if one must choose.*

TEACH

Evaluation

Point out that Machiavelli believed rulers could learn lessons from history. Ask students whether they agree with this idea. They may feel that although historical examples are often referred to in contemporary debates, history rarely teaches clear-cut lessons.

Comparison

Ask students to compare their view of human nature with that of Machiavelli. Challenge them to come up with examples that support their views. If they share Machiavelli's pessimism, they might use crime statistics to support the claim that people need to be strictly controlled. If they disagree with Machiavelli, they might point to the amount of charitable work people do.

Visualizing History

Cesare Borgia became famous throughout Italy as a brilliant but ruthless military tactician. When Machiavelli held Borgia up as a model ruler, many Italians were appalled.

Answer to Caption: *when it is not to his advantage or when his reasons for giving his word are no longer valid*

Interpretation

Discuss with students the implications of Machiavelli's ideas for a democracy. Some students may argue that if people are deceitful, a democracy is bound to fail. Others may argue that because people are deceitful, a democracy is the best way to check the power of individuals.

World Literature Selection 4

Linking Past and Present

Ethics Machiavelli pioneered the idea that rulers should be held to a looser moral standard because, to stay in power, they had to ignore ethics. Are politicians today held to a looser or stricter moral standard than ordinary citizens?

ASSESS

Assign **Responding to Literature** questions.

CAES·BORGIA·VALENTIN

Visualizing History This portrait of Cesare Borgia embodies the pride and confidence of the prince about whom Machiavelli wrote his political commentary. Borgia, the son of the controversial Pope Alexander VI, used his position as duke of Romagna to enhance papal political power. *When should a leader not keep his word, according to Machiavelli?*

but, since that is difficult, it is much safer to be feared than to be loved, if one must choose. For on men in general this observation may be made: they are ungrateful, fickle, and deceitful, eager to avoid dangers, and avid for gain, and while you are useful to them they are all with you, offering you their blood, their property, their lives, and their sons so long as danger is remote, as we noted above, but when it approaches they turn on you. Any prince, trusting only in their words and having no other preparations made, will fall to his ruin, for friendships that are bought at a price and not by greatness and nobility of soul are paid for indeed, but they are not owned and cannot be called upon in time of need. Men have less hesitation in offending a man who is loved than one who is feared, for love is held by a bond of

obligation which, as men are wicked, is broken whenever personal advantage suggests it, but fear is accompanied by the dread of punishment which never relaxes....

Hence a wise leader cannot and should not keep his word when keeping it is not to his advantage or when the reasons that made him give it are no longer valid. If men were good, this would not be a good precept, but since they are wicked and will not keep faith with you, you are not bound to keep faith with them....

So a prince need not have all the aforementioned good qualities, but it is most essential that he appear to have them. Indeed, I should go so far as to say that having them and always practicing them is harmful, while seeming to have them is useful. It is good to appear clement [merciful], trustworthy, humane, religious, and

ADDITIONAL LITERARY WORKS OF AND ABOUT THE PERIOD

Cao Xueqin. *Dream of the Red Chamber.* New York: Pantheon, 1958. Story of the problems faced by a well-to-do Chinese family in the 1700s.

Shakespeare, William. *Hamlet. Riverside Shakespeare.* Boston: Houghton Mifflin, 1974. Tragedy written in 1603 about a Danish prince and his Machiavellian uncle.

honest, and also to be so, but always with the mind so disposed that, when the occasion arises not to be so, you can become the opposite. It must be understood that a prince and particularly a new prince cannot practice all the virtues for which men are accounted good, for the necessity of preserving the state often compels him to take actions which are opposed to loyalty, charity, humanity, and religion. Hence he must have a spirit ready to adapt itself as the varying winds of fortune command him. As I have said, so far as he is able, a prince should stick to the path of good but, if the necessity arises, he should know how to follow evil.

A prince must take great care that no word ever passes his lips that is not full of the above mentioned five good qualities, and he must seem to all who see and hear him a model of piety, loyalty, integrity, humanity, and religion. Nothing is more necessary than to seem to possess this last quality, for men in general judge more by the eye than the hand; as all can see but few can feel. Everyone sees what you seem to be, few experience what you really are and these few do not dare to set themselves up against the opinion of the majority supported by the majesty of the state. In the actions of all men and especially princes, where there is no court of appeal, the end is all that counts. Let a prince then concern himself with the acquisition or the maintenance of a state; the means employed will always be considered honorable and praised by all, for the mass of mankind is always swayed by the appearances and by the outcome of an enterprise....

I am not ignorant of the fact that many have

Visualizing History *The Pier and the Ducal Palace* (detail) by Luca Carlevaris. *According to the principles of Machiavelli, why should a ruler carefully maintain the exterior of the palace?*

held and hold the opinion that the things of this world are so ordered by fortune and God that the prudence of mankind may effect little change in them, indeed is of no avail at all. On this basis it could be argued that there is no point in making any effort, but we should rather abandon ourselves to destiny. This opinion has been the more widely held in our day on account of the great variations in things that we have seen and are still witnessing and which are entirely beyond human conjecture. Sometimes indeed, thinking on such matters, I am minded to share that opinion myself. Nevertheless I believe, if we are to keep our free will, that it may be true that fortune controls half of our actions indeed but allows us the direction of the other half, or almost half....

Visualizing History Renaissance architecture revived the simplicity and symmetry of ancient Roman buildings. According to art historian Kenneth Clark, the buildings of Renaissance Italy are "an assertion of the dignity of man."
Answer to Caption: *because the exterior is the basis on which people form judgments about the ruler who lives inside*

CLOSE

Organize the class into small groups. Ask each group to prepare a rebuttal to Machiavelli's ideas. They could address his views of human nature, his analysis of politics, or the long-term effectiveness of his political tactics.

Contemporary Connection
Machiavelli says that a successful ruler must always appear good but can seldom afford to actually *be* good. Have students discuss the idea of appearances versus reality. Then have them write a short essay in which they analyze a person whose appearance belied his or her real nature.

Portfolio Project

Have students write an essay in which they discuss the qualities *they* believe a good political leader should have. Encourage them to support their assertions with examples from history and current events.

RESPONDING TO LITERATURE

1. Describe in your own words Machiavelli's view of human nature.
2. Write a brief essay giving an example that explains whether today's politicians follow Machiavelli's advice.
3. Propose an alternative principle to Machiavelli's view that "where there is no court of appeal, the end is all that counts."
4. **Making Judgments** Do you think individuals should follow Machiavelli's advice in dealing with their family, friends, and classmates? Why or why not?

Chapter 16 *Renaissance and Reformation* **429**

ANSWERS TO RESPONDING TO LITERATURE

1. Student answers should recognize that the view is largely pessimistic.
2. Essays should indicate that students understand Machiavelli's belief that politicians' lying is justified.
3. One alternative is the belief that immoral actions cannot lead to a moral end.
4. Answers will vary. Some students may realize that Machiavelli believed standards governing personal relationships differed from those he recommends to princes. Students should give supporting reasons for their views.

Have students use the **Chapter 16 Self-Check Quiz** at worldhistory.glencoe.com to prepare for the chapter test.

GLENCOE TECHNOLOGY

VIDEODISC

Use MindJogger to review the chapter.

MindJogger Videoquiz

Chapter 16
Disc 2 Side B

 Also available in VHS.

Answers

Using Key Terms

1. a	3. j	5. i
2. b	4. g	

Using Your History Journal

Suggest that students research one of the following: Mennonites, Puritans, Huguenots, or Quakers.

Reviewing Facts

1. architecture: returned to classical style of domes and columns, adorned buildings; painting: realistic style, frescoes, use of lighting and perspective, themes from classical mythology and Bible, gestures to convey emotions; sculpture: returned to classical ideals about human figure, biblical themes, studied anatomy

2. governed by wealthy families; nobles and bankers, middle class of shopkeepers and artisans, peasants and workers

3. Renaissance art and architecture were based on classical styles and were more realistic and more individualistic and worldly.

4. They caused greater religious diversity in Europe, aided in

---

WORLD HISTORY Online

Self-Check Quiz

Visit the *World History: The Human Experience* Web site at **worldhistory.glencoe.com** and click on *Chapter 16—Self-Check Quiz* to prepare for the Chapter Test.

Using Key Terms

Write the key term that completes each sentence. Then write a sentence for each term not chosen.

a. baroque	h. theocracy
b. humanism	i. doge
c. seminary	j. sonnet
d. vocations	k. châteaux
e. indulgences	l. secular
f. predestination	m. individualism
g. justification by faith	

1. The Catholic Reformation made use of a new style of art known as _____.
2. _____, or the Renaissance interest in the ancient classical writings, sparked an interest in human creativity and fulfillment.
3. A _____ was a Renaissance form of writing that developed that dealt with the theme of love.
4. _____ is the belief that a person could be made good simply by having faith in God's mercy and love.
5. The Italian city of Venice had a republican style of government headed by an elected official called a _____.

Technology Activity

Using a Computerized Card Catalog Make use of a library's computerized card catalog to choose a Renaissance artist to research. Find information about the person's life and achievements. Using your research, create an oral history about that person by role-playing him or her. Have the class ask you questions about your life and your contributions to the Renaissance. Your responses should reflect your researched information.

Using Your History Journal

One effect of the Reformation was the migration of thousands of people to colonial America. Research and write a brief history of one religious group's migration. Create a map that shows the origin and destination(s) of that group.

Reviewing Facts

1. **Culture** Use a chart like the one below to list the characteristics of Renaissance art.

Renaissance Art

Architecture	Painting	Sculpture

2. **Government/Culture** Explain how the city-states of Renaissance Italy were governed. What social classes were present in the typical city-state?
3. **Culture** Describe how the art and architecture of the Renaissance differed from the art and architecture of the Middle Ages.
4. **History** Discuss why the Protestant and Catholic Reformations were important turning points in the history of Europe.
5. **Culture** Explain why Henry VIII separated from the Catholic Church and created the Church of England.
6. **Culture** State how Ignatius of Loyola and Teresa of Avila helped to reform Catholicism.

Critical Thinking

1. **Apply** Why did the Medici rulers use tax revenues to fund public works projects that benefited all the citizens of Florence?
2. **Analyze** What were the causes of the Protestant Reformation? Could the Reformation have occurred without a reformer such as Luther?
3. **Evaluate** How did the religious reformations of the 1500s affect Europe? How might Europe's religious heritage affect efforts toward unity today?

---

reviving religious faith, and ushered in a period of religious warfare.

5. Henry wished to divorce Catherine of Aragon, and the pope denied permission.

6. Ignatius of Loyola founded the Jesuits, an order devoted to strengthening Catholicism and halting the spread of Protestantism; also promoted missionary work and education; Teresa of Avila encouraged religious devotion and founding of convents.

Critical Thinking

1. to win the loyalty of Florence's lower classes

2. dissatisfaction with church corruption; humanist questioning of church teaching; rise of princes and middle classes who resented church wealth and controls

3. They led to the division of Europe into Protestant and Catholic areas; students might note that religious differences play a smaller role in Europe's largely secular political life today.

4. Analyze Apollonio Giovanni, an Italian artist, painted the entry of a group of cavaliers into a town in the 1300s, shown below. In what ways does this painting show how Renaissance artists broke away from traditional forms?

Understanding Themes

1. Innovation Why did the Renaissance begin in Italy? How did the movement change European thought and culture?

2. Cultural Diffusion How did the people of northern Europe adapt Italian Renaissance ideas to their society?

3. Conflict Could the conflict between Luther and the pope have been resolved if either had reacted differently? Explain.

4. Cultural Diffusion What factors helped Protestant ideas to spread so rapidly?

5. Reaction In what ways could the Catholic Reformation be called the Counter-Reformation?

Skill Practice

Use the information in Chapter 16 to find evidence for each claim below. Then decide which claim you support.

1. Martin Luther was a sincere believer who only wanted to reform the Catholic Church.

2. Martin Luther was a rebel intent on splitting the Catholic Church.

Linking Past and Present

1. Do you think ancient Greek and Roman culture influences artists, architects, and writers as much today as it did during the Renaissance? Why or why not?

2. What ideas of the Protestant Reformation do you think affect the United States today?

Geography in History

1. Location What is the approximate location of the first Spanish bishopric in South America?

2. Region In what geographic region were most Spanish missions established during the 1500s?

3. Human/Environment Interaction Large areas of South America were unreached by missionaries in the first 200 years of Spanish, Portuguese, and French mission activity. What geographic feature contributed to this?

4. Place What river did Jesuit missionaries use as a means of gaining access to the interior of South America?

Catholic Missions in South America

---

4. **CULTURAL DIFFUSION** printing press, Bible in the vernacular, peasants wanting freedom from church oppression, rulers wanting church property

5. **REACTION** It was a response or reaction that countered the Protestant Reformation.

Skill Practice

Evidence for (1) may include the fact that Luther had had sincere struggles of conscience as a monk, had eventually become a priest, and had not proposed leaving the Church until after Worms; (2) may include the fact that Luther proclaimed his Ninety-five Theses in a challenging manner and made them as widely known as possible.

Linking Past and Present

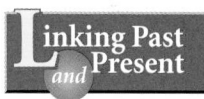

1. Yes: Western art is founded on styles developed by the Greeks and Romans. No: artists are exploring diverse influences and rejecting established rules in favor of individual expression.

2. Answers might mention separation of church and state and the value of diversity and toleration.

Geography in History

1. 66°W, 10°N

2. the northern and western coastal regions

3. tropical rain forests

4. Amazon

? Chapter Bonus Test Question

Ask students: Why was the time ripe for the Protestant Reformation? (*Answers may include: Italian humanism brought an emphasis on secular ideas, and Christian humanism in northern Europe focused on criticizing abuses in the Church and returning to the Church's piety.*)

---

4. figures and horses are lifelike and set off from the background; subject matter drawn from everyday life

Understanding Themes

1. **INNOVATION** Town life was stronger in Italy, enabling Italians to easily discard feudal ways and accept new ideas. Also, the classical tradition was stronger in Italy, once the center of the Roman Empire. The Renaissance led to a

focus on classical learning and the values of individualism and human achievement; society also became more secular in tone, although religious values were also held.

2. **CULTURAL DIFFUSION** Many added a religious emphasis to the classical ideals of the Italian Renaissance.

3. **CONFLICT** Possible answer: Luther might not have broken away from the Church had the pope responded thoughtfully to him.

A complete, 1-page lesson plan is provided for each section in the *Reproducible Lesson Plans* booklet.

Expanding Horizons

CHAPTER RESOURCES

	Reproducible Resources	Multimedia Resources
Chapter Opener	Chapter Themes: Graphic Organizer 17 Historical Significance Chapter Activity 17	MindJogger Videoquiz
Chapter Enrichment	Vocabulary Activity 17* Time Line Activity 17 Mapping History Activity 17 History Simulation 17 Geography and History Activity 17 Source Reading 17 People in World History Profiles 31, 32 World Art and Music Activity 17 Enrichment Activity 17 Critical Thinking Activity 17 Skill Reinforcement Activity 17 Building Skills in Geography Workbook, Unit 1, Lesson 11 Performance Assessment Activity 17 Standardized Test Practice Workbook Activity 17 Inclusion for the Social Studies Classroom Strategies and Activities	Focus on World Art Print 1, Jan Vermeer. *The Artist and His Model as Klio* World History and Art Transparencies 22, 23 Mapping History Overlay Transparency 11, *Triangular Trade Routes*; 12, *17th Century Latin American Viceroyalties* Chapter Transparency 17 NGS PicturePack Transparency Set: *The Age of Exploration, 1 & 2* Vocabulary PuzzleMaker Software NGS PictureShow CD-ROM: *The Age of Exploration, 1 & 2* Turning Points in World History World History Primary Source Document Library
Chapter Review/Reteaching	Reteaching Activity 17 Skill Reinforcement Activity 17 Spanish Chapter Summary 17	Chapter 17 Digest Audiocassette, Activity, Test* Vocabulary PuzzleMaker Software Interactive Tutor Self-Assessment Software MindJogger Videoquiz
Chapter Evaluation/Testing	Performance Assessment Activity 17 Chapter 17 Test, Forms A and B	ExamView® Pro Testmaker

0:00 OUT OF TIME? Assign the Chapter 17 Audiocassettes.

* *Also available in Spanish*

World History Primary Source Document Library

Make History Come Alive!

Engage your students with over 250 easily accessible primary source documents—available on this CD-ROM—that will give them real life insight into the important events of world history.

Block Schedule

Activities that are particularly suited to use within the block scheduling framework are identified throughout this chapter by the following designation.

KEY TO ABILITY LEVELS

Teaching strategies are coded for varying learning styles.

L1 BASIC activities for all students
L2 AVERAGE activities for average to above-average students
L3 CHALLENGING activities for above-average students
LEP LIMITED ENGLISH PROFICIENCY activities

Use Glencoe's *Presentation Plus!* multimedia teacher tool to easily present dynamic lessons that visually excite your students. Using Microsoft PowerPoint® you can customize the presentations to create your own personalized lessons.

Interactive Lesson Planner

Planning has never been easier! Using this CD-ROM, organize your week, month, semester, or year with all the help you need. The **Interactive Lesson Planner** gives you access to all of the blackline masters that accompany *World History: The Human Experience.*

SECTION RESOURCES

Daily Objectives	Reproducible Resources	Multimedia Resources
Section 1 **Early Explorations** Explain why Europeans risked dangerous ocean voyages to discover sea routes to other parts of the world.	Lecture Notes 17-1 Reproducible Lesson Plan 17-1 Vocabulary Activity 17* Guided Reading Activity 17-1* History Simulation 17 Time Line Activity 17 Source Reading 17 Section Quiz 17-1* Reading Essentials and Study Guide 17-1	Section Focus Transparency 17-1 Chapter Transparency 17 Interactive Tutor Self-Assessment Software Testmaker Turning Points in World History: *Age of Exploration*
Section 2 **Overseas Empires** Describe how Europeans exploited the lands and the peoples they found in Africa, Asia, and the Americas.	Lecture Notes 17-2 Reproducible Lesson Plan 17-2 Vocabulary Activity 17* Guided Reading Activity 17-2* People in World History Profiles 31, 32 Mapping History Activity 17 Geography and History Activity 17 Section Quiz 17-2* Reading Essentials and Study Guide 17-2	Section Focus Transparency 17-2 Mapping History Overlay Transparency 11, *Triangular Trade Routes*; 12, *17th Century Latin American Viceroyalties* NGS PicturePack Transparency Set: *The Age of Exploration, 1 & 2* Interactive Tutor Self-Assessment Software Testmaker NGS PictureShow CD-ROM: *The Age of Exploration, 1 & 2* Turning Points in World History: *Age of Exploration*
Section 3 **Changing Ways of Life** Analyze how increased trade and colonial expansion set the stage for a global economy.	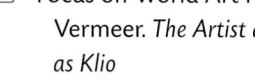 Lecture Notes 17-3 Reproducible Lesson Plan 17-3 Guided Reading Activity 17-3* Reteaching Activity 17 Enrichment Activity 17 Section Quiz 17-3* Performance Assessment Activity 17 Spanish Chapter Summary 17 Reading Essentials and Study Guide 17-3	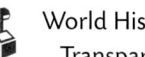 Focus on World Art Print 1, Jan Vermeer. *The Artist and His Model as Klio* Section Focus Transparency 17-3 World History and Art Transparency 22, *View of Toledo*; 23, *Mission San Xavier del Bac* Vocabulary PuzzleMaker Software Interactive Tutor Self-Assessment Software Testmaker

* Also available in Spanish

Chapter Activities

Performance Assessment Activity

A Court Case After students have studied the causes for and results of the era of exploration and mercantilism, have them demonstrate their understanding by taking the roles of modern-day government officials in one of the countries explored by Spain, England, and so on. Students who represent countries of the same empire should form groups to brainstorm ideas and plan a course of action intended to file suit in court and claim damages from the exploring country for lasting harm done to the explored country. Ideas may be presented in the form of a speech to a jury or testimony of experts in a role play, or letters laying out a plan of action.

Possible Rubric Features
Accuracy of content information, concept attainment, collaborative planning, argumentation, clarity of presentation (letter), and impact on audience

• *For an additional activity, refer to Activity 17 in the* Performance Assessment Strategies and Activities *booklet.*

ACTIVITY

From the Classroom of...

**Scott Shephard
Watertown Senior High School
Watertown, SD**

Why We Explore
Encourage students to think about the general reasons humans explore. This activity also encourages students to compare the motives of explorers from the age of exploration with those of explorers from other eras of investigation.

On the board, write the headings *Motives, Risks,* and *Significant Gains.* Ask students what they know about Christopher Columbus and fill in the chart with facts about his explorations.

Next, give students a list of famous explorers such as Neil Armstrong, Lewis and Clark, Yuri Gagarin, Marco Polo, and Edmund Hillary. Have students use classroom resources to find out about these people, then add facts about them to the chart on the board.

As a follow-up to this activity, ask students to draw some generalizations about the following: Why do we explore? Do the risks of exploration ever outweigh the gains? Was Columbus's voyage riskier than the *Apollo 11* moon mission? As a final evaluation, you might ask students to write an essay that compares and contrasts Columbus with another explorer they choose in the areas of motives, risks, and gains.

MULTIPLE LEARNING STYLES

Verbal/Linguistic
During the age of exploration, many Europeans believed in terrible sea monsters and odd beings that inhabited unknown lands. Have students research and report on some of these legends.

Logical/Mathematical
Have students create a time line of all the voyages of exploration and all the colonial activities described in this chapter.

Visual/Spatial
Have students research Columbus's life and create a mural that summarizes its highlights.

Auditory/Musical
Many old folk songs, such as "Upon Sir Francis Drake's Return," relate stories about the sea. Have students locate such folk songs and report on them. Students may refer to the *Oxford Book of Sea Songs,* edited by Roy Palmer (New York: Oxford University Press, 1986) or obtain recordings of some of the songs from the public library and play them for the class.

GLENCOE'S **ASSESSMENT** ADVANTAGE

Use the following to easily assess student learning in a variety of ways.

- Performance Assessment Strategies and Activities
- Section Quizzes
- Chapter and Unit Tests
- Interactive Tutor Self-Assessment Software
- Testmaker Software
- MindJogger Videoquiz
- SAT/SAT II Test Practice
- worldhistory.glencoe.com

Additional Resources

NATIONAL GEOGRAPHIC SOCIETY

Teacher's Corner

INDEX TO NATIONAL GEOGRAPHIC MAGAZINE

The following articles relate to this chapter:

- "Why Explore?" by Priit J. Vesilind, 2/98.
- "La Salle's Last Voyage," by Lisa Moore LaRoe, 5/97.
- "San Diego: An Account of Adventure, Deceit, and Intrigue," by Franck Goddio, 7/94.
- "African Slave Trade: The Cruelest Commerce," by Colin Palmer, 9/92.
- "Portugal's Sea Road to the East," by Merle Severy, 11/92.
- "La Isabela: Europe's First Foothold in the New World," by Kathleen A. Deagan, 1/92.
- "Pizarro: Conqueror of the Inca," by John Hemming, 2/92.
- "Track of the Manila Galleons," by Eugene Lyon, 9/90.

NATIONAL GEOGRAPHIC SOCIETY PRODUCTS AVAILABLE FROM GLENCOE

To order the following, call National Geographic Society at 1-800-368-2728:
- *PictureShow: The Age of Exploration, 1 & 2 (CD-ROM)*
- *Age of Exploration (Transparencies)*
- *PicturePack: The Age of Exploration (Transparencies)*

ADDITIONAL NATIONAL GEOGRAPHIC SOCIETY PRODUCTS

Access National Geographic's new dynamic MapMachine Web site and other geography resources at:
- http://www.nationalgeographic.com/
- http://www.nationalgeographic.com/maps/

BIBLIOGRAPHY

Literature of the Period
Las Casas, Bartolomé de. *A Short Account of the Destruction of the Indies.* Translated and edited by Nigel Griffin. New York: Penguin, 1992. A missionary's critical account, written in 1552, of the Europeans' actions.

Readings for the Student
Yue, Charlotte and David. *Christopher Columbus: How He Did It.* Boston: Houghton Mifflin, 1992. Describes the knowledge on which Columbus's voyages were based.

Readings for the Teacher
The Times Atlas of World Exploration: 3,000 Years of Exploring, Explorers, and Mapmaking. Edited by Felipe Fernandez-Armesto. New York: Harper Collins, 1991.

WORLD HISTORY Online

Use our Web site as an additional resource. All essential content is covered in the Student Edition.

You and your students can visit the *World History: The Human Experience* Web site at worldhistory. glencoe.com The student text directs students to the Web site for the following options:

- **Chapter Overviews**
- **Student Web Activities**
- **Self-Check Quizzes**

Answers are provided for you in a link entitled "Web Activity Lesson Plan." Additional Web Resources, Interactive Puzzles, and content updates are also available.

Visit the Glencoe Web site at socialstudies. glencoe.com for social studies activities, updates, and links to other resources.

LOCAL OBJECTIVES

_____
_____
_____
_____
_____
_____
_____
_____
_____
_____
_____
_____
_____
_____
_____

Expanding Horizons

CHAPTER THEMES

Chapter Themes are listed by section on this chapter opening page of the Student Edition. A corresponding theme-based activity is available under "TEACH," and a theme-based question is asked in the Section and Chapter Assessments.

The Storyteller

Historical Setting At first Columbus failed to persuade the monarchs of Portugal, England, and France to finance his plan of finding a sea route to Asia by sailing west across the Atlantic Ocean. The deeply religious Catholic queen, Isabella of Spain, was impressed by Columbus's stated intention to use the proceeds of his expedition to seize Jerusalem from the Muslims and to rebuild the Temple of the Jews there. A commission of the queen's experts rejected Columbus's plan. Only after Spain's conquest of Granada (January 1492) was Isabella persuaded (April 1492) by royal treasurer Luis de Santangel to seize the opportunity offered by Columbus's plan.

Historical Significance

Answer: *The age of exploration brought the people of Europe, Asia, the Americas, and Africa south of the Sahara into direct contact for the first time and led to a transfer of ideas and products. However, the European process of colonization took a great toll in human life and often had a negative impact on cultures that were conquered.*

Have students use the **Chapter 17 Overview** at worldhistory. glencoe.com as a prereading and postreading exercise for understanding chapter content.

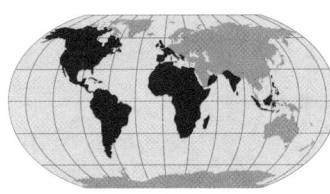

Chapter Themes

▶ **Innovation** European sailors borrow technological and navigational ideas from Asia. *Section 1*
▶ **Movement** European nations establish colonies in the lands they explore in Asia, Africa, and the Americas. *Section 2*
▶ **Change** The wealth of overseas colonies sparks the Commercial Revolution in Europe. *Section 3*

The Storyteller

On the night of October 11, 1492, Christopher Columbus scanned the horizon, praying that landfall was near. "About 10 o'clock at night, while standing on the sterncastle, I thought I saw a light to the west. It looked like a little wax candle bobbing up and down. It had the same appearance as a light or torch belonging to fishermen or travellers...."

The light flickered out, though, and the ship sailed on. The moon rose, but no land appeared. Two hours later, the boom of a cannon roared across the water. A sailor aboard the Pinta, the fastest of the expedition's three ships, had sighted land. For Spain and other nations of Europe, the land that appeared in the darkness was part of a far greater treasure. As a result of Columbus's voyage, contacts increased among Europeans, Native Americans, Africans, and Asians.

Historical Significance

How were Europe, Asia, Africa, and the Americas changed as the result of cross-cultural contacts from the 1400s to the 1700s?

1450	1500	1550	1600

1492 Christopher Columbus reaches America.

1521 Hernán Cortés conquers the Aztec Empire.

1599 The Dutch send first expedition to East Asia.

1607 The English establish a permanent settlement at Jamestown.

432

GEOGRAPHY CONNECTION

Location Using a world map or globe, have students locate Portugal, Spain, the Netherlands, England, France, North and South America, the islands of the Caribbean, Africa, the East Indies (now Indonesia), India, and the Philippines. Into what three major oceans are the great waters of the world divided? *(Pacific, Atlantic, Indian)* Which ocean is the largest and which the smallest? *(The Pacific is the largest and the Indian the smallest.)* Have students note the distances from Europe to India, the islands of Indonesia, and the coast of the Americas. **L1**

Although Dutch artists painted pictures with nautical subjects throughout the seventeenth century, English painters began to respond artistically to their country's nautical activity only at the beginning of the eighteenth century. English artists such as Samuel Scott put on canvas faithful depictions of actual scenes in English seaports.

Visualizing History This busy English port of the 1700s reveals England's position as one of Europe's major seafaring nations.

✔ **Performance Assessment**

Refer to the activity on page 432C of the Planning Guide.

📁 **For an additional activity, refer to Activity 17 in the *Performance Assessment Strategies and Activities* booklet.**

WORLD HISTORY
Online

apter Overview

sit the *World History: The Human Experience* eb site at **worldhistory.glencoe.com** and click **Chapter 17—Chapter Overview** to preview e chapter.

Your History Journal

Imagine crossing the Atlantic, the Pacific, or the Indian Ocean in the early 1600s. Compared to today, ships were small, and the journey was neither safe nor pleasant. Write a diary of a few days on such a voyage.

Using Your History Journal

Suggest that students consider such basic aspects of daily life aboard ship as diet, sleeping conditions, and sanitary facilities.

GLENCOE
TECHNOLOGY

VIDEODISC
Use MindJogger to preview chapter content.

MindJogger Videoquiz

Chapter 17
Disc 3 Side A

 Also available in VHS.

Chapter 17 *Expanding Horizons* **433**

➕ **EXTRA CREDIT PROJECT**

Issues in History Historians are still debating whether the early explorers should be viewed primarily as heroes or as exploiters. Have students research this question and report to the class not only on the contributions to knowledge that resulted from the voyages of exploration but also on their negative impact on Native American cultures. Suggested resources: H. Faber, *The Discoverers of America*; M. E. Jones, ed., *Christopher Columbus and His Legacy*; S. E. Morison, *The Great Explorers: The European Discovery of America*; and R. Wright, *Stolen Continents: The Americas Through Indian Eyes Since 1492*.

1400	1450	1500

1432 Prince Henry the Navigator's explorers reach the Azores.

1488 Bartholomeu Dias of Portugal sails to the tip of Africa.

1519 Magellan expedition sets sail from Seville, Spain.

Section 1

Early Explorations

Read to Find Out
Main Idea *Europeans risked dangerous ocean voyages to discover sea routes to other parts of the world.*

▶ **Terms to Define**
cartographer, line of demarcation, circumnavigation

▶ **People to Meet**
Prince Henry the Navigator, Bartholomeu Dias, Vasco da Gama, Christopher Columbus, Ferdinand Magellan

▶ **Places to Locate**
Cape of Good Hope, Strait of Magellan

The Storyteller

Spanish treasure

Wealth was on everyone's mind when they thought about the New World. Ferdinand and Isabella wrote, "We have commanded [Columbus] to return ... because thereby our Lord God is served, His Holy Faith extended and our own realms increased." The King and Queen offered financial incentives for accompanying Columbus: "Whatever persons wish to ... dwell in ... Hispaniola ... shall pay no tax whatsoever and shall have for their own ... the houses which they build and the lands which they work...." As a final enticement, Columbus insisted, "The Indians are the wealth of Hispaniola—for they perform all labor of men and beasts."

—adapted from *Ferdinand and Isabella*, Felipe Fernández-Armesto, 1975

In the 1400s European explorers tested uncharted oceans in search of a better trade route to Asia. They left their homelands filled with a desire for gold, glory, and for spreading Christianity. In just over 250 years, their ventures had destroyed and built empires at a great cost in human life. Their efforts, however, linked people of different cultures and ended forever the isolation of the world's major civilizations.

POINT

Age of Exploration

Europe in the 1300s had depended on spices from Asia. Such spices as pepper, cinnamon, and nutmeg were in great demand. Used chiefly to flavor and preserve meat, spices were also used for perfumes, cosmetics, and medicine.

The spice trade was controlled by Arab and Venetian merchants. Chinese and Indian traders sold spices to Arab merchants, who then reaped huge profits in the sale of the spices to the Venetians. Europeans, eager to amass quick fortunes through direct trade with Asians, began to look for quicker routes eastward. Because the Mongols by the mid-1300s could no longer guarantee safe overland passage, Europeans were forced to consider the possibility of sea routes to Asia.

Several motivations led Europeans into an era of exploration. Not only did merchants seek a profitable trade with Asia, but also church leaders sought to halt the expansion of Islam and to spread Christian teachings. Learning and imagination also played a part. Renaissance thinkers had expanded the European world view to include new possibilities for exploration and discovery.

Overseas voyages would end Europe's isolation and set it on the path of worldwide expansion. They would also prepare the way for the rise of the world's first global age.

European Knowledge of the World

Map Study In 1400 Europeans had only a limited knowledge of the world. Geographers agreed the world was round, but they disagreed on its size. **Human/Environment Interaction** What factors contributed to European geographers' knowledge of the world?

Technology of Exploration

Open-water ocean sailing—necessary to find a water route to Asia—required sailors trained in navigation, accurate maps, and oceangoing ships. For exploration to succeed, ships had to be able both to leave the coastal waters and sight of land and to return home. Ancient navigators stayed close to the coast, using landmarks to determine their position. Later, sailors who traveled beyond sight of land used the positions of stars and the sun to determine in which direction they were traveling. Hourglasses told them how long they had traveled. Keeping track of speed, direction, and time theoret-

ically enabled a captain to tell where the ship was. However, these calculations were very inaccurate.

The compass, of Chinese origin, enabled sailors to determine geographical direction. By 1100, sailors used the astrolabe—perfected by the Arabs—to determine the altitude of the sun or other heavenly bodies. But in practice, standing on the deck of a heaving ship, few ship captains had the skill and patience that the astrolabe required.

Maps were another problem for early navigators. Most maps were wildly inaccurate, drawn from scattered impressions of travelers and traders.

Chapter 17 *Expanding Horizons* **435**

TEACH

Guided Practice

THEME Innovation

Have students discuss the design innovations of the caravel that contributed to successful voyages by the Portuguese and Spanish. *(lateen sails, multiple masts, rudder at stern)* **L1**

Map Study

Answer
inventions such as the compass and the astrolabe, and the reappearance of Ptolemy's maps in Europe

POINT

Age of Exploration
What impact did European voyages of exploration have on the course of world history? *They ended Europe's long isolation and set it on the paths of global expansion and greater contact among different regions of the world. In the course of this expansion, indigenous peoples were greatly affected.*

VIDEODISC
Turning Points in World History

Side One
Chapter 9

Title: *Age of Exploration*

COOPERATIVE LEARNING ACTIVITY

Cultural Life Early Spanish and Portuguese explorers encountered many different cultures in the Americas (including Arawak, Carib, Maya, Aztec, Inca). Organize the class into small groups and have each group research and report on one of the indigenous American cultures. Remind students that each group member is responsible for contributing to the overall effort. Each student should be assigned one of the following areas to research: geographic location and method of subsistence, arts and crafts, religious beliefs, customs, and the effect of European contact on the culture. One or more students may illustrate the report. **L2**

Visualizing History

Visualizing History A caravel usually had three masts with lateen or both square and lateen sails. The *Niña* and the *Pinta*, two of Columbus's three ships for the historic 1492 voyage, were caravels. Astrolabes were in use as early as the sixth century but came into wide use by Europeans and Muslims from the early Middle Ages.
Answer to Caption: *Its rudder made it maneuverable, and it drew little water, allowing it to travel in shallow waters.*

Visualizing History The American artist J.L.G. Ferris painted *The Eve of Discovery*, showing a caravel as it may have appeared in the 1400s. *Why was the caravel a good ship for sailing up rivers?*

An astrolabe

Literature Have students read an excerpt from one of Columbus's journals. Discuss what the excerpt reveals about Columbus and his times. **L2**

 History Simulation 17

 Chapter Transparency 17

Independent Practice

 Guided Reading Activity 17-1 **L1**

 Time Line Activity 17

 Source Reading Activity 17

Global Gourmet

Americas Florida's citrus industry can be traced back to Columbus's second voyage to the Americas in 1493. The citrus seeds the navigator brought to the West Indies took root there and eventually made their way to Mexico and Florida.

Cartographers, or mapmakers, filled their parchments with lands found only in rumor or legend.

Cartographers' skills gradually improved. By about 1300, coastal charts showed the Mediterranean coastline with a great degree of accuracy. During the Renaissance, works by the Hellenistic astronomer Ptolemy reappeared in Europe. His maps, improved over the centuries by Byzantine and Arab scholars, gave Europeans a new picture of the world. Ptolemy also introduced the grid system of map references based on the coordinates of latitude and longitude still in use today all over the world.

Innovations were also made in the construction of ships. Late in the 1400s, shipwrights began to outfit ships with triangle-shaped lateen sails perfected by Arab traders. These sails made it possible for ships to sail against the wind, not simply with it. Shipwrights also abandoned using a single mast with one large sail. Multiple masts, with several smaller sails hoisted one above the other, made ships travel much faster. In addition, moving the rudder from the ship's side to the stern made ships more maneuverable.

In the 1400s a European ship called a caravel incorporated all these improvements. The caravel was up to 65 feet (20 m) in length with the capability of carrying about 130 tons (118 metric tons) of cargo. Because a caravel drew little water, it allowed explorers to venture up shallow inlets and to beach the ship to make repairs. A Venetian mariner called the caravels "the best ships that sailed the seas." The caravels also carried new types of weapons—rifles and cannons.

Portugal Leads the Way

Portugal was the first European country to venture out on the Atlantic Ocean in search of spices and gold. Between 1420 and 1580, Portuguese captains pushed farther and farther down the west coast of Africa in search of a sea route to Asia.

Although **Prince Henry the Navigator**, son of King John I of Portugal, was not a sailor—never making an ocean voyage—he brought together mapmakers, mathematicians, and astronomers to study navigation. He also sponsored many Portuguese exploratory voyages westward into the Atlantic and southward down Africa's west coast. In the early 1400s Henry's explorers discovered the Azores, the Madeira Islands, and the Cape Verde Islands. These discoveries were the foundation of what in the 1500s became the Portuguese Empire.

In August 1487 **Bartholomeu Dias** left Portugal, intent upon finding the southern tip of Africa. In 1488 his expedition discovered the southern tip of Africa, which was later named the **Cape of Good Hope**. Dias's voyage proved that ships could reach East Asia by sailing around Africa.

In 1497 four ships led by **Vasco da Gama** sailed from Portugal for India. The expedition rounded the Cape of Good Hope, made stops at trading centers along the east coast of Africa, and landed at Calicut on the southwest coast of India in 10 months. There da Gama found Hindus and Muslims trading fine silk, porcelain, and spices that made the glass beads and trinkets of the Portuguese appear shoddy.

MEETING SPECIAL NEEDS ACTIVITY

Learning Style: Visual/Spatial Have students work in pairs or small groups to summarize in pictures on poster board the achievements of Portugal and Spain described in this section. Try to pair competent illustrators with verbally proficient students. Tell students to discuss how the pictures should best convey the information. After the picture or pictures have been sketched and colored in, the groups should write labels summarizing the information the pictures convey. After the posters are completed, display them in the classroom. **L1 LEP**

Richard Schlecht

"Little Girl"

The *Niña*—"Little Girl"—was Christopher Columbus's favorite ship, a small, fast, seaworthy vessel about 67 feet long. Descriptions of the *Niña* discovered in a Spanish [docu]ment from the period have enabled historians to [draw] pictures of what the craft actually looked like. [The lines] drawing the lines in red show the *Niña's* sails [and] riggings. The document also revealed that the [ship] had four masts, not two or three, as previously [belie]ved. Columbus's beloved "Little Girl," the most [techni]cally advanced craft of her day, probably made [one] of his four voyages to the Americas.

[Th]e Europe of 1500 was on the brink of the modern era. Monarchs Isabella and Ferdinand of Spain could command Columbus and other explorers, who combined knowledge of sophisticated naval technologies with bravery and determination. In quick succession Columbus (1492), Vasco da Gama (1498), and Magellan (1519–21), among others, linked Europe with the rest of the world. The sea-sheltered Americas were invaded. The slave trade expanded and brought much of Africa into the shadow of the Americas. The Muslim peoples of Africa and Asia lost their central position as guardians of trade between Europe, Asia, and Africa. Within a few centuries, the whole world came within European explorers' reach. ⊕

Chapter 17 *Expanding Horizons* **437**

TEACH

Tell students that the fifteenth-century document describing the *Niña* is only one of many so-called Columbus documents. The documents include more than 2,500 notes Columbus wrote in the margins of his books, about 80 letters and notes, copies of the log from his first trip to the Americas, and his will. Ask students where they think most of the books and manuscripts are located. *(Spain)* Tell them that Columbus documents are also found in Italy, France, and the United States.

CURRICULUM CONNECTION

GEOGRAPHY

Columbus's seafaring interest may have been shaped by the geography of his birthplace, the seaport Republic of Genoa, in today's Italy. Lacking much fertile land and surrounded by powerful rival cities like Milan and Florence, many inhabitants of Genoa looked to the Mediterranean Sea in search of their fortunes.

WORLD HISTORY Online

Have students use the **Chapter 17 Student Web Activity** at worldhistory.glencoe.com for in-depth study of Amerigo Vespucci.

Biography®

The following videotape program is available from Glencoe:

- **Christopher Columbus: Explorer of the New World**

ASSESS

Check for Understanding

Assign Section 1 Assessment as homework or as an in-class activity.

🖳 Use Interactive Tutor Self-Assessment Software to review Section 1.

History & Art
After being dismissed in 1487 by advisers to Ferdinand and Isabella, Columbus did not allow the rejection to cause him to abandon his plan.
Answer to Caption: *He made three voyages after the initial voyage.*

Da Gama tried to persuade the ruler of Calicut and Muslim merchants in India to trade with the Portuguese. He had little success and returned home. In Portugal, however, da Gama was regarded as a national hero. He had pioneered a water route to India, and he had provided a glimpse of the riches that could come from direct trade with the East.

Spain's Quest for Riches

In the late 1400s Spain ended a long period of internal turmoil and wars against the Moors. Under King Ferdinand and Queen Isabella, Spain entered the race for Asian riches by backing the expeditions of an Italian navigator named **Christopher Columbus**.

Columbus Crosses the Atlantic

In 1492 Christopher Columbus approached Queen Isabella with an intriguing plan—to reach India by sailing west across the Atlantic. For years Columbus had tried unsuccessfully to persuade other European rulers to finance his voyage. With Queen Isabella his persistence paid off.

In August 1492 Columbus sailed from Spain with three small ships. He calculated the distance to India to be 700 leagues, about 2,200 nautical miles;

History & Art *Columbus Before the Queen* by Peter Rothermel, 1842. National Museum of American Art, Washington, D.C. *How many voyages did Columbus make to prove that he had found a new route to India?*

he knew that the actual distance might be greater. To calm the crew's fears, he showed them a log that understated the distance they had sailed.

The days out of sight of land wore on and on, and the terrified sailors begged Columbus to turn back. After a false sighting of land, the crews began to talk of mutiny. Columbus reluctantly agreed to turn back if they did not reach land within three days.

After midnight on the second day, the expedition sighted land. In the morning Columbus and his men went ashore, becoming the first Europeans to set foot on one of the islands of the Bahamas. Columbus wrote of the inhabitants:

> ❝ The islanders came to the ships' boats, swimming and bringing us parrots and balls of cotton thread … which they exchanged for … glass beads and hawk bells … they took and gave of what they had very willingly, but it seemed to me that they were poor in every way. They bore no weapons, nor were they acquainted with them, … ❞

Believing he was off the coast of India, Columbus called the islanders "Indians." Columbus spent the next three months exploring the islands Hispaniola (present-day Haiti and the Dominican Republic) and Cuba in search of gold. Although he found enough gold to raise Spanish hopes, he saw no evidence of the great civilizations of Asia.

When Columbus returned to Spain, Ferdinand and Isabella gave him the title "Admiral of the Ocean Sea, Viceroy and Governor of the Islands he hath discovered in the Indies." Columbus made three more voyages to the Caribbean islands and South America seeking proof that he had discovered a new route to Asia. In 1506 he died certain that he had.

Even without sure proof, it was difficult for anyone to dispute Columbus's claim. Maps of the time did not show any landmass between Europe and Asia. It was not until 1507 that another Italian explorer, Amerigo Vespucci (veh•SPOO•chee), suggested that Columbus had discovered a "New World." In honor of Vespucci, the name *America* began to appear on maps that included the newly discovered lands.

WORLD HISTORY Online

Student Web Activity 17

Visit the *World History: The Human Experience* Web site at worldhistory.glencoe.com and click on **Chapter 17—Student Web Activities** for an activity relating to Amerigo Vespucci.

MAKING CONNECTIONS ACTIVITIES

Technology Have students research and write a brief illustrated report on developments in ship design and construction from antiquity through the age of exploration. Make sure they include mention of Henry the Navigator's role in encouraging the building of new types of ships. **L2**

Cartography Ask students to research and write a brief report on the history of cartography from antiquity (beginning with Babylonian maps on clay tablets) through the age of exploration. Encourage them to focus on how the discoveries of explorers such as Columbus and Magellan transformed the world maps of those days. **L2**

Dividing the World

Both Spain and Portugal wanted to protect their claims in the Americas and turned to the pope for help. In 1493 the pope drew a line of demarcation, an imaginary line running down the middle of the Atlantic from the North Pole to the South Pole. Spain was to have control of all lands to the west of the line, while Portugal was to have control of all lands to the east of the line.

The Portuguese, however, feared that their line was so far to the east that Spain might take over their Asian trade. As a result, in 1494 Spain and Portugal signed the Treaty of Tordesillas (TAWR•duh•SEE•yuhs), an agreement to move the line of demarcation farther west. The treaty divided the entire unexplored world between just two powers, Spain and Portugal.

Voyage of Magellan

In 1519 an expedition led by **Ferdinand Magellan**, a Portuguese soldier of fortune, set sail from Seville under the Spanish flag to find a western route to Asia. The five ships and 260-man crew sailed across the Atlantic and made their way along the eastern coast of South America, searching every bay and inlet for this route.

Along the coast of Argentina, crews of three of the ships attempted a mutiny because Magellan had decided to halt the expedition until spring. Magellan executed the captain who had instigated the mutiny, regained control of the fleet, and resumed the expedition. Finally, near the southern tip of South America, the ships reached a narrow water passageway now called the **Strait of Magellan**. The ships threaded their way through the maze of rocky islands in the 350-mile- (504-km-) long strait. Strong currents and unpredictable gales separated one ship from the others, and its crew forced its return to Spain. Another was shipwrecked.

 Discovery of Magellan Strait (artist unknown). **By this point in Magellan's voyage, one ship foundered on the rocks and another turned back.** *What did the journey prove?*

The three remaining ships finally passed through the strait into the South Sea, discovered and named seven years earlier by Vasco Núñez de Balboa. Because the water was so calm, Magellan renamed it the Pacific Ocean. The fleet then sailed nearly four months before reaching land. Water and food ran out, and some sailors died before the ships reached the present-day Philippines. Caught in a skirmish between a local chief and his enemy, Magellan was killed. The surviving crew escaped and sailed for Spain.

In 1522, after three years at sea, the last ship with its 18 survivors arrived at Seville, completing the first circumnavigation, or circling of the globe. The spices they brought back barely covered the cost of the voyage, but the expedition had a value far beyond money. It proved that the world was round and much larger than anyone had believed, that the oceans of the world were connected, and that the lands discovered by Columbus were not part of Asia.

SECTION 1 ASSESSMENT

Main Idea
1. Use a web diagram like the one below to identify reasons why Europeans sought sea routes to other parts of the world.

Recall
2. **Define** cartographer, line of demarcation, circumnavigation.
3. **Identify** Prince Henry the Navigator, Bartholomeu Dias, Vasco da Gama, Christopher Columbus, Ferdinand Magellan.

Critical Thinking
4. **Synthesizing Information** Using your text as a resource, write a journal entry as though you had sailed on an expedition of Dias, Columbus, Magellan, or da Gama.

Understanding Themes
5. **Innovation** What sciences and new technologies developed at this time led to European voyages of exploration?

SECTION 1 ASSESSMENT ANSWERS

1. wanted better trade routes to Asia; Church leaders wanted to halt Islam and spread Christianity; Renaissance thinkers encouraged exploration and discovery of new lands
2. All terms are defined in the Glossary.
3. Henry, 436; Dias, 436; da Gama, 436; Columbus, 438; Magellan; 439
4. Students should include details of the expedition they select.
5. **INNOVATION** sciences: cartography, math, astronomy; technologies: compass, astrolabe, caravels

History & Art Until the opening of the Panama Canal (1914) shortened the water route from the Atlantic to the Pacific, the Strait of Magellan remained an important sailing-ship route.
Answer to Caption: *that the world was round and larger than previously believed, that the oceans were connected, and that the lands Columbus discovered were not part of Asia*

Evaluate

Section Quiz 17-1

Use the Testmaker to create a customized quiz for Section 1.

Reteach

Organize the class into two groups. Ask both groups to prepare a quiz based on the information discussed in this section. Then have the members of each group take the other group's quiz.

Reading Essentials and Study Guide 17-1

Enrich

Have students use library resources to research the expeditions of Amerigo Vespucci or Vasco Nuñez de Balboa. Then have them prepare a script about the explorer's expedition.

CLOSE

Write these headings on the chalkboard: *Country Financing Voyage, Explorer, Discovery, Date, Result.* Ask volunteers to provide the information for each heading.

1500 Pedro Alvares Cabral claims Brazil for Portugal.

1532 Francisco Pizarro of Spain invades the Inca Empire.

1608 France's Samuel de Champlain founds Quebec.

1640 English planters introduce sugarcane in the West Indies.

Section 2

Overseas Empires

Guide to Reading

Read to Find Out
Main Idea *The Europeans exploited the peoples of Africa, Asia, and the Americas.*

▶ **Terms to Define**
conquistador, triangular trade, the Middle Passage

▶ **People to Meet**
Pedro Alvares Cabral, Hernán Cortés, Montezuma II, Francisco Pizarro, Atahualpa, Henry Hudson, Jacques Cartier, Samuel de Champlain, John Cabot

▶ **Places to Locate**
Brazil, Peru, West Indies, Quebec, Jamestown

The Storyteller

Native Americans digging gold

John Sparke, who traveled with English admiral John Hawkins, wrote an account of the inhabitants of the Florida coast in 1589: "They have for apothecary [medicine] herbs, trees, roots, and gum, myrrh, and frankincense, with many others, whereof I know not the names.... Gold and silver they want [lack] not, for when the Frenchmen came, they offered it for little or nothing. They received for a hatchet two pounds of gold. The soldiers, being greedy, took it from them, giving them nothing for it." When the Floridians perceived that, they stopped wearing their gold ornaments, for fear they would be taken away.

—from *The Hawkins Voyages*, edited by Clements R. Markham, reprinted in *The Annals of America*, 1968

440 Chapter 17 *Expanding Horizons*

T he Treaty of Tordesillas claimed to divide the world between Spain and Portugal. Only Spain and Portugal, however, recognized the treaty. The Netherlands, France, and England soon joined them in a race to exploit wealth from the lands beyond Europe.

Portugal and Spain

Portugal's main interest lay in Africa and Asia, and in trade rather than colonization. When the Portuguese became the first Europeans to reach the Indian Ocean, they found themselves in waters already thoroughly explored by seafarers from Asian lands. Eager to seize control of the spice trade, the Portuguese reacted quickly to Vasco da Gama's voyage to India. In 1500, less than six months after da Gama's return, 13 ships were dispatched to Calicut. Led by **Pedro Alvares Cabral**, the Portuguese won a bloody trade war with Muslim merchants and defeated a large Arab fleet to establish Portuguese control of the Indian Ocean.

The Portuguese then built naval bases along the Indian Ocean—along the Persian Gulf and in Southeast Asia. They soon controlled shipping in the Indian Ocean. Next, they expanded eastward toward the Moluccas, or the Spice Islands. From the Spice Islands, the Portuguese established trading ports in China and Japan.

Portugal also colonized the area of present-day **Brazil**. Cabral claimed this territory as he swung west across the Atlantic to India in 1500. Because this area of South America juts east of the line of demarcation, it became Portuguese. The rest of South America had been claimed by Spain.

Settlers in Brazil grew income-producing crops such as sugarcane, tobacco, coffee, and cotton. Because the local population did not supply enough labor, enslaved people were brought from Africa. By the late 1500s, Brazil was one of Portugal's most important colonies.

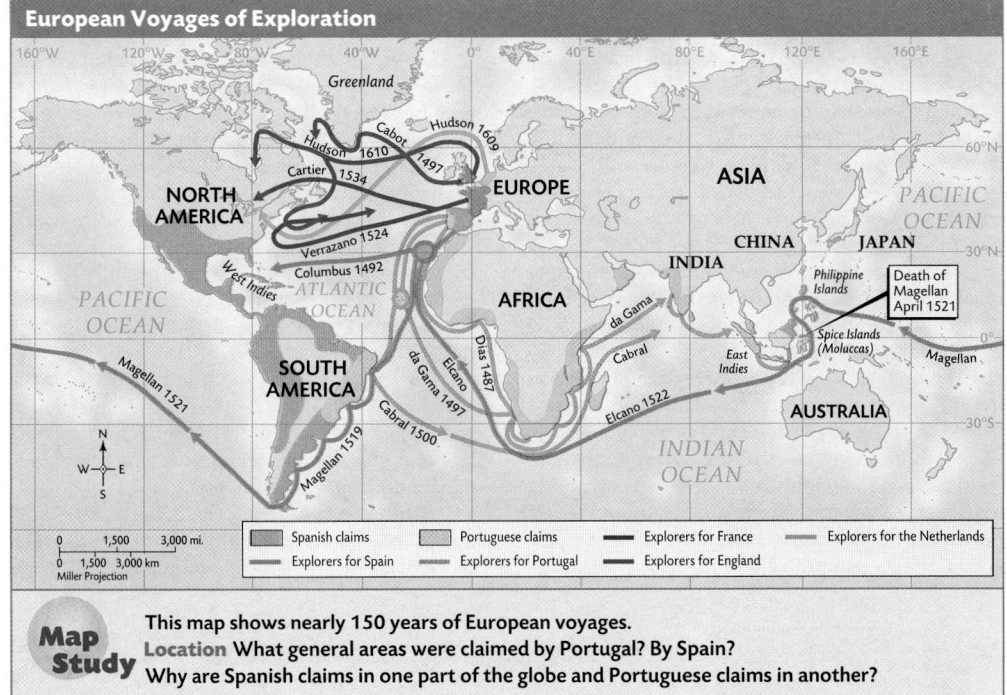

European Voyages of Exploration

Spanish claims
Portuguese claims
Explorers for France
Explorers for the Netherlands
Explorers for Spain
Explorers for Portugal
Explorers for England

0   1,500   3,000 mi.
0   1,500   3,000 km
Miller Projection

Map Study This map shows nearly 150 years of European voyages.
Location What general areas were claimed by Portugal? By Spain? Why are Spanish claims in one part of the globe and Portuguese claims in another?

TEACH

Guided Practice

THEME Movement

Have students discuss the movement of goods and people described in this section. Ask them to name some examples of colonies and trading settlements. (*Portugal: Brazil; Spain: West Indies and the Americas; the Netherlands: Indonesia and Africa*) Have students give examples of some of the goods exported from these areas. (*Brazil: sugarcane, tobacco, coffee, cotton; West Indies and the Americas: animal hides, sugar, tobacco; Indonesia: sugar, spices, coffee, tea*) **L1**

Map Study

Answer

Portugal's claims are primarily in Africa, India, Southeast Asia, and the tip of Brazil; Spain's claims are in the Americas and the Philippines; the Line of Demarcation set by the Treaty of Tordesillas divided the world between Spain and Portugal.

Map Skills Practice

Reading a Map How did the destinations change over time? (*After Columbus crossed the Atlantic, explorers searched for a western, rather than an eastern, route to the East Indies.*)

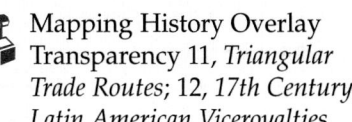 People in World History Profiles 31, 32

Mapping History Overlay Transparency 11, *Triangular Trade Routes*; 12, *17th Century Latin American Viceroyalties*

Spain

Spanish conquistadors, or conquerors, came to the Americas "to serve God and his Majesty, to give light to those who were in darkness and to grow rich as all men desire to do."

One conquistador, **Hernán Cortés**, landed in Mexico in 1519 with about 600 men, 16 horses, and a few cannons. Guided by Malinche (mah•LIHN•chay), a Native American woman who learned Spanish, Cortés allied with local enemies of the Aztecs and journeyed inland to Tenochtitlán. Meanwhile, in the Aztec capital, messengers told the Aztec ruler **Montezuma II** that the approaching soldiers were "supernatural creatures riding on hornless deer, preceded by wild animals on leashes, dressed in iron." Thinking that Cortés might be the long-awaited god-king Quetzalcoatl returning from the east, Montezuma offered gifts of gold.

Tenochtitlán's riches were beyond anything the Spaniards had ever seen. Soon fighting broke out. With the advantage of horses and guns, the Spanish force ultimately slaughtered thousands of Aztec people. Within three years, Aztec resistance had ended and Cortés ruled Mexico.

In 1532 another conquistador, **Francisco Pizarro**, invaded the Inca Empire in present-day

Peru. The Spaniards' arrival followed a conflict in which the Incan ruler **Atahualpa** (AH•tuh•WAHL•puh) won the throne from a brother. Aided by Native American allies, Pizarro captured Atahualpa and had thousands of Inca massacred. Although a ransom was paid for Atahualpa's release, the Spaniards killed him anyway. Inca resistance continued, but Spanish forces eventually conquered vast stretches of Inca territory in South America.

Building an Empire

By the 1600s, Spain's empire in the Americas included much of North America and South America as well as islands in the **West Indies**. Keeping close watch over their empire, Spanish monarchs named viceroys, or royal representatives, to rule local provinces with the advice of councils of Spanish settlers.

Spain had two goals for its American empire—to acquire its wealth and to convert Native Americans to Christianity. Farmers set up plantations, or large estates, for the growing of sugarcane; landowners drew gold and silver from mines. At the same time priests founded missions—settlements where many Native Americans lived, worked, and adopted European ways.

Chapter 17 *Expanding Horizons* **441**

COOPERATIVE LEARNING ACTIVITY

Research Organize the class into four research groups and ask each group to become experts on one period in the life of Rembrandt. One group might focus on the artist's early years (1606–1625), another the Leiden years (1625–1631), a third his Amsterdam years (1632–1640), and a fourth his last years (1640–1669). Each group member should have a specific assignment, with some students focusing on specific paintings, etchings, or drawings of each period. After individual students compile their research notes, each group should meet to plan a presentation format—panel discussion, poster presentation, or short dramatic sketch. Each group should make its presentation to the entire class. **L2**

NATIONAL GEOGRAPHIC SOCIETY

Use these materials to enrich student understanding of the age of exploration.

- **NGS PICTURESHOW CD-ROM**
  The Age of Exploration, 1 & 2
- **NGS PICTUREPACK TRANSPARENCY SET**
  The Age of Exploration, 1 & 2

Independent Practice

📁 Guided Reading Activity 17-2 **L1**

📁 Mapping History Activity 17

📁 Geography and History Activity 17

Religion Explain to the class that Spain and France were predominantly Roman Catholic countries. The English and Dutch were primarily Protestant. Ask students how much importance each nation placed on converting the native populations it encountered to Christianity. *(Jesuit missionaries from France and Spain were the most dedicated to conversion.)* **L2**

Biography

The following videotape is available from Glencoe:

- **Ponce de León: The First Conquistador**

Under the encomienda system, Spanish monarchs granted landowners the right to use Native American labor. Some Native Americans were enslaved and mistreated. Disease also took its toll. Exposed to diseases from Europe for the first time, millions of Native Americans died during the first 50 years of Spanish rule.

A few priests, such as Bartolomé de Las Casas, tried to protect the Native Americans. The Spanish government responded with laws meant to end abuses, but the laws were never enforced. In many cases, Native Americans resisted Spanish rule on their own by preserving their local cultures and by staging periodic revolts.

The decline in the Native American population led the Spaniards to bring over enslaved workers from Africa. As sugarcane production and profits soared, more and more Africans arrived to work in the fields and in various trades. In time, the coming together of African, Native American, and European peoples in Spain's American colonies gave rise to a new culture.

Colonies of the Netherlands

The Netherlands was also interested in expansion. In the late 1500s the Dutch won their independence from Spain. This small country on the North Sea had few natural resources and limited farmland. A large Dutch middle class saw commerce as the key to survival.

The period of the 1600s was the golden age of the Netherlands. Dutch ships were efficient, carrying more cargo and smaller crews than other ships. Amsterdam became the world's largest commercial city, and the Dutch enjoyed the world's highest standard of living.

The first Dutch expedition to East Asia returned in 1599. Three years later the Dutch chartered the Dutch East India Company to expand trade and ensure close relations between the government and enterprises in Asia.

In 1619 the company set up headquarters at Batavia on the island of Java in present-day Indonesia. Soon the Dutch controlled island trade

Images of the Times

The Dutch Republic

With no monarchy or aristocracy, the tastes and ideals of society as reflected in Dutch art were determined largely by the middle class.

The World Upside-down by Jan Steen, the son of a brewer, is representative of his earthy, humorous scenes of ordinary people.

The Flower Vendor and the Vegetable Vendor by Arnout de Muysor focuses on two important themes in Dutch painting of this period—middle-class life and trade.

442

Images of the Times

 The Dutch Republic

The formal name of the Dutch Republic was the United Provinces of the Netherlands. Formed in 1579, the republic experienced a golden age during the seventeenth century, when it was not only the center of a world colonial empire but also a center of international finance and culture. The comic perspective of Jan Steen (1626–1679) makes him unique among leading seventeenth-century Dutch painters. Gabriel Metsu (1629–1667) began painting religious subjects but found the life of the marketplace better suited to his personality. Rembrandt (1606–1669) movingly conveyed the human aspect of all his subjects, whether drawn from the Bible, history, mythology, or everyday life.

in sugar, spices, coffee, and tea. Using Batavia as a base, the Dutch pushed the Portuguese and English out of Asian outposts. After taking Malacca from the Portuguese in 1641, the Netherlands controlled all trade with the Spice Islands. The Dutch also used force against local Muslim rulers to win lands and ports in the region.

At the same time, the Dutch set out for North America. An English navigator, **Henry Hudson,** claimed land for the Dutch along the Atlantic coast of North America, and in 1621 the government chartered the Dutch West India Company to establish colonies in the Americas. The company founded New Amsterdam on Manhattan Island at the mouth of the Hudson River. This settlement was soon a center for European and colonial trade.

The Dutch established a colony in Africa as well. In 1652 Dutch farmers known as Boers settled at the Cape of Good Hope to provide fresh food and water for sailing ships. By the 1700s, however, Dutch power was declining, and England had emerged as Europe's leading maritime nation.

French and English Colonies

The French and the English played only a small part in the early voyages of exploration. Religious conflicts and civil wars kept their interests focused at home. During the 1500s, however, France and England searched for overseas trading colonies.

Thwarted by the Portuguese and later the Dutch control of Asian markets, England and France turned toward North America and the Caribbean. In general, the French companies sought quick profits from trade rather than the long-term investment of farming. For the English, colonies could provide the raw materials—lumber, fish, sugarcane, rice, and wheat—they would otherwise have to purchase from other countries.

France

In 1524 the French hired an Italian captain, Giovanni da Verrazano, to find a Northwest Passage through America to Asia. Da Verrazano explored the North American coast from North

Geography: Movement Have students work in pairs to locate information, including maps, about the explorations of Cartier, Champlain, Marquette, and Joliet. Ask them to draw maps showing each explorer's routes and claims in North America. **L3**

Linking Past and Present

Wall Street, the major financial center of the United States, gets its name from a wall built by the colonists of New Amsterdam in 1653. The wall, meant to protect the colonists from enemy attacks, fell down within a few years. When the colonists built a road in its place, it became known as Wall Street.

VIDEODISC
Turning Points in World History

Side One
Chapter 9

Title: *Age of Exploration*
Subject: As western Europeans sought new routes to Asia, they found lands unknown to them; Europeans seeking wealth and power conquered these lands.
Ask: In what ways was the age of exploration a turning point in history? *(Many indigenous peoples were mistreated, killed, or died from disease; new crops were brought to Europe, and other crops were introduced to the Americas.)*

Rembrandt van Rijn, the celebrated Dutch painter, earned fame with his portraits of himself and of his family. Although he died poor and forgotten, his paintings were of more spiritual depth than those of his contemporaries.

REFLECTING ON THE TIMES

1. How does Dutch art compare with art from a nation like France that had a monarch and nobility?
2. Why did Rembrandt's work receive greater acclaim after he died?

443

ANSWERS TO REFLECTING ON THE TIMES

1. Dutch art focuses on middle-class, not aristocratic, concerns.
2. People later responded to the spiritual depth of his portraits and paintings.

ASSESS

Check for Understanding

Assign Section 2 Assessment as homework or as an in-class activity.

 Use Interactive Tutor Self-Assessment Software to review Section 2.

Evaluate

Section Quiz 17-2

 Use the Testmaker to create a customized quiz for Section 2.

The following videotape program is available from Glencoe:

- **Pocahontas: Her True Story**

Carolina to Maine without success. About ten years later the French navigator **Jacques Cartier** continued the search and sailed up the St. Lawrence River to the site of the present-day city of Montreal. He claimed much of eastern Canada for France.

In 1608 **Samuel de Champlain**, a French mapmaker, founded **Quebec**, the first permanent French settlement in the Americas. In 1673 missionaries Jacques Marquette and Louis Joliet explored the Mississippi Valley. Later, Robert Cavelier, known as Sieur de La Salle, claimed the entire inland region surrounding the Mississippi River for France.

Like the Spanish, the French sent Jesuit missionaries to convert Native Americans to Christianity. French explorers traded the Native Americans blankets, guns, and wine for animal skins. Trapping, fishing, and lumbering were also profitable.

Some French settlers went to the West Indies, where they claimed the islands of St. Kitts, Martinique, and Guadeloupe. The French brought enslaved Africans to work on sugar and tobacco plantations on the islands. Although most of their interests were in North America, the French also established trading posts in India.

England

England also showed an interest in overseas trade. In 1497 the Italian-born navigator **John Cabot** explored the coast of present-day Newfoundland. During the 1500s, English sea captains, such as Francis Drake, raided Spanish ships for gold and silver. English overseas expansion, however, did not begin until the founding of the English East India Company in 1600. This trading enterprise set up posts in India and Southeast Asia.

During the 1600s, the English also founded settlements in the Americas. On West Indian islands, such as Jamaica, they introduced sugarcane, worked by enslaved African labor. **Jamestown**, the earliest English settlement in North America, was founded in 1607 in present-day Virginia. In 1620 devout Protestants, calling themselves Pilgrims, sought religious freedom by establishing Plymouth in present-day Massachusetts. Before landing, the Pilgrims set down rules for governing Plymouth in the Mayflower Compact:

> ❝ We, whose names are underwritten… having undertaken for the glory of God, and advancement of the Christian faith…a voyage to plant [a] colony…do…enact, constitute, and frame …just and equal Laws…as shall be

thought most [appropriate] and convenient for the general good of the colony. ❞

In the 1600s and 1700s, English settlements arose and thrived along the eastern coast of North America. In northern areas, family-operated farms emerged, while in southern areas, plantation farming based on African enslaved labor was established. Although English monarchs supervised these settlements by sending out governors, the English in North America enjoyed a large degree of self-government in their representative assemblies modeled on the English Parliament.

English settlement, however, pushed out the earlier inhabitants, the Native Americans. Concerned about land, the English had little desire to Christianize Native Americans, although they adopted Native American farming methods and foods, such as corn and beans. On the other side, Native Americans fought back to save their lands, but disease and food shortages had reduced their numbers. As the settlers expanded inland, they also came into conflict with the Dutch and the French. By 1765, after a series of wars, the English had emerged as the leading European power in much of North America.

Slave Trade

In the 1600s European territories in the Americas based their economies on agricultural products that required intensive labor. Enslaved Africans planted and harvested sugar, tobacco, and coffee crops. They also worked silver mines.

The Triangular Trade

The slave trade was part of what was called the triangular trade. Ships sailed the legs of a triangle formed by Europe, Africa, and the Americas. Typically, European ships left their home ports carrying manufactured goods—knives, swords, guns, cloth, and rum. In West Africa the ship captains traded their goods with local rulers for enslaved people, most of whom were war captives. During the second leg of the journey, the ships brought enslaved Africans across the Atlantic to various Caribbean islands or to mainland areas in North America and South America. The enslaved Africans were sold, and the money was used to buy sugar, molasses, cotton, and tobacco. Finally, the ships returned to Europe to sell the goods purchased in America.

The Middle Passage

An enslaved person's journey from Africa to the Americas was a ghastly ordeal called the Middle Passage. This middle leg of the triangular trade originated from ports along a 3,000-mile (4,800-km) stretch on the west coast of Africa. Captured by other Africans, enslaved Africans were sold to European slave traders along the coast for transport to American plantations.

Because large cargoes brought large profits, the slave traders packed the captives as tightly as possible. Below deck, each African occupied a space only 4 or 5 feet (122 cm to 153 cm) long and 2 or 3 feet (60 cm to 92 cm) high. Chained together, they could neither stand nor lie at full length. In the darkness and stifling heat, many Africans suffocated or died of disease.

Estimates of the number of enslaved Africans brought to America range from 10 to 24 million. One in five who began the trip did not survive it. Because of the enormous value of their "cargo," however, slave traders made some effort to keep the enslaved people alive. Psychological torment may have been worse than physical conditions. Some Africans committed suicide by jumping overboard. Others simply lost the will to live and refused to eat.

An Enslaved Person's Life

Africans who survived the long Middle Passage faced another terror when they arrived in American ports: the slave auction. Examined and prodded by plantation owners, most Africans were sold to work as laborers—clearing land, hoeing, planting, weeding, and harvesting. The work was hard, the hours long, and life expectancy short. Because many

Visualizing History A deck plan shows tightly packed ranks of enslaved people on a ship bound from Africa to the Americas. *What did enslaved people experience on the Middle Passage?*

Europeans believed that Africans were physically suited to hard labor, especially in hot, humid climates, the enslaved people were viewed as nothing more than a unit of labor to exploit for profit.

Resistance

In addition to its inhumanity, the slave trade wrenched untold numbers of young, productive Africans from their homelands. This population loss at least temporarily weakened many African societies. As a result, many Africans tried to resist the slave trade. For example, as a Christian, Affonso I, ruler of Kongo in central Africa, favored contact with Europeans but spoke out against the trade in human lives. The slave trading network, however, was too powerful for African opponents to end it.

Enslaved people also acted to obtain freedom. A few escaped their masters and got far enough away to set up their own free communities. The ultimate weapon, however, was mass rebellion because in many areas of the Americas enslaved people outnumbered free populations. The most successful uprising occurred in the French-ruled West Indian island of Saint Domingue. There, a prolonged rebellion in the 1790s led to the creation of the republic of Haiti in 1804. By the early 1800s, humanitarian concerns and fear of uprisings had fueled an anti-slavery movement that saw slavery as an evil bringing only violence, oppression, and suffering.

SECTION 2 ASSESSMENT

Main Idea
1. Use a chart like the one below to describe ways in which Europeans exploited land and peoples in Africa.

   European Exploitation of Africa

Recall
2. **Define** conquistador, triangular trade, the Middle Passage.
3. **Identify** Pedro Alvares Cabral, Hernán Cortés, Montezuma II, Francisco Pizarro, Atahualpa, Henry Hudson, Jacques Cartier, Samuel de Champlain, John Cabot.

Critical Thinking
4. **Making Comparisons** How did Spain, France, and England each treat Native American groups?

Understanding Themes
5. **Movement** Why did Europeans move to the Americas?

SECTION 2 ASSESSMENT ANSWERS

1. colonies established; used goods for trade and enslaved Africans, bringing them to the Americas to do labor
2. All terms are in the Glossary.
3. Cabral, 440; Cortés, 441; Montezuma II, 441; Pizarro, 441; Atahualpa, 441; Hudson, 443; Cartier, 444; Champlain, 444; Marquette and Joliet, 444; Cabot, 444
4. Spain converted, enslaved, and mistreated Native Americans; France traded with and converted them; England borrowed farming methods and foods and pushed out Native Americans.
5. **MOVEMENT** They sought national prestige, wealth, religious freedom, and religious converts.

Visualizing History Death was common on slave ships. The white spaces on the deck plans denote enslaved persons who died during the crossing. Sharks routinely trailed the slave ships, enticed by the large number of dead or dying Africans who were tossed overboard during the Middle Passage.
Answer to Caption: *Chained together into a tight space in darkness and heat, one in five suffocated or died of disease.*

Reteach

Work with students to make a chart showing European colonial possessions and the major goods each European power received from its colonies.

📁 Reading Essentials and Study Guide 17-2

Enrich

Many students will have seen the animated film very loosely based on the life of Pocahontas. Have students research the actual facts of her life and summarize their findings in short reports. If they have access to the film, have them include its factual inaccuracies in their reports.

CLOSE

Organize the class into five groups; each representing one country: Spain, Portugal, France, England, the Netherlands. Have each group summarize its colonial actions for the others.

1400	1500	1600
c. 1400s Increased trade leads to advanced banking methods.	**c. 1500s** The nation replaces the city and the village as Europe's primary economic unit.	**c. 1600** Europe's population reaches 100 million.

Section 3

Changing Ways of Life

Read to Find Out

Main Idea *Increased trade and colonial expansion set the stage for a global economy.*

▶ **Terms to Define**
joint-stock company, entrepreneur, mercantilism, bullion, balance of trade

▶ **Places to Locate**
Florence, Augsburg

SECTION THEME

▶ **Change** The wealth of overseas colonies sparks the Commercial Revolution in Europe.

Guide to Reading

For reading strategies to help students read effectively see pages 12–13.

Vocabulary Pre-check

 Use the Vocabulary PuzzleMaker for Chapter 17 to create a crossword puzzle to reinforce section terms. **L1 LEP**

Use Vocabulary Activity 17 to introduce vocabulary terms. **L1 LEP**

FOCUS

Section Objective

Analyze how increased trade and colonial expansion set the stage for a global economy.

The Storyteller

The English and French considered piracy against Spain practically a religious crusade. Pirates sometimes held Holy Communion before starting a raid on a Spanish ship! The strangest pirate fleet of all, based in England, attacked Spaniards passing anywhere near, and openly sold their stolen cargo in the market. Even their Spanish prisoners were publicly auctioned for prices set by the ransom money each one might bring. Public opinion finally forced Elizabeth I to put a stop to all this: She declared the pirates public outlaws—"Rascals of the Sea."

—adapted from *The Pirate Picture,* Rayner Thrower, 1980

Pirate ship

The age of exploration brought far-reaching changes to global cultures. Overseas trade and the conquest of empires expanded Europe's economy. This search for wealth led to the rise of free enterprise, or modern capitalism, an economic system in which money is invested in business to make profits.

The Commercial Revolution

By the 1600s the nation had replaced the city and village as the basic economic unit in Europe. Nations competed for markets and trade goods. New business methods were instituted for investing money, speeding the flow of wealth, and reducing risks in commercial ventures. These changes, which came to be known as the Commercial Revolution, formed the roots of modern financial and business life.

New Business Methods

Launching an overseas trading venture was a major undertaking. The financial backer of the voyage had to raise money for supplies and to hire a crew. Often several years passed before a fleet finished trading overseas and returned home. Only then could the initial investment be recovered. Governments and rich merchants alone had enough money to back such trading voyages, and even they needed financial assistance.

At first merchants turned to bankers for the money to finance their ventures. Families like the Medici of **Florence**, Italy, and the Fuggers of **Augsburg**, Germany, loaned money as part of their operations. By the 1500s these families were so wealthy that they accepted deposits, made loans, and transferred funds over long distances. Both banking families had branches in several European cities and also made loans to European monarchs.

BELLRINGER
Motivational Activity

Before taking roll at the beginning of the class period, project Section Focus Transparency 17-3 and have students answer the activity questions. Discuss students' responses.

This activity is also available as a blackline master.

SECTION RESOURCES

Reproducible Masters
- Lecture Notes 17-3
- Reproducible Lesson Plan 17-3
- Guided Reading Activity 17-3
- Reteaching Activity 17
- Enrichment Activity 17
- Section Quiz 17-3
- Performance Assessment Activity 17

- Spanish Chapter Summary 17
- Reading Essentials and Study Guide 17-3

Transparencies
- Section Focus Transparency 17-3
- World History and Art Transparency 22, *View of Toledo;* 23, *Mission San Xavier del Bac*

Multimedia
- Focus on World Art Print 1, Jan Vermeer. *The Artist and His Model as Klio*
- Vocabulary PuzzleMaker Software
- Interactive Tutor Self-Assessment Software
- Testmaker

Visualizing History This European port scene by Jan Griffier the Elder shows the mix of cultures that resulted from the increased trade between Europeans and the rest of the world. *How did merchants protect themselves against losses?*

By the 1600s, however, these banking families were beginning to be replaced by government-chartered banks. The banks accepted deposits of money and charged interest on loans. Before long the banks began to provide other services. They issued banknotes and checks, making large payments in heavy coins a thing of the past. They acted as money changers, exchanging currencies from other countries. The banks even provided official exchange rates for foreign currency.

Individual merchants who wanted to invest in exploration often raised money by combining their resources in joint-stock companies, organizations that sold stock, or shares, in the venture, enabling large and small investors to share the profits and risks of a trading voyage. If a loss occurred, investors would lose only the amount they had invested in shares. This sharing of risk provided a stable way of raising funds for voyages.

A few joint-stock companies became rich and powerful through government support. For example, the Dutch government gave the Dutch East India Company a monopoly in trade with Africa and the East Indies. It also gave the company the power to make war, to seize foreign ships, to coin money, and to establish colonies and forts. In return

the government received customs duties, or taxes on imported goods, from the company's trade.

Increase in Money

As gold and silver flowed into Europe from abroad, the supply of coined money increased. This, in turn, led to inflation, or a dramatic rise in prices. Money, however, became more widely available for large enterprises, and ideas changed about the nature and goals of business. Gradually, a sys-

Footnotes to History

Spanish Doubloons and Pieces of Eight

During the 1500s, Spanish ships called galleons sailed the seas loaded with gold doubloons and silver pieces of eight. Minted from the plunder of Central and South American mines, the coins were a favorite target for pirates of other nations. Today, marine archaeologists have explored a number of sunken galleons and recovered hundreds of doubloons and pieces of eight—still worth a fortune.

Chapter 17 *Expanding Horizons* **447**

TEACH

Guided Practice

THEME Change

Discuss how entrepreneurs could change the social structure of a nation that previously had a stable social hierarchy. Ask students what happens when common people can accumulate wealth that had previously been available only to nobility. *(Common people become empowered by wealth; they demand more rights from government.)* **L1**

Visualizing History In the early 1600s, the Dutch Republic modified the port city of Amsterdam to make it more suitable as a base for expanding sea power. Other nations, anxious to emulate the Netherlands' success as a commercial empire, imitated Dutch techniques of planning port cities.

Answer to Caption: *They combined resources in joint-stock companies, enabling them to share profits and risks.*

TURNING POINT

The Commercial Revolution
How did the Commercial Revolution transform Europe's economy?
The nation replaced the city and village as Europe's basic economic unit; new business institutions, such as joint-stock companies, opened opportunities for investment and increased the flow of wealth. The roots of modern business methods can be traced to the Commercial Revolution.

Focus on World Art Print 1, Jan Vermeer. *The Artist and His Model as Klio*

 World History and Art Transparency 22, *View of Toledo*; 23, *Mission San Xavier del Bac*

Independent Practice

📁 Guided Reading Activity 17-3 **L1**

Linking Past and Present

The Commercial Revolution

The founder of England's Royal Exchange was merchant and financier Sir Thomas Gresham (1518/19–1579). He had the Royal Exchange built in London in order to provide a convenient place for merchants and traders to conduct business. The Royal Exchange was first called the "Bourse," from the French word for purse. Queen Elizabeth issued a royal proclamation in 1571 that changed its name. Today the London International Financial Futures Exchange stands on the site of the original Royal Exchange.

ANSWER

Joint-stock companies shared risks and costs among several investors. Both joint-stock companies and corporations raise money through sale of stock to a number of investors; joint-stock companies were involved in overseas trading ventures and were forerunners of today's corporations, which are large-scale organizations involved in a number of business activities.

tem based on the belief that the goal of business was to make profits took shape. Individuals known as **entrepreneurs** combined money, ideas, raw materials, and labor to make goods and profits. Profits were then used to expand the business and develop new ventures.

An entrepreneur in the cloth industry, for example, would buy wool and employ spinners to make the wool into yarn. Weavers and dyers would also be hired to turn the yarn into cloth. The entrepreneur would then sell the cloth on the open market for a price that brought a profit. Of course, entrepreneurs took risks when they put up capital for businesses. They could lose their investment if prices fell or workers could not produce goods at a specified time or for a specific market.

In the 1600s the greatest increase in trade took place in the countries bordering the Atlantic Ocean—Portugal, Spain, England, and the Netherlands—in large part because they had the largest colonial empires. Italian cities such as Venice and Genoa, formerly the leading trade centers in Europe, found themselves cut out of overseas trade as trade routes and fortunes gradually moved westward toward the Atlantic Ocean and the Americas.

Mercantilism

A new theory of national economic policy called **mercantilism** also appeared. This theory held that a state's power depended on its wealth. Accordingly, the goal of every nation was to become as wealthy as possible.

Europeans believed that the measure of a nation's wealth was the amount of **bullion**, or gold and silver, it owned. One Venetian summed up the general feeling about bullion: "[It is] the sinews of all government, it gives it its pulse, its movement, its mind, soul, and it is its essence and its very life. It overcomes all impossibilities, for it is the master … without it all is weak and without movement."

Under mercantilism, nations could gain wealth by mining gold and silver at home or overseas. Thus, Spain sent conquistadors to the Americas to seize the silver and gold mines of the Aztec and Inca Empires. Governments could also gain wealth through trade. Nations sought to create a favorable **balance of trade** by exporting more goods than they imported. The gold and silver received for exports would exceed that paid for imports. This greater wealth meant greater national power and influence in the world.

CONNECTIONS Economics

The Commercial Revolution

Queen Elizabeth opens the Royal Exchange

Europe's economic prosperity during the 1500s and 1600s made European merchants eager to increase their fortunes. Overseas trade, however, was costly and dangerous. Individual merchants found it impossible to take the entire burden on themselves. If a voyage failed, the merchant would lose everything.

This uncertainty led to the rise of joint-stock companies, which shared expenses, risks, and profits by selling stock to many investors. Joint-stock companies became so popular that stock exchanges, where investors could buy and sell stock, developed in western Europe.

Setting up a joint-stock company involved getting a charter from the monarch, who controlled merchant trade. Charters became important in the founding

of settlements and trading ventures in the Americas. Also, with their emphasis on shared risk and gain, joint-stock companies were the forerunners of modern corporations. Today, the Hudson's Bay Company, chartered in 1670 to operate the fur trade in Canada, exists as a large retail corporation with many business interests.

Linking Past and Present — ACTIVITY

Explain why joint-stock companies were popular among merchants. Compare and contrast the joint-stock company of the 1600s with the modern corporation.

MEETING SPECIAL NEEDS ACTIVITY

Learning Style: Visual/Spatial Work with students who learn best by producing or decoding graphic information to prepare a balance-of-trade chart of a hypothetical nation's imports and exports. For example, under the heading *Imports*, students might list raw materials and goods. Put a hypothetical dollar value next to each entry. Under the heading *Exports*, they should list items and give a hypothetical dollar value for each item. Have students explain why a nation must have a balance of trade. Ask what happens if more money is spent for imported goods than is received for exported goods. *(The nation goes into debt.)* Ask students how this applies to nations today. **L2**

Visualizing History Coffeehouses, such as this one depicted in London in 1668, were places to converse about the news of the day—fires, feasts, riots, weddings, plays, and scandals. *Besides coffee, what other foods and drinks were introduced to Europe in this period?*

To increase national wealth, governments often aided businesses producing export goods. They sold monopolies, or the right to operate free of local competition, to producers in certain key industries. They also set tariffs, or taxes on imported goods, to protect local industries from foreign competitors.

Colonies, or overseas territories ruled by a parent country, were highly valued in the mercantilist system. They were both the sources of raw materials as well as vital markets for finished goods provided by the parent country. The primary reason for having colonies was to help make the parent country self-sufficient.

European Daily Life

The Commercial Revolution had a noticeable impact on European society. Merchants prospered most from the expansion of trade and empire. They began to surpass the nobility in both wealth and power. Hereditary nobles had to rely on rents from their lands for wealth, but rents did not rise as fast as prices.

The newly rich entrepreneurs set trends in lifestyles. Coffeehouses became their favorite gathering places where business and gossip were exchanged. A Spaniard described a coffeehouse in Amsterdam in 1688:

66 [They] are of great usefulness in winter, with their welcoming stoves and tempting pastimes; some offer books to read, others gaming-tables and all have people ready to converse with one; one man drinks chocolate, another coffee, one milk, another tea

and practically all of them smoke tobacco …In this way they can keep warm, be refreshed and entertained for little expense, listening to the news. 99

—Joseph de la Vega, *The Wheels of Commerce*, 1817

In the countryside, however, peasants lived as meagerly as they ever had. The French writer Jean de La Bruyère (LAH•broo•YEHR) remarked that European peasants worked like animals, lived in hovels, and survived on a diet of water, black bread, and roots.

TURNING POINT

A Global Exchange

During the Commercial Revolution, Europe's population grew rapidly. In 1450 Europe had about 55 million people; by 1650, Europeans numbered about 100 million. They also had become more mobile. Towns expanded outside their walls as more and more people left rural areas to be closer to centers of trade.

Europe's growing population demanded more goods and services. This demand was met by Europe's increasing contacts with the rest of the world. As Europe's trade expanded, it contributed to a worldwide exchange of people, goods, technologies, ideas, and even diseases that had profound consequences for the entire globe.

Known as the Columbian Exchange, after Christopher Columbus, the transfer of products from continent to continent brought changes in

Chapter 17 *Expanding Horizons* **449**

Visualizing History Until the middle of the nineteenth century, when daily newspapers and home mail delivery became the norm, London coffeehouses served as informal mail depots and suppliers of newspapers. **Answer to Caption:** *corn, potatoes, chocolate, and tea*

TURNING POINT

A Global Exchange
How did increased global trade after the 1400s affect the world's people?
A worldwide exchange of people, goods, technologies, ideas, and even diseases brought changes in ways of life throughout the world. New foods and crops helped increase population in Asia, Africa, Europe, and the Americas. European influences, however, often disrupted other cultures.

ASSESS

Check for Understanding
Assign Section 3 Assessment as homework or as an in-class activity.

▣ Use Interactive Tutor Self-Assessment Software to review Section 3.

Evaluate

 Section Quiz 17-3

▣ Use the Testmaker to create a customized quiz for Section 3.

MAKING CONNECTIONS ACTIVITIES

Cultural Life Have students research and prepare short reports comparing and contrasting the role of the coffeehouse in the cultural life of London with that of the café in Paris and Vienna. Students who wish to bring their reports up to date may also include speculations on why coffeehouses have become so popular in American cities today. **L2**

Religion Missionary work continues around the world today. Ask students to research and prepare short oral reports describing the nature of contemporary missionary activity. Encourage them to focus not only on Christian missionaries but also on efforts by eastern religions, Lubavitcher Hasidic Jews, and Muslims to attract converts. **L2**

Reteach

Have students work in small groups to list and discuss the most significant changes brought about by overseas empires and the Commercial Revolution.

 Reteaching Activity 17

📁 Reading Essentials and Study Guide 17-3

Enrich

Have students research and write short reports on the life of Sir Thomas Gresham, founder of the Royal Exchange.

📁 Enrichment Activity 17

CLOSE

Have students prepare a television talk show about the impact of overseas empires on Europe and on the indigenous peoples. Appoint one student as host and several students as experts. The rest of the class should act as audience. The host should direct a series of questions at the experts and encourage audience participation.

History & Art *Man-o'-War Firing a Salute* by Jan Porcellis. **Building an empire called for military strength in this period of intense European rivalry.** *What caused many Europeans to venture to America?*

ways of life throughout the world. Europeans brought wheat, grapes, and livestock to the Americas. From Native Americans, Europeans acquired foods such as corn, potatoes, tomatoes, beans, and chocolate. Easy-to-grow food crops, such as the potato, fed Europe's growing population. Some foods, such as corn, also spread to Asia and Africa. From Asia and Africa, Europeans acquired tropical products—bananas, coffee, tea, and sugarcane—and luxury goods, such as ivory, perfumes, silk, and gems.

New global trading links increased the movement of people and cultures from continent to continent. Europeans, seeking wealth or fleeing economic distress and religious persecution, moved to the Americas and other parts of the world. They exchanged food, ideas, and practices with the peoples living in these areas. European influences profoundly affected local cultures. Traders spread European languages, and missionaries taught Christianity and European values. Wealthy Europeans, in turn, developed an interest in the arts, styles, and foods of Asia. At the same time, the drastic decline of the Native American populations and the forcible removal of Africans to the Americas revealed that European expansion often had a disruptive effect on cultures in other parts of the world.

SECTION 3 ASSESSMENT

Main Idea
1. Use a diagram like the one below to show ways in which increased trade and colonial expansion resulted in a global economy.

```
[ ]
   ↓
[ ]
   ↓
[ ]
   ↓
Global
Economy
```

Recall
2. **Define** joint-stock company, entrepreneur, mercantilism, bullion, balance of trade.
3. **Identify** capitalism and discuss the changes of the Commercial Revolution that led to its rise.

Critical Thinking
4. **Synthesizing Information** Imagine that you are an entrepreneur of the 1700s. Invent a way for making profits by using your capital and talents. Appraise the potential risks and profits in your venture.

Understanding Themes
5. **Change** Which class of European society benefited most from the Commercial Revolution? Explain your answer.

Using a Computerized Card Catalog

By now you probably have been assigned several research reports. Skill in using a computerized card catalog will help you find the information you need to complete your assignment.

Learning the Skill

Go to the card-catalog computer in your school or local library. What information do you need? Type in the name of an author or performer (for tapes, cassettes, and CDs); the title of a book, videotape, audiocassette, or CD; or a subject heading. You will access the online, or computerized card catalog that lists all the library's resources for that topic. The computer will list on screen the title's author, or the information you requested.

The "card" that appears on screen will provide other information as well, including the year the work was published, who published it, what media type it is, and the language in which it is written or recorded. Use this information to determine if the material meets your needs. Then check to see if the item is available. In addition, find the classification (biography, travel, and so on) and call number under which it is shelved.

Practicing the Skill

This chapter discusses explorers. The following steps will help you use the computerized card catalog to find additional information on the subject "explorers":

1. Type "s/explorers."
2. From the list of subjects that appears on the screen, determine which might apply to European explorers from the 1400s to the 1700s.
3. Follow the instructions on the computer screen to display all the titles under each subject you selected. For example, the

instructions might be to type the line number next to the subject and press RETURN.

4. Determine which of the books, videos, audiocassettes, and CDs now on the screen you want to learn more about.
5. What do the instructions on the screen tell you to do to find more details?
6. What do the instructions on the screen tell you to do if you want to find out how many copies of the title the library owns and if and where a copy is available?

Applying the Skill

Use the computerized card catalog in your school or local library to identify four resources—books, videotapes, CDs, or audiocassettes—you can use to write two reports. Write one report on French explorer Jacques Cartier, and the other report on technological advances in exploration from 1400 to 1700.

For More Practice

Turn to the Skill Practice in the Chapter Assessment on page 453 for more practice in using a computerized card catalog.

TEACH

Using a Computerized Card Catalog This skill introduces the use of the computer in finding library materials. After students have read **Learning the Skill**, have them use the library computer to follow the instructions in **Practicing the Skill** and in **Applying the Skill.** If the school library does not have a computerized card catalog, make arrangements with the public library to work with students. You might arrange a class field trip to the library for that purpose.

Point out to students the advantage of a computerized card catalog—the ability of the computer to narrow the student's search for information. If the student does not know or remember the name of a specific book or author, the subject heading can guide the student in the right direction.

Additional Practice

📁 Skill Reinforcement Activity 17

ANSWERS TO PRACTICING THE SKILL

Answers will vary depending on the computer program in use and the resources available in the library system.

WORLD HISTORY
Online

Have students use the **Chapter 17 Self-Check Quiz** at worldhistory.glencoe.com to prepare for the Chapter Test.

TECHNOLOGY

 VIDEODISC
Use MindJogger to review the chapter.

MindJogger Videoquiz

Chapter 17
Disc 3 Side A

Also available in VHS.

Answers

Using Key Terms
1. g   3. b   5. h
2. a   4. e

Using Your History Journal
Advise students to find specific data for their journal entries by reviewing the material in Chapters 7, 14, and 15.

Reviewing Facts
1. merchants became richer than nobles; rich entrepreneurs set trends in lifestyle; no change in peasant life; population growth; expanding trade led to cultural exchange; greater movement of people between continents
2. Causes: European interest in a more direct trade route to Asia; improved navigational technology; European investment overseas; Effects: European overseas empires; exchange of ideas, products, and peoples among several continents; better food supplies and rising populations; enslavement of Africans and the spread of diseases that ravaged

WORLD HISTORY
Online

Self-Check Quiz

Visit the *World History: The Human Experience* Web site at **worldhistory.glencoe.com** and click on *Chapter 17—Self-Check Quiz* to prepare for the Chapter Test.

Using Key Terms
Write the key term that completes each sentence. Then write a sentence for each term not chosen.

    a. cartographers   g. Middle Passage
    b. circumnavigation   h. mercantilism
    c. conquistadors   i. balance of trade
    d. entrepreneurs   j. bullion
    e. joint-stock companies   k. triangular trade
    f. line of demarcation

1. An enslaved person's journey from Africa to the Americas was known as the _____.
2. As a result of discoveries made by early European explorers, _____ were able to draw maps with greater accuracy.
3. In 1522 Ferdinand Magellan's crew arrived at Seville, Spain, completing the first _____, or circling of the globe.
4. _____, or organizations that sold stock in ventures, enabled large and small investors to share the risks and profits of a trading voyage.
5. The theory of _____ held that a nation's power rested on its accumulated wealth.

Technology Activity

Using a Spreadsheet
Search the Internet or your local library for additional information about early European explorers and their achievements. Organize your information by creating a spreadsheet. Include headings such as name, regions of exploration, types of technology used, and contributions. Provide a map of the world labeling oceans, continents, and the routes that European explorers took in discovering the world.

Using Your History Journal
Exploration brought people from Europe into contact with the cultures of Asia, Africa, and the Americas for the first time in this period. Imagine and describe such a meeting. Remember that these people did not, when meeting, understand each other's language or culture.

Reviewing Facts

1. **History** Use a diagram like the one below to identify the major effects of the Commercial Revolution on European society.

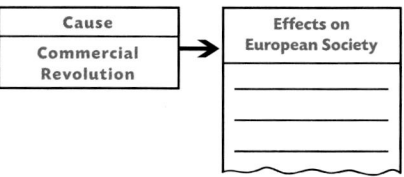

Cause		Effects on European Society
Commercial Revolution	→	_____ _____ _____

2. **History** Identify the causes and effects of European expansion in the 1500s.
3. **Technology** Describe the improvements that shipbuilders incorporated in the caravel.
4. **Economics** Explain why the Dutch turned to commerce instead of agriculture in the late 1500s.
5. **Government** Identify the Mayflower Compact and discuss politics in England's colonies.
6. **Citizenship** Describe what the Middle Passage was like for enslaved Africans.
7. **History** Explain in what ways the French and the English differed in their aims for their colonies.
8. **Economics** State how a joint-stock company enabled small investors to profit from a major voyage.

Critical Thinking

1. **Apply** Why did Columbus's plan to reach Asia by a western route appeal to Spain?
2. **Analyze** Were the English and the Spanish justified in colonizing the Americas? Why or why not?

Native Americans
3. triangular sails, multiple masts, a stern-operated rudder, and a shallow draft that enabled it to sail faster, sail against the wind, maneuver better, and go into inlets for repairs
4. They had limited land for agriculture and few natural resources. The large middle class was ready for commercial expansion.
5. Agreement signed by Pilgrims in 1620 that set down principles for governing their settle-

ment; colonists established their own representative assemblies apart from Parliament.
6. a terrifying psychological and physical ordeal
7. The French were interested in trade; the English sought raw materials.
8. It reduced the risk of individual investors.

Critical Thinking
1. Spain sought quicker routes to Asia's wealth.
2. Students should support their position.

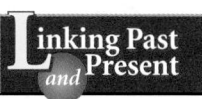
3. Evaluate How would the colonies have been different if Europeans had not used slave labor?

4. Synthesize Why is the era from the 1400s to the 1700s called the Age of Exploration? What are its major features? What was its impact?

5. Evaluate How did the influx of wealth from the colonies help bring about the Commercial Revolution in Europe?

6. Analyze What were the results of Ferdinand Magellan's circumnavigation?

7. Apply Why were the Dutch eager to establish overseas colonies?

Geography in History

1. Place What European city was the first to have potatoes for consumption?

2. Movement Why were potatoes introduced into Sweden and Finland so much later than they were in other nations?

3. Human/Environment Interaction How would new crops such as the potato affect agriculture?

Potato Introduced to Europe

Understanding Themes

1. Innovation How did Chinese and Arab discoveries aid European voyages of exploration?

2. Movement How did the Columbian Exchange affect changes in world populations?

3. Change How did the Commercial Revolution encourage more European voyages of exploration and colonization?

Linking Past and Present

1. History books used to say that Columbus "discovered" America. What did they mean, and why do we no longer see his voyage in this way?

2. Making profits motivated early entrepreneurs. Is this still the goal of entrepreneurs today?

3. Compare and contrast modern space explorations with European voyages of exploration. Consider the technologies used, the ways explorations were funded, and the impact of these ventures on human knowledge.

Skill Practice

Use the card catalog computer in your school library to find out more about Spain's empire from the 1500s to the 1700s.

1. Type "s/Spain."

2. From the list of subjects that appears on screen determine which might apply to Spain's empire from the 1500s to the 1700s.

3. Follow the instructions on the computer screen to display all the titles under each subject you selected. Which book on the screen do you want to learn more about?

4. Who is the author and publisher of the book and in what year was the book published?

5. What is the call number of the book?

6. Is the book available?

7. Go back to the screen that displays all the titles under the subject you selected. Are there any videotapes, audiocassettes, or CDs listed? If so, which resource do you want to learn more about? What is the call number? Is the resource available?

Understanding Themes

1. **INNOVATION** Europeans used the Chinese compass, the Arab astrolabe, and Muslim lateen sails.

2. **MOVEMENT** Africans brought to the Americas, Native American populations reduced.

3. **CHANGE** It made it easier to finance such voyages and for more people to profit from them.

Linking Past and Present

1. Before his voyages, Europeans were unaware of the Americas. Today we have a world perspective rather than a Eurocentric one.

2. Some students may agree, or may argue that entrepreneurs today, regulated by laws and conscience, may base their decisions on factors besides profit.

3. Technology—the development of shipping and navigation in early modern times and that of rockets, shuttles, and on-site planetary exploration craft today; funding—the role of government and private ventures then and now; human knowledge—increasing understanding of dimensions of earth and of solar system.

Skill Practice
Answers will vary depending on the resources available.

? Chapter Bonus Test Question

Ask students: How would the world be different if the age of exploration had never occurred? *(only local, or possibly, regional economies; no interracial problems; Native Americans would constitute entire population of North and South America; products and ideas would not have spread; geographical knowledge limited.)*

---

3. Possible answer: The colonies would have been less successful economically.

4. European explorers ventured overseas; exchange of goods, ideas, and peoples; European overseas empires established

5. Entrepreneurs needed expanded banking services for business outside Europe.

6. Magellan's voyage proved the world was round and larger than previously believed, that the oceans were connected, and that Columbus had not reached Asia.

7. The Dutch middle class saw trade as a means of survival.

Geography in History

1. Madrid

2. Sweden and Finland were more isolated from trade with the rest of Europe.

3. They added to, and sometimes replaced, crops that were being grown.

A complete, 1-page lesson plan is provided for each section in the *Reproducible Lesson Plans* booklet.

Empires of Asia

CHAPTER RESOURCES

	Reproducible Resources	Multimedia Resources
Chapter Opener	Chapter Themes: Graphic Organizer 18 Historical Significance Chapter Activity 18	MindJogger Videoquiz
Chapter Enrichment	Vocabulary Activity 18* Time Line Activity 18 Mapping History Activity 18 History Simulation 18 Geography and History Activity 18 Source Reading 18 People in World History Profiles 33, 34 World Art and Music Activity 18 Enrichment Activity 18 Critical Thinking Activity 18 Skill Reinforcement Activity 18 Performance Assessment Activity 18 Standardized Test Practice Workbook Activity 18 Inclusion for the Social Studies Classroom Strategies and Activities	Focus on World Art Print 10, Kitagawa Utamaro. *Reflected Beauty* World History and Art Transparency 24, *Taj Mahal*; 25, *Shah Jahan and One of His Sons Riding in Escort* Chapter Transparency 18 Vocabulary PuzzleMaker Software Picture Atlas of the World World Music: Cultural Traditions, Lessons 7, 8, 9 World History Primary Source Document Library
Chapter Review/Reteaching	Reteaching Activity 18 Skill Reinforcement Activity 18 Spanish Chapter Summary 18	Chapter 18 Digest Audiocassette, Activity, Test* Vocabulary PuzzleMaker Software Interactive Tutor Self-Assessment Software MindJogger Videoquiz
Chapter Evaluation/Testing	Performance Assessment Activity 18 Chapter 18 Test, Forms A and B	ExamView® Pro Testmaker

* *Also available in Spanish*

`0:00` **OUT OF TIME?** Assign the Chapter 18 Audiocassettes.

World History Primary Source Document Library
Make History Come Alive!
Engage your students with over 250 easily accessible primary source documents—available on this CD-ROM—that will give them real life insight into the important events of world history.

Block Schedule

Activities that are particularly suited to use within the block scheduling framework are identified throughout this chapter by the following designation.

KEY TO ABILITY LEVELS

Teaching strategies are coded for varying learning styles.
L1 BASIC activities for all students
L2 AVERAGE activities for average to above-average students
L3 CHALLENGING activities for above-average students
LEP LIMITED ENGLISH PROFICIENCY activities

Use Glencoe's *Presentation Plus!* multimedia teacher tool to easily present dynamic lessons that visually excite your students. Using Microsoft PowerPoint® you can customize the presentations to create your own personalized lessons.

 Interactive Lesson Planner

Planning has never been easier! Using this CD-ROM, organize your week, month, semester, or year with all the help you need. The **Interactive Lesson Planner** gives you access to all of the blackline masters that accompany *World History: The Human Experience.*

SECTION RESOURCES

Daily Objectives	Reproducible Resources	Multimedia Resources
Section 1 **Muslim Empires** Describe how Muslim rulers controlled and governed much of the Middle East, North Africa, and India between the 1500s and 1800s.	Lecture Notes 18-1 Reproducible Lesson Plan 18-1 Vocabulary Activity 18* Guided Reading Activity 18-1* Time Line Activity 18 History Simulation 18 People in World History Profile 33 Section Quiz 18-1* Reading Essentials and Study Guide 18-1	Section Focus Transparency 18-1 Chapter Transparency 18 World History and Art Transparency 24, *Taj Mahal*; 25, *Shah Jahan and One of His Sons Riding in Escort* Interactive Tutor Self-Assessment Software Testmaker World Music: Cultural Traditions, Lesson 7
Section 2 **Chinese Dynasties** Analyze why China flourished and then declined during the Ming and Qing dynasties.	Lecture Notes 18-2 Reproducible Lesson Plan 18-2 Vocabulary Activity 18* Guided Reading Activity 18-2* Section Quiz 18-2* Reading Essentials and Study Guide 18-2	Section Focus Transparency 18-2 Interactive Tutor Self-Assessment Software Testmaker World Music: Cultural Traditions, Lesson 8 Picture Atlas of the World
Section 3 **The Japanese Empire** Explain why Japan was more adaptable to changes than China before the 1800s.	Lecture Notes 18-3 Reproducible Lesson Plan 18-3 Vocabulary Activity 18* Guided Reading Activity 18-3* Geography and History Activity 18 People in World History Profile 34 Section Quiz 18-3* Reading Essentials and Study Guide 18-3	Focus on World Art Print 10, Kitagawa Utamaro. *Reflected Beauty* Section Focus Transparency 18-3 Interactive Tutor Self-Assessment Software Testmaker World Music: Cultural Traditions, Lesson 8
Section 4 **Southeast Asia** Explain how the Thai kingdom was able to keep its independence while other parts of Southeast Asia gradually came under European control.	Lecture Notes 18-4 Reproducible Lesson Plan 18-4 Guided Reading Activity 18-4* Reteaching Activity 18 Enrichment Activity 18 Section Quiz 18-4* Performance Assessment Activity 18 Spanish Chapter Summary 18 Reading Essentials and Study Guide 18-4	Section Focus Transparency 18-4 Vocabulary PuzzleMaker Software Interactive Tutor Self-Assessment Software Testmaker World Music: Cultural Traditions, Lesson 9

* *Also available in Spanish*

Chapter Activities

Performance Assessment Activity

Creating a Television Series Have students take the roles of producers who want to find the perfect location for a historical television series for a network. Students should work alone or in pairs to study the empires of Asia and develop proposals for the investors for the site they think people of today would find most interesting. The proposals should include descriptions of the setting, possible historical characters, possible problems for episode story lines, and the type of series that would be created. Students might present their proposals orally with visuals or in writing.

Possible Rubric Features
Accuracy of content information, concept attainment, decision-making process skills, creative thinking, clarity and organization of presentation or proposal

• *For an additional activity, refer to Activity 18 in the* Performance Assessment Strategies and Activities *booklet.*

ACTIVITY

From the Classroom of...

Jon Kilgore
Moline High School
Moline, IL

The Quest for Japan
Prepare a list of review questions about Chapter 18. Then divide an outline map of Japan into 10 or 12 sections. Assign each a value between 1 and 5 (representing a number of questions). Organize the class into five groups or families and assign each group one of the sections on the map as its family's home. The families are competing to take over the rest of Japan. Let each group in turn decide which section it wants to "enter." In order to gain that territory, the group must answer correctly the designated number of questions for the section. If a group chooses to enter an occupied section, it must compete with the group already there. The groups take turns answering questions until one answers incorrectly and loses. When all sections have been taken, the "family" with the most territory wins.

MULTIPLE LEARNING STYLES

Verbal/Linguistic
Have students debate the following proposition: Western influence on the countries of East Asia in the early modern period was more helpful than harmful.

Visual/Spatial
Select books on Indian and Persian art from the library and bring them to class. Have each student choose a different miniature painting and write a short description of it.

Kinesthetic
Have students prepare a large map of East and Southeast Asia, indicating on it some of the most important points of contact between Europeans and Asians, such as Macao, the Philippines, and Java. (They might use different colored tacks, push-pins, or labels to represent the various European countries.)

Use the following to easily assess student learning in a variety of ways.

• Performance Assessment Strategies and Activities
• Section Quizzes
• Chapter and Unit Tests
• Interactive Tutor Self-Assessment Software

• Testmaker Software
• MindJogger Videoquiz
• SAT/SAT II Test Practice
• worldhistory.glencoe.com

Additional Resources

NATIONAL GEOGRAPHIC SOCIETY — Teacher's Corner

INDEX TO NATIONAL GEOGRAPHIC MAGAZINE

The following articles relate to this chapter:

- "Sumo," by T. R. Reid, July 1997.
- "China's Gold Coast," by Mike Edwards, March 1997.
- "The New Saigon," April 1995.
- "Ibn Battuta: Prince of Travelers," by Thomas J. Abercrombie, December 1991.
- "The World of Süleyman the Magnificent," by Merle Severy, November 1987.
- "When the Moguls Ruled India," by Mike Edwards, April 1985.

NATIONAL GEOGRAPHIC SOCIETY PRODUCTS AVAILABLE FROM GLENCOE

To order the following, call Glencoe at 1-800-334-7344:

- *STV: World Geography (Videodisc)*
- *Picture Atlas of the World (CD-ROM)*
- *MapPack: Asia (Transparency Maps)*

ADDITIONAL NATIONAL GEOGRAPHIC SOCIETY PRODUCTS

To order the following, call National Geographic at 1-800-368-2728:

- *Asia (Laminated Desk Maps)*
- *Japan: Political/Historical (Map)*
- *Sumo Wrestlers of Japan: Dance of the Gargantuans (Video)*

Access National Geographic's new dynamic MapMachine Web site and other geography resources at:

- http://www.nationalgeographic.com/
- http://www.nationalgeographic.com/maps/

BIBLIOGRAPHY

Literature of the Period
Tsao Hsueh-Chin. *The Dream of the Red Chamber.* Westport, CT: Greenwood Press, 1975. Written in the eighteenth century, this is considered to be China's greatest novel.

Readings for the Student
Ebrey, Patricia B., ed. *Chinese Civilization: A Sourcebook, 2nd rev. ed.* New York: Free Press, 1993.

Readings for the Teacher
Savory, R.M., ed. *Introduction to Islamic Civilization.* New York: Cambridge University Press, 1976. Essays about Islam.

WORLD HISTORY Online

Use our Web site as an additional resource. All essential content is covered in the Student Edition.

You and your students can visit the *World History: The Human Experience* Web site at worldhistory.glencoe.com The student text directs students to the Web site for the following options:

- **Chapter Overviews**
- **Student Web Activities**
- **Self-Check Quizzes**

Answers are provided for you in a link entitled "Web Activity Lesson Plan." Additional Web Resources, Interactive Puzzles, and content updates are also available.

Visit the Glencoe Web site at socialstudies.glencoe.com for social studies activities, updates, and links to other resources.

LOCAL OBJECTIVES

_____
_____
_____
_____
_____
_____
_____
_____
_____
_____
_____
_____
_____
_____
_____
_____
_____
_____
_____

Empires
of Asia

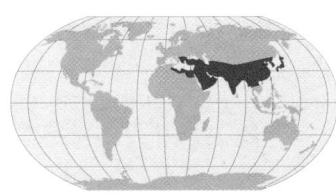

CHAPTER THEMES

Chapter Themes are listed by section on this chapter opening page of the Student Edition. A corresponding theme-based activity is available under "TEACH," and a theme-based question is asked in the Section and Chapter Assessments.

Storyteller

Historical Setting Suleiman had begun his campaign against Europe in 1521, soon after coming to power. (It was an Ottoman tradition for a new ruler to celebrate with a military campaign.) Although Suleiman was successful in his attacks on Hungary, well-organized resistance, coupled with supply difficulties and bad weather, contributed to his defeat in Vienna.

Chapter Themes

▶ **Movement** Muslim rulers govern empires that cover vast regions of Asia, North Africa, and Europe. *Section 1*
▶ **Cultural Diffusion** China is directly challenged by its contacts with western European cultures. *Section 2*
▶ **Reaction** Japan enforces isolationist policy to keep out Western influences. *Section 3*
▶ **Change** Southeast Asian lands face the growth of European trade and commerce in their region. *Section 4*

Storyteller

Within the city walls of Vienna, Austria, people quaked as thundering cannonballs signaled the beginning of the Turkish siege of the city on September 27, 1529. Occupying the surrounding hills were 100,000 Turkish soldiers led by their skilled commander Suleiman.

By mid-October, Turkish troops twice had broken through part of Vienna's walls, but failed to capture the city as the Austrians and their allies rushed to plug the breaches. This clash between European and Asian armies was one of many encounters between different civilizations during the early modern period.

Historical Significance

What kinds of empires arose in Asia during the early modern period? How did they respond to the arrival of Europeans in their areas?

Historical Significance

Answers: *One kind—represented by the Ottoman, Persian, and Mogul Empires—was founded by Muslim steppe peoples. New dynasties in China were characterized by a strong central government, while in Japan the ruling shoguns had lost much power to the daimyos. A new type of empire, the European colonial empire, began to transform Southeast Asia, although the Thai emperors managed to preserve their people's independence.*

Asian response to European arrivals ranged from cordial (Philippines) to suspicious (China) to hostile (Japan).

| 1300 | | 1500 | | 1700 | | 1900 |

1368 Ming dynasty begins in China.

1453 The Ottomans capture Constantinople.

1587 Hideyoshi outlaws Christianity in Japan.

454

— **WORLD HISTORY** —
Online

Have students use the **Chapter 18 Overview** at worldhistory. glencoe.com as a prereading and postreading exercise for understanding chapter content.

GEOGRAPHY CONNECTION

Region Use a wall map or one of the maps in the Atlas to review with students the distinguishing geographic features of the major regions discussed in this chapter: eastern Europe, western Asia, North Africa, South Asia, East Asia, and Southeast Asia. How might geography make it easier to govern Japan than the Ottoman Empire? *(Japan covers a relatively small area, whereas the Ottoman Empire stretched thousands of miles from the western Mediterranean to the Gulf of Aden.)* **L2**

History & Art This painting dates from the 1700s, when China was ruled by the Manchus, a non-Chinese people from Manchuria. Their empire—the largest in Chinese history—included Nepal, Outer Mongolia, Taiwan, and parts of Southeast Asia. What other rulers of China governed large empires? (the Han, around 200 B.C.–A.D. 200; and the Mongols, in the 1200s)

History & Art *Voyage of the Emperor Qianlong* (detail of a scroll), Qing dynasty. Musée Guimet, Paris, France

WORLD HISTORY Online

apter Overview

sit the *World History: The Human Experience* eb site at <u>worldhistory.glencoe.com</u> and click *Chapter 18—Chapter Overview* to preview e chapter.

Your History Journal

Research one of the following topics, make notes, and write an outline for a short paper: the Imam Mosque of Isfahan, the Taj Mahal, the Forbidden City, and the Imperial Palace of Tokyo.

Chapter 18 *Empires of Asia* **455**

Performance Assessment

Refer to the activity on page 454C of the Planning Guide.

For an additional activity, refer to Activity 18 in the *Performance Assessment Strategies and Activities* booklet.

Using Your History Journal

Headings might include *When* and *Where Built, Description* and *Culture/Values Reflected* for each of the places.

GLENCOE
TECHNOLOGY

VIDEODISC
Use MindJogger to preview chapter content.

MindJogger Videoquiz

Chapter 18
Disc 3 Side A

Also available in VHS.

1500   **1700**   **1900**

1526 Babur founds the Mogul dynasty in India.

c. 1740 Nader Shah expands the empire of Safavid Persia.

1856 The Hatt-I Humayun decree sets out reforms for the Ottoman Empire.

SECTION THEME

▶ **Movement** Muslim rulers govern empires that cover vast regions of Asia, North Africa, and Europe.

Guide to Reading

For reading strategies to help students read effectively see pages 12–13. Have students think about the main head as they read the subheads.

Vocabulary Pre-check

 Use the Vocabulary PuzzleMaker for Chapter 18 to create a crossword puzzle to reinforce section terms. **L1 LEP**

Use Vocabulary Activity 18 to introduce vocabulary terms. **L1 LEP**

FOCUS

Section Objective

Describe how Muslim rulers controlled and governed much of the Middle East, North Africa, and India between the 1500s and 1800s.

BELLRINGER
Motivational Activity

 Before taking roll at the beginning of the class period, project Section Focus Transparency 18-1 and have students answer the activity questions. Discuss students' responses.

This activity is also available as a blackline master.

Section 1

Muslim Empires

Guide to Reading

Read to Find Out
Main Idea *Muslim rulers controlled and governed much of the Middle East, North Africa, and India between the 1500s and 1800s.*

▶ **Terms to Define**
    sultan, grand vizier, janissary, *millet*

▶ **People to Meet**
    Suleiman I, Shah Abbas, Babur, Akbar

▶ **Places to Locate**
    Istanbul, Isfahan, Delhi

The Storyteller

    On the day that Jahangir was crowned emperor of the Moghuls [Moguls], favorable omens abounded. His coronation was a scene of splendor, illuminated by nearly three thousand wax lights in branches of gold and silver. By his command, the imperial crown was brought to him. On each of the twelve points of this crown was a single diamond.... At the point in the center was a single pearl ... and on different parts of the same were set two hundred rubies. The Emirs of his empire, waiting for Jahangir's commands, were covered from head to foot in gold and jewels.

    —adapted from *Memoirs of the Emperor Jahangir Written by Himself*, translated by David Price, reprinted in *The Human Record*, Alfred J. Andrea and James H. Overfield, 1990

Mogul warriors

    Between the 1400s and the 1800s, three Muslim empires—the Ottoman Empire, the Persian Empire, and the Mogul Empire—conquered and controlled much of eastern Europe, central Asia, and India respectively. Strong leaders used powerful armies to amass territory that gave them economic control over major trade routes. As these empires spread into new areas, the religion and culture of Islam also expanded.

The Ottoman Empire

    During the late 1200s, Turkish clans—calling themselves Ottoman Turks after their first leader, Osman—settled part of Asia Minor and began conquests to build an empire. They conquered much of Byzantine territory, making Constantinople their capital in 1453. Extending their Muslim empire even farther, by the 1500s the Ottomans controlled the Balkan Peninsula and parts of eastern Europe. By the end of their rule in the early 1900s, they had acquired much of the Middle East, North Africa, and the Caucasus region between the Black and Caspian Seas.

    The Ottoman Empire maintained a strong navy in the Mediterranean to protect the lucrative trade they controlled there. Alarmed by the threat to their trade and to Christianity, Europeans under Philip II of Spain fought and defeated the Ottoman fleet at the Battle of Lepanto in 1571. But the Ottomans rebuilt their navy and remained a significant seapower until the 1700s.

Suleiman I

    Suleiman I was one of the early Ottoman rulers who strengthened Muslim forces prior to the Battle of Lepanto. He was a multitalented man—a heroic military commander, a skillful administrator, and a patron of the arts. Ruling from 1520 to 1566, Suleiman received the name "The Lawgiver" for his work in organizing Ottoman laws.

SECTION RESOURCES

Reproducible Masters
- Lecture Notes 18-1
- Reproducible Lesson Plan 18-1
- Vocabulary Activity 18
- Guided Reading Activity 18-1
- Time Line Activity 18
- History Simulation 18
- People in World History Profile 33

- Section Quiz 18-1
- Reading Essentials and Study Guide 18-1

Transparencies
- Section Focus Transparency 18-1
- Chapter Transparency 18
- World History and Art Transparencies 24, 25

Multimedia
 Interactive Tutor Self-Assessment Software
Testmaker
World Music: Cultural Traditions, Lesson 7

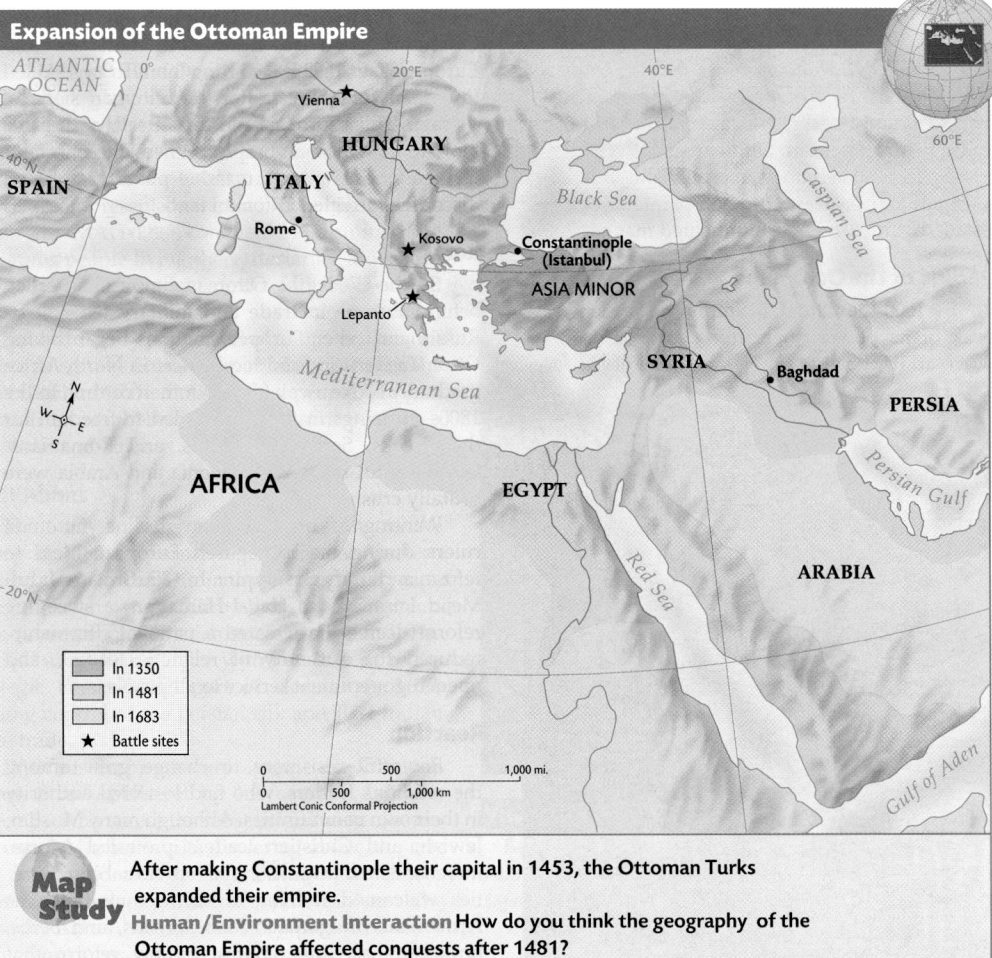

Expansion of the Ottoman Empire

After making Constantinople their capital in 1453, the Ottoman Turks expanded their empire.

Map Study **Human/Environment Interaction** How do you think the geography of the Ottoman Empire affected conquests after 1481?

Legend:
- In 1350
- In 1481
- In 1683
- ★ Battle sites

0 500 1,000 mi.
0 500 1,000 km
Lambert Conic Conformal Projection

Suleiman acted as both the sultan, or political ruler, and the caliph, or religious leader; he enjoyed absolute authority. To rule effectively, however, Suleiman needed support from his personal advisers, the bureaucracy, a group of religious advisers known as the Ulema, and a well-trained army. A grand vizier, or prime minister, headed the bureaucracy. The Ulema made rulings on questions of Islamic law, and the army held much power by conquering and controlling new territories.

The Ottomans recruited officers from among the conquered peoples of their empire. An elite corps of officers called janissaries came from the Balkans, where Christian families were required by the Ottomans to turn over young boys to the government. Converted to Islam, the boys received rigorous training that made them a loyal fighting force.

Ottoman Law

Because the empire was so large, Ottoman Muslims ruled diverse peoples, including Arabs, Greeks, Albanians, Slavs, Armenians, and Jews. The population was divided into several classes: a ruling class made up of the sultan's family and high government officials; the nobility, which administered agricultural estates; and the largest class, the peasants who worked on those estates.

To accommodate these diverse populations, the government made special laws affecting those who did not practice Islam, the empire's official religion. Non-Muslims were allowed to practice their faith. Ottoman law also permitted the empire's diverse religious groups to run affairs in their own *millets*, or communities, and choose their own leaders to present their views to the Ottoman government.

Chapter 18 *Empires of Asia* **457**

COOPERATIVE LEARNING ACTIVITY

Quiz Game Organize the class into three groups representing the Ottomans, Safavids, and Moguls. Have each team prepare questions about its empire. Encourage students to ask about the arts, foods, religious beliefs, and social codes of the cultures they represent. Each group should select one person to record the questions on note cards, with the answers on the back. Each team should choose ten questions and present these to the rest of the class as a quiz game. **L1**

TEACH

Guided Practice

THEME Movement

Ask students why Muslim peoples like the Ottomans, Persians, and Moguls might have wanted to expand their territory. *(to gain control of trade routes; to spread their religion; to protect the lands they already governed)* **L1**

Map Study

Answer
Much of Asia Minor is mountainous. Ottoman invaders had to be familiar with mountain passes and inaccessible areas before they attacked their enemies.

Map Skills Practice

Reading a Map Which modern countries, wholly or in part, were ruled by the Ottoman Empire at its greatest extent? *(Turkey, Bulgaria, Romania, Greece, Hungary, Egypt, Libya, Tunisia, Algeria, Saudi Arabia, Yemen, Syria, Jordan, Israel, Iraq)*

Religion Have students review the main tenets of Islam, with emphasis on the Five Pillars (Chapter 11). What is the main difference between Shiite and Sunni Muslims? *(Shiites believe that only a descendant of Muhammad possesses true spiritual [and political] power; Sunnis believe that any devout Muslim can hold this authority.)* **L2**

History Simulation 18

World History and Art Transparency 24, *Taj Mahal*; 25, *Shah Jahan and One of His Sons Riding in Escort*

Compare Ask students to compare the treatment of subject peoples by the Ottomans, Safavids, and Moguls. *(Ottomans: Non-Muslims could practice their own religion and run their own communities; Safavids: forced everyone to adopt Shiite Islam; Moguls: Akbar encouraged religious tolerance, but later Moguls persecuted Hindus.)* **L3**

 World Music: Cultural Traditions, Lesson 7

Who? What? Where? When?

The Janissaries By 1826 this military force had grown so large—135,000 strong—and so powerful that the sultan was forced to massacre all its members.

Independent Practice

 Guided Reading Activity 18-1 **L1**

 Time Line Activity 18

 People in World History Profile 33

Visualizing History

Although Suleiman was credited with many achievements, the governmental reforms of his reign were due largely to his vizier, Ibrahim Pasha, a man of Greek origin.
Answer to Caption: *They could practice their own religion and manage their own affairs.*

WORLD HISTORY Online

Have students use the **Chapter 18 Student Web Activity** at worldhistory.glencoe.com for in-depth study of Suleiman I.

The Ottoman Islamic civilization borrowed from the Byzantine, Persian, and Arab cultures they had absorbed. Mosques, bridges, and aqueducts reflected this blend of styles. The Christian city of Constantinople was transformed into a Muslim one and renamed **Istanbul**. Ottoman architects renovated Hagia Sophia into a mosque and built new mosques and palaces. Ottoman painters produced detailed miniatures and illuminated manuscripts.

Decline of the Ottomans

By 1600 the Ottoman Empire had reached the peak of its power; thereafter it slowly declined. Even at its height, however, the empire faced

 Portrait of Suleiman, "The Lawgiver," from the late 1600s. *What provision did the Ottoman law make for peoples of diverse religions?*

WORLD HISTORY Online

Student Web Activity 18

Visit the *World History: The Human Experience* Web site at **worldhistory.glencoe.com** and click on *Chapter 18—Student Web Activities* for an activity relating to Suleiman I.

enemies on its borders. Conquests ended as the Ottomans tried to fight both Persians and Europeans. In 1683 Polish King John III Sobieski led European forces in ending an Ottoman siege of Vienna. This European victory dealt a decisive blow to the Ottoman Empire. When Ottoman military conquests ceased, massive poverty and civil discontent afflicted Ottoman lands.

Reform

By the 1700s, the Ottoman Empire had fallen behind Europe in trade and military technology. Russia and other European nations began taking Ottoman territory, and local rulers in North Africa gradually broke away from Ottoman control. In the 1800s uprisings in the Balkans led to freedom for the Greeks, Serbs, Bulgarians, and Romanians. Unsuccessful revolts in Armenia and Arabia were brutally crushed.

Wanting to halt Ottoman decline, Ottoman rulers during the 1800s used European ideas to reform and unify the empire. In 1856 Sultan Abdul-Mejid I issued the **Hatt-I-Hamayun**, a sweeping reform decree that created a national citizenship, reduced the authority of religious leaders, and opened government service to all peoples.

Reaction

Powerful resistance to change grew among the religious leaders, who had lost civil authority in their own communities. Although many Muslim, Jewish, and Christian leaders protested reform, merchants and artisans in the individual communities welcomed it. Non-Turkish groups, such as Armenians, Bulgarians, Macedonians, and Serbs, however, had little interest in any reform that would save the empire. They wanted nation-states of their own.

After Abdul-Mejid's death in 1861, the reform movement lacked the strong leadership needed to guarantee its success. To gain public support, reformers known as the Young Ottomans overthrew the weak sultan Abdul-Aziz and replaced him with Abdul-Hamid II.

At first the new sultan went along with the reformers. In 1876 he proclaimed a new constitution. He affirmed the unity of the empire and promised individual liberties for his subjects. In 1877 the first Ottoman parliament met in Istanbul. But later that year Abdul-Hamid II suddenly dissolved the parliament and ended constitutional rule. He believed that liberalism would ruin the government. To further protect the empire from change, he exiled many of the Young Ottomans and imposed absolute rule.

MEETING SPECIAL NEEDS ACTIVITY

Study Strategy Have students work alone or in small groups to develop topic sentences for this section—first, for the section as a whole; second, for each of the three peoples discussed; and third, for each paragraph of the section. After they have developed their sentences, each one should be read aloud and discussed briefly. **L1**

Safavid Persia

To the east of the Ottoman Empire lay Persia, a land that had once been part of the Islamic Empire, but which had broken away because of religious differences. In the 1500s Shiite Muslims, bitter enemies of the Ottoman Turks, conquered the land of present-day Iran. The Shiite leader, Ismail (ihs•MAH•EEL), conquered and unified the numerous people living there, declaring himself to be the founder of the Safavid (sah•FAH•weed) dynasty.

Safavid rulers required all of their Persian subjects to accept the Shiite form of Islam. Belief in the Shia branch of Islam distinguished people living in Persia from neighboring Sunni Muslim peoples—the Arabs and Turks.

Shah Abbas

The Safavid leader **Shah Abbas** came to the throne in 1587. His army regained some western territory lost to the Ottomans in previous years. Then the shah sought allies against the Ottomans even among such Christian states as England. The English used their alliance with Persia to seize the strategic Persian Gulf port of Hormuz in 1622, gaining control of the Persian silk and East Indian spice trade.

With his empire secure against the Ottoman forces, Shah Abbas set up his court in **Isfahan**, which became one of the most magnificent cities in the entire Muslim world. Towering above the city was the blue dome of the Imam Mosque, which was covered with lacy white decorations. Near the mosque, Abbas had a three-story palace built for his personal use. He also ordered beautiful streets and parks constructed throughout the city.

During the reign of Abbas, Persian spread as the language of culture, diplomacy, and trade in most of the Muslim world. Later the language spread to India. Urdu, spoken in Pakistan today, is partly based on Persian.

Nader Shah

After the death of Shah Abbas in 1629, inept Safavid rulers weakened the empire, bringing on its decline. In 1736, after the Safavid decline, Nader Shah came to power. He expanded the Persian Empire to its greatest height since Darius. But after his assassination in 1747, territory was lost and the country was divided.

In the late 1700s another Turkic group, the Qajar dynasty, seized the Persian throne and established a new dynasty in Tehran. The Qajars ruled Persia until 1925.

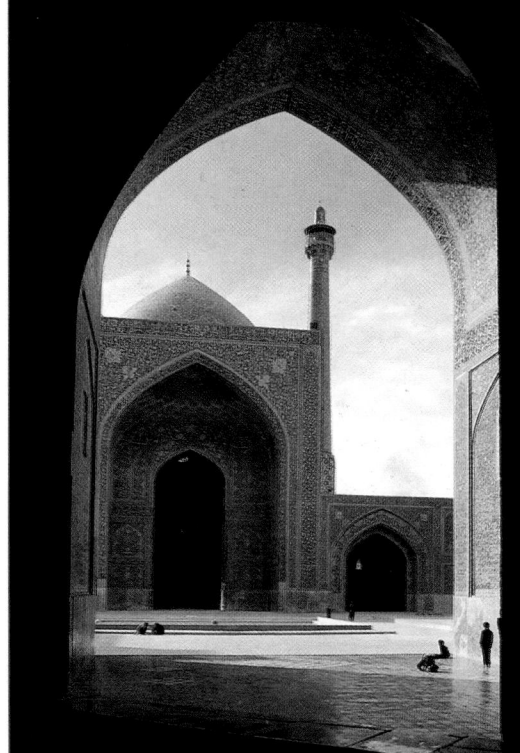

The Imam Mosque in Isfahan (in present-day Iran) was built by Shah Abbas during the early 1600s. *What cultural impact did Safavid Persia have on the Muslim world?*

The Mogul Empire

Even before the Ottomans and the Safavids built their empires, Islamic invaders from central Asia had conquered much of northern India by the 1100s. The invaders set up a sultanate, or Muslim kingdom, in **Delhi** in 1206. Once order was restored, northern India prospered economically and culturally. Traditional Hindu culture survived the invasions and blended with Islamic civilization.

Timur Lenk in India

By the late 1300s the Muslim Mongol ruler, Timur Lenk (Tamerlane), had conquered much of central Asia and made Samarkand the capital of his empire. Although a devout Muslim, Timur Lenk was also a ruthless leader. His forces sacked the city of Delhi in 1398, killing thousands and leaving the city in rubble. After Timur Lenk's death, his Islamic

Chapter 18 *Empires of Asia* **459**

Biography Have students write an article on Suleiman the Magnificent, Shah Abbas, Babur, or Akbar. Have them assume that they interviewed the ruler in order to write the article in a question-and-answer format. They should include information about the man's interests, religious beliefs, and political goals. **L2**

News Report Have students write a news report on the Battle of Lepanto or the Battle of Panipat. Remind them that news reports tell who, what, where, when, and why. **L3**

Global Gourmet

Middle East A favorite food for barbecues is shish kebab, meat and vegetables grilled on a skewer. The English term comes from Armenia, whose people adapted it from the Turkish words *sis* ("skewer") and *kebabi* ("roast mutton").

MAKING CONNECTIONS ACTIVITIES

Architecture One of Istanbul's most famous buildings, the Christian church of Hagia Sophia, has undergone several changes in its long history. Have students research these changes, ending with a description of the building today. **L2**

Religion Although Sikhs have never been as numerous as Hindus or Muslims in India, their religious group has played an important role in the country. Have students research the basic tenets of Sikhism and summarize the role Sikhs have played in Indian politics, especially in recent years. **L2**

TEACH

Tell students that the name of this tomb comes from the title of Shah Jahan's favorite wife, Mumtaz Mahal, which means "Chosen of the Palace." (Her actual name was Arjumand Banu.) For his own resting place, the emperor planned to build a replica of the Taj Mahal in black marble across the Jumna River from his wife's tomb. He lost his throne, however, before he could do so. Ask students for their responses to Tagore's description of the Taj Mahal.

Who?What?Where?When?

Shah Jahan was a conqueror as well as a builder, extending Mogul rule over areas of central India. But his reign ended unhappily, with his four sons struggling for the throne. His son Aurangzeb declared himself emperor in 1658 and confined his father to a fort for the last six years of his life.

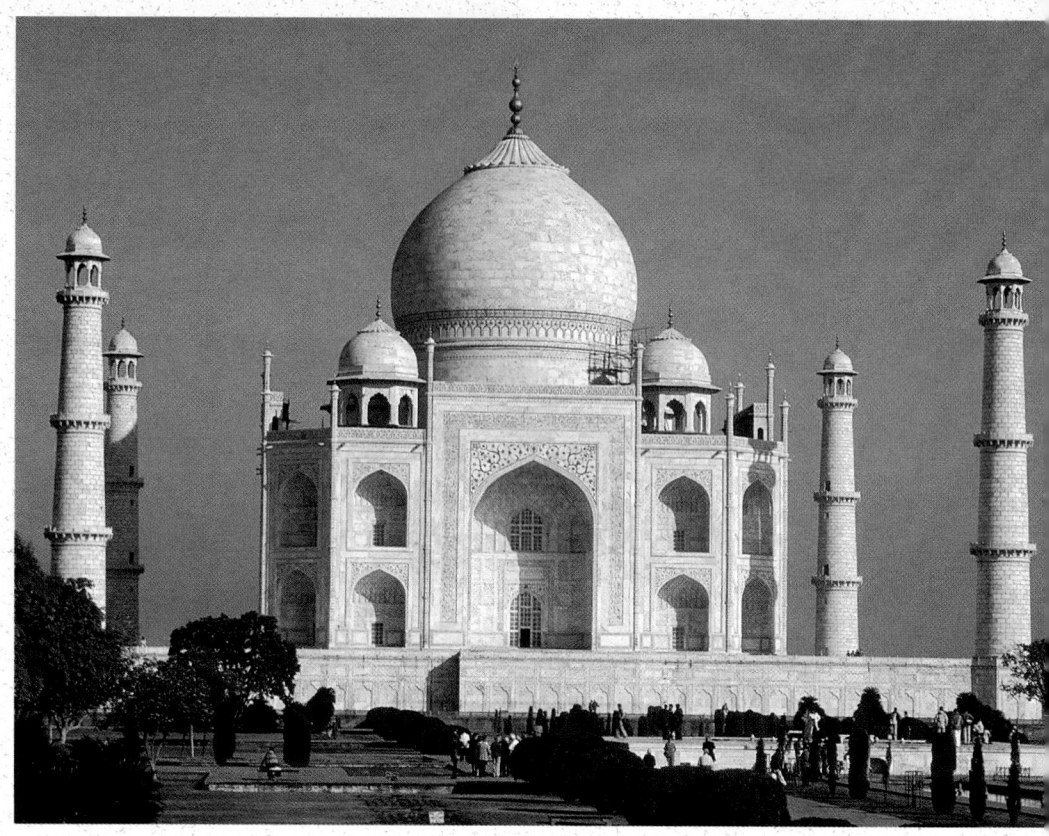

Taj Mahal

The beauty of the Taj Mahal has awed visitors for centuries. A pear-shaped dome crowns the square central building, complete with a reflecting pool. The marble surface glitters with semiprecious stones: jade from China; turquoise from Tibet; lapis lazuli from Afghanistan; chrysolite from Egypt; and mother-of-pearl from the Indian Ocean. Inside all this wealth and beauty lies Mumtaz Mahal, wife of the Mogul emperor of India, Shah Jahan, who ruled from 1628 to 1658. He fell in love with Mumtaz at 16 and adored his queen throughout her life. In 1629, shortly after Shah Jahan's reign began, Mumtaz died in childbirth, after giving birth to their 14th child. Her death left him in black despair, and in his grief he decide build the world's greatest tomb.

Or so goes the legend. Contemporary sch argue that Shah Jahan built the Taj Mahal not on a resting place for his well-loved wife—and late himself—but also as a symbol of his power wealth. The Moguls were Muslims—outsiders conquerors who ruled India in an absolute mona Their administration left India weak and, by 1800s, vulnerable to British conquest. In their ar architecture they gave India a more lasting le "The Taj Mahal," wrote Indian poet Rabindra Tagore, is "like a solitary tear suspended on the c of time." ⊕

460 Chapter 18 *Empires of Asia*

empire disintegrated; yet northern India would face other Muslim invasions.

Akbar the Great

In the early 1500s **Babur**, a descendant of Timur Lenk, led another attack on northern India. Using artillery and with cavalry riding elephants and horses, Babur conquered Delhi at the Battle of Panipat in 1526. Then he set up the Mogul dynasty, the Persian name for Mongol, which lasted three centuries in India. The Moguls encouraged orderly government, and they expanded the arts.

Babur's grandson, **Akbar**, was a benevolent ruler who brought peace and order to northern India. Recognizing that most of the people he ruled were Hindus, Akbar encouraged religious tolerance to end quarrels between Hindus and Muslims. Whereas Muslims believed in one God, Hindus worshiped many deities. Hindus and Muslims differed about sacred foods, social organization, and religious customs. To reduce tension among his people, Akbar repealed a tax on Hindus.

Akbar invited religious scholars of other faiths to his court to learn about other religions. He concluded that all religions revealed the same divine truth, whatever their external practices were. He tried to set up a new religion called Divine Faith, which included features of many of the world's religions such as Islam, Hinduism, and Christianity.

Mogul Civilization

Under Akbar's rule music, painting, and literature flourished in Mogul India. Mogul rulers made their lavish courts centers of art and learning. Although Akbar could not read, he understood the value of education and set up a large library, employing more than 100 court painters to illustrate the elegantly bound books.

Another Mogul ruler, Shah Jahan, created one of the world's most beautiful buildings—the Taj

 Akbar Hunting Tigers Near Gwalior by Husain Haqqash, c. 1580, from the *Akbar-Nama*. Victoria and Albert Museum, London, England *How did Akbar encourage religious tolerance?*

Mahal at Agra—a magnificent example of Muslim architecture. Muslim architects introduced the arch and dome to India, and in trading contacts with China, Muslim merchants brought gunpowder, paper, and Chinese porcelain to Mogul India.

Mogul Decline

During the late 1600s, Mogul rulers, such as Shah Aurangzeb, abandoned religious toleration. They persecuted India's Hindu majority as well as the Sikhs, followers of Sikhism (SEE•KIH•zuhm), a new religion founded by the teacher Nanak in the 1500s. Sikhism holds to a belief in one God and teaches that good deeds and meditation bring release from the cycle of reincarnation. Today there are about 14 million Sikhs, most of whom live in the northern Indian state of Punjab. During the late 1600s, both Sikhs and Hindus rebelled against the Moguls and helped weaken Mogul authority. As Mogul central government declined, local rulers became more independent.

SECTION 1 ASSESSMENT

Main Idea
1. Use a chart like the one below to list ways Ottoman Muslim rulers governed their empires.

Ottoman Ruler	How Governed

Recall
2. **Define** sultan, grand vizier, janissary, *millet*.
3. **Identify** Suleiman I, Hatt-I-Hamayun, Shah Abbas, Babur, Akbar.

Critical Thinking
4. **Making Comparisons** How did Shah Abbas's patronage of

the arts compare to that of a contemporary European monarch?

Understanding Themes
5. **Movement** How do you think the movement of Muslims into northern India affected the people already living there?

Chapter 18 *Empires of Asia* **461**

History & Art Akbar's interest in religion led him to invite Jesuit missionaries to his court, but they failed to convert him to Christianity. **Answer to Caption:** *by repealing a tax on Hindus*

ASSESS

Check for Understanding

Assign Section 1 Assessment as homework or as an in-class activity.

Use Interactive Tutor Self-Assessment Software to review Section 1.

Evaluate

Section Quiz 18-1

Use the Testmaker to create a customized quiz for Section 1.

Reteach

Have students review which territories were ruled by each of these peoples at their height: Ottomans, Safavids, Moguls.

Reading Essentials and Study Guide 18-1

Enrich

Have students research a famous landmark in Istanbul, Isfahan, or Delhi and write a description of it.

CLOSE

Ask: **Would you have preferred to live under Suleiman, Shah Abbas, or Akbar? Why?**

SECTION 1 ASSESSMENT ANSWERS

1. Suleiman I: acted as absolute ruler, was supported by bureaucracy and army, organized Ottoman laws; Abdul-Mejid I: introduced European ideas, such as a national citizenship and government service open to all; Abdul Hamid II: reimposed absolute rule

2. All terms are defined in the Glossary.
3. Suleiman I, 456; Hatt-I-Humayun, 458; Shah Abbas, 459; Babur, 461; Akbar, 461
4. Many contemporary rulers also encourage civic improvements.
5. **MOVEMENT** This movement led to conflicts with the people living

there, who were Hindu; eventually it led to the development of a new religion, Sikhism, which holds to beliefs in one God and reincarnation.

1400   1600   1800

1405 China begins first seagoing expedition.

1644 The Manchus establish the Qing dynasty.

1800 China's population reaches 350 million.

Section 2

Chinese Dynasties

Guide to Reading

Read to Find Out
Main Idea *China flourished and then declined during the Ming and Qing dynasties.*

▶ **Terms to Define**
junk, queue, labor-intensive farming

▶ **People to Meet**
Hong Wu, Yong Le, Zheng He, the Manchus

▶ **Places to Locate**
Beijing, the Forbidden City

The Storyteller

The examination process for civil servants was riddled with corruption. "There are too many men who claim to be pure scholars and yet are stupid and arrogant," K'ang-hsi [Kangxi] fumed. Incompetent examiners were set on memorization instead of independent thinking. Candidate lists were manipulated to favor specific provinces.

Some candidates even hired people to take the exams for them. As an active ruler K'ang-hsi was determined to have officials who were able and efficient. He addressed the problems by holding the exams under armed supervision and reading the exam papers himself.

—adapted from *Emperor of China: Self-Portrait of K'ang-hsi,* translated by Johnathan D. Spence, reprinted in *The Human Record,* Alfred J. Andrea and James H. Overfield, 1990

Han civil service exam

I n 1368, after the Yuan dynasty fell, a new era of reform began. The Ming and the Qing dynasties built strong central governments that implemented agricultural and public works projects. As food production and trade increased, so did China's population. At the same time, China looked to earlier achievements to invigorate its culture. After years of prosperity, Chinese emperors isolated themselves from their people and the outside, resulting in government corruption, rebellions, and decline.

The Ming Dynasty

After 89 years of Mongol rule, a military officer named Zhu Yuanzhang (JOO YOO•AHN•JAHNG) led a rebellion that overthrew the Yuan dynasty. Born into a poor peasant family, Zhu had been a Buddhist monk before entering the army. In 1368 he became emperor, taking the name **Hong Wu** and establishing his capital at Nanjing. For the first time in more than 1,000 years, the Son of Heaven was of peasant origin. Hong Wu gave the name *Ming* ("brilliant") to his dynasty, which would rule China for nearly 300 years.

Peace and Stability

The Ming dynasty brought peace and stability to China. Hong Wu and the early Ming rulers imposed new law codes, reorganized the tax system, and reformed local government.

The new law codes were harsher than those of previous Chinese dynasties. Scholars, traditionally exempt from corporal punishment, had to endure public whippings if they displeased the emperor and his officials. Formerly, the saying was that "a gentleman could be ordered to die but should never be humiliated."

462 Chapter 18 *Empires of Asia*

Visualizing History The Forbidden City in the heart of the city of Beijing contains hundreds of buildings. Many of these buildings housed the emperors of China and their imperial court from 1421 to 1911. *How did the Ming Emperor Yong Le contribute to Chinese scholarship?*

Chinese persons replaced Mongols in all civil service posts, and Confucianism again became the empire's official doctrine. The Ming dynasty restored the old examination system, making the tests even stricter than in earlier dynasties.

Strong rulers at the beginning of the dynasty enforced peace throughout the land. With peace and additional revenues from a reformed tax system, economic prosperity came to China. But northern China had been devastated by nomadic invaders. To encourage farmers to move there, the government offered free land, tools, seeds, and farm animals. Farmers reclaimed and restored much of the land in the north, and the policy helped secure the northern frontier from invaders.

With more land under cultivation, farmers could sell their surplus produce at local markets. Government workers repaired and maintained the canal system that connected local markets. Increased agricultural productivity also freed workers for nonfarming tasks. Artisans in larger numbers expanded the production of silk, textiles, tea, and porcelain to meet the demands of growing urban populations. Thus, trade within China

increased, enriching merchants in cities such as Shanghai and Guangzhou (GWONG•JOH).

As city merchants and artisans grew wealthier, they demanded more popular entertainments and learning. The third Ming emperor, **Yong Le**, ordered 2,000 scholars to compile a treasury of Chinese histories and literature. This massive library included neo-Confucian writings from the Song dynasty and also many Buddhist scriptures.

Ming writers preferred the novel to other forms of fiction. Their works were based largely on tales told over the centuries by storytellers. One of the most popular novels, *The Romance of the Three Kingdoms*, describes military rivalries at the end of the Han era.

Chinese Exploration

The early Ming emperors spent government money on a navy that could sail to foreign ports and collect tribute for the emperor. The ships,

Chapter 18 *Empires of Asia* **463**

COOPERATIVE LEARNING ACTIVITY

Chart Organize students into two teams, one to focus on the Ming dynasty, the other on the Qing. Each team should make a chart organizing the text information about its dynasty. Among the topics to be included are *Leaders, Religion, Trade Policies, Economics, European Contacts,* and *Cause of Decline.* Each team member should be responsible for one topic. The team members should jointly decide on the chart's format and organization. After completion, the charts should be displayed for the entire class. **L1**

Government Remind students that the Manchus formed a small minority in China. Ask how these non-Chinese exerted their control. *(by adopting some Chinese traditions, such as Confucian ideals; by favoring Manchus as officers and soldiers; by reserving top government jobs for Manchus and having Manchu supervisors for lesser employees)* **L3**

 World Music: Cultural Traditions, Lesson 8

 NATIONAL GEOGRAPHIC SOCIETY

⊙ **CD-ROM** *PICTURE ATLAS OF THE WORLD*

View traditional ceremonies that open games in Urumqi, a Muslim city deep in Central Asia, by clicking China's "Video" button.

Linking Past and Present

Chinese New Year Although China today uses the Gregorian calendar, its traditional New Year is still celebrated in both China and Chinese communities living outside China. Occurring on the second new moon after the winter solstice, it falls between January 21 and February 19. A time of clearing out the old, Chinese New Year has traditionally been an occasion for thorough housecleaning, paying debts, and giving charity to the poor.

---

known as **junks**, usually traveled along the coastline, but they could also venture into open water.

From 1405 to 1433, emperors sent out seven seagoing expeditions. Their purpose was "glorifying Chinese arms in the remote regions and showing off the wealth and power of the [Middle] Kingdom." The leader of the voyages was a Chinese Muslim named **Zheng He** (JUNG HUH).

Zheng He took his first fleet to the nations of Southeast Asia. In later voyages he reached India, sailed up the Persian Gulf to Arabia, and even visited eastern Africa. Everywhere he went, he demanded that the people submit to the emperor's authority. If they refused, he applied force; rulers who accepted were rewarded with gold or silk.

Zheng He brought back trade goods and tribute from many lands. From Africa he returned home with animals for the emperor's zoo. As a result of Zheng He's voyages, Chinese merchants settled in Southeast Asia and India and spread Chinese culture.

Later Ming emperors, however, did not follow through: ocean voyages were costly, and in the early 1400s China concentrated its funds on military forces to combat threats from nomadic tribes to the north. The emperor's officials saw no great benefit in exploring expeditions and halted them. The government discouraged trade with foreign countries partly because Confucian philosophy regarded trade as the lowest of occupations. The emperor even forbade construction of seagoing vessels.

Inside the Forbidden City

To help defend the northern border, Yong Le shifted his capital from Nanjing to Cambaluc, renaming it **Beijing** (BAY•JING), which means "northern capital." He ordered the city completely rebuilt, modeled after the great Tang capital of Changan. For 16 years, from 1404 to 1420, workers labored on its construction. On the Chinese New Year's Day in 1421, the government moved to Beijing.

A visitor entering Beijing walked through the great gate in the 30-foot-(9-meter-) high southern wall. Government workers passed through the Gate of Heavenly Peace to the offices of the Imperial City.

Images of the Times

Chinese Life

Under the stable, centralized rule of the Ming and Qing dynasties, crafts, industry, and agriculture flourished.

Breeding the silkworm required patience, but the reward was income from trade.

The Gate of Supreme Harmony at Beijing's Forbidden City is guarded well by a centuries-old lion.

Images of the Times

Chinese Life

China generally prospered in the early modern period. One development that helped the economy during the Qing dynasty was the growth of private banks. For the first time in Chinese history, merchants and traders were able to secure loans, transfer funds from one part of the empire to another, and use banknotes—along with coins—as payment.

Farther north, across a moat and through the Meridian Gate, stood **the Forbidden City**, where the emperor and his family lived. The Forbidden City had two main sections: one for the emperor's personal use and another for state occasions. The main courtyard outside the gate held 90,000 people. The emperor sometimes appeared before guests here, but ordinary people stayed out or faced a penalty of death.

The residential section of the Forbidden City consisted of many palaces with thousands of rooms. Pavilions and gardens gave comfort to the imperial family, who spent their days in fabulous splendor. Later Ming emperors devoted much of their time to pleasure. In the last 30 years of one emperor's reign, he met with his closest officials only five times.

Corrupt officials, eager to enrich themselves, took over the country. As law and order collapsed, Manchu invaders from Manchuria attacked the northern frontier settlements. Revenues for military spending were limited by the expenses of the lavish court. The Manchus managed to conquer a weakened China.

The Qing Dynasty

In 1644 **the Manchus** set up a new dynasty, called the Qing (CHING), or "pure." For only the second time in history, foreigners controlled all of China. The Manchus slowly extended their empire to the north and west, taking in Manchuria, Mongolia, Xinjiang (SHIN•JEE•ONG), and Tibet. The offshore island of Taiwan became part of the empire in 1683. For almost 300 years the Qing dynasty ruled over the largest Chinese empire that ever existed.

Adapting Chinese Culture

The Manchus had already accepted Confucian values before invading China. Their leaders understood that these precepts benefited the ruling class. Ruling over an empire in which Chinese outnumbered Manchus by at least 30 to 1, the Manchu rulers controlled their empire by making every effort to adopt many of the native Chinese customs and traditions.

Independent Practice

Guided Reading Activity 18-1 **L1**

Daily Life Have students prepare advertisements to encourage farmers during the Ming dynasty to move to northern China. In their ads, students should mention some of these government benefits: free land, tools, seeds, and farm animals. **L2**

Politics Have students brainstorm a list of topics related to the Taiping Rebellion. Examples are: Western reactions, the leader of the rebellion, the government's response to the rebellion. Ask each student to research one topic, taking notes on index cards. Have students make oral reports to the class and turn their cards in to you after the presentation. **L3**

> ### *Cultural Perspectives*
> **Foot-binding** The Manchus tried unsuccessfully to outlaw an ancient custom of foot-binding of girls. The Chinese not only admired small feet but also believed in restricting women's freedom. Long strips of cloth were used to turn the toes under and keep the feet three or four inches long. For centuries, only women who did heavy work could escape this painful procedure, for normal feet made a woman unfit for marriage. The practice did not die out until the 1900s.

A Ming porcelain bowl painted in underglaze displays the familiar blue willow pattern.

Iron workers decorate this Chinese vase preserved in the Golestan Palace, Tehran, Iran.

> **REFLECTING ON THE TIMES**
>
> 1. What artistic creation was done under the emperor's patronage?
> 2. How do these objects and scenes reflect life under the Ming and Qing dynasties?

465

ANSWERS TO REFLECTING ON THE TIMES

1. porcelain
2. China enjoyed stable government under emperors who patronized artists and architects. The Chinese also enjoyed economic prosperity based on trade and the production of practical and luxury items.

Feeding China

Providing for China's growing population was made easier by an innovation introduced by the Manchus—the use of storehouses in each province. By storing reserves of grain, these granaries helped avert famine in years when crops were poor.

ANSWER

In the past, farmers terraced the land and received new food products; and the government sponsored irrigation systems and canals. Today, government has encouraged the profit motive among farmers; dams, bridges, and other public works have been constructed. Answers may include: use of power-driven machinery to cultivate more land; extensive cultivation, however, can lead to soil erosion, and chemicals in fertilizers run off into vital water supplies and contaminate them.

Who?What?Where?When?

Matteo Ricci—known to the Chinese as Li Ma-tou—was the most famous Jesuit missionary to China. He and his fellow Jesuits impressed the Chinese not only with their knowledge of Chinese but also with their tolerance for Chinese customs. For example, they allowed their congregations to discharge fireworks during Mass, in accordance with Chinese religious practice.

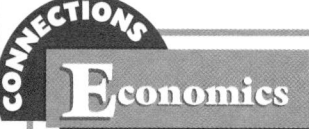

Economics

Feeding China

During the Ming and Qing eras, China expanded its agricultural production. Rapid population growth, particularly in eastern China, made it necessary for farmers to grow more food. Terracing—the steplike areas that farmers dug out of hillsides—helped them make full use of their lands. To help farmers water their crops and transport them to market, the government continued building canal and irrigation systems.

Chinese irrigation

Meanwhile, new crops from the Americas arrived in China on Chinese ships that traveled regularly to Southeast Asia. During the 1500s, Spanish ships brought sweet potatoes, maize, and peanuts as well as silver and gold from the Americas to the Philippines. There Chinese merchants exchanged silk or porcelain for the precious metals and exotic foods. All these factors helped make China's population the largest in the world.

Today, China is still the world's most populous country, despite government efforts to limit population growth. Farm production also has significantly risen because of better opportunities for farmers to make profits on the open market. Electricity reaches many villages, and a few rural households now operate small factories and businesses. Dam construction, bridge building, and other public works have transformed rural China, while new products have come to China through increased trade with other parts of the world.

 ACTIVITY

Discuss past and present ways used by the Chinese to expand food production. In doing so, how have they changed their environment? How have modern farming practices affected the environment in various parts of the world?

Manchus kept control by naming Manchus to the officer corps and by ensuring that most of the soldiers were Manchus. To control the Chinese civil service, Manchus reserved the top jobs in the government hierarchy for their people. Even Chinese officials in lower positions had a Manchu supervisor monitoring their work. Critical military and government positions thus remained loyal to the Manchu leadership.

In 1645 the Manchu emperor ordered all Chinese men to shave their heads leaving a single queue, or braid, at the back of their heads—or be executed. Among the people this order was known as "Keep your hair and lose your head" or "Lose your hair and keep your head." The upper classes had to adopt the Manchu tight, high-collared jacket and abandon their customary loose robes. But in spite of the many-layered controls, the Manchu rulers took on more elements of Chinese culture.

The Qing were fortunate in having able emperors in the first years of their rule. Emperor Kangxi, who ruled from 1661 to 1722, reduced taxes and undertook public works projects, such as flood control. Kangxi, himself a poet, also sponsored Chinese art. Other emperors secured new territory, extending the Qing Empire.

Daily Life

The Manchus made few changes in China's economy. The government-sponsored work projects and internal peace contributed to economic prosperity in the 1700s. Agricultural improvements increased food production, whereupon China's population exploded, from about 150 million in 1600 to 350 million in 1800. China was the most populous country in the world.

More than three-fourths of the Chinese people lived in rural areas. In the south where Chinese farmers worked as tenants, each family farmed its plot and paid rent to a landlord. In the north, more families owned their land. But because a family divided its land among its sons, over the generations the average peasant's share of land shrank.

As population increased, every inch of land had to be made productive. Although the Chinese had invented such simple machines as the wheelbarrow and paddle-wheel pumps, farmers depended on human labor for most farm tasks. In hill country, farm workers dug flat terraces into the hillsides where rice and other crops could be grown. Workers carried pails of water to fill the rice paddies. This labor-intensive farming, in which work

MEETING SPECIAL NEEDS ACTIVITY

Language Delayed To encourage active participation by students for whom English is a second language, organize the class into two groups. Have one represent a Chinese family in Beijing during the Ming dynasty, the other a Turkish family in Istanbul during the same period. Each group should prepare an itinerary for a visiting student from the other country. Tasks should include gathering information about the places on the itinerary and role-playing an interaction between the hosts and the visitor. Each student should participate by explaining at least one aspect of the culture or describing one historic place to the guest. **L1 LEP**

is performed by human effort, contrasts with agriculture in which the hard work is done by animals or machinery.

Subsistence farming was not a year-round occupation during the Qing dynasty. Many farmers grew cash crops such as cotton, rather than just their own food. A writer in the 1700s described the life of farm families in one district:

> **The country folk only live off their fields for the three winter months…. During the spring months, they … spin or weave, eating by exchanging their cloth for rice…. The autumn is somewhat rainy, and the noise of the looms' shuttles is once again to be heard everywhere in the villages…. Thus, even if there is a bad harvest … our country people are not in distress so long as the other counties have a crop of cotton [for them to weave].** 》

Silk production provided extra income for farm families. They grew mulberry trees, whose leaves provided food for silkworms. From the leaves women and girls plucked the cocoons and carefully unwound them. Then the silk was ready for those who spun it into thread and others who wove it into silk cloth.

Internal trade flourished during the Qing period. There was a lively exchange of goods within and between the various regions of China. Great merchant families made fortunes trading rice, silk, fish, timber, cloth, and luxury goods. The growth of trade prompted specialization. Some regions were famous for textiles; others for cotton, porcelain, tea, or silk. At Jingdezhen, the emperor's porcelain factory employed thousands of workers. Artists delicately painted vases, bowls, and plates. Others made chemical glazes that formed a hard, shiny surface on the pottery after it was fired in a hot kiln.

Contacts With Europeans

European demand for Chinese goods such as silk and porcelain was high, attracting European ships to China's coast. The first Europeans arrived in China during the Ming dynasty. In 1514 Portuguese caravels landed near Guangzhou. The Chinese officials refused to deal with them. Nonetheless, by 1557 the Portuguese had built a trading base at Macao.

Jesuit missionaries followed the Portuguese traders with the dream of converting China's huge population to Christianity. Although most Chinese officials were not interested in Christianity, the Jesuits' scientific knowledge impressed them. In 1611 the emperor placed a Jesuit astronomer in charge of the Imperial Calendar, and in years to come Jesuits gained other government positions. They also converted some court officials to Christianity. By the 1700s, however, Qing rulers worried that Jesuits were too involved in government affairs and forced the missionaries to leave. The Jesuits had failed to make China a Christian nation.

Qing Decline

During the 1700s corruption and internal rebellions forced the Qing dynasty into a slow decline. As the population grew, the government raised taxes to support public services. High-ranking officials, however, kept much of the revenue. Peasant rebellions followed.

By 1850 the Qing faced the Taiping Rebellion. The leader of this revolt came in contact with Christian missionaries and developed his version of Christianity. He organized many Chinese into a political movement to replace the Qing dynasty with a "Heavenly Kingdom of Great Peace." Lasting 14 years, the rebellion left much of southern China destroyed and the central government weakened. Thus undermined, the Qing faced new threats from foreign imperialistic powers.

SECTION 2 ASSESSMENT

Main Idea
1. Use a diagram like the one below to show the reasons for China's rise and decline during the Ming and Qing dynasties.

Ming/Qing Dynasties

Rise / \ Decline

Recall
2. **Define** junk, queue, labor-intensive farming.
3. **Identify** Hong Wu, Yong Le, Zheng He, the Forbidden City, the Manchus.

Critical Thinking
4. **Evaluating Information** How did the achievements of the Ming and Qing dynasties

differ? Did the Qing build on the successes of the Ming, or did they create a completely new civilization?

Understanding Themes
5. **Cultural Diffusion** What might have happened if the Chinese had continued moving westward? Would China have colonized as Europeans did?

ASSESS

Check for Understanding

Assign Section 2 Assessment as homework or as an in-class activity.

 Use Interactive Tutor Self-Assessment Software to review Section 2.

Evaluate

Section Quiz 18-2

Use the Testmaker to create a customized quiz for Section 2.

Reteach

Have students summarize the similarities between the Ming and Qing dynasties. (*Agricultural development was encouraged, internal trade thrived, the arts flourished, foreigners were met with suspicion, rulers accepted Confucian values.*)

Reading Essentials and Study Guide 18-2

Enrich

Have students research the way silk was produced in the 1500s and 1600s in China. Have them prepare diagrams and oral reports on the process.

CLOSE

Have students summarize relations between China and the rest of the world during the Ming and Qing dynasties.

SECTION 2 ASSESSMENT ANSWERS

1. Ming: rise: peace and stability; reformed local government; strong rulers; economic prosperity; exploration; decline: stopped exploring; discouraged trade; collapse of law and order; invaded; Qing: rise: adapted Chinese culture; economic prosperity; international trade; decline: corruption; raised taxes; internal rebellion

2. All terms are defined in the Glossary.
3. Hong Wu, 462; Yong Le, 463; Zheng He, 464; the Forbidden City, 464; the Manchus, 465
4. The Ming were known for their overseas voyages, the Qing for conquests that made the Chinese Empire the largest that ever existed. The Qing built on Ming successes.

5. **CULTURAL DIFFUSION** The Chinese would probably have met stiff resistance from the Ottomans, among others. It is unlikely that they would have set up colonies since they were interested mainly in internal development and protecting their borders.

1600

1600 Tokugawa Ieyasu wins the Battle of Sekigahara.

1636 Act of Seclusion forbids Japanese to leave the country.

c. 1700s Japanese cities grow in size and population.

1700

1800

Section 3

The Japanese Empire

Guide to Reading

Read to Find Out
Main Idea *Japan was more adaptable to changes than China was before the 1800s.*

▶ **Terms to Define**
sankin-kotai, metsuke, geisha, haiku

▶ **People to Meet**
Oda Nobunaga, Toyotomi Hideyoshi, Tokugawa Ieyasu, Francis Xavier, Matsuo Basho

▶ **Places to Locate**
Edo, Nagasaki

The Storyteller

Yamaga Soko bowed deeply. The shogun, Tokugawa Ieyasu, would determine if Yamaga was prepared to assume a samurai's responsibilities. "In peacetime, we should not be oblivious to the danger of war. Should we not then prepare ourselves for it?" asked Tokugawa. Yamaga understood that many considered the use of arms evil. "Beyond these military duties, we have other functions. We are examples for all society, leading simple and frugal lives," Yamaga responded. Not only would the samurai excel at death; they should also cultivate all aspects of life. Tokugawa spoke again, "A samurai's life calls for constant discipline. Are you, Yamaga Soko, prepared to devote yourself to this?"

—adapted from *Sources of Japanese Tradition,* reprinted in *The Human Record,* Alfred J. Andrea and James H. Overfield, 1990

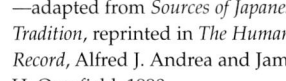
Samurai in combat

While China enjoyed stability in the 1400s and 1500s, Japan experienced a period of turmoil. The shogun was a mere figurehead, and the emperor performed only religious functions. Daimyos, who controlled their own lands, waged war against their neighbors as feudal lords had done in Europe in the 1400s. "The strongest eat and the weak become the meat" was a Japanese expression of the time. Warriors showed no chivalry or loyalty. This time of local wars left Japan with a political system known as the Tokugawa shogunate that combined a central government with a system of feudalism.

Tokugawa Shogunate

Oda Nobunaga (oh•DAH noh•boo•NAH•gah) was the first military leader to begin uniting the warring daimyos. He announced his ambition on his personal seal: "to bring the nation under one sword." After winning control of a large part of central Japan, Nobunaga led his army against the capital city of Kyoto in 1568. Five years later, amid the chaos caused by the weak Ashikaga (ah•shee•KAH•gah) family, Nobunaga deposed the Ashikaga shogun. Meanwhile, his forces had moved against Buddhist military strongholds around Kyoto. After a 10-year siege, he won and so became the most powerful man in the country. In 1582, however, a treacherous soldier murdered him.

Toyotomi Hideyoshi

Power then shifted to Nobunaga's best general, **Toyotomi Hideyoshi** (toh•yoh•TOH•mee HEE•day•YOH•shee), who rose from a peasant family to his high position in the military. By 1590 Hideyoshi had forced Japan's daimyos to pledge their loyalty to him. Acting as a military dictator, Hideyoshi furthered his goal of unity by disarming the peasants to prevent them from becoming warriors. In 1588 he ordered the "great sword hunt," demanding that all peasants turn in their weapons. To stabilize the daimyo realms he controlled, he imposed laws that prevented warriors from leaving their daimyo's service to become merchants or farmers. The laws also prevented farmers and merchants from becoming warriors.

Hideyoshi, planning to expand Japan's power abroad, invaded Korea as a step toward conquering China. The invasion had another purpose—to rid the country of warriors who could start rebellions at home. However, as you learned in Chapter 14, Admiral Yi's Korean turtle ships thwarted Hideyoshi's conquest.

Tokugawa Ieyasu

After Hideyoshi's death in 1598, a third leader, **Tokugawa Ieyasu** (toh•kuh•GAH•wah ee•YAH•soo), completed the work of unification. At the Battle of Sekigahara (seh•kee•gah•HAR•ah) in 1600, Ieyasu defeated the last of his opponents. Three years later, Ieyasu asked the emperor to make him shogun. The Tokugawa family retained the shogunate for 265 years.

Tokugawa Rule

Ieyasu established his government headquarters at the fishing village of **Edo**, present-day Tokyo. There he built a stone fortress protected by high walls and moats. Today, the fortress is the Imperial Palace, but during the Tokugawa shogunate, the Japanese emperor continued to live in Kyoto. Although the emperor remained the official leader of Japan, the shogun exercised the real power.

After taking control, Ieyasu reassigned the daimyos' lands. He divided the daimyos into three groups: Tokugawa relatives, longtime supporters of the Tokugawa family, and those who came to the Tokugawa side only after the Battle of Sekigahara. He issued the most productive lands near Edo to the Tokugawa relatives. The others—potential enemies—received less desirable lands in outlying areas of Japan.

To ensure daimyo loyalty, Ieyasu set up a system called *sankin-kotai*, or attendance by turn. Each daimyo had to travel to Edo every other year, bringing tribute and remaining in the shogun's service for a full year. Thus, half the daimyos were directly under the shogun's control at any one time. Even when the daimyos returned to their estates, they had to leave their families at Edo as hostages.

The daimyos spent much of their income traveling to and from Edo and maintaining several households. They also had to get the shogun's permission to marry and to repair or build their castles. *Sankin-kotai* kept them weak, obedient to the shogun, and less able to rebel against the government. Much like Louis XIV of France, the shogun turned his aristocracy into courtiers who were carefully watched and controlled.

Political System

The Tokugawa family and a select group of daimyos controlled the government. Together they made up the Council of Elders, the leading administrative body. Assisting the Council, as the "eyes and ears" of the state, was a group of officials known as the *metsuke*. The *metsuke* toured the country and reported on possible uprisings or plots against the shogun. A genuine bureaucracy began to develop, working on the principles of joint decision making and promotion based on talent and success.

Social Classes

Before 1600 there had been some social mobility between classes in Japan. Hideyoshi and Ieyasu

Visualizing History As a member of a professional class of women, a geisha might serve a samurai in song or dance, by playing a musical instrument, or engaging in stimulating conversation. *What were the symbols of authority permitted only to a samurai?*

TEACH

Guided Practice

THEME Reaction

Ask: Who were the first Europeans to arrive in Japan? When? (*the Portuguese; in 1543*) How did the Japanese react to the Portuguese arrival, both initially and later on? (*Initially they welcomed the Westerners; eventually they forced them to leave and initiated a policy of isolation.*) **L1**

Geography Give each student an outline map of Japan. Have students label the major islands: Hokkaido, Honshu, Kyushu, and Shikoku. Then ask them to add these cities: Edo (Tokyo), Osaka, Kyoto, and Nagasaki. **L1 LEP**

Focus on World Art Print 10, Kitagawa Utamaro. *Reflected Beauty*

World Music: Cultural Traditions, Lesson 8

Visualizing History When a geisha married, she retired from the profession.
Answer to Caption: *a sword and a distinctive topknot in the hair*

COOPERATIVE LEARNING ACTIVITY

Presentation Have students develop presentations on the samurai. Organize the class into small groups and have each one choose a particular topic to research. Possible topics: the rise of samurai, famous samurai, clothing and armor, daily life, combat techniques (such as kendo). Have each group decide on the format of its presentation, such as lecture, bulletin-board display, role play, or drawings. Plan class time for the students to give their presentations. **L2**

Independent Practice

📁 Guided Reading Activity 18-3 **L1**

📁 Geography and History Activity 18

📁 People in World History Profile 34

Art Have students use library resources to prepare a report on one of these Japanese artists: Hiroshige, Hokusai, or Utamaro. In their reports to the class, have them tell something about the artist, the style of art for which he was known, and the subject matter of his work. Encourage students to show examples of the artist's work. **L2**

Linking Past and Present

Kurosawa Feudal Japan has been brought to life in the movies of today. In dramatizing the past, few have excelled more than the great Japanese film director, Akira Kurosawa. His *Seven Samurai* tells the story of poor villagers who hire samurai to fight off bandits. Kurosawa's film was the basis for a popular American Western, *The Magnificent Seven*.

Visualizing History In the early 1700s, Edo's population of more than 1,000,000 made it the largest city in the world.
Answer to Caption: *samurai, farmers, artisans, and merchants*

---

had both risen to the top from lowly backgrounds. To maintain social stability and limit future rivals, they introduced measures that froze the Japanese social structure.

Under Tokugawa rule, the Japanese were divided into four social classes. At the top were the samurai, including the daimyos, who held all political power. They alone could wear symbols of authority: a sword and a distinctive topknot in their hair. The farmers, as major food producers, were the second-highest class. They were followed by artisans who made goods. Merchants were at the bottom of society, because they only exchanged goods and thus were not productive.

No one could change his social class or perform tasks that belonged to another class. One samurai recalled that his father took him out of school because he was taught arithmetic—a subject fit only for merchants. A character in a popular puppet play, written by the author Chikamatsu, described the proper order of society:

> **❝** A samurai's child is reared by samurai parents and becomes a samurai himself because they teach him the warrior's code. A merchant's child is reared by merchant parents and becomes a merchant because they teach him the way of commerce. A samurai seeks a fair name in disregard for profit, but a merchant, with no thought to his reputation, gathers profit and amasses a fortune. This is the way of life proper to each. This strict social order helped maintain peace and stability throughout Japan. **❞**

Visualizing History In Tokugawa Japan, cities became leading centers of Japanese culture. Artisans began to produce goods for a growing urban market. *What social classes made up Tokugawa Japan?*

Tokugawa Ethics

Tokugawa ethics placed loyalty to the shogun above the family. Duty and honor became the central values. Individuals had to develop strict inner discipline to live up to the requirements of their assigned place in life. These values gradually spread from the samurai through all social classes in Japan.

Over the course of time, Tokugawa rules for personal conduct evolved into complex rituals and etiquette. Minute details came to have heavy symbolic meaning. They became a way to maintain conformity and control. This was important for a society that had a large population and only a small area of productive land.

Contacts with the West

The peace and order of the Tokugawa shogunate were interrupted when the first Europeans—the Portuguese—arrived in Japan in 1543. Although the Japanese looked upon Europeans as barbarians, the warrior society saw that European weapons meant power. They purchased muskets and cannon to defeat their opponents.

Roman Catholic missionaries soon followed the Portuguese merchants. **Francis Xavier**, the earliest of the Jesuit priests who came to Japan, admired the Japanese people. To convert them, the Jesuits adopted their customs. Jesuit missionaries learned the subtleties of conversing in polite Japanese and set up a tea room in their houses so that they could receive their visitors properly.

After Xavier won the support of some local daimyos, Christianity spread rapidly. Oda Nobunaga himself lent support to the Christians, for during this time he was moving against the Buddhist monasteries that were serving as military strongholds. Jesuits trained Japanese priests to create a strong Japanese Christian church. By 1614 the Jesuits had converted 300,000 Japanese.

Many Japanese welcomed the first contact with Westerners, whose customs and styles became widespread in Japanese society. Even for Japanese who had not converted to Christianity, Christian symbols became fashionable. A missionary described non-Christian daimyos who would wear "rosaries of driftwood on their breasts, hang a

---

MEETING SPECIAL NEEDS ACTIVITY

Study Strategy Textbooks such as this one often use boldface type to call attention to terms, people, and places students should remember. As students read this chapter, have them make a list of the words in boldface, together with an identifying phrase or sentence to help them recall why the word is important. **L1**

Merchants from the West arrive in Japan accompanied by Jesuit missionaries. *How did Christian missionary activity end under Tokugawa rule?*

crucifix from their shoulder or waist … they think it good and effective in bringing success in daily life."

Hideyoshi began to suspect that Christian influence could be harmful to Japan. He had heard of Spanish missionaries in the Philippines who had helped establish Spain's control over the islands. In 1587 Hideyoshi outlawed Christianity. Although some priests were crucified, Hideyoshi generally did not enforce his ban on the religion.

Tokugawa Ieyasu and his successors also feared that Christianity threatened their power and so continued to persecute Christians, killing them or forcing them to leave Japan. When Japanese Christians in the port city of **Nagasaki** defied authorities and refused to disband, the government attacked their community in 1637 and finally wiped them out in 1638.

Japan barred all Europeans except the Dutch. Unlike the Spanish and the Portuguese, the Dutch were interested only in trade, not conquest or religious conversion of the Japanese. For this reason, after 1641 the Tokugawa government confined the Dutch to a tiny island in Nagasaki harbor where they and a few Chinese carried on a tightly regulated trade. Through the Dutch traders, a trickle of information about the West continued to flow into Japan.

Despite Japan's geographic isolation and the Tokugawa policy of isolation, Japan's society and economy continued to change internally. During the early Tokugawa period, agriculture brought wealth to daimyos and samurai, who profited from the rice produced on their lands. Merchants, in turn, grew wealthy by lending money to daimyos and samurai.

TURNING POINT

Japan's Policy of Isolation

The Tokugawa rulers, deciding that contact with outsiders posed too many dangers, laid down edicts. Their seclusion policy lasted 200 years. The Act of Seclusion of 1636 forbade any Japanese to leave the country and added, "All Japanese residing abroad shall be put to death when they return home." The government banned construction of ships large enough for ocean voyages.

Footnotes to History

Karate
Karate is unarmed combat in which a person uses primarily the hands or feet to strike a blow at an opponent. This martial art began on the island of Okinawa near Japan. During the 1600s, Okinawa's Japanese conquerors forbade the local people to own weapons. In response, many Okinawans learned to turn their hands and feet into fighting instruments.

Chapter 18 *Empires of Asia* **471**

CURRICULUM CONNECTION

THE ARTS

Japanese prints *(ukiyo-e)* influenced many European artists in the 1800s. Among the painters who admired and imitated their flat, decorative style were Vincent van Gogh, Henri de Toulouse-Lautrec, and Édouard Manet.

ASSESS

Check for Understanding

Assign Section 3 Assessment as homework or as an in-class activity.

▣ Use Interactive Tutor Self-Assessment Software to review Section 3.

Evaluate

 Section Quiz 18-3

Reteach

Have students make charts for the Tokugawa era (1600–1868). Use headings such as *Government, Society,* and *Foreign Relations* to summarize main events.

Reading Essentials and Study Guide 18-3

Enrich

Have students read the classic *A Book of Five Rings* and prepare a brief book report, including biographical material about the author, Miyamoto Musachi.

CLOSE

Discuss Japan's location and how it furthered a policy of isolation. Ask students what would be different in our society if Japan had remained isolated.

 AROUND THE WORLD First Public Opera House Opens

Venice, Italy, 1637
The Teatro San Cassiano—the world's first public opera house—opened in Venice in 1637. Early baroque operas consisted of recitatives, or informational parts, sung by soloists accompanied by one or two instruments. The arias, or solos expressing a character's feelings, allowed opera singers to show off their vocal skills. By the late 1600s, operas were being written and performed in England, France, and Germany. Italian opera, however, remained the accepted style.

Venice

As the daimyos became a debtor class, the merchant class became more powerful.

The system of *sankin-kotai* also helped merchants to prosper and trade to increase, because merchants provided the goods and services that the daimyos needed on their twice-yearly trips to Edo. To smooth the daimyos' journey, the government built roads, which also eased trade to distant regions. Rest stations along the roads often grew into large trading or administrative towns.

At the same time, the demands for increased taxes led the daimyos to increase agricultural yields. As agriculture became more efficient, farming required fewer people. Unemployed farmworkers moved to prosperous towns and cities, seeking work as artisans. In urban centers such as Edo, Kyoto, and Osaka, social order began to break down and class distinctions became less rigid.

Social life in the cities converged on bathhouses, restaurants, and theaters. Japanese merchants and samurai could relax in the company of geishas, women who were professional entertainers. Geishas were trained in the arts of singing, dancing, and conversation. Urban amusement centers also provided employment for playwrights, artists, and poets. At this time a new form of theater known as Kabuki developed. Kabuki became popular for its portrayal of historical events and emotion-filled domestic scenes. During this period the elaborate Japanese puppet theater called Bunraku, in which three-man teams manipulated each puppet as a backstage chorus sang a story, also arose.

A popular form of art called ukiyo-e developed from the demand for prints of famous actors and their plays. At first, ukiyo-e prints were black-and-white, but soon ornate, brightly colored prints appeared in street stalls. Printed on delicate rice paper, they are highly prized collectors' items today.

A new form of poetry called haiku (HY•koo) also became popular among city people. In only 17 syllables, the haiku was to express a thought that would surprise the reader. **Matsuo Basho**, one of the great haiku masters, wrote this haiku:

❝ **In my new clothing
I feel so different
I must
Look like someone else.** ❞

As cities grew in size and population during the 1700s and 1800s, the ban on foreign contacts was gradually relaxed. Some Japanese began to study Western medicine in books that the Dutch brought to Nagasaki. Their interest in the so-called Dutch learning spread to Western science and technology. However, it would not be until the other Europeans arrived in the 1800s that Japan would begin to absorb other Western ideas.

SECTION 3 ASSESSMENT

Main Idea
1. Use a diagram like the one below to show major changes in the Japanese political and social system from the 1400s to the 1800s.

1400s ————————————— 1800s

Recall
2. **Define** *sankin-kotai, metsuke,* geisha, haiku.
3. **Identify** Oda Nobunaga, Toyotomi Hideyoshi, Tokugawa Ieyasu, Francis Xavier, Matsuo Basho.

Critical Thinking
4. **Synthesizing Information** Imagine that you lived in Japan during the Tokugawa shogunate. Which social class would you have wanted to belong to? Explain.

Understanding Themes
5. **Reaction** Discuss Japan's rejection of Western ideas, its isolationist policy, and how this affected the country's development.

SECTION 3 ASSESSMENT ANSWERS

1. 1598 country unified; 1636 Act of Seclusion forbade people to leave country; economic prosperity; wealthy merchants lent money; increased trade; unemployed farm workers sought work as artisans; rise of Kabuki Theater, haiku
2. All terms are defined in the Glossary.
3. Oda Nobunaga, 468; Toyotomi Hideyoshi, 468; Tokugawa Ieyasu, 469; Francis Xavier, 470; Matsuo Basho, 472
4. Answers should reflect an understanding of social classes.
5. **REACTION** The Tokugawa rulers believed Western religious ideas were harmful; Japan was unaware of much Western thought and technology until the 1800s.

Using a Word Processor

There are several ways to create a professional looking printed document. You may use a word processor or a computer word processing software program. A word processor is a keyboard-operated terminal with a video display.

Learning the Skill

When you open most word processors, you are initially presented with a blank document. To create a new document, simply begin typing. Use the following tips to help you format the document to make it look the way you want:

1. Text fonts, or size and style of type, can be chosen. To choose font or size and style of type, click **Font** on your Standard toolbar.
2. Text can be made to appear **bold**, *italicized*, or underlined. To do this, first highlight the text (drag the cursor, or pointer, over the text with the left mouse button depressed). Then choose the modification mentioned above (the way you do this depends on the word processor you are using).
3. Press **Tab** to indent a paragraph. Press **Enter** to start a new paragraph.
4. To insert new text in a line, move the cursor to the point where you want the line to go and type. The word processing program moves the existing text to the right to make room for the new text.
5. When you finish typing, click the **Spell Check** button on the Standard toolbar to check the spelling of your document.

Practicing the Skill

This chapter focuses on the empires of Asia from 1350 through 1850. Create a newspaper article about an important event during one of these empires. Be sure to include a headline in your article. To use a word processor to create this document, complete the following steps.
1. Choose a font and the text size from the standard toolbar. Use a different text and size for your headline than you use for the rest of the text.
2. Type two or three paragraphs of copy about the event you chose for your article. As you type, make modifications to the text, such as bold, italics, or underlining.
3. Press **Tab** to indent a paragraph. Press **Enter** to start a new paragraph.
4. Insert new text in a line.
5. Use **Spell check** to check the spelling of your document.

Applying the Skill

Using a word processor, create an official-looking document that explains the Ottoman Laws described on pages 457–458 of this textbook.

For More Practice

Turn to the Skill Practice in the Chapter Assessment on page 479 for more practice in using a word processor.

ANSWERS TO PRACTICING THE SKILL

Answers will vary depending on the event chosen to write about. Check for accurate use of word processing functions, such as fonts, paragraph indents, spelling, and so on.

TEACH

Using a Word Processor If possible, schedule computer lab time so students can get practice in using a word processor. As students follow the instructions in **Learning the Skill,** point out that word processing programs automatically "wrap" the text to the next line when the text reaches the right margin. Tell them to make sure that they do not press **Enter** at the end of each line of text, unless they are starting a new paragraph.

Help students find the toolbar on the screen of their computer. Have them practice word processing techniques using the functions shown on the toolbar. For example, have them practice moving text around on a page. Have students move several lines of text. Say to students, "Highlight the text you wish to remove and then click the Cut button (or scissors icon) on the toolbar. Next, position your cursor (insertion point) in the location that you want to move the cut text and click the Paste button (or jar of paste icon). The cut text appears at your cursor. If you accidentally drag or paste text to the wrong place, click the Undo or Edit button on the toolbar."

To learn other word processing methods, have students read their word processor user's manual or click the Help button on their toolbar.

📁 Skill Reinforcement Activity 18

1500   1700   1900

1511 Portuguese seize port of Melaka on the Malay Peninsula.

1565 Spaniards found a colony in the Philippines.

1767 Troops from Burma seize Ayutthaya.

1868 Chulalongkorn becomes king of Siam.

SECTION THEME

▶ **Change** Southeast Asian lands face the growth of European trade and commerce in their region.

Guide to Reading

For reading strategies to help students read effectively see pages 12–13.

Vocabulary Pre-check

 Use the Vocabulary PuzzleMaker for Chapter 18 to create a crossword puzzle to reinforce section terms. **L1 LEP**

📁 Use Vocabulary Activity 18 to introduce vocabulary terms. **L1 LEP**

FOCUS

Section Objective

Explain how the Thai kingdom kept its independence while other parts of Southeast Asia gradually came under European control.

BELLRINGER
Motivational Activity

 Before taking roll at the beginning of the class period, project Section Focus Transparency 18-4 and have students answer the activity questions. Discuss students' responses.

📁 This activity is also available as a blackline master.

Section **4**

Southeast Asia

Guide to Reading

Read to Find Out
Main Idea *The Thai kingdom was able to keep its independence while other parts of Southeast Asia gradually came under European control.*

▶ **Terms to Define**
colony, *datus*, animism

▶ **People to Meet**
Trailok, Phraya Chakkri, Mongkut, Chulalongkorn

▶ **Places to Locate**
Manila, Java, Indochina, Bangkok

The Storyteller

The century-old Bayon Temple of Angkor swarmed with workers. Huge stone faces with faint, haunting smiles gazed in all directions. A European merchant stepped closer to examine the temple and nearly collided with a monk. When asked about the faces, the monk replied, "This old Hindu shrine will become a Buddhist temple. Jayavarman, our king, has adopted the Buddhist religion and wishes to introduce its teaching throughout our land. Sculptors have been commissioned to create new images on the temple. Most important is the image of boddhisattva, a compassionate being who looks everywhere for souls to save."

—freely adapted from *World History*, Volume 1, William Duiker and Jackson Spielvogel, 1994

Relief from Bayon Temple of Angkor

By the mid-1400s, Southeast Asia was carrying on extensive trade with other regions. This was partly because of its location on the water route between India and China. In addition, Southeast Asia produced valuable spices and woods that people in other parts of the world wanted to buy.

European Influences

In the early 1500s the first European explorers reached Southeast Asia in search of new trade routes and products. With the coming of the Europeans, Southeast Asian kingdoms faced a growing challenge to their independence and traditional ways of life.

The Portuguese Spice Trade

Coming from India, the Portuguese were the first Europeans to reach Southeast Asia in the early 1500s. They set out to control the region's lucrative spice trade which, for many years, had been controlled by Muslim traders. In 1511 Portuguese soldiers captured the most important of the Muslim ports—**Melaka**, on the west side of the Malay Peninsula.

During the next 25 years, the Portuguese built a number of new trading posts in Southeast Asia. They patrolled the seas near the islands of present-day Indonesia to keep out the ships of other countries. The Portuguese also tried to spread Catholicism in maritime Southeast Asia. They had little success, however, because most Southeast Asian islanders resented Portuguese disregard for their traditional cultures.

Spanish Rule in the Philippines

The Spaniards were eager to find their own route to the spices of Southeast Asia. In 1521 Ferdinand Magellan, exploring for Spain, reached Southeast Asia by sailing westward around the

---

SECTION RESOURCES

📁 **Reproducible Masters**
- Lecture Notes 18-4
- Reproducible Lesson Plan 18-4
- Guided Reading Activity 18-4
- Reteaching Activity 18
- Enrichment Activity 18
- Section Quiz 18-4
- Performance Assessment Activity 18

- Spanish Chapter Summary 18
- Reading Essentials and Study Guide 18-4

📖 **Transparencies**
- Section Focus Transparency 18-4

Multimedia
- Vocabulary PuzzleMaker Software
- Interactive Tutor Self-Assessment Software
- Testmaker
- World Music: Cultural Traditions, Lesson 9

Visualizing History During the 1600s, the Netherlands reached its height as a seafaring power. Dutch merchant ships sailed the seas from the Caribbean region to the East Indies (Indonesia). *How did the Dutch win control of the Indonesian island of Java?*

southern tip of South America. Magellan and his crew landed in the Philippines, becoming the first Europeans to visit these islands.

In 1565 the Spanish founded a colony, or overseas territory ruled by a parent country, in the Philippines. Although the Spanish did not find spices in the Philippines, they did find fertile land and an excellent location for trade. Spanish soldiers and officials established a fortified settlement at **Manila** on the island of Luzon. Manila's magnificent harbor made the Philippines a valuable link in Spain's trade with Asia and the Americas.

The Spaniards gradually expanded their control to other parts of the islands. They persuaded many of the *datus*, or local rulers, to pledge loyalty to Spain in return for keeping their regional powers. Under Spanish rule, most of the people of the Philippines—largely of Malay and Chinese descent—accepted many Spanish customs as well as the Roman Catholic faith. Spanish Roman

Catholic clergy established missions, learned the local languages, taught the people European agricultural methods, and introduced new crops—such as maize (corn) and cocoa—from the Americas. Spain's control of the Philippines would last well into the late 1800s.

Dutch Traders in Indonesia

By the end of the 1500s, English and Dutch traders were also wanting a share in the Southeast Asian spice trade. After breaking Portuguese control of the trade, they began to fight each other. During the 1620s, the Dutch finally succeeded in forcing the English to leave the islands that now make up present-day Indonesia. A further step toward Dutch control of the islands came in 1677 when the ruler of Mataram, a kingdom on the island of **Java**, asked the Dutch to help him defeat a rebel uprising. In return for their assistance, the Dutch received important trading rights and

Chapter 18 *Empires of Asia* **475**

COOPERATIVE LEARNING ACTIVITY

Debate Organize the class into two groups representing advisers to a Southeast Asian ruler. Europeans, who have been trading with their country, now want to establish a colony there. One group should argue in favor of the colony while the other group opposes it. Each participant should contribute specific reasons in support of their group's stand. **L2**

TEACH

Guided Practice

THEME Change

Ask students to list the foreigners who brought change to Southeast Asia beginning in the 1500s. *(Portuguese, Spanish, English, Dutch, French)* What goal did they all have in common? *(trade)* **L1 LEP**

Geography Using a wall map or a map in the Atlas of this book, review with the class the geographical features of the Southeast Asian regions of special concern in this chapter: the Malay Peninsula, Indonesia, the Philippines, Indochina, Siam (Thailand), and Burma (Myanmar). **L2**

Visualizing History During the golden age of the Netherlands—the 1600s—this small country was among the most powerful and influential nations on the earth.
Answer to Caption: *using force to get the English to leave; gaining concessions from local rulers in exchange for their help*

Economics Discuss with students the advantages and disadvantages to a parent country of having colonies. *(advantages: control over subject peoples, assured source of raw materials, assured market for goods from the home country; disadvantages: need for supervision by parent country, drain on parent country's resources)* **L3**

♩ World Music: Cultural Traditions, Lesson 9

Independent Practice

📁 Guided Reading Activity 18-4 **L1**

Daily Life Have students, as Spanish settlers living in the Philippines in the 1600s, write to friends in Spain urging them to emigrate and explaining why life as a colonist offers a good future. **L2**

Government Have students research the present-day Chakkri ruler of Thailand. In brief reports, have them summarize his role and compare it with that of the founder of the dynasty, Phraya Chakkri. **L3**

Linking Past and Present

The King and I In the 1860s King Mongkut employed a Welsh governess, Anna Leonowens, to tutor his children. Her story was told in a popular book of the 1940s, *Anna and the King of Siam*. The book in turn served as the basis for the musical *The King and I*, three movies, and a television serial.

Visualizing History

In a single year, King Trailok had 500 statues of the Buddha cast, hoping to prevent a repetition of the great famine that had devastated his country the year before.
Answer to Caption: *Hinduism and animism*

Javanese lands. Through similar agreements and by force, the Dutch had gained control of most of the other Indonesian islands by the late 1700s.

The French in Vietnam

The French were latecomers in the European pursuit of trade and colonies in Southeast Asia. Beginning in the 1600s, French traders based in India carried out only limited trade with the Vietnamese and other peoples in the Southeast Asian region of **Indochina**. Because of the weakness of this trade link, the Vietnamese and their Indochinese neighbors were able to keep the French from taking control of their area. Roman Catholic missionaries from France, however, converted many Vietnamese to Christianity.

By the early 1800s most of Indochina was ruled by local emperors who came from the region of Annam in present-day Vietnam. At this time, Indochina was predominantly Chinese in culture. Devoted to Confucian ideas, the Annamese emperors persecuted their Christian subjects and tried to keep Indochina closed to Europeans. Angered at the policies of the Annamese court, the French in 1858 returned to Southeast Asia in force. Their stated purpose was to protect local Christians from persecution. However, they also wanted Indochina's rubber, coal, and rice. In the 1860s the French began to colonize the region.

The Thai Kingdom

While European influence grew throughout Southeast Asia, the independent kingdom of Ayutthaya (ah•YU•tuh•yuh) continued to flourish in the area that is present-day Thailand. Under a series of powerful kings, the Thai people of Ayutthaya developed a rich culture based on Buddhism, Hinduism, and animism, the idea

Visualizing History This bronze bas-relief of the Buddha reveals the important role that Buddhism has played in unifying the Thai people and in supporting their rulers. *What other religious influences shaped the development of Thai culture?*

that both living and nonliving things have spirits or souls.

Trailok's Rule

One of the most powerful Ayutthaya monarchs was King **Trailok**, who ruled from 1448 to 1488. Trailok set up a strong central government with separate civil and military branches directly responsible to him. He also brought local leaders to Ayutthaya and put them in charge of new governmental offices. These officials were required to live in the capital where the king could easily oversee their work.

Trailok set up a rigid class system based on loyalty to the Thai monarchy. All male Thai were given the use of varying amounts of land according to their rank. Nobles and merchants were given as much as 4,000 acres (1,620 ha), while enslaved people, artisans, and other subjects with little status received 10 acres (4 ha) or less. Women were not included in this distribution of land.

Expansion

While the Ayutthaya kingdom set its internal affairs in order, Thai soldiers fought battles with neighboring peoples, such as the Khmer, Burmans, and Malays. Through conquests, the Ayutthaya kingdom grew to almost the size of present-day Thailand. In 1431 Thai soldiers from Ayutthaya captured Angkor Wat and destroyed it. They also overcame the Malays in the south as well as smaller Thai kingdoms in the north.

During the mid-1500s a border dispute led to war between the Ayutthaya kingdom and Burma (Myanmar). Soldiers from Burma briefly captured the city of Ayutthaya in 1569, but the Thai king Naresuan defeated Burma's ruler in the Battle of Nong Sarai in 1593.

European Contacts

The 1500s also saw the beginning of European contacts with Ayutthaya. The Portuguese and later the Dutch and the English sent delegations to the kingdom to encourage trade. For much of the 1600s, Thai rulers allowed Europeans the right to carry out trade in their territory. In 1612

MEETING SPECIAL NEEDS ACTIVITY

Learning Style: Kinesthetic Some students may need help understanding the nature of trade in Southeast Asia in early modern times. Organize the class into small groups and assign each one a Southeast Asian trade item, such as cloves, cinnamon, cassia, nutmeg, ebony, or rosewood. Have each group find an example of its item to bring to class. Also, have each group research its item, finding out where in the region it is from and how it was used by Europeans. **L1**

British traders took a letter from King James I to the Thai monarch. They reported back that the city of Ayutthaya, with its palaces and Buddhist temples, was as large and awesome as London.

The Thai, however, became concerned that Europeans wanted to colonize as well as trade. In 1688 a Thai group that opposed European influences took over the kingdom. The new rulers expelled most of the Europeans except for a few Dutch and Portuguese traders. The kingdom closed its ports to the West until 1826.

The Bangkok Era

Free of European influence, Thai rulers hoped for a period of calm. Burma, however, wanted to resume the conflict with Ayutthaya that it had lost in the late 1500s. In 1767 an army from Burma defeated the Thai and sacked and burned the city of Ayutthaya. The Thai, however, soon rallied after the disaster. Phraya Taksin (PRY•uh tahk•SEEN), a Thai general, led his troops against Burma's army and drove it out of the region.

After proclaiming himself king, Taksin forced rival Thai groups to accept his rule. He reigned until 1782, when rebel leaders overthrew him. The rebels called on General **Phraya Chakkri** (PRY•uh SHAH•kree) to be the new Thai monarch. Chakkri founded the royal dynasty that still rules Thailand today. Chakkri built a new capital called **Bangkok** on the Chao Phraya River. Under Chakkri's rule, the reborn Thai kingdom became known as Siam.

Reforming Monarchs

By the mid-1800s Europeans were pressuring Thai rulers to widen trade opportunities in Siam. King **Mongkut** recognized the threat that Western colonial nations posed to the independence of his kingdom. To protect Siam, he set foreign nations against one another through competition.

Mongkut achieved this goal by allowing many Western nations to have commercial opportunities

in the kingdom. The Thai king welcomed what he judged to be the positive influences of Western commerce on his country. He encouraged his people to study science and European languages with the Christian missionaries who had accompanied European traders to the kingdom.

After Mongkut's death in 1868, his son **Chulalongkorn** (choo•lah•LAHNG•kohrn) came to the throne. Like Mongkut, Chulalongkorn worked to modernize Siam while protecting the kingdom from European controls. He ended slavery, founded schools, encouraged his people to study abroad, and built railways and roads.

Visualizing History King Mongkut ruled Siam from 1851 to 1868. He increased the powers of the monarchy while supporting social reforms. *How did Mongkut work to preserve Siam's independence?*

Visualizing History Mongkut spent 25 years as a monk before he became king. He also studied Latin, English, mathematics, and astronomy. **Answer to Caption:** *By giving commercial opportunities to many different nations, he set them against one another and thus reduced their power.*

ASSESS

Check for Understanding

Assign Section 4 Assessment as homework or as an in-class activity.

▣ Use Interactive Tutor Self-Assessment Software to review Section 4.

Evaluate

 Section Quiz 18-4

▣ Use the Testmaker to create a customized quiz for Section 4.

Reteach

Have students review the role of European traders in Southeast Asia.

 Reteaching Activity 18

 Reading Essentials and Study Guide 18-4

Enrich

Have students research and report on the death of Magellan in the Philippine Islands.

 Enrichment Activity 18

CLOSE

Have students summarize how Southeast Asia in the late 1800s differed from what it had been in the early 1500s.

SECTION 4 ASSESSMENT

Main Idea

1. Use a diagram like the one below to identify reasons why the Thai kingdom stayed independent of European control.

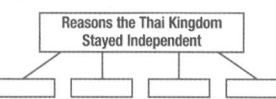

| Reasons the Thai Kingdom Stayed Independent |

Recall

2. **Define** colony, *datus*, animism.
3. **Identify** Melaka, Manila, Trailok, Phraya Chakkri, Bangkok, Mongkut, Chulalongkorn.

Critical Thinking

4. **Making Comparisons** How did the Spanish conquest of the

Philippine Islands differ from the Portuguese conquest of the Indonesian islands?

Understanding Themes

5. **Change** How did the Thai kings Mongkut and Chulalongkorn respond to the growth of Western influence in their region?

Chapter 18 *Empires of Asia* **477**

SECTION 4 ASSESSMENT ANSWERS

1. powerful kings; rich culture based on Buddhism, Hinduism, animism; strong central government; conquests of neighbors; closed ports to West until 1820s; mid 1800s set foreign nations against one another through competition
2. All terms are defined in the Glossary.
3. Melaka, 474; Manila, 475; Trailok, 476; Phraya Chakkri, 477; Bangkok, 477; Mongkut, 477; Chulalongkorn, 477
4. The Spanish established colonies, not just trading posts. Also, they had more success in spreading Christianity.
5. **CHANGE** welcomed some Western education and innovations but also protected Siam from foreign control

WORLD HISTORY *Online*

Have students use the **Chapter 18 Self-Check Quiz** at <u>worldhistory.glencoe.com</u> to prepare for the Chapter Test.

GLENCOE TECHNOLOGY

VIDEODISC
Use MindJogger to review the chapter.
MindJogger Videoquiz

Chapter 18
Disc 3 Side A

Also available in VHS.

Answers

Using Key Terms
1. h   3. d   5. k
2. g   4. c

Using Your History Journal

Remind students that they should back up any generalizations they make with specific details.

Reviewing Facts
1. Portugal; Spain; Netherlands; France
2. Ottoman, Safavid, Mogul
3. The Ottomans were Sunni Muslims; the Persians were Shiites and bitter enemies of the Ottomans.
4. The Moguls were Muslims, unlike their Hindu subjects. Rulers like Akbar were tolerant, but later Moguls persecuted Hindus.
5. to display China's wealth and to obtain trade and tribute
6. staffed army with Manchus; reserved top government jobs for Manchus; had Manchus monitor Chinese officials; enforced Manchu hair and clothing styles
7. Geishas were female professional entertainers who were trained in

478 Chapter 18 *Empires of Asia*

WORLD HISTORY *Online*

Self-Check Quiz

Visit the *World History: The Human Experience* Web site at **worldhistory.glencoe.com** and click on *Chapter 18—Self-Check Quiz* to prepare for the Chapter Test.

Using Key Terms

Write the key term that completes each sentence. Then write a sentence for each term not chosen.

a. geisha   g. labor-intensive farming
b. grand vizier   h. sultan
c. haiku   i. queue
d. janissaries   j. *datus*
e. *sankin-kotai* k. *millets*
f. colony

1. The Ottoman leader Suleiman I acted as both the _____, or political ruler, and the caliph, or religious leader.
2. During the Manchu dynasty, the Chinese practiced _____ in which workers dug flat terraces into hillsides to grow rice.
3. Ottoman sultans maintained a special corps of soldiers known as _____ who were noted as a fierce and loyal fighting force.
4. Japanese writers developed _____, a form of poetry made up of 17 syllables, that became popular among city people.
5. Ottoman law allowed religious groups to run affairs in their own _____, or communities.

Technology Activity

Using a Computerized Card Catalog Use a computerized card catalog to locate sources about traditional Japanese customs that are practiced in Japan today. Write an essay discussing how political power, leadership, and loyalty in traditional Japan compare to how these characteristics are viewed in modern democracies. Share your opinions with the rest of the class.

478   Chapter 18 *Empires of Asia*

Using Your History Journal

From your notes and outline write a three-page paper on one of the four sites listed on page 455. Discuss what that place reveals about the civilization that built it.

Reviewing Facts

1. **History** Use a chart like the one below to list the European countries that took control of an area in Southeast Asia.

European Countries
1.
2.
3.
4.

2. **History** Name the three great Muslim empires in eastern Europe, central Asia, and India.
3. **Culture** Define the relationship between Sunni Muslims and Shiite Muslims living in the Ottoman Empire and the Persian Empire.
4. **Culture** Explain how the Moguls' religion brought them into conflict with the majority of India's people. Describe how Mogul rulers reacted.
5. **History** Explain the purpose of the voyages of Zheng He.
6. **History** List the steps taken by the Manchus to maintain their control over China.
7. **Culture** Describe the role of geishas in Japan.
8. **Culture** Discuss the effects of the shogunate's policies on Japan's Christian population.

Critical Thinking

1. **Apply** How did religious differences cause strife between Muslim empires?
2. **Evaluate** Would you consider Suleiman I a successful ruler? Why was he called "The Lawgiver" by the Ottomans?
3. **Analyze** How did Akbar's religious tolerance in India differ from that of the Manchus in China?

---

the arts of singing, dancing, and conversation. They worked in expanding urban areas to entertain merchants and samurai.

8. Fearing the spread of Christian and Western influences, shoguns persecuted Christians, killing them or forcing them to leave Japan.

Critical Thinking

1. The Safavids, as Shiite Muslims, were bitterly opposed to the Ottomans, who were Sunnis.

2. yes; because of his work in organizing Ottoman laws

3. Akbar invited representatives of all faiths to his court because he was curious about different religions. The Manchus allowed Christian missionaries into China but were only interested in their scientific knowledge.

4. Answers should reflect knowledge of the various governments.

5. The Moguls (who were Muslims) conquered

4. Evaluate Which government described in this chapter was most successful in meeting its people's needs? Why?

5. Evaluate How did the movement of Islamic peoples affect northern India? What impact did Islam have on religion in this part of India?

6. Analyze What factors led to China's growth in both land and population during the Qing dynasty? How did government policies contribute to this growth?

7. Evaluate Was the Ming dynasty's policy of isolationism beneficial to China? Explain.

8. Analyze How did new urban centers in Japan influence growth in the arts and entertainment?

Geography in History

1. Region Refer to the map below that shows the political divisions of Japan about 1560. For more than a century, feudal lords fought for control of territory. How many daimyo clans ruled in Japan during this period?

2. Location What is the relative location of the Takeda domains?

3. Human/Environment Interaction What geographic conditions helped make it possible for Japan to enforce a policy of isolation from the rest of the world in the 1600s?

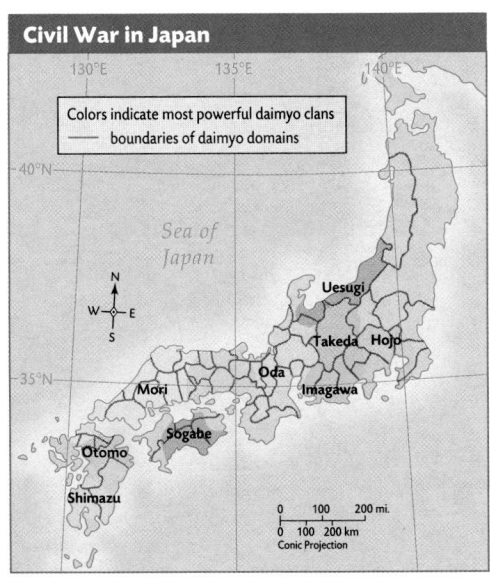

Civil War in Japan

Colors indicate most powerful daimyo clans
— boundaries of daimyo domains

Sea of Japan

Uesugi
Takeda Hojo
Oda
Mori Imagawa
Sogabe
Otomo
Shimazu

0   100   200 mi.
0 100 200 km
Conic Projection

Understanding Themes

1. Movement What areas of Asia came under the rule of the Muslim empires?

2. Cultural Diffusion How did Christianity spread to China? To Japan?

3. Reaction What good and bad effects resulted from Japan's policy of isolation?

4. Change What development was crucial in advancing Dutch control of the islands of Indonesia?

Linking Past and Present

1. Do you think it is possible for today's nations to follow a policy of isolation like Japan's in the early modern period? Have any tried to?

2. From the 1300s to the 1800s powerful Asian rulers took drastic measures to implement changes that they supported. Is a powerful ruler or a strong central government necessary today for technological advancement and economic prosperity? Give reasons to support your position.

Skill Practice

Using a word processor or a computer word processing software program, create a one-page professional-looking document using the subject of Japan's isolationist policy—The Act of Seclusion of 1636. For example, you might wish to create a letter written by the Tokugawa rulers to European rulers or create a handbill that was given out to European traders to warn them about the isolation policy. Be sure to complete the following steps while creating your document:

1. use more than one font and text size
2. use bold, italics, and underlining
3. include paragraph indents
4. run spell check
5. try other word processing techniques that help create a professional-looking document

2. CULTURAL DIFFUSION via Jesuit missionaries; by European Roman Catholic missionaries

3. REACTION Good: internal trade thrived and merchants became wealthy; roads were built; towns grew. Bad: Japan did not absorb many Western ideas until the 1800s.

4. CHANGE The ruler of Mataram asked for Dutch help in putting down rebels.

Linking Past and Present

1. Isolation is harder today because of modern communications; Albania, Cambodia, and North Korea.

2. Answers will vary.

Skill Practice

Answers will vary but content should include: Contact with outsiders posed too many dangers; Japanese were forbidden to leave Japan; the government banned construction of ships large enough for ocean voyages; Europeans, except Dutch, were barred from the country; Dutch were confined to a tiny island in Nagasaki harbor.

❓ Chapter Bonus Test Question

Ask students: In your view, what is the most important difference between the Muslim empires of western and South Asia and the older cultures of East Asia? *(In the former, Islam was a driving force, while in the latter, people maintained other religious traditions. The western and South Asian empires, at least in the beginning, resulted from expansive, outward thrusts; in East Asia, civilizations turned inward.)*

northern India, initiating a continuing conflict between Hinduism and Islam.

6. Manchus made conquests in the north and west; its population increased because of peace and improvements in agriculture.

7. yes; the Ming had the funds to fight off nomadic tribes because they had stopped putting money into ocean voyages

8. As cities grew and class divisions weakened, there was a larger market for entertainment.

Geography in History

1. nine

2. south of Uesugi territory, north of Imagawa lands, west of Hojo domains

3. It is an island nation.

Understanding Themes

1. MOVEMENT western Asia and South Asia

A complete, 1-page lesson plan is provided for each section in the *Reproducible Lesson Plans* booklet.

Royal Power and Conflict

CHAPTER RESOURCES

	Reproducible Resources	Multimedia Resources
Chapter Opener	Chapter Themes: Graphic Organizer 19 Historical Significance Chapter Activity 19	MindJogger Videoquiz
Chapter Enrichment	Vocabulary Activity 19* Time Line Activity 19 Mapping History Activity 19 History Simulation 19 Geography and History Activity 19 Source Reading 19 People in World History Profiles 35, 36 World Art and Music Activity 19 Enrichment Activity 19 Critical Thinking Activity 19 Skill Reinforcement Activity 19 Performance Assessment Activity 19 Standardized Test Practice Workbook Activity 19 Inclusion for the Social Studies Classroom Strategies and Activities	Focus on World Art Print 19, Jan Steen. *The Dancing Couple*; 20, Jean-Baptiste Simeon Chardin. *The Attributes of Painting* World History and Art Transparency 26, *The French Ambassadors*; 22, *View of Toledo* Chapter Transparency 19 Vocabulary PuzzleMaker Software Picture Atlas of the World World Music: Cultural Traditions, Lesson 3 World History Primary Source Document Library
Chapter Review/Reteaching	Reteaching Activity 19 Skill Reinforcement Activity 19 Spanish Chapter Summary 19	Chapter 19 Digest Audiocassette, Activity, Test* Vocabulary PuzzleMaker Software Interactive Tutor Self-Assessment Software MindJogger Videoquiz
Chapter Evaluation/Testing	Performance Assessment Activity 19 Chapter 19 Test, Forms A and B	ExamView® Pro Testmaker

* Also available in Spanish

0:00 OUT OF TIME? Assign the Chapter 19 Audiocassettes.

World History Primary Source Document Library
Make History Come Alive!
Engage your students with over 250 easily accessible primary source documents—available on this CD-ROM—that will give them real life insight into the important events of world history.

Block Schedule

Activities that are particularly suited to use within the block scheduling framework are identified throughout this chapter by the following designation.

KEY TO ABILITY LEVELS

Teaching strategies are coded for varying learning styles.
L1 BASIC activities for all students
L2 AVERAGE activities for average to above-average students
L3 CHALLENGING activities for above-average students
LEP LIMITED ENGLISH PROFICIENCY activities

Use Glencoe's *Presentation Plus!* multimedia teacher tool to easily present dynamic lessons that visually excite your students. Using Microsoft PowerPoint® you can customize the presentations to create your own personalized lessons.

Interactive Lesson Planner

Planning has never been easier! Using this CD-ROM, organize your week, month, semester, or year with all the help you need. The **Interactive Lesson Planner** gives you access to all of the blackline masters that accompany *World History: The Human Experience.*

SECTION RESOURCES

Daily Objectives	Reproducible Resources	Multimedia Resources
Section 1 Spain Explain why Philip II and other Spanish monarchs had difficulty ruling the Spanish Empire.	Lecture Notes 19-1 Reproducible Lesson Plan 19-1 Vocabulary Activity 19* Guided Reading Activity 19-1* Time Line Activity 19 Geography and History Activity 19 Section Quiz 19-1* Reading Essentials and Study Guide 19-1	Section Focus Transparency 19-1 Chapter Transparency 19 Interactive Tutor Self-Assessment Software Testmaker
Section 2 England Recognize how Tudor monarchs influenced English and European affairs.	Lecture Notes 19-2 Reproducible Lesson Plan 19-2 Vocabulary Activity 19* Guided Reading Activity 19-2* Section Quiz 19-2* Reading Essentials and Study Guide 19-2	Section Focus Transparency 19-2 World History and Art Transparency 22, *View of Toledo* Interactive Tutor Self-Assessment Software Testmaker World Music: Cultural Traditions, Lesson 3
Section 3 France Describe the kind of monarchy that developed in France under the Bourbon monarchs.	Lecture Notes 19-3 Reproducible Lesson Plan 19-3 Vocabulary Activity 19* Guided Reading Activity 19-3* Section Quiz 19-3* Reading Essentials and Study Guide 19-3	Focus on World Art Print 20, Jean-Baptiste Simeon Chardin. *The Attributes of Painting* Section Focus Transparency 19-3 World History and Art Transparency 26, *The French Ambassadors* Interactive Tutor Self-Assessment Software Testmaker
Section 4 The German States Examine how the Thirty Years' War differed from prior European wars.	Lecture Notes 19-4 Reproducible Lesson Plan 19-4 Vocabulary Activity 19* Guided Reading Activity 19-4* Section Quiz 19-4* Reading Essentials and Study Guide 19-4	Focus on World Art Print 19, Jan Steen. *The Dancing Couple* Section Focus Transparency 19-4 Interactive Tutor Self-Assessment Software Testmaker
Section 5 Russia Understand how the power of Russian czars differed from that of other European monarchs.	Lecture Notes 19-5 Reproducible Lesson Plan 19-5 Guided Reading Activity 19-5* History Simulation 19 Reteaching Activity 19 Enrichment Activity 19 Section Quiz 19-5* Performance Assessment Activity 19 Spanish Chapter Summary 19 Reading Essentials and Study Guide 19-5	Section Focus Transparency 19-5 Vocabulary PuzzleMaker Software Interactive Tutor Self-Assessment Software Testmaker Picture Atlas of the World

Chapter Activities

 Performance Assessment Activity

A Resume for a Political Candidate After students have studied the leaders in this chapter, have them think about their qualities and actions and then consider what they believe is required of our government leaders today. Each student should create a resume for a candidate for current office based on what they know of the real leaders presented in the chapter, choosing the qualities and actions that best support their vision for modern times. The task may be extended by having students make visual representations of their ideal candidates. Students should include a reflection that defines their vision of those qualities needed in a candidate today and why they chose specific qualities.

Possible Rubric Features
Accuracy of content information, appropriateness of choices for vision communicated, organization and format of resume, argumentation and level of support for qualities and actions chosen

• *For an additional activity, refer to Activity 19 in the* Performance Assessment Strategies and Activities *booklet.*

ACTIVITY

From the Classroom of...

Allan Solomonson
West High School
Wausau, WI

Power of Monarchs
Help students understand how monarchs consolidated their power and how they ensured that their monarchies would survive into the next generation.

Write the following words on an overhead transparency, the chalkboard, or a worksheet: *prestige, privilege, organization, personality, diplomacy, opulence, conflict.* Give each student a half sheet of paper or a large note card. Have them select the word that most accurately describes a monarch of their choosing. Using the paper or note card, students should write a short essay explaining why that word is most appropriate. This can be done in class or as a homework assignment.

Use the ideas of the students as a springboard for a discussion on the power of monarchs of this era. For example, ask students to consider what legacy these monarchs left that enabled the monarchy or the nation to survive.

MULTIPLE LEARNING STYLES

Verbal/Linguistic
Have students discuss and evaluate the positive and negative aspects of Louis XIV's reign.

Logical/Mathematical
Have students use the maps in this chapter to compute and compare the approximate areas of the Spanish Hapsburgs, Austrian Hapsburgs, Holy Roman Empire, Dutch Netherlands, and Brandenburg-Prussia at their largest.

Visual/Spatial
Have students create a mural that depicts major events in the reigns of Elizabeth I, Philip II, Louis XIV, and Peter the Great.

Kinesthetic
Have students draw a large outline map of Europe and hang it on the bulletin board. Using tacks and labels, identify the Hapsburg territories.

 GLENCOE'S ASSESSMENT ADVANTAGE

Use the following to easily assess student learning in a variety of ways.

- Performance Assessment Strategies and Activities
- Section Quizzes
- Chapter and Unit Tests
- Interactive Tutor Self-Assessment Software
- Testmaker Software
- MindJogger Videoquiz
- SAT/SAT II Test Practice
- worldhistory.glencoe.com

Additional Resources

NATIONAL GEOGRAPHIC SOCIETY

Teacher's Corner

INDEX TO NATIONAL GEOGRAPHIC MAGAZINE

The following articles relate to this chapter:

- "Hunting With Eagles," by Candice S. Millard, September 1999.
- "Catherine the Great," by Erla Zwingle, September 1998.
- "A Comeback for the Cossacks," by Mike Edwards, November 1998.
- "The Tale of the *San Diego*," by Frank Goddio, July 1994.
- "The Living Tower of London," by William R. Newcott, October 1993.
- "St. Petersburg: Capital of the Tsars," by Steve Raymer, December 1993.
- "Inside the Kremlin," by Jon Thompson, January 1990.
- "Shakespeare Lives at the Folger," by Merle Severy, February 1987.
- "Legacy from the Deep: Henry VIII's Lost Warship," by Margaret Rule, May 1983.

NATIONAL GEOGRAPHIC SOCIETY PRODUCTS AVAILABLE FROM GLENCOE

To order the following call Glencoe at 1-800-334-7344:

- *Picture Atlas of the World (CD-ROM)*

ADDITIONAL NATIONAL GEOGRAPHIC SOCIETY PRODUCTS

Access National Geographic's new dynamic MapMachine Web site and other geography resources at:

- http://www.nationalgeographic.com/
- http://www.nationalgeographic.com/maps/

BIBLIOGRAPHY

Literature of the Period
Shakespeare, William. *The Riverside Shakespeare.* Boston: Houghton Mifflin, 1974. Collection of all of Shakespeare's works.

Readings for the Student
Dumas, Alexandre. *The Three Musketeers.*
Translated by Jacques Le Clercq. New York: Random House, 1950. Tale of swashbucklers in the France of Louis XIII.

Readings for the Teacher
Fraser, Antonia. *The Weaker Vessel.* New York: Knopf, 1984. An exploration of women's roles in England during the 1600s.

WORLD HISTORY Online

Use our Web site as an additional resource. All essential content is covered in the Student Edition.

You and your students can visit the *World History: The Human Experience* Web site at worldhistory.glencoe.com The student text directs students to the Web site for the following options:

- **Chapter Overviews**
- **Student Web Activities**
- **Self-Check Quizzes**

Answers are provided for you in a link entitled "Web Activity Lesson Plan." Additional Web Resources, Interactive Puzzles, and content updates are also available.

Visit the Glencoe Web site at socialstudies.glencoe.com for social studies activities, updates, and links to other resources.

LOCAL OBJECTIVES

_____
_____
_____
_____
_____
_____
_____
_____
_____
_____
_____
_____
_____
_____
_____

CHAPTER THEMES

Chapter Themes are listed by section on this chapter opening page of the Student Edition. A corresponding theme-based activity is available under "TEACH," and a theme-based question is asked in the Section and Chapter Assessments.

𝒮toryteller

Historical Setting The opening text reveals one view of the social life of the upper class during the reign of Louis XIV. An evening at Versailles generally began at 6:00 P.M. and could last until 8:00 A.M. the next morning. During that time, activities might include eating two suppers, attending a comedy and a ballet, and dancing at a ball.

It is not surprising that Louis's sister-in-law went hunting—Louis kept 1,000 hounds at Versailles for that sport. France's poor, on the other hand, spent their days working on the estates of the rich, plowing fields, or working in cities at any job that would assure them food to eat and a roof over their heads.

Historical Significance

Answers: *Monarchs tried to strengthen the power of the throne, build up the national economy, and increase military strength. In Spain and France, monarchs also tried to promote a national culture.*

French expansion led to wars with Spain, the Netherlands, and Austria. Russian expansion led to wars with Poland, Sweden, and the Ottoman Empire.

Have students use the **Chapter 19 Overview** at worldhistory. glencoe.com as a prereading and postreading exercise for understanding chapter content.

Royal Power and Conflict

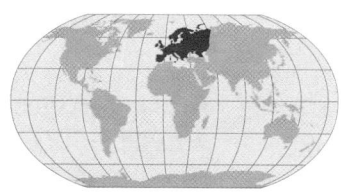

Chapter Themes

▶ **Conflict** Spanish and English monarchs engage in a dynastic struggle. *Section 1*
▶ **Change** Tudor monarchs bring stability and prosperity to England. *Section 2*
▶ **Uniformity** France's Louis XIV strengthens absolute monarchy and limits rights of dissenters. *Section 3*
▶ **Conflict** Dynastic and religious conflicts divide the German states. *Section 4*
▶ **Innovation** Peter the Great attempts to modernize Russian society. *Section 5*

𝒮toryteller

"We hunted all morning, got back around 3 o'clock in the afternoon, changed, went up to gamble until 7 o'clock, then to the play, which never ended before 10:30, then on to the ball until 3 o'clock in the morning…. So you see how much time I had for writing."

Princess Elizabeth-Charlotte, sister-in-law of France's King Louis XIV, described court life at the Palace of Versailles in a letter to a friend as an endless round of social activities. A man of tremendous energy and drive, Louis routinely devoted eight or nine hours daily to matters of state, regularly rode and hunted, ate with great enthusiasm, and expected courtiers, or members of his court, to do the same as well.

Historical Significance

How did monarchs build strong nation-states in early modern Europe? How did their efforts in national expansion contribute to Europe's legacy of territorial disputes and wars?

1500	1600	1700	1800

1509 Henry VIII begins rule in England.

1588 England defeats the Spanish Armada.

1643 Louis XIV becomes king of France.

1618 Thirty Years' War begins.

1762 Catherine the Great begins rule of Russia.

GEOGRAPHY CONNECTION

Location Use the Atlas to review with students the locations of England, Spain, Prussia, the Netherlands, Russia, Austria, and France. What is unique about England's geographical situation? *(England is an island.)* In what way is Russia different from other European countries? *(Russia covers a vast amount of land.)*

Visualizing History Versailles was so expensive to build that Louis XIV destroyed some of the bills to avoid criticism from his ministers. On several occasions during his reign, it was the scene of elaborate and enormously expensive festivals that lasted for as long as a week.

✔ Performance Assessment

Refer to the activity on page 480C of the Planning Guide.

For an additional activity, refer to Activity 19 in the *Performance Assessment Strategies and Activities* booklet.

Visualizing History The vast palace and grounds of Versailles lie outside of Paris, France. Versailles was home to France's monarchs and the royal court during the late 1600s and most of the 1700s.

Using Your History Journal

After students have finished their time lines, have them research the topic they find the most important or most interesting.

WORLD HISTORY Online

Chapter Overview

Visit the *World History: The Human Experience* Web site at **worldhistory.glencoe.com** and click on *Chapter 19—Chapter Overview* to preview the chapter.

Your History Journal

Choose a country from this chapter. As you read the section, create a time line of important events between 1500 and 1750. Include the reigning monarchs, expansions of territory, laws, and conflicts.

Chapter 19 *Royal Power and Conflict* **481**

GLENCOE TECHNOLOGY

 VIDEODISC
Use MindJogger to preview chapter content.

MindJogger Videoquiz
 Chapter 19
Disc 3 Side A

 Also available in VHS.

✚ EXTRA CREDIT PROJECT

Essay Many great writers wrote during the period covered here. These include Corneille, Racine, and Molière (France); Shakespeare (England); Cervantes (Spain); and Goethe (Prussia). Have students read excerpts from the works of two of these writers and write an essay comparing and contrasting their style and themes. Students may also draw conclusions, if warranted, about how any differences or similarities in the writers' styles reflect differences or similarities in the political, economic, and social life of the writers' homelands. **L3**

SECTION THEME

▶ **Conflict** Spanish and English monarchs engage in a dynastic struggle.

For reading strategies to help students read effectively see pages 12–13. Have students think about the main head as they read the subheads.

Vocabulary Pre-check

▣ Use the Vocabulary PuzzleMaker for Chapter 19 to create a crossword puzzle to reinforce section terms. **L1 LEP**

📁 Use Vocabulary Activity 19 to introduce vocabulary terms. **L1 LEP**

FOCUS

Section Objective

Explain why Philip II and other Spanish monarchs had difficulty ruling the Spanish Empire.

BELLRINGER
Motivational Activity

Before taking roll at the beginning of the class period, project Section Focus Transparency 19-1 and have students answer the activity questions. Discuss students' responses.

📁 This activity is also available as a blackline master.

Section 1

Spain

Read to Find Out
Main Idea *Philip II and other Spanish monarchs had difficulty ruling the Spanish Empire.*

▶ **Terms to Define**
absolutism, divine right, armada, inflation

▶ **People to Meet**
Philip II, the Marranos, the Moriscos, Charles II

▶ **Places to Locate**
El Escorial, Madrid

The Duke of Alva's son, ten-year-old Alejandro, was ecstatic. He had been appointed as a page to King Philip—an excellent beginning to a career with the Spanish court. Alejandro would learn to fence and to perform feats of horseman-

Philip II

ship, as well as the rudiments of reading and writing. In five or six years, when he completed his education, Alejandro would become a member of His Majesty's court and would be expected to serve at arms. That position was the fulfillment of most young men's desires. If he proved himself truly outstanding, he might become one of Philip's personal attendants, a position usually reserved for the sons of princes.

—from *Charles V and Philip His Son*, Marino Cavalli, reprinted in *The Portable Renaissance Reader*, Mary Martin McLaughlin, 1977

482 Chapter 19 *Royal Power and Conflict*

In the 1500s and 1600s, European monarchs sought to create powerful kingdoms in which they could command the complete loyalty of all their subjects. This form of government, known as absolutism, placed absolute, or unlimited, power in the monarch and his or her advisers. The strength of absolutism rested on divine right—the political idea that monarchs receive their power directly from God and are responsible to God alone for their actions. An absolute monarchy, it was reasoned, would unify diverse peoples and bring greater efficiency and control.

During the age of absolutism, the Hapsburgs remained Europe's most powerful royal family. But their lands were too scattered for any one person to rule effectively. To remedy this problem, Charles V retired in 1556 and divided the empire, leaving the Hapsburg lands in central Europe to his brother, Ferdinand, who became Holy Roman emperor. He gave Spain, the Netherlands, southern Italy, and Spain's overseas empire to his son, **Philip II**.

Philip II

Philip II, who ruled from 1556 to 1598, was the most powerful monarch in Spanish history. A devout Catholic, Philip saw himself as the leading defender of the faith. His efforts to end Protestantism in his domains made him the enemy of all Protestants. Son of the Holy Roman Emperor Charles V and Isabella of Portugal, Philip worked to increase the Hapsburg family's power throughout Europe. This effort led Philip to involve Spain in a number of costly European wars.

Known as the Prudent King, Philip II was cautious, hardworking, and suspicious of others. He built a granite palace called **El Escorial**, which served as royal court, art gallery, monastery, and tomb for Spanish royalty. There Philip spent most of his time at his desk, carefully reading and

---

SECTION RESOURCES

📁 **Reproducible Masters**
- Lecture Notes 19-1
- Reproducible Lesson Plan 19-1
- Vocabulary Activity 19
- Guided Reading Activity 19-1
- Time Line Activity 19
- Geography and History Activity 19

- Section Quiz 19-1
- Reading Essentials and Study Guide 19-1

📑 **Transparencies**
- Section Focus Transparency 19-1
- Chapter Transparency 19

Multimedia
▣ Interactive Tutor Self-Assessment Software
▣ Testmaker

---

responding to hundreds of documents from all over the empire. Bureaucrats advised him and handled routine matters, but he made all decisions and signed all papers that he received.

Unrest

Philip II faced many difficulties in ruling Spain. The Spanish kingdoms had united when Ferdinand of Aragon married Isabella of Castile in 1469. A uniform system of government for the entire country, however, had not been set up. Separate laws and local authorities remained in place, but the ways of Castile eventually came to dominate Spanish life. In the 1500s Castile had more territory, people, and wealth than any other part of Spain.

Philip II made Castile the center of Spain and the empire. **Madrid**, located in Castile, became the capital. The Castilian, or literary, form of Spanish was spoken at the royal court. Most of Philip's advisers came from Castile. Trade from the overseas empire was controlled by the Castilian city of Seville, and Castilian merchants benefited most from trade. Leaders in Aragon and other Spanish provinces resented the dominance of Castile, and in the 1590s Aragon revolted. The revolt was put down, but discontent continued into the 1600s.

Religious Policy

Philip had to deal with a number of troubling religious issues in his European domains. He was concerned about the loyalty of large religious minorities in Spain. These minorities included Protestants, **the Marranos** (Jews who had converted to Christianity), and **the Moriscos** (Muslims who had become Christians). Philip supported the Inquisition's efforts to uproot the heresies believed to exist among these groups. He personally attended several *autos da fé*, the elaborate public rituals of sentencing usually followed by executions. The Inquisition was so thorough that Protestantism never took hold in Spain. Its actions, however, led to a revolt by the Moriscos in 1569. The revolt was brutally crushed, and finally in 1609 the Moriscos were expelled from the country.

In 1567, when Philip had sought to impose Catholicism on the Netherlands, Dutch Protestants rebelled against his rule. This conflict proved to be long, bloody, and complex. The Dutch declared their independence in 1581, but the fighting continued. England gave support to the Dutch and to the English "sea dogs" who raided Spanish ships in their ports. Meanwhile, Philip extended his crusading zeal into the eastern Mediterranean, where in 1571 he defeated the Ottoman Turks in a naval battle at Lepanto off the coast of Greece.

 Visualizing History The Spanish Armada entered the English Channel in late July, 1588. *What advantages did the English fleet have over the Spanish Armada?*

Spanish Armada

Catholic Spain faced a growing challenge from Protestant England. Philip at first had supported Elizabeth I as England's queen against the pope's wishes. When Elizabeth aided the Dutch, Philip decided to act against her.

In 1586 Philip laid plans to invade England. In May 1588 a force of 130 ships and 33,000 men, known as the Spanish Armada, sailed for the English coast. (An armada is a fleet of warships organized to carry out a mission.) Two months later, the Armada entered the English Channel in crescent formation. The English had faster, more maneuverable ships and longer-range cannons than did the Spaniards. Yet they were unable at first to block the Spanish formation. English fire ships, however, were able to separate the Spanish vessels. Running out of shot and short of water, the Spanish fleet retreated to the stormy North Sea. After circling the northern tip of Great Britain, a number of Spanish ships later sank near the rocky coasts of Scotland and Ireland.

The defeat of the Armada not only ended Philip's plan to invade England, it also marked the beginning of Spain's decline as a sea power. During the next two centuries, the Dutch Netherlands, England, and France would gradually reduce Spanish might in Europe and around the world.

Chapter 19 *Royal Power and Conflict* **483**

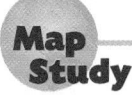

Map Study

Answer

primarily Spain, southern Italy, Sicily, Sardinia, the Netherlands

ASSESS

Check for Understanding

Assign Section 1 Assessment as homework or as an in-class activity.

 Use Interactive Tutor Self-Assessment Software to review Section 1.

Evaluate

Section Quiz 19-1

Use the Testmaker to create a customized quiz for Section 1.

Reteach

Ask volunteers to give oral summaries of important events during the rule of Philip II and during the decline of the Hapsburg rulers after his death.

Reading Essentials and Study Guide 19-1

Enrich

Have students make a time line reflecting the events of the section. Ask them to chart positive events above the line and negative events below it.

CLOSE

Write *Strengths* and *Weaknesses* on the chalkboard and ask students to list items under each heading for the Spanish Hapsburgs they have studied.

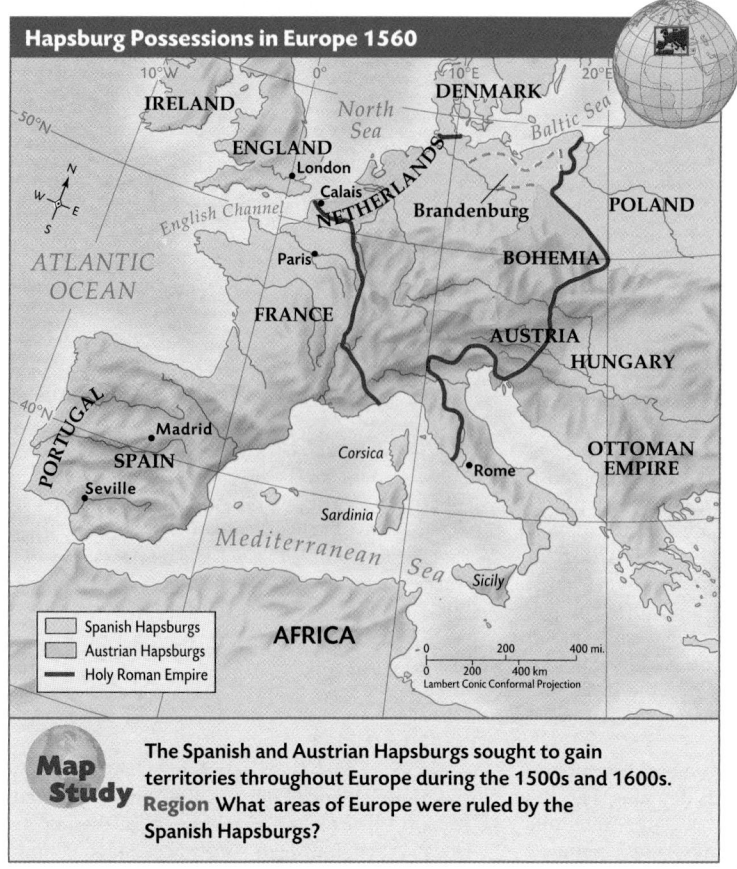

Hapsburg Possessions in Europe 1560

IRELAND

ENGLAND
London
Calais

DENMARK

North Sea

Baltic Sea

NETHERLANDS

Brandenburg

POLAND

English Channel

ATLANTIC OCEAN

Paris

FRANCE

BOHEMIA

AUSTRIA

HUNGARY

PORTUGAL

Madrid
SPAIN
Seville

Corsica

Rome

OTTOMAN EMPIRE

Sardinia

Mediterranean Sea

Sicily

AFRICA

☐ Spanish Hapsburgs
☐ Austrian Hapsburgs
— Holy Roman Empire

0   200   400 mi.
0   200   400 km
Lambert Conic Conformal Projection

Map Study The Spanish and Austrian Hapsburgs sought to gain territories throughout Europe during the 1500s and 1600s. **Region** What areas of Europe were ruled by the Spanish Hapsburgs?

Last of the Spanish Hapsburgs

The period from 1550 to 1650 is called Spain's cultural *siglo de oro,* or "golden century." Midway through this era, the Spanish author Miguel de Cervantes (suhr•VAN•teez) wrote *Don Quixote,* a novel about a landowner who imagines himself a knight called to perform heroic deeds. *Don Quixote*

presented a new kind of hero who did not conform to commonly accepted beliefs and practices.

Cervantes's novel also symbolized the steady decline of Spain as a European power. Despite Spain's profitable overseas empire, costly wars drained the national treasury, forcing the government to borrow money from foreign bankers. This, along with the flow of gold and silver from the Americas, led to inflation, an abnormal increase in currency resulting in sharp price rises. In addition, Spain's industry and agriculture declined. The government excessively taxed the industrious middle class. It also expelled the Muslims and Jews, many of whom were skilled artisans and merchants.

Philip II's successors lacked his political skills and turned the government over to corrupt and incompetent nobles. Spain became involved in a series of European wars, and overtaxed citizens rebelled. **Charles II,** who became king in 1665, was the last of the Spanish Hapsburgs. No one expected him to rule long, since he was physically and mentally weak. Although Charles later married, he did not have any children. With no heirs to the throne of Spain, European monarchs plotted to control the succession to the Spanish throne.

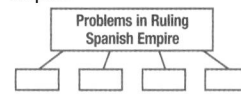

SECTION 1 ASSESSMENT

Main Idea
1. Use a chart like the one below to identify problems Spanish monarchs faced in ruling the empire.

Problems in Ruling Spanish Empire

Recall
2. **Define** absolutism, divine right, armada, inflation.
3. **Identify** Philip II, El Escorial, the Marranos, the Moriscos, Spanish Armada, Charles II.

Critical Thinking
4. **Analyzing Information** Why was the Spanish Armada sent out? What resulted?

Understanding Themes
5. **Conflict** What caused internal unrest under Philip II's rule? How did he respond?

484 Chapter 19 *Royal Power and Conflict*

SECTION 1 ASSESSMENT ANSWERS

1. dominance of Castile resented; revolt and rebellion; loyalties of religious minorities; challenge from England; defeat of armada; decline of Spain as sea power; costly war; industry and agriculture declined; incompetent rule after Philip
2. All terms are defined in the Glossary.
3. Philip II, 482; El Escorial, 482; Marranos,

483; Moriscos, 483; Spanish Armada, 483; Charles II, 484
4. Philip was angered by England's support of Protestants in the Netherlands.
5. **CONFLICT** resentment by other provinces of Castile's dominance, religious persecutions, declining economy; by crushing any revolts

1500   1550   1600

1547 Henry VIII dies.

1558 Elizabeth I becomes queen of England.

1597 Poor Law makes local areas responsible for care of the unemployed.

Section 2

England

Read to Find Out

Main Idea *Tudor monarchs strongly influenced English and European affairs.*

▶ **Terms to Define**
  gentry, yeoman, balance of power

▶ **People to Meet**
  Henry VII, Henry VIII, Edward VI, Mary, Elizabeth I, William Shakespeare, James I

▶ **Places to Locate**
  Scotland, Ireland

On this day, Elizabeth would be crowned Queen of England. London was arrayed with pavilions and bright banners, and the city's fountains offered wine, not the usual brackish water. Alison Crisp eagerly awaited the royal procession to Westminster Abbey. Although only six years of age, she would present a costly gift to Elizabeth from the Orphans Home board of directors. When the procession neared, the queen commanded her coachmen to stop. Alison flawlessly presented the gift. As the queen prepared to move on, Alison surprised her with another gift, a bouquet of flowers she had picked. With Elizabeth's acceptance of the child's humble offering, the rapport between the queen and her people strengthened.

—from *Description of Elizabeth I's Coronation Procession in 1559*, John Hayward, in *The Past Speaks*, L.B. Smith and J.R. Smith, 1993

Elizabeth I

ngland, like Spain, developed a strong monarchy. Its Tudor dynasty, which ruled from 1485 to 1603, brought unity to the country after a long period of decline and disorder. Tudor monarchs were hardworking, able, and popular. They greatly expanded the power and authority of the Crown. They were not, however, as absolute in their rule as other European monarchs. Instead, institutions such as Parliament and the courts of law set bounds to the authority that Tudor monarchs could exercise.

Early Tudors

Henry VII, the first Tudor monarch, became king in 1485 after the Wars of the Roses. He used shrewd maneuvering to disarm his rivals and to increase the prestige of his family. Most of Henry's close advisers came from the gentry and merchant classes. Titles were given to these officials, who formed a new aristocracy dependent on the king.

Henry VII helped rebuild England's commercial prosperity. He encouraged the expansion of foreign trade, especially the export of finished woolens to the Netherlands, Germany, and Venice. He promoted the improved collection of taxes as well as careful government spending. In foreign policy Henry avoided war, using diplomacy and the arrangement of suitable royal marriages to strengthen England's interests abroad.

Henry VIII

The second Tudor to rule was **Henry VIII**, son of Henry VII and the most powerful of all Tudor monarchs. Unlike his father, Henry VIII fought wars on the European continent and began to make England a great naval power. His personal life, however, would have a lasting effect on English history. In his pursuit of a male heir, Henry married six times. He worked with Parliament to obtain his personal goals and to break with the Catholic

For reading strategies to help students read effectively see pages 12–13.

Vocabulary Pre-check

Use the Vocabulary PuzzleMaker for Chapter 19 to create a crossword puzzle to reinforce section terms. **L1 LEP**

Use Vocabulary Activity 19 to introduce vocabulary terms. **L1 LEP**

FOCUS

Section Objective

Recognize how Tudor monarchs influenced English and European affairs.

BELLRINGER
Motivational Activity

Before taking roll at the beginning of the class period, project Section Focus Transparency 19-2 and have students answer the activity questions. Discuss students' responses.

This activity is also available as a blackline master.

SECTION RESOURCES

Reproducible Masters
- Lecture Notes 19-2
- Reproducible Lesson Plan 19-2
- Vocabulary Activity 19
- Guided Reading Activity 19-2
- Section Quiz 19-2
- Reading Essentials and Study Guide 19-2

Transparencies
- Section Focus Transparency 19-2
- World History and Art Transparency 22

Multimedia
- Interactive Tutor Self-Assessment Software
- Testmaker
- World Music: Cultural Traditions, Lesson 3

TEACH

Guided Practice

THEME Change

Tudor monarchs used their strong personalities and diplomatic skills to bring about change in England. Write *Henry VII, Henry VIII,* and *Elizabeth I* on the chalkboard. Ask students to name some of the changes each of these monarchs brought and list them on the chalkboard. *(Sample answers: Henry VII, expanded foreign trade; Henry VIII, established Anglican Church; Elizabeth I, ushered in one of England's greatest cultural periods.)* **L1 LEP**

Government Tudor rule differed from the absolute rule of Philip II. Both dynasties had successes and failures. Ask students to take a position on whether the Spanish Hapsburgs or the English Tudors were more successful in ruling their kingdoms and why. Students should consider the personal traits and public actions of monarchs. Ask volunteers to judge the positions and point out those with well-supported arguments. **L2**

Biography

The following videotape programs are available from Glencoe:
- **Elizabeth I: The Virgin Queen**
- **Henry VIII**

Church. As a result of this cooperation, the House of Commons increased its power during Henry VIII's reign. Henry, however, furthered support for his policies by seizing monastery lands and selling them to wealthy landowners.

Edward VI and Mary I

After Henry VIII's death in 1547, England entered a brief period of turmoil. **Edward VI,** Henry's son and successor, was only 9 years old when he became king. He died in 1553 after a short reign. Protestant nobles then plotted to prevent Edward's Catholic half sister, **Mary,** from becoming queen. The English people, however, supported Mary's claim to the Tudor throne.

Mary's Catholic policies soon offended the English. Despite strong opposition, Mary married Philip II of Spain in 1554. The next year, she restored Catholicism and had about 300 Protestants burned at the stake for heresy. At Philip's urging, Mary involved England in a war with France. As a result, England lost the port of Calais, its final

foothold on the European continent. Many English people feared that England would be controlled by Spain. Before this fear could be realized, Mary died childless, and the throne then passed to her Protestant half sister, Elizabeth.

Elizabeth I

Elizabeth I became queen in 1558, when she was 25 years old. She was shrewd, highly educated, and had a forceful personality. With a sharp tongue she asserted her iron will, causing sparks to fly in exchanges with Parliament. Elizabeth, however, used her authority for the common good of her people. On frequent journeys throughout the kingdom Elizabeth earned the loyalty and confidence of her subjects. During her travels, Elizabeth stayed at the homes of nobles who entertained her with banquets, parades, and dances.

Elizabeth's reign was one of England's great cultural periods. Poets and writers praised

Images of the Times

Tudor England

Under Tudor monarchs, England enjoyed a period of stability and relative prosperity.

Mary I married Philip II of Spain in 1554, against the wishes of her Protestant subjects. This coat of arms represents the marital union of the two monarchs.

486

Images of the Times — Tudor England

What was life like for the people? Houses of plaster and brick with thatched roofs now had glass windows, but people still needed candles or torches for light at night. Floors had no carpets, but tapestries were hung on walls. Furniture was strong and cut of walnut or oak to last for centuries. People of all classes had a garden by the house. Elizabethan England was an age of fashion. Men wore hats of many shapes and colors outside the home and in church. They wore their hair long and grew beards. Women often wore wigs, used cosmetics, wore jewelry, and had pierced ears. Both men and women wore pleated collars, called ruffs, made of fabric, pasteboard, and wire.

Elizabeth in their works. The theater flourished under playwrights such as **William Shakespeare**. During Elizabeth's reign, English was transformed into a language of beauty, grace, vigor, and clarity.

Marriage

People fully expected that Elizabeth would marry and that her husband would rule. The common attitude of the time was that only men were fit to rule and that government matters were beyond a woman's ability. Elizabeth, however, was slow in seeking a husband. She had learned from the lesson of her sister Mary: to marry a foreign prince would endanger England. At the same time, marrying an Englishman would cause jealousies among the English nobility. In the end, Elizabeth refused to give up her powers as monarch for the sake of marriage. To one of her suitors she stormed, "God's death! My lord, I will have but one mistress [England] and no master." Elizabeth's refusal to marry caused a great deal of speculation as to who would succeed her.

Court and Government

In matters of government, Elizabeth was assisted by a council of nobles. With her approval they drafted proclamations, handled foreign relations, and supervised such matters as the administration of justice and the regulation of prices and wages. These advisers were assisted by small staffs of professional but poorly paid bureaucrats.

Although Parliament did not have the power to initiate legislation, it could plead, urge, advise, and withhold approval. These powers gave Parliament some influence, especially when it was asked to consider tax laws.

The task of enforcing the queen's law was performed by unpaid respected community members known as justices of the peace. Most justices belonged to the rural landowning classes. They knew both the law and local conditions. They maintained peace, collected taxes, and kept the government informed of local problems. Their voluntary participation in support of the government was a key to its success.

The Court of Elizabeth I was known for its love of fashions and style. Noble men and women who served the queen wore elegant clothes and enjoyed music and the arts.

The Globe Theater in London was the site where many of William Shakespeare's plays—tragedies, comedies, and histories—were performed.

REFLECTING ON THE TIMES

1. Why is Elizabeth's reign considered one of England's great cultural eras?
2. Why was Mary I an unpopular ruler?

487

Chapter 19
Section 2

World History and Art Transparency 22, *View of Toledo*

World Music: Cultural Traditions, Lesson 3

Independent Practice
Guided Reading Activity 19-2 **L1**

Time Line Assign pairs of students to make a biographical time line of Tudor royalty. Using encyclopedias or biographical dictionaries, have them write brief descriptions of each Tudor ruler and place it next to the appropriate birth date on the time line. **L2 LEP**

Women in History Women were very influential during the Tudor reign. Have students research and report on one of the following: a wife of Henry VIII; Mary I; Elizabeth I; Mary, Queen of Scots; Margaret Pole; or Lady Jane Grey. **L3**

Linking Past and Present

Shakespeare's plays are as popular today as they were in Elizabethan England. Through the centuries, directors have adapted productions of the plays to fit contemporary situations. In some cases they have changed everything except the basic plot line. *Romeo and Juliet*, a story of ill-fated lovers in Verona, Italy, was transformed into *West Side Story*, a 1950s musical about lovers caught in the conflict between rival New York City gangs. Changes in time period and culture do not change the universal theme of the original play.

ANSWERS TO REFLECTING ON THE TIMES

1. It was a time when the English language, theater, art, and music all thrived.
2. People feared her Catholic policies and a loss of power because of her marriage to Philip of Spain.

ASSESS

Check for Understanding

Assign Section 2 Assessment as homework or as an in-class activity.

🔲 Use Interactive Tutor Self-Assessment Software to review Section 2.

you don't say...

"To take the chair," or to preside, is an expression that came from Tudor times. A chair with a back was a luxury then; most people sat on stools or benches. The chair, then, was reserved for the master or mistress of the house or the honored guest.

History & Art

 Elizabeth Tudor was an extraordinary individual who had had little security, hope, or love in her life. With the freedom of the throne, however, she was able to do as she chose. She chose to appeal to her subjects and earn their love.
Answer to Caption: *England developed a balance of power with European nations.*

CURRICULUM CONNECTION

ASTRONOMY

In his twenties, Edmund Halley published a paper on planetary orbits, financed Newton's first edition of *Principia*, and predicted that in 75 years there would be a reappearance of a comet that appeared in 1682. When the comet returned, it was named Halley's comet.

Social and Economic Policy

Elizabeth believed in the importance of social rank. During the late 1500s, English society was led by the queen and her court. Next were prominent nobles from the great landed families and a middle group of gentry, or lesser nobles, merchants, lawyers, and clergy. This group provided the source of Tudor strength and stability. The lowest social rank was comprised of yeomen, or farmers with small landholdings, and laborers.

Government laws and policies closely regulated the lives of the common people. The Statute of Apprentices of 1563 declared work to be a social and moral duty. It required people to live and work where they were born, controlled the movement of labor, fixed wages, and regulated apprenticeships. The Poor Laws of 1597 and 1601 made local areas responsible for their own homeless and unemployed. These laws included means to raise money for charity and to provide work for vagabonds.

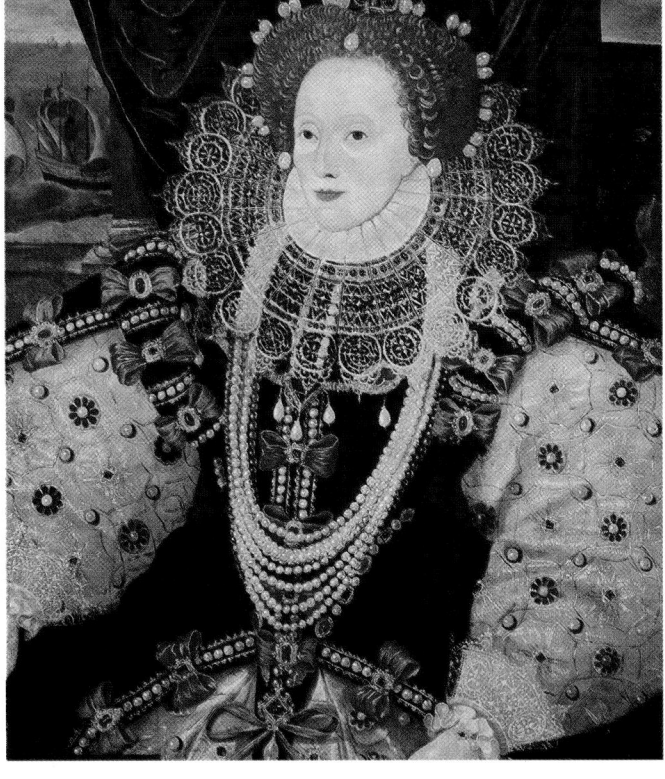

Elizabeth inherited a monarchy that was badly in debt. Royal revenues, which came from rents of royal land, fines in court cases, and duties on imports, barely covered annual expenses. The queen, however, spent lavishly on court ceremonies to show the power and dignity of the monarchy. In other matters, she showed the greatest financial restraint, leading many to call her a "pinchpenny."

To raise funds without relying on Parliament, Elizabeth sold off royal lands, offices, licenses, monopolies, and the right to collect customs. These measures helped but could not solve the problem. England faced the costs of war and mounting inflation. Elizabeth was therefore forced to turn to Parliament for funds. When she ended her reign, England remained badly in debt.

Foreign Policy

By Elizabeth's time, England had lost all of its possessions on the European continent. France was too powerful for England to defeat in order to regain territories. Although England could not completely withdraw from continental affairs, it developed a foreign policy suitable for a small island nation with limited resources.

For security, the English relied on the English Channel to protect their island from European invaders. Building and maintaining a strong navy was therefore important in defending the nation. For that reason, Elizabeth continued the efforts begun by her Tudor predecessors to build such a navy.

Spain and France posed the greatest naval threats to England. The attack of the Spanish Armada made England

History & Art *Elizabeth I* by George Glower, 1596. National Portrait Gallery, London, England **A woman of keen intellect, Elizabeth I was gifted in music, languages, and the arts. In addition, she was an excellent public speaker.** *What foreign policy strategy did England develop under Elizabeth I's reign?*

488 Chapter 19 *Royal Power and Conflict*

COOPERATIVE LEARNING ACTIVITY

Research Have students research Shakespeare, the Elizabethan theater, and London in the middle and late 1500s. Organize the class into several groups and ask each group to choose different tasks: write a biography of Shakespeare; make a model of the Globe or Black Friars theater; give an oral report or write a fictional diary entry describing London in the 1500s—its theater audience and its actors; stage a specific scene from a play (such as *Henry VIII*) to be discussed and performed; make drawings of costumes used on Shakespeare's stage. The class could combine their efforts in creating a Shakespeare Festival, including appropriate musical and dramatic recordings and samples of foods from the 1500s. **L2** 📖

realize the dangers of an alliance between Spain and France. England might be able to defeat one power, but certainly not both. As a result, the English relied on diplomacy as well as sea power to protect their interests.

During Elizabeth's reign, England worked to balance the power of European nations. In international affairs, balance of power refers to the system in which each nation helps to keep peace and order by maintaining power that is equal to, or in balance with, rival nations. If one nation becomes more powerful than the other, a third nation can reestablish the balance by supporting the second nation.

Under Elizabeth's rule, England operated as the third balancing nation. In the early part of Elizabeth's reign, England and Spain feared the power of the French. England cooperated with Spain in order to keep France out of the Netherlands. Later, when the Netherlands revolted against Philip II, the English supported the rebels and allied with the weaker power against the stronger one.

Scotland was largely Catholic and hostile toward England during the 1550s. Although part of **Ireland** was under English rule, the rest of the country resisted English armies. To protect English interests, Elizabeth sought to solidify her ties with Scotland and Ireland so they could not be used as bases for Spanish and French attacks on England.

In the 1560s, with Elizabeth's help, Scotland became Protestant and an ally of England. Mary Stuart, later known as Mary, Queen of Scots, was Elizabeth's cousin. She was forced to abdicate her position as queen of Scotland in 1567. She later fled to England, where her presence caused controversy. Mary was a Catholic and heir to the English throne. Many English Protestants feared she would try to replace Elizabeth. In 1586 Mary was accused of plotting with English and foreign Catholics against Elizabeth. In 1587 Elizabeth finally agreed to Mary's execution, although she was hesitant to sentence to death another monarch.

Visualizing History Sir Francis Drake was one of England's most famous explorers and military leaders. After sailing around the world, Drake was knighted in 1581 by Queen Elizabeth I. His naval warfare later helped make England a major sea power. *What European nation was England's primary enemy during the time of Elizabeth I and Francis Drake?*

In the 1590s, England carried out military campaigns in Ireland to conquer the Irish. With Scotland and Ireland allied with England, a period of temporary peace came to the British Isles.

Elizabeth died in 1603 at the age of 69. With her death came the end of the Tudor dynasty. King James VI of Scotland, the Protestant son of Mary, Queen of Scots, became the new monarch of England. As **James I**, he founded the Stuart dynasty and united Scotland and England under a common ruler.

SECTION 2 ASSESSMENT

Main Idea
1. Use a diagram like the one below to show the effects of Tudor rulers on European politics.

| Cause: Tudor Monarchy | → | Effects on European Politics |

Recall
2. **Define** gentry, yeomen, balance of power.
3. **Identify** Henry VII, Henry VIII, Edward VI, Mary, Elizabeth I, William Shakespeare, Poor Laws, James I.

Critical Thinking
4. **Evaluating Information** Contrast the effect on English government of Henry VIII's many marriages with the effect of Elizabeth I's refusal to marry.

Understanding Themes
5. **Change** How did the rule of the Tudor monarchs, especially the rule of Elizabeth I, affect the development of England?

Visualizing History Prospects of future Armada attacks on England and the subsequent financial burdens of war led Elizabeth to encourage Drake and his sea captains to attack foreign vessels carrying treasure from the Americas and claim the booty.
Answer to Caption: *Spain*

Evaluate

Section Quiz 19-2

Use the Testmaker to create a customized quiz for Section 2.

Reteach

Ask students to list the political tactics used by Tudor rulers. *(use of Parliament to grant favors, foreign policy based on diplomacy, a balance of power)*

Reading Essentials and Study Guide 19-2

Enrich

Have students assume the role of someone who might have lived between 1485 and 1603. Ask them to choose under which ruler—Henry VIII, Edward VI, Mary I, or Elizabeth I—they would like to have lived and why.

CLOSE

Hold a discussion on how religion affected the policies of the Tudors and whether this influence strengthened or weakened England.

SECTION 2 ASSESSMENT ANSWERS

1. England at war with France under Queen Mary; Elizabeth I worked to balance the power of European nations; Elizabeth cooperated with Spain against France; Elizabeth solidified ties with Scotland; conquered Ireland
2. All terms are defined in the Glossary.
3. Henry VII, 485; Henry VIII, 485; Edward VI, 486; Mary I, 486; Elizabeth I, 486; William Shakespeare, 487; Poor Laws, 488; James I, 489
4. Henry's marriages caused a split with the Catholic Church; Elizabeth's refusal to marry prevented foreign claims to the English throne.
5. **CHANGE** Elizabeth strengthened the monarch's ties with Parliament, subdued religious dissent, encouraged cultural development, and established a balance of power among European nations.

1550	1600	1650	1700

1598 Henry IV issues the Edict of Nantes. **1648** Fronde uprising grips Paris. **1661** Louis XIV takes sole charge of the government. **1701** War of the Spanish Succession begins.

SECTION THEME

▶ **Uniformity** France's Louis XIV strengthens absolute monarchy in France and limits rights of religious dissenters.

Guide to Reading

For reading strategies to help students read effectively see pages 12–13.

Vocabulary Pre-check

 Use the Vocabulary PuzzleMaker for Chapter 19 to create a crossword puzzle to reinforce section terms. **L1 LEP**

Use Vocabulary Activity 19 to introduce vocabulary terms. **L1 LEP**

FOCUS

Section Objective

Describe the kind of monarchy that developed in France under the Bourbon monarchs.

BELLRINGER
Motivational Activity

 Before taking roll at the beginning of the class period, project Section Focus Transparency 19-3 and have students answer the activity questions. Discuss students' responses.

This activity is also available as a blackline master.

Section 3

France

Guide to Reading

Read to Find Out
Main Idea *An absolute monarchy developed in France under the Bourbon monarchs.*

▶ **Terms to Define**
  Edict of Nantes, intendant

▶ **People to Meet**
  Henry IV, Cardinal Richelieu, Louis XIV

▶ **Places to Locate**
  Versailles

The Storyteller

A flourish of trumpets sounded. The crowd of courtiers bowed as King Louis entered the Grand Salon at Versailles, accompanied by his attendants. The Duke of Saint-Simon, one of many noblemen whose power Louis was systematically eclipsing, was nonetheless required to be present. He observed that the king "liked splendor, magnificence, and profusion in everything: you pleased him if you shone through the brilliancy of your houses, clothes, tables, equipages." Because everyone tried to emulate the king, a taste for extravagance and luxury was spreading through all classes of society.

—adapted from *The Memoires of the Duke of Saint-Simon*, reprinted in *Aspects of Western Civilization, Volume II*, Perry M. Rogers, 1988

Louis XIV's lavish court life

---

fter a period of religious conflict, peace was restored to most of France when Henry of Navarre became King **Henry IV** in 1589. He founded the Bourbon dynasty, which ruled France with some interruptions until the early 1800s. During most of that time, Bourbon kings maintained an absolute monarchy that was imitated by monarchs throughout Europe.

Henry IV

Henry IV was a Protestant, but he converted to Catholicism to quiet his Catholic opponents. Believing that people's religious beliefs need not interfere with their loyalty to the government, Henry issued the **Edict of Nantes** in 1598 to reassure the Huguenots, the name given to France's Protestants. The edict allowed Protestant worship to continue in areas where the Protestants were a majority, but barred Protestant worship in Paris and other Catholic strongholds. The edict granted Huguenots the same civil rights as Catholics.

These actions ended religious strife and enabled France to rebuild itself. With the help of his minister of finance, Henry restored the Crown's treasury, repaired roads and bridges, and supported trade and industry. He also tried to restore discipline in the army and bring order to the government bureaucracy. All of these royal policies were put into effect without the approval of the Estates-General and thus laid the foundation for the absolute rule of later Bourbon monarchs.

Cardinal Richelieu

When Henry IV was assassinated in 1610, his 9-year-old son, Louis XIII, became king. Louis's mother, Marie de Medici, was regent for the next 7 years. In 1617 Louis gained the throne by force and exiled his mother from court. A few years later, he

---

SECTION RESOURCES

Reproducible Masters
- Lecture Notes 19-3
- Reproducible Lesson Plan 19-3
- Vocabulary Activity 19
- Guided Reading Activity 19-3
- Section Quiz 19-3
- Reading Essentials and Study Guide 19-3

Transparencies
- Section Focus Transparency 19-3
- World History and Art Transparency 26

Multimedia
- Focus on World Art Print 20, Jean-Baptiste Simeon Chardin. *The Attributes of Painting*
- Interactive Tutor Self-Assessment Software
- Testmaker

gave power to one of her advisers, **Cardinal Richelieu**.

Gradually Louis gave complete control of the government to the cardinal, who set out to build an absolute monarchy in France. To realize this goal, Richelieu had to reduce the power of the nobles and the Huguenots.

When Louis XIII came to the throne, the nobility was in control of the provinces. Nobles collected taxes, administered justice, appointed local officials, and even made alliances with foreign governments. To end the nobles' power, Richelieu destroyed their fortified castles and stripped them of their local administrative functions. The nobility retained social prestige, while authority in local government affairs was given to special agents of the Crown known as intendants. Non-nobles, Richelieu believed, would not assert themselves and challenge the king's authority.

Richelieu also sought to take away the military and territorial rights given to the Huguenots by the Edict of Nantes. The Huguenots were seen as a threat to the French state. In 1625 radical Huguenots revolted against Louis XIII. After the defeat of Protestant forces at the seaport of La Rochelle in 1628, Richelieu took away the Huguenots' right to independent fortified towns. The Huguenots were, however, allowed to keep their religious freedom.

Having weakened the monarchy's internal enemies, Richelieu sought to make France the supreme power in Europe. He strengthened the French army and took steps to build up the economy. In order to strengthen national unity, he supported French culture. Under Richelieu's direction, France's leading writers in 1635 organized the French Academy. The Academy received a royal charter to establish "fixed rules for the language … and render the French language not only elegant but also capable of treating all arts and sciences." In the following century, French became the preferred language of European diplomacy and culture.

Louis XIV

Louis XIV is recognized as the most powerful Bourbon monarch. He became king in 1643 at the age of 5. At first, France was ruled by his two regents—his mother, Anne of Austria, and Cardinal Mazarin, Richelieu's successor. When Mazarin died in 1661, Louis announced that he would run his own government. He was then 23 years old.

The 72-year reign of Louis XIV was the longest in European history. It set the style for European

monarchies during the 1600s and 1700s. During his own lifetime, Louis was known as the Sun King, around whom the royalty and nobility of Europe revolved. He set up a lavish court and surrounded himself with pomp and pageantry. Louis's monarchy had power as well as style. Although Louis relied on a bureaucracy, he was the source of all political authority in France. In one of his audiences, he is said to have boasted, *"L'état, c'est moi!"* ("I am the state!").

Absolute Rule

Louis emphasized a strong monarchy because of his fear of disorder without it. As a child, he had lived through the Fronde, a series of uprisings by nobles and peasants that occurred between 1648 and 1653. During the Fronde, royal troops lost control of Paris and mobs rioted in the streets. The young Louis and his regents were called to give an account of their actions before the *Parlement*, or supreme court of law, in Paris. The Fronde was crushed, but Louis never forgot this attempt to limit royal power. As king, he intended never to let it happen again.

Louis XIV's feelings about absolute monarchy were later supported by Jacques Bossuet (ZHAHK baw•SWAY), the leading church official of France during the 1600s. Bossuet's defense of the divine

---

TEACH

Guided Practice

THEME Uniformity

The efforts of Cardinal Richelieu and Louis XIV brought uniformity of language, government, and religion to France. Discuss the importance of this uniformity and ask which institutions were unified. *(a predominant religion, common language, uniform currency, laws, taxes, culture, customs)* **L1**

Visualizing History Richelieu was devoted to his pursuit of power for France. He taxed the peasantry and used the taxes to build up the military in order to destroy the power of the Hapsburgs in Europe.
Answer to Caption: *He directed the establishment of the French Academy, which helped standardize and refine the French language.*

Science, Technology, and Society
Display pictures of the interior and exterior of Versailles from history, art, or architecture books. Ask students to comment on Versailles as a " perfect symbol" for Louis XIV and his court. Contrast Versailles with descriptions of French peasant life. **L1 LEP**

Politics Have students discuss the effects of Cardinal Richelieu's policies on France during the reign of Louis XIII. *(brought stability to government by ending powers of nobility, took away political power of Huguenots, built a strong army, strengthened economy, improved and standardized French language)* **L3**

COOPERATIVE LEARNING ACTIVITY

Research Organize the class into groups of four or five students. Assign a report on the life and actions of Henry Navarre (Henry IV), who converted to Catholicism and issued the Edict of Nantes to restore religious peace to France. Each group should decide on a thesis for their report. Individual students could research Henry's personal and political life, Huguenot beliefs, the St. Bartholomew's Day Massacre, consequences of the Edict of Nantes, or other information that would support the group's thesis. Each member should submit research notes to the person who will write the draft of the report. After group approval and editing, a member should copy the report in final form. **L2**

Louis XIV was a great patron of the arts and increased the number of paintings in his galleries from 200 to 2,500—many by French artists. He demanded that artists meet classical standards that reflected elegance, self-restraint, and polish. French art became the expression of the nation and the king, but not of the people. Its influence spread to ruling classes all over Europe.

Answer to Caption: *Answers will vary but should focus on the grandeur, splendor, and style of the monarchy that emphasized the position and power of the king as an absolute monarchy.*

 World History and Art Transparency 26, *The French Ambassadors*

Focus on World Art Print 20, Jean-Baptiste Simeon Chardin. *The Attributes of Painting*

Independent Practice

Guided Reading Activity 19-3 **L1**

Daily Life Ask students to assume the role of an English visitor to the court of Versailles. Have them compose a letter to a friend back home, describing life at court. Their letters could include information about famous acquaintances, fashion, food, the beauty of Versailles, and an audience with the king. **L2 LEP**

Global Gourmet

France By the time of Louis XIV, forks were in use, although the king used his fingers all of his life. People began to use napkins, and guests no longer had to use the tablecloth to wipe their fingers.

---

origins of monarchy became one of the most famous justifications of absolute rule. He wrote:

> **What grandeur that a single man should embody so much! … Behold this holy power, paternal and absolute, contained in a single head: you see the image of God in the king, and you have the idea of royal majesty.**

According to Bossuet, subjects had no right to revolt even if the king was unjust. Kings need account to no one except God, but they should act with humility and restraint.

Court Life

After the Fronde, Louis made plans to live outside of Paris. He moved his court and government to a new palace that he built at **Versailles**. No expense was spared, for Versailles was to demonstrate the wealth, power, and glory of France.

The palace had elegant royal apartments, sweeping staircases, mirrored halls, priceless tapestries, and lavish formal salons and dining rooms. There were offices for government bureaucrats as well as tiny, cramped rooms where officials lived. As many as 10,000 people lived at Versailles. Outside the palace were acres of formal gardens.

In this setting Louis felt secure from the danger of Parisian mobs. Here he had the nobility attend his court so that he could control them. Instead of using the nobles in government service, Louis had them wait on him in a round of daily court rituals. The nobility depended on the king's favor for pensions, court posts, and protection from creditors.

In exchange for ending the nobles' power, Louis freed them from taxation. To nobles and non-nobles alike, he sold many offices with salaries. The sale of offices provided needed royal income but became a long-term drain on the treasury.

Government Policies

Louis continued the efforts of Henry IV and Richelieu to strengthen the power of the monarch and the state. He followed the tradition of Richelieu and chose his top advisers not from the nobility, but from middle-class families.

Although Louis was an absolute monarch, he was not able simply to change the traditions of his country's feudal past. Legal systems varied throughout France. Private tolls and customs were levied on goods moving from one province to another. Weights and measures were not uniform. There were separate authorities and districts for financial, judicial, religious, and administrative affairs.

History & Art *Louis XIV of France* by Hyacinthe Rigaud, c. 1701, The Louvre, Paris, France **Louis XIV worked six to eight hours a day at what he called "the business of being king."** *How does this painting reflect the monarchy of Louis XIV?*

If Louis had tried to change these practices, it would have endangered his throne. Instead, the king kept the traditional ways, but added to them new administrative offices and practices. Two key people aided Louis XIV in his efforts—Jean-Baptiste Colbert (kohl •BEHR) and François Michel Le Tellier, the Marquis de Louvois (loov•WAH). As economic and financial minister, Colbert followed mercantilist policies to promote trade and industry. Louvois served as minister of war and helped make France's army the strongest in Europe.

Taxation

While reforming some aspects of government practice, Louis failed to adjust the complicated and unjust tax system. The poor carried most of the tax burden, while nobles, clergy, and government officials were exempt from many payments. Independent tax collectors often made large profits, but they were allowed to continue this practice since the money was needed to support the army.

The unreformed tax system heightened the economic differences between the regions of France. Since any visible improvement in one's farm or household might lead to higher tax payments, there was little desire to improve one's output. The tax system encouraged people to move from heavily

---

Mixed Learners As a challenge to some students and a help to others, organize the class into two teams. Have students plan a Who? What? When? Where? guessing game about people, places, and events they have studied in this section. Each team should write clues on cards and put the answers on the backs. One team can work on Who? and Where? clues while the other team prepares What? and When? cards. After each team has prepared about ten clue cards, students can take turns guessing the answers. At the end of the game, teams should give answers to clues not guessed. **L1**

---

taxed regions to regions with lower taxes. As a result, heavily taxed regions became poorer.

Religious Policy

Louis regarded the Huguenots as a threat to his absolute monarchy. Many Huguenots were military leaders and prosperous merchants. They often controlled local commerce. In spite of their high social standing, the Huguenots faced mounting persecution from Louis's government. The king wanted the Huguenots to accept Catholicism. He believed that, in this way, they would prove their loyalty to the throne. In 1685 the Edict of Nantes was repealed. Huguenots could no longer practice their religion and their children had to become Catholics.

The result of the king's policy was the emigration of about 200,000 Huguenots to such places as the Netherlands, England, and England's American colonies. Many of these people contributed to economic growth and prosperity where they settled.

Expansion

Louis XIV pursued a bold and active foreign policy. Other European rulers were fearful of Louis's desire for expansion and, as a result, allied in opposition to France.

At the end of Louis XIV's reign, Europe was concerned about the succession to the Spanish throne. It was expected that Charles II of Spain would die without an heir. Both France and Austria had claims to the throne. The rest of Europe was alarmed that the balance of power would be disrupted if France inherited Spain's vast empire. Prior to Spanish king Charles II's death, the

Student Web Activity 19

Visit the *World History: The Human Experience* Web site at **worldhistory.glencoe.com** and click on *Chapter 19—Student Web Activities* for an activity relating to the Huguenots.

European powers worked out a plan to divide the Spanish Empire. The will of Charles II upset this plan by stating that the entire empire should remain intact and pass to Louis XIV's grandson, Philip of Anjou. Louis XIV accepted the provisions of the will. When Charles II died in 1700, Philip of Anjou became King Philip V of Spain. As a result, Europe was plunged into a conflict known as the War of the Spanish Succession.

Conflict

The War of the Spanish Succession lasted from 1701 to 1713. During the conflict England, the Dutch Netherlands, and Austria led a Grand Alliance of nations against France and Spain.

Peace finally came with the **Treaty of Utrecht** in 1713. England and the Dutch Netherlands recognized Philip V as king of Spain, on the condition that France and Spain never be united under one crown. England gained trade advantages with the Spanish colonies. France, however, was forced to surrender Acadia (Nova Scotia) and Newfoundland to England. The War of the Spanish Succession drained the French treasury, increased poverty, and created opposition to Louis's rule.

Louis XIV's Legacy

France enjoyed one of its most brilliant cultural periods under Louis XIV. Builders and artisans designed and decorated palaces and churches. Artists and playwrights portrayed the daily life of the king's court, the nobility, and the lower classes. Louis's building projects and his wars, however, had left the country near financial ruin. The weakening of the French nobility also had its costs. The nobles lost their ability to govern, but not the desire for power. The peasants and the middle class resented the privileges and wealth of the nobles. After Louis XIV's death in 1715, the nobility sought to expand its power under Louis's great-grandson, Louis XV. Conflicts between the nobles and the middle and lower classes would bring France to the brink of revolution.

SECTION 3 ASSESSMENT

Main Idea
1. Use a web diagram like the one below to list characteristics of the Bourbon monarchy.

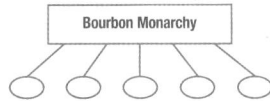

Recall
2. **Define** intendant.
3. **Identify** Henry IV, Edict of Nantes, Cardinal Richelieu, Louis XIV, Treaty of Utrecht.

Critical Thinking
4. **Evaluating Information** What do you think were the

successes and failures of Louis XIV's reign?

Understanding Themes
5. **Uniformity** What were Cardinal Richelieu's political goals? How did Richelieu reduce the power of the nobility? Of the Huguenots?

Check for Understanding

Assign Section 3 Assessment as homework or as an in-class activity.

▣ Use Interactive Tutor Self-Assessment Software to review Section 3.

Linking Past and Present

Molière was a great writer of comic theater during Louis XIV's reign. One of his plays, *L' Ecole des Femmes* or *School for Wives*, is considered the first great comedy of French theater and is still frequently performed. It is said that France loves Molière as England loves Shakespeare.

Reteach

Have students create a biographical outline, chronologically listing the major figures of this section and including examples of how each person helped or hindered France.

📁 Reading Essentials and Study Guide 19-3

Enrich

Have students research the decorative arts of this period in France and make a short oral report, including visuals.

Have students use the **Chapter 19 Student Web Activity** at worldhistory.glencoe.com for in-depth study of the Huguenots.

CLOSE

Have students explain how the reign of Louis XIV built on policies begun during the time of Louis XIII.

SECTION 3 ASSESSMENT ANSWERS

1. absolute rule; reduced power of nobles and Huguenots; lavish court; tax burden mostly on the poor; bold, active foreign policy; cultural achievements
2. All terms are defined in the Glossary.
3. Henry IV, 490; Edict of Nantes, 490; Cardinal Richelieu, 491; Louis XIV, 491; Treaty of Utrecht, 493

4. Louis XIV elevated French culture and brought every aspect of French life under his control; he antagonized nobility, Huguenots, and the poor.
5. **UNIFORMITY** Richelieu sought to build a strong monarchy; he stripped the nobles of their administrative powers and limited the rights of the Huguenots.

1600			1700		1800

1618 Czechs revolt against Hapsburg rule.

1648 Peace of Westphalia ends Thirty Years' War.

1740 Maria Theresa becomes empress of Austria.

1763 Seven Years' War ends.

Section 4

The German States

Guide to Reading

Read to Find Out
Main Idea *The Thirty Years' War involved more countries than prior European wars.*

▶ **Terms to Define**
pragmatic sanction, Peace of Westphalia

▶ **People to Meet**
Ferdinand of Styria, Maria Theresa, Frederick II

▶ **Places to Locate**
Austria, Prussia, Silesia

The Storyteller

Thomas Taylor traveled slowly and cautiously from Dresden to Prague. He was overwhelmed by a harshness he had never witnessed in his native England. Life all around him was insecure and uncomfortable. Violent outlaws roamed the highways, torture was part of the judicial process, executions were horrible, famine and disease were evident in every town. Taylor detoured around public refuse heaps, swarming with rats and carrion crows. He dodged the bodies of executed criminals dangling from the gallows. Taylor had heard rumors of war. If the rumors were true, he judged it would be long, brutal and terrible.

—freely adapted from *The Thirty Years' War*, C.V. Wedgwood, 1961

The Thirty Years' War

While the Bourbons were building the strongest monarchy in Europe, the Hapsburgs of Austria were trying to set up their own absolute monarchy in central and eastern Europe. Their efforts renewed tensions between Europe's Catholics and Protestants. This eventually led to yet another conflict—the Thirty Years' War. Though most of the fighting took place in Germany, all the major European powers except England became involved.

The Thirty Years' War

Conflicts between Catholics and Protestants had continued in Germany after the Peace of Augsburg in 1555. These disputes were complicated by the spread of Calvinism, a religion that had not been recognized by the peace settlement. Furthermore, the Protestant princes of Germany resisted the rule of Catholic Hapsburg monarchs.

In 1618 the Thirty Years' War began in Bohemia, where **Ferdinand of Styria** had become king a year earlier. Ferdinand was also the Hapsburg heir to the throne of the Holy Roman Empire. An enemy of Protestantism who wanted to strengthen Hapsburg authority, Ferdinand began his rule by curtailing the freedom of Bohemian Protestants, most of whom were Czechs. In 1618 the Czechs rebelled and took over Prague. Soon the rebellion developed into a full-scale civil war— Ferdinand and the Catholic princes against the German Protestant princes. Philip III of Spain, a Hapsburg, sent aid to Ferdinand.

The Czech revolt was crushed by 1620 and, over the next 10 years, the Czechs were forcefully reconverted to Catholicism. Instead of ending, however, the war continued. Protestant Denmark now fought against the Hapsburgs, hoping to gain German territory. The Danes were soon defeated and forced to withdraw. Then Sweden entered the war to defend the Protestant cause. By this time the war had been going on for 12 years, and religious issues were taking second place to political ones. In 1635, under Cardinal Richelieu, Roman Catholic France took up arms against the Roman Catholic Hapsburgs to keep them from becoming too powerful.

For 13 more years the war dragged on—rival armies plundering the German countryside and destroying entire towns. Historians estimate that Germany lost about one-third of its people.

When the conflict finally ended in 1648, the outcome was the further weakening of Germany and the rise of France as Europe's leading power. The **Peace of Westphalia** ending the war recognized Calvinism among the official religions and divided the Holy Roman Empire into more than 300 separate states. The Hapsburgs still ruled Austria and Bohemia, but their control of the other German states was in name only, thus ending their hope of establishing an absolute monarchy over all of Germany.

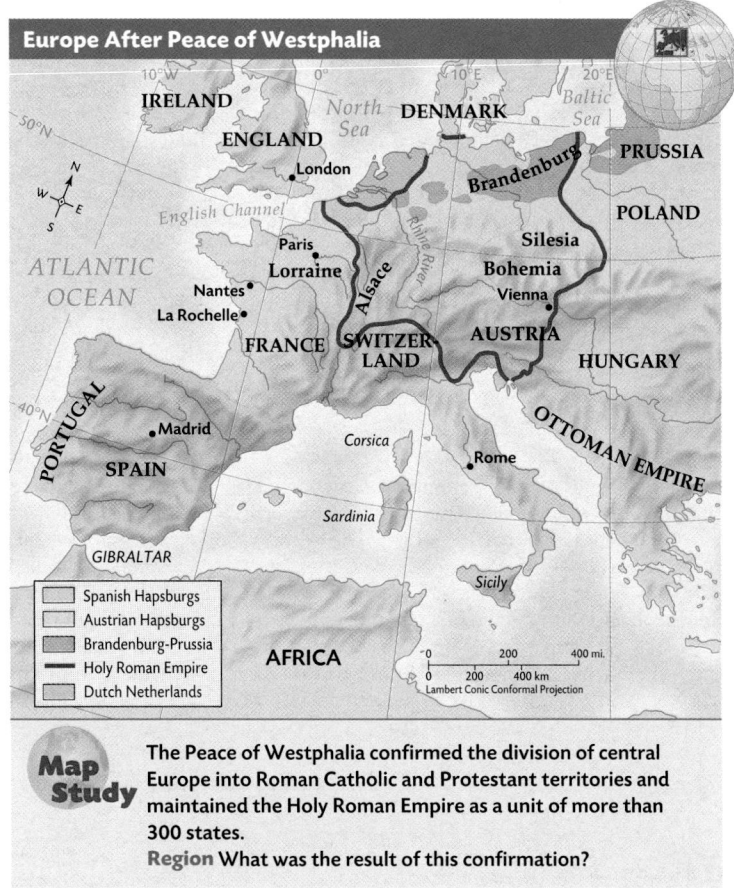

Europe After Peace of Westphalia

Spanish Hapsburgs
Austrian Hapsburgs
Brandenburg-Prussia
Holy Roman Empire
Dutch Netherlands

Map Study The Peace of Westphalia confirmed the division of central Europe into Roman Catholic and Protestant territories and maintained the Holy Roman Empire as a unit of more than 300 states.
Region What was the result of this confirmation?

Austria

After the Thirty Years' War, the Austrian Hapsburgs concentrated on building a strong monarchy in **Austria**, Hungary, and Bohemia. Austria was still the most powerful of the German states. In 1683 the Austrians, with the aid of the Poles, lifted an Ottoman siege of Vienna. By 1718, Austrian armies had regained territory in the Balkan Peninsula from the Ottomans. As a result of the War of the Spanish Succession, the Austrians received the Spanish Netherlands and acquired lands in Italy.

In 1740, 23-year-old **Maria Theresa** inherited the throne of Austria from her father, Holy Roman Emperor Charles VI. According to law and custom, women were not permitted to rule Austria. In 1718 Charles had convinced the monarchs of Europe to accept a pragmatic sanction, or royal decree having the force of law, by which Europe's rulers promised not to divide the Hapsburg lands and to accept

Footnotes to History

Tulip Mania

During the Thirty Years' War, western Europeans fell in love with tulips. Dutch traders brought tulip bulbs into Europe from Ottoman Turkey beginning in the 1500s, and gardeners in the Netherlands and other parts of Europe took a liking to the blossoms. This led to a public craze for tulips that reached a peak in the 1630s.

Section 4

TEACH

Guided Practice

THEME Conflict

In discussing the conflicts involved in the Thirty Years' War, ask students to recall religious conflicts that were a part of earlier periods. *(Romans and early Christians; Hindus and Muslims in India; Christians and Muslims in the Holy Land)* **L1**

Map Study

Answer
France became the leading power.

Map Skills Practice

Reading a Map What are the major cities in the Hapsburg territories? *(Madrid, Vienna)*

Geography Have students compare the map of the Hapsburg holdings in Section 1 on page 484 to the map in this section. Ask them to identify the changes that took place between the time represented by the earlier map and the time represented by this one. *(Holy Roman Empire is smaller; Hapsburg holdings smaller; Brandenburg-Prussia is new; Switzerland and Dutch Netherlands are now independent states; France is larger.)* **L2**

Focus on World Art Print 19, Jan Steen. *The Dancing Couple*

Maria Theresa of Austria not only ruled the foreign affairs of the Holy Roman Empire but also raised 16 children. One of her daughters, Marie Antoinette, became queen of France.

COOPERATIVE LEARNING ACTIVITY

Debate Have students hold a mock debate centering on Maria Theresa's right to rule the Hapsburg Empire after her father's death. Propose this question to debate: Should the Pragmatic Sanction have been honored by Austria's neighbors? Why or why not? Organize the class into two teams to take opposite positions. Direct each team to delegate a task to each member, such as finding outside resources, organizing data, creating questions and answers, and judging the outcome of the debate. Students should research the life and times of Maria Theresa, her father Charles VI, and also the status of women at that time. **L2**

Independent Practice

 Guided Reading Activity
19-4 **L1**

Political Cartoon Have students assume the role of a political cartoonist during the Austrian Succession or the Seven Years' War. Have them depict a major event in a cartoon for the *Prussian Press*. Subjects might include the fight over Silesia or alliances formed by different countries. **L2 LEP**

ASSESS

Check for Understanding

Assign Section 4 Assessment as homework or as an in-class activity.

⊙ Use Interactive Tutor Self-Assessment Software to review Section 4.

Linking Past and Present

The Sounds of Bach

In the Germany of Bach's time, music was taught in schools, and most people could play an instrument. The chief instrument was the organ, but string and keyboard (clavier) instruments were gaining in popularity. Bach favored the organ and composed 143 chorale preludes for it. Of these, 45 were compiled in a "little organ book" for his oldest son and other students.

ANSWERS

Bach's music was lively and complex in style. His work was largely neglected. Today, he is regarded as an esteemed musician and has had an impact on popular music ranging from Walt Disney classics to rock music.

---

female succession to the Austrian throne.

Maria Theresa had not received any training in political matters, yet she proved to be a clever and resourceful leader. Overcoming the opposition of the nobility and most of her ministers, Maria Theresa greatly strengthened the Austrian central government. She reorganized the bureaucracy, improved tax collection, and furthered the building of roads. Understanding that the unity of her empire depended on a strong economy, Maria Theresa ended trade barriers between Austria and Bohemia and encouraged exports. She also used government funds to boost the production of textiles and glass.

Prussia

Maria Theresa faced a number of enemies in Europe. One of these was France, the traditional rival of the Hapsburgs. In the 1700s a new European rival rose to prominence in northeastern Germany. Brandenburg-Prussia was ruled by the Hohenzollern family, which had governed the territory of Brandenburg since the 1400s. During the Thirty Years' War, they gained control of **Prussia** and other widely scattered lands in Germany.

Great Elector

One of the greatest of the Hohenzollern monarchs was Frederick William. He held the title "Great Elector." After the Thirty Years' War, Frederick William increased the strength of Brandenburg-Prussia by creating a permanent standing army. To meet the cost of his army, he proposed raising taxes. The Junkers, or nobles, opposed this plan. Frederick William then worked out a compromise with them. He permitted only Junkers to be landowners, freed them from taxes, and gave them full power over the peasants. In return, the Junkers agreed that Frederick William could tax townspeople and peasants. These two groups were too weak to organize and oppose this increased burden. In 1663 the Junkers further strengthened their ties to the Hohenzollerns. They pledged allegiance to Frederick William. As a result of this alliance with the Junkers, Frederick William was able to become an absolute ruler.

Frederick William was succeeded by his son Frederick I. Frederick aided the Austrian Hapsburgs against Louis XIV in the War of the Spanish Succession. As a reward, Frederick was given the title of king. He was, however, a weak ruler who did little to strengthen his country.

CONNECTIONS

The Arts

The Sounds of Bach

Johann Sebastian Bach

Born in Eisenach, Germany, in 1685, Johann Sebastian Bach was one of the world's most talented composers. He wrote music for the Lutheran Church, wealthy nobles, and other musicians. Bach's work reflects the baroque style of music, which reached its height during the early 1700s. Baroque music was characterized by lively, complex dramatic compositions that appealed to the listener's mind and emotions.

Bach is especially known for two types of baroque music—counterpoint and fugue. In counterpoint, two or more melodies are combined. In the fugue, several instruments or voices play together, each playing the same melodies but with variations.

For about 50 years after Bach's death in 1750, his work was neglected. Today Bach is esteemed as a brilliant musician, and his influence has touched even modern popular music and film. Walt Disney had Mickey Mouse conducting Bach's *Toccata and Fugue in D Minor* in the 1940 movie classic *Fantasia*. Bach's style is at least hinted at in the rock song *A Whiter Shade of Pale* and in rock musician Jethro Tull's jazz-like arrangement of the *Bourrée* from the *E Minor Lute Suite*.

Linking Past and Present ACTIVITY

Explain why Johann Sebastian Bach's work is called "baroque." How was he regarded after his death? How is he regarded today? What impact has Bach had on modern music?

MEETING SPECIAL NEEDS ACTIVITY

Learning Style: Visual/Spatial Help students who learn better visually to understand the conflicts involved between European powers during the Thirty Years' War or the War of the Austrian Succession by guiding them to make diagrams illustrating the actions and reactions, causes and effects, or problems and solutions of that time. For example, students might list problems or causes in one column, effects in another column, then draw arrows between the causes and effects. **L2 LEP**

Frederick William I

Frederick William I, who ruled from 1713 to 1740, was a powerful leader. He centralized the Prussian government, uniting all functions into one bureaucracy under his direct control. He supported production and trade and brought more revenue into the government treasury. Known as the Royal Drill Sergeant, Frederick William devoted his life to the Prussian army and made it the most efficient fighting force in Europe. He especially delighted in recruiting tall soldiers and formed a special "regiment of giants" that he drilled himself.

Frederick II

In 1740 **Frederick II**, Frederick William I's son, became king of Prussia. As king, Frederick adopted his father's military ways and set out to expand Prussian territory. Frederick the Great, as he became known, rejected Austria's pragmatic sanction and seized the Austrian province of **Silesia**.

Frederick's attack on Silesia began a conflict called the War of the Austrian Succession. Prussia's forces were stronger than Austria's. In spite of her disadvantage, the Austrian empress, Maria Theresa, decided to send her forces into battle. Spain and France backed Prussia, while Great Britain (formed in 1707 by the union of England and Scotland) and the Dutch Netherlands supported Austria.

After seven years of fighting, in 1748 the European powers signed the Treaty of Aix-la-Chapelle, which officially recognized Prussia's rise as an important nation. Frederick was allowed to keep Silesia; Maria Theresa was able to hold the rest of her domain: Austria, Hungary, and Bohemia.

The Austrian ruler, however, was not satisfied with the treaty and was determined to recover Silesia. To this end, Maria Theresa changed her alliance from Great Britain to France. She also gained the support of Russia since Prussia's Frederick II was an archenemy of Empress Elizabeth of Russia. These alliances set the stage for further conflict.

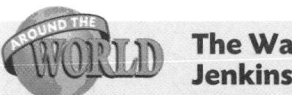

The War of Jenkins' Ear

Caribbean Sea, 1739

The War of Jenkins' Ear was part of a series of conflicts among European nations in the 1700s. In the waters off Florida, an English smuggler named Robert Jenkins lost his ear in a fight with Spaniards in 1731. Jenkins' appearance in Parliament in 1738 further incited public opinion against Spain. The result was war, declared in June 1739, over possession of Georgia and commercial rivalry at sea. Within a year, the War of Jenkins' Ear had become part of the more serious War of Austrian Succession.

The Seven Years' War—from 1756 to 1763—was a worldwide conflict in which Great Britain and France competed for overseas territory, and Prussia opposed Austria, Russia, France, and other nations. The war between Austria and Prussia erupted in 1756. After victories in Saxony—a German state and an ally of Austria—and after a later victory over the Austrians in Silesia, Frederick II signed a peace agreement that enabled him to retain most of Silesia.

The struggle between Great Britain and France in North America was known as the French and Indian War. The British and French also fought in India. At the Treaty of Paris in 1763, France gave up most of French Canada and its lands east of the Mississippi River to Great Britain. Great Britain also replaced France as the leading power in India. As a result of the Seven Years' War, Great Britain emerged as the strongest colonial empire and Prussia retained the province of Silesia.

SECTION 4 ASSESSMENT

Main Idea

1. Use a chart like the one below to identify the results of the Thirty Years' War.

Results of Thirty Years' War

Recall

2. **Define** pragmatic sanction.
3. **Identify** Ferdinand of Styria, Peace of Westphalia, Maria Theresa, Frederick II, Silesia.

Critical Thinking

4. **Analyzing Information** How did Empress Maria Theresa strengthen the central government in Austria and in her other territories?

Understanding Themes

5. **Conflict** How did the many conflicts among the German states affect the European balance of power?

Who?What?**Where?**When?

Sans Souci Frederick II planned and had built a one-story summer palace, Sans Souci. French for "without cares," Sans Souci was the king's favorite retreat. It was famous for its midnight suppers, at which Frederick surrounded himself with educated men.

Evaluate

Section Quiz 19-4

Use the Testmaker to create a customized quiz for Section 4.

Reteach

Have students work in small groups to write summaries of conflicts discussed in this section.

Reading Essentials and Study Guide 19-4

Enrich

Have students voice their opinions about the shifting of alliances in order to achieve political goals. Were these the decisions of a wise monarch or signs of disloyalty and ingratitude? *(Answers will vary. Students should mention the balance of power theory.)*

CLOSE

Ask students to offer opinions about the justification of war and bloodshed that raged throughout Europe before and during the Thirty Years' War. Ask how they might have reacted if they had lived in the 1600s.

SECTION 4 ASSESSMENT ANSWERS

1. further weakening of Germany; rise of France as Europe's leading power; Calvinism recognized as official religion; Holy Roman Empire divided into 300 separate states; Hapsburgs lost power
2. All terms are defined in the Glossary.
3. Ferdinand of Styria, 494; Peace of Westphalia, 495; Maria Theresa, 495; Frederick II, 497; Silesia, 497
4. Government took responsibilities for services such as public health, prisons, and roads; ended trade barriers; used government funds to encourage production of textiles and glass to build the economy.
5. **CONFLICT** weakened German states and allowed France to become dominant

| 1500 | 1600 | 1700 | 1800 |

1533 Ivan IV (the Terrible) begins rule.

1689 Peter I (the Great) becomes czar.

1721 Russia secures areas of Baltic coastline.

1796 Catherine II (the Great) dies.

Section 5

Russia

Guide to Reading

Read to Find Out
Main Idea *The power of Russian czars differed from that of other European monarchs.*

▶ **Terms to Define**
   boyar, *dvorianie*, serf

▶ **People to Meet**
   Ivan IV, the Romanovs, Peter I, Catherine II

▶ **Places to Locate**
   Poland, Siberia, St. Petersburg

The Storyteller

When first posted, no one could believe the decree. Czar Peter had ordered all children from the nobility and clerical classes [clergy] to study mathematics and geometry. Those who refused were forbidden to marry until they mastered the material. Such commands seemed absurd and many scoffed at the czar's ability to enforce his demands. However, teachers arrived in each district and local taxes were increased for support. Priests likewise received notification and no priest dared solemnize a marriage without proper certification. Father Konstantin looked sadly at the couple before him and explained, "You do not have the proper certification. I cannot marry you."

—adapted from *Decree on Compulsory Education of the Russian Nobility*, reprinted in *The Human Record, Volume 2*, Alfred J. Andrea and James H. Overfield, 1990

Russian Orthodox Bishop

Between 1500 and 1800, Russia made tremendous territorial gains and became a major European power. Slavs elsewhere lost ground and were taken over by other powers.

In southeastern Europe, the Ottoman Turks ruled most of the Balkan Peninsula and the Serbs, Bosnians, and Macedonians who lived there. Under the Ottomans, some of these Slavs converted to Islam, while the rest remained Eastern Orthodox. Hungary ruled the Croats (KROH•ATZ), and Austria controlled the Slovenes (SLOH•VEENZ). Both these Slavic peoples remained Roman Catholic and oriented to western Europe.

In central Europe, Austria ruled the Slovaks and Czechs. Neighboring **Poland** had been an important European power from the late 1300s. Polish monarchs created one of the larger states of Europe, but by the 1600s Poland had gradually weakened. Ukrainian subjects rebelled against Polish rule in the mid-1600s and allied with Russia. By 1764 almost all of Ukraine was under Russian control. In the late 1700s Prussia, Austria, and Russia divided Poland among themselves. The Belarus region and its people, the Belarussians, passed from Polish to Russian control at this time.

Rise of Russia

From the 1200s to the early 1700s, Russia was isolated from western European developments, such as the Crusades, the Renaissance, and the Reformation. Russia developed its own civilization based on the values of the Eastern Orthodox Church and the Byzantine Empire. The Russian monarchy became all-powerful and easily crushed its opponents. The nobility, the established church, and the towns—all of whom had posed repeated opposition to royal power elsewhere in Europe—never posed the same challenge in Russia.

498 Chapter 19 *Royal Power and Conflict*

Ivan IV

The most powerful of the early czars was **Ivan IV**, who ruled from 1533 to 1584. Known as Ivan "the Terrible" or "the Awesome," he was at once learned, religious, and cruel. Ivan became czar at the age of three. While growing up, he was caught between rival groups of nobles who sought to rule the country. He witnessed much cruelty and was never able to rid himself of his early memories. As an adult, Ivan saw treason everywhere and arrested, exiled, or executed many of his closest advisers. In a fit of rage, he even killed his own son.

Ivan took many steps against the boyars (boh•YAHRZ), or nobles, to reduce their potential threat to his throne. He seized their scattered lands and placed them under his direct control. The former owners were uprooted and dispersed. On the seized land, which made up about one-half of the country, Ivan placed his own loyal people. They became a secret police force, the *oprichniki*, (aw•PREECH•nee•kee) and terrorized the rest of the country.

Ivan IV also increased Russia's trade with western Europe and worked to expand his borders. Despite Russia's vast size, it had few seaports free of ice throughout the year. Gaining more access to the sea for trade and security became a major goal of Russian rulers. During the late 1500s, Ivan conquered Mongol lands east and south of Moscow but waged unsuccessful war against Poland, Lithuania, and Sweden for territory near the Baltic Sea.

The Time of Troubles

After Ivan's death in 1584, Russia drifted toward chaos. During the "Time of Troubles," from 1598 to 1613, noble feuds over the throne, peasant revolts, and foreign invasions plagued the country. Finally in 1613, an assembly of clergy, nobles, and townsmen named 17-year-old Michael Romanov as czar. Michael began **the Romanov dynasty** that ruled Russia until 1917.

During the 1500s and 1600s, Russian society experienced many changes. Boyars became more closely tied to the czar's service, townspeople lost what little influence they had on government, and peasants were bound to the land as a virtually enslaved workforce. To escape, many peasants moved to borderlands south of Moscow. In Ukraine, some formed self-governing villages of warrior pioneers and their families and became known as Cossacks. Peasants, traders, and adventurers also moved into **Siberia**, the vast stretch of land east of European Russia.

Visualizing History **Peter the Great, a man of restless energy and sometimes hasty decisions, attempted many reforms.** *What reforms did he introduce to make Russia more like western European nations?*

Peter the Great

In 1689 **Peter I**, known as Peter the Great, came to the throne. He was a towering figure, nearly 7 feet (2 m) tall. Peter had boundless energy and volcanic emotions. During his reign, he sought to bring Russia into the mainstream of European civilization.

Encounter With the West

As a young man, Peter enjoyed practical subjects, such as mechanics, geography, and military strategy. He sought out tutors among the foreign community in Moscow to learn the basic skills of navigation and shipbuilding. He discovered that Russian knowledge of the outside world was quite limited. Most Russians were illiterate peasants; only a few nobles were well educated.

After becoming czar, Peter took an 18-month study tour of England and the Netherlands. He visited shipyards, factories, mills, and laboratories. He learned carpentry and developed enough skill in surgery and dentistry to want to practice on others.

Chapter 19 *Royal Power and Conflict* **499**

Chapter 19
Section 5

TEACH

Guided Practice

THEME Innovation

Discuss and list on the chalkboard the changes that occurred in Russia between the time of Ivan the Terrible and Catherine the Great. Ask what advances were made in political control, the arts, science, and technology. (*Sample answers: nobility given land in exchange for government service; printing press introduced into Russia; new capital built; army and navy modernized*) **L1 LEP**

Visualizing History Because Peter had such stores of energy, he found relaxation difficult. Although hunting was a favorite sport of many monarchs, Peter refused to hunt; however, he sailed whenever he could. He also enjoyed playing chess and carried a folding leather chessboard with him so he could play with anyone at any time.

Answer to Caption: *required court members to wear Western-style clothes; included women in social gatherings; invited foreign experts to train Russians in sciences, naval warfare, shipbuilding, and foreign languages; increased the power of the central government*

Comparing Catherine the Great has been compared by historians to England's Elizabeth in her ability to rule and in the significance of her reign. Have students prepare a chart comparing the two rulers and their accomplishments. **L2**

 History Simulation 19

COOPERATIVE LEARNING ACTIVITY

Research Have students work in small groups to research and report on the daily life of women in Russia during the time of Peter the Great and Catherine the Great, as well as women in Russia today. Scholarly works on Russian feminism of the past and the present are available in local libraries. Have groups plan how to delegate the work—some students may research, and others may write the reports. Topics to consider might be family responsibilities, intellectual interests, types of work, and political concerns of the women. Copies of photographs from the resources will help the groups describe the life of women then and now. **L2**

TEACH

Explain to the class that the building of a city on the marshes of the Neva River was a major project. Peter hired hundreds of foreign architects and thousands of Russian workers to create a city described as the "Venice of the North." What feature unique to a city like Venice would be useful for a city built on a broad river and marshes? *(a network of canals)* Tell students that St. Petersburg became the country's main industrial center and one of the world's most brilliant cultural centers.

Who?What?Where?When?

St. Petersburg arrived late as a major city in the world. In the American colonies, New York was 79 years old, Boston was 73, and Philadelphia was 21. St. Petersburg was the capital of the Russian Empire for 200 years.

CD-ROM

PICTURE ATLAS OF THE WORLD

You and your students can see a skyline view of St. Petersburg and the Winter Palace (now the Hermitage Museum) by clicking Russia's "Photos" button.

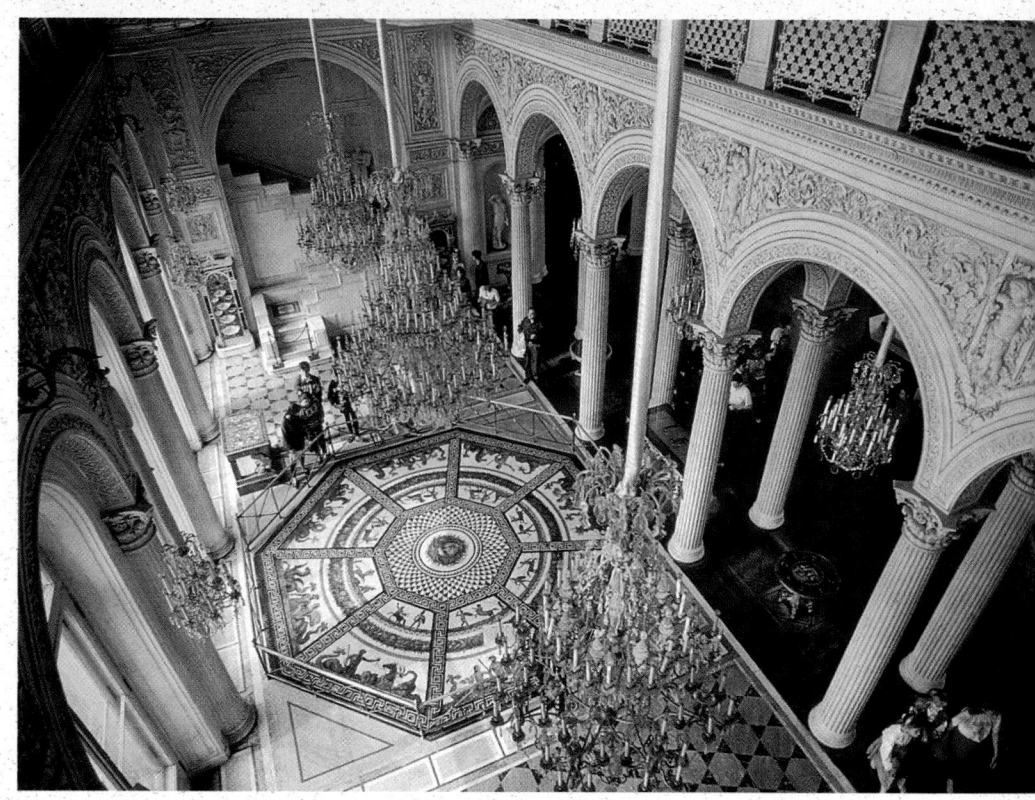

Peter's Great City

Where he first set foot on the Baltic coast, legend has it, Peter the Great proclaimed: "Here there shall be a town." On May 16, 1703, Russian workers laid the foundations for a fortress on the Baltic coast. The city of St. Petersburg soon spread out, and in 1712 Peter made it the new capital of Russia. A traveler in his youth, he was determined that his new capital would imitate the imposing European cities he had visited. St. Petersburg did not remain the capital of Russia, but the new city offered Peter the Great a chance to consolidate the power of the Russian central government and to drag Russia into the modern world. Many changes were inaugurated: He

G.D. Talbot

forbade men to wear beards dress in the traditional long called caftans. He simplifi Cyrillic alphabet. He was rel At times he even resorted to But he transformed Russia an his new city on the Baltic Sea dow to the West.

Today Peter's legacy is everywhere: in th yards, the research centers, and the architec ornate palaces such as the Winter Palace (c completed during the reign of Catherine the G 1762. "I have a whole labyrinth of rooms ... an them are filled with luxuries," she wrote of th ter Palace and the adjoining Hermitage, where ion Hall (top) fills one small corner. ⊕

500 Chapter 19 *Royal Power and Conflict*

When he returned home, Peter forced the Russian nobility to adopt the ways of western Europe. He ordered members of the court to wear western European clothing. Men entering Moscow were forced to shave their beards or pay a fine. Women, who had always been excluded from social gatherings, were ordered to attend parties.

Peter sent Russians abroad to study shipbuilding, naval warfare, mathematics, and foreign languages. He invited foreign experts to train Russians. His greatest effort to open Russia to Europe was the building of a new capital, which he named **St. Petersburg**. Located at the mouth of the Neva River near the Baltic Sea, St. Petersburg became Russia's "window to the West."

Foreign Policy

Peter's goal was to make Russia a European power. He expanded Russia's borders in the south, east, and northwest. In 1689 Russia forced China to accept Russian control of Siberia. In the early 1700s, the Danish navigator Vitus Bering claimed for Russia what became known as the Bering Strait between Siberia and Alaska. Russian settlements eventually started in Alaska and even California.

During much of Peter's reign, Russia fought Poland, Sweden, or the Ottoman Empire. Russian failures to win warm-water ports on either the Baltic or Black Seas convinced Peter to modernize the military. His reforms paid off in 1721, when Russia defeated Sweden and won control of the eastern end of the Baltic region.

Government Administration

Peter made sweeping changes in the Russian government. Borrowing ideas from France, he introduced a central bureaucracy and placed local governments under its control. Peter brought the Eastern Orthodox Church under his direct authority. In place of a single independent church leader, Peter created the Holy Synod, a council of bishops responsible to the government.

Peter also created a new class of nobles called *dvorianie* (DVOH•ree•YAH•nee•YUH), who, in return for government service, were allowed to own hereditary, landed estates. A noble's duty to the czar started at age 15 and continued until death.

Peter used privileges and force to make the established nobility accept government service. Nobles were given full control over the serfs, or peasant laborers who worked the estates and were bound to the land. While freedom for peasants had gradually increased in western Europe, the opposite was true in Russia.

Finally, Peter changed the tax laws to increase government income and efficiency. Under the plan, nobles paid no taxes. As in France, the tax burden fell on the poorest classes.

Economic Changes

To stimulate economic growth, Peter brought agriculture and craft production under strict government control. He gave incentives to increase production in favored areas such as mining and metalworking. New production centers were provided with land, money, and workers. Most of the workers were tied to their trades as the serfs were to the land.

Russian Expansion in Europe

	Moscow
	Acquired by 1505 (Death of Ivan III)
	Acquired by 1584 (Death of Ivan IV)
	Acquired by 1725 (Death of Peter)
	Acquired by 1796 (Death of Catherine)

0   150   300 mi.
0   150   300 km
Lambert Conic
Conformal Projection

Map Study Peter the Great and Catherine the Great looked westward to increase the power and influence of Russia. **Location** How did geography influence the foreign policy of Russian rulers?

Chapter 19 *Royal Power and Conflict* **501**

Independent Practice

 Guided Reading Activity 19-5 **L1**

Map Study

Answer

Russia was a vast northern country whose population centers were far from ports that were ice-free throughout the year; Russian rulers wanted to expand to acquire coastal areas with warm water outlets.

Map Skills Practice

Reading a Map The acquisition of Crimea gave Russia access to what important body of water? *(Black Sea)*

The following videotape program is available from Glencoe:

• **Secrets of the Romanovs**

To find classroom resources to accompany this video, check the following home page:

A&E Television: http://www.aetv.com

Linking Past and Present

City Renamed Peter the Great had the new city named St. Petersburg after himself. Later it was renamed Leningrad after the Communist revolutionary leader Vladimir Lenin. Today the city has been re-renamed and is again called St. Petersburg.

MEETING SPECIAL NEEDS ACTIVITY

Mixed Learners To help students who learn better by discussing a topic and also to help those who have limited use of the language, have students work in groups of three. Each student should select part of the section to study, outline, and then "teach" to the other members of the group. Suggest that they each write a short quiz for the others to take at the end of the teaching session. **L1 LEP**

ASSESS

Check for Understanding

Assign Section 5 Assessment as homework or as an in-class activity.

 Use Interactive Tutor Self-Assessment Software to review Section 5.

Evaluate

 Section Quiz 19-5

Reteach

Have students work in small groups to summarize the achievements and the acts of oppression of each major ruler in Section 5. Guide a class discussion based on their summaries.

 Reteaching Activity 19

 Reading Essentials and Study Guide 19-5

Enrich

Have students debate the following: Catherine the Great was not great.

 Enrichment Activity 19

CLOSE

Ask students which Russian monarch they would rather serve and in what capacity. *(Answers should reflect the ability and morality of the monarch.)*

History & Art *Portrait of Catherine the Great* by Alexandre Roslin. Musée des Beaux Arts, La Rochelle, France *What changed Catherine's mind about the equality of all people?*

Effects

Peter's reforms strengthened Russia's role in foreign affairs. In his own country, however, Peter had only limited success. His domestic policies broke the traditional Eastern Orthodox culture that had united nobles and peasants. With Peter's reign, a dangerous split developed between the few who accepted European ways and the many who clung to traditional values. Many of Peter's reforms were incomplete and hasty. Yet his measures brought Russia into the mainstream of western European civilization.

Catherine the Great

After Peter's death in 1725, Russia was ruled by a series of weak or ordinary monarchs. The next notable ruler was **Catherine II**. In 1762, Catherine seized the throne from her weak husband, Peter III, and ruled as empress of Russia until 1796. Although born a German princess, Catherine easily adopted Russian ways and earned the respect of her people.

As monarch, Catherine was greatly influenced by leading western European thinkers. She studied their works and corresponded with a number of them. For a time, she believed that all people were born equal and that it was "contrary to the Christian faith and to justice to make slaves of them."

Early in her reign, Catherine considered freeing the serfs. A peasant rebellion that threatened her rule, however, made Catherine change her mind. To ensure the continued support of the nobles, she released them from the government service required by Peter I. She also allowed the nobles to treat their serfs as they pleased. During Catherine's reign, more peasants were forced into serfdom than ever before, and their conditions worsened. Russia's common people had fewer rights than those in any other part of Europe. When groups of them revolted, Catherine brutally crushed the uprisings.

A successful foreign policy earned her the name Catherine the Great. She significantly expanded Russia's southern borders and secured a warm-water port on the Black Sea. In making this gain, Russian armies defeated the Ottoman Turks. In the west, Catherine acquired territory from Poland. Prussia and Austria took the rest of Poland, which then ceased to exist until 1919.

Catherine was the last of the great absolute monarchs of the 1700s. By the time of her death in 1796, new ideas of liberty and equality had spread throughout western Europe. These new ideas directly challenged and questioned the age-old institution of monarchy.

SECTION 5 ASSESSMENT

Main Idea
1. Use a chart like the one below to list the powers of the Russian czars.

Powers of Russian Czars
1.
2.

Recall
2. **Define** boyar, *dvorianie*, serf.
3. **Identify** Ivan IV, the Romanovs, Peter I, Catherine II.

Critical Thinking
4. **Synthesizing Information** How did the reigns of Romanov rulers Peter the Great and Catherine the Great affect the Russian nobility and the common people of the Russian Empire?

Understanding Themes
5. **Innovation** How did Peter the Great try to make Russian people of all ranks accept western European ideas and practices?

SECTION 5 ASSESSMENT ANSWERS

1. monarchy all-powerful; no threat posed by nobility, church, or towns; controlled land, church, culture, and politics; created secret police; created new nobles
2. All terms are defined in the Glossary.
3. Ivan IV, 499; the Romanovs, 499; Peter I, 499; Catherine II, 502
4. Peter used privileges and force to make the nobility accept government service; bound serfs to the land and granted nobles full control over them; Catherine released the nobles from government service; under her the lot of the common people worsened.
5. **INNOVATION** He brought foreign experts to teach the European ways and sent Russians abroad.

Recognizing a Stereotype

Emanuella asks her friend Ashley if she would date a football player. Ashley says, "No way. Football players are all muscle and no brains." Ashley has expressed a stereotype—an oversimplified description of a group. Because stereotypes may be both inaccurate and harmful, we must learn to recognize them in speaking, writing, and thinking.

Learning the Skill

A stereotype can describe any group—a gender, race, religion, country, region, city, neighborhood, school, or profession. Stereotypes blur or ignore the characteristics of individuals within the group. In the example above, Ashley may reject the friendship of a very considerate and intelligent person just because he plays football. While this is a negative stereotype, other stereotypes may have positive or neutral connotations. "Blondes have more fun" is a positive stereotype. Negative stereotypes, however, are the least accurate and most harmful.

Stereotypes can influence not only our attitude about a group's members, but also our behavior toward them. History is full of examples of oppression and persecution directed at particular groups of people. Negative stereotypes usually accompany these destructive acts.

Because stereotypes are so common, it is easy to ignore or accept them. Instead, learn how to recognize and evaluate them. Certain words, phrases, and thoughts signal the presence of stereotypes. In any kind of material, written or oral, first notice characteristics attributed to a particular group. Look for exaggerations, often indicated by words such as *all*, *none*, *every*, *always*, and *never*. Identify strong negative adjectives such as *lazy*, *sneaky*, *cruel*, and *corrupt*. Note a positive or negative tone to the description.

Once you recognize a stereotype, then evaluate its accuracy. Think about whether the stereotype puts a positive or negative slant on the information concerning a specific group. Ask yourself: Does this stereotype agree or disagree with what I know about individual members of this group?

Practicing the Skill

Each statement below contains a stereotype held from the 1500s to the 1700s. In each statement, identify any words or phrases that help you recognize the stereotype, and tell whether it has a negative, positive, or neutral connotation.

1. England is an isle fouled by heretics and barbarians. *(Spain, 1554)*
2. It is against the law, human and divine, that a woman should reign and have empire above men. *(England, 1560)*
3. The Italians are so jovial and addicted to music that nearly every countryman plays on the guitar, and will commonly go into the field with a fiddle. *(England, 1600)*
4. Do not put such unlimited power into the hands of husbands. Remember all men would be tyrants if they could. [We ladies] will not hold ourselves bound by any laws in which we have no voice, or representation. *(United States, 1776)*

Applying the Skill

Identify three stereotypes about groups within your community. For each one, write a paragraph evaluating its accuracy by recalling your own experiences with members of the group.

For More Practice

Turn to the Skill Practice in the Chapter Assessment on page 505.

The **Glencoe Skillbuilder Interactive Workbook**, Level 2 provides instruction and practice in key social studies skills.

TEACH

Recognizing a Stereotype Most students will understand and be aware of the problem of negative stereotypes. Suggest that they take time to consider positive stereotypes and the actual harm that can come from them, too. Ask students to brainstorm positive stereotype examples from television programs, movies, and magazine advertisements. For example, they might discuss the positive body images portrayed in the media, such as the scent ads, hairstyles, and fashions that are supposed to make life wonderful. Ask students to discuss the impact of these advertisements on young people and the problems they cause for self-esteem in the teenage population.

Additional Practice

Skill Reinforcement Activity 19

GLENCOE TECHNOLOGY

Glencoe's **Skillbuilder Interactive Workbook, Level 2**
This interactive CD-ROM promotes student mastery of key social studies skills.

ANSWERS TO PRACTICING THE SKILL

1. English people were opposed to Catholicism; words *fouled*, *heretics*, and *barbarians* are used for their negative connotations; a negative stereotype
2. only men should be rulers of countries; words "against the law" very absolute; a negative stereotype
3. Italians are happy and musical; *every* shows exaggeration; a positive stereotype
4. husbands, men in general, are not to be trusted with power; negative word *tyrants* and use of *all*; a negative stereotype

Chapter 19 Assessment

Have students use the **Chapter 19 Self-Check Quiz** at worldhistory.glencoe.com to prepare for the Chapter Test.

GLENCOE TECHNOLOGY

VIDEODISC
Use MindJogger to review the chapter.

MindJogger Videoquiz

Chapter 19
Disc 3 Side A

 Also available in VHS.

Answers

Using Key Terms
1. f   3. h   5. b
2. j   4. e

Using Your History Journal

Students should give supporting facts to explain their opinions.

Reviewing Facts

1. differences: Catherine seized throne from husband, acquired territory, and expanded Russia's border; Elizabeth inherited monarchy, relied on diplomacy and sea power to protect her country's interests; similarities: forceful rulers, well-educated
2. Hapsburgs, Spain and Austria; Tudors, England; Bourbons, France; Romanovs, Russia; Hohenzollern, Brandenburg-Prussia
3. European monarchs were at their pinnacle of power, emphasizing divine right—they unified their nations and built strong central government bureaucracies; they emphasized their wealth by building palaces and staging magnificent ceremonies.
4. by cooperating with Parliament

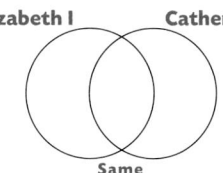

Self-Check Quiz

Visit the *World History: The Human Experience* Web site at **worldhistory.glencoe.com** and click on *Chapter 19—Self-Check Quiz* to prepare for the Chapter Test.

Using Key Terms

Write the key term that completes each sentence. Then write a sentence for each term not chosen.

a. absolutism	g. armada
b. balance of power	h. inflation
c. intendants	i. yeomen
d. serfs	j. pragmatic sanction
e. divine right	k. *dvorianie*
f. boyars	

1. Ivan IV of Russia took steps against the _____ to reduce their potential threat to his throne.
2. In 1718 the Holy Roman emperor Charles VI convinced Europe's monarchs to accept a _____ in which they promised to accept Maria Theresa as the future Hapsburg monarch.
3. During Spain's decline as a European power, its economy suffered from _____, an abnormal increase in currency resulting in sharp price increases.
4. During the 1600s and the 1700s, European monarchs claimed to rule by _____, the theory that monarchs derive their power from God.
5. During Elizabeth I's reign, England worked for a _____ on the Continent to prevent one European power from becoming too strong.

Technology Activity

Building a Database
Search the Internet or your library for additional information about European monarchies since the early 1500s. Build a database collecting biographical information about European monarchies from the 1500s to present day. Include information such as name of monarchy, country, date of coronation, achievements, and names of heirs.

504   **Chapter 19**   *Royal Power and Conflict*

Reviewing Facts

1. **Government** Use a diagram like the one below to identify similarities and differences between how Queen Elizabeth I ruled and Catherine the Great ruled.

Elizabeth I   Catherine the Great

Same

2. **History** List at least four European royal families and their countries during the period from about 1500 to about 1800.
3. **History** Identify major characteristics of Europe's age of absolutism.
4. **Government** Explain how England's Henry VIII strengthened support for his policies.
5. **Citizenship** State why Henry IV's issuing of the Edict of Nantes was a significant event.
6. **History** Identify the changes that Peter the Great brought to Russia.

Critical Thinking

1. **Analyze** How were the Hapsburg and Tudor monarchies of the 1500s similar? How were they different? Which one do you think was more successful?
2. **Synthesize** Imagine you are a soldier during the Thirty Years' War. Describe how you joined the army and what conditions were like during the war. What hopes do you have for the future?
3. **Evaluate** Consider the leadership style of Maria Theresa of Austria, who had no training in political matters. Can a person today be a successful political leader with no prior training or experience?

---

and selling monastery lands to wealthy landowners
5. It ended a long period of religious warfare in France; granted Protestants equal rights with Catholics; and moved toward acceptance of religious toleration.
6. He made St. Petersburg the capital; expanded Russia's borders; built a navy and factories; introduced newspapers and books and western European customs.

Critical Thinking

1. Similarities: both strong monarchies, sought to increase wealth, faced internal unrest. Differences: Hapsburg Empire vaster; Hapsburgs Catholic and Tudors Protestant; Hapsburgs a larger family with many branches.
2. I joined the army because it was the only way to escape hanging. Conditions during the war were terrible. I was hungry most of the time and often wounded; most of my friends died.

4. Evaluate Which of the monarchs described in this chapter do you most admire? Which one do you least admire? Explain your reasons.

5. Evaluate What does the portrait of Frederick the Great below reveal about the values and characteristics of the Prussian monarchy?

Understanding Themes

1. Conflict How did Spain's rivalry with England develop during the period from about 1500 to about 1750?

2. Change How did Tudor monarchs bring stability to England?

3. Uniformity How did Louis XIV try to strengthen French loyalty to his monarchy?

4. Conflict What dynastic and religious issues divided the German states?

5. Innovation Why did Peter the Great want to make innovations in government and society?

Skill Practice

The following lines from William Shakespeare's plays include stereotypes that were common in 16th-century England. Identify each stereotype and any words or phrases that helped you recognize it.

1. "Frailty, thy name is woman!"
2. "These Moors are changeable in their moods."
3. "This Hebrew will turn Christian; he grows kind."
4. "Today the French … all in gold, like heathen gods, shone down the English."

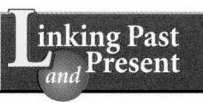

Linking Past and Present

1. European monarchs in the 1600s and 1700s resolved their territorial disputes and ambitions through war. How do present-day leaders resolve disputes? Explore the similarities and the differences between contemporary world leaders and monarchs in early modern Europe.

2. European monarchs in the 1600s and 1700s were powerful leaders who claimed to rule by divine right. What is the position of monarchs in Europe today? How is power exercised in modern European governments?

Geography in History

1. Location Refer to the map below. Along what body of water did Pomerania lie? What was the population loss over much of its area?

2. Place Of Bohemia, Saxony, and Silesia, which area had suffered the least population loss?

3. Region In general, what parts of the Holy Roman Empire retained the most population? Why do you think this was so?

Population Loss 1618–1648

Up to 15%	33–66%
15–33%	Over 66%

Boundary of Holy Roman Empire

4. CONFLICT Catholic Hapsburgs fought Protestant German princes; Catholic Bourbons fought Hapsburgs for power; Hohenzollerns of Prussia fought Austrian Hapsburgs.

5. INNOVATION He wanted to make Russia more like western Europe.

Skill Practice

1. all women are weak; woman used to mean "all women"; negative
2. Moors (Africans) are moody people; "these Moors" means "all Moors"; negative
3. Jews are not kind—kindness is a Christian trait; negative
4. the French looked splendid; *all in gold* and *gods* show exaggeration; positive

Linking Past and Present

1. Today leaders try to resolve disputes through negotiations and diplomacy, but sometimes conflicts still result in war.
2. Most European monarchs today are mainly figureheads with power exercised by a prime minister and national legislature.

Geography in History

1. Baltic Sea; over 66 percent
2. Saxony
3. western parts, Brunswick, and Saxony; there were more rebellions and wars in the other territories, depleting the population

Chapter Bonus Test Question

Ask students: If you could spend an evening with one of the rulers you have met in this chapter, who would it be and what would you do? *(Answers should reflect knowledge of the ruler's life and accomplishments.)*

I have little hope for the future because my home and land have been destroyed.

3. Students may conclude that political leaders need training in diplomacy and negotiation.

4. Students should give supporting facts to explain their answers.

5. reflects a dignified, serious, and strong leader

Understanding Themes

1. CONFLICT England supported the Dutch fight for independence against Spain and raided Spanish ships; Philip tried to invade England with Armada to rid himself of Elizabeth's interference.

2. CHANGE They unified the country, expanded foreign trade, and built a strong navy.

3. UNIFORMITY kept nation's traditional ways, chose top advisers from middle classes, repealed Edict of Nantes

FOCUS

This period of expansion and exploration brought challenges to traditional ideas in Europe. At the same time, Europe and Asia both experienced contact with outside influences.

TEACH

Reinforcing Vocabulary

Point out the **Vocabulary Preview** to students alerting them to words they will encounter that might be unfamiliar.

Erasmus's Description of Sir Thomas More

Interpreting the Primary Source
Ask students to interpret Erasmus's statements about More's piety such as the following: "He has set hours in which he offers to God not the customary prayers but prayers from the heart." *(Here and in the last line of the passage, Erasmus describes More as being much more devoutly religious than most men.)*

Evaluating the Primary Source
This primary source provides an extremely positive depiction of a man who was later executed for the very ideas applauded here. The reliability of this source is determined by the objectivity of its author. Because Erasmus was a friend of More's, he may have presented an overly reverent view of More or, by knowing More well, he may have been able to present a quite accurate view of him.

Unit 4

---·•·---

Between 1400 and the mid-1700s, European and Asian powers began exploring the world. This exploration and expansion often brought differing cultures into conflict with one another but also encouraged the exchange of ideas and technology.

---·•·---

◆ **VOCABULARY PREVIEW**

dexterity: the ability to adjust

piety: religious devotion

sovereignty: supreme leadership

For more primary sources to accompany this unit, use the *World History Primary Source Document Library CD-ROM.*

506 Unit 4 *Emergence of the Modern World*

Chapter 16
Erasmus's Description of Sir Thomas More

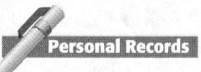 Personal Records

The Dutch scholar Desiderius Erasmus was one of the most influential writers of the Renaissance. Here Erasmus describes his friend Sir Thomas More, whose book Utopia *criticized society. Later, when More refused to recognize King Henry VIII's religious authority, he was executed. Erasmus wrote this description of Thomas More in 1519, 15 years before More's death.*

In human relations he looks for pleasure in everything he comes across, even in the gravest matters. If he has to do with intelligent and educated men, he takes pleasure in their brilliance; if with the ignorant and foolish, he enjoys their folly. He is not put out by perfect fools, and suits himself with marvellous dexterity to all men's feelings. For women generally, even for his wife, he has nothing but jests and merriment. . . .

He diligently cultivates true piety, while being remote from all superstitious observance. He has set hours in which he offers to God not the customary prayers but prayers from the heart. With his friends he talks of the life of the world to come so that one sees that he speaks sincerely and not without firm hope. Such is More even in the Court. And then there are those who think that Christians are to be found only in monasteries! . . .

Desiderius Erasmus c. 1466–1536

506 Unit 4 *Emergence of the Modern World*

Vespucci on South America

Interpreting the Primary Source
Ask students to react to Vespucci's statement that the native South Americans "live[d] according to nature." What implication does this carry?

(The implication is that they lived like animals, according to nature rather than reason. Some students will probably react by saying this is not a fair depiction of these people. Other students may feel that Vespucci meant "free" and unfettered by laws and conventions.)

Chapter 17
Vespucci on South America

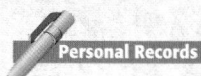
Personal Records

Amerigo Vespucci was the first person to suggest that the lands encountered by Columbus were part of a world unknown to Europeans. Here, in 1502, Vespucci describes Native Americans of Brazil.

Having no laws and no religious faith, they live according to nature. They understand nothing of the immortality of the soul. There is no possession of private property among them, for everything is in common. They have no boundaries of kingdom or province. They have no king, nor do they obey anyone. Each one is his own master. There is no administration of justice, which is unnecessary to them, because in their code no one rules. They live in communal dwellings, built [as] very large cabins. For people [without] metal, one can call their cabins truly miraculous . . .

Amerigo Vespucci 1454–1512

That which made me the more astonished at their wars and cruelty was that I could not understand from them why they made war upon each other, considering that they held no private property or sovereignty of empire and kingdoms and did not know any such thing as lust for possession, . . . which appear to me to [cause] wars. . . . When we requested them to state the cause, they did not know how to give any other cause than that this curse upon them began in ancient times . . .

Chapter 18
The Silk Industry in China

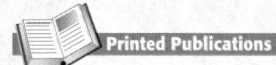
Printed Publications

During the 1600s Sung Ying-Hsing wrote a book on Chinese industry called the T'ien-kung K'ai-wu (Chinese Technology in the Seventeenth Century), which included sections on the production of silk.

. . . Members of the aristocracy are clothed in flowing robes decorated with patterns of magnificent mountain dragons, and they are the rulers of the country. Those of lowly stations would be dressed in hempen jackets and cotton garments to protect themselves from the cold in winter and cover their nakedness in summer, in order to distinguish themselves from the birds and beasts. Therefore Nature has provided the materials for clothing. Of these, the vegetable [plant] ones are cotton, hemp, *meng* hemp, and creeper hemp; those derived from birds, animals, and insects are furs, woolens, silk, and spun silk. . . .

But, although silk looms are to be found in all parts of the country, how many persons have actually seen the remarkable functioning of the draw-loom? Such words as "orderly government" [*chih*, i.e. the word used in silk reeling], "chaos" [*luan*, i.e. when the fibers are entangled], "knowledge or good policy" [*ching-lun*, i.e. the warp thread and the woven pattern] are known by every schoolboy, but is it not regrettable that he should never see the actual things that gave rise to these words? . . .

Interpreting Primary Sources

1. How would you describe Thomas More's behavior and personality?
2. What about the Native Americans surprised Vespucci the most? Why?
3. According to Sung, from what two sources was all clothing made?
4. **CRITICAL THINKING:** What do the excerpts about silk reveal about the importance of the weaving industry in Chinese society?

Applications Activity
Draw a map showing the route of the Silk Road, including the major cities that existed along it during the 17th century.

Evaluating the Primary Source
This primary source presents a description of an encounter with a foreign culture by a European explorer. The reliability of this source is determined by its author's objectivity. This is not a very objective report of a culture because Vespucci expresses so many cultural biases. For example, he assumes that the people he observes have no administration of justice because he saw no evidence of it. Although Vespucci seems to be truthful in his account, this does not also mean he was accurate.

The Silk Industry in China
Interpreting the Primary Source
Ask students whether silk was worn by all members of Chinese society or only some in particular. (*"Those of lowly station" are described only as wearing hempen and cotton clothes, so it seems silk was worn mainly by the aristocracy.*)

Evaluating the Primary Source
This primary source underscores the incredible importance of silk to the Chinese of this period. The reliability of the source is determined by the author's accuracy. If he, like so many Chinese, had not actually seen a silk loom, then it is possible that his commentary would not be accurate.

For the more complete version of each of these documents, see the World History Primary Source Document Library CD-ROM:

Document 75 *Erasmus's Description of Sir Thomas More*
Document 83 *Vespucci and the People of South America*
Document 88 *The Silk Industry in China*

ANSWER KEY

1. He enjoyed life, treated everyone with respect, and was a man of great faith and virtue.
2. He is mystified by their warlike behavior, as they have no private property or any other apparent reason to fight one another.
3. All clothing materials were derived from either plants or animals.
4. They reveal that the industry was so important that basic political ideas, such as chaos, orderly government, and good policy, were expressed by words borrowed from silk weaving.

APPLICATIONS ACTIVITY: Answers will vary but should accurately depict the route.

Answers and Analyses

1. **C** (History) The European Renaissance is discussed on pages 404–414. The pages mention the new importance of education, since it was thought that *people should develop their talents.* The rise of merchants and bankers, who constituted the new middle class, is also mentioned. Finally, page 409 discusses the use of perspective to give depth to paintings.

2. **H** (History) According to page 404, one of the tenets of humanism was a belief in *individualism, an emphasis on the dignity and worth of the individual person.* Therefore the correct answer should have something to do with the rights and abilities of individuals.

 TEST-TAKING TIP

Remind students to scrutinize the language of the question. It often contains valuable clues to the right answer. This question discusses *individualism.* Therefore the answer should be one that is consistent with individualist ideals.

3. **C** (History) According to the time line, a Portuguese explorer, Dias, was the first to discover the Cape of Good Hope, which was the first step on the way to finding a sea route to Asia.

4. **H** (History) Leonardo da Vinci is described on page 411 as having been not only an artist but also a skilled inventor as well as educated in *astronomy, mathematics, and anatomy.* This best supports choice H.

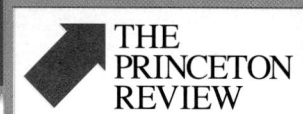

Standardized Test Practice

Directions: Choose the *best* answer to each of the following multiple choice questions. If you have trouble answering a question, use the process of elimination to narrow your choices. Write your answers on a separate piece of paper.

1. **Which of the following innovations is NOT associated with the European Renaissance?**

    A   The use of perspective in painting

    B   The increased interest in education

    C   The separation of church and state

    D   The development of a middle class

> **Test-Taking Tip:** Be careful—overlooking the words NOT or EXCEPT in a question is a common error. Look for the answer choice that does NOT fit with the question. For example, the use of perspective in painting *was* an important Renaissance development, so answer A cannot be the correct choice.

2. **The ideas of humanism and individualism most likely influenced which of Martin Luther's beliefs?**

    F   The sale of indulgences was unethical because it excluded peasants.

    G   The Bible was the final authority.

    H   Every individual Christian had the right to read and interpret the Bible.

    J   The pope should not be free from criticism for Church injustices.

> **Test-Taking Tip:** This question requires you to know the meaning of the words *humanism* and *individualism.* As you study, the glossary of your textbook can help you define unfamiliar terms. Remember, more than one answer will describe Luther's beliefs. Choose the answer that is most closely related to *humanism* and *individualism.*

Use the time line below to answer question 3.

European Exploration and Settlement

- **1497** Cabot (England) sails northern Atlantic to Newfoundland
- **1498** Da Gama (Portugal) reaches India after sailing around the Cape of Good Hope
- **1522** Magellan's crew (Spain) complete circumnavigation of the globe
- **1532** Pizarro (Spain) invades Inca Empire in Peru
- **1620** Pilgrims (England) found Plymouth colony
- **1488** Dias (Portugal) discovers and names the Cape of Good Hope
- **1492** Columbus (Spain) makes first trip to the West Indies
- **1519** Cortés (Spain) begins conquest of Aztec Empire in Mexico
- **1524** Verrazano (France) begins search for Northwest Passage to India
- **1608** Champlain (France) sets up colony in Quebec, Canada

3. **According to the time line above, which of these statements is true?**

    A   England did not send out explorers until the 1600s.

    B   Pizarro invaded India before Magellan's crew circumnavigated the globe.

    C   Portugal began the search for a sea route to Asia.

    D   France was interested primarily in setting up colonies in South America.

> **Test-Taking Tip:** Make sure that your answer is supported by information *on the time line.* Do not rely only on your memory for this type of question.

4. Leonardo da Vinci became known as a "Renaissance man" because

F   he was born in Italy during the time of the Italian Renaissance.

G   his paintings, such as the *Mona Lisa*, contributed to the rise of realism in the arts.

H   he developed talents in many fields, such as art, architecture, and engineering.

J   his ideas influenced many other Renaissance artists in Europe.

Test-Taking Tip: The terms *Renaissance man* and *Renaissance woman* are still used today. They are used to describe people who are often experts in several subject areas. Although more than one of the answer choices is certainly true, *only one* answer is directly related to the term *Renaissance man*.

5. The 1636 Japanese Act of Seclusion was

A   intended to prohibit contact between Japan and almost all other nations.

B   a brilliant policy that protected Japanese culture from Western influences.

C   never successful, since all Japanese citizens preferred foreign goods.

D   the most logical defense against a possible Mongol invasion.

Test-Taking Tip: The answer to this type of question must be a *fact*, not an *opinion*. A *fact* is a statement that can be proved; an *opinion* is a personal belief. To identify opinions, look for phrases such as *good*, *bad*, *greatest*, and *worst*. Which of these answer choices are *opinions*?

Use the following map to answer question 6.

Population Loss 1618–1648

Baltic Sea · North Sea · Pomerania · Brunswick · Brandenburg · POLAND · Saxony · Silesia · Bohemia · Palatinate · Bavaria · HUNGARY

Up to 15% · 15–33% · 33–66% · Over 66% · ---- Boundary of Holy Roman Empire

6. According to the map, which of the following statements is true?

F   Mountains divide Silesia and Bohemia.

G   Brunswick has more people than Pomerania.

H   Bavaria lost more people than Brunswick.

J   Bohemia and Bavaria had the same number of people.

Test-Taking Tip: Make sure that you look at the map's *title* and *key* so that you understand what it represents. It shows *population loss* in parts of Europe during the period 1618–1648. Since mountains are not shown on this map, you can eliminate answer F.

STOP

5. A (History) According to page 471, the Act of Seclusion was passed because the rulers decided *that contact with outsiders posed too many dangers.* In particular, *Japan barred all Europeans except the Dutch.*

THE PRINCETON REVIEW **TEST-TAKING TIP**

Students should be very wary of very strongly worded choices such as B and C. Unless such strong statements can be justified by their reading, they are probably incorrect.

6. H (Geography) Since this map does not show physical features or anything having to do with wars, choices F and J can be eliminated. The map does show political boundaries, but this is not the main point of the map. According to the legend, it shows population loss. Therefore choice G can be eliminated, and choice H is the best answer.

MORE PRACTICE

For additional practice, assign practice pages from:

📁   Glencoe Standardized Test Practice Workbook

📁   Glencoe SAT/SAT II Practice Book

Tested Objectives

Questions	Objective
1, 3	Evaluating Information
2	Making Inferences
4	Determining Cause and Effect
5	Distinguishing Fact from Opinion
6	Drawing Conclusions

0:00 **OUT OF TIME?**

If time does not permit teaching each chapter in Unit 5, you may use the Unit Digest Transparencies and Chapter Digest Audiocassettes with accompanying activities and tests.

Introducing the Unit

Unit 5 focuses on the revolutionary changes that transformed early modern Europe, including the Scientific Revolution and political revolutions in England, the United States, and France. The ideas of liberalism, nationalism, and democracy are also explored.

Unit Objectives

Students will be able to:
1. explain how the Scientific Revolution changed the way people looked at their world and how the Enlightenment advanced new ideas.
2. compare the causes and results of the English and American Revolutions.
3. understand the different phases of the French Revolution and trace the ways in which that revolution and the Napoleonic period transformed Europe.

**GLENCOE
TECHNOLOGY**

**Glencoe World History
Primary Source
Document Library**
Use the CD-ROM to access primary source documents related to the Age of Revolution.

Age of
Revolution

Chapter 20
Scientific Revolution

Chapter 21
English and American Revolutions

Chapter 22
The French Revolution

See pages 590–591 for primary source readings that accompany Unit 5.

*Then
& Now* *The discoveries and writings of the Age of Revolution ignited a fuse of knowledge that exploded in a scientific revolution so complete and far-reaching that the years from 1500 to 1830 are often called "the beginning of the modern age."*

Every time you have your temperature taken with a mercury thermometer, receive medication through a fine-needled syringe, let a doctor listen to your heartbeat through a stethoscope, or have your tooth drilled by a dentist, you are seeing instruments invented during the Age of Revolution. When you study a cell through a microscope or a star through a telescope, you are using equipment developed to fill the needs of sixteenth- and seventeenth-century scientists for precise, accurate scientific instruments. Even the simple multiplication symbol ✕ was proposed during this age of scientific revolution.

A Global Chronology

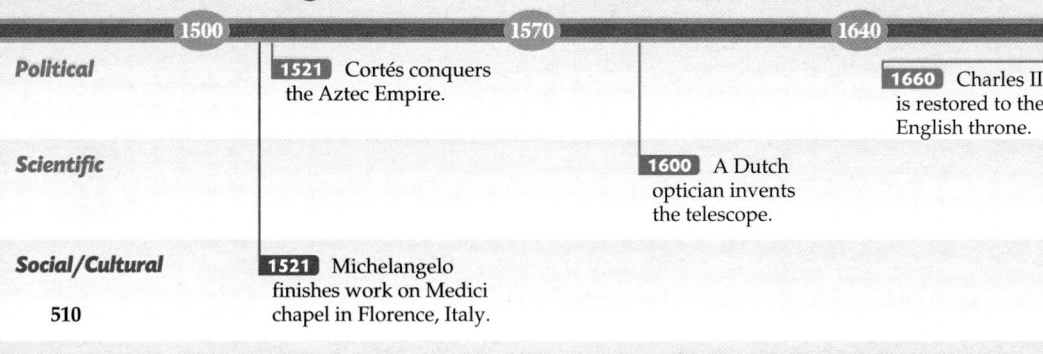

	1500	1570	1640
Political	**1521** Cortés conquers the Aztec Empire.		**1660** Charles II is restored to the English throne.
Scientific		**1600** A Dutch optician invents the telescope.	
Social/Cultural	**1521** Michelangelo finishes work on Medici chapel in Florence, Italy.		

510

*Then
& Now* **Science and Society** In this unit students will learn how breakthroughs in science and philosophy—the Scientific Revolution and the Enlightenment—eventually had repercussions on the political and social systems of Europe, North America, and elsewhere.

Have students think about the ways that science and technology influence the way we think and live today. How have scientific breakthroughs by NASA and the space shuttle program influenced our lives? *(Many breakthroughs in telecommunications, air travel, and computer science are*

World History and Art
Transparencies
- •27 *The Letter*
- •28 *Blue Boy*
- •29 *Napoleon Crossing the Alps*

VIDEODISC
Turning Points in World History

Side One,
Chapter 11

Title: *French Revolution*
Subject: French Revolution
Ask: What great changes in the way people thought about political rights and freedoms took place in this period? *(The idea of the divine right of monarchs to rule gave way to individual rights and rule by popular consent.)*

History & Art The Polish astronomer Copernicus (1473–1543) discredited the ancient idea that the earth was at the center of the solar system and that the sun moved around it. "I began to consider the mobility of the Earth," Copernicus wrote, "even though the idea seemed absurd."

Armillary sphere of the Copernican universe

History *and* You

Throughout the 18th century in France, great changes took place in the way people thought about political rights and freedoms, culminating in revolution.

To better understand the development of the French Revolution, view videodisc Chapter 11: *French Revolution* in Turning Points in World History.

Timeline

1710	1780	1850

1687 Isaac Newton states the theory of gravity.

1740 Frederick the Great introduces freedom of the press and of worship in Prussia.

1789 The French Revolution begins.

1799 Rosetta stone found in Egypt makes deciphering hieroglyphics possible.

1804 Ludwig van Beethoven composes his Third Symphony, the *Eroica.*

1832 The British Parliament passes the Reform Bill.

511

Glencoe Literature Library

The following literature from the **Glencoe Literature Library** may enrich this unit:
Frankenstein by M. Shelley
A Tale of Two Cities by C. Dickens

civilian applications of space program technology.) In what ways have computers and the information superhighway created new possibilities for political activity? *(Through the Internet and E-mail, individuals from around the world can communicate cheaply and instantly about issues that concern them.)* How does our knowledge about the transmission of diseases affect our behavior? *(We take precautions like washing our hands before eating, getting vaccinations, avoiding contact with blood and other body fluids.)*

TEACH

Introduction

This feature focuses on the movement of revolutionary ideas between Europe and the Americas. The challenge of early scientists such as Galileo to established authority led to the questioning of long-held ideas about government, religion, and society, as well as science. In the United States, France, and Haiti, revolutionaries tried to put new ideas about government into practice.

Background Notes

Linking Past and Present

Ideas of the 1700s continue to reverberate in this century. When Ho Chi Minh declared Vietnam's independence from France in 1945, his speech began: "All men are created equal. The Creator has given us certain inviolable Rights; the right to Life, the right to be Free, and the right to achieve Happiness. These immortal words are taken from the Declaration of Independence of the United States of America in 1776."

Who? What? Where? When?

Women played an important role in spreading the Enlightenment ideas that helped spark the French Revolution. Parisian intellectuals such as Madame du Deffand and Madame de Geoffrin brought together writers, artists, and nobles. The lively discussions in these salons helped popularize controversial ideas.

Revolution

*I*n the 1600s and 1700s, revolution bounced back and forth across the Atlantic. The pattern started with the arrival of the first English colonists in North America. They carried with them ideals born of the English Revolution. They believed that governments existed to protect the rights and freedoms of citizens.

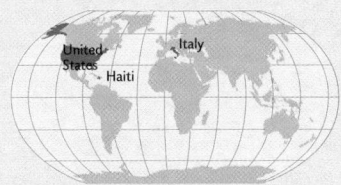

The United States
Revolutionary Ideas

In 1776 the colonists fought a revolution, making clear the principles of freedom and rights in the Declaration of Independence:

> We hold these truths to be self-evident, that all men are created equal, that they are endowed by their Creator with certain unalienable rights, that among these are life, liberty, and the pursuit of happiness.

These ideas bounced back across the Atlantic to influence the French Revolution. French rebels in 1789 fought in defense of *Liberté, Egalité, Fraternité* (Liberty, Equality, Fraternity). In drafting their declaration of freedom, French revolutionaries repeated the principles of the American Declaration of Independence: "Men are born and remain free and equal in rights."

Signing of the Declaration of Independence

COOPERATIVE LEARNING ACTIVITY

Wall Map and Display Have students work together to create a wall map and display that shows the origins of the ideas behind the American, French, and Haitian Revolutions. Organize the class into three groups, letting each group take one of the revolutions. Have members research their revolution, generating a list of philosophers, events, and other specific influences. For each item on the list, students should be sure to name the country of origin. When the lists have been completed, have students organize them by country in a format suitable for display. Have them mount the lists to the sides of a wall map, then use thumbtacks and colored yarn to show how various ideas traveled. **L2**

Italy
The Age of Revolution

The spread of ideas—specifically, revolutionary ideas—forms the subject of Unit 5. The spark that sent the spirit of revolution flashing across Europe and the Americas began in the minds of sixteenth-century European scientists. These thinkers challenged established ideas defended by the Roman Catholic Church. Church officials tried to stop the spread of new scientific ideas. But once unleashed, the ideas respected neither authority nor geographic boundary. Defiance of one authority, in this case, the Church, soon led people to question other authorities as well. The result was the intellectual and political upheavals that historians call the Age of Revolution.

Early telescope

Haiti
Exporting Revolution

In 1791 the ideals of the American and French Revolutions traveled across the Caribbean and the Atlantic to the French-held island colony of Saint Domingue. Inspired by talk of freedom, enslaved Africans took up arms. Led by Toussaint-Louverture, they shook off French rule. In 1804 Saint Domingue, present-day Haiti, became the second nation in the Americas to achieve independence from colonial rule. "We have asserted our rights," declared the revolutionaries. "We swear never to yield them to any power on earth."

Toussaint-Louverture

LINKING THE IDEAS

1. What was the role of government according to the American colonists?
2. What ideals did the Americans and the French share?

Critical Thinking

3. **Cause and Effect** Why do you think revolutionary ideas respect neither authority nor geographic boundaries?

Unit 5   *Age of Revolution*   513

Geography

Movement Americans living in France before the French Revolution actively promoted the principles of the new republic across the Atlantic. "Everyone here is trying their hands at forming declarations of rights," wrote Thomas Jefferson, whose advice was often sought by Lafayette and other moderate revolutionaries. Ask students to name other ways ideas of revolution may have traveled between the different locations of revolution shown on the map on page 512. (*Answers may include trade, newspapers, scholars exchanging books.*)

Cultural Diffusion

Containing Antislavery The success of the Haitian Revolution terrified American slaveholders, who feared that the overthrow of slavery in Haiti would inspire their own enslaved people to rebel. In the southern United States, tighter restrictions were placed on both enslaved and free African Americans. In 1802 Jefferson's postmaster general advised a senator from Georgia against letting enslaved people deliver the mail: "After the scenes which St. Domingo has exhibited to the world, we cannot be too cautious in attempting to prevent similar evils.... Everything which tends to increase their knowledge of natural rights ... or that affords them an opportunity ... of establishing a chain and line of intelligence, must increase your hazard."

ANSWERS TO LINKING THE IDEAS

1. to protect the rights and freedoms of citizens
2. belief in freedom and equal rights
3. Answers will vary. Students may feel that revolutionary ideas spread quickly when traditional authority has lost touch with the times. The desire for freedom and opportunity motivates people in all times and places.

A complete, 1-page lesson plan is provided for each section in the *Reproducible Lesson Plans* booklet.

Scientific Revolution

CHAPTER RESOURCES

	Reproducible Resources	Multimedia Resources
Chapter Opener	Chapter Themes: Graphic Organizer 20 Historical Significance Chapter Activity 20	MindJogger Videoquiz

Chapter Enrichment	Vocabulary Activity 20*
	Time Line Activity 20
	Mapping History Activity 20
	History Simulation 20
	Geography and History Activity 20
	Source Reading 20
	People in World History Profiles 37, 38
	World Art and Music Activity 20
	Enrichment Activity 20
	Critical Thinking Activity 20
	Skill Reinforcement Activity 20
	Performance Assessment Activity 20
	Standardized Test Practice Workbook
	    Activity 20
	Inclusion for the Social Studies Classroom
	    Strategies and Activities
		World History and Art
		    Transparency 27, *The Letter*
		
		Chapter Transparency 20
		Vocabulary PuzzleMaker Software
		Picture Atlas of the World
		Turning Points in World History:
		    The Scientific Revolution
		World History Primary Source
		    Document Library

Chapter Review/Reteaching	Reteaching Activity 20
	Skill Reinforcement Activity 20
	Spanish Chapter Summary 20
		Chapter 20 Digest Audiocassette,
		    Activity, Test*
		Vocabulary PuzzleMaker Software
		Interactive Tutor Self-Assessment
		    Software
		MindJogger Videoquiz

Chapter Evaluation/Testing	Performance Assessment Activity 20 Chapter 20 Test, Forms A and B	ExamView® Pro Testmaker

* Also available in Spanish

0:00 OUT OF TIME? Assign the Chapter 20 Audiocassettes.

World History Primary Source Document Library
Make History Come Alive!
Engage your students with over 250 easily accessible primary source documents—available on this CD-ROM—that will give them real life insight into the important events of world history.

Block Schedule
Activities that are particularly suited to use within the block scheduling framework are identified throughout this chapter by the following designation.

KEY TO ABILITY LEVELS
Teaching strategies are coded for varying learning styles.
- **L1 BASIC** activities for all students
- **L2 AVERAGE** activities for average to above-average students
- **L3 CHALLENGING** activities for above-average students
- **LEP LIMITED ENGLISH PROFICIENCY** activities

Use Glencoe's *Presentation Plus!* multimedia teacher tool to easily present dynamic lessons that visually excite your students. Using Microsoft PowerPoint® you can customize the presentations to create your own personalized lessons.

 Interactive Lesson Planner

Planning has never been easier! Using this CD-ROM, organize your week, month, semester, or year with all the help you need. The **Interactive Lesson Planner** gives you access to all of the blackline masters that accompany *World History: The Human Experience.*

SECTION RESOURCES

Daily Objectives	Reproducible Resources	Multimedia Resources
Section 1 New Scientific Ideas Discuss how scientific thought changed during the 1600s.	Lecture Notes 20-1 Reproducible Lesson Plan 20-1 Guided Reading Activity 20-1* Time Line Activity 20 People in World History Profile 37 Geography and History Activity 20 Section Quiz 20-1* Reading Essentials and Study Guide 20-1	Section Focus Transparency 20-1 Chapter Transparency 20 Vocabulary PuzzleMaker Software Interactive Tutor Self-Assessment Software Testmaker Turning Points in World History: *The Scientific Revolution*
Section 2 Impact of Science Analyze the effects that changes in scientific thought had on thinking in other fields.	Lecture Notes 20-2 Reproducible Lesson Plan 20-2 Vocabulary Activity 20* Guided Reading Activity 20-2* History Simulation 20 Section Quiz 20-2* Reading Essentials and Study Guide 20-2	Section Focus Transparency 20-2 Interactive Tutor Self-Assessment Software Testmaker Turning Points in World History: *The Scientific Revolution*
Section 3 Triumph of Reason Identify the factors that helped Enlightenment ideas spread throughout Europe.	Lecture Notes 20-3 Reproducible Lesson Plan 20-3 Guided Reading Activity 20-3* People in World History Profile 38 Reteaching Activity 20 Enrichment Activity 20 Section Quiz 20-3* Performance Assessment Activity 20 Spanish Chapter Summary 20 Reading Essentials and Study Guide 20-3	Section Focus Transparency 20-3 World History and Art Transparency 27, *The Letter* Vocabulary PuzzleMaker Software Interactive Tutor Self-Assessment Software Testmaker Turning Points in World History: *The Scientific Revolution*

* Also available in Spanish

Chapter 20 *Scientific Revolution* **514B**

Chapter Activities

 Performance Assessment Activity

A Last Will and Testament Have students think about the developments that occurred during the Scientific Revolution and list them in order of importance, giving a rationale for their choices. Students should then match each of the items on their list to a current-day group, individual, or country that would be a logical recipient of the invention or development if left to them in a will by the inventor or initiator. Students should then write a collective last will and testament for all of the people highlighted in the chapter. Wills should include a rationale with each beneficiary listed.

Possible Rubric Features
Accuracy of content information, argumentation and level of support, organization and clarity, research skills, ability to make logical connections

• For an additional activity, refer to Activity 20 in the Performance Assessment Strategies and Activities booklet.

ACTIVITY
From the Classroom of...

Ross Bennett Brown
Franklin K. Lane High School
Brooklyn, NY

The Scientific Method in Action
Have students employ the scientific method in order to solve a problem. One problem that works well involves a simple chemistry exercise. You will need some filter paper cut into 4-inch strips, paper clips, cups with about 1 inch of water in them, and green felt-tipped pens. Begin by drawing a dot about 1 inch from the end of a strip of filter paper. Ask students what will happen when the dot makes contact with water. This is their *hypothesis*. Most will suggest smearing. Pierce the other end of the filter paper with a paper clip and use the clip to suspend the paper in the cup so that the end with the dot is just touching the water, but the dot remains above the water. This is the *experiment*. The water is drawn up the filter paper, and when it reaches the dot, the green separates into blue and yellow. We could not know this without the process of hypothesis followed by the careful observation of events during the experiment.

Since the result is almost always different from students' hypotheses, it is likely to stimulate in the class the same sort of excitement that seventeenth-century scientists might have felt conducting their own experiments.

MULTIPLE LEARNING STYLES

Verbal/Linguistic
Ask each student to select a discovery or invention of the 1600s and write a promotional flyer or commercial promoting it. Have students present their commercials to the class.

Visual/Spatial
Have students draw political cartoons illustrating one of the controversies associated with the Enlightenment. Incorporate all the cartoons into a book.

Auditory/Musical
Have students listen to a recording of Leonard Bernstein's musical version of Voltaire's *Candide*. Ask them to write a sentence describing the connection between the lyrics of at least five songs and Enlightenment ideas.

Kinesthetic
Have students prepare models of the universe according to Aristotle and to Copernicus. Have them use diagrams in astronomy textbooks or other reference books as a guide.

GLENCOE'S ASSESSMENT ADVANTAGE

Use the following to easily assess student learning in a variety of ways.

• Performance Assessment Strategies and Activities
• Section Quizzes
• Chapter and Unit Tests
• Interactive Tutor Self-Assessment Software

• Testmaker Software
• MindJogger Videoquiz
• SAT/SAT II Test Practice
• worldhistory.glencoe.com

Additional Resources

NATIONAL GEOGRAPHIC SOCIETY
Teacher's Corner

INDEX TO NATIONAL GEOGRAPHIC MAGAZINE

The following articles may be used for research relating to this chapter:

- "Science—Asking Infinite Questions," by Joel L. Swerdlow, October 1999.
- "The Hubble Telescope," by William R. Newcott, April 1997.
- "Sir Joseph Banks," by T. H. Watkins, November 1996.
- "Information Revolution," by Joel L. Swerdlow, October 1995.
- "Humboldt's Way," by Loren McIntyre, September 1985.

NATIONAL GEOGRAPHIC SOCIETY PRODUCTS AVAILABLE FROM GLENCOE

To order the following product for use with this chapter, contact your local Glencoe sales representative, or call Glencoe at 1-800-334-7344:

- *Picture Atlas of the World (CD-ROM)*

ADDITIONAL NATIONAL GEOGRAPHIC SOCIETY PRODUCTS

Access National Geographic's new dynamic MapMachine Web site and other geography resources at:

- http://www.nationalgeographic.com/
- http://www.nationalgeographic.com/maps/

BIBLIOGRAPHY

Literature of the Period
Voltaire. *Candide and Other Stories.* Translated by Roger Pearson. New York: Oxford University Press, 1990. Voltaire's most popular philosophical novel and other stories.

Readings for the Student
Boorstin, Daniel. *The Discoverers: A History of Man's Search to Know His World and Himself.* New York: Random House, 1983. Contains much fascinating and readable information on Copernicus, Kepler, Galileo, Newton, and others.

Readings for the Teacher
Cohen, I. Bernard. *Science and the Founding Fathers: Science in the Political Thought of Thomas Jefferson, Benjamin Franklin, John Adams and James Madison.* New York: Norton, 1995. Explains how the Founders incorporated scientific reasoning into the Constitution.

WORLD HISTORY Online

Use our Web site as an additional resource. All essential content is covered in the Student Edition.

You and your students can visit the *World History: The Human Experience* Web site at worldhistory.glencoe.com The student text directs students to the Web site for the following options:

- **Chapter Overviews**
- **Student Web Activities**
- **Self-Check Quizzes**

Answers are provided for you in a link entitled "Web Activity Lesson Plan." Additional Web Resources, Interactive Puzzles, and content updates are also available.

Visit the Glencoe Web site at socialstudies.glencoe.com for social studies activities, updates, and links to other resources.

LOCAL OBJECTIVES

_____
_____
_____
_____
_____
_____
_____
_____
_____
_____
_____
_____
_____
_____
_____
_____
_____
_____
_____

Chapter
20
1600–1830
Scientific Revolution

CHAPTER THEMES

Chapter Themes are listed by section on this chapter opening page of the Student Edition. A corresponding theme-based activity is available under "TEACH," and a theme-based question is asked in the Section and Chapter Assessments.

Storyteller

Historical Setting Despite the fact that Leeuwenhoek never attended a university, he became one of the world's greatest scientific pioneers. Though England and Holland were trade rivals and enemies in several wars, Leeuwenhoek shared his scientific ideas with the Royal Society of London, one of the oldest scientific societies in Europe. In October 1678, in his eighteenth letter to the Royal Society, Leeuwenhoek described "these little animals" revealed by his microscope in a drop of water. Today scientists know they are not animals at all but rather bacteria. Leeuwenhoek also discovered red blood cells when he turned his microscope on a drop of human blood.

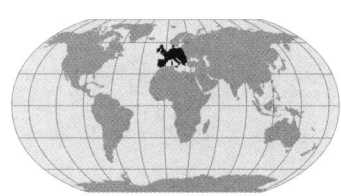

Chapter Themes

▶ **Innovation** European interest in science leads to discoveries and ideas based on reason. *Section 1*
▶ **Conflict** Changing views based on science and reason conflict with traditional beliefs. *Section 2*
▶ **Reaction** Reason and order are applied to many human endeavors. *Section 3*

Storyteller

Antonie van Leeuwenhoek, a Dutch cloth merchant in the late 1600s, found that his unusual hobby unlocked the door to an unknown world. By carefully grinding very small lenses out of clear glass, van Leeuwenhoek discovered that he could make things look much bigger than they appeared to the naked eye.

Soon the Dutch merchant turned his lenses to everything he could find—from the cloth he had just bought to the scales of his own skin. His most remarkable find was tiny microorganisms, which he described as "wretched beasties" with "incredibly thin feet" swimming through a tiny universe.

New technology such as van Leeuwenhoek's microscope and scientific study in general captured the imagination of many European people in the 1600s. A scientific revolution would lead to a new era in Western thought.

Historical Significance

How did the scientific revolution of the 1600s and 1700s transform European society? What impact has the growth of science had on the world today?

Historical Significance

Answers: *By introducing a philosophy of knowledge based on observation, experiment, and reason, the Scientific Revolution challenged faith and traditional ideas in many areas.*

New scientific discoveries and new applications continue to challenge accepted ideas and introduce new ways of life.

Have students use the **Chapter 20 Overview** at worldhistory. glencoe.com as a prereading and postreading exercise for understanding chapter content.

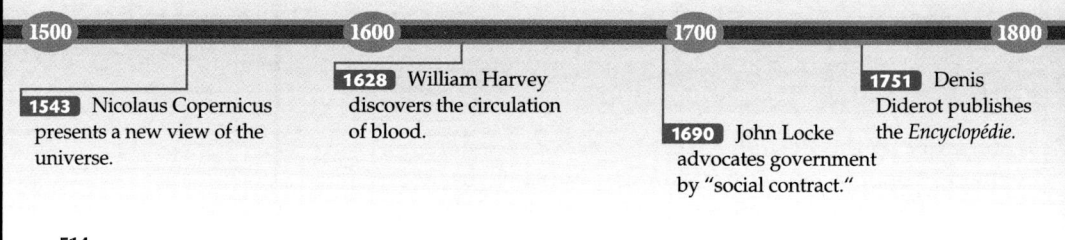

1500	1600	1700	1800

1543 Nicolaus Copernicus presents a new view of the universe.

1628 William Harvey discovers the circulation of blood.

1690 John Locke advocates government by "social contract."

1751 Denis Diderot publishes the *Encyclopédie.*

514

GEOGRAPHY CONNECTION

Movement Point out that scientific ideas traveled quickly and frequently between France, the Netherlands, and England. Have students locate these countries on a map. What route did ideas have to take between the two countries on the European continent and England? *(They had to cross the English Channel.)* How far across is the English Channel at its narrowest? *(about 20 miles [34 kilometers])* How did people cross the Channel at the time of the Scientific Revolution? *(by boat)* What options are available to people crossing the Channel today? *(boat, train, ferry, airplane, Chunnel)* **L1**

The Establishment of the Academy of Science and the Foundation of the Observatory by Louis XIV by Henri Testelin. Musée National du Chateau de Versailles, Versailles, France

Chapter Overview
Visit the *World History: The Human Experience* Web site at **worldhistory.glencoe.com** and click on *Chapter 20—Chapter Overview* to preview the chapter.

Your History Journal

Research a scientific discovery or invention from the 1600s. Write the story of the discovery or invention as it might have appeared in a publication at the time.

Chapter 20   *Scientific Revolution*   **515**

History & Art   Around 1662 a group of French scientists began to hold periodic private meetings in Paris. In 1666 the Royal Academy of Sciences was established to formalize those meetings. Construction of the observatory began the following year. Today the academy's building in Paris is headquarters of the International Time Bureau, which sets standard time for the world's observatories.

✔ Performance Assessment

Refer to the activity on page 514C of the Planning Guide.

📁   Refer to Activity 20 in the *Performance Assessment Strategies and Activities* booklet.

Using Your History Journal

Encourage students to include direct quotations from the scientists whose discoveries or inventions they choose. A good resource is Daniel J. Boorstin, *The Discoverers* (New York: Random House, 1983).

GLENCOE TECHNOLOGY

 VIDEODISC
Use MindJogger to preview chapter content.

MindJogger Videoquiz
   Chapter 20
Disc 3 Side A

   Also available in VHS.

➕ EXTRA CREDIT PROJECT

Oral Report Two new instruments, the microscope and the telescope, made possible many of the discoveries of the Scientific Revolution. Since the 1600s many improvements have been made in both. Have students research and report to the class on new types of microscopes developed in the twentieth century, including the electron microscope and the scanning tunneling microscope. Suggested resources: B. J. Ford, *The Leeuwenhoek Legacy*; G. B. Stewart, *Microscopes*. Or have them research and report on twentieth-century improvements in telescopes, such as camera telescopes and radio telescopes. **L2**

1600   1700   1800

1633 Galileo Galilei
stands trial for his ideas.

1687 Isaac Newton
publishes the *Principia*.

1774 Joseph Priestley
discovers oxygen.

SECTION THEME

▶ **Innovation** European interest in science leads to discoveries and ideas based on reason.

Guide to Reading

For reading strategies to help students read effectively see pages 12–13. Have students think about the main head as they read the subheads.

Vocabulary Pre-check

 Use the Vocabulary PuzzleMaker for Chapter 20 to create a crossword puzzle to reinforce section terms. **L1 LEP**

Use Vocabulary Activity 20 to introduce vocabulary terms. **L1 LEP**

FOCUS

Section Objective

Discuss how scientific thought changed during the 1600s.

BELLRINGER
Motivational Activity

 Before taking roll at the beginning of the class period, project Section Focus Transparency 20-1 and have students answer the activity questions. Discuss students' responses.
This activity is also available as a blackline master.

Section 1

New Scientific Ideas

Guide to Reading

Read to Find Out
Main Idea *The basis for scientific thought changed during the 1600s.*

▶ **Terms to Define**
hypothesis, ellipses, scientific method, calculus, alchemist

▶ **People to Meet**
Nicolaus Copernicus, Johannes Kepler, Galileo Galilei, Francis Bacon, René Descartes, Isaac Newton, Andreas Vesalius, William Harvey, Robert Hooke, Robert Boyle, Joseph Priestley, Antoine and Marie Lavoisier

▶ **Places to Locate**
Poland

The Storyteller

Christina, Grand Duchess of Tuscany, was intrigued. She had asked the renowned Galileo to describe his studies to her. "Nature," he explained in his letter, "never transgresses the laws imposed upon her, or cares whether her reasons and methods of operation are understandable to men." But Christina knew that others might find Galileo's opinions dangerous, for he also claimed that one could learn truth from these studies as much as from religion. "I do not feel obliged to believe that the same God who has endowed us with senses, reason, and intellect has intended us to forgo their use."

—adapted from *Letter to Christina of Tuscany*, reprinted in *Western Civilization: Sources, Images, and Interpretations*, Dennis Sherman, 1995

Galileo Galilei

agic, mysticism, and ancient writings ruled scientific thought in Europe throughout the Middle Ages. Scholars based their ideas on theories proposed almost a thousand years before by ancient Greek thinkers such as Aristotle, Ptolemy, and Galen. During the Middle Ages, most Europeans believed that the earth was flat, and they accepted the Catholic Church's view that the earth was the center of the universe. According to church doctrine, God created the universe to serve people. Therefore, the Church reasoned, the people's home—the earth—must be at the center of the universe.

In the 1600s, however, such ideas would topple as a scientific revolution spread throughout Europe. New technology, combined with innovative approaches to seeking knowledge, led to a breakthrough in Western thought. At the forefront of this scientific revolution was a Polish astronomer named **Nicolaus Copernicus.**

A Scientific Revolution

Copernicus started his scientific career at the University of Kraków in **Poland** in 1492—the same year in which Christopher Columbus reached the Americas. Like Columbus, Copernicus began his questioning in a time when few people dared to question age-old beliefs and superstitions.

As Copernicus delved into his studies, he became convinced that ideas commonly accepted about the universe were wrong. Copernicus believed that the earth was round and that it rotated on its axis as it revolved around the sun. The sun stayed still at the center of the universe.

Copernicus realized, however, that his ideas were revolutionary and even dangerous. Disputing or even questioning traditional views about the universe could mean persecution, excommunication, or even imprisonment. To avoid this risk, Copernicus worked in privacy, without publishing

SECTION RESOURCES

Reproducible Masters
• Lecture Notes 20-1
• Reproducible Lesson Plan 20-1
• Guided Reading Activity 20-1
• Time Line Activity 20
• People in World History Profile 37
• Geography and History Activity 20

• Section Quiz 20-1
• Reading Essentials and Study Guide 20-1

Transparencies
• Section Focus Transparency 20-1
• Chapter Transparency 20

Multimedia
 Vocabulary PuzzleMaker Software
 Interactive Tutor Self-Assessment Software
Testmaker
Turning Points in World History: *The Scientific Revolution*

Visualizing History In 1633, the Inquisition in Rome found Galileo guilty of heresy and sentenced him to life imprisonment. Recanting many of his views, Galileo was allowed to serve his sentence at home. *Why was Galileo charged with heresy?*

his ideas. The Polish scientist spent more than 30 years writing his treatise. Friends helped publish his work just before his death.

New Theories About the Universe

Other scientists took Copernicus's ideas and ventured even further into a scientific understanding of the universe. Copernicus had based his hypotheses, or theories that attempt to explain a set of facts, on study and observations. He could not provide proof, however, because the necessary mathematics was not available to him at the time. In the late 1500s, the Danish astronomer Tycho Brahe (TEE•koh BRAH•uh) set up an observatory to study heavenly bodies and accumulated much data on planetary movements. After Brahe's death, the German astronomer and mathematician **Johannes Kepler** used Brahe's data with the goal of providing mathematical proof for Copernicus's hypotheses.

Using mathematical formulas, Kepler did show that the planets revolve around the sun. His findings also refuted some of Copernicus's views. For example, Kepler proved that the planets move in oval paths called ellipses—not in circles as Copernicus had believed. He also found that planets move faster as they approach the sun and slower as they move away from it.

Challenging the Church

Kepler challenged the teachings of many academic and religious leaders. Because Kepler was a Protestant, however, he did not have to fear the Catholic Church. His Catholic contemporary, the Italian mathematician **Galileo Galilei**, did face considerable opposition from church leaders.

In 1609 Galileo built his own telescope and observed the night skies. His discovery of moons circling a planet convinced him that the Copernican theory about the earth revolving around the sun was correct. Because these moons revolved around Jupiter, Galileo reasoned, not all heavenly bodies revolved around the earth. It was possible that some planets did move around the sun.

In 1632 Galileo published his ideas. Soon afterward, the Catholic Church banned the book. The Church would not tolerate ideas that contradicted its own position. Pope Urban VIII demanded that Galileo come to Rome and stand trial.

Student Web Activity 20

Visit the *World History: The Human Experience* Web site at **worldhistory.glencoe.com** and click on *Chapter 20—Student Web Activities* for an activity relating to Nicolaus Copernicus.

Chapter 20 *Scientific Revolution* 517

TEACH

Guided Practice

THEME Innovation

New interest in science led to discoveries and philosophies based on reason. Guide students to a definition of reason. *(the power of acquiring intellectual knowledge based on facts or premises)* Ask students to give an example from this section of an innovator who used reason to advance an idea. *(Possible answer: Galileo reasoned that planets circle the sun.)* **L1**

Visualizing History Galileo's *Dialogue Concerning the Two Chief World Systems–Ptolemaic and Copernican*, published in 1632, had been approved by the censors. But after the Jesuits claimed that it could do more damage to Catholicism "than Luther and Calvin put together," the pope had Galileo prosecuted for "teaching or discussing Copernicanism in any way."

Answer to Caption: *He published ideas that contradicted the Church's earth-centered view of the universe.*

Chapter Transparency 20

Biography

The following videotape program is available from Glencoe:

- **Sir Isaac Newton: The Gravity of Genius**

Have students use the **Chapter 20 Student Web Activity** at worldhistory.glencoe.com for in-depth study of Nicolaus Copernicus.

COOPERATIVE LEARNING ACTIVITY

Readers' Theater and Discussion Organize the class into four groups. Have the members of three groups prepare five scenes each from Bertolt Brecht's *Life of Galileo* to read dramatically to the class. Have the members of the fourth group make an intensive study of the facts of Galileo's life. After the three groups have completed their classroom reading of the entire play, have members of the fourth group run a panel discussion comparing Brecht's dramatic treatment of characters and events with their actual historical models. **L3**

POINT

Newton's Universe

Why was Newton's thinking important in the scientific revolution?

Newton's work suggested that precise mathematical formulas could be used to describe an orderly universe. This idea greatly influenced the thinking of his own age and all later scientific thought.

ABCNEWS
INTERACTIVE

VIDEODISC
Turning Points in World History

Side One
Chapter 10

Title: *The Scientific Revolution*
Ask: What changes took place in European society in the seventeenth century that led to the Scientific Revolution? *(People began to challenge traditional thinking and began to see the world differently.)*

Independent Practice

📁 Guided Reading Activity 20-1 **L1**

📁 Time Line Activity 20

📁 People in World History Profile 37

📁 Geography and History Activity 20

Urban's threats of torture and death forced Galileo to recant many of his statements and publicly say that he had gone too far in some of his writing:

> ❝ I, Galileo Galilei, … swear that with honest heart and in good faith I curse … the said heresies and errors as to the movement of the earth around the sun and all other heresies and ideas opposed to the Holy Church; and I swear that I will never assert or say anything either orally or in writing, that could put me under such suspicion. ❞

Galileo continued his work after the trial. As he experimented with the motion of objects on the earth, he helped to establish the universal laws of physics. Among these was the law of inertia, by which an object remains at rest or in straight-line motion unless acted upon by an external force. Investigations into the workings of the pendulum advanced its use as a time controller in clocks.

New Ways of Thinking

As European scientists revolutionized the world of astronomy, philosophers such as **Francis Bacon** and **René Descartes** incorporated scientific thought into philosophy. Bacon, an English philosopher, claimed that ideas based solely on tradition or unproven facts should be discarded completely.

To Bacon, truth resulted only from a thorough investigation of evidence. He helped develop the scientific method. This method is made up of several steps. The scientist begins with careful observations of facts or things. Then the scientist tries to find a hypothesis to explain the observations. By experimenting, the scientist then tests the hypothesis under all possible conditions and in every possible way to see whether it is true. Finally, if repeated experiments show that the hypothesis does prove true under all conditions, it is considered a scientific law. In other words, a scientific truth is not assumed—it is deduced from observations and a series of thorough experiments.

Like Bacon, French philosopher and mathematician René Descartes believed that truth must be reached through reason. The inventor of analytic geometry, Descartes saw mathematics as the perfect model for clear and certain knowledge. In 1637 he published *Discourse on Method* to explain his philosophy. In the book, Descartes began by doubting everything except his own existence. He believed he had found one unshakable and self-evident truth in the statement "I think, therefore I am."

518 Chapter 20 *Scientific Revolution*

POINT

Newton's Universe

In 1642, after Bacon and Descartes had both transformed European thinking, one of the most influential figures in modern science was born in England. His name was **Isaac Newton**. Newton employed the scientific method in science and mathematics. He once commented, "Asking the correct question is half the problem. Once the question is formulated there remains to be found only proof…."

At Cambridge University, Newton was a below-average student with few friends. He almost left school without realizing his mathematical genius. But one of his teachers recognized his ability and began tutoring him. With this help Newton quickly became an eager and successful student. He explored the most complicated mathematics of his day, reading the writings of Copernicus and Galileo.

In 1665 an outbreak of the plague closed the university and forced Newton to return to his family's farm. There, he began his ground-breaking studies in mathematics and physics. The legend of Newton's apple originated during these years. It was claimed that while sitting in his garden one day, Newton watched an apple fall to the ground. The apple's fall led him to the idea of gravity.

Nearly 20 years later, in 1687, Newton published his theories about gravity and other scientific concepts in his book *Mathematical Principles of Natural Philosophy*, often called *Principia*. Newton offered in the *Principia* a new understanding of the universe, explaining and expanding the work of Copernicus, Galileo, and Kepler.

The book stated Newton's theory of universal gravitation, explaining why the planets move as they do. According to this theory, the force of gravity not only prevents objects from flying off the

Footnotes to History

The Circus
Identified by Newton, centripetal force pulls an object traveling in a circular path toward the center of the circle. In 1768 the English performer Philip Astley relied on centripetal force to perform stunts on horseback while the horse ran in a circle at full gallop. He took his horse show to Paris in 1774, beginning the first circus. *Circus* is the Latin word for "circle."

MEETING SPECIAL NEEDS ACTIVITY

Attention Deficiency To help students with attention problems organize and remember information about the people in this section, have them list these people's names. Tell students that remembering information is often easier if it is classified in some way. They can classify the names on their lists by scientific field. Organize students into small groups or pairs to identify the scientists' fields and then quiz each other; for example, "Who was Boyle?" "Boyle was a chemist." After students know these facts, have pairs add another fact about each person, then quiz each other again. For example, "Who was Boyle?" "Boyle was a chemist who is often called the founder of modern chemistry." **L1**

Science and Technology

Bubbling Waters

Have you ever sipped a fizzy soft drink to settle an upset stomach? People have long believed that bubbling waters contain healing properties. For centuries royalty and wealthy Europeans sought the health benefits of the mineral-rich, bubbling springs scattered throughout Europe.

Scientists in Europe and the United States attempted to reproduce these effervescent waters. In 1775 the French chemist Antoine Lavoisier identified the gaseous compound as carbon dioxide. In 1782 the English chemist Thomas Henry described how to make artificial carbonated waters commercially. Factories and bottling

Soft drink advertisement

plants soon began operating in London, Paris, Dublin, and Geneva.

"Soft drinks" were originally sold in drugstores in the United States as syrupy tonics used for medicinal purposes. In the early 1800s it became popular to combine these tonics with carbonated water. Bottled colas appeared on the market in the late 1800s.

Today mineral waters and carbonated beverages are popular throughout the world. People like the tangy, sparkling taste provided by carbonation, which also prevents spoilage.

 ACTIVITY

Determine whether or not carbonated soda has a positive or negative effect on your health. Can you think of any inventions or technologies that have been produced by the soft-drink industry?

 Linking Past and Present

Bubbling Waters

Soft drinks we enjoy today trace back to the eighteenth and nineteenth centuries. Jacob Schweppe, a jeweler in Geneva, began selling artificially carbonated mineral waters by 1794 and later started a carbonated beverage business in London. In 1886 John Pemberton, a pharmacist in Atlanta, Georgia, invented Coca-Cola.

ANSWERS

Students may assert that although carbonated beverages may not provide a direct medical benefit, doctors often recommend that patients drink them to help control nausea; overconsumption of sweetened beverages may increase tooth decay and lead to weight gain. Students may mention flavoring syrups; packaging in glass or plastic bottles, aluminum or plastic cans; vending machines.

Science Yesterday and Today

Have students prepare an illustrated poster with three types of information: key contributors to the Scientific Revolution, examples of their contributions at the time, and modern machines that may have resulted from their work. *(example: Galileo, telescope, Hubble Space Telescope)* Display completed posters in the classroom. **L3**

---

revolving earth, but it also holds the entire solar system together by keeping the sun and the planets in proper orbits. To prove his theory, Newton developed calculus, a system of mathematics that calculates changing forces or quantities.

Newton's work greatly influenced the thinking of his own age and all later scientific thought. It suggested that precise mathematical formulas could be used to describe an orderly universe.

Studying the Natural World

As astronomy, philosophy, and mathematics advanced at an incredible pace, so too did the sciences of anatomy and chemistry. Like astronomy and physics, anatomy had been based on ancient works. Most knowledge of anatomy had come from the work of Galen, an ancient Greek.

Because Roman law forbade the dissection of human corpses, Galen formulated his theories of human anatomy by dissecting dogs and apes. Galen did make many anatomical discoveries, such as the existence of blood within the arteries, but he also held many mistaken views. Galen believed, for example, that the liver digested food and processed it into blood. A thousand years would pass before anyone began to question his findings.

Investigating the Human Body

French lawmakers in the 1500s also considered dissecting human bodies illegal. This limitation, however, did not stop a young medical student from making great advances in anatomy. Self-assured and outspoken, **Andreas Vesalius** made it clear to his professors that because Galen's views were based on dissected apes and dogs, his beliefs about human anatomy could not be accepted as truth. By dissecting human bodies, Vesalius made groundbreaking discoveries in anatomy. In 1543 he published his work in *On the Structure of the Human Body.*

Almost 100 years later, English physician **William Harvey** made a discovery that also disproved many of Galen's hypotheses. From his direct observations of humans, Harvey concluded that blood circulates throughout the body, pumped by the heart and returning through the veins. His findings astounded a medical world that had based its beliefs about circulation on Galen.

As Vesalius and Harvey explained the workings of the human body, English scientist **Robert Hooke** made a more fundamental biological discovery—the cell. Using the newly invented microscope, Hooke recognized cells in vegetable tissue. He called them "cells" because they reminded him of the cells in a honeycomb.

Chapter 20 *Scientific Revolution* **519**

MAKING CONNECTIONS ACTIVITIES

Mathematics/Science Have students who are talented in math or physics do a demonstration for the rest of the class explaining one of Newton's laws of physics or the basic principle of calculus. Encourage students to use objects or chalkboard diagrams. **L3**

Social Life Antoine and Marie Lavoisier are only one pair of married scientific collaborators. Have students research and write short reports about the fruitful collaborative efforts of other scientist couples, such as Marie and Pierre Curie, Irène and Frédéric Joliot-Curie, or Carolyn and Eugene Shoemaker. **L2**

ASSESS

Check for Understanding

Assign Section 1 Assessment as homework or as an in-class activity.

 Use Interactive Tutor Self-Assessment Software to review Section 1.

Evaluate

Section Quiz 20-1

 Use the Testmaker to create a customized quiz for Section 1.

Reteach

Have students independently review the section and create a time line that lists important discoveries and persons. Discuss and create a class time line.

Reading Essentials and Study Guide 20-1

Enrich

Have students choose an innovator from the section, then choose a pivotal day in that innovator's life and write a journal entry in that person's voice for that day.

CLOSE

Write the words *before* and *after* on the chalkboard. Have students take turns choosing a person mentioned in this section and describing an accepted theory before and after this person's work.

 Franklin Experiments With Electricity

Philadelphia, Pennsylvania, 1752
American scientist and inventor Benjamin Franklin performed an experiment to prove his theory that lightning is electricity. During a thunderstorm, Franklin flew a homemade kite with a wire attached to it. A bolt of lightning struck the wire and traveled down the wet kite string to a key fastened at the end, where it caused an electric spark. Franklin reported the results in his pamphlet *Experiments and Observations in Electricity*.

Experimenting With Chemistry

European scientists working in the field of chemistry joined their peers in astronomy, mathematics, and medicine in challenging traditional ideas. By careful scientific experimentation, **Robert Boyle** was primarily responsible for taking chemistry from its mystical and unscientific origins and establishing it as a pure science.

When Boyle was born into an Irish noble family in 1627, the chemistry of the day was alchemy. People who practiced alchemy, called alchemists, spent much of their time trying to transform base metals, such as lead and copper, into precious metals, such as silver and gold. They also held to the age-old belief that all matter was made up of four elements: earth, fire, water, and air.

Boyle criticized alchemists and attacked the theory of the four elements in his book *The Skeptical Chymist*, published in 1661. Boyle proved that air could not be a basic element because it was a mixture of several gases. He also defined an element as a material that cannot be broken down into simpler parts by chemical means.

A century later, in 1774, an English chemist and clergyman named **Joseph Priestley** conducted further experiments into the properties of air and discovered the existence of oxygen. His study of the properties of carbon dioxide resulted in his invention of carbonated drinks. Toward the end of his career, Priestley wrote, "Every year of the last twenty or thirty has been of more importance to science ... than any ten in the preceding century."

In France, **Antoine Lavoisier** contributed still more to knowledge about oxygen. Lavoisier conducted scientific experiments that probed the nature of air and discovered that materials do not throw off a substance called phlogiston when burned, as commonly believed, but rather they consume oxygen. Lavoisier discovered the nature of combustion, which results from the chemical union of a flammable material with oxygen.

Marie Lavoisier contributed significantly to her husband's work. She translated English and Latin scientific essays and books for him. She also condensed articles so that he could be informed on many scientific subjects. Lastly, she illustrated her husband's writing.

Perhaps more significant than any single discovery in the 1700s was the application of the scientific view to an understanding of the world. Influenced by the discoveries in science, European philosophers in the 1700s began to apply the scientific method to all human ideas and practices. Most people, caught up in the daily struggle for survival, at first took little notice. In the years to come, however, science would profoundly alter humanity's view of the world.

SECTION 1 ASSESSMENT

Main Idea
1. Use a diagram like the one below to identify new scientific ideas that appeared during the 1600s.

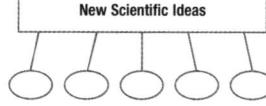

New Scientific Ideas

Recall
2. **Define** hypothesis, ellipses, scientific method, calculus, alchemist.
3. **Identify** Nicolaus Copernicus, Johannes Kepler, Galileo Galilei, Francis Bacon, René Descartes, Isaac Newton, Andreas Vesalius, William Harvey, Robert Hooke, Robert Boyle, Joseph Priestley, Antoine and Marie Lavoisier.

Critical Thinking
4. **Analyzing Information** Describe the scientific revolution and its effects on European thought.

Understanding Themes
5. **Innovation** How did Robert Boyle revolutionize chemistry by applying the scientific method?

SECTION 1 ASSESSMENT ANSWERS

1. earth is round and rotates on axis as it revolves; planets move in oval paths; planets move around sun; universal laws of physics; scientific method; gravity; calculus; discoveries in anatomy; discovery of cell; circulation of blood through body; advances in chemistry
2. The words are defined in the Glossary.
3. Copernicus, 516; Kepler, 517; Galileo, 517; Bacon, 518; Descartes, 518; Newton, 518; Vesalius, 519; Harvey, 519; Hooke, 519; Boyle, 520; Priestley, 520; Lavoisiers, 520
4. It was the use of reason, mathematics, and technology to understand the physical universe; they relied less on traditional authority, religion, and magic and turned to experimentation, individual experience, and the scientific method to understand the world around them.
5. **INNOVATION** Boyle used the scientific method to disprove the old theory of the four elements and define the true nature of an element, thereby establishing chemistry as a pure science.

1651 Thomas Hobbes publishes *Leviathan*.

1662 Charles II establishes the Royal Society of London.

1700s Deism becomes popular in Europe and America.

Section 2

Impact of Science

Guide to Reading

Read to Find Out
Main Idea *Changes in scientific thought also affected thinking in other fields.*

▶ **Terms to Define**
  natural law, natural rights, pacifism, deism

▶ **People to Meet**
  Thomas Hobbes, John Locke, Thomas Jefferson, Hugo Grotius, William Penn

▶ **Places to Locate**
  Pennsylvania

The Storyteller

Donald MacAdam bent forward to hear better. The lecturer was about to read from a new poem from the pen of Nicolas Boileau-Despreaux.

"What-e'er you write of Pleasant or Sublime,
Always let sense accompany your Rhyme:
Falsely they seem each other to oppose;
Rhyme must be made with Reason's Laws to
      close:
And when to conquer her you bend your force,
The Mind will Triumph in the Noble Course."

Donald wondered, how would poetry survive if it must always be so rational?

—adapted from *The Reasonableness of Poetry,* reprinted in *From Absolutism to Revolution,* edited by Herbert H. Rowen, 1964

European salon conversation

s scientists made revolutionary discoveries about people, nature, and the universe, popular interest in science spread throughout Europe. Using new technology such as the microscope, scientists and amateurs alike looked with wonder at the world inside a drop of pond water. Others tinkered and prodded in their home laboratories, studying gases and other substances. At social gatherings across Europe, people discussed the latest findings with lively interest.

Monarchs helped the new sciences by supporting scientific academies, observatories, and museums. In England Charles II established the Royal Society of London in 1662. The group included Isaac Newton and Robert Boyle among its members. In 1666 Louis XIV of France supported the founding of the French Academy of Science. These societies provided financial support to scientists and published scientific books and journals.

Exploring Political Ideas

The advances in science led philosophers and other thinkers to believe that if systematic laws governed the workings of nature and the universe, it followed that political, economic, and social relationships could also be understood through reasoned analysis. Scientific thought and method profoundly influenced political theory. Political philosophers believed in the idea of natural law, or a universal moral law that, like physical laws, could be understood by applying reason.

Two English philosophers, **Thomas Hobbes** and **John Locke**, grappled with their ideas of natural law and government during the 1600s, as England struggled with the political tensions of a civil war. The country was torn between people who wanted the king to have absolute power and those who thought the people have the right to govern themselves.

Chapter 20 *Scientific Revolution* **521**

TEACH

Guided Practice

THEME Conflict

Ask students how they would react if they encountered ideas that conflicted with their beliefs; for example, if someone argued that we descend from extraterrestrials. Have students list conflicts of ideas in this section. **L1**

 History Simulation 20

Picturing History ➡

Tell students that many historians of science challenge claims that Galileo was the first to disprove Aristotle's notions about the relationship between the speed of falling bodies and their weight. Medieval philosophers had pointed out Aristotle's mistake more than 1,000 years before Galileo, and other scientists in the 1500s had also challenged Aristotle's claim. Nonetheless, it is universally agreed that Galileo did make careful experiments of vertically falling objects by rolling balls down inclined planes. Scientists today study falling bodies by using equipment unavailable to Galileo: strobe lights and video cameras.

VIDEODISC

Turning Points in World History

Side One
Chapter 10

Title: *The Scientific Revolution*
Ask: What scientist perfected the telescope? *(Galileo)*

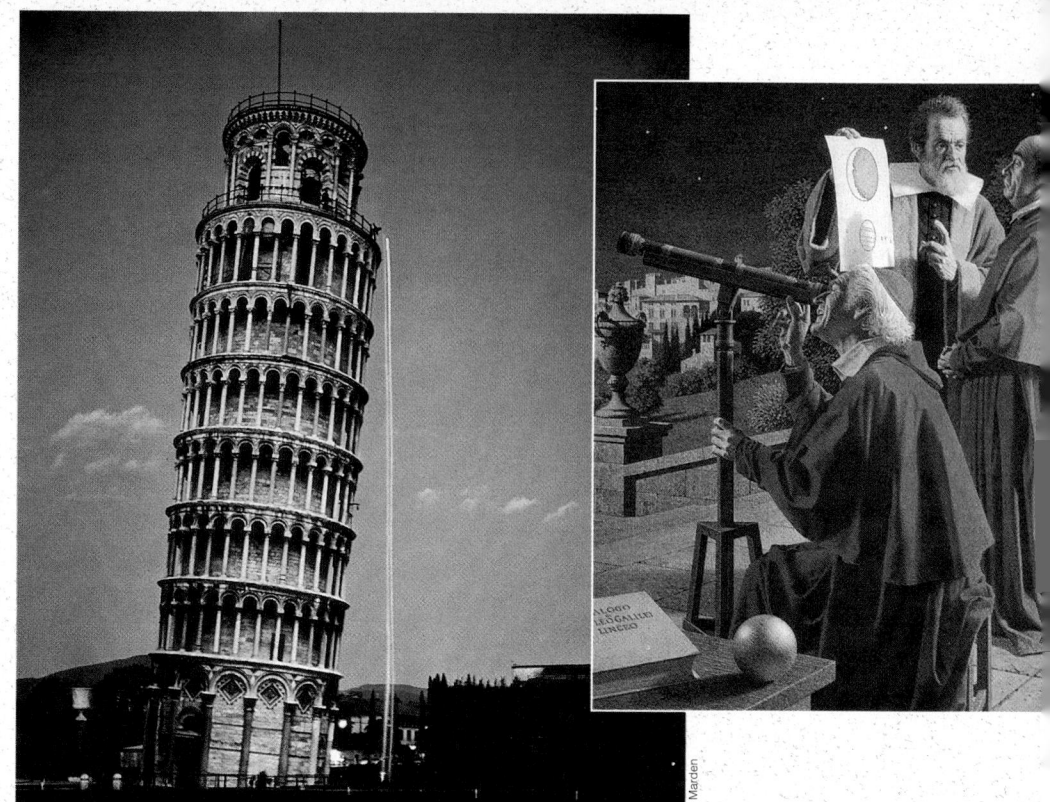

Luis Marden

Tower Physics

In a modern re-creation (left) of Galileo's famous experiment from the Leaning Tower of Pisa, two lighted plastic balls, one heavier than the other, plummet to the ground at once—a result the scientific community of Galileo's day refused to acknowledge. In 1591 Italian scientist Galileo Galilei (right) wanted to test the Aristotelian theory of motion—the idea that when two bodies of unequal weight are dropped simultaneously, the heavier object will hit the ground first. So he dropped a ten-pound weight and a one-pound weight from the top of the bell tower.

Galileo's experiment demonstrated that objects of different weights fell at the same rate—hit the ground at the same time—if one allowed for the impact of air resistance. Galileo proved Greek philos Aristotle's theory of motion wrong. In investi the science of the motion of bodies, Galileo w of the scientific revolution, a reformulation o that overturned those held by medieval thinke the Catholic Church. Scientists began carefull ing old theories of how the material world w they used careful measurements, exact observa and precise experiments. The conflict between new ideas and the power of the older theories the new scientists to develop techniques to their claims. Today we call this the scie method—and admire men like Galileo, who s to understand motion by dropping things fro tallest building in Pisa. ⊕

522 Chapter 20   *Scientific Revolution*

MORE ABOUT...

Science and Motion In July 1971, *Apollo 15* astronaut David Scott performed Galileo's demonstration on the moon, where there is no air. He dropped a hammer and a feather at the same time to show conclusively that in the absence of air resistance, a heavy object will hit the ground at the same time as a lighter one.

Hobbes Explores Government

Thomas Hobbes used the idea of natural law to argue that absolute monarchy was the best form of government. He believed that violence and disorder came naturally to human beings and that without an absolute government, chaos would occur. In his book *Leviathan*, published in 1651, Hobbes wrote about a state in which people lived without government. The book showed how "nasty, brutish, and short" life in such a world would be.

Hobbes believed that people should form a social contract, an agreement to give up their freedom and live obediently under a ruler. In this way, they would be governed by a monarch who would protect them and keep their world peaceful and orderly. According to Hobbes, people generally do not have the right to rebel against their government, no matter how unjust it might be.

Locke Offers a Different View

Another English philosopher, John Locke, also based his theories on the idea of natural law. Like Hobbes, Locke held that government was based on a social contract and that it was necessary to establish order. Unlike Hobbes, he believed that people in a state of nature are reasonable and moral and have natural rights, or rights belonging to all humans from birth. These included the right to life, liberty, and property.

In *Two Treatises of Government*, Locke stated that people created government to protect natural rights. A government functioned best when its powers were limited and it was accepted by all the citizens. If a government failed in its duty of protecting natural rights, the people had the right to overthrow it.

Locke's writings were widely read throughout Europe and the Americas. Ironically, many of the ideas that the American colonists later used to justify their independence from Britain came from Locke and other British thinkers. For example, **Thomas Jefferson** based much of the Declaration of Independence on Locke's ideas about the social contract and the right of people to overthrow an unjust government.

Reason Influences Law

As Europeans searched for new principles that would meet the standards of reason, great changes were made in the practice of law. Applying scientific or reasoned thought to the law helped to end unjust trials. Lawmakers placed less value on hearsay and on confessions made under torture in determining the guilt or innocence of suspected criminals.

In the 1600s attempts were made to create a body of international law. A Dutch jurist named **Hugo Grotius** called for an international code based on natural law. He believed that one body of rules could reduce the dealings of governments to a system of reason and order. In the American colonies, **William Penn**, founder of the Quaker colony of **Pennsylvania**, believed in pacifism, or opposition to violence as a means of settling disputes. Penn advocated an assembly of nations committed to world peace.

Examining Religion

Many Europeans also applied reason to religious beliefs. Members of the upper and middle classes increasingly turned away from traditional religious views, and Europe became a more secular society. In the 1700s a new religious philosophy called deism swept through Europe and America. Although believing in God, Deists often denounced organized religion, declaring that it exploited people's ignorance and superstitions. Deism was intended to construct a simpler and more natural religion based on reason and natural law. Its followers asserted the rightness of humanity's place in an orderly universe.

SECTION 2 ASSESSMENT

Main Idea
1. Use a diagram like the one below to list other fields of thought that were affected by new scientific thought.

Cause: New Scientific Thought

Effects:

Recall
2. **Define** natural law, natural rights, pacifism, deism.
3. **Identify** Thomas Hobbes, John Locke, Thomas Jefferson, Hugo Grotius, William Penn.

Critical Thinking
4. **Making Comparisons** Contrast Hobbes's and Locke's views.

Understanding Themes
5. **Conflict** What was deism's purpose, and how did it conflict with traditional religion?

Chapter 20 *Scientific Revolution* 523

SECTION 2 ASSESSMENT ANSWERS

1. political theory; the practice of law; international law; religion (deism)
2. The terms are defined in the Glossary.
3. Hobbes, 521; Locke, 521; Jefferson, 523; Grotius, 523; Penn, 523
4. Hobbes argued that people need absolute governments to prevent chaos. Locke argued that people may overthrow any government that denies them their natural rights.
5. **CONFLICT** Deism was based on reason and natural law. Deists claimed organized religion exploited people.

Independent Practice
 Guided Reading Activity 20-2 **L1**

ASSESS

Check for Understanding
Assign Section 2 Assessment as homework or as an in-class activity.

▣ Use Interactive Tutor Self-Assessment Software to review Section 2.

Evaluate
Section Quiz 20-2

▣ Use the Testmaker to create a customized quiz for Section 2.

Reteach
Review with students the concept of natural law, the political philosophies of the time, and the political changes that took place.

Reading Essentials and Study Guide 20-2

Enrich
Remind students that ideas covered in this section still affect today's world. Have students make a list of contemporary thinkers, ideas, and technologies they think will still affect the world 300 years from now.

CLOSE

Help students create a flowchart showing how the scientific method affected other areas of thought, such as politics, law, and religion. Incorporate material from Section 1 and leave room for additions from Section 3.

1700   **1750**   **1800**

c. 1736 John Wesley promotes religious revival in Great Britain.

1748 Baron de Montesquieu publishes *The Spirit of Laws.*

1780s Joseph II of Austria introduces Enlightenment reforms.

Section 3

Triumph of Reason

Guide to Reading

Read to Find Out

Main Idea *A number of cultural factors helped Enlightenment ideas to spread throughout Europe.*

▶ **Terms to Define**
philosophe, salon, enlightened despot, classicism, metaphysics, romanticism

▶ **People to Meet**
Madame de Pompadour, Denis Diderot, Baron de Montesquieu, Voltaire, Jean-Jacques Rousseau, Immanuel Kant, John Wesley

▶ **Places to Locate**
Paris

The notorious criminal Jean Chatel had just been executed. Moments before his death, the priests announced that the murderer had confessed all his sins and received absolution. Therefore, he had died in a state of grace and his soul would eventually reach Paradise. The proclamation greatly disturbed Joseph Leveque and his friends. They had just read Voltaire's comments about universal toleration. How could good and bad be defined in such absolute terms? They asked themselves and each other, would the Creator condemn Confucius and Socrates to limitless torment, while blessing a villain simply because he died according to a prescribed formula?

Voltaire

—adapted from *Treatise on Toleration,* Voltaire, reprinted in *The Human Record,* Alfred J. Andrea and James H. Overfield, 1990

524   Chapter 20   *Scientific Revolution*

C ompared to their ancestors, who lived in a world that seemed to be run by inexplicable forces and filled with magic, Europe's new thinkers believed that their scientific approach helped illuminate and clarify both the natural world and the study of human behavior. As a result, the period in Europe from the late 1600s through the 1700s came to be called the Age of Enlightenment.

Men and women of the Enlightenment studied the world as though they were looking at it for the first time. No longer held back by tradition, they defined the world in their own way, using science as their base. Natural scientists analyzed and classified thousands of animals, insects, and plants. Geologists drew maps of the earth's surface. Astronomers continued to make discoveries about the universe.

Largely due to reading Newton's *Principia*, Enlightenment thinkers perceived the universe as a machine governed by fixed laws. They saw God as the master mechanic of the universe—the builder of a machine who provided laws and then allowed it to run on its own, according to these orderly principles. They also believed in progress, or the idea that the world and its people could be improved.

Such radically new perceptions and ideas started a philosophical revolution. Jean Le Rond d'Alembert, a French mathematician, claimed that the new method of thinking and the enthusiasm that accompanied it had "brought about a lively fermentation of minds, spreading through nature in all directions like a river which has burst at its dams."

Spreading Ideas

The thinkers of the Enlightenment who spread these exciting new ideas came to be called philosophes (FEE•luh•ZAWFS), the French word for "philosopher." Most philosophes passionately believed in Locke's political philosophy and

Visualizing History This device is an orrery, or model of the solar system that demonstrates the motions of the planets about the sun. The typical orrery shows the planets as they appear from outside the solar system and provides an accurate scale model of the planets' periods of revolution. Earth, for example, completes a year's rotation in about 10 minutes. The first orrery was probably invented in England during the 1700s. *What English mathematician saw the universe as a machine governed by fixed laws?*

Newton's scientific theories. Most disapproved of superstition and religious opposition to new scientific endeavors. They believed in both freedom of speech and the individual's right to liberty. Many philosophes were talented writers whose essays and books helped to spread and popularize ideas and beliefs of the Enlightenment.

Activity in Paris

France was the most active center of ideas. In **Paris** especially, the new intellectuals delighted in gatherings called salons held in the homes of wealthy patrons. In a salon, writers, artists, and educated people of the growing middle class mingled with men and women of the nobility. Besides discussing the philosophies of the day, salon guests prized the art of conversation and often engaged in contests to see who had the sharpest wit.

Wealthy and influential women ran many of the popular salons. **Madame de Pompadour** was perhaps the most celebrated. A mistress to Louis XV, Pompadour's intelligence and courtly charm won the admiration of many philosophes.

A remarkable achievement compiled by some of the most prominent philosophes of the Enlightenment was the *Encyclopédie*. First published in 1751, these 28 volumes covered everything then known about the sciences, technology, and history in more than 3,000 pages crammed with illustrations.

The *Encyclopédie* was initially conceived to be simply a French translation of a two-volume English encyclopedia, but its editor, **Denis Diderot** (dee•DROH), had a work of much greater scope in mind. Diderot devoted much of his life to this project. Among other things, the *Encyclopédie* criticized the Church and government and praised religious tolerance.

The Catholic Church banned the *Encyclopédie*. When Diderot discovered that the printer, frightened by the controversial material in the volumes, had omitted passages that might offend the Church's leaders, he became enraged and screamed at the printer:

> ❝ You have massacred … the work of twenty good men who have devoted to you their time, their vigils, their talents, from a love of truth and justice, with the simple hope of seeing their ideas given to the public…. ❞

For their writings, Diderot and several others went to prison. Still, the *Encyclopédie* was widely read and its ideas spread all through Europe.

Montesquieu

A contributor to the *Encyclopédie* and one of the most learned of the philosophes in political matters was Charles-Louis de Secondat, the **Baron de Montesquieu** (MAHN•tuhs•KYOO). His masterwork, *The Spirit of Laws*, appeared in two volumes in 1748.

After studying various existing governments, Montesquieu wrote about his admiration for the English government and promoted the idea of separating governmental powers. Montesquieu believed that power should be equally divided among the branches of government: the legislative

Chapter 20 *Scientific Revolution* 525

TEACH

Guided Practice

THEME Reaction

Have students describe some of the different ways specific people reacted to Enlightenment ideas. Suggest that they consider the reactions of Madame de Pompadour, Diderot, Voltaire, Frederick II, Rousseau, and John Wesley. **L1**

Visualizing History The orrery gets its name from Charles Boyle, fourth earl of Orrery, who probably had the device invented by George Graham. **Answer to Caption:** *Newton*

Global Issues Ask students to restate Voltaire's words: "I disapprove of what you say, but I will defend to the death your right to say it." Then have them identify countries in which Voltaire's approach to free speech could and could not be practiced today. **L2**

Point of View To help students better understand opposition to the ideas of the Enlightenment, have them summarize the nature of the objections of Jean-Jacques Rousseau, Immanuel Kant, Count von Zinzendorf, and John Wesley. **L3**

World History and Art Transparency 27, *The Letter*

COOPERATIVE LEARNING ACTIVITY

Role Play Organize the class into two groups to plan a gathering in a salon. Have each student in one group select a favorite individual from this chapter. Have students in the other group choose roles as members of the middle class or the nobility. Students should research the individuals, the lifestyles of the different social classes, and the salons. They should then plan the setting and select a topic for the gathering. Remind students that salons were places where middle-class writers, artists, and educated people could mingle with the nobility. To stimulate conversation, you may wish to visit the salon in the guise of a noble person. **L2**

ABCNEWS
INTERACTIVE™

VIDEODISC
Turning Points in World History

Side One,
Chapter 10

Title: *The Scientific Revolution*
Ask: What is your interpretation of this statement, "If there is one evil in the world today for which there is no excuse, it is the evil of stupidity"? *(Students may suggest that the statement seems to say that there is no excuse for lacking knowledge, because everyone has the ability and opportunity to expand their knowledge.)*

Independent Practice

📁 Guided Reading Activity
20-3 **L1**

📁 People in World History
Profile 38

Critical Thinking Ask students to write a short paper stating whether they agree or disagree with Rousseau that human beings are naturally good. Ask them to give examples supporting their opinions. **L2**

Linking Past and Present

Encyclopedias—from the Greek words for "general education"—continue to be published along the lines of the French *Encyclopédie*. Although encyclopedias vary in length, format, and content, all aim at presenting up-to-date knowledge in a conveniently accessible form.

---

branch, which made the laws; the executive branch, which enforced them; and the judicial branch, which interpreted the laws and judged when they were violated.

Montesquieu strongly believed in the rights of individuals. His work powerfully influenced the writing of the constitutions in many countries, including the United States.

Voltaire

Perhaps the most celebrated of the philosophes was François-Marie Arouet, known to the world by his pen name, **Voltaire**. A French author and Deist, Voltaire wrote poetry, plays, essays, and books in a style that was entertaining and often satirical. *Candide*, his most celebrated satire, challenged the notion that everything that happens is for the best in "the best of all possible worlds."

In his youth, Voltaire twice served time in the Bastille, the notorious prison in Paris. His satirical works that mocked the Church and the royal court of France earned him one prison term; he received the other term when he was accused of insulting a nobleman. After his second offense, Voltaire was given a choice between further imprisonment and exile from France. He chose the latter. When Voltaire moved to England, he felt unfettered in an atmosphere of political and religious freedom.

During the three years he spent in England, Voltaire wrote books promoting Bacon's philosophy and Newton's science. Voltaire deeply admired the English ideal of religious liberty and its relative freedom of the press. Voltaire is credited with the famous statement in defense of free speech, "I disapprove of what you say, but I will defend to the death your right to say it."

Women and the Enlightenment

Enlightenment ideas about equality and freedom spread throughout Europe, but they were not

---

Images *of the* Times

Salon Society

During the Enlightenment, Europe's high society gathered in the salons of wealthy patrons to discuss the ideas and events of the day.

Upper-class society of the 1700s enjoyed card games as well as intellectual discussions.

Images *of the* Times
Salon Society

The salon of Marie-Thérèse Rodet Geoffrin (1699–1777), held in the Hôtel de Rambouillet from 1749 to 1777, drew artists and writers from France and beyond. Although she was the daughter of a valet and lacked a formal education, her native intelligence and her marriage to a rich manufacturer enabled her to be an excellent hostess. Madame Geoffrin underwrote the *Encyclopédie* project.

When Jeanne-Antoinette Poisson (1721–1764) became King Louis XV's mistress in 1745, he made her marchioness of Pompadour. A patron of the arts, Madame de Pompadour also introduced the pompadour hairstyle, in which the hair is raised up over the forehead in a roll.

Technology SKILLS

Developing Multimedia Presentations

You have been assigned a research report to present to your class. You want to really hold the attention of your classmates. How can you do this? One way is to use a variety of media.

Learning the Skill

At its most basic, a multimedia presentation involves using several types of media. To discuss the Age of Enlightenment, for example, you might show photographs or slides of the art, play and listen to recordings of the music or literature, or present a video of a play written during this time period.

You can also develop a multimedia presentation on a computer. Multimedia as it relates to computer technology is the combination of text, video, audio, and animation in an interactive program.

In order to create multimedia productions or presentations on a computer, you need to have certain tools. These may include traditional com-

puter graphic tools and draw programs, animation programs that make still images move, and authoring systems that tie everything together. Your computer manual will tell you which tools your computer can support.

Practicing the Skill

This chapter focuses on the Age of Revolution from 1500 to 1830. Ask yourself questions such as the following to develop a multimedia presentation on the politics of that era:

- Which forms of media do I want to include? Video? Sound? Animation? Photographs? Graphics? Other?
- Which of these media forms does my computer support?
- What kind of software programs or systems do I need? A paint program? A draw program? An animation program? A program to create interactive, or two-way, communication? An authoring system that will allow me to change images, sound, and motion?
- Is there a "do-it-all" program I can use to develop the kind of presentation I want?

Applying the Skill

Keeping in mind the four guidelines given above, write a plan describing a multimedia presentation you would like to develop. Indicate what tools you will need and what steps you must take to make the presentation an exciting reality.

For More Practice

Turn to the Skill Practice in the Chapter Assessment on page 533 for more practice in developing multimedia presentations.

ANSWERS TO PRACTICING THE SKILL

Answers will vary, depending on students' imaginations, the aspects of the topic they want to present, and the hardware and software available. Make sure that students have checked their computers' capabilities and the available software. You might give students the option of working in groups.

Technology SKILLS

TEACH

Developing Multimedia Presentations This skill helps students develop the ability to create multimedia presentations. Point out that this ability will do more than make for interesting classes. It might also prove helpful to them as they enter the workplace. Encourage students to look at this skill as an adventure. Have students brainstorm a list of possible forms of media that could be used in a multimedia presentation. Even suggestions that seem quite unusual may yield interesting possibilities.

Discuss the technologies pictured in the photograph. Also demonstrate some of the media appliances that are available to students in your school or local library. For example, you might play recordings of music from the Age of Enlightenment while you present a slide show of artwork from the same time period. You might ask staff members in the technology/media department of your school to help with the demonstration. Ask a guest speaker to discuss and demonstrate the development of multimedia presentations on a computer to your students. If possible, try to schedule computer lab time so that students can sample software and begin to build their own presentations.

Additional Practice

Skill Reinforcement Activity 20

Chapter 20 Assessment

GLENCOE TECHNOLOGY

VIDEODISC
Use MindJogger to review the chapter.

MindJogger Videoquiz

Chapter 20
Disc 3 Side A

   Also available in VHS.

Answers

Using Key Terms
1. f   3. g   5. j
2. e   4. b

Using Your History Journal
Encourage students to include personal as well as scientific details, just as a TV interviewer would.

Reviewing Facts
1. they saw it as overly rational; Rousseau criticized reliance on reason instead of emotion; Kant thought reason could not explain metaphysics; wanted religion to be more emotionally satisfying; artists wanted to celebrate emotion and the individual
2. Copernicus: sun-centered solar system; Galileo: observations support Copernican model; Kepler: planets move around sun in ellipses; Newton: gravity holds solar system together
3. sun is at the center of the solar system and the planets move around the sun; living matter composed of cells and blood circulates through body; truth of physical universe known through

532 Chapter 20 *Scientific Revolution*

Using Key Terms

Write the key term that completes each sentence. Then write a sentence for each term not chosen.

a. philosophes	g. pacifism
b. classicism	h. enlightened despots
c. salons	i. scientific method
d. hypotheses	j. deism
e. natural law	k. metaphysics
f. romanticism	l. natural rights

1. _____, with its emphasis on emotion and the individual, opposed the values of the Enlightenment.
2. Political philosophers of the Enlightenment believed in the idea of _____, or a universal moral law that, like physical laws, could be understood by applying reason.
3. William Penn believed in _____ and favored the creation of an assembly of nations committed to world peace.
4. Enlightenment writers, artists, and architects strove to achieve the ideals of _____, which to them represented ultimate order and reason.
5. The philosophy of _____ favored a simpler religion based on reason.

Technology Activity

Using a Word Processor
Search the Internet or a library for information about the achievements of European scientists during the scientific revolution. Use a word processor to organize your research into a chart. Include headings such as name of the scientist, country, year of discovery, and achievements. Write a paragraph explaining which discovery you believe had the greatest impact on modern civilization.

532 Chapter 20 *Scientific Revolution*

Reviewing Facts

1. **Culture** Use a chart like the one below to list reasons why some thinkers in Europe opposed the Enlightenment.

Opposition to the Enlightenment
_____
_____
_____
_____

2. **Science** Explain how Copernicus, Galileo, Kepler, and Newton each added something new to an understanding of the solar system.
3. **Culture** Describe the ways in which European thinking about the universe, philosophy, and law changed during the Enlightenment.
4. **History** Explain how the study of history was influenced by the Enlightenment.
5. **Government** State the political idea advocated by Montesquieu that can be found in the United States Constitution.
6. **Culture** Identify one philosopher whom you think embodies the ideas of the Enlightenment. What were his views?

Critical Thinking

1. **Apply** How did classical art reflect the values of the Enlightenment? Give examples to support your answer.
2. **Synthesize** Why do you suppose a belief in witches and ghosts largely became a thing of the past in Europe after the period of the Enlightenment?
3. **Evaluate** Were the 1700s an era of optimism or pessimism? Explain.

---

scientific method; use of reason to make laws just and workable
4. Possible answer: Historians began to use the scientific method, posing and testing hypotheses about the past.
5. the separation of powers, rights of individuals
6. Montesquieu studied governments and derived a system of breaking them into legislative, executive, and judicial branches that is the basis of many countries' constitutions. Voltaire

challenged the Church and royal court and believed in political and religious freedom. Mary Wollstonecraft favored equal education and societal contributions of men and women.

Critical Thinking
1. It emphasized form and order. Examples will vary; students may refer to classical architects' preference for squares and circles rather than elaborate swirls, or to David's

4. **Synthesize** Do scientific laws apply to human society in the way that they apply to the physical universe? Why or why not?
5. **Analyze** Why were the enlightened despots unable to carry out thorough reforms?
6. **Evaluate** Has science fulfilled the promise of progress that it seemed to hold in the 1700s? Why or why not? Give examples.

Geography in History

1. **Region** Refer to the map below. What conclusion can you draw about European interest in science and learning during the period of the 1500s and 1600s?
2. **Place** In what two nations were organizations founded for people interested in sharing scientific information?
3. **Movement** How do you think scientific ideas and theories spread from one nation of Europe into other nations?

Centers of Science A.D. 1500s and 1600s

ENGLAND — Francis Bacon, Isaac Newton, William Harvey, Royal Society of London
IRELAND — Robert Boyle
POLAND — Copernicus, University of Kraków
GERMANY — Johannes Kepler
FRANCE — René Descartes, Andreas Vesalius, French Academy of Science
ITALY — Galileo Galilei

Understanding Themes

1. **Innovation** How did the scientific revolution change the ways in which Europeans investigated the natural world?

2. **Conflict** Catholic Bishop Bossuet said that the skepticism of the philosophes was an "unending error, a risk-all boldness, a deliberate dizziness, in a word, a pride that cannot accept its proper cure, which is legitimate authority." Explain the bishop's view in your own words. What does he mean by "legitimate authority"?
3. **Reaction** What religious movements formed as a reaction to the ideas of the Enlightenment thinkers? Why?

Linking Past and Present

1. William Penn envisioned an assembly of nations working for world peace. What modern organization reflects Penn's idea?
2. Classical movements in music, art, and literature reflected the spirit of the Enlightenment. Does popular music, art, and literature reflect how people feel about society today? Why or why not? Give examples.
3. Do you agree or disagree with Jean-Jacques Rousseau's view that people are naturally good but that civilization and institutions make them evil? Give examples from modern life to support your viewpoint.

Skill Practice

Study the list of topics below. Choose one of the topics and explain how you would use at least three types of media in a presentation to best teach the topic to a class.

1. Michelangelo's work
2. The causes of the French Revolution
3. The American Revolution
4. The Scientific Revolution of the 1600s and 1700s
5. The Salon Society of the 1700s
6. Religious movements of the 1700s

Chapter 20 Assessment

in science.
2. England, France
3. Writers and traveling scholars and scientists spread ideas.

Understanding Themes

1. 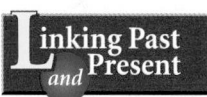 **INNOVATION** relied on observation, reason, and the scientific method instead of tradition
2. **CONFLICT** The philosophes should give up their questioning and accept the views of the Church, the "legitimate authority."
3. **REACTION** Methodism, the Moravian Brethren, and Hasidism formed. Each emphasized personal faith as opposed to emphasis on reason.

Linking Past and Present

1. the United Nations
2. Students should support claims.
3. Students should support claims.

Skill Practice

Answers will vary, depending on students' imaginations, the aspects of the topic they want to present, and the hardware and software available. Make sure that students have checked their computers' capabilities and the available software.

? Chapter Bonus Test Question

In 1611 English poet John Donne wrote that "new philosophy calls all in doubt." Similarly, in our times, many people are troubled by the destabilizing effects of new scientific methods. **Ask students:** What are three areas of scientific research today that some people find unsettling? (*Answers will vary but may include: manipulation of human reproduction, tinkering with genetic information.*)

---

concern for simplicity of form.
2. Superstition was replaced by observation, reason, and the scientific method.
3. Some may argue that it was an optimistic age because people looked favorably on new ideas and believed reason could provide the answers to many of life's problems.
4. Answers will vary. Some may argue that human emotions and actions vary too much to be predictable by law.

5. Many nobles felt threatened by the powers monarchs were giving common people, and so they frustrated reform efforts.
6. Answers will vary. Some may argue that scientific breakthroughs have enhanced the quality of life, others that new technologies have threatened environmental viability.

Geography in History
1. People all over Europe were interested

Chapter 20 *Scientific Revolution* **533**

Chapter 21 Planning Guide

A complete, 1-page lesson plan is provided for each section in the *Reproducible Lesson Plans* booklet.

English and American Revolutions

CHAPTER RESOURCES

	Reproducible Resources	Multimedia Resources
Chapter Opener	Chapter Themes: Graphic Organizer 21 Historical Significance Chapter Activity 21	MindJogger Videoquiz
Chapter Enrichment	Vocabulary Activity 21* Time Line Activity 21 Mapping History Activity 21 History Simulation 21 Geography and History Activity 21 Source Reading 21 People in World History Profiles 39, 40 World Art and Music Activity 21 Enrichment Activity 21 Critical Thinking Activity 21 Skill Reinforcement Activity 21 Writer's Guidebook, Lesson 11 Performance Assessment Activity 21 Standardized Test Practice Workbook Activity 21 Inclusion for the Social Studies Classroom Strategies and Activities	World History and Art Transparency 28, *Blue Boy* Mapping History Overlay Transparency 13, *European Claims in North America* Chapter Transparency 21 Vocabulary PuzzleMaker Software Picture Atlas of the World World Music: Cultural Traditions, Lesson 1 World History Primary Source Document Library
Chapter Review/Reteaching	Reteaching Activity 21 Skill Reinforcement Activity 21 Spanish Chapter Summary 21	Chapter 21 Digest Audiocassette, Activity, Test* Vocabulary PuzzleMaker Software Interactive Tutor Self-Assessment Software MindJogger Videoquiz
Chapter Evaluation/Testing	Performance Assessment Activity 21 Chapter 21 Test, Forms A and B	ExamView® Pro Testmaker

`0:00` **OUT OF TIME?** Assign the Chapter 21 Audiocassettes.

* Also available in Spanish

World History Primary Source Document Library

Make History Come Alive!

Engage your students with over 250 easily accessible primary source documents—available on this CD-ROM—that will give them real life insight into the important events of world history.

Block Schedule

Activities that are particularly suited to use within the block scheduling framework are identified throughout this chapter by the following designation.

KEY TO ABILITY LEVELS

Teaching strategies are coded for varying learning styles.

L1 BASIC activities for all students

L2 AVERAGE activities for average to above-average students

L3 CHALLENGING activities for above-average students

LEP LIMITED ENGLISH PROFICIENCY activities

Use Glencoe's **Presentation Plus!** multimedia teacher tool to easily present dynamic lessons that visually excite your students. Using Microsoft PowerPoint® you can customize the presentations to create your own personalized lessons.

Interactive Lesson Planner

Planning has never been easier! Using this CD-ROM, organize your week, month, semester, or year with all the help you need. The **Interactive Lesson Planner** gives you access to all of the blackline masters that accompany *World History: The Human Experience.*

SECTION RESOURCES

Daily Objectives	Reproducible Resources	Multimedia Resources
Section 1 **Civil War** Identify factors that led to civil war in England.	Lecture Notes 21-1 Reproducible Lesson Plan 21-1 Vocabulary Activity 21* Guided Reading Activity 21-1* Time Line Activity 21 History Simulation 21 People in World History Profile 40 Section Quiz 21-1* Reading Essentials and Study Guide 21-1	Section Focus Transparency 21-1 Chapter Transparency 21 Interactive Tutor Self-Assessment Software Testmaker
Section 2 **A King Returns to the Throne** Describe how England established a constitutional monarchy.	Lecture Notes 21-2 Reproducible Lesson Plan 21-2 Vocabulary Activity 21* Guided Reading Activity 21-2* Section Quiz 21-2* Reading Essentials and Study Guide 21-2	Section Focus Transparency 21-2 World History and Art Transparency 28, *Blue Boy* Interactive Tutor Self-Assessment Software Testmaker
Section 3 **Road to Revolt** Identify factors that led to disagreement and eventual conflict between the British and the American colonies.	Lecture Notes 21-3 Reproducible Lesson Plan 21-3 Vocabulary Activity 21* Guided Reading Activity 21-3* Geography and History Activity 21 Section Quiz 21-3* Reading Essentials and Study Guide 21-3	Section Focus Transparency 21-3 Interactive Tutor Self-Assessment Software Testmaker World Music: Cultural Traditions, Lesson 1
Section 4 **A War for Independence** Describe the kind of government Americans established after the American Revolution.	Lecture Notes 21-4 Reproducible Lesson Plan 21-4 Guided Reading Activity 21-4* People in World History Profile 39 Reteaching Activity 21 Enrichment Activity 21 Section Quiz 21-4* Performance Assessment Activity 21 Spanish Chapter Summary 21 Reading Essentials and Study Guide 21-4	Section Focus Transparency 21-4 Mapping History Overlay Transparency 13, *European Claims in North America* Vocabulary PuzzleMaker Software Interactive Tutor Self-Assessment Software Testmaker

* Also available in Spanish

Chapter Activities

 Performance Assessment Activity

A Time Capsule Have students suppose that they have found a time capsule from the era of the English and American Revolutions. Have them list and make visuals of artifacts they might find inside evoking revolutionary attitudes and events. Have them design a container and make a list with visuals of items they would select for a current-day time capsule representing a revolutionary activity of our time. Students should write a reflection explaining their choices for both capsules.

Possible Rubric Features

Concept attainment, accuracy of content information, decision-making process skills, analytical thinking, research skills, ability to make logical connections, organization and clarity of product

• *For an additional activity, refer to Activity 21 in the* Performance Assessment Strategies and Activities *booklet.*

ACTIVITY

From the Classroom of...

Mike Nitzel
Moline High School
Moline, IL

The Revolutionary Times
Organize the class into two groups—one group to write and assemble an American Revolution newspaper, the other group to write and assemble an English Revolution newspaper. Each newspaper should have three sections: Causes of the Revolution; Events of the Revolution; Effects of the Revolution.

Each student should write an article dealing with one of the three topics listed above. Articles should be typed in columns, with titles and by-lines, as in a real newspaper. Each student should also create an advertisement or political cartoon reflective of the period. Let each group put their newspaper together. Students may need to cut and paste and use a copy machine to give their newspapers a professional look. Make a copy of both newspapers for each student and have the class discuss how the American and English Revolutions were similar, how they were different, and how each advanced the ideas of limited government and/or democracy.

MULTIPLE LEARNING STYLES

Verbal/Linguistic
Have students write news reports about the American Revolution on such topics as George Washington, the Second Continental Congress, or a battle site.

Logical/Mathematical
Have students make a time line that shows steps in the English kings' loss of power and Parliament's increase in power. Ask students to display the time line on a bulletin board.

Visual/Spatial
Have students develop pictorial histories of the Glorious Revolution that illustrate the major events before, during, and after this revolution. Remind students to include captions. Encourage students to display completed projects.

Auditory/Musical
Have students listen to the Chapter 21 Digest Audiocassette, stopping at two-minute intervals to write summary sentences.

Kinesthetic
Have students research life in England under Cromwell. Then ask them to dramatize their research, showing the effects of Puritan rule on daily life.

GLENCOE'S ASSESSMENT ADVANTAGE

Use the following to easily assess student learning in a variety of ways.

• Performance Assessment Strategies and Activities
• Section Quizzes
• Chapter and Unit Tests
• Interactive Tutor Self-Assessment Software
• Testmaker Software
• MindJogger Videoquiz
• SAT/SAT II Test Practice
• worldhistory.glencoe.com

James I's greatest political weakness was his constant need to ask Parliament for money. He spent huge sums of money on the government as well as on himself and his advisers. After one of James's parties, a member of Parliament remarked that James had "given away more plate [money] than Queen Elizabeth did in her whole reign." When Parliament refused to vote him enough funds, James resorted to other means of raising money, such as selling titles of nobility.

Parliament also criticized the king's foreign policy. James's decision to end a war with Spain created outrage in Parliament. The war repayments that were part of the peace treaty put England deep into debt. Opposition to James's policies grew even stronger when James tried to arrange the marriage of his son, Charles, to a Spanish Catholic princess. Fearing the return of Catholics to power, the people celebrated when James's marriage plans for his son failed.

Religion and the Monarchy

England's unsettled religious issues only added to the tension between Parliament and the Crown. In the 1600s most English people belonged to the Church of England, but they had differences of opinion about the doctrine and rituals of the Church. One powerful group of dissenters, or opponents, within the Church was **the Puritans**. They wanted the Church to be "purified" of remaining Catholic rituals and symbols. Many Puritans in Parliament called for these reforms.

James I, as head of both church and government in England, thought that anyone who criticized the Church of England was not a loyal subject. When James had become king, the Puritans presented him with a petition asking for reforms to be made in the Church of England. Not only did James reject the suggested changes, he warned the Puritans that if they did not conform to the Church of England, he would "harry [force] them out of the land." When the king refused to support the Puritan cause, the Puritans turned against him. Because of James's policies, many Puritans left England and settled in North America.

Despite his controversial ways, James I made a lasting and important contribution to the religion and literature of the English-speaking world. In 1604 he had a group of scholars prepare a new translation of the Bible from Greek and Hebrew into English. The new version appeared in 1611 and became known as the "King James" Bible. Written in the eloquent prose and poetry of Shakespeare's time, it became the best-known English version of the Bible.

History & Art *Portrait of Charles I Hunting* by Anthony Van Dyck, c. 1636. The Louvre, Paris, France *Why were the English Parliament and people unhappy with Charles by 1628?*

Charles Inherits the Throne

When James I died in 1625, his son Charles became king. **Charles I** inherited the country's religious conflicts and political divisions. Like his father, Charles opposed the Puritans and believed in the divine right of kings. Adding to the tension, Charles eventually married a Catholic woman— Henrietta Maria, sister of France's King Louis XIII.

Early in his reign, Charles asked Parliament for money to fight a war against Spain and France. When it gave him only a fraction of the sum he had requested, the king dissolved Parliament immediately and tried to raise money without its consent. Charles then forced landowners to give "loans" to the government. When they refused, he put them in jail. People were outraged by the king's behavior.

People were also angered by Charles's demand to billet, or board and lodge, his troops in private homes. The king also placed some areas under martial law, or temporary military rule with limitations on individual rights. Thus, discontent ran high when Charles again called Parliament into session in 1628.

TEACH

Guided Practice

THEME Conflict

Tell students that the English Civil War was the result of the deep conflict between Parliament and James I and later Charles I. Help students identify the source of the conflict. (*James and Charles believed in the divine right of kings; Parliament wanted more control over government policy, raising money, and reforms in the Church of England.*) **L1**

History & Art Van Dyck was a Flemish artist who specialized in portraits of Flemish, Italian, Spanish, and English nobles. In 1632 King Charles I made Anton Van Dyck his court painter and knighted him Sir Anthony Van Dyck.

Answer to Caption: *Charles I had dissolved Parliament, tried to raise money without Parliament's consent, forced landowners to lend him money and put them in jail if they refused, forced people to lodge soldiers in their homes, and placed some areas of England under martial law.*

Politics Have students make a two-column chart that lists Parliament's grievances against James I and Charles I. **L2**

 Chapter Transparency 21

 History Simulation 21

Who?What?Where?When?

English Catholics In spite of England's anti-Catholic laws, about one-fourth of the population was Catholic in 1634.

COOPERATIVE LEARNING ACTIVITY

Role Play Organize students into three groups to stage the trial of Charles I: the prosecution, the defense, and witnesses for the prosecution and for the defense. Have students choose a classmate to play Charles and another to play Cromwell. Have students from the appropriate group research arguments for the prosecution, arguments for the defense, and background on witnesses. Have each group select a few representatives to work with the other groups' representatives to prepare dialogue for the role play. Encourage students to ad lib as well. If possible, videotape the students' presentation. **L2**

The Pilgrims were a dissenting sect that separated from the Church of England and left England on the *Mayflower* to start a new life in New England. In the Mayflower Compact, Pilgrim leaders agreed to form a government for the good of their colony. How did this differ from government in England? (*The king claimed to rule by divine right, and ordinary people had no role in government.*)

Answer to Caption: *Leaders of the Church of England persecuted Puritans and Pilgrims.*

Economics Have students discuss how collecting taxes became a point of conflict between Charles I and Parliament. (*When Parliament refused to give King Charles the money he asked for to fight France and Spain, the king tried to raise money without Parliament's consent. In exchange for approval of additional taxes, Parliament forced the king to sign the Petition of Right forbidding him from again collecting taxes without parliamentary consent.*) **L3**

Independent Practice

 Guided Reading Activity 21-1 **L1**

Time Line Activity 21

People in World History Profile 40

Political Cartoon Have students draw a political cartoon about the English Civil War, perhaps lampooning Charles I or Cromwell, expressing ideas of Roundheads or Cavaliers, or depicting the tragedy of civil war. **L2 LEP**

History & Art *Pilgrims Signing the Mayflower Compact* by Percy Moran, c. 1900. The Pilgrim Hall Museum, Plymouth, Massachusetts *Why did groups like the Pilgrims and the Puritans leave England?*

By this time England was at war with both France and Spain. Parliament, however, was now ready to press changes on the king. In return for its approval of additional taxes to support the war, Parliament forced Charles to sign the **Petition of Right**. The Petition severely limited Charles's power in four ways. First, the king was forbidden to collect taxes or force loans without Parliament's consent. Second, the king could not imprison anyone without just cause. Third, troops could not be housed in a private home against the will of the owner. Fourth, the king could not declare martial law unless the country was at war.

Charles's desire to maintain his power, however, was not checked by the Petition of Right. Nearly a year after Parliament had authorized funds in return for his signature on the document, Charles dissolved Parliament and vowed never to call it again. For the next 11 years, Charles ruled without the advice or consent of the Parliament. He continued to collect taxes and imprison opponents—ignoring the Petition of Right he had signed.

At the same time, Charles deepened the religious divisions within England. He named **William Laud** to be Archbishop of Canterbury, the leading official of the Church of England. Laud and Charles persecuted the Puritans. They denied Puritans the right to preach or to publish. They burned Puritan

writings, and punished outspoken Puritans with public whippings.

As a result, thousands of Puritans sought religious freedom in the English colonies in America. Their exodus from England from 1630 through 1643 is known as the Great Migration. Most Puritans, however, remained in their homeland, determined to fight Charles and others who opposed them.

Charles and Archbishop Laud then turned their attention to Scotland. In an effort to establish the Church of England in Scotland, the king and the archbishop tried to force the Calvinist Church of Scotland to accept the Church of England's prayer book. The Scots rejected the new prayer book and formed a National Covenant, or agreement, in which they pledged to preserve their religious freedom. Outraged by the king's actions, they were prepared to go to war to do so.

Beginnings of the Civil War

By 1640 the Scots had invaded England. In dire need of money, Charles was forced to recall a Parliament that he had ignored for 11 years. The members of Parliament, however, refused to discuss anything without first voicing their complaints about Charles's handling of religious and political issues. As a result, Charles dissolved this Parliament, known as the Short Parliament, after only 3 weeks.

Charles became so desperate for money that he had no choice but to summon Parliament once again. By this time members of Parliament were seething with anger and demanded to voice their complaints to the king. Controlled by Puritans, this session of Parliament, called the Long Parliament, would meet for almost 20 years.

The Long Parliament was determined to decrease Charles's power. The members abolished the special courts used to imprison Charles's opponents and passed a law requiring Parliament to be called every 3 years. They ended all forms of illegal taxation and jailed and later executed the hated Archbishop Laud.

While Parliament convened, trouble erupted in **Ireland**. Relations between England and Ireland had been strained since the 1100s. The Irish people remained Roman Catholic and refused to accept the Church of England. What angered the Irish most was the continuing English practice of seizing land from Irish owners and giving it to English and Scottish settlers. In 1641 the Irish rebelled. Faced with rebellion in both Scotland and Ireland, Charles was at the mercy of the Puritan-controlled Parliament.

538 Chapter 21 *English and American Revolutions*

MEETING SPECIAL NEEDS ACTIVITY

Learning Style: Visual/Spatial Collect several portraits of Charles I and Oliver Cromwell for students to analyze. Ask students to list the appearance, characteristics, qualities, and interests of each man as shown in their portraits. Let students discuss similarities and differences that they notice between the two men. Finally, ask students how their differences led to the conflict of the English Civil War. **L1 LEP**

As the Puritans grew stronger, a royalist, or pro-monarchy, group formed in Parliament. It was made up of people who supported the king and opposed Puritan control of the Church of England. As time went on, debates between Puritans and royalists became more heated.

Despite resistance by the royalists, Parliament in June 1642 sent Charles "Nineteen Propositions" that made Parliament the supreme power in England. Charles, however, refused to agree to its demands. With a dramatic personal appearance, Charles led troops into the House of Commons and attempted to arrest five of its leaders. The five were hidden and protected from capture. The king's use of force meant there could be no compromise. Both Charles and Parliament prepared for war.

The English Civil War

Charles gathered an army that included nobles and landowners in the north and west of the country. They were called **the Cavaliers** because many belonged to the king's cavalry, or armed horsemen. Supporters of Parliament and Puritans drew their strength from the south and east of England. They were called **the Roundheads** because many of them had close-cropped hair.

Parliament organized its military forces under the leadership of **Oliver Cromwell**. His rigorous training and firm discipline led to several decisive victories. After nearly four years of conflict, the royalist armies surrendered in May 1646. Parliament had won complete control of the English government. The Puritans removed their remaining opponents from Parliament, leaving behind what was known as the Rump Parliament.

After a failed attempt to escape from his enemies, Charles surrendered in 1647. The army then tried, sentenced, and executed the king in 1649. It was a shocking moment for many English people, no matter how they felt about Charles.

A New Government

After the execution, the Rump Parliament ended the monarchy and set up a republic known as a commonwealth, a state ruled by elected representatives. The new government faced much opposition. Cromwell's army crushed royalist uprisings in Scotland and Ireland. Many of Ireland's Catholic majority were killed or lost lands to Protestant landlords. In England, Cromwell and his officers later suppressed the Levellers, a group wanting the vote for all men.

Overseas, the republic's mercantilist policies advanced English trade. The Navigation Act (1651) required that imports be brought to England in English ships or in ships of the country producing the goods. This law angered the Dutch, who had grown rich from carrying goods to England on their ships. During the 1650s, however, English military victories over the Dutch and later the Spanish heightened England's position as a European power.

At home, Cromwell dismissed the ineffectual Rump Parliament and placed England under military rule, with himself as Lord Protector. Cromwell's government granted religious freedom to all non-Anglican Protestants, but enforced Puritan rules requiring people to attend church and to avoid drinking, swearing, and gambling. When Cromwell died in 1658, his son Richard was unable to maintain the government. Most English people were tired of military rule and unhappy with Puritan restrictions. In 1660 a newly elected Parliament restored the monarchy under Charles I's son, Charles II. Representative government and individual rights would survive, however. No English monarch would ever be able to claim absolute power again.

SECTION 1 ASSESSMENT

Main Idea
1. Use a diagram like the one below to identify causes of the English Civil War.

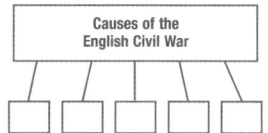

Causes of the English Civil War

Recall
2. **Define** divine right, martial law, royalist, commonwealth.
3. **Identify** James I, the Puritans, Charles I, Petition of Right, William Laud, the Cavaliers, the Roundheads, Oliver Cromwell.

Critical Thinking
4. **Analyzing Information** How did Elizabeth I, James I, and Charles I differ in getting what they wanted from Parliament? Whose methods were more effective? Why?

Understanding Themes
5. **Conflict** What problems did Parliament face before the English Civil War? After the war? Did Parliament achieve its political goals?

ASSESS

Check for Understanding

Assign Section 1 Assessment as homework or as an in-class activity.

◉ Use Interactive Tutor Self-Assessment Software to review Section 1.

Evaluate

🗁 Section Quiz 21-1

◉ Use the Testmaker to create a customized quiz for Section 1.

Reteach

Organize students into groups of six. Give each group six slips of paper with one of these roles on each slip: *James I, Charles I, Oliver Cromwell, a Puritan, a Cavalier,* and *Archbishop Laud.* Let students play charades with the roles on these slips of paper.

🗁 Reading Essentials and Study Guide 21-1

Enrich

Have students write a report comparing the structure of government under Charles I with government under Cromwell as Lord Protector.

CLOSE

Have students create a flowchart that traces events in England from 1603 to 1658.

SECTION 1 ASSESSMENT ANSWERS

1. Parliament opposed policies of James I; unsettled religious issues; Charles I dissolved Parliament; martial law under Charles I; Petition of Right limited king's power; Puritans persecuted; Long Parliament wanted to decrease Charles's power
2. All terms are defined in the Glossary.
3. James I, 536; the Puritans, 537; Charles I, 537; Petition of Right, 538; William Laud, 538; the Cavaliers, 539; the Roundheads, 539; Oliver Cromwell, 539
4. Elizabeth worked with Parliament; James I and Charles I insisted on their divine right as kings. Elizabeth's methods were more successful; Parliament usually did what she wanted whereas the Stuarts brought England into a civil war.
5. **CONFLICT** Answers will vary. Possible answer: No. Before the English Civil War, Parliament faced problems with an overbearing monarchy. After the war, it had to contend with Cromwell's autocratic rule.

1650   1700   1750

1688 The Glorious Revolution brings William III and Mary II to the English throne.

1707 The Act of Union unites England and Scotland.

1714 George I becomes king of Great Britain.

Section 2

A King Returns to the Throne

Guide to Reading

Read to Find Out
Main Idea *England established a constitutional monarchy.*

▶ **Terms to Define**
constitutional monarchy, habeas corpus, cabinet, prime minister

▶ **People to Meet**
Charles II, the Whigs, the Tories, William III, Mary II, George I, Sir Robert Walpole

▶ **Places to Locate**
London

The **Storyteller**

"What pillars and arches to be pulled down! What new ones to be erected! What scaffold and engines to lay the foundation of an endless and incalculable future expenditure." The authorities in charge of restoring St. Paul's Cathedral believed Christopher Wren's designs went too far and would cost too much. Just when it seemed as though the great architect would have to change his plans, disaster changed everything. In the Great Fire of London, buildings were demolished overnight. At St. Paul's Cathedral, heated stones flew like grenades and lead ran in rivers down the streets. Wren would design a new cathedral.

—adapted from *The Architecture of Wren*, Kerry Downes, 1982

Christopher Wren

As the son of Charles I, **Charles II** had faced danger throughout the English Civil War and Cromwell's rule. He risked death on the battlefield as he joined the royalist forces in their fight and in their defeat. He saw his father imprisoned and put to death. He narrowly escaped his own capture and execution by disguising himself as a servant and fleeing to the European continent.

In Europe, Charles wandered from country to country. While some European rulers received him as royalty, others threatened him with arrest as a fugitive. In his own country, the Puritans kept a close watch on Charles. Since he was the direct heir to the English throne, Charles posed a threat to their political power. By the time Parliament had restored the monarchy, Charles had learned a good deal about pleasing people he needed for support and safety. Charles willingly accepted a change from the absolute power of his ancestors.

The Merry Monarch

When Charles II returned to **London**, on May 29, 1660, the English people celebrated wildly. They felt released from a violent, unstable period followed by harsh Puritan rule. A court member described the happiness of the English people as they rejoiced in a lavish parade marking the king's return:

❝ **A triumph of above 20,000 horse and foot soldiers, brandishing their swords and shouting with inexpressible joy; the ways strewed with flowers, the bells ringing, the streets hung with tapestry, fountains running with wine.... I stood and beheld it, and blessed God.** ❞

This period, in which the House of Stuart was returned to the throne, is called the Restoration. In contrast to the severe and religious rule of Cromwell, Charles II was known as the Merry Monarch. He loved parties, games, and witty conversation. He supported the arts, science, and entertainment. People once again danced and enjoyed sports and theater. Charles married a Portuguese princess; and though they had no children, he fathered illegitimate children by his mistresses.

Dealing With Religious Questions

Outwardly, Charles was a member of the Church of England; secretly, however, he favored Catholicism. Although hoping for religious toleration, the king recognized that the settlement of England's religious divisions rested on Parliament. During the 1660s, the largely royalist Cavalier Parliament passed the Clarendon Code, a series of laws that made the Church of England once again the state religion. Only Church of England members could attend the universities, serve in Parliament, or hold religious services. Hundreds of Puritan clergy were driven from their churches.

During this time of troubles for the Puritans, the Puritan writer John Milton wrote *Paradise Lost* (1667), generally considered to be the greatest epic poem in the English language. *Paradise Lost* retells the biblical story of creation, the devil's revolt against God, and the fall of Adam and Eve.

Limiting Royal Power

In addition to its anti-Puritan policies, Parliament kept limits on royal power. All laws that Charles I had accepted, such as the Petition of Right, were still in effect. The Restoration thus gave England a constitutional monarchy, a form of government in which the monarch's powers are limited by a constitution. Rather than being a single document, however, England's constitution was made up of many documents—such as the Magna Carta and the Petition of Right—plus other laws and customs. Although Charles II disagreed with some of the reforms he never fought Parliament forcefully. Charles was determined to avoid his father's fate.

The French ambassador to England was astonished at the mood of the country. In France, the king had absolute power. The ambassador commented

---

The Arts

Rebuilding London

In 1666 a major fire destroyed much of London. Over the next decades, it was rebuilt as a beautiful capital. One of the men chosen to work on the commission rebuilding the city was Christopher Wren, a noted mathematician and astronomer at Oxford University. He is best known, however, as the architect of St. Paul's Cathedral, a London landmark begun in 1675.

The new St. Paul's Cathedral was the first major church built for Anglican worship, and Wren designed it to be an impressive, monumental structure. He used classical and baroque styles to produce a cathedral that combined orderliness with dramatic visual effects. Wren also designed other architecturally attractive churches for the city.

During World War II, the area around

St. Paul's Cathedral

St. Paul's Cathedral was heavily bombed by the German air force. St. Paul's was spared extensive damage, but other Wren churches were among the many buildings destroyed. Since then, heavily bombed areas, including some of these churches, have been rebuilt.

Today, skyscrapers rather than churches dominate the landscape of central London. As the city has built upward, it has also spread outward. A number of new towns have arisen in outlying areas, separated from central London by a greenbelt, a wide band of open country.

Linking Past and Present ACTIVITY

Discuss how Christopher Wren contributed to the architecture of London in the 1600s. How has the city's appearance changed since World War II? In what ways is London like, or unlike, other modern cities?

COOPERATIVE LEARNING ACTIVITY

Documentary Assign the class the task of producing a documentary television show about the London fire of 1666. Have students choose a producer to coordinate the class project. Then organize the class into teams. Have teams research, write, and present "hard news" about the fire, such as its origin, how far it spread, number of casualties, buildings destroyed, or plans for rebuilding. Ask other teams to prepare on-the-scene features about the fire, such as interviews with local residents, firefighters, or government officials. If possible, videotape the presentation for the basis of a class discussion later. **L2**

TEACH

Guided Practice

THEME Change

On the chalkboard, write the following column headings: *Monarchy's Power, Parliament's Power, Religious Problems*. Then write these row headings: *Charles II, James II, William and Mary, Anne, George I, George II*. Help students complete the chart to show how England's government changed between 1660 and 1760. **L1 LEP**

Critical Thinking Lead a discussion about why the English reestablished the monarchy yet limited the ruler's power through a constitutional monarchy. **L2**

 World History and Art Transparency 28, *Blue Boy*

Linking Past and Present

Rebuilding London

London builders and craftsmen took more than 30 years to complete St. Paul's Cathedral. The dome, its most famous feature, has an inner dome and a much taller outer dome. Light enters the cathedral through an opening in the middle of the inner dome.

ANSWERS

Christopher Wren built St. Paul's Cathedral and many other Anglican churches in London, combining baroque and classical styles. After World War II bombings, many areas of London were rebuilt; skyscrapers came to dominate churches; answers will vary, but should mention that like other modern cities, London has expanded upward and outward.

WORLD HISTORY Online

Have students use the **Chapter 21 Student Web Activity** at worldhistory.glencoe.com for in-depth study of Christopher Wren.

Independent Practice

 Guided Reading Activity 21-2 **L1**

Government Have students research to prepare a chart that compares rights in the English Bill of Rights with those in the United States Bill of Rights. Ask students to indicate on their charts the rights common to both countries' bills of rights. **L2**

CURRICULUM CONNECTION

EDUCATION

The College of William and Mary, founded in 1693 in Williamsburg, Virginia, was named for England's king and queen. It is the second oldest institution of higher learning in the United States. Harvard University is the oldest.

you don't say...

Tory comes from an Irish word for "robber" or "royalist outlaw." During the fight for the Exclusion Bill, Tory became an unflattering term for people who supported the monarchy and the Church of England.

 Religious Revolution in the Colonies

Maryland, 1689

The colony of Maryland had been founded as a refuge for Roman Catholics, with religious freedom for all people. Maryland Protestants resented having Roman Catholic Charles Calvert as the colony's owner. In 1689 Protestants took over Maryland and passed anti-Catholic legislation. The laws required children of mixed marriages to be raised as Protestants and imposed fines for sending children to Catholic schools abroad.

Maryland

on the changes in England in a letter to the French king, Louis XIV:

    66 This government has a monarchical appearance because there is a King, but at bottom it is far from being a monarchy.... The members of Parliament are ... allowed to speak their mind freely.... **99**

While the English celebrated the end of Puritan rule, two disasters struck. In 1665 the plague returned to London, killing about 100,000 people. Later, a raging fire destroyed much of London. Some people falsely blamed Catholics for setting the fire as part of a plan to gain control of the country.

Establishing Political Parties

Opposition to Catholicism helped to spark the growth of England's first political parties. The parties grew out of a debate over who would succeed Charles as the king of England. Because Charles had no legitimate children, James II, Charles's brother, was next in line to be king. James, who was a practicing Catholic, ignited the fears of a revival of Catholic power in England.

In 1679 Parliament tried to pass the Exclusion Bill, which would have kept James from becoming

 WORLD HISTORY Online

Student Web Activity 21

Visit the *World History: The Human Experience* Web site at **worldhistory.glencoe.com** and click on *Chapter 21—Student Web Activities* for an activity relating to Christopher Wren.

---

king. Those members of Parliament who wanted to exclude James from the throne were known as **the Whigs**. Those who defended the hereditary monarchy were referred to as **the Tories**.

In a compromise, the Tories agreed to defeat the Exclusion Bill by accepting another bill supported by the Whigs. The Whig-proposed bill established the principle of habeas corpus as law. According to habeas corpus, a person could not be held in prison without just cause or without a trial. It was another step that increased individual rights and reduced those of the Crown.

A Bloodless Revolt

When Charles II died in 1685, James II became king, effectively ending the peaceful relations between Parliament and the Crown. James wanted absolute power and claimed the right to suspend the law. Ignoring Parliament's religious laws, James appointed Catholics to government and university positions. He also allowed free worship by all Christians.

The Glorious Revolution

These actions alarmed many of the members of Parliament, but they tried to be patient. They were waiting for James to die and pass the throne to his Protestant daughter Mary, who was married to William of Orange, the ruler of the Netherlands.

In 1688, however, a royal birth prompted Parliament to take action. James's second wife bore a son, who would be raised a Catholic. He would inherit the throne, rather than Mary. Whig and Tory leaders united against James and invited William to invade England and take over the Crown. James fled to France when he realized he had little support in England. **William III** and **Mary II** gained the English throne without battles or bloodshed. This peaceful transfer of power was so welcome and so different from previous struggles that the English called it the Glorious Revolution.

New Limits on Royal Power

At previous coronations, English kings and queens had sworn to observe the laws and customs established by their royal ancestors. In 1689, however, William and Mary swore an oath that they would govern the people of England "according to the statutes in Parliament agreed upon, and the laws and customs of the same."

In that same year, Parliament further strengthened its power by passing the Bill of Rights. According to the Bill of Rights, the king could not

---

raise taxes or maintain an army without the consent of Parliament and could not suspend laws. Further, it declared that Parliament should be held often and that there should be freedom of debate in sessions of Parliament.

The Bill of Rights also guaranteed certain individual rights. It guaranteed the right to a trial by jury, outlawed cruel and unusual punishment for a crime, and limited the amount of bail money that could be required for a person to be temporarily released while awaiting trial. Citizens were given the right to appeal to the monarch and to speak freely in Parliament.

In 1689 the exiled James II landed in Ireland and led Irish Catholics in a revolt to recapture the Crown. Although the uprising failed a year later, English Protestants controlling Irish affairs began to exclude the Catholic majority in Ireland from government and business. This action only deepened the hatred Irish Catholics had for English policies.

Anti-Catholic feelings throughout the country also led the English Parliament in London to pass more legislation limiting the Crown's power. In the Act of Settlement (1701), Parliament excluded any Catholic from inheriting the English throne.

Parliament and the Crown

The Bill of Rights and the Act of Settlement made it clear that Parliament had won the long battle with the Crown. England was still a monarchy, but a king or queen could not rule without Parliament's consent.

England was not yet a true democracy, however. Although members of the House of Commons were elected, only male property owners—250,000 people out of 6 million, or 4 percent of the population—had the right to vote. Members of the House of Commons were not paid, so only the wealthy could afford to run for office. Parliament was controlled by people of property—nobles, gentry, wealthy merchants, and clergy.

Succession and Union

The power of Parliament further increased when Mary's sister Anne succeeded William in 1702. (Mary had died in 1694.) At the same time, Parliament had to establish a new order of succession to the throne. Since Anne had no living children to succeed her, she would be succeeded by the children of Sophia, a Protestant granddaughter of James I. Sophia was married to the German elector, or ruler, of Hanover. In short, the English throne

would pass to the heirs or heiresses from the German House of Hanover.

Yet there still remained a danger that the Scots might prefer a Stuart monarch to a member of the House of Hanover. Parliament also feared that the Scots would form an alliance with France against England. After negotiations with the Scots, who were militarily and economically weak, the two governments signed the Act of Union in 1707. It united the two countries into a new nation called Great Britain. Both the English and the Scots would now be "British." Although the Scots gave up their own parliament, they were given representation in the English Parliament. Scotland also retained its own Calvinist religion, and its own laws, courts, and educational system as well.

Visualizing History In 1688 Parliament presented the Crown of England to William and Mary. *Why did Parliament decide to give the Crown to the royal couple?*

Visualizing History Sixteen years before the Glorious Revolution, William had gained control of the Netherlands through another revolution. Although by right of birth the office of stadtholder should have been his (his father held it), it had fallen into the hands of Jan de Witt. A revolution in 1672 made William stadtholder.

Answer to Caption: *Parliament wanted England to have Protestant rulers instead of Catholic.*

ASSESS

Check for Understanding

Assign Section 2 Assessment as homework or as an in-class activity.

■ Use Interactive Tutor Self-Assessment Software to review Section 2.

MAKING CONNECTIONS ACTIVITY

The Arts After the long winter of Puritan rule, the arts blossomed in England during the Restoration period. Have students choose an area of the arts, such as architecture, drama, furniture design, music, or painting, and prepare an oral report about it in England from 1660 to 1760. Tell students to describe important people and works, how the works reflected the times, and whether these people and works have any impact on the arts today. Suggest that students illustrate their reports. Then display the illustrations on a classroom bulletin board. **L2**

Visualizing History
Robert Walpole wears a powdered wig in this portrait. This fashion spread from France to England in the late 1600s. Men with short hair did not want to be mistaken for Roundheads. **Answer to Caption:** *prime minister*

Evaluate

 Section Quiz 21-2

🖵 Use the Testmaker to create a customized quiz for Section 2.

Reteach

Have students discuss the evolution of England's constitutional monarchy from 1660 to 1760.

 Reading Essentials and Study Guide 21-2

Enrich

Have students write a research report on one of England's literary figures of this period, such as Alexander Pope, Jonathan Swift, Daniel Defoe, Richard Steele, or Joseph Addison.

CLOSE

Ask students to create a time line that includes important events and people discussed in Section 2. Have students write a brief explanation next to each event or person.

Visualizing History
Sir Robert Walpole directed policy as the leading cabinet official. *What title did the main cabinet official earn?*

Political Parties and the Cabinet

During Anne's reign (1702–1714), Parliament's political powers continued to increase. Anne was unskilled in British politics and sought guidance from a cabinet, a small group of advisers selected from the House of Commons. Because a cabinet made up of both Whigs and Tories often quarreled, it became the custom to choose cabinet members only from the party holding a majority of the seats in Parliament.

Anne died in 1714, and Sophia's son **George I** took the throne according to the Act of Settlement. George had been raised in Germany, and did not speak English very well.

George I relied on the cabinet more than Anne had. Eventually, **Sir Robert Walpole**, the leader of the Whigs, gained control of the cabinet. Walpole's position as head of the cabinet was later called prime minister, the chief executive of a parliamentary government. Walpole remained prime minister when a new king, George II, took the throne in 1727. With the king's encouragement, Walpole gradually took over many political responsibilities: managing finances, appointing government officials, and requesting the passage of laws. He helped avoid wars and allowed the North American colonies to grow without interference from the British government.

In 1760 George III, grandson of George II, became king at the age of 22. George III greatly expanded the British Empire through victory in a war against France. Great Britain gained Canada and all of France's territory east of the Mississippi River. The cost of waging the war—and the ways in which George III and his ministers tried to deal with that cost—would eventually lead to rebellion in Great Britain's American colonies.

SECTION 2 ASSESSMENT

Main Idea
1. Use a diagram like the one below to show the steps by which England established a constitutional monarchy.

How England Established Constitutional Monarchy	A.
	B.
	C.
	D.
	E.

Recall
2. **Define** constitutional monarchy, habeas corpus, cabinet, prime minister.
3. **Identify** Charles II, the Restoration, the Whigs, the Tories, William III, Mary II, Bill of Rights, George I, Sir Robert Walpole.

Critical Thinking
4. **Analyzing Information** How did the power of William and Mary compare with that of Charles II? How had Parliament's powers expanded by the time of William and Mary?

Understanding Themes
5. **Change** What individual rights were gained under constitutional monarchy?

SECTION 2 ASSESSMENT ANSWERS

1. House of Stuart returned to throne; Church of England state religion; Parliament kept limits on royal power; Bill of Rights, Act of Settlement, Act of Union passed; monarch relied on Cabinet headed by prime minister; political parties established

2. All terms are defined in the Glossary.
3. Charles II, 540; the Restoration, 541; the Whigs, 542; the Tories, 542; William III, 542; Mary II, 542; Bill of Rights, 542; George I, 544; Sir Robert Walpole, 544
4. Charles II accepted the Petition of Right and agreed not to be involved in church

affairs; William and Mary agreed to rule only with Parliament's consent.

5. **CHANGE** Individuals gained the right to a fair trial, freedom from cruel and unusual punishment, and the right to speak freely in Parliament.

c. 1730 Colonial assemblies win the right to limit royal governors' salaries.

1754 The French and Indian War begins.

1763 British proclamation bans colonial settlement west of the Appalachians.

1774 First Continental Congress meets in Philadelphia.

Section 3

Road to Revolt

Read to Find Out

Main Idea *Certain factors led to disagreement and eventual conflict between the British and the American colonies.*

▶ **Terms to Define**
duty, direct tax, boycott

▶ **People to Meet**
George Grenville, George III, John Adams, Patrick Henry, George Washington, Samuel Adams

▶ **Places to Locate**
New York City, Boston, Philadelphia

The Storyteller

Boston's newspapers announced that a ship bearing tea would arrive soon. All over town, this handbill appeared: "Friends! Brethren! Country–men! That worst of plagues, the detested tea, shipped for this port by the East India Company, is now arrived in this harbor; the hour of destruction or manly opposition to the machinations [schemes] of tyranny stares you in the face; every friend ... is now called upon ... to make a united and successful resistance. Boston, November 29, 1773."

—adapted from *Tea Leaves, Being a Collection of Letters and Documents Relating to the Shipment of Tea to the American Colonies ...*, 1970

Boston Tea Party

hile Great Britain struggled through civil war and a changing government, its colonies in America changed as well. By the mid-1700s, 13 colonies thrived on the eastern coast of North America. As more people migrated to North America to escape religious persecution or to gain a new start in life, the population of the colonies grew to more than 1.5 million by 1763.

Since most of the colonists were British, they shared a common language and political background. Although many radical political ideas—ideas about republicanism, universal suffrage, liberty, and equality—had died out in Great Britain, many political radicals had fled to the colonies. Here the old ideas stayed alive. In the colonies, there was no aristocracy. The hardships of life on the frontier and the easy availability of land tended to blur class divisions. Each American colony had a representative assembly, much like Parliament in Great Britain, and the colonists were used to governing themselves.

The British Empire in America

Except for regulating trade, the British government generally left the colonies alone. In the British mercantilist view, the American colonies were valuable to Great Britain only to the extent that they benefited British trade. The role of the colonies was to produce goods—mostly raw materials—that could not be produced in Great Britain, and to provide markets for British manufactured goods.

By the early 1700s, the colonies pulsated with economic activity. In the South, plantations produced tobacco, rice, and indigo with the labor of thousands of enslaved Africans. Settlers in the rich farming land of the Middle Colonies grew enough food to feed their families and trade throughout the year. New England colonists turned to the sea because of their poor soil and harsh climate. In 1673

Chapter 21 *English and American Revolutions* **545**

TEACH

Guided Practice

THEME Conflict

Have students recall acts of Parliament that caused conflicts in the colonies. *(Stamp Act, Declaratory Act, Intolerable Acts, Quebec Act, tax on tea)* Encourage students to discuss why the colonists disliked these acts. *(Colonists were not represented in Parliament.)* **L1 LEP**

Cause and Effect Help students make a flowchart on the chalkboard that shows the sequence of cause and effect from the Stamp Act to the First Continental Congress. *(For example: the Stamp Act caused colonists to call the Stamp Act Congress, whose actions in turn caused Parliament to repeal the Stamp Act.)* **L3**

Biography®

The following videotape programs are available from Glencoe:

- **King George III: Mad or Maligned?**
- **Patrick Henry: Voice of Liberty**

Who?What?Where?When?

Colony Names The colonies of Maryland, Virginia, North and South Carolina, and Georgia were named after the following English rulers: Henrietta Maria, wife of Charles I; Elizabeth I, who was known as the Virgin Queen; Charles I and Charles II; and George II.

---

a sea captain described busy Boston Harbor, reporting that "ships arrive dayly from Spain, France, Holland & Canarys bringing all sorts of wine, linens, silks, and fruits, which they transport to all the other plantations...."

To protect this profitable trade with its colonies, Parliament passed a series of Navigation Acts in the 1600s. According to these laws, the colonists were required to export certain products only to Great Britain or to other British colonies. In addition, all goods going to the colonies had to first pass through Great Britain, where a duty, or tax, had to be paid before shipment to the colonies. Finally, all goods going to or coming from the colonies were to be carried by ships built in British or colonial ports.

The colonists did not suffer as much as one might imagine from the effects these laws had on trade. Actually, the Navigation Acts had some benefits. Some colonies were able to develop a strong shipping industry, and some businesses grew prosperous in the absence of foreign competition. Moreover, the British government was never able to adequately enforce these laws. Smuggling goods in and out of ports along the coast became a major part of colonial trade.

Colonial Political Power

As people in the colonies grew more settled and economically secure, they also became more involved in their government. Most of the colonies were managed by a governor appointed by the king. The royal governor then appointed judges and other officials, but each colony also had an elected assembly. Voting in the colonies was restricted to men who owned property or paid taxes, as it was in Great Britain. In the colonies, however, it was much easier to acquire land. A much greater percentage of the population therefore could vote for their government.

The assemblies often struggled with the royal governors for power in the same way that Parliament and the Crown struggled in Great

Images *of the* Times

Colonial America

The colonies became prosperous and began to drift away from Great Britain. When the British Parliament tried to take control, Americans revolted.

A creche doll with a wooden face and glass inset eyes looked much like an adult. Colonists treated their children as miniature adults.

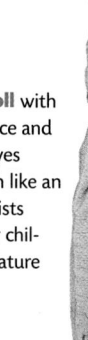

A New England dame school fulfilled the Massachusetts General Court's requirement for public school financed by taxes.

546

Images *of the* Times — Colonial America

Teaching children how to read so they could understand the Bible on their own was the main purpose of early New England schools. The *New England Primer*, the principal textbook, taught children their ABC's starting with "Adam" and ending with "Zaccheus." Prayers were also part of the *New England Primer*. Both boys and girls went to dame schools. When it came time to learn how to write, however, the boys advanced to grammar schools, whereas education ended for most girls.

Britain. These power struggles were often over money. In the early 1700s assemblies won the right to limit the salaries of governors and judges. If a governor would not do as colonists desired, the assembly would reduce or withhold his salary for the next year. In 1731 the New Hampshire assembly refused to pay the governor's salary for five years.

The assemblies also held fast to their right to approve any taxes requested by the Crown or governors. This issue would become a central point of conflict between the colonies and Great Britain. Just as the British Parliament had fought hard for its right to approve or refuse any taxes, so too would the American colonists.

Tightening Colonial Controls

A bitter rivalry between Great Britain and France for territory in North America would eventually lead the British government to interfere more actively in the colonial economy. A dispute over French and British land claims in North America as well as rights to the rich North American fur trade led France and Great Britain to war in 1754. The conflict, called the French and Indian War, brought French troops and French Canadian colonists against British forces and the American colonists. Some Native Americans fought on behalf of the British, while others supported the French.

After six years of war, the British-led forces finally defeated the French in 1760. Three years later, a treaty was signed in Paris. Under the treaty's terms, Great Britain acquired nearly all of France's possessions in North America, including Canada and lands in the area that lay west of the Appalachian Mountains.

Great Britain's empire had grown both in size and in power, but at a considerable cost. The war strained the British economy, and defending the huge new lands they had gained would cost the British even more.

George Grenville, whom **George III** appointed First Lord of the Treasury in 1763, took the first

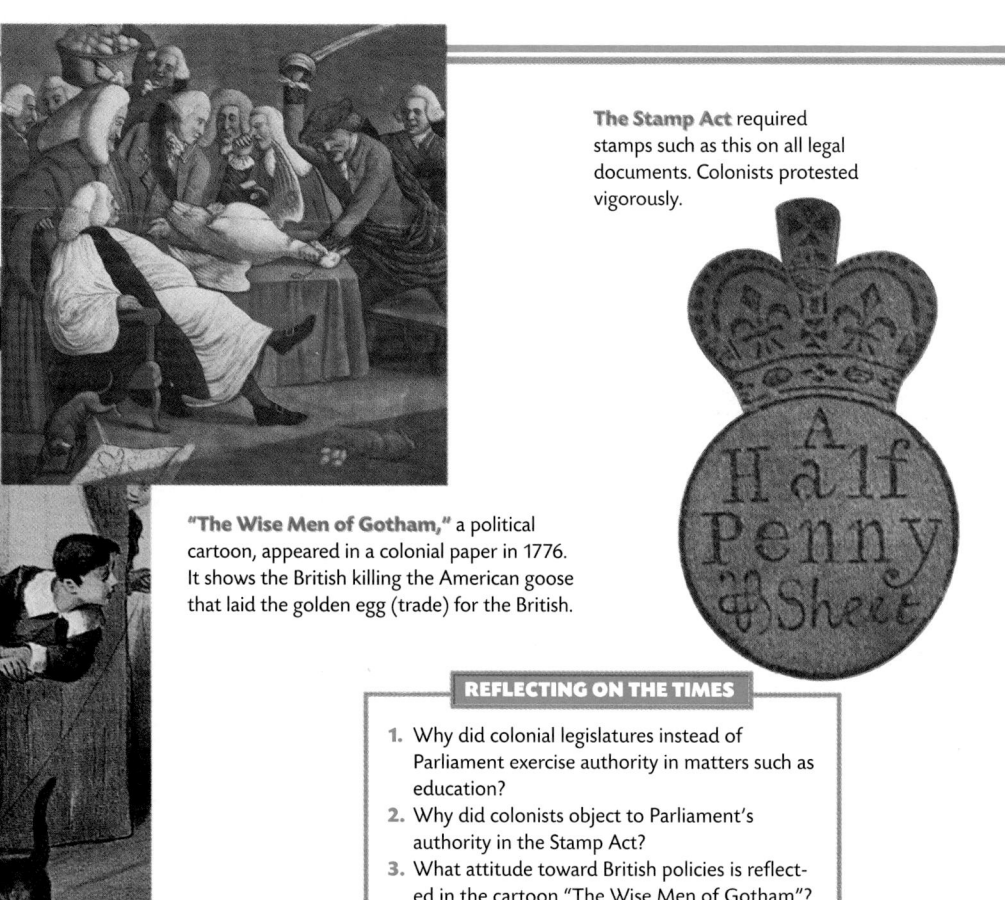

"The Wise Men of Gotham," a political cartoon, appeared in a colonial paper in 1776. It shows the British killing the American goose that laid the golden egg (trade) for the British.

The Stamp Act required stamps such as this on all legal documents. Colonists protested vigorously.

REFLECTING ON THE TIMES

1. Why did colonial legislatures instead of Parliament exercise authority in matters such as education?
2. Why did colonists object to Parliament's authority in the Stamp Act?
3. What attitude toward British policies is reflected in the cartoon "The Wise Men of Gotham"?

547

📁 Geography and History Activity 21

🎵 World Music: Cultural Traditions, Lesson 1

Independent Practice

📁 Guided Reading Activity 21-3 **L1**

Economics Have students write paragraphs explaining why Great Britain wanted to control colonial imports and exports. *(to protect colonial trade from competition with other countries)* **L2**

Foreign Affairs Have students use outside resources to write an essay on why the French believed they had a right to the land in the Ohio Valley during the French and Indian War. **L3**

Who?What?**Where?**When?

Paris has served as the site for the signing of several peace treaties. In addition to the treaty that ended the French and Indian War, the treaties that ended both the American Revolution and United States involvement in the Vietnam War were signed there. The treaty that ended World War I was signed at Versailles, a few miles from Paris.

Global Gourmet

America Native Americans invented succotash, a stew made of corn, lima beans, and meat from bears or wild birds. Colonists soon learned how to make this one-dish meal.

Visualizing History Bitter feelings erupted in bloodshed on March 5, 1770, in Boston, when British soldiers fired into a crowd and killed five people. This incident became known to the colonists as the Boston Massacre. *What happened as a result of the unrest in Boston?*

Who?What?Where?When?

John Peter Zenger In the early 1700s, colonial newspapers did not criticize government officials. When John Peter Zenger's *New York Weekly Journal* printed letters against New York's governor, Zenger was arrested. When Zenger's lawyer produced evidence proving the truth of the criticisms, a jury acquitted Zenger. Zenger's acquittal is usually viewed as the first American case to uphold freedom of the press.

ASSESS

Check for Understanding

Assign Section 3 Assessment as homework or as an in-class activity.

 Use Interactive Tutor Self-Assessment Software to review Section 3.

Evaluate

Section Quiz 21-3

Use the Testmaker to create a customized quiz for Section 3.

---

steps to solve these problems. Grenville issued a proclamation that said the colonists could not, for the time being, settle in the lands west of the Appalachians. This move, he hoped, would avoid wars with Native Americans until Great Britain had the area under control and could gradually open the land to settlers. The colonists, however, were eager to build new settlements in the west, and they were outraged by this attempt to stop them.

Grenville also believed that colonists should help pay the costs of their own defense. He began raising money by enforcing the Navigation Acts with the British navy. British warships hunted down smugglers, who were then tried in British military courts rather than in colonial courts. Another new law allowed British troops to be housed in colonists' homes.

It was the Stamp Act, however, that most infuriated the colonists. Passed in 1765, the Stamp Act was different from previous tax measures because it was a direct tax—a tax paid directly to the government rather than being included in the price of goods. It required that all printed materials, from newspapers and shipping documents to playing cards, bear a stamp to show that a tax had been paid to Great Britain. Colonial lawyers, tavern owners, merchants, and printers were most affected by the Stamp Act.

Colonial Protests

Colonists reacted to these measures quickly. They protested with a boycott—a refusal to buy British goods. They attacked stamp agents and burned stamps in the streets. In 1765 nine colonies sent 28 representatives to a Stamp Act Congress in

New York City. The Congress resolved that Parliament could not tax the colonies because the colonies did not have representatives in Parliament. They rallied under the cry "No taxation without representation!" and insisted that only their own colonial assemblies had the right to tax them. The British Parliament repealed the Stamp Act in 1766. The struggle for control of the colonies, however, had begun in earnest. **John Adams**, a colonial leader from Massachusetts, wrote in his diary:

> 66 The people have become more attentive to their liberties, ... and more determined to defend them.... Our presses have groaned, our pulpits have thundered, our legislatures have resolved, our towns have voted; the crown officers have everywhere trembled, and all their little tools and creatures been afraid to speak and ashamed to be seen. 99

Unrest in Boston

The British Parliament reasserted its right to pass laws governing the colonies in the Declaratory Act of 1766. The next year Great Britain placed new taxes on glass, lead, paper, and tea coming into the colonies. Royal agents trying to enforce these laws pleaded for British soldiers to protect them from the angry colonists.

In 1770 the first clash between the Americans and British troops took place. Two regiments of British troops had been sent to **Boston** to support the governor. One evening a squad of soldiers was harassed by a Boston crowd throwing snowballs and rotten eggs. Gunfire erupted, and five people died in what became known as the Boston Massacre.

Because of the unrest in Boston, Parliament repealed most of the taxes but kept the tax on tea.

COOPERATIVE LEARNING ACTIVITY

Posters Organize the class into small groups to research and make posters about colonial scientists, doctors, and inventors, such as John Lining, John Winthrop, Benjamin Franklin, James Logan, Benjamin Banneker, Samuel Higby, Thomas Cadwalader, David Rittenhouse, or others that students choose. Ask students to include written information and illustrations about these people's lives, discoveries, and inventions on their posters. When each group has decided on a subject, the tasks of research, writing, and illustration should be divided up among group members. Have students display completed posters around the classroom. Allow time for students to examine the posters and write one interesting fact that they learned from each poster. **L2**

Anne S. K. Brown Military Collection, Brown University Library

Tarred and Feathered

This 1774 British cartoon depicting the tarring and feathering of a British customs officer made a simple point: The American rebels were not men of goodwill simply petitioning parliamentary representation. The American [colonis]ts, the cartoon implied, were revolutionaries [deter]mined to upset the prevailing order in both the [Ame]ricas and Europe.

[In] January 1774 a mob took a customs officer [name]d John Malcolm, tarred and feathered him, and beat him with clubs and ropes until he agreed to speak against His Majesty's government. Even then the mob did not let him go but led him half-naked through the snow for four hours. By then the skin hung off his back in strips and his body was frozen solid—or so the British governor of Massachusetts wrote in his report to the British secretary of state. The men of Massachusetts thus earned a reputation for violence and disorder. The cartoon of Malcolm's ordeal made good anticolonial propaganda in Great Britain, and the idea of hot tar on human flesh still sears our imaginations with the violence of the Revolutionary period. ⊕

Chapter 21 *English and American Revolutions* **549**

TEACH

Tell students that the Boston Tea Party took place on December 16, 1773, and that this British cartoon is a response to that event. Have students carefully examine the cartoon. What activity is going on in the background? *(the Boston Tea Party)* What other colonial protest is referred to in the cartoon? *(protest against the Stamp Act)* What do you think the noose hanging from the tree might have symbolized? *(that the cause of liberty might require that people die)*

Linking Past and Present

Propaganda in the form of cartoons and stories is still used to make an enemy look like a monster and to rally citizens behind a cause. During the Persian Gulf War, stories and cartoons showed Saddam Hussein as a baby killer. Iraqi troops were supposed to have killed Kuwaiti babies by taking them out of incubators and removing the incubators to Iraq. The stories were later found to be incorrect.

Linking Past and Present

Patriots and Minutemen Colonists who favored American independence were called Patriots. New England's minutemen were volunteer soldiers who could be assembled quickly. Today *Minuteman* and *Patriot* continue to be used by the United States military as names for modern missile systems. Patriot missiles helped defeat Iraq in the Persian Gulf War in 1991.

Visualizing
History During the
American Revolution, the states and
local militias adopted their own
flags. The rattlesnake with the warning "Don't Tread on Me" appeared
on several of these flags.
Answer to Caption: *At the Congress, leaders from the different colonies
met face to face for the first time and
were united for a common cause.*

Reteach

Have students make a chart
about events that led to the
American Revolution. Help them
fill in information under the following headings: *Event, Date,
What Happened, Outcome of Event.*

📁 Reading Essentials and
Study Guide 21-3

Enrich

Have students read a book—fiction or nonfiction—related to
events of this section, write a
report, and deliver their report
orally to the class.

CLOSE

Ask students to imagine they are
attending a protest meeting at the
Old South Meetinghouse. Have
two students give brief speeches
about the "tyranny" of the British,
addressing some specific issue,
such as the Boston Massacre.
Have other students act as participants at the meeting "speaking
their minds" about the issues.

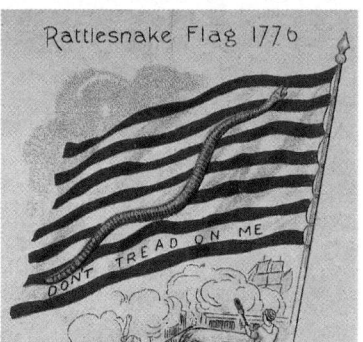
Rattlesnake Flag 1776

Visualizing
History **The Rattlesnake Flag with 13 alternating red and white stripes warns: "Don't
Tread on Me."** *What was the significance of most colonies
sending delegates to the First Continental Congress?*

In 1772 the law was changed to permit the British
East India Company to export tea directly to
America and sell it in wholesale markets. Although
this law meant much cheaper prices for tea, colonists
reacted against the 3-cents-per-pound tax. Some
American ports turned tea ships away. At Boston,
colonists disguised as Native Americans boarded the
ships and dumped the chests of tea into the harbor.

The British quickly punished the Massachusetts colonists for the Boston Tea Party by passing what the colonists called the Intolerable Acts.
These laws closed Boston Harbor until the tea had
been paid for and required colonists to feed and
house British soldiers in their homes. The acts also
greatly reduced the colonists' right of self-government. Town meetings, for example, could not be
held more than once a year without special permission from the royal governor. Parliament also
passed the Quebec Act, placing Canada and territories north of the Ohio River under a separate
government, thus closing the area to colonists.

The First Continental Congress

The latest repressive measures of the British
convinced the thirteen colonies to form a union of
resistance. On September 5, 1774, 56 colonial delegates met at **Philadelphia** at the First Continental
Congress. The Congress marked an important
event in colonial affairs in which leaders from different colonies met face to face. Usually, most
colonies considered their differences with Great
Britain individually. Now they were united as a
group. **Patrick Henry**, a leading statesman from
Virginia, commented: "There are no differences
between Virginians, Pennsylvanians, New Yorkers,
and New Englanders. I am not a Virginian but an
American." **George Washington** of Virginia and
Samuel Adams of Massachusetts were among the
leading members of the Congress.

The Congress, which met for more than 7
weeks, resolved that the "English colonists ... are
entitled to a free and exclusive power of legislation
in their several provincial legislatures." In other
words, only the colonial assemblies should have
the right to make laws in the colonies. Although the
Congress recognized Parliament's right to regulate trade, the Congress agreed that the colonies
would not import goods from Great Britain after
December 1774. After September 1775, they
resolved not to send colonial goods to Great Britain.

Many colonists, however, were determined to
take more radical steps to end British rule. In every
colony a volunteer army was organized and
weapons collected. In New England, minutemen
(so named because they could be ready for battle on
a minute's notice) drilled on village greens, while
the town officials stored ammunition, weapons,
and food. In the Southern Colonies, planters
recruited soldiers at their own expense. It began to
appear that the dispute between Great Britain and
the colonies would be settled only by force.

SECTION 3 ASSESSMENT

Main Idea
1. Use a diagram like the one
   below to identify causes of
   conflict between Great Britain
   and the American colonies.

   Causes of British-American
   Colonial Conflict

Recall
2. **Define** duty, direct tax, boycott.
3. **Identify** Navigation Acts,
   French and Indian War, George
   Grenville, George III, Stamp Act,
   John Adams, First Continental
   Congress, Patrick Henry, George
   Washington, Samuel Adams.

Critical Thinking
4. **Evaluating Information** Was
   Grenville right in expecting the

colonists to pay for their
colonies' defense? What else
could he have done?

Understanding Themes
5. **Conflict** Compare and contrast Parliament's struggles for
   power with the king with the
   American colonists' later struggle for control of their own
   affairs. What were the key
   issues in each case?

550 **Chapter 21** *English and American Revolutions*

SECTION 3 ASSESSMENT ANSWERS

1. Navigation Acts; power struggles
   between assemblies and governors;
   Britain active in colonial economy; Stamp
   Act; Declaratory Act; Intolerable Acts
2. All terms are defined in the Glossary.
3. Navigation Acts, 546; French and Indian
   War, 547; George Grenville, 547; George
   III, 547; Stamp Act, 548; John Adams,

548; First Continental Congress, 550;
Patrick Henry, 550; George Washington,
550; Samuel Adams, 550
4. Answers may include that colonists
   should have paid something for the
   French and Indian War, but Grenville
   should have consulted colonial legislatures
   about acceptable ways to raise money.

5. **CONFLICT** Both struggles
   were for more control over the taxing
   power and for protection of rights. The
   difference was that Parliament fought to
   limit the power of the king and change
   the government, whereas the colonists
   wanted more representation within the
   established British government.

Outlining

To sketch a scene, first you would draw the rough shape, or outline, of the picture. Then you would fill in this rough shape with details. Outlining written material is a similar process. You begin with the rough shape of the material and gradually fill in the details.

Learning the Skill

Outlining has two key functions. When studying written material, it helps you identify main ideas and group together related facts. In writing, it helps you put information in a logical order.

There are two kinds of outlines–formal and informal. An informal outline is similar to taking notes. You write only words and phrases needed to remember ideas. Under the main ideas, jot down related but less important details. This kind of outline is useful for reviewing for a test.

A formal outline has a standard format. In a formal outline, label main heads with Roman numerals, subheads with capital letters, and details with Arabic numerals. Each level would have at least two entries and should be indented from the level above. All entries use the same grammatical form. If one entry is a complete sentence, all other entries at that level must also be complete sentences.

When outlining written material, first read the material to identify the main ideas. In textbooks, section heads provide clues to main topics. Then identify the subheads. Place details supporting subheads under the appropriate head.

Practicing the Skill

Study the outline below of Chapter 21, Section 1 and then answer these questions.
1. Is this a formal or an informal outline?
2. What are the three main headings?
3. How do subheads under the heading "Commonwealth" relate to this main idea?
4. Give two examples of grammatical consistency in this outline.

I. Monarchy
  A. James I
    1. Believed in the divine right of kings
    2. Fought with Parliament over money and religion
  B. Charles I
    1. Continued to believe in divine right
    2. Tried to rule without Parliament
    3. Lost the Civil War and was beheaded
II. Commonwealth
  A. England ruled by Parliament
  B. Army led by Cromwell
III. Military dictatorship
  A. Headed by Oliver Cromwell
  B. Enforced Puritan rules

Applying the Skill

Write a formal outline for Section 2 of this chapter.

For More Practice

Turn to the Skill Practice in the Chapter Assessment on page 557 for more practice in outlining.

Oliver Cromwell

The **Glencoe Skillbuilder Interactive Workbook, Level 2** provides instruction and practice in key social studies skills.

ANSWERS TO PRACTICING THE SKILL

1. formal outline
2. Monarchy, Commonwealth, Military dictatorship
3. The subheads describe affairs in England during the Commonwealth.
4. The main headings are nouns and the numbered subheads are verb phrases.

TEACH

Outlining On the chalkboard, write the following main headings for an informal outline about activities of a typical school day: *Morning, Afternoon, Evening.* Have students add indented subheads and further indented supporting details under each main head. For example: *At home* and *At school* could be subheads under *Morning. Get up, Get dressed*, and *Eat breakfast* could be details under *At home.* Be sure students have at least two subheads under each head and at least two details under each subhead. Students should maintain grammatical consistency within each level of the outline. Convert students' outlines to formal outlines by placing Roman numerals, capital letters, and Arabic numerals in the appropriate places. Then have students read the skill and complete the practice questions.

Additional Practice

📁 Skill Reinforcement Activity 21

📁 Writer's Guidebook, Lesson 11

GLENCOE TECHNOLOGY

 Glencoe's **Skillbuilder Interactive Workbook, Level 2**
This interactive CD-ROM promotes student mastery of key social studies skills.

1775   1780   1785   1790

1775 British and American forces exchange fire at Lexington and Concord.

1781 British General Cornwallis surrenders at Yorktown.

1783 Great Britain recognizes American independence.

1787 Delegates in Philadelphia write the United States Constitution.

Section 4

A War for Independence

Guide to Reading

Read to Find Out
Main Idea *The Americans established a new kind of government after the American Revolution.*

▶ **Terms to Define**
revolution, confederation, federal system

▶ **People to Meet**
Paul Revere, George Washington, Thomas Paine, Thomas Jefferson

▶ **Places to Locate**
Yorktown

The Storyteller

Mercy Warren lived through the American Revolution and wrote about its horrors. "The roads [were] filled with frighted women and children; some in carts with their tattered furniture, others on foot fleeing into the woods. But what added greatly to the horrors of the scene, was our passing through the bloody field at Monotong, which was strewed with mangled bodies. We met one affectionate father with a cart, looking for his murdered son.... " She concluded one of her letters, "Be it known unto Britain, even American daughters are politicians and patriots, and will aid the good work with their female efforts."

—adapted from *The Women of the American Revolution*, Elizabeth F. Ellet, 1850

Powder horn

ostilities between the American colonists and the British broke out near Boston in 1775. People there were outraged by the British government. Their seaport was still closed because of the Boston Tea Party, causing many Bostonians to lose their jobs. As British troops filled the city, rumors accusing the "redcoats" of robberies and murders swept through shops, inns, and other meeting places.

Sensing the tension in the city, the British Parliament ordered the governor of Massachusetts, General Thomas Gage, to seize the colonists' military supplies. Before dawn on April 19, 1775, Gage sent a troop of 700 British soldiers to destroy weapons collected in the town of Concord, about 18 miles (29 km) from Boston.

Colonists **Paul Revere** and William Dawes learned of the British plan and rode to warn the colonial minutemen. As the British marched into Lexington on their way to Concord, they found about 70 farmers and villagers blocking their path. When the colonists refused to put down their guns, a shot was fired, though no one knows which side fired first. In the skirmish, British soldiers killed 8 colonists; later at Concord, the "redcoats" held off a sharp attack by more minutemen.

As the British troops marched back toward Boston, colonists fired at them from behind buildings, trees, and stone walls. The next day, almost 300 British soldiers and nearly 100 colonists lay dead. The British were humiliated. No one expected the colonists to be any match for the professional British soldiers.

Moving Toward Separation

News of the colonial attack on the British troops spread throughout the American colonies.

Signing of the Declaration of Independence by John Trumbull, c. 1825. The Yale University Art Gallery, New Haven, Connecticut **To the British, those who signed the Declaration of Independence committed an act of treason.** *How did the document justify revolution?*

When the Second Continental Congress gathered in Philadelphia one month after the battles at Lexington and Concord, it immediately organized an army and named **George Washington** as military commander.

Many colonists, however, still resisted the idea of declaring war on Great Britain. The Congress tried one last time to arrange a peaceful compromise with Parliament and the king. They sent a proposal, called the Olive Branch Petition, to King George III. When the British government refused the petition, chances of a peaceful settlement between Great Britain and the American colonies grew dimmer. To more and more colonists, independence seemed the only answer.

A Call to Part

The most stirring arguments in favor of independence came from the pen of colonist **Thomas Paine**. Paine, who recently had come to the American colonies from Great Britain, wrote a pamphlet called *Common Sense* in January 1776. In it he called upon the colonists to break away from Great Britain. Paine promoted independence for economic, social, and moral reasons:

❝ Every thing that is right begs for separation from [Great] Britain. The Americans who have been killed seem to say, 'TIS TIME TO PART. England and America are located a great distance apart. That is itself strong and natural proof that God never expected one to rule over the other. ❞

—Thomas Paine, *Common Sense*, 1776

Common Sense circulated widely and helped to convince thousands of American colonists that it was "time to part." The delegates to the Congress sensed the changing mood in the colonies and

assigned five of their best thinkers and writers to prepare a declaration of independence that would clearly state their resolve.

The Declaration of Independence

Thomas Jefferson, a young Virginian, was the principal author of the colonists' declaration of independence. The document set forth the colonists' reasons for separation from Great Britain. Jefferson, like many other colonial leaders, knew and valued the works of John Locke and other Enlightenment thinkers. He incorporated many of their ideas into the Declaration of Independence.

The Declaration stated that individuals have certain basic rights that cannot be taken away by any government. Focusing on John Locke's concept of the "social contract," the Declaration announced that governments are created by an agreement, or contract, between the rulers and those ruled. If a ruler loses the support of the people by taking away basic rights, the people have a right to change the government through rebellion. The beginning of the Declaration reads:

❝ We hold these truths to be self-evident, that all men are created equal, that they are endowed by their Creator with certain unalienable Rights, that among these are Life, Liberty, and the pursuit of Happiness. That to secure these rights, Governments are instituted among Men, deriving their just powers from the consent of the governed; that whenever any Form of Government becomes destructive of those ends, it is the Right of the People to alter or to abolish it.... ❞

The Declaration continued with a long list of the ways in which Great Britain and George III had

Chapter 21 *English and American Revolutions* **553**

TEACH

Guided Practice

THEME Revolution

Help students arrive at a definition of revolution as used in this section. *(violent overthrow of the government)* Have them explain how the American Revolution fits their definition. **L1 LEP**

 History & Art Trumbull served as George Washington's aide-de-camp during the war and did not start this painting until 1789. To portray Jefferson correctly, Trumbull made sketches of him in France where Jefferson served as United States ambassador.
Answer to Caption: *It said revolution was justified if a ruler took away basic rights of the people, which King George III had.*

Comparison Have students list the advantages and the disadvantages of the Americans and the British during the American Revolution. **L2**

Mapping History Overlay Transparency 13, *European Claims in North America*

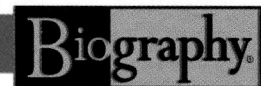

The following videotape programs are available from Glencoe:

- **Paul Revere: The Midnight Rider**

- **Thomas Jefferson: Philosopher of Freedom**

COOPERATIVE LEARNING ACTIVITY

Dramatization Organize the class into two groups and have each group prepare a play dramatizing the debate about and writing of either the Declaration of Independence or the Constitution. Be sure that each student has a task, such as researching Enlightenment ideas that influenced the documents, investigating background information on the main participants who wrote and debated the documents, writing dialogue that includes a discussion of the Enlightenment ideas, or acting in the drama. After each dramatization has been presented, allow the audience to ask questions. **L2**

Independent Practice

 Guided Reading Activity 21-4 **L1**

 People in World History Profile 39

Daily Life Have students research the daily routine of American or British soldiers during the American Revolution. Ask them to draw pictures or to write a first-person narrative describing a soldier's experiences. **L2 LEP**

POINT

United States Government
Why was the formation of the United States government an important event in world history?
Formed in an age of monarchy, the United States was a republic with a written constitution. The Constitution of the United States was an example of a social contract based on popular sovereignty, separation of powers among government branches, and guarantees for protecting citizen's rights. The American republic became a model for people everywhere seeking freedom.

ASSESS

Check for Understanding

Assign Section 4 Assessment as homework or as an in-class activity.

◉ Use Interactive Tutor Self-Assessment Software to review Section 4.

Evaluate

 Section Quiz 21-4

◉ Use the Testmaker to create a customized quiz for Section 4.

---

abused their power and concludes that "these United Colonies are and of Right ought to be Free and Independent States."

On July 4, 1776, the Congress adopted the Declaration of Independence. A few days later, George Washington had the Declaration read to his troops to inspire them and give them hope as war loomed ahead. Cheers went up from the ranks when the reading was done. That night some of the troops joined a crowd of townspeople who pulled down a statue of George III.

The War for Independence

The Declaration of Independence made a reconciliation with the British impossible. The only course open to the colonists was revolution, the violent overthrow of a government. For the revolutionary leaders, now seen as traitors to the British king, failure would mean death. As Benjamin Franklin said, "Yes, we must, indeed, all hang together, or, most assuredly, we shall all hang separately."

The War of Independence was long and bitter. The Americans did not have an army that could face the British in the open field, but they did have a skillful general in Washington. They also had military help from the French, who wanted to revenge the losses of the Seven Years' War. France, however, did not enter the conflict until American victory seemed certain.

The British had the disadvantage of trying to fight a long-distance war. Also, they had to conquer the whole country to win. The Americans had only to hold out until the British admitted defeat.

The turning point came in October 1777 with a British defeat at Saratoga, New York. The

Footnotes to History

"Yankee Doodle"
The song "Yankee Doodle" was first sung by the British to mock the American colonists:
"Yankee Doodle came to town,
    Riding on a pony;
He stuck a feather in his cap
    And called it macaroni."
"Macaroni" was a term used for British men who thought they dressed in style but actually looked ridiculous. The colonists loved the tune and added verses of their own to make it a song of defiance.

American victory persuaded France to come in on the American side. Spain followed in 1779. Faced with a naval war against France and Spain, Great Britain became less interested in defeating its rebellious colonies. In October 1781 the Americans forced the British army to surrender at **Yorktown**, Virginia.

 ## POINT

United States Government

In 1783 Great Britain recognized American independence. At first, the United States was a confederation, or a loose union of independent states, under the Articles of Confederation. Its central government, however, was too weak to deal effectively with national problems. In 1787 the nation's leaders meeting in Philadelphia wrote the Constitution of the United States, a strong, but flexible, framework for a new national government.

The Constitution

The Constitution set up a federal system, in which political authority was divided between the national government and state governments. It also provided for a separation of powers among the national government's executive, legislative, and judicial branches, an idea that came directly from Montesquieu's *The Spirit of Laws.* A system of checks and balances enabled each branch to limit the power of the other branches.

Under the Constitution, the United States was a republic with an elected president instead of a hereditary monarch. Elections held in 1789 made George Washington the first President of the United States. Yet, at the time, only white males who met certain property qualifications could vote in elections. Among the groups excluded were women, African Americans, and Native Americans. Not until this century would the right to vote—and other civil rights—be extended to all adult Americans.

In 1789, however, the United States was closer to democratic rule than any other country in the world. That same year, a Bill of Rights was added to the Constitution in the form of ten amendments. It affirmed the principle that people had basic liberties that government must protect. These liberties included freedom of religion, speech, and the press, as well as the right to private property and to trial by jury. As in the case of the vote, not all Americans at first had equal protection under the law but would later be included.

MEETING SPECIAL NEEDS ACTIVITY

Study Strategy Have students outline this section using the following Roman numeral heads: *I. The move toward separation, II. The War of Independence, III. The new government.* Help students correctly place the following subheads in the outline: *Olive Branch Petition, Common Sense, Declaration of Independence, American advantages and disadvantages, British advantages and disadvantages, Articles of Confederation, Constitution.* Then have students find at least two details to place under each subhead. **L1**

North America 1763

Russian
British
Spanish
French

0   500   1,000 mi.
0 500 1,000 km
Albers Azimuthal Equal-Area Projection

North America 1783

0   500   1,000 mi.
0 500 1,000 km
Albers Azimuthal Equal-Area Projection

Russian   French
British   United States
Spanish   Disputed

Map Study These maps reflect the changes in European territorial control as a result of the American Revolution.
Place What portion of North America did Great Britain control after the American Revolution?

The Republic's Significance

The creation of the American republic proved that Enlightenment values could work in practice. Based on the ideas of Locke, Montesquieu, and Rousseau, the Constitution of the United States was an example of a social contract based on the sovereignty of the people, with separation of powers among government branches and guarantees for protecting natural rights. Since their writing, the Constitution and the Declaration of Independence both have inspired peoples throughout the world seeking freedom from oppression. In the 1700s and 1800s, many Europeans and Latin Americans appealed to these American documents of liberty in ending absolute monarchy and creating new forms of government. In the 1900s people in many lands throughout the world did the same in their struggles against empires and dictators.

SECTION 4 ASSESSMENT

Main Idea
1. Use a chart like the one below to identify key aspects of the government set up by the American colonists.

New American Government
_____
_____
_____
_____
_____
_____

Recall
2. **Define** revolution, confederation, federal system.
3. **Identify** Paul Revere, George Washington, Thomas Paine, Thomas Jefferson, the Declaration of Independence.

Critical Thinking
4. **Evaluating Information** If Great Britain had treated the colonists differently, would they have been content with British rule? Support your answer.

Understanding Themes
5. **Revolution** Compare the Americans' attempts to organize a new form of government with those of the English after executing King Charles I. Did both governments ensure representation and individual rights?

SECTION 4 ASSESSMENT ANSWERS

1. federal system; separation of powers; system of checks and balances; republic with constitution and elected president; Bill of Rights
2. All terms are defined in the Glossary.
3. Paul Revere, 552; George Washington, 553; Thomas Paine, 553; Thomas Jefferson, 553; Declaration of Independence, 553
4. Answers may vary. Possible answer: If the British government had compromised, the Americans would not have revolted.
5. **REVOLUTION** After the English Civil War, Cromwell suspended Parliament, became a military dictator, and placed the people under strict laws. After the American Revolution, the United States wrote a new Constitution to which was added the Bill of Rights to protect individual liberties.

Answers

Using Key Terms

1. a   3. l   5. e
2. b   4. i

Using Your History Journal

Suggest that students examine constitutions from several school or community organizations as models.

Reviewing Facts

1. 1765: Stamp Act Congress; 1770: Boston Tea Party; 1774: First Continental Congress; 1775: Battle of Lexington and Concord; 1776: *Common Sense* published; 1776: Declaration of Independence approved; 1781: British surrender at Yorktown; 1783: Britain recognizes American independence; 1787: Constitution written; 1789: Washington elected president
2. royal powers were limited and certain individual rights were guaranteed
3. Harsh rule made the people eager to restore the monarchy.
4. Both parties united against James II and invited William and

WORLD HISTORY Online

Self-Check Quiz

Visit the *World History: The Human Experience* Web site at **worldhistory.glencoe.com** and click on *Chapter 21—Self-Check Quiz* to prepare for the Chapter Test.

Using Key Terms

Write the key term that completes each sentence. Then write a sentence for each term not chosen.

a. habeas corpus   g. constitutional monarchy
b. divine right   h. federal system
c. duty   i. royalists
d. prime minister   j. direct tax
e. commonwealth   k. confederation
f. revolution   l. martial law

1. According to the principle of _____, a person cannot be held in prison by the government without just cause or without a trial.
2. A rift between James I and Parliament grew deeper when the king publicly professed his belief in _____.
3. During times of _____, military authorities are given temporary rule and individual rights are limited.
4. In the English Civil War, supporters of the monarchy were known as _____.
5. When the monarchy was abolished in 1649, England became a _____, a state governed by elected representatives.

Technology Activity

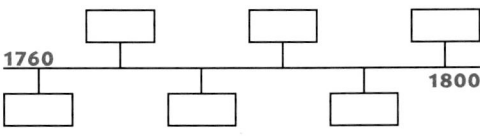

Using the Internet Access the Internet to locate a Web site about the history of the English Civil War. Use a search engine to help focus your search by using words such as *charles I, oliver cromwell,* or *english civil war.* Based on your research, write a position paper addressing whether you agree that monarchs should have divine right, or whether parliament should have more control over government policy, raising money, and reforms in the Church of England.

Reviewing Facts

1. **History** Use a time line like the one below to position key events in America's struggle for independence and the establishment of the Republic.

```
1760                                          1800
```

2. **Government/Citizenship** State the changes brought by the English Bill of Rights.
3. **Government** Discuss how the military rule of Oliver Cromwell helped set the stage for the Restoration in 1660.
4. **Government** Describe the Glorious Revolution.
5. **History** Identify the causes and effects of the English Civil War. How did it change England? How did it later affect America?
6. **History** State the causes and effects of the American Revolution. What was its impact?

Critical Thinking

1. **Apply** What political ideas transformed England and America during the 1600s and 1700s? Are these ideas relevant today? Explain.
2. **Contrast** How has American voting changed since the 1700s? What factors do you think have brought about this change?
3. **Evaluate** How were the ideas of separation of powers and checks and balances applied to the government of the United States? Why were these ideas adopted by the framers of the Constitution? How do they affect you today?

Mary of Orange to rule England.
5. Causes: Quarrels over religion, taxes, and royal power; Effects: temporary creation of republic; long-term limits on royal power and emergence of parliamentary supremacy; England became a constitutional monarchy. Idea of limited government spread to America.
6. Causes: rift between England and colonies over taxation, representation, and trade; Effects: U.S. became an independent republic

Critical Thinking

1. social contract theory, government by the people, separation of powers, constitutional government; these ideas are at the heart of modern democratic government
2. Today all adult Americans may vote; the belief in equality for all citizens
3. The federal government was divided into legislative, executive, and judicial branches. Checks and balances allowed each branch to

4. Synthesize How did the Enlightenment influence the American Revolution?

Geography in History

1. Region Refer to the map below. One of Great Britain's major challenges in the American Revolution was to control rebellion over a wide area. How far is it from the Battle of Saratoga to the Battle of Camden, South Carolina?

2. Movement Why did most British troop movement from one location to another occur by sea?

3. Region The dates and stars identify major Revolutionary battles. How do these battles indicate a shift in the region of the most significant battles from the earliest to the latest period?

Major Battles of the American Revolution

Understanding Themes

1. Conflict What factors caused the conflict between Parliament and the Stuart monarchs?

2. Change Why do you think the English restored the monarchy after the Commonwealth? What changes came to the monarchy after 1660?

---

3. Conflict How did the British punish Massachusetts colonists after the Boston Tea Party?

4. Revolution Why did the American Revolution lead to a stable republic in the colonies, while the English Civil War did not do so in England?

inking Past and Present

1. Some of the Revolutionary quarrels concerned taxes. In what ways does the United States today struggle with the issue of fair taxation?

2. After 1945, many peoples won their freedom from Great Britain. Compare their struggles with that of Americans in the 1700s.

3. The United States and Great Britain today are both democracies. How are their governments similar? How are they different? To what extent do they base their political principles on the events of the 1600s and 1700s?

Skill Practice

Complete the following formal outline for Section 3, "Road to Revolt."

I. Great Britain's American Empire
  A. Economic relationship between Great Britain and colonies
  B. _____
    1. Some colonial products exported only to Great Britain
    2. _____
    3. No foreign-made ships in colonies
II. _____
  A. Structure of colonial governments
    1. _____
    2. Elected assemblies
  B. Early power struggles
    1. Limited salaries of officials
    2. _____
III. Tightening British Control
  A. Effects of French and Indian War
    1. _____
    2. _____
  B. Stamp Acts
IV. _____
  A. Boston Massacre
  B. _____
  C. First Continental Congress

---

4. REVOLUTION After the Revolution, the Americans worked together to form a stable government. After the English Civil War, Cromwell ruled as a dictator.

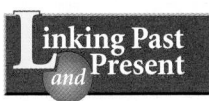

inking Past and Present

1. Congress makes some changes in the tax laws in response to various groups' calls for fairness.

2. Some places in the British Empire (Canada) achieved independence gradually and without revolution, while other places (India and Kenya) engaged in some kind of struggle.

3. Both have representative governments. Britain has a constitutional monarchy; the U.S. has a president. Both are influenced by Enlightenment ideas.

Skill Practice

I.B. Navigation Acts
I.B.2. All goods going to colonies first pass through Great Britain
II. Colonial Political Power
II.A.1. Governors appointed by king
II.B.2. Had right to approve taxes requested by the Crown or governors
III.A.1. Land west of the Appalachians closed to colonists
III.A.2. Navigation Acts enforced
IV. Events Leading to War
IV.B. Intolerable Acts

Chapter Bonus Test Question

Ask students: Why did England restore the monarchy after an era of conflict while the Americans set up a constitutional government after their revolution? (*The English, tired of Puritan ways and political uncertainty, favored royal tradition. The Americans set up a government to secure newly-won freedom.*)

---

limit the powers of the other branches. Student answers will reflect experiences.

4. The social contract was the basis of the Declaration of Independence.

Geography in History

1. about 700 miles [about 1,126 kilometers]
2. It was easier and faster to move by sea.
3. They show that the war started in the northern colonies and moved south.

Understanding Themes

1. CONFLICT Disagreement over the king's power and religion.

2. CHANGE They were tired of conflicts in Parliament and of harsh Puritan rule; it became a constitutional monarchy.

3. CONFLICT passed the Intolerable Acts, required colonists to quarter British soldiers, reduced self-government, and closed land north of Ohio River

A complete, 1-page lesson plan is provided for each section in the *Reproducible Lesson Plans* booklet.

The French Revolution

CHAPTER RESOURCES

	Reproducible Resources	Multimedia Resources
Chapter Opener	Chapter Themes: Graphic Organizer 22 Historical Significance Chapter Activity 22	MindJogger Videoquiz
Chapter Enrichment	Vocabulary Activity 22* Time Line Activity 22 Mapping History Activity 22 History Simulation 22 Geography and History Activity 22 Source Reading 22 People in World History Profiles 41, 42 World Literature Selection 5 World Art and Music Activity 22 Enrichment Activity 22 Critical Thinking Activity 22 Skill Reinforcement Activity 22 Building Skills in Geography Workbook, Unit 2, Lesson 8 Performance Assessment Activity 22 Standardized Test Practice Workbook Activity 22 Inclusion for the Social Studies Classroom Strategies and Activities	World History and Art Transparency 29, *Napoleon Crossing the Alps* Mapping History Overlay Transparency 14, *France and Europe* Chapter Transparency 22 Vocabulary PuzzleMaker Software Turning Points in World History: *French Revolution* World History Primary Source Document Library
Chapter Review/Reteaching	Reteaching Activity 22 Skill Reinforcement Activity 22 Spanish Chapter Summary 22	Chapter 22 Digest Audiocassette, Activity, Test* Vocabulary PuzzleMaker Software Interactive Tutor Self-Assessment Software MindJogger Videoquiz
Chapter Evaluation/Testing	Performance Assessment Activity 22 Chapter 22 Test, Forms A and B	ExamView® Pro Testmaker

0:00 OUT OF TIME? Assign the Chapter 22 Audiocassettes.

* *Also available in Spanish*

World History Primary Source Document Library
Make History Come Alive!
Engage your students with over 250 easily accessible primary source documents—available on this CD-ROM—that will give them real-life insight into the important events of world history.

Block Schedule

Activities that are particularly suited to use within the block scheduling framework are identified throughout this chapter by the following designation.

KEY TO ABILITY LEVELS

Teaching strategies are coded for varying learning styles.
L1 BASIC activities for all students
L2 AVERAGE activities for average to above-average students
L3 CHALLENGING activities for above-average students
LEP LIMITED ENGLISH PROFICIENCY activities

Use Glencoe's *Presentation Plus!* multimedia teacher tool to easily present dynamic lessons that visually excite your students. Using Microsoft PowerPoint® you can customize the presentations to create your own personalized lessons.

Interactive Lesson Planner

Planning has never been easier! Using this CD-ROM, organize your week, month, semester, or year with all the help you need. The **Interactive Lesson Planner** gives you access to all of the blackline masters that accompany *World History: The Human Experience.*

SECTION RESOURCES

Daily Objectives	Reproducible Resources	Multimedia Resources
Section 1 The Old Order Explain how France's class structure contributed to the French Revolution.	Lecture Notes 22-1 Reproducible Lesson Plan 22-1 Vocabulary Activity 22* Guided Reading Activity 22-1* Time Line Activity 22 People in World History Profile 41 Section Quiz 22-1* Reading Essentials and Study Guide 22-1	Section Focus Transparency 22-1 Chapter Transparency 22 Interactive Tutor Self-Assessment Software Testmaker Turning Points in World History: *French Revolution*
Section 2 Constitutional Government List the political reforms the National Assembly adopted for France.	Lecture Notes 22-2 Reproducible Lesson Plan 22-2 Vocabulary Activity 22* Guided Reading Activity 22-2* Source Reading 22 Section Quiz 22-2* Reading Essentials and Study Guide 22-2	Section Focus Transparency 22-2 Interactive Tutor Self-Assessment Software Testmaker Turning Points in World History: *French Revolution*
Section 3 Dawn of a New Era Explain why the French Revolution led to war between France and its neighbors.	Lecture Notes 22-3 Reproducible Lesson Plan 22-3 Vocabulary Activity 22* Guided Reading Activity 22-3* History Simulation 22 People in World History Profile 42 Section Quiz 22-3* Reading Essentials and Study Guide 22-3	Section Focus Transparency 22-3 Interactive Tutor Self-Assessment Software Testmaker Turning Points in World History: *French Revolution*
Section 4 Napoleon's Empire Relate how Napoleon built and then lost an empire.	Lecture Notes 22-4 Reproducible Lesson Plan 22-4 Vocabulary Activity 22* Guided Reading Activity 22-4* Geography and History Activity 22 World Art and Music Activity 22 Section Quiz 22-4* Reading Essentials and Study Guide 22-4	Section Focus Transparency 22-4 World History and Art Transparency 29, *Napoleon Crossing the Alps* Mapping History Overlay Transparency 14, *France and Europe* Interactive Tutor Self-Assessment Software Testmaker
Section 5 Peace in Europe Evaluate the success of the plans of the reactionaries to thwart the spread of liberalism in Europe.	Lecture Notes 22-5 Reproducible Lesson Plan 22-5 Guided Reading Activity 22-5* Reteaching Activity 22 Enrichment Activity 22 Section Quiz 22-5* Performance Assessment Activity 22 Spanish Chapter Summary 22 Reading Essentials and Study Guide 22-5	Section Focus Transparency 22-5 Mapping History Overlay Transparency 14, *France and Europe* Vocabulary PuzzleMaker Software Interactive Tutor Self-Assessment Software Testmaker

* Also available in Spanish

Chapter Activities

Performance Assessment Activity

A Concerned Citizen Speaks to the Government This chapter provides an example of how isolated incidents of conflict can spread. Ask students to think of analogous situations today (for example, gangs, crime families, political factions). Have each student assume the role of a citizen who is concerned about one of these situations and would like to bring its seriousness to the attention of the city council, state legislature, or United Nations. In their speeches, students should refer to the French Revolution for historical perspective, making connections with details in their modern-day examples. Have students deliver their speeches to collaborative groups of eight, with the listeners assuming the roles of members of the body being addressed.

Possible Rubric Features
Concept attainment, research skills, ability to make connections, clarity and impact of speech, accuracy of content information, appropriateness of speech to audience

• *For an additional activity, refer to Activity 22 in the* Performance Assessment Strategies and Activities *booklet.*

ACTIVITY

From the Classroom of...

Susan E. Szachowicz
Brockton High School
Brockton, MA

The Congress of Vienna Convenes
Organize the class into five groups, representing Austria, Great Britain, Russia, Prussia, and France, and direct each group to select one spokesperson to be Metternich, Castlereagh, Alexander I, Frederick William III, and Talleyrand. Provide each group with an overview of the Congress and its purpose; information specific to their country, which includes their delegate's role at the Congress and their country's goals, vital interests, and demands; and an outline map of Europe at the height of Napoleon's power. Each group should now develop their lists of demands and redraw the map of Europe as they would like to see it. Then convene the Congress by having the representative from each group offer their proposals and maps to the entire class. Questioning and negotiating should proceed until a plan acceptable to all is developed. Finally, the class plan should be compared to the actual decision made at the Congress of Vienna and similarities and differences noted.

MULTIPLE LEARNING STYLES

Verbal/Linguistic
Have students research and then debate the following question: Was Napoleon's legacy positive or negative?

Logical/Mathematical
Have students create a time line of major events that occurred during the French Revolution.

Visual/Spatial
Students may create a comic book that chronicles the life of a French peasant family living outside Paris at the time of the French Revolution. Each section should focus on a particular event that occurred in Paris between 1789 and 1815.

Kinesthetic
Have students draw a large outline map of Europe and hang it on the bulletin board. Using thumbtacks and labels, identify locations of major events during the French Revolution.

Use the following to easily assess student learning in a variety of ways.

- Performance Assessment Strategies and Activities
- Section Quizzes
- Chapter and Unit Tests
- Interactive Tutor Self-Assessment Software
- Testmaker Software
- MindJogger Videoquiz
- SAT/SAT II Test Practice
- worldhistory.glencoe.com

Additional Resources

NATIONAL GEOGRAPHIC SOCIETY — Teacher's Corner

INDEX TO NATIONAL GEOGRAPHIC MAGAZINE

The following articles may be used for research relating to this chapter:

- *France: Bicentennial of the Great Revolution, Special Issue,* July 1989.
- "Two Revolutions," by Charles McCarry, July 1989.
- "Napoleon," by John J. Putman, February 1982.

NATIONAL GEOGRAPHIC SOCIETY PRODUCTS AVAILABLE FROM GLENCOE

To order the following product for use with this chapter, contact your local Glencoe sales representative, or call Glencoe at 1-800-334-7344:

- *Picture Atlas of the World (CD-ROM)*

ADDITIONAL NATIONAL GEOGRAPHIC SOCIETY PRODUCTS

To order the following product for use with this chapter, call National Geographic Society at 1-800-368-2728:

- *Democratic Government Series: France (Video)*

Access National Geographic's new dynamic MapMachine Web site and other geography resources at:

- http://www.nationalgeographic.com/
- http://www.nationalgeographic.com/maps/

BIBLIOGRAPHY

Literature of the Period
Dickens, Charles. *A Tale of Two Cities.* New York: Dutton, 1970. A romantic novel that takes place during the French Revolution.

Readings for the Student
Forester, C. S. *Mr. Midshipman Hornblower.* Boston: Little, Brown, 1940. The first of eleven sea stories set in the era of the Napoleonic Wars.

Readings for the Teacher
Evenson, Norma. *Paris: A Century of Change, 1878–1978.* New Haven: Yale University Press, 1979. Historical and social changes in France as reflected in the city of Paris, from its rebuilding under Napoleon III.

WORLD HISTORY *Online*

Use our Web site as an additional resource. All essential content is covered in the Student Edition.

You and your students can visit the *World History: The Human Experience* Web site at worldhistory.glencoe.com The student text directs students to the Web site for the following options:

- **Chapter Overviews**
- **Student Web Activities**
- **Self-Check Quizzes**

Answers are provided for you in a link entitled "Web Activity Lesson Plan." Additional Web Resources, Interactive Puzzles, and content updates are also available.

Visit the Glencoe Web site at socialstudies.glencoe.com for social studies activities, updates, and links to other resources.

LOCAL OBJECTIVES

_____
_____
_____
_____
_____
_____
_____
_____
_____
_____
_____
_____
_____
_____
_____
_____
_____

Chapter Themes are listed by section on this chapter opening page of the Student Edition. A corresponding theme-based activity is available under "TEACH," and a theme-based question is asked in the Section and Chapter Assessments.

The Storyteller

Historical Setting Marie-Victoire Monnard was one of 15 children in her family. She was also one of thousands of young women who sewed hats and dresses in workshops throughout Paris.

Monnard is writing during a phase of the French Revolution called the Reign of Terror. From September 1793 to July 1794, revolutionaries declared a policy of terror against anyone who publicly disagreed with their policies. In time, hundreds of thousands of suspects filled French jails, and revolutionary courts handed down more than 17,000 death sentences.

Historical Significance

Answers: *Waves of violence and bloodshed swept across France during the revolution. In time, people became desensitized to the cruelties.*

The French Revolution destroyed the entire structure of royal absolutism and ended the social order based on aristocratic privilege. It set the stage for democratic movements around the world during the next century.

WORLD HISTORY Online

Have students use the **Chapter 22 Overview** at worldhistory. glencoe.com as a prereading and postreading exercise for understanding chapter content.

Chapter
22
1700–1830
The French Revolution

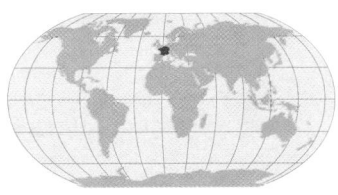

Chapter Themes

▶ **Revolution** The French overthrow their absolute monarchy. *Section 1*
▶ **Change** The National Assembly establishes a constitutional government. *Section 2*
▶ **Conflict** The new French Republic faces enemies at home and abroad. *Section 3*
▶ **Movement** Napoleon becomes France's emperor and conquers much of Europe. *Section 4*
▶ **Reaction** European leaders try to reestablish the old order. *Section 5*

The Storyteller

In 1792 the violence of the French Revolution filled the streets of Paris, where a young seamstress named Marie-Victoire Monnard lived and worked. Walking back to her workshop one afternoon, Marie-Victoire saw six large carts coming toward her. The 13-year-old girl later wrote in her diary, "The carts were full of men and women who had just been slaughtered … legs and arms and heads nodded and dangled on either side of the carts."

The next year she wrote again about the carts, "People just went on working in the shops when they passed by, often not even bothering to raise their heads to watch or to turn their backs to avoid the grisly sight."

Historical Significance

What happened during the French Revolution that allowed people to become accustomed to the bloodied bodies? How did the French Revolution alter society in Europe? What lasting effects did it have on the rest of the world?

| 1760 | 1780 | 1800 | 1820 |

1763 Treaty of Paris ends Seven Years' War.

1774 Louis XVI becomes king.

1789 The Bastille falls.

1815 Napoleon loses Battle of Waterloo.

1804 Napoleon names himself Emperor of the French.

558

Location Have students locate France, England, Spain, the Netherlands, and their capitals on a map in the Atlas of their textbook. What is the distance from Paris to each of these capitals? Have students compare these distances to those between Washington, D.C., and Cleveland, Ohio; and New York City and Dallas, Texas. How did geography affect relations among these nations in Europe? *(Because the nations were so close together, anything that one nation did affected its neighbors. National rivalries were intense.)* **L2**

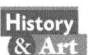
Assault on the Bastille, (artist unknown)
Musée National du Chateau de Versailles, Versailles, France

History & Art On July 14, 1789, an angry mob stormed the Bastille, a Paris prison. Bastille Day is a national holiday in France, much like July 4th in the United States, because the revolt that followed overthrew the French monarchy. What evidence of violence does the painting contain? *(The mob has weapons, there are bodies on the ground, and there is smoke in the air.)*

✔ Performance Assessment

Refer to the activity on page 558C of the Planning Guide.

📁 For an additional activity, refer to Activity 22 in the *Performance Assessment Strategies and Activities* booklet.

Using Your History Journal

Journal entries may be in diary form. Have students keep a diary of their reactions to various events of the French Revolution.

WORLD HISTORY *Online*

Chapter Overview

Visit the *World History: The Human Experience* Web site at **worldhistory.glencoe.com** and click on *Chapter 22—Chapter Overview* to preview the chapter.

Your History Journal

Imagine living through the tumultuous events of the French Revolution. Choose a point of view represented by one of the following: a Catholic bishop, a landed aristocrat, a wealthy merchant, a poor artisan, or a peasant. From your chosen viewpoint, describe your reactions to three major events of the times as you read the chapter.

Chapter 22 *The French Revolution* **559**

GLENCOE TECHNOLOGY

 VIDEODISC
Use MindJogger to preview chapter content.

MindJogger Videoquiz
 Chapter 22
Disc 3 Side B

 Also available in VHS.

➕ **EXTRA CREDIT PROJECT**

Report Interesting events and first-person accounts of the French Revolution are available in many books. Have students research and report to the class on an event of the French Revolution that is not detailed in the chapter. Suggest that students use vivid quotations from the first-person accounts. **L1**

1770   1780   1790   1800

1774 Louis XVI becomes king of France.

1786 Banks refuse to lend money to the government.

1789 Great Fear breaks out.

SECTION THEME

▶ **Revolution** The French overthrow their absolute monarchy.

Guide to Reading

For reading strategies to help students read effectively see pages 12–13. Have students think about the main head as they read the subheads.

Vocabulary Pre-check

 Use the Vocabulary PuzzleMaker for Chapter 22 to create a crossword puzzle to reinforce section terms. **L1 LEP**

Use Vocabulary Activity 22 to introduce vocabulary terms. **L1 LEP**

FOCUS

Section Objective

Explain how France's class structure contributed to the French Revolution.

BELLRINGER
Motivational Activity

Before taking roll at the beginning of the class period, project Section Focus Transparency 22-1 and have students answer the activity questions. Discuss students' responses.

This activity is also available as a blackline master.

Section 1

The Old Order

Guide to Reading

Read to Find Out
Main Idea *France's class system was a cause of the French Revolution.*

▶ **Terms to Define**
    estate, tithe, bourgeoisie

▶ **People to Meet**
    Louis XVI, Marie Antoinette

▶ **Places to Locate**
    Versailles, Paris, the Bastille

The Storyteller

Fear tightened young Claudette Leroux's throat as she waited for the questioning. She could not deny that she was smuggling salt. She could only explain that the gabelle—the tax on salt—made the cost ten times what it should be. French peasants simply could not afford the Farmers General's prices. She wondered who gave these corrupt officials the power to store, inspect, tax, register, and force people to buy their salt. Did anyone understand the peasants' plight?

—adapted from *Citizens: A Chronicle of the French Revolution*, Simon Schama, 1989

Peasant woman's burden

At its height, the absolute monarchy in France controlled the richest and possibly the most powerful state in Europe. The French aristocracy set European trends in literature, clothing, art, and ideas for change. Yet the majority of the people did not share the wealth or privileges of the aristocracy. Working men and women who had few rights yearned for a better way of life. The success of the American Revolution fueled their desire for change.

French Society Divided

The source of the unhappiness lay within France's class system, which fostered great inequalities among the French people. All French people belonged to one of three estates, or orders of society. The estates determined a person's legal rights and status. The Catholic clergy formed the First Estate. The nobility formed the Second Estate. Everyone else, 97 percent of the French people, made up the Third Estate.

Members of the Third Estate deeply resented the privileges that members of the First and Second Estates enjoyed. For example, neither the First Estate nor the Second Estate was required to pay taxes. The nobility received high positions in the Church, in the government, and in the army, and they could also hunt and carry swords. Third Estate members enjoyed none of these social and political privileges. No matter how successful and well-educated Third Estate members became, they were always excluded from the First and Second Estates—simply because of the families into which they were born.

The First Estate

The First Estate consisted of Roman Catholic clergy and made up about 1 percent of the population. The First Estate comprised two groups: the higher clergy and the lower clergy.

SECTION RESOURCES

Reproducible Masters
- Lecture Notes 22-1
- Reproducible Lesson Plan 22-1
- Vocabulary Activity 22
- Guided Reading Activity 22-1
- Time Line Activity 22
- People in World History Profile 41

- Section Quiz 22-1
- Reading Essentials and Study Guide 22-1

Transparencies
- Section Focus Transparency 22-1
- Chapter Transparency 22

Multimedia
- Interactive Tutor Self-Assessment Software
- Testmaker
- Turning Points in World History: *French Revolution*

History & Art *The City and Port of Tolone* (Toulon) by Joseph Vernet. The Louvre, Paris, France **The bourgeoisie in French cities enjoyed wealth and leisure, but few political rights.** *Where had they learned about freedom and social justice?*

Bishops and abbots, noblemen by birth, made up the higher clergy. These powerful men controlled between 5 and 10 percent of the land in France and enjoyed many privileges. At their disposal were the revenues from their land as well as a tithe, or a 10 percent tax on income, from each church member. Although this money was used to support schools, aid poor people, and maintain church property, it also paid for the grand lifestyles the higher clergy enjoyed, often at the expense of their religious duties.

The lower clergy, made up of parish priests, came from poorer backgrounds and were socially more a part of the Third Estate. Many lower clergy members who carried out religious duties, ran schools, and cared for the poor resented the luxurious lifestyles of the higher clergy.

The Second Estate

The nobility, the Second Estate, formed about 2 percent of the population and owned about 25 percent of the land in France. Like the upper clergy, the members of the Second Estate enjoyed many privileges and lived in great style.

The nobility held high posts in the government and the military. Some resided in the palace at **Versailles**. Others lived in lavish homes on inherited land, some of which they rented to peasants to farm. The Second Estate's main income came from the feudal dues they collected from the peasants who lived on and worked their land.

The Third Estate

The Third Estate made up the largest social group in France during the late 1700s. Peasants and artisans, as well as members of the bourgeoisie (BURZH•WAH•ZEE), or middle class, belonged to the Third Estate. Yet they had very few political rights or privileges.

The doctors, lawyers, merchants, and business managers of the bourgeoisie generally lived in the towns and cities. Educated and well-to-do, they had read Enlightenment works and believed in freedom and social justice.

Other members of the Third Estate, such as thousands of poor artisans and their families, also lived in the cities. Artisans worked for low wages and in poor working conditions. Many lived in the slums of **Paris**.

The peasants, the Third Estate's largest group, lived in rural areas. Although they owned 40 percent of the land, they were very poor because of the payments they had to make to the other estates. These payments included a tithe to the clergy; feudal dues and fines to the nobles; and a land tax to the king. Although members of the Third Estate worked hard, they had no effective voice in the government.

Growing Unrest

Unhappy with this unfair social structure, the people of the Third Estate began to call for change. An Englishman traveling in France saw this growing unrest reflected in a conversation he had with a peasant woman:

❝ Walking up a long hill ... I was joined by a poor woman who complained of the times, and that it was a sad country; ... she said her husband had but a morsel of land, one cow, and a poor little horse, yet they had [42 lbs.] of wheat and three chickens to pay as rent to one [lord], and [4 lbs.] of oats, one chicken and 1s. [shilling] to pay to another, besides very heavy tailles and other taxes. ❞

—Arthur Young, from *Travels*, 1789

Chapter 22 *The French Revolution* **561**

TEACH

Guided Practice

THEME Revolution

Ask students to brainstorm definitions of the term *revolution*. When are people justified in choosing revolution as a solution to political problems? **L1**

History & Art Toulon, on the southeast coast of France, is the principal site of modern-day France's Mediterranean fleet. **Answer to Caption:** *They had read Enlightenment works.*

VIDEODISC
Turning Points in World History

Side One
Chapter 11

Title: *French Revolution*
Ask: Why was 1789 considered "the best of times" for some and "the worst of times" for others in France? *(It was the best of times for the clergy and nobility because they had power and privileges while paying no taxes. It was the worst of times for peasants who went hungry and paid high taxes.)*

Religion Ask students to define the phrase "separation of church and state." *(Religions do not have a formal say in government decisions, and the government has no control over religions.)* Then discuss the relationship between church and state in France and its results. **L3**

COOPERATIVE LEARNING ACTIVITY

Debate Explain that the French government faced heavy debt in 1789. To pay the debt, the king wanted to increase taxes. The clergy and nobility had been exempt from taxation. Would they accept some of the burden now? Organize students into three groups, representing the First, Second, and Third Estates. Each group should prepare a statement and choose a person to present its position on taxation. Allow time for discussion, then vote on each proposal for tax apportionment. Each estate receives one vote. Members of each estate must arrive at a consensus before voting. **L3**

Chapter Transparency 22

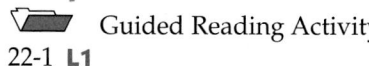

The following videotape program is available from Glencoe:

• **Marie Antoinette: Tragic Queen**

Independent Practice

 Guided Reading Activity 22-1 **L1**

Time Line Activity 22

People in World History Profile 41

Have students use the **Chapter 22 Student Web Activity** at worldhistory.glencoe.com for in-depth study of the Bastille.

Linking Past and Present

Tricolor The French revolutionaries established the red, white, and blue flag, called the tricolor, that France continues to use today.

ASSESS

Check for Understanding

Assign Section 1 Assessment as homework or as an in-class activity.

Use Interactive Tutor Self-Assessment Software to review Section 1.

As a growing population put increasing demands on resources, and the cost of living in France increased, the peasants' anger rose. Nobles also charged the peasants higher fees for the use of such equipment as mills and wine presses.

At the same time, artisans in the cities faced higher prices while their wages stayed the same. Although members of the bourgeoisie were prosperous, they wanted more political power. Nobles resented the king's absolute power and wanted to increase their political influence in the government.

A growing financial crisis in government only added to the country's problems. The 1700s had begun with debts from Louis XIV's wars. Louis XV's extravagant court had enlarged this debt.

In 1774 **Louis XVI**, the 19-year-old grandson of Louis XV, took the throne. His wife, **Marie Antoinette**, was a year younger. In spite of his inexperience, the young king recognized the growing financial crisis. Supporting the American Revolution had only increased his debt. After initiating government cost-cutting measures, Louis saw no option other than taxing the nobility and the clergy. Both groups, however, refused to be taxed.

By 1786 banks began to refuse to lend money to the ailing government. Crop failures caused bread shortages in 1788 and 1789. When the privileged classes refused to aid the government, Louis summoned the Estates-General to Versailles in May 1789. Only in this way could he get additional taxes.

Calling the Estates Together

The Estates-General, which had not met since 1614, was made up of delegates representing each estate. The king hoped that the gathering would agree to new taxes on the First and Second Estates. The nobles, however, intended to use the Estates-General to protect their privileges, weaken royal power, and gain control of the government. Because each estate in the Estates-General had a single vote, the nobles hoped that the First and Second Estates together could easily dominate the Third Estate.

Members of the Third Estate refused this plan. Claiming that they had more right to represent the

Student Web Activity 22

Visit the *World History: The Human Experience* Web site at **worldhistory.glencoe.com** and click on *Chapter 22—Student Web Activities* for an activity relating to the French Revolution.

---

nation than either the clergy or the nobles, Third Estate delegates called for a joint meeting of the three estates, with each delegate voting as an individual. The Third Estate was as large as the other two combined, and many reform-minded nobles and clergymen supported their views. A mass meeting would give the Third Estate a majority vote. A clergy member who supported the Third Estate, the Abbé Sieyès (see•AY•YEHS), wrote:

❝ Therefore, what is the Third Estate? Everything; but an everything shackled and oppressed. What would it be without the privileged order? Everything, but an everything free and flourishing. Nothing can succeed without it, everything would be infinitely better without the others. ❞

The king, however, insisted that the estates meet separately. Refusing the king's demands, the representatives of the Third Estate, most of whom were members of the bourgeoisie, were eventually locked out of the Estates-General. They named themselves the National Assembly and gathered at a nearby indoor tennis court with deputies from the other estates who supported their cause. Here the representatives took an oath, known as the Tennis Court Oath, promising not to disband until they had written a constitution for France.

The king recognized the danger of letting the Third Estate alone draw up a constitution. He ordered the first two estates to join the Third Estate in the National Assembly. Fearing trouble, he also called for troops to concentrate in areas around Paris.

A Call to Revolt

In the National Assembly, delegates voiced their unhappiness with the rigid French social order and the government. While the upper clergy and nobility fought to keep their privileges, some members of the Third Estate called for complete social equality. Debates also raged on streets and in cafes.

The king added to the anxiety by gathering more troops in Versailles. Fearing that he planned to dissolve the National Assembly and halt reforms, the citizens reacted. They focused their action on a Paris prison called **the Bastille** (ba•STEEL).

The Fall of the Bastille

To many French people, the Bastille symbolized the injustices of the monarchy. On July 14, 1789, a huge mob surrounded the Bastille in an attempt to

---

History & Art Some members of the First and Second Estates joined the Third Estate at the royal indoor tennis court at Versailles. Ask students why they may have decided to do that. *(to show support for the Third Estate or to try to prevent radicals from taking over the National Assembly)* **Answer to Caption:** *The king had gathered troops at his palace in Versailles.*

Evaluate

Section Quiz 22-1

Use the Testmaker to create a customized quiz for Section 1.

Reteach

Have students review the groups that made up each of the three estates and the privileges, rights, and responsibilities of each group that led to the revolution.

Reading Essentials and Study Guide 22-1

Enrich

Have students draw a political cartoon depicting a member of the Second Estate responding to Louis XVI's idea of taxing the nobility.

CLOSE

Have students create a flowchart documenting the events in France that led to the storming of the Bastille.

The Oath of the Tennis Court, detail from a painting by L.C.A. Couder **The National Assembly, locked out of the meeting hall for three days, resumed their meeting at an indoor tennis court.** *What caused members to fear that the National Assembly would be dissolved by force?*

steal weapons needed to defend the National Assembly. Tensions grew as the angry crowd tried to force its way into the fortress.

The prison commander finally lowered a drawbridge. The mob, however, angrily pressed forward into the main courtyard. Armed with axes, they freed the 7 prisoners held in the Bastille. The soldiers opened fire, killing 98 rioters. The prison commander and several soldiers were also killed as the rioters took over the prison. This outbreak led to the formation of a revolutionary government in Paris.

Violence in the Countryside

The storming of the Bastille released a wave of violence throughout France called the Great Fear. When rumors spread wildly that nobles had hired robbers to kill peasants and seize their property, the peasants armed themselves. No robbers came, but fear fanned the peasants' anxiety into violence. Peasants drove some landlords off their property, broke into manor houses, robbed granaries, and destroyed feudal records. The first wave of the French Revolution had struck.

SECTION 1 ASSESSMENT

Main Idea
1. Use a web diagram like the one below to show the causes of the French Revolution.

Causes of the French Revolution

Recall
2. **Define** estate, tithe, bourgeoisie.
3. **Identify** Louis XVI, Marie Antoinette, National Assembly, Tennis Court Oath.

Critical Thinking
4. **Analyzing Information** July 14, Bastille Day, is celebrated in France like an independence

day. Why is it an important national event?

Understanding Themes
5. **Revolution** When did events in France, which started as a protest by the people, become a revolution? Give specific evidence to support your reasoning.

Chapter 22 *The French Revolution* **563**

1788   1790   1792   1794

1789 National Assembly adopts Declaration of the Rights of Man and of the Citizen.

1791 New French constitution is presented to the people.

1792 France declares war on Austria.

Section 2

Constitutional Government

Guide to Reading

Read to Find Out

Main Idea *The National Assembly adopted many political reforms for France.*

▶ **Terms to Define**
unicameral legislature, émigré

▶ **People to Meet**
Pope Pius VI

The Storyteller

Sharp differences of political opinion disrupted the Paris opera. At a performance of Iphigenia the chorus sang "Let us honor our Queen." Royalists applauded, but the opposing party booed. Lainez, an actor who remarked that "every good Frenchman should love the king and queen," was thrown a laurel wreath. Two days later, the revolutionaries would not let Lainez act until he had trampled that wreath underfoot.

—adapted from *Blood Sisters, The French Revolution in Women's Memory,* Marilyn Yalom, 1993

French social groups

As violence swept the countryside, the National Assembly worked to form a new government. This task was complicated by power struggles among royalists, moderates, and radicals. Most royalists still favored absolute monarchy, but a growing number of moderates wanted the king to share power with a new legislature. Their leader was the Marquis de Lafayette, who had aided the colonists in the American Revolution. A radical group, the Paris Commune, won control of Paris's city government and pushed for an end to the monarchy.

End of the Old Order

Peasant unrest and urban violence finally forced the National Assembly to make reforms. On August 4, 1789, the nobles in that body voted to end their privileges. In a session lasting until 2 A.M., deputies wept and cheered as the last remains of feudalism in France were destroyed. The nobles gave up feudal dues as well as their exemption from taxation. They also agreed that all male citizens could hold government, army, or church office.

The Declaration of Rights

With the old order abolished, the deputies turned to ensuring the equality of all citizens before the law. Inspired by the American Declaration of Independence and Constitution, as well as the English Bill of Rights, the National Assembly composed the Declaration of the Rights of Man and of the Citizen in late August 1789. It is in the French Constitution today.

The Declaration of Rights, which incorporated the ideas of Enlightenment writers Locke, Montesquieu, and Rousseau, stated that all people are equal before the law. It also guaranteed freedom of speech, press, and religion, and protected against arbitrary arrest and punishment.

The Declaration, however, did not grant equal rights to women. When the journalist Olympe de Gouges and other women called for equality, revolutionary leaders rejected their demands. Women did, however, benefit from reforms that made divorce easier and allowed them to inherit property.

March to Versailles

The king refused to accept the new reforms and the Declaration of Rights. This rejection raised the fears of the citizens of Paris that he would take action against the National Assembly. The people wanted Louis to move to Paris from his countryside palace in the town of Versailles to show his support for the Assembly.

In October 1789 thousands of women demanding bread marched in the rain to the king's palace in Versailles. Wielding sticks and pitchforks, the angry mob surrounded the palace, shouting for the king and queen. As the cries grew louder and armed guards were not able to hold back the surging crowd, the king declared at last, "My friends, I will go to Paris with my wife and children."

That afternoon, women waving banners and loaves of bread on bayonets surrounded the king's carriage as it drove from Versailles to Paris. In Paris, fervent anti-royalists watched the king, Marie Antoinette, and their two children. A few days later the National Assembly moved to Paris.

A New France

With the king and the National Assembly settled in Paris, government affairs began to move forward again. The delegates could turn their attention to political reforms.

Political Reforms

One problem faced by the National Assembly was government financing. With the backing of a liberal bishop, Maurice de Talleyrand, the Assembly in 1790 voted to take and sell church lands to pay off the huge government debt. To weaken the power of the Catholic Church, it also passed the Civil Constitution of the Clergy, a measure that placed the French Church under government control and turned the clergy into elected, salaried officials. The Civil Constitution created a deep rift between the Church and the Revolution. **Pope Pius VI** condemned the legislation, and many clergy refused to accept it. Other opponents of the Civil Constitution were many conservative peasants in the provinces.

The Constitution of 1791

In 1791 the National Assembly presented a new constitution to the people. The constitution kept the monarchy but limited royal powers. It set up a uni-cameral legislature, or one-house assembly, whose members were to be chosen by voters. Although equal rights were declared for all, the suffrage, or

Visualizing History *Louis XVI Arrested at Varennes* (engraving) After an attempted escape in June 1791, the royal family was watched closely in Paris. *Why did revolutionary leaders declare war on Austria?*

Chapter 22   *The French Revolution*   **565**

TEACH

Guided Practice

THEME Change

Have students create a chart listing changes brought about by the National Assembly in the right-hand column and the corresponding state of affairs before the revolution in the left-hand column. **L1**

Critical Thinking Write the following sentence on the chalkboard: *I am king, and I have the God-given right to rule France. Signed, Louis XVI.* Discuss how this belief influenced events in France. **L2**

VIDEODISC
Turning Points in World History

Side One
Chapter 11

Title: *French Revolution*
Ask: What American document inspired the "Rights of Man"? *(the Declaration of Independence)*

Visualizing History Louis XVI and his family planned to cross the border into the Austrian Netherlands, northeast of France, and put down the revolution with help from Austrian troops stationed there. Marie Antoinette was from Austria.
Answer to Caption: *They feared Austria would try to reinstate Louis XVI as an absolute monarch.*

COOPERATIVE LEARNING ACTIVITY

Newspaper Have the class work together to plan the front page of *The Revolutionary Times*, a newspaper chronicling the events of the French Revolution through Louis XVI's failed flight to Varennes. After students have read Section 2, organize them into groups and have each group list the stories and visuals they would put on the front page. Students may get ideas for visuals from illustrations in Chapter 22. Groups can decide which event gets the top headline and where the other lead articles and visuals should go. Then, as a class, have groups decide on final placement of stories and visuals. **L2**

Independent Practice

 Guided Reading Activity
22-2 **L1**

 Source Reading 22

Government Have students research what *left wing* and *right wing* mean in politics today. Then have students write two or three paragraphs in which they define the terms and describe which groups were on the left and on the right in France in 1791. **L3**

ASSESS

Check for Understanding

Assign Section 2 Assessment as homework or as an in-class activity.

🖲 Use Interactive Tutor Self-Assessment Software to review Section 2.

Evaluate

 Section Quiz 22-2

🖲 Use the Testmaker to create a customized quiz for Section 2.

Reteach

Have students create a chart on the chalkboard listing the different political groups in France and their goals.

 Reading Essentials and Study Guide 22-2

Enrich

Have students prepare speeches that might have been made by women organizing the march to Versailles in 1789. Speeches should include reasons for the march.

CLOSE

Have students name important events in France for each year from 1789 through 1792. Then let them discuss the significance of each event.

 Revolution in Saint Domingue

August 12, 1791
The French National Assembly, supporting human rights, decided to give the vote to enslaved Africans and people of mixed race in the French colony of Saint Domingue (Haiti). When the planters on the island refused to comply, a major controversy broke out. Enslaved Africans rose in revolt against the plantation owners. Nearly 100,000 of the colony's half million enslaved people participated in the rebellion.

Saint Domingue

the right to vote, was limited to only males who paid a minimum tax.

To the moderates, the Constitution of 1791 had achieved their goals. It guaranteed basic rights and created a limited monarchy largely controlled by the wealthy middle class and freed from the power of the Church and the nobles. However, many French people were not happy with the Constitution. For some, the reforms had gone too far; for others, not far enough. Delegates in the newly elected Legislative Assembly were seated according to their political beliefs: the reactionary royalists on the right; the moderates in the center; and the radicals, who wanted a republic, on the left. Today political scientists use the terms *right*, *center*, and *left* to describe similar political positions.

As political groups became more divided, France entered one of the most tumultuous periods in its history. Disagreements led to unrest and violence. Many upper-class people feared the breakdown of law and order.

Decline of the Monarchy

Living in Paris, Louis XVI and Marie Antoinette were aware of the unrest. In June 1791 they decided to flee to Austria, where the queen's brother was emperor. Disguised as ordinary people, the royal family left Paris in a carriage late at night.

A bystander recognized the king at a road stop in Varennes, a town east of Paris. Soldiers immediately arrested the royal family, returning them to Paris. A virtual prisoner, Louis reluctantly accepted the limited monarchy established by the National Assembly. The limited monarchy, though, had little chance of success, for the people distrusted the king and were leaning toward a republic.

As news of the revolt against the French monarchy spread, German and Austrian monarchs began to worry about the stability of their own governments. French émigrés (EH•mih•GRAY), nobles who had fled France, hoped to restore Louis XVI to full power. The émigrés tried to convince the leaders of these governments that their own rule would be threatened unless they halted the revolution.

Meanwhile French revolutionary leaders, fearing that Austria would try to reinstate Louis, declared war on Austria in 1792. Austria was soon supported by other monarchies, including Prussia and Sardinia.

War threw France into total upheaval. In August 1792, Paris crowds attacked the king's palace and killed many royal guards. Seeking protection, the king and his family fled to the Legislative Assembly. There they were given no safety; instead the radicals voted for their imprisonment. A month later, Paris mobs carried out the "September massacres," killing imprisoned nobles and priests accused of political crimes. Meanwhile, the radicals took over the Assembly and called for a National Convention to create a new constitution. They also extended the vote to all males, whether or not they owned property.

SECTION 2 ASSESSMENT

Main Idea
1. Use a diagram like the one below to list the political reforms adopted by the French National Assembly.

Political Reforms of National Assembly

Recall
2. **Define** unicameral legislature, émigré.
3. **Identify** the Declaration of the Rights of Man and of the Citizen, Civil Constitution of the Clergy, Pope Pius VI.

Critical Thinking
4. **Analyzing Information** What type of government did French moderates and radicals each want?

Understanding Themes
5. **Change** How did the Civil Constitution of the Clergy affect church-government relations?

 SECTION 2 ASSESSMENT ANSWERS

1. nobles gave up feudal dues and exemption from taxation; all male citizens could hold government, army, or church office; all men equal before law; Civil Constitution of the Clergy; could take and sell Church land to pay debt; Constitution of 1791; limited monarchy
2. All terms are defined in the Glossary.
3. Declaration, 564; Civil Constitution, 565; Pope Pius VI, 565
4. Moderates favored a limited monarchy; radicals wanted a republic.
5. **CHANGE** It placed the French Church under government control and created a deep rift between the Church and the revolutionary government.

1793 King Louis XVI is beheaded on the guillotine.

1795 The Directory comes to power in France.

1799 Napoleon helps to overthrow the Directory.

Section 3

Dawn of a New Era

Guide to Reading

Read to Find Out
Main Idea *The French Revolution led to war between France and its neighbors.*

▶ **Terms to Define**
conscription, coup d'état

▶ **People to Meet**
Jacobins, Girondists, Napoleon Bonaparte

▶ **Places to Locate**
Prussia, Valmy

The Storyteller

Paul Lemieux was both excited and anxious. At age 16 he had just received a notice that he would be one of the 3,000 young citizens to attend the new School of Mars. The Committee of Public Safety created the new school for learning and public military instruction. He read the Committee's report, "Loyalty to your own families must end when the great family calls you. The Republic leaves to parents the guidance of your first years, but as soon as your intelligence develops, it loudly proclaims the right it has over you. You are born for the Republic and not to be the pride of family despotism or its victims...." Paul wondered how this choice would affect his life.

A sans-culotte

—from *The Era of the French Revolution, 1789-1799*, Leo Gershoy, 1957

In September 1792 the French revolutionary leaders faced the result of their declaration of war on Austria and **Prussia**. Prussian troops had taken the major French fort of Verdun, and the road to Paris was now open for them. As fear gripped the country, Georges-Jacques Danton, a revolutionary orator, exclaimed: "All are burning with a desire to fight! We need boldness ... and France will be saved."

In response to Danton's words, thousands of volunteers came forward to defend the revolution. A week later, thoughts of defeat vanished when the French army won an astonishing victory at **Valmy**, less than 100 miles (161 km) from Paris. The French commander later wrote in his diary:

> ❝ Our soldiers were badly clothed, they had no straw to sleep on, no blankets, they sometimes went two days without bread. I never once saw them complain.... The tiredness and hardship they have suffered have been rewarded. The enemy has [yielded] to the season, misery, and illness. Its formidable army is in flight, its numbers halved.... ❞
>
> —Commander Dumouriez, 1792

The victory at Valmy boosted the spirits of the revolutionaries. French forces had halted the powerful armies of Europe's monarchs and had saved the revolution for the time being.

TURNING POINT

The French Republic

As cannons thundered at Valmy, the National Convention met in Paris to create a new government for France. Shouts of "Long live the Nation!" echoed through the chamber as the delegates ended the monarchy and made France a republic.

Chapter 22 *The French Revolution* **567**

▶ **Conflict** The new French Republic faces enemies at home and abroad.

Guide to Reading

For reading strategies to help students read effectively see pages 12–13.

Vocabulary Pre-check

▣ Use the Vocabulary PuzzleMaker for Chapter 22 to create a crossword puzzle to reinforce section terms. **L1 LEP**

📁 Use Vocabulary Activity 22 to introduce vocabulary terms. **L1 LEP**

FOCUS

Section Objective
Explain why the French Revolution led to war between France and its neighbors.

BELLRINGER
Motivational Activity

Project Section Focus Transparency 22-3 and have students answer the questions.
📁 Available as a blackline master.

TURNING POINT

The French Republic
What were the achievements of the first French Republic? *France received its first democratic constitution and introduced the metric system.*

SECTION RESOURCES

📁 **Reproducible Masters**
- Lecture Notes 22-3
- Reproducible Lesson Plan 22-3
- Vocabulary Activity 22
- Guided Reading Activity 22-3
- History Simulation 22
- People in World History Profile 42
- Section Quiz 22-3
- Reading Essentials and Study Guide 22-3

🔖 **Transparencies**
- Section Focus Transparency 22-3

Multimedia
▣ Interactive Tutor Self-Assessment Software
▣ Testmaker
▣ Turning Points in World History: *French Revolution*

Chapter 22 *The French Revolution* **567**

TEACH

Guided Practice

THEME Conflict

Have students imagine that the classroom is the National Convention. Tell students at the back that they are sitting on high benches. Which groups do you represent? What are the views of these groups? (*sans-culottes and Jacobins; radical*) Tell students at the front that they are Girondists and those in the middle that they are the Plain. Have these two groups explain their views. Then ask students from the front and back to try to persuade the middle to support their points of view on the revolution. **L2**

Literature Write the following quote from the opening of Charles Dickens's *A Tale of Two Cities* on the chalkboard: "It was the best of times, it was the worst of times …" Discuss how this quote applies to the French Revolution. **L2**

History & Art

The Trianon and its gardens, a royal retreat on the grounds at Versailles complete with a theater, lake, river, and village, became a symbol of the excesses of Marie Antoinette. Why did the French people resent the queen's lifestyle? (*She continued her luxurious life while ordinary citizens did not have enough to eat.*)
Answer to Caption: *They began dressing more simply—men wearing long, plain trousers and women wearing long, straight dresses.*

The National Convention met from 1792 to 1795. Its members—who were all male and mostly lawyers, doctors, and other middle-class professionals—passed into law a number of democratic reforms. The Convention wrote France's first democratic constitution. The constitution placed political power in a single national legislature based on universal male suffrage, meaning that every man could vote, whether or not he owned property. Convention members also replaced the monarchy's confusing system of weights and measures with the metric system still used throughout the world today.

The National Convention also adopted a new calendar, naming September 22, 1792—the date of the republic's creation—as the first day of the Year I of Liberty. The year was divided into months with such names as *Nivôse* ("the snowy month"), *Germinal* ("seed time"), and *Thermidor* ("the warm month"). Although this calendar did not last, it and the other democratic reforms expressed the French people's hope that the republic would be the dawn of a new era of freedom.

Death of a King

Before it could enter the republican era, the Convention had to deal with the legacy of the past. Its first task was to decide Louis XVI's fate. In November 1792 a large iron box holding Louis's secret correspondence with foreign monarchs was found in the royal palace. Although the letters provided little evidence against Louis, the radicals successfully used them to discredit the royal family.

In December 1792 Louis was tried before the Convention and convicted of having "conspired against the liberty of the nation." In January 1793 he was beheaded on the guillotine—a killing machine the revolutionaries had adopted as a humane means of execution. As he faced execution, the king reportedly said:

> **I forgive my enemies; I trust that my death will be for the happiness of my people, but I grieve for France and I fear that she may suffer the anger of the Lord.**

History & Art *Marie Antoinette in the Park of Trianon* by Antoine Vestier **Because of her extravagance, the people referred to the queen as "Madame Deficit."** *How did Parisians show their feelings about elaborate clothes?*

Parisian crowds joyously celebrated the king's death. For them, it meant that there was no turning back; the republic would remain.

Toward the Future

In the days that followed, republican enthusiasm swept the country. Parisians were the most fervent. The *sans-culottes*—Paris's shopkeepers, artisans, and workers—saw themselves as heroes and heroines and demanded respect from the upper classes.

Soon even wealthy Parisians addressed each other as "citizen" or "citizeness" rather than "mister" or "madame." They rejected elaborate clothes and powdered wigs in favor of simple styles. Men wore long trousers instead of knee-length breeches (hence the name *sans-culottes,* meaning "without breeches"); women wore long dresses in the style of ancient Rome.

While the nation celebrated the republic, debate over the revolution's future erupted in the Convention. There, supporters of the *sans-culottes* and extreme radicals called the **Jacobins** (JA•kuh•buhns) formed the Mountain, so called because its members sat on high benches at the rear of the hall. Under leaders such as Maximilien Robespierre, Georges-Jacques Danton, and Jean-Paul Marat, the Mountain saw itself as the defender of the revolution and as the voice of the people.

Across the aisle was a group of moderates known as **Girondists** (juh•RAHN•dihsts), because many of them came from the Gironde, a region in southwestern France. The Girondists felt that the revolution had gone far enough and wanted to

---

COOPERATIVE LEARNING ACTIVITY

Role Play Organize the class into three or four groups and have each group create a television interview program in which ordinary citizens during the French Revolution talk about the times in which they live. Have each group select a television host and individuals to act as guests. The guests could be a shopkeeper, a Jacobin, a Girondist, a *sans-culottes*, a farm woman, a soldier in the French army, and a housewife. The host and students acting as the audience should prepare questions through which the guests reveal important historical developments and how these events affected them. **L2**

Spectrum of Political Opinion

Left		Center	Right	
Radical	**Liberal**	**Moderate**	**Conservative**	**Reactionary**
Favors extreme change in policy	Favors some change in policy	Open to minor change in policy	Favors maintaining the status quo	Favors a return to past policies

Chart Study To the three political groups in the French Legislative Assembly, political scientists today add two—liberal and conservative. Which group represents those who supported limited monarchy in 1791?

protect the wealthy middle class from radical attacks. They organized support to resist the growing strength of the Mountain in Paris.

Seated between these two rivals on the main floor was a group called the Plain. It was made up of undecided deputies who were a majority of the Convention. As the influence of the *sans-culottes* increased during 1793, members of the Plain came to support the Mountain. Together, they helped make the revolution more radical, more open to extreme and violent change.

Spreading the Revolution

Meanwhile, Europe's monarchs viewed events in France with horror. After Louis's execution, they feared democratic revolutions could spread from France and endanger their thrones and their lives. In January 1793 the monarchs of Great Britain, the Netherlands, Spain, and Sardinia joined those of Austria and Prussia in an alliance against the revolutionary government of France.

French Expansion

At the same time, France's leaders were determined to overthrow royalty everywhere. Early in 1793 Danton declared that "the kings in alliance try to frighten us, [but] we hurl at their feet, as a gage of battle, the French king's head." He then called upon French forces to expand France's territories to their natural frontiers: the Alps, the Pyrenees, the Rhine River, and the Mediterranean Sea.

In response to this call, an army made up of volunteers poured outward from France, eager to seize the natural frontiers and to bring "liberty, equality, and fraternity" to Europe's peoples. Although poorly trained, the French forces often caught the enemy off guard and won many battles. The enemy's professional soldiers, however, soon inflicted on the French a string of defeats. In despair, the French commander in chief abandoned his troops and surrendered.

As French forces retreated, the National Convention took steps to repel the foreign invasion. It formed the Committee of Public Safety to direct the entire war effort. In the summer of 1793 the Committee adopted conscription, or the draft, calling up all men between the ages of 18 and 45 for military service. It also called upon the skills and resources of all civilians, both men and women. The Committee turned the conflict into what has been called the world's first "people's war."

The Revolution in Crisis

While waging war, France's revolutionaries had to struggle with problems at home. A fierce civil war raged in western France as royalist peasants revolted against the revolutionaries. They were angered by the drafting of their sons to fight a war they opposed. Mobs in French cities rioted to protest rising food prices and food shortages.

Meanwhile, the government itself was embroiled in a political crisis. The Girondists accused the Jacobins of seeking the favor of the mob. The Jacobins responded by charging that the Girondists were secretly royalists. The Jacobins in the Mountain won control of the Convention and arrested Girondist delegates.

In retaliation Girondist supporters rebelled against the Jacobins in the Convention. During the uprising Charlotte Corday, a loyal Girondist supporter, killed the Jacobin leader Marat and was sent to the guillotine.

Footnotes to History

The Wax Museum A young Swiss woman living in Paris immortalized the revolution's leaders by making wax models of them. She escaped to London, where she opened a museum—Madame Tussaud's Exhibition—that is open today.

Chapter 22 *The French Revolution* **569**

Independent Practice

📁 Guided Reading Activity 22-3 **L1**

📁 People in World History Profile 42

Time Line Have students create a time line of events in Section 3. Ask students to write a paragraph describing each event and its significance. **L1**

Biography Have students choose a person from the French Revolution and write a short biography of him or her. Tell students to include information from Section 3 as well as from other sources. **L2 LEP**

Global 🌐 Gourmet

Paris Bread was the mainstay in the diet of the average Parisian in 1789. A typical French worker ate a four-pound loaf a day. Supplying bread for the city's more than 600,000 inhabitants was a major production. It is not surprising that it was often a problem as well. Bread shortages played a significant role in the onset of the French Revolution.

---

you don't say...

Jacobin was originally used to refer to priests of the Dominican order whose first religious house in Paris was on the Rue St. Jacques. When the radical group made up of Robespierre, Marat, and others met in a former Dominican religious house, the French radicals became known as Jacobins. Today the word is used to refer to people with radical views.

The Reign of Terror

Overwhelmed by enemies at home and abroad, the Jacobins set out to crush all opposition within France. This effort, known as the Reign of Terror, lasted from July 1793 to July 1794.

Crushing Opposition

During the Terror, neighborhood watch committees hunted down suspected traitors and turned them over to the courts. Pressured by mobs, the courts carried out swift trials and handed down harsh sentences. Innocent people often suffered—many of them sentenced because of false statements made by hostile neighbors. Among the victims of the Terror was Marie Antoinette, Louis XVI's wife. Royalty and aristocrats, however, were only a few of those killed. Historians estimate that about 85 percent of the 40,000 people who died were probably commoners—merchants, laborers, and peasants. The Committee of Public Safety ruled France, and Robespierre ruled the committee.

Republic of Virtue

Meanwhile, the Jacobin-controlled Committee of Public Safety went about setting up the "Republic of Virtue." By this the Jacobins meant a democratic republic made up of good citizens. Toward this end, the Committee opened new schools and promoted the idea of universal elementary education. In economic matters, it issued pamphlets to teach farmers agricultural skills and introduced temporary wage and price controls to halt inflation. In the area of human rights, it abolished slavery in France's colonies and encouraged religious toleration.

Radical revolutionaries, however, bitterly opposed Catholicism because of its traditional links with monarchy and its claim to be the sole source of religious truth. They closed churches or turned them into "temples of reason." Fearing a further loss of support for the revolution among believers, the Committee opposed these actions. Robespierre himself sponsored the worship of a Supreme Being in an effort to unite Catholics, deists, and nonbelievers.

Images *of the* Times

Revolutionary Life

Although the causes of the French Revolution had existed for years, the events of 1789 sparked the beginning of the revolution.

After a failed harvest caused bread prices to increase, about 6,000 Parisian women marched on Versailles.

Tri-color badge

570

Images *of the* Times
Revolutionary Life

The *bonnet rouge* or red liberty cap became a symbol of loyalty to the revolution. The cap came from the head wrap used by enfranchised formerly enslaved Romans. At first, the caps were held high on poles during meetings and ceremonies. Then the Jacobins started wearing them to their meetings. Soon they became the obligatory headgear of all French patriots. Citizens were forced to wear them under pain of beating or death. The king even wore one after the invasion of the Tuileries Palace.

End of the Terror

By the spring of 1794, the French had taken the offensive in the war. With the republic out of danger, Danton and his supporters called for an end to the Terror. Robespierre, however, accused them of treason and had them sent to the guillotine. Fearing for their own safety, other leaders then turned against Robespierre and had him executed. The day after the execution, a Paris newspaper expressed the relief that everyone felt: "We are all throwing ourselves into each other's arms."

After Robespierre's death, the Jacobins lost power and the Terror came to an end. A reaction against Jacobin ideas began, and the wealthier middle class took control of the Convention. Fashions changed as people rebelled against the "Republic of Virtue." Once again, people wore knee breeches, luxurious dresses, and wigs. Price controls were relaxed, and prices rose sharply, causing hardship for the poor. Riots broke out, but the leaderless lower classes were easily put down by the army. By mid-1794, many people even favored a restoration of the monarchy.

The Directory

After Robespierre's fall the Convention briefly carried on as France's government. In 1795 it wrote a new constitution. Universal male suffrage was ended; only citizens who owned property could vote. This constitution, in effect, brought the government under the control of the wealthy middle class. The constitution also set up an executive council of five men called directors. The Directory, as the council was called, ruled with a two-house legislature.

Once in power the Directory faced many enemies. Despite the Terror, enough royalists remained to threaten a takeover. Even more alarming was the growing discontent of the radical *sans-culottes*, angered by food shortages and rising prices. During its rule from 1795 to 1799, the Directory used the army to put down uprisings by both groups.

Meanwhile, the Directory made little effort to resolve a growing gap between the rich and the poor people of France. It was having its own problems: the revolutionary government was on the

Symbols of the revolution carried the message of liberty, equality, and fraternity—or death.

UNITE·INDIVISIBILITE
DE·LA·REPUBLIQUE
LIBERTE·EGALITE
FRATERNITE·OU·LA·MORT

REFLECTING ON THE TIMES

1. Why would these images cause European monarchs to react in horror?
2. How might peasants in neighboring European countries react?

571

Cultural Perspectives

Revolutionary Titles Just as the French revolutionaries addressed every person as "Citizen" rather than by titles such as "Sir" or "Madam," the Communists during the Russian Revolution addressed one another as *"Tovarishch"* (meaning "Comrade"). In both cases, the attempt was to show equality of people within a cause. "Comrade" later came to mean a member of the Communist party, not just a citizen of the country.

Who?What?Where?When?

The revolutionary calendar helped secularize revolutionary France by not including Sundays and church feast days. The new calendar contained 12 months, each with 30 days broken into 3 weeks made up of 10 days each. The remaining 5 days of the year were feast days dedicated to the *sans-culottes*. France reverted to the Gregorian calendar on January 1, 1806.

ASSESS

Check for Understanding

Assign Section 3 Assessment as homework or as an in-class activity.

🔲 Use Interactive Tutor Self-Assessment Software to review Section 3.

Evaluate

📁 Section Quiz 22-3

🔲 Use the Testmaker to create a customized quiz for Section 3.

TEACH

Tell students that the inventor of the guillotine, Dr. Joseph Ignace Guillotin, was a member of the Constituent Assembly and was regarded as a kindly man. Up until the revolution, the punishment of decapitation was viewed as a privilege reserved for nobles. Dr. Guillotin proposed that it be the punishment for anyone accused of a capital crime, regardless of class. He developed his machine to make the process as quick and painless as possible. Point out that people's concepts of "cruel and unusual punishments" have changed over the years. Ask students what they feel constitutes cruel and unusual punishment today.

Linking Past and Present

Guillotine Dr. Guillotin's invention was not the first such machine. Similar decapitating machines had been used in Germany and Italy; in Yorkshire, England; and in Scotland. The guillotine continued to be used in France until 1981, when the French abolished capital punishment.

CURRICULUM CONNECTION

TECHNOLOGY

The Legislative Assembly assigned the guillotine project to a committee that hired a German mechanic to build the machine. To make sure that the new beheading machine worked properly, experiments were conducted on dead bodies at a Paris hospital.

James L. Stanfield

Guillotine

This dreaded machine, pictured here in eerie stillness, embodies the violence and upheaval of the French Revolution. Yet this device used to chop off heads represents not only the terror of the revolution but also its reforms. The guillotine was adopted as a more humane form of capital punishment, a civilized advance over hanging or the executioner's ax. The swift, sharp blade was, according to its French inventor, Dr. Joseph-Ignace Guillotin, "a cool breath on the back of the nec[k]

A saga of social and political upheaval, the Fr[ench] Revolution transformed the people of France [from] subjects of an absolute monarch to citizens [of a] nation. The revolution marked the beginning o[f a] modern age in Europe. "It roused passions," said [19th-] century French writer Alexis de Tocqueville, "revolutions had never before excited." In France [peo]ple still argue over its importance and meaning.

brink of bankruptcy, and the directors were beset by financial and moral scandals in their personal lives. As the Directory appeared more and more inept, French people of all classes looked to the power of the army to save France from ruin.

Napoleon Takes Over

As the Directory faced growing unpopularity at home, the French army won victories in the continuing war with the European monarchies. One of the many able French military leaders who attracted public attention was a young general named **Napoleon Bonaparte**.

Napoleon's Early Fame

During the French Revolution, Napoleon's great military skills won him quick promotion to the rank of general. In 1795, at age 26, he crushed an uprising against the Directory. Napoleon placed his artillery so that he cleared the streets of Paris "with a whiff of grapeshot."

A year later Napoleon married Josephine de Beauharnais, a leader of Paris society. Using Josephine's connections, he won command of the French army that was fighting the Austrians in Italy. Upon arriving, Napoleon improved the soldiers' conditions and mustered their support.

Massing French forces at weak points on the enemy's line, Napoleon defeated the Austrians and forced them to give France most of northern Italy. Napoleon, France's leading general, was now ready to influence events at home.

Napoleon's Bold Move

In 1799 Napoleon seized his opportunity. For more than a year, he had been fighting the British in Egypt, hoping to cut off Britain's trade with the Middle East and India. Napoleon won victories on land against Egyptian forces. However, the British

 Napoleon Crossing the Great St. Bernard by Jacques-Louis David. Chateau de Malmaison, Ruiel-Malmaison, France **Known for his classical style, David was the leading artist of the French Revolution.** *How does David portray Napoleon?*

navy under Admiral Horatio Nelson destroyed the French fleet that was located at a harbor east of Alexandria. French forces were left stranded among the Pyramids. Hearing of the troubled political situation back home, Napoleon abandoned his army in Egypt and returned to France.

Napoleon landed unannounced on the French Mediterranean coast in October 1799. He was greeted in Paris by cheering crowds. Quickly, Napoleon joined leaders in a coup d'état, or a quick seizure of power, against the Directory.

History & Art Napoleon commissioned this painting in 1800. Napoleon spread his image throughout Europe with copies of this portrait and others by David. **Answer to Caption:** *as a heroic military leader, larger than life*

Reteach

Ask students to explain the relevance of each of the following to the French Revolution: National Convention, death of Louis XVI, Jacobins, Robespierre, Reign of Terror, Directory, Napoleon.

📁 Reading Essentials and Study Guide 22-3

Enrich

Have students explain the political significance of the *sans-culottes'* dress. *(celebration of the common citizen)* Ask students to give modern examples of dress reflecting social change.

CLOSE

Have students summarize the conditions in France that made Napoleon's rise to power possible. List the leading conditions on the chalkboard. *(food shortages, rising prices, growing gap between rich and poor, government financial problems, scandals among the directors)*

SECTION 3 ASSESSMENT

Main Idea
1. Use a diagram like the one below to show how the French Revolution led to war between France and its neighbors.

French Revolution

→ War Between France and Neighbors

Recall
2. **Define** conscription, coup d'état.
3. **Identify** Jacobins, Girondists, Reign of Terror, Napoleon Bonaparte.

Critical Thinking
4. **Applying Knowledge** Describe how one revolutionary leader succeeded—

or failed—in carrying out the ideals of "liberty, equality, and fraternity."

Understanding Themes
5. **Conflict** What conditions led to the Reign of Terror? Why did the French revolutionaries use such violent and drastic measures?

SECTION 3 ASSESSMENT ANSWERS

1. fear of revolution led to many European countries allying against French government; French leaders wanted to overthrow royalty everywhere; volunteer army tried to expand France's territories to natural frontiers
2. All the terms are defined in the Glossary.

3. Jacobins, 568; Girondists, 568; Reign of Terror, 570; Napoleon Bonaparte, 573
4. Answers will vary. Possible answer: Leaders such as Robespierre failed in carrying out the revolutionary ideals because they persecuted many innocent people.
5. **CONFLICT** The Reign of

Terror was the outgrowth of the revolutionaries' fears that the revolution would be overthrown. Because they were desperate and the government was in such a chaotic state, the revolutionaries resorted to violence to maintain their power.

1800   1810   1820

1802 France signs Treaty of Amiens with Great Britain.

1804 Napoleon names himself Emperor of the French.

1812 Napoleon invades Russia.

1815 Duke of Wellington wins Battle of Waterloo.

Section 4

Napoleon's Empire

Guide to Reading

Read to Find Out

Main Idea *Napoleon built and then lost an empire.*

▶ **Terms to Define**
dictatorship, plebiscite, nationalism

▶ **People to Meet**
Duke of Wellington, Alexander I, Louis XVIII

▶ **Places to Locate**
Trafalgar, Moscow, Waterloo

The Storyteller

Carl von Clausewitz, a military theoretician, analyzed the French disaster in Russia: "[Napoleon] had hoped from that centre [Moscow], to influence by opinion [St.]Petersburg and the whole of Russia.... He reached Moscow with 90,000 men, he should have reached it with 200,000. This would have been possible if he had handled his army with more care and forbearance. But these were qualities unknown to him.... It is, moreover, to be considered as a great neglect ... to have made so little preparation as he did for retreat."

—translated from *Campaign of 1812 in Russia*, Carl von Clausewitz, 1835

Napoleon Bonaparte

In 1804 Napoleon named himself Emperor of the French. At the brilliant coronation ceremony in Paris, the people witnessed an astonishing act. Napoleon took the crown from the pope's hands and placed it on his own head. Napoleon's action spoke loudly of his intention to be a strong ruler. How had the French government been transformed from a democracy to an empire in five short years?

The Consulate

After his successful overthrow of the Directory in 1799, Napoleon had proclaimed a new constitution, which theoretically established a republic. The constitution actually set up a dictatorship, a government headed by an absolute ruler. The executive branch was a committee of three members, called consuls, who took their title from ancient Rome. Napoleon, however, became First Consul and quickly concentrated power in his own hands.

Restoring Order

Napoleon wanted to bring order to the country. One of his first goals was to restructure the government. Although he tried to keep many of the revolutionary reforms, Napoleon replaced elected local officials with men he appointed himself. He also placed education under the control of the national government, creating technical schools, universities, and secondary schools. The secondary schools, called lycées (lee•SAY), were designed to provide well-educated, patriotic government workers. Although students who attended the lycées came mostly from wealthy families, some poorer students received scholarships. In this way the French schools were a step toward a public school system open to all children.

Napoleon also changed the country's financial system. He created the Bank of France and required that every citizen pay taxes. The collected taxes

History & Art *The Consecration of Emperor Napoleon I and the Coronation of the Empress Josephine* (detail) by Jacques-Louis David. The Louvre, Paris, France
In imitation of Pepin and Charlemagne, Napoleon seized the crown from Pope Pius VII and placed it on his own head in 1804. A virtual dictator, Napoleon had the support of most people in France. *How had Napoleon earlier made peace with the Catholic Church?*

were deposited in the bank and used by the government to make loans to businesses. These changes gradually brought inflation and high prices under control.

Napoleon's many supporters welcomed his strong government and the peace and order it brought. In 1802 Napoleon named himself Consul for life. This move was overwhelmingly approved by a plebiscite, or popular vote.

The Napoleonic Code

Many historians say that Napoleon made his greatest impact on French law. Old feudal and royal laws were often contradictory and confusing. To make French law clear and consistent, Napoleon had a new law code written. Commonly known as the Napoleonic Code, it was based on Enlightenment ideas, such as the equality of all citizens before the law, religious toleration, and advancement based on merit. However, the Code placed the state above the individual. For example, it limited freedom of speech and press by allowing the censorship of books, plays, and pamphlets. Women also lost

many of the rights they had gained during the revolution. Male heads of households were given extensive authority over wives and minor children.

The Church

Napoleon also made peace with the Catholic Church. Realizing that French Catholics had objected to the Civil Constitution of the Clergy, he negotiated an agreement called the Concordat of 1801 with Pope Pius VII. In this agreement Napoleon acknowledged that Catholicism was the religion of the majority of French people but affirmed religious toleration for all. Napoleon did, however, retain the right to name all bishops, who had to swear allegiance to the state. The pope agreed to accept the loss of church lands; in return the state agreed to pay salaries to the Catholic clergy.

Building an Empire

Although Napoleon proved that he was an able administrator, he was more interested in building

Chapter 22 *The French Revolution* **575**

Independent Practice

📁 Guided Reading Activity
22-4 **L1**

📁 Geography and History
Activity 22

📁 World Art and Music
Activity 22

Diary Have students write a diary entry or draw an illustration from the viewpoint of a French soldier involved in the march toward Moscow or in the retreat from Russia. **L2 LEP**

Judgment Have students label two columns *Positive* and *Negative* on a sheet of paper. Ask students to list Napoleon's actions, placing them under the appropriate heading. Some actions may be viewed as both positive and negative. *(example: replaced turmoil of revolution with orderly government—positive; put himself at head of a dictatorship —negative)* **L3**

Who? What? Where? When?

Metric System During the revolution French scientists developed the metric system. Before that, France had no uniform system of weights and measures. In 1801 the government made the metric system France's only system of weights and measures. Since then, the metric system has spread to most countries in the world.

---

an empire. Soon after becoming First Consul, Napoleon commanded the French forces that defeated both Italy and Austria. He also persuaded Russia to withdraw from the war. Though Napoleon was not able to defeat the British navy, the British were ready for peace because their commerce had suffered during the war. The two powers signed the Treaty of Amiens in March 1802.

Over the next few years Napoleon combined his talents as a masterful military leader and brilliant diplomat to build an empire. In 1804 he named himself Emperor of the French and soon set his armies on the road to conquest.

The Battle of Trafalgar

Despite his successes on the continent of Europe, Great Britain remained Napoleon's most tenacious enemy. By 1805 Napoleon felt he was ready to invade Great Britain from the English Channel; his fleet never made it that far, however. In October 1805 at the Battle of **Trafalgar**, off the southern coast of Spain, the British admiral Lord Nelson soundly defeated the French navy, removing once and for all the possibility of a French invasion of Great Britain.

Economic Blockades

After Trafalgar, Napoleon decided to use economic warfare against the British. He believed he could defeat Great Britain by destroying its economic lifeline—trade. In a plan called the Continental System, Napoleon ordered all European nations he had conquered to stop trade with the British. In another decree he forbade British imports entry to the European ports that he controlled. Napoleon also required Russia and Prussia to go along with the blockade of British goods.

Meanwhile, Great Britain responded to the trade blockade with a counterthreat: Any ship on its way to a European port had to stop first at a British port. Napoleon responded that he would seize any ship that did so.

This conflict put the United States and other neutral nations in a difficult position. The United States relied heavily on its trade with both Great Britain and France. If the United States ignored the British threat, American ships would be seized by the British navy. If the United States obeyed the British, the French navy would seize its ships. This conflict on the seas was one of the causes that eventually led to the War of 1812 between the United States and Great Britain.

Despite the blockades, the aggressive British navy did maintain control of the seas, and Napoleon's Continental System failed. French trade

suffered, and the French economy worsened. Yet Napoleon's empire kept growing as he continued to win battles on land.

Napoleonic Europe

By 1812 Napoleon controlled most of Europe. France's boundaries now extended to the Russian border. Through successful French military conquests, Napoleon became king of Italy, his brother Joseph became king of Naples and later Spain, and his other brother, Louis, became king of Holland. Napoleon then abolished the Holy Roman Empire and created the Confederation of the Rhine, a loose organization of the German states. This move led Prussia to declare war on France, but the French easily crushed the weak Prussian army.

The people who lived in the countries under Napoleon's rule resented paying taxes to France and sending soldiers to serve in Napoleon's armies. This resentment ignited in the conquered people a feeling of nationalism, the yearning for self-rule and restoration of their customs and traditions. Nationalism helped stir revolts against French rule throughout Europe.

The first signs of trouble appeared in Spain, where Spanish forces carried out guerrilla warfare, or hit-and-run attacks, on French forces. In 1812, aided by British troops under the command of Arthur Wellesley (later named **Duke of Wellington**), the Spaniards overthrew their French occupiers. They reinstated their old king under a system of limited monarchy. Prussia also joined in the revolt against Napoleon, as nationalist leaders rebuilt its army and amassed political support in the hope of ridding themselves of French rule.

Downfall of the Empire

When Russia joined the movement against Napoleon, it signaled the end of the empire. Czar **Alexander I** of Russia viewed Napoleon's control of Europe as a threat to Russia. Additionally, Napoleon's Continental System had hurt the Russian economy. In 1811 Alexander withdrew from the Continental System and resumed trade with Great Britain.

The Invasion of Russia

Alexander's withdrawal outraged Napoleon, leading him to invade Russia. Napoleon assembled a massive army of 600,000 soldiers from countries

---

MEETING SPECIAL NEEDS ACTIVITY

Learning Style: Auditory/Musical Tell students that the composer Beethoven had greatly admired Napoleon, seeing the general as the embodiment of the spirit of the French Revolution. Beethoven originally dedicated his Third Symphony to Napoleon. He retracted the dedication when Napoleon proclaimed himself emperor, renaming the work "Heroic Symphony to celebrate the memory of a great man." It has become known as the *Eroica*. Have students who are strong auditory/musical learners listen to the Third Symphony. Have them select segments that they feel especially express the spirit of Napoleonic or revolutionary France and play these for the rest of the class. **L2 LEP**

Europe at Height of Napoleon's Power 1812

Legend:
- Napoleon's empire
- Under Napoleon's control
- Napoleon's allies
- Napoleon's campaign in Russia

0   150   300 mi.
0   150   300 km
Lambert Conic Conformal Projection

Map Study

Before he invaded Russia, Napoleon dominated most of Europe.

1. **Location** What geographic factors helped to protect Great Britain and Russia from Napoleon's armies?
2. **Movement** How far would a foot soldier have traveled walking from Paris to Moscow?

Map Study

Answers

1. *Great Britain: the English Channel; Russia: harsh winters*
2. *about 1,700 miles (2,700 kilometers)*

Map Skills Practice

Reading a Map What countries were Napoleon's allies? *(Norway, Denmark, Prussia, Austrian Empire)*

Linking Past and Present

Napoleonic Code France exported the Napoleonic Code to its empire in Europe and its colonies in North America. Today Louisiana, once part of France's lands in America, is the only state with laws still based on the Napoleonic Code.

ASSESS

Check for Understanding

Assign Section 4 Assessment as homework or as an in-class activity.

 Use Interactive Tutor Self-Assessment Software to review Section 4.

Evaluate

Section Quiz 22-4

 Use the Testmaker to create a customized quiz for Section 4.

---

throughout Europe. The long French march toward **Moscow** began in May 1812. The Russians, however, refused to yield to Napoleon's threat. They retreated to central Russia, adopting a "scorched-earth policy" in which they burned everything as they went. On September 14, one of Napoleon's men finally saw the city of Moscow from a nearby hill. But the day after the French entered Moscow, a giant fire, probably started by Russian patriots, destroyed most of the city.

Shortly afterward the harsh Russian winter began to set in, and the French army could not remain in Russia without shelter. Despite the difficult conditions, Napoleon delayed before ordering a retreat. When the French troops finally did withdraw, the Russians relentlessly attacked them. Amid the extreme conditions the retreat became a rout. Of the 600,000 soldiers who entered Russia, about 400,000 died of battle wounds, starvation, and exposure.

Defeat

The Russian blow to Napoleon's power ruined him. Russians, Prussians, Spaniards, English, and Austrians sent armies against him. Russia and Prussia announced a War of Liberation. Joined by Austria, they defeated Napoleon at Leipzig in Saxony, part of present-day Germany, in October 1813.

By March 1814 the allies were in Paris, forcing Napoleon to surrender and abdicate as emperor. The victors restored the French throne to **Louis XVIII**, the brother of Louis XVI. Napoleon was exiled to Elba, an island off the coast of Italy. The boundaries of France were reduced to those of 1792.

Still determined to rule, Napoleon returned to France on March 1, 1815, and easily won support. The troops of Louis XVIII deserted to their former commander when Napoleon announced, "Your general, summoned to the throne by the prayer of the people and raised upon your shields, is now restored to you; come and join him." In a period

Chapter 22 *The French Revolution* **577**

MAKING CONNECTIONS ACTIVITY

Daily Life During the years of the French Empire, clothing and furniture were made in what became known as the Empire style. Have students prepare an oral report about this style, using reference materials in a local library on the history of fashion and furniture. Encourage them to find out how this style became popular, if it spread to other countries, if it influenced other styles, and if it remained popular in later years. Ask students to make sketches or use pictures showing the Empire style in their reports. **L1 LEP**

Linking Past and Present

Music of Revolutions

Claude-Joseph Rouget de Lisle's marching song received the title "The Marseillaise" four months after he wrote it. Troops from Marseilles sang it as they stormed the Tuileries on August 10, 1792.

ANSWER

It appeals to people's emotions, music unites them in a common cause; answers may include high school and college "fight songs" or songs such as "We Are the World."

Reteach

Have students summarize Napoleon's greatest accomplishments and greatest defeats. *(for example, accomplishments: legal and educational reforms; defeats: defeat at Trafalgar, retreat from Russia)*

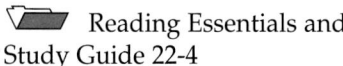 Reading Essentials and Study Guide 22-4

Enrich

Have students discuss what Napoleon could have done differently to make his return from Elba a success.

CLOSE

Let students discuss what they consider the most important changes in Europe caused by Napoleon's rule in France.

The Arts

Music of Revolutions

The French Revolution found its voice in a rousing march written in 1792 by Joseph Rouget de Lisle, a young captain in the army engineers. The march, later known as "The Marseillaise," rallied French citizens:

Rouget de Lisle Singing "The Marseillaise" at Dietrich's by Isidore Pils

> *To arms, citizens!*
> *Form your battalions,*
> *Let us march, let us march!*

"The Marseillaise" became the French national anthem in 1795. Because of its revolutionary character, it was banned under the reigns of Napoleon, Louis XVIII, and Napoleon III. It once again became the national anthem in 1879.

The best-known and most enduring song of the American Revolution was "Yankee Doodle." The British had originally used the term "yankee" as an insult. Singing "Yankee Doodle" as they marched, the British showed scorn for the American soldiers. The American colonists, however, turned the insult into a battle cry for freedom.

Revolutionary and protest groups today use music to gain public support. For example, since the 1960s, "We Shall Overcome" has been a unifying force in movements for freedom throughout the world.

Linking Past and Present ACTIVITY

Examine ways in which revolutionary music can be used to motivate people. Can you think of cases today where music is used to unite people?

known as the Hundred Days, Napoleon again reigned as emperor. To avoid war he announced that France wanted no more territory.

The European governments, however, feared that Napoleon might regain his former strength. Determined to stop him, the armies of Prussia, Great Britain, and the Netherlands advanced toward France under the command of the Duke of Wellington. Napoleon met them at **Waterloo** in the Austrian Netherlands in June 1815; the French troops were decisively defeated. Napoleon was placed under house arrest on the island of Saint Helena in the South Atlantic. He died there in 1821.

Napoleon's Legacy

Napoleon did not allow true representative government. He did, however, secure the revolution in France and spread throughout Europe ideas such as equality before the law, religious toleration, and advancement by merit rather than by birth. Napoleon's rule also set uniform standards of government, reformed tax systems, promoted education, and improved agriculture and industry. After the collapse of Napoleon's empire, many Europeans still wanted to keep these benefits from the French Revolution. They especially did not forget their taste of freedom from absolute monarchy.

SECTION 4 ASSESSMENT

Main Idea
1. Use a diagram like the one below to identify reasons for the rise and fall of Napoleon's empire.

Napoleon's Rise and Fall

Rise ↗ _____ ↘ Fall

Recall
2. **Define** dictatorship, plebiscite, nationalism.
3. **Identify** the Napoleonic Code, the Continental System, Duke of Wellington, Alexander I, Louis XVIII, Waterloo.

Critical Thinking
4. **Making Comparisons** Compare Napoleon's rule

after the French Revolution to Cromwell's rule after the English Civil War.

Understanding Themes
5. **Movement** How did the principles of the French Revolution spread throughout Europe and contribute to the rise of nationalism in other countries?

SECTION 4 ASSESSMENT ANSWERS

1. **Rise:** defeated Italy and Austria; persuaded Russia to withdraw from war; Treaty of Amiens with British; great diplomat and military leader; **Fall:** Russia joined movement against Napoleon and defeated his army; army attacked by all of France's enemies; 1814 throne restored to Louis XVIII; final defeat at Waterloo

2. All terms are defined in the Glossary.
3. Napoleonic Code, 575; Continental System, 576; Duke of Wellington, 576; Alexander I, 576; Louis XVIII, 577; Waterloo, 578
4. Both were stern military leaders who restored order after political chaos.
5. **MOVEMENT**   While emperor,

Napoleon helped spread the principles of the French Revolution; however, he also aroused resentment in the peoples he conquered by making them pay taxes to France and provide soldiers for his armies. This resentment, coupled with the inspiration of the new ideals of liberty, led to the development of nationalism.

Social Studies
SKILLS

Interpreting Graphs

When you divide a pizza among four people, it is easy to estimate where the circle should be sliced. A circle graph is similar to a round pizza. Circle graphs are useful for showing percentages, such as 25 percent of a pizza. A line or bar graph, however, can be used to show changes over a period of time.

Most graphs also use words to identify or label information. These steps will help you interpret graphs.
- Read the title.
- Read the captions and text.
- Determine the relationships among all sections of the graph.

Learning the Skill

The circle on the right visually compares the time periods from the information about revolution and empire in France between 1789 and 1815.

1. **Estates-General and National Assembly**
   May 1789–September 1791
   Limited constitutional monarchy
2. **Legislative Assembly**
   October 1791–September 1792
   New constitution; delegates seated according to political beliefs
3. **National Convention**
   September 1792–October 1795
   King executed; Reign of Terror
4. **Directory**
   October 1795–November 1799
   New constitution with bicameral legislature, five executive directors; Napoleon seizes control
5. **Consulate**
   December 1799–May 1804
   New constitution sets up three consuls; Napoleon rules
6. **Empire**
   May 1804–June 1815
   Napoleon I, emperor until overthrown

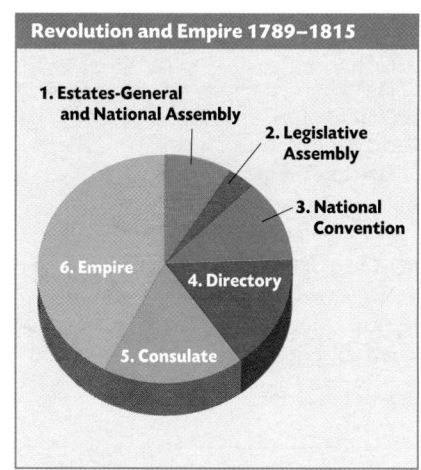

Revolution and Empire 1789–1815

1. Estates-General and National Assembly
2. Legislative Assembly
3. National Convention
4. Directory
5. Consulate
6. Empire

Practicing the Skill

Study the graph and answer the following:
1. What was the longest of the six periods of the French Revolution?
2. What was the shortest of the six periods?
3. About what percentage of the total time did Napoleon rule France (during the Consulate and Empire)?
4. About what percentage of the time did the Directory rule?

Applying the Skill

Draw a circle graph showing the major divisions of your day.

For More Practice

Turn to the Skill Practice in the Chapter Assessment on page 589.

The **Glencoe Skillbuilder Interactive Workbook**, Level 2 provides instruction and practice in key social studies skills.

TEACH

Interpreting Graphs Conduct a class survey by counting the number of students who travel to school on foot, by bicycle, on a school bus, by public transportation, or by car. (Have students choose the method they use the most often.) Note the results on the chalkboard and call on volunteers to convert these numbers into percentages. Next, draw a circle on the chalkboard and explain that it represents the whole class, or 100 percent. Divide the circle into sections to represent the percentages of the subgroups. Have students note how the circle illustrates the relationship of the parts to the whole. Then have students read the skill and complete the practice questions.

Additional Practice

📁 Skill Reinforcement Activity 22

📁 Building Skills in Geography Workbook, Unit 2, Lesson 8

GLENCOE
TECHNOLOGY

 Glencoe's **Skillbuilder Interactive Workbook, Level 2** This interactive CD-ROM promotes student mastery of key social studies skills.

ANSWERS TO PRACTICING THE SKILL

1. Empire
2. Legislative Assembly
3. about 66 percent
4. about 15 percent

1810	1815	1820	1825

1814 Congress of Vienna meets.

1819 Carlsbad Decrees impose censorship in Prussia.

1821 Greek nationalists revolt against Turkish rule.

Section 5

Peace in Europe

Read to Find Out
Main Idea *The plans of the reactionaries to thwart the spread of liberalism in Europe were fairly successful.*

▶ **Terms to Define**
buffer state, reactionary, liberalism

▶ **People to Meet**
Prince Klemens von Metternich

▶ **Places to Locate**
Vienna

The **Storyteller**

Vienna, native city of Haydn, home of Brahms, and host to Europe's greatest musicians, was known for its opera and its pageantry. The medieval streets of the old city, dominated by the tall Gothic tower of St. Stephen's Cathedral, were once occupied by Napoleon's troops. Now Vienna would host the victorious assembled aristocracies. The czar of Russia, the kings of Prussia, Denmark, Bavaria, and Saxony, and the nobility dined at forty lavish tables in the Hofburg. Colorful military parades, fireworks, balls in the Grand Hall, and Beethoven's concerts all served to disguise the serious discussions that would establish Europe's "balance of power."

The Old University in Vienna

—adapted from *Western Civilization, an Urban Perspective,* F. Roy Willis, 1973

Walking along the streets of **Vienna,** Austria, in the autumn of 1814 were the kings, princes, and diplomats who had gathered for a peace conference known as the Congress of Vienna. With Napoleon in exile, the delegates had come to Vienna to restore order and stability in Europe after nearly 25 years of war.

The Congress met from September 1814 to June 1815. Nearly every European nation sent delegates, but the Congress's main work was done by Austria's **Prince Klemens von Metternich** of Austria, Russia's Czar Alexander I, and Great Britain's Lord Robert Castlereagh (KAS•uhl•ray). Prince Maurice de Talleyrand, once a bishop, represented defeated France.

The Congress of Vienna

Austria's chief minister, Prince Klemens von Metternich, served as host to the Congress and presided over it. Metternich believed that in order to establish European stability, Europe should be restored to the way it was before the French Revolution. To achieve his goal, Metternich maintained that settlements reached at Vienna would be guided by three principles: compensation, legitimacy, and balance of power. Compensation meant that all countries should be repaid for the expenses they incurred while fighting the French. By legitimacy, Metternich meant restoring to power the royal families who had ruled before Napoleon. Finally, balance of power meant that no country should ever again dominate continental Europe.

Redrawing the Map
As the victors of the war claimed their rewards, they redrew the map of Europe. France was forced to give up its recently gained territory and to pay a large indemnity, or compensation, to other countries for war damages. Although Great Britain did not gain land in continental Europe, it took from France most of its remaining islands in the West

---

Europe After Congress of Vienna 1815

— German Confederation

NORWAY
SWEDEN
DENMARK
GREAT BRITAIN
NETHERLANDS
PRUSSIA
POLAND
RUSSIA
GERMAN STATES
Troppau
Vienna
AUSTRIAN EMPIRE
FRANCE
SWITZER-LAND
PORTUGAL
SPAIN
ITALIAN STATES
OTTOMAN EMPIRE
Constantinople
Greece
North Sea
Baltic Sea
ATLANTIC OCEAN
Black Sea
Mediterranean Sea

0   200   400 mi.
0   200   400 km
Lambert Conic Conformal Projection

Map Study

European powers at the Congress of Vienna divided much of Napoleon's territory without regard to the national interests of the people living there. Compare the map on page 577 showing Europe at the height of Napoleon's power.

1. **Place** How did the new boundaries created at the Congress of Vienna affect Polish hopes for a united nation?
2. **Region** What was the purpose of the new alliance formed in 1815?

Indies. Austria gained the Italian provinces of Lombardy and Venetia as well as territory on the eastern coast of the Adriatic Sea.

At the conference Prussia and Russia also made it known that they wanted to expand their borders by seizing formerly French-held lands. Yet Great Britain and Austria feared that increased Prussian and Russian influence in central Europe would lead to an imbalance of power on the continent. To put pressure on Prussia and Russia, Great Britain and Austria made an agreement with France. The agreement bound the three powers—Great Britain, Austria, and France—to resist any further Prussian or Russian territorial expansion in Europe by armed force if it was necessary.

In the end a compromise was reached. Prussia received extensive territories along the Rhine River and almost half the kingdom of Saxony for its compensation. Russia received most of the Polish

territory formerly held by Prussia and Austria. This increased the Polish territory held by Russia. A new kingdom of Poland was then formed under the czar.

Restoring the Monarchies

Once the territorial compensation was settled, delegates at the Congress of Vienna turned to stabilizing European governments. Believing that divine-right monarchy was necessary for proper order, the delegates made settlements based on legitimate claims to the throne and restored the absolute monarchs who ruled Europe before Napoleon. The Congress reestablished royal dynasties in France, Spain, Portugal, Naples, Sardinia, and Sicily. In France the Congress officially recognized the Bourbon heir Louis XVIII as the legitimate, or legal, ruler.

To safeguard other ruling dynasties, the Congress placed further controls on France. It

Chapter 22 *The French Revolution* **581**

TEACH

Guided Practice

THEME Reaction

Have students describe reactionary measures taken by the Congress of Vienna to restore Europe to pre-French Revolution status. *(restored absolute monarchies, formed an alliance to keep liberalism and nationalism in check)* **L1**

Map Study

Answers

1. *Poland's hopes were crushed; Polish lands were divided among Russia, Prussia, and Austria.*
2. *to prevent democratic revolutions in Europe*

Map Skills Practice

Reading a Map Compare this map with the map on page 577. Which European states gained French land in 1815? *(the Netherlands, Prussia, German States, and Italian States)*

Geography: Movement Using the map showing Europe after the Congress of Vienna in 1815, have students describe how the map of Europe was redrawn. *(Prussia received territories along the Rhine, almost half of Saxony; Russia received Polish territory formerly held by Prussia and Austria, increased Polish territory held by Russia.)* **L3**

 Mapping History Overlay Transparency 14, *France and Europe*

COOPERATIVE LEARNING ACTIVITY

Report Organize the class into three groups. Have one group create a large map of Europe after the Congress of Vienna, using the map in their book as a guide. Have the second group make a wall chart listing countries that participated in the Congress of Vienna, the major leaders who represented each country, and the terms of the Quadruple Alliance. Have the third group make a wall chart listing countries and leaders who reacted against the Congress of Vienna's work and the results of their reactions. Remind students to use library resources when needed. Have groups display their work on a "Congress of Vienna" bulletin-board display. **L2**

Independent Practice

📁 Guided Reading Activity 22-5 **L1**

Foreign Affairs Have students create a chart with three columns titled *Holy Alliance, Quadruple Alliance,* and *Concert of Europe.* In each column, have students write short statements describing the alliance. *(for example: Holy Alliance: by order of Czar Alexander I, called for Christian rulers in Europe to cooperate as a union of monarchs)* **L1**

Essay Have students write a short essay explaining what the Carlsbad Decrees were and why they were instituted. **L3**

Linking Past and Present

Carlsbad Decrees The repressive measures of the 1819 Carlsbad Decrees ended student protests for reform. Students in the 1980s and 1990s also used protests as a way to achieve change. Student protests in China were brutally put down; but in South Africa and Eastern Europe, protests and pressure from other countries helped bring about change.

Visualizing History
Parties, balls, and pageantry reminded delegates of what life had been like before the revolution.
Answer to Caption: *to establish peace and stability in Europe*

ASSESS

Check for Understanding

Assign Section 5 Assessment as homework or as an in-class activity.

---

reduced French borders to those of 1790 and established buffer states, or neutral territories, around French territory. To the north of France, the Austrian Netherlands and the Dutch Netherlands became one country under the Dutch ruler. Thirty-nine independent German states formed the German Confederation, headed by Austria. Switzerland regained its neutrality and independence as a federal league of states. The Italian kingdom of Piedmont united with the Mediterranean island of Sardinia.

Forces Changing Europe

The diplomats responsible for most of the agreements made at the Congress of Vienna were reactionaries, people who opposed change and wanted to return things to the way they had been in earlier times. They strongly felt that Europe could maintain peace only by returning to the tradition of strong absolute monarchies in effect before the French Revolution.

The reactionaries hoped that their plans would thwart the spread of liberalism, a political philosophy influencing European peoples in the 1800s. The liberals accepted the ideas of the Enlightenment and the democratic reforms of the French Revolution. Believing in individual freedom, liberals supported ideas such as freedom of speech, freedom of the press, and religious freedom—which had led to revolution.

The reactionaries also hoped to crush the rise of nationalism throughout Europe. When they redrew national boundaries, the delegates reflected the wishes of the rulers rather than those of the people they governed. The new boundaries thwarted the nationalistic hopes of many European groups. For example, the boundaries crushed the Polish people's hopes for a united nation of their own. Instead, their land was parceled out among their neighbors: Austria, Prussia, and Russia.

Alliances

The diplomats knew that nationalistic desires for independence, democratic rule, and national unity could well lead to revolution, and revolution threatened everything they believed in. To prevent democratic revolutions, they agreed to form new alliances. Great Britain, Austria, Prussia, and Russia joined in the Quadruple Alliance to maintain the settlements of Vienna. The four powers concluded the alliance in November 1815. France was admitted three years later, when the members of the alliance met for the first time at Aix-la-Chapelle.

According to the alliance agreement, representatives of the great powers were to meet periodically to discuss the security of Europe. Their goals included preservation of territorial boundaries set at the Congress of Vienna, exclusion of Napoleon Bonaparte and his heirs from French rule, and prevention of any revolutionary movements from taking hold in Europe.

With the goals of securing international order based on "Justice, Christian Charity, and Peace," Czar Alexander I of Russia created the Holy Alliance. Issued in the name of the czar, the Prussian king, and the Austrian emperor, the Holy Alliance called for Christian rulers in Europe to cooperate as a union of monarchs. Metternich dismissed the idea as "a loud-sounding nothing." Nevertheless, all the invited rulers joined the Holy Alliance except Pope Pius VII and the British government. The pope had said that "from time immemorial the papacy had been in possession of Christian truth and needed no new interpretation of it." The British government

Visualizing History The serious work of the Congress of Vienna was nearly overshadowed by lavish entertainment—plays, musicals, and balls. *What did Metternich want to achieve by a balance of power?*

582

---

excused itself on the grounds that, without approval by Parliament, such an alliance would violate the British constitution.

The Concert of Europe

The two alliances encouraged European nations to work together to preserve the peace. The members decided to have regular meetings, which became known as the Concert of Europe. This system helped to avoid major European conflicts by resolving local problems peacefully.

For nearly 30 years, Metternich used the system set up by the Congress of Vienna to achieve his own political goals: to oppose liberalism and nationalism and to defend absolute monarchies in Europe. His beliefs came to be known as the Metternich system.

Metternich's political goals and the Concert of Europe did not go unchallenged, however. In Germany university students demonstrated for liberal reforms and national unity. In response Metternich persuaded King Frederick William III of Prussia to pass a series of repressive measures in 1819. These Carlsbad Decrees imposed strict censorship on all publications and suppressed freedom of speech. Metternich managed to end agitation in Germany, but new challenges arose in other areas.

Liberal reformers in Spain, for example, forced their monarch to agree to constitutional government in 1820. Metternich pressured members of the Quadruple Alliance to intervene in European countries and their territories to prevent the spread of liberalism. Great Britain, with a tradition of liberalism in government, opposed the action and broke from the alliance. Metternich's system did prevail, however, as French troops restored the Spanish king to full power. But the spirit of revolt did not die, for Spanish colonies in Latin America successfully revolted against Spanish control during the 1820s.

Visualizing History Metternich pushed for the creation of the Quadruple Alliance. *What was the alliance's major role?*

The Greeks also fought for their independence in 1821 against Turkish rule. Metternich intervened by attempting to stop other countries from aiding the rebellion. The British and the French assisted the Greek nationalists despite Metternich's threats. Greece finally won independence in 1829.

The stable political system Metternich envisioned throughout Europe would soon be under attack. The nationalistic spirit fostered by the French Revolution would not die in Europe.

SECTION 5 ASSESSMENT

Main Idea
1. Use a chart like the one below to list ways in which reactionaries wanted to stop liberalism's spread in Europe.

Ways to Stop Liberalism

Recall
2. **Define** buffer state, reactionary, liberalism.
3. **Identify** the Congress of Vienna, Prince Klemens von Metternich, Quadruple Alliance.

Critical Thinking
4. **Making Comparisons** Compare and contrast the political philosophies of a liberal and a reactionary in the 1800s.

Understanding Themes
5. **Reaction** Why was the Congress of Vienna made up mostly of reactionaries? What effect did their views and policies have on the spread of liberalism and nationalism throughout Europe?

Visualizing History Metternich dominated European politics for 30 years after the Congress of Vienna. **Answer to Caption:** *maintaining the settlements made in Vienna*

 Use Interactive Tutor Self-Assessment Software to review Section 5.

Evaluate

 Section Quiz 22-5

 Use the Testmaker to create a customized quiz for Section 5.

Reteach

Have students summarize how the alliances formed after 1814 contributed to peace in Europe.

📁 Reteaching Activity 22
📁 Reading Essentials and Study Guide 22-5

Enrich

Have students research the effect of Great Britain withdrawing from the Quadruple Alliance.

📁 Enrichment Activity 22

CLOSE

Ask students to make a wall chart summarizing the work of the Congress of Vienna and the Concert of Europe.

SECTION 5 ASSESSMENT ANSWERS

1. principle of compensation to repay countries for expense of fighting the French; restoration of absolute monarchies; principle of balance of power; sought to crush rise of nationalism; formed new alliance to prevent democratic revolution

2. All terms are defined in the Glossary.
3. Congress of Vienna, 580; Prince Klemens von Metternich, 580; Quadruple Alliance, 582
4. Liberals accepted the ideas of the Enlightenment and the French Revolution. Reactionaries wanted to reestablish absolute monarchies.

5. **REACTION** They were the ones wanting to restore peace to Europe.

Block Schedule

Team Teaching This excerpt from *Les Misérables* may be presented in a team-teaching context, in conjunction with English or Language Arts.

Les Misérables

Historical Connection

This excerpt from Hugo's novel portrays the social conflicts that wracked France in the 1820s. The bitter argument between the young man and his grandfather reflects the division between monarchists and supporters of the French Republic that persisted long after Napoleon's death.

Background Information

Setting The scene takes place in 1827. Napoleon died in 1821, and the French monarchy has been restored. The spirit of republicanism, here represented by the memory of Marius's father, continues to influence the younger generation.

Characters Monsieur Gillenormand: grandfather of Marius, a bourgeois supporter of the monarchy; Marius: an 18-year-old who is beginning to develop political consciousness.

Plot Marius's grandfather and aunt search his belongings and find a note stating that Napoleon had made Marius's father a baron. When Marius arrives, the grandfather ridicules all republicans as bandits; Marius in turn insults the French monarchy. The scene ends with Gillenormand ordering Marius from his home.

from
Les Misérables
by Victor Hugo

As we have seen, literature can be a bridge to the past, transporting us to a world that may seem strange or obscure at first, but that has much in common with our own. Across the gap between then and now we can see faces that we recognize, situations that are familiar, hopes that we share. The selection that follows was written by one of France's most celebrated writers, Victor Hugo. Hugo lived from 1802 to 1885, a time of dramatic and violent change for France. In this scene, Monsieur Gillenormand snoops through the belongings of his grandson, Marius. Assisting the grandfather is Marius's aunt. Marius's father has recently died.

M. Gillenormand, who had risen early like all the elderly who are in good health, had heard [Marius] come in, and hurried as fast as he could with his old legs, to climb to the top of the stairs where Marius's room was, to give him a kiss, question him while embracing him, and find out something about where he had come from.

But the youth had taken less time to go down than the old man to go up, and when Grandfather Gillenormand went into the garret room, Marius was no longer there.

The bed had not been disturbed, and on it were trustingly laid the coat and the black ribbon.

"I like that better," said M. Gillenormand.

And a moment later he entered the drawing room [room for receiving guests] where Mlle. Gillenormand the elder was already seated, embroidering her carriage wheels.

The entrance was triumphant.

In one hand M. Gillenormand held the coat and in the other the neck ribbon, and cried out, "Victory! We are about to penetrate the mystery! We shall know the end of the mystery, unravel the wanton ways of our rascal! Here we are right to the core of the romance. I have the portrait!"

In fact, a black shagreen box, rather like a medallion, was fastened to the ribbon.

The old man took this box and looked at it for some time without opening it, with that air of desire, delight, and anger, with which a poor,

ABOUT THE AUTHOR

Victor Hugo expressed in his writing his concern for the poor, his belief in democracy, and his desire for social reform. In the mid-1840s, he won election to the French Chamber of Peers, where he advocated public funding of education and the broadening of the voting franchise. After the republican government of France was overthrown, he left the country to live in Belgium and Great Britain. In the middle of his almost twenty-year exile, he published *Les Misérables*. In 1870 he returned to France. By then, he was a successful and well-known writer. When Hugo died, huge throngs of Parisians marched in his funeral procession.

hungry devil sees an excellent dinner pass right under his nose, when it is not for him.

"For it is clearly a portrait. I know all about these things. They are worn tenderly against the heart. What fools they are! Some abominable floozy, probably enough to bring on the shudders! Young people have such bad taste nowadays!"

"Let's see, father," said the old maid.

The box opened by pressing a spring. They found nothing in it but a piece of paper carefully folded.

"More and more predictable," said M. Gillenormand, bursting with laughter. "I know what that is. A love letter!"

"Ah! Then let's read it!" said the aunt.

And she put on her spectacles. They unfolded the paper and read this:

"*For my Son.*—The emperor made me a baron on the battlefield of Waterloo. Since the Restoration contests this title I have bought with my blood, my son will take it and bear it. I need not say that he will be worthy of it."

The feelings of the father and daughter are beyond description. They felt chilled as by the breath of a death's head [skull]. They did not exchange a word. M. Gillenormand, however, said in a low voice, and as if talking to himself, "It is the handwriting of that bandit."

The aunt examined the paper, turned it over every which way, then put it back in the box.

At that very moment, a little rectangular package wrapped in blue paper fell out of the coat pocket. Mademoiselle Gillenormand picked it up and unwrapped the blue paper. It was Marius's hundred

[calling] cards. She passed one of them to M. Gillenormand, who read: *Baron Marius Pontmercy.*

The old man rang. Nicolette [the chambermaid] came. M. Gillenormand took the ribbon, the box, and the coat, threw them all on the floor in the middle of the drawing room, and said:

"Take those things away."

A full hour passed in complete silence. The old man and the old maid sat with their backs turned to one another, and were probably each individually thinking over the same things. At the end of that hour, Aunt Gillenormand said, "Pretty!"

A few minutes later, Marius appeared. He was just coming home. Even before crossing the

Visualizing History A French salon displays the wealth of the bourgeoisie. With the end of the revolution, the return of social class distinctions accompanied the restoration of the monarchy. *Why was Monsieur Gillenormand angry about Marius's calling cards?*

Literary Elements Repetition is the use of a word or phrase over and over to achieve some effect. In his tirade against the republicans, the grandfather repeats "I don't know" and "all," revealing that he has strong opinions but little knowledge.

Irony is the use of a word in a way that conveys the opposite of its usual meaning. When Marius's aunt says, "Pretty!" she means that the situation has become unpleasant and uncomfortable.

FOCUS

Point out to students that Gillenormand and Marius still harbor passionate feelings more than a decade after Napoleon's defeat. By showing that the conflict between monarchists and republicans had not disappeared, what is Hugo saying about the issues at stake in the French Revolution? (*that they were crucial, life-or-death matters*) Are there issues or events that arouse such strong emotion today? (*Answers will vary.*)

Visualizing History The literal meaning of the French word *salon* is "room" or "chamber." Later it came to refer to gatherings of intellectuals.
Answer to Caption: *He probably felt that only the king, not a usurper like Napoleon, had the right to make Marius's father a baron.*

OTHER WORKS BY VICTOR HUGO

Cobb, Walter J., trans. *The Hunchback of Notre Dame.* New York: New American Library, 1965.

The Works of Victor Hugo. New York: W.J. Black, 1928.

TEACH

Literary Analysis

Ask students to consider Monsieur Gillenormand's statement that a bourgeois like himself cannot live under the same roof with a baron. *Why is it ironic that Marius would have a higher social position than his grandfather? (because Marius and his father are supposedly republicans, not aristocrats)*

Visualizing History

In 1848 a wave of rebellions and near-revolutions challenged the old regimes of Europe. In France, the failed popular movement paved the way for the rise of Napoleon III, the nephew of Napoleon Bonaparte, who ruled as emperor from 1852 to 1870. **Answer to Caption:** *Gillenormand seems coldhearted.*

Evaluation

To describe the rage that Marius feels when his father is insulted, Hugo compares him to a priest and to a fakir. Discuss with students why Hugo compared Marius to religious figures. Many supporters of the revolution were not religious; Hugo may be implying that their politics had become a religion.

Literary Analysis

Discuss how Hugo builds tension in the final scene in the excerpt. By describing how the grandfather walks across the room, Hugo draws the scene out and involves the reader in the conflict.

 World Literature Selection 5

Visualizing History A republican club meets in Paris in 1848. Victor Hugo's concern for the common people underlies much of his writing. Social commentary and support for democratic movements mark his works in the 1850s and 1860s. *How does the character of Monsieur Gillenormand portray aristocracy?*

threshold of the drawing room, he saw his grandfather holding one of his cards in his hand; the old man, on seeing him, exclaimed with his crushing air of sneering bourgeois superiority, "Well! Well! Well! Well! Well! So you are a baron now. My compliments. What does this mean?"

Marius blushed slightly, and answered, "It means I am my father's son."

M. Gillenormand stopped laughing, and said harshly, "Your father; I am your father."

"My father," resumed Marius with downcast eyes and stern manner, "was a humble and

heroic man, who served the Republic and France gloriously, who was great in the greatest history that men have ever made, who lived a quarter of a century in the camps, under fire by day, and by night in the snow, in the mud, and the rain, who captured colors [flags], who was twenty times wounded, who died forgotten and abandoned, and who had but one fault; that was to have too dearly loved two ingrates [ungrateful persons], his country and me."

This was more than M. Gillenormand could bear. At the word, "Republic," he rose, or rather, sprang to his feet. Every one of the words

586 Chapter 22 *The French Revolution*

ADDITIONAL LITERARY WORKS OF THE PERIOD

Brontë, Charlotte. *Jane Eyre.* New York: Modern Library, 1993. Story of bright, self-possessed young woman of humble origins who falls in love with a troubled, wealthy Englishman.

Dickens, Charles. *Oliver Twist.* New York: Penguin, 1966. Novel about a poor English boy struggling to survive in the slums of London.

Stowe, Harriet Beecher. *Uncle Tom's Cabin.* New York: Penguin, 1981. Antislavery novel that helped turn Northerners against the institution of slavery.

Swift, Jonathan. *Gulliver's Travels.* New York: Oxford, 1977. Biting satire about English society and the human race in general.

Marius had just spoken, produced on the old royalist's face the effect of a blast from a bellows on a burning coal. From dark he had turned red, from red to purple, and from purple to flaming.

"Marius!" he exclaimed, "abominable child! I don't know what your father was! I don't want to know! I know nothing about him and I don't know him! But what I do know is that there was never anything but miserable wretches among them! That they were all beggars, assassins, thieves, rabble in their red bonnets! I say all of them! I say all of them! I don't know anybody! I say all of them! Do you hear, Marius? Look here, you are as much a baron as my slipper! They were all bandits, those who served Robespierre! All brigands who served Bu-o-na-parté! All traitors who betrayed, betrayed, betrayed! Their legitimate king! All cowards who ran from the Prussians and English at Waterloo! That's what I know. If your father is among them I don't know him, I'm sorry, so much the worse. Your humble servant, sir!"

In turn, it was Marius who now became the coal, and M. Gillenormand the bellows. Marius shuddered in every limb, he had no idea what to do, his head was burning. He was the priest who sees all his wafers thrown to the winds, the fakir [member of a Muslim religious order] seeing a passerby spit on his idol. He could not allow such things to be said before him. But what could he do? His father had just been trodden underfoot and stamped on in his presence, but by whom? By his grandfather. How could he avenge the one without outraging the other? It

was impossible for him to insult his grandfather, and it was equally impossible for him not to avenge his father. On one hand a sacred tomb, on the other a white head. For a few moments he felt dizzy and staggering with all this whirlwind in his head; then he raised his eyes, looked straight at his grandfather, and cried in a thundering voice: "Down with the Bourbons, and that great hog Louis XVIII!"

Louis XVIII had been dead for four years; but that made no difference to him.

Scarlet as he was, the old man suddenly turned whiter than his hair. He turned toward a bust of the Duc de Berry that stood on the mantel and bowed to it profoundly with a sort of peculiar majesty. Then he walked twice, slowly and in silence, from the fireplace to the window and from the window to the fireplace, covering the whole length of the room and making the parquet creak as if an image of stone were walking over it. The second time, he bent toward his daughter, who was enduring the shock with the stupor of an aged sheep, and said to her with a smile that was almost calm, "A baron like Monsieur and a bourgeois like myself cannot remain under the same roof."

And all at once straightening up, pallid, trembling, terrible, his forehead swelling with the fearful radiance of anger, he stretched his arm towards Marius and cried out, "Be off!"

Marius left the house.

The next day, M. Gillenormand said to his daughter, "You will send sixty pistoles [old gold coins] every six months to that blood drinker, and never speak of him to me again."

RESPONDING TO LITERATURE

1. What political conflict of the period does the heated clash between Marius and his grandfather represent?
2. What sort of person is Monsieur Gillenormand?
3. If Marius's father had not been a hero at the Battle of Waterloo, do you think Marius still would have become a revolutionary? Explain your answer.
4. **Supporting an Opinion** Was the era of the French Revolution and Napoleon "the greatest history that men have ever made," as Marius claims? Support your answer with evidence.

ANSWERS TO RESPONDING TO LITERATURE

1. Marius was a republican, a supporter of political reform, while his grandfather was a conservative royalist.
2. Answers might include that he is nosy, brash, unprincipled, and insulting, but that he does plan to send money to his grandson after throwing him out.
3. Students may feel that because of his temperament, Marius would be a republican whether or not his father had fought with Napoleon.
4. Answers will vary; students may say that the fact that the revolution dramatically changed not only French but also European history makes this claim justified.

Linking Past and Present

Les Misérables was made into one of the most popular musical plays of the 1990s. Students may be interested in listening to the soundtrack of the play.

ASSESS

Assign **Responding to Literature** questions.

CLOSE

After students have read the excerpt, ask them to discuss the high-handed treatment that Marius receives from his grandfather. Are conflicts between older and younger people common today? What issues lead to disagreements between them? (*Answers will vary.*)

Contemporary Connection

The musical *Les Misérables* has been playing on Broadway for more than 10 years. *Les Misérables* has also been made into five movies, including a 1935 version starring Charles Laughton and Fredric March. The universal appeal of its themes has extended for more than 100 years. The themes of Hugo's popular story—conflicting political loyalties and generation gaps—are as applicable today as when the book was published.

Portfolio Project

Write a script for a brief dialogue between a member of the older generation and yourself. The subject could be a political or social issue.

Chapter 22 Assessment

WORLD HISTORY Online

Have students use the **Chapter 22 Self-Check Quiz** at worldhistory.glencoe.com to prepare for the Chapter Test.

GLENCOE TECHNOLOGY

VIDEODISC
Use MindJogger to review the chapter.

MindJogger Videoquiz

Chapter 22
Disc 3 Side B

Also available in VHS.

Answers

Using Key Terms

1. j   3. c   5. l
2. i   4. k

Using Your History Journal

Students should consider how the lives of the characters they chose and how France changed as a result of Napoleon's reign.

Reviewing Facts

1. Causes: inequality of the estates; influence of Enlightenment and American Revolution; cost of living increases; government financial crisis; Effects: creation of constitutional government and Declaration of Rights; fall of the monarchy; establishment of republic; Reign of Terror; European wars; rise of Napoleon; spread of nationalism throughout Europe
2. to permanently destroy the French monarchy
3. abolition of feudal dues and tithes, taxation of nobles, Declaration of Rights of Man and of

---

WORLD HISTORY Online

Self-Check Quiz

Visit the *World History: The Human Experience* Web site at **worldhistory.glencoe.com** and click on *Chapter 22—Self-Check Quiz* to prepare for the Chapter Test.

Using Key Terms

Write the key term that completes each sentence. Then write a sentence for each term not chosen.

a. bourgeoisie
b. buffer states
c. conscription
d. coup d'état
e. émigrés
f. estate
g. dictatorship
h. liberalism
i. nationalism
j. plebiscite
k. reactionaries
l. tithe
m. unicameral legislature

1. Napoleon Bonaparte's move to become Consul for life was supported by a _____ , or popular vote.
2. Intense feelings of _____ caused people to fight for self-rule and a return to their traditional customs.
3. French revolutionaries resorted to _____ , or drafting civilians, in their fight against European powers.
4. _____ wanted to return absolute monarchs to Europe after the collapse of Napoleon's empire in 1814.
5. Before the revolution the Catholic Church in France was supported by a _____ , or a 10 percent tax on income.

Technology Activity

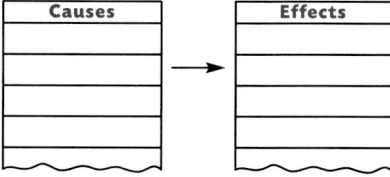

Developing a Multimedia Presentation Use a computerized card catalog or the Internet to find information about the French Revolution and the American Revolution. Using images from the Internet, create a short multimedia presentation comparing the two revolutions. Include a plan describing the type of multimedia presentation you would like to develop and the steps you will take to ensure its success.

Reviewing Facts

1. **History** Use a chart like the one below to identify the causes and effects of the French Revolution.

Causes		Effects
	→	

2. **History** Explain why Louis XVI was executed.
3. **Government** List three accomplishments of the French National Assembly.
4. **Citizenship** Describe the role of women, peasants, and urban workers in the French Revolution.
5. **History** Describe the Concert of Europe.

Critical Thinking

1. **Apply** Why was the creation of a French republic a significant turning point in history?
2. **Apply** What Enlightenment ideas affected the French Revolution?
3. **Synthesize** What circumstances, if any, justify a violent revolution? What other means could be used to change an unfair or tyrannical system of government?
4. **Evaluate** In your opinion, did Napoleon's thirst for power help or hurt France? Europe?

---

the Citizen
4. Women were involved in street protests and demanded equal rights; peasants revolted in countryside to end feudal remnants; workers and artisans in towns favored republican government and pushed the revolution toward greater equality and social changes.
5. meetings of members of the Quadruple Alliance and the Holy Alliance to keep peace in Europe

Critical Thinking

1. France was the first large European state that overthrew a monarchy and established a democratic republic. It became a model for democratic government elsewhere.
2. rule by the people expressed in extension of voting rights, equality of all citizens before the law, written constitutions and declarations of citizens' rights, and representative government with elected officials

Geography in History

1. **Location** Refer to the map below. What is the global address of Paris?
2. **Place** What role did agriculture play in starting the French Revolution?
3. **Movement** Why did Napoleon want to prevent British ships from trading at various European ports?

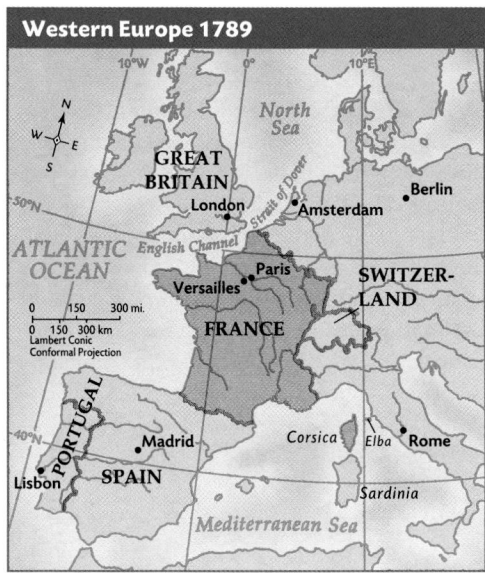

Western Europe 1789

Understanding Themes

1. **Revolution** What similarities and differences do you see between the American and the French Revolutions?
2. **Change** What specific rights did the Declaration of Rights apply to French citizens? How did the Declaration and other revolutionary events affect the position of French women?
3. **Conflict** How did violence and fear among the French people contribute to Napoleon's seizure of power?
4. **Movement** How did the desire to expand his European empire help to bring about the downfall of Napoleon?
5. **Reaction** How did the Congress of Vienna show itself to be a strong reaction to revolutionary ideals?

Linking Past and Present

1. Napoleon tried to use military force to unite Europe under his rule. What attempts have been made in this century to forcibly bring Europe or large areas of Europe under one form of government?
2. Unity remains a goal of many Europeans. What recent efforts are peacefully uniting the countries of Europe?

Skill Practice

The diagram below shows the growth of the French army in the early years of the French Revolution. The graph is divided into sizes relative to the additions made to the army between 1791 and 1793. Study the diagram and answer the following questions.

1. How large was the French army in the summer of 1792?
2. How many troops were added to France's army in 1793?
3. What was the total number of French troops called into service during this period?
4. If this information were on a bar graph, the horizontal axis (line) would list the dates. The vertical axis would have labels in units of 100,000 each. What would each bar represent?

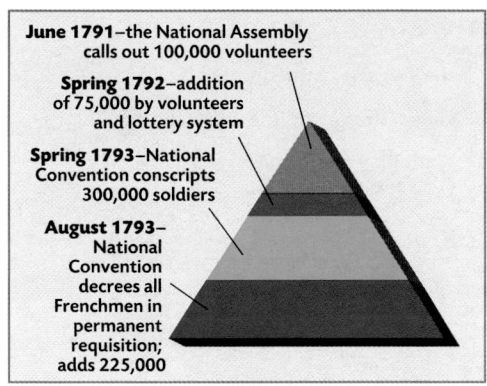

June 1791–the National Assembly calls out 100,000 volunteers

Spring 1792–addition of 75,000 by volunteers and lottery system

Spring 1793–National Convention conscripts 300,000 soldiers

August 1793–National Convention decrees all Frenchmen in permanent requisition; adds 225,000

---

tion to other countries.
2. **CHANGE** All people were equal before the law; freedom of speech, press, religion; freedom from arbitrary arrest and punishment; the Declaration of Rights did not grant women equality with men. Women did benefit from reforms that made divorce easier and allowed them to inherit property. The Napoleonic Code later removed some of these rights.
3. **CONFLICT** Napoleon was able to use his popularity and success as a military leader to seize political power.
4. **MOVEMENT** It led to many wars and finally to defeat.
5. **REACTION** Its actions restored monarchies and built alliances to prevent democratic revolutions.

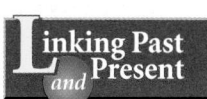
Linking Past and Present

Answers might mention Hitler's conquest of Europe during World War II and the USSR's control of Eastern Europe after World War II; union of East and West Germany and the European Community.

Skill Practice

1. 175,000 soldiers
2. 300,000 soldiers
3. 700,000 soldiers
4. number of soldiers

Chapter Bonus Test Question

Ask students: Why was the time ripe for revolution in France in 1789? (*widespread knowledge of Enlightenment ideas; example of the successful American Revolution; high national debt plus several poor harvests; seeming indifference of king, queen, and nobles for plight of peasants and workers*)

---

3. Possible answer: suppression of basic rights; work within the system or nonviolent protest
4. Possible answer: Napoleon's thirst for power led to France's downfall; French conquests antagonized other Europeans but in doing so stimulated the rise of nationalism among them.

Geography in History

1. about 48°N, about 2°E
2. Poor wheat harvests that made peasants'

financial conditions worse and caused bread shortages in cities fueled the discontent.
3. Napoleon wanted to destroy the lifeline of the British economy, which was trade.

Understanding Themes

1. **REVOLUTION** Similarities: People fought for political representation and rights. Differences: Americans did not go through a period of terror or try to spread the revolu-

FOCUS

During this period, both scientific and political revolutions took place, creating an atmosphere of action and reaction throughout the West.

TEACH

Reinforcing Vocabulary

Point out the **Vocabulary Preview** to students alerting them to words they will encounter that might be unfamiliar.

William Harvey

Interpreting the Primary Source
Ask students why people so strongly disagreed with Harvey and thought he was crazy for his ideas about the circulation of blood. (*Harvey's ideas disproved ancient theories. People often criticize anything that challenges tradition for fear of having been wrong in their understanding.*)

Evaluating the Primary Source
This primary source presents a description of Harvey written by a close friend many years after Harvey had been so strongly criticized. The reliability of this source is determined by the objectivity the writer could have in writing about a friend and in writing years after the time discussed. Additionally, in this passage Dick recounts Harvey's opinion, which may have been a subjective judgment of events.

The English Bill of Rights

Interpreting the Primary Source
Ask students to identify sections of the Bill of Rights in which it is clear to them which of King James II's actions were the inspiration for those particular laws.

Unit 5

Between 1600 and the early 1800s, Western civilization was transformed by scientific discoveries and new political ideas. In the 1600s, members of the English Parliament took radical measures to restrict the power of the monarchy, while in the 1800s the growing desire for democracy led to political revolution in America and in France.

✦ VOCABULARY PREVIEW

the vulgar: the uneducated

vindicating: justifying or defending

scaffold: a platform on which execution takes place

 For more primary sources to accompany this unit, use the *World History Primary Source Document Library CD-ROM.*

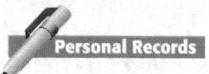

Chapter 20
William Harvey

Personal Records

In the 1600s William Harvey, the English anatomist, discovered that blood circulates through the human body, pumped by the heart and returning through the veins. This discovery, which disproved ancient medical theories, was at first ridiculed but later accepted by the scientific world. O.L. Dick, a friend of Harvey, wrote this personal account of the great doctor.

I have heard him say, that after his Booke of the *Circulation of the Blood* came out, that he fell mightily in his Practize, and that 'twas beleeved by the vulgar that he was crack-brained; and all the Physitians were against his Opinion, and envyed him; many wrote against him. With much ado at last, in about 20 or 30 yeares time, it was received in all the Universities in the world; and Mr. Hobbes says in his book *De Corpore*, he is the only man, perhaps, that ever lived to see his owne Doctrine established in his life-time. . . .

Illustration from Harvey's book Circulation of the Blood

(*The first and second rights both refer to "regal authority"—i.e., King James II—having suspended or dispensed with laws by "pretended power."*)

Evaluating the Primary Source
This primary source reveals the way the English Parliament solved a problem through legal means, bloodlessly. It indicates what rights were important to people of the time and indicates a progressive weakening of the British monarchy. The reliability of this source is determined by the truth behind Parliament's accusations against King James II. If he did behave in the ways this Bill of Rights accuses him of,

Chapter 21
The English Bill of Rights

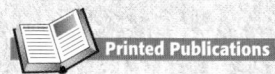

In 1688, Parliament deposed the autocratic king James II and replaced him with William and Mary. In the following year, Parliament passed the Bill of Rights, which guaranteed certain individual rights.

And thereupon the said lords spiritual and temporal, and commons, pursuant to their respective letters and elections, being now assembled in a full and free representative of this nation, taking into their most serious consideration the best means for attaining the aforesaid; do in the first place (as their ancestors in like case have usually done) for the vindicating and asserting their ancient rights and liberties, declare:

1. That the pretended power of suspending of laws, or the execution of laws, by regal authority, without consent of parliament, is illegal.

2. That the pretended power of dispensing with laws, or the execution of laws, by regal authority, as it hath been assumed and exercised of late, is illegal. . . .

5. That it is the right of the subjects to petition the King, and all committments and prosecutions for such petitioning are illegal.

6. That the raising or keeping a standing army within the kingdom in time of peace, unless it be with consent of parliament, is against the law. . . .

8. That election of members of parliament ought to be free.

9. That the freedom of speech, and debates or proceedings in parliament, ought not to be impeached or questioned in any court or place out of parliament.

10. That excessive bail ought not to be required, nor excessive fines imposed; nor cruel and unusual punishments inflicted. . . .

Chapter 22
The Execution of Louis XVI

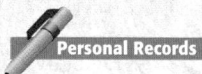

During the French Revolution, King Louis XVI was executed on charges of conspiring with foreign powers. This eyewitness account was written by Henry Essex Edgeworth de Firmont, a priest in the royal household.

I saw [the king] cross with a firm foot the breadth of the whole scaffold; silence, by his look alone, fifteen or twenty drums . . . ; and in a voice so loud, . . . I heard him pronounce distinctly these memorable words: "I die innocent of all the crimes laid to my charge; I pardon those who have occasioned my death; and I pray to God that the blood you are going to shed may never be visited on France."

Many voices were at the same time heard encouraging the executioners. They seemed reanimated themselves, in seizing with violence the most virtuous of Kings, they dragged

Execution of Louis XVI

him under the axe of the guillotine, which with one stroke severed his head from his body. . . . At first an awful silence prevailed; at length some cries of "Vive la République!" [Long Live the Republic] were heard. . . . this cry . . . became the universal shout of the multitude. . . .

Interpreting Primary Sources

1. What was the initial reaction to Dr. Harvey's discovery?
2. What are some freedoms granted by the English Bill of Rights?
3. How did King Louis XVI of France behave in his last moments?
4. **CRITICAL THINKING:** How would you explain the "awful silence" after the king's execution?

Applications Activity

Create a political cartoon that represents your feelings about the description of the beheading of King Louis XVI.

---

then the Bill is a reliable source of commentary on the king's actions.

The Execution of Louis XVI

Interpreting the Primary Source
Ask students to assess what impression of the king de Firmont gives in the first paragraph of this passage. *(De Firmont's presentation is a sympathetic one in which he tries to create the impression of a noble man walking to his death with honor.)*

Evaluating the Primary Source
This primary source depicts the actions and reactions of King Louis XVI and his executioners during the moments just before and after his death. The reliability of the source can be judged by an assessment of de Firmont's goal in writing this description. Because de Firmont was a priest in the king's household, he may have been loyal to the king and thus may have presented the king in an unrealistically sympathetic light.

For the more complete version of each of these documents, see the World History Primary Source Document Library CD-ROM:

ANSWER KEY

1. People thought that he was crazy.
2. People may petition the king; freedom of speech and debate in Parliament is guaranteed; people cannot be subject to excessive bail or fines or cruel and unusual punishments.
3. He behaved with dignity and even compassion, forgiving his enemies and hoping that the French would not be punished for his death.
4. Perhaps the execution of a king was such an unprecedented act that the people were shocked by what they had done.

APPLICATIONS ACTIVITY: Answers will vary. Students should be sure to represent the emotions of the king before his execution or the actions and emotions of the crowd.

Answers and Analyses

1. B (History) According to page 517, Galileo's discoveries with his telescope *convinced him that the Copernican theory about the earth revolving around the sun was correct.* If the earth revolved around the sun, it would not be the center of the universe.

 TEST-TAKING TIP

Remind students to use process of elimination and to guess aggressively. If all students remember is that Copernicus and Galileo were astronomers (among other things), they can eliminate choices A, C, and D.

2. F (History) Pages 524–526 state that the Enlightenment was characterized by people who were *No longer held back by tradition, they defined the world in their own way, using science as their base . . . they believed in both freedom of speech and the individual's right to liberty.* This information best supports choice F. No mention is made of church thinkers, and pages 526–527 state that Enlightenment ideas *were not applied to women.* Choice J is tempting, but no mention is made of enlightened despots in the discussion of the Renaissance.

3. D (Economics) According to the chart, the difference between imports and exports in 1750 was approximately 500. However, the axis states that this figure is expressed in thousands of pounds, so this amounts to about 500,000 pounds.

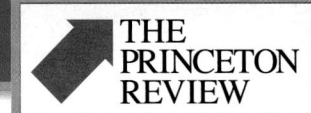
THE PRINCETON REVIEW

Standardized Test Practice

Directions: Choose the *best* answer to each of the following multiple choice questions. If you have trouble answering a question, use the process of elimination to narrow your choices. Write your answers on a separate piece of paper.

1. The work of Copernicus and Galileo questioned which of the following beliefs inherited from the Middle Ages?

- A The superiority of European civilization
- B The earth as the center of the universe
- C The evolution of humankind
- D The role of religion in society

> **Test-Taking Tip:** This question requires you to remember a fact about these two scientists. However, there are also clues in the question that can help you to eliminate wrong answers. For example, the question specifies that the belief was *inherited from the Middle Ages.* Since *evolution* was not a belief held during that time, answer C must be incorrect.

2. The 1700s in Europe was an Age of Enlightenment. In what way were the ideas of the Enlightenment similar to the ideas of the Renaissance?

- F Both periods stressed the worth of the individual.
- G Both periods increased the opportunities and liberties of women.
- H Church leaders were influential thinkers during both periods.
- J Ideas were promoted by *enlightened despots* during both periods.

> **Test-Taking Tip:** This question asks for a *comparison* between two time periods. Make sure that your answer choice is true for *both* eras. Since answer J is true only for the Enlightenment, but not for the Renaissance, it can be eliminated.

Use the graph below to answer question 3.

Value of American Exports and Imports with England, 1700–1750

(In thousands of pounds sterling)

Year

Exports Imports

Source: *Historical Statistics of the United States: Colonial Times to 1970*

3. In 1750, the difference between imports and exports was

- A more than 400 pounds sterling.
- B more than 4000 pounds sterling.
- C more than 40,000 pounds sterling.
- D more than 400,000 pounds sterling.

> **Test-Taking Tip:** Make sure that you look carefully at the labels on both axes of a bar graph. The horizontal axis (bottom) shows different dates, while the vertical axis (side) shows numbers *in thousands of pounds sterling.* At first glance, the difference between imports and exports would seem to be about 400 pounds sterling (answer A), but since this number represents *thousands of pounds sterling,* it must be multiplied by 1000.

4. The English Bill of Rights and the American Bill of Rights grant citizens certain rights and set specific limits on the powers of government. Which of the following provisions is contained in the English, but NOT the American, Bill of Rights?

F Citizens have freedom of speech.

G People accused of crimes have the right to a jury trial.

H The government is not allowed to impose cruel or unusual punishments.

J The king is not allowed to suspend laws.

Test-Taking Tip: This question requires a comparison, but unlike question 2, it is looking for a *difference,* not a similarity. Since free speech *is* a provision in the American Bill of Rights, it cannot be the correct answer. Look for the answer that relates only to *England.*

5. The purpose of the Declaration of Independence was to

A outline colonists' reasons for separating from Great Britain.

B establish the first royal government in North America.

C set forth the rights and duties of the President.

D grant religious freedom to all citizens.

Test-Taking Tip: Think about the meaning of the words *Declaration of Independence.* Eliminate answer choices that don't match the *meaning* of these words. Since answer C does not directly relate to *declaring independence,* it should be eliminated.

Use the map below to answer question 6.

6. According to the map above, which of the following is true?

F The battle at Moscow was unsuccessful for Napoleon.

G Napoleon controlled most of the nations west of the Prime Meridian.

H Napoleon did not conquer Great Britain.

J The Ottoman Empire included Sardinia.

Test-Taking Tip: Look at the *map key* to understand how the map is organized. Can you see which countries are allied with Napoleon? Which countries are independent? Make sure that your answer choice is supported by information *on the map.* Do not rely only on your memory for this type of question.

Unit 5 *Age of Revolution* 593

4. J (Civics) Page 543 states that the English Bill of Rights provided for the right to trials by jury, banned cruel and unusual punishment, and protected the right to speak freely in Parliament. Since Americans have no king, there is no provision in the American Bill of Rights that limits the power of kings.

5. A (Civics) Page 553 states that the Declaration *set forth the colonists' reason for separation from Great Britain.*

Remind students to scrutinize the language in the question for clues, and to use their common sense. The question asks about the Declaration of Independence. Independence is always freedom from something else, so choices B and C are implausible.

6. H (Geography) According to the map, Great Britain remained independent and was not subject to Napoleon's rule.

MORE PRACTICE

For additional practice, assign practice pages from:

Glencoe Standardized Test Practice Workbook

Glencoe SAT/SAT II Practice Book

Tested Objectives	
Questions	**Objective**
1	Making Generalizations
2	Making Comparisons
3, 4	Evaluating Information
5	Identifying Central Issues
6	Analyzing Information

Industry and Nationalism

Introducing the Unit

Unit 6 focuses on the Industrial
Revolution and the world's rapid
political, social, and cultural
changes in the 1700s and 1800s.

Unit Objectives

After reading Unit 6, students
will be able to:

1. understand the technological
   innovations and new economic developments of the Industrial Revolution.
2. trace new political, economic,
   and scientific ideas and the
   growth of popular culture.
3. describe the revolutionary
   and reform movements that
   reshaped politics of Europe
   and the Americas in the 1800s.
4. explain how nationalists unified Italy and Germany and
   challenged autocracy in Russia and Austria-Hungary.
5. discuss the effects of imperialism in Asia, Africa, and Latin
   America.

PRIMARY SOURCES
Library

See pages 728–729 for
primary source readings
that accompany Unit 6.

Then & Now For centuries wealthy landowners in Europe controlled a static agricultural economy. Peasant fami-
lies farmed strips of land, and small industries and trades met local
needs. Then, in England in the late 1700s, innovations in farming
made agriculture a profitable business. An agricultural revolution
helped start a revolution in industry, beginning in textiles. The factory system expanded the power and wealth of the middle class.
While scientific and medical advances improved life for many, in
much of Europe the poor remained powerless.

How long would it take you to walk to school? The railroad
began the revolution in transportation. When a German engineer
redesigned the internal combustion engine to run on gasoline, the
automobile took center stage. Within a few decades the automobile
would transform society in every industrial country.

A Global Chronology

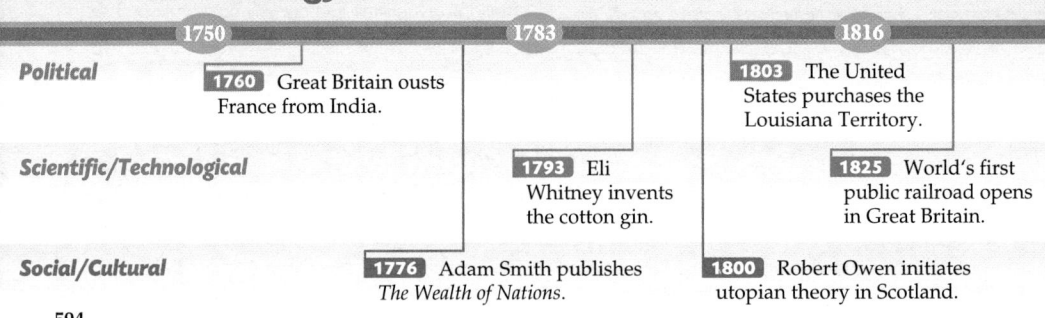

	1750		1783		1816
Political		**1760** Great Britain ousts France from India.			**1803** The United States purchases the Louisiana Territory.
Scientific/Technological			**1793** Eli Whitney invents the cotton gin.		**1825** World's first public railroad opens in Great Britain.
Social/Cultural			**1776** Adam Smith publishes *The Wealth of Nations*.		**1800** Robert Owen initiates utopian theory in Scotland.

594

Then & Now **Nationalism** In this unit students will learn about the rise of nationalism in
Europe, including nationalist movements in the Balkans (pages 697–698). Ask
students to discuss regions of the world where nationalism has led to violence
in recent years. Why is nationalism such a powerful feeling throughout the
world? *(Answers will vary. Some students may feel that nationalism or patriotism is a natural feeling.)* In
what ways has nationalism been a positive force in recent history? *(It led to dramatic restructuring*

Steam locomotive and wood car

History *and the* Humanities

📖 Focus on World Art Prints
- 5 *Palace, Partially Destroyed*
- 22 *Hospital at Saint-Rémy*

🎨 World History and Art Transparencies
- 30 *Le Moulin de la Galette*
- 31 *In the Garden*
- 34 *Starry Night*
- 35 *Ono Waterfall*

🎵 World Music: Cultural Traditions, Lessons 2, 3, 4, 6, 9

ABCNEWS INTERACTIVE™

 VIDEODISC
Turning Points in World History

Side Two, Chapter 3
Title: *The Industrial Revolution*
Ask: How was the railroad instrumental in the new industrial economy? (*It transported goods being made in the factories.*)

Visualizing History
Rail lines spread across Europe and North America after 1820, opening up new markets and spurring growth.

History and You

The Industrial Revolution started in the late 1700s and changed the way people lived. The introduction of modern machines and the building of factories brought technical advancement but also a new set of problems.

📺 To examine the social issues related to the Industrial Revolution, view videodisc Chapter 3: *The Industrial Revolution* in Turning Points in World History.

1849	**1882**	**1915**

1871 Bismarck unifies Germany.

1911 Revolution topples Qing dynasty in China.

1876 Alexander Graham Bell invents the telephone.

1914 Panama Canal opens.

1848 Karl Marx publishes *The Communist Manifesto.*

1874 French impressionists hold first major exhibition in Paris.

595

 Glencoe Literature Library

The following literature from the **Glencoe Literature Library** may enrich this unit:
The Brothers Karamazov by F. Dostoevsky
Great Expectations by C. Dickens
Wuthering Heights by E. Brontë

of the Soviet Union and the Communist regimes of Eastern Europe.) Where has nationalism led to violence in recent years? (former Soviet Union, former Yugoslavia, Rwanda, Liberia) Why has nationalism sometimes led to violence? (Answers will vary. Students may mention that political boundaries often do not correspond to distribution of ethnic groups.) Do you think that every distinct ethnic group should form its own nation? Why or why not? (Answers will vary. Students may realize that the idea would lead to the splitting up of nearly all nations that now exist.)

The Spread of Ideas

TEACH

Introduction

This feature focuses on the spread of the Industrial Revolution from its beginnings in Great Britain to the United States and Japan.

Background Notes

Linking Past and Present

Today, industrial technology moves quickly from one country to another. For example, computer software, microelectronics, and industrial chemicals, once produced almost entirely in Europe, Japan, and the United States, are now exported from Brazil, India, Korea, and Taiwan. The reduction in trade barriers under GATT (General Agreement on Tariffs and Trade) has made the movement of technology even easier.

Geography

Movement The Industrial Revolution caused unprecedented movement among people as farmers in many lands left their farms to work in factories, often in far-off places. Skilled European workers came to the United States in the early 1800s to work in cotton mills like the one Slater built in Pawtucket. In the 1820s one observer noted that a mix of workers from different parts of Britain made problems for one mill owner: "I cannot conceive a more uncomfortable situation than … to be surrounded by a mixture of Irish, Yorkshire, and west of England workmen. Whatever advice he might receive from the one party would be condemned by the others…."

The Spread of Ideas

Industrialization

*T*he rise of industry changed the world forever. So dramatic were the changes that historians have labeled the period the Industrial Revolution. Although the revolution began in Britain, it respected neither time nor place. The revolution traveled beyond Britain to touch every nation on earth.

Great Britain
Workshop of the World

The birth of industry needed certain preconditions: the science, incentive, and money capital to build machines; a labor force to run them; raw materials and markets to make the system profitable; and efficient farms to feed a new group of workers. At the start of the 1700s, Great Britain possessed all these conditions. Here industrialism first took root.

As with the development of agriculture, no one person can be credited with the invention of industry. Instead, it grew from the innovations of individuals who developed machines to do work formerly done by humans and animals. One inventor built on the ideas of another. In 1705, for example, Thomas Newcomen devised a crude steam engine to pump water out of coal mines. In 1769 James Watt improved upon Newcomen's work and built a more efficient steam engine. Other inventors adapted Watt's engine to run cloth-making machines. Business owners soon brought machines and workers together in a single place called a factory.

By the 1800s, industry had catapulted Great Britain into a position of world leadership. "[Britain has] triumphantly established herself as the workshop of the world," boasted one leader. It was impossible to monopolize this idea. Workshops began to hum in America.

James Watt

Watt's steam engine

COOPERATIVE LEARNING ACTIVITY

Reports Have students brainstorm a list of important technologies today (prompt them if necessary to consider semiconductors, satellites, fiber optics, biotechnology, software, and high-resolution television). Then organize the class into groups and have each group research and prepare an oral report on one technology. Reports should indicate, if possible, where the technology was first developed and where it is produced today. Then have students from each group present their report to the class. Encourage students to include visuals in their reports. **L2**

The United States
The Revolution Spreads

Great Britain tried to keep the secrets of industry locked up. It forbade the export of industrial machines. It also barred the people who built and operated the machines from leaving the country. In 1789, however, a young factory supervisor named Samuel Slater found a way to escape. He disguised himself as a farm-hand and boarded a ship for New York.

Working entirely from memory, Slater built a mill in Pawtucket, Rhode Island. On December 20, 1790, the mill turned out the first machine-made cotton yarn produced in America.

Within two years, Slater had sales offices in Salem, New York City, Baltimore, and Philadelphia. As Slater's mills turned out cotton, the United States began churning out its own brilliant industrial inventors. They produced more than just machines. They came up with new industrial principles such as Eli Whitney's use of standardized parts and Henry Ford's use of the assembly line. Together these two ideas gave the world mass production—a concept that would revolutionize people's lives around the globe.

Matthew Perry's steamboat in Tokyo Bay

Samuel Slater's mill

Japan
The Search for Markets

In 1853, the Industrial Revolution traveled to Japan in the form of a fleet of United States steamships sent to open the island to trade. "What we had taken as a fire at sea," recalled one Japanese observer, "was really smoke coming out of their smokestacks."

The military power produced by United States industry shook the Japanese. Recalled the same observer, "What a joke, the steaming teapot fixed by America—Just four cups [ships], and we cannot sleep at night."

The Japanese temporarily gave in to American demands. But they also vowed that they too would possess industry. By the start of the 1900s, Japan had joined other industrial nations in the search for markets. By 1914 Japan's merchant fleet was the sixth largest in the world and their foreign trade had increased one hundred-fold in value in fifty years.

LINKING THE IDEAS

1. How was the idea for a cotton mill brought from Great Britain to the United States?
2. What feature of the American fleet most impressed the Japanese in 1853?

Critical Thinking

3. **Drawing Conclusions** Why did the British want to control the spread of an idea that made production of goods easier?

Unit 6 *Industry and Nationalism* 597

ANSWERS TO LINKING THE IDEAS

1. Samuel Slater memorized the mill design and left England by pretending to be a farmer.

2. their steam engines
3. Britain wanted to maintain a monopoly over industrial production.

A complete, 1-page lesson plan is provided for each section in the *Reproducible Lesson Plans* booklet.

Age of Industry

CHAPTER RESOURCES

	Reproducible Resources	Multimedia Resources
Chapter Opener	Chapter Themes: Graphic Organizer 23 Historical Significance Chapter Activity 23	MindJogger Videoquiz
Chapter Enrichment	Vocabulary Activity 23* Time Line Activity 23 Mapping History Activity 23 History Simulation 23 Geography and History Activity 23 Source Reading 23 People in World History Profiles 43, 44 World Art and Music Activity 23 Enrichment Activity 23 Critical Thinking Activity 23 Skill Reinforcement Activity 23 Performance Assessment Activity 23 Standardized Test Practice Workbook Activity 23 Inclusion for the Social Studies Classroom Strategies and Activities	World History and Art Transparency 30, *Le Moulin de la Galette* Chapter Transparency 23 Vocabulary PuzzleMaker Software Turning Points in World History: *The Industrial Revolution* World History Primary Source Document Library
Chapter Review/Reteaching	Reteaching Activity 23 Skill Reinforcement Activity 23 Spanish Chapter Summary 23	Chapter 23 Digest Audiocassette, Activity, Test* Vocabulary PuzzleMaker Software Interactive Tutor Self-Assessment Software MindJogger Videoquiz
Chapter Evaluation/Testing	Performance Assessment Activity 23 Chapter 23 Test, Forms A and B	ExamView® Pro Testmaker

0:00 OUT OF TIME? Assign the Chapter 23 Audiocassettes.

* Also available in Spanish

World History Primary Source Document Library
Make History Come Alive!
Engage your students with over 250 easily accessible primary source documents—available on this CD-ROM—that will give them real life insight into the important events of world history.

Block Schedule

Activities that are particularly suited to use within the block scheduling framework are identified throughout this chapter by the following designation.

KEY TO ABILITY LEVELS

Teaching strategies are coded for varying learning styles.

L1 **BASIC** activities for all students
L2 **AVERAGE** activities for average to above-average students
L3 **CHALLENGING** activities for above-average students
LEP **LIMITED ENGLISH PROFICIENCY** activities

Use Glencoe's *Presentation Plus!* multimedia teacher tool to easily present dynamic lessons that visually excite your students. Using Microsoft PowerPoint® you can customize the presentations to create your own personalized lessons.

Interactive Lesson Planner

Planning has never been easier! Using this CD-ROM, organize your week, month, semester, or year with all the help you need. The **Interactive Lesson Planner** gives you access to all of the blackline masters that accompany *World History: The Human Experience.*

SECTION RESOURCES

Daily Objectives	Reproducible Resources	Multimedia Resources
Section 1 **Living From the Land** Describe what daily life was like before the rise of modern industry.	Lecture Notes 23-1 Reproducible Lesson Plan 23-1 Vocabulary Activity 23* Guided Reading Activity 23-1* Time Line Activity 23 Section Quiz 23-1* Reading Essentials and Study Guide 23-1	Section Focus Transparency 23-1 Chapter Transparency 23 Interactive Tutor Self-Assessment Software Testmaker Turning Points in World History: *The Industrial Revolution*
Section 2 **The Beginnings of Change** Explain why the Industrial Revolution began in Great Britain.	Lecture Notes 23-2 Reproducible Lesson Plan 23-2 Vocabulary Activity 23* Guided Reading Activity 23-2* Geography and History Activity 23 Section Quiz 23-2* Reading Essentials and Study Guide 23-2	Section Focus Transparency 23-2 Interactive Tutor Self-Assessment Software Testmaker Turning Points in World History: *The Industrial Revolution*
Section 3 **The Growth of Industry** Analyze how new technology advanced the growth of industry.	Lecture Notes 23-3 Reproducible Lesson Plan 23-3 Guided Reading Activity 23-3* People in World History Profiles 43, 44 History Simulation 23 Section Quiz 23-3* Reading Essentials and Study Guide 23-3	Section Focus Transparency 23-3 Vocabulary PuzzleMaker Software Interactive Tutor Self-Assessment Software Testmaker Turning Points in World History: *The Industrial Revolution*
Section 4 **A New Society** Describe how the Industrial Revolution affected people's lives.	Lecture Notes 23-4 Reproducible Lesson Plan 23-4 Vocabulary Activity 23* Guided Reading Activity 23-4* Reteaching Activity 23 Enrichment Activity 23 Section Quiz 23-4* Performance Assessment Activity 23 Spanish Chapter Summary 23 Reading Essentials and Study Guide 23-4	Section Focus Transparency 23-4 World History and Art Transparency 30, *Le Moulin de la Galette* Interactive Tutor Self-Assessment Software Testmaker Turning Points in World History: *The Industrial Revolution*

* *Also available in Spanish*

Chapter Activities

 Performance Assessment Activity

Students as Inventors Have students assume the roles of modern-day inventors who have identified a clear need for a new product. Ask them to draw up plans for an invention to fill the need, determine an area of the world in which to manufacture it, and suggest possible ways to finance the project. Students will then create a proposal including a diagram and map of manufacturing and distribution. Included in the proposal should be the likely impact of the manufacturing in the area under consideration. As an alternative, you might suggest the type of invention needed, have several groups come up with proposals, then debate the relative merits of their proposals for location and investment.

Possible Rubric Features

Accuracy of research; thoroughness in meeting criteria for labor force, capital, natural resources, and need; organization and clarity of presentation and visuals

• *For an additional activity, refer to Activity 23 in the* Performance Assessment Strategies and Activities *booklet.*

ACTIVITY
From the Classroom of...

**Edward Thomas
Elmont Memorial High
School
Elmont, NY**

Analyzing Effects of Industrialization

Ask students what products or inventions have been important during the 1990s. Have students discuss the ways each product or invention has affected their lives and society as a whole, both positively and negatively. Then have students list products and inventions from the Age of Industry, along with their effects in both rural and urban regions. Use these lists as a springboard for a general discussion of the changes in lifestyle brought about by industrialization. Be sure students mention the movement of many people from rural to urban areas. Ask students if any of the problems brought about by industrialization are still present in society.

MULTIPLE LEARNING STYLES

Verbal/Linguistic
Have students read Charles Dickens's *Hard Times* and write a book report analyzing how the novel presents relations between industrialists and workers. Have them consider these questions: Who are the heroes? Who are the villains? How does Dickens's portrayal compare with this chapter's discussion of the situation?

Logical/Mathematical
Have students select one or more stocks and follow their progress on the stock market for several days or weeks. If possible, they should research the companies they select and learn something about their development.

Visual/Spatial
Have students construct a graph showing the growth of Europe's population from 1600 to 1900.

Kinesthetic
Have students select an invention of the period and prepare a model or detailed diagram showing how it works.

 GLENCOE'S ASSESSMENT ADVANTAGE

Use the following to easily assess student learning in a variety of ways.

- Performance Assessment Strategies and Activities
- Section Quizzes
- Chapter and Unit Tests
- Interactive Tutor Self-Assessment Software
- Testmaker Software
- MindJogger Videoquiz
- SAT/SAT II Test Practice
- worldhistory.glencoe.com

Additional Resources

Teacher's Corner

NATIONAL GEOGRAPHIC SOCIETY

INDEX TO NATIONAL GEOGRAPHIC MAGAZINE

The following articles may be used for research relating to this chapter:

- "Robot Revolution," by Curt Suplee, July 1997.
- "Information Revolution" by Joel L. Swerdlow, October 1995.
- "George Washington's Patowmack Canal," by Wilbur E. Garrett, June 1987.

ADDITIONAL NATIONAL GEOGRAPHIC SOCIETY PRODUCTS

To order the following products for use with this chapter, call National Geographic Society at 1-800-368-2728:

- *Wired World* (Video)
- *Inventors and Inventions* (Video)
- *Technology's Price* (Video)

Access National Geographic's new dynamic MapMachine Web site and other geography resources at:

- http://www.nationalgeographic.com/
- http://www.nationalgeographic.com/maps

BIBLIOGRAPHY

Literature of the Period
Trollope, Anthony. *The Way We Live Now.* London: Trollope Society, 1992. Witty dissection of English society in the Industrial Age.
Zola, Émile. *Germinal.* New York: Vintage Books, 1994. Outspoken attack on harsh conditions in French coal mines.
Readings for the Student
Dickens, Charles. *Oliver Twist.* New York: Dodd, Mead, 1984. An orphan's adventures in seamy, industrial London.
Readings for the Teacher
Avery, Gillian. *The Echoing Green: Memories of Victorian Youth.* New York: Viking, 1974. Diaries and memoirs re-create life in the 1800s.

WORLD HISTORY Online

Use our Web site as an additional resource. All essential content is covered in the Student Edition.

You and your students can visit the *World History: The Human Experience* Web site at worldhistory.glencoe.com The student text directs students to the Web site for the following options:

- **Chapter Overviews**
- **Student Web Activities**
- **Self-Check Quizzes**

Answers are provided for you in a link entitled "Web Activity Lesson Plan." Additional Web Resources, Interactive Puzzles, and content updates are also available.

Visit the Glencoe Web site at socialstudies.glencoe.com for social studies activities, updates, and links to other resources.

LOCAL OBJECTIVES

_____
_____
_____
_____
_____
_____
_____
_____
_____
_____
_____
_____
_____
_____
_____
_____
_____
_____
_____
_____

CHAPTER THEMES

Chapter Themes are listed by section on this chapter opening page of the Student Edition. A corresponding theme-based activity is available under "TEACH," and a theme-based question is asked in the Section and Chapter Assessments.

The Storyteller

Historical Setting Children had worked for centuries before the onset of the Industrial Revolution. They had worked on their families' farms and had been apprenticed at a variety of skilled crafts. But with the advent of the industrial age, working children's lives were little better than those of enslaved peoples. They worked in factories and in mines. They toiled long hours in the cold and the dark, handling dangerous machinery for very low wages.

Historical Significance

Answers: *Many nations developed urban industrial economies. New inventions led to the growth of factories, and these in turn led to the growth of manufacturing cities. The middle class expanded in size and wealth. Harsh conditions for working people led to the development of labor unions.*

Today industrialized nations have advanced technology and high standards of living; nonindustrialized nations try to gain these benefits by industrializing.

—WORLD HISTORY *Online* —

Have students use the **Chapter 23 Overview** at worldhistory. glencoe.com as a prereading and postreading exercise for understanding chapter content.

Chapter
23
1700–1914
Age of Industry

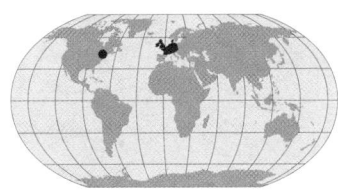

Chapter Themes

▶ **Relation to Environment** Before the Industrial Revolution most Europeans live in isolated rural villages and depend on the land. *Section 1*
▶ **Innovation** Inventions and new procedures in agriculture and industry transform economies in Europe and North America. *Section 2*
▶ **Change** Throughout the Western world, new urban centers based on industry develop along with the rise of new social classes. *Section 3*
▶ **Conflict** Workers in Europe and North America organize to gain better wages and improved working conditions. *Section 4*

The Storyteller

Change swept through Europe and North America as new coal mines and iron works began to dominate rural landscapes. Susan Pitchforth, an 11-year-old British girl, was just one of the millions of men, women, and children who left farming villages to find work in these growing industries.

Like countless others, Susan suffered difficult and dangerous industrial working conditions. When the British Parliament investigated horrible conditions in coal mines, young Susan told them her story:

"I have worked at this pit going on two years … I walk a mile and a half to my work, both in winter and summer. I run 24 [loads] a day; I cannot come up till I have done them all."

Historical Significance

What changes took place in Europe and North America during the Industrial Revolution? How does the Industrial Revolution affect life throughout the world today?

| 1750 | 1800 | 1850 | 1900 |

1787 Edmund Cartwright develops power loom.

1760s James Watt perfects steam engine.

1855 Henry Bessemer obtains patent for mass-producing steel from iron.

1903 Wright brothers make first airplane flight.

598

GEOGRAPHY CONNECTION

Location Have students locate Great Britain (England, Scotland, Wales) in the Atlas in their textbook or on a wall map. What geographic features do you see? *(Britain is an island nation; there are many harbors and rivers.)* How might these features help stimulate industry? *(Isolation from continental Europe would protect Britain from invasion and warfare; harbors and rivers aid transportation.)* **L1**

Coalbrookdale by Night by Philip de Loutherberg.
Science Museum, London, England

 WORLD HISTORY *Online*

Chapter Overview

Visit the *World History: The Human Experience*
Web site at **worldhistory.glencoe.com** and
click on **Chapter 23—Chapter Overview**
to preview the chapter.

Your History Journal

*Build a time line of inventions of the
Industrial Revolution beginning with John
Kay's improved loom and ending with the
first airplane.*

✚ EXTRA CREDIT PROJECT

Biography Have students investigate one of
the men who helped bring about the agricultural revolution: Robert Bakewell, Charles
Townshend, or Jethro Tull in England, or John
Deere in the United States. Students should
report, orally or in writing, on what the man
contributed and the difference his contribution
made to agricultural production. **L2**

Introducing
Chapter 23

History & Art Tell students that
Coalbrookdale was an important
center of English industrialization. It
was here, in the early 1700s, that
entrepreneur Abraham Darby first
used coke—a coal product—to smelt
iron. Previously, manufacturers had
used charcoal, a wood product, with
the result that England's forests
were being depleted.

✔ Performance Assessment

Refer to the activity on page
598C of the Planning Guide.

🗁 For an additional
activity, refer to Activity 23 in
the *Performance Assessment
Strategies and Activities* booklet.

Using Your History Journal

Students may use different colors
for different industries, such as textiles, iron and steel, and transportation and communication.

GLENCOE
TECHNOLOGY

VIDEODISC
Use MindJogger to preview
chapter content.

MindJogger Videoquiz
   Chapter 23
Disc 3 Side B

  Also available in VHS.

1700   1750   1800

c. 1700s Domestic system is widespread in European towns and villages.

c. 1750 About 75 percent of Europeans live in rural areas.

Section 1

Living From the Land

Guide to Reading

Read to Find Out
Main Idea *Daily life was based around villages and agriculture before the rise of modern industry.*

▶ **Terms to Define**
domestic system

▶ **People to Meet**
Charles Dickens

▶ **Places to Locate**
London

The Storyteller

Landlords increased their income by removing common farmers from their rented fields. An anonymous poem passed judgment on the enclosure of Thornborough landlords in 1798:

Ye Thornbro' youths bewail with me;
Ye shepherds lay your pipes aside,
       No longer tune the merry
           glee,
       For we are rob'd of all
           our pride.
       The time alas will soon
           approach,
       When we must all our
           pasture yield;
       The wealthy on our
           rights encroach
       And will enclose our
           common field.

Haymaking in rural England

—adapted from *English Parliamentary Enclosure*, Michael Turner, 1980

During the 1700s and 1800s, a series of innovations in agriculture and industry led to profound economic and social change throughout Europe and the United States. Urban industrial economies emerged in these areas and eventually spread around the world. This transformation, which became known as the Industrial Revolution, began when power-driven machinery in factories replaced work done in homes—altering the way people had lived and worked for hundreds of years.

Cloth making provides a dramatic example of the far-reaching effects of the Industrial Revolution. In the 1700s a home weaver worked many hours to produce a yard of cloth. A century later, a worker operating machines in a textile mill could make 50 times more cloth.

As adventurous businesspeople brought machines and workers together in factories, industries produced mass quantities of goods. Millions of people in search of new opportunities to make a living left rural villages to find factory work in growing towns and cities. A new era of mechanization had arrived.

A Harsh Way of Life

Before the dawn of the Industrial Revolution in the 1700s, people lived in much the same way their ancestors had lived for hundreds of years. Nature's seasons and religious traditions measured time, and social change was rare. Relying almost solely on farming to make a living, people planted and harvested fields, hoped for good weather, and lived always under the threat of disease.

Families, both rich and poor, remained relatively small because of a very high infant death rate. One baby in three died in his or her first year of life,

600   **Chapter 23**   *Age of Industry*

and only one in two people reached age 21. Life expectancy hovered around age 40. People expected life to be short and harsh. As one mother in the 1770s said after her baby's death, "One cannot grieve after her much, and I have just now other things to think of."

Only 25 percent of Europeans lived in towns or cities in the 1700s. **London** was the largest city in Europe in 1750 with about 700,000 people. Yet it too had a rural character. The famous British novelist **Charles Dickens** described a London morning in the early 1800s:

> ❝ By degrees, other shops began to be unclosed, and a few scattered people were met with. Then, came straggling groups of labourers going to their work; then men and women with fish baskets on their heads; donkey carts laden with vegetables; chaise carts filled with livestock or whole carcasses of meat, milk women with pails; an unbroken concourse of people…. ❞
>
> —Charles Dickens, *Oliver Twist*, 1837

Most people in preindustrial times lived in country villages consisting of a few hundred people. Many never went beyond their villages. When braver people traveled to other cities and towns, their tales delighted their less worldly neighbors.

Village Life

Virtually all rural villagers were farmers. Wealthy landowners controlled the majority of the village land, renting most of it to small farming families. Families owned or rented small strips of land in several areas of the village. This practice ensured both fair land distribution and economic protection should disaster strike any one field. Farmers worked the land cooperatively, jointly deciding what crops to grow and when to plant and harvest.

In most of the villages, private and public lands were not separated or fenced off. The public lands, called the village commons, consisted of woodlands, pastures, and less fertile land near the village. For centuries, farmers could gather wood and

History & Art *Harvest Scene* by George Vicat Cole. Christie's, London, England **What were the village commons?**

graze their livestock on the commons. Poorer farmers even used these public lands for raising crops.

Village economies were limited largely to the local area because transporting goods to other areas was difficult and unprofitable. Rain turned the few roads into muddy rivers. For this reason, villages had to be nearly self-sufficient. People grew enough food for their families and perhaps a small amount to sell to nearby towns. They made their own homes, clothes, and tools from products raised in the fields or gathered from the land.

The richest rural landowners lived on sprawling country estates with a huge main house, cottages, several barns, and extensive fields. Landowners and their families lived lavishly. Servants ran the households and catered to the families' needs.

People who rented land from the landowners lived quite differently. Most lived in small, smoky, poorly lighted cottages with dirt floors. Since the poorest farming families often did not have barns, they sometimes shared their cramped living quarters with farm animals.

All daily activities revolved around farming, an occupation dominated by tradition. Farmers used the same simple methods and tools their ancestors had used and relied on nature to provide good growing seasons. Nature, however, was never predictable, and harvests ranged from plentiful to disastrously small.

Everyone in the farming family worked hard. From morning to night, husband, wife, and children worked together. Boys helped their fathers in

Chapter 23 *Age of Industry* **601**

TEACH

Guided Practice

THEME Relation to Environment

Ask students to identify some positive features—perhaps things they lack in their own lives—of life in a preindustrial farm village. (*Answers will vary but might include a feeling of community, little crime, and a sense of accomplishment that comes with self-reliance.*) **L1**

History & Art Before the Industrial Revolution, Britain produced almost all its own foodstuffs except for sugar.
Answer to Caption: *land that all villagers could use*

Daily Life Have half the class take the role of magazine reporter and the other half that of a village inhabitant—landowner, farmer, and so on. Reporters should interview villagers about what it is like to live in the village. **L2**

VIDEODISC
Turning Points in World History

Side Two, Chapter 3
Title: *The Industrial Revolution*
Ask: What kinds of power did inventors use to run new machines? (*water, steam, coal*)

 Chapter Transparency 23

Independent Practice

 Guided Reading Activity 23-1 **L1**

 Time Line Activity 23

Technology Have students make a flowchart of the steps involved in creating a woolen garment under the domestic system. **L2**

ASSESS

Check for Understanding

Assign Section 1 Assessment as homework or as an in-class activity.

 Use Interactive Tutor Self-Assessment Software to review Section 1.

Evaluate

 Section Quiz 23-1

 Use the Testmaker to create a customized quiz for Section 1.

Reteach

Have groups of students list the key characteristics of preindustrial farming, preindustrial mining, and the early wool industry. As the groups share their lists, write major points on the board.

 Reading Essentials and Study Guide 23-1

Enrich

Have students draw cartoons showing the best and worst features of rural life in the preindustrial age.

CLOSE

Remind students that people often use the phrase "the good old days" out of nostalgia for the past. Have them write an essay explaining whether the preindustrial era could be considered good.

---

the fields or at the workbench. Girls helped their mothers with chores such as milking cows, churning butter, and preparing meals.

Early Industries

In addition to farming, many people worked in small industries or in coal mines. These industries met local needs for goods such as coal, glass, iron, and clothing and employed a small number of workers. Since many workers were also farm workers, work schedules were coordinated with the agricultural cycle.

During harvest time nail makers, glassblowers, ironworkers, and miners helped farmers with the crops; likewise, in the winter farmworkers worked in the mines and in the workshops. This close relationship between farming and industry provided a steadier income to workers than either farming or industry alone.

Making Wool

In Great Britain, the woolen industry had for centuries been second only to farming in the numbers of people it employed and in the volume of trade it created. In the 1700s the demand for wool grew so great that merchants hired workers to produce woolens in their own homes. This system of labor, called the domestic system, spread to other industries such as leather working and was widely used throughout Europe in the 1700s.

The domestic system depended on a network of workers. In the case of wool, a merchant first bought the raw fiber and divided it among several families. Women and children usually cleaned, sorted, and spun the fiber into thread or yarn. Men usually did the actual weaving. Then the merchant collected the yarn, paid the spinner a fee, and took the yarn to a weaver. The material next went to a fuller, who shaped and cleaned the material, and at last to the dyer for coloring. Finally, the merchant took the finished products to market and sold them for the highest possible price.

The domestic system had many benefits. Workers set their own hours and could tend to duties at home during work breaks. Women cared for children, tended vegetable gardens, and cooked meals while they earned money at home. Men carried on farming tasks, such as plowing and planting fields. Children also helped their parents. In one British region, children attended special schools to learn the art of lace making. With this skill they contributed to the family income. The domestic system provided work and income during hard times, saving many families from starvation. It later became the basis on which the technology and skills of the Industrial Revolution were built.

Mining Coal

The domestic system also had its place in coal mining. Coal fields often lay under farmland. The people who worked the mines often became farm laborers during the harvest, and farm horses pulled coal wagons from the pits. In some coal fields, women and children even hauled baskets of coal from the pits. One observer described these loaded baskets, saying it was "frequently more than one man could do to lift the burden."

With the money earned from mining or farmwork, country people might buy the few things they could not manufacture. Craftspeople sold handmade guns, furniture, and clothing in their small shops. Some craftspeople sent their goods to foreign markets in exchange for imported goods and traded the rest for food from nearby farmers and products from other local craftspeople.

Yet changes to this way of life were on the horizon. The development of new machinery and sources of power would soon upset the domestic system, transforming forever the way people lived and worked.

SECTION 1 ASSESSMENT

Main Idea
1. Use a diagram like the one below to list aspects of life before the rise of industry.

Aspects of Life:
Preindustrial Times

Recall
2. **Define** the domestic system.
3. **Identify** the Industrial Revolution, Charles Dickens.

Critical Thinking
4. **Predicting Trends** As a result of the Industrial Revolution, many traditions were abandoned in Europe. How could abandoning tradition help

Europe's small farming villages? How might it hurt them?

Understanding Themes
5. **Relation to the Environment** Where did most people live during the period of history before the rise of industry? What was the most important occupation during preindustrial times?

SECTION 1 ASSESSMENT ANSWERS

1. relied on farming; small families; high infant mortality; life expectancy of 40 years; most people lived in rural villages; rich landowners lived well, renters lived poorly; people also worked in small industries or coal mines
2. All terms are defined in the Glossary.
3. Industrial Revolution, 600; Charles Dickens, 601

4. It might help them by increasing production and raising the standard of living; it might harm them by weakening community ties.
5. **RELATION TO ENVIRONMENT**
   in rural villages; farming

c. 1700s British landowners extend enclosures and displace farmers.

1787 Edmund Cartwright develops power loom.

 1807 Robert Fulton designs first practical steamboat.

Section 2

The Beginnings of Change

Guide to Reading

Read to Find Out
Main Idea *The Industrial Revolution began in Great Britain.*

▶ **Terms to Define**
enclosure movement, capital, entrepreneur, factory system

▶ **People to Meet**
James Hargreaves, Richard Arkwright, Edmund Cartwright, Eli Whitney, James Watt, Henry Bessemer, Robert Fulton

The Storyteller

About 210,000 men built the first railroads in Britain. They called themselves "navvies." Mostly the men worked in silence. The only British navvies whose singing was noticed were the Welsh, whose songs were mainly hymns. Most other songs that navvies sang while they worked have disappeared. One tune, however, heard on the railway in 1859 gives some insight into the navvies' lives:

> *…I'm a navvy on the line.*
> *I get me five-and-twenty bob a week,*
> *Besides me overtime.*
> *Roast Beef and boiled beef*
> *An' puddin' made of eggs….*

—adapted from *The Victorian Railway*, Jack Simmons, 1991

Early train

For hundreds of years, British farmers had planted crops and kept livestock on unfenced private and public lands. Village society depended on this age-old system of farming and grazing. By the late 1700s, however, wealthy British landowners would end this open-field system, which had been slowly giving way to private ownership since the 1100s.

The landowners felt that larger farms with enclosed fields would increase farming efficiency and productivity. Parliament supported this enclosure movement, passing laws that allowed landowners to take over and fence off private and common lands. In the 1700s the enclosure movement transformed rural Great Britain. Many small farmers dependent on village lands were forced to move to towns and cities to find work. At the same time, landowners practiced new, more efficient farming methods.

To raise crop yields, landowners mixed different kinds of soils and used new crop rotation systems. One landowner, Lord Charles Townshend, urged the growing of turnips to enrich exhausted soil. Another reformer, Robert Bakewell, bred stronger horses for farm work and fatter sheep and cattle for meat. The inventor Jethro Tull developed a seed drill that enabled farmers to plant seeds in orderly rows instead of scattering them over the fields. As innovation and competition replaced traditional methods, agriculture underwent a revolution that improved the quality, quantity, and profitability of farm goods.

Great Britain Leads the Way

This agricultural revolution helped Great Britain to lead the Industrial Revolution. Successful farming businesses provided landowners with money to invest in growing industries. Many

Chapter 23 *Age of Industry* **603**

TEACH

Guided Practice

THEME Innovation

Ask students why they think textiles were in the forefront of technological innovation. (*A British textile industry already existed but could not meet the increasing demand for cloth.*) **L1**

Visualizing History One indication of the enormous growth of the textile industry was the increase in cotton imports: in the 1760s Britain imported 4 million pounds (1,816 kilograms) of cotton yearly; by the 1830s it was importing 300 million pounds (13,620,000 kilograms). **Answer to Caption:** *by passing laws that helped business*

Economics Ask students why the British had surplus capital to invest in the late 1700s. (*Landowners benefited from new large-scale farming; they and others also profited from overseas commerce, including the slave trade.*) **L2**

Time Line Have students construct a time line of important eighteenth-century developments in the textile industry. **L2**

Who?What?Where?When?

James Hargreaves (who may have named the spinning jenny after his wife) tried to keep his invention secret. But other spinners became suspicious because his family produced so much yarn. They burst into his house, destroyed his machine, and forced the family to move away.

Visualizing History The task of beating cotton by hand was replaced by a beating and lapping machine in the 1700s. *How did Parliament encourage investment in industry?*

displaced farmers became industrial workers. These factors added to the key elements for industrial success that Great Britain already possessed—capital, natural resources, and labor supply.

Money and Industry

Capital, or money to invest in labor, machines, and raw materials, is essential for the growth of industry. Many British people became very wealthy during the 1700s. Landowners and other members of the aristocracy profited not only from new large-scale farming but also from overseas commerce and the slave trade, as you learned in Chapter 17. At the same time, an emerging middle class of British merchants and shopkeepers had grown more prosperous from trade.

Industry provided the aristocracy and the middle class with new opportunities to invest their money. By investing in growing industries, they stood a good chance of making a profit. Parliament encouraged investment by passing laws that helped the growing businesses.

Natural Resources

Great Britain's wealth also included its rich supply of natural resources. The country had fine harbors and a large network of rivers that flowed year-round. Water provided power for developing industries and transported raw materials and finished goods.

Great Britain also had huge supplies of iron and coal, the principal raw materials of the Industrial Revolution. Iron and the steel made from it proved to be the ideal materials for building industrial machinery. An abundance of coal also helped to fuel industry.

Large Labor Supply

Perhaps the country's greatest natural resource was its growing population of workers. Improvements in farming led to an increased availability of food. Better, more nutritious food allowed people to enjoy longer, healthier lives. In just one century, England's population nearly doubled, growing from about 5 million in 1700 to about 9 million in 1800.

The changes in farming also helped to increase the supply of industrial workers. With the introduction of machinery such as the steel plow, farms needed fewer workers. Former farmworkers left their homes to find jobs in more populated and industrialized areas.

Ambitious British people in the middle and upper classes organized and managed the country's growing industries. These risk-taking entrepreneurs (AHN•truh•pruh•NUHRS), or businesspeople, set up industries by bringing together capital, labor, and new industrial inventions.

By the mid-1700s, the British domestic system was ready for change. The textile industry led the way.

Growing Textile Industries

In the 1700s people in Great Britain and overseas were eager to buy cool, colorful cotton cloth. Since the domestic system could not meet the demand, cotton merchants looked for new ways to expand production. A series of technological advances would revolutionize cloth production.

Advances in Machinery

One of the first innovations in cloth making occurred at the dawn of the Industrial Revolution. Weaving cloth was difficult and time-consuming work. Weavers had to push a shuttle back and forth across a loom by hand. Then they had to beat the

604 Chapter 23 *Age of Industry*

COOPERATIVE LEARNING ACTIVITY

Research Organize the class into groups. Have each group research innovations in one of these areas: farming, textiles, power sources, transportation. Each team member should be assigned a specific topic; for example, a student in the group examining power sources could research the use of wood or coal.

After completing their research, the groups should meet to share their findings. Each team member should summarize his or her research for the group. Then each team should create a general summary, to be delivered orally by one member. **L2** woof—the threads that run crosswise—down tightly against the previous row. The width of the fabric was limited by the distance a weaver could "throw" the shuttle.

In 1733 British clock maker John Kay improved the loom with his "flying shuttle." Instead of pushing the shuttle by hand, the weaver simply pulled sharply on a cord, and the shuttle "flew" across the loom. Wider fabrics could be woven at a faster pace.

Using the flying shuttle, weavers could produce two to three times more material; thus they needed more yarn than ever from the spinners. To answer this need, **James Hargreaves**, a weaver-carpenter, in the 1760s invented a more efficient spinning machine that he called the spinning jenny. Early models of the spinning jenny enabled one person to spin 6 to 7 threads at a time; later refinements increased this number to 80 threads.

While the spinning jenny revolutionized spinning in the home, another invention revolutionized spinning in factories and industrial settings. In 1768 **Richard Arkwright**, a struggling barber with a great interest in machines, developed the water frame, a huge spinning machine that ran continually on waterpower.

By 1779 spinner Samuel Crompton combined the best features of the spinning jenny and the water frame into a new machine called the "spinning mule." It produced strong thread that could be woven into high-quality muslin cloth. Until this time, such fine cloth had to be imported from Asia.

Producing More Cloth

The new spinning machines produced more yarn or thread than there were weavers to use it. In 1787 **Edmund Cartwright**, a British poet and minister, answered this shortage of weavers with the development of a power loom. Running on horse, water, or steam power, the mechanical loom made it possible for weavers to keep up with the amount of yarn produced.

These new inventions created a growing need for raw cotton. Yet raw cotton was expensive because cleaning the seeds out of it was a slow and tedious job. In 1793 **Eli Whitney**, an American inventor, developed a machine that cleaned cotton 50 times more quickly than a person could. The cotton gin helped the booming British textile industry to overcome its last major hurdle on its journey toward full mechanization.

ABCNEWS INTERACTIVE™

VIDEODISC
Turning Points in World History

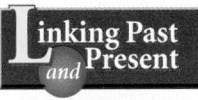

Side Two, Chapter 3
Title: *The Industrial Revolution*
Ask: How did the Industrial Revolution change settlement patterns? *(People moved to the cities to work in factories.)*

Independent Practice

📁 Guided Reading Activity 23-2 **L1**

📁 Geography and History Activity 23

Telecast Ask students to imagine they are TV journalists to present a "telecast" about a technological development in Britain. **L2**

Linking Past and Present

An Industrial City

Cities grew at an incredible pace as Britain industrialized. In 1801, only Manchester's and London's populations exceeded 100,000. In only 20 years, they were joined by Glasgow, Edinburgh, Liverpool, and Birmingham.

ANSWERS

It was close to coal fields, at the junction of three rivers, and on a canal that connected to the sea; yes, in purely material terms; no, if quality of life is considered; answers will vary

---

Geography

An Industrial City

The growth of industrial cities depended on geographic factors such as the availability of raw materials and accessible routes. The city of Manchester in northern England has had many geographic advantages. It lies close to coal fields and the Irwell and Mersey rivers. A canal connects the city to the Irish Sea, making Manchester an inland port.

Despite being a wool trade center, Manchester retained a rural atmosphere in the 1700s. Merchants lived in city townhouses, and people enjoyed sailing on the Irwell River. During the 1800s, Manchester grew into a textile-manufacturing city with world markets. Mills and warehouses replaced private homes in many areas, and

Manchester, England

the Irwell became so polluted it was described as "a flood of liquid manure." Some Britons at the time saw Manchester's transformation as evidence of the evils of industrialization. Others, however, saw the change as a symbol of progress.

During the first half of the 1900s, Manchester's production of textiles declined steadily. The growth of other businesses, however, helped the city and its surrounding communities to retain their economic importance in the British economy. Today, Manchester is England's third largest urban area, after London and Birmingham, and is still a major center of trade and finance.

Linking Past and Present ACTIVITY

Discuss how Manchester became an industrial city. Do you think that what happened to Manchester can be called "progress"? How do cities today compare/contrast with cities of the 1800s?

Chapter 23 *Age of Industry* **605**

MEETING SPECIAL NEEDS ACTIVITY

Mixed Learners To help students grasp the timesaving quality of technological innovations, organize the class into three groups. Have one group make up mathematical problems and keep a record of the time spent solving them by members of the second and third groups. The second group should do the math problems with pencil and paper, the third with electronic calculators. Rotate the three tasks, so that each group gets to perform each task. **L2 LEP**

WORLD HISTORY *Online*

Have students use the **Chapter 23 Student Web Activity** at worldhistory.glencoe.com for in-depth study of steel production.

Visualizing History The cotton gin made cotton more profitable, stimulating production and thus entrenching slavery in the South. **Answer to Caption:** *It removed the seeds from the cotton.*

TURNING POINT

The Factory System
How did the factory system transform production?
It brought workers and machines together under managers to produce goods in greater quantity and with more efficiency.

ASSESS

Check for Understanding

Assign Section 2 Assessment as homework or as an in-class activity.

Use Interactive Tutor Self-Assessment Software to review Section 2.

Evaluate

Section Quiz 23-2

Use the Testmaker to create a customized quiz for Section 2.

Reteach

Have students review the three main reasons Britain led the way in industrialization.

Reading Essentials and Study Guide 23-2

Enrich

Have students debate which innovation discussed in this section they think was most important.

CLOSE

Ask students why they think the Industrial Revolution is sometimes called the Machine Age.

Visualizing History Eli Whitney's original cotton gin was a simple device that one person could turn by hand. *What task did the cotton gin perform?*

TURNING POINT

The Factory System

Since the new textile machinery was too large and costly for most workers to use in their homes, cloth production gradually moved into large buildings built near major waterways. This marked the

WORLD HISTORY Online

Student Web Activity 23

Visit the *World History: The Human Experience* Web site at **worldhistory.glencoe.com** and click on *Chapter 23—Student Web Activities* for an activity relating to steel production.

beginning of the factory system, which brought workers and machines together under the control of managers. The waterways powered the machines and provided transportation routes.

As the factory system spread, manufacturers required more power than horses and water could provide. In the 1760s a Scottish mathematician named **James Watt** designed an efficient steam engine, which helped to set the Industrial Revolution in full motion. Factories could now run continuously on steam power. They also could be built far from waterways.

Industrial Developments

The use of factory machinery increased demand for iron and steel. In response, the iron industry developed new technologies. In the mid-1800s William Kelly, an American ironworker, and **Henry Bessemer**, a British engineer, developed methods to inexpensively produce steel from iron. Steel answered industry's need for a sturdy, workable metal.

Meanwhile, private companies began building and paving roads. Two Scottish engineers, Thomas Telford and John McAdam, established better drainage systems and the use of layers of crushed rock.

Water transportation also improved. In 1761 British workers dug one of the first modern canals to link coal fields with the industrial city of Manchester. Soon, a canal building craze began both in Europe and the United States.

A combination of steam power and steel soon revolutionized both land and water transportation. In 1801 British engineer Richard Trevithick devised a steam-powered carriage and, three years later, a steam locomotive that ran on rails. Later, in 1807 **Robert Fulton**, an American inventor, designed the first practical steamboat. Railroads and steamboats laid the foundations for a global economy and opened up new forms of investment.

SECTION 2 ASSESSMENT

Main Idea
1. Use a diagram like the one below to list the causes of the Industrial Revolution.

Causes	Effect
	Industrial Revolution

Recall
2. **Define** enclosure movement, capital, entrepreneur, factory system.
3. **Identify** James Hargreaves, Richard Arkwright, Edmund Cartwright, Eli Whitney, James Watt, Henry Bessemer, Robert Fulton.

Critical Thinking
4. **Synthesizing Information** Write a diary entry for a British farmer who has lost land due to the enclosure movement.

Understanding Themes
5. **Innovation** Is an Industrial Revolution still happening? If so, how have its developments changed modern life?

606 Chapter 23 *Age of Industry*

SECTION 2 ASSESSMENT ANSWERS

1. landowners had money to invest in growing industries; improved technology; farmers became industrial workers; had the needed capital, natural resources, and large labor supply
2. All terms are defined in the Glossary.
3. James Hargreaves, 605; Richard Arkwright, 605; Edmund Cartwright, 605; Eli Whitney, 605; James Watt, 606; Henry Bessemer, 606; Robert Fulton, 606
4. Entries might express nostalgia, sadness, or anger.
5. **INNOVATION** Developments in communications, medicine, and high-speed transportation have resulted in global interdependence and longer life span.

1839 Germany builds its first major railway.

1870 The Standard Oil Company is formed in the United States.

1895 Guglielmo Marconi develops wireless telegraph.

Section 3

The Growth of Industry

Read to Find Out

Main Idea *New technology advanced the growth of industry.*

▶ **Terms to Define**
  industrial capitalism, interchangeable parts, division of labor, partnership, corporation, depression

▶ **People to Meet**
  Eli Whitney, Frederick Taylor, Henry Ford, Samuel Morse, Guglielmo Marconi, Alexander Graham Bell, Thomas Edison, Rudolf Diesel, Wilbur and Orville Wright

The people on the street in Paris waited impatiently for word from inside the store. "It works!" cried a spectator suddenly. Someone held up a hand. "Not so much noise. The people in Brantford [Canada] are talking ... and singing. It can be heard as plain as day." Now everyone wanted a turn at the receiver. Finally, at eleven o'clock the crowd went home. Mr. Bell's telephone was a success.

—adapted from *The Chord of Steel, The Story of the Invention of the Telephone*, Thomas B. Costain, 1960

Alexander Graham Bell's telephone

In 1789 a tall, ruddy young British worker boarded a ship bound for New York, listing his occupation in the ship's record as farmer. Although he looked like the farmer he claimed to be, Samuel Slater was actually a smuggler. Slater was stealing a valuable British commodity—industrial know-how. The 21-year-old spinner headed for the United States with the knowledge of how to build an industrial spinning wheel. When he arrived two months later, Slater introduced spinning technology to the United States.

By keeping spinning and other technologies secret, Great Britain had become the most productive country in the world. To maintain its position, Parliament passed laws restricting the flow of machines and skilled workers to other countries. Until 1824 the law that Samuel Slater had ignored prohibited craftspeople from moving to other countries. Another law made it illegal to export machinery. Nonetheless, by the late 1820s many mechanics and technicians had left Great Britain, carrying industrial knowledge with them.

Spread of Industry

As British workers left the country, Great Britain gave up trying to guard its industrial monopoly. Wealthy British industrialists saw that they could make money by spreading the Industrial Revolution to other countries.

In the mid-1800s, financiers funded railroad construction in India, Latin America, and North America. In Europe, British industrialists set up factories, supplying capital, equipment, and technical staff. The industrialists earned Great Britain the nickname "the workshop of the world." In other lands, however, large-scale manufacturing based on the factory system did not really take hold

Chapter 23 *Age of Industry* **607**

SECTION THEME

▶ **Change** Throughout the Western world, new urban centers based on industry develop along with the rise of new social classes.

Guide to Reading

For reading strategies to help students read effectively see pages 12–13.

Vocabulary Pre-check

🔲 Use the Vocabulary PuzzleMaker for Chapter 23 to create a crossword puzzle to reinforce section terms. **L1 LEP**

📁 Use Vocabulary Activity 23 to introduce vocabulary terms. **L1 LEP**

FOCUS

Section Objective

Analyze how new technology advanced the growth of industry.

BELLRINGER
Motivational Activity

Before taking roll at the beginning of the class period, project Section Focus Transparency 23-3 and have students answer the activity questions. Discuss students' responses.

📁 This activity is also available as a blackline master.

SECTION RESOURCES

📁 Reproducible Masters
- Lecture Notes 23-3
- Reproducible Lesson Plan 23-3
- Guided Reading Activity 23-3
- People in World History Profiles 43, 44
- History Simulation 23
- Section Quiz 23-3
- Reading Essentials and Study Guide 23-3

🔳 Transparencies
- Section Focus Transparency 23-3

Multimedia
- 🔲 Vocabulary PuzzleMaker Software
- 🔲 Interactive Tutor Self-Assessment Software
- 🔲 Testmaker
- 🔳 Turning Points in World History: *The Industrial Revolution*

TEACH

Guided Practice

THEME Change

Write the headings *Topic* and *Changes* on the chalkboard. Under *Topic*, list *Communications, Energy, Production Methods,* and *Business Organization.* Have a volunteer complete the chart as you elicit information from the class. **L1**

VIDEODISC
Turning Points in World History

Side Two, Chapter 3
Title: *The Industrial Revolution*
Ask: What happened to housing as a result of the mass movement of people to cities? *(Housing became hard to find, resulting in the outgrowth of slums.)*

Growth of Big Business
What factors enabled big business to achieve economic growth?
use of machines, development of mass production and division of labor, and formation of new types of business organization

History & Art   Although Germany and France lagged behind Britain in the Industrial Revolution, they soon made rapid progress.
Answer to Caption: *Great Britain, Germany, and the United States*

608 Chapter 23   *Age of Industry*

---

until 1870 or later. The major exceptions were France, Germany, and the United States.

Because the French government encouraged industrialization, France developed a large pool of outstanding scientists. In spite of this, France's industrialization was slow-paced. The Napoleonic Wars had strained the economy and depleted the workforce. For a long time the French economy depended more on farming and small businesses than on new industries. Yet with the growth of mining and railway construction, railway lines radiated in every direction from Paris by 1870.

Germany's efforts to industrialize proved more successful. Before 1830 Germans brought in some machinery from Britain and set up a few factories. In 1839 they used British capital to build the country's first major railway. In the following decade, strong coal, iron, and textile industries emerged. Even before the German states united in 1871, government funding had helped industry to grow.

At the same time, industrialization increased in the United States, especially in the Northeast. British capital and machinery, combined with American mechanical skills, promoted new indus-try. In time, shoe and textile factories flourished in New England. Coal mines and ironworks expanded in Pennsylvania. By 1870 the United States ranked with Great Britain and Germany as one of the world's three most industrialized countries.

Growth of Big Business

A major factor in spurring industrial growth was free enterprise, or capitalism, the economic system in which individuals and private firms, not the government, own the means of production—including land, machinery, and the workplace. In a capitalist system, individuals decide how they can make a profit and determine business practices accordingly.

Industrialists practiced industrial capitalism, which involved continually expanding factories or investing in new businesses. After investing in a factory, industrial capitalists used profits to hire more workers and buy materials and machines.

History & Art   *Beirmeister and Wain Steel Forge* by P. S. Kroyer. Statens Museum, Copenhagen, Denmark   **Industrialization spread throughout Europe.** *What were the three most industrialized nations in 1870?*

608   Chapter 23   *Age of Industry*

COOPERATIVE LEARNING ACTIVITY

Report   Organize the class into groups. Have each group study innovations in transportation during the Industrial Revolution: railroads, steamships, and automobiles. Assign each team member a specific topic, such as method of operation, economic impact, and most common uses. After completing their research, team members should share information. Each team should then combine individual reports into a summary. One member of each team should present the group's summary. **L2**

Mass Production

Looking to increase their profits, manufacturers invested in machines to replace more costly human labor. Fast-working, precise machines enabled industrialists to mass-produce, or to produce huge quantities of identical goods.

In the early 1800s **Eli Whitney**, inventor of the cotton gin, contributed the concept of interchangeable parts that increased factory production. Whitney's system involved machine-made parts that were exactly alike and easily assembled or exchanged. In the past, handmade parts were not uniform—each differed from the next to some degree.

By the 1890s industrial efficiency had become a science. **Frederick Taylor** encouraged manufacturers to divide tasks into detailed and specific segments of a step-by-step procedure.

Using Taylor's plan, industrialists devised a division of labor in their factories. Each worker performed a specialized task on a product as it moved by on a conveyor belt. The worker then returned the product to the belt where it continued down the line to the next worker. Because products were assembled in a moving line, this method was called the assembly line.

American automobile manufacturer **Henry Ford** used assembly-line methods in 1913 to mass-produce his Model T automobiles. Ford described the assembly line this way:

> ❝ The man who places a part does not fasten it. The man who puts in a bolt does not put in a nut; the man who puts on the nut does not tighten it. Every piece of work in the shop moves; it may move on hooks, on overhead chains…. No workman has anything to do with moving or lifting anything. Save ten steps a day for each of the 12,000 employees, and you will have saved fifty miles of wasted motion and misspent energy. ❞

—Henry Ford, *Ford*, 1913

As Ford produced greater quantities of his cars, the cost of producing each car fell, allowing him to drop the price. Millions of people could then buy what earlier only a few could afford.

Organizing Business

As production increased, industrial leaders developed various ways to manage the growing business world and to ensure a continual flow of capital for business expansion. In addition to individual and family businesses, many people formed partnerships. A partnership is a business organization involving two or more entrepreneurs who can raise more capital and take on more business than if each had gone into business alone. Partners share management responsibility and debt liability.

Corporations take the idea of partnership many steps further. Corporations are business organizations owned by stockholders who buy shares in a company. Stockholders vote on major decisions concerning the corporations. Each vote carries weight according to the number of shares owned. Shares decrease or increase in value depending on the profits earned by the company. In the late 1800s, as industries grew larger, corporations became one of the best ways to manage new businesses.

Business Cycles

As market needs grew more complex, individual businesses concentrated on producing a particular kind of product. This increase in specialization made growing industries dependent on each other. When one industry did well, other related industries also flourished. A great demand for cars, for example, led to expansion in the petroleum industry. Likewise, bad conditions in one industry often spread rapidly to other related industries.

The economic fate of an entire country came to rest on business cycles, or alternating periods of business expansion and decline. Business cycles follow a certain sequence, beginning with expansion. In this "boom" phase, buying, selling, production, and employment rates are high. When expansion ends, a "bust" period of decreased business activity follows. The lowest point in the business cycle is a depression, which is characterized by bank failures and widespread unemployment. As industry increasingly dominated the economy, more people suffered during "bust" periods.

Science and Industry

Amateur inventors relying heavily on trial and error produced most industrial advances at the beginning of the Industrial Revolution. By the late 1800s, manufacturers began to apply more scientific findings to their businesses.

Communications

Science played an important role in the development of communications. In the 1830s **Samuel Morse**, an American inventor, assembled a working model of the telegraph. Using a system of dots and dashes, the telegraph carried information at high speeds. Soon telegraph lines linked most European and North American cities.

 History Simulation 23

Bio**graphy**®

The following videotape programs are available from Glencoe:

- **Henry Ford: Tin Lizzy Tycoon**
- **J. Pierpont Morgan: Emperor of Wall Street**
- **Wilbur & Orville Wright: Dreams of Flying**

Independent Practice

Guided Reading Activity 23-3 **L1**

People in World History Profiles 43, 44

Who?What?Where?When?

The corporation had its roots in the joint-stock companies that were formed during the Commercial Revolution of the 1600s. Most joint-stock companies were simple trading companies, however. A corporation, like a person, can own property, buy and sell goods, and bring lawsuits. Its stockholders have limited liability. This means that, if the corporation fails, no stockholder is liable for more than his or her original investment.

Business Have students research and report on a contemporary stock exchange, such as the New York Stock Exchange. Students' reports should summarize how the exchange is organized and how it works. **L3**

MEETING SPECIAL NEEDS ACTIVITY

Language Delayed Have students interview their parents and/or grandparents about technological changes that have occurred during their lifetimes. (They may wish to tape the interviews.) Have them find out what changes have most impressed the interviewees and how the changes have affected their lives. **L1 LEP**

TEACH

Remind students that the chief metal for centuries was iron. But cast iron, though hard, was brittle, and wrought iron was malleable but soft. People knew that steel was better—hard but not brittle—but it was expensive to make. Only with the Bessemer process, developed in the mid-nineteenth century, did inexpensive steel become widely available. Ask students if they think Benton's mural is a realistic portrayal of steel manufacturing. *(Answers will vary. Some may say it represents a romantic view of a mill.)*

CURRICULUM CONNECTION

MATHEMATICS

As industrialization spread, a common system of weights and measures became necessary. Most countries of the world adopted the metric system, first developed in France in the 1790s. Its basic measurement, the meter, equals one ten-millionth of the distance along a meridian from the Equator to one of the Poles.

Detail from "Steel," mural by Thomas Hart Benton. The New School for Social Research, NY

Steel

Coal, iron, and steel; railroads, steamships, and airplanes; factories, skyscrapers, and steel forges: This was the new world of the age of industry depicted by artist Thomas Hart Benton in this mural painted in 1930. This section, called "Steel," was taken from a drawing Benton had sketched of a Maryland steel plant. The workers in the mural are skilled and strong, the kind of American citizens who will make the American democracy, originally designed for an agricultural world, thrive in the industrial environment.

The Industrial Revolution began in Great Brita the late 1700s. By applying steam power to machinery the British profoundly transformed things were made. These new industries bega change how people worked, where they lived, they ate, and what they needed to know in ord survive. After 1870 the United States and Ger began to take the lead in industrialization, and became the most important metal used in indust this mural Benton welded a new industrial image older republican ideal. ⊕

Other communications advances occurred. In 1864 British physicist James Clerk Maxwell theorized that electromagnetic waves travel through space at the speed of light. In 1895 Italian inventor **Guglielmo Marconi** devised the wireless telegraph, later modified into the radio. The invention of the telephone in 1876 is credited to **Alexander Graham Bell,** a Scottish-born American teacher of the deaf.

Electricity

By the early 1900s, scientists were able to harness electrical power. As a result, electricity replaced coal as the major source of industrial fuel. In 1831 British physicist **Michael Faraday** had discovered that a magnet moving through a coil of copper wire produced an electric current. In the 1870s, this principle led to the development of an electric generator. During the same decade, American inventor **Thomas Edison** developed the phonograph, which reproduced sound. He also invented incandescent lightbulbs, making electric lighting cheap and accessible.

Energy and Engines

Advances also occurred in the making of engines. In the late 1880s, Gottlieb Daimler, a German engineer, redesigned the internal-combustion engine to run on gasoline. The small portable engine produced enough power to run vehicles and boats. Another German engineer, **Rudolf Diesel,** developed an oil-burning internal-combustion engine that could run factories, ships, and locomotives. These inventions ushered in the age of the motor car.

Gasoline engines influenced aviation technology. In the 1890s Germany's Ferdinand von Zeppelin streamlined the dirigible, a balloonlike invention that could carry passengers. Other scientists experimented with flying heavier aircraft. In 1903, the American inventors **Wilbur** and **Orville Wright**

Milestones of Free Enterprise

Modern free enterprise, or capitalism, which has its roots in medieval Europe, has increased the production of goods, raised standards of living, and advanced trade throughout the world. Below are some milestones of capitalist development in world history.

- **1200s–1500s** European merchants use currency instead of barter and develop banking procedures.

- **1500s–1700s** European joint-stock companies finance large ventures for overseas exploration, colonization, and trade.

- **1700s–1800s** Beginning in Great Britain, entrepreneurs bring together energy sources, machines, and workers to form factories that allow for efficient and increased production.

- **1800s–1900s** Large corporations in North America and Europe unify management, limit individual investment risk, and rely on banks for large amounts of capital.

- **1900s** Multinational corporations link activities in an emerging global economy. North America, Europe, and Asia's Pacific Rim are leading centers of free enterprise.

carried out the first successful flight of a motorized airplane. Five years later, the brothers flew their wooden airplane a distance of 100 miles (161 km).

Vehicles needed a steady supply of fuel for power and rubber for tires. As a result, petroleum and rubber industries skyrocketed. Advances in transportation, communications, and electricity sped the world into an era of increasing mechanization.

SECTION 3 ASSESSMENT

Main Idea
1. Use a diagram like the one below to list new technologies that advanced the growth of industry.

New Technologies

Recall
2. **Define** industrial capitalism, interchangeable parts, division of labor, partnership, corporation, depression.
3. **Identify** Eli Whitney, Frederick Taylor, Henry Ford, Samuel Morse, James Clerk Maxwell, Guglielmo Marconi, Alexander Graham Bell, Michael Faraday, Thomas Edison, Rudolf Diesel, Wilbur and Orville Wright.

Critical Thinking
4. **Synthesizing Information** Imagine you are living in the early 1900s. Describe how one invention mentioned in this section has changed your life.

Understanding Themes
5. **Change** What effects do you think industrial advancements, such as mass production and the assembly line, have had on workers' lives?

ASSESS

Check for Understanding

Assign Section 3 Assessment as homework or as an in-class activity.

 Use Interactive Tutor Self-Assessment Software to review Section 3.

Who?What?Where?When?

Guglielmo Marconi, inventor of the wireless telegraph, was inspired to experiment with science after reading a biography of Benjamin Franklin.

Evaluate

Section Quiz 23-3

 Use the Testmaker to create a customized quiz for Section 3.

Reteach

Have students review the growth of big business.

Reading Essentials and Study Guide 23-3

Enrich

Ask students to give oral reports on how internal-combustion engines are used today.

CLOSE

Have students show how capital was necessary to develop innovations summarized in this section.

SECTION 3 ASSESSMENT ANSWERS

1. communication: telegraph, radio, telephone; electricity: incandescent lightbulb; energy and engines: internal-combustion engine ran on gasoline, oil-burning internal-combustion engine, motorized airplane
2. All terms are defined in the Glossary.
3. Eli Whitney, 609; Frederick Taylor, 609;

Henry Ford, 609; Samuel Morse, 609; James Clerk Maxwell, 611; Guglielmo Marconi, 611; Alexander Graham Bell, 611; Michael Faraday, 611; Thomas Edison, 611; Rudolf Diesel, 611; Wilbur and Orville Wright, 611
4. Answers should reflect a knowledge of inventions in this section.

5. **CHANGE** Students may say that in many cases, industrial advancements have led to boredom and dissatisfaction; however, by lowering product costs, they have enabled more workers to buy more products.

c. 1800 Combination Acts passed by British Parliament ban labor unions.

1845 Massachusetts mill workers petition state for better working conditions.

1870 British Parliament legalizes labor's right to strike.

c. 1900 Labor union membership grows steadily in Europe and North America.

SECTION THEME

▶ **Conflict** Workers in Europe and North America organize to gain better wages and improved working conditions.

Guide to Reading

For reading strategies to help students read effectively see pages 12–13.

Vocabulary Pre-check

◉ Use the Vocabulary PuzzleMaker for Chapter 23 to create a crossword puzzle to reinforce section terms. **L1 LEP**

▨ Use Vocabulary Activity 23 to introduce vocabulary terms. **L1 LEP**

FOCUS

Section Objective

Describe how the Industrial Revolution affected people's lives.

BELLRINGER
Motivational Activity

Before taking roll at the beginning of the class period, project Section Focus Transparency 23-4 and have students answer the activity questions. Discuss students' responses.

▨ This activity is also available as a blackline master.

Section 4

A New Society

Guide to Reading

Read to Find Out
Main Idea *The Industrial Revolution affected people's lives greatly.*

▶ **Terms to Define**
   labor union, collective bargaining

▶ **Places to Locate**
   Massachusetts

The Storyteller

Factory inspectors interviewed a little boy who worked carrying coal early in the Industrial Revolution:

    I don't know how old I am; father is dead; mother is dead also. I began to work when I was about 9. I first worked for a man who used to hit me with the belt or with tools and fling coals at me. I left him and went to see if I could get another job. I used to sleep in the old pits that had no more coal in them; I laid upon the shale all night. I used to eat whatever I could get; I ate for a long time the candles that I found in the pits. I work now for a man who serves me well; he pays me with food and drink.

      —freely adapted from *Hard Times, Human Documents of the Industrial Revolution*, E. Royston Pike, 1966

Child at work

Before the Industrial Age, a person's position in life was determined at birth, and most people had little chance of rising beyond that level. Few managed to rise above their inherited place in the rigid European society.

As the Industrial Revolution progressed throughout the 1700s and 1800s, however, new opportunities made the existing social structure more flexible. Many people, such as inventor Richard Arkwright, used their talents and the opportunities presented by the Industrial Age to rise from humble beginnings to material success.

The youngest of 13 children of poor parents, Arkwright trained to become a barber. Yet machines, not his barbershop, occupied his time and energy. Spurred by the developments in the textile industry, Arkwright developed the huge water-frame spinning wheel that was powered by water and spun continuously. Arkwright persuaded investors to join him in establishing textile mills throughout Great Britain.

Soon Arkwright's mills employed more than 5,000 people. He amassed a great fortune, became active in politics, and was eventually knighted by Great Britain's King George III.

The Rise of the Middle Class

Although few businesspeople in Europe and America prospered as Arkwright had, industrialization did expand the size, power, and wealth of the middle class. Once made up of a small number of bankers, lawyers, doctors, and merchants, the middle class now also included successful owners of factories, mines, and railroads. Professional workers such as clerks, managers, and teachers added to the growing numbers.

Many wealthy manufacturers and other members of the middle class strongly believed in education as the key to business success. Politically

---

SECTION RESOURCES

active, they became involved in many reform efforts, including education, health care, prison improvements, and sanitation.

Middle-Class Lifestyles

As European and American middle-class men rose in society and assumed the role of sole provider for families, family life began to change. By the end of the late 1800s, stereotypes emerged from the middle class that created and reinforced the idea that men and women occupied different roles based on differences in their characters. Men centered their energy on the workplace, while women concentrated their efforts on maintaining the home and bringing up children.

Visualizing History During the late 1800s, the middle classes in North America and Great Britain stressed the importance of leisure activities shared by the entire family. *How did middle-class male and female roles differ?*

As soon as the family could afford it, a middle-class woman would hire domestic help. The number of her servants increased with her wealth. In 1870 an English guidebook listed the sequence in which women hired new help. First she "hires a washerwoman occasionally, then a charwoman, then a cook and housemaid, a nurse or two, a governess, a lady's maid, a housekeeper…." Servants, usually women, did the more difficult and unpleasant household chores, such as carrying loads of wood and coal, washing laundry, and cleaning house.

As middle-class women freed themselves from more tedious labor, they devoted their time to other occupations, such as educating their children, hand-sewing and embroidering, and planning meals. Magazines for women proliferated at this time, instructing housewives in everything from cooking and housekeeping to geography and natural science.

A typical day for one American middle-class woman in the early 1800s began at 6:00 A.M. and lasted until after 10:00 P.M. After waking up the family, the woman fed her infant son and then sat down to breakfast with her family. She read the Bible to her other three children, prayed with the servants, and then ordered the meals for the day. During the day she wrote letters, took one child to the park, and supervised the older daughters in feeding the younger children and folding up the laundry. The woman's schedule continued after nightfall. "After tea," she wrote, "read to [the children] till bedtime…."

Middle-class parents sent their boys to school to receive training for employment or preparation for higher education. Sons often inherited their fathers' positions or worked in the family business. Most daughters were expected to learn to cook, sew, and attend to all the workings of the household so that they would be well prepared for marriage.

Lives of the Working Class

As the middle class in Europe and America grew, so too did the working class in even greater numbers. The members of this class enjoyed few of the new luxuries that the upper and middle classes could now afford. Most people in the working classes had once labored on rural farms and now made up the majority of workers in new industries. Workers depended solely on the money they earned to buy what they needed. Unlike in earlier days, they did not grow or make what their families needed.

Footnotes to History

Shampoo
In the early 1900s, 25-year-old Joseph Breck tried in vain to find a cure for premature baldness. His efforts, however, led to a full line of hair care products that replaced the harsh soaps used at that time. Breck's businesses soon led the United States in shampoo production.

Chapter 23 *Age of Industry* **613**

TEACH

Guided Practice

THEME Conflict

Discuss the conflicts between industrialists and workers. Why did conflict arise between mill owners and the workers in their factories? *(Industrialists wanted to maximize profits by keeping wages low and hours long; laborers wanted to improve their quality of life by doing the opposite.)* **L1**

Visualizing History Along with music, middle-class families enjoyed reading aloud, playing card games such as whist, and acting out charades.
Answer to Caption: *Men focused on the workplace, while women concentrated on the home.*

Daily Life Ask students to compare the roles of men and women in the middle class with those of working-class men and women. *(Middle-class men and women had very different roles, the men involved in the world of work and the women caring for the children and the house. Among the working classes, both men and women worked long hours.)* **L2**

Biography

The following videotape program is available from Glencoe:
• **The Astors: High Society**

World History and Art Transparency 30, *Le Moulin de la Galette*

Economics Have students assume the role of entrepreneur, imagining that they are starting their own business. They should choose a form of business organization—individual ownership, partnership, or corporation—and explain why it is best for their particular enterprise. **L3**

 VIDEODISC
Turning Points in World History

Side Two, Chapter 3
Title: *The Industrial Revolution*
Ask: What were working conditions like for children? *(Children worked long hours for low pay in terrible conditions.)* How did workers express their opposition to poor work conditions? *(They formed unions and lobbied for government regulation to protect workers.)*

Independent Practice

Guided Reading Activity 23-4 **L1**

Music Have students prepare an oral report on a labor song such as "Sixteen Tons." (Several such songs can be found in the *Folksinger's Wordbook*.) Students should present the lyrics of the songs and summarize the background of the specific events and people mentioned. **L2**

At the Mercy of Machinery

When British and American industrialists first established mill towns such as Lowell, Manchester, Sheffield, and Fall River, work conditions were tolerable. As industrial competition increased, however, work became harder and increasingly more dangerous. Managers assigned workers more machines to operate and insisted that workers perform their tasks as fast as possible throughout the day.

Under the system of division of labor, workers did the same tasks over and over again, and did not have the satisfaction of seeing the completed work. The combination of monotonous work and heavy, noisy, repetitive machinery made the slightest interruption in the work potentially dangerous. Many workers—often children—lost fingers and limbs, and even their lives, to factory machinery.

Time ruled the lives of the industry workers down to the second. On the farms, workers' days had followed the sun and the weather. Now rigid schedules clocked by ringing bells commanded their every minute. One woman who worked in a Lowell, **Massachusetts**, textile mill wrote about her frustration in 1841:

> **❝ I am going home, where I shall not be obliged to rise so early in the morning, nor be dragged about by the factory bell, nor confined in a close noisy room from morning to night. I shall not stay here…. Up before day, at the clang of the bell—and out of the mill by the clang of the bell—into the mill, and at work in obedience to that ding-dong of a bell—just as though we were so many living machines. ❞**
>
> —anonymous worker, *The Lowell Offering*

In the textile mills, workers spent 10 to 14 hours a day in unventilated rooms filled with lint and dust. Diseases such as pneumonia and tuberculosis spread throughout the factories, killing many workers. In coal mines, workers faced the danger of working with heavy machinery and of breathing in coal dust in the mines.

Images *of the* Times

The Industrial Age

Industrialization brought new products and leisure activities to many people. It also produced terrible working conditions that gave rise to labor unions.

A badge of an early labor union represents the cooperative efforts of workers to seek fair wages and a more humane workplace.

614

Images *of the* Times The Industrial Age

The courtyard shown here was ringed by tiny houses. In complexes like this, a house usually had just two rooms, one per family. The only light and air came through the courtyard, for other houses backed up to the ones shown. There was no running water. A common tap and a single toilet in the courtyard served all the families that lived there. In American cities such as New York, old houses were subdivided into tiny, dark apartments. Several families often lived in a single room. In New York's Lower East Side, 290,000 people lived in one square mile. Yet rents were 25 to 30 percent higher than in middle-class neighborhoods uptown.

For these long hours at dangerous work, employees earned little to support themselves and their families. Factory owners kept workers' wages low so that their businesses could make profits. Women often made half the wages as men for the same job. Children were paid even less.

Workers' Lives

To earn enough money, whole families worked in the factories and mines, including small children as young as 6 years old. Children often worked 12-hour shifts, sometimes longer and through the night, with only a short break to eat a small meal.

Working-class children did not usually go to school, spending most of the day working instead. Many became crippled or ill from working under unhealthful and dangerous conditions. In 1843 an observer wrote that a child worker in the brick-fields "works from 6 in the morning till 8 or 9 at night … Finds her legs swell sometimes … and [suffers] pains and aches between the shoulders, and her hands swell."

For many women, the industries offered new opportunities for independence. For centuries, women's choices were limited almost entirely either to marriage or to life in a convent. Now they could earn a living. Textile mills in New England, for example, provided young single women an opportunity to make money while making new friends. These "mill girls" lived together in mill boardinghouses where they often gathered in study groups devoted to reading and discussing literature.

Yet for the majority of working-class women and their families, life consisted of a difficult working life and an uncomfortable home life. Workers often lived in crowded, cold apartments in poorly constructed tenement housing near factories. Sometimes whole families lived in one or two rooms.

Because the mill owners often owned the workers' housing, they controlled the rent and decided when and whether to improve living conditions. New urban problems complicated life. Human and industrial waste contaminated water supplies and spread diseases such as cholera and typhoid.

Edison's Vitascope, an early type of motion picture projector, fascinated large audiences.

Children of the working class were often underfed and without schooling. Many in this London tenement lived with discouraged parents. Others worked alongside adults.

REFLECTING ON THE TIMES

1. Why did labor unions organize in the industrial period?
2. How did the Industrial Revolution tend to divide people into separate classes?

615

ANSWERS TO REFLECTING ON THE TIMES

1. because workers on their own could not effectively stand up to the powerful mill owners
2. It enabled the middle class to get richer but made workers' lives poorer and harsher; also, the wealth of the middle class was gained by exploiting laborers.

Daily Life Have students research and report on men's and women's clothing during some period of the Industrial Revolution. Their reports should answer such questions as: Did social classes dress differently, and if so, how? Ask students what conclusions they can draw about the period by studying its clothing. **L3**

Who?What?Where?When?

Luddites, who were named after a (probably legendary) worker named Ned Ludd, organized an early protest against industrialization. In the early 1800s, these English laborers smashed textile machines that were putting them out of work. Some of the Luddites were hanged, and others were transported to Australia.

Cultural Perspectives

Women's Rights Middle-class married women during the industrial age benefited from domestic help, but they had few legal rights. In England, for example, a woman forfeited to her husband not only her property but also her right to control it. A man could will his wife's property to someone without her consent.

ASSESS

Check for Understanding

Assign Section 4 Assessment as homework or as an in-class activity.

◉ Use Interactive Tutor Self-Assessment Software to review Section 4.

Chapter 23
Section 4

THE I.W.W. is COMING!

JOIN THE ONE BIG UNION

Visualizing History Through posters, early labor unions called for unity, realizing that the individual worker was powerless. *How did factory owners try to prevent unionization?*

Workers Unite

Although governments in western Europe began to recognize the workers' complaints and initiate reforms, workers still labored under harsh conditions. Only through forming organized labor groups were workers able to begin to improve their working conditions in the late 1800s and early 1900s.

Workers knew that they could not fight successfully as individuals against the factory owners. They had to join together into groups to make their problems heard. In Great Britain, many workers joined to form worker associations, which were groups dedicated to representing the interests of workers in a specific industry. The associations hoped to improve the wages and working conditions of their members. Eventually these worker associations developed into labor unions both in Europe and in the United States in the 1800s.

Union Tactics

Workers in labor unions protested in many ways. They organized strikes, in which every worker refused to work. In sit-down strikes, workers stopped working but refused to leave the work area.

Despite these efforts, unions faced great opposition. Manufacturers complained that the shorter hours and higher wages would add to production costs, increase the price of goods, and hurt business. To discourage workers from joining unions, factory owners added the names of suspected union members to a blacklist to prevent them from getting jobs throughout the industry. The British Parliament even banned unions in the Combination Acts of 1799 and 1800.

Yet British workers kept their cause alive, and in the 1820s Parliament agreed that workers could meet to discuss working hours and wages. In the following years, skilled British workers formed unions based on a specific trade or craft. Because they had valuable skills, trade union members were able to bargain with employers. When union leaders meet with an employer to discuss problems and reach an agreement, they practice collective bargaining. The British unions' power increased in the 1870s after Parliament legalized strikes.

Following the skilled trade unions' success, unskilled workers formed unions in the late 1880s. By the beginning of the 1900s, union membership grew steadily in Europe and the United States.

SECTION 4 ASSESSMENT

Main Idea
1. Use a diagram like the one below to list effects of the Industrial Revolution on people's lives.

Effects On	
Middle Class	Working Class

Recall
2. **Define** labor unions, collective bargaining.
3. **Identify** Combination Acts.

Critical Thinking
4. **Analyzing Information** Why were industrialists in western Europe and the United States often able to subject factory workers to poor working conditions?

Understanding Themes
5. **Conflict** What were some of the social and economic problems that early factory workers faced? Why did they form labor unions to solve these problems?

SECTION 4 ASSESSMENT ANSWERS

1. middle class: increase in size, power, wealth; growing emphasis on education; involved in political reform; men in workplace; women at home; working class: worked in new industries; low wages; children uneducated; uncomfortable homelife; organized labor unions to improve working conditions
2. All terms are defined in the Glossary.
3. Combination Acts, 616
4. because factory workers were unskilled and many others would be willing to take their place
5. **CONFLICT** They faced harsh working conditions and formed unions to gain strength in numbers.

TURNING POINT

Workers Unite
How did industrial workers unite to deal with labor and social issues that affected their lives?
They formed workers associations and labor unions to demand better pay and working conditions either through strikes or collective bargaining.

Visualizing History The I.W.W. (Industrial Workers of the World) was a militant American labor organization of the early 1900s.
Answer to Caption: *Among other things, they circulated blacklists.*

Evaluate
 Section Quiz 23-4

Use the Testmaker to create a customized quiz for Section 4.

Reteach
Have students form two groups. Have one group present a skit showing typical middle-class life; have the other group present a skit showing working-class life during the time.

 Reteaching Activity 23

Reading Essentials and Study Guide 23-4

Enrich
Have students draw a cartoon expressing a factory worker's dissatisfaction.

 Enrichment Activity 23

CLOSE

Have students summarize the social changes that accompanied the Industrial Revolution.

Detecting Bias

Suppose you see a billboard showing two happy customers shaking hands with "Honest Harry," the owner of a used-car sales business. The ad says, "Visit Honest Harry for the best deal on wheels." That evening you see a television program that investigates used-car sales businesses. The report says that many of these businesses cheat their customers.

Each message expresses a bias—an inclination or prejudice that inhibits impartiality. Most people have preconceived feelings, opinions, and attitudes that affect their judgment on many topics. For this reason, ideas stated as facts may be opinions. Detecting bias enables us to evaluate the accuracy of information.

Learning the Skill

In detecting bias, first identify the writer's or speaker's purpose. For example, a billboard ad is a marketing tool for selling cars. We would expect that it has a strong bias.

Another clue to identify bias is emotionally charged language such as *exploit, terrorize,* and *cheat.* Also look for visual images that provoke an emotional response. For example, in the television report an interview with a person who bought a "lemon" automobile may elicit a strong response.

Look for overgeneralizations such as *unique, honest,* and *everybody.* Notice italics, underlining, and punctuation that highlights particular ideas. Finally, examine the material to determine whether it presents equal coverage of differing views.

Practicing the Skill

Industrialization produced widespread changes in society and widespread disagreement on its effects. While many people hailed the abundance of manufactured goods, others criticized its impact on working people. Karl Marx and Friedrich Engels presented their viewpoint on industrialization in the *Communist Manifesto* in 1848. Read the following excerpt and then answer these questions.

1. What is the purpose of this manifesto?
2. What are three examples of emotionally charged language?
3. According to Marx and Engels, which is more inhumane—the exploitation by feudal lords or by the bourgeoisie? Why?
4. What bias about industrialization is expressed in this excerpt?

66 **The bourgeoisie** *[the class of factory owners and employers]* **... has put an end to all feudal, patriarchal, idyllic relations. It has pitilessly torn asunder the motley feudal ties that bound man to his "natural superiors," and has left remaining no other nexus** *[link]* **between man and man than naked self-interest, than callous "cash payment." It has drowned the most heavenly of ecstasies of religious fervor, of chivalrous enthusiasm ... in the icy water of egotistical calculation.... In one word, for exploitation, veiled by religious and political illusions, it has substituted naked, shameless, direct, brutal exploitation.** 99

Applying the Skill

Find written material about a topic of interest in your community. Possible sources include editorials, letters to the editor, and pamphlets from political candidates and interest groups. Write a short report analyzing the material for evidence of bias.

For More Practice

Turn to the Skill Practice in the Chapter Assessment on page 619.

The **Glencoe Skillbuilder Interactive Workbook**, Level 2 provides instruction and practice in key social studies skills.

TEACH

Detecting Bias Point out that everyone is biased. Without using reason, people rely on gut emotional reactions, favoring some things—a sports team, a political party—and disapproving of others—a nationality, a breed of dog. Have students list, anonymously, two biases of theirs, either positive or negative. After collecting these, read some of them aloud for class discussion. Which are positive and which negative? How might they be helpful or harmful?

Additional Practice

📁 Skill Reinforcement Activity 23

GLENCOE TECHNOLOGY

Glencoe's **Skillbuilder Interactive Workbook, Level 2** This interactive CD-ROM promotes student mastery of key social studies skills.

ANSWERS TO PRACTICING THE SKILL

1. to arouse negative feelings about capitalists and capitalism
2. Emotionally charged language includes: *idyllic, pitilessly, naked, callous, heavenly, ecstasies, chivalrous, egotistical, shameless, brutal.*
3. exploitation by the bourgeoisie; at least feudal relations were accompanied by religious faith and chivalry
4. It is a totally negative force. It has destroyed all ties between people except for the "naked self-interest" expressed through a cash nexus.

WORLD HISTORY *Online*

Have students use the **Chapter 23 Self-Check Quiz** at worldhistory.glencoe.com to prepare for the Chapter Test.

GLENCOE TECHNOLOGY

VIDEODISC
Use MindJogger to review the chapter.
MindJogger Videoquiz

Chapter 23
Disc 3 Side B

Also available in VHS.

Answers

Using Key Terms
1. l   3. f   5. k
2. d   4. c

Using Your History Journal

Students could discuss the telephone, electricity, and the automobile.

Reviewing Facts

1. industrial capitalism; mass production: interchangeable parts, division of labor, assembly line methods; organizing business; partnerships and corporations; boom and bust periods
2. the widespread change from human labor to machines; Causes: agricultural revolution providing more food for more people; availability of capital for investment; development of factory system based on steam power; Effects: more and cheaper goods, new social classes, growth of cities, short-term suffering for workers, but long term improvement in standards of living
3. It provided a source of power that enabled factories to be built in more locations.
4. Women and children worked long hours in dangerous conditions.

WORLD HISTORY *Online*

Self-Check Quiz

Visit the *World History: The Human Experience* Web site at **worldhistory.glencoe.com** and click on *Chapter 23—Self-Check Quiz* to prepare for the Chapter Test.

Using Key Terms

Write the key term that completes each sentence. Then write a sentence for each term not chosen.

a. factory system
b. partnership
c. division of labor
d. corporation
e. enclosure movement
f. collective bargaining
g. industrial capitalism
h. entrepreneurs
i. labor unions
j. domestic system
k. capital
l. depression

1. The lowest point in the business cycle is a _____, which is characterized by bank failures and widespread unemployment.
2. A _____ is a business organization owned by stockholders who buy shares in the company and vote on major decisions concerning the future of the business.
3. When union leaders and an employer meet together to discuss problems and reach an agreement, they practice _____.
4. Under a _____, workers perform a particular task on a product as it is moved by on a conveyor belt.
5. Money invested in labor, machines, and raw materials is known as _____.

Technology Activity

Using E-mail Locate an E-mail address for your chamber of commerce. Compose a letter requesting information about various industries in your area. Create an illustrated pamphlet of information about area industries. Include advancement of technology within these industries, and their impact on the community. Provide a circle graph illustrating the percentage of people employed by specific industries within your community.

Using Your History Journal

From your time line of inventions choose one invention that you believe affects your life every day. How would people live today without this invention? Write a paragraph describing life without it.

Reviewing Facts

1. **Technology/Society** Use a chart like the one below to list factors that contributed to the growth of big business during the Industrial Revolution.

Factors in the Growth of Big Business
1. _____
2. _____
3. _____
4. _____

2. **Technology/Society** Identify the Industrial Revolution, and list its causes and effects.
3. **Technology** Explain the role of steam engine in the development of the factory system.
4. **Technology/Society** Discuss the impact of industrialization on working-class women and children.
5. **Science** Identify three inventors in industry, transportation, and communication, and list their individual contributions.
6. **Technology/Society** Track the spread of industry. How did industrialization differ from country to country?

Critical Thinking

1. **Apply** How did the Industrial Revolution affect Great Britain's social structure?
2. **Analyze** In what ways did the life of a farm laborer differ from the life of a factory worker?
3. **Synthesize** Great Britain had an early lead in industrialization. Which factor was the most critical in this development? Why?
4. **Evaluate** What do you see as the positive and negative effects of the Industrial Revolution?

---

5. (Industry) James Watt, the steam engine; (Transportation) Robert Fulton, first practical steamboat; (Communication) Alexander Graham Bell, telephone
6. Great Britain lost its industrial monopoly as its ideas and products spread abroad; France's industrial development was slow, as farming and small businesses dominated its economy; with government aid, industry forged ahead in Germany; the United States

developed its industry in the Northeast, using British capital and local mechanical skills; Japan developed into an industrial power by 1914.

Critical Thinking

1. It increased social mobility and enlarged both the middle class and the working class.
2. Farm laborers worked in accordance with the seasons and the days, not a fixed time

5. **Evaluate** How can consumer demand influence technological development?

Geography in History

1. **Region** Refer to the map below. Why did England have an advantage in developing heavy industry?
2. **Place** What industrial center is closest to several iron ore and coal fields?
3. **Movement** Railways in northern Scotland and Ireland were not built for transporting iron and coal. How can you tell this from the map? What may have been transported on these railways?

Industrial Revolution: England 1850–1870

- **I** Iron ore fields
- Coal fields
- Railways, 1850
- Railways developed, 1850-1870
- □ Industrial centers

SCOTLAND

Glasgow

North Sea

Belfast

Stockton

IRELAND

Dublin   Liverpool   Leeds

Manchester   Sheffield

WALES

Birmingham

ATLANTIC OCEAN

Cardiff

London

ENGLAND

Understanding Themes

1. **Relation to Environment** How were industry and farming related during the period before the Industrial Revolution?
2. **Innovation** It is often said that "necessity is the mother of invention." Using one invention in

this chapter, illustrate this statement.
3. **Change** Do you think that progress is a necessary result of change? Give examples.
4. **Conflict** How have differences between employers and workers produced positive effects for workers in the modern world?

Linking Past and Present

1. What effects do you see from the Industrial Revolution in your everyday life?
2. What changes and challenges has industry presented society in recent years?
3. The Industrial Revolution replaced many handcrafted items with mass-produced ones. What things that we use today are made mostly by hand?

Skill Practice

Read the following excerpt from "The Gospel of Wealth," an 1889 essay by Andrew Carnegie. Then answer the questions that follow.

66 The contrast between the palace of the millionaire and the cottage of the laborer with us today measures the changes which had come with civilization. The change, however, is not to be deplored, but welcomed as highly beneficial. It is well, nay, essential for the progress of the race that the houses of some should be homes for all that is highest and best in literature and the arts, and for all the refinements of civilization, rather than that none should be so. Much better this great irregularity than universal squalor. 99

1. Does the term *cottage* coincide with the description of how workers lived that is found on page 615?
2. How does Carnegie's use of this term indicate bias?
3. How does Carnegie justify large differences in lifestyle between rich and poor?
4. How does Carnegie describe the condition of most of humanity, except the wealthy?

Chapter 23 *Age of Industry* **619**

the domestic system.
2. **INNOVATION** The textile industry offers many good examples.
3. **CHANGE** Possible answer: No, the factory system brought with it exploitation of workers, child labor, and slums.
4. **CONFLICT** In industrialized nations, unions and government regulation have helped workers achieve good wages, benefits, and decent working conditions.

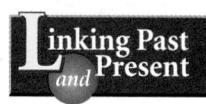

Linking Past and Present

1. rapid transportation, instant communication, and a huge range of inexpensive mass-produced items
2. the need to adapt to electronic technology, to protect the environment, to lessen the gap between industrialized and nonindustrialized nations
3. some items of clothing and furnishings, works of art, some musical instruments

Skill Practice
1. Answers will vary.
2. He infers that all laborers live in cottages or squalor.
3. as a progress of civilization
4. universal squalor

---

schedule; they also had greater autonomy.
3. capital, natural resources, or labor force
4. positive—growth of cities, higher standard of living; negative—exploitation of labor, degradation of environment
5. If enough people want a good or service, individuals or businesses will try to develop it.

Geography in History
1. England had plenty of iron ore and coal.

2. Birmingham
3. Neither of these areas has iron or coal fields. The railways may have carried agricultural products to industrial areas and industrial goods to Ireland and Scotland.

Understanding Themes
1. **RELATION TO ENVIRONMENT** Often, families were engaged in both part-time farming and part-time industry through

? Chapter Bonus Test Question

Ask students: In "exporting" the Industrial Revolution to nonindustrialized nations, what do you think would be the single most important element of the nineteenth-century revolution described in this chapter to introduce? *(Technological innovations might include steel manufacturing, electric power, good roads, labor unions.)*

Chapter 23 *Age of Industry* **619**

A complete, 1-page lesson plan is provided for each section in the *Reproducible Lesson Plans* booklet.

Cultural Revolution

CHAPTER RESOURCES

	Reproducible Resources	Multimedia Resources
Chapter Opener	Chapter Themes: Graphic Organizer 24 Historical Significance Chapter Activity 24	MindJogger Videoquiz
Chapter Enrichment	Vocabulary Activity 24* Time Line Activity 24 Mapping History Activity 24 History Simulation 24 Geography and History Activity 24 Source Reading 24 People in World History Profiles 38, 45, 46 World Literature Selection 6 World Art and Music Activity 24 Enrichment Activity 24 Critical Thinking Activity 24 Skill Reinforcement Activity 24 Performance Assessment Activity 24 Standardized Test Practice Workbook Activity 24 Inclusion for the Social Studies Classroom Strategies and Activities	Focus on World Art Prints 2, 5, 22 World History and Art Transparency 31, *In the Garden*; 32, *Sunday Afternoon on the Island of La Grande Jatte*; 34, *Starry Night* Mapping History Overlay Transparency 16, *Global Ancestry of Americans* Chapter Transparency 24 Vocabulary PuzzleMaker Software Turning Points in World History: *The Industrial Revolution* Communism and the Cold War: • *Perspectives on Capitalism* • *Perspectives on Communism* World History Primary Source Document Library
Chapter Review/Reteaching	Reteaching Activity 24 Skill Reinforcement Activity 24 Spanish Chapter Summary 24	Chapter 24 Digest Audiocassette, Activity, Test* Vocabulary PuzzleMaker Software Interactive Tutor Self-Assessment Software MindJogger Videoquiz
Chapter Evaluation/Testing	Performance Assessment Activity 24 Chapter 24 Test, Forms A and B	ExamView® Pro Testmaker

* Also available in Spanish

0:00 OUT OF TIME? Assign the Chapter 24 Audiocassettes.

World History Primary Source Document Library

Make History Come Alive!

Engage your students with over 250 easily accessible primary source documents—available on this CD-ROM—that will give them real life insight into the important events of world history.

Block Schedule

Activities that are particularly suited to use within the block scheduling framework are identified throughout this chapter by the following designation.

KEY TO ABILITY LEVELS

Teaching strategies are coded for varying learning styles.

L1 BASIC activities for all students

L2 AVERAGE activities for average to above-average students

L3 CHALLENGING activities for above-average students

LEP LIMITED ENGLISH PROFICIENCY activities

Use Glencoe's *Presentation Plus!* multimedia teacher tool to easily present dynamic lessons that visually excite your students. Using Microsoft PowerPoint® you can customize the presentations to create your own personalized lessons.

Interactive Lesson Planner

Planning has never been easier! Using this CD-ROM, organize your week, month, semester, or year with all the help you need. The **Interactive Lesson Planner** gives you access to all of the blackline masters that accompany *World History: The Human Experience.*

SECTION RESOURCES

Daily Objectives	Reproducible Resources	Multimedia Resources
Section 1 **New Ideas** Explain why Karl Marx advocated doing away with the capitalist system.	Lecture Notes 24-1 Reproducible Lesson Plan 24-1 Guided Reading Activity 24-1* People in World History Profile 38 Time Line Activity 24 Section Quiz 24-1* Reading Essentials and Study Guide 24-1	Section Focus Transparency 24-1 Chapter Transparency 24 Vocabulary PuzzleMaker Software Interactive Tutor Self-Assessment Software Testmaker Communism and the Cold War: • *Perspectives on Communism* • *Perspectives on Capitalism*
Section 2 **The New Science** List advances made in science between 1750 and 1914 that have improved life today.	Lecture Notes 24-2 Reproducible Lesson Plan 24-2 Guided Reading Activity 24-2* People in World History Profiles 45, 46 Section Quiz 24-2* Reading Essentials and Study Guide 24-2	Section Focus Transparency 24-2 Vocabulary PuzzleMaker Software Interactive Tutor Self-Assessment Software Testmaker
Section 3 **Popular Culture** Analyze why the population grew dramatically in Europe and North America during the 1800s.	Lecture Notes 24-3 Reproducible Lesson Plan 24-3 Vocabulary Activity 24* Guided Reading Activity 24-3* Geography and History Activity 24 Section Quiz 24-3* Reading Essentials and Study Guide 24-3	Section Focus Transparency 24-3 Mapping History Overlay Transparency 16, *Global Ancestry of Americans* Interactive Tutor Self-Assessment Software Testmaker Turning Points in World History: *The Industrial Revolution*
Section 4 **Revolution in the Arts** Describe how writers and artists in Europe and North America reflected changes in society between 1750 and 1914.	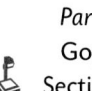 Lecture Notes 24-4 Reproducible Lesson Plan 24-4 Guided Reading Activity 24-4* History Simulation 24 Reteaching Activity 24 Enrichment Activity 24 Section Quiz 24-4* Performance Assessment Activity 24 Spanish Chapter Summary 24 Reading Essentials and Study Guide 24-4	Focus on World Art Print 2, Franz Marc. *Stables*; 5, Paul Klee. *Palace, Partially Destroyed*; 22, Vincent van Gogh. *Hospital at Saint-Rémy* Section Focus Transparency 24-4 World History and Art Transparency 31, *In the Garden*; 32, *Sunday Afternoon on the Island of La Grande Jatte*; 34, *Starry Night* Vocabulary PuzzleMaker Software Interactive Tutor Self-Assessment Software Testmaker

* Also available in Spanish

Chapter Activities

Performance Assessment Activity

Reform Inquiry and Projection Reforms covered in this chapter took place in government, working conditions, medicine, education, art, and urban life. Have students research reform efforts today in the same areas in order to complete a compare-and-contrast matrix. After students have drawn conclusions about the continuity and change in these areas, ask them to predict the reform movements that might occur after another 50 to 100 years. As a concluding activity, students can create a collage, mural, chart, or multimedia slide show including symbols and illustrations of the past, present, and future reform movements.

Possible Rubric Features
Accuracy of content information; accuracy, relevance, and degree of research; plausibility of predictions; originality, impact, and clarity of visuals

• *For an additional activity, refer to Activity 24 in the* Performance Assessment Strategies and Activities *booklet.*

ACTIVITY

From the Classroom of...

Charles Dixon
High School Redirection
Brooklyn, NY

Rise of Socialism Round Robin

Have students read from "A Better Society" to the end of Section 1 in the text (pages 623–625) and outline the ideas of the different reformers. Ask students to head a sheet of paper *During the 1800s socialism began to ...* , then write an end to the sentence, using information from their outlines.

Have students exchange papers six times (each time with someone new). After each exchange have students add a sentence to the paper they have just received. On the last exchange instruct students to write concluding sentences. Have several students read their completed paragraphs and use these as a springboard for discussion.

MULTIPLE LEARNING STYLES

Logical/Mathematical
Have students create a time line that tracks the major social, cultural, and scientific developments of the period. Students should include details from the text and from class discussions and activities.

Visual/Spatial
Have students produce an art journal filled with their own drawings and paintings done in the different artistic styles presented in this chapter.

Auditory/Musical
Have students listen to Schiller's "Ode to Joy," sung as part of Beethoven's Ninth Symphony. Ask them to write new words of their own that seem appropriate to the music.

Kinesthetic
Have students plan and attend a field trip to a nearby museum whose collection includes works by the artists discussed in this chapter. If possible, arrange to be led through the collection by a docent.

GLENCOE'S ASSESSMENT ADVANTAGE

Use the following to easily assess student learning in a variety of ways.

• Performance Assessment
  Strategies and Activities
• Section Quizzes
• Chapter and Unit Tests
• Interactive Tutor
  Self-Assessment Software

• Testmaker Software
• MindJogger Videoquiz
• SAT/SAT II Test Practice
• worldhistory.glencoe.com

Additional Resources

Teacher's Corner

INDEX TO NATIONAL GEOGRAPHIC MAGAZINE

The following articles may be used for research relating to this chapter:

- "Secrets of the Gene," by James Shreeve, October 1999.
- "Feeding the Planet," by T.R. Reid, October 1998.
- "Vincent van Gogh," by Joel L. Swerdlow, October 1997.
- "Sir Joseph Banks," by T. H. Watkins, November 1996.
- "Viruses," by Peter Jaret, July 1994.
- "Paris: La Belle Epoque," by Eugen Weber, July 1989.
- "The World of Tolstoy," by Peter T. White, June 1986.

ADDITIONAL NATIONAL GEOGRAPHIC SOCIETY PRODUCTS

To order the following product for use with this chapter, call National Geographic Society at 1-800-368-2728:

- *Capitalism, Socialism, Communism Series (Videos)*

ADDITIONAL NATIONAL GEOGRAPHIC SOCIETY PRODUCTS

Access National Geographic's new dynamic MapMachine Web site and other geography resources at:

- http://www.nationalgeographic.com/
- http://www.nationalgeographic.com/maps/

BIBLIOGRAPHY

Literature of the Period
Dreiser, Theodore. *Sister Carrie.* Edited by Donald Pizer. New York: Norton, 1970. Includes backgrounds, sources, and criticism in addition to an authoritative text of the naturalist novel.
Readings for the Student
Briggs, Asa. *A Social History of England: From the Ice Age to the Channel Tunnel.* London: Weidenfeld and Nicolson, 1994. Offers the human side of change, drawing on artistic, economic, and political developments.
Readings for the Teacher
Heilbroner, Robert L. *The Worldly Philosophers.* New York: Simon and Schuster, 1980. Discusses Smith, Ricardo, Malthus, Marx, and the utopian Socialists.

WORLD HISTORY Online

Use our Web site as an additional resource. All essential content is covered in the Student Edition.

You and your students can visit the *World History: The Human Experience* Web site at worldhistory.glencoe.com The student text directs students to the Web site for the following options:

- **Chapter Overviews**
- **Student Web Activities**
- **Self-Check Quizzes**

Answers are provided for you in a link entitled "Web Activity Lesson Plan." Additional Web Resources, Interactive Puzzles, and content updates are also available.

Visit the Glencoe Web site at socialstudies.glencoe.com for social studies activities, updates, and links to other resources.

LOCAL OBJECTIVES

_____
_____
_____
_____
_____
_____
_____
_____
_____
_____
_____
_____
_____
_____
_____
_____
_____
_____

Chapter Themes are listed by section on this chapter opening page of the Student Edition. A corresponding theme-based activity is available under "TEACH," and a theme-based question is asked in the Section and Chapter Assessments.

Historical Setting Dreiser (1871–1945) wrote this description of Chicago in his first novel, *Sister Carrie.* Dreiser is considered a member of the literary movement of naturalism, which began in the mid-1800s in France. According to Dreiser and other naturalists, social, economic, and biological forces control human actions and destinies. Dreiser lived and worked in Chicago for several years. Although Dreiser believed that cities were the source of power and wealth, he also believed that most city-dwellers were fated to lives of poverty and degradation.

Historical Significance

Answers: *Economic reformers developed theories of socialism and Marxism as alternatives to capitalism; scientists began to understand the nature of living matter and of the atom, and they made advances in medicine. Improved nutrition, sanitation, and medical practices resulted in healthier, longer-lived populations. People became more mobile, and many moved to cities. Artists reacted to the changes in society through movements such as romanticism, realism, symbolism, and impressionism.*

— **WORLD HISTORY** —
Online

Have students use the **Chapter 24 Overview** at worldhistory. glencoe.com as a prereading and postreading exercise for understanding chapter content.

Chapter
24
1750–1914
Cultural Revolution

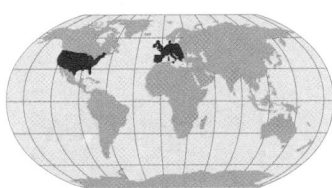

Chapter Themes

▶ **Change** Political and economic philosophies attempt to make sense of a changing industrial world. *Section 1*
▶ **Innovation** Scientific discoveries lead to better health and revolutionary views on the natural world and human society. *Section 2*
▶ **Movement** People move from rural to urban areas and from continent to continent. *Section 3*
▶ **Innovation** Western artists and writers reflect the changes in urban industrial society. *Section 4*

Storyteller

A new world was in the making. Factories boomed. Cities grew. By the late 1800s, steamships and trains allowed people to move in search of better lives. American novelist Theodore Dreiser described the excitement that drew people to Chicago:

"Its many and growing commercial opportunities gave it widespread fame, which made of it a giant magnet, drawing to itself, from all quarters, the hopeful and the hopeless.... It was a city of over 500,000 with the ambition, the daring, the activity of a metropolis of a million."

The Industrial Revolution also brought challenges to Europeans and North Americans. Cities became overcrowded, and the gap between rich and poor widened. People struggled to make sense of an increasingly complex society.

Historical Significance

What changes occurred in the economics, the sciences, and the arts of the West between 1750 and 1914? How did these changes alter people's values and daily lives?

1750	1800	1850	1900

1776 Adam Smith writes *The Wealth of Nations.*

1858 Louis Pasteur discovers that bacteria cause disease.

1880 Education is made compulsory in Great Britain.

1900 Max Planck creates quantum theory.

620

GEOGRAPHY CONNECTION

Location Have students locate Chicago on a map. What two great North American waterways does the Chicago River lie between? *(It empties into Lake Michigan, and its arms nearly reach the drainage basin of the Mississippi River.)* Explain to students that several factors helped transform Chicago into the interior land and water hub of the expanding United States: The opening of the Erie Canal in 1825 connected the Atlantic Ocean and the Great Lakes; the completion of the Illinois and Michigan Canal in 1848 linked the Great Lakes and Mississippi River systems; and the railroad system in 1856 turned the city into the nation's chief rail center.

Boulevard Des Capuchines and Théâtre de Vaudeville, 1889, by Jean
Beraud. Musée Carnavalet, Paris, France

History & Art Tell students that
easy movement through the streets
of Paris in 1889, as depicted in the
painting, was a result of the city
planning efforts of Baron Georges-
Eugène Haussmann (1809–1891). At
the request of Napoleon III, he eliminated constricted streets, cutting
large straight boulevards through
them.

 **Performance
Assessment**

**Refer to the activity on page
620C of the Planning Guide.**

 **For an additional
activity, refer to Activity 24 in
the *Performance Assessment
Strategies and Activities*
booklet.**

WORLD HISTORY Online

Chapter Overview

Visit the *World History: The Human Experience*
Web site at **worldhistory.glencoe.com** and
click on **Chapter 24—Chapter Overview**
to preview the chapter.

Your History Journal

*This chapter introduces thinkers and
reformers who wanted to create a better
society. Write an essay suggesting ways to
improve the society in which we live today.*

**Using Your History
Journal**

Suggest that students research the
goals of some reformers active in the
United States today, such as Ralph
Nader or Amory Lovins.

 **GLENCOE
TECHNOLOGY**

 VIDEODISC
Use MindJogger to pre-
view chapter content.

MindJogger Videoquiz

  Chapter 24
Disc 3 Side B

  Also available in VHS.

Chapter 24   *Cultural Revolution*   621

 EXTRA CREDIT PROJECT

Socialist Reformers Have students research
and report to the class on the life and work of
one of the early French utopian Socialist
reformers, such as Count Claude Henri de
Saint-Simon (1760–1825) or Charles Fourier
(1772–1837). Suggested resources: A. J. Booth,
Saint-Simon and Saint-Simonism; F. E. Manuel, *The
Prophets of Paris*; A. Gray, *The Socialist Tradition.*

Chapter 24   *Cultural Revolution*   **621**

1800   1850   1900

1817 David Ricardo writes about the "iron law of wages."

1847 British Parliament passes the Ten Hours Act.

1867 Karl Marx publishes *Das Kapital*.

Section 1

New Ideas

Read to Find Out
Main Idea *Karl Marx advocated doing away with the capitalist system.*

▶ **Terms to Define**
laissez-faire, utilitarianism, socialism, proletariat, bourgeoisie, communism

▶ **People to Meet**
Adam Smith, David Ricardo, Jeremy Bentham, John Stuart Mill, Robert Owen, Karl Marx, Friedrich Engels

The Storyteller

Karl Marx, the chief architect of communism, was always and everywhere a student. At an early age his withdrawal from all university activities except the intellectual brought stern advice from his father:

Karl Marx

"My clever and gifted son Karl passes wretched and sleepless nights, wearying body and mind with cheerless study…. But what he builds today he destroys again tomorrow…. At last the body begins to ail and the mind gets confused, whilst ordinary folk … attain their goal if not better at least more comfortably than those who condemn youthful pleasures and undermine their health…."

—from *The Life and Teaching of Karl Marx*, M. Beer, 1921

nglish essayist William Hazlitt, writing in the early 1800s, described Europe in the critical years after the French Revolution:

❝ There was a mighty ferment in the heads of statesmen and poets, kings and people. According to the prevailing notions, all was to be natural and new. Nothing that was established was to be tolerated…. The world was to be turned topsy-turvy. ❞

The Western world did appear to be turning upside down, as society underwent a transformation. In little more than 100 years, the Industrial Revolution converted Europe from a farming economy centered in the country to an industrial economy based in urban areas.

Industry in the short term brought great wealth to a few and imposed hardships on the many. In the long run, however, it provided material benefits to all people. Still, the gap between "haves" and "have nots" remained to create unrest in many societies.

Capitalist Ideas

During the Industrial Revolution, European thinkers for the first time studied and explained how capitalism worked. Rejecting mercantilism with its government controls, many supported laissez-faire (LEH•SAY•FAHR), a policy allowing business to operate without government interference. Laissez-faire, from a French term meaning "let them alone," was developed in France during the 1700s by the Physiocrats. These thinkers valued land as the primary source of national wealth. They held that fewer taxes and regulations would enable farmers to grow more produce. In the early 1800s, the middle-class owners of railroads, factories, and mines began supporting laissez-faire. They believed that freedom from government controls would mean a growing economy with material progress for all people.

Adam Smith

Industrial leaders relied on the ideas of **Adam Smith**, a Scottish economist who set down the workings of a laissez-faire economy. In *The Wealth of Nations* (1776), Smith stated that an economy works best when the natural forces of supply and demand operate without government interference. In such a free market, individual sellers and buyers act on self-interest. Smith did not think this was necessarily bad, believing that a natural order in the universe made all individual striving for self-interest add up to the common good. Businesses compete to produce goods as inexpensively as possible, and consumers buy the best goods at the lowest prices. Efficient producers make more profit, hire more workers, and continue to expand, to everyone's benefit.

As the Industrial Revolution gathered momentum and spread throughout the world, Smith's ideas profoundly influenced economic thought and practice. By the 1850s, Great Britain, the world's leading industrial power, had adopted free trade and other laissez-faire policies.

Malthus and Ricardo

Not all thinkers, however, held Smith's optimism about the future. Thomas Malthus, an Anglican clergyman, wrote in *An Essay on the Principle of Population* (1798) that poverty, famine, and misery were unavoidable because population was increasing faster than the food supply. Influenced by Malthus, the British economist **David Ricardo** stated in his "iron law of wages" that rapid population growth would lead only to fierce competition for jobs, lower wages, and higher unemployment. Continual poverty was all that was in store for the working class. As strong believers in laissez-faire, both Malthus and Ricardo opposed government aid to the poor. Instead, they believed that the poor could help themselves by working hard, saving their earnings, and having fewer children.

Because of these gloomy theories, people in the 1800s called economics "the dismal science." However, the forecasts of Malthus and Ricardo were not fulfilled. Population continued to rise, but as a result of the agricultural revolution, the food supply grew even faster. By the 1900s, higher living standards and lower birthrates prevailed in many

Visualizing History Grim-faced young coal mine workers in Kingston, Pennsylvania, pose for the camera. *How would photographs such as this support criticism of laissez-faire economics?*

Western countries such as Great Britain, the United States, and Germany. Yet, industrialization benefited some more than others and fueled demands for reforms that would create a more just society.

A Better Society

During the 1800s, reformers set out to improve the lives of the disadvantaged, especially enslaved people and the urban poor. At the same time, a new generation of thinkers questioned laissez-faire and urged government to work for a better society.

Evangelicals and Reform

During the late 1700s and early 1800s, a series of religious awakenings swept through the Protestant churches. The outcome of these revivals was Evangelicalism, a movement that joined personal faith with social improvement. Some Evangelicals supported strict laissez-faire; others, however, believed that government needed to involve itself in the lives of the disadvantaged. One of the most noted participants in the Evangelical cause was William Wilberforce, a member of Parliament. Opposed to slavery, Wilberforce had Parliament pass a bill in 1807 that ended the British slave trade. Later, in 1833—the year of Wilberforce's death—Parliament abolished slavery throughout the British Empire.

Chapter 24 *Cultural Revolution* **623**

TEACH

Guided Practice

THEME Change

Have students brainstorm things they would change about present-day society if they could create their own utopian community. At the end of the brainstorming session, have students vote on the changes they would make. **L1**

Visualizing History Not until 1916 did the U.S. Congress pass the first federal child labor law. Among other provisions, that law set the minimum age for work in mines at 16. **Answer to Caption:** *It depicts the dismal life of children exploited by the system.*

ABCNEWS INTERACTIVE™

VIDEODISC Communism and the Cold War

Side One, Chapter 7
Frames 13483–14256
Title: *Perspectives on Capitalism*
Ask: What is the underlying idea behind capitalism? *(individual initiative)*

Side One, Chapter 8
Frames 14264–14893
Title: *Perspectives on Communism*
Ask: In communism, what was "the ideal society"? *(one in which everyone is happy, no competition)*

COOPERATIVE LEARNING ACTIVITY

Newsletters Organize the class into several groups. Have each group prepare the front page of a newsletter advocating an economic policy presented in this section, such as laissez-faire or socialist economics. Each group should choose a name for its newsletter that suggests its point of view (for example, *Voice of the People* for a socialist perspective) and select a time period between 1750 and 1914. The groups should research economic issues of that time, which might include unionization, worker strikes, or labor reform. After selecting topics for a number of front-page stories, group members should write the articles or illustrate them. Completed front pages can be displayed in class. **L3**

Visualizing History Many socialist groups used posters and cartoons to win support for the overthrow of Europe's monarchies as well as the capitalist system. *What were two other goals of the socialist movement?*

Another Evangelical leader, Lord Shaftesbury, promoted laws to limit working hours for women and children. Aiding Shaftesbury's efforts were parliamentary commissions investigating factories and mines. Commission reports detailing miserable working conditions raised a public outcry. Parliament responded with the first factory laws of the industrial era. Passed during the 1830s and 1840s, these measures regulated child employment in factories, prohibited women and children from working in underground mines, and established a 10-hour day in textile factories for children under 18 and women.

Utilitarian Reformers

Many secular social reformers also believed that laissez-faire policies should be changed to allow for some government involvement in economic and social affairs. British philosopher **Jeremy Bentham** promoted utilitarianism, the idea that society should work for "the greatest happiness for the greatest number" of citizens. To Bentham, laws should be judged by their usefulness, whether they advanced human happiness and reduced human misery. To this end, Bentham called for a better code of law, education for all, a public health service, and improved prisons.

Bentham's follower, **John Stuart Mill**, challenged strict views of laissez-faire economics, calling on government to distribute national wealth more justly by taxing income. However, he also held a firm belief in individual freedom. In works such as *On Liberty*

624 Chapter 24 *Cultural Revolution*

(1859), Mill stated that freedom of thought and discussion promoted social progress and supported extending the vote to all adults. A believer in full democracy, Mill advocated equal rights for women.

TURNING POINT

Rise of Socialism

Not everyone in Europe agreed with the capitalist way of thinking in the early 1800s. Some people believed that ending the misery of workers required eliminating capitalism completely. They advocated socialism—the belief that the means of production—capital, land, raw materials, and factories—should be owned and controlled by society, either directly or through the government. In this way, wealth could be distributed equally among all citizens.

Early Socialism

Some early advocates of socialism planned and built communities where everyone was supposed to share equally in the benefits of the industrial age. Among the first to establish such a community was **Robert Owen**, a wealthy Welsh manufacturer. Owen believed that competition caused society's problems. Thus, he reasoned that if cooperation replaced competition, life would improve.

In 1800 Owen set out to prove his point in New Lanark, a dreary Scottish mill town. In time he reconstructed it into a model industrial community. Although he did not turn the textile mill completely over to the workers, he greatly improved their living and working conditions. In 1825 Owen stopped managing New Lanark and bought New Harmony, Indiana, where he tried to set up a cooperative community. New Harmony, however, did not meet with the same success as New Lanark. Feuding among Owen and the residents led Owen to return to Great Britain.

Marx and Engels

German philosopher **Karl Marx** dismissed the ideas of the early socialists as impractical and set out to provide a scientific basis for socialism. The son of a prosperous German lawyer, Marx received a doctorate in history and philosophy. When his radical views got him into trouble with the Prussian government, he fled to Paris. There in 1844 he met **Friedrich Engels**. Engels was on his way home from one of his father's factories in Manchester, England. Horrified by what he saw there, Engels wrote a classic book called *The Condition of the Working Class in England*.

Marx later settled in London, and he and Engels became lifelong friends and collaborators. Engels, a successful businessman, supported Marx, who devoted his life to writing about economics.

Marx's Theories

Marx based his ideas in part on the teachings of the German philosopher G.W.F. Hegel. Hegel taught that changing ideas were the major force in history. As ideas clashed, new ideas emerged. This produced new changes, conflicts, and ideas.

Like Hegel, Marx believed that history advanced through conflict. In Marx's view, however, economics was the major force for change. Production was at the base of every social order.

The most important aspect of the economic base was the division of society into classes. The class that controlled production became the ruling class. The only way to make the ruling class give up control was through revolution. Therefore, conflict between classes was inevitable. Marx stated "class struggle" was what pushed history forward.

Marx argued that Europe had moved through four stages of economic life—primitive, slave, feudal, and capitalist. During the primitive stage, people produced only what they needed to live. There was no exploitation, or unfair use of a person for one's own advantage. Once tools were developed, however, and people could produce a surplus, they became exploitable. From then on, history was a class struggle. It was the "haves" against the "have–nots."

Marx believed that capitalism was only a temporary phase. As the makers of goods, the proletariat, or the working class, was the true productive class. An economic crisis in one of the advanced industrial countries would give the proletariat the chance to seize control from the bourgeoisie (BURZH•WAH•ZEE), or middle class. The proletariat would then build a society in which the people owned everything. Without private property, classes would vanish, and the government would wither away. In this last stage, known as communism, the governing principle would be "from each according to his ability, to each according to his need."

Marx and Engels published their views in *The Communist Manifesto* in 1848. In it they appealed to the world's workers:

> **Let the ruling classes tremble at a Communist revolution. The proletarians have nothing to lose but their chains. They have a world to win. Working men of all countries, unite!**

In 1867 Marx developed his ideas further in the work *Das Kapital*.

The Socialist Legacy

History did not proceed by Marx's plan. When Marx was writing, workers' poverty contrasted sharply with industrialists' wealth. By 1900 workers could buy more with their wages than they could 50 years earlier. Rather than overthrow their governments, workers gained the right to vote and used it to correct the worst social ills. They also remained loyal to their own nations rather than ally with workers in other countries to promote revolution.

In time, democratic socialism developed in western Europe. Democratic Socialists urged public control of some means of production, but they respected individual values and favored democratic means to implement Socialist policies.

In the early 1900s, however, revolution swept Russia, an agricultural society. A small group of Marxist revolutionaries had developed a radical form of socialism called "communism." In power, the Russian communists imposed their beliefs on the country and shunned democratic values.

SECTION 1 ASSESSMENT

Main Idea
1. Use a diagram like the one below to show the process in Marxist theory by which capitalism would be replaced by communism.

Communism   Capitalism

Recall
2. **Define** laissez-faire, utilitarianism, socialism, proletariat, bourgeoisie, communism.
3. **Identify** Adam Smith, David Ricardo, Jeremy Bentham, John Stuart Mill, Robert Owen, Karl Marx, Friedrich Engels.

Critical Thinking
4. **Making Comparisons** How are the viewpoints of the Evangelicals and the Utilitarians similar? How are they different?

Understanding Themes
5. **Change** Why did industrialization make people think about the causes and cures of poverty? Can poverty be totally eliminated? Explain.

Chapter 24 *Cultural Revolution* **625**

**Chapter 24
Section 2**

Vocabulary Pre-check

 Use the Vocabulary PuzzleMaker for Chapter 24 to create a crossword puzzle to reinforce section terms. **L1 LEP**

 Use Vocabulary Activity 24 to introduce vocabulary terms. **L1 LEP**

FOCUS

Section Objective

List advances made in science between 1750 and 1914 that have improved life today.

BELLRINGER
Motivational Activity

 Before taking roll at the beginning of the class period, project Section Focus Transparency 24-2 and have students answer the activity questions. Discuss students' responses.

📁 This activity is also available as a blackline master.

1750   1800   1850   1900

1796 Edward Jenner invents smallpox vaccine.

1803 John Dalton develops atomic theory.

1859 Charles Darwin publishes *On the Origin of Species*.

1898 Marie Sklodowska Curie and Pierre Curie discover radium.

Section 2

The New Science

Guide to Reading

Read to Find Out
Main Idea *Many of the advances made in science between 1750 and 1914 have improved life today.*

▶ **Terms to Define**
cell theory, evolution, genetics, atomic theory, sociology, psychology

▶ **People to Meet**
Charles Darwin, Gregor Mendel, Edward Jenner, Louis Pasteur, John Dalton, Marie Sklodowska Curie, Pierre Curie, Ivan Pavlov, Sigmund Freud

The Storyteller

Dr. Hugh Barrett's hands shook with anger as he met with the industrial board of directors. They had requested his presence because many workers were falling ill and dying, costing them loss of labor. They hoped that modern medicine could offer a cure. Dr. Barrett tried to explain. "Cholera and typhoid will continue to rage as long as elementary hygiene is impossible. The congested, unsanitary housing—all your workers can afford on the wages you give them—is a breeding ground for disease." His persuasive words fell on deaf ears. What good is it, he wondered, to explain how disease is transmitted, if his recommendations were not to be followed?

—freely adapted from *History of Private Life, Volume 4, From the French Revolution to the Great War*, edited by Michelle Perrot, 1987

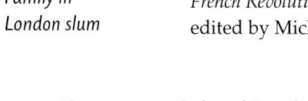
Family in London slum

During the 1800s and early 1900s, scientific discoveries were beginning to unravel some intriguing mysteries. Not only did discoveries help our understanding of life and the universe, they also led to medical advances, longer life spans, and cures for deadly diseases.

New Look at Living Things

In the 1600s scientists had observed under a microscope the cells that make up living things, but they did not understand what they saw. It was not until 1838 that German botanist Mathias Schleiden and biologist Theodor Schwann formulated the cell theory: All living things are made up of tiny units of matter called cells. They also discovered that all cells divide and multiply, causing organisms to grow and mature.

The Diversity of Life

Cell theory could not explain why the world has so many kinds of plants and animals. In the 1800s scientists proposed the theory that all plants and animals descended from a common ancestor by evolution over millions of years. During that time, they said, plants and animals had evolved from simple to complex forms.

In France, the scientist Jean-Baptiste de Lamarck observed similarities between fossils and living organisms. He found that an animal's parts—its legs, for example—might grow larger or smaller depending on how much it used them. He suggested that living things adapt to their environment and then pass the changes on to the next generation. Lamarck's theory, though later disproved, influenced **Charles Darwin**, a British naturalist who would build his own theory of evolution.

In December 1831 Charles Darwin set off on a world voyage on HMS *Beagle*, a British naval ship. While traveling he became curious about the great

---

variety of plants and animals. He also wondered why some kinds had become extinct while others lived on.

Influenced by the theories of Malthus, Darwin developed a theory of evolution based on natural selection. In his book *On the Origin of Species*, Darwin stated that most animal groups increase faster than the food supply and are constantly struggling for survival. The plants and animals that survive are better adapted to their environment, so that they alone live on, producing offspring having the same characteristics. In another book, *The Descent of Man*, Darwin traced human evolution from animal species. Darwin's writings created controversy because many religious leaders believed that his views contradicted the biblical account of creation and ignored divine purpose in the universe.

Development of Genetics

In the 1860s **Gregor Mendel** wondered how plants and animals pass characteristics from one generation to another. Mendel, an Austrian monk, experimented with pea plants. He concluded that characteristics are passed from one generation to the next by tiny particles. The particles were later called genes, and Mendel's work became the basis for genetics, the science of heredity.

Medical Advances

Through most of history, diseases have killed more people than famines, natural disasters, and wars. In the 1800s knowledge of living organisms brought medical advances that would give people longer, healthier lives.

Fighting Disease

Smallpox, which killed millions of people over the centuries, was one of the most dreaded diseases. In 1796 **Edward Jenner**, an English doctor, noticed that dairy workers who had contracted cowpox, a mild disease, never caught smallpox. Jenner hypothesized that he could prevent smallpox by injecting people with cowpox. To prove his theory, Jenner injected a boy with cowpox serum and later with smallpox serum. As Jenner expected, the boy contracted cowpox but not smallpox. Jenner had given the world's first vaccination.

About 50 years later, **Louis Pasteur**, a French chemist, learned why Jenner's vaccination worked. In the 1850s Pasteur discovered bacteria, or germs, and proved that they cause infectious diseases. He also discovered that bacteria do not appear spontaneously, but instead reproduce like other living

Science and Technology

Triumph Over an Ancient Enemy

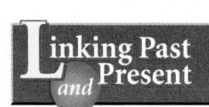
Louis Pasteur

When a wine maker asked his friend French scientist Louis Pasteur to find out why some wines turned sour as they fermented, science and medicine vaulted into a new era. Pasteur discovered that the wines would not sour if they were heated to a specific temperature and bottled without contact with the air.

With his microscope, Pasteur saw that tiny microbes were destroyed in this heating, later called pasteurization. He had proved that the germs that caused contamination came from an outside source. Pasteur worked to show that bacteria were carried in the air, on hands or clothes, and in other ways. He developed the theory that bacteria can cause disease, and he argued that bacteria could be killed only by heat or other means.

Pasteur applied his knowledge of bacteria to fighting diseases. In the 1880s he developed a successful vaccine against rabies. That same decade, the Pasteur Institute was founded in Paris, with Pasteur as director. Today, as one of the world's leading research centers, the Institute has been involved in medical breakthroughs to control many deadly diseases. In 1983 Institute researchers were the first to isolate the AIDS virus.

 ACTIVITY

Discuss how Pasteur developed the germ theory of disease and changed people's thinking about illness. How does his work influence the world today?

Chapter 24 *Cultural Revolution* **627**

TEACH

Guided Practice

THEME Innovation

Guide students in a discussion about innovations in today's society caused by modern scientific breakthroughs. **L1 LEP**

Linking Past and Present

Triumph Over an Ancient Enemy

Although as a child Pasteur (1822–1895) seemed interested only in drawing, he went on to become a major contributor to science and industry. In 1854, as dean of the science faculty at the University of Lille, he not only offered evening classes for the workers of that industrial city but also exposed his day students to the factories. In 1857 he became director of scientific studies at France's most prestigious university, the École Normale Supérieure, but after a decade he devoted himself to research. He helped the French economy by finding the bacteria threatening the silk industry. His groundbreaking work in the prevention of rabies led to the opening of the Pasteur Institute in Paris, which he headed until his death.

ANSWER
While investigating why some wines turned sour, Pasteur learned that germs that cause contamination come from an outside source. Once people knew that bacteria can cause disease, they could take protective measures. Pasteur's lasting legacy is the Pasteur Institute.

things. Pasteur knew then that they could be killed and that many diseases could be prevented.

New Approaches to Surgery

Surgery benefited from advances in chemistry. Until the mid-1800s, surgeons could operate only when their patients were forcibly held down. The experience was gruesome and often fatal. In the 1840s a Boston dentist demonstrated surgery using ether. When ether was administered, patients slept through their operations, feeling no pain. Sir James Simpson, a professor at the University of Edinburgh, investigated another sleep-producing chemical, chloroform. The anesthetics ether and chloroform led to painless surgery.

Still, many people died after surgery because of infection introduced during the procedure. Joseph Lister, an English surgeon, searched for a way to destroy bacteria and make surgery safe. He found that carbolic acid could be used to sterilize medical instruments, which moved surgery into a new era.

Breakthroughs in Physics

The explosion of ideas also advanced the physical sciences. Expanding the ideas of Galileo and Newton, scientists created our modern ideas about atomic energy. Atomic theory is the idea that all matter is made up of tiny particles called atoms.

John Dalton, an English chemist, provided proof of this theory. He discovered that elements are composed of atoms, and that all atoms of an element are identical and unlike the atoms of any other element. Dalton then determined formulas showing which atoms make up specific elements.

Until the 1890s scientists believed that atoms were solid and indivisible; then in 1895 German physicist Wilhelm K. Roentgen discovered X rays, or high-energy electromagnetic waves that could penetrate solid matter. Later scientists showed that X rays are made up of particles of electricity called electrons, which are part of every atom.

These beginnings led scientists to frame modern physics. In 1898 the physicists **Marie Sklodowska** (skluh•DAWF•skuh) **Curie** and **Pierre Curie** discovered the highly radioactive element of radium and proved that it emits energy. In 1900 German physicist Max Planck theorized that energy is not continuous, but is released in separate units called quanta. Another German scientist, Albert Einstein, developed his theory of relativity, changing ideas about time, space, mass, and motion.

Social Sciences

Meanwhile, other scientists used the scientific method to study human behavior. This led to the development of two new social sciences—sociology, the study of human behavior in groups, and psychology, the science of human behavior in individuals. The French thinker Auguste Comte (KOHNT) was one of the founders of sociology. Comte believed that society, like nature, operated by certain laws. He stated that once these laws were discovered, people could apply scientific methods to the study of human social groups.

In the 1890s **Ivan Pavlov**, a Russian researcher, experimented with animals to see what effects outside stimuli had on their behavior. His findings suggested that human actions were unconscious reactions to stimuli and could be changed by training. The Austrian physician **Sigmund Freud** (FROYD) held that an unconscious part of the mind governs human behavior. Freud's theories led to psychoanalysis, a method of treatment to discover people's motives.

SECTION 2 ASSESSMENT

Main Idea
1. Use a diagram like the one below to identify scientific advances made between 1750 and 1914.

Scientific Advances
1750–1914

Recall
2. **Define** cell theory, evolution, genetics, atomic theory, sociology, psychology.
3. **Identify** Charles Darwin, Gregor Mendel, Edward Jenner, Louis Pasteur, John Dalton, Marie Sklodowska Curie, Pierre Curie, Ivan Pavlov, Sigmund Freud.

Critical Thinking
4. **Applying Information** Explain how a scientist discussed in Section 2 helped to change the ideas of the day.

Understanding Themes
5. **Innovation** How are the scientific understandings of the 1800s and early 1900s being expanded today? How do they impact your life?

1837 Mary Lyon opens the first women's college in the United States.

1858 Frederick Law Olmsted designs New York City's Central Park.

c. 1890s Many Russian Jews flee persecution and settle in the United States.

Chapter 24 Section 3

Section 3

Popular Culture

Guide to Reading

Read to Find Out

Main Idea *Population grew dramatically in Europe and North America during the 1800s.*

▶ **Terms to Define**
  emigration, immigration, urbanization

▶ **People to Meet**
  Frederick Law Olmsted, Mary Lyon

▶ **Places to Locate**
  London, New York City, Paris

The Storyteller

A book titled Host and Guest *described dining for wealthy Europeans in the late 1800s:*
"*The first course consists of soups and fish, followed by boiled poultry, ham or tongue, roasts, stew, etc.; with vegetables … curries, hashes, cutlets, patties, etc. For the second course, roasted poultry or game at the top and bottom, with dressed vegetables, omelets, macaroni, jellies, creams, salads, preserved fruit, and all sorts of sweet things and pastry are employed…. The third course consists of game, confectionary, the more delicate vegetables dressed in the French way….*" *Dessert, of course, followed.*

—adapted from Manners and Morals in the Age of Optimism, 1848-1914, James Laver, 1966

Dining scene in Victorian England

As the 1900s began, the new science and technology were making a difference throughout Europe and North America. Most people could now expect a longer and healthier life. The rate of infant mortality dropped in the late 1800s, and life expectancy climbed. In 1850 the average person lived about 40 years; by 1900 most people could expect to live beyond 50.

Thus, as industrialization grew, so did world population. At the beginning of the Industrial Revolution, 140 million people lived in Europe. By 1850, about 100 years later, Europe's population had soared to 266 million. In Europe and the United States, the first industrialized areas, the rate of population growth was highest.

Improved Living Conditions

The medical advances of the 1800s were partly responsible for this dramatic growth in population. So too was the availability of more and better food. Before 1740 many people died of starvation and of diseases caused by vitamin deficiency such as rickets. At that time a person's entire daily diet might have consisted of three pounds of bread.

In the 1800s, however, bread ceased to be the staple it had been for centuries. With new machinery and scientific methods, farmers could produce many kinds of foods. Potatoes, nutritious and easy to grow, became popular. Methods for preserving foods, including canning and eventually refrigeration, enabled people to take advantage of the greater variety of food that was available.

One observer of working-class life in London during the late 1890s wrote: "A good deal of bread is eaten and tea is drunk especially by the women and children, but … bacon, eggs and fish appear regularly in the budgets. A piece of meat cooked on Sundays serves also for dinner on Monday and Tuesday." Some Europeans imported corn from the

Chapter 24 *Cultural Revolution* **629**

SECTION THEME

▶ **Movement** People move from rural to urban areas and from continent to continent in search of better lives.

Guide to Reading

For reading strategies to help students read effectively see pages 12–13.

Vocabulary Pre-check

 Use the Vocabulary PuzzleMaker for Chapter 24 to create a crossword puzzle to reinforce section terms. **L1 LEP**

Use Vocabulary Activity 24 to introduce vocabulary terms. **L1 LEP**

FOCUS

Section Objective

Analyze why the population grew dramatically in Europe and North America during the 1800s.

BELLRINGER Motivational Activity

 Before taking roll at the beginning of the class period, project Section Focus Transparency 24-3 and have students answer the activity questions. Discuss students' responses.
This activity is also available as a blackline master.

SECTION RESOURCES

Reproducible Masters
- Lecture Notes 24-3
- Reproducible Lesson Plan 24-3
- Vocabulary Activity 24
- Guided Reading Activity 24-3
- Geography and History Activity 24
- Section Quiz 24-3
- Reading Essentials and Study Guide 24-3

Transparencies
- Section Focus Transparency 24-3
- Mapping History Overlay Transparency 16, *Global Ancestry of Americans*

Multimedia
- Interactive Tutor Self-Assessment Software
- Testmaker
- Turning Points in World History: *The Industrial Revolution*

TEACH

Guided Practice

THEME Movement

Guide students in discussing the positive and negative aspects of population movement. *(positive: new opportunities; negative: newcomers often face discrimination)* Ask students for examples from other periods and from personal experiences. **L1**

Critical Thinking Organize the class into groups such as the working poor, industrialists, and government officials. Have students role-play a public meeting on urban health and housing during the 1800s. Encourage students to discuss health issues such as housing and clean air. **L3**

VIDEODISC
Turning Points in World History

Side Two
Chapter 3

Title: *The Industrial Revolution*
Ask: What was the "price" of the Industrial Revolution? *(Some negative effects include pollution, overcrowding in cities, exploitation of workers.)*

Mapping History Overlay Transparency 16, *Global Ancestry of Americans*

United States and fruit and frozen meat from Australia and New Zealand.

Seeking a Better Life

As the population grew, people became more mobile. Railroads revolutionized not only the food people ate, but also the way they lived. In 1860 London's Victoria Station opened, making it easier for Londoners to leave their crowded city. Steamships carried people to other countries and continents in search of a better life. Between 1870 and 1900, more than 25 million people left Europe for the United States; others moved to South America, South Africa, and Australia.

For a number of reasons, some Europeans chose emigration, leaving their homelands to settle elsewhere. Some looked for higher-paying jobs and better working conditions. Others sought to escape discrimination and persecution by oppressive governments. Still others hoped to escape famine.

Advertisements of steamship companies, along with low fares, lured many immigrants to the United States. Industries looking for cheap labor offered additional encouragement. Some American industrialists sent recruiters whose task was to urge people to leave Europe and obtain permanent jobs and homes in the United States.

Twelve-year-old Mary Antin joined thousands of Russian Jews fleeing persecution in 1894. Many years earlier Mary's father had decided on immigration, or coming to settle permanently in a foreign land. His new homeland was the United States. Mary, her mother, and her brothers and sisters endured a harrowing journey across Europe and the Atlantic Ocean to join him in Boston, Massachusetts. Mary wrote of her experiences: "And so suffering, fearing, brooding, and rejoicing, we crept nearer and nearer to the coveted shore until on a glorious May morning … our eyes beheld the Promised Land and my father received us in his arms."

Most people left their homelands knowing that they would never see their parents or their birthplace again. The ocean voyage often proved a frightening experience. One youngster

Images *of the* Times

Leisure Time

An urban environment offered many people new opportunities for leisure activities.

A Bicycle was a fashionable new means of getting around, for those who could afford it.

630

Perth Station, Going South by George Earl captures the happy confusion of a London holiday.

Images *of the* Times   Leisure Time

Bicycles were exhibited as early as 1818, but the first to become popular was the 1861 machine produced by a French father-and-son team. The bicycle soon gave rise to such leisure-time activities as bicycle touring and bicycle racing.

Railway travel had become very popular in England by the 1840s. British writer Sydney Smith said in an 1842 letter to *The Morning Leader*, "Railway travelling is a delightful improvement of human life."

Iced desserts originated in Asia, but the ice-cream soda was first served in 1874 in Philadelphia, and the ice-cream cone had its debut at the St. Louis World's Fair in 1904.

remembered "the howling darkness, the white rims of the mountain-high waves speeding like maddened dragons toward the tumbling ship."

When the immigrants reached their new homes, many learned that their troubles had only begun. Now they had to find housing and jobs in strange surroundings where they did not know the culture or the language. Some people took advantage of the European immigrants, who seemed to them strange "foreigners."

From Country to City

During the 1800s and early 1900s, many people moved within their own country. Cities around the world were absorbing newcomers who were moving from rural villages to find new opportunities. As farms grew larger and more mechanized, they needed fewer workers. The growing industries in or near the cities offered new and challenging ways to make a living.

Although the new city dwellers faced no language barriers, some of their problems were similar to those of the European immigrants. Their old life was gone, with its known boundaries, familiar people, and established routines. Although work was plentiful, living quarters in the cities were often cramped, and neighbors might be less friendly than people they had known. British poet Lord Byron summed up the feelings of many newcomers to the city:

> ❝ I live not in myself, but I become a
> Portion of that around me: and to me
> High mountains are a feeling, but the hum
> Of human cities torture. ❞

Growth of Cities

The movement of people into the cities resulted in the urbanization, or the spread of city life, of the industrialized countries. A country is urbanized when more people live in cities than in rural areas. Great Britain is a prime example. In 1800 **London**

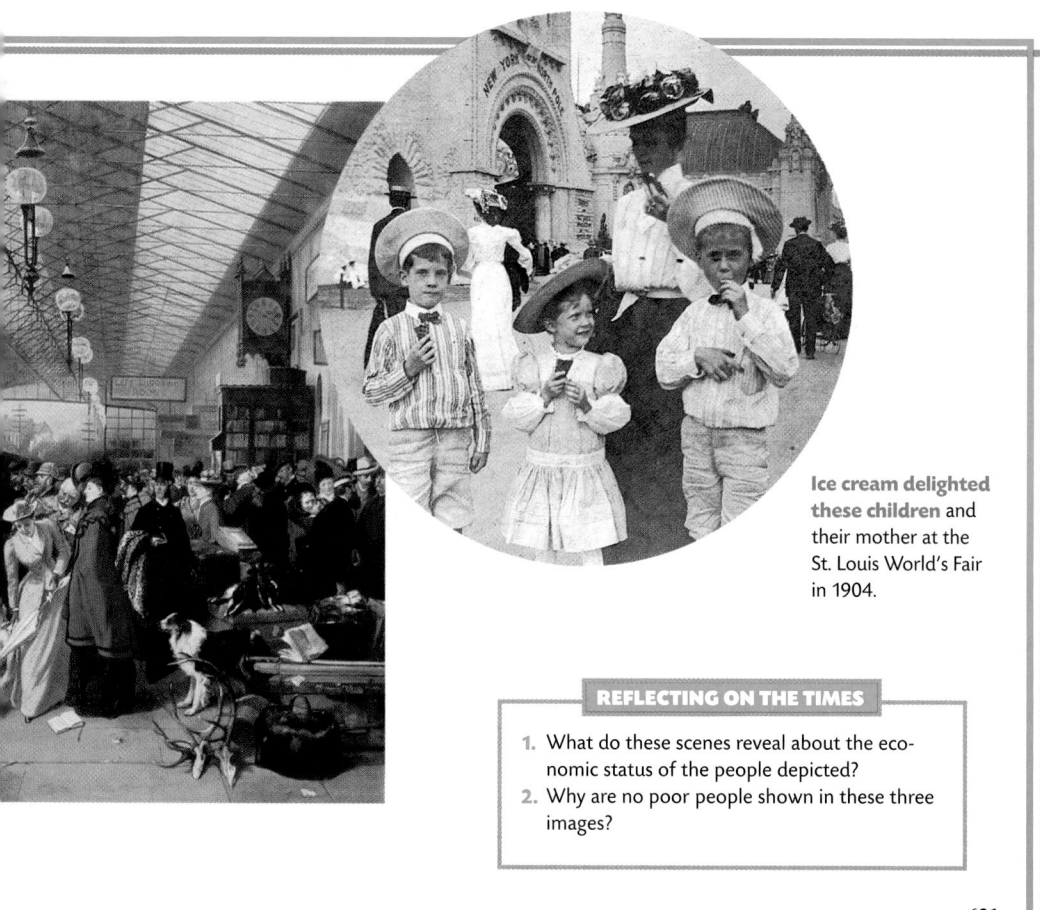

Ice cream delighted these children and their mother at the St. Louis World's Fair in 1904.

REFLECTING ON THE TIMES

1. What do these scenes reveal about the economic status of the people depicted?
2. Why are no poor people shown in these three images?

631

ANSWERS TO REFLECTING ON THE TIMES

1. All the people are sufficiently wealthy to be able to take time off from work and to pay for excursions and treats.
2. The poor had no disposable income to pay for leisure-time activities or treats.

Biography

The following videotape programs are available from Glencoe:

- **The Rockefellers**
- **The Pulitzers**
- **P. T. Barnum: American Dreamer**

Independent Practice

📁 Guided Reading Activity 24-3 **L1**

📁 Geography and History Activity 24

Brochure Ask students to investigate one of the cultural institutions founded during this period, such as the Louvre or the Royal Albert Hall. Have students create a brochure for the institution, describing its most interesting features and encouraging people to visit it. **L1**

Environmental Issues Have students do further research into the environmental conditions in the large cities of the period, such as London. Have them write letters to the editor as urban dwellers protesting the conditions they see around them. **L2**

Who?What?Where?When?

Pogroms, or government-sponsored attacks against Jews, led two million East European Jews to seek refuge in the United States between 1881 and the outbreak of World War I. This massive migration accounted for 10 percent of the movement between Europe and America during that period.

was its only city with a population of more than 100,000. By 1851 Britain had 9 such cities. In the same year, and for the first time, slightly more than half of the British people lived in cities. By 1914 that figure had reached 80 percent.

Urbanization also took place elsewhere. In 1914, 60 percent of Germans, 50 percent of Americans, and 45 percent of French were city dwellers.

As people moved to cities, they began to marry earlier. Children could increase a family's income by working in factories. As a result, people had more children, adding to the population.

The cities' growth soon outpaced their ability to provide needed housing and sanitation. Few cities had building codes that mandated adequate housing. Houses were built close together in long rows. The workers crowded together in damp, cold, unsanitary rooms, with fire a constant danger.

The factories added to the unpleasant city environment. Here is a report on the working conditions of British miners in 1843: "Sheffield is one of the dirtiest and most smoky towns I ever saw. The town is also very hilly, and the smoke ascends the streets, instead of leaving them...."

City Services

City governments in Europe and the United States began to look for solutions to the overwhelming troubles. They saw that one of the most

Student Web Activity 24

Visit the *World History: The Human Experience* Web site at **worldhistory.glencoe.com** and click on ***Chapter 24—Student Web Activities*** for an activity relating to Frederick Law Olmsted.

Moving to the Suburbs
During the late 1800s, suburbs, or small communities next to large cities, grew in Europe and the United States along with the development of streetcar lines and railroads. Middle-class people could afford to live in less urban areas and ride the trolley or train to their jobs in the city. In the United States, suburban growth greatly increased in the 1950s as more and more families were able to buy one or two automobiles.

pressing problems was sanitation. An observer in the British city of Leeds reported, "The ashes, garbage, and filth of all kinds are thrown from the doors and windows of the houses upon the surface of the streets and courts." Ditches and open sewers carried waste from public toilets. Polluted water encouraged epidemics of cholera and other diseases, especially in the crowded slums.

In the late 1800s, the germ theory and the newly invented iron pipe spurred city leaders to clean up their cities. They installed closed sewer lines and improved garbage collection. Police and fire protection created safer cities.

As city planning progressed, city governments set aside areas as parks. In **New York City**, landscape architect **Frederick Law Olmsted** saw the need for "a simple, broad, open space of clean greensward [grassy turf]" enclosed by a large enough green space to "completely shut out the city." With architect and landscape designer Calvert Vaux, Olmsted designed Central Park in 1858.

Leisure Time

Leisure time activities expanded for the middle classes and for the working classes. People enjoyed more cultural activities. Newspapers helped to make people interested in places and events outside of their own neighborhoods and communities.

In the 1700s the fine arts were available only to the upper classes. Concerts were performed in palaces, grand homes, or churches. Wealthy aristocrats, prosperous merchants, and religious leaders commissioned cultural events and artworks to commemorate events or to honor special people.

In the 1800s, fine art and music became available to middle- and working-class people in the city. City governments in Europe and North America built concert halls and opera houses, such as London's vast Royal Albert Hall, erected in 1871. Cities sponsored the opening of art museums, such as the Louvre (LOOV) Museum in **Paris**.

When people were not visiting libraries and museums, they went to amusement parks. Sports such as soccer and rugby began to be organized between cities and around the nation. Many people also enjoyed archery, lawn tennis, and cricket.

New Interest in Education

In the early 1800s, when governments began to support public schools, their reasons were political. For example, the Prussian government established public schools to train its people in citizenship and in devotion to the monarchy and the army. In the

United States, government support for public schools grew out of a desire to foster national unity after the Revolutionary War.

By the late 1800s, as people grew more and more interested in improving their lives, they became more actively involved in promoting education. Both in Europe and the United States, believing education would improve their children's chances for a better life, they supported education funded by the government and available to everyone. Schools and colleges were also established to provide better training for teachers.

The new kind of society—urbanized and industrialized—also benefited from the cause of public education. Industrialists needed employees who could read and write. Advanced technologies based on science depended on workers who had scientific training. Many people came to see that an ever more complex society would demand a well-educated populace. People were needed who could participate intelligently in public affairs.

Education for Women

Education for women was a hotly debated topic in the 1800s. Some felt that women's roles as wives and homemakers did not require education. Others believed women should be given the same educational opportunities as men. Girls were included in the laws providing education to all. Still, they could usually attend only elementary schools; secondary education was limited to the wealthy.

Determined to offer higher education to women, some people began to open secondary schools and colleges especially for them. In 1837 American educator **Mary Lyon** opened the first women's college, the Mount Holyoke Female Seminary, which later became Mount Holyoke College in Massachusetts. In 1874 the London School of Medicine was opened, and after two years of bitter debate, the British Parliament finally allowed women to be registered as doctors.

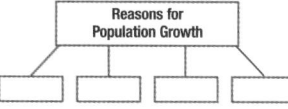 *Piccadilly Circus, 1912* by Charles Ginner. Tate Gallery, London, England **Piccadilly Circus was built near the shopping district of London.** *By 1914, what percent of the British lived in cities?*

Results of Education

The advances in education made magazines and books popular. Libraries with large collections opened as early as the 1840s in major cities such as Paris and London. Lending libraries loaned books for small fees.

Mass-circulation newspapers were first printed at this time, and by 1860, more than 3,000 newspapers were published in the United States. Newspaper publishers benefited from the combination of rapid communication provided by the telegraph, cheaper printing methods, and improved distribution by railroad and steamship.

SECTION 3 ASSESSMENT

Main Idea
1. Use a diagram like the one below to list reasons for population growth in Europe and North America in the 1800s.

Reasons for Population Growth

Recall
2. **Define** emigration, immigration, urbanization.
3. **Identify** Frederick Law Olmsted, Mary Lyon.

Critical Thinking
4. **Making Comparisons** How do attitudes about women's education today differ from attitudes in the late 1800s? Explain reasons for the differences.

Understanding Themes
5. **Movement** Why did many people in Europe and North America move to new places in the late 1800s and early 1900s?

History & Art Tell students that in England, a *circus* is an open circle, square, or plaza where several streets converge. Six busy streets meet at Piccadilly Circus, which, together with Trafalgar Square, is one of two huge intersections in London's West End.
Answer to Caption: *80 percent*

Evaluate

Section Quiz 24-3

Use the Testmaker to create a customized quiz for Section 3.

Reteach

Have students meet in small groups of five or six to discuss the review questions. Circulate to monitor progress.

Reading Essentials and Study Guide 24-3

Enrich

Have students research the popular culture of their town or city during the 1800s and report on topics such as entertainment, economic growth, and population shifts.

CLOSE

Tell students to imagine they are immigrants living in a large city in the late 1800s. Have them write a letter to friends at home describing their new homeland.

SECTION 3 ASSESSMENT ANSWERS

1. infant mortality decreased; life expectancy increased; improved living conditions; more and better food; people in cities married earlier and had more children
2. All terms are defined in the Glossary.
3. Olmsted, 632; Lyon, 633
4. Most people today believe that all opportunities available to men should also be available to women; to enable women to take advantage of these opportunities on equal terms, they need an equivalent education. Many people in the 1800s felt a woman's role as wife and homemaker did not require an education. Reasons for the differences will vary but may include that seeing women perform successfully in such formerly all-male roles as doctors, lawyers, and engineers has changed people's thinking.
5. **MOVEMENT** Answers should include the search for better jobs and working conditions and the need to escape from discrimination, famine, and persecution. Similar reasons apply today.

TEACH

Using E-Mail As electronic communication becomes an ever-increasing part of our daily lives, students almost inevitably will find that they must know how to send and receive E-mail. You might begin discussion of this feature by taking a class survey to find out if anyone frequently corresponds in this fashion. Also discuss the advantages of sending E-mail rather than phoning or sending messages through the post office. *(faster and cheaper)*

In discussing components of an E-mail system, mention that it is possible to attach documents and other kinds of files to E-mail messages. For example, a student can send an essay to a friend without typing it again as part of a message itself.

Demonstrate sending a message and opening and printing a received message. Then demonstrate how to send a message with an attached file and opening and printing a received message with an attached file. If possible, schedule time in the computer lab so that students can send E-mail on their own.

Additional Practice

Skill Reinforcement Activity 24

Using E-Mail

Sharing information, thoughts, and feelings with others is communication. *Telecommunication* refers to communicating at a distance through the use of a telephone, video, or computer. How can you communicate using your computer?

Learning the Skill

In order to use your computer to telecommunicate, you must add two parts to it. The first part is a piece of hardware called a *modem*. A modem is a device that enables computers to communicate with each other through telephone lines.

The second part is *communications software* which lets your computer prepare and send information to the modem. It also lets your computer receive and understand the information it receives from the modem.

Electronic mail, or *E-mail*, for short, is one way of sending and receiving messages electronically. Anyone who is part of an E-mail network can send and receive private messages.

Before you can send or receive E-mail, you must obtain an E-mail address. This address identifies the location of your electronic "mailbox"—the place where you receive your E-mail. To send an E-mail message to another person you must include that person's E-mail address, just as you might address an envelope. There is no central listing of E-mail addresses. The best way to find out an address is to ask the person for their address.

Many corporations are using E-mail communications, which makes some environmentalists happier. More electronic communication means less use of paper and more saved trees.

Practicing the Skill

To send a message to a friend on an E-mail network, complete the following steps.

1. Select the "message" function from your communications software.
2. Type in the E-mail address.
3. Type in your message. Proofread it for errors.
4. Select the "send" function.

The E-mail system places the message in the receiver's "mailbox." He or she can read the message at any time—and then send you a reply.

Applying the Skill

Many scientific discoveries took place in the mid-1700s to the early 1900s. Use E-mail to contact a librarian. Ask for recommendations of young adult books related to scientific discoveries from 1750–1914.

For More Practice

Turn to the Skill Practice in the Chapter Assessment on page 645 for more practice in using E-mail.

ANSWERS TO PRACTICING THE SKILL

If possible, have students who are familiar with E-mail help you guide novices through the process of sending a message. Because of computer availability, you may find it more practical to have groups of students work together on the activity.

1750 ------- **1800** ------- **1850** ------- **1900**

c. 1780 Romanticism becomes a leading cultural movement.

1854 Charles Dickens writes *Hard Times*.

c. 1873 Impressionist movement begins in France.

c. 1890 Symbolist movement reacts against industrial civilization.

Section 4

Revolution in the Arts

Guide to Reading

Read to Find Out
Main Idea *Writers and artists in Europe and North America reflected changes in society between 1750 and 1914.*

▶ **Terms to Define**
romanticism, realism, symbolism, impressionism, Postimpressionism

▶ **People to Meet**
Peter Tchaikovsky, Johann Wolfgang von Goethe, George Sand, Honoré de Balzac, Charles Dickens, Leo Tolstoy, Claude Monet, Vincent van Gogh

▶ **Places to Locate**
Paris

The Storyteller

Gustave frowned as he read his mother's letter. "I am tired of seeing your talent receive no recognition. You must acknowledge what people want. You need to cater to the popular taste ... paint imaginary scenes of Roman or medieval heroes. Then your paintings might win prizes or be purchased by influential collectors."
Gustave Courbet would not follow the crowd or popular tastes, just because others were doing it. He would paint images of his own time.

—freely adapted from *Realism*, Linda Nochlin, 1971

Landscape
by Gustave Courbet

uropean and American artists in the 1800s mirrored society's mixed feelings about the rapid disappearance of the old order and the uncertainty of the new. A growing middle class created a larger audience for music, literature, and poetry. Formerly, artists had depended on patronage by the wealthy. Now, although some artists sought support in the new industrial society, others rebelled against middle-class values and shunned patronage of any kind, preferring to work independently. Those who rebelled would dominate the arts in the late 1700s and early 1800s.

The Romantic Movement

By the late 1700s, artists had begun to react to the Enlightenment's emphasis on order and reason. The French philosopher Jean-Jacques Rousseau taught that people were naturally good and needed only to be free. In rejecting society's formal structures and rules, Rousseau anticipated romanticism, a movement in which artists would emphasize human emotion and imagination over reason.

Romantic artists tried to free themselves from the rigid forms and structures of neoclassical art. Rejecting the mechanization and ugliness of industrialized society, many turned to nature, glorifying its awesome power and quiet beauty.

Many romantic artists looked to the past, admiring the mythical heroes of old. They felt compassion for the weak and oppressed, and they celebrated the lives of "simple peasants." The struggle for personal freedom and heroic rebellion against society's established rules are frequent themes in their works. The French poet Charles Baudelaire described the movement: "Romanticism is precisely situated neither in choice of subject nor in exact truth, but in a way of feeling."

Chapter 24 *Cultural Revolution* **635**

SECTION THEME

▶ **Innovation** Artists and writers in the Western world reflect the changes in urban industrial society.

Guide to Reading

For reading strategies to help students read effectively see pages 12–13.

Vocabulary Pre-check

⊡ Use the Vocabulary PuzzleMaker for Chapter 24 to create a crossword puzzle to reinforce section terms. **L1 LEP**

◤ Use Vocabulary Activity 24 to introduce vocabulary terms. **L1 LEP**

FOCUS

Section Objective
Describe how writers and artists in Europe and North America reflected changes in society between 1750 and 1914.

**BELLRINGER
Motivational Activity**

Before taking roll, project Section Focus Transparency 24-4 and have students answer the activity questions.
◤ This activity is also available as a blackline master.

SECTION RESOURCES

◤ **Reproducible Masters**
• Lecture Notes 24-4
• Reproducible Lesson Plan 24-4
• Guided Reading Activity 24-4
• History Simulation 24
• Reteaching Activity 24
• Enrichment Activity 24
• Section Quiz 24-4

• Performance Assessment Activity 24
• Spanish Chapter Summary 24
• Reading Essentials and Study Guide 24-4

✑ **Transparencies**
• Section Focus Transparency 24-4
• World History and Art Transparencies 31, 32, 34

Multimedia
▭ Focus on World Art Prints 2, 5, 22
⊡ Vocabulary PuzzleMaker Software
⊡ Interactive Tutor Self-Assessment Software
⊡ Testmaker

TEACH

Guided Practice

THEME Innovation

Ask students to scan the section and provide examples of innovations in art. *(They may point out any of the movements discussed or specific examples within them, such as the emphasis on emotion and imagination by the romantics.)* Ask students to cite examples of innovations in art, music, or literature that they have noticed in their lifetimes. **L1**

History *and the* Humanities

Focus on World Art Prints
•2 Franz Marc. *Stables*
•5 Paul Klee. *Palace, Partially Destroyed*
•22 Vincent van Gogh. *Hospital at Saint-Rémy*

World History and Art Transparencies
•31 *In the Garden*
•32 *Sunday Afternoon on the Island of La Grande Jatte*
•34 *Starry Night*

History Simulation 24

 Tell students that a fjord is a long, narrow arm of the sea bordered by steep cliffs.
Answer to Caption: *It is dramatic and celebrates nature and freedom of the human spirit.*

Romantic Music

The composers of the Enlightenment had emphasized form and order, but romantic composers departed from traditional forms and styles. They often fused music with imaginative literature, creating operas—dramas set to music—and *lieder* (LEED•uhr)—art songs, or poems set to music.

Romantic music was meant to stir the emotions—whether in large works, such as symphonies by German composer Ludwig van Beethoven (BAY•TOH•vuhn) or Russian composer **Peter Tchaikovsky** (chy•KAWF•skee), or in smaller, more intimate works, such as piano pieces by Poland's Frédéric Chopin (SHOH•PAN) or the *lieder* of Austria's Franz Schubert. Melodies from folk music added emotional power to romantic music, as in works by Czech composer Antonín Dvořák (DVAWR•ZHANK), whose *Symphony From the New World* echoes American spirituals.

Romantic Literature

Like romantic composers, romantic writers created emotion-filled, imaginative works. Early leaders of the romantic movement in literature

include German writers Friedrich von Schiller and **Johann Wolfgang von Goethe** (GUHR•tuh). Schiller glorified freedom fighters, such as the legendary hero William Tell. His drama with that title is about the medieval Swiss struggle for freedom. Goethe is best known for *Faust*, a drama about human striving and the need for redemption.

France produced some of the most popular romantic writers. Alexandre Dumas's novel *The Three Musketeers* recounts the exploits of three dashing adventurers in the 1600s. Aurore Dupin, better known as **George Sand**, made peasants and workers heroes in her fiction. The novels of Victor Hugo, the foremost French romanticist, include *The Hunchback of Notre Dame* and *Les Misérables*, tales portraying human suffering with compassion and power.

Romanticism also influenced Great Britain. Scots writer Sir Walter Scott won a huge following with his historical novels *Ivanhoe, Quentin Durward,* and *The Talisman*. Another Scot, Robert Burns, showed deep feeling for nature and romantic love in his poetry. English poet and painter William Blake attacked the growing results of industrialization in *Songs of Innocence* and *Songs of Experience*. Similar themes fill the works of English poets Samuel Taylor Coleridge, William Wordsworth, John Keats, Percy Bysshe Shelley, and Lord Byron.

Romantic Painting

Painters, like writers, reflected romantic ideals. Turning from the order, clarity, and balance of the neoclassical style, painters began to portray exotic, powerful subjects in a dramatic and colorful way. For example, the painting *Liberty Leading the People,* by Eugène Delacroix (DEH•luh•KWAH), shows the figure of Liberty as a brave woman carrying a flag and leading patriots through the streets of **Paris**. Like many other romantic works, the painting was meant to stir the emotions, not appeal to the intellect.

The Turn Toward Realism

In the mid-1800s, some artists began to reject the sentimentality of romanticism. They sought to portray life in a realistic manner. In France, painter Gustave Courbet (kur•BAY) expressed the idea behind this style, known as realism: "Painting ... does not consist of anything but the presentation of real and concrete things." Realist painters and writers wished to portray life as it was, not to escape from it.

Courbet's own large, somber canvases called attention to the less fortunate members of society and their difficult circumstances. *Burial at Ornans*

COOPERATIVE LEARNING ACTIVITY

Art Magazine Have students work together to produce a magazine displaying their literary and artistic accomplishments. Contributions must be in the style of one of the artistic movements of the period described in this section and may include paintings, drawings, poetry, songs, and so on. Some students should be responsible for assembling and organizing the materials by movement. Others may do interviews of the contributors or write articles evaluating the works. **L2 LEP**

National Gallery of Art

French Impressionists

urest of the impressionists, Claude Monet captured the essence of light and air. A stiff breeze swirls through *Woman With a Parasol—Madame Monet and Her Son*, painted between and 1878. "His pictures always were too draughty e!" commented fellow impressionist Edgar Degas. had been any worse, I should have had to turn up coat collar." Unlike Monet and other French essionists who insisted on painting from life, s was the master of the fleeting moment. He relied uick sketches and his memory of posture, light, color, and painted later at his studio.

One of Monet's paintings entitled *Impression—Sunrise*, exhibited in a Paris art show gave impressionism its name. An art critic reviewing the show ridiculed the painting and invented the term "impressionism." French impressionists such as Monet, Degas, and others rebelled against the strict traditions and rules of the art world of the late 1800s to capture the natural appearances of objects. Using dabs and strokes of primary colors, they tried to give the impression of actual reflected light. They often painted outdoors, trying to capture natural light, shadow, and color on canvas. ⊕

Chapter 24 *Cultural Revolution* **637**

TEACH

The impressionist style is said to have had its origins at a French riverside café called La Grenouillière, where Monet and Renoir began meeting in 1869. Until that time, both men had employed an ordinary naturalist style in their work. But upon gazing out at the sun sparkling on the rippling river waters, they felt that a new technique was needed to capture that delightful play of light. From then on Monet began to work at finding ways of rendering an *impression* of the many different effects of light. "Light is the principal person in the picture," he once said. **What characteristics of impressionist painting can you see in "Woman With a Parasol"?** *(Students may point to the pattern of separate brushstrokes, the brilliant color, the feathery lightness.)*

CURRICULUM CONNECTION

POLITICS

Many artists of the time took sides in the Dreyfus affair, a military-political scandal that polarized French society during the last half of the 1890s. Monet and Pissarro were among the artists believing that the charge of treason against Captain Alfred Dreyfus, the only Jew on the General Staff of the French army, was unfounded (as in fact it proved to be). Cézanne, Rodin, Renoir, and Degas believed in Dreyfus's guilt.

Independent Practice

Biography Have students research the life of one of the artists of the period and write a brief biography. Tell students to include information on education, training, major works, and public acceptance. **L1**

The following videotape program is available from Glencoe:

• **The Hunchback of Notre Dame**

The Arts Have students assemble copies of paintings from the period covered in this section and report to the class on the techniques and subject matter of the different artists. Instruct them to identify the movement each work represents and to point out characteristics of the movement. **L3**

ASSESS

Check for Understanding

Assign Section 4 Assessment as homework or as an in-class activity.

Use Interactive Tutor Self-Assessment Software to review Section 4.

Evaluate

Section Quiz 24-4

Use the Testmaker to create a customized quiz for Section 4.

Futabatei Publishes *The Drifting Clouds*

Japan, 1889

Beginning in the 1880s, Western ideas began to influence Japanese writing. A group of Japanese authors, who had been educated in Western languages, broke from traditional forms of literature. These writers believed that Japan's technological development should be accompanied by the development of modern European-style literary works. In 1889 Futabatei Shimei produced a novel titled *The Drifting Clouds* which helped establish the novel as a respected form of Japanese literature.

portrayed peasants from his hometown standing around the grave of a loved one. By the end of the 1850s, other French artists had joined Courbet in painting realistically. Among the most notable were Honoré Daumier (doh•MYAY) and Jean-François Millet (mee•YAY).

Realism in Literature

Realism also flourished in literature. French writer **Honoré de Balzac** grouped about 90 of his novels and short stories of French life in the 1800s into a collection he called *The Human Comedy*. Many described frankly the greed and stupidity that Balzac saw in the growing middle class. Gustave Flaubert (floh•BEHR), another French writer, portrayed the conflict between dreary realities and romantic dreams in *Madame Bovary*, the story of a young woman married to a dull provincial doctor.

The English novelist, Mary Ann Evans wrote under the pen name George Eliot. Her novels portrayed the rigidity and senselessness of the British social order. **Charles Dickens**, the foremost English realistic writer, spoke out on behalf of the poor. Dickens focused on the deplorable conditions in the prisons, hospitals, and poorhouses of London. In his novel *Hard Times*, he attacked the materialism of Coketown, a fictional city.

Russian writers came to be known for their penetrating novels about the human spirit. The novels of Russian writer **Leo Tolstoy** also reflected his compassion for the peasants and gave his analysis of social customs. *War and Peace* is a family novel in which Tolstoy takes five families through the

stages of life. It is also a historical novel about Napoleon's invasion of Russia in 1812.

The works of American novelist Theodore Dreiser belong to a pessimistic style of realism called naturalism, in which writers tried to apply scientific methods to imaginative writing. In Dreiser's novel *An American Tragedy*, a young man is executed for killing his pregnant girlfriend. To Dreiser, the man is a victim whose tragedy results from circumstances over which he has no control.

Symbolism

Some writers became disgusted with what they viewed as the ugly and brutal realities of European industrial civilization. To escape, they created a world of shadowy images evoked by symbols. This movement, called symbolism, began in France and was led by the poet Stéphane Mallarmé (MA•LAHR•MAY), who believed that "to name an object is to destroy three-quarters of the enjoyment of a poem, which is made up of the pleasure of guessing little by little." He and his followers, Paul Verlaine (vehr•LAYN) and Arthur Rimbaud (ram•BOH), gave impressions by suggestion rather than by direct statement.

Symbolism spread to the other arts and to other countries. The symbolists focused on the exotic, using imagery to suggest the world of the spirit. Intellectuals applauded this effort, but the average person found symbolism difficult to understand.

New Trends in Painting

Intense competition and rigid, traditional standards characterized the artistic world in the 1800s. An artist's works had to be considered "correct" and the subject matter "proper" by judges at London's Royal Academy of Art or Paris's École des Beaux-Arts (School of Fine Arts). Acceptance by those schools and a place in their yearly exhibitions were crucial to a beginning artist's success.

In 1863 the École turned down more than 3,000 of the 5,000 works that were submitted for its approval—the highest proportion of rejections that anyone could remember. Napoleon III, the French emperor at the time, decided to hold an exhibit to let the public see the paintings that had been rejected by the École. Those paintings delighted many people and gave the painters renewed hope that their works would win recognition.

Impressionism

During the 1870s, a group of French artists developed a style called impressionism. The

---

MEETING SPECIAL NEEDS ACTIVITY

Learning Style: Logical/Mathematical Have students with good computer skills access information from the World Wide Web on the artistic movements described in this section. Ask them to print out the information they find and distribute it to the class. Then they can explain to the class how they located the information and point out ways it enhances the coverage available in the text. **L2**

impressionist painters abandoned many of the rules on which earlier painters had based their art—rules about proper subject matter and traditional techniques of line, perspective, and studio lighting. Fascinated by color and light, the impressionists sought to capture the momentary impression a subject made on their senses. They moved out of the studio and into the real world, choosing to work outdoors, in theaters, and in cafes.

Pierre-Auguste Renoir (REHN•WAHR) painted idealized portraits of women and children and outdoor scenes. **Claude Monet** (moh•NAY) painted series of paintings on the same subject to show variations in light and color over time.

Postimpressionism

In the late 1880s some artists turned away from impressionism. Known as Postimpressionists, they formed independent styles to express in different ways the chaos and complexity around them. One of their leaders was Paul Cézanne (say•ZAN). Earlier, he had identified with romanticism and impressionism. By the 1880s he had laid the foundation for Postimpressionism by stating, "I do not want to reproduce nature, I want to recreate it."

Georges Seurat (suh•RAH) applied science to his paintings. He developed pointillism, the placing of small dabs of color close together to produce a three-dimensional effect. His painting *A Sunday Afternoon on the Island of La Grande Jatte* consists of thousands of different-colored dots.

Paul Gauguin (goh•GAN) moved to the Pacific island of Tahiti, where he painted *Where do we come from? What are we? Where are we going?* It was an attempt to find universal truths in the symbols of a nonindustrial culture.

The son of a Dutch minister, **Vincent van Gogh** (van GOH) turned to painting after failing at the ministry. Within two years, he produced most of the paintings for which he is known, using brilliant

 The Swing by Pierre-Auguste Renoir, 1876. Musée d'Orsay, Paris, France *What did impressionist painters seek to capture in their works?*

colors and distorted forms to make intense emotional statements.

Henri de Toulouse-Lautrec (tu•LOOZ loh•TREHK) painted Paris nightlife using bright colors to catch the reality of lives he portrayed. His use of line and color in posters of Paris's Moulin Rouge nightclub attracted worldwide attention.

History & Art The Musée d'Orsay is situated in the former Gare d'Orsay, a railroad station in Paris. After being remodeled, the building was reopened in 1986 as a museum specializing in the different schools of French art—middle to late 1800s. **Answer to Caption:** *They sought to capture the momentary impression a subject made on their senses.*

Reteach

Ask each student to write three questions on the section's content. Then have students meet in groups and exchange questions.

Reteaching Activity 24

Reading Essentials and Study Guide 24-4

Enrich

Have students who are musically inclined research trends in postromantic music of the late 1800s and early 1900s. Have them summarize their findings in brief reports to the class that include taped excerpts of compositions.

Enrichment Activity 24

CLOSE

Have students write a brief paragraph explaining which artistic movement described in this section they find most visually pleasing and which they like least.

SECTION 4 ASSESSMENT

Main Idea
1. Use a diagram like the one below to show the new movements in painting that reflected social change between 1750 and 1914.

```
Writers/Artists
Reflected Social
Change
```

Recall
2. **Define** romanticism, realism, symbolism, impressionism, Postimpressionism.
3. **Identify** Peter Tchaikovsky, Johann Wolfgang von Goethe, George Sand, Honoré de Balzac, Charles Dickens, Leo Tolstoy, Claude Monet, Vincent van Gogh.

Critical Thinking
4. **Analyzing Information** How might the painting *Liberty Leading the People* have influenced French attitudes about revolution?

Understanding Themes
5. **Innovation** How was nature a significant theme in romantic art?

Chapter 24 *Cultural Revolution* **639**

SECTION 4 ASSESSMENT ANSWERS

1. romanticism; realism; symbolism; impressionism; Postimpressionism
2. All terms are defined in the Glossary.
3. Tchaikovsky, 636; Goethe, 636; Sand, 636; Balzac, 638; Dickens, 638; Tolstoy, 638; Monet, 639; van Gogh, 639
4. Answers will vary. Possible answer:

The patriotic emotions it stirred might have encouraged people to revolt against a government that seemed unresponsive to the people's needs.
5. **INNOVATION** Answers will vary but might include the idea that nature's awesome power and quiet beauty

inspired artists who rejected industrialized society's mechanization and ugliness.

Block Schedule

Team Teaching This excerpt from *The Beggar* may be presented in a team-teaching context, in conjunction with English or Language Arts.

The Beggar

Historical Connection

Industrialization increased the number of poor city dwellers. Societies had to decide how to treat those unable to support themselves.

Background Information

Setting The story is set in a Russian city in the late 1800s. During this period many Russians moved to the city to find work and escape the poverty and tedium of rural life.

Characters Lushkoff: a poor alcoholic who survives by begging; Skvortsoff: a wealthy lawyer who prides himself on his compassion for the needy; Olga: Skvortsoff's cook who often supervises Lushkoff

Plot Skvortsoff, though angered by Lushkoff's lies, hires him to cut wood and do other chores. Eventually Lushkoff is able to find a better job as a notary. Years later the two men meet again at the theater, where Skvortsoff takes credit for teaching Lushkoff the value of work. The former beggar confesses that he never chopped any wood; Olga did it all.

from
The Beggar
by Anton Chekhov

*A*nton Chekhov, who died in 1904 at age 44, wrote several plays and short stories that became classics of Russian literature. The issue he confronts in the following excerpt—how to help those in need—remains a vital issue today. A wealthy lawyer, Skvortsoff, is angered by the lies a beggar tells to win sympathy and money from passersby. Skvortsoff complains to the beggar that "you could always find work if you only wanted to, but you're lazy and spoiled and drunken!"

*B*y God, you judge harshly!" cried the beggar with a bitter laugh. "Where can I find manual labor? It's too late for me to be a clerk because in trade one has to begin as a boy; no one would ever take me for a porter because they couldn't order me about; no factory would have me because for that one has to know a trade, and I know none."

"Nonsense! You always find some excuse! How would you like to chop wood for me?"

"I wouldn't refuse to do that, but in these days even skilled wood-cutters find themselves sitting without bread."

"Huh! You loafers all talk that way. As soon as an offer is made you, you refuse it. Will you come and chop wood for me?"

"Yes, sir; I will."

"Very well; we'll soon find out. Splendid—we'll see—"

Skvortsoff hastened along, rubbing his hands, not without a feeling of malice, and called his cook out of the kitchen.

"Here, Olga," he said, "take this gentleman into the wood-shed and let him chop wood."

The tatterdemalion [clothed in ragged garments] scarecrow shrugged his shoulders, as if in perplexity, and went irresolutely after the cook. It was obvious from his gait that he had not consented to go and chop wood because he was hungry and wanted work, but simply pride and shame, because he had been trapped by his own words. It was obvious, too, that his strength had been undermined by vodka and

ABOUT THE AUTHOR

Anton Chekhov grew up in Taganrog, a city on the Black Sea. His father, a recently freed serf, struggled to make a living as a grocer. From this childhood poverty, Chekhov developed a sympathy for the poor and working classes. He worked as a medical doctor among the poor during his adult life. His real interest, however, was writing. As a young man, Chekhov began writing short humorous tales to add to his income. As he grew older, he wrote plays and more serious short stories. He occasionally wrote nonfiction, including an account of convicts on Russia's Sakhalin Island. Often ill, Chekhov died of tuberculosis in 1904.

that he was unhealthy and did not feel the slightest inclination for toil.

Skvortsoff hurried into the dining room. From its windows one could see the wood-shed and everything that went on in the yard. Standing at the window, Skvortsoff saw the cook and the beggar come out into the yard by the back door and make their way across the dirty snow to the shed. Olga glared wrathfully at her companion, shoved him aside with her elbow, unlocked the shed, and angrily banged the door.

"We probably interrupted the woman over her coffee," thought Skvortsoff. "What an ill-tempered creature!"

Next he saw the pseudo-teacher, pseudo-student seat himself on a log and become lost in thought with his red cheeks resting on his fists. The woman flung down an ax at his feet, spat

angrily, and, judging from the expression of her lips, began to scold him. The beggar irresolutely pulled a billet [log] of wood toward him, set it up between his feet, and tapped it feebly with the ax. The billet wavered and fell down. The beggar again pulled it to him, blew on his freezing hands, and tapped it with his ax cautiously, as if afraid of hitting his overshoe or of cutting off his finger. The stick of wood again fell to the ground.

Skvortsoff's anger had vanished and he now began to feel a little sorry and ashamed of himself for having set a spoiled, drunken, perchance sick man to work at menial labor in the cold.

"Well, never mind," he thought, going into his study from the dining room. "I did it for his own good."

An hour later Olga came in and announced

History & Art *Religious Procession in the Province of Kursk* by Ilya Repin. Tretyakov Gallery, Moscow, Russia **Ilya Repin painted realistic scenes of everyday Russian life.** *How does Chekhov portray Russian life in his story "The Beggar"?*

OTHER WORKS BY ANTON CHEKHOV

Frayn, Michael, trans. *Chekhov: Plays.* Methueun UK: Heinemann, 1988.
Garnett, Constance, trans. *The Duel and Other Stories.* New York: Echo Press, 1984.

Garnett, Constance, trans. *The Steppe.* Gloucester: Sutton, 1987.
Mamet, David, ed. *Uncle Vanya.* New York: Grove Press, 1988.

Literary Element Irony is the contrast between what is anticipated and what actually occurs. The unexpected twist at the end of the story—that Lushkoff did little work for Skvortsoff—makes the lawyer's comments about the value of hard work ironic.

FOCUS

Ask students how they respond when they see someone asking for money. Discuss how they feel toward the individual and whether they think about why the person might have to beg.

History & Art In the late 1800s when Chekhov wrote, Russia was still a vast, overwhelmingly agrarian society. There was a sharp contrast between the urban lifestyle of city dwellers in Moscow and St. Petersburg and the way that poor, deeply religious former serfs lived in the countryside.
Answer to Caption: *Students may feel Russia was marked by strong class differences but that members of different classes still had regular contact and that there was some social mobility.*

TEACH

Literary Analysis

Students may recall being told by English teachers to avoid the passive voice, a sentence structure in which the writer does not make clear who carried out an action. However, Chekhov, or the translator of this story, used the passive voice to good effect. When Olga enters, she "announced that the wood had been chopped." The construction avoids stating who actually chopped the wood, which the reader does not learn until the end of the story.

History & Art

In the late 1800s Russian women had few rights. A wife had no legal rights except through her husband; a widow was entitled to inherit only one-seventh of her husband's real estate.
Answer to Caption: *Unknown to Skvortsoff, Olga, his cook, played the key role in reforming Lushkoff.*

Interpretation

Point out to students that Skvortsoff obviously considers himself a good judge of character. Yet he misunderstands both his cook, whom he calls "ill-tempered" but who is actually very kind, and Lushkoff, who he believes was reformed by hard work but was actually changed by the cook's sympathy. Ask students what Chekhov might have been saying about how well upper-class Russians understood the poor. (*They did not understand the poor well at all.*)

World Literature
Selection 6

History & Art *Female Farmers* by Kazimir Malevich. Russian State Museum, St. Petersburg, Russia **Malevich used modern painting techniques to portray the life of peasant women in rural Russia.** *What role does Olga play in Chekhov's story?*

that the wood had all been chopped.

"Good! Give him half a ruble [the Russian unit of currency]," said Skvortsoff. "If he wants to he can come back and cut wood on the first day of each month. We can always find work for him."

On the first day of the month the waif made his appearance and again earned half a ruble, although he could barely stand on his legs. From that day on he often appeared in the yard and every time work was found for him. Now he would shovel snow, now put the wood-shed in order, now beat the dust out of rugs and mattresses. Every time he received from twenty to forty kopecks [one kopeck equals one-hundredth of a ruble], and once, even a pair of old trousers were sent out to him.

When Skvortsoff moved into another house he hired him to help in the packing and hauling of the furniture. This time the waif was sober, gloomy, and silent. He hardly touched the furniture, and walked behind the wagons hanging his head, not even making a pretense of appearing busy. He only shivered in the cold and became embarrassed when the carters jeered at him for his idleness, his feebleness, and his tattered, fancy overcoat. After the moving was over Skvortsoff sent for him.

"Well, I see that my words have taken effect," he said, handing him a ruble. "Here's for your pains. I see you are sober and have no objection to work. What is your name?"

"Lushkoff."

"Well, Lushkoff, I can now offer you some

ADDITIONAL LITERARY WORKS OF THE PERIOD

Futabatei, Shimei. *Ukigumo.* Novel about Japanese modernization.
Hernandez, José. *Martin Fierro.* Epic poem about an Argentinian gaucho.

London, Jack. *Call of the Wild.* Tale of a dog that returns to the wilderness.
Wharton, Edith. *Ethan Frome.* Tragic novel set in rural New England.

other, cleaner employment. Can you write?"

"I can."

"Then take this letter to a friend of mine tomorrow and you will be given some copying to do. Work hard, don't drink, and remember what I have said to you. Good-bye!"

Pleased at having put a man on the right path, Skvortsoff tapped Lushkoff kindly on the shoulder and even gave him his hand at parting. Lushkoff took the letter, and from that day forth came no more to the yard for work.

Two years went by. Then one evening, as Skvortsoff was standing at the ticket window of a theater paying for his seat, he noticed a little man beside him with a coat collar of curly fur and a worn sealskin cap. This little individual timidly asked the ticket seller for a seat in the gallery and paid for it in copper coins.

"Lushkoff, is that you?" cried Skvortsoff, recognizing in the little man his former wood-chopper. "How are you? What are you doing? How is everything with you?"

"All right. I am a notary [a clerk who certifies legal documents] now and get thirty-five rubles a month."

"Thank Heaven! That's fine! I am delighted for your sake. I am very, very glad, Lushkoff. You see, you are my godson, in a sense. I gave you a push along the right path, you know. Do you remember what a roasting I gave you, eh? I nearly had you sinking into the ground at my feet that day. Thank you, old man, for not forgetting my words."

"Thank you, too," said Lushkoff. "If I hadn't come to you then I might still have been calling myself a teacher or a student to this day. Yes, by flying to your protection I dragged myself out of a pit."

"I am very glad, indeed."

"Thank you for your kind words and deeds. You talked splendidly to me then. I am very grateful to you and to your cook. God bless that good and noble woman! You spoke finely then, and I shall be indebted to you to my dying day; but, strictly speaking, it was your cook, Olga, who saved me."

"How is that?"

"Like this. When I used to come to your house to chop wood she used to begin: 'Oh, you sot [drunkard], you! Oh, you miserable creature! There's nothing for you but ruin.' And then she would sit down opposite me and grow sad, look into my face and weep. 'Oh you unlucky man! There is no pleasure for you in this world and there will be none in the world to come. You drunkard! You will burn in hell. Oh, you unhappy one!' And so she would carry on, you know, in that strain. I can't tell you how much misery she suffered, how many tears she shed for my sake. But the chief thing was—she used to chop the wood for me. Do you know, sir, that I did not chop one single stick of wood for you? She did it all. Why this saved me, why I changed, why I stopped drinking at the sight of her I cannot explain. I only know that, owing to her words and noble deeds a change took place in my heart; she set me right and I shall never forget it. However, it is time to go now; there goes the bell."

Lushkoff bowed and departed to the gallery.

RESPONDING TO LITERATURE

1. Explain how the beggar Lushkoff's character and behavior change between the beginning of Chekhov's story and the conclusion of the story.
2. Contrast Skvortsoff's plan for helping Lushkoff improve his life and what actually helped Lushkoff.
3. What advice do you think Chekhov would give to people today who want to help the poor?
4. **Predicting an Outcome** What might have happened if Skvortsoff had found out immediately that Olga was chopping the wood for Lushkoff?

ANSWERS TO RESPONDING TO LITERATURE

1. Lushkoff stops drinking and begging and takes a respectable job as a notary.
2. Skvortsoff thought he would help Lushkoff by giving him work. Instead, Olga helped him by showing real concern.
3. Students may feel Chekhov was saying that people should help the poor out of genuine compassion, not a sense of superiority.
4. He probably would have stopped hiring Lushkoff. He probably would have scolded Olga.

ASSESS

Assign **Responding to Literature** questions.

CLOSE

After students have read the excerpt, point out to them that Chekhov came from a very humble background. Ask them to discuss whether Chekhov was sympathetic to Lushkoff when he was a beggar. Does Chekhov seem to blame society in general or Lushkoff himself for Lushkoff's poverty? (*Since Lushkoff reforms through his own efforts, Chekhov seems to point to individual responsibility for poverty in this story.*)

Contemporary Connection

The Cherry Orchard and other Chekhov plays are often presented by regional theater companies. Students may also be interested in watching the film *Uncle Vanya on 42nd Street*, a play within a play that deals with a production of the famous drama by Chekhov, directed by Louis Malle.

Portfolio Project

Have students interested in issues of unemployment, poverty, and substance abuse choose and research a specific topic in one of these areas and write a brief essay.

Chapter 24 Assessment

WORLD HISTORY *Online*

Have students use the **Chapter 24 Self-Check Quiz** at worldhistory.glencoe.com to prepare for the Chapter Test.

GLENCOE TECHNOLOGY

VIDEODISC
Use MindJogger to review the chapter.

MindJogger Videoquiz

Chapter 24
Disc 3 Side B

Also available in VHS.

Answers

Using Key Terms
1. f   3. i   5. c
2. g   4. l

Using Your History Journal

Encourage students to comment on the universality and timelessness of Chekhov's subject.

Reviewing Facts

1. people married earlier and had more children; population increased; inadequate housing and sanitation; factories caused pollution; police, fire protection; city parks; more leisure-time activities for middle and working classes; emphasis on education
2. They preferred not to have the government restrict their ability to make money.
3. Smith's analysis of capitalism shaped people's understanding of capitalist economies worldwide; Marx's views influenced revolutionaries.
4. Marie and Pierre Curie discovered radium; Max Planck theorized that energy is released in units known as quanta; Albert

644 Chapter 24 *Cultural Revolution*

WORLD HISTORY *Online*

Self-Check Quiz

Visit the *World History: The Human Experience* Web site at **worldhistory.glencoe.com** and click on *Chapter 24—Self-Check Quiz* to prepare for the Chapter Test.

Using Key Terms

Write the key term that completes each sentence. Then write a sentence for each term not chosen.

a. atomic theory	g. socialism
b. evolution	h. sociology
c. laissez-faire	i. genetics
d. immigration	j. emigration
e. impressionism	k. urbanization
f. realism	l. psychology

1. In the mid-1800s artists and writers in Europe and North America developed a style called _____ that often called attention to the less fortunate members of society.
2. Supporters of _____ believe that society, directly or through the government, should own the means of production.
3. The research of Gregor Mendel laid the foundation for the development of _____, the science of heredity.
4. Freud's theory that human actions grew out of subconscious motives led to the development of the science of _____.
5. Supporters of _____ believed that people should be able to buy and sell, hire and fire, free from government interference.

Technology Activity

Using the Internet Search the Internet for a Web site that provides additional information about the history of Marxism. Use a search engine to help focus your search by using words such as *karl marx*, *history*, and *socialism*. Write a research report based on your findings. Explain Marx's stages toward true communism, and provide examples of governments that were influenced by Karl Marx's ideas.

644 Chapter 24 *Cultural Revolution*

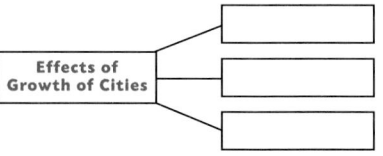
Your History Journal

After reading the literature selection from "The Beggar" by Anton Chekhov, write a review of the piece. Do you agree or disagree with Chekhov's assumptions about the poor? Why?

Reviewing Facts

1. **Society** Use a diagram like the one below to show how the growth of cities affected daily life.

Effects of Growth of Cities	
	_____
	_____
	_____

2. **Economics** Explain why business leaders during the 1800s promoted laissez-faire economics.
3. **Economics** Discuss the impact of the ideas of Adam Smith and Karl Marx on world history.
4. **Science** List the contributions of Marie Curie and other physicists and state their impact.
5. **Economics** Identify the factors that led to the rise and spread of socialism in the 1800s.
6. **Culture** Describe one work by each of these writers: Hugo, Tolstoy, Dreiser.

Critical Thinking

1. **Apply** What are three examples of the romantics' emphasis on emotion?
2. **Analyze** How did Charles Darwin's theories answer his question about the great variety of living things?
3. **Synthesize** A frame of reference is a set of ideas that determines how something will be understood. Explain how the Industrial Revolution would be viewed from a capitalistic frame of reference and a Marxist frame of reference.
4. **Evaluate** Write a letter to the editor of an 1800s newspaper, expressing your views on secondary-school education for women.

Einstein developed his theory of relativity. They laid the foundations of modern physics and the nuclear age.

5. the belief that capitalism could not remedy social ills and that equal distribution of wealth was needed; when capitalism brought some social improvements, many socialist movements discarded revolution and favored democratic means to introduce socialist reforms
6. Hugo's *Les Misérables*: romantic novel portraying human suffering with compassion; Tolstoy's *War and Peace*: realistic historical novel about Napoleon's 1812 invasion of Russia; Dreiser's *An American Tragedy*: naturalistic novel about a young man executed for killing his pregnant girlfriend

Critical Thinking

1. Answers may include examples from painting, literature, or music.

5. Analyze The painting *Dinner at Haddo House* shows the lifestyle of the wealthy. How did this show of wealth further separate social classes?

Understanding Themes

1. Change According to Karl Marx, what steps would societies follow in moving toward the goal of communism?

2. Innovation Describe one innovation of the 1800s and early 1900s in each of these sciences: biology, physics, psychology. How did each innovation affect people's lives?

3. Movement How did improved methods of transportation affect the movement of people and products?

4. Innovation Select a cultural movement such as romanticism, realism, symbolism, impressionism, or Postimpressionism, and explain how the movement reflected the way people felt about changes in the 1800s.

Explain why modern Russia has turned to capitalism from the radical Socialism born during the Industrial Revolution.

Skill Practice

Using your communications software, type a message to another student naming your favorite writer or artist from one of the following artistic movements. Explain why this artist is your favorite.
- Romanticism
- Realism
- Symbolism
- Impressionism
- Postimpressionism

Geography in History

1. Place Refer to the map "Population Growth in the United Kingdom." What were the major industrial cities of the United Kingdom by 1900?

2. Place How much did the population per square mile in the London and Bristol areas grow during this period?

Chapter 24 *Cultural Revolution* 645

2. **INNOVATION** discovery of bacteria led to new approaches in disease prevention; discovery of X rays led to new diagnostic methods in medicine; theory of the unconscious led to psychoanalysis

3. **MOVEMENT** People became more mobile. Railroads enabled people to eat food grown elsewhere and encouraged travel.

4. **INNOVATION** Answers should reflect an understanding of cultural movements.

Answers should mention the strengths of the free market in promoting economic growth and material prosperity, while communism with its controls failed to provide incentives for work and the goods and services that people wanted.

Skill Practice
Messages will vary depending on the writer or artist chosen by the students. Make sure the students have used the steps for sending E-mail as described on page 634.

Geography in History
1. London, Bristol, Liverpool, Glasgow, Dublin
2. London: from over 100 people per square mile to over 200 per square mile; Bristol: by no more than 20 people per square mile

Chapter Bonus Test Question

Ask: How would you respond to the romantic poet Keats's famous statement, "Beauty is truth, truth beauty,—that is all/Ye know on earth, and all ye need to know"? *(Keats's statement reflects the romantics' rejection of the increasing mechanization of industrialized society.)*

2. Natural selection explained that only those species best adapted to their environment survive.

3. Answers should mention the capitalist's faith in the self-regulating marketplace to provide benefits for all with minimal government involvement and the Marxist belief in the importance of class conflict, the revolutionary overthrow of capitalism by the workers, and the creation of a classless society.

4. Answers may focus on the equality of men and women.

5. It emphasized the great gap between rich and poor.

Understanding Themes
1. **CHANGE** primitive, slave, feudal, and capitalist—before the proletariat seized control, creating a society without private property, class distinctions, or government

Chapter 24 *Cultural Revolution* 645

A complete, 1-page lesson plan is provided for each section in the *Reproducible Lesson Plans* booklet.

Democracy and Reform

CHAPTER RESOURCES

	Reproducible Resources	Multimedia Resources
Chapter Opener	Chapter Themes: Graphic Organizer 25 Historical Significance Chapter Activity 25	MindJogger Videoquiz
Chapter Enrichment	Vocabulary Activity 25* Time Line Activity 25 Mapping History Activity 25 History Simulation 25 Geography and History Activity 25 Source Reading 25 People in World History Profiles 47, 48 World Art and Music Activity 25 Enrichment Activity 25 Critical Thinking Activity 25 Skill Reinforcement Activity 25 Performance Assessment Activity 25 Standardized Test Practice Workbook Activity 25 Inclusion for the Social Studies Classroom Strategies and Activities	World History and Art Transparency 33, *The Banjo Lesson* Mapping History Overlay Transparency 16, *Global Ancestry of Americans* Chapter Transparency 25 Vocabulary PuzzleMaker Software World Music: Cultural Traditions, Lessons 1, 2, 3, 10 Lessons of War: *Why Soldiers Fight* World History Primary Source Document Library
Chapter Review/Reteaching	Reteaching Activity 25 Skill Reinforcement Activity 25 Spanish Chapter Summary 25	Chapter 25 Digest Audiocassette, Activity, Test* Vocabulary PuzzleMaker Software Interactive Tutor Self-Assessment Software MindJogger Videoquiz
Chapter Evaluation/Testing	Performance Assessment Activity 25 Chapter 25 Test, Forms A and B	ExamView® Pro Testmaker

* Also available in Spanish

0:00 OUT OF TIME? Assign the Chapter 25 Audiocassettes.

World History Primary Source Document Library

Make History Come Alive!

Engage your students with over 250 easily accessible primary source documents—available on this CD-ROM—that will give them real life insight into the important events of world history.

Block Schedule

Activities that are particularly suited to use within the block scheduling framework are identified throughout this chapter by the following designation.

KEY TO ABILITY LEVELS

Teaching strategies are coded for varying learning styles.

L1   BASIC activities for all students
L2   AVERAGE activities for average to above-average students
L3   CHALLENGING activities for above-average students
LEP   LIMITED ENGLISH PROFICIENCY activities

Use Glencoe's *Presentation Plus!* multimedia teacher tool to easily present dynamic lessons that visually excite your students. Using Microsoft PowerPoint® you can customize the presentations to create your own personalized lessons.

Interactive Lesson Planner

Planning has never been easier! Using this CD-ROM, organize your week, month, semester, or year with all the help you need. The **Interactive Lesson Planner** gives you access to all of the blackline masters that accompany *World History: The Human Experience.*

SECTION RESOURCES

Daily Objectives	Reproducible Resources	Multimedia Resources
Section 1 **Reform in Great Britain** Describe how political change came to Great Britain during the 1800s.	Lecture Notes 25-1 Reproducible Lesson Plan 25-1 Vocabulary Activity 25* Guided Reading Activity 25-1* Time Line Activity 25 History Simulation 25 Section Quiz 25-1* Reading Essentials and Study Guide 25-1	Section Focus Transparency 25-1 Chapter Transparency 25 Interactive Tutor Self-Assessment Software Testmaker World Music: Cultural Traditions, Lesson 3
Section 2 **The Dominions** Relate how new societies emerged in Canada, Australia, and New Zealand.	Lecture Notes 25-2 Reproducible Lesson Plan 25-2 Vocabulary Activity 25* Guided Reading Activity 25-2* Geography and History Activity 25 Section Quiz 25-2* Reading Essentials and Study Guide 25-2	Section Focus Transparency 25-2 Interactive Tutor Self-Assessment Software Testmaker World Music: Cultural Traditions, Lesson 10
Section 3 **Political Struggles in France** Identify the changes in government that France underwent during the 1800s.	Lecture Notes 25-3 Reproducible Lesson Plan 25-3 Vocabulary Activity 25* Guided Reading Activity 25-3* Section Quiz 25-3* Reading Essentials and Study Guide 25-3	Section Focus Transparency 25-3 Interactive Tutor Self-Assessment Software Testmaker
Section 4 **Expansion of the United States** Explain how the United States changed during the 1800s.	Lecture Notes 25-4 Reproducible Lesson Plan 25-4 Vocabulary Activity 25* Guided Reading Activity 25-4* People in World History Profile 47 Section Quiz 25-4* Reading Essentials and Study Guide 25-4	Section Focus Transparency 25-4 World History and Art Transparency 33, *The Banjo Lesson* Mapping History Overlay Transparency 16, *Global Ancestry of Americans* Interactive Tutor Self-Assessment Software World Music: Cultural Traditions, Lesson 1 Lessons of War: *Why Soldiers Fight*
Section 5 **Latin American Independence** Relate how the countries of Latin America won independence.	Lecture Notes 25-5 Reproducible Lesson Plan 25-5 Guided Reading Activity 25-5* People in World History Profile 48 Reteaching Activity 25 Enrichment Activity 25 Section Quiz 25-5* Performance Assessment Activity 25 Spanish Chapter Summary 25 Reading Essentials and Study Guide 25-5	Section Focus Transparency 25-5 Vocabulary PuzzleMaker Software Interactive Tutor Self-Assessment Software Testmaker World Music: Cultural Traditions, Lesson 2

* Also available in Spanish

Chapter Activities

 Performance Assessment Activity

An Import/Export Company Organize students into groups that will assume the roles of owners of an import/export company. First, each group will review the expansions and reforms of the era and predict how various parts of the world would be different today if none of these had occurred—including differences today in government, foreign affairs, trade, language, travel and tourism, and economics. Each group will then create five scenarios of how they would acquire merchandise for their companies from different parts of the world studied in this chapter. Each scenario should reflect the long-term effects of one of the expansions or reforms.

Possible Rubric Features
Accuracy of content information; collaborative skills; logical predicting; plausibility of scenarios; and thoroughness in including criteria related to government, trade, language, foreign affairs, economics, and tourism

• *For an additional activity, refer to Activity 25 in the* Performance Assessment Strategies and Activities *booklet.*

ACTIVITY

From the Classroom of...

**Chuck Kloes
Beverly Hills High
School
Beverly Hills, CA**

**The Irish Question: A
Solution Satisfactory to
Whom?**

Prepare "point of view" sheets for both sides of the Irish question—Sheet A listing four to five arguments in support of granting home rule to all of Ireland, and Sheet B listing four to five arguments in support of maintaining British control over Northern Ireland. Organize the class into A and B groups to debate the question and pass out the sheets. Give the groups 15 minutes to study the sheets, collect data, and prepare their presentations. Have each group select two students to be spokespersons, with you acting as moderator. After the debate, hold a class discussion about what students learned from the exercise.

MULTIPLE LEARNING STYLES

Verbal/Linguistic
Tell students to imagine going on a tour of Europe and North and South America during the 1800s. Have them keep a journal of their travels and record their impressions of culture, environment, society, and special events.

Logical/Mathematical
Have students create a time line that tracks the major political, social, and cultural struggles of the period. Ask students to include details from the text as well as class presentations.

Visual/Spatial
Have students make a large wall map of the Oregon, Santa Fe, and California Trails. Have them mark key physical geographic features and main stopping places.

Auditory/Musical
Ask students to research and report on the music of this period in Europe, the British dominions, the United States, or Latin America. They might select a sample from each area or concentrate on just one location. They may present their findings to the class.

GLENCOE'S ASSESSMENT ADVANTAGE

Use the following to easily assess student learning in a variety of ways.

- Performance Assessment Strategies and Activities
- Section Quizzes
- Chapter and Unit Tests
- Interactive Tutor Self-Assessment Software
- Testmaker Software
- MindJogger Videoquiz
- SAT/SAT II Test Practice
- worldhistory.glencoe.com

Additional Resources

NATIONAL GEOGRAPHIC SOCIETY — Teacher's Corner

INDEX TO NATIONAL GEOGRAPHIC MAGAZINE

The following articles relate to this chapter:

- "El Libertador: Simón Bolívar," by Bryan Hodgson, March 1994.
- "The Itch to Move West: Life and Death on the Oregon Trail," by Boyd Gibbons, August 1986.
- "The Travail of Ireland," by Joseph Judge, April 1981.

NATIONAL GEOGRAPHIC SOCIETY PRODUCTS AVAILABLE FROM GLENCOE

To order the following call Glencoe at 1-800-334-7344:

- *GTV: The American People (Videodiscs)*
- *GTV: A Geographic Perspective on American History (Videodiscs)*

ADDITIONAL NATIONAL GEOGRAPHIC SOCIETY PRODUCTS

To order the following call National Geographic at 1-800-368-2728:

- *Heritage of the Black West (Video)*
- *Democratic Government Series: France, United Kingdom (Videos)*
- *Australia's Aborigines (Video and Videodisc)*

Access National Geographic's new dynamic MapMachine Web site and other geography resources at:

- http://www.nationalgeographic.com/
- http://www.nationalgeographic.com/maps/

BIBLIOGRAPHY

Literature of the Period
Eliot, George. *The Mill on the Floss.* New York: Bantam, 1987. Novel explores family relationships while taking a critical look at British middle-class values.

Readings for the Student
Davis, William C., ed. *Touched by Fire: A Photographic Portrait of the Civil War.* Boston: Little, Brown, 1985. Portrays the tragedy of the American Civil War.

Readings for the Teacher
Hoppen, K. Theodore. *Ireland Since 1800: Conflict and Conformity.* White Plains, NY: Longman, 1989. This survey of Irish history examines the social, economic, and political aspects of recent Irish history.

WORLD HISTORY Online

Use our Web site as an additional resource. All essential content is covered in the Student Edition.

You and your students can visit the *World History: The Human Experience* Web site at worldhistory. glencoe.com The student text directs students to the Web site for the following options:

- **Chapter Overviews**
- **Student Web Activities**
- **Self-Check Quizzes**

Answers are provided for you in a link entitled "Web Activity Lesson Plan." Additional Web Resources, Interactive Puzzles, and content updates are also available.

Visit the Glencoe Web site at socialstudies. glencoe.com for social studies activities, updates, and links to other resources.

LOCAL OBJECTIVES

_____
_____
_____
_____
_____
_____
_____
_____
_____
_____
_____
_____
_____
_____
_____
_____
_____
_____
_____

Storyteller

Historical Setting Richard Cobden, an English political leader and economist, became a great supporter of the democratic movement and of laws to protect the interests of the middle class. Cobden worked for peace and argued against the British foreign policy of intervention to maintain the balance of power. He was a strong advocate of free trade and played a key role in the fight to repeal the Corn Law.

Historical Significance

Answers: *Ideals of individual liberty and self-government spread among the middle and working classes who demanded the vote and social reforms; Latin Americans broke with Spain and set up independent republics; however, democracy was often elusive.*

Have students use the **Chapter 25 Overview** at worldhistory. glencoe.com as a prereading and postreading exercise for understanding chapter content.

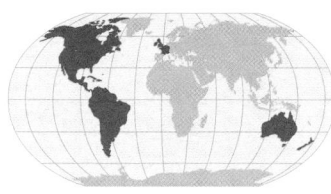

Chapter
25 1800–1914
Democracy and Reform

Chapter Themes

▶ **Change** Great Britain carries out democratic reforms. *Section 1*
▶ **Movement** Immigrants settle Canada, Australia, and New Zealand. *Section 2*
▶ **Revolution** France undergoes political upheaval during the 1800s. *Section 3*
▶ **Change** The United States extends its borders and develops its economy. *Section 4*
▶ **Nationalism** Latin American nations achieve self-government. *Section 5*

Storyteller

British politician Richard Cobden stood before the House of Commons in 1845. In a loud voice, he demanded that the middle and working classes be given more representation in a government that unfairly favored the landed aristocracy. Cobden declared:

"I say without being revolutionary … that the sooner the power of this country is transferred from the landed ruling class, which has so misused it, and is placed absolutely … in the hands of the intelligent middle and industrious classes, the better for the condition and destinies of this country."

While Cobden worked for change within the British political system, people in Europe and Latin America faced fiercer and often bloody struggles for democratic reform. By the end of the 1800s, democracy had triumphed in many parts of the world.

Historical Significance

Why did democratic reform movements develop and flourish in Europe and other parts of the world? How did independence change the lives of people in Latin America?

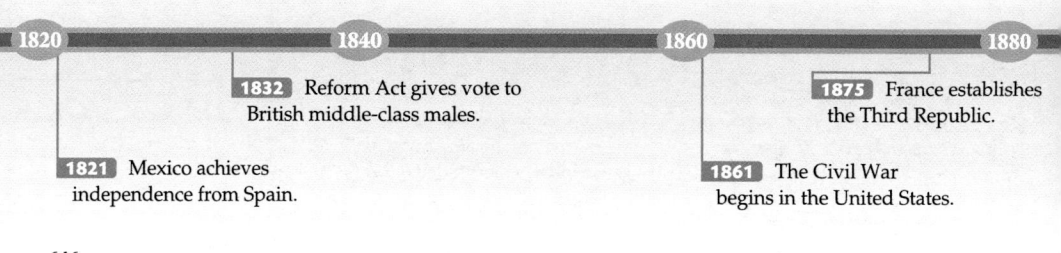

1820	1840	1860	1880

1832 Reform Act gives vote to British middle-class males.

1875 France establishes the Third Republic.

1821 Mexico achieves independence from Spain.

1861 The Civil War begins in the United States.

646

GEOGRAPHY CONNECTION

Location Using a world map, have students use a scale of miles to estimate distance between Great Britain and Australia *(approximately 8,000 miles [13,000 km])* and the distance between Spain and Ecuador *(approximately 6,000 miles [10,000 km])*. Ask students what effect these distances might have on the relationship between the country and the colony. *(It might have made it difficult for the countries to govern their distant colonies efficiently or knowledgeably; it might have increased the colonies' desire for independence.)*

Celebration of the Concorde of May 21, 1848 by Jean Jacques Champin. Musée de la Ville de Paris, Musée Carnavalet, Paris, France

History & Art The work to build the Place de la Concorde began in 1755. Almost a hundred years later, during the reign of Louis-Philippe, it was completed with the addition of the Egyptian obelisk. The Place de la Concorde has been the arena for many historic events including guillotine executions in the 1790s.

✔ Performance Assessment

Refer to the activity on page 646C of the Planning Guide.

📂 For an additional activity, refer to Activity 25 in the *Performance Assessment Strategies and Activities* booklet.

Using Your History Journal

Suggest that students use colored pencils or pens to color code the territories on their maps. They should label neatly with black pen.

WORLD HISTORY Online

Chapter Overview

Visit the *World History: The Human Experience* Web site at **worldhistory.glencoe.com** and click on **Chapter 25—Chapter Overview** to preview the chapter.

Your History Journal

On an outline map of the world, draw and label all the territories once held by Great Britain and the dates when they became self-governing, or independent.

GLENCOE TECHNOLOGY

 VIDEODISC
Use MindJogger to preview chapter content.

MindJogger Videoquiz

 Chapter 25
Disc 4 Side A

 Also available in VHS.

➕ EXTRA CREDIT PROJECT

Research To further their understanding of the period covered in this chapter, have students investigate one of the following topics: the potato famine of 1845–1847, schools and education on the frontier, the California gold rush, the Dreyfus affair, or the penal colonies of Australia. Ask students to prepare an outline first, then write the report and present it to the class. **L2**

1825	1850	1875	1900

1837 Victoria becomes queen of Great Britain.

1867 Reform Act extends vote to all male homeowners and renters.

1886 Gladstone introduces Irish home rule legislation.

1900 Trade unionists and Socialists begin to form the Labour party.

SECTION THEME

▶ **Change** Great Britain carries out democratic reforms.

Guide to Reading

For reading strategies to help students read effectively see pages 12–13. Have students think about the main head as they read the subheads.

Vocabulary Pre-check

■ Use the Vocabulary PuzzleMaker for Chapter 25 to create a crossword puzzle to reinforce section terms. **L1 LEP**

▢ Use Vocabulary Activity 25 to introduce vocabulary terms. **L1 LEP**

FOCUS

Section Objective

Describe how political change came to Britain during the 1800s.

BELLRINGER
Motivational Activity

Before taking roll at the beginning of the class period, project Section Focus Transparency 25-1 and have students answer the activity questions. Discuss students' responses.

▢ This activity is also available as a blackline master.

Section 1

Reform in Great Britain

Guide to Reading

Read to Find Out
Main Idea *Political change came peacefully to Great Britain during the 1800s.*

▶ **Terms to Define**
apportion, disenfranchised, suffragette, home rule

▶ **People to Meet**
the Chartists, Queen Victoria, William Gladstone, Benjamin Disraeli, the Fabians, Emmeline Pankhurst, Charles Stewart Parnell

▶ **Places to Locate**
Ireland

S_toryteller_

When women first lobbied for voting rights, some critics feared that if they won the vote, men would become women's servants. Political cartoons and works of art appeared that showed sour-faced men caring for babies and wringing out dirty laundry, while women happily rode around in carriages or talked excitedly around the ballot box. Other opponents claimed that if women won the vote, they would spend all their time at the polls. One poster nicknamed a woman who ran for office "Susan Sharp-Tongue, the Celebrated Man Tamer."

Woman suffrage rally

—adapted from *On To Victory, Propaganda Plays of the Woman Suffrage Movement,* edited by Bettina Friedl, 1987

olitical change in Great Britain took place gradually and peacefully. The British government moved toward greater democracy through evolution rather than revolution. By the 1800s Great Britain was a limited constitutional monarchy. The monarch's authority consisted only of the rights to encourage, to warn, and to be consulted by those who really governed Great Britain. Actual executive power belonged to the Cabinet led by the prime minister, while Parliament maintained legislative control.

Although all British people in theory were represented in the House of Commons, the British government was not a true democracy in the early 1800s. Political power remained with the landed aristocracy, while the middle and working classes had no voting rights.

Electoral Reforms

In the early 1800s some rural districts were well represented in the House of Commons, while growing industrial areas had little representation. Factory workers, farm laborers, and the middle class began to demand that they receive a greater political voice. The liberal minority party, the Whigs, continually introduced bills to give voting rights to more people and to apportion, or divide and share, electoral districts more fairly. The Whigs' efforts were repeatedly defeated by the Tory party, which opposed such bills.

When the Whigs came to political power in 1830, however, their demands could no longer be ignored. In 1832 the Whigs forced the king to announce that he would create as many new lords as necessary to give the reform bill a majority in the House of Lords. To avoid this action, the lords gave in and passed the bill.

SECTION RESOURCES

▢ **Reproducible Masters**
- Lecture Notes 25-1
- Reproducible Lesson Plan 25-1
- Vocabulary Activity 25
- Guided Reading Activity 25-1
- Time Line Activity 25
- History Simulation 25

- Section Quiz 25-1
- Reading Essentials and Study Guide 25-1

Transparencies
- Section Focus Transparency 25-1
- Chapter Transparency 25

Multimedia
■ Interactive Tutor Self-Assessment Software
■ Testmaker
♫ World Music: Cultural Traditions, Lesson 3

The Reform Act of 1832

The Reform Act of 1832 lowered the property qualifications for voting and gave more middle-class males the right to vote. The proportion of voters increased from 1 in 100 to 1 in 32 men. The act also took representation rights away from areas that had declined in population. With 143 seats freed in the House of Commons, the heavily populated cities finally increased their representation. One observer recalled the moments after the passing of the reform bill:

❝ We shook hands and clapped each other on the back, and went out laughing, crying ... into the lobby. And no sooner were the outer doors opened than another shout answered that within the House. All the passages ... were thronged by people who had waited till four in the morning to know the issue [outcome]. ❞

Reform Movements

While the Reform Act gave middle-class men the right to vote, it only frustrated the industrial and farm workers, who remained disenfranchised, or deprived of the right to vote. These disenfranchised citizens banded together to demand further reforms. In a document called *A People's Charter*, **the Chartists**, an important reform group of the working class, proposed political changes. The Chartists' demands included voting rights for all adult men, no property qualifications for voting, a secret ballot, salaries for members of Parliament so that the middle and lower classes could take seats, and equal electoral districts.

The Chartists submitted two petitions to Parliament, one with more than a million signatures and the other with more than 3 million. Parliament rejected both petitions. After the defeat, the Chartists had little success and their movement faded by the 1850s. Parliament did, however, eventually pass many of their reforms.

Another reform movement, the Anti-Corn Law League, was supported by the middle class. The aim of the League was to repeal the Corn Law, which since 1815 had severely limited and taxed the importation of foreign grain. Wealthy landowners benefited from the law, as it ensured them a profitable hold on the grain market. Middle-class industrialists fought the Corn Law because it forced them to pay higher wages to workers to enable them to buy bread.

The League—the first major political pressure group in Great Britain—captured public attention with lectures, pamphlets, books, and meetings.

Visualizing History In this British cartoon, Prime Minister Benjamin Disraeli presents the crown of India to Queen Victoria. *What other noted prime minister served during Victoria's reign?*

When an Irish crop failure forced Great Britain to import much grain, Parliament responded to the pressure and repealed the Corn Law.

Political Parties

One result of electoral reform was more elaborate organization of political parties. Before 1800 both parties—the Tories and the Whigs—represented wealthy landowners. They had no formal organization. They were actually loose groups of politicians with common interests. As more middle-class men gained voting rights, the old parties reorganized to win support from the new voters. After 1832 the Tory and Whig parties began to change into the modern Conservative and Liberal parties.

Support for the Conservative party came largely from the aristocracy and members of the old Tory party. The industrial and commercial classes and members of the old Whig party supported the Liberal party. Both parties eventually competed for middle-class and working-class votes.

Political Leadership

This era of political reform took place during the reign of **Queen Victoria**. She came to the throne in 1837 at age 18 and reigned for 64 years. Two brilliant prime ministers—**William Gladstone** and **Benjamin Disraeli**—served during Victoria's reign. Both men offered dynamic leadership for the

Chapter 25 Democracy and Reform **649**

Chapter 25 Section 1

TEACH

Guided Practice

THEME Change

Work with students to create a chart on the chalkboard listing the changes caused by the Reform Act of 1832. **L1 LEP**

Visualizing History The rise of British political cartoons came with the movement toward greater democracy. These caricatures became a popular way to communicate political messages and influence voters. In this cartoon the artist is commenting on the well-known fact that Queen Victoria was very fond of Disraeli and had offered him a peerage.
Answer to Caption: *William Gladstone*

Diagram Have students list events that influenced the democratic reform movement in Great Britain during the 1800s. *(Whigs coming to power in 1830, formation of the Chartists)* Help students make a diagram showing the cause-and-effect relationships between these events and specific reforms. **L2**

Debate Have students take the following roles: industrial workers, middle-class landowners, and members of the House of Lords. Lead an impromptu debate on the Reform Act of 1832. **L3**

📁 History Simulation 25

🔖 Chapter Transparency 25

🎵 World Music: Cultural Traditions, Lesson 3

COOPERATIVE LEARNING ACTIVITY

Role Play Have students form groups to role-play a visit to Ireland by members of the British Parliament. Tell students to imagine that they are living in the mid-1800s and that some members of Parliament are visiting Ireland to hear the people's views on home rule. Select one group of five or six students to be observers. Have remaining students represent: members of Parliament who oppose or favor home rule, Irish Catholics, and a group of Irish Protestants. Have students who have assumed roles debate the issue of home rule. At the conclusion of the debate, have the observers comment on the effectiveness of each faction's arguments. **L2**

Independent Practice

 Guided Reading Activity 25-1 **L1**

Time Line Activity 25

Geography: Location Using the Atlas in their textbook, have students locate Ireland and write a brief paragraph about the conflict between the Irish and the British, focusing especially on the locations of the places. **L1 LEP**

Women Ask students to investigate the Women's Social Political Union or the lives of Emmeline, Christabel, and Sylvia Pankhurst and report on the women's rights movements. Ask them to describe the strategies used to gain public support and then tell whether they agree with the strategies. **L2**

Critical Thinking Have students recall the cultural, economic, and political history of Great Britain and how it may have contributed to a male, landowner-dominated political system. Ask them to list specific changes that may have brought about the reevaluation of this political system in the 1800s. *(the Industrial Revolution)* **L3**

Linking Past and Present

Protests To publicize their cause, British suffragists went to extraordinary lengths, including arson, bombing of monuments, window smashing, and hunger strikes. These tactics were also used by Vietnam War protesters in the 1960s.

Have students use the **Chapter 25 Student Web Activity** at worldhistory.glencoe.com for in-depth study of Queen Victoria.

Liberal and Conservative parties. With their help Great Britain continued toward democracy.

William Gladstone

William Gladstone of the Liberal party served 4 times as prime minister between 1868 and 1894. His first term, from 1868 to 1874, became known as the Great Ministry because of his many social reforms. Deeply religious, Gladstone always sought to apply morality to politics.

Gladstone directed reforms in such areas as government administration, education, and elections. A civil service reform of 1870 made appointments to most civil service positions dependent on competitive examinations. The Education Act of 1870 divided the country into school districts maintained by local control. The Ballot Act of 1872 satisfied the old Chartist demand for the secret ballot. The Redistribution Act of 1885 created electoral districts almost equal in population.

Benjamin Disraeli

Benjamin Disraeli of the Conservative party first gained fame in Great Britain as a novelist and later as a politician. He served two terms as prime minister—briefly in 1868 and from 1874 to 1880.

Disraeli believed the Conservative party could save aristocratic traditions while adopting democratic reforms. He realized that blocking change would hurt the Conservative party, whose primary support came from the upper middle class.

In 1867 Disraeli had introduced a Conservative-backed reform bill. By lowering property qualifications for voters, it extended the vote to all male homeowners and most men who rented property. The bill increased the electorate by about 1 million men, adding to it many working-class voters.

Growth of Democracy

The British government changed in the last quarter of the 1800s. As steps were taken toward democracy, the working class, women, and Irish Catholics began to influence political life.

Student Web Activity 25

Visit the *World History: The Human Experience* Web site at **worldhistory.glencoe.com** and click on *Chapter 25—Student Web Activities* for an activity relating to Queen Victoria.

Rise of Labor

Political reforms inspired many groups to fight for increased rights. Labor unions had been steadily growing and gaining political strength since the mid-1700s. By the time of Gladstone's Great Ministry, unions had become a way of life among the working classes. Laborers from nearly every trade organized into unions, which achieved great gains by staging strikes and demonstrations.

At the same time that labor unions were growing stronger, socialism was also gaining followers. In 1884 a group of middle-class intellectuals formed the Fabian Society with the aim of peacefully and gradually preparing the way for a Socialist government. Through education, its members promoted social justice such as improved conditions for workers. Unlike unions, **the Fabians** favored parliamentary action over strikes and demonstrations.

In 1900 trade unionists and Socialists laid the foundation for a new political party—the Labour party—to speak for the working class. Labour party supporters backed the reform-minded Liberal government elected in 1906. Together the Liberal and Labour members of Parliament promoted government reform to improve workers' lives. Between 1906 and 1914, new legislation provided the working classes with old-age pensions, a minimum wage, unemployment assistance, and health and unemployment insurance.

A Constitutional Crisis

To finance these measures, the Liberal government called for higher taxes in the budget of 1909. The largely Conservative House of Lords vehemently opposed the proposed taxation, because it directly threatened the wealth of the aristocracy.

The contest ended when the 1911 Parliament Act narrowed the powers of the House of Lords by removing money bills from their control. This action symbolized the aristocracy's political decline.

Women Demand Greater Rights

Women also sought to benefit from Great Britain's move toward more representative democracy. British women, mostly from the middle class, spoke out for political and social equality in the mid-1800s. In the 1850s women's rights activists fought to win property rights for married women. The Married Women's Property Acts of 1870 and 1882 gave women increased legal control over a family's earnings and property.

Achieving women's voting rights came more slowly. Although women had gained the right to vote in local elections in 1869, they still could not vote on a national level. In 1903 **Emmeline**

Mixed Learners Because of the large amount of information conveyed in this chapter, allow students with learning disabilities to work in study groups. Help them to graphically organize the material by using time lines, charts, and diagrams to show relationships and to serve as study aids. Encourage students who need challenges to explore the section topics in detail. Direct them to key events that had major repercussions or that typify other similar situations. Have students look for cause-and-effect relationships. Establish a forum by which students can share their research with the class in a meaningful way, such as by a panel discussion. **L2**

Pankhurst and her two daughters, Christabel and Sylvia, founded the Women's Social and Political Union (WSPU). They led a voting rights campaign on behalf of all British women and became known as suffragettes. The WSPU attracted attention to its cause through street demonstrations and hunger strikes. The violence cost the movement much support. Nevertheless, the movement grew. In 1918 Parliament finally granted women over 30—along with all men—the right to vote. Ten years later, it gave the vote to all women over 21.

Ireland

Like others in the British Isles, Irish Catholics sought greater participation in government. Their ultimate goal, however, was to govern themselves. For centuries, English and Scottish Protestants who had settled in **Ireland** enjoyed almost total political and economic control. They owned much land, which they rented at high prices to Irish Catholic peasants, who were prohibited from purchasing it. Most Irish people lived in poverty. Ireland was predominantly Catholic, and a law requiring Catholics to pay taxes to the Anglican Church of Ireland only intensified anti-British feeling.

In 1801 Parliament had passed the Act of Union, joining Ireland and Great Britain. This union entitled Ireland to representation in Parliament, but it was not until 1829 that Catholics in the British Isles won the right to vote and hold office. Although these acts increased their rights, most Irish people still demanded to rule themselves.

Irish hatred of British rule heightened when a disastrous potato famine known as the "Great Hunger" hit the country in the 1840s. Because peasants were forced to export the grain they grew in order to pay their high rents, they came to rely on the potato as their main source of food. In 1845 a

Visualizing History Irish activists seeking home rule riot in Belfast in 1872. *What minority group controlled most of the land in Ireland for centuries?*

deadly fungus destroyed much of the potato crop, and the British government sent inadequate aid. In four years, at least one million Irish died of starvation and disease. Millions more emigrated to the United States, Canada, and Australia.

Various groups fought for Irish rights. **Charles Stewart Parnell** led Irish nationalists seeking a debate on home rule, or self-government, in Parliament. Liberal Prime Minister Gladstone tried to pass legislation granting Irish home rule, but the measure was defeated. In 1914 Parliament finally passed a home rule bill, but it never went into effect. Irish Protestants threatened to fight British troops if Parliament enforced it.

SECTION 1 ASSESSMENT

Main Idea

1. Use a diagram like the one below to show how Great Britain changed politically in the 1800s.

Political Change in Great Britain

Recall

2. **Define** apportion, disenfranchised, suffragette, home rule.
3. **Identify** the Chartists, Anti-Corn Law League, Queen Victoria, William Gladstone, Benjamin Disraeli, the Fabians, Emmeline Pankhurst, Charles Stewart Parnell.

Critical Thinking

4. **Synthesizing Information** Imagine that you are an Irish Catholic farmworker in Ireland in the 1800s. Express your feelings and attitudes about British rule.

Understanding Themes

5. **Change** What might have happened if Parliament had opposed democratic reform?

Chapter 25 *Democracy and Reform* 651

SECTION 1 ASSESSMENT ANSWERS

1. voting rights for more people; electoral districts apportioned more fairly; growth of reform groups, democracy, labor unions, socialism; political parties better organized; power of House of Lords narrowed
2. All terms are defined in the Glossary.
3. Chartists, 649; Anti-Corn Law League, 649; Queen Victoria, 649; William Gladstone, 649; Benjamin Disraeli, 649; the Fabians, 650; Emmeline Pankhurst, 651; Charles Stewart Parnell, 651
4. Answers will vary but should include a sense of anger and frustration.
5. **CHANGE** Possible answer: British lower classes might have staged a revolution against the ruling classes.

ASSESS

Check for Understanding

Assign Section 1 Assessment as homework or as an in-class activity.

◉ Use Interactive Tutor Self-Assessment Software to review Section 1.

Visualizing History The population of the city of Belfast in 1872 was largely Protestant with much opposition to home rule.
Answer to Caption: *English and Scottish Protestants*

Evaluate

📂 Section Quiz 25-1

◉ Use the Testmaker to create a customized quiz for Section 1.

Reteach

Have students review the material and write one sentence that summarizes the key idea under each heading in the section.

📂 Reading Essentials and Study Guide 25-1

Enrich

Have students imagine that they are journalists working for a political magazine in the 1830s. Have them write an article on the growth of democracy in Great Britain, focusing on the people who have recently been given the vote and those who are still struggling to obtain it.

CLOSE

Have students write six newspaper headlines that report the main ideas discussed in this section.

1850   1875   1900   1925

1840 Treaty of Waitangi guarantees Maori rights in New Zealand.

1867 British North America Act forms the Dominion of Canada.

1885 Canadian Pacific Railway links eastern and western parts of Canada.

1901 Australia becomes a dominion in the British Empire.

SECTION THEME

▶ **Movement** Immigrants from Great Britain and other countries settle Canada, Australia, and New Zealand.

Guide to Reading

For reading strategies to help students read effectively see pages 12–13.

Vocabulary Pre-check

 Use the Vocabulary PuzzleMaker for Chapter 25 to create a crossword puzzle to reinforce section terms. **L1 LEP**

Use Vocabulary Activity 25 to introduce vocabulary terms. **L1 LEP**

FOCUS

Section Objective

Relate how new societies emerged in Canada, Australia, and New Zealand.

BELLRINGER
Motivational Activity

 Before taking roll at the beginning of the class period, project Section Focus Transparency 25-2 and have students answer the activity questions. Discuss students' responses.

This activity is also available as a blackline master.

Section 2

The Dominions

Guide to Reading

Read to Find Out
Main Idea *New societies emerged in Canada, Australia, and New Zealand.*

▶ **Terms to Define**
   dominion

▶ **People to Meet**
   the Loyalists, Lord Durham, John A. Macdonald, the Aborigines, the Maori

▶ **Places to Locate**
   Canada, Australia, New Zealand

 The Storyteller

On the long sea voyage to Australia, first-class passengers could go anywhere on board; other passengers, traveling more cheaply, were more restricted. Seamen were most restricted of all, and after three months on board, got their revenge for staying below-deck in curious ways. Sometimes the crew would protest their rights by tossing a pig or sheep down among the cabins at night, to invade the passengers' space and keep them awake. One emigrant wrote in her diary: "From every quarter of the cabin you could hear the 'Ma, Ma' during the greater part of the night."

—adapted from *Sailing to Australia*, Andrew Hassam, 1994

Immigrant mother and children

As Great Britain moved toward greater democracy, the British Empire reached its height. With its colonies making up one-fourth of the world's land and people, Great Britain became the richest and most powerful country in the world. Political changes also took place in the empire, especially in territories largely inhabited by British settlers. Colonies such as **Canada**, **Australia**, and **New Zealand** sought self-government.

Canada

By the mid-1800s, Canada consisted of a number of British colonies dependent on the British government. The colonial population was ethnically divided. One part was French, another immigrant British, and a third part descendants of **the Loyalists**—Americans loyal to Great Britain during the American Revolution. Most Britons and Loyalists lived in Nova Scotia, New Brunswick, and near the Great Lakes. The French were concentrated in the Saint Lawrence River valley.

In 1763, as a prize for their victory in the French and Indian War, the British gained control of Quebec, which included most of French Canada. From that time, the French in Quebec firmly resisted British colonial rule. The predominantly Catholic French population were irritated by the influx of British immigrants, English-speaking and Protestant, that began about 1760.

To solve the growing English and French problem, the British government passed the Constitutional Act of 1791. This law divided Quebec into two colonies: Lower Canada and Upper Canada. Lower Canada remained French-speaking, but Upper Canada became English. Each colony had an assembly whose laws were subject to veto by a governor appointed by the British government. This arrangement worked until political differences brought rebellion in each colony.

Visualizing History Quebec City, founded in 1608, is Canada's oldest city. Located on the St. Lawrence River, Quebec City was a major lumber and ship-building center during the 1800s. *What three groups contributed to the founding of Canada?*

By the late 1830s the French began to feel threatened by the growing English-speaking minority. Meanwhile, the British-Loyalist community was divided by disagreements between the conservative upper-class leadership and a group of liberal reformers who wanted a share in government. In 1837 unrest triggered rebellions in both colonies.

Canadian Self-Government

Uprisings in both Upper Canada and Lower Canada convinced the British that they had a serious problem in North America. In 1838 the British Parliament ordered **Lord Durham** to Canada to investigate. In a report to Parliament, Durham urged granting virtual self-government to Canada. Durham insisted that the real authority should be an elected assembly, not a British-appointed governor-general or the British government in London. With acceptance of the Durham report by the British Parliament, self-government developed in Canada. This pattern was later adopted by other territories of the British Empire.

In 1867 the British Parliament passed the British North America Act. This law established Canada as a dominion, or a self-governing territory owing allegiance to the British king or queen. The British North America Act joined Upper Canada (Ontario), Lower Canada (Quebec), Nova Scotia, and New Brunswick in a confederation called the Dominion of Canada. This act became the basis of the modern nation of Canada. In that same year, Canadian voters elected their first parliament. The first Canadian prime minister was **John A. Macdonald**, a Scottish-born lawyer.

Expanding Canadian Territory

At first the Dominion of Canada consisted of four provinces in the southeast, extending from the Great Lakes to the Atlantic Ocean. Then, in 1869 the dominion acquired the Northwest Territory, which extended west across vast prairies and forestlands and north to the Arctic wilderness. Most of this area was populated by Native Americans and European and American fur traders. Following sporadic violence between traders and Native Americans, the Canadian government set up and sent westward a special law-keeping force known as the Northwest Mounted Police. The police largely won the respect and loyalty of the Native Americans before the arrival of large numbers of Canadian settlers.

Canada further expanded its territory during the late 1800s. From the eastern part of the Northwest Territory, the province of Manitoba was formed in 1870. In 1871 British Columbia, a separate British colony on the Pacific coast, became a province. In 1873 tiny Prince Edward Island near the Atlantic Ocean joined Canada. To link the eastern provinces with the western provinces, the Canadian Pacific Railway was completed in 1885. This made possible the development of the Canadian prairies. In 1905 the prairie provinces of Saskatchewan and Alberta were added to the dominion.

Australia and New Zealand

On the other side of the world—in the south and southwest Pacific—the British colonies of Australia and New Zealand also sought self-government.

Chapter 25 *Democracy and Reform* **653**

TEACH

Guided Practice

THEME Movement

Ask students to recall other periods or places where two cultures clashed as a result of colonization. *(the Spanish and the Aztec; British colonists and Native Americans)* Point out that culture clashes occurred in the British dominions. Ask students to predict how these clashes might affect the indigenous peoples in the Dominions. *(Colonization usually results in negative effects on native peoples.)* **L2**

Visualizing History It was in the mid-1820s that unemployment in Britain and Ireland spurred a great migration to Canada. Many of the people who came were fairly wealthy and educated.
Answer to Caption: *French-speaking settlers, American Loyalists and their descendants, and British settlers*

🎵 World Music: Cultural Traditions, Lesson 10

THE HISTORY CHANNEL®

The following videotape program is available from Glencoe:

• **Transcontinental Railroads**

To find classroom resources to accompany this video, check the following home page:

The History Channel: http://www.historychannel. com

Independent Practice

 Guided Reading Activity 25-2 **L1**

 Geography and History Activity 25

Multicultural Have students imagine themselves as settlers in one of the Dominions. Ask them to write letters describing their lives to friends in Great Britain. Suggest that students describe their work, their relationship with native people, their remoteness from England, and the rigors of living on a frontier. **L2**

ASSESS

Check for Understanding

Assign Section 2 Assessment as homework or as an in-class activity.

◉ Use Interactive Tutor Self-Assessment Software to review Section 2.

Evaluate

 Section Quiz 25-2

◉ Use the Testmaker to create a customized quiz for Section 2.

Reteach

Have students create a time line documenting the development of the British dominions.

 Reading Essentials and Study Guide 25-2

Enrich

Have students research the working of modern government in Canada, Australia, or New Zealand.

CLOSE

Ask students to write an essay summarizing changes in the Dominions during the 1800s.

654 Chapter 25 *Democracy and Reform*

Footnotes *to* **H**istory

Australian Language
Australian English has its own unique words: some come from the Aboriginal languages; others from the experiences of European settlers in the outback—the dry, open Australian interior. "Waltzing Matilda," Australia's best-known song, captures the flavor of Australian speech in this region:

"Once a jolly swagman [hobo] camped by a billabong [waterhole]
Under the shade of a coolibah tree,
And he sang as he watched and waited till his billy [milkpail] boiled
Who'll come a-waltzing Matilda [tramp the roads carrying a blanket roll] with me?"

Australia

Initially, Great Britain established Australia as a prisoners' colony to relieve overcrowded British jails. By 1860, after a gold rush lured new immigrants, the population reached 1 million, and the practice of transporting prisoners to Australia was abolished.

In settling, Europeans came into contact with **the Aborigines**, the original people of Australia. Many settlers treated the Aborigines badly, occupied their land, and killed them. Large numbers of Aborigines died from European diseases.

The increase in European settlement called for a better administration. By the late 1800s Australia was made up of six colonies—New South Wales, Victoria, Queensland, Tasmania, Western Australia, and South Australia. In 1901 Parliament made Australia a dominion that included the colonies plus a region known as the Northern Territory.

New Zealand

The first Europeans to settle in New Zealand were from James Cook's expedition in 1770. Hunters from Great Britain and the United States set up whaling stations during the 1790s. New Zealand also attracted timber traders.

Foreigners brought many problems to the original inhabitants, known as **the Maori**. Firearms, for example, increased warfare among the Maori tribes. Foreigners also brought diseases to which the Maori had no immunity, causing an almost 50 percent reduction in the Maori population in 20 years.

In an effort to provide law for the Maori and the settlers, British naval officers and Maori chiefs concluded the Treaty of Waitangi in 1840. The treaty protected Maori rights while the Maori gave the British sovereignty over New Zealand. In 1840 the first permanent British settlements were founded at Wellington and Wanganui, based on wool exports to British markets.

As with Australia, New Zealand's British population was small until the discovery of gold. The gold discovery also brought conflict between the newcomers and the Maori.

Prospectors unsuccessful in finding gold in New Zealand remained to farm. To gain more land, they violated those Maori land rights guaranteed by the treaty with the British. During the Maori Wars in the mid-1800s, the New Zealand government sided with the newcomers and seized some Maori land for public use.

New Zealand received a constitution from Great Britain in 1852 and became largely self-governing. In the 1890s, the New Zealand government carried out extensive social reforms, such as pensions for the elderly and protection of workers' rights. At this time Great Britain had not yet introduced many of these reforms. In 1907 New Zealand finally became a dominion within the British Empire.

SECTION 2 ASSESSMENT

Main Idea
1. Use a chart like the one below to explain how and when new societies emerged in Canada, Australia, and New Zealand.

Canada	Australia	New Zealand

Recall
2. **Define** dominion.
3. **Identify** the Loyalists, Lord Durham, John A. Macdonald, British North America Act, Northwest Mounted Police, the Aborigines, the Maori, Treaty of Waitangi.

Critical Thinking
4. **Evaluating Information** The Canadians at first wanted to

call their confederation "the Kingdom of Canada." The British government suggested the term *dominion* to avoid offending the United States. Why might that have offended Americans?

Understanding Themes
5. **Movement** What was the original purpose for British settlement of Australia?

---

654 Chapter 25 *Democracy and Reform*

SECTION 2 ASSESSMENT ANSWERS

1. Canada: British North America Act in 1867 made it a dominion; Canadian Territory expanded in 19th and early 20th century; Australia: in 1901 Parliament made it a dominion; New Zealand: Constitution from Great Britain in 1852; became a dominion in 1907
2. All terms are defined in the Glossary.
3. Loyalists, 652; Durham, 653; Macdonald,

653; British North America Act, 653; Mounted Police, 653; Aborigines, 654; Maori, 654; Waitangi, 654
4. Americans had fought to be independent from the "kingdom" of Great Britain and favored republican governments.
5. **MOVEMENT** Australia was a prisoners' colony.

1800 ———— **1850** ———— **1900**

1830 Revolution overthrows Bourbon dynasty.

1848 Voters elect Louis-Napoleon president.

1870 Revolutionaries establish Commune of Paris.

1890s The Dreyfus affair divides French society.

Section 3

Political Struggles in France

Guide to Reading

Read to Find Out

Main Idea *France underwent serious changes in government during the 1800s.*

▶ **Terms to Define**
ultraroyalist, coup d'état, plebiscite

▶ **People to Meet**
Charles X, Louis Philippe, Louis-Napoleon, General Georges Boulanger, Alfred Dreyfus

▶ **Places to Locate**
Paris

The Storyteller

Louis-Napoleon Bonaparte (Emperor Napoleon III) had grand ideas for the government of France—including a grand role for himself. Of course, he would not revive the excesses of royalty that France had groaned under before. Still, Frenchmen could not help but notice that his plans for the new constitution of France included the following ideas: "The executive power vests in the Emperor alone. The Emperor is the supreme head of the state; he commands the national forces both on land and sea; declares war, makes treaties of peace, of alliance, and of commerce...."

—adapted from *The Political and Historical Works of Louis Napoleon Bonaparte*, Volume 1, 1852

Louis-Napoleon Bonaparte

The Congress of Vienna sought to reduce France's might and restore traditional monarchs to their thrones. Although the European balance of power was restored, Congress delegates found their plans for monarchy frustrated as liberal and nationalist ideas spread among the peoples of Europe. The clash between old and new ideologies, or systems of thought and belief, sparked revolutions throughout Europe from the 1820s to the 1840s.

Revolt in France

Because of its revolutionary traditions, France was the center point of these upheavals. In 1815 the Congress of Vienna restored the Bourbon monarchy under Louis XVIII. Many French republicans accepted Louis because he was willing to rule as a constitutional monarch.

After Louis's death in 1824, his brother and successor **Charles X** set out to restore absolute monarchy—with help from the ultraroyalists—nobles favoring a return to the old order. When Charles tried to repay nobles for lands lost during the revolution, liberals in the legislative assembly opposed him. The king then dissolved the assembly and held new elections; but voters only elected more liberals to reject Charles's policies. Finally the king issued the July Ordinances, measures designed to dissolve the assembly, end press freedom, and restrict voting rights.

On July 27, 1830, angry Parisian workers and students rose up against the king. By July 29, after *Les Trois Glorieuses* (three glorious days) they forced

Chapter 25 *Democracy and Reform* **655**

TEACH

Guided Practice

THEME Revolution

Based on their knowledge of the French Revolution, guide students in a discussion about how the events described in this section can be called a continuation of the original French Revolution of 1789. *(French people revolted against monarchy installed after Napoleon's downfall.)* **L1 LEP**

TURNING POINT

Revolt in France

Why were political developments in France during the early 1800s influential in other areas of Europe?
France became a model of democratic political action. Upheavals there against monarchical government sparked similar uprisings against royal authority in other parts of Europe.

Visualizing History The 1848 uprising lasted three days. Louis Philippe had called the National Guard to keep order, but they sided with the rioters, and the municipal police force was too small to control the citizens. The mobs took over. This was considered a fairly bloodless revolution as revolutions go.
Answer to Caption: *It was replaced by an empire headed by Louis-Napoleon Bonaparte.*

Chart Guide students in making a chart to organize the succession of French governments presented in this section. Use the following heads: *French Leader, Form of Government, Cause of Downfall.* **L2**

Visualizing History The Revolution of 1848 that began in France triggered revolts throughout Europe. *What happened to the Second Republic within four years of its constitution?*

Charles X to give up his right as monarch and abdicate the throne. The fallen king fled to Great Britain.

The "Citizen-King"

After the chaos had subsided, revolutionary leaders set up a new constitutional monarchy that did not have close ties to the old aristocracy. **Louis Philippe**, a cousin of Charles, accepted the throne. Because he dressed and behaved like a middle-class person, Louis Philippe became known as the "Citizen-King" and won the support of the growing middle class.

From 1830 to 1848, however, many French people became discontented with Louis Philippe's government. At heart, the "Citizen-King" favored the wealthy, and many working-class citizens began to demand political reforms, especially voting rights.

Louis Philippe refused their demands. When they appealed to Prime Minister François Guizot (gee•ZOH), he too refused. Frustrated, leaders organized political banquets, where they called for an extended vote and Guizot's resignation.

The Revolution of 1848

In 1848 Guizot canceled a banquet, fearing a demonstration. This order, however, came too late. On February 22, crowds flooded the streets, singing "The Marseillaise" and shouting protests against Guizot. Louis Philippe called in troops, but the soldiers sympathized with the rebels and joined them. Over the next days, at least 52 civilians were killed or wounded. The disturbances forced Louis Philippe to abdicate and flee to Great Britain. The Revolution of 1848 ended with the rebels proclaiming France a republic.

656   Chapter 25   *Democracy and Reform*

Inspired by events in France, revolutionaries in other European countries also fought for greater political rights. Political discontent in Austria, Italy, and Prussia was particularly significant. In these areas, however, the political status quo was more or less maintained despite the uprisings.

The Second Empire

When the political turmoil in France had finally subsided, the revolutionary leaders proclaimed the Second Republic of France and set out to create a new constitution. The French constitution featured many democratic reforms, including a legislative branch called the National Assembly, the election of a president, and an extension of voting rights to all adult men. Nine million men eagerly set off to the polls to elect a new National Assembly in the spring of 1848. Only briefly, however, would the French enjoy the freedoms brought by the Second Republic.

The Rise of Louis-Napoleon

In presidential elections held in December 1848, French voters gave **Louis-Napoleon Bonaparte**, the nephew of Napoleon Bonaparte, an overwhelming victory. Louis-Napoleon's popularity came more from his name than from his political skills. The name "Napoleon" reminded the French people of the greatness their nation had once enjoyed under Napoleon I.

Although Louis-Napoleon presented himself as a democratic reformer, the president hoped to use his popularity to make himself an emperor. To guarantee victory, Louis-Napoleon worked to win

---

COOPERATIVE LEARNING ACTIVITY

News Broadcast Organize students into broadcast teams to provide coverage of the revolutions in France. Each team should divide up responsibility to research and prepare stories that provide a rounded picture of events in one of the revolutions. Each team member should have a role as a news anchor, on-the-scene reporter, or subject of an interview. Have teams report on events, reactions of royalists, republicans, leaders, and the person-in-the-street. Remind students to base their reports on actual events and actual people when possible. Have them write scripts and present their broadcasts to the class. You may want to videotape the presentations. **L2**

the support of powerful groups in France—the army, the Church, the middle class, and the peasants. For example, in 1849 he won the confidence of French Catholics by ordering French troops to help the pope suppress an attempt by Italian nationalists to set up a republic in Rome. He also gave the Church more control over French education.

This support for the Catholics, however, created an uproar in **Paris**. Demonstrators opposing support for the pope filled the streets. Alarmed by the mob action, the National Assembly restricted people's rights in order to keep law and order. They also revoked voting rights for about a third of the voters.

Louis-Napoleon used this uproar to his advantage by convincing the French people that the republic was a failure. Deciding to take control of the French government, Louis-Napoleon directed a coup d'état, or a quick seizure of power, on December 2, 1851. He dissolved the National Assembly and arrested many of his opponents. With shrewd planning, he won popular support by reestablishing voting rights for all French men.

Louis-Napoleon then called for a plebiscite, or national vote, asking the people to give him the power to create a new French constitution. The people enthusiastically gave him their support. Now Louis-Napoleon had complete legislative and executive control, and the people appeared happy with the order and stability he provided. In a second plebiscite, a large percentage of the people approved the transformation of the French republic into a hereditary empire. In 1852 Louis-Napoleon became Napoleon III, Emperor of France.

Although Napoleon III restricted the press and limited civil liberties, he had a successful economic program. During the 1850s French industrial growth doubled and foreign trade tripled. France built new railroads and roads, including Paris's famous wide boulevards.

The Crimean War

In 1854 Napoleon III led France into the Crimean War. The war pitted France and Great Britain against Russia and arose from the interests that all three countries had in the Ottoman Empire. The immediate cause of the conflict was a dispute between France and Russia over which of them had the right to protect Christians in the empire or those visiting the Holy Land. In this dispute the Ottoman emperor sided with France.

Angered by the decision, Russia's Czar Nicholas I in July 1853 seized Ottoman territory in the Balkans. This Russian invasion upset both Great Britain and France, who wanted to protect their trade and financial interests in the Middle East. After the

Ottoman Empire declared war on Russia in October 1853, Great Britain, France, and the tiny Italian kingdom of Sardinia eventually joined the conflict.

In the fall of 1854, French and British armies invaded the Russian-ruled Crimean Peninsula on the north shore of the Black Sea. At first, little fighting occurred as the armies battled cold, violent storms, and disease. By war's end, disease would cause more deaths on both sides than war injuries. Among British forces, however, a nurse, Florence Nightingale, improved hospital care and saved many lives. In the fall of 1855, French and British forces finally defeated the Russians, who lacked supplies, reinforcements, and railroads. The 1856 Treaty of Paris ending the war made Russia return some of the Ottoman territory it had seized and banned warships and forts around the Black Sea.

End of the Empire

In 1870 conflict with Prussia ended Napoleon III's empire. Alarmed by Prussia's growing power, Napoleon made his most costly error in judgment: he declared war on the Prussians on July 19, 1870.

Few French or foreign observers anticipated the quick and relatively easy defeat of France in the Franco-Prussian War. The French armies were slow to mobilize, and German forces crossed into France with little armed resistance. The Prussians defeated the French in just over six weeks. On September 2, after winning a decisive victory at Sedan, the Prussians took Napoleon III as prisoner.

History & Art *The Siege of Paris* by Ernest Meissonier. The Louvre, Paris, France *What impact did the Franco-Prussian conflict of 1870–1871 have on France and the government of Napoleon III?*

Chapter 25 *Democracy and Reform* **657**

Independent Practice

📁 Guided Reading Activity 25-3 **L1**

Daily Life Have students work in small groups and take the roles of ordinary French people in the late 1800s. Have them role-play casual conversations in which they reveal the average person's thoughts about the political events of the day. **L2**

Critical Thinking Ask students to list factors that contributed to the revolutions described in this section. **L3**

History & Art Two million Parisians were cut off from all contact with the outside world during the siege. The Prussians formed a continuous front of about 52 miles with 150,000 men and 700 guns. How might the four-month siege have affected people's daily lives? *(They would have been cut off from food and fuel supplies and suffered severe hardships.)*
Answer to Caption: *France was easily defeated by Prussia, and the government of Napoleon III collapsed.*

Who?What?Where?When?

Florence Nightingale became a nurse at a time when it was not considered a noble profession, and in 1854 led a group of British nurses to the Crimean War. Her efforts at the battle zone transformed the appalling conditions and won her worldwide fame. In 1864 she helped inspire the organization of the International Red Cross.

MEETING SPECIAL NEEDS ACTIVITY

Study Strategy To help students learn the information in this section, suggest that they outline it. They should list each major head and any subheads, leaving space under these heads to write the key figures, dates, and events as they read about them. They should look up words they do not understand and write the definitions to reinforce remembering them. They might continue this strategy with other chapters. **L1**

The Development of Photography

Tell students that in 1839 in France, photographs were displayed for the first time. By the 1850s, photographers were heading west in the United States and recording the frontier. They carried bulky cameras and used glass plates for negatives instead of small rolls of film as are used today. The photographer's covered wagon served as a darkroom.

ANSWER

Photography provided them with exact images of people and events. Answers will vary. Possible answer: Photography has a major influence on people's lives given the importance of television.

When the news of the emperor's capture reached Paris on September 4, crowds filled the streets and forced the collapse of the Second Empire. The people of Paris endured a Prussian siege for four months before a truce was signed.

Making Peace With Prussia

The French people elected a new National Assembly, dominated by royalists, to make peace with Prussia. The Assembly surrendered the provinces of Alsace and Lorraine and agreed to pay 5 billion francs—the equivalent of 1 billion dollars—to Prussia. Prussian forces further humiliated France by staging a victory march through Paris. The people of Paris, strong republicans who wanted a renewal of the war with Prussia instead of peace, were angered by the peace terms. They sank into despair after their loss.

In March the National Assembly set about restoring order in France, particularly in Paris. The provisional government inspired an angry outcry when it demanded that Parisians pay the rents and the debts that had been suspended during the siege. At the same time, the Assembly stopped payments to the National Guard, which many Parisian workers had joined during the Prussian siege. These drastic measures led to unrest and to an uprising in Paris.

The Commune of Paris

During the revolt, the workers established a Socialist government known as the Commune of Paris. The leaders of the Commune refused to recognize the National Assembly and called for the conversion of France into a decentralized federation of independent cities. The Commune declared war on the propertied classes and the Church. It advocated an end to government support for religion, the adoption of a new revolutionary calendar, and the introduction of a 10-hour workday.

In a bitter civil war, the National Assembly took the offensive and reasserted its control over Paris. Armies pushed past the Commune's barricades throughout the strife-ridden city. In defiance, the supporters of the Commune burned public buildings, including the Tuileries Palace and the City Hall. During the "Bloody Week" in May 1871, the Assembly's powerful military forces arrested nearly 40,000 people and killed more than 20,000. The horror of rebellion set back the political and social advances made by workers and caused distrust between France's middle and working classes.

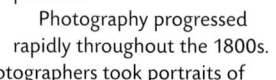

The Development of Photography

For centuries scientists tried to record lasting images, but it was not until 1826 that the world's first camera was made. Its inventor, the Frenchman Joseph Niépce, produced a blurry image of a farmyard by coating a metal plate with a light-sensitive chemical. In 1837 Louis Daguerre perfected Niépce's methods and fixed an image on silver-coated copper. Daguerreotypes, as these images were called, produced detailed pictures.

Early Camera

Photography progressed rapidly throughout the 1800s. Some photographers took portraits of wealthy families. Others risked their lives photographing the horrors of war. Gradually scientific and technical discoveries made cameras more efficient and easier to operate. In 1888 George Eastman developed the small, lightweight, and relatively inexpensive box camera. Mass-produced, the box camera put photography into the hands of millions.

Today, a picture can be taken simply by aiming the camera and pressing a button. In sophistication, cameras range from simple fixed-focus models to ones that have many lenses and built-in features.

ACTIVITY

Discuss how photography helped people record their lives in the 1800s. In what ways does photography affect events today? Consider the power of the media.

MAKING CONNECTIONS ACTIVITIES

Science and Technology Have students investigate the photographic process. Have them present their findings to the class in the form of a detailed diagram that shows the stages of the printing process. **L2**

Photography Students can research the lives and the work of pioneers in photography. Examples include Mathew Brady and his photographs during the Civil War, George Eastman and the development of the Eastman-Kodak company, or Julia Cameron, a British pioneer of portrait photography. Have students present their findings to the class. **L2**

The Third Republic

After the fall of the Commune, the dispirited French again tried to rebuild their government. This proved to be a difficult task, as royalists and republicans alike fought bitterly over the form the government should take.

Finally, in 1875 a new constitution made France once again a republic. The Third Republic's constitution provided for a two-house legislature. The two houses elected a president, who served for four years and who had little real power. Every official act required the full support of both houses of the legislature to be signed into law. A cabinet of ministers was responsible for government policy, and the post of premier was created to handle all executive business.

Threats to the Republic

Although France had finally established itself as a republic, the new government was particularly vulnerable to attack. One of its greatest threats came from **General Georges Boulanger** (BOO •lahn•ZHAY), who was a popular war hero. Boulanger won great support from royalists and others who opposed the republic. In 1889 his supporters urged him to overthrow the Third Republic with a coup d'état. When the government ordered him arrested for treason, Boulanger fled the country to Belgium. Without the direction of its popular leader, the Boulanger movement collapsed.

A second threat to the republic in the early 1890s centered around the construction of a canal through Panama. The canal would provide France with a waterway connecting the Atlantic and Pacific Oceans.

When the Panama Company collapsed and the Panama project failed, thousands of French stockholders lost all of the money they had invested. Charges of dishonesty and poor managerial practices erupted. The scandal spread as members of both houses were accused of accepting bribes to get more funding for the troubled project. The Panama scandal partly benefited France's growing Socialist movement. In 1893 nearly 50 Socialists won seats in the national legislature.

The Dreyfus Affair

The 1890s saw the Third Republic's greatest crisis—the Dreyfus affair. In 1894 **Alfred Dreyfus**, a French army officer, was convicted by a military court of selling military secrets to the Germans and sentenced to a life term on Devil's Island, a prison colony off the coast of French Guiana in South America. The French army was, at the time, influenced by anti-Semitic views, and its suspicion had fallen on Dreyfus, who was Jewish.

Dreyfus, however, protested his innocence and it soon became known that another officer was the real traitor and that the official evidence used in Dreyfus's trial had been forged. In an article, "*J'accuse* (I Accuse)", the novelist Émile Zola took a strong stand in support of Dreyfus. In 1899 a new trial was ordered, but the military court, unable to admit error, found Dreyfus guilty once again. This time, Dreyfus won a presidential pardon, and a civilian court later declared him innocent.

While it lasted, the Dreyfus affair deeply divided France. Republicans, Socialists, and anti-Catholics united to defend Dreyfus and to discredit the military. Wanting to uphold the army's honor, royalists, nationalists, and many Catholics joined anti-Semites—those hostile to Jews—in regarding Dreyfus as guilty.

The Dreyfus affair proved that republican government could survive in France. Its immediate effect was to bring to power radical republicans and Socialists, who carried out changes such as the separation of church and state in 1905.

SECTION 3 ASSESSMENT

Main Idea
1. Use a chart like the one below to identify French governmental changes of the 1800s.

French Governmental Changes of the 1800s

Recall
2. **Define** ultraroyalist, coup d'état, plebiscite.
3. **Identify** Charles X, Louis Philippe, Louis-Napoleon, Commune of Paris, General Georges Boulanger, Alfred Dreyfus.

Critical Thinking
4. **Analyzing Information** Why was the government of the Third Republic especially vulnerable to political opposition?

Understanding Themes
5. **Revolution** What sparked revolutions in France in 1830 and 1848? How did these revolutions impact Europe?

Chapter 25 *Democracy and Reform* **659**

1800   1850   1900

1803 The United States gains the Louisiana Purchase.

1846 War begins between the United States and Mexico.

1865 The Civil War ends.

c. 1890s Immigrants arrive in the United States from eastern and southern Europe.

SECTION THEME

▶ **Change** The United States extends its borders and develops its economy.

Guide to Reading

For reading strategies to help students read effectively see pages 12–13.

Vocabulary Pre-check

 Use the Vocabulary PuzzleMaker for Chapter 25 to create a crossword puzzle to reinforce section terms. **L1 LEP**

Use Vocabulary Activity 25 to introduce vocabulary terms. **L1 LEP**

FOCUS

Section Objective

Explain how the United States changed during the 1800s.

BELLRINGER
Motivational Activity

 Before taking roll at the beginning of the class period, project Section Focus Transparency 25-4 and have students answer the activity questions. Discuss students' responses.

This activity is also available as a blackline master.

Section 4

Expansion of the United States

Guide to Reading

Read to Find Out

Main Idea *The United States grew in size, wealth, and power during the 1800s.*

▶ **Terms to Define**
   sectionalism, secede, ratify

▶ **People to Meet**
   Thomas Jefferson, Abraham Lincoln, Susan B. Anthony, Woodrow Wilson

▶ **Places to Locate**
   Louisiana Purchase, Gadsden Purchase

The Storyteller

During the Civil War when Confederate casualties returned in large numbers from the front, buildings quickly became makeshift hospitals. Miss Sally Tomkins was one of the most tireless workers among the many brave women who served in the overcrowded places of mercy. As a "soldier without a gun," she received a commission in the Confederate Army as well as a commendation—the only such commission ever issued to a woman, and a unique "first" for any American army. In a note to the War Department, she said: "I accepted the commission … but would not allow my name to be placed on the payroll of the army."

—adapted from *A Pictorial History of the Confederacy*, Lamont Buchanan, 1951

Civil War nurse and patient

hile many political upheavals shook Europe during the 1800s, the United States grew in size, wealth, and power. The vast area of forests and plains west of the original colonies lured American settlers by the thousands, and no European powers with colonial interests blocked their westward drive. The conflicts between European countries during the early years of the nation had created opportunities for the United States to acquire more territory.

The Young Nation Grows

The United States gained its biggest territorial prize as a result of Napoleon I's desire to conquer his most hated enemy, Great Britain. In 1803 Napoleon was preparing to go to war against Great Britain and needed money to finance it. Desperate for money, Napoleon offered to sell the French-owned Louisiana territory to the United States. With a quick stroke of the pen and a payment of $15 million, President **Thomas Jefferson** acquired the **Louisiana Purchase**—all the land between the Mississippi River and the Rocky Mountains. The area eventually formed 13 states.

The United States also gained land as a result of Spain's internal conflicts. Weakened by political and financial problems, Spain ceded, or gave up, Florida in 1819.

Later acquisitions of new land from other nations proved to be not so easy or peaceful. In 1845 the Republic of Texas was annexed to the United States. By 1846 this territorial gain resulted in a conflict between the United States and Mexico that escalated into war. The United States defeated the Mexicans in 1848, and in the resulting treaty Mexico gave up a vast area that later formed all of California, Utah, and Nevada and parts of

---

SECTION RESOURCES

Reproducible Masters
- Lecture Notes 25-4
- Reproducible Lesson Plan 25-4
- Vocabulary Activity 25
- Guided Reading Activity 25-4
- People in World History Profile 47
- Section Quiz 25-4
- Reading Essentials and Study Guide 25-4

Transparencies
- Section Focus Transparency 25-4
- World History and Art Transparency 33
- Mapping History Overlay Transparency 16, *Global Ancestry of Americans*

Multimedia
- Interactive Tutor Self-Assessment Software
- Testmaker
- World Music: Cultural Traditions, Lesson 1
- Lessons of War: *Why Soldiers Fight*

Denver Public Library, Western History Department

Pioneers

You can see the fatigue in the faces of these pioneers, moving West in Conestoga wagons. Prairie stretched behind them, mountains ahead—and an unbearable distance to [fro]m the settlement of Jamestown in 1607 to the [settleme]nt of the West two centuries later, Americans [mov]ed, moved, and endured unspeakable hardships. [J]ourneys stretched their endurance, as they bat[tled hu]nger, Native Americans, and the difficulties of [the te]rrain itself. The West was dry: Wood shrank; [rim]s fell off wagons; and the hooves of oxen split. [Dust] is two or three inches in depth and as fine as [flour,] one pioneer wrote. "We cannot see the wagons

next to us...." Settled into new homes, the pioneers' hardships did not end. Families lived through winters so harsh that cows, sheathed in ice, had to be brought inside. Summers brought plagues of grasshoppers and prairie fires. And always there was isolation and loneliness.

By 1860 the United States stretched from the Atlantic to the Pacific. But expansion brought problems for the nation as well as benefits. The territory won in the Mexican-American War (1846–1848) shifted the issue of slavery into the political mainstream with such force that it took the Civil War to resolve the conflict between North and South. ◉

Chapter 25 *Democracy and Reform* **661**

TEACH

Tell students that the first wagon trains to go West set out in 1841 from one of a number of towns in Missouri along the Missouri River called "jumping-off places." They headed toward Oregon or California. Supplies were fresh, animals were healthy, the Kansas prairie was flat, and this beginning part of the trip was the easiest. Hardships and fatigue came later on the trails. How do you think this pioneer life affected the lives of children? (*Answers will vary but may include that children grew up faster because they faced so many dangers and hardships at a young age and because they had to shoulder adult responsibilities for the good of their families.*)

Who?What?Where?When?

Willa Cather was a journalist and novelist who wrote many stories about the plains of Nebraska. At the age of nine, she had to move with her parents from Virginia to the West. She portrays the psychological trauma of that move in *My Ántonia.*

TEACH

Guided Practice

 THEME Change

Discuss with students the changes that occurred in the United States as it expanded rapidly. Emphasize the impact of rapid expansion and westward migration on daily life. Help them to visualize heading West without knowing much about your destination. **L1**

POINT

Rise of the United States
How did the United States increase its political power during the 1800s?
It expanded democratic rights, used its resources to build an economy based on agriculture and industry, and overcame divisions, although by means of a bloody civil war.

Geography: Movement Have students recall how the colonists slowly expanded their settlements along the east coast. Have students describe the stages in westward expansion. Point out that between 1607 and 1890, the idea of expansion was part of the American consciousness. Ask students what people mean today when they think of expansion. **L3**

🎵 World Music: Cultural Traditions, Lesson 1

📦 World History and Art Transparency 33, *The Banjo Lesson*

📦 Mapping History Overlay Transparency 16, *Global Ancestry of Americans*

Colorado, Arizona, Wyoming, and New Mexico. This large acquisition of territory added a sizable Hispanic population to the United States.

Farther north, the United States argued with Great Britain over the borders of the Oregon Country. In a treaty with Great Britain, the United States gained part of this area. Oregon, Washington, and Idaho, as well as parts of Wyoming and Montana, were later created from this territory.

By the mid-1800s, only one step remained in the country's move across the continent. In 1853 James Gadsden, the American ambassador to Mexico, gave Mexico $10 million for 45,000 square miles (116,550 sq. km) of land in southern New Mexico and Arizona, south of the Rio Grande.

With the **Gadsden Purchase**, the United States finally stretched from "sea to shining sea." This westward expansion brought new opportunities to settlers, who forged communities and built states in the new lands. The expansion also brought suffering—loss of land, culture, and often life—to Native Americans who had inhabited lands in the West for centuries.

Rise of the United States

As Americans moved westward, democratic rights in the United States expanded. When the nation was first founded, the right to vote and hold public office was generally restricted to white male property owners.

The people of the West sought to extend these voting rights. All of the new states adopted constitutions that granted the right to vote to all men. These new states gradually gained power in Congress, and, over time, their liberal policies influenced the country. By 1856 every state had granted all white men the vote.

An Expanding Economy

Many factors contributed to the rapid growth of the American economy. The Industrial Revolution, which began in Great Britain, spread to

---

Images of the Times

The Civil War

There had always been economic and cultural differences between the North and the South. In 1861 these differences led to the American Civil War, or the War Between the States.

Union naval forces took New Orleans in May 1862. In the Civil War, both North and South suffered heavy losses, but the North's industrial strength gave it an advantage over the agricultural South.

Antislavery feeling in the North was stimulated by Harriet Beecher Stowe's *Uncle Tom's Cabin*, a novel portraying slavery at its worst. The book sold 300,000 copies in 1852, its first year of publication.

135,000 SETS, 270,000 VOLUMES SOLD.
UNCLE TOM'S CABIN
FOR SALE HERE.
AN EDITION FOR THE MILLION, COMPLETE IN 1 Vol., PRICE 37 1/2 CENTS.
IN GERMAN, IN 1 Vol. PRICE 50 CENTS.
IN 2 Vols., CLOTH, 4 PLATES, PRICE $1.50.
SUPERB ILLUSTRATED EDITION, IN 1 Vol., WITH 153 ENGRAVINGS,
PRICES FROM $2.50 TO $5.00.
The Greatest Book of the Age.

662

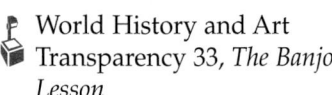
Images of the Times
The Civil War

Harriet Beecher Stowe wrote most of *Uncle Tom's Cabin* in Brunswick, Maine; she had spent exactly one weekend in a slave state. Stowe said that the powerful death scene of Uncle Tom came to her in a vision while she was in church.

Although slavery was the primary moral issue dividing the North and the South, the abolition of slavery was not the main reason that hundreds of thousands of men joined the Northern army in the early days of the war. Most of them did not agree with the abolitionists; they viewed their own efforts as a struggle to preserve the Union.

the United States. Busy commercial regions filled with factories and heavily populated cities characterized the North. Irish, German, and Scandinavian immigrants joined the Northern workforce, settling in cities and farmlands. Northern workers received pay for their labor, as well as the right to leave their jobs for better ones. This system of work was called free labor.

In contrast, the South became the chief producer of raw cotton for the booming British textile industry. The South's economy remained primarily agricultural and depended on the labor of enslaved African Americans. Most white Southerners, even those who held no enslaved people, believed in slave labor. As the United States expanded, it was clear that the different economic interests of the two regions would cause conflict.

A Nation Divided

The differences in their economies led the two regions, the North and the South, to take widely different positions on many political and economic issues. The result was sectionalism, the devotion to the political and economic interest of a region or a section of the country. The most divisive issue, however, was slave labor. The South wanted to expand slavery into the territories gained during the Mexican War. The North wanted these new western areas to remain territories employing free labor.

By 1860 the United States consisted of 18 free states and 15 slave states. In the presidential election of 1860, proslavery and antislavery forces vied for power. When **Abraham Lincoln** won the presidency, the South feared he would abolish slavery.

To protest the election, South Carolina decided to secede, or withdraw, from the Union. Other Southern states followed suit. By February 8, 1861, seven states had joined to form their own nation, the Confederate States of America. In Washington, D.C., Congress worked on a compromise, but to no avail. When Lincoln was sworn in as President in March, he declared that "no state, upon its own mere motion, can lawfully get out of the Union." By April the divided nation was at war. The Civil

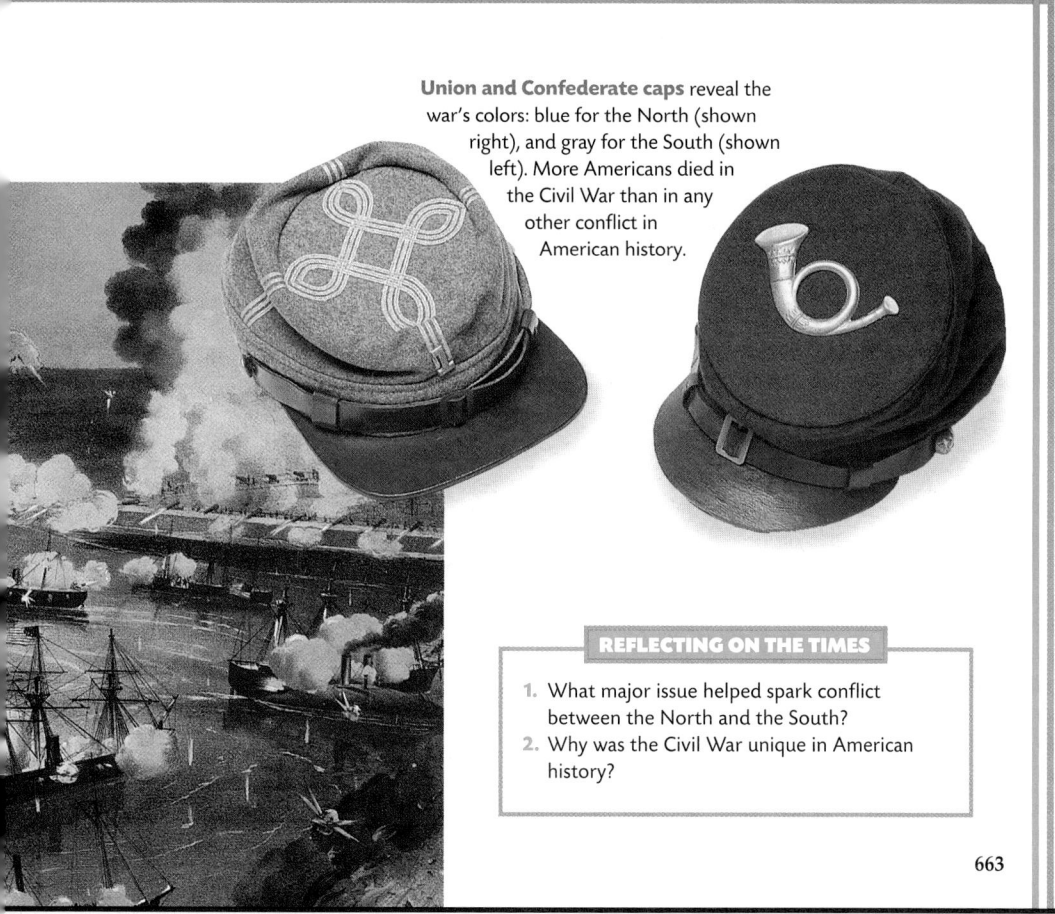

Union and Confederate caps reveal the war's colors: blue for the North (shown right), and gray for the South (shown left). More Americans died in the Civil War than in any other conflict in American history.

REFLECTING ON THE TIMES

1. What major issue helped spark conflict between the North and the South?
2. Why was the Civil War unique in American history?

663

Biography

The following videotape programs are available from Glencoe:

- **Lewis & Clark**
- **Crazy Horse**
- **Frederick Douglass**
- **Susan B. Anthony: Rebel for a Cause**

Independent Practice

Guided Reading Activity 25-4 **L1**

People in World History Profile 47

Critical Thinking Organize students into small groups to consider whether a state should have the right to withdraw from the United States. Have each group take one side of the issue and gather information. Then each group should choose a member to participate in a class debate on the issue. **L3**

Linking Past and Present

States' Rights Today United States government officials continue to disagree about whether certain issues, such as school integration, should be controlled by the federal or by the state government.

ANSWERS TO REFLECTING ON THE TIMES

1. slavery
2. More Americans died in the Civil War than in any other conflict in American history.

Map Study

Answer

France, Spain, Britain, Russia

Map Skills Practice

Reading a Map Which acquisitions allowed the United States to stretch from "sea to shining sea"? (*Oregon Country, 1846; Mexican Cession, 1848; Gadsden Purchase, 1853*)

VIDEODISC

Lessons of War

Side One, Chapter 4
Frames 8662–11204

Title: *Why Soldiers Fight*

Subject: Discussion and images of what motivates soldiers to fight

Ask: What motivates people to volunteer in the armed services?

(*Most volunteer because they feel a sense of patriotic duty and loyalty to their country.*)

ASSESS

Check for Understanding

Assign Section 4 Assessment as homework or as an in-class activity.

▣ Use Interactive Tutor Self-Assessment Software to review Section 4.

Evaluate

🗁 Section Quiz 25-4

Territorial Expansion of the United States

Webster-Ashburton Treaty with Great Britain 1842 adjusted boundary

Convention of 1818 (with Britain)

CANADA

Treaty of Paris ending Revolutionary War 1783

Compromise line (Treaty of 1846 with Britain)

Oregon Country (Joint Possession by United States and Britain 1818-1846)

Boundary established by part of Adams-Onís Treaty with Spain 1819

Boundary established by Treaty of Paris ending Revolutionary War 1783

Area claimed by Original 13 States

Louisiana Purchase 1803 from France

Mexican Cession from Mexico by Treaty of Guadalupe Hidalgo 1848

Gadsden Purchase from Mexico 1853

ATLANTIC OCEAN

Disputed United States and Spain 1783-1795

Disputed with Mexico 1845-1848

Annexation of the Republic of Texas 1845

Florida Spanish Cession by Adams-Onís Treaty 1819

MEXICO

1810 1813

Adams-Onís Treaty 1819

Secured by U.S. troops

Alaska (Purchased from Russia 1867)

Hawaii (Annexed 1898)

PACIFIC OCEAN

Gulf of Mexico

0   250 mi.
0   250 km

0   100 mi.
0   100 km

0   100   200 mi.
0   100   200 km
Lambert Azimuthal Equal-Area Projection

Map Study The United States stretched from the Atlantic Ocean to the Pacific Ocean by 1848. Territory was added by purchase, conquest, and treaty.

Region From what four European nations did the United States acquire most of its territory?

War, pitting North against South and lasting from 1861 to 1865, was one of the bloodiest struggles of the 1800s.

Although the North had 22 million people and the South only 9 million, of which nearly a third were enslaved, Southern forces won many early victories under skilled military leaders such as Robert E. Lee. Later, however, the North threw the full weight of its massive resources against the South.

After four years of war that claimed the lives of more than 600,000 Americans, the Northern forces defeated the Confederate forces. After the war, Congress passed three amendments to the Constitution of the United States. These amendments abolished slavery and gave formerly enslaved African Americans citizenship and equal protection under the law, as well as the right to vote. The nation set about to rebuild itself. 🔫

A New Society

After the Civil War, the growth of industries and cities in the United States continued with new vigor. Across the country textile mills, lumberyards, mines, and factories increased their output. In 1900 oil fields provided about 130 times more oil than they had in 1860, ironworks 10 times more iron, and steelworks almost 60 times more steel. The "captains of industry" who developed and invested in these thriving industries amassed great fortunes and gained widespread admiration.

664   Chapter 25   *Democracy and Reform*

COOPERATIVE LEARNING ACTIVITY

Discussion Groups Organize the class into groups to discuss the ways American life might be different if the Civil War had not been fought and the country had remained divided into two separate nations. Have each group focus on a different topic, such as economy, international relations, labor, government, or culture. One person from each group should take notes on the discussion and report the group's ideas to the class. Encourage students from the other groups to ask questions after each presentation. **L1** 🗊

Immigration

As industry grew, so did the nation's population. Between 1870 and 1900, the number of Americans doubled from approximately 38 million to 76 million. Immigrants contributed significantly to this growth. Before the Civil War, most immigrants had come from northern Europe, mainly the British Isles, Germany, and Scandinavia. The Irish potato famine of the 1840s brought nearly 1 million Irish people to the United States. The failed German revolution of 1848 had prompted many disappointed liberals and intellectuals to leave their homeland.

After the Civil War, immigration from northern Europe decreased, while immigration from southern and eastern Europe increased. By 1900, immigrants from Italy, Russia, and Austria-Hungary made up more than three-fourths of the United States's foreign-born population. Most of these immigrants headed for urban areas to work.

Along the West coast by the late 1800s, communities of Asian immigrants thrived. Chinese immigrants first came to California in the late 1840s to find gold and stayed to work in the mines and build railroads. By 1900, immigrants from Japan had also arrived. Anti-Asian feelings, however, led to legal limits or bans on further Asian immigration. Asian Americans also faced widespread discrimination, which lasted well into the 1900s.

Women's Rights

As women gained economic opportunities, they also demanded political equality. A women's rights movement had flourished in the 1850s under leaders such as Lucretia Mott and Sojourner Truth. During the late 1800s, women known as suffragists fought hard for women's right to vote. Forming organizations such as the National Woman Suffrage Association (NWSA), suffragists such as Elizabeth Cady Stanton and **Susan B. Anthony** wrote books,

Visualizing History During the late 1800s and early 1900s, suffragists pushed for an amendment to the Constitution granting women the right to vote. *By 1918, in which states could women vote?*

testified before state legislatures, and spoke at public meetings to urge votes for women.

Slowly women achieved the right to vote at the state level, beginning with Wyoming, Colorado, and Utah. By 1918 women had gained full suffrage in many Western states, Michigan, Illinois, and New York. Finally, because of their contributions in World War I, politicians could not ignore women's demands. In September 1918 President **Woodrow Wilson** asked Congress to pass a constitutional amendment guaranteeing the vote to all United States citizens 21 years of age and older regardless of their sex. In 1920 the states acted to ratify, or approve, the Nineteenth Amendment.

SECTION 4 ASSESSMENT

Main Idea
1. Use a diagram like the one below to identify ways in which the United States's geography changed in the 1800s.

U. S. Geographical Changes in 1800s

Recall
2. **Define** sectionalism, secede, ratify.
3. **Identify** Thomas Jefferson, Louisiana Purchase, Abraham Lincoln, the Civil War, Susan B. Anthony, Woodrow Wilson.

Critical Thinking
4. **Analyzing Information** How did the Industrial Revolution in the North contribute to the outbreak of the Civil War?

Understanding Themes
5. **Change** How and why did the United States economy change in the late 1800s?

Chapter 25 *Democracy and Reform* 665

Visualizing History Susan B. Anthony joined Elizabeth Cady Stanton in working for women's rights and forming the NWSA. They fought for other legal rights in addition to suffrage.
Answer to Caption: *in every Western state, Michigan, and New York*

Use the Testmaker to create a customized quiz for Section 4.

Reteach

Have each student write a question about the material under each head in this section. Then have students work in pairs to answer each other's questions, looking up answers as necessary.

Reading Essentials and Study Guide 25-4

Enrich

Ask students to assess how one of the territorial acquisitions benefits the United States today looking at the population, economy, political leadership, and cultural diversity. Have students write an editorial on the acquisition merits.

CLOSE

Have students write one-paragraph summaries of how the United States changed in each of the following areas during the 1800s: territory, economy, industry, population, human rights.

SECTION 4 ASSESSMENT ANSWERS

1. gained land between Mississippi River and Rocky Mountains in the Louisiana Purchase; Spain ceded Florida; won and bought vast southwestern region from Mexico; gained northwestern lands from Great Britain
2. All terms are defined in the Glossary.
3. Thomas Jefferson, 660; Louisiana Purchase, 660; Abraham Lincoln, 663; the Civil War, 664; Susan B. Anthony, 665; Woodrow Wilson, 665
4. It caused the North to build factories and rely on free labor. Cotton farming boomed in the South to meet demands from British textile industry. The South relied on slave labor. These economic differences led to the Civil War.
5. **CHANGE** The economy boomed in the late 1800s; it was caused by the increase in production that began during the Civil War.

1800 **1820** **1840**

1804 Haiti proclaims
its independence.

1819 Simón Bolívar defeats
Spaniards at the Battle of Boyacá.

1825 Portugal recognizes
Brazil's independence.

SECTION THEME

▶ **Nationalism** Latin American
nations achieve self-government.

Guide to Reading

For reading strategies to help
students read effectively see
pages 12–13.

Vocabulary Pre-check

☑ Use the Vocabulary
PuzzleMaker for Chapter 25 to
create a crossword puzzle to
reinforce section terms. **L1 LEP**

📁 Use Vocabulary Activity
25 to introduce vocabulary terms.
L1 LEP

FOCUS

Section Objective

Relate how the countries of Latin
America won independence.

**BELLRINGER
Motivational Activity**

Before taking roll at the
beginning of the class
period, project Section
Focus Transparency 25-5
and have students answer
the activity questions. Discuss
students' responses.
📁 This activity is also available as a blackline master.

Section **5**

Latin American Independence

Guide to Reading

**Read to Find Out
Main Idea** *The countries of Latin America won independence in a variety of ways.*

▶ **Terms to Define**
peninsulares, creoles, mestizos

▶ **People to Meet**
François Toussaint-Louverture,
Miguel Hidalgo, Simón Bolívar,
José de San Martín, Pedro I

▶ **Places to Locate**
Haiti, Mexico, Central America,
Venezuela, Argentina, Chile, Peru, Brazil

The Storyteller

Simón Bolívar sent a joyous letter to a fellow general on January 8, 1822, displaying his belief in a unified America. He wrote, "America's greatest day has not yet dawned. We have indeed driven out our oppressors, smashed the tablets of their

tyrannical laws, and established legitimate institutions; but we have yet to lay the foundation … that will make of this part of the world a nation of republics." Bolívar was confident that this unified America would impress Europe: "Who shall oppose an America united in heart, subject to one law, and guided by the torch of liberty?"

—adapted from *Selected Writings of
Bolívar,* compiled by Vicente Lecuna
and edited by Harold A. Bierck, Jr.,
1951

Simón Bolívar

or 300 years Spain and Portugal held
colonies in the Americas without facing
serious threats to their rule. In the early
1800s, however, the situation changed. Inspired by
the American and French Revolutions, Latin
Americans sought an end to colonial rule and
joined independence movements.

Ruling the Colonies

Like other European nations, Spain and
Portugal regarded their Latin American colonies
with a mercantilist view—the idea that colonies
existed chiefly to increase the home countries'
wealth. Mexico, Peru, and Brazil contained large
deposits of gold and silver as well as forests that
yielded valuable exotic woods such as mahogany
and ebony.

Farming provided another major source of
colonial income. Spanish and Portuguese monarchs
granted huge tracts of fertile land to explorers and
nobles for the growing of cash crops, such as corn,
sugar, and cocoa. The landowners then forced the
Native Americans to work the farms. When they
died from forced labor and diseases that the
Europeans had introduced to the Americas, the
Spanish and the Portuguese imported large numbers of enslaved Africans.

The Catholic Church also played a critical role
in the colonial economies, strengthening Spanish
and Portuguese rule in Latin America. Both the
Spaniards and the Portuguese brought the Catholic
religion with them to the Americas. Priests and
monks converted the Native Americans who
worked on the farms to Catholicism and taught
them loyalty to the Crown.

The colonial governments and the clergy
worked very closely together. Clergymen held high

666 **Chapter 25** *Democracy and Reform*

SECTION RESOURCES

📁 **Reproducible Masters**
• Lecture Notes 25-5
• Reproducible Lesson Plan 25-5
• Guided Reading Activity 25-5
• People in World History Profile 48
• Reteaching Activity 25
• Enrichment Activity 25
• Section Quiz 25-5

• Performance Assessment Activity 25
• Spanish Chapter Summary 25
• Reading Essentials and Study Guide 25-5

🔦 **Transparencies**
• Section Focus Transparency 25-5

Multimedia
☑ Vocabulary PuzzleMaker Software
☑ Interactive Tutor Self-Assessment
Software
☑ Testmaker
🎵 World Music: Cultural Traditions,
Lesson 2

government offices. The government, in turn, supported the Church. By 1800 the Catholic Church controlled almost half the wealth of Latin America.

Over the years, colonists became increasingly unhappy with colonial rule. They resented the trade restrictions and high taxes Spain and Portugal imposed upon them. Most of all, they resented the rigid colonial social structure.

A Rigid Social Order

Social classes based on privilege divided colonial Latin America. Colonial leaders, called *peninsulares*, were born in Spain or Portugal and stood at the top level of the social order. Appointed by the Spanish and Portuguese governments, the *peninsulares* held all important military and political positions. Below them were the colonial-born white aristocrats, called creoles. Although they controlled most of the land and business in the colonies, the creoles were regarded as second-class citizens by the *peninsulares*. The creoles envied the privileged leadership positions that were held exclusively by the *peninsulares*.

At the bottom of the colonial social pyramid were the majority of Latin Americans. Some were Native Americans. Others were of African or African and European ancestry. The largest of this group, however, were mestizos (meh•STEE•zohz), Latin Americans of mixed Native American and European ancestry. Spurned by the ruling white classes, these Latin Americans faced social and racial barriers in colonial society. They worked as servants for *peninsulares* and creoles, and as unskilled laborers and carpenters. Some worked as plantation overseers and farmhands.

Growing Discontent

In the 1800s Latin Americans began to challenge the rigid social order and its controls with revolts throughout Latin America. The creoles played the largest leadership roles in these conflicts. Wealthy and well educated, many were well versed in the liberal political philosophies of the Enlightenment, but their colonial birth prevented them from holding the highest government positions. The creoles were eager to take control of Latin American affairs.

Uprising in Haiti

Although the Spanish and Portuguese colonies were ripe for revolt, the first successful uprising in the Latin American colonies took place in the French colony of **Haiti** (Saint Domingue), on the island of

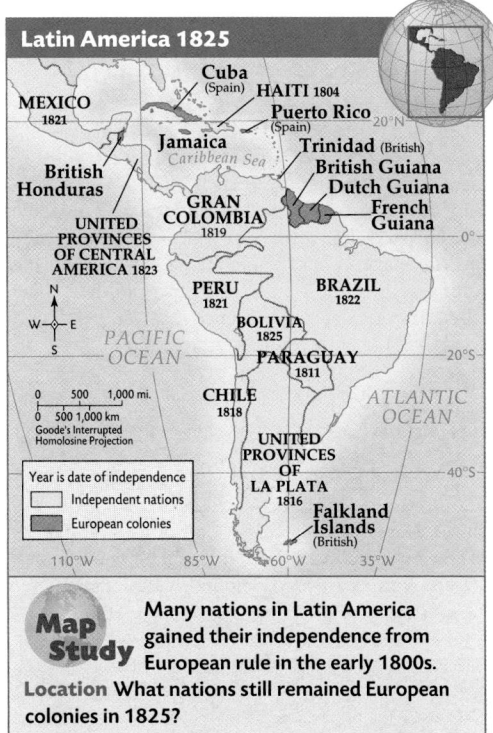

Latin America 1825

Map Study

Many nations in Latin America gained their independence from European rule in the early 1800s.
Location What nations still remained European colonies in 1825?

Hispaniola in the Caribbean Sea. Huge plantations of sugar, cotton, and coffee spread across the mountains and valleys of the lush tropical land. France and many other countries depended on the tiny colony for their supply of sugar and coffee.

The plantations were owned by French planters and worked by the colony's enslaved African population. More than 500,000 of the 560,000 people living in Haiti in the late 1700s were enslaved or had been. The few French planters who controlled the French colony often went to severe and brutal extremes to control the African majority.

Unrest erupted in the early 1790s when enslaved Africans led by a formerly enslaved man named **François Toussaint-Louverture** (TOO•SAN LOO•vuhr•TYUR) revolted, setting fire to plantation homes and fields of sugarcane. One observer described the horrifying scene:

❝ Picture to yourself the whole horizon a wall of fire, from which continually rose thick vortices [whirling columns] of smoke, whose huge black volumes could be likened only to those frightful storm-clouds ... for nearly three weeks we could

Chapter 25 *Democracy and Reform* **667**

TEACH

Guided Practice

THEME Nationalism

Review with students the definition of *nationalism*. (*the feeling that people of the same culture should have their own nation*) Ask students how nationalism can lead to revolution. (*People revolt against foreign governments in an effort to rule themselves.*) Have students cite examples of present-day or historic nationalistic struggles. (*Answers may include: Palestinian Arabs; Bosnians in former Yugoslavia.*) **L1**

Map Study

Answer
Cuba, British Honduras, Trinidad, British Guiana, Dutch Guiana, French Guiana, Falkland Islands, Puerto Rico

Map Skills Practice

Reading a Map What is the only Latin American country that is completely landlocked? (*Paraguay*)

Multicultural Discuss the rigid social order in South American colonies. Ask students to compare this with the Estate system that existed before the French Revolution of 1789. (*Both were rigid social orders that a person was born into; the small number of people in the top classes created discontent.*) **L3**

🎵 World Music: Cultural Traditions, Lesson 2

COOPERATIVE LEARNING ACTIVITY

Creating a Constitution Organize students into teams: priests, *peninsulares*, mestizos, and Creoles. Tell students that their colony has just achieved independence from Spain and they now have the opportunity to form a new government. Have students research the social and economic interests and goals of their groups. Next have the groups discuss their concerns and draw up a platform stating their positions and their goals for the new government. Then have the teams meet in a constitutional convention to create the laws for their new government. Allow students to debate their needs and draw up a constitution. Emphasize the importance of negotiation and compromise throughout the activity. **L2**

barely distinguish between day and night, for so long as the rebels found anything to feed the flames, they never ceased to burn.... **99**

In 1802 Napoleon sent forces to take control of the colony. Captured by French officers, Toussaint-Louverture was imprisoned in France, where he died in 1803. Then a wave of yellow fever aided the revolutionaries. The epidemic swept across the colony, killing thousands of French soldiers. The rebel army defeated the French, and in 1804 Haiti proclaimed its independence.

Mexico Struggles for Freedom

One of the earliest uprisings against Spanish rule occurred in **Mexico**, which at that time was part of New Spain. In 1810 a Catholic priest named **Miguel Hidalgo** led the fight against the Spanish government in Mexico. Hidalgo cared deeply for

History & Art *Father Miguel Hidalgo*, a fresco by José Clemente Orozco, 1937. Governor's Mansion, Guadalajara, Mexico *What two groups made up the rebel force that Hidalgo led against the Spanish army?*

the poverty-stricken Native Americans and mestizos in his parish of Dolores. In addition to political freedom, he also wanted to end slavery and to improve living conditions for Mexico's poor. To Hidalgo, revolt was the only way to bring change to Mexico.

On September 16, 1810, Hidalgo gave a stirring address that became known as "el Grito de Dolores" —the cry of Dolores. In the speech, he called on Mexicans to fight for "Independence and Liberty." Hidalgo then led Native Americans and mestizos on a freedom march to Mexico City that eventually turned into an armed movement. In spite of early advances, Hidalgo and his forces faced mounting opposition from the Spaniards and their Mexican creole allies. In 1811 the well-trained Spanish army finally overwhelmed the rebels, and Hidalgo was captured and executed.

Another priest, José María Morelos, took charge of the revolution after Hidalgo died. Morelos captured a large portion of southern Mexico. In 1813 he called a conference that declared Mexico's independence from Spain. Morelos's forces fought the Spaniards but were defeated in 1815. Like Hidalgo, Morelos was executed.

Despite many battles, Mexico did not gain full independence until 1821. That year, a liberal revolt in Spain threatened to overthrow the monarchy and establish a constitution. This reform frightened wealthy Mexican creoles, who feared such a change might infringe on their own privileges. To make sure this did not happen, they declared independence from Spain in 1821.

Ironically, their leader was Agustín de Iturbide (EE•TUR•BEE•thay), the army officer who had crushed Morelos's movement. Iturbide made himself emperor in 1822, but opposition to his oppressive rule developed. The Mexican people soon deposed Iturbide and declared their country a republic in 1823.

When Mexico became a republic, the Central American provinces in New Spain declared their independence. In Guatemala, representatives established the United Provinces of **Central America**. In the 1830s leaders divided the region into the countries of Costa Rica, El Salvador, Guatemala, Honduras, and Nicaragua.

Spanish South America

Creoles in the Spanish colonies of South America gained an opportunity for independence in 1808 when Napoleon seized control of the Spanish government. The refusal of the Spanish

American colonists to acknowledge Napoleon's government resulted in revolts throughout the empire. In addition, Spain's fight against France, together with the colonies' isolation from their home country, left the Spanish weak and vulnerable to attack. Three outstanding leaders—Simón Bolívar, José de San Martín, and Bernardo O'Higgins—led South American colonies in their fight against Spanish rule.

Simón Bolívar, a creole from **Venezuela**, led many colonies to independence. Bolívar believed in equality and saw liberty as "the only object worth a man's life." Bolívar had witnessed the reforms of the French Revolution. Called "the Liberator," Bolívar devoted his life to freedom for Latin Americans.

In 1810 Bolívar started a revolt against the Spaniards in Caracas. After nearly 9 years of fighting, Bolívar crushed Spain's power in northern South America at the Battle of Boyacá in 1819. During the next 20 years, Bolívar and his forces won freedom for the present-day countries of Venezuela, Colombia, Panama, Bolivia, and Ecuador.

While Bolívar fought in Venezuela, another revolutionary leader, **José de San Martín** of **Argentina**, led Latin American armies over the Andes Mountains and into **Chile**. In Chile, San Martín joined Bernardo O'Higgins. Together, their forces successfully achieved independence for Chile in 1818. San Martín then set off to free **Peru** in 1820. Within a year he captured Lima and declared Peru independent.

In July 1822 San Martín and Bolívar met in the Ecuadorian port of Guayaquil (GWY•uh•KEEL) to discuss the future of Latin America. Though they shared a common goal, they could not agree on strategy and policy. San Martín finally decided to withdraw from the revolt and allowed Bolívar to take command. By 1826 Bolívar and his armies had liberated all of South America.

Brazil Gains Independence

Brazil achieved its independence without the bloodshed that accompanied the liberation of Spanish America. In 1808 Napoleon's French army had invaded Portugal, causing the Portuguese royal family to flee to Brazil.

King João transferred his monarchy to Brazil, declaring Rio de Janeiro capital of the Portuguese Empire. João immediately introduced governmental reforms in Brazil. He reinstated more favorable trade laws by opening Brazil's ports to the world. João also worked to make the agriculture and

mining industries more profitable. Soon both industry and commerce were flourishing.

The liberal ruler brought Brazilians increasing opportunities by funding public education, including military academies, an art school, and medical schools. With these reforms Brazil moved quickly toward independence, and in 1815 João made Brazil a self-governing kingdom within the Portuguese Empire.

King João came to love the semitropical land of mountains and endless forests; he chose to remain there after Napoleon was defeated in 1815. In 1820, however, liberals took over the Portuguese government. Determined to save his throne, he returned to Portugal. He left Brazil in the hands of his 23-year-old son, Dom Pedro.

The new Portuguese government fought to make Brazil a colonial possession again. Leaders ended free trade and many of the other advantages Brazil had enjoyed under João's monarchy. They also demanded that Dom Pedro abandon his rule and immediately return to Portugal. Supported by his father, Dom Pedro declared that he would remain in Brazil. Dom Pedro defied Portuguese leaders by calling a constitutional convention and answered their angry response with a cry of "Independence or death!"

In September 1822 Brazil won full independence from Portugal. Three months later Dom Pedro was

Greeks Fight for Independence

Greece, 1821
Greece's struggle for independence from the Ottoman Turks began in 1821 when Greek fighters gained control of the Peloponnesus and many islands in the Aegean Sea. But in 1825, a combined army of Turks and Egyptians regained these regions. France, Great Britain, and Russia came to Greece's aid in 1827 and defeated the Turkish-Egyptian fleet in the Battle of Navarino. By 1829 both the Turks and the Egyptians left Greece, and Greece became independent that year.

Greece

Cultural Perspectives
Other Revolts The spirit of revolt also swept through China during the 1800s. The Taiping Rebellion (1850–1864) tore the country apart when a group combining Christian and ancient Chinese beliefs attempted to create a perfect society with an equal division of land among the people. In 1899–1900, a Chinese group led the Boxer Rebellion in which they tried to protect their traditions against Western influences.

Who?What?Where?When?
Brazil is the fifth-largest country in the world. It encompasses an area greater than that of the 48 contiguous states of the United States.

ASSESS

Check for Understanding
Assign Section 5 Assessment as homework or as an in-class activity.

🔲 Use Interactive Tutor Self-Assessment Software to review Section 5.

MAKING CONNECTIONS ACTIVITY

Religion The Roman Catholic Church was extremely powerful in Latin America in the nineteenth century. Have students investigate the role of the Church in Latin America today and answer the question: How has the role of the Church changed in Latin America during the past 150 years? Students should research the Church's role in the social affairs of the people, in economics, and in political affairs. After doing the research, students should present the information in a panel presentation. **L2**

Evaluate

 Section Quiz 25-5

 Use the Testmaker to create a customized quiz for Section 5.

Reteach

Ask students to imagine they have to write a history of the Latin American independence movement. Ask them to create an outline of the topics and key information they would include in their book.

 Reteaching Activity 25

 Reading Essentials and Study Guide 25-5

Enrich

Remind students that the main reason European powers wanted colonies was for their raw materials. Ask students to report on how the economies of selected Latin American countries have changed since the days of colonialism.

 Enrichment Activity 25

CLOSE

Have students make lists of general causes for revolutions based on revolutions they have studied thus far. Have them write a brief explanation of how the Latin American revolutions were similar to and different from others they have studied.

---

crowned Emperor **Pedro I** of Brazil. With Pedro ruling the empire under a constitution, Brazil became the only independent country in South America to freely choose a constitutional monarchy as its form of government.

Meanwhile, João maintained his support of his beloved Brazil by refusing to allow the Portuguese government to send new military forces to fight the rebels. Great Britain also pressured Portugal to end its battle. In 1825 Portugal finally recognized Brazil's independence.

Challenges to Growth

By the mid-1820s most Latin American countries had won their independence. Their next task was to achieve national unity and a stable government. These goals, however, were difficult to reach. Simón Bolívar, who had dreamed of uniting all of northern South America into one large and powerful state, became so disappointed and disillusioned that he wrote, "Those who have toiled for liberty in South America have plowed the sea."

Common Problems

In trying to build stable and prosperous nations, Latin Americans faced a number of challenges. One obstacle was the geography of Central and South America. High mountains and thick jungles made transportation and communication difficult, hindering trade and economic growth. Vast areas of fertile land remained undeveloped. Population centers, separated by physical barriers, became rivals instead of allies.

Other problems were part of Latin America's colonial heritage. Spanish and Portuguese rule had given the Latin Americans little practice in governing themselves. Instead, they were used to authoritarian government, which was not responsible to the people and demanded obedience from them.

In the colonial system, political power was in the hands of the executive branch of government. The judicial branch was weak and limited, and the legislative branch was practically nonexistent. Latin Americans had strong, well-educated leaders, but they had no experience in the legislative process. Simón Bolívar complained that the colonial system had kept his people in a state of "permanent childhood" with regard to knowledge of running a government.

Independence did not bring about much change in social conditions in Latin America. Catholicism remained the official religion, and Church and government continued to be closely tied. The new countries also continued to maintain a separation between upper and lower classes. The dominant group was now the creoles instead of the *peninsulares*. Creoles owned the best land and controlled business and government. Their privileged position was resented, especially by the mestizos.

Continuing Political Conflicts

Soon after independence, political conflicts increased. Liberals called for separation of Church and state, the breakup of large estates, higher taxes on land, public social services, and civilian control of the government. Most of the liberals were mestizos, intellectuals, or merchants who wanted free trade. Opposed to this group were the creoles, most of whom were rich landowners, church leaders, and military officers. These conservatives favored strong central government and a powerful Church and army.

The decades that followed the wars for independence saw an ongoing struggle for economic strength and social justice. Although many South American governments were republics in appearance, many actually were military dictatorships. Today, there still remains in many Latin American countries a vast gap between the ruling rich and the underprivileged poor.

SECTION 5 ASSESSMENT

Main Idea
1. Use a diagram like the one below to describe ways in which Latin American countries won independence.

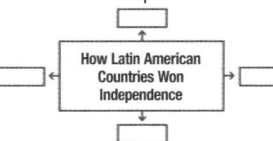

Recall
2. **Define** *peninsulares*, creoles, mestizos.
3. **Identify** François Toussaint-Louverture, Miguel Hidalgo, Simón Bolívar, José de San Martín, Pedro I.

Critical Thinking
4. **Making Comparisons** How did the independence move-

ment in Mexico differ from the independence movement in Brazil?

Understanding Themes
5. **Nationalism** Did the coming of independence from European rule bring social and political advances to many Latin American countries? Why or why not?

SECTION 5 ASSESSMENT ANSWERS

1. Haiti: revolted against France, gained independence in 1804; Mexico: revolution led to independence in 1821; Spanish South America: revolts led by Simón Bolívar and José de San Martín; by 1826, Bolívar liberated all of South America; Brazil: Portuguese king's son declared

Brazil's independence in 1822
2. All terms are defined in the Glossary.
3. François Toussaint-Louverture, 667; Miguel Hidalgo, 668; Simón Bolívar, 669; José de San Martín, 669; Pedro I, 670
4. The independence movement in Mexico was violent; in Brazil, the king granted

independence without violence.
5. **NATIONALISM** Answers will vary. Possible answer: No, there was still separation between upper and lower classes; creoles assumed the positions formally held by the *peninsulares* and ignored the needs of the mestizos.

Reading a Cartogram

On most maps, land area is drawn in proportion to actual surface area. On some maps, however, a small country may appear large, and a large country may look small. Even the shapes of the countries may look different. Why do these maps seem so distorted?

Learning the Skill

Maps that distort country size and shape are called **cartograms**. In a cartogram, country size reflects some value *other* than a land area, such as population or gross national product. For example, on a conventional map Canada appears much larger than India. In a cartogram showing world population, however, India would appear larger than Canada because it has a much larger population. The cartogram is a tool for making visual comparisons. At a glance, you can see how each country or region compares with another in a particular value.

To use a cartogram, first read the title and key to identify what value the cartogram illustrates. Then examine the cartogram to see which countries or regions appear. Find the largest and smallest countries. Compare the cartogram with a conventional land-area map to determine the degree of distortion of particular countries. Finally, draw conclusions about the topic.

Practicing the Skill

Study the cartogram shown at the top right and answer these questions.

1. What is the subject of the cartogram?
2. Which country appears largest on the cartogram? Which appears smallest?
3. Compare the cartogram to the map of Europe found in the Atlas. Which countries are most distorted in size compared to a land-area map?
4. What accounts for these distortions?

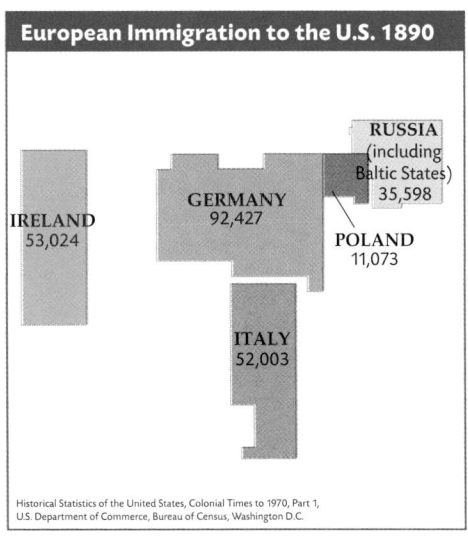

European Immigration to the U.S. 1890

IRELAND 53,024

GERMANY 92,427

RUSSIA (including Baltic States) 35,598

POLAND 11,073

ITALY 52,003

Historical Statistics of the United States, Colonial Times to 1970, Part 1,
U.S. Department of Commerce, Bureau of Census, Washington D.C.

Applying the Skill

At the library, find statistics that compare some value for different states or countries. For example, you might compare the number of farms in each state, or annual oil consumption of countries in North America.

Convert these statistics into a simple cartogram. Determine the relative size of each country or state according to the chosen value. If the United States consumes five times more oil than does Mexico, then the United States should appear five times larger.

For More Practice

Turn to the Skill Practice in the Chapter Assessment on page 673.

The **Glencoe Skillbuilder Interactive Workbook**, Level 2 provides instruction and practice in key social studies skills.

TEACH

Reading a Cartogram Suggest that students imagine they are members of a city school board charged with the responsibility of planning where the city needs new schools. The standard city map shows the various residential areas and the borders of school districts. Ask students to consider how a cartogram would help them. Suggest that if it showed at a glance the relative numbers of school-age children in each district, this would help them to judge the capacity needs. Ask students to brainstorm other situations where a cartogram would be helpful.

Additional Practice

 Skill Reinforcement Activity 25

GLENCOE TECHNOLOGY

 Glencoe's **Skillbuilder Interactive Workbook, Level 2**
This interactive CD-ROM promotes student mastery of key social studies skills.

ANSWERS TO PRACTICING THE SKILL

1. European immigration to the United States in 1890
2. Germany; Poland
3. Ireland and Russia
4. the number of immigrants these nations sent to the United States relative to their size

CHAPTER 25 ASSESSMENT

—WORLD HISTORY
Online

Have students use the **Chapter 25 Self-Check Quiz** at worldhistory.glencoe.com to prepare for the Chapter Test.

GLENCOE
TECHNOLOGY

 VIDEODISC
Use MindJogger to review the chapter.

MindJogger Videoquiz

Chapter 25
Disc 4 Side A

Also available in VHS.

Answers

Using Key Terms
1. c   3. j   5. b
2. l   4. k

Using Your History Journal

Have students refer to the maps they made of Britain's territories and choose one to write about. Be sure they supply details and sources.

Reviewing Facts
1. 1801: Act of Union joins Ireland and Great Britain; 1829: Catholics win right to vote; 1840s: potato famine; 1845: potato crop destroyed; 1914: home rule bill passed, never put into effect
2. most British middle-class men; British working-class men, women
3. Middle-class felt that Louis Philippe favored the rich; they overthrew his government.
4. Napoleon felt that Prussia was gaining too much power; the Prussians defeated the French, and Napoleon's empire collapsed.
5. Louisiana Purchase; Mexican Cession; Oregon Country; Gadsden Purchase
6. Toussaint-Louverture, Hidalgo, Bolívar, San Martín, O'Higgins

---

WORLD HISTORY *Online*

Self-Check Quiz

Visit the *World History: The Human Experience* Web site at **worldhistory.glencoe.com** and click on *Chapter 25—Self-Check Quiz* to prepare for the Chapter Test.

Using Key Terms

Write the key term that completes each sentence. Then write a sentence for each term not chosen.

a. creoles
b. disenfranchised
c. dominion
d. home rule
e. seceded
f. ratify
g. *peninsulares*
h. sectionalism
i. ultraroyalists
j. suffragettes
k. plebiscite
l. mestizos

1. A self-governing country other than Great Britain that recognizes the British monarch as its head of state is called a _____.
2. _____ are Latin Americans of mixed Native American and European ancestry.
3. Women in Great Britain who led a voting rights campaign for women became known as _____.
4. In 1851 Louis-Napoleon called for a _____, or national vote, asking the French people to give him support to create a new constitution.
5. While the Reform Act of 1832 gave middle-class men the right to vote, agricultural laborers, factory workers, and women remained _____.

Technology Activity

Using a Computerized Card Catalog Use the computerized card catalog in your school or local library to locate sources about Latin American countries. Research current information about a country from that region. Organize your research into a fact sheet. Include headings such as history, culture, religion, demographics, economics, and government. Provide a map of your country illustrating features such as mountain ranges, bodies of water, natural resources and major cities.

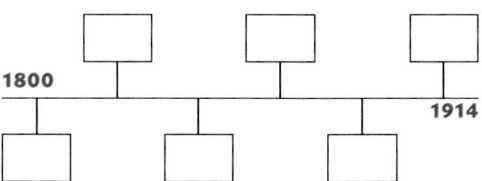

Using Your History Journal

Write a short report on a political issue in one of Great Britain's former territories, such as Hong Kong's return to Chinese rule in 1997, or the movement for an independent Quebec.

Reviewing Facts

1. **History** Use a time line like the one below to identify key events in the struggle for Irish rights.

1800 _____ 1914

2. **Citizenship** List the groups in Great Britain that gained the right to vote under the Reform Act of 1832. What groups were still excluded from voting?
3. **Government** Explain why many French people came to oppose the constitutional monarchy of Louis Philippe. How did this opposition affect Louis Philippe's rule?
4. **History** Explain why France went to war in 1870. What was the result of the conflict?
5. **Geography** Identify three land acquisitions that significantly expanded the territorial borders of the United States in the 1800s.
6. **Government** Name three leaders who helped win freedom for Latin American countries.

Critical Thinking

1. **Apply** Compare the movement toward democratic reform in Great Britain with similar movements in France under Louis Philippe. How were they alike? How did they differ?
2. **Synthesize** How did expansion and the Civil War affect the growth of democracy and civil rights in the United States?

Critical Thinking

1. Alike: Reform movements in both countries sought to expand voting rights to the working class. Different: The British democratic movements were peaceful; the French movement was violent.
2. Settlers moving west pressed for extension of voting rights, and their liberal policies soon influenced the country; the Civil War ended slavery and ushered in constitutional guaran-

tees of civil rights for African Americans.
3. With European nations involved in conflict, the United States was able to expand its territory with few prohibitions. European countries were willing to sell North American land to raise money for their wars at home.

Geography in History
1. Great Britain
2. United States

3. Evaluate How did conflict in Europe in the 1800s contribute to the development of the United States?

Geography in History

1. Movement Refer to the map below. Which European nation lost the most emigrants in this period?
2. Movement To which nation did most Europeans migrate during this period?
3. Human/Environment Interaction What caused many Irish people to migrate to the United States in the 1840s?
4. Region What circumstances in Europe caused millions of people to migrate during this period?

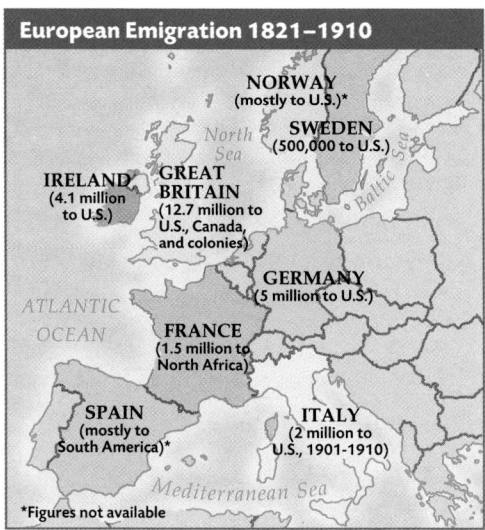

European Emigration 1821–1910

NORWAY (mostly to U.S.)*

SWEDEN (500,000 to U.S.)

IRELAND (4.1 million to U.S.)

GREAT BRITAIN (12.7 million to U.S., Canada, and colonies)

GERMANY (5 million to U.S.)

FRANCE (1.5 million to North Africa)

SPAIN (mostly to South America)*

ITALY (2 million to U.S., 1901–1910)

ATLANTIC OCEAN

North Sea

Baltic Sea

Mediterranean Sea

*Figures not available

Understanding Themes

1. Change From your reading, would you say that the method of gradual reform was the best way that the British could have taken to change their government and society in the 1800s?
2. Movement How did British settlement of the dominions affect the original inhabitants?
3. Revolution Why do you think revolutions are often followed by governments led by dictators?
4. Change How did immigration affect the economic growth of the United States?

5. Nationalism How did the American Revolution affect Latin America in the early 1800s?

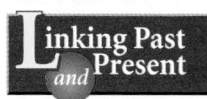

Linking Past and Present

1. British and American women fought to win the right to vote. What rights do women seek today? Are their methods today similar to or different from past methods?
2. After slavery was abolished in the United States, African Americans and other groups still had to struggle for equality. What educational and employment opportunities do some Americans seek today?
3. The Irish were granted home rule in 1914, but it never went into effect. How does this relate to the politics in Ireland today?

Skill Practice

Study the cartogram below and then answer these questions.

1. What is the subject of the cartogram?
2. Which country appears largest on the cartogram? Which appears smallest?
3. Compare the cartogram to a world map or globe. Which countries are most distorted in size compared to a land-area map?
4. What accounts for these distortions?

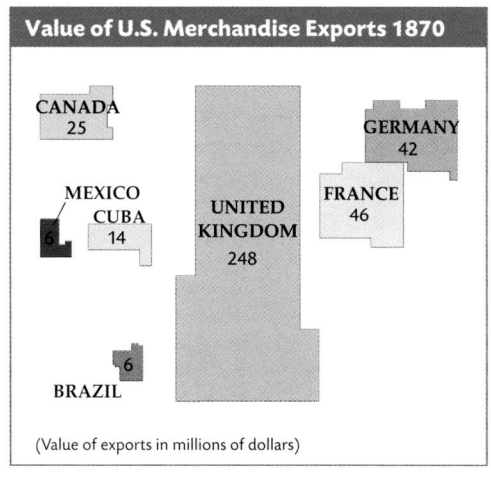

Value of U.S. Merchandise Exports 1870

CANADA 25

GERMANY 42

MEXICO

CUBA 14

FRANCE 46

UNITED KINGDOM 248

6

6

BRAZIL

(Value of exports in millions of dollars)

4. **CHANGE** Immigrants provided the workforce for the expanding United States industries.
5. **NATIONALISM** The example of the American Revolution inspired Latin Americans to end colonial rule and join independence movements.

Linking Past and Present

1. Possible answer: Women still seek equal pay for equal work and an end to sex discrimination. Methods used today by the women's movement are less dramatic and violent.
2. Possible answer: African Americans continue to seek legislation to fight discrimination.
3. The Irish Catholics in Northern Ireland continue to resent British rule, and some of them use terrorism to protest.

Skill Practice

1. value of United States merchandise exports in 1870
2. United Kingdom; Mexico or Brazil
3. Canada, the United Kingdom, Brazil
4. the value of these countries' United States merchandise exports relative to their size

? Chapter Bonus Test Question

Ask students: What political, social, economic, or other conditions make it easiest for a country to achieve democratic government with civil rights for all citizens? What conditions make it most difficult? *(Answers may include that some history of self-government or of limitations on monarchical power make it easiest; traditions of absolute rule and a rigid social class structure make it most difficult.)*

3. the potato famine
4. Possible answers: the revolts in Europe; economic instability; colonization of territory.

Understanding Themes

1. **CHANGE** Possible answer: It seems that Great Britain's way of achieving democracy was the smoothest, most stable, and longest lasting.

2. **MOVEMENT** It brought them deadly diseases, took away their land, and led to conflicts that killed many native peoples.
3. **REVOLUTION** Possible answer: The people have been used to being ruled by an autocratic government and may not know how to go about ruling themselves. It may be difficult for opposing factions to agree on the best way of establishing the new government.

A complete, 1-page lesson plan is provided for each section in the *Reproducible Lesson Plans* booklet.

Reaction and Nationalism

CHAPTER RESOURCES

	Reproducible Resources	Multimedia Resources
Chapter Opener	Chapter Themes: Graphic Organizer 26 Historical Significance Chapter Activity 26	MindJogger Videoquiz
Chapter Enrichment	Vocabulary Activity 26* Time Line Activity 26 Mapping History Activity 26 History Simulation 26 Geography and History Activity 26 Source Reading 26 People in World History Profiles 49, 50 World Art and Music Activity 26 Enrichment Activity 26 Critical Thinking Activity 26 Skill Reinforcement Activity 26 Writer's Guidebook, Lesson 9 Performance Assessment Activity 26 Standardized Test Practice Workbook Activity 26 Inclusion for the Social Studies Classroom Strategies and Activities	Mapping History Overlay Transparency 17, *Revolutionary Centers in Europe 1820–1848* Chapter Transparency 26 Vocabulary PuzzleMaker Software Turning Points in World History: *The Russian Revolution* World History Primary Source Document Library
Chapter Review/Reteaching	Reteaching Activity 26 Skill Reinforcement Activity 26 Spanish Chapter Summary 26	Chapter 26 Digest Audiocassette, Activity, Test* Vocabulary PuzzleMaker Software Interactive Tutor Self-Assessment Software MindJogger Videoquiz
Chapter Evaluation/Testing	Performance Assessment Activity 26 Chapter 26 Test, Forms A and B	ExamView® Pro Testmaker

* Also available in Spanish

0:00 OUT OF TIME? Assign the Chapter 26 Audiocassettes.

World History Primary Source Document Library
Make History Come Alive!
Engage your students with over 250 easily accessible primary source documents—available on this CD-ROM—that will give them real life insight into the important events of world history.

Block Schedule
Activities that are particularly suited to use within the block scheduling framework are identified throughout this chapter by the following designation.

KEY TO ABILITY LEVELS
Teaching strategies are coded for varying learning styles.
- **L1 BASIC** activities for all students
- **L2 AVERAGE** activities for average to above-average students
- **L3 CHALLENGING** activities for above-average students
- **LEP LIMITED ENGLISH PROFICIENCY** activities

Use Glencoe's **Presentation Plus!** multimedia teacher tool to easily present dynamic lessons that visually excite your students. Using Microsoft PowerPoint® you can customize the presentations to create your own personalized lessons.

Interactive Lesson Planner

Planning has never been easier! Using this CD-ROM, organize your week, month, semester, or year with all the help you need. The **Interactive Lesson Planner** gives you access to all of the blackline masters that accompany *World History: The Human Experience.*

SECTION RESOURCES

Daily Objectives	Reproducible Resources	Multimedia Resources
Section 1 **The Unification of Italy** Explain how nationalism led to a united Italy in the 1860s.	Lecture Notes 26-1 Reproducible Lesson Plan 26-1 Vocabulary Activity 26* Guided Reading Activity 26-1* History Simulation 26 Time Line Activity 26 Section Quiz 26-1* Reading Essentials and Study Guide 26-1	Section Focus Transparency 26-1 Chapter Transparency 26 Interactive Tutor Self-Assessment Software Testmaker
Section 2 **The Unification of Germany** Identify the methods Bismarck used to unite the German states.	Lecture Notes 26-2 Reproducible Lesson Plan 26-2 Vocabulary Activity 26* Guided Reading Activity 26-2* Section Quiz 26-2* Reading Essentials and Study Guide 26-2	Section Focus Transparency 26-2 Interactive Tutor Self-Assessment Software Testmaker
Section 3 **Bismarck's Realm** Analyze how Bismarck's policies affected the German Empire.	Lecture Notes 26-3 Reproducible Lesson Plan 26-3 Vocabulary Activity 26* Guided Reading Activity 26-3* Section Quiz 26-3* Reading Essentials and Study Guide 26-3	Section Focus Transparency 26-3 Interactive Tutor Self-Assessment Software Testmaker
Section 4 **Empire of the Czars** Explain why revolutionary movements developed in Russia.	Lecture Notes 26-4 Reproducible Lesson Plan 26-4 Guided Reading Activity 26-4* Geography and History Activity 26 Section Quiz 26-4* Reading Essentials and Study Guide 26-4	Section Focus Transparency 26-4 Vocabulary PuzzleMaker Software Interactive Tutor Self-Assessment Software Testmaker Turning Points in World History: *The Russian Revolution*
Section 5 **Austria-Hungary's Decline** Describe how the growth of nationalistic feelings affected the empire of Austria-Hungary.	Lecture Notes 26-5 Reproducible Lesson Plan 26-5 Vocabulary Activity 26* Guided Reading Activity 26-5* Reteaching Activity 26 Enrichment Activity 26 Section Quiz 26-5* Performance Assessment Activity 26 Spanish Chapter Summary 26 Reading Essentials and Study Guide 26-5	Section Focus Transparency 26-5 Mapping History Overlay Transparency 17, *Revolutionary Centers in Europe 1820–1848* Interactive Tutor Self-Assessment Software Testmaker

* Also available in Spanish

Chapter Activities

Performance Assessment Activity

A Portfolio of Examples The concepts featured in this chapter include sectionalism, nationalism, and empire. Ask students to make connections with their own lives by creating a portfolio of contemporary examples of these concepts. For each example, have students discuss the positive and negative roles played by diversity and unity in the situation. Students may include examples from politics, business, city, and the family. As a concluding activity, have students write a reflection in their portfolios in which they explain how diversity and unity affect their lives.

Possible Rubric Features
Concept attainment for concepts and themes studied, organization and classification of portfolio, analytical skills, clarity and detail of reflection

• *For an additional activity, refer to Activity 26 in the* Performance Assessment Strategies and Activities *booklet.*

ACTIVITY

From the Classroom of...

**Kimberly C. Felder
Frederick Douglass
Academy
New York, NY**

Nationalism Then and Now
Organize students into four groups: Germany, Italy, Russia, and Austria-Hungary. Have each group use the text to review the nationalistic struggle in its country, or provide groups with fact sheets. Then have each group write a letter to the editor of a newspaper in their country, arguing a nationalistic position.

Distribute magazine and newspaper articles about current nationalistic struggles (try to include letters to the editor). Have the entire class compare the late twentieth-century struggles with the nationalistic movements of the nineteenth century.

MULTIPLE LEARNING STYLES

Verbal/Linguistic
Have students write an essay comparing the effects of war on the governments of Italy, Germany, Russia, Austria-Hungary, and the Ottoman Empire during the last half of the 1800s. Ask students to consider how war strengthened or weakened the governments and what political changes war caused.

Logical/Mathematical
Have students make a time line that shows the main events in the spread of nationalism through Italy, Germany, Russia, Austria-Hungary, and the Ottoman Empire.

Visual/Spatial
Have students create a picture gallery of the many personalities mentioned in the chapter. Have them accompany each copy of a portrait with a thumbnail sketch of the person.

Auditory/Musical
Have students develop a musical collage of works by Richard Wagner, Giuseppe Verdi, and Modest Mussorgsky that show the spirit of nationalism.

Kinesthetic
Have students create a board game that uses Bismarck's domestic and foreign strategies to bring about a unified Germany.

GLENCOE'S ASSESSMENT ADVANTAGE

Use the following to easily assess student learning in a variety of ways.

- Performance Assessment Strategies and Activities
- Section Quizzes
- Chapter and Unit Tests
- Interactive Tutor Self-Assessment Software
- Testmaker Software
- MindJogger Videoquiz
- SAT/SAT II Test Practice
- worldhistory.glencoe.com

Additional Resources

NATIONAL GEOGRAPHIC SOCIETY

Teacher's Corner

INDEX TO NATIONAL GEOGRAPHIC MAGAZINE

The following articles may be used for research relating to this chapter:

- "Reinventing Berlin," by Peter Ross Range, December 1996.
- "Crimea: Pearl of a Fallen Empire," by Peter T. White, September 1994.
- "St. Petersburg: Capital of the Tsars," by Steve Raymer, December 1993.
- "The Morning After: German Revisited," by William S. Ellis, September 1991.
- "Berlin's Ode to Joy," by Priit J. Vesilind, April 1990.

ADDITIONAL NATIONAL GEOGRAPHIC SOCIETY PRODUCTS

To order the following products for use with this chapter, call National Geographic Society at 1-800-368-2728:

- *The Democratic Government Series: Germany (Video)*
- *Russia's Last Tsar (Video)*

Access National Geographic's new dynamic MapMachine Web site and other geography resources at:

- http://www.nationalgeographic.com/
- http://www.nationalgeographic.com/maps/

BIBLIOGRAPHY

Literature of the Period
Dostoyevsky, Fyodor. *The Possessed.* Translated by Constance Garnett. New York: Modern Library, 1963. A Russian novel about nineteenth-century revolutionaries.

Readings for the Student
Snyder, L. L. *A Comparative History of Nationalism.* New York: Holt, 1976. An introduction to the different varieties of nationalism.

Readings for the Teacher
Knapton, Ernest John, and Thomas Kingston Derry. *Europe: 1815–1914.* New York: Scribners, 1965. Comprehensive history of Europe that includes cultural, social, and economic trends as well as political, diplomatic, and military themes.

WORLD HISTORY Online

Use our Web site as an additional resource. All essential content is covered in the Student Edition.

You and your students can visit the *World History: The Human Experience* Web site at worldhistory.glencoe.com The student text directs students to the Web site for the following options:

- **Chapter Overviews**
- **Student Web Activities**
- **Self-Check Quizzes**

Answers are provided for you in a link entitled "Web Activity Lesson Plan." Additional Web Resources, Interactive Puzzles, and content updates are also available.

Visit the Glencoe Web site at socialstudies.glencoe.com for social studies activities, updates, and links to other resources.

LOCAL OBJECTIVES

_____
_____
_____
_____
_____
_____
_____
_____
_____
_____
_____
_____
_____
_____
_____
_____
_____
_____

CHAPTER THEMES

Chapter Themes are listed by section on this chapter opening page of the Student Edition. A corresponding theme-based activity is available under "TEACH," and a theme-based question is asked in the Section and Chapter Assessments.

Storyteller

Historical Setting Giuseppe Mazzini, born in Genoa in 1805, founded Young Italy, a secret society whose goal was the unification of Italy. Mazzini spent most of his life in exile under a sentence of death. While in Switzerland, he and exiles from Poland and Germany founded Young Europe. Their vision was a Europe of many free nations coming together through an elected assembly that would regulate matters of common interest.

Historical Significance

Answers: *French nationalism under Napoleon brought parts of Europe into the French Empire. When the Congress of Vienna broke up the French Empire and divided much of Europe among Prussia, Russia, and Austria, it set the stage for nationalist movements in those lands.*

Nationalist feelings in the Balkans led to World War I and to the recent war in Bosnia; Hitler's nationalistic program to unite the German people and create a German Empire led to World War II; nationalist feelings in Africa and Asia broke up the British and French Empires.

— **WORLD HISTORY** —
Online

Have students use the **Chapter 26 Overview** at worldhistory. glencoe.com as a prereading and postreading exercise for understanding chapter content.

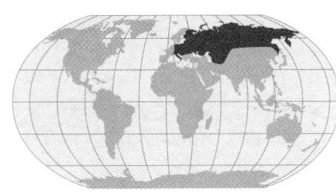

Chapter
26 1815–1914
Reaction and Nationalism

Chapter Themes

▶ **Nationalism** The rise of nationalism contributes to the unification of Italy. *Section 1*
▶ **Conflict** Bismarck uses war and diplomacy to bring unity to Germany. *Section 2*
▶ **Change** Bismarck's German Empire allows for economic growth but limits political freedoms. *Section 3*
▶ **Reaction** Czars oppose the forces of liberalism and nationalism in the Russian Empire. *Section 4*
▶ **Diversity** The empire of Austria-Hungary contains many nationalities seeking self-rule. *Section 5*

Storyteller

One Sunday in 1821, 16-year-old Giuseppe Mazzini walked along a street in Genoa, Italy. Suddenly a tall, black-bearded stranger approached him. With a piercing look, the stranger held out his hand for money and said, "for the refugees of Italy." Everyone knew that the refugees were those who had recently rebelled against the Austrians to win independence for Italy.

Forty years later, Mazzini—now a leader of the Italian nationalist movement—wrote of this incident: "That day was the first in which ... [I realized that] ... we Italians could and therefore ought to struggle for the liberty of our country." During the early 1800s feelings of nationalism similar to Mazzini's began to stir all across Europe.

Historical Significance

How has the force of nationalism repeatedly changed the map of Europe? What impact has nationalism had on European and world developments in the twentieth century?

1795	1835	1875	1915

1861 Alexander II frees serfs in Russia.

1912 War breaks out in the Balkans.

1815 Congress of Vienna creates German Confederation.

1848 Revolutions sweep Europe.

1890 Bismarck resigns.

674

GEOGRAPHY CONNECTION

Location On a historical map of Europe of about 1860, have students locate the independent Italian states and German states, the Russian Empire, Austria-Hungary, and the Ottoman Empire. Why would Austria-Hungary and Russia be interested in land in the Ottoman Empire? *(The Ottoman Empire bordered both Austria-Hungary and Russia.)* Then have students compare the historical map with a present-day map of Europe. What area in present-day Italy remains part of the Papal States? *(Vatican City)*

History & Art In 1860 Giuseppe Garibaldi had conquered the Kingdom of the Two Sicilies in southern Italy, while Victor Emmanuel II had brought most of northern Italy into his kingdom. When the two men met at the bridge of Teano, Garibaldi surrendered his conquests to Victor Emmanuel and hailed him as king of Italy.

 Performance Assessment

Refer to the activity on page 674C of the Planning Guide.

For an additional activity, refer to Activity 26 in the *Performance Assessment Strategies and Activities* booklet.

History & Art *Meeting at Teano* by Cesare Maccari. Palazzo Pubblico, Siena, Italy
A desire to unite Italy brought together Sardinia's King Victor Emmanuel II (left) and the revolutionary leader Giuseppe Garibaldi (right).

WORLD HISTORY *Online*

Chapter Overview

Visit the *World History: The Human Experience* Web site at **worldhistory.glencoe.com** and click on **Chapter 26—Chapter Overview** to preview the chapter.

Your History Journal

Write a report on a subtopic from "Powder Keg in the Balkans" in Section 5 of this chapter. Suggested titles: Decline of the Ottoman Empire, The Crimean War, Russo-Turkish War, The Congress of Berlin, Russian Objectives in the Balkans, British Objectives in the Balkans.

Using Your History Journal

Have students research one of the suggested report topics by using outside sources. Suggest that they take notes for their report in their journals.

 GLENCOE TECHNOLOGY

 VIDEODISC
Use MindJogger to preview chapter content.

MindJogger Videoquiz

 Chapter 26 Disc 4 Side A

Also available in VHS.

Chapter 26 *Reaction and Nationalism* 675

✚ EXTRA CREDIT PROJECT

Oral Report Have students use outside sources to do in-depth research on one of the people mentioned in this chapter or on a person or group not mentioned in the chapter that was involved in a European nationalist movement during the 1800s. Suggest that they cover the background, education, social position, political ideas, and political actions of the person or group. Ask them to analyze the success or failure of their person or group.

1820   1860   1900

1831 Giuseppe Mazzini founds Young Italy.

1861 Italians establish a united kingdom.

1871 Victor Emmanuel II moves the capital from Florence to Rome.

SECTION THEME

▶ **Nationalism** The rise of nationalism contributes to the unification of Italy.

Guide to Reading

For reading strategies to help students read effectively see pages 12–13. Have students think about the main head as they read the subheads.

Vocabulary Pre-check

🔲 Use the Vocabulary PuzzleMaker for Chapter 26 to create a crossword puzzle to reinforce section terms. **L1 LEP**

📁 Use Vocabulary Activity 26 to introduce vocabulary terms. **L1 LEP**

FOCUS

Section Objective

Explain how nationalism led to a united Italy in the 1860s.

**BELLRINGER
Motivational Activity**

Before taking roll at the beginning of the class period, project Section Focus Transparency 26-1 and have students answer the activity questions. Discuss students' responses.

📁 This activity is also available as a blackline master.

Section 1

The Unification of Italy

Guide to Reading

Read to Find Out
Main Idea *Nationalism led to a united Italy in the 1860s.*

▶ **Terms to Define**
nationalism, nation-state, guerrilla warfare

▶ **People to Meet**
Giuseppe Mazzini, Charles Albert, Victor Emmanuel II, Count Camillo di Cavour, Giuseppe Garibaldi

▶ **Places to Locate**
Florence, Genoa, Sicily, Sardinia, Rome

ⓈT<small>The</small>oryteller

*As the crowd shouted "Viva Verdi!",
Giuseppe Verdi smiled. He understood the phrase's double meaning. Although the throng appreciated his operas, they were actually demonstrating for a unified Italy. The* Risorgimento, *those wishing for a unified Italy, adopted Verdi's music as a rally-cry supporting Victor Emmanuel, the king of Sardinia. When people cheered "Viva Verdi," the occupying Austrians thought they were praising the musician. But the words meant* Viva Vittorio Emanuele, Re D'Italia—*long live Victor Emmanuel, king of Italy.*

—adapted from *A History of Western Music,* Donald J. Grout and Claude V. Palisca, 1988

The Musician Giuseppe Verdi *by Boldini*

676 Chapter 26 *Reaction and Nationalism*

---

rom about the 1100s to the 1800s, central Europe was made up of numerous kingdoms, principalities, and free cities. Stimulated by the desire for economic growth, by the success of the American Revolution, and by the experience of the Napoleonic Wars, a small but dedicated group of Italians and Germans worked to unify these territories into nations in the 1800s. The desire for national independence that inspired them, known as nationalism, became one of the most powerful forces at work in Europe during the 1800s.

In 1815 the modern nation of Italy did not yet exist. At that time the Italian Peninsula was divided into a number of independent states, many of which had foreign rulers. A French Bourbon monarch ruled the Kingdom of the Two Sicilies, while Austria controlled Lombardy and Venetia and the pope controlled the Papal States.

In addition to political divisions, cultural and economic differences divided the regions of the Italian Peninsula. Not only did people speak different dialects of the Italian language, but trade barriers and poor transportation discouraged the flow of goods and people. To move goods the 200 miles (322 km) from **Florence** to Milan often took 8 weeks.

While cultural and economic divisions continued into the 1900s, a growing unification movement eventually swept aside the political divisions on the Italian Peninsula. By the 1860s, Italy had become a single country.

Early Attempts

The name given to the movement for Italian unity was *Risorgimento* (ree•ZAWR•jih•MEHN •toh), meaning the "resurgence" or "revival."

SECTION RESOURCES

📁 **Reproducible Masters**
- Lecture Notes 26-1
- Reproducible Lesson Plan 26-1
- Vocabulary Activity 26
- Guided Reading Activity 26-1
- History Simulation 26
- Time Line Activity 26

- Section Quiz 26-1
- Reading Essentials and Study Guide 26-1

🔖 **Transparencies**
- Section Focus Transparency 26-1
- Chapter Transparency 26

Multimedia
🔲 Interactive Tutor Self-Assessment Software
🔲 Testmaker

Giuseppe Mazzini was its most effective speaker. A native of **Genoa** and a bold and active leader in the fight for Italian independence, Mazzini founded in 1831 a secret society called Young Italy. The goal of this society was to transform Italy into an independent sovereign nation. According to Mazzini, the nation-state, a political organization consisting of one nationality rather than several nationalities, was very important. Through it, people in one unified country with common ideals could best contribute their efforts to the well-being of all its citizens.

In January 1848, Mazzini-inspired nationalists led a republican revolution in **Sicily**. Some weeks later, news of larger revolutions in France and Austria sparked uprisings throughout the Italian Peninsula. When fighting began against Austrian forces in Lombardy and Venetia, King **Charles Albert** of the Kingdom of **Sardinia** joined the war to expel the foreigners. Nationalists pressured the rulers of Naples, Tuscany, and the Papal States to send troops against the Austrians.

By April 1848 the united Italian forces had almost succeeded in driving the Austrians from the peninsula. Then, saying that he opposed a war with another Catholic country, Pope Pius IX suddenly withdrew his troops. Naples followed suit. Their withdrawal enabled Austria to defeat the army of Charles Albert and reestablish its control over Lombardy and Venetia.

The pope's decision infuriated Italian nationalists. In November 1848 angry mobs forced the pope to flee the city. Nationalists proclaimed **Rome** a republic and summoned Mazzini to the capital to head the government. The expulsion of the pope, however, aroused the Catholic governments of Naples, Spain, and France. As a result, Louis-Napoleon sent a French army to Rome. His troops occupied the city and restored the pope to power.

The events of 1848 caused many Italians to lose faith in Mazzini's revolutionary methods. They became more conservative and turned to Charles Albert, who had earned their respect with his brave stand against the Austrians. Nationalists now looked to Sardinia to lead the struggle for Italian unification.

Count Cavour's Diplomacy

In 1849 **Victor Emmanuel II**, Charles Albert's son, became king of Sardinia. During the next few years Victor Emmanuel II toiled to keep popular support for the unity movement alive. He was greatly helped in his efforts by a shrewd and determined adviser named **Count Camillo di Cavour**.

Italian Unification 1871

Map Study

The unification of Italy was largely accomplished between 1859 and 1870.

Place What territories were added in 1860?

Map legend:
- Sardinia before 1859
- Territory added 1859
- Territory added 1860
- Territory added 1866
- Territory added 1870

Physically, Cavour was not impressive, as this description by a contemporary illustrates:

> The squat ... pot-bellied form; the small, stumpy legs; the short, round arms, with the hands stuck constantly in the trousers' pockets ... and the sharp grey eyes, covered by the goggle spectacles ... The dress itself seemed a part and property of the man.

Cavour's looks were deceptive, however. Hidden behind the rumpled clothes and strange appearance was a bold, intelligent man of great personal charm. By the time of the Crimean War in 1854, Cavour dominated Sardinia's council of ministers. His major goals were the promotion of rapid industrial growth, the reduction of the Catholic Church's influence, and the advancement of Sardinia's national interests in foreign affairs.

The defeat of Sardinia in 1848 convinced Cavour that the kingdom needed the aid of a foreign power to expel Austria and achieve Italian

Chapter 26 *Reaction and Nationalism* **677**

Chapter 26
Section 1

TEACH

Guided Practice

THEME Nationalism

Help students define *nationalism*. Discuss how nationalism can unify people in a country or can lead to war and to discrimination against minority groups. Conclude by asking students to give examples of nationalism at work in the world today. **L1**

Map Study

Answer
Parma, Modena, Tuscany, part of the Papal States, and the Kingdom of the Two Sicilies

Map Skills Practice

Reading a Map When did Venetia become part of Italy? *(1866)*

Geography: Place Refer students to the map on this page. Have students identify the changing political loyalties of the major islands west of Italy. Which ones became part of a unified Italy? *(Sardinia and Sicily)* Which one did not? *(Corsica)* Let students discuss the importance of political loyalties of islands. *(important for trade and military strategy)* **L2**

Critical Thinking Have students discuss whether Cavour's problems with Garibaldi were justified. *(No; Garibaldi surrendered his conquests to Victor Emmanuel II.)* **L2**

 Chapter Transparency 26

 History Simulation 26

COOPERATIVE LEARNING ACTIVITY

Time Line Organize students into three groups to construct a chronology showing the unification of Italy. Have one group gather information on key people, writing short descriptions of their roles. Have the second group prepare short written descriptions about key events and their dates. Have the third group design and draw the time line, incorporating information from the other two groups. Have this group post the time line on a classroom bulletin board or wall. Encourage the class to use the time line as a reference. **L1**

Independent Practice

📁 Guided Reading Activity
26-1 **L1**

📁 Time Line Activity 26

Chart Have students create a chart with the following column headings: *Mazzini, Count Cavour, Victor Emmanuel II, Garibaldi.* Include the following topics for rows: *Goals and Ideals, Events and Dates, Impact on Unification.* Suggest students use outside sources to complete the chart. **L2 LEP**

Biography Have students research the life of Pope Pius IX and write a short biography. Suggest that students include the following topics in their biographies: Pius IX's early reforms, his views on and role in Italian unification, his removal from Rome, the doctrine of papal infallibility. **L3**

you don't say...

Carbonari means "charcoal burners" in Italian. It was the name of one of the first Italian secret societies for the overthrow of foreign governments in Italy. Although charcoal is black, it gives off a bright glow when burning. This was associated with the light of freedom and liberty.

unity. To win such aid, Cavour decided to support France and Britain in the Crimean War. One historian later called this action "one of the most brilliant strokes of statecraft in the nineteenth century."

By sending an army to the Crimea in 1854, Sardinia established a claim to equality with the other warring nations. Participating in the war also won Sardinia admittance to the Congress of Paris, which settled treaty matters after the war.

War With Austria

Not long after the Crimean War, in the summer of 1858, Cavour met secretly with Napoleon III at Plombiéres-les-Bains in France. There Napoleon III promised to aid Sardinia in expelling Austria if Sardinia found itself at war. In return, Sardinia agreed that it would give the provinces of Savoy and Nice to France in the event of an Italian-French victory over Austria. Cavour next forced Austria to declare war against Sardinia. He did this by encouraging nationalist groups in Lombardy to revolt. When Austria demanded that Sardinia withdraw

its support of the rebels, Sardinia refused. Austria declared war in April 1859. As he had promised, Napoleon III led a force of 120,000 French soldiers to aid Sardinia.

The combined forces of France and Sardinia defeated the Austrians at Magenta and Solferino in June 1859. Austria was on the run. The French suffered heavy losses, however, and Napoleon III feared the loss of public support at home if the fighting in Italy continued.

Without consulting Cavour, Napoleon III withdrew from the fighting in July and signed a treaty with Emperor Francis Joseph of Austria. By the terms of the treaty, Austria gave Lombardy to Sardinia but retained control of Venetia. When Cavour read these terms, he became furious. He insisted that Victor Emmanuel II continue to fight. Believing that victory was impossible without France, the king refused.

The fighting, however, did not stop. People in Tuscany, Parma, Modena, and the papal province of Romagna overthrew their rulers in late 1859 and

Images *of the* Times

Uniting Italy

Before 1860 Italy was made up of many separate states. After 1860 it became a united kingdom but remained culturally and economically divided. The deepest division was between northern and southern parts of the country.

Southern Italy remained a leading rural and agricultural area. Traditional customs were strong, and artisans excelled in various crafts.

678

Images *of the* Times

Uniting Italy

"We have made Italy, now we have to make Italians," remarked Massimo d'Azeglio, a former prime minister of the Piedmont, after 1860. This task was especially hard to accomplish in southern Italy, where few local people had actively taken part in the fight for unification. Many of the peasants who lived in this region had to scratch out a living working as laborers or as tenants on large estates. Poverty and unemployment were common throughout the south, and the new government lacked revenue for relief, job programs, and education. Because of lack of work, many southern Italians migrated to North Africa and the Americas. From there, they sent money home to their families.

early 1860. Their new governments demanded the right to unite with Sardinia. To gain Napoleon III's consent for this unification, Cavour gave Savoy and Nice to France. In April 1860 Victor Emmanuel II accepted the territories into his kingdom.

Garibaldi Seizes the South

Southern Italy remained isolated from the revolutionary fever sweeping the rest of the peninsula, but at the death of Ferdinand II, ruler of the Kingdom of the Two Sicilies, Italian nationalists prepared for a revolution. Their leader was charismatic military commander **Giuseppe Garibaldi**.

Forced into exile after taking part in the 1830 uprisings, Garibaldi went to South America. There he became an expert in guerrilla warfare, a method of warfare using hit-and-run tactics. Garibaldi returned to Italy in 1848 and took part in Mazzini's short-lived Roman Republic. When that fell in 1849, Garibaldi fled to the United States.

Sensing that the people of the Kingdom of the Two Sicilies were ready to revolt, Garibaldi returned to Italy in 1860. After collecting volunteers in Genoa, he set out for Sicily. When his troops faltered, Garibaldi rallied them to victory. In a few weeks, he gained control of the island.

He then crossed to the mainland and advanced toward Naples. The army of the Kingdom of the Two Sicilies proved no match for Garibaldi's Red Shirts, named for the color of their uniforms. Naples fell, and the king of the Two Sicilies fled.

WORLD HISTORY Online

Student Web Activity 26

Visit the *World History: The Human Experience* Web site at **worldhistory.glencoe.com** and click on *Chapter 26—Student Web Activities* for an activity relating to Giuseppe Garibaldi.

Northern Italy became a highly urbanized and industrialized region. The city of Milan was known both for its economic prosperity and its festive outdoor celebrations.

Tuscany, a region in north-central Italy, was known for its picturesque villages and vineyards as well as the cultural city of Florence.

> **REFLECTING ON THE TIMES**
>
> 1. How was Italy organized politically before 1860?
> 2. What economic and social differences distinguished northern Italy from southern Italy?

679

Who?What?Where?When?

Giuseppe Garibaldi Between 1850 and 1860, Garibaldi lived on Staten Island in New York City. He made a meager living working in a friend's candle factory.

Linking Past and Present

Guerrilla warfare, such as that which Garibaldi's Red Shirts were known for, has been used since biblical times. During the American Revolution, Francis Marion, the "Swamp Fox," led guerrilla groups against the British in South Carolina. More recently, guerrilla warfare proved effective during the Vietnam War.

ASSESS

Check for Understanding

Assign Section 1 Assessment as homework or as an in-class activity.

Use Interactive Tutor Self-Assessment Software to review Section 1.

WORLD HISTORY Online

Have students use the **Chapter 26 Student Web Activity** at worldhistory.glencoe.com for in-depth study of Giuseppe Garibaldi.

> **ANSWERS TO REFLECTING ON THE TIMES**
>
> 1. Italy was divided into several independent states.
> 2. Northern Italy became highly industrialized and urbanized; southern Italy remained a rural, agricultural area.

Visualizing History

  Tell students that Garibaldi left Sicily at Messina, crossed the Straits of Messina, and entered the mainland at Reggio. The army of the Kingdom of the Two Sicilies—although 30,000 strong—offered little resistance to Garibaldi's 4,000 men.
Answer to Caption: *guerrilla warfare*

Evaluate

Section Quiz 26-1

Use the Testmaker to create a customized quiz for Section 1.

Reteach

Have students write five paragraphs summarizing information in Section 1. Suggest that students organize each paragraph around one of the section's headings.

Reading Essentials and Study Guide 26-1

Enrich

Have students discuss the role foreign nations played in the unification of Italy. Ask students to decide which nation had the most influence on unification.

CLOSE

Use the map on page 677 to summarize the steps by which Italian unification was achieved.

Visualizing History After gaining control of Sicily in 1860, Giuseppe Garibaldi left for the Italian mainland. *What type of warfare did Garibaldi carry out on behalf of Italian national unity?*

Garibaldi's successes in the south made Cavour nervous. To prevent Garibaldi from further victories, Cavour sent an army into the Papal States. On September 18 the forces of Sardinia defeated the papal army at Castelfidaro. Cavour kept control of the campaign for national unity.

When voters in southern Italy supported union with Sardinia in October 1860, Garibaldi surrendered his conquests to Victor Emmanuel II. By February 1861 the whole peninsula, with the exception of Rome and Venetia, was united under one government. Victor Emmanuel II was now king of the newly created constitutional monarchy of Italy.

Building a New Nation

Three months after the unification of Italy, Count Cavour died. His last words were "Italy is made. All is safe." However, many difficult problems confronted the new nation. National unification had not erased the profound cultural and economic divisions that separated the south and north. The south was poor and agricultural, while the north had begun to industrialize. The gap in the standards of living between the two regions fueled discontent and hampered unification efforts.

In the name of national unity, Sardinia often tried to force its laws and customs onto the other Italian states. This tactic only fanned resentment. Former rulers also encouraged discontent. When some of these rulers tried to regain their thrones, bloody civil wars erupted.

Gradually the government developed a unified military and a national educational system. It built railroads, linking not only the south with the north but also Italy with the rest of Europe. These were important steps toward unification, but cultural and economic barriers remained.

Another problem concerned the location of the nation's capital. Most Italians thought that **Rome** should be the capital of the new nation. During the 1860s, however, the pope still ruled the city. In addition, the Austrians continued to control Venetia.

Italy again sought foreign help to solve a political problem. In 1866 Italy allied itself with Prussia in a war against Austria. In return, Prussia promised to give Venetia to Italy. Although Austria defeated Italian forces in the conflict, the Prussian victory was so overwhelming that Prussia gave Venetia to Italy anyway.

Foreign intervention also played a role in helping Italy win Rome. When war broke out between France and Prussia in 1870, Napoleon III withdrew French troops that had been protecting the pope. Italian troops then entered Rome and conquered the pope's territory. In 1871 Victor Emmanuel II moved the national capital from Florence to Rome. The political unification of Italy was finally complete.

SECTION 1 ASSESSMENT

Main Idea
1. Use a diagram like the one below to show how nationalism led to a united Italy in the 1860s.

> Nationalism
> ↓
> ↓
> United Italy

Recall
2. **Define** nationalism, nation-state, guerrilla warfare.
3. **Identify** Giuseppe Mazzini, Charles Albert, Victor Emmanuel II, Count Camillo di Cavour, Giuseppe Garibaldi.

Critical Thinking
4. **Applying Information** How did one Italian nationalist further the movement's aims?

Understanding Themes
5. **Nationalism** How did the papacy and the Catholic Church respond to the rise of Italian nationalism?

SECTION 1 ASSESSMENT ANSWERS

1. Mazzini founded Young Italy; republican revolt in Sicily; uprisings in Italian Peninsula; Pope Pius IX's loss to Austria infuriated nationalists, who proclaimed Rome a republic; Louis-Napoleon restored Pope to power; Cavour favored Italian unity; Italian government united with Sardinia; Garibaldi seized south; southern Italy supported union with Sardinia in 1860; Italy won Rome, Venetia
2. All terms are defined in the Glossary.
3. Mazzini, 677; Charles Albert, 677; Victor Emmanuel II, 677; Cavour, 677; Garibaldi, 679
4. Answers will vary but should reveal an understanding of how selected leader furthered Italian unification.
5. **NATIONALISM** At first Pope Pius IX supported the war against Austria, but later he withdrew the forces of the Papal States, opposing warfare with another Catholic state. This earned him the dislike of Italian nationalists, who staged an uprising against the pope in Rome.

1820 ——————— 1840 ——————— 1860 ——————— 1880

1834 German states create the *Zollverein*.

1866 Prussia and Austria fight Seven Weeks' War.

1871 William I becomes emperor of a united Germany.

Section 2

The Unification of Germany

SECTION THEME

▶ **Conflict** Bismarck uses war and diplomacy to bring unity to Germany.

Guide to Reading

Read to Find Out

Main Idea *Bismarck used war and diplomacy to unite the German states.*

▶ **Terms to Define**
  realpolitik, kaiser, chancellor

▶ **People to Meet**
  William I, Otto von Bismarck

▶ **Places to Locate**
  Frankfurt, Austria, Prussia, Schleswig, Holstein

The Storyteller

Klaus von Erlach was impressed by Otto von Bismarck's message, although many of Klaus's fellow aristocrats disliked the Iron Chancellor, considering him a traitor to his class. Who other than a great leader, Klaus wondered, would be able to defend a change of political opinion? As Bismarck stated, "The man who does not learn also fails to progress and cannot keep abreast of his time. People are falling behind when they remain rooted in the position they occupied two years ago." If Germany was to progress, the old systems would have to adapt.

—adapted from "Professorial Politics," Otto von Bismarck, reprinted in *Sources of World History*, Mark A. Kishlansky, 1995

Otto von Bismarck

ermany was the last of the great European powers to achieve complete political unity. In 1815, 39 independent German states stretched north and south from the Baltic Sea to the Alps, and east and west from the Rhine River to the Russian Empire. Political rivals Austria and Prussia were the most powerful of these German states.

While Great Britain and France were developing as strong industrial nations, Germany remained divided and economically disadvantaged. The Reformation and the Thirty Years' War contributed to Germany's social and political divisions. Antagonisms between Protestant and Catholic states ran deep. By 1871, however, the German states—excluding Austria and Switzerland—had united into a single nation.

Steps Toward Unity

The Congress of Vienna had created the German Confederation in 1815 as a buffer against possible future French expansion. This first major step toward German unity established closer economic ties between the German states and helped pave the way for greater political union.

The German Confederation loosely tied together the numerous German states with a diet, or assembly, sitting at **Frankfurt**. **Austria** dominated the confederation. Its position as head of the diet eventually brought it into conflict with **Prussia**. Neither Austria nor the smaller German states wanted to see a united Germany. Austria feared the economic competition, while the smaller states feared domination by Prussia.

The largest of the German states, Prussia had a well-organized government and a strong economy. Political power in Prussia lay in the hands of

Chapter 26 *Reaction and Nationalism* **681**

Guide to Reading

For reading strategies to help students read effectively see pages 12–13.

Vocabulary Pre-check

◉ Use the Vocabulary PuzzleMaker for Chapter 26 to create a crossword puzzle to reinforce section terms. **L1 LEP**

📁 Use Vocabulary Activity 26 to introduce vocabulary terms. **L1 LEP**

FOCUS

Section Objective

Identify the methods Bismarck used to unite the German states.

BELLRINGER
Motivational Activity

Before taking roll at the beginning of the class period, project Section Focus Transparency 26-2 and have students answer the activity questions. Discuss students' responses.

📁 This activity is also available as a blackline master.

SECTION RESOURCES

📁 **Reproducible Masters**
• Lecture Notes 26-2
• Reproducible Lesson Plan 26-2
• Vocabulary Activity 26
• Guided Reading Activity 26-2
• Section Quiz 26-2
• Reading Essentials and Study Guide 26-2

🔖 **Transparencies**
• Section Focus Transparency 26-2

Multimedia
◉ Interactive Tutor Self-Assessment Software
◉ Testmaker

Chapter 26
Section 2

TEACH

Guided Practice

THEME Conflict

Have students make a chart on the chalkboard that shows the participants, purpose, and outcomes of the war against Denmark, the Seven Weeks' War, and the Franco-Prussian War. **L1 LEP**

Map Study

Answers
1. *Prussia*
2. *a well-organized government and a strong economy*

Map Skills Practice

Reading a Map For what practical reason would Prussia want a united Germany? *(to unite the two parts of Prussia)*

Economics Lead a discussion about economic issues involved in unification. Have students include the *Zollverein* and Bismarck's budget for the army. **L2**

Government Hold an informal class debate on the advantages and disadvantages of Bismarck's policy of realpolitik. Conclude the debate by having students discuss whether realpolitik is a force in political policy today. Encourage students to give examples of realpolitik from current events. **L3**

influential aristocratic landowners called Junkers (YUN•kuhrs), but members of the rising business class demanded a share of political power. To reduce trade barriers, German states in 1834 formed a *Zollverein*, or economic union. This step toward unity strengthened the influence of Prussia, while weakening that of Austria, in German affairs.

In 1848, as revolutions swept Europe, power in the German states shifted to the liberals. From all parts of Germany, delegates met in the Frankfurt Assembly to unite the country under a liberal constitution. Internal feuding, however, weakened this effort, allowing the conservatives to regain control. In 1849 the Prussian military forced the Assembly's closure and later put down street revolts. Many liberal and radical Germans fled abroad, especially to the United States. During the 1850s, in Germany as in other parts of Europe, conservatives in many cases came to control nationalist causes.

Rise of Bismarck

German conservatives looked to Prussia for help in uniting Germany. In 1861 **William I** became king of Prussia. Opposed to liberal ideas, William believed in a strong military and took steps to expand the Prussian army. Liberal German nationalists, however, saw no use for a strong military except to control the Prussian people. They wanted the king to adopt democratic policies to gain support from the other German states. As a result, liberal deputies in the Prussian assembly overwhelmingly defeated new taxes to support a larger army.

Frustrated by the defeat, the king appointed as his new prime minister a man who shared his views on army reconstruction. That man was **Otto von Bismarck**. A Junker himself, Bismarck had served in the Prussian assembly and as ambassador to Russia and France. He shared the king's view that Prussia needed a strong government and army to achieve German unity. A brilliant negotiator, Bismarck embraced the policy of realpolitik, the right of the nation-state to pursue its own advantage by any means, including war and the repudiation of treaties.

In September 1862 Bismarck defied the finance committee of the Prussian assembly. He declared that the great issues of the times would not be decided "by speeches and majority decisions ... but by blood and iron." When the lower house again refused to approve the new army budget, Bismarck pushed the program through by simply collecting the necessary taxes without authorization.

German Confederation 1815

Map Study The German Confederation consisted of many small independent states in 1815.
1. Location Which was the largest and most important of these states?
2. Place What characteristics of the largest state in the German Confederation made it so important?

Three Wars

Bismarck once said, "Show me an objective worthy of war and I will go along with you." As prime minister, he found several worthy objectives. His initial goal was to raise money for army expansion. Then he wanted Prussia to use its military and economic power to reduce Austrian influence among the German states. Finally, he planned to arrange the unification of all German states except Austria and Switzerland under Prussian domination. To accomplish these objectives, Bismarck went to war three times.

War Against Denmark

By inheritance, the king of Denmark ruled the territories of **Schleswig** and **Holstein**. Schleswig's population was part German and part Danish; Holstein's population was entirely German. When King Christian IX proclaimed Schleswig a Danish province in 1863, Germans in both territories appealed to the larger German states for support.

682 Chapter 26 *Reaction and Nationalism*

COOPERATIVE LEARNING ACTIVITY

Role Play Organize the class into six groups to role-play the diplomatic stands taken by Germany and its rivals in the war with Denmark, the Seven Weeks' War, and the Franco-Prussian War. Have three groups research Germany's position in each war and the other three groups each research Denmark's, Austria's, and France's positions. Suggest that students gather data about their assigned country's goals and relations with their opposing country. Then have each pair of rival groups present their dramatizations in the order in which they occurred: the war with Denmark, the Seven Weeks' War, and the Franco-Prussian War. **L2**

To prevent Danish annexation of Schleswig, Bismarck persuaded Austria to join Prussia in declaring war against Denmark in 1864. Prussia and Austria soon won this war and forced Denmark out of the disputed provinces. By mutual agreement, Prussia took control of Schleswig, and Austria took over the administration of Holstein. This arrangement strained the relationship between these rival powers.

The war accomplished two of Bismarck's objectives. First, it made Europe aware of Prussia's military might and influence. Second, the tension resulting from the war settlement gave Bismarck the excuse he wanted for going to war with Austria.

Seven Weeks' War

One month before the invasion of Schleswig, Bismarck wrote to his envoy in Paris:

❝ You do not trust Austria. Neither do I. But I consider it the correct policy at present to have Austria with us. Whether the moment of parting will come, and on whose initiative, we shall see…. I am not in the least afraid of war, on the contrary … you may very soon be able to convince yourself that war also is included in my program. ❞

Bismarck prepared for war by stripping Austria of possible allies. He gained Russia's goodwill by offering the czar aid against Polish rebels in 1863. He offered France possible "compensations" for its neutrality in case of an Austro-Prussian war. He also forged an alliance with Italy by supporting its claim to Venetia in return for military support against Austria.

Bismarck gained public support for his actions when Austria sided with the duke of Augustenburg, who claimed title to Schleswig and Holstein. To prevent an alliance between Austria and the duke, Bismarck ordered Prussian troops into Austrian-occupied Holstein. When Austria then asked the German Confederation to take military action against Prussia for this invasion, Bismarck responded by declaring war against Austria.

The war between Austria and Prussia began on June 15, 1866, and ended in a Prussian victory just seven weeks later. For Bismarck, the conflict had been a limited war with limited objectives. Its purpose was to separate Austria from Germany and

Geography

A Divided Land

Germany's geography has made it a country of distinct regions. Throughout German history, rivers have drawn people in different directions. The north-flowing Rhine, Weser, and Oder Rivers have linked the peoples of these river valleys to the northern plains. In southern Germany, the Danube River has oriented people of that region to the southeast.

Mountains and highland areas—especially the Alps and the Central Highlands—have isolated populations and strengthened local dialects and traditions.

In the past, political and religious conflict heightened divisions; Swabians considered Westphalians as foreigners, and Bavarians regarded Prussians as archrivals. This regionalism led Germans to resist political unity until the late 1800s. In the 1900s, the German defeat in World War II and the rivalry between the United States and the Soviet Union caused Germany's division into eastern and western parts. With communism's fall, Germany finally reunited in 1990.

A divided Berlin

Linking Past and Present ACTIVITY

Discuss the geographical and historical factors contributing to German regionalism. What has been the relationship between regionalism and national unity in the United States?

Chapter 26 *Reaction and Nationalism* 683

Linking Past and Present

German Unification Bismarck used three wars to unify Germany, but another German-caused war—World War II—left Germany divided for 45 years. In 1990 West Germany and East Germany were reunited as one country.

Independent Practice

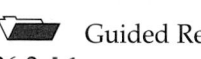 Guided Reading Activity 26-2 **L1**

Comic Strip Have students draw an action comic strip of the major events that led to German unification. Suggest that they include the German Confederation, *Zollverein*, rise of Bismarck, the three wars, William I, the Ems telegram, and the government of the empire. **L2**

A Divided Land

Germany is made up of three major geographic areas: the northern Lowlands, the Central Highlands, and the southern mountains. These physical divisions hindered political unification of the German states.

ANSWER

Geographic factors: mountains, highlands, and flow of major rivers; historical: political and religious strife. Because of its large size and varied geography, regionalism has also existed in the United States; regional differences between North and South led to the Civil War; since the late 1800s, a growing economy and common beliefs in liberty and democracy, however, have united the country while respecting regional differences.

MEETING SPECIAL NEEDS ACTIVITY

Study Strategy Organize students into four groups, with the most students in group three. Assign each group one of the four main headings in the section. Ask each group to prepare an outline of its part of the section. Remind students to include important dates and explanations of why certain people, places, and events were important to German unification. Make photocopies of each group's outline to distribute to students in all the groups. **L2**

Map Study

Answer

to unite the eastern and western parts of Prussia

Map Skills Practice

Reading a Map To which central European country did a united Germany pose the biggest threat? *(Austria-Hungary)*

CURRICULUM CONNECTION

MILITARY HISTORY

In 1841 Johann Nikolas Dreyse designed the Prussian needle gun. Using this breech-loading rifle, the Prussian army defeated the Austrian army at the Battle of Sadowa in 1866 during the Seven Weeks' War. Lying down on the ground, Prussian soldiers outfired the standing Austrians who used muzzle-loading rifles.

Cultural Perspectives

German Dialects The German language has many dialects. When Germany was first united, speakers of Low German dialects had trouble understanding Swabians in southern Germany. Eastern Rhinelanders could not easily communicate with southwestern Saxons. In addition, minority groups spoke French, Lithuanian, Polish, and Danish.

ASSESS

Check for Understanding

Assign Section 2 Assessment as homework or as an in-class activity.

---

end the chance for a united Germany under Austrian control. In the end, Bismarck did not want to destroy Austria with a harsh peace settlement. He knew that he would probably need an alliance with Austria in the future.

The treaty ending the war was negotiated in the city of Prague. The settlement dissolved the German Confederation and gave Holstein to Prussia and Venetia to Italy. The treaty also called for "a new organization of Germany without the participation of Austria."

This "new organization" became the North German Confederation in 1867. It embraced all the German states north of the Main (MYN) River. The Confederation's constitution gave each state the right to manage its domestic affairs, but put foreign policy and national defense in the hands of Prussia. Legislative authority was vested in a federal council composed of representatives from the various governments and a diet, or assembly, elected by universal male suffrage.

The establishment of a strong confederation by Prussia made Bismarck a hero among German nationalists. Bismarck's work of uniting Germany, however, was not finished.

The Franco-Prussian War

The southern German states, which were largely Catholic, remained outside the new German confederation. Most of them feared Protestant Prussia's military strength and its control of Germany. The kingdoms of Bavaria and Württenberg (WUHR•tehm•BUHRG), in particular, steadfastly opposed German unification under Prussian rule. They would accept German unification only if Prussia gave up some of its authority in a united government. Prussia would not agree to this, however.

France posed the most serious obstacle to a united Germany. Napoleon III would not accept German unification unless France received some territory—its compensation for not joining Austria in the Seven Weeks' War. To resolve the situation, Bismarck again chose war.

Some historians believe that Bismarck was responsible for the Franco-Prussian War. In his memoirs, Bismarck had written that "a Franco-German [Prussian] war must take place before the construction of a united Germany could be realized." If Napoleon III had not wanted war as much as Bismarck, however, the war may never have taken place. Bismarck knew that he could not invade France without public support. Instead, he had to lure France into war, taking advantage of Napoleon III's weakness in foreign policy and of the French public's current anti-Prussian feeling.

German Unification 1871

Map showing German Unification 1871, with labels including SWEDEN, DENMARK, Schleswig, Holstein, NETHERLANDS, Mecklen-burg, Hanover, Berlin, RUSSIA, BELGIUM, Hesse, Ems, Frankfurt, Saxony, POLAND, LUXEMBOURG, Lorraine, Württem-berg, Bavaria, AUSTRIA-HUNGARY, FRANCE, Baden, ALPS, SWITZERLAND. Legend: Prussia before 1866; Territory added 1867; Territory added 1871.

Map Study Bismarck succeeded in unifying Germany in just 15 years. **Location** Why do you think it was important to Prussia to add northern Germany to its territory?

Bismarck's chance came in 1870 in connection with the Hohenzollern candidacy for the Spanish throne.

A revolution in 1868 had deposed Queen Isabella of Spain. The Spanish government offered the throne to Prince Leopold of Hohenzollern, a Catholic cousin of William I of Prussia. Fearing a Spanish-German alliance against France, Napoleon III protested the offer. William brushed aside this protest, but Leopold later voluntarily declined the throne.

In July 1870, France demanded a promise from William that a Hohenzollern would never sit on the Spanish throne. William, who was vacationing at the German resort of Ems, refused. In a telegram to Bismarck, he described the details of his meeting with the French ambassador. To make it appear that William had deliberately insulted the French envoy, Bismarck altered the Ems telegram and released it to the press. Newspaper coverage of the supposed insult enraged the French, leading Napoleon to declare war on Prussia.

The fighting began on July 19, 1870. More anti-French than anti-Prussian, the southern German states allied with Prussia. With highly efficient military forces, the Prussians easily defeated the French.

MAKING CONNECTIONS ACTIVITY

Music and Literature Have students research and write brief reports on one of the following German composers or writers: Richard Wagner, Johannes Brahms, Gustav Mahler, Anton Bruckner, Friedrich Nietzsche, Gustav Freytag, Leopold von Ranke, or Heinrich von Treitschke. Ask students to include the major works and main ideas of the person chosen and to discuss the person's views about the unification of Germany. **L2**

Otto von Bismarck by Franz von Lenbach, Art History Museum, Vienna, Austria **Otto von Bismarck poses in military uniform with a Prussian helmet. He came from the Junker class of Prussia and supported a strong monarchy.** *What does Bismarck's style of dress reveal about the German Empire formed in 1871?*

Bismarck then gained support from all the German states for the unification of Germany under Prussia.

Formation of an Empire

On January 18, 1871, William I assumed the title of kaiser, or emperor, of a united Germany. He ruled over a domain that stretched from the Baltic Sea in the north to the Alps in the south. Bismarck became the German chancellor, or chief minister.

The new empire united 25 German states into one federal union. Although each state had its own ruler, and some had their own armies and diplomatic staffs, the kaiser headed the national government. He had authority to make appointments, command the military in time of war, and determine foreign policy. Prussian Junkers now shared power with wealthy industrialists. Unification did not make Germany a model democratic state.

William's son, Crown Prince Frederick of Prussia, was a liberal and a supporter of reform. He deplored the means Bismarck used to bring about the unification of Germany. In his diary, he wrote of his despair: "We are no longer looked upon as the innocent victims of wrong, but rather as arrogant victors." While he foresaw many of the consequences of Bismarck's policies, Frederick did nothing to change them.

SECTION 2 ASSESSMENT

Main Idea
1. Use a chart like the one below to show the steps Bismarck took to unite the German states.

How Bismarck United the German States
1. _____
2. _____
3. _____
4. _____

Recall
2. **Define** realpolitik, kaiser, chancellor.
3. **Identify** William I, Otto von Bismarck.

Critical Thinking
4. **Synthesizing Information** Imagine that you are a member of the Prussian assembly opposed to Otto von Bismarck's policy for German unification. What alternative policy would you have suggested to William I?

Understanding Themes
5. **Conflict** Compare Bismarck's methods for achieving the unification of Germany with Cavour's methods for bringing about the unification of Italy.

Fashionable parties in the German Empire were not complete without officers attired in imperial uniforms. Bismarck even wore his uniform in the parliament.
Answer to Caption: *It shows that the German Empire was founded on militaristic, authoritarian values.*

 Use Interactive Tutor Self-Assessment Software to review Section 2.

Evaluate
Section Quiz 26-2

Use the Testmaker to create a customized quiz for Section 2.

Reteach

Have students orally summarize material under each of the section's major headings.

Reading Essentials and Study Guide 26-2

Enrich

Have students write a brief essay on why the Junkers felt that Bismarck had betrayed his class by giving the industrial, business class a share in political power.

CLOSE

Have students discuss whether Germany could have been unified without war.

SECTION 2 ASSESSMENT ANSWERS

1. collected taxes for army expansion with no authorization; wanted Prussia to use power to reduce Austrian influence among German states; arranged unification of German states except Austria and Switzerland under Prussian domination; used wars to achieve his goals: against Denmark, Seven Weeks' War against Austria, Franco-Prussian War
2. All terms are defined in the Glossary.
3. William I, 682; Otto von Bismarck, 682
4. Answers will vary but may include that offering people greater participation in government rather than threats of force might have gained their support for unification.
5. **CONFLICT** Both Cavour and Bismarck planned the unification of their respective countries; both used military means to achieve their objective; both used foreign help to achieve unification—although Bismarck relied more on his own Prussian army than on foreign troops.

1870   1885   1900   1915

1872 Bismarck expels Jesuits from Germany.

1883 German government provides health insurance to workers.

1888 William II becomes emperor of Germany.

1913 Germany's standing army numbers more than 800,000 soldiers.

Section 3

Bismarck's Realm

Guide to Reading

Read to Find Out
Main Idea *Bismarck's policies greatly affected the German Empire.*

▶ **Terms to Define**
  papal infallibility, militarism

▶ **People to Meet**
  Pope Pius IX, Ferdinand Lassalle, William II

The Storyteller

Erich Klein's Uncle Karl enjoyed talking politics and was eager to explain the German political system to his American nephew. "Germany consists of twenty-six different states that were once independent but now are united. Each state has its own governmental officials and hereditary princes, but they are all subject to Kaiser [William] I." Erich remarked, "This government sounds similar to the United States." Uncle Karl agreed, but mentioned an important difference: "The Kaiser was not elected. He was acclaimed by the various princes who were willing to concede their power so that aristocracy by birth would remain within the German government."

Kaiser William I

—adapted from *Im Vaterland [In the Fatherland]*, Paul V. Bacon, 1910

Victory on the battlefield brought about Germany's political unity, but the Germans were not united as a people. Religious, economic, social, and political divisions remained. German leaders now had to encourage a sense of common purpose in the population.

Bismarck became the key figure in early German nation building. With the support of Kaiser William I, Bismarck took charge of policy in the German Empire. Over the years, he faced several direct challenges to the German nation-state and his own political authority.

Bismarck and the Church

One of the first challenges Bismarck faced was with the Catholic Church in the so-called Kulturkampf (kul•TUR•KAHMF), or cultural struggle, between Church and state. After German unification, Catholics in Germany organized the Center party to represent their interests in opposition to the predominantly Protestant Prussians.

Bismarck viewed Catholicism as an antinationalist force and consequently supported the Protestants in political affairs. In part, he was annoyed at the popularity of the Center party. He was also worried about an 1870 proclamation by Catholic bishops in Rome declaring papal infallibility—the doctrine that the pope, when speaking on matters of faith and morals, is infallible, or free from error.

Since the Jesuits, in Bismarck's eyes, were papal agents working to destroy the German Empire, the chancellor launched his campaign against the Church by expelling the Jesuits from Germany in 1872. One year later, the German legislature began passing a series of laws aimed at destroying Catholic influence in Germany. These so-called May Laws deprived Catholic bishops of much of their authority and even required that weddings be performed by secular officials. In response,

---

Pope Pius IX declared the laws invalid and broke diplomatic ties with Germany.

Bismarck soon realized that he was fighting a losing battle. Instead of weakening the Center party, Bismarck's repressive measures strengthened it. In the legislative elections of 1877, the Center party gained even more seats. Even the Junker-controlled Conservative party began to oppose Bismarck's policies. Knowing that he needed the support of the Center party to defeat a serious challenge from the Socialists, Bismarck sought to make peace with the Catholics.

When Pope Pius IX died in 1878, his successor, Leo XIII, made an effort to heal the rift with Germany. Eventually, the German legislature repealed most laws directed against Catholics. By 1881 the Kulturkampf was over.

Germany's Industrial Growth

Prior to unification, Germany was not a great industrial nation. Primarily agricultural, the German states lagged far behind Great Britain in the production of textiles, coal, iron, and steel. Knowing that Germany's position as a major political and military power depended on a strong economy, German political and business leaders worked to expand the nation's industry. By the mid-1800s, advances in many areas began to transform Germany's economy. The establishment of the *Zollverein* had already encouraged economic growth and spurred efforts to improve transportation. After unification, investment capital from Great Britain, France, and Belgium helped to modernize industrial production and establish a mechanized factory system.

The development of deep-pit coal mining in the provinces along the Rhine and the opening of new coal mines in the Saar made available large reserves of cheap fuel for the new plants. Cities grew rapidly. Many young men and women streamed in from the villages to work in the new factories. As a result, at the end of the 1800s, Germany finally became a major industrial power.

The economic changes sweeping Germany conferred on at least some of its people the highest standard of living in Europe. The middle class and the business leaders benefited enormously from the rapid industrialization of the country. Every improvement in factory machinery, however, resulted in lower wages and higher unemployment for many German workers. They lived in crowded, filthy tenements and toiled long hours under dangerous working conditions.

Visualizing History Pope Leo XIII took a more conciliatory approach to new forms of secular government than did earlier popes. *What effect did Leo's papacy have on church relations with Bismarck's Germany?*

Workers and Socialism

Poor wages, long workdays, and job uncertainty made German workers receptive to a more hopeful vision of the future. They looked forward to a democratic social order in which they would no longer be exploited. To help bring about this new order in Germany, **Ferdinand Lassalle**, a writer and labor leader, founded the Universal German Workingmen's Association in 1863. Although he called himself a Socialist and a disciple of Karl Marx, Lassalle did not preach revolution. Whereas Marx called for the workers of the world to revolt against capitalism, Lassalle advocated mass political action to change the system.

Lassalle was a national celebrity who knew Bismarck and lectured him on the workers' plight. He did not live long enough, however, to finish the fight, for he was killed in a duel in 1864. The party he founded grew slowly until it merged with the Social Democratic party in 1875 and became a major political force.

Chapter 26 *Reaction and Nationalism* **687**

TEACH

Guided Practice

THEME Change

Have students make two lists, one showing economic changes in the German Empire under Bismarck, the other showing social changes. **L1 LEP**

Visualizing History Although Pope Leo XIII worked to reconcile with Germany, he continued to support the papacy's conservative political views, remaining opposed to freedom of speech, freedom of conscience, freedom of worship, and separation of church and state. **Answer to Caption:** *Pope Leo XIII worked to heal the rift between the papacy and Germany. German laws against Catholics were repealed and Kulturkampf ended by 1881.*

Religion Have students discuss the goals and outcome of Bismarck's Kulturkampf with the Catholic Church. **L2**

Cause and Effect Have students identify the causes and effects of the rise of socialism in the German Empire. **L3**

Independent Practice

Guided Reading Activity 26-3 **L1**

ASSESS

Check for Understanding

Assign Section 3 Assessment as homework or as an in-class activity.

Use Interactive Tutor Self-Assessment Software to review Section 3.

COOPERATIVE LEARNING ACTIVITY

Research Organize the class into five groups to research the reign of Kaiser William II. Have each group select one of the following topics to research: economic growth, William II and chancellors after Bismarck, the growth of the German navy, foreign affairs, and the rise of anti-Semitism. Ask each group to compile a written report of their research and to choose one group member to present the group's findings to the class. After all groups have given their reports, encourage students to compare Germany under William II with Germany under Bismarck. **L3**

TEACH

Tell students that to get Ludwig II to join the German Empire, Bismarck promised Bavaria its own post office and a separate peacetime army. Bismarck also had Ludwig send William I a letter inviting him to be emperor of Germany. Ludwig received the equivalent of $45,000 a year in exchange for the letter. **What do you think he spent the money on?** *(castles)* Within a week of being declared insane in 1886, Ludwig was found drowned in a lake near Neuschwanstein.

Linking Past and Present

Neuschwanstein Today close to 1 million people tour Neuschwanstein each year. Many more people see a model of Ludwig's famous castle at the Disney theme parks. Cinderella's castle, the heart of Fantasyland, was patterned after Neuschwanstein.

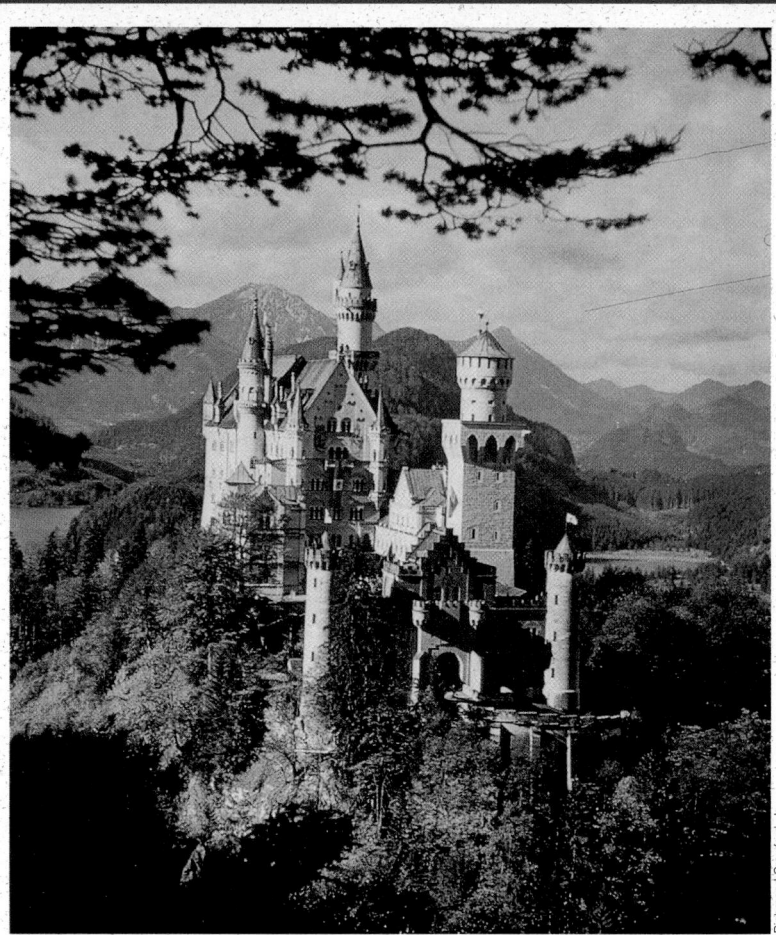

Richmond Crawford, Jr.

Mad Ludwig's Castle

Ludwig II, King of Bavaria, ruled the independent German kingdom of Bavaria until 1871 and built for himself the storybook Neuschwanstein castle. He came to the throne unprepared to rule but enthusiastic about indulging his two passions: opera and palaces. Ludwig's castles were based on his romantic vision of the past. In each new mansion, rooms were decorated to look like scenes from the famous operas of nineteenth-century composer Richard Wagner. Ludwig's dreamy castles glorified and enshrined a bygone Germany. Ludwig's ministers, who had to f cash to pay for his follies, finally had him d insane and removed from power. Today his c one of Germany's leading tourist attractions.

While Ludwig dreamed and listened to ro operas, Count Otto von Bismarck set about the German Confederation and creating a German nation through military strength. "Th questions of the age," Bismarck once remarke not settled by speeches and majority votes ... iron and blood." ⊕

688 **Chapter 26** *Reaction and Nationalism*

Bismarck and the Socialists

Despite his association with Lassalle, Bismarck believed that any Socialist party was out to change the government and that it therefore posed a serious threat to the German Empire. To destroy the Socialist movement in Germany, he set out to crush its organization. In 1878 the German legislature passed an anti-Socialist bill introduced by Bismarck. Although the bill did not outlaw the party itself, it banned all Socialist meetings and publications.

Bismarck's efforts to suppress the Socialists met with only temporary success. Consequently, Bismarck changed his tactics. He tried to show the workers that the government, and not the Socialists, had their true interests at heart. He directed the passage of several bills that gave workers some measure of comfort and security. In 1883, for example, the Sickness Insurance Law gave limited compensation to those who missed work because of illness. In 1889 the Old Age Insurance Law protected industrial workers in retirement.

Bismarck's reform efforts, however, did not go far enough to end the popularity of the Socialists. In 1890 the Social Democratic party won 35 seats in the legislature, which then refused to renew Bismarck's anti-Socialist law.

The Fall of Bismarck

In 1888 Kaiser William I died at the age of 91. Crown Prince Frederick, his liberal-minded son, succeeded him. Frederick III, however, died about 100 days after his coronation. **William II**, his son, succeeded him as emperor in 1888.

Only 29 years old at the time of his coronation, William II was a man of great energy and strong conservative opinions. Like his grandfather, William I, he favored militarism, or support for a powerful military prepared for war. His belief in the absolute authority of the emperor immediately brought him into conflict with Bismarck.

Under William I, Bismarck often got his way by threatening to resign. When Bismarck offered his resignation in 1890, the kaiser accepted it. Much to Bismarck's surprise, William II "sent the veteran pilot over the side," as a popular cartoon of the time illustrated Bismarck's dismissal.

Bismarck's policies had left Germany strong, but his strict rule prevented the development of a parliamentary democracy. With Bismarck gone, William II was free to pursue his own policies. During his reign Germany became one of the world's major industrial and military powers.

Visualizing History After governing the German Empire for almost 30 years, Bismarck resigned in 1890, when this cartoon was published. *What is the cartoon saying about Bismarck's relationship with Kaiser William II?*

SECTION 3 ASSESSMENT

Main Idea
1. Use a diagram like the one below to list ways in which Bismarck's policies affected the German Empire.

Cause — Effects

German Empire

Bismarck's Policies →

Recall
2. **Define** papal infallibility, militarism.
3. **Identify** Kulturkampf, Pope Pius IX, Ferdinand Lassalle, William II.

Critical Thinking
4. **Evaluating Information** Predict what might have happened

if Frederick III had not died so soon after becoming kaiser of a united Germany.

Understanding Themes
5. **Change** What tactics did Bismarck use in his attempt to block challenges from Catholicism and the Socialist movement?

Visualizing History
Tell students that after William II accepted Bismarck's resignation, William made Bismarck a duke, offered him a gift of cash, and sent Bismarck a portrait. Bismarck accepted the title and portrait but refused the money.
Answer to Caption: *Bismarck, the dignified elder statesman, is being dismissed by the young, upstart kaiser.*

Evaluate
Section Quiz 26-3

Use the Testmaker to create a customized quiz for Section 3.

Reteach
Have students make a chart that shows how Bismarck influenced political, economic, social, and religious developments in the German Empire.

Reading Essentials and Study Guide 26-3

Enrich
Have students write a brief essay on Bismarck's Kulturkampf, which includes their views of separation of church and state.

CLOSE

Have students discuss struggles Bismarck had with the legislature during his years as chancellor. *(Kulturkampf alienated many legislators; legislature refused to renew anti-Socialist laws introduced by Bismarck.)*

SECTION 3 ASSESSMENT ANSWERS

1. campaigned against Catholic Church, then made peace; worked to expand nation's industry; set out to suppress Socialist movement; passed Sickness Insurance Law and Old Age Insurance Law to win over workers
2. All terms are defined in the Glossary.

3. Kulturkampf, 686; Pope Pius IX, 687; Ferdinand Lassalle, 687; William II, 689
4. Answers may vary but should include that since Frederick was liberal-minded, he might have promoted liberal reforms.
5. **CHANGE** Bismarck expelled the Jesuits and deprived bishops of their

authority, encouraged passage of anti-Catholic and anti-Socialist laws, and directed passage of laws that gave workers some measure of comfort and security as a way to blunt the Socialist challenge.

| 1815 | | 1845 | | 1875 | | 1905 |

1825 The Decembrist uprising fails. **1855** Nicholas I dies. **c. 1870** Populist movement reaches out to peasants. **1905** Nicholas II issues the October Manifesto.

Section 4

Empire of the Czars

Guide to Reading

Read to Find Out
Main Idea *A number of factors caused revolutionary movements to develop in Russia.*

▶ **Terms to Define**
autocracy, emancipation, zemstvo, anarchy, nihilist, Russification, pogrom, soviet, duma

▶ **People to Meet**
Alexander I, Nicholas I, Alexander II, Nicholas II, Empress Alexandra, Mensheviks, Bolsheviks, Lenin

▶ **Places to Locate**
Poland, St. Petersburg

The Storyteller

Prince Peter Kropotkin, a student in the Corps of Pages for the sons of the aristocracy, went to the opera with his friends the evening after Czar Alexander proclaimed an end to serfdom. The students planned to sing the hymn "God Save the Czar," and expected that everyone would join them. When they arrived they found the band of the opera was already playing the hymn, which was drowned immediately in enthusiastic cheers from all parts of the hall. This night, Prince Kropotkin thought, was undoubtedly the czar's finest hour.

—adapted from *A Source Book for Russian History from Early Times to 1917*, reprinted in *Sources of World History*, Mark A. Kishlansky, 1995

Czar Alexander II

In the early 1800s the Russian Empire stretched from Europe to the Pacific Ocean. More than 60 nationalities, speaking over 100 different languages, populated this vast territory. Although Slavs, including Russians, comprised nearly two-thirds of the population, many other European, Middle Eastern, and Asiatic peoples lived within the empire.

The agricultural economy of the Russian Empire was more oppressive but not much more effective than it had been during the Middle Ages. Serfdom, long in decline in western Europe, still bound the peasants living and working in rural areas. As a result of this entrenched agricultural system, Russia's level of industrialization remained lower than that of western Europe.

As an autocracy, a government in which one person rules with unlimited authority, the political structure of the Russian Empire had also remained much as it was in the days of Peter the Great. The forces of reform, already at work in western Europe in the early 1800s, soon threatened this traditional economic and political order of the Russian Empire.

Autocracy on the Defensive

Alexander I, who ruled from 1801 to 1825, dreamed of improving Russia's system of government and even granted a constitution to Russian-ruled **Poland** for a brief period of time. Convinced by the Napoleonic Wars that he was the savior of Europe, Alexander soon lost his desire to improve social, political, and economic conditions within his country.

The Russian officers who fought in the Napoleonic Wars were impressed by the reforms they saw in western Europe. Many of these officers joined secret societies to discuss the need in their country for economic reform, for a constitutional government, and for freeing the serfs. In December

690 Chapter 26 *Reaction and Nationalism*

SECTION RESOURCES

🗀 Reproducible Masters
- Lecture Notes 26-4
- Reproducible Lesson Plan 26-4
- Guided Reading Activity 26-4
- Geography and History Activity 26
- Section Quiz 26-4
- Reading Essentials and Study Guide 26-4

🕯 Transparencies
- Section Focus Transparency 26-4

Multimedia
- ◉ Vocabulary PuzzleMaker Software
- ◉ Interactive Tutor Self-Assessment Software
- ◉ Testmaker
- ◈ Turning Points in World History: *The Russian Revolution*

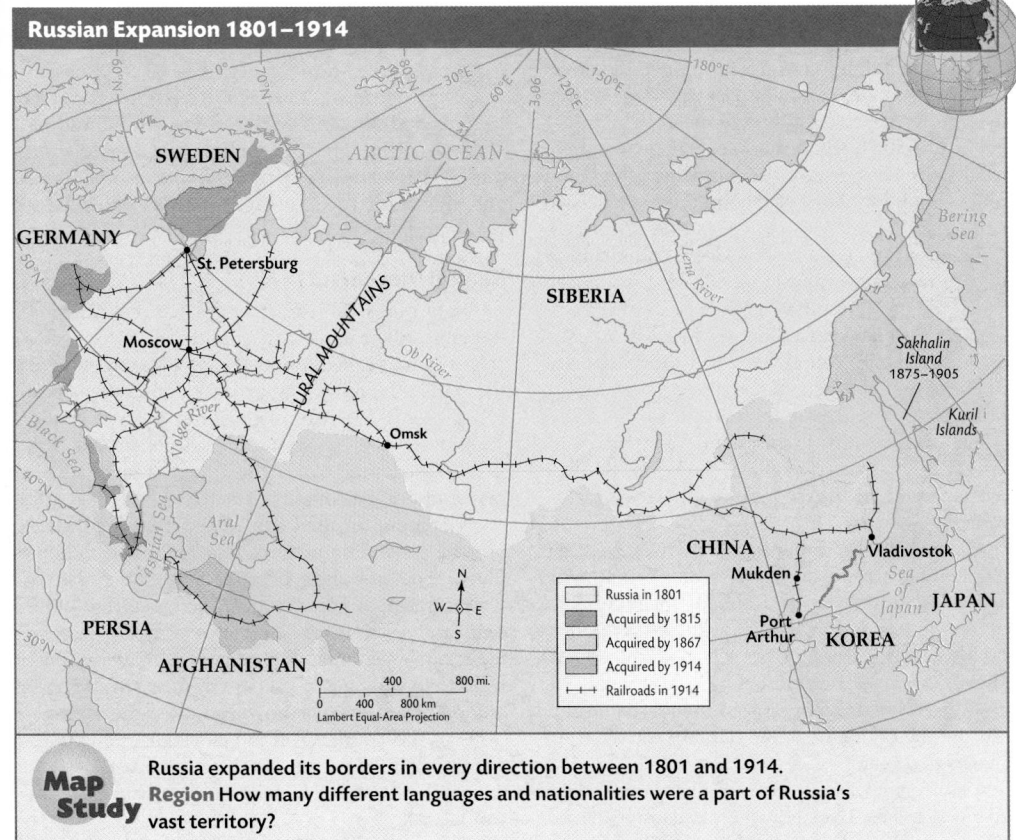

Russian Expansion 1801–1914

SWEDEN · GERMANY · St. Petersburg · Moscow · URAL MOUNTAINS · Ob River · Omsk · Black Sea · Volga River · Aral Sea · Caspian Sea · PERSIA · AFGHANISTAN · ARCTIC OCEAN · SIBERIA · Lena River · Sakhalin Island 1875–1905 · Kuril Islands · Bering Sea · CHINA · Mukden · Vladivostok · Sea of Japan · JAPAN · Port Arthur · KOREA

Russia in 1801
Acquired by 1815
Acquired by 1867
Acquired by 1914
Railroads in 1914

0   400   800 mi.
0   400   800 km
Lambert Equal-Area Projection

Map Study Russia expanded its borders in every direction between 1801 and 1914. **Region** How many different languages and nationalities were a part of Russia's vast territory?

1825, some of these officers took advantage of the uncertainty about the transfer of power after Alexander I's death and staged a military revolt.

Although the government quickly crushed the so-called Decembrist Revolt, the uprising had two very different effects. Its leaders were seen as martyrs and inspired later generations of revolutionaries. In the short term, however, the uprising hardened the determination of Alexander I's successor, **Nicholas I**, to strengthen the autocracy and suppress all opposition.

Under Nicholas I, the secret police had unlimited power to arrest and imprison people without trial and to censor the press. Despite Nicholas I's efforts to resist change, demands for reform persisted during the 1830s and 1840s. Russian losses in the Crimean War underscored the fact that the Russian Empire was in serious trouble. Nicholas, however, was too ill to begin any reforms. Following Nicholas I's death in 1855, his son **Alexander II** undertook the task of saving the autocracy and preventing a revolution.

Alexander II and Reforms

Russia's humiliating defeat in the Crimean War revealed the extent to which the nation lagged behind the other European powers militarily and economically. One major reason for Russia's backwardness was its system of serf labor. To progress, Russia needed to industrialize, but to industrialize, the factories needed a steady source of cheap labor. Only the serfs could provide this labor force, but they were not free to leave the land.

On March 3, 1861, Alexander II decreed the emancipation, or freeing, of the serfs. Although the serfs attained legal freedom, they received no land individually. Their village communities, called mirs, were granted varying amounts of the landlords' holdings, for which they had to undertake a 50-year mortgage. Peasants could not leave the mirs without paying their share, so they were still bound to the worst land and had an additional tax to pay. The landlords kept the best land and

Chapter 26 *Reaction and Nationalism* **691**

Chapter 26 *Reaction and Nationalism* **691**

Chapter 26 Section 4

TEACH

Guided Practice

THEME Reaction

Help students recall the definition of *reaction* as it applies to government and politics. *(a maintenance of or return to a former political or social order)* Have students discuss how this definition fits the Russian czars. *(The czars suppressed all opposition.)* **L1 LEP**

Map Study

Answer
People of 60 nationalities speaking 100 different languages lived in the Russian Empire.

Map Skills Practice

Reading a Map What does the heavy concentration of railroads in the western part of the empire indicate? *(That part of Russia was the most heavily populated, the most urban, and the most industrial.)*

Critical Thinking Have students compare the methods of Russia's anarchists, nihilists, Mensheviks, and Bolsheviks. Ask what goal all four groups had in common. *(ending the autocracy)* **L3**

COOPERATIVE LEARNING ACTIVITY

Panel Discussion Organize the class into five groups and have each group research the following groups of Russian society: the aristocracy, the landowners, the intellectuals, the urban workers, and the peasants. Have each group assemble a composite portrait of its class. Suggest that students include in their portraits the major characteristics, occupations, interests, and problems of the class. Have each group assign one of those topics to one or more group members to present in a panel discussion. After each group has presented its panel, encourage students to predict possible outcomes of these class differences for Russia. **L2**

VIDEODISC
Turning Points in World History

Side Two
Chapter 5

Title: *The Russian Revolution*
Ask: Why was the Russian Revolution a turning point in history? *(A Communist government was established.)*

Independent Practice

 Guided Reading Activity 26-4 **L1**

 Geography and History Activity 26

Who?What?Where?When?

Fabergé Eggs In the 1880s, Alexander III appointed Peter Carl Fabergé jeweler to the imperial court. Each Easter, Fabergé's workshop designed a special Easter egg for the czar to present to the czarina. These eggs, made of jewels and precious metals, opened to reveal a surprise, such as a miniature peacock or basket of flowers.

Global Gourmet

Russia Beef stroganoff, made of thinly sliced beef, onions, sour cream, and seasonings served with egg noodles, is a popular dish in Europe and the United States. It was created for Count Paul Stroganov, a liberal adviser of Alexander I.

---

received compensation from the government for their losses.

Many peasants gave up farming rather than return to bondage. Landless peasants moved from the farms to the cities, adding to the growing numbers of unskilled urban workers. Their discontent revealed itself in occasional minor uprisings and produced new stirrings of revolutionary activity in the Russian Empire.

Because the emancipation decree took control of the provinces away from the landowners, it also created the need for a new system of local government. An 1864 law created this new system. Locally elected assemblies called zemstvos took charge of provincial matters such as schools and health care. Three groups could vote in zemstvo elections: the nobility, the wealthy townspeople, and the peasants. The vote was weighted, however, so that noblemen and rich taxpayers dominated the local assemblies.

Czar Alexander II became known as the Czar Liberator for freeing the serfs and for his many reforms. In addition to those already mentioned, he limited the use and authority of the secret police, eased restrictions on the press, modernized the judicial system, and expanded the educational system. Alexander also reorganized the Russian army, reducing the period of active military service from 25 years to 6 years.

Unfortunately, the reforms of Alexander II satisfied few Russians. The landowners had lost both land and power. The peasantry had made few economic gains. Conservatives feared weakening of the autocracy, while reformers pushed for even greater changes. Designed to stem discontent, the reforms failed to halt the growth of revolutionary movements.

Footnotes to History

A Sickly Prince
In 1904 Czar Nicholas II and Empress Alexandra finally had a son—an heir to the throne— after four girls. Tragically, Alexis suffered from hemophilia, an inherited disease preventing the normal clotting of blood. To ease her son's agonies, Alexandra relied on a mystic healer named Grigori Rasputin (ra•SPYOO•tuhn). Rasputin's apparent success in helping Alexis gave him great political influence over the czar. This in turn increased Nicholas's isolation from his people and the forces of change sweeping his empire.

---

692 Chapter 26 *Reaction and Nationalism*

Terror and Reaction

Among the most vocal critics of the Russian government during Alexander II's reign were intellectuals and students from the upper and middle classes. Although these reformers had strong ideals, they had little practical political experience and almost no direct contact with the Russian people, especially the peasants.

Radical Movements

Some radical reformers, such as Michael Bakunin, advocated anarchy, or the absence of government, and called for the complete destruction of the state, the family, law, property, and other institutions. Nihilists (from the Latin *nihil*, meaning "nothing") also rejected all traditions, believing that Russia would have to destroy the czarist autocracy and build a completely new society.

Beginning in the early 1870s, many reformers became active in a new movement known as populism. The populists believed that the peasants would eventually lead a revolution, overthrow the czar, and establish a socialist society. To further their cause, groups of students and intellectuals went to the villages to prepare the peasants for revolution. The peasants, however, often grew suspicious of the young revolutionaries and sometimes even turned them over to the police. Frustrated by their lack of success, many populists turned to violent tactics.

The most radical faction of the revolutionaries plotted the assassinations of key officials in order to frighten the government into making radical reforms. Beginning in 1866, revolutionaries made several attempts to assassinate Alexander II. Although Alexander insisted that these radicals be crushed, he eventually responded to popular pressure by drafting a plan to establish a national assembly. Before the plan could be enacted, however, a young revolutionary killed the czar with a bomb in 1881.

Alexander III

Alexander III, who succeeded his father, vowed to maintain the old order and crush revolutionaries. He warned that he would not tolerate a constitution and reduced the powers of the zemstvos. Reversing his father's reforms, he abolished autonomy in the schools, restored censorship of the press, and extended the powers of the secret police.

To protect the autocracy, Alexander III used a resurgence of nationalism to promote a policy of Russification. Designed as an attempt to unite the empire's many peoples, Russification instead

---

MEETING SPECIAL NEEDS ACTIVITY

Learning Style: Visual/Spatial Have students who are visual learners research outside sources and then draw a picture depicting one of the following people in czarist Russia: a member of the imperial family, a wealthy landowner, a revolutionary intellectual, an urban worker, or a peasant. Suggest that students characterize the position of the person through clothing, hairstyle, facial expression, surroundings, and tools or equipment. Set aside space on a bulletin board for completed drawings. **L1 LEP**

Moscow workers, students, and intellectuals fought czarist troops during the 1905 Revolution. *How did the czarist government under Alexander III and Nicholas II deal with its opponents?*

Visualizing History In August 1905 the czar proposed to give peasants, but not urban workers, the right to vote for duma representatives. In response, urban workers and students led a general strike for 10 days in October that has often been described as the most effective strike in history. Why was this a successful strike? *(The czar issued the October Manifesto making Russia a constitutional monarchy.)*
Answer to Caption: *It vowed to maintain the old order and cracked down on revolutionary opposition, extending the powers of the secret police.*

became an official policy of intolerance and persecution of non-Russian peoples. Anyone who questioned the czar's authority, who spoke a language other than Russian, or who followed a religion other than Eastern Orthodoxy risked prosecution.

Russification singled out the Jews in particular for persecution. Government decrees deprived Jews of the right to own land and forced them to live in a certain area of the empire called the Pale. The government also encouraged bloody pogroms, or organized massacres of a minority group, in Jewish communities.

The Revolution of 1905

After Alexander III's death in 1894, many Russians were disappointed when his son **Nicholas II** stated he would also rule as an autocrat. The new czar, however, lacked the strong will to make absolute rule effective. He was easily influenced by those around him, particularly his wife, **Empress Alexandra**, who wanted their son to inherit an autocracy.

During the reign of Nicholas II, a revolutionary mood swept over Russia. Peasants grew increasingly dissatisfied; national minorities called for an end to persecution; and middle-class reformers pushed for a constitutional monarchy. At the same time, the emancipation of the serfs and rapid industrialization had resulted in a marked increase in the size of the urban working class. Russian factories at the turn of the century lacked proper lighting, ventilation, and sanitation. Workers toiled long hours for little pay and lived in terrible, overcrowded housing. Not surprisingly, then, urban workers joined the ranks of the dissatisfied.

Russian Marxists

By the early 1900s several revolutionary groups in Russia followed the teachings of Karl Marx. Their members believed that the working class, not the peasants, would lead the revolution. The **Mensheviks** believed that Russia needed to develop into an industrial state with a sizable working class before a socialist revolution could occur. The more radical **Bolsheviks**, led by Vladimir Ilyich Ulyanov—commonly known as **Lenin**—believed that a small party of professional revolutionaries

The Revolution of 1905
How did the Revolution of 1905 affect Russian government under the czars?
It nearly overthrew the monarchy, forcing the autocratic czar to grant concessions to liberals and revolutionaries, especially the creation of a legislature.

Linking Past and Present

Secret police have been known since Greek and Roman times. In 1825 the Russian czar established the first modern version of the secret police, giving them the power not only to arrest but also to try and to punish anyone who opposed the czar's power. From 1954 to 1991, the KGB was the Soviet Union's secret police, questioning and trying suspects and sending those with questionable loyalty to forced labor camps, psychiatric hospitals, and prisons. With the USSR's collapse, the KGB was overhauled.

MAKING CONNECTIONS ACTIVITY

Literature Have students research and present an oral report on one of the following Russian writers: Aleksandr Pushkin, Mikhail Lermontov, Nikolay Gogol, Ivan Turgenev, Fyodor Dostoyevsky, or Leo Tolstoy. Ask students to include the following information in their reports: the writer's education and social, economic, and political background; titles of major works; how the writer portrayed Russian history and society in the works; and the writer's lasting impact on Russian culture. **L3**

ASSESS

Check for Understanding

Assign Section 4 Assessment as homework or as an in-class activity.

 Use Interactive Tutor Self-Assessment Software to review Section 4.

Evaluate

Section Quiz 26-4

 Use the Testmaker to create a customized quiz for Section 4.

Reteach

Have students make an outline of Section 4 showing czarist reforms and reactions. Tell students to use the names of the five czars discussed in this section as the main headings for their outlines.

Reading Essentials and Study Guide 26-4

Enrich

Have students do further research and then write an essay about the events and outcome of the Revolution of 1905.

CLOSE

Have students draw evidence from Section 4 to support the following statement: Czarist reforms were incomplete, aroused opposition, and were always followed by reactionary measures.

---

could use force to bring about a socialist society in the near future.

Upheavals

War between Russia and Japan in 1904 over control of Manchuria furthered the Socialists' cause. Russian land forces suffered major setbacks, and a Russian fleet attempting to deliver supplies lost many ships in a Japanese attack. With the mediation of the United States, the war-exhausted empires finally concluded a peace agreement in 1905.

Russia's humiliating military performance heightened opposition to the czar's government by urban workers, middle-class thinkers, and peasants. The war had strained the Russian economy, raising food prices while keeping wages low.

Spontaneous strikes began to break out in many cities throughout the empire. On Sunday, January 22, 1905, about 200,000 workers marched in a peaceful procession to the czar's palace in **St. Petersburg** to present a petition for reform. Palace soldiers opened fire on the crowd, killing hundreds of workers. Bloody Sunday, as the demonstration was called, set off a wave of political protests.

Middle-class organizations drew up programs for political reform. The zemstvos issued lists of demands. In the spring of 1905, the first soviets, or workers' councils, formed to voice workers' grievances. From all reformist and revolutionary groups came the cry for the establishment of a representative government elected by universal suffrage.

In October 1905, angry workers seized control of the major cities in a general strike. As disorder and violence in the cities and rural areas continued, Nicholas II announced a law providing for the election of a national duma, or legislature. The czar, however, proposed that the Duma serve as an advisory council rather than a genuine legislative body. Instead of appeasing the Russian people, the measure set off more nationwide strikes.

Slavery Is on Its Way Out

Washington, D.C., 1863
During the American Civil War, President Abraham Lincoln issued the Emancipation Proclamation that eventually led to the end of slavery in the United States. This historic document declared freedom for all enslaved people in the Confederacy—the states that were in rebellion against the Union. The Emancipation Proclamation strengthened the Union's war effort and made the war a fight against slavery. It also weakened the Confederacy by discouraging France and England from entering the war.

The events of October forced Nicholas to yield reluctantly to the demands of his people. The czar issued the October Manifesto, granting civil rights to citizens and allowing the Duma to make laws. In theory, Russia became a constitutional monarchy; in practice, Nicholas kept his powers. Stern measures to restore order, including pogroms against the Jews and the arrests of peasant and labor leaders, took place. When the Duma tried to act independently, Nicholas dissolved it.

Nicholas II's ability to silence opposition was only temporary. Russia's many serious troubles had not been resolved. On the eve of World War I, growing numbers of peasants, workers, national minorities, and middle-class reformers supported an immediate end to the autocracy. Their demands and the stress of war would soon bring revolution to the Russian Empire.

SECTION 4 ASSESSMENT

Main Idea
1. Use a diagram like the one below to list reasons why Russian revolutionary movements developed.

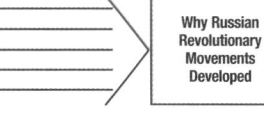

Recall
2. **Define** autocracy, emancipation, zemstvo, anarchy, nihilist, Russification, pogrom, soviet, duma.
3. **Identify** Alexander I, Nicholas I, Alexander II, Nicholas II, Empress Alexandra, Mensheviks, Bolsheviks, Lenin.

Critical Thinking
4. **Applying Information** Select one of the Russian czars and tell how his policies affected the Russian Empire.
Understanding Themes
5. **Reaction** Why was effective reform difficult to achieve in Russia during the reign of Nicholas II?

SECTION 4 ASSESSMENT ANSWERS

1. Russian officers impressed by reforms in western Europe; discontent of landless peasants; Alexander II's reforms did not satisfy Russia; growth of populism; national minorities called for end of persecution; middle-class reformers wanted constitutional monarchy; large, dissatisfied urban working class; rise of Russian Marxists; humiliating war with Japan added to anti-government feeling
2. All terms are defined in the Glossary.
3. Alexander I, 690; Nicholas I, 691; Alexander II, 691; Nicholas II, 693; Empress Alexandra, 693; Mensheviks, 693; Bolsheviks, 693; Lenin, 693
4. Answers may vary but should include both the reforms and reactionary measures.
5. **REACTION** Answers may vary but should include that Nicholas II gave in to reforms only when he was forced to but remained determined to maintain his power and the autocracy of the czars.

1867 Austria and Hungary form a dual monarchy.

1878 Congress of Berlin settles Russo-Turkish War.

1913 Treaty of Bucharest ends Balkan conflict.

Section 5

Austria-Hungary's Decline

Guide to Reading

Read to Find Out
Main Idea *The growth of nationalistic feelings strongly affected the empire of Austria-Hungary.*

▶ **Terms to Define**
dual monarchy, jingoism

▶ **People to Meet**
Francis Joseph, Francis Deak

▶ **Places to Locate**
Austria, Vienna, Hungary, Bohemia, Moravia, Serbia, Bulgaria, Romania, Montenegro, Bosnia and Herzegovina

The Storyteller

Josef Heismann knew that the army was edgy. Once a powerful force, Austria was now regarded as second-rate. Inflammatory newspaper articles called for Austria to annex Bosnia, Serbia, and other Slav republics. Josef read an army newspaper article calling for an immediate invasion: "On us depends the future of our Empire. If we return victorious, we shall not only have conquered a foreign land: we shall have won back Austrian self-respect, given new life to the Imperial idea and vanquished ... the enemy in our midst."

—adapted from *The Origins of World War I*, Roger Parkinson, 1970

Austrian soldiers of the 1860s

In the early 1800s, in addition to Russia and the Ottoman Empire, there was a third dominant power in eastern Europe: **Austria**. The Austrian Empire at this time contained more than 11 different national groups, including the Germans of Austria and the Magyars of Hungary.

Like Russia, Austria lacked national and geographical unity. Also as in Russia, life in Austria remained almost feudal at the beginning of the 1800s. A powerful landed nobility controlled a large peasant population and resisted any change in the old agricultural system. Through strict censorship and the arrest and intimidation of protesters, the government sought to stem the forces of nationalism and revolution sweeping through Europe.

The Revolution of 1848

As you learned in Chapter 22, the principal political figure in Austria during the early 1800s was Prince Klemens von Metternich, who held the office of minister of foreign affairs from 1809 to 1848. Metternich believed that democratic and nationalist movements would destroy the Austrian Empire and threaten peace in Europe. As a result, Metternich worked to crush all revolutionary activity, both within and outside the empire.

Despite Metternich's conservative policies, however, the revolutionary movement that had begun in France in 1848 spread to Austria the same year. Throughout the empire, nationalist groups demanded freedom of speech and press, peasant relief from feudal dues, and a representative government. The Austrian Empire seemed on the verge of collapse.

The tide of revolutionary activity was to turn once more, however. Infighting among nationalist groups and within radical factions with different

Chapter 26 *Reaction and Nationalism* **695**

SECTION THEME

▶ **Diversity** The large empire of Austria-Hungary contains many different nationalities seeking self-rule.

Guide to Reading

For reading strategies to help students read effectively see pages 12–13.

Vocabulary Pre-check

Use the Vocabulary PuzzleMaker for Chapter 26 to create a crossword puzzle to reinforce section terms. **L1 LEP**

Use Vocabulary Activity 26 to introduce vocabulary terms. **L1 LEP**

FOCUS

Section Objective
Describe how the growth of nationalistic feelings affected the empire of Austria-Hungary.

BELLRINGER
Motivational Activity

Before taking roll at the beginning of the class period, project Section Focus Transparency 26-5 and have students answer the activity questions. Discuss students' responses.

This activity is also available as a blackline master.

SECTION RESOURCES

Reproducible Masters
- Lecture Notes 26-5
- Reproducible Lesson Plan 26-5
- Vocabulary Activity 26
- Guided Reading Activity 26-5
- Reteaching Activity 26
- Enrichment Activity 26
- Section Quiz 26-5

- Performance Assessment Activity 26
- Spanish Chapter Summary 26
- Reading Essentials and Study Guide 26-5

Transparencies
- Section Focus Transparency 26-5
- Mapping History Overlay Transparency 17, *Revolutionary Centers in Europe 1820–1848*

Multimedia
- Interactive Tutor Self-Assessment Software
- Testmaker

TEACH

Guided Practice

THEME Diversity

Have students list the national groups that were part of Austria-Hungary by 1914. **L1 LEP**

Geography: Regions Have students use the map on page 697 to name the areas that bordered the Austro-Hungarian Empire. (*Germany, Russia, Romania, Serbia, Montenegro, Italy, Switzerland*) Have students discuss how cultural ties between these neighbors and ethnic groups within Austria-Hungary could threaten the coherence of the empire. **L2**

Analyzing Information Have students explain how the Congress of Berlin and the Treaty of Bucharest set the stage for further conflict in the Balkans. **L3**

📖 Mapping History Overlay Transparency 17, *Revolutionary Centers in Europe 1820–1848*

Visualizing History Although Francis Joseph was both an emperor and a king, he has been described as being at heart "a simple soul with Spartan tastes." Francis Joseph was usually painted wearing the white jacket and red trousers of the Austrian army.
Answer to Caption: *the transformation of Austria-Hungary into a dual monarchy, with Hungary as an independent kingdom on an equal level with Austria*

---

political ideas enabled conservative forces to strike back. In **Vienna**, for example, conflict between middle-class moderates who wanted to reform the political system and radical workers who wanted to overthrow it weakened the revolutionary movement. By October 1848, the government once more occupied the capital. When Emperor Francis Ferdinand resigned his throne, his nephew, **Francis Joseph**, became emperor at the age of 18.

Francis Joseph moved quickly to restore the conservative order. He dissolved the revolutionary assembly and rejected the new constitution. Although threatened, the old regime had managed to withstand revolutionary change by playing one nationalist faction against another.

Throughout his 68-year reign, Francis Joseph struggled to maintain a unified empire. Neither repressive measures nor reforms, however, helped ease the nationalist tensions that threatened Austria. At the same time, a series of foreign crises further weakened the empire. In 1859 Austria was forced to give up the Italian province of Lombardy. Then in 1866, during the Seven Weeks' War with Prussia, Austria lost its influence over its German states as well.

The Dual Monarchy

Francis Joseph's efforts to strengthen his authority were most effectively challenged by the Magyars of **Hungary**. In 1848 Hungarian nationalists led by Louis Kossuth declared Hungary an independent republic, but this achievement was short-lived. With Russian help, Austrian forces defeated the Hungarian nationalists, and Hungary was restored to the Austrian Empire. After Austria's defeat in the Seven Weeks' War (1866), however, Francis Joseph realized that his empire's stability depended on better relations with the Hungarians. He met with Hungarian leader **Francis Deak** to see if a compromise could be worked out.

After months of negotiations, Austria and Hungary finally reached an agreement in 1867. The *Ausgleich* (OWS•glyk), or Compromise, restored Hungary's independence and divided the Austrian Empire into a dual monarchy: the empire of Austria and the kingdom of Hungary. Francis Joseph remained ruler of both areas. He kept his title as emperor of Austria, and the Hungarians crowned him king of Hungary.

In addition to sharing a monarch, the two states had common ministries of foreign affairs, war, and finance. A system of committees handled other matters of mutual concern. In internal affairs, however, Austria and Hungary were completely independent of each other. Each had its own constitution, prime minister, and parliament.

While Austria and Hungary were independent politically, they were dependent on each other economically. Industrialized Austria supplied manufactured goods for the peoples of the dual

Visualizing History Francis Joseph ruled the Austrian Empire for 68 years. When he came to the throne in 1848, Europe was in the midst of revolutions. When he died in 1916, Europe was in the midst of World War I. *What change did Francis Joseph agree to in 1867 in order to save his empire?*

696 Chapter 26 *Reaction and Nationalism*

COOPERATIVE LEARNING ACTIVITY

Fact File Organize the class into groups of two or three students to research and prepare fact files on the following ethnic groups in the Austro-Hungarian Empire: Germans, Magyars, Italians, Romanians, Czechs, Serbs, Croatians, Slovaks, Poles, Slovenes, and Ukrainians. Have each group gather information on the culture, language, religion, traditions, national dress, and political goals of one ethnic group. Tell students to organize this information on no more than two sheets of paper. Choose a few students to compile each group's information into a "Fact File on Ethnic Groups in Austria-Hungary." Make the Fact File available to the class as a source of information.
L1 👐

monarchy. Agricultural Hungary supplied food products. Their cooperation, however, was not without conflict. Disputes inevitably developed between Austria and Hungary over foreign trade, tariffs, and currency.

During the mid-1800s, Austrian industrial growth had been slow. After the creation of the dual monarchy, however, the empire's production of coal, iron, steel, and manufactured goods grew rapidly. The territories of **Bohemia** and **Moravia** became the empire's leading industrial centers, producing machine tools, textiles, armaments, shoes, and chemicals. The concentration of industry in Bohemia and Moravia caused a more rapid urbanization in those areas.

The dual monarchy was satisfactory to both the Austrian-Germans, who maintained power in Austria, and the Magyars, who controlled Hungary. Other nationalities remained discontented. Three-fifths of the population of Austria-Hungary were Slavs—Poles, Czechs, Slovaks, Serbs, and Bosnians— who had no voice in the government. Many Slavic nationalist groups dreamed of breaking free from the Austro-Hungarian Empire and forming a large Slav kingdom. Their discontent became a threat to the empire's unity.

Powder Keg in the Balkans

By the mid-1800s, the Ottoman Empire had declined to a weakened and diminished state. In 1829 Greece won its independence. By 1850 the Ottomans had lost the provinces of Moldavia and Wallachia to Russia and Algeria to France. In addition, Egypt, Arabia, and several Balkan territories had gained their autonomy.

Foreign powers watched the decline of the Ottoman Empire closely. Austria hoped to expand into the Balkan region. France sought to protect persecuted Catholics within the empire. Great Britain feared disruption of its Mediterranean trade. The primary objective of these foreign powers, though, was to prevent Russian expansion into the region. "We have a sick man on our hands," declared Czar Nicholas I, referring to Turkey, and Russia stood ready to contribute to its final collapse.

During the Crimean War, from 1854 to 1856, France, Great Britain, and Sardinia helped defend the Ottoman Empire against Russia's advances. Although the Ottoman allies defeated Russia in this war, the empire continued to lose power and territory. In 1875 nationalists in the Balkan states of **Serbia**, **Bulgaria**, and **Romania** rose up in revolt, demanding immediate independence from Turkey. The Turks brutally suppressed these revolts with widespread massacres.

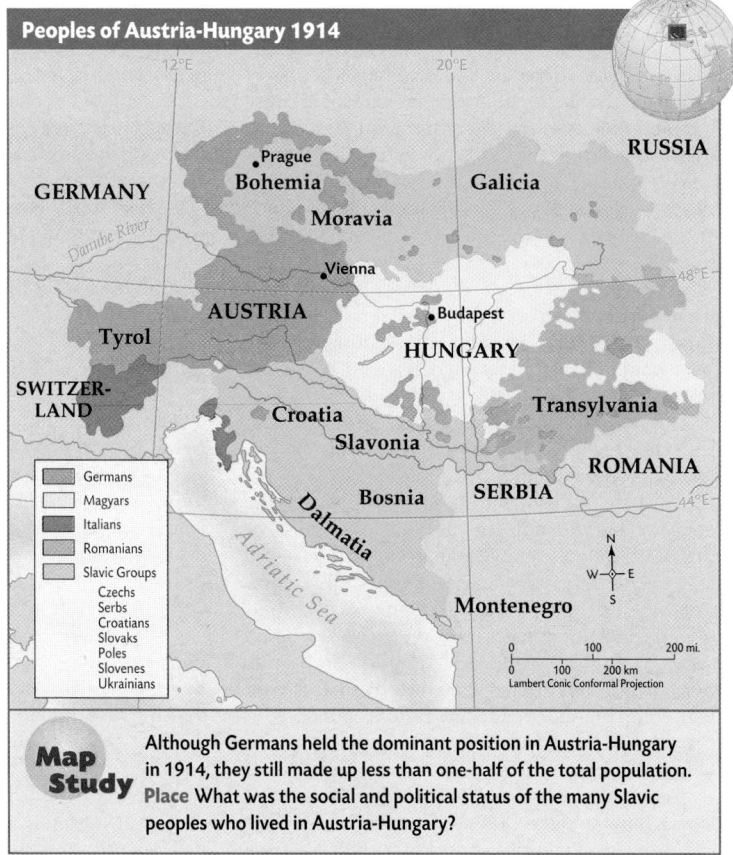

Peoples of Austria-Hungary 1914

Germans
Magyars
Italians
Romanians
Slavic Groups
  Czechs
  Serbs
  Croatians
  Slovaks
  Poles
  Slovenes
  Ukrainians

0   100   200 mi.
0 100 200 km
Lambert Conic Conformal Projection

Map Study Although Germans held the dominant position in Austria-Hungary in 1914, they still made up less than one-half of the total population. **Place** What was the social and political status of the many Slavic peoples who lived in Austria-Hungary?

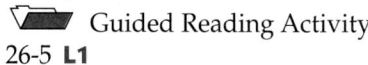

Map Study

Answer
They had no voice in their government.

Map Skills Practice

Reading a Map Which nationality group lived throughout Austria-Hungary? *(the Germans)*

Independent Practice

 Guided Reading Activity 26-5 **L1**

Multicultural Have students research and write a brief history on one of the following ethnic groups from early times through the present: Magyars, Romanians, Serbs, Croatians, Bosnians, Poles, Lithuanians, Slovaks, Bohemians, Moravians, or Slovenes. **L2**

Global Gourmet

Hungary Hungary's first people, the Magyars, were nomads. As such they needed food that traveled well without spoiling. *Gulyás*, cubes of seasoned, cooked, dried meat added to hot water and any local vegetables, became an instant soup or stew. Today the ingredients in *gulyás*, or goulash, are fresh.

ASSESS

Check for Understanding

Assign Section 5 Assessment as homework or as an in-class activity.

☐ Use Interactive Tutor Self-Assessment Software to review Section 5.

MEETING SPECIAL NEEDS ACTIVITY

Learning Style: Visual/Spatial To help students better visualize the location of ethnic groups in the Austro-Hungarian and Ottoman Empires, have them work in pairs using a historical atlas to draw a map of these areas. Ask students to label the map with the ethnic groups. Then have students compare their maps with a map of present-day Europe. Help students identify the countries in which these ethnic groups now live. **L2 LEP**

Linking Past and Present

Ethnic Cleansing From the 1890s to the 1920s, Turkish officials led massacres to suppress the Christian Armenians; more than 1.5 million Armenians died. In the 1990s, Bosnian Serbs who followed Orthodox Christianity led a similar program of "ethnic cleansing" against the Muslims who lived in Bosnia.

Evaluate

 Section Quiz 26-5

⬛ Use the Testmaker to create a customized quiz for Section 5.

Reteach

Have students make a time line from 1848 to 1913 of major events covered in Section 5.

 Reteaching Activity 26

 Reading Essentials and Study Guide 26-5

Enrich

Have students redraw the map on page 697 to show how they would have divided Austria-Hungary into independent countries based on nationality.

 Enrichment Activity 26

CLOSE

Have students discuss why the Balkans were called "the powder keg of Europe."

The Congress of Berlin

In 1877 Russia went to war on behalf of the Slavic people in the Balkan Peninsula. Publicly embracing the Slavic nationalist movement because it suited the government's imperial ambitions, Russia used the conflict known as the Russo-Turkish War to justify its expansion into Balkan territory. The Treaty of San Stefano (1878), which ended the war, created a large Russian-controlled Bulgarian state.

As news of Russian victories reached Great Britain, the public cried out for war. A popular slogan at the time captured the sentiment: "We don't want to fight, but by jingo, if we do, we've got the men, we've got the ships, we've got the money, too." From this slogan came the term jingoism, describing extreme patriotism, usually provoked by a perceived foreign threat.

The great European powers protested the Treaty of San Stefano. In the end a congress of European leaders met in Berlin, Germany, to revise it. At the meeting, which began in June 1878, representatives of the European powers divided Bulgaria into three parts, one of which remained under Ottoman rule. Neighboring Serbia, **Montenegro**, and Romania, on the other hand, won their complete independence. Britain gained control of Cyprus, and Austria-Hungary won the Balkan provinces of **Bosnia** and **Herzegovina**.

The Congress of Berlin satisfied few. Russia lost its war gains, and the Ottoman Empire lost much of its European territory. In addition, the congress dealt with the Balkan states inequitably, granting independence for some, but not all, of the people of any given nationality.

Balkan Conflict

By 1912 the Balkan states had joined forces and moved to free members of their respective nationalities from Ottoman rule. Encouraged by Italy's easy victory over the Turks in North Africa, the Balkan League—consisting of Bulgaria, Greece, Montenegro, and Serbia—declared war on Turkey in 1912. As a result of the war, the Ottomans lost all of their European territory with the exception of Istanbul and a small surrounding area.

Unity among members of the Balkan League was short-lived. No sooner had the Balkan states won the war than they began to fight among themselves over the lands they had gained. Before the war, Serbia and Bulgaria had secretly arranged for land distribution in case of victory. After the war, Bulgaria refused to go along with the plan, not wanting to give up territory won directly in battle.

To keep their land, the Bulgarians in June 1913 attacked Greek and Serb forces in the disputed area. In this second Balkan War, Montenegro and Greece sided with Serbia against Bulgaria. Romania joined the fighting when it saw the opportunity to win land from Bulgaria. The Balkan conflict brought new hope to the Ottomans. Seeing the chance to recover its own lost European territory, the Ottoman Empire attacked Bulgaria.

The fighting ended in 1913 with the Treaty of Bucharest, and the disputed land was redistributed. Bulgaria, which lost the war, surrendered much of the land it had previously won from the Ottomans.

The Treaty of Bucharest did not bring lasting peace to the Balkans. Serbia's increased power encouraged nationalism among Slavs and threatened Austria-Hungary. Russia, in supporting the pan-Slavic movement, sought to extend its own influence in the Balkans. The French, British, and German governments tried to preserve the existing balance of power to prevent either Austria-Hungary or Russia from gaining greater influence in the area. Writers of the time called the Balkans "the powder keg of Europe" because it seemed inevitable that events there would sooner or later explode into a major European war.

SECTION 5 ASSESSMENT

Main Idea
1. Use a diagram like the one below to list effects of nationalism on Austria-Hungary.

Cause → Effects

Nationalism in Austria-Hungary → ▢ ▢ ▢

Recall
2. **Define** dual monarchy, jingoism.
3. **Identify** Francis Joseph, Francis Deak, the Congress of Berlin.

Critical Thinking
4. **Analyzing Information** How did the empires of Austria-Hungary and Russia differ from the Balkan countries in their reasons for intervening in the Ottoman Empire's problems?

Understanding Themes
5. **Diversity** Explain how ethnic diversity and rising nationalism contributed to the decline of Austria-Hungary. Could this decline have been avoided? Why or why not?

SECTION 5 ASSESSMENT ANSWERS

1. demands for freedom of speech and press, peasant relief from feudal dues, and representative government; nationalist tensions threatened Austria; Hungarian nationalists declared Hungary an independent republic in 1848, were defeated by Austria; Slavic nationalists wanted independence

2. All terms are defined in the Glossary.
3. Francis Joseph, 696; Francis Deak, 696; Congress of Berlin, 698
4. The Balkan countries wanted to win independence from the Ottoman Empire. Austria-Hungary and Russia wanted to expand their control into the Balkans.

5. **DIVERSITY** Answers will vary but should include that the many ethnic groups in the empire had more allegiance to their own group than to the empire. Because nationalism was spreading across Europe, the Austrian Empire's decline probably could not have been avoided.

Selecting and Using Research Sources

You have to write a report, so you head to the library. There you are surrounded by shelves of books. Where do you begin?

Learning the Skill

Libraries contain many kinds of research sources. Understanding the content and purpose of each type will help you find relevant information more efficiently. Here are brief descriptions of important sources:

Reference Books Reference books include encyclopedias, biographical dictionaries, atlases, and almanacs.

An encyclopedia is a set of books with short articles on many subjects arranged alphabetically. General encyclopedias present a wide range of topics, while specialized encyclopedias have articles on a theme—e.g., an encyclopedia of music.

A biographical dictionary provides brief biographies listed alphabetically by last names. Each biography gives data such as place and date of birth, occupation, and achievements.

An atlas is a collection of maps and charts for locating geographical features and places. An atlas can be general or thematic. An atlas contains an alphabetical index of place names that directs you to the map(s) where that place appears.

An almanac is an annually updated reference that provides current statistics together with historical information on a wide range of subjects.

Card Catalog The library's catalog, on computer or cards, lists every book in the library. Each listing gives the book's author, title, subject, call number, and location. Computer catalogs also show whether the book is available.

Many libraries have joined networks. A library network usually has a single computer catalog listing all the books in the network. A patron can borrow any book in the system.

Periodical Guides A periodical guide is a set of books listing topics covered in magazine and newspaper articles.

Computer Databases Computer databases provide collections of information organized for rapid search and retrieval.

If you have trouble finding the needed information, ask the librarian for help.

Practicing the Skill

Suppose you are going to Germany and want to learn more about the country before you go. Read the research questions below. Then decide which of the following sources you would use to answer each question and why.

a. encyclopedia
b. atlas
c. historical atlas
d. almanac
e. biographical dictionary
f. catalog entry: Germany—travel
g. catalog entry: Germany—modern history
h. periodical guide

1. Locate each city on the trip itinerary.
2. What are the places of interest in each city?
3. What have been the major events in German history since 1800?
4. What political issues face Germany today?

Applying the Skill

Use research resources from your school or local library to research the following topic:

What medical treatment was given to Czarevitch Alexis, son of Nicholas II and Alexandra? How has medical care of hemophiliacs improved since 1910? List your sources.

For More Practice

Turn to the Skill Practice in the Chapter Assessment on page 701.

 The **Glencoe Skillbuilder Interactive Workbook**, Level 2 provides instruction and practice in key social studies skills.

ANSWERS TO PRACTICING THE SKILL

1. atlas; provides collection of maps
2. catalog entry: Germany—travel; entry deals with travel in Germany
3. encyclopedia; provides information on many subjects; catalog entry: Germany—modern history
4. periodical guide; lists article topics covered in current magazines and newspapers

— **WORLD HISTORY** *Online* —

Have students use the **Chapter 26 Self-Check Quiz** at worldhistory.glencoe.com to prepare for the Chapter Test.

GLENCOE TECHNOLOGY

VIDEODISC
Use MindJogger to review the chapter.

MindJogger Videoquiz

 Chapter 26
Disc 4 Side A

Also available in VHS.

Answers

Using Key Terms

1. a   3. f   5. j
2. g   4. h

Using Your History Journal

Suggest that students use the encyclopedia to gain an understanding of the history of the conflict in Bosnia.

Reviewing Facts

1. 1829: Greece independent; 1854-56: Crimean War; 1875: Serbia, Bulgaria, Romania revolt; 1877: Russo-Turkish War; 1878: Treaty of San Stefano; 1878: Congress of Berlin; 1912: Balkan League declares war on Turkey; 1913: Second Balkan war, Treaty of Bucharest

2. After the events of 1848, Italian nationalists lost faith in Mazzini and turned to the king of Sardinia to lead the struggle for unification.

3. Mazzini, Cavour, Victor Emmanuel II, Garibaldi

4. The *Zollverein* was an economic union that established a uniform tariff among the German states. By forming the *Zollverein* and being the largest German state, Prussia outmaneuvered Austria.

— **WORLD HISTORY** *Online* —

Self-Check Quiz

Visit the *World History: The Human Experience* Web site at **worldhistory.glencoe.com** and click on **Chapter 26—Self-Check Quiz** to prepare for the Chapter Test.

Using Key Terms

Write the key term that completes each sentence. Then write a sentence for each term not chosen.

a. anarchy	g. dual monarchy
b. duma	h. nihilists
c. jingoism	i. kaiser
d. nationalism	j. pogroms
e. Russification	k. emancipation
f. autocracy	l. zemstvo

1. In the 1800s some radical reformers in Russia called for _____, the complete destruction of the government, the family, law, property, and other institutions.

2. In 1867 Austria and Hungary reached an agreement to transform the Austrian Empire into a _____, consisting of two separate but interrelated kingdoms.

3. During the 1800s the Russian Empire was an _____, a government in which one person rules with unlimited authority.

4. Among Russian revolutionaries, the _____ rejected all traditions, believing that Russia would have to completely build a new society.

5. The Russian government encouraged bloody _____, or organized massacres, in Jewish communities of the Russian Empire.

Technology Activity

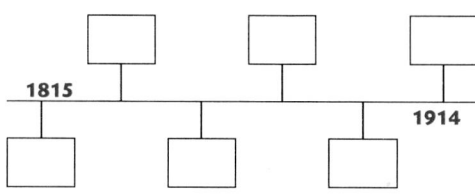

Using a Word Processor
Search the Internet or your local library for sources about the history of Russian czars. Using a word processor or software, create a genealogy chart of the Romanov dynasty. Include a short report explaining why the empire of the czars ended and how it impacted Russian culture.

Using Your History Journal

Read two or three recent news magazine reports on Bosnia and Herzegovina. Write an essay about how to achieve lasting peace in the Balkans.

Reviewing Facts

1. **History** Use a time line like the one below to show key events in the Balkan conflicts between 1815 and 1914.

1815 ———————————————— 1914

2. **Government** Explain how Sardinia gained control of the Italian struggle for unification.

3. **Government** Identify the leaders of Italy's unification movement.

4. **Economics** Describe the *Zollverein*. How did it help Prussia lead the German Confederation?

5. **Government** List the challenges that faced the new German state.

6. **Government** Explain why the reforms of Alexander II satisfied few Russians.

7. **History** State the effects of the 1905 Revolution on Russian government and society.

Critical Thinking

1. **Apply** How did foreign powers help Italians achieve independence?

2. **Contrast** How did the problems that Italy faced after unification differ from the problems that Germany faced?

3. **Synthesize** Why do you think Austria agreed to the compromise with Hungary that established the dual monarchy?

4. **Evaluate** What do you think might have happened if Russia's Czar Nicholas II had given the Duma full legislative power?

---

5. economic, social, religious, political, and cultural divisions

6. Landowners lost land and power; peasants made few gains; conservatives feared autocracy was weakened; reformers wanted greater reforms.

7. Strikes forced the czar to grant a national legislature and civil rights; however, after the uprisings were suppressed, he tried to return to autocratic rule.

Critical Thinking

1. Britain and France recognized Italy's sovereignty; France agreed to help the Italians expel Austria from the peninsula; Prussia agreed to give Italy Venetia.

2. Germany faced divisions based on religion and dialects; Italy was threatened by former rulers of the Italian states and Austria still controlled some Italian land.

3. After losing the Seven Weeks' War, Austria

Geography in History

1. **Place** Refer to the map below. In what two areas was most of the fighting during the Russo-Japanese War?
2. **Movement** Across what two bodies of water were Japanese troops transported to the war zone?
3. **Movement** What railway helped in moving Japanese forces north?
4. **Region** What effect did Russia's setback in this region have on the czar's government?

Russo–Japanese War

Understanding Themes

1. **Nationalism** How did the rise of nationalism spur the unification movement in Italy?
2. **Conflict** How did Bismarck promote his goal of German unification?
3. **Change** What changes came to Germany's economy after unification?
4. **Reaction** How did the policies of Alexander III affect the Jews and other non-Russian groups within the Russian Empire?
5. **Diversity** How did the great diversity of nationalities in the Austrian Empire lead to the establishment of the dual monarchy in the mid-1800s?

Linking Past and Present

1. Bismarck had the difficult task of forging a strong, united German nation. What problems did he face? What problems have confronted German leaders since the early 1990s in reuniting Germany today after nearly 50 years of division into Communist and democratic areas?
2. Alexander III carried out a policy of Russification that led to intolerance and persecution of non-Russian groups in the Russian Empire. Are similar policies carried out today in Russia and the other countries of the former Soviet Union? Explain your answer.

Skill Practice

For each research question below, decide which of these sources would provide relevant information.

a. encyclopedia
b. atlas
c. historical atlas
d. almanac
e. biographical dictionary
f. catalog entry: European history 19th century
g. catalog entry: nationalism
h. periodical guide

1. How have the borders of the countries discussed in Chapter 26 changed since World War I?
2. What are the latest population statistics for Germany, Italy, Austria, Hungary, and Russia?
3. What were Otto von Bismarck's greatest accomplishments?
4. What nationalist struggles have occurred in Europe in the last decade?

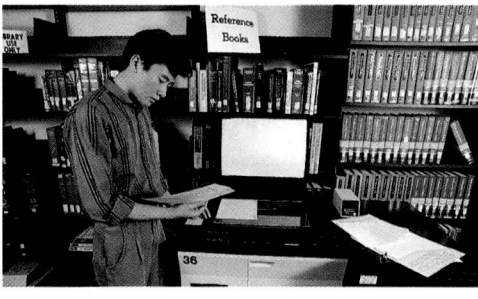

strong and prosperous industrial economy.
4. **REACTION** Alexander III tried to force Russian language and ways on the non-Russian peoples; he exerted strong pressure on the Jews who were singled out for persecution. The government forced Jews to live in the Pale and encouraged bloody massacres of Jewish communities.
5. **DIVERSITY** The nationalist movements of the empire's many ethnic groups had left Austria in a weakened position. When the Magyars in Hungary asked for greater independence, Francis Joseph agreed to the dual monarchy.

Linking Past and Present

1. Bismarck faced problems with the Catholic Church and Socialists. Since 1990, Germany has faced economic differences between former East and West Germans and has had to protect foreign minority workers.
2. yes; Russia's move against the Chechen independence movement

Skill Practice

1. c   3. e
2. d   4. g, h

Chapter Bonus Test Question

Ask students: How did the goals of nationalism differ between the people in Italy and Germany and the people in the Austrian, Russian, and Ottoman Empires? *(Nationalism in Italy and Germany sought to unite the separate states in each of those countries, but nationalism in the Austrian, Russian, and Ottoman Empires sought independence for their various ethnic groups.)*

was in a weakened bargaining position.
4. Russia might have evolved into a constitutional monarchy.

Geography in History

1. along the coast of the Yellow Sea; along the South Manchurian Railway
2. Sea of Japan, Yellow Sea
3. South Manchurian Railway
4. It weakened the government.

Understanding Themes

1. **NATIONALISM** caused the Italian people to move toward independence from foreign countries and to unite the Italian states into one country
2. **CONFLICT** He carried out a policy of realpolitik, using a combination of war and diplomacy to advance the interests of the Prussian state.
3. **CHANGE** Germany developed a

A complete, 1-page lesson plan is provided for each section in the *Reproducible Lesson Plans* booklet.

The Age of Imperialism

CHAPTER RESOURCES

	Reproducible Resources	Multimedia Resources
Chapter Opener	Chapter Themes: Graphic Organizer 27 Historical Significance Chapter Activity 27	MindJogger Videoquiz
Chapter Enrichment	Vocabulary Activity 27* Time Line Activity 27 Mapping History Activity 27 History Simulation 27 Geography and History Activity 27 Source Reading 27 People in World History Profiles 51, 52 World Art and Music Activity 27 Enrichment Activity 27 Critical Thinking Activity 27 Skill Reinforcement Activity 27 Performance Assessment Activity 27 Standardized Test Practice Workbook Activity 27 Inclusion for the Social Studies Classroom Strategies and Activities	World History and Art Transparency 35, *Ono Waterfall* Chapter Transparency 27 Vocabulary PuzzleMaker Software World History Primary Source Document Library
Chapter Review/Reteaching	Reteaching Activity 27 Skill Reinforcement Activity 27 Spanish Chapter Summary 27	Chapter 27 Digest Audiocassette, Activity, Test* Vocabulary PuzzleMaker Software Interactive Tutor Self-Assessment Software MindJogger Videoquiz
Chapter Evaluation/Testing	Performance Assessment Activity 27 Chapter 27 Test, Forms A and B	ExamView® Pro Testmaker

* Also available in Spanish

0:00 OUT OF TIME? Assign the Chapter 27 Audiocassettes.

World History Primary Source Document Library
Make History Come Alive!
Engage your students with over 250 easily accessible primary source documents—available on this CD-ROM—that will give them real life insight into the important events of world history.

Block Schedule

Activities that are particularly suited to use within the block scheduling framework are identified throughout this chapter by the following designation.

KEY TO ABILITY LEVELS

Teaching strategies are coded for varying learning styles.
- **L1 BASIC** activities for all students
- **L2 AVERAGE** activities for average to above-average students
- **L3 CHALLENGING** activities for above-average students
- **LEP LIMITED ENGLISH PROFICIENCY** activities

Use Glencoe's *Presentation Plus!* multimedia teacher tool to easily present dynamic lessons that visually excite your students. Using Microsoft PowerPoint® you can customize the presentations to create your own personalized lessons.

Interactive Lesson Planner

Planning has never been easier! Using this CD-ROM, organize your week, month, semester, or year with all the help you need. The **Interactive Lesson Planner** gives you access to all of the blackline masters that accompany *World History: The Human Experience.*

SECTION RESOURCES

Daily Objectives	Reproducible Resources	Multimedia Resources
Section 1 **Pressures for Expansion** Identify the political, economic, and social causes of imperialism.	Lecture Notes 27-1 Reproducible Lesson Plan 27-1 Vocabulary Activity 27* Guided Reading Activity 27-1* Time Line Activity 27 Section Quiz 27-1* Reading Essentials and Study Guide 27-1	Section Focus Transparency 27-1 Chapter Transparency 27 Interactive Tutor Self-Assessment Software Testmaker
Section 2 **The Partition of Africa** List the effects imperialism had on the continent of Africa.	Lecture Notes 27-2 Reproducible Lesson Plan 27-2 Vocabulary Activity 27* Guided Reading Activity 27-2* People in World History Profile 52 History Simulation 27 Section Quiz 27-2* Reading Essentials and Study Guide 27-2	Section Focus Transparency 27-2 Interactive Tutor Self-Assessment Software Testmaker
Section 3 **The Division of Asia** Describe how the countries of Asia responded to imperialism.	Lecture Notes 27-3 Reproducible Lesson Plan 27-3 Guided Reading Activity 27-3* Geography and History Activity 27 People in World History Profile 51 Section Quiz 27-3* Reading Essentials and Study Guide 27-3	Section Focus Transparency 27-3 World History and Art Transparency 35, *Ono Waterfall* Vocabulary PuzzleMaker Software Interactive Tutor Self-Assessment Software Testmaker
Section 4 **Imperialism in the Americas** Explain how Latin Americans responded to the growth of American influence in their region.	Lecture Notes 27-4 Reproducible Lesson Plan 27-4 Vocabulary Activity 27* Guided Reading Activity 27-4* Reteaching Activity 27 Enrichment Activity 27 Section Quiz 27-4* Performance Assessment Activity 27 Spanish Chapter Summary 27 Reading Essentials and Study Guide 27-4	Section Focus Transparency 27-4 Interactive Tutor Self-Assessment Software Testmaker

* Also available in Spanish

Chapter Activities

 Performance Assessment Activity

Conducting a Draft Assign students to cooperative groups, with each group representing a world power of the era discussed in the chapter. The whole class should brainstorm a list of all of the areas of the world that once were under the control of these powers. Then give each group approximately 30 minutes to organize a strategy for drafting countries or areas from this list for their empires. On the second day, the actual draft, patterned after the NFL or NBA drafts, will occur with agreed upon draft rules for when the country is removed from the list. Groups of world powers may work out trades among themselves as well. The groups should submit a record sheet of each of their transactions and drafts with a rationale for each.

Possible Rubric Features

Accuracy of content information, decision-making skills, collaborative skills, concept attainment for imperialism and empires, organization of plan

• *For an additional activity, refer to Activity 27 in the* Performance Assessment Strategies and Activities *booklet.*

ACTIVITY

From the Classroom of...

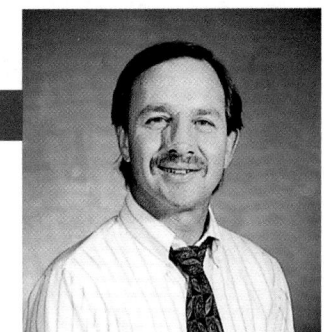

**Scott L. Miles—
Teacher of the Year,
Wisconsin Council for
the Social Studies
Wausau West High
School Wausau, WI**

Establishing Colonies in Africa
Assign small groups a European nation and give them a list of goals for the country's colonial activities in Africa. (For example, Portugal: secure African coastal areas to help develop secure trade routes with Asia.)

Spread out a large piece of paper on the classroom floor and draw a large outline map of Africa. Provide each nation (small group) with a length of yarn based on their relative strength. Some suggested lengths are: Portugal (9 ft.), England (26 ft.), France (22 ft.), Germany (12 ft.), Spain (6 ft.), and Italy (6 ft.). You may wish to use a separate color for each nation. Then ask students to place the yarn on the map to mark off territory in such a way as to meet their country's objectives.

Compare the map with an actual colonial map of the continent. How accurate was your country in fulfilling its objectives? How do colonial boundaries (maps) compare with current national boundaries? What problems would this cause for African nations?

MULTIPLE LEARNING STYLES

Verbal/Linguistic
As a newspaper editor during the 1800s, have students prepare editorials entitled either "The Case for Imperialism" or "The Case Against Imperialism." Their editorials should include examples that support their opinion.

Logical/Mathematical
Have students create a circle graph showing how much of Africa was controlled by the colonial powers during the Age of Imperialism. Have them obtain rough area figures by comparing colonial boundaries with those of modern nations. Areas can be converted to percentages of the total area of the continent.

Visual/Spatial
Have students trace the continents of Europe, Asia, Africa, and the Americas, including the Pacific islands. Have them label countries discussed in the chapter and create a key using different colors to indicate the European power that ruled each country and then color their maps.

Auditory/Musical
Have students prepare a short musical skit about one of the events described in this chapter, such as the Sepoy Rebellion or U.S. involvement in Mexico from 1914 until 1917.

GLENCOE'S ASSESSMENT ADVANTAGE

Use the following to easily assess student learning in a variety of ways.

- Performance Assessment Strategies and Activities
- Section Quizzes
- Chapter and Unit Tests
- Interactive Tutor Self-Assessment Software
- Testmaker Software
- MindJogger Videoquiz
- SAT/SAT II Test Practice
- worldhistory.glencoe.com

Additional Resources

NATIONAL GEOGRAPHIC SOCIETY	Teacher's Corner

INDEX TO NATIONAL GEOGRAPHIC MAGAZINE

The following articles relate to this chapter:

- "Remember the *Maine*?" by Thomas B. Allen, February 1998.
- "Malaysia," by T.R. Reid, August 1997.
- "French Polynesia," by Peter Benchley, June 1997.
- "India," by Geoffrey C. Ward, May 1997.
- "Hong Kong," by Mike Edwards, March 1997.
- "Burma, the Richest of Poor Countries," by Joel L. Swerdlow, July 1995.
- "Hagi: Where Japan's Revolution Began," by N. Taylor Gregg, June 1984.

NATIONAL GEOGRAPHIC SOCIETY PRODUCTS AVAILABLE FROM GLENCOE

To order the following, call Glencoe at 1-800-334-7344:

- *PicturePack: Physical Geography of the World (Transparencies)*

ADDITIONAL NATIONAL GEOGRAPHIC SOCIETY PRODUCTS

To order the following call National Geographic at 1-800-368-2728:

- *China: Beyond the Clouds (Video)*
- *The Great Indian Railway (Video)*
- *World (Laminated Desk Maps)*

Access National Geographic's new dynamic MapMachine Web site and other geography resources at:

- http://www.nationalgeographic.com/
- http://www.nationalgeographic.com/maps/

BIBLIOGRAPHY

Literature of the Period
Forster, E. M. *A Passage to India.* New York: Harcourt Brace, 1989. A novel about life in India under British rule.
Readings for the Student
Conrad, Joseph. *Heart of Darkness.* New York: Norton, 1987. A story of one man's journey up the Congo River.
Readings for the Teacher
Said, Edward W. *Culture and Imperialism.* New York: Knopf, 1993. A study of the links between imperialism and literature.

WORLD HISTORY Online

Use our Web site as an additional resource. All essential content is covered in the Student Edition.

You and your students can visit the *World History: The Human Experience* Web site at worldhistory.glencoe.com The student text directs students to the Web site for the following options:

- **Chapter Overviews**
- **Student Web Activities**
- **Self-Check Quizzes**

Answers are provided for you in a link entitled "Web Activity Lesson Plan." Additional Web Resources, Interactive Puzzles, and content updates are also available.

Visit the Glencoe Web site at socialstudies.glencoe.com for social studies activities, updates, and links to other resources.

LOCAL OBJECTIVES

_____
_____
_____
_____
_____
_____
_____
_____
_____
_____
_____
_____
_____
_____
_____
_____
_____
_____

CHAPTER THEMES

Chapter Themes are listed by section on this chapter opening page of the Student Edition. A corresponding theme-based activity is available under "TEACH," and a theme-based question is asked in the Section and Chapter Assessments.

Storyteller

Historical Setting The incident that led to the Sepoy Rebellion reveals how Great Britain in the 1800s imposed its own culture and values on its colonized peoples. Imperialists were often contemptuous of the sacred beliefs and rituals of the people in their colonies. Where colonized peoples tried to resist imperialist pressures to discard traditional ways of life, tension—and sometimes fighting—occurred. In many cases, simple ignorance or thoughtlessness about local customs and beliefs created hostile feelings between imperialists and colonial peoples.

Historical Significance

Answers: *Colonized people were introduced to Western traditions and technologies—sometimes against their will. Often, they were also led to reject native customs and beliefs. Imperialists exploited laborers and sometimes split up families and villages.*

Western rule inspired nationalist movements that led to independence.

— WORLD HISTORY
Online

Have students use the **Chapter 27 Overview** at worldhistory.glencoe.com as a prereading and postreading exercise for understanding chapter content.

Chapter
27
1800–1914
The Age of Imperialism

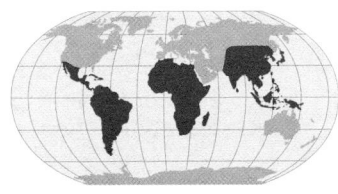

Chapter Themes

▶ **Movement** Political, economic, and social factors lead to the Age of Imperialism. *Section 1*
▶ **Change** European powers divide most of Africa into colonies, and Africans resist European intervention and colonialism. *Section 2*
▶ **Reaction** India and China come under European control or influence, while Japan tries to meet the Western challenge. *Section 3*
▶ **Nationalism** Nationalism intensifies in Latin America as United States involvement in the region increases. *Section 4*

Storyteller

No one knows how the rumor started, but it spread quickly. The bullets for the new rifles, the story went, were greased with the fat of cows and pigs. The sepoys, Indian soldiers in the British army, were outraged. Because Hindus regarded the cow as sacred and Muslims could not touch pork, using these bullets would violate the beliefs of both groups. As a result, the sepoys started a rebellion in May 1857 that soon engulfed much of India.

The Indian Revolt of 1857 was not an isolated incident. As European powers acquired new territories in the 1800s, conflicts between colonial rulers and colonial peoples developed. By the early 1900s European nations ruled large parts of Asia and Africa, while the United States was expanding its interests in Latin America.

Historical Significance

How did the spread of empires affect peoples in Asia, Africa, and Latin America? How did colonial peoples respond to Western rule?

1850	1875	1900	1925

1869 Suez Canal opens.

1911 China becomes a republic.

1853 Commodore Perry lands in Japan.

1885 European powers meet in Berlin to divide Africa into colonies.

702

GEOGRAPHY CONNECTION

Location Have students locate on a world map some of the regions in which the British acquired possessions during the Age of Imperialism, including South Africa, India, and the Pacific islands. Then have them locate the British dominions they studied in Chapter 25, including Canada, Australia, and New Zealand. What was required to rule such a large and far-flung empire? *(Answers may include: a large navy and merchant fleet, a sizable army, many adventurous and loyal citizens.)* **L1**

Visualizing History An Indian prince hosts a British officer at a nautch (a form of entertainment by professional dancers).

Visualizing History Lower-ranking Indian princes were called rajas, while higher-ranking ones were known as maharajas. Unlike Western ballet, which emphasizes the action of the legs, in Indian dance the legs are usually bent and the feet flat.

✔ Performance Assessment

Refer to the activity on page 702C of the Planning Guide.

📁 For an additional activity, refer to Activity 27 in the *Performance Assessment Strategies and Activities* booklet. 📦

Using Your History Journal

Suggest that students choose any single African country (for example, Bechuanaland), research its history, and summarize in their journals what interest imperialist powers had in it and how the country attained independence. 📦

WORLD HISTORY Online

Chapter Overview

Visit the *World History: The Human Experience* Web site at **worldhistory.glencoe.com** and click on *Chapter 27—Chapter Overview* to preview the chapter.

Your History Journal

Draw or copy the map "Imperialism in Africa 1914" on page 710 of this chapter. Then, using the map of modern Africa in the Atlas as a guide, write in the new national names and draw in present boundaries.

Chapter 27 *The Age of Imperialism* **703**

GLENCOE TECHNOLOGY

 VIDEODISC
Use MindJogger to preview chapter content.

MindJogger Videoquiz

 Chapter 27 Disc 4 Side A

📼 Also available in VHS.

➕ EXTRA CREDIT PROJECT

Oral Report Ask students to search for an explanation of why India's struggle for independence lasted 90 years. To find their answers, students should research the phases of that struggle. Have them summarize their findings **L2** 📦 for the class in a brief oral report. Suggested resources: C. A. Galbraith and R. Mehta, *India: Now and Through Time*; S. Ashton, *Indian Independence*; S. Wolpert, *A New History of India*.

1800   1850   1900

c. 1800 Age of Imperialism begins.

c. 1840s French citizens settle in Algeria.

1899 British author Rudyard Kipling writes the poem "The White Man's Burden."

SECTION THEME

▶ **Movement** Political, economic, and social factors lead to a new period of expansion known as the Age of Imperialism.

Guide to Reading

For reading strategies to help students read effectively see pages 12–13. Have students think about the main head as they read the subheads.

Vocabulary Pre-check

◉ Use the Vocabulary PuzzleMaker for Chapter 27 to create a crossword puzzle to reinforce section terms. **L1 LEP**

🗀 Use Vocabulary Activity 27 to introduce vocabulary terms. **L1 LEP**

FOCUS

Section Objective

Identify the political, economic, and social causes of imperialism.

BELLRINGER
Motivational Activity

Before taking roll at the beginning of the class period, project Section Focus Transparency 27-1 and have students answer the activity questions. Discuss students' responses.
🗀 This activity is also available as a blackline master.

Section 1

Pressures for Expansion

Guide to Reading

Read to Find Out
Main Idea *There were political, economic, and social causes of imperialism.*

▶ **Terms to Define**
imperialism, colony, protectorate, sphere of influence

▶ **People to Meet**
Cecil Rhodes, Rudyard Kipling

▶ **Places to Locate**
Algeria, Australia, New Zealand, Rhodesia (Zimbabwe)

The Storyteller

In India, British schools taught English and required students to adopt Christianity. The wife of a British official described attending a graduation ceremony in the year 1886. "The proceedings began with a hymn. The children sang pretty well, though in a harsh voice…. Then a boy stood up, put his hands together, and repeated the Lord's Prayer. Others followed him, and then Mr.

Summers [the teacher] read a chapter from the Old Testament about Adam and Eve…. We could just tell he was speaking of the various nations—English, Parsee, [Muslim], Hindu, all came from Adam and Eve, we were all one family here."

—adapted from *An Indian Journal,* Nora Scott, 1994

Indians and British

The term imperialism is a Latin word from the days of the Roman Empire. Imperialism means one country's domination of the political, economic, and social life of another country. About 2,000 years ago, imperial Rome controlled most of the Mediterranean world. By the end of the 1800s, a handful of European countries, together with the United States, controlled nearly the entire world. Not surprisingly, the era between 1800 and 1914 has come to be known as the Age of Imperialism.

The imperialism of the 1800s resulted from three key factors. First, nationalism prompted rival European nations to build empires in their competitive quests for power. Second, the Industrial Revolution created a tremendous demand for raw materials and expanded markets, which prompted industrialized nations to seek new territories. Finally, both religious fervor and feelings of racial and cultural superiority inspired Europeans to impose their cultures on distant lands.

Political Rivalries

In the mid-1800s European countries saw themselves as actors on the world stage, and each country wanted to play a starring role. If Great Britain started a small colony in distant Asia or Africa, France had to start one too—and so did Belgium, Germany, Italy, Holland, Spain, Portugal, and Russia.

Once begun, the quest for colonies became a continuing enterprise that seemed to have no limits. Slow and difficult communication between remote territories and European capitals often enabled colonial governors and generals to take matters into their own hands. If a colony's borders did not provide military security, for instance, military officials

SECTION RESOURCES

🗀 **Reproducible Masters**
- Lecture Notes 27-1
- Reproducible Lesson Plan 27-1
- Vocabulary Activity 27
- Guided Reading Activity 27-1
- Time Line Activity 27
- Section Quiz 27-1
- Reading Essentials and Study Guide 27-1

📑 **Transparencies**
- Section Focus Transparency 27-1
- Chapter Transparency 27

Multimedia
◉ Interactive Tutor Self-Assessment Software
◉ Testmaker

Visualizing History In this cartoon Bismarck (representing Germany), John Bull (representing Great Britain), and Uncle Sam (representing the United States) decide the fate of Samoa. *What phrase described Great Britain's vast overseas holdings?*

based in the colony used their armies to expand the colony's borders. This strategy worked well enough until colonial governments started claiming the same territories. Then new conflicts arose, and European troops found themselves facing off on remote battlefields in Africa and Asia.

Desire for New Markets

The Industrial Revolution of the 1800s knew no borders. Factories in Europe and the United States consumed tons of raw materials and churned out thousands of manufactured goods. The owners and operators of these factories searched constantly for new sources of raw materials and new markets for their products. They hoped to find both in foreign lands.

Rubber, copper, and gold came from Africa, cotton and jute from India, and tin from Southeast Asia. These raw materials spurred the growth of European and American industries and financial markets, but they represented only the tip of the iceberg. Bananas, oranges, melons, and other exotic fruits made their way to European markets. People in Paris, London, and Berlin drank colonial tea, coffee, and cocoa with their meals and washed themselves with soap made from African palm oil.

The colonies also provided new markets for the finished products of the Industrial Revolution. Tools, weapons, and clothing flowed out of the factories and back to the colonies whose raw materials had made them possible.

Seeking New Opportunities

Imperialism involved more than just guns, battles, raw materials, and manufactured goods. Colonies needed people who were loyal to the imperialist country. Great Britain, France, and Germany needed British, French, and German citizens to run their newly acquired territories and keep them productive.

Throughout the 1800s European leaders urged their citizens to move to far-off colonies. Many of them responded. In the 1840s, for example, thousands of French citizens sailed across the Mediterranean Sea to **Algeria**, where they started farms and estates on lands seized from local Algerian farmers.

The British, meanwhile, emigrated to the far corners of the globe, hoping to find opportunities not available at home. Many rushed to **Australia** and **New Zealand** in the 1850s in search of gold. As the British government continued to acquire vast tracts of land in Africa, Asia, and the Pacific, the phrase "the sun never sets on the British Empire" became a popular way of describing Great Britain's vast holdings.

Strong-minded individuals saw emigration as a chance to strike it rich or make a name for themselves. Perhaps the most spectacular success story of the era belonged to **Cecil Rhodes**, a British adventurer who made a fortune from gold and diamond mining in southern Africa. Rhodes went on to found a colony that bore his name: **Rhodesia** (now **Zimbabwe**).

Chapter 27 *The Age of Imperialism* **705**

COOPERATIVE LEARNING ACTIVITY

Oral Reports Organize students into groups of three or four. Assign each group a topic that has something to do with daily life in India under the British (for example, Indian ceremonies, Indian religious life, the role of Indian women, transportation, agriculture, tiger hunts). Have each group member take on a specific task, such as library work, note taking, or presenting. Have the spokesperson for each group present a 10-minute report. Then open the topic for class discussion.

L2

TEACH

Guided Practice

THEME Movement

Have students begin a discussion of the concept of movement during the Age of Imperialism by first considering their own personal travels. Ask them how traveling to new places has changed their views of the world, of other people, and of themselves. **L1**

Visualizing History John Bull, who first appeared as a literary character in 1712, later became the caricaturist's symbol for England. He was usually portrayed as a solid and jovial figure. The original Uncle Sam is said to have been Samuel Wilson, a businessman from Troy, New York, who supplied beef to the army during the War of 1812. *Why are the three men not looking at one another? (The cartoonist seems to imply that each country stubbornly resisted the others' arguments.)*
Answer to Caption: *"The sun never sets on the British Empire."*

Economics Discuss the close connection between the Industrial Revolution in Europe and America and the rise of imperialism. Review the effects of industrialization discussed in Chapter 23. Include the idea that the colonies that provided raw materials also became new markets for mass-produced goods. **L3**

 Chapter Transparency 27

Independent Practice

Guided Reading Activity 27-1 **L1**

Time Line Activity 27

Chapter 27 *The Age of Imperialism* **705**

Essay Have students write an essay summarizing the causes and effects of imperialism. The essays should include an introduction; a paragraph each for political, economic, and social causes and effects; and a conclusion. **L1**

ASSESS

Check for Understanding

Assign Section 1 Assessment as homework or as an in-class activity.

◉ Use Interactive Tutor Self-Assessment Software to review Section 1.

Evaluate

 Section Quiz 27-1

◉ Use the Testmaker to create a customized quiz for Section 1.

Reteach

Have students create an outline for Section 1 using the main headings and subheadings. Go over the outlines in class, creating a group outline on the chalkboard so that students can check their understanding.

 Reading Essentials and Study Guide 27-1

Enrich

Assign each student a person or event to research (for example, Cecil Rhodes or Perry's opening of Japan). Have them summarize their research in a three-minute class presentation.

CLOSE

Ask students how their own views on imperialism have changed after reading Section 1. Is it possible that imperialism led to progress? How? Why?

"Civilizing" Mission

Some emigrants had motives that went beyond mere personal glory and profit. Religious and humanitarian impulses inspired many individuals to leave their secure lives at home and head for the distant colonies. The desire to spread Western technology, religion, customs and traditions also fueled colonial expansion.

During the Age of Imperialism, growing numbers of Catholic and Protestant missionaries decided to bring the Christian message to the most remote corners of Africa and Asia. Over the decades they set up hundreds of Christian missions and preached to thousands of Africans and Asians. Like many other Europeans and Americans of this period, these missionaries believed that Christianity and Western civilization together could benefit and transform the world.

The missionaries were not military conquerors, but they did try to change people's beliefs and practices. They believed that, in order to become "civilized," the people of Africa and Asia would have to reject their old religions and convert to Christianity. To achieve this goal, missionaries built churches and taught Christian doctrine. Missionaries often set up schools and hospitals as well.

Other Europeans also believed that Western civilization was superior to the civilizations of colonial peoples. As a result, some colonial officials tried to impose Western customs and traditions on the people they conquered. These officials insisted that their colonial subjects learn European languages, and they encouraged Western lifestyles as well. They also discouraged colonial peoples from practicing traditional customs and rituals.

Some Europeans seized on the theory of social Darwinism as proof of their cultural superiority. This theory adapted Darwin's ideas about the evolution of animals—particularly his notion of "the survival of the fittest"—to explain differences among human beings. Social Darwinists believed that white Europeans were the "fittest" people in the world and that they had a duty to spread Western ideas to "backward" peoples.

In 1899 the British writer **Rudyard Kipling** captured the essence of the imperialist attitude in his famous poem "The White Man's Burden." Kipling addressed the poem to the United States, which at this time had just begun to acquire and govern colonies of its own:

> ❝ Take up the White Man's burden—
> Send forth the best ye breed—
> Go bind your sons to exile
> To serve your captives' need;
> To wait in heavy harness
> On fluttered folk and wild—
> Your new-caught, sullen peoples,
> Half-devil and half-child. ❞

Forms of Imperialism

Imperial nations gained new lands through treaties, purchases, and military conquest. Once in power, they used several forms of territorial control. A colony was a territory that an imperial power ruled directly through colonial officials. A protectorate had its own government, but its policies were guided by a foreign power. A sphere of influence was a region in which the imperial power had exclusive investment or trading rights.

Within these general forms of control, each imperial nation exercised its power differently. The French used their colonial officials to govern, to spread French culture, and to make territories overseas extensions of France. The British, by contrast, focused strictly on administration and were less apt to convert colonial peoples to British ways. The British often allowed local rulers to govern territories as their representatives.

SECTION 1 ASSESSMENT

Main Idea
1. Use a diagram like the one below to identify the economic and social causes of imperialism.

Causes of Imperialism

Economic	Social

Recall
2. **Define** imperialism, colony, protectorate, sphere of influence.
3. **Identify** Cecil Rhodes, Rudyard Kipling.

Critical Thinking
4. **Evaluate** What does the Kipling poem reveal about his attitude toward Africans and Asians?

Understanding Themes
5. **Movement** Explain why the period from 1800 to 1914 is the Age of Imperialism.

SECTION 1 ASSESSMENT ANSWERS

1. economic: Industrial Revolution led to need for raw materials and new markets so industrialized nations sought new territories; social: emigration from Europe to colonies; desire to spread Western technology, religion, customs, and traditions
2. All terms are defined in the Glossary.
3. Rhodes, 705; Kipling, 706

4. The colonists were childlike, in need of discipline and instruction.
5. **MOVEMENT** During this period, European powers extended their control over people and territories overseas to acquire new markets, to spread European values, and to provide security in the face of increasing power rivalries.

1870   1890   1910

c. 1870 David Livingstone explores Africa.

1896 The Ethiopians defeat the Italians in the battle of Adowa.

1904 The French win special rights in Morocco.

1910 The British form the Union of South Africa.

Section 2

The Partition of Africa

Guide to Reading

Read to Find Out
Main Idea *Imperialism greatly affected the continent of Africa.*

▶ **Terms to Define**
  partition

▶ **People to Meet**
  David Livingstone, Abd al-Qadir, Muhammad Ali, Samory Touré, Menelik II, the Afrikaners, Shaka

▶ **Places to Locate**
  Morocco, Egypt, the Sudan, Liberia, Ethiopia, Union of South Africa

The Storyteller

An eyewitness to the opening ceremonies for the Suez Canal reported: "Fireworks in front of the Viceroy's Palace. Open house everywhere.... Luxurious dinners, vintage wines, exquisite fish, partridges, wild duck. Seven or eight thousand people sitting down to dinner in the middle of the desert. It was like something out of the Arabian Nights.... *At last I got back to my houseboat....*

Opening of Suez Canal

All through the night I could hear the noise of the fair—the sound of music, the banging of fireworks, and the shouting of happy revelers."

—adapted from *World Ditch, The Making of the Suez Canal,* John Marlowe, 1964

Until the 1800s Europeans knew little of Africa beyond its northern, western, and southern coasts. Then, in the mid-1800s, a few brave explorers began to venture into the African interior. The most famous of these was Scottish doctor and missionary **David Livingstone**, who first went to Africa in 1840. For the next 30 years, Livingstone explored wide tracts of central and eastern Africa, setting up Christian missions and sending back to Great Britain detailed reports of his discoveries, such as Victoria Falls.

When Europeans temporarily lost touch with Livingstone late in the 1860s, the *New York Herald* hired a British journalist and explorer named Henry M. Stanley to track him down. Their famous meeting in 1871 is best remembered for Stanley's understated greeting, "Dr. Livingstone, I presume?" With help from European financial backers, Stanley went on to lead several major expeditions through central Africa himself.

The publicity surrounding the explorations of Livingstone and Stanley generated new interest in Africa throughout Europe. This interest swelled when subsequent explorers sent back excited reports about the continent's abundance of resources. Reports such as these helped set off a mad European scramble for Africa between 1880 and 1914. One European country after another laid claim to parts of Africa. In 1885, 14 nations met in Berlin, Germany, and agreed to partition, or divide, the prize King Leopold II of Belgium called "this magnificent African cake." By 1914 European nations controlled 90 percent of the continent.

North Africa

The world's largest desert—the Sahara—stretches across North Africa from the Atlantic

Chapter 27   *The Age of Imperialism*   **707**

SECTION THEME

▶ **Change** European powers divide most of Africa into colonies, and Africans resist European intervention and colonialism.

Guide to Reading

For reading strategies to help students read effectively see pages 12–13.

Vocabulary Pre-check

🔲 Use the Vocabulary PuzzleMaker for Chapter 27 to create a crossword puzzle to reinforce section terms. **L1 LEP**

📁 Use Vocabulary Activity 27 to introduce vocabulary terms. **L1 LEP**

FOCUS

Section Objective

List the effects imperialism had on the continent of Africa.

BELLRINGER Motivational Activity

Before taking roll at the beginning of the class period, project Section Focus Transparency 27-2 and have students answer the activity questions. Discuss students' responses.
📁 This activity is also available as a blackline master.

SECTION RESOURCES

📁 **Reproducible Masters**
- Lecture Notes 27-2
- Reproducible Lesson Plan 27-2
- Vocabulary Activity 27
- Guided Reading Activity 27-2
- People in World History Profile 52
- History Simulation 27

- Section Quiz 27-2
- Reading Essentials and Study Guide 27-2

📜 **Transparencies**
- Section Focus Transparency 27-2

Multimedia
🔲 Interactive Tutor Self-Assessment Software
🔲 Testmaker

TEACH

Guided Practice

THEME Change

Discuss the changes brought to Africa as a result of imperialist expansion and conflict. Focus on changes involving local inhabitants, land, and culture. Ask students to explain which changes they perceive as good and which they view as bad. *(Students may point to new products and the establishment of better transportation and trade routes as good; they may point to the inhumane treatment of Africans by people such as Leopold II and the land devastation caused by wars as bad.)* **L1**

Visualizing History The historic meeting between Livingstone and Stanley took place in Ujiji, in Central Africa, on November 10, 1871. **Answer to Caption:** *British recognition of French control of Morocco*

Critical Thinking Ask students to speculate on Italy's reasons for "settling" Libya. Why was controlling Libya better than having no imperialist claim at all? *(Possible answer: It gave Italy a foot in the door to further expansion in Africa—to Ethiopia, for example.)* **L3**

History Simulation 27

Independent Practice

Guided Reading Activity 27-2 **L1**

 People in World History Profile 52

Visualizing History British explorer Sir Henry Morton Stanley finds missionary David Livingstone in Africa. *What ended Britain's imperialist dispute with France over the Sudan?*

Ocean to the Red Sea. Most of the people in North Africa live on a thin strip of land located north of the Sahara along the Mediterranean coast. Here the land is fertile and the climate mild. In the early 1800s Muslim Arabs under the authority of the Ottoman ruler in Istanbul governed the large territories west of Egypt, which at that time were called Tripoli, Tunis, and Algiers. Today Tripoli, Tunis, and Algiers are the independent North African countries of Libya, Tunisia, and Algeria.

The French in North Africa

In 1830 King Charles X of France ordered an invasion of Algiers with the aim of colonizing that country. French troops encountered stiff resistance from the Algerians, whose leader was **Abd al-Qadir** (AB•duhl KAH•duhr). About 10 years passed before 100,000 French soldiers finally subdued the determined Algerians. After conquering Algiers, the French seized neighboring Tunis in 1881 and secured special rights in **Morocco** in 1904. About 1 million French people settled in North Africa during these years of struggle.

Britain and Egypt

During the early 1800s, Ottoman **Egypt** was virtually independent under its governor, **Muhammad Ali**. Muhammad Ali's armies conquered neighboring lands, making Egypt a power in the eastern Mediterranean. To modernize Egypt, Ali reformed tax and land systems, encouraged industry, and supported irrigation projects to boost cotton production. Under Ali's successors, however, Egypt's debts rose along with European influence.

In 1859 a French entrepreneur, Ferdinand de Lesseps, set up a company to build the Suez Canal. Joining the Mediterranean and Red Seas, this waterway became a vital shortcut between Europe and Asia and was especially valued by the British as an important link to India. In 1875 Great Britain gained effective control of the canal when Egypt sold its canal shares to the British to pay off its debts. During the next few years, British influence increased over Egypt. In 1882 British forces put down a revolt led by nationalist leader Ahmed Arabi, and Egypt became a British protectorate.

Meanwhile, in **the Sudan**, south of Egypt, a Muslim revival stirred nationalist feelings. Since the 1880s, the Sudanese, under their leader the Mahdi, had challenged British expansion. In 1898, however, British forces, using Maxim machine guns, defeated the more simply armed Sudanese army at the Battle of Omdurman. Soon after the battle, the British also confronted a French force at Fashoda, bringing Great Britain and France to the brink of war. In the end, the French withdrew their army and their claim to the Sudan when the British recognized French control of Morocco.

Italy Seizes Libya

Libya lies between Egypt on the east and Algeria and Tunisia on the west. Known as Tripoli in the 1800s, the country had almost no economic value, but it was coveted by Italy, the nearest European nation. Entering the imperialist race late, Italy was eager to establish an African empire. After seeking guarantees of neutrality from other European nations, Italy in 1911 declared war on the Ottoman Empire, which ruled Tripoli. Italy easily

708 Chapter 27 *The Age of Imperialism*

---

defeated the Ottoman Turks and took Tripoli as a colony, renaming it Libya. Libya was the last country in North Africa to be conquered by European nations.

West, Central, and East Africa

West, Central, and East Africa have varied landscapes: mountains, plains, deserts, and rain forests. During the 1800s, these regions consisted of many territories, each with its own history and traditions. Europeans, however, exploited the Africans' lack of political unity and swallowed up most of these lands in the late 1800s.

West Africa

In the 1500s and 1600s Europeans traded along the coasts of Africa. From West African coastal trading posts, they carried out the transatlantic slave trade that provided labor for plantations and mines in the Americas. West African states traded salt, gold, and iron wares with the Europeans, but some local rulers also supplied prisoners of war to the slave trade.

During the early 1800s, many Western nations declared an end to the slave trade and abolished slavery. Slave trading, however, continued as Arab and African traders sent people from Central and East Africa to perform slave labor in the Middle East and Asia. Meanwhile, West African states, weakened by the population losses of the slave trade, traded natural products, such as palm oil, ivory, rubber, cotton, and cacao beans, for European manufactured goods.

To control this trade and to expand their coastal holdings, European nations began to push inland in the 1870s. Before this time, Europeans had avoided inland Africa because of the difficult terrain and deadly diseases, such as malaria. In the late 1800s, the discovery of the natural ingredient, quinine, to fight malaria and the use of steamships for river transportation made European exploration of inland Africa easier. By 1900, European powers, especially Great Britain and France, had acquired vast new territories in West Africa.

European expansion, however, did not go unchallenged. In the 1890s West African rulers, such as **Samory Touré** (sah•MOHR•ree too•RAY) and Behanzin, led armies against the French. In the Gold Coast, the Ashanti queen Yaa Asantewaa rallied her people against British expansion. All of these efforts were defeated by well-armed European forces. By 1900, **Liberia** was the only remaining independent state in West Africa. Established in 1822 by free African Americans, Liberia became a republic in 1847. Its ties to the United States made it off limits to European expansion.

Central and East Africa

In 1877 the explorer Henry M. Stanley reached the mouth of the Congo River. He later described the river as a "grand highway of commerce to … Central Africa." As a result of Stanley's exploration, Belgium's King Leopold II claimed the Congo region as his own private plantation. He enslaved the Congolese people and had them cut down forests for rubber trees and kill elephant herds for ivory tusks. In pursuing his ambitions, Leopold stripped the Congo of many people and resources.

Leopold's brutal control of the Congo lasted about 20 years, despite the world's outrage. In 1908 he finally agreed to give his plantation to the Belgian government in return for a large loan. Thus, in that year, the Congo region owned by Leopold became the Belgian Congo.

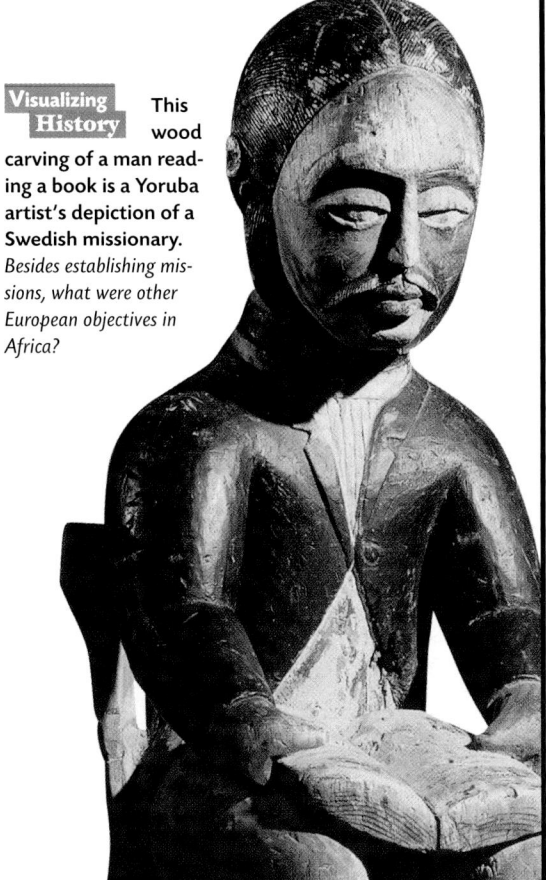

Visualizing History This wood carving of a man reading a book is a Yoruba artist's depiction of a Swedish missionary. *Besides establishing missions, what were other European objectives in Africa?*

Role Play Ask students to assume the persona of Henry Stanley, David Livingstone, or Cecil Rhodes and write letters describing the details of everyday life and their discoveries. **L2**

Multicultural The imperialists, with their desire to colonize and control Africa, often clashed with the diverse indigenous groups. Have students research some of the original inhabitants of Africa and their relations with the imperialists and report to the class on their findings. This exercise may be done in small groups. **L3**

Literature Have students read Joseph Conrad's *Heart of Darkness* as background for studying imperialism in the Congo. Have them prepare written reports. Some may wish to work together to prepare a class presentation on different aspects of imperialism as presented in Conrad's story. **L3**

Visualizing History Southwestern Nigeria is home to the Yoruba peoples. Yoruba sculptures of humans are distinctive for their bulging eyes and flat lips.
Answer to Caption: *to exploit the continent's resources for their own purposes, to control trade to their own advantage, and to enhance their national prestige by increasing their overseas possessions*

Linking Past and Present

Apartheid, the South African policy of segregation, has taken on a more general meaning. The word is sometimes used to refer to any practice anywhere that separates people by race, social class, gender, and so on.

you don't say...

Trek, an arduous journey, comes from the Afrikaans word meaning "to draw a vehicle or to migrate." In South Africa a trek is also a stage of a journey, between two stopping places.

Map Study

Answer

It shortened the distance between Europe and Asia; it was a vital link between the British and their Indian empire.

Map Skills Practice

Reading a Map Which two European imperialist powers controlled the most territory in Africa in 1914? *(France, Great Britain)*

While the Belgians were claiming the Congo Basin, the British, the Germans, and the Italians were doing the same in East Africa. The only country in East Africa to remain independent during this period was **Ethiopia**, located in a remote region known as the Horn of Africa. Beginning in the 1880s, Italy tried to conquer this country, but the Italians underestimated the determination of their opponent, Ethiopia's Emperor **Menelik II**. As emperor, Menelik had conquered many small kingdoms and reunified the Ethiopian Empire.

When the Italians attacked Ethiopia in 1896, Menelik's well-trained forces crushed the invaders at the battle of Adowa. His victory was so devastating

Imperialism in Africa 1914

Spanish Morocco
Morocco
Tunisia
Mediterranean Sea
Suez Canal
Algeria
Libya
Egypt
Red Sea
Rio de Oro
Gambia
French West Africa
Portuguese Guinea
Sierra Leone
Nigeria
Anglo-Egyptian Sudan
Eritrea
French Somaliland
British Somaliland
ETHIOPIA
LIBERIA
Gold Coast
Togo
Cameroon
French Equatorial Africa
Rio Muni
Uganda
British East Africa
Italian Somaliland
Belgian Congo
Cabinda
German East Africa
INDIAN OCEAN
ATLANTIC OCEAN
Angola
Northern Rhodesia
Nyasaland
Mozambique
Madagascar
German Southwest Africa
Bechuana-land
Southern Rhodesia
Union of South Africa

Legend:
Independent — German
French — Spanish
British — Portuguese
Italian — Belgian

0   500   1,000 mi.
0   500   1,000 km
Miller Stereographic Projection

Map Study
By 1914 only two independent countries remained in all of Africa.
Movement How did the Suez Canal affect global trading patterns?

MAKING CONNECTIONS ACTIVITY

The Arts Have some students watch the video *Out of Africa* (1985), which takes place around the time of World War I, when discontented European settlers moved in waves to East Africa. Ask students to summarize what the film shows about the effects of imperialism on both Africans and Europeans of the time. Have other students watch movies set in South Africa, such as *Sarafina!* (1992), *A World Apart* (1988), *Overindulgence* (1987), and the more recent *Cry, the Beloved Country* (1996). Ask them to write brief reviews of the movies, focusing on the long-lasting effects of imperialism on the country's inhabitants. Use students' reactions to the various movies as a springboard for a general discussion of the effects of imperialism in Africa. **L2**

Visualizing History King Menelik is shown here with his chiefs. *How did Ethiopia's emperor prevent Italy and other nations from establishing imperialist control of Ethiopia?*

Visualizing History Sahle Miriam (1844–1913) took the title Menelik II when he assumed the imperial crown of Ethiopia in 1889. Menelik I was the son of the Bible's Solomon and the queen of Sheba.
Answer to Caption: *Menelik crushed the invading Italians so effectively that no Europeans dared invade Ethiopia again during his lifetime.*

...at no Europeans dared invade his country again ...uring his lifetime. Ethiopia and Liberia were the ...nly two African nations to escape European domi-...ation completely during the Age of Imperialism.

Southern Africa

Dutch settlers came to southern Africa in 1652 ...nd established the port of Cape Town. For the next ...50 years, **the Afrikaners**, as these settlers came to ...e called, conquered the lands around the port, ...hich eventually became known as Cape Colony.

Before construction of the Suez Canal, the ...uickest sea route to Asia from Europe was around ...he Cape of Good Hope at the southern tip of ...frica. Sensing the strategic value of Cape Colony, ...he British seized it during the Napoleonic Wars in ...he early 1800s. The Afrikaners resented British ...ule, particularly laws that forbade slavery. They ...elieved that they were superior to black Africans ...nd that God had ordained slavery.

In the 1830s about 10,000 Afrikaners, whom the ...British called *Boers* (the Dutch word for "farmers"), ...ecided to leave Cape Colony rather than live ...nder British rule. In a move known as the Great ...rek, the Afrikaners migrated northeast into the ...nterior. Here they established two independent ...epublics, the Transvaal and the Orange Free State. ...he constitution of the Transvaal stated, "There ...hall be no equality in State or Church between ...white and black."

The Afrikaners fought constantly with their ...eighbors. First they battled the powerful Zulu ...ation for control of the land. Under their king ...haka, the Zulu in the early 1800s had conquered a ...arge empire in southern Africa. The Zulu and ...oers were unable to win a decisive victory. Finally, ...n 1879, the British became involved in battles with

the Zulu. Under their king, Cetywayo, the Zulu at first defeated British forces. With guns and greater numbers, however, the British eventually destroyed the Zulu Empire.

Conflict also developed between the British and the Boers. During the 1880s, British settlers moved into the Boer-ruled Transvaal in search of gold and diamonds. Eager to acquire this wealth for Great Britain, Cecil Rhodes—the prime minister of Cape Colony—and other British leaders wanted all of South Africa to come under British rule. They began pressuring the Boers to grant civil rights to the British settlers in the Transvaal. Growing tension finally erupted in 1899 into the Anglo-Boer War, which the British won three years later.

In 1910 Great Britain united the Transvaal, the Orange Free State, Cape Colony, and Natal into the **Union of South Africa**. The constitution of this British dominion made it nearly impossible for nonwhites to win the right to vote. As one black African writer of the time said, "The Union is to be a Union of two races, namely the British and the Afrikaners—the African is to be excluded."

Racial equality became a dominant issue in South African affairs after the formation of the Union. Several nonwhite South African groups tried to advance their civil rights against the white minority government. Mohandas K. Gandhi, a lawyer from India, worked for equality for Indians in South Africa. He urged the Indians to disobey laws that discriminated against them. Gandhi's efforts brought some additional rights for the Indian community.

South Africa's black majority also took action against racial injustices. In 1912 black South Africans founded the South African Native National Congress (SANNC), whose goal was to work for black rights in South Africa. In 1923 the SANNC became the African National Congress (ANC).

Chapter 27 *The Age of Imperialism* **711**

ASSESS

Check for Understanding
Assign Section 2 Assessment as homework or as an in-class activity.

 Use Interactive Tutor Self-Assessment Software to review Section 2.

Evaluate
Section Quiz 27-2

Use the Testmaker to create a customized quiz for Section 2.

Reteach
Ask students to identify the role each of the following played in the imperialist expansion in Africa: Stanley and Livingstone, Suez Canal, Leopold II, Afrikaners, gold and palm oil, Liberia.

Reading Essentials and Study Guide 27-2

Enrich
Have each student select an important figure from the section to impersonate and use information from the text to prepare a brief speech to deliver in class. Challenge the class to identify the person each student represents.

Recognizing Ideologies On the chalkboard write these statements quoted on page 711: "There shall be no equality in State or Church between white and black" and "The Union is to be a Union of two races, namely the British and the Afrikaners—the African is to be excluded." Without glossing over American racial problems, ask students to suggest some aspects of American national ideology that enabled more rapid advances in the civil rights movement in this country than in South Africa. *(Students may point to the assertion in the Declaration of Independence "that all Men are created equal, that they are endowed by their Creator with certain unalienable Rights....")* **L3**

Coastal Trading Centers

Scottish-born Mungo Park (1771–1806) was trained as a surgeon and began his explorations in 1792 as medical officer of a ship bound for trade in the East Indies. Park survived many adventures, which he recounted in the popular book *Travels in the Interior Districts of Africa* (1797). He died by drowning in 1806, when his second expedition to the Niger was attacked.

ANSWERS

He was interested in establishing the Niger River as a trading route for the British. They were places where European trading ships could unload manufactured goods in exchange for raw materials transported from the African interior; growing cities with increasing population and ports that supply crude oil to world industrial centers.

CLOSE

Many countries vied for Africa during the Age of Imperialism. Have students summarize five or six main reasons for the scramble for Africa.

CONNECTIONS Geography

Coastal Trading Centers

Dakar, Senegal

"The king of the white people wishes to find out a way by which we may bring our own merchandise to you and sell everything at a much cheaper rate," said British explorer Mungo Park to a West African king in 1805. Park was interested in the possibilities of trade on the Niger River.

Like the other great rivers of Africa—the Congo, the Nile, and the Zambezi—the Niger flows to the sea. To the European traders of the 1800s, few places were more important than the mouth of a river. These were the only places where the large trading ships could unload European manufactured goods in exchange for African raw materials.

At the mouth of the Niger in the late 1800s, trade centered on palm oil. The British used the oil for making soap. Barrels of the precious oil were floated down the Niger and collected at depots, or ports, with names like Calabar and Port Harcourt.

Today these ports are growing cities that draw people from all parts of Nigeria. Port Harcourt now has a population of 400,000 inhabitants, while Calabar has about 160,000. Both ports still provide oil to the world, but today it is crude oil, the lifeblood of the world's industries and transportation.

Linking Past and Present ACTIVITY

Explain why Mungo Park was interested in Africa. Why did the mouths of African rivers become centers of trade with Europeans? Describe African port cities today.

Effects of Imperialism

Imperialism had profound effects on Africa. These effects varied from colony to colony, but they centered mainly on economic and social life. The imperialists profited from the colonies by digging mines, starting plantations, and building factories and ports. They hired Africans at low wages and imposed taxes that had to be paid in cash. Men were often housed in dormitories away from their families and subjected to brutal discipline.

Schools set up by Europeans taught Africans that European ways were best. In some cases, African traditions declined, although most Africans held on to their cultures while accepting some European ways. For example, many Africans came to accept some form of Christianity.

By the early 1900s, a western-educated elite had emerged in many European colonies in Africa. These Africans condemned imperialism as contrary to western ideals of liberty and equality. They founded nationalist groups to push for self-rule. By the end of the twentieth century, Africa's peoples had won their political independence from European rule.

SECTION 2 ASSESSMENT

Main Idea
1. Use a diagram like the one below to identify effects of imperialism on Africa.

> Effects of Imperialism on Africa

Recall
2. **Define** partition.
3. **Identify** David Livingstone, Abd al-Qadir, Muhammad Ali, Samory Touré, Menelik II, the Afrikaners, Shaka.

Critical Thinking
4. **Analyzing Information** How did European rule affect civil rights in South Africa? What steps did Africans and Asians take to bring about change?

Understanding Themes
5. **Change** What were the main causes and effects of the partition of Africa by European countries?

SECTION 2 ASSESSMENT ANSWERS

1. imperialists profited from African mines, factories, ports, plantations; paid low wages; brutality; broke up families; some African traditions declined; many Africans accepted some form of Christianity; European culture stressed
2. All terms are defined in the Glossary.
3. Livingstone, 707; al-Qadir, 708; Muhammad Ali, 708; Touré, 709; Menelik, 710; Afrikaners, 711; Shaka, 711
4. The Afrikaners imposed slavery on Africans; the British abolished slavery but Africans did not have full rights with whites; Asians practiced disobedience against discriminatory laws while Africans formed the South African Native National Congress, later African National Congress, to work for black rights.
5. **CHANGE** It resulted from European rivalries and interest in Africa's resources and potential markets. The imperialists hired Africans at low wages, laid waste their land, and destroyed traditional ways of life.

Section 3

The Division of Asia

Guide to Reading

Read to Find Out
Main Idea *The countries of Asia responded in varying ways to imperialism.*

▶ **Terms to Define**
sepoy, viceroy, sphere of influence, culture system, westernization

▶ **People to Meet**
Ci Xi, Sun Yat-sen, Matthew C. Perry, Mutsuhito, Diponegoro, Emilio Aguinaldo

▶ **Places to Locate**
Beijing, the East Indies, the Philippines, Indochina

The Storyteller

"Until the year 1924 I was the only foreigner privileged to witness and to participate in the great ceremonies...." So wrote Reginald Johnston, Professor of Chinese at the University of London, and witness to the end of an empire in the "Palace of Cloudless Heaven" within the Forbidden City. *"It was not without difficulty that even the emperor was able to ... invite a few 'ocean-men' to witness the New Year ceremonial which took place on February 5, 1924. It turned out to be the last occasion on which the ceremony was performed.*

Before another year had passed, the life of the Manchu court had come to an end."

—adapted from *Twilight in the Forbidden City*, Reginald F. Johnston, 1934

China's Forbidden City

$\mathcal{I}$n his book *Description of the World*, written in 1298, Italian explorer Marco Polo relates the many stories he heard about Zipangu, an East Asian island with a supposedly inexhaustible supply of gold. Polo never did visit Zipangu, now called Japan, but his description of its imagined treasures, and of the Asian riches he did see, inspired generations of Europeans. They looked eastward to Asia, dreaming of wealth.

The British in India

European trade with Asia opened up in the 1500s as sea routes replaced difficult overland routes. British involvement in India dates back to this period, when English traders first sailed along India's coast. In 1600 some of these traders formed the East India Company, which later became one of the richest and most powerful trading companies the world had ever known.

After its founding, the East India Company built trading posts and forts in strategic locations throughout India. The French East India Company did the same and challenged the British for control of the India trade. In 1757 Robert Clive, a British East India Company agent, used an army of British and Indian troops to defeat the French at the Battle of Plassey. During the next hundred years, the British expanded their territory in India through wars and commercial activity.

The Sepoy Rebellion

As a result of steady expansion, the East India Company came to control most of India by 1857. Their power was tested that year, however, when the sepoys, or Indian soldiers, rebelled against their British commanders. Long before the greased bullet rumor discussed at this chapter's beginning triggered the Indian Revolt of 1857, sepoy resentment had been growing over British attempts to impose Christianity and European customs on them.

Chapter 27 *The Age of Imperialism* **713**

SECTION THEME

▶ **Reaction** India and China come under European control or influence, while Japan adopts reforms to meet the Western challenge.

Guide to Reading

For reading strategies to help students read effectively see pages 12–13.

Vocabulary Pre-check

⊙ Use the Vocabulary PuzzleMaker for Chapter 27 to create a crossword puzzle to reinforce section terms. **L1 LEP**

📁 Use Vocabulary Activity 27 to introduce vocabulary terms. **L1 LEP**

FOCUS

Section Objective
Describe how the countries of Asia responded to imperialism.

BELLRINGER
Motivational Activity

Before taking roll at the beginning of the class period, project Section Focus Transparency 27-3 and have students answer the activity questions. Discuss students' responses.
📁 This activity is also available as a blackline master.

SECTION RESOURCES

📁 **Reproducible Masters**
- Lecture Notes 27-3
- Reproducible Lesson Plan 27-3
- Guided Reading Activity 27-3
- Geography and History Activity 27
- People in World History Profile 51
- Section Quiz 27-3
- Reading Essentials and Study Guide 27-3

▯ **Transparencies**
- Section Focus Transparency 27-3
- World History and Art Transparency 35, *Ono Waterfall*

Multimedia
⊙ Vocabulary PuzzleMaker Software
⊙ Interactive Tutor Self-Assessment Software
⊙ Testmaker

TEACH

Guided Practice

THEME Reaction

Write the words *China* and *Japan* on the chalkboard. Lead students in a comparison and contrast of Chinese and Japanese reactions to Western influence. Summarize student comments on the appropriate place on the chalkboard. *(China: People rebelled, first in the Opium War, then in the Boxer Rebellion, but foreign influence increased; Japan: New leaders worked to make Japan a great power capable of competing with modern, industrialized Western nations.)* **L1**

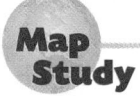

Map Study

Answer

Kashmir, the Rajput States, Hyderabad, Mysore

Map Skills Practice

Reading a Map In which period did Great Britain seize the largest amount of territory in India? *(1805–1856)*

Economics Discuss the importance of the Chinese opium trade to the merchants in imperialist countries. What were the effects of smuggling opium into China besides the exchange of merchandise? *(war between Britain and China)* What effects do you think this trade had on the Chinese people? *(The use of opium led to illness and less productive lives.)* **L2**

India Under British Rule

	Territory under British rule in 1805
	Added by 1856
	Added by 1886
	Princely states

0   150   300 mi.
0 150 300 km
Lambert Conic Conformal Projection

Map Study By 1886 the British had gained control of most of India. **Region** What areas remained free of British rule?

telegraph lines and dug irrigation canals; and it established schools and universities.

At the same time, British colonial officials discriminated against Indians and forced them to change their ancient ways, often with tragic results. Indian farmers, for example, were told to grow cotton instead of wheat, because British textile mills needed cotton. The lack of wheat then led to severe food shortages that killed millions of Indians during the 1800s.

Outraged by the food shortages and other problems, many Indians wanted to move toward self-rule. In 1885 a group of Indian business and professional leaders formed the Indian National Congress. Accepting western ideas such as democracy and equality, the Congress at first used peaceful protest to urge the British to grant more power to Indians. Later, as the Congress party, it led the long struggle for complete independence.

The sepoy rebellion spread across northern and central India, in some places resulting in the massacre of British men, women, and children. Within a year, British forces put down the uprising. In revenge for the massacres, they killed thousands of unarmed Indians. The revolt left bitterness on both sides and forced the British to tighten their control of India. In 1858 Parliament ended the East India Company and sent a **viceroy** to rule as the monarch's representative. Treaties secured the loyalty of the remaining independent Indian states.

Indian Nationalism

The British government tried to quell further unrest in India by spending vast amounts of money on India's economic development. It built paved roads and an extensive railway system; it installed

China Faces the West

While the British increased their hold on India, they and other Europeans developed trade with China. During the 1500s, Chinese civilization had been highly advanced, and the Chinese at that time had little interest in European products. There was only limited trade between China and Europe during the next 300 years. During this period, while technological changes transformed Europe, China's political, economic, and military position weakened under the Qing dynasty. Qing emperors ruled China from 1644 to 1912.

The Unequal Treaties

In the early 1800s, British merchants found a way to break China's trade barriers and earn huge

714   Chapter 27   *The Age of Imperialism*

COOPERATIVE LEARNING ACTIVITY

Debate Have students prepare a debate between the British officials who ruled India and the Indian National Congress. Have students on one team portray members of the British government and defend their rule in India by citing the progress they have brought to the country. Have students on the other team portray the Indians who dispute this assertion and cite the problems they face as a result of British rule. Have each group member contribute by gathering data, forming arguments, or suggesting practice questions. **L3**

rofits. In exchange for Chinese tea, silk, and porce-
[i]n—and to avoid paying cash—the merchants
[sm]uggled a drug called opium, which they obtained
[fr]om India and Turkey, into China. In 1839 Chinese
[tr]oops tried to stop the smuggling. When the British
[re]sisted, war broke out. The British used gunboats
[to] bombard Chinese ports and easily defeated the
[C]hinese, who lacked modern weapons.

British victory in the Opium War in 1842 led to
[th]e Treaty of Nanking, the first of many "unequal
[tr]eaties" that forced China to yield many of its
[ri]ghts to Western powers. The Nanking treaty
[g]ranted the British payment for war losses as well
[a]s the island of Hong Kong. British citizens in
[C]hina also gained extraterritoriality, the right to
[li]ve under their own laws and courts. Over the next
[5]0 years, the "unequal treaties" increased foreign
[i]nfluence in China and weakened the Qing dynasty.
[C]ivil wars, such as the Taiping Rebellion (1850–
[18]64), also eroded the dynasty's control.

By the 1890s, European powers as well as Japan
[c]laimed large sections of China as spheres of
[in]fluence—areas where they had exclusive trading
[ri]ghts. Coming late to the imperialist scramble, the
[U]nited States did not claim a sphere of influence.
[In]stead, it tried to open China to the trade of all
[n]ations through the Open Door Policy. Deadlocked
[b]y their own rivalries, the other powers reluctantly
[a]greed to this policy in 1899.

Chinese Responses

To modernize China, some reformers during
[t]he late 1800s began a "self-strengthening" move-
[m]ent. This program involved importing both
[W]estern technology and educational methods. They
[a]lso worked to improve agriculture, strengthen the
[a]rmed forces, and end the European practice of
[e]xtraterritoriality.

Lack of government support stalled these
[e]fforts. Chinese weakness was only further exposed
[i]n an 1894 war against a modernizing Japan that
[e]nded in China's defeat and loss of territory. From
[C]hina, Japan gained the island of Taiwan and the
[L]iaodong Peninsula as well as trading benefits in
[C]hinese territory. The Japanese also ended China's
[in]fluence in Korea.

After this setback, reformers regained influence
[w]ith the support of the young emperor Guang Xu
[g]wawng SHYOO). They launched the Hundred
[D]ays of Reform to modernize the government and
[e]ncourage new industries. However, conservatives
[l]ed by the emperor's mother, **Ci Xi** (TSUH•SEE),
[r]eturned to power, arrested the emperor, and halt-
[e]d the reforms.

China 1900

Spheres of Influence
- British
- German
- French
- Russian
- Japanese

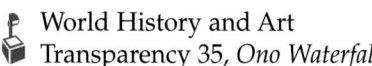

Map Study

The European powers divided China into spheres of influence in the late 1800s.

Location Which of these powers controlled Manchuria in 1900?

By the late 1890s, anti-foreign feelings in China
had led to the formation of secret societies dedicated to removing diplomats, entrepreneurs, missionaries, and other foreigners from the country. One
group, the Righteous and Harmonious Fists, practiced a Chinese form of boxing, and Westerners
named its members Boxers. In 1900 the Boxers carried out attacks against foreigners and Chinese
Christians, besieging foreign communities in
Beijing, the Chinese capital. In response, the
Western powers and Japan sent a multinational
force that ended the uprising. The empress, who
had supported the Boxers, reversed her policy.

The Revolution of 1911

After the Boxer Uprising, Ci Xi struggled to
hold on to power. She agreed to allow foreign
troops to remain in China and gave in to some of
her people's demands for change. For example, she
established schools and reorganized the government. But it was too little, too late. Many Chinese
believed that a modern republic should replace the
Qing dynasty. In their view, the only way to achieve
this goal was through revolution.

Chapter 27 *The Age of Imperialism* **715**

Map Study

Answer
Russia controlled Manchuria in 1900.

Map Skills Practice

Reading a Map Which non-European nation had a sphere of influence in China? *(Japan)*

Critical Thinking Have students analyze and discuss the reasons the British dissolved the East India Company. What were their main concerns? *(fear of rebellion and of conflict with local inhabitants)* What seems to have concerned them least about the Sepoy Rebellion? *(the feelings and sacred beliefs of the sepoys)* **L3**

World History and Art Transparency 35, *Ono Waterfall*

Who? What? Where? When?

Surendranath Banerjea The history of the brilliant Indian Surendranath Banerjea (1848–1925) sheds light both on impe-rialist oppression and on the rise of colonial nationalism. Although Banerjea scored higher on the Indian Civil Service exam than most British test takers, every effort was made to prevent him from having a successful career. After giving up on British justice, Banerjea founded a nationalist political organization. His politi-cal persistence combined with the pronunciation of his first name led to his nickname, "Surrender Not."

MEETING SPECIAL NEEDS ACTIVITY

Learning Style: Visual/Spatial Ask students who learn best by producing and decoding graph-ic information to depict events such as the Sepoy Rebellion or the Dutch presence in Southeast Asia in drawings, graphs, or political cartoons. Encourage them to share their work with the class as a way of reinforcing the section's main ideas. **L2**

Independent Practice

 Guided Reading Activity 27-3 **L1**

 Geography and History Activity 27

 People in World History Profile 51

TURNING POINT

Modernization of Japan
How did Meiji leaders transform Japan during the late 1800s?
They created a parliamentary form of government, industrialized the economy, and built up the military, making Japan a world power by the early 1900s.

Interview Have students research Matthew Perry's dealings with the Japanese and prepare a television interview with questions and answers for Perry and the Japanese shoguns who signed treaties with him. Have students prepare and present a "Special News Report" for U.S. citizens eager to know the outcome of Perry's dealings with the Japanese. Some students can take the role of reporters and others can represent Perry, members of his crew, and the Japanese. **L2**

Who?What?Where?When?

Shogun James Clavell's novel *Shogun*, and the 10-hour television miniseries based on it, tell the story of Blackthorne, an English sailor shipwrecked among the feudal Japanese.

The revolutionaries wanted China to regain its former power and influence. One of them, a doctor named **Sun Yat-sen**, wrote in the early 1900s: "Today we are the poorest and weakest nation in the world and occupy the lowest position in international affairs. Other men are the carving knife and serving dish; we are the fish and the meat."

In 1905 Sun and other revolutionaries formed the United League (later known as the *Guomindang*, or Nationalist party). Their goal was to modernize China on the basis of the "Three Principles of the People": nationalism (freedom from foreign control), democracy (representative government), and livelihood (economic well-being for all Chinese). The revolutionary cause was strengthened in 1908 when Ci Xi died, and two-year-old Prince Pu Yi became emperor. Three years later, revolution swept China as peasants, workers, soldiers, and court officials turned against the weak dynasty. Sun Yat-sen hurried home from a fund-raising tour of the United States. In January 1912, he became the first president of the new Chinese republic.

TURNING POINT

Modernization of Japan

Japan's dealings with the European power began in much the same way as China's, but the ended differently. European traders first came t the island country in the 1500s. Like the Chinese the Japanese were uninterested in European products, and they cut off almost all trade with Europ in the early 1600s. At the time a military commander called a shogun ruled Japan. Although th country also had an emperor, he had no real powe

Japan did not trade again with the outsid world until 1853, when four American warship commanded by Commodore **Matthew C. Perr** sailed into the bay at Edo (present-day Tokyo Perry wanted Japan to begin trading with th United States. The shogun, knowing what had hap pened to China in the recent Opium War, decide early in 1854 to sign a treaty with Perry.

Images of the Times

The British Empire

From the late 1700s to the early 1900s, Great Britain ruled the world's largest overseas empire. British territories were found in every continent.

British naval forces demonstrated British power in countries that were not directly under Queen Victoria's crown. Here a British ship attacks Chinese warships off the coast of China.

716

Images of the Times   The British Empire

The period of British rule in India is often called the Raj, from the Sanskrit word for "rule" or "king." It comes from the same root as *raja*, an Indian prince, yet during the Raj, the princes' powers were limited by the British. India was considered "the jewel in the crown," that is, Great Britain's prize possession.

The canopied elephant saddle is called a howdah. The Australian outback is called the bush.

The Meiji Leaders

In the first five years after Perry's arrival, the shogun signed trade treaties with Britain, France, Holland, Russia, and the United States. Since the treaties favored the imperialist powers, the Japanese people called them unequal treaties, just as the Chinese had. Unhappiness with the treaties led to the overthrow of the shogun in 1868. A group of samurai gave its allegiance to the new emperor, **Mutsuhito**, but kept the real power to themselves. Because Mutsuhito was known as the Meiji (MAY•jee), or "Enlightened" emperor, Japan's new rulers were called the Meiji leaders.

The Meiji leaders tried to make Japan a great power capable of competing with Western nations. Adopting the slogan "Rich country, strong military" they brought the forms of parliamentary government to Japan, strengthened the military, and worked to transform the nation into an industrial society. The Meiji leaders established a system of universal education designed to produce loyal, skilled citizens who would work for Japan's mod-ernization. In this way, the Japanese hoped to create a new ruling class based on talent rather than birth.

Industrialization

In the 1870s Japan began to industrialize in an effort to strengthen its economy. The Japanese did this with little outside assistance. They were reluctant to borrow money from the West, fearing foreign takeovers if loans could not be repaid. In any case, most Western banks were not interested in making loans to Japan, because they considered the country a poor financial risk.

The Japanese government laid the groundwork for industrial expansion. It revised the tax structure to raise money for investment. It also developed a modern currency system and supported the building of postal and telegraph networks, railroads, and port facilities.

Beginning in the late 1880s, Japan's economy grew rapidly. A growing population provided a continuing supply of cheap labor. The combination of new technological methods and cheap labor

Literature Have students choose a work by Rudyard Kipling, such as *Plain Tales from the Hills, Kim, Soldiers Three and Other Stories, The Man Who Would Be King,* or a collection of his poems. Have them write a report on the work, concentrating on Kipling's literary uses of Indian culture, people, and geography. **L3**

Cultural Perspectives

Madama Butterfly Puccini's popular opera *Madama Butterfly,* which was first performed in 1904, dramatizes some of the consequences of Japan's relationship with the West. It is the tragic story of the love affair between a young Japanese girl and Lieutenant Pinkerton, an officer in the United States Navy. The opera provided the model for the modern musical *Miss Saigon,* though set in a different location and historical period.

Global Gourmet

India Chutney, whose name comes from the Hindi word *chatni,* is a relish that originated in east India. Chutney, which has remained popular in Great Britain since the Age of Imperialism, usually combines mangoes or other fruits with onions, raisins, sugar, and spices. Indian curry is typically served with one or more chutneys.

India was the most important British possession. This painting shows a British military officer traveling by elephant through northern India with his cavalry and foot soldiers.

Australia drew many British settlers, who made their homes in the harsh outback, or semi-dry interior, as well as in coastal areas.

REFLECTING ON THE TIMES

1. What types of people were found throughout Great Britain's empire?
2. In the 1800s, people often said that "the sun never sets on the British Empire." What do you think this phrase meant?

717

ANSWERS TO REFLECTING ON THE TIMES

1. Europeans: military officials, adventurers, missionaries, ordinary settlers; indigenous peoples: laborers, minor officials, soldiers
2. Britain's imperial holdings covered such a vast portion of the globe that, when it was nighttime in one part of the holding (Canada and the Caribbean), it was daytime in another part (India and Australia).

Who?What?Where?When?

The Philippines Spanish explorers who colonized the Philippines in the 1500s named the island country after King Philip II of Spain (1527–1598).

Global Gourmet

The Philippines Typical of Filipino food are two items made of fermented seafood: *bagoong* is a fish paste, and *patis* is a flavoring sauce. Both have a sour-salty taste.

ASSESS

Check for Understanding

Assign Section 3 Assessment as homework or as an in-class activity.

 Use Interactive Tutor Self-Assessment Software to review Section 3.

Evaluate

Section Quiz 27-3

Use the Testmaker to create a customized quiz for Section 3.

Reteach

Create a group outline of the section on the board. Have students contribute oral summaries of each part for a class discussion.

Reading Essentials and Study Guide 27-3

---

allowed Japan to produce low-priced goods. Wars at the turn of the century further stimulated Japan's economy and helped it enter new world markets. By 1914 Japan had become one of the world's leading industrial nations.

Japan as a World Power

By the 1890s the Meiji leaders had taken great strides toward creating a modern nation. Japan had acquired an efficient government, a vigorous economy, and a strong military. Needing more natural resources, the Japanese government began to establish its own overseas empire. The first prize it attempted to take was Korea.

When the people of Korea revolted against their Chinese rulers in 1894, Japan decided to intervene. Japanese troops easily defeated the Chinese army in the Sino-Japanese War. Although Korea officially became independent, Japan gained partial control of its trade. Over the next few years, thousands of Japanese settled in Korea.

Korea also figured in Japan's next war. The Russian Empire had interests in Korea as well, and its interests began to clash with Japan's. Even more important was neighboring Manchuria, where the Russians kept troops and had a naval base at Port Arthur. In 1904 the Japanese navy launched a surprise attack on Port Arthur. Few people expected Japan to win the Russo-Japanese War, but the Japanese piled up victory after victory. The conflict ended in 1905, when Russia signed a treaty granting the country of Japan control over Korea and other nearby areas.

Japan's victory over Russia inspired non-Western nationalist leaders throughout the world. It proved that the European empires could be defeated if one had the will and determination. On the other hand, Japan had now become an imperialist country itself. It annexed Korea as a colony in 1910 and continued to expand its empire for the next 35 years.

Footnotes to History

A Teenage Emperor Mutsuhito was only 15 when he became Japan's emperor in 1867. During his 44-year reign, he often led the way in adopting Western customs. He cut his traditional topknot, a tuft of hair on the top of the head, and wore European-style clothes. While previous emperors lived apart from the people, Mutsuhito rode around Tokyo in an open carriage and toured the countryside.

Southeast Asia

Southeast Asia consists of two distinct geographic areas. Island Southeast Asia is made of two archipelagos, or groups of islands: **the East Indies** and **the Philippines**. To the north and west lies mainland Southeast Asia. It includes all of the territories that occupy the Indochinese and Malay Peninsulas.

The growth of imperialism in these areas followed a familiar pattern. Beginning in the 1500s, imperialist powers came, saw, and conquered. Over the next 400 years Portugal, Spain, the Netherlands, Great Britain, France, and the United States all set up colonies in that region. They ranged in size from the huge Dutch East Indies that included thousands of islands to the tiny British settlements on the island of Singapore.

The Islands of Southeast Asia

For centuries, the island region of Southeast Asia had attracted foreign traders and colonizers. At the beginning of the 1800s, the Dutch controlled most of the East Indies and Spain controlled the Philippines.

The Dutch East Indies, present-day Indonesia, had many natural resources, including rich soil. Farmers grew coffee, pepper, cinnamon, sugar, indigo, and tea; miners dug for tin and copper; loggers cut down ebony, teak, and other hardwood trees. The Dutch government used a method of forced labor called the culture system to gather all these raw materials. The Dutch also discouraged westernization, or the spread of European civilization. The enormous profits the Dutch received from the East Indies made the colony the envy of the imperialist powers.

Diponegoro, a native prince from the East Indian island of Java, started a revolt against the Dutch in 1825. Although it lasted 10 years, this revolt eventually ended in failure, and the Dutch encountered little real opposition for the next 80 years. One of the Dutch governors put it this way: "We have ruled here for 300 years with the whip and the club and we shall still be doing it in another 300 years." In the early 1900s, the Dutch won control of the entire archipelago, extending their rule into northern Sumatra and the Celebes. But within a generation, nationalist forces would bring the Dutch East Indian empire to its knees.

The Spanish rule of the Philippines resembled the Dutch rule of the Dutch East Indies. Native Filipinos worked for very low wages, if any, on tobacco and sugar plantations owned by wealthy Spaniard landowners. During the 1800s the

---

Daily Life Ask students to research and then write short reports on the similarities and differences among the cuisines of China, Japan, India, and Southeast Asia. **L1**

Science, Technology, and Society Have students research the improvements made by the Japanese under the Meiji leaders. Have students pay particular attention to modern Japanese business philosophy and its influence on American corporations. **L2**

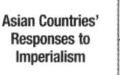
This view of Whampoa Reach in China (about 1860) shows an English barque and an American ship. *How did Western trade and commerce affect Southeast Asia?*

Filipinos' resentment grew until it finally exploded into revolution in 1896.

When the United States declared war on Spain in 1898, the American government promised to free the Philippines in return for the rebels' help against the Spanish. After winning the Spanish-American War, the United States broke its promise and ruled the Philippines as a colony. The Filipinos led by **Emilio Aguinaldo** (ah•gee•NAHL•doh) then arose against American rule, but United States troops defeated them two years later.

Mainland Southeast Asia

The mainland region of Southeast Asia consisted of several large territories in the early 1800s, including Burma (present-day Myanmar), Malaya, Vietnam, Siam (Thailand), Cambodia, and Laos. All through the 1800s, Great Britain and France struggled for domination of the area—more for military, than for economic, reasons.

The British swept into Burma from India in the 1820s. Over the next 60 years, they took full control of Burma and Malaya. Meanwhile, the French were slowly conquering **Indochina**, including present-day Vietnam, Cambodia, and Laos. They took complete control in the 1880s.

Squeezed between the two growing blocks of British and French territory lay the kingdom of Siam. In 1893 the French invaded Siam, sending forces into Bangkok, the capital city. Great Britain and France avoided armed conflict, however, when they agreed to define their spheres of influence in Southeast Asia. As a result of the agreement, Siam remained independent.

European rivalries for control of resources brought much disturbance to mainland Southeast Asia. Western influences changed traditional ways of life. Colonial landowners and trading companies forced local farmers and workers to grow cash crops, mine coal, and cut teak trees.

SECTION 3 ASSESSMENT

Main Idea
1. Use a diagram like the one below to identify ways in which Asian countries responded to imperialism.

> Asian Countries' Responses to Imperialism

Recall
2. **Define** sepoy, viceroy, sphere of influence, culture system, westernization.
3. **Identify** Ci Xi, Sun Yat-sen, Matthew C. Perry, Mutsuhito, Diponegoro, Emilio Aguinaldo.

Critical Thinking
4. **Synthesizing Information** How did European imperialism differ in India, China, and Southeast Asia?

Understanding Themes
5. **Reaction** How did Japan avoid extensive Western interference, while China did not?

SECTION 3 ASSESSMENT ANSWERS

1. India: rebellion, nationalism; China: nationalism, revolution, attacks on foreigners and westernization; Japan: trade treaties with western nations; strengthened economy through industrialization to become a competitive world power; Southeast Asia: revolt

2. All terms are defined in the Glossary.
3. Ci Xi, 715; Sun Yat-sen, 716; Perry, 716; Mutsuhito, 717; Diponegoro, 718; Emilio Aguinaldo, 719
4. In India, Britain ruled closely and developed Western institutions. In China, various European powers held spheres of influence.

In Southeast Asia, a number of European powers ruled colonies in a variety of ways; make sure students use specific facts.

5. **REACTION** Japan industrialized and created a strong military, becoming a power in its own right.

TEACH

Using the Internet The Internet is a powerful research tool. It can provide students with more recent information than would appear in books or magazines. The Internet offers access to a world of resources that may not be available in students' school or local libraries. The Internet also gives students an interactive way to learn.

Discuss the need for an Internet provider. Students probably have heard of such providers as America OnLine and Prodigy. Use the yellow pages to mention a few local Internet services as well. If possible, ask a representative from a local provider to speak to the class about the Internet. Discuss various World Wide Web browsers. If you have access to the Internet at school, demonstrate and supervise its use.

As you talk about URLs— Web page addresses—point out that although they all start with http://, that prefix is not always followed by *www.* Also mention some of the domain designations that may end a URL—*.com* for a commercial organization, and *.gov* for a government organization.

Additional Practice

Skill Reinforcement Activity 27

Technology SKILLS

Using the Internet

Have you heard the expression, "surfing the Net"? This means you can search through the Internet to find information on many subjects. You won't get wet, but you sure can learn a lot and have fun!

Learning the Skill

The Internet is a global computer network that offers many features, including the latest news and weather, stored information, E-mail, and on-line shopping. Before you can connect to the Internet and use the services it offers, however, you must have three things: a computer, a modem, and a service provider. A service provider is a company that, for a fee, gives you entry to the Internet.

Once you are connected, the easiest and fastest way to access sites and information is to use a "Web browser," a program that lets you view and explore information on the World Wide Web. The Web consists of many documents called "Web pages," each of which has its own address, or Uniform Resource Locator (URL). Many URLs start with the keystrokes *http://*

Practicing the Skill

This chapter focuses on the Age of Imperialism, when the Panama Canal and the Suez Canal were completed. Surf the Internet to learn about the history of these canals.
1. Log on the Internet and access one of the World Wide Web search tools, such as Yahoo at website http://www.yahoo.com *or* Lycos at http://www.lycos.com *or* WebCrawler at http:/www.webcrawler.com
2. Search by category or by name. If you search by category in Yahoo, for example, click on *Social* Science. To search by name, type in *Panama Canal and Suez Canal.*

3. Scroll the list of Web pages that appears when the search is complete. Select a page to bring up and read or print it. Repeat the process until you have enough information you can use to develop a short report on the two major canals completed during the Age of Imperialism.

Applying the Skill

Go through the steps just described to search the Internet for information on the Sepoy Rebellion in India. Based on the information, write an article for your school newspaper or magazine about your topic.

For More Practice

Turn to the Skill Practice in the Chapter Assessment on page 727 for more practice in using the Internet.

ANSWERS TO PRACTICING THE SKILL

Some report details about the Panama and Suez canals will vary and will arise from varying information. You might have groups of students use different search tools and later discuss the helpfulness of each one.

320 ————————————— **1870** ————————————— **1920**

1823 The United States
proclaims the Monroe Doctrine.

1898 The United States
declares war on Spain.

1914 The Panama
Canal opens.

Section 4

Imperialism in the Americas

Read to Find Out
Main Idea *Latin Americans largely opposed the growth of American influence in their region.*

▶ **Terms to Define**
   arbitration

▶ **People to Meet**
   James Monroe, José Martí, William McKinley, Theodore Roosevelt, Benito Juárez, Porfirio Díaz, Emiliano Zapata, Francisco "Pancho" Villa, Venustiano Carranza, Woodrow Wilson

▶ **Places to Locate**
   Cuba, Puerto Rico, the Virgin Islands, Isthmus of Panama, Mexico

The Storyteller

Frederic Remington was one of the first "foreign correspondents"—a journalist in Cuba during the Spanish-American War. He wrote: "At night I lay up beside the road outside of Siboney, and cooked my supper by a soldier fire, and lay down under a mango-tree on my raincoat, with

my haversack for a pillow. I could hear the shuffling of the marching troops, and see by the light of the fire near the road the ... sweaty men."

—adapted from *Frederic Remington and the Spanish-American War*, Douglas Allen, 1971

Teddy Roosevelt and the Rough Riders

On the floor of the Senate in 1898, United States Senator Albert J. Beveridge delivered a stirring speech on America's growing role as a world power:

❝ Fate has written our policy for us; the trade of the world must and shall be ours. We will establish trading-posts throughout the world as distributing-points for American products.... Great colonies governing themselves, flying our flag and trading with us, will grow about our posts of trade. ❞

Senator Beveridge's grand ambition capped a half-century of growing American influence in world affairs. The imperialist powers of Europe had already laid claim to much of the world. Now that the United States had grown considerably in size, wealth, and power, it was determined to use the Monroe Doctrine to block the spread of European imperialism in neighboring Latin America, an area that includes Mexico, the Caribbean islands, Central America, and South America. In doing so, the United States was also promoting its own brand of imperialism that involved the penetration of new economic markets and the acquisition of overseas territories.

POINT

The Monroe Doctrine

Even before the independence of all the Latin American countries was well established, Spain had sought the support of other European powers in reconquering its former colonies. Both the United States and Great Britain opposed Spain's

Chapter 27 *The Age of Imperialism* **721**

TEACH

Guided Practice

THEME Nationalism

Ask students to write a definition of *nationalism*. Discuss students' ideas about nationalism and refer to nationalist leaders discussed in the section (Martí, Juárez, Díaz, Carranza, "Pancho" Villa, Zapata). Then ask students to name some locations where nationalist movements have arisen recently. *(former Yugoslav republics, republics of the former Soviet Union, the West Bank and Gaza Strip under Israeli control, Basque separatists in Spain)* What do nationalist movements hope to gain or preserve? *(cultural and political independence)* **L1**

Visualizing History

A U.S. military government controlled Cuba from 1898 to 1902. In 1903 Cuba signed a treaty granting the United States a permanent lease on Guantánamo Bay, where it built a large naval base. From 1906 to 1909, American forces occupied Cuba again.

Answer to Caption: *Cuba's sugar and tobacco plantations were important to Spain's economy.*

TURNING POINT

The Monroe Doctrine
Why was the Monroe Doctrine an important statement of American foreign policy? *It warned against further European influence in the Western Hemisphere and was later used to justify American involvement in the region.*

 Visualizing History United States Marines hoist the American flag in Cuba. *What was Spain's economic interest in Cuba?*

plan. The United States did not want a strong European power so close to its borders. Great Britain had developed good trade relations with the Latin Americans and did not feel that its commercial interests would be served by the return of Spanish control to the Americas.

Great Britain suggested to the United States that a joint warning be issued to the various European powers. However, President **James Monroe** and Secretary of State John Quincy Adams decided to act alone. In 1823 Monroe warned the European powers not to interfere in the countries of the Western Hemisphere. The Monroe Doctrine, as it was later called, contained two major points:

> 1. **The American continents, by the free and independent condition which they have assured and maintain, are hence forth not to be considered as subjects for future colonization by any European powers.**
>
> 2. **We should consider any attempt on their part to extend their system to any portion of this hemisphere as dangerous to our peace and safety.**

At the time the Monroe Doctrine was declared, it was not clear what the United States would do if European powers tried to conquer any part of Latin America. The support of the British Royal Navy, however, ensured that the infant states of Latin America would remain free to determine their own political destinies.

As the United States grew in strength during the late 1800s and early 1900s, it began to make its power felt in Latin America. In 1895, when Great Britain was in conflict with Venezuela over the boundaries of British Guiana, the United States urged that the dispute be submitted to arbitration, or settlement by a third party that is agreeable to both sides. Appealing to the Monroe Doctrine, the United States Department of State issued a strong warning to the British to pressure them into accepting arbitration. Aware of the power of the United States and involved with problems in its empire, Great Britain agreed to a peaceful settlement.

The Spanish-American War

Soon after the Guiana border dispute was settled, the United States turned its attention to **Cuba**. Cuba and the neighboring island of **Puerto Rico** were still Spanish colonies in the late 1800s. Cuba was particularly important to Spain, which reaped huge profits from the island's many sugar and tobacco plantations.

In 1895 **José Martí**, a writer and political activist, led Cubans in a revolution against Spanish rule. Cuba's Spanish leaders embarked on a bloody attack on the rebel forces. Martí was killed in a battle against the Spaniards, and Spanish troops rounded up thousands of Cubans and sent them to prison camps where conditions were brutal. Disease and starvation soon claimed more than 400,000 Cuban lives.

Remember the *Maine*!

The struggle of the Cubans for freedom attracted much sympathy in the United States. American newspapers printed vivid stories describing the cruelty and killings in Cuba. Soon, prominent American politicians began clamoring for war with Spain. Businesspeople who had invested in Cuba also joined in. Finally, in January 1898, President **William McKinley** ordered the battleship *Maine* to Havana, the capital of Cuba, to demonstrate growing American interest in Cuban affairs. A few weeks later, an explosion ripped through the *Maine* while it was still anchored in Havana harbor, sinking the ship and killing 260 American sailors.

The cry "Remember the *Maine!*" swept across the United States. American newspapers left little doubt that Spain was responsible for the disaster. In April 1898, under pressure from all sides, McKinley asked Congress to declare war on Spain. The Spanish-American War lasted four months and ended with a victory for the United States.

COOPERATIVE LEARNING ACTIVITY

Research Organize students into several small groups. Have each group research U.S. relations with the Philippines during one of these time periods: immediately after the Spanish-American War (the period discussed in this section), during World War I, during World War II, during the cold war, and at the present time. Have each group divide the tasks of gathering data, preparing summaries of the material, providing a time line to accompany the summaries, and exhibiting the material in a class presentation. **L2**

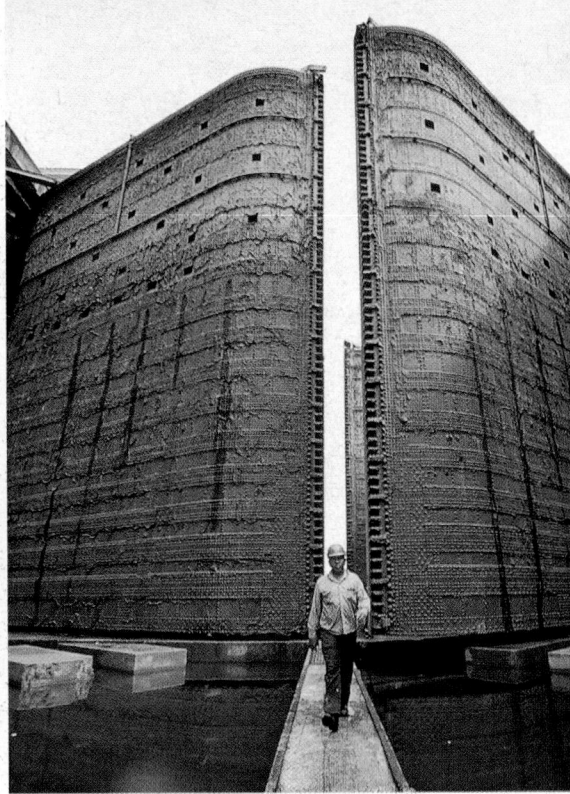

George F. Mobley

Panama Canal

The Panama Canal was a testament to the skill of American engineers. The enormous lock gates (under construction, left) made of steel plates attached to a ton of steel girders. (Note the size of en working around these gates.) Each veighed 700 tons (784 short tons) but ollow and could float. Because they buoyant, the gates exerted less stress eir hinges as the gates were opened closed. Without the significant ces made in technology during the s, this canal could not have been built. thout President Theodore Roosevelt (center) the

Harvard College Library

Panama Canal would not have been built. During his presidency he decided that the United States would build a canal across the Isthmus of Panama— and he made it happen. Roosevelt wanted to boost American power and to compete more effectively with the imperial powers of Europe and Japan. The Panama Canal helped accomplish this goal by strengthening the military posture of the United States. The canal eliminated 7,800 miles (12,550 km) from the sea voyage between New York and San Francisco. It cost $380 million and tens of thousands of lives, and took ten years to complete.

Chapter 27 *The Age of Imperialism* **723**

TEACH

Tell students that there were several reasons for Lesseps's failure to build a Panama Canal. The French not only did not have the necessary tools for implementing such a huge task of digging but also lacked the medical knowledge needed to control the epidemics of tropical disease that decimated the laborers. In addition, dishonest political backers of Lesseps siphoned off cash from the company, which went bankrupt in 1889.

CURRICULUM CONNECTION

MEDICINE
Beginning in 1904, Colonel William C. Gorgas, the U.S. physician who had wiped out yellow fever in Havana, Cuba, after the Spanish-American War, began an effort to eliminate malaria, yellow fever, and bubonic plague from the Isthmus of Panama. By destroying the mosquitoes that carry the first two diseases and the rats that carry the third, Gorgas dramatically lowered the death toll.

Linking Past and Present

Teddy Bears The stuffed bears that generations of children have cherished are named for President Theodore Roosevelt. After a cartoonist depicted him with a bear cub, toymakers began to produce the stuffed animals that are still called teddy bears.

Independent Practice

 Guided Reading Activity 27-4 **L1**

Cartoon Have students draw political cartoons depicting a major event from the section and present them to the class. **L2**

Foreign Policy Have students research and write short reports on public reaction to a more recent attempt by the United States to shape political events in Latin America by supporting the Nicaraguan *contras*. Ask students to consider how attitudes toward American intervention have changed over the century. **L3**

ASSESS

Check for Understanding

Assign Section 4 Assessment as homework or as an in-class activity.

📀 Use Interactive Tutor Self-Assessment Software to review Section 4.

Evaluate

 Section Quiz 27-4

📀 Use the Testmaker to create a customized quiz for Section 4.

Reteach

Ask students to explain the importance of the Monroe Doctrine and the Roosevelt Corollary to U.S. imperialism providing examples of the influence each had on the events covered in Section 4.

📁 Reteaching Activity 27

📁 Reading Essentials and Study Guide 27-4

— WORLD HISTORY
Online

Have students use the **Chapter 27 Student Web Activity** at worldhistory.glencoe.com for in-depth study of United States imperialism.

American Territorial Gains

During the late 1800s, the United States made many significant territorial gains. In 1867 it purchased Alaska from Russia, and in 1898 annexed Hawaii, shortly after American entrepreneurs on the islands had overthrown the Hawaiian queen Liliuokalani (lee•lee•oo•oh•kah•LAH•nee). As a result of the Spanish-American War, the United States gained from Spain territories in the Pacific Ocean (the Philippines and Guam) and in the Caribbean Sea (Puerto Rico). Although independent, Cuba was under American protection. In 1917 the United States purchased **the Virgin Islands** (St. Thomas, St. John, and St. Croix) from Denmark.

The Panama Canal

Victory in the Spanish-American War made the United States a world power. It needed to be able to move its fleet quickly between the Pacific and Atlantic Oceans. What was needed was a canal across the **Isthmus of Panama**, a narrow neck of land that linked Central America and South America.

For centuries, Europeans and Americans had dreamed of building a canal across Central America. In the 1880s the Frenchman Ferdinand de Lesseps, who had built the Suez Canal, tried—and failed—to build a canal in Panama. Thirteen years after the bankruptcy of de Lesseps's company, United States President **Theodore Roosevelt** received the backing of Congress to acquire the Panama canal rights and property.

In 1902 Panama was part of Colombia. Roosevelt tried to negotiate a treaty with Colombia that year that would give the United States land to build the canal in Panama. When Colombia refused, Roosevelt and the American public were outraged.

Roosevelt soon developed a plan, however. With his approval, American agents encouraged the people of Panama to revolt against the government of Colombia. They did so on the night of November 3, 1903, with the help of the United States Navy. The rebellion was over by the next day, and the new Republic of Panama quickly signed a treaty granting the United States the land to build the Panama Canal.

Student Web Activity 27

Visit the *World History: The Human Experience* Web site at **worldhistory.glencoe.com** and click on *Chapter 27—Student Web Activities* for an activity relating to United States imperialism.

Construction of the canal began in 1904 and took 10 years and more than 40,000 workers to complete. Many of the workers, however, died of malaria and yellow fever. This problem was eventually solved by implementing a sanitation program to control disease-carrying mosquitoes. When the first ship finally steamed through the canal in August 1914, the canal was hailed as one of the world's great engineering feats.

Possession of the Panama Canal gave the United States even more of a stake in Latin America. Thus, the United States continued to exert its power in the region throughout the early 1900s. In 1904 President Theodore Roosevelt extended the Monroe Doctrine in what became known as the Roosevelt Corollary. Now the United States would actively force Latin American countries to honor their foreign debts. During the next two decades, United States forces intervened in countries such as the Dominican Republic, Haiti, and Nicaragua. The United States hoped its interventions would provide stability and prepare the way for democracy. Most Latin Americans viewed American actions as moves to turn their countries into "colonies" of the United States and to protect foreign businesses that were exploiting their resources.

Mexico

During the 1800s and early 1900s, the United States became deeply involved in the affairs of its southern neighbor, **Mexico**. During the 1830s, opposition to the dictatorial rule of General Antonio López de Santa Anna grew in the Mexican state of Texas, where many Americans had settled. In 1835 the Americans and some Mexicans in Texas revolted and the next year set up an independent republic. Texas in 1845 joined the American republic as a state, and conflict soon developed between Mexico and the United States. Mexico lost the Mexican War, and in the Treaty of Guadalupe Hidalgo (1848), lost nearly half of its territory to the United States.

Reform and Conflict

After the Mexican War, Mexico entered an era of change known as La Reforma. In 1855 Mexican voters chose **Benito Juárez**, a lawyer of Native American background, as president. Juárez reduced the power of the military, separated church and state, and improved the lot of impoverished farmers. In 1863, when Mexico could not pay its foreign debts, French troops occupied Mexico City. Juárez fled the capital to organize a guerrilla movement in the countryside. In 1864 Mexican conservatives, supported by the French, named Austrian Archduke

Language Delayed Some students who speak English as a second language may come from families with personal experiences in countries fighting against outside intervention. Ask these students to interview a parent or an acquaintance with such experience. Have them write the interviews in their native language. Then work with them individually as they translate their interviews into English. Read some of the translated interviews to the class as a basis for class discussion. **L1 LEP**

Maximilian emperor of Mexico. In 1867 the French, under American pressure, withdrew their troops from Mexico, and Juárez returned to power after his forces had ousted and executed Maximilian.

Four years after Juárez's death in 1872, General **Porfirio Díaz** seized power. To ensure "Order and Progress," Díaz strengthened the army and limited individual freedoms. Under Díaz's harsh rule, however, Mexico made economic advances, building railroads, developing industries, expanding farmlands, and opening new mines. Unfortunately for the Mexican people, most profits went to foreign investors and wealthy landowners. While the rich prospered, most Mexicans remained poor.

The Mexican Revolution

Discontent with Díaz eventually led to revolution. From 1910 to 1920, Mexico was engulfed by the first major social upheaval in modern Latin America. During this time, armies of farmers, workers, ranchers, and even *soldaderas*, or women soldiers, fought the authorities and each other across Mexico. The unrest also sparked a wave of Mexican immigration to the United States.

The revolution began when Francisco Madero, a liberal reformer, and his supporters overthrew Díaz in 1911. Once in power, Madero was murdered by one of his generals, Victoriano Huerta. A year later, Huerta himself was toppled from power by Mexican revolts and American intervention.

No strong leader emerged to take Huerta's place. Instead, three revolutionary leaders—**Emiliano Zapata**, **Francisco "Pancho" Villa**, and **Venustiano Carranza**—competed for power. Using the battle cry, "*Tierra y Liberdad!*" (Land and Liberty!), Zapata and his followers fought for the

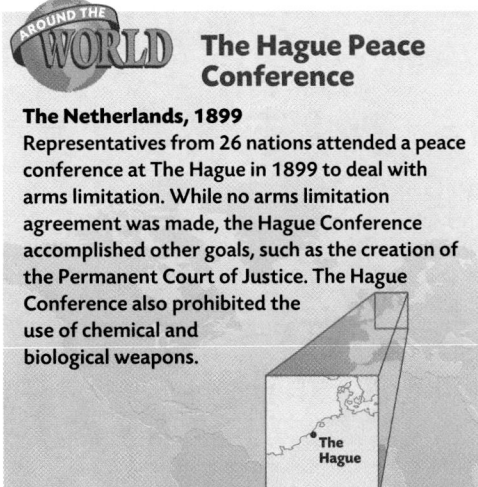

The Hague Peace Conference

The Netherlands, 1899
Representatives from 26 nations attended a peace conference at The Hague in 1899 to deal with arms limitation. While no arms limitation agreement was made, the Hague Conference accomplished other goals, such as the creation of the Permanent Court of Justice. The Hague Conference also prohibited the use of chemical and biological weapons.

rights of impoverished farmers. Like Zapata, Villa proposed radical reforms. The more conservative Carranza, however, was able to become president in 1915 with American support. In retaliation, Villa crossed the border into New Mexico and killed 18 Americans. United States President **Woodrow Wilson** then sent American troops into Mexico to capture Villa. American entry into World War I in 1917 led to the withdrawal of these troops.

That same year, Carranza reluctantly introduced a liberal constitution but was slow in carrying out reforms. In 1919 a pro-Carranza military officer murdered Zapata, who had protested Carranza's disregard of land reform. A year later, Carranza was killed and General Álvaro Obregón came to power. As the violence began to subside in the 1920s, relations between Mexico and the United States were less tense. The memory of American intervention, however, lingered in Mexican minds.

The Mexican Revolution
Why was the Mexican revolution a major development in Latin American history?
It was the first major social upheaval in modern Latin America, resulting in reforms to benefit peasants and workers.

Enrich

Arrange for students to see a video of *Viva Zapata!*, the 1952 film chronicling the life of the Mexican revolutionary leader. Ask students to imagine they are newspaper or television movie critics and to write a review of the film for submission or for class presentation.

Enrichment Activity 27

CLOSE

Have students divide a sheet of paper into three columns. In one column have them summarize their reactions to imperialism as if they were supporters of Woodrow Wilson in 1914–1916. In the second column have them summarize their reactions to imperialism as if they were supporters of "Pancho" Villa in 1914–1916. In the third column have them summarize their reactions to imperialism in their own voices.

SECTION 4 ASSESSMENT

Main Idea
1. Use a diagram like the one below to list ways in which Latin American countries reacted to American influence.

Recall
2. **Define** arbitration.
3. **Identify** James Monroe, Monroe Doctrine, José Martí, William McKinley, Theodore Roosevelt, Benito Juárez, Porfirio Díaz, Emiliano Zapata, Francisco "Pancho" Villa, Venustiano Carranza, Woodrow Wilson.

Critical Thinking
4. **Analyzing Information** Why do you think the United States government was so concerned about maintaining its influence in Latin America during the late 1800s and early 1900s?

Understanding Themes
5. **Nationalism** What factors led to the Mexican Revolution?

SECTION 4 ASSESSMENT ANSWERS

1. American intervention in countries viewed as attempt to colonize; efforts at protecting exploitive foreign businessmen resented; Mexicans resented American support of Carranza and attempt to capture Villa.
2. All terms are defined in the Glossary.
3. Monroe, 722; Monroe Doctrine, 722; Martí, 722; McKinley, 722; Roosevelt, 724; Juárez, 724; Díaz, 725; Zapata, 725; "Pancho" Villa, 725; Carranza, 725; Wilson, 725
4. It wanted to establish itself as a contender in the imperialist competition.
5. **NATIONALISM** pent-up grievances after years of dictatorship under Díaz; demands for social justice for mestizos and Native Americans

GLENCOE TECHNOLOGY

VIDEODISC

Use MindJogger to review the chapter.

MindJogger Videoquiz

Chapter 27
Disc 4 Side A

 Also available in VHS.

Answers

Using Key Terms

1. a   3. e   5. c
2. f   4. i

Using Your History Journal

Suggest that students use the same nation they chose to highlight when they began the chapter.

Reviewing Facts

1. Monroe: Monroe Doctrine to halt European imperialism in Latin America; McKinley: sent battleship to Havana to show American interest in Cuba; Roosevelt: encouraged Panamanians to revolt; built Panama Canal; Roosevelt Corollary to force Latin American repayment of debts; Wilson: sent troops to capture Pancho Villa
2. through treaties, purchases, and conquest; French: spread their culture overseas; British: allowed local rulers to represent them
3. Suez (Asia/Africa): joined Mediterranean and Red Seas and facilitated trade between Europe and Asia; Panama (Central America): linked Caribbean Sea and

---

Using Key Terms

Write the key term that completes each sentence. Then write a sentence for each term not chosen.

a. sepoys	f. imperialism
b. protectorate	g. spheres of influence
c. partition	h. viceroy
d. arbitration	i. culture system
e. westernization	j. colony

1. Before revolting in 1857, _____ had resented British attempts to impose Christianity and European customs on them.
2. _____ means one country's control of the political, economic, and social life of another country.
3. The acquisition of colonies by Europeans led to _____, or the spread of European civilization to other parts of the world.
4. In the East Indies, the Dutch used a method of forced labor called the _____ to gather raw materials and harvest crops.
5. In 1885, 14 nations met in Berlin, Germany, and agreed to _____ the continent of Africa among themselves.

Technology Activity

Using the Internet Search the Internet for a Web site that provides a map of the world around 1900 that includes political boundaries and a distance scale. Color code all countries that the British Empire controlled. Describe the relative location of the countries that were part of the British Empire in terms of the approximate distance from each country to Great Britain. Use the distance scale on the map. Then organize your findings in a chart. In addition, find out which countries remain under British control today.

Reviewing Facts

1. **History** Use a diagram like the one below to identify different responses of U.S. Presidents to events in Latin America.

Responses to Latin America	
Monroe	McKinley
Roosevelt	Wilson

2. **History** Explain how imperial nations acquired and ruled overseas lands. In what ways did the British and the French differ in ruling their empires?
3. **Geography** Identify the locations and state the significance of the Suez and Panama Canals.
4. **Culture** Describe the role of religion in the spread of Western values during the 1800s.
5. **History** Identify how Asians, Africans, and Latin Americans reacted to Western imperialism after the mid-1800s.

Critical Thinking

1. **Apply** How did science, industry, and technology aid the growth of imperialism?
2. **Evaluate** Why was Japan able to establish itself as an imperial and military power?
3. **Synthesize** How did imperialism affect peoples in Africa, Asia, and Latin America? What impact did imperialism have on the peoples of Europe and North America?
4. **Analyze** Contrast the ways in which the Age of Imperialism contributed to the growth of unity in the world with the ways in which it contributed to disunity.

Pacific Ocean; helped U.S. Navy to guard the nation's two coasts.

4. Missionaries set up schools and hospitals; they also spread European ways.
5. Asians: China did not readily adapt Western ways; Japan modernized into an imperial power; Africa: resisted colonization; western-educated elite formed nationalist movements; Latin America: resisted U.S. intervention and sought social justice; Mexican Revolution

Critical Thinking

1. New mass-produced weapons of war enabled Europeans to defeat non-European peoples that had simpler technologies.
2. It modernized its government and schools, and built industry and a strong military.
3. Africans and Asians faced cultural challenges from European rule; however, they often used western values to condemn imperialism. Latin Americans opposed United States

Geography in History

1. **Place** Refer to the map below. What two large bodies of water does the Panama Canal connect?
2. **Human/Environment Interaction** Why do you think engineers chose this particular location in which to build the canal?
3. **Location** Why is the Pacific Ocean located on the southeast side of this map?
4. **Region** What geographic features of this region made building the canal difficult?

The Panama Canal

Caribbean Sea
Colón
Cristobal
Madden Lake
Gatun Locks
Chagres River
Gatun Lake
Gaillard Cut
Pedro Miguel Locks
Miraflores Locks
Balboa — Panama
PACIFIC OCEAN

Legend:
- Canal Zone
- Canal route
- Railroad
- Locks

0   5   10 mi.
0   5   10 km

Understanding Themes

1. **Movement** What factors stimulated outward expansion by the European powers in the Age of Imperialism?
2. **Change** How did Africans react to the changes brought by the spread of imperialism in Africa?
3. **Reaction** In what two ways did Indian nationalists respond to British rule in India?

4. **Nationalism** Trace the events of the Mexican Revolution. Why was the Revolution an important development in modern Latin America?

Linking Past and Present

1. Historical context refers to the setting in which an event occurs. Throughout the 1900s the United States continued to intervene in Latin America. Investigate three recent interventions, and explain how the historical context surrounding American interventions has changed from 1900 to the present.
2. Have attitudes about imperialism changed from the 1800s to the present time? Explain. What factors do you think account for any changes?
3. Does imperialism exist in some form today? What factors do you think account for any changes? If imperialism exists today, does it differ from the imperialism of the 1800s?
4. Examine the role of the South African Native Congress (SANNC) in South Africa after its founding in 1912. As the African National Congress (ANC) after 1923, how did the organization's involvement change under independent white-dominated South African governments from the 1920s to the early 1990s? How does the ANC influence developments in South Africa today?

Skill Practice

Using the steps described on page 720, search the Internet for information about one of the following topics from the Age of Imperialism. Write an article for the school newspaper or magazine based on the information you retrieved about your topic.

- writings of Rudyard Kipling
- establishment of Liberia
- African Imperialism 1914
- Cecil Rhodes
- Russo-Japanese War
- Spanish-American War

with limited self-government.
3. **REACTION** They revolted during the Sepoy Rebellion, and they later formed the Indian National Congress to fight for Indian independence.
4. **NATIONALISM** The Revolution started as a revolt against dictatorship; it became a social upheaval; leaders sought social justice, especially land reform. It was the first social upheaval in modern Latin America.

Linking Past and Present

1. After 1945 the cold war affected U.S. involvements in Latin America. About 1900 the U.S. focused on intervention by traditional European powers. During the entire period U.S. concerns included regional stability, democracy, and protection of U.S. interests.
2. Opinions should be supported.
3. A typical response: imperialism still exists in an economic sense, because many politically free but economically weak nations rely on other nations for aid.
4. SANNC was founded to work for black rights. As the ANC, it continued this goal after the introduction of apartheid. By the 1960s, ANC militancy rose as government crackdowns grew harsh; the ANC is the largest political party in South Africa.

Skill Practice
Articles will vary depending on the topic and information found.

intervention; Europeans and North Americans believed their ways were superior.
4. It promoted unity by bringing people from around the world into closer contact; it promoted disunity by sparking conflicts.

Geography in History
1. Atlantic and Pacific Oceans
2. for the shortest distance across the continent
3. because the isthmus bends where the Panama Canal was dug, putting the Pacific Ocean south and east of the Atlantic
4. its jungles, hills, and swamps

Understanding Themes
1. **MOVEMENT** national rivalries, the desire for raw materials and markets, search for new opportunities, a "civilizing" mission
2. **CHANGE** Leaders fought Europeans; some Africans accepted European rule

Chapter Bonus Test Question

Ask students: How did the motives behind the age of exploration differ from those behind the Age of Imperialism? *(less pressure to find sources of raw materials and new markets for products during the age of exploration)*

FOCUS

With the Industrial Revolution came a push to make social and political changes both within the countries of the West and in other areas affected by the West. Such changes were revealed in actions taken and ideologies formed.

TEACH

Reinforcing Vocabulary

Point out the **Vocabulary Preview** to students alerting them to words they will encounter that might be unfamiliar.

Women's Right to Vote

Interpreting the Primary Source
Ask students to describe the "very, very unpleasant situation" to which Pankhurst refers. (*The very unpleasant situation for women demanding rights was that of strong opposition to and often ridicule of their movement.*)

Evaluating the Primary Source
This primary source reveals the vehement opposition of a woman to the exclusion of women from legal rights given to men. The source is a useful historical document because it illuminates the source and nature of the complaints of early 20th-century British and American women about their treatment under the law.

Unit 6

Between the late 1700s and the early 1900s, the nations of Europe and North America entered an Industrial Revolution which had far-reaching effects. Many people pushed for social and political reforms. Meanwhile, Western nations gradually extended their imperialism.

✦ VOCABULARY PREVIEW

admonitions: warnings

consumption: use

tyranny: oppression imposed by government

enunciated: spoken clearly

debouched: emerged

 For more primary sources to accompany this unit, use the *World History Primary Source Document Library CD-ROM.*

Chapter 25
Women's Right to Vote

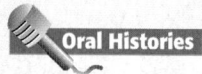 **Oral Histories**

In the United States and Great Britain women struggled for decades to gain the right to vote. Here, Emmeline Pankhurst, a leader of this cause in England, speaks to women in Connecticut in 1913.

. . . We found that all the fine phrases about freedom and liberty were entirely for male consumption, and that they did not in any way apply to women. When it was said . . . "Taxation of men without representation is tyranny," everybody quite calmly accepted the fact that women had to pay taxes and even were sent to prison if they failed to pay them—quite right. We found that "Government of the people, by the people and for the people" . . . was again only for male consumption; half of the people were entirely ignored; it was the duty of women to pay their taxes and obey the laws and look as pleasant as they could under the circumstances; in fact, every principle of liberty enunciated in any civilized country on earth, with very few exceptions, was intended entirely for men; and when women tried to force the putting into practice of these principles, for women, then they discovered they had come into a very, very unpleasant situation indeed. . . .

Emmeline Pankhurst 1858–1928

Garibaldi Liberates Palermo

Interpreting the Primary Source
Ask students to surmise from this passage whether the *London Times* was a newspaper that supported or opposed Garibaldi's nationalist revolt. (*The reference to Garibaldi's men as "the brave fellows who led the way" is one clear instance of support for Garibaldi's cause.*)

Evaluating the Primary Source
This primary source reveals a journalistic attempt to do two things: present only the facts but also indicate the political stance of the newspaper it was printed in. The reliability of this source can be judged by assessing whether the newspaper's desire to support the movement was strong

Chapter 26
Garibaldi Liberates Palermo

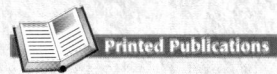
Printed Publications

From 1859 to 1870, a series of wars led to Italy's unification. One nationalist leader was Giuseppe Garibaldi, whose attack on Palermo, Sicily, in 1860 is recorded in this eyewitness account written by London Times correspondent Nandor Eber.

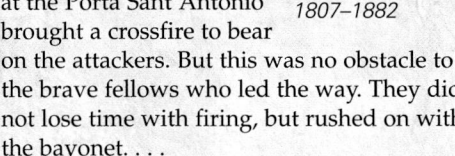
Giuseppe Garibaldi
1807–1882

. . . The Neapolitan fort at the gate, considerably reinforced, opened a hot fire, . . . while at the same time the two guns and the troops posted at the Porta Sant'Antonio brought a crossfire to bear on the attackers. But this was no obstacle to the brave fellows who led the way. They did not lose time with firing, but rushed on with the bayonet. . . .

Close to the Porta di Termini is the Vecchia Fiera—the old marketplace. This was the first point where Garibaldi stopped. One must know these Sicilians to have an idea of the frenzy, screaming, shouting, crying, and hugging; all would kiss his hand and embrace his knees. Every moment brought new masses, which debouched in troops from one of the streets, anxious to have their turn. As the Cacciatori gradually cleared the lower part of the town most of the inhabitants came to have a look, and give a greeting to the liberator of Palermo and Sicily. . . .

Chapter 27
Myth of Kintu

Oral Histories

In this folktale Kintu, legendary founder of Buganda (in present-day Uganda), becomes engaged to marry Nambi, the daughter of the sky god Ggulu. The story also explains how Death enters the world.

Ggulu gives his admonitions

He then called Nambi and said to Kintu: "Take my daughter who loves you, marry her and go back to your home [the earth]. . . . You must hurry away and go back before Death (Walumbe) comes, because he will want to go with you and . . . he will only cause you trouble and unhappiness." . . .

Kintu and Nambi then took leave of Ggulu, who said: "Be sure if you have forgotten anything not to come back, because Death will want to go with you. . . ."

They started off. . . . On the way Nambi remembered that she had forgotten the grain for the fowl, and said to Kintu: "I will hurry back and get it without anyone seeing me." He said: "Your brother Walumbe will . . . see you." She would not listen to her husband, but went back and said to her father: "I have forgotten the grain of the fowl. . . ." He replied: "Did I not tell you that you were not to return if you forgot anything, because . . . Walumbe would see you, and want to go with you? Now he will accompany you. . . ."

Interpreting Primary Sources

1. What, to Pankhurst, is ironic about the meaning of "liberty"?
2. How did the people of Palermo react to Garibaldi's arrival there?
3. According to the myth of Kintu, how did Death enter the world?
4. **CRITICAL THINKING:** Why do you think Pankhurst's message was considered so radical at that time?

Applications Activity
Create a political cartoon that depicts either Garibaldi's liberation of Palermo or the struggle for voting rights for women.

enough to sway its report from the facts.

Myth of Kintu

Interpreting the Primary Source
Ask students to decide whether they think this mythical story was intended to be an explanation of events or a way of teaching a life lesson, or both. *(As an explanation, the story explains how Death entered the world; as a life lesson, it teaches that there are serious ramifications to disobedience.)*

Evaluating the Primary Source
This primary source presents one culture's myth of how Death entered the world while also revealing that culture's valuing of obedience. This source is a useful historical document because of the cultural values and outlooks it reveals. It is clear from the myth that death is viewed not with acceptance but with wariness, while disobedience is viewed as a mistake bringing about the downfall of people.

For the more complete version of each of these documents, see the World History Primary Source Document Library CD-ROM:

Document 134 *Women's Right to Vote*
Document 136 *Garibaldi Liberates Palermo*
Document 140 *Myth of Kintu*

ANSWER KEY

1. Pankhurst says that "liberty" means liberty only for men—not for women.
2. The people of Palermo greeted Garibaldi joyously as their liberator.
3. Death came into the world because the daughter of the sky god disobeyed her father.
4. It suggested that men and women should be equals, at least politically. Her message threatened the structure of power in society and challenged men's traditional domination of women.

APPLICATIONS ACTIVITY: Students' cartoons will vary but should demonstrate an understanding of the events and situations being depicted.

Answers and Analyses

1. **C** (Economics) The development of the power loom is discussed on page 605. There it states that there was more thread than weavers could use until the power loom was invented, which *made it possible for weavers to keep up with the amount of yarn produced.*

2. **F** (Economics) According to pages 622–623, Great Britain *adopted free trade and other laissez-faire policies,* which means that the government allows *businesses to operate without government interference.*

 TEST-TAKING TIP

Even if students do not remember the specific fact being tested, they should still rely on their general historical knowledge to aggressively eliminate choices. In general, high duties and state ownership of factories leads to a reduction in productivity and stifles capitalism. Therefore choices G and H can be eliminated.

---

3. **C** (History) Page 615 states that *Because mill owners often owned the workers' housing, they controlled the rent and decided when and whether to improve living conditions.* Because of laissez-faire policies, governments were slow to regulate business: they did not do so until the 1830s and 1840s, according to page 624. Finally, the ability of employers to blacklist workers depends on a surplus of workers. Therefore choices A, B, and D can be eliminated.

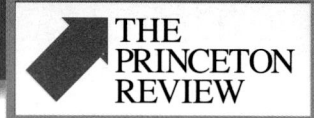

Standardized Test Practice

Directions: Choose the *best* answer to each of the following multiple choice questions. If you have trouble answering a question, use the process of elimination to narrow your choices. Write your answers on a separate piece of paper.

1. The invention of the power loom in 1787 led to

A an increase in cloth imports from Asia.

B an increase in the need for skilled craftspeople.

C an increase in productivity.

D an increase in the price of finished cloth.

> **Test-Taking Tip:** The phrase *led to* indicates that this question is looking for a *cause and effect* relationship. In general, the machinery developed during the Industrial Revolution *reduced* the need for skilled craftspeople, so answer B is an unlikely effect of this invention.

2. The Industrial Revolution led to the growth of capitalism. In which of the following ways did the government help capitalism flourish?

F By establishing few regulations

G By setting duties on imports and exports

H By requiring state ownership of factories

J By enacting laws protecting workers

> **Test-Taking Tip:** This question requires you to remember the meaning of the word *capitalism*. Since capitalism is an economic system in which individuals and private firms—not the government—own the means of production, answer H does not make sense. Look for the answer that would help make businesses *profitable*.

3. Early factory workers faced dangerous conditions and unfair practices. Busines owners exploited workers for all the following reasons EXCEPT that

A there were more workers than available jobs.

B business controlled housing and jobs.

C labor unions did not focus on safety.

D governments were slow to interfere with capitalism.

> **Test-Taking Tip:** Be careful—this question is looking for the *exception*. Do not simply choose the first answer that "makes sense." Look for the answer that does NOT fit. Since answer A is true, it cannot be the *exception*.

Read the quotation from *The Communist Manifesto* and answer the question that follows.

Let the ruling classes tremble at a Communist revolution. The proletarians have nothing to lose but their chains. They have a world to win. Working men of all countries, unite!

4. Engels and Marx wrote *The Communist Manifesto* to advocate

F freedom for political prisoners.

G a revolution of the working class against the bourgeoisie.

H the growth of their empire.

J democratic ideals and civil rights.

> **Test-Taking Tip:** Make sure that your answer is supported by information *in the quotation*. Do not rely only on your memory. Remember also that *proletarians* means "members of the working class."

Use the graph below to answer question 5.

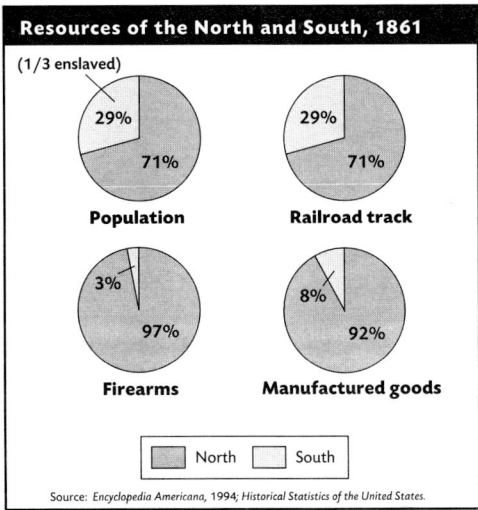

Resources of the North and South, 1861

(1/3 enslaved)

29% / 71% — **Population**

29% / 71% — **Railroad track**

3% / 97% — **Firearms**

8% / 92% — **Manufactured goods**

☐ North   ☐ South

Source: *Encyclopedia Americana, 1994; Historical Statistics of the United States.*

Use the following map to answer question 6.

Central Africa: Land Use and Resources

Agriculture
☐ Subsistence farming
■ Manufacturing area

Resources
🪨 Coal
🪨 Copper
◆ Diamonds
🌲 Forest
Gold
⚡ Hydroelectric power
● Manganese
Petroleum
▼ Tin
❄ Uranium

0   250   500 mi.
0   250   500 km

5. According to the graph

A the North had more people and firearms, but the South had more manufactured goods.

B the North had more railroad tracks, but the South had more farmland and bank deposits.

C the North had more manufactured goods, but the South had more people and railroad tracks.

D None of the above

Test-Taking Tip: Double check all the answer choices against the information on the graph. Make sure that you look at the *key* to determine how North and South are represented. Remember that the sections of a circle graph are different sizes for a *reason.*

6. Which area of Central Africa produces manganese?

F Democratic Republic of the Congo

G Gabon

H Congo

J Cameroon

Test-Taking Tip: Use the map's *key,* or *legend,* to identify the symbols used on the map. Make sure that you double check all answers against the information *on the map.*

 STOP

4. G (History) This excerpt discusses a revolution on the part of the working class. The choice that best matches this idea is G.

 THE PRINCETON REVIEW **TEST-TAKING TIP**

Whenever students are given a quotation or excerpt, they should look very carefully at the language. This excerpt does not mention political prisoners, democratic ideals, or an empire. Instead, it discusses a *revolution,* the *proletarians,* and *Working men of all countries.* These ideas best match choice G.

5. D (Economics) According to the chart, the North had more manufactured goods, more bank deposits, and more railroads. Therefore choices A, B, and C are all incorrect.

6. G (Geography) According to the map, the country that produces manganese is Gabon.

MORE PRACTICE

For additional practice, assign practice pages from:

📁 Glencoe Standardized Test Practice Workbook

📁 Glencoe SAT/SAT II Practice Book

Tested Objectives

Questions	Objective
1	Determining Cause and Effect
2	Making Inferences
3	Evaluating Information
4	Synthesizing Information
5, 6	Analyzing Information

Introducing the Unit

Unit 7 focuses on the political movements and global conflicts that gripped the world between 1914 and 1945, including the rise of fascism and communism in Europe, the growth of nationalism in the developing world, and World War I and World War II.

Unit Objectives

After reading Unit 7, students will be able to:
1. discuss the causes, events, and results of World War I.
2. trace the growth of fascist and Communist dictatorships in Italy, Germany, and the Soviet Union.
3. explain the upsurge of nationalism in Asia, Africa, and Latin America from 1919 to 1939.
4. discuss the causes of World War II and the major political realignments that followed the war.

GLENCOE TECHNOLOGY

Glencoe World History Primary Source Document Library
Use the CD-ROM to access primary source documents related to world conflicts.

Unit 7

1914–1945

World in Conflict

See pages 854–855 for primary source readings that accompany Unit 7.

Then & Now Nationalism and imperialism had dire consequences for Europe and the world. When national pride and the scramble for overseas territories dictated foreign relations among industrial states, conflict was inevitable. Two world wars resulted. Never before in the history of civilization had the world endured devastation on such a massive scale.

When you climb aboard a jetliner, you may reflect on the technology of air travel developed in this period. After World War II, many people hoped that the refined instruments of war could be turned to peaceful purposes. The power of the atom could be used to produce energy rather than bombs. Airplanes, developed in World War I and refined in World War II, could become a major means of transportation.

A Global Chronology

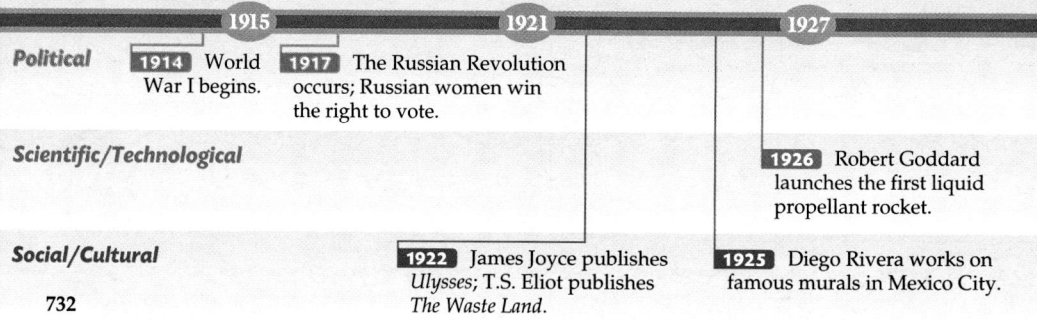

1915   **1921**   **1927**

Political   **1914** World War I begins.   **1917** The Russian Revolution occurs; Russian women win the right to vote.

Scientific/Technological   **1926** Robert Goddard launches the first liquid propellant rocket.

Social/Cultural   732   **1922** James Joyce publishes *Ulysses*; T.S. Eliot publishes *The Waste Land*.   **1925** Diego Rivera works on famous murals in Mexico City.

Then & Now **Why War?** In this unit, students will learn how democracy and peace broke down twice in Europe during the first half of the twentieth century, leading to the bloodiest conflicts in world history.

Ask students to think about the causes of war in general, particularly more recent conflicts involving the United States such as the Vietnam War and the Persian Gulf War. What are the main reasons that nations go to war? *(Answers will vary. Students may feel that*

A 1938 Zenith console radio

History and You

World War I erupted as the first major conflict to involve most of the world's nations. Global participation was sparked by the assassination of the Austro-Hungarian Archduke.

To examine the role of the archduke's assassination in instigating World War I, view videodisc Chapter 4: **Assassination Ignites the World** in **Turning Points in World History.**

Timeline

1933

1933 Adolf Hitler comes to power in Germany.

1928 Alexander Fleming discovers penicillin.

1935 Jews lose rights of citizenship in Germany.

1939

1939 World War II begins.

1942 Enrico Fermi produces the first controlled nuclear chain reaction.

1940 Charlie Chaplin makes the movie *The Great Dictator.*

1945

1945 The United States drops an atomic bomb on Hiroshima.

733

History and the Humanities

World History and Art Trans.
- 37 *I Want You for the U.S. Army*
- 38 *Migrant Mother*
- 40 *Zapatistas*
- 41 *Turkestan Oriental Rug*

World Music: Cultural Traditions, Lessons 1, 2, 6, 9

ABCNEWS INTERACTIVE™

VIDEODISC
Turning Points in World History

Side Two
Chapter 4

Title: *Assassination Ignites World War I*
Ask: Why did the assassination of the archduke plunge Europe into war? *(European alliances caused major nations to declare war.)*

Visualizing History

The first commercial radio station began to broadcast in the United States in 1920; only two years later more than 500 stations were broadcasting throughout the country.

Glencoe Literature Library

The following literature from the **Glencoe Literature Library** may enrich this unit:
Animal Farm by G. Orwell
The Chosen by C. Potok
A Separate Peace by J. Knowles

---

conflicting ideologies or interests between two nations, or aggressive actions by one nation, are the main causes of war.) Are democratic governments more or less likely to go to war than dictatorships? Why? *(Some students may feel that democracies are less likely to resort to war; others may point out that Britain and the United States, the world's oldest democracies, have fought many wars.)* Is war ever justified as a way of achieving foreign policy goals? *(Answers will vary; some students may feel that at times war cannot be avoided or is the lesser of two evils; others may respond that war is never justified.)*

The Spread of Ideas

TEACH

Introduction

This feature focuses on efforts by the international community to achieve collective security, first through the League of Nations, established after World War I, and later through the United Nations, set up in the aftermath of World War II.

Background Notes

Linking Past and Present

As students will read on pages 762–764, American President Woodrow Wilson was the prime mover of the League of Nations; the failure of the Senate to approve American participation was a blow to Wilson and the League. In contrast, today the United States is a leading funder and supporter of the United Nations, even though there is often heated debate in Congress about American participation in UN peacekeeping missions.

Geography

Movement Since 1989, troops from around the world have participated in UN observer and peacekeeping missions in Latin America, Africa, and Europe. Among the most important have been observer groups to monitor elections in Nicaragua, Haiti, and South Africa and peacekeeping missions in the former Yugoslavia, the republic of Georgia, and Somalia. Ask students what problems the growing number of UN missions in recent years may have created. (*The UN has been burdened with ballooning costs and funding shortages.*)

The Spread of Ideas

International Peacekeeping

*T*he 1900s taught people the meaning of world war. No previous century in history had ever seen conflicts that literally spanned the globe. In addition to numerous regional conflicts, the 20th century witnessed two world wars. As the scope of war grew, so did the commitment to collective security—the principle in which a group of nations join together to promote peace.

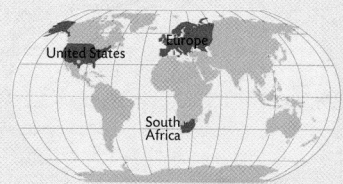

Europe
The League of Nations

As early as 1828, an American named William Ladd sought to establish a Congress of Nations to settle international disputes and avoid war. Nearly a century later, at the end of World War I, the victorious nations set up a "general association of nations" called the League of Nations.

By 1920 42 nations had sent delegates to the League's headquarters in Geneva, Switzerland. Another 21 nations eventually joined, but conspicuously absent was the United States. Opponents in the United States Senate had argued that membership in the League went against George Washington's advice against "entangling alliances."

When the League failed to halt warlike acts in the 1930s, these same opponents pointed to the failure of collective security. The League was a peacekeeper without a sword—it possessed neither a standing army nor members willing to stop nations that used war as a method of diplomacy.

UN distribution center in the Gaza Strip

COOPERATIVE LEARNING ACTIVITY

Role Play Have students brainstorm a list of international conflicts today. Then organize students into small groups. Assign each group a conflict from the list. Have them role-play an attempt by the United Nations to resolve the situation. In each group, have some students represent the two parties in conflict and others represent UN mediators. Have students discuss the sources of the conflict, then draw up and if possible agree to a peace treaty. Each group can describe its dilemma to the class and explain whether—and why—they could or could not resolve it. **L3**

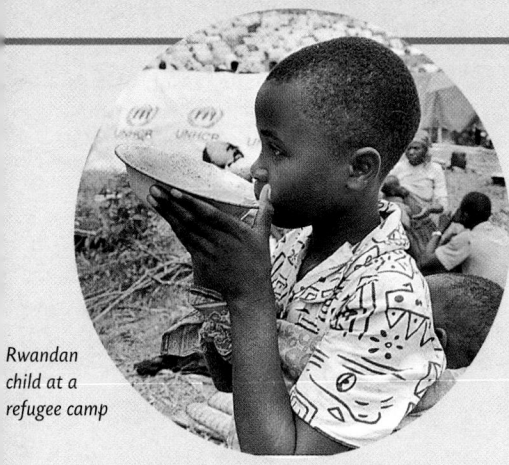

Rwandan child at a refugee camp

The United States
The United Nations

Non-membership in the League did not protect the United States from the horrors of war. The Japanese air attack on Pearl Harbor, Hawaii, ended the notion that the United States could isolate itself from the rest of the world.

As World War II drew to a close, the United States hosted a meeting in San Francisco to create a new global peacekeeping organization. Here delegates from 50 nations hammered out the Charter of the United Nations. The document's Preamble sets forth a formula for international peace:

We the peoples of the United Nations, determined to save succeeding generations from the scourge of war, which twice in our lifetime has brought untold sorrow to mankind and to reaffirm faith in fundamental human rights ... and to promote social progress and to better standards of life and to promote our strength to maintain international peace and security, and to ensure ... that armed force shall not be used, save in the common interest ... have resolved to combine our efforts to accomplish these aims.

In the years following, the United Nations (UN) attempted to eliminate the root causes of war. In 1946 it founded the UN Educational, Scientific, and Cultural Organization (UNESCO) and the UN Children's Fund (UNICEF). These agencies promoted global education and the well-being of children. Two years later, in 1948, United States delegate Eleanor Roosevelt convinced the UN to adopt The Universal Declaration of Human Rights. This committed the UN to the elimination of oppression wherever it existed.

South Africa
The Power of World Opinion

Like the League of Nations, the UN could be only as strong as its members were prepared to make it. The development of atomic weapons, however, was a powerful incentive for members to cooperate. By 1995, the UN had taken part in 35 peacekeeping missions—some successful, some failures. It also had provided protection for more than 30 million refugees.

The UN's ability to use world opinion to promote justice was perhaps best tested in South Africa. In 1977 the UN urged nations to use an arms embargo and economic sanctions against South Africa until apartheid was lifted. In 1994 South Africa held its first all-race elections. Many believed this was a major triumph for collective international action.

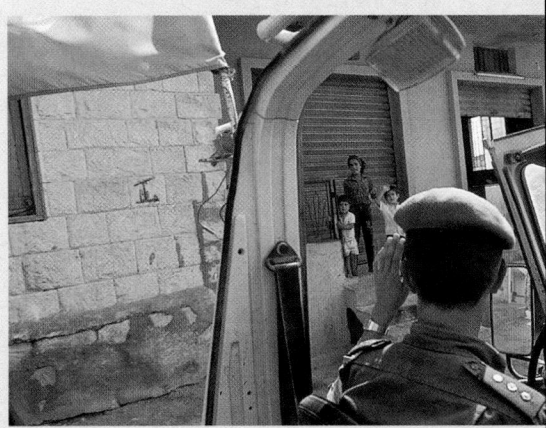

UN troops in Beirut, Lebanon

LINKING THE IDEAS

1. What factors made it difficult for the League of Nations to promote world peace?
2. What methods has the United Nations used to encourage peace?

Critical Thinking

3. **Forming Opinions** The United Nations Declaration of Human Rights sees injustice in one part of the world as a threat to peace in all parts of the world. Do you agree? Why or why not?

Unit 7 *World in Conflict* 735

The Spread of Ideas

Cultural Diffusion

International Cooperation and Popular Music Since the 1970s the spirit of international cooperation has influenced the world of rock music. In the early 1970s, a number of rock musicians, including George Harrison and Bob Dylan, held a concert to raise money for famine victims in the newly created nation of Bangladesh (formerly part of Pakistan). In the 1980s Bob Geldof of the Boomtown Rats organized Band Aid, featuring many recording artists such as Sting and Phil Collins, to raise money for famine relief in Ethiopia.

ANSWERS TO LINKING THE IDEAS

1. It had no army, and its members were not willing to use force to stop aggression.
2. The UN has tried to eliminate the causes of war through UNESCO and UNICEF and has used peacekeeping missions, arms embargoes, and economic sanctions to promote peace.
3. Answers will vary. Some students may feel that injustice creates instability that can lead to war.

A complete, 1-page lesson plan is provided for each section in the *Reproducible Lesson Plans* booklet.

World War I

CHAPTER RESOURCES

	Reproducible Resources	Multimedia Resources
Chapter Opener	Chapter Themes: Graphic Organizer 28 Historical Significance Chapter Activity 28	MindJogger Videoquiz
Chapter Enrichment	Vocabulary Activity 28* Time Line Activity 28 Mapping History Activity 28 History Simulation 28 Geography and History Activity 28 Source Reading 28 People in World History Profiles 53, 54 World Art and Music Activity 28 Enrichment Activity 28 Critical Thinking Activity 28 Skill Reinforcement Activity 28 Performance Assessment Activity 28 Standardized Test Practice Workbook Activity 28 Inclusion for the Social Studies Classroom Strategies and Activities	World History and Art Transparency 36, *Three Musicians*; 37, *I Want You for the U.S. Army* Mapping History Overlay Transparency 18, *World War I* Chapter Transparency 28 Vocabulary PuzzleMaker Software Turning Points in World History: *Assassination Ignites World War I* Lessons of War: *How Wars Begin–World War I* Communism and the Cold War: *Perspectives on Communism* World History Primary Source Document Library
Chapter Review/Reteaching	Reteaching Activity 28 Skill Reinforcement Activity 28 Spanish Chapter Summary 28	Chapter 28 Digest Audiocassette, Activity, Test* Vocabulary PuzzleMaker Software Interactive Tutor Self-Assessment Software MindJogger Videoquiz
Chapter Evaluation/Testing	Performance Assessment Activity 28 Chapter 28 Test, Forms A and B	ExamView® Pro Testmaker

0:00 OUT OF TIME? Assign the Chapter 28 Audiocassettes.

* *Also available in Spanish*

World History Primary Source Document Library
Make History Come Alive!
Engage your students with over 250 easily accessible primary source documents—available on this CD-ROM—that will give them real life insight into the important events of world history.

Block Schedule
Activities that are particularly suited to use within the block scheduling framework are identified throughout this chapter by the following designation.

KEY TO ABILITY LEVELS
Teaching strategies are coded for varying learning styles.
L1 BASIC activities for all students
L2 AVERAGE activities for average to above-average students
L3 CHALLENGING activities for above-average students
LEP LIMITED ENGLISH PROFICIENCY activities

Use Glencoe's *Presentation Plus!* multimedia teacher tool to easily present dynamic lessons that visually excite your students. Using Microsoft PowerPoint® you can customize the presentations to create your own personalized lessons.

Interactive Lesson Planner

Planning has never been easier! Using this CD-ROM, organize your week, month, semester, or year with all the help you need. The **Interactive Lesson Planner** gives you access to all of the blackline masters that accompany *World History: The Human Experience.*

SECTION RESOURCES

Daily Objectives	Reproducible Resources	Multimedia Resources
Section 1 **The Seeds of War** Identify the underlying causes of World War I.	Lecture Notes 28-1 Reproducible Lesson Plan 28-1 Vocabulary Activity 28* Guided Reading Activity 28-1* Time Line Activity 28 Section Quiz 28-1* Reading Essentials and Study Guide 28-1	Section Focus Transparency 28-1 Chapter Transparency 28 Interactive Tutor Self-Assessment Software
Section 2 **The Spark** Describe the series of events that provided the spark that ignited World War I.	Lecture Notes 28-2 Reproducible Lesson Plan 28-2 Vocabulary Activity 28* Guided Reading Activity 28-2* Section Quiz 28-2* Reading Essentials and Study Guide 28-2	Section Focus Transparency 28-2 Interactive Tutor Self-Assessment Software Turning Points in World History: *Assassination Ignites World War I*
Section 3 **The War** Specify where and how World War I was fought.	Lecture Notes 28-3 Reproducible Lesson Plan 28-3 Guided Reading Activity 28-3* History Simulation 28 Geography and History Activity 28 Section Quiz 28-3* Reading Essentials and Study Guide 28-3	Section Focus Transparency 28-3 Mapping History Overlay Transparency 18, *World War I* World History and Art Transparency 36, *Three Musicians;* 37, *I Want You for the U.S. Army* Vocabulary PuzzleMaker Software Interactive Tutor Self-Assessment Software Lessons of War: *How Wars Begin—WWI*
Section 4 **The Russian Revolution** Summarize the events that led to the Russian Revolution.	Lecture Notes 28-4 Reproducible Lesson Plan 28-4 Vocabulary Activity 28* Guided Reading Activity 28-4* Section Quiz 28-4* Reading Essentials and Study Guide 28-4	Section Focus Transparency 28-4 Interactive Tutor Self-Assessment Software Communism and the Cold War: *Perspectives on Communism*
Section 5 **Peace at Last** Explain why the Treaty of Versailles was ultimately unsuccessful.	Lecture Notes 28-5 Reproducible Lesson Plan 28-5 Guided Reading Activity 28-5* Reteaching Activity 28 Enrichment Activity 28 Section Quiz 28-5* Performance Assessment Activity 28 Spanish Chapter Summary 28 Reading Essentials and Study Guide 28-5	Section Focus Transparency 28-5 Vocabulary PuzzleMaker Software Interactive Tutor Self-Assessment Software Testmaker

* Also available in Spanish

Chapter Activities

 Performance Assessment Activity

A Chain of Events Have students assume the role of scriptwriters for a television episode about a time traveler. Each student will think of one event of the World War I era to change, then predict the chain of events that would have flowed from the changed event and describe how the war would have been different because of it. Then have students write a brief summary of the chain of events, choose real actors to play the parts of the significant individuals, decide on how the time traveler will be able to make the proposed change, and choose locations for the scenes (either real or with designed sets). Students will then present their ideas to a group whose members play the roles of producers.

Possible Rubric Features

Accuracy of content information, logical predictions, appropriateness of sets and locales for events, clarity of presentation, originality, and summarization skills

• For an additional activity, refer to Activity 28 in the Performance Assessment Strategies and Activities booklet.

ACTIVITY

From the Classroom of...

**Kathleen M. Slane
Rockville High School
Vernon, CT**

World War I Propaganda Posters

Show the class a number of World War I propaganda posters, designed by members of both the Allied Powers and the Central Powers. Explain to students that they will design propaganda posters for either the Allied forces or the Central forces. Number slips of paper with a 1 or 2, representing the Allied or Central forces. Place the slips of paper in a container and have each student (or group of students) pick one to determine the alliance system for which they will create a poster.

Students may create posters that demonstrate the following: (1) support for the Red Cross, (2) women's roles in wartime, (3) financial support through the purchase of war bonds, (4) fear of the opposing forces, (5) savagery of the opposing forces, (6) patriotism for their country and loyalty to the cause.

Display the completed posters in the classroom. Have students study each poster and answer the following questions: Which country or alliance system designed this propaganda poster? How do you know? What was the important message of the poster? Can you think of examples of propaganda that present-day countries utilize?

MULTIPLE LEARNING STYLES

Verbal/Linguistic
Have students select poems from the World War I era and read them aloud in class as a basis for discussion.

Logical/Mathematical
Have students debate the following proposition: War unites the people of a country as nothing else can.

Auditory/Musical
Have students listen to a tape or CD of World War I songs. On the basis of these, ask what generalizations they can make about the armies and/or civilians of the time.

Kinesthetic
Have students use models or diagrams to explain to the rest of the class the workings of one of the new pieces of military technology used in World War I. They might choose machine guns, tanks, submarines, or fighter planes.

GLENCOE'S ASSESSMENT ADVANTAGE

Use the following to easily assess student learning in a variety of ways.

• Performance Assessment Strategies and Activities
• Section Quizzes
• Chapter and Unit Tests
• Interactive Tutor Self-Assessment Software
• Testmaker Software
• MindJogger Videoquiz
• SAT/SAT II Test Practice
• worldhistory.glencoe.com

Additional Resources

NATIONAL GEOGRAPHIC SOCIETY — Teacher's Corner

INDEX TO NATIONAL GEOGRAPHIC MAGAZINE

The following articles relate to this chapter:

- "Riddle of the Lusitania," by Robert D. Ballard, April 1994.
- "The Bolshevik Revolution: Experiment That Failed," by Dusko Doder, October 1992.

NATIONAL GEOGRAPHIC SOCIETY PRODUCTS AVAILABLE FROM GLENCOE

To order the following call Glencoe at 1-800-334-7344:

- *PicturePack: World War I Era (Transparencies)*
- *PictureShow: World War I Era (CD-ROM)*
- *GTV: The American People (Videodiscs)*
- *GTV: A Geographic Perspective on American History (Videodiscs)*
- *MapPack: Europe (Transparency Maps)*

ADDITIONAL NATIONAL GEOGRAPHIC SOCIETY PRODUCTS

To order the following, call National Geographic at 1-800-368-2728:

- *Europe (Laminated Desk Maps)*
- *1914–1918: World War I (Video)*
- *1917: Revolution in Russia (Video)*
- *The Rise and Fall of the Soviet Union (Video)*

Access National Geographic's new dynamic MapMachine Web site and other geography resources at:

- http://www.nationalgeographic.com/
- http://www.nationalgeographic.com/maps/

BIBLIOGRAPHY

Literature of the Period
Hemingway, Ernest. *A Farewell to Arms.* New York: Macmillan, 1988. A romantic novel by a writer who served as an ambulance driver during the war.
Readings for the Student
Taylor, A.J.P. *The First World War: An Illustrated History.* New York: Perigee, 1980. Includes many photographs and an informative commentary.
Readings for the Teacher
Tuchman, Barbara W. *The Guns of August.* New York: Bantam, 1980. A vivid account of the crucial first six weeks of World War I.

WORLD HISTORY Online

Use our Web site as an additional resource. All essential content is covered in the Student Edition.

You and your students can visit the *World History: The Human Experience* Web site at worldhistory.glencoe.com The student text directs students to the Web site for the following options:

- **Chapter Overviews**
- **Student Web Activities**
- **Self-Check Quizzes**

Answers are provided for you in a link entitled "Web Activity Lesson Plan." Additional Web Resources, Interactive Puzzles, and content updates are also available.

Visit the Glencoe Web site at socialstudies.glencoe.com for social studies activities, updates, and links to other resources.

LOCAL OBJECTIVES

_____
_____
_____
_____
_____
_____
_____
_____
_____
_____
_____
_____
_____
_____
_____
_____
_____
_____
_____
_____

CHAPTER THEMES

Chapter Themes are listed by section on this chapter opening page of the Student Edition. A corresponding theme-based activity is available under "TEACH," and a theme-based question is asked in the Section and Chapter Assessments.

Storyteller

Historical Setting Erich Maria Remarque, author of *All Quiet on the Western Front*, was 18 when he was drafted into the German army. He saw action on the Western Front, where he was wounded.

The novel's hero, Paul Baumer, volunteers enthusiastically for the army but is soon disillusioned by the carnage. "How senseless is everything," he says, "when such things are possible.... A hospital alone shows what war is." Baumer is killed on the Western Front, on a day that is otherwise "all quiet."

Historical Significance

Answers: *It differed in scope (fought on several continents), scale (heavy casualties), and the destructiveness of the weapons used, including poison gas and machine guns.*

The war ended several empires and created many small countries. Among its legacies were the decimation of a generation of young men, widespread impoverishment, and lasting resentments and animosities.

— WORLD HISTORY
Online

Have students use the **Chapter 28 Overview** at worldhistory. glencoe.com as a prereading and postreading exercise for understanding chapter content.

Chapter
28 1914–1920
World War I

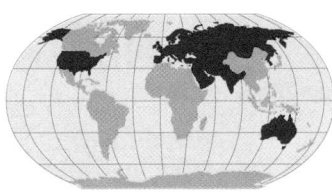

Chapter Themes

▶ **Cooperation** European powers form a series of alliances before World War I. *Section 1*
▶ **Conflict** Tensions between the two European alliances erupt into a European-wide conflict. *Section 2*
▶ **Conflict** The European war grows to engulf much of the world; the conflict directly affects civilians as well as soldiers. *Section 3*
▶ **Revolution** The Russian czar is overthrown and Lenin and the Bolsheviks take power. *Section 4*
▶ **Internationalism** The Treaty of Versailles provides for the creation of a League of Nations to mediate international disputes. *Section 5*

Storyteller

To survive days of bombardment on the Western Front during World War I, men crouched down in deep ditches. During these times there was nothing to do but wait and watch. Finally, they would receive orders to attack:

"Suddenly the nearer explosions cease. The shelling continues but it has lifted and falls behind us, our trench is free. We seize the hand-grenades, pitch them out in front of the dug-out and jump after them. The bombardment has stopped and a heavy barrage now falls behind us. The attack has come."

In this passage from All Quiet on the Western Front, *Erich Maria Remarque captures the chaos and horror of what is now called World War I. When this war broke out in the summer of 1914, most Europeans thought it would be over by Christmas. Instead, it lasted four long years and changed Europe and the world forever.*

Historical Significance

In what ways was World War I different from previous wars? How did it affect the countries and peoples involved? What impact did it have on the future course of the 1900s?

1905   1910   1915   1920

1907 The Triple Entente forms to counter the Triple Alliance.

1914 Major European powers declare war.

1917 United States enters the war; Bolsheviks seize power in Russia.

1918 Germans sign armistice.

736

GEOGRAPHY CONNECTION

Location On a wall map, have students locate the countries that became the Central Powers: Germany, Austria-Hungary, the Ottoman Empire, and Bulgaria. Then have them locate the countries that became the (European) Allies: Britain, France, Russia, Belgium, Serbia, Montenegro, and later, Romania, Greece, Portugal, and Italy. **L1 LEP**

History & Art

American Troops Arriving in Paris July 14, 1918 by J. F. Foucher. West Point Museum, West Point, New York

History & Art Tell students that although the United States was late in entering World War I, its participation made a big difference. Note that this parade is being held on Bastille Day, the French national holiday. What is the mood of this painting? (*upbeat, excited, with bands playing and flags flying*)

✔ Performance Assessment

Refer to the activity on page 736C of the Planning Guide.

 For an additional activity, refer to Activity 28 in the *Performance Assessment Strategies and Activities* booklet.

Using Your History Journal

The main participants were Ypres: Germans and British; *Lusitania*: Germans, British, Americans; Verdun: Germans, French.

WORLD HISTORY Online

...pter Overview

...the *World History: The Human Experience* site at **worldhistory.glencoe.com** and ... on *Chapter 28—Chapter Overview* ...review the chapter.

Your History Journal

Write a letter home as a first-person account of one of the following events: Poison gas at Ypres, the Sinking of the Lusitania, the Battle of Verdun.

GLENCOE TECHNOLOGY

VIDEODISC
Use MindJogger to preview chapter content.

MindJogger Videoquiz

Chapter 28
Disc 4 Side A

 Also available in VHS.

Chapter 28 *World War I* 737

➕ **EXTRA CREDIT PROJECT**

Deadly Influenza In the last months of the war, the world was struck by a pandemic of influenza that killed more people than the war itself. Have students research and report on the pandemic: where and when it began; how the disease manifested itself; and the total number of casualties.

1882 Italy joins Germany and Austria-Hungary to form the Triple Alliance.

1894 France and Russia become allies to counter the Triple Alliance.

c. 1900 Germany has the most powerful weapons and the best army in Europe.

1905 France and Ge come close to war ove

SECTION THEME

▶ **Cooperation** European powers form a series of alliances before World War I.

Guide to Reading

For reading strategies to help students read effectively see pages 12–13. Have students think about the main head as they read the subheads.

Vocabulary Pre-check

🔲 Use the Vocabulary PuzzleMaker for Chapter 28 to create a crossword puzzle to reinforce section terms. **L1 LEP**

🗂 Use Vocabulary Activity 28 to introduce vocabulary terms. **L1 LEP**

FOCUS

Section Objective

Identify the underlying causes of World War I.

BELLRINGER
Motivational Activity

Before taking roll at the beginning of the class period, project Section Focus Transparency 28-1 and have students answer the activity questions. Discuss students' responses.

🗂 This activity is also available as a blackline master.

Section 1

The Seeds of War

Guide to Reading

Read to Find Out
Main Idea *Several key factors caused World War I.*

▶ **Terms to Define**
militarism, conscription, alliance system, *entente*

▶ **People to Meet**
Otto von Bismarck

▶ **Places to Locate**
Morocco, Alsace-Lorraine, Bosnia-Herzegovina

The Storyteller

Herbert Marlow, foreign editor for a large United States newspaper, was amazed. His correspondents in Paris, Vienna, and Berlin had all wired similar reports concerning European nationalism and attitudes favoring war. Roland Doregelès wrote, "No more poor or rich … there were only Frenchmen." Stefan Zweig in Vienna observed, "As never before, thousands and hundreds of thousands felt what they should have felt in peacetime, that they belonged together." Marlow reread Philipp Scheidermann's dispatch from Berlin, resolving to use it as his headline. Scheidermann had noted Germans proclaiming "It is the hour we yearned for."

German military parade

—adapted from articles reprinted in *Sources of the Western Tradition*, edited by Marvin Perry, 1991

738 **Chapter 28** *World War I*

In the summer of 1914, an assassination took place in the Austro-Hungarian province of Bosnia in the Balkans. Although some people mourned, there was no broad sense of outrage or alarm. There had been other assassinations in the recent past with no major consequences.

Within weeks, it became apparent that this assassination was different. By August, the major European powers were at war with each other. The war was to last from 1914 to 1918; it led to the development of new weapons that changed warfare forever. By the time it was over, the war had involved most nations of the world and was the largest that the world had ever seen.

It was known as the Great War, the "war to end all wars." The name by which it was called was not important. The changes it brought about were. The way of life that had existed before the war was destroyed. Empires were swept away, and governments toppled. European dominance of the world was shaken. The war marked the close of a long era of international peace.

European Rivalries

Since the mid-1800s, rivalries had been building up and intensifying among some of the countries of Europe. As Western nations industrialized, each sought the most favorable conditions for economic growth. This led to intense competition. As industrialization spread, the competition grew keener. One by one, Great Britain, France, Germany, Austria-Hungary, Russia, and Italy sought to acquire new markets and to establish and expand global empires.

Great Britain wanted to maintain the lifelines of its empire and keep open the sea-lanes it needed for trade. It also wanted to make sure no other nation became strong enough to attack it. France was intent on adding mineral-rich **Morocco** to its gains.

SECTION RESOURCES

🗂 Reproducible Masters
- Lecture Notes 28-1
- Reproducible Lesson Plan 28-1
- Vocabulary Activity 28
- Guided Reading Activity 28-1
- Time Line Activity 28
- Section Quiz 28-1
- Reading Essentials and Study Guide 28-1

📖 Transparencies
- Section Focus Transparency 28-1
- Chapter Transparency 28

Multimedia
- 🔲 Interactive Tutor Self-Assessment Software
- 🔲 Testmaker

Race to the South Pole

Antarctica, 1911
Two European explorers–Roald Amundsen of Norway and Robert Scott of Great Britain–became engaged in a dramatic race to reach the South Pole. Amundsen and his companions began crossing the Ross Ice Shelf on October 19, 1911. They traveled on skis and used dogsleds to carry their supplies. They arrived at the South Pole on December 14. Scott and his party reached the Pole in January to find a Norwegian flag and a message from Amundsen. Then tragically, Scott and all his companions died on the return trip.

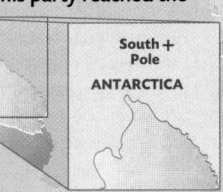

Germany hoped to gain economic control of the declining Ottoman Empire. Austria-Hungary set out to gain territorial access through the Balkans to the Aegean Sea. Russia aspired to take control of the Bosporus and the Dardanelles near the Black Sea and to extend the influence it already had over Manchuria in East Asia.

Competition turned to hostility as one power crossed another in its efforts to accomplish its goals. In 1898, for example, Great Britain and France confronted one another over rival claims in Egypt and the Sudan. The following year, Germany started to build the Berlin-Baghdad railway, which created resentment among both the British and the Russians. The British feared that the railroad would interfere with their interests in India and reduce traffic through the Suez Canal. The Russians thought the railroad interfered in their traditional areas of interest. In 1905, 1908, and 1911, Germany and France came close to war over control of Morocco.

Nationalism

Contributing to the tension was a growing spirit of nationalism. Nationalism had unified Germany and was rapidly becoming popular in France. There, French nationalists sought revenge against Germany for depriving France of the border provinces of **Alsace-Lorraine** in the 1870–1871 Franco-Prussian War.

The French novelist Victor Hugo urged France to "have but one thought: to reconstitute her forces, gather her energy, nourish her sacred anger.... Then one day she will be irresistible. Then she will take back Alsace-Lorraine." This put the Germans on their guard. They were well aware that the issue of Alsace-Lorraine was not settled permanently.

Slavic Nationalism

In Austria-Hungary, nationalism was creating the most violent tensions in Europe. The empire's Slavs were attracted to Pan-Slavism, the idea that the Slavs had a historic mission to develop their culture and unite into an empire. Slavic nationalists in neighboring Serbia supported the Slavs of Austria-Hungary. They wanted their own country to be the center of a South Slav, or Yugoslav, nation. This new Slavic state would be formed out of Slavic territories in Austria-Hungary.

Austria-Hungary was alarmed by Serbian activities in the Balkans. It feared that the idea of a Yugoslav state would attract restless Slavic groups in Austria-Hungary. Such a development would harm the security of the empire and lead to its eventual breakup.

In 1908 Austria-Hungary annexed the Slavic territories of **Bosnia-Herzegovina**, once the provinces of the Ottoman Empire. Angered at the Austro-Hungarian move, Serbia called on Russia, its traditional protector, for help. Russia, however, was still weak from the Russo-Japanese War and was not ready to fight again. In addition, Russia had made a secret deal with the Austro-Hungarians. The Russians had agreed to let Austria-Hungary have Bosnia-Herzegovina in exchange for the right for Russian warships to go through the Dardanelles. So, Russia persuaded the Serbs to restrain themselves. Then, Russia discovered that Austria-Hungary had made its move before Russia could get its part of the deal. As a result, the Russians were bitter.

Balkan Wars

The first Balkan war in 1912 further inflamed the Serbs. One of Serbia's war aims had been to acquire Albania, a small territory along the coast of the Adriatic Sea, an arm of the Mediterranean Sea. This would give Serbia the water outlet it desired. When, after winning the war, Serbia did not get Albania, Serb resentment grew even stronger.

In 1913 a second Balkan war broke out. Albania was made independent, frustrating once again Serbian ambitions. In this war, as in the last one, the Russians had not been able to support Serbia. This upset the Serbs and humiliated the Russians. Austria-Hungary, meanwhile, became increasingly worried about its future role in European affairs.

Chapter 28 *World War I* **739**

TEACH

Guided Practice

THEME Cooperation
Ask students to suggest different reasons why nations cooperate. (*Possible answers: for protection against mutual enemies, to help poorer nations, to increase trade and wealth, to manage common natural resources wisely.*) Ask which of these reasons are most likely to lead to war. (*protection against mutual enemies*) **L1**

Militarism Have students name the main components of militarism in the period before World War I. (*winning allies, increasing military spending, stockpiling arms, conscription, universal military training*) Ask which of these elements can be found in societies today. (*Answers will vary, but students may mention high levels of military spending.*) **L2**

Time Line Have students create a time line of the alliance systems formed between 1872 and 1907. Ask a volunteer to record the time line on the chalkboard. **L2**

 Chapter Transparency 28

Who? What? Where? When?

Slavs, modern descendants of an ancient people, are related mainly by their similar languages. Slavs include the Russians, Ukrainians, Belorussians, Poles, Czechs, Slovaks, Bulgarians, Croats, Slovenes, Serbs, and Macedonians.

COOPERATIVE LEARNING ACTIVITY

Roundtable Organize the class into small groups. Each group should represent one of the major nations that eventually became the Central Powers and the Allies. Have each "nation" list its grievances and fears vis-à-vis the others. Then have them reevaluate their lists in light of one factor changing–for example, if Germany agreed to return Alsace-Lorraine to France. Discuss how small incidents can lead to major shifts in alignments. **L3**

Independent Practice

 Guided Reading Activity 28-1 **L1**

 Time Line Activity 28

Competition Have students explain briefly why each of the following caused tension among the European powers: Berlin-Baghdad railway; Morocco; Alsace-Lorraine; Dardanelles. **L2**

ASSESS

Check for Understanding

Assign Section 1 Assessment as homework or as an in-class activity.

◙ Use Interactive Tutor Self-Assessment Software to review Section 1.

Evaluate

Section Quiz 28-1

◙ Use the Testmaker to create a customized quiz for Section 1.

Reteach

Have students summarize the chief factors that constituted the "seeds" of war.

Reading Essentials and Study Guide 28-1

Enrich

Have students list the alliances the United States maintains today.

CLOSE

Have students point out on a map the main areas of tension in Europe, the Middle East, and Africa in 1914. For each area, have students indicate whether the tensions were due principally to nationalistic feelings or imperialist rivalries.

Militarism

As tensions began to rise, so did militarism, the glorification of war and the military. The European powers assessed each other's military strength. They compared military training programs and levels of spending. They also looked at levels of industrialization and tried to estimate how fast a nation could ready its troops for battle.

Diplomats maneuvered to win new allies. Military leaders argued for increased military spending and more arms. After 1870, all the powers except Great Britain adopted conscription, the compulsory call-up of civilians for military service, and universal military training. They were sure that their national security depended on the technology, skill, and readiness of their military forces.

Each nation's actions caused a reaction in the other nations. For example, when Germany decided in 1898 to expand its navy, Great Britain felt threatened. The Germans argued that they needed a larger navy to protect colonial and merchant shipping and "for the general purpose of greatness." Great Britain claimed that as an island nation that depended on trade for many vital supplies, it had to be able to control the seas. To do this, said the British, they had to maintain a navy as large as the combined fleet of their two nearest rivals.

Alliances

Along with militarism came a hardening of the alliance systems, or the defense agreements among nations. In 1873 **Otto von Bismarck** created the Three Emperors' League, which united Germany, Austria-Hungary, and Russia. His purpose was to isolate France. The Emperors' League, however, did not last very long because of Austrian-Russian rivalry in the Balkans. Bismarck then created a new and stronger alliance with Austria-Hungary.

In 1882 Italy joined the Austrian-German alliance, and it became known as the Triple Alliance. Italy joined because it wanted allies against France. The Italians were angry with the French for occupying Tunis, or present-day Tunisia, in North Africa. They also were afraid that the French might send an army to defend the pope, with whom they were having a dispute. The three powers of the Triple Alliance agreed that if any one member became involved in a war with two or more enemies, the others would provide support.

In 1890 another alliance began to evolve as Russia and France developed friendlier relations. In 1894 Russia and France signed a military alliance in which they agreed to come to each other's aid in case of an attack by either Germany or Austria-Hungary, or by both powers. This was followed in 1904 by the Entente Cordiale between France and Great Britain. The term *entente* refers to a friendly understanding between two nations that, at the same time, lacks the binding commitments of a full-fledged alliance.

All of these agreements developed into the Triple Entente, a loose alliance between France, Russia, and Great Britain. Russia, an autocratic monarchy, and France, a democratic republic, were willing to ally out of a common fear of Germany and Austria-Hungary. Great Britain, a democratic monarchy, was willing to join because it was alarmed by Germany's naval-building program. It felt hard pressed to protect its empire on its own.

Thus, by 1907, the great powers of Europe had aligned themselves in two opposing combinations. On one side stood the Triple Alliance. On the other stood the Triple Entente. Instead of making their members more secure, however, these alliances threatened the peace of the continent. Given the conditions of the Triple Alliance and the Triple Entente, a minor conflict between rival nations had the potential to involve all major European powers in war.

SECTION 1 ASSESSMENT

Main Idea
1. Use a diagram like the one below to identify main causes of World War I.

Causes of World War I

Recall
2. **Define** militarism, conscription, alliance system, *entente.*
3. **Identify** Otto von Bismarck, Triple Alliance, Triple Entente.

Critical Thinking
4. **Evaluating Information** What were the factors that led

to the formation of alliances before the outbreak of World War I?

Understanding Themes
5. **Cooperation** Given the conditions that existed in Europe before 1914, could the nations of that continent have avoided a major war? If so, how?

SECTION 1 ASSESSMENT ANSWERS

1. European rivalries for economic and political influence; nationalism: French nationalists sought revenge against Germany, Slavic nationalism, Balkan Wars in 1912 and 1913; militarism; alliances: Triple Alliance, Triple Entente
2. All terms are defined in the Glossary.
3. Otto von Bismarck, 740; Triple Alliance,

740; Triple Entente, 740
4. fear of military threats from rival powers; nationalistic rivalries; imperialistic rivalries
5. **COOPERATION** Answers will vary. Possible answer: They probably could have avoided a major war if some differences had been negotiated.

JUNE 28, 1914 Slav nationalist assassinates Austria's Archduke Francis Ferdinand.

JULY 28, 1914 Austria-Hungary declares war on Serbia.

AUGUST 1, 1914 Germany declares war on Russia.

AUGUST 4, 1914 Great Britain declares war on Germany.

Section 2

The Spark

Read to Find Out
Main Idea *A series of events provided the spark that ignited World War I.*

▶ **Terms to Define**
ultimatum, mobilization

▶ **People to Meet**
Francis Ferdinand, Gavrilo Princip, William II, Nicholas II

▶ **Places to Locate**
Sarajevo, Serbia

Nearly one month after Archduke Francis Ferdinand was assassinated at the Bosnian capital of Sarajevo, some European leaders suspected that the crisis would pass. Newspaper headlines carried other stories. Cabinet minister Lloyd George of Britain told the House of Commons: "I cannot help thinking that civilization which is able to deal with disputes among individuals and small communities ... should be able to extend its operations to the larger sphere of disputes among states." Before he finished his address, Austria had delivered an ultimatum to Serbia. World War I was about to begin.

Assassination at Sarajevo

—adapted from *The Modern World*, edited by Esmond Wright, 1979

Until 1914, a false optimism prevailed in Europe. Although military buildups continued, most Europeans did not really think there would be a major war. Almost a century of relative peace had followed the Congress of Vienna. The absence of a major war for so long a period had lulled many Europeans into believing that such a war would not ever happen again.

Major social reforms and important scientific advances during the 1800s reinforced the belief that the world was improving steadily and that people had outgrown the need for war to solve their problems. Most countries were enjoying economic prosperity. A war would destroy what had been built up over the years. Despite this optimism, war did come, triggered by the assassination in the Balkans. That event set in motion the diplomatic moves that ended in war.

TURNING POINT

Trouble in the Balkans

On June 28, 1914, Archduke **Francis Ferdinand**, nephew and heir to Austro-Hungarian Emperor Francis Joseph, paid a visit to **Sarajevo** (SAR•uh•YAY•voh), the capital of Bosnia-Herzegovina. Francis Ferdinand planned, upon becoming emperor, to give the Slavs of Bosnia-Herzegovina and other parts of the empire a voice in the government equal to that of the Austrians and Hungarians. This political action might have defused the movement for a separate Slavic state.

Before the archduke and his wife, Sophie, began their ride through the streets of Sarajevo in an open car, seven young assassins had already taken their places along the route. All were members of a secret nationalist group based in **Serbia** known as the Black Hand, or Union of Death. Although the archduke and Sophie survived the first assassin's attempt, their luck did not hold.

Chapter 28 *World War I* **741**

SECTION THEME

▶ **Conflict** Tensions between the two European alliances erupt into a European-wide conflict.

Guide to Reading

For reading strategies to help students read effectively see pages 12–13.

Vocabulary Pre-check

◉ Use the Vocabulary PuzzleMaker for Chapter 28 to create a crossword puzzle to reinforce section terms. **L1 LEP**

📁 Use Vocabulary Activity 28 to introduce vocabulary terms. **L1 LEP**

FOCUS

Section Objective
Describe the series of events that provided the spark that ignited World War I.

BELLRINGER
Motivational Activity

Project Section Focus Transparency 28-2 and have students answer the questions.
📁 This activity is also available as a blackline master.

TURNING POINT

Trouble in the Balkans
What was the significance of the assassination of Austrian Archduke Ferdinand?
It triggered World War I by bringing the two rival European alliances into conflict.

Chapter 28 *World War I* **741**

SECTION RESOURCES

Reproducible Masters
- Lecture Notes 28-2
- Reproducible Lesson Plan 28-2
- Vocabulary Activity 28
- Guided Reading Activity 28-2
- Section Quiz 28-2
- Reading Essentials and Study Guide 28-2

🎞 **Transparencies**
- Section Focus Transparency 28-2

Multimedia
◉ Interactive Tutor Self-Assessment Software
◉ Testmaker
◉ Turning Points in World History: *Assassination Ignites World War I*

TEACH

Guided Practice

THEME Conflict

Have students study the map on page 742, then create a list of all the possible sources of conflict between the major powers in Europe at this time. Discuss how one of these sources of conflict might have led to World War I if Archduke Ferdinand had not been assassinated. **L1**

Map Study

Answer

Triple Entente countries, they surrounded the Triple Alliance countries and had better access to the sea

Map Skills Practice

Reading a Map What geographic advantages did the Central Powers have over the Allied Powers? *(They had better access to western Asia; also, because they were centrally located, they could move troops quickly from one theater of war to another.)*

VIDEODISC
Turning Points in World History

Side Two
Chapter 4

Title: *Assassination Ignites World War I*

Ask: Why did the assassination of the archduke plunge Europe into war? *(A web of European alliances caused most major nations to declare war.)*

Europe in 1917

- Central Powers
- Allied Powers
- Neutral nations

Map Study
World War I split Europe into two armed camps.
Location Which side do you think had the better strategic location: the Triple Alliance or the Triple Entente countries?

When the couple's car took a wrong turn, 19-year-old **Gavrilo Princip** (gah•VREE•loh PREEN•seep) fired his gun, fatally wounding them both.

German Support

Although the assassination had not occurred in Serbia, Austro-Hungarian leaders held the Serbians responsible. They were encouraged in this line of thinking by their German allies and by Count Leopold Berchtold, the Austro-Hungarian foreign minister. On July 5, Berchtold sent an envoy to Berlin to talk to the German emperor, **William II**. William assured the envoy that Germany would give its full support to any actions Austria-Hungary might take against Serbia. The next day, the German chancellor officially repeated this promise to the Austro-Hungarian government. In effect, Germany gave Austria-Hungary permission to do with Serbia as it pleased.

Declaration of War

On July 23, Austria-Hungary gave Serbia an ultimatum, a set of final conditions that must be accepted to avoid severe consequences. The ultimatum demanded that Serbia allow Austro-Hungarian officials into the country to suppress all subversive movements there and to lead an investigation into the archduke's murder. Austria-Hungary gave Serbia 48 hours to agree to these terms or face war. Berchtold knew, however, that the ultimatum "would be wholly impossible for the Serbs to accept."

Although the ultimatum outraged Serbian leaders, they knew that their nation was not ready for war with Austria-Hungary. Therefore, on July 25, they responded in a conciliatory manner. They rejected, however, the demand that Austro-Hungarian officials take part in the investigation and trial of those involved in the assassination.

COOPERATIVE LEARNING ACTIVITY

Dramatization Organize students into small groups and have them stage a series of radio or television newscasts devoted to the outbreak of World War I. Each group should select a critical date from June 28 to August 4. They should incorporate researched information with the text material. Have groups include comments by participants, descriptions of citizen responses, and speculation as to what will happen next. **L3**

The Serbian answer did not satisfy Austria-Hungary. Consequently, on July 28, 1914, exactly one month after the assassination of Archduke Ferdinand, Austria-Hungary declared war on Serbia. Both countries immediately issued general orders for mobilization, the gathering and transport of military troops and fighting equipment in preparation for war. News of these mobilizations spread quickly across the European continent.

A European War

Many Europeans still believed war could be avoided. The major European powers pushed each other to the brink of war, believing that the other side would back down at the last minute. They were tragically mistaken.

Russia was the first to act once Austria-Hungary declared war. Knowing it had lost face often in the past, the Russian government had to support Serbia now or risk the bitter hatred of all the Slavs in the Balkan region. Although the czar was convinced that Germany would fight, he had also been assured through diplomatic channels that France would support Russia.

Consequently, on July 30, Czar **Nicholas II** ordered a general mobilization of his armed forces against both Austria-Hungary and Germany. Austria-Hungary mobilized against Russia the following day.

On July 31, Germany issued Russia an ultimatum to cancel its mobilization order or face war. On the same day, Germany gave France 18 hours to decide whether or not it would remain neutral if Germany went to war with Russia. France's answer was to give its support to Russia. When Czar Nicholas did not even reply to Germany's ultimatum, Germany declared war on Russia on August 1. Germany declared war on France two days later.

The British, meanwhile, were undecided on the question of going to war. They still hoped to use negotiations to avoid conflict. They did not make it clear whether or not they would support France and Russia. Germany hoped that Great Britain would stay neutral.

The same day that Germany declared war on Russia, however, the German army marched into Luxembourg. The Germans then demanded passage across Belgium, claiming that France intended to invade that country at any moment. Belgium was a neutral country whose borders and neutrality had been guaranteed in an 1839 treaty signed by Great Britain, Russia, France, and Germany.

The Belgians refused the Germans entry into their territory and appealed to Great Britain for help. When the Germans invaded Belgium on August 3, Britain protested and demanded withdrawal of German forces from Belgium. The German chancellor responded by calling the 1839 treaty "a scrap of paper." This left the British little choice. On August 4, Britain declared war on Germany.

The outbreak of war in August 1914 was generally greeted with confidence and rejoicing by the peoples of Europe. In an outburst of patriotic enthusiasm, crowds gathered in the streets, squares, and railway stations of European cities to cheer on the military forces of their respective nations. As the conflict unfolded, most Europeans believed in the war as a matter of defending their country's honor or upholding "right against might."

Few people, however, imagined how long or how devastating a war between the powers of Europe could be. Designed to protect nations against their enemies, the European alliance systems instead dragged a whole continent into war. What began as a local dispute between Austria-Hungary and Serbia eventually became a global conflict that had no clear, limited objective.

SECTION 2 ASSESSMENT

Main Idea
1. Use a diagram like the one below to identify the series of events that led to World War I.

↓
↓
↓
World War I

Recall
2. **Define** ultimatum, mobilization.
3. **Identify** Francis Ferdinand, Gavrilo Princip, William II, Nicholas II.

Critical Thinking
4. **Evaluating Information** Historians have long argued over which European nation was most responsible for the start of World War I. Using examples to support your statements, explain which country you think was most responsible for World War I.

Understanding Themes
5. **Conflict** Why do you think World War I came as a surprise to many Europeans?

SECTION 2 ASSESSMENT ANSWERS

1. Archduke assassinated; Austria-Hungary gave ultimatum to Serbia, Serbia rejected it; war against Serbia declared; Germany declared war on Russia and France, invaded Belgium; Britain declared war on Germany
2. The terms are defined in the Glossary.
3. Francis Ferdinand, 741; Gavrilo Princip, 742; William II, 742; Nicholas II, 743

4. Possibilities: Austria-Hungary, because of its rigid ultimatum; Germany, because of the tacit permission it gave Austria-Hungary.
5. **CONFLICT** The period preceding it was one of optimism. Europeans were proud of their material progress. Also, there had been no major wars since Napoleon.

Time Line Have students create a time line on the chalkboard listing events from the assassination of Francis Ferdinand (June 28) to Britain's declaration of war against Germany (August 4). **L2**

Independent Practice

Guided Reading Activity 28-2 **L1**

Biography Have students research Gavrilo Princip and write a short biographical sketch of him, including what happened to him after the assassination of Archduke Francis Ferdinand. **L2**

ASSESS

Check for Understanding

Assign Section 2 Assessment as homework or as an in-class activity.

Use Interactive Tutor Self-Assessment Software to review Section 2.

Evaluate

Section Quiz 28-2

Use the Testmaker to create a customized quiz for Section 2.

Reteach

Have students recount in their own words the causes of World War I.

Reading Essentials and Study Guide 28-2

Enrich

Have students write an essay on how World War I might have been avoided.

CLOSE

Have students discuss why the Balkans have been called "the powder keg of Europe."

Section 3

The War

SECTION THEME

▶ **Conflict** The European war is transformed into a war that engulfs much of the world; the global conflict directly affects many civilians as well as soldiers.

Guide to Reading

For reading strategies to help students read effectively see pages 12–13.

Vocabulary Pre-check

 Use the Vocabulary PuzzleMaker for Chapter 28 to create a crossword puzzle to reinforce section terms. **L1 LEP**

Use Vocabulary Activity 28 to introduce vocabulary terms. **L1 LEP**

FOCUS

Section Objective

Specify where and how World War I was fought.

BELLRINGER
Motivational Activity

 Before taking roll at the beginning of the class period, project Section Focus Transparency 28-3 and have students answer the activity questions. Discuss students' responses.

This activity is also available as a blackline master.

Guide to Reading

Read to Find Out
Main Idea *World War I was fought in many areas and with an array of methods and weapons.*

▶ **Terms to Define**
belligerent, propaganda, war of attrition, trench, contraband

▶ **People to Meet**
Alfred von Schlieffen, Helmuth von Moltke, Joseph Jacques Joffre, Henri-Philippe Pétain, Winston Churchill, Woodrow Wilson

▶ **Places to Locate**
Paris, Tannenberg, Verdun, Gallipoli

The Storyteller

François was only 8 years old when war's realities entered his small French village. Gendarmes delivered the official notice of death on the field of honor to the towns, villages, and farms. A hush fell when the names were read. Then the word spread. "Gustave was killed, the little clerk who had looked so handsome in his cavalryman's uniform. Alcide, Jules, Léon, Maurice, Rèmi, Raoul—all killed." In horror, François

 watched his neighbors' grief. Childhood playmates, cousins, the only sons of families, and brothers all perished in battle. "They remained on their battlefields in the great military cemeteries, neat and orderly, hidden forever."

French soldiers in the trenches

—adapted from "World War I: A Frenchman's Recollections," reprinted in *The Global Experience*, vol. 2, 1987

By August 1914 the major powers of Europe had lined up against each other. Germany and Austria-Hungary, joined by the Ottoman Empire and Bulgaria, became known as the Central Powers. Great Britain, France, Russia, Serbia, Belgium, and, later, Japan and Montenegro, became known as the Allied Powers, or Allies. Claiming that Austria-Hungary and Germany had acted aggressively rather than defensively, Italy remained neutral.

In spite of their military buildups, none of the European powers was fully prepared for what lay ahead. For example, cavalry and horse-drawn vehicles still played an important role in each nation's army—traditions that were quickly discarded. Nations from both sides also seriously underestimated the length of the war. No country had stockpiled enough war materials or ammunition to last more than six months. The widespread feeling among Europeans was that the war would be over by Christmas.

The Schlieffen Plan

Germany's invasion of Belgium on August 3 had been part of the Schlieffen Plan, a war strategy that German General **Alfred von Schlieffen** (SHLEE•fuhn) drew up in 1905. Germany's main problem was that it had enemies in both the east and the west. Schlieffen assumed, however, that Russia would be slow to mobilize. As a result, Schlieffen believed that the Germans could reach Paris and defeat the French in six weeks and then move on to the Eastern Front and fight against Russian forces.

Schlieffen's plan ran into problems from the beginning. First, German Commander **Helmuth von Moltke** led his troops through an area of Belgium that proved to be heavily fortified. Second, Moltke encountered far stronger resistance than anyone had expected; the German advance was

744 Chapter 28 *World War I*

---

delayed until August 20. Third, the Russian army mobilized far more quickly than Schlieffen had estimated, necessitating the movement of two German divisions to the Eastern Front.

The Germans were held up further when they met British forces in the north of France. British troops eventually had to retreat, but they fought expertly and inflicted heavy losses on the Germans. At the same time, the French attacked another wing of the German army in Alsace-Lorraine. The French offensive eventually collapsed but not before delaying the German advance yet again.

The Battle of the Marne

France struggled to recover after the defeat at Alsace-Lorraine. The French chief of command, General **Joseph Jacques Joffre**, pulled back his troops to protect **Paris**. While many Parisians fled the city, General Joseph Simon Gallieni strengthened the army in Paris to the point that it was able to launch a counterattack. To speed troops into position, the French army requisitioned several hundred Parisian taxis.

On September 5 the French and German armies collided in northeastern France in the Battle of the Marne. After four days of shelling, the French finally pushed the Germans back a distance of about 50 miles (80 km) from Paris. The attack saved Paris from the Germans and boosted French morale. Although German forces continued to hold much of France's heavily industrialized areas, the German retreat from the Battle of the Marne signified the abandonment of the Schlieffen Plan. It also made it clear that neither side was capable of defeating the other quickly or easily.

A Russian Disaster

Russia, meanwhile, kept its word to the French and sent troops into battle even before its military was fully mobilized. The speed with which the Russians moved surprised Germany and Austria-Hungary. By August 13 the Russians had invaded East Prussia from the south and from the east. This attack diverted German troops from the attack against the French and British during the first critical weeks of the war.

Russia's success did not last long. At the end of August, Russian and German troops met at **Tannenberg** in present-day Poland. There the Russians suffered a disastrous defeat from which they never fully recovered. At Tannenberg, the Germans were able to encircle and destroy the Russian army. They killed more than 30,000 Russian soldiers and took 92,000 prisoners. German casualties numbered only about 13,000.

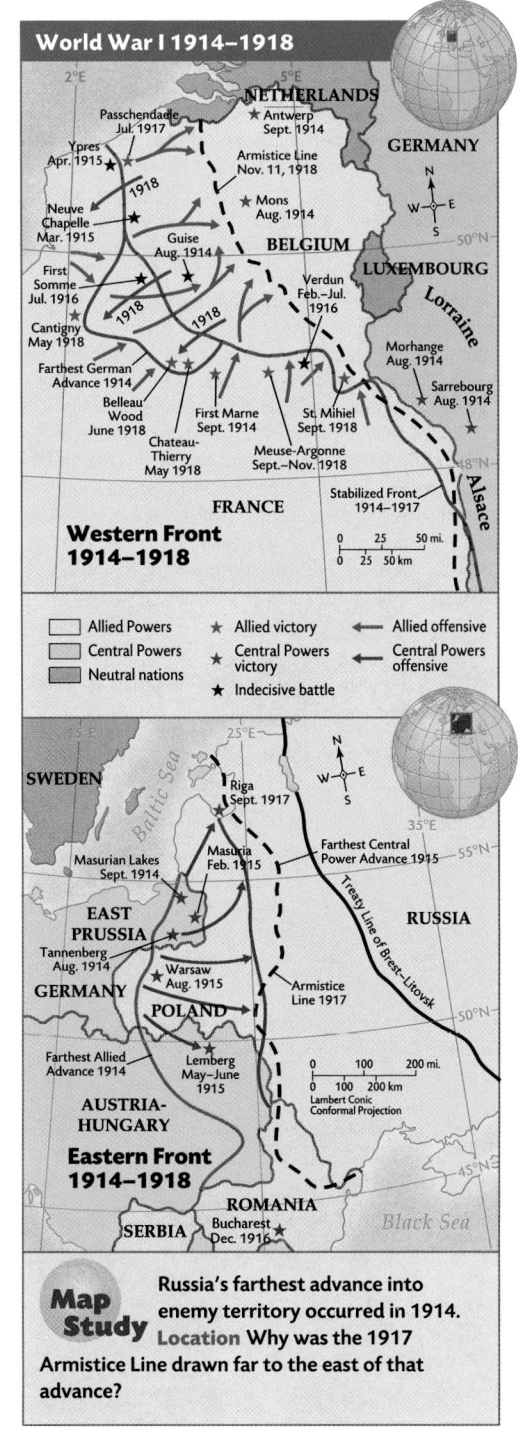

World War I 1914–1918

Western Front 1914–1918

☐ Allied Powers	★ Allied victory	⟵ Allied offensive
☐ Central Powers	★ Central Powers victory	⟵ Central Powers offensive
☐ Neutral nations	★ Indecisive battle	

Eastern Front 1914–1918

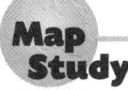

Map Study Russia's farthest advance into enemy territory occurred in 1914. **Location** Why was the 1917 Armistice Line drawn far to the east of that advance?

TEACH

Guided Practice

THEME Conflict
Have students write several reasons trench warfare was so deadly. Discuss these reasons as a class. Focus especially on how trench warfare resulted in a state of deadlock. (*Machine guns made successful offenses almost impossible; neither side had a way to break through the other's lines.*) **L1**

Military History Have students explain the significance of the Battle of the Marne. (*It signified the end of the Schlieffen Plan and also showed that the war would not end quickly.*) **L2 LEP**

Geography: Location Ask students why they think the Germans attacked the Allies through Belgium rather than more directly across Alsace and Lorraine. (*France probably expected a German attack from the east and so fortified its eastern boundary more heavily than its northern border with Belgium. Also, Alsace and Lorraine, once French, might have been more hostile to the Germans than Belgium was.*) **L3 LEP**

Map Study

Answer
By 1917 the Central Powers had pushed the front that far to the east.

Map Skills Practice

Reading a Map What aspects of fighting on the Western Front did not characterize the Eastern Front? (*indecisive battles, a stabilized front*)

COOPERATIVE LEARNING ACTIVITY

Report Have students research and present an oral report on the first six weeks of World War I. Assign each of five groups one of the following: the invasion of Belgium, the German sweep through France toward Paris, the retreat of the Allies, Russian mobilization and early victories ending at Tannenberg, and the Battle of the Marne. Individual students should gather information on a specific topic within his or her group. Then ask each group to present its report to create a composite picture. **L2**

Years of Deadlock

After the Battle of the Marne, the Germans and the Allies began a series of battles known as "the race to the sea," with each attempting to reach the North Sea first and outflank the other. As the Germans advanced toward the ports of Dunkirk and Calais, they ran into British troops at Ypres (EEPR), a town in western Belgium. The battle that followed brought high casualties to both sides. Despite the heavy sacrifices, there were no breakthroughs. At this point the war in the west settled into a stable front from the Swiss border to the North Sea coast. By November 1914 the war had already reached a stalemate.

All of the belligerent, or warring, nations now had to adjust their plans. To produce the needed ships, guns, food, ammunition, and medicines, large numbers of civilians had to enter the war effort. To raise morale, newspapers gave even the smallest victories big headlines. In addition, governments used propaganda—ideas or rumors used to harm an opposing cause—to portray the enemy as beastly and inhuman. Making peace with such an enemy seemed unthinkable.

Trench Warfare

By early 1915 the war on the Western Front had turned into a deadly war of attrition, in which each side tried to wear down the other side by constant attacks. To protect themselves, soldiers on both

Footnotes to History

Holiday Cheer
On Christmas Day, 1914, fighting stopped, and British and German soldiers met in "no-man's-land" to chat, play soccer, and pose for photographs! Officers, however, quickly ended these goodwill meetings, and the soldiers returned to their positions to take up firing at one another again.

Images of the Times

Industry Generates War Materials

More than any previous war, World War I demanded large-scale industrial production of military and transportation equipment.

This German officer's helmet and the English gas mask and pack were produced by their respective war industries.

746

Images of the Times
Industry Generates War Materials

The Allies faced problems in supplying their troops because they had expected the war to be short and mobile. But when soldiers dug in on the Western Front, they needed much larger quantities of war materials, especially ammunition, than had been foreseen. Not only were supplies short, but hundreds of the skilled male workers needed to produce more shells had volunteered for or been drafted into the army. For many of the warring nations, women workers provided vital help in war industries.

sides dug trenches, or ditches. Eventually, two parallel trenches stretched for about 500 miles (805 km) in an unbroken line from Switzerland to the North Sea. Land mines and barbed wire protected the area in front of each trench. The desolate area that separated the two sides, which could vary from a half a mile to a few yards, was known as "no-man's-land."

Soldiers lived in the trenches for weeks at a time, fighting boredom and terror. They endured cold, mud, rats, and disease. To attack, the soldiers charged "over the top" of their own trenches and ran across "no man's land" to the enemy's trenches. As attackers struggled through the barbed wire, their opponents mowed them down with heavy artillery and machine guns.

Throughout 1915, battle followed battle, and casualties mounted. At the battle of Ypres, the Germans introduced a new weapon—poison gas. From cylinders in their trenches, they released yellow-green chlorine gas. The wind carried the gas into French trenches, causing blindness, choking, vomiting, torn lungs, and death. Wilfred Owen, an English poet and soldier, described the horrors of poison gas in his poem "Dulce et Decorum Est" (1916):

    ❝ Gas! Gas! Quick, boys!—An ecstasy of
        fumbling,
    Fitting the clumsy helmets just in time;
    But someone still was yelling out and
        stumbling
    And flound'ring like a man in fire or lime …
    Dim, through the misty panes and thick
        green light,
    As under a green sea, I saw him drowning. ❞

Verdun and the Somme

The year 1916 opened with the war on the Western Front still stalemated. Although Italy had denounced the Central Powers six months earlier and entered the war on the side of the Allies, it had gained little ground after four battles against the Austro-Hungarians. Then in February 1916, the Germans made a move. They staged a surprise

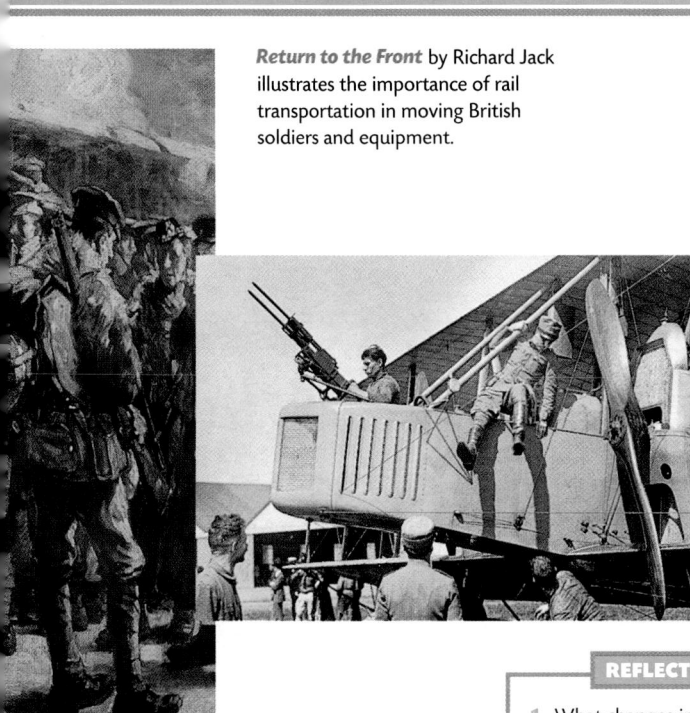

Return to the Front by Richard Jack illustrates the importance of rail transportation in moving British soldiers and equipment.

Training begins on a military airplane in Mineola, New York. At the beginning of the war Germany had more planes than did the United States. Most American pilots flew French and English planes.

REFLECTING ON THE TIMES

1. What changes in production take place in industrial nations during war?
2. How does developing technology affect the training of a nation's armed forces?

747

ANSWERS TO REFLECTING ON THE TIMES

1. They must switch from making peacetime goods to meeting wartime needs. They have to do so quickly, since lives are at stake.
2. Troops must be trained in the use of new and unfamiliar technologies; specialization is often the result, with specific personnel trained to use specific equipment.

Chapter 28
Section 3

Who?What?Where?When?

"Dulce et Decorum Est" The title of Wilfred Owen's poem is the first phrase of a line from the Latin poet Horace, "Dulce et decorum est pro patria mori," meaning "It is sweet and honorable to die for one's country." Owen's use is ironic—fitting for a man who himself was killed on the battlefield.

Independent Practice

📁 Guided Reading Activity 28-3 **L1**

📁 Geography and History Activity 28

Science, Technology, and Society Have students research and report on the use of poison gas in World War I—the different types used, when and where employed, effects, and effectiveness. **L2**

Who?What?Where?When?

Edith Cavell, an English nurse working in Belgium, was an Allied heroine of World War I. After the Germans occupied the country, she helped Belgian, French, and British soldiers escape. Arrested in 1915, she confessed and was sentenced to die by the firing squad. Her execution in October, though legally justified, aroused worldwide condemnation.

Propaganda Have students research and report on the propaganda issued by both sides during World War I. If possible, they should bring examples, such as posters, to class. **L2**

you don't say...

Blimp The German dirigibles known as zeppelins, which were used to drop bombs on London, had their counterpart in British balloons known as blimps. The English word comes from the original designation—*B* for balloon and *limp* indicating that the gas bag was not rigid, having no metal framework.

inking Past and Present

Flaming Coffins

Because World War I aircraft were so vulnerable, the men who flew them were widely admired. Pilots who shot down five enemy planes were known as "aces." Among the best-known aces of the war were Georges Guynemer of France, Manfred von Richthofen of Germany, "Mick" Mannock of England, and Eddie Rickenbacker of the United States.

ANSWERS
They were flimsily built and had no brakes. There was no radio communication, either. Modern planes are safer, faster, and more maneuverable, with jet engines, thinner and flatter wings, and heat-resistant materials.

attack against French forces at **Verdun**, a massive fortress in northeastern France on the Meuse River. The French, under General **Henri-Philippe Pétain** (PAY•TAN), rallied to the cry "They shall not pass." After six months, the French still held firm, and the Germans finally abandoned the attack. The Battle of Verdun was one of the bloodiest of the war. Before the struggle ended, both sides had suffered more than a half million casualties.

Later that year, the British, aided by a small French force, launched a similar offensive against the Germans in the Somme River valley in northern France. The Battle of the Somme turned out to be as terrible and inconclusive as the one at Verdun, costing the Germans about 500,000 men, the British 400,000, and the French 200,000. Although the British introduced another new weapon during this battle—an armored vehicle called the tank—it made little difference to the outcome of the struggle. Tanks were still too clumsy and slow to be an effective weapon, and the generals on both sides did not yet understand how best to use them.

The Eastern Front

The Eastern Front in Russia was less entrenched than the Western Front in France; the war there was far more mobile, involving constant changes in battlefield positions. Neither side, however, was able to achieve a complete victory.

In 1915 Germany and Austria-Hungary made determined efforts to remove Russia from the war. As the least industrialized of the European powers, Russia did not have the resources and skills to fight a modern conflict. By year's end, the Russians had been forced to give up territory greater than the whole of France. In addition to suffering a staggering number of casualties, they had lost ammunition and guns equal to the amount they had possessed when the war began. The Allies, however, had promised Russia control of Constantinople and the Dardanelles if their side won the war.

Inspired by this agreement, the Russians went to work rebuilding their army. In March 1916 they launched an offensive against the Germans but made little headway. A few months later, however, they fared much better against Austria-Hungary. In addition to capturing many cities, they took several hundred thousand prisoners. They paid a heavy toll in the process, however, losing more than a million men and most of their supplies.

Although morale in the Russian army suffered greatly as a result of the 1916 offenses, their efforts

CONNECTIONS

Science and Technology

Flaming Coffins

Airplanes added a new dimension to fighting in World War I. For the first time, combat took place not only on land and at sea but also in the air. Crude but operational, these noisy, pitching, and bucking machines were not built with the pilot's safety foremost in mind. The typical plane was made of thin wood reinforced by steel wire. Its body and wings were covered by cloth coated with a highly flammable liquid. The pilot sat on a seat directly over the fuel tank. Fire was such a constant danger that airplanes were often referred to as "flaming coffins."

Battle between German and British planes

Brakes did not exist on World War I-era planes. On takeoff, the crew had to hold the plane back while the pilot revved the engine. On landing, the pilot had to turn the engine off and on to slow the approach. Once the pilot was airborne, contact with the ground was possible only if an unwieldy Morse code transmitter was on board.

Today, military aircraft are safer, faster, and more maneuverable. For example, the development of jet engines has enabled planes to fly much faster than before. Other recent innovations increasing the speed and range of planes include the development of thinner and flatter wings and the use of more effective heat-resistant materials.

inking Past and Present ACTIVITY

In what sense were World War I airplanes "crude" vehicles? Compare World War I-era military aircraft with that of today.

748   Chapter 28   *World War I*

MEETING SPECIAL NEEDS ACTIVITY

Mixed Learners Encourage students needing extra reinforcement to summarize the material under each subhead in this section in a manner of their own choosing. Some students may elect to prepare oral summaries. Students may be divided into small groups. Each group would assign a subsection to pairs of students who would prepare the summaries.

Visual learners might draw a series of cartoons depicting such subjects as the battles, the weapons used, or trench warfare. Gifted students may use outside resources to enhance their summaries. This activity may be done in groups or individually. **L2 LEP**

Visualizing History The Gallipoli Campaign took a savage toll on both sides. The Allies lost more than a quarter of a million men as casualties. Turkish losses were almost as great.

Answer to Caption: *to supply Russia and strengthen Serbia through the Dardanelles; to take Constantinople and thus end Ottoman participation in the war; to precipitate the collapse of Austria-Hungary*

Visualizing History These heavy guns were not enough to overcome the resistance of the Turks at Gallipoli. *What were Churchill's three main goals in attacking Turkey?*

Who?What?Where?When?

Mustafa Kemal was the commander of the Turkish forces at Gallipoli. After the war he became the first president of the newly created nation of Turkey.

Linking Past and Present

Wristwatches were first introduced in Switzerland in 1790. For over a century, however, they were worn only by women. Men traditionally used pocket watches. It was not until World War I, when pocket watches were impractical at the front, that men started to wear wristwatches.

ASSESS

Check for Understanding
Assign Section 3 Assessment as homework or as an in-class activity.

⚬ Use Interactive Tutor Self-Assessment Software to review Section 3.

Evaluate
▭▱ Section Quiz 28-3

helped the Allies on the Western Front. The Germans had to transfer several divisions from the west to the east, hampering the effectiveness of their attack at Verdun.

Gallipoli Campaign

As the war dragged on and casualties soared, each side tried to find ways to turn the war in its favor. In Great Britain, **Winston Churchill**—head of the British navy—asked, "Are there not other alternatives than sending our armies to chew barbed wire in Flanders?" Churchill favored opening an offensive on the Dardanelles strait, which Turkey controlled. This strait was the only practical means of supplying Russia and of strengthening Serbia. From there, the Allies could take Constantinople and possibly put the Ottoman Empire out of the war. This offensive, Churchill believed, might also lead to the collapse of Austria-Hungary.

The Allies' initial offensive in early 1915 nearly succeeded, but a lack of planning and reinforcements gave the Turks time to rearm. When the Allies followed up in April with a land attack on the peninsula of **Gallipoli** (guh•LIH•puh•lee), the Turks drove them back. On January 9, 1916, the Allies finally withdrew the last of their troops.

On the Seas

The British, meanwhile, had been dominating the seas. They were determined to keep the Germans from invading Great Britain and to keep war materials from reaching the Central Powers by sea. The Germans were just as determined to disrupt Allied shipping. Both Great Britain and Germany depended heavily on the seas for their food and war materials. Without those goods, neither country could continue the war.

Great Britain blockaded all ports under German control at the start of the war. The blockade was so effective that Germany had to receive most of its supplies through the neutral countries of Holland, Denmark, Sweden, and Norway. The Germans protested that the blockade violated international law and called it "the hunger blockade." Ignoring these protests, the British also stopped ships they suspected of carrying contraband, or prohibited goods. They escorted these ships into port and seized their cargoes.

Chapter 28 *World War I* **749**

MAKING CONNECTIONS ACTIVITIES

Daily Life Have students research and report on the effects of the war on civilians. Among the subjects they might investigate are: rationing; restrictions on transportation; and the role of popular entertainment. **L2**

Economics Have students research and report on how the war was paid for, with special attention to the sale of war bonds. **L3**

TEACH

Tell students that the main line of trenches on the Western Front was established by November 1914. It ran almost 500 miles from the North Sea to Switzerland. One reason it became relatively fixed as soon as it did was that both sides were too exhausted and too short of war materials to launch major offensives in the fall; over the winter, troops had an opportunity to dig in and make their positions more defensible. Ask students why both sides were in such bad shape after only four months of war. *(They expected a short war and had not stockpiled enough arms and ammunition.)*

Linking Past and Present

Gallipoli One of the most effective movies ever made about World War I is *Gallipoli* (1981). It tells the story of two Australian soldiers who take part in the unsuccessful Allied attack on the Turkish peninsula.

In the Trenches

In the Dardanelles Campaign of 1915 these soldiers of the British Empire fought to capture Gallipoli. Held by the Ottoman Empire, Gallipoli was a strategic location for supplying Russia and the Eastern Front of the war. These troops have hastily dug a trench on their way up a hillside. There they could make use of periscopes and wait for their officers to decide whether they should go "over the top." Three of the men in this photo are Australian. The heavy losses sustained by Australian troops in the Gallipoli Campaign fostered a new sense of Australian identity.

It was on the Western Front, however, in Fr and Belgium, that trench warfare was most g some. In ditches and tunnels called trenches armies of the Allies and the Central Powers se into a war of position. The units of horse cavalry had pranced proudly into war were replaced by soldiers hunkered into trenches, facing the en across a no-man's-land of barbed wire. Stuck in and water, soldiers lived alongside lice and rats a the smell of dead horses and dead men. It was a British poet Wilfred Owen wrote, "obscene as cer" and "bitter as ... vile." ⊕

Submarine Warfare

To wear down British sea power, the Germans introduced submarine warfare. At first, German submarines, or U-boats, struck only warships. In 1915 they also began to strike civilian and commercial ships, many of which were carrying supplies to the Allies. In May 1915 a German U-boat torpedoed the British passenger liner *Lusitania*. About 1,200 people, including 128 Americans, were killed. The Germans argued that the *Lusitania* carried weapons.

By March 1916, German U-boats had sunk other British and French ships. This led President **Woodrow Wilson** to threaten to sever diplomatic relations if Germany did not agree to stop attacking passenger and freight vessels. The Germans responded by ending unrestricted submarine warfare for a while.

In May 1916, the only major battle between the British and German fleets took place off the coast of Denmark. Both sides claimed victory, but the Battle of Jutland, as it was called, still left the British in control of the seas and the Germans bound by the British blockade.

United States Enters War

One of the most important events of 1917 was United States's decision to enter the war. Until this point, American public opinion was divided about the conflict in Europe. Many Irish Americans were staunchly anti-British, and many German Americans sided with the Central Powers. Other Americans, mostly of English, Scottish, and Scots-Irish descent, favored the Allies. The majority of Americans, however, agreed with President Wilson that the war was strictly a European conflict. While

incidents such as the sinking of the *Lusitania* in 1915 angered them, Americans were not ready to take an active part in the war.

Meanwhile, the Germans did not want the Americans to enter the war. At the same time, they were determined to break the British blockade and end British control of the seas. They believed that the way to do this was by resuming a policy of unrestricted submarine warfare. Germany announced that beginning February 1, 1917, it would sink any merchant ships heading to British or western European ports. President Wilson responded by breaking off diplomatic relations with Germany.

Tensions between the two countries grew worse in March 1917 when American newspapers printed a message from the German foreign minister, Arthur Zimmermann, to his ambassador in Mexico. Zimmermann promised that, in return for Mexican support, Germany would help Mexico to regain New Mexico, Texas, and Arizona. The British had passed on the Zimmermann telegram to the American government, and the message's publication heightened anti-German attitudes in the United States.

After the German sinking of four American merchant ships, President Wilson on April 2, 1917, asked Congress for a declaration of war and called upon Americans to help "make the world safe for democracy." American financial aid and military intervention led to an eventual Allied victory.

Student Web Activity 28

Visit the *World History: The Human Experience* Web site at **worldhistory.glencoe.com** and click on *Chapter 28—Student Web Activities* for an activity relating to World War I propaganda.

SECTION 3 ASSESSMENT

Main Idea
1. Use a chart like the one below to list warfare methods and weapons used in World War I.

World War I

Methods	Weapons

Recall
2. **Define** belligerent, propaganda, war of attrition, trench, contraband.
3. **Identify** Alfred von Schlieffen, Helmuth von Moltke, Joseph Jacques Joffre, Henri-Philippe Pétain, Winston Churchill, Woodrow Wilson.

Critical Thinking
4. **Synthesizing Information** Determine the main factors working against the avoidance of a stalemate in trench warfare.

Understanding Themes
5. **Conflict** Explain how World War I was a new kind of war. Consider objectives, strategy, and technology.

Chapter 28 *World War I* **751**

United States Enters War
How did American entry into World War I affect the conflict? *It added military and economic strength to the Allies at a time when they were being exhausted.*

Use the Testmaker to create a customized quiz for Section 3.

Reteach

Discuss the major events on the Western and Eastern Fronts, and at sea; technological advances used, and their effects; events prior to and following the entrance of the United States into the war.

Reading Essentials and Study Guide 28-3

Enrich

Have students read Mark Helprin's *A Soldier of the Great War*. Have them select several passages to read aloud in class.

CLOSE

Have students summarize the situations of the Allies and the Central Powers in the spring of 1917. *(The prospect of victory was slim for both sides at this point.)*

Have students use the **Chapter 28 Student Web Activity** at worldhistory.glencoe.com for in-depth study of World War I propaganda.

SECTION 3 ASSESSMENT ANSWERS

1. methods: trench warfare, blockades, submarine warfare, infantry attacks, naval battles; weapons: poison gas, tanks, airplanes, submarines
2. All terms are defined in the Glossary.
3. Alfred von Schlieffen, 744; Helmuth von Moltke, 744; Joseph Jacques Joffre, 745; Henri Pétain, 748; Winston Churchill, 749; Woodrow Wilson, 751
4. Answers will vary but should show an understanding of trench warfare.
5. **CONFLICT** Old strategies did not take into account the contingencies of war and surprise moves by the enemy. In World War I, strategists had to react to many new situations as they arose; new technology—machine guns, land mines, submarines, tanks, airplanes—made it possible to kill people in unprecedented numbers.

The Lusitania

Special Report Summary

In 1915 a German submarine sank the British luxury liner *Lusitania*, killing more than 1,000 people and helping draw the United States into World War I.

To clear up questions about the sinking, scientists used a robot vehicle to examine the wreck on the ocean floor.

Although the ship was carrying arms, the team found that the weapons had not exploded when a torpedo struck the *Lusitania*. This disproved a once-popular theory of why the ship sank so fast.

The team hypothesized that the powerful secondary explosion that caused the ship to sink in only 18 minutes was probably caused by the ignition of coal dust in a storage compartment.

Passengers boarding the British liner R.M.S. *Lusitania* in New York on May 1, 1915, for the voyage to Liverpool, England, knew of Germany's threat to sink ships bound for the British Isles. England and Germany had been fighting for nine months. Still, few passengers imagined that a civilized nation would attack an unarmed passenger steamer without warning.

Built eight years earlier, the *Lusitania* was described as a "floating palace." German authorities, however, saw her as a threat. They accused the British government of using the *Lusitania* to carry ammunition and other war materials across the Atlantic.

With her four towering funnels, the liner looked invincible as she left New York on her last voyage. Six days later, at 2:10 p.m. on May 7, 1915, Walther Schwieger, the 30-year-old commander of the German submarine U 20, fired a single torpedo at the *Lusitania* from a range of about 750 yards.

Captain William Turner of the *Lusitania* saw the torpedo's wake from the navigation bridge just before impact. It sounded like a "million-ton hammer hitting a ste boiler a hundred feet high," one senger said. A second, more pow ful explosion followed, sending a geyser of water, coal, and debris high above the deck.

Listing to starboard, the liner began to sink rapidly at the bow, sending passengers tumbling dov her slanted decks. Lifeboats on th port side were hanging too far inboard to be readily launched, while those on the starboard side

752 Chapter 28 *World War I*

TEACHER NOTES

_____
_____
_____
_____
_____

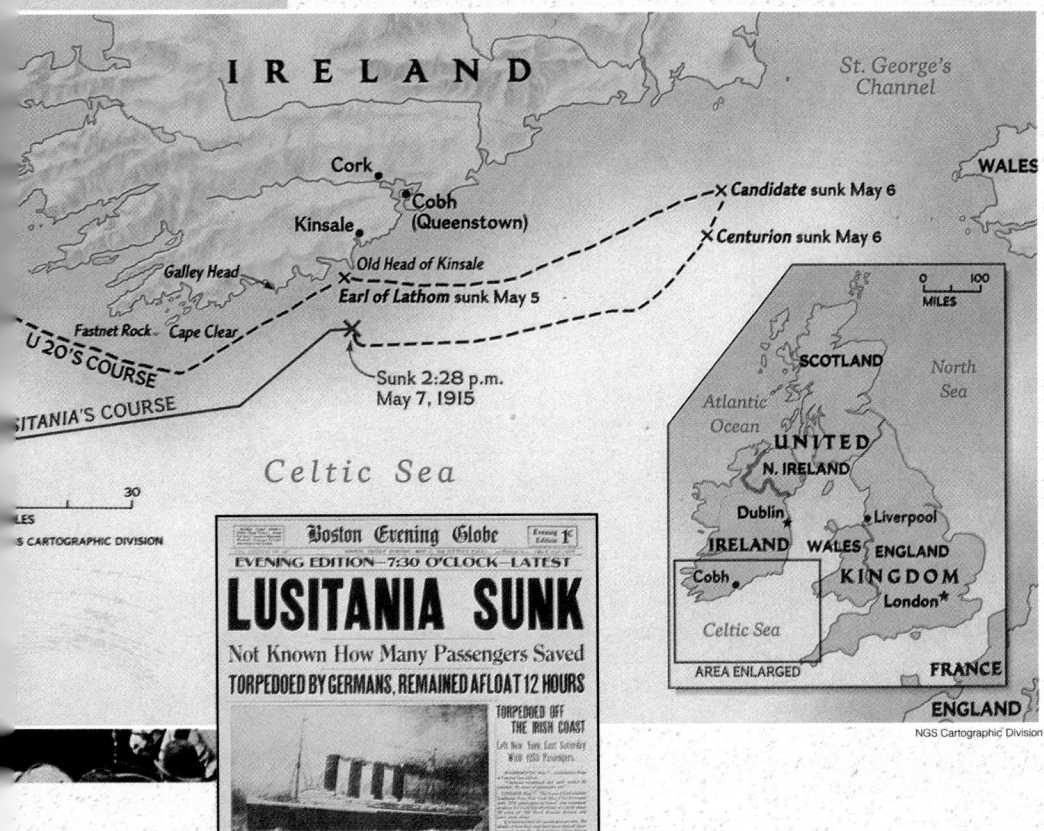

Boston Evening Globe

EVENING EDITION—7:30 O'CLOCK—LATEST

LUSITANIA SUNK

Not Known How Many Passengers Saved

TORPEDOED BY GERMANS, REMAINED AFLOAT 12 HOURS

TORPEDOED OFF THE IRISH COAST

Titanic Historical Society Inc.

NGS Cartographic Division

TEACH

Points to Discuss

After students have read the feature, ask the following: Why did the sinking of the *Lusitania* anger many Americans? *(because sinking the unarmed passenger vessel killed more than 1,000 civilians, including* 128 Americans) What questions were raised about the sinking? *(Was the ship warned about German submarines? Why did one torpedo sink it so fast? Was it armed, as Germany claimed? What caused a second explosion?)* What did researchers learn by examining the wreck with a robot vehicle? *(They found that weapons carried by the* Lusitania *had not exploded, and they hypothesized that the second explosion was caused by the ignition of coal dust.)*

e too far out to be easily board- Several overfilled lifeboats spilled upants into the sea. The great r disappeared under the waves in 18 minutes, leaving behind a ble of swimmers, corpses, deck rs, and wreckage. Looking back n the scene from his submarine, n German commander Schwieger shocked. He later called it the st horrible sight he had ever seen. News of the disaster raced across Atlantic. Of 1,959 people aboard, y 764 were saved. The dead uded 94 children and infants. Questions were immediately ed. Did the British Admiralty

give the *Lusitania* adequate warning? How could one torpedo have sunk her? Why did she go down so fast? Was there any truth to the German claim that the *Lusitania* had been armed?

From the moment the *Lusitania* sank, she was surrounded by controversy. Americans were outraged by the attack, which claimed the lives of 128 U.S. citizens. Newspapers called the attack "deliberate murder" and a "foul deed," and former President Theodore Roosevelt demanded revenge against Germany. The attack on the *Lusitania* is often credited with drawing the United States into

■ The Lusitania *arrives in New York on her maiden voyage in 1907 (opposite page).*

■ *In the two days prior to the attack on the* Lusitania, *the German submarine U 20 had sunk three ships off Ireland's southern coast. Yet the captain of the* Lusitania, *who had received warnings by wireless from the British Admiralty, took only limited precautions as he approached the area. Headlines in Boston and New York report the terrible news of the sinking of the* Lusitania *on May 7, 1915 (above).*

Chapter 28 *World War I* **753**

Cultural Perspectives

Rules of War Although the *Lusitania* carried arms in its hold, under the rules of war at the time, it was not considered a legitimate target. Even so, before the *Lusitania* sailed, Germany published a warning in American newspapers: "NOTICE! Travellers … are reminded that a state of war exists … that the zone of war includes the waters adjacent to the British Isles; that … vessels flying the flag of Great Britain, or of any of her allies, are liable to destruction."

FUN FACTS

- Woodrow Wilson's secretary of state, William Jennings Bryan, resigned rather than sign a strongly worded protest Wilson sent to Germany after the *Lusitania*'s sinking.
- The name of the ship came from the ancient Roman province of Lusitania, which made up the region that is now Portugal and western Spain.
- The cargo of arms and ammunition that the *Lusitania* was carrying weighed about 173 tons.
- The British admiralty had recommended that the *Lusitania* follow a zigzag course, changing direction every few minutes, to avoid torpedo attacks.

Linking Past and Present

Shipwrecks In recent years a number of wrecked ships have been raised from the ocean bottom by scientists and entrepreneurs. The salvage operations have generated controversy about the ownership of the materials recovered, which can be worth millions of dollars.

Among the better-known cases are the Padre Island wrecks in Texas and the case of *Nuestra Señora de la Atocha* in Florida.

CURRICULUM CONNECTION

SCIENCE AND TECHNOLOGY

The first submarine to be used in combat was built by an American, David Bushnell, in 1776, and was used during the Revolutionary War. It was made of wood and moved by means of a hand-turned propeller. (The craft was used in an unsuccessful attempt to blow up a British warship in New York harbor.) By the late 1800s, an American engineer named Simon Lake had made considerable advances in submarine technology, including the use of horizontal rudders for diving and water ballast for submergence. However, the U.S. Navy was slow to see the merits of Lake's work. It wasn't until several European governments had made use of Lake's ideas in the early 1900s that he was hired by the United States.

World War I. President Woodrow Wilson—though he had vowed to hold Germany responsible for its submarine attacks—knew that the American people were not ready to go to war. It was almost two more years before the United States joined the conflict in Europe.

A British judge laid full blame on the German submarine commander, while the German government claimed that the British had deliberately made her a military target. Tragically, inquiries following the sinking of the *Lusitania* revealed that Captain Turner had received warnings by wireless from the British Admiralty, but took only limited precautions as he approached the area where U 20 was waiting.

Rumors of diamonds, gold, and valuables locked away in *Lusitania's* safes have prompted salvage attempts over the years. To date, no treasure has ever been reported.

Perhaps the biggest puzzle has been the hardest to solve: Why did the liner sink so fast? Newspapers speculated that the torpedo had struck ammunition in a cargo hold, causing the strong secondary explosion. Divers later reported a huge hole in the port side of the bow, opposite where munitions would have been stored.

HOPING TO SETTLE the issue, a team from the Woods Hole Oceanographic Institution, sponsored by the National Geographic Society, sent their robot vehicle Jason down to photograph the damage. Fitted with cameras and powerful lights, the robot sent video images of the wreck by fiber-optic cable to a control room on the surface ship, *Northern Horizon*. A pilot maneuvered Jason with a joystick, while an engineer relayed instructions to the robot's computers. Other team members watched for recognizable

objects on the monitors. In addition to using Jason to make a visual survey of the *Lusitania*, the team of researchers and scientists also used sonar to create a computerized, three-dimensional diagram of how the wreck looks today.

From this data, it was discovered that the *Lusitania's* hull had been flattened—in part by the force of gravity—to half its original width. When Jason's cameras swept across the hold, looking for the hole reported by divers shortly after the sinking, there was none to be found. Indeed, no evidence was found that would indicate that the torpedo had detonated an explosion in a cargo hold, undermining one theory of why the liner sank.

Questions about her cargo have haunted the *Lusitania* since the day she went down. Was she carrying illegal munitions as the Germans have always claimed? In fact, she was. The manifest for her last voyage included wartime essentials such as motorcycle parts, metals, cotton goods, and food, as well as 4,200 cases of rifle ammunition, 1,250 cases of shrapnel (not explosive), and 18 boxes of percussion fuses. The investigation conducted by the Woods Hole team and Jason suggested that these munitions did not cause the secondary blast that sent the *Lusitania* to the bottom. So what did?

One likely possibility was a coal-dust explosion. The German torpedo struck the liner's starboard side about ten feet below the waterline, rupturing one of the long coal bunkers that stretched along both sides. If that bunker, mostly empty by the end of the voyage, contained explosive coal dust, the torpedo might have ignited it. That would explain all the coal found scattered on the seafloor near the wreck.

The *Lusitania's* giant funnels have long since turned to rust, an eerie

Brown Brothers

UPI/Bettmann

marine growth covers her hull, a her superstructure is ghostly wre age. Yet the horror and fascinatio surrounding the sinking of the g liner live on. With today's high-te nology tools, researchers and sci tists at Woods Hole and the Natio Geographic Society have provide another look—and some new answers—to explain the chain of events that ended with the *Lusita* at the bottom of the sea.

MORE ABOUT...

German U-Boat Attacks After the sinking of the *Lusitania*, German submarines continued to torpedo merchant vessels without warning. In March 1916, fearing the United States would enter the war, Germany stopped the attacks. With the war stalemated, however, Germany resumed unrestricted submarine attacks in February 1917, sinking four American ships in just two months. Wilson cited German violations of "freedom of the seas" as a reason for entering the war in April 1917.

ENLIST

Bowman Gray Collection, University of North Carolina, Chapel Hill

Jonathan Blair

Jonathan Blair

Captain William Turner of the Lusitania, (opposite page, top); Walther Schwieger, commander of the German submarine U 20 (opposite page, bottom).

Homer, a small robot, (left) explores a hole in the stern of the Lusitania that was cut by a salvage crew to recover silverware and other items.

A provocative poster (left) depicted drowning innocents and urged Americans to enlist in the armed forces. For the women pictured above, the image was all too real. Alice Drury (above left) was a young nanny for an American couple on the Lusitania. She and another nanny were caring for the couple's children: Audrey, Stuart, Amy, and Susan. Alice was about to give Audrey a bottle when the torpedo hit. Alice wrapped Audrey in a shawl, grabbed Stuart, and headed for the lifeboats. A crewman loaded Stuart, but when Alice tried to board, the sailor told her it was full. Without a life jacket and with Audrey around her neck, Alice jumped into the water. A woman in the lifeboat grabbed her hair and pulled her aboard. Audrey's parents were rescued too, but Amy, Susan, and the other nanny were lost. Alice and Audrey Lawson Johnston (above right) have remained close ever since.

Chapter 28 *World War I* **755**

you don't say...

"There is such a thing as a man being too proud to fight," President Wilson explained on May 10. Although Wilson had sent several stern diplomatic notes to Germany following the *Lusitania*'s sinking, he had stopped short of delivering an ultimatum that would lead to war. Most Americans were horrified by the attack, but they supported Wilson's measured response.

Portfolio Project

Have students discuss the effect of the *Lusitania*'s sinking on U.S. public opinion. Organize the class into two groups and have each write a short newspaper editorial either for or against going to war with Germany as a result of the attack on the *Lusitania*.

TEACHER NOTES

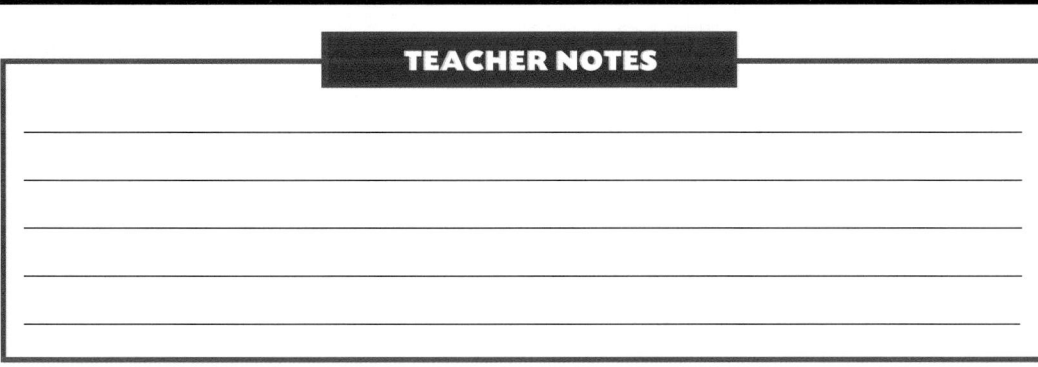

SECTION THEME

▶ **Revolution** Revolution in Russia overthrows the czar and brings Lenin and the Bolsheviks to power.

Guide to Reading

For reading strategies to help students read effectively see pages 12–13.

Vocabulary Pre-check

🔲 Use the Vocabulary PuzzleMaker for Chapter 28 to create a crossword puzzle to reinforce section terms. **L1 LEP**

📁 Use Vocabulary Activity 28 to introduce vocabulary terms. **L1 LEP**

FOCUS

Section Objective

Summarize the events that led to the Russian Revolution.

**BELLRINGER
Motivational Activity**

Before taking roll at the beginning of the class period, project Section Focus Transparency 28-4 and have students answer the activity questions. Discuss students' responses.
📁 This activity is also available as a blackline master.

1916　　　　　　1918　　　　　　1920

1917 Czar Nicholas II abdicates.

1918 Bolshevik Russia and Germany sign Treaty of Brest-Litovsk.

1919 Reds and Whites fight civil war.

Section 4

The Russian Revolution

Guide to Reading

**Read to Find Out
Main Idea** *A series of key events led to the Russian Revolution.*

▶ **Terms to Define**
provisional government, communism

▶ **People to Meet**
Nicholas II, Grigori Rasputin, Alexander Kerensky, Vladimir Ilyich Lenin, Leon Trotsky

▶ **Places to Locate**
Petrograd, Siberia, Poland, Ukraine

The Storyteller

Thousands filled the hall, waiting for Trotsky's speech. The crowd was tense, waiting. When Trotsky appeared, they applauded, but

Leon Trotsky

briefly, so as to hear that much sooner what he would say. Trotsky spoke of current conditions, and then continued. "The Soviet government will give everything the country contains to the poor and the men in the trenches. You, bourgeois, have two fur caps!—give one of them to the soldier, who's freezing in the trenches." The crowd surrounding Trotsky was aroused almost to ecstasy. This, actually, was already an insurrection. A transformation had begun.

—adapted from *The Russian Revolution,* N. N. Sukharov, translated by Joel Carmichael, 1917

756 Chapter 28 *World War I*

orld War I proved to be the breaking point for czarist rule in Russia. By 1917, morale in the Russian army had reached bottom. As many as one-fourth of the Russian soldiers, having no weapons of their own, had to pick up the guns of dead soldiers. Inadequate transport made grave food shortages even worse. Almost all of the country's resources went to supply the army, making the human and financial costs of war increasingly unbearable.

A nurse at the Russian front in 1917 described the situation that helped bring about the collapse of the autocracy and the establishment of a Communist state:

❝ **Discontent among the masses in Russia is daily becoming more marked. Disparaging statements concerning the Government are being voiced…. "Bring the men home!" "Conclude peace!" "Finish this interminable war once and for all!" Cries such as these penetrate to the cold and hungry soldiers in their bleak earthworks, and begin to echo among them. Now that food has grown scarce in Petrograd (St. Petersburg) and Moscow, disorder takes the shape of riots and insurrections. We are told that mobs of the lower classes parade the streets shouting 'Peace and Bread!'** ❞

Fall of the Czar

Events leading to the fall of the czar began to accelerate in the last half of 1916. Czar **Nicholas II** and his wife, Alexandra, had already become unpopular because of the czar's political incompetence and the couple's reliance on the mystic healer **Grigori Rasputin** (ra•SPYOO•tuhn). Wanting to

SECTION RESOURCES

📁 **Reproducible Masters**
• Lecture Notes 28-4
• Reproducible Lesson Plan 28-4
• Vocabulary Activity 28
• Guided Reading Activity 28-4
• Section Quiz 28-4
• Reading Essentials and Study Guide 28-4

📱 **Transparencies**
• Section Focus Transparency 28-4

Multimedia
📀 Interactive Tutor Self-Assessment Software
📀 Testmaker
💿 Communism and the Cold War: *Perspectives on Communism*

ave the monarchy, two relatives of the czar assist-
d in killing Rasputin in December 1916.

Rasputin's death did not solve the monarchy's
roblems. Public anger against the government
nounted as a result of food and fuel shortages, and
trikes erupted across the country. On March 8,
917, and for the next few days, hundreds of thou-
ands of men and women gathered in the streets of
etrograd (the Russian name given to St. Peters-
urg). Demanding food and an end to the war, the
rowds shouted, "Down with the czar!" On March
1 and 12, the troops the government ordered to put
lown the riots refused to fire on the crowds. Many
oldiers joined the protesters.

When the czar ordered his generals at the front
o crush the rebellion, they told him that any troops
hey might send to the capital would also join the
ioters. With the country sinking into chaos, the
zar finally abdicated on March 15, ending the 300-
ear-old Romanov dynasty. The March revolution
vas a spontaneous uprising of working people and
oldiers. It caused the loss of relatively few lives
and took place, surprisingly, without the leadership
f its revolutionary intellectuals, most of whom
vere living in exile abroad.

The Provisional Government

After Czar Nicholas II's abdication, political
uthority in Russia passed into the hands of a
temporary central government known as the
provisional government. This new regime called
for elections later in the year to choose a constituent, or constitutional, assembly. The constituent assembly would then establish a permanent government.

The provisional government, which consisted
of middle-class Duma representatives, soon had a
rival for power—the Petrograd Soviet of Workers'
and Soldiers' Deputies. Members of the Petrograd
Soviet were workers and peasants belonging to different socialist groups. The majority were either
Mensheviks or Social Revolutionaries, the political
heirs of the Populists. A smaller, more radical group
was the Bolsheviks.

One man who moved easily between the provisional government and the Petrograd Soviet was
Alexander Kerensky (keh•REHN•skee). A moderate socialist, Kerensky served first as the provisional government's minister of justice and then as its
prime minister. He also belonged to the executive
committee of the Petrograd Soviet.

The Petrograd Soviet became a model for the
founding of other soviets throughout Russia.

Together, the soviets called for an immediate peace,
the transfer of land to the peasants, and the control
of factories by workers. As the Russian economy
continued to collapse under the war effort, this
three-point program gained great popularity
among the Russian masses.

In spite of the suffering and anger of the
Russian people, however, the provisional government did not withdraw from the war. Desertion,
worsening transportation problems, and a drop in
already low armament production plagued the
Russian army. Preoccupied with war policy, the
provisional government could not carry out the
social reforms proposed by the soviets. As a result,
the government lost much of its popular support, a
factor that contributed to its eventual downfall.

Lenin

As the provisional government struggled to
maintain order, a variety of revolutionary groups
vied to fill the power vacuum. Since their split into
two factions in 1903, the Mensheviks and the
Bolsheviks had competed for control of Russia's
revolutionary movement. By 1917 the Mensheviks
far outnumbered the Bolsheviks. Because they
believed that a socialist revolution would be the
work of the masses, however, the Mensheviks did
not make concrete plans to seize control of the
Russian government.

The more radical Bolsheviks, on the other hand,
believed that a socialist society could be introduced
immediately by force. They claimed that a small
group of dedicated revolutionaries could carry out
the revolution with the help of a relatively small
working class and the peasants. They also believed
that Russia's revolution would spread worldwide.
Their leader, **Vladimir Ilyich Lenin**, urged them to
make plans to topple the provisional government
from power.

Born in 1870, Lenin came from a middle-class
provincial background. When Lenin was in high
school, his older brother, Alexander, became
involved in a plot to assassinate Czar Alexander III,
the father of Nicholas II. The attempt failed, however, and the government hanged Lenin's brother
and four fellow conspirators in 1887. Alexander's
death made a powerful impression on Lenin, who
dedicated his life to promoting a revolution.

In 1895 the Russian government arrested Lenin
for his activities and exiled him to **Siberia**. After his
release, he went to Germany, Great Britain, and
Switzerland, where he wrote revolutionary articles
and kept a close eye on the political situation in

Chapter 28 *World War I* **757**

TEACH

Guided Practice

THEME Revolution

Have students review the earlier
Russian Revolution, that of 1905.
*How was the situation different
in 1917? (widespread dissatisfaction
caused by Russian participation in
World War I)* **L1**

*The following videotape program is
available from Glencoe:*

• **Rasputin: The Mad Monk**

Independent Practice

 Guided Reading Activity
28-4 **L1**

SCIENCE

After the execution of Czar
Nicholas II and his family, their
bodies were disfigured by acid
and thrown into unmarked
graves. Not until the 1990s were
systematic efforts made to locate
and identify the Romanovs.
When some likely remains were
found, they were subjected to
DNA analysis. Prince Philip, husband of Britain's Queen Elizabeth
II, also was tested. DNA from his
blood matched DNA from a bone
fragment, proving that one of the
bodies was that of Philip's relative, Czarina Alexandra.

COOPERATIVE LEARNING ACTIVITY

Biographies Organize the class into four groups and assign each one a major figure in the
Russian Revolution: Czar Nicholas II, Kerensky, Lenin, and Trotsky. Have each group research its
assigned individual—his background, education, beliefs, and so on—and prepare a written or oral
report to present to the class. If possible, the report should be accompanied by illustrations. **L2**

VIDEODISC
Communism and the Cold War

Side One, Chapter 8
Frames 14264–14893
Title: *Perspectives on Communism*
Subject: Discussion of the ideals of communism
Ask: What did the Soviet Union feel it could teach the world? *(It felt the world needed to be taught to work collectively.)*

Literature Have students research and report on one of the following: Maksim Gorky, a champion of the revolutionary movement in Russia; Alexander Blok, who wrote "The Twelve," a poem about the revolution; or Vladimir Mayakovsky, who popularized the revolution. **L3**

The Bolshevik Revolution
What change did the Bolshevik Revolution bring to Russia and the rest of the world?
It established the world's first Communist state in Russia and promoted the spread of communism elsewhere.

Russia. After hearing the news of the March 1917 revolution, he wanted to return to Russia as soon as possible. Since Germany wanted Russia out of the war and knew that Lenin would promote a withdrawal, it provided him with a special "sealed" train that allowed no one to enter or exit during the trip. Lenin's goal upon his arrival in Russia was to organize the Bolsheviks and seize power from the provisional government.

Lenin realized that the provisional government could not maintain the support of the soldiers, peasants, and workers. His slogan, "Peace, Land, and Bread," promised the Russian people that Russia would withdraw from the war, that the peasants would be given land, and that everyone would have enough to eat. Another point in Lenin's program was that the soviets should become the nation's only government. This goal was summed up in the slogan "All power to the soviets!"

The Bolshevik Revolution

During the summer of 1917, a number of demonstrations against the provisional government broke out across Russia. Blaming these demonstrations on the Bolsheviks and calling Lenin a German agent, the government issued arrest warrants for all Bolshevik leaders, forcing Lenin into hiding. By late August, however, the Bolsheviks started to show new strength in local elections, and by mid-September they had gained control of the Petrograd Soviet.

In November 1917, the Bolsheviks staged a coup d'etat in Petrograd, overthrowing the provisional government. Bolshevik soldiers, workers, and sailors took over the main post office, the telephone system, electrical generating plants, and train stations. When the Bolsheviks turned the guns of the battleship *Aurora* against the Winter Palace, the former home of the czar, the ministers of the provisional government surrendered. As a result, the revolution was relatively bloodless.

In spite of the Bolshevik coup, the election for the constituent assembly still took place in late November. Of those elected, 420 seats went to the Social Revolutionaries and only 225 to the Bolsheviks. When the assembly met in Petrograd in January 1918, however, the Bolsheviks dissolved it after only one day.

Claiming absolute power, the Bolsheviks laid the foundation of a socialist state—ending private ownership of property, distributing land among the peasants, and giving workers control of factories

and mines. The Bolsheviks began calling themselves Communists and their political viewpoint based on the ideas of Marx and Lenin, communism. The Communists and their supporters in other countries created an international movement to spread their revolution throughout the world.

Civil War

In addition to building a socialist state, Lenin also sought peace with Germany. At a heavy price, Russia in March 1918 signed the Treaty of Brest-Litovsk, losing much western territory and a third of the population. Meanwhile, powerful nationalist movements set up independent governments in Estonia, Latvia, Lithuania, **Poland**, **Ukraine**, and the Caucasus lands of Armenia, Georgia, and Azerbaijan. Although in theory allowing these countries to break away from Russia, the Communists in practice used force to gain control in Ukraine and the Caucasus.

Reds and Whites

During the early months of 1918, Russia also slipped into a devastating civil war between the Communists and their political opponents. In this conflict, the Communists were called Reds, because they favored the red flag of revolution. Their opponents—royalists, liberal democrats, and moderate socialists—became known as the Whites.

Lenin's government was determined not to yield power. Under the Communist leader, **Leon Trotsky**, the Red Army was organized to defend the Communist state. Trotsky used force and education to foster loyalty to communism.

The Whites promised to defeat the Reds quickly and get Russia back into World War I against the Central Powers. As a result, they received military aid from the Allies and the United States. This did little to help the Whites, but it stirred Russian nationalist support for the Communists and increased Communist distrust of the West.

For three grim years, the fighting raged across the vast landscape. Both sides burned villages and killed civilians. When the Whites captured an area, they killed all suspected Communists. The Reds did the same to "counter-revolutionaries," or those believed to be opposed to communism. In the meantime, workers and peasants were starving and the nation's economy was crumbling.

The Terror

During the upheaval, the Communists further tightened their hold on Russia. They imposed a

---

Study Strategy Students may have trouble following the events in the chaotic period of the Russian Revolution. Have them construct a chart with dates (from 1916 to 1922) along the side and these headings across the top: *Leader(s) of Government; Political/Social Events.* **L3**

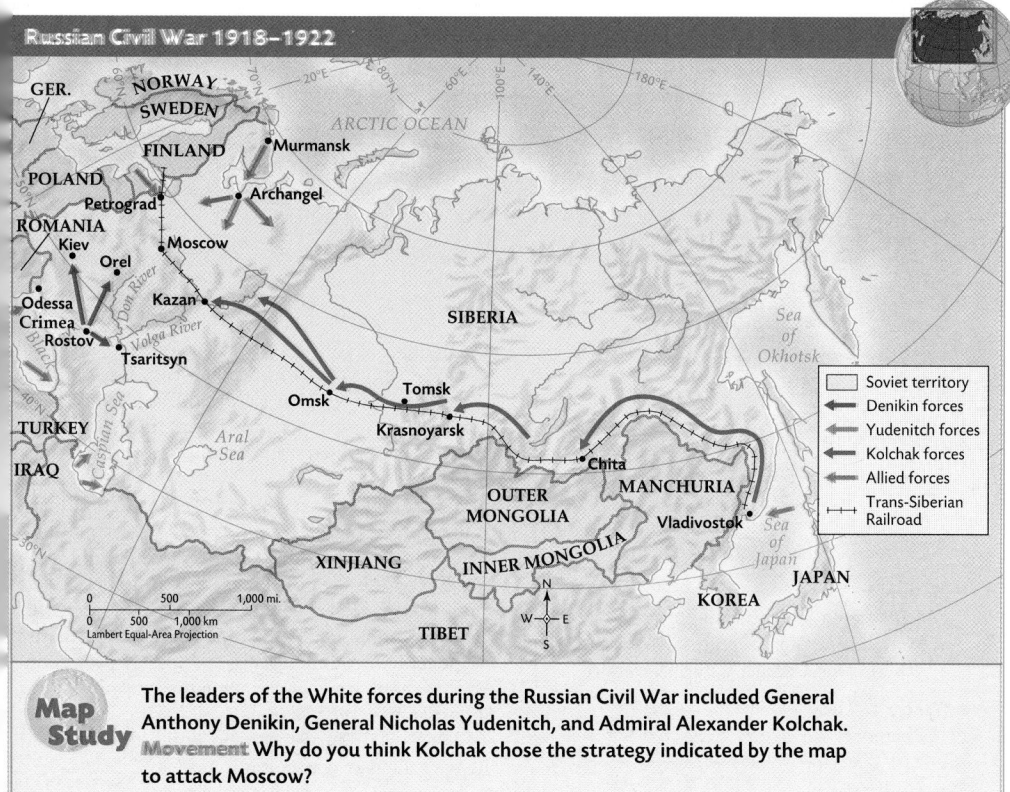

Russian Civil War 1918-1922

☐	Soviet territory
←	Denikin forces
←	Yudenitch forces
←	Kolchak forces
←	Allied forces
⊢⊢⊢	Trans-Siberian Railroad

Map Study The leaders of the White forces during the Russian Civil War included General Anthony Denikin, General Nicholas Yudenitch, and Admiral Alexander Kolchak. **Movement** Why do you think Kolchak chose the strategy indicated by the map to attack Moscow?

Map Study

Answer
He hoped that if he could seize control of the Trans-Siberian Railroad, he could control an important supply line and transport his troops to the main theater of action.

Map Skills Practice

Reading a Map From what regions did Denikin and Yudenitch attack? *(Denikin: from the Crimea, south of Moscow; Yudenitch: from the Baltic region, in the north)*

policy called "war communism"—taking direct control of industry and forcing peasants to send food to the starving cities. Lenin also used terror as a weapon against his opponents. In 1918 Communist soldiers killed the imprisoned czar and his family. A secret police force, the Cheka, arrested anyone considered an "enemy of the revolution." In keeping with communism's anti-religious viewpoint, Lenin placed severe restrictions on the Russian Orthodox Church.

Many Socialists who had backed Lenin's revolution now withdrew their support and fled Russia. At the same time, the Whites suffered from a lack of unity among their royalist, liberal, and moderate socialist supporters. Outnumbered, disorganized, and poorly equipped, the White armies finally admitted defeat. By 1921 Lenin had extended Communist control throughout the war-ravaged country.

SECTION 4 ASSESSMENT

Main Idea
1. Use a diagram like the one below to identify the events leading to the Russian Revolution.

```
        Russian
       Revolution
    ○            ○
  ○                ○
    ○            ○
```

Recall
2. **Define** provisional government, communism.
3. **Identify** Nicholas II, Grigori Rasputin, Alexander Kerensky, Vladimir Ilyich Lenin, Leon Trotsky.

Critical Thinking
4. **Evaluating Information** Do you think Vladimir I. Lenin was justified in closing down the democratically elected constituent assembly in January 1918? Why or why not?

Understanding Themes
5. **Revolution** What impact did the events of the Russian Revolution have on Russian and global affairs?

SECTION 4 ASSESSMENT ANSWERS

1. czar and wife unpopular; public anger over food and fuel shortages; March revolution; czar abdicated; provisional government; government struggled to maintain power; rise of Lenin; Bolshevik Revolution 1917
2. The terms are defined in the Glossary.
3. Nicholas II, 756; Rasputin, 756; Kerensky, 757; Lenin, 757; Trotsky, 758
4. Answers should show understanding of

Bolsheviks' political beliefs.
5. **REVOLUTION** It led to the collapse of one of the world's most powerful monarchies and the foundation of the first socialist state. Communism became the ideological basis of the Soviet Union, which sought to export revolution and/or expand its territory. This contributed to the rivalry with the United States.

ASSESS

Check for Understanding

Assign Section 4 Assessment as homework or as an in-class activity.

🔘 Use Interactive Tutor Self-Assessment Software to review Section 4.

Evaluate

▱ Section Quiz 28-4

🔘 Use the Testmaker to create a customized quiz for Section 4.

Reteach

Have students review the goals of the Bolsheviks and discuss why they appealed to the Russian people.

▱ Reading Essentials and Study Guide 28-4

Enrich

Have the class watch the film *Dr. Zhivago* and discuss its message and impact.

CLOSE

Have students summarize the effects of World War I on the Russian Revolution.

1917 United States declaration of war raises Allied morale.

1918 President Woodrow Wilson presents Fourteen Points.

1919 Allies sign Treaty of Versailles.

1917　　　　　　　　　1918　　　　　　　　　1919

SECTION THEME

▶ **Internationalism** The Treaty of Versailles provides for the creation of a League of Nations to mediate international disputes.

Guide to Reading

For reading strategies to help students read effectively see pages 12–13.

Vocabulary Pre-check

🔲 Use the Vocabulary PuzzleMaker for Chapter 28 to create a crossword puzzle to reinforce section terms. **L1 LEP**

📁 Use Vocabulary Activity 28 to introduce vocabulary terms. **L1 LEP**

FOCUS

Section Objective

Explain why the Treaty of Versailles was ultimately unsuccessful.

BELLRINGER
Motivational Activity

Before taking roll at the beginning of the class period, project Section Focus Transparency 28-5 and have students answer the activity questions. Discuss students' responses.

📁 This activity is also available as a blackline master.

Section 5

Peace at Last

Guide to Reading

Read to Find Out
Main Idea *Ultimately, the Treaty of Versailles was unsuccessful.*

▶ **Terms to Define**
convoy, armistice, reparation, mandate, cordon sanitaire

▶ **People to Meet**
T.E. Lawrence, Ferdinand Foch, Woodrow Wilson, Georges Clemenceau, David Lloyd George, Vittorio Orlando

▶ **Places to Locate**
Fiume

The **Storyteller**

    Four officers of France, Great Britain, America, and Italy marched into the Palace of Versailles to sign the treaty ending World War I. Harold Nicholson described the ceremony in his diary: "And then, isolated and pitiable, come the two German delegates, Dr. Muller and Dr. Bell. The silence is terrifying…. They keep their eyes fixed away from those two thousand staring eyes, fixed upon the ceiling. They are deathly pale…. Suddenly from outside comes the crash of guns thundering a salute. It announces to Paris that the second Treaty of Versailles had been signed….
    We kept our seats while the Germans were conducted like prisoners from the dock, their eyes still fixed upon some distant point of the horizon."

—adapted from *Peacemaking*, Harold Nicholson, reprinted in *Western Civilization, an Urban Perspective*, F. Roy Willis, 1973

German officer's helmet

760　Chapter 28　*World War I*

    Russia's withdrawal from the war was offset by the entry of the United States into the conflict. American intervention boosted Allied morale and gave the Allies much needed resources, both industrial and human. It took time for the Americans to build and train an army, but the American navy was of immediate help. United States Admiral William S. Sims introduced the idea of the convoy to guard Allied ships from German U-boats. Under the successful convoy system, merchant ships crossed the Atlantic in clusters surrounded by warships for protection. At the same time, improvements in mines and underwater explosives—as well as the use of the airplane for air surveying and bombing—changed the way the war was being fought.

Turning the Tide

    Until American forces arrived, the fighting along the trench lines in the Western Front continued without lasting gains for either side. In April 1917 a French offensive stalled, leading to losses so great that French forces mutinied. The British, in order to keep the Germans from taking advantage of French weakness, launched an offensive into Flanders, a coastal region of northern France and southwestern Belgium. Heavy rains, however, made the clay soil of Flanders an impassable expanse of mud. In November, the fighting finally came to an end at Passchendaele (PAH•shehn•dayl). Casualties were so enormous that both the British and the Germans were reaching the end of their reserves.

Total War

    By 1917, the pressures of war had brought notable changes to the societies of fighting countries. The demands of a large-scale mechanized war required the efficient use of human and natural resources. Governments therefore carried out the principle of total war, directing all people and resources to the

---

SECTION RESOURCES

📁 **Reproducible Masters**
- Lecture Notes 28-5
- Reproducible Lesson Plan 28-5
- Guided Reading Activity 28-5
- Reteaching Activity 28
- Enrichment Activity 28
- Section Quiz 28-5
- Performance Assessment Activity 28

- Spanish Chapter Summary 28
- Reading Essentials and Study Guide 28-5

🔖 **Transparencies**
- Section Focus Transparency 28-5

Multimedia
🔲 Vocabulary PuzzleMaker Software
🔲 Interactive Tutor Self-Assessment Software
🔲 Testmaker

war effort. Greatly increasing their powers, governments on both sides recruited, drafted, trained, and supplied large armies. They raised taxes and borrowed vast sums of money. They also placed controls on capitalist economies, setting prices and wages, rationing goods, and banning strikes. Even in democratic countries, censorship of the press and other media was imposed in an effort to control public opinion and to keep morale high.

Women also played an important role in the war effort. As millions of men went to the battlefields, many women took their places in factories making weapons and supplies. Other women became military nurses or joined special branches of the armed forces. War work proved the abilities of women in areas once limited to men. Although women had to leave many jobs after the war, their contributions had boosted their self-confidence and in the long term aided the ongoing struggle for women's rights. By war's end, many countries were ready to grant the vote to women.

Global War

World War I reached beyond Europe to other parts of the world. European imperialist nations obtained badly needed resources from their empires. They also turned to recruits from their overseas possessions to fight on the Western Front. Meanwhile, in parts of Asia and Africa, Allied forces, including those of Japan, won victories that enabled them to take control of German colonies.

For their services, colonial Asians and Africans expected citizenship or independence at war's end; however, they were often disappointed when European empires were not only preserved but often extended at their expense. In the Middle East, the Arabs, seeking freedom from Ottoman rule, backed the Allied cause. While the war on the Western Front was deadlocked, they helped the British advance in the Middle East and finally conquer the Ottoman Turks. For example, Arab guerilla fighters, led by **T.E. Lawrence**, a young British officer, harassed the Ottoman Turks and gave the British information about important Turkish military positions. Unknown to the Arabs, however, the British and the French had in the 1916 Sykes-Picot Agreement already determined to divide the defeated Ottoman Empire among themselves.

End of Fighting

In July 1918 an Allied breakthrough on the Western Front finally came. Under the unified command of French General **Ferdinand Foch** (FAWSH), Allied forces stopped a huge German offensive that had moved them back to within 40 miles (60 km) of

Visualizing History More than 2 million American soldiers made up of 42 infantry divisions served in France before the war ended in 1918. *How did the arrival of American troops affect the war's outcome?*

Paris. Aided by the arrival of American forces, the Allies then launched a counterattack that pushed the exhausted Germans back to the border of Germany. In September, German generals told Kaiser Wilhelm II that the war could not be won.

The collapse of other Central Powers followed. The Ottoman Turks asked for peace after an Allied drive through the Balkans, and the Austro-Hungarians surrendered following their defeat by the Italians at Vittorio Veneto in northern Italy. The Austro-Hungarian military collapse led to the revolt of the empire's many nationalities and the end of the Hapsburg monarchy.

Although the German army stood firm, morale in Germany gave way. On November 9, 1918, the kaiser abdicated, and a German republic was proclaimed. On November 11, the Germans signed an armistice, or agreement to end the fighting.

Effects of the War

The war shattered Europe's aristocratic order and increased political and social instability. Boundaries had to be redrawn in various parts of the world. Human misery also had become commonplace. Nearly 9 million soldiers were dead, and another 21 million of them were wounded.

Chapter 28 World War I **761**

Chapter 28
Section 5

TEACH

Guided Practice

THEME Internationalism

Ask students to define *internationalism. (having to do with two or more nations)* Then have them list the goals of the United States, Britain, and France in drafting a peace settlement after World War I. **L1 LEP**

Visualizing History U.S. soldiers, known as the American Expeditionary Force, were commanded by General John J. Pershing. This was the first American army ever sent to Europe.
Answer to Caption: *They helped bolster Allied morale and provided much needed human and industrial resources.*

Geography: Location Have students look at the map on page 764 and locate the new European nations created after the war. *(Finland, Estonia, Latvia, Lithuania, Poland, Czechoslovakia, Austria, Hungary, Yugoslavia)* **L2 LEP**

Linking Past and Present

Lafayette After the first U.S. troops landed in France, an American officer announced: "Lafayette, we are here." He was referring to the services rendered to the colonists during the American Revolution by a French aristocrat, the Marquis de Lafayette, who served as a valuable aide to George Washington.

COOPERATIVE LEARNING ACTIVITY

Presentation Organize the class into three groups to research and report on World War I in the Middle East. One group should research the life of T. E. Lawrence. The second group should research Britain's role on the Middle Eastern front, including its broken promise of Arab independence. The third group should research the goals and participation of the Arab peoples involved. All three groups should then meet to share their data in a presentation to the rest of the class.

L3

Graph Study

Answers

Russia; the United States; Russia was the least industrialized of the great powers and was ill-equipped to fight a mechanized war; the United States entered the war later and its troops had a powerful industrial economy behind them.

Practice

Reading a Chart Which side had the heavier casualties, the Allies or the Central Powers? *(the Allies)*

Independent Practice

 Guided Reading Activity 28-5 **L1**

Time Line Ask students to create a time line of events that led to Allied victory. They should begin with May 1917 (the first convoy) and end with the armistice in November 1918. **L2 LEP**

Biography

The following videotape program is available from Glencoe:

- **Woodrow Wilson: Reluctant Warrior**

Linking Past and Present

November 11, 1918—the day World War I ended—is a time when members of the armed services are honored in many of the former Allied countries. It is called Veterans Day in the United States, Remembrance Day in Canada, and Armistice Day in Britain.

Military Casualties in World War I

Dead

United States 116,000
Serbia-Montenegro 48,000
Others 25,000
Germany 1,773,000
Austria-Hungary 1,200,000
Ottoman Empire 325,000
Romania 336,000
Italy 650,000
British Empire 908,000
France 1,385,000
Russia 1,700,000
Bulgaria 87,000

Wounded

United States 234,000
Serbia-Montenegro 143,000
Others 80,000
Germany 4,216,000
Austria-Hungary 3,620,000
Ottoman Empire 400,000
Romania 120,000
Italy 947,000
British Empire 2,090,000
France 4,266,000
Russia 4,950,000
Bulgaria 152,000

☐ Central Powers
☐ Allied Powers

Graph Study The casualties resulting from World War I were worse than those of any other war before that time.
Which major power suffered the worst combined casualties? The least combined casualties? Why?

In addition, about 13 million civilians were dead of disease and starvation. Mass deaths or killings on a grand scale, such as those of the Armenians under the rule of the Ottoman Turks in 1915, added to the list of horrors.

Angry at Armenian support for the Allies and fearful of Armenian nationalism, the Turkish government decided to use the war as an excuse to end the long history of animosity between Turks and Armenians. The Turkish army first removed all Armenian soldiers from its ranks and deported them to labor camps. Then they rounded up Armenian civilians, roped them together, and drove them into the desert to starve. In other cases they destroyed whole Armenian villages and shot the inhabitants. Some historians have estimated that more than 1 million Armenians lost their lives in this slaughter.

Restoring the Peace

The hopes of many Europeans and North Americans focused on United States President **Woodrow Wilson**. Even before the war ended,

Wilson had put forth his Fourteen Points, a peace plan whose terms included international recognition of freedom of the seas and of trade, limitations on arms, and an end to all secret alliances. Wilson's plan also called for just settlements of colonial claims, the right of self-rule for all nations, and the establishment of a "general assembly of nations" to settle future problems peacefully. It was these points that Germany thought would be the basis of peace negotiations.

For the most part, everyone seemed to agree that Wilson's points should be the guiding framework for the peace settlement. There were only two major reservations—one was Great Britain's. Control of the seas had been a major British war aim vital to British interests. Great Britain depended on foreign trade for its survival and still ruled a vast overseas empire. The British, therefore, objected to the idea of open seas. The other reservation was held by France. Wilson had stated that there should be "no annexations, no contributions, and no punitive damages" as a result of the war. France believed that some statement demanding reparations, or payments for damages, should be included in any peace settlement.

MEETING SPECIAL NEEDS ACTIVITY

Learning Style: Visual/Spatial Have students compare the map of Europe in 1919 on page 764 with the map of Europe in 1915 on page 742. Ask them to make a list of all the ways Europe changed as a result of World War I. **L1 LEP**

The Paris Peace Conference

In January 1919, delegates from 27 nations gathered in Paris to work out 5 separate peace treaties known as the Peace of Paris. The Allies did not invite representatives from the defeated Central Powers or Russia. In a break with tradition, heads of state attended the conference. President Wilson represented the United States; Prime Minister Georges Clemenceau (KLEH•muhn•SOH), France; Prime Minister **David Lloyd George**, Britain; and Prime Minister **Vittorio Orlando**, Italy. Most of the decisions were made by these "Big Four."

It soon became clear that there was a large gap between the idealistic goals of Wilson and the nationalistic goals of the French, British, and Italian leaders. Lloyd George and Clemenceau wanted to make Germany pay for the war. Wilson's chief aim was to win support for his idea of an international assembly of nations. The League of Nations, as Wilson called it, became a bargaining point. Again and again, Wilson gave in on other issues to ensure the acceptance of the League of Nations.

The Treaty of Versailles

The Treaty of Versailles, the most important treaty of the Peace of Paris, spelled out the details of the Allied settlement with Germany. Lloyd George and Clemenceau prevailed in their goal to punish Germany. Militarily, the treaty reduced the German army and banned conscription and the manufacture of major war weapons.

The treaty reduced Germany in size as well. Germany had to return Alsace-Lorraine, seized in the Franco-Prussian War of 1870, to France. For a period of 15 years, France would also control the coal-rich Saar Basin, while Allied forces together would occupy the Rhineland region of Germany.

In the east, Germany had to renounce the Treaty of Brest-Litovsk. The Allies also reestablished an independent Poland out of lands held by Germany, Austria-Hungary, and Russia. So that it had access to the Baltic Sea, Poland received the Polish Corridor, a strip of land separating East Prussia from the rest of Germany.

The Treaty of Versailles stripped Germany of its overseas colonies as well. The Allies received Germany's overseas possessions as mandates, territories administered by other countries. Great Britain and France divided the African colonies, Australia and New Zealand split the Pacific islands south of the Equator, and Japan took the Pacific islands north of the Equator.

Although these terms were harsh, France and Great Britain were still not satisfied. The Allies also demanded that Germany accept blame for causing

the war and that it pay reparations for Allied war costs and damages.

The Allies signed the treaty at the Palace of Versailles on June 28, 1919. Only four of Wilson's Fourteen Points and nine supplementary principles emerged intact in the treaty. The most important of these was the Covenant of the League of Nations.

Other Settlements

The Allied Powers signed separate peace agreements with Austria, Bulgaria, Hungary, and Turkey. In them, the greatest attention was given to territorial matters. The Allies recognized the breakup of Austria-Hungary. Austria was left a small, economically weak country. Italy received from Austria German-speaking areas near the Brenner Pass in the Alps. Italy also wanted the port of **Fiume** on the Adriatic, but Wilson refused to agree.

New nations emerged in eastern Europe from the ashes of the old German, Russian, and Austro-Hungarian empires. These included Finland, Estonia, Latvia, Lithuania, Poland, Czechoslovakia, and Yugoslavia. The Allies, particularly France, regarded these countries as a cordon sanitaire (kawr•DOHN sah•nee•TEHR), or quarantine line, against potential threats from Russia or Germany. In creating Yugoslavia, the Serbs achieved their goal of forming a nation of South Slavic peoples. Hungary lost territory to Yugoslavia, Czechoslovakia, and Romania, while Bulgaria lost land to Yugoslavia, Greece, and Romania.

In the Middle East, the Allies divided what was left of the Ottoman Empire. The Arabs did not receive the independence that Great Britain had promised them. Instead, Palestine, Transjordan, and Iraq became British mandates. At the same time, Lebanon and Syria became French mandates.

Bitter Fruits

A general disillusionment set in after World War I. Slogans such as "the war to end all wars" and "to make the world safe for democracy" rang hollow after years of slaughter. In addition to killing millions of people, the war destroyed the homes and lives of millions more. Many people suddenly found themselves to be minorities within newly formed nations. Others who believed they would become the citizens of independent nations found their hopes dashed by the settlements. Those whose lands were defeated were embittered by the loss of territory and prestige.

The Germans felt an especially deep sense of resentment about their loss in World War I. Because

Cultural Perspectives

Anti-German feeling reached near-hysteria in many of the Allied countries during World War I. In the United States, German-language instruction was dropped from schools. In Britain, King George V changed his family name from the Germanic name "Saxe-Coburg-Gotha" to the English name "Windsor."

CURRICULUM CONNECTION

SCIENCE

Vitamins had been isolated before World War I. Only with the war, when medical examinations of draftees revealed widespread malnourishment, did people realize how important they were. Of 2.5 million British draftees examined in 1917–1918, 41 percent were in poor health, mainly because of inadequate nutrition.

ASSESS

Check for Understanding

Assign Section 5 Assessment as homework or as an in-class activity.

Use Interactive Tutor Self-Assessment Software to review Section 5.

MAKING CONNECTIONS ACTIVITY

Literature For writers who took part in World War I, the war was an unforgettable experience. Have students research and write brief biographies of writers who wrote fiction or memoirs about their experiences. Possible subjects include Robert Graves, Siegfried Sassoon, e. e. cummings, John Dos Passos, and Ernest Hemingway. Encourage students to read an actual work by their subject as well. **L2**

Map Study

Answer

Russia

Map Skills Practice

Reading a Map What European countries created after World War I no longer exist today? *(Czechoslovakia, Yugoslavia)*

Evaluate

 Section Quiz 28-5

 Use the Testmaker to create a customized quiz for Section 5.

Reteach

Have students list the major participants at the Paris Peace Conference and summarize the aims of each.

 Reteaching Activity 28

 Reading Essentials and Study Guide 28-5

Enrich

Have students research and write an essay on the history and activities of the present-day United Nations as an outgrowth of the earlier League of Nations. Ask students to compare the UN and the League in terms of their effectiveness.

 Enrichment Activity 28

CLOSE

Have a roundtable discussion about the ways the Treaty of Versailles prepared the way for World War II. Include the provisions of the treaty and the role that U.S. isolationism played in the aftermath.

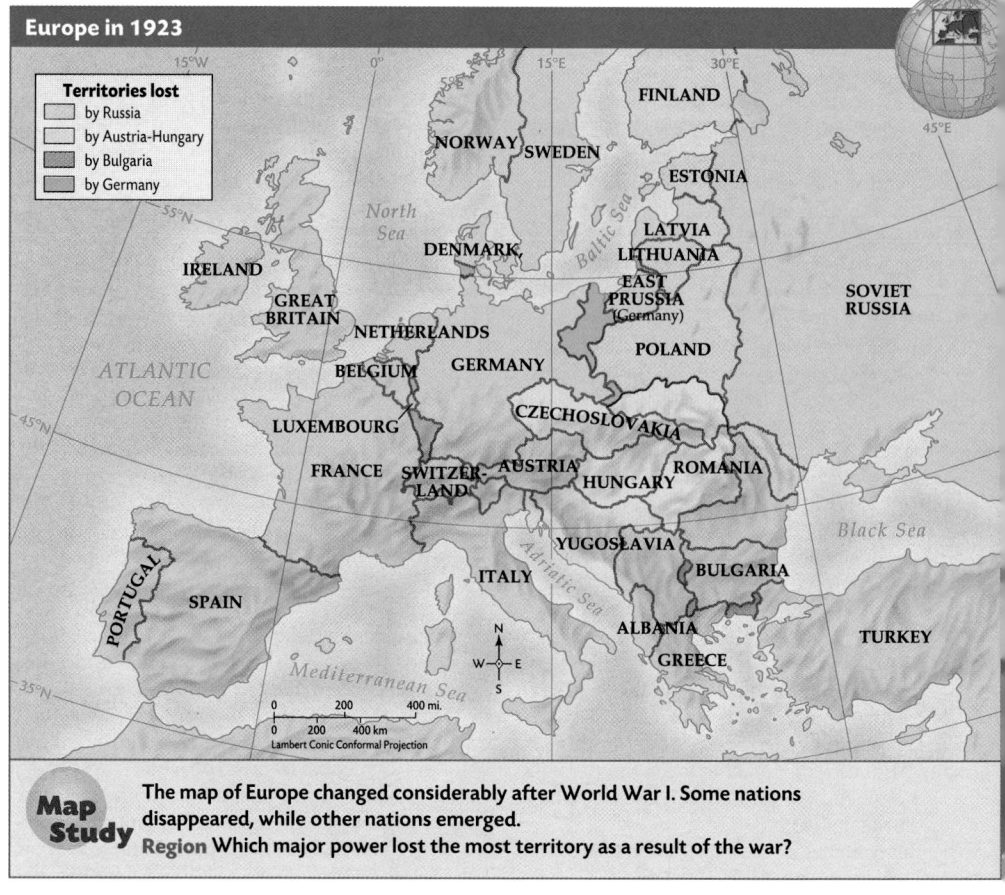

Europe in 1923

Territories lost
- by Russia
- by Austria-Hungary
- by Bulgaria
- by Germany

Map Study

The map of Europe changed considerably after World War I. Some nations disappeared, while other nations emerged.

Region Which major power lost the most territory as a result of the war?

they had fought mostly on foreign territory and used resources from other countries to supplement their own, German economic strength remained largely intact. The harsh provisions of the Treaty of Versailles, however, left Germany weakened and humiliated as well as deprived of great-power status. This made reconciliation with the Allies very difficult. The Germans' festering resentment burst forth upon the world with an even greater violence two decades later in the form of Nazism.

SECTION 5 ASSESSMENT

Main Idea

1. Use a diagram like the one below to give reasons why the Treaty of Versailles was not successful.

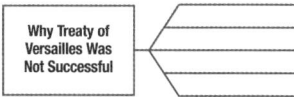

Why Treaty of Versailles Was Not Successful

Recall

2. **Define** convoy, armistice, reparation, mandate, cordon sanitaire.

3. **Identify** T. E. Lawrence, Ferdinand Foch, Woodrow Wilson, the Fourteen Points, Georges Clemenceau, David Lloyd George, Vittorio Orlando.

Critical Thinking

4. **Analyzing Information** How would a German citizen in 1919 have felt about the Treaty of Versailles?

Understanding Themes

5. **Internationalism** How could the Treaty of Versailles have been written to prevent another international conflict?

764 Chapter 28 *World War I*

SECTION 5 ASSESSMENT ANSWERS

1. Germany resented loss in World War I; Treaty deprived Germany of great-power status; German reconciliation with allies difficult; German resentment led to rise of Nazism

2. The terms are defined in the Glossary.

3. T. E. Lawrence, 761; Foch, 761; Wilson, 762; the Fourteen Points, 762; Clemenceau, 763; George, 763; Orlando, 763

4. angry, humiliated, vengeful

5. **INTERNATIONALISM** If punishments had been lessened, or if Germany had been present at the peace conference, future conflict might have been avoided.

Interpreting Military Movements on Maps

Although wars begin over many different issues, they all end up as fights to control territory. Because wars are basically fought over land, maps are particularly good tools for seeing the "big picture" of a war.

Learning the Skill

The map key is essential in interpreting military maps. The key explains what the map's colors and symbols represent. Use the following steps to study the key:

- Determine the meanings of the colors on the map. Usually, colors represent different sides in the conflict.
- Identify all symbols. These may include symbols for battle sites, victories, types of military units and equipment, and so on.
- Study the arrows, which show the direction of military movements. Because these movements occur over time, some maps give dates showing when and where troops advanced and retreated.

Once you have studied the key and the map, follow the progress of the campaign that is shown. Notice where each side began, in which direction it moved, where the two sides fought, and which side claimed victory.

Practicing the Skill

The map on this page shows the Middle East front during World War I. Study the map and then answer the following questions.

1. On which side did Arabia and Egypt fight?
2. Who won the battle of the Dardanelles?
3. Describe the movement of the Central Powers offensive.
4. When did the Allied Powers win the most battles in the Middle East?

Applying the Skill

Choose one of the maps on page 745. Study your map selection carefully. Then write a para-

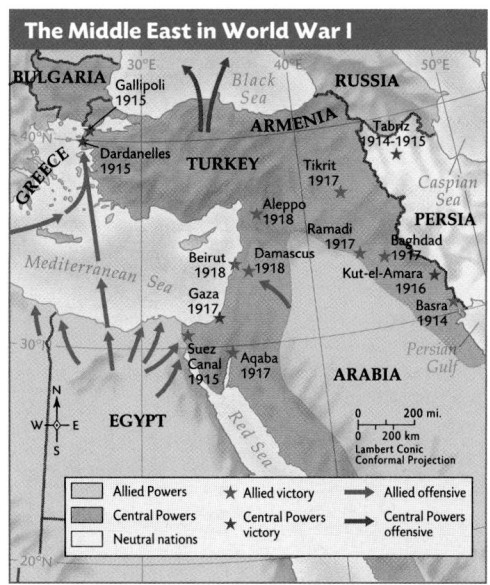

The Middle East in World War I

☐ Allied Powers	★ Allied victory	→ Allied offensive
☐ Central Powers	★ Central Powers victory	→ Central Powers offensive
☐ Neutral nations		

graph answering the following questions.

1. Where did most of the fighting occur?
2. Which side made the most significant advance in 1914?
3. How did each side progress on this front as the war continued?
4. Did either side win a decisive victory on this front?

For More Practice

Turn to the Skill Practice in the Chapter Assessment on page 767 for more practice in interpreting military movements on maps.

The **Glencoe Skillbuilder Interactive Workbook**, Level 2 provides instruction and practice in key social studies skills.

TEACH

Interpreting Military Movements on Maps Ask students to make their own military maps of an engagement in an imaginary war. They should use two different colors to represent the opposing sides; different symbols or colors for the victories of each side; and arrows to show the direction of troop movements. The students should label land and water areas and a few important towns or cities. The map should also include a key explaining what the various colors and symbols represent.

Additional Practice

📁 Skill Reinforcement Activity 28

GLENCOE TECHNOLOGY

Glencoe's **Skillbuilder Interactive Workbook, Level 2** This interactive CD-ROM promotes student mastery of key social studies skills.

ANSWERS TO PRACTICING THE SKILL

1. on the Allied side
2. the Central Powers
3. from Turkey (the Ottoman Empire) north across the Black Sea toward Russia
4. 1917

Have students use the **Chapter 28 Self-Check Quiz** at worldhistory.glencoe.com to prepare for the Chapter Test.

GLENCOE
TECHNOLOGY

VIDEODISC
Use MindJogger to review the chapter.

MindJogger Videoquiz

Chapter 28
Disc 4 Side A

Also available in VHS.

Answers

Using Key Terms
1. i   3. b   5. f
2. d   4. k

Using Your History Journal
Remind students to write their letters at the appropriate time.

Reviewing Facts
1. increase in political and social instability; large war casualties; mass slaughter; territorial boundaries redrawn
2. 1914: assassination of Archduke Ferdinand and beginning of World War I; 1917: United States entry into World War I, the Russian Revolution; 1918: Armistice ending World War I
3. It abandoned the Schlieffen Plan.
4. about 30 million soldiers; about 13 million civilians
5. Peace: Russian withdrawal from the war; Land: land to the peasants; Bread: enough food for everyone. "All power to the soviets" meant that these local organizations would govern Russia.
6. freedom of the seas; freedom of trade; arms limitations; an end

---

WORLD HISTORY Online

Self-Check Quiz
Visit the *World History: The Human Experience* Web site at **worldhistory.glencoe.com** and click on *Chapter 28—Self-Check Quiz* to prepare for the Chapter Test.

Using Key Terms

Write the key term that completes each sentence. Then write a sentence for each term not chosen.

a. armistice	g. trenches
b. contraband	h. alliance system
c. convoy	i. provisional government
d. entente	j. reparations
e. propaganda	k. communism
f. mobilization	l. ultimatum

1. After Czar Nicholas's abdication, political authority in Russia passed into the hands of a _____.
2. In 1904, Great Britain and France signed an _____ that settled key colonial disputes.
3. The British stopped ships on the high seas that they suspected carried _____, or prohibited goods.
4. The Bolsheviks founded an international revolutionary movement based on _____, the political viewpoint stemming from the ideas of Marx and Lenin.
5. Warring countries issued general orders for _____, the gathering and transport of military troops and fighting equipment.

Technology Activity

Using E-mail Use your local library or access the Internet to locate an E-mail address for an organization that deals with World War I. Compose a letter requesting information about World War I submarine warfare. Using your response, create a bulletin board of the history of the American submarine during the Great War. Provide pictures and captions showing different types of submarines.

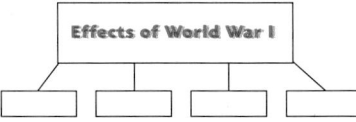

Reviewing Facts

1. **History** Use a diagram like the one below to identify the major effects of World War I.

Effects of World War I

2. **History** State the significance of the following dates: 1914, 1917, and 1918.
3. **History** Explain how Germany's war strategy changed after the Battle of the Marne.
4. **History** State how many soldiers were killed or wounded in World War I. How many civilians died of disease or starvation?
5. **Culture** Explain the social changes promised by the Bolshevik slogans.
6. **History** List five of the Fourteen Points that United States President Woodrow Wilson presented at the Paris peace conference in 1919.
7. **Culture** State the role and contributions of women during World War I. What was their standing in society after the war?

Critical Thinking

1. **Evaluate** How did Lenin's beliefs and goals differ from those of Wilson? Which leader has had the greater impact on world history?
2. **Apply** How did sea power have a major effect on the outcome of World War I?
3. **Analyze** How were technological advances in weaponry most responsible for the military stalemate during much of World War I?

---

to secret alliances; just settlement of colonial claims; self-rule for all nations; "general assembly of nations"
7. Large numbers of women entered the labor force; others became nurses or served in armed forces; their post-war contributions led to obtaining the vote.

Critical Thinking
1. Lenin's stress on revolution and dictatorial

government v. Wilson's affirmation of democratic values, self-determination, and free institutions.
2. The British maintained an extremely effective blockade of Germany. Germany's submarine warfare did extensive damage but also brought the United States into the war.
3. Machine guns, heavy artillery, and trenches made it hard for either side to mount a decisive offensive attack on the other.

Understanding Themes

1. **Cooperation** Why do you think Great Britain, France, and Russia put aside their differences to form the Triple Entente?
2. **Conflict** Name a war goal for each of these countries: Serbia, Austria-Hungary, Russia, and France. Discuss a situation today where a conflict over national goals might lead to war.
3. **Conflict** What were the causes of World War I? What key events affected its outcome? How did World War I affect global affairs?
4. **Revolution** Name the main causes of the Russian Revolution of 1917. How did the Russian Revolution differ from the American Revolution in its causes and global impact?
5. **Internationalism** Do you think the peace settlement after World War I promoted the success of the League of Nations? Explain.

Skill Practice

Study the map "Russian Civil War 1918–1922" and answer the questions that follow.

1. From which direction did the Allied forces invade Russia?

Russian Civil War 1918–1922

2. Where did Denikin's forces begin and in what direction did they move?
3. Why do you think Kolchak chose his route to Moscow?
4. Which military group advanced on Russian territory from an area near Poland?

Geography in History

1. **Place** Refer to the map below. What five European nations had built up the largest standing armies during World War I?
2. **Location** How do you think Germany's location affected its military strategy?
3. **Movement** When war broke out, which side had the more challenging task of moving troops and materials, the Allies or the Central Powers? Why?

Mobilized Forces During World War I

1. How do conflicts in the Balkans before World War I compare with those in the region today?
2. The ideal of self-determination was not granted to European colonies after World War I. Where do struggles for self-determination continue today? How are they faring?

---

munism as opposed to spread of democracy
5. **INTERNATIONALISM** No, it created bad feeling and weakened cooperation.

Skill Practice

1. from the northwest; south
2. Denikin's forces began in the Crimea and moved north.
3. He hoped to seize control of the Trans-Siberian Railroad, which would give him control of an important supply line into Russia and enable him to use the railroad to transport his troops.
4. Yudenitch forces

Geography in History

1. Germany, Russia, Great Britain, France, Austria-Hungary
2. It had to worry about two fronts.
3. the Allies, because their territories were split in two by the Central Powers

1. Students should stress ethnic and national rivalries as the cause of conflicts.
2. Chechens in the Russian Federation; Basques in Spain; Kurds in the Middle East; Tamils in Sri Lanka; Kashmiris in South Asia; and Tibetans in China.

Chapter Bonus Test Question

Ask students: One clause of the Versailles Treaty put all the blame for causing World War I on Germany. Do you think this was just? *(Yes: War might have been avoided if Germany had not given Austria-Hungary permission to do with Serbia as it pleased. No: The intransigence of Austria-Hungary was also to blame, and without the terrorism of Serbian nationalists, the war might not have broken out at all.)*

Understanding Themes

1. **COOPERATION** because they were all afraid of Germany
2. **CONFLICT** Serbia: to be the center of a new South Slav nation; Austria-Hungary: to gain territory through the Balkans to the Aegean Sea and to contain Slavic nationals; Russia: the Dardanelles; France: return of Alsace-Lorraine; possibilities include the former Yugoslavia and the former Soviet Union.

3. **CONFLICT** militarism, rivalries among alliances, imperialist expansion; total war, Russian Revolution, entry of the United States; rise of new nations in Europe, end of European global dominance, economic and social upheaval, totalitarianism

4. **REVOLUTION** shortages of food and fuel, dissatisfaction with the monarchy, war casualties; Russian upheaval based on social as well as political grievances; spread of com-

A complete, 1-page lesson plan is provided for each section in the *Reproducible Lesson Plans* booklet.

Between Two Fires

CHAPTER RESOURCES

	Reproducible Resources	Multimedia Resources
Chapter Opener	📁 Chapter Themes: Graphic Organizer 29 📁 Historical Significance Chapter Activity 29	💿 MindJogger Videoquiz

Chapter Enrichment	📁 Vocabulary Activity 29*
	📁 Time Line Activity 29
	📁 Mapping History Activity 29
	📁 History Simulation 29
	📁 Geography and History Activity 29
	📁 Source Reading 29
	📁 People in World History Profiles 55, 56
	📁 World Art and Music Activity 29
	📁 Enrichment Activity 29
	📁 Critical Thinking Activity 29
	📁 Skill Reinforcement Activity 29
	📁 Writer's Guidebook, Lesson 10
	📁 Performance Assessment Activity 29
	📁 Standardized Test Practice Workbook
	    Activity 29
	📁 Inclusion for the Social Studies Classroom
	    Strategies and Activities
		📖 Focus on World Art Print 3, Thomas Hart Benton. *The Wreck of the Ole '97*; 4, Sargent Johnson. *Forever Free*; 23, René Magritte. *The Human Condition 1*
		🎞 World History and Art Transparency 38, *Migrant Mother*; 39, *Bird in Space*; 43, *The Persistence of Memory*
		🎞 Chapter Transparency 29
		💿 Vocabulary PuzzleMaker Software
		🎵 World Music: Cultural Traditions, Lesson 1
		💿 Lessons of War: *The Enemy*
		💿 Communism and the Cold War: *Growing Up Communist*
		💿 World History Primary Source Document Library

Chapter Review/Reteaching	📁 Reteaching Activity 29 📁 Skill Reinforcement Activity 29 📁 Spanish Chapter Summary 29	🎧 Chapter 29 Digest Audiocassette, Activity, Test* 💿 Vocabulary PuzzleMaker Software 💿 Interactive Tutor Self-Assessment Software 💿 MindJogger Videoquiz
Chapter Evaluation/Testing	📁 Performance Assessment Activity 29 📁 Chapter 29 Test, Forms A and B	💿 ExamView® Pro Testmaker

* Also available in Spanish

0:00 OUT OF TIME? Assign the Chapter 29 Audiocassettes.

World History Primary Source Document Library
Make History Come Alive!
Engage your students with over 250 easily accessible primary source documents—available on this CD-ROM—that will give them real life insight into the important events of world history.

Block Schedule
Activities that are particularly suited to use within the block scheduling framework are identified throughout this chapter by the following designation. 📦

KEY TO ABILITY LEVELS
Teaching strategies are coded for varying learning styles.
L1 BASIC activities for all students
L2 AVERAGE activities for average to above-average students
L3 CHALLENGING activities for above-average students
LEP LIMITED ENGLISH PROFICIENCY activities

Use Glencoe's *Presentation Plus!* multimedia teacher tool to easily present dynamic lessons that visually excite your students. Using Microsoft PowerPoint® you can customize the presentations to create your own personalized lessons.

Interactive Lesson Planner

Planning has never been easier! Using this CD-ROM, organize your week, month, semester, or year with all the help you need. The **Interactive Lesson Planner** gives you access to all of the blackline masters that accompany *World History: The Human Experience.*

SECTION RESOURCES

Daily Objectives	Reproducible Resources	Multimedia Resources
Section 1 **The Postwar World** Describe the trends that dominated the arts and popular culture from 1919 to 1939.	Lecture Notes 29-1 Reproducible Lesson Plan 29-1 Vocabulary Activity 29* Guided Reading Activity 29-1* Time Line Activity 29 Chapter Themes: Graphic Organizer 29 Section Quiz 29-1* Reading Essentials and Study Guide 29-1	Focus on World Art Print 3, Thomas Hart Benton. *The Wreck of the Ole '97*; 4, Sargent Johnson. *Forever Free*; 23, René Magritte. *The Human Condition 1* Section Focus Transparency 29-1 Chapter Transparency 29 World History and Art Transparency 39, *Bird in Space*; 43, *The Persistence of Memory* Interactive Tutor Self-Assessment Software Testmaker World Music: Cultural Traditions, Lesson 1
Section 2 **The Western Democracies** Explain why democratic government survived in the United States, Great Britain, and France during the post-World War I era.	Lecture Notes 29-2 Reproducible Lesson Plan 29-2 Vocabulary Activity 29* Guided Reading Activity 29-2* Section Quiz 29-2* Reading Essentials and Study Guide 29-2	Section Focus Transparency 29-2 World History and Art Transparency 38, *Migrant Mother* Interactive Tutor Self-Assessment Software Testmaker
Section 3 **Fascist Dictatorships** Identify the factors that led to the rise of Fascist dictatorships in Italy and Germany after World War I.	Lecture Notes 29-3 Reproducible Lesson Plan 29-3 Guided Reading Activity 29-3* History Simulation 29 Geography and History Activity 29 Section Quiz 29-3* Reading Essentials and Study Guide 29-3	Section Focus Transparency 29-3 Vocabulary PuzzleMaker Software Interactive Tutor Self-Assessment Software Testmaker Lessons of War: *The Enemy*
Section 4 **The Soviet Union** Examine how Joseph Stalin's rule transformed the Soviet Union.	Lecture Notes 29-4 Reproducible Lesson Plan 29-4 Guided Reading Activity 29-4* Reteaching Activity 29 Enrichment Activity 29 Section Quiz 29-4* Performance Assessment Activity 29 Spanish Chapter Summary 29 Reading Essentials and Study Guide 29-4	Section Focus Transparency 29-4 Vocabulary Puzzlemaker Software Interactive Tutor Self-Assessment Software Testmaker Communism and the Cold War: *Growing Up Communist*

* Also available in Spanish

Chapter Activities

Performance Assessment Activity

Newsreel Explain that in the 1920s and 1930s (before television), movie theaters showed newsreels along with the feature film. Newsreels included narration and footage of what was happening nationally and around the world, and they often included propaganda. Have small groups of students choose an important event and write newsreel scripts, including headlines and visuals. Then groups can combine their scripts into a 10- or 15-minute production. One student from each group may narrate its segment.

Possible Rubric Features

Accuracy of content information, concept attainment, originality and creativity of product, clarity, organization of ideas, and collaborative skills

• *For an additional activity, refer to Activity 29 in the* Performance Assessment Strategies and Activities *booklet.*

ACTIVITY

From the Classroom of...

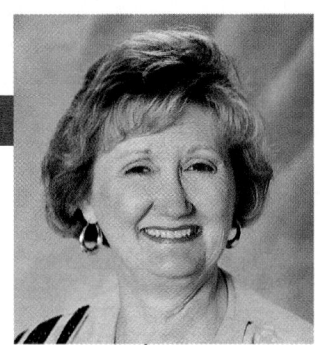

Loretta Smithson
Elsinore High School
Lake Elsinore, CA

Experiencing the Holocaust

Organize the class into small groups to research the roots and results of anti-Semitism. Assign each group a different area to research: (1) a history of the Hebrew people, including the Diaspora (A.D. 70); (2) a history of Jewish expulsion from European countries (e.g., Spain, 1493); (3) excerpts of writings or speeches by famous people (e.g., Martin Luther); (4) excerpts from books or stories of the Holocaust (e.g., *The Blue Tattoo*); (5) reasons given by Nazis for their treatment of European Jews; and (6) world reactions to Nazi treatment of the Jews.

Provide students with the condensed materials they need for their categories, and encourage them to prepare their information in interesting ways for group presentations, such as charts, maps, diagrams, slides.

After group presentations, let students share their analyses of the materials provided, then conduct a class discussion on the meaning of genocide and its implications for world events today (in Bosnia, for example).

MULTIPLE LEARNING STYLES

Verbal/Linguistic
Have students create a front page for a postwar-period newspaper. Allow students to divide the work: writing, editing, laying out the copy, printing, and distributing.

Visual/Spatial
For a mock international TV news special, have students imagine they are reporters in one of the following: Great Britain, France, Germany, Italy, or the Soviet Union. They are to cover a postwar event or a special feature on daily life.

Auditory/Musical
Suggest that students collect both popular and classical music from the 1920s and present a sampling as a concert for the class. They should include a program for the audience that lists the composers, songwriters, and musicians along with brief biographical sketches, and the names of the works.

Kinesthetic
Ask students to research the currency of each of the countries mentioned in the chapter and collect samples, either real or photocopied. Remind students that some of the nations may have had a change in currency during the postwar period. Have students create a display for the class.

GLENCOE'S
ASSESSMENT
ADVANTAGE

Use the following to easily assess student learning in a variety of ways.

- Performance Assessment Strategies and Activities
- Section Quizzes
- Chapter and Unit Tests
- Interactive Tutor Self-Assessment Software
- Testmaker Software
- MindJogger Videoquiz
- SAT/SAT II Test Practice
- <u>worldhistory.glencoe.com</u>

Additional Resources

NATIONAL GEOGRAPHIC SOCIETY — Teacher's Corner

INDEX TO NATIONAL GEOGRAPHIC MAGAZINE

The following articles may be used for research relating to this chapter:

- "Our Man in China," by Mike Edwards, January 1997.
- "U.S.S. Macon: Lost and Found," by J. Gordon Vaeth, January 1992.

NATIONAL GEOGRAPHIC SOCIETY PRODUCTS AVAILABLE FROM GLENCOE

To order the following products for use with this chapter, contact your local Glencoe sales representative, or call Glencoe at 1-800-334-7344:

- *GTV: The American People (Videodiscs)*
- *GTV: A Geographic Perspective on American History (Videodiscs)*

ADDITIONAL NATIONAL GEOGRAPHIC SOCIETY PRODUCTS

To order the following product for use with this chapter, call National Geographic Society at 1-800-368-2728:

- *1929–1941: The Great Depression (Video)*

Access National Geographic's new dynamic MapMachine Web site and other geography resources at:

- http://www.nationalgeographic.com/
- http://www.nationalgeographic.com/maps/

BIBLIOGRAPHY

Literature of the Period
Hemingway, Ernest. *The Sun Also Rises.* New York: Scribner, 1926. A novel about English and American expatriates in France and Spain after World War I.
Readings for the Student
Laqueur, Walter. *Stalin: The Glasnost Revelations.* New York: Scribner, 1990. A review of a new body of evidence about Stalin and modern-day Russia.
Readings for the Teacher
Garraty, John. *The Great Depression.* San Diego: Harcourt, 1986. Focuses on the events of the Great Depression from a global perspective.

WORLD HISTORY Online

Use our Web site as an additional resource. All essential content is covered in the Student Edition.

You and your students can visit the *World History: The Human Experience* Web site at worldhistory.glencoe.com The student text directs students to the Web site for the following options:

- **Chapter Overviews**
- **Student Web Activities**
- **Self-Check Quizzes**

Answers are provided for you in a link entitled "Web Activity Lesson Plan." Additional Web Resources, Interactive Puzzles, and content updates are also available.

Visit the Glencoe Web site at socialstudies.glencoe.com for social studies activities, updates, and links to other resources.

LOCAL OBJECTIVES

_____
_____
_____
_____
_____
_____
_____
_____
_____
_____
_____
_____
_____
_____
_____
_____
_____
_____

Between Two Fires

Storyteller

Historical Setting Hitler was a master speechmaker. His personal architect, Albert Speer, recalled in his memoirs that when he first heard Hitler speak, he was immediately charmed by his style. He had expected a fanatic man dressed in uniform. Instead Hitler appeared in a blue suit and seemed almost shy. He had a gift for adjusting to his audience. Hitler spoke with hypnotic persuasiveness that cast a mood that transformed his listeners.

Historical Significance

Answers: *Economic depressions, unemployment, and social unrest led to the rise of dictatorships in postwar Europe.*

Democratic governments had to become involved in social reforms, adapt to changing technology, and (except for the United States) deal with major debts and rebuild damaged territory.

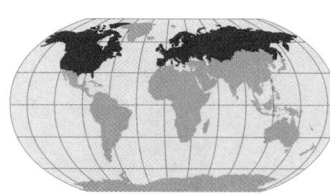

Chapter Themes

▶ **Innovation** The period after World War I brings revolutionary changes in science, the arts, and popular culture. *Section 1*
▶ **Change** The Great Depression forces governments in Europe and North America to increase their involvement in social and economic affairs. *Section 2*
▶ **Uniformity** Fascist governments in Italy and Germany limit individual liberties and stress loyalty to the state. *Section 3*
▶ **Uniformity** Communists in the Soviet Union impose state control and crush opposition. *Section 4*

Storyteller

From early evening until long past midnight, Nazi stormtroopers and youth groups marched in disciplined columns through Berlin. For many of the young people in that torchlight parade in the 1930s, their marching was only a beginning. They looked forward to a bright future, playing important roles in creating a new Germany out of the confusion and trouble that surrounded them. To them, Hitler seemed like a deliverer who would restore Germany's greatness.

Years later, a number of them looked back on that night, appalled at how little they really knew about the Nazis. But the economic and political chaos caused by World War I and the Great Depression led many Europeans to support powerful dictators during the 1920s and 1930s.

Historical Significance

What factors led to the rise of dictatorships in Europe after World War I? How were democratic nations affected by the social and economic crises that came after the end of World War I?

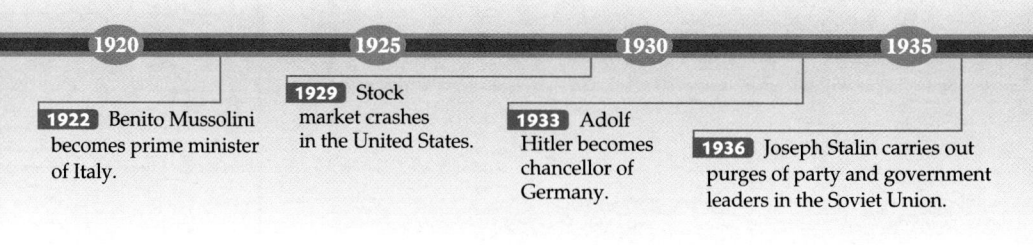

1920	1925	1930	1935
1922 Benito Mussolini becomes prime minister of Italy.	**1929** Stock market crashes in the United States.	**1933** Adolf Hitler becomes chancellor of Germany.	**1936** Joseph Stalin carries out purges of party and government leaders in the Soviet Union.

768

GEOGRAPHY CONNECTION

Location To help students realize where events of this chapter took place, have them find the United States, Great Britain, France, Germany, the Commonwealth of Independent States, and Italy on a world map. What geographic factor made it possible for the United States to escape economic problems and get on with life immediately after World War I? *(Its distance from battle sites kept it from being physically damaged and allowed people to isolate themselves from Europe's problems.)*

Automat, Edward Hopper, 1927. Des Moines Art Center Permanent Collection, Des Moines, Iowa

History & Art

Edward Hopper (1882–1967) was an American artist known for his realistic paintings of loneliness and boredom. He depicted characters in all-night restaurants or in lonely settings such as this automat. The world he revealed was stark and impersonal. What detail in this picture tells you that the setting is not a modern fast-food restaurant? *(radiator)*

Performance Assessment

Refer to the activity on page 768C of the Planning Guide.

For an additional activity, refer to Activity 29 in the *Performance Assessment Strategies and Activities* booklet.

Using Your History Journal

Students might find it helpful to tape-record the interview. This will allow them to capture all of the details and get accurate quotes.

WORLD HISTORY Online

apter Overview

it the *World History: The Human Experience* b site at <u>worldhistory.glencoe.com</u> and :k on *Chapter 29—Chapter Overview* preview the chapter.

Your History Journal

Interview an older person about his or her feelings and perceptions in the period between 1930 and 1941. Use the chapter to formulate questions about events. Take notes during the interview, or write down your impressions soon afterward.

Chapter 29 *Between Two Fires* **769**

GLENCOE TECHNOLOGY

VIDEODISC
Use MindJogger to preview chapter content.

MindJogger Videoquiz
 Chapter 29
Disc 4 Side B

 Also available in VHS.

➕ EXTRA CREDIT PROJECT

The Commonwealth Students might research the history of Canada or Australia during the postwar years. They should find out about the relationship with Great Britain, the economies, social issues, Canadians' relationship with France, and developments in literature, the arts, and sciences in those countries. Have students prepare reports to share with the whole class.

SECTION THEME

▶ **Innovation** The period after World War I brings revolutionary changes in science, the arts, and popular culture.

Guide to Reading

For reading strategies to help students read effectively see pages 12–13. Have students think about the main head as they read the subheads.

Vocabulary Pre-check

 Use the Vocabulary PuzzleMaker for Chapter 29 to create a crossword puzzle to reinforce section terms. **L1 LEP**

☞ Use Vocabulary Activity 29 to introduce vocabulary terms. **L1 LEP**

FOCUS

Section Objective

Describe the trends that dominated the arts and popular culture from 1919 to 1939.

BELLRINGER
Motivational Activity

 Before taking roll at the beginning of the class period, project Section Focus Transparency 29-1 and have students answer the activity questions. Discuss students' responses.

☞ This activity is also available as a blackline master.

Section 1

The Postwar World

Guide to Reading

Read to Find Out
Main Idea *New styles dominated the arts and popular culture from 1919 to 1939.*

▶ **Terms to Define**
    cubism, surrealism, jazz, choreographer

▶ **People to Meet**
    Albert Einstein, Sigmund Freud, T.S. Eliot, Pablo Picasso, Sergey Prokofiev, Walter Gropius

▶ **Places to Locate**
    Hollywood

The Storyteller

    There was trouble in Hollywood. One of Tinseltown's biggest names, with a bigger screen following than 90 percent of the stars, according to columnist Louella Parsons, had "fallen afoul of the censors in a big way." Censor boards throughout the nation were receiving vigorous complaints about the "devilish, naughty" behavior of this national celebrity. Terry Ramsaye wrote in the Motion Picture Herald, "It's the old, old story. If nobody knows you, you can do anything, and if everybody knows you, you can't do anything—except what everyone approves." The star was Mickey Mouse.

    —adapted from *Of Mice and Magic*, Leonard Maltin, 1987

Hollywood landmark

"**A**RMISTICE SIGNED, END OF THE WAR!" proclaimed *The New York Times* headline on November 11, 1918. In the United States and Europe, people exploded in a frenzy of celebration. The critic and author Malcolm Cowley wrote later of the feeling of euphoria that marked the end of the war: "We danced in the streets, embraced old women and pretty girls, swore blood brotherhood with soldiers in little bars...." But the excitement did not last. "On the next day," continued Cowley, "...we didn't know what to do."

    World War I marked the great divide between the old and the new. The war changed the way many people looked at the world, and the disillusionment it caused led artists and intellectuals on a restless search for something new. The postwar period was a time for breaking with tradition and experimenting with new styles in politics and culture.

Changing Patterns of Life

    Warren Harding was elected President of the United States in 1920, promising a "return to normalcy." But there was no going back to the past. The war had changed the world too much for that to be possible. Instead, people in both North America and Europe began to experiment with new customs and ways of life.

New Trends in Culture and Style

    In the postwar era, women gained a new level of independence. With the ratification of the Nineteenth Amendment in 1920, women in the United States won the right to vote at last. Women also won the vote in most other Western countries following the war.

    Many women now demanded other freedoms as well. Throwing off the inhibitions of the prewar era, some women in the United States and western

---

SECTION RESOURCES

☞ **Reproducible Masters**
- Lecture Notes 29-1
- Reproducible Lesson Plan 29-1
- Vocabulary Activity 29
- Guided Reading Activity 29-1
- Time Line Activity 29
- Chapter Themes: Graphic Organizer 29

- Section Quiz 29-1
- Reading Essentials and Study Guide 29-1

Transparencies
- Section Focus Transparency 29-1
- Chapter Transparency 29
- World History and Art Transparencies 39, 43

Multimedia
- Focus on World Art Prints 3, 4, 23
- Interactive Tutor Self-Assessment Software
- Testmaker
- World Music: Cultural Traditions, Lesson 1

Europe began to use rouge and lipstick openly. Their skirts rose from a few inches above the ankle to an inch above the knee. They cropped their hair to a shingle bob and aimed for a carefree, little-boy look. Thus attired, the "flapper" created a revolution in manners and morals.

In the postwar era, not only the flapper but people in general disdained the familiar and the commonplace. They wanted heroes who were larger than life. Babe Ruth, the "Sultan of Swat," was the king of baseball. Tennis champions Big Bill Tilden and Helen Wills Moody became national heroes. When Gertrude Ederle swam the English Channel and Charles Lindbergh flew nonstop from Long Island to Paris, the public saluted them with tumultuous ticker-tape parades on Broadway.

Amid all the hoopla, bankers and business leaders were having a heyday. The war had opened new prospects for economic development. President Calvin Coolidge neatly summed up the nation's focus in the 1920s when he said, "The business of America is business."

The Impact of Technology

New forms of technology altered people's lifestyles and brought people closer together in the 1920s. The decade following World War I witnessed a revolution in transportation and communication throughout the world.

The automobile had perhaps the greatest impact on European and American society. A network of highways began to crisscross Europe and the United States. People could now move easily from place to place, and move they did. The United States, in particular, became an increasingly mobile society. Americans traveled farther afield on vacations and moved from rural areas to cities.

Radio also brought about dramatic changes. By exposing millions of people to the same news and entertainment shows, radio helped to produce a more homogeneous, or uniform, culture. Through its advertisements, radio also stimulated the public's desire for consumer goods. Advertisers learned the art of motivation, and ads now played on people's insecurities and self-doubts. "Why had he changed so in his attentions?" queried a forlorn-looking woman in an ad for a leading mouthwash.

Many products of the new technology eased the burden of the homemaker. With the advent of packaged foods, refrigerators, vacuum cleaners, and electric irons, people had more leisure time. Instead of working at home, they could take a drive, listen to the radio, or go out dancing. Millions spent their idle moments with another new product of technology: the movies.

A Revolution in Ideas

New inventions had an enormous impact on people's daily lives in the postwar period. At the same time, exciting new ideas in physics and psychology transformed the way people looked at themselves and the world.

Physics

In 1905 German physicist **Albert Einstein** introduced his theories of relativity, shattering Newton's view of the universe as a machine that operated by universal laws. According to Einstein, there are no absolutes in measuring time and space. Time and space instead depend on the relative motion of bodies in space. For example, the speed of two trains appears differently to bystanders on the station platform than it does to passengers on the trains.

Einstein also held that the speed of light is constant, and that all matter has energy. If matter could be broken down and changed into energy, the amount of energy would be enormous. Einstein's formula $E=MC^2$ was finally supported in 1945 when scientists tested the first atomic bomb in New Mexico.

Although too difficult for the average person to understand, Einstein's views had an impact beyond physics. To many people, his views seemed to reinforce the idea that there were no absolutes in any field of knowledge or in moral values.

Psychology

The Austrian physician **Sigmund Freud** (FROYD) revolutionized people's ideas about how the human mind works. After observing many patients, Freud concluded that the unconscious mind plays a major role in shaping behavior. The unconscious, he said, is full of memories of events from early childhood. If the memories are especially painful, people sometimes suppress them. Such suppression may lead to a variety of mental disorders.

When Freud first introduced his theories in the late 1800s, many people ridiculed or attacked them. By the 1920s, however, his ideas about human

> **Footnotes to History**
>
> **Fads**
> The 1920s was a time when many fads swept the United States. These ranged from crossword puzzles, to stunts, such as sitting on the top of flagpoles for days at a time, to parlor games, such as mah-jongg, a Chinese version of rummy played with tiles.

Chapter 29 *Between Two Fires* **771**

TEACH

Guided Practice

THEME Innovation

Ask students to review the section and identify the innovations of the postwar years. *(automobile, radio, refrigerator, new ideas in science and the arts)* Discuss with the class how these changes made a difference in people's lives. **L1 LEP**

Economics Initiate a class debate focused on Calvin Coolidge's words, "The business of America is business." Ask students to analyze whether his words are still applicable today. Should economic development be the main focus of the United States? What else are Americans concerned about? *(peace, human rights, the environment)* **L2**

 Chapter Transparency 29

 History *and the* Humanities

 World Music: Cultural Traditions, Lesson 1

World History and Art Transparency 39, *Bird in Space;* 43, *The Persistence of Memory*

Focus on World Art Print 3, Thomas Hart Benton. *The Wreck of the Ole '97;* 4, Sargent Johnson. *Forever Free;* 23, René Magritte. *The Human Condition 1*

 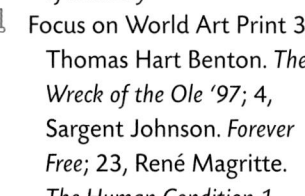

Chapter 29
Section 1

Independent Practice

 Guided Reading Activity 29-1 **L1**

Time Line Activity 29

Chapter Themes: Graphic Organizer 29

History & Art Picasso did not complete Stein's face during the actual sitting. When he did finish it, he painted the face from memory in a sculptural, masklike style. This was indicative of the move Picasso would soon make into cubism. **Answer to Caption:** *Artists and writers broke with long-established traditions and experimented with new styles, media, and subject matter.*

Biography

The following videotape programs are available from Glencoe:

- **Amelia Earhart: Queen of the Air**
- **Admiral Richard Byrd**

you don't say...

Cubism, as a name, had its origin in a comment by art critic Louis Vauxhouses. Vauxhouses described Georges Braque's works as reducing things to "geometrical schemas, to cubes." Although there were no cubes in cubist painting, the name stuck.

History & Art *Gertrude Stein* by Pablo Picasso, 1906. The Metropolitan Museum of Art, New York, New York **The Spanish painter Pablo Picasso and the American writer Gertrude Stein were two of the major cultural figures of the 1920s and 1930s.** *What were two major characteristics of the arts during the period between the world wars?*

psychology had become more accepted and influential. Freud's theories eventually led to new approaches in the treatment of mental illness, in child rearing, and in education.

Upheaval in the Arts

The break between old and new following World War I was perhaps most sharply defined in the arts. In painting, music, literature, and dance, artists abandoned long-accepted traditions. The avant-garde experimented with new styles, media, and subject matter. Often the public greeted their pioneering efforts with cries of shock and protest.

Literature

Many of the period's writers had been disillusioned by World War I and its aftermath. The war had destroyed their belief in the traditional values of middle-class society. In expressing that disillusionment, they broke new literary ground.

In his poems *The Waste Land* and "The Hollow Men," for example, American-born poet **T.S. Eliot** used a patchwork style that juxtaposed different literary, religious, and historical references to convey a sense of despair about life. German novelist Thomas Mann, Czech novelist Franz Kafka, and British novelist Virginia Woolf also experimented

with new literary techniques. Both in terms of their style and content, all of these writers represented a sharp break with the literature of the past.

While they echoed Eliot's sense of disenchantment, American writers such as Ernest Hemingway and F. Scott Fitzgerald developed markedly different literary styles. For instance, in his 1926 novel *The Sun Also Rises*, Hemingway used a lean, straightforward style to tell the tale of Americans and Britons who roamed France and Spain, living for the moment while trying to find meaning in their lives. In contrast, Fitzgerald used a more elaborate poetic style in his 1925 novel *The Great Gatsby* to explore the atmosphere and excesses of the Roaring Twenties.

Several years earlier, in 1922, Irish novelist James Joyce had published *Ulysses*, an in-depth account of a day in the lives of three ordinary people in Dublin. *Ulysses* was a landmark in the development of the modern novel. Influenced by Freud's theories, Joyce developed a style known as "stream of consciousness" in which he presented the inner thoughts—rather than just the external actions—of his characters. Joyce's psychological emphasis and his earthy language caused a storm of protest, which led to a number of court battles over the publication of his novel.

In the late 1920s and the 1930s, many writers became interested in important social issues of the

---

Mixed Learners Review the headings that appear in Section 1. Help students understand that each heading introduces the specific topic or change that will be covered. Organize the class into small groups. Ask each group to select a heading and prepare an oral presentation about that topic for the class. Encourage students to find ways to illustrate the topic either with photographs from books or magazines or with drawings. These oral presentations should provide additional help in reviewing the material for students. **L2 LEP**

day. Langston Hughes, Claude McKay, and Zora Neale Hurston, who belonged to an African American literary movement known as the Harlem Renaissance, explored the African American experience in America. In *The Grapes of Wrath*, John Steinbeck described the plight of Oklahoma farmers who, in the midst of a severe drought, abandoned their farms and moved to California. John Dos Passos's *U.S.A.* trilogy was a broader social criticism of conditions in American society during the postwar period.

Painting

The postwar world also saw a revolution in the visual arts. Artists no longer tried to be realistic in their works. Instead they developed radical new styles and redefined the nature of painting. In 1907, the Spanish painter **Pablo Picasso** created an uproar in the art world when he painted *Les Demoiselles d'Avignon*. The painting was the earliest example of cubism, an abstract art form that uses intersecting geometric shapes. Cubist painters transform their subjects by flattening them, cutting them up, rearranging different portions of them, and altering shapes and colors to fit their own vision. As Picasso explained: "Art is a lie that makes us realize the truth."

Another development was Dada, an art form that aimed to shock middle-class viewers. Dada stressed absurdity and the role of the unpredictable in life. For example, the paintings and poems of Dada consisted of meaningless and random arrangements of objects and words. Dada's reliance on the imagination led to surrealism, an art form that used dreamlike images and unnatural combinations of objects. Influenced by Freud, surrealist painters tried to find a new reality by exploring the unconscious mind. The Spanish painter Salvador Dali created such realistically impossible images as limp watches set in bleak landscapes.

In the tradition of Steinbeck and Dos Passos, other artists used their talents to attack social problems. In their paintings and photographs, social realists such as Ben Shahn, Peter Blume, and Dorothea Lange showed the human suffering caused by the Depression of the 1930s. Although not a realist, Pablo Picasso protested the horrors of Spain's civil war in his symbolic painting *Guernica*.

Music and Dance

Composers also broke new ground after the war. Several eastern European composers transformed the classical form. **Sergey Prokofiev**

(sehr•GAY pruh•KAWF•yuhf), a Russian, composed driving and dissonant music that lacked the familiar harmonies of traditional forms. Critics dubbed him the "age of steel composer." Prokofiev, however, later composed more pleasant sounding symphonies and operas.

Arnold Schoenberg (SHUHN•BUHRG), a self-taught Austrian composer, made radical changes in music theory. Instead of harmonies based on the traditional eight-note scale, he proposed new musical arrangements based on 12 equally valued notes. In his groundbreaking composition, *Pierrot Lunaire* (1912), Schoenberg used harsh, dissonant music to express what he regarded as the decay of Western civilization. His composition outraged conservative audiences.

Meanwhile, in the United States, musicians were creating their own distinctive sound. The 1920s was "the golden age of jazz." What some have called the only art form to originate in the United States, jazz is a mixture of American folk songs, West African rhythms, harmonies from European classical music, and work songs from the days of slavery. Trumpet player Louis Armstrong, blues singer Bessie Smith, and pianist Jelly Roll Morton popularized the new music which soon spread throughout the world.

The postwar era also saw a transformation in the art of dance. Performing barefoot in a loose tunic, the American dancer Isadora Duncan changed people's ideas about dance. Another American, Martha Graham, expanded on Duncan's style and turned modern dance into a striking new art form.

Visualizing History Pablo Picasso's mural painting *Guernica* expresses the horror of the bombing of the town of Guernica during the civil war that devastated Spain in the 1930s. *What changes developed in the visual arts after World War I?*

ASSESS

Check for Understanding

Assign Section 1 Assessment as homework or as an in-class activity.

Use Interactive Tutor Self-Assessment Software to review Section 1.

Evaluate

Section Quiz 29-1

Use the Testmaker to create a customized quiz for Section 1.

Reteach

Have students independently review the section and list important dates, discoveries, movements, and people on a time line. Discuss the time lines in class and combine them to make a class time line.

Reading Essentials and Study Guide 29-1

Visualizing History Picasso, in addition to creating lasting works of art, also expanded our definition of what art could be. His art was very influential among artists during his own lifetime and remains so among artists today.

Answer to Caption: *Artists turned from realism to abstraction, showing basic artistic forms and probing the subconscious rather than portraying everyday scenes. They also commented on social problems in their works.*

MAKING CONNECTIONS ACTIVITY

The Arts Motion pictures became a major industry in the 1920s. One of the earliest silent film stars was British comedian Charlie Chaplin. Sound was added to films in the late 1920s. Have students research the movie industry and the technological advances it made during the postwar decade. Have students work in pairs to write a report on their findings and then design a poster advertising a movie of the era. This was the time of *Dracula* with Bela Lugosi, Greta Garbo in *Mata Hari*, Jeanette MacDonald and Nelson Eddy in *Rose Marie*, and Fred Astaire and Ginger Rogers in *Top Hat*. Suggest that students bring to class a video of one of the old films; groups of students could plan a small film festival. **L2**

NATIONAL GEOGRAPHIC PICTURING HISTOR

TEACH

Point out that the people in the status symbol cars wearing fancy dresses and tuxedos were the wealthy set. Entertainment for millions of others often centered around a more modest piece of technology—the radio. By 1925 the listening audience was put at 50 million, and radio advertising was making an incredible impact. *What radio shows or stars have you heard about from that era? (some shows: "Fibber McGee and Molly," "Baby Snooks," "Flash Gordon," "Little Orphan Annie," "Inner Sanctum"; stars: Jack Benny, Burns and Allen, Edgar Bergen and Charlie McCarthy, Kate Smith)*

you don't say...

Clarence Darrow also defended Nathan Leopold and Richard Loeb, two university students accused of murdering a classmate, in 1924. Darrow did not believe in capital punishment, even though the men admitted to the murder. Darrow introduced psychiatrists and neurologists to the courtroom battle and opened a new era in murder trials by entering the first "temporary insanity" plea.

Flying High

Racing down a dark road, the young men and women in this photograph enjoy a new freedom. Cars were important throughout the industrialized world of Europe and North America, and the American auto industry led the global market. The automobile brought mobility to many Americans during the years following World War I. It was all part of a new lifestyle called the Roaring Twenties.

Behind the gaiety and frivolity, however, the 1920s was a decade in which a new urban style of living came into conflict with an older rural v life. In the United States this conflict was play again and again: Politician and orator W Jennings Bryan battled lawyer Clarence Darr the famous Scopes trial over whether or not schools should teach Darwinian science. failed and farmers lost their land, while the s of the new prosperity played on radios in their rooms. The new city slickers were jazz age fla like the ones here, racing along unpaved road fancy new Stutz Bearcat. ⊕

Sergey Diaghilev (dee•AH•guh•LEHF), the Russian impresario, or sponsor, developed modern ballet, which blended modern dance with classical ballet. When Russian composer Igor Stravinsky wrote *The Rite of Spring* (1913) for Diaghilev and his company of dancers, the Ballets Russes, it was a turning point for ballet. The leaping dance steps that ballet star Vaslav Nijinsky (VAHT•slahv nuh•ZHIHN•skee) performed to Stravinsky's music created a sensation. George Balanchine, who had been a choreographer, or dance arranger, with the Ballets Russes, expanded on Diaghilev's work after moving from the Soviet Union to the United States.

Architecture

The 1920s and 1930s saw striking new designs in buildings and furnishings. **Walter Gropius** founded the Bauhaus (BOW•HOWS) school of design in Weimar (VY•MAHR), Germany. He and his followers created a simple, unornamented style of design. Linking beauty to practicality, Gropius pioneered geometric concrete and glass structures in both Germany and the United States.

In the United States, Frank Lloyd Wright blended his structures with their natural surroundings. Because of their low horizontal form, his houses seem to grow out of the ground. Instead of creating boxlike rooms, Wright reduced the number of walls so that one room flowed into another.

Popular Culture

While the revolutionary developments taking place in art and music may not have had an immediate effect on the lives of ordinary people, films and big bands did. In the postwar era, **Hollywood** productions dominated the movie screens of the world. The movies reflected the new morality of the "Jazz Age" and the doctrine of living for the moment. During the 1930s the public flocked to movie theaters, where for 10 cents they could escape the harsh realities of hard economic times.

In the early part of the century, the creative use of the camera elevated the motion picture to an art form. In *The Last Laugh*, a silent film directed by German filmmaker F.W. Murnau, the camera work is so expressive that the story is told entirely without subtitles. British actor and director Charlie Chaplin also broke new ground in his films while delighting millions of moviegoers with his humor.

In 1927 *The Jazz Singer*, starring American actor Al Jolson, changed motion pictures overnight and signaled the end of silent films. During the early 1930s American musicals, gangster movies, and horror movies were popular. However, some filmmakers tried to educate as well as entertain their audiences. *I Am a Fugitive From a Chain Gang* (1932) was a forceful indictment of the Southern penal system, while *Mr. Smith Goes to Washington* (1939) showed the effects of political corruption.

The public also sought escape from their troubles on the ballroom floor. In the 1930s and 1940s, dance bands reached their greatest popularity. Tommy Dorsey, Count Basie, Benny Goodman, Duke Ellington, Artie Shaw, and their swing bands performed in ballrooms and hotels all across America. Swing was the new word for music played with a happy, relaxed jazz beat. But if swing was not everyone's cup of tea, there were alternatives. The bands of Guy Lombardo and Sammy Kaye played traditional waltzes and fox-trots.

Obviously, the social upheavals and economic hardships that World War I created did not dampen the creative spirit following the war. During this era artists introduced new styles in every major art form. They took little interest in politics and reform. Many cried out against conformity and retreated into individualism. At times it seemed as if they were transforming the world with their radical new visions of life. But the euphoria did not last. The stock market crash that took place on Wall Street in late October 1929 brought on an economic depression that had devastating and deadly consequences.

Cultural Perspectives

Jazz, created by African American musicians in the United States, incorporated many sources. It grew out of spiritual music, old ballads, children's jingles, minstrel music, and the ragtime piano music of the early 1920s. In New Orleans it was common for bands in funeral processions to play hymns on the way to the funeral and then break out in joyful jazz tunes afterward. Singing and dancing crowds would tag along after the band. Today jazz is a popular form of music throughout the world.

Enrich

Have students choose one of the literary works or paintings mentioned in the section, read or study it, and report on it to the class.

CLOSE

Discuss with students how World War I changed the way people viewed the world. Review the artistic and scientific advances and cultural movements of the time. Help students conclude that the postwar world had adopted a style of "living for the moment."

SECTION 1 ASSESSMENT

Main Idea
1. Use a chart like the one below to identify trends in the arts from 1919 to 1937.

Trends in the Arts
1.
2.

Recall
2. **Define** cubism, surrealism, jazz, choreographer.
3. **Identify** Albert Einstein, Sigmund Freud, T.S. Eliot, Pablo Picasso, Sergey Prokofiev, Walter Gropius.

Critical Thinking
4. **Analyzing Information** The era after World War I was a time for breaking with tradition. How could abandoning traditions help a society? How might it harm a society?

Understanding Themes
5. **Innovation** What impact did technological advances in transportation and communication have on American culture in the 1920s?

SECTION 1 ASSESSMENT ANSWERS

1. literature: stream of consciousness, social issues in writing; painting: Cubism, Dada, Surrealism, artists attacked social problems; music: dissonant music (12 equally valued notes), jazz; dance: modern dance, modern ballet; architecture: Bauhaus School, Frank Lloyd Wright

2. All terms are defined in the Glossary.
3. Albert Einstein, 771; Sigmund Freud, 771; T. S. Eliot, 772; Pablo Picasso, 773; Sergey Prokofiev, 773; Walter Gropius, 775
4. Answers will vary. Possible answer: New creative spirit can spur inventions and

improvements; however, some traditions are still valuable and should not be abandoned.
5. **INNOVATION** They made society more homogeneous, brought people together more easily, and made life easier so there was more leisure time.

1920   1925   1930   1935

1926 The General Strike paralyzes Great Britain.

1933 Franklin D. Roosevelt introduces the New Deal.

1936 French voters elect a Socialist government.

SECTION THEME

▶ **Change** The Great Depression forces Western governments to increase their involvement in social and economic affairs.

Guide to Reading

For reading strategies to help students read effectively see pages 12–13.

Vocabulary Pre-check

◙ Use the Vocabulary PuzzleMaker for Chapter 29 to create a crossword puzzle to reinforce section terms. **L1 LEP**

� Use Vocabulary Activity 29 to introduce vocabulary terms. **L1 LEP**

FOCUS

Section Objective

Explain why democratic government survived in the United States, Great Britain, and France during the post-World War I era.

BELLRINGER
Motivational Activity

Before taking roll at the beginning of the class period, project Section Focus Transparency 29-2 and have students answer the activity questions. Discuss students' responses.

▸ This activity is also available as a blackline master.

Section 2

The Western Democracies

Guide to Reading

Read to Find Out
Main Idea *Democratic government was able to survive in the United States, Great Britain, and France during the post-World War I era.*

▶ **Terms to Define**
disarmament, general strike, coalition

▶ **People to Meet**
Franklin D. Roosevelt, Ramsay MacDonald, Eamon De Valera, Léon Blum

▶ **Places to Locate**
Washington, D.C., Irish Free State

The Storyteller

Throughout 1932 the lines had grown. They formed at banks, as investors tried to withdraw their savings before the bank collapsed. They formed at factory gates and employment offices. Men lost their jobs, lost their homes. They swallowed their pride and formed another line—for relief. If there was none to be found, another line waited. As one eyewitness reported, "We saw a crowd of some 50 men fighting over a barrel of garbage which had been set outside the back door of a restaurant."

Depression-era food line

—adapted from *Since Yesterday*, Frederick Lewis Allen, 1939

---

eace brought neither stability nor lasting prosperity to the Western democracies, which paid a heavy price for their victory in World War I. Although the United States suffered comparatively minor financial losses, huge war debts threatened the economic and political stability of Great Britain and France. The West did enjoy a brief period of prosperity in the 1920s, but a global economic depression soon followed. This depression further weakened the Western democracies in the 1930s, making it difficult for them to counter the rising totalitarian threat in Italy and Germany.

The United States

The United States emerged from World War I in better shape than its allies. No battles were fought on American soil, and because of its late entry into the conflict, America suffered far fewer casualties than the other nations. Moreover, unlike the economies of many European countries, the American economy remained strong until 1929.

Cutting Foreign Ties

President Woodrow Wilson wanted the United States to assume a greater role in world affairs following the war. Americans, however, were weary of war and of the foreign entanglements that had dragged the nation into war. They wanted to return to a life of isolation, free from international problems.

An idealistic man, Wilson had seized on the notion of a League of Nations as the cornerstone of a lasting peace. But the newly elected Republican majorities in Congress had no wish to accommodate the Democratic President. When Congress failed to ratify the Treaty of Versailles in 1919, it also rejected American membership in the League. The absence of the United States significantly weakened the

---

SECTION RESOURCES

▸ Reproducible Masters
- Lecture Notes 29-2
- Reproducible Lesson Plan 29-2
- Vocabulary Activity 29
- Guided Reading Activity 29-2
- Section Quiz 29-2
- Reading Essentials and Study Guide 29-2

⚑ Transparencies
- Section Focus Transparency 29-2
- World History and Art Transparency 38, *Migrant Mother*

Multimedia
- ◙ Interactive Tutor Self-Assessment Software
- ◙ Testmaker

League's effectiveness as a strong international peacekeeping organization.

Meanwhile, many Americans feared the effects of communism on the United States. In 1919 and 1920 this "red scare" led to the expulsion of suspected foreign-born radicals. Some native-born Americans also opposed immigration from southern and eastern Europe. In response, Congress enacted limits to immigration from Europe. Earlier laws had already excluded or limited Asian immigration.

From Boom to Depression

Unlike Europe, the United States emerged from the war with a dynamic industrial economy. It was now a nation lending, instead of borrowing, money. American industries produced a major share of the world's manufactured goods, and many industrial workers earned higher wages. As a result of this prosperity, more Americans were willing to take risks. Some bought expensive goods on credit. Others entered the stock market, buying stocks on margin, that is, they paid only part of the cost and borrowed the rest from brokers.

Despite the soaring "bull market," the economy had underlying weaknesses. Most farmers faced hardships because of falling farm prices. Also, in certain industries, workers did not see their wages rise as fast as the production of goods. As a result, many people held back from buying goods that factories were rapidly turning out. This combination of slow demand and overproduction paved the way for an economic crisis.

In late October 1929, concern about the economy led brokers to call in loans. When investors were unable to pay, a financial panic began. Stock prices tumbled, wiping out the fortunes of many investors. This stock market crash sparked the Great Depression of the 1930s. In the three years after the crash, prices fell and many businesses and banks closed. Sales dropped off, forcing a production slump. Salaries and wages also fell, and many workers lost their jobs. By 1933 more than 13 million American workers were unemployed—nearly one-fourth of the nation's workforce.

Many Americans believed that direct relief for the needy was the responsibility of the individual, the family, and the local community. Government-funded relief, they held, would destroy American self-reliance and lead to socialism. However, in these desperate times, not everyone agreed.

The Dust Bowl

American farmers in the 1930s suffered greatly from the Great Depression, but their hardships also came from a devastating drought that afflicted the central United States from 1933 to 1937. As the Great Plains became powder-dry, winds lifted vital topsoil in clouds of dust that turned day into night. Dust storms had swept over the area before, but never on such a large and destructive scale.

The roots of this disaster lay well in the past. Ranchers' cattle overgrazed an area that experienced scant rainfall. The ranchers were followed by farmers, who planted wheat. These early settlers plowed land that should never have been cultivated, and they farmed

Dust Bowl scene

it badly. They did not use contour plowing to check erosion, rotate their crops, or plant trees as windbreaks to hold the soil.

Ruined by drought, about 200,000 farm families headed West, especially to California. They found little relief in their new home—only low-paying jobs and the resentments of local residents opposed to their coming. It took many years of normal rainfall and improved farming methods to transform the Great Plains into productive land again. In addition to agriculture, the region today prospers from petroleum and coal mining.

Linking Past and Present ACTIVITY

Describe the factors that created the Dust Bowl. What did many Dust Bowl farmers do in the 1930s? How has the region developed since that time?

COOPERATIVE LEARNING ACTIVITY

Interviews Organize the class into small groups. Ask students in each group to interview people who lived through the Great Depression of the 1930s. (If some students have no such contacts, direct them to local retirement or nursing homes.) Within each group, students should choose a topic (memories of Hoover and Roosevelt, New Deal programs, family experiences) and assign tasks such as planning the interview questions, selecting people to be interviewed, and deciding how to present the interviews. Remind students to have questions ready, listen well, and take accurate notes. If possible, students should tape-record the interviews. Have each group share the interviews with the class. **L2**

TEACH

Guided Practice

THEME Change

Discuss how the aftermath of the war changed the economies in France, Great Britain, and the United States. Ask students to comment on the drastic change in the United States when the stock market crashed. **L1**

From Boom to Depression

How did the Great Depression affect people's ideas about the role of government in society? *With large numbers of workers unemployed and on relief, people during the Great Depression began to expect government to take a greater role in finding solutions to social and economic problems.*

The Dust Bowl

Lead students in a discussion of how the weather and other natural phenomena affect business, the economy, and daily life. Ask them to consider how heavy rains and flooding, unexpected snow and freezing, and hurricanes affect farmers and orchard growers.

ANSWERS

overgrazing of land, drought, poor farming methods; they headed west to find work in California; normal rainfall and improved farming methods restored productivity and petroleum and coal mining also became important to the region's economy

World History and Art Transparency 38, *Migrant Mother*

Independent Practice

 Guided Reading Activity 29-2 **L1**

Visualizing History A general strike is labor's strongest weapon, and when it occurs society can be thrown into upheaval. Winston Churchill had prepared for such a strike in 1926. Police were mobilized, troops dispatched, and thousands of upper- and middle-class volunteers drove trucks, taxis, and locomotives.
Answer to Caption: *The war had reduced Great Britain's standing in world markets; its foreign trade was upset by challenges from new competitors; it became a debtor nation.*

Broadcast Have students write the script for a 1930s radio news broadcast. They may use facts from the text or conduct additional research. The broadcast should also include weather or sports or some other features. **L2 LEP**

Linking Past and Present

"Happy Days Are Here Again," the popular jingle that Franklin D. Roosevelt used as his 1932 campaign song, is still played today at the Democratic party's national conventions.

WORLD HISTORY Online

Have students use the **Chapter 29 Student Web Activity** at worldhistory.glencoe.com for in-depth study of the New Deal.

Visualizing History During the 1920s and 1930s, economic downturns led to labor unrest in many western democracies, especially Great Britain. *What was Great Britain's economic standing after World War I?*

The New Deal

In 1932 voters elected **Franklin D. Roosevelt** President, who had campaigned on the promise of "a new deal" for the American people. He wanted the federal government to aid the stricken economy and provide relief for the unemployed.

Roosevelt sent a number of bills to Congress that quickly became laws. These measures regulated the banks and stock market and established production guidelines for industry and agriculture. To put people back to work, the government established public works projects to build roads, dams, bridges, homes, and parks. Later New Deal legislation provided for social security and unemployment insurance. Roosevelt's New Deal policies did much to restore the nation's confidence.

Student Web Activity 29

Visit the *World History: The Human Experience* Web site at **worldhistory.glencoe.com** and click on **Chapter 29—Student Web Activities** for an activity relating to the New Deal.

Foreign Affairs

The American government was concerned with more than just domestic affairs during the 1920s and 1930s. Despite its rejection of the League of Nations and binding alliances, the United States did take steps to prevent a future world war. In 1922 in **Washington, D.C.**, it hosted an international conference on disarmament, the reduction of military weapons. There the United States signed a treaty with Japan and Great Britain limiting the number of naval warships each could stockpile. The leading powers at the conference also agreed to seek peaceful solutions to disagreements.

In 1928 the United States and France signed the Kellogg-Briand Pact, which denounced war as a means of settling disputes. Eventually, nearly all the nations of the world signed this agreement. Unfortunately, it was nothing more than a statement of intentions and had no powers of enforcement.

Great Britain

Although World War I increased the United States's economic and political influence, it cost Great Britain its position as a leading economic

---

MEETING SPECIAL NEEDS ACTIVITY

Physical Disability For students who have chronic illnesses and are absent from classes fairly often, it is helpful to provide materials that can be used at home or in the hospital. If there are special oral class presentations, tape them for home use. Assign a special book report or research project to make up for missed class lectures. When a cooperative learning activity has a task that can be done at home, assign it to the student who must be absent often. **L2**

---

power in the world. Before the war British banks lent money to nations all over the globe. But the war was costly, and Great Britain was forced to borrow heavily from the United States. As a result, Great Britain became a debtor instead of a creditor nation.

The war also cost Great Britain its privileged position in world trade. American and Japanese companies captured many British overseas markets during the war. In addition, Great Britain's factories were old and the equipment outdated. Countries like the United States and Japan, which had industrialized later, had newer factories and more modern equipment. Consequently, they could produce goods at a lower cost. Many factories in Great Britain closed or cut back production after the war. By 1921 more than 2 million workers had lost their jobs.

The General Strike

Great Britain's economic woes reached a crisis point in 1926. Coal miners were engaged in a bitter strike for higher wages that year. For months the coal companies had refused to give in to their demands. In an effort to end the stalemate, the coal miners convinced many other trade union workers to join in a general strike, a strike involving all or a large number of a nation's workers. On May 4 all transport workers, dockers, public utility employees, and workers in the building trades and heavy industry walked off their jobs. The government declared a state of emergency and called out the troops to run essential services.

In the end, the General Strike was a failure. By December 1926 the coal strike had also collapsed. In 1927 Parliament passed the Trade Disputes Act, which made general strikes illegal.

Rise of the Labour Party

Despite the failure of the General Strike, British workers gained political strength during the 1920s. The Labour party became the second leading party in the country after the Conservatives. In 1924 and again in 1929, Labour governments were elected to office. Each time, King George V named Scottish Labour leader Ramsay MacDonald prime minister. Because the Labour party supported Socialist policies, its rise to power alarmed the Conservatives and their wealthy supporters. However, once in power, MacDonald and other Labour leaders tempered many of their radical demands.

The Dominions and Ireland

During the 1920s and 1930s, Great Britain held on to most of its empire. However, dominions, such as Canada and Australia, became independent states. In 1931 Parliament passed the Statute of

 Irish nationalist leader Michael Collins, speaking here to crowds in the Irish capital of Dublin, negotiated a 1921 treaty with the British. *What changes did the treaty bring to Ireland?*

Westminister, establishing the Commonwealth of Nations, a voluntary association linking Great Britain and its former colonies on an equal basis.

One of Great Britain's major problems was its relationship with Ireland. Unwilling to wait for home rule, militant Irish nationalists on Easter 1916 had revolted against the British. The brutal crushing of the Easter Uprising by British forces increased Irish support for full independence. In 1921 moderate leaders in Ireland and Great Britain signed a compromise. The Catholic southern part of Ireland became a dominion known as the **Irish Free State**. The largely Protestant north remained joined to Great Britain as Northern Ireland.

Wanting full independence for all of Ireland, Irish radicals, led by **Eamon De Valera**, revolted against the Irish Free State. The Irish government suppressed this uprising, but Irish elections in 1932 brought De Valera to power. Five years later, the country's name was changed to Eire, and a president replaced the British monarch as head of state.

France

World War I had an even more devastating effect on France than on Great Britain. In the four years of fighting, the combatants had destroyed thousands of square miles of farmland and forests and reduced villages and cities to rubble. French casualties were enormous. Half of the males between the ages of 18 and 32 had been killed.

Chapter 29 *Between Two Fires* **779**

The following videotape programs are available from Glencoe:

- **FDR: The Years of Crisis**
- **Eleanor Roosevelt: A Restless Spirit**

ASSESS

Check for Understanding

Assign Section 2 Assessment as homework or as an in-class activity.

 Use Interactive Tutor Self-Assessment Software to review Section 2.

Evaluate

Section Quiz 29-2

Use the Testmaker to create a customized quiz for Section 2.

Reteach

Write the headings *Causes* and *Effects* on the chalkboard and create a class chart to help students review the causes and effects of World War I.

Reading Essentials and Study Guide 29-2

Enrich

Have students use the chart from **Reteach** to write a short report on what they think were the most important effects of World War I on the Western democracies.

CLOSE

Lead a discussion about why democracy survived in the United States, Great Britain, and France after World War I despite serious economic and political problems.

 Jordan Gains Independence

Jordan, 1921

After World War I, lands east and west of the Jordan River were administered by Great Britain. In 1921 the territory east of the Jordan gained partial self-government. This land—then called Transjordan—won full independence in 1946 as a monarchy under King Abdullah. The country was renamed Jordan after it annexed the West Bank of the Jordan River following the 1948–1949 Arab-Israeli war.

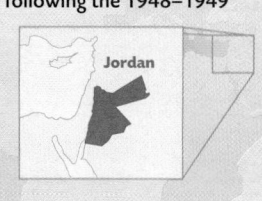

Troubled Years

Like Great Britain, France faced severe economic problems after the war. High unemployment and soaring inflation caused terrible hardships. The French government was nearly bankrupt, and its war debts were staggering. As a result of these financial problems, France's factories, railways, and canals could not be quickly rebuilt.

The political picture was as bleak as the economic one. Many political parties competed for votes. Since each party received seats in the national legislature according to its percentage of the vote, no party ever won a majority of seats. In order to form a government, several parties had to band together into a coalition, or alliance of factions, but the coalition governments often fell apart quickly.

Extremist groups on both the left and the right also threatened the political stability of the nation.

Communists and Socialists struggled for power against Fascists, extreme nationalists favoring a strong government, and outbreaks of violence were common.

The Popular Front

In 1934 the political crisis reached a head. Fascist groups rioted in Paris, killing several people. Fearing a Fascist takeover, the Communists appealed to leaders of the Socialist party for "a broad Popular Front to combat fascism and for work, liberty, and peace."

The new coalition won enough votes in a 1936 election to form a government. **Léon Blum**, the Socialist leader, became prime minister. The Popular Front was in power for about a year, but in that short time it passed many new laws that benefited workers and farmers.

Foreign Policy

Exhausted and drained by World War I, France wanted, above all else, to prevent another war. Consequently, the French government supported the League of Nations in the postwar years and worked to create a series of alliances to contain Germany. But it also sought friendly ties with Germany's new democratic Weimar Republic. In 1925 France signed the Locarno Treaties with Germany, Italy, Belgium, and Great Britain that appeared to ensure a lasting peace.

As added insurance against a future German invasion, France built a series of fortifications that were 200 miles (320 km) long called the Maginot (MA•zhuh•NOH) Line. This stretch of concrete bunkers and trenches extended along France's border with Germany. French military leaders boasted that the Maginot Line could never be crossed. What they failed to consider was that past German invasions had come through Belgium, whose border with France remained virtually undefended.

SECTION 2 ASSESSMENT

Main Idea
1. Use a diagram like the one below to give reasons why democratic government survived in the U.S., Great Britain, and France during the post-World War I era.

U.S.	Great Britain	France

Recall
2. **Define** disarmament, general strike, coalition.
3. **Identify** Franklin D. Roosevelt, Ramsay MacDonald, Commonwealth of Nations, Eamon De Valera, Léon Blum.

Critical Thinking
4. **Evaluating Information** How did British workers

expect a general strike to improve working conditions in the coal mines?

Understanding Themes
5. **Change** How did President Franklin D. Roosevelt's New Deal policies change the role the federal government played in American society after 1933?

SECTION 2 ASSESSMENT ANSWERS

1. Students may conclude that democracy was more firmly established in these countries or that the governments of these nations took bold new steps to meet citizens' needs.
2. All terms are defined in the Glossary.
3. Roosevelt, 778; MacDonald, 779; Commonwealth of Nations, 779; De Valera, 779; Blum, 780

4. They thought that if the majority of the nation's workers refused to work, the government would have to appease their demands for higher wages in order to make them resume work.
5. **CHANGE** The federal government became more actively involved in domestic affairs.

1924 Italy's Benito Mussolini assumes dictatorial powers.

1933 Adolf Hitler becomes chancellor of Germany.

1935 Nuremberg Laws in Germany deprive Jews of rights.

Section 3

Fascist Dictatorships

Guide to Reading

Read to Find Out
Main Idea *Fascist dictatorships arose in Italy and Germany.*

▶ **Terms to Define**
totalitarianism, fascism, corporate state, syndicate, *Kristallnacht*, concentration camp

▶ **People to Meet**
Benito Mussolini, Adolf Hitler

▶ **Places to Locate**
Weimar

The Storyteller

Alice Hamilton was dismayed. Twenty-five years earlier, she had spent a year in Frankfurt as a student. She now returned to visit the city only to find the lovely Römer Platz draped with Nazi flags. The city's children and young people also had changed. Formerly they played games; now they marched in regular ranks. Where tuneful songs had been sung in public houses, militant music blared forth. Mrs. Hamilton understood why this transformation had taken place. Hitler was inspiring Germany's impoverished, hopeless youth to believe they were the elect of the earth.

—adapted from "The Youth Who Are Hitler's Strength," *New York Times Magazine*, October 8, 1933. Alice Hamilton. Reprinted in *Sources of the Western Tradition*, Marvin Perry, 1991

Nazi poster

After World War I, political, economic, and social strife engulfed many Western nations. Long-established democracies remained strong in the United States and Great Britain, but in Italy, Germany, and Russia, a new form of dictatorship known as totalitarianism emerged. Totalitarian governments aimed at total control over every aspect of citizens' lives. Under totalitarianism, the individual was viewed as a servant of the state and was allowed few personal freedoms. Books, radio, films, the arts, and the schools were used to promote the government's political philosophy.

Totalitarianism grew out of World War I. To fight a total war, democratic and autocratic governments alike had temporarily assumed sweeping powers. After the war, totalitarian dictatorships extended such powers further, using their vast authority to remodel entire societies and conquer other lands. In seeking these goals, totalitarian governments came into conflict with each other and with the Western democracies. Their actions set the stage for the beginning of another world war.

Rise of Fascism in Italy

After World War I, a general mood of dissatisfaction gripped the people of Italy. Italian nationalists were outraged that the Paris peace treaties had not given Italy huge portions of territory from the Central Powers. Returning veterans found no work, workers went on strike or took over factories, and peasants seized land. Reeling from an economic downturn, the government was unable to relieve the mounting discontent.

These chaotic conditions favored the rise of **Benito Mussolini** (MOO•suh•LEE•nee). Born in 1883, Mussolini came from a working-class family. As a young journalist, he was active in Socialist politics; but during the war, he switched loyalties and became an ardent nationalist.

Chapter 29 *Between Two Fires* **781**

SECTION THEME

▶ **Uniformity** Fascist governments in Italy and Germany limit individual liberties and stress loyalty to the state.

Guide to Reading

For reading strategies to help students read effectively see pages 12–13.

Vocabulary Pre-check

▣ Use the Vocabulary PuzzleMaker for Chapter 29 to create a crossword puzzle to reinforce section terms. **L1 LEP**

📁 Use Vocabulary Activity 29 to introduce vocabulary terms. **L1 LEP**

FOCUS

Section Objective
Identify factors that led to the rise of Fascist dictatorships in Italy and Germany after World War I.

BELLRINGER
Motivational Activity

Before taking roll at the beginning of the class period, project Section Focus Transparency 29-3 and have students answer the activity questions. Discuss students' responses.

📁 This activity is also available as a blackline master.

SECTION RESOURCES

📁 **Reproducible Masters**
• Lecture Notes 29-3
• Reproducible Lesson Plan 29-3
• Guided Reading Activity 29-3
• History Simulation 29
• Geography and History Activity 29
• Section Quiz 29-3
• Reading Essentials and Study Guide 29-3

🗐 **Transparencies**
• Section Focus Transparency 29-3

Multimedia
▣ Vocabulary PuzzleMaker Software
▣ Interactive Tutor Self-Assessment Software
▣ Testmaker
◉ Lessons of War: *The Enemy*

TEACH

Guided Practice

THEME Uniformity

Ask students if they would like to live in a uniform society. Have them give examples from Fascist Italy and Nazi Germany to illustrate the effects of imposed uniformity. List these examples on the chalkboard as they are given. **L1**

Visualizing History

Point out what effect Mussolini's military attire and disciplined stance would have on the people. When *Il Duce* was in power there were no purges, but he was able to intimidate people with the threat of terror.

Answer to Caption: *Mussolini promised "something to everyone," then used street violence and political pressure to destroy his opponents and get himself named prime minister.*

Recognizing Ideologies Write two headings on the chalkboard: *What the People Wanted* and *What Mussolini Had to Offer*. Encourage students to fill in the chart during class discussion. Ask students to make a similar chart for Adolf Hitler. **L2**

Biography

The following videotape program is available from Glencoe:

- **Mussolini: Italy's Nightmare**

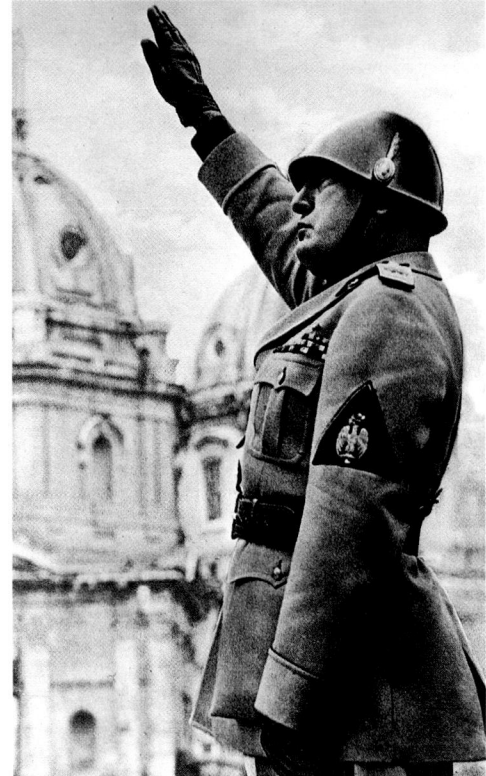

Visualizing History Italian dictator Benito Mussolini salutes soldiers at a military parade. He dreamed of making Italy a great nation and reviving the Roman Empire. *How did Mussolini come to power in Italy?*

Mussolini formed a new political party in 1919 called the *Fasci di Combattimento*, or Fascist party. Fascism (FA•SHIH•zuhm) is a political philosophy that advocates the glorification of the state, a single-party system with a strong ruler, and an aggressive form of nationalism. Like communism, fascism gave the state absolute authority. But fascism defended private property, although with some government regulation, and the class structure. According to its principles, the nation's cause was to be advanced at all cost even by war.

Mussolini's Road to Power

Conditions in Italy continued to deteriorate in the months following the war. The value of the lira

declined steadily, the price of bread rose, and a shortage of coal hampered industrial production. To express their dissatisfaction, workers staged a series of strikes that paralyzed the country. In September 1920, workers in Lombardy and Piedmont took over the factories. Mussolini showed his support for the strikers in a speech at Trieste:

> **❝ I demand that the factories increase their production. If this is guaranteed to me by the workers in place of the industrialists, I shall declare without hesitation that the former have the right to substitute themselves … [for] the latter. ❞**

The unrest spread to rural Italy. Peasants seized land from wealthy landowners, and tenant farmers refused to pay their rents. The situation was so chaotic that the middle and upper classes feared a Communist revolution. Ever the politician, Mussolini offered "a little something to everyone." To appease the landowners, he vowed to end the unrest and protect private property. To woo the workers, he promised full employment and workers' benefits. He pleased nationalists by pledging to restore Italy to its former greatness.

By 1922 the Fascists were ready to use force in a bid for power. The Blackshirts, as Mussolini's followers were called, did not rely on verbal assaults alone to achieve their goals. They physically attacked political opponents in the streets and drove elected officials from office.

Believing that fascism was a useful way of controlling the Socialists and workers, the democratic government did nothing to stop the Blackshirts. As a result, Mussolini grew even bolder. In October 1922 the Fascists staged a march on Rome. Mussolini waited in Milan to see how the government would react. Believing that the Fascists were planning to seize power, the cabinet asked King Victor Emmanuel III to declare martial law. The king refused, and the cabinet resigned. Instead of calling for new elections, the monarch named Mussolini prime minister.

Mussolini's Dictatorship

Mussolini quickly put an end to democratic rule in Italy. In a 1924 election, Blackshirts used their now familiar brutal tactics to make sure that Italians voted for Fascist candidates. As a result, Fascists won a majority of seats in the Italian parliament. The Fascist-controlled parliament gave Mussolini sweeping new powers. After this election Mussolini began calling himself *Il Duce* (eel DOO•chay), "The Leader."

To consolidate his power, Mussolini reorganized the Italian government and established a corporate state. Under the corporate state, Mussolini hoped to bring workers and employers together and consequently to end the political quarreling that he associated with a democratic, multiparty system. To this end, he banned non-Fascist parties and ordered that syndicates, or corporations of workers and employers, be formed in each industry. Each syndicate sent representatives to a legislature in Rome that set policies on wages, production, and distribution. In theory, the corporate state was a new form of democracy; in practice, it was a political tool expressly designed for strengthening Mussolini's power.

Many Italians bitterly opposed fascism. They mourned the loss of democracy and individual freedoms. The Fascists arrested, assaulted, and murdered any who dared speak out against the abuses. "The masses must obey," thundered Mussolini. "They cannot afford to waste time searching for truth."

A majority of Italians, however, supported Mussolini. They believed he had done Italy a great service by preventing a Communist revolution and had brought order to the nation. After all, they said, he "made the trains run on time."

By building up Italy's armed forces, Mussolini did solve the unemployment problem. Even more important, he rekindled the feelings of patriotism and nationalism that had lain dormant in the Italian people. He made it clear to Italians that it was in their destiny to recapture all the greatness that had made the glory of ancient Rome. He would use all the economic and human resources available to make Italy a great power again.

The Weimar Republic

While Mussolini was establishing fascism in Italy, the Allies were preoccupied with ensuring that Germany would never again threaten peace. As a result, the Treaty of Versailles limited the size of Germany's armed forces and required the Germans to form a democratic government. While many Germans believed that democracy had become inevitable after the breakdown of the monarchy, few really believed in it.

In early 1919 Germans went to the polls and elected delegates to a national assembly. Meeting in **Weimar**, the assembly drafted a constitution for Germany establishing a democratic republic. The republic, which lasted from 1919 to 1933, was called the Weimar Republic.

Soon after the Weimar Republic became a reality, political instability and violence threatened to overwhelm it. In 1920 nationalist army officers tried to overthrow the government in a coup d'état. Like many other Germans, they claimed that Weimar leaders had betrayed the nation by accepting the Treaty of Versailles. Although the revolt was suppressed, the government failed to overcome widespread opposition to its policies.

Reparations

More than just political problems threatened Germany. Great Britain and France promised their citizens that the German government would pay reparations for the full cost of the war. The Allies set this cost at $35 billion. Already beset by serious economic problems, the German government in 1922

The blockade of Germany in World War I and postwar reparations on Germany brought hardships to many German citizens. These women in Berlin are searching in a garbage pile for food. *What form of government did Germany have between 1919 and 1933?*

Chapter 29 *Between Two Fires* **783**

Daily Life Ask students to list some freedoms that we take for granted that would be suppressed under Fascist rule. Have a student read the United States Bill of Rights to stimulate a follow-up discussion. **L3**

History Simulation 29

Visualizing History German citizens struggled to survive in a time of increasing inflation. People in the United States were also finding food hard to get and spent hours waiting in breadlines or at soup kitchens.
Answer to Caption: *a democratic republic*

MEETING SPECIAL NEEDS ACTIVITY

Reading Comprehension Suggest that students who have difficulty reading the text take notes as they read. Have them list the headings and write any important ideas, events, and people under the headings. They should also write words they are unsure of and look them up in a dictionary as they study. By the end of the chapter, students will have completed a guide for studying. **L1**

TURNING POINT

Rise of Nazism
How did the rise of Nazism affect Germany and the world?
It ended democracy and established a totalitarian state in Germany; it persecuted opponents and sought to destroy the Jews; its expansionist program set the stage for World War II.

Independent Practice

📁 Guided Reading Activity 29-3 **L1**

📁 Geography and History Activity 29

Biography Have students list the steps in Hitler's rise to power. They may begin with his forming the Brownshirts and conclude with his taking the title of *Der Führer*. **L1 LEP**

Critical Thinking Have students write short essays comparing and contrasting the ways Hitler and Mussolini rose to power. Instruct students to include the conditions that favored each ruler's coming to power. **L2**

Economics Ask students to research the topic of inflation. Have them find or calculate what the inflation rate of the German mark was in 1923, then compare that figure to the current inflation rates in Germany and the United States. **L3**

Global 🍲 Gourmet

Italy is known for its traditional pasta dishes but it also has some foods that reflect German influence. Northeastern Italy has such dishes as sauerbraten, wurst, and strudel (marinated meat, sausage, and a pastry).

announced that it could not under present circumstances meet its obligations.

France, however, insisted that Germany pay its debt. To ensure this result, French troops marched into Germany's industrial Ruhr Valley in 1923 and took control of the coal mines and steel mills. Angered at the French invasion, German workers went on strike while their government paid them. With income from Ruhr industries going to France, Germany had lost an important asset.

Inflation

To meet expenses, the German government printed more and more paper money. As a result, inflation soared. Before the war, 4 marks equaled 1 American dollar. By late 1923, it took 4 trillion marks to equal 1 dollar. Inflation wiped out the savings of many middle-class Germans.

In the mid-1920s, Germany finally saw some relief ahead from its troubles. The French reached a compromise with the Germans that eased payments, and they left the Ruhr. Freed of debt and strengthened by American loans, Germany entered a five-year period of relative prosperity. But the seeds of discontent had already been sown.

TURNING POINT

Rise of Nazism

Among the political parties challenging the Weimar Republic was the National Socialist Workers' party, or Nazi party. One of its first recruits was World War I veteran **Adolf Hitler**. Born in Austria in 1889, Hitler failed in his efforts to become a successful artist. After the war, he settled in Munich and joined the Nazi party.

Hitler soon formed the Brownshirts, a private army of young veterans and street thugs. During the inflationary crisis of 1923, Hitler made an attempt to seize power. With armed Brownshirts outside, Hitler jumped on a table in a Munich beer hall and announced, "The revolution has begun!"

Images *of the* Times

Life in Nazi Germany

During the 1930s, Hitler's National Socialist party ruled Germany with an iron hand. Many Germans accepted the Nazi dictatorship, believing that it would solve the country's problems. Other Germans, however, suffered under Hitler's rule.

Adolf Hitler at a Nazi rally accepts flowers from a German child. German children were taught in schools to honor Hitler as Germany's savior.

German young people joined Nazi youth groups where they participated in parades and athletics and learned Nazi ideas.

784

Images *of the* Times

Life in Nazi Germany

When the Nazis took power in 1933, terror against the Jews escalated. November 9, 1938—*Kristallnacht* (named "The Night of Broken Glass" because of the shattered glass strewn all over German cities)—marked the beginning of the Nazis' open persecution of the Jews. Almost 8,000 Jewish businesses were destroyed, homes were broken into and looted, and 177 synagogues were gutted. Main streets everywhere were littered with glass. This night of terror was the start of massive arrests and transportation of Jews to concentration camps.

When the police intervened and arrested Hitler, however, the revolt quickly collapsed.

While in prison, Hitler wrote his autobiography, *Mein Kampf (My Struggle)*. In Hitler's view, the Germans were not responsible for losing the war. He blamed the Jews and the Communists for the German defeat. He also declared that the Germans were a "master race" whose destiny was to rule the world. Hitler saw himself as the leader who would unite all German-speaking people into a new empire that would dominate other groups.

After his release from prison, Hitler resumed his activities. When the Great Depression struck in 1929, he appealed to German workers and industrialists alike with his promise to end unemployment and restore Germany's military might. In the early 1930s, the Nazis won a large number of seats in the multiparty Reichstag, or legislative lower house. With the government paralyzed by divisions, conservative politicians decided to back Hitler and use him for their own ends. In 1933 Hitler became chancellor. Through entirely legal means, the Nazis had come to power.

Hitler in Power

Hitler's goal all along was the creation of a totalitarian state. Because the Nazis were still a minority in the Reichstag, however, he planned to hold a new election. But a week before it was to be held, the Reichstag building mysteriously caught fire and burned to the ground. Hoping to reduce Communist support among the workers, Hitler blamed the Communists for the fire. In the election, the Brownshirts forced German voters to back the Nazis. When the Nazi-dominated Reichstag met after the election, it voted Hitler emergency powers to deal with the "Communist threat."

Hitler used his new powers to crush his opponents and consolidate his rule. All political parties, except the Nazi party were banned, and constitutional guarantees of freedom of speech, assembly, press and religion were ended. The Nazi government took over the labor unions and regulated production and wages. It also tried to control the Christian churches and silence clergy who opposed Nazi policies.

The Jews of Germany were persecuted by the Nazis. Nazi groups often terrorized Jewish people and vandalized Jewish-owned businesses.

REFLECTING ON THE TIMES

1. How were Germany's young people influenced by the Nazis?
2. How did Nazi rule affect Germany's Jews?

785

ASSESS

Check for Understanding

Assign Section 3 Assessment as homework or as an in-class activity.

 Use Interactive Tutor Self-Assessment Software to review Section 3.

Evaluate
Section Quiz 29-3

Reteach

Review with students the differences in postwar life in the United States, Great Britain, France, Italy, and Germany. Discuss the reasons democracy continued in the United States, France, and Great Britain, but not in Italy and Germany.

Reading Essentials and Study Guide 29-3

Enrich

Show students a documentary film of Nazi rallies in the 1930s such as the Nazi propaganda film *Triumph of the Will* or the American propaganda film *Nazi Strike*. Discuss the feelings they have after seeing and hearing Hitler speak.

Who?What?Where?When?

The Sound of Music, the Rodgers and Hammerstein musical, depicts the Nazi takeover of Austria.

ANSWERS TO REFLECTING ON THE TIMES

1. Young people were taught Nazi ideas at school and in youth groups.
2. Hitler's rule led to the persecution of Germany's Jews.

Linking Past and Present

Anne Frank was a Jewish girl who kept a diary during the two years she spent hiding with her family in an attic in Amsterdam. She was arrested in 1944 and sent to the Nazi death camp at Bergen-Belsen, where she died at the age of 15. Her account, *The Diary of a Young Girl*, was published in 1952. More than thirty years later, in 1987, Miep Gies, the woman who hid the Frank family, wrote her own story, *Anne Frank Remembered*, about life under Nazi occupation and what she remembers of Anne Frank.

Visualizing History

Point out the Hitler salute in the photo and explain that this "Heil Hitler" salute became a famous gesture associated with Hitler.

Answer to Caption: *Hitler wanted to expand German territory and make it into a mighty world power.*

CLOSE

Hold a class discussion to help students outline what led to the rise of Fascist dictatorships in Italy and Germany. For each country, have students create a flowchart of the events on the chalkboard. Encourage students to copy the flowchart and use it for reference.

Attacks on the Jews

Hitler directed his most bitter attacks against the Jews. In 1935 the Nuremberg Laws stripped Jews of their citizenship and their right to hold public office. The laws barred Jewish students from schools and destroyed Jewish businesses. In the *Kristallnacht* of November 9 and 10, 1938, Nazis attacked Jews on the streets and vandalized Jewish property. Hitler's secret police, the Gestapo, arrested Jews and political opponents by the thousands. Many were shot. Others were sent to concentration camps, large prison camps where people were confined under harsh conditions.

Hitler was suspicious of even his closest supporters. He particularly feared radical members among the Brownshirts and set out to weaken their ranks. On June 30, 1934, the "Night of Long Knives," Hitler had hundreds of Brownshirts and their leaders shot.

The Third Reich

Assured of absolute power, Hitler took the title of *der Führer* (duhr FYUR•uhr), "the Leader." He called his government the Third Reich (RYK), or Third Empire, and boasted it would last 1,000 years. To reach this end, he set about restoring Germany's military might. He ignored the provisions of the Versailles Treaty, which limited the size of the German army, and ordered German factories to begin turning out guns, ammunition, airplanes, tanks, and other weapons. He made no secret of his ambitions to expand Germany's territory: "Today, Germany; tomorrow, the world!"

Hitler also brought all intellectual and artistic activity in Germany under his control and imposed his own ideas on the arts. To glorify Nazism, he made plans to rebuild Berlin in the style of monumental classical architecture. He discouraged the artistic experimentation that had flourished during the 1920s. As a result, many of Germany's most talented artists and scientists—such as Walter Gropius, Arnold Schoenberg, Sigmund Freud, and Albert Einstein—fled the country.

Hitler actively used the media to flood Germany with propaganda praising the Nazi cause. The government stressed the importance of a strong military and devotion to the nation and its leader. Hitler also set up organizations for young people between the ages of 6 and 18 to mold German youth to accept Nazi ideas.

SECTION 3 ASSESSMENT

Main Idea
1. Use a diagram like the one below to list factors that led to the rise of dictatorship in Italy.

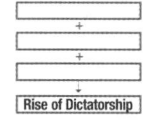

Recall
2. **Define** totalitarianism, fascism, corporate state, syndicate, *Kristallnacht*, concentration camp.
3. **Identify** Benito Mussolini, Weimar, Adolf Hitler.

Critical Thinking
4. **Analyzing Information** Why did fascism appeal to many Italians and Germans in the decade following World War I?

Understanding Themes
5. **Uniformity** Analyze the Nazi government. What were its goals?

SECTION 3 ASSESSMENT ANSWERS

1. chaotic conditions after World War I (no work, peasants seized land, economic downturn); Mussolini formed Fascist party; workers staged strikes, Mussolini supported them; Fascists tried to please all dissatisfied factions; king refused to dictate martial law and named Mussolini prime minister

2. All terms are defined in the Glossary.
3. Benito Mussolini, 781; Weimar, 783; Adolf Hitler, 784
4. because the economic and social chaos created by war and depression made both Italy and Germany ripe for Fascist-style revolution
5. **UNIFORMITY** Germany was a totalitarian state under the Nazi party led by Adolf Hitler. All other political parties were banned; constitutional freedoms were ended; controls were placed on all aspects of society; goals were to make Germany militarily strong, end the depression in Germany, and eliminate Jews/various opponents from Germany.

Analyzing Political Cartoons

Do you enjoy reading the comics section in the newspaper? Most people do. Cartoons also appear on the editorial page. These give opinions on political issues. Political cartoons are good historical sources because they reflect opinions on current affairs.

Learning the Skill

Using caricature and symbols, political cartoonists help readers see relationships and draw conclusions about events. A caricature exaggerates a detail such as a subject's features. Cartoonists use caricature to create a positive or negative impression. For example, if a cartoon shows one figure three times larger than another, it implies that one figure is more powerful than the other.

A symbol is an image or object that represents something else. For example, a cartoonist may use a crown to represent monarchy. Symbols often represent nations or political parties. Uncle Sam is a common symbol for the United States.

To analyze a political cartoon, first identify the topic and principal characters. Read labels and messages. Note relationships between the figures and symbols. Review your knowledge of the cartoon's topic to determine the cartoonist's viewpoint and message.

Practicing the Skill

The political cartoon on this page, published in 1938, makes a statement about the dictatorships that developed in Europe after World War I and the reaction of the Western democracies toward them. Study the cartoon and then answer these questions.

1. What do the figures represent?

2. Why is the standing figure so large?
3. What is the standing figure holding and what is it attached to?
4. What is the message of the cartoon?

Applying the Skill

Choose a current issue on which you hold a strong opinion. Draw a political cartoon expressing your opinion on this issue. Show it to a friend to find out if the message is clear. If not, revise the cartoon to clarify its point.

For More Practice

Turn to the Skill Practice in the Chapter Assessment on page 793 for more practice in analyzing a political cartoon.

The **Glencoe Skillbuilder Interactive Workbook**, Level 2 provides instruction and practice in key social studies skills.

WOULD YOU OBLIGE ME WITH A MATCH PLEASE?

TEACH

Analyzing Political Cartoons

Bring some political cartoons to class, such as the ones that appear on the editorial page of many newspapers. Before having the class read the skill, distribute copies of the cartoons. What is each cartoon's message and how did you figure it out? After a short class discussion, ask students to read the skill and complete the practice questions.

Ask students to look for political cartoons in newspapers and magazines and bring them to class. Have students apply what they learned about analyzing political cartoons to explain the cartoons to the class.

Additional Practice

Skill Reinforcement Activity 29

GLENCOE TECHNOLOGY

Glencoe's **Skillbuilder Interactive Workbook, Level 2** This interactive CD-ROM promotes student mastery of key social studies skills.

ANSWERS TO PRACTICING THE SKILL

1. The seated figure represents Western democracies. The standing figure represents the dictatorships.
2. The standing figure is large because it implies that dictatorships are becoming more powerful than democracies.
3. The standing figure is holding a rope that is attached to a bomb.
4. The dictatorships are setting the stage for the beginning of another world war with Western democracies.

Chapter 29 *Between Two Fires* **787**

1921 Lenin announces New Economic Policy.

1928 Stalin promotes collective farms.

1932 "Terror famine" sweeps Ukraine.

Section 4

The Soviet Union

Guide to Reading

Read to Find Out

Main Idea *Joseph Stalin's rule transformed the Soviet Union.*

▶ **Terms to Define**
nationalization, dictatorship of the proletariat, collectivization, kulak, purge, Socialist realism

▶ **People to Meet**
Vladimir Ilyich Ulyanov (Lenin), Leon Trotsky, Joseph Stalin, Maksim Gorky

▶ **Places to Locate**
Georgia, Ukraine

The Storyteller

It was 35 degrees below zero when the team set out for work at Magnitogorsk. They would weld fittings to the blast furnaces 100 feet off the

Soviet construction project, 1930s

ground. It was hazardous work, for ice coated every surface. Three hours into the day a rigger fell off the scaffolding. Badly injured, he was carried to the first-aid station. His shaken companions talked of the need to improve the scaf-folding. The foreman, how-ever, blamed the workers. "You ploughboys don't know how to be careful. You don't pay as much attention as you should. People will fall, but we are building blast furnaces all the same, aren't we?"

—adapted from *Behind the Urals: An American Worker in Russia's City of Steel*, John Scott, reprinted in *The Global Experience*, Volume 2, 1987

By 1921 Russia had endured the horrors of world war, revolution, and civil war. In the course of seven years of conflict, 27 million people had perished. Most had died on the battlefields and in countless guerrilla engagements, but millions had died of disease and starvation as well. In addition, the nation's transport system was in ruins, the peasants were in open revolt, and the economy was plunging toward collapse. At the Tenth Party Congress, Red Army director Leon Trotsky proclaimed: "We have destroyed the country in order to defeat the Whites."

Lenin in Power

In their struggle for survival during the civil war, **Vladimir Ilyich Ulyanov** (ool•YAH•nuhf), also known as **Lenin**, and the Bolsheviks had introduced an economic policy called war communism in 1918. Under war communism, the government carried out a policy of nationalization, in which it brought under state control all major industries. Applying the principle that those who would eat must work, the government required everyone between the ages of 16 and 50 to hold a job. It also erected a huge bureaucratic administration that wielded tremendous power but was extremely inefficient.

In 1921 Lenin tried to bring order out of the chaos that both war and government policy had caused. He announced a plan called the New Economic Policy, or NEP. Major industries such as steel, railroads, and large-scale manufacturing remained under government control. But in an attempt to stimulate the economy, Lenin allowed some private businesses to operate. In a startling departure from Marxist theory, NEP permitted small manufacturers and farmers to own their own businesses and to sell what they produced for a profit.

In 1922 the Communists changed the official name of the country from Russia to the Union of

---

Soviet Socialist Republics (USSR), or the Soviet Union. During this time, Lenin and other Communist leaders also completed a new constitution. This constitution stated that the USSR was a Socialist state, meaning that the government controlled the means of production.

In theory this state, called the dictatorship of the proletariat, was controlled by workers. But in practice the leadership of the Communist party controlled the workers. It was, as German Communist party member Rosa Luxemburg observed: "... a dictatorship, to be sure, not the dictatorship of the proletariat, however, but only the dictatorship of a handful of politicians." The classless society envisioned by Marx was, in the Soviet Union, a pyramid, with the party boss at the top and the peasants at the bottom.

The non-Russian nationalities in the USSR did not fare much better than the peasants. Because Lenin did not want to break up the old Russian Empire into independent states, he gave each major nationality its own republic with its own bureaucracy. In reality, however, the central government in Moscow still made the important decisions for these republics. In spite of the government's talk about equality for all nationalities, the Russians remained the dominant group in the Soviet Union and largely determined its policies.

Trotsky and Stalin

In 1922 Lenin suffered two strokes that left him permanently disabled. He died two years later at the age of 54.

The struggle to succeed Lenin began during his final illness. The two main contenders for the position were **Leon Trotsky** and **Joseph Stalin**. Next to Lenin, Trotsky had been the most important person in the Communist party. He had played a key role in the Bolshevik Revolution and had built the Red Army into a powerful fighting force. Trotsky came from a middle-class background and was a scholar who contributed many new ideas to the Marxist movement. He was also a speaker of great power and eloquence.

Born in **Georgia**, a territory south of Russia, Stalin was the son of artisans. A seminary student in his youth, Stalin was punished for reading books about revolution and social conditions, including novels such as *Les Misérables*. Stalin later renounced Russian Orthodoxy and became a Marxist revolutionary. Unlike Trotsky, Stalin was a skilled administrator. In 1922 he rose to the post of general secretary of the Communist party.

Visualizing History Lenin's New Economic Policy (NEP) helped put the Soviet Union's economy back on its feet in the early 1920s. *In what way did NEP depart from Marxist theory?*

Trotsky and Stalin held fundamentally different views about the path the Soviet Union should follow. Like Lenin, Trotsky believed in the theory of a "permanent revolution." He believed that only when the Russian Revolution had touched off uprisings all over the world could Socialists build an ideal society in the Soviet Union. Stalin, in contrast, declared it possible and necessary to "build socialism in a single country." By this he meant that the Soviet Union should concentrate on growing strong first, before it tried to spread revolution around the world.

Trotsky was better known than Stalin, both at home and in the Comintern (Communist International), an organization of Communist parties from all over the world. Moreover, Trotsky had been closer to Lenin. Nevertheless, Stalin managed to outmaneuver Trotsky politically. As general secretary, Stalin had the authority to appoint and remove officials. He gradually gained control of the party bureaucracy. As soon as he was securely in power, Stalin exiled Trotsky to Siberia and then expelled him from the Soviet Union. Trotsky eventually settled in Mexico City, where he continued to write about communism and the Soviet Union. An assassin acting on Stalin's orders murdered Trotsky in 1940.

Chapter 29 *Between Two Fires* **789**

TEACH

Guided Practice

THEME Uniformity

Ask students to imagine the United States government taking total control of all industrial and agricultural production. Have students tell ways such control would change daily life. (*Average citizens could not own businesses; the government would control the supply of food and industrial products.*) Ask students how they would react to such a government. **L1**

Visualizing History Lenin's New Economic Policy was a radical change that opened the way for a modified form of capitalism. Whereas selling for profit had once been a crime against the state, it was now officially encouraged. However, along with Lenin's strategy to get the economy moving came a new tightening of discipline.
Answer to Caption: *It allowed small manufacturers and farmers to own businesses and sell their products for a profit.*

Literature Lead a discussion on Socialist realism, or the literary and artistic style that became obligatory under Stalin's rule. Ask what the aim of art was under Socialist realism. Discuss how this style stifled artistic expression. **L3**

Independent Practice

📁 Guided Reading Activity 29-4 **L1**

COOPERATIVE LEARNING ACTIVITY

Advertising Plans Organize the class into three groups and have each group create an advertising plan. One group's plan should promote the Bolshevik policy of communism, or government control over all major industries; another group should promote Lenin's New Economic Policy (NEP), which allowed some private businesses to operate but maintained government control over steel, railroads, and large-scale manufacturing; the last group should create an advertisement to support Stalin's Five-Year Plan, which set Soviet economic goals for that period and brought industrial and agricultural production under government control. Each group should research its topic, create an advertisement, and select someone to present it. **L2**

VIDEODISC
Communism and the Cold War

Side One, Chapter 9
Frames 14929–17326
Title: *Growing Up Communist*
Ask: What did the leaders of the Soviet Union feel they could teach the world? *(to work collectively)*

Answer
This land gave Russia greater access to the Black Sea and created a larger buffer between Germany and Russia.

Stalin's Dictatorship
What were the major features of Stalin's dictatorship?
One of the world's most brutal governments, Stalin's dictatorship employed terror through the secret police, purged Old Bolshevik leaders and secured mastery of the Communist party, and sought control of the arts.

ASSESS

Check for Understanding

Assign Section 4 Assessment as homework or as an in-class activity.

■ Use Interactive Tutor Self-Assessment Software to review Section 4.

Russia 1914–1922

Russian border, 1914
Area lost at Brest-Litovsk, 1918
Area regained, 1922

Map Study
Russia gave up a vast amount of territory in the 1918 Treaty of Brest-Litovsk.
Region Why was the land Russia regained by 1922 particularly valuable to the nation?

Five-Year Plans

Fearing war with the West, Stalin wanted to rapidly transform the Soviet Union into an industrial power. In 1928 he declared an end to NEP and announced the first of his Five-Year Plans, a program that set economic goals for a five-year period. The plan brought all industrial and agricultural production under government control. It also provided for housing, health care, and other services.

While promising a better future, Stalin demanded sacrifices from the Soviet people. The first Five-Year Plan concentrated on building heavy industry. Consumer goods were produced in small amounts and were of inferior quality.

Responsibility for administering the plan lay in the hands of bureaucrats in Moscow. Theirs was a difficult task requiring tight control and careful planning. Not surprisingly, they made plenty of mistakes. For example, one Soviet enterprise

purchased its nail supply from a nail factory many miles away, while a nail factory across the street was shipping its goods a similar distance. Despite the mistakes, the first Five-Year Plan was a success in spurring industrial growth.

Collective Farms

In agriculture, Stalin's plan called for collectivization, a system of farming in which the government owned the land and used peasants to farm it. Stalin believed that collective farms would be more efficient. They would not only produce food for the Soviet people but produce it for export as well. By increasing agricultural exports, Stalin hoped to pay for Soviet industrialization without borrowing from the capitalist West.

Stalin also planned to use collectivization to intimidate the Soviet Union's peasant majority, most of whom were fiercely anti-Communist. Kulaks, or the most prosperous peasants, especially opposed collectivization. They had prospered under NEP and did not want to give up their land, livestock, and machinery. Fighting broke out in the countryside when the government tried to impose its plans. Thousands of peasants and their families were killed or arrested and sent to labor camps in Siberia. Stalin also took measures to crush anti-Communist resistance in **Ukraine**. By seizing the region's grain during the terrible winter of 1932, Stalin promoted a "terror famine," causing the deaths of millions of Ukrainian peasants.

Results

The first Five-Year Plan transformed the Soviet Union into an industrial power, but the human cost of the plan was enormous. Industrial workers received low wages, or none at all, and food was often limited in quantity. Millions of people died because of rural unrest, and collective farms were often unable to provide enough grain to feed the nation's population.

Stalin's Dictatorship

Stalin ruled the Soviet Union from the mid-1920s until his death in 1953. During this period he established one of the most brutal dictatorships the world has ever seen. Stalin demanded complete obedience from the people he ruled and got it through an effective use of terror. He granted the secret police immense power, which they used to scrutinize every aspect of the nation's social and

---

MEETING SPECIAL NEEDS ACTIVITY

Study Strategy To visually clarify the information in this section, have students create a chart that summarizes the changes brought about by Lenin and Stalin in the Soviet Union. Headings for one axis of the chart might include *Major Industries, Small Businesses, Agriculture, Non-Russian Nationalities, Communist Party, The Arts, Comintern.* Headings for the other axis would be *Stalin, Lenin.*
L2

political life. Secret police agents encouraged workers to spy on each other and children to spy on their parents. Those accused of disloyalty were shot or sent to labor camps in Siberia. The secret police and their activities helped to create a climate of fear in Soviet society.

Purges

In the 1930s Stalin began a methodical attack upon his potential enemies, which even members of the Communist party did not escape. In the year 1934 an unknown assailant, probably acting on Stalin's orders, assassinated a high party official. Stalin used the event to rid himself of opponents and strengthen his hold on the party. He had millions of party members expelled, arrested and put in labor camps, or shot.

Stalin then turned against the Old Bolsheviks. These officials had been associates of Lenin and Stalin in the early days of the movement. Because some of them had sided with Trotsky, Stalin moved in 1936 to purge, or remove, them from any position where they could threaten his leadership. He had them arrested and put on trial. In open court in Moscow, with foreign reporters looking on, they pleaded guilty to false charges of treason, murder, and other crimes. Although these prisoners showed no signs of mistreatment, many Western experts have since concluded that the secret police used psychological torture to break their wills.

The Arts

Stalin also set out to put all artistic and cultural activities under the Communist party's control. In

Visualizing History The Soviet government used posters to glorify Soviet achievements and to urge people to carry out the goals of the Communist party. *How did Stalin strengthen his hold on the Soviet Union and the Communist party?*

1934 he put **Maksim Gorky**, one of the Soviet Union's leading writers, in charge of all Soviet culture. Gorky promoted a new literary style that soon became obligatory in the arts: Socialist realism. Writers and artists created a "new reality" by glorifying Soviet heroes and achievements, while denouncing the rumors about forced labor and terror. Artists who violated these dictates faced exile or imprisonment in labor camps.

Stalin's restrictions had a chilling effect on Soviet artists. Although talented writers and artists struggled to survive, most official artistic works were predictable and uninspiring.

The Comintern

In 1919 Lenin had established the Communist International, or Comintern. The goal of the Comintern was to encourage Communist parties in other countries to overthrow their governments by any means and to establish Soviet-style regimes. While Stalin at first gave low priority to Comintern affairs, he later took them more seriously. However, Stalin decided to dissolve the Comintern in 1943, to win the favor of the Western Allies during World War II.

---

spread propaganda by bombarding the Soviets with his portraits—they were hung in schoolrooms and every public building.
Answer to Caption: *He used terror tactics to demand obedience. He expelled millions of Communists from the party. All Soviet citizens accused of disloyalty were arrested.*

Evaluate

  Section Quiz 29-4

🔲 Use the Testmaker to create a customized quiz for Section 4.

Reteach

Review with students the economic and cultural changes that took place under Lenin and Stalin. Discuss these items from the points of view of the leaders and the general public.

Reteaching Activity 29

Reading Essentials and Study Guide 29-4

Enrich

Books and music can bring the period to life. Suggest that students read *And Quiet Flows the Don* by Mikhail Sholokov or listen to the music of Rimsky-Korsakov or Shostakovich.

  Enrichment Activity 29

CLOSE

Have students discuss what postwar life was like for the average citizen in the Soviet Union. Have students compare this picture to postwar life in Italy, Germany, and the Western democracies.

SECTION 4 ASSESSMENT

Main Idea
1. Use a diagram like the one below to identify ways in which Stalin's rule changed the Soviet Union.

How Stalin's Rule Changed Soviet Union

Recall
2. **Define** nationalization, dictatorship of the proletariat, collectivization, kulak, purge, Socialist realism.
3. **Identify** Vladimir Ilyich Ulyanov (Lenin), Leon Trotsky, Joseph Stalin, Georgia, Ukraine, Maksim Gorky.

Critical Thinking
4. **Analyzing Information** What effects did Stalin's policies have on the Soviet people? Are these effects still felt today? Explain.
Understanding Themes
5. **Uniformity** Predict what might have happened if Trotsky had succeeded Lenin.

SECTION 4 ASSESSMENT ANSWERS

1. government control of all industrial and agricultural production; few consumer goods produced; collectivization; secret police; labor camps for dissenters; purges of enemies and members of Communist party; Communist control of artistic and cultural acts; dissolved Comintern
2. All terms are defined in the Glossary.
3. Lenin, 788; Trotsky, 789; Stalin, 789; Georgia, 789; Ukraine, 790; Gorky, 791
4. Many peoples died or suffered hardships from harsh government policies; yes, society is freer but more disorganized.
5. **UNIFORMITY** Answers will vary. Students may conclude that Trotsky's regime may have been less repressive.

CHAPTER 29 ASSESSMENT

WORLD HISTORY *Online*

Have students use the **Chapter 29 Self-Check Quiz** at worldhistory.glencoe.com to prepare for the Chapter Test.

GLENCOE
TECHNOLOGY

VIDEODISC
Use MindJogger to review the chapter.

MindJogger Videoquiz

Chapter 29
Disc 4 Side B

 Also available in VHS.

Answers

Using Key Terms

1. i 3. d 5. c
2. b 4. k

Using Your History Journal

Be sure students have used some quotes from the interviews.

Reviewing Facts

1. banned political parties except Nazi party; ended freedom of speech, assembly, religion, press; took over labor unions; tried to control churches and end opposition; attacked Jews; Nuremberg Laws; concentration camps; intellectual activity under his control; organizations to make youth accept Nazism
2. automobiles, radios, vacuum cleaners, packaged foods, refrigerators, movies, and electric irons
3. T. S. Eliot, new style of writing; Pablo Picasso, cubism; Arnold Schoenberg, 12-note scale
4. Americans were weary of war and international problems.
5. nationalist outrage; strikes; peasant seizure of lands; economic downturn; political paralysis; high unemployment; influence

WORLD HISTORY *Online*

Self-Check Quiz

Visit the *World History: The Human Experience* Web site at **worldhistory.glencoe.com** and click on *Chapter 29—Self-Check Quiz* to prepare for the Chapter Test.

Using Key Terms

Write the key term that completes each sentence. Then write a sentence for each term not chosen.

a. cubism
b. coalition
c. surrealism
d. fascism
e. purge
f. kulaks
g. concentration camps
h. disarmament
i. corporate state
j. nationalization
k. *Kristallnacht*
l. general strike

1. Under the _____, Mussolini hoped to bring workers and employers together.
2. Because there were numerous political parties, the formation of a government in France required a _____ of several parties.
3. _____ is a political philosophy that glorifies the state, supports a single-party system under a strong leader, and promotes an aggressive form of nationalism.
4. In the _____, members of the Nazi party attacked Jews on the streets and vandalized Jewish businesses, homes, and synagogues.
5. The art form of _____ used dreamlike images and unnatural combinations of objects.

Technology Activity

Developing a Multimedia Presentation Search the Internet or your local library for sources on World War I. Based on your research, create a multimedia presentation about the economic effects of World War I on Western countries. Use images from the Internet in your presentation. Include a plan describing the type of presentation you would like to develop and the steps you will take to ensure a successful presentation.

Using Your History Journal

Use your notes from the interview of a person who lived through the period between the wars. Write an account of how events affected ordinary people's lives.

Reviewing Facts

1. **Government** Use a diagram like the one below to show governmental actions Hitler took after coming to power.

Hitler's Actions	

2. **Technology** List the technological advances in the 1920s and 1930s that impacted people.
3. **Culture** Identify three artists who produced changes in literature, art, music, or architecture. Describe the contributions each made.
4. **History** Explain why the United States retreated into isolationism after World War I.
5. **Culture** Explain the rise of fascism in Italy.
6. **Culture** Discuss how Hitler rose to power.
7. **Government** Explain how Hitler and Mussolini strengthened their political power.
8. **Economics** Identify Lenin's NEP.
9. **Government** Describe how Stalin defeated Trotsky.

Critical Thinking

1. **Apply** Why was World War I a watershed event in the twentieth century?
2. **Apply** How did Einstein's theories affect twentieth-century science and culture?
3. **Analyze** Compare totalitarianism and democracy. Why did totalitarian governments rise to power after World War I?
4. **Analyze** How does the term "Night of Terror" describe *Kristallnacht*?

---

of Mussolini
6. Hitler fostered belief in German supremacy.
7. Mussolini gave the state absolute authority; Hitler crushed Communist opponents until he gained control.
8. put major industries under government control but permitted small manufacturers and farmers to own businesses
9. Stalin was a more skilled administrator and used his post to gain control politically.

Critical Thinking

1. It radically changed the way people looked at the world.
2. Einstein's theories laid the foundation of modern physics with his understanding of relativity and atomic theory; made possible the development of uses for atomic energy.
3. Totalitarianism sees individual as a servant of the state, while democracy sees government as the servant of individuals. Totalitarian gov-

5. Synthesize To aid Germany's economic recovery after World War I, how might the Allies have structured the peace settlements?

6. Compare How does fascism differ from communism? How do both differ from capitalism?

7. Analyze Salvador Dali was influenced by Sigmund Freud. How is Freud's influence evident in *The Persistence of Memory* (1931)?

*The Persistence of Memory, Salvador Dali.
Museum of Modern Art, New York, New York*

Understanding Themes

1. Innovation How did new movements in literature and the arts reflect changes after World War I?

2. Change How was Roosevelt's New Deal similar to Stalin's Five-Year Plan? How was it different?

3. Uniformity Why did the Nazis try to control labor unions and the Christian churches? Why did they mistreat Germany's Jewish population?

4. Uniformity How did Lenin try to unify all non-Russian republics under one government?

Linking Past and Present

During the 1920s and 1930s the automobile, motion pictures, and the radio transformed the way Americans lived. What technological advances shape our lives today? Are they negative or positive? Explain.

Skill Practice

Study the cartoon and answer the questions.

1. Who is the figure in the cartoon?
2. What country does the flag represent?
3. What is the message of the cartoon?

Geography in History

1. **Place** In which countries did Fascist governments come to power during the 1930s?
2. **Region** In what region of Europe were 10 of the 11 democracies in the 1930s?

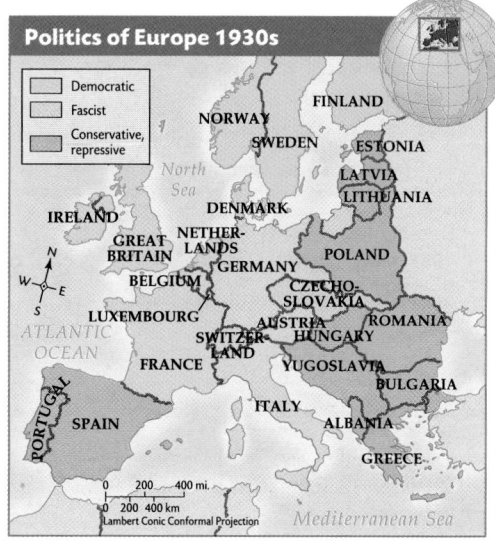

Politics of Europe 1930s

---

7. Answers should mention that the bizarre images reflect Dali's attempt to explore the unconscious mind.

Understanding Themes

1. **INNOVATION** reflected disillusionment and search for new ideas and ways of portraying the world

2. **CHANGE** Both plans brought enormous changes in the two countries and increased the governments' involvement in social and economic affairs. The New Deal did not demand great sacrifices from the people.

3. **UNIFORMITY** to create a totalitarian state; because they blamed the Jews for German defeat in World War I and saw the Jews as inferior.

4. **UNIFORMITY** gave each nationality its own republic but had Moscow make the important decisions

Linking Past and Present

the computer, lasers, microwaves, and televisions; answers will vary

Skill Practice

1. Communists
2. United States
3. Americans did not want Communists in the United States.

Geography in History

1. Germany, Austria, Italy
2. northwestern Europe

? Chapter Bonus Test Question

Ask students: Given the state in which Germany, Italy, and Russia found themselves after World War I, could they have achieved economic health and national self-respect by any means other than totalitarianism? Explain your answer.

---

ernments arose in countries that had many social and economic problems and weak democratic traditions. The conditions of war had increased government powers (temporarily) even in democracies.

4. It describes the terrorizing and assault on Jews and their property by the Nazis.

5. Possible answer: The Allies should have imposed milder terms on Germany and reduced its war debt payments.

6. Fascism defended private property and class structure and made the nation supreme. Communism, in theory, did away with private property and class division and worked for a workers' revolution. Fascism and communism both emphasize the role of the state in all areas of life, especially in the economy. Capitalism, although limited by some regulations, allows a free market of private owners who make their own economic decisions.

A complete, 1-page lesson plan is provided for each section in the *Reproducible Lesson Plans* booklet.

Nationalism in Asia, Africa, and Latin America

CHAPTER RESOURCES

	Reproducible Resources	Multimedia Resources
Chapter Opener	Chapter Themes: Graphic Organizer 30 Historical Significance Chapter Activity 30	MindJogger Videoquiz

Chapter Enrichment	Vocabulary Activity 30*
	Time Line Activity 30
	Mapping History Activity 30
	History Simulation 30
	Geography and History Activity 30
	Source Reading 30
	People in World History Profiles 57, 58
	World Literature Selection 7
	World Art and Music Activity 30
	Enrichment Activity 30
	Critical Thinking Activity 30
	Skill Reinforcement Activity 30
	Performance Assessment Activity 30
	Standardized Test Practice Workbook
	    Activity 30
	Inclusion for the Social Studies Classroom
	    Strategies and Activities
		World History and Art
		    Transparency 40, *Zapatistas*; 41,
		    Turkestan Oriental Rugs
		Chapter Transparency 30
		Vocabulary PuzzleMaker Software
		In the Holy Land: *Arab violence*
		    1919–1921
		Lessons of War:
		    Philosophy of Nonviolence
		World History Primary Source
		    Document Library

Chapter Review/Reteaching	Reteaching Activity 30
	Skill Reinforcement Activity 30
	Spanish Chapter Summary 30
		Chapter 30 Digest Audiocassette,
		    Activity, Test*
		Vocabulary PuzzleMaker Software
		Interactive Tutor Self-Assessment
		    Software
		MindJogger Videoquiz

Chapter Evaluation/Testing	Performance Assessment Activity 30 Chapter 30 Test, Forms A and B	ExamView® Pro Testmaker

* Also available in Spanish

`0:00` OUT OF TIME? Assign the Chapter 30 Audiocassettes.

World History Primary Source Document Library

Make History Come Alive!

Engage your students with over 250 easily accessible primary source documents—available on this CD-ROM—that will give them real life insight into the important events of world history.

Block Schedule

Activities that are particularly suited to use within the block scheduling framework are identified throughout this chapter by the following designation.

KEY TO ABILITY LEVELS

Teaching strategies are coded for varying learning styles.

L1 BASIC activities for all students

L2 AVERAGE activities for average to above-average students

L3 CHALLENGING activities for above-average students

LEP LIMITED ENGLISH PROFICIENCY activities

Use Glencoe's *Presentation Plus!* multimedia teacher tool to easily present dynamic lessons that visually excite your students. Using Microsoft PowerPoint® you can customize the presentations to create your own personalized lessons.

Interactive Lesson Planner

Planning has never been easier! Using this CD-ROM, organize your week, month, semester, or year with all the help you need. The **Interactive Lesson Planner** gives you access to all of the blackline masters that accompany *World History: The Human Experience.*

SECTION RESOURCES

Daily Objectives	Reproducible Resources	Multimedia Resources
Section 1 **New Forces in the Middle East and Africa** Identify how the forces of nationalism affected events in the Middle East and Africa after World War I.	Lecture Notes 30-1 Reproducible Lesson Plan 30-1 Vocabulary Activity 30* Guided Reading Activity 30-1* People in World History Profile 58 Section Quiz 30-1* Reading Essentials and Study Guide 30-1	Section Focus Transparency 30-1 Chapter Transparency 30 Interactive Tutor Self-Assessment Software Testmaker In the Holy Land: *Arab violence 1919–1921*
Section 2 **India's Struggle for Independence** State the methods Gandhi used in India's struggle for independence from British rule.	Lecture Notes 30-2 Reproducible Lesson Plan 30-2 Vocabulary Activity 30* Guided Reading Activity 30-2* Section Quiz 30-2* Reading Essentials and Study Guide 30-2	Section Focus Transparency 30-2 Interactive Tutor Self-Assessment Software Testmaker Lessons of War: *Philosophy of Nonviolence*
Section 3 **China's Drive for Modernization** Explain the factors that divided and the factors that united nationalist forces in China.	Lecture Notes 30-3 Reproducible Lesson Plan 30-3 Vocabulary Activity 30* Guided Reading Activity 30-3* Time Line Activity 30 Section Quiz 30-3* Reading Essentials and Study Guide 30-3	Section Focus Transparency 30-3 Interactive Tutor Self-Assessment Software Testmaker
Section 4 **Militarism in Japan** Describe how militarism shaped the development of Japan after World War I.	Lecture Notes 30-4 Reproducible Lesson Plan 30-4 Vocabulary Activity 30* Guided Reading Activity 30-4* History Simulation 30 Mapping History Activity 30 Section Quiz 30-4* Reading Essentials and Study Guide 30-4	Section Focus Transparency 30-4 Interactive Tutor Self-Assessment Software Testmaker
Section 5 **Nationalism in Latin America** Analyze why nationalism in Latin America brought conflict with the United States.	Lecture Notes 30-5 Reproducible Lesson Plan 30-5 Vocabulary Activity 30* Guided Reading Activity 30-5* World Art and Music Activity 30 People in World History Profile 57 Reteaching Activity 30 Enrichment Activity 30 Section Quiz 30-5* Performance Assessment Activity 30 Spanish Chapter Summary 30 Reading Essentials and Study Guide 30-5	Section Focus Transparency 30-5 World History and Art Transparency 40, *Zapatistas* Interactive Tutor Self-Assessment Software Testmaker

Chapter Activities

Performance Assessment Activity

Point/Counterpoint For the concepts of pacifism and militarism, organize students into groups of four to role-play a point/counterpoint segment on public television. Each group will research a current problem that has led to violence or that threatens to erupt in violence in Asia, Africa, the Middle East, or Latin America. After groups have gathered information from newspapers or magazines, have two students from each group present the pacifist response to solving the problem and two students present the militarist perspective. During the role play, students should refer to principles or historical examples to justify their positions.

Possible Rubric Features
Concept attainment, accuracy of content information, clarity of oral presentation, effect on audience, collaborative skills, persuasion and argumentation skills

• *For an additional activity, refer to Activity 30 in the* Performance Assessment Strategies and Activities *booklet.*

ACTIVITY

From the Classroom of...

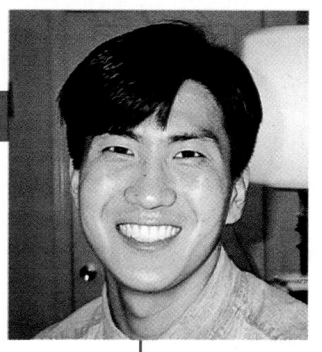

**James Kim
Polytechnic
Preparatory Country
Day School
Brooklyn, NY**

China's Drive for Modernization

Have students create either a Nationalist (Guomindang) or Communist newspaper. Once they have read the chapter, have each student select a topic for an article. After researching their topics at the library, students should write rough drafts, then use peer editing to edit the drafts and prepare final versions of their articles. Have students type the articles, select a name for their paper, and lay out the copy. The newspaper can be photocopied or printed for distribution and display.

MULTIPLE LEARNING STYLES

Verbal/Linguistic
Have students imagine that they live in one of the countries in this chapter during the time period under study. Ask them to write a letter to the editor of a newspaper expressing their opinions about an incident.

Visual/Spatial
As they read the chapter, have students fill in the names of the countries, continents, and regions on an outline map of the world. Then put an enlarged version of the outline map on the bulletin board. Organize the class into two teams and hold a geography bee. Have teams take turns trying to identify places mentioned in the chapter.

Auditory/Musical
Have students write and present a short class musical based on the rise of nationalism in one of the countries described in this chapter.

Kinesthetic
Have students choreograph and perform a dance that displays through movement the struggle for independence in one of the countries described in this chapter.

GLENCOE'S ASSESSMENT ADVANTAGE

Use the following to easily assess student learning in a variety of ways.

- Performance Assessment Strategies and Activities
- Section Quizzes
- Chapter and Unit Tests
- Interactive Tutor Self-Assessment Software
- Testmaker Software
- MindJogger Videoquiz
- SAT/SAT II Test Practice
- worldhistory.glencoe.com

Additional Resources

NATIONAL GEOGRAPHIC SOCIETY — Teacher's Corner

INDEX TO NATIONAL GEOGRAPHIC MAGAZINE

The following articles relate to this chapter:

- "The Promise of Pakistan," by John McCarry, October 1997.
- "India," by Geoffrey C. Ward, May 1997.
- "African Gold," by Carole Beckwith and Angela Fisher, October 1996.
- "Eritrea Wins the Peace," by Charles E. Cobb, Jr., June 1996.
- "Simon Bolívar," by Bryan Hodgson, March 1994.
- "Who Are the Palestinians?" by Tad Szulc, June 1992.

ADDITIONAL NATIONAL GEOGRAPHIC SOCIETY PRODUCTS

To order the following call National Geographic at 1-800-368-2728:

- *The Mexicans: Through Their Eyes (Video)*
- *The Great Indian Railway (Video)*
- *China: Beyond the Clouds (Video)*
- *Jerusalem: Within These Walls (Video and Videodisc)*
- *National Geographic: Eyewitness to the Twentieth Century (Book)*

Access National Geographic's new dynamic MapMachine Web site and other geography resources at:

- http://www.nationalgeographic.com/
- http://www.nationalgeographic.com/maps/

BIBLIOGRAPHY

Literature of the Period
Malraux, André. *Man's Fate.* Translated by Haakon M. Chevalier. New York: Random, 1990. First published in 1933, this French novel is based on the struggle between the Communist Reds and Chiang Kai-shek's Blues in 1927.

Readings for the Student
Paz, Octavio. *The Labyrinth of Solitude: The Other Mexico, Return to the Labyrinth of Solitude, Mexico and the U.S.A., The Philanthropic Ogre.* Translated by Lysander Kemp, Vara Milos, and Rachel Phillips Belash. New York: Grove Press, 1985. Perceptive studies of Mexican character and culture.

Readings for the Teacher
Rose, Norman. *Chaim Weizmann: A Biography.* New York: Viking, 1986. Life of the Zionist leader whose work in England led to the Balfour Declaration.

WORLD HISTORY Online

Use our Web site as an additional resource. All essential content is covered in the Student Edition.

You and your students can visit the *World History: The Human Experience* Web site at worldhistory.glencoe.com The student text directs students to the Web site for the following options:

- **Chapter Overviews**
- **Student Web Activities**
- **Self-Check Quizzes**

Answers are provided for you in a link entitled "Web Activity Lesson Plan." Additional Web Resources, Interactive Puzzles, and content updates are also available.

Visit the Glencoe Web site at socialstudies.glencoe.com for social studies activities, updates, and links to other resources.

LOCAL OBJECTIVES

_____
_____
_____
_____
_____
_____
_____
_____
_____
_____
_____
_____
_____
_____
_____
_____
_____
_____

Chapter Themes are listed by section on this chapter opening page of the Student Edition. A corresponding theme-based activity is available under "TEACH," and a theme-based question is asked in the Section and Chapter Assessments.

The Storyteller

Historical Setting U.S. Marines had occupied Nicaragua in 1912. In 1925 they left, but civil war soon broke out. When liberal forces under Sandino seized American property, the Marines returned. Sandino then led his forces to the mountains. His ability to evade capture by U.S. forces and the Nicaraguan National Guard not only turned Sandino into a popular hero but also encouraged anti-American sentiment. After the Marines withdrew in 1933, Sandino attended a peace conference with the head of the National Guard, Anastasio Somoza, who abducted and murdered the guerrilla leader. In 1962 the Sandinista National Liberation Front was formed with the goal of overthrowing the Somoza family dictatorship. The Sandinistas did so in July 1979 and governed Nicaragua until 1990.

Historical Significance

Answer: *World War I shattered the old order in Europe while the Versailles peace conference raised hopes for self-determination in many colonies.*

WORLD HISTORY Online

Have students use the **Chapter 30 Overview** at worldhistory. glencoe.com as a prereading and postreading exercise for understanding chapter content.

Chapter

30
1919–1939

Nationalism in Asia, Africa, and Latin America

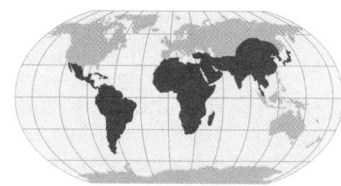

Chapter Themes

▶ **Nationalism** Hope for a new world after World War I leads to the rise of nationalism in the Middle East and Africa. *Section 1*
▶ **Change** Gandhi calls for non-violence in India's struggle for independence. *Section 2*
▶ **Conflict** Nationalists, Communists, and the Japanese compete for control of China. *Section 3*
▶ **Conflict** Japan's militarism and expansionism place it on a collision course with the West. *Section 4*
▶ **Change** Nationalist forces in Latin America oppose increased American intervention. *Section 5*

The Storyteller

"I swear before country and history that my sword will defend our nation's dignity, that it will be a sword for the oppressed. I accept the invitation to fight.... The last of my soldiers, the soldiers of freedom for Nicaragua, may die; but before that, more than a battalion of your blond invaders will have bitten the dust of my wild mountains."

With these fighting words, General Augusto César Sandino challenged the United States Marines in 1927. Sandino was trying to drive out the "blond invaders" who had occupied Nicaragua for 15 years. In the years following World War I, nationalist leaders such as Sandino struggled to end foreign control and win independence for their countries around the globe.

Historical Significance

What factors led to the growth of nationalist and independence movements in Asia, Africa, and Latin America between 1919 and 1939?

1920 | **1930** | **1940**

1921 Harry Thuku organizes nationalists in Kenya.

1930 Mohandas K. Gandhi leads salt-tax march in India.

1934 Chinese Communists carry out the Long March.

1938 Mexico nationalizes oil wells.

794

GEOGRAPHY CONNECTION

Location Have students use a globe to locate the Middle East, Africa, India, China, Japan, and Central America. In which hemisphere does each region or country lie? (*Central America is in the Western Hemisphere; all the other locations are in the Eastern Hemisphere.*)

The Destruction of the Old Order by José Clemente Orozco.
National Preparatory School, Mexico City, Mexico

WORLD HISTORY *Online*

apter Overview

sit the *World History: The Human Experience*
eb site at **worldhistory.glencoe.com** and click
Chapter 30—Chapter Overview to preview
e chapter.

Your History Journal

*Choose a major event that occurred
after 1930 in one of the nations featured
in this chapter. Write a short radio news
report describing the event for broadcast
in the United States.*

Chapter 30 *Nationalism in Asia, Africa, and Latin America* **795**

History & Art Orozco is considered
the most important modern muralist to work in fresco, the technique
of applying watercolors to a moist
plaster surface. While he did not
fight in the Mexican Revolution, his
political cartoons rallied support for
General Venustiano Carranza. Orozco lived in the U.S. on several occasions, and in 1932–1934 he painted
a series of frescoes at Dartmouth
College in Hanover, New Hampshire.

Performance Assessment

Refer to the activity on page
794C of the Planning Guide.

Refer to Activity 30 in
the *Performance Assessment Strategies and Activities* booklet.

Using Your History Journal

If possible, have students listen to
Edward R. Murrow's radio broadcasts
on the recording, *I Can Hear It Now,
1919–1949: 30 Years of Audible
History.*

GLENCOE TECHNOLOGY

VIDEODISC
Use MindJogger to pre-
view chapter content.

MindJogger Videoquiz

Chapter 30
Disc 4 Side B

 Also available in VHS.

➕ EXTRA CREDIT PROJECT

Oral Report Ask students to research the
events leading to the Balfour Declaration, the
importance of that document in the establishment of Israel, and Britain's short-lived commitment to it. Have students summarize their
findings in a brief oral report. Suggested
resources: R. Sanders, *The High Walls of
Jerusalem: A History of the Balfour Declaration and
the Birth of the British Mandate for Palestine;* W.
Laqueur, *A History of Zionism.*

1917

1917 The British issue
the Balfour Declaration.

1927

1929 Nigerian women
oppose British tax.

1937

1936 Egypt becomes
independent.

▶ **Nationalism** Hope for a new
world after World War I leads
to the rise of nationalism in the
Middle East and Africa.

Guide to Reading

For reading strategies to help
students read effectively see
pages 12–13. Have students
think about the main head as
they read the subheads.

Vocabulary Pre-check

 Use the Vocabulary
PuzzleMaker for Chapter 30
to create a crossword puzzle to
reinforce section terms. **L1 LEP**

 Use Vocabulary Activity
30 to introduce vocabulary terms.
L1 LEP

FOCUS

Section Objective

Identify how the forces of nationalism affected events in the Middle
East and Africa after World War I.

BELLRINGER
Motivational Activity

Before taking roll at the
beginning of the class
period, project Section
Focus Transparency 30-1
and have students answer
the activity questions. Discuss
students' responses.
This activity is also available as a blackline master.

Section 1

New Forces in the Middle East and Africa

Guide to Reading

Read to Find Out
Main Idea *The forces of nationalism
affected events in the Middle East and
Africa after World War I.*

▶ **Terms to Define**
self-determination, fez, shah

▶ **People to Meet**
Kemal Atatürk, Reza Shah Pahlavi,
Theodor Herzl, Saad Zaghlul, Harry
Thuku, Jomo Kenyatta, Nnamdi Azikiwe

▶ **Places to Locate**
Turkey, Iran, Palestine, Egypt, Kenya,
Nigeria

The
Storyteller

*Fawaz Khourey listened as a delegate at the
Arab Students Congress in Paris read the committee report. "I am an Arab.
I believe Arabs constitute one
nation. This nation's sacred
right is to be sovereign in her
own affairs. Her ardent
nationalism drives her to lib-
erate our homeland, uniting
all parts, and finding political, economic, and social
institutions more sound and
more compatible than existing
ones."*

—adapted from *Arab
Nationalism: An Anthology,*
edited by Sylvia G. Haim,
reprinted in *Documents in
World History,* Volume 2, 1988

Paris mosque

At the end of World War I, European
powers continued to control most of
the Middle East and Africa. Many
colonies had assisted the Allies during the war,
hoping to gain their independence as a reward.
President Woodrow Wilson of the United States
raised their hopes in 1918 by endorsing the concept
of self-determination: the right of national groups
to set up independent nations.

But instead of relaxing their grip, the European
powers tightened it. Nationalists prepared to fight
for independence and organized political demonstrations. They were eager to establish modern
countries where their own cultures could flourish.

Turkey

For nearly 500 years, Turkish emperors called
sultans ruled the vast Ottoman Empire, which at
one time included parts of eastern Europe, the
Middle East, and North Africa. During the 1800s,
however, large sections of this empire broke away
or were conquered. When World War I began, the
Ottomans joined forces with Germany, hoping to
save their remaining lands.

War With Greece

The Allied victory in World War I dashed
Ottoman hopes. The Ottoman sultan, or ruler, lost
all of his lands except the area of present-day
Turkey. In 1919 the Greeks invaded Turkey in an
attempt to complete the destruction of the Ottoman
Empire. Turkish general Mustafa Kemal, however,
rallied forces to his country's defense. Kemal led a
political group known as the Young Turks who
wanted reforms to modernize Turkey. Turkish
armies under Kemal counterattacked and defeated
the Greeks in 1922.

796 Chapter 30 *Nationalism in Asia, Africa, and Latin America*

SECTION RESOURCES

 Reproducible Masters
• Lecture Notes 30-1
• Reproducible Lesson Plan 30-1
• Vocabulary Activity 30
• Guided Reading Activity 30-1
• People in World History Profile 58
• Section Quiz 30-1
• Reading Essentials and Study Guide 30-1

🕯 **Transparencies**
• Section Focus Transparency 30-1
• Chapter Transparency 30

Multimedia
 Interactive Tutor Self-Assessment
Software
🔲 Testmaker
🌐 In the Holy Land: *Arab violence
1919–1921*

The Turkish victory led to dramatic changes. The sultan gave up his throne, and the Turks formed a new country, the Republic of Turkey. Kemal became its first president. The new government moved the capital from Istanbul to Ankara, a city near the center of the country. Believing that Turkey needed to industrialize in order to assert its role in world affairs, Kemal's government established industries and planned their growth. Tariffs on imports were raised to protect the new industries from foreign competition and to reduce dependence on foreign countries.

Kemal's Reforms

Kemal carried out a number of radical reforms in Turkish society. As a result of Kemal's policies, Turkey adopted a Western way of life. The Turks began using the Western calendar, the Latin alphabet, and the metric system. Kemal ordered men to stop wearing the fez, a traditional hat, and he tried to rid the country of the custom of veiling among women. He also urged Turks to use Western-style last names. To Westernize the government, he reformed the legal code and separated government and religion.

Some of Kemal's changes were designed to promote national pride among the Turks. For example, he urged Turks to "purify" their language by ridding it of all words that had Persian or Arabic origins. He also changed his own name to **Kemal Atatürk** (keh•MAHL AT•uh•TUHRK), which means "father of the Turks."

In defense of his reforms, Kemal said: "We have suffered much. This is because we have failed to understand the world. Our thoughts and our mentality will become civilized from head to toe." Kemal ruled Turkey with an iron fist until his death in 1938. His policies were not always popular, but he changed Turkey from an ancient empire into a modern nation.

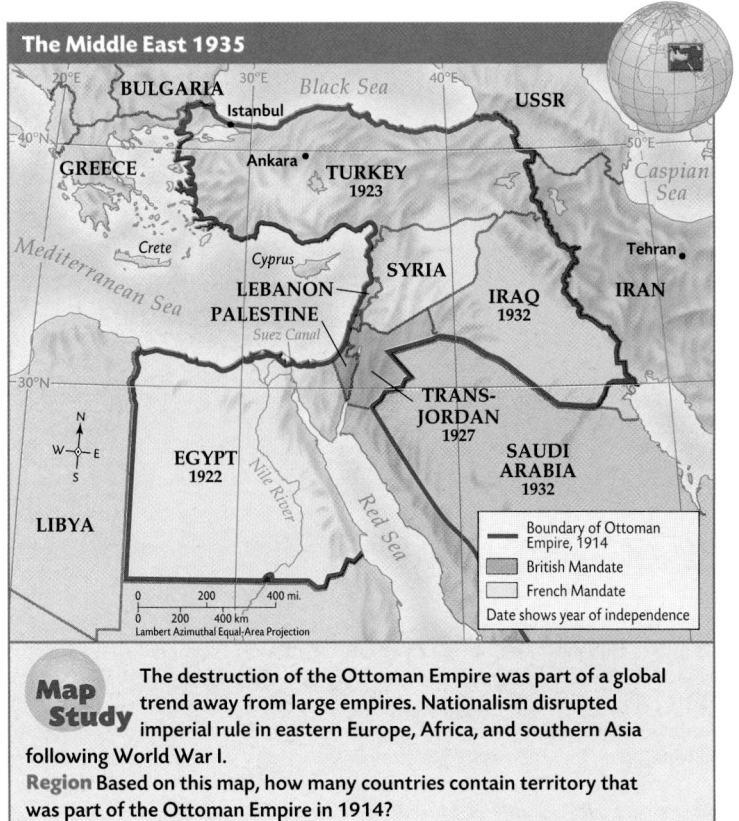

The Middle East 1935

Boundary of Ottoman Empire, 1914
British Mandate
French Mandate
Date shows year of independence

Map Study The destruction of the Ottoman Empire was part of a global trend away from large empires. Nationalism disrupted imperial rule in eastern Europe, Africa, and southern Asia following World War I.

Region Based on this map, how many countries contain territory that was part of the Ottoman Empire in 1914?

Iran

Located between Turkey and Pakistan, **Iran** is a land of mountains, deserts, and oil. At the end of World War I this land, known by its historic name of Persia, was ruled by a shah, or king. However, Great Britain and the Soviet Union each had controlling interests in Persia's oil fields.

In 1921 nationalist forces led by Reza Khan, an army officer, wanted to cut back the foreign influence on their government and economy. The nationalists overthrew the shah and set up a new government. Like Atatürk, Reza Khan built schools, roads, and hospitals, and he allowed women more freedom. Improved communications helped unite the diverse groups in the country. Although adopting many Western ways, he tried to reduce Western political influence in Persia.

Reza wanted to change the Persian monarchy into a republic. However, traditional Muslim leaders opposed this change, so Reza ruled as a dictator. Later, in 1925, he declared himself shah and

---

TEACH

Guided Practice

THEME Nationalism

Write on the chalkboard Sandino's statement quoted on page 794: "I swear before country and history that my sword will defend our nation's dignity, that it will be a sword for the oppressed." Although the statement was made by a Nicaraguan general, it may have been echoed by nationalist leaders in other areas of the world. Have students explain how Sandino's statement might have rallied the support of Nicaraguans. **L1**

 People in World History Profile 58

Map Study

Answer
eight countries

Map Skills Practice

Reading a Map Which region did Britain control through a mandate? *(Palestine)*

Geography: Location Have students study the map on this page. What body of water lies west of Palestine? *(Mediterranean Sea)* What country now exists in the area that was a British mandate? *(Israel)* What nations bordered Syria in 1935? *(Turkey, Iraq, Transjordan, Palestine, Lebanon)* **L2**

Chapter Transparency 30

Independent Practice

Guided Reading Activity 30-1 **L1**

COOPERATIVE LEARNING ACTIVITY

Posters Organize the class into two groups and assign one group Turkey and the other Iran. Have each group list the ways its country modernized and adopted certain elements of Western countries following World War I. Then ask the groups to research the subsequent history of each country, including the reaction against westernization in Iran. Have students create posters illustrating daily life in Turkey and Iran today. Encourage students to use photographs from magazines or newspapers to illustrate their posters. When the posters are completed, have students discuss how life in secular Turkey differs from life in Iran's Islamic republic. **L3**

**Chapter 30
Section 1**

Visualizing History

Although he served in a series of governments that collaborated with the British, Zaghlul (1857–1927) became a nationalist when he realized that Britain had no intention of granting independence to Egypt.
Answer to Caption: *Kemal Atatürk of Turkey and Reza Shah Pahlavi of Iran*

Linking Past and Present

Iran In 1979 a revolutionary movement led by Muslim religious leader Ayatollah Ruholla Khomeini overthrew Reza Shah's son, Mohammad Reza Pahlavi, and declared Iran an Islamic republic. Although Khomeini died in 1989, Iran continues to follow his anti-Western orientation and commitment to Muslim fundamentalism.

VIDEODISC
In the Holy Land

Side One, Chapter 15
Frame: 20841
Title: *Arab violence 1919–1921*
Subject: Jewish and Palestinian perspectives of anti-Jewish rioting and violence
Ask: As a result of the Balfour Declaration, Jewish immigration to Israel increased. What was the effect of this on the Arabs? *(They felt threatened because others were claiming their homeland. This resulted in riots, strikes, and violence.)*

Visualizing History In 1919 Egyptian nationalists protested the arrest of their leader Saad Zaghlul by the British. *What two other nationalist leaders rose to prominence in the Middle East after World War I?*

adopted the new name **Reza Shah Pahlavi** (rih•ZAH SHAH PAL•uh•vee). Pahlavi was the name of the ancient Persian language. Reza Shah Pahlavi earned money from Persia's oil fields and factories and from his vast royal estates.

During the 1930s, Reza Shah Pahlavi aligned his country with Germany. He admired Hitler, in part because he believed that Germans and Persians shared a common ancestry in the ancient Aryan, or Indo-European, peoples. In 1935 he changed the country's name from Persia to Iran, a variation of the word *Aryan*. In 1941, when Great Britain and the Soviet Union were at war with Germany, British and Soviet forces deposed Reza Shah Pahlavi and replaced him with his son, Mohammad Reza Pahlavi. The new ruler permitted British and Soviet troops to remain in Iran.

Palestine

While Iran was trying to free itself from European control, another Middle Eastern region was just coming under British domination. After World War I, the newly formed League of Nations gave Great Britain a mandate over **Palestine**. This region had been part of the Ottoman Empire. Britain was eager to benefit from control of Palestine's strategic location at the eastern end of the Mediterranean Sea.

In Palestine, the nationalism of two groups—Jews and Arabs—came into conflict. The Jews claimed the land on the basis of their biblical heritage and the continuing presence of Jews in the area since ancient times. Arabs pointed out that their ancestors had lived there for many centuries also. During this period, Palestine's small number of Jews and large number of Arabs lived together peacefully most of the time.

Beginning in the late 1800s, the number of Jews in Palestine began increasing. European Jews, facing harsh anti-Jewish pogroms in Russia and stirred by a growing sense of nationalism, believed they should reestablish a Jewish national homeland in Palestine. This movement, known as Zionism, became an organized political force in the late 1890s under the leadership of **Theodor Herzl**, a prominent Austrian Jewish writer and journalist. By World War I, about 500,000 Arabs and 85,000 Jews lived in Palestine.

During World War I, the British government promised independence to the Arabs in return for their help against the Ottoman Turks and also promised a homeland to the Jews. The Balfour Declaration—a letter from British Foreign Secretary Arthur Balfour in 1917 to the English Zionist Federation—promised Great Britain's help in establishing "a national home for the Jewish people" in Palestine. Great Britain's pledge of support, however, was on the condition that the civil and religious rights of other communities be protected. In September 1923, the British mandate officially came into force in Palestine in spite of Great Britain's conflicting promises to the area's Jewish and Arab communities.

798 Chapter 30 *Nationalism in Asia, Africa, and Latin America*

MEETING SPECIAL NEEDS ACTIVITY

Learning Disability To check the progress of students with learning problems, ask them to identify the country described in each of the following statements:
1. In 1922 the British granted this country limited independence. *(Egypt)*
2. It was originally known as Persia. *(Iran)*
3. Greece invaded this country in 1919. *(Turkey)*
4. Reza Khan became its leader and eventually declared himself shah. *(Iran)*
5. Mustafa Kemal introduced radical reforms here. *(Turkey)* **L1**

Under the British mandate, tensions heightened between Arabs and Jews. As the persecution of Jews in Nazi Germany increased, so did Jewish immigration to Palestine. As more Jews moved into a region long inhabited by Arabs, the two groups clashed. Riots broke out, resulting in hundreds of casualties. When Great Britain tried to limit Jewish immigration, Zionists responded in anger. By the end of the 1930s, Great Britain's ambiguous promises had angered both Jews and Arabs, and the conflict in Palestine was worsening.

Egypt

Palestine's neighbor **Egypt** also confronted troubles after World War I. Under British occupation since 1882, Egypt was beginning to feel the power of nationalism. **Saad Zaghlul** (zag•LOOL) led the nationalist forces in Egypt demanding independence. The British tried to weaken the nationalist cause by arresting Zaghlul, but their action only sparked riots and violence. Finally, in 1922, Great Britain granted Egypt limited independence. However, the British kept control of the Suez Canal.

Tensions continued over the next decade between Egypt and Great Britain. But when Italy invaded Ethiopia in 1935, the British decided they needed Egypt's help to prevent further Italian aggression. As a result, the British government granted Egypt its complete independence in 1936 and helped it become a member of the League of Nations the following year. Great Britain also withdrew all British troops from Egypt, except for those in the Suez Canal zone.

Kenya

South of Egypt, in central East Africa, lay another part of Great Britain's empire: **Kenya**. During World War I, about 45,000 Kenyans died while helping the British fight the Germans in East Africa. The survivors returned home after the war with dreams of independence and a new life. However, instead of granting Kenya its independence, the British allowed European settlers to seize the land of many Kenyans in order to start large coffee plantations and other agricultural operations. The settlers hired Kenyans at low wages and made them work under harsh conditions. Resentment of British rule in Kenya gave rise to a

Geography

Imperialist Boundaries

During the late 1800s, European powers carved up Africa without respect to the continent's historic ethnic boundaries. Colonial boundary lines split groups of people and joined them to other groups with different religious beliefs, customs, and languages. This often led to unwanted rivalries and hostilities. Nowhere was this problem more evident than in Nigeria.

Nigeria is home to more than 250 separate ethnic groups. The three largest are the Hausa, the Yoruba, and the Ibo. In the days before colonial rule, each group controlled its own territory. When the British united the region in 1914, Hausa,

Nigerian nationalist Nnamdi Azikiwe

Yoruba, and Ibo peoples were part of the same country for the first time. They eyed each other with suspicion.

After independence arrived in 1960, the struggle for unity continued in Nigeria. However, hostilities flared into warfare in 1967. Eastern Nigeria seceded and established the independent state of Biafra. The Nigerian government eventually won the war and reclaimed Biafra, but the country remains haunted by the prophetic words that nationalist leader Obafemi Awolowo spoke in 1947: "Nigeria is not a nation. It is a mere geographical expression."

 ACTIVITY

Explain the statement: "Nigeria is not a nation. It is a mere geographical expression." Why have Nigerians been reluctant to unite?

Linking Past and Present

Imperialist Boundaries

Awolowo (1909–1987) himself was a leader of the Yoruba people. He studied law in London, where he wrote *Path to Nigerian Freedom* (1947), a call for his homeland's independence. Upon his return to Nigeria, he founded the Action Group, a Yoruba political party. After Nigeria attained independence in 1960, Awolowo turned to socialism and spent some years in prison.

ANSWERS

Nigeria's nationhood is based on place, not on a common culture. Ethnic groups formerly in control of their own territories were reluctant to live as one people.

ASSESS

Check for Understanding

Assign Section 1 Assessment as homework or as an in-class activity.

⦿ Use Interactive Tutor Self-Assessment Software to review Section 1.

Chapter 30 *Nationalism in Asia, Africa, and Latin America* **799**

MAKING CONNECTIONS ACTIVITIES

The Arts Have students watch videos of *Lawrence of Arabia*, the 1962 screen biography of T. E. Lawrence, the British leader of the Arab revolt against the Ottoman Empire, and *Exodus*, the 1960 film about the last days of the British mandate in Palestine and the clash of Arab and Zionist nationalists there after the birth of Israel.

Have students write brief reports in which they evaluate the complex British role in the region as depicted in the two films. **L2**

Politics Have students research and write brief reports comparing the lives and political goals of Theodor Herzl, founder of political Zionism, and Yasir Arafat, leader of the Palestine Liberation Organization. **L2**

Evaluate

 Section Quiz 30-1

Use the Testmaker to create a customized quiz for Section 1.

Reteach

Have students explain why the experience of World War I promoted the concept of self-determination among colonial peoples of Africa and the Middle East. *(Many hoped to receive their independence in exchange for fighting with the Allies.)*

Reading Essentials and Study Guide 30-1

Enrich

Ask students to imagine that they are one of the nationalist leaders described in this section. Have them write a short speech directed at a European audience, demanding independence for their homeland.

CLOSE

Write the following on the chalkboard: *No matter how small or weak, every nation has the right to decide its own form of government and to manage its own affairs.* Ask students to discuss whether they agree or disagree with this statement.

protest movement in 1921 led by **Harry Thuku** (THOO•koo). The protesters complained about high colonial taxes and strict British labor laws. Colonial officials promptly arrested Thuku, and in the riot that followed, British troops killed about 25 Kenyans. The British then exiled Thuku.

In Thuku's absence, **Jomo Kenyatta** took over the growing nationalist movement. Instead of fighting the British in Kenya for independence, Kenyatta took his struggle to the center of British power in London. By meeting with government officials in the 1920s and 1930s, he made progress—but very slowly. He later recalled his frustrations:

> 66 By driving [the African] off his ancestral lands, the Europeans have robbed him of the material foundations of his culture, and reduced him to a state of serfdom incompatible with human happiness.... It is not in his nature to accept serfdom forever. He realizes that he must fight unceasingly for his own complete emancipation; for without this he is doomed to remain the prey of rival imperialisms. 99

—Jomo Kenyatta, *Facing Mount Kenya*, 1938

In spite of Kenyatta's efforts, when World War II began, Kenya remained firmly in British hands.

Nigeria

Across the continent from Kenya, on the west coast, lies **Nigeria**. The British controlled this region as well, and they made large fortunes from its rubber, oil, and tin. As in Kenya, the British imposed heavy taxes on men and strict labor laws.

In 1929 Nigerian women learned that they too would be taxed. When a group of unarmed women

Visualizing History Jomo Kenyatta wrote a book, *Facing Mount Kenya*, that explained how British rule had disrupted his country's culture. *How did Kenyatta try to obtain Kenya's independence?*

protested by attacking British goods and property, police fired on them, killing 50.

The violent end of the women's uprising drove many Nigerians to adopt nonviolent methods in their struggle. **Nnamdi Azikiwe** (eh •nahm•dee ah•zee•KEE•WEE), started the newspaper *The West African Pilot* in 1937. He wrote many articles in favor of independence for all of Africa. "Africa needs a pilot," he wrote once. "Those who follow the true pilot, believing they are on the right track, will find their way to their destination."

SECTION 1 ASSESSMENT

Main Idea
1. Use a diagram like the one below to identify effects of nationalism on Africa after World War I.

> Effects of Nationalism on Africa

Recall
2. **Define** self-determination, fez, shah.
3. **Identify** Kemal Atatürk, Reza Shah Pahlavi, Theodor Herzl, Saad Zaghlul, the Balfour Declaration, Harry Thuku, Jomo Kenyatta, Nnamdi Azikiwe.

Critical Thinking
4. **Evaluating Information** The British in Kenya said they

were "exercising a trust on behalf of the African population." What does this imply about Great Britain's attitude toward Africans?

Understanding Themes
5. **Nationalism** What factors contributed to the rise of nationalist feeling in the Middle East and Africa at the end of World War I?

SECTION 1 ASSESSMENT ANSWERS

1. Egypt gained complete independence in 1936; in Kenya a nationalist movement toward independence formed, and Kenyatta took the struggle to the government in London; in Nigeria nonviolent methods were adopted to gain independence
2. All terms are defined in the Glossary.
3. Atatürk, 797; Reza Shah Pahlavi, 798;

Balfour Declaration, 798; Herzl, 798; Zaghlul, 799; Thuku, 800; Kenyatta, 800; Azikiwe, 800
4. The British thought they knew what was best for Africans.
5. **NATIONALISM** Colonial peoples wanted to establish modern nations where their own cultures could flourish.

1919 The Amritsar Massacre heightens anti-British feeling in India.

1930 Mohandas K. Gandhi leads protest against British rule.

1935 The British Parliament passes the Government of India Act.

Section 2

India's Struggle for Independence

Read to Find Out

Main Idea *Gandhi used nonviolent methods in India's struggle for independence from British rule.*

▶ **Terms to Define**
pacifist, civil disobedience, satyagraha

▶ **People to Meet**
Mohandas K. Gandhi, Mohammed Ali Jinnah, Jawaharlal Nehru

▶ **Places to Locate**
India, Amritsar, Ahmadabad

The Storyteller

Riswati and Kamala, once friendly neighbors in Bombay, had not spoken to each other for months—since relations between Muslims and Hindus had deteriorated. The British could use the problem as an excuse for delaying Indian independence. The two women had argued over which group, Muslims or Hindus, was more to blame. Kamala recalled the example of Mohandas Gandhi and resolved to visit Riswati and renew their friendship. Perhaps she could quote Gandhi saying, "It does not matter to me that we see things from different angles of vision." Kamala caught sight of Riswati at the market. Quickly she crossed the square toward her old friend.

—adapted from *Communal Unity*, M.K. Gandhi, reprinted in *World Civilizations*, Volume 2, 1994

Mohandas Gandhi

When World War I began, the most important territory in the British Empire was **India**. As in the Middle East and Africa, nationalism was spreading in India. Some Indians wanted independence. Many were willing to remain in the British Empire but demanded home rule. Two of the largest nationalist organizations were the Indian National Congress and the Muslim League.

During World War I, Indian nationalists supported Great Britain and its allies. More than a million Indian soldiers fought on the battlefields of the Middle East and Africa. Indian wheat fed the Allied troops, and Indian cotton kept them clothed. In return for this aid, Great Britain promised in 1917 to support eventual self-rule for India.

The Amritsar Massacre

Independence did not come easily to India. After the war, the Indian National Congress staged demonstrations to protest British rule. The nationalist movement, however, was divided by religion. The Hindu majority and the Muslim minority did not trust each other. The British authorities in India encouraged that distrust.

A second difficulty was British opposition. Many Britons were unwilling to see their empire's power reduced and staunchly opposed freeing India. In 1919 Great Britain imposed on India harsh laws intended to stifle opposition to British rule. British officials could arrest nationalists without cause and jail them without trial.

British repression reached an extreme in the Punjabi city of **Amritsar** in April 1919. The British had outlawed all large gatherings and declared that they would respond to any violation with force. When 10,000 unarmed Indians assembled in a

Chapter 30 *Nationalism in Asia, Africa, and Latin America* **801**

SECTION THEME

▶ **Change** Gandhi calls for nonviolence in India's struggle for independence from British rule.

Guide to Reading

For reading strategies to help students read effectively see pages 12–13.

Vocabulary Pre-check

■ Use the Vocabulary PuzzleMaker for Chapter 30 to create a crossword puzzle to reinforce section terms. **L1 LEP**

▶ Use Vocabulary Activity 30 to introduce vocabulary terms. **L1 LEP**

FOCUS

Section Objective

State the methods Gandhi used in India's struggle for independence from British rule.

BELLRINGER
Motivational Activity

Before taking roll at the beginning of the class period, project Section Focus Transparency 30-2 and have students answer the activity questions. Discuss students' responses.

▶ This activity is also available as a blackline master.

SECTION RESOURCES

Reproducible Masters
• Lecture Notes 30-2
• Reproducible Lesson Plan 30-2
• Vocabulary Activity 30
• Guided Reading Activity 30-2
• Section Quiz 30-2
• Reading Essentials and Study Guide 30-2

Transparencies
• Section Focus Transparency 30-2

Multimedia
■ Interactive Tutor Self-Assessment Software
■ Testmaker
◉ Lessons of War: *Philosophy of Nonviolence*

TEACH

Guided Practice

THEME Change

Discuss the purpose of the boycott led by Gandhi. Ask students to explain why this tactic might be more effective at achieving change than a demonstration. How did the boycott attack the underlying logic of imperialism? *(The empire was supposed to benefit England economically.)* **L1**

The Indian National Congress, founded in 1885, led the movement for independence, and was also India's ruling party from 1947 to 1977.
Answer to Caption: *South Africa*

Gandhi's Campaign
How did Gandhi's campaign affect India's relationship with Great Britain?
His use of nonviolence weakened British authority and helped lead to India's independence.

VIDEODISC
Lessons of War

Side Two, Chapter 6
Frames 12636–20751
Title: *Philosophy of Nonviolence*
Ask: Identify two people in history who exemplified nonviolent protest. *(Mohandas Gandhi and Martin Luther King, Jr.)*

Visualizing History During the 1920s and 1930s, Gandhi was India's leading nationalist. He worked to promote unity between Hindus and Muslims in the Indian National Congress party. *Where did Gandhi first use nonviolent methods to protest injustices?*

walled garden in Amritsar for a political meeting, the local commander decided that the British needed to demonstrate their authority. Without warning, British troops blocked the only entrance to the garden and began firing into the trapped crowd. When the firing ceased, nearly 400 people, including many children, lay dead. Another 1,200 people were wounded. Criticized for his action, the British commander declared:

> **❝** I fired and continued to fire until the crowd dispersed, and I consider this is the least amount of firing which would produce the necessary moral effect.... If more troops had been at hand, the casualties would have been greater. **❞**

 Gandhi and the West
Mohandas K. Gandhi has had a profound influence on people in the West. He served as a model for Martin Luther King, Jr. King led the African American civil rights struggle until his assassination in 1968. Like Gandhi, King protested injustice with nonviolent boycotts and marches.

Indians across the country were shocked by the brutal massacre and the general's justification of it. In large numbers, they came together in meeting after meeting, more determined than ever to drive the British out of their land. However, they needed a strong leader to spearhead their struggle.

Gandhi's Campaign

In the months following the Amritsar Massacre, **Mohandas K. Gandhi** became the leading Indian nationalist. Born in India of middle-class parents in 1869, Gandhi had been educated in England. He later practiced law in South Africa, where he and other Indians experienced mistreatment because of their dark skin.

Until 1914 Gandhi lived in South Africa and led protests against racial discrimination. He was a pacifist, a person opposed to using war and other violence to settle disputes. In keeping with his beliefs, Gandhi used protest methods based on civil disobedience, or the refusal to obey laws that are considered unjust.

When Gandhi returned to India, he began working with the Indian National Congress and led a nonviolent movement for self-government and for greater tolerance among the country's many social and religious groups. Gandhi urged Indians to reject much of Western civilization for its use of brute force, its worship of money, and its prejudicial attitudes toward non-Western peoples. Gandhi's understanding of India's problems made him popular throughout the country. The Indian people called Gandhi *Mahatma*, meaning "great soul."

Gandhi's doctrine of moral nonviolent protest won him international attention. He believed that one could force an evil person or government to change by challenging it directly, but without violence. Gandhi used the term satyagraha (suh•TYAH•gruh•huh), which means "truth force," to describe the nonviolent protests he led after the Amritsar Massacre. One effective form of protest was the boycott, in which Indians refused to buy British cloth and other manufactured goods. As a step toward independence, Gandhi urged Indians to begin spinning their own cloth.

Gandhi practiced what he preached by spinning cloth for a half hour every day. He made the spinning wheel the symbol of the National Congress, and he wore nothing but simple homespun clothes for the rest of his life.

COOPERATIVE LEARNING ACTIVITY

Debate Organize the class into two groups to debate the following statement: "Gandhi's nonviolent philosophy made India's independence movement less effective than it would have been, had force been used." Each group should research the issue and organize its argument before the debate takes place, dividing the work into research, organization of information, and presentation of information, and assigning these tasks to subgroups. You might want to have students conduct this debate before another class and let the members of that class vote on the more persuasive argument. **L2**

Gandhi's courage inspired millions of Indians to protest. In 1922, however, the British arrested Gandhi, and he disappeared from active protest for the rest of the decade. Undaunted, the Indian National Congress continued to protest, but it achieved little success until Gandhi's return in 1930.

Toward Independence

Gandhi planned his next major protest around salt. In India's hot climate, the millions of people who worked in fields and factories needed salt to replace what they lost daily in sweat. The British controlled the salt mines and the ocean salt fields. They taxed every grain of salt they sold and jailed Indians who gathered salt on their own.

In 1930 Gandhi protested the salt tax. First he led thousands of his followers on a 200-mile (322-km) march from **Ahmadabad** to the sea, where they made salt from sea water. One month later, Gandhi openly defied British authority by wading into the sea and picking up a lump of salt. The British did not dare arrest him, but they did arrest thousands who followed his example. To quell the mounting protests, they arrested him a month later, but the protests only increased. Webb Miller, a British journalist, described one such protest, in which a group marched on a heavily guarded salt mine: "Although every one knew that within a few minutes he would be beaten down, perhaps killed, I could detect no signs of wavering or fear.... [T]he marchers simply walked forward until struck down."

This pattern continued throughout the 1930s. As Indians protested, the British responded with guns and clubs. Their violence could not stop the millions of people motivated by nationalism.

Limited Self-Rule

Under pressure from the nationalist movement, the British began to give Indians more political power. In 1935 the British Parliament passed the Government of India Act, which created a constitution for India. This measure gave provincial legislatures control over the making of law in the provinces. Areas such as agriculture, education, public health, and public works came under the control of the provincial governments. The British government retained control of national lawmaking, finance, defense, and foreign affairs.

The majority of Indian nationalists rejected the act, wanting complete independence. However, the Indian National Congress, at the insistence of Gandhi, finally accepted it as the first step toward self-rule. The Indian historian K.M. Panikkar states that with this act, "British authority in India was in full retreat, in the administrative field no less than in the political and economic fields." Nevertheless, independence was not yet won.

Hindu-Muslim Relations

Even as India moved toward independence in the 1930s, conflicts among Indians increased. For every Muslim, India had three Hindus. As independence approached, the Muslims began worrying about their future treatment by the Hindus, and many joined the Muslim League.

In 1937 the Indian National Congress, controlled by Hindu, won election majorities in 7 out of 11 provinces. Muslims came to power in the others. This heightened bitter feelings. The Muslim League, headed by **Mohammed Ali Jinnah**, split with the Congress party. It demanded a separate Muslim nation for the millions of Muslims in India. The Hindus, led by **Jawaharlal Nehru**, a follower of Gandhi, wanted a united India.

Although a Hindu, Gandhi was concerned about the deepening rift between Hindus and Muslims. His pleas for toleration were largely ignored by both groups. As 1939 ended, the nationalist movement had split in two, and not even Gandhi could put it together again.

SECTION 2 ASSESSMENT

Main Idea
1. Use a diagram like the one below to identify specific methods Gandhi used in India's struggle for independence.

Gandhi's Methods

Recall
2. **Define** pacifist, civil disobedience, satyagraha.
3. **Identify** Mohandas K. Gandhi, Mohammed Ali Jinnah, Jawaharlal Nehru.

Critical Thinking
4. **Synthesizing Information** What could India's Hindus have

done to keep Muslims united with them against their British rulers?

Understanding Themes
5. **Change** How did Mohandas K. Gandhi's nonviolent methods keep Indian nationalism from being defeated by Great Britain?

SECTION 2 ASSESSMENT ANSWERS

1. civil disobedience; non-violent protests; boycott of British cloth and other goods; urging Indians to spin their own cloth; marching to sea to protest salt tax
2. All terms are defined in the Glossary.
3. Gandhi, 802; Jinnah, 803; Nehru, 803
4. Answers will vary but may include the

guarantee of a voice for Muslims in political decisions or support of strong civil rights laws.
5. **CHANGE** Their success motivated people to keep hope even against British attacks.

Independent Practice

Guided Reading Activity 30-2 **L1**

Critical Thinking Have students discuss under what conditions, if any, it is proper to break the law. Ask them to consider whether someone who breaks an unjust law should accept punishment.

ASSESS

Check for Understanding
Assign Section 2 Assessment as homework or as an in-class activity.

🔲 Use Interactive Tutor Self-Assessment Software to review Section 2.

Evaluate
Section Quiz 30-2

🔲 Use the Testmaker to create a customized quiz for Section 2.

Reteach
Have students write one question for each of the major parts of this section. Ask students to exchange their questions and answer each other's.

Reading Essentials and Study Guide 30-2

Enrich
Have students watch a video of the 1982 screen biography *Gandhi*. Ask them to write a brief review as if they were a critic.

CLOSE

Have students create two lists on the chalkboard, one of British actions to prevent Indian independence, and the other of measures taken by Indian nationalists to win self-rule.

1919   1929   1939

1919 Chinese students protest Treaty of Versailles.   **1928** Chiang Kai-shek sets up government at Nanjing.   **1939** Japan controls most of eastern China.

Section 3

China's Drive for Modernization

Guide to Reading

Read to Find Out
Main Idea *Nationalist forces in China were both divided and united.*

▶ **Terms to Define**
warlord

▶ **People to Meet**
Sun Yat-sen, Yuan Shigai, Chiang Kai-shek, Mao Zedong

▶ **Places to Locate**
Nanjing, Guangzhou, Manchuria

The Storyteller

Wai Zhou watched a small man addressing a group in the square. "China has become a colony of all the Powers," he proclaimed. This was nothing new, Wai Zhou thought, just another agitator seeking an audience. But the man continued, "Foreigners often refer to the Chinese nation as a bowl of loose sand. To revive nationalism we must expand our small group loyalty to a very large group. The people must learn to read and write. China must become a democracy. Those who till the soil should own it." The speaker outlined a plan for Chinese independence. Completely won over, Wai Zhou asked a bystander who the speaker was. "I heard him called Sun Yat-sen," the man replied.

—adapted from *Lectures on Nationalism*, Sun Yat-sen, reprinted in *Lives and Times*, James P. Holoka and Jiu-Hwa Lo Upshur, 1995

Sun Yat-sen

nlike India, China was never entirely controlled by a European country. However, despite its independence and population size, China did not have the military power to command respect. That they lacked the respect of Europeans was shown by the final terms of the Versailles peace conference that followed World War I. The Versailles Treaty had a provision granting Japan economic control of the Shandong (SHON•DOONG) Peninsula of northeastern China. This provision was a humiliating and surprising blow to the Chinese. During and after World War I, China was torn apart by internal divisions, and the foreign powers took advantage of China's weakness.

The Chinese Republic

As you read in Chapter 27, the Chinese revolutionary leader **Sun Yat-sen** formally declared China a republic in January 1912. Sun dreamed of a free, democratic society. However, just two months after taking office, he was ousted by **Yuan Shigai** (YOO•AHN SHUR•GIE). Yuan quickly turned the new republic into a dictatorship. Meanwhile, Sun organized and formed the nationalist Guomindang (KWOH•MIHN•DAHNG) party, tried and failed to overthrow Yuan, and then fled to Japan.

When Yuan died in 1916, China slipped into chaos. Local military leaders called warlords divided the vast country among themselves. An almost continual state of civil war followed.

Sun Yat-sen returned to China in 1917 and tried in vain to restore strong central government and rebuild the Guomindang party. Then in 1923, with aid from the Soviet Union and an officer named **Chiang Kai-shek** (JEE•AHNG KY•SHEHK), the Guomindang army grew rapidly in strength. Sun Yat-sen died in 1925.

Three years later, Chiang led the army to victory over the warlords and established a government in the city of **Nanjing**.

Though undemocratic, government under the Guomindang promoted economic development by building schools, roads, and railways. However, the Guomindang did very little to raise the living standards of China's many peasants.

Rivalry With the Communists

Many peasants, along with intellectuals and urban workers, supported another party that opposed the warlords: the Communists. During Chiang's drive against the warlords, Communist soldiers provided him with crucial military support. But in 1927 the Communists attempted to take over the Guomindang party and failed. Chiang turned against the Communists and tried to wipe them out. In Shanghai, **Guangzhou**, and other cities, Guomindang soldiers killed tens of thousands of Communists.

As Chiang began his purge, tens of thousands of Communists fled to the mountains in the southern province of Jiangxi (jee•AHNG•SHEE). Here they gathered their strength and formed the Red Army, led by the son of a prosperous peasant family, **Mao Zedong** (MOW DZUH•DOONG). Mao believed that the Communists could still triumph with the help of China's millions of peasants:

❝ In a very short time, in China's central, southern, and northern provinces, several hundred million peasants will rise like a mighty storm, like a hurricane, a force so swift and violent that no power, however great, will be able to hold it back. ❞

—Mao Zedong, *Report on an Investigation,* 1926

Living conditions for China's peasants had changed little over the centuries. They worked small plots of land and turned over most of their crops to wealthy landlords. The Red Army gained popular support by overthrowing local landlords and distributing their land to the peasants. Soon, the Red Army included nearly 30,000 peasant troops.

The success of the Red Army worried Chiang. In the early 1930s he ordered "extermination campaigns" to destroy this rival army. Mao fought back with his own strategies: "The enemy advances, we retreat; the enemy camps, we harass; the enemy tires, we attack; the enemy retreats, we pursue."

Mao's military plans worked at times, but by October 1934, the Guomindang had nearly surrounded the Communists with a million troops. Mao decided to retreat once again, leading about 100,000 followers out of Jiangxi Province.

Student Web Activity 30

Visit the *World History: The Human Experience* Web site at **worldhistory.glencoe.com** and click on *Chapter 30—Student Web Activities* for an activity relating to Republican China.

TEACH

Guided Practice

THEME Conflict

Have students discuss the difficulties faced by Sun Yat-sen in creating a new China. *(ousted shortly after taking office; failed in his attempt to overthrow Yuan with his Guomindang party; failed to restore strong central government)* **L1**

Visualizing History Chiang (1887–1975) encouraged a movement to teach Confucian morals. **Answer to Caption:** *the Communists*

Independent Practice

 Guided Reading Activity 30-3 **L1**

Time Line Activity 30

Politics Have students imagine that they are members of the Red Army trying to gain the support of peasants in the countryside. Have them write a short speech directed at Chinese peasants. **L2**

Linking Past and Present

Taiwan After Mao won control of the Chinese mainland, Chiang headed the Nationalist government in exile on Taiwan from 1949 until his death in 1975. China continued to regard Taiwan as a renegade province. Although tensions between the two eased in the late 1980s, they intensified again in the 1990s.

Have students use the **Chapter 30 Student Web Activity** at worldhistory.glencoe.com for in-depth study of Republican China.

COOPERATIVE LEARNING ACTIVITY

Reports Organize the class into two groups to report on the influence of Chinese students on the politics of China. Each group member should have a specific task, such as researching, organizing, or summarizing. Have one group examine the political role Chinese students played in the early part of this century and the other group research the role Chinese students have played in politics in recent years, including the Tiananmen Square demonstrations of June 1989. **L2**

ASSESS

Check for Understanding

Assign Section 3 Assessment as
homework or as an in-class activity.

 Use Interactive Tutor Self-
Assessment Software to review
Section 3.

Evaluate

Section Quiz 30-3

 Use the Testmaker to create a
customized quiz for Section 3.

Reteach

Have students list statements on
the chalkboard summarizing the
main events in China's drive for
unity and modernization.

Reading Essentials and
Study Guide 30-3

Enrich

Have students watch a video of
the 1987 film *The Last Emperor*.
Have them write reports analyzing the way the film uses the
story of Pu Yi as a mirror reflecting China's passage from feudalism through revolution toward a
modern society.

CLOSE

Have students create a time line
covering the key events in Chinese history from 1919 to 1939.
Have them write summary statements describing the political situations in China.

Visualizing
History **Mao Zedong led the Communist**
retreat known as the Long March.
From what Chinese force were the Communists fleeing?

The Long March

Mao's retreat from Jiangxi lasted for one year
and covered about 6,000 miles (9,600 km). The Red
Army marched an average of 16 miles (26 km) a
day, across rivers and mountains, and defeated 10
provincial armies while being chased by Guomin-

dang military forces. The Chinese Communists
called the arduous undertaking the Long March.

At times the line of marching Communist
soldiers stretched out for nearly 50 miles (80 km).
One of these soldiers later recalled the march:

> If it was a black night and the enemy far
> away, we made torches from pine branch-
> es or frayed bamboo, and then it was
> truly beautiful. At the foot of a mountain,
> we could look up and see a long column
> of lights coiling like a fiery dragon up
> the mountainside. From the summit we
> could look in both directions and see
> miles of torches moving forward like a
> wave of fire. A rosy glow hung over the
> whole route of the march. 99

Conditions on the Long March were far from
rosy, however. Many soldiers froze or starved to
death, and others died in battle. Of the original
100,000 troops, fewer than 8,000 survived.

Threat From Japan

While Chiang and Mao battled each other in
1931, the Japanese had conquered the large section
of northeast China known as **Manchuria**. Now it
appeared that Japan wanted even more land, and
Chiang's advisers urged him to confront the
Japanese. Mao offered assistance but was rejected
by Chiang. Manchurian forces then kidnapped
Chiang and held him prisoner until he finally
agreed to end his war with the Communists.

However, unity between Chiang and Mao
could not stop the Japanese invasion that came
eight months later. By 1939 Japan controlled most of
eastern China. Chiang withdrew to the interior of
the country, where Mao was awaiting the proper
moment to strike back. Before that moment arrived,
the entire world was at war.

SECTION 3 ASSESSMENT

Main Idea
1. Use a chart like the one below to
identify factors that divided and
united nationalist forces in China.

Nationalist Forces	
Divided By:	United By:

Recall
2. **Define** warlord.
3. **Identify** Sun Yat-sen,
Yuan Shigai, Chiang Kai-shek,
Mao Zedong.

Critical Thinking
4. **Analyzing Information** Why
do you think Mao Zedong and

the Communists decided to
undertake the Long March?
What other choices did they
have?

Understanding Themes
5. **Conflict** What conflicts kept
China in turmoil after World
War I?

SECTION 3 ASSESSMENT ANSWERS

1. divided by: Guomindang did not help peasants; Communists, under Mao, needed
peasants' help for Red Army; rivalry
between Communists and Guomindang;
united by: opposition to warlords; opposition to Japan
2. All terms are defined in the Glossary.
3. Sun Yat-sen, 804; Yuan Shigai, 804; Chiang

Kai-shek, 804; Mao Zedong, 805
4. Possible answer: Mao may have believed
the Long March would build solidarity
among members of the Red Army.
5. **CONFLICT** Fighting occurred
among the warlords, between the Guomindang and the Communists, and against the
Japanese.

1915 Japan forces China to accept the Twenty-One Demands.

1925 Japanese parliament grants vote to all males.

1932 Army officers assassinate Japanese prime minister.

Section 4

Militarism in Japan

Read to Find Out
Main Idea *Militarism shaped Japan during the period after World War I.*

▶ **Terms to Define**
population explosion, heavy industry, *zaibatsu*

▶ **People to Meet**
Hirohito

▶ **Places to Locate**
Manchuria

Japan's Total War Research Institute drafted a secret strategy for the Japanese government. Called the "Greater East Asia Co-Prosperity Sphere," the plan outlined the establishment of a "zone of peaceful living and common prosperity for the peoples of East Asia." Japan would be the stabilizing power. The influence of all other nations would be driven out. The "New Order of East Asia" was an idea that did not include independence based on national self-determination. Instead, Japan would establish a new morality whose basic principle would be the Imperial Way.

—adapted from *Sources of the Japanese Tradition*, edited by W.T. deBary, reprinted in *Sources of World Civilization*, Volume 2, 1994

Japanese cavalry in China

Like China, Japan, an independent country, had fought on the side of the Allies in World War I. During the conflict, the Japanese supplied weapons to their European partners, particularly to Russia. At the same time, they took advantage of the war to expand their economic and political influence in East Asia. In addition to ruling Korea and Taiwan, Japan pressed for an enlargement of its role in China. In 1915 Japanese diplomats forced the Chinese government to accept a list of terms known as the Twenty-One Demands. The Twenty-One Demands, in effect, made China a Japanese protectorate.

Japan and the West

When World War I ended, Japan received Germany's Pacific islands north of the Equator as mandates from the League of Nations. The Japanese also entered into a series of military and commercial agreements with the Western powers. A disarmament conference held in Washington, D.C., in 1922 led to a five-power agreement among Japan, Great Britain, the United States, Italy, and France that allowed Japan to become the world's third-largest naval power after Great Britain and the United States. Yet, in spite of this and other gains, the Japanese were bitter toward the West.

First, Japan felt that the West did not accept it as an equal. In 1919 the League of Nations, dominated by Western powers, refused to accept Japan's demand for a statement on racial equality in the League's charter. The Japanese regarded this rejection as a humiliation. In 1924 the United States banned further Japanese immigration to its shores. In response, the Japanese staged demonstrations and boycotted American goods.

The Japanese were angered further by the West's refusal to support Japanese policy in China. Japan wanted to tie China closer to itself; the West wanted to retain the Open Door policy. As a result

▶ **Conflict** Japan's militarism and expansionism place it on a collision course with the West.

For reading strategies to help students read effectively see pages 12–13.

Vocabulary Pre-check

🔲 Use the Vocabulary PuzzleMaker for Chapter 30 to create a crossword puzzle to reinforce section terms. **L1 LEP**

📁 Use Vocabulary Activity 30 to introduce vocabulary terms. **L1 LEP**

FOCUS

Section Objective

Describe how militarism shaped the development of Japan after World War I.

BELLRINGER
Motivational Activity

Before taking roll at the beginning of the class period, project Section Focus Transparency 30-4 and have students answer the activity questions. Discuss students' responses.

📁 This activity is also available as a blackline master.

SECTION RESOURCES

📁 **Reproducible Masters**
• Lecture Notes 30-4
• Reproducible Lesson Plan 30-4
• Vocabulary Activity 30
• Guided Reading Activity 30-4
• History Simulation 30
• Mapping History Activity 30

• Section Quiz 30-4
• Reading Essentials and Study Guide 30-4

🖹 **Transparencies**
• Section Focus Transparency 30-4

Multimedia
🔲 Interactive Tutor Self-Assessment Software
🔲 Testmaker

TEACH

Guided Practice

THEME Conflict

To help students understand how population density encouraged Japanese expansionism, have them consider the relative areas of Japan (145,856 square miles [377,767 square km]) and California (158,706 square miles [411,049 square km]). By 1925 Japan's population was about 60 million; have students find out the current population of California. Ask students to discuss how Japan's growth led to aggressive policies. **L1**

Visualizing History

After Chiang Kai-shek's Nationalist government made Nanking (now Nanjing) the capital of a united China in 1928, the city thrived. When the city fell to the Japanese in 1937, between 40,000 and 300,000 civilians were killed. From then until Japan's defeat in World War II, Nanjing was ruled by puppet governments. **Answer to Caption:** *His advisers feared the emperor would be removed and that extremism would increase if he opposed militarism.*

Independent Practice

 Guided Reading Activity 30-4 **L1**

 History Simulation 30

Mapping History Activity 30

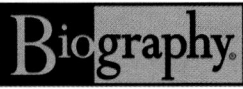

The following videotape program is available from Glencoe:

• **Hirohito**

Visualizing History **Young Japanese students celebrate the fall of Nanjing to Japanese forces in 1938.** *Why was Emperor Hirohito unable to thwart the spread of militarism in Japan?*

of Western pressure, Japan had to abandon the Twenty-One Demands and recognize Western interests in China.

Social and Political Tensions

After World War I, Japan faced social and economic challenges at home. Of major concern was a population explosion, or dramatic increase in population. Japan's population had increased from nearly 35 million in 1872 to about 60 million in 1925. This rate of increase was a challenge because of the already high density of population on the Japanese islands.

Japan's Industrial Growth

Since emigration was cut off to such places as the United States, the Japanese looked for other ways to cope. They placed new emphasis on manufacturing and foreign trade. It was hoped that new factories and markets would provide employment for large numbers of people.

Government-controlled banks provided the needed capital to encourage the expansion of heavy industry, or the manufacture of machinery and equipment needed for factories and mines. Industries important to national defense, especially

steel and the railroads, were owned by the government, but most of the Japanese economy was in the hands of large privately owned businesses known together as the *zaibatsu* (zy•BAHT•soo).

During the 1920s and 1930s Japan's industry grew rapidly, and Japanese manufactured goods began to flood world markets. Increased manufacturing, however, stimulated the desire for raw materials. Since Japan had few mineral resources of its own, it was forced to look overseas for them.

Social and Political Changes

Meanwhile, Japan's working class increased in importance. Because of overpopulation in the countryside, land already scarce was continually subdivided among farmers. Rural economic woes enabled farm villages to provide the bulk of labor for the new urban industries. Along with male workers, many young women from rural areas found jobs in the factories.

Labor unions became more powerful and increased their membership to more than 300,000 members by the end of the 1920s. The growth of the urban, working-class population produced movements demanding social changes. Several efforts by intellectuals to organize Socialist groups, however, were speedily met with police repression.

During this period, the urban middle class expanded as well. Japanese cities became great metropolitan areas and centers of middle-class culture. The Tokyo-Yokohama area, devastated by a terrible earthquake in 1923, took on a new appearance as Western influences increasingly shaped the tempo of urban life. American music, dancing, and sports especially became popular, and rising standards of living and expectations produced the need for more and better higher education.

With the growth of the working and middle classes, steps were taken toward greater political democracy. In 1925 the Japanese parliament granted universal male suffrage; voters increased from 3 million to 14 million. Japanese women, however, did not receive the right to vote until 1947.

Political Weaknesses

In spite of these gains, democracy remained very limited in Japan. Political power was actually in the hands of nobles and urban industrialists. The emperor, **Hirohito**, was a constitutional monarch. However, he was a powerful symbol of traditional authority. Behind the emperor was an influential group of military leaders, who were opposed to democratic reforms.

The appeal of antidemocratic nationalist groups increased as the economy deteriorated in

---

COOPERATIVE LEARNING ACTIVITY

Roundtable Discussion Have students make a list of the social and economic problems that Japan faced after World War I. The list should include rapid population growth, need for raw materials, scarce farmland, limited democracy, and political repression. Organize the class into groups and have each group think of several possible solutions to one problem. Then hold a roundtable discussion in which representatives from each group try to work out peaceful solutions to Japan's challenges. **L2**

the 1930s. A worldwide fall in prices caused by the Great Depression devastated Japan's silk factories and other industries. Millions of workers lost their jobs and could not find new ones. Some began to starve, and children went begging in the streets. In November 1930 an assassin from a secret society shot Prime Minister Osachi Hamaguchi (oh•SAH •chee hah•mah•GOO•chee). Teetering on the brink of economic chaos, many impoverished farmers and workers in Japan looked to strong-minded military leaders such as Hashimoto Kingoro (hah•shee•MOH•toh keen•GOH•roh) for answers:

❝ We are like a great crowd of people packed into a small and narrow room, and there are only three doors through which we might escape, namely emigration, advance into world markets, and expansion of territory. The first door … has been barred to us by the anti-Japanese immigration policies of other countries. The second door … is being pushed shut by tariff barriers.… Japan should rush upon the last door [expansion of territory]. ❞

—Hashimoto Kingoro, *Addresses to Young Men*

Militarism and Daily Life

During the 1930s, militarism began to influence all aspects of Japanese life. Supporters of the military program opposed the spread of Western lifestyles in Japan and favored traditional Japanese ways. Military dress, including items such as the samurai swords, appealed to nationalist sentiments. Young children even carried out military drills in schools and participated in parades.

Military Expansion

In September 1931 the Japanese military demonstrated just how powerful it had become.

Without seeking approval from the government, army leaders invaded the northeastern region of China known as **Manchuria**. It was clear that the Japanese government could no longer control its own army. In five months the powerful Japanese army had conquered Manchuria.

The conquest of Manchuria was a clear sign of the plans of the military to dominate the Japanese government at home and expand Japanese influence abroad. The principal opposition to democratic government came from young military officers. Largely from rural backgrounds, they opposed the urban luxuries of the politicians and readily accepted extremist ideas.

By the early 1930s extremist groups in the military were ready to use violence to bend the government to their will. In 1932 army officers assassinated a prime minister who dared to oppose their views. Then, in 1936, another group of officers led an armed revolt against the government. Although the revolt collapsed, it did not halt the steady takeover of government policy making by the military. By early 1937 the army and the government had become one and the same.

Many democratically minded Japanese hoped that Emperor Hirohito would thwart the spread of militarism. As a crown prince, the emperor had traveled in the West and had a keen appreciation of Western ways. Palace advisers, however, feared that a strong stand by the emperor would increase the military leaders' extremism. They feared that the emperor would be removed from office and that the Japanese monarchy would be abolished.

As international criticism of Japan's expansion grew, many Japanese rallied to the support of their soldiers and the military leaders. With no powerful political opposition at home, Japan's military leaders looked forward to conquering all of Asia. Their dreams of a mighty Japanese empire—like the dreams of German and Italian rulers—brought the world to war.

Linking Past and Present

Japan's Military The Japanese Constitution of 1947 abolished the country's army and navy and pledged that Japan would abandon war as a political tool. The prohibition was observed so strictly that it was not until February 1996 that 45 Japanese soldiers joined UN forces peacekeeping operations in the Golan Heights.

ASSESS

Check for Understanding

Assign Section 4 Assessment as homework or as an in-class activity.

🖱 Use Interactive Tutor Self-Assessment Software to review Section 4.

Evaluate

📁 Section Quiz 30-4

🖱 Use the Testmaker to create a customized quiz for Section 4.

Reteach

Have students state how Japan's geography contributed to its problems during the late 1800s and early 1900s.

📁 Reading Essentials and Study Guide 30-4

Enrich

Have students imagine that they are Japanese civilians opposed to militarism living in Tokyo during the 1930s. Have them write diary entries responding to key events.

CLOSE

Have students make two lists, one of the problems that Japan confronted in the 1920s and 1930s, and one of solutions pursued by Japanese militarists.

SECTION 4 ASSESSMENT

Main Idea
1. Use a diagram like the one below to list militarism's influences on Japanese society after World War I.

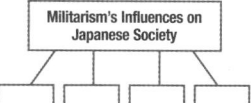
Militarism's Influences on Japanese Society

Recall
2. **Define** population explosion, heavy industry, *zaibatsu*.
3. **Identify** Hirohito.
Critical Thinking
4. **Synthesizing Information** Imagine you are an unemployed worker in Japan during the depression of the 1930s.

Would you support the new military policies of Japan's government? Why or why not?

Understanding Themes
5. **Conflict** What steps did the military take to increase its hold on the Japanese government?

Chapter 30 *Nationalism in Asia, Africa, and Latin America* **809**

SECTION 4 ASSESSMENT ANSWERS

1. opposed spread of Western lifestyles; favored tradition; military dress; military drills in schools and parades; military expansion
2. All terms are defined in the Glossary.
3. Hirohito, 808
4. Answers will vary. Students might suggest that a strong military government might

provide work through expanding war industries.
5. **CONFLICT** invaded Manchuria without government approval in 1931, assassinated a prime minister who opposed it in 1932, rebelled against the government in 1936, and steadily took over government policy making

TEACH

Identifying an Argument In preparation for this lesson, find two newspaper editorials or opinion pieces that make opposing arguments on the same issue. Before having the class read the skill, distribute copies of the pieces. After students have read the editorials, ask them to identify the argument and supporting reasons in each piece. Now have students read the skill and complete the practice questions.

Additional Practice

 Skill Reinforcement Activity 30

GLENCOE
TECHNOLOGY

GO TO

Glencoe's **Skillbuilder Interactive Workbook, Level 2**
This interactive CD-ROM promotes student mastery of key social studies skills.

Critical Thinking SKILLS

Identifying an Argument

Have you ever argued with someone about a political or social issue? In everyday conversation, the word *argument* refers to a conflict involving two or more opinions. However, in writing and in formal debate, an argument is the full presentation of a single opinion. It is important to learn how to identify an argument to fully evaluate the position.

Learning the Skill

The main idea of an argument is its thesis, or the writer's basic position or viewpoint on the subject. In some arguments the thesis is stated explicitly. In others, you must read carefully to determine the writer's position.

The writer supports the thesis with reasons and supports the reasons with examples or facts. For instance, suppose your parents have said that it would be better if you did not have a car to drive until after your 18th birthday. They support their thesis with these reasons: 1) other forms of transportation are available; and 2) you will be a more mature and better driver by that age. They support the first reason with these facts: you live in a city with good public transportation; your best friend has a car and frequently drives you to school. They support the second reason with accident statistics of younger and older drivers.

Before accepting or rejecting an argument, evaluate its strengths and weaknesses. How well is each reason supported by facts and examples? Does the author's bias invalidate the argument? In our example, your parents may be biased; they may want to protect your safety and keep their car insurance rates low for another year. Despite this bias, they still may have a strong argument if the supporting facts are true.

Practicing the Skill

Read the following quotation from Jomo Kenyatta, and review the discussion of Kenya in Section 1, pages 799–800. Then answer the following questions.

1. What is Kenyatta's thesis?
2. What reasons does Kenyatta give to support this thesis?
3. What facts support Kenyatta's statement that Europeans have robbed Africans of their birthright?
4. What bias does Kenyatta show in his statement? Do the facts outweigh his bias? Why or why not?

❝ **By driving [the African] off his ancestral lands, the Europeans have robbed him of the material foundations of his culture, and reduced him to a state of serfdom incompatible with human happiness.... It is not in his nature to accept serfdom forever. He realizes that he must fight unceasingly for his own complete emancipation; for without this he is doomed to remain the prey of rival imperialisms.** ❞

—Jomo Kenyatta, *Facing Mount Kenya*, 1938

Applying the Skill

Find a recent article that states an argument about a political or historical issue. Identify the thesis of the argument and major reasons and evidence supporting it. Decide whether you accept or reject this argument and explain why.

For More Practice

Turn to the Skill Practice in the Chapter Assessment on page 823.

GO TO

The **Glencoe Skillbuilder Interactive Workbook**, Level provides instruction and practic in key social studies skills.

ANSWERS TO PRACTICING THE SKILL

1. Europeans have robbed Africans of the material foundations of their culture.
2. Europeans drove Africans from their lands, reducing them to serfdom. Unless Africans emancipate themselves, they will continue to be subject to outside powers.
3. Britain refused to grant independence to Kenya and violently suppressed protests; Europeans settled on African lands and employed Africans on plantations for very low wages.
4. Kenyatta reveals an anti-European bias with emotional words such as *robbed, serfdom, emancipation, prey*. Student evaluations may differ, but point out that, despite his bias, the facts support Kenyatta's thesis.

1917 Mexico ratifies a new constitution.

1930 José F. Uriburu leads successful coup in Argentina.

 1934 Lázaro Cárdenas becomes president of Mexico.

Chapter 30 Section 5

Section 5

Nationalism in Latin America

Guide to Reading

Read to Find Out

Main Idea *Nationalism in Latin America brought conflict with the United States.*

▶ **Terms to Define**
cooperatives, nationalization

▶ **People to Meet**
Lázaro Cárdenas, Juan Vicente Gómez, Hipólito Irigoyen, José F. Uriburu, Getúlio Vargas, Augusto César Sandino

▶ **Places to Locate**
Mexico, Venezuela, Argentina, Brazil, Nicaragua

The Storyteller

"Let us forget the marble of the Acropolis and the towers of the Gothic cathedrals. We are the sons of the hills and the forests. Stop thinking of Europe. Think of America!" The words of Ronald de Carvallo, a Brazilian nationalist, rang in Lucio Costa's ears. He resolved to break with traditional forms and create architecture appropriate for Brazil. He visualized a style integrating art and nature—murals, sculptures, and tiles with gardens and decorative painting.

—adapted from
Latin America, A Concise Interpretive History, E. Bradford Burns, 1994

Palacio Do Ilamarati, Brasilia

A fter World War I, economic change and nationalism swept Latin America. Although the region's economy remained basically agricultural, the oil and mineral industries became increasingly important. Much of the investment that developed these resources was from the United States, Great Britain, France, Germany, and Italy. Anger at foreign influence led to growing nationalism among Latin Americans of all backgrounds. Rubén Darío, a noted Nicaraguan writer, had expressed the view of many Latin Americans:

❝ The United States is grand and powerful.
Whenever it trembles, a profound shudder runs down the enormous backbone of the Andes.
If it shouts, the sound is like the roar of a lion....
But our own America, which has had poets since the ancient times ...
and has lived, since the earliest moments of its life,
in light, in fire, in fragrance, and in love—
the America of Moctezuma and Atahualpa, the aromatic America of Columbus,
Catholic America, Spanish America ...
our America lives. And dreams. And loves.
And it is the daughter of the Sun. Be careful.
Long live Spanish America! ❞

—Rubén Darío, "To Roosevelt," 1903

Economic Changes

In the 20 years following World War I, Latin Americans continued to grow coffee, bananas,

▶ **Change** Nationalist forces in Latin America oppose increased American intervention in the region.

Guide to Reading

For reading strategies to help students read effectively see pages 12–13.

Vocabulary Pre-check

🔲 Use the Vocabulary PuzzleMaker for Chapter 30 to create a crossword puzzle to reinforce section terms. **L1 LEP**

📁 Use Vocabulary Activity 30 to introduce vocabulary terms. **L1 LEP**

FOCUS

Section Objective

Analyze why nationalism in Latin America brought conflict with the United States.

BELLRINGER Motivational Activity

 Before taking roll at the beginning of the class period, project Section Focus Transparency 30-5 and have students answer the activity questions. Discuss students' responses.

📁 This activity is also available as a blackline master.

SECTION RESOURCES

📁 **Reproducible Masters**
- Lecture Notes 30-5
- Reproducible Lesson Plan 30-5
- Vocabulary Activity 30
- Guided Reading Activity 30-5
- World Art and Music Activity 30
- People in World History Profile 57
- Reteaching Activity 30

- Enrichment Activity 30
- Section Quiz 30-5
- Performance Assessment Activity 30
- Spanish Chapter Summary 30
- Reading Essentials and Study Guide 30-5

💡 **Transparencies**
- Section Focus Transparency 30-5
- World History and Art Transparency 40, *Zapatistas*

Multimedia
💿 Interactive Tutor Self-Assessment Software
💿 Testmaker

TEACH

Guided Practice

THEME Change

Write on the chalkboard the following line from Rubén Darío's poem quoted on page 811: *"Whenever it trembles, a profound shudder runs down the enormous backbone of the Andes."* Ask students to interpret the sentence. How did economic changes in Latin America after World War I make the poem even more relevant? *(Latin America became even more tied to global markets.)* **L1**

Global Issues Ask students to discuss the ways in which the United States was involved in Latin America following World War I. *(It kept a military presence in Nicaragua, Haiti, the Dominican Republic, Panama; it was involved in the economies of many countries through ownership of oil wells and other businesses.)* **L2**

Politics Have students explain what the United States promised to do under the Good Neighbor policy. *(not to interfere militarily in the affairs of other countries)* Initiate a discussion of why this was a change from the actions of the United States before this time. *(The United States had formerly kept a strong military presence in Latin America.)* **L3**

📁 World Art and Music Activity 30

📌 World History and Art Transparency 40, *Zapatistas*

---

wheat, corn, beans, sugarcane, and other crops in large amounts. However, industrial growth—particularly in the United States and western Europe—increased the demand for tin, copper, silver, oil, and other raw materials from Latin America. As mineral exports increased, Latin Americans had more cash with which to buy imports. More and more of the Latin American economy became tied to global markets.

When world prices for raw materials increased, Latin American economies improved. However, in the 1920s, prices for coffee, sugar, and other raw materials plunged. The price declines foretold the global economic depression that was soon to occur. Like much of the world, Latin America suffered high unemployment and low prices for its products in the decade of the Great Depression, 1929–1939.

Mexico's Oil Economy

Oil was one of the vital resources for growing industries, and **Mexico** was an important source of oil. Mexico entered the postwar era, still reeling from its own bloody and divisive revolution that had begun in 1910. However, a stable, one-party system was evolving that seemed able to maintain order and unity. Mexico's constitution, ratified in 1917, authorized the government to protect workers from exploitation and to require private property owners to act in the public interest.

Despite the constitution, reforms came slowly until 1934. In that year, **Lázaro Cárdenas** (KAHR•duhn•AHS) was elected to the presidency. Over the next six years, his government carried out other reforms in the spirit of the 1910 revolution. First, Cárdenas directed the redistribution of vast tracts of land to landless peasants. To increase agricultural production, the Mexican government also encouraged the formation of cooperatives, farm organizations operated by and for the peasants. By 1940 more than half of all Mexicans farmed land they could finally call their own.

Cárdenas's main goal, however, was to make Mexico economically independent of foreign countries. His government especially wanted to bring

Images of the Times

Mexican Murals

During the 1930s, Mexican artists painted colorful murals showing key themes and events in Mexico's history. Many of these murals still decorate outer and inner walls of government buildings, theaters, universities, and hospitals throughout the country.

Distribution of the Land by Diego Rivera. Court of Fiestas, Secretaria de Educacion Publica, Mexico City, Mexico

812

Images of the Times   Mexican Murals

Mexican murals won world renown after World War I, and controversy made Diego Rivera (1886–1957) the best-known Mexican muralist. A mural he was commissioned to paint for the Detroit Institute of Arts was attacked for being antireligious, and a fresco he did for New York's Rockefeller Center was ultimately destroyed because it included a portrait of the Bolshevik leader Lenin.

Siqueiros (1896–1974) also used his art to convey his radical political beliefs. Over the course of his lifetime, his Communist sympathies and work for labor unions landed him in jail and drove him into exile at different times.

the industrial economy under Mexican control. In 1937 Cárdenas supported an oil workers' strike. At the time, many Mexican workers had gone on strike against their British and American employers, demanding higher wages and better working conditions. Cárdenas urged the oil companies to meet their demands, but the companies refused. After a year of futile negotiations, Cárdenas carried out a policy of nationalization of foreign-owned oil wells on March 18, 1938, declaring them the property of the government. He explained his actions by reaching all the way back to a colonial law written by the Spanish king in 1783, which had been retained in the new constitution: "The Mines are the property of My Royal Crown, [including] all bitumens [minerals] and juices of the earth."

The British and American companies were furious, but the Mexican people were ecstatic. They celebrated March 18 as the day of their "Declaration of Economic Independence." Cárdenas, meanwhile, defused the crisis by offering to pay a fair price for the oil wells. With World War II looming on the horizon, Great Britain and the United States soon accepted this offer. They did not want an angry Mexico to sell its oil to Japan and Germany.

The nationalization of Mexico's oil fields signaled the arrival of economic nationalism in Latin America. For Mexico it was a clean break from the economic dependence of the past.

Changes in Venezuela

Another oil-rich country, **Venezuela**, followed a course unlike that of Mexico, but more like that of other Latin American countries that had a single source of wealth. Between 1908 and 1935, President **Juan Vicente Gómez** ruled Venezuela as a dictator. During this period, engineers discovered oil along Venezuela's Caribbean coast. By the late 1930s Venezuela was the third-largest oil-producing country in the world. However, British, Dutch, and American oil companies controlled the Venezuelan oil industry. Gómez, instead of nationalizing the oil companies, worked closely with them. He, his

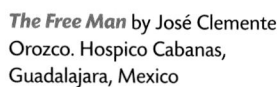

The Free Man by José Clemente Orozco. Hospicio Cabañas, Guadalajara, Mexico

From Porfirio's Dictatorship to the Revolution (detail with Martyrs) by David Alfaro Siqueiros. Museo Nacional de Historia, Castillo de Chapultepec, Mexico City, Mexico

REFLECTING ON THE TIMES

1. What three leading Mexican artists painted murals during the 1930s?
2. Based on the murals, what do you think are some major themes in Mexican history?

813

ANSWERS TO REFLECTING ON THE TIMES

1. Diego Rivera, José Clemente Orozco, and David Alfaro Siqueiros
2. transforming Mexico into a more independent and equitable society, economically as well as politically

Independent Practice

📁 Guided Reading Activity 30-5 **L1**

Economics Organize students into two groups. Have one group write a pamphlet in favor of the nationalization of foreign-owned oil wells in Mexico, and the other a pamphlet against nationalization. Tell students to support their arguments by forecasting the long-term effects of state ownership of the wells. **L2**

The Arts Have students research Latin American artists and writers whose work dealt with nationalist issues. Then ask students to deliver brief oral reports describing how the artists' political beliefs shaped their work. Suggest that they bring in reproductions of artwork if possible. **L3**

📁 People in World History Profile 57

you don't say...

Latin America The region consisting of Mexico, Central America, South America, and the islands of the Caribbean gets its name from the Latin language. When Europeans began to settle the area during the late 1400s, they brought their languages and customs with them. These languages—Spanish, Portuguese, and French—all derived from ancient Latin. They are the main languages of Latin America to this day.

Visualizing History By the 1930s, Buenos Aires had become a city of wide avenues and public buildings. Its prosperity rested on the export of beef and other agricultural products. *How did the Great Depression affect Argentina's political life during the 1930s?*

political allies, and oil companies prospered, but most Venezuelans did not.

Gómez used the oil profits to strengthen his government. He paid off his country's huge national debt to European bankers and created a strong army. He also used some of the profits for his personal benefit.

After Gómez died in 1935, workers and students around the country rioted to protest the domination of their country by foreign oil companies and their Venezuelan partners. The army intervened to stop the protests and remained in charge of the country for the next several decades.

Democracy and the Military

Venezuela was one of many Latin American countries in which a small group of people prospered from the natural wealth found in the country. It was also typical in that the military intervened to put down protests that threatened business interests. Argentina and Brazil are two of the other countries in which democracy failed to take hold.

Argentina Becomes Fascist

In 1916 **Argentina** held its first open presidential election in which every male could vote. The winner, **Hipólito Irigoyen** (ee•PAW•lee•TOH IHR•ih•GOH•YEHN), obtained most of his support from urban workers and the middle class. They elected him because of his party's success in achieving electoral reforms. During his first administration, Irigoyen carried through social reforms that improved factory conditions, boosted workers' wages, and regulated working hours. He advocated other democratic reforms and efforts to help the poor. After serving six years as president, Irigoyen proudly claimed:

> ❝ We have held public office in obedience to the popular mandate and inspired by the duty to make reparation ... for all the injustices, moral and political, collective and individual, that have long dishonored the country. ❞

In 1928 Irigoyen was again elected president. His second term, however, aroused widespread opposition, and he did not complete his term in office. Although he was personally popular, his government had often been ineffective. He was slow to make decisions, so that official documents needing his attention piled up on his desk awaiting action. More important, corrupt aides stole money from the national treasury. In addition, few Argentinians believed any more in the democratic process by which Irigoyen had won office.

Angered by inefficiency and corruption and opposed to democracy, General **José F. Uriburu** led a successful coup against Irigoyen in 1930. With the coming of the Great Depression, Argentina was divided between Socialist and Fascist political

National Archives

Sending in the Marines

American marines in Nicaragua unload a cannon to help defend their military position. The United States has a history of military intervention in the Central American nation of Nicara-
in the early years of the 1900s American interest
Nicaragua increased with the building of the
ma Canal, with growing pressure to defend
emisphere against British and German threats,
with expanding United States involvement in

Central American trade.

In 1912, U.S. Marines landed in Nicaragua to ensure the payment of its debts and remained there for the next 13 years. In 1927, American forces again intervened to put down an uprising by nationalist leader Augusto César Sandino (left, center figure). Sandino fought American involvement in his country's domestic affairs—and failed. American forces remained in Nicaragua until 1933.

During the years between the two world wars the empires of Europe began to crumble. In the Western Hemisphere President Hoover pulled American troops out of Nicaragua, and President Franklin D. Roosevelt declared a Good Neighbor policy with Latin America. Nevertheless, imperialism endured until after World War II. ⊕

Chapter 30 *Nationalism in Asia, Africa, and Latin America* **815**

TEACH

Tell students that for many years before the United States began construction of the Panama Canal, Americans had hoped to build a canal across Nicaragua to link the Atlantic and Pacific Oceans. What was the political group that controlled Nicaragua from 1979 until 1990 called, and why? (*They were called Sandinistas in honor of Nicaragua's nationalist hero, Sandino.*)

 CURRICULUM CONNECTION

THE ARTS
Nicaraguan poet and essayist Rubén Darío (1867–1916) was a founder of the literary movement called modernism. Many literary historians date the birth of modernism to the 1888 publication of *Azul*, Darío's first major work, and the movement's peak to the 1896 publication of his *Prosas profanas*.

ASSESS

Check for Understanding

Assign Section 5 Assessment as homework or as an in-class activity.

🖲 Use Interactive Tutor Self-Assessment Software to review Section 5.

Evaluate

🗁 Section Quiz 30-5

🖲 Use the Testmaker to create a customized quiz for Section 5.

Reteach

Write this heading on the chalk-board: *Latin America and the Global Economy.* Have students list facts that show how the world market affected Latin America. *(Lists might include increased U.S. and European demand for raw materials from Latin America; sale of exports increased Latin American purchases of imports; U.S. investment in Latin America led to interventions to protect American interests.)*

🗁 Reading Essentials and Study Guide 30-5

Major Oil Discovery

Saudi Arabia, 1938
In 1933 the government of Ibn Saud granted an American oil company the right to explore for oil in the newly united kingdom of Saudi Arabia. After a major oil deposit was discovered on the Arabian Peninsula, other oil companies joined to form the Arabian American Oil Company (Aramco) in 1944. After World War II, large-scale oil production brought immense wealth to Saudi Arabia and enabled Ibn Saud's government to build roads, schools, and hospitals throughout the country.

Saudi Arabia

movements. To maintain social order, the army began to assume an important role in the Argentine government.

Uriburu, like Italy's Mussolini, believed in fascism. He cancelled elections and tried to abolish the congress. For the remainder of the 1930s, military men and their sympathizers ruled Argentina. They faked elections, suppressed their opponents, and consolidated their power. Democracy was dead in Argentina, destroyed by the military.

Brazil's Popular Dictator

Brazil, like Argentina, fell under an authoritarian government. In 1930 President **Getúlio Vargas** took power. Seven years later, Vargas proclaimed a new constitution that made him a virtual dictator. He strengthened the government by transferring powers from the cities and states to the national government. He won support from many Brazilians for his willingness to oppose the interests of large businesses. To gain working-class support, Vargas's administration increased wages, shortened working hours, and gave unions the right to organize. Vargas's supporters called him "father of the poor" for these efforts.

Vargas, with the support of the military, was able to keep Brazil united and stable until 1945. In that year, a democratic revolt threw him out of power. When Vargas refused to leave office, military leaders stepped in and forced Vargas out of office. Although the military did not actually rule in Brazil, their support was crucial in deciding who did.

Ties With the United States

During the 1920s and 1930s, the mineral wealth of Latin America attracted American investment. To protect its economic interests, the United States intervened militarily in Central America and the Caribbean countries.

Increased American Intervention

In 1912 United States Marines had invaded **Nicaragua** when the country failed to pay its debts. American forces landed again during the 1920s to protect United States interests. Rebel forces led by General **Augusto César Sandino** tried to force a United States withdrawal. To help the American soldiers, the United States government trained a loyal Nicaraguan army called the National Guard. By the mid-1930s the National Guard was able to defeat the rebels. Its leader, Anastasio Somoza, seized power in 1936. The Somoza family ruled Nicaragua with American support until 1979.

During the early 1900s, American troops also occupied Haiti and the Dominican Republic. This military intervention, as well as the growth of American economic influence, was deeply resented by many Latin Americans. Latin American nationalists particularly opposed the Roosevelt Corollary. They stated that no country had the right to intervene in the affairs of another. They also claimed that, while the United States was exploiting their raw materials, Latin America was getting few economic benefits in return. Anti-Americanism was especially strong during the Great Depression. At this time, prices for raw materials fell sharply. This decline increased hardships among Latin Americans dependent on trade with North America and Europe.

Good Neighbor Policy

Aware of growing resentment, the United States tried to improve relations with its southern neighbors. Following his election in 1928, United States President Herbert Hoover went on a good-will tour of Latin America. He hoped to show that the United States regarded its Latin American neighbors as equals. At the same time, Undersecretary of State Joshua Reuben Clark began to restate the meaning of the Monroe Doctrine. In a memorandum issued in December 1928, Clark held that the Monroe Doctrine's warning that European powers could not interfere in Latin America did not mean that the United States had the right to interfere.

In 1933 President Franklin D. Roosevelt, Hoover's successor, announced the Good Neighbor policy toward Latin America. He declared, "I

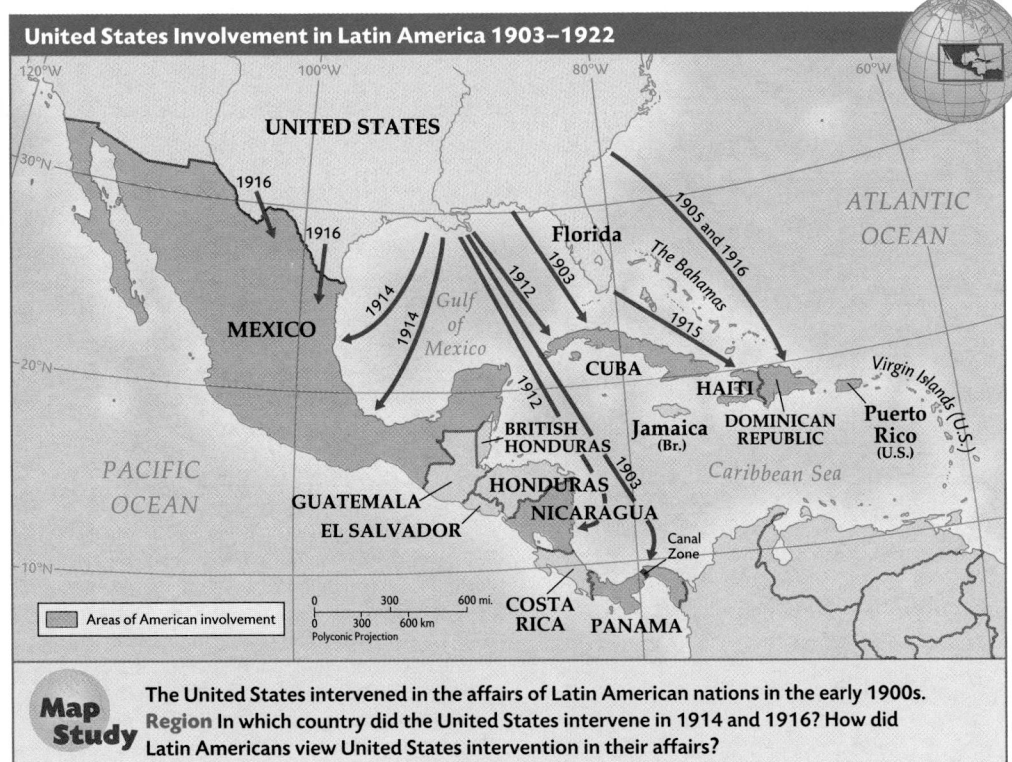

United States Involvement in Latin America 1903–1922

UNITED STATES

MEXICO

PACIFIC OCEAN

GUATEMALA
EL SALVADOR

Gulf of Mexico

Florida

The Bahamas

ATLANTIC OCEAN

CUBA

HAITI

BRITISH HONDURAS

Jamaica (Br.)

DOMINICAN REPUBLIC

Virgin Islands (U.S.)

Puerto Rico (U.S.)

Caribbean Sea

HONDURAS
NICARAGUA

Canal Zone

COSTA RICA

PANAMA

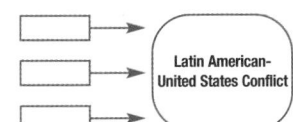

Areas of American involvement

0   300   600 mi.
0   300   600 km
Polyconic Projection

Map Study
The United States intervened in the affairs of Latin American nations in the early 1900s. **Region** In which country did the United States intervene in 1914 and 1916? How did Latin Americans view United States intervention in their affairs?

Map Study

Answer
Mexico; Latin Americans resented U.S. interference in their national affairs.

Map Skills Practice

Reading a Map What nations border Costa Rica? *(Nicaragua and Panama)*

 Reteaching Activity 30

Enrich

Have students select one leader from this section and research his life. Have them write a brief essay about the leader that focuses on whether he was good or bad for his country.

 Enrichment Activity 30

CLOSE

Review with students the political and economic changes that were occurring in Latin America during the period after World War I. *(the revolution in Mexico, struggles for economic independence, conflicts over freedom from interference by the United States)*

---

would dedicate this nation to the policy of the good neighbor—the neighbor who resolutely respects himself, and because he does so, respects the rights of others." This policy renounced past United States military intervention in the region. Roosevelt also ended American restrictions on Cuba's sovereignty and ordered the withdrawal of American troops from Haiti and Nicaragua.

In 1933 the United States took another step toward improving its relationship with Latin America. Diplomats from the United States joined with their Latin American counterparts at the Pan American conference in Montevideo, Uruguay. After much discussion, all parties signed an agreement stating: "No state has the right to intervene in the internal or external affairs of another."

SECTION 5 ASSESSMENT

Main Idea
1. Use a diagram like the one below to show the factors that caused conflict between Latin America and the United States.

Latin American-United States Conflict

Recall
2. **Define** cooperatives, nationalization.
3. **Identify** Lázaro Cárdenas, Juan Vicente Gómez, Hipólito Irigoyen, José F. Uriburu, Getúlio Vargas, Augusto César Sandino, the Good Neighbor policy.

Critical Thinking
4. **Making Comparisons** How did the governments of Mexico

and Venezuela differ in their response to European and American control of their oil industries?

Understanding Themes
5. **Change** Does the United States government have the right to intervene in the domestic affairs of other countries? Explain, using recent examples.

Chapter 30 *Nationalism in Asia, Africa, and Latin America* **817**

SECTION 5 ASSESSMENT ANSWERS

1. Mexico's nationalization of foreign-owned oil wells in 1938 angered American companies; Latin American countries' opposition to American military intervention, American economic influence, and Roosevelt Corollary
2. All terms are defined in the Glossary.
3. Cárdenas, 812; Gómez, 813; Irigoyen, 814;

Uriburu, 814; Vargas, 816; Sandino, 816; the Good Neighbor policy, 817
4. Mexico nationalized its oil industry; Venezuela worked closely with foreign oil companies.
5. **CHANGE** Answers will vary but might include discussions of U.S. intervention in Somalia, Haiti, or Bosnia.

Literature

Block Schedule

Team Teaching This excerpt from *Gifts of Passage* may be presented in a team-teaching context, in conjunction with English or Language Arts.

Gifts of Passage

Historical Connection

British rule dramatically affected Indian society. In British schools, government offices, and elsewhere, the diverse peoples of India met and interacted with the British but not on terms of equality.

Background Information

Setting The incident takes place in the Indian city of Zorinabad about 1928. The British still ruled India, but the Indian independence movement was growing stronger.

Characters Santha: a five-year-old girl from whose point of view the story is told; Premila: Santha's eight-year-old sister; Headmistress: the Englishwoman who runs the Anglo-Indian school; Mother: the mother of Santha and Premila

Plot Santha and Premila start to attend an Anglo-Indian school, where the headmistress assigns them British names because she does not think she can pronounce Indian names. When Premila takes her first test, her teacher separates the Indian students because she thinks they will cheat. Premila, with Santha, leaves the school in anger.

Literature

from

Gifts of Passage

by Santha Rama Rau

antha Rama Rau, born in Madras, India, in 1923, spent her childhood in India, England, and South Africa. In each place, she closely watched the way people from different backgrounds related with one another. Advances in transportation and communication have sharply increased the interactions of people from different cultures. Today these interactions shape the world more than ever before. In the following excerpt, Rau recalls her early experiences at a school for English and Indian children in India.

*A*t the Anglo-Indian day school in Zorinabad to which my sister and I were sent when she was eight and I was five and a half, they changed our names. On the first day of school, a hot, windless morning of a north Indian September, we stood in the headmistress's study and she said, "Now you're the *new* girls. What are your names?"

My sister answered for us. "I am Premila, and she"—nodding in my direction—"is Santha."

The headmistress had been in India, I suppose, fifteen years or so, but she still smiled her helpless inability to cope with Indian names. Her rimless half-glasses glittered, and the precarious bun on the top of her head trembled as she shook her head. "Oh, my dears, those are much too hard for me. Suppose we give you pretty English names. Wouldn't that be more jolly? Let's see, now—Pamela for you, I think." She shrugged in a baffled way at my sister. "That's as close as I can get. And for *you*," she said to me, "how about Cynthia? Isn't that nice?"

My sister was always less intimidated than I was, and while she kept a stubborn silence, I said "Thank you," in a very tiny voice.…

That first day at school is still, when I think of it, a remarkable one. At that age, if one's name is changed, one develops a curious form of dual personality. I remember having a certain detached and disbelieving concern in the actions of "Cynthia," but certainly no responsibility. …

ABOUT THE AUTHOR

Santha Rama Rau is the daughter of an Indian government official. When she was young, India was still part of the British Empire. Many Indian leaders and administrators, including Rau's father, were strongly influenced by British culture. Her father, for example, was educated in England. Rau herself attended Wellesley College in Massachusetts. She has written a number of novels and nonfiction works, including essays about her childhood and her extensive travels, as well as a stage play based on the novel *A Passage to India*, by E. M. Forster.

During the years of British rule, the Indian subcontinent had a wealthy upper class of princes and their families. This upper-class Indian family of the 1940s practiced traditional ways but was also familiar with the customs of the British aristocracy. *What are the British teachers' attitudes toward ordinary Indians in the story by Santha Rama Rau?*

Accordingly, I followed the thin, erect back of the headmistress down the veranda [porch] to my classroom feeling, at most, a passing interest in what was going to happen to me in this strange, new atmosphere of School….

I can't remember too much about the proceedings in class that day, except for the beginning. The teacher pointed to me and asked me to stand up. "Now, dear, tell the class your name."

I said nothing.

"Come along," she said, frowning slightly. "What's your name, dear?"

"I don't know," I said, finally.

The English children in the front of the class—there were about eight or ten of them—giggled and twisted around in their chairs to look at me. I sat down quickly and opened my eyes very wide, hoping in that way to dry them off. The little girl with the braids put out her hand and very lightly touched my arm. She still didn't smile.

Most of the morning I was rather bored. I looked briefly at the children's drawings pinned to the wall, and then concentrated on a lizard clinging to the ledge of the high, barred window behind the teacher's head. Occasionally it would shoot out its long yellow tongue for a fly, and then it would rest, with its eyes closed and its belly palpitating, as though it were swallowing several times quickly. The lessons were mostly concerned with reading and writing and simple numbers—things that my mother had already taught me—and I paid very little attention. The teacher wrote on the easel blackboard words like

Chapter 30 *Nationalism in Asia, Africa, and Latin America* **819**

OTHER WORKS BY SANTHA RAMA RAU

The Adventuress. New York: Harper, 1970.
East of Home. New York: Harper, 1950.
Home to India. New York: Harper, 1945.
My Russian Journey. New York: Harper, 1959.

Remember the House. New York: Harper, 1956.
This Is India. New York: Harper, 1954.
View to the Southeast. New York: Harper, 1957.

Visualizing History Many upper-class Indians strongly supported the movement for independence. Like the Latin American creoles who fought for independence from Spain in the early 1800s, members of this upper class had the most to gain from independence since they would become the ruling elite of the new nation.
Answer to Caption: *superficially friendly but condescending and mistrustful*

Literary Element Imagery consists of the words and phrases that a writer uses to evoke particular sights, sounds, smells, or other sensations for the reader. In this excerpt, for example, Rau helps readers picture the headmistress by describing her "rimless half-glasses" and "precarious bun."

FOCUS

As students read, ask them to think about the importance of name giving in the story. Santha and her sister are given British names, as is Santha's friend, Nalini. But other characters, such as the headmistress and the teachers, are not referred to by name at all. Discuss what Rau may have intended by not giving names to certain characters. Why might Rau have chosen to focus on names, and their significance, at this moment in Indian history? *(Names establish identity, and the struggle for an Indian identity was part of the independence movement.)*

TEACH

Literary Analysis

Rather than simply tell the reader that she was bored during her first day in school, Rau describes a lizard on the wall in vivid detail. The description of the lizard takes the reader's mind off the classwork, just as the actual lizard distracted Santha.

Comparison

Discuss the difference between Santha's view of games and that of the British children. The way the children played reflected their basic values about individual achievement and group cooperation. Discuss how games today may reflect the values of students in schools in the United States.

Clarification

Discuss how social-class relationships affect even school students. Rau, even as a five-year-old child, knew that friendship between Indian and British or Anglo-Indian children was "out of the question." Have students consider how Rau knew that social equality between British and Indian students was impossible.

📖 World Literature
Selection 7

"bat" and "cat," which seemed babyish to me; only "apple" was new and incomprehensible.

When it was time for the lunch recess, I followed the girl with braids out onto the veranda. There the children from the other classes were assembled. I saw Premila at once and ran over to her, as she had charge of our lunchbox. The children were all opening packages and sitting down to eat sandwiches. Premila and I were the only ones who had Indian food—thin wheat chapatties [a type of bread], some vegetable curry, and a bottle of buttermilk. Premila thrust half of it into my hand and whispered fiercely that I should go and sit with my class, because that was what the others seemed to be doing....

I had never really grasped the system of competitive games. At home, whenever we played tag or guessing games, I was always allowed to "win"—"because," Mother used to tell Premila, "she is the youngest, and we have to allow for that." I had often heard her say it, and it seemed quite reasonable to me, but the result was that I had no clear idea of what "winning" meant.

When we played twos-and-threes that afternoon at school, in accordance with my training, I let one of the small English boys catch me, but was naturally rather puzzled when the other children did not return the courtesy. I ran about for what seemed like hours without ever catching anyone, until it was time for school to close. Much later I learned that my attitude was called "not being a good sport," and I stopped allowing myself to be caught, but it was not for years that I really learned the spirit of the thing....

It was a week later, the day of Premila's first test, that our lives changed rather abruptly. I was sitting at the back of the class, in my usual inattentive way, only half listening to the teacher. I had started a rather guarded friendship with the girl with the braids, whose name turned out to be Nalini (Nancy, in school). The three other Indian children were already fast friends. Even at that age it was apparent to all of us that friendship with the English or Anglo-Indian children was out of the question. Occasionally, during the class, my new friend and I would draw pictures and show them to each other secretly.

The door opened sharply and Premila marched in. At first, the teacher smiled at her in a kindly and encouraging way and said, "Now, you're little Cynthia's sister?"

Premila didn't even look at her. She stood with her feet planted firmly apart and her shoulders rigid, and addressed herself directly to me. "Get up," she said. "We're going home."

I didn't know what happened, but I was aware that it was a crisis of some sort. I rose obediently and started to walk toward my sister.

"Bring your pencils and your notebook," she said.

I went back for them, and together we left the room. The teacher started to say something just as Premila closed the door, but we didn't wait to hear what it was.

In complete silence we left the school grounds and started to walk home. Then I asked Premila what the matter was. All she would say was "We're going home for good."...

When we got to our house the ayah [maid] was just taking a tray of lunch into Mother's room. She immediately started a long, worried questioning about what are you children doing back here at this hour of the day.

Mother looked very startled and very concerned, and asked Premila what had happened.

Premila said, "We had our test today, and she made me and the other Indians sit at the back of the room, with a desk between each one."

Mother said, "Why was that, darling?"

"She said it was because Indians cheat," Premila added. "So I don't think we should go back to that school."

Mother looked very distant, and was silent a long time. At last she said, "Of course not, darling." She sounded displeased.

We all shared the curry she was having for lunch, and afterward I was sent off to the beautifully familiar bedroom for my siesta. I could hear Mother and Premila talking through the open door.

Mother said, "Do you suppose she understood all that?"

ADDITIONAL LITERARY WORKS OF THE PERIOD

Mistral, Gabriela. *Feeling.* Poems for children by one of Chile's most famous writers.
Natsume, Sóseki. *The Three-Cornered World.* Story of a Japanese artist who visits a small village.
Tagore, Rabindranath. *Gitanjali.* Poetry about India, religion, and nationalism.

Visualizing History These Indian women are dressed in the sari, a garment of several yards of material draped so that one end forms a skirt and the other a shoulder or head covering. *How do you think the two Indian girls in the story dressed for their classes at the British school?*

Premila said, "I shouldn't think so. She's a baby."

Mother said, "Well, I hope it won't bother her."

Of course, they were both wrong. I understood it perfectly, and I remember it all very clearly. But I put it happily away, because it had all happened to a girl called Cynthia, and I never was really particularly interested in her.

RESPONDING TO LITERATURE

1. Why did Santha and her sister leave school?
2. Explain why Santha was unable to tell the class her name.
3. When the headmistress gives Santha and her sister new names, what can you determine the headmistress thought of Indian culture?
4. **Demonstrating Reasoned Judgment** Explain why Santha's mother would or would not keep her children home permanently from the Anglo-Indian school.

ANSWERS TO RESPONDING TO LITERATURE

1. because a British teacher assumed that Indian students cheated
2. Answers may vary but might suggest that Santha had not accepted her British name but realized her real name would not be accepted by the teacher.
3. The headmistress does not value Indian culture and feels it should be replaced by British customs.
4. Answers will vary. Students may say that the mother is forced to face the fact that to get a good, that is British, education, her daughters must confront British racism.

WORLD HISTORY *Online*

Have students use the **Chapter 30 Self-Check Quiz** at worldhistory.glencoe.com to prepare for the Chapter Test.

GLENCOE
TECHNOLOGY

 VIDEODISC
Use MindJogger to review the chapter.

MindJogger Videoquiz

|||||||||| Chapter 30
Disc 4 Side B

Also available in VHS.

Answers

Using Key Terms
1. a   3. b   5. d
2. i   4. c

Using Your History Journal

Suggest that students model their feature on radio news broadcasts.

Reviewing Facts
1. population exploded; working class more important; rural workers became laborers in urban industries; women took factory jobs; labor unions grew; urban middle class grew
2. soldiers, wheat, and cotton; greater governmental control
3. Kemal Atatürk, Reza Shah, Chiang Kai-shek, Mao Zedong, and José Uriburu, among others
4. Gandhi's nonviolent protest effectively undermined British claims to rule India.
5. Atatürk separated government and religion and had Turks follow Western ways. Reza Shah built schools, roads, and hospitals.
6. Nigerian women held protests against British taxes.

WORLD HISTORY *Online*

Self-Check Quiz

Visit the *World History: The Human Experience* Web site at **worldhistory.glencoe.com** and click on *Chapter 30—Self-Check Quiz* to prepare for the Chapter Test.

Using Key Terms

Write the key term that completes each sentence. Then write a sentence for each term not chosen.

a. warlords	f. heavy industry
b. nationalization	g. shah
c. pacifist	h. population explosion
d *zaibatsu*	i. self-determination
e. cooperatives	j. civil disobedience

1. After Yuan Shigai's death in 1916, local military leaders called _____ divided China among themselves.
2. United States President Woodrow Wilson raised the hopes of colonial peoples by endorsing the principle of _____.
3. In 1938 the Mexican government carried out a policy of _____ in which it took over the foreign-owned oil industries.
4. Mohandas K. Gandhi was a _____, a person opposed to using war and other means of violence to settle disputes.
5. The privately owned part of the Japanese economy in the 1920s and 1930s was largely in the hands of large companies known as _____.

Technology Activity

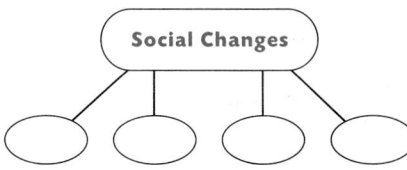

Using a Computerized Card Catalog Use a computerized card catalog to locate information about nationalism in Asia, Africa, and Latin America after World War I. Using your research, create a bulletin board focusing on the themes of "global nationalism." Include time lines for each region, showing significant events related to nationalism. List similarities and differences you see among the nationalist movements.

Using Your History Journal

Write a three-minute radio news feature about the setting and causes of the event you described in Your History Journal news report at the beginning of the chapter.

Reviewing Facts

1. **Culture** Use a diagram like the one below to identify social changes in Japan after World War I.

```
        Social Changes
       /    |    |    \
     (  ) (  ) (  ) (  )
```

2. **History** Name the contributions that India made to the war effort in World War I. What did Great Britain promise India in return?
3. **Government** Identify three leaders who would agree with the statement "Political power grows out of the barrel of a gun."
4. **History** Describe the influence of Gandhi on India's struggle for freedom.
5. **History** List the reforms introduced by Kemal Atatürk in Turkey and Reza Shah in Iran.
6. **Culture** Discuss the role of women in the nationalist movement in Nigeria after World War I.
7. **History** Identify the major event in 1938 that marked the arrival of economic nationalism in the countries of Latin America.

Critical Thinking

1. **Apply** How does political control relate to economic control? Give examples from Egypt or India.
2. **Apply** How did religious differences hamper the Indian independence movement? Give examples to support your opinion.

---

7. Mexican President Cárdenas nationalized foreign oil wells.

Critical Thinking
1. The two forms work together. In Egypt, Britain asserted political control in order to retain the Suez Canal. In India, Britain's political control maintained a profitable trade in raw materials.
2. Differences split the independence move-

ment just as it was gaining power.
3. Nationalist movements had to grow stronger so that the cost of retaining colonial control outweighed the profits of imperialism.
4. Students might discuss such themes as revolution and social justice. These themes first appeared in Western art during the 1800s and have since become international.
5. Possible answer: While Egypt, India, and other countries either won or moved toward

- **Analyze** In 1939 most of Africa and much of Asia were European colonies. What conditions needed to change before self-determination could be achieved by all countries? Give examples to support your answer.
- **Synthesize** Name a 1930s Mexican mural and state its theme. Could artists of other cultures and eras have also used this theme? Explain.
- **Evaluate** Did the global influence of the West become more or less widespread in the two decades after World War I? Give examples to support your opinion.

Geography in History

1. **Location** Refer to the map below. What is the relative location of the Sea of Japan?
2. **Movement** Approximately how many miles would the Japanese military have had to transport troops across the Sea of Japan to invade Manchuria (Northeast Plain) in 1931?
3. **Region** Along what major rivers might the Japanese have traveled to gain access to central China? What obstacles would they have faced?

China and Japan

Understanding Themes

1. **Nationalism** In what countries of Africa and the Middle East did nationalism lead to self-

determination in the period 1919 to 1939?
2. **Change** How did the British respond to Gandhi's campaign for Indian independence?
3. **Conflict** Do you think Mao Zedong and Chiang Kai-shek were wise to put aside their differences and unite against Japan? Explain.
4. **Conflict** What were the main areas of disagreement that resulted in conflict between Japan and the West after World War I?
5. **Change** How did nationalism change Latin America following World War I?

Linking Past and Present

1. Review Gandhi's major criticisms of Western civilization. Were they accurate? Do they apply today?
2. Do you think nationalism is stronger or weaker throughout the world today than it was in the 1920s and 1930s? Give examples from current events that support your opinion.

Skill Practice

Read the quotation below by Hashimoto Kingoro and review the discussion of Japan in Section 4, pages 807–809. Then answer the questions below.

❝ **We are like a great crowd of people packed into a small and narrow room, and there are only three doors through which we might escape, namely emigration, advance into world markets, and expansion of territory. The first door ... has been barred to us by the anti-Japanese immigration policies of other countries. The second door ... is being pushed shut by tariff barriers ... Japan should rush upon the last door [expansion of territory].** ❞

—Hashimoto Kingoro, *Addresses to Young Men*

1. What is Kingoro's thesis in this argument?
2. What reasons does he give to support this thesis?
3. What evidence in Section 4 supports Kingoro's thesis?
4. Do you accept or reject Kingoro's argument? Explain your answer.

breaking free of the West's political control, countries such as Iran and Turkey adopted many elements of Western culture.

Geography in History

1. It lies between Japan to the east and Korea and China to the west.
2. about 600 miles (965 km)
3. Huang He, Wei He, Chang Jiang, Xi Jiang; mountains

Understanding Themes

1. **NATIONALISM** Turkey, Iran, and Egypt
2. **CHANGE** They arrested Gandhi, keeping him from active protest and weakening the Indian National Congress.
3. **CONFLICT** Even though the Chinese could not stop Japan, they were more likely to be effective as a united force.
4. **CONFLICT** Japan felt humiliated by the League of Nations' rejection of its

---

demand for a statement on racial equality, by the U.S. ban on Japanese immigration, and by the West's insistence that Japan abandon the Twenty-One Demands and recognize Western interests in China.

5. **CHANGE** Mexico nationalized its oil fields, breaking with past economic dependence; Nicaraguans fought U.S. Marines; anti-Americanism spread throughout the region.

Linking Past and Present

1. the West's violence, materialism, and self-righteousness; answers will vary.
2. Answers will vary. Students should support their answers.

Skill Practice

1. To support its large population, Japan must expand its territory.
2. Japan is overcrowded. The only solutions are emigration, capturing world markets, or expanding its territory. The first two options are closed by hostile foreign powers, leaving only the third.
3. Japan had a population explosion; the United States banned Japanese immigration in 1924; Western countries forced Japan to abandon the Twenty-One Demands on China.
4. Answers may vary.

? Chapter Bonus Test Question

Ask students: How does Mao's statement, "Political power grows out of the barrel of a gun," apply to the revolutions discussed in this chapter? *(Answers may include: Not all the revolutions were violent, but brute force played a key role in many of them.)*

A complete, 1-page lesson plan is provided for each section in the Reproducible Lesson Plans booklet.

World War II

CHAPTER RESOURCES

Chapter	Reproducible Resources	Multimedia Resources
Chapter Opener	Chapter Themes: Graphic Organizer 31 Historical Significance Chapter Activity 31	MindJogger Videoquiz
Chapter Enrichment	Vocabulary Activity 31* Time Line Activity 31 Mapping History Activity 31 History Simulation 31 Geography and History Activity 31 Source Reading 31 People in World History Profiles 59, 60 World Art and Music Activity 31 Enrichment Activity 31 Critical Thinking Activity 31 Skill Reinforcement Activity 31 Performance Assessment Activity 31 Standardized Test Practice Workbook Activity 31 Inclusion for the Social Studies Classroom Strategies and Activities	World History and Art Transparency 42, *The Red Stairway* Mapping History Overlay Transparencies 19, 20, 21 Chapter Transparency 31 Vocabulary PuzzleMaker Software Turning Points in World History: • *The Holocaust* • *Dropping the Atomic Bomb* Lessons of War: • *Can a Battle Change History?* • *Appeasement: Munich Pact* • *At the Front* • *Laws of War* World History Primary Source Document Library
Chapter Review/Reteaching	Reteaching Activity 31 Skill Reinforcement Activity 31 Spanish Chapter Summary 31	Chapter 31 Digest Audiocassette, Activity, Test* Vocabulary PuzzleMaker Software Interactive Tutor Self-Assessment Software MindJogger Videoquiz
Chapter Evaluation/Testing	Performance Assessment Activity 31 Chapter 31 Test, Forms A and B	ExamView® Pro Testmaker

* *Also available in Spanish*

0:00 OUT OF TIME? Assign the Chapter 31 Audiocassettes.

World History Primary Source Document Library
Make History Come Alive!
Engage your students with over 250 easily accessible primary source documents—available on this CD-ROM—that will give them real life insight into the important events of world history.

Block Schedule
Activities that are particularly suited to use within the block scheduling framework are identified throughout this chapter by the following designation.

KEY TO ABILITY LEVELS
Teaching strategies are coded for varying learning styles.
L1 BASIC activities for all students
L2 AVERAGE activities for average to above-average students
L3 CHALLENGING activities for above-average students
LEP LIMITED ENGLISH PROFICIENCY activities

Additional Resources

NATIONAL GEOGRAPHIC SOCIETY

Teacher's Corner

INDEX TO NATIONAL GEOGRAPHIC MAGAZINE

The following articles relate to this chapter:

- "The Last Dive," by Priit J. Vesilind, October 1999.
- "The Battle of Midway," by Thomas B. Allen, April 1999.
- "Hiroshima," by Ted Gup, August 1995.
- "Blueprints for Victory," by John F. Shupe, May 1995.
- "The Wings of War," by Thomas B. Allen, March 1994.
- "Pearl Harbor: A Return to the Day of Infamy," by Thomas B. Allen, December 1991.
- "Remembering the Blitz," by Cameron Thomas, July 1991.
- "Ghosts of War in the South Pacific," by Peter Benchley, April 1988.

NATIONAL GEOGRAPHIC SOCIETY PRODUCTS AVAILABLE FROM GLENCOE

To order the following, call Glencoe at 1-800-334-7344:

- *PictureShow: World War II Era (CD-ROM)*
- *PicturePack: World War II Era (Transparencies)*
- *GTV: The American People (Videodisc)*
- *GTV: A Geographic Perspective on American History (Videodisc)*

ADDITIONAL NATIONAL GEOGRAPHIC SOCIETY PRODUCTS

Access National Geographic's new dynamic MapMachine Web site and other geography resources at:

- http://www.nationalgeographic.com/
- http://www.nationalgeographic.com/maps/

BIBLIOGRAPHY

Literature of the Period
Frank, Anne. *The Diary of a Young Girl.* New York: Doubleday, 1972. First-person account of a young Jewish girl and her family who spent years hiding from the Nazis.
Readings for the Student
Ryan, Cornelius. *The Longest Day.* New York: Simon and Schuster, 1984. Detailed, exciting account of D-Day and the Normandy invasion.
Readings for the Teacher
Leckie, Robert. *Delivered from Evil: The Saga of World War II.* New York: Harper, 1987. A complete history of World War II told in the style of a novel.

Use our Web site as an additional resource. All essential content is covered in the Student Edition.

You and your students can visit the *World History: The Human Experience* Web site at worldhistory.glencoe.com The student text directs students to the Web site for the following options:

- **Chapter Overviews**
- **Student Web Activities**
- **Self-Check Quizzes**

Answers are provided for you in a link entitled "Web Activity Lesson Plan." Additional Web Resources, Interactive Puzzles, and content updates are also available.

Visit the Glencoe Web site at socialstudies.glencoe.com for social studies activities, updates, and links to other resources.

LOCAL OBJECTIVES

_____
_____
_____
_____
_____
_____
_____
_____
_____
_____
_____
_____
_____
_____
_____
_____
_____
_____
_____

Introducing
Chapter 31

CHAPTER THEMES

Chapter Themes are listed by section on this chapter opening page of the Student Edition. A corresponding theme-based activity is available under "TEACH," and a theme-based question is asked in the Section and Chapter Assessments.

The Storyteller

Historical Setting The invasion of Normandy launched by the Allies in June 1944 was not their first invasion of German-occupied France. In 1942 the Allies launched a raid on the seaport town of Dieppe. About two-thirds of the 6,000 soldiers who took part in this attack were killed, wounded, captured, or reported missing. However, the defeat at Dieppe did provide the Allies with valuable information that was used two years later when planning the D-Day invasion.

Historical Significance

Answers: *By the end of World War II, the balance of power had shifted away from Europe.*

The United States and the Soviet Union held the balance of power.

WORLD HISTORY Online

Have students use the **Chapter 31 Overview** at worldhistory. glencoe.com as a prereading and postreading exercise for understanding chapter content.

World War II

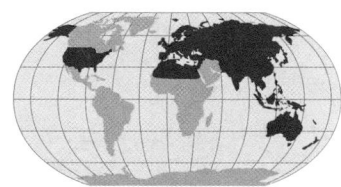

Chapter Themes

▶ **Movement** Japan, Italy, and Germany carry out expansionist policies. *Section 1*
▶ **Cooperation** The United States and Great Britain move slowly toward an alliance, while Germany and Italy make major territorial gains in Europe and the Mediterranean. *Section 2*
▶ **Conflict** Two separate and opposing alliances, the Allies and the Axis, wage a worldwide war. *Section 3*
▶ **Conflict** The Allies make major gains against the Axis Powers. *Section 4*
▶ **Innovation** New military technologies, such as the atomic bomb, affect the war's outcome. *Section 5*

The Storyteller

On June 6, 1944, the Allies mounted an all-out attack against German forces in Normandy, France. Years later an American soldier named Elliott Johnson could still vividly recall the events of the day:

"I remember going up to the highest part of that ship and watching the panorama around me unfold. In my mind's eye, I see one of our ships take a direct hit and go up in a huge ball of flames. There were big geysers coming up where the shells were landing and there were bodies floating, face down, face up."

The invasion of Normandy was one of the key events of World War II. Although the war began in 1939, it had its roots in the peace treaties that settled World War I.

Historical Significance

How did World War II affect the world balance of power? What nations emerged from conflict as world powers?

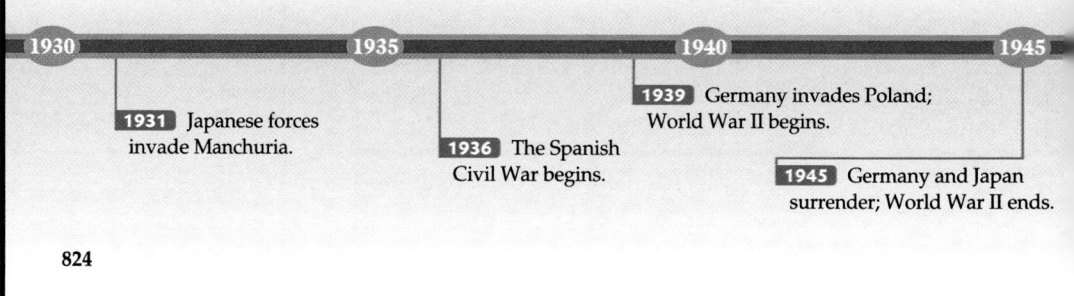

| 1930 | 1935 | 1940 | 1945 |

1931 Japanese forces invade Manchuria.

1936 The Spanish Civil War begins.

1939 Germany invades Poland; World War II begins.

1945 Germany and Japan surrender; World War II ends.

824

GEOGRAPHY CONNECTION

Location On a large wall map of the world or on the world map in the Atlas of their textbook, have students locate the following countries that took part in World War II: Germany, Italy, Japan, China, Poland, Finland, Norway, Denmark, France, the former Soviet Union (now the Commonwealth of Independent States), the United States, Egypt, Libya, and the Philippines. Why was this war called a world war? *(World War II involved countries in all parts of the world.)*

Visualizing History
Allied forces led by the United States land in the Pacific island of Bougainville, the largest of the Solomon Islands.

WORLD HISTORY Online

Chapter Overview

Visit the *World History: The Human Experience* Web site at **worldhistory.glencoe.com** and click on **Chapter 31—Chapter Overview** to preview the chapter.

Your History Journal

Create a two-column chart that shows the significance of ten key events in World War II. In column one list the event and date. In column two write a short statement of why the event was important to the outcome of the war.

Chapter 31   *World War II*   825

Visualizing History   The United States entered World War II on December 8, 1941, one day after Japan's surprise attack on the American naval and air base at Pearl Harbor in Hawaii. The victory at Bougainville was part of America's strategy of "island-hopping" to capture Japanese-held islands in the Pacific.

✔ Performance Assessment

Refer to the activity on page 824C of the Planning Guide.

📁 Refer to Activity 31 in the *Performance Assessment Strategies and Activities* booklet.

Using Your History Journal

Tell students to note major events and turning points in World War II as they read the chapter. Then, from their notes, ask them to select the ten most significant events and tell why they were important to the outcome of the war.

GLENCOE TECHNOLOGY

VIDEODISC
Use MindJogger to preview chapter content.

MindJogger Videoquiz

Chapter 31
Disc 4 Side B

 Also available in VHS.

➕ EXTRA CREDIT PROJECT

Prisoners of War Have students use outside sources to do in-depth research on a prisoner-of-war camp run by the Germans, the Japanese, or the Allies. Have them write a report that includes information on general living conditions, work done by prisoners, chances for recreational activities, escape attempts, and compliance with international law on treatment of prisoners of war. 📦

Chapter 31   *World War II*   **825**

SECTION THEME

▶ **Movement** Japan, Italy, and Germany carry out expansionist policies.

Guide to Reading

For reading strategies to help students read effectively see pages 12–13. Have students think about the main head as they read the subheads.

Vocabulary Pre-check

■ Use the Vocabulary PuzzleMaker for Chapter 31 to create a crossword puzzle to reinforce section terms. **L1 LEP**

🗁 Use Vocabulary Activity 31 to introduce vocabulary terms. **L1 LEP**

FOCUS

Section Objective

Explain in what sense World War II was a product of World War I.

BELLRINGER
Motivational Activity

Before taking roll at the beginning of the class period, project Section Focus Transparency 31-1 and have students answer the activity questions. Discuss students' responses.

🗁 This activity is also available as a blackline master.

Section 1

The Path to War

Guide to Reading

Read to Find Out
Main Idea *World War II was partially a product of World War I.*

▶ **Terms to Define**
collective security, sanctions, appeasement

▶ **People to Meet**
Chiang Kai-shek, Benito Mussolini, Haile Selassie, Francisco Franco, Adolf Hitler, Joseph Stalin, Neville Chamberlain

▶ **Places to Locate**
Manchuria, Ethiopia, Spain, the Rhineland, Austria, Czechoslovakia

The Storyteller

Joseph Stalin

Joseph Stalin sent an invitation to formal negotiations to Adolf Hitler, the Nazi dictator. Hitler read the note and drummed both fists against the wall, exclaiming, "Now I have the world in my pocket." German Foreign Minister Joachim von Ribbentrop and Stalin arranged the division of Europe and agreed never to attack each other, then celebrated with an elaborate dinner. Each side toasted the other and told jokes the other side did not find funny. After dinner, in a final show of hospitality, Stalin drew the German foreign minister aside and told him that he personally could guarantee, on his word of honor, that the Soviet Union would not betray its partner.

—adapted from *Joseph Stalin: Man and Legend*, Ronald Hingley, 1974

826 **Chapter 31** *World War II*

In the 1930s the Western democracies watched uneasily as militaristic dictatorships came to power in Europe and Asia. Despite their fears, Britain, France, and the United States could not agree on what steps to take to ensure their collective security, or what was needed to defend their common interests against enemy attack. Much of the unrest in Europe and Asia can be traced to the peace settlements made at the end of World War I. Great Britain, France, and the United States were substantially satisfied with these settlements; however, Japan, Italy, and Germany were not.

Japan's Expansion in Asia

Japan was the first of the nondemocratic powers to reveal its territorial ambitions in the interwar period. With limited natural resources of its own, Japan depended heavily on foreign sources for raw materials and on foreign markets for finished goods. To acquire more of these materials and markets, Japan sought new territories for conquest.

The Japanese military used a bomb explosion on the South Manchurian Railway in September 1931 as an excuse to overrun **Manchuria**. The following year Japan established Manchuria as an independent state, renamed it Manchukuo, and set up former Chinese emperor Pu Yi as puppet ruler.

When China protested in the League of Nations about Japan's actions, the League ordered a commission under British statesman Lord Lytton to investigate the affair. Lytton's commission laid the blame squarely on Japan and ordered the Japanese government to return Manchuria to China. The League voted overwhelmingly in favor of this recommendation, to which Japan responded in March 1933 by withdrawing from the League. The Manchurian incident not only revealed that the League of Nations was powerless, but also boosted the expansionist ambitions of Italy and Germany.

SECTION RESOURCES

🗁 Reproducible Masters
• Lecture Notes 31-1
• Reproducible Lesson Plan 31-1
• Vocabulary Activity 31
• Guided Reading Activity 31-1
• Chapter Themes: Graphic Organizer 31
• People in World History Profile 59
• Time Line Activity 31

• Section Quiz 31-1
• Reading Essentials and Study Guide 31-1

🕯 Transparencies
• Section Focus Transparency 31-1
• Chapter Transparency 31

Multimedia
■ Interactive Tutor Self-Assessment Software
■ Testmaker
🌐 Lessons of War:
Appeasement: Munich Pact

In the early 1930s, the Japanese military wanted to acquire the rich oil reserves of the East Indies to supply its ships and airplanes. But to control the East Indies, Japan needed Chinese ports. Consequently, in the summer of 1937, Japanese forces invaded China and captured major eastern and southern cities. In the capital of Nanjing, they engaged in mass brutality, killing over 200,000 civilians. Meanwhile, the Nationalist government of **Chiang Kai-shek** retreated inland and later allied with the Western powers. From 1937 to 1945, the Nationalists, the Chinese Communists, and the Japanese fought each other for control of China.

Visualizing History Haile Selassie (center) appealed to the League of Nations for action against Italian aggression in Ethiopia. The League's failure to halt Axis expansion led to its own downfall. *Why were the League's sanctions against Italy ineffective?*

Italy's Conquest of Ethiopia

The relative ease with which Japan acquired Manchuria encouraged Italy to make a similar move. Italy's goal was to secure control of the ancient kingdom of **Ethiopia** in eastern Africa. In 1934 Italian and Ethiopian forces clashed in a disputed zone on the border of Ethiopia and Italian Somaliland. When the Italian dictator, **Benito Mussolini**, demanded an apology and reparations, the Ethiopians responded by asking the League of Nations to investigate the matter. The League decided that because each side viewed the area where the incident took place as its own territory, either side was to blame.

The League's decision did not satisfy Mussolini, who thought an Ethiopian colony would enhance Italy's image as a world power. Consequently, in October 1935, Mussolini ordered the Italian army to invade Ethiopia. In a dramatic appearance at the League of Nations, Ethiopian Emperor **Haile Selassie** appealed for help. This time the League condemned the action and voted to impose economic **sanctions**, measures designed to stop trade and other economic contacts, against Italy. The League forbade its members to sell Italy arms and certain raw materials. But the sanctions did not include oil, coal, and iron, all vital to Italy's war efforts.

Once again the League's actions were ineffective. Mussolini completed his conquest of Ethiopia, and in May 1936 he formally annexed the African nation.

Spanish Civil War

A civil war in **Spain** further inflamed the international situation in the 1930s. After presiding over years of social and economic chaos, King Alfonso XIII abdicated in 1931, and Spain became a republic. The new republican government immediately began a program of social reforms. It ended the Catholic Church's role in educating Spanish youth and redistributed land from nobles to peasants.

As a result of these and other reforms, many right-wing groups in Spain opposed the republic and wished to restore the old order. In July 1936 right-wing army chiefs staged an uprising in Spanish Morocco that soon spread to Spain. For three years the conservative Spanish Nationalists, led by General **Francisco Franco**, and the left-wing Loyalists, or Spanish Republicans, battled for control of Spain.

Early in the fighting several foreign powers intervened in the Spanish war. The Soviets supported the Loyalists, while the Germans and Italians aided the Nationalists. Volunteers from Britain, France, the United States, and other countries around the world flocked to Spain to join the International Brigade and fight for the Republican cause against fascism. The governments of the Western democracies, however, refused to intervene because they feared a general European war.

Germany's dictator, **Adolf Hitler**, viewed German participation in the Spanish Civil War as a

Chapter 31 *World War II* **827**

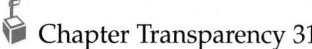

COOPERATIVE LEARNING ACTIVITY

Oral Report Organize students into groups of four to six to research how the world reacted to the expansion of Japan, Italy, or Germany into Manchuria, Nanjing, Ethiopia, the Rhineland, Austria, and Czechoslovakia, respectively. Have each group choose one area and find reports about that conquest. Encourage students to use quotations that reveal the point of view of the reporter toward the conquest. Then have each group present its report to the class. **L2**

VIDEODISC
Lessons of War

Side Two, Chapter 3
Frames 3466–5635
Title: *Appeasement: Munich Pact*
Subject: British Prime Minister Neville Chamberlain's attempt to keep peace with Germany in 1938
Ask: What did Hitler demand at the Munich Conference?
(that the Sudetenland be given to Germany)

Global Issues Have students imagine that they are newspaper editors in 1938. Ask them to list the events that have pushed the world toward another war. Then have them write an editorial titled "On the Brink of War" that offers suggestions on how to diffuse the powder keg. **L3**

THE HISTORY CHANNEL

The following videotape program is available from Glencoe:

• **World War II: The War Chronicles** (Seven Video Set)

To find classroom resources to accompany this video, check the following home page:

The History Channel: http://www.historychannel.com

---

way to strengthen ties with Italy and to secure a vital supply of Spanish iron ore and magnesium. Hermann Goering, head of the Luftwaffe—or German air force—saw an opportunity "firstly, to prevent the further spread of Communism; secondly, to test my young Luftwaffe in this or that technical aspect." To accomplish these goals, Goering formed the Condor Legion, an all-German air and ground force. They used Spanish towns and cities as testing grounds for new weapons and military tactics, such as the combined use of fire and high-explosive bombs.

By the summer of 1936, the Nationalists had taken most of western Spain. When the Soviets stopped sending aid to the Loyalists in 1938, Franco launched his final offensive. In March 1939 Franco entered Madrid, the last of the Loyalist strongholds. The civil war had ended, but more than half a million Spaniards had died, and much of the country lay in ruins. Although Spain joined Italy and Germany as countries headed by fascist dictators, Franco did not ally himself with Italy and Germany.

Hitler on the Offensive

The same year the Spanish Civil War broke out, Hitler made his move in Germany. The German dictator was convinced that Germany needed more *lebensraum*, or living space, for its expanding population. In his book, *Mein Kampf (My Struggle)*, Hitler wrote:

> 66 Only an adequate large space on this earth assures a nation freedom of existence....We must hold unflinchingly to our aim ... to secure for the German people the land and soil to which they are entitled.... 99

Footnotes to History

Writers at War
The Spanish Civil War became a crusade for many writers. In *For Whom the Bell Tolls*, American writer Ernest Hemingway describes an idealistic American fighting the Fascist forces in Spain. The English novelist George Orwell, in *Homage to Catalonia*, presents his experiences on the Aragon front and his nearly fatal gunshot wound.

Occupying the Rhineland

Since 1919, the Versailles Treaty had forbidden German troops in **the Rhineland**, a German region between the Rhine and the French border. This ban was designed to provide security to France. Hitler gambled that if he violated the treaty, France and Great Britain would do nothing to stop him. In March 1936, therefore, Hitler sent troops into the Rhineland. France had the right to take military action, and Britain had the obligation to back France with its own armed forces. Neither country acted, however, because neither was willing to risk a war.

In October 1936, Hitler and Mussolini agreed to the Rome-Berlin Axis, an alliance that they hoped would be the "axis" around which world affairs would turn. Known thereafter as the Axis Powers, Italy and Germany later joined Japan in the Anti-Comintern Pact, an alliance against Soviet communism. Viewing the Pact as a threat to his country, the Soviet dictator **Joseph Stalin** urged the West to unite against the Axis. But the West, fearing war and distrusting Stalin, refused.

Seizing Austria

Hitler, meanwhile, grew bolder. For a long time he had dreamed of *Anschluss* (ANSH•luhs)—the joining of **Austria** to Germany. "German-Austria must return to the great mother country," he wrote. "One blood demands one Reich."

In 1934 Hitler had tried to take over Austria but backed down when Mussolini responded by mobilizing Italy's troops. In 1938, now that Germany and Italy were allies, Hitler tried again. He invited the Austrian chancellor to Berchtesgaden, his mountain retreat in the German Alps, and bullied him into appointing Nazis to key posts in Austria. The Austrian chancellor appealed to Britain and France for help, but once more the two major democracies in Europe did nothing. In March 1938 Hitler sent German troops into Austria and then proclaimed it part of Germany. He insisted that he was only promoting political stability in central Europe by uniting German-speaking peoples into one country. The Western democracies, however, refused to take military action.

Tension Builds in Europe

Austria was the first victim of Hitler's policy of expansion. **Czechoslovakia** was the next. In the late 1930s, Czechoslovakia was the only democratic nation in central Europe. It held a key strategic position in the region. Its standard of living was second only to that of

---

MEETING SPECIAL NEEDS ACTIVITY

Learning Style: Visual/Spatial Have students who are strong visual learners work together to review information in Section 1 and plan political cartoons based on these topics: Japan sets up puppet government in Manchuria; Italy takes Ethiopia; Condor Legion bombs Spain; League of Nations fails to stop aggression; Hitler grabs Austria. Display completed cartoons on the bulletin board and hold a class discussion on what the cartoons say about events of the 1930s. **L2**

Germany. Czechoslovakia also had a strong army and alliances with France and the Soviet Union.

The nation of Czechoslovakia was created by treaty at the end of World War I. In addition to Czechs and Slovaks, it had 1 million Hungarians, half a million Ruthenians, and more than 3 million Germans. During the 1930s these minorities began to demand more freedom than they had received under the terms of the treaties, creating serious problems for the Czechoslovak government. Hitler took advantage of Czechoslovakia's ethnic problems to destroy the country.

Sudeten Crisis

On September 12, 1938, Hitler demanded that the Germans of the Sudetenland, a heavily fortified region in northwestern Czechoslovakia, be given the right of self-determination. Czechoslovak leaders responded by proclaiming martial law. In an effort to avert an international crisis, British Prime Minister **Neville Chamberlain** suggested to Hitler that they meet to discuss the matter. France supported his request.

Chamberlain met with Hitler in Germany on September 15, 1938. There Hitler demanded that the Sudetenland be given to Germany. At a second meeting a week later, Chamberlain accepted Hitler's demands. He thought that a policy of appeasement, granting concessions to maintain peace, would stabilize Europe. As the British and their French allies searched for a peaceful solution, Hitler raised his demands. The Sudetenland, he stated, must be united with Germany.

The Munich Conference

On September 29, Chamberlain met with Hitler a third time in Munich, Germany. Also attending were French Premier Édouard Daladier and Italy's dictator Benito Mussolini. Czechoslovakia and the Soviet Union were not represented.

Mussolini offered a "compromise" that gave Germany control over the Sudetenland. In return, Hitler promised to respect Czechoslovakia's sovereignty. He also promised not to take any more European territory and to settle future disputes by peaceful negotiation. Still hoping to avoid war,

In May 1938 Adolf Hitler (left) visited Rome, Italy, to meet with his Italian ally Benito Mussolini (right). The visit was designed to demonstrate the unity of the Rome-Berlin Axis. *What role did Mussolini play in the Czech crisis later that year?*

Great Britain and France accepted the terms. On September 30, Czechoslovakia reluctantly accepted the Munich Agreement.

Chamberlain returned home to cheering crowds, proclaiming that he had ensured "peace in our time." He trusted Hitler and believed that the Nazis would cause no more trouble. Events soon proved him wrong. On March 15, 1939, Hitler sent his armies into Czechoslovakia and took control of the western part of the country. The eastern part, Slovakia, became a German puppet state. After the takeover the Western democracies could no longer maintain their illusions about Hitler's plans and began to prepare for war.

The Coming of War

More German demands followed the Munich agreement. In March 1939 Hitler turned his attention to eastern Europe. He forced Lithuania to give up the German-speaking city of Memel. Next the German dictator put pressure on Poland, threatening to take over the Baltic port of Danzig

Chapter 31 *World War II* **829**

ASSESS

Check for Understanding

Assign Section 1 Assessment as homework or as an in-class activity.

 Use Interactive Tutor Self-Assessment Software to review Section 1.

Evaluate

Section Quiz 31-1

Use the Testmaker to create a customized quiz for Section 1.

Reteach

Have students explain the connection of the following people to acts of aggression in the 1930s: Pu Yi, Benito Mussolini, Haile Selassie, Francisco Franco, Adolf Hitler, Joseph Stalin, and Neville Chamberlain.

Reading Essentials and Study Guide 31-1

Enrich

Have students write a paragraph explaining why Germany, Italy, and Japan eventually became allies.

CLOSE

Have students summarize how aggressive expansion, a weak League of Nations, appeasement, and secret treaties led to the outbreak of war in 1939.

---

and the Polish Corridor, a narrow strip of Polish land that separated the German region of East Prussia from the rest of Germany. Great Britain and France promised to help Poland defend its borders if it became necessary. The Polish government accepted the support of the Western democracies and firmly rejected Hitler's demands.

The West and the Soviets

To defend Poland, the democracies had to consider the Soviet Union, Poland's neighbor but also its traditional enemy. During the late 1930s, Stalin had urged the Western powers to do something about Hitler. He suspected that the Munich Agreement was an attempt by the British and the French to turn Hitler's attention away from the West and toward the Soviet Union. Chamberlain, on the other hand, did not trust Stalin. He suspected that the Soviet leader wanted to extend his influence in eastern Europe. This confusion as to whether the Fascists or the Communists were the greater enemy contributed to the coolness of the British and the French toward Stalin.

Despite Chamberlain's suspicions and his lack of faith in the fighting ability of the Soviet army, he asked the Soviets to join Britain and France in an alliance to contain Nazism. Stalin agreed on the condition that the West acknowledge the Soviet right to occupy a broad zone stretching from Finland to Bulgaria. Chamberlain refused the request, deepening Stalin's suspicion that the West would like nothing better than to see Germany and the Soviet Union destroy each other.

Nazi-Soviet Talks

Stalin believed that Hitler's desire for "living space" would eventually lead the German dictator to move into the rich agricultural areas of eastern Europe. Because he doubted that the West would come to his country's aid if Germany threatened it, Stalin began secret talks with the Germans. On August 23, 1939, the Soviet Union and Germany signed the Nazi-Soviet Nonaggression Pact.

According to the agreement, Germany and the Soviet Union pledged that they would never attack each other. Moreover, each would remain neutral if the other became involved in a war. Stalin and Hitler also secretly agreed to create spheres of influence in eastern Europe. Germany would occupy the western part of Poland, while the Soviets would govern the eastern part. They agreed to include Finland, part of Romania, Estonia, Latvia, and Lithuania in the Soviet sphere of influence.

Neither Stalin nor Hitler had any illusions about their agreement. They were long-term enemies who, for their own purposes, needed a short-term arrangement. Stalin still believed that war with Germany was inevitable. But he thought that the pact would improve Soviet security. If nothing else, it would buy the Soviets time to prepare for war. Hitler saw the pact as a means of securing Germany's eastern border.

The pact shocked Western leaders, who realized that it destroyed the last barrier to war. The West had also lost a potential ally, and Hitler had won a pledge of neutrality that freed him to pursue his military objectives regarding Poland. Hitler remained convinced, however, that the West would do nothing if he moved against Poland. "The men of Munich," he said, "will not take the risk." With this thought in mind, Hitler sent his armies across the Polish frontier on September 1, 1939. However, he had finally misjudged what the Western leaders would do. Two days after Hitler's invasion of Poland, Great Britain and France declared war on Germany. World War II had begun.

SECTION 1 ASSESSMENT

Main Idea

1. Use a chart like the one below to identify ways in which World War II was a product of World War I.

How WWII Was a Product of WWI
1.
2.
3.

Recall

2. **Define** collective security, sanctions, appeasement.
3. **Identify** Chiang Kai-shek, Benito Mussolini, Haile Selassie, Francisco Franco, Adolf Hitler, Joseph Stalin, Neville Chamberlain.

Critical Thinking

4. **Evaluating Information** Why did Stalin make a pact with Hitler rather than the United States or Great Britain?

Understanding Themes

5. **Movement** How was the response of the League of Nations to Japanese expansion in 1933 similar to the response of the Western democracies to German expansion in 1938? How was it different? Explain your response.

SECTION 1 ASSESSMENT ANSWERS

1. Japan, Italy, and Germany were left unsatisfied with the World War I peace settlements; as a result they wanted to expand their territories and regain lost power.
2. All terms are defined in the Glossary.
3. Chiang Kai-shek, 827; Benito Mussolini, 827; Haile Selassie, 827; Francisco Franco, 827; Adolf Hitler, 827; Joseph Stalin, 828; Neville Chamberlain, 829
4. because he feared German invasion and expected not to receive any Western support against Hitler, he saw the pact as a way to improve Soviet security
5. **MOVEMENT** The response of both the League of Nations and the Western democracies was so weak and ineffective that it encouraged more aggression.

1939 The Soviet Union fights Finland.

1940 France surrenders to Germany; the Battle of Britain begins.

1941 Franklin D. Roosevelt and Winston Churchill issue the Atlantic Charter.

1939 ⬤ 1940 ⬤ 1941 ⬤

1939 The Soviet Union fights Finland.

1940 France surrenders to Germany; the Battle of Britain begins.

1941 Franklin D. Roosevelt and Winston Churchill issue the Atlantic Charter.

Section 2

War in Europe

Guide to Reading

Read to Find Out
Main Idea *Hitler took over most of Europe, sparking responses from Great Britain and the United States.*

▶ **Terms to Define**
blitzkrieg, blitz, cash-and-carry policy, lend-lease

▶ **People to Meet**
Winston Churchill, Charles de Gaulle, Franklin D. Roosevelt

▶ **Places to Locate**
Finland, Norway, London, Libya

The Storyteller

Saturday night, August 24th, 1940, the first German bombs fell on London. That September, bombing became more frequent and deadly as waves of planes came over the city. For hours bombers would attack; then, to fight the fires, thousands of firefighters went into action. Many Londoners lost their homes. An observer reported that boats normally used by tourists on vacation became evacuation boats "chugging along the riverside … defying high explosive and incendiary bombs, walls of flame, and clouds of choking

fumes.… With a few bundles of clothes the refugees climbed aboard and were taken by river to the safety zone or ferried across to the opposite bank."

—adapted from *The Lost Treasures of London,* William Kent, 1947

German bombers

On September 1, 1939, the German Luftwaffe roared toward its targets in Poland, spreading panic and confusion with its bombs. At the same time, armored tank divisions known as panzers swept across the Polish border. Next came the infantry, a million and a half strong, in motorized vehicles. This was blitzkrieg, or "lightning war," a new German strategy aimed at taking the enemy by surprise.

The blitzkrieg worked with speed and efficiency, devastating Poland in a few weeks. Great Britain and France could not move fast enough to send troops to Poland. The Soviet Union, meanwhile, quickly moved its forces to occupy the eastern half of that nation.

Stalin also forced the Baltic republics of Latvia, Lithuania, and Estonia to accept Soviet military bases. When he tried to do the same with **Finland**, war broke out. The Finns held out heroically until March before the Soviets forced them to surrender. As a result of their victory, the Soviets moved their frontier 70 miles (112 km) to the west, making the city of Leningrad less vulnerable to German attack.

Hitler Looks to the West

All through the winter and spring of 1939–1940, the western front was quiet. The Germans called this period the "sit-down war," or *Sitzkrieg*, while the West dubbed it the "phony war." Many hoped that an all-out war could still be avoided.

When Finland capitulated to the Soviets, however, the British took steps to ensure that the same fate would not befall **Norway**. In early April 1940, they mined Norwegian waters to block any ships trading with Germany. Hitler used the mining to support his claim that the Allies were about to invade Scandinavia. He delivered an ultimatum to Norway and Denmark, demanding that they accept the "protection of the Reich." The Danes accepted his demands; the Norwegians did not.

Chapter 31 *World War II* **831**

TEACH

Guided Practice

THEME Cooperation

Have students find examples in Section 2 of countries cooperating, or working together for their common good. (*Britain mined Norwegian waters to keep German ships out, helped the French, and sent troops to Belgium; the United States supplied food and weapons to Britain; Hitler sent Rommel to help the Italians in Libya.*) **L1**

Map Study

Answer

Ireland, Portugal, Spain, Switzerland, Turkey, Sweden

Map Skills Practice

Reading a Map What countries did Germany invade in 1941? (*Yugoslavia, Lithuania, Latvia, Estonia, the Soviet Union, Bulgaria, Greece, Finland*)

Military History Have students compare the fall of France with the Battle of Britain. **L2**

Politics Have students examine the reasons for the downfall of Neville Chamberlain and discuss why Great Britain's attitude toward Germany changed when Winston Churchill became prime minister. **L3**

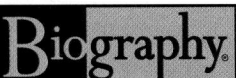

The following videotape program is available from Glencoe:

- **The Complete Churchill**
  (Four Video Set)

Axis Expansion Into Europe 1935–1941

- Allied nations
- Neutral nations
- Axis nations
- Occupied by Germany
- Occupied by Italy
- Vichy France and colonies
- → Axis offensive
- Siegfried Line
- Maginot Line

Map Study By the end of 1941, Germany had seized control of much of Europe.
Location Which European nations chose to remain neutral during the war?

The Invasion of Scandinavia

In the early morning hours of April 9, three small German transports steamed into the harbor of Copenhagen, the Danish capital. After meeting little resistance, the Germans took control of Denmark. That same morning, German forces also landed along the coast of Norway. British forces had been busy laying mines in Norwegian waters in an effort to cut off German shipment of iron ore from neighboring Sweden. Within hours, however, the Germans had seized Norway's major cities, including the capital of Oslo.

Although Germany now controlled Norway, the Norwegian invasion proved costly. Germany

lost a large number of destroyers and cruisers. On the other hand, Hitler won the outlet to the Atlantic that he needed to ensure that the German navy would not be bottled up in the Baltic Sea like it had in World War I.

News of the fall of Norway and Denmark caused an uproar in the British House of Commons. The Labour and Liberal opposition strongly attacked Prime Minister Neville Chamberlain and his policies. Knowing that he had lost the confidence of his own Conservative party as well, Chamberlain stepped down. On May 10, 1940, King George VI summoned **Winston Churchill** to Buckingham Palace and asked him to form a new

832 Chapter 31 *World War II*

COOPERATIVE LEARNING ACTIVITY

Video Presentation Organize the class into three groups to create a 15-minute video documentary about Germany's early military offensives in World War II. Assign each group one of the following topics: the conquest of Poland, fall of France (include the Low Countries and Dunkirk), or the Battle of Britain. Suggest that students use pictures of events and people, sound effects, "interviews," speeches, and songs in their films. Each group should choose a narrator for its segment, and one student to act as a coordinator with the other groups. When the documentaries are completed, have students present them to other classes. **L3**

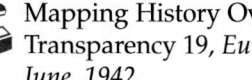
overnment. Churchill, one of the few politicians to arn of the Nazi danger in the 1930s, was now rime minister.

he Fall of France

On that same momentous date, the war began a earnest on the western front. Along the Maginot ine, the British and French watched and waited. he Maginot Line was impressive, but it had one najor flaw. It had a 50-mile (80-km) gap in the ardennes. Although the Germans had invaded hrough Belgium and the Ardennes during World War I, the French still believed that the forests, wamps, and hills of that region were a sufficient arrier. A French tank commander, **Charles de Gaulle**, pleaded for more tanks and planes, but the rench command insisted that the Maginot Line vas impenetrable.

Hitler, meanwhile, carried out a massive attack in the Low Countries—Luxembourg, the Netherlands, and Belgium. Before dawn on May 10, 940, German troops parachuted into the Netherlands. It was the first large-scale airborne attack in the history of warfare and caught the Dutch by surprise. Five days after the start of the invasion, the Dutch capitulated.

On the same day that Germany invaded the Netherlands, Britain and France moved their best roops into Belgium. German panzers swept into he Ardennes and began to encircle them. Other panzer divisions drove through Luxembourg and raced toward France.

Dunkirk

Although the Belgian forces fought valiantly, hey did not hold out as long as had been expected. The Germans were now rolling through undefended open country. They pushed westward toward the English Channel, trapping the Belgian, British, and French forces in the northwest corner of France. The only hope for the Allies was an evacuation by sea from the French port of Dunkirk. With German forces within sight of the coast, the rescue of 300,000 Allied soldiers seemed impossible. But for reasons never entirely understood, Hitler ordered his forces to halt.

The British Admiralty began a desperate rescue operation at Dunkirk on May 26. A ragtag armada of 850 vessels, ranging from destroyers and cruisers to trawlers, tugs, yachts, and fishing boats, left England and set sail for Dunkirk. Civilians operated many of the smaller boats. Over the next nine days, under fierce air and ground attack, this hastily assembled fleet rescued the Allied armies.

The evacuation of Dunkirk was a stunning

military achievement, but as Churchill said, "wars are not won by evacuations." Faced with an unprepared French army and a confused French government, the Germans continued their sweep into France and on June 14 entered Paris. A week later France signed an armistice with Germany.

Vichy and the Free French

By the terms of the armistice, the Germans occupied all of northern France and the Atlantic coastline to the Spanish border. In southern France, the Nazis set up a puppet government in the city of Vichy under French Marshal Henri Pétain. Pétain and other officials in the so-called Vichy government collaborated with the Germans. Many French citizens, on the other hand, continued to fight for freedom. In Britain, de Gaulle organized a Free French government, while in France many joined the French Resistance, an underground movement that opposed the German occupation.

Battle of Britain

All that stood between Hitler and German domination of western Europe was Winston Churchill and the determined British people. Hitler expected that Britain would seek peace with Germany, but he misjudged the resolve of the British. Alone and only partially prepared, Britain faced the mightiest military machine the world had ever seen.

Chemist Invents Nylon

Wilmington, Delaware, 1938
Wallace H. Carothers, a chemist at the DuPont Company in Wilmington, Delaware, created fiber from coal or petroleum in a solution form in the early 1930s. These early products melted at a temperature that was too low to make them useful for textiles. Carothers came up with a product called nylon 66–the first completely synthetic textile fiber. One of its most common uses was in women's stockings. During World War II, nylon was widely used for making parachutes.

Wilmington

DELAWARE

Chapter 31 *World War II* **833**

📂 Mapping History Overlay Transparency 19, *Europe in June, 1942*

Who?What?Where?When?

Radar The invention of radar, an early-warning system against incoming aircraft, by physicist Robert Watson-Watts in 1935 helped the British defeat the German Luftwaffe in the Battle of Britain.

Independent Practice

📁 Guided Reading Activity 31-2 **L1**

📁 People in World History Profile 60

Art Have students research and write a brief report on the work of a World War II correspondent or photojournalist such as Edward R. Murrow, Alan Moorehead, Robert Capa, Margaret Bourke-White, Max Alpert, or Henri Cartier-Bresson. **L2**

Literature Have students research Winston Churchill's World War II speeches and write a brief report that explains how Churchill's oratory rallied the British people. Ask students to use quotations from Churchill in their reports. **L3**

Cultural Perspectives

Finland In the war between Finland and the Soviet Union (November 1939–March 1940), Finnish ski patrols in white camouflage maneuvered over Finland's snow-covered fields. They cut off Soviet supplies, isolated Soviet patrols, and stranded entire brigades. Eventually, 1,000,000 Soviet troops were massed against Finland's army of 200,000.

MEETING SPECIAL NEEDS ACTIVITY

Study Strategy To help students better understand terms used in Section 2, have them make a minidictionary for the following words: *blitzkrieg, sitzkrieg, capitulate, ultimatum, panzer, armada, Luftwaffe, neutrality, cash-and-carry policy,* and *lend-lease.* Tell them first to alphabetize the words, then find them in Section 2 and either determine their meaning from context or look them up in the dictionary or the Glossary of their textbook. Then have students write a good definition for each word and use each in a sentence. **L1**

VIDEODISC
Lessons of War

Side One, Chapter 12
Frames 46153–50167
Title: *Laws of War*
Subject: The rules that place limits on the types of weapons that can be used in war and against whom they can be used
Ask: What rule is supposed to protect civilians? *(Civilians should not be "injured or killed on purpose"; there should be no attacks on residential areas.)*

you don't say...

Quisling, a word that means "traitor," comes from the name of Vidkun Quisling, a Norwegian Nazi who helped the Germans take over Norway in 1940. During the war Quisling headed Norway's government under direction from Germany.

THE HISTORY CHANNEL.

The following videotape program is available from Glencoe:

- **Churchill & the Cabinet War Rooms**

To find classroom resources to accompany this video, check the following home page:

The History Channel: http://www.historychannel.com

On May 13, 1940, Churchill delivered his first speech before the House of Commons. He told the Commons that he had "nothing to offer but blood, toil, tears, and sweat" and ended with these words:

> **You ask, what is our policy? I will say: it is to wage war, by sea, land, and air, with all our might and with all the strength that God can give us: to wage war against a monstrous tyranny, never surpassed in the dark, lamentable catalogue of human crime. That is our policy. You ask, what is our aim? I can answer in one word: Victory—victory at all costs, victory in spite of all terror, victory, however hard and long the road may be; for without victory, there is no survival.**

Immediately after France fell, Hitler began making plans to invade Great Britain. Hitler and the German High Command soon realized that this invasion depended on winning air supremacy over the English Channel and destroying British airfields and vital industries. The Luftwaffe began to bomb Britain's southern coast in August 1940. The bombings damaged four aircraft factories and five Royal Air Force (RAF) airfields, but British fighter planes known as Hurricanes and Spitfires shot down 75 German planes. Hermann Goering, head of the German air force, then focused his attacks on the RAF. From August 24 to September 6, Goering sent over 1,000 planes a day. The RAF lost 466 fighters and 103 pilots, but the Germans lost even more.

Seeking to do better, the Luftwaffe switched to night bombings of **London.** From September 7 to November 3, German bombers pounded London in its great blitz, or series of air raids. In one night alone, the Luftwaffe dropped 70,000 fire bombs. The devastation was enormous, killing and injuring thousands of civilians, damaging light, power, and gas lines and destroying buildings, roads, and railways. But the bombings did not break British morale.

The Luftwaffe never did gain air supremacy over Britain. While incurring heavy losses the RAF

Images of the Times

The Blitz

During World War II, German bombers rained destruction on London and strategic targets in an attempt to knock out Great Britain's defenses and force the British to surrender.

Many London school children were evacuated to safer parts of Great Britain and even overseas to escape the bombing.

Public shelters were set up throughout London in subway tunnels and other protected areas. At the height of the blitz, 1 out of 7 Londoners slept in a shelter.

834

Images of the Times

The Blitz

During the war, about two million children were evacuated to the countryside from London and other British cities. There, many of these city children played on grass and climbed trees for the first time. The government paid the children's hosts for their care. Some children lived in cottages, while others stayed at large country estates. Parents and children were reunited periodically when the government offered reduced train fares to the country. Knowing that their children were safe helped parents carry on with the war effort.

downed more than 1,700 German aircraft during the Battle of Britain, blocking Hitler's invasion. Churchill spoke for all Britons when he said of the RAF pilots: "Never in the field of human conflict was so much owed by so many to so few."

Anglo–American Cooperation

Throughout the early phase of the war, the United States was determined to remain neutral. Even before the fighting began, Congress had enacted laws designed to prevent American involvement. The Neutrality Acts, passed in 1937, prohibited arms shipments, loans, and credit to belligerent nations. Congress later banned the export of armaments to either side in the Spanish Civil War.

President **Franklin D. Roosevelt**, however, became convinced that Germany's expansion endangered American security and that Britain and France could not stop Hitler without American aid.

Throughout his presidential campaign in 1940, Roosevelt tried to rally national opinion. As they listened to news of German aggression, Americans became more sympathetic to Britain's plight.

After Dunkirk, Churchill appealed to the United States for help. Roosevelt gave the British 50 old American naval destroyers in return for the right to maintain American bases in Newfoundland, Bermuda, and the British West Indies. He also convinced Congress that a cash-and-carry policy—in which Great Britain traded cash for greatly needed supplies—would allow the

WORLD HISTORY Online

Student Web Activity 31

Visit the *World History: The Human Experience* Web site at **worldhistory.glencoe.com** and click on *Chapter 31—Student Web Activities* for an activity relating to the Battle of Britain.

The Royal Air Force (RAF) won the Battle of Britain, the first battle ever fought to control the air. RAF pilots intercepted German planes with the help of ground radar stations that warned of the German planes' approach.

The bombing of London, which lasted nightly beginning in September 1940, caused much ruin, but failed to break the determined spirit of the British people.

REFLECTING ON THE TIMES

1. What did the Germans achieve by bombing London during World War II?
2. How did the British people respond to the German attacks?

835

ANSWERS TO REFLECTING ON THE TIMES

1. They destroyed some of Britain's aircraft factories and airfields and damaged light, power, and gas lines as well as buildings, roads, and railways.
2. The German air attacks pulled the British people together and made them more determined to defeat the Nazis.

Visualizing History Rommel had trained his troops for desert warfare on a sandy peninsula on the Baltic Sea. To prepare them for desert conditions, Rommel housed them in overheated barracks and held them to strict rations of food and water. **Answer to Caption:** *to stop German troops that were sweeping through Yugoslavia and Greece*

Evaluate

Section Quiz 31-2

Use the Testmaker to create a customized quiz for Section 2.

Reteach

Have students write paragraphs that summarize the information under each main heading in Section 2.

Reading Essentials and Study Guide 31-2

Enrich

Have students write short essays about the resistance movement against the Nazis in occupied France.

CLOSE

Call on volunteers to trace the major events in World War II from September 1939 to April 1941 in chronological order on a map of Europe and North Africa. Ask other students to tell the significance of each event.

United States to supply the British, without risking the loss of American neutrality. Throughout 1940 the British imported American food and armaments. They paid cash and transported the goods on their own.

But the cost of the war drained the British treasury. Britain ordered 12,000 airplanes from the United States in 1940 but could not pay for them. On Roosevelt's urging, Congress approved a policy of lend-lease. It authorized the President to lend war equipment to any country whose defense he deemed vital to national security.

On August 9, 1941, Churchill met with Roosevelt on a British battleship off the Newfoundland coast to discuss war aims. The leaders issued a joint declaration called the Atlantic Charter. It upheld freedom of trade and the right of people to choose their own government. But it also called for the "final destruction of Nazi tyranny."

Eastern Europe and Africa

While Hitler was conquering much of western Europe, Mussolini was dreaming of building a Mediterranean empire for Italy. On June 10, 1940, Mussolini declared war on France and Britain. Italy's armies in **Libya** were poised for an attack on the British forces guarding Egypt and the Sudan. Although vastly outnumbered, the British attacked the Italians on December 9. In the following weeks they scored victory after victory along Libya's north coast.

Churchill, however, halted this advance and diverted some of the troops to stop a German advance in southeast Europe that had already claimed Romania, Bulgaria, and Hungary. It was a fatal decision. German forces, sweeping through Yugoslavia and Greece in April 1941, forced the British into a second Dunkirk. Although most British troops escaped by sea, they left behind their tanks and 12,000 men. Meanwhile, Hitler sent Erwin Rommel, a brilliant general who had led the 7th Panzer Division in France, to command a tank force in Libya and to rescue the Italians. By April 11, Rommel had pushed the British out of northern Libya, except for a small force at Tobruk.

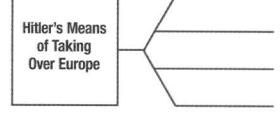

SECTION 2 ASSESSMENT

Main Idea
1. Use a diagram like the one below to list the means by which Hitler took over most of Europe.

> Hitler's Means of Taking Over Europe

Recall
2. **Define** blitzkrieg, blitz, cash-and-carry policy, lend-lease.
3. **Identify** Winston Churchill, Charles de Gaulle, Franklin D. Roosevelt.

Critical Thinking
4. **Analyzing Information** What mistakes did French military

leaders make that led to the fall of France?

Understanding Themes
5. **Cooperation** How did the United States government in the early 1940s move from a policy of isolationism to a policy of openly assisting the British in the war effort against the Nazis?

SECTION 2 ASSESSMENT ANSWERS

1. blitzkrieg in Poland; invaded Denmark and Norway; attacked Low Countries (Luxembourg, Netherlands, Belgium); occupied all of northern France and the Atlantic coastline, set up puppet government in Vichy

2. All terms are defined in the Glossary.
3. Winston Churchill, 832; Charles de Gaulle, 833; Franklin D. Roosevelt, 835
4. French military leaders assumed that the Maginot Line would stop an invasion even though Germany had invaded

through Belgium in World War I.

5. **COOPERATION** Because Roosevelt believed that German aggression threatened American security, he convinced Congress to adopt the cash-and-carry and lend-lease policies.

Synthesizing Information

A school wants to cut funding for one of its programs. If you talk to parents, read newspaper articles, and watch TV reports, you can put together, or synthesize, the information to better understand the issue.

Learning the Skill

When synthesizing information, we combine information from separate sources. To write a research report, you study several sources—encyclopedias, books, and articles. Eventually, you synthesize this information into a report.

Before synthesizing information, analyze each source separately. Determine the value and reliability of each source. Then, look for connections and relationships among the different sources.

Practicing the Skill

Study the passage and the map on this page. Then answer the following questions.
1. What is the main idea of the passage?
2. What does the map tell about this topic?
3. By synthesizing the two sources, what conclusion can you draw about the extent of the Nazis' "final solution."

66 I have received a report which is of the greatest importance.... It is stated in this report that very large numbers of … Jews first deported to Poland or directly sent to [Auschwitz-] Birkenau in the well-known cattle-trucks from Germany, France, Belgium, Holland, Greece, etc. have been killed in these establishments. The bodies have been burnt in specially constructed stoves and the ashes have been used as fertilizers. All those who died by starvation or ill-treatment in the various labour-camps nearby were also burned in these stoves. 99

—Letter from Richard Lichtheim of the Jewish Agency, June 19, 1944

Applying the Skill

Find two sources of information on the same topic and write a short report. In your report, answer these questions: What kinds of sources did you use—primary or secondary? What are the main ideas in these sources? How does each source add to your understanding of the topic? Do the sources support or contradict each other?

For More Practice

Turn to the Skill Practice in the Chapter Assessment on page 853 for more practice in synthesizing information.

 The **Glencoe Skillbuilder Interactive Workbook**, Level 2 provides instruction and practice in key social studies skills.

Nazi Concentration and Death Camps

TEACH

Synthesizing Information Ask students to write detailed directions from your classroom to the principal's office, to the cafeteria, or to the gym. Have students exchange directions with a classmate. Then pass out copies of a school map. Have students compare the written directions with the map. How do the two sources differ? *(For example: The written directions are more personal; the map gives options of other routes.)* Does the information from each source lead to the same locations? *(yes)* Tell students that when they prepare material for reports, they must first synthesize, or combine, information from several sources. Then have students read the skill and complete the practice questions.

Additional Practice

▱ Skill Reinforcement Activity 31

GLENCOE
TECHNOLOGY

GO TO ▸ Glencoe's **Skillbuilder Interactive Workbook, Level 2**
This interactive CD-ROM promotes student mastery of key social studies skills.

ANSWERS TO PRACTICING THE SKILL

1. It describes the systematic extermination of Jews in Nazi concentration camps.
2. The map shows the location of Auschwitz-Birkenau and other concentration camps and killing centers.
3. This was happening not only at Auschwitz but also at camps throughout occupied Europe.

SECTION THEME

▶ **Conflict** Two separate and opposing alliances, the Allies and the Axis, wage a worldwide war.

Guide to Reading

For reading strategies to help students read effectively see pages 12–13.

Vocabulary Pre-check

 Use the Vocabulary PuzzleMaker for Chapter 31 to create a crossword puzzle to reinforce section terms. **L1 LEP**

 Use Vocabulary Activity 31 to introduce vocabulary terms. **L1 LEP**

FOCUS

Section Objective

Describe how the Soviet Union and the United States entered World War II.

**BELLRINGER
Motivational Activity**

Before taking roll at the beginning of the class period, project Section Focus Transparency 31-3 and have students answer the activity questions. Discuss students' responses.

This activity is also available as a blackline master.

MAY 1941	AUG. 1941	NOV. 1941	FEB. 1942
JUNE 1941 German forces invade the Soviet Union.	**JULY 1941** The Nazis order the mass killing of Europe's Jews.	**NOV. 1941** German forces reach the outskirts of Moscow.	**DEC. 1941** Japan stages surprise attack on Pearl Harbor; the United States enters World War II.

Section 3

A Global Conflict

Guide to Reading

Read to Find Out
Main Idea *Particular events led the Soviet Union and the United States to enter World War II.*

▶ **Terms to Define**
scorched-earth policy, Holocaust, genocide

▶ **People to Meet**
Isoroku Yamamoto

▶ **Places to Locate**
Moscow, Kiev, Leningrad, Dachau, Warsaw, Auschwitz, Pearl Harbor

toryteller

In 1942 a young Jewish woman wrote: "Of course, it is our complete destruction they want! But let us bear it with grace.... And a camp needs a poet, one who experiences life there, even there

Surviving in a concentration camp

... and is able to sing about it.... At night, as I lay in the camp on my plank bed ... I was sometimes filled with an infinite tenderness, and lay awake for hours letting all the many, too many impressions of a much too long day wash over me, and I prayed, 'Let me be the thinking heart of these barracks.' And that is what I want to be again. The thinking heart of a whole concentration camp."

—from *An Interrupted Life, the Diaries of Etty Hillesum, 1941–1943*, translated by Arno Pomerans, 1983

In the spring of 1941, Great Britain stood alone against Nazi Germany, which now controlled almost all of western Europe. In Africa, the Nazi General Erwin Rommel had succeeded in pushing the British back and had taken control of most of Libya. In Asia, meanwhile, the Japanese held Manchuria and controlled much of China. By the end of 1941, the expansive war would grow even larger. Events since June drew two more major powers into the conflict: the Soviet Union and the United States.

Invasion of the Soviet Union

Having failed in his attempt to defeat Great Britain, Hitler now turned his attention to the Soviet Union. Only by conquering the vast Soviet steppe, Hitler reasoned, could the "living space" believed vital to Germany's future be gained. He also wanted the wheat of Ukraine and the oil reserves of the Caucasus region.

On June 22, 1941, Hitler launched Operation Barbarossa, a massive attack on the Soviet Union. Despite British warnings and the massing of German troops along the border, the invasion took Stalin by surprise. In the first few days of fighting, the Germans destroyed the greater part of the Soviet air force, disabled thousands of Soviet tanks, and captured half a million Soviet soldiers. As German divisions advanced deeper into Soviet territory, Stalin appealed to his people to resist the invasion and issued his famous scorched-earth policy. If the Germans forced Soviet forces to retreat, Stalin ordered, Soviet citizens should destroy everything that could be of use to the invaders.

By November 1941 German armies had pushed 600 miles (960 km) inside the Soviet Union to the outskirts of **Moscow**. In addition to controlling 40 percent of the Soviet population, the Germans had captured **Kiev** and begun the siege of **Leningrad**. Yet the Soviets refused to surrender. Young Soviet

---

SECTION RESOURCES

Reproducible Masters
- Lecture Notes 31-3
- Reproducible Lesson Plan 31-3
- Vocabulary Activity 31
- Guided Reading Activity 31-3
- History Simulation 31
- Section Quiz 31-3
- Reading Essentials and Study Guide 31-3

Transparencies
- Section Focus Transparency 31-3

Multimedia
- Interactive Tutor Self-Assessment Software
- Testmaker
- Lessons of War: *At the Front*
- Turning Points in World History

soldiers rallied to the cry, "Behind us is Moscow—there is no room left for retreat!" The Germans faced not only a steely Soviet resistance but another equally formidable foe—the Russian winter. A German soldier described the conditions:

> " We had no gloves. We had no winter shoes. We had no equipment whatsoever to fight or withstand the cold…. We lost a considerable part of our equipment…. Due to the cold we lost a lot of people who got frost-bitten, and we had not even the necessary amount of ointments, or the most simple and primitive things to fight in…. Guns didn't fire anymore. Even our wireless equipment didn't work properly anymore because the batteries were frozen hard…. "

On December 2, 1941, German troops began an assault on Moscow, and in just one day they drew within sight of the city's center. It was as far as they ever got. When all seemed lost, the Soviets staged a counterattack and forced a German retreat.

The Nazi Order

Hitler wanted to conquer the Soviet Union as part of his plan to create a "New Order" in Europe. In the new world that Hitler envisioned, the Nazis would rule Europe and exploit its resources. In addition to enslaving the conquered peoples and forcing them to work for the German "master race," the Nazis would exterminate "undesirable elements" such as the Jews and the Slavs.

The Nazis began to implement Hitler's plan by plundering the occupied countries. They seized art treasures, raw materials, and factory equipment. At the same time, the Nazis drove millions into forced labor and concentration camps and massacred millions more. Between 1939 and 1944, about 7.5 million people were deported to Germany and put to work in factories, fields, and mines. Many people in the occupied countries, however, joined underground resistance movements to combat the Nazis.

The Holocaust

Beginning in 1941, Nazi leaders carried out a plan that aimed at the complete extermination of all Jews in Europe. During the next four years, the

Visualizing History The powerful German panzers were no match for the harsh Soviet winter of 1941. The intense cold froze lubricating oil and cracked engine blocks. *What other problems did the German invaders encounter during that winter?*

Nazis murdered more than 6 million Jews. This mass destruction of the Jewish people based on racial grounds has become known as the Holocaust. Another 6 million people, including the Slavs and Gypsies, also were killed by the Nazis.

Beginnings

In mid-1940, the Nazis began to persecute Jews in the lands they had conquered. They expelled Jews from jobs and schools and forced them to wear yellow badges showing the Star of David, an ancient Jewish symbol. Some Jews managed to flee Nazi-occupied Europe; others went into hiding; but many more failed to escape and were sent to concentration camps, such as **Dachau** (DAH•KOW) in southern Germany.

The largest number of Jews in Nazi-occupied Europe lived in areas of Poland and the Soviet Union. To control this sizable Jewish population, the Nazis at first forced the Jews into specially designated areas of towns and cities called ghettos. The largest ghetto was in **Warsaw**, where almost half a million Jews were kept.

Life in the ghettos was unbearable. Families had to crowd into unsanitary housing, and contagious diseases spread rapidly. The Nazis deliberately tried to starve residents by allowing only small amounts of food. As a result, tens of thousands died in the ghettos from hunger, disease, and the cold. Despite their suffering, many people courageously tried to live as normally as possible. For example, many young people carried out their education by attending secret classes organized and taught by adults.

Chapter 31 *World War II* **839**

TEACH

Guided Practice

THEME Conflict

Remind students that World War II began as a European conflict but expanded to become a global conflict by the end of 1941. Have students point out on a map of the world the areas involved in the war by December 8, 1941. **L1 LEP**

Visualizing History Have students review Napoleon's invasion of Russia in the winter of 1812. Remind students that geography often plays a vital role in war. In what ways did Napoleon and Hitler make the same mistakes? *(They underestimated the effects of the Russian winter and the resistance of the Russian people.)* **Answer to Caption:** *They were without winter clothing and medical supplies.*

The Holocaust
Why was the Holocaust a major development in twentieth-century world affairs? *Hitler's murder of 6 million European Jews is an example of genocide. It reflected the extent to which totalitarian governments violated human rights in pursuing their ideological goals.*

 VIDEODISC
Turning Points in World History

 Side Two
Chapter 6

Title: *The Holocaust*

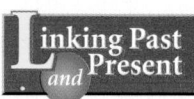
The Killing Squads

The German invasion of the Soviet Union in June 1941, proved to be a turning point in the Nazi mistreatment of the Jews. At that time, the Nazis turned from the forced emigration and imprisonment of Jews to the mass murder of them. Special units of Nazi soldiers known as the SS moving with the German army acted quickly to kill any Jews they could find in occupied Soviet territory. Captured Jews had to surrender their valuables and were forcibly marched to open areas on the outskirts of captured towns and cities. There they were shot, and their bodies dumped into mass graves. The killing squads murdered more than a million Jews and hundreds of thousands of other innocent people. At Babi Yar, near Kiev in Ukraine, about 35,000 Jews were murdered in two days of shooting.

The Final Solution

In January 1942, Nazi party and German government leaders secretly agreed to what they called "the final solution to the Jewish question in Europe." The "final solution" was the Nazi code word for the destruction of all European Jews. Never before had a modern state set out on a campaign of genocide, the deliberate, carefully planned killing of an entire people on the basis of race, politics, or culture.

Beginning in the summer of 1942, the Nazis arrested and rounded up Jews throughout occupied Europe by the hundreds of thousands. The Jews then were transported by train or trucks to death camps, such as **Auschwitz** (AUSH•VIHTS) in Poland, where most eventually died. Many of the people in the camps were murdered in poison gas chambers. Others died of starvation or were the victims of cruel experiments carried out by Nazi doctors.

Response and Resistance

The Nazis tried to keep the killings and death camps secret from the world. Even European Jews at first had been unaware of the fate in store for them. But once they became aware of Nazi intentions, Jews fought back in Warsaw and other European ghettos. However, Jewish resistance groups in the ghettos were outnumbered and lacked the arms to fight the Germans. In spite of their heroic efforts, Jewish resistors were easily defeated.

Some Jews who succeeded in escaping from the ghettos formed fighting units in densely forested areas of eastern Europe. Others joined regular

---

Let Us Never Forget

From 1941 to 1945, Jewish artists, musicians, and writers in the Theresienstadt concentration camp created moving artistic expressions of their Holocaust experiences. Since World War II, their works—and those of others—have stirred hearts and consciences of people everywhere about one of the most horrifying events of our century.

In his memoir called *Night* (1958), the Romanian-born writer Elie Wiesel (vee•ZEHL), a Holocaust survivor, described the horrors he witnessed in the Auschwitz and Buchenwald camps. Another writer, the Australian Thomas Keneally, in his 1982 novel

Concentration camp survivors

Schindler's List, tells a powerful true story about Oskar Schindler, a German manufacturer who saved his Jewish workers from the Holocaust. The American filmmaker Steven Spielberg later turned Keneally's novel into an Oscar Award-winning movie in 1993.

Another 1993 event relating to the Holocaust was the opening of the United States Holocaust Memorial Museum in Washington, D.C. Through exhibits, videos, and special lectures, the museum commemorates the millions of Jews and others murdered by the Nazis during World War II.

inking Past and Present   ACTIVITY

Explain how people in the Theresienstadt concentration camp tried to cope with their ordeal. How has the Holocaust been artistically commemorated since World War II?

CRITICAL THINKING ACTIVITY

Identifying Alternatives Remind students that Churchill and Roosevelt feared that Stalin would impose Communist governments on the countries liberated by the Soviets from German control. Have students research the events in East Germany, Poland, Hungary, Czechoslovakia, Romania, Bulgaria, and Yugoslavia from 1945 to 1950. Encourage them to discuss other ways the fate of Eastern Europe might have been handled at the Yalta Conference. **L3**

Visualizing History When the Nazis advanced throughout Europe in 1939 and 1940, they rounded up Jews—such as these residents of Warsaw, Poland—and forced them to work as slave laborers. Later, the Nazis killed or imprisoned millions of Jews. *How did the Allies react to the Nazi persecution and killing of Europe's Jews?*

Visualizing History In October 1940 the Nazis forced all 400,000 of Warsaw's Jews to move into a walled, 1-square-mile (2.6-square-kilometer) area known as the Warsaw Ghetto. Warsaw's Jews resisted the Nazis, but more than 300,000 died in the ghetto or were deported to Nazi labor or death camps. On April 18, 1943, Nazi forces blew up the ghetto's synagogue, killing 14,000 people. The remaining 42,000 Jews were sent to labor camps.

Answer to Caption: *Rumors of Nazi atrocities had reached the Allies, but little action was taken on behalf of the Jews. Many governments did not believe the rumors and devoted their main attention to winning the war.*

Allied forces fighting the Nazis. One Jewish resistance fighter was Hannah Senesh, a Hungarian Jew who had emigrated to Palestine in 1939. Allied forces dropped her and other parachutists into German-controlled Hungary to organize resistance efforts. Before she could accomplish her mission, she was captured and executed.

A major factor hindering Jewish resistance both in the ghettos and the forests was the widespread lack of support for the Jews. Anti-Semitic Europeans in occupied areas helped the Nazis hunt down Jews, and pro-Nazi governments, such as those of France, Italy, and Hungary, sent tens of thousands of Jews to the death camps. Even banks in neutral Switzerland accepted and profited from the money and valuables stolen from Jews by the Nazis. Even as late as the 1990s, much of this wealth had yet to be returned to the families of the rightful owners.

Most people in occupied areas, however, did nothing, thinking that the plight of the Jews did not concern them or fearing punishment if they got involved. Despite dangers, a small number of courageous people did provide help to the Jews and other persecuted people. Denmark, alone among the occupied countries, actively resisted the Nazi regime's efforts to remove its Jewish citizens.

During the Holocaust, evidence reached the outside world about the Nazi mistreatment of Jews and other groups. However, little action was taken.

Allied governments believed that fighting the war and defeating the Nazis was the only way they could help those suffering from Nazi injustices. The full horror of the Holocaust was not realized until Allied forces had liberated the concentration camps and death camps in 1945.

Japanese Expansion

After seizing much of China in the 1930s, Japan shifted its attention to the European colonies in East and Southeast Asia and their stores of raw materials. Taking advantage of Hitler's offensive in Europe, the Japanese acquired many of these territories. The collapse of France and the Low Countries left French Indochina and the Dutch East Indies virtually defenseless. And when the Germans threatened to invade Great Britain, the British withdrew their fleet from Singapore, leaving that colony open to attack as well.

In July 1940 the Japanese government announced its plan to create a "new order in greater East Asia." Proclaiming "Asia for the Asiatics," Japan moved to establish the "Greater East Asia Co-prosperity Sphere," an appeal to Asians who wanted to rid their lands of European rule. First, it asked France for the right to build airfields and station troops in northern Indochina. After gaining this foothold, Japan invaded southern Indochina.

Chapter 31 *World War II* **841**

History Simulation 31

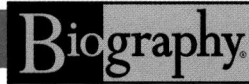

The following videotape program is available from Glencoe:
- **FDR: The War Years**

Independent Practice
Guided Reading Activity 31-3 **L1**

TEACHER NOTES

_____

_____

_____

_____

_____

TEACH

Tell students that on February 19, 1942, President Roosevelt signed Executive Order 9066, which authorized the War Department to move 112,000 Japanese American men, women, and children from the West Coast to crude internment camps farther inland. These Americans lost their constitutional rights, property, businesses, and homes. Despite this policy, Japanese Americans remained loyal to the United States. None were ever brought to trial for espionage or sabotage. Why do you think Roosevelt signed this order?

Linking Past and Present

Reparations Not until 1988 did the U.S. government acknowledge the wrong done to Japanese Americans during World War II. That year, President Ronald Reagan signed a bill that gave surviving internees a formal apology and reparations for their suffering during internment.

VIDEODISC
Lessons of War

Side Two, Chapter 8
Frames 25814–28652
Title: At the Front
Subject: Contributions of minorities in World War II
Ask: How did the Japanese American 442nd Regimental Combat Team of World War II prove themselves during the war? (This regiment was even more successful than the other units.)

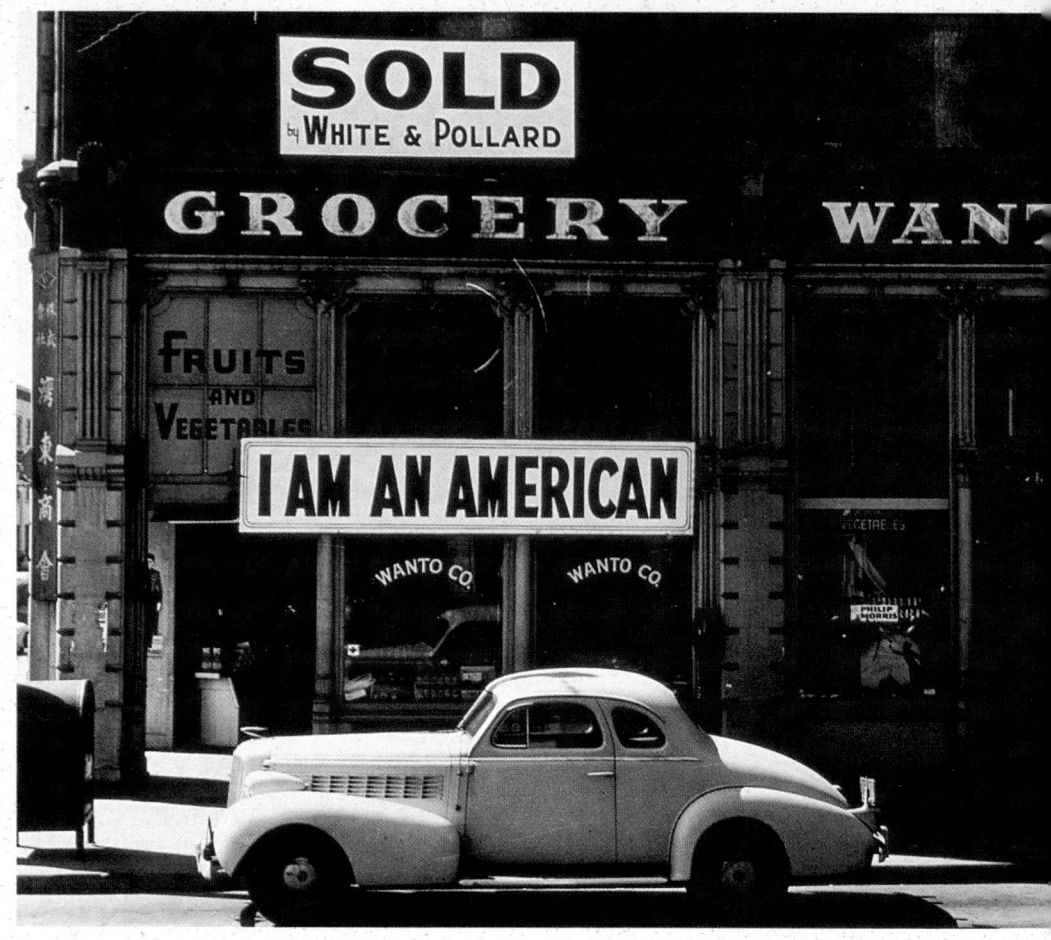

Japanese Americans

D uring World War II Japanese Americans were feared and hated by many other Americans, especially those living on the West Coast. In Oakland, California, the Japanese American owner of this small store—in an attempt to prevent its burning or looting—put up a sign asserting his loyalty: "I am an American." This very American scene emphasizes the cruelty of persecuting Japanese American businessmen. After the Japanese bombed Pearl Harbor, U.S. politicians spoke with fiery rhetoric, and newspapers ran hate stories that fanned the fe antagonism against Japanese Americans.

This campaign of hate was a symptom of the tality of the war in the Pacific. Both sides, Japanes American, found it necessary to demonize the e so that their own soldiers could fight a long an war, and their own civilian populations could support their country's war effort, despite wa shortages, extra-long working hours, or family bers killed in the war. ⊕

MORE ABOUT...

Japanese American Soldiers The 442nd Regimental Combat Team, a Japanese American unit, helped the Allies win control of Italy. Altogether, almost 26,000 Japanese Americans fought for the United States during World War II.

The United States retaliated by placing an embargo, or ban, on the sale of scrap iron to Japan. In response, Japan signed the Tripartite Pact with Germany and Italy on September 27, 1940. Under this pact, the three powers affirmed the right of every nation to "receive the space to which it is entitled" and pledged to cooperate to reach that goal as well as to come to one another's aid if attacked.

Pearl Harbor

When the Japanese invaded southern Indochina on July 24, 1941, President Roosevelt demanded that they withdraw—not only from Indochina but also from China. Congress also placed an embargo on oil and froze all Japanese assets in the United States. Negotiations with the Japanese government continued through the fall.

Japan decided to go to war with the United States because it believed the United States stood in the way of its expansion in the East. To defeat American military forces, however, Japanese leaders knew they had to destroy the American Pacific fleet based at **Pearl Harbor** in Hawaii. Although most American and Japanese leaders believed that Pearl Harbor was safe from attack, Admiral **Isoroku Yamamoto**, the commander of the Japanese navy, did not agree. He convinced Japanese leaders that bombers taking off from aircraft carriers and equipped with newly designed torpedos for use in shallow water could effect a successful surprise attack on Pearl Harbor. In November 1941 the Japanese fleet set sail for Hawaii.

Meanwhile, negotiations between the United States and Japan had broken down. By now Roosevelt knew that the Japanese were "poised for attack," but was convinced that Japan's move would be in Southeast Asia. As a precaution, United States military leaders sent all aircraft carriers and half the army's planes from Pearl Harbor.

On the morning of December 7, the Japanese attack squadron took off from their carrier decks and began the attack on Pearl Harbor. Within the first 25 minutes of the attack, they sank or damaged the battleships *Arizona, Utah, Oklahoma, West Virginia,* and *California.* The Japanese success was even greater than they had hoped. In all, they sank or disabled 19 American ships and destroyed 188 airplanes. They also killed more than 2,400 people and wounded 1,100. Fortunately for the United States, its aircraft carriers were at sea and escaped the attack. Calling December 7 "a date which will live in infamy," President Roosevelt, in an appearance before Congress the next day, asked for and received a declaration of war against Japan.

The Allies

The United States was now officially at war. On December 11, 1941, Germany and Italy honored their pledge to Japan in the Tripartite Pact by declaring war on the United States. Great Britain, backing the United States, declared war on Japan.

Although mistrust still lingered between the Western democracies and the Soviet Union, they put aside their differences to defeat their common enemy. Meanwhile, the fighting in the Soviet Union remained fierce. Vast areas of the country were under German occupation. The Germans had completely surrounded Leningrad, trapping 3 million people. Within two years, nearly 1 million of its people died from cold, hunger, and starvation.

Stalin urged the Allies to open a "second front" in Europe as quickly as possible. Although President Roosevelt favored this, Winston Churchill was opposed to it. He knew that Great Britain would have to bear the brunt of any second-front operation. Consequently, the two Allied leaders postponed plans for an invasion of Europe. Instead, they planned campaigns in North Africa and the Mediterranean.

Pearl Harbor
How did Pearl Harbor change the course of World War II?
The Japanese attack brought the United States, with its powerful military potential, into World War II.

ASSESS

Check for Understanding
Assign Section 3 Assessment as homework or as an in-class activity.

🖲 Use Interactive Tutor Self-Assessment Software to review Section 3.

Evaluate
📁 Section Quiz 31-3

🖲 Use the Testmaker to create a customized quiz for Section 3.

Reteach
Have students summarize the events that brought the Soviet Union and the United States into World War II.

📁 Reading Essentials and Study Guide 31-3

Enrich
Have students research the raw materials Japan gained by invading French Indochina and the Dutch East Indies.

CLOSE

Have students discuss how the entry of the Soviet Union and the United States into the war changed the balance of forces between the Allies and the Axis.

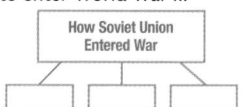
SECTION 3 ASSESSMENT

Main Idea
1. Use a diagram like the one below to identify the events that caused the Soviet Union to enter World War II.

How Soviet Union Entered War

Recall
2. **Define** scorched-earth policy, Holocaust, genocide.
3. **Identify** Isoroku Yamamoto.

Critical Thinking
4. **Analyzing Information** How did the proposed "New Order" that Germany's Adolf Hitler wanted to create in Nazi-

occupied Europe affect different groups of people living on that continent?

Understanding Themes
5. **Conflict** What political and economic issues caused the conflict between the governments of Japan and the United States?

Chapter 31 *World War II* **843**

SECTION 3 ASSESSMENT ANSWERS

1. Hitler launched Operation Barbossa, a massive attack on the Soviet Union; after initial defeat, Stalin instigated a scorched-earth policy, refusing to surrender; succeeded in forcing German retreat
2. All terms are defined in the Glossary.
3. Isoroku Yamamoto, 843
4. Hitler's "New Order" exploited the resources

of the conquered countries and enslaved or exterminated the conquered people.
5. **CONFLICT** Japan's expansionism in Asia and plans for a "new order"; U.S. embargo on scrap iron to Japan; Tripartite Act with Germany and Italy; U.S. embargo on oil and freezing of Japanese assets in U.S.

1941   **1942**   **1943**

MAY 1941 British naval forces sink German battleship *Bismarck*.

October 1942 British halt German advance in North Africa at El Alamein, Egypt.

FEB. 1943 German forces at Stalingrad surrender to the Soviets.

Section 4

Turning Points

SECTION THEME

▶ **Conflict** The Allies make major gains against the Axis powers.

Guide to Reading

For reading strategies to help students read effectively see pages 12–13.

Vocabulary Pre-check

 Use the Vocabulary PuzzleMaker for Chapter 31 to create a crossword puzzle to reinforce section terms. **L1 LEP**

Use Vocabulary Activity 31 to introduce vocabulary terms. **L1 LEP**

FOCUS

Section Objective

Explain how the tide of war turned in favor of the Allies during 1942 and 1943.

BELLRINGER
Motivational Activity

 Before taking roll at the beginning of the class period, project Section Focus Transparency 31-4 and have students answer the activity questions. Discuss students' responses.

This activity is also available as a blackline master.

Guide to Reading

Read to Find Out

Main Idea *The tide of war turned in favor of the Allies during 1942 and 1943.*

▶ **Terms to Define**
kamikaze

▶ **People to Meet**
Erwin Rommel, Bernard Montgomery, Dwight D. Eisenhower, Douglas MacArthur, Chester W. Nimitz

▶ **Places to Locate**
Stalingrad, Casablanca, Sicily, Guadalcanal

The Storyteller

A kamikaze attack on an American aircraft carrier, the Hornet, was recorded in photographs and by eyewitness accounts such as this one: "His [plane] already with flame blossoming on its underside, appeared high above the Hornet's starboard quarter. Perhaps dead or dying, [the pilot] did not release his bomb but kept coming directly at the carrier. He did not miss.... Ruptured fuel tanks sprayed the signal bridge with burning gasoline, while the wrecked airplane smashed into the flight deck...." The impact and burning fuel killed and maimed many men, and fires blazed for two hours.

Japanese kamikaze pilot

—adapted from *The First Team and the Guadalcanal Campaign*, John B. Lundstrom, 1994

In the early months of 1942, the war was going badly for the Allies. By destroying much of the American fleet at Pearl Harbor, Japan had gained control of the Pacific Ocean and cleared the way for a seaborne invasion of American, British, and Dutch territories in that region. In December 1941 Japanese forces had captured the British colony of Hong Kong and invaded the Malay Peninsula. In the West, meanwhile, Rommel controlled a large area of North Africa, and German forces held the upper hand in the Soviet Union as well.

Despite these successes, the Axis powers would never again enjoy such a strong position. By the end of 1942, the tide of the war had begun to turn in favor of the Allies.

Sea and Air Battles

Even before the United States entered the war, it was shipping food and war supplies to Britain under the Lend-Lease Act. But German submarines, or U-boats, threatened this vital lifeline across the Atlantic. By the end of 1939, U-boats had already sunk 114 Allied and neutral ships. German air attacks also took their toll.

To make matters worse for the Allies, the new German battleship *Bismarck*, accompanied by the new cruiser *Prinz Eugen*, entered the fight in May 1941. With 11 Allied convoys either at sea or about to sail, the British hastily dispatched several ships to intercept the Nazis. On May 23 they sighted the two German ships in the Denmark Strait between Iceland and Greenland and opened fire. In the battle that followed, the *Bismarck* sank the British battle cruiser *Hood* and damaged a new British battleship before slipping away to safety.

Three days later, on May 26, a British patrol plane spotted the *Bismarck* about 600 miles (965 km) off the French coast. In the battle that followed, the *Bismarck* sustained at least eight

---

SECTION RESOURCES

Reproducible Masters
- Lecture Notes 31-4
- Reproducible Lesson Plan 31-4
- Vocabulary Activity 31
- Guided Reading Activity 31-4
- Geography and History Activity 31
- Section Quiz 31-4
- Reading Essentials and Study Guide 31-4

Transparencies
- Section Focus Transparency 31-4
- Mapping History Overlay Transparency
  20, *Southeast Asia Prior to World War II*

Multimedia
- Interactive Tutor Self-Assessment Software
- Testmaker
- Lessons of War: *Can a Battle Change History?*

orpedo hits before it finally sank. With this crucial victory, the British put an end to German efforts to win the Battle of the Atlantic with surface ships. Gradually, the Allies devised new methods for protecting their convoys against U-boats as well.

As they fought for control of the Atlantic, the Allies carried out an air offensive against Germany. These attacks were directed at factories, railroads, dockyards, and cities and towns. Their purpose was to destroy German war industries and weaken the will of the civilian population to continue the war.

POINT
Stalingrad

In July 1942 the military situation in the Soviet Union looked desperate. With the Soviet army in full retreat, the Germans were approaching **Stalingrad**, a major industrial center on the Volga River. In angry exchanges with Churchill, Stalin continued to press for a second front in the West to take some of the military pressure off his nation. But in August Churchill went to Moscow to tell Stalin that there would be no second front in 1942.

On August 22 the Germans attacked Stalingrad. Because it was named after Stalin, losing the city would have been a blow to Soviet morale. As determined to protect Stalingrad as Hitler was to take it, Stalin ordered that the city be held at all costs.

The Soviets launched a counterattack in September and encircled the German troops threatening the city. They cut off German supply lines. Although the Soviets and the frigid winter weather were closing in on the Germans, Hitler refused to allow his troops to retreat. By the time German officers finally surrendered in February 1943, the German army had lost the best of its troops. Many historians now view the Soviet victory at Stalingrad as the major turning point of World War II. By killing about 100,000 German soldiers, capturing 80,000 more, and seizing large quantities of German military equipment, the Soviet Union broke the back of the Nazi military machine.

War in the Desert

In January 1942 Allied forces in North Africa were struggling to regain ground lost to the Germans. They faced a formidable foe. **Erwin Rommel,** commander of the Afrika Korps, applied blitzkrieg tactics to warfare in the desert. His exploits earned him the nickname "the Desert Fox."

Eastern Front 1941–1944

	Soviet victory
Axis holdings, Dec. 1941	★ Soviet victory
Axis conquest, 1941–1943	★ Axis victory
Unoccupied Soviet territory	

Map Study Some of the fiercest battles of World War II took place on the eastern front in the Soviet Union.
Place How did the German offensive affect the city of Leningrad?

In the spring of 1942, Rommel pushed the British two-thirds of the way back to the Egyptian frontier. He struck again at the end of May, but the British, under General **Bernard Montgomery,** stopped him two months later at El Alamein (EL A•luh•MAYN), a railway junction about 70 miles (112 km) from Alexandria. In October Montgomery launched a counterattack that forced the Germans back across the Egyptian-Libyan frontier and ended with the British capture of Tripoli, the capital of Libya, in January 1943.

As Montgomery was advancing westward, the Allies were landing troops in Morocco and Algeria as part of a planned offensive against Rommel. By advancing from the east and from the west, the Allies hoped to trap Rommel with their "pincers" strategy. But the Allied landings met with heavy resistance from the Vichy French, who governed French North Africa. To end the fighting, Allied commander **Dwight D. Eisenhower** struck a deal with Admiral François Darlan, a Vichy official. In

Chapter 31 *World War II* **845**

TEACH
Guided Practice

THEME Conflict

List the following events on the chalkboard: the sinking of the *Bismarck*; victory at Stalingrad; the battle of El Alamein in North Africa; the invasion of Sicily; the capture of Malaya, Singapore, Burma, Dutch East Indies, Guam, Wake Island, and the Philippines; Battles of the Coral Sea, Midway, and Guadalcanal. Have students identify the combatants and the victors of each event. **L1 LEP**

Map Study

Answer
It was surrounded by German forces who laid siege to the city. Within two years, about 1 million people died from cold, starvation, and disease.

POINT

Stalingrad
Why was Stalingrad a major turning point in World War II? *The Battle of Stalingrad put the Germans on the defensive on the Eastern Front and marked the beginning of the turning of the tide in favor of the Allies.*

Mapping History Overlay Transparency 20, *Southeast Asia Prior to World War II*

Independent Practice

Guided Reading Activity 31-4 **L1**

Geography and History Activity 31

COOPERATIVE LEARNING ACTIVITY

Biographies Organize the class into two groups. Have one group use outside sources to prepare a biography of Franklin Roosevelt, and the other group to do the same for Winston Churchill. Tell students to focus on how each man developed the qualities he needed to serve as a wartime leader. Students should examine factors such as education, military experience, personality traits, charisma, oratory skills, and ideals. Have both groups present their reports and then have them draw up a list of leadership qualities shared by FDR and Churchill. **L2**

Map Study

Answer

The Allies invaded Italy from Tunisia because it was the closest point to Italy.

Map Skills Practice

Reading a Map Where in North Africa did the Allies win victories in 1943? (*Tripoli, Kasserine Pass, Tunis, Bizerte*)

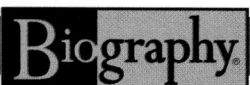

The following videotape programs are available from Glencoe:

- **General Douglas MacArthur: Return of a Legend**
- **Dwight D. Eisenhower: Commander-in-Chief**

North African and Italian Campaigns 1942–1945

Under Axis control, July 1943
Neutral nations
★ Allied victory
← Allied offensive

Map Study Before the Allies could invade Italy, they had to defeat the Italians and Germans for control of North Africa.
Region From which country in this region did the Allies eventually launch their invasion, and why did they choose this region?

return for Allied support of his claim to French North Africa, Darlan ordered an end to the resistance. With the armistice concluded in November 1942, the Free French, under Charles de Gaulle, joined the Allies in Africa. Meanwhile, in a series of powerful attacks, the Allies began closing the pincers. When Rommel flew to Berlin to tell Hitler that the situation was hopeless, the Nazi dictator rejected his general's assessment and barred Rommel from returning to Africa. But Rommel was right. In May 1943, General von Arnim, the new commander of the German forces in Tunisia, surrendered. The Allies now controlled all of North Africa.

Invasion of Italy

In early 1943, the American and British chiefs of staff and political leaders met at **Casablanca** in Morocco to discuss their next move. Because they wanted to secure communications in the Mediterranean and intensify the pressure on Italy, they decided to invade **Sicily**, the large island near the southern tip of the Italian Peninsula.

Under the command of General Eisenhower, the Allies began a combined air and sea attack on **Sicily** in July 1943. The seaborne landings met little

resistance at first, but when the Allies approached Messina, on the extreme northeastern tip of the island, the Germans put up a stronger fight to cover their withdrawal across the Strait of Messina. In six days nearly 40,000 German and 70,000 Italian troops escaped to Italy.

The conquest of Sicily led quickly to Mussolini's downfall. On July 25, King Victor Emmanuel III, pressed into action by antiwar factions, fired Mussolini and had him arrested. The new prime minister, Marshal Pietro Badoglio, soon dissolved the Fascist party and on September 3 signed a secret act of surrender.

That same day, Allied forces crossed the Strait of Messina and landed in Calabria on the Italian mainland. The broadcast announcement of Badoglio's unconditional surrender caught the Germans by surprise, but they recovered in time to occupy Rome two days later, forcing the king and Badoglio to withdraw to the south. The Germans later rescued Mussolini and put him in control of northern Italy.

For the remaining months of 1943 and early months of 1944, the Allies fought their way up the Italian Peninsula. Allied troops could not penetrate the German defenses at Monte Cassino, a sixth-century monastery located on a mountaintop that dominated the road to Rome. In the end it took a

MEETING SPECIAL NEEDS ACTIVITY

Learning Style: Kinesthetic Have students who are kinesthetic learners create a "war map" showing one of the following conflicts of the war: the Soviet offensive, the war in the desert, the invasion of Italy, or the war in the Pacific. Tell students to re-create the area of conflict and then illustrate how the Allied forces took the offensive and achieved victory. Suggest that they use markers, flags, or pictures to illustrate the actions in the conflict. Display completed maps in the classroom and encourage students to explain their maps. **L2 LEP**

massive artillery bombardment and almost five months for the Allies to dislodge the Germans in May 1944. One month later, on June 4, Allied forces entered Rome.

Pacific War

While war raged in Europe, Japan took over much of Southeast Asia and the Pacific. At first welcomed as liberators, the Japanese soon were hated by local peoples for their killing of civilians and taking of property. Resistance groups arose to fight Japanese forces.

Meanwhile, the Allies were able to make some gains. In May 1942, in the Battle of the Coral Sea, the Allies claimed a victory. And in June, at the Battle of Midway, the Americans defeated the Japanese navy and ended Japanese naval superiority in the Pacific.

Japanese Empire 1910–1945

Area held by Japan in 1910
To 1931
To 1941
To 1942
Anglo-American advances, 1943-1945
Soviet advances, 1945
★ Allied victory

Map Study Between 1910 and 1942, Japan took over large areas of East Asia, Southeast Asia, and the Pacific.
Region Why were the Japanese able to seize the European colonies in this region so easily in 1941 and 1942?

To follow up this victory, the Americans launched an attack against the Pacific island of **Guadalcanal** in early August. While troops under General **Douglas MacArthur** attacked the Japanese on land, naval forces under Admiral **Chester W. Nimitz** confronted them at sea. The six-month land, sea, and air battle ended in victory for the Allies. Guadalcanal was the first in a series of island battles the Americans fought as they leapfrogged their way north to Japan. Their strat-

egy was to capture some islands and bypass others. Those bypassed would be cut off from supplies and made to "wither on the vine."

After Guadalcanal, the Americans paused to build up their Pacific forces. When the American advance resumed in November 1943, Japanese pilots known as kamikazes volunteered for suicide missions, crashing their bomb-laden aircraft into Allied bases and ships. The Japanese were far from ready to surrender.

SECTION 4 ASSESSMENT

Main Idea
1. Use a chart like the one below to list the events of 1942 and 1943 that turned the war to the Allies' favor.

Events of 1942 and 1943
1.
2.

Recall
2. **Define** kamikaze.
3. **Identify** Erwin Rommel, Bernard Montgomery, Dwight D. Eisenhower, Douglas MacArthur, Chester W. Nimitz.

Critical Thinking
4. **Synthesizing Information** How did Adolf Hitler's political

and military decisions contribute to Nazi Germany's defeats in both Stalingrad and North Africa?

Understanding Themes
5. **Conflict** Why did the Allies decide to "leapfrog" their way to Japan rather than launch a direct attack?

Chapter 31 *World War II* **847**

SECTION 4 ASSESSMENT ANSWERS

1. Soviet victory at Battle of Stalingrad; allies victorious over Germany in North Africa; conquest of Sicily and eventually the rest of Italy; Pacific war victories at battles of the Coral Sea, Midway, and Guadalcanal
2. The word is defined in the Glossary.
3. Erwin Rommel, 845; Bernard Montgomery, 845; Dwight D. Eisenhower, 845; Douglas MacArthur, 847; Chester W. Nimitz, 847

4. Hitler refused to allow the German forces to withdraw from Stalingrad and refused to end the North African campaign even after it had become hopeless.
5. **CONFLICT** By capturing some islands and leapfrogging over others, the Allies hoped to cut off supplies to the bypassed islands, forcing them to surrender.

Map Study

Answer
The European powers were preoccupied with Hitler.

ASSESS

Check for Understanding
Assign Section 4 Assessment as homework or as an in-class activity.

🖭 Use Interactive Tutor Self-Assessment Software to review Section 4.

Evaluate
🗁 Section Quiz 31-4

🖭 Use the Testmaker to create a customized quiz for Section 4.

Reteach
Using a large wall map, have students show Allied progress in the Atlantic, Soviet Union, North Africa, Italy, and the Pacific in 1942–1943.

🗁 Reading Essentials and Study Guide 31-4

Enrich
Have students watch the film *North Star* (also called *Armored Attack*), made in 1943, which shows the German invasion of the Soviet Union. Have students write a short essay describing the attitude toward the Soviet Union reflected in the film.

CLOSE

Organize the class into two groups. Have each group make a list in chronological order of ten key events from this section. Combine the two lists into one top-ten list.

JUNE 6, 1944 (D-Day) Allies land in Normandy.

DEC. 16, 1944 Battle of the Bulge begins.

MAY 8, 9, 1945 V-E (Victory in Europe) Day celebrated in Allied countries.

AUG. 6, 1945 The United States drops atomic bomb on Hiroshima, Japan.

Section 5

Allied Victories

Guide to Reading

Read to Find Out
Main Idea *New technology affected the conduct and outcome of World War II.*

▶ **Terms to Define**
D-Day, partisan

▶ **People to Meet**
George Patton, Harry S Truman, Clement Attlee

▶ **Places to Locate**
Rhine River, Berlin, Yalta, Potsdam, Hiroshima, Nagasaki

The Storyteller

An American woman, living in Russia, later recalled how hope for Allied rescue was everywhere in Russia during the spring of 1944:

"They knew it must come this summer, for the war was already in Europe.... On a day in early June the air was split by a radio announcement: 'Stand by for a special broadcast at 1:45.' We knew what it would be. Everybody knew. 'Today, June 6, 1944, early in the morning, General Eisenhower's forces began landing operations on the northern coast of France.'" The long-awaited second front was a reality. People laughed and slapped each other on the back.

American troops land in Normandy

—adapted from *Fifty Russian Winters, An American Woman's Life in the Soviet Union*, Margaret Wettlin, 1992

To fight the Axis, Allied democracies geared their economies for war production, rationed goods, and regulated prices and wages. The wartime emergency limited citizens' rights, but unemployment ended as factories turned out weapons and supplies. With men joining the military, women in large numbers entered industry and served in supporting roles in the armed forces. Outside of the democracies, women supported the Allied cause by fighting in the resistance forces of occupied Europe; in the Soviet Union, they saw combat as ground soldiers and pilots.

POINT

D-Day

At a 1943 conference in Tehran, Iran, Roosevelt and Churchill told Stalin about their plan to open a second front the following spring. Meanwhile, General Eisenhower assembled a force of 176,000 soldiers, 600 warships, and 10,000 aircraft in England for Operation Overlord, the invasion of France. On June 6, 1944, D-Day, or the day of attack, convoys carrying troops and equipment sailed across the English Channel to the French province of Normandy. British bombers attacked German coastal defenses, and Allied airborne troops parachuted into France to assist the invasion. As battleship guns pounded German positions, Allied soldiers moved from their landing craft onto the beaches, fighting their way forward amid German machine-gun fire.

Despite the battle's confusion and the heavy German resistance, the invasion was a success. From their Normandy foothold, the Allies launched an offensive against the Germans. By early August, American tank commander General **George Patton** and his forces were racing across northern France. At the same time, in Paris, French resistance fighters rose up against the occupying Germans.

848 Chapter 31 *World War II*

Allied Offensive in Europe June 1944–May 1945

Legend:
← Allied offensive
← German offensive
☐ Land held by Allies, Sept. 1944
☐ Land held by Allies, Jan. 1945
☐ Land held by Allies, May 1945
☐ Land held by Germans, May 1945

Map Study From D-Day in June 1944 to its surrender in May 1945, Germany was in full retreat on both the western and eastern fronts. **Location** Where did the one German offensive occur during this period?

Pressured on all sides, German forces retreated, and on August 25, Allied troops, led by Free French forces, entered Paris.

Victory Over Germany

Months before D-Day, Soviet forces advanced steadily toward Germany from the east. By the summer of 1944, they had pushed the Germans out of Soviet territory and were moving into eastern Europe. Despite the Allied gains, Hitler was convinced that a surprise offensive in the west might still reverse the Allied advance. In December 1944, the Germans cut through the center of the American forces, creating a bulge in the Allied line of troops. The Allies finally checked the German drive at Bastogne, Belgium, and in March 1945, stormed across the **Rhine River**, Germany's historic defense barrier. By this time, Germany's cities had undergone repeated Allied air attacks, which destroyed industrial centers and killed hundreds of thousands of people.

Meanwhile, from the east, the Soviets inflicted a savage revenge on the German population and fought their way into the city of **Berlin**. In late April, American and Soviet troops met on the Elbe

---

COOPERATIVE LEARNING ACTIVITY

Mapmaking Organize the class into five groups. Each group will be responsible for mapping one of the following military campaigns from June 1944 to August 1945: Operation Overlord, the Battle of the Bulge, the Soviet advances, the Pacific Campaign, and the bombing of Japan. Instruct each group to create a map of their campaign using poster paper and markers. Suggest that they use maps from the text as well as from other sources as guides. Tell them to show the locations of battles, troop movements, flight patterns, and strategies. Have each group prepare a brief written summary that explains the campaign. When the maps are completed, ask each group to present its map and summary to the class. **L3 LEP**

TEACH

Guided Practice

THEME Innovation

Have students describe how strategies used in the D-Day invasion and in capturing Pacific islands helped the Allies, and how the atomic bomb quickly ended the war. **L1**

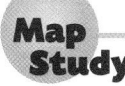
Map Study

Answer
the Battle of the Bulge

Cultural Perspectives

Navajo Code Talkers In 1943 the U.S. Marines recruited the Navajo to develop a military code that the Japanese could not break. Based on their oral language, the Navajo code talkers created the only unbreakable code in military history.

 Mapping History Overlay Transparency 21, *Battle Sites in the Pacific*

 World History and Art Transparency 42, *The Red Stairway*

 CURRICULUM CONNECTION

TECHNOLOGY
After D-Day, PLUTO (Pipe-Line Under The Ocean), a pipeline under the English Channel, supplied 700 tons of gasoline a day for Allied trucks and tanks advancing across Europe.

Independent Practice

📁 Guided Reading Activity 31-5 **L1**

ABCNEWS INTERACTIVE™

VIDEODISC
Turning Points in World History

Side Two
Chapter 7

Title: *Dropping the Atomic Bomb*
Ask: What cities were bombed?
(Hiroshima and Nagasaki, Japan)

TURNING POINT

Victory Over Japan
How did the way in which the United States defeated Japan affect future world events?
For the first time, the atomic bomb was used in warfare, forcing Japan's surrender. It opened the atomic age, in which nuclear weapons played a role in global rivalry.

ASSESS

Check for Understanding

Assign Section 5 Assessment as homework or as an in-class activity.

◉ Use Interactive Tutor Self-Assessment Software to review Section 5.

Visualizing History
The Soviet army, coming from the east, fought for nine days to win control of Berlin. On April 30, 1945, Soviet tanks reached the Reichstag, the German parliament building, which they bombarded until afternoon.
Answer to Caption: *The Western Allies crossed the Rhine and by April 11 reached the Elbe, where they later met Soviet armies coming from the east.*

River. On May 7, the Germans surrendered unconditionally, and the next day was proclaimed V-E (Victory in Europe) Day in the Allied democracies; May 9 was celebrated as V-E Day in the Soviet Union. With the German surrender, the war in Europe had finally ended. The end also came for the Fascist dictators. Italian partisans, or resistance fighters, had shot Mussolini, and Hitler had committed suicide in an underground chamber in Berlin.

Yalta and Potsdam

In February 1945, Roosevelt, Churchill, and Stalin had met at **Yalta**, a Black Sea resort in the Soviet Union, to discuss issues affecting the postwar world. The Allied leaders proposed that France and China join their countries in forming the United Nations, a permanent international organization to maintain peace after the war. They also agreed to divide Germany, as well as the city of Berlin, into four zones that Great Britain, France, the United States, and the Soviet Union would occupy.

 Celebrating the Red Army's capture of Berlin, a group of Soviet troops unfurl the Soviet flag over the ruins of the German parliament building. *What advances were made by the Western Allies during the spring of 1945?*

Roosevelt and Churchill obtained from Stalin a promise to hold free elections in Soviet-occupied eastern Europe. In return, they gave Stalin the eastern part of Poland. Poland would receive German land in return for yielding its eastern territory.

To hasten the end of the Pacific conflict, the Western leaders sought and received Stalin's promise to declare war on Japan. In return, Stalin gained the Kuril Islands and the southern part of Sakhalin Island. These islands, located off the coast of Siberia in the northern Pacific Ocean, were ruled by Japan.

Six months later, the Allies met in **Potsdam** in Germany, but by this time some of the key participants had changed. After Franklin D. Roosevelt died in April, **Harry S Truman** succeeded him as President. Although Churchill was there at the opening, his Conservative party lost the general election, and **Clement Attlee** of the Labour party replaced him as prime minister halfway through the conference.

The atmosphere at Potsdam was also quite different from that at Yalta. The Allies made plans for the occupation of Germany and issued an ultimatum to Japan demanding unconditional surrender. However, more issues were raised than were settled. New tensions over the future of Europe were beginning to pull apart the wartime alliance.

TURNING POINT
Victory Over Japan

By end of 1944, an Allied victory over Japan seemed inevitable. American planes bombed Japanese cities, and General Douglas MacArthur regained the Philippines. In early 1945, the Americans defeated the Japanese in bloody battles on the Pacific islands of Iwo Jima and Okinawa, and the British completed the destruction of Japanese forces in Southeast Asia. Despite setbacks, Japan's military leaders, such as General Hideki Tojo, refused to surrender.

When Japan rejected an American ultimatum in July, President Truman decided to use a new secret weapon—the atomic bomb. His stated reason for using the bomb against Japan was to end the war swiftly and to avoid the enormous loss of life that would have resulted from an American invasion of the Japanese home islands. Concerned about growing Soviet-American rivalry, Truman also may have used the bomb to impress the Soviets with American military might.

On August 6, 1945, an American plane dropped an atomic bomb on **Hiroshima**, a munitions center. The blast leveled most of the city. When no response

---

Visualizing History In February 1945, Allied leaders Winston Churchill, Franklin D. Roosevelt, and Joseph Stalin met at Yalta on the USSR's Crimean Peninsula. They discussed a number of issues related to the post-war Europe. *What major agreement was made at Yalta regarding the war against Japan?*

Visualizing History At Yalta, Churchill, Roosevelt, and Stalin also agreed that each of the five permanent members of the United Nations Security Council would have veto power over matters brought before the Council. During the early years of the United Nations, the Soviet Union often used its veto to prevent UN action against Soviet actions in Eastern Europe.
Answer to Caption: *The Soviets agreed to join the war against Japan. In return they received the Japanese-owned Kuril Islands and the southern part of Sakhalin Island.*

came from Japan, three days later the Americans dropped a second atomic bomb on the port city of **Nagasaki**. Altogether, about 200,000 Japanese died in both cities. In the following months, many more would die from the blasts' radioactivity.

On August 14, 1945, Japan finally surrendered. A few weeks later, on September 2 (proclaimed V-J—or Victory over Japan—Day by the Allies) Japanese officials signed the official surrender document on board the American battleship *Missouri* anchored in Tokyo Bay. World War II was over.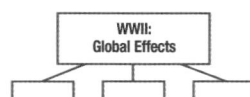

Effects of the War

More than 70 million people fought in World War II. The casualties were staggering. Altogether, some 55 million people perished because of the conflict. The Soviet Union lost 22 million people, Germany almost 8 million, Japan 2 million, and the United States almost 300,000. In addition, millions of people in Europe and Asia died in campaigns of genocide.

After the war the Allies began to address the wrongs committed by the Axis Powers. Between November 1945 and September 1946, trials held at Nuremburg, Germany, brought many Nazi leaders to justice for pursuing "aggressive war" and for "committing crimes against humanity." Similar war crimes trials were held in Japan and Italy.

In addition to the casualties, many areas of Europe and Asia lay in ruins. The use of deadly new weapons made World War II the most destructive war in history. Heavy aerial bombing and shifting battlelines left as many as 12 million people homeless. Food, medicine, and clothing were in short supply. One Japanese student recalls life after the war:

66 **When winter came we were really miserable. We had neither food nor clothing.... We were told to go to the countryside and find food wherever we could. There was nothing in Tokyo.** 99

For millions of people the suffering and hardships lasted long after the war's end.

Evaluate
 Section Quiz 31-5

▣ Use the Testmaker to create a customized quiz for Section 5.

Reteach
Have students compare the end of the European war with the conclusion of the war in the Pacific.

 Reteaching Activity 31

 Reading Essentials and Study Guide 31-5

Enrich
Have students research the controversy surrounding the commemoration of the dropping of atomic bombs on Hiroshima and Nagasaki on the fiftieth anniversary of those events in 1995.

▱ Enrichment Activity 31

CLOSE

Have students discuss why World War II is seen as a turning point in United States history.

SECTION 5 ASSESSMENT

Main Idea
1. Use a diagram like the one below to identify the global effects of World War II.

> WWII:
> Global Effects

Recall
2. **Define** D-Day, partisan.
3. **Identify** George Patton, Harry S Truman, Clement Attlee.

Critical Thinking
4. **Analyzing Information** War crimes trials after World War II held Axis leaders responsible

for actions in wartime. Give examples of similar trials after recent conflicts.

Understanding Themes
5. **Innovation** What factors made World War II the most destructive war in the history of the world?

Chapter 31 *World War II* **851**

SECTION 5 ASSESSMENT ANSWERS

1. 55 million people killed; much of Europe and Asia in ruins; 12 million people left homeless; food, medicine, and clothing in short supply
2. The terms are defined in the Glossary.
3. George Patton, 848; Harry S Truman, 850; Clement Attlee, 850
4. Students should mention war crimes trials in Bosnia and in Rwanda, dealing with

"ethnic cleansing" atrocities.
5. **INNOVATION** Answers will vary but should include that World War I was mainly a trench war fought between armies. In World War II, both the Axis and Allied powers used tanks and air power, especially aerial bombing against civilian as well as military targets; the atomic bomb.

WORLD HISTORY *Online*

Have students use the **Chapter 31 Self-Check Quiz** at worldhistory.glencoe.com to prepare for the Chapter Test.

GLENCOE
TECHNOLOGY

VIDEODISC
Use MindJogger to review the chapter.

MindJogger Videoquiz

Chapter 31
Disc 4 Side B

Also available in VHS.

Answers

Using Key Terms
1. d   3. l   5. k
2. j   4. h

Using Your History Journal
Remind students to use examples.

Reviewing Facts
1. Similarities: involved Allies; purpose was to discuss postwar issues; differences: participating heads of state changed; different atmospheres: decisions and plans were made at Yalta while at Potsdam more issues were raised than answered
2. It could only make recommendations and impose sanctions. The Japanese treated conquered peoples cruelly, killing civilians and seizing property.
3. Austria and Czechoslovakia
4. Causes: ineffective World War I peace treaties; dislocations caused by economic depression; Fascist expansionist policies; weakness of the League of Nations; United States isolationism; Effects: loss of life, misery, homelessness; weakening of European powers and their

---

WORLD HISTORY *Online*

Self-Check Quiz

Visit the *World History: The Human Experience* Web site at **worldhistory.glencoe.com** and click on *Chapter 31—Self-Check Quiz* to prepare for the Chapter Test.

Using Key Terms

Write the key term that completes each sentence. Then write a sentence for each term not chosen.

a. blitzkrieg	g. D-Day
b. sanctions	h. scorched-earth policy
c. lend-lease	i. genocide
d. appeasement	j. Holocaust
e. kamikazes	k. collective security
f. partisan	l. cash-and-carry policy

1. British Prime Minister Chamberlain pursued _____ with Nazi Germany in hopes of stabilizing Europe.
2. In the _____, the Nazis murdered almost 6 million Jews during the war.
3. The _____ allowed the United States to supply the British in return for payment without risking American neutrality.
4. Joseph Stalin tried to thwart the German invasion of his country by a _____.
5. During the 1930s, the Western democracies were unable to agree on what steps to take to ensure their _____.

Technology Activity

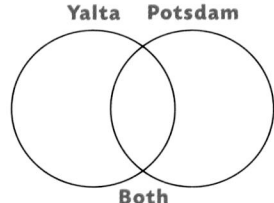

Using the Internet Search the Internet for a World War II Web site that includes memoirs or excerpts from Holocaust survivors. Copy or print a part of the memoirs that you find especially moving. Create a bulletin board about the Holocaust. Post the excerpts on the bulletin board under the heading "Voices of World War II." Include pictures of the Holocaust with captions underneath providing explanations.

Reviewing Facts

1. **History** Use a diagram like the one below to show similarities and differences between the conferences at Yalta and Potsdam.

Yalta   Potsdam

Both

2. **Citizenship** Explain why the League of Nations could not stop Japan's expansion. How did Japan treat its conquered peoples?
3. **History** List the countries that Germany occupied before the outbreak of war.
4. **History** Identify the causes and effects of World War II.
5. **History** Explain Japan's attack on Pearl Harbor.
6. **Citizenship** Identify the Holocaust and discuss the different stages of its implementation.

Critical Thinking

1. **Apply** Why did the Western democracies let Hitler overrun much of Europe before trying to stop him?
2. **Analyze** What factors account for the response the world gave to the Holocaust?
3. **Synthesize** If the Japanese had not bombed Pearl Harbor, would the United States have entered the war? Explain your position.
4. **Evaluate** Was the United States justified in using the atomic bomb to end the war with Japan?

---

empires; rise of the superpowers; development of nuclear weapons; the United Nations
5. The U.S. hindered Japan's expansionist policy. As war with the U.S. was inevitable, Japan wanted to destroy its Pacific fleet.
6. It was the deliberate attempt by the Nazis to exterminate Europe's Jews and also other groups such as Slavs and Gypsies. At first the Nazis used forced emigration and imprison-

ment. After the invasion of the Soviet Union, Nazi SS forces rounded up and shot large numbers of Jews. Finally, the Jews were sent to the death camps for extermination.

Critical Thinking
1. They thought that by appeasing Hitler they could maintain peace.
2. Within Nazi-occupied areas, anti-Semitic people helped the Nazis round up Jews;

Understanding Themes

1. **Movement** What were Hitler's objectives in Europe? What were Japan's objectives in Asia?
2. **Cooperation** What assistance did the United States provide to Great Britain before American entry into the conflict?
3. **Conflict** Why did Stalin press the Allies to establish a second front in Europe?
4. **Conflict** Why did the Western Allies at Yalta agree to give Stalin the Kuril Islands and the southern part of Sakhalin Island?
5. **Innovation** What effect did new technology have on the war?

Geography in History

1. **Location** Refer to the map below. What were the relative locations of territories held in France by the Allies in September 1944?
2. **Region** What areas touching the Mediterranean Sea were in Allied control by September 1944?
3. **Movement** Beginning in June 1944, the Allied strategy was to pressure Germany on two fronts —East and West. How does the map show that the plan was a successful way to end the war?
4. **Location** Where did Soviet and American forces meet in April 1945?

The Allies Regain Europe

Land held by Allies, Sept. 1944
Land held by Allies, Jan. 1945
Land held by Allies, May 1945
Land held by Germans, May 1945

0   150   300 mi.
0 150 300 km
Lambert Conic Conformal Projection

Linking Past and Present

1. To avert war with Germany, the European democracies allowed Hitler to occupy Czechoslovakia. How did the United Nations react to Iraq's occupation of Kuwait in 1990? Do you think the United Nations made the correct decision? Explain.
2. In the 1940s, several publications called Churchill "Man of the Century." Do you think he still deserves the title? Explain.

Skill Practice

Reread the section of Chapter 31 that describes the bombing on Hiroshima, pages 850–851. Then read the passage on this page written six years later by a survivor. Use the two sources to answer the questions below.

" I was eating breakfast … when there was bright light in front of my eyes and an indescribable orange light surged in…. It must have been ten or fifteen minutes later when I recovered consciousness…. but I could see nothing because the place was filled with white smoke…. I tried to stand up and fell again…. What on earth had happened? …

I looked over my shoulder and saw our house was a flattened wreck, and at the back waves of swirling flames were threatening to sweep down on us at any moment…. I suddenly heard my sister's voice calling, 'Someone help me! …' She was my own sister but the sight of her was horrifying. Her dark hair which reached her shoulders, that hair was now pure white. At the side of her mouth was a crescent-shaped gash through which her gums were pitifully exposed, and from which bright red blood flowed… When I saw this figure my sister had been transformed into, for a fleeting moment, I just couldn't think that it was her. I was afraid even to go near her. "

—Eiko Matsunaga, 11th grade girl, 1951

1. What is the topic of the two sources?
2. What information does the textbook give about this topic?
3. How does the passage add to your understanding of this topic?

Chapter 31   *World War II*   853

4. **CONFLICT** in exchange for Stalin's promise to enter the war against Japan
5. **INNOVATION** New technology extended the scope of the war and increased its devastation.

Geography in History

1. northwest and southeast France
2. southeastern France, Corsica, Sardinia, Italy, Sicily, North Africa
3. It shows that the Allies steadily gained territory on both the eastern and western fronts throughout late 1944 and early 1945.
4. in Germany

Linking Past and Present

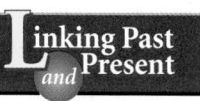

1. The UN sent a multinational force to the Middle East to expel Iraq from Kuwait. Answers will vary but should include that Iraqi aggression might have continued had the UN not responded as it did.
2. Answers might state that Churchill's firm stand in the Battle of Britain gave the British the courage to face the Nazis.

Skill Practice

1. the dropping of the atomic bomb on Hiroshima
2. why the bomb was dropped; extent of damage, and outcome
3. It makes the personal suffering very real.

? Chapter Bonus Test Question

Ask students: How were the gains made by Stalin at Yalta similar to those made by Hitler at the Munich conference? *(Both men got what they wanted in exchange for promises they didn't keep: Hitler got the Sudetenland and then took over the rest of Czechoslovakia; Stalin got Poland but instead of holding elections made Poland a Communist state.)*

---

most people did nothing, fearing punishment or believing that it was none of their concern; Allied governments did nothing, believing that carrying out the war was the only way to eliminate Nazi injustice.
3. Yes; because of the Atlantic Charter.
4. Students should explain their opinions.

Understanding Themes

1. **MOVEMENT** Hitler wanted to control all of Europe, including the Soviet Union, to obtain "living space" for the "master race." Japan wanted to establish a "Greater East Asia Co-Prosperity Sphere."
2. **COOPERATION** It gave the British old destroyers, supplied food and weapons through the cash-and-carry policy, and lent war equipment through the lend-lease policy.
3. **CONFLICT** because the Soviet Union was fighting the Nazis alone

FOCUS

During this period of worldwide political upheavals, the daily lives of the general public and of political figures were drastically altered. People were faced with all sorts of new challenges, and their experiences in coping with them varied greatly.

TEACH

Reinforcing Vocabulary

Point out the **Vocabulary Preview** to students alerting them to words they will encounter that might be unfamiliar.

The Great Depression

Interpreting the Primary Source
Ask students to discern from this description of the Depression a societal value that was lost due to the Depression. (*Being able to survive independently, without having to ask for public aid in the forms of money, food, or shelter, was valued, because the description reveals shame at people not being able to do that any longer.*)

Evaluating the Primary Source
This primary source reveals the regret and discouragement with which the Great Depression was viewed not only by the public but also by political officials. This source provides insight into the challenges of the Depression, both for the general public who were struggling to survive and for the officials who were trying to solve the everyday problems faced in the cities of the United States.

Unit 7

During the first half of the 1900s, two destructive wars raged throughout the world and brought about tremendous political and social change. World War I destroyed the power of European monarchies and led to a Communist revolution in Russia. Nazi aggression in Germany eventually led to World War II—the most destructive war in history.

◆ **VOCABULARY PREVIEW**

incinerator: a furnace that burns waste

paralysis: a state of being powerless to act

abstention: deliberate avoidance

annihilation: complete destruction

For more primary sources to accompany this unit, use the *World History Primary Source Document Library CD-ROM.*

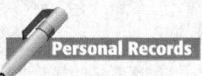

Chapter 29
The Great Depression

Personal Records

In October 1929 the United States's stock market crashed—investors were ruined, businesses were destroyed, and millions of people lost their jobs. The 1930s brought a period of economic gloom, poverty, and despair. Joseph L. Heffernan, an Ohio mayor, describes life during the Great Depression in this excerpt.

As time went on, business conditions showed no improvement. Every night hundreds of homeless men crowded into the municipal incinerator, where they found warmth even though they had to sleep on heaps of garbage. In January 1931, I obtained the cooperation of the City Council to convert an abandoned police station into a "flophouse." The first night it was filled, and it has remained filled ever since. . . .

Men receiving soup during the Depression

This descent from respectability, frequent enough in the best of times, has been hastened immeasurably by two years of business paralysis, and the people who have been affected in this manner must be numbered in millions. . . . I have seen thousands of these defeated, discouraged, hopeless men and women, cringing and fawning as they come to ask for public aid. It is a spectacle of national degeneration. . . .

Gandhi on Nonviolence

Interpreting the Primary Source
Ask students to interpret Gandhi's comment that both India and England were living in an "unnatural state." (*Gandhi seemed to view the cooperation with evil that he saw within each of these countries as unnatural; he thus must have thought that non-cooperation with evil was* not only morally right but also the natural state of humans.)

Evaluating the Primary Source
This primary source reveals Gandhi's explanations for his actions at the same time as it reveals his condemnation of the actions taken by others around him. The reliability

Chapter 30
Gandhi on Nonviolence

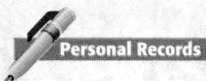
Personal Records

After World War I, protests against British rule in India began to spread, and Mohandas K. Gandhi became the leader of the independence movement. Gandhi developed a nonviolent form of civil disobedience that was later adopted in other parts of the world. While on trial in 1922, Gandhi made the following statement explaining his theories of nonviolent civil disobedience.

Mohandas Gandhi
1869–1948

In fact, I believe that I have rendered a service to India and England by showing in non-cooperation the way out of the unnatural state in which both are living. In my humble opinion, non-cooperation with evil is as much a duty as is cooperation with good. But in the past, non-cooperation has been deliberately expressed in violence to the evildoer. I am endeavoring to show to my countrymen that violent non-cooperation only multiplies evil and that as evil can only be sustained by violence, withdrawal of support of evil requires complete abstention from violence. Nonviolence implies voluntary submission to the penalty for non-cooperation with evil. I am here, therefore, to invite and submit cheerfully to the highest penalty that can be inflicted upon me for what in law is a deliberate crime and what appears to me to be the highest duty of a citizen. . . .

Chapter 31
Surviving the Nazi Concentration Camps

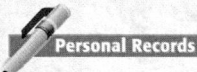
Personal Records

During World War II the Nazis sent millions of Jews, Slavs, Gypsies, and others to concentration camps, where they were tortured and murdered. In this excerpt, one of the few Jewish survivors describes how prisoners managed to stay alive.

The most horrible things happened to you as well as to others. Later, from reading Bruno Bettelheim's work, I learned about the strange experiences, protective mechanisms, called "derealization" and "depersonalization." Derealization is when reality is not experienced as reality: this cannot be true; this doesn't exist. And depersonalization, that is the phenomenon of a split of the personality: . . . You are the object of your own observation, and at the same time, you are the subject who walks off, or who is hungry, or who is suffering. . . .

The goal of the SS was, aside from physical annihilation, to degrade a person . . . to make you into a rag, without any will. Because of the isolation, . . . you didn't know anything about the outside world, but you also didn't know anything about the "inside" world. You didn't know what you would do the next day, what they were up to—whether the doors of the gas chamber would open for you the next day. . . .

Interpreting Primary Sources

1. Why does Heffernan say people needed public aid in the 1930s?
2. Why did Gandhi refuse to resort to violence?
3. What did the SS try to do to the prisoners? Why?
4. **CRITICAL THINKING:** Why were "derealization" and "depersonalization" so crucial to concentration camp prisoners' survival?

Applications Activity

Imagine that you are a mayor of a city during the Great Depression. Prepare a list of proposals you would make to get people working again.

ANSWER KEY

1. There were no jobs, and people were impoverished.
2. Gandhi felt that violence toward the evildoer only multiplies evil.
3. The SS tried to degrade each person, to destroy self-respect, and to confuse the prisoners, which would make the prisoners easier to control and unable to fight back.
4. The prisoners found a way of distancing themselves from their suffering; otherwise they might have been completely unable to cope with and survive their situation.

APPLICATIONS ACTIVITY: Answers will vary but should show an understanding of some of the major problems of the crisis.

---

of this source is determined by the fairness of the condemnations Gandhi made. It was his belief that violence was evil, but if one were to disagree with that belief, then one would also disagree with his opinion that India and England were living in unnatural states of cooperation with evil.

Surviving the Nazi Concentration Camps

Interpreting the Primary Source
Ask students what they think the effects of writing such a document as this might have been on its author. *(The writing of this document might have served to help the author sort through her personal reactions to her experiences; it might also have served to strengthen or vindicate her by knowing she would bring many people to understanding the torment so many people were put through during the Holocaust.)*

Evaluating the Primary Source
The reliability of this source is determined by the accuracy with which the author's generalizations fit the experiences of all women in Nazi concentration camps. The source provides insight into the experiences of one woman; the events she encountered and thoughts she had may well have been shared by many others during the Holocaust. Experiences of concentration camp prisoners may also have varied to some degree.

For the more complete version of each of these documents, see the World History Primary Source Document Library CD-ROM:

Document 162 *The Great Depression*
Document 168 *Gandhi on Nonviolence*
Document 175 *Surviving the Nazi Concentration Camps*

Answers and Analyses

1. **A** (History) The entry of the United States into the war is discussed on page 751. There it states that the *sinking of four American merchant ships* by German U-boats, in addition to the Zimmermann telegram, encouraged the United States to enter the war.

2. **H** (History) According to page 759, *Lenin also used terror as a weapon against his opponents . . . A secret police force . . . arrested anyone considered an "enemy of the revolution."*

 TEST-TAKING TIP

Even if students do not remember the specific fact being tested, they should still rely on their general historical knowledge to aggressively eliminate choices. In general, communist governments do not grant more personal freedoms, and the Russians faced hardships during the early years of communist power. Therefore choices F and G can be eliminated.

---

3. **C** (Economics) According to page 771, *The automobile had perhaps the greatest impact on European and American society . . . People could now move more easily from place to place . . . Americans traveled farther afield on vacations and moved from rural areas to cities.*

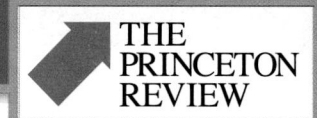

Standardized Test Practice

Directions: Choose the *best* answer to each of the following multiple choice questions. If you have trouble answering a question, use the process of elimination to narrow your choices. Write your answers on a separate piece of paper.

1. **The United States did not enter World War I until 1917. Which of the following was the most important factor in convincing the American public to support the war?**

   A German submarine attacks against American merchant ships

   B Continued loss of troops and land by the Russian army

   C Failure of the British and French to defeat Germany

   D The threat of a German invasion

   > **Test-Taking Tip:** This question requires you to remember a *fact* about World War I. Since the majority of Americans favored an isolationist policy, answer C is not a strong enough reason to change public opinion.

2. **Under the Communist government established by Lenin, which of the following changes were made to Russian society?**

   F Working conditions and wages improved.

   G People were granted more personal freedoms.

   H There was no tolerance for political dissent.

   J The economy improved because of public ownership.

   > **Test-Taking Tip:** Eliminate answers that you know are incorrect. Lenin's policy of "war communism" placed more *restrictions* on people, which is the opposite of answer G.

3. **Which of the following new technologies, developed in the 1920s, had the greatest impact on settlement patterns in the United States?**

   A The radio

   B The semiconductor

   C The automobile

   D The motion picture

   > **Test-Taking Tip:** The important phrases in this question are *greatest impact* and *settlement patterns*. Although the radio certainly had an important effect on modern life, it is not the answer most closely related to *settlement patterns*.

4. **The rise of dictatorial governments in Italy and Germany in the 1920s and 1930s was a result of all of the following EXCEPT**

   F the land divisions created under the Treaty of Versailles.

   G middle-class fears of social disorder.

   H severe economic downturns.

   J the new appeal of religion.

   > **Test-Taking Tip:** Be careful—questions containing the words NOT or EXCEPT are a common source of error. Remember, three choices *will* fit with the question. Choose the answer that *does not* fit.

Read the passage below and answer questions 5 and 6 that follow.

Mohandas K. Gandhi was a pacifist. In keeping with his beliefs, Gandhi used protest methods based on civil disobedience, or the refusal to obey laws that are considered unjust.

In 1930 Gandhi protested the salt tax. First he led thousands of his followers on a 200-mile march from Ahmadabad to the sea, where they made salt from sea water. One month later, Gandhi openly defied British authority by wading into the sea and picking up a lump of salt. Gandhi and thousands of followers were eventually arrested by the British.

5. **The movement for freedom from British rule in India was similar to the American Revolution in which of the following ways?**

   A   Both used nonviolence as a means to achieve freedom.

   B   Both involved long marches to gain attention.

   C   Both were fueled by British arrest of a local leader.

   D   Both used a tactic of a symbolic protest over the taxation of a common food.

> **Test-Taking Tip:** This question asks for a *comparison.* Although it is clear from the passage that *nonviolence* was a strategy used in the movement for freedom in India (answer A), this statement is *not* true for the American Revolution. Choose the answer that applies to *both* conflicts.

6. **Gandhi's protest against the British tax on salt resulted in**

   F   Gandhi's arrest and execution.

   G   no action by the British.

   H   Gandhi's arrest and the arrest of thousands of his followers.

   J   the British leaders repealing the salt tax.

> **Test-Taking Tip:** Make sure your answer is supported by information in the passage. For example, choice F asks you to draw a conclusion from information not given, and thus is incorrect.

7. **Which of the following was a turning point in Europe during World War II?**

   A   The Munich Conference

   B   The Spanish Civil War

   C   The defeat of the Germans by the Russians at Stalingrad

   D   The bombing of Pearl Harbor

> **Test-Taking Tip:** Be aware of the order of events asked about in a question. This question specifically asks about World War II in Europe. Both choices A and B are events that occured before the war had begun, and are thus incorrect.

 STOP

Tested Objectives

Questions	Objective
1	Making Generalizations
2, 4	Evaluating Information
3	Drawing Conclusions
5	Making Inferences
6, 7	Analyzing Information

4. **J** (History) The rise of fascism is discussed on pages 781–785. There it states that Italians *were outraged that the Paris peace treaties had not given Italy huge portions of territory from the Central Powers.* Further, in Italy *The value of the lira declined steadily, the price of bread rose,* leading to unrest. Likewise, the German government had *serious economic problems,* and fear of communists encouraged Germans to give Hitler wide authority.

 THE PRINCETON REVIEW **TEST-TAKING TIP**

Students can often answer EXCEPT and NOT questions by association. All of these choices are associated with the events of the 1920s and 1930s in Italy and Germany, with the exception of choice J. Religious concerns had very little to do with the rise of fascism, so this is the choice that does NOT fit with the others.

5. **D** (History) Each of the choices can be found in the excerpt, but only choice D is true of the American Revolution as well.

6. **H** (History) According to page 803, the British *did arrest thousands of* [Gandhi's] *follow-ers . . . To quell the mounting protests, they arrested* [Gandhi] *a month later.*

7. **C** (History) Students can answer questions by process of elimination. Choice A and B occurred in Europe but took place before the war had begun. Although U.S. involvement was critical to the war's outcome, choice D took place in the Pacific, not Europe. Thus, choice C is the obvious answer.

If time does not permit teaching each chapter in Unit 8, you may use the Unit Digest Transparencies and Chapter Digest Audiocassettes with accompanying activities and tests.

Introducing the Unit

Unit 8 focuses on the political trends of the post-World War II era, including the origins and effects of the cold war; decolonization in Asia, Africa, and the Middle East; and the decline of communism and the end of the cold war since 1989.

Unit Objectives

After reading Unit 8, students will be able to:

1. summarize the causes and impact of the cold war.
2. describe conflicts in Asia and the region's emergence as an economic powerhouse.
3. analyze the legacy of colonial rule in Africa and the challenges facing that continent.
4. examine the rival nationalisms of the Middle East and the region's search for peace.
5. identify political and economic trends in Latin America.
6. analyze factors that are leading toward globalization.

GLENCOE
TECHNOLOGY

Glencoe World History Primary Source Document Library
Use the CD-ROM to access primary source documents related to the 20th-century balance of power.

The Contemporary World

See pages 1026–1027 for primary source readings that accompany Unit 8.

Then & Now *International tension continued after World War II. Two blocs of nations aligned themselves behind the United States and the Soviet Union to dominate world politics. The two sides fought a cold war using economic powers, diplomacy, espionage, and the threat of nuclear war. When the cold war ended, leaders struggled to address the long-standing problems of nationalism, poverty in the developing nations, unequal distribution of resources, and environmental damage.*

The pace of scientific and technological change quickened. Satellite communications and computers linked in a global network offered undreamed of challenges and opportunities. When you turn on your computer, remember that it has been just a few years since this technology was invented. No one can guess the nature or degree of change it will bring to your future.

A Global Chronology

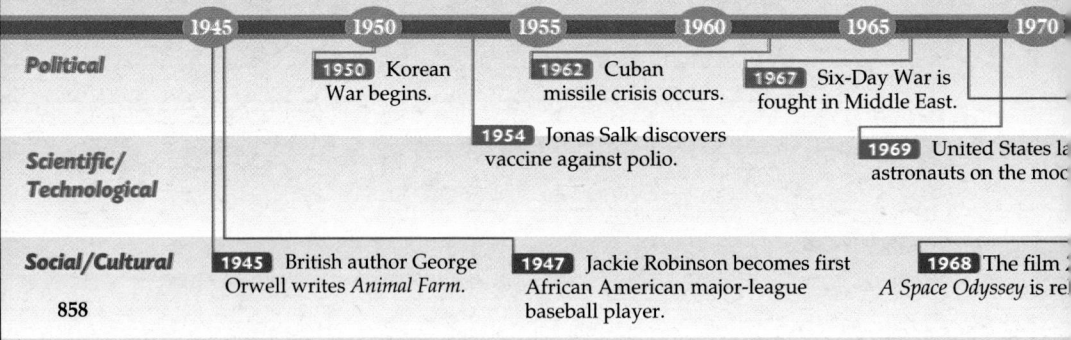

	1945	1950	1955	1960	1965	1970
Political		**1950** Korean War begins.	**1962** Cuban missile crisis occurs.		**1967** Six-Day War is fought in Middle East.	
Scientific/ Technological			**1954** Jonas Salk discovers vaccine against polio.		**1969** United States la astronauts on the moc	
Social/Cultural	**1945** British author George Orwell writes *Animal Farm.*	**1947** Jackie Robinson becomes first African American major-league baseball player.		**1968** The film *A Space Odyssey* is re		

858

Declaring Independence In this unit, students will learn about the problems faced by the newly independent nations of Africa, the Middle East, and Asia, as well as efforts by Latin American countries to end their economic dependency on the industrialized nations.

Point out to students that the nations that have emerged from colonial rule since World War II won their independence nearly 200 years after the United States became the first colony in modern history to become a sovereign nation. What are the main problems that newly independent nations face in the modern world? *(Answers will vary. Students may say that setting up a representative*

Computer Pentium chip

History and You

In the twentieth century, the space race developed as a competition between countries to excel in developing space technology, resulting in the landing of a man on the moon.

To better understand this time period, view videodisc Chapter 8: *The Moon Landing* in **Turning Points in World History.**

| 1975 | 1980 | 1985 | 1990 | 1995 | 2000 |

1973 U. S. troops leave Vietnam; oil embargo begins.

1989 Berlin Wall falls.

1991 Soviet Union breaks up; cold war ends.

1993 Czechoslovakia divides into Czech Republic and Slovakia.

1971 Invention of the microprocessor launches computer revolution.

1986 Disaster at USSR's Chernobyl nuclear power plant leaks radiation into the atmosphere.

1999 The world population reaches six billion.

1978 John Paul II becomes first pope from Poland.

859

government and creating a vigorous, independent economy are main challenges.) How do the challenges facing new nations today differ from those faced by the United States after 1776? (Answers will vary. Students may say that the economy was simpler in the 1700s; the United States did not have to worry about the technology gap. On the other hand, as the world's first constitutional democracy the United States had to pioneer an untested system of government.) How did the cold war affect the transition of many colonies to independence? (Answers will vary. Some students may realize that in Vietnam, Algeria, and elsewhere independence movements backed by the Soviet Union were opposed by the United States and its allies, leading to bloody wars.)

History and the Humanities

- Focus on World Art Print
- •24, Bridget Riley. *Current*
- World History and Art Transparencies
- •43 *The Persistence of Memory*
- •47 *Iranian Mihrab*
- •48 *The Twelve Tribes of Israel*
- •50 *Diego and I*
- •51 *Vietnam Memorial*
- World Music: Cultural Traditions, Lessons 1, 2, 3, 4, 5, 6

ABCNEWS INTERACTIVE™

VIDEODISC
Turning Points in World History

Side Two
Chapter 8

Title: *The Moon Landing*
Ask: Competition between what two countries led to the space race? *(the United States and Soviet Union)*

Visualizing History

Computers have revolutionized the world economy. A single pentium chip holds more computing capacity than did the earliest mainframe computers.

Glencoe Literature Library

The following literature from the **Glencoe Literature Library** may enrich this unit:
A House for Mr. Biswas by V.S. Naipaul
Nectar in a Sieve by K. Markandaya
One Day in the Life of Ivan Denisovich by A. Solzhenitsyn

The Spread of Ideas

TEACH

Introduction

This feature focuses on the political consequences of the development of modern international communications through satellite broadcasting and the Internet.

Background Notes

Linking Past and Present

The early days of the space race that was triggered by the Soviet launching of *Sputnik I* are the subject of Tom Wolfe's novel *The Right Stuff* and the popular film by the same title. Students interested in learning more about the period may want to read the book or watch a video of the movie.

Geography

Movement The United States is the leading source of television programs and films for the world market. Many countries have taken steps to limit the consumption of American cultural products in order to support their own film and television industries. Attempts by European nations to limit imports from the United States have led to conflicts under GATT (General Agreement on Tariffs and Trade), which seeks to open markets and reduce trade restrictions.

The Spread of Ideas

Communications

The invention of writing reshaped history. So did Johannes Gutenberg's use of movable type. Today electronics technology is moving communications forward at a startling rate. Two of the biggest changes have been the linking of people around the world via satellite broadcasts and the creation of a vast computer network known as the Internet.

The United States
Satellite Communications

In October 1957, a special announcement interrupted radio broadcasts across the United States. "Listen now … for the sound which forever separates the old from the new," said the broadcaster. Then a transmission from outer space—an eerie beep … beep … beep.

The former Soviet Union had taken the lead in space exploration by launching a tiny communications satellite named *Sputnik I*. A crudely simple device by today's standards, the first satellite could do little more than beam back radio signals. In the cold war era, however, it sent shock waves through American society.

Three years later, the United States launched *Echo* and *Courier*. Instead of beeps, these satellites relayed telephone calls between Europe and the United States. In 1962, the United States launched *Telstar*—the first satellite to relay live television programs from one place to another. By the 1980s people around the world with satellite dish antennas could tune in to hundreds of television programs. The effect was revolutionary. Repressive governments in Eastern Europe and elsewhere could not legislate against free speech beamed down from the skies.

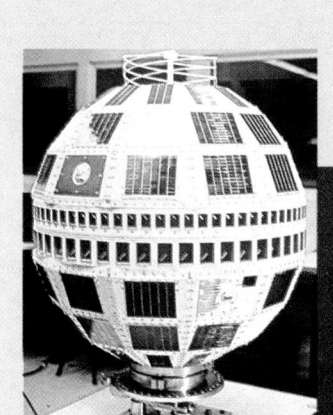

Telstar

Scientist and Soviet Sputnik I

860 Unit 8

COOPERATIVE LEARNING ACTIVITY

Multimedia Presentation Organize students into small groups and have each group select one medium of communication, such as films, television, radio, newspapers, CD-ROM, or the Internet. Then ask each group to choose a current international news story and create a news feature on that topic for the medium they have chosen. Have each group present its report, explaining the features of the presentation that were specially adapted to the medium they chose, and estimating the size and nature of the audience they hoped to reach. **L3**

China
Satellite Dishes

In the 1990s, satellite dishes sprouted like mushrooms across the People's Republic of China. Star TV, a pan-Asian satellite service, boomed down Mandarin-speaking rappers out of Hong Kong, English broadcasts of CNN News, NFL football games, and movies from Japan. The uncensored broadcasts enraged government officials. However, a 1993 ban against satellite dishes proved nearly impossible to enforce. Even while officials tried to dismantle the thousands of large dishes, kits for smaller dishes were being smuggled into the country.

The example of China was repeated in other nations with repressive policies. Iran, Myanmar (Burma), and other countries tried and failed to ban satellite reception. Even free governments, such as India, expressed concern about the "cultural invasion," but satellite television, a part of the information age, was here to stay.

Satellite dish

Africa
The Internet

A telephone line, a modem, and a personal computer—that is all someone needs to jump on the information super-highway. Internet Web sites can be accessed globally, connecting computer users on every continent.

In Africa, UNESCO is helping the Pan-African News Agency to link to the Internet. The project will help Africans overcome one of the legacies of imperialism—a communications system that linked African nations with European capitals rather than with each other. The driving force behind the project, a Senegalese journalist named Babacar Fall, sees the Internet as one of the keys to unlocking Africa's economic potential. "Without information," explained Fall, "there can be no development."

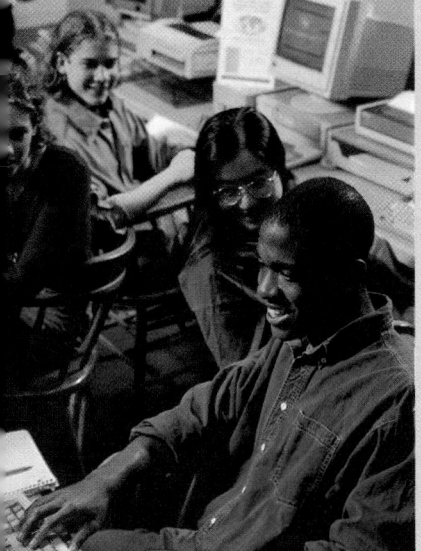

school students accessing the Internet

LINKING THE IDEAS

1. How did the revolution in satellite communications get its start?
2. How has this revolution affected nondemocratic political systems?

Critical Thinking

3. **Drawing Conclusions** How has the revolution in communications made our world more interdependent?

Who? What? Where? When?

Sputnik I The launching of *Sputnik I* in 1957 created near-panic in the United States. One senator called the Soviet breakthrough "a devastating blow to the prestige of the United States as the leader in the scientific and technical world," while *The New Republic* said it proved "that the Soviet Union gained a commanding lead in certain vital sectors of the race for world scientific and technological supremacy."

Cultural Diffusion

Hollywood Abroad The internationalization of the film industry has changed the content of Hollywood films. Many American films now earn as much or more money in foreign distribution as they do inside the United States. Since these films are either dubbed or subtitled, those based on action and adventure rather than dialogue tend to be more successful. This phenomenon in part explains the trend toward producing Hollywood blockbuster action thrillers.

ANSWERS TO LINKING THE IDEAS

1. The Soviet Union launched *Sputnik I* in 1957.
2. They have been unable to stop the flow of information from democratic nations that comes via satellites and the Internet.
3. Sharing of information has been greatly enhanced by satellite technology and the Internet, bringing all parts of the world into closer communication. Development and growth are frequently dependent on this shared information.

> A complete, 1-page lesson plan is provided for each section in the *Reproducible Lesson Plans* booklet.

The Cold War

CHAPTER RESOURCES

	Reproducible Resources	Multimedia Resources
Chapter Opener	Chapter Themes: Graphic Organizer 32 Historical Significance Chapter Activity 32	MindJogger Videoquiz
Chapter Enrichment	Vocabulary Activity 32* Time Line Activity 32 Mapping History Activity 32 History Simulation 32 Geography and History Activity 32 Source Reading 32 People in World History Profiles 61, 62 World Art and Music Activity 32 Enrichment Activity 32 Critical Thinking Activity 32 Skill Reinforcement Activity 32 Building Skills in Geography Workbook, Unit 1, Lesson 10 Performance Assessment Activity 32 Standardized Test Practice Workbook Activity 32 Inclusion for the Social Studies Classroom Strategies and Activities	Focus on World Art Print 24, Bridget Riley. *Current* World History and Art Transparency 43, *The Persistence of Memory* Mapping History Overlay Transparency 22, *The United Nations*; 23, *The Commonwealth of Nations* Chapter Transparency 32 Vocabulary PuzzleMaker Software World Music: Cultural Traditions, Lessons 3, 4 Turning Points in World History Lessons of War Communism and the Cold War World History Primary Source Document Library
Chapter Review/Reteaching	Reteaching Activity 32 Skill Reinforcement Activity 32 Spanish Chapter Summary 32	Chapter 32 Digest Audiocassette, Activity, Test* Vocabulary PuzzleMaker Software Interactive Tutor Self-Assessment Software MindJogger Videoquiz
Chapter Evaluation/Testing	Performance Assessment Activity 32 Chapter 32 Test, Forms A and B	ExamView® Pro Testmaker

0:00 OUT OF TIME? Assign the Chapter 32 Audiocassettes.

* Also available in Spanish

World History Primary Source Document Library
Make History Come Alive!
Engage your students with over 250 easily accessible primary source documents—available on this CD-ROM—that will give them real life insight into the important events of world history.

Block Schedule
Activities that are particularly suited to the block scheduling framework are identified throughout this chapter by the following designation.

KEY TO ABILITY LEVELS
Teaching strategies are coded for varying learning styles.
L1 **BASIC** activities for all students
L2 **AVERAGE** activities for average to above-average students
L3 **CHALLENGING** activities for above-average students
LEP **LIMITED ENGLISH PROFICIENCY** activities

Use Glencoe's *Presentation Plus!* multimedia teacher tool to easily present dynamic lessons that visually excite your students. Using Microsoft PowerPoint® you can customize the presentations to create your own personalized lessons.

 Interactive Lesson Planner

Planning has never been easier! Using this CD-ROM, organize your week, month, semester, or year with all the help you need. The **Interactive Lesson Planner** gives you access to all of the blackline masters that accompany *World History: The Human Experience.*

SECTION RESOURCES

Daily Objectives	Reproducible Resources	Multimedia Resources
Section 1 **The East-West Split** Identify the events that caused and heightened the cold war.	Lecture Notes 32-1 Reproducible Lesson Plan 32-1 Guided Reading Activity 32-1* Time Line Activity 32 Geography and History Activity 32 Section Quiz 32-1* Reading Essentials and Study Guide 32-1	Section Focus Transparency 32-1 Chapter Transparency 32 World History and Art Transparency 43, *The Persistence of Memory* Mapping History Overlay Transparency 22, *The United Nations* Vocabulary PuzzleMaker Software Interactive Tutor Self-Assessment Software Testmaker World Music: Cultural Traditions, Lesson 4 Communism and the Cold War
Section 2 **The Communist Bloc** Explain how the Soviet Union carried out Communist policies after the death of Stalin.	Lecture Notes 32-2 Reproducible Lesson Plan 32-2 Vocabulary Activity 32* Guided Reading Activity 32-2* Section Quiz 32-2* Reading Essentials and Study Guide 32-2	Section Focus Transparency 32-2 Interactive Tutor Self-Assessment Software Testmaker Communism and the Cold War
Section 3 **Western Europe** Describe how Western Europe moved toward greater political and economic unity during the cold war.	Lecture Notes 32-3 Reproducible Lesson Plan 32-3 Vocabulary Activity 32* Guided Reading Activity 32-3* History Simulation 32 Section Quiz 32-3* Reading Essentials and Study Guide 32-3	Focus on World Art Print 24 Section Focus Transparency 32-3 Mapping History Overlay Transparency 23, *The Commonwealth of Nations* Interactive Tutor Self-Assessment Software Testmaker
Section 4 **The United States and Canada** Trace the political and social changes that the people of the United States and Canada experienced during the cold war years.	Lecture Notes 32-4 Reproducible Lesson Plan 32-4 Guided Reading Activity 32-4* Reteaching Activity 32 Enrichment Activity 32 Section Quiz 32-4* Performance Assessment Activity 32 Spanish Chapter Summary 32 Reading Essentials and Study Guide 32-4	Section Focus Transparency 32-4 Vocabulary PuzzleMaker Software Interactive Tutor Self-Assessment Software Testmaker Communism and the Cold War Turning Points in World History Lessons of War

* Also available in Spanish

Chapter Activities

✓ Performance Assessment Activity

Another Berlin Wall Assign students to groups of four to create an expressive version of the Berlin Wall. Give each group a piece of poster board to use for their wall. On one side of the wall, have students use visuals, words, and graffiti to represent sentiments and beliefs held by the Soviet Union. On the other side, have students represent beliefs held by the West. Important events of the era should also be included. Have the students write an individual reflection listing and explaining each item included on their wall.

Possible Rubric Features

Accuracy of content information, concept attainment, originality and creativity of product, collaborative skills, thoroughness of explanation

• *For an additional activity, refer to Activity 32 in the* Performance Assessment Strategies and Activities *booklet.*

ACTIVITY

From the Classroom of...

Robert W. Gardner
New Canaan High School
New Canaan, CT

Preventing the Cold War

On the chalkboard, list the leaders of the United States and the Soviet Union who played key roles during the cold war era: Harry Truman, Joseph Stalin, Nikita Khrushchev, Leonid Brezhnev, Dwight Eisenhower, John Kennedy, Lyndon Johnson, and Richard Nixon.

Have partners pick an issue, event, or crisis faced by these leaders during the cold war. One student analyzes the problem from the point of view of the American president at the time, the other from the perspective of the Soviet leader. Have students attempt to negotiate a solution to the problem and describe it in a paragraph.

Have pairs present the problem, the world leaders they represent, and the solution they agreed on. Then have the class discuss whether the cold war could have been avoided, or at least ameliorated.

MULTIPLE LEARNING STYLES

Verbal/Linguistic
Have students obtain and read short selections from a collection of *samizdat*—underground literature circulated by Soviet dissidents.

Logical/Mathematical
Have students debate the following proposition: The United States and the Soviet Union were equally to blame for the cold war.

Visual/Spatial
Have students create a poster, based on conditions in the early days of the cold war, warning Americans against the "Communist menace."

Auditory/Musical
Have students listen to a tape or CD of music from the early era of rock and roll, featuring such performers as Chuck Berry and Elvis Presley. Discussion might focus on why this music aroused so much opposition from mainstream America at the time.

GLENCOE'S ASSESSMENT ADVANTAGE

Use the following to easily assess student learning in a variety of ways.

- Performance Assessment Strategies and Activities
- Section Quizzes
- Chapter and Unit Tests
- Interactive Tutor Self-Assessment Software
- Testmaker Software
- MindJogger Videoquiz
- SAT/SAT II Test Practice
- worldhistory.glencoe.com

Additional Resources

Teacher's Corner

INDEX TO NATIONAL GEOGRAPHIC MAGAZINE

The following articles relate to this chapter:

- "Kaliningrad," by Priit J. Vesilind, March 1997.
- "The New Saigon," by Tracy Dahlby, April 1995.
- "East Europe's Dark Dawn," by Jon Thompson, June 1991.
- "Bikini: A Way of Life Lost," by William S. Ellis, June 1986.

NATIONAL GEOGRAPHIC SOCIETY PRODUCTS AVAILABLE FROM GLENCOE

To order the following, call Glencoe at 1-800-334-7344:

- *GTV: The American People (Videodisc)*
- *GTV: A Geographic Perspective on American History (Videodisc)*

ADDITIONAL NATIONAL GEOGRAPHIC SOCIETY PRODUCTS

To order the following, call National Geographic at 1-800-368-2728:

- *1945–1989: The Cold War (Video)*
- *Capitalism, Socialism, Communism Series: Communism (Video)*
- *Europe: The Road to Unity (Video)*
- *Racing for Home: The Jackie Robinson Story (Video)*

Access National Geographic's new dynamic MapMachine Web site and other geography resources at:

- http://www.nationalgeographic.com/
- http://www.nationalgeographic.com/maps/

BIBLIOGRAPHY

Literature of the Period
Ellison, Ralph. *The Invisible Man.* New York: Random House, 1952. An idealistic young African American man meets disappointment in Harlem.

Readings for the Student
le Carré, John. *The Spy Who Came in from the Cold.* New York: Coward-McCann, 1964. Classic espionage fiction set in postwar Europe.

Readings for the Teacher
Patterson, Thomas G. *On Every Front: The Making and Unmaking of the Cold War.* New York: Norton, 1992. Objective explanation of the motives and tactics of both sides.

WORLD HISTORY Online

Use our Web site as an additional resource. All essential content is covered in the Student Edition.

You and your students can visit the *World History: The Human Experience* Web site at worldhistory. glencoe.com The student text directs students to the Web site for the following options:

- **Chapter Overviews**
- **Student Web Activities**
- **Self-Check Quizzes**

Answers are provided for you in a link entitled "Web Activity Lesson Plan." Additional Web Resources, Interactive Puzzles, and content updates are also available.

Visit the Glencoe Web site at socialstudies. glencoe.com for social studies activities, updates, and links to other resources.

LOCAL OBJECTIVES

_____
_____
_____
_____
_____
_____
_____
_____
_____
_____
_____
_____
_____
_____
_____
_____
_____
_____
_____

Chapter Themes are listed by section on this chapter opening page of the Student Edition. A corresponding theme-based activity is available under "TEACH," and a theme-based question is asked in the Section and Chapter Assessments.

Storyteller

Historical Setting The Allies had made a mistake by failing to arrange for a safe land corridor through East Germany to West Berlin. But their prompt, decisive action in supplying the city by airlift during the Berlin blockade was an important cold war victory for the West.

Historical Significance

Answers: *the lowering of the iron curtain in Eastern Europe; the division of Germany; the Berlin blockade; the formation of rival military and economic alliances*

It led to an arms race and to competition by the superpowers for power and influence on a global scale.

Have students use the **Chapter 32 Overview** at worldhistory. glencoe.com as a prereading and postreading exercise for understanding chapter content.

Chapter

32

1945–1979

The Cold War

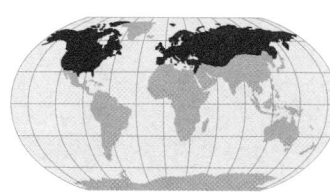

Chapter Themes

▶ **Conflict** A cold war develops between the United States and the Soviet Union, the two superpowers after World War II. *Section 1*
▶ **Change** The Soviet Union tries to move away from the legacy of Stalin while maintaining its control over Eastern Europe. *Section 2*
▶ **Regionalism** Western European democracies develop closer regional unity. *Section 3*
▶ **Cooperation** The United States and Canada build strong economies and forge closer ties. *Section 4*

Storyteller

In 1948 the city of West Berlin was an island in the middle of a hostile sea. The Soviets had cut off all land routes into the German city in the hope of driving out the Western Allies. For 11 months the United States airlifted food to 2 million stranded residents in West Berlin.

One day while his plane was on the ground in West Berlin, an American pilot, Lieutenant Gale S. Halvorsen, met a group of German children. Although they had received few sweets to eat during the blockade, they did not beg. He told them to wait for his plane at the end of the airport runway the next day. The children came, and, to their delight, packets of gum and chocolate showered down from Halvorsen's plane.

Soon other pilots joined "Operation Little Vittles," and the crowds of children grew. The children named Halvorsen "the Chocolate Pilot."

Historical Significance

What developments led to a cold war between the Western democracies and the Soviet Union? How did this East-West split affect world affairs during the next 40 years?

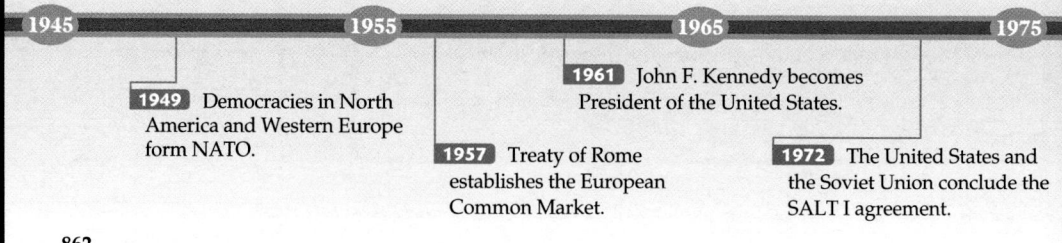

1945	1955	1965	1975

1949 Democracies in North America and Western Europe form NATO.

1957 Treaty of Rome establishes the European Common Market.

1961 John F. Kennedy becomes President of the United States.

1972 The United States and the Soviet Union conclude the SALT I agreement.

862

Location Ask students to locate Moscow, Berlin, Bonn, Paris, and London in the Atlas of their textbooks or on a wall map. What were the Eastern European countries that fell behind the iron curtain? *(Albania, Bulgaria, Czechoslovakia, East Germany, Hungary, Poland, Romania, Yugoslavia)* **L1**

Visualizing History Point out that
May Day has been the "labor day"
for Socialist and Communist countries since 1889. What message is
conveyed by a parade like this one?
(that the country is prepared militarily;
it has the latest weapons; its people are
united behind it) Kremlinologists used
to study the lineup of leaders at
these parades to see, by their positions (or nonappearance), who was
in favor and who was not.

Visualizing History During the Soviet era, vast numbers of military vehicles and marchers paraded past Soviet leaders in Moscow's famous Red Square to celebrate May Day (May 1st), the Communist workers' holiday.

✔ Performance Assessment

Refer to the activity on page 862C of the Planning Guide.

📁 For an additional activity, refer to Activity 32 in the *Performance Assessment Strategies and Activities* booklet.

WORLD HISTORY Online

Chapter Overview

Visit the *World History: The Human Experience* Web site at **worldhistory.glencoe.com** and click on *Chapter 32—Chapter Overview* to preview the chapter.

Your History Journal

Interview people who can remember the early period of the cold war. Evaluate the reliability of their accounts by ana-lyzing their background, biases, and closeness to the events.

Using Your History Journal

Students may want to make an audiocassette or videotape of their interview.

GLENCOE TECHNOLOGY

💿 **VIDEODISC**
Use MindJogger to pre-view chapter content.

MindJogger Videoquiz

Chapter 32
Disc 4 Side B

 Also available in VHS.

Chapter 32 *The Cold War* 863

✚ EXTRA CREDIT PROJECT

Report Almost as soon as the war ended, the Allies began trials of several leading Nazis at Nuremberg, Germany. The men were accused of murder, enslavement, and other crimes against humanity. Have students research and report on the Nuremberg trials and their out-come. They should also deal with the contro-versy surrounding the trials—the first in which a nation's leaders were tried for war crimes.

SECTION THEME

▶ **Conflict** A cold war develops between the United States and the Soviet Union, the two superpowers that emerged after World War II.

Guide to Reading

For reading strategies to help students read effectively see pages 12–13. Have students think about the main head as they read the subheads.

Vocabulary Pre-check

 Use the Vocabulary PuzzleMaker for Chapter 32 to create a crossword puzzle to reinforce section terms. **L1 LEP**

Use Vocabulary Activity 32 to introduce vocabulary terms. **L1 LEP**

FOCUS

Section Objective

Identify the events that caused and heightened the cold war.

BELLRINGER
Motivational Activity

 Before taking roll at the beginning of the class period, project Section Focus Transparency 32-1 and have students answer the activity questions. Discuss students' responses.

This activity is also available as a blackline master.

Section 1

The East-West Split

Guide to Reading

Read to Find Out
Main Idea *Key events caused and heightened the cold war.*

▶ **Terms to Define**
superpower, cold war, satellite, iron curtain, containment, arms race, ideology, bloc

▶ **People to Meet**
Joseph Stalin, Harry S Truman, George C. Marshall

▶ **Places to Locate**
San Francisco, Greece, West Berlin

The Storyteller

Nikita Khrushchev recalled the beginning of the arms race: "We are surrounded by American air bases.... For many years after the war, bombers were to represent the major threat in our enemy's arsenal of weapons. It took time and a great deal of work for us to develop a bomber force on our own.... Two of our famous designers ...

developed the MiG-15, which in time was acknowledged as the best jet fighter in the world.... However, our superiority was short-lived. During the Korean War the U.S. started making a jet fighter that was better than the MiG-15, and soon the Americans ruled the air over Korea."

—from *Khrushchev Remembers, The Last Testament*, translated and edited by Strobe Talbott, 1974

Nikita Khrushchev

The United States and the Soviet Union emerged from World War II as the world's two superpowers. No other countries were equal to them in military power or political influence. Differences in political beliefs and policies soon pulled the two superpowers apart and led to a struggle between them known as the cold war. In the cold war, each superpower sought world influence by means short of total war. This was because the possibility of nuclear war made the costs of a "hot" war too high. The "weapons" used in the cold war included the threat of force, the use of propaganda, and the sending of military and economic aid to weaker nations.

The United Nations

In the closing months of World War II, the Allies started planning for the postwar world. To handle future global problems, they had agreed at Yalta to replace the League of Nations with the United Nations, a new, permanent international organization. The purpose of the United Nations (UN) was to maintain peace by guaranteeing the security of member nations. It would foster good relations among nations based on the principles of equal rights and self-determination. It would also encourage cooperation on economic, cultural, and humanitarian problems.

In April 1945, representatives from 50 nations gathered in **San Francisco** to draft the Charter of the United Nations, which was completed and signed in June. The United Nations, headquartered in New York City, held its first sessions in 1946.

Although the UN Charter provided for six major bodies, it assigned the bulk of power to only two of them—the Security Council and the General Assembly. The Security Council, established to decide diplomatic, political, and military disputes, was made up of 11 members. The five permanent members were Great Britain, China, France, the

---

SECTION RESOURCES

Reproducible Masters
- Lecture Notes 32-1
- Reproducible Lesson Plan 32-1
- Guided Reading Activity 32-1
- Time Line Activity 32
- Geography and History Activity 32
- Section Quiz 32-1
- Reading Essentials and Study Guide 32-1

Transparencies
- Section Focus Transparency 32-1
- Chapter Transparency 32
- World History and Art Transparency 43, *The Persistence of Memory*
- Mapping History Overlay Transparency 22, *The United Nations*

Multimedia
- Vocabulary PuzzleMaker Software
- Interactive Tutor Self-Assessment Software
- Testmaker
- World Music: Cultural Traditions, Lesson 4
- Communism and the Cold War

Visualizing History All seemed well when American and Soviet forces met at the Elbe River in April 1945. *What events in Eastern Europe changed the American attitude toward the Soviet Union?*

United States, and the Soviet Union. Each was given the right to veto any Security Council decision. The other six members served two-year terms. The General Assembly, the policy-making body, was made up of representatives from all UN member nations. Each nation had one vote.

The third body, the Economic and Social Council, oversaw the fights against poverty, ignorance, and disease. The fourth, the International Court of Justice, handled international legal disputes. The fifth, the Trusteeship Council, promoted the welfare of people in colonial territories and helped them toward self-rule. The sixth, the Secretariat, handled the UN's administrative work.

During the postwar period, the UN effectively resolved many crises. However, the right of veto given to the Security Council's permanent members made the UN powerless to resolve any dispute involving the United States and the Soviet Union. The United Nations became deadlocked. It was criticized as being a "debating society"—far from what the signers of the Charter had hoped it would be.

From Allies to Arch Enemies

After World War II, the Western Allies—the United States, Great Britain, and France—believed the best way to achieve security was to strengthen democracy and to build prosperous economies in Europe. The Soviets, however, had different goals. Historically, they had well-justified fears of invasion and had lost more than 20 million people in

World War II. The Soviet dictator **Joseph Stalin** wanted to establish pro-Soviet governments in Eastern Europe not only to prevent any future attacks but also to expand his empire. He made sure Eastern Europe's Communist parties were loyal to him and worked to strengthen their position throughout the region.

President Franklin D. Roosevelt had believed that postwar cooperation with Stalin was possible, although he was starting to change his mind shortly before his death in April 1945. In the months afterward, Roosevelt's successor, President **Harry S Truman**, and other leaders adopted a much darker view of Stalin. They concluded that the Soviet dictator wanted to control Eastern Europe with the same ruthlessness that he used to govern the Soviet Union.

The Iron Curtain

Eastern Europe thus became the first region where Soviet and Western interests came into conflict. In Albania and Yugoslavia, local Communist parties, which had led the resistance against Axis forces in their countries, took control with little help from the Soviets. In Poland, Romania, and Bulgaria, where Soviet troops were in full command, the Soviet Union made sure that government ministries included Communists. Later, breaking his promise made at Yalta, Stalin refused to allow free elections. Non-Communists were ousted from governments, and Communists took charge. By 1947, most of the nations of the region had become Soviet satellites, controlled by the Soviet Union.

Chapter 32 *The Cold War* **865**

Chapter 32 *The Cold War* **865**

Map Study

Answer
Austria, Finland, Republic of Ireland, Spain, Sweden, Switzerland

Map Skills Practice

Reading a Map What Communist nation did not join the Warsaw Pact? *(Yugoslavia)*

Regionalism Ask students to explain how the circumstances of Soviet expansion differed in: (1) Albania, Yugoslavia, and Czechoslovakia; (2) Poland, Romania, Bulgaria, and Hungary; and (3) East Germany. *(1: Local Communists took control; 2: Soviet troops occupied during the war; 3: originally agreed on as the Soviet zone.)* **L3**

Who? What? Where? When?

Harry S Truman, a little-known senator from Missouri before he became Franklin Roosevelt's Vice President, had relatively little experience in foreign affairs. When he succeeded to the presidency on Roosevelt's death, he had been Vice President only 82 days and had met with the President just twice.

Independent Practice

 Guided Reading Activity 32-1 **L1**

Time Line Activity 32

Geography and History Activity 32

Literature Have students read George Orwell's *Animal Farm*, the satire of Russian totalitarianism. Some of them may want to read selected portions to the class for discussion. **L2**

Europe 1945–1955

Warsaw Pact member
Communist nation outside Soviet bloc
Neutral nation
NATO member

Map Study
After World War II, Europe became divided between the Soviet and Western spheres of influence.
Place What nations of Europe remained neutral?

Stalin's actions in Eastern Europe convinced President Truman that the United States had to resist further Soviet moves. Truman was backed by British statesman Winston Churchill. In March 1946, Churchill had first used the phrase "iron curtain" in a speech in Fulton, Missouri: "From Stettin in the Baltic to Trieste in the Adriatic an iron curtain has descended across the continent of Europe." Thereafter, iron curtain referred to the Soviet-made divider that split Europe into non-Communist Western Europe and Communist Eastern Europe.

Containing Communism

To counter any expansionist threat from the Soviet Union, the United States developed a new foreign policy in 1947. The idea for the new policy was presented in early 1947 by George Kennan, a State Department expert on the Soviet Union. Believing that the Soviets sought to expand their territory without war, he suggested a policy of containment—holding back the spread of communism. By standing firm, the United States hoped to keep communism inside its existing borders.

The Truman Doctrine

In the spring of 1947, President Truman applied the containment policy for the first time in the eastern Mediterranean. In **Greece**, local Communists were fighting a guerrilla war against the pro-Western monarchy. They were aided by Communists from neighboring Yugoslavia and Albania. The West feared that the fall of Greece to

---

MEETING SPECIAL NEEDS ACTIVITY

Study Strategy Events unfolded rapidly in the early years of the cold war. To understand the events that were happening in many parts of Europe, students can construct a chart. Along the side, suggest that they put the years 1945 to 1947, divided into two- or three-month intervals. Along the top, students should enter the names of the countries most involved in the cold war, either alphabetically or by region. At the appropriate place, they should then indicate important events in the cold war. **L2**

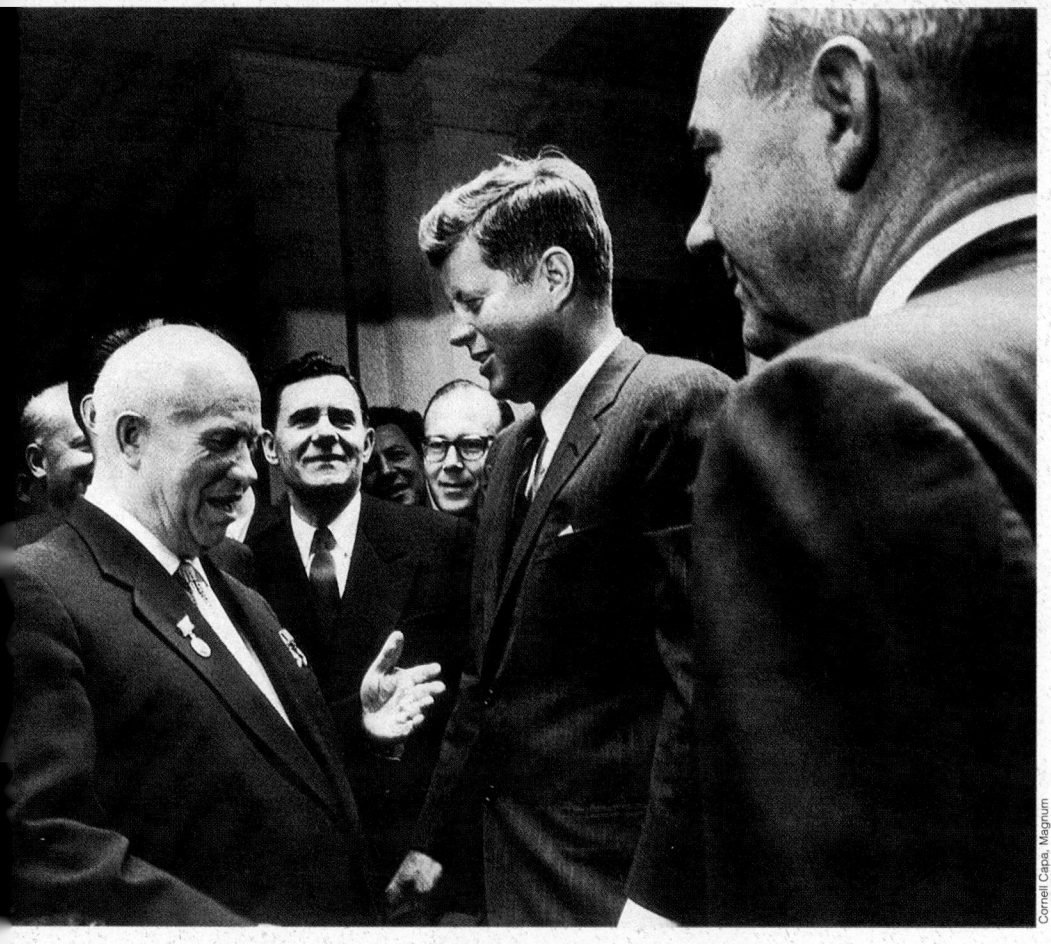

Cornell Capa, Magnum

Cold War

1961 Soviet Premier Nikita Khrushchev (left) d United States President John F. Kennedy held cold war meeting. Khrushchev insisted that ɔops of the Soviet Union's former World War II –France, Great Britain, and the United States— ave West Berlin. The Allies' part of Berlin was y inside East Germany, a nation separate from Germany and an ally of the Soviet Union. dy refused, believing that the Soviets would take l over West Berlin if the Allies departed. Two s later the Soviets shocked the people of both

Berlins—and the world—by building the Berlin Wall.

The Berlin Wall became an important symbol of the cold war. For nearly a half century after the end of World War II the world's two superpowers, the United States and the Union of Soviet Socialist Republics, dominated the world and fought a "cold" war. In fact, it was not always cold. The two powers fought a number of regional conflicts either directly or through allies, including the Korean and Vietnam Wars. In 1989 the Berlin Wall was torn down; in 1991, the Soviet Union crumbled and the cold war came to an end. ⊕

Chapter 32 *The Cold War* **867**

TEACH

Tell students that, although the United States could not prevent the building of the Berlin Wall, American leaders never abandoned their goal of reuniting Germany. Two years after this meeting, in June 1963, Kennedy appeared before a huge outdoor rally in West Berlin and delivered an address that included this famous declaration: "All free men, wherever they may live, are citizens of Berlin, and, therefore, as a free man, I take pride in the words 'Ich bin ein Berliner' (I am a Berliner)."

Linking Past and Present

Green Berets One tactic advanced by the West against the East during the cold war was counterinsurgency—organized military action to counteract revolutionary activity. A prime U.S. counterinsurgent force, the Green Berets, received its name because of its distinctive headgear, specifically authorized by President Kennedy.

VIDEODISC
Communism and the Cold War

Side One, Chapter 15
Frames 26867–29413
Title: *Berlin Wall*
Ask: What reason did the Soviets give for blockading East and West Berlin? *(They were attempting to keep agents from the West from coming into the Soviet Union.)*

you don't say...

"Iron curtain" was an expression that Winston Churchill popularized but did not originate. As long ago as the early 1800s, it was used to refer to a fireproof curtain in theaters, installed to prevent the spread of flames between the stage area and the audience.

communism would endanger Western influence in the eastern Mediterranean region.

Great Britain was the traditional defender of the eastern Mediterranean. Economic weaknesses, however, prevented the British from continuing their commitment. In February 1947, Great Britain asked the United States to assume British responsibilities in the area. A month later, Truman asked Congress for a $400 million aid program for Greece and Turkey. In asking Congress for support, Truman made a new statement of foreign policy that became known as the Truman Doctrine:

> **❝I believe that it must be the policy of the United States to support free peoples who are resisting attempted subjugation by armed minorities or by outside pressures.... [W]e must assist free peoples to work out their own destiny in their own way. ❞**

Congress approved Truman's aid request. With the Truman Doctrine, the United States took on international responsibilities as the leader of the Western world. American military aid would now be available to any nation threatened by communism. As a result, Greece was able to defeat the Communist guerrillas and the spread of communism in the eastern Mediterranean was blocked.

The Marshall Plan

Conditions in Europe posed immediate and long-term challenges for the United States. World War II had severely weakened European economies. The Truman administration feared that a European economic collapse would open Europe to communism. It believed that the military and economic security of the United States depended on a strong and democratic Europe.

Therefore, the United States government devised a new approach to aiding Europe. On June 5, 1947, Secretary of State **George C. Marshall** proposed an aid program known as the **Marshall Plan**. Its purpose was to restore "the confidence of European people in the economic future of their

Images of the Times

Rebuilding Europe

Fearing the spread of communism, the United States adopted strong economic programs to rebuild Europe after World War II. The Soviets responded with a rival plan in Eastern Europe.

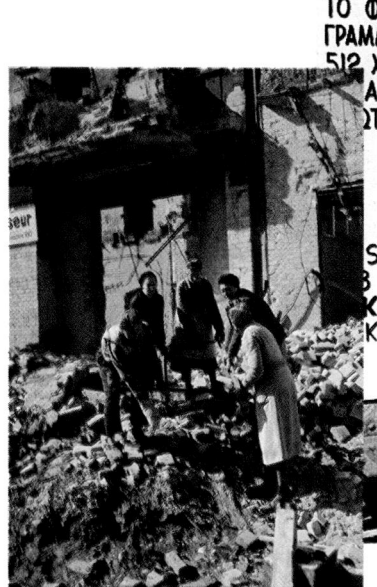

Devastation in the divided city of Berlin challenged the resolve of the West to restore not only the structures but the spirit of the people.

868

Images of the Times
Rebuilding Europe

By 1946 Europe had begun to recover from the war. But an extremely harsh winter in 1947 caused a setback. For this reason, economic aid such as the Marshall Plan was crucial. By the mid-1960s, European industrial output totaled more than two and a half times what it had been before the war.

wn countries." For the plan to work, Marshall urged a united effort to determine Europe's economic needs and how the United States could help.

Western European countries responded enthusiastically to the Marshall Plan; however, the Soviet Union refused to participate in the plan and forced its Eastern European allies to do the same. Despite their great need for economic aid, the Soviets felt they could not afford to give out information about their economy. They also opposed linking their Communist economy with capitalist ones.

The Marshall Plan was a great success. Western European nations worked together to boost productivity, reduce trade barriers, and use resources efficiently. They received about $13 billion in aid during the next four years. By 1951, Western Europe's economies were prospering, and Communist prospects in these countries had declined.

The Marshall Plan extended American influence in Western Europe and helped unite the region into a single economic group to counter the Soviets. In reaction to the Marshall Plan, in 1949 the Soviet Union set up a rival plan known as the Council for Mutual Economic Assistance, or COMECON. Eastern Europe was thus formed into a competing economic group led by the Soviet Union.

Germany Divided

In 1945, Germany had been divided into four zones, controlled by Great Britain, France, the United States, and the Soviet Union. The zones of the Western Allies included the western part of Germany, while the Soviet zone encompassed eastern Germany. The city of Berlin, deep within the Soviet zone, was also divided into four sectors.

WORLD HISTORY Online

Student Web Activity 32

Visit the *World History: The Human Experience* Web site at **worldhistory.glencoe.com** and click on **Chapter 32—Student Web Activities** for an activity relating to the Marshall Plan.

Modern Warsaw finally emerged from behind the iron curtain when Poland overthrew its Communist government in 1989.

Threatened by revolt, Greece received economic aid under the Truman Doctrine until the Marshall Plan went into effect.

REFLECTING ON THE TIMES

1. Why was it difficult for the United States to send supplies into Berlin in 1948?
2. What is the purpose of the large sign on the railway car delivering goods in Greece?
3. Why did the Soviet Union prevent its allies from participating in the Marshall Plan?

869

ANSWERS TO REFLECTING ON THE TIMES

1. The Soviet Union had cut off access by land.
2. to publicize the role of the United States in bringing about European recovery
3. The Soviets did not want to give out information about their economy, and they did not want to link their economies with the non-Communist West.

Cooperation The UN, which began with 51 members, now has 188. Have students research the changes in membership and what these changes have meant to the operation of the United Nations. **L3**

Who?What?Where?When?

Denazification After the war the Allies agreed that Nazis should be punished—a process called denazification. One aspect of this process consisted of trials of wartime leaders. But many low-level collaborators were also purged—some tried and executed or imprisoned, many simply fired from their jobs.

 VIDEODISC
Communism and the Cold War

Side One, Chapter 6
Frames 11768–13455
Title: *The Arms Race*
Subject: Development of the arms race between the United States and the Soviet Union
Ask: What was the arms race? *(It was a competition between the United States and the Soviet Union in the development of high-tech weaponry.)*

WORLD HISTORY Online

Have students use the **Chapter 32 Student Web Activity** at worldhistory.glencoe.com for in-depth study of the Marshall Plan.

Map Study

Answer

the Soviet zone

Map Skills Practice

Reading a Map In what zone was the port city of Bremen? (*U.S. zone*)

Linking Past and Present

NATO Although the Warsaw Pact came to an end in 1991, NATO continues to flourish. In 1999 three Warsaw Pact countries—the Czech Republic, Hungary, and Poland—were admitted to NATO.

ASSESS

Check for Understanding

Assign Section 1 Assessment as homework or as an in-class activity.

◻ Use Interactive Tutor Self-Assessment Software to review Section 1.

Evaluate

 Section Quiz 32-1

◻ Use the Testmaker to create a customized quiz for Section 1.

Occupation of Germany and Austria 1945

Map Study
Germany and Austria were divided into zones. In 1955, Austria reunited as a neutral country.
Place What zone surrounded Berlin?

Zones of Occupation

The Western Allies and the Soviets could not reach agreement on a final peace treaty for Germany. As relations with Stalin soured, the United States, Great Britain, and France decided to include their zones in the Marshall Plan as means to contain communism.

While the Soviets stripped their German zone of its industrial resources and equipment, the three Western powers aided their zones toward economic recovery. Free elections for local governments were held in the Western zones. The United States, Great Britain, and France also agreed to combine their sectors of Berlin to form what became known as the city of **West Berlin**. They also planned to form an independent West German state by joining their zones of occupation.

The Berlin Blockade

In June 1948, the Soviets tried to block this merger plan by cutting all land access from the West into West Berlin. Two million Berliners depended on the Western Allies for all their food, fuel, and other needs. The United States and other Western countries considered and rejected the idea of using force to regain access to Berlin. Instead, they came up with a plan to airlift needed supplies

to the isolated city.

To keep the city alive, at least 4,000 tons of supplies were needed every day. Airplanes surpassed this goal by landing every three minutes at West Berlin's two airports. At the peak of the airlift, 13,000 tons were landed in one day. The airlift would continue for 11 months. Its success finally forced the Soviets to lift the blockade in May 1949.

That same month, the Western Allies went ahead with their plans to form an independent West German state. A constitution was approved that set up a federal system of 10 states. In the fall of 1949, the Federal Republic of Germany, or West Germany, was proclaimed. Its capital was Bonn. The Soviets then set up the German Democratic Republic, or East Germany, with its capital East Berlin. Thus, Germany was divided into two separate countries.

New Alliances

Just before the Berlin blockade, another crisis had occurred in Europe. In February 1948, Czechoslovakia was taken over by Communists and incorporated into the Soviet alliance system. The Czechoslovak and Berlin crises heightened Western concerns about military defense. In April 1949, shortly before the end of the Berlin blockade, the North Atlantic Treaty Organization (NATO) was formed by the United States, Great Britain, France, Belgium, the Netherlands, Luxembourg, Italy, Portugal, Denmark, Iceland, Norway, and Canada. NATO expanded to include Greece and Turkey in 1952 and West Germany in 1955. Members of this military alliance agreed that an attack on one would be considered an attack on all. In response to NATO, the Soviet Union and its Eastern European allies signed a military agreement known as the **Warsaw Pact** in 1955.

Later events showed that the purpose of the Warsaw Pact was as much to strengthen the Soviet

---

MAKING CONNECTIONS ACTIVITIES

Military History The United States has stationed troops in Germany ever since the end of World War II. Have students research and report on the reasons for their presence; the location of the main bases; and troop totals and how they have varied over the years. **L2**

Daily Life At its height the cold war had a strong impact on many nonpolitical aspects of life, including sports. Have students research and report on how the cold war affected the Olympic Games. **L1**

hold on Eastern Europe as to defend it. Soviet troops stationed in Hungary under the terms of the Warsaw Pact were used to suppress a 1956 uprising there. In 1968 the Soviet Union appealed to the treaty to justify its invasion of Czechoslovakia, which had introduced a liberal form of communism.

Worldwide Struggle

The cold war soon turned into a global struggle. In 1949, the Soviets successfully exploded their first atomic bomb. International tensions further increased as the two superpowers engaged in an **arms race**, or a competition to strengthen their armed forces and weapons systems.

Meanwhile, communism made rapid advances in Asia. In the late 1940s, Communist governments came to power in China and North Korea. In 1950, the North Koreans, allied to the Soviet Union and Communist-ruled China, attacked South Korea, a pro-Western republic. Although the North Koreans were forced back to their territory, the Korean conflict fed Western fears that in communism, it faced a single, powerful enemy seeking world conquest.

Beginning in the 1950s, the cold war also came to be not only a test of military strength, but also a test of the superpowers' competing **ideologies**, or political and economic philosophies—democratic capitalism on the part of the United States, and communism on the part of the Soviet Union. Military buildups, space exploration, and local and regional conflicts around the globe became entangled in the cold war as the two superpowers sought to win support and to block gains by the other.

Germany

Germany became a critical flashpoint in the cold war during the 1950s and 1960s. Nikita Khrushchev (krush•CHAWF), who became Soviet leader in the mid-1950s, set out to test the resolve of the new United States President, John F. Kennedy, in 1961 by threatening to force the Allies out of West Berlin. Stating that the West would defend West Berlin's freedom, Kennedy bolstered the United States military presence, and Khrushchev did not act on his threats.

Meanwhile, large numbers of East Germans were fleeing to West Berlin, which was easily accessible to them. In an effort to halt the drain of its workforce, the East German government, with Soviet backing, built a concrete wall across the divided city in August 1961. The Berlin Wall stemmed the flow of East Germans fleeing communism and raised East-West tensions. It became a symbol of the cold war and the hostile confrontation between democracy and communism.

The Developing World

After the early 1960s, superpower competition directly affected developing nations in Asia, Africa, and Latin America. In most areas, such as in Africa and the Caribbean, the superpowers provided aid to their allies in the particular region. Sometimes—as in the case of the Soviet Union in Afghanistan and the United States in Vietnam—they became militarily involved themselves.

By the late 1970s, however, the division of the world into two **blocs**, or groups of nations, each headed by a superpower, was coming to an end. The United States, wary of military involvements, faced growing challenges to its hold on world markets. Western Europe and Japan, less dependent on the United States, were prosperous economic powers in their own right. The Soviet Union, faltering economically, was facing internal pressures for change. Finally, many smaller nations, aligned with neither superpower, were following their own paths of development. All of these events marked the move away from a world dominated by the superpowers to one in which there were many competing groups of countries.

Worldwide Struggle
What made the cold war a unique development?
It was a long struggle between global superpowers that involved all means short of all-out war. The conditions of the cold war were set by the superpowers' possession of nuclear weapons and their fear of mass destruction in the event of these weapons being used.

Reteach

Have students review the events that precipitated the cold war by brainstorming a list on the chalkboard and then putting the events in chronological order.

Reading Essentials and Study Guide 32-1

Enrich

Have students watch a video of a film made during the cold war such as *Fail Safe, Dr. Strangelove,* or *The Russians Are Coming! The Russians Are Coming!* Have them write an analysis of the film's view of U.S.–Soviet relations.

CLOSE

Have students list, in order, the American Presidents who held office during the cold war and the major events related to the cold war that took place during their administrations.

SECTION 1 ASSESSMENT

Main Idea
1. Use a diagram like the one below to identify key events that caused and intensified the cold war.

Recall
2. **Define** superpower, cold war, satellite, iron curtain, containment, arms race, ideology, bloc.
3. **Identify** Joseph Stalin, Harry S Truman, George C. Marshall, the Marshall Plan, NATO, Warsaw Pact.

Critical Thinking
4. **Analyzing Information** What geographic factor made the Berlin blockade possible?

Understanding Themes
5. **Conflict** What were some of the "weapons" of the cold war? What did the superpowers hope to accomplish with them?

SECTION 1 ASSESSMENT ANSWERS

1. Key events: iron curtain; U.S. containment policy; Truman Doctrine; Marshall Plan; Berlin Blockade; NATO formed; arms race; military buildups; local and regional conflicts; Soviet threat to force allies from West Berlin; creation of Berlin Wall

2. All terms are defined in the Glossary.
3. Joseph Stalin, 865; Harry S Truman, 865; George C. Marshall, 869; Marshall Plan, 869; NATO, 870; Warsaw Pact, 870
4. West Berlin was totally surrounded by the Soviet zone.

5. **CONFLICT** Weapons: transforming governments into Communist or democratic states; active military intervention; aid and trade links. Goals included extending actual rule or at least influence.

1955   1965   1975

1955 Nikita Khrushchev becomes the dominant leader in the Soviet Union.

1968 The Soviets invade Czechoslovakia.

1972 Soviet and American leaders hold summit meeting in Moscow.

Section 2

The Communist Bloc

Guide to Reading

Read to Find Out
Main Idea *The Soviet Union continued Communist policies after the death of Stalin.*

▶ **Terms to Define**
  peaceful coexistence, intercontinental ballistic missile (ICBM), dissident, detente

▶ **People to Meet**
  Nikita Khrushchev, Leonid Brezhnev, Josip Broz Tito, Alexander Dubček

▶ **Places to Locate**
  Yugoslavia, East Germany, Poland, Hungary, Czechoslovakia

The Storyteller

Peter Hauptman and Willi Pfeiffer had been best friends since childhood. Although their homes were only two blocks apart, they lived in different sectors of Berlin. Now, literally overnight, their frequent visits ended. The Soviet sector was walled off. Not just a barricade or a lowered gate, it was a wall, protected by barbed wire and concrete blocks. Peter stood on the western side of the wall, straining to catch a glimpse of Willi. But it was to no avail. Everyone living near the wall's eastern side had been forcibly relocated, and the nearby apartment doors and windows were sealed shut.

—adapted from *People and Politics: The Years 1960–1975,* translated and edited by Strobe Talbott, 1974

Children play near the Berlin Wall

The cold war affected the internal policies of the Soviet Union and its Eastern European satellites. During the late 1940s and early 1950s, Joseph Stalin believed that a full-scale conflict with the West was inevitable. To confront the West, the Soviet leader increased his control over the Soviet Union and Eastern Europe. He purged Communist parties of officials suspected of disloyalty. He also forbade writers and artists to use Western ideas in their works.

The Soviet Union

After World War II, Stalin worked to rebuild the Soviet Union's heavy industry and to boost its military strength. The Soviet Union surpassed its prewar rates of production in several major products, including coal, steel, and oil. It continued a high level of military spending and exploded its first nuclear bomb. In spite of the country's military prestige, life for the average Soviet citizen was difficult. Towns and cities destroyed by the war were rebuilt but consumer goods, food, and clothing remained in short supply because of high military spending.

Stalin died in March 1953. He was succeeded by a collective leadership of top Communist officials. **Nikita Khrushchev,** who served as Communist party secretary, emerged as the dominant leader in 1955.

De-Stalinization

In the following year, the 20th Congress of the Soviet Communist Party was held in Moscow. At a secret session, Nikita Khrushchev gave a controversial speech about Stalin. He denounced the Soviet dictator for the purges in the 1930s, in which thousands of loyal party members had been tortured

---

President Eisenhower (right) hosts Premier Nikita Khrushchev in Washington, D.C., in 1959. *What prevented the four-power summit meeting planned for May 1960 from taking place?*

and condemned to death or sent to labor camps. He also accused Stalin of creating a "cult of personality," in which he boosted his own image at the expense of the Communist party.

Khrushchev's anti-Stalin speech was part of a broader program of de-Stalinization, which he undertook from 1956 to 1964 to reverse some of the policies that had existed under Stalin. Khrushchev understood that many Soviet citizens wanted a relaxation of government controls and an improved standard of living. While keeping Stalin's Five-Year Plans and collective farms, he promised better wages and more consumer goods. He gave artists and intellectuals more freedom. He also reduced the terror of the secret police and freed many political prisoners from labor camps.

Cold War "Thaw"

By the mid-1950s, both American and Soviet leaders were interested in reducing cold-war tensions. Khrushchev called for a policy of peaceful coexistence in which the Soviets would compete with the West but avoid war. He stated the Soviet Union would surpass the West economically and encouraged other countries to follow the Communist model.

To make the Soviet Union more economically competitive, Khrushchev tried to boost production by improving working conditions. He sought to improve housing and to increase the production of consumer goods. The Soviet leader also put new emphasis on technological research. This paid off in 1957 with the launch of *Sputnik I,* the world's first space satellite. *Sputnik* stunned the United States and boosted the prestige of the Soviet Union and its leader.

Despite the cold war "thaw," both superpowers continued a massive military buildup. In the late 1950s, the Americans and Soviets successfully tested long-range rockets known as intercontinental ballistic missiles, or ICBMs, and added them to their arsenals. ICBMs for the first time could target locations in both countries. A nuclear war would result in what was known as mutual assured destruction—that is, the certain destruction of both nations.

Even as they pursued this deadly race, United States and Soviet leaders sought to maintain peace. Summit meetings were the most visible of many contacts between Soviets and the United States. United States President Dwight Eisenhower and Soviet Premier Khrushchev met in Geneva, Switzerland, in 1955 and again in 1959 at Camp David, in Maryland. They recognized the deadly threat of nuclear war and agreed on the need to end the arms race. They planned a four-power summit for Paris in May 1960 and Khrushchev invited Eisenhower to visit the Soviet Union later in the year. But shortly before the Paris summit, the Soviets shot down an American U-2 spy plane over their territory and captured its pilot. Facing criticism from the Soviet military, Khrushchev strongly

Footnotes to History

The Kitchen Debate
In 1959 Vice President Richard M. Nixon, on a tour of the Soviet Union, visited an exhibition of American products with Soviet leader Nikita Khrushchev. The two leaders soon got into a heated argument on the merits of capitalism versus communism. The argument became known as the "kitchen debate" because the two men were standing in front of a model kitchen display.

Chapter 32 *The Cold War* 873

TEACH

Guided Practice

THEME Change
After Stalin's death in 1953, the Soviet leadership instituted some changes to ease living conditions. What were the most important aspects of de-Stalinization? *(promises of higher wages and more consumer goods; more freedom for artists and intellectuals; a lessening of secret police activities; and the release from labor camps of many political prisoners)* **L1 LEP**

Visualizing History On this 1959 trip, Khrushchev dined at the White House, visited a farm in Iowa, and dropped in on a supermarket in San Francisco. In Hollywood he watched a rehearsal of the movie *Can Can,* later criticizing it as immoral.
Answer to Caption: *An American U-2 spy plane was shot down by Soviets.*

VIDEODISC
Communism and the Cold War

Side One, Chapter 14
Frames 24964–26834
Title: *Sputnik Launches the Space Race*
Subject: The beginning of the space race
Ask: Why did the United States panic when the Soviet Union unveiled *Sputnik*? *(The U.S. feared that the enemy was more technologically prepared.)*

COOPERATIVE LEARNING ACTIVITY

Press Conference Organize the class into two groups, one to represent reporters and the other to play the roles of President Eisenhower and his staff. The teams should research to plan questions and answers for a news conference after the announcement of the shooting down of the U-2 spy plane. Encourage students to address the larger issues of the cold war. The conference should be enacted as if it were actually happening, and you may want to videotape it. **L3**

denounced the United States and canceled Eisenhower's visit. Relations soon worsened further.

The Cuban Missile Crisis

The Soviet Union and the United States came to the brink of nuclear war in 1962. In 1961, Eisenhower was succeeded as United States President by John F. Kennedy, who adopted a dynamic foreign policy to impress the Soviets with American strength and boost American prestige abroad. Testing Kennedy's resolve, Khrushchev used pressure to try to remove the Allies from Berlin. Then in 1962 he secretly began to install nuclear missiles on Cuba 90 miles (145 km) from Florida. In his gamble, the Soviet leader hoped to offset American missiles based in Turkey that were aimed at the Soviet Union. He also wanted to get from Kennedy a promise not to overthrow Cuba's Communist government. Devising a strong response short of attack, Kennedy blockaded Cuba. Khrushchev then agreed to withdraw the missiles; and in return, Kennedy pledged not to invade Cuba.

The Cuban missile crisis was one of the most significant events in the cold war. Having come so close to nuclear conflict, the superpowers decided to establish a better relationship. In 1963, a telephone "hot line" linked Washington and Moscow to provide instant communication. That same year, the Soviets and the Western Allies also signed a treaty banning nuclear weapons tests in the atmosphere.

Meanwhile, Khrushchev's position within the Soviet Union weakened. In addition to his poor handling of the Cuban missile crisis, relations with China had soured, and Khrushchev's economic policies were in trouble. Heavy spending on technology, defense, and heavy industry had left little for improving agriculture and consumer goods. Far from surpassing the United States, the Soviet Union was forced to import grain from the United States. Sharply rising meat and butter prices provoked angry public demonstrations. In October 1964, Khrushchev was removed from office.

The Brezhnev Era

The Communist party chose a new collective leadership: Aleksei Kosygin (kuh•SEE•guhn) was premier and **Leonid Brezhnev** (BREHZH•NEHF) was general secretary of the party. By the mid-1970s, Brezhnev emerged as the dominant leader. He remained in control until his death in 1982.

Cautious and traditional, Brezhnev reversed Khrushchev's de-Stalinization policies. He clamped down again on intellectuals and dissidents—those who criticized the party or regime. Two prominent

dissidents refused to be silenced. Alexander Solzhenitsyn (SOHL•zhuh•NEET•suhn), author of many works including *The Gulag Archipelago*, an account of the horrors of Soviet prison camps, was eventually deported and settled in the United States. Dr. Andrei Sakharov (SAH•kuh•RAWF), scientist and developer of the Soviet hydrogen bomb, later denounced the arms race and was sentenced to internal exile in Gorki.

Brezhnev's military and economic policies were similar to Khrushchev's. Concerned that there was a missile gap with the United States, he greatly increased the Soviet nuclear arsenal and its supplies of conventional weapons. He felt that military power gave the Soviet Union a stronger position in world diplomacy.

Under Brezhnev, economic conditions, however, worsened in the Soviet Union. Heavy military spending stifled growth in other sectors of the economy. Soviet workers had to make do with outdated equipment. Technologically, many industries were at least 20 years behind the times. Consumer goods were shoddy and in short supply. Farmers were only one-sixth as productive as their American counterparts. Poor harvests forced the Soviet Union to again import grain from the West.

Detente

By 1972, Brezhnev was ready to reduce tensions with the West. He hoped to find a way to cut military spending without falling behind the United States militarily. He also needed access to Western technology, grain, and consumer goods.

The United States was ready for Brezhnev's policy of detente. Derived from the French word meaning "relaxation," detente referred to an improvement of American-Soviet relations. A 1972 summit meeting between Brezhnev and United States President Richard Nixon in Moscow began a period of detente that lasted seven years. The Brezhnev-Nixon summit led to the signing of the SALT (Strategic Arms Limitation Talks) treaty, under which both sides agreed to limit the number of nuclear warheads and missiles each country could maintain. SALT did not reduce the number of weapons or end the arms race; it did slow it significantly.

Detente did not end the rivalry between the United States and the Soviet Union. The countries continued to compete for influence in various parts of the world. In 1979, the Soviets invaded neighboring Afghanistan to reinforce local Communist control. The move shocked the West and marked the end of detente. It also drew the Soviet Union into a 10-year guerrilla war against tough Afghan

While the Soviets constructed the Berlin Wall in 1961, Russian and American tanks maneuvered within sight of each other. *What was the real purpose of the wall?*

nationalists. The occupation of Afghanistan drained the Soviet national treasury, brought about the deaths of thousands of young Soviet soldiers, and became extremely unpopular at home.

Soviet Satellites

For most of the cold war, the Soviet Union maintained tight control over its Eastern European satellites. The peoples of these nations resented Soviet domination, but were largely powerless against the secret police and Soviet troops.

Yugoslavia

After World War II, **Yugoslavia** became the only large Communist state in Eastern Europe to resist Soviet control. Its leader, **Josip Broz Tito**, had participated in the resistance against the Nazis. As much a nationalist as a Communist, Tito insisted on developing his own national policies. Angered by Tito's independence, Stalin expelled Yugoslavia from the international Communist movement. Throughout Eastern Europe, Stalin waged a propaganda war against what he called Titoism, or the

tendency of some Communists to place their national interests above those of the Soviet Union. With the support of his people, Tito resisted Soviet pressure, developed his own form of communism, held together the different religious and ethnic groups of the country, and won aid from the West. He led Yugoslavia until his death in 1980.

East Germany

Although it recovered from World War II more slowly than West Germany, **East Germany** became the most prosperous of the Soviet satellites. Its people deeply resented Soviet controls, however. In the aftermath of Stalin's death in 1953, East German workers went on strike and rioted when the government tried to lengthen the work day without an increase in wages. Soviet troops and tanks easily put down the revolt.

In the years that followed, nearly 3 million East Germans migrated to West Germany, by way of West Berlin, the only safe access available once the Soviets sealed the East German-West German border. A large percentage of the migrants were well-educated professionals who were attracted by West Germany's higher standard of living and greater

Chapter 32 *The Cold War* **875**

VIDEODISC
Communism and the Cold War

Side One, Chapter 10
Frames 17333–20021
Title: *Rebellion Behind the Iron Curtain*
Subject: Discussion of rebellions in Soviet satellite nations, Soviet reaction, and why the United States did not support the rebellion acts
Ask: Why would the Soviet Union not allow democratic reforms in Czechoslovakia and Hungary? *(due to the fear that the reform movements would spread into the Soviet Union)*

---

freedoms. This "brain drain" was an embarrassment to the Soviets and an economic blow to the nation.

East Germany's problems contributed to a new cold war crisis in 1959. By then, West Germany had recovered from the war and was fully armed with tanks, bombs, and guns. It also had nuclear weapons on its soil under the control of NATO command. Alarmed at this development, Khrushchev called for negotiations on European security and on a nuclear-free Germany. He also demanded that the Western powers withdraw from Berlin.

Frustrated by the lack of a settlement and the continuing flight of East Germans, Khrushchev ordered the construction of what became the notorious Berlin Wall. In 1961, East German soldiers began work on the wall, a massive concrete structure 26 miles (42 km) long and up to 15 feet (4.6 m) high, topped with electrified wire.

The stated purpose of the wall was to keep Westerners out, but its true purpose was to halt the exodus of East Germans from East Berlin. To escape to West Berlin, people now had to get past mined trenches, guard dogs, and self-activating guns. Then they had to scale the wall itself. Stories reached the West of heroic escapes, but scores of East Germans died trying to run to freedom. The Berlin Wall halted the flow of East German refugees, and it became the most visible and powerful physical symbol of the iron curtain.

Poland

Under Communist rule, **Poland** industrialized and, among the satellites, became second in manufacturing only to East Germany. Poles, however, resented Soviet controls. They were angered by the government's efforts to collectivize farms and by its anti-Catholic policies. In June 1956 workers demanding better wages rioted in the city of Poznan. Upheavals in other cities forced Poland's Communist leaders to remove hard-line officials from office.

Poland's new leader was Wladyslaw Gomulka (VLAH•dee•slah goh•MUL•kuh), a popular Communist who had been accused of anti-Soviet activities and jailed during the late 1940s. Gomulka freed political prisoners, ended forced collectivization, and eased relations with the Catholic Church. He retained close ties with the Soviet Union, however. By the mid-1960s many of the Polish freedoms had again been lost.

In the 1970s, there was a new wave of anti-government strikes, with workers demanding better living conditions, and political and economic reforms. Gomulka resigned under the pressure.

Continued economic problems led to food riots in 1976 and the growth of an underground anti-Soviet movement, aided by the Catholic Church.

Hungary

Hungary, a largely agricultural nation, experienced harsh Communist rule after 1947. The Hungarian government required peasants to join collective farms, and nationalized banking, trade, and industry. Central planners emphasized heavy industry, at the expense of consumer goods. The Communist leadership silenced or disbanded potential opposition groups, such as trade unions or other political parties. Catholic Church property was seized, and Church schools were taken over by the government. Opponents within the Communist party were purged and executed.

After Stalin's death in 1953, Hungary's Communist leaders eased controls for two years and then reimposed them when the economy did not reach its goals. Bitter opposition turned into full revolt in the fall of 1956. As in Poland, worker uprisings brought a liberal Communist government to power. However, Imre Nagy, the new Hungarian prime minister, went further than the Polish leaders. He announced Hungary's neutrality and its withdrawal from the Warsaw Pact. This raised the danger the Soviet Union feared most—the loss of Soviet control over Eastern Europe.

Two days after Nagy's announcement, Soviet tanks and troops poured into Hungary to crush the revolt. Realizing that intervention could cause World War III, the West sympathized with the Hungarians, but did nothing to help. Order in Hungary was restored under a Soviet-controlled government led by János Kádár. More than 200,000 Hungarian refugees fled to the West.

During the 1960s and 1970s, Hungary's Communist government tried to increase production, sometimes tightening controls, while at other times encouraging initiative through small private enterprises. Support of economic reform would eventually spur political reform efforts in the 1980s.

Czechoslovakia

Czechoslovakia, with its developed industry and democratic traditions, was the last Eastern European country to become Communist. After the Communist takeover in 1948, the country was forced to conform to the Soviet model, like Hungary. Purges against officials in Czechoslovakia were the bloodiest outside of the Soviet Union. The Czechoslovak leader, Antonin Novotny, kept the country under such rigid control that

---

CRITICAL THINKING ACTIVITY

Identifying Cause and Effect The cold war period was one of shifting policies and frequent international crises. Identifying cause-and-effect relationships makes these events easier to understand. For example, the death of Stalin and Khrushchev's desire to lessen discontent were causes that led to the effect of de-Stalinization. Have students write short essays that identify the causes of each of the following: the policies of peaceful coexistence and of detente and Soviet military intervention in East Germany, Hungary, and Czechoslovakia; the building of the Berlin Wall. **L2**

Czech citizens reacted in anger and defiance when Soviet and other Warsaw Pact troops invaded Prague. *How did the Soviets justify the invasion?*

de-Stalinization did not begin in Czechoslovakia until the 1960s.

At this time, public pressure for reform finally gained strength because of Czechoslovakia's economic stagnation. A liberal Communist reformer, **Alexander Dubček** (DOOB•chehk), replaced Novotny as leader in 1968 when Brezhnev signaled his approval. For a brief time, known as "the Prague spring," reform was allowed. Dubček eased press censorship and began to allow some political groups to meet freely.

Although Dubček assured the Soviets that Czechoslovakia was still loyal to the Warsaw Pact and to communism, the Soviets became alarmed at the direction the reform movement was taking. Many Czechoslovak thinkers wanted more freedom, and there were hints that opposition parties might

be allowed to operate. To the Soviets, their hold on Eastern Europe again seemed threatened.

On August 20, 1968, about 500,000 troops from the Soviet Union and its Warsaw Pact allies invaded Czechoslovakia. They took control of Prague and sent Dubček and other Czechoslovak leaders to Moscow. Most of Dubček's reforms were withdrawn and a new constitution was put into effect. In April 1969, Dubček was replaced as party leader. In 1970 he was expelled from the party entirely.

The Soviet Union declared its right to intervene in Communist states to counter any opposition that threatened communism or the unity of the Soviet bloc. This principle, called **the Brezhnev Doctrine**, was the basis for relations between the Soviet Union and its Eastern European satellites for the next 20 years.

SECTION 2 ASSESSMENT

Main Idea
1. Use a diagram like the one below to identify how the Soviet Union carried out Communist policies.

```
        Soviet Union's
         Communist
          Policies
       ╱  ╱  │  ╲  ╲
      ○  ○  ○  ○  ○
```

Recall
2. **Define** peaceful coexistence, intercontinental ballistic missile (ICBM), dissident, detente.
3. **Identify** Nikita Khrushchev, Leonid Brezhnev, Josip Broz Tito, Alexander Dubček, the Brezhnev Doctrine.

Critical Thinking
4. **Analyzing Information** How did Communist rule affect religion in Eastern Europe?

Understanding Themes
5. **Change** What impact did de-Stalinization have in the satellites of Eastern Europe?

Chapter 32 *The Cold War* **877**

SECTION 2 ASSESSMENT ANSWERS

1. de-Stalinization; promised better wages, more goods, more freedom for artists and intellectuals; reduced terror of secret police; freed political prisoners; peaceful with the U.S.; Cuban missile crisis; detente; controlled Eastern European satellites
2. All terms are defined in the Glossary.
3. Nikita Khrushchev, 872; Leonid Brezhnev,

874; Josip Broz Tito, 875; Alexander Dubček, 877; the Brezhnev Doctrine, 877
4. Communism opposed religious practices, seized church property, and closed church schools.
5. **CHANGE** It probably raised hopes for greater freedom and may have encouraged dissident activities.

ASSESS

Check for Understanding
Assign Section 2 Assessment as homework or as an in-class activity.

◘ Use Interactive Tutor Self-Assessment Software to review Section 2.

Evaluate
◥ Section Quiz 32-2

◘ Use the Testmaker to create a customized quiz for Section 2.

Reteach
Have students use an outline map of the world to locate, date, and label hot spots during the cold war.

◥ Reading Essentials and Study Guide 32-2

Enrich
Have students draw political cartoons criticizing Soviet control over its satellites.

CLOSE

Have students create a time line that includes the major events discussed in this section.

SECTION THEME

▶ **Regionalism** Western European democracies develop closer regional unity.

Guide to Reading

For reading strategies to help students read effectively see pages 12–13.

Vocabulary Pre-check

◉ Use the Vocabulary PuzzleMaker for Chapter 32 to create a crossword puzzle to reinforce section terms. **L1 LEP**

🗁 Use Vocabulary Activity 32 to introduce vocabulary terms. **L1 LEP**

FOCUS

Section Objective

Describe how Western Europe moved toward greater political and economic unity during the cold war.

BELLRINGER
Motivational Activity

Before taking roll at the beginning of the class period, project Section Focus Transparency 32-3 and have students answer the activity questions. Discuss students' responses.

🗁 This activity is also available as a blackline master.

1945 ——— 1955 ——— 1965 ——— 1975

1945 Great Britain elects a Labour party government.

1958 Charles de Gaulle heads France's Fifth Republic.

1963 Konrad Adenauer retires as West German chancellor.

1978 Spain introduces a new democratic constitution.

Section 3
....

Western Europe

Guide to Reading

Read to Find Out

Main Idea *Western Europe moved toward greater political and economic unity during the period of the cold war.*

▶ **Terms to Define**
welfare state, coalition

▶ **People to Meet**
Clement Attlee, Charles de Gaulle, Valéry Giscard d'Estaing, Konrad Adenauer, Willy Brandt

▶ **Places to Locate**
Rome

The Storyteller

Paris street disturbance

Jacques LeMoine nervously held the rifle issued to him just that morning. Like many other citizens of Paris, the 17-year-old had been pressed into service, guarding the city's perimeter. President de Gaulle's announced plans to guide Algeria to independence had aroused furious opposition. In reaction to the independence policy for Algeria, a threat had been received: Paris would be invaded. Paratroopers under the leadership of four retired French generals had seized key overseas bases and planned to bring citizens like Jacques LeMoine to defend the city.

—adapted from *The 1962 World Year Book,* "France," Fred J. Pannwitt, 1962

878 Chapter 32 *The Cold War*

After World War II, the non-Communist nations of Western Europe were concerned about two major issues: economic recovery and military security. They came to realize that only through united action would they be able to improve their economies, strengthen the Western Alliance, and contribute to world affairs.

Great Britain

After World War II, Great Britain's position as a world power further declined. The British had bankrupted themselves to win the war. Therefore, they had to sharply reduce their worldwide military, political, and economic role.

A Reduced Role

Even with financial cutbacks, Great Britain's recovery was slow. Many British industries were too inefficient and outdated to compete successfully in world markets that were increasingly dominated by the United States, Japan, and other Western European nations.

Because of economic weakness, the British passed on many of their international obligations to the United States. To maintain its pride and a level of independent security, Great Britain, however, developed its own nuclear force. It also maintained a close relationship with other members of the Western Alliance.

Loss of Empire

The British also could no longer afford to support a vast global empire. During the 1950s and 1960s, many of Great Britain's important Asian and African colonies became independent. Most of these new nations joined as equals with Great Britain in the Commonwealth of Nations, an organization that promoted cooperation among the nations of the former British Empire.

SECTION RESOURCES

🗁 **Reproducible Masters**
• Lecture Notes 32-3
• Reproducible Lesson Plan 32-3
• Vocabulary Activity 32
• Guided Reading Activity 32-3
• History Simulation 32
• Section Quiz 32-3
• Reading Essentials and Study Guide 32-3

🖳 **Transparencies**
• Section Focus Transparency 32-3
• Mapping History Overlay Transparency 23, *The Commonwealth of Nations*

Multimedia
🖳 Focus on World Art Print 24, *Current*
◉ Interactive Tutor Self-Assessment Software
◉ Testmaker

The Welfare State

Internally, Great Britain underwent many changes after World War II. In 1945 Churchill and the Conservatives were voted out of office. They were replaced by the Labour party, which appealed to many Britons who wanted greater economic equality. Under Prime Minister **Clement Attlee**, the Labour government continued wartime restrictions to improve the economy. However, it also promised a better standard of living for all British citizens.

Carrying out a moderate Socialist program, the Labour government nationalized the coal, steel, and transportation industries. Greater freedom was given to labor unions to strike and to participate in political activities. Like many other Western European governments, Britain's Labour government created a welfare state, a system in which the national government provides programs for the well-being of its citizens. Social security was expanded to provide lifetime benefits for the needy. Free education was provided to all children up to the age of 16. The government also introduced a national health service that provided free medical care for everyone.

As the economic situation improved in the early 1950s, the Conservatives returned to power and ruled until 1964. Although they ended many government controls over the economy, Conservative prime ministers, such as Winston Churchill, Anthony Eden, and Harold Macmillan, did not eliminate the social welfare programs introduced by the Labour party.

The Monarchy

In 1952, the popular wartime monarch, George VI, died and was succeeded by his elder daughter, Elizabeth. As queen, Elizabeth II had little, if any, power. But, for many Britons, she served as a reassuring symbol of traditional British values during a period of rapid, and sometimes discouraging, change. For other Britons, however, the monarchy represented all that they believed was wrong with Great Britain—its preoccupation with past imperial glories and its failure to discard the trappings of an outdated class system.

France

Germany's occupation of France during World War II had ended the Third French Republic created in 1870. After the war, a new constitution established the Fourth French Republic. Like the Third Republic, it had a strong legislature and a weak presidency.

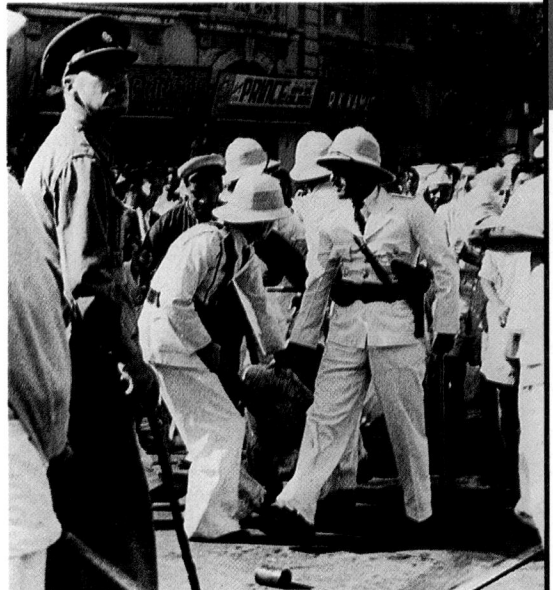

Visualizing History Riots between Hindus and Muslims led to the division of British India in 1947 into two nations: India and Pakistan. Both joined the Commonwealth of Nations. *What was the Commonwealth of Nations?*

The Fourth French Republic

In spite of economic growth, France in the 1950s was plagued with domestic and international problems. The existence of many political parties undermined hopes for a stable government. No single political party was strong enough to obtain a working majority in the National Assembly. Cabinets were formed by coalitions, or temporary alliances, of several parties. When one of the parties disagreed with policy, the cabinet members had to resign and form a new government.

Overseas, France's Asian and African colonies demanded their independence. Unlike Great Britain, France at first clung to its empire. It fought, and lost, expensive and bloody wars in Indochina and North Africa.

The Fifth French Republic

In 1958, the threat of civil war in the North African colony of Algeria resulted in the downfall of France's ineffective Fourth Republic. **Charles de Gaulle**, leader of the French Resistance during World War II, was called from retirement to head an emergency government. De Gaulle asked the

---

TEACH

Guided Practice

THEME Regionalism

Ask students to discuss what regionalism means to them. They should focus on the concept as it applies to their own area. *What region do you live in? How do people in this region cooperate with one another? With other regions?* **L1 LEP**

Visualizing History In a 1942 speech, Prime Minister Winston Churchill declared proudly: "I have not become the King's First Minister in order to preside over the liquidation of the British Empire." But the process began under his successor and was almost complete by the mid-1960s.

Answer to Caption: *an organization to promote cooperation among former nations of the British Empire*

Who?What?Where?When?

Vatican II This general council of the Roman Catholic Church, held from 1962 to 1965, had far-reaching consequences for Catholics worldwide. Among the changes it instituted was the substitution, in the Mass, of local languages for the Latin that had been used for centuries.

COOPERATIVE LEARNING ACTIVITY

Debate Organize the class into two groups and have students debate this proposition: The British monarchy should be abolished. Both sides should gather information to bolster their cases. Possible points to discuss include cost of the monarchy and functions of the royal family. **L3**

The following videotape program is available from Glencoe:

- **Her Majesty, The Queen Mother**

Economics Britain, France, and West Germany all instituted programs to promote citizens' well-being during the cold war period. What programs in the United States provide for our well-being? *(Answers might include Social Security, medicare, medicaid, and welfare.)* **L2**

Movement Since World War II, millions of Africans, Asians, and West Indians have resettled in the former colonial powers, especially Britain and France. Since the 1970s, Germany has allowed millions of Turks to settle in Germany to ease labor shortages. Today the presence of non-Europeans in these countries has led to racist violence. Have students investigate and report on the situation of immigrants in Europe. **L3**

 History Simulation 32

Focus on World Art Print 24, Bridget Riley. *Current*

Mapping History Overlay Transparency 23, *The Commonwealth of Nations*

Independent Practice

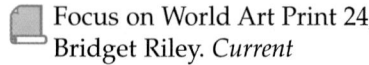 Guided Reading Activity 32-3 **L1**

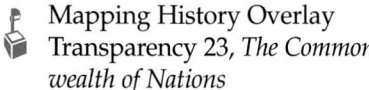 De Gaulle saw himself as the personification of France. "There were many things I would have liked to do but could not," he once said, "for they would not have been fitting for General de Gaulle."
Answer to Caption: *He allowed Algeria to become independent.*

French people to approve a new constitution providing for a strong presidency. French voters overwhelmingly responded to de Gaulle's appeal. Thus, the Fifth French Republic was born.

De Gaulle became the first president of the Fifth Republic. His political party, the Gaullist Union, formed a working majority in the National Assembly. As president, de Gaulle recognized that France could not stubbornly hold on to its empire against strong nationalist opposition. In the early 1960s, he allowed France's African colonies, including Algeria, to become independent.

With the loss of France's empire, de Gaulle worked to strengthen French cultural and economic influence in Europe and throughout the rest of the world. His strongly nationalistic policies angered France's allies, especially Great Britain and the United States. In 1963, de Gaulle blocked Great Britain's application for membership in the European Common Market. Three years later, the French president decided to withdraw all French troops from NATO's military command and requested that all NATO bases and headquarters be removed from French soil. At the same time, he insisted on maintaining France's political ties to NATO. De Gaulle's ultimate expression of nationalism was the building of an independent French nuclear force.

De Gaulle's successor, Georges Pompidou (PAHM•pih•DOO), by contrast, worked to build

Visualizing History France gave Charles de Gaulle broad presidential powers and election by direct popular vote. *How did de Gaulle solve the problem of nationalist opposition in Algeria?*

880 Chapter 32 *The Cold War*

closer relations with Great Britain and the United States. He also focused on economic growth rather than on nationalistic projects. After Pompidou's death in 1974, **Valéry Giscard d'Estaing** (zhihs •KAHR dehs•TAN) was elected president. Giscard continued Pompidou's domestic and international policies. He set out to lessen state economic controls and to encourage the expansion of French private enterprise. Giscard's pro-business policies, however, were crippled by the worldwide economic downturn of the 1970s.

Germany

During the postwar years, West Germany rebuilt its economy and became Western Europe's leading industrial nation. Many experts called West Germany's reconstruction an "economic miracle." New industries used the latest in modern equipment, and industrial production more than tripled in the 1950s. Prosperity enabled West Germany to create a welfare state closely resembling those in Great Britain and France. West Germany also absorbed 10 million refugees from Eastern Europe. Another 1 million people settled in Germany from other parts of the continent.

The Adenauer Years

West Germany's democratic political system was dominated by two parties: the Christian Democrats and the Social Democrats. In 1949, the Christian Democrats, led by **Konrad Adenauer** (A•duhn•OWR), formed the first West German government. They created a capitalist economy with close ties to the West. In 1955 West Germany joined NATO and developed its own armed forces.

As chancellor, Adenauer was known as a strong leader devoted to the Western Alliance, European unity, and the reunification of Germany under a democratic government. During his tenure, West Germany became one of the world's most stable democracies. Adenauer retired in 1963. He was succeeded as chancellor by the economic minister Ludwig Erhard, who served until 1966.

Willy Brandt

During the 1960s, the Christian Democrats lost support to the Social Democrats, a moderate socialist party led by West Berlin's mayor, **Willy Brandt**. The Social Democrats maintained strong support for NATO while seeking improved relations with the Soviet bloc.

Brandt became chancellor of Germany in 1969. During the 1970s, he worked to reduce tensions

---

MEETING SPECIAL NEEDS ACTIVITY

Reading Comprehension Organize the class into four groups, one for each major subsection of Section 3. Then have each group develop a topic sentence for each paragraph in its subsection. After completing the sentences, each group should share its list with other students, then review and comment on their topic sentences. **L2**

between West Germany and the Soviet bloc. This policy, known as *Ostpolitik* (German for "Eastern policy") led West Germany to reach agreements to normalize relations with the Soviet Union and Poland in 1972. Brandt's initiative eventually led to the establishment of diplomatic ties between West Germany and East Germany a year later.

European Unity

Throughout Europe's history, local disputes between two or more nations often drew the entire continent into war. In the twentieth century, developments in technology, such as nuclear weapons, made it clear that future wars could lead to global catastrophe. This possibility prompted leaders to seek regional solutions to European issues.

As World War II ended, European leaders discussed plans for the postwar unification of European countries. These plans included organizations for economic cooperation and the resolution of disputes. Some even raised the idea of a United States of Europe. Others proposed that each nation retain its national identity but hand over control of defense and foreign policy to an all-European government. This arrangement, it was felt, would prevent European nations from waging war on each other.

To coordinate economic policies, six nations— France, Italy, West Germany, Belgium, the Netherlands, and Luxembourg established the European Coal and Steel Community in 1952. The organization's goal was to create a tariff-free market for European coal and steel products. By ending trade barriers and developing uniform standards, the European Coal and Steel Community would further European industrial growth.

The Community was so successful that the same countries decided to bring together the rest of their economies. In 1957, representatives of the six nations meeting in **Rome**, Italy, signed the Treaty of

 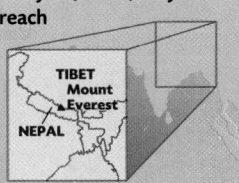

Edmund Hillary Climbs Mount Everest

Nepal-Tibet, 1953
Located in the Himalayas, on the Nepal-Tibet border, Mount Everest is the world's highest peak. A British expedition set out in 1953 to scale the south slope, which was considered unclimbable. The climbers established a series of camps as they advanced up the mountain. The last camp was set up by Edmund Hillary of New Zealand and Tenzing Norgay of Nepal. On May 29, 1953, they became the first climbers to reach the top of Mount Everest. Queen Elizabeth II knighted Hillary for his achievement.

Rome. This agreement created the **European Economic Community**, also known as the Common Market. The six members of the Common Market planned to abolish all tariffs among themselves and form a single economic market by 1970. During the 1960s and 1970s, Great Britain, attracted by the Common Market's success, ended its traditional aloofness from European affairs and sought membership in the European organization.

The Common Market benefited Western Europe in several ways. By promoting economic cooperation among individual European nations, it reduced the threat of conflict and contributed to European prosperity. It also enabled Western Europe to pursue cooperative technological programs in fields such as space research and nuclear energy. These programs were too expensive for any one nation to pursue on its own. Finally, it enabled Europe to compete on an equal basis with North America and East Asia in world markets.

SECTION 3 ASSESSMENT

Main Idea
1. Use a chart like the one below to show how Western Europe was united economically during the cold war.

Economic Unity
1.
2.

Recall
2. **Define** welfare state, coalition.
3. **Identify** Clement Attlee, Charles de Gaulle, Valéry Giscard d'Estaing, Konrad Adenauer, Willy Brandt, *Ostpolitik*, European Economic Community.

Critical Thinking
4. **Synthesizing Information** What factors contributed to Western Europe's postwar economic recovery?

Understanding Themes
5. **Regionalism** Explain advantages and disadvantages of a United States of Europe.

Regionalism Have students research and report on the following European regions in the cold war period: Scandinavia, Italy, Spain. **L3**

ASSESS

Check for Understanding

Assign Section 3 Assessment as homework or as an in-class activity.

☐ Use Interactive Tutor Self-Assessment Software to review Section 3.

Evaluate

📁 Section Quiz 32-3

☐ Use the Testmaker to create a customized quiz for Section 3.

Reteach

Have students review the factors that moved Western Europe toward greater cooperation in the postwar period.

📁 Reading Essentials and Study Guide 32-3

Enrich

Have students watch a video of the film *The Mouse That Roared* and then discuss the European attitude toward the United States that is reflected in the film.

CLOSE

Have students summarize the ways Western democracies cooperated during the cold war era.

SECTION 3 ASSESSMENT ANSWERS

1. 1952: European Coal and Steel Community created tariff-free market for European coal and steel products; 1957: Treaty of Rome created Common Market to end all tariffs among six European nations and to form single economic market by 1970
2. All terms are defined in the Glossary.
3. Clement Attlee, 879; Charles de Gaulle, 879; Valéry Giscard d'Estaing, 880; Konrad Adenauer, 880; Willy Brandt, 880; *Ostpolitik*, 881; European Economic Community, 881
4. the Marshall Plan, the European Coal and Steel Community, and the Common Market
5. **REGIONALISM** Answers will vary but might include the following ideas. Advantages: lower trade barriers, cooperative research and development in industry, pooling of resources. Disadvantages: loss of sovereignty, weakening of national identity

882 Chapter 32 The Cold War

SECTION THEME

▶ **Cooperation** The United States and Canada build strong economies and forge closer ties.

Guide to Reading

For reading strategies to help students read effectively see pages 12–13.

Vocabulary Pre-check

 Use the Vocabulary PuzzleMaker for Chapter 32 to create a crossword puzzle to reinforce section terms. **L1 LEP**

Use Vocabulary Activity 32 to introduce vocabulary terms. **L1 LEP**

FOCUS

Section Objective

Trace the political and social changes that the people of the United States and Canada experienced during the cold war years.

BELLRINGER
Motivational Activity

 Before taking roll at the beginning of the class period, project Section Focus Transparency 32-4.

This activity is also available as a blackline master.

1945 ⎯⎯⎯⎯⎯⎯⎯⎯ **1955** ⎯⎯⎯⎯⎯⎯⎯⎯ **1965** ⎯⎯⎯⎯⎯⎯⎯⎯ **1975**

1947 U.S. Congress conducts hearings on Communist influence in American life.

1955 Martin Luther King, Jr., begins nonviolent civil rights campaign for African Americans.

1967 Canada celebrates 100th anniversary of nationhood.

1974 Richard M. Nixon becomes the first United States President to resign his office.

Section 4

The United States and Canada

Guide to Reading

Read to Find Out

Main Idea *The United States and Canada experienced a number of political and social changes during the cold war years.*

▶ **Terms to Define**
automation, racial segregation, imperial presidency, stagflation, embargo, double-digit inflation, trade deficit, middle power, multicultural, separatism

▶ **People to Meet**
Dwight D. Eisenhower, John F. Kennedy, Lyndon B. Johnson, Richard M. Nixon, Martin Luther King, Jr., Gerald R. Ford, Jimmy Carter, Lester B. Pearson, Pierre Elliott Trudeau

▶ **Places to Locate**
Vietnam, Cambodia, Washington, D.C., St. Lawrence Seaway, Toronto, Montreal, Quebec

 The **Storyteller**

By the time President Eisenhower began his first term, 33,629 Americans had been killed in the Korean War. Then on March 5, 1953, Joseph Stalin died. Hearing of Stalin's death, Eisenhower asked his associates, "Well, what do you think we can do about this?" He was advised to seek improved relations with Russia. The new Soviet leaders also wanted reduced tensions. As a result, a truce ending the war in Korea was signed on July 28th.

—adapted from *The Glorious Burden*, Stefan Lorant, 1968

President Dwight D. Eisenhower

B ecause they were spared the destruction of their territory in World War II, the United States and Canada both emerged from the war with prosperous economies. During the postwar era, the stunning technological achievements of the United States, its high standard of living, and business success were admired and envied around the globe.

In the 1960s and the 1970s, however, the United States was shaken by domestic political crises, economic difficulties, and its involvement in the Vietnam War. By the 1980s other nations were catching up economically, but the United States retained its role as the leader of the non-Communist world.

During this time, the United States's northern neighbor, Canada, sought to maintain unity between its French-speaking and English-speaking populations. It also attracted immigrants from all parts of the world. Moving away from its traditional British connection, Canada sought a new identity in international affairs and developed closer economic ties with the United States.

American Prosperity

After World War II, the United States entered an era of economic growth that brought material wealth to a larger group of Americans. Demand for American goods was high, and business responded to meet this need. Production soared, and new industries appeared. Higher wages and better benefits gave Americans more money to spend. American shoppers pushed up demand as they eagerly purchased consumer goods that had been scarce during the war. Future prospects were also bright. The postwar "baby boom," or soaring birthrate, added to the potential number of consumers and promised increased economic growth.

SECTION RESOURCES

Reproducible Masters
- Lecture Notes 32-4
- Reproducible Lesson Plan 32-4
- Guided Reading Activity 32-4
- Reteaching Activity 32
- Enrichment Activity 32
- Section Quiz 32-4
- Performance Assessment Activity 32

- Spanish Chapter Summary 32
- Reading Essentials and Study Guide 32-4

Transparencies
- Section Focus Transparency 32-4

Multimedia
- Vocabulary PuzzleMaker Software
- Interactive Tutor Self-Assessment Software
- Testmaker
- Communism and the Cold War
- Turning Points in World History
- Lessons of War

Science and Technology

During the postwar years, the United States made spectacular leaps in the field of science and technology. With more money to spend, an increase in the number of university-trained scientists, and a growing commitment to the future, the United States led the world in new technological developments.

During the 1950s and 1960s, American factories and industries began to use automation, the technique of operating a production system using mechanical or electronic devices. With automated methods of production, goods could be produced more efficiently than with human workers.

Beginning in the 1950s, the use of computers began to revolutionize American industry. Businesses used computers for many purposes, including billing and inventory control. Computers were also used for such things as making hotel reservations, sorting bank checks, tracking space satellites, forecasting weather conditions, and setting type for printing. Automation and computers in the workplace caused many workers to lose their jobs. In the long run, however, computers and automation created more jobs than they eliminated. In addition, the new jobs usually demanded a higher level of education.

American technological skills brought the United States into competition with the Soviet Union in space exploration and missile development. The two superpowers experimented with moon probes, weather and communications satellites, and extended flights of humans orbiting the earth. The grand prize of the "space race" was putting a human on the moon. United States astronaut Neil Armstrong won that honor on July 20, 1969.

Social Changes

Many social changes came to the United States during the period from the late 1940s to the late 1970s. In the 1950s the automobile changed the face of America. No longer did people have to live near their places of work. Those who lived and worked in the city could move to less-crowded places. This migration of city residents caused the rapid growth of suburbs.

In the years after World War II, American cities became ringed by seemingly endless housing developments carved out of the less densely settled country land. Shopping centers with vast parking lots were built to serve the new suburban population. Businesses and factories also began relocating from the cities to the suburbs, where their workers now lived. The Highway Act of 1956 contributed to the growth of the suburbs by adding 41,000 miles (66,000 km) to the interstate highway system.

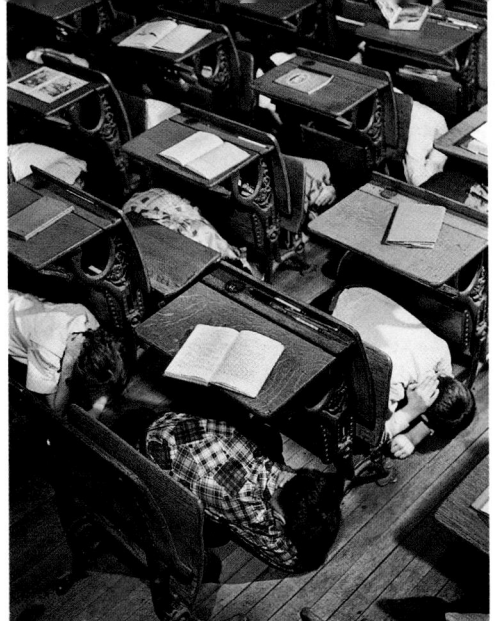

Visualizing History Cold war tensions and fear of nuclear attack led to "duck and cover" drills in public schools. *How did the government react to the fear of the "enemy within"?*

In addition to the automobile, another symbol of American prosperity was the television set. In 1945, fewer than 1 in 20,000 people had a television. But within a few years, televisions were everywhere, and they were almost as common as telephones. Some critics worried that television would make Americans desire entertainment more than solid information. However, other experts pointed out the positive impact of television in making people directly aware of national and international events.

The Cold War at Home

Despite this time of prosperity, the cold war created deep political divisions in the United States. During the late 1940s and early 1950s, conservatives blamed President Harry S Truman and State Department officials for allowing the Communists to make gains in Eastern Europe and Asia. They also charged that Communists were serving in high government positions. A "red scare" swept the country. The growing fear of the "enemy within"—of subversion within the United States government and society—helped to launch a controversial anti-Communist crusade to discover and expose

---

TEACH

Guided Practice

THEME Cooperation

The United States and Canada had a cooperative relationship throughout the twentieth century. What factors served to promote this relationship? *(geographic proximity, a common language, and similar political and social institutions based on British models)* **L1 LEP**

Visualizing History In the late 1950s, some Americans called for the construction of an extensive network of fallout shelters to protect civilians in case of atomic attack. Congress and state legislatures, however, refused to appropriate the massive funds needed.

Answer to Caption: *Congress investigated suspected Communists, and many people lost their jobs.*

Daily Life Fear of Communist influence was very strong in American society during the cold war years. Ask students whether they think attitudes are different today, and if so, why. **L2**

ABCNEWS INTERACTIVE™

VIDEODISC
Turning Points in World History

Side Two, Chapter 8
Title: *The Moon Landing*
Ask: Who was aboard *Apollo 11* in 1969 when it headed to the moon? *(Neil Armstrong, Edwin "Buzz" Aldrin, and Michael Collins)*

COOPERATIVE LEARNING ACTIVITY

The Anti-Communist Crusade Organize the class into small groups, one for each year from 1947 through 1954, the years of the post-World War II "red scare." Have each group research and report on relevant anti-Communist activities in its year. Then have groups work together to agree on a format to present their information; suggest either radio or TV reports. **L3**

VIDEODISC
Communism and the Cold War

Side One, Chapter 11
Frames 20050–21335
Title: *Communists in Our Midst: McCarthyism*
Ask: How were Americans who believed in Communist ideas treated in the 1940s and 1950s? *(They were investigated, shunned, and considered treasonous.)*

Abstract Painting

European abstract painting of the early 1900s tended to be cool and geometrical. What was new in the 1940s, when American painters set the trend, was a heightened, energetic emotionalism—in other words, abstract *expressionism*. While some artists dripped paint on canvas (Pollock), others experimented with wild colors (Willem de Kooning) or used thin washes that allowed the canvas to show through (Mark Rothko).

ANSWERS
It is a highly emotional form of abstract (nonobjective) painting. Answers will vary but might include dissatisfaction with realism and reaction against European traditions.

---

suspected Communists. The search focused on diplomats, intellectuals, labor leaders, and entertainers believed to be tolerant of communism.

Congressional Investigations

A congressional body, the House Committee on Un-American Activities, investigated Communist influences. Alger Hiss, a former government official, denied that he had tried to pass secrets to the Soviets in the 1930s. Brought to trial, Hiss was not prosecuted because too much time had passed since the events had occurred. However, he was found guilty of lying and was sent to prison. Later, Julius and Ethel Rosenberg, both Communists, were accused of spying. They claimed innocence but were tried, convicted, and executed.

In the early 1950s, Senator Joseph McCarthy of Wisconsin charged that Communists were conspiring within the federal government. The Senate Committee on Investigation, which McCarthy headed, called government workers to testify. McCarthy never proved his charges, but the public mood was such that even the accusation alone was enough to label someone a Communist, and many lost their jobs. The term *McCarthyism* came to mean making charges of disloyalty without regard to evidence.

Forming Alliances

Between the 1950s and the 1980s, the cold war influenced national political campaigns, and many aspects of domestic policy, as well as most major foreign policy decisions of the United States. In its dealings with Eastern Europe, Africa, the Middle East, Latin America, and Asia, the United States saw its diplomacy as an extension of the struggle against communism.

During the 1950s, the United States expanded the nation's network of alliances in order to contain communism. In Western Europe, the Americans took a leading role in NATO. In Southeast Asia, the United States helped to create the Southeast Asia Treaty Organization (SEATO). In the Middle East, the United States counted on the cooperation of the Central Treaty Organization (CENTO), and in Latin America, the United States promoted the Organization of American States (OAS). These alliances created a formidable counterbalance to the influence of the Soviet Union.

Military Buildup

When necessary, American Presidents also used espionage and military power to fight the cold war. During the 1950s, the effort to contain

---

CONNECTIONS
The Arts

Abstract Painting

Abstract expressionism was a movement in American painting that flourished from the mid-1940s to the mid-1950s. Abstract expressionist artists rejected many of the rules of earlier art. Instead of showing recognizable subject matter in their works, they emphasized the techniques or basic elements of painting, such as color, brush-strokes, lines, and shapes.

One of the important abstract expressionist painters was Jackson Pollock. His usual painting technique involved placing a huge canvas on the floor and then dripping paint from above onto it. The drippings formed sweeping, rhythmic

Out of the Web by Jackson Pollock

patterns that seemed to move across the surface. About his highly unusual method of painting, Pollock said, "I feel nearer, more a part of the painting, since this way I can walk around it, work from the four sides, and literally be in the painting."

Although abstract expressionist styles differed, all of the artists in the movement believed that art should express immediate personal feelings and attitudes toward life. Their nontraditional, revolutionary approach to art has influenced painters throughout the world.

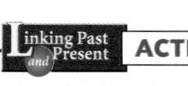 **ACTIVITY**

Explain how abstract expressionist painting differs from traditional forms of art. Why do you think abstract expressionist art developed in the United States during the cold war era?

MEETING SPECIAL NEEDS ACTIVITY

Mixed Learners List on the chalkboard some key terms that occur in this section, including all or some of the following: *baby boom, computers, television, Communist subversion, McCarthyism, abstract expressionism, military-industrial complex, teach-ins, Vietnamization, Watergate scandal.* Have students define each term and tell why it is relevant to a discussion of the cold war period. **L2 LEP**

communism, strongly backed by the American public, caused the United States to send troops to fight Communist forces in Korea. It also led President **Dwight D. Eisenhower** in 1954 to agree to shoulder France's efforts to stop Communist military activity in **Vietnam**. The United States engaged in an unprecedented military buildup during this time, even during the cold war "thaw" in the late 1950s.

By the closing months of his presidency, Dwight D. Eisenhower, though a proponent of a strong military, was deeply concerned about the global arms race, or the competition between the superpowers for new and better weapons. On leaving office in 1961, he warned of a growing "military-industrial complex" in the United States. According to Eisenhower, the superpower rivalry, the competition for sophisticated weapons, and the role of arms production in supporting economic growth had created a built-in incentive to increase military spending.

Battle of Ideas

John F. Kennedy, a young senator from Massachusetts, succeeded Eisenhower as President in 1961. During the 1960 presidential race, Kennedy had campaigned on the theme of restoring the strength and prestige the United States had lost after the embarrassments of the U-2 spying incident and *Sputnik*.

Kennedy engaged in cold-war maneuvering on several fronts. He acted quickly to create the Peace Corps, a program that sent young American volunteers overseas to help impoverished countries that

were open to Communist influence. Kennedy's cold-war views influenced his actions in several major foreign policy crises, including the building of the Berlin Wall and the Cuban missile crisis.

The Vietnam War

Kennedy's assassination in 1963 brought **Lyndon B. Johnson** to the White House. Johnson supported civil rights laws and reforms in education and social welfare to achieve what he

Nuclear Battlefield

Map Study

By the 1980s the United States and the Soviet Union each had more than 12,000 ICBMs aimed at the other. The Distant Early Warning Line (DEW Line) was a radar system built in 1957 to detect incoming missiles. It was replaced in 1994 with a more sophisticated North Warning System.

Region Why were DEW Line radars placed in northern Canada rather than along the east and west coasts of the United States?

Map Study

Answer

the most direct path of the missiles would be over the North Pole

Map Skills Practice

Reading a Map Why are the Soviet Union's missile sites located mostly on its western borders? *(located near Europe and NATO forces)*

Independent Practice

Guided Reading Activity 32-4

Who? What? Where? When?

Eleanor Roosevelt A moderate voice in the controversial postwar period was that of Eleanor Roosevelt, who continued her public career after the death of her husband, Franklin, in 1945. As a member of the UN Commission on Human Rights, she tried to meet the Russians halfway. "All of us are going to die together or we are going to learn to live together," she said, "and if we are to live together we have to talk."

Report Two notable trials of the cold war era were those of Alger Hiss, accused of Communist ties, and Julius and Ethel Rosenberg, convicted of spying for Russia. Have students research and report on one of these trials. **L3**

Chapter 32   *The Cold War*   **885**

MAKING CONNECTIONS ACTIVITIES

Military History One of the most notorious incidents of the Vietnam War was the My Lai massacre of 1968. Have students research and report on the event and on the subsequent trial of William L. Calley, Jr., the American officer accused of responsibility for it. **L2**

Architecture Few war monuments have moved and inspired Americans as much as the Vietnam Veterans Memorial in Washington, D.C. Have students research and report on this structure: who designed it, what it looks like, when it was dedicated, and the controversy about its design. If possible, they should include illustrations to show the class or post on the bulletin board. **L2**

VIDEODISC
Communism and the Cold War

Side Two, Chapter 8
Title: *Vietnam War*
Ask: In what way did the United States view Vietnam as a conflict not between North and South Vietnam but rather between the United States and the Soviet Union? *(The United States believed they were also fighting the Soviet Union because of Soviet military/economic support for North Vietnam.)*

POINT

Struggle for Civil Rights
How did the civil rights struggle of the 1960s affect American society?
It brought greater equality to African Americans and other marginalized groups and helped alter American attitudes toward race, discrimination, and poverty.

you don't say...

Hawks and doves are terms that were used widely in the 1960s. Supporters of the Vietnam War were called hawks, while opponents were known as doves. The use of *hawk* to describe a warlike person goes back to the War of 1812. Doves have long been thought of as peaceful; the symbolism was reinforced by a poster by Pablo Picasso that was popular during the 1950s and 1960s.

called the Great Society. However, the consuming issue during Johnson's five years in office became the Vietnam War, in which the United States assisted South Vietnam in resisting a Communist takeover.

American involvement in Vietnam, described in Chapter 33, began under Presidents Eisenhower and Kennedy and grew out of their desire to keep communism from spreading throughout Southeast Asia. During the Eisenhower and Kennedy years, American civilian and military advisers had arrived in Vietnam to aid the South Vietnamese. The role of the United States in the Southeast Asian nation was later expanded into full-scale participation by President Johnson. During Johnson's administration, large numbers of American combat soldiers were sent to fight in Vietnam.

Opposition to the War

By 1968, large-scale American intervention had not been able to overcome the Communist Vietnamese forces. As a result, domestic opposition to the war became widespread, and Vietnam became the central issue in the presidential race of that year. President Johnson, condemned for his handling of the lengthy, costly, and indecisive war, decided not to run for reelection. Former Vice President **Richard M. Nixon**, a strong anti-Communist, won the election with his pledge to stop the war and bring the American people together.

President Nixon soon found that ending the war was difficult. As he struggled to find a politically acceptable solution, his administration was besieged by the antiwar forces that had overwhelmed Johnson's presidency.

Although many young Americans believed that it was their duty to serve in the military if they were called, others stated that they would refuse to serve. Some young men eligible for the draft—the mandatory enrollment in the United States armed forces—burned their draft cards, which was an illegal act. Others fled to Canada to avoid the draft, choosing to spend years in exile from their country rather than fight in the war. Demonstrators marched in front of the White House, carrying signs and shouting antiwar slogans. College professors cancelled classes and held antiwar protests called "teach-ins." Most protests across the country were peaceful, but many incidents of violence occurred, including the bombing of military facilities and other institutions that symbolized America's political and military power.

Ending the War

President Nixon's plans for ending the war for the United States was called "Vietnamization"—a

gradual withdrawal of American troops while handing over control of war operations to South Vietnam. In a November 1969 speech, the President tried to counter the antiwar protests by appealing to what he called the silent majority of Americans whom he said supported his policies.

Simultaneously with the American withdrawal from Vietnam, Nixon ordered fierce bombing raids on neighboring **Cambodia**. The bombings prompted renewed protests, creating a superheated atmosphere of anger and distrust between supporters and opponents of the war. The situation exploded tragically in May 1970, when National Guard soldiers fired into a crowd of demonstrators at Kent State University in Ohio, killing four students.

In 1973, the last of the active American forces withdrew from Vietnam, and the Paris Accords were signed. Of the 2,700,000 Americans who served in Vietnam, about 58,000 died and more than 300,000 were wounded. The war cost the United States $150 billion. In addition, it made the nation more cautious of foreign involvement.

POINT

Struggle for Civil Rights

Despite the general economic prosperity of the United States after World War II, millions of Americans continued to live in poverty. The poor included members of all ethnic groups, but the plight of the nation's poor in the African American community seemed especially critical. Ever since emancipation in the 1860s, African Americans in both the North and the South had faced discrimination in jobs, housing, education, and other areas. After World War II, an increasing number of Americans realized that continuing poverty and racial discrimination were at odds with the basic American values of equality and justice for all. A civil rights movement begun by African Americans in the early 1900s gained momentum and affected many areas of American life.

Changing Social Attitudes

Changing social attitudes helped civil rights advances. The war against Germany played a part. The horrifying racism of the Nazis helped to make some Americans more sensitive to racism in their own country. They began to realize that not only African Americans, but also Asian Americans, Hispanic Americans, and other ethnic groups had been treated unfairly and denied social and educational opportunities.

CRITICAL THINKING ACTIVITY

Making Comparisons Write two headings on the chalkboard, *United States* and *Canada*. Under each, have students enter data given in this section, supplemented by research in reference works. Data should include size, population, major resources, and main ethnic groups. **L2**

ourt Decisions

During the 1940s and 1950s, African Americans orked hard to gain civil rights. The war years saw e membership of the National Association for the dvancement of Colored People (NAACP) increase om 100,000 to 351,000. In the late 1940s, the AACP hired teams of able lawyers to bring a eries of lawsuits to the federal courts to end viola- ons of the constitutional rights of African merican citizens.

This effort resulted in several United States upreme Court decisions that attacked discrimina- on. In the best known case, *Brown v. Board of ducation of Topeka, Kansas* (1954), the United States upreme Court ruled that racial segregation, or the eparation of the races, in public schools was ille- al. President Eisenhower used federal agencies to nforce the Court's decision.

Martin Luther King, Jr.

In the following years, the civil rights move- ent broadened and changed tactics. **Martin uther King, Jr.**, a Baptist minister, advocated the se of nonviolent sit-ins and marches to focus ttention on discrimination in housing, public acilities, and voting. Media coverage of the segre- ationist opposition to the movement's efforts elped convince many Americans of the injustice of iscrimination.

In 1963, more than 200,000 African Americans, vhites, and people of many ethnic groups con- erged on Washington, D.C., for the largest civil ights demonstration in the nation's history. At the Lincoln Memorial, the marchers heard eloquent peeches, especially from Martin Luther King, Jr., who, in a famous address, described his dream of reedom and equality for all people:

> **❝ I have a dream that one day this nation will rise up and live out the true meaning of its creed: 'We hold these truths to be self-evident; that all men are created equal'.... And when this happens, and when we allow freedom to ring, when we let it ring from every village and hamlet, from every state and every city, we will be able to speed up that day when all God's children ... [will] join hands and sing in the words of the old ... spiritual: 'Free at last, Free at last, Thank God Almighty, we're free at last.' ❞**

The civil rights movement peaked in the 1960s with the passage of major civil rights laws under President Johnson. These measures banned dis- crimination in public places and education as well as strengthened the right to vote. In addition to helping African Americans, the civil rights legisla- tion also advanced opportunities for other groups, such as Hispanic Americans.

After Martin Luther King, Jr.'s assassination in 1968, the civil rights movement faced the loss or delay of some of its hard-won gains. Beginning in the late 1960s, much of the United States govern- ment's social policies shifted to the right, away from earlier liberal policies. However, despite the setback, the movement for civil rights continued. It strongly influenced other groups in the United States—women, Hispanic Americans, and Native Americans—that wanted better opportunities and social equality. It also was an inspiration to civil rights groups in other parts of the world.

Visualizing History Dr. Martin Luther King, Jr., spoke to more than 200,000 people on the 100th anniversary of the Emancipation Proclamation. *What civil rights did legislation in the 1960s address?*

Chapter 32 *The Cold War* 887

CURRICULUM CONNECTION

SCIENCE
A great scientific breakthrough of the cold war period was the conquest of polio. This disease had menaced both children and adults all over the world for cen- turies. (Franklin D. Roosevelt was one of its most prominent victims.) An inoculation, pio- neered by Jonas Salk, was pro- nounced safe in 1955. An oral vaccine, developed by Albert Sabin, was approved in 1961. Today polio has been all but eliminated globally.

Visualizing History King came to prominence in 1955, when African Americans in Montgomery, Alaba- ma, began a boycott against the local bus company, which practiced discrimination in seating and hiring. **Answer to Caption:** *the right to vote, the right to education, and the use of public accommodations without dis- crimination*

MORE ABOUT...

The Civil Rights Struggle Students and other young people played a key role in the civil rights struggle. In 1960 college students in North Carolina organized the first sit-ins, occupying seats at a segregated lunch counter as a form of protest. The following year many students took part in free- dom rides, demonstrating against segregated buses. In 1964 three young men—two white (Michael Schwerner and Andrew Goodman) and one black (James Chaney)—were murdered while organiz- ing voter registration in Mississippi.

Visualizing History

The embargo affected many sectors of the American economy, from home heating to a range of products that depended on petroleum—synthetic fabrics, plastics, cosmetics, and even toothpaste. **Answer to Caption:** *It made them rise.*

Who? What? Where? When?

Accidental Executives When Gerald Ford became President, he named Nelson Rockefeller, former governor of New York, as his Vice President. For the first time in history, the two Chief Executives of the United States occupied their offices by appointment rather than by election.

ABCNEWS INTERACTIVE™

VIDEODISC
Lessons of War

Side Two, Chapter 6
Frames 12636–20751
Title: *Philosophy of Nonviolence*
Subject: The philosophies of Mohandas Gandhi and Martin Luther King, Jr., and how their philosophies were used in protests and demonstrations
Ask: For what cause did Martin Luther King, Jr., peacefully protest? *(civil rights)*

Visualizing History

Long lines formed at gasoline stations because of shortages when OPEC placed an embargo on oil exports. *How did the embargo affect the prices of other goods?*

The Changing Presidency

During the cold war, United States Presidents gradually began to exercise powers beyond those spelled out in the United States Constitution. Claiming a need for a quick military response to counter communism, Presidents began to assume the war-making powers of Congress, committing American military forces to combat without congressional approval. The two largest commitments to undeclared wars were in Korea and Vietnam.

The Imperial Presidency

As the cold war continued into the 1960s and 1970s, many people felt that the increased presidential power was subject to abuses and a violation of the Constitution. The term imperial presidency came into use, reflecting this concern.

The term was most often applied to Presidents Lyndon B. Johnson and Richard M. Nixon, both of whom expanded the conflict in Vietnam without a congressional declaration of war, as called for in the Constitution, and often kept their actions secret from Congress. In 1973 Congress overrode Nixon's veto to pass the War Powers Limitation Act. The measure required the President to consult Congress before committing United States troops to combat.

888 Chapter 32 *The Cold War*

The Watergate Scandal

Political scandals rocked the United States during the 1970s. Investigations revealed many cases of corruption in local and state government, but the country's attention focused primarily on charges of corruption in the federal government. Early in President Nixon's second term, scandal engulfed his administration. Vice President Spiro Agnew was accused of taking bribes when he was governor of Maryland and was forced to resign. Then the President himself came under fire in a scandal that became known as Watergate.

The Watergate scandal began on June 17, 1972, when five men were caught trying to plant electronic listening devices in the offices of the Democratic National Committee, located in the Watergate building in downtown **Washington, D.C.** The break-in was traced to Nixon's reelection committee.

A congressional probe revealed that the White House knew of the burglary and tried to cover it up. The President denied the charges at first, but tape recordings of Oval Office conversations proved that he had participated in the cover-up. Under the threat of impeachment, Nixon resigned on August 9, 1974. He was the first United States President ever to do so.

Gerald R. Ford, the Republican congressman from Michigan who had replaced Spiro Agnew as Vice President, became President when Nixon stepped down. Ford was the first United States President not to have been elected to either of the nation's top two offices. He assumed a presidency that had been weakened and tarnished. Watergate had shaken public confidence in the American political system. In addition, Ford had no personal mandate from the voters, since he had not been elected to the presidency. As a former congressman, Ford maintained close ties with Congress. That, coupled with his acknowledged personal integrity, enabled him to function effectively. Both Ford and his Democratic successor, **Jimmy Carter**, a former governor of Georgia, worked to restore ethics to the presidency. In addition, as a result of Watergate, the media became far more vigilant in pursuing wrongdoing of public officials.

The Economy

During the late 1960s and 1970s, the United States economy was buffeted by the effects of the cold war and a changing world economy. The country suffered serious inflation in the 1970s as a result of the costs of the Vietnam War and increased

TEACHER NOTES

_____

_____

_____

_____

_____

overnment spending for social programs. Administrations and congressional leaders were reluctant to offset spiraling costs with either cuts in programs or tax increases. Meanwhile, inflation combined with high unemployment to produce an economic trend called stagflation. Low productivity in factories and increased competition from foreign companies also slowed the American economy.

Soaring gas prices were part of an energy crisis that crippled economies around the world during the 1970s. In the United States, rapid economic growth had been dependent on cheap, abundant oil. Wanting to gain from increased world oil prices, OPEC (Organization of Petroleum Exporting Countries) countries in 1973 refused to ship oil to foreign customers. This oil embargo was damaging to American—and world—economic stability because it increased the cost of producing a wide range of goods.

Sharp rises in the price of oil and gasoline contributed to double-digit inflation, or a rise in the general level of prices of 10 percent or more. By 1980 it cost more than $200 to purchase the same goods that $100 would have bought only 10 years earlier. At the same time, the United States government raised interest rates to all-time highs in an effort to discourage borrowing and bring the economy under control. These policies helped reduce inflation but caused a severe recession.

During the 1970s, the United States also experienced a trade deficit, or importing more goods than it was exporting, and the steady loss of American jobs. As other nations in the world became more industrialized, they began to compete with American companies for sales to American consumers. In the late 1970s, for example, rising gasoline prices led Americans to buy more fuel-efficient Japanese cars rather than larger American cars. The shift of American factories abroad to take advantage of cheaper, talented labor also had a chilling impact on the employment situation in the United States.

Canada

Canada thrived economically after World War II. By 1960, it had changed from a primarily agricultural country to one of the world's most important industrial nations. As in the United States, production in Canada boomed after World War II as consumers demanded household goods and new homes. The exploitation of Canada's rich mineral resources also enabled the Canadian economy to flourish. Foreign investors, mainly from the neighboring United States, financed the development of many new industries.

Improved communications and transportation strengthened Canada's trade links with the United States. One significant joint venture of both countries in the 1950s was the completion of the **St. Lawrence Seaway**, a system of locks and canals that allows ships to travel between the Great Lakes and the Atlantic Ocean.

Canada's World Role

Traditionally linked to Great Britain, Canada's loyalties to the parent country gradually diminished as British global influence plummeted after World War II. Meanwhile, Canada's new and growing economic strength convinced many Canadians that their country needed to play a more active, independent role in world affairs. In 1945, Canada became a founding member of the United Nations and sent troops to Korea as part of the UN forces in 1950. Canada also joined NATO when it was formed in 1949. During the 1950s, cold-war tensions brought the United States and Canada into a close defensive partnership.

In pursuing their foreign policy, Canadians were suspicious of a world dominated by superpowers. Over time, Canada advanced a role for itself as a middle power—that is, one that is strong economically, if not militarily. The Canadians used what military strength they had to promote peace. In 1956, Canada helped to bring about peace in the Middle East after Great Britain, France, and Israel had invaded Egypt. **Lester B. Pearson**, Canada's secretary of state for external affairs, won the 1957 Nobel Peace Prize for proposing and organizing a UN peacekeeping force for the troubled area.

A National Identity

In internal affairs, Canada struggled to find its own national identity during the period after World War II. While breaking many of their traditional ties to Europe, Canadians found themselves increasingly influenced by American ideas and practices. Most Canadians favored a continued close relationship to the United States. However, there were growing concerns that the "Americanization" of Canada posed a threat to Canada's newly emerging culture. In 1963, Pearson became Canada's prime minister. His administration expanded the country's social welfare programs and worked to strengthen Canadian national identity. Pearson achieved a personal goal when the Canadian parliament in 1965 adopted a new national flag, one that featured a red maple leaf as a symbol of Canada. The maple leaf soon became very popular

Global Gourmet

United States An American innovation that has spread around the world is the fast-food restaurant. From humble origins in hot-dog stands in the 1950s, fast-food outlets began to grow into a multibillion-dollar industry. Although their staple fare has been the American hamburger with fries and soft drinks, they now sell everything from minestrone soup to burritos. One of the factors encouraging fast-food growth has been an increase in the number of women who work outside the home.

Who?What?Where?When?

Ice Hockey More than 25 countries now play ice hockey, a game that originated in Canada. The sport began in military garrisons in the 1800s, when soldiers had time—and a lot of winter weather—on their hands.

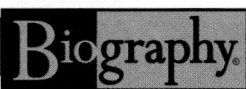

The following videotape programs are available from Glencoe:

- **John F. Kennedy: A Personal Story**
- **Jimmy Carter**

ASSESS

Check for Understanding

Assign Section 4 Assessment as homework or as an in-class activity.

Use Interactive Tutor Self-Assessment Software to review Section 4.

TEACHER NOTES

_____

_____

_____

_____

_____

Evaluate

 Section Quiz 32-4

🖳 Use the Testmaker to create a customized quiz for Section 4.

Reteach

Have students brainstorm a list of similarities and differences between the experiences of the United States and Canada during the cold war years.

 Reteaching Activity 32

📁 Reading Essentials and Study Guide 32-4

Enrich

Have students view one or more episodes of *Eyes on the Prize*, the public television series about the civil rights movement. Then have them describe their reactions to the video.

📁 Enrichment Activity 32

CLOSE

Have students discuss which they think was the most important event or development in the United States and in Canada during the cold war period.

Visualizing History The movement for an independent Quebec continued to gain strength through the 1990s. *How ethnically diverse is the population of Canada?*

among Canadians, who for years had honored some form of the Union Jack, or the British flag.

In 1967, Pearson presided over celebrations marking Canada's 100th anniversary of its nationhood. Many Canadians were especially proud of the fact that Canada had become a multicultural country, made up of people from many different ethnic groups. From 1945 to 1956, more than a million people from Germany, Italy, and other war-torn European countries had moved to farms or to **Toronto, Montreal**, and other large Canadian cities. In addition, other Canadians claimed Native American, Asian, African, or Latin American ancestry. Canada's population, however, was still

about 35 percent of British descent and about 30 percent of French descent.

Separatism

While celebrating their nationhood, Canadians also faced a growing challenge to their country's unity. During the 1960s, French Canadians began a movement to defend their rights throughout Canada. They also wanted English-speaking Canadians to recognize and respect their culture in the province of **Quebec**, where 80 percent of the people are French-speaking.

A growing debate arose over the issue of separatism, a movement favoring the establishment of Quebec as an independent country. The issue gave rise to the Parti Quebecois (kay•beh•KWAH), or Quebec party, sometimes known as the Separatist party. Opposing the separatist drive for Quebec independence was Canadian Prime Minister **Pierre Elliott Trudeau**, himself a French Canadian, who had been elected to office in 1968. Trudeau promised to protect French Canadian language and cultural rights while supporting a strong united Canada. In 1969, he had the Canadian parliament pass the Official Languages Act. This law required federal government offices to provide service in both French and English if 10 percent of the people in a particular area spoke either language.

The Official Languages Act brought many changes to Canada's government. However, it had little effect on the growing separatist movement. In 1976, the Parti Quebecois won control of Quebec's government and declared French the province's official language. It also promised to hold an election to decide Quebec's future.

SECTION 4 ASSESSMENT

Main Idea
1. Use a chart like the one below to identify social changes in the United States and Canada during the cold war.

United States	Canada
Social Changes	Social Changes

Recall
2. **Define** automation, racial segregation, imperial presidency, stagflation, embargo, double-digit inflation, trade deficit, middle power, multicultural, separatism.
3. **Identify** Dwight D. Eisenhower, John F. Kennedy, Lyndon B. Johnson, Richard M. Nixon, Martin Luther King, Jr., Gerald

R. Ford, Jimmy Carter, Lester B. Pearson, Pierre Elliott Trudeau.
Critical Thinking
4. **Analyzing Information** Why did President Eisenhower believe the military-industrial complex to be dangerous?
Understanding Themes
5. **Cooperation** Why did the United States and Canada develop close ties after 1945?

SECTION 4 ASSESSMENT ANSWERS

1. U.S.: increased automobile use; rapid growth of suburbs; greater TV use; Canada: Americanization; more social welfare programs; stronger national identity; multicultural country; separatism
2. All terms are defined in the Glossary.
3. Dwight D. Eisenhower, 885; John F. Kennedy, 885; Lyndon B. Johnson, 885;

Richard M. Nixon, 886; Martin Luther King, Jr., 887; Gerald R. Ford, 888; Jimmy Carter, 888; Lester B. Pearson, 889; Pierre Elliott Trudeau, 890
4. He believed that it encouraged increasing military spending to expand the arms race.
5. **COOPERATION** Because Canada's ties with Europe had weakened.

Understanding World Time Zones

Imagine that you work in New Jersey and call a client in London at 2:00 P.M. No one answers. Why? When it is 2:00 P.M. in New Jersey, it is already 7:00 P.M. in London.

Learning the Skill

In 1884 an international conference established standard world time zones. The Prime Meridian (0° longitude), which runs through Greenwich, England, became the reference point. The conference divided the world into 24 time zones. Traveling east from Greenwich, the time is one hour later in each time zone. Traveling west from Greenwich, the time is one hour earlier per zone.

The International Date Line is at 180° longitude. When crossing this line from west to east, you lose one day; when crossing in the opposite direction, you gain a day.

The map on this page illustrates the world time zones. Locate a reference point and note its time. Then locate the place for which you wish to know the time. Determine whether this place lies east or west of the reference point. Then count the number of time zones and add or subtract as needed. If the International Date Line lies between two points, add or subtract a day.

Practicing the Skill

Use the map to calculate these times.
1. If it is 3:00 P.M. in Greenwich, what time is it in Moscow?
2. If it is 9:00 A.M. in Cape Town, what time is it in Washington, D.C.?
3. If it is Tuesday, 4:30 P.M. in Japan, what day and time is it in Honolulu?
4. If it is Friday, 8:15 A.M. in Rio de Janeiro, what day and time is it in Beijing?

The **Glencoe Skillbuilder Interactive Workbook**, Level 2 provides instruction and practice in key social studies skills.

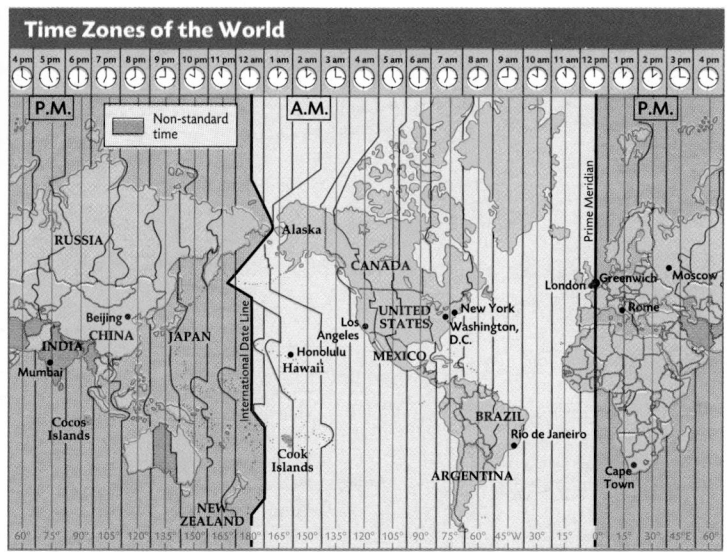

Time Zones of the World

Applying the Skill

Make up four time zone problems and compute the answers. Exchange your problems with a friend.

For More Practice

Turn to the Skill Practice in the Chapter Assessment on page 893 for more practice in understanding world time zones.

TEACH

Understanding World Time Zones
Point out that the United States has had standard time zones only since 1883, when they were instituted by America's railroads, which found the 100 different time zones in that era too difficult to cope with. Have students use the hour your class begins and then figure out what the time would be in the following places: Washington, D.C.; Toronto, Ontario; Budapest, Hungary; and Cairo, Egypt.

Additional Practice

📁 Skill Reinforcement Activity 32

📁 Building Skills in Geography Workbook, Unit 1, Lesson 10

GLENCOE TECHNOLOGY

Glencoe's **Skillbuilder Interactive Workbook, Level 2**
This interactive CD-ROM promotes student mastery of key social studies skills.

ANSWERS TO PRACTICING THE SKILL

1. 6 P.M.
2. 3 A.M.
3. Students will either answer Monday, 9:00 P.M. or Monday, 9:30 P.M. depending on which Japanese island student is using to count.
4. Saturday, 7:15 P.M.

WORLD HISTORY
Online

Have students use the **Chapter 32 Self-Check Quiz** at worldhistory.glencoe.com to prepare for the Chapter Test.

GLENCOE
TECHNOLOGY

VIDEODISC
Use MindJogger to review the chapter.

MindJogger Videoquiz

Chapter 32
Disc 4 Side B

Also available in VHS.

Answers

Using Key Terms
1. d 3. f 5. i
2. b 4. g

Using Your History Journal

Headings may include *Politics*, *The Economy*, and *Daily Life*.

Reviewing Facts
1. Great Britain: economically weak; welfare state; ruling monarch; gave colonies independence; France: growing economy; weak President, strong legislature; fought colonial independence
2. It provided financial aid to Europe to further stability. It spurred economic recovery.
3. to try to force the Western powers out of Berlin
4. In Albania, Yugoslavia, and Czechoslovakia, local communists took control. In Poland, East Germany, and Bulgaria, it was Soviet troops. Communist governments imposed Soviet government on their countries.
5. eased censorship; let some political groups meet freely

WORLD HISTORY
Online

Self-Check Quiz

Visit the *World History: The Human Experience* Web site at **world history.glencoe.com** and click on *Chapter 32—Self-Check Quiz* to prepare for the Chapter Test.

Using Key Terms

Write the key term that completes each sentence. Then write a sentence for each term not chosen.

a. cold war	g. dissidents
b. containment	h. separatism
c. ICBMs	i. racial segregation
d. iron curtain	j. imperial presidency
e. welfare states	k. peaceful coexistence
f. stagflation	l. middle power

1. The term _____ referred to the Soviet-made barrier that divided Europe into non-Communist and Communist areas.
2. To counter any expansionist threat from the Soviet Union, the Truman administration in 1947 developed a policy known as _____.
3. In the 1970s, inflation combined with high unemployment to produce _____.
4. Soviet leader Leonid Brezhnev applied harsh measures to _____ who criticized the Communist party or the Soviet government.
5. In *Brown* v. *Board of Education of Topeka, Kansas,* the United States Supreme Court ruled that _____ in public schools was illegal.

Technology Activity

Using E-mail One by-product of the computer revolution is the hundreds of new computer-related words we have added to our language, such as *surfing* and *modem.* Using E-mail, compose and send a message to a publisher of dictionaries, such as Merriam Webster, requesting a list of words that probably did not exist before computers were invented in the 1950s. Share your responses with the class.

Using Your History Journal

From your notes on the interviews with the people who remember the events of the 1950s or early 1960s, write a newspaper feature piece titled "Living Through the Cold War."

Reviewing Facts

1. **History** Use a chart like the one below to compare political and economic aspects of France and Great Britain after World War II.

Great Britain	France

2. **History** Explain the purpose of the Marshall Plan. In what ways was the plan effective?
3. **History** Explain why Joseph Stalin ordered the Berlin blockade.
4. **Government** Describe how Communists came to power in Eastern Europe. How did they govern?
5. **History** Identify the reforms that Dubček introduced in Czechoslovakia.
6. **History** Explain the meaning of *McCarthyism.*
7. **Citizenship** Identify the role of Martin Luther King, Jr., in the civil rights struggle.

Critical Thinking

1. **Apply** What postwar developments launched the cold war?
2. **Analyze** In your view, why did the United States assume global responsibility for containing communism?
3. **Synthesize** Create a time line showing major events in the spread of communism from 1945 to 1979. What effect did Communist expansion have on global affairs during this period?
4. **Evaluate** Was Americans' fear of communism during the 1950s justified? Do you think the actions that Congress took to counter

---

6. accusation of political subversion without regard to evidence
7. He protested discrimination nonviolently.

Critical Thinking
1. the Soviet imposition of communism in Eastern Europe; the division of Germany; the Berlin blockade; the formation of alliances
2. because it was a democratic superpower, firmly opposed to the spread of communism

3. Time line should show dates for communist takeovers, formation of Warsaw Pact, Korean War, and revolutions in China and Cuba. It contributed to the cold war competition in arms and diplomatic alliances.
4. Some students may feel communism posed little threat to the United States; others may say the Soviet Union was engaged in aggression. Congressional actions seem inappropriate because they exposed minimal Communist

communism were appropriate? Explain your reasoning.

5. Apply How do you think the cold war affected politics in Western European countries?

6. Synthesize Compare the economic systems of the United States, Great Britain, and the Soviet Union during the cold war era.

7. Apply Is the United States presidency today an imperial presidency? Why or why not?

8. Apply What was the major source of tension that led to French Canadian separatism?

Understanding Themes

1. Conflict By the 1950s the superpowers had enough nuclear weapons to eliminate each other. What effect did this power have on super-power relations during the cold war?

2. Change What might have happened if the Soviet Union had not used force to keep its Eastern European satellite countries under control?

3. Regionalism How did the European Common Market benefit member countries?

4. Cooperation How did the foreign policy of Canada compare and contrast with that of the United States during the cold war era?

Linking Past and Present

1. Key cold war issues continued until about 1989, when they reached a dramatic conclusion. Name these issues and explain their link to recent events.

2. Name a previous period in history when Europe was united. When did the continent become fragmented again?

3. Is containment an important or pressing issue in American foreign policy today? Explain your reasoning.

Geography in History

1. Location Refer to the map of Berlin on this page. What side of the city of Berlin became the Soviet sector after World War II?

2. Place What nations maintained army head-quarters in Berlin following the war?

Berlin After World War II

3. Movement Approximately how long was the wall that the Soviets built to keep East Germans from crossing to the West?

4. Location How many control points were located along the Berlin Wall?

Skill Practice

Refer to the map of World Time Zones on page 891 to answer the following questions.

1. Name some areas of the world in which you find non-standard time.

2. You are in New York and you want to call someone in Rome, Italy, at noon Rome time. When would you call?

3. Assume that flying from New York to London requires 6 hours. When would a flight leaving New York on a Wednesday at 6:00 P.M. arrive in London?

4. You are flying from Los Angeles to Moscow. You leave Los Angeles at 10:00 A.M. on Saturday and you arrive in Moscow on Sunday at 9:00 A.M. How many hours did you actually spend flying?

5. You are planning a flight from Mumbai, India, to Washington, D.C., that must connect through several cities. You will leave Mumbai on August 2, at 8:00 A.M., and will continue directly through Beijing and Los Angeles to Washington, D.C. What time is it in Washington, D.C., when you begin your trip? What will be the date when you arrive in Washington, D.C.?

able, sought ways to limit the arms race.

2. **CHANGE** They might have broken away and become independent or allied themselves with the West.

3. **REGIONALISM** It reduced conflict, lessened trade barriers, and raised the standard of living.

4. **COOPERATION** Although Canada joined the UN and NATO, it saw itself as a middle power and thus a peace-keeper.

Linking Past and Present

1. The iron curtain lifted and the Berlin Wall fell in 1989; Eastern Europe abandoned communism and instituted democratic reforms; the Warsaw Pact was dissolved.

2. under the Roman Empire; after the death of Charlemagne

3. No; the cold war is over, as is the threat of Soviet expansion.

Geography in History
1. east
2. France, Britain, United States, Soviet Union
3. approximately 26 miles (42 km)
4. 7

Skill Practice
1. Cook Islands, Newfoundland, Suriname, area north of Iceland, Saudi Arabia, Afghanistan, India and the Bay of Bengal, Cocos Islands, central Australia
2. 6:00 A.M.
3. 5:00 A.M. Thursday
4. 12 hours
5. 10 P.M. August 1; August 2

danger while destroying many careers.

5. It heightened fears of Soviet intervention while encouraging moves toward European unity.

6. U.S. had a prosperous free enterprise system, with recurring challenges of inflation and balancing budgets; Great Britain practiced democratic Socialism with some government economic controls and a welfare state; the Soviet Union had a government-run economy based on heavy industry with consumer goods

in short supply.

7. Some may feel the President has great power; others may say that the system of checks and balances works to limit the presidency.

8. Quebecois fear that their culture would not be recognized and respected

Understanding Themes
1. **CONFLICT** Both sides, realizing that using nuclear weapons was unaccept-

Chapter Bonus Test Question

Ask students: Could the cold war have been prevented? *(Yes, if the West had acted quickly after Stalin's first takeovers in Eastern Europe; no, Stalin would risk war to get what he wanted.)*

A complete, 1-page lesson plan is provided for each section in the *Reproducible Lesson Plans* booklet.

Asia and the Pacific

CHAPTER RESOURCES

	Reproducible Resources	Multimedia Resources
Chapter Opener	Chapter Themes: Graphic Organizer 33 Historical Significance Chapter Activity 33	MindJogger Videoquiz

Chapter Enrichment	Vocabulary Activity 33*
	Time Line Activity 33
	Mapping History Activity 33
	History Simulation 33
	Geography and History Activity 33
	Source Reading 33
	People in World History Profiles 63, 64
	World Art and Music Activity 33
	Enrichment Activity 33
	Critical Thinking Activity 33
	Skill Reinforcement Activity 33
	Performance Assessment Activity 33
	Standardized Test Practice Workbook Activity 33
	Inclusion for the Social Studies Classroom Strategies and Activities
		World History and Art Transparency 44, *Sydney Opera House*
		Mapping History Overlay Transparency 24
		Chapter Transparency 33
		Vocabulary PuzzleMaker Software
		World Music: Cultural Traditions, Lessons 7, 8, 9, 10
		Lessons of War: *Philosophy of Nonviolence*
		Communism and the Cold War:
		  • *Revolution in China*
		  • *Korean War*
		  • *Vietnam War*
		  • *Tiananmen Square*
		World History Primary Source Document Library

Chapter Review/Reteaching	Reteaching Activity 33 Skill Reinforcement Activity 33 Spanish Chapter Summary 33	Chapter 33 Digest Audiocassette, Activity, Test* Vocabulary PuzzleMaker Software Interactive Tutor Self-Assessment Software MindJogger Videoquiz
Chapter Evaluation/Testing	Performance Assessment Activity 33 Chapter 33 Test, Forms A and B	ExamView® Pro Testmaker

* *Also available in Spanis*

0:00 OUT OF TIME? Assign the Chapter 33 Audiocassettes.

World History Primary Source Document Library
Make History Come Alive!
Engage your students with over 250 easily accessible primary source documents—available on this CD-ROM—that will give them real life insight into the important events of world history.

Block Schedule

Activities that are particularly suited to use within the block scheduling framework are identified throughout this chapter by the following designation.

KEY TO ABILITY LEVELS

Teaching strategies are coded for varying learning styles.
L1 BASIC activities for all students
L2 AVERAGE activities for average to above-average students
L3 CHALLENGING activities for above-average students
LEP LIMITED ENGLISH PROFICIENCY activities

Use Glencoe's *Presentation Plus!* multimedia teacher tool to easily present dynamic lessons that visually excite your students. Using Microsoft PowerPoint® you can customize the presentations to create your own personalized lessons.

Interactive Lesson Planner

Planning has never been easier! Using this CD-ROM, organize your week, month, semester, or year with all the help you need. The **Interactive Lesson Planner** gives you access to all of the blackline masters that accompany *World History: The Human Experience.*

SECTION RESOURCES

Daily Objectives	Reproducible Resources	Multimedia Resources
Section 1 **Japan's Economic Rise** List the factors that have contributed to the economic success of Japan.	Lecture Notes 33-1 Reproducible Lesson Plan 33-1 Vocabulary Activity 33* Guided Reading Activity 33-1* History Simulation 33 Section Quiz 33-1* Reading Essentials and Study Guide 33-1	Section Focus Transparency 33-1 Mapping History Overlay Transparency 24, *Trade Between the U.S. and Japan* Chapter Transparency 33 Interactive Tutor Self-Assessment Software World Music: Cultural Traditions, Lesson 8
Section 2 **China in Revolution** Explain how communism has affected the domestic and international affairs of China since the late 1940s.	Lecture Notes 33-2 Reproducible Lesson Plan 33-2 Vocabulary Activity 33* Guided Reading Activity 33-2* Geography and History Activity 33 Section Quiz 33-2* Reading Essentials and Study Guide 33-2	Section Focus Transparency 33-2 Interactive Tutor Self-Assessment Software World Music: Cultural Traditions, Lesson 8 Communism and the Cold War
Section 3 **A Divided Korea** Describe how South Korea and North Korea have differed in their political and economic development.	Lecture Notes 33-3 Reproducible Lesson Plan 33-3 Vocabulary Activity 33* Guided Reading Activity 33-3* Section Quiz 33-3* Reading Essentials and Study Guide 33-3	Section Focus Transparency 33-3 Interactive Tutor Self-Assessment Software Communism and the Cold War
Section 4 **Southeast Asia** Explain how nationalism, the cold war, and the rise of a global economy have affected Southeast Asia.	Lecture Notes 33-4 Reproducible Lesson Plan 33-4 Vocabulary Activity 33* Guided Reading Activity 33-4* Section Quiz 33-4* Reading Essentials and Study Guide 33-4	Section Focus Transparency 33-4 Interactive Tutor Self-Assessment Software World Music: Cultural Traditions, Lesson 9 Communism and the Cold War
Section 5 **South Asia** Identify the challenges that have faced the countries of South Asia since independence.	Lecture Notes 33-5 Reproducible Lesson Plan 33-5 Vocabulary Activity 33* Guided Reading Activity 33-5* Section Quiz 33-5* Reading Essentials and Study Guide 33-5	Section Focus Transparency 33-5 Interactive Tutor Self-Assessment Software World Music: Cultural Traditions, Lesson 7 Lessons of War
Section 6 **The Pacific** List the factors that have helped Pacific nations develop prosperous economies and new national identities since World War II.	Lecture Notes 33-6 Reproducible Lesson Plan 33-6 Guided Reading Activity 33-6* Reteaching Activity 33 Enrichment Activity 33 Section Quiz 33-6* Performance Assessment Activity 33 Spanish Chapter Summary 33 Reading Essentials and Study Guide 33-6	Section Focus Transparency 33-6 World History and Art Transparency 44, *Sydney Opera House* Vocabulary PuzzleMaker Software Interactive Tutor Self-Assessment Software Testmaker World Music: Cultural Traditions, Lesson 10

Chapter Activities

✓ Performance Assessment Activity

A Page on the Internet Many of the physical and ideological conflicts in Korea, Vietnam, and China, as well as the economic conflicts the United States has had with Japan, still affect Americans today. Many people have lived through these times, and others have strong opinions about them. Have students design a page for the Internet giving information about one of these historical conflicts, their own opinions, information regarding interviews they have had with Americans who have experiences to share, and current laws or reforms that can be traced back to these conflicts.

Possible Rubric Features

Research skills, interviewing techniques, accuracy of content information, appropriateness to audience and purpose, clarity and organization, and use of technology

• *For an additional activity, refer to Activity 33 in the* Performance Assessment Strategies and Activities *booklet.*

ACTIVITY

From the Classroom of...

**Anna Mae Grimm
Homestead High School
Mequon, WI**

Leading a Developing Republic

Students will play the roles of the newly elected president and cabinet of a fictitious developing country, to gain a perspective on the complexities involved in national development. Students should take the roles of president; military leader; ministers of health, industry, finance, trade, agriculture, public works; leaders of two religious groups; farmers; businesspeople; feminists; and the unemployed—all of them with competing interests.

   Have students participate in a roundtable discussion and try to create a national structure that keeps everyone happy. Students should keep in mind that their country is poor, with health and literacy problems. It does, however, have abundant untapped natural resources. Remind students that their contribution to the discussion should reflect the interests of their chosen role. Ask students to discuss whether their discussion gave them insight into the complexities involved in industrializing a developing country.

MULTIPLE LEARNING STYLES

Verbal/Linguistic

Ask students to conduct an interview of a veteran of the Korean or Vietnam War, focusing on wartime experiences and postwar reflections. Have students write up the interview for possible classroom presentation.

Visual/Spatial

Have students draw the national flag for each country in this chapter. Ask them to research the meaning of any symbols, colors, and wording on the flags.

Auditory/Musical

Have the class listen to a tape or CD of *Miss Saigon*, the musical about the relationship between a young Vietnamese woman and an American soldier in 1975 at the end of the Vietnam War.

Kinesthetic

Have students investigate the degree to which Western styles of dress have been adopted in the countries discussed in this chapter and the extent to which traditional styles are still worn. Suggest that students make drawings illustrating existing traditional styles.

GLENCOE'S **ASSESSMENT** ADVANTAGE

Use the following to easily assess student learning in a variety of ways.

- Performance Assessment Strategies and Activities
- Section Quizzes
- Chapter and Unit Tests
- Interactive Tutor Self-Assessment Software
- Testmaker Software
- MindJogger Videoquiz
- SAT/SAT II Test Practice
- worldhistory.glencoe.com

Additional Resources

Teacher's Corner

INDEX TO NATIONAL GEOGRAPHIC MAGAZINE

The following articles relate to this chapter:

- "Kashmir: Trapped in Conflict," by Lewis M. Simons, September 1999.
- "The New Saigon," by Tracy Dahlby, April 1995.
- "Shanghai: Where China's Past and Future Meet," by William S. Ellis, March 1994.
- "Kyushu: Japan's Southern Gateway," by Tracy Dahlby, January 1994.
- "Taiwan: The Other China Changes Course," by Arthur Zich, November 1993.

ADDITIONAL NATIONAL GEOGRAPHIC SOCIETY PRODUCTS

To order the following, call National Geographic at 1-800-368-2728:

- *The Democratic Government Series: Japan (Video)*
- *China: Sichuan Province (Video)*
- *Australia's Aborigines (Video)*
- *Nations of the World Series: Australia, Japan (Videos)*
- *Asia Political (Map)*
- *Australia and Oceania (Laminated Desk Maps)*

Access National Geographic's new dynamic MapMachine Web site and other geography resources at:

- http://www.nationalgeographic.com/
- http://www.nationalgeographic.com/maps/

BIBLIOGRAPHY

Literature of the Period

Oe, Kenzaburo. *Nip the Buds, Shoot the Kids.* Translated by Paul St. John Mackintosh and Maki Sugiyama. New York: Marion Boyars, 1995. This first novel by the winner of the 1994 Nobel Prize in literature tells the story of a band of teenage delinquents in wartime.

Readings for the Student

Marrin, Albert. *America and Vietnam: The Elephant and the Tiger.* New York: Viking, 1992. The causes and effects of the Vietnam War.

Readings for the Teacher

Paik, Sun Yup. *From Pusan to Panmunjom.* New York: Macmillan, 1992. A South Korean commander describes his involvement in the Korean War.

WORLD HISTORY Online

Use our Web site as an additional resource. All essential content is covered in the Student Edition.

You and your students can visit the *World History: The Human Experience* Web site at worldhistory.glencoe.com The student text directs students to the Web site for the following options:

- **Chapter Overviews**
- **Student Web Activities**
- **Self-Check Quizzes**

Answers are provided for you in a link entitled "Web Activity Lesson Plan." Additional Web Resources, Interactive Puzzles, and content updates are also available.

Visit the Glencoe Web site at socialstudies.glencoe.com for social studies activities, updates, and links to other resources.

LOCAL OBJECTIVES

_____
_____
_____
_____
_____
_____
_____
_____
_____
_____
_____
_____
_____
_____
_____
_____
_____
_____
_____
_____

Chapter Themes are listed by section on this chapter opening page of the Student Edition. A corresponding theme-based activity is available under "TEACH," and a theme-based question is asked in the Section and Chapter Assessments.

Storyteller

Historical Setting Although the kimono is universally recognized as a Japanese garment, this familiar ankle-length gown with long, wide sleeves actually derives from a Chinese robe. The transformation of the kimono into a work of art, however, is attributable to Japanese designers of the 1600s and 1700s. Their stylistic prowess turned a simple garment into one of the world's most beautiful articles of clothing. Although Japanese men and women have worn the kimono since the Early Nara period (A.D. 645–724), the broad sash, or obi, that holds the buttonless garment together is of more recent origin, dating from the 1700s.

Historical Significance

Answers: *The countries of Asia play an important role in world politics, economics, and culture.*

Several Asian nations have emerged as economic models; Asian cinema, music, and religion have had a growing influence; and world peace has been affected by Asia since 1945.

Have students use the **Chapter 33 Overview** at <u>worldhistory. glencoe.com</u> as a prereading and postreading exercise for understanding chapter content.

Chapter

33

1945–Present

Asia and the Pacific

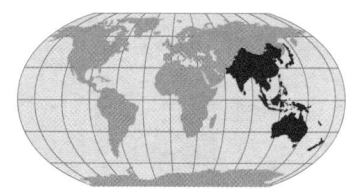

Chapter Themes

▶ **Change** Japan builds a democracy and a strong economy. *Section 1*
▶ **Revolution** Communists in China introduce socialist measures, and then promote a limited free enterprise economy. *Section 2*
▶ **Regionalism** After decades of conflict and cold war tensions, North Korea and South Korea take first steps toward unification. *Section 3*
▶ **Conflict** The rise of nationalism and cold war competition leads to conflict in Southeast Asia. *Section 4*
▶ **Diversity** A diversity of religious and ethnic groups challenges the unity in South Asia. *Section 5*
▶ **Cultural Diffusion** Changing political and economic roles open the nations of the Pacific to other parts of the globe. *Section 6*

Storyteller

"My methods are old," declares Japanese artist Kako Muriguchi, *"but my designs are new."* Muriguchi designs innovative patterns for kimonos, the traditional Japanese garment for women. The people of Japan have such respect for his contributions to their heritage that they have declared him a *"living national treasure."* As a result of this designation, Muriguchi is entitled to lifetime national support for his art. Like Muriguchi, Japan and other countries in Asia have found success by combining old and new. Traditional values that encourage education and hard work, combined with modern developments, such as computer technology, have brought prosperity to many countries in Asia since the end of World War II.

Historical Significance

What role do the countries of Asia and the Pacific play in the contemporary world? How have they contributed to the world's economy, culture, and politics since 1945?

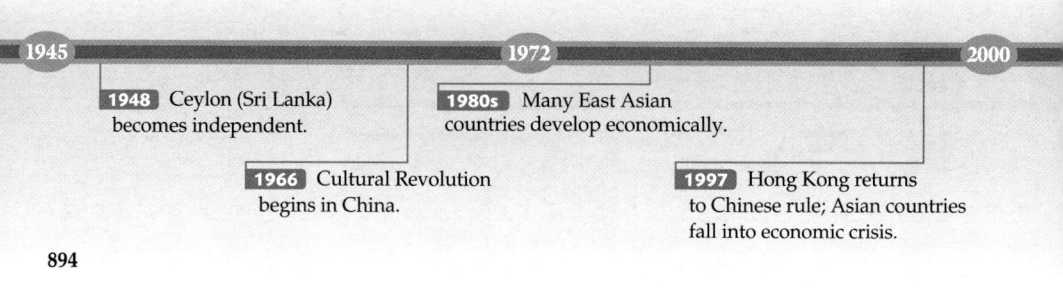

| 1945 | | 1972 | | 2000 |

1948 Ceylon (Sri Lanka) becomes independent.

1980s Many East Asian countries develop economically.

1966 Cultural Revolution begins in China.

1997 Hong Kong returns to Chinese rule; Asian countries fall into economic crisis.

894

GEOGRAPHY CONNECTION

Location Have students use a globe to locate the countries discussed in this chapter: Japan, China, Taiwan, North Korea, South Korea, India, Pakistan, Bangladesh, Myanmar, Sri Lanka, Vietnam, Cambodia, Laos, Thailand, Indonesia, Singapore, the Philippines, Australia, and New Zealand. Which of the countries are large? *(China, India, Australia)* Do you think that size is a measure of a country's power or importance? *(No. India is relatively big, but much of its population is poor. Japan is small but economically advanced.)*

Visualizing History Hong Kong's skyline is aglow with lights in celebration of the territory's return to Chinese rule on June 30, 1997.

Visualizing History

On June 30, 1997, ceremonies were held to commemorate the transfer of Hong Kong from British to Chinese rule. A band of Scots Guards played "God Save the Queen" as Britain's Union Jack flag was lowered. On the other side of the stage, the Chinese flag was raised as a band played the Chinese national anthem. The festivities were televised throughout China.

Performance Assessment

Refer to the activity on page 894C of the Planning Guide.

For an additional activity, refer to Activity 33 in the *Performance Assessment Strategies and Activities* booklet.

WORLD HISTORY Online

Chapter Overview

Visit the *World History: The Human Experience* Web site at **worldhistory.glencoe.com** and click on *Chapter 33—Chapter Overview* to preview the chapter.

Your History Journal

Interview someone who migrated to the United States from an Asian or Pacific nation, or research the culture of an Asian or Pacific nation. Write a short report on the cultural adjustments a person from that nation would make to live in the United States.

Using Your History Journal

Advise students to prepare a specific list of questions they want to have answered before they begin their interviews.

GLENCOE TECHNOLOGY

VIDEODISC
Use MindJogger to preview chapter content.

MindJogger Videoquiz

Chapter 33
Disc 5 Side A

 Also available in VHS.

Chapter 33 *Asia and the Pacific* 895

+ EXTRA CREDIT PROJECT

Oral Report Ask students to research the industrial and economic development of China from the Communist takeover to the present. Advise them to consider the effects of the First Five-Year Plan, the Great Leap Forward, the Cultural Revolution, and the reform measures introduced following Mao's death. Have students summarize their findings in a brief oral report. Suggested resources: J. K. Fairbank, *China: A New History*; Feng Jicai, *Voices from the Whirlwind: An Oral History of the Chinese Cultural Revolution*; W. Overholt, *The Rise of China*; R. Terrill, *China in Our Time.*

1945   **1972**   **2000**

1947 Japan adopts democratic constitution.

1980s Japan has one of the world's most successful economies.

1995 Severe earthquake strikes Kobe area.

Section 1

Japan's Economic Rise

Guide to Reading

Read to Find Out
Main Idea *Certain factors have contributed to the economic success of Japan.*

▶ **Terms to Define**
gross domestic product, pollution, sect, quota

▶ **People to Meet**
Douglas MacArthur, Hirohito

▶ **Places to Locate**
Tokyo, Kobe

The Storyteller

Kyoichi Tabuchi's plane landed in Bangkok, the city he would now call home. He had accepted a position as manager of an industrial complex. The Thai government eagerly received Tabuchi and his fellow Japanese for establishing economic opportunities. The age of Heisei, or peaceful achievement, had begun. Japan's economy was booming; her industry was welcomed throughout the region she had occupied militarily just 50 years earlier. As Tabuchi drove to the Japanese district, he heard the radio play a song that clearly defined the beneficial situation: "The Samurai Are Here."

—adapted from "Japan's Sun Rises Over the Pacific," *National Geographic*, November, 1995, Arthur Zich

Ascendant electronics

The end of World War II brought dramatic changes to Asia; Japan was stripped of the lands it had conquered. Great Britain, France, and the Netherlands were forced to withdraw from their Asian colonies, and new nations arose. Communists won control in China and North Korea, and the cold war affected the entire region. Out of the turmoil, vigorous industrial powers have emerged. Japan's transformation into a global economic giant has been one of the most important changes of the post-World War II era.

Occupation and Reform

Japan, a proud nation with a long history of self-reliance, ended World War II with its pride crushed, its economy wrecked, and its people demoralized by the humiliating defeat. The victorious countries established an occupation government, the Supreme Command of the Allied Powers (SCAP), to govern Japan after the war. Although planned as a joint venture of the Allies, the occupation government became entirely a United States enterprise, headed by General **Douglas MacArthur**. The general was determined not to plant the seeds of future war by imposing an unjust and unworkable system on the Japanese. MacArthur's reform policies affected Japan's political and economic spheres, and Japan made a remarkable recovery.

A New Constitution

SCAP required Japan to adopt a new constitution in 1947. The constitution stripped the imperial family of its political power and gave it to the Japanese citizens. No longer could Japanese emperors rule by their claim to divine authority. Instead, Emperor **Hirohito** remained in office as a symbol of the state. The constitution also established a cabinet based on the British model. Both houses of the Diet, or legislature, were made elective, and citizens over the age of 20 could vote. A bill of rights guaranteed basic freedoms.

The new constitution included an unusual provision. Article 9 barred Japan from all warfare except for defense—"The Japanese people forever renounce war as a sovereign right of the nation.... land, sea, and air forces, as well as other war potential, will never be maintained." SCAP hoped that this would prevent Japan from ever threatening its neighbors again. The United States agreed to protect Japan militarily. In the late 1990s, the United States still had troops—47,000 in all—stationed on Japanese territory, most of them on the island of Okinawa. This military arrangement enabled Japan to concentrate more of its resources on consumer goods than on military equipment. It also reassured other nations of the region who feared the revival of a militarily strong Japan.

Economic Reform

SCAP also set out to decentralize Japanese agriculture and industry. Landlords not living on their property could own only 2.5 acres (1.1 ha) of land. The law required them to sell off holdings above this figure at very low prices. Those who actually farmed the soil were permitted to own up to 7.5 acres (3.1 ha). Decentralization changed the face of Japanese agriculture, resulting in the transfer of more than 5 million acres (2 million ha). Although Japanese farmers have prospered, small-scale farming has been costly and inefficient. Today, the Japanese government subsidizes farmers by buying their crops at high prices to cover farmers' costs and then resells the crops to consumers at a loss.

SCAP took steps to decentralize the *zaibatsu*, the giant industrial and banking organizations that controlled Japanese industry. General MacArthur believed that removal of *zaibatsu* control would prevent Japan from rearming. The Korean War, however, led the United States to change this policy and gave renewed life to Japan's large industrial organizations. It was hoped by the United States that a strong Japanese economy would help contain the spread of communism in Asia.

Japan's Dramatic Recovery

Japan's shattered economy recovered quickly in the early 1950s with assistance from the United States. The Korean War created a vast need for all kinds of war supplies, ranging from trucks to uniforms and medical supplies. To have sources of supply close at hand, the United States poured $3.5 billion into Japan—an amount nearly equal to what

Visualizing History **Japan's Emperor Hirohito (center) reigned from 1926 until his death in 1989. His son, Akihito, succeeded him.** *What changes came to Japan's government during the late 1940s?*

the United States gave Germany under the Marshall Plan. The United States also provided training in management skills so that Japan was able to rebuild its factories to the latest standards. Japanese shipbuilders, car manufacturers, electronics and pharmaceutical industries all benefited from American aid and later became major leaders in the global economy.

As part of its recognition of Japan's support to the United States during the Korean War, a formal peace treaty with Japan was reached in 1951 and the American occupation of Japan ended.

Government-Business Cooperation

The Japanese government and Japan's well-educated workforce took advantage of the boom created by the United States. Although Japan had to import most of its raw materials, the Japanese economy expanded quickly. Japan's engineers, managers, and laborers worked hard to boost the country's prosperity. The Japanese government worked closely with large corporations to plan and promote industrial growth. They brought vision to long-range planning and then followed through on their

---

TEACH

Guided Practice

THEME **Change**

Have students give examples of political, economic, and cultural reforms instituted by MacArthur in Japan. Ask students if they think making these changes was easy. **L1**

Visualizing History Hirohito was the longest-reigning ruler in Japan's history. From the outset, the period of his rule was named *Showa*, or "Enlightened Peace." Even though World War II took place during Hirohito's reign, he wound up accepting the Allied terms of surrender. A few months later he renounced the tradition of conferring divine status on Japan's emperors.

Answer to Caption: *A new constitution stripped the imperial family of its political power, established a cabinet based on the British model, and barred Japan from all warfare except for defense.*

Japan's Dramatic Recovery
What changes came to Japan's economy after World War II? *American aid and Japanese know-how enabled Japan to rebuild its economy. Japan's government and business leaders invested heavily in electronics and automobiles for export. By the 1970s Japan had become a leader in the world market.*

The Arts Arrange a classroom showing of the Japanese director Akira Kurosawa's *Rhapsody in August*, about the bombing of Nagasaki during World War II. After viewing the film, have the class discuss it. **L2**

COOPERATIVE LEARNING ACTIVITY

TV Interview Organize the class into two groups: one group to prepare interview questions to ask General MacArthur, the other group to prepare questions for Emperor Hirohito. Questions should be based on research of topics such as demilitarization, government, economic reform, and world affairs. Have students from both groups meet to combine their questions into a satisfactory list. Then appoint students to act as MacArthur, Hirohito, and an interviewer, and have them practice role-playing a TV interview. When students are prepared, invite another class or families to attend the mock broadcast. **L3**

Visualizing History By 1980, Japan had overtaken West Germany, France, Great Britain, and the United States to become the world's leading automotive producer.
Answer to Caption: *Japan increased its share of world automobile production from 3 percent in 1960 to 29 percent in 1980.*

Geography: Location Have students locate Japan, China, Taiwan, Korea, and Indonesia on a map. Point out how proximity would cause these countries to be involved in one another's affairs. Have students note examples of this involvement as study of the chapter proceeds. **L2 LEP**

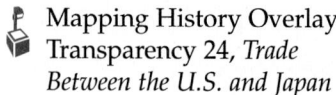 Mapping History Overlay Transparency 24, *Trade Between the U.S. and Japan*

 Chapter Transparency 33

 History Simulation 33

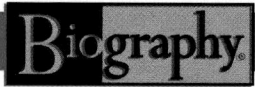 World Music: Cultural Traditions, Lesson 8

Biography

The following videotape program is available from Glencoe:
• **Hirohito**

Independent Practice
Guided Reading Activity 33-1 **L1**

decisions. For example, in the late 1950s government and industry agreed to invest heavily in research and development in the home electronics field. By the early 1970s, Japanese radios, televisions, stereos, and other items were challenging American dominance in the world market.

Similarly, the Japanese government and industrial leaders targeted the automobile industry as one they thought could help bring prosperity to Japan. The government helped fund researchers who developed dependable, high-mileage automobiles. Managers and laborers worked together to develop newer and more efficient production techniques. As a result of these innovations, Japan began producing high-quality cars at competitive prices, and sales of Japanese automobiles around the world soared. Japan increased its share of world automobile production from 3 percent in 1960 to a full 29 percent in 1980.

By 1980 Japan had one of the world's most successful economies. Although only as big as California, Japan's gross domestic product (GDP)—the sum value of all goods and services it produced—was about half that of the United States. Its per capita GDP, the amount of production per individual, was among the highest in the industrialized world.

Japan's rapid growth continued through the 1980s. Between 1988 and 1992, the annual growth rate was 5 percent, one of the highest rates in the world. Japanese businesses invested heavily overseas in real estate, banks, and factories.

In 1997, a severe economic slump affected Japan and several other Asian nations. Because of Japan's role as a major lending nation, Japanese banks were especially hard hit. Japanese companies also faced losses, and unemployment increased. Concerned about the global impact of the economic

crisis, the United States and other industrial nations urged Japan to stimulate its economy by cutting taxes and ending regulations that restricted production and trade.

Side Effects of Growth

Like many other industrialized countries, postwar Japan had solid economic growth that raised the standard of living of its citizens. However, the spread of industry also caused environmental damage. Japan's industries clustered along a narrow coastal belt between the city of **Tokyo** and the southernmost Japanese island, Kyushu. Along with industry came a dense concentration of people and automobiles and pollution, or the release of impure or poisonous substances into land, water, and air. In addition, rapid industrial development had created severe housing shortages in urban areas. Government and business leaders began to take steps to balance industrial growth with environmental protection.

Politics and Government

Until recently, Japan's economic growth had been bolstered by an extraordinary level of political stability. From 1955 to 1993, one political party dominated the Japanese government. Despite its name, the Liberal Democratic Party (LDP) is a conservative, pro-business party that has had broad Japanese support. The LDP has traditionally been strong among Japan's farming population, but it also receives heavy financial support from the country's large corporations. Voters liked the party's dependability, especially during the uncertainty of the cold war.

Learning Style: Logical/Mathematical Have students create a time line of important events in Japan's history between World War II and the present. Before advising students on the appropriate scale to use (for example, three inches per year), determine how much wall space you have available to display the five time lines that students will generate as they study other sections in this chapter. Tell students to include political, religious, economic, and cultural events, as well as natural disasters such as the 1995 Kobe earthquake. **L1**

In 1993, Japanese voters voted out the scandal-weakened LDP. With the collapse of the Soviet Union and the end of the cold war, it seemed safe to support the chief opposition party, the Social Democratic Party of Japan (SDPJ). The splintered SDPJ was forced to form a coalition government and to include many LDP leaders in the cabinet.

Because of its political diversity, the new government had difficulty steering Japan through a number of crises. In January 1995, a severe earthquake struck the area around the port city of **Kobe**. It was one of the deadliest natural disasters to hit Japan in the twentieth century. Political opponents criticized the government for not responding rapidly to provide relief to the quake victims.

Japan also encountered the ugly face of terrorism. In March 1995, a Japanese sect, or small religious group, carried out a nerve gas attack in Tokyo's subway system, leaving 12 people dead and 5,000 injured. A month later, another gas attack in a railroad station in the city of Yokohama injured more than 300 people. The two attacks stunned most Japanese, who considered their society violence-free, and heightened security concerns among government officials and business leaders.

In early 1996 the LDP regained its influence over Japanese politics. A new prime minister, Ryutaro Hashimoto (ree•you•TAH•roh hah•shee•MOH•toh), promised to rid Japan's government of corruption and promote economic growth. Hashimoto failed to achieve his goals, however, and was forced to resign in 1998. He was replaced by Keizo Obuchi (KY•zo oh•BU•shee).

Japan in World Affairs

As a result of its economic growth since World War II, once self-reliant and isolated Japan became tightly interwoven in the world economy. Economic power has made Japan a world political leader as well, but the Japanese have been unsure how to use their power in world affairs.

Trade Tensions

Japan's economic prosperity has created tensions with other countries in the area of trade. Japan today exports more products than it imports. It therefore has trade surpluses with many countries. By contrast, Japan's major trading partners—the United States, Europe, and neighboring Asian

Chapter 33
Section 1

Linking Past and Present

Religion and Government In 1868 the Japanese government set up an official religion, State Shinto, which emphasized loyalty to the nation and worship of the emperor as a god. When the government abolished State Shinto after World War II in a historic radio broadcast on January 1, 1946, Hirohito claimed that the emperor was not a divine being. Thirteen years later, in 1959, Hirohito's son, Akihito, broke a 1,500-year-old tradition when he married a commoner, Shoda Michiko. Akihito became emperor upon Hirohito's death in 1989.

Economics

Japan's Steel Industry

Japan's steel industry was devastated by World War II. Steel, like other Japanese industries, needed a major rebuilding effort.

Beginning in the 1950s Japan poured capital into new steelmaking facilities. An efficient method of continuous casting, computer-controlled production systems, and speed smelting made Japanese plants the most efficient in the world.

With the advantage of greater productivity, Japan began to sell steel at lower prices on the world market. By the 1980s, American steelmakers who had dominated world production were complaining that the Japanese were dumping underpriced steel on the market.

The United States responded with voluntary restraint agreements to hold imported steel to 20 percent of its domestic market. Japanese companies began to buy into United States steel companies.

By the year 2000, Japan's economic growth slowed, and American steel companies regained the lead in productivity. Then Japanese and American steelmakers started joint ventures to find even more efficient methods of making steel.

Japanese steel mill

ACTIVITY

Discuss three methods that enabled Japan to become the world's most efficient steel producer. How did competition in the making of steel change from the 1980s to the 1990s?

Linking Past and Present

Japan's Steel Industry

Japan has proved that by industrializing, non-Western nations can become not only the equals of the Western powers but also economically superior to some of the strongest.

ANSWERS

continuous casting, computer-controlled production systems, and speed smelting; Japanese and American steelmakers competed against each other in the 1980s, but in the 1990s they began joint steelmaking ventures

MAKING CONNECTIONS ACTIVITIES

Science, Technology, and Society The Japanese have a deep reverence for nature and longevity. Both are reflected in the ancient Japanese art of bonsai, in which trees are carefully pruned to be no more than a few feet tall and may live for centuries. Have students research the techniques used in bonsai and do a demonstration for the class. **L3**

Earthquakes Have students use *Readers' Guide to Periodical Literature* to find articles about Japan's reaction to the 1995 Kobe earthquake and the United States's reaction to the 1989 San Francisco earthquake. Ask them to write a comparison and contrast of the national responses to the two events. **L2**

ASSESS

Check for Understanding

Assign Section 1 Assessment as homework or as an in-class activity.

 Use Interactive Tutor Self-Assessment Software to review Section 1.

Evaluate

Section Quiz 33-1

Use the Testmaker to create a customized quiz for Section 1.

Reteach

Ask students to explain the relevance of each of the following to the modern history of Japan: SCAP, 1947 constitution, and decentralization. (*The Supreme Command of the Allied Powers, or SCAP, governed postwar Japan; the new constitution provided democratic reforms; business and agricultural monopolies were decentralized right after the war, dramatically changing the face of Japanese agriculture.*)

Reading Essentials and Study Guide 33-1

Enrich

Have students write short biographical sketches of the two recent Japanese winners of the Nobel Prize in literature: Yasunari Kawabata (1968) and Kenzaburo Oe (1994).

CLOSE

Have students write one or two paragraphs assessing whether it was right for MacArthur to impose his political views on an entire nation. (*Answers will vary. Students may point to the great success Japan enjoys today and say that the end justifies the means.*)

---

lands—have trade deficits with Japan. That is, they import more goods from Japan than they export to it. Because of this trade imbalance, other industrialized countries have pressured Japan to change its trade laws to make it easier for their companies to sell their products to Japanese consumers.

Japanese government regulations limit the ability of foreign companies to sell goods in Japan. Japanese retailers have long-standing ties with local producers that they want to maintain. Japanese farmers want to continue trade protection for their crops and livestock rather than face competition from lower-priced imports. Japanese consumers often prefer to purchase goods made in Japan because the goods are well made and because they wish to protect the jobs of Japanese citizens.

Overcoming Japanese trade barriers has been difficult and frustrating for foreigners. In 1995 a trade war between the United States and Japan was prevented by a compromise agreement. In the accord, the United States agreed not to impose trade quotas, or specified restrictions, on Japanese goods. In return, Japan agreed to encourage its auto companies to increase purchases of American car parts and to step up production at their plants in the United States. Since 1997 Japan has taken steps to open markets in a variety of industries.

Military Issues

Since the early 1950s, Japan has relied on the United States for its national security. However, the fall of Soviet communism in 1991 greatly reduced Japanese fears of an attack from the Russians. Today most Japanese still expect American help in any emergency, but many of them question the need for large numbers of American troops in their country. Tensions have flared on Okinawa between local residents and American troops. In 1996 Japan and the United States agreed that some of the American military sites on Okinawa would be returned to Japan by 2003. In the meantime, American troop strength would remain the same.

Japan also faces the issue of taking on more responsibility for its own defense and that of other parts of Asia. Some American leaders claim that Japan's low defense budget gives Japan an economic advantage in non-defense industries. They also believe that Japan's economic strength requires that it play a part in maintaining peace in Asia. Many Japanese, however, oppose an expansion of the country's military role. In 1990, when the Middle Eastern country of Iraq invaded its neighbor Kuwait, the United States called upon Japan to help force Iraq out of Kuwait. The Japanese government responded with a financial contribution to the military effort but refused to send troops. Two years later, however, Japan did send troops overseas as part of a United Nations peacekeeping mission in war-torn Cambodia.

In 1997 Japan cautiously took steps to increase its role in the military alliance with the United States. It stated that, in any emergency, the Japanese military would support American forces with sea operations, facilities, equipment, and fuel. In return for changes in the alliance, Japan wants a permanent seat on the UN Security Council.

Japan and Its Neighbors

With the most advanced economy in East Asia, Japan since the 1970s has increased its influence in the region. Beginning in 1978, Japan improved relations and forged new trading links with China. Today large amounts of Japanese aid and investment flow to the Chinese. Japan also has developed ties with South Korea, but is more hesitant with Communist North Korea because of concerns that North Korea is intent on pursuing aggressive policies in Asia. Since the late 1970s, the Japanese have greatly expanded trade and investment links with Southeast Asia, one of their fastest growing markets. Still Japan's past continues to trouble relations with its neighbors. Many people in China, Korea, and Southeast Asia recall with bitterness Japan's harsh occupation of their lands during World War II. They fear a renewal of Japanese power in East Asia, whether economic or military.

SECTION 1 ASSESSMENT

Main Idea
1. Use a diagram like the one below to show factors contributing to Japan's economic success.

Japan's Economic Success

Recall
2. **Define** gross domestic product, pollution, sect, quota.
3. **Identify** Douglas MacArthur, Hirohito, Liberal Democratic Party.

Critical Thinking
4. **Synthesizing Information** Imagine how Japan's modern

history might have been different if General MacArthur had wanted to punish the Japanese for their actions in World War II.

Understanding Themes
5. **Change** What economic policies have promoted Japan's prosperity since World War II?

SECTION 1 ASSESSMENT ANSWERS

1. Korean War created need for war supplies; U.S. gave $3.5 billion and management training to Japan; engineers and managers worked hard; industrial growth promoted; electronics and auto developments
2. All terms are defined in the Glossary.
3. MacArthur, 896; Hirohito, 896; LDP, 898

4. Answers will vary. Students might suggest that the Japanese may have resented MacArthur and returned to militarism.
5. **CHANGE** Japan has focused on building a strong economy and the government has worked closely with large corporations to promote industrial growth.

1949 Communists proclaim the People's Republic of China.

1972 United States President Richard M. Nixon visits China.

1989 Chinese students in Beijing call for democracy.

Section 2

China in Revolution

Guide to Reading

Read to Find Out
Main Idea *Communism has affected the domestic and international affairs of China since the late 1940s.*

▶ **Terms to Define**
communes, pragmatists, special economic zone

▶ **People to Meet**
Chiang Kai-shek, Mao Zedong, Deng Xiaoping, Jiang Jing, Zhou Enlai, Jiang Zemin, Dalai Lama

▶ **Places to Locate**
Beijing, Taiwan, Taipei, Shanghai, Tibet, Hong Kong

The Storyteller

Wang Xin had heard his father and grandfather talk about the old days in China. As peasants, they owned no land. If someone was unable to work, he was dismissed by the landlord and had to beg or live off his family. But when Wang was a small boy, things changed. The peasants became masters, receiving shares of farmland. They were no longer starving. Wang's family of 10 people moved from a three-room house to one with seven rooms and a tile roof. For the rest of his life, Wang Xin would remember how happy the peasants were that spring of 1950.

—adapted from "A Peasant Maps His Road to Wealth," *Beijing Review*, reprinted in *Documents in World History*, Peter Stearns, 1988

Chinese peasant's house

A fter World War II, the Nationalists under **Chiang Kai-shek** and the Communists led by **Mao Zedong** fought a bitter civil war in China. By 1949, Mao's Communist forces had defeated the Nationalists. That year, the Communists proclaimed the People's Republic of China, with **Beijing** as the capital. The defeated Nationalists fled to the offshore island of **Taiwan**, where they set up the new capital of the Republic of China at **Taipei**.

Mao's revolution was one of the major upheavals of the century. It succeeded in part because the Communists' self-proclaimed patriotism and sense of duty appealed to many Chinese citizens disgusted with foreign controls and the corruption of Chiang's officials. Above all, Mao won over China's peasants with his promises of land reform and an end to oppression by landlords.

The Mao Era

After coming to power, the Chinese Communists worked to remake Chinese society along totalitarian Communist lines. Having absolute control of the Chinese government, the Communist party set out to impose its will on the country. Its leaders were determined to uproot both traditional Chinese and Western attitudes in the process.

In theory, the Chinese Communists promoted equality. Women, for example, were made equal with men under the law and benefited from social reforms, such as state-run nurseries that provided child care. They also were expected to enter the workplace alongside men; however, few women were freed from traditional household chores, and even fewer gained top positions in government and industry.

Chapter 33 *Asia and the Pacific* **901**

TEACH

Guided Practice

THEME Revolution

Write *Five-Year Plan, Great Leap Forward, Red Guards, Gang of Four, Four Modernizations,* and *Tiananmen Square* on the chalkboard. Ask students to describe the role each played in initiating or preserving revolutionary change in China. **L1**

The Mao Era

How did Mao Zedong's rule affect China and its place in world affairs?

Mao imposed a Communist system on China and tried to uproot traditional ways. Mao's China later became an independent Communist power, and in the 1970s began to normalize relations with the West.

VIDEODISC
Communism and the Cold War

Side Two, Chapter 4
Frames 5825–7229
Title: *Revolution in China*
Subject: Transformation of China into a Communist country
Ask: Why was it a shock to the U.S. when China became Communist? *(During World War II, the U.S. backed the Nationalist Chiang Kai-shek and believed that China would be an ally after the war.)*

Building a New Economy

One of the major Communist goals was China's transformation into a modern industrial and agricultural nation. In rural areas, the Communists drove landlords from their property and distributed land to the peasants. Several million people may have died in this often bloody struggle.

Once in power, the Communists worked to improve living conditions and education in the countryside. Health workers and teachers loyal to communism set up clinics and schools in villages.

China's Communist government also set out to establish a state-controlled economy that would advance industrial and agricultural development. In 1953 it launched its first Soviet-style Five-Year Plan, which stressed heavy industry and agricultural efficiency. The Plan brought private industries under government control and had peasants merge their individual landholdings into large cooperatives. With Soviet help, the Chinese Communists built roads, railroads, factories, and canals. While industrial output rose significantly under this first Plan, agricultural production improved more slowly.

The Great Leap Forward

In 1958 the Chinese launched an ambitious economic plan known as the **Great Leap Forward**. Under this plan the cooperatives were merged into larger government-controlled units called communes. Human labor was stressed over complex technology. Members of communes worked in production brigades on tasks ranging from farming

Free Speech Movement

Berkeley, California, 1964
In 1964 officials at the University of California at Berkeley prohibited political activities on campus, including the distribution of literature promoting various causes near the school's main gate. The Free Speech Movement was a reaction against these restrictions. In December, students took over the college administration building, then proclaimed a strike. More than 800 students were arrested, but the movement succeeded in forcing the school's president and chancellor out of office.

Berkeley

CALIFORNIA

---

to making steel in small backyard furnaces.

The Great Leap Forward was a disaster. Food shortages, mismanagement, and peasant resistance to communes brought the program to a halt. It also caused massive suffering—as many as 20 million people died of starvation.

The Cultural Revolution

After the Great Leap Forward, a deep division occurred within the Chinese Communist party. Pragmatists, headed by **Deng Xiaoping** (DUNG SHOW•PIHNG), party general secretary, wanted practical reforms. Radicals, led by Mao and his wife **Jiang Jing**, insisted on strict obedience to revolutionary principles.

To end the influence of the pragmatists, Mao in 1966 launched the **Cultural Revolution.** In response to Mao's direction, young people formed bands of Red Guards. Waving copies of the "Little Red Book" of Mao's sayings, the Red Guards attacked local politicians, teachers, and other leaders for betraying Mao and the revolution. The accused were denounced, publicly humiliated, and sometimes killed.

The Cultural Revolution was a time of disorder and confusion. Schools closed, factory production dropped, and violence erupted. Finally, in 1968, Mao called on the army to restore order. By then, however, the lives of millions of people had been disrupted, and tens of thousands of people had died.

China's Foreign Policy

After the Communist victory in 1949, Mao Zedong opposed capitalist countries. In the early 1950s, China supported Communist North Korea in its war against American-backed South Korea. In 1954 Chinese Premier **Zhou Enlai** (joh ehn•LY) took part in talks that ended French rule in Indochina and paved the way for a Communist northern Vietnam.

During the late 1950s, Chinese-Soviet relations soured and led to an open split. Mao's version of Marxism, based on Chinese experience, held that peasants, rather than workers, were the leaders of revolutions in largely agricultural societies. The Soviets viewed Mao's ideas as a threat to their leadership of world communism. Mao demanded that

Student Web Activity 33

Visit the *World History: The Human Experience* Web site at **worldhistory.glencoe.com** and click on *Chapter 33—Student Web Activities* for an activity relating to the Great Leap Forward.

COOPERATIVE LEARNING ACTIVITY

Oral-Visual Presentations Have students form five groups to research one of the following topics: the 1949 civil war, the Five-Year Plans of the 1950s, the Cultural Revolution of the 1960s, the pragmatists versus the Gang of Four in the 1970s, and the Tiananmen Square crackdown in 1989.

Tell students to use their texts as well as outside research materials. After they have completed their research, they can make charts and other visuals to present their findings. Each group should then choose one student to present its research orally, using the visual materials. **L2** the Soviets take a firmer line against the West. The two Communist powers soon became rivals for influence in the developing world. They also disputed their long border, with China wanting back the territory seized from it by Russia in the late 1600s. In 1960 the Soviets finally withdrew their advisers from China, and the alliance ended.

During the 1960s, internal upheavals largely isolated China from the rest of the world. The Chinese, however, were able in 1964 to explode their first atomic bomb. By the 1970s the desire for advanced technology made the Chinese reach out to other countries, especially the United States. Since 1949, the United States had regarded China as an aggressive Communist power and maintained ties with the Nationalist government on Taiwan. But the Chinese-Soviet split gave the United States and China an opportunity to improve relations. In 1972 United States President Richard Nixon made a historic visit to China, and seven years later the United States and China established diplomatic ties.

The Deng Era

After Mao's death in 1976, the pragmatists under Deng Xiaoping gained power. They arrested the Gang of Four, Jiang Jing and three of her radical supporters. Deng then began to move China in a new direction. The Communist party maintained political control. In making economic policy, however, Deng was willing to learn from the capitalist West if it could contribute to China's well-being.

The Four Modernizations

Deng backed a plan called the Four Modernizations that stressed the need for improvements in agriculture, industry, science, and defense. To boost food production, the government replaced the communes with the rural "responsibility system," in which families farmed individual plots. The government received some of the produce; the family could keep or sell the rest.

Although the government still controlled major industries, factory managers were encouraged to make plants more efficient. They could now base production on supply and demand rather than by government decree. In addition, economic reforms allowed some privately owned small businesses and private property.

Deng also welcomed foreign businesses and technology to China. European, American, and Japanese investment flowed into the country,

Visualizing History **Students at a commune perform a play supporting Mao Zedong.** *What was the role of the Red Guards in the Cultural Revolution?*

and the Chinese set up special economic zones where foreigners could own and operate businesses with little government interference.

The Four Modernizations sparked economic growth and raised standards of living. For the first time, many Chinese were able to buy consumer goods, such as televisions and household appliances. The reforms, however, created a social gap between a new wealthy class and the rest of the population. Other problems included increased crime and corruption, more unemployment, and rising prices. By the late 1980s, discontent was stirring in China despite the progress that had been made.

Tiananmen Square Massacre

While Deng encouraged some free enterprise, he refused to grant political freedoms. By the late 1980s, students and intellectuals in Beijing, **Shanghai**, and other Chinese cities had organized movements to demand a more open political system. In May and June 1989, more than 100,000 people rallied for democracy and other reforms in Beijing's **Tiananmen Square**. Determined to maintain control, government

 Footnotes to History

Chinese Students Abroad

In the spirit of improving and expanding relations with Western countries, the Chinese government allowed more students to study in foreign countries. By 1999 there were about 50,000 Chinese students studying in American universities.

 WORLD HISTORY *Online*

Have students use the **Chapter 33 Student Web Activity** at worldhistory.glencoe.com for in-depth study of the Great Leap Forward.

Visualizing History The Red Guards were named for the real army units Mao had organized in 1927. The Red Guard movement subsided by 1969.
Answer to Caption: *They spread the Cultural Revolution throughout the country, using such methods as burning books and destroying treasures of traditional Chinese culture, as well as harassing and arresting their opponents.*

♪ World Music: Cultural Traditions, Lesson 8

POINT

The Deng Era
Why was Deng Xiaoping an important leader of China?
He promoted modernization of China's economy by allowing some free enterprise and extending contacts with the West. However, he maintained the Communist party's hold over political affairs and suppressed a pro-democracy movement.

Independent Practice

📁 Guided Reading Activity 33-2 **L1**
📁 Geography and History Activity 33

Literature Have students read a work by a Chinese American writer, such as Amy Tan or Maxine Hong Kingston. Ask them to write a report about how the writer incorporates historical events into her work. **L2**

MEETING SPECIAL NEEDS ACTIVITY

Learning Style: Logical/Mathematical Have students work together to create a time line of important events in China's history between World War II and the present. This time line will be displayed along with the time line they completed for Japanese history of the same period, so students should use the same scale for this project. Tell students to include political, economic, and cultural events. **L1**

Visualizing History Tiananmen Square has been used for student demonstrations since 1919. Ironically, the square's name means "Gate of Heavenly Peace." It is named for the huge stone (formerly the main gate of the Imperial Palace) located at its northern end.
Answer to Caption: *Deng sent in tanks and troops to break up the demonstration, killing or wounding many protesters.*

VIDEODISC
Communism and
the Cold War

Side Two, Chapter 19
Frames 46766–49626
Title: *Tiananmen Square*
Ask: What were the protests in Tiananmen Square about? *(students and others protesting for democratic reform in China)*

Linking Past and Present

"Ownership" of Taiwan Taiwan, originally called Formosa, was "discovered" by Portugal, then controlled by the Dutch and later by Spain. Still later it was acquired by China, then Japan, then China again. Taiwanese moves toward independence are strongly resisted by China. In early March 1996, as a threat, China launched 3 unarmed missiles in the water only 20 miles (32 km) from Taiwan's coast.

Visualizing History Demonstrating for more freedoms, students carry a hastily constructed model of the Statue of Liberty through Tiananmen Square. *How was this demonstration broken up?*

leaders sent in troops and tanks when the demonstrators refused to disperse. Thousands of demonstrators were killed or wounded. Throughout the country, those who supported political change were shot, imprisoned, tortured, or silenced.

The Tiananmen Square massacre damaged China's prestige abroad. The United States and other democratic nations condemned Deng's use of force. Fearing political instability, foreign investors backed off from doing business with the Chinese. Later, they resumed dealings when the Chinese government continued with economic reforms.

China After Deng

Following the Tiananmen Square massacre, Deng Xiaoping, elderly and in poor health, named Chinese President **Jiang Zemin** as his successor. Deng, however, retained power from behind the scenes until his death in 1997. Deng at that time was hailed worldwide for his free enterprise reforms, but he was criticized for his use of force against the pro-democracy movement.

The Economy

Since Deng's death, China's economic growth has remained strong, but uneven. A gap has widened between prosperous industrial areas on the coast and less wealthy agricultural regions of the interior. Since the 1980s, millions of peasants have moved to

the cities seeking work. This mass migration has put pressure on housing and various city social services.

Deng's successors have continued his emphasis on capitalist-style economic reforms. In 1997 Jiang Zemin allowed ailing state-run industries to sell stock, although the government would hold the majority of shares. Chinese authorities also moved ahead with the world's largest public works project: the Three Gorges Dam on the Chang Jiang in central China. When completed in 2009, the dam is expected to prevent dangerous flooding and will provide electricity for new commercial ventures. Almost 2 million people will be relocated before the dam's giant reservoir covers up farms, villages, and canyons. Critics charge that the project is destroying one of the world's most scenic areas.

Human Rights

China's leaders continue to affirm Communist party control over government and the military. However, they have also raised the possibility that they might consider some political reforms. One of the challenges faced by Chinese leaders is growing unrest among China's many ethnic groups. Of every 100 people in China, 93 are Chinese; the remainder are from at least 55 other groups, including Kazakhstanis, Mongols, Uyghurs, and Tibetans. Opposition to Chinese Communist rule is particularly strong in **Tibet**, a mountainous region in the southwestern part of the country. Once an independent Buddhist kingdom, Tibet came under direct Chinese

MAKING CONNECTIONS ACTIVITY

International Affairs Have students research to find out about China's behavior as a permanent member of the United Nations Security Council. Ask them to write short reports summarizing their findings. Make sure they include information comparing China's use of the veto with that of the Soviet Union and the United States. **L3**

control in 1950. Since an unsuccessful Tibetan rebellion in 1959, the **Dalai Lama**, the spiritual leader of Tibet, has led a worldwide movement in support of Tibetan rights from his place of exile in India.

International Relations

During most of the 1990s, China's relations with the West were strained. China wanted Western trade and investment but resented Western pressures on human rights and United States support for the Nationalists on Taiwan. As the new century dawns, these issues remain dominant. In addition, some nations are concerned about China's efforts to beef up its military muscle. Tensions between China and the United States grew in 1999 following charges that China had stolen United States nuclear information. However, late in the year, an agreement was signed paving China's eventual entry in the World Trade Organization (WTO).

Despite these difficulties, China has expanded contacts with its neighbors in East Asia. China has ties to Japan, North Korea, and South Korea, and has developed friendly relations with Russia since the fall of the Soviet Union. It also has expanded trade with various countries in Southeast Asia.

Hong Kong and Taiwan

Economic growth has increased Chinese national pride. In recent years, China's leaders have set as their goal the return of all separated territories to the Chinese homeland. In 1997, they regained **Hong Kong** from the British; in 1999, they acquired the port of Macao from the Portuguese. Their most controversial demand, however, is the reuniting of Taiwan with the People's Republic of China.

Hong Kong

In 1997 Hong Kong, one of the world's major ports and financial centers, became part of China after 156 years of British rule. Under a "one country, two systems" plan, Hong Kong keeps its capitalist system and some of its freedoms for 50 years after its return to China. Many Hong Kong residents, however, are concerned about their territory's future under Communist control.

During the early 1990s, Great Britain introduced democratic reforms such as a freely elected legislative council. The Chinese Communists, however, opposed these reforms and developed their own institutions for the territory. On June 30, 1997, the date of transfer, Tung Chee-hwa, a local businessman favored by Beijing, became Hong Kong's leader. A China-backed provisional legislature replaced the democratically elected legislative council. Although China promises to respect Hong Kong's unique status, many Hong Kong residents resent the limits on their political rights.

Taiwan

The status of Taiwan has been a prominent issue in Chinese affairs since 1949. Both the Chinese Nationalists and the Chinese Communists believe that Taiwan is a province of China. Each government claims to be the legal ruler of all of China.

Under Chiang Kai-shek and his son Chiang Ching-kuo, Taiwan prospered from the export of manufactured goods. In 1988 Lee Teng-hui became president of the country. He moved Taiwan toward democracy by allowing other political parties to challenge the Nationalists. Popular with voters, Lee Teng-hui in 1997 was reelected in Taiwan's first democratic presidential race.

Today, Taiwan's economy remains strong, but its political future is uncertain. In recent years, many Taiwanese have come to accept separation from China as a fact and want to declare Taiwan an independent country. The Chinese government in Beijing, however, opposes such a move and has threatened to use force against Taiwan if the island declares its independence.

Who? What? Where? When?

Dalai Lama For his nonviolent struggle to end China's rule of Tibet, the Dalai Lama was awarded the 1989 Nobel Peace Prize.

ASSESS

Check for Understanding

Assign Section 2 Assessment as homework or as an in-class activity.

 Use Interactive Tutor Self-Assessment Software to review Section 2.

Evaluate

Section Quiz 33-2

 Use the Testmaker to create a customized quiz for Section 2.

Reteach

Assign one student to be timekeeper and organize the rest of the class into two teams. Play a game in which you give the teams names or terms such as Mao Zedong, Taipei, and the First Five-Year Plan. Have students explain the importance of each term or name within 10 seconds. Score one point for a correct answer.

Reading Essentials and Study Guide 33-2

Enrich

Have students write and perform skits that dramatize events in this section. Each scene should show how the event affected a segment of society, such as students, peasants, or factory workers.

CLOSE

Have students write a paragraph summarizing China's current position in world affairs.

SECTION 2 ASSESSMENT

Main Idea
1. Use a diagram like the one below to list communism's effects on China's international affairs.

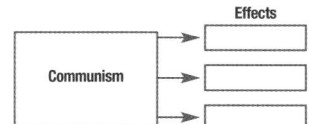

Recall
2. **Define** communes, pragmatists, special economic zone.
3. **Identify** Chiang Kai-shek, Mao Zedong, Great Leap Forward, Cultural Revolution, Deng Xiaoping, Jiang Jing, Zhou Enlai, Tiananmen Square, Jiang Zemin, Dalai Lama.

Critical Thinking
4. **Making Comparisons** How did Mao's economic development policies differ from MacArthur's?
Understanding Themes
5. **Revolution** How can a country's political struggles always be viewed as a battle between pragmatists and radicals?

Chapter 33 *Asia and the Pacific* **905**

SECTION 2 ASSESSMENT ANSWERS

1. opposition to U.S. after 1949; split with Soviet Union in 1950s; improved U.S. relations in 1970s; Deng welcomed foreign business, technology; relationship with West strained in 1990s; expanded East Asian contacts
2. All terms are defined in the Glossary.
3. Chiang Kai-shek, 901; Mao Zedong, 901; Great Leap Forward, 902; Cultural Revolu-
tion, 902; Deng Xiaoping, 902; Jiang Jing, 902; Zhou Enlai, 902; Tiananmen Square, 903; Jiang Zemin, 904; Dalai Lama, 905
4. They also promoted equality and economic reform but were harsh and repressive.
5. **REVOLUTION** Answers should include earlier examples such as the French or Russian Revolutions.

1945 .... 1972 .... 200C

1945 Soviets and Americans divide Korea at the 38th parallel.

1950 North Koreans invade South Korea.

1953 Korean War ends.

1997 Nort and South F in prelimina

A Divided Korea

Read to Find Out
Main Idea *South Korea and North Korea have differed in their political and economic development.*

▶ **Terms to Define**
    stalemate, referendum

▶ **People to Meet**
    Kim Il Sung, Kim Young Sam, Kim Jong Il

▶ **Places to Locate**
    Pyongyang, Seoul

Storteller

South Korean government officials watched as teams from 161 nations marched into the stadium. It was a proud day for South Korea, host of the 1988 Olympic games. North Korea had called for a boycott, had even threatened violence, but only 6 national teams had chosen to stay at home. In fact, most Communist states had openly supported the Seoul Olympics. Even now, as the torch entered the stadium, American, Japanese, and Soviet ships off the peninsula kept North Korea under surveillance. As South Koreans

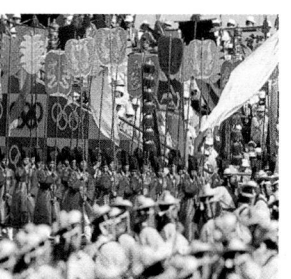

watched 300 of China's finest athletes in the opening ceremonies, they wondered, was it a sign of a new era dawning?

—adapted from "The Politics of the Olympics," *The World and I*, October 1988

1988 Olympics in Seoul

Korea's modern history has beer heavily shaped by international politics. In 1910 the Korean Peninsula was annexed by the Japanese, who ruled it as a colony until the end of World War II, when Japan was stripped of its territorial possessions.

During the war, the Allied powers had agreed that Korea was to be temporarily occupied. In 1945 Soviet troops moved into the northern part of Korea down to the 38th parallel. United States forces occupied the southern area. The occupation was to end as soon as a Korean government could be freely elected. The Soviets and Americans, however, could not agree on procedures for the election.

By 1948, two separate governments had emerged, each claiming to be the legal ruler of all of Korea. North Korea, officially called the Democratic People's Republic of Korea, with its capital at **Pyongyang**, kept close ties with the Soviet Union and China. South Korea, officially the Republic of Korea, established its capital at **Seoul**. It maintained links with the United States. The Soviets withdrew their troops from North Korea in late 1948, and the United States withdrew their troops from South Korea in mid-1949.

 POINT

The Korean War

In June 1950, North Korea, hoping to unify the country under a Communist government, invaded South Korea. The United Nations Security Council immediately voted to condemn the invasion and organized an army to oppose it. At that time the Soviets could not use their veto because of their absence from the Council in protest against the United Nations' refusal to recognize Communist China. While 16 countries contributed troops to the UN force, more than 90 percent of the soldiers came from the United States.

906 **Chapter 33** *Asia and the Pacific*

▶ **Regionalism** After decades of conflict and cold war tensions, North Korea and South Korea take first steps toward unification.

Guide to Reading

For reading strategies to help students read effectively see pages 12–13.

Vocabulary Pre-check

Use the Vocabulary PuzzleMaker for Chapter 33 to create a crossword puzzle to reinforce section terms. **L1 LEP**

Use Vocabulary Activity 33 to introduce terms. **L1 LEP**

FOCUS

Section Objective

Describe how South Korea and North Korea have differed in their political and economic development.

BELLRINGER
Motivational Activity

Before taking roll at the beginning of the class period, project Section Focus Transparency 33-3 and have students answer the activity questions.
    This activity is also available as a blackline master.

Reproducible Masters
• Lecture Notes 33-3
• Reproducible Lesson Plan 33-3
• Vocabulary Activity 33
• Guided Reading Activity 33-3
• Section Quiz 33-3
• Reading Essentials and Study Guide 33-3

Transparencies
• Section Focus Transparency 33-3

Multimedia
Interactive Tutor Self-Assessment Software
Testmaker
Communism and the Cold War: *Korean War*

In the first months of the war, the North Koreans swept southward, conquering almost all of South Korea. However, in September 1950, the UN troops led by United States General Douglas MacArthur counterattacked. MacArthur launched a surprise invasion at **Inchon,** along Korea's west coast and far behind North Korean lines. The daring move gave UN forces the offensive they needed. Within six weeks, the UN forces had pushed the North Koreans out of South Korea and had advanced into North Korea, reaching the Yalu River at the Chinese border.

At this point in the war, Communist China came to the aid of North Korea. Chinese forces crossed into Korea in such large numbers that the UN forces were forced to retreat southward. By mid-1951, each army dug in along a line near the 38th parallel. There the fighting reached a *stalemate*, a situation in which two opponents are unable to move significantly or make further gains. Talks between the two sides began in July 1951 and lasted until July 1953, when a truce was signed. After the deaths of nearly 5 million people and the devastation of much of Korea, the fighting ended with Korea once again divided near the 38th parallel.

Korea Since 1953

The stalemate in the Korean War for a long time was matched by a stalemate in diplomacy. The two Koreas continued to draw economic and military aid from their respective sponsors, the United States and China.

North Korea

From 1948 to 1994, North Korea was led by the Communist dictator **Kim Il Sung**. A cult of personality developed around Kim, and North Koreans revered him as a god-like figure. Called the "Great Leader," Kim established a repressive and tightly controlled government that largely isolated North Korea from the rest of the world.

Like the Soviet Union and China, North Korea implemented a Communist program of economic development. Under Kim's direction, all of the country's farmland was organized into collective farms between 1953 and 1956. In 1954 the North Korean government announced the first Five-Year Plan for building an industrial economy. North Korea stressed the growth of heavy industry and built up its military power.

Until the early 1990s, North Korea made some progress in developing its economy, but it did not match South Korea's growth. About 20 percent of North Korea's gross domestic product (GDP) was

Map: Korean War 1950–1953

North Korean advances
United Nations advances

CHINA
NORTH KOREA
UN maximum advance Nov. 24, 1950
Chosan
Chinese intervention Nov. 1950
An-tung
Unsan
Hungnam
Wonsan
Pyongyang
UN forces
armistice line July 27, 1953
Kaesong
Panmunjom
38th Parallel
Inchon
Seoul
Chinese and North Korean maximum advance Jan. 25, 1951
landing of UN forces Sept. 15, 1950
SOUTH KOREA
North Korean maximum advance Sept. 15, 1950
Taegu
Pusan
0 25 50 mi.
0 25 50 km
Bonne Projection
Sea of Japan
Yalu River

Map Study Each side of the Korean War occupied virtually the entire Korean Peninsula at various times.
Movement Why was MacArthur's Inchon landing so effective?

annually devoted to military expenditures, including the development of nuclear capabilities. Improvements in the standard of living were limited by this heavy military spending.

In the mid-1990s, another factor limiting North Korea's growth was widespread crop failure. This agricultural collapse was due to floods, drought, and government policies that provided few incentives for farmers to produce. The resulting food shortages brought starvation to many of North Korea's people. As catastrophe loomed on the horizon, the Communist government reluctantly admitted its need for foreign aid. In 1997 relief organizations in the United States and other countries began sending food to North Korea.

South Korea

In contrast, South Korea after the mid-1960s enjoyed tremendous economic success. By the mid-1980s, the South Korean economy was growing at the remarkable rate of 10 percent a year. To promote

COOPERATIVE LEARNING ACTIVITY

An Exchange of Letters One of the most controversial episodes of the Korean War was President Truman's firing of General Douglas MacArthur, head of the UN forces in Korea. Organize students into two groups, one to research Truman's role in the war and the other to research MacArthur's role. Direct them to study the two men's personalities, political views, and leadership styles. Then have the groups plan and write mock dispatches between the two men— one exchange following the Inchon landing and another during the dismissal. The letters should contain historical detail and reflect knowledge of war strategy. Choose students to read the letters to the class. **L3**

TEACH

Guided Practice

THEME Regionalism

Discuss ways that life in North Korea and South Korea are different as a result of their different forms of government.

Map Study

Answer
The surprise attack cut off enemy troops behind their front lines.

Independent Practice

 Guided Reading Activity 33-3 **L1**

TURNING POINT

The Korean War
Why was the Korean conflict a significant event in the cold war?
It was the first "hot" conflict of the cold war, pitting American-led UN forces against those of Communist North Korea and China. The fighting ended in a stalemate that kept Korea divided at the 38th parallel.

VIDEODISC
Communism and the Cold War

Side Two, Chapter 7
Frames 16806–18713
Title: *Korean War*
Ask: What was the policy of containment? (*U.S. policy to stop the spread of communism*)

Visualizing History Founded in 1392, the city of Seoul was heavily damaged during the Korean War and has been extensively rebuilt. The city was the site of the 1988 summer Olympics.
Answer to Caption: *dealing with government corruption scandals, the effects of the 1997 financial crisis, and a slowdown in economic growth*

ASSESS

Check for Understanding

Assign Section 3 Assessment as homework or as an in-class activity.

 Use Interactive Tutor Self-Assessment Software to review Section 3.

Evaluate

Section Quiz 33-3

 Use the Testmaker to create a customized quiz for Section 3.

Reteach

Write the following dates on the chalkboard and ask students to identify their significance in Korean history: June 25, 1950 (*North Korea invades South Korea*); September 15, 1950 (*Inchon invasion*); July 27, 1953 (*both sides accept a temporary armistice line*); October 1990 (*unification talks begin*); December 1991 (*a treaty is signed, officially ending the state of war*).

Reading Essentials and Study Guide 33-3

Enrich

Have students research the life and career of Douglas MacArthur in a brief biographical essay.

CLOSE

Have students write a summary of Korea's history from 1945 to the present.

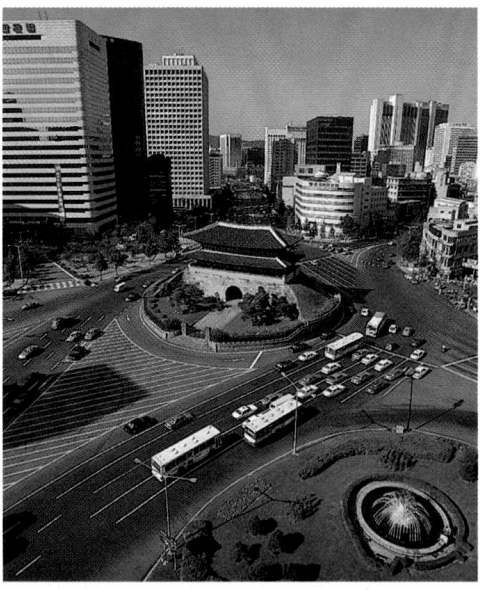

Visualizing History The central area of Seoul, South Korea, reflects the city's economic prosperity in recent years. *What challenges face South Korea as it approaches the year 2000?*

prosperity, the South Korean government strongly encouraged the export of electronics products, textiles, ships, trucks, automobiles, and other industrial goods.

South Korea's economic boom, however, was achieved under repressive governments. Beginning in the early 1960s, the military used the Communist threat to play a strong role in the government. Despite elections, South Korea's president was essentially a military-backed dictator.

During the 1980s, massive student protests led to greater democracy. In 1987 a new constitution allowing almost complete political freedoms was adopted by referendum, an election in which all voters approve or disapprove a measure. That same year, South Korean voters for the first time elected a new president—Roh Tae Woo—by direct vote instead of indirectly by an electoral college. Six years later, the same method was used to select **Kim Young Sam** as president.

During Kim's term, South Korea was plagued by strikes, political scandals, and economic setbacks. When a number of leading companies and banks collapsed, the South Korean government turned to the International Monetary Fund (IMF), an international lending agency, for a $57 billion bailout. Under IMF controls, the South Koreans were forced to reform their economy. In the short term, this meant industrial cutbacks, lower wages, and higher unemployment. As discontent mounted, South Korean voters in December 1997 elected Kim Dae Jung, a leading government opponent, as president.

North-South Relations

The end of the cold war raised hopes for uniting the two Koreas. Both countries took halting steps toward better relations, but continuing resentments hampered progress. The death of Kim Il Sung in 1994 and uncertainty about the intentions of his son and successor, **Kim Jong Il**, further delayed movement toward peace.

By the late 1990s, however, the food crisis had forced North Korea to increase contacts with the outside world. In 1997 North Korea began talks with South Korea, the United States, and China aimed at exploring ways to end the state of war still existing between the two Koreas. The North Koreans also hoped to receive food in return for scaling back their weapons program. Much to their neighbors' alarm, however, North Korea continues to strengthen its military muscle.

SECTION 3 ASSESSMENT

Main Idea
1. Use a chart like the one below to list some factors involved in the development of North Korea's economy.

Factors in North Korean Economic Development

Recall
2. **Define** stalemate, referendum.
3. **Identify** Inchon, Kim Il Sung, Kim Young Sam, Kim Jong Il.

Critical Thinking
4. **Making Comparisons** How are North Korea and South Korea similar? In what ways are

the two Koreas different?

Understanding Themes
5. **Regionalism** How might the two Koreas' futures be influenced by recent global events such as the end of the cold war and the rise of a global economy?

SECTION 3 ASSESSMENT ANSWERS

1. collective farms; 1954, first Five-Year Plan for building industrial economy; growth of heavy industry; limited improvement in standard of living due to military build-up; agricultural collapse led to severe food shortage
2. All terms are defined in the Glossary.
3. Inchon, 907; Kim Il Sung, 907; Kim Young Sam, 908; Kim Jong Il, 908
4. Both have had stable, authoritarian governments. South Korea has prospered more than North Korea and has also moved toward democracy.
5. **REGIONALISM** The easing of tensions and weakening of communism might promote reunification.

1949 Indonesia wins its independence from Dutch rule. **1954** Vietminh defeats French forces at Dien Bien Phu. **1965** U.S. President Johnson sends first American ground troops to Vietnam. **1994** Cambodia establishes a democracy.

1997 Economic cri begins in Southeast

Section 4

Southeast Asia

Guide to Reading

Read to Find Out
Main Idea *Nationalism, the cold war, and the rise of a global economy have affected Southeast Asia.*

▶ **Terms to Define**
domino theory, refugee

▶ **People to Meet**
Ho Chi Minh, Norodom Sihanouk, Pol Pot, Aung San Suu Kyi, Achmed Sukarno, Suharto, Lee Kuan Yew

▶ **Places to Locate**
Vietnam, Cambodia, Laos, Thailand, Myanmar, Indonesia, Malaysia, Singapore

The Storyteller

Once again it was Tet. Tran Van Dinh could recall when that most joyous of Vietnamese holidays was the background for twenty-six days of bloody fighting between American and Viet Cong forces. Thousands had died. But throughout Vietnam's history, whether independent or under foreign domination, Tet was an occasion to meditate on the past, enjoy the present, and contemplate the future. Tran, who had made his life in France since 1968, bought flowers from the street vendor to mark the new beginning. It was deeply satisfying to return to his native city of Hue for the celebration.

—adapted from "Hue: My City, Myself," *National Geographic*, November 1989, Tran Van Dinh.

Celebrating Tet

During the cold war years, Southeast Asia was thrust into the middle of the super-power contest and also suffered because of regional hostilities. The ongoing struggle between Communists and anti-Communists brought instability and war to much of the region of Southeast Asia known as Indochina. Only in recent years have Indochinese countries such as **Vietnam** and **Cambodia** begun to recover from earlier conflicts.

Struggle for Indochina

Before Japan conquered Southeast Asia in World War II, France ruled most of Indochina as a colony. When Japanese forces withdrew following the war, France attempted to reestablish its control. By then, however, nationalist movements demanding independence had gained strength. Vietnamese nationalists in the Indochinese Communist party, later known as the Vietminh, declared the formation of the independent Democratic Republic of Vietnam in 1945. The Vietminh were supported by the Soviet Union and the Communist Chinese.

The Vietminh, under the leadership of **Ho Chi Minh**, and the French could not reach an agreement on how to share power. In 1946 the two sides went to war. The United States, fearing Ho's Communist ties and wanting to support its ally France, provided military and financial aid to France to subdue the Vietminh. Despite American aid, the French could not win a military victory. In May 1954 the Vietminh defeated French forces in the decisive battle at Dien Bien Phu. After their loss, the French agreed to a cease-fire and decided to pull out of Vietnam completely.

A month before the battle, the Vietminh, the French, the United States, and several other countries had agreed to meet in Geneva, Switzerland, to negotiate a settlement to the Vietnam conflict. Negotiators divided Vietnam along the 17th parallel, creating a Communist North Vietnam and a

Chapter 33 *Asia and the Pacific* **909**

SECTION THEME

▶ **Conflict** The rise of nationalism and cold war competition leads to conflict in post-World War II Southeast Asia.

Guide to Reading

For reading strategies to help students read effectively see pages 12–13.

Vocabulary Pre-check

🔲 Use the Vocabulary PuzzleMaker for Chapter 33 to create a crossword puzzle to reinforce section terms. **L1 LEP**

📁 Use Vocabulary Activity 33 to introduce vocabulary terms. **L1 LEP**

FOCUS

Section Objective

Explain how nationalism, the cold war, and the rise of a global economy have affected Southeast Asia.

BELLRINGER
Motivational Activity

Before taking roll at the beginning of the class period, project Section Focus Transparency 33-4 and have students answer the activity questions. Discuss students' responses.
📁 This activity is also available as a blackline master.

SECTION RESOURCES

📁 **Reproducible Masters**
• Lecture Notes 33-4
• Reproducible Lesson Plan 33-4
• Vocabulary Activity 33
• Guided Reading Activity 33-4
• Section Quiz 33-4
• Reading Essentials and Study Guide 33-4

🖺 **Transparencies**
• Section Focus Transparency 33-4

Multimedia
🔲 Interactive Tutor Self-Assessment Software
🔲 Testmaker
💿 World Music: Cultural Traditions, Lesson 9
◉ Communism and the Cold War: *Vietnam War*

TEACH

Guided Practice

THEME Conflict

Have students examine the map of Vietnam on page 912. Describe the physical outline of the country. *(long and narrow)* What influence might Vietnam's shape have had on its conflicts? *(It was difficult to integrate the territory of Vietnam. Few roads or railroads connected the north with the south. Internal divisions within the nation increased.)* **L1**

The Vietnam War
Why was the Vietnam War fought?
Communist Vietnamese forces sought to overthrow the pro-American government of South Vietnam and unify all of Vietnam under Communist rule. In its effort to contain communism, the United States sent troops to support the non-Communist government of South Vietnam.

VIDEODISC
Communism and the Cold War

Side Two, Chapter 8
Frames 18729–22891
Title: *Vietnam War*
Ask: Why was Vietnam known as a television war? *(For the first time, a war was televised. Showing the reality of war proved detrimental to public support.)*

pro-Western South Vietnam. This arrangement was to last only until elections could be held in 1956. With United States approval, Ngo Dinh Diem, South Vietnam's leader, rejected the proposed elections. He claimed that the Communists would not allow fair elections in North Vietnam. Diem also may have feared that elections would reveal Ho's popularity. Guerrillas in South Vietnam, known as the Viet Cong, fought Diem in hope of uniting Vietnam under Ho. The United States sent financial aid and several hundred advisers to help Diem.

However, Diem was a weak and unpopular leader. In 1963 the South Vietnamese military, despairing of Diem's leadership and fearing that the South would fall to the Communists, staged a coup in which Diem was killed. This was done with the quiet approval of the United States government and President John F. Kennedy.

Reflecting on France's earlier troubles in Vietnam, French President Charles de Gaulle urged Kennedy to withdraw. "I predict you will sink step by step into a bottomless quagmire," he warned.

The Vietnam War

Since the early 1950s, American officials had accepted the domino theory—that if one Southeast Asian land fell to communism, its neighbors would fall as well. To halt communism, the United States moved deeper into the conflict. By late 1963, 16,000 American advisers were in Vietnam.

In 1964 the United States approved secret South Vietnamese naval raids against North Vietnam. On August 2, 1964, United States President Lyndon Johnson announced that North Vietnam had fired on two American destroyers off the coast of Vietnam. Although the incident could not be confirmed, Johnson used it to increase American involvement in the war. He ordered air strikes on North Vietnam. At his request Congress passed the Gulf of Tonkin Resolution, which gave the

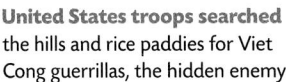

Images of the Times

Vietnam War, 1964–1975

Americans, forced to consider the cost of war in terms of human and economic sacrifice, debated for years before withdrawing troops in 1973.

United States troops searched the hills and rice paddies for Viet Cong guerrillas, the hidden enemy.

910

Images of the Times
Vietnam War, 1964–1975

The human costs of the war included 58,000 Americans killed in action and an additional 305,000 wounded. Vietnamese military casualties were much higher (about 3 million North Vietnamese and Viet Cong; 900,000 South Vietnamese), and many civilians were killed by bombs. The economic costs of the war were also high. For the United States, the cost of the war has been estimated at $200 billion. The war also had devastating effects on Vietnamese agriculture, business, and industry.

The Viet Cong concentrated their efforts on the countryside, where their guerrilla tactics included ambush, terrorism, and sabotage.

resident broad war powers. In March 1965 Johnson nt the first ground troops to Vietnam.

By 1968, American forces numbered more than 0,000, and United States planes were bombing ietnam heavily. The South Vietnamese army numered about 800,000; the Viet Cong and their North ietnamese allies had about 300,000. The Soviet nion and China sent aid but no troops to help orth Vietnam. North Vietnam sent troops and upplies southward over the Ho Chi Minh Trail. espite greater numbers and advanced technology, e Americans could not defeat the Communists, ho relied on surprise and mobility and avoided pen battle. As the war intensified, antiwar attitudes pread within the United States and overseas.

he Tet Offensive

The turning point in the war came in early 1968. he Viet Cong launched a major military offensive uring the Vietnamese New Year holiday, Tet. lthough they failed to capture any major cities, the itter fighting made more and more Americans real-ize that several years of United States involvement had failed to significantly weaken the Viet Cong. Opposition to Johnson's war policy became so fierce that Johnson decided not to seek reelection in 1968.

Ending the War

Opposition to the war grew rapidly during the Nixon presidency. As a result, the United States began withdrawing its troops. With the war becoming costly to both sides, South Vietnam, the United States, and the Communists in 1973 agreed to a cease-fire, and the last United States troops left Vietnam. The war resumed in 1975, however, and North Vietnamese and Viet Cong forces defeated the South Vietnamese.

After more than 20 years of fighting, Vietnam was reunited under the Communists. However, at least 2 million people, including 58,000 Americans, had died in the conflict. About 10 million South Vietnamese were refugees, people who flee to another country for safety from danger or disaster. In addition, large areas of Vietnam lay devastated.

South Vietnamese villagers from Quang Tri Province assemble at a refugee camp. Many hope to leave Vietnam.

Student war protest demonstrations on United States college campuses became common in the early 1970s.

REFLECTING ON THE TIMES

1. Why did college students play a significant role in the antiwar protest movement?
2. Why was the war so difficult for a powerful nation like the United States to win?

911

ANSWERS TO REFLECTING ON THE TIMES

1. Many college students who opposed the war did not want to serve in the army.
2. American soldiers did not know the terrain of Vietnam as well as the Viet Cong—a necessity for the guerrilla-style war the Viet Cong waged.

Chapter 33
Section 4

Daily Life Have students plan a reenactment of a 30-minute radio broadcast on a particular day in the United States in the late 1960s or early 1970s. Advise them to look through old newspapers to find the events of the day they want to report. In addition to news bulletins reporting that day's significant events, have students include popular music and ads for foods, fashions, and fads. **L2**

World Music: Cultural Traditions, Lesson 9

Independent Practice

Guided Reading Activity 33-4 **L1**

The Arts Have students watch films involving the Vietnam War, such as *Apocalypse Now; Born on the Fourth of July; The Deer Hunter; Good Morning, Vietnam;* and *Platoon.* Then have them write reports that compare and contrast the points of view of the different directors. **L2**

Critical Thinking Have students compare and contrast the Vietnam War with the Korean War. As resources, suggest J. C. Goulden, *Korea: The Untold Story of the War* and S. Karnow, *Vietnam: A History.* Ask students to write a short report summarizing the similarities and differences between the two conflicts. **L3**

Global Gourmet

Indonesia *Nasi goreng* is similar to Chinese fried rice, but instead of the meat and vegetables being cooked together with the rice, the individual ingredients surround a pile of fried rice. In the course of eating, the diner mixes them together.

Map Study

Answer

Cambodia and Laos

Map Skills Practice

Reading a Map What is the name of the trail used by North Vietnam and Vietcong forces for transport and communication among North and South Vietnam, Laos, and Cambodia? *(Ho Chi Minh Trail)*

Linking Past and Present

Cambodia The 1984 film *The Killing Fields* told the story of the relationship between an American reporter covering the invasion of Cambodia and a local translator, Dith Pran, who was caught and tortured by the Khmer Rouge but escaped. Even though Haing S. Ngor, the Cambodian refugee who played the latter role, was a physician with no acting experience, his portrayal was so convincing that he won an Academy Award for best supporting actor. In February 1996, Ngor was shot to death outside his Los Angeles home. He had spent his years in the United States helping survivors of the Khmer Rouge and trying to bring to justice those responsible for the Cambodian massacres.

Who?What?Where?When?

The Year of Living Dangerously (1983) was set in Indonesia in the mid-1960s, when the Sukarno regime was unstable and the war in Vietnam was intensifying. The film stars Mel Gibson as a foreign correspondent from Australia and Sigourney Weaver as a British attaché.

Vietnam War 1964–1975

- Viet Cong Sanctuary
- Tet Offensive 1968

0 75 150 mi.
0 75 150 km
Lambert Conic Conformal Projection

Map Study The negotiated division of Vietnam, unlike in Korea, did not hold. **Place** In what two countries did the Viet Cong find sanctuary to stage their attacks on South Vietnam?

Vietnam's Relations With the West

Since the war, Vietnam has faced economic difficulties. To improve the economy, the government in the late 1980s encouraged limited private enterprise and sought contacts with the West.

In recent years, relations between the United States and Vietnam have begun to improve. The Vietnamese government has helped locate and return many of the bodies of American soldiers killed in Vietnam. Unfortunately, the remains of many United States soldiers have not been found. Some former American soldiers have returned to Vietnam to help disarm land mines they planted during the war.

A major step toward normal relations was made in 1995 when the United States and Vietnam established diplomatic ties. Vietnam also moved to improve its relations and trade with the industrial-

ized nations of western Europe as a way to gain funds to rebuild and strengthen its desperately poor economy.

A Legacy of Violence

The Vietnam War affected many areas of Southeast Asia other than Vietnam. Fighting and civil war engulfed Vietnam's neighbors, Laos and Cambodia. Other countries of Southeast Asia, such as Thailand, escaped combat but were flooded by refugees. Since the late 1970s, the region has slowly recovered from the effects of conflict.

Cambodia

In 1953 Cambodia won its independence from France. The country became a constitutional monarchy led by King **Norodom Sihanouk** (noo•roh•DAHM SEE•ah•nuk), a member of Cambodia's historic ruling family. In 1955 Sihanouk abdicated the Cambodian throne in order to become prime minister.

Sihanouk refused to take sides in cold war power struggles. However, as the war intensified in Vietnam, Cambodia became an unwilling participant. In 1969 American planes began to bomb Cambodia in an effort to destroy Viet Cong bases there. The bombings were also intended to stop the flow of supplies and troops moving through Cambodia from North Vietnam to South Vietnam.

The bombing failed to achieve its objectives but did intensify the conflict between Cambodian Communists and Sihanouk's government. In 1970 an American-backed army officer, Lon Nol, ousted Sihanouk. Lon Nol charged that Sihanouk was not battling the Communists aggressively enough.

Civil war broke out after the American bombings and Lon Nol's seizure of power. Cambodian Communists, known as the Khmer Rouge, finally defeated Lon Nol's forces in 1975. Khmer Rouge troops, under the leadership of **Pol Pot**, took control of Cambodia's capital, Phnom Penh.

The Khmer Rouge wanted Cambodia, which they renamed Kampuchea, to become an independent, self-sufficient agricultural country. In the attempt to achieve this goal, the Khmer Rouge devastated the country. They destroyed all money and books. Soldiers forced city residents into the countryside to work on farms. Troops murdered civil servants, teachers, and students who may have supported the old system. Starvation, torture, and executions by the brutal government killed more than 3 million people—nearly one-third of the entire Cambodian population.

COOPERATIVE LEARNING ACTIVITY

Research Organize students into groups. Assign each group one of the countries studied in this chapter. Tell them to research types of arts and crafts produced in these countries. As much as possible, divide each country's art forms and crafts among group members. Make sure that each student has a specific role to play in the research effort. Have each group prepare a short presentation summarizing its findings, using visual examples wherever possible. **L1 LEP**

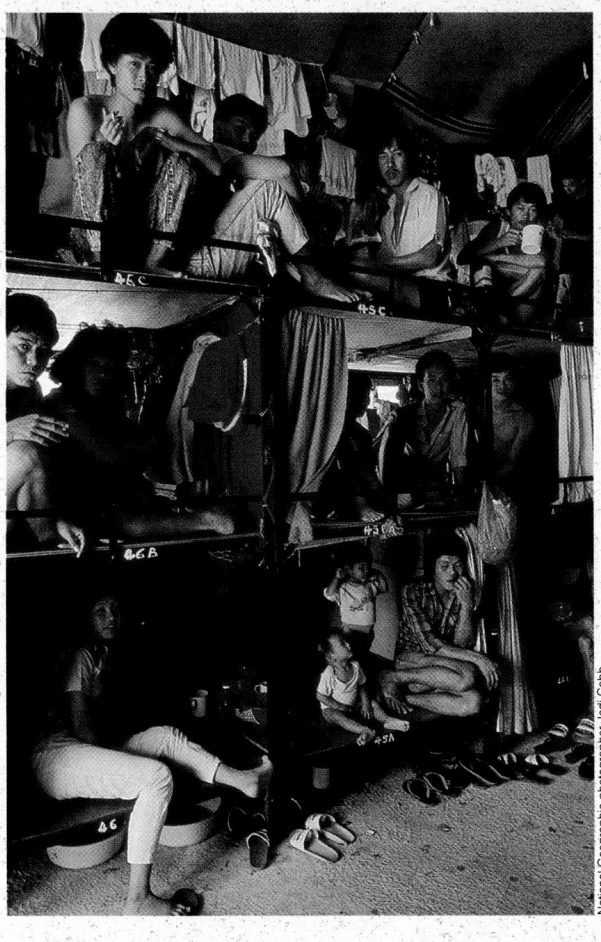

National Geographic photographer Jodi Cobb

Boat People

wo decades after the Vietnam War, Vietnamese refugees waiting to go elsewhere remained stranded in Hong Kong. In this photograph, Vietnamese refugees in Kong live inside huge concrete-and-metal dories where whole families sleep together in -like bunks.

tnam suffered decades of war. In the 1800s the was colonized by the French, who often proved to utal masters of rubber plantations and tin works. he beginning of the 1900s an independence movement had begun in Vietnam. Not until 1975 did Vietnam free itself from foreign interference. But the price was high: economic devastation and domination of South Vietnam by North Vietnam. During the second half of the 1970s—years of poverty and political persecution—hundreds of thousands of Vietnamese left their country, many by boat. Untold numbers died. Some came to the United States; others scattered across Asia. By the end of the century most of the boat people had returned to Vietnam, either voluntarily or through force. ⊕

Chapter 33 *Asia and the Pacific* **913**

TEACH

Tell students that sometimes the boat people fled political tensions only to find themselves caught up in ethnic tensions. For example, in 1979, Vietnamese boat people who were mostly ethnic Chinese arrived in Malaysia, already an ethnically diverse country. So intense was the fear that the arrival of the Vietnamese would upset the country's ethnic balance that, instead of welcoming the newcomers, the Malaysian government issued orders to shoot any boat person found landing on Malaysian shores. What current movement in the United States reflects Malaysia's response to the boat people? *(the movement to put an end to immigration)*

Linking Past and Present

Racial tensions between Malays and ethnic Chinese have been a problem in Malaysia since its formation in 1963. In May 1969, race riots between Malays and Chinese led to a state of emergency that lasted for nearly two years, with the suspension of parliamentary rule. Differences in income between the two groups remain a serious problem, with Malays forming a majority in five of Malaysia's six poorest states.

Visualizing
History
Suu Kyi's commitment to her beliefs is evidenced in the following quote from an essay she wrote, "Fearlessness may be a gift, but perhaps more precious is the courage acquired through endeavor, courage that comes from cultivating the habit of refusing to let fear dictate one's actions, courage that could be described as 'grace under pressure'—grace renewed repeatedly in the face of harsh unremitting pressure."
Answer to Caption: *the military*

The following videotape program is available from Glencoe:

• **Vietnam/Cuban Missile Crisis**

To find classroom resources to accompany this video, check the following home page:
A&E Television: http://www.aetv.com

ASSESS

Check for Understanding

Assign Section 4 Assessment as homework or as an in-class activity.

🖥 Use Interactive Tutor Self-Assessment Software to review Section 4.

Visualizing
History
Aung San Suu Kyi addresses a pro-democracy rally in Yangon, Myanmar's capital. *What group rules Myanmar?*

In 1978, after a series of border incidents, Vietnam invaded Cambodia and ousted Pol Pot. Cambodian Communists friendly to Vietnam took control of the government, but other Communist groups continued the civil war. In October 1991, representatives of the four major political groups in Cambodia signed an agreement that ended the civil war and called for an election under UN peace-keeping forces.

Cambodian voters in 1993 elected a government under Prince Norodom Ranariddh. However, Hun Sen, a political rival, demanded a role in the government. He gradually forced his way into power, finally removing the prince in 1997. In 1998 his party won national elections. Hun Sen formed a coalition government in which ousted Prince Ranariddh serves as president of the National Assembly.

Laos

Laos became independent of France in 1954. While war raged in neighboring Vietnam, Laos had its own civil war between Laotian Communists and the American-backed government.

After United States forces withdrew from the region, Laos fell under the domination of Vietnam, in 1975. A Communist government was formed,

and the economy was reorganized along socialist lines. The Lao People's Revolutionary party abandoned those policies 20 years later after the collapse of the Soviet Union. They have reintroduced private land ownership and free markets. With investments from Thailand, Australia, and other foreign countries, the Lao government has built new roads, bridges, and railroads to advance regional trade and to gain access to timber and mineral resources.

Thailand

Thailand's post-World War II history was less violent than that of its neighbors. It had not been a European colony. It did not have to fight a war of national independence or struggle to forge a new national identity. The monarchy continued as a stabilizing force in Thai society, but the real power was often held by top military leaders.

During the 1980s, Thailand had one of Southeast Asia's fast-growing "tiger" economies, with a yearly growth rate of 8 percent. By 1997, however, high foreign borrowing and slow export growth had cast a dark shadow over the Thai economy. As hardships mounted for the Thai people, the government devalued its currency to make Thai exports cheaper and relied on an international loan.

Myanmar

Myanmar is the northernmost country of Southeast Asia. Once called Burma, it was for many years part of British India but became a separate independent republic in 1948. The new Burmese government faced opposition from Communists and various ethnic groups. To restore order, military leaders took control of the country in 1962.

During the 1960s and 1970s, the military leadership turned Myanmar into a dictatorship. The government took control of the economy and forbade any criticism of its policies. It also limited Myanmar's contacts with the outside world.

During the late 1980s, large numbers of Burmese began to protest the government's policies and call for democracy. Military leaders finally promised free elections in 1990, but before the voting took place they arrested the leader of the main opposition party, **Aung San Suu Kyi** (AWNG SAHN SOO SHE). In spite of her arrest, her party won the elections.

The military leaders refused to accept the election results, but Aung San Suu Kyi won increased international support. While under house arrest, she received the 1991 Nobel Peace Prize. Released in 1995, she has continued efforts to achieve democracy in Myanmar.

MEETING SPECIAL NEEDS ACTIVITY

Learning Style: Logical/Mathematical Have students work together to create a time line of important events in Vietnam's history from World War II to the present. Advise students to use the same scale for this project, so that their time lines for Japanese, Chinese, and Vietnamese history can be juxtaposed, making simultaneous events easy to see. **L1**

Rim of Southeast Asia

Indonesia, Malaysia, Singapore, and the Philippines won their independence following World War II. They went through periods of turmoil and have emerged 50 years later with stable, booming economies. Their people and leaders are optimistic about the future of their countries.

Indonesia

Under Dutch rule for nearly 350 years, **Indonesia** won its freedom in 1949. Largely Muslim in religion, the new nation was very diverse in other ways. It consisted of a string of 14,000 islands stretching 3,000 miles (4,827 km) as well as nearly 80 million people of many cultures and languages. Therefore, forging a national identity was an early goal. Indonesia's first president, **Achmed Sukarno**, did much to unite the country. He ensured the adoption of a national language that put all Indonesians on an equal footing.

In 1965 Indonesia's Communists tried to seize power. In a bloody crackdown, the army killed about 300,000 allegedly pro-Communist ethnic Chinese. The anti-Communist General **Suharto** then replaced Sukarno as ruler.

Suharto at first brought economic growth, but his long dictatorial rule increased the national debt and political corruption. In 1998, Indonesia's economic collapse drove Suharto from office. A year later, voters freely elected a new parliament, and an assembly of political leaders named Abdurrahman Wahid as president. Relying on the army, the new government worked to rebuild the economy and to dampen ethnic and religious unrest that threatened national unity.

Suharto's Indonesia was known for human rights abuses. In 1975 Indonesian forces had seized East Timor, once a colony of Portugal. During the next 24 years, about 200,000 East Timorese died resisting Indonesian rule. In 1999, East Timor voted freely for independence. Indonesian forces opposing the results then staged violent attacks throughout the territory. Global pressure forced Indonesia to allow UN peacekeeping forces to restore order.

Malaysia

Created by the merger of several former British colonies in 1963, **Malaysia** is made up of territory on the Malay Peninsula and on the island of Borneo. Conflict between Malays and Chinese—the country's two largest ethnic groups—has been a frequent source of tension.

Since the 1970s, Malaysia has enjoyed a strong economy, thanks to its rich natural resources, a well-educated labor force, and large amounts of foreign investment. This growth slowed, however, in the late 1990s as a result of rising national debt and the effects of Asia's financial crisis.

Singapore

Singapore is a small island republic off the tip of the Malay Peninsula. Independent since 1965, Singapore is a leading international port and commercial center, involved in shipping, banking, insurance, and telecommunications. Today, Singapore's people are well-educated and prosperous. Their standard of living is second only to Japan's in Asia.

Singapore's modern economic growth occurred under the authoritarian leadership of **Lee Kuan Yew** (lee kwahn yoo), who was prime minister from 1965 to 1990. The government focused on encouraging high-technology industries and welcomed foreign business investment. A prosperous economy and the high rate of savings by Singapore citizens helped finance quality housing, health care, and education. In spite of having these benefits, Singapore's people have had limits placed on their freedom of speech and other rights.

1945   1972   2000

1947 India and Pakistan become independent nations.

1971 Civil war in Pakistan leads to independence of Bangladesh.

1998 India and Pakistan conduct tests of nuclear weapons.

Section 5

South Asia

Guide to Reading

Read to Find Out
Main Idea *The countries of South Asia have faced many challenges since independence.*

▶ **Terms to Define**
   nonaligned

▶ **People to Meet**
   Muhammad Ali Jinnah, Jawaharlal Nehru, Indira Gandhi, Atal Behari Vajpayee

▶ **Places to Locate**
   India, Pakistan, Kashmir, Bangladesh, Sri Lanka

The Storyteller

Pradeep Bandhari was deeply shaken. Yet another Indian leader had been assassinated. Confused and distressed, he asked his professor to explain why visionary leaders were repeatedly struck down. "I have no immediate answer to give," replied the professor. "However, you might find some meaning in the eulogy for Mohandas Gandhi written by Jawaharlal Nehru." Pradeep was struck by the timeliness of the message:

"Long ages afterwards history will judge of this period we have passed through. We are too near to be proper judges and to understand what has happened and what has not happened."

—adapted from *Independence and After*, "A Glory Has Departed," Jawaharlal Nehru, reprinted in *Great Speeches from Pericles to Kennedy*, 1965

Nehru and Mohandas Gandhi

*B*ritish rule of South Asia came to an end after World War II. The creation of independent states in the region, however, was marred by religious and ethnic conflicts. The cold war also had an impact. In recent years, dramatic changes in the world have made South Asian nations rethink their policies and relationships.

TURNING POINT

Dividing the Subcontinent

After World War II, the British finally agreed to give **India** its freedom. Growing political disunity, however, divided the subcontinent. **Muhammad Ali Jinnah**, leader of the Muslim League, wanted Muslims to have their own state. Riots between Hindus and Muslims finally persuaded the British to partition, or divide, India. In early 1947, Lord Louis Mountbatten, a World War II military hero, became British India's last viceroy. He and other officials quickly drew borders for two separate states, a difficult task because many Hindus and Muslims lived side by side. Heavily Muslim areas in the far west and far east became **Pakistan**. The vast area in between, where most of the people were Hindus, became India.

On August 15, 1947, independence came to both countries, but not peace. The division of the subcontinent led to one of the largest single mass movements of people in history. About 12 million Hindus and Muslims crossed the borders of India and Pakistan in both directions. Centuries of mistrust between religious groups led to violence that resulted in the deaths of a million or more people. Tragically, another casualty of the conflict was Mohandas Gandhi, killed in January 1948 by a Hindu extremist angered at Gandhi's call for peace and reconciliation.

The migrations and the killings did not end the conflicts between Hindus and Muslims. More than

916 Chapter 33 *Asia and the Pacific*

---

60 million Muslims remained in India, ensuring future tensions. Bitter hostilities between India and Pakistan would also continue.

India

India's first prime minister was **Jawaharlal Nehru** (jah•wah•HAR•lahl NAY•roo), a British-educated lawyer who had led the fight for freedom along with Gandhi. Nehru headed India's government, from 1947 until his death in 1964.

The Nehru "Dynasty"

For 40 years after independence, India was ruled by a member of the Nehru family. Jawaharlal Nehru aimed to make India a modern, industrialized state based on secular ideas. His government worked for religious freedom and greater social equality. India's constitution granted universal suffrage, and aimed to ban caste distinctions and improve the status of women.

Nehru favored a mixed economy of privately owned and government-run businesses. Attention was also given to raising food production. Increased food supplies, however, were accompanied by rapid population growth and the increased migration of people from rural areas to the cities.

Under Nehru, India became a leader among the new nations of Asia and Africa. Nehru argued that recently independent countries such as India should not participate in the cold war. By remaining nonaligned—that is, tied to neither superpower—the less powerful countries of the world could forge their own way in global affairs. In the early 1960s, however, tense relations with China helped bring India into a closer relationship with China's new rival, the Soviet Union.

Two years after Nehru's death in 1964, his daughter, **Indira Gandhi,** became prime minister. An energetic leader, Gandhi continued her father's policies; however, her crackdown on political opponents in 1977 made her unpopular and eventually swept her from office.

When Gandhi returned to power in 1980, India faced growing religious and ethnic unrest. In the Punjab region of northern India, some Sikhs wanted their own state. Sikh separatists occupied the Golden Temple of Amritsar, Sikhism's holiest shrine. When talks failed, Indira Gandhi in 1984 drove out the separatists with troops and tanks. Outraged at the shrine's violation, two of Gandhi's bodyguards, themselves Sikhs, later assassinated her.

Gandhi's son, Rajiv Gandhi, served as prime minister from 1984 to 1989. In 1991 he was assassi-

Visualizing History Indira Gandhi had been a leader in the Congress party and minister of information and broadcasting in India before becoming prime minister. *Why did she lose the 1977 election?*

nated while campaigning to become prime minister again. Rajiv's death seemed to mark the end of the Nehru "dynasty" in politics.

However, in 1998 the Italian-born widow of Rajiv Gandhi, Sonia Gandhi, took over the leadership of the Congress Party. Many Indians hoped she would carry on the Gandhi legacy.

A New Course

In the 1990s India's prime ministers did not have the influence or power of the Nehru "dynasty." However, with workable parliamentary institutions, India's democracy may have been strengthened. Although India still struggles with poverty, disease, and illiteracy, recent reforms have improved its economy by promoting free enterprise, less government regulation, and increased trade.

A major challenge still facing India is religious and ethnic conflict, which brought **Atal Behari Vajpayee,** the leader of the nationalist Bharatiya Janata Party (the BJP), to power in 1998. His party's desire to promote Hindu principles disturbed many non-Hindu Indians, who viewed it as a threat to India's secular government.

Since 1947, India has faced periodic conflicts with Pakistan. A major source of hostility between the two countries has been the disputed northern territory of **Kashmir.** Although most of Kashmir's people are Muslim, two-thirds of the territory is governed by India. Since the 1980s, Muslims in the

TEACH

Guided Practice

THEME Diversity
Ask students to read the section, looking for signs of how diversity contributed to developments in this region. *(Not only did British India break up into India and Pakistan because of religious differences, but Bangladesh later broke off from Pakistan because of language and cultural differences. Religious and ethnic diversity within India, Pakistan, and Sri Lanka continues to create unrest.)* **L1**

Visualizing History One of Indira Gandhi's assassins died soon after the assassination. The second, as well as a third coconspirator, was tried and sentenced to death.
Answer to Caption: *She had moved away from democracy toward authoritarian rule.*

POINT

Dividing the Subcontinent
How was independence finally achieved in South Asia?
The British withdrew from the subcontinent, but religious differences resulted in the formation of two independent states: India and Pakistan.

♫ World Music: Cultural Traditions, Lesson 7

Independent Practice
Guided Reading Activity 33-5 **L1**

COOPERATIVE LEARNING ACTIVITY

Research Organize the class into four teams, one for each country being studied—India, Pakistan, Bangladesh, and Sri Lanka. Each team should assign individual members to research one of the following topics: religion, economy, language, education, government (type, current leadership, and perceived strengths and weaknesses). Instruct each team to create a chart in poster form that will summarize what they learn about their assigned country. Have students display the completed charts and compare and contrast the four nations. **L1**

Map Study

Answer

The large number of island nations made regional unity difficult to achieve.

Map Skills Practice

Reading a Map Which country achieved independence most recently? *(Brunei)*

Critical Thinking Have students research and summarize the militant activities of the Sikhs since Indian independence in order to explain the Sikh wish to establish a separate nation.

VIDEODISC
Lessons of War

Side Two, Chapter 6
Frames 12636–20751
Title: *Philosophy of Nonviolence*
Subject: The philosophies of Mohandas Gandhi and Martin Luther King, Jr., and how their philosophies were used in protests and demonstrations
Ask: What form of demonstration did Mohandas Gandhi stress? *(nonviolent protest)*

ASSESS

Check for Understanding

Assign Section 5 Assessment as homework or as an in-class activity

■ Use Interactive Tutor Self-Assessment Software to review Section 5.

Postwar Independence in Asia

[Map of Asia showing postwar independence dates: USSR, MONGOLIA, KOREA (PDR) 1948, AFGHANISTAN, CHINA (PEOPLE'S REPUBLIC), KOREA (ROK) 1948, JAPAN, PAKISTAN 1947, NEPAL, BHUTAN, BANGLADESH 1971, INDIA 1947, MYANMAR (BURMA) 1948, Macao, TAIWAN, Hong Kong, GOA (to India) 1961, LAOS 1954, THAILAND, VIETNAM 1945, CAMBODIA 1953, PHILIPPINES 1946, GUAM, SRI LANKA 1948, BRUNEI 1984, MALAYSIA 1963, MALDIVES 1965, SINGAPORE 1965, INDONESIA 1949, PAPUA NEW GUINEA 1975]

Map Study With the crumbling of the European colonial empires after World War II, a large portion of the world's population came under self-rule.
Region Why would regional cooperation in Asia be difficult for these nations to achieve?

Indian section of Kashmir have organized to oppose Indian rule.

In the 1990s, a nuclear arms race developed between India and Pakistan. In May 1998 India successfully tested its first nuclear weapons. Within a few days, Pakistan responded by testing its own nuclear weapons. The following year tensions between the two countries rose again, after fighting broke out along the Indo-Pakistani border.

Pakistan and Bangladesh

After independence in 1947, Pakistan faced difficulties in joining two distinct regions separated by over 1,000 miles (1,609 km) of Indian territory. West Pakistan was a dry, mountainous region in which most people spoke Urdu. East Pakistan was a wet

lowlands region in which most people spoke Bengali. The religion of Islam was their only bond.

In 1971, civil war broke out between the two regions of Pakistan. Fighting began when forces from West Pakistan tried to quell riots in the eastern region. India soon joined the war in support of East Pakistan. This military action spread the conflict to West Pakistan and Kashmir. The war ended quickly, and East Pakistan won its independence as the republic of Bangladesh.

Bangladesh

Bangladesh is one of the most densely populated nations of the world. More than 125 million people live in an area about the size of New York State. Most people live in rural areas where illiteracy and the birthrate are high and life expectancy is low.

MEETING SPECIAL NEEDS ACTIVITY

Learning Style: Logical/Mathematical Have students work together to create two time lines, one of important events in India's history between World War II and the present, and the second of important events in Pakistan's history over the same period. Tell students to include political, economic, and cultural events. Advise students to use the same scale for this project so that their five time lines can be studied together. **L1**

Achieving stable rule has been difficult in Bangladesh. Since independence, two leaders of the country have been assassinated, and military officials often have controlled the government. Beginning in 1991, free elections have been held, however, and political power has alternated between the female leaders of the two major parties. In 1996 Sheik Hasina Wazid became prime minister.

In spite of economic growth and substantial foreign aid, the future of Bangladesh remains uncertain. The average annual per capita (per person) income of $240 is one of the world's lowest. The country also is subject to intense summer storms and flooding.

Pakistan Since 1971

During the 1970s and 1980s, Pakistan allied with the United States in order to counter India's ties with the Soviet Union. The Pakistani government allowed the Americans to channel military arms to anti-Soviet rebels in neighboring Afghanistan. It also permitted Afghani fighters to use Pakistan as a base, and sheltered 3 million Afghani refugees. Despite United States aid, the presence of so many refugees was costly and worsened ethnic tensions within Pakistan.

Pakistan suffered from political instability and military rule after the 1971 civil war. A move toward a stable democracy seemed likely in 1993 when Benazir Ali Bhutto became prime minister. In 1996, however, her government fell as a result of corruption charges. Elections brought to power the opposition party under Nawaz Sharif. Sharif's mishandling of the economy again brought military rule in 1999.

Military spending has taken a large share of Pakistan's budget because of tensions with India. This has drained resources that could have been used for the economic development of the country. Partly as a result of such spending, Pakistan remains very poor.

Visualizing History **Sheik Hasina Wazid became prime minister of Bangladesh in 1996. Her father, Sheik Mujibur Rahman, is regarded as Bangladesh's founder.** *What challenges does Bangladesh face?*

Sri Lanka

In 1948, the year after the partition of India, Great Britain granted independence to Ceylon, known since 1972 as **Sri Lanka**. This beautiful island off the southeast coast of India has been the site of ethnic civil war since the 1980s. The Sinhalese, who make up about about 75 percent of the population, are Buddhists. The Tamils, who make up about 20 percent, are Hindus. In recent years the Tamils, complaining of discrimination against them by the Sinhalese, have demanded their own state within Sri Lanka. At least 50,000 people have died as a result of conflicts between government troops and Tamil guerrillas.

SECTION 5 ASSESSMENT

Main Idea

1. Use a diagram like the one below to identify challenges South Asian countries have faced since independence.

Challenges Since Independence

Recall

2. **Define** nonaligned.
3. **Identify** Muhammad Ali Jinnah, Jawaharlal Nehru, Indira Gandhi, Atal Behari Vajpayee.

Critical Thinking

4. **Analyzing Information** What do you think are the underlying causes of continuing political tensions in Indian society today?

Understanding Themes

5. **Diversity** Has the division of the Indian subcontinent into the separate countries of India and Pakistan been beneficial? Explain your answer.

Chapter 33 *Asia and the Pacific* **919**

SECTION 5 ASSESSMENT ANSWERS

1. Indian independence led to mass migration and religious conflicts; rapid population growth in India; Hindu nationalist party opposed to India's secular government; India and Pakistan in conflict over Kashmir; civil war within Pakistan and Sri Lanka; political instability in Kashmir and Pakistan
2. All terms are defined in the Glossary.
3. Muhammad Ali Jinnah, 916; Jawaharlal Nehru, 917; Indira Gandhi, 917; Atal Behari Vajpayee, 917
4. Answers will vary but should refer to religious and ethnic conflict.
5. **DIVERSITY** Answers will vary. The division allowed groups more autonomy but left a legacy of conflict.

Visualizing History Sheik Hasina Wazid graduated from Dhaka University in 1973. Despite a forced exile and the deaths of her family members, she returned to Bangladesh to become its second female prime minister.
Answer to Caption: *Bangladesh has a low GDP and a high birthrate. It is vulnerable to drought and floods.*

Evaluate

Section Quiz 33-5

Use the Testmaker to create a customized quiz for Section 5.

Reteach

Have students locate India, Pakistan, Bangladesh, and Sri Lanka on a map. Ask them to identify the year each country achieved independence and to summarize the contemporary challenges each country faces.

Reading Essentials and Study Guide 33-5

Enrich

Have students each choose one of the 22 states of India and write a short report on its ethnic, cultural, and religious aspects. Some students may organize the class findings visually as a poster.

CLOSE

Have students write a short paragraph summarizing modern history and contemporary problems of each of the four countries studied in this section.

1945   1972   2000

1946 The Philippines wins independence from the United States.

1970s Australia admits non-British European and Asian immigrants for the first time.

1995 Pacific nations protest French nuclear testing.

Section 6

The Pacific

Guide to Reading

Read to Find Out
Main Idea *A variety of factors have helped Pacific nations develop prosperous economies and new national identities since World War II.*

▶ **Terms to Define**
  archipelago

▶ **People to Meet**
  Ferdinand Marcos, Corazon Aquino, Paul Keating, David Lange, Jim Bolger

▶ **Places to Locate**
  the Philippines, Australia, New Zealand, Papua New Guinea

The Storyteller

Toby Doust knew what to expect between the Great Sandy Desert and the Gibson Desert in northwestern Australia—and it wasn't water. Earlier explorers had expected water, but Lake Disappointment had water only when a rare inland cyclone brought a spattering shower to the dry bed. Toby, however, was prospecting for more commercial materials—iron, zinc, bauxite—to sell throughout the Pacific Basin. Perhaps there was even gold or uranium. One thing Toby never lacked was nerve. Nearing a remote outcrop, he unstrapped his bag and got out his metal detector, ready to strike it rich.

—adapted from "Journey into the Daytime," *National Geographic,* January 1991

Australia's Uluru (Ayers Rock)

The Pacific region east and south of Asia contains Australia, the world's only island continent, and numerous other islands that spread out across millions of square miles of the Pacific Ocean. Until recently, long distances and rugged landscapes kept many parts of the region isolated from each other and the rest of the world. Beginning in the 1700s, Western powers exercised a strong influence in the region. Since World War II, the Pacific countries, now mostly independent, have forged new identities from a mix of European, traditional Pacific, and Asian cultures. Many of them have close trading ties to Japan, Singapore, and other nations of the Pacific Rim, a region of economically prosperous countries bordering the Pacific Ocean.

The Philippines

The Philippines is an archipelago, or group of islands, in the Pacific Ocean east of Vietnam. The Philippines faced severe challenges when it became independent from the United States in 1946. Philippine Communists, known as the Huks, pressed for land reform and tried to take over the government. The Philippine army defeated them in 1954, but the Huks have arisen periodically to challenge later leaders.

Between 1965 and 1986, the Philippines was led by President **Ferdinand Marcos**. Marcos at first was popular because he tried to improve education and transportation. Evidence of corruption later fueled bitter protests against him. Marcos's downfall finally came about as a result of his suspected involvement in the killing of the political opposition leader, Benigno Aquino, Jr.

A massive public outcry over the assassination forced new elections, which Marcos won by fraud. Popular outrage at his deceit forced Marcos to flee the country. **Corazon Aquino**, the widow of the assassinated opposition leader, became the new president.

920 **Chapter 33** *Asia and the Pacific*

President Corazon Aquino pledged to restore democracy to the Philippines under a new constitution in 1987. *What four groups opposed her rule?*

Guided Practice

THEME Cultural Diffusion

Ask students to list the cultural influences that have affected the development of Australia *(population: Aborigines, British, other European, Asian; military: United States; trade: United States, Europe, Japan, Southeast Asia)*, New Zealand *(population: Maori, British, other European; trade: Japan, Australia, Europe)*, and Papua New Guinea *(population: ethnic groups speaking nearly 700 different languages)*. **L1**

Visualizing History Corazon Aquino called for only nonviolent demonstrations, boycotts, and strikes to protest the corrupt Marcos regime.
Answer to Caption: *Marcos supporters, the Huks, the military, and nationalist Filipinos opposed to American military bases in the Philippines*

World History and Art Transparency 44, *Sydney Opera House*

World Music: Cultural Traditions, Lesson 10

Hopes for reform faded, however, as Aquino faced opposition from Marcos supporters, the Huks, the military, and nationalists opposed to American military bases in the country. An attempt to overthrow Aquino failed due to American support. In the 1990s her successors, Fidel Ramos and later, Joseph Estrada, worked to promote economic growth and to reduce crime.

In 1992 the United States withdrew from its last military base in the Philippines. Although this was the desire of the Philippine government, the loss of revenue to the Philippine economy was substantial. Japan has since become the foreign country with the most economic influence in the Philippines.

Australia

Before World War II, **Australia** was a largely agricultural country dependent on Great Britain. Beef, wool, wheat, and dairy products were the country's main exports. Since 1945, Australia has changed to an industrial economy with close links to the United States and Asian countries. With the help of foreign investment, Australians have developed assembly and manufacturing plants for consumer goods, processed foods, paper, textiles, and transportation equipment.

Since the 1970s, Australia has strengthened ties with Japan and Southeast Asia. Today more than 60 percent of Australia's trade is with Asian countries. Meanwhile, Australia is gradually ending its links

to Great Britain and the monarchy. **Paul Keating**, who was prime minister in the early 1990s, pushed for the creation of an Australian republic. Voters in 1999, however, rejected this proposal.

Australia's shift from Great Britain to its Asian and Pacific neighbors has been influenced by the country's changing population. After World War II, large numbers of southern and eastern Europeans—Greeks, Italians, and Slavs—made new homes in Australia. Then, in the 1970s, the Australian government liberalized its immigration laws and allowed Asian immigrants into the country. Today, about 50 percent of immigrants to Australia each year come from neighboring Asian countries. By the end of the 1990s, only about 35 percent of Australians were of British descent, down from 75 percent in 1949.

On the World Stage

Since World War II Australia has sought a greater role in world affairs. It became a founding member of the United Nations in 1945. Five years later, Australian troops joined the UN forces fighting in the Korean War. In 1951 Australia signed the **ANZUS** treaty, which linked Australia, New Zealand, and the United States in a mutual defense pact. As part of the effort to contain communism, Australia sent forces to fight alongside the United States in the Vietnam War. It later backed the UN effort against Iraq in 1990 by sending Australian warships to the Persian Gulf.

Australians continue to support close military ties with the United States but are concerned about

Chapter 33 *Asia and the Pacific* **921**

COOPERATIVE LEARNING ACTIVITY

The Arts Organize the class into four groups to research Australian, Melanesian, Polynesian, and Micronesian art. Each group member should have a specific area to research, such as visual art, music, dance, literature, or specific crafts. When the groups have completed their research, ask them to prepare class presentations combining oral commentary with visual and aural examples. After all the groups have made their presentations, hold a class discussion in which students compare and contrast Australian, Melanesian, Polynesian, and Micronesian arts and crafts. **L2**

Linking Past and Present

Philippine Government In February 1986, Marcos dispatched columns of tanks against a group of rebel soldiers in Manila. They were stopped by the crowds assembled at the corner of Ortigas Avenue and the highway. In February 1996, Filipinos celebrated the tenth anniversary of the "People Power" revolution against Marcos. President Fidel V. Ramos addressed a rally at that corner.

Independent Practice

 Guided Reading Activity 33-6 **L1**

Literature Have students choose a book by Australian novelist Patrick White, who won the 1973 Nobel Prize in literature. Ask them to write a book report that focuses on life in Australia. **L2**

ASSESS

Check for Understanding

Assign Section 6 Assessment as homework or as an in-class activity.

📀 Use Interactive Tutor Self-Assessment Software to review Section 6.

Evaluate

 Section Quiz 33-6

📀 Use the Testmaker to create a customized quiz for Section 6.

Reteach

Have students write one-sentence identifications of each of the terms, people, and places listed in "Setting the Scene," on page 920.

 Reteaching Activity 33

 Reading Essentials and Study Guide 33-6

Enrich

Have students locate articles about recent antinuclear activities in the Pacific region. Ask them to summarize their findings in a brief written report.

 Enrichment Activity 33

CLOSE

Have students write a short paragraph for each of the countries covered in this section (the Philippines, Australia, New Zealand, and Papua New Guinea) summarizing recent developments.

the presence of nuclear weapons in the Pacific region. Australia has been a major sponsor of a South Pacific Nuclear-Free Zone. Even so, it sided with the United States in the United States dispute with New Zealand about American nuclear-armed vessels entering New Zealand waters.

New Zealand

Consisting of two major islands and many small ones, **New Zealand** lies about 1,000 miles (1,600 km) to the southeast of Australia. Most of New Zealand's 3.5 million people are of British, other European, or Maori descent. Like Australia, New Zealand traditionally was joined by trade, politics, and culture to Great Britain. After World War II, it began to ally itself more closely with the United States and Asian countries.

New Zealand also added more variety to its economy. While agriculture—mainly sheep and dairy farming—remains important, New Zealand now has many manufacturing and service industries. It trades with Japan, Australia, the United States, and the countries of Western Europe.

Fear of Japanese attack during World War II made New Zealand turn to the United States for defense after the war. In 1951, New Zealand joined the ANZUS alliance and participated in the Korean and Vietnam conflicts.

Since the 1980s, however, New Zealand's opposition to nuclear weapons has strained its relationship with the United States and has drawn it closer to other Pacific countries that also oppose nuclear weapons. In 1985, New Zealand Prime Minister **David Lange** announced that ships carrying nuclear weapons, including those from the United States, could no longer enter New Zealand ports. In the early 1990s, Lange's successor as prime minister, **Jim Bolger**, worked to improve relations with the United States on the nuclear issue.

South Pacific Island Countries

Thousands of islands dot the Pacific Ocean. Many are small and uninhabited. Others were first settled thousands of years ago by various Asian and Pacific peoples. Their descendants today belong to three major groups: Melanesians, Micronesians, and Polynesians.

Nations and Colonies

Since World War II, some South Pacific islands—such as Fiji—have become independent of Western rule. Other islands—such as Tahiti—continue to be held by Western powers for military reasons. France, for example, in 1995 conducted nuclear tests on an atoll, or ring-shaped coral island, in French Polynesia. France's actions aroused antinuclear protests and boycotts of French goods.

Papua New Guinea

Among the larger island countries in the Pacific region is **Papua New Guinea**. Made up of 700 islands, Papua New Guinea has most of its territory on the eastern half of the island of New Guinea. Formerly held by Germany and Great Britain, and later by Australia, Papua New Guinea became independent in 1975.

Papua New Guinea faces many challenges in its efforts to achieve national unity. Its population is made up of many ethnic groups that speak nearly 700 different languages. This ethnic diversity makes tensions and conflict common, so that Papua New Guinea has little sense of nationhood.

In addition, most of Papua New Guinea's people are poor and illiterate. Copper and gold mining has boosted the economy since the 1980s, but other economic sectors remain to be developed. The government of Papua New Guinea is working to interest companies in Japan, the United States, China, and Singapore to invest in the country.

SECTION 6 ASSESSMENT

Main Idea
1. Use a chart like the one below to list factors that have helped New Zealand develop a prosperous economy since World War II.

New Zealand
1.
2.
3.
4.

Recall
2. **Define** archipelago.
3. **Identify** Ferdinand Marcos, Corazon Aquino, Paul Keating, ANZUS, David Lange, Jim Bolger.

Critical Thinking
4. **Analyzing Information** How has the economy of Australia changed since the end of World War II?

Understanding Themes
5. **Cultural Diffusion** What political, economic, and cultural influences have affected the development of island countries in the vast region of the South Pacific?

SECTION 6 ASSESSMENT ANSWERS

1. closer alliance with U.S. and Asia; more variety to economy; increase in manufacturing and service industry; opposition to nuclear weapons
2. The term is defined in the Glossary.
3. Ferdinand Marcos, 920; Corazon Aquino, 920; Paul Keating, 921; ANZUS, 921; David Lange, 922; Jim Bolger, 922

4. It has changed from a largely agricultural country dependent on Great Britain to an industrial economy with close links to the United States and Asia.
5. **CULTURAL DIFFUSION** independence; foreign investment; ethnic diversity: Melanesian, Micronesian, Polynesian, and European

Using a Spreadsheet

Electronic spreadsheets can help people manage numbers quickly and easily. You can use a spreadsheet any time a problem involves numbers that can be arranged in rows and columns.

Learning the Skill

A spreadsheet is an electronic worksheet. All spreadsheets follow a basic design of rows and columns. Each *column* (vertical) is assigned a letter or number. Each *row* (horizontal) is assigned a number. Each point where a column and row intersect is called a *cell*. The cell's position on the spreadsheet is labeled according to its corresponding column and row—Column A, Row 1 (A1); Column B, Row 2 (B2), and so on.

Spreadsheets use *standard formulas* to calculate the numbers. You create a simple mathematical equation that uses these standard formulas and the computer does the calculations for you.

Practicing the Skill

Suppose you want to know the population densities (population per square mile) of the countries in South Asia. Use these steps to create a spreadsheet that will provide this information.

1. In cell A1 type *Country*, in cell B1 type *Population*, in cell C1 type *Land Area (square miles)*, and in cell D1 type *Population per square mile*.
2. In cells A2-A5 respectively, type one of the following country's name: *India*, *Pakistan*, *Bangladesh*, and *Sri Lanka*. In cell A6, type the words *Total for South Asia*.
3. In cells B2-B5, enter the population area of each country shown in cells A2-A5.
4. In cells C2-C5, enter the land area (square miles) of each country shown in cells A2-A5.
5. In cell D2, create a formula to calculate the population per square mile. The formula for the equation tells what cells (B1 ÷ C1) to divide. Copy this formula into cells D3-D5.

6. Use the process in step 5 to create and copy a formula to calculate the total population of South Asia (B2 + B3 + B4 + B5) for cell B6; to calculate the total Land Area of South Asia (C2 + C3 + C4 + C5) for cell C6.
7. Use the process in step 5 to create and copy a formula to calculate the population per square mile of South Asia (B6 ÷ C6) for cell D6.

Applying the Skill

Use a spreadsheet to enter your test scores and your homework grades. At the end of the grading period, the spreadsheet can calculate your average grade.

For More Practice

Turn to the Skill Practice in the Chapter Assessment on page 925 for more practice in using a spreadsheet.

TEACH

Using a Spreadsheet **This skill teaches students to work with a spreadsheet program on the computer. Review Learning the Skill with students. What types of information could be placed on spreadsheets?** (*Budgets, grades, schedules, populations, temperatures, amount of precipitation, and so on.*) Next review **Practicing the Skill** with students. Then allow them computer time to apply the directions. Students can find the information they need to complete **Practicing the Skill** in *The World Almanac, Statesmen's Yearbook,* and *The Population Data Sheet* from the Population Bureau, Inc.

Additional Practice

📁 Skill Reinforcement Activity 33

ANSWERS TO PRACTICING THE SKILL

Students will create a spreadsheet that shows the population density of the countries of South Asia as well as the average population density of all of South Asia. The population densities will vary depending on the population figures (year) used in the calculations.

WORLD HISTORY Online

Have students use the **Chapter 33 Self-Check Quiz** at worldhistory.glencoe.com to prepare for the Chapter Test.

GLENCOE TECHNOLOGY

VIDEODISC
Use MindJogger to review the chapter.

MindJogger Videoquiz

Chapter 33
Disc 5 Side A

  Also available in VHS.

Answers

Using Key Terms

1. i   3. f   5. a
2. j   4. h

Using Your History Journal

Suggest that students reflect on political, cultural, and economic changes they confront as new immigrants.

Reviewing Facts

1. 1945: Democratic Republic of Vietnam founded; 1946: France and Vietminh go to war; 1963: Diem killed in coup; 16,000 military advisors in Vietnam; 1964: Gulf of Tonkin resolution; first U.S. ground troops in Vietnam; 1973: cease-fire; 1975: defeat of South Vietnam
2. Indira Gandhi (prime minister, India); Benazir Ali Bhutto (prime minister, Pakistan); Sheik Hasina Wazid (prime minister, Bangladesh)
3. He is the spiritual leader of Tibet.
4. Mao Zedong established a totalitarian Communist regime that suppressed human rights; he

WORLD HISTORY Online

Self-Check Quiz

Visit the *World History: The Human Experience* Web site at **worldhistory.glencoe.com** and click on *Chapter 33—Self-Check Quiz* to prepare for the Chapter Test.

Using Key Terms

Write the key term that completes each sentence. Then write a sentence for each term not chosen.

a. referendum
b. stalemate
c. archipelago
d. refugee
e. quota
f. pragmatists
g. sect
h. special economic zones
i. domino theory
j. nonaligned
k. pollution
l. gross domestic product

1. In the 1960s the growing American role in Vietnam was justified by those who accepted the _____.
2. Jawaharlal Nehru believed if India and other less powerful countries remained _____ in the cold war, they could provide alternatives to the superpowers.
3. In China, a group known as _____ favored modernizing China through increased trade and contacts with the West.
4. The Chinese government has allowed foreign privately owned businesses to flourish in _____ located in southeastern China.
5. In a _____, voters are asked to accept or reject a measure.

Technology Activity

Using a Word Processor
Locate resources about present-day North Korea and South Korea. Organize your findings by creating a fact sheet comparing the two countries. Use a word processor to create a chart. Headings to include are population, type of economy, GDP, type of government, currency, infant mortality rate, literacy rate, and official religion. Provide a map of each country that shows political boundaries, major cities, and natural resources.

Reviewing Facts

1. **History** Use a time line like the one below to identify key events in the struggle for control of Indochina.

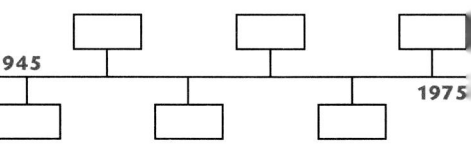

2. **Culture** Identify examples of women who have been successful in Asian politics.
3. **Culture** Explain the role of the Dalai Lama.
4. **History** Discuss the policies of Mao Zedong and Deng Xiaoping, and describe their effects on the Chinese people.
5. **Citizenship** Identify examples of how human rights have advanced and how they have been violated in Asia since World War II.
6. **History** Identify the causes and outcome of the Korean War.
7. **History** Describe the impact of the Vietnam War on Southeast Asia and the United States.

Critical Thinking

1. **Apply** Using examples from Asia, explain whether a country's economic progress is related to its form of government.
2. **Analyze** What impact did Japan's recovery after World War II have on global affairs?
3. **Synthesize** Explain how events in Asia since 1945 have influenced the population profile of the people of the United States.
4. **Analyze** How do you think the return of Hong Kong to China has affected China and Hong Kong?

raised living standards but his policies killed millions. Deng introduced market reforms but kept Communist controls.

5. Advances: Aquino's victory in the Philippines; India's maintenance of democratic rule; Violations: the Khmer Rouge atrocities in Cambodia; suppression of democracy in Myanmar, the Tiananmen Square massacre in China
6. North Korea's aim to unite Korea under communism; cold war tensions; stalemate

with truce talks. Korea remained divided at 38th parallel.
7. Asia: Vietnam destroyed, taken over by Communists, problems in Laos and Cambodia; United States: defeat, fear of international involvement

Critical Thinking

1. Countries with relatively stable governments—such as Singapore and Japan—have

5. Analyze United States President Richard Nixon visited China in 1972. What historic change in United States foreign policy did this visit signal?

Understanding Themes

1. Change What factors account for Japan's economic recovery and prosperity after World War II?

2. Revolution What changes did the Communist takeover of 1949 bring to China during the 1950s? How have policies changed since the 1970s?

3. Regionalism What basic reason keeps Korea divided into two nations?

4. Conflict How did the United States get involved in the war in Vietnam?

5. Diversity Why was India partitioned in 1947? Why did Pakistan later split into two separate nations?

6. Cultural Diffusion What new national and ethnic groups have come to once predominantly British Australia as a result of changes in immigration since World War II?

1. The era from about 1950 to the present and on into the twenty-first century has been called the Asian Century. Explain what name you would give to the 100 years prior to 1950.

2. The involvement by the United States in Vietnam was based on the domino theory and the Truman Doctrine, both of which declared the United States commitment to containing communism. What circumstances, if any, do you think would justify United States involvement overseas today?

Geography in History

1. Region Refer to the map on this page. What generalization describes the diverse economies of East Asia and the Pacific?

2. Place What nations make up the middle-income economies group?

3. Region What do the economies of Japan and Australia have in common according to the map?

East Asia and the Pacific Economies

Low-income economies
Middle-income economies
High-income economies

Skill Practice

Look at the weather page in a newspaper or on the Internet. Choose a city in Asia or the Pacific that is listed in the weather report for international cities. Using an electronic spreadsheet over a 4-week period, note both the high and low temperature for each day. Insert an equation to calculate the average temperature for the first day. Copy the equation to calculate the average temperature for each day. Using your spreadsheet software, create a line graph showing the daily high, daily low, and the daily average temperature for this 4-week period.

Chapter 33 *Asia and the Pacific* **925**

---

fears its military threat.

4. **CONFLICT** support of its ally, France in Indochina

5. **DIVERSITY** because of differences between Hindus and Muslims; a civil war between West Pakistan and East Pakistan

6. **CULTURAL DIFFUSION** southern and eastern Europeans, Asians

Linking Past *and* Present

1. The American Century or the European Century, because of their economic and political dominance.

2. prevention of genocide and other types of humanitarian aid

Geography in History

1. Most are low-income; only 3 high-income

2. South Korea, Taiwan, Thailand, Malaysia, Philippines, Brunei, Papua New Guinea

3. high-income economies

Skill Practice

Answers will vary depending on the city chosen to track.

Chapter Bonus Test Question

Ask students: How convincing are arguments by developing nations that democracy should be sacrificed in the name of promoting economic growth and public safety? Discuss countries studied in this chapter. *(The end justifies the means, and countries such as Singapore are cleaner and safer than the United States, with a higher general standard of living, even if there is political repression; or, the end does not justify the means, and people are better served by democratic countries, even if some citizens do not have an economic safety net.)*

---

had the greatest economic success.

2. Japan's creation of an export economy has made Japan an economic giant.

3. Turmoil in Southeast Asia caused a large immigration to the United States.

4. Hong Kong's economic power may further open China to outside influences; or China may limit Hong Kong's liberties.

5. It led to the establishment of diplomatic relations with the People's Republic of China.

Understanding Themes

1. **CHANGE** MacArthur's policies, Japanese government-business cooperation, political stability

2. **REVOLUTION** the 1950s: state-run economy, close ties to Soviets; since the 1970s: split with Soviets, closer ties to West, market reforms with Communist political controls

3. **REGIONALISM** North Korea remains a Communist dictatorship, and South Korea

A complete, 1-page lesson plan is provided for each section in the *Reproducible Lesson Plans* booklet.

Africa

CHAPTER RESOURCES

	Reproducible Resources	Multimedia Resources
Chapter Opener	Chapter Themes: Graphic Organizer 34 Historical Significance Chapter Activity 34	MindJogger Videoquiz
Chapter Enrichment	Vocabulary Activity 34* Time Line Activity 34 Mapping History Activity 34 History Simulation 34 Geography and History Activity 34 Source Reading 34 People in World History Profiles 65, 66 World Art and Music Activity 34 Enrichment Activity 34 Critical Thinking Activity 34 Skill Reinforcement Activity 34 Writer's Guidebook, Lesson 12 Performance Assessment Activity 34 Standardized Test Practice Workbook Activity 34 Inclusion for the Social Studies Classroom Strategies and Activities	World History and Art Transparency 45, *The Liberated African Woman*; 46, *Bedouin Woman's Headpiece* Chapter Transparency 34 NGS PicturePack Transparencies: Physical Geography of the World Vocabulary PuzzleMaker Software Picture Atlas of the World World Music: Cultural Traditions, Lesson 6 Turning Points in World History: *End of Apartheid* STV: World Geography, Vol. 2, *Africa* World History Primary Source Document Library
Chapter Review/Reteaching	Reteaching Activity 34 Skill Reinforcement Activity 34 Spanish Chapter Summary 34	Chapter 34 Digest Audiocassette, Activity, Test* Vocabulary PuzzleMaker Software Interactive Tutor Self-Assessment Software MindJogger Videoquiz
Chapter Evaluation/Testing	Performance Assessment Activity 34 Chapter 34 Test, Forms A and B	ExamView® Pro Testmaker

* Also available in Spanish

0:00 OUT OF TIME? Assign the Chapter 34 Audiocassettes.

World History Primary Source Document Library

Make History Come Alive!

Engage your students with over 250 easily accessible primary source documents—available on this CD-ROM—that will give them real life insight into the important events of world history.

Block Schedule

Activities that are particularly suited to use within the block scheduling framework are identified throughout this chapter by the following designation.

KEY TO ABILITY LEVELS

Teaching strategies are coded for varying learning styles.

L1 **BASIC** activities for all students
L2 **AVERAGE** activities for average to above-average students
L3 **CHALLENGING** activities for above-average students
LEP **LIMITED ENGLISH PROFICIENCY** activities

Use Glencoe's *Presentation Plus!* multimedia teacher tool to easily present dynamic lessons that visually excite your students. Using Microsoft PowerPoint® you can customize the presentations to create your own personalized lessons.

Interactive Lesson Planner

Planning has never been easier! Using this CD-ROM, organize your week, month, semester, or year with all the help you need. The **Interactive Lesson Planner** gives you access to all of the blackline masters that accompany *World History: The Human Experience.*

SECTION RESOURCES

Daily Objectives	Reproducible Resources	Multimedia Resources
Section 1 **African Independence** Describe how African nations won their independence after World War II.	Lecture Notes 34-1 Reproducible Lesson Plan 34-1 Vocabulary Activity 34* Guided Reading Activity 34-1* Time Line Activity 34 People in World History Profile 65 Section Quiz 34-1* Reading Essentials and Study Guide 34-1	Section Focus Transparency 34-1 Chapter Transparency 34 World History and Art Transparency 46, *Bedouin Woman's Headpiece* NGS PicturePack Transparencies: Physical Geography of the World Interactive Tutor Self-Assessment Software Testmaker Picture Atlas of the World
Section 2 **Africa Today** Explain what kinds of governments ruled in Africa from the 1970s to the 1990s.	Lecture Notes 34-2 Reproducible Lesson Plan 34-2 Vocabulary Activity 34* Guided Reading Activity 34-2* People in World History Profile 66 Section Quiz 34-2* Reading Essentials and Study Guide 34-2	Section Focus Transparency 34-2 Interactive Tutor Self-Assessment Software Testmaker World Music: Cultural Traditions, Lesson 6 Picture Atlas of the World Turning Points in World History: *End of Apartheid*
Section 3 **Africa's Challenges** Identify the challenges faced by modern African nations in their quest for political and economic independence.	Lecture Notes 34-3 Reproducible Lesson Plan 34-3 Guided Reading Activity 34-3* Reteaching Activity 34 Enrichment Activity 34 Section Quiz 34-3* Performance Assessment Activity 34 Spanish Chapter Summary 34 Reading Essentials and Study Guide 34-3	Section Focus Transparency 34-3 World History and Art Transparency 45, *The Liberated African Woman* Vocabulary PuzzleMaker Software Interactive Tutor Self-Assessment Software Testmaker Picture Atlas of the World STV: World Geography, Vol. 2, *Africa*

* *Also available in Spanish*

Chapter Activities

 Performance Assessment Activity

A Letter to a Young African Have students write letters to a high school student in Africa who is living with the challenges addressed in this chapter. Have students organize their letters around the question of why political independence was easier to achieve than economic independence for most African nations. Ask students to suggest reasons why it is sometimes easier to solve political problems than economic problems and have them give examples from their own experiences or from recent United States history.

Possible Rubric Features

Concept attainment, critical thinking, elaboration and organization of letter, analysis of relationships, persuasion

• *For an additional activity, refer to Activity 34 in the* Performance Assessment Strategies and Activities *booklet.*

ACTIVITY
From the Classroom of...

Anna Mae Grimm
Homestead High School
Mequon, WI

Experiencing Apartheid

For one class period, designate about half the students in the class to be part of an "underclass" that will not be allowed to participate in activities with the rest of the class. Have the "underclass" sit at the back of the room. Provide an interesting activity for the rest of the class, and assign the separated students routine worksheets. Hold an election during the class period (for example, elect a discussion leader) and exclude the separated students from the voting.

During the next class period, discuss how students felt during the simulation—both those in the "underclass" and those in the mainstream. Use this as a springboard for discussing apartheid in South Africa.

MULTIPLE LEARNING STYLES

Verbal/Linguistic

Have students read and write brief reviews of a short story, play, novel, or poem by a contemporary African author.

Visual/Spatial

Have students create a piece of art based on an African model.

Auditory/Musical

Have students find recordings of modern African music by such popular artists as King Sunny Ade and Babatunde Olanji of Nigeria, Baaba Maal or Youssou N'Dour of Senegal, Ladysmith Black Mambazo of South Africa, or Thomas Mapfumo of Zimbabwe and play selected songs for the class.

Kinesthetic

Have students plan and attend a field trip to a nearby museum that displays African art and artifacts.

GLENCOE'S ASSESSMENT ADVANTAGE

Use the following to easily assess student learning in a variety of ways.

- Performance Assessment Strategies and Activities
- Section Quizzes
- Chapter and Unit Tests
- Interactive Tutor Self-Assessment Software
- Testmaker Software
- MindJogger Videoquiz
- SAT/SAT II Test Practice
- worldhistory.glencoe.com

Additional Resources

NATIONAL GEOGRAPHIC SOCIETY

Teacher's Corner

INDEX TO NATIONAL GEOGRAPHIC MAGAZINE

The following articles relate to this chapter:

- "Masai Passage to Manhood," by Carol Beckwith, September 1999.
- "Down the Zambezi," by Paul Theroux, October 1997.
- "African Gold," by Carol Beckwith and Angela Fisher, October 1996.
- "Ndoki—The Last Place on Earth," by Douglas Chadwick, July 1995.

NATIONAL GEOGRAPHIC SOCIETY PRODUCTS AVAILABLE FROM GLENCOE

To order the following, call Glencoe at 1-800-334-7344:

- *STV: World Geography, Vol. 2, Africa (Videodisc)*
- *Picture Atlas of the World (CD-ROM)*
- *Physical Geography of the World (Transparencies)*
- *MapPack: Africa (Transparency Maps)*

ADDITIONAL NATIONAL GEOGRAPHIC SOCIETY PRODUCTS

To order the following, call National Geographic at 1-800-368-2728:

- *South Africa: After Apartheid (Video)*
- *Baka: People of the Forest (Video)*
- *Africa (Laminated Desk Maps)*

Access National Geographic's new dynamic MapMachine Web site and other geography resources at:

- http://www.nationalgeographic.com/
- http://www.nationalgeographic.com/maps/

BIBLIOGRAPHY

Readings for the Student
Davidson, Basil. *The Black Man's Burden: Africa and the Curse of the Nation-State.* New York: Times Books, 1992. Underlying causes of political conflict and instability in Africa since independence.

Readings for the Teacher
Malan, Rian. *My Traitor's Heart: A South African Exile Returns to Face His Country, His Tribe, and His Conscience.* New York: Atlantic Monthly Press, 1990. Reflections on South Africa by a descendant of one of the builders of apartheid.

WORLD HISTORY Online

Use our Web site as an additional resource. All essential content is covered in the Student Edition.

You and your students can visit the *World History: The Human Experience* Web site at worldhistory. glencoe.com The student text directs students to the Web site for the following options:

- **Chapter Overviews**
- **Student Web Activities**
- **Self-Check Quizzes**

Answers are provided for you in a link entitled "Web Activity Lesson Plan." Additional Web Resources, Interactive Puzzles, and content updates are also available.

Visit the Glencoe Web site at socialstudies. glencoe.com for social studies activities, updates, and links to other resources.

LOCAL OBJECTIVES

_____
_____
_____
_____
_____
_____
_____
_____
_____
_____
_____
_____
_____
_____
_____
_____
_____

CHAPTER THEMES

Chapter Themes are listed by section on this chapter opening page of the Student Edition. A corresponding theme-based activity is available under "TEACH," and a theme-based question is asked in the Section and Chapter Assessments.

Historical Setting Mandela, born in 1918, spent 28 years (1962–1990) in prison for conspiring to overthrow the white-minority government of South Africa. During those years, his wife, Winnie, helped focus the world's attention on Mandela and make him a symbol of the struggle against apartheid. After his release from prison, his negotiations with white leaders led to the end of apartheid and establishment of a nonracial government system. For their joint efforts to end apartheid, Mandela and F. W. de Klerk, his predecessor as president of South Africa, shared the 1993 Nobel Peace Prize.

Historical Significance

Answers: *The European colonial empires in Africa were replaced by independent nations.*

Africa has become an international force, wielding more than a third of the votes in the United Nations General Assembly.

— WORLD HISTORY Online —

Have students use the **Chapter 34 Overview** at worldhistory. glencoe.com as a prereading and postreading exercise for understanding chapter content.

Chapter
34 1945–Present
Africa

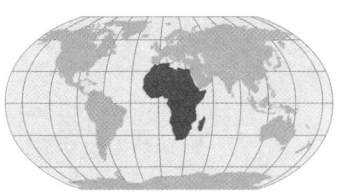

Chapter Themes

▶ **Nationalism** European empires crumble, and independent nations emerge in Africa. *Section 1*
▶ **Change** Some African nations move toward democracy and free enterprise economies. *Section 2*
▶ **Change** Ethnic, cultural, environmental, and economic challenges face newly independent African nations. *Section 3*

Storyteller

From April 26 to 29, 1994, South Africa held its first election in which all of its citizens, regardless of race, could vote. The outcome was a landslide victory for nationalist leader Nelson Mandela and his African National Congress party.

On May 10, during his inauguration as South Africa's first black president, Mandela declared, "The people of South Africa ... want change.... Our plan is to create jobs, promote peace and reconciliation and to guarantee freedom for all South Africans." Mandela's rise to office signaled a joyous dawn of freedom after decades of white-minority rule and racial discrimination in South Africa.

By the 1990s nearly 700 million people in more than 50 African countries had thrown off various forms of colonial rule and were charting new courses as independent nations.

Historical Significance

What sweeping changes came to Africa after World War II? What role does Africa play in world affairs today?

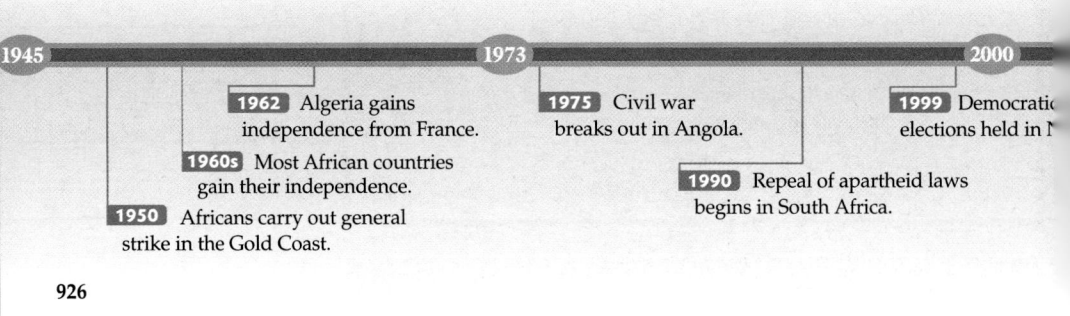

1945	1973	2000

1962 Algeria gains independence from France.

1975 Civil war breaks out in Angola.

1999 Democratic elections held in N

1960s Most African countries gain their independence.

1990 Repeal of apartheid laws begins in South Africa.

1950 Africans carry out general strike in the Gold Coast.

926

GEOGRAPHY CONNECTION

Location Have students use a world map to locate Africa. Compare the size of Africa with the size of the United States. *(It is much larger, closer to the size of North America.)* Show students a landform or vegetation map of Africa and ask them to describe the continent. *(About one-third is desert; it has grasslands, rain forests, and hot, dry savannas.)*

In 1991 fighting broke out among rebel groups in Somalia. By late 1992 the fighting had led to the deaths of about 30,000 people and had disrupted food production, threatening millions with starvation. With UN authorization, a coalition of military forces from several countries, led by the United States, went into Somalia to provide security for relief organizations distributing food. U.S. troops were withdrawn in March 1994, and the remaining UN forces left Somalia in March 1995.

Performance Assessment

Refer to the activity on page 926C of the Planning Guide.

For an additional activity, refer to Activity 34 in the *Performance Assessment Strategies and Activities* booklet.

Visualizing History Children in Somalia were doing their daily schoolwork in the midst of civil war, when UN troops arrived in 1992.

WORLD HISTORY *Online*

Chapter Overview

Visit the *World History: The Human Experience* Web site at **worldhistory.glencoe.com** and click on ***Chapter 34—Chapter Overview*** to preview the chapter.

Your History Journal

Watch for current articles about African nations in newspapers and magazines. Clip and paste or write headlines and paraphrase short excerpts from these articles in your History Journal.

Chapter 34 *Africa* **927**

GLENCOE TECHNOLOGY

VIDEODISC
Use MindJogger to preview chapter content.

MindJogger Videoquiz

Chapter 34
Disc 5 Side A

Also available in VHS.

Using Your History Journal

Advise students to concentrate on a single country or region of Africa.

+ EXTRA CREDIT PROJECT

Oral Report Ask students to choose three African countries, one in western Africa, one on the Mediterranean Sea, and one in eastern or central Africa. Have them research the economic problems each country faces and the policies each country is adopting to solve them. Have students summarize their findings in a brief oral report. Suggested resources: C. Wekesser and C. Pierce, *Africa: Opposing Viewpoints*; S. Baynham, *Africa from 1945*; B. Davidson, *The Black Man's Burden: Africa and the Curse of the Nation-State*; S. J. Ungar, *Africa: The People and Politics of an Emerging Continent.*

1948 South Africa introduces apartheid policies.

1957 Ghana becomes independent.

1970 Biafran conflict ends in Nigeria.

SECTION THEME

▶ **Nationalism** European empires crumble, and independent nations emerge in Africa.

Guide to Reading

For reading strategies to help students read effectively see pages 12–13. Have students think about the main head as they read the subheads.

Vocabulary Pre-check

 Use the Vocabulary PuzzleMaker for Chapter 34 to create a crossword puzzle to reinforce section terms. **L1 LEP**

Use Vocabulary Activity 34 to introduce vocabulary terms. **L1 LEP**

FOCUS

Section Objective

Describe how African nations won their independence after World War II.

BELLRINGER
Motivational Activity

 Before taking roll at the beginning of the class period, project Section Focus Transparency 34-1 and have students answer the activity questions. Discuss students' responses.

This activity is also available as a blackline master.

Section 1

African Independence

Guide to Reading

Read to Find Out

Main Idea *Many African nations won their independence after World War II.*

▶ **Terms to Define**
colons, general strike, apartheid

▶ **People to Meet**
Muammar al-Qaddafi, Kwame Nkrumah, Ahmed Sékou Touré, Jomo Kenyatta, Nelson Mandela, Desmond Tutu

▶ **Places to Locate**
Sudan, Algeria, Ghana, Nigeria, Congo (Zaire), Kenya, Angola, Mozambique, Malawi, Zambia, Zimbabwe, South Africa

The Storyteller

Meeting in an open field at Kliptown, South Africa, 3,000 delegates adopted the Freedom Charter in 1955. The Charter held out hope for a democratic nation: "We the people of South Africa, declare for all our country and the world to know: that South Africa belongs to all who live in it, black and white, and that no government can claim authority unless it is based on the will of all the people ... that our country will never be prosperous and free until all people live in brotherhood, enjoying equal rights and opportunities."

—from *South Africa, Challenge and Hope,* American Friends Service Committee, Lyle Tatum, editor, 1987

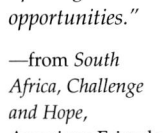

First free election in South Africa

After World War II, the desire for liberation that found expression in Asia spread to Africa. On the vast African continent in 1945, only Egypt, Ethiopia, and Liberia were independent states. South Africa, although independent, was governed by a white minority that withheld freedom from most of the country's population. In other areas, Great Britain, France, Portugal, Spain, and Belgium still exercised direct colonial rule.

By the mid-1960s, most African colonies had gained independence from European countries. The southern part of Africa remained the only area of the continent where liberation movements encountered obstacles—in this case, from sizable European settler populations. The path to independence in Africa was often bloody, and once free, the new nations faced the enormous task of building modern societies.

 POINT

A Changing Africa

Since the beginning of the colonial era, nationalist groups in Africa had resisted European rule, often violently. But following World War II, these relatively small efforts for freedom swelled into powerful mass movements.

Opposition to Empire

The democratic ideals for which the Allies fought in the war—self-rule and freedom from tyranny—inspired Africans, many of whom had fought in the Allied armies. "[We] overseas soldiers are coming back home with new ideas," wrote Nigerian Theo Ayoola, stationed with British troops in India. "We have been told what we fought for. That is freedom! We want freedom, nothing but freedom!"

Many people throughout the world were recognizing the hypocrisy and injustice of European

---

SECTION RESOURCES

Reproducible Masters
- Lecture Notes 34-1
- Reproducible Lesson Plan 34-1
- Vocabulary Activity 34
- Guided Reading Activity 34-1
- Time Line Activity 34
- People in World History Profile 65
- Section Quiz 34-1

- Reading Essentials and Study Guide 34-1

Transparencies
- Section Focus Transparency 34-1
- Chapter Transparency 34
- World History and Art Transparency 46
- NGS PicturePack Transparencies:
  Physical Geography of the World

Multimedia
- Interactive Tutor Self-Assessment Software
- Testmaker
- Picture Atlas of the World

tions continuing to rule African populations while professing democratic values. In addition to the moral argument against colonialism, European nations faced political and economic changes that made it impractical to retain their African possessions. The European continent itself was devastated by World War II, and debt-ridden Europeans could scarcely afford to maintain empires abroad. Even so, the imperial nations of Europe as a matter of pride clung stubbornly to the idea of empire, making the inevitable changes more painful.

African Nationalism

What European imperial nations did not recognize were the changes occurring throughout Africa. In many colonies, nationalism was growing among the European-educated African elite who worked in colonial governments and in businesses. In the late 1940s, leaders emerged among this group, and rallied support for African independence.

Nationalist leaders found a ready audience for their ideas among workers in the fields, mines, and factories owned by overseas investors. World demand for African minerals and crops boomed after World War II, but Africa's European-owned industries appropriated the profits. Africans saw little change in their conditions, and their resentment of foreign rule grew.

North Africa

The movement for independence from European rule saw its first successes in North Africa. Italy ruled Libya, a large country west of Egypt, under a UN trusteeship. France ruled colonial possessions—Tunisia, Algeria, and Morocco—in the rest of North Africa. These three states are also known

as the Maghrib states. All of the territories of North Africa were Muslim and shared in a common Arab culture.

The only exception was **Sudan**—ruled jointly by Great Britain and Egypt—which had a large non-Muslim African population in its southern part. Sudan eventually became independent in 1956.

Libya

In 1951, Libya, once an Italian colony, became an independent monarchy. The discovery of oil in Libya in 1959 transformed the country from a poor, desert nation into a wealthy one. Widespread discontent against the monarchy and the ruling class owning the oil wealth led to a military takeover in 1969 under Colonel **Muammar al-Qaddafi** (kuh•DAH•fee). Qaddafi established a socialist government to redistribute the national wealth. He also sought to spread his radical brand of nationalism to other parts of Africa and the Arab world.

Chapter 34 *Africa* **929**

African Independence

MOROCCO 1956
TUNISIA 1956
ALGERIA 1962
LIBYA 1951
EGYPT 1922
Western Sahara (Disputed Territory)
MAURITANIA 1960
SENEGAL 1960
GAMBIA 1965
MALI 1960
BURKINA FASO 1960
NIGER 1960
GUINEA-BISSAU 1974
GUINEA 1958
BENIN 1960
CHAD 1960
SUDAN 1956
ERITREA 1993
DJIBOUTI 1977
GHANA 1957
TOGO 1960
SIERRA LEONE 1961
CÔTE D'IVOIRE 1960
NIGERIA 1960
CENTRAL AFRICAN REPUBLIC 1960
ETHIOPIA*
LIBERIA 1847
CAMEROON 1960
EQUATORIAL GUINEA 1968
CONGO 1960
RWANDA 1962
UGANDA 1962
KENYA 1963
SOMALIA 1960
SÃO TOMÉ AND PRÍNCIPE 1975
GABON 1960
DEMOCRATIC REPUBLIC OF THE CONGO 1960
Cabinda (Angola)
BURUNDI 1962
TANZANIA 1961
SEYCHELLES 1976
CAPE VERDE 1975
ANGOLA 1975
MALAWI 1964
MOZAMBIQUE 1975
COMOROS 1975
ZAMBIA 1964
ZIMBABWE 1980
MADAGASCAR 1960
MAURITIUS 1968
NAMIBIA 1990
BOTSWANA 1966
SWAZILAND 1968
SOUTH AFRICA 1931
LESOTHO 1966
Ethiopia was invaded by Italy in 1935 but regained independence in 1941.
Azimuthal Equal-Area Projection

Map Study Between 1951 and 1993 more than 50 African colonies achieved independence. **Place** What four African nations were independent before 1950?

TEACH

Guided Practice

THEME Nationalism

Write on the chalkboard the following sentence from the statement of Theo Ayoola quoted on page 928: "[We] overseas soldiers are coming back home with new ideas." Ask students to describe some of the postwar ideas that led to the rise of African nationalism. *(realization that ideals for which the Allies fought the war were not being applied to Africans; realization that Africans were not sharing in wealth resulting from postwar demands for African resources)* **L1**

Map Study

Answer
Liberia, Egypt, Ethiopia, South Africa

Map Skills Practice

Reading a Map What African nations have gained their independence in the 1990s? *(Eritrea, Namibia)*

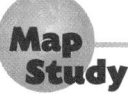

POINT

A Changing Africa
How did Africa change after World War II?
European empires came to an end, and independent states emerged in Africa after World War II.

 Chapter Transparency 34

 World History and Art Transparency 46, *Bedouin Woman's Headpiece*

COOPERATIVE LEARNING ACTIVITY

Geographical Map Have students separate the countries of Africa into five regions: north, west, central, east, and south. Organize the class into five teams, assigning one region to each team. Have the class create a wall-size map of the African continent, with each group researching its area and coordinating with other groups to produce the final map. Students should research the climate, landforms, and waterways of their region. Have team members illustrate the map and present a short oral presentation about their region. **L2**

TEACH

Tell students that the city of Banjul was formerly called Bathurst, after Henry Bathurst, who was British colonial secretary in 1816. In that year the British established a military post on the Gambia River to stop the slave trade and to serve as a trade center. Why does the Gambian woman's dress include the portrait of a Senegalese leader? *(The Gambia is completely surrounded by Senegal, and relations between the two countries have always been close.)*

CURRICULUM CONNECTION

THE ARTS

Tell students that only recently has the influence of African art on modern European art been fully recognized. Have students look at reproductions of traditional African sculptures and masks and then compare these works with the sculpture and painting of European modernists such as Picasso, Matisse, Brancusi, and Braque.

NATIONAL
GEOGRAPHIC
SOCIETY

PHYSICAL GEOGRAPHY OF THE WORLD TRANSPARENCIES

Display and discuss the physical features shown on the following transparencies:

41. Atlas Mountains, Morocco
42. Sahara in North Africa
44. Nile River, Egypt
51. Namib Desert, Namibia
53. Rain Forest, Dem. Rep. of the Congo
57. Lake Victoria in East Africa

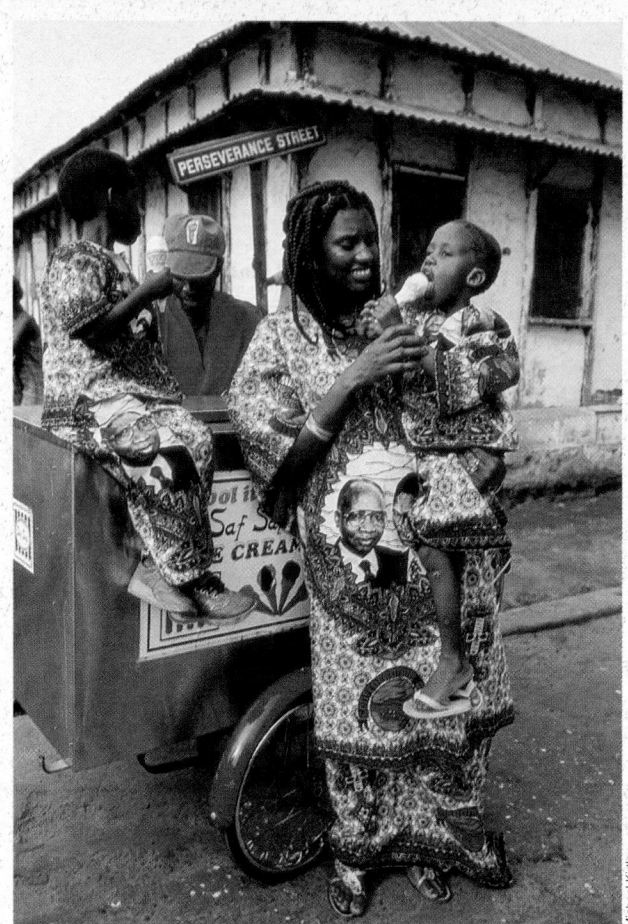

Michael Kirtley

Africa and Independence

This mother in Banjul, capital of The Gambia, combines something old and something new. She wears a traditional West African dress stamped with the colors of Africa: red, black, yellow, and green. Printed on the fabric is a portrait of two of Africa's independence leaders. On the left is Sir Dawda Jawara, who led The Gambia to independence in 1965. He remained president until 1994, when Captain Yahya Ajj Jammeh took power. On the right is President Abdou Diouf, who succeeded Senegal's great independence leader Léopold Sédar Senghor in 1981.

Keeping local traditions and languages—t in being African—while discarding the years nial rule and white supremacy became the ta new leaders of West Africa. Where once ther colonial empires, today there are 14 sovereig in the region.

Independence from France, Great Brita Portugal was won peacefully. The task that mains is to create and to sustain ex economies. This is the hope of all West A including this young mother and her chil Perseverance Street in The Gambia's capital.

lgeria

The French colonies of Morocco, Tunisia, and Algeria also wanted independence. France reluctantly granted independence to Morocco and Tunisia in 1956, but refused to do so in the case of Algeria.

Freedom for **Algeria** came only after one of the most costly wars in African colonial history. French settlers, called colons, had been coming to Algeria since the 1830s. By 1940 nearly 1 million colons had taken the best land and jobs in Algeria, ignoring the needs of 9 million Muslim Algerians.

Backed by Egypt, Morocco, and Tunisia, Algerian guerrilla fighters launched a war for independence in 1954. In response to guerrilla raids, French troops destroyed Algerian property, herded people into concentration camps, and used helicopters and heavy artillery to hunt down the rebels.

Despite French firepower, the guerrillas fought on. The controversial war forced the collapse of France's government, the Fourth Republic. After General Charles de Gaulle became president in May 1958, he promised self-determination for Algeria. Despite fierce resistance from the colons, de Gaulle arranged talks with the rebels that led to independence on July 3, 1962. The price of freedom had been eight years of warfare and more than 1 million deaths.

Ghana

In Africa south of the Sahara, mass independence movements pressured the colonial powers to relinquish control. Great Britain's richest colony, the Gold Coast, traveled a relatively easy road to independence, raising the hopes of other African nations for a smooth transition.

Before World War II ended, the British had begun to give the Africans of the Gold Coast more political rights. By then, well-educated African leaders had organized an independence movement. In 1947 the group asked the political activist **Kwame Nkrumah** (kwah•may ehn•KROO•muh) to lead them. Three years later, Nkrumah led a general strike, in which a large number of workers pressured the British for independence.

For his role in the strike, Nkrumah was jailed, but his efforts were effective. He soon moved from his jail cell to head a new government. In 1957 the

Visualizing History Kwame Nkrumah celebrates independence. Ten years of struggle had won freedom for Ghana and inspired other African nations to form national movements. *What led to Nkrumah's loss of power in Ghana?*

Gold Coast, now renamed **Ghana**, became the first African nation south of the Sahara to gain full independence after World War II.

The Nkrumah years came to represent the best and the worst in African leadership after independence. Ghana got off to a strong start, exporting cocoa, gold, and diamonds. It also had a skilled labor force. The Nkrumah government, however, mismanaged the economy. After Nkrumah was ousted by the army in 1966, one regime after another ruled Ghana, forcing the nation into a slow decline.

Guinea

Nationalist movements also took hold in France's African colonies south of the Sahara. Seeking to head off another "Algeria-like" conflict, France's President de Gaulle in 1958 proposed the creation of a French Community. Under this plan, France's African colonies south of the Sahara could choose to remain linked to France, with their foreign and economic policies under French control. The other option was for them to become completely

---

Visualizing History After the army deposed Nkrumah, President Sékou Touré of Guinea not only gave him political asylum but also declared him cohead of state.
Answer to Caption: *He was ousted by the army in 1966.*

Compare Remind students that American colonists had to fight for their independence from Britain and that Latin Americans fought Spain to create independent nations in the early 1800s. By the 1950s, why had European powers not learned that colonized people prefer independence over foreign rule? *(Students may realize that imperialism brought economic and other advantages that Europeans would not easily give up.)* **L2**

Independent Practice

📁 Guided Reading Activity 34-1 **L1**

📁 Time Line Activity 34

📁 People in World History Profile 65

Literature Have students read Wole Soyinka's short drama *Death and the King's Horseman* and write a brief report describing the contrast it develops between Yoruba culture and British power. **L3**

Who?What?Where?When?

Buchi Emecheta was born in 1944 near Lagos, Nigeria, and moved to London in 1962. Her 1976 novel, *The Bride Price*, focuses on an intelligent Nigerian girl who confronts conflicts with her family when she elopes with a low-caste schoolmaster.

MEETING SPECIAL NEEDS ACTIVITY

Learning Style: Visual/Spatial Have students who learn best by producing graphic information create a "home page" for several African nations. Each page should consist of the country's flag, a picture of its ruler, a map and legend showing the major cities and geographic features, and other references appropriate to a web site. Have students share their home pages with the class. **L2**

Visualizing History Crowds in eastern Nigeria celebrate Nigeria's independence in 1960 with a folk-dancing and sports festival. *Why was the path to Nigerian independence easier than that of other African countries?*

independent—with no economic support from France.

Only Guinea (GIH•nee) under its nationalist leader, **Ahmed Sékou Touré** (ah•MEHD SEH•koo TOO•ray), wanted full independence. De Gaulle swiftly ordered all French officials out of Guinea and vowed not to help the new nation. The Soviet Union, however, promised aid to the new nation.

In a world dominated by the cold war, Sékou Touré's link to the Soviets angered de Gaulle, who feared that other African colonies would follow suit. To prevent this, France gave its remaining African colonies independence in 1960, this time with French help.

Nigeria

In the West African country of **Nigeria**, Africa's most populous nation, few Europeans had settled during the period of British colonial rule. The path to independence was therefore easier there than in the colonies that had sizable European minorities. With little resistance, the Nigerians won independence from Great Britain in 1960. Creating

a stable democratic nation was far more difficul however.

Because Nigeria was contained within ol colonial boundaries, the country's population con sisted of 250 ethnic groups speaking 395 languages as well as 3 major religious groups. Muslims dom inated the north, followers of traditional Africa religions the east, and Christians the west. From 1960 to 1965, first one group, then another seize control of the central government.

By the mid-1960s, ethnic conflict drove the Ib to set up the independent Republic of Biafra in th eastern part of Nigeria. After the creation of Biafra civil war ravaged Nigeria for three years, killing more than 600,000. About 2 million Biafrans died o hunger as a result of the fighting. Biafra surren dered in January 1970. The Nigerian governmen then turned to rebuilding the country, developing the nation's rich oil reserves.

Congo

By the late 1950s the vast Belgian Congo in central Africa was ready for change. Belgian authorities, however, responded slowly to the independence movement and imprisoned nationalist leaders who demanded radical changes. Following riots in 1959, however, Belgium hastily granted independence in June 1960. The new country was called **Congo**. In the 1970s, it became known as **Zaire**.

Civil war broke out in Congo following independence between rival political groups and different regions. The rich copper-mining province of Katanga (now the Shaba region) seceded from the new nation in July 1960. UN peacekeeping forces arrived in Congo to prevent the superpowers from becoming involved. After settling differences with the central government, Katanga finally returned to Congolese rule, and UN forces withdrew in 1964. However, conflicts among rival political and ethnic groups continued to divide the country. Not until General Joseph D. Mobutu became dictator in 1965 was order restored.

East Africa

After World War II, nationalism also swept the East African countries of Uganda, Tanzania, and Kenya, all ruled by Great Britain. Uganda, which won independence in 1962, fell prey to ethnic conflicts and brutal military dictatorship.

By contrast, Tanzania, independent in 1961, developed a stable government that followed cialist principles. **Kenya** attracted considerable lobal attention because of a combination of unique eographic and political characteristics.

Under British colonial rule, Kenya was ominated by European settlers who held control the fertile highlands of central Kenya. The kuyu, the local African ethnic group, regarded is region as their homeland. Moreover, the uropeans banned all Africans from owning land. his discrimination fanned the flames of national-m in Kenya.

During the postwar period, the nationalist ader **Jomo Kenyatta**, who had been living in Great ritain, brought his battle for independence home Kenya. By this time, nationalist feelings in Kenya ad become intense. A political movement for inde-endence—the Kenya African Union—was formed, nd it chose Kenyatta as its president in 1947.

Meanwhile, some Kenyans had formed an nderground freedom movement, which the uropeans called the Mau Mau. The movement ought to unite Kenya's many African ethnic roups against British rule. In the early 1950s, it car-ied out attacks on European settlers, and the ritish government took military action against the novement. British authorities jailed thousands of ationalists, including Kenyatta, whom they ccused of leading the rebellion. By 1956, the upris-ng had been crushed, but calls for freedom contin-ed. The British finally granted Kenya its indepen-ence in 1963.

Kenyatta was elected Kenya's first president in 964 and held office until 1978. He maintained a ree market economy and made Kenya a popular pot for tourists and international businesses.

Angola and Mozambique

Portugal ruled the southern African countries f **Angola** and **Mozambique** with an iron hand. The Portuguese, governed by a dictatorship at nome, refused to listen to nationalist demands and reated conditions for brutal uprisings.

Starting in 1961 in Angola and 1964 in Mozambique, rebel groups waged guerrilla wars against Portugal. For over a decade, Portuguese troops were able to suppress the guerrillas. In 1974, nowever, Portugal itself underwent a revolution that overthrew the dictatorship. The new demo-cratic Portuguese government, facing many prob-lems at home, freed Angola and Mozambique in 1975. Both African countries eventually came under Marxist governments that took complete control of their economies.

Malawi, Zambia, and Zimbabwe

Throughout the late 1950s and early 1960s, Great Britain slowly gave up control of its other African colonies. In 1964, Nyasaland became **Malawi** (mah•LAH•wee), and Northern Rhodesia became **Zambia**. The future, however, remained uncertain for Rhodesia, with 4 million Africans and 250,000 Europeans.

As European Rhodesians saw new African nations coming into existence in the 1960s, they formed a party called the Rhodesian Front. Two years later, the Front took control of Rhodesian pol-itics to keep Africans from gaining power.

Great Britain opposed the Front's goals and asked that Africans be given a greater share of polit-ical power. White Rhodesians were enraged. In 1965 Rhodesian Prime Minister Ian Smith declared Rhodesia independent. Although most of the world refused to recognize or trade with Rhodesia, the country did get support from South Africa, where a white minority also ruled.

In the 1970s, bands of guerrilla fighters began attacking Rhodesia's Europeans. European settlers began to flee, and the nation's economy was dis-rupted. In 1979 Smith agreed to negotiate with the African majority, and in 1980, Rhodesia—renamed **Zimbabwe**—won its freedom.

South Africa

After World War II, independent **South Africa** was governed by a white minority—most of British and Afrikaner descent—that denied basic freedoms to other minorities and the majority African popu-lation. British and pro-British Afrikaner South Africans controlled the government until elections in 1948 brought to power the nationalist Afrikaners. The nationalist Afrikaner government opposed

Footnotes to History

The Great Zimbabwe Having won freedom, many African nations took new names with great meaning for their people. Zimbabwe, for example, refers to the 1,000-year-old city of Great Zimbabwe. Massive, protective stone walls gave the city its name—*zimbabwe*—which means "stone enclosure."

Global Gourmet

South Africa Among the tradi-tional specialties eaten by white South Africans is *boerewors*, an Afrikaner sausage dish. A staple food for black South Africans is *mealies*, a corn porridge.

Who?What?Where?When?

The *lukasa*, or memory board, is a small rectangular wooden panel produced by the Luba people of the Democratic Republic of the Congo (formerly Zaire). Each *lukasa* is used to store the history of the Luba kings, who reigned from the 1600s to the early 1900s.

CD-ROM

PICTURE ATLAS OF THE WORLD

You and your students can see and read about the physical fea-tures of Africa by clicking the "Photos" and "Essay" buttons of individual countries in the region.

ASSESS

Check for Understanding

Assign Section 1 Assessment as homework or as an in-class activity.

📱 Use Interactive Tutor Self-Assessment Software to review Section 1.

Evaluate

 Section Quiz 34-1

📱 Use the Testmaker to create a customized quiz for Section 1.

CRITICAL THINKING ACTIVITY

Synthesizing Information Have students reread the section and write two sentences for each of the countries discussed, summarizing how each attained independence. Then ask students to write a paragraph that answers the "Read to Find Out" question on page 928. **L2**

Visualizing History The Soweto uprising began as a protest against a government order that students in the township's high schools be taught in Afrikaans, which blacks associated with their oppressors. **Answer to Caption:** *The inhabitants of the township, like other black South Africans, were oppressed economically and politically.*

Reteach

Have students state the country associated with the following names or terms: colons (*Algeria*); Nkrumah (*Ghana*); Sékou Touré (*Guinea*); Lumumba, Tshombe, Mobutu (*Democratic Republic of the Congo, formerly Zaire*); Ibo, Biafra (*Nigeria*); Kenyatta (*Kenya*); Smith, Mugabe (*Zimbabwe*); apartheid, Afrikaners, ANC, Mandela, Botha, de Klerk (*South Africa*).

Reading Essentials and Study Guide 34-1

Enrich

Have students write a report on *Things Fall Apart*, the first novel of Nigerian author Chinua Achebe, or watch the film *The Camp at Thiaroye* by Ousmane Sembene, Africa's premier director.

CLOSE

Have students write one paragraph in which they describe the main differences between pre-World War II Africa and Africa today. (*Answers should include mention of independence and the independent nations' attempts to establish more economic autonomy and diversification, increased political involvement of the population, and accelerated modernization of national infrastructures.*)

South Africa's remaining ties to Great Britain and had a strong belief in its divine right to rule the country. Committed to white supremacy, the nationalist Afrikaners legalized and strengthened a policy of racial separation between blacks and whites called apartheid.

Enforcement of Apartheid

Under apartheid—meaning "apartness"—white, black, and mixed races were strictly segregated. Black South Africans suffered the worst under this legalized segregation. Apartheid laws defined whom blacks could marry and where they could travel, eat, and go to school. Blacks could not vote or own property. To enforce segregation, the government moved thousands of blacks to desolate rural areas called "homelands," where jobs and food were scarce. Those who were able to get low-paying jobs in the cities were forced to live in wretched, fenced-in townships, like Soweto, on the outskirts of Johannesburg. Blacks had to carry identity cards at all times. Under the repressive police state, blacks could be jailed indefinitely without cause.

African Resistance

Black nationalist groups, such as the African National Congress (ANC), peacefully demanded reforms, but the government refused. By the 1960s ANC leader **Nelson Mandela** was leading a military operation to press for change. In 1962 he was jailed on charges of treason, becoming a symbol of the struggle for freedom in South Africa.

International criticism of apartheid led to South Africa's increasing political isolation from the 1960s to the 1980s. South Africa, for example, was not welcome in the Commonwealth of Nations, the United Nations, and the Olympics. Many nations eventually imposed sanctions on South Africa, moves designed to hurt South Africa's economy. Within South Africa itself, massive protests developed after police fired on a student march in the black township of Soweto in 1976. During the 1980s, Archbishop **Desmond Tutu**, the head of South Africa's Anglican Church, emerged as a major advocate of nonviolence and interracial reconciliation in the struggle against apartheid. In 1984 he was awarded the Nobel Peace Prize.

SECTION 1 ASSESSMENT

Main Idea
1. Use a chart like the one below to show how one country in North Africa, in East Africa, and in South Africa achieved independence.

Country	Country	Country

Recall
2. **Define** colons, general strike, apartheid.
3. **Identify** Muammar al-Qaddafi, Kwame Nkrumah, Ahmed Sékou Touré, Jomo Kenyatta, Nelson Mandela, Desmond Tutu.

Critical Thinking
4. **Applying Information** How did populations of European descent affect African nationalist movements?

Understanding Themes
5. **Nationalism** What impact did nationalist movements have on Africa after World War II?

SECTION 1 ASSESSMENT ANSWERS

1. North Africa: Libya independent in 1951; France freed Morocco and Tunisia in 1956; Algeria won freedom in 1962. East Africa: Uganda won freedom in 1962; Tanzania independent in 1961; Great Britain freed Kenya in 1963. Southern Africa: Portugal freed Mozambique and Angola in 1975; Malawi and Zambia independent in 1964; Zimbabwe won freedom in 1980
2. The terms are defined in the Glossary.
3. Qaddafi, 929; Nkrumah, 931; Sékou Touré, 932; Kenyatta, 933; Mandela, 934; Tutu, 934
4. White colonists resisted efforts to give black majorities political control.
5. **NATIONALISM** Nationalist movements paved the way for independence.

1970   1980   1990   2000

1978   Daniel T. arap Moi becomes president of Kenya.

 1994   African National Congress wins South Africa's first open, multiracial elections.

Section 2

Africa Today

Guide to Reading

Read to Find Out
Main Idea *Different kinds of governments ruled in Africa from the 1970s to the 1990s.*

▶ **Terms to Define**
genocide, clan

▶ **People to Meet**
Abdelaziz Bouteflica, Hassan II, Mohammed VI, Mobutu Sese Seko, Olusegum Obasanjo, Laurent Kabila, Daniel T. arap Moi, Nelson Mandela, Thabo Mbeki

▶ **Places to Locate**
Namibia, Eritrea, Libya, Democratic Republic of the Congo, Somalia

The Storyteller

Fidele Nshogoza had been monitoring gorillas for 18 years. In the gorilla parks of the Virunga volcano range of east central Africa, he worked to prevent war and poaching from wiping out the animals he loved. "Gorillas are better than us," he explained. "They are peaceful. They have no tribes. When they fight it is for good reason." Fidele knew the horror of warfare. An ethnic Hutu, he fled over the volcanoes after the 1994 Tutsi victory. Two of his children almost died in a refugee camp—one of seven huge camps in Zaire [now the Democratic Republic of the Congo] that sheltered more than 700,000 ethnic Hutu.

Hutu children in a refugee camp

—adapted from "Gorillas and Humans: An Uneasy Truce," by Paul F. Salopek in *National Geographic*, October 1995.

*B*y the year 2000, Africa had experienced both setbacks and gains. Beginning in the early 1980s, devastating droughts ravaged large areas of the continent. The ups and downs of the world economy as well as political and ethnic conflict also negatively affected African nations.

Still there were reasons for celebration. Since the late 1970s, three new nations had emerged—Zimbabwe and **Namibia** in southern Africa (1980 and 1990), and **Eritrea** in the northeastern part of the continent (1993). Progress also was made in settling some of the civil wars that ravaged the continent. The most remarkable achievement was the end of apartheid in the Republic of South Africa.

North Africa

The 1980s and 1990s saw widespread economic and political unrest in the North African countries of Algeria, Morocco, and Tunisia. A soaring population and increased industrialization led to the growth of the cities. Urban growth rates were further heightened as people from the countryside crowded into urban areas in hope of finding food, shelter, and work. When governments proved unable to provide decent housing and steady jobs, many people turned to radical political movements in an effort to solve their problems.

Algeria

The greatest challenge to established government in the region took place in Algeria. In a free election in 1992, the people of Algeria elected to the national legislature a majority of members who favored strict application of Islamic laws and values. The more secular government, however, ignored the election results and dissolved the legislature. Military leaders then took control of Algeria. They banned the Islamic movement and arrested many of its members.

Chapter 34   *Africa*   **935**

TEACH

Guided Practice

THEME Change

On the chalkboard copy the section's opening sentence from page 935: "By the late 1990s, Africa had experienced both setbacks and gains." Underneath it, create two columns headed *Setbacks* and *Gains*. As you work through the section with the class, have students enter events in the appropriate columns. **L1**

Government Ask students to discuss the aftermath of the elections of 1992 in Algeria as described on pages 935–936. **Was the military's banning of the Islamic movement justified in any way?** *(Some students might argue that the end—the suppression of theocratic rule—justified the means. Others might argue that denying power to the Islamic movement only further radicalized its supporters, and any subversion of democracy is wrong.)* **L2**

VIDEODISC
Turning Points in World History

Side Two
Chapter 10

Title: *End of Apartheid*
Ask: What did the international community do to show disapproval of South African apartheid policies? *(South Africa was banned from the UN and Olympic Games and boycotted.)*

Fighting soon developed between the government and the Islamic opposition. By 1999, more than 70,000 people had been killed. In that year, however, newly elected President **Abdelaziz Bouteflica** sought reconciliation and promised new legislative elections. The guerrillas called off their uprising and promised to cooperate.

Morocco, Tunisia, and Libya

During the 1980s and 1990s, Morocco and Tunisia had strong, stable governments. Morocco, however, seized neighboring West Sahara despite opposition from many West Saharans. A UN-backed vote, set for 2000, was expected to determine the territory's future. In 1999, Morocco's King **Hassan II**, who had ruled for 38 years, died and was succeeded by his reform-minded son **Mohammed VI**.

Meanwhile, the ruler of **Libya**, Muammar al-Qaddafi, accused the West of plotting against him. The West in turn claimed that Qadaffi was backing terrorism. In 1999, Libya agreed to turn over two fugitives accused of blowing up a Pan Am airliner in 1988. By this gesture, Qadaffi hoped to improve relations with the West.

Nigeria

After independence, Nigeria and other nations in West Africa faced political conflicts and economic hardships. Some relied on military leaders or one-party systems to maintain order. By the late 1980s, a trend toward democracy and stability had emerged in the region. Nigeria, the most populous West African country, continued to remain under military rule, however. After the Biafran war of the 1960s, Nigeria's military leaders worked to rebuild the country. They relied on oil for economic prosperity. As oil prices rose in the 1970s, Nigeria grew wealthy. Its military leaders set as their goals industrial development, new schools, improved transportation, and development programs to raise the standard of living of all Nigerians.

Images of the Times

Toward a New Africa

Beyond independence, African nations work to promote economic growth, while preserving cultural traditions and developing democracy.

An earth satellite station 30 miles (48 km) from Nairobi, Kenya, signals Africa's connection to the telecommunications revolution.

936

Images of the Times
Toward a New Africa

As in other parts of the developing world, Africans experience sharp contrasts between older ways of life and the latest technological developments. In the continent's rapidly growing cities, newcomers from small villages encounter movies, fax machines, and computers for the first time.

One sign that the telecommunications revolution has not yet saturated the African countryside is the fact that on average, there is only one television set for every 25 Africans. In the United States, by contrast, more than 98 percent of households have at least one television. In most of rural Africa, radios, not televisions or computers, are the lifeline to the rest of the world.

Hopes for progress, however, were dashed by instability in the global oil market and government mismanagement of the economy. During the 1980s and 1990s, pro-democracy groups called for an end to military rule. Although promising to work for reform, the government of ruthless military dictator Sani Abachi instead ignored election results and cracked down on its opponents. In 1997, it even brought treason charges against exiled writer Wole Soyinka, winner of the Nobel Prize for Literature.

After Abachi's death, in 1998, Nigeria made the transition from military to civilian rule. In 1999 democratic elections were held, and **Olusegum Obasanjo** was elected president.

Democratic Republic of the Congo

From the 1970s to the 1990s Congo continued under the rule of Mobutu, who took the name **Mobutu Sese Seko** and changed the country's name to Zaire. During his rule, copper prices rose and fell, bringing a boom and then a decline to Zaire's economy. Meanwhile, Mobutu ruled as a dictator, stole from the country's resources, and banned rival political groups.

Angered by Mobutu's misrule, guerrilla forces led by **Laurent Kabila** began a rebellion in late 1996. During the next several months, they took control of most of Zaire with little opposition from demoralized government forces. In May 1997, Mobutu gave up power and fled abroad. Kabila's forces then entered the capital, Kinshasa, where he named himself the new leader and changed the country's name to the **Democratic Republic of the Congo**. Kabila promised that there would be eventual elections, but his commitment to democracy was held in question when he banned political parties.

In 1998 rebels tried to overthrow Kabila. In an effort to try to end the conflict, peace talks began in 1999.

Modern office buildings rise above a newly built monument and public garden in Pretoria, South Africa.

Tea pickers toil on a plantation in Kenya. Tea is one of Kenya's chief cash crops and a major export.

REFLECTING ON THE TIMES

1. In what ways could the connection to global telecommunications affect African economies? Cultural traditions?
2. Why are export products key to economic development?

937

ANSWERS TO REFLECTING ON THE TIMES

1. Access to global telecommunications might make Africa a more inviting place for international business and thus might strengthen African economies. The widespread exposure to foreign media might further erode African cultural traditions.
2. Exports bring in foreign capital and strengthen a country's balance of trade, although reliance on a single export makes the economies of some African countries dangerously sensitive to changes in world market prices.

World Music: Cultural Traditions, Lesson 6

Who?What?Where?When?

The Nobel Prize in literature was awarded to two Africans in recent years, Nigeria's Wole Soyinka (1986) and South Africa's Nadine Gordimer (1991).

Independent Practice

Guided Reading Activity 34-2 **L1**

People in World History Profile 66

Human Rights Have students use *Readers' Guide to Periodical Literature* to find articles about the execution in 1995 of Nigerian author Ken Saro-Wiwa and the role played by the oil industry in that controversial event. Ask them to summarize their findings in a brief oral report. **L2**

The following videotape program is available from Glencoe:

- **Nelson Mandela: Journey to Freedom**

NATIONAL GEOGRAPHIC SOCIETY

CD-ROM

PICTURE ATLAS OF THE WORLD

Click the "Video" button of Tanzania to view the Masai people and Serengeti National Park.

Global Gourmet

Ethiopia A popular Ethiopian food now being served in Ethiopian restaurants in the United States is a thick stew called *wat*. Vegetarian *wats* are made with lentils or chickpeas flavored with spices. Other *wats* contain chicken or meat and are sometimes served with hard-cooked egg. Most *wats* are flavored with a very spicy berbere sauce.

ASSESS

Check for Understanding

Assign Section 2 Assessment as homework or as an in-class activity.

 Use Interactive Tutor Self-Assessment Software to review Section 2.

Evaluate

Section Quiz 34-2

 Use the Testmaker to create a customized quiz for Section 2.

Visualizing History
Nelson Mandela served as president of South Africa from 1994 until 1999.
What event in 1994 was a turning point in South Africa's history?

East Africa

In East Africa, ethnic unrest tore apart some countries. Others, however, enjoyed political stability. Uganda, after a period of harsh rule in the 1970s under dictator Idi Amin, moved toward a one-party system that at the same time encouraged free enterprise. Uganda's southern neighbor, Tanzania, combined a tradition of stable government with socialism. Economic difficulties in the 1990s, however, moved Tanzania toward free enterprise.

Kenya

From the early 1960s to the late 1970s, Kenya enjoyed political stability and economic prosperity under a one-party system. After President Kenyatta's death in 1978, **Daniel T. arap Moi** became the leader. In the 1980s, Moi dealt harshly with political opponents wanting a multiparty system. A decade later, he allowed a multiparty election in which he won endorsement. However, critics charged that the elections were not free or fair. In 1997 a powerful reform movement led by opposition politicians, human rights activists, and Christian and Muslim religious leaders pressured Moi to carry out genuine

democratic reforms. Moi was reelected in 1998 but under questionable circumstances.

Rwanda and Burundi

During the 1990s, ethnic tensions in Rwanda and Burundi led to violent conflict. Most people in Rwanda and Burundi belong to the Hutu and the Tutsi ethnic groups. The Hutu are the largest group in both countries. Under Belgian colonial rule, the Tutsi were favored over the Hutu. Since the independence of Rwanda and Burundi in 1962, the Hutu have worked to regain power.

In 1994 the Hutu-led Rwandan government battled Tutsi-led guerrillas. In a genocide, or the deliberate killing of a racial or cultural group, Hutu forces killed more than 500,000 people, mostly Tutsi, before the Tutsi guerrillas declared victory. Another 2 million people fled Rwanda and settled in camps on the border of Zaire and neighboring countries.

In 1996, conflict broke out in Burundi between the Tutsi-led government and Hutu rebels. Meanwhile, about 1.2 million Rwandan Hutu refugees in eastern Zaire faced mass starvation as ethnic and political conflict erupted in that country. Another human catastrophe was avoided when hundreds of thousands of refugees voluntarily returned to Rwanda. In 1997, tribunals in Tanzania and Rwanda began bringing to justice people accused of participating in the 1994 genocide.

Ethiopia and Somalia

In Ethiopia, military leaders in 1974 ousted Emperor Haile Selassie I and installed a Marxist dictatorship. The new leaders carried out land reforms, but killed many of their opponents. These actions led to civil war and movements for independence in the regions of Tigre and Eritrea.

By the early 1990s, civil war and drought led to the fall of the dictatorship. In 1991, rebel forces took control and moved Ethiopia toward democracy. As a result of this victory, Eritrea became independent in 1993.

Since 1998, Eritrea and Ethiopia have been waging a brutal war over disputed territory. Tens of thousands of people have died in the war, and hundreds of thousands of people have been displaced.

Drought and civil war also ravaged Ethiopia's neighbor, **Somalia**. There, in the 1980s, rival clans, or groups of people related to one another, fought for control of the government. When a drought struck a few years later, many Somalis starved. Other countries sent food, but the fierce fighting kept much of it from reaching the starving.

In 1992, a UN-sponsored coalition of military forces led by the United States arrived in Somalia to

938 Chapter 34 *Africa*

COOPERATIVE LEARNING ACTIVITY

The Arts Have students form five teams, one for each region of Africa: north, west, central, east, and south. Individual team members should choose different types of African art to research within their region, such as painting, pottery, metal and wood sculpture, textiles, body ornamentation, and music. Have students find examples of each type of art and copy or record them to bring to class. Have the teams work together to create a classroom or hallway exhibit, complete with captions explaining the display. Organize the exhibit by region or by type of art. **L2 LEP**

...rotect relief organizations that were distributing food to needy Somalis. A year later, UN forces replaced most of the coalition troops. Tensions heightened when fighting broke out between the UN soldiers and the forces of one of the Somali clan leaders. By 1995, foreign troops, including United States forces, had withdrawn from Somalia after the worst of the famine had ended, and rival clan leaders had signed a peace settlement. Continued fighting, however, delayed progress toward stability.

South Africa

From the 1970s to the 1990s, South Africa and its neighbors Mozambique, Angola, and Zimbabwe experienced many sweeping changes. After a period of civil wars between Marxist and non-Marxist groups, Mozambique, Angola, and Zimbabwe moved toward peace and gradually abandoned socialism for free enterprise.

In South Africa, mounting pressure from the antiapartheid movement and from foreign countries brought a gradual end to apartheid. During the 1980s, the white-dominated South African government lifted the ban on interracial marriage, and the nation's sizable population of Asian and mixed-race people won voting rights.

In February 1990, South African President F. W. de Klerk surprised the world by releasing the black nationalist leader **Nelson Mandela** from prison. During the next few years, the South African government repealed the remaining apartheid laws. Talks began in 1992 between white and black political groups that paved the way for a constitution, ending apartheid, and granting political equality to all South Africans regardless of race. A year later, black South Africans won full voting rights.

Kwanzaa Celebrates African American Culture

United States, 1966
Kwanzaa is a holiday based on a traditional African harvest festival. Developed in the United States in 1966 by Maulana Karenga, an African American cultural leader, Kwanzaa begins on December 26 and lasts for seven days. Each day is dedicated to one of the seven principles of African American culture that Karenga established. African American families celebrate Kwanzaa by lighting candles and exchanging gifts.

In April 1994, South Africa held its first election open to all races. The African National Congress won nearly two-thirds of the seats in the national legislature, and the legislature then elected Nelson Mandela president. Mandela recognized the importance of reconciling racial and ethnic groups and bridging the social and economic gap that separated white and nonwhite South Africans. He faced the challenge of raising the standard of living of disadvantaged South Africans while maintaining economic growth.

In 1997 South Africa began to prepare for a transition of power from Mandela to his successor. **Thabo Mbeki** was elected president in 1999, and the African National Congress again won just under two-thirds of the legislative seats.

Chapter 34
Section 2

POINT

South Africa
Why was 1994 a significant year for South Africa?
South Africa held its first election open to all races. For the first time, after years of apartheid, the country's black majority had a fair voice in the country's political life.

Reteach

Have students write a sentence to define each term and to identify each individual and each country listed in "Guide to Reading" on page 935.

📁 Reading Essentials and Study Guide 34-2

Enrich

Have students watch the 1992 film *Sarafina!*, based on a popular antiapartheid stage musical, and write a brief review.

CLOSE

Have students list ten countries discussed in this section (*Algeria, Libya, Nigeria, Democratic Republic of the Congo, Kenya, Rwanda, Burundi, Ethiopia, Somalia, South Africa*) and write a sentence for each that summarizes the changes it has undergone since the 1980s.

SECTION 2 ASSESSMENT

Main Idea
1. Use a diagram like the one below to identify the kinds of government that ruled Africa from the 1970s to 1990s.

```
Kinds of Government in Africa
1970s – 1990s
```

Recall
2. **Define** genocide, clan.
3. **Identify** Abdelaziz Bouteflica, Hassan II, Mohammed VI, Mobutu Sese Seko, Daniel T. arap Moi, Olusegum Obasanjo, Laurent Kabila, Nelson Mandela, Thabo Mbeki.

Critical Thinking
4. **Synthesize** If you were a

citizen of South Africa today, how would you describe recent political and social changes there?

Understanding Themes
5. **Change** What worldwide factors do you think account for a growing trend toward democracy and free enterprise in Africa?

Chapter 34 *Africa* **939**

SECTION 2 ASSESSMENT ANSWERS

1. Algeria: after 1992, military-ruled government. Nigeria: military rule. Congo: dictatorship overthrown in 1997 by Laurent Kabila; democracy established. Uganda: one-party system. Tanzania: stable socialist government; 1990s, movement toward free enterprise. Kenya: one-party system; 1990s pressure for democracy. Ethiopia: Marxist dictatorship until 1990s–push for democracy. South Africa; apartheid until 1994 open elections
2. All terms are defined in the Glossary.
3. Bouteflica, 936; Hassan II, 936; Mohammed VI, 936; Mobutu Sese Seko, 937; Olusegum Obasanjo, 937; Laurent Kabila, 937; Daniel T. arap Moi, 938; Nelson Mandela, 939; Thabo Mbeki, 939
4. Answers will vary depending on the race of the South African described.
5. **CHANGE** Answers will vary. Students might feel that the democratic trend has been encouraged by global technology and the end of the cold war.

TEACH

Writing a Research Report Have students review the process of choosing a topic. Practice this process with them by suggesting a number of general topics about Africa that students must narrow down. General topics might include Africa since the cold war, Africa's natural resources, democracy in Africa, or the role of women in Africa. These could be narrowed down to Angola since the cold war, northern Africa's natural resources, democracy in Algeria, and African women in politics.

Additional Practice

 Skill Reinforcement Activity 34

 Writer's Guidebook, Lesson 12

GLENCOE TECHNOLOGY

GO TO Glencoe's **Skillbuilder Interactive Workbook, Level 2**
This interactive CD-ROM promotes student mastery of key social studies skills.

Writing a Research Report

Writing a research report is a complex task. There are tools to use, skills to master, and steps to follow.

Learning the Skill

Select a topic that interests you. Brainstorming, skimming books and magazines, and talking with classmates can help.

Do preliminary research to determine whether your topic is too broad or too specific. Suppose you've chosen "Problems Facing Africa Today." The library's computers list more than 100 books on this topic. A more manageable topic might be: "Environmental Problems in the Sahara."

As early as possible, write a statement defining what you want to prove, discover, or illustrate in your report. For this topic, your statement might be: "Deforestation is the greatest environmental threat to North Africa."

- **Prepare to do research**. Formulate a list of main idea questions.
- **Research your topic and take notes**. At the library, use the computerized referral service to find suitable research sources. Note cards are a great tool for preparing a research report. They let you record and combine related facts and ideas from several sources. Prepare note cards on each main idea question listing the source information. Keep all the facts for each main idea together.
- **Organize your information**. Build an outline or another kind of organizer to follow in writing a rough draft.
- **Write a rough draft**. A research report should have three main parts: the introduction, the body, and the conclusion. The introduction briefly presents the topic and gives your thesis statement. The body develops the important ideas in your argument. Connect these ideas with transitions. The conclusion summarizes and restates your findings.

Write the rough draft as quickly as possible without editing. Imagine that you are explaining your findings and ideas to an interested listener.

Revise the draft into a final report. Put it away for a day or so; then reread it with the cold, clear eye of an editor. Does the report have a clear structure—an introduction, a body, and a conclusion? Does the body contain all the main ideas arranged logically? Are there transitions to lead the reader from one thought to the next? If not, revise it and repeat the writing process. Correct spelling, punctuation, and grammar. Finally, make a clean copy.

Practicing the Skill

Suppose you are writing a report on recent changes in South Africa. Answer the following questions about the writing process.

1. How could you narrow this topic?
2. What are three main idea questions to use?
3. Name three possible sources of information.
4. What are the next two steps in the process of writing a research report?

Applying the Skill

Choose a topic and prepare note cards. Continue your research on this topic, organize your information, and write a short report.

For More Practice

Turn to the Skill Practice in the Chapter Assessment on page 947.

GO TO The **Glencoe Skillbuilder Interactive Workbook**, Level provides instruction and practi in key social studies skills.

ANSWERS TO PRACTICING THE SKILL

1. Answers will vary. Possible answers include: end of apartheid; voting rights for black South Africans; the African National Congress; Nelson Mandela; challenges for future government
2. Answers will vary depending on the topic.
3. Sources include books, magazines, and newspapers.
4. After selecting sources, students should prepare note cards, organize them, and then write a rough draft.

1945   1973   2000

1963 African nations form Organization of African Unity (OAU).

1980s Famine ravages Ethiopia, Somalia, and other areas of Africa.

1990s A trend develops in Africa toward democracy and free enterprise.

Section 3

Africa's Challenge

Guide to Reading

Read to Find Out
Main Idea *Modern African nations have faced multiple challenges in their quest for political and economic development.*

▶ **Terms to Define**
Pan-Africanism, cash crop, subsistence farmer, desertification, literacy rate, negritude

▶ **People to Meet**
Kofi Annan, Léopold Sédar Senghor

▶ **Places to Locate**
the Sahel

The Storyteller

The Sahara has its own voices. The abrupt changes from darkness to daylight are often accompanied by the shattering of the desert rocks, with a grating sound or a loud noise. Even the sand dunes talk: wind or even the pressure of a human foot will cause shocks and tremblings; then the countless grains of sand, rubbing gently together, will make a strange snoring noise.

According to legend, these mysterious noises

Desert oasis

are the bursts of laughter of a genie named Rul—the bad angel of strayed travelers. When the wanderer has lost his way, when fatigue and thirst begin to confuse the mind, then the traveler is tormented by "the laughter of Rul."

—adapted from *Sahara, the Great Desert,* Emile Felix Gautier, 1935

African nations have seen enormous changes in less than half a century. In that short time, a largely rural continent has become increasingly urban, with ties to all parts of the globe. By the mid-1990s, African economies were growing at an average rate of nearly 5 percent, faster than for two decades. Africa also has become an international force, wielding more than a third of the votes in the United Nations General Assembly. In 1997 **Kofi Annan**, a career diplomat from the West African nation of Ghana, became secretary-general of the United Nations. He is the first African from south of the Sahara to serve in the post.

Search for Unity

After the excitement of independence celebrations had passed, Africa's new nations entered a difficult period. Many of them adopted the political borders that had been drawn by the colonial powers. These boundaries divided people with similar customs and faiths. Old ruling families and ethnic groups began to struggle for power, and civil wars erupted in many places.

National Unity

African politicians and parliaments were unable to stop the violence that sprang from these ethnic divisions. At first, many leaders in Africa governed through political systems inherited from their colonial predecessors—systems that were unfamiliar to many Africans. Often these systems did not work for African countries in the postindependence years. All too often, a nation's most powerful group, the military, stepped in to restore order.

By the 1970s, military leaders or one-party dictatorships ruled about half of Africa's newly freed nations. In some, like Nigeria, dividing strong regional groups into smaller states helped to break down some regional rivalry. By the late 1980s, however, military rule and one-party political systems

Chapter 34 *Africa* **941**

SECTION THEME

▶ **Change** Ethnic, cultural, environmental, and economic challenges face newly independent African nations.

Guide to Reading

For reading strategies to help students read effectively see pages 12–13.

Vocabulary Pre-check

📀 Use the Vocabulary PuzzleMaker for Chapter 34 to create a crossword puzzle to reinforce section terms. **L1 LEP**

📁 Use Vocabulary Activity 34 to introduce vocabulary terms. **L1 LEP**

FOCUS

Section Objective

Identify the challenges faced by modern African nations in their quest for political and economic independence.

BELLRINGER
Motivational Activity

Before taking roll at the beginning of the class period, project Section Focus Transparency 34-3 and have students answer the activity questions. Discuss students' responses.

📁 This activity is also available as a blackline master.

SECTION RESOURCES

📁 Reproducible Masters
- Lecture Notes 34-3
- Reproducible Lesson Plan 34-3
- Guided Reading Activity 34-3
- Reteaching Activity 34
- Enrichment Activity 34
- Section Quiz 34-3
- Performance Assessment Activity 34

- Spanish Chapter Summary 34
- Reading Essentials and Study Guide 34-3

🎞 Transparencies
- Section Focus Transparency 34-3
- World History and Art Transparency 45, *The Liberated African Woman*

Multimedia
📀 Vocabulary PuzzleMaker Software
📀 Interactive Tutor Self-Assessment Software
📀 Testmaker
💿 Picture Atlas of the World
🎦 STV: World Geography, Vol. 2

TEACH

Guided Practice

THEME Change

Write on the chalkboard each of the terms listed in "Guide to Reading" on page 941. Ask students to explain the relationship between each term and a change Africa has undergone in recent times. **L1**

Visualizing History The modern city takes its name from *Enkare Nairobi*, or "cold water," referring to a freshwater spring that used to be located on the site.
Answer to Caption: *the creation of an all-African common market to promote Africa's economic growth and development*

NATIONAL GEOGRAPHIC SOCIETY

VIDEODISC
STV: WORLD GEOGRAPHY, VOLUME 2

Side 1
Frames 00001–49739
Title: *Africa* (in its entirety)
Subject: Describes the geographic contrasts and how people and animals have affected the natural environment of Africa
Ask: What desert in Africa is the world's largest? *(the Sahara)* What kind of technique is used to clear the land for planting? *(slash-and-burn)*

 World History and Art Transparency 45, *The Liberated African Woman*

Visualizing History The Kenyatta Conference Center, named after Jomo Kenyatta—Kenya's first president, reflects the rapid growth and modernity of Nairobi, Kenya's capital. Founded in the late 1890s as a small railway settlement, Nairobi today is a busy metropolis of more than 1.5 million people. *What major goal has been set by the Organization of African Unity?*

had failed to fulfill their promises of order and economic progress. They were in decline in certain countries of Africa. Meanwhile, the end of the cold war and the collapse of the Soviet Union discredited the socialist economic model once popular among many African leaders. By the mid-1990s, some African countries had adopted multiparty systems and free enterprise approaches to economic development.

Pan-Africanism

Through a movement called Pan-Africanism, African leaders have sought to promote cooperation among all nations of the continent. In 1963, 32 African nations formed the **Organization of African Unity** (OAU) in Addis Ababa, Ethiopia. Although the original vision of creating a United

Student Web Activity 34

Visit the *World History: The Human Experience* Web site at **worldhistory.glencoe.com** and click on *Chapter 34—Student Web Activities* for an activity relating to the Organization of African Unity.

States of Africa failed, the OAU did help to build a strong African identity and establish defense and health policies.

Since its founding, the OAU has increased its influence in African and global affairs. During the 1970s and 1980s, member nations of the OAU pledged to remain neutral in cold war politics. To rid Africa of colonialism, the OAU backed nationalist movements in Angola, Mozambique, and Zimbabwe. As part of this undertaking, OAU members put pressure on white-ruled South Africa to end apartheid. A major achievement of the OAU during this period was the settlement of border disputes among member states.

In addition to working through the OAU, African states have cooperated on a regional level. In 1996, the Economic Community of West African States (ECOWAS) provided a 10,000-strong peacekeeping force to implement a cease-fire between warring groups in the West African nation of Liberia. Their efforts helped end a seven-year civil war that had killed 150,000 of Liberia's 2.4 million people and had left the country in ruins.

As they look to the twenty-first century, the OAU and other African organizations have set as their major goal Africa's economic growth and development. Member states of the OAU eventually plan to create an all-African free trade area.

Economic Development

In addition to creating a united continent, post-independence leaders of Africa worked to build strong economies in their nations. To move Africa's rural economies into the world of mining, manufacturing, and service industries, millions of people

---

COOPERATIVE LEARNING ACTIVITY

Debate Have pairs of students select one African country to represent at a mock session of the UN General Assembly. Before the session, have students brainstorm a list of issues they will discuss; these should include economic development, the environment, foreign aid, free trade, and urbanization. Have students research their country so they can represent its interests at the General Assembly session. **L2**

ad to learn to read and write. Workers who made living with their hands had to learn to operate machines in factories. Governments had to repair ging phone lines, railroads, and highways. Tanzania's President Julius Nyerere in the 1960s tated, "While the great powers are trying to get to he moon, we are trying to get to the village."

Legacy of Colonialism

After independence, most African countries suffered from the economies created by colonial rule. As you remember from Chapter 27, Europeans obtained raw materials in Africa for their home industries and developed little industry in Africa. Under colonial rule, some Africans worked on European-owned plantations that produced cash crops, or crops grown for profit and exported. Most, however, were subsistence farmers, who grew only enough food to meet the needs of a family or village.

After independence, African leaders tried to remedy the imbalance between farming and industry. Many African countries were rich in one or two key resources or crops, but their economies could not provide the basic needs of their populations.

One-product economies, such as Ghana with cocoa and Burundi with coffee, were constantly at the mercy of changing prices for products on world markets. In addition, internal conflicts left some countries with ruined land and heavy war debts.

Economic Challenges

To bring economic advancement, African leaders decided to push the export of cash crops and raw materials while promoting industrialization. A lack of capital, skilled workers, and transportation systems, however, stood in the way of industrial growth. Seeking to overcome these obstacles, African countries turned to foreign governments and banks for loans to build factories, airports, harbors, and roads.

Reliance on foreign aid, however, provoked different reactions among Africans. Some nations followed a capitalist model and developed close ties with the West. Resource-rich nations, such as Nigeria with its oil wealth, tried to fund development from their exports of minerals and other raw materials. To assert their sovereignty, other nations decided to organize various kinds of

Geography

The Moving Sahara

Deep in the Sahara, ancient rock paintings show grazing cattle and grasses where now there is only rock and sand. In recent times, farmers also grazed cattle in areas bordering the Sahara. But now those grasslands too are giving way to desert.

Before Africa was colonized, farmers cultivated fields until the soil was exhausted. When they moved to new plots of land, they let the old ones lie fallow, replenishing the soil. Under colonialism, better medical care caused a population boom and a growing demand for food. Europeans pushed Africans to grow big cash crops for export.

The encroaching desert

Destruction of the land increased. Farmers cut down trees to open up new fields and farmed land year after year without allowing the fields to lie fallow. Droughts in the 1980s brought disaster. People had to use grains for food instead of for seed. Without plants to anchor the soil, tons of topsoil washed or blew away. The mixture of overfarming, overgrazing, cutting trees, and drought pushed the Sahara south as fast as 90 miles (145 km) a year.

The solution to this problem lies with individual farmers. By planting trees, terracing fields, and fertilizing the soil, they may be able to slow the shifting of the Sahara.

Linking Past and Present — ACTIVITY

Examine what is causing the Sahara to spread south. Why do you think it is difficult to get individual farmers to change their agricultural practices?

Chapter 34 *Africa* 943

Chapter 34 *Africa* 943

Linking Past and Present

The Moving Sahara

Tell students that the name *Sahara* comes from *sahrá*, the Arabic word for "desert." From the late 1800s through the mid-1900s, France, Spain, Italy, and Britain occupied parts of the Sahara. In 1976 Spain became the last European country to give up control of the portion of the Sahara it claimed as its own.
ANSWERS
drought and poor farming practices; students may suggest that individual farmers may not understand the larger problems caused by their methods

— WORLD HISTORY *Online* —

Have students use the **Chapter 34 Student Web Activity** at worldhistory.glencoe.com for in-depth study of African Unity.

Independent Practice

📁 Guided Reading Activity 34-3 **L1**

Economics Have students compare the current economic situations in five African countries. Students should look up such information as per capita income and percentage of the labor force in agriculture and industry in a current almanac or other reference work. Have students display their data in chart form. **L2**

NATIONAL GEOGRAPHIC SOCIETY

CD-ROM

PICTURE ATLAS OF THE WORLD

You and your students can see apartheid's legacy by clicking the "Video" button of South Africa.

MEETING SPECIAL NEEDS ACTIVITY

Mixed Learners Have language-delayed students and visual learners identify the different African nations by researching the current flags of several nations from different African regions. On a large sheet of paper or poster board, have students draw and color each nation's flag and describe briefly what the colors and the symbols mean. Encourage students to display their completed work in the classroom. **L1 LEP**

Visualizing
History The attempt to
improve educational opportunities
in Africa is challenged in a variety of
ways. New schools cannot be built
quickly enough to keep up with the
population growth, there is a shortage of trained teachers in many
regions, and many families cannot
afford to send their children to
school instead of to work.
Answer to Caption: *They are rising
in many countries and falling in others.*

Linking Past and Present

African Music American musician Paul Simon has helped to popularize African pop music around
the world. Simon worked with
black South African musicians to
create his 1986 album, *Graceland.*

ASSESS

Check for Understanding

Assign Section 3 Assessment as
homework or as an in-class activity.

 Use Interactive Tutor Self-
Assessment Software to review
Section 3.

Evaluate

Section Quiz 34-3

 Use the Testmaker to create a
customized quiz for Section 3.

Visualizing History The education of children like these kindergarten students in Angola is the key to the
nation's future. *What is happening with literacy rates in Africa?*

government-controlled economies. This turn to
socialism pleased many nationalists, who equated
capitalism with colonialism.

No matter how they organized their economies, however, many countries failed to develop
agriculture in their push to industrialize. Soon food
crops for the domestic markets began to suffer and
thousands of unskilled rural people moved to the
cities, searching in vain for jobs. With many people
out of work and unable to buy the products of new
African industries, economies suffered.

Africa's soaring population also caused problems for economic growth. With economies geared
for export, not enough food was produced for
domestic needs. Governments had to increase borrowing from foreign sources, often to buy food, and
their debts grew. As a result, not enough money
was available to develop health care, food production, and industry necessary to improve overall
standards of living.

Disease and Famine

Disease and famine have affected parts of
Africa in recent years. Despite efforts to improve
health care, African governments have not been
able to limit the spread of AIDS. By 2000, this epidemic, which also has had an impact on people

elsewhere in the world, became a major
concern in Africa, where millions were
infected. African countries need massive
global assistance to deal with this health
challenge.

Severe droughts also hindered
African development, causing food
shortages and starvation. The situation
worsened with **desertification**, or the
transformation of fertile areas into desert,
taking place. The most serious case of
desertification was in **the Sahel**, a West
African grassland bordering the Sahara,
Africa's largest desert. In addition,
human activities, such as grazing livestock, planting, and harvesting trees,
exposed land in this area to erosion.

Signs of Hope

In the 1980s, Africa was a continent in
crisis. A World Bank study showed that
21 of the world's 34 poorest countries
were in Africa. More than 60 percent of all
Africans received too little food each day,
and more than 5 million children died
every year. Relying on foreign help to
remedy these problems, sub-Saharan
African nations by the end of the 1990s were $300
billion in debt.

As a new century begins, the problems of inadequate food, growing populations, and foreign debt
still plague Africa, but some hopeful signs exist.
More Africans than ever are attending school.
Literacy rates, or the percentages of people who
can read and write, have risen. Through education,
many Africans are developing the skills needed to
improve their standard of living.

In various parts of the continent, Africans are
cooperating to improve their economies. To break
their dependency on foreign countries, some
African nations have formed regional associations
that promote trade and economic contacts. An
example of this type of organization is the
Economic Community of West African States
(ECOWAS), in which a number of West African
nations have agreed to barter among themselves,
trading products for oil instead of for scarce cash. In
late 1992 Ugandan President Yoweri Museveni
expressed a viewpoint that had become increasingly widespread in Africa: "We have to go back to the
year 1500 [prior to colonialism], where we left off
building an African economy, able to produce its
own food, its own tools, its own weapons.... In
short, we have to rely on ourselves."

944 Chapter 34 *Africa*

MAKING CONNECTIONS ACTIVITIES

Languages More than 800 languages are spoken in Africa. Ask
students to research and write a short report on Swahili or other
native African languages; Amharic or other Afro-Asian languages;
or Afrikaans, which is an Indo-European language. **L2**

Marriage Ask students to research and write a short report on
marriage practices in different parts of Africa, including dowries
and bride wealth. **L1**

African American children celebrate Kwanzaa, a festival held in late December since 1966. *What is the purpose of such poems as "My Africa"?*

African Identity

In 1963 the African American poet Langston Hughes gathered nearly 100 African poems into a collection called *Poems from Black Africa*. It includes this one by Dei-Anang, a poet and government official in Ghana.

> **❝ I love a world,
> This priceless world,
> Sweet home of haunting melodies
> And roll of tom-toms—
> My Africa. ❞**
>
> —Michael Dei-Anang,
> from the poem "My Africa"

The poetry of Dei-Anang, like that of other Africans, had begun to rekindle a deep pride among Africans in their heritage.

During the colonial era, Africans had learned much, both good and bad, from Europeans. There remained the idea, although not accepted by all Africans, that European culture was superior to African culture in art, music, literature, and technology.

As independent nations emerged on the continent, many African leaders stressed the need to take pride in Africa. In Senegal, a former French colony, President **Léopold Sédar Senghor** published poems that expressed his love of Africa. Because Africans had never lost touch with nature, he thought, they could help restore "a world that has died of machines and cannons." Senghor helped found a poetry movement called negritude, an effort to recapture black Africa's past dignity.

During the decades since independence, African artists and writers have built on this foundation of pride. Theater groups, filmmakers, novelists, painters, and others have explored the pain of colonialism as well as the modern problems of corruption and hunger.

Open now to influences from around the globe, Africans have also created exciting new art forms. Congolese music, for instance, a mix of African, Latin American, and Caribbean styles, brings pleasure and delight to people in all of Africa and around the world.

Visualizing History The word *Kwanzaa* comes from a Swahili phrase meaning "first fruits." The holiday, based on a traditional harvest festival, celebrates seven principles of African culture: unity, self-determination, collective work and responsibility, cooperative economics, purpose, creativity, and faith. Holiday customs include candle lighting and the exchange of gifts.
Answer to Caption: *to instill pride in African culture*

Reteach

Ask students to explain (1) the relevance of the Pan-African movement and the OAU to Africa's search for political unity; (2) the causes and significance of drought in Africa; and (3) the role of negritude in the formation of an African identity.

 Reteaching Activity 34

 Reading Essentials and Study Guide 34-3

Enrich

Have students read a work by Nobel laureates Wole Soyinka or Nadine Gordimer and write a short report describing the novel's treatment of challenges facing Africa in recent times.

📁 Enrichment Activity 34

CLOSE

Have students write one paragraph in which they summarize the main challenges facing African countries today. *(Answers should include a search for unity, economic development, and the preservation of an African identity.)*

SECTION 3 ASSESSMENT

Main Idea

1. Use a chart like the one below to identify challenges faced by African nations in search of economic development.

Challenges to Economic Development
1. _____
2. _____

Recall

2. **Define** Pan-Africanism, cash crop, subsistence farmer, desertification, literacy rate, negritude.

3. **Identify** Kofi Annan, Organization of African Unity, Economic Community of West African States, Léopold Sédar Senghor.

Critical Thinking

4. **Evaluating Information** What might have happened if African nations had grown more food for their people instead of growing cash crops and industrializing their economies?

Understanding Themes

5. **Change** What trend influenced African political systems by the early 1990s?

SECTION 3 ASSESSMENT ANSWERS

1. lack of capital, skilled workers, and transportation systems hindered industrial growth; need for foreign aid; lack of agricultural development hurt domestic market; unemployment; population growth; government debt; drought; famine
2. The terms are defined in the Glossary.
3. Annan, 941; OAU, 942; Economic Community, 944; Senghor, 945
4. A better balance between food and export crops might have reduced hunger and lessened dependence on foreign governments and banks for loans.
5. **CHANGE** The new trend favored multiparty systems and free enterprise approaches.

CHAPTER 34 ASSESSMENT

WORLD HISTORY *Online*

Have students use the **Chapter 34 Self-Check Quiz** at worldhistory.glencoe.com to prepare for the Chapter Test.

GLENCOE TECHNOLOGY

VIDEODISC
Use MindJogger to review the chapter.

MindJogger Videoquiz

Chapter 34
Disc 5 Side A

Also available in VHS.

Answers

Using Key Terms

1. e   3. h   5. j
2. f   4. i

Using Your History Journal

Suggest that students write as if it were the year 2020 and that they are looking back on how their chosen nation has fared since 2000.

Reviewing Facts

1. 1948: nationalist Afrikaners in power in South Africa; 1951: Libya independent; 1957: Ghana independent; 1962: Algeria independent; Mandela jailed; 1969: Qaddafi takes over Libya; 1960: Nigeria, Congo independent; 1962: Uganda independent; 1966: Ghana's ruler overthrown by army; 1976: police fire on student march in Soweto; 1980: Zimbabwe independent; 1980s: Tutu opposes apartheid
2. The democratic ideals of the Allies inspired Africans. African nationalists found support among workers who resented foreign exploitation of Africa.
3. opposition politicians, human

WORLD HISTORY *Online*

Self-Check Quiz

Visit the *World History: The Human Experience* Web site at **worldhistory.glencoe.com** and click on *Chapter 34—Self-Check Quiz* to prepare for the Chapter Test.

Using Key Terms

Write the key term that completes each sentence. Then write a sentence for each term not chosen.

a. general strike   f. desertification
b. colons   g. cash crops
c. clans   h. apartheid
d. negritude   i. genocide
e. Pan-Africanism   j. literacy rate

1. Through the movement of _____, African nations seek to promote oneness and cooperation throughout the continent.
2. _____, or the transformation of fertile land into desert land, affected countries near the Sahara.
3. In 1948, the South African government began legalizing and strengthening a policy of racial separation known as _____.
4. The deliberate killing of a racial, ethnic, or national group is known as _____.
5. _____, the percentage of people who can read and write, has increased in Africa in recent years.

Technology Activity

Using a Spreadsheet
Search the Internet or a library for sources about the independence of three African countries. Use a spreadsheet to organize your information. Include headings such as name of country, highlights of colonial history, year of independence, how independence was attained, current economy, and present form of government. Include a map showing the political borders of the three countries and their capitals.

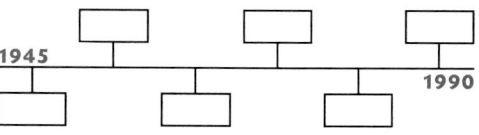

Using Your History Journal

Review your news clippings on Africa. Write a short essay on the future of an African nation. What are the challenges that your chosen nation faces? What are the prospects for peace and progress?

Reviewing Facts

1. **History** Use a time line like the one below to identify key events in the African nations' quest for independence after World War II.

1945 [time line] 1990

2. **History** Discuss the reasons for the growth of nationalism in Africa after 1945.
3. **Culture** Identify the groups that pressed for reform in Kenya during the 1990s.
4. **Economics** Explain the reason for Libya's postwar economic prosperity.
5. **History** Discuss the events leading to Zimbabwe's late independence in 1980.
6. **History/Culture** Describe the roles of Nelson Mandela and Desmond Tutu in South Africa from the 1960s to the 1990s. What was the outcome of their efforts?
7. **History** Discuss developments in Somalia during the 1980s and early 1990s.
8. **Culture** Identify the changes that are occurring in African culture.

Critical Thinking

1. **Analyze** What are the benefits and drawbacks of Africa's cultural and ethnic diversity?
2. **Apply** How would you solve the problem of food shortages in various parts of Africa?
3. **Analyze** How did the political boundaries drawn by European colonial powers cause

---

rights activists, and Christian and Muslim religious leaders
4. Oil was discovered there in 1959.
5. The Rhodesian Front thwarted Britain's wish to share political power with Africans and in 1965 declared independence; guerrilla warfare caused European settlers to flee and the economy to crumble, driving the Front to negotiate with the African majority and leading to the emergence of a free Zimbabwe.

6. Both led the struggle against apartheid in South Africa; ANC president Mandela carried out military operations, was jailed, and became a symbol of the struggle; Tutu was Anglican archbishop of Cape Town and urged nonviolent action and interracial reconciliation. Their efforts helped to bring an end to apartheid and the founding of genuine democracy in South Africa.
7. Rival clans fought for control of the government, keeping food aid from reaching famine

problems for many African nations after they gained independence?

4. **Synthesize** How would you respond if you were living under the system of apartheid?

5. **Apply** How has migration of people from the countryside to cities affected many African countries?

6. **Analyze** In the photograph below Nigerian farmers irrigate a field. How does this show the transition to a new Africa?

Understanding Themes

1. **Nationalism** What was the purpose of the African National Congress (ANC) in South Africa? How has its role changed since 1994?

2. **Change** What political changes came to Angola and Mozambique between the 1970s and 1990s?

3. **Change** How has the Organization of African Unity (OAU) affected African affairs since its founding in 1963?

Skill Practice

Exchange with another student the research reports you completed in "Applying the Skill" for this chapter. Critique the reports using the following questions. For each question, find examples in the report and present them to the author.

1. Does the report have an introduction, body, and conclusion?

2. Does the introduction define the writer's thesis or main point of the report?

3. Is the body of the report organized in a logical way?

4. Are there clear transitions between ideas? Give an example of a good transition and a weak one.

5. Does the conclusion restate and summarize the thesis of the report?

Geography in History

1. **Region** Refer to the map below. What is the largest uninhabited region of Africa?

2. **Human/Environment Interaction** Why is a narrow strip of land in northeast Africa heavily populated?

3. **Location** The heaviest population in South Africa is near what city?

Population Density of Africa

Rabat, Algiers, Tunis, Casablanca, Tripoli, Alexandria, Cairo, Dakar, Khartoum, Accra, Ibadan, Abidjan, Lagos, Douala, Addis Ababa, Nairobi, Kinshasa, Dar es Salaam, Luanda, Harare, Johannesburg, Maputo, Cape Town

ATLANTIC OCEAN
INDIAN OCEAN

Uninhabited
Less than 2
2-25
26-60
61-125
126-250
more than 250
○ Metropolitan areas more than 1,000,000 population

0   1,000 mi.
0   1,000 km
Azimuthal Equal-Area Projection

1. In the 1980s, droughts brought widespread famine to Africa. What efforts to relieve food shortages continue there today?

2. In 1994, power passed relatively peacefully from the white minority government of South Africa to a multi-racial government that includes black South Africans. How might the South African solution serve as a model for solving political problems in other countries that are torn by ethnic unrest?

Chapter 34   *Africa*   **947**

Understanding Themes

1. **NATIONALISM** to press the white government for reform; since 1994 it has been the country's ruling party

2. **CHANGE** After civil war, they moved toward peace and gradually abandoned socialism for free enterprise.

3. **CHANGE** It urged its members to remain neutral during the cold war, put pressure on South Africa to end apartheid, supported pro-independence movements, and settled boundary disputes among member nations.

Skill Practice

Answers will vary but should be based on critical evaluation of the written report and on the elements of the lesson on page 940.

Geography in History

1. North Africa
2. It borders the Nile River.
3. Johannesburg

Linking Past and Present

1. Students might mention international relief programs and attempts to improve agricultural productivity in the Sahel.

2. Students might argue that if blacks and whites can overcome the racial divide, Hutus and Tutsis and different Somali clans should be able to live in peace also.

? Chapter Bonus Test Question

Ask students: What situations elsewhere in the world suggest that optimism about Africa's future is warranted? What situations suggest otherwise? *(Answers will vary but may include: Peace developments in the Middle East suggest that optimism is warranted. Ongoing ethnic conflicts elsewhere suggest otherwise.)*

victims. UN forces sent in to protect the distribution of food were withdrawn because they were becoming involved in the fighting.

8. African artists have been developing art expressing pride in their heritage.

Critical Thinking

1. Benefits may include a variety of perspectives with which to approach problems. Drawbacks include conflict and a lack of unity.

2. Solutions may include short-term relief efforts or long-term agricultural reform.

3. Old boundaries often divided ethnic and religious groups; divisions created factionalism.

4. Answers should reflect familiarity with South Africa's former racial policies.

5. Unskilled rural people remain unemployed and unable to buy African products, weakening national economies.

6. shows more advanced agricultural techniques

Chapter 34   *Africa*   **947**

A complete, 1-page lesson plan is provided for each section in the *Reproducible Lesson Plans* booklet.

The Middle East

CHAPTER RESOURCES

	Reproducible Resources	Multimedia Resources
Chapter Opener	Chapter Themes: Graphic Organizer 35 Historical Significance Chapter Activity 35	MindJogger Videoquiz
Chapter Enrichment	Vocabulary Activity 35* Time Line Activity 35 Mapping History Activity 35 History Simulation 35 Geography and History Activity 35 Source Reading 35 People in World History Profiles 67, 68 World Literature Selection 8 World Art and Music Activity 35 Enrichment Activity 35 Critical Thinking Activity 35 Skill Reinforcement Activity 35 Writer's Guidebook, Lessons 9, 13 Performance Assessment Activity 35 Standardized Test Practice Workbook Activity 35 Inclusion for the Social Studies Classroom Strategies and Activities	World History and Art Transparency 47, *Iranian Mihrab*; 48, *The Twelve Tribes of Israel* Chapter Transparency 35 Vocabulary PuzzleMaker Software World Music: Cultural Traditions, Lesson 5 Turning Points in World History: *Middle East Peace Accords* In the Holy Land: • *State of Israel Proclaimed: 1948* • *Six-Day War: Scenes* • *Intifadah (The Uprising)* World History Primary Source Document Library
Chapter Review/Reteaching	Reteaching Activity 35 Skill Reinforcement Activity 35 Spanish Chapter Summary 35	Chapter 35 Digest Audiocassette, Activity, Test* Vocabulary PuzzleMaker Software Interactive Tutor Self-Assessment Software MindJogger Videoquiz
Chapter Evaluation/Testing	Performance Assessment Activity 35 Chapter 35 Test, Forms A and B	ExamView® Pro Testmaker

* Also available in Spanish

0:00 **OUT OF TIME?** Assign the Chapter 35 Audiocassettes.

World History Primary Source Document Library
Make History Come Alive!
Engage your students with over 250 easily accessible primary source documents—available on this CD-ROM—that will give them real life insight into the important events of world history.

Block Schedule
Activities that are particularly suited to use within the block scheduling framework are identified throughout this chapter by the following designation.

KEY TO ABILITY LEVELS
Teaching strategies are coded for varying learning styles.
L1 **BASIC** activities for all students
L2 **AVERAGE** activities for average to above-average students
L3 **CHALLENGING** activities for above-average students
LEP **LIMITED ENGLISH PROFICIENCY** activities

Use Glencoe's *Presentation Plus!* multimedia teacher tool to easily present dynamic lessons that visually excite your students. Using Microsoft PowerPoint® you can customize the presentations to create your own personalized lessons.

Interactive Lesson Planner

Planning has never been easier! Using this CD-ROM, organize your week, month, semester, or year with all the help you need. The **Interactive Lesson Planner** gives you access to all of the blackline masters that accompany *World History: The Human Experience.*

SECTION RESOURCES

Daily Objectives	Reproducible Resources	Multimedia Resources
Section 1 Nationalism in the Middle East Explain how nationalism established independent nations and created conflict in the Middle East after World War II.	Lecture Notes 35-1 Reproducible Lesson Plan 35-1 Vocabulary Activity 35* Guided Reading Activity 35-1* Time Line Activity 35 Section Quiz 35-1* Reading Essentials and Study Guide 35-1	Section Focus Transparency 35-1 Chapter Transparency 35 Interactive Tutor Self-Assessment Software Testmaker In the Holy Land: *State of Israel Proclaimed: 1948*
Section 2 War and Peace in the Middle East Summarize how issues of peace and war have been decided in the Middle East since the mid-1960s.	Lecture Notes 35-2 Reproducible Lesson Plan 35-2 Vocabulary Activity 35* Guided Reading Activity 35-2* People in World History Profile 68 Geography and History Activity 35 Section Quiz 35-2* Reading Essentials and Study Guide 35-2	Section Focus Transparency 35-2 World History and Art Transparency 47, *Iranian Mihrab;* 48, *The Twelve Tribes of Israel* Interactive Tutor Self-Assessment Software Testmaker World Music: Cultural Traditions, Lesson 5 Turning Points in World History: *Middle East Peace Accords* In the Holy Land: • *Six-Day War: Scenes* • *Intifadah (The Uprising)*
Section 3 Challenges Facing the Middle East Describe how people in the Middle East have handled the conflict between traditional ways and modern values.	Lecture Notes 35-3 Reproducible Lesson Plan 35-3 Guided Reading Activity 35-3* People in World History Profile 67 Reteaching Activity 35 Enrichment Activity 35 Section Quiz 35-3* Performance Assessment Activity 35 Reading Essentials and Study Guide 35-3	Section Focus Transparency 35-3 Vocabulary PuzzleMaker Software Interactive Tutor Self-Assessment Software Testmaker

* Also available in Spanish

Chapter Activities

 Performance Assessment Activity

An Awareness Campaign Events in the Middle East affect the United States in major ways. Have students work through the following steps: (1) list Middle East conflicts and events that have affected the United States in the past; (2) list the areas and issues of continued tensions in the region; (3) for each tension, predict future problems or implications for Americans; and (4) prioritize the list according to the degree of impact on Americans.

Have students work in groups to create an awareness campaign to inform Americans about the severity of the issues. This campaign may include talk-shows, leaflets, newspaper ads, interviews on the evening news, and so on. For each venue chosen, have students explain what would be said or shown, or have them actually create the visual product.

Possible Rubric Features

Concept attainment, accuracy of content information, plausibility of predictions, analysis skills, originality of products, elaboration and detail, persuasion, and collaborative skills

• *For an additional activity, refer to Activity 35 in the* Performance Assessment Strategies and Activities *booklet.*

ACTIVITY

From the Classroom of...

Peter Twomey
Brockton High School
Brockton, MA
Israel/Palestine—
A Solution?

Assign each student a Middle Eastern or North African country to research. Then, utilizing the text, library books, and current newspaper articles, each student should write a brief history of his or her country from the end of World War II to the present, including an economic profile. Supply each student with a summary sheet of Arab-Israeli conflicts from 1948 to the present accompanied by maps of the Israeli-Palestinian area in 1948, 1967, and today. When students' research is completed, call a peacekeeping meeting. In round one, each country introduces itself and gives an oral summary of its recent history, including an economic profile. In round two, the countries give their views on the question at hand: What should be the nature of the Israeli and Palestinian states? Why?

To conclude, students should compare their views with current Israeli and Palestinian politicians.

MULTIPLE LEARNING STYLES

Verbal/Linguistic
Have students find different types of modern Middle Eastern literature and present oral reports that explain how the literature reflects life in the the Middle East.

Logical/Mathematical
Have students make charts that show the per capita income and the literacy rate of each country in the Middle East. Ask students to compare the charts of several countries.

Visual/Spatial
Students may research the flags of Middle Eastern countries and then draw them on poster board, including the meaning of each flag's colors and symbols.

Auditory/Musical
Have students collect recordings of Middle Eastern music and play them for the class. Ask students to point out similarities and differences between this music and Western music.

Kinesthetic
Ask students to construct a model that shows the strategies and outcome of the Six-Day War and the Persian Gulf War.

 GLENCOE'S **ASSESSMENT** ADVANTAGE

Use the following to easily assess student learning in a variety of ways.

- Performance Assessment Strategies and Activities
- Section Quizzes
- Chapter and Unit Tests
- Interactive Tutor Self-Assessment Software
- Testmaker Software
- MindJogger Videoquiz
- SAT/SAT II Test Practice
- worldhistory.glencoe.com

Additional Resources

NATIONAL GEOGRAPHIC SOCIETY
Teacher's Corner

INDEX TO NATIONAL GEOGRAPHIC MAGAZINE

The following articles relate to this chapter:

- "Lawrence of Arabia," by Don Belt, January 1999.
- "Beirut Rising," by Peter Theroux, September 1997.
- "Syria Behind the Mask," by Peter Theroux, July 1996.
- "Israel's Galilee: Living in the Shadow of Peace," by Don Belt, June 1995.
- "Water: The Middle East's Critical Resource," by Priit J. Vesilind, May 1993.
- "Struggle of the Kurds," by Christopher Hitchens, August 1992.
- "Who Are the Palestinians?" by Tad Szulc, June 1992.

ADDITIONAL NATIONAL GEOGRAPHIC SOCIETY PRODUCTS

To order the following, call National Geographic at 1-800-368-2728:

- *Nations of the World Series: Egypt. (Video)*
- *Nations of the World Series: Israel. (Video)*
- *Jerusalem: Within These Walls (Video and Videodisc)*

Access National Geographic's new dynamic MapMachine Web site and other geography resources at:

- http://www.nationalgeographic.com/
- http://www.nationalgeographic.com/maps/

BIBLIOGRAPHY

Literature of the Period
Yesoshea, A. B. *Mr. Mani.* Translated by Hillel Halkin. New York: Harcourt, 1992. This contemporary Israeli novel gives a great deal of history on the Zionist movement and Israel today.
Readings for the Student
Moore, Molly. *A Woman at War: Storming Kuwait with the U.S. Marines.* New York: Macmillan, 1993. Eyewitness account from the battlefield of the Persian Gulf War by a reporter.
Readings for the Teacher
Decosse, David E., ed. *But Was It Just? Reflections on the Morality of the Persian Gulf War.* New York: Doubleday, 1992. Five essays from differing points of view on the war's justness.

WORLD HISTORY Online

Use our Web site as an additional resource. All essential content is covered in the Student Edition.

You and your students can visit the *World History: The Human Experience* Web site at worldhistory.glencoe.com The student text directs students to the Web site for the following options:

- **Chapter Overviews**
- **Student Web Activities**
- **Self-Check Quizzes**

Answers are provided for you in a link entitled "Web Activity Lesson Plan." Additional Web Resources, Interactive Puzzles and content updates are also available.

Visit the Glencoe Web site at socialstudies.glencoe.com for social studies activities, updates, and links to other resources.

LOCAL OBJECTIVES

_____
_____
_____
_____
_____
_____
_____
_____
_____
_____
_____
_____
_____
_____
_____
_____
_____
_____
_____

Chapter

35 1945–Present

The Middle East

CHAPTER THEMES

Chapter Themes are listed by section on this chapter opening page. A corresponding theme-based activity is available under "TEACH," and a theme-based question is asked in the Section and Chapter Assessments.

The Storyteller

Historical Setting Both Yitzhak Rabin and Yasir Arafat were born in Jerusalem, Palestine. Rabin fought the British to form an independent Israeli state and led the defense of Jerusalem during Israel's war for independence (1947–1949). Rabin later became a leader of Israel's Labor party and an opponent of the PLO.

Yasir Arafat left Jerusalem in 1948 when Israel became a nation. He led raids into Israel, became a leader of the PLO, and dreamed of a new state of Palestine. In 1993 after secret negotiations, these two old enemies signed a peace accord.

Historical Significance

Answers: *Protecting the Middle East's waterways and oil resources caused the Western powers and the Soviet Union to back opposing Middle Eastern countries during the cold war. The United Nations administered the partition of Palestine in 1947 and has sent peacekeeping troops to the Middle East. The United States helped negotiate peace between Israel and its Arab neighbors.*

Egypt, Jordan, and the Palestinians have signed peace agreements with Israel, and Syria has begun negotiations.

— WORLD HISTORY Online —

Have students use the **Chapter 35 Overview** at worldhistory. glencoe.com as a prereading and postreading exercise for understanding chapter content.

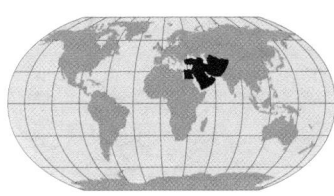

Chapter Themes

▶ **Nationalism** The cold war and rival nationalisms affect the politics of the Middle East. *Section 1*
▶ **Cooperation** Middle Eastern nations take steps toward peace after years of conflict. *Section 2*
▶ **Cultural Diffusion** Middle Eastern countries search for a reconciliation between traditional and modern values. *Section 3*

The Storyteller

In the fall of 1993, a remarkable event occurred that, to many people, seemed like a miracle. Yitzhak Rabin, the prime minister of Israel, and Yasir Arafat, the chairman of the Palestine Liberation Organization (PLO) signed an agreement to end the decades-long conflict between Israel and the Palestinian Arabs.

In 1995 Rabin's assassination stunned Israel and the world, revealing that the quest for peace is often an uphill struggle marked by tragedy. Since 1945 the Middle East has shown itself to be a complex region where violence has been a constant feature of life but where hopes for peace remain unquenchable.

Historical Significance

How have Middle Eastern developments affected world affairs since 1945? What steps have the nations of the Middle East taken to resolve their differences?

1944   1972   2000

1956 Egypt's President Gamal Abdel Nasser nationalizes the Suez Canal.

1948 State of Israel established.

1995 Israel's prime minister Yitzhak Rabin is assassinated.

1980 Iran-Iraq War begins.

948

GEOGRAPHY CONNECTION

Region Point out the locator map of the Middle East on page 948. What has long made the Middle East an important region of the world? *(The Middle East links Europe, Asia, and Africa.)* What makes it an especially important region today? *(its plentiful oil reserves)* Have students turn to the map of the Middle East in the Atlas in their textbook. Ask them to make a list of the 15 countries in the Middle East and their capitals. Also ask them to write down one characteristic of each country. *(For example: The Nile River flows through Egypt; Kuwait borders the Persian Gulf.)*

Visualizing
History Istanbul (formerly Constantinople) is Turkey's largest city and one of the busiest ports in the Middle East.

WORLD HISTORY Online

Chapter Overview

Visit the *World History: The Human Experience* Web site at **world history.glencoe.com** and click on *Chapter 35—Chapter Overview* to preview the chapter.

Your History Journal

Create an illustrated time line of conflicts and peace conferences or accords in the Middle East beginning in 1948 and ending at the present. Illustrate your time line with symbols of peace and war.

Chapter 35 *The Middle East* **949**

➕ EXTRA CREDIT PROJECT

Country Fact Booklet Have students select one of the Middle Eastern countries, conduct in-depth research on it, and compile a fact booklet. Tell students to include the following types of information in their booklets: geography (bordering countries, physical features, plants, animals); government, politics, and army; economy (agriculture, natural resources, industry, trade); society (social classes, religion, education, daily life, literature, the arts, sports and recreation, role of women, role of children and teens); and history. 📦

Visualizing History

Tell students that Istanbul straddles the Bosporus Strait that divides Europe from Asia. As Constantinople, the city was once the capital of the Byzantine Empire and then the Ottoman Empire. Today the city is a shipbuilding center and a major center for the manufacture of cement, cigarettes, and leather products. Why has Istanbul's location made it an important city throughout history? *(It has been a link between Europe and Asia.)*

✔️ Performance Assessment

Refer to the activity on page 948C of the Planning Guide.

📁 Refer to Activity 35 in the *Performance Assessment Strategies and Activities* booklet. 📦

Using Your History Journal

Suggest that students also include on their time lines the names, and if possible, the pictures of people important in the conflicts and peace conferences. 📦

GLENCOE TECHNOLOGY

 VIDEODISC
Use MindJogger to preview chapter content.

MindJogger Videoquiz

 Chapter 35
Disc 5 Side A

 Also available in VHS.

Chapter 35 *The Middle East* **949**

1945   1955   1965

1948 Israel and Arab states fight first conflict.

1951 Iran nationalizes foreign-owned oil industries.

1958 Political crisis engulfs Lebanon.

SECTION THEME

▶ **Nationalism** The cold war and rival nationalisms affect the politics of the Middle East.

Guide to Reading

For reading strategies to help students read effectively see pages 12–13. Have students think about the main head as they read the subheads.

Vocabulary Pre-check

 Use the Vocabulary PuzzleMaker for Chapter 35 to create a crossword puzzle to reinforce section terms. **L1 LEP**

Use Vocabulary Activity 35 to introduce vocabulary terms. **L1 LEP**

FOCUS

Section Objective

Explain how nationalism established independent nations and created conflict in the Middle East after World War II.

BELLRINGER
Motivational Activity

 Before taking roll at the beginning of the class period, project Section Focus Transparency 35-1 and have students answer the activity questions.

This activity is also available as a blackline master.

Section 1

Nationalism in the Middle East

Guide to Reading

Read to Find Out
Main Idea *Nationalism helped to establish independent nations and create conflict in the Middle East after World War II.*

▶ **Terms to Define**
Pan-Arabism, kibbutzim, nationalize, pact

▶ **People to Meet**
David Ben-Gurion, Gamal Abdel Nasser, Hussein I, Mohammad Reza Pahlavi, Mohammad Mossadeg

▶ **Places to Locate**
Egypt, Iraq, Lebanon, Syria, Jordan, Saudi Arabia, Yemen, Israel, Suez Canal, Turkey, Iran

The Storyteller

In spite of the separate living arrangements, members of a kibbutz family do not become strangers to one another.… Kibbutz parents spend a great deal of their free time with their children.… Parents and children enjoy each other all the more

when they meet just for fun and companionship. Kibbutz-niks [residents of a kibbutz] take good care of their elderly parents, too. There is less friction among kibbutz grandparents, parents, and children.… There is less divorce—fewer marriage problems.

—adapted from *Israel Today,* Harry Essrig and Abraham Segal, 1977

Children in a kibbutz

In the decades after World War II, nationalist movements took hold in the Middle East. For more than 20 years, Great Britain and France had governed much of the area under the terms of post–World War I agreements. Gradually the presence of foreign officials and troops on Middle Eastern soil revived the desire for independence, as it did in Asia and Africa.

While most Middle Eastern countries shook off European control in the postwar years, foreign influence in the region remained strong. With its valuable waterways and oil reserves, the Middle East became the scene of superpower maneuvering for influence during the cold war.

Arab Independence

Several Arab countries, such as **Egypt** and **Iraq**, had achieved independence before World War II. During the 1940s, other European-ruled Arab territories followed. The Mediterranean coastal lands of **Lebanon** and **Syria** won their freedom from France. In Lebanon, Christian and Muslim leaders agreed to share power under a new constitution, while Syria elected its first parliamentary government. The largely desert kingdom of Transjordan (present-day **Jordan**) gained its independence from Great Britain. In all of these new states, however, Western influences remained strong after independence.

As independent Arab states emerged, Pan-Arabism, a movement aimed at building closer cultural and political ties among Arabs, grew stronger, especially among the educated urban middle class. In 1945, leaders of Egypt, Iraq, Transjordan, Syria, Lebanon, **Saudi Arabia**, and **Yemen** formed the Arab League. Its mission was to unify the Arab world.

SECTION RESOURCES

Reproducible Masters
- Lecture Notes 35-1
- Reproducible Lesson Plan 35-1
- Vocabulary Activity 35
- Guided Reading Activity 35-1
- Time Line Activity 35
- Section Quiz 35-1
- Reading Essentials and Study Guide 35-1

Transparencies
- Section Focus Transparency 35-1
- Chapter Transparency 35

Multimedia
- Interactive Tutor Self-Assessment Software
- Testmaker
- In the Holy Land: *State of Israel Proclaimed: 1948*

Formation of Israel

By 1947, Palestine remained the only significant European-ruled territory in the region. Arabs, who had lived in Palestine for centuries, wanted the British to honor their promise of freedom made in the early 1900s. Zionist Jews wanted to build a Jewish state on the same land—land that their ancestors had claimed since Biblical times and that the British had also promised to them.

The Holocaust in Nazi-occupied Europe had boosted support in Western countries for the Zionist movement. Fearing that the British would allow increased Jewish immigration, Arabs in Palestine increased attacks on Jewish settlers. Many of Palestine's Jews lived on kibbutzim, or collective farms, where they struggled to turn swamps and boulder-strewn hillsides into productive farms. To defend themselves, Jewish settlements relied on a military force called the Haganah. Meanwhile, Jewish underground forces carried out attacks on British soldiers and Palestinian Arabs. As hostilities mounted, Great Britain admitted its inability to keep the peace and turned Palestine over to the United Nations in 1947.

For months, world leaders debated the future of Palestine. The United States, the Soviet Union, and much of the West wanted to divide Palestine into a Jewish and an Arab state. Arab nations, along with several European and Pacific nations, rejected the idea and called for a single Palestinian state. On November 29, 1947, the General Assembly voted to partition Palestine and to place Jerusalem under UN control.

Jewish leaders were quick to accept the UN partition plan, while embittered Arab leaders rejected it. Great Britain relinquished control of Palestine on May 14, 1948, as Prime Minister **David Ben-Gurion** proclaimed the new state of **Israel**. Within 24 hours, the armies of Syria, Lebanon, Iraq, Egypt, and Transjordan attacked the new Jewish state. With foreign aid and effective civilian and military organization, the Israelis defeated the Arab forces in nine months.

When the fighting ended in early 1949, Israel held more territory. Jerusalem was divided, with the eastern part of the city in Arab hands. Transjordan annexed East Jerusalem and the West Bank of the Jordan River. Egypt held the Gaza Strip. The war was a resounding victory for Israel. To the Arabs, the war spelled disaster. As a result of partition, more than 700,000 Palestinians became homeless. Many fled to neighboring Arab lands, where a large number settled in refugee camps hoping to eventually return home.

Visualizing History Despite British restrictions on immigration, Jews aboard the *Exodus* tried to migrate to Palestine in 1947. *Why did Great Britain turn Palestine over to the United Nations in 1947?*

Arab Unity

The 1948–1949 war had other serious consequences for the Arab world. In Egypt, many people blamed rich, corrupt King Farouk for the Arab defeat and the country's weak economy. In 1952 army officers seized control of the government and proclaimed a republic. Within a year, Colonel **Gamal Abdel Nasser**, a leader of the coup, took over as president.

Nasser profoundly disliked Western influence in the Middle East, and quickly launched new policies through which he hoped Egypt would lead the Arab world to greatness. In an extremely popular move, Nasser broke up the estates of wealthy Egyptian landowners and gave plots of land to the peasants. Then he negotiated the British withdrawal from the **Suez Canal**. Finally, he set out to modernize Egypt and build up its military muscle to confront Israel.

The Suez Crisis

Nasser wanted to help Egypt by building a dam at Aswan in the Upper Nile River valley. Known as the Aswan High Dam, the massive structure—36 stories high and more than 2 miles (3 km) wide—would end flooding, increase irrigation, and give farmers two extra harvests a year. Electricity generated by the dam would power new industries.

Seeking political influence, the United States offered Egypt a $270 million loan to build the dam. However, Nasser also wanted weapons to modernize his army, but the West refused to sell arms to him. Nasser then made an arms deal with the Soviets. This caused the United States to angrily

TEACH

Guided Practice

THEME Nationalism

Help students recall the meaning of *nationalism*. (*the desire of a people to achieve independence from foreign control and to govern themselves*) Lead students in a discussion on how Egypt's seizure of the Suez Canal increased the spirit of Arab nationalism in the Middle East. (*Nasser emerged from the Suez crisis as a powerful Arab leader and his brand of nationalism spread throughout the Arab world.*) **L1**

Visualizing History Tell students that the British did not allow the *Exodus* to disembark its 4,500 Jewish refugee passengers in Palestine. After the ship was badly damaged by British destroyers, its passengers were taken by other ships to France and Germany.
Answer to Caption: *Great Britain was unable to keep the peace between Jewish settlers and Arabs in Palestine.*

Politics Have students make a chart that shows the parties involved, the goals, and the outcomes of the following events: the Israeli war of independence (1948–1949), the Suez crisis, the civil war in Lebanon (1958), the crisis in Iran (early 1950s). **L2**

 Chapter Transparency 35

International Relations Have students compare the role the United States played in Turkish affairs with its role in Iranian affairs. **L3**

Independent Practice

 Guided Reading Activity 35-1 **L1**

Time Line Activity 35

COOPERATIVE LEARNING ACTIVITY

Time Line Organize students into nine groups and assign each group one of the following countries mentioned in this section: Egypt, Iraq, Lebanon, Syria, Jordan, Saudi Arabia, Israel, Turkey, Iran. Have each group make a horizontal time line of significant events that occurred in the country from the 1940s to the present. Have representatives from each group get together to determine a standard length for the time lines. Remind the groups to assign members to research or to place information on the time lines. Display completed time lines one above the other so that students can determine what occurred in each country at a particular time. **L2**

Map Study

Answer

It is a crucial waterway linking the Persian Gulf and the Arabian Sea. Through it pass oil tankers and other commercial vessels.

Map Skills Practice

Reading a Map What nations border Israel? (*Egypt, Jordan, Lebanon, Syria*)

Daily Life Have students research life in a Palestinian refugee camp or in an Israeli kibbutz. Ask students to write diary entries for a week from the point of view of a teenager in a camp or on a kibbutz. **L2**

Geography: Movement Have students draw a map that shows the route of a ship from Jiddah, Saudi Arabia, to Marseilles, France, before and after the closing of the Suez Canal. Ask students to estimate the difference in distance between the two routes and research the difference in travel time. **L3 LEP**

VIDEODISC
In the Holy Land

Side One, Chapter 20
Frame: 27441
Title: *State of Israel Proclaimed: 1948*
Ask: What was the significance of the founding of the State of Israel? (*Now there was a Jewish nation.*)

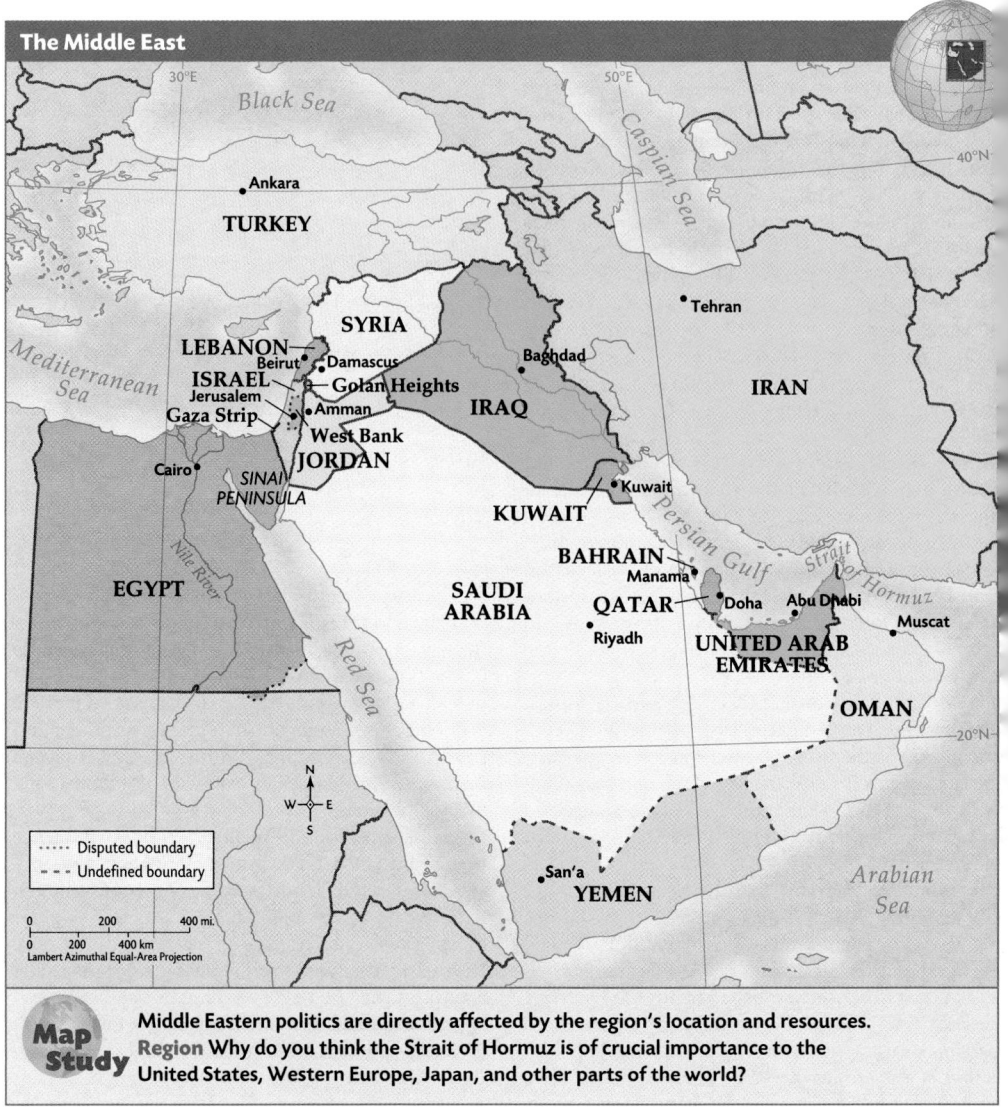

The Middle East

Map Study

Middle Eastern politics are directly affected by the region's location and resources.
Region Why do you think the Strait of Hormuz is of crucial importance to the United States, Western Europe, Japan, and other parts of the world?

withdraw its offer. In July 1956 Nasser retaliated against the Western powers by nationalizing, or bringing under government control, the Suez Canal. He vowed to use millions of dollars in canal fees to finance the building of the dam.

President Eisenhower was opposed to Western intervention, and the United States tried to negotiate an end to the crisis. Great Britain and France, however, feared that Nasser might close the canal and cut off shipments of oil between the Middle East and Western Europe. In October, the two European powers joined Israel in invading Egypt. Great Britain and France hoped to overthrow Nasser and seize the canal. Israel wanted to end Egyptian guerrilla attacks on its borders. The United States immediately sponsored a United Nations resolution calling for British and French withdrawal from Egypt. The Russians threatened rocket attacks on British and French cities. Eisenhower, opposed to Soviet interference, put the Strategic Air Command on alert. In face of this pressure, the three nations pulled out of Egypt. United Nations forces were sent to patrol the Egyptian-Israeli border. Nasser then accepted the Soviet offer to build the Aswan High Dam.

MEETING SPECIAL NEEDS ACTIVITY

Study Strategy Have students make a flash card for each of the following countries: Egypt, Iraq, Syria, Lebanon, Jordan, Israel, Turkey, and Iran. Tell students to write the country's name on one side of the card. On the other side, they should write the names of the main leaders from 1948 to 1960; the leaders' positions—pro-Western or pro-Arab, pro-Nasser, and so forth; and main crises or events for the country during those years. **L2**

Arab Nationalism

Nasser emerged from the Suez crisis as a powerful Arab leader. He had embarrassed Great Britain and France, won control of the Suez Canal, and had stopped Israel from taking more territory. Pro-Nasser parties began forming throughout the Arab world. It seemed that Nasser might rise to lead a unified Arab world.

In early 1958 Syria and Egypt merged to form a Nasser-led state called the **United Arab Republic** (UAR). The union lasted about three years. At that point, Syrian leaders had grown resentful of the loss of their power, and Syria withdrew from the UAR.

That same year, Nasser's brand of Arab nationalism seemed to be taking hold in Iraq. There, King Faisal II, Nasser's strongest Arab opponent and a friend of the West, was killed by radical political and military forces who set up a one-party regime like Nasser's and broke ties with the West.

In the face of pro-Nasser pressure, some Arab leaders turned to the West for support. Jordan's **Hussein I** asked for British and American help when pro-Nasser forces threatened his government. In Lebanon, violence broke out between the Christians, who dominated the nation, and a huge Muslim population that sympathized with Nasser and the UAR. Christian President Camille Chamoun, a supporter of the West, sought election to a new term. Anti-Western elements revolted, and a civil war followed. Chamoun asked for Western help to stop the violence. At first, Eisenhower refused. However, when an unexpected coup overthrew the government of Iraq, Eisenhower decided to uphold political stability in the region. He sent 15,000 Marines to Lebanon in July 1958. When order was restored that fall, the troops pulled out.

By 1960 Arab nationalism had made gains, but the Middle East was in a state of uncertainty. A fragile truce held between Arabs and Israelis; competing Arab groups were at an impasse; and neither superpower had managed to achieve dominance in the region.

Pro-Western Tier

Two other Middle Eastern countries, **Turkey** and **Iran**, experienced the upheaval of nationalism and rapid modernization. Both bordered the Soviet Union, making them pawns in cold war struggles.

Turkey

At the end of World War II, Turkey received American aid to modernize its economy and to ward off Soviet advances. During the 1950s, the Turks joined NATO and the Baghdad Pact, alliances aimed at blocking Soviet expansion. Turkey also made strides toward democracy, encouraged foreign investment, and strengthened its capitalist economy. By the 1960s, however, government corruption, inflation, and a huge international debt discredited Turkey's ruling politicians and increased the political influence of the military.

Iran

By contrast, Western influence in oil-rich Iran was shaken after World War II. The young shah, **Mohammad Reza Pahlavi**, relied on Western help to block Soviet influence. Many Iranian people, however, resented the West. For decades, the British had grown rich on Iranian oil at Iran's expense.

In 1951, a wealthy politician, **Mohammad Mossadeg**, became prime minister. He nationalized the British-owned oil industry and declared that all oil money would be used for social and economic reforms. Great Britain called for a world boycott of Iranian oil. As Iranians began to suffer, their hatred of the West and the shah grew.

In 1953 growing support for Mossadeg forced the shah to flee the country. He returned after a military coup—promoted by the United States—deposed Mossadeg. The shah increased his ties to the United States and signed the Baghdad Pact. A **pact** is a treaty between two or more nations. He also signed an agreement with Western oil companies. The shah was firmly in control by the 1960s.

SECTION 1 ASSESSMENT

Main Idea
1. Use a web diagram like the one below to identify effects of nationalism in the Middle East after World War II.

Effects of Nationalism

Recall
2. **Define** Pan-Arabism, kibbutzim, nationalize, pact.
3. **Identify** David Ben-Gurion, Gamal Abdel Nasser, United Arab Republic, Hussein I, Mohammad Reza Pahlavi, Mohammad Mossadeg.

Critical Thinking
4. **Applying Information** How did the Holocaust contribute to the development of Israel?

Understanding Themes
5. **Nationalism** How was Nasser viewed by the Arab world after he nationalized the Suez Canal?

ASSESS

Check for Understanding

Assign Section 1 Assessment as homework or as an in-class activity.

Use Interactive Tutor Self-Assessment Software to review Section 1.

Global Gourmet

Middle East Pita bread, or pocket bread, began with nomads in the Middle East. After pitching their tents at the end of the day, they mixed powdered grain and water to form a dough, patted it into flat rounds, and baked them over an open fire.

Evaluate

Section Quiz 35-1

Use the Testmaker to create a customized quiz for Section 1.

Reteach

Have students identify the relation of the following people to a Middle Eastern country and to major events in the Middle East: David Ben-Gurion, King Farouk, Gamal Abdel Nasser, Hussein I, Camille Chamoun, Mohammad Reza Pahlavi, and Mohammad Mossadeg.

Reading Essentials and Study Guide 35-1

Enrich

Have students research and write a short report explaining how and why Lebanon's government was divided between Christians and Muslims.

CLOSE

Have students summarize the results of anti-Western feelings in Egypt, Iraq, Lebanon, and Iran.

1965   1975   1985   199

1967 Israel and Arab nations fight Six-Day War.

1979 Revolution establishes Islamic republic in Iran.

1990 Iraq invades Kuwait.

1993 Israelis and Palestinians agree to end their conflict:

Section 2

War and Peace in the Middle East

Guide to Reading

Read to Find Out
Main Idea *Since the mid-1960s, issues of peace and war in the Middle East have been decided both violently and diplomatically.*

▶ **Terms to Define**
disengagement, cartel, *intifada*, embargo

▶ **People to Meet**
Yasir Arafat, Anwar el-Sadat, Menachem Begin, Hosni Mubarak, Yitzhak Rabin, Shimon Peres, Ehud Barak, Abdullah II, Ayatollah Ruhollah Khomeini, Saddam Hussein

▶ **Places to Locate**
Gaza Strip, Golan Heights, West Bank, Beirut, Strait of Hormuz, Kuwait

The **S**toryteller

When Shah Mohammad Reza Pahlavi was overthrown in 1979, Iran had male tailors fitting women's clothes and male teachers in girls' classrooms. The revolutionaries, however, refused to allow unrelated men and women to work closely together. The result: many more job opportunities for women. In the media, for example, the need for women to cover women's sports opened jobs for directors and reporters.

—adapted from *Nine Parts of Desire, The Hidden World of Islamic Women*, Geraldine Brooks, 1995

Shah Mohammad Reza Pahlavi

954   **Chapter 35**   *The Middle East*

From the 1960s to the 1990s, many sweeping changes came to the Middle East Wars broke out between various nations and groups in the region, but hopes for peace were also high, especially in the early 1990s.

As the 1960s opened, the most bitter dispute was between Israel and its Arab neighbors, especially the Palestinians. In their struggle for nationhood, the Palestinians in 1964 formed the Palestine Liberation Organization (PLO) to eliminate Israel and to create a Palestinian state. Later, however, many Palestinians and Israelis favored a two-state solution: a state for Israelis and a state for Palestinians.

TURNING POINT

Arab-Israeli Conflict

The cease-fire between Israel and its Arab neighbors fell apart during the 1960s. A new radical regime in Syria sought the end of Israel and the creation of an Arab Palestine. Syrian and Israeli troops engaged in border clashes in early 1967. Egypt's President Nasser aided Syria by closing the Gulf of Aqaba to Israel and by having United Nations forces removed from the Israeli-Egyptian border.

Six-Day War
Fearing possible attack, Israel responded with force on June 5, 1967. At 8:45 A.M., Israeli fighter jets bore down on 17 Egyptian airfields, destroying 300 of Egypt's 350 warplanes. Hundreds of miles away, Israeli jets also demolished the air forces of Iraq, Jordan, and Syria. Israeli land troops invaded parts of Egypt and Syria. The war ended on June 11.

In the Six-Day War, Israeli forces tripled Israel's land holdings, seizing the Sinai Peninsula and the **Gaza Strip** from Egypt, and the **Golan Heights** from Syria. When Jordan entered the war, Israeli troops also took East Jerusalem.

In a move that spawned decades of upheaval, Israel occupied the **West Bank** of the Jordan River. The West Bank was land that had been designated as part of Arab Palestine in the United Nations partition plan in 1947. Palestinian Arabs had never achieved self-rule, however; they had been under Jordanian rule ever since 1949, when Jordan annexed the West Bank. Now, as a result of the Six-Day War, the area's more than 1 million Palestinians found themselves under Israeli military occupation.

Thousands more Palestinians fled to neighboring countries such as Lebanon. They turned more than ever to the PLO and its militant leader, **Yasir Arafat**, who vowed to use armed struggle to establish a Palestinian state.

The United Nations asked Israel to pull out of occupied territories and asked Arab nations to recognize Israel's right to exist. Both sides refused. Terrorist attacks and border raids continued for many years.

Oil and Conflict

Nasser died in 1970. His successor, President **Anwar el-Sadat**, led Arab forces in a new war against Israel. On October 6, 1973, Egyptian and Syrian forces launched a surprise attack on Israeli military positions on the Jewish holy day of Yom Kippur and during the Muslim holy month of Ramadan. In early battles, many Israeli planes were shot down. Egyptian troops crossed over into the Sinai, and Syria moved into the Golan Heights. With an American airlift of weapons, Israel struck back. Israeli troops crossed the Suez Canal and occupied Egyptian territory. The fighting raged until the UN negotiated a cease-fire. Secretary of State Henry Kissinger negotiated a disengagement, or military withdrawal, agreement in early 1974.

American support of Israel during the 1973 war angered Arab countries. Attempting to halt Western support, Arab oil countries imposed an embargo on oil sales to Israel's allies in 1973. Additional pressure came from the Organization of Petroleum Exporting Countries (OPEC), a cartel, or group of businesses formed to regulate production and prices among its members. OPEC, which included Arab and non-Arab oil producers, quadrupled the price of oil. However, the embargo threatened such dire economic problems for the world, including Arab countries, that it was lifted in 1974.

The Camp David Accords

In 1977, Egypt's President Sadat acted independently to break the deadlock. He accepted an invitation to visit Israel, becoming the first Arab

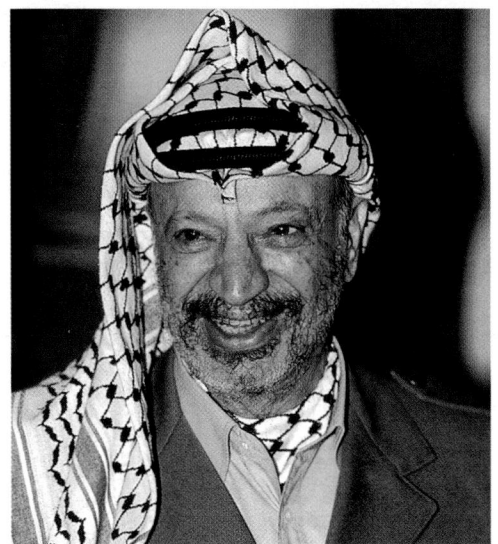

Yasir Arafat became chairman of the Palestine Liberation Organization (PLO) in 1969. He is now president of the Palestinian Authority. *Why was the PLO formed?*

leader to step in peace on Israeli soil. In a speech before Israel's parliament, Sadat called for Arab acceptance of Israel, a just solution to the Palestinian problem, and an end to hostilities between Israelis and Arabs.

The next year Sadat accepted an invitation from United States President Jimmy Carter to meet with Israeli Prime Minister **Menachem Begin** (BAY•gihn). The 12 days of meetings at Camp David in Maryland resulted in the Camp David Accords, the basis for an Arab-Israeli peace treaty.

Sadat and Begin signed the treaty in March 1979—the first time an Arab nation recognized Israel's right to exist. In return, Israel gave up the Sinai Peninsula. Many nations applauded Sadat's actions, but several Arab states broke ties with Egypt. Sadat's separate peace with Israel, they said, threatened Arab unity.

In 1981 Muslim extremists assassinated Sadat, and **Hosni Mubarak** succeeded him as president. Mubarak supported Egypt's peace with Israel but also worked to improve Egypt's relations with other Arab nations in the region. At home, he faced economic pressures caused by Egypt's soaring population and lack of resources. Another challenge to Mubarak came from a growing opposition movement led by Islamicist groups that wanted to end Western influences in Egypt.

Chapter 35   *The Middle East*   **955**

COOPERATIVE LEARNING ACTIVITY

Group Presentations Organize the class into five groups. Have each group choose a slip of paper from a box with one of the following types of people on it: Palestinians who took part in the *intifada*; Israelis who participated in the Six-Day War; Lebanese Christian merchants during Lebanon's civil war; American hostages during Iran's revolution; or Kuwaiti civilians during the Persian Gulf War. Have each group research to present its people's view of the cause of violence in the Middle East. Let each team decide the format of its presentation—skit, interview, role playing, or lecture. Suggest that one person from the group record on the chalkboard the main points of the presentation. **L2**

VIDEODISC
In the Holy Land

Side One, Chapter 26
Frame: 36164
Title: *Six-Day War: Scenes*
Ask: In 1967, which areas were captured by Israeli forces? *(the Sinai Peninsula, Golan Heights, the West Bank of Jordan River, and East Jerusalem)*

Side Two, Chapter 6
Frame: 9840
Title: *Intifadah (The Uprising)*
Subject: Different perspectives
Ask: What were the Palestinians' reasons for the uprising? *(They felt that Israeli policies had been repressive.)* How did the Israeli soldier feel about putting down the Palestinian uprising? *(He said he had been trained to fight military enemies, not civilians, and that it was very difficult.)*

The Palestinian Issue

For 20 years after the 1967 war, Arabs and Israelis could not agree on the future of the West Bank and Gaza Strip. Resenting Israeli rule, Palestinians lived in a smoldering rage. Most could get only low-paying jobs; those who protested could be arrested. During this time, the PLO staged hijackings and bombings in Israel and in foreign countries.

In 1987 the Palestinians carried out an *intifada*, or uprising, against the Israelis. The uprising spread from the Gaza Strip to the West Bank. Workers went on strike, and protesters hurled stones at Israeli soldiers and civilians. The *intifada* focused world attention on the Palestinian issue.

In 1988 the PLO's leader Arafat stated that he would renounce terrorism and accept Israel's right to exist. However, believing that Arafat would not be true to his word, Israel refused to hold talks with the PLO and to halt the growth of Jewish settlements in the West Bank.

The Peace Process

Despite continuing tensions in the Middle East, the United States pressed the Arabs and Israelis to hold peace talks beginning in 1991 in Madrid, Spain. The Israeli Prime Minister **Yitzhak Rabin** (YIHT•zahk rah•BEEN), elected in 1992, agreed in principle to exchange some of the occupied land for security guarantees and to accept self-rule by the Palestinians. Many Arab leaders also showed a new flexibility in their positions.

In 1993, Israel and the PLO recognized each other and agreed to eventual self-rule for Palestinians in the West Bank and the Gaza Strip. The Israelis also stated they would gradually withdraw militarily from both areas. By mid-1996, the Palestinians had gained significant self-rule with Yasir Arafat as their first president.

The peace process also reached out to Israel's Arab neighbors: Jordan and Syria. In 1994, Israel and Jordan signed a peace treaty, the first such agreement between Israel and an Arab country since the Israeli-Egyptian peace treaty of 1979. Syria

Images of the Times

Living in the Middle East

Daily life in the Middle East today is a blend of modern and traditional ways as well as urban and rural lifestyles.

Beirut, Lebanon, is rebuilding its neighborhoods after a long period of civil war.

Jiddah, Saudi Arabia, is a modern port city on the Red Sea that has prospered from the country's oil wealth.

956

Images of the Times

Living in the Middle East

Money from oil provides most of Kuwait's income. These oil revenues pay for medical care, education, and social security for the Kuwaitis. Kuwaitis pay no taxes other than customs duties. Because Kuwaiti families share in the country's oil wealth, they can afford to hire household help. This help and workers in other service industries come from immigrants from Asian and other Arab countries. As a result of immigration, the ethnic Kuwaiti population now makes up a minority of only 45 percent. To keep Kuwait for the Kuwaitis, the government limits voting rights to males born in the country or naturalized after 20 years of residence.

and Israel began talks, but a major obstacle between them was the future status of the Golan Heights, occupied by Israel since the 1967 war.

Increased Tensions

Although many Israelis and Palestinians supported the peace process, a large number on both sides opposed it. Some Palestinians feared that peace would lead to a less-than-independent Palestinian state subject to Israeli restrictions. Israeli opponents of the process feared that a self-governing Palestinian state could threaten Israel.

Unexpectedly, in November 1995, Rabin was shot to death by an Israeli student who opposed the peace process. Rabin's successor, **Shimon Peres** (shee•MOHN PEHR•ehs), pledged to continue efforts toward peace, and Yasir Arafat made the same commitment. However, events followed that heightened tensions and hardened positions on both sides.

Opposed to the peace process, the militant Palestinian group Hamas in early 1996 began a series of suicide bombings that killed a number of Israelis. Shocked by the violence, Israeli voters that May narrowly elected Benjamin Netanyahu (neh•tahn•YAH•hoo), leader of the conservative Likud party, over Peres and the Labor party.

After the Israeli elections, Hamas stepped up its attacks on Israeli citizens. To keep would-be bombers out of Israeli cities, Netanyahu closed off Palestinian areas from Israel. He refused to carry out promises to withdraw military forces from remaining Palestinian areas (except for the town of Hebron) until the bombings stopped.

During the late 1990s, Israelis feared continued attacks, while Palestinians protested what they felt were Israeli efforts to block progress toward their freedom. Palestinians especially opposed Jewish settlements in the West Bank. As turmoil threatened, the United States tried to get the two sides together.

With the help of Jordan's King Hussein, talks held outside of Washington, D.C., in late 1998 finally moved the peace process forward. In the Wye

World Music: Cultural Traditions, Lesson 5

World History and Art Transparency 47, *Iranian Mihrab*; 48, *The Twelve Tribes of Israel*

ABCNEWS INTERACTIVE™

VIDEODISC
Turning Points in World History

Side Two
Chapter 11

Title: *Middle East Peace Accords*
Ask: Why is it likely that the Middle East peace talks will be ongoing? *(The disputes are centuries old and many difficult issues are involved; thus, negotiations will likely take a long time.)*

Kuwait on the Persian Gulf has an economy based on oil. An increasing number of women in the Middle East, as in other areas of the world, earn university degrees and work in businesses.

The Galilee region of Israel has areas where swamps and lakes have been drained to create productive farmlands.

you don't say...

Intifada literally translated means "shaking off." The Palestinians in the Israeli-controlled East Jerusalem, the Gaza Strip, and the West Bank tried to "shake off" Israeli control and end the expansion of Jewish settlements in these areas.

REFLECTING ON THE TIMES

1. What impact has oil had on various countries of the Middle East?
2. What country in the Middle East is rebuilding after a long period of civil war?

957

Who? What? Where? When?

Nobel Peace Prizes were awarded in 1978 to Anwar el-Sadat and Menachem Begin for signing the Camp David Accords and in 1994 to Yasir Arafat, Yitzhak Rabin, and Shimon Peres for starting the peace process between Israel and the PLO.

ANSWERS TO REFLECTING ON THE TIMES

1. The economies of countries such as Kuwait and Saudi Arabia are based on oil. Oil production has brought prosperity to these countries.
2. Lebanon

Visualizing History
Ehud Barak is the most decorated soldier in Israel's history. He was the commander of an elite commando unit and later head of military intelligence.
Answer to Caption: *Barak wanted to resume peace talks with Syria and the Palestinians.*

Independent Practice

📁 Guided Reading Activity 35-2 **L1**

Multicultural Have students research to make a chart that shows the majority religion, official language, and current leader of Egypt, Israel, Iran, Iraq, Jordan, Lebanon, and Syria. **L2**

Literature Have students write a one-page report on the extent of censorship under the Shiite regime in Iran, using as an example the case of the novelist Salman Rushdie. **L3**

Linking Past and Present

The Hanging Gardens of Babylon, one of the Seven Wonders of the Ancient World, were built about 2,600 years ago by Nebuchadnezzar. In the 1980s, Saddam Hussein started rebuilding the gardens using 15 million bricks baked in the ancient way. The Persian Gulf War ended this ambitious project.

Visualizing History Israel's most decorated war hero, **Ehud Barak**, was elected prime minister in 1999. *What was Barak's position regarding the peace process?*

River Memorandum, Israel agreed to hand over more land to the Palestinians, and the Palestinians agreed to combat terrorism.

Progress seemed to fade, however, when Netanyahu refused to turn over the agreed-upon land. Another setback was the Jordanian king's death in early 1999.

In May of 1999, Israelis elected a new leader, **Ehud Barak**. The former chief of staff of the Israeli Defense Forces, Barak promised to renew the peace process. Jordan's new King **Abdullah II** also pledged to work toward this goal.

Lebanon

The Palestinian issue also affected neighboring Lebanon. In 1975 a civil war broke out between Lebanon's Christian and Muslim groups. As the Muslim population grew to outnumber Christians, unrest had spread. Adding to these tensions was the presence of armed PLO forces in the country. Most Lebanese Muslims supported the PLO; most Lebanese Christians did not.

As fighting erupted, the weakened Lebanese government asked Syria to send in troops to keep

order. In 1982 the Israelis invaded southern Lebanon to wipe out PLO bases housing Israel's attackers. A multinational peacekeeping force finally arranged a PLO withdrawal to other Arab countries; however, private armies continued fighting among themselves. After foreign troops became victims of terrorist bombings, the peacekeeping force departed by 1985.

In the early 1990s, some signs of hope appeared. Lebanon agreed to give Muslims an equitable say in the political process, and the various private armies in **Beirut** pulled out of the city, which made rapid strides in rebuilding. By the mid-1990s, Lebanon had made progress toward stability. Tensions remained, however, and both Syria and Israel kept troops in the country.

Iran's Revolution

During the 1960s and 1970s, Iran became a major military power in the Persian Gulf area. Shah Mohammad Reza Pahlavi worked to build a modern industrial economy based on oil. Shiite Muslim religious leaders, however, disliked the influx of Western values into Iran and called for a return to Muslim traditions. The shah silenced all protests and dissent.

In the late 1970s, anti-shah forces rallied around **Ayatollah Ruhollah Khomeini** (ko•MAY•nee), a powerful Shiite Muslim leader, living in exile in France. Khomeini had long preached the overthrow of the shah and the creation of a republic. By January 1979, widespread unrest forced the shah to flee Iran. Khomeini returned to form a government based on Islamic laws and traditions.

Iranian hatred for the shah was also directed at the United States. The Americans had long supported the shah, valuing Iran as a major supplier of oil and a reliable buffer against Soviet expansion. Anti-American feelings were so strong that on November 4, 1979, militants stormed the American embassy in Tehran, the capital, and took 52 Americans hostage. United States President Carter's efforts to free the hostages were unsuccessful, thus sealing his defeat in the 1980 presidential election. Only after his successor, Ronald Reagan, was sworn in on January 20, 1981, did Iran release the Americans.

During most of the 1980s, Iran fought a devastating war with neighboring Iraq. The Iraqis first seized a disputed border area and then pushed into Iran. The Iranians, hoping to spread their revolution into Iraq, responded with a fierce counterattack. The Iraqis had superior weapons and used poison gas; the Iranians, however, had more troops.

MEETING SPECIAL NEEDS ACTIVITY

Study Strategy Give students outline maps of the Middle East. Have them locate and label the following places mentioned in this section: Syria, Israel, Egypt, Lebanon, Iran, Iraq, Kuwait, Saudi Arabia, Sinai Peninsula, Golan Heights, Gaza Strip, West Bank, Gulf of Aqaba, Suez Canal, Persian Gulf, Beirut, and Baghdad. Remind students to title their map and to make a legend. **L1 LEP**

Curry, Magnum

Mohsen Shandiz, SYGMA

Mortal Enemies

This giant portrait of Iraqi President Saddam Hussein (left) overlooks a Baghdad street. An inscription under the portrait in red Arabic characters praises the Arab forces in [its] struggle with its Islamic but non-Arab enemy [neigh]bor, Iran. In Iran the stern gaze of the Ayatollah [Ru]ollah Khomeini peers from a mural behind [wom]en attending the departure of soldiers for the bat[tlefro]nt in September 1988. With his zealous view of [Isla]m, Khomeini, who died in 1989, regarded the sec[ular] Saddam Hussein as both an enemy and an infidel.

The Middle East has changed profoundly since World War II. What was once an area largely held by the Ottoman Empire and then by European colonial powers is now a region of independent nations. With the end of imperialism came the rise of nationalism. At the same time parts of the Islamic world have witnessed the rise of a fiercely held fundamentalism that views the secular world, even the Muslim secular world, as evil and corrupt. In this context Iran and Iraq fought a long and devastating war that lasted from 1980 to 1988. ⊕

Chapter 35   *The Middle East*   **959**

TEACH

Tell students that the dispute between Iran and Iraq was about religious and political issues more than it was a struggle over territory. Before the ayatollah came to power in Iran, he listed his enemies as, "First the Shah; then the American Satan; then Saddam Hussein and his infidel Ba'ath party." Iraq's Ba'ath party was made up of Sunni Muslims and promoted pan-Arabism. It was also the party in charge of expelling Khomeini in 1978 at the request of the shah of Iran. Iran is not an Arab country, and most of its people are Shiite Muslims. Most Arabs are Sunni Muslims.

Linking Past and Present

Iran and Iraq The present-day countries of Iran and Iraq were sites of ancient empires and kingdoms that are often called "cradles of civilization." Iran was part of the Persian Empire; Iraq, part of ancient Mesopotamia, is heir to the civilizations of Sumer, Akkad, Babylonia, and Assyria. The two peoples clashed in ancient times also. In 539 B.C., Cyrus the Great, founder of the Persian Empire, captured the city of Babylon and conquered the Babylonian Empire.

People in World History
Profile 68

 Geography and History
Activity 35

ASSESS

Check for Understanding

Assign Section 2 Assessment as homework or as an in-class activity.

Use Interactive Tutor Self-Assessment Software to review Section 2.

Evaluate

Section Quiz 35-2

Use the Testmaker to create a customized quiz for Section 2.

Reteach

Have students take turns summarizing major events in Israel, Egypt, Lebanon, Iran, and Iraq from 1967 to the present.

Reading Essentials and Study Guide 35-2

Enrich

Have students research and give a short oral report on how the 1973 oil embargo affected daily life in the United States.

CLOSE

Have students create a time line on the chalkboard that shows major events in the Middle East from 1967 to the present.

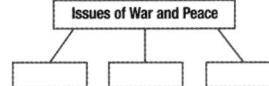

Footnotes **to H**istory

War and the Environment

During the Persian Gulf War, Iraqi troops spilled an estimated 250 million gallons (947 million l) of Kuwait's oil into the Persian Gulf. Thousands of birds, fish, and other marine life perished when the oil spill spread for 350 miles (563 km) along the Persian Gulf coastline.

When both sides targeted commercial vessels in the Persian Gulf, the United States sent naval forces to protect the vital shipping lanes running through the **Strait of Hormuz**. In 1988 Iran and Iraq, both exhausted, agreed to end the fighting.

After Khomeini's death a year later, Iran's leaders worked to rebuild Iran's crippled economy. In 1997 a moderate religious leader, Mohammad Khatami, became president. Khatami supported a reduction in press censorship and closer economic ties with the West. Some Iranian leaders, however, opposed Khatami's liberalization measures. A struggle between the moderates who support Khatami and the militant conservatives continues to preoccupy Iran.

Iraq's Bid for Power

The war with Iran left Iraq near collapse and in debt to its small, but oil-rich, neighbor, **Kuwait**. In August 1990, Iraq's President **Saddam Hussein** sent Iraqi forces into Kuwait, claiming that the country was a historic part of Iraq. In occupying Kuwait, Hussein also wanted to expand Iraq's influence in the Persian Gulf region.

The Persian Gulf War

Fearing an Iraqi attack, oil-rich Saudi Arabia asked the United States for protection. United States President George Bush responded by sending troops to the Saudi desert. Eight Arab nations also sent forces to Saudi Arabia. At the urging of the UN, Western nations, the Soviet Union, and Japan imposed a trade embargo, or a ban on the export of goods, against Iraq.

In January 1991, after a UN deadline for an Iraqi withdrawal expired, the United States rained medium-range missiles on the Iraqi capital of Baghdad. During the next month, coalition forces from the United States, Great Britain, France, Syria, Saudi Arabia, Egypt, and Kuwait conducted a massive air war against Iraq. Iraq responded by launching missiles against Saudi Arabia and Israel. Iraqi forces in Kuwait also set fire to oil fields. When Iraq still refused to withdraw, coalition land forces moved into Iraq and Kuwait, defeating the Iraqis after a mere 100 hours of fighting. With Kuwait freed, a cease-fire went into effect. Allied war deaths totaled just over 100, with tens of thousands of Iraqi soldiers believed killed.

Iraq After the War

After their victory, coalition forces withdrew from Iraq. Saddam Hussein, however, remained in power. He brutally crushed Kurdish and Shiite groups in Iraq that used the war to rebel against his authority. He also appeared to be rebuilding his stocks of chemical and biological weapons.

In 1997 a prolonged confrontation with Saddam Hussein began after Iraq expelled the American members of the UN team monitoring Iraq for chemical and biological weapons. The following year, Iraq expelled the entire UN monitoring team, in violation of UN agreements signed after the end of the Persian Gulf War.

In 1998 and 1999 the United States and Britain attacked Iraq in an operation known as Desert Fox. The purpose of the strikes was to hit military and security targets that allow Iraq to produce, store, maintain, and deliver weapons of mass destruction.

SECTION 2 ASSESSMENT

Main Idea
1. Use a diagram like the one below to summarize the issues of peace and war in the Middle East since the mid-1980s.

Issues of War and Peace

Recall
2. **Define** disengagement, cartel, *intifada*, embargo.
3. **Identify** Yasir Arafat, Anwar el-Sadat, Menachem Begin, Hosni Mubarak, Yitzhak Rabin, Shimon Peres, Ehud Barak, Abdullah II, Ayatollah Ruhollah Khomeini, Saddam Hussein.

Critical Thinking
4. **Analyzing Information** How did the Persian Gulf War affect the Middle East?

Understanding Themes
5. **Cooperation** What were the major points of the 1993 agreement between Israel and the Palestinians?

SECTION 2 ASSESSMENT ANSWERS

1. Issues of war: Arab-Israeli conflict led to Six-Day War; conflict led to war between Israel, Egypt, and Syria in 1973; Arab countries imposed an oil embargo against Israel's allies; Israeli rule caused Palestinian uprisings and terrorist attacks; religious tensions caused civil war in Lebanon; Iran and Iraq fought in the 1980s; Persian Gulf War resulted from Iraqi aggression. Issues of peace: withdrawal agreement ended 1973 war; Camp David Accords led to Arab-Israeli peace treaty; Arab-Israeli peace-talks held during the 1990s

2. All terms are defined in the Glossary.

3. Arafat, 955; Sadat, 955; Begin, 955; Mubarak, 955; Rabin, 956; Peres, 957; Barak, 958; Abdullah II, 958; Khomeini, 958; Hussein, 960

4. It reduced Iraq's power in the region.

5. **COOPERATION** Israel and the PLO recognized each other and agreed to eventual self-government for Palestinians in the West Bank and the Gaza Strip and a gradual withdrawal of Israeli forces.

Preparing a Bibliography

In the last chapter, you wrote a research report on some topic of interest. To complete your report, you have one more step—preparing a bibliography.

Learning the Skill

A bibliography is a list of sources used in a research report. These sources include: books; articles from newspapers, magazines, and journals; interviews; films, videotapes, audiotapes, and compact discs.

There are two main reasons to write a bibliography. First, those who read your report may want to learn more about the topic. Second, a bibliography supports the reliability of your report.

A bibliography should follow a definite format. The entry for each source must contain all the information needed to find that source: author, title, publisher information, and publication date. You should have this information already on note cards.

In a bibliography, arrange entries alphabetically by the author's last name. The following are accepted formats for bibliography entries, followed by sample entries.

Books

Author's last name, first name. <u>Full Title</u>. Place of publication: publisher, copyright date.
Holiday, Laurel. <u>Children of Israel, Children of Palestine: Our Own True Stories</u>. New York: Washington Square Press, 1999.

Articles

Author's last name, first name. "Title of Article." <u>Name of Periodical</u> in which article appears, Volume number (date of issue): page numbers.
Watson, Bruce. "The New Peace Corps in the New Kazakhstan." <u>Smithsonian</u>, Vol. 25 (August 1994): pp. 26–35.

Other Sources

For other kinds of sources, adapt the format for book entries.

Practicing the Skill

Review the sample bibliography below for a report on Mexico. Then answer the questions that follow.

Castañeda, Jorge G. <u>The Mexican Shock: Its Meaning for the United States</u>. New York: The New Press, 1995.
Oppenheimer, Andres. Bordering on Chaos: Mexico's Roller-Coaster Journey to Prosperity. New York, New York, Little, Brown & Co, 1998.
Cockburn, A., "The Fire This Time." <u>Condé Nast Traveller</u>, Vol. 30 (June 1995): pp. 104–113.
Smith, G. "The Brave New World of Mexican Politics." Business Week (August 28, 1995) pp. 42–44.

1. Are the bibliography entries in the correct order? Why or why not?
2. What is wrong with the second book listing?
3. What is missing from the second article listing?

Applying the Skill

Compile a bibliography for your research report. Include at least five sources, preferably a mix of books and articles. Exchange bibliographies with another student and check each other for proper format and arrangement.

For More Practice

Turn to the Skill Practice in the Chapter Assessment on page 971 for more practice in preparing a bibliography.

 The **Glencoe Skillbuilder Interactive Workbook**, Level 2 provides instruction and practice in key social studies skills.

TEACH

Preparing a Bibliography Write the following list on the chalkboard: *Author's name, Title, Place of publication, Publisher, Date of publication.* Ask students to find this information for their textbook. If necessary, guide students to the title and copyright pages. Have volunteers write the correct information from their text opposite the five categories on the chalkboard. Then tell students that this information is required for books in a bibliography. Direct students to read the skill and complete the practice questions to learn more about the purposes and formats of a bibliography.

Additional Practice

 Skill Reinforcement Activity 35

Writer's Guidebook, Lessons 9, 13

GLENCOE
TECHNOLOGY

Glencoe's **Skillbuilder Interactive Workbook, Level 2** This interactive CD-ROM promotes student mastery of key social studies skills.

ANSWERS TO PRACTICING THE SKILL

1. No; the entries should be in alphabetical order by author's last name.
2. The title of the book should be underlined.
3. The volume number is missing, and the title of the periodical should be underlined.

1945 Arab nations form the Arab League.

1979 Israel and Egypt sign peace treaty.

1994 Jordan and Israel end their state of war.

1999 King Hussein of Jordan dies.

Section 3

Challenges Facing the Middle East

Guide to Reading

Read to Find Out
Main Idea *People in the Middle East have handled the conflict between traditional culture and modern values in various ways.*

▶ **Terms to Define**
sovereignty, desalination, fundamentalism

▶ **People to Meet**
Shimon Peres, Hafez al-Assad, Benjamin Netanyahu, Golda Meir, Tansu Çiller

▶ **Places to Locate**
West Bank, Gaza Strip, Jerusalem, Golan Heights, Saudi Arabia, Cairo, Turkey, Euphrates River

The Storyteller

An Israeli observer records the expulsion of Arabs from Israeli-held territory: "Masses of people marched on behind the next. Women bore bundles and sacks on their heads; mothers dragged children after them. From close up it was sad to watch this trek of thousands going into exile. As soon as they left the city, they began to divest themselves of things … and the roads were cluttered with the belongings that people had abandoned to make their walk easier."

—from *The People of Nowhere*, Danny Rubenstein, 1991

Palestinian Arabs in exile

962 **Chapter 35** *The Middle East*

The tragic cycle of violence, wars between nations, and civil wars within nations have brought much suffering to the people of the Middle East since the end of World War II. Since 1948 Israelis and Arabs have fought four major wars. The civil war in Lebanon largely destroyed the country and killed and wounded thousands of civilians. Besides the lost lives, billions of dollars of precious resources are spent each year on weapons. If you speak to Middle Easterners about their hopes for the future, they consistently include peace and stability. But peace and stability have been hard to achieve.

War and Peace

Since Egypt and Israel agreed to peace in 1979, major steps have been taken in ending the state of war between Israel and the rest of the Arab world. In 1993, the Israelis and the Palestinians signed an agreement known as the Oslo Accords. A year later, Jordan and Israel finally ended their conflict. Contacts also began between Israel and Syria for the settlement of issues related to the Six-Day War.

West Bank and Gaza Strip

After successful peace efforts in the early 1990s, Israeli-Palestinian relations worsened in 1997. Hamas bombings and the tough position of Israel's conservative government threatened the peace process. Increasing tensions delayed indefinitely any resolution of the major issues dividing Israelis and Palestinians. These issues include the timing of Israeli military withdrawals from Palestinian areas in the **West Bank** and **Gaza Strip**, the status of **Jerusalem**, and the future of Israeli Jewish settlers on the West Bank. The election of Ehud Barak, however, raised hopes and gave the peace process a new momentum.

SECTION THEME

▶ **Cultural Diffusion** Middle Eastern countries search for a reconciliation between traditional and modern values.

Guide to Reading
For reading strategies to help students read effectively see pages 12–13.

Vocabulary Pre-check

◉ Use the Vocabulary PuzzleMaker for Chapter 35 to create a crossword puzzle to reinforce section terms. **L1 LEP**

📁 Use Vocabulary Activity 35 to introduce vocabulary terms. **L1 LEP**

FOCUS

Section Objective
Describe how people in the Middle East have handled the conflict between traditional ways and modern values.

BELLRINGER
Motivational Activity

Before taking roll at the beginning of the class period, project Section Focus Transparency 35-3 and have students answer the activity questions.

📁 This activity is also available as a blackline master.

SECTION RESOURCES

📁 **Reproducible Masters**
- Lecture Notes 35-3
- Reproducible Lesson Plan 35-3
- Guided Reading Activity 35-3
- People in World History Profile 67
- Reteaching Activity 35
- Enrichment Activity 35
- Section Quiz 35-3

- Performance Assessment Activity 35
- Spanish Chapter Summary 35
- Reading Essentials and Study Guide 35-3

📗 **Transparencies**
- Section Focus Transparency 35-3

Multimedia
◉ Vocabulary PuzzleMaker Software
◉ Interactive Tutor Self-Assessment Software
◉ Testmaker

Still another major issue is the resettlement of Palestinians who fled their homes beginning in the 1948 Arab-Israeli conflict. Today, more than 6 million Palestinian Arabs live in the Middle East, North Africa, Europe, and the Americas. About 2 million Palestinians live in the West Bank and Gaza Strip. In addition, about 850,000 Israeli Arabs live inside Israel itself and try to combine Israeli citizenship with their Arab heritage.

Golan Heights and Lebanon

Relations between Israel and its northern neighbor, Syria, also need to improve before a general peace can be achieved. The **Golan Heights**, which has been in Israeli hands since 1967, is a major area of dispute. Israeli Prime Minister **Shimon Peres** and Syrian President **Hafez al-Assad** committed themselves to settling this issue, but talks between Israel and Syria were deadlocked after the election of Israeli Prime Minister **Benjamin Netanyahu** in 1996. Three years later, Ehud Barak's election enabled negotiations to resume.

In neighboring Lebanon, the civil war has ended, and the country is fast rebuilding its economy. In the south of Lebanon, Israeli forces hold a strip of land for security purposes. They are opposed by Shiite Muslim guerrillas. Attacks occur repeatedly between the two sides.

The Elusive Dream

Unity among Arab people has long been a powerful desire. For centuries, people throughout the Arab world have shared strong cultural ties, such as language, traditions, religious beliefs, and a common history. British and French imperialism in the 1800s and 1900s increased division among the Arabs and created numerous states with artificial boundaries. Many Arabs thought that with independence from foreign powers they would be able to achieve unity. They began to take steps to strengthen the common links among them.

In 1945 political unity seemed within reach when Egypt, Transjordan (present-day Jordan), Syria, Lebanon, Iraq, **Saudi Arabia**, and Yemen formed the **Arab League**. By 1995 its membership had grown to 22 participants (including the PLO), with a population of about 200 million. But disputes among nations and their unwillingness to give up sovereignty, or independent decision-making powers, blocked moves toward further unity.

Some political leaders and government officials have advocated a cautious move toward

Banking and financial services are important to the economies of many Middle Eastern countries. *In what other ways have Middle Eastern economies changed in the past 40 years?*

unity. They formed cooperative councils among their countries to coordinate trade, economic development, and travel. Peoples' aspirations and political realities, in time, may lead to some type of loose union in which each state retains independence and contributes to stability in the region.

Economic Developments

In the past 40 years the Middle East has seen greatly changed economic and social conditions. Light and heavy industry has been developed in most countries of the region. Irrigation for agriculture spread as hydroelectric projects were constructed on major rivers. At the same time as production rose and jobs became available, the region's population grew rapidly. If the current rate of increase continues, the population will double in the next 25 years. The increase has been most apparent in major urban centers. By the year 2000, more than 7 cities had populations exceeding 3 million each. The largest is **Cairo**, Egypt's capital, with 12 million people. It is also the largest city on the entire African continent. The needs and the challenges of rapidly growing populations are on the minds of every major leader in the Middle East.

Oil and Water

Oil-producing countries of the Middle East have built wealthy and highly developed societies

Chapter 35 *The Middle East* **963**

TEACH

Guided Practice

THEME Cultural Diffusion

Remind students that cultural diffusion is the spread of ideas or ways of living from one culture to another. Help students find examples of cultural diffusion in this section. (*Arabs in Israel combining Israeli citizenship with Arab heritage; goods and ideas from the West changing Islamic society*) **L1 LEP**

Visualizing History Have students differentiate between the modern and traditional styles of clothing shown in the picture. Tell students that the long, loose robe, called a *thwab*, and the head covering, a *keffiyah*, are suited to the climate of the Middle East.
Answer to Caption: *Industry has developed in most Middle Eastern countries. Agricultural production has increased because of irrigation.*

Economics Have students make a flowchart that shows how economic development (industrialization, improved agriculture) in the Middle East has led to challenges (increase in population, gap between oil-producing and non-oil-producing countries, water shortages). **L2**

COOPERATIVE LEARNING ACTIVITY

Panel Discussions Organize the class into five groups. Have each group choose one of the following topics: role of women in Muslim nations; dam building on the Nile and Euphrates Rivers; Middle Eastern desalination projects; dispersal of oil wealth among citizens in oil-producing countries; or the debate about moving toward more democratic government in Kuwait and Saudi Arabia. Tell students to research their topic using recent newspaper, magazine, and journal indexes. Suggest that each group break its topic into subtopics so that each group member has a specific topic to research. Before each group presents its panel discussion, have students choose a moderator for their panel. **L3**

Have students use the **Chapter 35 Student Web Activity** at worldhistory.glencoe.com for in-depth study of the Euphrates River.

Independent Practice

 Guided Reading Activity 35-3 **L1**

People in World History Profile 67

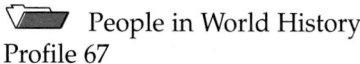 Linking Past and Present

Water from the Euphrates

Because Turkey had not worked out an agreement with Syria and Iraq for sharing water from the Euphrates, the World Bank refused to extend Turkey a loan to build Ataturk Dam. Turkey obtained independent financing to build the dam.

ANSWERS

Answers will vary but should mention shadoofs and other early technology compared to modern dams and reservoirs; ancient peoples include Sumerians, Babylonians, and Persians; modern lands: Turkey, Syria, Iraq. Turkey needs water to irrigate farmland to supply food for its people, but its dams should not hurt the people of Iraq and Syria.

 CURRICULUM CONNECTION

GOVERNMENT

The royal family of Saudi Arabia holds daily *majlis*, audiences with citizens who come to petition for help in settling disputes or to receive special aid from the government. The royal princes receive up to 300 people a day; the king, far fewer and on a less regular basis.

964 Chapter 35 *The Middle East*

---

in recent years. The region's highest per capita incomes, or the total national incomes divided by the number of people in each nation, are found in the Persian Gulf countries. Their prosperity, however, contrasts sharply with the poverty of some other countries in the region. Hoping to lessen the gap between rich and poor nations, oil-producing countries have invested in and loaned large sums of money to the non-oil producing countries.

Another valuable, but scarce, resource in the Middle East is water. The region has long had critical water shortages caused by an unequal distribution of water. However, as Middle Eastern countries develop industrially and face population increases, they are working to meet their water needs. For example, **Turkey** has built dams and other water facilities on the **Euphrates River** to irrigate fertile, but dry, areas.

Other countries with water shortages include Israel, Syria, and Jordan. If all three countries settle their political differences, they will be able to coordinate their water resources and build plants for desalination, the removal of salt from seawater to make it usable for drinking and farming. In 1997 Israel and Jordan settled a dispute about the sharing of water. At present, both countries are constructing dams on the Yarmuk River, which serves as part of the Jordanian-Israeli border.

Social Change

Throughout the Middle East, modernization has turned traditional societies upside down. With the discovery of oil, desert cities bloomed and new industrial areas were created. Urban areas now contain high-rise offices, shopping centers, and freeways. Foreign investment has created new jobs and raised living standards. New wealth has led to

Student Web Activity 35

Visit the *World History: The Human Experience* Web site at **world history.glencoe.com** and click on *Chapter 35—Student Web Activities* for an activity relating to the Euphrates River.

 Science and Technology

Water From the Euphrates

Like their ancient ancestors, people in the Middle East today rely on the Euphrates River for water. The technology used for obtaining the water, however, has changed considerably over the centuries. To ensure their water supply, the people of Turkey today rely on a series of huge dams on the Euphrates. The dams' reservoirs provide water for Turkey's expanding industries and urban centers.

Turkey's solution for its water problem, however, deprives Syria and Iraq of water from the same river. Iraq potentially is the worst off because it is the last country that is situated along the river.

The Turks claim they need the river to better their economy. They hope to turn more of the Anatolian Peninsula into farmland. Crops grown there are needed to feed Turkey's growing population, they say.

Syria and Iraq claim that Turkey does not own the entire Euphrates River. They point out that not only will they lose water from the reduced flow, but that more will be lost through evaporation from the Turkish reservoirs.

Experts state that this crisis can be eased by all three countries repairing existing equipment, improving irrigation and water conservation methods, expanding water recycling, and sharing water equitably. The countries also need to grow some crops that do not require so much water. Above all, experts state that the countries need to better manage their population growth.

Turkish dam on the Euphrates River

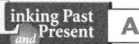 Linking Past and Present **ACTIVITY**

Compare water technology today with that used in the past. What peoples relied on the Euphrates in ancient times? What lands depend on the Euphrates today? Does Turkey have a right to build dams on the river?

964 Chapter 35 *The Middle East*

MEETING SPECIAL NEEDS ACTIVITY

Learning Style: Visual/Spatial Have students create a bulletin-board display of various aspects of traditional Islamic life. They might include drawings of traditional dress for both men and women and photographs of Islamic religious rituals or such rituals of daily life as eating, entertaining, and shopping. Be sure all images are clearly labeled with explanatory captions. **L1 LEP**

better education and health care. In addition, women in the region have made a growing impact on business and politics. In politics, for example, **Golda Meir** (meh•IHR), who served as Israeli prime minister from 1969 to 1974, was the modern Middle East's first female head of government. In the early 1990s **Tansu Çiller** (TAHN•soo see•LAHR) of Turkey became the first female prime minister to govern a Middle Eastern Muslim country.

Challenges

Rapid change in the Middle East also had its negative side. Crime rose, and the gap between the rich and the poor grew. The greater independence of family members led to a loosening of traditional family ties. The availability of cars, TVs, VCRs, and personal computers brought a new materialism to daily life. Many people in the Middle East blamed the West for the new social trends that they did not like.

Saudi Arabia

In Saudi Arabia, the birthplace of Islam, most people have fiercely resisted undesirable Western cultural influences. For hundreds of years, the land that is now Saudi Arabia was divided among many tribes. During the early 1900s, these groups joined together under the Saud family to form the kingdom of Saudi Arabia. Beginning in the mid-1900s, the Saudi royal family used income from the oil industry to support modernization programs. However, the family, despite its conservative policies, faces opposition from traditional Saudis who resist change. By contrast, more liberal lifestyles prevail in Iraq, Lebanon, Syria, Jordan, Egypt, and Israel.

A Return to Religion

In recent years many Middle Easterners have sought solutions to their problems in fundamentalism, or adherence to traditional religious values. This development has also occurred, although in different ways, in other parts of the world. In the United States, conservative Protestantism has flourished and has expressed itself politically; in India, Hindu nationalists have won much support.

Some observers view fundamentalism as a natural reaction by people who are overwhelmed by massive change and desire security in long-valued traditions. Other experts, however, point out that the continued growth of religious fundamentalism deepens mistrust and hardens divisions at a time when the world's peoples need to develop greater understanding and cooperation.

In the Middle East, the revival of traditional religion has increased the political influence of Islam in many countries. Since 1979, Shiite Muslim religious leaders have ruled Iran. In Turkey, Egypt, and Jordan, the political power of Islam poses a serious challenge to secular forms of government. Israel's Jewish right-wing religious parties, although small in size, have contributed to the rising strength of political conservatism and nationalism there.

The most direct confrontation in the Middle East between traditional religion and secularism has occurred in Turkey. In 1996 Necmettin Erbakan became Turkey's first prime minister from an Islamic party. Military leaders, however, saw Erbakan's pro-Islamicist policies as a threat to Turkey's secular political traditions. They forced Erbakan from power in 1997, and secular politicians then formed a new government. Many of the new leaders believe that the country's Islamic schools promote militancy among students. They have proposed a plan that would force the closing of many Islamic schools. Islamicist supporters have protested this plan as a violation of their religious freedom.

Egypt also has seen religious conflict. Since 1992, groups in southern Egypt have sought to oust President Hosni Mubarak's secular government and establish a government based on Islamic principles. By 2000, stability seemed to have come to Egypt as the government placed more emphasis on economic growth and social well-being.

ASSESS

Check for Understanding

Assign Section 3 Assessment as homework or as an in-class activity.

 Use Interactive Tutor Self-Assessment Software to review Section 3.

Evaluate

Section Quiz 35-3

 Use the Testmaker to create a customized quiz for Section 3.

Reteach

Have students make charts that describe the positive and the negative aspects of the political, economic, and social changes that have taken place since the 1970s in the Middle East.

Reteaching Activity 35

Reading Essentials and Study Guide 35-3

Enrich

Have students write a short report on the effect of Islamic militant groups on the Israel-PLO peace process since 1994.

Enrichment Activity 35

CLOSE

Have students hold a mock UN meeting in which they offer possible solutions to Middle East problems.

SECTION 3 ASSESSMENT

Main Idea
1. Use a chart like the one below to show how Middle Eastern countries dealt with conflict between traditionalism and modernism.

Traditionalism vs. Modernism

Political Response	Religious Response

Recall
2. **Define** sovereignty, desalination, fundamentalism.
3. **Identify** Shimon Peres, Hafez al-Assad, Benjamin Netanyahu, Arab League, Golda Meir, Tansu Çiller.

Critical Thinking
4. **Applying Information** How has religious fundamentalism impacted the Middle East?

Understanding Themes
5. **Cultural Diffusion** How have foreign influences affected modern Middle Eastern society?

SECTION 3 ASSESSMENT ANSWERS

1. Political response: censorship in Saudi Arabia; more liberal lifestyle in Iraq, Lebanon, Syria, Jordan, Egypt, and Israel. Religious response: rise of religious fundamentalism; Shiite Muslim leaders have ruled Iran; threat to secular government from Islam in Turkey, Egypt, and Jordan

2. All terms are defined in the Glossary.
3. Peres, 963; Assad, 963; Netanyahu, 963; Arab League, 963; Meir, 964; Çiller, 965
4. Muslim fundamentalists have taken control of the government in Iran and pose a challenge to secular governments in other nations. Fundamentalist Jewish parties have contributed to the rise of political conservatism in Israel.

5. **CULTURAL DIFFUSION** Foreign investment and material goods have affected Middle Eastern society. Many Middle Easterners blame the West for materialistic values that threaten cherished traditions.

Block Schedule

Team Teaching This selection of modern poems may be presented in a team-teaching context, in conjunction with English or Language Arts.

Modern Poems

Historical Connection

The three poems in this feature were written by poets from developing countries: Mexico, Turkey, and Nigeria. The increasing prominence in the West of literature from developing nations suggests that people in Europe and the United States are more aware of the achievements of people in other parts of the world.

Background Information

Setting The setting for each poem appears to be the homeland of the poet. Students may wish to discuss, however, whether these poems could be set in another country just as well.

Literary Elements Personification means giving human characteristics to an inanimate object. For example, in "The Window," Torres Bodet talks about the world issuing a "great, rough, hoarse cry." Giving the world the power of speech is personification.

A stanza is a collection of lines in a poem, separated from other lines or stanzas. In "Once Upon a Time," most stanzas are six lines long. In modern poetry, stanza length varies.

Metaphor is a comparison of two objects. For example, Nazim Hikmet compares the earth to "a mere toy next to the sun."

966 Chapter 35 *The Middle East*

Literature

from

Modern Poems

by
Jaime Torres Bodet,
Nazim Hikmet, and
Gabriel Okara

*M*odern poets have continued to explore both universal themes, such as friendship and loneliness, as well as individual preferences for a particular place or group of people.

*T*he following poem was written by one of Mexico's greatest writers, Jaime Torres Bodet, who was born in 1902 and was active in politics. Bodet served the government as an administrator and diplomat. In this poem, Bodet urges people to take risks in their lives. Bodet died in 1974.

The Window

Translated from Spanish by George Kearns

You closed the window, And it was the world,
the world that wanted to enter, all at once,
the world that gave that great shout,
that great, deep, rough cry
you did not want to hear—and now
will never call to you again as it called today,
asking your mercy!

The whole of life was in that cry:
the wind, the sea, the land
with its poles and its tropics,
the unreachable skies,
the ripened grain in the resounding wheat field,
the thick heat above the wine presses,
dawn on the mountains, shadowy woods,
parched lips stuck together longing for
cool water condensed in pools,
and all pleasures, all sufferings,
all loves, all hates,
were in this day, anxiously
asking your mercy …

But you were afraid of life,
And you remained alone,
behind the closed and silent window,
not understanding that the world calls to a man
only once that way, and with that kind of cry,
with that great, rough, hoarse cry!

*A*BOUT THE AUTHOR

Jaime Torres Bodet was supervisor of Mexico's libraries in the 1920s. Later he served as director-general of the United Nations Educational, Scientific, and Cultural Organization (UNESCO).

Nazim Hikmet's outspoken views on behalf of the poor and oppressed in Turkey led to his imprisonment by the government. When he was released in 1951, he left the country. Many of his works were not published in Turkey during his lifetime, yet he became a popular hero there.

Gabriel Okara received little formal schooling in Nigeria. He learned enough on his own, however, to become a widely respected writer. He usually writes in his native language, Ijaw.

Nazim Hikmet, who lived from 1902 to 1963, often criticized the government of his native Turkey for serving only the wealthy. In 1951 he left Turkey, never to return, and settled in Europe. His sympathy for the peasants of his country, his love of nature, and his hope for humanity are all suggested in the following poem.

The World, My Friends, My Enemies, You, and the Earth

*Translated from Turkish by
Randy Blasing and Mutlu Konuk*

I'm wonderfully happy I came into the world,
I love its earth, its light, its struggle, and its bread.
Even though I know its dimensions from pole to pole to the
    centimeter,
and while I'm not unaware that it's a mere toy next to the sun,
the world for me is unbelievably big.
I would have liked to go around the world
and see the fish, the fruits, and the stars that I haven't seen.
However,
I made my European trip only in books and pictures.
In all my life I never got one letter
        with its blue stamp canceled in Asia.
Me and our corner grocer,
we're both mightily unknown in America.
Nevertheless,
from China to Spain, from the Cape of Good Hope to Alaska,
in every nautical mile, in every kilometer, I have friends and
       enemies.
Such friends that we haven't met even once—
we can die for the same bread, the same freedom, the same dream.
And such enemies that they're thirsty for my blood,
        I am thirsty for their blood.
My strength
is that I'm not alone in this big world.
The world and its people are no secret in my heart,
      no mystery in my science.
Calmly and openly
    I took my place
        in the great struggle.
And without it,
    you and the earth
       are not enough for me.
And yet you are astonishingly beautiful,
      the earth is warm and beautiful.

Nazim Hikmet

FOCUS

Before students read the poems, have them speculate about what writers from such different countries as Mexico, Turkey, and Nigeria might have in common. Have them read the biographical statement about each poet and then ask them to consider what the poets' attitudes might be toward European culture, political change, economic development, and nationalism. After they have read the poems, ask them if the works have anything in common. *(Students may say that, in distinct ways, each poet deals with his attitude toward the wider world.)*

CURRICULUM CONNECTION

POLITICS

Many writers from developing countries are actively involved in their countries' politics. Other politically active Latin American, Middle Eastern, and African writers include Mario Vargas Llosa, Carlos Fuentes, Naguib Mahfouz, Chinua Achebe, and Wole Soyinka.

OTHER WORKS BY THE AUTHORS

Other Works by Jaime Torres Bodet
Karser, Sonja, trans. *Selected Poems.*
Bloomington: Indiana University Press, 1964.
Other Works by Nazim Hikmet
The Moscow Symphony and Other Poems.
Chicago: Swallow Press, 1971.

Blasing, Randy, and Mutlu Konuk, trans.
Things I Didn't Know I Loved. New York:
Persea Books, 1975.
Other Works by Gabriel Okara
The Voice. New York: Africana Publishing
Corp., 1970.

TEACH

Interpretation

Ask students to decide for which age group Torres Bodet wrote this poem. *(Possible answer: Young people trying to choose a direction in life might benefit from the challenge he presents, but the message can apply to people of any age.)*

Definition

Hikmet's claim to know the dimensions of the world "to the centimeter" is an example of hyperbole. Discuss with students how Hikmet uses overstatement as a way of suggesting his love of the world.

Literary Analysis

Okara effectively uses the technique of repetition when he lists the many faces that one must learn to wear as one grows older. Ask students to cite other examples of repetition in the poem. Have volunteers read the verses aloud and guide them to see how repetition gives the verses a certain rhythm.

Evaluation

Ask students to choose their favorite poem of the three and to write a paragraph on why they like it. Tell them to support their view with specific details.

 World Literature Selection 8

Gabriel Okara, born in 1921, is one of many Nigerian writers to achieve international acclaim since the 1960s. Others include Chinua Achebe, Christopher Okigbo, and Wole Soyinka. Some of Okara's poems deal with the problems of living in a country that is influenced by European culture. Others deal with family, friends, and daily life.

Once Upon a Time

Once upon a time, son,
they used to laugh with their hearts
and laugh with their eyes;
but now they only laugh with their teeth,
while their ice-block-cold eyes
search behind my shadow.

There was a time indeed
they used to shake hands with their hearts;
but that's gone, son.
Now they shake hands without hearts
while their left hands search
my empty pockets.

"Feel at home," "Come again,"
they say, and when I come
again and feel
at home, once, twice,
there will be no thrice—
for then I find doors shut on me.

So I have learned many things, son.
I have learned to wear many faces
like dresses—homeface,
officeface, streetface, hostface, cock-
tailface, with all their conforming smiles
like a fixed portrait smile.

And I have learned, too,
to laugh with only my teeth
and shake hands without my heart.
I have also learned to say, "Goodbye,"
when I mean, "Good-riddance";
to say "Glad to meet you,"
without being glad; and to say "It's been
nice talking to you," after being bored.

ADDITIONAL LITERARY WORKS OF THE PERIOD

García Márquez, Gabriel. *One Hundred Years of Solitude.* A mystical novel by a prominent Colombian writer about life in a Latin American village.

Head, Bessy. *A Question of Power.* A powerful and disturbing novel by one of South Africa's leading women writers.

Mahfouz, Naguib. *The Beginning and the End.* A novel by one of Egypt's greatest writers, winner of the 1988 Nobel Prize in literature.

Senghor, Léopold Sédar. *Poems.* Poetry about African culture by a West African.

Visualizing History Nigeria's people belong to more than 250 ethnic groups.
Answer to Caption: *as happy times*

Visualizing History National unity has been difficult for Nigeria to achieve because of its diverse ethnic groups. *How does the author remember his childhood years before strife divided the country?*

But believe me, son.
I want to be what I used to be
when I was like you. I want
to unlearn all these muting things.
Most of all, I want to relearn
how to laugh, for my laugh in the mirror
shows only my teeth like a snake's bare fangs!

So show me, son,
how to laugh; show me how
I used to laugh and smile
once upon a time when I was like you.

RESPONDING TO LITERATURE

1. In your own words, define "the great struggle" that Hikmet refers to near the end of his poem.
2. Explain whether you think the poem by Bodet is written just to the people of Mexico or whether it applies to people throughout the world.
3. What is the main point of the poem by Okara?
4. **Demonstrating Reasoned Judgment** How does each poet view individuals who are willing to act boldly?

Chapter 35 *The Middle East* **969**

ASSESS

Assign **Responding to Literature** questions.

CLOSE

After students have read the poems, ask them if they think that writers and artists in the developing world have special responsibilities to their people.

Contemporary Connection

Students interested in learning more about the culture of Nigeria can listen to the music of such world-famous "Afropop" musicians as King Sunny Ade, Fela Anikulapo Kuti, Babatunde Olatunji, or Shina Peters.

Portfolio Project

Have students read a poem on one of the themes touched on in these selections but written by a Western poet. Walt Whitman and T.S. Eliot are two possible choices. Then have students write an essay comparing the two poems. Have them answer these questions: Do you think any of the differences between the two poems can be traced to the differences in the poets' backgrounds? Is poetry a universal language?

ANSWERS TO RESPONDING TO LITERATURE

1. Answers will vary. Some students may feel Hikmet means that life itself is a struggle, while others may feel he refers to class struggle between the rich and poor.
2. Torres Bodet's challenge seems directed to people everywhere but may have special significance for people in Mexico and other developing countries.
3. Students may feel the poet is reflecting on the insincerity that comes with success in the world.
4. Each poet seems to value boldness: Torres Bodet criticizes one who is "afraid of life"; Hikmet praises those who dared to struggle; Okara is nostalgic for the honesty of his early years.

Chapter 35
Assessment

WORLD HISTORY Online

Have students use the **Chapter 35 Self-Check Quiz** at worldhistory.glencoe.com to prepare for the Chapter Test.

GLENCOE TECHNOLOGY

VIDEODISC

Use MindJogger to review the chapter.

MindJogger Videoquiz

Chapter 35
Disc 5 Side A

Also available in VHS.

Answers

Using Key Terms

1. a	3. e	5. d
2. g	4. c	

Using Your History Journal

Have students use their time lines on conflicts, peace conferences, and accords as a basis for essays.

Reviewing Facts

1. Positive: discovery of oil led to new cities and industrial areas; more jobs; higher standard of living; better education; women in business and politics. Negative: rise of city crime; gap between rich and poor growing; breakdown of traditional family ties; materialism; anti-Western feelings
2. As a strategic crossroads and with its valuable waterways, the Middle East was affected.
3. After U.S. refusal to help build the Aswan Dam, Nasser took over the Suez Canal.
4. He invited Egyptian and Israeli leaders to Camp David, where they worked out accords.
5. These places, still held by Israel,

970 Chapter 35 *The Middle East*

WORLD HISTORY Online

Self-Check Quiz

Visit the *World History: The Human Experience* Web site at **worldhistory.glencoe.com** and click on *Chapter 35—Self-Check Quiz* to prepare for the Chapter Test.

Using Key Terms

Write the key term that completes each sentence. Then write a sentence for each term not chosen.

a. disengagement
b. nationalized
c. fundamentalism
d. *intifada*
e. kibbutzim
f. embargo
g. sovereignty
h. Pan-Arabism
i. pact
j. desalination
k. cartel

1. In 1974 United States Secretary of State Henry Kissinger negotiated a _____, or military withdrawal, agreement between Egypt and Israel.
2. In the quest for regional unity, some Arab nations refuse to yield their _____ to an international body.
3. Some Jewish immigrants to Palestine settled on _____, or collective farms.
4. In recent years, some Middle Easterners have supported religious _____ in their efforts to defend traditional values and to oppose governments they dislike.
5. In 1987, Palestinians in the West Bank and Gaza Strip carried out an _____ to oppose Israeli rule of their areas.

Technology Activity

Using the Internet Use the Internet to search for an on-line newspaper with current articles about the Middle East. Find a recent article pertaining to any news from the Middle East. Evaluate your findings by writing a report that contains the source of information, title, date, and summary of the article. Include an opinion of whether or not this particular current event impacts your life.

970 Chapter 35 *The Middle East*

Using Your History Journal

Write an essay about an unresolved Middle Eastern issue shown on your time line. Gather information about the issue, consider ways of solving the problems it poses, and evaluate which resolution you believe is most effective.

Reviewing Facts

1. **History** Use a diagram like the one below to identify positive and negative effects of modernization in the Middle East.

Positive Effects	Negative Effects
————	————
———— Modernization ————
———— in ————
———— Middle East ————

2. **Geography** Discuss how geography helped make the Middle East a scene of cold war rivalry.
3. **History** Explain the link between the Aswan High Dam and the Suez crisis of 1956.
4. **History** Describe United States President Jimmy Carter's role in improving relations between Israel and Egypt.
5. **Geography** Explain the importance of the West Bank, the Gaza Strip, and the Golan Heights.
6. **History** Explain why the United States gave support to Turkey and to Iran.
7. **History** State the reasons for Saddam Hussein's invasion of Kuwait in 1990.
8. **Citizenship** Discuss why Iran's Muslim leaders opposed the rule of the shah.
9. **Citizenship** Describe the factors that sparked the outbreak of the Palestinian *intifada*.

Critical Thinking

1. **Evaluate** Do you think that terrorism can be justified as a means of attaining political goals? Why or why not?

---

were taken in the 1967 war. Peace depends on Israel handing over their control.
6. to ward off Soviet influence
7. He claimed that Kuwait was part of Iraq.
8. because of his emphasis on Western values
9. anger at Israeli rule and poor jobs

Critical Thinking

1. Some will argue that taking innocent lives is wrong. Others will argue that terrorism may

---

be the only way for a small group to win power from a large one.
2. more opportunities for education and jobs, some advances in business and politics; general progress in women's rights worldwide, although some areas have progressed faster than others
3. Israel is a democracy, but Palestinians point out violation of their rights. Turkey and Lebanon are democratic, but the military has

. Apply How have women's roles changed in the Middle East in recent years? Compare the position of women in the Middle East today with those of women in other parts of the world.

. Evaluate To what degree do you think human rights and democratic government have made advances in the Middle East since 1945?

. Evaluate Saddam Hussein justified Iraq's invasion of Kuwait, in part, on the grounds of nationalism and Arab unity. Analyze this reasoning. Do you think it is justified?

Geography in History

1. Place Refer to the map below. What country of the Middle East produced the most oil?

2. Location The four main producers of oil in the Middle East all border what body of water?

3. Region What correlation is there between the size, in area, and the amount of oil produced in the countries shown?

Major Oil Producers in the Middle East

TURKEY 4

SYRIA 23

IRAQ 101

IRAN 159

Mediterranean Sea

KUWAIT 60

EGYPT 44

SAUDI ARABIA 320

UNITED ARAB EMIRATES 102

Persian Gulf

Red Sea

10 million metric tons per year

0   400   800 mi.
0   400   800 km
Lambert Conic Conformal Projection

Arabian Sea

Understanding Themes

1. Nationalism How did the cold war contribute to the development of the Suez crisis in 1956?

2. Cooperation Why can the Camp David Accords be considered a turning point in the history of the modern Middle East?

3. Cultural Diffusion Do you think Saudi Arabia

will succeed in resisting unwanted foreign influences while developing its economy and society? Explain.

Linking Past and Present

1. When the state of Israel was founded in 1948, Israelis and Palestinians were bitter enemies. What was the basic issue that divided them in 1948? By 1999, how had their relationship changed? What issues continue to divide them?

2. Religion continues to influence life in the Middle East. What recent developments reflect this influence? How have religious ideas and movements shaped events in other parts of the world since World War II? What impact will they have in the future?

Skill Practice

Review the sample bibliography below for a report on the South American country of Brazil. Then answer the questions that follow.

Page, Joseph A. The Brazilians. Perseus Press, 1996.

McGowan, Chris and Ricardo Pessanha. The Brazilian Sound: Samba, Bossa Nova, and the Popular Music of Brazil. Philadelphia: Temple University Press, 1998.

Skidmore, Thomas. Brazil: Five Centuries of Change. Oxford University Press, 1999.

J. F. Hage, "Fulfilling Brazil's Promise: a Conversation with President Cardoso." Foreign Affairs, Vol. 74, July–August 1995: pp. 62–75.

Levine, J. "The Dance Drink: Brazil's Samba Soft Drink to be Marketed in the U.S." Vol. 154: p. 232.

1. The entries presented above are not listed in the correct order. What author do you think should be listed first?

2. What is missing from the Joseph A. Page book listing?

3. What is wrong and/or missing in the Thomas Skidmore book listing?

4. Rewrite the J. F. Hage article listing correctly.

5. What do you think is missing from the J. Levine listing?

and Israel. They laid the foundation for later agreements.

3. CULTURAL DIFFUSION Students might point out the difficulty of isolating a country in the age of CNN and the World Wide Web.

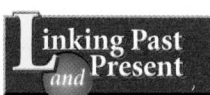

Linking Past and Present

1. partition into Jewish and Arab states; by 1995, both sides working toward a settlement; Palestinian's desire for more land, status of Jerusalem

2. Islam's influence in Iran and Turkey, Orthodox Judaism's support of West Bank settlements, Catholic opposition to communism in Eastern Europe. In the future, religious intolerance may cause conflicts.

Skill Practice

1. J. F. Hage

2. The title should be underlined, and the place of publication is missing.

3. The author's name should not be underlined, and the place of publication is missing.

4. Hage, J. F. "Fulfilling Brazil's Promise: A Conversation with President Cardoso." Foreign Affairs, Vol. 74 (July–August 1995): pp. 62–75.

5. the title of the periodical and the date

Chapter Bonus Test Question

Ask students: What role did the end of the cold war play in the formation of the coalition of nations that opposed Iraq in the Persian Gulf War? *(If the cold war had not ended, the Soviet Union might have backed Iraq against the United States, Saudi Arabia, and Kuwait.)*

influence. Iran and Iraq have authoritarian regimes.

4. No country or people should be forced to become part of another country.

Geography in History

1. Saudi Arabia

2. Persian Gulf

3. Generally, the larger the country, the more oil it produces.

Understanding Themes

1. NATIONALISM superpower desire for influence; Soviet grant of weapons led to U.S. refusal to help build Aswan High Dam; Nasser seized Suez Canal to obtain its fees

2. COOPERATION They represented the first break in the cycle of war between Israel and its Arab neighbors and led to the first peace treaty between an Arab state (Egypt)

A complete, 1-page lesson plan is provided for each section in the *Reproducible Lesson Plans* booklet.

Latin America

CHAPTER RESOURCES

	Reproducible Resources	Multimedia Resources
Chapter Opener	Chapter Themes: Graphic Organizer 36 Historical Significance Chapter Activity 36	MindJogger Videoquiz
Chapter Enrichment	Vocabulary Activity 36* Time Line Activity 36 Mapping History Activity 36 History Simulation 36 Geography and History Activity 36 Source Reading 36 People in World History Profiles 69, 70 World Art and Music Activity 36 Enrichment Activity 36 Critical Thinking Activity 36 Skill Reinforcement Activity 36 Performance Assessment Activity 36 Standardized Test Practice Workbook Activity 36 Inclusion for the Social Studies Classroom Strategies and Activities	World History and Art Transparency 49, *Figura*; 50, *Diego and I* Chapter Transparency 36 Vocabulary PuzzleMaker Software Communism and the Cold War: • *Perspectives on Communism* • *Bay of Pigs* • *Cuban Missile Crisis* • *Revolution in Cuba* • *Nicaragua* • *El Salvador* • *Chile* World History Primary Source Document Library
Chapter Review/Reteaching	Reteaching Activity 36 Skill Reinforcement Activity 36 Spanish Chapter Summary 36	Chapter 36 Digest Audiocassette, Activity, Test* Vocabulary PuzzleMaker Software Interactive Tutor Self-Assessment Software MindJogger Videoquiz
Chapter Evaluation/Testing	Performance Assessment Activity 36 Chapter 36 Test, Forms A and B	ExamView® Pro Testmaker

0:00 **OUT OF TIME?** Assign the Chapter 36 Audiocassettes.

World History Primary Source Document Library
Make History Come Alive!
Engage your students with over 250 easily accessible primary source documents—available on this CD-ROM—that will give them real life insight into the important events of world history.

* *Also available in Spanish*

Block Schedule
Activities that are particularly suited to use within the block scheduling framework are identified throughout this chapter by the following designation.

KEY TO ABILITY LEVELS
Teaching strategies are coded for varying learning styles.
L1 **BASIC** activities for all students
L2 **AVERAGE** activities for average to above-average students
L3 **CHALLENGING** activities for above-average students
LEP **LIMITED ENGLISH PROFICIENCY** activities

Use Glencoe's *Presentation Plus!* multimedia teacher tool to easily present dynamic lessons that visually excite your students. Using Microsoft PowerPoint® you can customize the presentations to create your own personalized lessons.

 Interactive Lesson Planner

Planning has never been easier! Using this CD-ROM, organize your week, month, semester, or year with all the help you need. The **Interactive Lesson Planner** gives you access to all of the blackline masters that accompany *World History: The Human Experience.*

SECTION RESOURCES

Daily Objectives	Reproducible Resources	Multimedia Resources
Section 1 **Latin American Challenges** List the social and political challenges facing Latin America after World War II.	Lecture Notes 36-1 Reproducible Lesson Plan 36-1 Vocabulary Activity 36* Guided Reading Activity 36-1* Time Line Activity 36 Section Quiz 36-1* Reading Essentials and Study Guide 36-1	Section Focus Transparency 36-1 Chapter Transparency 36 Interactive Tutor Self-Assessment Software Testmaker Communism and the Cold War: *Perspectives on Communism*
Section 2 **Mexico and the Caribbean** Describe the political and economic crises faced by Mexico and the Caribbean after World War II.	Lecture Notes 36-2 Reproducible Lesson Plan 36-2 Vocabulary Activity 36* Guided Reading Activity 36-2* History Simulation 36 People in World History Profile 70 Section Quiz 36-2* Reading Essentials and Study Guide 36-2	Section Focus Transparency 36-2 World History and Art Transparency 49, *Figura*; 50, *Diego and I* Interactive Tutor Self-Assessment Software Testmaker Communism and the Cold War: • *Bay of Pigs* • *Cuban Missile Crisis* • *Revolution in Cuba*
Section 3 **Central America** Summarize the factors that led to conflicts in Central America from the 1970s to the 1990s.	Lecture Notes 36-3 Reproducible Lesson Plan 36-3 Vocabulary Activity 36* Guided Reading Activity 36-3* Mapping History Activity 36 Section Quiz 36-3* Reading Essentials and Study Guide 36-3	Section Focus Transparency 36-3 Interactive Tutor Self-Assessment Software Testmaker Communism and the Cold War: • *Nicaragua* • *El Salvador*
Section 4 **South America** Explain how democracy has advanced in South America since the late 1980s.	Lecture Notes 36-4 Reproducible Lesson Plan 36-4 Vocabulary Activity 36* Guided Reading Activity 36-4* People in World History Profile 69 Reteaching Activity 36 Enrichment Activity 36 Section Quiz 36-4* Performance Assessment Activity 36 Spanish Chapter Summary 36 Reading Essentials and Study Guide 36-4	Section Focus Transparency 36-4 Interactive Tutor Self-Assessment Software Testmaker Communism and the Cold War: *Chile*

* Also available in Spanish

Chapter Activities

Performance Assessment Activity

A Conversation Among Immigrants Have students list situations and locations from the postwar era that produced refugees or immigrants. In each instance have them identify reasons people would want to immigrate to the United States. Students should then role-play a conversation among a group of refugees representing several of the countries from their list. In the conversation students should use information from their lists, from the chapter, and from their own research. The conversation should include opinion statements about standing policies or potential laws that could affect them.

Possible Rubric Features

Accuracy of content information, concept attainment, elaboration and detail, research skills, analytical skills, and persuasion

• *For an additional activity, refer to Activity 36 in the* Performance Assessment Strategies and Activities *booklet.*

ACTIVITY

From the Classroom of...

Mark Manning
Egg Harbor Township
High School
Egg Harbor Township, NJ

Value of the Amazon Rain Forest

After students have read about the Amazon region, organize the class into two groups. Have one group research the economic potential of the rain forest, while the other investigates the region's unique ecology. Then have the class generate two lists comparing the economic and ecological worth of the Amazon region.

Have the full class discuss both sides of the issue of developing the Amazon rain forest. Given the struggling economies of the nations of the region, should economic development be a priority? Can economic development and ecological preservation be balanced?

MULTIPLE LEARNING STYLES

Verbal/Linguistic
Have students locate Latin American literature, including folktales, poetry, drama, nonfiction, novels, and short stories. Direct them to create an annotated bibliography.

Visual/Spatial
Have students draw or reproduce the flag of each nation studied. Ask them to find out what the flag symbols mean and to provide a key to them. They should then display the flags to the class.

Auditory/Musical
Play recordings of the music of several of the countries studied and ask students to compare musical styles. Possible examples include reggae from Jamaica, merengue from the Dominican Republic, tango from Argentina, and samba from Brazil.

Kinesthetic
Show the class examples of murals by such Latin American artists as Diego Rivera and José Orozco. Have students choose aspects of life in Latin America and illustrate them. Create a colorful classroom mural, using all of the illustrations.

GLENCOE'S ASSESSMENT ADVANTAGE

Use the following to easily assess student learning in a variety of ways.

- Performance Assessment Strategies and Activities
- Section Quizzes
- Chapter and Unit Tests
- Interactive Tutor Self-Assessment Software
- Testmaker Software
- MindJogger Videoquiz
- SAT/SAT II Test Practice
- worldhistory.glencoe.com

Additional Resources

NATIONAL GEOGRAPHIC SOCIETY

Teacher's Corner

INDEX TO NATIONAL GEOGRAPHIC MAGAZINE

The following articles relate to this chapter:

- "Cuba," by John J. Putnam, June 1999.
- "Popocatépetl," by A. R. Williams, January 1999.
- "Peru Begins Again," by John McCarry, May 1996.
- "El Salvador," by Mike Edwards, September 1995.
- "Buenos Aires: Making Up for Lost Time," by John J. Putman, December 1994.

ADDITIONAL NATIONAL GEOGRAPHIC SOCIETY PRODUCTS

To order the following, call National Geographic at 1-800-368-2728:

- *Capitalism, Socialism, Communism Series: Communism (Video)*
- *Nations of the World Series: Mexico (Video)*
- *Nations of the World Series: Central America (Video)*
- *Physical Geography of the Continents Series: South America (Video)*
- *The Mexicans: Through Their Eyes (Video)*

Access National Geographic's new dynamic MapMachine Web site and other geography resources at:

- http://www.nationalgeographic.com/
- http://www.nationalgeographic.com/maps/

BIBLIOGRAPHY

Literature of the Period
García Márquez, Gabriel. *One Hundred Years of Solitude.* New York: Harper, 1970. The rise and fall of the fictional town of Macondo is an allegory of Colombian history.
Vargas Llosa, Mario. *The Time of the Hero.* New York: Grove Press, 1966. Adolescents struggle for survival in a military school.
Readings for the Student
Guillermoprieto, Alma. *The Heart That Bleeds: Latin America Now.* New York: Knopf, 1994. Personal encounters in major cities.
Readings for the Teacher
Winn, Peter. *Americas: The Changing Face of Latin America and the Caribbean.* New York: Pantheon, 1992. Past and present, with an emphasis on human interest.

Use our Web site as an additional resource. All essential content is covered in the Student Edition.

You and your students can visit the *World History: The Human Experience* Web site at worldhistory.glencoe.com The student text directs students to the Web site for the following options:

- **Chapter Overviews**
- **Student Web Activities**
- **Self-Check Quizzes**

Answers are provided for you in a link entitled "Web Activity Lesson Plan." Additional Web Resources, Interactive Puzzles, and content updates are also available.

Visit the Glencoe Web site at socialstudies.glencoe.com for social studies activities, updates, and links to other resources.

LOCAL OBJECTIVES

_____
_____
_____
_____
_____
_____
_____
_____
_____
_____
_____
_____
_____
_____
_____
_____
_____
_____

Chapter
36

1945–Present
Latin America

The **Storyteller**

Historical Setting Fidel Castro came from a family of well-to-do landowners. But he claimed that his "vocation" was "being a revolutionary." As a young man, he took part in an unsuccessful invasion of the neighboring Dominican Republic to try to overthrow that nation's dictator, and he organized riots that disrupted the 1948 Pan-American Conference at Bogotá, Colombia.

Historical Significance

Answers: *They have tried to institute democratic reforms and industrialize their countries, as well as joining economic and political alliances.*

Countries have become more democratic, and their economies have grown. Their populations have also skyrocketed.

— **WORLD HISTORY** —
Online

Have students use the **Chapter 36 Overview** at worldhistory. glencoe.com as a prereading and postreading exercise for understanding chapter content.

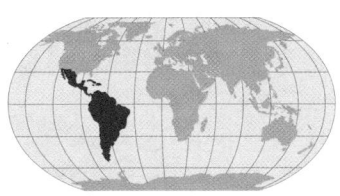

Chapter Themes

▶ **Cooperation** New organizations promote economic ties in Latin America. *Section 1*
▶ **Revolution** The overthrow of dictatorial government in Cuba opens the door to communism in the Western Hemisphere. *Section 2*
▶ **Conflict** Calls for land reform and political freedom lead to civil wars in Latin America. *Section 3*
▶ **Change** Latin American countries work to develop their struggling economies and to establish democracies. *Section 4*

The **Storyteller**

On New Year's Day, 1959, the island of Cuba went mad with joy. Tall, bearded Fidel Castro, a lawyer turned soldier, and his band of guerrillas had overthrown dictator Fulgencio Batista.

Along the road to Santiago, crowds of people waved and cheered as Castro's ragtag troops passed by in battered jeeps and trucks. "Viva, Fidel! Viva la revolución!" they cried. So delirious were the throngs, so swept away by the power of the moment, that a friend of Castro's later recalled, "It was like a messiah arriving. We were walking on a cloud."

Castro's revolution was not the first in Latin America, nor the last. Over the next few decades, tensions between rich and poor would erupt in violence repeatedly as the nations of Latin America struggled toward economic and political development.

Historical Significance

How have Latin American countries worked toward political reform and economic growth? What changes have come to Latin America since the end of the cold war?

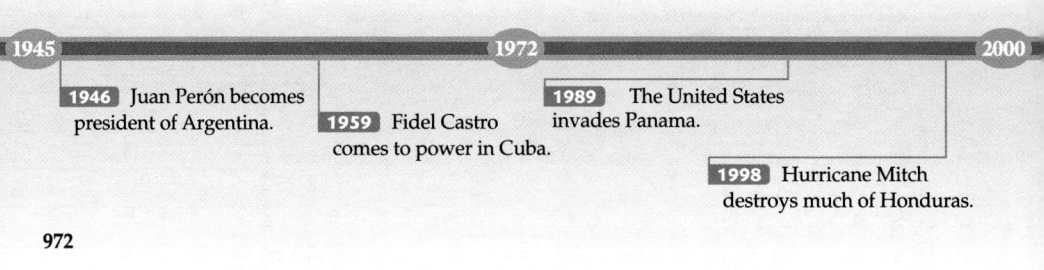

1945 **1972** **2000**

1946 Juan Perón becomes president of Argentina.
1959 Fidel Castro comes to power in Cuba.
1989 The United States invades Panama.
1998 Hurricane Mitch destroys much of Honduras.

972

GEOGRAPHY CONNECTION

Location Have students locate Latin America on a map. Ask them to point out the following: Mexico; the Caribbean region; Central America; South America; the Isthmus of Panama. What major American cities are closest to the Caribbean, Mexico, and Central America? (*Answers include Miami, New Orleans, Houston, San Antonio, and Los Angeles.*) Why is this region called Latin America? (*Except for indigenous people, most of the inhabitants of this region speak Spanish, Portuguese, or French—languages based on Latin.*)

**Visualizing
History** Portuguese
sailors named Rio de Janeiro; the
words mean "river of January."
Arriving on January 1, 1502, they
thought that Guanabara Bay was the
mouth of a river. What is special
about the culture of Brazil? *(Brazil
is the only South American country
where Portuguese, not Spanish or
French, is spoken.)*

**Visualizing
History** Amid the glow of night lights, Sugarloaf Mountain overlooks
the city of Rio de Janeiro, Brazil.

**Performance
Assessment**

**Refer to the activity on page
972C of the Planning Guide.**

For an additional activity,
refer to Activity 36 in the
*Performance Assessment Strategies
and Activities* booklet.

**Using Your History
Journal**

Suggest that students use a current
almanac or recent encyclopedia for
up-to-date statistics.

WORLD HISTORY *Online*

Chapter Overview

Visit the *World History: The Human Experience*
Web site at **worldhistory.glencoe.com** and
click on *Chapter 36—Chapter Overview* to
preview the chapter.

Your History Journal

*Research population statistics of
either Central or South American
nations. Draw a cartogram that shows
the relative population sizes of these
nations today.*

GLENCOE
TECHNOLOGY

VIDEODISC
Use MindJogger to pre-
view chapter content.

MindJogger Videoquiz

Chapter 36
Disc 5 Side A

 Also available in VHS.

Chapter 36 *Latin America* **973**

➕ **EXTRA CREDIT PROJECT**

Native Americans In pre-Columbian times,
Latin America had the most advanced Native
American cultures in the Western Hemisphere
and the largest population of Native Americans. Ask students what has happened to the
descendants of the Maya, Aztec, Inca, and
other indigenous peoples. Have them research
and report on the Native Americans of Latin
America today—where most of them are concentrated and how they live.

SECTION THEME

▶ **Cooperation** New organizations promote economic ties in Latin America.

Guide to Reading

For reading strategies to help students read effectively see pages 12–13. Have students think about the main head as they read the subheads.

Vocabulary Pre-check

 Use the Vocabulary PuzzleMaker for Chapter 36 to create a crossword puzzle to reinforce section terms. **L1 LEP**

Use Vocabulary Activity 36 to introduce vocabulary terms. **L1 LEP**

FOCUS

Section Objective

List the social and political challenges facing Latin America after World War II.

BELLRINGER
Motivational Activity

 Before taking roll at the beginning of the class period, project Section Focus Transparency 36-1 and have students answer the activity questions. Discuss students' responses.

This activity is also available as a blackline master.

1945 | **1972** | **2000**

1948 The United States and Latin American nations form the Organization of American States (OAS).

1968 Catholic clergy in Latin America support social reform efforts.

1990s Civilian democratic governments begin to replace military rule throughout Latin America.

Section 1

Latin American Challenges

Guide to Reading

Read to Find Out
Main Idea *Latin America faced social and political challenges after World War II.*

▶ **Terms to Define**
campesino, elite, liberation theology, free trade

▶ **People to Meet**
Luis Echeverría, Jacobo Arbenz Guzmán

▶ **Places to Locate**
Mexico City, Brazil, Rio de Janeiro

The Storyteller

The university student volunteers reached the Guatemalan Indian village after nightfall. Eating tortillas and drinking fresh milk around the fire came first; then the cursillo *began—city and mountain people coming together to talk about liberation. The program included talks about the common good, the right of people to organize, and how to organize for greater strength. Standing before the gathering, Juan took a stick and snapped it. "Alone we are like this," he said. Then he picked up a bundle of sticks that he could not break. "Together we are like this. You and I and your children."*

—adapted from *Guerrillas of Peace, Liberation Theology and the Central America Revolution*, Blase Bonpane, 1985

Guatemalan village

In the years after World War II, powerful changes began to reshape Latin America. Between 1940 and 1970, many Latin American nations industrialized as rapidly as did the United States in the late 1800s. Social changes followed this economic transformation. For example, schools and health-care facilities spread, and women won the right to vote.

Yet a dark cloud hung over these bright and hopeful achievements. Much of the region's newfound wealth flowed into the hands of the well-to-do, leaving millions of farmers and workers in the grip of desperate poverty. As the gap between rich and poor widened, the huge peasant class grew hungry and angry. Communism, with its appeal to the oppressed and its promise of social and economic equality, won many converts. As the peasants' demands increased, strong military dictators emerged to quell political upheaval through repression and terror.

These military leaders, in turn, were unable to solve mounting political and economic problems during the 1970s, and their failures inspired calls for democratic reform. By the early 1990s, new civilian democratic governments had replaced many of the old, harsh regimes in a number of Latin American countries.

Population Growth

Since World War II, Latin America's population has skyrocketed. In 1940 Latin America's population was 126 million. With a growth rate of about 1.8 percent a year—about three times the rate of the United States and other industrialized countries—the region's population may expand to nearly 600 million by the year 2010.

Rapid growth has resulted from a combination

974 Chapter 36 *Latin America*

Visualizing History Deforestation by slash-and-burn methods and by excessive logging threatens the rain forests of Latin America. Despite increased agricultural acreage, there are not enough jobs in rural areas. *Where do people from these areas go to find work?*

Guided Practice

THEME Cooperation
Have students list ways the United States and Latin America can cooperate and the benefits that would result for each region. *(The United States can help Latin American nations become economically stable, enabling them to improve living conditions, prevent environmental degradation, and repay their debts to U.S. banks. Cooperating to curb the drug trade would reduce crime in both regions.)* **L1 LEP**

Visualizing History In some cases, deforestation is aimed at clearing land on which to graze cattle (often for export to the Northern Hemisphere). Elsewhere, it is done to create more farmland; unfortunately, much of the cleared soil lacks fertility. **Answer to Caption:** *to cities*

Population A major challenge to development in Latin America has been its growing population. How does population growth in Latin America compare with that in the United States? *(It is about three times as great in Latin America.)* **L2**

 Chapter Transparency 36

Independent Practice

 Guided Reading Activity 36-1 **L1**

 Time Line Activity 36

---

f tradition and progress. Traditionally, families had many children. But because so many died in infancy, the population grew slowly. Latin American women still have many children. The average number of births per 1,000 Latin American women is twice the number in the United States, but improved health care has sharply lowered the infant mortality rate.

The rate of infant deaths, though five times that in the United States, is lower than in the past. Thus, more babies live to adulthood, and Latin America's population is increasing.

The population growth of Latin America has strained its economic and political systems. The expanding population requires increased supplies of food, clean drinking water, housing, schools, health care, jobs, and transportation.

Urbanization

As the population of rural areas expanded, the poor farmers—known as campesinos—headed to cities in search of work in factories or stores and of better living conditions. With more schools, medical facilities, and other social services than rural areas have, larger cities continue to attract many rural people. In the 1950s about 10 percent of Latin Americans lived in a city of at least 1 million people. Today, over 25 percent do; another 45 percent live in smaller cities.

Cities, however, could not easily absorb the heavy flow of campesinos. The new residents clustered in sprawling, dilapidated shantytowns, many with no electricity, running water, or sanitary

facilities. In his 1969 book *A Death in the Sanchez Family*, Oscar Lewis captured the bleakness of life in one such **Mexico City** slum:

> ❝ The [place] where she [Guadalupe] lived consisted of a row of 14 one-room adobe huts about 10 feet by 15 feet, built along the left side and across the back of a 30-foot-wide bare lot.... Five of the dwellings had makeshift sheds, constructed by setting up two poles and extending the kitchen roofs of tarpaper, tin, and corrugated metal over the low front doorways.... Toward the rear of the yard, two large cement water troughs, each with a faucet, were the sole sources of water for the 84 inhabitants. ❞

Such miserable surroundings offered little comfort or hope for the future. Even so, thousands of campesinos kept coming. The president of Venezuela observed, "The poor country peasant would rather come to the city and try to make a living selling lottery tickets than remain in the [countryside] where he has absolutely nothing."

Social Inequality

Latin America's social structure—masses of poor people dominated by a small but wealthy class of elite—was established during the colonial period. Today the elite includes large landowners, industrialists, top church officials, and military leaders. Many of the elite in Latin America today

Chapter 36 *Latin America* **975**

Posters Have students form five teams, each one to make a poster graphically representing one of the challenges faced by Latin America: population growth, urbanization, economic development, the growth of democracy, and foreign relations. Students should focus on these aspects: background of the challenge, a clear statement of the issue, key individuals or countries involved with the issue, and possible solutions. **L2**

Cooperation The Organization of American States (OAS), formed in 1948, has worked to encourage political and economic ties among its members. Have students research and report on how this organization is set up and how it operates. **L2**

Economics Land reform has been a controversial issue in many Latin American countries for many years. Have students research and report on land-reform efforts since World War II. They may wish to choose a specific country. **L3**

Who?What?Where?When?

Woman Suffrage For decades, left-wing politicians in Latin America opposed woman suffrage because they thought that women would vote for right-wing candidates. In Ecuador, the first Latin American country to give women the vote, voting was mandatory for men but optional for women.

Linking Past and Present

Booming Buenos Aires

Visitors to the city enjoy shopping—especially for fine woolens and leather goods—eating steak dinners at reasonable prices (Argentina remains a major beef producer); and dancing the tango, the Argentine national dance.

ANSWERS

its pleasant climate and its prosperity as a commercial and industrial center; students may suggest that growth will likely increase pollution and strain city services

---

are the descendants of the Europeans who colonized the region centuries ago. The increase in wealth brought by industrialization in this century simply made these families richer. By the late 1980s, 50 percent of the newly generated wealth in **Brazil** flowed into the hands of the wealthiest 10 percent of the people. As of 1997, 42 million Brazilians, about 30 percent of the population, lived in extreme poverty.

The majority of Latin America's population consists of poor people: peasants, landless farm workers, and factory workers. Many countries in recent decades have a small but growing middle class consisting of professionals, managers, clerks, and government workers.

A more important change has been in the development of the role of women in Latin America. Traditionally women had important but restricted roles in society. They were expected to work at home and raise children. In the late 1800s, women established their right to get an education and to enter a variety of careers. However, not until the mid-1960s did all Latin American women win the right to vote.

CONNECTIONS
Geography

Booming Buenos Aires

Latin America is one of the world's most rapidly urbanizing continents. For example, today more than 13 million people—well over one-third of all Argentinians—live in the port city and capital of Buenos Aires. One attractive feature of the city is the pleasant, temperate climate. The people of Buenos Aires, called *porteños*, or port dwellers, are descendants of immigrants from all over the world—Spain, Italy, England, France, Poland, and the Middle East.

In the mid-1800s, British and Argentinian investors built a network of rail lines spreading outward from Buenos Aires. On these rail lines, wheat, corn, cattle, and

Downtown Buenos Aires

sheep are now sent to Buenos Aires for export. Building on its foundation of trade in agricultural products, Buenos Aires grew into a prosperous industrial center. Among the major industries are food processing and textiles.

Buenos Aires' rapid growth typifies the recent expansion of cities throughout the region. In 1909 Buenos Aires topped the 1 million mark. Immigration from overseas and from rural areas in Argentina added to the population in the succeeding decades. During the 1940s, Buenos Aires had 4.5 million people, and in forty years the population had nearly tripled, reaching about 13 million.

Linking Past and Present ACTIVITY

Discuss the features of Buenos Aires that have attracted immigrants. What effects do you think continued growth will have on Buenos Aires' future?

Economic Development

In recent decades many Latin American leaders pushed for increased industrialization. They hoped that their countries could manufacture their own products instead of importing them, thereby reducing their trade deficits. In just a few decades, Latin American steel production grew by 20 percent while the production of metals, machines, and energy rose by 10 percent. Manufacturers flooded the markets with consumer products aimed at the upper and middle classes—fashions, sports cars, toys, and appliances. Since industrialization did little to increase the buying power of the poor, the market for consumer goods was limited to the small elite. Latin American firms quickly produced more than they could sell at home, so they turned to exporting goods to stay in business.

The efforts at industrialization brought results. Between 1950 and 1995, Latin America achieved a remarkable economic growth rate. Much of the money to finance industrial growth, however, came from large multinational corporations and banks. For every dollar they invested in Latin America,

---

MEETING SPECIAL NEEDS ACTIVITY

Mixed Learners Students with learning disabilities and those with limited English proficiency will benefit from organizing the chapter information in a visual way. Have students create wall maps of Latin America to reinforce the location of each country. Have students find, copy, or create images of important aspects of life in the various countries: people, places, farming, industry, and so on. Gifted students may write captions explaining the meaning and importance of the images for each country. **L1 LEP**

ese business and banking enterprises took out ore than three dollars in profits and dividends.

Agricultural growth did not match industrial rowth. More land was allocated for growing cash rops for export, such as coffee, bananas, and coca, hich is used to make cocaine. But as farmers con- erted more land to growing cash crops, they grew ss food for the local population. Although the ndowners prospered from selling their crops broad, local people had to pay more to buy food rom farther away. Most campesinos remained poor.

Hoping to stimulate economic growth, many atin American leaders borrowed heavily from large anks in the United States and other countries. Be- ween 1975 and 1985, Latin American debt to other arts of the world rose 318 percent. By the 1980s, a worldwide recession made matters worse—cutting lobal demand for Latin American products and urther raising interest rates and Latin American ebts. By 1984, the region's debt totaled $350 billion; y 1993, it had climbed to over $465 billion.

In spite of economic improvements in the 990s, Latin American debt remains a major prob- em for the region. If debts are not paid, banks may ail, threatening the stability of the global economy. n the mid-1990s, a political and economic crisis in Mexico nearly led to Mexico's failure to meet its international debt payments. The United States came to Mexico's rescue with an aid package to bol- ster the Mexican economy. The United States gov- ernment has also worked with Latin American countries to reschedule international loan pay- ments to avoid potential crises.

Another economic area in which the United States and Latin America work together is the war on drugs. Powerful dealers profit from international trading in illegal drugs made from certain crops grown in Latin America. The United States and Latin American governments both aim to end the illegal drug trade, but difficulties often hamper cooperation. The United States often expresses concern about the corrupt influence drug dealers have on Latin Amer- ican governments, while Latin American countries claim the United States needs to take stronger mea- sures at home to lessen the demand for drugs.

Growth of Democracy

The economic problems of Latin America made the growth of democracy almost impossible. In most countries, the elite controlled the government as well as the economy. The elite did not trust the masses enough to allow any form of majority rule to take hold. The majority of people, long dominat-

Visualizing History Workers load bananas for shipment in Ecuador, where petroleum and agricultural products are the main exports. *How did the emphasis on production of cash crops affect the campesinos?*

ed by a few powerful leaders, had little experience in making decisions or choosing leaders.

Political conflicts in most of Latin America were between liberals and conservatives. Liberals tried to help the masses through land and tax reforms. Conservatives wanted to maintain the tra- ditional social structure and opposed any redistrib- ution of wealth. Clashes between liberals and con- servatives have often been bloody.

The failure of democracy and social reform prompted calls for more radical change. Armed guer- rilla movements that sought to change society by force emerged in many countries. These groups often relied on the support and protection of campesinos. Many guerrilla organizations included at least some Communists. In countries such as Cuba and Nicaragua, guerrilla movements success- fully overthrew governments and took power themselves.

Fear of communism combined with outrage at the poverty of so many people caused changes in the Catholic Church. Since colonial times, the Church had generally supported rule by elites in most Latin American countries. Individual priests sometimes called for reforms to help the poor, but they were exceptions. After a meeting of Latin American bishops in Colombia in 1968, however, an increasing number of Catholic clergy began sup- porting land reform, democracy, and other changes that campesinos and workers had long demanded. They began emphasizing the role of Christianity in

Chapter 36 *Latin America* **977**

VIDEODISC
Communism and the Cold War

Side One, Chapter 8
Frames 14264–14893
Title: *Perspectives on Communism*
Subject: Discussion of the ideals of communism
Ask: In Communist philosophy, what was the ideal society? *(The ideal society was one in which every- one was happy; in which all were "master and owner of everything" with no competition.)*

MAKING CONNECTIONS ACTIVITIES

Literature Latin American literature has gained worldwide fame in recent decades. The first writer from this region to win the Nobel Prize was the Chilean poet Gabriela Mistral, in 1945. Have students research her work or the poetry of such writers as Pablo Neruda, Octavio Paz, or Derek Walcott and then present selections to the class, reading in both Spanish (where relevant) and English if possible. **L3**

History Several Nazi leaders fled to South America after the defeat of Germany in World War II. One of the best known was Adolf Eichmann, who was arrested in Argentina in 1960. Have stu- dents research and report on how he was found and captured and his subsequent fate. **L3**

ASSESS

Check for Understanding

Assign Section 1 Assessment as homework or as an in-class activity.

 Use Interactive Tutor Self-Assessment Software to review Section 1.

Evaluate

Section Quiz 36-1

Use the Testmaker to create a customized quiz for Section 1.

Reteach

Have students brainstorm a list of the main challenges facing Latin America in the post-World War II period and then rank them by importance.

Reading Essentials and Study Guide 36-1

Enrich

Have students watch the 1983 movie *El Norte*, a moving depiction of illegal immigrants who make a dangerous journey from Guatemala to California, and write a short essay on why immigrants are willing to take great risks to reach the United States.

CLOSE

Have students list all the organizations through which Latin American nations cooperate for economic, social, and political progress.

---

liberating people from oppression. Their beliefs became known as liberation theology. One Latin American religious worker explained the new movement this way:

❝ For example, if, as the book of Genesis teaches, human beings have been created in God's image, they have a great dignity; hence, to torture another human being is to disfigure God's image. If the Lord gave the Earth to Adam and Eve, he meant it for all—not just a few plantation owners. ❞

—Philip Berryman, *Inside Central America*, 1985

The combined pressure of guerrillas, liberal Catholic clergy, and organized citizens began to bring changes in the 1980s. Argentina, Brazil, Chile, and other countries threw off their dictators and adopted democratic governments. However, these young democracies inherited international debts, widespread poverty, and social unrest. The most controversial issue has been land reform, which is still opposed by the military and landowners.

International Relations

Since the end of World War II, Latin American nations have forged new trading relationships with Western Europe, Asia, Africa, and Japan. In addition, many Latin American leaders have taken more active and prominent roles in world diplomacy. For example, in the 1970s during the Cold War, Mexico's president, **Luis Echeverría** (AY•chuh•vuh•REE•uh), was a leader in the non-aligned movement.

The most important relations of Latin American nations, however, have been with each other and with the United States. In **Rio de Janeiro**, Brazil, in 1947, representatives of the United States and most of the Latin American nations signed the Rio Treaty. This defense pact provided that any attack on one member would be considered an attack on all members.

A year later, the Organization of American States (OAS) was set up to develop political and economic ties among the nations of the Western Hemisphere. One of its most important successes was in 1995, when OAS members Brazil, the United States, Argentina, and Chile intervened to stop a war between Peru and Ecuador.

Relations between Latin America and the United States were shaped by the cold war. The United States often provided military aid to conservative regimes while undermining left-wing governments. In 1954 the U.S. CIA helped overthrow a left-wing government in Guatemala led by **Jacobo Arbenz Guzmán.** Arbenz's efforts to redistribute land to the peasants was viewed as a threat to American business interests.

Another way to fight communism was through financial assistance. In 1961 President John F. Kennedy launched the **Alliance for Progress.** It provided $10 billion for Latin American industry, housing, medical care, and military development. However, much of the money sent to Latin America was used to buy American-made goods.

As the cold war ended in the 1980s nations in the Americas began working toward free trade, or the elimination of trade barriers among countries. Throughout the Western Hemisphere, groups of countries formed regional economic pacts, such as the North American Free Trade Agreement (NAFTA), the Andean Pact, the Southern Common Market (Mercosur), the Caribbean Community and Common Market (Caricom), and the Central American Common Market.

Western Hemisphere governments also took steps to bring together all of the region's free trade organizations. In 1994 leaders from 34 Western Hemisphere nations planned to establish a free trade area by the year 2005.

SECTION 1 ASSESSMENT

Main Idea

1. Use a chart like the one below to identify social and political challenges in Latin America after World War II.

Social Challenges	Political Challenges

Recall

2. **Define** campesino, elite, liberation theology, free trade.
3. **Identify** Luis Echeverría, Jacobo Arbenz Guzmán, Alliance for Progress, NAFTA.

Critical Thinking

4. **Evaluating Information** How has the cause of human

rights advanced in Latin American countries since the 1980s?

Understanding Themes

5. **Cooperation** How might increased United States-Latin American trade affect the lives of the campesinos of Latin America?

SECTION 1 ASSESSMENT ANSWERS

1. Social challenges: rapid population growth; increased migration from rural to urban areas; social inequalities between rich and poor. Political challenges: dictatorships; liberal-conservative conflicts; guerrilla movements; many conversions to communism; Catholic clergy supported land reform and democracies; adoption of democratic governments

2. All terms are defined in the Glossary.

3. Luis Echeverría, 978; Jacobo Arbenz Guzmán, 978; Alliance for Progress, 978; NAFTA, 978

4. Students might discuss the return of democratic rule in Chile, Argentina, and various Central American nations that had poor human rights records in the 1970s.

5. **COOPERATION** It might benefit them if the increased income is distributed more widely than in the past; if only the rich profit, campesinos will make no progress.

1961 U.S.-trained exiles stage Bay of Pigs invasion in Cuba.

1971 The first Duvalier presidency ends in Haiti.

1993 United States, Mexico, and Canada enact NAFTA.

Section 2

Mexico and the Caribbean

Read to Find Out
Main Idea *Mexico and the Caribbean faced political and economic crises after World War II.*

▶ **Terms to Define**
standard of living, privatization

▶ **People to Meet**
Carlos Salinas de Gortari, Zapatistas, Ernesto Zedillo Ponce de León, Fidel Castro, Jean Bertrand Aristide

▶ **Places to Locate**
Mexico, Cuba, Dominican Republic, Haiti

S_toryteller_

The revolutionary leader Fidel Castro spoke of revolutionaries: *"Whoever stops to wait for ideas to triumph among the majority of the masses before initiating revolutionary action will never be a revolutionary.... It is obvious that in Latin America there are already in many places a number of men who ... have started revolutionary action. And what distinguished the true revolutionary from the false revolutionary is precisely this: one acts to move the masses, the other waits for the masses to have a conscience already before starting to act."*

—*Fidel Castro Speaks*, edited by Martin Kenner and James Petras, 1969

Castro as a young rebel fighter

*A*fter World War II, Mexico and the Caribbean nations of Cuba, the Dominican Republic, and Haiti were ruled frequently by either a single political party or by dictators. Mexico's single-party government controlled much of its economy, while American businesses played an important role in the Caribbean economies. In Cuba, a Communist government took power in 1959, bringing the cold war to the Western Hemisphere. In recent decades, Mexico and the Caribbean countries have tried to reform their political systems and develop their economies. Growing populations and political turmoil, however, have made these goals difficult to reach.

Mexico

Of all the countries in Latin America, **Mexico** was among the most stable after World War II. Since 1929, it had been dominated by one political party, the Institutional Revolutionary Party (PRI). Restricted by the constitution to single, six-year terms, strong PRI presidents, using their appointment powers, kept tight control over national and local governments. State-controlled businesses produced rapid industrialization and a growing middle class.

From the late 1940s to the 1960s, Mexico's standard of living—the overall wealth of its people—increased. Industrial growth was concentrated in the central region of the country around Mexico City. There, more goods and services were available to a growing number of people. Rural areas, especially in the south, lagged far behind, and millions of peasants remained desperately poor. Today 40 percent of Mexico's population lives in poverty.

Chapter 36 *Latin America* **979**

▶ **Revolution** The overthrow of dictatorial government in Cuba opens the door to communism in the Western Hemisphere.

For reading strategies to help students read effectively see pages 12–13.

Vocabulary Pre-check

◉ Use the Vocabulary PuzzleMaker for Chapter 36 to create a crossword puzzle to reinforce section terms. **L1 LEP**

🗁 Use Vocabulary Activity 36 to introduce vocabulary terms. **L1 LEP**

FOCUS

Section Objective

Describe the political and economic crises faced by Mexico and the Caribbean after World War II.

BELLRINGER
Motivational Activity

Before taking roll at the beginning of the class period, project Section Focus Transparency 36-2 and have students answer the activity questions. Discuss students' responses.
🗁 This activity is also available as a blackline master.

SECTION RESOURCES

🗁 **Reproducible Masters**
• Lecture Notes 36-2
• Reproducible Lesson Plan 36-2
• Vocabulary Activity 36
• Guided Reading Activity 36-2
• History Simulation 36
• People in World History Profile 70

• Section Quiz 36-2
• Reading Essentials and Study Guide 36-2

🕯 **Transparencies**
• Section Focus Transparency 36-2
• World History and Art Transparency 49, *Figura*; 50, *Diego and I*

Multimedia
◉ Interactive Tutor Self-Assessment Software
◉ Testmaker
◉ Communism and the Cold War:
  • *Bay of Pigs*
  • *Cuban Missile Crisis*
  • *Revolution in Cuba*

TEACH

Guided Practice

THEME Revolution

Cuba's government was overthrown in 1959. What dissatisfactions led to this uprising? *(foreign domination of the economy, together with Batista's repressive and corrupt rule)* **L1 LEP**

Linking Past and Present

Three Cultures Mexico City boasts a dramatic example of how the present builds on the past. The Plaza of the Three Cultures contains the ruins of Aztec temples, the remains of a Spanish colonial church, and a modern housing complex.

Politics In spite of economic progress under Mexico's President Salinas, his regime faced opposition. What were three causes of this opposition? *(Economic benefits were slow to reach the poor; many resented the political domination of the PRI; many opposed NAFTA, fearing the loss of their lands.)* **L2**

 History Simulation 36

World History and Art Transparency 49, *Figura*; 50, *Diego and I*

Who?What?Where?When?

Zapata The name of Emiliano Zapata is written in gold in Mexico's chamber of deputies. An uneducated, landless Native American, Zapata became a powerful spokesperson for others like himself. In 1919, during the violence of the Mexican Revolution, he was assassinated by political foes.

Economic Problems

In the 1970s, oil seemed to offer Mexico a way to prosperity. New oil discoveries and rising world oil prices brought profits to the state-owned Mexican oil industry and boosted the Mexican economy. The government borrowed money from foreign sources to finance economic development, assuming that oil revenues would make repaying the loans easy.

Global recession in the early 1980s and increased oil supplies caused world oil prices to drop. The Mexican government was forced to cut back jobs and services to save money. To boost exports, the value of the peso, the Mexican unit of currency, was cut by nearly half. Some wealthy Mexicans responded by fleeing the country with their money.

Mexico soon faced an economic crisis, owing foreign investors $100 billion, one of the highest national debts in the developing world. The gap between rich and poor widened, as the population continued to grow rapidly. The growing demand for jobs, goods, and services could not be m Then in 1985, a devastating earthquake hit Mex City, the capital, killing thousands of people a causing billions of dollars in damages.

Relations worsened with the United States d ing this period, too, as a result of controversy ov drug smuggling and illegal immigration. T United States wanted the Mexican government do more to stop the flow of illegal drugs ir United States territory. In addition, growing nur bers of Mexicans and Central Americans we crossing the United States-Mexico border witho visas in hopes of finding work.

The Salinas Era

In 1988 Mexican president **Carlos Salinas** **Gortari** promised broad reforms. To improve re tions with the United States, he pledged to cra down on drug smuggling and illegal immigratio He also rolled back the policy of government ow ership of major industries. With privatization, or shift to private ownership of businesses, Salin

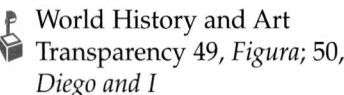

Mexico Today

Mexico faces economic, social, and political change as the nation attempts to provide a better living for its growing population.

Native Mexican crafts delight shoppers in the Sunday craft market in Oaxaca.

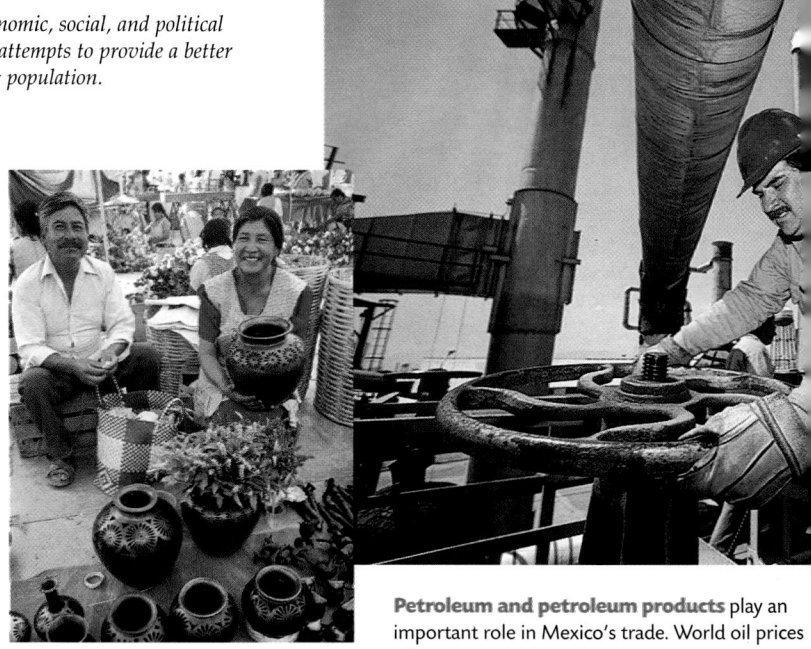

Petroleum and petroleum products play an important role in Mexico's trade. World oil prices affect the nation's economy.

980

Images *of the* Times   Mexico Today

Every year some 800,000 people move to Mexico City. This migration has made the city the largest metropolitan area in the world. Almost one-fourth of the Mexican people live in the *distrito federal*— on less than one-half of one percent of the country's land.

oped that Mexican industries would be run more efficiently.

Salinas also sought to create jobs for Mexicans by attracting more foreign investment. The centerpiece of his effort was NAFTA, the North American Free Trade Agreement. Begun in 1993, NAFTA committed Mexico, Canada, and the United States to removing trade barriers among all three countries over a 15-year period.

While Salinas's reforms were expected to succeed in the long run, Mexico at first faced setbacks. Economic benefits were slow to reach the poorest Mexicans. In addition, there was growing opposition to the PRI's hold on political power. In 1994 a guerrilla army of Native American peasants in the southern Mexican state of Chiapas rebelled against the government. Calling themselves the **Zapatistas**, after the revolutionary leader Emiliano Zapata, they demanded that the government aid the poor and advance democracy. They also vehemently opposed NAFTA, which they feared would hand their lands over to large corporations.

Zedillo and Reform

Also in 1994, the PRI candidate for president was assassinated during the campaign. **Ernesto Zedillo Ponce de León**, the new PRI candidate, won easily, but there was widespread dissatisfaction about the extent of government corruption, which allegedly reached even to the Salinas family.

As president, Zedillo continued free enterprise reforms, while promising to improve the lot of the poor. In late 1994, however, he faced a trade deficit that forced him to devalue the peso, a move that shook international business confidence in Mexico. American financial aid helped support Mexico's economy, but Mexican government cutbacks in jobs and services imposed hardships on many Mexicans.

To counter growing public discontent, Zedillo held talks with the Zapatistas and opened up the political system to other political parties. In 1997 elections, the PRI, for the first time since 1929, lost its majority in the lower house of the Mexican legislature. The two major opposition parties—the

Independent Practice

📁 Guided Reading Activity 36-2 **L1**

📁 People in World History Profile 70

Biography

The following videotape program is available from Glencoe:

• **Fidel Castro: El Commandante**

you don't say...

Buckaroos—and more Mexicans were the first cowboys, so many of the words we associate with the American West are of Spanish origin. They include *buckaroo* (*vaquero*, cowboy), *bronco* (rough, unruly), *chaps* (*chaparejos*), *corral* (enclosed yard), *lariat* (*la reata*), and *ranch* (*rancho*).

Who?What?Where?When?

Ernesto "Che" Guevara, an Argentinian, was one of Castro's ablest guerrilla fighters. After Castro came to power, Guevara occupied several important posts until 1965, when he dropped out of public life in Cuba. Apparently Guevara went to South America to preach revolution. He was captured and shot in Bolivia in 1967. His eloquent writings made him a hero to revolutionaries everywhere.

Mexico City, home to more than 20 million people and one of the world's most rapidly growing cities, faces pollution, crime, and inadequate housing.

Ballet Folklórico enhances the cultural life of Mexico City, the nation's leading business, industrial, and cultural center.

REFLECTING ON THE TIMES

1. How do world oil prices affect Mexico's economy?
2. What challenges does Mexico City face because of its rapidly growing population?

981

ANSWERS TO REFLECTING ON THE TIMES

1. Since Mexico is a prime oil producer, high world prices help its economy and low ones harm it.
2. dealing with pollution, crime, and inadequate services

Map Study

Answer
about 2,300 miles (3,700 kilometers)

Cuba and the Cold War

Why did Cuba become an important "flash point" in the cold war?

The United States saw Fidel Castro's Communist revolution in Cuba as a threat to the rest of Latin America. The Soviet Union sought to protect Cuba from the Americans by installing missiles in the island republic. To defuse the Cuban missile crisis, the United States promised not to invade Cuba in return for Soviet withdrawal of the missiles.

VIDEODISC
Communism and the Cold War

Side Two, Chapter 13
Frames 30190–31200
Title: *Bay of Pigs*
Ask: What does this footage portray? *(American forces in Cuba as a result of the threat of communism.)*

Side One, Chapter 16
Frames 29427–32782
Title: *Cuban Missile Crisis*
Ask: What part of the United States was in the most danger from the missiles? *(the southeastern United States)*

Map Study The Cuban missile crisis of 1962 brought the United States and the Soviet Union to the brink of a nuclear conflict.
Region From east to west, how large was the area covered by the United States blockade of Cuba?

conservative National Action Party (PAN) and the leftist Democratic Revolutionary Party (PRD) gained a significant influence in national politics.

Meanwhile, United States-Mexican relations remained strained. Mexican nationalists were angered by American doubts about Mexico's commitment to the war against drugs. They also opposed a new United States law that sought to crack down on illegal immigration.

Cuba

From 1952 to 1959, the Caribbean island nation of **Cuba** was ruled by the dictator Fulgencio Batista. Batista's government—often accused of employing corrupt practices—allowed American corporations to dominate the Cuban economy. By the early 1950s, United States companies owned or controlled many of Cuba's mines and ranches as well as much of the oil and sugar industries.

In 1956 a young lawyer named **Fidel Castro** began a guerrilla movement against Batista. Castro opposed Batista's repressive and corrupt practices. For three years, he and his soldiers attacked Batista's forces. On January 1, 1959, Batista fled the country, and Castro took control. Many former

982 Chapter 36 *Latin America*

political officials and army officers were tried and executed. Independent newspapers were closed. Many Cubans who opposed Castro left the country and settled in the United States.

Castro's Domestic Policies

Castro promised democratic reforms and a better standard of living for the Cuban people. However, Castro suspended elections. He did improve wages, health care, and basic education. He took control of the land and nationalized plantations and major industries. Castro's seizure of American-owned property and his disregard of Cuban civil liberties angered the United States.

In retaliation, the United States cut off all sugar imports from Cuba in 1960. Castro meanwhile allied Cuba with the Soviet Union. Soviet Premier Nikita Khrushchev agreed to buy Cuban sugar and to sell arms to Cuba. Castro's dictatorship was openly Communist two years after the revolution.

Cuba and the Cold War

Castro's friendship with the Soviet Union made Cuba the focal point of the cold war in the Western Hemisphere. Castro supported revolutions in Latin America and Africa by supplying military aid and troops and by urging people to join the cause:

> **The revolution will triumph in America and throughout the world, but it is not for revolutionaries to sit in the doorways of their houses waiting for the corpse of imperialism to pass by.**
>
> —From a 1962 speech by Fidel Castro

Castro's defiance of the United States put him in danger. During this period the Central Intelligence Agency (CIA), the intelligence-gathering agency of the United States government, made many attempts to assassinate Castro.

In April 1961 the United States tried and failed to overthrow Castro in a secretly planned invasion. About 1,500 anti-Castro exiles trained by the CIA landed in Cuba at the Bay of Pigs, hoping to rally the Cubans to revolt. At the last moment, United States President John F. Kennedy barred open American military support for the effort. The Cuban people failed to revolt, and Castro's forces captured or killed most of the invaders. Kennedy's new presidency and the global image of the United States were badly damaged.

COOPERATIVE LEARNING ACTIVITY

Debate Have students hold a debate about the Cuban missile crisis of 1962. Organize the students into two groups, one taking the position that Soviet missiles had to be removed from Cuba at any cost, the other defending a negotiated settlement or even allowing the missiles to remain. Refer students to Samuel Dinerstein, *The Making of a Missile Crisis*, October 1962; Robert A. Divine, *The Cuban Missile Crisis*; and Robert F. Kennedy, *Thirteen Days: A Memoir of the Cuban Missile Crisis*.
L2

James L. Stanfield

Rich Heritage

Havana, the capital city of Cuba, dates to the 1500s. The Old City has endured, essentially unchanged for four centuries. Today more than 900 buildings—including palaces, churches, mansions, and humble [dwell]ings—remain so uniquely preserved that the [Unite]d Nations has classified Old Havana as a world [herit]age site. This palace, being restored from [the gr]ound up, reveals the faded grandeur and splen[dor o]f the colonial era. Once home to a Spanish [conqu]istador's widow and later to orphans, the

building now houses one of the few restaurants in Old Havana.

In 1959 Fidel Castro led a successful Cuban Revolution. After the United States rejected Castro, he turned to the Soviet Union, and for the next 30 years Cuba was a critical stronghold of communism in the Western Hemisphere. Castro's revolution kept out modern developers—along with tourist dollars. But it is partly as a result of Cuba's poverty and relative isolation that the island has preserved its heritage of architectural wonders like the building above. ⊕

Chapter 36 *Latin America* **983**

TEACH

Tell students that Havana is also famous for fortresses originally built by Spain to defend the port city. One of them, Morro Castle, has become the symbol of Havana. Another, the Castillo de la Fuerza, was begun in 1538 and is the oldest colonial military building in the Americas. What historic sites are preserved in or near your community? *(Examples might include birthplaces or residences of famous people; forts or other military installations; and buildings of architectural interest.)*

Linking Past and Present

Cuban Exiles More than half a million Cubans fled to the United States after the Cuban Revolution. The vast majority settled in south Florida, where they transformed Miami into "Little Havana." The annual Calle Ocho (formerly Eighth Street) Festival draws as many as a million visitors.

ABCNEWS
INTERACTIVE™

 VIDEODISC
Communism and the Cold War

Side Two, Chapter 12
Frames 28259–30174
Title: *Revolution in Cuba*
Ask: According to Gennadi Gerasimov, how did the United States push Fidel Castro toward communism? *(by trying to stop the revolution instead of supporting it)*

ASSESS

Check for Understanding

Assign Section 2 Assessment as homework or as an in-class activity.

 Use Interactive Tutor Self-Assessment Software to review Section 2.

Evaluate

Section Quiz 36-2

Use the Testmaker to create a customized quiz for Section 2.

Reteach

Review with the class key events in relations between the United States and Cuba since the 1950s.

Reading Essentials and Study Guide 36-2

Enrich

Have students draw a cartoon from the point of view of another Latin American country that reacts to the Cuban missile crisis.

CLOSE

Have students discuss whether the United States should lift the economic embargo it placed on Cuba in 1962.

Have students use the **Chapter 36 Student Web Activity** at worldhistory.glencoe.com for in-depth study of the Cuban missile crisis.

A year later, the Cuban missile crisis brought the world to the brink of nuclear war. Soviet leader Khrushchev's installation of nuclear missiles on Cuba met with stiff American opposition. President Kennedy ordered nearly 200 American warships to blockade Cuba and stop military shipments from the Soviet Union. American B-52 bombers with nuclear warheads took to the skies, and American forces worldwide went on full alert.

Four days later, after tense negotiations, the crisis ended. Khrushchev agreed to dismantle the bases and withdraw the missiles if the United States promised never to attack Cuba again. Separately the United States agreed to remove American missiles in Turkey aimed at the Soviet Union. The most dangerous confrontation of the cold war was over. Castro, however, was outraged at Khrushchev's yielding to American pressure.

United States–Cuban relations also continued to be icy. In 1962, the United States imposed an economic embargo on Cuba. Travel between the two countries was tightly restricted. Due to its ties with the Communist world, Cuba was isolated by other countries in the Western Hemisphere.

For brief periods, in 1980 and 1994, Castro allowed thousands of Cubans to sail to the United States. Most of these people were opponents of Castro's authoritarian rule. Others were criminals, mentally ill, or impoverished peasants.

Cuba After the Cold War

In the 1970s, Cuba sent troops to Africa to aid Marxists in Angola. With the fall of Soviet communism two decades later, the Cubans could no longer export revolution. Loss of Soviet aid, poor sugar harvests, and the U.S. embargo meant they had to attend primarily to their devastated economy.

Despite setbacks, Castro still clung to communism. However, he allowed limited free enterprise to obtain foreign investment. He also permitted some religious freedom after a 1998 visit by Pope John Paul II. The United States, however, refused to end the embargo. As a result, Cuba remained the last remnant of the cold war.

Haiti

East of Cuba is the large, mountainous island of Hispaniola, which is divided into two nations. The eastern two-thirds of the island is the **Dominican Republic**, a Spanish-speaking country. The western third is French-speaking **Haiti**. The two countries are among the poorest in the Western Hemisphere. Relations between the two countries have often been tense because of their cultural differences.

Haiti has been ruled by dictatorships during much of its recent history. The dictator François Duvalier (du•VAL•YAY) ruled from 1957 to 1971. His son, Jean-Claude Duvalier, then became Haiti's leader but was overthrown in 1986. After four years of strife, **Jean Bertrand Aristide** (ah•reh•STEED), a popular reform-minded priest, was elected president. A military coup forced Aristide to flee the country in 1991. With broad international support, and the intervention of U.S. military forces, Aristide returned to power in 1994. A UN peacekeeping mission helped in the country's transition from military rule to democracy. Mistrust and violence among rival political groups, however, slowed progress toward stable government and economic recovery. In December 1995 René Preval was elected to succeed Aristide as president of Haiti. The transition to democracy has been a difficult one, however, and by 1999 political violence had returned to the troubled island nation.

Student Web Activity 36

Visit the *World History: The Human Experience* Web site at **worldhistory.glencoe.com** and click on *Chapter 36—Student Web Activities* for an activity relating to the Cuban missile crisis.

SECTION 2 ASSESSMENT

Main Idea

1. Use a chart like the one below to show how Mexico has reacted to two political or economic crises since World War II.

Crisis	Reaction
1.	
2.	

Recall

2. **Define** standard of living, privatization.
3. **Identify** Carlos Salinas de Gortari, Zapatistas, Ernesto Zedillo Ponce de León, Fidel Castro, Jean Bertrand Aristide.

Critical Thinking

4. **Analyzing Information** How was citizens' participation in government advanced in Mexico during the 1990s?

Understanding Themes

5. **Revolution** Explain why revolution is common in the Caribbean and Latin America.

SECTION 2 ASSESSMENT ANSWERS

1. to improve relations with the U.S., Salinas cracked down on drug smuggling and illegal immigration; to run industry more efficiently, Salinas shifted to privatization and created jobs by attracting foreign investments; because of world recession and trade deficit, the peso was devalued; to counter public discontent, Zedillo opened political system to other parties
2. All terms are defined in the Glossary.
3. Carlos Salinas de Gortari, 980; Zapatistas, 981; Ernesto Zedillo Ponce de León, 981; Fidel Castro, 982; Jean Bertrand Aristide, 984
4. Zedillo opened up the one-party system to other political parties. In 1997 the opposition parties together won a majority of seats in the lower house of the national legislature.
5. **REVOLUTION** The region has been dominated, politically and economically, by elites or dictators; it has also been subject to foreign intervention.

1979 The Sandinistas overthrow Somoza rule in Nicaragua.

1990 War in Nicaragua ends.

1999 Panama takes control of Panama Canal.

Chapter 36 Section 3

Section 3

Central America

Read to Find Out
Main Idea *Multiple factors led to conflicts in Central America from the 1970s to the 1990s.*

▶ **Terms to Define**
  covert, death squad

▶ **People to Meet**
  Anastasio Somoza Debayle, Sandinistas, contras, Oscar Arias, Violeta Chamorro, Oscar Romero, Manuel Noriega

▶ **Places to Locate**
  Nicaragua, El Salvador, Panama

The Storyteller

An American journalist interviewed a Nicaraguan mother whose daughter, a school-teacher, had been killed. The teacher, who had volunteered to help young children in a small remote village in the war zone, was ambushed by the contras. "My daughter gave her life fighting for freedom, like my son who died in the insurrection. Losing a child is like losing your life." She stopped for a moment to wipe her cheeks, and then looked up again. "My children were my whole life," she said. "My daughter never hurt anyone. All she was doing was teaching poor children in the mountains how to read."

Contra soldiers

—adapted from
Blood of Brothers, Life and War in Nicaragua, Stephen Kinzer, 1991

lthough independent since the 1800s, the nations of Central America have suffered from wars, civil unrest, and interference by foreign powers. Ruled by wealthy elites, several nations were gripped by revolution and civil war from the late 1970s. Only in the early 1990s was some stability restored to the region. This achievement gave hope that the desperate needs of the people could finally be addressed.

Nicaragua

Nowhere was the hold of the wealthy elite tighter than it was in **Nicaragua**. There the Somoza family took power in 1937, and, with the exception of one four-year period, remained in control, backed by the American-trained army known as the National Guard until 1979. By 1967, when **Anastasio Somoza Debayle** took over the presidency, the Somoza family owned one-quarter of the land in Nicaragua and most of the country's industries, banks, and businesses.

The Somozas' rule of Nicaragua caused increasing resentment; and by the late 1970s, the United States had ended its support. In 1978 peasants, Catholic priests, business people, and Marxists united to challenge Somoza. Leading the anti-Somoza alliance was the Sandinista National Liberation Front (FSLN). The **Sandinistas** took their name from Augustino Sandino, the popular hero who had waged guerrilla attacks on American occupation forces in Nicaragua in the 1920s. Sandino had been killed by the father of Anastasio Somoza in 1934.

After the Revolution

The rebel alliance succeeded in overthrowing Somoza in 1979. Although the majority of Nicaraguans cheered the revolution, they differed on how the new government should operate. Some Nicaraguans believed in capitalism and wanted to

Chapter 36 *Latin America* **985**

TEACH

Guided Practice

THEME Conflict

The United States played a key part in the conflicts in both Nicaragua and El Salvador. Which side did the United States aid in Nicaragua? (*the* contras) Which side did the United States help in El Salvador? (*the government*) What was its motive in both cases? (*fear of communism*) **L1 LEP**

Map Study

Answer

Guatemala, Nicaragua, and El Salvador

Map Skills Practice

Reading a Map Besides the three countries that experienced civil wars in the 1980s, what nations are located in Central America? (*Panama, Honduras, Costa Rica, Belize, Mexico*)

Independent Practice

📁 Guided Reading Activity 36-3 **L1**

Critical Thinking One of the slogans of FMLN supporters was "no justice, no peace." Ask students what the slogan meant in the context of El Salvador's civil war and whether it might be relevant in other parts of Latin America. **L2**

📁 Mapping History Activity 36

Latin America

Map Study

Powerful wealthy minorities ruled Central American countries, fueling revolutions.

Region What three nations in Central America were torn by civil wars in the 1980s?

---

maintain close ties with the United States. Others called for socialism and a lessening of dependence on the United States.

The Sandinistas, many of whom were Socialists or Communists, held control and began a series of popular reforms. They seized land that belonged to Somoza supporters and turned it over to peasant groups. With Castro's help, they taught people to read and write and improved rural health care.

Within a year after taking power, however, the new Nicaraguan government faced growing opposition. Upper- and middle-class Nicaraguans who had lost property to the Sandinistas opposed the creation of what they saw as a socialist dictatorship. Many of them fled to the United States. Meanwhile, disgruntled former allies of the Sandinistas joined forces with former Somoza supporters to try to overthrow the government. These opponents were called the **contras**, from the Spanish word meaning "against."

Civil War

The Nicaraguan government received financial and military aid from Cuba, the Soviet Union, and

---

many Western European countries. The United States, fearing the influence of the Soviets and the Cubans, decided to support the contras. In 1981 the United States government sent $19.5 million to the contras, the first official aid to the rebels. By 198_ contra forces numbered approximately 12,000 soldiers. From bases in Honduras and Costa Rica, the attacked Nicaraguan military bases and businesses

By 1985 the American public began to fear that the United States would be drawn into another conflict like that in Vietnam. The United State Congress banned military aid to the contras Despite the ban, members of President Ronald Reagan's staff continued to send covert, or secret funds to the contras. This illegal use of funds was part of the so-called Iran-Contra scandal that became public in 1987, embarrassing the Reagan administration and leading to indictments of some of the President's staff. Critics charged that an undercover foreign policy was being carried out against the express will of Congress.

Through negotiations, which were led by Costa Rican president **Oscar Arias**, the contras and the Nicaraguan government agreed to a cease-fire and to hold presidential elections in 1990. With American financial and political backing, **Violeta Chamorro**, the widow of a popular newspaper editor killed by Somoza in 1978, won the election. Chamorro led a wide-ranging coalition of parties. After her victory, she faced immense challenges. Her inclusion of key Sandinistas in her government cost her support among the conservative opposition. Despite efforts to introduce reforms, Nicaragua by the mid-1990s had a staggering foreign debt, high inflation, and massive unemployment. In 1996 Arnoldo Aleman, a conservative, was elected president over his Sandinista challenger, Daniel Ortega. After a campaign marked by bitter political rivalry, the new president called for national unity to solve Nicaragua's problems.

Footnotes to History

Nicaragua's Literacy Campaign

In 1980 over one-half of adult Nicaraguans were unable to read or write. The Nicaraguan government decided that those who were literate must help those who were not literate. Over the next 5 months, almost 100,000 students helped teach 500,000 people, most of whom were peasants. At the end of the period, Nicaragua's illiteracy rate was less than 15 percent.

COOPERATIVE LEARNING ACTIVITY

News Coverage Organize students into three teams, one each for Nicaragua, El Salvador, and Guatemala. Have each team investigate news coverage about its country. Students should listen to radio news broadcasts, watch TV news broadcasts, and read newspapers and newsmagazines. They may use *Readers' Guide to Periodical Literature* to find stories that have appeared recently. Students should summarize the information they gather and share it with the class. As a wrap-up, have the class discuss how well and how fairly these countries are covered by the media. **L2**

El Salvador

By the early 1970s, **El Salvador** was one of the most industrialized countries in Central America, boasting modern highways, railroads, airports, and office buildings. However, nearly 90 percent of the country's wealth was held by a small group of landowning families. About 40 percent of the population consisted of landless peasants.

The unequal distribution of wealth led to demands for change. Fearing a revolution, wealthy landowners hired death squads—bands of killers who murdered their political opponents. As many as 1,000 people were killed a month. One of the main critics of the murder of innocent civilians was Roman Catholic archbishop **Oscar Romero**. When a death squad killed him as he celebrated Mass on March 24, 1980, the country erupted into a civil war.

Moderates in the Salvadoran government supported land reform but were powerless to stop the death squads. As the killing continued, the Farabundo Martí National Liberation Front (FMLN)—a coalition of leftist guerrilla groups—won greater popular support. The United States, fearing Communist influence within the FMLN, gave military aid to the Salvadoran government. In 1992 the government and the FMLN finally agreed to a peace settlement. Over 70,000 people had died in the 12-year civil war. Another 1.5 million became refugees. Since the end of fighting, the government has made progress toward economic recovery and cooperation with its Central American neighbors.

Honduras

Following the overthrow of Somoza in Nicaragua in 1979, the military in neighboring Honduras moved to return power to civilian rulers. General elections were held in 1981, and a new constitution was approved the following year. Five democratically elected presidents have served Honduras since democracy was restored.

Although its government is stable, Honduras remains one of the poorest and least developed countries in the Western Hemisphere. Efforts to improve conditions were dealt a crushing blow in 1998, when Hurricane Mitch, the worst natural disaster in the area during the twentieth century, hit the country. The hurricane killed at least 7,000 Hondurans and forced hundreds of thousands from their homes. Mitch also destroyed more than half of all the agricultural crops in the country, severely reducing Honduras's exports.

In response to the natural disaster, foreign governments, the UN, and nonprofit organizations sent aid to Honduras and other countries affected by Hurricane Mitch. Despite that aid, however, the hurricane has had a devastating effect on the economy.

Guatemala

In recent decades Guatemala, the northernmost Central American country, has been torn by conflict arising from deep-rooted ethnic and social divisions. Most Guatemalans are rural Native Americans, but political and economic power has long been held by Spanish-speaking urban dwellers. Beginning in the 1960s, the wide social gap between rich and poor contributed to tensions

 Visualizing History Destruction of homes was widespread in Honduras, Nicaragua, Guatemala, and Belize during Hurricane Mitch in 1998. *How did the world respond to the crisis?*

Visualizing History Hurricane Mitch was the deadliest hurricane to hit the Western Hemisphere in two centuries. Damage was particularly devastating because clearing of hillsides for farming had left slopes vulnerable to mudslides. Without better land use, a similar tragedy could occur again.
Answer to Caption: *Individuals and national governments sent money to help the victims. The United States sent soldiers to help with relief efforts.*

ABC NEWS INTERACTIVE™

VIDEODISC
Communism and the Cold War

Side Two, Chapter 15
Frames 33016–35726
Title: *Nicaragua*
Ask: Why did Nicaragua *contra rebels* fight? *(because they believed the Communist regime was taking over Nicaragua)*

Side Two, Chapter 16
Frames 35749–38013
Title: *El Salvador*
Ask: What threat did San Salvador represent to the United States, according to President Reagan? *(Communist influence in close proximity to the United States)*

Chapter 36   *Latin America*   **987**

Visualizing History Until 1999, the U.S. controlled the Panama Canal, which links the Atlantic and Pacific oceans. *Why did the U.S. give up control of the canal?*

Visualizing History The Panama Canal is one of the greatest engineering marvels of all time. Ships at the canal are raised 85 feet above sea level. Each ship passing through the canal uses 52 million gallons of fresh water.
Answer to Caption: *It wanted a new relationship with Panama based on friendship and mutual respect.*

ASSESS

Check for Understanding

Assign Section 3 Assessment as homework or as an in-class activity.

 Use Interactive Tutor Self-Assessment Software to review Section 3.

Evaluate

Section Quiz 36-3

Use the Testmaker to create a customized quiz for Section 3.

Reteach

Review with the class the various motives behind U.S. intervention in Central America.

Reading Essentials and Study Guide 36-3

Enrich

Have students watch the 1989 film *Romero*, starring Raul Julia, which tells the story of the Salvadoran archbishop murdered in 1980, and write a short essay on the role of the Catholic Church in El Salvador's civil war.

CLOSE

Have students debate whether they think U.S. intervention helped or harmed the three Central American countries discussed in this section.

between these two groups. A small number of Europeanized families owned most of the nation's wealth, while the majority of the Native American population were landless and faced discrimination.

In the early 1960s, leftist guerrillas supporting land reform took up arms against the Guatemalan government. The conflict heightened in the 1970s and 1980s as the guerrillas strengthened their hold on the countryside. In response, the military harshly treated rural villagers, whom it suspected of aiding the guerrillas.

In the late 1980s, the government and the guerrillas agreed to talks. The 36-year civil war finally ended with a peace agreement in 1996. Although making no promises about land reform, the government agreed to reduce the military's size and to end discrimination against native peoples. The guerrillas in turn agreed to disarm and return to their homes. As a result of the conflict, more than 100,000 people had died, 46,000 others were missing, and about 1 million civilians were refugees.

Panama

Despite periods of dictatorship, **Panama** was relatively prosperous and peaceful after World War II. Much of this prosperity came from the American-owned Panama Canal. Many Panamanians, however, resented what they saw as foreign domination. In 1977 United States President Jimmy Carter and Panamanian President Omar Torrijos (toh•REE•hohs) signed the Panama Canal Treaties. According to the agreements, Panama would take control of the canal by December 31, 1999, the canal would remain open to the ships of all nations, and the United States would have the right to protect the canal's neutrality.

In 1988 General **Manuel Noriega** took power as president. Despite Noriega's former position as a CIA agent, his role in drug smuggling increased tensions with the United States. When Noriega arrested Americans in Panama, United States President George Bush sent American troops into the country in December 1989. Noriega was seized a month later and taken to Florida, where in 1992 he was tried and convicted of drug smuggling. Seven years later, Panama elected a female president, Mireya Moscoso, and also gained the Panama Canal from the United States.

SECTION 3 ASSESSMENT

Main Idea
1. Use a diagram like the one below to show what caused political conflicts in Central America from the 1970s to the 1990s.

Causes → Effect: Political Conflicts in Central America

Recall
2. **Define** covert, death squad.
3. **Identify** Anastasio Somoza Debayle, Sandinistas, contras, Oscar Arias, Violeta Chamorro, Oscar Romero, Manuel Noriega.

Critical Thinking
4. **Applying Information** John Kennedy once said of Central America: "Those who make peaceful change impossible make violent change inevitable." Show how events in El Salvador support this observation.

Understanding Themes
5. **Conflict** What role do you think the United States and other countries should play in Central America?

SECTION 3 ASSESSMENT ANSWERS

1. ethnic and social divisions; unequal distribution of wealth; drug trafficking; foreign intervention; dictatorships
2. All terms are defined in the Glossary.
3. Anastasio Somoza Debayle, 985; Sandinistas, 985; contras, 986; Oscar Arias, 986; Violeta Chamorro, 986; Oscar Romero, 987; Manuel Noriega, 988

4. The elite resisted demands for change and used death squads to silence opposition; the result was a violent revolution.
5. **CONFLICT** Answers should consider the security of other Western Hemisphere nations, fears of elites, and poverty of the masses.

Developing a Database

Do you have a collection of sports cards or CDs? Have you ever kept a list of the names, addresses, and phone numbers of friends and relatives? If you have collected information and kept some sort of list or file, then you have created a database.

Learning the Skill

An electronic database is a collection of facts that are stored in a file on the computer. The information is organized in fields.

A database can be organized and reorganized in any way that is useful to you. By using a database management system (DBMS)—special software developed for record keeping—you can easily add, delete, change, or update information. You give commands to the computer telling it what to do with the information, and it follows your commands. When you want to retrieve information, the computer searches through the file, finds the information, and displays it on the screen.

Practicing the Skill

Fidel Castro is one of the Latin American leaders discussed in this chapter. Follow these steps to build a database of the political events that have taken place during his years as Cuba's leader.

1. Determine what facts you want to include in your database.
2. Follow instructions in the DBMS that you are using to set up fields. Then enter each item of data in its assigned field.
3. Determine how you want to organize the facts in the database—chronologically by the date of the event, or alphabetically by the name of the event.
4. Follow the instructions in your computer program to place the information in order of importance.

5. Check that the information in your database is all correct. If necessary, add, delete, or change information or fields.

Applying the Skill

Bring to class current newspapers. Using the steps just described, build a database of current political events in Latin American countries. Explain to a partner why the database is organized the way it is and how it might be used in this class.

For More Practice

Turn to the Skill Practice in the Chapter Assessment on page 995 for more practice in developing a database.

TEACH

Developing a Database Students who know how to use and construct a database will have a valuable skill that can save them time in locating specific facts and figuring out relationships among facts. Begin a discussion of this page by taking a class survey to find out if any students have done computer database searches. (Students who have used a computerized card catalog at the library have used a database.)

When discussing the information in **Learning the Skill,** give students some examples of *fields*—for example, the year that an event takes place, the name of the event, or the main people connected with the event. Then explain that all of the data fields related to the same subject make up a record, and that a collection of records is a data file. If possible, show students examples of data files, records, and fields on a computer as well as the use of a database management system.

You might have students work in pairs to complete **Applying the Skill.** Have students share information about the organization and use of their databases. Point out notable similarities and differences.

Additional Practice

📁 Skill Reinforcement Activity 36

ANSWERS TO PRACTICING THE SKILL

Have students review Chapter 36—noting the references to Cuba and Fidel Castro—before they choose their facts. If students work at school computers, spot-check their progress, offering advice as requested. Invite students to share information about their completed databases. Point out the fields that are used most often, as well as ideas that are original and practical.

Section 4

South America

Guide to Reading

Read to Find Out
Main Idea *Democracy has advanced in South America since the late 1980s.*

▶ **Terms to Define**
   hyperinflation, cartel

▶ **People to Meet**
   Juan Perón, Eva Perón, Carlos Menem, Salvador Allende, Augusto Pinochet, Alberto Fujimori

▶ **Places to Locate**
   Argentina, Falkland Islands, Chile, Colombia, Peru, Brazil

The Storyteller

Eva Perón expressed herself about many topics, including feminismo, *the women's movement in Argentina:* "I felt that the women's movement in my country and all over the world had a

Eva Perón

sublime mission to fulfill … and everything I knew about feminism seemed to me ridiculous. For, not led by women but by those who aspired to be men, it ceased to be womanly and was nothing: feminism had taken the step from the sublime to the ridiculous. And that is the step I always try to avoid taking."

—from *Feminismo!* by Marifran Carlson, 1988

*S*ince the end of World War II, South America has become a region of sharp contrasts. Rapidly growing cities have sprawling slum areas as well as suburbs for the well-to-do and glamorous tourist resorts. While new industries have developed in the coastal urban areas, traditional forms of agriculture still dominate much of the interior of the continent. Despite areas of modernization and prosperity, widespread poverty continues to shape the politics and social structures of South American nations.

Argentina

Before a world depression and the rise of fascism in **Argentina** in the 1930s, the country was one of the 10 wealthiest in the world. Since then, the country has often been under military rule, and its prosperity has declined.

The Perón Era

The dominant political figure in Argentina from the 1940s to the 1970s was Colonel **Juan Perón** (pay•ROHN). When he was first elected president in 1946, Perón enjoyed great popularity, even though he was an authoritarian ruler. Perón and his glamorous wife, **Eva Perón**, a former film and radio star, became the heroes of the downtrodden. By increasing the military budget and supporting pay raises for union members, Perón won the loyalty of soldiers and workers. By nationalizing foreign-owned industries, he appealed to Argentinian pride over controlling its own resources. Eva supported construction of hospitals, schools, clinics, and nursing homes and distributed millions of shoes, sewing machines, and other household goods to the poor.

However, Perón's popularity began to wane in the 1950s. The much-loved Eva died in 1952. Perón's policy of taxing agriculture to fuel industrial growth led to a decline in food production. As the economy declined, anti-Perón protests increased.

990 Chapter 36 *Latin America*

Visualizing History More than 100,000 people rally in Buenos Aires, Argentina, in support of democratic government in 1987. The nation has had long periods of military rule interrupted by brief intervals of constitutional government. *Why has the military often seized power?*

In 1973, after almost 20 years of military rule, Perón returned briefly to power. When he died in 1974, his new wife Isabel took over, becoming the first woman president in the Americas. Economic problems led the military to oust her in 1976.

Argentina's military leaders sparked an economic recovery but ruled brutally. Death squads roamed the country, torturing and killing those who dissented. About 20,000 people simply disappeared. Mothers of missing children brought these human rights abuses to the world's attention through their weekly silent protest in Buenos Aires.

Toward Democracy

In 1982, in an effort to unite Argentina and to end one of the last outposts of colonialism, the military leadership sent Argentinian troops to seize the **Falkland Islands**, also known as the Malvinas. These islands off the coast of Argentina had been controlled by the British since 1833. Seventy-four days later, the Argentinians returned home defeated by the British forces.

After the Falklands humiliation, the military was discredited, and democracy was gradually restored. Economically, Argentina came dangerously close to collapse. In 1988 inflation reached 388 percent. This hyperinflation—extremely sharp and rapid price increases—caused a severe depression, and much of the middle class fell into poverty.

In 1989 Argentinians elected **Carlos Menem** as president. Menem brought inflation under control, attracted foreign investment, and sold off inefficient state-owned industries. During Menem's presidency, Argentina expanded its role in world affairs. It joined with Brazil, Paraguay, and Uruguay to form Mercosur, a free trade area. Despite successes, Argentinians worried about high unemployment, government corruption, and social inequality. With Menem expected to retire, voters in 1999 elected opposition leader **Fernando de la Rua** as president.

Chile

Once a stable democracy, **Chile** has faced political challenges in recent years. In 1970 **Salvador Allende** (ah•YEHN•day) was elected president, becoming the first Marxist in the Americas to win power peacefully. Allende applied socialist principles to the faltering economy—nationalizing industries and distributing land to the poor.

Chapter 36 *Latin America* **991**

TEACH

Guided Practice

THEME Change

Beginning in the late 1980s, many South American countries formerly controlled by the military changed to civilian rule. What factors led to this change in Argentina, Chile, and Brazil? *(Argentina: Falklands defeat discredited the military; Chile: popular dissatisfaction with repression; Brazil: military agreed to democratic rule.)* **L1 LEP**

Visualizing History In 1987 Argentine army officers staged an antigovernment revolt, but it was quelled, with strong public support.
Answer to Caption: *because of the country's economic problems and political turmoil*

Economics High inflation rates affect the price of everything. In Argentina in 1988, the annual inflation rate was 388 percent. For a $5 movie ticket, how much will the increase be? *($19.40)* How would people cope with increases like this? *(Wages would also rise, but usually not enough to compensate.)* **L2**

CURRICULUM CONNECTION

SCIENCE

Charles Darwin's study of animals in the Galápagos Islands, an Ecuadorean possession in the Pacific, were crucial to his theory of evolution. In his journal, Darwin noted that animal species he observed there were the "origin of all my views."

Visualizing History In the four months after Pinochet's 1973 coup, 250,000 people were detained for political reasons, and concentration camps appeared throughout Chile. **Answer to Caption:** *Pinochet was charged with human rights violations, including many of the disappearances and deaths that occurred during his rule.*

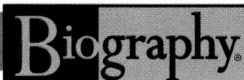

The following videotape program is available from Glencoe:

- **Evita: The Woman Behind the Myth**

Independent Practice

 Guided Reading Activity 36-4 **L1**

 People in World History Profile 69

VIDEODISC
Communism and the Cold War

Side Two, Chapter 14
Frames 31217–32996
Title: *Chile*
Subject: Inauguration of President Salvador Allende
Ask: To what does President Nixon refer by saying that Latin America will be all "red" eventually due to the election of a Marxist leader in Chile? *(He believes Chile will spread communism across Latin America.)*

Visualizing History There was much angry protest against the actions of General Augusto Pinochet, who ruled Chile between 1973 and 1990, and was arrested in 1998. *Of what crimes was he accused?*

Allende's programs had mixed success and made him powerful enemies. Wealthy Chileans invested their money abroad instead of at home. The United States, wary of Allende's ties to Cuba, funded opposition groups within Chile and blocked international loans to the country. By 1973, Chile's economy was near collapse.

At this time, Chilean military leaders backed by the CIA led a coup against Allende that resulted in his death. General **Augusto Pinochet** (PEE•noh•CHEHT), head of the new government, then dissolved Congress and canceled civil liberties. Many Chileans were killed or were imprisoned during this assault on Chilean democracy.

To improve the Chilean economy, Pinochet imposed higher taxes and encouraged foreign investment. Despite economic progress, opposition to Pinochet remained strong. In 1990 Pinochet resigned and a freely elected president, Patricio Aylwin, took office. After the return of democracy, Chile developed one of Latin America's strongest economies and sought to join NAFTA. In 1998 Pinochet was arrested in London, where he was living at the time, on charges of torturing opponents during his years in power.

Venezuela

Since the 1940s, **Venezuela** has been one of the world's major oil producers. In recent years, however, it has suffered a prolonged economic recession because of declining global oil prices. Frustrated with the lack of economic improvement, Venezuelan voters in 1998 elected **Hugo Chavez**, a political outsider and former military leader, as president.

Chavez pledged to rid Venezuela of corruption, rewrite the constitution, and promote economic recovery. In 1999, a constitutional assembly, made up largely of Chavez supporters, set out to increase presidential powers and reduce those of Congress and the Supreme Court. Critics charged that Chavez wanted to become a dictator.

In the midst of this political wrangling, Venezuela in December 1999 was hit with torrential rains that caused floods and mudslides. More than 50,000 people died in what was viewed as Latin America's worst natural disaster of the twentieth century. Responding to the crisis, the constitutional assembly gave Chavez sweeping powers to rebuild Venezuela.

Colombia

Since World War II, **Colombia** has had long periods of instability. Between the late 1940s and the mid-1960s, battles between liberals and conservatives caused the deaths of about 200,000 people. Colombians refer to this period as *La Violencia*, or the Violence.

During the 1970s and 1980s, the ever-growing power of drug dealers infected Colombian politics. Drugs, including marijuana and cocaine, became Colombia's largest export. Drug dealers in the city of Medellín amassed tremendous fortunes. They murdered more than 350 judges and prosecutors who tried to stop the drug business. By the mid-1990s, some progress was made in curtailing the power of the Colombian drug cartels, associations formed to establish an international monopoly by price fixing and regulating production. The illegal trade continued to flourish, however.

Learning Disability Students who have difficulty reading and understanding standard text material may respond well to music. Play selections from the works of the Brazilian composer Heitor Villa-Lobos and have students create drawings to illustrate their responses to the music. **L1 LEP**

Peru

Since World War II, **Peru** has experienced both military and civilian rule. In the early 1970s, military leaders distributed land to peasants, nationalized foreign-owned industries, and aided the urban poor. However, inflation and unemployment remained high. By the early 1980s, democracy had been restored under a new constitution.

In 1990, and again in 1995, Peruvians elected **Alberto Fujimori**, the son of Japanese immigrants, as president. Although criticized for his dictatorial ways, Fujimori worked to improve government efficiency and increase free enterprise. Under his leadership, Peru increased economic links with other Pacific countries, especially Japan.

In 1995 Fujimori ended the 15-year civil war with a Marxist guerrilla group known as the Shining Path. Some 25,000 Peruvians had been killed by the guerrillas and billions of dollars worth of property destroyed.

Brazil

From the late 1940s to the early 1960s, **Brazil** was generally a democracy. During this period, Brazil's economy expanded, as foreign investors opened steel plants and auto factories. In the early 1960s, labor unions helped elect leaders who promoted social reforms. However, military leaders, afraid reforms would lead to communism, took control of the government in 1964.

In the late 1960s, Brazil's military rulers pressed for greater industrial growth. They reduced social programs, increased foreign investment, and weakened labor unions. Although the economy prospered, wages stayed low and poverty was widespread.

By the late 1980s, increasing opposition at home and abroad forced the military to gradually return Brazil to democracy. Hopes for both economic growth and social reforms were raised with the election of Fernando Collor de Mello as president in 1990. Collor's concern for the environment, including efforts to slow the destruction of the Amazon rain forest, won him international support. However, in 1992 Collor resigned amid charges of corruption.

Brazil's new president, Fernando Henrique Cardoso, was forced to deal with serious economic problems. In 1998 the Brazilian currency lost more than a third of its value, and the economy was in a deep recession. Millions of Brazilians lost their jobs and sank into poverty.

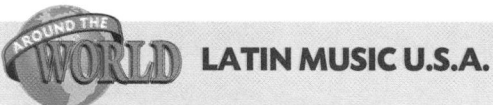 LATIN MUSIC U.S.A.

Hollywood, California, 1999
After his hit appearance at the 1999 Grammys, Puerto Rican-born singer Ricky Martin had the number one song in the United States. By the late 1990s, major American record companies were courting Martin and other Hispanic singing stars, such as Marc Anthony and Jennifer Lopez. Spanish-language radio in the United States was also booming. Many observers were forecasting that Latin pop music would be the sound of the future.

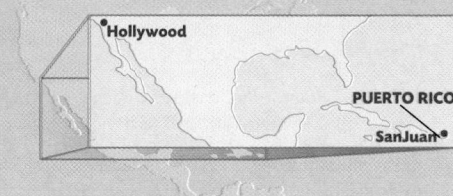

SECTION 4 ASSESSMENT

Main Idea
1. Use a diagram like the one below to show how democracy has advanced in South America since the late 1980s.

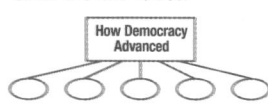
How Democracy Advanced

Recall
2. **Define** hyperinflation, cartel.
3. **Identify** Juan Perón, Eva Perón, Carlos Menem, Salvador Allende, Augusto Pinochet, Alberto Fujimori.

Critical Thinking
4. **Making Comparisons** How do the economies of Chile and Cuba differ?

Understanding Themes
5. **Change** How did military governments both improve and damage various South American nations?

Chapter 36   *Latin America*   **993**

ASSESS

Check for Understanding
Assign Section 4 Assessment as homework or as an in-class activity.

 Use Interactive Tutor Self-Assessment Software to review Section 4.

Evaluate
Section Quiz 36-4

 Use the Testmaker to create a customized quiz for Section 4.

Reteach
Have students review the changes in government in Argentina, Chile, and Brazil since the 1980s.

Reteaching Activity 36

Reading Essentials and Study Guide 36-4

Enrich
Have students watch the 1982 film *Missing*, starring Jack Lemmon and Sissy Spacek, based on the true story of an American who disappeared in Chile after Allende's overthrow in 1973.

 Enrichment Activity 36

CLOSE

Have students list the challenges facing the countries of South America today.

CHAPTER 36 ASSESSMENT

WORLD HISTORY *Online*

Have students use the **Chapter 36 Self-Check Quiz** at worldhistory.glencoe.com to prepare for the Chapter Test.

GLENCOE TECHNOLOGY

VIDEODISC
Use MindJogger to review the chapter.
MindJogger Videoquiz

Chapter 36
Disc 5 Side A

Also available in VHS.

Answers

Using Key Terms
1. c   3. g   5. d
2. e   4. i

Using Your History Journal

Explain that gross domestic product (GDP) is the total goods and services produced in a year, while gross national product (GNP) is GDP plus income from foreign investments.

Reviewing Facts

1. trade relationships with western Europe, Asia, Africa and Japan; leadership positions in world diplomacy; 1947 Rio treaty; OAS established in 1948; U.S. military aid to conservative governments and undermining of left-wing governments; Alliance for Progress; in the 1980s began working toward free trade
2. population growth, urbanization, domination by elites, foreign intervention and debt
3. Politically, PRI control has somewhat relaxed; economically, Mexico has privatized some industries and joined NAFTA.
4. Nicaragua: Somoza family

WORLD HISTORY *Online*

Self-Check Quiz

Visit the *World History: The Human Experience* Web site at **worldhistory.glencoe.com** and click on *Chapter 36—Self-Check Quiz* to prepare for the Chapter Test.

Using Key Terms

Write the key term that completes each sentence. Then write a sentence for each term not chosen.

a. campesinos   f. free trade
b. death squads   g. liberation theology
c. elite   h. covert
d. privatization   i. cartels
e. standard of living j. hyperinflation

1. Since colonial times, Latin American society has consisted of masses of poor people dominated by a small but wealthy _____.
2. From 1945 to the 1960s, Mexico's _____— the overall wealth of its people—increased.
3. Beginning in the 1960s, many Catholics in Latin America supported social change and promoted the ideas of _____.
4. Since the 1970s, Colombia has been affected by the drug _____, who control the illegal drug trade by fixing prices and regulating production.
5. By the mid-1980s, Mexico and other Latin American countries were supporting programs of _____, shifting control of industry from governments to private owners.

Technology Activity

Creating a Multimedia Presentation Locate information about the history of colonialism in Central America. Create a multimedia presentation about an individual country from that region. Include information about the history of colonialism, cultural influences of colonial powers and how that country achieved its independence. Before you begin, plan the type of multimedia presentation you would like to develop and the steps you will need to take. Cite all electronic resources used.

Reviewing Facts

1. **History** Use a diagram like the one below to show aspects of Latin America's international relations since the end of World War II.

```
    Latin America's
  International Relations
  ◯    ◯    ◯    ◯
```

2. **Government/Economics** List various political and economic challenges that confront Latin American countries.
3. **Government** Describe Mexico's political and economic system since the 1980s.
4. **History** List the causes of the civil wars in Nicaragua and El Salvador.
5. **History** Discuss political developments in Haiti since the fall of the Duvaliers.
6. **History** Explain how the Soviet collapse affected Cuba.
7. **History** Explain the purpose of the Organization of American States (OAS).
8. **Culture** Discuss the role of women in the struggle for human rights in Argentina.
9. **History** State why Juan and Eva Perón were popular in Argentina.

Critical Thinking

1. **Evaluate** How did the policies of the United States and Canada differ in the mid-1990s regarding Cuba? Which country do you think had the better approach in dealing with Castro?
2. **Apply** How would you solve the problem of the illegal drug trade between Colombia and criminals in the United States?

---

owned one-quarter of the land and most industry, banks, and businesses. El Salvador: A small group of families controlled 90 percent of the country's wealth.
5. After four years of turmoil, Aristide was elected president but was forced to flee; reinstated in 1994, he served until 1995, when a successor was elected.
6. Soviet aid ended and economy suffered
7. to develop political and economic ties

among nations of Western Hemisphere
8. Mothers of missing persons staged a weekly silent vigil in Buenos Aires, winning world attention for the plight of Argentine citizens.
9. They increased funds for the military and unionized workers, built public facilities, aided the poor, and stimulated national pride.

Critical Thinking
1. The U.S. believed in isolating Castro with an

3. **Synthesize** Imagine that you were a citizen of Nicaragua in the 1970s and 1980s. How would you feel about the Somoza government? The Sandinistas? The contras?
4. **Synthesize** Describe the goal of NAFTA. What are the advantages and disadvantages of NAFTA to Mexico and to the United States?

Geography in History

1. **Region** Refer to the map below. What large area of South America has an economy largely based on hunting, fishing, and gathering?
2. **Movement** Why are most manufacturing and commercial areas located along the seacoast?
3. **Place** Judging from the type of economic activity, where are South America's largest plains?

Economic Activity in South America

PACIFIC OCEAN

ATLANTIC OCEAN

0 250 500 mi.
0 250 500 km
Goode's Interrupted
Homolosine Projection

Agriculture
Forestry
Hunting, fishing, gathering
Little economic activity
Manufacturing and Commerce
Mining
Stock raising

Understanding Themes

1. **Cooperation** How has Latin America's interdependence with global and hemispheric markets affected its ability to develop economically?
2. **Revolution** How did Cuba's revolution affect the United States and the Soviet Union?
3. **Conflict** How did the cold war affect revolutions and civil wars in Central America?
4. **Change** How have South American countries changed politically and economically since the late 1980s and early 1990s?

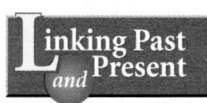

Linking Past and Present

1. How have American responses to Latin American crises today differed from American responses a century ago? How do you think the United States might respond in years to come?
2. In both the Monroe Doctrine and the Rio Treaty of 1947, the United States pledged to protect Latin American nations from outside powers. In the Falkland Islands War, however, the United States supported Great Britain. How do you think Latin Americans responded to this?

Skill Practice

Prepare a database of the major political events in South America from the 1970s to the 1990s. Include the following information in your database.
- Year
- Country
- Event

Be sure to follow these steps to build your database.
1. Determine what facts to include.
2. Follow instructions in the DBMS that you are using. Then enter each item in its assigned field.
3. Determine how you want to organize the facts in the database.
4. Place the information in order of importance.
5. Check the accuracy of the information. Make necessary changes.

Chapter 36 Assessment

materials and finished goods
3. east and southeast

Understanding Themes

1. **COOPERATION** It has brought industry and more exports.
2. **REVOLUTION** It brought the cold war to Latin America. The U.S. worked to rid Cuba of Castro and to deter revolutionary ideas in Latin America through the Alliance for Progress and the Peace Corps; the Soviet Union gained a foothold in the Americas and used Cuba to further its foreign policy interests.
3. **CONFLICT** U.S. fear of communism led it to intervene in many countries.
4. **CHANGE** Several countries have become democratic. Inflation has been brought under control.

Linking Past and Present

1. Answers will vary but should suggest that current and future policy will depend on cooperation rather than force.
2. Some saw it as a violation of U.S. pledges; others did not object since they had never supported Argentina's move.

Skill Practice
Databases will vary depending on events.

? Chapter Bonus Test Question

Ask students: Which of the three regional groupings in this chapter—Mexico and the Caribbean, Central America, or South America—do you think has the best prospects for the future? *(When predicting, students should keep in mind the region's history, government, economic resources, and social structure.)*

---

embargo; Canada traded with Castro, hoping that contact would move Cuba toward reforms. Answers will vary.
2. Suggestions may include education, interdiction, eradication, or legalization.
3. The Somozas dictatorially ruled Nicaragua for decades, the Sandinistas were a left-wing alliance that overthrew the Somozas, and the contras were U.S.-backed right-wing groups organized to oppose the new leftist regime.

4. NAFTA removes trade barriers among the U.S., Mexico, and Canada. Mexico: economic growth; expansion of agro-businesses; loss of traditions; environmental and labor concerns; U.S.: more trade and markets; job losses and gains; environmental and labor concerns

Geography in History
1. the north
2. for access to the sea for easy transport of raw

A complete, 1-page lesson plan is provided for each section in the *Reproducible Lesson Plans* booklet.

The World in Transition

CHAPTER RESOURCES

	Reproducible Resources	Multimedia Resources
Chapter Opener	Chapter Themes: Graphic Organizer 37 Historical Significance Chapter Activity 37	MindJogger Videoquiz
Chapter Enrichment	Vocabulary Activity 37* Time Line Activity 37 Mapping History Activity 37 History Simulation 37 Geography and History Activity 37 Source Reading 37 People in World History Profiles 71, 72 World Art and Music Activity 37 Enrichment Activity 37 Critical Thinking Activity 37 Skill Reinforcement Activity 37 Building Skills in Geography Workbook, Unit 2, Lesson 11 Performance Assessment Activity 37 Standardized Test Practice Workbook Activity 37 Inclusion for the Social Studies Classroom Strategies and Activities	World History and Art Transparencies 51, 52 Mapping History Overlay Transparency 25 Chapter Transparency 37 Vocabulary PuzzleMaker Software Picture Atlas of the World Turning Points in World History: *Fall of the Berlin Wall* Lessons of War: *The Nature of Violence* Communism and the Cold War: • *A New Soviet Union: Communist Rule Ends* • *Challenge of Reform* World History Primary Source Document Library
Chapter Review/Reteaching	Reteaching Activity 37 Skill Reinforcement Activity 37 Spanish Chapter Summary 37	Chapter 37 Digest Audiocassette, Activity, Test* Vocabulary PuzzleMaker Software Interactive Tutor Self-Assessment Software MindJogger Videoquiz
Chapter Evaluation/Testing	Performance Assessment Activity 37 Chapter 37 Test, Forms A and B	ExamView® Pro Testmaker

* Also available in Spanish

0:00 OUT OF TIME? Assign the Chapter 37 Audiocassettes.

World History Primary Source Document Library

Make History Come Alive!

Engage your students with over 250 easily accessible primary source documents—available on this CD-ROM—that will give them real life insight into the important events of world history.

Block Schedule

Activities that are particularly suited to use within the block scheduling framework are identified throughout this chapter by the following designation.

KEY TO ABILITY LEVELS

Teaching strategies are coded for varying learning styles.
L1 BASIC activities for all students
L2 AVERAGE activities for average to above-average students
L3 CHALLENGING activities for above-average students
LEP LIMITED ENGLISH PROFICIENCY activities

Use Glencoe's *Presentation Plus!* multimedia teacher tool to easily present dynamic lessons that visually excite your students. Using Microsoft PowerPoint® you can customize the presentations to create your own personalized lessons.

Interactive Lesson Planner

Planning has never been easier! Using this CD-ROM, organize your week, month, semester, or year with all the help you need. The **Interactive Lesson Planner** gives you access to all of the blackline masters that accompany *World History: The Human Experience.*

SECTION RESOURCES

Daily Objectives	Reproducible Resources	Multimedia Resources
Section 1 **The End of the Cold War** Identify the developments that changed the relationship of the superpowers by the mid-1990s.	Lecture Notes 37-1 Reproducible Lesson Plan 37-1 Guided Reading Activity 37-1* Section Quiz 37-1* Reading Essentials and Study Guide 37-1	Section Focus Transparency 37-1 Chapter Transparency 37 World History and Art Transparency 51, *Vietnam Memorial* Vocabulary PuzzleMaker Software Interactive Tutor Self-Assessment Software Communism and the Cold War: *A New Soviet Union: Communist Rule Ends*
Section 2 **The Crumbling Wall** Describe how Soviet Communist controls came to an end in Eastern Europe.	Lecture Notes 37-2 Reproducible Lesson Plan 37-2 Vocabulary Activity 37* Guided Reading Activity 37-2* People in World History Profile 71 Section Quiz 37-2* Reading Essentials and Study Guide 37-2	Section Focus Transparency 37-2 Interactive Tutor Self-Assessment Software Turning Points in World History: *Fall of the Berlin Wall* Communism and the Cold War: *Challenge of Reform*
Section 3 **Toward a European Union** Identify the steps Western European nations have taken to unify their governments and economies.	Lecture Notes 37-3 Reproducible Lesson Plan 37-3 Vocabulary Activity 37* Guided Reading Activity 37-3* Section Quiz 37-3* Reading Essentials and Study Guide 37-3	Section Focus Transparency 37-3 Interactive Tutor Self-Assessment Software Testmaker Picture Atlas of the World
Section 4 **National and Ethnic Conflicts** Recognize the areas of the world that have been in ethnic discord since the end of the cold war.	Lecture Notes 37-4 Reproducible Lesson Plan 37-4 Vocabulary Activity 37* Guided Reading Activity 37-4* People in World History Profile 72 Section Quiz 37-4* Reading Essentials and Study Guide 37-4	Section Focus Transparency 37-4 Interactive Tutor Self-Assessment Software Testmaker Lessons of War: *The Nature of Violence*
Section 5 **Global Interdependence** Explain how recent advances in technology have affected the world's cultures.	Lecture Notes 37-5 Reproducible Lesson Plan 37-5 Guided Reading Activity 37-5* Geography and History Activity 37 History Simulation 37 Reteaching Activity 37 Enrichment Activity 37 Section Quiz 37-5* Performance Assessment Activity 37 Spanish Chapter Summary 37 Reading Essentials and Study Guide 37-5	Section Focus Transparency 37-5 World History and Art Transparency 52, *Sky Above Clouds II* Mapping History Overlay Transparency 25, *World Population Growth* Vocabulary PuzzleMaker Software Interactive Tutor Self-Assessment Software Testmaker

* Also available in Spanish

Chapter Activities

 Performance Assessment Activity

An Awards Ceremony Have the students take the roles of producers and judges of a competition of persons and developments of the last 20 years. Have students create a name for the awards ceremony and identify the different types of awards that might be given, the nominees for each award (based on accomplishments found in the chapter or researched), and the winners (as determined by greatest impact). As a final product, students should create one of the following: (1) a newspaper article summarizing the awards ceremony, giving the categories, nominees and winners; (2) a videotape of the actual awards program; or (3) a set of radio interviews with the winners.

Possible Rubric Features
Accuracy of content information, decision-making skills, originality, ability to analyze relationships and classify information, oral presentation skills (if applicable), clarity of writing (if applicable)

• *For an additional activity, refer to Activity 37 in the* Performance Assessment Strategies and Activities *booklet.*

ACTIVITY
From the Classroom of...

Trent Steele
Kearney High School
Kearney, NE

[Name]'s Excellent Adventure!
Organize the class into five teams and give each team a current physical/political map of Europe with roads and train routes. Each team must plan a trip across modern-day Europe; for example, from London to Athens. Each group must plot the route on a map, following major roadways, trains, and water routes. Then, on poster paper, each group should list all countries, major cities, and major physical geographic features they will encounter on their journey, as well as at least ten major points of interest. Finally, each group should provide an approximate mileage [kilometer] figure for the entire trip. Have each group present the details of their journey to the class. After comparing current maps of Europe with some older ones, have the class draw conclusions about European geography. How has Europe changed? What features have stayed the same?

MULTIPLE LEARNING STYLES

Verbal/Linguistic
Have students choose one of the global concerns covered in this chapter (political, economic, social, or environmental), research the problem, and prepare a report to share with the class.

Logical/Mathematical
Have students who are computer buffs create a "bibliography" of interesting and useful web sites from around the world.

Visual/Spatial
Have students create a series of cartoons focusing on global environmental problems.

Kinesthetic
Ask students to make a time line banner for the bulletin board or wall that covers the years 1980 to 2000. They should fill in events and places from this chapter and leave spaces for filling in current events and predictions.

GLENCOE'S
ASSESSMENT
ADVANTAGE

Use the following to easily assess student learning in a variety of ways.

• Performance Assessment Strategies and Activities
• Section Quizzes
• Chapter and Unit Tests
• Interactive Tutor Self-Assessment Software

• Testmaker Software
• MindJogger Videoquiz
• SAT/SAT II Test Practice
• worldhistory.glencoe.com

Additional Resources

NATIONAL GEOGRAPHIC SOCIETY

Teacher's Corner

INDEX TO NATIONAL GEOGRAPHIC MAGAZINE

The following articles relate to this chapter:

- "Global Culture," by Joel L. Swerdlow, 8/99.
- "Barcelona," by T.D. Allman, 12/98.
- "A New Day for Romania," by Ed Vulliamy, 9/98.
- "Russia's Iron Road," by Fen Montaigne, 6/98.
- "Nenets: Surviving on the Siberian Tundra," by Fen Montaigne, 3/98.
- "A Dream Called Nunavut," by Michael Parfit, 9/97.
- "Sri Lanka," by Priit J. Vesilind, 1/97.
- "Information Revolution," by Joel L. Swerdlow, 10/95.

NATIONAL GEOGRAPHIC SOCIETY PRODUCTS AVAILABLE FROM GLENCOE

To order the following, call Glencoe at 1-800-334-7344:

- *GTV: The American People (Videodisc)*
- *GTV: A Geographic Perspective on American History (Videodisc)*
- *Picture Atlas of the World (CD-ROM)*

ADDITIONAL NATIONAL GEOGRAPHIC SOCIETY PRODUCTS

To order the following, call National Geographic at 1-800-368-2728:

- *The Rise and Fall of the Soviet Union (Video)*
- *Europe: The Road to Unity (Video)*
- *Technology's Price (Video)*

Access National Geographic's new dynamic MapMachine Web site and other geography resources at:

- http://www.nationalgeographic.com/
- http://www.nationalgeographic.com/maps/

BIBLIOGRAPHY

Literature of the Period
Shields, Carol. *The Stone Diaries.* New York: Penguin Books, 1993. A novel of a woman's journey through life in the changing twentieth century.

Readings for the Student
Weiner, Jonathan. *The Next One Hundred Years.* New York: Bantam Books, 1990. Prospects for life on this planet in light of the accelerated changes of the twentieth century.

Readings for the Teacher
Walker, Martin. *The Cold War.* New York: Henry Holt, 1993. An overview of the origins and course of the cold war.

WORLD HISTORY Online

Use our Web site as an additional resource. All essential content is covered in the Student Edition.

You and your students can visit the *World History: The Human Experience* Web site at worldhistory. glencoe.com The student text directs students to the Web site for the following options:

- **Chapter Overviews**
- **Student Web Activities**
- **Self-Check Quizzes**

Answers are provided for you in a link entitled "Web Activity Lesson Plan." Additional Web Resources, Interactive Puzzles, and content updates are also available.

Visit the Glencoe Web site at socialstudies. glencoe.com for social studies activities, updates, and links to other resources.

LOCAL OBJECTIVES

_____
_____
_____
_____
_____
_____
_____
_____
_____
_____
_____
_____
_____
_____
_____
_____
_____
_____
_____
_____
_____
_____

The World in Transition

CHAPTER THEMES

Chapter Themes are listed on this chapter opening page. A corresponding theme-based activity is available under "TEACH," and a theme-based question is asked in the Section and Chapter Assessments.

Storyteller

Historical Setting More than a year had passed since a group of Soviet economists had prepared a 500-day plan for transition to a semifree market based on Western economic support and cuts in Soviet defense spending. Opposition came from the Soviet military and directors of the defense industries. Gorbachev also failed to get Western financial support.

Historical Significance

Answers: *Glasnost, perestroika, and military concessions to the West; the growing influence of blocs of nations other than the United States and the Soviet Union, helped end the cold war.*

The Soviet Union broke up, and the former Soviet republics formed a commonwealth. Communist systems collapsed in Eastern Europe. Nationalist sentiments led to war in the Balkans and ethnic conflicts in CIS republics and elsewhere. The movement for European unity resulted in the European Union.

Nations became more interdependent economically. European and Pacific Rim nations are now economic giants.

Have students use the **Chapter 37 Overview** at worldhistory. glencoe.com as a prereading and postreading exercise for understanding chapter content.

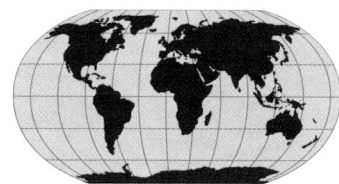

Chapter Themes

▶ **Change** The end of the cold war transforms the relationship of the United States and the Soviet Union. *Section 1*
▶ **Change** The weakening of the Soviet Union and the rise of reform movements bring an end to Soviet control in Eastern Europe. *Section 2*
▶ **Cooperation** The European Union works to create a united European economic power. *Section 3*
▶ **Conflict** National and ethnic conflicts intensify worldwide after the end of the cold war. *Section 4*
▶ **Cultural Diffusion** New technology and an integrated world communications system speed the transfer of ideas. *Section 5*

Storyteller

On December 25, 1991, Soviet President Mikhail Gorbachev resigned his office in a speech on national television:

"We live in a new world. The Cold War has ended, the arms race has stopped, as has the insane militarization that mutilated our economy, public psyche and morals. The threat of world war has been removed....

We opened ourselves to the rest of the world, abandoned the practices of interfering in others' internal affairs ..., and we were reciprocated with trust, solidarity, and respect.... "

With these words, Gorbachev pronounced the end of the cold war. The road that had led to the end of this war was long and dangerous. The last ten years were no exception. Now, amid the jubilation and hope, the question was raised: "Where do we go from here?"

Historical Significance

What developments brought about the end of the cold war? How has the world changed politically and economically since the beginning of the 1980s?

1980	**1990**	**2000**

1991 The Soviet Union and its Communist system collapse after a failed coup attempt.

1980 The Solidarity movement presses for reforms in Poland.

1993 Treaty of Maastricht creates the European Union.

1999 Pol. Hungary, the Czech Republic join NATC

996

GEOGRAPHY CONNECTION

Location Display a world map. Before studying each section of the chapter, ask students to find the region covered on the map. Have students put markers on the map for the areas of ongoing conflict as they study them. How does the location of European countries present a special problem not encountered by the United States? *(They are so close together that they are in the midst of each other's conflicts; uprisings can easily spread beyond national boundaries. The United States, by contrast, is physically removed.)*

Visualizing History New technology has helped advance space exploration. The earth's people now can view the earth as a single unit with a shared environment.

Visualizing History Space has become a laboratory in which scientists can assess what is happening to our planet. Spacecraft can orbit the earth and photograph areas of the planet to monitor changes. Scientists hope to be able to "watch the planet breathe" and study global change with the aim of preventing more damage to the earth.

 Performance Assessment

Refer to the activity on page 996C of the Planning Guide.

 For an additional activity, refer to Activity 37 in the *Performance Assessment Strategies and Activities* booklet.

WORLD HISTORY *Online*

apter Overview

it the *World History: The Human Experience* eb site at **worldhistory.glencoe.com** and ck on *Chapter 37—Chapter Overview* preview the chapter.

Your History Journal

Choose a region of the world that is having difficulty keeping peace. Imagine that you are part of a delegation of diplomats from the United Nations who have been sent to the region to talk with leaders. Write your opening statement.

Using Your History Journal

Remind students to think first about how the people native to the region they are visiting differ from them culturally. Remind them of the need to be sensitive to and respect their values and needs.

Chapter 37 *The World in Transition* **997**

GLENCOE TECHNOLOGY

 VIDEODISC
Use MindJogger to preview chapter content.

MindJogger Videoquiz

 Chapter 37
Disc 5 Side B

 Also available in VHS.

➕ EXTRA CREDIT PROJECT

Global Issues Daily newspapers, television broadcasts, and newsmagazines cover and update most of the topics in this chapter. Have students gather up-to-the-minute information on the issues, people, and places they study and compile articles to put into a "Global Issues" newspaper. They can work in groups or individually; one or two students might volunteer to be the editors and oversee the articles coming in. By the end of the chapter, they should have current information on most of the topics to print in the newspaper for class distribution.

1980 Ronald Reagan is elected President of the United States.

1985 Mikhail Gorbachev becomes leader of the Soviet Union.

1991 Former Soviet republics form the CIS.

1995 Russian and American soldiers take part in NATO-led Bosnian peacekeeping mission.

Section 1

The End of the Cold War

SECTION THEME

▶ **Change** The end of the cold war and the collapse of communism transform the relationship of the United States and the Soviet Union.

Guide to Reading

For reading strategies to help students read effectively see pages 12–13. Have students think about the main head as they read the subheads.

Vocabulary Pre-check

☒ Use the Vocabulary PuzzleMaker for Chapter 37 to create a crossword puzzle to reinforce section terms. **L1 LEP**

📁 Use Vocabulary Activity 37 to introduce vocabulary terms. **L1 LEP**

FOCUS

Section Objective

Identify the developments that changed superpower relations by the mid-1990s.

BELLRINGER
Motivational Activity

Before taking roll at the beginning of the class period, project Section Focus Transparency 37-1 and have students answer the activity questions. Discuss students' responses.
📁 This activity is also available as a blackline master.

Guide to Reading

Read to Find Out
Main Idea *Certain developments changed superpower relations by the mid-1990s.*

▶ **Terms to Define**
trade deficit, budget deficit, glasnost, perestroika, privatization

▶ **People to Meet**
Ronald Reagan, George Bush, Bill Clinton, Madeleine Albright, Mikhail Gorbachev, Boris Yeltsin, Vladimir Putin

▶ **Places to Locate**
Moscow, Latvia, Lithuania, Estonia, Russia, Ukraine, Belarus, Kazakhstan, Georgia, Armenia, Azerbaijan, Uzbekistan, Tajikistan, Turkmenistan

The Storyteller

As the U.S. government's deficit soared out of control, the budget became the focus of debate.

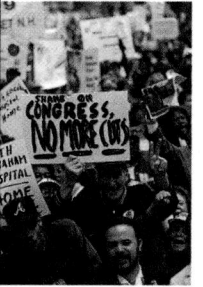

Aaron Wildavsky explained what may be the heart of the problem: "There are times when an agency wishes to cut its budget…. If the agency [has] effective clientele groups (special interests), however, it may not only fail in this purpose but may actually see the appropriation increased as this threat mobilizes the affected interests."

—from "Political Implications of Budgetary Reform," Aaron Wildavsky in *Classic Readings in American Politics,* 1986

U.S. group protesting budget cuts

998 Chapter 37 *The World in Transition*

n the early 1980s, cold war tensions between the United States and the Soviet Union increased dramatically. However, the world had changed since the 1950s when the superpowers competed alone in the arena of world affairs. Now other blocs of nations, with their own separate concerns, were influencing global developments. In addition, the two superpowers faced growing political and economic problems at home. Together, domestic and international changes would lead to the end of the cold war.

The United States

By the early 1980s, the United States was losing its dominance of the global market. It had changed from a lending nation to a borrowing nation. America also experienced trade deficits, buying more from foreign nations than it sold in foreign markets. As other industrialized lands developed powerful economies, their industries competed with American industries in making sales to American consumers.

Reinventing Government

Meanwhile, the United States government found it difficult to live within its means. In 1980 Republican **Ronald Reagan** won the presidency partly on his promise to reduce the budget deficit, or the difference between the amount of money the government collects in revenues and what it spends. As President, Reagan cut spending on social programs and lowered taxes to stimulate economic growth. During his two terms, inflation slowed and the economy improved. However, increased military spending by Reagan and his Republican successor, **George Bush**, pushed the budget deficit to new heights.

SECTION RESOURCES

📁 **Reproducible Masters**
• Lecture Notes 37-1
• Reproducible Lesson Plan 37-1
• Guided Reading Activity 37-1
• Section Quiz 37-1
• Reading Essentials and Study Guide 37-1

🖥 **Transparencies**
• Section Focus Transparency 37-1
• Chapter Transparency 37
• World History and Art Transparency 51, *Vietnam Memorial*

Multimedia
🖥 Vocabulary PuzzleMaker Software
🖥 Interactive Tutor Self-Assessment Software
🖥 Testmaker
🖥 Communism and the Cold War: *A New Soviet Union: Communist Rule Ends*

In 1992 Democrat **Bill Clinton** was elected President. Clinton favored both moderate deficit reduction and increased spending. Attacking Clinton for favoring costly government programs, Republicans in 1994 won control of both houses of Congress. After strong disagreements, Clinton and Congress finally worked out a plan to balance the budget and to move people from welfare to jobs. By 1998, government cutbacks and the robust economy turned the budget deficit into a surplus.

Meanwhile, new technology and increased efficiency had boosted the American economy. This success enabled Clinton to win reelection in 1996 over his Republican opponent, Robert Dole, and Reform party candidate Ross Perot.

Clinton's second term in office, however, was plagued with problems. In 1998 a scandal involving the President's relationship with a White House intern engulfed the nation. The House of Representatives voted impeachment, or formal charges of misconduct, against the President, and a trial was held in the Senate. Clinton was acquitted by the Senate and continued to serve as President.

American Foreign Policy

During the 1980s and 1990s, sweeping changes in the world affected American foreign policy. In the early 1980s, President Reagan called the Soviet Union an "evil empire" and increased military spending. The Soviets also intensified the arms race, and they continued to occupy Afghanistan. By mid-decade, new Soviet leaders saw the dangers of the arms race to their economy and signaled their desire for change.

With the Soviet collapse in 1991, the United States developed a new foreign policy for the post-cold war world. Presidents Bush and Clinton supported the growth of democracy in Russia and other former Communist nations. They also pushed for the expansion of NATO to include former Soviet satellites in Eastern Europe. Meanwhile, the United States—as the world's sole superpower—participated in efforts to solve regional conflicts in the Middle East, Northern Ireland, Somalia, Haiti, and the Balkans.

One of the architects of the new foreign policy was **Madeleine Albright**, who in 1997 became the first woman to serve as Secretary of State. She used diplomacy, mediation, and economic pressure where possible, but did not avoid using force in the Balkans when negotiations broke down.

American Society

At the turn of the century, many opportunities and challenges face the United States. The technological revolution has created opportunities for workers trained in new skills. However, workers without such training have not always benefited. By the late 1990s, the income gap between rich and poor had become wider than at any time since the 1930s. As a result, Americans now recognize the need for more effective ways to improve education and provide people with relevant job skills.

Crime and violence present another challenge. In 1995 the bombing of a federal office building in Oklahoma City claimed 168 lives and focused national attention on the violent anti-government feelings of private American militia groups. In 1999 two high school students in Colorado planted bombs and opened fire on their classmates. The gunmen and 13 people were killed, setting off a national debate about guns and youth violence.

In the 1990s there were new or increased risks to the health of Americans. Diseases such as AIDS (acquired immunodeficiency syndrome) killed thousands in the United States. Drug addiction continues to be a concern, which causes many to demand more governmental solutions.

Immigration became a pressing issue in the 1990s, when economic and political ills around the world brought a new tide of immigrants to the United States. Some newcomers were illegal aliens, people who enter a country without a permit. Many Americans blamed increased immigration for loss of jobs and higher taxes. In 1996 Congress passed legislation that imposed new restrictions on both legal and illegal immigrants. The new rules, however, were opposed by civil rights groups.

Related to immigration is the question of diversity. Some Americans believe that the different peoples who make up the United States should retain their individual cultural heritage. Others believe that the United States should be a melting-pot society in which immigrants from around the world blend into one unique people.

Gorbachev's USSR

In the mid-1980s, **Mikhail Gorbachev**, a reform-minded leader, came to power in the Soviet Union. To transform the inefficient, state-run economy and halt the decay of Soviet society, Gorbachev was willing to make drastic changes. Under his policy of glasnost, meaning "openness," Gorbachev allowed freedom of expression for Soviet citizens and eased harsh measures against critics of the Soviet system.

Departing from rigid state controls, Gorbachev also pushed for a rebuilding of the Soviet economy, a policy the Soviets called perestroika (PEHR•uh•

TEACH

Guided Practice

THEME Change

Put the heads *U.S.* and *USSR* on the chalkboard and ask students to list the economic problems these countries faced in the 1980s and the changes leaders sought. **L1 LEP**

Critical Thinking With the freedom to leave the Soviet Union, Soviet Jews poured into Israel in the early 1990s. Ask students to suggest what problems Israel faced as a result of this influx. *(shortage of jobs, newcomers don't understand the language or such basic things as the banking system; inadequate housing)* **L3**

The following videotape programs are available from Glencoe:

- **Ronald Reagan: The Role of a Lifetime**

- **George Bush: A Sense of Duty**

VIDEODISC
Communism and the Cold War

Side One, Chapter 21
Frames 38662–44504
Title: *A New Soviet Union: Communist Rule Ends*
Ask: What changes were made by Gorbachev's reforms? *(The people were allowed to vote, political prisoners were set free, and the ruling party was no longer required to be Communist.)*

COOPERATIVE LEARNING ACTIVITY

Geography: Place Organize the class into small groups. Assign each group one of the republics of the Soviet Union to research and prepare an oral report. Students should find out about the geographic features, the people, the resources, the cities, and daily life. Suggest that each group divide the tasks and prepare information, including a map or copies of photographs, about one aspect of their republic. When the research is complete, ask each group to give a class presentation on its assigned republic. **L2**

Chapter Transparency 37

 World History and Art
Transparency 51, *Vietnam
Memorial*

Independent Practice

Guided Reading Activity
37-1 **L1**

**Visualizing
History** By speaking
directly with citizens and listening to
their complaints and hopes, Gorbachev sought to soften the government's image and encourage greater
citizen participation.
Answer to Caption: *He wanted to
publicly acknowledge the nation's problems and rebuild the Soviet economy,
moving toward greater reliance on free
enterprise.*

TURNING POINT

The Soviet Breakup
How did communism in the
Soviet Union come to an end?
*Gorbachev's efforts to reform the
Communist system led only to
the Soviet Union's further decay.
Attempts by hard-liners to
regain power led to public resistance and the complete collapse
of Soviet communism.*

Critical Thinking Gorbachev has
written that the end of the cold
war "… has also brought to the
fore tensions that were latent,
frozen as it were, during the confrontation between global
alliances. Many of these tensions
have exploded into bloody conflicts." Have students comment
on this statement in view of
material in this section. **L3**

Soviet leader Mikhail Gorbachev
(center) and his wife Raisa (left)
greet Soviet citizens at a public meeting. *What
changes did Gorbachev want to make in 1985?*

STROY•kuh). Gorbachev encouraged limited
moves toward free enterprise. He began to dismantle the national bureaucracy that controlled
industrial production, allowing more decision making at local levels.

Gorbachev's Foreign Policy

Facing the enormous American military
buildup under President Reagan, Gorbachev needed to negotiate new arms-reduction agreements
with the United States. Since Soviet economic
progress depended on military cutbacks, Gorbachev
made large concessions to settle long-stalled treaty
negotiations. His offers to cancel nuclear tests and to
withdraw Soviet missiles from Eastern Europe were
so sweeping that they took Western leaders by surprise. To further ease global tensions, Gorbachev
withdrew Soviet troops from Afghanistan.

Gorbachev also encouraged Eastern European
Communist leaders to carry out reforms. His policies inspired discontented majorities in these
repressed countries. Scattered demands for democracy grew into a wave of anti-Communist protest
that eventually brought down the Iron Curtain.

New Challenges

Gorbachev's fresh outlook and friendly personality made him popular in the Western countries he
visited. At home, however, Gorbachev was increasingly criticized. Economic problems continued, and
even worsened, while reforms stalled. At the same
time, the conservative bureaucracy and military

resisted change, fearing the loss of jobs and the
weakening of Soviet might. To maintain control,
Gorbachev zigzagged between reformist and hard-line positions, creating uncertainty throughout government and business.

By 1990, perestroika's slow pace had brought
forward rivals to Gorbachev's leadership. The most
powerful of these challengers was **Boris Yeltsin**, a
former Gorbachev ally. Wanting to increase the
pace of reforms, Yeltsin took his case to the people,
winning election to the presidency of the Russian
Republic, the largest of the Soviet republics. As an
elected leader, Yeltsin had a stronger base of support than did Gorbachev.

TURNING POINT

The Soviet Breakup

While Gorbachev faced mounting opposition
from political rivals, nationalist and ethnic unrest
began to sweep the Soviet Union. As its name
reflected, the Union of Soviet Socialist Republics
(USSR) was a union of 15 separate republics, or
states. The largest was Russia, which included the
Soviet capital, **Moscow**. The non-Russian republics
resented the dominance of the Russians over their
affairs. A strong Soviet secret police and army had
long kept opposition and nationalist groups under
control. But in the relaxed atmosphere of glasnost,
old hatreds resurfaced. Throughout the republics
there were strong demands for self-rule, if not outright secession. In 1990 **Latvia**, **Lithuania**, and
Estonia became the first republics to declare their
independence from the Soviet Union.

A Dangerous Course

To appease the conservatives who feared a
breakup of the Soviet Union, Gorbachev began a
rollback of glasnost in the early 1990s and adopted
new hard-line positions. Among them were the
tightening of controls on the Soviet press to curb
dissent and the restoration of powers to the secret
police. Some of Gorbachev's reform-minded political aides resigned in protest, and Soviet citizens, led
by Yeltsin, called for Gorbachev to step down.

The Coup Attempt

In August 1991 events in the Soviet Union finally reached a climax. Hard-liners in the military and
secret police staged a coup to remove Gorbachev
from power and to restore the old order. In three
tense days the coup unraveled. Early support for the
coup evaporated in the face of the heroic leadership

Boris Yeltsin in Moscow. Resistance spread to other parts of the country. Military units refused to carry out the orders of the coup leaders.

The coup turned out to be the turning point for the Soviet Union. Gorbachev was seen as unable to solve the country's problems and unable to shake off his Communist roots. Yeltsin became the real leader of the Soviet Union. Popular anger at the Communist Party and the secret police swept the land, and the party dissolved. Statues of party leaders were torn down; many cities chose to return to their pre-1917 names. One such city was Leningrad, which had given birth to the 1917 Bolshevik Revolution. It took back its historic name —St. Petersburg.

Independent Republics

By late September all the Soviet republics had announced their independence from the Soviet Union. Gorbachev failed to win their support for a Union Treaty guaranteeing the republics greater self-rule within the old Soviet framework. Yeltsin, however, chose another plan to maintain unity among the republics. In December 1991, the three Slavic republics—**Russia**, **Ukraine**, and **Belarus**—announced the formation of the Commonwealth of Independent States (CIS), a loose association of republics. Other republics quickly joined. Mikhail Gorbachev, now a man without a country to govern, resigned the Soviet presidency.

Foreign Policy

After the Soviet collapse, Russia and the other nuclear CIS republics—Ukraine, Belarus, and Kazakhstan—took steps to secure their nuclear arsenals. They agreed that Russia would assume control of all their nuclear arms. Ukraine later dismantled its arsenal and declared itself nuclear-free. Meanwhile, the United States and Russia agreed on a mutual reduction in nuclear weapons. By 1997 both nations were no longer targeting warheads at each other.

Russia's weakened global position, however, made it wary of Western intentions on many different fronts. Yeltsin opposed NATO's admission of three Eastern European nations–Poland, Hungary, and the Czech Republic–all former Soviet satellites. The Soviet president later accepted NATO's eastward

Map Study

Russia and the Independent Republics

By December 1991 all the republics had declared independence from the Soviet Union. Beginning in 1994, Russia fought a war against the breakaway republic of Chechnya.
Place What independent republic has the best access to warm water ports?

Map Study

Answer
Russia

Map Skills Practice

Reading a Map What bodies of water does Russia border? (*Baltic Sea, Barents Sea, Black Sea, Caspian Sea, Sea of Japan, Sea of Okhotsk, Bering Sea, Arctic Ocean*)

Who? What? Where? When?

Soviet Exodus With glasnost came the freedom for Soviet Jews to emigrate. Half a million Jews moved to Israel between 1989 and 1992.

Linking Past and Present

Alexander Pushkin, perhaps Russia's greatest poet, was born in 1799 and lived only 37 years, but he is an enduring part of Russian culture. He was a champion of liberty and wrote drama and some prose as well as poetry. His masterpiece, *Eugene Onegin*, inspired an opera by Tchaikovsky and was translated into English by Vladimir Nabokov. Russian poet Yevgeny Yevtushenko, a modern-day champion of freedom, says, "Pushkin stands out as that rare Russian, an independent man."

ASSESS

Check for Understanding

Assign Section 1 Assessment as homework or as an in-class activity.

Use Interactive Tutor Self-Assessment Software to review Section 1.

Chapter 37 *The World in Transition* **1001**

MAKING CONNECTIONS ACTIVITY

Environment One of the largest lakes in the world, the Aral Sea, is located in the republics of Uzbekistan and Kazakhstan and is drying up. Many have recognized this as a major environmental tragedy. The Aral Sea has already lost a volume of water equal to one and a half times that of Lake Erie and continues to shrink. Have students research this topic and prepare a written report on the problem and the environmental impact it is having on the inhabitants of the area. **L2**

TEACH

Explain that the new freedom of expression allowed under Gorbachev opened a floodgate after years of repression. Ask students to try to imagine the courage it took, after such ingrained habits of watching one's words, to openly confront a Russian colonel as the man in this photograph is doing. What other forms of protest could people make under glasnost? *(open display of banners of protest, telegrams of criticism to politicians, publicly airing grievances through demonstrations, publishing books critical of the government, even jokes about the system)*

Who? What? Where? When?

Mikhail Gorbachev, who is now president of the International Foundation for Socio-Economic and Political Studies in Moscow, has written a book called *The Search for a New Beginning: Developing a New Civilization*. The views expressed in the book reflect a man who has taken a careful look at the past, has learned from it, and has changed. About the early years of glasnost and perestroika, he says: "... we formulated the principle 'Start perestroika with yourself.' In fact, however, we rushed to change society while leaving the change of ourselves for later ... the root cause of many of our ... failures."

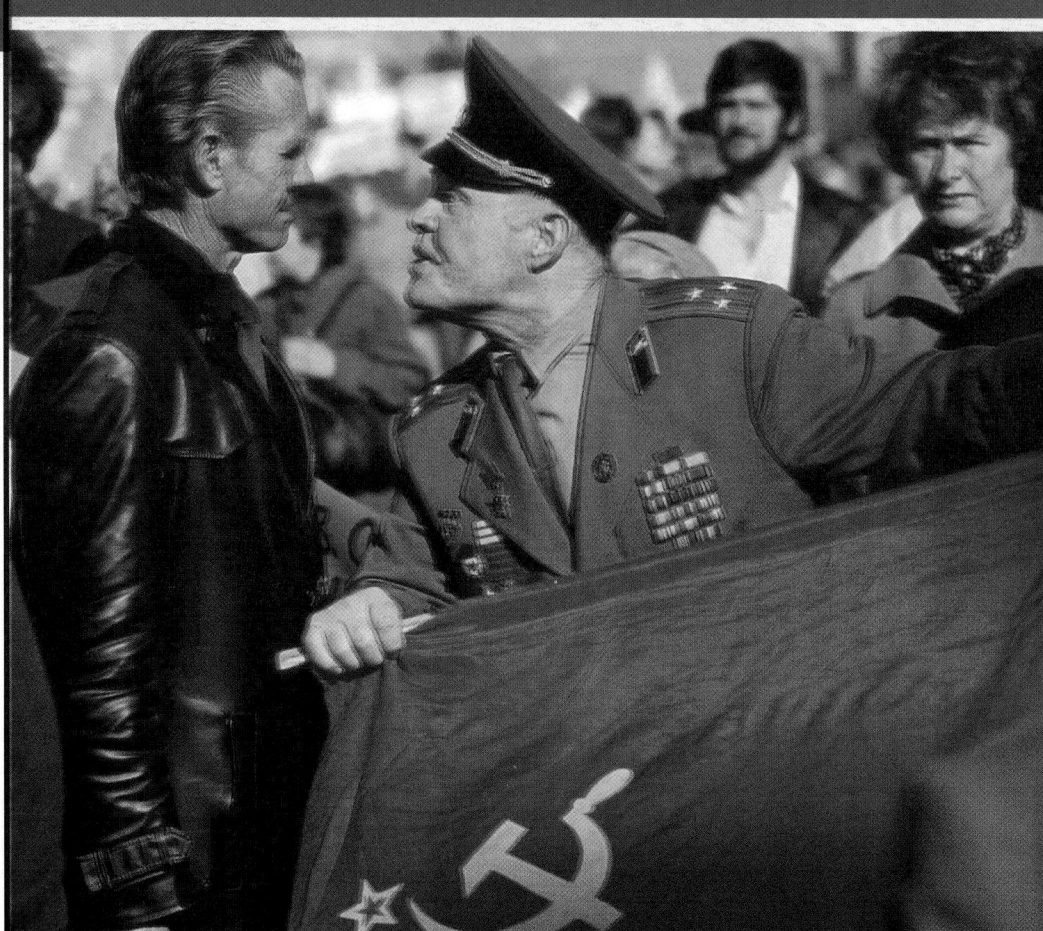

Seeing Red

Traitor! A flag-waving Russian colonel shouts at a demonstrator who wants to end the 70-year-long rule of communism in the Soviet Union. Opposing visions divided the Russian people as they faced their uncertain future in the spring of 1990. Would their children live in the Union of Soviet Socialist Republics where they had grown up? Would communism prevail, after all the sacrifices made in the name of Lenin or Stalin? Would the state plan a national economy, or would the forces of the market prevail? Who would win and who would lose?

Communism first began to crumble in th nations of Eastern Europe. As early as Hungarians revolted, and in 1968 the Czech In these early years of the cold war the C regime was strong enough to withstand thos In 1989 Germany's Berlin Wall crumbled. I Soviet Union itself began to fall apart, fi Baltic States and then throughout the coun various republics proclaimed their independ wonder anger and fear line the faces of the pictured above, as they confront the end of they know. ⊕

1002   Chapter 37   *The World in Transition*

expansion but won Western assurances that no nuclear missiles would be placed in Eastern Europe. Russia also joined discussions held by the world's major free enterprise democracies known as the Group of Eight.

In the late 1990s, Russia's relations with the West, however, threatened to break down over NATO's military involvement in the Balkans. Russia has long regarded this area as its sphere of influence. Only intense diplomacy prevented a complete rupture in Soviet-Western ties.

Economic and Social Changes

At home, Yeltsin introduced reforms to move Russia's economy from government control to free enterprise. These measures included removing price controls, closing inefficient factories, and promoting privatization, the setting up of privately owned businesses. The immediate result, however, was an increase in both prices and unemployment, causing much discontent. Many of the other CIS countries—for example, **Ukraine**, **Georgia**, **Armenia**, **Azerbaijan**, **Uzbekistan**, **Tajikistan**, and **Turkmenistan**—pushed similar economic reforms while facing unrest among their populations.

By the mid-1990s, some progress had been made in stabilizing prices, and new businesses and a new middle class were growing in the former Soviet republics. Yet many reforms were stalled or had little immediate impact. In Russia, production fell sharply, and the government lacked funds, mainly due to mismanagement, corruption, and difficulty in collecting taxes. To receive needed aid from abroad,

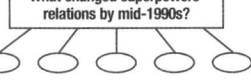
Russian President Boris Yeltsin tried to promote free enterprise reforms but had mixed results. *What economic problems did Russia face in the 1990s?*

Yeltsin had to cut spending for the military. In 1998, Russia faced a serious economic crisis, and the currency was devalued.

Social conditions also worsened for most Russians. A third of the country fell below the poverty line. Street violence, organized crime, and ethnic unrest increased fears about declining law and order. Pollution caused by Soviet-era industrialization presented a major health risk.

By the late 1990s, Yeltsin's health, as well as public confidence in his leadership, had declined. Then in 1999, Yeltsin increased military pressure on the breakaway republic of Chechnya. This show of Russian power came after alleged Chechen terrorist attacks in Russian cities. The chief architect of the "get tough" policy was Yeltsin's newly-appointed prime minister, **Vladimir Putin**. In a surprise move in January 2000, Yeltsin resigned, handing over the presidency to Putin a few weeks in advance of presidential elections.

SECTION 1 ASSESSMENT

Main Idea

1. Use a diagram like the one below to identify developments that changed the superpowers' relations by the mid-1990s.

> What changed superpowers' relations by mid-1990s?

Recall

2. **Define** trade deficit, budget deficit, glasnost, perestroika, privatization.
3. **Identify** Ronald Reagan, George Bush, Bill Clinton, Madeleine Albright, Mikhail Gorbachev, Boris Yeltsin, Vladimir Putin.

Critical Thinking

4. **Applying Information** Why has the transition to free enterprise been difficult in the former Soviet republics?

Understanding Themes

5. **Change** How did Gorbachev's policy of glasnost allow for independence movements?

Chapter 37 *The World in Transition* 1003

**Chapter 37
Section 1**

Visualizing History Yeltsin had the support of both urban and rural sectors in the 1990 elections. In the 1991 coup, he showed the courage and populist instincts that made them rally behind him.
Answer to Caption:
declining productivity, lack of funds, corruption

Evaluate

Section Quiz 37-1

Use the Testmaker to create a customized quiz for Section 1.

Reteach

Lead the class in discussing the main points covered in this section about the United States, the Soviet breakup, and the new Commonwealth of Independent States. Ask volunteers to name the key people involved and write them on the chalkboard.

Reading Essentials and Study Guide 37-1

Enrich

Have students find music, art, or literature from Eastern Europe in the late twentieth century and compile a resource list for the class.

CLOSE

Ask students to consider what problems they think the end of the cold war solved and what new problems it may have created.

SECTION 1 ASSESSMENT ANSWERS

1. U.S. foreign policy based on diplomacy or economic pressure; Soviet policy of perestroika; U.S. and Russia negotiated nuclear weapons reduction agreements; breakup of Soviet Union; fall of Iron Curtain; Russia strengthened economic and political ties with West

2. All terms are defined in the Glossary.
3. Ronald Reagan, 998; George Bush, 998; Bill Clinton, 999; Madeleine Albright, 999; Mikhail Gorbachev, 999; Boris Yeltsin, 1000; Vladimir Putin, 1003
4. Answers will vary. Possible answer: Not all people favor the change and some

have wanted to block the transition.
5. **CHANGE** It allowed people to express discontent and admit problems; rigid controls were dropped and old resentments resurfaced.

1980   1990   2000

1983 Polish labor leader Lech Walesa
is awarded the Nobel Peace Prize.

1989 Uprisings topple
Communist governments
in Eastern Europe.

1999 NATO forces
intervene in Kosovo.

Section 2

The Crumbling Wall

Guide to Reading

Read to Find Out
Main Idea *Soviet Communist controls came
to an end in Eastern Europe.*

▶ **Terms to Define**
autonomy

▶ **People to Meet**
Pope John Paul II, Lech Walesa, Nicolae
Ceauşescu, Václav Havel, Slobodan
Milosevic

▶ **Places to Locate**
Poland, Gdansk, East Germany, Hungary,
Romania, Bulgaria, Berlin, the Czech
Republic, Slovakia, Albania, Bosnia-
Herzegovina, Croatia, Macedonia,
Slovenia, Serbia, Montenegro, Kosovo

The Storyteller

The wall was coming down. West Berliners
chipped away at it with hammers and chisels,
while impatient East Berliners used heavy equipment. Finally a gap opened and a crowd of people
surged through. Young people who had never
visited the West sampled the
goods of a market economy.
Older people looked for
friends whom they had not
seen for nearly three decades.
"It's been so long, it's a wonder we recognized each
other!" With joyful exclama-
tions, two old friends met by
the ruins of the wall that had
separated them as teenagers.

—adapted from "Berlin's Ode
to Joy," Priit J. Vesilind in
National Geographic, April 1990

*Fall of the Berlin
Wall*

During the 1980s, the Communist nations
of Eastern Europe, like the Soviet Union,
faced massive problems. Their government-controlled economies failed to produce high-
quality consumer goods and had fallen far behind
the economies of the West. Reform had to be tried,
but the Communist system was too flawed. When
the Soviet Union began to change and signaled that
it would not object to changes in Eastern Europe,
the Communist systems collapsed.

The Rise of Solidarity

The final round of unrest in Eastern Europe
began in the 1970s and continued into the 1980s. In
Poland, the antigovernment movement had
received a strong boost in 1978, when the Roman
Catholic Church selected a Polish church leader,
Karol Wojtyla (voy•TEE•wah), as its pope. The ele-
vation of **Pope John Paul II**, a staunch anti-
Communist, inspired confidence among the largely
Catholic Poles and enabled them to take further
steps toward liberation from Communist control.

In 1980 Polish workers in the Baltic port of
Gdansk organized a trade union called **Solidarity**.
Lech Walesa (lehk vah•LEHN•suh), an electrical
worker at the Lenin Shipyard in Gdansk, was a
founder and leader of Solidarity.

Solidarity backed up its demands for better living and working conditions with strikes, including
one led by Walesa at the Gdansk shipyards. In a
remarkable victory, the strikers forced the Polish
government to recognize Solidarity in October
1980. Until this time, self-governing trade unions
independent of Communist control had not been
allowed to exist in Communist countries.

Under Walesa's leadership, Solidarity demanded free elections and a voice for workers in forming
government policy. The Polish government
responded by demanding that strikes and other
"antistate" activities be ended. Under pressure

1004   Chapter 37   *The World in Transition*

Left margin teacher column

▶ **Change** The weakening of the
Soviet Union and the rise of
reform movements bring an
end to Soviet control in Eastern
Europe.

Guide to Reading

For reading strategies to help
students read effectively see
pages 12–13.

Vocabulary Pre-check

▣ Use the Vocabulary
PuzzleMaker for Chapter 37
to create a crossword puzzle to
reinforce section terms. **L1 LEP**

📁 Use Vocabulary Activity
37 to introduce vocabulary terms.
L1 LEP

FOCUS

Section Objective

Describe how Soviet Communist
controls came to an end in Eastern Europe.

BELLRINGER
Motivational Activity

Before taking roll at the
beginning of the class
period, project Section
Focus Transparency 37-2
and have students answer
the activity questions. Discuss
students' responses.

📁 This activity is also available as a blackline master.

Lech Walesa began his career as an electrician and eventually became ~oland's first democratically elected president of the ~ost-Communist era. *What role did Walesa have in Polish ~ffairs during the early 1980s?*

~rom the Soviet Union, Polish authorities outlawed ~he union 16 months later and jailed many of its ~eaders. Despite this, Walesa and others continued ~heir activities underground.

Although Solidarity's activities were not immediately successful, the courage of its members ~nspired people in other Eastern European coun-~ries. Walesa became a symbol of freedom and an international hero. He was awarded the Nobel ~Peace Prize in 1983. By the end of the decade, the ~Soviet Union itself was changing under Gorbachev, ~and unrest had spread across Eastern Europe.

POINT

1989: A Year of Miracles

By the late 1980s, reduced production, decreas-es in labor productivity, high inflation, and trade deficits had virtually paralyzed the economies of Eastern Europe. This meant fewer goods at ever-increasing prices. The highly centralized economies, out of touch with consumer needs, caused widespread food shortages. Dissent against communism reached its peak in 1989.

Soviet Policies

As democratic movements gathered force across Eastern Europe during the late 1980s, many people wondered: Would Mikhail Gorbachev exer-

cise the terms of the Brezhnev Doctrine and put down rebellions? In a speech in January 1989, Gorbachev announced that he had ordered a cut-back of 500,000 troops in the Soviet army—about half of that number to come from troops stationed in Eastern Europe. The troops had been put there to keep the Soviet satellites in line.

In March he pledged not to interfere with democratic reforms in Hungary. Referring to the 1956 and 1968 invasions of Hungary and Czechoslovakia, Gorbachev declared that "all pos-sible safeguards should be provided so that no external force can interfere in the domestic affairs of socialist countries."

Gorbachev decided that most Eastern-bloc gov-ernments—which lacked popular support—would continue to provoke opposition. The Soviet Union would be forced to intervene militarily at great cost. Soviet interests would be better served if he simply let these governments fall. Gorbachev would then establish friendly relations with new governments.

Collapse of Communism

In 1989 Communist governments in Eastern Europe crumbled under the weight of staggering problems. All the satellite countries had ruined economies. Many had terrible environmental dam-age that had been ignored in the push to industrial-ize. Other countries, such as Yugoslavia, were being shaken by internal ethnic conflicts.

As economic and political instability increased, Communist regimes either resigned or were over-turned in **East Germany**, Czechoslovakia, **Hun-gary**, Poland, **Romania**, and **Bulgaria**. Throughout this remarkable year of 1989, Gorbachev astounded the world by not only refusing to intervene in democratic uprisings, but actually encouraging reform in the region.

In mid-1989 Hungary, which had been quietly moving toward democratic reform for more than a decade, opened its sealed borders. A flood of East German refugees poured through this new "hole" in the Iron Curtain, seeking sanctuary in the West. The exodus called attention to the failed govern-ment of East Germany's leader, Erich Honecker.

The Wall's Fall

Amid mass demonstrations and calls for demo-cratic reform, Honecker's government was toppled in October and replaced by a more moderate Communist administration. The move did not satisfy the reform movement but made its supporters bolder and more demanding. The next month, in an attempt to defuse the situation, the government lift-ed all travel restrictions between East and West. It

TEACH

Guided Practice

THEME Change

Write *1989: A Year of Miracles* on the chalkboard and ask students to list the events and changes from this section that made 1989 a year of "miracles." **L1 LEP**

 Walesa was jailed for his involvement with Soli-darity, and after his release suffered harassment from the government. Influenced by its economic prob-lems, however, in 1988 the govern-ment agreed to recognize Solidarity and to allow the union to have seats in the legislature.
Answer to Caption: *He led the drive for free elections and became a symbol of freedom.*

POINT

1989: A Year of Miracles
Why was 1989 a significant year in the history of Eastern Europe?
Economic decline and popular unrest, aided by Gorbachev's disinclination to intervene, led to the collapse of Communist governments in Eastern Europe.

COOPERATIVE LEARNING ACTIVITY

Television Broadcast Organize the class into news teams and assign one team to cover West Germany, one to cover East Germany, and one to represent the team in the news studio in the United States. Each team will need to research the November 1989 reuniting of Berlin as the wall came down. Students are to conduct interviews to get firsthand reactions and accounts of reunited families and friends. (Teams should decide what parts each member will play.) The studio team should research details about the people in the West and the East and alert news teams about the questions they might ask when they air the show. If possible, have a video camera available to tape the broadcast. **L2**

Government Guide students in naming the different countries mentioned in this section whose Communist regimes ended. *(Poland, East Germany, Hungary, Romania, Bulgaria, Czechoslovakia, Albania, Yugoslavia)* Have students create a chart on the chalkboard that lists the names of the rulers involved in each country and that tells whether the change in each country was peaceful or violent. **L2 LEP**

Critical Thinking Ask students to discuss the issues of freedom and control. Point out how difficult it has been for the newly freed countries to build democracies and stability without new outbreaks of fighting and chaos. Ask students to give examples from this section of the results of too much control and of the results of sudden freedom. **L3**

ABCNEWS
INTERACTIVE™

VIDEODISC
Turning Points in World History

Side Two
Chapter 9

Title: *Fall of the Berlin Wall*
Subject: The building of the Berlin Wall, its symbolic and literal 28-year division between East and West Germany, the fall of the wall as a symbol of the failure of communism
Ask: What was desirable about the West for East Germany's people? *("Good wages, affordable homes, and most of all freedom.")* What did the fall of the wall represent to Germany? *(that East and West Germany were unified once again)*

hoped the refugees would remain in East Germany under a reformed but still Communist government.

On the evening of November 9, 1989, the famous Brandenburg Gate at the **Berlin** Wall was opened. All through the night East Germans and West Germans, hearing the wall had been opened, rushed there to see for themselves, overwhelming the guards and passing through the gate in both directions. Others swarmed over the wall, dancing and singing atop it.

In the following days, people on both sides of the wall attacked it with picks and shovels, opening huge holes—even selling chunks as souvenirs. More gates were opened, and the flow of people increased. Families and friends who had not seen each other in decades were reunited. The government, helpless before this popular uprising, ordered the rest of the wall torn down.

Violence in Romania

The fall of communism in Eastern Europe was, for the most part, nonviolent. The one grim chapter in the story took place in Romania. There, dictator **Nicolae Ceaușescu** (NEE•koh•lay chow•SHEHS•koo) brutally fought his opponents but was later ousted, tried, and executed in December 1989. Crowds throughout Europe celebrated Ceaușescu's fall. They were also celebrating the end of Soviet control in Eastern Europe and, in a larger sense, the end of the cold war.

Facing Challenges

Following the downfall of Communist governments, reformers looked for new leaders to bring democracy and stability to their countries. In October 1990, the two parts of Germany were quickly reunited under Chancellor Helmut Kohl. Also that year, Poland made a choice that surprised no one: Lech Walesa was elected president. In Czechoslovakia, a dissident playwright, **Václav Havel** (VAHT•SLAHF HAH•vehl), became president. Despite Havel's respected leadership, ethnic

Images *of the* Times

A New Era

A wave of unrest swept Eastern Europe in the late 1980s, leading to the fall of hard-line Communist governments. By the mid-1990s, some countries in the region had become sound democracies; others, plagued by economic uncertainties, turned to nationalist or former Communist leaders.

Solidarity led the movement for democracy in Poland. The labor union began in the shipyards of the Baltic port of Gdansk and soon spread to other parts of the country.

1006

Images *of the* Times

A New Era

With the fall of communism and rise of nationalism came ethnic conflicts that have resulted in a major international problem: refugees. The UN founded an agency known as the United Nations High Commissioner for Refugees (UNHCR) after World War II. Its mission is to assist people who are refugees, including those living like refugees in their own country. The UNHCR staff attempts to get food and medicine to refugees. It has airlifted supplies to Kurds, Rwandans, and to the people in the former Yugoslavia.

fferences led in 1993 to Czechoslovakia's split to two nations: **the Czech Republic** and **lovakia**.

he Communist Inheritance

Once in power, new Eastern European leaders .ced the awesome task of moving from communism to democracy and free enterprise. They had .herited a host of problems from the Communist .ra: inefficient or outdated industries, huge nation-.l debts, workforces paid regardless of the quality f their work, artificially low prices for basic goods, .nd currencies considered worthless by the rest of .ne world. In addition, little investment was avail-ble in Eastern Europe to modernize old industries r to fund new ones. To attract foreign investment .nd financial aid, new governments set out to .eform their economies. They cut spending, closed r sold off many state-run firms, and began training .vorkers in new skills.

Reforms and Stability

With their strong industrial bases, the Czech Republic, Hungary, and Poland were the most like-ly to succeed in the transition from communism to capitalism. However, even in these lands, econom-ic reforms imposed hardships on citizens, with many workers facing unemployment and reduc-tions in social benefits. In Hungary and Poland, dis-satisfied voters in the mid-1990s returned ex-Communists to power. By decade's end, however, voters moved back toward the political center. In 1997 Solidarity and other non-Communist candi-dates triumphed over ex-Communist opponents in Poland's parliamentary elections. Encouraging this trend was the decision of NATO to admit Poland, Hungary, and the Czech Republic in 1999.

Upheavals

The end of communism brought not only economic hardships but political upheavals to

**Chapter 37
Section 2**

Independent Practice

Guided Reading Activity 37-2 **L1**

People in World History Profile 71

Daily Life Have students research and depict in a letter to a newspaper what everyday life is like in one of the Eastern European countries studied in this section. **L2**

Refugees push across the border from Hungary into Austria after Hungary in 1989 became the first Communist state to open its sealed borders.

A reunited Germany was celebrated by throngs of people near Berlin's Brandenburg Gate on October 3, 1990.

REFLECTING ON THE TIMES

1. How did the fall of communism in Eastern Europe affect Germany?
2. What movement rallied public support for democracy in Poland?

1007

Linking Past and Present

Nazi War Crimes Germans have decided to remember the victims of Nazi war crimes by establishing January 27, the anniversary of the liberation of Auschwitz by Red Army troops, as a national day of commemor-ation. In establishing this day, the German president expressed the desire that young people who did not experience the Nazi regime maintain awareness of racism and totalitarianism in order to resist them.

 VIDEODISC
Communism and the Cold War

Side Two, Chapter 17
Frames 38033–42654
Title: *Challenge of Reform*
Subject: Challenges facing East-ern European countries
Ask: What happened as Poland tried to establish a free market system? (*Prices and unemployment rose.*)

ANSWERS TO REFLECTING ON THE TIMES

1. It led to the reunification of Germany.
2. Solidarity movement

Critical Thinking Have students research Yugoslavia and its collapse. Ask them to study resources other than newspapers and to analyze the factors that led to its collapse. **L3**

Who?What?Where?When?

Women from East Germany have lost benefits with reunification. They were used to working with a year's paid maternity leave and free day-care centers. The unemployment after unity has left many jobless.

ASSESS

Check for Understanding

Assign Section 2 Assessment as homework or as an in-class activity.

 Use Interactive Tutor Self-Assessment Software to review Section 2.

Evaluate

Section Quiz 37-2

Use the Testmaker to create a customized quiz for Section 2.

---

countries in the southern part of Eastern Europe. There, democratic traditions were weaker, and economies had only recently been industrialized. In **Albania**, Eastern Europe's poorest country, democracy and free enterprise were nearly engulfed in chaos. The collapse of investment schemes in 1997 wiped out the life savings of many Albanians. As citizens blamed the government for the collapse, rival groups throughout the country fought each other with weapons looted from arsenals. A UN-sponsored peacekeeping force finally restored order, and new elections were held. The new government stated that it could not pay back investors but that it would work to revive the economy.

War in the Balkans

After communism's fall, Eastern Europe experienced a rebirth of nationalist feeling. The most serious outbreak of nationalist conflict occurred in Yugoslavia. For centuries, tensions had existed among Yugoslavia's many ethnic groups. However, these hatreds were muted under the Communist leadership of Josip Broz Tito. After Tito's death in 1980, Communist controls gradually weakened, and in 1990, opposition political parties were allowed to form.

Multiparty elections in Yugoslavia were held later that year. Non-Communist parties won most seats in the parliaments of **Bosnia-Herzegovina**, **Croatia**, **Macedonia**, and **Slovenia**. In **Serbia** and **Montenegro**, the former Communist parties, renamed as Socialist parties, won majorities. The leader of Serbia, **Slobodan Milosevic** (sloh•boh•dahn mee•LAH•soh•veech), renounced communism but was intent on expanding his power. After the elections, the most industrialized republics—Croatia and Slovenia—charged that Serbia sought to dominate the rest of the country. In 1991, when Serbia opposed any restructuring of Yugoslavia that would give the other republics more *autonomy*, or self-rule, Slovenia and Croatia declared their independence.

Fighting in Croatia

Fighting then broke out in Croatia between the Croat army and ethnic Serbs who refused to be under Croat rule. Serbia and Montenegro, which together became known as Yugoslavia, backed the ethnic Serbs of Croatia. With this aid, ethnic Serb forces gained control of one-third of Croatia's territory.

A cease-fire in 1992 finally ended much of the fighting in Croatia, and UN peacekeeping forces patrolled the borders between Serb-held and Croat-

held areas. A Croat offensive in 1995 finally brought the Serb-held territory back into Croatia. Since then, international human rights groups have accused the Croat government of abuses in its treatment of the ethnic Serbs in Croatia.

Bosnia-Herzegovina

In the fall of 1991, another republic, Macedonia, declared its independence. The following year, most of the Muslim population and the ethnic Croats in still another republic—Bosnia-Herzegovina—voted for independence from Serb-controlled Yugoslavia. Ethnic Serbs living in Bosnia-Herzegovina opposed the election and its outcome.

Fighting then broke out between the ethnic Serbs in Bosnia-Herzegovina and the rest of the population—the Bosnian Muslims and the Croats. Yugoslavia provided aid to the Bosnian Serbs, who soon controlled most of Bosnia-Herzegovina.

In 1994 the exhausted Bosnian Muslims and Croats formed a federation, and the United States asked the Bosnian Serbs to end the fighting and join as well. After military pressure from Croatia's land forces and NATO air strikes, the Bosnian Serbs accepted a cease-fire and American-sponsored peace talks. In 1995 the leaders of Bosnia-Herzegovina, Yugoslavia, and Croatia met at Dayton, Ohio, and agreed to set up a Bosnian state divided into separate Croat-Muslim and Serb regions.

Kosovo

In 1998 a new crisis in the region erupted. Until 1991 people of Albanian descent living in the southern province of **Kosovo** had enjoyed autonomy, or limited independence. At that time, Milosevic decided to suppress uprisings in Kosovo and strip the people of their autonomy. His actions inflamed support for the Kosovo Liberation Army (KLA), an armed group that sought to create an independent Kosovo by attacking Serbian troops there.

Under pressure from NATO, the Serbs and the Kosovar Albanians met at Rambouillet (rahm•bwee•YAY), France, in 1998. The Albanian negotiators signed an agreement that would have allowed considerable autonomy for Kosovo. The Serbs, objecting to having foreign troops on their soil, rejected the agreement.

After negotiations and pleas to Serbia to remove their troops from Kosovo failed, the United States and other NATO countries began bombing Belgrade, the Yugoslav capital, and later other parts of Yugoslavia as well. As bombing continued, the Serbs forced hundreds of thousands of ethnic Albanians out of Kosovo and into refugee camps in Albania and Macedonia (the former Yugoslav

---

MEETING SPECIAL NEEDS ACTIVITY

Reading Comprehension To help students who learn best by hearing words and information first and then writing, organize the class into small study groups. Suggest that each group list the names of the people and places in this section. Have them first say the names aloud, practicing difficult pronunciations, before they write their lists. You may also want to have students read the sections aloud and discuss them in their study groups. **L1 LEP**

Visualizing
History In 1999 Serbs forced hundreds of thousands of ethnic Albanians from their homes in Kosovo, creating a massive refugee crisis. *Why were the Kosovars forced to flee?*

Republic of Macedonia). Thousands remained missing, and there were fears that the Serbs had engaged in mass executions.

In May 1999 the international war crimes tribunal indicted Slobodan Milosevic and four other senior Serb officials for war crimes against humanity, including the murder, forced deportation, and persecution of ethnic Albanians. The move represented the first time in history that a sitting head of state had been indicted as a war criminal.

At the UN's urging, the Serbs agreed to remove their forces from Kosovo in June of 1999. NATO ended its bombing and installed troops throughout Kosovo to maintain peace as ethnic Albanians began to return to their homes. However, concerns about future peacekeeping remained as ethnic Albanians and Serb neighbors again attempted to co-exist.

Serbia

Dissatisfaction with Slobodan Milosevic led to discord in Serbia. In 1996 Milosevic tried to block opposition wins in local elections. Protests later forced him to accept the results, but Milosevic continued to strengthen his power. In 1999, after the Serb withdrawal from Kosovo, many Serbs again protested against Milosevic's rule. This political opposition, however, was too disunited to pose a major threat to the Serb leader.

Reteach

Have the class make a flowchart documenting what happened to Eastern Europe after the collapse of the Soviet Union.

📁 Reading Essentials and Study Guide 37-2

Enrich

Ask students to collect information from the library or a travel agency about the historic sights and the natural beauties of the Eastern European countries before civil wars changed some of them.

CLOSE

Ask students to summarize the recent changes in the Balkans and predict what might change in Eastern Europe in the next decade.

SECTION 2 ASSESSMENT

Main Idea
1. Use a diagram like the one below to show how Soviet Communist control in Eastern Europe was ended.

> End of Soviet Communism in Eastern Europe ⟩

Recall
2. **Define** autonomy.
3. **Identify** Pope John Paul II, Solidarity, Lech Walesa, Nicolae Ceauşescu, Václav Havel, Slobodan Milosevic.

Critical Thinking
4. **Applying Information** What kinds of changes have

occurred rapidly in Eastern European countries? Which changes are occurring slowly?

Understanding Themes
5. **Change** What political changes came to the Yugoslav area with the collapse of communism in the late 1980s and early 1990s?

Chapter 37 *The World in Transition* **1009**

SECTION 2 ASSESSMENT ANSWERS

1. rise of Solidarity trade union in Poland; democratic movements in Eastern Europe strengthened in late 1980s; economic and political instability ended Communist regimes; East German government toppled; Berlin Wall torn down; revolt in Romania
2. All terms are defined in the Glossary.

3. Pope John Paul II, 1004; Solidarity, 1004; Lech Walesa, 1004; Nicolae Ceauşescu, 1006; Václav Havel, 1007; Slobodan Milosevic, 1008
4. The collapse of Communist systems and establishment of new governments was rapid; privatization and the establishment of a free market has

been a slower process.
5. **CHANGE** Individual republics declared independence, fighting broke out in Croatia and Bosnia-Herzegovina, a Bosnian state with two separate regions was established, and ethnic Albanians were forced to flee Kosovo.

Chapter 37 *The World in Transition* **1009**

1980   1990   2000

1986 Spain and Portugal join the European Community.

1990 East Germany and West Germany reunite.

1998 Peace agreement on Northern Ireland signed.

1999 Eleven European countries adopt single currency.

Guide to Reading

For reading strategies to help students read effectively see pages 12–13.

Vocabulary Pre-check

◉ Use the Vocabulary PuzzleMaker for Chapter 37 to create a crossword puzzle to reinforce section terms. **L1 LEP**

📁 Use Vocabulary Activity 37 to introduce vocabulary terms. **L1 LEP**

FOCUS

Section Objective

Identify the steps Western European nations have taken to unify their governments and economies.

**BELLRINGER
Motivational Activity**

Before taking roll at the beginning of the class period, project Section Focus Transparency 37-3 and have students answer the activity questions.

📁 This activity is also available as a blackline master.

Section 3

Toward a European Union

Guide to Reading

Read to Find Out
Main Idea *Western European nations have taken steps to unify their governments and economies.*

▶ **Terms to Define**
referendum, collective security

▶ **People to Meet**
Margaret Thatcher, John Major, Tony Blair, François Mitterrand, Jacques Chirac, Juan Carlos I, Gerhard Schröder, José Maria Aznar

▶ **Places to Locate**
Northern Ireland, Cyprus

The Storyteller

Paddy Ashdown believed in the European Union. As a businessman and a member of Parliament, he saw the benefits of Britain's participation. Already he had seen imports and exports move more freely, unhampered by restrictive tariffs. The last remaining hurdle was that of a common currency. Ashdown took the floor of Parliament to argue for the proposition. "We face the prospect of either joining an imperfect monetary union at a later date, or staying out altogether. This is exactly what happened over the EU itself. We must not make the same mistake twice."

European Union currency

—adapted from "The Case for a Single Currency," Paddy Ashdown, in *The Economist Newspaper, Ltd.*, March 4, 1995

1010 Chapter 37 *The World in Transition*

---

*S*ince the 1970s, Western European nations have faced economic recession, budget deficits, and high unemployment. However, they also have worked to modernize their societies and to balance economic growth with the social needs of their peoples. By 1995, Western Europe as a whole had made great strides toward full economic and political unity. Yet it faced a number of economic and political challenges resulting from economic restructuring, increasing immigration, the reunification of Germany, the collapse of the Soviet bloc, and the outbreak of fierce ethnic conflict in the Balkans.

Great Britain

During the 1970s, Great Britain's economic woes continued under Labour governments. In 1979 voters, dissatisfied with a weak economy, high taxes, and trade union strikes, brought the Conservative party into a long period of power.

From Thatcher to Blair

Great Britain's first woman prime minister, Conservative party leader **Margaret Thatcher** aggressively introduced free market measures. She privatized state-owned industries, scaled back welfare programs, and limited trade union powers. Although Thatcher's policies aided business growth, they created high unemployment. Declining popularity and the loss of Conservative support led to her resignation in 1990.

Thatcher's successor, **John Major**, led a Conservative party increasingly divided over Great Britain's ties to Europe. Some Conservatives wanted British participation in a united Europe, while others feared a future European union would mean a loss of British independence.

Visualizing History Political murals cover buildings in both Protestant and Catholic Northern Ireland neighborhoods. *What issue led to conflict in Northern Ireland?*

During the 1990s, the British economy continued to grow, with falling unemployment and relatively low inflation. Despite the relatively strong economy, however, after nearly 18 years of Conservative rule, voters wanted a change and in 1997 brought the Labour party to power. Known for his youthful, energetic style, the new prime minister, **Tony Blair**, moved away from Labour's traditional socialism and favored low taxes, tightly controlled social spending, and closer ties to Europe.

The most innovative of Blair's plans was the reform of British government. In response to growing nationalism in Scotland and Wales, Blair favored home rule for these parts of Great Britain.

In 1997 Scottish voters approved creation of their own parliament to tax and legislate on local issues. Welsh voters backed plans for a less powerful assembly that would spend funds provided by the British Parliament.

Ireland

A major European issue from the 1970s to the 1990s was the status of **Northern Ireland**, the British-ruled province torn by divisions between Protestants and Catholics. The Protestant majority wanted to remain British, while the Catholic minority wanted to become part of the Republic of Ireland. Long-standing Protestant discrimination of Catholics in the province had led to civil rights protests during the 1960s. As clashes between the two communities increased, the British government sent troops to Northern Ireland and imposed direct rule during the early 1970s. Meanwhile, the outlawed Irish Republican Army (**IRA**), a terrorist group, attacked British military forces and Protestant civilians in Northern Ireland and England.

Thousands of people died in the conflict, which the local people refer to as "the Troubles." Finally, in 1998, following tough negotiations moderated by former U.S. Senator George Mitchell, Catholics and Protestants agreed to make peace. The agreement, known as the Good Friday Agreement, was endorsed by the people of both Northern Ireland and the Republic of Ireland, each of which held a referendum on the issue. Despite the peace agreement, violence continued. However, at the end of 1999, home-rule was established in Northern Ireland, with a government consisting of members of both sides of the conflict.

France

France enjoyed political stability from the 1970s to the 1990s. In 1981 French voters elected **François Mitterrand** as France's first Socialist president. Mitterrand nationalized major industries and funded new social programs. His measures, however, increased inflation, and he eventually was forced to make cutbacks.

In 1995 **Jacques Chirac**, the conservative mayor of Paris, was elected president of France. Chirac promised a referendum, or popular vote, on France's future relationship with a united Europe. He also tried to balance the budget by further cuts in government spending. To protest Chirac's economic policies, workers and students staged nationwide strikes and demonstrations. In 1997 a majority of voters rebuffed Chirac and elected Socialists and other leftists to France's legislature. A period of difficult relations began between the conservative president and the leftist legislature. Chirac pushed for less spending and more business growth, while his Socialist opponents stressed jobs for unemployed workers and the protection of social benefits.

Germany

During the 1970s West Germany, under Chancellor Willy Brandt and his successor, Helmut Schmidt, enjoyed prosperity. But the early 1980s saw a growth of inflation and unemployment. Promising better times, a conservative chancellor, Helmut Kohl, came to power. In 1990 Kohl presided

Chapter 37 *The World in Transition* **1011**

Independent Practice

Guided Reading Activity 37-3 **L1**

Politics Have students draw cartoons about one of the political situations discussed in this section. Each cartoon should express a specific point of view. **L2 LEP**

Linking Past and Present

Madrid's Plaza Mayor This Spanish city square was built in the seventeenth century and served as the site for public tortures during the Spanish Inquisition. Today it is a place of pleasure, where people enjoy refreshments and conversation at its courtyard cafés.

Civil Strife Ask students to look at a map showing Turkey and Greece in relation to Cyprus. Ask volunteers to research and report to the class about the conflicts in Cyprus between the Greek and Turkish communities. **L2**

NATIONAL GEOGRAPHIC SOCIETY

CD-ROM

PICTURE ATLAS OF THE WORLD

You and your students can view the streets of London, the moors of the United Kingdom, the vineyards of Germany, and the hillsides of Greece by clicking the "Video" button of selected countries.

---

over the reunification of Germany following the collapse of communism in Eastern Europe. He made preparations for the transfer of the German capital from Bonn to Berlin by the year 2000. In 1998 the leader of the Social Democrats, **Gerhard Schröder**, defeated Chancellor Kohl and promised to reform and modernize his country.

When the excitement of reunification wore off, Germans realized that the economic costs of reunification were far higher than anyone had foreseen. Eastern Germany's economic rebuilding after years of Communist rule required vast expenditures, and Germans in the western part had to pay higher taxes to support this restructuring. In eastern Germany, the closing of inefficient industries caused unemployment to soar, although economic rebuilding in the long term would provide eastern Germany with the most modern technology in Europe.

By 1997, unemployment was at its highest level throughout Germany since the 1930s. Meanwhile, the government faced the dilemma of trying to maintain generous welfare programs while controlling its budget deficit. Further progress toward greater European economic unity required Germany to keep its deficit under control, but workers opposed any government effort to roll back price supports for certain goods.

Social and political unrest accompanied economic difficulties throughout Germany. Neo-Nazis and other right-wing Germans protested immigration from southern Europe and the Middle East. Some of them attacked and killed foreigners. Many Germans protested the attacks, but the German parliament in 1993 amended the constitution to reduce the flow of immigrants into Germany.

That same year, Germany's highest court ruled that German troops could take part in international peacekeeping missions. Until then, the constitution had banned all military activities except those related to collective security, or joint agreement by nations to protect themselves from attack.

Mediterranean Europe

Mediterranean Europe made great strides in political and economic development from the 1970s to the 1990s. Dictatorships fell and democracies arose in Spain and Portugal. Economic recession, however, hurt the Mediterranean countries.

Italy

From the 1970s to the 1990s, a variety of economic, social, and political problems plagued Italy. Among these were the uneven distribution of wealth, especially between north and south; an inefficient government bureaucracy; and constantly changing governments.

During the 1970s, Italy had the largest Communist party in Western Europe. The party was popular in part because it promoted a less authoritarian view of communism. It sought to share power with the ruling conservative Christian Democrats. Many conservative Italians, however, were alarmed at this prospect. Adding to the political uncertainty was a wave of murders, kidnappings, and bombings by leftist groups.

Christian Democrats, later renamed the Populists, controlled the government during the late 1980s and early 1990s. During this time, the leftist parties—Communists and Socialists—suffered from policy disputes and political scandals. By the late 1990s, government power shifted back and forth between conservative and leftist coalitions.

Spain and Portugal

After nearly 35 years of dictatorship under Francisco Franco, Spain in the late 1970s entered a new era of democracy guided by its new king, **Juan Carlos I**. For most of the 1980s and 1990s, Spain's democratic government was in the hands of the Socialists and their leader, Felipe González. In 1996 Spanish voters replaced the Socialists with a conservative government under **José Maria Aznar**.

Since the restoration of democracy, the Spanish government has granted the Basque Provinces and other regions of Spain increased self-rule after years of repression under Franco. In foreign affairs, Spain has increased its links to the rest of Europe after joining NATO and the European Community in the 1980s. It also has strengthened traditional relations with Latin America and North Africa.

Footnotes to History

Berlin: Back to the Future? The return of Germany's capital to Berlin by 2000 marked the return of the Bundestag, or German Parliament, to its former home in the Reichstag. This legislative building had lost much of its grandeur in a 1933 fire that ushered in the Nazi era. Now rebuilt, with a modern glass and concrete dome, the Reichstag sparks debate. Some Germans say it represents the new democratic Germany; others claim it reminds them of Germany's militaristic past.

1012 Chapter 37 *The World in Transition*

MEETING SPECIAL NEEDS ACTIVITY

Language Delayed Have students trace an outline map of Europe. Ask them to label the countries studied in this section and then color-code each country. Have them make a color-code key for the map and in the key give specific information about each country, such as political leaders, important dates and events, and any other details they want to include. **L1 LEP**

A turn toward democracy also occurred in Portugal. There, dictatorship ended with a military coup in 1974, and two years later the nation held its first free elections in 50 years. During this time, Portugal freed most of its African and Asian colonies and in 1986 joined the European Community.

Greece

From the mid-1960s to the early 1970s, Greece was ruled by a repressive military government. In 1974 democracy was restored, and for the next two decades the country was ruled by either conservatives or Socialists. In 1981 the Socialists under Premier Andreas Papandreou (pah•pahn•DRAY•yoo) brought Greece into the European Community.

In recent years, Greece has had differences with neighboring Turkey over **Cyprus**, a Mediterranean island republic divided between feuding Greek and Turkish communities. Since 1974, Turkish forces have occupied northern Cyprus, while the southern part of the island remains under an internationally recognized government led by Greek Cypriots.

A United Europe

During the 1980s and 1990s, the Common Market broadened its activities to include political and financial affairs and became known as the European Community. In 1992 European Community members met in Maastricht, the Netherlands, and signed the **Treaty of Maastricht**, setting up the European Union (EU). This new body aimed to establish closer ties among member nations.

In 1993 another measure—the Single Europe Act—ended most barriers to trade among EU members. Two years later, seven EU nations allowed their citizens to travel freely from one member country to another without passports. The year

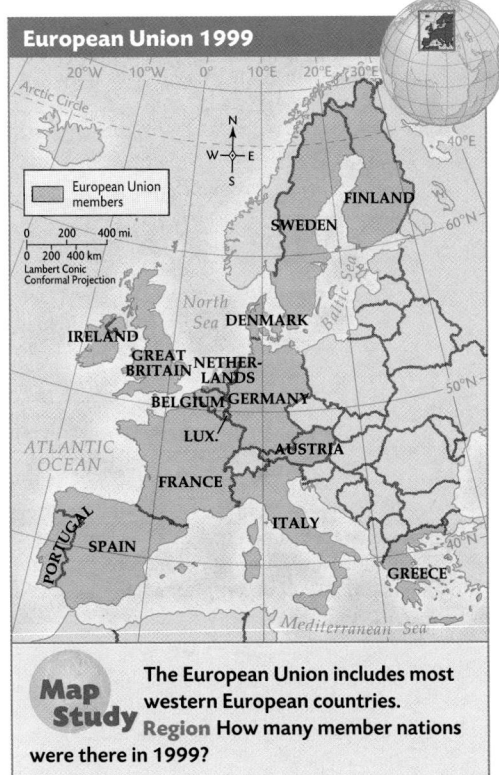

European Union 1999

European Union members

0   200   400 mi.
0 200 400 km
Lambert Conic
Conformal Projection

 The European Union includes most western European countries. Region **How many member nations were there in 1999?**

1995 also saw the admission of Austria, Finland, and Sweden to the EU.

In 1999 EU countries created an Economic and Monetary Union (EMU) and set up a European Central Bank and a common European currency called the euro. Although qualified, Britain, Denmark, and Sweden have not yet joined. Euro coins and notes, which will begin circulation in January 2002, will be used by about 300 million people.

SECTION 3 ASSESSMENT

Main Idea
1. Use a time line like the one below to list events leading to Western European political and economic unity.

1980 _____ 2000

Recall
2. **Define** referendum, collective security.
3. **Identify** Margaret Thatcher, John Major, Tony Blair, IRA, François Mitterrand, Jacques Chirac, Gerhard Schröder, Juan Carlos I, Treaty of Maastricht, José Maria Aznar.

Critical Thinking
4. **Applying Information** Why has Great Britain not fully participated in the EU?

Understanding Themes
5. **Cooperation** Compare relationships among EU countries with those among U.S. states.

SECTION 3 ASSESSMENT ANSWERS

1. 1980s: Common Market becomes European Community; 1992: European Union set up; 1993: Single Europe Act; 1995: citizens can travel freely among seven EU countries; 1995: EU membership grows; 1999: common currency adopted
2. The terms are defined in the Glossary.
3. Thatcher, 1010; Major, 1010; Blair, 1011; IRA, 1011; Mitterrand, 1011; Chirac, 1011; Schröder, 1012; Juan Carlos I, 1012; Aznar, 1012; Maastricht, 1013
4. Great Britain fears a loss of independence.
5. **COOPERATION** Countries in the EU do not share a common government or legal system, as U.S. states do. Both allow free trade and movement among members.

Chapter 37
Section 3

Map Study

Answer
15 member nations

POINT

A United Europe
Why was the signing of the Treaty of Maastricht an important event for Europeans?
It created the European Union (EU), which furthered the economic and political union of member nations.

ASSESS
Check for Understanding
Assign Section 3 Assessment as homework or as an in-class activity.

Use Interactive Tutor Self-Assessment Software to review Section 3.

Evaluate
Section Quiz 37-3

Reteach
Create a diagram or chart with the students identifying the countries and the leading political groups discussed in this section and the problems they faced in the 1980s and 1990s.

Reading Essentials and Study Guide 37-3

Enrich
Have students research the European Union and create a chart of its current members. Summarize any goals it has for further unity.

CLOSE
Ask students to write a brief summary of the evidence of growing cooperation among European countries since 1990.

SECTION THEME

▶ **Conflict** National and ethnic conflicts intensify worldwide after the end of the cold war.

Guide to Reading

For reading strategies to help students read effectively see pages 12–13.

Vocabulary Pre-check

☑ Use the Vocabulary PuzzleMaker for Chapter 37 to create a crossword puzzle to reinforce section terms. **L1 LEP**

📁 Use Vocabulary Activity 37 to introduce vocabulary terms. **L1 LEP**

FOCUS

Section Objective

Recognize the areas of the world that have been in ethnic discord since the end of the cold war.

BELLRINGER
Motivational Activity

Before taking roll at the beginning of the class period, project Section Focus Transparency 37-4 and have students answer the activity questions. Discuss students' responses.
📁 This activity is also available as a blackline master.

1980 ——————————— **1990** ——————————— **2000**

| **1982** Canada enacts new constitution. | **1992** Civil war begins in Bosnia. | **1994** Russian troops enter Chechnya. |

Section 4
National and Ethnic Conflicts

Guide to Reading

Read to Find Out
Main Idea *Many areas of the world have been in ethnic discord since the end of the cold war.*

▶ **Terms to Define**
ethnic cleansing, atrocity, embargo, enclave

▶ **People to Meet**
Slobodan Milosevic, Alija Izetbegovic, Franjo Tudjman, the Chechens, the Ossetians, the Abkhazians, the Kurds, the Sinhalese, the Tamils, Brian Mulroney, Jean Chretien

▶ **Places to Locate**
Sarajevo, Dayton, Chechnya, Nagorno-Karabakh, Sri Lanka, Quebec, Nunavut

The Storyteller

Zahid Olorcic remembered how things had been just a few years ago. People in Sarajevo had gotten along with their neighbors. Even though coming from diverse backgrounds, the city's multiethnic population lived in harmony. Then the situation changed as radical groups stirred up ethnic hatred. Zahid recalled earlier times:

"Funerals, weddings, birthdays, we never counted how many Muslims were there, how many Serbs, how many Croats. The only important thing was to be together.... "

—adapted from "Bosnians Recall Karadzic, a Neighbor Turned Enemy," Tracy Wilkinson in *The Los Angeles Times,* July 23, 1995

War damage in Sarajevo

The end of the cold war brought about communism's fall and the triumph of democracy. A new world was at hand—or so it seemed. The aftermath has proven to be more complex. During the cold war, even regional conflicts were often linked to the East-West struggle. Now that the superpower rivalry was over, each issue stood on its own terms, and predictability and stability had given way to uncertainty and confusion.

During the 1990s, long-hidden national and ethnic rivalries flared into violence in various parts of the world. The threats to peace included not only fighting, but also human tragedies such as starvation and the flow of refugees. Often, the global community, through the United Nations and other organizations, seemed helpless in dealing with these crises. However, there were bright spots—for example, South Africa, the Balkans, and the Middle East. In all three places, the 1990s saw efforts, either fulfilled or in progress, to peacefully resolve disputes or deeply rooted injustices.

Fighting in Bosnia

Bitter ethnic fighting took place in Bosnia-Herzegovina, where the creation of an independent state led to conflict among Croats, Muslims, and Serbs in the early 1990s. With the support of neighboring Serbia and Montenegro, the Bosnian Serbs conquered most of Bosnia-Herzegovina. In April 1992, they began a siege of **Sarajevo**, the Bosnian capital, which was controlled largely by Muslims. Following a policy called ethnic cleansing, the Serbs ruthlessly expelled rival ethnic groups from the areas taken by their army. The Croats and Muslims also carried out atrocities, or cruel actions, against the Serbs.

1014 Chapter 37 *The World in Transition*

SECTION RESOURCES

📁 **Reproducible Masters**
• Lecture Notes 37-4
• Reproducible Lesson Plan 37-4
• Vocabulary Activity 37
• Guided Reading Activity 37-4
• People in World History Profile 72
• Section Quiz 37-4
• Reading Essentials and Study Guide 37-4

🕯 **Transparencies**
• Section Focus Transparency 37-4

Multimedia
💻 Interactive Tutor Self-Assessment Software
💻 Testmaker
💿 Lessons of War: *The Nature of Violence*

The UN imposed an embargo, a ban on trade, against Serbia in 1992, hoping to get the Serbs to stop supplying the ethnic Serbs in Bosnia. UN peacekeeping forces also arrived in the war-torn republic to protect food and medicine sent to the Bosnian people. Since the war began, thousands of Bosnians had been killed, and hundreds of thousands left homeless.

The United States and other UN members also reported human rights abuses in Bosnia. The reports indicated that Bosnian Serbs had tortured and killed Bosnian Muslims and Croats in detention camps. In 1995 an international court charged Bosnian Serb leaders with genocide for operating Nazi-style concentration camps and ruthlessly attacking civilian populations.

Steps Toward Peace

In 1994 Serbia, hurting from the effects of the UN embargo, called on Bosnian Serbs to cease fighting. Later that year, the United States offered a peace plan that proposed dividing Bosnia between the Serbs and a new Muslim-Croat federation. Hostilities, however, continued into 1995. When Bosnian Serbs stepped up their attacks on Sarajevo, NATO responded with air attacks on Serb positions around the city. Meanwhile, Croatia completed a land offensive to regain land held by its own Serb minority. With a possible defeat looming, the Bosnian Serbs finally decided to negotiate.

In November 1995, three presidents—**Slobodan Milosevic** (sloh•boh•dahn mee•LAH•soh•veech) of Serbia, **Alija Izetbegovic** (ah•LEE•hah ee•zeht•BEH•goh•veech) of Bosnia-Herzegovina, and **Franjo Tudjman** (FRAHN•hoh TOOZH•mahn) of Croatia—met in **Dayton**, Ohio, and agreed to the partition of Bosnia into distinct Serb and Muslim-Croat areas. In December the Dayton Treaty was signed in Paris, ending the Bosnian conflict. In response to the agreement, the UN Security Council voted to lift the embargo on Serbia. By the time of the Dayton agreement, the Bosnian conflict had resulted in the deaths of 200,000 people and the forced removal of 3 million people from their homes.

Keeping the Peace

To safeguard the peace, a 60,000-strong NATO-led force arrived in Bosnia to replace the exhausted UN troops. American and Russian troops served as part of the peacekeeping force. In 1996 Bosnian voters elected Muslim, Serb, and Croat leaders to serve on a three-person panel that would govern the country. Despite these steps toward peace, the three Bosnian communities disputed territory and

blocked refugees from returning to their homes. Another problem was the difficulty in bringing indicted war criminals to justice. However, in 1997 as conflicts erupted between moderate and extremist Bosnian Serbs, NATO forces began attacks against positions held by the war criminals and their supporters.

By the end of the century, the situation in Bosnia had become relatively quiet. NATO forces, including 8,000 United States troops, kept the three major ethnic groups from fighting, and a fragile peace was maintained.

Unrest in the CIS

During the Soviet era, the Russian-dominated government in Moscow had repressed the nationalism of non-Russian ethnic groups. This policy increased resentment among many peoples. With the collapse of communism, fierce ethnic hatreds boiled to the surface in Russia and the other CIS republics.

Russia and the CIS

Even after the Soviet collapse, relations among the Commonwealth republics were strained. Russia was clearly the most powerful nation, and European republics, such as Ukraine, were reluctant to concede their hard-won independence to a Russian-dominated federation. During the late 1990s, however, Russia worked to improve relations with these countries in order to offset NATO's eastward expansion. In 1997 Russia and Ukraine signed a treaty that recognized Ukrainian rule over the Crimea and divided the disputed Black Sea naval fleet between them. Also that year, Russia and Belarus forged a close union, allowing Russian and Belarussian citizens to move freely between the two countries, own property in either country, and vote in each other's local elections.

Wary of Russia, the Central Asian republics and those in the Caucasus region balanced ties to Russia with new links to Middle Eastern and Western countries. Largely Muslim in religious background, the Caucasus republic of Azerbaijan and the Central Asian republics rediscovered the spiritual and cultural traditions they shared with the Middle East. Rich in oil deposits awaiting development, these lands also were eager to attract Western businesses.

Although Commonwealth ties were often weak, the CIS remained intact as member nations worked together to resolve conflicts between them and within their territories. Since the Soviet collapse, ethnic unrest had also arisen within some of the

TEACH

Guided Practice

THEME Conflict

Trace the steps of the Bosnian conflict with the class, making a time line on the chalkboard as students list events from this section. Start the time line with Bosnian independence in 1992. **L1 LEP**

Summarize Ask students to summarize the pressures applied by the UN against Serbia and the peace plan that was finally agreed on. **L2**

Critical Thinking Have students discuss the stand Boris Yeltsin took against Chechnya. Have them suggest how they think Yeltsin should have responded to the Chechens. **L3**

VIDEODISC
Lessons of War

Side Two, Chapter 10
Title: *The Nature of Violence*
Subject: Various perspectives concerning the nature of violence
Ask: Is violence inherent in human nature? *(Answers will vary, but one theory is that if provoked, all humans are capable of violence.)* How can violence be stopped? *(perhaps through peaceful negotiations)*

COOPERATIVE LEARNING ACTIVITY

Global Peace Union Organize students into small groups to plan and organize a cooperative international effort to educate people in techniques for peaceful resolution of conflicts. First students should brainstorm ideas in their small groups, then have a joint meeting of all the groups and write guidelines for the organization and a plan of action for use in future conflicts. **L2**

Independent Practice

📁 Guided Reading Activity 37-4 **L1**

📁 People in World History Profile 72

Visualizing History The Russian military took over Grozny and expanded into the countryside. According to some reports, the Russians' "total-war strategy" in Chechnya made it a terrifying war zone.
Answer to Caption: *He wanted to prevent the breakup of Russia that might occur if other ethnic groups followed the example of the Chechens.*

Culture Have students research Sri Lanka and prepare a bulletin-board display of the land, its people, and its culture. **L2**

Who?What?**Where?**When?

Village Divided On the border between the United States and Canada, a village is divided. On the United States side, in Escourt Station, Maine, live five French-speaking families and an American wildlife warden. On the Canadian side is Escourt, Quebec. One of the households in the village is bisected by the border line.

ASSESS

Check for Understanding

Assign Section 4 Assessment as homework or as an in-class activity.

📀 Use Interactive Tutor Self-Assessment Software to review Section 4.

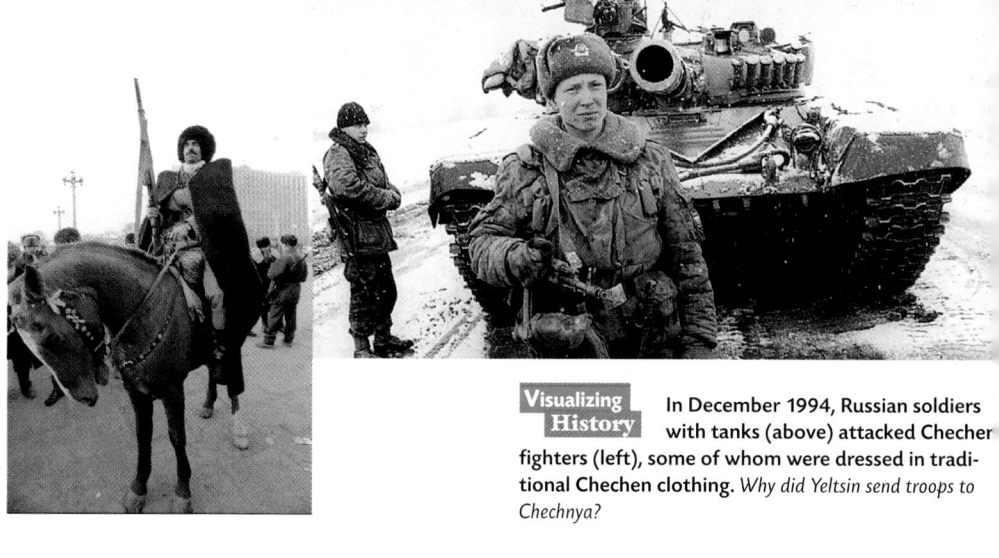

Visualizing History In December 1994, Russian soldiers with tanks (above) attacked Chechen fighters (left), some of whom were dressed in traditional Chechen clothing. *Why did Yeltsin send troops to Chechnya?*

individual CIS republics. Each republic had dominant ethnic groups and many smaller ones. Many of these groups were concentrated in a particular area and had their own local governments. With the collapse of Soviet power, they asserted pride in their traditions and demanded greater self-rule.

The Chechens

The **Chechens** are among the ethnic groups of Russia. Their territory, **Chechnya** (chechh•NYA), lies in southern Russia near the Caspian Sea. In 1994 the Chechens declared their independence from Russia. Fearing Russia's breakup if other groups did the same, Russian leader Boris Yeltsin sent Russian troops into Chechnya. He was widely criticized at home and abroad for the invasion, in which hundreds of civilians were killed in bombing attacks.

The Chechens fought well against poorly trained and disheartened Russian forces. Meanwhile, the conflict divided the Russian people and further strained the economy. In 1996, fierce Chechen resistance forced Russia to agree to peace talks. The resulting treaty did not grant independence, but the Chechens claimed victory and set up their own separate state. In 1999, they aided anti-Russian forces in neighboring Russian-ruled Dagestan. This aid, as well as alleged Chechen terrorist attacks within Russia itself, renewed fighting between Russia and Chechnya.

The Caucasus Republics

Ethnic conflicts troubled other republics in the CIS. In the Caucasus region, Armenia and Azerbaijan both claimed ownership of the enclave of **Nagorno-Karabakh**. An **enclave** is a small territory entirely surrounded by another territory. Nagorno-Karabakh lies entirely within Azerbaijan, but its majority population of Armenians wanted it to separate from Azerbaijan and join Armenia. In 1993 Armenia and Azerbaijan went to war over Nagorno-Karabakh. Armenian forces took control of much of the disputed territory.

Neighboring Georgia has faced separatist uprisings by minority ethnic groups, such as **the Ossetians** and **the Abkhazians**. In 1994 the Abkhazians declared their region an independent republic. Meanwhile, Georgia has received support from Russia in the effort to preserve its national unity. The Russians hold three military bases in Georgia and train and equip the Georgian army.

Africa and Asia

During the 1990s, ethnic conflicts erupted in various parts of Africa and Asia. In Africa, full-scale fighting broke out between Hutu and Tutsi peoples in the East African republics of Rwanda and Burundi. (See Chapter 34.) The unleashed hatreds led to genocides, and the violence spilled over into neighboring Zaire, later called the Democratic Republic of the Congo. Other ethnic divisions contributed to civil wars in West Africa, especially in the nations of Sierra Leone and Liberia.

The Kurds

In the Middle East, one of the most divisive ethnic disputes was between **the Kurds** and the governments of Iraq and Turkey. The 30 million Kurds are Sunni Muslims and live mostly in

---

MEETING SPECIAL NEEDS ACTIVITY

Attention Deficiency Suggest that students who find it easier to break up study into short sessions concentrate on the information under one subhead for a short time, then go to the resource center and find additional information about that subject. This physical activity will help them to focus again when they return to studying. These students could be responsible for gathering current information about conflicts for the newspaper project suggested for this chapter. **L1**

Armenia, Iran, Iraq, Syria, and Turkey. They have never had their own nation but have long sought their freedom. In the 1980s and 1990s, the Kurds of Turkey and Iraq carried out separate revolts against their respective governments. In 1982 Saddam Hussein used poison gas against the Kurds in Iraq, killing hundreds of men, women, and children. He has continued to attack the Kurds since then. Turkish forces have staged offensives against Turkish Kurdish bases in remote mountain areas along the border of Turkey and Iran.

In 1999 the Turkish authorities captured Abdullah Ocalan (OH•jah•lahn), the Kurdish terrorist leader. He was convicted and sentenced to death for treason.

Sri Lanka

Another place torn by ethnic discord was the Indian Ocean island republic of **Sri Lanka**. Sri Lanka's 18 million people largely belong to two ethnic groups. **The Sinhalese**, who make up about 75 percent of the population, are Buddhist. **The Tamils**, most of whom are Hindus, form about 18 percent of the population and live in northern and eastern areas of Sri Lanka.

For decades, the Tamils had resented discrimination by the Sinhalese-controlled government. In 1983 fighting broke out between Tamil guerrillas and Sinhalese government troops. Despite peace efforts, the fighting continued into the 1990s. More than 50,000 were killed, and hundreds of thousands of Tamil refugees fled to India.

Canada's Fragile Unity

During the 1980s and 1990s, Canada faced growing uncertainty about its future. Many French-speaking people in the province of **Quebec** wanted independence from English-speaking Canada. When Quebec voters in 1980 narrowly defeated an independence proposal, the Canadian federal government worked to strengthen national unity while respecting regional differences. In 1982 a new Canadian constitution was enacted that granted more power to the provinces and guaranteed the language and cultural rights of all Canadians.

Quebec, however, rejected the constitution because it did not allow individual provinces to veto future amendments. Prime Minister **Brian Mulroney**, whose Conservative party came to power in 1984, tried in vain to get English-speaking Canada to accept a special status for Quebec. Ten years later, the Liberal party won parliamentary elections, and **Jean Chretien** (ZHAWN cray•TYEHN) became prime minister. Although a French-speaking Quebecer, Chretien believed in national unity and opposed Quebec separatism.

In 1995 Quebec voters again turned down independence for the province, but only by a minute margin. Canada in theory remained united, but the referendum left Canada's people deeply divided.

In June 1997 Canadian voters elected a new parliament, splitting their vote along regional lines. Running on its record of reducing government spending, Prime Minister Jean Chretien's Liberal party captured a majority of seats—19 fewer than it held before the vote.

In second place was the conservative Reform party, which had strong support in the western provinces where opposition to a special status for Quebec was strongest. The Bloc Quebeçois, the Quebec separatist party, was third. Because of deep divisions between them these two opposition parties could not effectively unite against the Liberals.

Canada was faced with further, although more positive, division when in 1992 a referendum was passed authorizing the establishment of the eastern half of the Northwest Territories as a new autonomous territory. Called **Nunavut** (NOO-na-voot), "Our Land" in the Inuit language, the region came into being as an 85-percent Inuit territory in April 1999.

Linking Past and Present

United Nations Fiftieth Anniversary On June 26, 1945, fifty nations joined to sign the UN Charter. Fifty years later there were 185 members planning a celebration in New York City at the UN headquarters. This organization has received the Nobel Peace Prize numerous times. Although it has not succeeded in resolving some major conflicts, most members believe that the problems countries face are too great for any one nation to solve alone.

Evaluate

Section Quiz 37-4

Use the Testmaker to create a customized quiz for Section 4.

Reteach

Ask students to write five opening statements for a national TV news broadcast covering issues in this section.

Reading Essentials and Study Guide 37-4

Enrich

Have students scan newspapers and magazines for articles related to the regions or issues mentioned in this section. Then have them share the articles with the class.

CLOSE

Ask students to discuss which conflicts that they have studied in this section cause them the greatest concern and why.

SECTION 4 ASSESSMENT

Main Idea

1. Use a diagram like the one below to identify areas of the world that experienced ethnic discord after World War II.

Areas of Ethnic Discord

Recall

2. **Define** ethnic cleansing, atrocity, embargo, enclave.

3. **Identify** Slobodan Milosevic, Alija Izetbegovic, Franjo Tudjman, the Chechens, the Ossetians, the Abkhazians, the Kurds, the Sinhalese, the Tamils, Brian Mulroney, Jean Chretien, Nunavut.

Critical Thinking

4. **Making Comparisons** Compare Quebec's expression of dissatisfaction with Canada to that of the Tamils with Sri Lanka.

Understanding Themes

5. **Conflict** Why did the Bosnian Serbs in 1992 oppose the creation of an independent Bosnian state?

Chapter 37 *The World in Transition* **1017**

SECTION 4 ASSESSMENT ANSWERS

1. the Balkans; southern Russia and the Caucasus; central Africa; Turkey; Iraq; Sri Lanka; Canada

2. All terms are defined in the Glossary.

3. Milosevic, 1015; Izetbegovic, 1015; Tudjman, 1015; Chechens, 1016; Ossetians, 1016; Abkhazians, 1016; Kurds, 1016; Sinhalese, 1017; Tamils, 1017; Mulroney, 1017; Chretien, 1017; Nunavut, 1017

4. Quebec sought separation from Canada through the election process; the Tamils' discord was expressed through violent fighting. Possible reasons why: responding to an unjust blocking of basic opportunities for education and employment; people in Quebec were not having rights withheld.

5. **CONFLICT** Bosnian Serbs feared domination by the Croatians and Muslims if Bosnia became independent. Bosnian Serbs agreed to peace talks because it looked like they would be defeated and would lose territory.

SECTION THEME

▶ **Cultural Diffusion** New technology and an integrated world communications system speed the transfer of ideas and practices throughout the world.

Guide to Reading

For reading strategies to help students read effectively see pages 12–13.

Vocabulary Pre-check

 Use the Vocabulary PuzzleMaker for Chapter 37 to create a crossword puzzle to reinforce section terms. **L1 LEP**

📁 Use Vocabulary Activity 37 to introduce vocabulary terms. **L1 LEP**

FOCUS

Section Objective

Explain how recent advances in technology have affected the world's cultures.

BELLRINGER
Motivational Activity

 Before taking roll at the beginning of the class period, project Section Focus Transparency 37-5 and have students answer the activity questions.

📁 This activity is also available as a blackline master.

1980		1990		200(

1987 The Montreal Protocol calls for global reduction of chemical pollutants.

1992 The first Earth Summit is held in Rio de Janeiro, Brazil.

1995 The United States space shuttle *Atlantis* docks with the Russian space station *Mir*.

Section 5

Global Interdependence

 Guide to Reading

Read to Find Out
Main Idea *Recent advances in technology have affected the world's cultures.*

▶ **Terms to Define**
interdependent, developing nations, developed nations, deforestation, Internet, genetic engineering

▶ **People to Meet**
Neil Armstrong, Jean Paul Sartre, Mother Teresa

▶ **Places to Locate**
Montreal, Rio de Janeiro

The Storyteller

Robert "Hoot" Gibson, the American astronaut, carefully maneuvered Atlantis closer to Mir, the Russian space station. Finally, just after 9:00 A.M. eastern standard time, June 29, 1995, Gibson gently docked the 100-ton shuttle with the Mir's central docking port. On Earth, at the Russian mission control, NASA chief Dan Goldin leaped from his seat to hug his Russian counter-

part, Yuri Koptev. When the hatch was opened, Gibson floated along the pathway into the Russian ship. After decades of competition, American and Russian space programs had launched a promising partnership.

Partnership in space

—adapted from "Mir Reflections," Frank Sietzen in *Final Frontier*, November/December 1995

1018 **Chapter 37** *The World in Transition*

I n 1900 most of the world's people knev little about other people in distant place on the planet. By the year 2000, howeveï people communicate instantly with others thou sands of miles away and access vast amounts o information with their fingertips. Today, we shaï in a technological and communications revolutior that has made people increasingly interdependent or reliant on each other.

The Global Community

Today's nations have become economically interdependent through world trade, which now exceeds $9 trillion per year. Since World War II, technological advances and the removal of tariff and other barriers to free trade have led to a tremendous increase in the global exchange of goods and services. The forging of new trade links among different regions has ensured that an economic boom or bust in one region will impact economies in other parts of the world.

The world's economic superpowers include the United States, the European Union, and Japan. These areas, along with South Korea, Taiwan, and other countries of Asia's Pacific Rim, are the leading competitors in international markets.

Developing and Developed Nations

With the rise of the global economy, some observers claim that the nation-state is no longer the key economic and political institution it was a hundred years ago. They point out that large multinational organizations and corporations now have greater control over international flows of people, goods, funds, and technology. Others believe that nation-states are still crucial in making and carrying out basic economic policies.

One of the major global issues involving nations is the gap between rich and poor countries. Developing nations in Asia, Africa, and Latin

---

SECTION RESOURCES

📁 **Reproducible Masters**
• Lecture Notes 37-5
• Reproducible Lesson Plan 37-5
• Guided Reading Activity 37-5
• Geography and History Activity 37
• History Simulation 37
• Reteaching Activity 37
• Enrichment Activity 37

• Section Quiz 37-5
• Performance Assessment Activity 37
• Spanish Chapter Summary 37
• Reading Essentials and Study Guide 37-5
📖 **Transparencies**
• Section Focus Transparency 37-5
• World History and Art Transparency 52, *Sky Above Clouds II*

• Mapping History Overlay Transparency 25, *World Population Growth*
Multimedia
 Vocabulary PuzzleMaker Software
 Interactive Tutor Self-Assessment Software
 Testmaker

merica are newly industrializing countries, and many of their people still follow traditional ways of life. These developing nations are dependent on *developed nations*, such as the United States, that have long been industrialized and have the technology to produce a great quantity and variety of goods.

Building Strong Economies

To raise standards of living, developing nations often try to diversify, or increase the variety of, the goods they supply to the world. This enables them to avoid relying on a single crop or product. The transition to a diversified economy, however, can be difficult because of lack of funds and skilled workers. Developing countries often rely on outside lending sources for funding. The World Bank and the International Monetary Fund (IMF) were set up after World War II to assist global economic development. Private banks and international corporations also invest in developing nations.

Borrowing funds for economic growth has placed many countries in monumental debt. When loans cannot be paid, banks suffer huge losses that hurt businesses. Many strategies have been tried to solve international debt problems. In some cases, banks have issued new loans to enable developing countries to pay off old debts. While such practices have helped to offset immediate concerns, debt remains a threat to the world's economic health.

Population Growth

The number of people on our planet affects both human well-being and the environment. Developed nations point to the rapid growth of population in developing countries as a major cause in straining world resources. As much as 97 percent of the world's population growth occurs in the developing world. Families are large in very poor countries in part because many children are needed to help earn money and to assist parents in their old age. At the present rate of growth, the world's population is expected to increase from the present 6 billion to about 12 billion by 2050.

People in developing countries consume far less per person than do people in developed countries. However, the large populations in the developing world are exhausting the resources of many areas. In Africa and Asia, for example, population pressures have forced farmers to make a living on fragile, poorly productive lands. In some places erosion and landslides have caused irreversible environmental damage. Throughout the developing world, millions of people leave the countryside each year and crowd into cities in the hope of

Visualizing History Hong Kong is one of the busiest ports of Asia's Pacific Rim. *In addition to Asia's Pacific Rim, what other prosperous area of the world trades extensively with the United States?*

improving their lives. Urban growth has been so rapid that cities cannot keep up with the needs for shelter, food, and jobs. To remedy these problems, developing countries are working to link population, development, and environmental needs.

The Environment

Protecting the environment is another global challenge. For much of human history, the abundance of the earth's resources was taken for granted. Today, however, human use and abuse of resources—especially the high consumption of resources in the

Student Web Activity 37

Visit the *World History: The Human Experience* Web site at **worldhistory.glencoe.com** and click on *Chapter 37—Student Web Activities* for an activity relating to the global economy.

Chapter 37 *The World in Transition* **1019**

TEACH

Guided Practice

THEME Cultural Diffusion
Have students discuss how increasing economic interdependence can hasten the spread of different cultures. (*Answers may include that an increase in international trade encourages foreign travel by businesspeople and brings people into contact with the goods from other countries.*) **L1**

Visualizing History

Answer to Caption: *Western Europe*

Economics Explain that the World Bank is a specialized agency that the United Nations founded to provide loans to developing countries to help their economic growth. Discuss the issues this bank would have to consider in making such loans. (*environmental concerns, human rights, political upheavals*) **L2**

Critical Thinking Ask students to consider the problem and effects of overpopulation at the individual and family level. Have some students participate in an impromptu panel discussion about how overcrowding can affect people's daily lives. **L3**

History Simulation 37

COOPERATIVE LEARNING ACTIVITY

Environmental Responsibilities Display Have students choose an environmental concern (for example, energy conservation, deforestation, species extinction) and make one poster graphically dramatizing the problem and another poster displaying a possible solution. Have students gather visual materials to go with the posters and make a wall display to promote environmental awareness. They should include global as well as local examples. **L1 LEP**

— **WORLD HISTORY** Online —
Have students use the **Chapter 37 Student Web Activity** at worldhistory.glencoe.com for in-depth study of the global economy.

World History and Art Transparency 52, *Sky Above Clouds II*

 Mapping History Overlay Transparency 25, *World Population Growth*

Independent Practice

📁 Guided Reading Activity 37-5 **L1**

📁 Geography and History Activity 37

Economics Have students do a survey of where the foods they eat and other things they purchase or consume are produced. Have them bring labels to class and use these as a basis for making a rough assessment of how the world is catching up to the United States in trade. **L2**

Linking Past and Present

Global Economy

China is another Asian nation on its way to becoming an economic giant. Its economy is expected to boom in the twenty-first century. It has been growing rapidly and is expected to expand to $6 trillion over the next 25 years, a nearly tenfold growth since 1994. With this explosion of growth, however, has come increased pollution; in 1991, industries there created more polluted water than those in the entire Western world.

ANSWERS

to increase trade and coordinate economic growth among members; possible answer: They help the global economy since they help member nations achieve economic health and stability.

---

developed world—has reached such levels that the planet may no longer be able to heal itself.

Land and Water

Vast areas of the earth's land have been destroyed by overgrazing, pesticides, and deforestation, the widespread clearing of forests for logging or farming. Particularly at risk are semi-arid areas near the edge of deserts. Since the 1970s, developing countries have lost much of their farmland, making it difficult to raise enough food for growing populations.

Another challenge to the earth comes from pollution. Some scientists believe that increasing amounts of certain industrial chemicals in the air are gradually warming the earth. This global warming, they claim, will raise global temperatures a few degrees during the 2000s. Glaciers and parts of ice caps may melt, increasing sea level throughout the world.

The oceans and freshwater resources of the planet are also showing signs of overuse and abuse. Poisonous industrial wastes, sewage, and pesticides are polluting coastal waters and soil. Environmental damage is seen in increasing num-

bers of diseased fish and wildlife and in the dec of coral reefs.

Meanwhile, demand for fresh water has grow Disputes over water usage have developed in dri areas of the world, such as the Middle East. Effor are under way to achieve some fair distribution scarce water supplies among countries, as well between rural and urban areas.

Environmental Awareness

Since the 1970s, the world's people have becom increasingly aware of environmental issues, and number of international gatherings have stressed th urgency of dealing with the environmental crisis. 1987 delegates from 46 countries met in **Montrea** Canada, and signed the **Montreal Protocol**, whic called for reductions in the use of chemicals damag ing to the earth's atmosphere. Other important gath erings were the 1992 Earth Summit in **Rio d Janeiro**, Brazil, and the follow-up 1997 Eart Summit+5 in New York City. These UN-sponsored conferences called on nations to plan economi growth to meet present global needs without sacri ficing the environmental needs of future generations

---

CONNECTIONS
 Economics

Global Economy

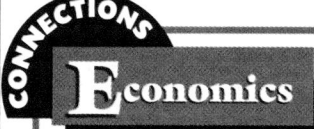

Japanese cars for export

Since 1945, many of the world's nations have joined to create large regional economic markets. The goal of each of these markets is to increase trade and to coordinate economic growth among member nations.

In North America the United States, Canada, and Mexico have implemented the North American Free Trade Agreement (**NAFTA**). In southern South America several nations participate in the Southern Common Market (Mercosur), while in the Caribbean region a number of countries form the Association of Caribbean States (ACS).

Western European nations have not only promoted economic interdependence among themselves. In the 1993 Treaty of Maastricht, they also took steps toward political unity by creating the European Union.

The creation of large economic blocs in the Americas and in Europe in part stems from the increasing competition these two regions have faced from the growing economic might of the countries of Asia's Pacific Rim. During the past few decades Japan, South Korea, Taiwan, and Hong Kong have become economic giants that are active in world trade. In the near future, China, (now including Hong Kong) and the Association of Southeast Asian Nations (**ASEAN**) will powerfully impact the global economy.

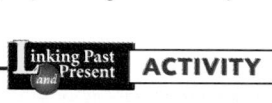 Linking Past and Present **ACTIVITY**

Explain why individual countries have joined in forming large regional economic markets. Do you think regional economic blocs benefit or hinder the global economy?

MEETING SPECIAL NEEDS ACTIVITY

Language Delayed Students with a need for help with language would benefit by making a set of flash cards for the names of places and the special vocabulary in this section. They might want to go on to compile a set of cards for the entire chapter and use them in studying the material. **L1 LEP**

The Technological Revolution

Since 1945 the world has undergone a technological revolution as dramatic as the Industrial Revolution. Computers are at the heart of this transformation. They process data about a nation's economy, forecast the weather, and calculate the flight path of a rocket. The "brain" driving the computer is the microchip, a mesh of circuits etched on a silicon wafer.

Computers: The Internet and Y2K

Computers are important in today's explosion of global communications. The Internet, a web of tens of thousands of computer networks linked by telephone lines, swiftly sends data around the world and links users to a vast wealth of resources. Using a computer with a modem, a device linking two computers through a telephone line, you can research and share information on the World Wide Web, the major Internet network. You can also send a message through E-mail, or electronic mail, to any place in the world in seconds.

In the 1990s, computer programmers faced a serious challenge. In order to save memory space, computers had been programmed to shorten the four-digit year into two—for example, recognizing "99" as the year 1999. The possibility existed, however, that "00" would be recognized as the year 1900 instead of the year 2000. Many people therefore wondered if the coming of the new millennium would bring a flood of computer errors, plunging much of the world into chaos. Over $400 billion were spent to solve what became known as the "Y2K (the year 2000) bug." When 2000 finally arrived, greeted with celebrations around the world, computer problems appeared to be minimal.

Space Exploration

Computers and other new technologies have made space exploration possible. Since the Soviet launching of *Sputnik*, the first satellite into orbit, in 1957, the Americans and Russians have sent hundreds of satellites and human-operated spacecraft into space. In July 1969 American astronaut **Neil Armstrong** became the first human to step on the moon's surface. In the early 1980s, American scientists developed the space shuttle, a reusable spacecraft that takes off like a rocket and lands like an airplane. From the shuttle, astronauts can launch, retrieve, and repair satellites. Throughout the 1990s

Air pollution from factories is a problem in industrialized countries. In this scene, clouds containing industrial pollutants cover an area in Germany. *How has pollution affected the planet's water?*

the American space shuttle *Atlantis* docked with the Russian space station *Mir*. Symbolizing a new era of space cooperation, this linkage raised hopes for the building of an internationally operated space station. The United States also sent many space vehicles to other planets, finally successfully landing the space probe *Pathfinder* on Mars in 1997.

Medical Advances

Medical science also has benefited from technological progress. Lasers, or devices that emit narrow, powerful beams of light, allow doctors to perform surgery with minimal discomfort to patients. Medicines correct chemical imbalances in the brain, treating severe depression. Kidney and liver transplants are performed frequently, and many people now live for years with transplanted hearts.

Recent DNA (deoxyribonucleic acid) technology has led to the new field of genetic engineering, a process that involves the alteration of cells to

ASSESS

Check for Understanding

Assign Section 5 Assessment as homework or as an in-class activity.

 Use Interactive Tutor Self-Assessment Software to review Section 5.

Evaluate

 Section Quiz 37-5

Reteach

Lead a class discussion on developments of the last decade in communications technology, medicine, environment, and cultural global interdependence.

 Reteaching Activity 37

Reading Essentials and Study Guide 37-5

Enrich

Have students prepare written reports on an international environmental issue. Allow an opportunity for them to share these studies.

Enrichment Activity 37

CLOSE

Have students create a wall chart showing the major technological changes in communication and transportation that occurred in the twentieth century.

---

produce new life-forms. Further molecular research may yield insights into the origins and cure of diseases such as cancer and AIDS that affect millions of people worldwide.

The Global Culture

Technological advances have hastened the growth of a global culture. Jet travel, television, and communications satellites have spread ideas and practices from one part of the globe to another. Today the cultures of various regions meet and blend. American rock music now echoes in clubs around the world. Asian folk dancers perform their artistry on tour in Europe, while Latin American poets recite their works before audiences in Japan.

The Search for Life's Meaning

Today's rapid and often complex changes have sent many people on a search for life's meaning. After World War II, the French thinker **Jean Paul Sartre** stated a viewpoint known as existentialism that became popular among intellectuals in the West. According to Sartre, each person is essentially alone but free to choose his or her path in life.

Individual freedom became a key goal during the last half of the twentieth century. Civil rights movements have advanced racial equality in the United States and South Africa; and in many countries, the women's movement has altered traditional female roles and opportunities.

While secular viewpoints have spread, religious individuals and groups have sought to meet society's needs. For example, the Vatican Council II (1962–1965) related Roman Catholic teaching to modern life and simplified many church practices. The Roman Catholic nun **Mother Teresa** inspired many people with her care of the needy in the slums of Calcutta, India. Also, the Dalai Lama,

Tibet's Buddhist leader, and Desmond Tutu, South African Anglican archbishop, spoke out for human rights. Within Islam and Protestant Christianity, powerful conservative movements have attracted many followers. Although religious hostilities persist in areas such as the Balkans and South Asia, efforts have increased to promote understanding among global religions.

Human Rights

In recent decades, the issue of human rights has captured world attention. According to human rights groups, despite democratic advances since the 1980s, many governments still imprison and abuse people for speaking their minds. Among the countries accused of human rights violations are China, Indonesia, the Democratic Republic of the Congo, Afghanistan, and Myanmar. Others such as Iran, Iraq, Cuba, Libya, North Korea, and Sudan have also been charged with sponsoring terrorist acts outside of their borders.

The good news is that human rights abuses are more carefully monitored than they were. In South Africa, Haiti, and El Salvador, for example, national truth commissions have investigated abuses of past governments, and international tribunals for Bosnia and Rwanda have called individuals to account for their war crimes. The increased visibility of each government's actions and the accompanying accountability that many nations and groups feel is showing results.

In 1948 the United Nations adopted what has become the most important human-rights document of the postwar years—the Universal Declaration of Human Rights. Addressing social and economic as well as political rights, the Declaration is a statement not of the way things are, but of the way they should be. As new technologies develop, more will have to be done to provide the basic needs and a decent quality of life for the planet's inhabitants.

SECTION 5 ASSESSMENT

Main Idea

1. Use a diagram like the one below to list the effects of recent technological advances on world cultures.

Recall

2. **Define** interdependent, developing nations, developed nations, deforestation, Internet, genetic engineering.

3. **Identify** ASEAN, Montreal Protocol, Neil Armstrong, Jean Paul Sartre, Mother Teresa.

Critical Thinking

4. **Analyze** Why do environmental dangers to the planet require global solutions?

Understanding Themes

5. **Cultural Diffusion** What is the most powerful source of cultural diffusion today? Explain the reasoning behind your answer.

SECTION 5 ASSESSMENT ANSWERS

1. computers: process complex information quickly; Internet: expands global communication; space exploration: new era of space cooperation; medical advances: laser surgery, organ transplants, genetic engineering
2. All terms are defined in the Glossary.
3. ASEAN, 1020; Montreal Protocol, 1020; Neil Armstrong, 1021; Jean Paul Sartre, 1022; Mother Teresa, 1022
4. Damage to one part of the planet affects other parts of the planet, as all environments are interconnected.
5. **CULTURAL DIFFUSION** Answers will vary. Possible answer: Computer technology has made instant global communication possible, which has allowed the sharing of art, language, and science within seconds.

Interpreting Statistics

Statistics seem to support a claim or an opinion with a ring of authority. We have heard that statistics can be misleading, but do we really understand how to interpret statistics?

Learning the Skill

Statistics are sets of tabulated information that may be gathered through surveys and other sources. When studying statistics, consider each of the following:

Biased sample A sample, or group of the total population surveyed, may affect the results. A sample that does not represent the entire population is called a biased sample. An unbiased sample is called a representative sample.

Correlation Two sets of data may be related or unrelated. If they are related, we say that there is a correlation between them. For example, there is a positive correlation between academic achievement and wages. There is a negative correlation, however, between smoking and life expectancy. Statistics may seem to show a correlation when none exists. For example, a report that "people who go fishing are less likely to get cancer" may be statistically true but lack any correlation.

Statistical Significance Using statistics, researchers determine whether the data support a generalization or whether the results are due to chance. If the probability that the results were due to chance is less than 5 percent, researchers say that the result is statistically significant.

Practicing the Skill

Study the table below (the amount of economic freedom is shown on a scale from 0–8, with 8 being most free). Then answer the questions that follow.

1. Is there a correlation between wage rates and the percentage of government employees? Explain.
2. What statistics deny a correlation between the percentage of government employees and the index of economic freedom?

 The **Glencoe Skillbuilder Interactive Workbook**, Level 2 provides instruction and practice in key social studies skills.

Applying the Skill

Create a survey with two questions for which you believe the answers may show a correlation. For example, "How many hours of television do you watch per day?" and "How many hours of sleep do you average per night?" Gather a representative sample of responses. Tabulate and evaluate your statistics.

For More Practice

Turn to the Skill Practice in the Chapter Assessment on page 1025 for more practice in interpreting statistics.

Wages, Government Employment, and Economic Freedom

Nation	Hourly Wage Rate (1994)	Government Employees as Percent of Total	Index of Economic Freedom 1993–1995*
Germany	$27	16.2	6.5
Japan	$21	8.4	7.0
Sweden	$19	33.2	5.5
United States	$17	15.4	7.5
Great Britain	$14	18.1	7.0
New Zealand	$10	15.3	8.0
South Korea	$6	na	7.0
Mexico	$5	31.8	5.5

* Index compiled by survey of economists for "Economic Freedom of the World: 1975–1995," James Gwartney, Robert Lawson, and Walter Block.

TEACH

Interpreting Statistics Explain to students that finding a correlation does not mean you have found its cause. When two things are correlated, you cannot tell whether one factor causes the other. For example, if students who did particularly well on an exam were found to have consumed more caffeine the night before, it would not mean that this was the reason for the better performance. The real reason might have been that these students spent more time studying. Remind students to be on guard against inferring a causative relationship where none exists when analyzing statistical data.

Additional Practice

📁 Skill Reinforcement Activity 37

📁 Building Skills in Geography Workbook, Unit 2, Lesson 11

GLENCOE
TECHNOLOGY

 Glencoe's **Skillbuilder Interactive Workbook, Level 2** This interactive CD-ROM promotes student mastery of key social studies skills.

ANSWERS TO PRACTICING THE SKILL

1. No; wages are highest in Germany, but percentage of government employees is highest in Sweden.
2. They all do. For example, Sweden has the highest percentage of government employees but its index is 5.5; Japan has the lowest percentage of government employees and its index is high, 7.0.

Chapter 37
Assessment

GLENCOE TECHNOLOGY

VIDEODISC
Use MindJogger to review the chapter.

MindJogger Videoquiz

Chapter 37
Disc 5 Side B

Answers
Using Key Terms
1. a   3. d   5. k
2. f   4. e

Using Your History Journal
Students should include several specific issues with their effects.

Reviewing Facts
1. Challenges: shift from communism to democracy and free enterprise; state-run economies in collapse; debt; worthless currencies; no foreign investment. Solutions: cut spending; balance budgets; sell off state-run farms; retrain workers
2. U.S. free enterprise economy had trade deficits and high inflation and unemployment, but was basically sound; the Soviet Union had a state-run economy, inefficient and in decay.
3. He worked for reform and agreements with the West.
4. **1980:** Solidarity strikes in Poland; **1985:** Gorbachev comes to power; **1989:** Communist governments fall in Eastern Europe;

Using Key Terms

Write the key term that completes each sentence. Then write a sentence for each term not chosen.

   a. interdependent   g. Internet
   b. glasnost   h. referendum
   c. privatization   i. perestroika
   d. genetic engineering   j. trade deficit
   e. developing nations   k. enclave
   f. ethnic cleansing   l. deforestation

1. The growth of technology, communications, and transportation since 1945 has made the regions of the world increasingly _____.
2. In Bosnia and Kosovo, ethnic Serb forces carried out _____, a policy of forcibly removing rival ethnic groups.
3. Through _____, scientists can now alter cells to produce new life-forms.
4. _____ have established new industries, but many of their people still follow traditional ways of earning a living.
5. The territory of Nagorno-Karabakh is an _____ completely surrounded by Azerbaijan.

Technology Activity

Using the Internet Search the Internet for information about the latest technological innovations that are influencing our global culture. Use a search engine to focus your search by using phrases such as *information technology innovations, global communications,* and *technology revolution.* Create a bulletin board using the information retrieved on the Internet. Include illustrations or pictures of the latest technological innovations.

Using Your History Journal

How will world events affect your future? Write an essay entitled "The World's Future and My Own" identifying important international issues and explaining how events could affect your life.

Reviewing Facts

1. **Government** Use a diagram like the one below to identify challenges faced by new Eastern European governments and how they have dealt with them.

    Problems   **Solutions**

2. **Economics** Describe the economic challenges faced by Americans and Soviets during the 1980s.
3. **History** Explain how Mikhail Gorbachev differed from earlier Soviet leaders.
4. **History** List in chronological order, the significant events that led to the fall of communism.
5. **Economics** Discuss Boris Yeltsin's economic policy and its effects on Russia.
6. **History** Describe how the Soviet collapse and the fall of communism affected global affairs.
7. **Culture** Explain the role of religion in the anti-Communist movements of Eastern Europe during the late 1970s and early 1980s.
8. **Geography** Explain how developed and developing nations affect the environment.
9. **History** Describe the roles of Pope John Paul II, the Dalai Lama, and Mother Teresa.
10. **Citizenship** Discuss the advances made in human rights since World War II. How has the UN dealt with this issue?
11. **Science/Technology** Explain how the cold war affected space exploration.

   Aug. 1991: Failed coup in Moscow; **Dec. 1991:** End of Soviet Union
5. Yeltsin removed price controls, closed inefficient factories, and backed free enterprise; this increased prices and unemployment, then led to business and middle-class growth.
6. The Soviet collapse led to new republics, the end of the cold war, and free enterprise.
7. John Paul II inspired Catholic Poles and other

Europeans to resist communism.
8. developed nations consume more resources than do developing countries; developing countries cannot afford clean technologies
9. John Paul II inspired activities in Eastern Europe; the Dalai Lama spoke for Tibet; Mother Teresa cared for poor
10. Despite violations, greater awareness, monitoring of governments, and use of tribunals

Critical Thinking

Analyze Is Europe less stable now than it was during the cold war? Why or why not?

Analyze How would you identify the era after 1989? What are its major features?

Evaluate How does a global economy affect developing nations?

Analyze How have recent developments in medical technology affected humans?

Geography in History

Region Refer to the map below. What continent has the largest population?

Place Why do economists believe that the Pacific Rim is likely to become the world's fastest-growing market in the next decades?

Human/Environment Interaction How does this map help to identify regions of extreme climate and unsuitable living conditions?

Eastern Hemisphere Population Density

Population per square kilometer
| 0–19 | 20–49 | 50–199 | 200 or more | Data not available |

Understanding Themes

1. **Change** What factors do you think led both superpowers to seek an end to the cold war?
2. **Change** Evaluate Mikhail Gorbachev's response to the uprisings in Eastern Europe. What might have happened if he had tried to stop the changes?

3. **Cooperation** What is the most recent achievement of the European Union?
4. **Conflict** What was the cause of the conflict in Yugoslavia?
5. **Cultural Diffusion** What factors have led to the emergence of a global culture?

Linking Past and Present

1. How have many people's attitudes toward natural resources and their use changed over the past 50 years?
2. Placing a person on the moon was the primary goal of the space race between the United States and the Soviet Union. Has a new goal for the space programs of the United States and Russia emerged? Explain.

Skill Practice

Study the statistics in the chart below and answer the questions that follow.

1. Is there a correlation between energy consumed and per capita GDP?
2. What factors may explain the correlation between energy consumption and GDP?
3. Is the sample of countries used in the chart statistically significant? Explain.

Energy Use and Per Capita GDP

Country	Electricity Consumed* per capita (kilowatts)	GDP** per capita
United States	13,732	$30,200
New Zealand	9,889	$17,700
Bahrain	7,640	$13,700
Netherlands	4,968	$22,000
Poland	3,360	$7,250
Argentina	1,960	$9,700
Thailand	1,295	$8,800
India	427	$1,600
Sudan	43	$875

* Figures for 1995.
** Gross Domestic Product: the sum of all goods and services produced within the country (1997).
Source: CIA World Factbook 1998.

Geography in History

1. Asia
2. because it has such a large population
3. They have low population densities.

Understanding Themes

1. **CHANGE** political and economic problems at home
2. **CHANGE** Uprisings may have occurred anyway but would have been violent.
3. **COOPERATION** a common currency called the euro
4. **CONFLICT** by dividing Bosnia into Serb and Muslim-Croat areas
5. **CULTURAL DIFFUSION** jet travel, TV, computers

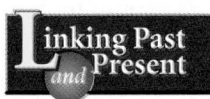

Linking Past and Present

1. People have become concerned about using up world resources.
2. Yes, advancing scientific knowledge or developing space stations.

Skill Practice

1. In most cases, the higher GDP, the more energy consumed.
2. The higher the GDP, the better off people are likely to be, thus the use of more energy-consuming devices.
3. It looks like a fairly good cross section from all over the world.

Chapter Bonus Test Question

Ask students: What do you think is the future of communism as an international political ideology? (*Students should discuss the overthrowing of Communist regimes in the former Soviet Union and Eastern Europe and of recent events in these countries, such as the election of former Communists in Hungary and Poland.*)

---

to punish violators; UN has defined human rights and supported peacekeeping missions.

11. It sparked a rivalry to land a human on the moon.

Critical Thinking

1. Answers may vary. Threat of war with the Soviet Union is gone, but turmoil in that region is greater than it was under communism.
2. Answers should relate to end of cold war;

cessation of superpower rivalry, rise of non-communist governments, expansion of democracy and free enterprise, global economy, communications revolution.

3. It means they must be more competitive.
4. Lasers allow doctors to perform delicate surgery with minimal discomfort; drugs can help relieve depression; organs can be transplanted; genetic engineering may lead to cures for diseases such as cancer and AIDS.

FOCUS

Following World War II, the United States and the Soviet Union exerted the strongest worldwide influence of all countries. However, by the 1990s, many other countries found themselves assessing the state of the world around them and making decisions about how that world should be.

TEACH

Reinforcing Vocabulary

Point out the **Vocabulary Preview** to students alerting them to words they will encounter that might be unfamiliar.

Khrushchev's Secret Speech

Interpreting the Primary Source
Ask students to describe the change in mindset that Khrushchev hoped to bring about with his process of de-Stalinization. (*In dismantling Stalin's legacy, Khrushchev hoped to alter people's belief that those tortured into confessions by Stalin had committed any legitimate crimes.*)

Evaluating the Primary Source
This primary source presents the view of Stalin's actions held by his opposition and voiced after his death. The reliability of this source is determined by the political goals of Khrushchev in giving this speech. As an opposition force, Khrushchev may have wanted to make Stalin look as bad as possible and thus fabricated his own horrifying details. However, he may also have been exposing the frightening truth of the details of Stalin's reign.

Unit 8

After World War II the balance of power in the world shifted dramatically. Many nations came under the political and ideological influence of the United States, which promoted capitalism, or the Soviet Union, which promoted communism. The long period of tension and conflict between these superpowers and their allies is known as the "cold war." By the 1990s the cold war had ended, but civil wars and ethnic conflicts in various parts of the world were a new cause for anxiety and alarm.

✦ VOCABULARY PREVIEW

saboteur: a person who commits deliberate acts of destruction

fabricated: made up

pre-ordained: destined; already decided

colleague: professional associate

 For more primary sources to accompany this unit, use the World History Primary Source Document Library CD-ROM.

Chapter 32
Khrushchev's Secret Speech

 Oral Histories

Nikita Khrushchev began a process of de-Stalinization. In 1956 he delivered a secret speech, denouncing Stalin and his brutal regime, to the 20th Congress of the Soviet Communist Party in Moscow.

Stalin organized the concept "enemy of the people." This term automatically rendered it unnecessary that the ideological errors [mistaken beliefs] of a man or men engaged in a controversy be proven; this term made possible the use of the most cruel repression, violating all norms of revolutionary legality, against anyone who in any way disagreed with Stalin, against those who were only suspected of hostile intent, against those who had bad reputations in the main, and in actuality, the only proof of guilt used, against all norms of current legal science, was the "confession" of the accused himself; and . . . "confessions" were acquired through physical pressures against the accused.

Nikita Khrushchev 1894–1971

It was determined that of the 139 members and candidates of the party's Central Committee who were elected at the seventeenth congress, 98 persons, that is, 70 percent, were arrested and shot. . . .

Now, when the cases of some of these so-called "spies" and "saboteurs" were examined, it was found that all their cases were fabricated. Confessions of guilt of many arrested and charged with enemy activity were gained with the help of cruel and inhuman tortures. . . .

Mandela's Farewell Speech

Interpreting the Primary Source
Ask students why Mandela made a point of stating that "these social ills . . . are not a pre-ordained result of the forces of nature or the product of a curse of the deities." (*It is likely that those in opposition to Mandela's con-*

demnation would cite the ways of nature or of a god as reasons for the injustices that Mandela has highlighted.)

Evaluating the Primary Source
The primary source presents Mandela's criticism of the state of social affairs in the

Chapter 34
Mandela's Farewell Speech

Oral Histories

In 1990 South Africa's anti-apartheid leader Nelson Mandela was released from a long imprisonment and, in the first election open to all races, was elected president. In 1998 Mandela retired from public life. This excerpt is from his farewell speech to the United Nations.

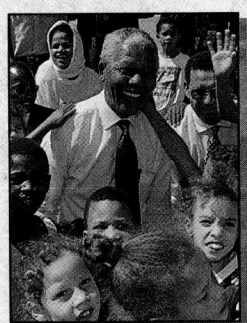
Nelson Mandela
b. 1918

The failure to achieve the vision contained in the Universal Declaration of Human Rights finds dramatic expression in the contrast between wealth and poverty which characterises . . . countries in all hemispheres.

It is made especially poignant and challenging by the fact that this coexistence of wealth and poverty, the perpetuation of the practice of the resolution of inter- and intra-state conflicts by war and the denial of the democratic right of many across the world, all result from the acts of commission and omission particularly by those who occupy positions of leadership. . . .

. . . all these social ills which constitute an offence against the Universal Declaration of Human Rights are not a pre-ordained result of the forces of nature or the product of a curse of the deities.

They are the consequence of decisions which men and women take or refuse to take . . .

Chapter 35
Hussein's Eulogy for Rabin

Oral Histories

Prime Minister Yitzhak Rabin worked to establish peace with Israel's Arab neighbors. In 1995 Rabin was assassinated by an opponent of the peace process. King Hussein I of Jordan paid him tribute with this eulogy.

. . . I had never thought that the moment would come like this when I would grieve the loss of a brother, a colleague and a friend—a man, a soldier who met us on the opposite side of a divide whom we respected as he respected us. A man I came to know because I realized, as he did, that we have to cross over the divide, establish a dialogue, . . . and strive to leave for those who follow us a legacy that is worthy of them. And so we did. And so we became brethren and friends. . . .

King Hussein I
1935–1999

You lived as a soldier, you died as a soldier for peace. . . . We belong to the camp of peace. We believe in peace. We believe that our one God . . . wishes peace upon us, for these are His teachings to all the followers of the three great monotheistic religions, the children of Abraham. . . .

Interpreting Primary Sources

1. How did Stalin obtain evidence of guilt for those he accused?
2. What does Mandela say about the causes of economic inequality and warfare?
3. For what reason does King Hussein believe in peace?
4. **CRITICAL THINKING:** What causes does Mandela believe create poverty, war, and the denial of democratic rights? Do you agree or disagree?

Applications Activity
Devise a constitution for your school that would protect students from forms of persecution such as teasing and racism.

---

world and his accusations of who is to blame for that. This source is a useful historical document because it reveals a situation that seemed so dire to Mandela that he felt he needed to make an emphatic message heard.

Hussein's Eulogy for Rabin
Interpreting the Primary Source
Ask students what important legacy Hussein refers to as having been established by himself and Rabin. (*Hussein refers to the legacy of dialogue across distance, of understanding and cooperating so as to maintain peace.*)

Evaluating the Primary Source
This primary source presents a heroic impression of a dead leader as crafted by a colleague and friend into a sermon on peace. The reliability of the source is determined by Hussein's purpose in giving this speech. If, in addition to giving a eulogy, Hussein saw himself in a position to make a public statement, he may have valorized Rabin in order to hold him up as a martyr for the peace process. However, he may also have made heartfelt statements about Rabin out of true respect for the leader.

For the more complete version of each of these documents, see the World History Primary Source Document Library CD-ROM:

Document 190 *Khrushchev's Secret Speech*
Document 209 *Mandela's Farewell Speech*
Document 227 *King Hussein's Eulogy for Yitzhak Rabin*

ANSWER KEY

1. He extracted "confessions" through torture.
2. Mandela cites the contrast between the wealthy and the poverty-stricken.
3. Hussein believes God has called for peace and that the three great monotheistic religions of Judaism, Christianity, and Islam teach us to live in peace.
4. Mandela refuses to believe that these inequalities and calamities are caused by the forces of nature or by God or the gods but that they are caused by human decisions.

APPLICATIONS ACTIVITY: Answers will vary, but students' constitutions should indicate ways in which students' rights could be safeguarded.

Answers and Analyses

1. **A** (History) The Marshall Plan is described on pages 868–869. There it states that *The Truman administration feared that a European economic collapse would open Europe to communism. It believed that the military and economic security of the United States depended on a strong and democratic Europe.*

2. **F** (History) According to page 890, the separatist movement aimed *to protect French Canadian language and cultural rights.*

 TEST-TAKING TIP

If students recall only that the separatist movement was concerned with cultural, instead of economic or other, ideas they can narrow their search down to a couple of plausible choices. They should then guess from among the choices that remain.

3. **C** (History) Page 887 states that the *Brown* decision ruled that *racial segregation, or the separation of the races, in public schools was illegal.*

4. **J** (History) The Cultural Revolution is discussed on page 902. There it states that *Red Guards attacked local politicians, teachers, and other leaders . . . The accused were denounced, publicly humiliated, and sometimes killed . . . Schools closed, factory production dropped, and violence erupted.*

 THE PRINCETON REVIEW

Standardized Test Practice

Directions: Choose the *best* answer to each of the following multiple choice questions. If you have trouble answering a question, use the process of elimination to narrow your choices. Write your answers on a separate piece of paper.

1. **The primary purpose of the Marshall Plan was to prevent a European economic collapse that would open the door to communism. Which of the following was a secondary purpose?**

   A To build a strong Europe on which American economic security could depend

   B To shift the balance of power away from Asian nations

   C To encourage and reward European Allied efforts in World War II

   D To prevent the Soviet Union from becoming a major economic power

   > **Test-Taking Tip:** This question requires you to remember a *fact* about the Marshall Plan. By reading the question carefully, you can find clues about the Marshall Plan. It was an *economic* program—that is, it provided money to help rebuild European economies. Which answer fits best with this information?

2. **In the 1960s, a movement developed in Quebec to separate that province from the rest of Canada. What was the main issue behind the movement?**

   F Differing cultural identities

   G Religious conflict

   H Differing systems of education

   J Conflicting systems of taxation

   > **Test-Taking Tip:** Separatism in Quebec developed as a result of *differences* between that province and the rest of Canada. Since education is not the primary source of this conflict, you can easily eliminate answer H.

3. **In *Brown* v. *Board of Education of Topeka, Kansas,* the U.S. Supreme Court ruled that Topeka's school district had engaged in which unconstitutional practices?**

   A They had prohibited school prayer.

   B They had transported students to schools far from their homes.

   C They had set up different schools for white and African American students.

   D They had refused to offer bilingual education.

   > **Test-Taking Tip:** The important word in this question is *unconstitutional*. Transporting students great distances seems inconvenient, but it is not specifically banned by the U.S. Constitution. Therefore, you can eliminate answer B.

4. **The Chinese Cultural Revolution of the 1960s resulted in**

   F a greater emphasis on the arts.

   G the translation of classic literature into Chinese.

   H greater political and social freedoms for Chinese women.

   J a decrease in productivity and an increase in human rights abuses.

   > **Test-Taking Tip:** This question is tricky— if you do not remember the term *Cultural Revolution*, it may be tempting to choose answers F or G, since they both relate to *cultural improvements*. However, the Cultural Revolution refers specifically to Mao Zedong's ideas for remaking Chinese society as a Communist regime.

se the following map to answer questions 5, , and 7.

West African Independence

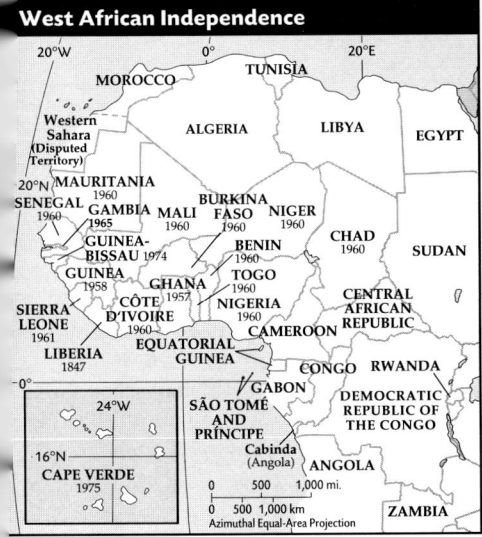

5. By which year had most West African nations gained their independence?

A 1945

B 1950

C 1955

D 1965

Test-Taking Tip: Double check each answer choice against the information *on the map.* Do not rely only on your memory.

6. According to the map, what do Burkina Faso, Mauritania, and Nigeria have in common?

F They are all located in South Africa.

G They all gained their independence in 1958.

H They all gained their independence in 1960.

J They all have coastline borders.

Test-Taking Tip: When looking at a map, be sure to pay attention to the title. Since this is a map of West Africa, you can eliminate choice F as a possible correct answer.

7. Which West African country lies directly north of the Central African Republic?

A Sierra Leone

B Nigeria

C Mauritania

D Chad

Test-Taking Tip: The *compass rose* can help you find cardinal directions. Although north is *usually* at the top of a map, it is not always: make sure that you check before choosing an answer!

5. D (History) According to the map, Mauritania, Mali, Niger, Chad, Nigeria, Togo, Ghana, Guinea, Senegal, Sierra Leone, Liberia, Côte D'Ivoire, and others were independent between 1956 and 1963.

 TEST-TAKING TIP

All the information required to answer this question is on the map itself; students simply need to work carefully to avoid mistakes.

6. H (Geography) According to the map, all three countries gained independence in 1960.

7. D (Geography) According to the map, Chad is directly north of the Central African Republic.

MORE PRACTICE

For additional practice, assign practice pages from:

📁 Glencoe Standardized Test Practice Workbook

📁 Glencoe SAT/SAT II Practice Book

Tested Objectives

Questions	Objective
1	Making Generalizations
2	Evaluating Information
3	Determining Cause and Effect
4, 5, 7	Analyzing Information
6	Making Comparisons

APPENDIX

GLOSSARY

abbess – belligerent

abbess the director of a convent (p. 305)

abbot the head of a monastery (p. 304)

absolutism political system in which a monarch (or group) holds supreme, unlimited power or theory that supports such a system (p. 482)

acupuncture traditional technique of Chinese medicine using thin needles at vital body points (p. 232)

age set in traditional Africa, a group of males or females of similar age who learn skills and go through life stages together (p. 188)

ahimsa (uh•HIHM•sah) Hindu doctrine of nonviolence toward all living things (p. 207)

alchemist person who practiced alchemy, an early form of chemistry emphasizing changes in substances, such as lead into gold (p. 520)

alliance system series of defense agreements involving two or more nations (p. 740)

alphabet system of symbols or characters that represent the sounds of a language (p. 82)

amphora a tall, two-handled Greek vase (p. 131)

anarchy absence of political authority (p. 692)

animism belief that spirits are found in both living and nonliving things (pp. 351, 476)

anthropologist (an•thruh•PAH•luh•jihst) scientist who studies physical and cultural characteristics of humans and their ancestors (p. 20)

apartheid official policy of strict racial separation and discrimination practiced in South Africa from 1948 to the early 1990s (p. 934)

appeasement policy of granting concessions to a potential enemy in order to maintain peace (p. 829)

apportion to divide into assigned shares (p. 648)

apprentice person who works for a master to learn a trade, art, or business (p. 325)

aqueduct a channel built to carry water (p. 168)

arabesque (ar•uh•BEHSK) complex designs typical of Islamic art, combining intertwining plants and geometric patterns (p. 286)

"Arabic numerals" counting symbols (1-9) devised by mathematicians in Gupta India (p. 214)

arbitration process of settling a dispute by submitting it to an impartial third party (p. 722)

archaeologist (ahr•kee•AHL•uh•jihst) scientist who studies earlier peoples and cultures (p. 20)

archipelago a group or chain of islands (pp. 351, 920)

aristocrat member of the nobility or the upper class (p. 113)

armada (ahr•MAH•duh) a fleet of warships (p. 483)

armistice an agreement to stop fighting (p. 761)

arms race the cold war competition between the U.S. and Soviet Union to build up their respective armed forces and weapons (p. 871)

artifact a historic object made or used by humans, such as a tool, ornament, or pottery (p. 20)

artisan person skilled in a craft (p. 33)

atomic theory scientific idea that all matter is made up of tiny particles called atoms (p. 628)

atrocity a cruel and evil action, such as torture (p. 1014)

autocracy government ruled by one person with unlimited authority (p. 690)

automation process in which electronic devices or machines do work once done by humans (p. 883)

autonomy self-government (p. 1008)

balance of power the distribution of power among rival nations so that no one is dominant (p. 489)

balance of trade difference in value between what a nation imports and what it exports over a period of time (p. 448)

bard a poet who tells stories by singing (p. 108)

baroque (buh•ROHK) ornate, dramatic artistic style developed in Europe in the 1550s (p. 423)

barter a system of trade in which goods, not money, are exchanged (p. 82)

bazaar marketplace in an Islamic city (p. 284)

belligerent engaged in fighting or war (p. 746)

bishop a regional leader of the early Christian Church, with authority over a diocese and other clergy (p. 174)

blitz a series of intensive air raids (p. 834)

blitzkrieg (German, "lightning war") a swift, sudden Nazi offensive (p. 831)

bloc a group of political factions or nations acting together (p. 871)

bourgeoisie (boorzh•wah•ZEE) the middle class, between aristocrats and workers (pp. 561, 625)

boyar a landowning noble of early Russia (pp. 260, 499)

boycott a refusal to buy or use certain goods as a protest against an action (p. 548)

budget deficit the amount by which government spending exceeds government income (p. 998)

buffer state neutral territory between rival powers, intended to prevent conflict (p. 582)

bullion gold or silver in the form of bars or plate (p. 448)

bureaucracy a group of government officials headed by an administrator (p. 48)

C

cabinet group of advisers to a ruler or head of state (p. 544)

calculus system of mathematics developed by Newton to analyze changing quantities (p. 519)

caliph (KAY•lihf) supreme leader of Islam, chosen as the "successor" of Muhammad (p. 277)

calligraphy the art of beautiful handwriting (p. 286)

campesino (kahm•puh•SEE•noh) a poor Latin American farm worker (p. 975)

capital money available to invest in business (p. 604)

cardinal high-ranking official of Roman Catholic Church, appointed by the pope (p. 306)

cartel (kahr•TELL) an association of businesses supplying the same product that regulates its members' prices and production (pp. 955, 992)

cartographer person who makes maps (p. 436)

cash-and-carry policy World War II program allowing Great Britain to pay cash and transport needed supplies from the U.S. (p. 835)

cash crop farm product grown to be sold or traded, not used by the farmer (p. 943)

cavalry soldiers mounted on horseback (p. 221)

cell theory scientific theory that small units called cells make up all living things (p. 626)

chancellor title of the chief minister of some European countries (p. 685)

charter formal document granting the right of self-rule (p. 326)

châteaux (sing., chateau [Fr.]) castles (p. 413)

chinampas artificial islands built by the Aztecs for use as gardens (p. 388)

chivalry code of conduct for medieval knights, based on ideals of honor and courtesy (p. 301)

choreographer person who creates dances (p. 775)

chronicle an account that records events in the order in which they happened (p. 288)

circumnavigation sailing completely around something, such as the world (p. 439)

citizen in ancient Greece, a person who took part in the government of a city-state (p. 112)

city-state an independent state consisting of a city and the surrounding land and villages (p. 59)

civil disobedience nonviolent refusal to obey a law or practice thought unjust (p. 802)

civil service system by which government offices are given on the basis of examinations (p. 224)

civilization highly organized society marked by advanced knowledge of trade, government, arts, science, and often written language (p. 32)

clan group based on family ties (pp. 342, 938)

classical describing the artistic style of ancient Greece and Rome, characterized by balance, elegance, and simplicity (p. 130)

classicism style and attitudes derived from the ideals of ancient Greece and Rome (p. 528)

clergy persons, such as priests, given authority to conduct religious services (p. 249)

coalition a temporary alliance of differing political factions (pp. 780, 879)

cold war era of political tension in which the United States and the Soviet Union competed for world influence without actual armed conflict (p. 864)

collective bargaining negotiations between union representatives and employers (p. 616)

collective security the common defense interests of several nations against an enemy (pp. 826, 1012)

collectivization under Stalin, a system to combine land into large farms owned by the government and worked by peasants (p. 790)

colon (koh•LOHN) a French settler in the colony of Algeria (p. 931)

colony a settlement of people outside their homeland, linked with the parent country by trade and direct government control (pp. 82, 475, 706)

comedy story or play intended to entertain and amuse, usually with a happy ending (p. 134)

common law body of English law based on tradition and court decisions, not specific laws (p. 309)

commonwealth a nation or state governed by the people or their representatives (p. 539)

commune – dictatorship of the proletariat

commune people who live communally, with collective ownership and use of property (p. 902)

communism in the theories of Marx and Engels, a society without class distinctions or private property (pp. 625, 758)

concentration camp prison camp where political prisoners or refugees are held (p. 786)

confederation a loose alliance or union of several states or groups (pp. 82, 378, 554)

conquistador (kon•KEES•tuh•dohr) a Spanish "conqueror" or soldier in the Americas (p. 441)

conscription compulsory call to military service; the draft (pp. 569, 740)

constitution plan of government (p. 117)

constitutional monarchy state in which a monarch's power is limited by a constitution (p. 541)

consul in ancient Rome, one of two officials who headed the executive branch (p. 157)

containment U.S. policy designed to prevent the spread of communism (p. 866)

contraband goods that may not legally be transported, particularly during wartime (p. 749)

convoy group of merchant ships traveling together with warships for safety (p. 760)

cooperative a farm organization owned and managed by members, who share profits (p. 812)

cordon sanitaire (kawr•dahn sah•nee•TEHR) a line of "quarantine" or buffer states (p. 763)

corporate state Mussolini's concept of a government with representation by industrial corporations, not political parties (p. 783)

corporation business organization that is owned by stockholders who buy shares, and is run by professional managers (p. 609)

cortes (KOR•tays) assembly of nobles, clergy, and town officials in medieval Spain; also, the parliament of modern Spain (p. 332)

count a noble who acted as a local official within the Frankish empire (p. 295)

coup d'état (koo day•TAH) sudden overthrow of government leaders by a small group (pp. 573, 657)

covenant a solemn pledge or agreement (p. 83)

covert (KOH•vert) secret (p. 986)

Creole a person of European ancestry born in colonial Latin America (p. 667)

Crusades military expeditions by European Christians in the 11th–13th centuries to regain the Holy Land from the Muslims (p. 318)

cubism 20th-century art style that abstracts natural forms into geometric shapes (p. 773)

cultural diffusion the exchange of goods, ideas, and customs among different cultures (p. 34)

culture the way of life of a given people at a given time, including language, behavior, and beliefs (p. 24)

culture system in Dutch colonies in Asia, a system of forced labor to get raw materials (p. 718)

cuneiform (kyoo•NEE•uh•fawrm) Sumerian system of writing using wedge-shaped markings (p. 60)

czar (from "caesar") title taken by rulers of Russia beginning in the late 1400s (p. 264)

D

D-Day the day of the Allied invasion of Normandy, France (June 6, 1944)(p. 848)

daimyo (DY•mee•oh) a powerful local noble in feudal Japan (p. 363)

datus local rulers in the Philippines (p. 475)

death squad in Central America, a band of killers hired by landowners to murder political opponents (p. 987)

deforestation process of cutting trees and clearing forests on large areas of land (p. 1020)

deism religious philosophy of the 1700s based on reason and the idea of natural law (p. 523)

deity a god or goddess (p. 31)

democracy form of government in which the citizens hold power (p. 114)

depression economic situation characterized by a business slump and unemployment (p. 609)

desalination process of removing salt from seawater to produce drinkable water (p. 964)

desertification process of fertile land becoming desert (p. 944)

detente (day•TAHNT) the relaxing of tensions between the United States and the Soviet Union in the 1970s (p. 874)

developed nation an industrialized nation with advanced technology (p. 1019)

developing nation a country in the process of industrializing, where people often follow traditional lifestyles (p. 1018)

dharma duties and rights of members of each class in traditional Hindu society (p. 205)

Diaspora (dye•AS•pur•uh) term for the scattering of communities of Jews outside their original homeland after the Babylonian captivity (p. 86)

dictator in ancient Rome, a leader given temporary absolute power during a crisis (p. 157)

dictatorship government headed by a ruler with absolute authority (p. 574)

dictatorship of the proletariat in the former Soviet Union, theoretical control of the state by the working class (p. 789)

direct tax a tax paid directly to the government (p. 548)

disarmament limiting or reducing military forces and weapons (p. 778)

disciple an active follower of a teacher (p. 172)

disenfranchised denied the right to vote (p. 649)

disengagement act of freeing oneself or withdrawing from a situation (p. 955)

dissident a person who openly criticizes the policies of his or her government (p. 874)

divine right political theory that a ruler derives his or her power directly from God and is accountable only to God (pp. 482, 536)

division of labor production technique in which each worker does one specialized task (p. 609)

doge (DOHJ) the elected leader of the republic in the city-states of Venice and Genoa (p. 408)

domain territory held by a ruler (p. 142)

domesticate to tame animals or plants to serve human needs (p. 30)

domestic system early industrial labor system in which workers produced goods at home (p. 602)

dominion a self-governing nation within the British Empire, later the Commonwealth (p. 653)

domino theory Cold War belief that if one nation became Communist, its neighbors would follow (p. 910)

double-digit inflation a quick rise in prices of 10 percent or more (p. 889)

dual monarchy two states with one monarch (p. 696)

duma the Russian national legislature (p. 694)

duty a tax on imports (p. 546)

dvorianie (dvoh•ree•YAH•nee•yuh) new class of Russian landed nobility established by Peter the Great (p. 501)

dynasty a line of rulers who belong to the same family (p. 47)

E

economy system by which goods and services are produced and distributed to meet people's needs (p. 33)

elite a select group of people (p. 975)

ellipse an oval (not round) closed curve (p. 517)

emancipation legally granting freedom (p. 691)

embargo an order restricting trade (pp. 889, 960, 1015)

emigration leaving one's home country or region to settle elsewhere (p. 630)

émigré (EH•mih•GRAY) person who fled France during the Revolution (p. 566)

empire group of territories or nations ruled by a single ruler or government (p. 49)

enclave (EHN•klayv) a small territory entirely surrounded by the territory of another country or group (p. 1016)

enclosure movement the trend for large landowners gradually to fence and include public and private common lands in their own estates (p. 603)

enlightened despot a monarch who began social changes based on Enlightenment ideas (p. 527)

entente (ahn•TAHNT) an agreement, but not a formal alliance, between nations (p. 740)

entrepreneur person who undertakes risks to establish a business (pp. 448, 604)

epic long poem celebrating the deeds of a legendary or historical hero (p. 203)

estate one of three distinct social classes in France during the 1700s: clergy, nobility, and commoners (the Third Estate) (p. 560)

ethics a system of moral principles that guide behavior (p. 225)

ethnic cleansing term used in the Bosnian conflict for a policy of forcibly removing or killing members of another ethnic group (p. 1014)

evolution theory that species of living things change over long periods of time (p. 626)

excommunication formal exclusion from membership or participation in a church (p. 306)

exodus the departure of a large group of people (p. 84)

extended family family group including several generations as well as other relatives (p. 229)

F

factory system method of production in which goods are made by workers and machines in one location (a factory) outside their homes (p. 606)

fascism (FASH•ihz•uhm) political philosophy based on nationalism and an all-powerful state (p. 782)

federal system form of government in which power is divided between a central authority and its political subdivisions (p. 554)

feudalism medieval political system in which monarchs and lesser nobles made alliances based on exchanging land grants for loyalty (p. 298)

fez traditional hat worn by Turkish men (p. 797)

fief under feudalism, an estate with its peasant workers granted to a noble in exchange for loyalty and military help (p. 298)

filial piety children's respect for their parents, an important principle in Confucian ethics (p. 226)

free trade – inflation

free trade the elimination of trade barriers between nations (p. 978)

friar member of a Catholic order who preached in towns and practiced poverty (p. 307)

fundamentalism movement emphasizing adherence to traditional religious laws and practices (p. 965)

G

geisha Japanese woman trained as a professional entertainer (p. 472)

general strike a strike involving workers from many parts of a nation's economy (pp. 779, 931)

genetic engineering scientific field in which cell structures can be altered to produce new or different organisms (p. 1021)

genetics the study of biological heredity (p. 627)

genocide deliberate attempt to kill all members of a racial, cultural, or ethnic group (pp. 840, 938)

gentry in Elizabethan England, the social group including minor nobility and landowners (p. 488)

ghana title of the ruler of a region in ancient Africa, later applied to the kingdom (p. 189)

glasnost Russian term for the policy of "openness" and free expression introduced by Mikhail Gorbachev (p. 999)

grand jury in English law, group of people who decide whether the evidence of a crime justifies bringing a person to trial (p. 309)

grand vizier (vih•ZEER) prime minister to the sultan of a Muslim country (p. 457)

gross domestic product (GDP) total value of goods and services produced within a country in a year (p. 898)

guerrilla warfare method of fighting in which small groups strike unexpectedly (p. 679)

guild medieval business association of merchants or craftsworkers (p. 324)

H

habeas corpus legal principle that requires authorities to show reasons why a person should be held in custody and to provide a speedy trial (p. 542)

haiku (HY•koo) Japanese poetry form with 17 syllables, usually in three lines (p. 472)

hajj pilgrimage to Makkah that every able-bodied Muslim is expected to make at least once (p. 276)

heavy industry the manufacture of machines and equipment for factories and mines (p. 808)

heresy disagreement with or denial of the basic teachings of a religion (p. 306)

hierarchy group of people organized according to levels of rank or importance (pp. 228, 389)

hieroglyphics ancient Egyptian writing system using picture symbols for ideas or sounds (p. 52)

Holocaust name given to the Nazis' mass murder of European Jews in World War II (p. 839)

homage formal ceremony establishing feudal ties between a lord and a vassal (p. 299)

home rule self-government, especially when granted to a dependent country (p. 651)

hominid (HAH•muh•nihd) member of the group that includes human beings and earlier human-like creatures (p. 20)

humanism Renaissance movement based on the literature and ideas of ancient Greece and Rome, such as the worth of each individual (p. 404)

hygiene the science of good health (p. 138)

hyperinflation an extreme form of inflation, with sharp, rapid price increases (p. 991)

hypothesis solution proposed to explain a set of facts, which can be tested (p. 517)

I

icon a Christian religious image or picture (p. 249)

iconoclast ("image breaker") an opponent of the use of icons in Byzantine churches, who thought they encouraged the worship of idols (p. 250)

ideology the system of beliefs and attitudes that guides the actions of a group or nation (p. 871)

illuminated manuscript book page decorated by hand with elaborate designs, beautiful lettering, or miniature paintings (p. 253)

imam (ih•MAM) a Muslim prayer leader (p. 276)

immigration entering a new country or region to settle permanently there (p. 630)

imperialism policy of building an empire (p. 704)

imperial presidency term for a President and executive branch who assume powers beyond those defined in the Constitution (p. 888)

impressionism artistic style of the late 1800s in which painters tried to capture quick impressions and the effects of light (p. 638)

indemnity payment for damages or losses (p. 160)

individualism emphasis on the dignity and worth of the individual person (p. 404)

indulgence pardon sold by the Catholic Church to reduce one's punishment for sins (p. 416)

industrial capitalism economic system in which individuals continually reinvest profits and expand their businesses (p. 608)

inflation situation in which prices rise quickly while the value of money decreases (pp. 176, 484)

intendant an agent representing the king of France in local government (p. 491)

interchangeable parts production method using identical, easy-to-assemble parts (p. 609)

intercontinental ballistic missile (ICBM) a long-range rocket carrying a warhead (p. 873)

interdependent relying on one another (p. 1018)

Internet popular term for the advanced communications network linking people and computers around the world (p. 1021)

intifada the 1987 uprising by Palestinians against Israeli occupation (p. 956)

iron curtain term coined by Winston Churchill for the political barrier isolating Soviet-dominated Eastern Europe from Western Europe (p. 866)

J

jaguar spotted wild cat of Mesoamerica (p. 380)

janissary member of an elite corps of soldiers in the Ottoman Empire (p. 457)

jati groups based on occupation formed within larger social classes (varna) in ancient India, each with its own rules and customs (p. 204)

jazz American musical style incorporating African rhythms with American and European sounds (p. 773)

jihad (jih•HAHD) Muslim struggle to introduce Islam to other lands (p. 278)

jingoism attitude of extreme patriotism, usually directed toward a foreign power (p. 698)

joint-stock company trading venture that sold shares to divide costs and profits (p. 447)

journeyman craftsworker who has finished an apprenticeship and works for pay (p. 325)

junk a Chinese sailing ship (p. 464)

justification by faith a concept developed by Martin Luther that says faith alone is enough to bring salvation (p. 415)

K

kaiser title of the German emperor (p. 685)

kamikaze in World War II, the Japanese pilots who crashed bomb-filled planes in suicide attacks on Allied targets (p. 847)

karma in Hinduism, the idea that one's actions in life determine one's destiny and future (p. 207)

khan an absolute ruler of the Mongols (p. 344)

kibbutz (pl. kibbutzim) a collective farm community in Israel (p. 951)

Kristallnacht ("night of broken glass") Nazi terrorist attacks, November 9-10, 1938, on Jewish property in Germany and Austria (p. 786)

kulak a well-to-do peasant in the USSR (p. 790)

L

labor-intensive farming agriculture that relies on human labor, not animals or machines (p. 466)

labor union organization of workers formed to pressure business owners to improve wages and working conditions (p. 616)

labyrinth a complex, confusing series of connected passages (p. 107)

laissez-faire (leh•say•FAYR) economic principle that government should not regulate businesses (p. 622)

laity church members who are not clergy (p. 249)

lay investiture medieval practice in which secular rulers appointed and inaugurated church officials such as bishops (p. 306)

lend-lease World War II policy allowing the loan of equipment to friendly countries (p. 836)

liberalism political philosophy that promotes social change and individual freedoms (p. 582)

liberation theology movement led by Catholic clergy in Latin America emphasizing the Church's role in improving people's lives (p. 978)

line of demarcation imaginary line in the Atlantic Ocean, drawn by the pope in 1493 to divide the world's lands between Spain and Portugal (p. 439)

literacy rate the percentage of a country's adult population who can read and write (p. 944)

logic the science of reasoning and establishing proof for arguments (p. 135)

M

madrasa Muslim school of theology and law (p. 283)

maize corn native to the Americas (p. 374)

mandarin member of the elite class of civil servants in Chinese government (pp. 224, 348)

mandate (1) in ancient China, authority granted by heaven to deserving rulers, called the Mandate of Heaven (p. 71); (2) a territory administered by another nation before independence (p. 763)

manorialism medieval economic system linking nobles and the peasants on their land (p. 301)

martial law temporary military rule, limiting rights such as free speech (p. 537)

martyr person who dies for a belief (p. 173)

master skilled artisan who owned a shop and employed other craftsworkers (p. 325)

matrilineal tracing family descent through the mother and her ancestors (p. 187)

mayor of the palace Frankish official who, by A.D. 700, held real power in government (p. 294)

mercantilism economic policy of European nations in the 1600s, equating wealth and power (p. 448)

mercenary a soldier who serves a foreign country for pay (p. 124)

meritocracy system in which people gain success on the basis of ability and performance (p. 347)

messiah in Judaism, a savior promised by the Hebrew prophets, who would bring peace (p. 171)

mestizo (meh•STEE•zoh) in Latin America, a person of Native American and European ancestry (p. 667)

metaphysics aspects of philosophy dealing with basic questions of existence and reality (p. 530)

metsuke group of officials who gathered information for the Tokugawa shoguns (p. 469)

middle class class of society that originally fell between nobility and peasants, earning their income from business and trade (p. 310)

Middle Passage middle section of the triangular trade, in which enslaved Africans were brought by ship to the Americas (p. 445)

middle power a nation that is economically strong but not a military power (p. 889)

militarism national policy based on military strength and glorification of war (pp. 689, 740)

millet community of non-Muslims within the Ottoman Empire (p. 457)

missionary person who travels to carry the ideas of a religion to others (p. 254)

mobilization act of assembling and preparing troops and equipment for war (p. 743)

monarchy rule by a king or a queen (p. 47)

monastery a community of men who have taken religious vows (p. 254)

money economy economic system in which money (not barter) is used to buy and sell (p. 323)

monopoly control of all (or almost all) trade or production of a given good (p. 194)

monotheism belief in one God (pp. 83, 189)

monsoon seasonal wind that affects climates and ways of life in southern Asia (p. 66)

mosaic picture made up of tiny pieces of colored glass, tile, or stone set in mortar (p. 253)

mosque a Muslim house of worship (pp. 191, 276)

multicultural representing several different cultural and ethnic groups (pp. 195, 890)

myth a traditional story that explains natural events (p. 35)

N

nationalism pride in one's own nation; desire for independence (pp. 576, 676)

nationalization placing a privately owned business under government ownership (p. 813)

nationalize to bring a private industry under government control (p. 952)

nation-state a political state whose people also share the same language and culture (p. 677)

natural law a universal truth or principle that 17th-century thinkers believed could be found through reason (p. 521)

natural rights rights belonging to all persons from birth (p. 523)

negritude a modern literary movement that emphasizes and takes pride in the cultural heritage of Africa (p. 945)

nihilist member of a Russian political movement of the late 1800s that rejected all authority and advocated terrorism (p. 692)

nirvana in Buddhism, a state of oneness with the universe, the end of the cycle of rebirth (p. 210)

nomad member of a group of people with no fixed home, who travel constantly to find food and water (p. 22)

nonaligned not taking sides with either of the superpowers in the cold war (p. 917)

nuclear family family group consisting only of parents and children (p. 229)

O

obsidian black volcanic glass (p. 383)

oligarchy form of government in which a small group holds political power (p. 114)

oral tradition the legends and history of a culture preserved by word of mouth (p. 184)

P

pacifism opposition to war or violence as a way to settle disputes (p. 523)

pacifist a believer in pacifism (p. 802)

pact a treaty between several nations (p. 953)

paleontologist (pay•lee•ahn•TAH•luh•jihst) scientist who studies fossil remains (p. 20)

Pan-Africanism movement encouraging unity and cooperation among African nations (p. 942)

Pan-Arabism movement intended to build cultural and political ties among Arabs (p. 950)

papal infallibility Roman Catholic doctrine that the pope cannot make an error in speaking about faith and morals (p. 686)

partisan World War II term for an underground resistance fighter, especially in Italy and Yugoslavia (p. 850)

partition to divide a region (p. 707)

partnership business owned by two or more entrepreneurs who share management, profits, and losses (p. 609)

patriarch in the early Christian Church, one of five powerful bishops in major cities (p. 174)

patrician a member of the wealthy aristocratic class of ancient Rome (p. 156)

peaceful coexistence Soviet policy of competing with the United States while avoiding war (p. 873)

peninsulares officials born in Spain or Portugal who led society in colonial Latin America (p. 667)

perestroika (pehr•uh•STROY•kuh) Russian term for "restructuring," the changes in the Soviet economy that were begun by Mikhail Gorbachev (p. 1000)

perspective an artistic technique for showing relationships and space between objects (p. 131)

petit jury group of people who determine the guilt or innocence of a person on trial (p. 309)

phalanx in ancient Greece, a military formation in which foot soldiers stood so that their shields overlapped (p. 114)

pharaoh title of rulers of ancient Egypt (p. 49)

philosophe (fee•luh•ZAWF) a social or political thinker of the Enlightenment (p. 524)

philosopher a thinker or lover of wisdom (p. 135)

pilgrimage journey to a holy place (p. 334)

plateau a relatively flat region of land higher than the surrounding area (p. 185)

plebeian (plih•BEE•uhn) a citizen of ancient Rome who was not an aristocrat (p. 156)

plebiscite (PLEB•uh•syt) a direct popular vote on a program or issue (pp. 575, 657)

pogrom organized persecution of a minority group, usually Jews, in czarist Russia (p. 693)

polis city-state of ancient Greece (p. 112)

pollution putting toxic or impure substances into the air, land, or water (p. 898)

polytheism worship of many gods (p. 52)

pope the bishop of Rome, later the head of the Roman Catholic Church (p. 174)

population explosion a large, sudden increase in the human population (p. 808)

Postimpressionism artistic movement whose members experimented with form and color (p. 639)

potlatch feast held by Native Americans of the Pacific Northwest to display their wealth (p. 376)

pragmatic sanction decree issued by a ruler on an important question (p. 495)

pragmatist in China, a moderate who advocated economic reform and trade with the West (p. 902)

predestination doctrine of John Calvin that each person's fate is predetermined by God (p. 419)

prehistory time before written history (p. 20)

prime minister the chief executive of a parliamentary government (p. 544)

principality territory ruled by a prince (p. 260)

privatization the return of government-owned industries to private owners (pp. 980-81, 1003)

proletariat in Marxist theory, the working class (p. 625)

propaganda news and information intended to influence people's feelings about a cause (p. 746)

prophet a person who preaches or interprets what are thought to be messages from God (p. 83)

protectorate a country whose policies are guided by a foreign nation (p. 706)

provisional government a temporary government set up while waiting for elections (p. 757)

psychology study of behavior and its causes (p. 628)

purge an official effort to remove people that a government considers undesirable (p. 791)

Q

queue (KYOO) single braid of hair at the back of the head (p. 466)

quinoa grain grown in the Andes (p. 390)

quota a specified number or amount (p. 900)

R

racial segregation the social separation of people according to their race (p. 887)

radiocarbon dating modern scientific method for telling the age of once-living material by measuring the amount of radioactive carbon remaining in it (p. 21)

rajah an Aryan tribal chief in ancient India; later the ruler of an Indian state (p. 202)

ratify to give formal approval (p. 665)

reactionary one who opposes progress or change and wants to return to earlier ways (p. 582)

realism artistic and literary style of the mid-1800s that pictured the realities of everyday life (p. 636)

realpolitik political theory that national success justifies the use of any means (p. 682)

referendum a direct popular vote on a measure or proposed law (pp. 908, 1011)

refugee person who must leave his or her home and flee elsewhere for safety (p. 911)

regent — stalemate

regent person who acts as a temporary ruler (p. 251)

reincarnation the rebirth of the soul or spirit in different bodies over time (p. 206)

reparation compensation for war damage (p. 762)

republic a government in which citizens elect the leaders (p. 156)

revelation a vision of divine truth, such as those attributed to Muhammad (p. 272)

revolution a sudden, radical change; change of government by force (p. 554)

rhetoric art of effective public speaking (p. 119)

romanticism artistic movement emphasizing individuality and emotion (pp. 530, 635)

royalist person who supports a monarchy (p. 539)

Russification policy of imposing Russian language and customs on other peoples (p. 692)

S

sacrament one of the established formal rituals of the Roman Catholic Church, such as baptism, holy communion, or matrimony (p. 303)

salon in France, a gathering where Enlightenment intellectuals met for conversation (p. 525)

samurai class of landowning warriors in feudal Japan, who pledged loyalty to a daimyo (p. 363)

sanctions penalties and restrictions imposed on a nation for breaking international law (p. 827)

sanctuary building used for worship (p. 130)

sankin-kotai ("alternate attendance") in feudal Japan, system in which a daimyo had to spend every other year at the shogun's court (p. 469)

satellite a country politically dominated by a nearby power (p. 865)

satrap governor of a Persian province (p. 91)

satyagraha ("truth force") term for nonviolent protests led by Gandhi (p. 802)

savanna a flat grassland, with few trees, in tropical or subtropical regions (p. 185)

schism (SIH•zuhm) the division of the Christian Church in 1054 that separated the Roman Catholic Church and the Eastern Orthodox Church (p. 250)

scholasticism medieval school of thought that tried to bring together Aristotle's philosophy and the teachings of Church scholars (p. 326)

scientific method steps to find scientific truth through observation and experiments (p. 518)

scorched-earth policy Stalin's order for the Soviet people to destroy buildings, land, and anything that Nazi invaders could use (p. 838)

secede to withdraw formally from membership in a political organization (p. 663)

sect a subgroup with distinct beliefs within a larger religious group (pp. 171, 899)

sectionalism overemphasis on the political and economic interests of one's own region (p. 663)

secular worldly, not overtly or specifically religious (p. 404)

self-determination the right of a people to decide their own political status or government (p. 796)

seminary school for educating priests, as ordered by the Council of Trent (p. 423)

separatism in Canada, a political movement favoring the independence of Quebec (p. 890)

sepoy an Indian soldier in the British army (p. 713)

serf a peasant laborer legally bound to the lands of a noble (pp. 302, 501)

shah the ruler of a Middle Eastern country (p. 797)

shamanism belief that spirits inhabit living and nonliving things, communicating with humans through priests called shamans (p. 358)

shari'ah (shuh•REE•uh) Islamic code of law that includes rules for all aspects of life (p. 275)

sheikh (SHAYK) chief of a bedouin tribe (p. 271)

shogun military ruler of feudal Japan (p. 363)

shogunate government established by a shogun's family and followers in feudal Japan (p. 363)

simony the selling of official positions in the medieval Roman Catholic Church (p. 335)

slash-and-burn farming farming method in which land for crops is cleared by cutting and burning trees to fertilize the soil (p. 380)

socialism political theory that society as a whole should control the means of production, such as factories and land (p. 624)

Socialist realism under Stalin, an artistic style that glorified the Soviet way of life (p. 791)

sociology study of human group behavior (p. 628)

sonnet poetry form with 14 lines and a fixed pattern of rhyme and meter (p. 405)

sovereignty the independent decision-making power of a group or nation (p. 963)

soviet a workers' council formed early in the Russian Revolution; later, a unit of government in the Soviet Union (p. 694)

special economic zone areas of China where foreign businesses and a free market were allowed to operate in the 1990s (p. 903)

sphere of influence area in a country where a foreign power has exclusive rights to trade or invest (pp. 706, 715)

stagflation slow growth with high inflation and unemployment (p. 889)

stalemate a deadlock, or situation in which neither of two opponents can move further (p. 907)

standard of living a general measure of people's overall wealth and quality of life (p. 979)

steppe wide, grassy, semiarid plains of Eurasia, from the Black Sea to the Altai Mountains (p. 258)

stupa a dome-shaped Buddhist shrine built over relics or bones of a holy person (p. 210)

subcontinent landmass that is part of a continent but distinct from it, such as India (p. 66)

subsistence farmer farmer who grows only enough to supply a family or village (p. 943)

suffragette woman who actively worked to win voting rights for women (p. 651)

sultan political leader with absolute authority over a Muslim country (p. 457)

superpower a powerful, influential nation with a bloc of allies; specifically, the United States and the Soviet Union during the cold war (p. 864)

surrealism 20th-century art movement using distorted, surprising images (p. 773)

symbolism antirealism artistic movement that focused on dreamlike images and symbols (p. 638)

symposium in ancient Athens, a gathering of men that featured eating, drinking, entertainment, and intellectual discussions (p. 123)

syndicate under fascism, an organization of workers and employers in an industry (p. 783)

T

technology the skills and knowledge used by people to make tools and do work (p. 24)

theocracy government headed by religious leaders or a leader regarded as a god (pp. 48, 418)

theology study of religious questions (p. 251)

tithe a 10 percent tax on income, paid to the clergy (p. 561)

totalitarianism idea that a dictatorial government should control all aspects of citizens' lives (p. 781)

tournament medieval sport in which knights competed to show their fighting skills (p. 299)

trade deficit the economic imbalance when a country's imports exceeds its exports (pp. 889, 998)

tragedy story or play in which the central character struggles against destiny but meets an unhappy end (p. 132)

trench a ditch dug to protect soldiers (p. 747)

triangular trade three-directional trade route between Europe, Africa, and America in the 1600s (p. 444)

tribune in ancient Rome, an official who represented the plebeians (p. 157)

triumvirate in ancient Rome, a three-person ruling group (p. 162)

troubadour poet-musician of the Middle Ages, who traveled from court to court (p. 327)

tyrant in ancient Greece, a person who seized power and established one-man rule (p. 114)

U **V**

ultimatum a final demand or statement of terms, implying a threat of serious penalties (p. 742)

ultraroyalist an extremely conservative aristocrat in France in the 1820s (p. 655)

unicameral legislature assembly or lawmaking body with one house (p. 565)

urbanization the spread of cities and city living (p. 631)

utilitarianism economic philosophy, developed by Jeremy Bentham, that social and political actions should be useful and helpful to humanity (p. 624)

varna one of four main social classes in Aryan society of ancient India (p. 203)

vassal in feudalism, a noble who held land from and served a higher-ranking lord (p. 299)

vernacular the language of everyday speech, not of scholars, in a country or region (p. 328)

viceroy governor representing a monarch (p. 714)

vocation a calling from God to take up certain work (p. 417)

W **X** **Y** **Z**

war of attrition conflict in which each side tries to win by wearing down the other (p. 746)

warlord local military leader in China (p. 804)

weir net or trap placed across a river to catch fish (p. 376)

welfare state government system in which the state provides programs to protect people's social and economic well-being (p. 879)

westernization the spread of European culture (p. 718)

yasa Mongol law code of Genghis Khan (p. 344)

yeoman (YOH•mun) in English society, a farmer who owned land (p. 488)

yin and yang in Chinese thinking, the opposing principles present in all nature (p. 227)

yurt large, round, portable tent used by nomads of central Asia (p. 343)

zaibatsu (zy•BAHT•soo) large Japanese industrial firms owned by a few families (p. 808)

zemstvo local assembly in czarist Russia (p. 692)

Italicized page numbers refer to illustrations. Preceding the page number, abbreviations refer to a map (m), chart (c), photograph or other picture (p), graph (g), cartoon (crt), painting (ptg). Quoted material is referenced with the abbreviation (q) before the page number.

abbess/abadesa superiora de un convento (pág. 305)

abbot/abad superior de un monasterio (pág. 304)

absolutism/absolutismo sistema político en el cual un monarca (o grupo) tiene poder supremo e ilimitado, o teoría que sustenta tal sistema (pág. 482)

acupuncture/acupuntura técnica tradicional de la medicina china que utiliza agujas finas en puntos vitales del cuerpo (pág. 232)

age set/grupo etario en el África tradicional, un grupo de varones o hembras de edad semejante que adquieren destrezas y siguen juntos a través de las distintas etapas de la vida (pág. 188)

ahimsa/ahimsa doctrina hindú de no-violencia hacia todo lo que tiene vida (pág. 207)

alchemist/alquimista persona que practica la alquimia, forma primitiva de la química, que enfatizaba cambios en las sustancias, como la conversión del plomo en oro (pág. 520)

alliance system/sistema de alianzas serie de acuerdos sobre la defensa en que participan dos o más naciones (pág. 740)

alphabet/alfabeto sistema de símbolos o caracteres que representan los sonidos de un lenguaje (pág. 82)

amphora/ánfora jarrón griego alto, de dos asas (pág. 131)

anarchy/anarquía ausencia de autoridad política (pág. 692)

animism/animismo creencia de que los espíritus residen tanto en los seres vivos como en las cosas inanimadas (págs. 351, 476)

anthropologist/antropólogo científico que estudia las características físicas y culturales de los seres humanos y sus antecesores (pág. 20)

apartheid/apartheid política oficial de estricta segregación y discriminación racial practicada en África del Sur desde 1948 hasta principios de la década de 1990 (pág. 934)

appeasement/apaciguamiento la política de hacer concesiones a un enemigo en potencia a fin de mantener la paz (pág. 829)

apportion/prorratear dividir en partes proporcionales (pág. 648)

apprentice/aprendiz persona que trabaja para un maestro a fin de aprender un oficio, arte o negocio (pág. 325)

aqueduct/acueducto canal construido para conducir las aguas (pág. 168)

arabesque/arabesco complejos diseños típicos del arte islámico que combinaban plantas entrelazadas y patrones geométricos (pág. 286)

"Arabic numerals"/números arábigos símbolos de numeración diseñados por matemáticos en Gupta, India (pág. 214)

arbitration/arbitraje proceso de poner fin a una disputa sometiéndola a una tercera parte imparcial (pág. 722)

archaeologist/arqueólogo científico que estudia pueblos y culturas de la Antigüedad (pág. 20)

archipelago/archipiélago grupo o cadena de islas (págs. 351, 920)

aristocrat/aristócrata miembro de la nobleza o de la clase alta (pág. 113)

armada/armada escuadra de buques de guerra (pág. 483)

armistice/armisticio acuerdo para dar fin a una guerra (pág. 761)

arms race/carrera armamentista la competencia durante la Guerra Fría entre Estados Unidos y la Unión Soviética para fortalecer sus respectivas fuerzas militares y armamentos (pág. 871)

artifact/artefacto histórico objeto fabricado o usado por los humanos, tal como una herramienta, adorno o artículo de alfarería (pág. 20)

artisan/artesano persona diestra en un arte manual (pág. 33)

atomic theory/teoría atómica idea científica de que la materia está hecha de partículas pequeñas llamadas átomos (pág. 628)

atrocity/atrocidad acción cruel y maligna, tal como la tortura (pág. 1014)

autocracy/autocracia gobierno regido por una persona con poder ilimitado (pág. 690)

automation/automatización proceso por el cual dispositivos electrónicos o máquinas hacen el trabajo antes realizado por humanos (pág. 883)

autonomy/autonomía gobierno propio (pág. 1008)

balance of power/equilibrio de poder la distribución del poder entra naciones rivales de modo que ninguna predomine (pág. 489)

balance of trade/equilibrio comercial diferencia en valor entre lo que una nación importa y lo que exporta durante un período de tiempo (pág. 448)

bard/bardo poeta que narra cuentos por medio del canto (pág. 108)

baroque/barroco estilo artístico recargado y dramático, desarrollado en Europa a mediados del siglo XVI (pág. 423)

barter/trueque sistema de comercio en el cual se

bazaar — classical

intercambiaban bienes y no dinero (pág. 82)

bazaar/bazar mercado público en una ciudad islámica (pág. 284)

belligerent/beligerante enfrascado en una guerra (pág. 746)

bishop/obispo jefe regional de la Iglesia Cristiana primitiva, con autoridad sobre una diócesis y otros miembros del clero (pág. 174)

blitz/ataque relámpago serie de ataques aéreos intensos (pág. 834)

blitzkrieg/guerra relámpago ofensiva nazi rápida e inesperada (pág. 831)

bloc/bloque grupo de facciones políticas o agrupación de naciones que actúan conjuntamente (pág. 871)

bourgeoisie/burguesía la clase media, entre los aristócratas y los trabajadores (págs. 561, 625)

boyar/boyardo un noble propietario de tierras en la Rusia primitiva (págs. 260, 499)

boycott/boicot rechazo a comprar ciertos productos como protesta por alguna acción (pág. 548)

budget deficit/déficit presupuestario la cantidad por la cual los gastos del gobierno exceden a sus ingresos (pág. 998)

buffer state/estado parachoques territorio neutral entre potencias rivales, destinado a prevenir un conflicto (pág. 582)

bullion/lingote oro o plata en forma de barras o planchas (pág. 448)

bureaucracy/burocracia un grupo de funcionarios del gobierno encabezado por un administrador (pág. 48)

C

cabinet/gabinete grupo de consejeros de un gobernante o jefe de estado (pág. 544)

calculus/cálculo sistema de matemáticas desarrollado por Newton para analizar cantidades variables (pág. 519)

caliph/califa líder supremo de Islam, escogido como sucesor de Mahoma (pág. 277)

calligraphy/caligrafía el arte de escribir con letra hermosa (pág. 286)

campesino/campesino agricultor pobre de Latinoamérica que trabaja en una finca (pág. 975)

capital/capital dinero disponible para invertir en negocios (pág. 604)

cardinal/cardenal eclesiástico de alto rango en la Iglesia Católica designado por el Papa (pág. 306)

cartel/cartel convenio entre empresas que ofrecen el mismo producto, que regula los precios de sus

miembros y su producción (págs. 955, 992)

cartographer/cartógrafo persona que dibuja mapas (pág. 436)

cash-and-carry policy/política de compra al contado programa de la Segunda Guerra Mundial que permitía a Gran Bretaña pagar en efectivo y transportar desde los Estados Unidos las mercancías que necesitara (pág. 835)

cash crop/cosecha comercial producto agrícola cultivado para la venta o el intercambio, no usado por el agricultor (pág. 943)

cavalry/caballería cuerpo de soldados a caballo (pág. 221)

cell theory/teoría celular teoría científica que sostiene que las pequeñas unidades llamadas células constituyen todas las cosas vivas (pág. 626)

chancellor/canciller título del primer ministro en algunos países europeos (pág. 685)

charter/carta constitucional documento formal que concede el derecho al gobierno propio (pág. 326)

chateaux/castillos un tipo de fortaleza (pág. 413)

chinampas/chinampas islas artificiales construidas por los aztecas para utilizar como jardines (pág. 388)

chivalry/caballería código de conducta de los caballeros medievales basado en ideales de honor y cortesía (pág. 301)

choreographer/coreógrafo persona que crea bailes (pág. 775)

chronicle/crónica relación que registra eventos en el orden en que éstos sucedieron (pág. 288)

circumnavigation/circunnavegación viaje marítimo completamente alrededor de algo, como por ejemplo, el mundo (pág. 439)

citizen/ciudadano en la antigua Gracia, persona que participaba del gobierno en una ciudad-estado (pág. 112)

city-state/ciudad-estado un estado independiente que consistía en una ciudad y las tierras y aldeas que la rodeaban (pág. 59)

civil disobedience/desobediencia civil rechazo sin violencia a obedecer una ley o práctica considerada injusta (pág. 802)

civil service/servicio civil sistema mediante el cual puestos del gobierno son concedidos mediante exámenes (pág. 224)

civilization/civilización sociedad altamente organizada caracterizada por el conocimiento avanzado del comercio, gobierno, artes, ciencia y a menudo, lenguaje escrito (pág. 32)

clan/clan grupo unido por lazos familiares (págs. 342, 938)

classical/clásico que describe el estilo artístico de las antiguas Gracia y Roma, caracterizado por el equilibrio, la elegancia y la simpleza (pág. 130)

classicism/clasicismo estilo y actitudes derivadas de los ideales de las antiguas Gracia y Roma (pág. 528)

clergy/clero personas, tales como los sacerdotes, que tienen autoridad para conducir servicios religiosos (pág. 249)

coalition/coalición alianza temporal de facciones políticas en desacuerdo (págs. 780, 879)

cold war/Guerra Fría período de tensión política en el que Estados Unidos y la Unión Soviética rivalizaron por obtener el dominio mundial sin llegar a un conflicto armado real (pág 864)

collective bargaining/convenios colectivos negociaciones entre los delegados sindicales y los patronos acerca de asuntos (pág. 616)

collective security/seguridad colectiva los intereses de defensa comunes a varias naciones frente a un enemigo (págs. 826, 1012)

collectivization/colectivización bajo Stalin, sistema de unificar tierras en grandes fincas que pertenecían al gobierno y las trabajaban los campesinos (pág. 790)

colon/colon colonizador francés en la colonia de Algeria (pág. 931)

colony/colonia establecimiento de personas que están fuera de su país, enlazado a la madre patria por el comercio y el control directo del gobierno (págs. 82, 475, 706)

comedy/comedia historia o representación que se propone entretener y divertir usualmente con un desenlace feliz (pág. 134)

common law/derecho consuetudinario sistema de leyes inglesas basadas en la tradición y decisiones de la corte, no en leyes específicas (pág. 309)

commonwealth/mancomunidad nación o estado gobernado por el pueblo o representantes del mismo (pág. 539)

commune/comuna Un grupo de personas que viven en comuna, con posesión y uso colectivo de la sociedad (pág. 902)

communism/comunismo según las teorías de Marx y Engels, una sociedad sin distinciones de clases ni propiedad privada (págs. 625, 758)

concentration camp/campo de concentración recinto donde se encierra a prisioneros políticos o a refugiados (pág. 786)

confederation/confederación alianza flexible o unión de varios estados o grupos (págs. 82, 378, 554)

conquistador/conquistador aventurero o soldado español en las Américas (pág. 441)

conscription/reclutamiento llamado obligatorio al servicio militar (págs. 569, 740)

constitution/constitución plan de gobierno (pág. 117)

constitutional monarchy/monarquía constitucional estado en el cual el poder del monarca está limitado por una constitución (pág. 541)

consul/cónsul en la antigua Roma, un magistrado que dirigía al poder ejecutivo (pág. 157)

containment/contención política de Estados Unidos proyectada para prevenir la propagación del comunismo (pág. 866)

contraband/contrabando mercancías que no pueden ser transportadas legalmente, particularmente en tiempo de guerra (pág. 749)

convoy/convoy grupo de naves mercantes que viajan junto a buques de guerra para su seguridad (pág. 760)

cooperative/cooperativa sociedad de fincas que pertenece y es administrada por sus miembros, los cuales comparten sus ganancias (pág. 812)

cordon sanitaire/cordón sanitario línea de cuarentena o estados "parachoques" (pág. 763)

corporate state/estado corporativo concepto de Mussolini de un gobierno con representación de corporaciones, y no de partidos políticos (pág. 783)

corporation/corporación organización de empresas que es propiedad de socios que compran acciones y que es dirigida por administradores profesionales (pág. 609)

cortes/cortes asamblea de los nobles, el clero y los funcionarios del pueblo en la España medieval; el parlamento en la España moderna (pág. 332)

count/conde noble que actuaba como funcionario local dentro del imperio de los francos (pág. 295)

coup d'état/golpe de estado derrocamiento repentino de líderes del gobierno por un pequeño grupo (págs. 573, 657)

covenant/convenio pacto o acuerdo solemne (pág. 83)

covert/encubierto secreto (pág. 986)

Creole/criollo persona de ascendencia europea nacida en la América Latina colonial (pág. 667)

Crusades/Cruzadas expediciones militares por cristianos europeos en los siglos XI al XIII para conquistar la Tierra Santa de manos de los musulmanes (pág. 318)

cubism/cubismo estilo artístico del siglo XX que representa las formas naturales por medio de formas geométricas (pág. 773)

cultural diffusion/difusión cultural intercambio de bienes, ideas y costumbres entre diferentes culturas (pág. 34) culture — dual monarchy

culture/cultura modo de vida de un pueblo en un tiempo determinado, que incluye su lenguaje, conducta y creencias (pág. 24)

culture system/sistema de cultivo en las colonias holandesas en Asia, sistema de trabajos forzados para obtener materias primas (pág. 718)

cuneiform/cuneiforme sistema de escritura sumerio que utilizaba símbolos en forma de cuña (pág. 60)

czar/zar (de "caesar") título adoptado por los gobernantes de Rusia desde finales del siglo XV (pág. 264)

D

D-Day/Día D día de la invasión de Normandía, Francia por los Aliados (junio 6 de 1944)(pág. 848)

daimyo/daimyo poderoso noble local en el Japón feudal (pág. 363)

datus/datus gobernantes locales en las Filipinas (pág. 475)

death squad/escuadrón de la muerte en la América Central, una banda de asesinos contratados por terratenientes para asesinar a sus contrincantes políticos (pág. 987)

deforestation/deforestación proceso de talar los árboles y desmontar los bosques en grandes extensiones de tierra (pág. 1020)

deism/deísmo filosofía religiosa del siglo XVIII basada en la razón y en la idea de leyes naturales (pág. 523)

deity/deidad un dios o diosa (pág. 31)

democracy/democracia forma de gobierno en la cual los ciudadanos ejercen el poder (pág. 114)

depression/depresión situación económica caracterizada por la quiebra de los negocios y el desempleo (pág. 609)

desalination/desalinización proceso de extraer la sal del agua de mar para producir agua potable (pág. 964)

desertification/desertización proceso por el cual una tierra fértil se convierte en un desierto (pág. 944)

detente/detente la relajación de las tensiones entre los Estados Unidos y la Unión Soviética en la década de 1970 (pág. 874)

developed nation/nación desarrollado nación industrializada, con una tecnología avanzada (pág. 1019)

developing nation/nación en desarrollo nación en proceso de industrialización, donde el pueblo mantiene frecuentemente los estilos de vida tradicionales (pág. 1018)

dharma/dharma deberes y derechos de los miembros de cada clase en la sociedad hindú tradicional (pág. 205)

Diaspora/Diáspora término que se refiere a la dispersión de las comunidades judías fuera de su patria original después de la Cautividad de Babilonia (pág. 86)

dictator/dictador en la antigua Roma, líder a quien se daba poder temporal absoluto durante una crisis (pág. 157)

dictatorship/dictadura gobierno encabezado por un gobernante con poder absoluto (pág. 574)

dictatorship of the proletariat/dictadura del proletariado en la antigua Unión Soviética, control teórico del estado por la clase trabajadora (pág. 789)

direct tax/impuesto directo impuesto pagado directamente al gobierno (pág. 548)

disarmament/desarme limitación o reducción de las fuerzas militares y de las armas (pág. 778)

disciple/discípulo activo seguidor de un maestro (pág. 172)

disenfranchised/privado del derecho al sufragio negado el derecho al voto (pág. 649)

disengagement/desembarazo acto de liberarse o retirarse uno mismo de una situación (pág. 955)

dissident/disidente persona que critica abiertamente las maneras de actuar de su gobierno (pág. 874)

divine right/derecho divino teoría politica que mantiene que un gobernante deriva su autoridad directamente de Dios y es responsable de sus actos sólo ante Dios (págs. 482, 536)

division of labor/división del trabajo técnica de producción en la cual cada obrero realiza un trabajo especializado (pág. 609)

doge/dux líder electo de la república en las ciudades-estados de Venecia y Génova (pág. 408)

domain/dominio territorio perteneciente a un gobernante (pág. 142)

domesticate/domesticar adiestrar animales o adaptar plantas para satisfacer necesidades humanas (pág. 30)

domestic system/sistema doméstico sistema primitivo de trabajo industrial en el cual los obreros producían los bienes en sus hogares (pág. 602)

dominion/dominio nación de gobierno propio dentro del Imperio Británico; más tarde, mancomunidad (pág. 653)

domino theory/teoría del dominó creencia de la época de la Guerra Fría por la que si una nación se hacía comunista, sus vecinos seguirían el ejemplo (pág. 910)

double-digit inflation/inflación de dos dígitos rápida elevación de los precios en un diez por ciento o más (pag. 889)

dual monarchy/monarquía dual dos estados con un

solo monarca (pág. 696)

duma/duma legislatura nacional rusa (pág. 694)

duty/arancel de aduana impuesto sobre productos importados (pág. 546)

dvorianie/dvorianie nueva clase de nobleza rusa dueña de tierras, establecida por Pedro I el Grande (pág. 501)

dynasty/dinastía sucesión de gobernantes que pertenecen a la misma familia (pág. 47)

E

economy/economía sistema por el cual bienes y servicios son producidos y distribuidos para satisfacer las necesidades del pueblo (pág. 33)

elite/elite un grupo de personas selecto (pág. 975)

ellipse/elipse curva cerrada ovalada (no redonda) (pág. 517)

emancipation/emancipación acción de conceder la libertad legalmente (pág. 691)

embargo/embargo orden restringiendo el tráfico comercial (págs. 889, 960, 1015)

emigration/emigración abandono del país o región natal para establecerse en otro lugar (pág. 630)

émigré/émigré emigrado o persona que huyó de Francia durante la Revolución (pág. 566)

empire/imperio grupo de territorios o naciones regidos por un solo emperador o gobierno (pág. 49)

enclave/enclave pequeño territorio completamente rodeado por el territorio de otro país o grupo (pag. 1016)

enclosure movement/expansión por apropiación tendencia de los grandes terratenientes a cercar e incluir tierras comunes públicas y privadas en sus propios terrenos (pág. 603)

enlightened despot/déspota iluminista monarca que comenzaba cambios sociales basados en las ideas del iluminismo (pág. 527)

entente/entente acuerdo, pero no alianza formal, entre naciones (pág. 740)

entrepreneur/empresario persona que corre riesgos para fundar un negocio (págs. 448, 604)

epic/poema épico poema extenso que celebraba las hazañas de un héroe legendario o histórico (pág. 203)

estate/estado una de las tres clases sociales distintas en Francia durante el Siglo XVIII: el clero, la nobleza y los plebeyos (el Tercer Estado) (pág. 560)

ethics/ética sistema de principios morales que guían la conducta (pág. 225)

ethnic cleansing/limpieza étnica término usado en el conflicto de Bosnia, para referirse a una política de traslado forzoso o de dar muerte a los miembros de otro grupo étnico (pág. 1014)

evolution/evolución teoría de que las especies de seres vivos se transforman a través de largos períodos de tiempo (pág. 626)

excommunication/excomunión exclusión formal de la membresía o de su participación en una iglesia (pág. 306)

exodus/éxodo emigración de un grupo numeroso de personas (pag. 84)

extended family/familia completa grupo familiar que incluye a varias generaciones así como a otros parientes (pág. 229)

F

factory system/sistema de fábrica método de producción en el cual los bienes son producidos por obreros y máquinas en un local (una fábrica) fuera de sus hogares (pág. 606)

fascism/fascismo filosofía política basada en el nacionalismo y en un estado todopoderoso (pág. 782)

federal system/sistema federal forma de gobierno en la cual el poder se halla dividido entre la autoridad central y sus subdivisiones políticas (pág. 554)

feudalism/feudalismo sistema político medieval en el cual los monarcas y los nobles menores hacían alianzas basadas en el intercambio de concesiones de tierras por lealtad (pág. 298)

fez/fez sombrero tradicional usado por los hombres turcos (pág. 797)

fief/feudo bajo el feudalismo, una tierra con sus labriegos concedida a un noble a cambio de lealtad y ayuda militar (pág. 298)

filial piety/piedad filial respeto de los hijos hacia sus padres, un principio importante en la filosofía moral de Confucio (pág. 226)

free trade/comercio libre la eliminación de barreras comerciales entre naciones (pág. 978)

friar/fraile miembro de una orden religiosa católica que predicaba en los pueblos y practicaba la pobreza (pág. 307)

fundamentalism/fundamentalismo movimiento que enfatiza el cumplimiento de las leyes y prácticas religiosas tradicionales (pág. 965)

G

geisha/geisha mujer japonesa adiestrada profesionalmente para entretener (pág. 472)

general strike/huelga general huelga en que participan obreros de muchas áreas de la economía de la nación (págs. 779, 931)

genetic engineering/ingeniería genética campo científico en el cual la estructura de las células puede ser alterada para producir organismos nuevos o distintos (pág. 1021)

genetics/genética el estudio de la herencia biológica (pág. 627)

genocide/genocidio intento deliberado de matar a todos los miembros de un grupo racial, cultural o étnico (págs. 840, 938)

gentry/gentry en la Inglaterra isabelina, el grupo social que incluía a la nobleza menor y a los terratenientes (pág. 488)

ghana/ghana título del gobernante de una región en el África antigua, que más tarde fue aplicado al reinado (pág. 189)

glasnost/glasnost palabra rusa aplicada a la política de "apertura" o "transparencia" y de libre expresión, introducida por Mijail Gorbachov (pág. 999)

grand jury/gran jurado en la ley inglesa, grupo de personas que deciden si la evidencia de un crimen justifica llevar a una persona a juicio (pag. 309)

grand vizier/gran visir primer ministro del sultán de un país musulmán (pág. 457)

gross domestic product/producto territorial bruto valor total de las mercancías y los servicios producidos en un país en un año (pág. 898)

guerrilla warfare/guerra de guerrillas método de lucha en el cual pequeños grupos atacan de modo inesperado (pág. 679)

guild/gremio asociación comercial medieval de mercaderes o artesanos (pág. 324)

habeas corpus/hábeas corpus principio legal que requiere que las autoridades muestren las razones por las cuales una persona debe ser detenida y garanticen un juicio rápido (pág. 542)

haiku/hai kai forma de poesía japonesa generalmente con tres versos de 17 sílabas (pág. 472)

hajj/hajj peregrinación a La Meca que todo musulmán en buenas condiciones físicas se supone realice por lo menos una vez en su vida (pág. 276)

heavy industry/industria pesada la manufactura de máquinas y equipo para fábricas y minas (pág. 808)

heresy/herejía desacuerdo con la enseñanzas básicas de una religión o negación de las mismas (pág. 306)

hierarchy/jerarquía grupo de personas organizadas de acuerdo con niveles de rango o importancia (págs. 228, 389)

hieroglyphics/jeroglíficos sistema egipcio antiguo de escritura que utilizaba símbolos pictóricos para representar ideas o sonidos (pág. 52)

Holocaust/Holocausto nombre dado al asesinato en masa de judíos europeos por los nazis en la Segunda Guerra Mundial (pág. 839)

homage/homenaje ceremonia formal que establecía lazos feudales entre un señor y un vasallo (pág. 299)

home rule/autonomía local gobierno propio, especialmente cuando se concede a un país dependiente (pág. 651)

hominid/homínido miembro del grupo que incluye a los seres humanos y a las criaturas primates primitivas (pág. 20)

humanism/Humanismo movimiento renacentista basado en la literatura e ideas de las antiguas Grecia y Roma, tales como el valor de cada individuo (pág. 404)

hygiene/higiene la ciencia de la buena salud (pág. 138)

hyperinflation/hiperinflación forma extrema de inflación, con aumentos violentos y rápidos de los precios (pág. 991)

hypothesis/hipótesis solución propuesta para explicar una serie de hechos, que puede ser probada (pág. 517)

icon/ícono imagen religiosa cristiana o cuadro que representa a un santo u otra persona sagrada (pág. 249)

iconoclast/iconoclasta ("destructor de imágenes") un opositor al uso de íconos en las iglesias bizantinas, que pensaba que éstos estimulaban la adoración de ídolos (pág. 250)

ideology/ideología sistema de creencias y actitudes que guían las acciones de un grupo o nación (pág. 871)

illuminated manuscript/manuscrito iluminado página de un libro, decorada con elaborados diseños, hermosas letras, o pinturas en miniatura (pág. 253)

imam/imán un guía de oraciones musulmanas (pág. 276)

immigration/inmigración entrada a un nuevo país o región para asentarse allí permanentemente (pág. 630)

imperialism/imperialismo política de erigir un imperio para extender el poderío y el territorio de una nación (pág. 704)

imperial presidency/presidencia imperial término

aplicado a un presidente y al poder ejecutivo que asumen poderes que van más allá de los estipulados en la Constitución (pág. 888)

impressionism/impresionismo estilo artístico del Siglo XIX en el cual los pintores trataban de captar impresiones rápidas y los efectos de la luz (pág. 638)

indemnity/indemnización pago por daños y pérdidas (pág. 160)

individualism/individualismo énfasis en la aignidad de la persona (pág. 404)

indulgence/indulgencia perdón vendido por la Iglesia Católica para reducir el castigo de pecados (pág. 416)

industrial capitalism/capitalismo industrial sistema económico en en cual individuos continuamente reinvierten sus ganancias y expanden sus negocios (pág. 608)

inflation/inflación situación en la cual los precios suben rápidamente mientras que el valor del dinero disminuye (págs. 176, 484)

intendant/intendente agente que representaba al rey de Francia en el gobierno local (pág. 491)

interchangeable parts/piezas intercambiables método de producción que utiliza piezas idénticas, fáciles de ensamblar (pág. 609)

intercontinental ballistic missile (ICBM)/misil balístico intercontinental un cohete de combate de largo alcance que lleva una carga explosiva en la punta (pág. 873)

interdependent/interdependiente confianza mutua (pág. 1018)

Internet/Internet término popular para la red avanzada de comunicación que vincula a personas y computadoras a nivel mundial (pág. 1021)

intifada/intifada el levantamiento de los palestinos contra la ocupación israelita (pág. 956)

iron curtain/Cortina de Hierro término acuñado por Winston Churchill para referirse a la barrera política que aislaba a la Europa Oriental dominada por los soviéticos de la Europa Occidental (pág. 866)

J

jaguar/jaguar gato salvaje con manchas en la piel, de América Central (pág. 380)

janissary/jenízaro miembro del cuerpo más selecto de soldados del Imperio Otomano (pág. 457)

jati/jati grupos formados dentro de las mayores clases sociales *(varna)* en la antigua India según las ocupaciones de sus miembros y con sus propias reglas y costumbres (pág. 204)

jazz/jazz estilo de música de Estados Unidos que incorpora ritmos africanos a sonidos estadounidenses y europeos (pág. 773)

jihad/jihad lucha mahometana para introducir el islamismo en otras tierras (pág. 278)

jingoism/jingoísmo actitud de patriotismo extremo, usualmente dirigida hacia un poder extranjero (pág. 698)

joint-stock company/compañía por acciones empresa comercial que vende acciones para dividir entre los participantes los costos y las ganancias (pág. 447)

journeyman/jornalero artesano que ha terminado su aprendizaje y trabaja por un jornal (pág. 325)

junk/junco embarcación china (pág. 464)

justification by faith/justificación por la fe concepto de Martín Lutero de que la fe por sí sola es suficiente para alcanzar la salvación (pág. 415)

K

kaiser/káiser el emperador de Alemania (pág. 685)

kamikaze/kamikaze en la Segunda Guerra Mundial, pilotos japoneses que hacían estallar aviones llenos de bombas en ataques suicidas contra objetivos Aliados (pág. 847)

karma/karma en el hinduismo, la idea de que las acciones en la vida de los hombres y las mujeres determinaban el destino y el futuro (pág. 207)

khan/kan gobernante de los mongoles (pág. 344)

kibbutz/kibbutz comunidad de granjas colectivas en Israel (pág. 951)

Kristallnacht/la noche de las vidrieras rotas ataques terroristas nazis en noviembre 9 y 10 de 1938, contra propiedades judías en Alemania y Austria (pág. 786)

kulak/kulak labriego en la Unión Soviética que vivía holgadamente (pág. 790)

L

labor-intensive farming/agricultura manual intensiva agricultura en la que se utiliza el trabajo humano, no animales o máquinas (pág. 466)

labor union/sindicato obrero organización de obreros formada para presionar a los dueños de los negocios a que mejoren los salarios y las condiciones en el trabajo (pág. 616)

labyrinth/laberinto conjunto complejo y confuso de pasajes que se conectan (pág. 107)

laissez-faire/laissez-faire doctrina económica según la cual el gobierno no debe regular los negocios (pág. 622)

laity/el estado seglar miembros de una iglesia que

no pertenecen al clero (pág. 249)

lay investiture/investidura seglar práctica medieval en la cual las autoridades seglares designaban e investían a funcionarios de la iglesia tales como los obispos (pág. 306)

lend-lease/préstamo-arriendo política de la Segunda Guerra Mundial de permitir el préstamo de equipo a países amigos (pág. 836)

liberalism/liberalismo filosofía política que promueve el cambio social y las libertades individuales (pág. 582)

liberation theology/teología de la liberación movimiento dirigido por el clero católico en la América Latina que enfatizaba el papel de la Iglesia en el mejoramiento de las vidas humanas (pág. 978)

line of demarcation/línea de demarcación línea imaginaria en el Océano Atlántico, trazada por el papa en 1493 para dividir las tierras del mundo entre España y Portugal (pág. 439)

literacy rate/tasa de alfabetización el porcentaje de población adulta de un país que sabe leer y escribir (pág. 944)

logic/lógica la ciencia del razonamiento y del establecimiento de pruebas en los debates (pág. 135)

M

madrasa/madrasa escuela musulmana de teología y leyes (pág. 283)

maize/maíz el maíz nativo de la América (pág. 374)

mandarin/mandarín miembro de la clase más selecta de funcionarios en el gobierno chino (págs. 224, 348)

mandate/mandato (1) en la antigua China, la autoridad concedida por el cielo a gobernantes merecedores de ello, llamada el Mandato del Cielo (pág. 71); (2) territorio administrado por otra nación antes de su independencia (pág. 763)

manorialism/economía feudal sistema económico medieval que ataba a los nobles y a los campesinos a su tierra (pág. 301)

martial law/ley marcial ley militar temporal, que limita derechos tales como la libertad de expresión (pág. 537)

martyr/mártir persona que sufre y muere por una creencia (pág. 173)

master/maestro artesano hábil que era el propietario de un taller y empleaba a otros artesanos (pág. 325)

matrilineal/línea materna que traza el origen de una familia a través de la madre y los ancestros de ésta (pág. 187)

mayor of the palace/jefe del palacio dignatario franco que, alrededor del siglo VIII d.C. tenía poder en el gobierno (pág. 294)

mercantilism/mercantilismo política económica de las naciones europeas en el Siglo XVII, que igualaba la riqueza al poder (pág. 448)

mercenary/mercenario soldado que sirve a un país extranjero por dinero (pág. 124)

meritocracy/sistema de ascenso por méritos sistema en el cual las personas obtienen éxito a base de su habilidad y actuación (pág. 347)

messiah/mesías en el judaísmo, el salvador prometido por los profetas hebreos, quien traería la paz (pág. 171)

mestizo/mestizo en América Latina, persona de ancestro indígena americano y europeo (pág. 667)

metaphysics/metafísica aspectos de la filosofía relativos a los problemas básicos de la existencia y la realidad (pág. 530)

metsuke/metsuke grupo de funcionarios que recolectaban información para los shogúnes de Tokugawa (pag. 469)

middle class/clase media clase social que originalmente estaba entre la nobleza y el campesinado, y que se ganaba la vida por medio de actividades comerciales (pág. 310)

Middle Passage/Paso Central sección intermedia del comercio triangular, en el cual los africanos esclavizados eran traídos a la América por barco (pág. 445)

middle power/potencia mediana nación que es fuerte económicamente pero que no es una potencia militar (pág. 889)

militarism/militarismo política nacional basada en la fuerza militar y la glorificación de la guerra (págs. 689, 740)

millet/millet comunidad de los no-musulmanes dentro del imperio otomano (pág. 457)

missionary/misionero persona que viaja para llevar las principios de una religión a otras personas (pág. 254)

mobilization/movilización acción de reunir y preparar tropas y equipo para la guerra (pág. 743)

monarchy/monarquía gobierno de un rey o una reina (pág. 47)

monastery/monasterio comunidad de hombres que han tomado votos religiosos (pág. 254)

money economy/economía monetaria sistema económico en el cual se usa el dinero y no el trueque para comprar y vender (pág. 323)

monopoly/monopolio control de todo (o casi todo) el comercio o la producción de un producto determinado (pág. 194)

monotheism/monoteísmo creencia en un solo dios (págs. 83, 189)

monsoon/monzón viento periódico que afecta el clima y las formas de vida en el sur de Asia (pág. 66)

mosaic/mosaico cuadro hecho de pedazos de vidrio de colores, barro cocido o piedra unidos con mortero (pág. 253)

mosque/mezquita templo mahometano (págs. 191, 276)

multicultural/multicultural que representa varios grupos culturales y étnicos diferentes (págs. 195, 890)

myth/mito relato tradicional que explica sucesos naturales (pág. 35)

nationalism/nacionalismo orgullo en la nación o grupo propios y sus tradiciones; deseo de independencia de un gobierno extranjero (págs. 576, 676)

nationalization/nacionalización traspaso de un negocio de propiedad privada al gobierno (pág. 813)

nationalize/nacionalizar traspasar una industria privada al control del gobierno (pág. 952)

nation-state/estado-nación un estado político cuyos habitantes comparten también el mismo idioma y la misma cultura (pág. 677)

natural law/ley natural verdad o principio universal que los pensadores del Siglo XVII creían podía ser hallado mediante la razón (pág. 521)

natural rights/dereches naturales derechas que poseen todas las personas al nacer (pág. 523)

negritude/negritud movimiento literario que enfatiza y se enorgullece de la herencia cultural del África (pág. 945)

nihilist/nihilista miembro de un movimiento político ruso de finales del Siglo XIX que rechazaba toda autoridad y abogaba a favor del terrorismo (pág. 692)

nirvana/nirvana en el budismo, estado de unidad con el universo; el final del ciclo de renacimiento (pág. 210)

nomad/nómada miembro de un grupo de personas sin hogar fijo, que viajan constantemente para buscar comida y agua (pág. 22)

nonaligned/no alineado que no toma partido con ninguna de las superpotencias en una guerra fría (pág. 917)

nuclear family/núcleo familiar grupo familiar que incluye sólo a padres e hijos (pág. 229)

obsidian/obsidiana cristal volcánico negro (pág. 383)

oligarchy/oligarquía forma de gobierno en la cual un grupo pequeño ejerce el poder político (pág. 114)

oral tradition/tradición oral las leyendas e historia de una cultura preservada de viva voz (pág. 184)

P

pacifism/pacifismo oposición a la guerra o a la violencia como medio de resolver disputas (pág. 523)

pacifist/pacifista creyente en el pacifismo (pág. 802)

pact/pacto tratado entre varias naciones (pág. 953)

paleontologist/paleontólogo científico que estudia los fósiles (pág. 20)

Pan-Africanism/Panafricanismo movimiento que aboga por la unidad y la cooperación entre las naciones africanas (pág. 942)

Pan-Arabism/Panarabismo movimiento de mediados del siglo XX que pretendía construir lazos culturales y políticos entre los árabes (pág. 950)

papal infallibility/infalibilidad papal doctrina católica romana que sostiene que el papa no puede cometer un error al hablar acerca de la fe y la moral (pág. 686)

partisan/partisano en la Segunda Guerra Mundial, término aplicado a un guerrillero de la resistencia clandestina, especialmente en Italia y Yugoeslavia (pág. 850)

partition/partición división de una región (pág. 707)

partnership/sociedad negocio que es propiedad de dos o más empresarios que comparten el manejo, las ganancias y las pérdidas (pág. 609)

patriarch/patriarca en la Iglesia cristiana primitiva, uno de los cinco obispos poderosos en las ciudades importantes (pág. 174)

patrician/patricio miembro de una clase aristocrática acaudalada en la antigua Roma (pág. 156)

peaceful coexistence/coexistencia pacífica política soviética de competir con los Estados unidos para evitar la guerra (pág. 873)

peninsulares/peninsulares funcionarios nacidos en España o Portugal que dirigían la sociedad en la América Latina colonial (pág. 667)

perestroika/perestroika término ruso que significa "reestructuración"; los cambios en la economía soviética iniciados por Mijail Gorbachov (pág. 1000)

perspective/perspectiva técnica artística que muestra las relaciones entre los objetos (pág. 131)

petit jury/jurado menor grupo de personas que determinan la culpabilidad o la inocencia de una persona procesada (pág. 309)

phalanx/falange en la antigua Grecia, una formación militar en la cual soldados de infantería se colocaban de tal modo que sus escudos quedaban superpuestos (pág. 114)

pharaoh/faraón título de los gobernadores del antiguo Egipto (pág. 49)

philosophe/filósofo pensador social o político del Siglo de las Luces (pág. 524)

philosopher/filósofo un pensador o un amante de la sabiduría (pág. 135)

pilgrimage/peregrinación viaje a un lugar sagrado (pág. 334)

plateau/altiplanicie región relativamente llana más elevada que el área circundante (pág. 185)

plebeian/plebeyo ciudadano de la antigua Roma que no era un aristócrata (pág. 156)

plebiscite/plebiscito voto popular directo sobre un programa o asunto (págs. 575, 657)

pogrom/pogrom persecución organizada de un grupo minoritario, usualmente judíos, en la Rusia de los zares (pág. 693)

polis/polis ciudad-estado de la antigua Grecia (pág. 112)

pollution/contaminación incorporación de sustancias tóxicas o impuras en el aire, tierra o agua (pág. 898)

polytheism/politeísmo adoración de varios dioses (pág. 52)

pope/papa el obispo de Roma, más tarde el jefe de la Iglesia Católica Romana (pág. 174)

population explosion/explosión demográfica aumento grande y repentino de la población humana (pág. 808)

Postimpressionism/Posimpresionismo movimiento artístico cuyos miembros experimentaban con la forma y el color (pág. 639)

potlatch festín celebrado por los americanos nativos del Noroeste del Pacífico (pág. 376)

pragmatic sanction/sanción pragmática decreto emitido por un gobernante sobre un asunto importante (pág. 495)

pragmatist/pragmatista en China, una persona moderada que abogaba por reformas económicas y por el comercio con Occidente (pág. 902)

predestination/predestinación doctrina de John Calvin (fundador del calvinismo) que predicaba que el destino de una persona estaba predeterminado por Dios (pág. 419)

prehistory/prehistoria tiempo anterior a la historia escrita (pág. 20)

prime minister/primer ministro jefe ejecutivo de un gobierno parlamentario (pág. 544)

principality/principado territorio gobernado por un príncipe (pág. 260)

privatization/privatización la devolución de industrias que eran propiedad del gobierno, a dueños privados (págs. 980-81, 1003)

proletariat/proletariado según la teoría marxista, la clase trabajadora (pág. 625)

propaganda/propaganda noticias e información destinadas a influir en los sentimientos de las personas hacia una causa (pág. 746)

prophet/profeta persona que predica o interpreta lo que se cree son mensajes de Dios (pág. 83)

protectorate/protectorado país cuya política es dirigida por una nación extranjera (pág. 706)

provisional government/gobierno provisional gobierno temporal establecido mientras se espera por un proceso electoral (pág. 757)

psychology/psicología estudio del comportamiento y sus causas (pág. 628)

purge/purga esfuerzo oficial para eliminar a las personas que un gobierno considera indeseables (pág. 791)

Q

queue/coleta trenza de pelo única en la parte posterior de la cabeza (pág. 466)

quinoa/quinua grano cultivado en los Andes (pág. 390)

quota/cuota número o cantidad específica (pág. 900)

R

racial segregation/segregación racial separación social de las personas de acuerdo a su raza (pág. 887)

radiocarbon dating/datación de carbono radioactivo método científico moderno para determinar la edad de un sustancia que tuvo vida, midiendo la cantidad de carbono que permanece en ella (pág. 21)

rajah/rajá jefe tribal ario en la antigua India; más tarde el gobernante de un estado indio (pág. 202)

ratify/ratificar dar aprobación oficial (pág. 665)

reactionary/reaccionario el individuo que se opone al progreso o al cambio y desea retornar a costumbres antiguas (pág. 582)

realism/realismo estilo y literatura de mediados del Siglo XIX, que reflejaba las realidades de la vida cotidiana (pág. 636)

realpolitik/realpolitik teoría política según la cual el

éxito nacional justifica el uso de cualquier medio (pág. 682)

referendum/referéndum voto popular directo para ratificar una disposición o una ley propuesta (págs. 908, 1011)

refugee/refugiado persona que tiene que abandonar su patria y escapar a otro lugar buscando seguridad (pág. 911)

regent/regente persona que actúa como gobernante temporal (pág. 251)

reincarnation/reencarnación el renacimiento del alma o el espíritu en diferentes cuerpos a través del tiempo (pág. 206)

reparation/indemnización de guerra compensación por daños producidos durante una guerra (pág. 762)

republic/república gobierno en el cual los ciudadanos eligen a sus dirigentes (pág. 156)

revelation/revelación visión de una realidad divina, como las atribuidas a Mahoma (pág. 272)

revolution/revolución cambio de gobierno mediante la fuerza (pág. 554)

rhetoric/retórica el arte de hablar en público de manera efectiva (pág. 119)

romanticism/romanticismo movimiento artístico de principios del siglo XIX, que enfatizaba la individualidad y la emoción (págs. 530, 635)

royalist/realista persona que apoya una monarquía (pág. 539)

Russification/rusificación política de imponer la lengua y costumbres rusas a otros pueblos (pág. 692)

S

sacrament/sacramento uno de los rituales formales establecidos por la Iglesia Católica Romana, tales como el bautismo, la sagrada comunión o el matrimonio (pág. 303)

salon/salón en Francia, tertulia donde los intelectuales del Siglo de las Luces se reunían para conversar (pág. 525)

samurai/samurai clase de guerreros terratenientes en el Japón feudal que juraban lealtad a un *daimyo* (pág. 363)

sanctions/sanciones penalidades y restricciones impuestas a una nación por haber infringido la ley internacional (pág. 827)

sanctuary/santuario edificio considerado sagrado, usado para la adoración (pág. 130)

sankin-kotai/sankin-kotai ("presencia alterna") en el Japón feudal, el sistema en el cual un *daimyo* tenía que residir en años alternos en la corte de un shogún (pág. 469)

satellite/satélite país dominado políticamente por un poder vecino (pág. 865)

satrap/sátrapa el gobernador de una provincia persa (pág. 91)

satyagraha/satyagraha ("fuerza de la verdad") término para referirse a las protestas no violentas guiadas por Ghandi (pág. 802)

savanna/sabana llanura cubierta de vegetación, con pocos árboles, en las regiones tropicales o subtropicales (pág. 185)

schism/Cisma de Oriente la división de la Iglesia cristiana en 1054, que separó a la Iglesia Católica Romana de la Iglesia Ortodoxa Oriental (pág. 250)

scholasticism/escolasticismo enseñanza medieval que trataba de combinar la filosofía de Aristóteles con las enseñanzas de los sabios de la Iglesia (pág. 326)

scientific method/método científico pasos para descubrir la verdad científica por medio de la observación y la experimentación (pág. 518)

scorched-earth policy/política de tierra arrasada orden dada por Stalin para que el pueblo soviético destruyera edificios, tierras y cualquier cosa que pudiera ser usada por los invasores nazis (pág. 838)

secede/separarse retirarse formalmente de la membresía de una organización política (pág. 663)

sect/secta subgrupo con sus propias creencias dentro de un grupo religioso mayor (págs. 171, 899)

sectionalism/regionalismo énfasis exagerado en los intereses políticos y económicos de la región propia (pág. 663)

secular/seglar mundano, que no es abierta o específicamente religioso (pág. 404)

self-determination/autodeterminación el derecho de un pueblo de decidir su propio gobierno o estado político (pág. 796)

seminary/seminario escuela destinada para la enseñanza de los sacerdotes, según ordenó el Concilio de Trento (pág. 423)

separatism/separatismo en el Canadá, movimiento político que favorecía la independencia de Quebec (pág. 890)

sepoy/cipayo soldado natural de la India en el ejército británico (pág. 713)

serf/siervo campesino labrador que dependía de las tierras de un noble (págs. 302, 501)

shah/sha el soberano de un país del Oriente Medio (pág. 797)

shamanism/chamanismo creencia de que los espíritus habitan en cosas vivas y muertas, y que se comunican con los humanos a través de unos sacerdotes llamados chamanes (pág. 358) *shari'ah/shari 'ah* código islámico de leyes que contiene reglas para todos los aspectos de la vida (pág. 275)

sheikh/jeque jefe de una tribu beduina (pág. 271)

shogun/shogún gobernador militar en el Japón feudal (pág. 363)

shogunate/shogunado gobierno fundado por la familia de un shogún y sus seguidores en el Japón feudal (pág. 363)

simony/simonía venta de cargos oficiales en la Iglesia Católica Romana medieval (pág. 335)

slash-and-burn farming/sistema de quema y siembra método de labranza en el cual la tierra cosechable se limpia talando y quemando los árboles para fertilizar el terreno (pág. 380)

socialism/socialismo teoría política que propugna que la sociedad como un todo debe tener el control de los medios de producción, tales como las fábricas y la tierra (pág. 624)

Socialist realism/realismo socialista bajo Stalin, un estilo artístico que glorificaba el modo de vida soviético (pág. 791)

sociology/sociología el estudio del comportamiento de grupos humanos (pág. 628)

sonnet/soneto composición poética de 14 versos y con un patrón de rima y métrica (pág. 405)

sovereignty/soberanía el poder independiente de un grupo o nación de tomar sus propias decisiones (pág. 963)

soviet/soviet un consejo de trabajadores formado al principio de la Revolución Rusa; más tarde, una unidad del gobierno en la Unión Soviética (pág. 694)

special economic zone/zona económica especial áreas de China donde se han permitido que negocios extranjeros y un mercado libre desarrollaran sus actividades en la década de 1990 (pág. 903)

sphere of influence/esfera de influencia área de un país donde una potencia extranjera tiene derechos exclusivos para comerciar o hacer inversiones (págs. 706, 715)

stagflation/estanflación tendencia económica que combina el estancamiento con la elevada inflación y el desempleo (pág. 889)

stalemate/estancamiento una detención o una situación en la que ninguna de las dos partes opuestas pueden avanzar (pág. 907)

standard of living/nivel de vida la medida general de la riqueza global de las personas y su calidad de vida (pág. 979)

steppe/estepa llanuras de Eurasia, extensas, herbáceas, semiáridas, que se extienden desde el Mar Negro hasta los montes Altai (pág. 258)

stupa/estupa capilla budista con bóveda semiesférica, construida sobre las reliquias o los huesos de un santo (pág. 210)

subcontinent/subcontinente porción de tierra que es parte de un continente pero bien diferenciada del mismo, tal como la India (pág. 66)

subsistence farmer/agricultor de subsistencia campesino que cultiva sólo lo suficiente para mantener a su familia o a una aldea (pág. 943)

suffragette/sufragista mujer que trabajaba activamente para obtener el derecho al voto femenino (pág. 651)

sultan/sultán líder político con autoridad absoluta sobre un país mahometano (pág. 457)

superpower/superpotencia nación poderosa e influyente, con un bloque de aliados, específicamente, los Estados Unidos y la Unión Soviética durante la Guerra Fría (pág. 864)

surrealism/surrealismo movimiento artístico que utilizaba sorpresivas imágenes distorsionadas (pág. 773)

symbolism/simbolismo movimiento artístico antirrealista que se centraba alrededor de imágenes y símbolos fantásticos (pág. 638)

symposium/simposio en la antigua Atenas, reunión que se celebraba con banquetes, entretenimiento y discusiones literarias (pág. 123)

syndicate/sindicato bajo el fascismo, agrupación de obreros y patronos en una industria (pág. 783)

technology/tecnología las habilidades y conocimientos empleados por las personas para fabricar herramientas y trabajar (pág. 24)

theocracy/teocracia gobierno encabezado por líderes religiosos o por un líder considerado como un dios (págs. 48, 418)

theology/teología el estudio de temas religiosos (pág. 251)

tithe/diezmo contribución de un 10 por ciento de los ingresos que se pagaba al clero (pág. 561)

totalitarianism/totalitarismo idea en que un gobierno dictatorial debe controlar todos los aspectos de la vida de los ciudadanos (pág. 781)

tournament/torneo deporte medieval en el cual los caballeros competían para mostrar sus habilidades en la lucha (pág. 299)

trade deficit/déficit comercial el desequilibrio económico que ocurre cuando el valor de las importaciones excede el valor de las exportaciones (págs. 889, 998)

tragedy/tragedia historia o representación teatral en la que el personaje central lucha contra el destino pero que desemboca en un final trágico (pág. 132)

trench/trinchera zanja cavada para dar protección a los soldados (pág. 747)

triangular trade/comercio triangular ruta de tres direcciones entre Europa, África y América en el Siglo XVII (pág. 444)

tribune/tribuna en la antigua Roma, magistrado que representaba a los plebeyos (pág. 157)

triumvirate/triunvirato en la antigua Roma, grupo de tres personas gobernando (pág. 162)

troubadour/trovador músico y poeta de la Edad Media que viajaba de corte en corte (pág. 327)

tyrant/tirano en la antigua Grecia, persona que usurpaba el poder y establecía un gobierno unipersonal (pág. 114)

ultimatum/ultimátum última disposición o declaración de condiciones, que implica una amenaza de penalidades severas (pág. 742)

ultraroyalist/ultrarrealista aristócrata extremadamente conservador en la Francia de principios del Siglo XIX (pág. 655)

unicameral legislature/legislatura unicameral asamblea o cuerpo legislativo de una sola cámara (pág. 565)

urbanization/urbanización la expansión de las ciudades y la vida citadina (pág. 631)

utilitarianism/utilitarismo filosofía económica desarrollada por Jeremy Bentham que considera que las acciones sociales y políticas deben ser de utilidad y ayuda a la humanidad (pág. 624)

varna/varna una de las cuatro clases sociales principales en la sociedad aria de la antigua India (pág. 203)

vassal/vasallo en el feudalismo, noble que ocupaba la tierra de un señor de más alto rango y le servía (pág. 299)

vernacular/vernáculo el lenguaje del habla diaria, no de los eruditos, en un país o región (pág. 328)

viceroy/virrey gobernante que representa a un monarca (pág. 714)

vocation/vocación llamado de Dios para asumir cierto trabajo (pág. 417)

war of attrition/guerra de desgaste conflicto en el cual cada bando trata de ganar agotando al contrario (pág. 746)

warlord/señor de la guerra líder militar local en China (pág. 804)

weir/nasa red o trampa colocada a lo ancho de un río para coger peces (pág. 376)

welfare state/estado de proteccionismo social sistema de gobierno en el cual el estado provee programas para proteger el bienestar económico y social del pueblo (pág. 879)

westernization/occidentalización la expansión de la cultura europea (pág. 718)

yasa/yasa código de leyes de Gengis Kan (pág. 344)

yeoman/campesino propietario en la sociedad inglesa, un campesino que poseía tierras (pág. 488)

yin and yang/yin y yan en el pensamiento chino, los principios opuestos presentes en toda naturaleza (pág. 227)

yurt/yurta tienda de campaña portátil grande y redonda que usaban los nómadas del Asia central (pág. 343)

zaibatsu/zaibatsu grandes firmas industriales japonesas que pertenecían a varias familias (pág. 808)

zemstvo/zemstvo asamblea local en la Rusia zarista (pág. 692)

ACKNOWLEDGMENTS

Text

Grateful acknowledgment is given authors and publishers for permission to reprint the following copyrighted material.
58 W.G. Lambert, Shamash Hymn from Babylonian Wisdom Literature, Copyright © 1960. Reprinted by permission Oxford University Press; **72** Reprinted by permission of Houghton Mifflin Co. All rights reserved; **146** From "Antigone" in *Sophocles, the Oedipus Cycle: An English Version* by Dudley Fitts and Robert Fitzgerald, copyright 1939 by Harcourt Brace & Company and renewed 1967 by Dudley Fitts and Robert Fitzgerald, reprinted by permission of Harcourt Brace & Company. CAUTION: All rights, including professional, amateur, motion picture, recitation, lecturing, performance, public reading, radio broadcasting, and television are strictly reserved. Inquiries on all rights should be addressed to Harcourt Brace & Company, Permissions Dept., Orlando, FL 32887; **366** Li Bo, "On a Quiet Night" from The Works of Li Bo the Chinese Poet, translated by Shigeyoshi Obata. Published in 1965 by Paragon Book Reprint Corp.; **366** Li Bo, "Taking Leave of a Friend" from Personae by Ezra Pound. Copyright 1926 by Ezra Pound. Reprinted by permission of New Directions Publishing Corporation; **367** "Hard Is the Journey" and **368** Li Bo, "Letter to His Two Small Children Staying in Eastern Lu at Wen Yang Village Under Turtle Mountain" from Li Bo and Tu Fu, translated by Arthur Cooper. Translation copyright © 1973 by Arthur Cooper. Reprinted by permission of Viking-Dutton, Inc.; **388** from "The Broken Spears" by Miguel Leon-Portilla, Copyright © 1962, 1990 by Beacon Press, Reprinted by permission of Beacon Press; **426** Niccolò Machiavelli, The Prince, translated and edited by Thomas G. Bergin. Copyright © 1947 by F. S. Crofts & Co. Inc. Reprinted by permission of Viking-Dutton, Inc.; **584** From *Les Misérables* by Victor Hugo, translated by Lee Fahnestock and Norman MacAfee. Translation copyright © 1987 by Lee Fahnestock and Norman MacAfee. Used by permission of Dutton Signet, a division of Penguin Books USA Inc.; **640** "The Beggar" from *The Short Stories of Anton Chekhov* by Anton Chekhov, edited with introduction by Robert Linscott. Copyright © 1932 and renewed 1960 by The Modern Library, Inc. Reprinted by permission of Random House, Inc.; **747** "Dulce et Decorum Est" by Wilfred Owen, from *The Collected Poems of Wilfred Owen*. Copyright © 1963 by Chatto & Windus. Reprinted by permission of New Directions Publishing Corp.; **818** From "By Any Other Name" from *Gifts of Passage* by Santha Rama Rau. Copyright © 1951 by Vasanthi Rama Rau Bowers. Copyright renewed. Reprinted by permission of HarperCollins Publishers, Inc. "By Any Other Name" originally appeared in The New Yorker; **837** From *Central Zionist Archives, Jerusalem 1939–1945*, edited by Francis R. Nicosia, Volume 4 of the *Archives of the Holocaust*, Garland Publishing, 1990; **985** Michael Dei-Anang, "My Africa" from Poems from Black Africa, edited by Langston Hughes. Copyright © 1963 by Langston Hughes. Reprinted by permission of Indiana University Press; **966** Jaime Torres Bodet, "The Window," translated by George Kearns. Translation copyright © 1974, 1963 by the McGraw-Hill Book Company, Inc.; **967** "The World, My Friends, My Enemies, You, and the Earth" from *Things I Didn't Know I Loved* by Nazim Hikmet, translated by Randy Blasing and Mutlu Konuk, copyright © 1975 by Randy Blasing and Mutlu Konuk. Reprinted by permission of Persea Books, Inc.; **968** Gabriel Okara, "Once Upon a Time," from African Voices, edited by Howard Sergeant. Copyright © 1973 by Howard Sergeant. Used by permission of Evans Brothers Ltd, London; **987** "Because I Want Peace" by Claribel Alegría, from *El Salvador: Testament of Terror*, edited by Joe Fish and Cristina Sganga. Copyright © 1988. Reprinted by permission of Interlink Publishing Group, Inc.

Maps

Cartographic Services provided by Ortelius Design, and GeoSystems Global Corp.

Photographs

Cover i Mark D. Phillips/Photo Researchers; **iv** Erich Lessing/Art Resource, NY; **v** (t)Palazzo Ducale, Mantua, Italy/M. Magliari/SuperStock, (b)National Gallery of Art, Washington DC; **vi** (t)Scala/Art Resource, NY, (b)Christies, London/SuperStock; **vii** AFP/Bettmann; **viii** (l)David David Gallery, Philadelphia/SuperStock, (r)Heraklion Museum, Crete/Kurt Scholz/SuperStock; **ix** Scala/Art Resource, NY; **0** Lauros-Giraudon/Art Resource, NY; **2** NASA; **8** Simon Fraser/Science Photo Library/Photo Researchers; **13** The Metropolitan Museum of Art, The Michael C. Rockefeller Collection, Gift of Nelson A. Rockefeller, 1972 (1978.412.310); **15** National Museum, Belgrade/E.T. Archives, London/SuperStock; **16-17** Anthony Howard/Woodfin Camp & Associates; **16** Heraklion Museum, Crete/Kurt Scholz/SuperStock; **17** (t)David David Gallery, Philadelphia/SuperStock, (b)National Museum, Lagos, Nigeria/Kurt Scholz/SuperStock; **19** Jean Clottes/Sygma; **20** Esias Baitel/Gamma-Liaison; **21** John Reader/Science Photo Library/Photo Researchers; **26** Boltin Picture Library; **27** John Reader/Science Photo Library/Photo Researchers; **28-29** Erich Lessing/Art Resource, NY; **28** Boltin Picture Library; **29** Scala/Art Resource, NY; **31** Ara Guler/Magnum; **32** Scala/Art Resource, NY; **33** Borromeo/Art Resource, NY; **35** Ira Block/The Image Bank; **36** Scala/Art Resource, NY; **45** The British Museum, London/Bridgeman Art Library/SuperStock; **46** Giraudon/Art Resource, NY; **47** (t)Sylvain Grandadam/Photo Researchers, (b)Erich Lessing/Magnum; **49** John Heaton/Westlight; **51** Michael Holford; **52** Boltin Picture Library; **58** Boltin Picture Library; **59** Ancient Art & Architecture Collection Ltd.; **60 through 62** Boltin Picture Library; **63** (l)Aleppo Museum, Syria/E.T. Archives, London/SuperStock, (r)Museum of Baghdad, Iraq/Silvio Fiore/SuperStock; **64** Musee de Louvre, Paris/E.T. Archives, London/SuperStock; **66** Borromeo/Art Resource, NY; **68** Scala/Art Resource, NY; **69** Courtesy the Institute of History and Philology; **70-71** Bridgeman/Art Resource, NY; **72 74 79** Michael Holford; **80** Giraudon/Art Resource, NY; **83** Laura Zito/Photo Researchers; **85** David Forbert/SuperStock; **86** Brent Turner; **88** Boltin Picture Library; **90-91** SEF/Art Resource, NY; **90 91** Erich Lessing/Art Resource, NY; **93** H. Linke/SuperStock; **97** (l) Royal Ontario Museum, Ontario, (r) Robert Harding Picture Library; **101** Scala/Art Resource, NY; **102-103** Bettmann Archive; **103** Joseph Nettis/Photo Researchers; **105** Scala/Art Resource, NY; **106** Erich Lessing/Art Resource, NY; **107** SuperStock; **108** Alberto Incrocci/The Image Bank; **110** Museo Capitolino, Rome/E.T. Archives, London/SuperStock; **111** House of Masks, Delos, Greece/Bridgeman Art Library/SuperStock; **112** William Katz/Photo Researchers; **113** Giraudon/Art Resource, NY; **115** Michael Holford; **116-117** Bill Bachmann/Photo Researchers; **116** Nimatallah/Art Resource, NY; **117** Art Resource, NY; **118** The Brooklyn Museum, Charles Wilbour Fund; **120 122** Scala/Art Resource, NY; **123** Foto Marberg/Art Resource, NY; **127** Bettmann Archive; **129** Scala/Art Resource, NY; **130** Scala/Art Resource, NY; **131** Werner Forman Archive/Art Resource, NY; **134** Museo Delle Terme, Rome/E.T. Archives, London/SuperStock; **135** Scala/Art Resource, NY; **136** Museo Capitolino, Rome/E.T. Archives, London/SuperStock; **138** Erich Lessing/Art Resource, NY; **140** Scala/Art Resource, NY; **141** Musee du Louvre, Paris/E.T. Archives, London/SuperStock; **142-143** Erich Lessing/Art Resource, NY; **142** (r)Staatliche Antikensammlung, Munich/Bridgeman Art Library/Art Resource, NY, (l)The Metropolitan Museum of Art, Bequest of Walter C. Backer, 1972 (1972.118.95); **143** (l)Art Resource, NY, (r)Giraudon/Art Resource, NY; **144** Boltin Picture Library; **145** Eric Lessing/Art Resource; **146 147 148** Art Resource, NY; **153** Erich Lessing/Art Resource, NY; **154 through 159** Scala/Art Resource, NY; **160** Prenestino Museum, Rome/E.T. Archives, London/SuperStock; **161** Scala/Art Resource, NY; **162** Archaeological Museum, Venice/E.T. Archives, London/SuperStock; **164** Robert Emmett Bright/Photo Researchers; **166-167** Scala/Art Resource, NY; **166** (c)Villa of the Mysteries, Pompeii/Euramax/SuperStock, (l)The Metropolitan Museum of Art, Rogers Fund, 1903 (03.14.5); **167** Alinari/Art Resource, NY; **168 171** Scala/Art Resource, NY; **172** Erich Lessing/Art Resource, NY; **173** Werner Forman/Art Resource, NY; **174** Scala/Art Resource, NY; **175** Robert Frerck/Tony Stone Images; **176** (l)Erich Lessing/Art Resource, NY; **179** Scala/Art Resource, NY; **181** The Metropolitan Museum of Art, Fletcher Fund, 1924 (24/97.21ab) **183** Tassili N'Ajjer Plateau, Algeria/Holton Collection/SuperStock; **184** Roger K. Burnard; **185** Egyptian Expedition of The Metropolitan Museum of Art, The Rogers Fund, 1930 (30.4.21); **186** file photo; **189** The Metropolitan Museum of Art, The Michael C. Rockefeller Collection, Gift of Nelson A. Rockefeller, 1972 (1978.412.310); **190** The British Museum, London/Bridgeman Art Library/SuperStock; **190-191** The Elliott Elisofon Archives, Museum of African Art, The Smithsonian Institution; **191** The Metropolitan Museum of Art, The Michael C. Rockefeller Memorial Collection, Gift of Nelson A. Rockefeller, 1964

(1978.412.352). Photo by Schecter Lee; **194** H. von Meiss/Photo Researchers; **195** Dave G. Houser; **196** M.P. Kahl/Photo Researchers; **197** Mark Burnett; **199** The Metropolitan Museum of Art, The Michael C. Rockefeller Collection, Gift of Nelson A. Rockefeller, 1972 (1978.412.310); **201** Scala/Art Resource, NY; **202** Toby Molenaar/ The Image Bank; **204** Robert Harding Picture Library; **204-205** B. Kapbor/SuperStock; **205** Art Resource, NY; **207** Victoria & Albert Museum, London/Art Resource, NY; **208** Christies, London/ Bridgeman Art Library/SuperStock; **211** Ancient Art & Architecture Collection; **213** Gueorgui Pinkhassov/Magnum Photos, Inc.; **214** James P. Blair/National Geographic Image Collection; **215** Borromeo/ Art Resource, NY; **217** Jon Gardey/Robert Harding Picture Library Ltd.; **219** Tony Stone Images; **220** Bettmann Archive; **225** Bibliotheque Nationale, Paris/Bridgeman Art Library/SuperStock; **226** Michael Holford; **227** Giraudon/Art Resource, NY; **228** Paul Biddle & Tim Malyon/Science Photo Library/Photo Researchers; **230** Bibliotheque Nationale, Paris; **231** (l)Giraudon/Art Resource, NY, (r)Bettmann Archive; **232** Bettmann Archive; **233** Mark Burnett; **236** Ancient Art & Architecture Collection; **237** The Cleveland Museum of Art, Sundry Purchase Fund, 1972. 43; **241** Jacksonville Museum of Contemporary Art, FL/SuperStock; **242** Erich Lessing/Art Resource; **243** (l)The Smithsonian Institution, (c)Archive Photos, (r)Ancient Art & Architecture Collection, **245 246 248** Scala/Art Resource, NY; **249** SuperStock; **251** Hagia Sophia, Istanbul, Turkey/E.T. Archives, London/SuperStock; **252** (l)Michael Holford, (r)Ancient Art & Architecture Collection; **253 255** Ancient Art & Architecture Collection; **256** SEF/Art Resource, NY; **258** Roy/Explorer/Photo Researchers; **260** Art Wolfe/Tony Stone Images; **262 263** Bettmann Archive; **264** Richard Bergman/Photo Researchers; **265** Michael Holford; **267** Ancient Art & Architecture Collection; **269** Bettmann Archive; **270** British Library, London/Bridgeman Art Library International Ltd; **272** AKG Berlin/SuperStock; **273** Ancient Art & Architecture Collection; **275** Werner Forman/Art Resource, NY; **276** Michael Holford; **277** Bibliotheque Nationale, Paris/The Bridgeman Art Library International Ltd; **278-279** Lerner Fine Art Collection/ SuperStock; **278** Courtesy of the Arthur M. Sackler Gallery, Smithsonian Institution, Washington, D.C.; **279** Ancient Art & Architecture Collection; **282 286** Bettmann Archive; **287** Michael Holford; **288** SuperStock; **293** San Francisco, Assisi/Canali PhotoBank, Milan/SuperStock; **294** Bettmann Archive; **295** Scala/ Art Resource, NY; **298** British Library, London/Bridgeman Art Library/SuperStock; **299** Ancient Art & Architecture Collection; **301** The Metropolitan Museum of Art, Munsey Fund, 1932(32.130.6); **303** Robert Smith/Ancient Art & Architecture Collection; **304-305** Art Resource, NY; **304** (l)Ronald Sheridan/Ancient Art & Architecture, (r)Abbey of Monteoliveto Maggiore, Sienna/E.T. Archives, London/ SuperStock; **304-305** Art Resource, NY; **305 306** Ronald Sheridan/ Ancient Art & Architecture Collection; **307** Museo del Prado, Madrid/E.T. Archives, London/SuperStock; **308** Ronald Sheridan/ Ancient Art & Architecture Collection; **309** Erich Lessing/Art Resource, NY; **313** Robert Smith/Ancient Art & Architecture Collection; **317** Scala/Art Resource, NY; **318** Ancient Art & Architecture Collection; **319** Giraudon/Art Resource, NY; **321** Erich Lessing/Art Resource, NY; **322** O. Troisfontaines/SuperStock; **323** The British Library, London/Bridgeman Art Library/SuperStock; **324-325** Scala/Art Resource, NY; **325** Ancient Art & Architecture Collection; **327** Giraudon/Art Resource, NY; **328** Scala/Art Resource, NY; **329** British Library, London/E.T. Archives, London/SuperStock; **330** Erich Lessing/Art Resource, NY; **334** Ancient Art & Architecture Collection; **336** Bridgeman Art Library/Art Resource, NY; **341** Bibliotheque Nationale, Paris/AKG Berlin/SuperStock; **342** Laurie Platt Winfrey, Inc.; **344** J. Bertrand/Photo Researchers; **345** SEF/Art Resource, NY; **346** Naomi Duguid/Asia Access; **347** Laurie Platt Winfrey, Inc.; **351** Wolfgang Kaehler; **352-353** Ernest Manewal/ SuperStock; **352** (l)George Holton/Photo Researchers, (r)Frederick Ayer/Photo Researchers; **353** R. Rowan/Photo Researchers; **355** A. Hubrich/H. Armstrong Roberts; **356** Jim Steinberg/Photo Researchers; **358** T. Iwamiya/Photo Researchers; **359** Rick Browne/Photo Researchers; **360** Masao Hayashi/Dunq/Photo Researchers; **361** Bettmann Archive; **363** Private Collection/Bridgeman Art Library/ SuperStock; **364** Freer Gallery; **365** Paul Chesley/Tony Stone Images; **366** Mary Evans Picture Library; **367** The Metropolitan Museum of Art, Edward Elliott Family Collection. Purchase, the Dillon Fund Gift, 1982. !982.2.2; **368 369** Bettmann Archive; **371** file photo; **373**

Boltin Picture Library; **374** Steve Smith/Westlight; **376-377** Mark Burnett; **376** Georgia Department of Natural Resources; **377** (l)Cranbrook Institute of Science, (r)Bettmann Archive; **378** J. Warden/SuperStock; **379** S. Vidler/SuperStock; **380** Museum of Mankind/E.T. Archives, London/SuperStock; **381** W. Bertsch/H. Armstrong Roberts; **383** Jacksonville Museum of Contemporary Art, FL/SuperStock; **388** Michael Zabe/Art Resource, NY; **391** Woodfin Camp & Associates; **393** Loren McIntyre/Woodfin Camp & Associates; **394** Mohamed Lounes/Liaison; **395** Private Collection/Bridgeman Art Library/SuperStock; **399** Scala/Art Resource, NY; **400** The British Museum; **401-402** Scala/Art Resource, NY; **401** Wolfgang Kaehler; **403** Palazzo Ducale, Mantua, Italy/M. Magliari/SuperStock; **404** Sistine Chapel, Vatican, Rome/Bridgeman Art Library/SuperStock; **406-407** Vatican Museums & Galleries, Rome/Fratelli Alinari/ SuperStock; **406** Galleria Dell'Academia, Florence/Scala/ SuperStock; **407** Erich Lessing/Art Resource, NY; **408** Scala/Art Resource, NY; **410** Victor R. Boswell, Jr.; **411** Vatican Museums & Galleries, Rome/Canali PhotoBank, Milan/SuperStock; **412** AKG, Berlin/SuperStock; **413** Scala/Art Resource, NY; **414** Erich Lessing/ Art Resource, NY; **415** SuperStock; **416** Erich Lessing/Art Resource, NY; **417** (l)Erich Lessing/Art Resource, NY, (r)National Museum, Copenhagen/E.T. Archives, London/SuperStock; **418** Mary Evans Picture Library/Photo Researchers; **420** Scala/Art Resource, NY; **421** Erich Lessing/Art Resource, NY; **422** Michael Holford; **423** Giraudon/Art Resource, NY; **425** Werner Forman Archive/Art Institute of Chicago/Art Resource, NY; **426 through 429** Scala/Art Resource, NY; **431** Erich Lessing/Art Resource, NY; **433** National Maritime Museum; **434** Karen Kasmauski/Woodfin Camp & Associates; **436** (l)SuperStock, (r)Michael Holford; **438** National Museum of American Art, Washington DC/Art Resource, NY; **439 440** AKG, Berlin/SuperStock; **442-443** Alinari/Art Resource, NY; **442** Erich Lessing/Art Resource, NY; **443** (t)Scala/Art Resource, NY, (b)Brent Turner/BLT Productions; **445** Bettmann Archive; **446 447** SuperStock; **448** Bridgeman/Art Resource, NY; **449** Michael Holford; **450** Bridgeman/Art Resource, NY; **455 456** Giraudon/Art Resource, NY; **458** Art Resource, NY; **459** Adam Woolfitt/Woodfin Camp & Associates; **461** by courtesy of the Board of Trustees of the Victoria & Albert Museum, London/Bridgeman Art Library/SuperStock; **462** Bibliotheque Nationale, Paris; **463** Dallas & John Heaton/Westlight; **464-465** Philadelphia Free Library/AKG, Berlin/SuperStock; **464** G. Hunter/SuperStock; **465** (l)Art Trade, Bonhams, London/Bridgeman Art Library/SuperStock, (r)SEF/Art Resource, NY; **466** D.E. Cox/Tony Stone Images; **468** Werner Forman Archive/Art Resource, NY; **469** Culver Pictures Inc./SuperStock; **470** Kita-In Saitumi/Werner Foreman Archive/Art Resource, NY; **471** Michael Holford; **473** Doug Martin; **474** George Holton/Photo Researchers; **475** SuperStock; **476** Scala/Art Resource, NY; **477** Bettmann Archive; **481** Giraudon/Art Resource, NY; **482** Bridgeman Art Library, London/SuperStock; **483** Bettmann Archive; **485** Victoria & Albert Museum/Art Resource, NY; **486** Michael Holford; **487** (l)Bridgeman/Art Resource, NY, (r)National Portrait Gallery, London; **488 489** National Portrait Gallery, London/SuperStock; **490** Giraudon/Art Resource, NY; **491** Lauros-Giraudon/Art Resource, NY; **492** A&F Pears Ltd., London/ SuperStock; **494** Museum of Art History, Vienna/AKG, Berlin/ SuperStock; **496** AKG, Berlin/SuperStock; **498** Novosti from Sovfoto; **499** Michael Holford; **502** Giraudon/Art Resource, NY; **505** Bridgeman/Art Resource, NY; **506** Musee du Louvre, Paris/Art Resource; **507** Corbis-Bettman; **511** Scala/Art Resource, NY; **512** Architect of the Capitol, Washington D.C.; **513** Bettmann Archive; **515** Giraudon/Art Resource, NY; **516** Royal Society of London **517** Private Collection/Bridgeman Art Library/SuperStock; **519** Bettmann Archive; **521** (detail)Erich Lessing/Art Resource, NY; **524** Giraudon/Art Resource, NY; **525** Derby Museum and Art Gallery, England/Bridgeman Art Library/SuperStock; **526** Christies, London/SuperStock; **526-527** Erich Lessing/Art Resource, NY; **527** Bettmann Archive; **528 529** Ronald Sheridan/Ancient Art & Architecture Collection; **530 531** Archive Photos; **535** Bridgeman/Art Resource, NY; **536** Ronald Sheridan/Ancient Art & Architecture Collection; **537** Bettmann Archive; **538** courtesy The Pilgrim Society; **540** National Portrait Gallery, London/SuperStock; **541 543** Ronald Sheridan/Ancient Art & Architecture Collection; **544** Bettmann Archive; **545** Scala/Art Resource, NY; **546-547** Bettmann Archive; **546** Historic Deerfield Inc.: photo by Amanda Merullo; **547** (l)John Carter Brown Library, Brown University, (r)Massachusetts Historical Society;

548 Bettmann Archive; 550 Archive Photos; 551 Ronald Sheridan/Ancient Art & Architecture Collection; 552 Chicago Historical Society; 553 Yale University Art Gallery; 559 AKG, Berlin/SuperStock; 560 Bettmann Archive; 561 Scala/Art Resource, NY; 563 Mary Evans Picture Library/Photo Researchers; 564 Bettmann Archive; 565 Giraudon/Art Resource, NY; 567 Photo Researchers; 568 AKG, Berlin/SuperStock; 570-571 Stock Montage; 570 Photo Researchers; 571 Archiv/Photo Researchers; 573 Erich Lessing/Art Resource, NY; 574 Bettmann Archive; 575 578 Giraudon/Art Resource, NY; 580 Photo Researchers; 582 583 Bettmann Archive; 584 Giraudon/Art Resource, NY; 585 The Metropolitan Museum of Art, Gift of Mrs. Herbert N. Straus, 1942(42.203.1) Photo by Derry Moore; 586 Mary Evans Picture Library/Photo Researchers; 590 The Wellcome Institute Library, London; 591 Cabinet des Estampes, Bibliotheque Nationale de France/Laurie Platt Winfrey, Inc.; 595 L. Berger/SuperStock; 596 Stock Montage; 597 (t)Library of Congress, (b)Laurie Platt Winfrey, Inc.; 599 The Science Museum, London; 600 Waterhouse and Dodd, London/Bridgeman Art Library/SuperStock; 601 Christies, London/SuperStock; 603 Archive Photos; 604 Ronald Sheridan/Ancient Art & Architecture Collection; 605 file photo; 606 607 The Smithsonian Institution; 608 Royal Museum of Fine Arts, Copenhagen/Bridgeman Art Library/SuperStock; 612 International Museum of Photography/George Eastman House; 613 614 Collection of Picture Research Consultants; 614-615 Snark/Art Resource, NY; 615 Library of Congress; 616 Courtesy Labor Archives and Research Center, San Francisco State University; 621 622 Giraudon/Art Resource, NY; 623 Library of Congress; 624 file photo; 626 Bettmann Archive; 627 Erich Lessing/Art Resource, NY; 629 National Portrait Gallery, London/SuperStock; 630-631 Christies, London/SuperStock; 630 Library of Congress; 631 Missouri Historical Society; 633 Tate Gallery, London/Art Resource, NY; 635 Gemaldegalerie, Dresden, Germany/A.K.G., Berlin/SuperStock; 636 Christies, London/SuperStock; 639 Erich Lessing/Art Resource, NY; 640 Archive Photos; 641 Scala/Art Resource, NY; 642 Russian State Museum, St. Petersburg/Bourkatouskey/SuperStock; 645 National Portrait Gallery, London/SuperStock; 647 Giraudon/Art Resource, NY; 648 Library of Congress; 649 Snark/Art Resource, NY; 651 652 Bettmann Archive; 653 Archive Photos; 655 Erich Lessing/Art Resource, NY; 656 Stock Montage; 657 Giraudon/Art Resource, NY; 658 660 662 Bettmann Archive; 662-663 Scala/Art Resource, NY; 663 Mark Burnett; 665 Library of Congress; 666 Bettmann Archive; 668 Schalkwijk/Art Resource, NY; 675 676 Scala/Art Resource, NY; 678-679 Giraudon/Art Resource, NY; 679 (l)Scala/Art Resource, NY, (r)Vince Streano/Tony Stone Images; 680 Bettmann Archive; 681 Archive for Art & History, Berlin/AKG, Berlin/SuperStock; 683 Bryan F. Peterson/The Stock Market; 685 Erich Lessing/Art Resource, NY; 686 FPG International; 687 SuperStock; 689 Bettmann Archive; 690 FPG International; 693 Bettmann Archive; 695 Corbis-Bettmann; 696 SEF/Art Resource, NY; 701 Mark Burnett; 703 Bridgeman/Art Resource, NY; 704 Laurie Platt Winfrey, Inc.; 705 Bettmann Archive; 707 Archive Photos/Popperfoto; 708 Bettmann Archive; 709 Werner Forman Archive/Art Resource, NY; 711 Bettmann Archive; 712 Thierry Prat/Sygma; 713 Stock Concepts; 716-717 Bridgeman/Art Resource, NY; 717 (l)Bettmann Archive, (r)Bridgeman Art Library/Art Resource, NY; 719 Bettmann Archive; 720 file photo; 721 722 Bettmann Archive; 727 Historical Picture Service; 728 Corbis-Bettmann; 729 Stock Montage, Chicago; 733 Aaron Haupt; 734 UPI/Bettmann Archive; 735 (t)AP/Wide World Photos, (b)Lena Kara/SIPA; 737 West Point Museum/Joshua Nefsky; 738 SuperStock; 741 Bettmann Archive; 744 Archive Photos; 746-747 Bridgeman/Art Resource, NY; 746 Collection of Colonel Stuart S. Corning. Photo: Rob Huntley: Lightstream; 747 UPI/Bettmann Archive; 748 Erich Lessing/Art Resource, NY; 749 Bettmann Archive; 756 Snark/Art Resource, NY; 757 AP/Wide World Photos; 760 Collection of Colonel Stuart S. Corning. Photo: Rob Huntley:Lightstream; 761 Bettmann Archive; 769 Des Moines Art Center Permanent Collection, 1958.2. Photo: Craig Anderson; 770 Archive Photos; 772 The Metropolitan Museum of Art, bequest of Gertrude Stein, 1946(47.106); 773 Centro de Arte Reina Sofia, Madrid, Spain/Giraudon, Paris/SuperStock; 776 Archive Photos; 777 National Museum of American Art/Art Resource, NY; 778 Bettmann Archive; 779 UPI/Bettmann; 781 AKG, Berlin/SuperStock; 782 L'Illustration/Sygma; 783 784 Bettmann Archive; 784-785 AP/Wide World Photos; 785 Bettmann Archive; 786 Hugo Jaeger/LIFE Magazine, Time Inc.; 787 David Low/London Evening Standard/Solo Syndication Limited; 788 Sovfoto; 789 791 Bettmann Archive; 793 (l) Museum of Modern Art, New York/Bridgeman Art Library/SuperStock, Demart Pro Arte, Geneva/Artists' Rights Society, NY; (r) Stock Montage, Inc.; 795 Schalkwijk/Art Resource, NY; 796 Archive Photos; 798 UPI/Bettmann; 799 Eliot Elisofon National Museum of African Art, Eliot Elisofon Archives, Smithsonian Institution; 800 John Moss/Black Star; 801 Bridgeman/Art Resource, NY; 802 file photo; 804 Keystone, Paris/Sygma; 805 AP/Wide World Photos; 806 SIPA Press; 807 808 Bettmann Archive; 810 John Moss/Black Star; 811 SuperStock; 812 813 Schalkwijk/Art Resource, NY; 814 818 UPI/Bettmann; 819 Laurie Platt Winfrey, Inc.; 821 Rudi Von Briel; 825 U.S. Naval Photographic Center; 826 UPI/Bettmann; 827 AP/Wide World Photos; 829 Sygma; 831 Archive Photos; 834-835 UPI/Bettmann; 834 AP/Wide World Photos; 835 (l)Bettmann Archive, (r)Archive Photos; 836 Popperfoto/Archive Photos; 838 839 842 UPI/Bettmann; 846 Archive Photos; 848 RIA-Novosti/Sovphoto; 849 UPI/Bettmann; 850 Archive Photos; 851 UPI/Bettmann; 854 Corbis-Bettmann; 855 Corbis-Bettmann; 859 Chuck O'Rear/Westlight; 860 (l)UPI/Corbis-Bettmann, (r)Sovfoto/Eastfoto; 861 (l)T. Rosenthal/SuperStock; (r)The Granger Collection; 863 Sovfoto/Eastfoto; 864 Archive Photos; 865 SuperStock; 868-869 AP/Wide World Photos; 868 UPI/Bettmann; 869 S. Vidler/SuperStock; 872 Archive Photos; 873 UPI/Bettmann; 875 Black Star; 877 UPI/Bettmann; 878 Roger-Viollet; 879 AP/Wide World Photos; 880 UPI/Bettmann; 882 Bettmann Archive; 883 UPI/Bettmann; 884 SIPA Press; 887 AP/Wide World Photos; 888 UPI/Corbis-Bettmann; 890 Reuters/Bettmann; 895 M. Setboun/Sygma; 896 P. Amranand/SuperStock; 897 T. Matsumoto/Sygma; 898 Tom Wagner/SABA; 899 Michael Yamashita/Westlight; 901 George Matchneer; 903 Bettmann Archive; 904 Langevin/Sygma; 906 Duclos/Guichard/Gouver/Gamma-Liaison; 908 R. Ian Lloyd/The Stock Market; 909 UPI/Bettmann; 910-911 file photo; 911 UPI/Bettmann; 914 Howard/Spooner/Gamma; 916 Sygma; 917 UPI/Bettmann; 919 V. Miladinovic/Sygma; 920 G.R. Robert; 921 925 Sygma; 927 Klaus Reisinger/Black Star; 928 Louis Gubb/JB Pictures; 931 UPI/Bettmann; 932 Archive Photos/Express News/D.E.1; 934 David Keith Jones/Images of Africa Photobank; 935 Haviv/SABA; 936 937 (l)David Keith Jones/Images of Africa Photobank; 938 Alain Buu/Gamma-Liaison Network; 940 Mark Burnett; 941 J.M. Bertrand/SuperStock; 942 David Travers/The Stock Market; 943 Doug Menuez/SABA; 944 P. Schmidt/SuperStock; 945 Lawrence Migdale/Tony Stone Images; 947 Betty Press/Woodfin Camp & Associates; 949 Robert Frerck/Woodfin Camp & Associates; 950 Jesse Nemerofsky/Photoreporters; 951 Sygma; 954 L. de Raemy/Sygma; 955 UPPA/Photoreporters; 956 957 Barry Iverson/Woodfin Camp & Associates; 957 (l)Penny Tweedie/Woodfin Camp & Associates, (r)Esaias Baitel/Gamma-Liaison; 958 Chip Hires/Gamma-Liaison; 962 Reuters/Bettmann; 963 Tony Stone Images; 964 Ed Kashi; 967 AP/Wide World Photos; 969 Dennis Stock/Magnum; 973 Ary Diesendruck/Tony Stone Images; 974 Alain Keler/Sygma; 975 David L. Perry; 976 Neil Beer/Tony Stone Images; 977 Carrion/Sygma; 979 Bettmann Archive; 980-981 Sergio Dorantes/Sygma; 980 Robert Frerck/Tony Stone Images; 981 (l)Robert Frerck/Woodfin Camp & Associates, (r)Russell Cheyne/Tony Stone Images; 985 Javier Bauluz/SABA; 987 Noel Quidu/Gamma-Liaison; 988 Max Hunn/Archive Photos; 989 Gary Payne/Gamma-Liaison; 990 UPI/Bettmann; 991 Reuters/Bettmann; 992 Martin Thomas/Gamma-Liaison; 997 NASA; 998 Les Stone/Sygma; 1000 Novosti/Gamma-Liaison; 1003 1004 Reuters/Bettmann; 1005 AP/Wide World Photos; 1006 1007 Reuters/Bettmann; 1009 Archive Photos; 1010 AP/Wide World Photos; 1011 Peter Turnley/Black Star; 1014 AP/Wide World Photos; 1016 (l)AP/Wide World Photos, (r)Reuters/Bettmann; 1018 NASA/Gamma-Liaison; 1019 SuperStock; 1020 J.L. Atlan/Sygma; 1021 Hans Peter Merten/Tony Stone Images; 1026 Vince Finnegan/Hulton Getty/Gamma-Liaison; 1027 (l) Reuters/Mike Hutchings/Archive Photos, (r) Reuters/Yannis Behrakis/Archive Photos.